THE NEW AMERICAN EPHEMERIS
2007 to 2020

Longitude, Declination, Latitude and Daily Aspectarian

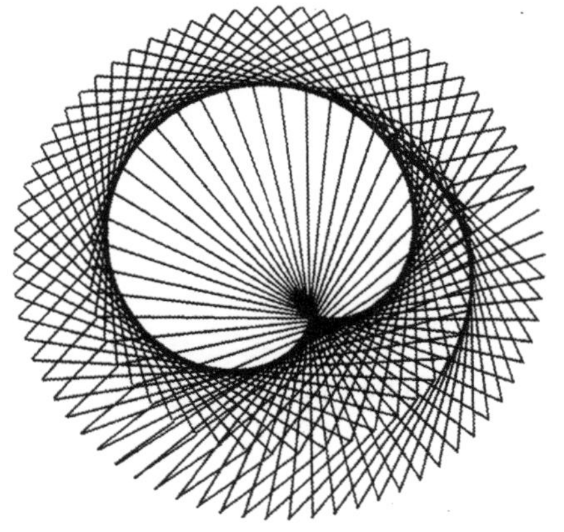

Compiled and Programmed by
Rique Pottenger

based on the earlier work of
Neil F. Michelsen

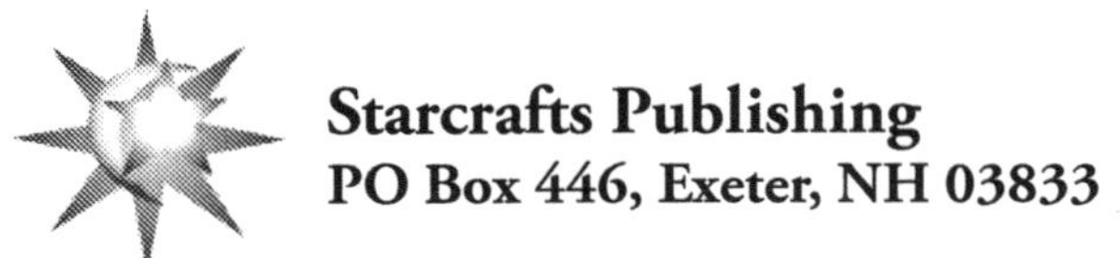

Starcrafts Publishing
PO Box 446, Exeter, NH 03833

The New American Ephemeris 2007-2020
Longitude, Declination & Latitude

First Printing 2007

Compiled and Programmed by Rique Pottenger
Based on the earlier work of Neil F. Michelsen

Cover by Maria Kay Simms

The mandala shown on cover and title page is from
Neil F. Michelsen's *Tables of Planetary Phenomena.*
It shows the heliocentric orbital pattern made by Venus and Earth.

Library of Congress Control Number: 2007932613

International Standard Book Number: ISBN 978-0-9762422-8-4

Published by Starcrafts Publishing, Starcrafts LLC
PO Box 446, Exeter, NH 03833-0446
http://www.starcraftspublishing.com

Printed in the United States of America

Introducing *The New American Ephemeris 2007-2020*

This book is a substantially revised and updated version of a series of 10-year ephemerides beginning with ***The American Ephemeris 1931-1940***, compiled and programmed by Neil F. Michelsen and published by his company, ACS Publications. Earlier, in 1976, Neil had published the first fully computer-generated ephemeris ***The American Ephemeris 1931 to 1980 & Book of Tables.*** More versions followed over the years until Michelsen's death in 1990. Since then, Rique Pottenger has revised and updated all of the Michelsen references as needed. He first extended Michelsen's last version for 1981-1990 by programming and compiling ***The American Ephemeris 1991-2000*** for ACS. With this new publication, Rique has included new features that he'd added to Starcrafts Publishings 2006 release, ***The New American Ephemeris for the 21st Century, 2000-2100 at Midnight*** and has added even more new features unique to this book.

Books from the "decade ephemeris" series, as we who were then at ACS always referred to the 10 year publications, have always been particular favorites of mine. Even though I've always had the full century books in multiples at both home and office, I've found the current decade book to be the easiest to have close at hand during a consultation, or to take along on a trip, for quick reference to transits. This thinner, lightweight book is easy to slip into my briefcase. Most valuable of all, though, to a great many astrologers, is that these books include not only the daily longitude tables found in all ephemerides in the series, but they also have declination and latitude tables and a daily aspectarian.

The New American Ephemeris Features

Because of interest in the features included in our prior full 21st century "New American," the most obvious difference in this volume is that it's a "decade plus." We decided to include the remainder of the current decade so that those using this book for quick scans of transits will have the new features of the full 21st century book easily at hand in this version, too. For a continuation of the series past 2020 we'd revert to 10 years only, for 2021-2030.

You'll find Ceres and Chiron added to all daily longitude positions, and the position of very slowly moving Eris shown once per month. New in this volume, you'll find asteroids Pallas, Juno and Vesta shown at five day intervals. In the Declination and Latitude tables, Uranus through Pluto were formerly shown at five day intrervals. Now you'll also find Chiron, the three asterods and Eris there. The Daily Aspectarian now includes Ceres and Chiron. Other features include the improved calculation formula for the Galactic Center. The table below is provided for those who wish to use it to convert from UT to ET, and Rique has updated it with values for the added years. We have omited other tables included in the back of former versions as unnecessary today for most users. We hope that you will find this book to be a valuable addition to your reference library.

—Maria Kay Simms

Universal to Ephemeris Time Correction (ΔT)

Add to Universal Time Entries for January 1st

YEAR	SECONDS	YEAR	SECONDS	YEAR	SECONDS
1860	8	1910	10	1960	33
1861	8	1911	12	1961	34
1862	8	1912	13	1962	34
1863	7	1913	15	1963	34
1864	6	1914	16	1964	35
1865	6	1915	17	1965	36
1866	5	1916	18	1966	37
1867	4	1917	19	1967	37
1868	3	1918	20	1968	38
1869	2	1919	21	1969	39
1870	2	1920	21	1970	40
1871	0	1921	22	1971	41
1872	-1	1922	22	1972	42
1873	-1	1923	23	1973	43
1874	-3	1924	23	1974	44
1875	-3	1925	24	1975	45
1876	-4	1926	24	1976	46
1877	-5	1927	24	1977	48
1878	-5	1928	24	1978	49
1879	-5	1929	24	1979	50
1880	-5	1930	24	1980	51
1881	-5	1931	24	1981	51
1882	-5	1932	24	1982	52
1883	-5	1933	24	1983	53
1884	-5	1934	24	1984	54
1885	-6	1935	24	1985	54
1886	-6	1936	24	1986	55
1887	-6	1937	24	1987	55
1888	-6	1938	24	1988	56
1889	-6	1939	24	1989	56
1890	-6	1940	24	1990	57
1891	-6	1941	25	1991	58
1892	-6	1942	25	1992	58
1893	-7	1943	26	1993	59
1894	-6	1944	26	1994	60
1895	-6	1945	27	1995	61
1896	-6	1946	27	1996	62
1897	-6	1947	28	1997	62
1898	-5	1948	28	1998	63
1899	-4	1949	29	1999	63
1900	-3	1950	29	2000	64
1901	-2	1951	30	2001	64
1902	0	1952	30	2002	64
1903	1	1953	30	2003	64
1904	3	1954	31	2004	65
1905	4	1955	31	2005	65
1906	5	1956	31	2006	65
1907	6	1957	32	2007	65
1908	8	1958	32		
1909	9	1959	33		

About Rique Pottenger

Rique Pottenger was born September 16, 1949, in Tucson, Arizona at 6:18 am. He has a B.Sc. in Math and Astronomy from the University of Arizona and an M.S. in Computer Science from UCLA. Though never formally trained in astrology, he has absorbed quite a bit of it over the years, as he is the eldest son of Zipporah Dobyns, and Maritha Pottenger is his sister. Rique had intended to become a mathematician until he discovered computer programming, and he has now been a programmer for more than 30 years. He has written programs for machines from 8 to 32 bits, running under many different operating systems.

From 1984 to 2004, Rique was employed at Astro Computing Services and ACS Publications where he programmed some of the company's most popular interpreted reports. After the death of founder Neil F. Michelsen in 1990, Rique became responsible for maintaining and improving Astro's production programs. This included his taking the major role in implementing Michelsen's wishes to switch from main frame computers to a modern and faster Windows based PC network. After designing and programming the new system, and recommending new equipment, Rique then trained the staff in how to use the new system. Later, Rique progammed the company's Electronic Astrologer software series. He also assumed responsibility for maintaining and improving the ACS Atlas database.

Now semi-retired, Rique continues to do astrological programming for a small list of clients. He lives in Opelika, Alabama with his beloved wife, Zowie Wharton, and their two cats. In their spare time they work at home-improvement projects (both have lots of Virgo), play computer games on their home network, and do puzzles together.

Other Books by Rique Pottenger

The Asteroid Ephemeris 1900-2050 with Chiron and the Black Moon
The American Ephemeris 2001-2010
The International Atlas, Expanded Sixth Edition (with Thomas C. Shanks)
The New American Ephemeris for the 21st Century 2000-2100 at Midnight
The New American Midpoint Ephemeris 2006-2020

and

Revisions to:

The American Ephemeris for the 20th Century, Revised 5th Edition
The American Ephemeris for the 21st Century, 2000-2050, at Midnight, Expanded 2nd Edition,
The American Ephemeris for the 21st Century, 2000-2050, at Noon, Revised Second Edition
Tables of Planetary Phenomena, Second Edition

KEY TO THE EPHEMERIS
EPHEMERIDENSCHLÜSSEL
COMMENT COMPRENDRE LES EPHEMERIDES
CLAVE PARA LAS EFEMERIDES

Planets
☉ Sun
☽ Moon
☊ Moon's node
☿ Mercury
♀ Venus
♂ Mars
♃ Jupiter
♄ Saturn
♅ Uranus
♆ Neptune
♇ Pluto
⚳ Ceres
⚴ Pallas
⚵ Juno
⚶ Vesta

Signs
♈ Aries
♉ Taurus
♊ Gemini
♋ Cancer
♌ Leo
♍ Virgo
♎ Libra
♏ Scorpio
♐ Sagittarius
♑ Capricorn
♒ Aquarius
♓ Pisces

Major Aspects
☌ conjunction
⚹ sextile
□ square
△ trine
☍ opposition

Minor Aspects
⚼ sesquisquare
⚻ quincunx
⚺ semisextile
∠ semisquare

Aspects in Declination
∥ parallel
contraparallel

Planeten
☉ Sonne
☽ Mond
☊ Knotenpunkt des Mondes
☿ Merkur
♀ Venus
♂ Mars
♃ Jupiter
♄ Saturn
♅ Uranus
♆ Neptun
♇ Pluto
⚳ Ceres
⚴ Pallas
⚵ Juno
⚶ Vesta

Tierkreiszeichen
♈ Widder
♉ Stier
♊ Zwillinge
♋ Krebs
♌ Löwe
♍ Jungfrau
♎ Waage
♏ Skorpion
♐ Schütze
♑ Steinbock
♒ Wassermann
♓ Fische

Wichtige Aspekte
☌ Konjunktion
⚹ Sextaler
□ Quadratisch
△ Trigon
☍ Opposition

Unwichtige Aspekte
⚼ Anderthalbquadratisch
⚻ Quincunx
⚺ Halbsextal
∠ Halbquadratisch

Aspekte in Deklination
∥ Parallel
Gegenparallel

Planètes
☉ Soleil
☽ Lune
☊ Le noeud lunaire
☿ Mercure
♀ Vénus
♂ Mars
♃ Jupiter
♄ Saturne
♅ Uranus
♆ Neptune
♇ Pluton
⚳ Ceres
⚴ Pallas
⚵ Juno
⚶ Vesta

Signes
♈ Bélier
♉ Taureau
♊ Gémeaux
♋ Cancer
♌ Lion
♍ Vierge
♎ Balance
♏ Scorpion
♐ Sagittaire
♑ Capricorne
♒ Verseau
♓ Poissons

Aspects Majeurs
☌ conjonction
⚹ sextil
□ carré
△ trigon
☍ opposition

Aspects Mineurs
⚼ sesquicarré
⚻ quinconce
⚺ semisextil
∠ semicarré

Aspects en declination
∥ paralléle
contreparalléle

Los Planetas
☉ El Sol
☽ La luna
☊ El nodo lunar
☿ Mercurio
♀ Venus
♂ Marte
♃ Júpiter
♄ Saturno
♅ Urano
♆ Neptuno
♇ Plutón
⚳ Ceres
⚴ Pallas
⚵ Juno
⚶ Vesta

Los Signos
♈ Aries
♉ Tauro
♊ Géminis
♋ Cáncer
♌ Leo
♍ Virgo
♎ Libra
♏ Escorpion
♐ Sagitario
♑ Capricornio
♒ Acuario
♓ Piscis

Los aspectos mayores
☌ la conjunción
⚹ el sextil
□ la cuadratura
△ el trígono
☍ la oposición

Los aspectos menores
⚼ la sesquicuadratura
⚻ el quinconce
⚺ el semisextil
∠ el semicuadratura

Los aspectos en declinación
∥ paralelo
contraparalelo

In the Longitude box, shaded positions are retrograde, and unshaded positions are direct. D indicates stationary going direct. R indicates stationary going retrograde, except on the second day of the month, where it merely indicates retrograde, unless the first day of the month is not shaded, in which case the R indicates stationary going retrograde after all.

Im Länge Kasten, Positionen mit die Schattierung rückläufig sind, und Positionen ohne Schattierung direkt sind. D zeigt feststehend geht direkt an. R zeigt feststehend geht rückläufig an, außer auf dem zweiten Tag des Monats, wo es nur rückläufig anzeigt, es sei denn der erste Tag vom Monat keine Schattierung hat, in dem der R doch feststehend geht rückläufig anzeigt.

Dans la boîte de Longitude, les positions avec ombragers sont rétrogrades, et les positions sans ombragers pas sont directes. D indique tourner à l'arrêt direct. R indique tourner à l'arrêt rétrograde, sauf sur le deuxième jour du mois, où il indique simplement rétrograde, à moins que le premier jour du mois n'est pas ombragé, dans lequel reconnaît le R indique tourner à l'arrêt rétrograde après tout.

En la caja de la Longitud, las posiciones dadas sombra son las posiciones retrógradas y sin sombrear son directas. D indica la curva inmóvil dirige. R indica la curva inmóvil retrógrado, menos en el segundo día del mes, donde solamente indica retrógrado, a menos que el primer día del mes no sea dado sombra, en que embala la R indica la curva inmóvil retrógrado.

Moon Phenomena
● new Moon
☽ first quarter
○ full
☾ third quarter
Solar eclipse
T = Total
P = Partial
A = Annular
Lunar eclipse
T = Total
P = Partial
A = Appulse

Mondersheinungen
Neumond
erstes Viertel
Vollmond
letztes Viertel
Sonnenfinsternis
T = totale
P = partielle
A = ringförmig
Mondfinsternis
T = totale
P = partielle
A = appulse

Phénomènes Lunaires
nouvelle Lune
premier quartier
pleine Lune
dernier quartier
éclipse du Soleil
T = totale
P = partielle
A = annulaire
éclipse de la Lune
T = totale
P = partielle
A = appulse

Fenómenos Lunares
la luna nueva
la creciente
la luna llena
la luna menguante
el eclipse solar
T = total
P = parcial
A = annular
el eclipse lunar
T = total
P = parcial
A = acercamiento

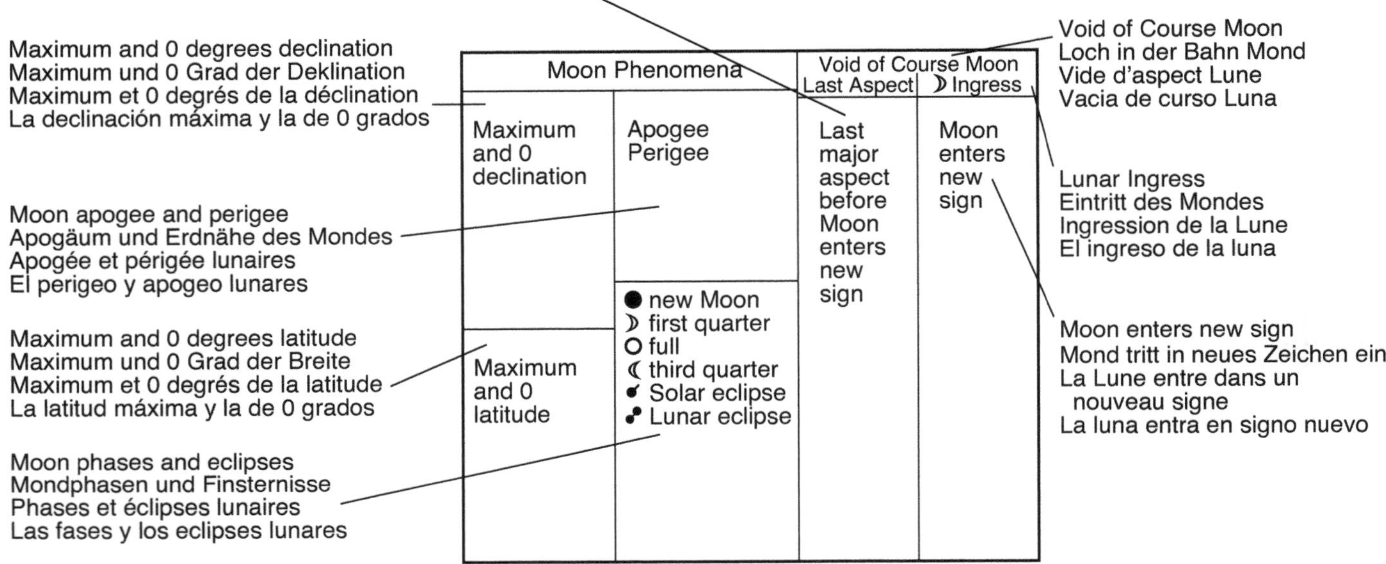

Sidereal Times are given for midnight (0h) Ephemeris Time at 0° longitude (Greenwich).
All planetary positions are given for midnight (0h) Ephemeris Time except Moon 12 hour positions which are given for noon Ephemeris Time.
Aspect and Moon phenomena times are given in Ephemeris Time.

Sternzeiten sind für Null Uhr Mitternacht (0h) Ephemeriden–Zeit bei 0° geographische Länge (Greenwich) angegeben.
Alle Stellungen der Gestirne für 0 Uhr Mitternacht Ephemeriden–Zeit mit Ausnahme der Mond 12–Stunden Positionen, die für 12 Uhr mittags Ephemeriden–Zeit angegeben sind.
Aspekt– und Monderscheinungszeiten sind in Ephemeriden–Zeit angegeben.

Temps Sidéraux donnés pour minuit (0h) Temps Ephéméride a 0° de longitude (Greenwich).
Toutes les positions planétaires sont données pour minuit (0h) Temps Ephéméride, sauf pour les positions lunaires de 12 Heures indiquées pour midi, Temps Ephéméride.
Les heures des aspects et des phénomènes lunaires sont données en Temps Ephéméride.

El Tiempo sidereal dado es el de medianoche (0h) Tiempo de Efemérides a 0° longitud (en Greenwich).
Todas las posiciones planetarias son calculadas a la medianoche (0h) Tiempo de Efemérides, con la excepción de las posiciones de la luna de 12 horas calculadas al mediodía Tiempo de Efemérides.
La hora de los fenómenos de la luna y de los aspectos es dada en Tiempo de Efemérides.

LONGITUDE — January 2007

Day	Sid.Time	☉	☽	☽ 12 hour	Mean☊	True☊	☿	♀	♂	⚳	♃	♄	⚷	♅	♆	♇
	h m s	° ' "	° ' "	° ' "	° '	° '	° '	° '	° '	° '	° '	° '	° '	° '	° '	° '
1 M	6 41 04	10♑10 24	7♊24 41	14♊22 13	19♓40.1	18♓50.6	6♑30.5	26♑03.4	18♐25.7	0♓59.3	8♐11.6	24♌27.6	7♒46.9	11♓32.3	18♒06.8	27♐01.6
2 Tu	6 45 01	11 11 32	21 17 12	28 09 09	19 36.9	18R 39.8	8 05.9	27 18.6	19 09.1	1 19.5	8 23.9	24R 24.8	7 51.3	11 34.4	18 08.8	27 03.8
3 W	6 48 58	12 12 40	4♋57 36	11♋42 07	19 33.7	18 28.0	9 41.6	28 33.7	19 52.6	1 39.8	8 36.2	24 22.0	7 55.8	11 36.5	18 10.7	27 06.0
4 Th	6 52 54	13 13 49	18 22 21	24 58 03	19 30.5	18 16.7	11 17.6	29 48.9	20 36.1	2 00.3	8 48.4	24 19.0	8 00.3	11 38.6	18 12.6	27 08.2
5 F	6 56 51	14 14 57	1♌29 00	7♌55 09	19 27.4	18 06.8	12 54.0	1♒04.1	21 19.7	2 20.8	9 00.5	24 15.9	8 04.8	11 40.8	18 14.6	27 10.3
6 Sa	7 00 47	15 16 05	14 16 31	20 33 14	19 24.2	17 59.3	14 30.8	2 19.2	22 03.3	2 41.4	9 12.6	24 12.7	8 09.3	11 43.0	18 16.5	27 12.5
7 Su	7 04 44	16 17 13	26 45 32	2♍53 43	19 21.0	17 54.3	16 08.0	3 34.4	22 46.9	3 02.1	9 24.6	24 09.5	8 13.9	11 45.2	18 18.5	27 14.6
8 M	7 08 40	17 18 21	8♍58 12	14 59 27	19 17.8	17D 52.0	17 45.6	4 49.5	23 30.6	3 22.8	9 36.5	24 06.2	8 18.4	11 47.5	18 20.5	27 16.7
9 Tu	7 12 37	18 19 29	20 58 00	26 54 25	19 14.7	17 51.6	19 23.5	6 04.6	24 14.3	3 43.7	9 48.4	24 02.7	8 23.0	11 49.8	18 22.6	27 18.8
10 W	7 16 34	19 20 38	2♎49 20	8♎43 25	19 11.5	17 52.3	21 01.9	7 19.7	24 58.1	4 04.7	10 00.2	23 59.2	8 27.6	11 52.2	18 24.6	27 21.0
11 Th	7 20 30	20 21 46	14 37 20	20 31 45	19 08.3	17R 53.2	22 40.8	8 34.8	25 41.9	4 25.7	10 11.9	23 55.7	8 32.3	11 54.6	18 26.6	27 23.0
12 F	7 24 27	21 22 54	26 27 23	2♏24 54	19 05.1	17 53.2	24 20.0	9 49.9	26 25.8	4 46.8	10 23.6	23 52.0	8 36.9	11 57.1	18 28.7	27 25.1
13 Sa	7 28 23	22 24 02	8♏24 56	14 28 08	19 02.0	17 51.5	25 59.7	11 04.9	27 09.7	5 08.0	10 35.2	23 48.3	8 41.6	11 59.5	18 30.8	27 27.2
14 Su	7 32 20	23 25 11	20 35 05	26 46 16	18 58.8	17 47.8	27 39.8	12 20.0	27 53.6	5 29.3	10 46.7	23 44.5	8 46.3	12 02.0	18 32.9	27 29.3
15 M	7 36 16	24 26 19	3♐02 10	9♐23 09	18 55.6	17 41.7	29 20.4	13 35.0	28 37.6	5 50.7	10 58.2	23 40.6	8 51.0	12 04.6	18 35.0	27 31.3
16 Tu	7 40 13	25 27 27	15 49 28	22 21 16	18 52.4	17 33.8	1♒01.3	14 50.1	29 21.6	6 12.1	11 09.6	23 36.6	8 55.7	12 07.2	18 37.1	27 33.3
17 W	7 44 09	26 28 34	28 58 37	5♑41 26	18 49.3	17 24.8	2 42.7	16 05.1	0♑05.7	6 33.7	11 20.9	23 32.6	9 00.4	12 09.8	18 39.3	27 35.4
18 Th	7 48 06	27 29 42	12♑29 30	19 22 29	18 46.1	17 15.5	4 24.4	17 20.1	0 49.8	6 55.3	11 32.1	23 28.5	9 05.1	12 12.5	18 41.4	27 37.4
19 F	7 52 03	28 30 49	26 19 58	3♒21 24	18 42.9	17 07.1	6 06.5	18 35.0	1 33.9	7 16.9	11 43.2	23 24.4	9 09.9	12 15.1	18 43.6	27 39.4
20 Sa	7 55 59	29 31 55	10♒26 13	17 33 44	18 39.7	17 00.5	7 48.8	19 50.0	2 18.1	7 38.7	11 54.3	23 20.2	9 14.6	12 17.9	18 45.8	27 41.3
21 Su	7 59 56	0♒33 01	24 43 19	1♓54 16	18 36.6	16 56.1	9 31.3	21 05.0	3 02.3	8 00.5	12 05.3	23 15.9	9 19.4	12 20.6	18 48.0	27 43.3
22 M	8 03 52	1 34 05	9♓05 57	16 17 48	18 33.4	16D 54.0	11 14.0	22 19.9	3 46.5	8 22.4	12 16.1	23 11.6	9 24.2	12 23.4	18 50.2	27 45.2
23 Tu	8 07 49	2 35 09	23 29 16	0♈39 54	18 30.2	16 53.9	12 56.7	23 34.8	4 30.8	8 44.3	12 26.9	23 07.2	9 28.9	12 26.2	18 52.4	27 47.1
24 W	8 11 45	3 36 12	7♈49 19	14 57 11	18 27.0	16 55.0	14 39.3	24 49.7	5 15.1	9 06.3	12 37.6	23 02.8	9 33.7	12 29.0	18 54.6	27 49.0
25 Th	8 15 42	4 37 14	22 03 17	29 07 25	18 23.8	16R 56.3	16 21.7	26 04.5	5 59.5	9 28.4	12 48.3	22 58.3	9 38.5	12 31.9	18 56.8	27 50.9
26 F	8 19 38	5 38 14	6♉09 25	13♉09 11	18 20.7	16 56.9	18 03.8	27 19.3	6 43.9	9 50.5	12 58.8	22 53.8	9 43.3	12 34.8	18 59.0	27 52.8
27 Sa	8 23 35	6 39 14	20 07 38	27 01 38	18 17.5	16 56.0	19 45.2	28 34.2	7 28.3	10 12.7	13 09.2	22 49.2	9 48.1	12 37.7	19 01.2	27 54.6
28 Su	8 27 32	7 40 13	3♊54 08	10♊44 02	18 14.3	16 53.3	21 25.8	29 48.9	8 12.8	10 34.9	13 19.5	22 44.6	9 52.9	12 40.6	19 03.5	27 56.5
29 M	8 31 28	8 41 10	17 31 14	24 15 36	18 11.1	16 48.8	23 05.4	1♓03.7	8 57.3	10 57.2	13 29.8	22 40.0	9 57.7	12 43.6	19 05.7	27 58.3
30 Tu	8 35 25	9 42 06	0♋57 02	7♋35 23	18 08.0	16 43.0	24 43.5	2 18.4	9 41.8	11 19.6	13 39.9	22 35.3	10 02.5	12 46.6	19 08.0	28 00.1
31 W	8 39 21	10♒43 02	14 10 33	20 42 23	18♓04.8	16♓36.6	26♒19.8	3♓33.1	10♑26.4	11♓42.0	13♐49.9	22♌30.6	10♒07.3	12♓49.6	19♒10.3	28♐01.8

1st of Month

Julian Day # 2454101.5
Obliquity 23°26'26"
SVP 5♓09'40"
GC 26♐56.2
Eris 20♈13.5R

Day	⚴	Day	⚵	Day	⚶
1	1♒33.4	1	22♎32.6	1	13♏03.5
6	3 17.4	6	23 36.5	6	15 20.7
11	5 01.8	11	24 34.4	11	17 35.8
16	6 46.5	16	25 25.9	16	19 48.5
21	8 31.3	21	26 10.4	21	21 58.5
26	10 16.0	26	26 47.5	26	24 05.5
31	12 00.6	31	27 16.8	31	26 09.2

DECLINATION and LATITUDE

Day	☉ Decl	☽ Decl	☽ Lat	☽ 12h Decl	☿ Decl	☿ Lat	♀ Decl	♀ Lat	♂ Decl	♂ Lat	⚳ Decl	⚳ Lat	♃ Decl	♃ Lat	♄ Decl	♄ Lat
1 M	23S03	26N25	4N56	27N31	24S45	1S28	22S15	1S20	23S14	0S18	19S31	8S60	20S59	0N42	14N30	1N12
2 Tu	22 58	28 10	5 02	28 24	24 44	1 32	22 02	1 21	23 19	0 19	19 22	8 58	21 01	0 42	14 31	1 12
3 W	22 53	28 11	4 50	27 32	24 42	1 37	21 48	1 23	23 23	0 19	19 13	8 56	21 03	0 42	14 33	1 13
4 Th	22 47	26 30	4 22	25 07	24 38	1 41	21 33	1 24	23 26	0 20	19 04	8 55	21 05	0 42	14 34	1 13
5 F	22 41	23 25	3 41	21 27	24 33	1 45	21 18	1 25	23 30	0 21	18 55	8 53	21 07	0 42	14 35	1 13
6 Sa	22 34	19 15	2 49	16 51	24 27	1 48	21 02	1 26	23 33	0 21	18 46	8 52	21 09	0 42	14 36	1 13
7 Su	22 27	14 19	1 50	11 40	24 19	1 52	20 46	1 27	23 37	0 22	18 37	8 50	21 11	0 42	14 37	1 13
8 M	22 19	8 56	0 47	6 09	24 09	1 55	20 29	1 28	23 40	0 23	18 28	8 49	21 12	0 42	14 39	1 14
9 Tu	22 11	3 20	0S17	0 29	23 59	1 57	20 11	1 29	23 42	0 23	18 19	8 48	21 14	0 42	14 40	1 14
10 W	22 03	2S20	1 19	5S08	23 46	1 60	19 53	1 30	23 45	0 24	18 10	8 46	21 16	0 42	14 41	1 14
11 Th	21 54	7 53	2 18	10 35	23 32	2 02	19 35	1 31	23 47	0 25	18 01	8 45	21 18	0 42	14 43	1 14
12 F	21 45	13 11	3 12	15 41	23 17	2 03	19 15	1 31	23 49	0 25	17 52	8 43	21 19	0 42	14 44	1 14
13 Sa	21 35	18 03	3 57	20 16	22 60	2 05	18 55	1 32	23 51	0 26	17 42	8 42	21 21	0 42	14 45	1 14
14 Su	21 25	22 17	4 33	24 05	22 41	2 06	18 35	1 33	23 52	0 27	17 33	8 41	21 23	0 42	14 47	1 15
15 M	21 14	25 37	4 57	26 51	22 21	2 06	18 14	1 33	23 53	0 27	17 24	8 39	21 24	0 42	14 48	1 15
16 Tu	21 03	27 46	5 06	28 18	21 59	2 06	17 53	1 34	23 54	0 28	17 15	8 38	21 26	0 42	14 50	1 15
17 W	20 52	28 27	5 00	28 10	21 36	2 06	17 31	1 34	23 55	0 29	17 05	8 37	21 27	0 42	14 51	1 15
18 Th	20 40	27 28	4 38	26 20	21 11	2 05	17 08	1 34	23 56	0 29	16 56	8 36	21 29	0 42	14 53	1 15
19 F	20 28	24 27	3 58	22 51	20 45	2 04	16 45	1 34	23 56	0 30	16 47	8 34	21 30	0 42	14 54	1 15
20 Sa	20 15	20 34	3 04	17 59	20 17	2 02	16 22	1 35	23 56	0 31	16 38	8 33	21 32	0 42	14 56	1 16
21 Su	20 02	15 07	1 57	12 03	19 47	1 60	15 58	1 35	23 56	0 31	16 28	8 32	21 33	0 42	14 57	1 16
22 M	19 49	8 49	0 42	5 27	19 17	1 57	15 34	1 35	23 55	0 32	16 18	8 31	21 35	0 42	14 59	1 16
23 Tu	19 35	2 02	0N36	1N24	18 44	1 53	15 09	1 35	23 54	0 33	16 09	8 30	21 36	0 42	15 01	1 16
24 W	19 21	4N48	1 51	8 08	18 11	1 49	14 44	1 35	23 53	0 33	15 60	8 28	21 37	0 42	15 02	1 16
25 Th	19 07	11 21	2 59	14 25	17 35	1 44	14 19	1 34	23 52	0 34	15 50	8 27	21 39	0 42	15 04	1 16
26 F	18 52	17 16	3 55	19 53	16 59	1 39	13 53	1 34	23 51	0 35	15 41	8 26	21 40	0 42	15 05	1 16
27 Sa	18 37	22 13	4 37	24 14	16 22	1 33	13 26	1 34	23 49	0 35	15 31	8 25	21 41	0 42	15 07	1 17
28 Su	18 21	25 53	5 03	27 09	15 43	1 26	12 60	1 34	23 47	0 36	15 21	8 24	21 43	0 42	15 09	1 17
29 M	18 05	28 00	5 10	28 26	15 03	1 18	12 33	1 33	23 45	0 37	15 12	8 23	21 44	0 42	15 10	1 17
30 Tu	17 49	28 27	5 01	28 03	14 23	1 10	12 06	1 33	23 42	0 37	15 02	8 22	21 45	0 42	15 12	1 17
31 W	17S33	27N15	4N36	26N05	13S42	1S01	11S38	1S32	23S40	0S38	14S53	8S21	21S46	0N42	15N14	1N17

Day	⚷ Decl	⚷ Lat	♅ Decl	♅ Lat	♆ Decl	♆ Lat	♇ Decl	♇ Lat
1	12S06	6N26	7S56	0S45	15S37	0S13	16S32	6N53
6	12 01	6 25	7 52	0 45	15 34	0 13	16 32	6 52
11	11 56	6 25	7 47	0 45	15 31	0 13	16 33	6 52
16	11 51	6 24	7 42	0 45	15 28	0 13	16 33	6 52
21	11 45	6 23	7 37	0 45	15 24	0 14	16 33	6 52
26	11 39	6 23	7 32	0 45	15 21	0 14	16 33	6 52
31	11S33	6N23	7S26	0S44	15S17	0S14	16S33	6N53

Day	⚴ Decl	⚴ Lat	⚵ Decl	⚵ Lat	⚶ Decl	⚶ Lat	Eris Decl	Eris Lat
1	0N33	20N50	6S02	2N57	9S58	6N04	5S20	14S17
6	0 33	20 29	6 10	3 14	10 32	6 10	5 20	14 16
11	0 36	20 10	6 15	3 30	11 04	6 16	5 19	14 15
16	0 41	19 52	6 18	3 48	11 33	6 22	5 18	14 14
21	0 49	19 34	6 16	4 07	11 60	6 29	5 17	14 13
26	0 58	19 18	6 12	4 26	12 24	6 36	5 16	14 12
31	1N09	19N03	6S03	4N46	12S46	6N43	5S14	14S12

Moon Phenomena

Max/0 Decl
dy hr mn
2 12:00 28N23
9 14:05 0 S
16 22:17 28S27
23 7:07 0 N
29 18:29 28N30

Max/0 Lat
dy hr mn
1 19:37 5N02
8 17:45 0 S
16 3:05 5S06
22 13:00 0 N
28 22:52 5N10

Perigee/Apogee
dy hr m kilometers
10 16:30 a 404333
22 12:33 p 366927

PH dy hr mn
○ 3 13:59 12♋48
☾ 11 12:46 20♎54
● 19 4:02 28♑41
☽ 25 23:03 5♉36

Void of Course Moon

Last Aspect	☽ Ingress
2 10:07 ♇ ☍	♋ 2 15:15
3 13:59 ☉ ☍	♌ 4 21:15
7 0:57 ♇ △	♍ 7 6:19
9 12:52 ♇ □	♎ 9 18:16
12 1:57 ♇ ⚹	♏ 12 7:09
14 15:51 ☿ ⚹	♐ 14 18:12
16 21:30 ♇ ☌	♑ 17 1:50
19 4:02 ☉ ☌	♒ 19 6:17
21 5:02 ♇ ⚹	♓ 21 8:49
23 7:12 ♇ □	♈ 23 10:53
25 9:51 ♇ △	♉ 25 13:30
27 16:09 ♀ □	♊ 27 17:11
29 18:41 ♇ ☍	♋ 29 22:17

DAILY ASPECTARIAN

1 M: ☽△⚷ 0:38; ☽☍♃ 1:22; ☉⊼☽ 5:08; ☽Q♀ 6:54; ☽□♅ 7:08; ♀∠♅ 9:29; ☽△♆ 18:32; ♀⊻♇ 19:09; ☽☍♂ 20:05; ☿⊻⚷ 20:10

2 Tu: ☽Q⚷ 2:45; ☿⊻♃ 5:12; ☽⚹♄ 5:26; ☉⚹♅ 9:17; ☽☍♇ 10:07; ☽⊼♀ 11:35; ☽△⚳ 18:02; ☿Q♄ 19:14; ☽Q♆ 20:50

3 W: ☽⊼⚷ 5:18; ☽⊼♃ 6:34; ☽∠♄ 7:48; ☽☍☿ 9:33; ☽△♅ 11:52; ☉☍☽ 13:59; ☽Q⚳ 21:28; ☽⊼♆ 23:42

4 Th: ♀ ♒ 3:32; ☽⊼♂ 4:17; ☿⚹♅ 5:20; ☽Q♃ 10:02; ☽⊻♄ 10:46; ☽Q♅ 15:07; ☽#☿ 16:01; ☽⊼♇ 16:01; ☽☍♀ 23:09; ☽#♂ 23:28

5 F: ☽⊼⚳ 1:39; ☉#☽ 4:49; ☽Q♂ 9:34; ☽☍⚷ 12:23; ☽#♀ 13:39; ☽#♃ 13:47; ☽△♃ 14:16; ♀∥♃ 15:32; ☽⊼♅ 19:08; ☽Q♇ 20:04

6 Sa: ☽⊼☿ 0:31; ☉⊼☽ 2:03; ☽#⚳ 2:33; ☽☍♆ 7:39; ♀⊻⚳ 9:45; ☽#♇ 13:33; ☽△♂ 15:49; ☽#♆ 18:14; ☽☌♄ 18:59; ☽∥♄ 22:37

7 Su: ☽△♇ 0:57; ☉☌☿ 6:06; ☉Q☽ 9:39; ☽Q☿ 9:51; ☽#⚷ 10:35; ☽☍⚳ 12:38; ☽⊼♀ 14:52; ♂∠⚷ 16:32; ☽⊼⚷ 22:41

8 M: ☽□♃ 1:17; ☽#♅ 4:47; ☽☍♅ 5:38; ☿⊻♆ 8:46; ☿∠⚳ 11:37; ♂△♄ 18:06; ☉△☽ 18:11; ☽⊼♆ 18:46; ☽△☿ 20:20

9 Tu: ☽Q♀ 0:15; ☉⊻♆ 1:15; ☽Q⚷ 4:54; ☽⊻♄ 6:11; ☽□♂ 7:02; ☽□♇ 12:52; ☉∠⚳ 14:28

10 W: ☽Q♆ 1:12; ☿∥♂ 2:10; ☽⊼⚳ 2:38; ☽△♀ 10:15; ☽△⚷ 11:32; ☽∠♄ 12:28; ☽⚹♃ 14:51; ☽⊼♅ 18:28; ♀☌⚷ 23:09; ☽∥♅ 23:33

11 Th: ☽△♆ 7:47; ☽Q⚳ 10:04; ☉□☽ 12:46; ☿⊼♄ 17:29; ☽∥⚷ 18:07; ☽⚹♄ 18:47; ☽□☿ 19:01; ☽∠♃ 21:49; ☽⚹♂ 23:57

12 F: ☽Q♅ 1:00; ☽⚹♇ 1:57; ☽#♄ 7:24; ☽∥♆ 11:05; ♀⚹♃ 12:46; ☽∥♇ 16:17; ☽△⚳ 17:15; ☿∠♃ 17:20; ☽∥⚳ 22:16

13 Sa: ☽□⚷ 0:33; ☽∥♀ 4:17; ☽⊻♃ 4:23; ☽□♀ 5:55; ☽△♅ 7:08; ☽∠♂ 7:55; ☽∠♇ 8:02; ♂☌♇ 10:03; ☿∠♅ 14:43; ♀⊻♅ 18:04; ☽∥♃ 18:26; ☉∥☽ 18:53; ☽□♆ 20:00; ☿⊻♇ 21:25

14 Su: ☽∥☿ 2:21; ♀∠♇ 3:03; ☉∥♃ 4:07; ☿⊻♂ 5:51; ☉⚹☽ 6:01; ☽□♄ 6:06; ☉⊼♄ 7:07; ☽∥♂ 10:35; ☽⊻♇ 13:25; ☽⊻♂ 15:03; ☽⚹☿ 15:51

15 M: ♀∠♂ 1:59; ☽□⚳ 5:29; ☿ ♒ 9:26; ☽⚹⚷ 11:04; ☉∠☽ 13:09; ☽☌♃ 15:11; ☽□♅ 17:06; ☽⚹♀ 21:58

16 Tu: ☽∠☿ 0:25; ☽⚹♆ 5:10; ☽△♄ 14:13; ☽∠⚷ 14:57; ☉⊻☽ 19:07; ☉∠♃ 20:17; ♂ ♑ 20:55; ☽☌♇ 21:30

17 W: ☽☌♂ 2:07; ☽∠♀ 4:10; ☽⊻☿ 7:40; ☿∥♃ 8:02; ☽∠♆ 8:24; ☽⚹⚳ 13:55; ☉∠♅ 16:55; ☽Q♄ 16:58; ☽⊻⚷ 17:58; ☽⊻♃ 22:18; ☽⚹♅ 23:30

18 Th: ☉⊻♇ 3:07; ☽⊻♀ 9:18; ☽⊻♆ 10:50; ☽∠⚳ 16:51; ☽⊼♄ 19:00; ♀∥⚳ 21:27

19 F: ☽∠♃ 0:40; ☽∠♅ 1:35; ☽⊻♇ 2:16; ♀☌♆ 2:49; ☉☌☽ 4:02; ☽∥♂ 5:35; ☽⊻♂ 9:27; ♀∥♇ 12:39; ☽☌☿ 18:57; ☽⊻⚳ 19:09; ☽∥♃ 19:12; ☿⊻⚳ 21:00; ☽☌⚷ 21:58

20 Sa: ☽∥☿ 1:34; ☉∥☽ 1:38; ☽⚹♃ 2:31; ☉∥☿ 2:45; ☽⊻♅ 3:09; ☽∠♇ 3:49; ☉ ♒ 11:02; ⚳∥♇ 11:04; ☽∠♂ 12:11; ☽☌♆ 14:03; ☽☌♀ 17:19; ☽∥♇ 18:07; ☽∥⚳ 18:19; ☽∥♀ 20:17; ☿☌⚷ 21:04; ☽☍♄ 21:34; ☽∥♆ 22:50

21 Su: ☽#♄ 0:39; ☽⚹♇ 5:02; ☉⊻☽ 10:29; ☽∥⚷ 13:09; ☽⚹♂ 14:39; ☽☌⚳ 22:45

22 M: ☽⊻⚷ 0:31; ♂∠♆ 2:04; ☽⊻☿ 4:02; ☽∥♅ 4:23; ☽□♃ 5:21; ☽☌♅ 5:30; ♀∥♆ 10:13; ☉∠☽ 13:24; ♀☍♄ 15:39; ☿⚹♃ 16:14; ☽⊻♆ 16:17; ☿⊻♅ 16:40; ♃□♅ 21:43; ☿∠♇ 21:44; ☽⊼♄ 23:23

23 Tu: ☽⊻♀ 0:10; ☽∠⚷ 1:40; ☽□♇ 7:12; ♀#♄ 7:44; ☽∠☿ 8:27; ☉⚹☽ 16:23; ☽∠♆ 17:25; ☽□♂ 19:27

24 W: ☽Q♄ 0:23; ☽⊻⚳ 2:13; ☽⚹⚷ 2:56; ☽∠♀ 3:42; ☽⊻♅ 7:52; ☽△♃ 8:11; ☽#♅ 9:53; ☽⚹☿ 13:04; ☽⚹♆ 18:44

25 Th: ☽#⚷ 1:13; ☽△♄ 1:33; ☽∠⚳ 4:13; ☽⚹♀ 7:29; ☽∠♅ 9:19; ☽△♇ 9:51; ☽Q♃ 9:53; ☽#♀ 10:47; ⚳⊻⚷ 14:00; ☽∥♄ 14:42; ☽#♆ 15:50; ☽#⚳ 17:22; ☽#♇ 20:52; ☽#☿ 22:52; ☉□☽ 23:03

26 F: ☽△♂ 1:02; ☽□⚷ 6:08; ☽⚹⚳ 6:29; ☉#☽ 6:49; ♀⚹♇ 11:00; ☽⚹♅ 11:03; ☽Q♇ 11:33; ☽⊼♃ 11:51; ☿☌♆ 13:21; ☿∥♇ 16:46; ☽#♃ 21:07; ☽□♆ 22:07; ☽□☿ 23:18

27 Sa: ☽Q♂ 4:19; ☽□♄ 4:40; ☽#♂ 9:18; ♂Q♄ 10:15; ☽⊼♇ 13:34; ☽□♀ 16:09

28 Su: ♀ ♓ 3:33; ⚳∥♆ 5:19; ☉△☽ 7:08; ☽⊼♂ 8:00; ☽△⚷ 10:34; ☽□⚳ 12:04; ☿∥♆ 14:28; ☽□♅ 15:29; ☽☍♃ 16:47; ☿∥⚳ 17:09; ☿☍♄ 18:08; ☿#♄ 19:56

29 M: ☽△♆ 2:48; ⚳#♄ 3:29; ☽⚹♄ 9:06; ☽△☿ 11:17; ☉Q☽ 11:52; ☽Q⚷ 13:20; ☽☍♇ 18:41; ☿∠♂ 23:15; ☉⊻♂ 23:33

30 Tu: ☽△♀ 2:42; ☽Q♆ 5:45; ☉☌⚷ 8:42; ☽∠♄ 11:56; ♂⊻⚷ 12:28; ☽⊼⚷ 16:33; ☽☍♂ 16:46; ☉⊼☽ 17:10; ☽Q☿ 18:05; ☽△⚳ 19:21; ☽△♅ 21:32; ☽⊼♃ 23:22

31 W: ♀∥⚷ 4:10; ☽Q♀ 8:53; ☽⊼♆ 9:12; ☽⊻♄ 15:14; ☽Q⚳ 23:48

February 2007

LONGITUDE

Day	Sid.Time	☉	☽	☽ 12 hour	Mean ☊	True ☊	☿	♀	♂	⚳	♃	♄	⚷	♅	♆	♇
	h m s	° ' "	° ' "	° ' "	° '	° '	° '	° '	° '	° '	° '	° '	° '	° '	° '	° '
1 Th	8 43 18	11♒43 56	27♋10 49	3♌35 47	18♓01.6	16♓30.4	27♒53.9	4♓47.8	11♑11.0	12♓04.5	13♐59.9	22♌25.9	10♒12.1	12♓52.7	19♒12.5	28♐03.6
2 F	8 47 14	12 44 48	9♌57 12	16 15 07	17 58.4	16R 25.0	29 25.2	6 02.4	11 55.6	12 27.0	14 09.7	22R 21.1	10 16.9	12 55.8	19 14.8	28 05.3
3 Sa	8 51 11	13 45 40	22 29 33	28 40 36	17 55.3	16 21.1	0♓53.4	7 17.0	12 40.3	12 49.5	14 19.4	22 16.4	10 21.6	12 58.8	19 17.1	28 07.0
4 Su	8 55 07	14 46 31	4♍48 26	10♍53 16	17 52.1	16D 18.8	2 17.7	8 31.6	13 25.0	13 12.1	14 29.0	22 11.6	10 26.4	13 02.0	19 19.3	28 08.7
5 M	8 59 04	15 47 20	16 55 21	22 55 00	17 48.9	16 18.1	3 37.5	9 46.1	14 09.7	13 34.8	14 38.5	22 06.7	10 31.2	13 05.1	19 21.6	28 10.3
6 Tu	9 03 01	16 48 09	28 52 36	4♎48 34	17 45.7	16 18.8	4 52.1	11 00.6	14 54.5	13 57.5	14 47.9	22 01.9	10 36.0	13 08.2	19 23.9	28 12.0
7 W	9 06 57	17 48 56	10♎43 22	16 37 30	17 42.5	16 20.3	6 00.7	12 15.1	15 39.4	14 20.2	14 57.2	21 57.0	10 40.7	13 11.4	19 26.2	28 13.6
8 Th	9 10 54	18 49 43	22 31 32	28 26 01	17 39.4	16 22.2	7 02.7	13 29.5	16 24.2	14 43.0	15 06.4	21 52.2	10 45.5	13 14.6	19 28.4	28 15.2
9 F	9 14 50	19 50 28	4♏21 34	10♏18 48	17 36.2	16 23.9	7 57.1	14 43.9	17 09.1	15 05.9	15 15.4	21 47.3	10 50.2	13 17.8	19 30.7	28 16.7
10 Sa	9 18 47	20 51 13	16 18 20	22 20 48	17 33.0	16R 24.8	8 43.4	15 58.3	17 54.0	15 28.7	15 24.3	21 42.4	10 55.0	13 21.1	19 33.0	28 18.3
11 Su	9 22 43	21 51 57	28 26 48	4♐36 57	17 29.8	16 24.7	9 20.7	17 12.7	18 39.0	15 51.7	15 33.2	21 37.5	10 59.7	13 24.3	19 35.3	28 19.8
12 M	9 26 40	22 52 39	10♐51 47	17 11 49	17 26.7	16 23.5	9 48.5	18 27.0	19 24.0	16 14.6	15 41.8	21 32.6	11 04.4	13 27.6	19 37.6	28 21.3
13 Tu	9 30 36	23 53 21	23 37 29	0♑09 08	17 23.5	16 21.3	10 06.2	19 41.3	20 09.0	16 37.6	15 50.4	21 27.7	11 09.1	13 30.8	19 39.8	28 22.7
14 W	9 34 33	24 54 01	6♑47 02	13 31 19	17 20.3	16 18.4	10R 13.5	20 55.5	20 54.1	17 00.7	15 58.9	21 22.9	11 13.8	13 34.1	19 42.1	28 24.2
15 Th	9 38 30	25 54 40	20 21 58	27 18 52	17 17.1	16 15.3	10 10.3	22 09.7	21 39.2	17 23.7	16 07.2	21 18.0	11 18.5	13 37.5	19 44.4	28 25.6
16 F	9 42 26	26 55 18	4♒21 43	11♒30 05	17 14.0	16 12.4	9 56.5	23 23.9	22 24.3	17 46.8	16 15.4	21 13.1	11 23.1	13 40.8	19 46.7	28 27.0
17 Sa	9 46 23	27 55 55	18 43 23	26 00 54	17 10.8	16 10.1	9 32.5	24 38.1	23 09.4	18 10.0	16 23.4	21 08.3	11 27.8	13 44.1	19 48.9	28 28.3
18 Su	9 50 19	28 56 30	3♓21 49	10♓45 15	17 07.6	16D 08.8	8 58.9	25 52.2	23 54.6	18 33.2	16 31.4	21 03.5	11 32.4	13 47.5	19 51.2	28 29.7
19 M	9 54 16	29 57 03	18 10 15	25 35 51	17 04.4	16 08.5	8 16.5	27 06.2	24 39.8	18 56.4	16 39.2	20 58.7	11 37.0	13 50.8	19 53.4	28 31.0
20 Tu	9 58 12	0♓57 35	3♈01 07	10♈25 09	17 01.2	16 09.0	7 26.3	28 20.2	25 25.1	19 19.6	16 46.8	20 53.9	11 41.6	13 54.2	19 55.7	28 32.2
21 W	10 02 09	1 58 05	17 47 09	25 06 25	16 58.1	16 10.0	6 29.9	29 34.2	26 10.3	19 42.9	16 54.3	20 49.1	11 46.2	13 57.6	19 57.9	28 33.5
22 Th	10 06 05	2 58 33	2♉22 20	9♉34 25	16 54.9	16 11.1	5 28.6	0♈48.1	26 55.6	20 06.2	17 01.7	20 44.4	11 50.7	14 01.0	20 00.2	28 34.7
23 F	10 10 02	3 59 00	16 42 18	23 45 44	16 51.7	16 12.0	4 24.1	2 02.0	27 40.9	20 29.5	17 08.9	20 39.7	11 55.3	14 04.4	20 02.4	28 35.9
24 Sa	10 13 59	4 59 24	0♊44 34	7♊38 45	16 48.5	16R 12.4	3 18.1	3 15.8	28 26.3	20 52.8	17 16.0	20 35.0	11 59.8	14 07.8	20 04.6	28 37.0
25 Su	10 17 55	5 59 47	14 28 16	21 13 12	16 45.4	16 12.3	2 12.3	4 29.6	29 11.7	21 16.2	17 23.0	20 30.4	12 04.2	14 11.2	20 06.9	28 38.2
26 M	10 21 52	7 00 08	27 53 41	4♋29 53	16 42.2	16 11.8	1 08.3	5 43.3	29 57.1	21 39.6	17 29.8	20 25.8	12 08.7	14 14.6	20 09.1	28 39.3
27 Tu	10 25 48	8 00 26	11♋01 58	17 30 07	16 39.0	16 10.9	0 07.4	6 57.0	0♒42.5	22 03.0	17 36.5	20 21.3	12 13.1	14 18.0	20 11.3	28 40.4
28 W	10 29 45	9♓00 43	23 54 34	0♌15 30	16♓35.8	16♓09.9	29♒10.8	8♈10.6	1♒27.9	22♓26.5	17♐43.0	20♌16.8	12♒17.5	14♓21.4	20♒13.5	28♐41.4

1st of Month

Julian Day #
2454132.5
Obliquity
23°26'27"
SVP 5♓09'34"
GC 26♐56.3
Eris 20♈16.4

Day	⚴	⚵	⚶
1	12♒21.4	27♎21.7	26♏33.5
6	14 05.6	27 41.1	28 32.7
11	15 49.2	27 51.8	0♐27.9
16	17 32.3	27 53.4R	2 18.6
21	19 14.6	27 45.8R	4 04.2
26	20 56.0	27 28.8R	5 44.2

DECLINATION and LATITUDE

Day	☉ Decl	☽ Decl	☽ Lat	☽ 12h Decl	☿ Decl	☿ Lat	♀ Decl	♀ Lat	♂ Decl	♂ Lat	⚳ Decl	⚳ Lat	♃ Decl	♃ Lat	♄ Decl	♄ Lat
1 Th	17S16	24N35	3N56	22N47	12S60	0S51	11S10	1S31	23S37	0S38	14S43	8S20	21S47	0N42	15N15	1N17
2 F	16 59	20 44	3 06	18 28	12 18	0 40	10 42	1 30	23 33	0 39	14 33	8 19	21 48	0 42	15 17	1 17
3 Sa	16 42	16 01	2 07	13 25	11 36	0 28	10 13	1 30	23 30	0 40	14 24	8 18	21 50	0 42	15 19	1 18
4 Su	16 24	10 43	1 03	7 56	10 54	0 16	9 45	1 29	23 26	0 40	14 14	8 17	21 51	0 42	15 20	1 18
5 M	16 06	5 07	0S03	2 15	10 13	0 03	9 16	1 28	23 22	0 41	14 04	8 16	21 52	0 42	15 22	1 18
6 Tu	15 48	0S36	1 09	3S26	9 33	0N11	8 47	1 27	23 18	0 42	13 55	8 15	21 53	0 42	15 24	1 18
7 W	15 30	6 14	2 10	8 59	8 55	0 26	8 17	1 26	23 13	0 42	13 45	8 14	21 54	0 42	15 25	1 18
8 Th	15 11	11 39	3 06	14 12	8 18	0 41	7 47	1 24	23 09	0 43	13 35	8 13	21 55	0 42	15 27	1 18
9 F	14 52	16 39	3 54	18 56	7 43	0 56	7 18	1 23	23 04	0 44	13 25	8 12	21 56	0 42	15 29	1 18
10 Sa	14 33	21 04	4 33	22 59	7 11	1 12	6 48	1 22	22 59	0 44	13 16	8 11	21 57	0 42	15 30	1 18
11 Su	14 13	24 41	4 60	26 07	6 42	1 29	6 17	1 21	22 53	0 45	13 06	8 10	21 58	0 42	15 32	1 18
12 M	13 53	27 15	5 14	28 03	6 16	1 45	5 47	1 19	22 48	0 46	12 56	8 10	21 59	0 42	15 34	1 18
13 Tu	13 34	28 29	5 12	28 32	5 54	2 01	5 16	1 18	22 42	0 46	12 46	8 09	21 59	0 42	15 35	1 19
14 W	13 13	28 11	4 55	27 24	5 37	2 17	4 46	1 16	22 35	0 47	12 37	8 08	22 00	0 42	15 37	1 19
15 Th	12 53	26 12	4 21	24 35	5 24	2 33	4 15	1 14	22 29	0 48	12 27	8 07	22 01	0 42	15 39	1 19
16 F	12 32	22 35	3 31	20 13	5 16	2 47	3 44	1 13	22 22	0 48	12 17	8 06	22 02	0 42	15 40	1 19
17 Sa	12 12	17 31	2 26	14 33	5 12	3 00	3 13	1 11	22 15	0 49	12 07	8 06	22 03	0 42	15 42	1 19
18 Su	11 51	11 22	1 10	7 60	5 14	3 12	2 42	1 09	22 08	0 50	11 57	8 05	22 03	0 42	15 44	1 19
19 M	11 29	4 30	0N11	0 57	5 20	3 23	2 11	1 07	22 01	0 50	11 47	8 04	22 04	0 42	15 45	1 19
20 Tu	11 08	2N37	1 32	6N08	5 31	3 31	1 39	1 05	21 53	0 51	11 38	8 03	22 05	0 42	15 47	1 19
21 W	10 46	9 33	2 46	12 49	5 45	3 37	1 08	1 03	21 46	0 52	11 28	8 03	22 06	0 42	15 48	1 19
22 Th	10 25	15 53	3 49	18 42	6 04	3 42	0 37	1 01	21 38	0 52	11 18	8 02	22 06	0 42	15 50	1 19
23 F	10 03	21 14	4 36	23 27	6 26	3 43	0 05	0 59	21 29	0 53	11 08	8 01	22 07	0 42	15 51	1 19
24 Sa	9 41	25 17	5 06	26 44	6 50	3 43	0N26	0 57	21 21	0 53	10 58	8 01	22 08	0 42	15 53	1 19
25 Su	9 19	27 47	5 17	28 24	7 16	3 40	0 57	0 54	21 12	0 54	10 48	7 60	22 08	0 42	15 55	1 19
26 M	8 56	28 36	5 10	28 23	7 43	3 36	1 29	0 52	21 03	0 55	10 38	7 59	22 09	0 43	15 56	1 19
27 Tu	8 34	27 46	4 48	26 46	8 10	3 29	2 00	0 50	20 54	0 55	10 28	7 59	22 09	0 43	15 58	1 19
28 W	8S11	25N27	4N11	23N48	8S37	3N21	2N31	0S47	20S45	0S56	10S19	7S58	22S10	0N43	15N59	1N20

Day	⚷ Decl	⚷ Lat	♅ Decl	♅ Lat	♆ Decl	♆ Lat	♇ Decl	♇ Lat
1	11S32	6N23	7S25	0S44	15S17	0S14	16S33	6N53
6	11 26	6 23	7 19	0 44	15 13	0 14	16 33	6 53
11	11 19	6 23	7 12	0 44	15 10	0 14	16 32	6 53
16	11 13	6 23	7 06	0 44	15 06	0 14	16 32	6 54
21	11 06	6 24	6 59	0 44	15 03	0 14	16 32	6 54
26	10S59	6N25	6S53	0S44	14S59	0S14	16S31	6N55

Day	⚴ Decl	⚴ Lat	⚵ Decl	⚵ Lat	⚶ Decl	⚶ Lat	Eris Decl	Eris Lat
1	1N12	19N00	6S01	4N50	12S50	6N44	5S14	14S11
6	1 25	18 46	5 49	5 11	13 09	6 51	5 13	14 11
11	1 40	18 33	5 32	5 32	13 25	6 59	5 12	14 10
16	1 57	18 21	5 12	5 54	13 39	7 06	5 10	14 09
21	2 15	18 10	4 48	6 17	13 51	7 14	5 09	14 08
26	2N34	17N59	4S21	6N40	14S00	7N22	5S07	14S07

Moon Phenomena

Max/0 Decl
dy hr mn
5 21:28 0 S
13 7:28 28S34
19 15:12 0 N
25 23:48 28N36

Max/0 Lat
dy hr mn
4 22:46 0 S
12 10:27 5S15
18 20:43 0 N
25 3:00 5N17

Perigee/Apogee
dy hr m kilometers
7 12:40 a 404991
19 9:35 p 361439

PH dy hr mn
○ 2 5:46 12♌59
☾ 10 9:52 21♏16
● 17 16:15 28♒37
☽ 24 7:57 5♊19

Void of Course Moon

Last Aspect			☽ Ingress	
30 21:32	♅	△	♌	1 5:16
3 10:56	♇	△	♍	3 14:35
5 22:38	♇	□	♎	6 2:16
8 11:40	♇	⚹	♏	8 15:11
10 10:40	♄	□	♐	11 3:02
13 8:46	♇	☌	♑	13 11:43
15 3:25	♀	⚹	♒	15 16:36
17 16:15	☉	☌	♓	17 18:31
19 16:44	♇	□	♈	19 19:07
21 17:43	♇	△	♉	21 20:04
23 19:48	♂	△	♊	23 22:43
26 1:23	♇	☍	♋	26 3:49
27 6:04	♅	△	♌	28 11:31

DAILY ASPECTARIAN

1 Th ☽⚼♅ 1:18; ☽⚻☿ 1:31; ☽⚻♇ 1:39; ☿⚹♇ 2:34; ☽⚼♃ 3:26; ☽#♂ 6:50; ☉⚺⚳ 12:50; ♄#♆ 15:01; ☽⚻♀ 15:48; ☽#♃ 17:55

2 F ☽☍⚷ 0:38; ☽⚻♂ 3:59; ☉⚺♅ 4:33; ☽⚻⚳ 4:53; ☽⚻♅ 5:41; ☉☍☽ 5:46; ☽⚼♇ 5:58; ☽△♃ 8:07; ☉∠♇ 8:19; ☿ ♓ 9:21; ☽☍♆ 17:48; ☉#☽ 20:31; ☽#♇ 21:26; ☽☌♄ 23:35

3 Sa ☽∥♄ 3:17; ☽#♆ 3:34; ☿∥⚷ 3:49; ☽#⚳ 7:47; ♂⚹⚳ 10:02; ☽⚼♂ 10:41; ♂⚹♅ 10:42; ☽△♇ 10:56; ⚳☌♅ 11:28; ☉∥♇ 12:19; ☉⚹♃ 15:48; ☽☍☿ 18:27; ☽#⚷ 20:41; ☽#☿ 23:03

4 Su ☽#♀ 4:39; ☽☍♀ 8:10; ☽⚻⚷ 11:11; ☽#♅ 14:35; ☽☍♅ 16:20; ☽☍⚳ 17:08; ☽△♂ 18:08; ☽□♃ 19:24; ☉⚻☽ 21:32

5 M ☽⚻♆ 4:53; ☽⚺♄ 10:19; ♀⚺⚷ 15:31; ☽⚼⚷ 17:21; ♂⚺♃ 19:31; ☽□♇ 22:38

6 Tu ☉⚼☽ 6:28; ☽⚼♆ 11:12; ☽⚻☿ 13:27; ☽∠♄ 16:24; ☽△⚷ 23:55

7 W ☽⚻♀ 3:28; ☽∥♅ 4:33; ☽⚻♅ 5:02; ☉#♄ 5:07; ☽⚻⚳ 7:35; ☽∥♀ 8:11; ☽⚹♃ 8:43; ☽∥☿ 10:29; ☽□♂ 10:42; ☉△☽ 15:47; ☽△♆ 17:47; ♀☌♅ 18:59; ☽⚹♄ 22:40; ☉∥♆ 22:48; ☽∥⚷ 22:50; ☽⚼☿ 22:56

8 Th ☽∥⚳ 8:46; ☽⚹♇ 11:40; ☽⚼♅ 11:40; ☽⚼♀ 13:32; ☽⚼⚳ 15:05; ☽∠♃ 15:35; ☉∥☽ 15:43; ☉☌♆ 15:53; ☽∥♆ 16:45; ☽#♄ 18:08; ☽∥♇ 23:29

9 F ♀∥♅ 2:16; ☽△☿ 7:47; ♀☌⚳ 10:13; ♀□♃ 11:32; ☽□⚷ 13:08; ⚳□♃ 16:27; ☽∠♇ 17:59; ☽△♅ 18:04; ⚶ ♐ 18:30; ☿∥♅ 21:45; ☽⚺♃ 22:11; ☽△⚳ 22:18; ☽△♀ 23:15

10 Sa ☽⚹♂ 3:23; ☽∥♃ 5:21; ☽□♆ 6:29; ☉□☽ 9:52; ☽□♄ 10:40; ☽∥♂ 11:38; ☉☍♄ 18:43; ☽⚺♇ 23:46

11 Su ☽∠♂ 10:47; ☽□☿ 21:55

12 M ☽⚹⚷ 0:24; ☽□♅ 4:58; ♂⚺♆ 7:37; ☽☌♃ 9:17; ☽□⚳ 10:31; ☽□♀ 15:53; ☽⚹♆ 16:36; ☽⚺♂ 17:08; ☽△♄ 20:00; ♀⚺♆ 23:31

13 Tu ☉⚹☽ 0:32; ☽∠⚷ 4:42; ☽☌♇ 8:46; ☽∠♆ 20:15; ♀⚹♂ 22:48; ☽⚼♄ 23:17

14 W ☿ R 4:37; ☉∠☽ 6:01; ☽⚹☿ 6:09; ☽⚺⚷ 7:59; ♀⚻♄ 8:18; ⚵ R 9:49; ☽⚹♅ 12:08; ♂⚻♄ 13:50; ☽⚺♃ 16:30; ☽⚹⚳ 18:40; ☽⚺♆ 22:54

15 Th ☽⚻♄ 1:37; ☽☌♂ 2:22; ☽⚹♀ 3:25; ☽∠☿ 8:13; ☉⚺☽ 10:20; ☽⚺♇ 13:56; ☽∠♅ 14:18; ☽∠♃ 18:41; ☽∠⚳ 21:15

16 F ☽∥♂ 1:09; ☽∥♃ 2:56; ☽∠♀ 7:27; ☽⚺☿ 9:10; ☽☌⚷ 11:52; ☽∠♇ 15:16; ☽⚺♅ 15:42; ☽⚹♃ 20:06; ☽⚺⚳ 23:03

17 Sa ☽☌♆ 1:49; ☽☍♄ 3:58; ☽∥♇ 4:07; ☽#♄ 7:28; ☽⚺♂ 7:42; ☉∥⚳ 9:48; ☽∥♆ 9:56; ☽⚺♀ 10:38; ☉⚹♇ 13:08; ☽⚹♇ 16:03; ☉☌☽ 16:15; ☽∥⚳ 21:47; ☉∥☽ 22:08

18 Su ☽∥⚷ 0:42; ☿∠♂ 1:14; ☽☌☿ 8:44; ☽∠♂ 9:30; ☽⚺⚷ 13:21; ♀∠⚷ 13:55; ♂∥♃ 14:37; ☽∥♅ 15:18; ☽☌♅ 16:59; ☽∥☿ 21:14; ☽□♃ 21:31

19 M ☉ ♓ 1:10; ☽☌⚳ 1:17; ☽⚺♆ 2:47; ☽⚻♄ 4:31; ☽∥♀ 8:30; ☽⚹♂ 11:03; ☽∠⚷ 13:43; ☽☌♀ 15:45; ☽□♇ 16:44; ☉⚺☽ 20:26; ☽#♀ 21:00

20 Tu ☉∥⚷ 0:38; ☽∠♆ 3:06; ♀□♇ 3:58; ☽⚼♄ 4:38; ☽⚺☿ 6:45; ☽#☿ 10:13; ☽⚹⚷ 14:09; ☽#♅ 15:02; ☽⚺♅ 17:44; ☽△♃ 22:33; ☉∠☽ 22:34

21 W ☽⚺⚳ 3:14; ☽⚹♆ 3:34; ☉#☽ 4:13; ☽△♄ 4:56; ☽#⚷ 5:38; ☽∠☿ 5:41; ☽#⚳ 6:48; ♀ ♈ 8:22; ☽□♂ 14:30; ⚳⚺♆ 17:10; ☽△♇ 17:43; ☽∠♅ 18:25; ☽#♆ 20:37; ☽⚺♀ 21:09; ☽⚼♃ 23:26; ☽∥♄ 23:49

22 Th ☉⚹☽ 1:05; ☽#♇ 2:39; ☽∠⚳ 4:40; ☽⚹☿ 4:48; ☽□⚷ 15:54; ☽⚼♇ 18:45; ☽⚹♅ 19:32

23 F ☽∠♀ 0:37; ☽⚻♃ 0:45; ☽#♂ 1:15; ☽#♃ 4:35; ☉☌☿ 4:47; ☽□♆ 5:40; ☽⚹⚳ 6:36; ☽□♄ 6:41; ⚳⚻♄ 8:45; ⚳∥⚷ 12:32; ☽△♂ 19:48; ☽⚻♇ 20:20

24 Sa ☿⚺♀ 0:24; ☽□☿ 4:06; ☽⚹♀ 4:48; ☿∥♅ 5:17; ♂⚺♇ 5:50; ☉□☽ 7:57; ☽△⚷ 19:44; ☽⚼♂ 23:29; ☽□♅ 23:30; ♂∠♅ 23:43

25 Su ☽☍♃ 5:12; ☽△♆ 10:03; ☽⚹♄ 10:40; ☽□⚳ 12:27; ♀∠♆ 12:30; ♀⚼♄ 18:38; ☽⚼⚷ 22:38

26 M ☽☍♇ 1:23; ♂ ♒ 1:33; ☽⚻♂ 3:57; ☽△☿ 5:27; ☽⚼♆ 13:14; ☽∠♄ 13:38; ☽□♀ 15:43; ☿⚺♂ 15:59; ☉△☽ 17:58

27 Tu ☽⚻⚷ 2:12; ☿R♒ 3:02; ☽△♅ 6:04; ☽⚼☿ 7:03; ☉∥☿ 11:30; ☽⚻♃ 12:18; ☽⚻♆ 17:04; ☽⚺♄ 17:14; ☽△⚳ 21:09

28 W ☉⚼☽ 0:13; ☽⚻♇ 9:02; ☽⚻☿ 9:18; ☽⚼♅ 10:20; ♄☍♆ 12:02; ☿⚹♇ 13:10; ☽☍♂ 15:12; ☽⚼♃ 16:49; ☽#♃ 22:22

LONGITUDE — March 2007

Day	Sid.Time	☉	☽	☽ 12 hour	Mean ☊	True ☊	☿	♀	♂	⚳	♃	♄	⚷	♅	♆	♇
	h m s	° ' "	° ' "	° ' "	° '	° '	° '	° '	° '	° '	° '	° '	° '	° '	° '	° '
1 Th	10 33 41	10♓00 58	6♌33 09	12♌47 41	16♓32.6	16♓09.0	28♒19.5	9♈24.2	2♒13.4	22♓49.9	17♐49.3	20♌12.3	12♒21.9	14♓24.9	20♒15.6	28♐42.4
2 F	10 37 38	11 01 10	18 59 18	25 08 14	16 29.5	16R 08.3	27R 34.2	10 37.7	2 58.9	23 13.4	17 55.5	20R 07.9	12 26.2	14 28.3	20 17.8	28 43.4
3 Sa	10 41 34	12 01 21	1♍14 38	7♍18 44	16 26.3	16 07.9	26 55.4	11 51.2	3 44.4	23 36.9	18 01.6	20 03.6	12 30.6	14 31.8	20 20.0	28 44.3
4 Su	10 45 31	13 01 30	13 20 43	19 20 49	16 23.1	16D 07.7	26 23.4	13 04.6	4 29.9	24 00.4	18 07.5	19 59.3	12 34.9	14 35.2	20 22.1	28 45.3
5 M	10 49 28	14 01 37	25 19 14	1♎16 15	16 19.9	16 07.8	25 58.4	14 17.9	5 15.5	24 23.9	18 13.2	19 55.0	12 39.1	14 38.6	20 24.2	28 46.1
6 Tu	10 53 24	15 01 42	7♎12 07	13 07 08	16 16.8	16 07.9	25 40.4	15 31.2	6 01.1	24 47.5	18 18.8	19 50.8	12 43.3	14 42.1	20 26.4	28 47.0
7 W	10 57 21	16 01 46	19 01 37	24 55 55	16 13.6	16R 07.9	25 29.2	16 44.4	6 46.7	25 11.0	18 24.3	19 46.7	12 47.5	14 45.5	20 28.5	28 47.8
8 Th	11 01 17	17 01 48	0♏50 25	6♏45 32	16 10.4	16 07.9	25D 24.7	17 57.6	7 32.3	25 34.6	18 29.5	19 42.6	12 51.7	14 48.9	20 30.6	28 48.6
9 F	11 05 14	18 01 48	12 41 42	18 39 23	16 07.2	16 07.7	25 26.6	19 10.7	8 18.0	25 58.2	18 34.6	19 38.6	12 55.8	14 52.4	20 32.6	28 49.4
10 Sa	11 09 10	19 01 47	24 39 06	0♐41 20	16 04.0	16 07.4	25 34.6	20 23.8	9 03.7	26 21.8	18 39.6	19 34.7	12 59.9	14 55.8	20 34.7	28 50.1
11 Su	11 13 07	20 01 44	6♐46 38	12 55 32	16 00.9	16 07.1	25 48.4	21 36.7	9 49.4	26 45.4	18 44.4	19 30.8	13 04.0	14 59.2	20 36.8	28 50.8
12 M	11 17 03	21 01 39	19 08 35	25 26 19	15 57.7	16D 07.0	26 07.7	22 49.7	10 35.1	27 09.0	18 49.0	19 27.0	13 08.0	15 02.7	20 38.8	28 51.5
13 Tu	11 21 00	22 01 33	1♑49 14	8♑17 47	15 54.5	16 07.1	26 32.1	24 02.5	11 20.9	27 32.6	18 53.4	19 23.3	13 12.0	15 06.1	20 40.8	28 52.1
14 W	11 24 57	23 01 25	14 52 25	21 33 26	15 51.3	16 07.5	27 01.4	25 15.4	12 06.7	27 56.3	18 57.7	19 19.6	13 16.0	15 09.5	20 42.8	28 52.7
15 Th	11 28 53	24 01 15	28 21 05	5♒15 30	15 48.2	16 08.1	27 35.1	26 28.1	12 52.5	28 19.9	19 01.8	19 16.1	13 19.9	15 12.9	20 44.8	28 53.3
16 F	11 32 50	25 01 04	12♒16 40	19 24 24	15 45.0	16 08.9	28 13.1	27 40.8	13 38.3	28 43.6	19 05.8	19 12.6	13 23.7	15 16.3	20 46.8	28 53.8
17 Sa	11 36 46	26 00 51	26 38 24	3♓58 07	15 41.8	16 09.6	28 55.1	28 53.4	14 24.1	29 07.3	19 09.5	19 09.2	13 27.6	15 19.7	20 48.8	28 54.3
18 Su	11 40 43	27 00 36	11♓22 52	18 51 50	15 38.6	16R 10.0	29 40.8	0♉06.0	15 10.0	29 30.9	19 13.1	19 05.8	13 31.4	15 23.1	20 50.7	28 54.8
19 M	11 44 39	28 00 19	26 24 00	3♈58 15	15 35.4	16 09.9	0♓29.9	1 18.4	15 55.8	29 54.6	19 16.5	19 02.6	13 35.1	15 26.5	20 52.6	28 55.3
20 Tu	11 48 36	29 00 00	11♈33 24	19 08 15	15 32.3	16 09.2	1 22.3	2 30.9	16 41.7	0♈18.3	19 19.7	18 59.4	13 38.8	15 29.9	20 54.5	28 55.7
21 W	11 52 32	29 59 39	26 41 36	4♉12 18	15 29.1	16 07.8	2 17.8	3 43.2	17 27.6	0 42.0	19 22.8	18 56.3	13 42.5	15 33.3	20 56.4	28 56.0
22 Th	11 56 29	0♈59 16	11♉39 21	19 01 51	15 25.9	16 06.0	3 16.1	4 55.5	18 13.5	1 05.7	19 25.7	18 53.3	13 46.1	15 36.6	20 58.3	28 56.4
23 F	12 00 25	1 58 51	26 19 05	3♊30 29	15 22.7	16 04.1	4 17.2	6 07.7	18 59.4	1 29.3	19 28.4	18 50.4	13 49.7	15 39.9	21 00.1	28 56.7
24 Sa	12 04 22	2 58 23	10♊35 42	17 34 32	15 19.6	16 02.4	5 20.8	7 19.8	19 45.3	1 53.0	19 30.9	18 47.6	13 53.2	15 43.3	21 01.9	28 57.0
25 Su	12 08 19	3 57 53	24 26 55	1♋12 57	15 16.4	16D 01.4	6 26.9	8 31.8	20 31.2	2 16.7	19 33.2	18 44.9	13 56.7	15 46.6	21 03.7	28 57.2
26 M	12 12 15	4 57 21	7♋52 50	14 26 51	15 13.2	16 01.2	7 35.2	9 43.8	21 17.2	2 40.4	19 35.3	18 42.2	14 00.2	15 49.9	21 05.5	28 57.4
27 Tu	12 16 12	5 56 47	20 55 22	27 18 47	15 10.0	16 01.8	8 45.8	10 55.7	22 03.1	3 04.1	19 37.3	18 39.7	14 03.5	15 53.2	21 07.3	28 57.6
28 W	12 20 08	6 56 10	3♌37 34	9♌52 08	15 06.8	16 03.1	9 58.5	12 07.5	22 49.1	3 27.7	19 39.1	18 37.3	14 06.9	15 56.5	21 09.0	28 57.8
29 Th	12 24 05	7 55 31	16 02 58	22 10 30	15 03.7	16 04.7	11 13.2	13 19.2	23 35.0	3 51.4	19 40.7	18 34.9	14 10.2	15 59.7	21 10.7	28 57.9
30 F	12 28 01	8 54 49	28 15 10	4♍17 24	15 00.5	16 06.2	12 29.8	14 30.8	24 21.0	4 15.0	19 42.1	18 32.7	14 13.4	16 03.0	21 12.4	28 58.0
31 Sa	12 31 58	9♈54 05	10♍17 35	16 16 03	14♓57.3	16♓07.1	13♓48.3	15♉42.3	25♒07.7	4♈38.7	19♐43.3	18♌30.5	14♒16.6	16♓06.2	21♒14.1	28♐58.0

1st of Month

Julian Day # 2454160.5
Obliquity 23°26'27"
SVP 5♓09'30"
GC 26♐56.4
Eris 20♈27.4

Day	⚴		Day	⚵		Day	⚶
1	21♒56.3		1	27♎14.2R		1	6♐41.4
6	23 35.9		6	26 42.6R		6	8 11.5
11	25 14.3		11	26 02.4R		11	9 34.7
16	26 51.4		16	25 14.0R		16	10 50.3
21	28 26.8		21	24 18.4R		21	11 57.5
26	0♓00.6		26	23 16.9R		26	12 55.5
31	1 32.4		31	22 10.7R		31	13 43.8

DECLINATION and LATITUDE

Day	☉ Decl	☽ Decl	☽ Lat	☽12h Decl	☿ Decl	☿ Lat	♀ Decl	♀ Lat	♂ Decl	♂ Lat	⚳ Decl	⚳ Lat	♃ Decl	♃ Lat	♄ Decl	♄ Lat
1 Th	7S49	21N54	3N23	19N46	9S04	3N11	3N03	0S45	20S35	0S57	10S09	7S57	22S11	0N43	16N00	1N20
2 F	7 26	17 26	2 25	14 56	9 30	2 60	3 34	0 42	20 25	0 57	9 59	7 57	22 12	0 43	16 02	1 20
3 Sa	7 03	12 18	1 22	9 35	9 55	2 48	4 05	0 39	20 15	0 58	9 49	7 56	22 12	0 43	16 03	1 20
4 Su	6 40	6 47	0 15	3 57	10 18	2 35	4 36	0 37	20 05	0 58	9 39	7 56	22 12	0 43	16 05	1 20
5 M	6 17	1 05	0S51	1S47	10 39	2 21	5 07	0 34	19 55	0 59	9 29	7 55	22 13	0 43	16 06	1 20
6 Tu	5 54	4S37	1 54	7 24	10 58	2 07	5 38	0 31	19 44	0 60	9 19	7 54	22 13	0 43	16 07	1 20
7 W	5 31	10 07	2 53	12 45	11 15	1 53	6 08	0 29	19 33	1 00	9 10	7 54	22 13	0 43	16 09	1 20
8 Th	5 07	15 16	3 44	17 38	11 29	1 39	6 39	0 26	19 22	1 01	8 60	7 53	22 14	0 43	16 10	1 20
9 F	4 44	19 51	4 25	21 53	11 42	1 25	7 09	0 23	19 11	1 02	8 50	7 53	22 14	0 43	16 11	1 20
10 Sa	4 21	23 42	4 56	25 17	11 52	1 11	7 40	0 20	18 59	1 02	8 40	7 52	22 15	0 43	16 13	1 20
11 Su	3 57	26 35	5 13	27 35	12 01	0 58	8 10	0 17	18 48	1 03	8 30	7 52	22 15	0 43	16 14	1 20
12 M	3 33	28 16	5 17	28 35	12 07	0 44	8 40	0 14	18 36	1 03	8 20	7 51	22 15	0 43	16 15	1 20
13 Tu	3 10	28 31	5 06	28 04	12 11	0 31	9 09	0 11	18 24	1 04	8 11	7 51	22 16	0 43	16 16	1 20
14 W	2 46	27 13	4 39	25 58	12 13	0 18	9 39	0 08	18 12	1 04	8 01	7 51	22 16	0 43	16 17	1 20
15 Th	2 22	24 20	3 55	22 19	12 13	0 06	10 08	0 05	17 59	1 05	7 51	7 50	22 16	0 43	16 18	1 20
16 F	1 59	19 57	2 57	17 16	12 11	0S06	10 37	0 02	17 47	1 06	7 41	7 50	22 17	0 43	16 20	1 20
17 Sa	1 35	14 18	1 46	11 06	12 07	0 17	11 06	0N01	17 34	1 06	7 31	7 49	22 17	0 43	16 21	1 20
18 Su	1 11	7 42	0 27	4 11	12 02	0 28	11 35	0 05	17 21	1 07	7 22	7 49	22 17	0 43	16 22	1 20
19 M	0 48	0 34	0N56	3N04	11 54	0 39	12 03	0 08	17 08	1 07	7 12	7 49	22 17	0 43	16 23	1 20
20 Tu	0 24	6N40	2 16	10 09	11 45	0 49	12 31	0 11	16 55	1 08	7 02	7 48	22 18	0 43	16 24	1 20
21 W	0 00	13 30	3 26	16 37	11 34	0 59	12 59	0 14	16 41	1 08	6 52	7 48	22 18	0 43	16 25	1 20
22 Th	0N24	19 28	4 21	21 60	11 22	1 08	13 26	0 17	16 28	1 09	6 43	7 48	22 18	0 43	16 26	1 20
23 F	0 47	24 09	4 58	25 54	11 08	1 17	13 53	0 21	16 14	1 10	6 33	7 47	22 18	0 43	16 26	1 20
24 Sa	1 11	27 14	5 15	28 06	10 52	1 25	14 20	0 24	16 00	1 10	6 23	7 47	22 18	0 43	16 27	1 20
25 Su	1 35	28 32	5 13	28 31	10 35	1 32	14 47	0 27	15 46	1 11	6 14	7 47	22 18	0 44	16 28	1 20
26 M	1 58	28 05	4 54	27 16	10 16	1 40	15 13	0 31	15 32	1 11	6 04	7 46	22 19	0 44	16 29	1 20
27 Tu	2 22	26 05	4 20	24 35	9 56	1 46	15 39	0 34	15 17	1 12	5 54	7 46	22 19	0 44	16 30	1 20
28 W	2 45	22 48	3 34	20 47	9 34	1 52	16 04	0 37	15 03	1 12	5 45	7 46	22 19	0 44	16 30	1 20
29 Th	3 09	18 33	2 38	16 09	9 11	1 58	16 29	0 41	14 48	1 13	5 35	7 45	22 19	0 44	16 31	1 20
30 F	3 32	13 36	1 37	10 57	8 46	2 04	16 54	0 44	14 33	1 13	5 26	7 45	22 19	0 44	16 32	1 20
31 Sa	3N55	8N12	0N32	5N24	8S21	2S08	17N18	0N47	14S19	1S14	5S16	7S45	22S19	0N44	16N32	1N20

Day	⚷ Decl	⚷ Lat	♅ Decl	♅ Lat	♆ Decl	♆ Lat	♇ Decl	♇ Lat
1	10S55	6N25	6S49	0S44	14S57	0S14	16S31	6N55
6	10 49	6 26	6 42	0 44	14 54	0 14	16 30	6 56
11	10 42	6 27	6 36	0 44	14 51	0 14	16 30	6 56
16	10 35	6 28	6 29	0 44	14 47	0 14	16 29	6 57
21	10 29	6 30	6 22	0 44	14 44	0 14	16 28	6 58
26	10 22	6 31	6 16	0 44	14 42	0 14	16 28	6 58
31	10S16	6N33	6S10	0S44	14S39	0S14	16S27	6N59

Day	⚴ Decl	⚴ Lat	⚵ Decl	⚵ Lat	⚶ Decl	⚶ Lat	Eris Decl	Eris Lat
1	2N47	17N53	4S03	6N54	14S05	7N27	5S06	14S07
6	3 08	17 44	3 30	7 17	14 11	7 35	5 05	14 06
11	3 30	17 36	2 55	7 39	14 15	7 43	5 03	14 06
16	3 54	17 28	2 17	8 01	14 17	7 52	5 02	14 05
21	4 18	17 21	1 38	8 23	14 18	7 60	5 00	14 05
26	4 42	17 14	0 57	8 42	14 17	8 08	4 59	14 04
31	5N07	17N09	0S16	9N01	14S15	8N15	4S57	14S04

Moon Phenomena

Max/0 Decl
dy hr mn
5 4:32 0 S
12 16:15 28S36
19 1:53 0 N
25 5:34 28N35

Perigee/Apogee
dy hr m kilometers
7 3:36 a 405853
19 18:49 p 357818

PH dy hr mn
○ 3 23:18 13♍00
◐ 3 23:22 T 1.233
☾ 12 3:55 21♐11
● 19 2:44 28♓07
◐ 19 2:33 P 0.876
☽ 25 18:17 4♋43

Max/0 Lat
dy hr mn
4 5:33 0 S
11 18:12 5S18
18 7:41 0 N
24 9:18 5N16
31 11:42 0 S

Void of Course Moon

Last Aspect			☽ Ingress	
2 19:04	♇	△	♍	2 21:33
5 6:57	♇	□	♎	5 9:26
7 19:52	♇	✱	♏	7 22:18
10 1:52	☿	□	♐	10 10:38
12 18:28	♇	☌	♑	12 20:36
14 20:22	♀	□	♒	15 2:53
17 4:02	♀	✱	♓	17 5:31
19 4:00	♇	□	♈	19 5:43
21 3:34	♇	△	♉	21 5:16
22 15:13	♆	□	♊	23 6:07
25 7:58	♇	☍	♋	25 9:50
26 14:37	♅	△	♌	27 17:05
30 1:25	♇	△	♍	30 3:28

DAILY ASPECTARIAN

1 Th
☽⚼⚳ 2:32
☽△♀ 6:04
☉⚻☽ 7:14
☽⋕♂ 7:50
☽☍⚷ 11:14
☽⚼♇ 13:47
☽⚻♅ 15:12
☽△♃ 21:55
♂∠♃ 21:58

2 F
☽☌♄ 2:13
☽☍♆ 2:33
☽⋕♇ 4:30
☽∥♄ 6:46
☽⚻⚳ 8:32
☽⋕♆ 11:59
☽⚼♀ 14:24
☽☍☿ 15:54
☽△♇ 19:04
☿∥⚳ 19:53

3 Sa
☿∠♀ 0:56
☽⚻♂ 5:15
☽⋕⚷ 6:22
☽⋕☿ 9:52
☽⋕⚳ 11:19
☉⚺⚷ 12:33
♀✱⚷ 13:41
☉⚺♀ 18:26
☉∥♅ 18:47
☽⚻⚷ 22:28
☉☍☽ 23:18
☽⚻♀ 23:24

4 Su
☽⋕♅ 0:09
☉⋕☽ 0:31
☽☍♅ 2:29
☽∥♀ 8:29
☽□♃ 9:38
☽⚼♂ 13:08
☽⚺♄ 13:12
☽⚻♆ 14:05
☽☍⚳ 22:05

5 M
☽⚻☿ 1:17
☽⚼⚷ 4:43
☽□♇ 6:57
♀⚺♅ 7:07
☿∥⚷ 13:02
☉☌♅ 15:41
☽∠♄ 19:16
☽⚼♆ 20:25
☽△♂ 21:26

6 Tu
☽⋕♀ 4:47
☉∥☽ 5:09
☽⚼☿ 6:54
☉⋕♀ 7:14
☽∥♅ 8:57
☽△⚷ 11:16
☽⚻♅ 15:17
☉⚻☽ 17:21
☽☍♀ 18:49
☽∥⚳ 19:52
☽✱♃ 22:44

7 W
☽✱♄ 1:31
☽△♆ 2:57
☽∥⚷ 3:01
☽∥☿ 5:22
☽⚻⚳ 12:56
☽△☿ 13:01
☿⚺⚳ 14:56
☽✱♇ 19:52
☽⚼♅ 21:55
☽∥♆ 22:08

8 Th
♀⋕♅ 0:29
☉⚼☽ 2:38
☽⋕♄ 4:31
☿ D 4:45
☽∠♃ 5:25
☽∥♇ 6:10
♀△♃ 11:17
☽□♂ 14:31
☽⚼⚳ 20:24
☽∥♂ 20:24

9 F
☽□⚷ 0:29
☽∠♇ 2:17
☽△♅ 4:25
♀△♄ 8:42
☉△☽ 11:43
☽⚺♃ 11:55
☽□♄ 13:54
☽∥♃ 14:12
☉□♃ 14:20
☽⚻♀ 14:32
☽□♆ 15:50

10 Sa
☽□☿ 1:52
☽△⚳ 3:32
♀✱♆ 3:42
☽⚺♇ 8:20
☉⚻♄ 12:22
☽⚼♀ 23:38

11 Su
☽✱♂ 6:21
♀⋕⚳ 12:20
☽✱⚷ 12:20
☉⚺♆ 14:32
☽□♅ 16:04
☽☌♃ 23:22

12 M
☽△♄ 0:35
☽✱♆ 2:53
☉□☽ 3:55
☽△♀ 7:48
☽∠♂ 13:04
☽✱☿ 13:44
☽□⚳ 15:43
☽∠⚷ 17:11
☽☌♇ 18:28

13 Tu
☽⚼♄ 4:45
☽∠♆ 7:12
☽∠☿ 18:37
☽⚺♂ 18:40
☽⚺⚷ 21:04

14 W
☽✱♅ 0:31
☽⚺♃ 7:24
☽⚻♄ 7:59
☽⚺♆ 10:31
☉✱☽ 15:46
☽□♀ 20:22
☽⚺☿ 22:36
⚳∠⚷ 23:55
☽✱⚳ 23:58

15 Th
☽⚺♇ 0:56
☽∠♅ 3:16
☽∠♃ 9:56
☽∥♃ 12:14
♂☌⚷ 15:41
☉∠☽ 19:52
♀⋕⚷ 22:26

16 F
☽☌⚷ 1:54
☽☌♂ 2:26
☽∠⚳ 2:31
☽∠♇ 2:45
☽⚺♅ 5:05
♂∠⚳ 5:45
♂∠♇ 8:14
☽∥♂ 10:11
⚳□♇ 10:37
☽✱♃ 11:32
☽☍♄ 11:37
☽☌♆ 14:19
☽∥♇ 15:16
☽⋕♄ 15:52
☽∥♆ 22:07
♃△♄ 22:43
☉⚺☽ 22:54
☿✱♇ 23:35

17 Sa
♀△♇ 0:19
☿✱♀ 1:24
☽✱♇ 3:44
☽☌☿ 3:57
☽✱♀ 4:02
☽⚺⚳ 4:11
♀⚺⚳ 6:48
☽∥☿ 8:21
☽⋕♀ 11:10
☿⚺⚳ 13:46
☽∥⚷ 13:57
♀ ♉ 22:02

18 Su
☽∥⚳ 1:13
☽⚺⚷ 3:28
☽∥♅ 4:22
♀∠♅ 5:58
☽⚺♂ 6:24
☽☌♅ 6:27
☽∠♀ 6:30
♂⚺♅ 7:27
☿ ♓ 9:36
☽⚻♄ 12:20
☽□♃ 12:37
☽⚺♆ 15:12
☿⋕♀ 18:13
☉∥☽ 23:13

19 M
☉☌☽ 2:44
☽∠⚷ 3:29
☽□♇ 4:00
☉⋕☽ 4:16
⚳ ♈ 5:28
☽☌⚳ 5:43
☽⚺☿ 6:53
☽∠♂ 7:34
☽⚺♀ 8:27
☽⚼♄ 12:04
☉∠⚷ 14:55
☽∠♆ 15:03
☉□♇ 22:15
☽⋕♅ 23:07

20 Tu
☽⋕⚳ 1:14
☽✱⚷ 3:19
☽⚺♅ 6:16
☽∠☿ 8:06
☽✱♂ 8:34
☽△♄ 11:44
☽△♃ 12:21
☽⋕⚷ 13:10
☽✱♆ 14:50
☽⋕☿ 17:12
☽∥♀ 21:58

21 W
☉ ♈ 0:08
☽△♇ 3:34
☽⋕♆ 4:41
☉⚺☽ 5:38
☽∠♅ 6:11
☽⚺⚳ 6:34
☽✱☿ 9:33
☽∥♄ 11:13
☽⋕♇ 11:26
☽⋕♂ 11:51
☽☌♀ 12:12
☽⚼♃ 12:19
♀⚼♃ 13:42
♂∥♇ 22:54

22 Th
☽□⚷ 3:26
♂⋕♄ 3:33
☽⚼♇ 3:42
☉☌⚳ 4:16
☽✱♅ 6:27
☽∠⚳ 7:24
☉∠☽ 7:33
☽□♂ 11:16
☽□♄ 11:44
☽⚻♃ 12:41
☽⋕♃ 13:36
☽□♆ 15:13
♂☍♄ 19:35

23 F
☽⚻♇ 4:22
☽✱⚳ 8:52
☉✱☽ 10:08
☽□☿ 14:22
♂✱♃ 16:02
☽⚺♀ 17:56

24 Sa
☽△⚷ 5:40
☽□♅ 8:50
⚳∥♅ 13:21
☽✱♄ 14:04
☽☍♃ 15:25
☽△♂ 16:43
☽△♆ 18:03
☉⚼♄ 18:58
♄⋕♇ 19:23
♀⋕♆ 19:59
☽∠♀ 22:14

25 Su
♇∠⚷ 3:43
☽☍♇ 7:58
☽⚼⚷ 7:59
☽□⚳ 14:19
☿∥⚷ 15:13
☽∠♄ 16:29
♂☌♆ 17:40
☉□☽ 18:17
☽⚼♆ 20:45
☽⚼♂ 20:56
♀ ♓ 23:17
☽△☿ 23:25

26 M
☽✱♀ 3:42
☽⚻⚷ 11:14
♀⋕♂ 11:20
☽△♅ 14:37
☽⚺♄ 19:48
☽⚻♃ 21:34

27 Tu
☽⚻♆ 0:22
☽⚻♂ 2:15
☉∠♆ 4:22
☽⚼☿ 5:52
☽⚻♇ 15:07
☽⚼♅ 18:51
☽△⚳ 23:41

28 W
☽⚼♃ 1:58
☽⋕♃ 3:02
☉△☽ 6:54
⚳⚼♄ 8:48
☽⚻☿ 13:33
☽□♀ 18:07
☽⚼♇ 19:56
☽☍⚷ 20:19
♀⋕♇ 22:33
☽⚻♅ 23:54

29 Th
♀∥♄ 2:11
☽☌♄ 4:56
☽⚼⚳ 5:40
☽△♃ 7:07
☽∥♀ 9:33
☽☍♆ 10:04
☽∥♄ 10:09
☽⋕♇ 10:28
♀⚼♇ 12:58
♂∥♆ 13:53
☉⚼☽ 14:40
☽☍♂ 15:46
♀□⚷ 17:54
☽⋕♆ 19:04
☽⋕♂ 19:19

30 F
☽△♇ 1:25
☽⚻⚳ 12:19
☽⋕⚷ 14:56
☉⚻☽ 23:09
☽⋕☿ 23:20

31 Sa
☽☍☿ 7:56
☽⚻⚷ 8:02
♀✱♅ 8:23
☽⋕♅ 8:48
☿⚺⚷ 8:52
☽☍♅ 11:43
☽△♀ 12:04
☽⋕⚳ 12:58
☽⚺♄ 16:28
☉∥☽ 17:08
☽□♃ 18:59
☽⚻♆ 22:04
♇ R 22:46
☉∠♂ 23:23

April 2007

LONGITUDE

Day	Sid.Time	☉	☽	☽ 12 hour	Mean☊	True☊	☿	♀	♂	⚳	♃	♄	⚷	♅	♆	♇
	h m s	° ' "	° ' "	° ' "	° '	° '	° '	° '	° '	° '	° '	° '	° '	° '	° '	° '
1 Su	12 35 55	10♈53 19	22♍13 11	28♍09 15	14♓54.1	16♓07.1	15♓08.7	16♉53.8	25♒53.0	5♈02.3	19♐44.3	18♌28.5	14♒19.8	16♓09.4	21♒15.7	28♐58.0
2 M	12 39 51	11 52 31	4♎04 34	9♎59 24	14 51.0	16R 05.8	16 30.8	18 05.1	26 39.0	5 26.0	19 45.2	18R 26.5	14 22.9	16 12.6	21 17.3	28R 58.0
3 Tu	12 43 48	12 51 41	15 54 00	21 48 37	14 47.8	16 03.2	17 54.6	19 16.4	27 25.0	5 49.6	19 45.9	18 24.7	14 25.9	16 15.7	21 18.9	28 57.9
4 W	12 47 44	13 50 49	27 43 30	3♏38 53	14 44.6	15 59.3	19 20.1	20 27.5	28 11.0	6 13.2	19 46.3	18 23.0	14 28.9	16 18.9	21 20.5	28 57.9
5 Th	12 51 41	14 49 55	9♏35 01	15 32 09	14 41.4	15 54.4	20 47.2	21 38.6	28 57.0	6 36.8	19 46.6	18 21.3	14 31.8	16 22.0	21 22.0	28 57.8
6 F	12 55 37	15 48 59	21 30 36	27 30 37	14 38.2	15 49.1	22 16.0	22 49.6	29 43.0	7 00.4	19R 46.7	18 19.8	14 34.7	16 25.1	21 23.6	28 57.6
7 Sa	12 59 34	16 48 01	3♐32 33	9♐36 45	14 35.1	15 43.9	23 46.4	24 00.5	0♓29.1	7 24.0	19 46.6	18 18.3	14 37.5	16 28.2	21 25.1	28 57.4
8 Su	13 03 30	17 47 02	15 43 33	21 53 23	14 31.9	15 39.3	25 18.3	25 11.2	1 15.1	7 47.5	19 46.4	18 17.0	14 40.3	16 31.3	21 26.5	28 57.2
9 M	13 07 27	18 46 00	28 06 40	4♑23 48	14 28.7	15 36.0	26 51.8	26 21.9	2 01.2	8 11.1	19 45.9	18 15.8	14 43.0	16 34.3	21 28.0	28 57.0
10 Tu	13 11 23	19 44 57	10♑45 15	17 11 28	14 25.5	15D 34.2	28 26.9	27 32.5	2 47.2	8 34.7	19 45.3	18 14.7	14 45.7	16 37.3	21 29.4	28 56.7
11 W	13 15 20	20 43 52	23 42 52	0♒19 52	14 22.4	15 33.8	0♈03.5	28 43.0	3 33.3	8 58.2	19 44.4	18 13.7	14 48.3	16 40.3	21 30.8	28 56.4
12 Th	13 19 17	21 42 46	7♒02 49	13 52 01	14 19.2	15 34.6	1 41.7	29 53.4	4 19.3	9 21.7	19 43.4	18 12.8	14 50.9	16 43.3	21 32.1	28 56.1
13 F	13 23 13	22 41 38	20 47 40	27 49 52	14 16.0	15 36.0	3 21.4	1♊03.6	5 05.4	9 45.2	19 42.2	18 12.0	14 53.4	16 46.3	21 33.5	28 55.7
14 Sa	13 27 10	23 40 27	4♓58 32	12♓13 30	14 12.8	15R 37.3	5 02.7	2 13.8	5 51.4	10 08.7	19 40.8	18 11.3	14 55.8	16 49.2	21 34.8	28 55.3
15 Su	13 31 06	24 39 15	19 34 20	27 00 28	14 09.6	15 37.6	6 45.5	3 23.9	6 37.4	10 32.2	19 39.2	18 10.7	14 58.2	16 52.1	21 36.1	28 54.9
16 M	13 35 03	25 38 02	4♈31 07	12♈05 19	14 06.5	15 36.3	8 29.9	4 33.8	7 23.5	10 55.6	19 37.5	18 10.2	15 00.5	16 55.0	21 37.3	28 54.4
17 Tu	13 38 59	26 36 46	19 41 57	27 19 46	14 03.3	15 33.1	10 15.8	5 43.7	8 09.5	11 19.0	19 35.5	18 09.8	15 02.7	16 57.8	21 38.5	28 54.0
18 W	13 42 56	27 35 29	4♉57 25	12♉33 35	14 00.1	15 28.1	12 03.4	6 53.4	8 55.6	11 42.4	19 33.4	18 09.6	15 04.9	17 00.6	21 39.7	28 53.4
19 Th	13 46 52	28 34 09	20 06 58	27 36 20	13 56.9	15 21.8	13 52.5	8 03.0	9 41.6	12 05.8	19 31.0	18D 09.4	15 07.1	17 03.4	21 40.9	28 52.9
20 F	13 50 49	29 32 48	5♊00 39	12♊19 02	13 53.8	15 15.1	15 43.2	9 12.5	10 27.6	12 29.2	19 28.5	18 09.4	15 09.1	17 06.2	21 42.0	28 52.3
21 Sa	13 54 46	0♉31 25	19 30 50	26 35 34	13 50.6	15 08.9	17 35.6	10 21.9	11 13.6	12 52.5	19 25.8	18 09.4	15 11.2	17 08.9	21 43.1	28 51.7
22 Su	13 58 42	1 29 59	3♋33 00	10♋23 06	13 47.4	15 04.1	19 29.5	11 31.1	11 59.6	13 15.8	19 23.0	18 09.6	15 13.1	17 11.6	21 44.2	28 51.1
23 M	14 02 39	2 28 31	17 05 59	23 41 55	13 44.2	15 01.0	21 25.0	12 40.3	12 45.6	13 39.1	19 20.0	18 09.9	15 15.0	17 14.3	21 45.3	28 50.4
24 Tu	14 06 35	3 27 01	0♌11 17	6♌34 34	13 41.1	14D 59.7	23 22.1	13 49.3	13 31.5	14 02.4	19 16.7	18 10.3	15 16.8	17 16.9	21 46.3	28 49.8
25 W	14 10 32	4 25 29	12 52 19	19 05 06	13 37.9	15 00.0	25 20.8	14 58.1	14 17.5	14 25.6	19 13.4	18 10.8	15 18.6	17 19.5	21 47.3	28 49.0
26 Th	14 14 28	5 23 55	25 13 33	1♍18 15	13 34.7	15 01.1	27 21.1	16 06.8	15 03.4	14 48.8	19 09.8	18 11.4	15 20.3	17 22.1	21 48.2	28 48.3
27 F	14 18 25	6 22 18	7♍19 49	13 18 51	13 31.5	15R 02.2	29 22.8	17 15.4	15 49.4	15 12.0	19 06.1	18 12.1	15 21.9	17 24.6	21 49.1	28 47.5
28 Sa	14 22 21	7 20 40	19 15 54	25 11 29	13 28.3	15 02.4	1♉25.9	18 23.8	16 35.3	15 35.1	19 02.2	18 12.9	15 23.5	17 27.1	21 50.0	28 46.7
29 Su	14 26 18	8 18 59	1♎06 05	7♎00 10	13 25.2	15 00.9	3 30.4	19 32.0	17 21.2	15 58.2	18 58.1	18 13.8	15 25.0	17 29.6	21 50.9	28 45.9
30 M	14 30 15	9♉17 16	12 54 06	18 48 16	13♓22.0	14♓57.1	5♉36.2	20♊40.2	18♓07.1	16♈21.3	18♐53.9	18♌14.9	15♒26.4	17♓32.0	21♒51.7	28♐45.0

1st of Month

Julian Day # 2454191.5
Obliquity 23°26'27"
SVP 5♓09'27"
GC 26♐56.4
Eris 20♈45.7

Day	⚴	⚵	⚶
1	1♓50.5	21♎57.1R	13♐52.2
6	3 19.8	20 47.6R	14 27.9
11	4 46.8	19 37.0R	14 52.4
16	6 11.4	18 27.1R	15 05.0
21	7 33.3	17 19.5R	15 05.2R
26	8 52.2	16 16.0R	14 53.0R

DECLINATION and LATITUDE

Day	☉ Decl	☽ Decl	☽ Lat	☽ 12h Decl	☿ Decl	☿ Lat	♀ Decl	♀ Lat	♂ Decl	♂ Lat	⚳ Decl	⚳ Lat	♃ Decl	♃ Lat	♄ Decl	♄ Lat
1 Su	4N19	2N34	0S34	0S16	7S54	2S13	17N42	0N51	14S03	1S14	5S06	7S45	22S19	0N44	16N33	1N20
2 M	4 42	3S06	1 37	5 55	7 25	2 17	18 05	0 54	13 48	1 15	4 57	7 45	22 19	0 44	16 34	1 19
3 Tu	5 05	8 40	2 36	11 20	6 56	2 20	18 28	0 57	13 33	1 15	4 47	7 44	22 19	0 44	16 34	1 19
4 W	5 28	13 55	3 29	16 22	6 25	2 23	18 50	1 01	13 17	1 16	4 38	7 44	22 19	0 44	16 35	1 19
5 Th	5 51	18 40	4 12	20 48	5 52	2 25	19 12	1 04	13 02	1 16	4 29	7 44	22 19	0 44	16 35	1 19
6 F	6 13	22 43	4 45	24 25	5 19	2 27	19 34	1 07	12 46	1 17	4 19	7 44	22 19	0 44	16 36	1 19
7 Sa	6 36	25 51	5 05	27 00	4 45	2 28	19 55	1 10	12 30	1 17	4 10	7 44	22 19	0 44	16 36	1 19
8 Su	6 59	27 51	5 12	28 21	4 09	2 29	20 15	1 14	12 14	1 18	4 00	7 43	22 19	0 44	16 36	1 19
9 M	7 21	28 30	5 05	28 18	3 32	2 30	20 35	1 17	11 58	1 18	3 51	7 43	22 19	0 44	16 37	1 19
10 Tu	7 43	27 42	4 43	26 44	2 54	2 29	20 55	1 20	11 42	1 19	3 42	7 43	22 19	0 44	16 37	1 19
11 W	8 06	25 24	4 06	23 42	2 15	2 29	21 14	1 23	11 26	1 19	3 32	7 43	22 19	0 44	16 37	1 19
12 Th	8 28	21 39	3 15	19 17	1 35	2 28	21 32	1 26	11 10	1 20	3 23	7 43	22 19	0 44	16 38	1 19
13 F	8 50	16 38	2 11	13 43	0 54	2 26	21 50	1 30	10 53	1 20	3 14	7 43	22 19	0 44	16 38	1 19
14 Sa	9 11	10 35	0 58	7 16	0 12	2 24	22 07	1 33	10 37	1 20	3 05	7 43	22 18	0 44	16 38	1 19
15 Su	9 33	3 48	0N21	0 15	0N31	2 21	22 24	1 36	10 20	1 21	2 56	7 43	22 18	0 44	16 38	1 19
16 M	9 55	3N20	1 41	6N54	1 15	2 18	22 40	1 39	10 03	1 21	2 46	7 43	22 18	0 44	16 38	1 19
17 Tu	10 16	10 24	2 54	13 44	2 00	2 14	22 56	1 42	9 46	1 22	2 37	7 43	22 18	0 44	16 38	1 19
18 W	10 37	16 52	3 56	19 44	2 46	2 10	23 11	1 45	9 29	1 22	2 28	7 43	22 18	0 44	16 38	1 19
19 Th	10 58	22 16	4 40	24 24	3 33	2 06	23 25	1 48	9 12	1 22	2 19	7 43	22 18	0 44	16 38	1 19
20 F	11 19	26 07	5 04	27 22	4 20	2 00	23 39	1 50	8 55	1 23	2 10	7 43	22 17	0 44	16 38	1 19
21 Sa	11 39	28 09	5 08	28 26	5 08	1 55	23 52	1 53	8 38	1 23	2 01	7 43	22 17	0 44	16 38	1 19
22 Su	11 60	28 17	4 53	27 41	5 57	1 49	24 05	1 56	8 21	1 24	1 52	7 43	22 17	0 44	16 38	1 19
23 M	12 20	26 41	4 22	25 20	6 47	1 42	24 17	1 59	8 04	1 24	1 43	7 43	22 17	0 44	16 38	1 18
24 Tu	12 40	23 40	3 38	21 44	7 37	1 35	24 28	2 01	7 46	1 24	1 34	7 43	22 16	0 44	16 38	1 18
25 W	12 60	19 35	2 45	17 15	8 27	1 27	24 39	2 04	7 29	1 25	1 26	7 43	22 16	0 44	16 37	1 18
26 Th	13 19	14 46	1 45	12 09	9 18	1 19	24 49	2 06	7 12	1 25	1 17	7 43	22 16	0 44	16 37	1 18
27 F	13 39	9 28	0 41	6 42	10 09	1 11	24 58	2 09	6 54	1 25	1 08	7 43	22 16	0 44	16 37	1 18
28 Sa	13 58	3 54	0S23	1 05	11 00	1 02	25 07	2 11	6 37	1 26	0 59	7 43	22 15	0 44	16 37	1 18
29 Su	14 17	1S45	1 25	4S33	11 52	0 52	25 15	2 14	6 19	1 26	0 51	7 43	22 15	0 44	16 36	1 18
30 M	14N35	7S18	2S24	10S00	12N43	0S43	25N22	2N16	6S01	1S26	0S42	7S43	22S15	0N44	16N36	1N18

Day	⚷ Decl	⚷ Lat	♅ Decl	♅ Lat	♆ Decl	♆ Lat	♇ Decl	♇ Lat
1	10S15	6N33	6S09	0S44	14S38	0S14	16S27	6N59
6	10 09	6 35	6 03	0 44	14 36	0 14	16 26	6 60
11	10 04	6 37	5 57	0 44	14 34	0 15	16 26	7 00
16	9 58	6 39	5 51	0 45	14 32	0 15	16 25	7 01
21	9 53	6 41	5 46	0 45	14 30	0 15	16 25	7 01
26	9 49	6 43	5 41	0 45	14 28	0 15	16 24	7 02

Day	⚴ Decl	⚴ Lat	⚵ Decl	⚵ Lat	⚶ Decl	⚶ Lat	Eris Decl	Eris Lat
1	5N13	17N08	0S08	9N04	14S15	8N17	4S57	14S04
6	5 38	17 03	0N33	9 20	14 12	8 24	4 55	14 04
11	6 04	16 58	1 12	9 34	14 08	8 30	4 54	14 04
16	6 30	16 54	1 48	9 46	14 04	8 35	4 53	14 03
21	6 56	16 51	2 22	9 55	14 00	8 39	4 51	14 03
26	7 21	16 48	2 53	10 02	13 57	8 41	4 50	14 03

Moon Phenomena

Max/0 Decl
dy hr mn
1 10:51 0 S
8 23:09 28S30
15 12:50 0 N
21 13:41 28N26
28 16:35 0 S

Max/0 Lat
dy hr mn
7 23:55 5S12
14 17:34 0 N
20 16:50 5N09
27 15:29 0 S

Perigee/Apogee
dy hr m kilometers
3 8:40 a 406330
17 5:50 p 357140
30 10:57 a 406210

PH dy hr mn
○ 2 17:16 12♎35
☾ 10 18:05 20♑29
● 17 11:37 27♈05
☽ 24 6:37 3♌43

Void of Course Moon

Last Aspect			☽ Ingress	
1 13:39	♇	□	♎	1 15:44
4 2:31	♇	⚹	♏	4 4:37
6 2:56	♀	☍	♐	6 16:58
9 1:37	♇	☌	♑	9 3:37
11 9:58	♀	△	♒	11 11:24
13 13:51	♇	⚹	♓	13 15:40
15 15:03	♇	□	♈	15 16:48
17 14:28	♇	△	♉	17 16:12
19 2:30	♆	□	♊	19 15:52
21 15:53	♇	☍	♋	21 17:51
23 9:11	☿	□	♌	23 23:39
26 7:03	♇	△	♍	26 9:25
28 19:15	♇	□	♎	28 21:46

DAILY ASPECTARIAN

1 Su ☽⚻♂ 7:55 · ☽□♇ 13:39 · ☽⚼⚷ 14:27 · ☿☌♅ 18:31 · ☽⚼♀ 21:46 · ☽∠♄ 22:43

2 M ☽☍⚳ 2:51 · ☽⚼♆ 4:30 · ♀□♄ 7:02 · ☉#☽ 7:17 · ☽∥⚳ 7:39 · ☉#⚳ 11:14 · ☽∥♅ 12:52 · ☽⚼♂ 16:26 · ☽∥☿ 17:02 · ☉☍☽ 17:16 · ☽△⚷ 21:00

3 Tu ☽⚻♅ 0:44 · ☽⚻☿ 4:38 · ☽⚹♄ 5:05 · ☽∥⚷ 6:53 · ☽⚻♀ 7:37 · ☽⚹♃ 7:51 · ☿⚻♄ 8:20 · ♀⚻♃ 10:01 · ☽△♆ 11:01 · ☽∥♂ 21:12

4 W ☽△♂ 1:00 · ☽⚹♇ 2:31 · ☽∥♆ 3:23 · ☿□♃ 7:18 · ☽⚼♅ 7:18 · ⚳∠♆ 7:56 · ☽∥♇ 12:25 · ☽#♄ 13:07 · ☽∠♃ 14:17 · ☽⚼☿ 15:15 · ☿∥♅ 15:22 · ☉⚹⚷ 16:16 · ☽⚻⚳ 17:48 · ♀□♆ 18:17 · ♀∠⚳ 23:05

5 Th ♂⚹♇ 0:23 · ☉#☿ 0:45 · ☽#♀ 3:12 · ☽∠♇ 8:50 · ☿⚺♆ 9:38 · ☽□⚷ 10:01 · ☉⚻☽ 11:32 · ☉#♅ 13:02 · ☽△♅ 13:44 · ☽□♄ 17:38 · ☽⚺♃ 20:32 · ☽∥♃ 21:23 · ☽□♆ 23:46

6 F ☽⚼⚳ 1:02 · ♃R 1:24 · ☽△☿ 1:44 · ☽☍♀ 2:56 · ♂ ♓ 8:51 · ☽⚺♇ 14:53 · ☉⚺♅ 15:30 · ☽□♂ 17:31 · ☉⚼☽ 20:14

7 Sa ☽△⚳ 7:53 · ☿⚹♀ 16:11 · ☽⚹⚷ 21:56

8 Su ☽□♅ 1:34 · ☉△☽ 4:22 · ☽△♄ 4:59 · ☿∥⚳ 7:29 · ☽☌♃ 7:53 · ☽⚹♆ 11:09 · ☉△♄ 11:57 · ☽⚻♀ 20:18 · ☽□☿ 21:16

9 M ☽☌♇ 1:37 · ☽∠⚷ 3:05 · ☽⚹♂ 7:58 · ☽⚼♄ 9:50 · ☽∠♆ 15:57 · ☽□⚳ 19:47

10 Tu ☉△♃ 0:08 · ☽⚼♀ 3:41 · ☿□♇ 7:26 · ☽⚺⚷ 7:31 · ☽⚹♅ 10:59 · ☽∠♂ 13:56 · ☽⚻♄ 13:56 · ☽⚺♃ 16:43 · ☉□☽ 18:05 · ☽⚺♆ 19:58 · ☿∠⚷ 20:09 · ☿ ♈ 23:08

11 W ♀⚻♇ 4:34 · ☽⚺♇ 9:29 · ☽△♀ 9:58 · ☽⚹☿ 13:07 · ☽∠♅ 14:28 · ☽⚺♂ 18:52 · ☉⚹♆ 19:34 · ☽∠♃ 19:52 · ☽∥♃ 20:19

12 Th ☽#♀ 0:35 · ♀ ♊ 2:16 · ☽⚹⚳ 4:13 · ☽∠♇ 12:07 · ☽☌⚷ 13:45 · ☽⚺♅ 17:02 · ☽∠☿ 19:13 · ☽☍♄ 19:32 · ☿⚼♄ 21:46 · ☽⚹♃ 22:08

13 F ☽#♄ 0:02 · ☽∥♇ 0:53 · ☽☌♆ 1:19 · ☉⚹☽ 3:30 · ☽∠⚳ 6:58 · ☽∥♆ 8:41 · ☽⚹♇ 13:51 · ☽□♀ 19:00 · ☽∥♂ 23:54

14 Sa ☽⚺☿ 0:08 · ☽☌♂ 1:33 · ☽∥⚷ 2:08 · ☉#☽ 4:50 · ☉∠☽ 6:35 · ☽⚺⚳ 8:49 · ♀#♃ 15:40 · ☽⚺⚷ 16:29 · ☽∥♅ 16:51 · ☽☌♅ 19:35 · ☿⚺♂ 20:39 · ☽⚻♄ 21:44 · ☿∠♆ 21:47

15 Su ☽□♃ 0:08 · ☽∥⚳ 3:02 · ☽⚺♆ 3:17 · ☉⚺☽ 8:48 · ☽#☿ 10:03 · ☽□♇ 15:03 · ☽∥☿ 16:14 · ☽∠⚷ 16:47 · ☽⚼♄ 21:51 · ☽#⚳ 22:09

16 M ☽⚹♀ 0:05 · ☽∠♆ 3:21 · ☉#⚷ 3:55 · ☽⚺♂ 4:48 · ☉#♂ 5:24 · ☽☌☿ 7:09 · ♂∥⚷ 7:30 · ☽#♅ 8:24 · ☽☌⚳ 10:26 · ☽⚹⚷ 16:39 · ☽⚺♅ 19:41 · ☽△♄ 21:35 · ☽#♂ 21:55 · ☽#⚷ 22:28 · ☉∥☽ 23:31 · ☽△♃ 23:50

17 Tu ☽∠♀ 1:45 · ☽⚹♆ 3:04 · ☽∠♂ 5:44 · ☉☌☽ 11:37 · ☽△♇ 14:28 · ☽#♆ 14:55 · ☿#⚳ 16:16 · ☿☌⚳ 18:04 · ☽∠♅ 19:21 · ☽#♇ 22:12 · ☽∥♄ 23:04 · ☽⚼♃ 23:22

18 W ☽⚺♀ 3:18 · ☽⚹♂ 6:35 · ☽⚺⚳ 10:56 · ☽⚺☿ 12:44 · ☽⚼♇ 14:06 · ⚶R 14:12 · ☽□⚷ 16:02 · ☽⚹♅ 19:07 · ☽□♄ 20:53 · ☽⚻♃ 23:03

19 Th ☽#♃ 0:10 · ☽□♆ 2:30 · ☽∥♀ 6:36 · ☉△♇ 7:36 · ☽∠⚳ 11:29 · ☽⚻♇ 14:03 · ☉⚺☽ 14:31 · ☽∠☿ 16:02 · ☿⚹⚷ 16:30 · ♄D 21:25

20 F ☽☌♀ 7:28 · ☽□♂ 9:26 · ☉ ♉ 11:08 · ☽⚹⚳ 12:37 · ☽△⚷ 16:45 · ☉∠☽ 16:50 · ☿⚺♅ 18:11 · ☽□♅ 20:01 · ☽⚹☿ 20:18 · ☽⚹♄ 21:43 · ☽☍♃ 23:52

21 Sa ☽△♆ 3:43 · ☿△♄ 7:10 · ☽☍♇ 15:53 · ☿#♅ 18:03 · ☽⚼⚷ 18:13 · ☉⚹☽ 20:10 · ☿△♃ 22:40 · ☽∠♄ 23:19

22 Su ☽⚼♆ 5:35 · ☽⚺♀ 15:19 · ☽△♂ 15:45 · ☽□⚳ 17:38 · ☉∠♅ 17:52 · ☽⚻⚷ 20:40

23 M ☽△♅ 0:15 · ☽⚺♄ 1:55 · ☽⚻♃ 4:01 · ☿⚹♆ 4:12 · ♀□♂ 5:31 · ☽⚻♆ 8:27 · ☽□☿ 9:11 · ☽∥♀ 18:44 · ☽⚼♂ 20:43 · ☽∠♀ 21:12 · ☽⚻♇ 21:28

24 Tu ☿#♂ 3:28 · ☽⚼♅ 3:56 · ☉□☽ 6:37 · ♀⚹⚳ 6:53 · ☽⚼♃ 7:38 · ☽#♃ 8:48 · ☉⚼♃ 19:18

25 W ☽⚼♇ 1:49 · ☽⚻♂ 2:54 · ☽△⚳ 3:05 · ☽⚹♀ 4:26 · ☽☍⚷ 4:42 · ♀△⚷ 7:20 · ♂⚺⚳ 8:33 · ☽⚻♅ 8:37 · ☽☌♄ 10:15 · ☽△♃ 12:13 · ☽∥♄ 15:05 · ☽#♇ 16:08 · ☽☍♆ 17:17

26 Th ☽#♆ 1:21 · ☽△☿ 5:01 · ☉∥☽ 6:18 · ☽△♇ 7:03 · ♂⚺⚷ 9:07 · ☽⚼⚳ 9:21 · ☿#⚷ 14:09 · ☿△♇ 17:07 · ☽∥☿ 21:22 · ☉△☽ 21:55 · ☽#⚷ 22:31

27 F ♀□♅ 3:21 · ☿ ♉ 7:17 · ⚳⚹⚷ 11:05 · ☽#♂ 11:45 · ☽⚻⚷ 16:10 · ☽⚻⚳ 16:19 · ☽#♅ 16:31 · ☽⚼☿ 17:05 · ☽☍♂ 18:13 · ♀⚹♄ 20:08 · ☽☍♅ 20:19 · ☽⚺♄ 21:53 · ☽□♀ 22:04 · ☽□♃ 23:32

28 Sa ☿∠♂ 2:53 · ☽⚻♆ 5:12 · ☉⚼☽ 6:47 · ☿∠♅ 12:04 · ☽#⚳ 12:42 · ♀☍♃ 12:45 · ☽□♇ 19:15 · ☽∥⚳ 20:16 · ☽⚼⚷ 22:36

29 Su ☽∠♄ 4:20 · ♂☌♅ 4:38 · ☿⚼♃ 5:08 · ☽⚻☿ 5:57 · ☽⚼♆ 11:42 · ☉#♆ 13:48 · ☉⚻☽ 15:59 · ☽∥♅ 16:39 · ☽∥♂ 18:41

30 M ☿∠♀ 1:37 · ♂⚻♄ 4:11 · ☽△⚷ 5:10 · ☽☍⚳ 7:15 · ☽⚻♅ 9:27 · ☽∥⚷ 10:51 · ☽⚹♄ 10:53 · ☽⚻♂ 11:20 · ☽⚹♃ 12:07 · ☽△♀ 17:28 · ☽△♆ 18:14 · ♂□♃ 22:22

LONGITUDE

May 2007

Day	Sid.Time	☉	☽	☽ 12 hour	Mean ☊	True ☊	☿	♀	♂	⚳	♃	♄	⚷	♅	♆	♇
	h m s	° ' "	° ' "	° ' "	° '	° '	° '	° '	° '	° '	° '	° '	° '	° '	° '	° '
1 Tu	14 34 11	10♉15 32	24♎42 58	0♏38 30	13♓18.8	14♓51.0	7♉43.1	21♊48.1	18♓52.9	16♈44.3	18♐49.5	18♌16.0	15♒27.8	17♓34.4	21♒52.5	28♐44.2
2 W	14 38 08	11 13 46	6♏35 05	12 32 57	13 15.6	14R 42.6	9 51.1	22 55.9	19 38.8	17 07.3	18R 45.0	18 17.2	15 29.1	17 36.8	21 53.3	28R 43.3
3 Th	14 42 04	12 11 58	18 32 17	24 33 15	13 12.5	14 32.5	11 59.8	24 03.5	20 24.6	17 30.3	18 40.3	18 18.6	15 30.3	17 39.1	21 54.0	28 42.3
4 F	14 46 01	13 10 08	0♐36 00	6♐40 41	13 09.3	14 21.6	14 09.2	25 11.0	21 10.5	17 53.2	18 35.5	18 20.0	15 31.5	17 41.4	21 54.7	28 41.4
5 Sa	14 49 57	14 08 17	12 47 29	18 56 34	13 06.1	14 10.7	16 19.0	26 18.3	21 56.3	18 16.1	18 30.5	18 21.6	15 32.6	17 43.6	21 55.4	28 40.4
6 Su	14 53 54	15 06 24	25 08 05	1♑22 17	13 02.9	14 00.9	18 28.9	27 25.5	22 42.1	18 39.0	18 25.3	18 23.2	15 33.7	17 45.9	21 56.1	28 39.4
7 M	14 57 50	16 04 29	7♑39 23	13 59 38	12 59.7	13 52.9	20 38.8	28 32.4	23 27.8	19 01.8	18 20.1	18 25.0	15 34.7	17 48.0	21 56.7	28 38.4
8 Tu	15 01 47	17 02 34	20 23 21	26 50 48	12 56.6	13 47.4	22 48.2	29 39.2	24 13.6	19 24.6	18 14.6	18 26.9	15 35.6	17 50.2	21 57.2	28 37.3
9 W	15 05 44	18 00 36	3♒22 20	9♒58 16	12 53.4	13 44.4	24 57.0	0♋45.8	24 59.3	19 47.4	18 09.1	18 28.8	15 36.4	17 52.3	21 57.8	28 36.3
10 Th	15 09 40	18 58 38	16 38 57	23 24 40	12 50.2	13D 43.4	27 04.8	1 52.2	25 45.0	20 10.1	18 03.4	18 30.9	15 37.2	17 54.4	21 58.3	28 35.2
11 F	15 13 37	19 56 38	0♓15 42	7♓12 13	12 47.0	13R 43.6	29 11.4	2 58.5	26 30.7	20 32.8	17 57.5	18 33.1	15 37.9	17 56.4	21 58.8	28 34.1
12 Sa	15 17 33	20 54 37	14 14 21	21 22 06	12 43.9	13 43.9	1♊16.4	4 04.5	27 16.4	20 55.4	17 51.6	18 35.3	15 38.6	17 58.4	21 59.2	28 32.9
13 Su	15 21 30	21 52 34	28 35 17	5♈53 38	12 40.7	13 43.1	3 19.6	5 10.3	28 02.0	21 18.0	17 45.5	18 37.7	15 39.1	18 00.3	21 59.6	28 31.8
14 M	15 25 26	22 50 30	13♈16 38	20 43 37	12 37.5	13 40.3	5 20.8	6 16.0	28 47.6	21 40.6	17 39.3	18 40.2	15 39.7	18 02.2	22 00.0	28 30.6
15 Tu	15 29 23	23 48 25	28 13 43	5♉45 56	12 34.3	13 34.9	7 19.7	7 21.4	29 33.2	22 03.1	17 33.0	18 42.7	15 40.1	18 04.1	22 00.4	28 29.4
16 W	15 33 19	24 46 19	13♉19 06	20 51 59	12 31.2	13 26.9	9 16.1	8 26.7	0♈18.7	22 25.5	17 26.6	18 45.4	15 40.5	18 05.9	22 00.7	28 28.2
17 Th	15 37 16	25 44 11	28 23 18	5♊51 48	12 28.0	13 17.1	11 10.0	9 31.7	1 04.3	22 47.9	17 20.0	18 48.2	15 40.8	18 07.7	22 01.0	28 27.0
18 F	15 41 13	26 42 02	13♊16 19	20 35 50	12 24.8	13 06.5	13 01.0	10 36.5	1 49.7	23 10.3	17 13.4	18 51.0	15 41.0	18 09.4	22 01.2	28 25.7
19 Sa	15 45 09	27 39 51	27 49 27	4♋56 31	12 21.6	12 56.4	14 49.2	11 41.1	2 35.2	23 32.6	17 06.7	18 54.0	15 41.2	18 11.1	22 01.4	28 24.4
20 Su	15 49 06	28 37 39	11♋56 36	18 49 25	12 18.5	12 47.8	16 34.5	12 45.4	3 20.6	23 54.9	16 59.9	18 57.1	15R 41.3	18 12.8	22 01.6	28 23.2
21 M	15 53 02	29 35 25	25 34 57	2♌13 20	12 15.3	12 41.5	18 16.6	13 49.5	4 06.0	24 17.1	16 52.9	19 00.2	15 41.4	18 14.4	22 01.8	28 21.8
22 Tu	15 56 59	0♊33 09	8♌44 49	15 09 50	12 12.1	12 37.7	19 55.7	14 53.3	4 51.3	24 39.2	16 45.9	19 03.4	15 41.3	18 15.9	22 01.9	28 20.5
23 W	16 00 55	1 30 52	21 28 53	27 42 33	12 08.9	12D 36.0	21 31.5	15 56.9	5 36.6	25 01.3	16 38.9	19 06.8	15 41.2	18 17.5	22 02.0	28 19.2
24 Th	16 04 52	2 28 34	3♍51 28	9♍56 18	12 05.7	12R 35.7	23 04.1	17 00.2	6 21.9	25 23.4	16 31.7	19 10.2	15 41.1	18 18.9	22 02.0	28 17.8
25 F	16 08 49	3 26 13	15 57 42	21 56 23	12 02.6	12 35.8	24 33.4	18 03.2	7 07.1	25 45.4	16 24.5	19 13.7	15 40.8	18 20.4	22R 02.0	28 16.5
26 Sa	16 12 45	4 23 51	27 52 58	3♎48 07	11 59.4	12 35.0	25 59.4	19 05.9	7 52.3	26 07.3	16 17.2	19 17.3	15 40.5	18 21.8	22 02.0	28 15.1
27 Su	16 16 42	5 21 28	9♎42 26	15 36 27	11 56.2	12 32.5	27 22.1	20 08.4	8 37.4	26 29.2	16 09.9	19 21.0	15 40.2	18 23.1	22 02.0	28 13.7
28 M	16 20 38	6 19 03	21 30 43	27 25 42	11 53.0	12 27.6	28 41.3	21 10.5	9 22.5	26 51.0	16 02.5	19 24.8	15 39.7	18 24.4	22 01.9	28 12.3
29 Tu	16 24 35	7 16 37	3♏21 47	9♏19 22	11 49.9	12 19.9	29 57.1	22 12.4	10 07.5	27 12.7	15 55.0	19 28.7	15 39.2	18 25.6	22 01.8	28 10.8
30 W	16 28 31	8 14 10	15 18 45	21 20 10	11 46.7	12 09.6	1♋09.4	23 13.9	10 52.6	27 34.4	15 47.6	19 32.6	15 38.7	18 26.8	22 01.7	28 09.4
31 Th	16 32 28	9♊11 41	27 23 50	3♐29 55	11♓43.5	11♓57.3	2♋18.1	24♋15.1	11♈37.5	27♈56.0	15♐40.0	19♌36.7	15♒38.1	18♓28.0	22♒01.5	28♐08.0

1st of Month

Julian Day # 2454221.5
Obliquity 23°26'27"
SVP 5♓09'23"
GC 26♐56.5
Eris 21♈05.2

Day	⚴	⚵	⚶
1	10♓08.0	15♎17.9R	14♐28.5R
6	11 20.4	14 26.1R	13 52.3R
11	12 29.1	13 41.7R	13 05.2R
16	13 33.8	13 05.1R	12 08.4R
21	14 34.2	12 36.9R	11 04.0R
26	15 29.9	12 17.2R	9 54.3R
31	16 20.7	12 06.1R	8 42.1R

DECLINATION and LATITUDE

Day	☉ Decl	☽ Decl	☽ Lat	☽12h Decl	☿ Decl	☿ Lat	♀ Decl	♀ Lat	♂ Decl	♂ Lat	⚳ Decl	⚳ Lat	♃ Decl	♃ Lat	♄ Decl	♄ Lat
1 Tu	14N54	12S37	3S16	15S07	13N34	0S33	25N29	2N18	5S44	1S27	0S33	7S43	22S14	0N44	16N36	1N18
2 W	15 12	17 29	4 00	19 42	14 24	0 23	25 35	2 20	5 26	1 27	0 25	7 43	22 14	0 44	16 35	1 18
3 Th	15 30	21 43	4 34	23 32	15 14	0 12	25 41	2 22	5 08	1 27	0 16	7 43	22 13	0 44	16 35	1 18
4 F	15 48	25 05	4 55	26 22	16 03	0 02	25 45	2 24	4 50	1 27	0 08	7 44	22 13	0 44	16 34	1 18
5 Sa	16 05	27 21	5 04	28 00	16 51	0N09	25 49	2 26	4 32	1 28	0N01	7 44	22 13	0 44	16 34	1 18
6 Su	16 22	28 19	4 58	28 16	17 38	0 19	25 53	2 28	4 15	1 28	0 09	7 44	22 12	0 44	16 33	1 18
7 M	16 39	27 51	4 38	27 04	18 24	0 30	25 56	2 30	3 57	1 28	0 17	7 44	22 12	0 44	16 32	1 18
8 Tu	16 56	25 55	4 05	24 26	19 07	0 40	25 58	2 31	3 39	1 28	0 26	7 44	22 11	0 44	16 32	1 18
9 W	17 12	22 36	3 18	20 28	19 49	0 50	25 59	2 33	3 21	1 29	0 34	7 44	22 11	0 44	16 31	1 18
10 Th	17 28	18 03	2 19	15 23	20 29	1 00	25 60	2 34	3 03	1 29	0 42	7 45	22 10	0 44	16 30	1 18
11 F	17 44	12 29	1 11	9 24	21 07	1 10	26 00	2 36	2 45	1 29	0 50	7 45	22 10	0 44	16 30	1 17
12 Sa	17 59	6 10	0N03	2 48	21 42	1 19	25 60	2 37	2 27	1 29	0 59	7 45	22 09	0 44	16 29	1 17
13 Su	18 14	0N38	1 18	4N06	22 15	1 28	25 58	2 38	2 09	1 30	1 07	7 45	22 09	0 44	16 28	1 17
14 M	18 29	7 33	2 30	10 55	22 46	1 36	25 56	2 39	1 51	1 30	1 15	7 46	22 08	0 44	16 27	1 17
15 Tu	18 44	14 10	3 33	17 12	23 14	1 43	25 54	2 40	1 33	1 30	1 23	7 46	22 08	0 44	16 26	1 17
16 W	18 58	19 59	4 22	22 27	23 39	1 50	25 51	2 41	1 15	1 30	1 31	7 46	22 07	0 44	16 26	1 17
17 Th	19 12	24 32	4 52	26 12	24 02	1 56	25 47	2 42	0 57	1 30	1 38	7 46	22 07	0 44	16 25	1 17
18 F	19 25	27 23	5 02	28 05	24 22	2 02	25 43	2 42	0 39	1 30	1 46	7 47	22 06	0 44	16 24	1 17
19 Sa	19 38	28 17	4 52	28 01	24 40	2 06	25 38	2 43	0 21	1 31	1 54	7 47	22 06	0 44	16 23	1 17
20 Su	19 51	27 17	4 24	26 09	24 55	2 10	25 32	2 43	0 03	1 31	2 02	7 47	22 05	0 43	16 22	1 17
21 M	20 04	24 40	3 42	22 51	25 08	2 13	25 26	2 43	0N14	1 31	2 10	7 48	22 04	0 43	16 21	1 17
22 Tu	20 16	20 48	2 49	18 31	25 19	2 16	25 19	2 43	0 32	1 31	2 17	7 48	22 04	0 43	16 20	1 17
23 W	20 28	16 04	1 49	13 29	25 27	2 17	25 12	2 43	0 50	1 31	2 25	7 48	22 03	0 43	16 19	1 17
24 Th	20 39	10 49	0 46	8 04	25 33	2 18	25 04	2 43	1 08	1 31	2 32	7 49	22 03	0 43	16 17	1 17
25 F	20 51	5 16	0S18	2 27	25 37	2 17	24 55	2 43	1 26	1 31	2 40	7 49	22 02	0 43	16 16	1 17
26 Sa	21 01	0S23	1 20	3S11	25 39	2 16	24 46	2 43	1 44	1 31	2 47	7 49	22 01	0 43	16 15	1 17
27 Su	21 12	5 58	2 18	8 41	25 39	2 14	24 36	2 42	2 01	1 31	2 55	7 50	22 01	0 43	16 14	1 17
28 M	21 22	11 20	3 10	13 52	25 37	2 11	24 26	2 42	2 19	1 31	3 02	7 50	21 60	0 43	16 13	1 17
29 Tu	21 32	16 18	3 54	18 35	25 34	2 08	24 15	2 41	2 37	1 31	3 09	7 51	21 59	0 43	16 11	1 16
30 W	21 41	20 42	4 28	22 36	25 29	2 03	24 04	2 40	2 54	1 31	3 16	7 51	21 59	0 43	16 10	1 16
31 Th	21N50	24S17	4S50	25S42	25N23	1N58	23N52	2N39	3N12	1S31	3N24	7S51	21S58	0N43	16N09	1N16

Day	⚷ Decl	⚷ Lat	♅ Decl	♅ Lat	♆ Decl	♆ Lat	♇ Decl	♇ Lat
1	9S44	6N45	5S36	0S45	14S27	0S15	16S24	7N02
6	9 41	6 47	5 32	0 45	14 26	0 15	16 23	7 03
11	9 37	6 50	5 28	0 45	14 25	0 15	16 23	7 03
16	9 34	6 52	5 24	0 45	14 25	0 15	16 23	7 03
21	9 32	6 54	5 21	0 46	14 25	0 15	16 23	7 03
26	9 30	6 56	5 18	0 46	14 25	0 15	16 23	7 03
31	9S29	6N58	5S16	0S46	14S25	0S16	16S23	7N03

Day	⚴ Decl	⚴ Lat	⚵ Decl	⚵ Lat	⚶ Decl	⚶ Lat	Eris Decl	Eris Lat
1	7N46	16N46	3N19	10N07	13S54	8N42	4S49	14S03
6	8 11	16 44	3 41	10 10	13 52	8 40	4 48	14 03
11	8 34	16 42	3 59	10 11	13 51	8 35	4 47	14 04
16	8 57	16 41	4 13	10 11	13 52	8 27	4 46	14 04
21	9 18	16 40	4 22	10 09	13 54	8 17	4 46	14 04
26	9 39	16 39	4 27	10 06	13 58	8 03	4 45	14 04
31	9N57	16N39	4N28	10N02	14S05	7N46	4S44	14S05

Moon Phenomena

Max/0 Decl
dy hr mn
6 4:16 28S20
12 21:48 0 N
18 23:19 28N17
25 22:22 0 S

Perigee/Apogee
dy hr m kilometers
15 15:12 p 359394
27 22:09 a 405460

Max/0 Lat
dy hr mn
5 2:36 5S04
11 23:08 0 N
17 23:57 5N02
24 17:17 0 S

PH dy hr mn
○ 2 10:10 11♏38
◐ 10 4:28 19♒09
● 16 19:28 25♉33
◑ 23 21:04 2♍21

Void of Course Moon

Last Aspect			☽ Ingress
1 8:08	♇	✱	♏ 1 10:42
3 6:43	♆	□	♐ 3 22:49
6 6:47	♇	☌	♑ 6 9:22
8 7:36	♂	✱	♒ 8 17:49
10 21:48	♀	□	♓ 10 23:33
12 23:54	♇	□	♈ 13 2:20
15 0:25	♇	△	♉ 15 2:49
16 19:28	☉	☌	♊ 17 2:35
19 0:58	♇	☍	♋ 19 3:39
21 7:47	☉	✱	♌ 21 7:58
23 13:10	♇	△	♍ 23 16:27
26 0:45	♇	□	♎ 26 4:17
28 16:18	☿	△	♏ 28 17:12
30 17:13	♀	△	♐ 31 5:08

DAILY ASPECTARIAN

1 Tu
♀△♆ 1:35
☽#☿ 5:24
☽✱♇ 8:08
☽∥♆ 8:44
♂∥♅ 10:46
☉#☽ 11:38
☽⚼♅ 15:57
☽∠♃ 18:19
☽∥♇ 18:22
☽#♄ 19:20
☽⚼♂ 19:49

2 W
☿#♆ 1:10
☽⚼♀ 3:00
☽☍☿ 8:01
☉☍☽ 10:10
☽∠♇ 14:20
☽□⚷ 17:55
☽⊼⚳ 21:52
☽△♅ 22:13
☽□♄ 23:33

3 Th
☽⊻♃ 0:16
☽∥♃ 3:11
☽△♂ 4:00
☉☌☿ 4:07
☽□♆ 6:43
⚳⊻♅ 10:14
☉∥☿ 11:50
☽⊼♀ 12:09
☿⚼♇ 18:53
☽⊻♇ 20:13

4 F
☽⚼⚳ 4:40
☽#♀ 6:06
☿#♇ 10:00
☉⚼♇ 12:41
☿∥♄ 15:08
☿□⚷ 15:22
♂⊻♆ 23:33

5 Sa
☉⊼☽ 2:52
☽✱⚷ 5:23
⚳△♄ 6:09
☽⊼☿ 8:21
☽□♅ 9:40
☽△♄ 10:53
☽△⚳ 11:02
☽☌♃ 11:05
⚳△♃ 12:18
☿✱♅ 15:54
☽✱♆ 17:48
☽□♂ 18:59
☿□♄ 22:56
☿⊼♃ 23:22

6 Su
☉#♇ 1:52
☿⊻⚳ 2:15
☽☍♀ 4:51
☽☌♇ 6:47
♃△♄ 7:12
☉⚼☽ 10:23
☽∠⚷ 10:28
☉□⚷ 11:28
☉∥♄ 14:57
☽⚼♄ 15:54
☽⚼☿ 19:23
☽∠♆ 22:39

7 M
♀☍♇ 2:07
☿□♆ 14:29
☽⊻⚷ 15:00
☉△☽ 17:13
☽✱♅ 19:13
☽⊻♃ 20:01
☽⊼♄ 20:22
☽□⚳ 22:07
☽#♀ 23:38

8 Tu
☽⊻♆ 2:55
☽△☿ 5:24
♀ ♋ 7:29
☽✱♂ 7:36
☽⊻♇ 15:15
☽⊼♀ 18:47
☉✱♅ 20:26
♀⚼⚷ 20:34
☽∠♅ 23:05
☽∠♃ 23:36

9 W
☿✱♂ 0:40
☽∥♃ 2:31
☉⊼♃ 3:11
☉□♄ 12:06
☽∠♂ 12:46
☽#☿ 13:26
☽∠♇ 18:31
☽☌⚷ 22:10

10 Th
☽⚼♀ 0:26
☽⊻♅ 2:15
☽✱♃ 2:29
☉#☽ 2:37
☽☍♄ 3:20
☉□☽ 4:28
☽✱⚳ 6:27
☽#♄ 7:06
☽∥♇ 7:37
☽☌♆ 9:28
☽∥♆ 16:05
☿⊼♇ 16:58
☽⊻♂ 17:04
☽✱♇ 21:03
☽□☿ 21:48

11 F
♃□♅ 3:33
☽△♀ 5:07
☿ ♊ 9:18
☽∠⚳ 9:24
☽∥⚷ 11:11
♀∠♄ 13:01

12 Sa
☉⊻⚳ 0:33
☽⊻⚷ 2:23
☽∥♅ 2:34
☽□♃ 6:04
☽☌♅ 6:19
☽⊼♄ 7:22
☽⊻⚳ 11:33
☉✱☽ 12:03
☽⊻♆ 13:02
☽∥♂ 13:50
☽#⚳ 18:03
☿#♃ 19:16
☽☌♂ 23:02
☽□♇ 23:54

13 Su
☽∥⚳ 1:41
☉□♆ 2:57
☽∠⚷ 3:24
☽#♂ 5:02
☽⚼♄ 8:19
☽✱☿ 9:03
☽□♀ 11:41
☽∠♆ 13:48
☉∠☽ 14:33
♂□♇ 15:17
☽#♅ 16:36

14 M
☽✱⚷ 3:51
☽△♃ 7:01
☽#⚷ 7:13
☽⊻♅ 7:42
☽△♄ 8:43
☽∠☿ 13:08
☽☌⚳ 13:52
☽✱♆ 14:03
♀⚼♆ 16:14
☉⊻☽ 16:27
☿∠⚳ 19:50
⚳✱♆ 21:05

15 Tu
☽△♇ 0:25
☿⊻♀ 0:49
☽#♆ 0:58
☽⊻♂ 2:13
☽⚼♃ 6:50
☽∠♅ 7:43
☽#♇ 8:40
☽∥♄ 8:53
♂#⚳ 9:43
♂ ♈ 14:07
☽✱♀ 15:39
☽⊻☿ 16:38
☉∥☽ 19:14

16 W
☽⚼♇ 0:14
☽∠♂ 3:20
☽□⚷ 3:45
☽⊼♃ 6:30
☽✱♅ 7:37
☽□♄ 8:40
☽#♃ 10:16
♂∠⚷ 11:32
☽□♆ 13:50
☽⊻⚳ 14:51
☽∠♀ 17:21
☉☌☽ 19:28
☽∥☿ 20:34

17 Th
☽⊼♇ 0:06
☽✱♂ 4:32
☽∥♀ 8:33
☽∠⚳ 15:31
☽⊻♀ 19:20
☽☌☿ 23:32

18 F
☽△⚷ 3:56
☽☍♃ 6:24
☽□♅ 8:00
☽✱♄ 9:09
☽△♆ 14:21
☽✱⚳ 16:41
☉⊻☽ 23:43

19 Sa
♄#♇ 0:04
☽☍♇ 0:58
☽⚼⚷ 4:48
☽□♂ 8:28
☽∠♄ 10:16
☿△⚷ 11:47
☽⚼♆ 15:33
☉⊼♇ 18:07

20 Su
⚷ R 0:00
☽☌♀ 1:32
☉∠☽ 3:08
☿☍♃ 5:32
☽⊼⚷ 6:30
☽⊼♃ 8:43
☽⊻☿ 9:13
☽△♅ 10:57
☽⊻♄ 12:16
☽⊼♆ 17:40
☽∥♀ 17:55
☽∥☿ 20:40
♂⚼♄ 20:43
☽□⚳ 21:37
☿□♅ 23:27

21 M
☽⊼♇ 5:00
☉✱☽ 7:47
☉ ♊ 10:13
☿✱♄ 10:49
☽⚼♃ 11:17
☽⚼♅ 13:53
☽∠☿ 15:57
☽△♂ 16:23
☽#♃ 16:46

22 Tu
☿∥♀ 0:35
☉∥☽ 2:45
☽⚼♇ 8:34
☽⊻♀ 12:32
☽☍⚷ 12:59
☽△♃ 14:53
☽⊼♅ 17:54
♀⊼⚷ 18:06
☽☌♄ 19:28
☽⚼♂ 22:14
☽#♇ 22:32
☽∥♄ 22:52

23 W
☽✱☿ 0:06
☽☍♆ 1:03
☽△⚳ 7:01
☽#♆ 7:48
☿△♆ 7:48
☽△♇ 13:10
♀⊼♃ 14:18
☽∠♀ 20:01
☉□☽ 21:04

24 Th
☽⊼♂ 5:15
☽#⚷ 5:42
☽⚼⚳ 13:18
♂∠♆ 21:19
☽⊼⚷ 23:26
☽#♅ 23:47

25 F
☽□♃ 0:53
♆ R 1:09
☽✱♀ 4:35
☽☍♅ 4:46
☽⊻♄ 6:35
♀△♅ 6:43
☽∥⚳ 10:49
☽⊼♆ 12:11
☽∥♂ 15:29
☽□☿ 19:39
☽⊼⚳ 20:19

26 Sa
☽□♇ 0:45
☿✱⚳ 3:02
♀⊻♄ 4:38
☽⚼⚷ 5:39
☽#♂ 6:02
☽#⚳ 10:30
☽∠♄ 13:03
☉△☽ 14:23
☽⚼♆ 18:34
☽∥♅ 21:06
☽☍♂ 21:39

27 Su
☽△⚷ 12:07
☽✱♃ 13:00
☿☍♇ 15:14
☽∥⚷ 15:39
☽⊼♅ 17:41
☽✱♄ 19:43
☽□♀ 23:15
☉⚼☽ 23:34

28 M
☽△♆ 1:03
☽☍⚳ 11:10
☽✱♇ 13:33
☽∥♆ 14:36
☽△☿ 16:18
☽∠♃ 19:07
♀⊼♆ 19:54
☽#♄ 23:26

29 Tu
☽⚼♅ 0:08
☽∥♇ 0:22
☿ ♋ 0:57
☉⊼☽ 8:35
☿⚼⚷ 13:45
☽⊼♂ 14:31
☽∠♇ 19:42

30 W
☽□⚷ 0:40
☽⊻♃ 0:57
☉∠♀ 1:50
☽⚼☿ 1:52
☉#☽ 6:16
☽△♅ 6:16
☽∥♃ 7:51
☽□♄ 8:29
☽□♆ 13:22
☽△♀ 17:13
☽#♀ 21:02
☽⚼♂ 22:23

31 Th
☽⊼⚳ 1:05
☽⊻♇ 1:27
♃✱⚷ 6:55
☽#☿ 8:43
☽⊼☿ 10:36
⚳△♇ 12:26
☉#♃ 20:53

June 2007

LONGITUDE

Day	Sid.Time	☉	☽	☽ 12 hour	Mean ☊	True ☊	☿	♀	♂	⚳	♃	♄	⚷	♅	♆	♇
	h m s	° ' "	° ' "	° ' "	° '	° '	° '	° '	° '	° '	° '	° '	° '	° '	° '	° '
1 F	16 36 24	10♊09 11	9♐38 30	15♐49 41	11♓40.3	11♓44.0	3♋23.2	25♋15.9	12♈22.5	28♈17.6	15♐32.5	19♌40.8	15♒37.4	18♓29.1	22♒01.3	28♐06.5
2 Sa	16 40 21	11 06 41	22 03 31	28 20 01	11 37.2	11R 30.7	4 24.6	26 16.4	13 07.3	28 39.1	15R 24.9	19 45.0	15R 36.6	18 30.2	22R 01.0	28R 05.0
3 Su	16 44 18	12 04 09	4♑39 14	11♑01 10	11 34.0	11 18.6	5 22.3	27 16.5	13 52.2	29 00.5	15 17.3	19 49.3	15 35.8	18 31.2	22 00.8	28 03.6
4 M	16 48 14	13 01 37	17 25 52	23 53 23	11 30.8	11 08.7	6 16.1	28 16.3	14 37.0	29 21.9	15 09.7	19 53.6	15 34.9	18 32.2	22 00.5	28 02.1
5 Tu	16 52 11	13 59 03	0♒23 48	6♒57 12	11 27.6	11 01.5	7 06.1	29 15.7	15 21.7	29 43.2	15 02.0	19 58.1	15 34.0	18 33.1	22 00.1	28 00.6
6 W	16 56 07	14 56 29	13 33 44	20 13 31	11 24.5	10 57.2	7 52.1	0♌14.7	16 06.4	0♉04.4	14 54.4	20 02.6	15 33.0	18 34.0	21 59.8	27 59.1
7 Th	17 00 04	15 53 54	26 56 45	3♓43 36	11 21.3	10 55.3	8 34.0	1 13.3	16 51.1	0 25.6	14 46.7	20 07.2	15 31.9	18 34.8	21 59.4	27 57.5
8 F	17 04 00	16 51 19	10♓34 13	17 28 46	11 18.1	10 54.9	9 11.8	2 11.5	17 35.7	0 46.7	14 39.1	20 11.9	15 30.7	18 35.6	21 59.0	27 56.0
9 Sa	17 07 57	17 48 42	24 27 20	1♈29 57	11 14.9	10 54.8	9 45.3	3 09.3	18 20.2	1 07.7	14 31.5	20 16.7	15 29.5	18 36.3	21 58.5	27 54.5
10 Su	17 11 53	18 46 06	8♈36 34	15 47 02	11 11.7	10 53.8	10 14.6	4 06.6	19 04.7	1 28.6	14 23.8	20 21.5	15 28.3	18 37.0	21 58.0	27 53.0
11 M	17 15 50	19 43 29	23 01 03	0♉18 12	11 08.6	10 50.9	10 39.4	5 03.5	19 49.1	1 49.5	14 16.2	20 26.4	15 27.0	18 37.7	21 57.5	27 51.4
12 Tu	17 19 47	20 40 51	7♉37 55	14 59 29	11 05.4	10 45.3	10 59.8	5 59.9	20 33.5	2 10.3	14 08.6	20 31.4	15 25.6	18 38.2	21 56.9	27 49.9
13 W	17 23 43	21 38 13	22 22 05	29 44 47	11 02.2	10 37.2	11 15.6	6 55.8	21 17.8	2 31.0	14 01.1	20 36.5	15 24.1	18 38.8	21 56.4	27 48.3
14 Th	17 27 40	22 35 34	7♊06 34	14♊26 27	10 59.0	10 27.2	11 27.0	7 51.3	22 02.1	2 51.6	13 53.6	20 41.6	15 22.6	18 39.3	21 55.8	27 46.8
15 F	17 31 36	23 32 55	21 43 24	28 56 30	10 55.9	10 16.2	11R 33.7	8 46.2	22 46.3	3 12.2	13 46.1	20 46.9	15 21.1	18 39.7	21 55.1	27 45.2
16 Sa	17 35 33	24 30 15	6♋04 56	13♋08 00	10 52.7	10 05.6	11 35.9	9 40.6	23 30.4	3 32.6	13 38.7	20 52.1	15 19.5	18 40.1	21 54.5	27 43.7
17 Su	17 39 29	25 27 35	20 05 11	26 56 05	10 49.5	9 56.4	11 33.6	10 34.4	24 14.5	3 53.0	13 31.3	20 57.5	15 17.8	18 40.5	21 53.8	27 42.1
18 M	17 43 26	26 24 54	3♌40 33	10♌18 32	10 46.3	9 49.5	11 26.9	11 27.7	24 58.5	4 13.3	13 24.0	21 02.9	15 16.1	18 40.8	21 53.0	27 40.5
19 Tu	17 47 22	27 22 12	16 50 11	23 15 43	10 43.2	9 45.2	11 15.9	12 20.4	25 42.5	4 33.5	13 16.7	21 08.4	15 14.3	18 41.0	21 52.3	27 39.0
20 W	17 51 19	28 19 29	29 35 34	5♍50 09	10 40.0	9D 43.1	11 00.7	13 12.4	26 26.3	4 53.6	13 09.5	21 13.9	15 12.4	18 41.2	21 51.5	27 37.4
21 Th	17 55 16	29 16 45	12♍00 03	18 05 50	10 36.8	9 42.8	10 41.6	14 03.9	27 10.1	5 13.6	13 02.4	21 19.6	15 10.5	18 41.4	21 50.7	27 35.8
22 F	17 59 12	0♋14 01	24 08 10	0♎07 41	10 33.6	9R 43.1	10 18.9	14 54.6	27 53.8	5 33.5	12 55.4	21 25.2	15 08.6	18 41.5	21 49.9	27 34.3
23 Sa	18 03 09	1 11 16	6♎05 04	12 00 59	10 30.5	9 43.1	9 53.0	15 44.7	28 37.5	5 53.3	12 48.4	21 31.0	15 06.6	18R 41.5	21 49.0	27 32.7
24 Su	18 07 05	2 08 30	17 56 06	23 51 02	10 27.3	9 41.8	9 24.1	16 34.0	29 21.1	6 13.0	12 41.5	21 36.8	15 04.5	18 41.5	21 48.1	27 31.2
25 M	18 11 02	3 05 44	29 46 23	5♏42 43	10 24.1	9 38.5	8 52.8	17 22.6	0♉04.6	6 32.7	12 34.8	21 42.6	15 02.4	18 41.5	21 47.2	27 29.6
26 Tu	18 14 58	4 02 57	11♏40 33	17 40 22	10 20.9	9 32.9	8 19.6	18 10.4	0 48.0	6 52.2	12 28.1	21 48.6	15 00.3	18 41.4	21 46.3	27 28.0
27 W	18 18 55	5 00 10	23 42 33	29 47 28	10 17.7	9 25.0	7 45.0	18 57.4	1 31.4	7 11.6	12 21.5	21 54.6	14 58.0	18 41.3	21 45.3	27 26.5
28 Th	18 22 51	5 57 22	5♐55 24	12♐06 34	10 14.6	9 15.2	7 09.6	19 43.6	2 14.7	7 30.9	12 15.0	22 00.6	14 55.8	18 41.1	21 44.3	27 25.0
29 F	18 26 48	6 54 34	18 21 07	24 39 09	10 11.4	9 04.5	6 34.0	20 28.9	2 57.9	7 50.1	12 08.6	22 06.7	14 53.5	18 40.9	21 43.3	27 23.4
30 Sa	18 30 45	7♋51 45	1♑00 41	7♑25 41	10♓08.2	8♓53.8	5♋58.8	21♌13.3	3♉41.1	8♉09.2	12♐02.4	22♌12.9	14♒51.1	18♓40.6	21♒42.2	27♐21.9

1st of Month

Julian Day # 2454252.5
Obliquity 23°26'26"
SVP 5♓09'18"
GC 26♐56.6
Eris 21♈22.3

Day	⚴
1	16♓30.2
6	17 14.5
11	17 53.0
16	18 25.2
21	18 50.7
26	19 09.2

Day	⚵
1	12♎04.8R
6	12 03.7
11	12 10.5
16	12 25.1
21	12 47.0
26	13 15.9

Day	⚶
1	8♐27.5R
6	7 15.8R
11	6 07.4R
16	5 04.9R
21	4 10.5R
26	3 26.2R

DECLINATION and LATITUDE

Day	☉ Decl	☽ Decl	☽ Lat	☽12h Decl	☿ Decl	☿ Lat	♀ Decl	♀ Lat	♂ Decl	♂ Lat	⚳ Decl	⚳ Lat	♃ Decl	♃ Lat	♄ Decl	♄ Lat
1 F	21N58	26S50	4S60	27S38	25N16	1N52	23N40	2N38	3N29	1S31	3N31	7S52	21S57	0N42	16N07	1N16
2 Sa	22 07	28 06	4 55	28 13	25 07	1 45	23 27	2 36	3 47	1 31	3 38	7 52	21 56	0 42	16 06	1 16
3 Su	22 14	27 57	4 36	27 19	24 57	1 37	23 14	2 35	4 04	1 31	3 45	7 53	21 56	0 42	16 05	1 16
4 M	22 22	26 19	4 03	24 57	24 46	1 28	23 00	2 33	4 21	1 31	3 52	7 53	21 55	0 42	16 03	1 16
5 Tu	22 29	23 16	3 16	21 16	24 34	1 19	22 46	2 31	4 39	1 31	3 58	7 54	21 54	0 42	16 02	1 16
6 W	22 35	18 58	2 19	16 26	24 21	1 09	22 32	2 29	4 56	1 31	4 05	7 54	21 54	0 42	16 00	1 16
7 Th	22 42	13 41	1 13	10 44	24 08	0 58	22 17	2 27	5 13	1 31	4 12	7 55	21 53	0 42	15 59	1 16
8 F	22 47	7 38	0 02	4 25	23 53	0 46	22 01	2 25	5 30	1 31	4 19	7 55	21 52	0 42	15 57	1 16
9 Sa	22 53	1 07	1N11	2N14	23 39	0 34	21 45	2 22	5 47	1 31	4 25	7 56	21 51	0 41	15 56	1 16
10 Su	22 58	5N34	2 21	8 52	23 23	0 21	21 29	2 20	6 04	1 31	4 32	7 56	21 51	0 41	15 54	1 16
11 M	23 03	12 05	3 23	15 10	23 07	0 07	21 13	2 17	6 21	1 31	4 38	7 57	21 50	0 41	15 53	1 16
12 Tu	23 07	18 02	4 13	20 39	22 51	0S08	20 56	2 14	6 38	1 31	4 45	7 57	21 49	0 41	15 51	1 16
13 W	23 11	22 58	4 46	24 54	22 35	0 23	20 39	2 11	6 54	1 31	4 51	7 58	21 48	0 41	15 49	1 16
14 Th	23 14	26 26	5 00	27 30	22 19	0 38	20 21	2 07	7 11	1 31	4 58	7 59	21 48	0 41	15 48	1 16
15 F	23 17	28 05	4 55	28 11	22 02	0 54	20 03	2 04	7 27	1 31	5 04	7 59	21 47	0 41	15 46	1 16
16 Sa	23 20	27 49	4 31	26 59	21 46	1 10	19 45	1 60	7 44	1 30	5 10	7 60	21 46	0 41	15 44	1 16
17 Su	23 22	25 45	3 51	24 08	21 30	1 27	19 27	1 56	8 00	1 30	5 16	8 00	21 45	0 40	15 42	1 16
18 M	23 24	22 14	2 59	20 03	21 14	1 44	19 08	1 52	8 16	1 30	5 22	8 01	21 45	0 40	15 41	1 16
19 Tu	23 25	17 40	1 58	15 07	20 58	2 00	18 49	1 47	8 32	1 30	5 28	8 02	21 44	0 40	15 39	1 16
20 W	23 26	12 27	0 51	9 41	20 42	2 17	18 30	1 43	8 48	1 30	5 34	8 02	21 43	0 40	15 37	1 16
21 Th	23 26	6 52	0S12	4 01	20 28	2 33	18 11	1 38	9 04	1 30	5 40	8 03	21 42	0 40	15 35	1 16
22 F	23 26	1 10	1 16	1S41	20 13	2 50	17 51	1 33	9 20	1 29	5 46	8 04	21 42	0 40	15 33	1 16
23 Sa	23 26	4S29	2 15	7 15	19 60	3 05	17 31	1 28	9 36	1 29	5 51	8 04	21 41	0 39	15 31	1 16
24 Su	23 25	9 56	3 09	12 32	19 47	3 20	17 11	1 23	9 51	1 29	5 57	8 05	21 40	0 39	15 30	1 16
25 M	23 24	15 02	3 54	17 23	19 35	3 34	16 51	1 17	10 07	1 29	6 03	8 06	21 40	0 39	15 28	1 16
26 Tu	23 23	19 35	4 29	21 36	19 24	3 47	16 31	1 11	10 22	1 28	6 08	8 07	21 39	0 39	15 26	1 15
27 W	23 21	23 25	4 52	24 58	19 14	3 60	16 11	1 05	10 38	1 28	6 14	8 07	21 38	0 39	15 24	1 15
28 Th	23 18	26 16	5 03	27 15	19 05	4 11	15 50	0 59	10 53	1 28	6 19	8 08	21 38	0 39	15 22	1 15
29 F	23 16	27 54	4 59	28 12	18 57	4 20	15 30	0 53	11 08	1 28	6 24	8 09	21 37	0 38	15 20	1 15
30 Sa	23N12	28S07	4S41	27S40	18N50	4S28	15N09	0N46	11N23	1S27	6N30	8S10	21S36	0N38	15N18	1N15

Day	⚷ Decl	⚷ Lat	♅ Decl	♅ Lat	♆ Decl	♆ Lat	♇ Decl	♇ Lat
1	9S29	6N59	5S16	0S46	14S25	0S16	16S23	7N03
6	9 28	7 01	5 14	0 46	14 25	0 16	16 23	7 03
11	9 28	7 03	5 13	0 46	14 26	0 16	16 23	7 03
16	9 28	7 05	5 12	0 47	14 27	0 16	16 23	7 02
21	9 29	7 06	5 12	0 47	14 29	0 16	16 23	7 02
26	9 30	7 08	5 12	0 47	14 30	0 16	16 24	7 01

Day	⚴ Decl	⚴ Lat	⚵ Decl	⚵ Lat	⚶ Decl	⚶ Lat	Eris Decl	Eris Lat
1	10N00	16N38	4N28	10N02	14S06	7N42	4S44	14S05
6	10 17	16 38	4 24	9 57	14 16	7 22	4 44	14 05
11	10 31	16 37	4 17	9 52	14 27	6 59	4 44	14 06
16	10 42	16 36	4 06	9 47	14 41	6 34	4 43	14 06
21	10 51	16 35	3 53	9 41	14 57	6 08	4 43	14 07
26	10 56	16 33	3 36	9 35	15 15	5 41	4 43	14 07

Moon Phenomena

Max/0 Decl

dy	hr mn	
2	9:28	28S13
9	4:01	0 N
15	8:22	28N12
22	4:55	0 S
29	15:46	28S13

Max/0 Lat

dy	hr mn	
1	3:55	5S00
8	0:36	0 N
14	5:16	5N01
20	19:32	0 S
28	6:20	5S03

Perigee/Apogee

dy	hr m		kilometers
12	17:14	p	363781
24	14:29	a	404538

PH	dy	hr mn	
○	1	1:05	10♐12
☾	8	11:44	17♓19
●	15	3:14	23♊41
☽	22	13:16	0♎46
○	30	13:50	8♑25

Void of Course Moon

Last Aspect			☽ Ingress		
2 11:30	♇	☌	♑	2	15:10
4 21:45	♀	☍	♒	4	23:16
7 1:48	♇	⚹	♓	7	5:25
9 5:53	♇	□	♈	9	9:27
11 7:58	♇	△	♉	11	11:30
12 23:18	♆	□	♊	13	12:25
15 10:00	♇	☍	♋	15	13:46
17 7:40	♂	□	♌	17	17:26
19 21:23	☉	⚹	♍	20	0:47
22 6:51	♇	□	♎	22	11:45
24 19:24	♇	⚹	♏	25	0:28
26 20:24	♄	□	♐	27	12:25
29 17:09	♇	☌	♑	29	22:06

DAILY ASPECTARIAN

1 F: ☉☍☽ 1:05; ☽⚼♀ 1:19; ♂∥⚳ 3:29; ☽△♂ 5:39; ☽⚼⚳ 7:18; ☽☌♃ 11:20; ☽⚹⚷ 11:35; ☽□♅ 17:09; ☽△♄ 19:32; ☽⚹♆ 23:55

2 Sa: ☽⚻♀ 8:46; ☿∠♄ 8:58; ☽☌♇ 11:30; ☽△⚳ 12:58; ☽∠⚷ 16:19

3 Su: ☽⚼♄ 0:19; ☽☍☿ 1:28; ☽∠♆ 4:27; ☉⚻☽ 15:06; ♀⚻♇ 18:24; ☽□♂ 18:25; ☽⚺♃ 19:48; ☽⚺⚷ 20:33

4 M: ☽⚹♅ 2:04; ☽⚻♄ 4:37; ⚵ D 5:08; ☽⚺♆ 8:31; ☽#☿ 14:21; ♂△♃ 14:59; ☽⚺♇ 19:37; ☿⚼♆ 21:03; ☉⚼☽ 21:12; ☽☍♀ 21:45; ☽□⚳ 22:43; ☽∠♃ 23:20

5 Tu: ☽#♀ 3:20; ☉#☽ 4:46; ☽∠♅ 5:48; ♂⚹⚷ 6:26; ☽∥♃ 8:20; ☽⚻☿ 13:03; ⚳⚼♃ 15:39; ♀⚼♃ 16:40; ♀□⚳ 17:27; ♀ ♌ 18:00; ⚳ ♉ 19:00; ☉∥♀ 19:43; ☽∠♇ 22:57; ☉☍♃ 23:14

6 W: ☽⚹♃ 2:24; ☉△☽ 2:41; ☽☌⚷ 3:35; ☽⚹♂ 4:52; ☉∠⚳ 5:15; ☽⚺♅ 9:02; ☽☍♄ 11:44; ☽∥♇ 12:16; ☽#♄ 14:00; ☉△⚷ 14:58; ☽☌♆ 15:10; ☽⚼☿ 17:40; ☽∥♆ 20:49

7 Th: ♂#♅ 0:57; ☽⚹♇ 1:48; ☽⚹⚳ 6:20; ☽⚻♀ 8:10; ☽∠♂ 9:12; ☽∥⚷ 16:58; ☽△☿ 21:29

8 F: ☽□♃ 7:02; ☽#♂ 7:39; ☽⚺⚷ 8:35; ☽∥♅ 9:02; ☽∠⚳ 9:17; ☉□☽ 11:44; ☽#⚳ 12:10; ☽⚼♀ 12:22; ☽⚺♂ 12:53; ☽☌♅ 13:56; ♀#♃ 14:43; ☽⚻♄ 16:47; ☽⚺♆ 19:45

9 Sa: ☽□♇ 5:53; ♂⚺♅ 8:50; ☽∠⚷ 10:17; ♀⚼♅ 11:27; ☽⚺⚳ 11:39; ☽△♀ 15:52; ☽⚼♄ 18:30; ☉□♅ 20:09; ☽∥⚳ 20:12; ☽∠♆ 21:14; ☽#♅ 22:43

10 Su: ☽∥♂ 1:52; ☽□☿ 2:50; ☽△♃ 9:36; ☽⚹⚷ 11:28; ☽#⚷ 14:10; ☽⚺♅ 16:43; ☉⚹☽ 18:10; ☽☌♂ 18:25; ☽△♄ 19:43; ☽⚹♆ 22:15

11 M: ☉∥☿ 5:49; ☽△♇ 7:58; ☽#♆ 9:07; ☽⚼♃ 10:13; ☉⚹♂ 10:28; ☽∥♄ 14:50; ☽☌⚳ 14:51; ☽#♇ 16:59; ☽∠♅ 17:28; ☉⚹♄ 19:41; ☉∠☽ 20:35; ☽□♀ 21:09; ♂△♄ 22:44

12 Tu: ☽⚹☿ 5:36; ☽⚼♇ 8:28; ☽⚻♃ 10:32; ☽∥♀ 12:37; ☽□⚷ 12:41; ☽#♃ 17:46; ☽⚹♅ 17:57; ☽□♄ 21:07; ☽∥☿ 22:01; ☽⚺♂ 22:10; ☉⚺☽ 22:44; ☽□♆ 23:18

13 W: ☉∥☽ 1:13; ☽∠☿ 6:25; ☉△♆ 7:31; ☽⚻♇ 8:50; ☽⚺⚳ 16:54; ♂⚹♆ 20:36; ☽∠♂ 23:52

14 Th: ☽⚹♀ 1:18; ☽⚺☿ 7:10; ☽☍♃ 11:00; ☽△⚷ 13:31; ☽∠⚳ 18:03; ☽□♅ 18:57; ☽⚹♄ 22:26

15 F: ☽△♆ 0:19; ☽⚹♂ 1:50; ☉☌☽ 3:14; ☽∠♀ 3:37; ☽☍♇ 10:00; ☽⚼⚷ 14:20; ☽⚹⚳ 19:37; ☽∠♄ 23:38; ☿ R 23:42; ☿#♃ 23:47

16 Sa: ☽⚼♆ 1:24; ☽⚺♀ 6:31; ⚳#♅ 7:17; ⚳∠♅ 8:59; ☽☌☿ 9:22; ☽⚻♃ 12:46; ☽⚻⚷ 15:44; ☽△♅ 21:33

17 Su: ☽⚺♄ 1:32; ☽⚻♆ 3:09; ☽□♂ 7:40; ☉⚺☽ 10:07; ☽⚻♇ 13:20; ☽⚼♃ 14:41; ☉∥☽ 16:58; ☿⚺♀ 23:41

18 M: ☽⚼♅ 0:00; ☽□⚳ 1:00; ☽#♃ 2:48; ☽∥☿ 6:03; ☽⚺☿ 13:54; ☉∠♀ 14:58; ☽☌♀ 15:07; ☉∠☽ 15:07; ☽⚼♇ 16:18; ☽△♃ 17:30; ☽∥♀ 17:56; ☽☍⚷ 21:03

19 Tu: ☽⚻♅ 3:26; ☽#♇ 6:08; ☉☍♇ 6:50; ☽☌♄ 8:05; ♀⚼♇ 8:17; ☽☍♆ 9:23; ☽∥♄ 9:39; ☽#♆ 14:59; ☽∠☿ 17:20; ☽△♂ 17:38; ☽△♇ 20:15; ☉⚹☽ 21:23; ♀△♃ 22:49

20 W: ☽△⚳ 10:28; ☽#⚷ 12:54; ☽∥♂ 15:05; ☽⚹☿ 21:31

21 Th: ☽⚼♂ 0:21; ☽□♃ 2:01; ☽⚺♀ 4:21; ☽∥⚳ 5:01; ☽⚻⚷ 6:13; ☽#♅ 7:05; ☽☍♅ 13:10; ♂△♇ 13:38; ☽⚼⚳ 16:41; ☉ ♋ 18:08; ☽⚺♄ 18:33; ☽⚻♆ 19:25; ☉⚼⚷ 21:48

22 F: ♂⚼♃ 0:43; ♀☍⚷ 6:25; ☽□♇ 6:51; ☽⚻♂ 8:01; ☽⚼⚷ 12:00; ☽∠♀ 12:26; ☉□☽ 13:16; ♂#⚷ 14:07; ☽⚻⚳ 23:36

23 Sa: ☽∠♄ 0:53; ☽⚼♆ 1:29; ☽∥♅ 3:02; ☽#⚳ 6:01; ☽□☿ 7:23; ☽⚹♃ 13:28; ♅ R 14:44; ☽△⚷ 18:13; ☽⚹♀ 21:01; ☽∥⚷ 22:00; ☽#♂ 23:36

24 Su: ☽⚻♅ 1:32; ☽⚹♄ 7:31; ☽△♆ 7:50; ☽⚹♇ 19:24; ☽∠♃ 19:36; ☽∥♆ 21:22; ♂ ♉ 21:28

25 M: ☽☍♂ 0:39; ☽#♄ 2:07; ☽∥♇ 6:51; ☉△☽ 7:18; ☽⚼♅ 7:55; ☽#♀ 8:35; ☽☍⚳ 14:04; ♄☍♆ 15:55; ☽△☿ 17:34; ☽#☿ 22:56

26 Tu: ☽⚺♃ 1:34; ☽∠♇ 1:35; ☽□⚷ 6:39; ♀#♇ 8:23; ☽∥♃ 12:13; ☽□♀ 13:54; ☽△♅ 14:02; ♀⚻♅ 15:44; ☉⚼☽ 16:01; ☽□♆ 20:08; ☽□♄ 20:24; ☽⚼☿ 22:11; ☉#☽ 23:32

27 W: ☽⚺♇ 7:22; ☿⚹⚳ 14:40; ☽⚻♂ 16:22

28 Th: ☉⚻☽ 0:04; ☽⚻☿ 2:18; ☽⚻⚳ 3:11; ☿∠♄ 5:11; ☽☌♃ 12:10; ☽⚹⚷ 17:23; ☿⚼♆ 17:33; ☉☌☿ 18:41; ☉⚼♆ 19:21; ☽⚼♂ 23:13

29 F: ☽□♅ 0:38; ☽△♀ 4:19; ☉∠♄ 5:42; ☽⚹♆ 6:25; ☽△♄ 7:14; ☽⚼⚳ 8:46; ♀∥♄ 13:01; ☽☌♇ 17:09; ☿∠♀ 19:35; ☽∠⚷ 21:50; ♂∠♅ 23:44

30 Sa: ☽△♂ 5:19; ☽☍☿ 8:54; ☽⚼♀ 10:20; ☽∠♆ 10:38; ☉⚹⚳ 10:59; ☽⚼♄ 11:42; ☽△⚳ 13:41; ☉☍☽ 13:50; ♀☍♆ 15:32; ☽⚺♃ 20:24

LONGITUDE — July 2007

Day	Sid.Time	☉	☽	☽ 12 hour	Mean ☊	True ☊	☿	♀	♂	⚳	♃	♄	⚷	♅	♆	♇
	h m s	° ' "	° ' "	° ' "	° '	° '	° '	° '	° '	° '	° '	° '	° '	° '	° '	° '
1 Su	18 34 41	8♋48 57	13♑54 07	20♑25 51	10♓05.0	8♓44.0	5♋24.6	21♌56.8	4♉24.1	8♉28.2	11♐56.2	22♌19.1	14♒48.8	18♓40.3	21♒41.2	27♐20.4
2 M	18 38 38	9 46 08	27 00 46	3♒38 43	10 01.9	8R 36.1	4R 52.0	22 39.3	5 07.1	8 47.1	11R 50.2	22 25.3	14R 46.3	18R 39.9	21R 40.1	27R 18.8
3 Tu	18 42 34	10 43 19	10♒19 34	17 03 09	9 58.7	8 30.5	4 21.6	23 20.8	5 50.0	9 05.9	11 44.3	22 31.6	14 43.8	18 39.5	21 39.0	27 17.3
4 W	18 46 31	11 40 30	23 49 21	0♓38 04	9 55.5	8 27.4	3 53.9	24 01.3	6 32.9	9 24.6	11 38.5	22 38.0	14 41.3	18 39.0	21 37.8	27 15.8
5 Th	18 50 27	12 37 42	7♓29 12	14 22 42	9 52.3	8D 26.5	3 29.4	24 40.7	7 15.6	9 43.1	11 32.8	22 44.4	14 38.7	18 38.5	21 36.7	27 14.3
6 F	18 54 24	13 34 53	21 18 28	28 16 29	9 49.2	8 26.9	3 08.5	25 19.0	7 58.3	10 01.5	11 27.3	22 50.9	14 36.1	18 37.9	21 35.5	27 12.8
7 Sa	18 58 21	14 32 05	5♈16 41	12♈18 58	9 46.0	8R 27.8	2 51.7	25 56.1	8 40.9	10 19.8	11 21.9	22 57.4	14 33.5	18 37.3	21 34.3	27 11.4
8 Su	19 02 17	15 29 17	19 23 14	26 29 20	9 42.8	8 28.0	2 39.2	26 32.0	9 23.4	10 38.0	11 16.7	23 04.0	14 30.8	18 36.6	21 33.1	27 09.9
9 M	19 06 14	16 26 30	3♉37 02	10♉46 03	9 39.6	8 26.7	2 31.4	27 06.7	10 05.8	10 56.1	11 11.6	23 10.6	14 28.1	18 35.9	21 31.8	27 08.4
10 Tu	19 10 10	17 23 43	17 56 02	25 06 30	9 36.4	8 23.5	2D 28.4	27 40.1	10 48.1	11 14.0	11 06.6	23 17.2	14 25.3	18 35.2	21 30.6	27 07.0
11 W	19 14 07	18 20 56	2♊16 59	9♊26 53	9 33.3	8 18.2	2 30.5	28 12.2	11 30.3	11 31.8	11 01.8	23 23.9	14 22.5	18 34.4	21 29.3	27 05.6
12 Th	19 18 03	19 18 10	16 35 34	23 42 32	9 30.1	8 11.4	2 37.7	28 42.8	12 12.5	11 49.5	10 57.1	23 30.7	14 19.7	18 33.6	21 28.0	27 04.1
13 F	19 22 00	20 15 25	0♋46 44	7♋47 56	9 26.9	8 03.9	2 50.2	29 12.1	12 54.5	12 07.0	10 52.6	23 37.5	14 16.8	18 32.7	21 26.7	27 02.7
14 Sa	19 25 56	21 12 39	14 45 25	21 38 41	9 23.8	7 56.5	3 08.1	29 39.8	13 36.5	12 24.4	10 48.3	23 44.3	14 14.0	18 31.8	21 25.3	27 01.3
15 Su	19 29 53	22 09 54	28 27 20	5♌11 01	9 20.6	7 50.2	3 31.2	0♍06.0	14 18.3	12 41.7	10 44.1	23 51.2	14 11.0	18 30.8	21 24.0	27 00.0
16 M	19 33 50	23 07 09	11♌49 33	18 22 50	9 17.4	7 45.5	3 59.8	0 30.5	15 00.1	12 58.8	10 40.1	23 58.1	14 08.1	18 29.8	21 22.6	26 58.6
17 Tu	19 37 46	24 04 25	24 50 54	1♍13 53	9 14.2	7 42.8	4 33.7	0 53.4	15 41.7	13 15.8	10 36.2	24 05.0	14 05.1	18 28.7	21 21.2	26 57.2
18 W	19 41 43	25 01 40	7♍32 00	13 45 34	9 11.0	7D 42.0	5 13.0	1 14.6	16 23.2	13 32.6	10 32.5	24 12.0	14 02.1	18 27.6	21 19.8	26 55.9
19 Th	19 45 39	25 58 56	19 54 59	26 00 44	9 07.9	7 42.6	5 57.5	1 33.9	17 04.7	13 49.2	10 29.0	24 19.0	13 59.1	18 26.5	21 18.4	26 54.6
20 F	19 49 36	26 56 12	2♎03 19	8♎03 17	9 04.7	7 44.0	6 47.3	1 51.4	17 46.0	14 05.7	10 25.7	24 26.1	13 56.0	18 25.3	21 16.9	26 53.3
21 Sa	19 53 32	27 53 28	14 01 14	19 57 47	9 01.5	7 45.5	7 42.3	2 07.0	18 27.2	14 22.1	10 22.5	24 33.2	13 52.9	18 24.1	21 15.5	26 52.0
22 Su	19 57 29	28 50 44	25 53 33	1♏49 11	8 58.3	7R 46.3	8 42.4	2 20.6	19 08.3	14 38.3	10 19.5	24 40.3	13 49.8	18 22.8	21 14.0	26 50.7
23 M	20 01 25	29 48 01	7♏45 17	13 42 27	8 55.2	7 46.0	9 47.5	2 32.1	19 49.3	14 54.3	10 16.6	24 47.4	13 46.7	18 21.5	21 12.5	26 49.5
24 Tu	20 05 22	0♌45 18	19 41 18	25 42 21	8 52.0	7 44.2	10 57.6	2 41.6	20 30.2	15 10.2	10 14.0	24 54.6	13 43.6	18 20.1	21 11.0	26 48.2
25 W	20 09 19	1 42 35	1♐46 09	7♐53 08	8 48.8	7 40.9	12 12.6	2 48.9	21 10.9	15 25.9	10 11.5	25 01.8	13 40.4	18 18.8	21 09.5	26 47.0
26 Th	20 13 15	2 39 53	14 03 44	20 18 16	8 45.6	7 36.3	13 32.4	2 53.9	21 51.6	15 41.5	10 09.2	25 09.1	13 37.3	18 17.3	21 08.0	26 45.8
27 F	20 17 12	3 37 11	26 37 02	3♑00 13	8 42.5	7 31.0	14 56.8	2R 56.8	22 32.1	15 56.8	10 07.1	25 16.4	13 34.1	18 15.9	21 06.4	26 44.7
28 Sa	20 21 08	4 34 30	9♑27 55	16 00 11	8 39.3	7 25.5	16 25.7	2 57.3	23 12.6	16 12.0	10 05.2	25 23.7	13 30.9	18 14.4	21 04.9	26 43.5
29 Su	20 25 05	5 31 50	22 36 58	29 18 08	8 36.1	7 20.5	17 58.9	2 55.5	23 52.9	16 27.0	10 03.4	25 31.0	13 27.7	18 12.8	21 03.4	26 42.4
30 M	20 29 01	6 29 10	6♒03 28	12♒52 43	8 32.9	7 16.6	19 36.3	2 51.3	24 33.1	16 41.9	10 01.8	25 38.3	13 24.5	18 11.3	21 01.8	26 41.3
31 Tu	20 32 58	7♌26 30	19 45 33	26 41 37	8♓29.7	7♓14.1	21♋17.5	2♍44.8	25♉13.1	16♉56.5	10♐00.4	25♌45.7	13♒21.2	18♓09.7	21♒00.2	26♐40.2

1st of Month

Julian Day # 2454282.5
Obliquity 23°26'26"
SVP 5♓09'12"
GC 26♐56.6
Eris 21♈32.1

Day	⚴
1	19♓20.1
6	19 23.2R
11	19 18.2R
16	19 04.6R
21	18 42.3R
26	18 11.3R
31	17 31.9R

Day	⚵
1	13♎51.2
6	14 32.6
11	15 19.6
16	16 11.9
21	17 09.0
26	18 10.6
31	19 16.4

Day	⚶
1	2♐53.0R
6	2 31.5R
11	2 22.2R
16	2 25.0
21	2 39.9
26	3 06.4
31	3 43.7

DECLINATION and LATITUDE

Day	☉ Decl	☽ Decl	☽ Lat	☽ 12h Decl	☿ Decl	☿ Lat	♀ Decl	♀ Lat	♂ Decl	♂ Lat	⚳ Decl	⚳ Lat	♃ Decl	♃ Lat	♄ Decl	♄ Lat
1 Su	23N09	26S50	4S09	25S38	18N45	4S35	14N49	0N39	11N37	1S27	6N35	8S10	21S36	0N38	15N16	1N15
2 M	23 05	24 04	3 22	22 10	18 41	4 40	14 28	0 32	11 52	1 27	6 40	8 11	21 35	0 38	15 14	1 15
3 Tu	23 00	19 58	2 24	17 30	18 38	4 44	14 08	0 25	12 07	1 26	6 45	8 12	21 35	0 38	15 12	1 15
4 W	22 56	14 48	1 17	11 54	18 37	4 46	13 47	0 17	12 21	1 26	6 50	8 13	21 34	0 38	15 09	1 15
5 Th	22 50	8 50	0 05	5 40	18 37	4 46	13 26	0 09	12 35	1 26	6 55	8 14	21 33	0 37	15 07	1 15
6 F	22 45	2 24	1N09	0N55	18 39	4 45	13 06	0 01	12 49	1 25	6 59	8 14	21 33	0 37	15 05	1 15
7 Sa	22 39	4N13	2 19	7 30	18 42	4 43	12 46	0S07	13 03	1 25	7 04	8 15	21 32	0 37	15 03	1 15
8 Su	22 32	10 42	3 22	13 46	18 46	4 39	12 25	0 16	13 17	1 24	7 09	8 16	21 32	0 37	15 01	1 15
9 M	22 26	16 40	4 12	19 22	18 51	4 34	12 05	0 25	13 31	1 24	7 13	8 17	21 31	0 37	14 59	1 15
10 Tu	22 19	21 47	4 48	23 52	18 58	4 28	11 45	0 34	13 45	1 24	7 18	8 18	21 31	0 36	14 57	1 15
11 W	22 11	25 36	5 05	26 55	19 05	4 20	11 25	0 43	13 58	1 23	7 22	8 19	21 30	0 36	14 54	1 15
12 Th	22 03	27 48	5 04	28 13	19 14	4 11	11 05	0 53	14 11	1 23	7 27	8 20	21 30	0 36	14 52	1 15
13 F	21 55	28 10	4 43	27 39	19 23	4 02	10 46	1 03	14 24	1 22	7 31	8 21	21 29	0 36	14 50	1 15
14 Sa	21 46	26 42	4 06	25 22	19 33	3 51	10 27	1 13	14 37	1 22	7 35	8 21	21 29	0 36	14 48	1 15
15 Su	21 37	23 40	3 16	21 40	19 43	3 40	10 08	1 24	14 50	1 21	7 40	8 22	21 28	0 35	14 45	1 15
16 M	21 28	19 24	2 15	16 57	19 55	3 28	9 49	1 34	15 03	1 21	7 44	8 23	21 28	0 35	14 43	1 15
17 Tu	21 18	14 19	1 09	11 35	20 06	3 16	9 31	1 45	15 15	1 20	7 48	8 24	21 28	0 35	14 41	1 15
18 W	21 08	8 45	0 01	5 53	20 17	3 03	9 13	1 57	15 28	1 20	7 52	8 25	21 27	0 35	14 38	1 15
19 Th	20 57	2 59	1S06	0 05	20 29	2 50	8 55	2 08	15 40	1 19	7 55	8 26	21 27	0 35	14 36	1 15
20 F	20 46	2S47	2 08	5S36	20 40	2 36	8 38	2 20	15 52	1 19	7 59	8 27	21 27	0 34	14 34	1 15
21 Sa	20 35	8 22	3 04	11 02	20 52	2 22	8 21	2 32	16 04	1 18	8 03	8 28	21 26	0 34	14 31	1 15
22 Su	20 24	13 36	3 52	16 03	21 02	2 07	8 05	2 44	16 16	1 18	8 06	8 29	21 26	0 34	14 29	1 15
23 M	20 12	18 21	4 30	20 28	21 12	1 53	7 50	2 56	16 27	1 17	8 10	8 30	21 26	0 34	14 27	1 15
24 Tu	19 59	22 24	4 56	24 07	21 21	1 39	7 34	3 09	16 39	1 17	8 13	8 31	21 26	0 34	14 24	1 15
25 W	19 47	25 34	5 09	26 44	21 29	1 24	7 20	3 22	16 50	1 16	8 17	8 32	21 26	0 33	14 22	1 16
26 Th	19 34	27 36	5 09	28 08	21 36	1 10	7 06	3 35	17 01	1 15	8 20	8 33	21 26	0 33	14 19	1 16
27 F	19 21	28 18	4 54	28 05	21 41	0 56	6 53	3 48	17 12	1 15	8 23	8 34	21 25	0 33	14 17	1 16
28 Sa	19 07	27 30	4 24	26 31	21 44	0 42	6 40	4 01	17 23	1 14	8 27	8 36	21 25	0 33	14 15	1 16
29 Su	18 53	25 09	3 40	23 26	21 46	0 28	6 28	4 15	17 33	1 13	8 30	8 37	21 25	0 33	14 12	1 16
30 M	18 39	21 23	2 42	19 01	21 46	0 15	6 17	4 28	17 44	1 13	8 33	8 38	21 25	0 33	14 10	1 16
31 Tu	18N25	16S23	1S34	13S31	21N43	0S02	6N07	4S41	17N54	1S12	8N36	8S39	21S25	0N32	14N07	1N16

Day	⚷ Decl	⚷ Lat	♅ Decl	♅ Lat	♆ Decl	♆ Lat	♇ Decl	♇ Lat
1	9S32	7N09	5S12	0S47	14S32	0S16	16S24	7N00
6	9 35	7 11	5 13	0 47	14 34	0 16	16 25	6 60
11	9 37	7 12	5 15	0 48	14 36	0 16	16 26	6 59
16	9 41	7 13	5 17	0 48	14 38	0 16	16 27	6 58
21	9 44	7 13	5 19	0 48	14 40	0 16	16 28	6 57
26	9 48	7 14	5 22	0 48	14 43	0 16	16 29	6 56
31	9S52	7N14	5S25	0S48	14S45	0S17	16S30	6N54

Day	⚴ Decl	⚴ Lat	⚵ Decl	⚵ Lat	⚶ Decl	⚶ Lat	Eris Decl	Eris Lat
1	10N58	16N31	3N18	9N30	15S36	5N14	4S43	14S08
6	10 56	16 27	2 57	9 24	15 58	4 47	4 44	14 08
11	10 50	16 23	2 34	9 19	16 23	4 20	4 44	14 09
16	10 39	16 17	2 10	9 14	16 49	3 54	4 44	14 09
21	10 23	16 09	1 44	9 09	17 16	3 29	4 45	14 10
26	10 02	15 59	1 16	9 04	17 45	3 05	4 46	14 11
31	9N36	15N46	0N48	9N00	18S14	2N43	4S46	14S11

Moon Phenomena

Max/0 Decl

dy	hr mn	
6	8:42	0 N
12	16:45	28N15
19	12:22	0 S
26	23:32	28S18

Perigee/Apogee

dy	hr m		kilometers
9	21:43	p	368528
22	8:41	a	404148

Max/0 Lat

dy	hr mn	
5	1:40	0 N
11	9:58	5N07
18	0:19	0 S
25	11:32	5S11

PH	dy	hr mn	
☾	7	16:55	15♈12
●	14	12:05	21♋41
☽	22	6:30	29♎06
○	30	0:49	6♒31

Void of Course Moon

Last Aspect				☽ Ingress		
1	8:46	♅	✶	♒	2	5:25
4	6:04	♇	✶	♓	4	10:53
6	10:10	♇	□	♈	6	14:58
8	13:07	♇	△	♉	8	17:55
10	16:55	♀	□	♊	10	20:11
12	21:13	♀	✶	♋	12	22:40
14	12:05	☉	☌	♌	15	2:44
17	3:56	♇	△	♍	17	9:40
19	13:45	♇	□	♎	19	19:54
22	6:30	☉	□	♏	22	8:19
24	10:31	♄	□	♐	24	20:31
27	0:14	♇	☌	♑	27	6:22
29	2:24	♂	△	♒	29	13:15
31	11:57	♇	✶	♓	31	17:42

DAILY ASPECTARIAN

1 Su ☽⊻⚷ 1:40 · ☽✶♅ 8:46 · ☽⊻♆ 14:17 · ♀☌♄ 14:39 · ☽⊼♄ 15:34 · ☽⊼♀ 15:37 · ☿✶♂ 19:09 · ♀#♆ 19:14 · ☽∠♃ 23:41

2 M ☽⊻♇ 0:33 · ☉#☽ 6:36 · ☽∠♅ 12:02 · ☽⊼☿ 13:40 · ☽∥♃ 15:24 · ☽□♂ 15:29 · ☽□⚳ 21:45

3 Tu ☉⊼☽ 0:46 · ☽✶♃ 2:30 · ☽∠♇ 3:30 · ☽#☿ 6:39 · ☽☌⚷ 7:51 · ☽⊻♅ 14:51 · ☽⚼☿ 15:33 · ☽∥♇ 16:57 · ☽☌♆ 20:08 · ☽☍♄ 21:53 · ☽#♄ 22:27 · ☉⊼♃ 23:14

4 W ☽☍♀ 0:22 · ☽∥♆ 1:04 · ☽#♀ 4:34 · ☉⚼☽ 5:25 · ☽✶♇ 6:04 · ☽#♂ 9:47 · ☽△☿ 17:12 · ☽∥⚷ 21:12 · ☽✶♂ 23:35

5 Th ☽✶⚳ 3:59 · ☽□♃ 7:02 · ☽#⚳ 7:14 · ☉△☽ 9:37 · ⚴ R 10:25 · ☽⊻⚷ 12:26 · ☽∥♅ 13:38 · ☽☌♅ 19:23

6 F ☽⊻♆ 0:29 · ☽⊼♄ 2:41 · ☽∠♂ 3:02 · ☽∠⚳ 6:33 · ☽⊼♀ 7:14 · ☽□♇ 10:10 · ♀∥♂ 11:30 · ☽∠⚷ 14:14 · ☽□☿ 19:56

7 Sa ☉⊼⚷ 0:34 · ☽∠♆ 2:12 · ☽#♅ 3:40 · ☽⚼♄ 4:37 · ☽⊻♂ 6:07 · ☽⊻⚳ 8:49 · ☽⚼♀ 10:05 · ☽△♃ 10:19 · ☽∥⚳ 10:33 · ☽✶⚷ 15:46 · ☉□☽ 16:55 · ☽#⚷ 19:49 · ☽⊻♅ 22:41

8 Su ☽✶♆ 3:39 · ☽△♄ 6:16 · ☽∥♀ 6:19 · ☽∥♂ 10:28 · ☽⚼♃ 11:34 · ☽△♀ 12:35 · ☽△♇ 13:07 · ☽#♆ 15:16 · ☽∥♄ 16:57 · ☽✶☿ 22:10 · ☽#♇ 22:56 · ☽∠♅ 23:58

9 M ♀△♇ 1:10 · ☽∥☿ 9:50 · ☽☌♂ 11:26 · ☽☌⚳ 12:32 · ☽⊼♃ 12:38 · ☽⚼♇ 14:17 · ⚳⊼♃ 16:13 · ☽□⚷ 18:08 · ☽#♃ 22:36 · ☉✶☽ 23:02 · ☽∠☿ 23:14

10 Tu ☽✶♅ 1:05 · ☿ D 2:15 · ☉∥☽ 2:48 · ☽□♆ 5:58 · ☽□♄ 9:01 · ♂⊼♃ 9:25 · ☽⊼♇ 15:20 · ☽□♀ 16:55

11 W ☽⊻☿ 0:23 · ♂☌⚳ 1:27 · ☉∠☽ 1:55 · ☉△♅ 5:34 · ☽☍♃ 14:34 · ☽⊻⚳ 15:49 · ☽⊻♂ 16:15 · ♂⚼♇ 19:24 · ☽△⚷ 20:12

12 Th ☽□♅ 3:18 · ☉⊻☽ 4:54 · ⚶ D 7:37 · ☽△♆ 8:12 · ☽✶♄ 11:46 · ☽∠⚳ 17:39 · ☽☍♇ 17:40 · ⚳⚼♇ 18:33 · ☽∠♂ 18:52 · ☽✶♀ 21:13 · ☽⚼⚷ 21:28

13 F ☽☌☿ 3:34 · ☽⚼♆ 9:40 · ☽∠♄ 13:32 · ☽⊼♃ 17:12 · ☽✶⚳ 19:51 · ☽✶♂ 21:54 · ☽⊼⚷ 23:06 · ♂#♆ 23:37 · ☽∠♀ 23:50

14 Sa ☉⊼♆ 5:11 · ☽△♅ 6:33 · ☽⊼♆ 11:36 · ☉☌☽ 12:05 · ☽⊻♄ 15:48 · ♂∥♄ 16:13 · ♀ ♍ 18:25 · ☽⚼♃ 19:13 · ♂□⚷ 20:05 · ☽⊼♇ 21:26

15 Su ☽⊻♀ 3:01 · ☽⚼♅ 9:00 · ☽⊻☿ 9:20 · ☉∥☽ 12:43 · ☽#♃ 13:05 · ☽∥☿ 21:32 · ☽△♃ 21:54 · ☉#♃ 22:58

16 M ☽⚼♇ 0:16 · ☽□⚳ 2:09 · ☽☍⚷ 4:12 · ☽□♂ 6:07 · ♀#⚷ 10:46 · ☽⊼♅ 12:12 · ☽∠☿ 13:43 · ☽#♇ 14:21 · ☽☍♆ 17:30 · ☽∥♂ 19:58 · ☽∥♄ 22:24 · ☉⊻☽ 22:26 · ☽☌♄ 22:34 · ☽#♆ 22:35

17 Tu ☉⊻♄ 0:17 · ☽△♇ 3:56 · ☽☌♀ 11:41 · ♄#♆ 18:52 · ☽✶☿ 19:19 · ☽#⚷ 20:02 · ☽∥♀ 21:58

18 W ☽∥⚳ 3:44 · ☉∠☽ 5:11 · ☽□♃ 5:45 · ☽△⚳ 11:51 · ☉⚼♃ 12:11 · ☽⊼⚷ 12:29 · ☽#♅ 14:25 · ☽△♂ 18:07 · ☽☍♅ 21:07

19 Th ☽⊼♆ 2:43 · ☽⊻♄ 8:44 · ☿⚼♆ 10:04 · ⚳□⚷ 12:02 · ☉✶☽ 12:58 · ☽□♇ 13:45 · ☽⚼⚷ 17:49 · ☽⚼⚳ 17:58 · ☉⊼♇ 22:48 · ☽⊻♀ 23:36

20 F ☽⚼♂ 1:30 · ☉∥☿ 6:15 · ☽⚼♆ 8:26 · ☽□☿ 10:13 · ☽∥♅ 10:46 · ☽∠♄ 14:55 · ☽✶♃ 16:41 · ♂✶♅ 22:14 · ☽#⚳ 22:36 · ☽△⚷ 23:43 · ☽#♀ 23:59

21 Sa ☽⊼⚳ 0:43 · ☽∥⚷ 6:08 · ☽∠♀ 6:22 · ☽⊼♅ 8:50 · ☽⊼♂ 9:30 · ☽△♆ 14:35 · ☽✶♄ 21:30 · ♀∥⚳ 22:30 · ☽∠♃ 22:51

22 Su ☽✶♇ 1:56 · ☽#♄ 4:13 · ☽∥♆ 5:14 · ☉□☽ 6:30 · ☽✶♀ 13:17 · ☽#♂ 13:39 · ☽∥♇ 14:07 · ☽⚼♅ 15:08 · ☿∠♄ 23:58

23 M ♂#♇ 1:19 · ☽△☿ 4:33 · ☉ ♌ 5:01 · ☽⊻♃ 5:04 · ☽∠♇ 8:12 · ☿⊼♃ 9:48 · ☉#☽ 9:53 · ☽□⚷ 12:05 · ☽☍⚳ 14:44 · ☽#☿ 17:03 · ☽∥♃ 17:49 · ☽△♅ 21:18

24 Tu ☽☍♂ 1:44 · ☽□♆ 2:59 · ☽□♄ 10:31 · ☿#♃ 13:51 · ☽⚼☿ 13:56 · ☽⊻♇ 14:09 · ♂□♆ 23:11 · ☉△☽ 23:52

25 W ☽□♀ 2:05 · ☽☌♃ 16:27 · ☽⊼☿ 22:52 · ☽✶⚷ 23:09

26 Th ☿⊼⚷ 1:22 · ☽⊼⚳ 3:13 · ☉⊻♀ 6:17 · ☉⚼☽ 7:31 · ☽□♅ 8:07 · ☽✶♆ 13:33 · ☉⚼♅ 15:18 · ☽⊼♂ 15:49 · ☽△♄ 21:26

27 F ☽☌♇ 0:14 · ☽∠⚷ 3:40 · ☽⚼⚳ 8:19 · ☽△♀ 11:55 · ☉⊼☽ 14:12 · ♀ R 17:29 · ☽∠♆ 17:45 · ☿✶⚳ 19:39 · ☽⚼♂ 21:33

28 Sa ☽⊻♃ 1:09 · ☽⚼♄ 1:44 · ☽⊻⚷ 7:25 · ☽△⚳ 12:36 · ☽☍☿ 14:28 · ☽⚼♀ 15:32 · ☽✶♅ 16:03 · ☽⊻♆ 21:11 · ☿∠♀ 23:10

29 Su ☽△♂ 2:24 · ☿△♅ 3:26 · ☽∠♃ 4:23 · ☽⊼♄ 5:16 · ☽⊻♇ 7:21 · ☽⊼♀ 18:22 · ☽∠♅ 18:56 · ☽#☿ 21:51 · ☽∥♃ 23:45

30 M ☉☍☽ 0:49 · ☽✶♃ 6:59 · ☽∠♇ 9:54 · ☽☌⚷ 12:53 · ☉#☽ 14:23 · ☽#♂ 17:25 · ☽□⚳ 19:01 · ☿⊼♆ 20:01 · ☽⊻♅ 21:14 · ☽∥♇ 23:30

31 Tu ☽☌♆ 2:09 · ☽⊼☿ 3:02 · ☽∥♆ 6:53 · ☽#♄ 9:36 · ☽□♂ 9:56 · ☽☍♄ 10:29 · ☽✶♇ 11:57 · ☽☍♀ 22:10

August 2007

LONGITUDE

Day	Sid.Time	☉	☽	☽ 12 hour	Mean ☊	True ☊	☿	♀	♂	⚳	♃	♄	⚷	♅	♆	♇
	h m s	° ' "	° ' "	° ' "	° '	° '	° '	° '	° '	° '	° '	° '	° '	° '	° '	° '
1 W	20 36 54	8♌23 52	3♓40 30	10♓41 49	8♓26.6	7♓13.1	23♋02.5	2♍35.8	25♉53.1	17♉11.0	9♐59.2	25♌53.1	13♒18.0	18♓08.0	20♒58.6	26♐39.1
2 Th	20 40 51	9 21 14	17 45 07	24 50 02	8 23.4	7D 13.4	24 50.8	2R 24.5	26 32.9	17 25.3	9R 58.2	26 00.5	13R 14.8	18R 06.3	20R 57.1	26R 38.1
3 F	20 44 48	10 18 38	1♈56 10	9♈03 07	8 20.2	7 14.5	26 42.2	2 10.8	27 12.6	17 39.4	9 57.4	26 07.9	13 11.5	18 04.6	20 55.5	26 37.0
4 Sa	20 48 44	11 16 02	16 10 33	23 18 08	8 17.0	7 15.9	28 36.4	1 54.7	27 52.2	17 53.3	9 56.7	26 15.4	13 08.3	18 02.9	20 53.9	26 36.0
5 Su	20 52 41	12 13 28	0♉25 33	7♉32 32	8 13.9	7R 17.1	0♌32.9	1 36.4	28 31.7	18 07.0	9 56.2	26 22.9	13 05.0	18 01.1	20 52.2	26 35.1
6 M	20 56 37	13 10 55	14 38 48	21 44 03	8 10.7	7 17.4	2 31.6	1 15.8	29 11.0	18 20.5	9 55.9	26 30.4	13 01.8	17 59.3	20 50.6	26 34.1
7 Tu	21 00 34	14 08 24	28 48 03	5♊50 31	8 07.5	7 16.8	4 31.9	0 53.0	29 50.2	18 33.8	9D 55.8	26 37.9	12 58.5	17 57.5	20 49.0	26 33.2
8 W	21 04 30	15 05 54	12♊51 10	19 49 45	8 04.3	7 15.2	6 33.6	0 28.2	0♊29.2	18 46.9	9 55.9	26 45.4	12 55.3	17 55.6	20 47.4	26 32.3
9 Th	21 08 27	16 03 25	26 46 00	3♋39 36	8 01.2	7 12.7	8 36.2	0 01.4	1 08.1	18 59.7	9 56.1	26 53.0	12 52.0	17 53.7	20 45.8	26 31.4
10 F	21 12 23	17 00 58	10♋30 20	17 17 55	7 58.0	7 09.9	10 39.5	29♌32.7	1 46.9	19 12.4	9 56.6	27 00.5	12 48.8	17 51.8	20 44.1	26 30.5
11 Sa	21 16 20	17 58 31	24 02 09	0♌42 47	7 54.8	7 07.2	12 43.1	29 02.3	2 25.5	19 24.8	9 57.2	27 08.1	12 45.6	17 49.8	20 42.5	26 29.7
12 Su	21 20 17	18 56 06	7♌19 41	13 52 42	7 51.6	7 04.9	14 46.8	28 30.4	3 04.0	19 37.0	9 58.0	27 15.7	12 42.3	17 47.8	20 40.9	26 28.9
13 M	21 24 13	19 53 42	20 21 47	26 46 53	7 48.4	7 03.4	16 50.3	27 57.0	3 42.3	19 49.0	9 59.0	27 23.3	12 39.1	17 45.8	20 39.2	26 28.1
14 Tu	21 28 10	20 51 20	3♍08 02	9♍25 20	7 45.3	7D 02.7	18 53.3	27 22.5	4 20.5	20 00.7	10 00.2	27 30.9	12 35.9	17 43.8	20 37.6	26 27.4
15 W	21 32 06	21 48 58	15 38 55	21 49 01	7 42.1	7 02.8	20 55.7	26 47.0	4 58.5	20 12.2	10 01.6	27 38.5	12 32.7	17 41.7	20 36.0	26 26.7
16 Th	21 36 03	22 46 37	27 55 52	3♎59 48	7 38.9	7 03.6	22 57.3	26 10.7	5 36.3	20 23.5	10 03.1	27 46.1	12 29.5	17 39.6	20 34.3	26 26.0
17 F	21 39 59	23 44 18	10♎01 11	16 00 25	7 35.7	7 04.7	24 58.0	25 33.8	6 14.0	20 34.5	10 04.9	27 53.7	12 26.4	17 37.5	20 32.7	26 25.3
18 Sa	21 43 56	24 41 59	21 57 59	27 54 21	7 32.6	7 05.9	26 57.7	24 56.6	6 51.5	20 45.3	10 06.8	28 01.3	12 23.2	17 35.3	20 31.1	26 24.7
19 Su	21 47 52	25 39 42	3♏50 02	9♏45 37	7 29.4	7 07.0	28 56.2	24 19.3	7 28.9	20 55.8	10 08.9	28 09.0	12 20.1	17 33.2	20 29.4	26 24.1
20 M	21 51 49	26 37 26	15 41 38	21 38 41	7 26.2	7R 07.6	0♍53.5	23 42.2	8 06.1	21 06.0	10 11.2	28 16.6	12 17.0	17 31.0	20 27.8	26 23.5
21 Tu	21 55 46	27 35 11	27 37 20	3♐38 11	7 23.0	7 07.9	2 49.5	23 05.5	8 43.1	21 16.0	10 13.6	28 24.2	12 13.9	17 28.8	20 26.2	26 22.9
22 W	21 59 42	28 32 57	9♐41 48	15 48 43	7 19.8	7 07.7	4 44.2	22 29.4	9 19.9	21 25.8	10 16.3	28 31.9	12 10.8	17 26.6	20 24.6	26 22.4
23 Th	22 03 39	29 30 44	21 59 29	28 14 33	7 16.7	7 07.1	6 37.7	21 54.1	9 56.6	21 35.2	10 19.1	28 39.5	12 07.8	17 24.4	20 22.9	26 21.9
24 F	22 07 35	0♍28 33	4♑34 22	10♑59 17	7 13.5	7 06.4	8 29.7	21 19.9	10 33.1	21 44.4	10 22.1	28 47.2	12 04.8	17 22.1	20 21.3	26 21.4
25 Sa	22 11 32	1 26 22	17 29 36	24 05 29	7 10.3	7 05.7	10 20.5	20 47.0	11 09.4	21 53.4	10 25.2	28 54.8	12 01.8	17 19.8	20 19.7	26 21.0
26 Su	22 15 28	2 24 13	0♒47 04	7♒34 18	7 07.1	7 05.0	12 09.9	20 15.5	11 45.6	22 02.0	10 28.6	29 02.4	11 58.8	17 17.6	20 18.2	26 20.6
27 M	22 19 25	3 22 05	14 27 04	21 25 08	7 04.0	7 04.6	13 57.9	19 45.7	12 21.5	22 10.4	10 32.1	29 10.0	11 55.9	17 15.3	20 16.6	26 20.2
28 Tu	22 23 21	4 19 59	28 28 07	5♓35 32	7 00.8	7D 04.5	15 44.6	19 17.7	12 57.3	22 18.5	10 35.8	29 17.7	11 53.0	17 13.0	20 15.0	26 19.9
29 W	22 27 18	5 17 54	12♓46 50	20 01 19	6 57.6	7 04.4	17 30.0	18 51.6	13 32.9	22 26.3	10 39.6	29 25.3	11 50.1	17 10.6	20 13.4	26 19.6
30 Th	22 31 15	6 15 51	27 18 17	4♈36 56	6 54.4	7R 04.5	19 14.1	18 27.6	14 08.3	22 33.8	10 43.6	29 32.9	11 47.2	17 08.3	20 11.9	26 19.3
31 F	22 35 11	7♍13 49	11♈56 30	19 16 11	6♓51.2	7♓04.5	20♍56.9	18♌05.8	14♊43.5	22♉41.0	10♐47.8	29♌40.5	11♒44.4	17♓05.9	20♒10.3	26♐19.0

1st of Month

Julian Day # 2454313.5
Obliquity 23°26'26"
SVP 5♓09'06"
GC 26♐56.7
Eris 21♈32.7R

Day	⚴
1	17♓23.0R
6	16 33.7R
11	15 36.9R
16	14 33.3R
21	13 24.0R
26	12 10.6R
31	10 54.3R

Day	⚵
1	19♒30.0
6	20 40.3
11	21 54.1
16	23 11.0
21	24 31.0
26	25 53.6
31	27 18.7

Day	⚶
1	3♐52.4
6	4 41.8
11	5 40.6
16	6 48.1
21	8 03.7
26	9 26.7
31	10 56.4

DECLINATION and LATITUDE

Day	☉ Decl	☽ Decl	☽ Lat	☽ 12h Decl	☿ Decl	☿ Lat	♀ Decl	♀ Lat	♂ Decl	♂ Lat	⚳ Decl	⚳ Lat	♃ Decl	♃ Lat	♄ Decl	♄ Lat
1 W	18N10	10S28	0S19	7S16	21N39	0N10	5N57	4S55	18N04	1S11	8N38	8S40	21S25	0N32	14N05	1N16
2 Th	17 55	3 58	0N57	0 36	21 31	0 22	5 49	5 08	18 14	1 11	8 41	8 41	21 25	0 32	14 02	1 16
3 F	17 40	2N47	2 11	6N08	21 22	0 33	5 41	5 22	18 24	1 10	8 44	8 42	21 25	0 32	13 60	1 16
4 Sa	17 24	9 24	3 18	12 33	21 09	0 44	5 35	5 35	18 34	1 09	8 46	8 43	21 26	0 31	13 57	1 16
5 Su	17 08	15 33	4 12	18 20	20 54	0 53	5 29	5 48	18 43	1 09	8 49	8 45	21 26	0 31	13 55	1 16
6 M	16 52	20 51	4 50	23 04	20 36	1 02	5 24	6 01	18 52	1 08	8 51	8 46	21 26	0 31	13 52	1 16
7 Tu	16 35	24 57	5 11	26 26	20 16	1 10	5 20	6 13	19 01	1 07	8 54	8 47	21 26	0 31	13 50	1 16
8 W	16 18	27 31	5 13	28 09	19 53	1 17	5 17	6 26	19 10	1 06	8 56	8 48	21 26	0 30	13 47	1 16
9 Th	16 01	28 20	4 56	28 05	19 28	1 24	5 15	6 38	19 19	1 06	8 58	8 49	21 26	0 30	13 45	1 16
10 F	15 44	27 24	4 23	26 18	18 60	1 29	5 14	6 49	19 28	1 05	9 01	8 50	21 27	0 30	13 42	1 16
11 Sa	15 27	24 50	3 35	23 03	18 30	1 34	5 14	6 60	19 36	1 04	9 03	8 52	21 27	0 30	13 40	1 16
12 Su	15 09	20 58	2 37	18 39	17 58	1 38	5 15	7 10	19 44	1 03	9 05	8 53	21 27	0 30	13 37	1 16
13 M	14 51	16 08	1 31	13 28	17 24	1 41	5 18	7 20	19 52	1 02	9 06	8 54	21 28	0 29	13 34	1 16
14 Tu	14 33	10 42	0 22	7 50	16 48	1 43	5 21	7 29	20 00	1 02	9 08	8 55	21 28	0 29	13 32	1 16
15 W	14 14	4 56	0S47	2 01	16 11	1 45	5 24	7 38	20 08	1 01	9 10	8 56	21 29	0 29	13 29	1 16
16 Th	13 55	0S54	1 53	3S47	15 32	1 46	5 29	7 45	20 15	0 60	9 12	8 58	21 29	0 29	13 27	1 16
17 F	13 37	6 37	2 52	9 22	14 52	1 46	5 35	7 52	20 23	0 59	9 13	8 59	21 29	0 29	13 24	1 16
18 Sa	13 17	12 01	3 44	14 33	14 10	1 45	5 41	7 58	20 30	0 58	9 15	9 00	21 30	0 28	13 22	1 17
19 Su	12 58	16 57	4 25	19 11	13 28	1 44	5 48	8 03	20 37	0 57	9 16	9 01	21 30	0 28	13 19	1 17
20 M	12 38	21 14	4 55	23 05	12 45	1 42	5 56	8 07	20 44	0 56	9 18	9 03	21 30	0 28	13 16	1 17
21 Tu	12 19	24 42	5 12	26 03	12 01	1 40	6 05	8 11	20 51	0 55	9 19	9 04	21 31	0 28	13 14	1 17
22 W	11 59	27 07	5 16	27 52	11 17	1 37	6 14	8 13	20 57	0 54	9 20	9 05	21 32	0 28	13 11	1 17
23 Th	11 39	28 17	5 06	28 21	10 32	1 33	6 23	8 15	21 04	0 53	9 21	9 06	21 33	0 28	13 09	1 17
24 F	11 18	28 03	4 41	27 21	9 46	1 30	6 33	8 16	21 10	0 53	9 22	9 08	21 33	0 27	13 06	1 17
25 Sa	10 58	26 17	4 02	24 51	9 01	1 25	6 44	8 16	21 16	0 52	9 23	9 09	21 34	0 27	13 03	1 17
26 Su	10 37	23 02	3 08	20 54	8 15	1 21	6 54	8 15	21 22	0 51	9 24	9 10	21 35	0 27	13 01	1 17
27 M	10 16	18 27	2 02	15 43	7 28	1 16	7 05	8 13	21 28	0 50	9 25	9 12	21 35	0 27	12 58	1 17
28 Tu	9 55	12 45	0 48	9 35	6 42	1 10	7 16	8 10	21 33	0 48	9 26	9 13	21 36	0 27	12 56	1 17
29 W	9 34	6 17	0N32	2 52	5 56	1 05	7 27	8 07	21 39	0 47	9 26	9 14	21 37	0 26	12 53	1 17
30 Th	9 13	0N37	1 50	4N05	5 10	0 59	7 38	8 03	21 44	0 46	9 27	9 15	21 37	0 26	12 50	1 17
31 F	8N51	7N30	3N02	10N50	4N24	0N53	7N49	7S58	21N49	0S45	9N28	9S17	21S38	0N26	12N48	1N18

Day	⚷ Decl	⚷ Lat	♅ Decl	♅ Lat	♆ Decl	♆ Lat	♇ Decl	♇ Lat
1	9S53	7N14	5S26	0S48	14S46	0S17	16S30	6N54
6	9 58	7 14	5 29	0 48	14 49	0 17	16 31	6 53
11	10 02	7 14	5 33	0 48	14 51	0 17	16 32	6 51
16	10 07	7 13	5 37	0 49	14 54	0 17	16 33	6 50
21	10 12	7 12	5 42	0 49	14 57	0 17	16 35	6 49
26	10 17	7 11	5 46	0 49	14 59	0 17	16 37	6 47
31	10S22	7N10	5S51	0S49	15S02	0S17	16S38	6N45

Day	⚴ Decl	⚴ Lat	⚵ Decl	⚵ Lat	⚶ Decl	⚶ Lat	Eris Decl	Eris Lat
1	9N30	15N44	0N42	8N59	18S20	2N38	4S46	14S11
6	8 57	15 28	0 12	8 55	18 50	2 17	4 47	14 12
11	8 18	15 09	0S18	8 52	19 20	1 57	4 48	14 12
16	7 34	14 47	0 49	8 48	19 50	1 38	4 49	14 13
21	6 44	14 21	1 21	8 45	20 20	1 20	4 50	14 13
26	5 50	13 52	1 52	8 43	20 50	1 03	4 51	14 14
31	4N52	13N20	2S25	8N41	21S19	0N47	4S52	14S14

Moon Phenomena

Max/0 Decl
dy hr mn
2 14:07 0 N
8 23:17 28N20
15 20:16 0 S
23 8:01 28S22
29 21:54 0 N

Max/0 Lat
dy hr mn
1 6:03 0 N
7 14:28 5N14
14 7:27 0 S
21 18:57 5S17
28 14:28 0 N

Perigee/Apogee
dy hr m kilometers
3 23:54 p 368891
19 3:22 a 404617
31 0:04 p 364171

PH dy hr mn
☾ 5 21:21 13♉05
● 12 23:04 19♌51
☽ 20 23:55 27♏35
○ 28 10:36 4♓46
☊ 28 10:38 T 1.476

Void of Course Moon

Last Aspect				☽ Ingress		
2	15:38	♂	⚹	♈	2	20:44
4	17:32	♇	△	♉	4	23:17
7	1:51	♂	☌	♊	7	2:02
9	5:28	♀	⚹	♋	9	5:37
10	12:58	♅	△	♌	11	10:43
13	13:35	♀	☌	♍	13	18:04
15	21:03	♇	□	♎	16	4:05
18	12:22	♄	⚹	♏	18	16:14
21	1:35	♄	□	♐	21	4:45
23	12:55	♄	△	♑	23	15:21
24	23:42	♅	⚹	♒	25	22:36
28	1:25	♄	☍	♓	28	2:35
29	22:23	♇	□	♈	30	4:26

DAILY ASPECTARIAN

1 W
♂□♄ 0:00
☽∥⚷ 2:11
☉∥♂ 5:27
☽∦⚳ 6:50
☽⚼☿ 8:33
☉⚻☽ 8:40
☽□♃ 10:47
☽⚺⚷ 16:22
☽∦♀ 17:09
☽∥♅ 18:39
☽⚹⚳ 23:26

2 Th
☽☌♅ 0:36
☿⚼♃ 1:36
♂⚻♇ 3:02
☽⚺♆ 5:25
☉⚼☽ 12:00
☽△☿ 13:49
☽⚻♄ 14:07
☽□♇ 15:02
☉△♃ 15:13
☿∦♃ 15:17
☽⚹♂ 15:38
☿⚺♄ 16:10
☽∠⚷ 17:42
☿⚻♇ 22:55

3 F
☽⚻♀ 0:24
☽∠⚳ 1:14
☽∠♆ 6:43
☽∦♅ 9:35
☿⚹♂ 9:54
☽∥♀ 10:14
☽△♃ 13:31
☉△☽ 15:08
☽⚼♄ 15:39
☽∠♂ 18:10
☽⚹⚷ 18:54
☽∥⚳ 21:39

4 Sa
☽⚼♀ 1:13
☽∦⚷ 1:59
☽⚺⚳ 2:56
☽⚺♅ 3:09
☽⚹♆ 7:56
☉⚼♇ 8:13
☽⚼♃ 14:45
⚳⚹♅ 14:50
☽△♄ 17:08
☿ ♌ 17:16
☽∥♄ 17:23
☽△♇ 17:32
☽⚺♂ 20:39
☽∦♆ 20:56

5 Su
♀∦♅ 0:10
☽□☿ 0:14
☽△♀ 1:57
☽∦♇ 4:04
☽∠♅ 4:22
☉∥☽ 6:24
☿⚺♀ 11:02
☽∥♂ 14:12
☽⚻♃ 16:02
☽⚼♇ 18:48
☉☍⚷ 20:23
☽□⚷ 21:17
☉□☽ 21:21
☽∥☿ 22:51

6 M
☽∦♃ 2:59
☿⚼♅ 5:28
☽⚹♅ 5:38
☽☌⚳ 6:21
☽□♆ 10:28
♄△♇ 10:36
☽⚻♇ 20:11
☽□♄ 20:17

7 Tu
☽☌♂ 1:51
♃ D 2:05
☽□♀ 3:27
☉∦♇ 5:34
♂ ♊ 6:02
☽⚹☿ 11:24
☽☍♃ 19:00
♀□♂ 23:37

8 W
☽△⚷ 0:07
☉⚹☽ 4:08
☽□♅ 8:42
☽⚺⚳ 10:21
☽△♆ 13:38
☽∠☿ 17:34
☽☍♇ 23:35

9 Th
☽⚹♄ 0:12
♀R♌ 1:11
☽⚼⚷ 1:54
☽⚹♀ 5:28
☿∥♂ 5:49
☽⚺♂ 7:58
☉∠☽ 8:01
☽∠⚳ 12:47
☿△♃ 15:37
☽⚼♆ 15:39
☽⚻♃ 23:01

10 F
☽⚺☿ 0:19
☽∠♄ 2:40
☽⚻⚷ 4:03
☽∠♀ 6:52
☿⚼♇ 9:51
☽∠♂ 11:38
☉⚺☽ 12:23
☽△♅ 12:58
☽⚹⚳ 15:38
☽⚻♆ 18:04
☉⚻♅ 20:29

11 Sa
☿☍⚷ 0:28
☽⚼♃ 1:39
☽⚻♇ 4:24
☽⚺♄ 5:37
☽⚺♀ 8:38
☽⚼♅ 15:47
☽⚹♂ 15:52
☽∦♃ 21:17

12 Su
☽△♃ 4:50
☽∥♂ 6:19
☽⚼♇ 7:35
☽☍⚷ 9:48
☽☌☿ 16:14
☽∥☿ 17:19
☽⚻♅ 19:11
☉□⚳ 21:32
☽∦♇ 22:05
☉∦♆ 22:08
☽□⚳ 22:58
☉☌☽ 23:04

13 M
☽☍♆ 0:32
☽∦♆ 5:45
☉∥☽ 6:14
☿⚻♅ 10:38
☽△♇ 11:24
☽∥♄ 11:39
☽☌♄ 13:16
☽☌♀ 13:35
☉☍♆ 18:27
♀☌♄ 19:17

14 Tu
☽□♂ 2:25
☽∦⚷ 2:33
☽∥⚳ 6:31
☿∦♇ 9:32
☽□♃ 13:08
☿□⚳ 14:35
☽⚻⚷ 18:02
☿☍♆ 20:10
☽∦♅ 21:13
☽∥♀ 22:04

15 W
☽☍♅ 3:57
☽△⚳ 8:59
☽⚻♆ 9:36
☽⚺☿ 12:18
☉⚺☽ 13:01
♀△♇ 13:45
☉☌☿ 19:57
☽⚺♀ 20:43
☽□♇ 21:03
☽⚼⚷ 23:08
☽⚺♄ 23:41

16 Th
☽⚼⚳ 15:00
☽⚼♆ 15:06
☽△♂ 16:02
☽∦♀ 19:31
☽∥♅ 19:49
⚳□♆ 20:32
☉∠☽ 21:13
☿∦♆ 22:18
☽∠☿ 23:52

17 F
☽⚹♃ 0:07
☽∠♀ 1:02
☽△⚷ 4:49
☿☌♀ 5:28
☽∠♄ 5:49
☽∦⚳ 11:26
♀∦♅ 14:27
☽⚻♅ 15:12
☽∥⚷ 15:31
☿△♇ 17:24
☉∥♄ 18:01
☽△♆ 21:05
☽⚻⚳ 21:31
☽⚼♂ 23:46

18 Sa
☉☌♀ 3:42
☉∦☽ 5:37
☽⚹♀ 5:43
☉⚹☽ 6:00
☽∦♄ 6:14
☽∠♃ 6:22
☽∦☿ 8:55
☽⚹♇ 8:58
☽⚹☿ 12:07
☽⚹♄ 12:22
☿☌♄ 13:45
☽∥♆ 13:49
☽⚼♅ 21:25
☽∥♇ 22:05

19 Su
☿∥♄ 5:26
☽⚻♂ 7:48
☽⚺♃ 12:50
☿ ♍ 13:02
☽∠♇ 15:18
☽□⚷ 17:08
☉△♇ 18:15
☽∦♂ 20:51

20 M
☽∥♃ 1:43
☽△♅ 3:40
☉∥☿ 6:29
☽□♆ 9:36
☽☍⚳ 11:04
☽□♀ 15:21
☽⚺♇ 21:31
☉□☽ 23:55

21 Tu
☽□♄ 1:35
☽□☿ 12:21
☽☍♂ 23:15
☉☌♄ 23:29

22 W
☽☌♃ 1:08
☽⚹⚷ 4:52
☽□♅ 15:08
☽⚹♆ 20:54
☽⚻⚳ 23:13
☽△♀ 23:50

23 Th
☽☌♇ 8:24
☿∦⚷ 9:01
☽∠⚷ 9:50
♀□⚳ 10:20
☉ ♍ 12:09
☽△♄ 12:55
☉△☽ 15:37
♂☍♃ 16:04

24 F
☽∠♆ 1:28
☽⚼♀ 3:10
☽⚼⚳ 4:07
☽△☿ 8:36
☽⚺♃ 10:53
☽⚻♂ 11:44
☿∥⚳ 12:19
☽⚺⚷ 13:58
☽⚼♄ 17:21
☉⚼☽ 21:55
☽⚹♅ 23:42

25 Sa
☿□♃ 1:04
☽⚺♆ 5:10
☽⚻♀ 5:46
☽△⚳ 8:06
☽∠♃ 14:27
☿□♂ 16:00
☽⚺♇ 16:04
☽⚼♂ 16:28
☽⚼☿ 16:31
☽⚻♄ 20:52
☿⚻⚷ 21:38
♀☍♆ 21:49

26 Su
☽∠♅ 2:40
☉⚻☽ 3:06
♂△⚷ 8:09
☽∥♃ 8:22
☽∦♂ 9:19
☽⚹♃ 17:09
☽∠♇ 18:35
☽☌⚷ 19:38
☽△♂ 20:12
☉∦⚷ 21:52
☽⚻☿ 23:02

27 M
☽⚺♅ 4:50
☽∥♇ 8:10
☽☍♀ 8:51
☿∥♀ 9:57
☽☌♆ 10:01
☽□⚳ 13:25
☽∥♆ 14:59
☽⚹♇ 20:23
☽∦♄ 23:18

28 Tu
☽☍♄ 1:25
☽∥⚷ 9:15
☉☍☽ 10:36
☉∦☽ 11:23
☽∦⚳ 12:34
♂∦♃ 14:12
☿☍♅ 19:40
☽∦♀ 19:56
☽□♃ 20:27
☽⚺⚷ 22:26

29 W
☽□♂ 1:20
☽∦☿ 1:22
☽∥♅ 1:39
☿∦♅ 3:43
☽☌♅ 7:17
☉∥⚳ 8:28
☽☍☿ 8:54
☽⚻♀ 9:48
☽⚺♆ 12:19
☿⚺♀ 15:13
☽⚹⚳ 16:08
☽□♇ 22:23
☽∠⚷ 23:09

30 Th
☽⚻♄ 3:43
☽⚼♀ 9:51
☽∠♆ 12:56
☿⚻♆ 13:15
☽∥☿ 14:11
☉⚻☽ 15:44
☽∠⚳ 16:58
☽∦♅ 18:07
☽△♃ 22:07
☽⚹⚷ 23:40

31 F
☽∥♀ 1:07
☽⚼♄ 4:31
☉∥☽ 4:34
☽⚹♂ 4:45
☽∥⚳ 7:00
☽⚺♅ 8:25
☽△♀ 9:51
☽∦⚷ 10:20
☽⚹♆ 13:27
☽⚻☿ 16:41
☽⚺⚳ 17:44
☉⚼☽ 18:03
☽∥♄ 19:13
☽⚼♃ 22:49
☽△♇ 23:33

LONGITUDE — September 2007

Day	Sid.Time	☉	☽	☽ 12 hour	Mean ☊	True ☊	☿	♀	♂	⚳	♃	♄	⚷	♅	♆	♇
	h m s	° ' "	° ' "	° ' "	° '	° '	° '	° '	° '	° '	° '	° '	° '	° '	° '	° '
1 Sa	22 39 08	8♍11 49	26♈35 14	3♉52 57	6♓48.1	7♓04.4	22♍38.4	17♌46.2	15♊18.5	22♉47.9	10♐52.2	29♌48.1	11♒41.7	17♓03.6	20♒08.8	26♐18.8
2 Su	22 43 04	9 09 51	11♉08 43	18 21 58	6 44.9	7R 04.3	24 18.6	17R 28.9	15 53.3	22 54.5	10 56.7	29 55.6	11R 38.9	17R 01.2	20R 07.2	26R 18.6
3 M	22 47 01	10 07 55	25 32 14	2♊39 10	6 41.7	7 04.1	25 57.6	17 14.1	16 27.9	23 00.7	11 01.4	0♍03.2	11 36.2	16 58.9	20 05.7	26 18.4
4 Tu	22 50 57	11 06 01	9♊42 29	16 41 58	6 38.5	7D 04.0	27 35.4	17 01.6	17 02.3	23 06.7	11 06.2	0 10.8	11 33.5	16 56.5	20 04.2	26 18.3
5 W	22 54 54	12 04 10	23 37 32	0♋29 06	6 35.4	7 04.1	29 12.0	16 51.6	17 36.5	23 12.4	11 11.2	0 18.3	11 30.9	16 54.1	20 02.7	26 18.2
6 Th	22 58 50	13 02 20	7♋16 40	14 00 17	6 32.2	7 04.5	0♎47.3	16 44.0	18 10.5	23 17.7	11 16.4	0 25.8	11 28.3	16 51.7	20 01.2	26 18.2
7 F	23 02 47	14 00 32	20 40 00	27 15 56	6 29.0	7 05.0	2 21.5	16 38.8	18 44.2	23 22.7	11 21.7	0 33.3	11 25.8	16 49.3	19 59.8	26D 18.1
8 Sa	23 06 44	14 58 46	3♌48 12	10♌16 53	6 25.8	7 05.8	3 54.4	16D 36.0	19 17.7	23 27.3	11 27.2	0 40.8	11 23.3	16 46.9	19 58.3	26 18.1
9 Su	23 10 40	15 57 02	16 42 08	23 04 05	6 22.7	7 06.5	5 26.2	16 35.6	19 51.0	23 31.6	11 32.9	0 48.3	11 20.8	16 44.5	19 56.9	26 18.1
10 M	23 14 37	16 55 20	29 22 51	5♍38 34	6 19.5	7R 06.9	6 56.8	16 37.5	20 24.0	23 35.6	11 38.7	0 55.8	11 18.4	16 42.1	19 55.5	26 18.2
11 Tu	23 18 33	17 53 39	11♍51 23	18 01 28	6 16.3	7 07.0	8 26.1	16 41.7	20 56.8	23 39.3	11 44.6	1 03.2	11 16.0	16 39.7	19 54.1	26 18.3
12 W	23 22 30	18 52 01	24 08 56	0♎14 00	6 13.1	7 06.5	9 54.3	16 48.2	21 29.4	23 42.5	11 50.7	1 10.6	11 13.7	16 37.3	19 52.7	26 18.4
13 Th	23 26 26	19 50 24	6♎16 51	12 17 42	6 09.9	7 05.3	11 21.3	16 56.8	22 01.6	23 45.5	11 57.0	1 18.0	11 11.4	16 34.9	19 51.3	26 18.6
14 F	23 30 23	20 48 49	18 16 49	24 14 27	6 06.8	7 03.5	12 47.1	17 07.6	22 33.7	23 48.0	12 03.4	1 25.4	11 09.2	16 32.5	19 50.0	26 18.7
15 Sa	23 34 19	21 47 16	0♏10 55	6♏06 35	6 03.6	7 01.3	14 11.6	17 20.5	23 05.4	23 50.3	12 10.0	1 32.7	11 07.0	16 30.1	19 48.6	26 19.0
16 Su	23 38 16	22 45 44	12 01 48	17 57 01	6 00.4	6 59.0	15 34.9	17 35.4	23 36.9	23 52.1	12 16.7	1 40.0	11 04.9	16 27.8	19 47.3	26 19.2
17 M	23 42 13	23 44 15	23 52 38	29 49 10	5 57.2	6 56.8	16 56.8	17 52.3	24 08.2	23 53.6	12 23.5	1 47.3	11 02.8	16 25.4	19 46.0	26 19.5
18 Tu	23 46 09	24 42 46	5♐47 06	11♐46 58	5 54.0	6 55.0	18 17.5	18 11.2	24 39.1	23 54.7	12 30.5	1 54.6	11 00.8	16 23.0	19 44.7	26 19.8
19 W	23 50 06	25 41 20	17 49 19	23 54 44	5 50.9	6D 54.0	19 36.8	18 31.8	25 09.8	23 55.5	12 37.7	2 01.8	10 58.8	16 20.6	19 43.5	26 20.2
20 Th	23 54 02	26 39 56	0♑03 45	6♑16 57	5 47.7	6 53.8	20 54.6	18 54.3	25 40.2	23R 55.9	12 44.9	2 09.0	10 56.9	16 18.3	19 42.3	26 20.5
21 F	23 57 59	27 38 33	12 34 52	18 58 00	5 44.5	6 54.5	22 11.0	19 18.5	26 10.3	23 55.9	12 52.3	2 16.2	10 55.0	16 16.0	19 41.1	26 21.0
22 Sa	0 01 55	28 37 11	25 26 50	2♒01 45	5 41.3	6 55.8	23 25.9	19 44.4	26 40.1	23 55.5	12 59.9	2 23.3	10 53.2	16 13.6	19 39.9	26 21.4
23 Su	0 05 52	29 35 52	8♒43 04	15 30 59	5 38.2	6 57.3	24 39.1	20 12.0	27 09.6	23 54.8	13 07.6	2 30.4	10 51.5	16 11.3	19 38.7	26 21.9
24 M	0 09 48	0♎34 34	22 25 36	29 26 50	5 35.0	6 58.5	25 50.6	20 41.1	27 38.8	23 53.7	13 15.4	2 37.5	10 49.8	16 09.0	19 37.6	26 22.4
25 Tu	0 13 45	1 33 17	6♓34 29	13♓48 08	5 31.8	6R 59.1	27 00.3	21 11.7	28 07.7	23 52.2	13 23.4	2 44.5	10 48.1	16 06.7	19 36.4	26 22.9
26 W	0 17 42	2 32 03	21 07 14	28 31 01	5 28.6	6 58.5	28 08.1	21 43.8	28 36.3	23 50.3	13 31.4	2 51.5	10 46.6	16 04.4	19 35.3	26 23.5
27 Th	0 21 38	3 30 50	5♈58 36	13♈28 57	5 25.5	6 56.6	29 13.9	22 17.3	29 04.5	23 48.1	13 39.7	2 58.5	10 45.1	16 02.2	19 34.3	26 24.1
28 F	0 25 35	4 29 40	21 00 57	28 33 25	5 22.3	6 53.6	0♏17.5	22 52.2	29 32.5	23 45.4	13 48.0	3 05.4	10 43.6	15 59.9	19 33.2	26 24.7
29 Sa	0 29 31	5 28 31	6♉05 10	13♉35 04	5 19.1	6 49.7	1 18.7	23 28.4	0♋00.1	23 42.4	13 56.5	3 12.3	10 42.2	15 57.7	19 32.2	26 25.4
30 Su	0 33 28	6♎27 25	21 02 05	28 25 16	5♓15.9	6♓45.6	2♏17.5	24♌05.9	0♋27.3	23♉39.0	14♐05.0	3♍19.1	10♒40.9	15♓55.5	19♒31.2	26♐26.1

1st of Month

Julian Day # 2454344.5
Obliquity 23°26'27"
SVP 5♓09'02"
GC 26♐56.8
Eris 21♈23.7R

Day	⚴		Day	⚵		Day	⚶
1	10♓38.9R		1	27♎35.9		1	11♐15.1
6	9 21.4R		6	29 03.7		6	12 52.0
11	8 04.8R		11	0♏33.5		11	14 34.5
16	6 50.8R		16	2 05.2		16	16 22.1
21	5 41.0R		21	3 38.6		21	18 14.4
26	4 36.8R		26	5 13.4		26	20 10.9

DECLINATION and LATITUDE

Day	☉ Decl	☽ Decl	☽ Lat	☽ 12h Decl	☿ Decl	☿ Lat	♀ Decl	♀ Lat	♂ Decl	♂ Lat	⚳ Decl	⚳ Lat	♃ Decl	♃ Lat	♄ Decl	♄ Lat
1 Sa	8N30	14N00	4N01	16N58	3N38	0N46	7N59	7S53	21N54	0S44	9N28	9S18	21S39	0N26	12N45	1N18
2 Su	8 08	19 41	4 45	22 06	2 52	0 40	8 10	7 47	21 59	0 43	9 28	9 19	21 40	0 26	12 43	1 18
3 M	7 46	24 10	5 11	25 51	2 06	0 33	8 21	7 41	22 03	0 42	9 29	9 20	21 41	0 25	12 40	1 18
4 Tu	7 24	27 07	5 17	27 58	1 21	0 26	8 31	7 34	22 08	0 41	9 29	9 21	21 41	0 25	12 37	1 18
5 W	7 02	28 21	5 04	28 17	0 36	0 18	8 41	7 27	22 12	0 40	9 29	9 23	21 42	0 25	12 35	1 18
6 Th	6 40	27 48	4 34	26 54	0S09	0 11	8 50	7 19	22 16	0 39	9 29	9 24	21 43	0 25	12 32	1 18
7 F	6 18	25 38	3 50	24 02	0 53	0 03	8 59	7 11	22 20	0 37	9 29	9 25	21 44	0 25	12 30	1 18
8 Sa	5 55	22 07	2 54	19 58	1 37	0S04	9 08	7 03	22 24	0 36	9 29	9 26	21 45	0 25	12 27	1 18
9 Su	5 33	17 35	1 51	15 03	2 21	0 12	9 16	6 54	22 28	0 35	9 29	9 28	21 46	0 24	12 25	1 18
10 M	5 10	12 21	0 43	9 34	3 04	0 20	9 24	6 45	22 32	0 34	9 29	9 29	21 47	0 24	12 22	1 18
11 Tu	4 47	6 43	0S26	3 49	3 46	0 28	9 32	6 36	22 35	0 33	9 29	9 30	21 48	0 24	12 19	1 19
12 W	4 24	0 54	1 33	1S60	4 28	0 36	9 39	6 27	22 39	0 31	9 28	9 31	21 49	0 24	12 17	1 19
13 Th	4 01	4S51	2 34	7 39	5 10	0 44	9 45	6 17	22 42	0 30	9 28	9 32	21 50	0 24	12 14	1 19
14 F	3 38	10 23	3 28	12 59	5 51	0 52	9 51	6 08	22 45	0 29	9 27	9 33	21 51	0 23	12 12	1 19
15 Sa	3 15	15 29	4 13	17 49	6 31	0 60	9 57	5 58	22 48	0 27	9 27	9 34	21 52	0 23	12 09	1 19
16 Su	2 52	19 59	4 46	21 57	7 11	1 08	10 01	5 48	22 51	0 26	9 26	9 35	21 53	0 23	12 07	1 19
17 M	2 29	23 42	5 07	25 12	7 50	1 16	10 06	5 39	22 54	0 25	9 26	9 36	21 54	0 23	12 04	1 19
18 Tu	2 06	26 26	5 15	27 23	8 28	1 24	10 09	5 29	22 57	0 23	9 25	9 37	21 55	0 23	12 02	1 19
19 W	1 43	28 01	5 10	28 19	9 05	1 32	10 13	5 19	22 59	0 22	9 24	9 38	21 56	0 23	11 59	1 20
20 Th	1 20	28 16	4 50	27 52	9 42	1 40	10 15	5 09	23 02	0 21	9 23	9 39	21 57	0 22	11 57	1 20
21 F	0 56	27 06	4 16	25 58	10 18	1 48	10 17	4 59	23 04	0 19	9 22	9 40	21 58	0 22	11 54	1 20
22 Sa	0 33	24 28	3 29	22 38	10 53	1 55	10 19	4 49	23 06	0 18	9 21	9 41	21 60	0 22	11 52	1 20
23 Su	0 10	20 29	2 29	18 01	11 27	2 03	10 20	4 40	23 08	0 16	9 20	9 42	22 01	0 22	11 50	1 20
24 M	0S14	15 17	1 19	12 19	12 00	2 10	10 20	4 30	23 10	0 15	9 19	9 43	22 02	0 22	11 47	1 20
25 Tu	0 37	9 08	0 02	5 48	12 33	2 18	10 19	4 20	23 12	0 13	9 18	9 44	22 03	0 22	11 45	1 20
26 W	1 00	2 21	1N17	1N11	13 04	2 25	10 19	4 10	23 14	0 12	9 17	9 44	22 04	0 22	11 42	1 20
27 Th	1 24	4N42	2 32	8 11	13 34	2 32	10 17	4 01	23 16	0 10	9 16	9 45	22 05	0 21	11 40	1 21
28 F	1 47	11 34	3 38	14 47	14 03	2 38	10 15	3 51	23 18	0 09	9 15	9 46	22 06	0 21	11 38	1 21
29 Sa	2 11	17 47	4 29	20 29	14 30	2 45	10 12	3 42	23 19	0 07	9 13	9 46	22 08	0 21	11 35	1 21
30 Su	2S34	22N51	5N01	24N50	14S57	2S51	10N09	3S32	23N21	0S06	9N12	9S47	22S09	0N21	11N33	1N21

Day	⚷ Decl	⚷ Lat	♅ Decl	♅ Lat	♆ Decl	♆ Lat	♇ Decl	♇ Lat
1	10S23	7N10	5S51	0S49	15S02	0S17	16S38	6N45
6	10 28	7 08	5 56	0 49	15 05	0 17	16 40	6 44
11	10 33	7 07	6 01	0 49	15 07	0 17	16 41	6 42
16	10 38	7 05	6 05	0 49	15 09	0 17	16 43	6 40
21	10 42	7 03	6 10	0 49	15 11	0 17	16 45	6 39
26	10 46	7 01	6 14	0 49	15 13	0 17	16 46	6 37

Day	⚴ Decl	⚴ Lat	⚵ Decl	⚵ Lat	⚶ Decl	⚶ Lat	Eris Decl	Eris Lat
1	4N40	13N13	2S31	8N40	21S24	0N44	4S52	14S14
6	3 38	12 37	3 03	8 38	21 52	0 29	4 53	14 14
11	2 34	11 57	3 35	8 37	22 18	0 15	4 55	14 15
16	1 29	11 16	4 07	8 36	22 42	0 02	4 56	14 15
21	0 24	10 33	4 39	8 35	23 05	0S10	4 57	14 15
26	0S41	9 48	5 10	8 34	23 26	0 22	4 58	14 15

Moon Phenomena

Max/0 Decl

dy	hr mn	
5	4:19	28N22
12	3:44	0 S
19	16:28	28S21
26	8:00	0 N

Perigee/Apogee

dy	hr m		kilometers
15	21:11	a	405642
28	1:44	p	359420

Max/0 Lat

dy	hr mn	
3	19:36	5N17
10	14:50	0 S
18	2:14	5S15
25	0:41	0 N

PH	dy	hr mn	
☾	4	2:33	11♊12
●	11	12:45	18♍25
● (eclipse)	11	12:32	P 0.751
☽	19	16:49	26♐22
○	26	19:46	3♈20

Void of Course Moon

Last Aspect				☽ Ingress		
1	5:20	♄	△	♉	1	5:36
3	0:48	☿	△	♊	3	7:31
5	11:02	☿	□	♋	5	11:09
6	17:05	♅	△	♌	7	17:00
9	18:08	♇	△	♍	10	1:11
12	4:15	♇	□	♎	12	11:32
14	16:11	♇	✶	♏	14	23:38
16	23:42	☉	✶	♐	17	12:22
19	16:49	☉	□	♑	19	23:53
22	6:16	☉	△	♒	22	8:19
24	9:15	♂	△	♓	24	12:56
26	12:32	♂	□	♈	26	14:24
28	14:00	♂	✶	♉	28	14:18
30	5:11	♀	□	♊	30	14:35

DAILY ASPECTARIAN

1 Sa: ☿△⚳ 2:25; ☽#♆ 4:05; ☽△♄ 5:20; ☽∠♂ 6:22; ☽∠♅ 8:58; ☽#♇ 10:37; ☉△☽ 20:29; ☽⚼☿ 20:34; ☉∥♀ 22:29; ☽⚻♃ 23:40

2 Su: ☽⚼♇ 0:16; ☽□⚷ 0:50; ☽⚺♂ 8:12; ☽✶♅ 9:44; ☽#♃ 9:44; ☽□♀ 10:21; ☽∥♂ 11:33; ♄ ♍ 13:50; ☽□♆ 14:54; ☽☌⚳ 19:44

3 M: ☽△☿ 0:48; ☽⚻♇ 1:18; ☿□♇ 5:05; ☽□♄ 7:40; ☿⚼⚷ 9:11; ♂□♅ 20:10; ♀✶♂ 23:37

4 Tu: ☉□♃ 0:05; ☽☍♃ 2:24; ☉□☽ 2:33; ☽△⚷ 3:09; ☉⚻⚷ 10:52; ☽□♅ 12:23; ☽✶♀ 12:24; ☽☌♂ 13:07; ♀⚻♅ 15:13; ☽△♆ 17:48; ☽⚺⚳ 23:16

5 W: ☽☍♇ 4:40; ☽⚼⚷ 5:02; ☽□☿ 11:02; ☽✶♄ 11:48; ☿ ♎ 12:03; ☽∠♀ 14:17; ☿⚺♄ 18:06; ☽⚼♆ 20:00

6 Th: ☽∠⚳ 1:49; ☽⚻♃ 7:10; ☽⚻⚷ 7:27; ☉✶☽ 11:04; ☿∠♀ 13:35; ☽∠♄ 14:42; ☽⚺♀ 16:47; ☽△♅ 17:05; ☽⚺♂ 20:22; ☽⚻♆ 22:47

7 F: ☽✶⚳ 4:57; ☽⚻♇ 10:14; ☽⚼♃ 10:25; ♃✶⚷ 12:10; ♇ D 14:56; ☉∠☽ 16:24; ☽⚺♄ 18:12; ☽⚼♅ 20:17; ☉#♅ 20:59; ☽∥♂ 22:21

8 Sa: ☽✶☿ 0:13; ☽∠♂ 0:57; ☽#♃ 2:10; ☽⚼♇ 13:54; ☽☍⚷ 14:01; ☽△♃ 14:17; ♀ D 16:15; ☿⚼♆ 16:26; ☉⚺☽ 22:28; ☽☌♀ 23:48

9 Su: ☽⚻♅ 0:04; ⚵ ♏ 3:31; ♂△♆ 4:06; ☽#♇ 4:22; ☽☍♆ 6:06; ☽✶♂ 6:11; ☽∠☿ 7:59; ☽#♆ 11:43; ☽□⚳ 12:56; ☉⚺♀ 16:18; ☽△♇ 18:08; ☉☍♅ 18:47; ☽∥♄ 23:57

10 M: ♇∠⚷ 1:49; ☽☌♄ 2:59; ☽#⚷ 7:52; ☽∥⚳ 12:23; ☽∥♀ 12:25; ♀∥⚳ 13:37; ☽⚺☿ 16:29; ♀⚻♅ 17:37; ☽⚻⚷ 22:52; ☽□♃ 23:47

11 Tu: ☽#♅ 2:54; ☿⚼⚳ 3:41; ☉∥☽ 8:33; ☽☍♅ 9:19; ☽⚺♀ 9:29; ☽#☿ 10:52; ☉☌☽ 12:45; ☽⚻♆ 15:38; ☽□♂ 18:32; ☉#☿ 22:32; ☽△⚳ 23:08

12 W: ☽⚼⚷ 4:05; ☽□♇ 4:15; ☽⚺♄ 14:01; ☽∠♀ 15:17; ☉#☽ 20:42; ☽⚼♆ 21:10; ☿△⚷ 21:19

13 Th: ☉⚻♆ 0:22; ☽∥☿ 1:28; ☽⚼⚳ 4:57; ☽∥♅ 5:04; ☽△⚷ 9:46; ☿✶♃ 10:44; ☽✶♃ 11:25; ☽☌☿ 11:30; ☽#⚳ 19:54; ☽∠♄ 20:14; ☽⚻♅ 20:31; ☽#♀ 21:37; ☽✶♀ 21:39

14 F: ☽∥⚷ 1:00; ☽△♆ 3:07; ☉⚺☽ 5:33; ☿∥♅ 7:51; ☽#♄ 8:14; ☽△♂ 9:01; ☽⚻⚳ 11:09; ☽✶♇ 16:11; ☽∠♃ 17:51; ☽∥♆ 22:21

15 Sa: ☽⚼♅ 2:40; ☽✶♄ 2:47; ☽∥♇ 6:15; ☉∠☽ 14:34; ☽⚼♂ 16:46; ☽□⚷ 22:05; ☽∠♇ 22:34

16 Su: ☽⚺♃ 0:30; ☽⚺☿ 8:09; ☽△♅ 8:57; ☽□♀ 11:32; ☽∥♃ 11:39; ♂⚺⚳ 12:15; ☿⚻♅ 15:00; ☽□♆ 15:42; ☽#♂ 18:15; ☿∠♄ 20:55; ☉✶☽ 23:42

17 M: ☽☍⚳ 0:02; ☽⚻♂ 0:33; ☉△⚳ 3:56; ☽⚺♇ 4:57; ☽□♄ 16:08; ☽∠☿ 18:22; ☉□♂ 20:50; ☿✶♀ 21:29

18 Tu: ☽✶⚷ 10:26; ☽☌♃ 13:35; ☽□♅ 21:05

19 W: ☽△♀ 1:27; ☿△♆ 2:01; ☽✶♆ 3:45; ☽✶☿ 3:58; ☉⚼⚷ 6:55; ☿#⚳ 11:54; ☽⚻⚳ 12:02; ☽☍♂ 15:04; ☽∠⚷ 16:00; ☉□♇ 16:01; ☽☌♇ 16:45; ☉□☽ 16:49

20 Th: ☽△♄ 4:05; ☽⚼♀ 7:40; ☽∠♆ 8:57; ♂⚼⚷ 12:30; ⚳ R 13:06; ☽⚼⚳ 17:04; ☽⚺⚷ 20:51; ☿#♀ 23:27

21 F: ☽⚺♃ 0:33; ☽✶♅ 6:55; ♂☍♇ 8:41; ☽⚼♄ 8:55; ☽⚻♀ 13:04; ☽⚺♆ 13:19; ☿∥⚷ 16:49; ☽□☿ 19:54; ♀☍♆ 20:04; ☽△⚳ 21:12

22 Sa: ☽⚺♇ 1:40; ☽⚻♂ 2:20; ☽∠♃ 4:43; ☉△☽ 6:16; ☽#♂ 9:05; ☿⚻⚳ 9:35; ☽∠♅ 10:31; ☽⚻♄ 12:46; ☽∥♃ 15:43

23 Su: ☽☌⚷ 3:47; ☽∠♇ 4:42; ☽⚼♂ 6:20; ☽✶♃ 7:53; ☉ ♎ 9:52; ☉⚼☽ 11:11; ☽⚺♅ 13:08; ☿#♄ 14:56; ☽∥♇ 17:40; ☽☌♆ 19:10; ☽☍♀ 20:53

24 M: ☽∥♆ 0:21; ☽□⚳ 2:31; ☽△☿ 6:24; ☽✶♇ 6:46; ☽△♂ 9:15; ☿✶♇ 10:57; ☽∥☿ 12:07; ☽#♄ 14:07; ☉⚻☽ 14:56; ☽☍♄ 17:31; ☽∥⚷ 17:58; ☽#♀ 19:34; ☽#⚳ 23:22

25 Tu: ☽⚺⚷ 7:01; ☽⚼☿ 9:48; ☽∥♅ 10:27; ☽□♃ 11:25; ☽☌♅ 15:46; ☽⚺♆ 21:30

26 W: ☽⚻♀ 1:02; ☉∥☽ 4:20; ☽✶⚳ 4:25; ☽∠⚷ 7:33; ☽□♇ 8:34; ☉⚺♄ 9:01; ☿∠♃ 9:36; ☉#☽ 12:05; ☽⚻☿ 12:18; ☽□♂ 12:32; ☿△♂ 17:54; ☽⚻♄ 19:09; ☉☍☽ 19:46; ☽∠♆ 21:45

27 Th: ☽⚼♀ 2:11; ☽∠⚳ 4:31; ☽#♅ 5:19; ☽✶⚷ 7:38; ☽△♃ 12:24; ☽∥⚳ 15:43; ☽⚺♅ 16:02; ☿ ♏ 17:19; ☽∥♀ 19:16; ☽⚼♄ 19:18; ☽#⚷ 21:13; ☽✶♆ 21:41

28 F: ☽∥♄ 0:12; ☉⚼♆ 1:26; ☽△♀ 3:04; ☽⚺⚳ 4:21; ☽△♇ 8:36; ☽#☿ 9:54; ☽⚼♃ 12:30; ☽#♆ 13:43; ☽✶♂ 14:00; ☽☍☿ 15:51; ☽∠♅ 15:51; ☿⚼♅ 15:57; ☽△♄ 19:22; ☽#♇ 19:55; ☉⚻☽ 22:57; ♂ ♋ 23:56

29 Sa: ☽□⚷ 7:22; ♀□⚳ 8:21; ☽⚼♇ 8:33; ☽⚻♃ 12:42; ☽∠♂ 14:44; ☽✶♅ 15:47; ☽#♃ 20:13; ☽□♆ 21:33

30 Su: ☉⚼☽ 0:44; ☽∥♂ 2:49; ☽☌⚳ 4:13; ☽□♀ 5:11; ☽⚻♇ 8:46; ☽⚺♂ 15:49; ☿∥♆ 16:56; ☽⚻☿ 19:36; ☽□♄ 20:11

October 2007

LONGITUDE

Day	Sid.Time	☉	☽	☽ 12 hour	Mean ☊	True ☊	☿	♀	♂	⚳	♃	♄	⚷	♅	♆	♇
	h m s	° ' "	° ' "	° ' "	° '	° '	° '	° '	° '	° '	° '	° '	° '	° '	° '	° '
1 M	0 37 24	7♎26 21	5♊43 53	12♊57 18	5♓12.7	6♓42.0	3♏13.5	24♌44.6	0♋54.3	23♉35.3	14♐13.7	3♍25.9	10♒39.6	15♓53.3	19♒30.2	26♐26.8
2 Tu	0 41 21	8 25 20	20 05 08	27 07 07	5 09.6	6R 39.3	4 06.5	25 24.5	1 20.8	23R 31.1	14 22.6	3 32.7	10R 38.4	15R 51.2	19R 29.3	26 27.6
3 W	0 45 17	9 24 21	4♋03 08	10♋53 14	5 06.4	6D 38.1	4 56.4	26 05.6	1 47.0	23 26.6	14 31.5	3 39.4	10 37.2	15 49.0	19 28.4	26 28.4
4 Th	0 49 14	10 23 24	17 37 35	24 16 24	5 03.2	6 38.1	5 42.8	26 47.8	2 12.8	23 21.6	14 40.6	3 46.0	10 36.1	15 46.9	19 27.5	26 29.2
5 F	0 53 11	11 22 30	0♌50 00	7♌18 45	5 00.0	6 39.3	6 25.4	27 31.0	2 38.2	23 16.3	14 49.8	3 52.6	10 35.1	15 44.8	19 26.6	26 30.0
6 Sa	0 57 07	12 21 37	13 43 02	20 03 14	4 56.9	6 40.9	7 03.8	28 15.2	3 03.3	23 10.6	14 59.1	3 59.2	10 34.2	15 42.7	19 25.8	26 30.9
7 Su	1 01 04	13 20 47	26 19 46	2♍32 59	4 53.7	6R 42.3	7 37.8	29 00.4	3 27.9	23 04.5	15 08.5	4 05.7	10 33.3	15 40.7	19 25.0	26 31.8
8 M	1 05 00	14 20 00	8♍43 15	14 50 56	4 50.5	6 42.7	8 06.8	29 46.6	3 52.1	22 58.1	15 18.0	4 12.2	10 32.4	15 38.7	19 24.2	26 32.8
9 Tu	1 08 57	15 19 14	20 56 19	26 59 41	4 47.3	6 41.6	8 30.5	0♍33.6	4 15.9	22 51.3	15 27.7	4 18.6	10 31.7	15 36.7	19 23.5	26 33.7
10 W	1 12 53	16 18 31	3♎01 18	9♎01 25	4 44.1	6 38.6	8 48.4	1 21.5	4 39.3	22 44.1	15 37.4	4 25.0	10 31.0	15 34.7	19 22.7	26 34.7
11 Th	1 16 50	17 17 49	15 00 13	20 57 55	4 41.0	6 33.5	8 59.9	2 10.3	5 02.2	22 36.5	15 47.3	4 31.3	10 30.3	15 32.8	19 22.0	26 35.8
12 F	1 20 46	18 17 10	26 54 44	2♏50 51	4 37.8	6 26.7	9R 04.7	2 59.9	5 24.7	22 28.6	15 57.3	4 37.5	10 29.8	15 30.8	19 21.4	26 36.8
13 Sa	1 24 43	19 16 33	8♏46 28	14 41 50	4 34.6	6 18.6	9 02.2	3 50.2	5 46.7	22 20.4	16 07.3	4 43.7	10 29.3	15 29.0	19 20.8	26 37.9
14 Su	1 28 39	20 15 58	20 37 09	26 32 42	4 31.4	6 10.0	8 52.0	4 41.3	6 08.3	22 11.8	16 17.5	4 49.8	10 28.8	15 27.1	19 20.2	26 39.0
15 M	1 32 36	21 15 24	2♐28 47	8♐25 44	4 28.3	6 01.6	8 33.7	5 33.2	6 29.3	22 02.8	16 27.8	4 55.9	10 28.5	15 25.3	19 19.6	26 40.2
16 Tu	1 36 33	22 14 53	14 23 55	20 23 44	4 25.1	5 54.3	8 07.0	6 25.7	6 49.9	21 53.6	16 38.2	5 01.9	10 28.2	15 23.5	19 19.1	26 41.3
17 W	1 40 29	23 14 23	26 25 37	2♑30 04	4 21.9	5 48.8	7 31.8	7 18.9	7 10.0	21 44.0	16 48.6	5 07.9	10 27.9	15 21.8	19 18.6	26 42.5
18 Th	1 44 26	24 13 56	8♑37 35	14 48 43	4 18.7	5 45.3	6 48.2	8 12.8	7 29.6	21 34.1	16 59.2	5 13.8	10 27.8	15 20.1	19 18.1	26 43.8
19 F	1 48 22	25 13 30	21 03 59	27 23 58	4 15.5	5D 43.9	5 56.4	9 07.3	7 48.7	21 23.8	17 09.9	5 19.6	10D 27.7	15 18.4	19 17.6	26 45.0
20 Sa	1 52 19	26 13 06	3♒49 13	10♒20 15	4 12.4	5 44.1	4 57.2	10 02.4	8 07.2	21 13.3	17 20.6	5 25.4	10 27.7	15 16.8	19 17.2	26 46.3
21 Su	1 56 15	27 12 43	16 57 33	23 41 32	4 09.2	5 45.1	3 51.6	10 58.1	8 25.2	21 02.5	17 31.5	5 31.1	10 27.7	15 15.2	19 16.9	26 47.6
22 M	2 00 12	28 12 22	0♓32 31	7♓30 40	4 06.0	5R 46.0	2 40.9	11 54.3	8 42.7	20 51.4	17 42.4	5 36.7	10 27.8	15 13.6	19 16.5	26 49.0
23 Tu	2 04 08	29 12 03	14 36 03	21 48 30	4 02.8	5 45.7	1 26.8	12 51.1	8 59.6	20 40.1	17 53.4	5 42.3	10 28.0	15 12.1	19 16.2	26 50.3
24 W	2 08 05	0♏11 46	29 07 39	6♈32 58	3 59.7	5 43.6	0 11.4	13 48.5	9 16.0	20 28.5	18 04.6	5 47.8	10 28.3	15 10.6	19 15.9	26 51.7
25 Th	2 12 02	1 11 30	14♈03 36	21 38 34	3 56.5	5 39.0	28♎56.8	14 46.4	9 31.7	20 16.6	18 15.8	5 53.2	10 28.6	15 09.1	19 15.7	26 53.1
26 F	2 15 58	2 11 16	29 16 39	6♉56 31	3 53.3	5 32.2	27 45.5	15 44.8	9 46.9	20 04.5	18 27.0	5 58.5	10 29.0	15 07.7	19 15.5	26 54.6
27 Sa	2 19 55	3 11 04	14♉36 42	22 15 45	3 50.1	5 23.8	26 39.4	16 43.7	10 01.5	19 52.2	18 38.4	6 03.8	10 29.4	15 06.3	19 15.3	26 56.0
28 Su	2 23 51	4 10 55	29 52 17	7♊24 57	3 46.9	5 14.7	25 40.8	17 43.0	10 15.5	19 39.7	18 49.9	6 09.0	10 29.9	15 05.0	19 15.1	26 57.5
29 M	2 27 48	5 10 47	14♊52 40	22 14 29	3 43.8	5 06.2	24 51.1	18 42.9	10 28.8	19 27.0	19 01.4	6 14.2	10 30.5	15 03.7	19 15.0	26 59.1
30 Tu	2 31 44	6 10 42	29 29 42	6♋37 52	3 40.6	4 59.2	24 11.8	19 43.1	10 41.6	19 14.1	19 13.0	6 19.2	10 31.2	15 02.5	19 14.9	27 00.6
31 W	2 35 41	7♏10 39	13♋38 45	20 32 18	3♓37.4	4♓54.5	23♎43.5	20♍43.9	10♋53.6	19♉01.0	19♐24.7	6♍24.2	10♒31.9	15♓01.3	19♒14.9	27♐02.2

1st of Month

Julian Day #
2454374.5
Obliquity
23°26'27"
SVP 5♓08'59"
GC 26♐56.8
Eris 21♈08.3R

Day	⚴
1	3♓39.3R
6	2 49.5R
11	2 08.0R
16	1 35.4R
21	1 11.8R
26	0 57.5R
31	0 52.0R

Day	⚵
1	6♏49.6
6	8 27.1
11	10 05.6
16	11 45.1
21	13 25.4
26	15 06.3
31	16 47.8

Day	⚶
1	22♐11.2
6	24 15.0
11	26 22.1
16	28 32.1
21	0♑44.9
26	3 00.0
31	5 17.4

DECLINATION and LATITUDE

Day	☉ Decl	☽ Decl	☽ Lat	☽ 12h Decl	☿ Decl	☿ Lat	♀ Decl	♀ Lat	♂ Decl	♂ Lat	⚳ Decl	⚳ Lat	♃ Decl	♃ Lat	♄ Decl	♄ Lat
1 M	2S57	26N23	5N12	27N29	15S22	2S57	10N05	3S23	23N22	0S04	9N11	9S47	22S10	0N21	11N31	1N21
2 Tu	3 20	28 07	5 04	28 17	15 45	3 02	10 00	3 14	23 24	0 02	9 09	9 48	22 11	0 21	11 28	1 21
3 W	3 44	28 00	4 38	27 17	16 07	3 08	9 55	3 05	23 25	0 01	9 08	9 48	22 12	0 20	11 26	1 21
4 Th	4 07	26 11	3 56	24 43	16 27	3 12	9 50	2 56	23 26	0N01	9 06	9 49	22 13	0 20	11 24	1 22
5 F	4 30	22 57	3 03	20 55	16 45	3 16	9 43	2 47	23 27	0 03	9 05	9 49	22 15	0 20	11 21	1 22
6 Sa	4 53	18 39	2 02	16 13	17 01	3 20	9 36	2 38	23 29	0 04	9 03	9 49	22 16	0 20	11 19	1 22
7 Su	5 16	13 37	0 56	10 55	17 15	3 23	9 29	2 29	23 30	0 06	9 01	9 49	22 17	0 20	11 17	1 22
8 M	5 39	8 08	0S11	5 17	17 26	3 25	9 21	2 21	23 31	0 08	8 60	9 50	22 18	0 20	11 15	1 22
9 Tu	6 02	2 25	1 17	0S27	17 36	3 26	9 13	2 12	23 32	0 10	8 58	9 50	22 19	0 20	11 12	1 22
10 W	6 25	3S19	2 18	6 07	17 42	3 27	9 03	2 04	23 33	0 11	8 56	9 50	22 21	0 19	11 10	1 22
11 Th	6 48	8 52	3 12	11 32	17 45	3 26	8 54	1 56	23 34	0 13	8 55	9 50	22 22	0 19	11 08	1 23
12 F	7 10	14 04	3 58	16 29	17 45	3 24	8 44	1 48	23 35	0 15	8 53	9 49	22 23	0 19	11 06	1 23
13 Sa	7 33	18 44	4 33	20 48	17 41	3 21	8 33	1 40	23 36	0 17	8 51	9 49	22 24	0 19	11 04	1 23
14 Su	7 55	22 40	4 56	24 18	17 34	3 17	8 22	1 32	23 37	0 19	8 49	9 49	22 25	0 19	11 02	1 23
15 M	8 18	25 40	5 07	26 46	17 23	3 11	8 10	1 24	23 38	0 21	8 47	9 48	22 27	0 19	10 60	1 23
16 Tu	8 40	27 34	5 04	28 03	17 07	3 04	7 58	1 17	23 39	0 23	8 46	9 48	22 28	0 19	10 58	1 24
17 W	9 02	28 11	4 48	27 60	16 47	2 55	7 45	1 09	23 40	0 25	8 44	9 47	22 29	0 18	10 56	1 24
18 Th	9 24	27 28	4 19	26 35	16 22	2 44	7 32	1 02	23 41	0 27	8 42	9 47	22 30	0 18	10 54	1 24
19 F	9 46	25 22	3 37	23 48	15 53	2 31	7 18	0 55	23 42	0 29	8 40	9 46	22 31	0 18	10 52	1 24
20 Sa	10 07	21 56	2 43	19 46	15 19	2 17	7 04	0 48	23 43	0 31	8 38	9 45	22 32	0 18	10 50	1 24
21 Su	10 29	17 20	1 39	14 38	14 42	2 01	6 50	0 41	23 44	0 33	8 36	9 44	22 34	0 18	10 48	1 24
22 M	10 50	11 43	0 28	8 36	14 01	1 43	6 35	0 34	23 45	0 35	8 35	9 43	22 35	0 18	10 46	1 25
23 Tu	11 11	5 20	0N47	1 57	13 18	1 24	6 19	0 27	23 46	0 38	8 33	9 42	22 36	0 18	10 44	1 25
24 W	11 32	1N31	2 02	5N00	12 32	1 04	6 03	0 20	23 47	0 40	8 31	9 41	22 37	0 17	10 42	1 25
25 Th	11 53	8 28	3 10	11 50	11 47	0 44	5 47	0 14	23 48	0 42	8 29	9 40	22 38	0 17	10 40	1 25
26 F	12 14	15 03	4 06	18 03	11 02	0 23	5 30	0 08	23 49	0 44	8 28	9 38	22 39	0 17	10 39	1 25
27 Sa	12 35	20 45	4 45	23 06	10 19	0 02	5 13	0 02	23 50	0 47	8 26	9 37	22 40	0 17	10 37	1 26
28 Su	12 55	25 03	5 03	26 33	9 39	0N17	4 55	0N04	23 51	0 49	8 24	9 35	22 41	0 17	10 35	1 26
29 M	13 15	27 33	4 60	28 03	9 04	0 36	4 37	0 10	23 53	0 51	8 23	9 34	22 42	0 17	10 33	1 26
30 Tu	13 35	28 04	4 37	27 35	8 33	0 53	4 19	0 16	23 54	0 54	8 21	9 32	22 43	0 17	10 32	1 26
31 W	13S55	26N41	3N58	25N23	8S08	1N09	4N00	0N22	23N55	0N56	8N19	9S30	22S45	0N17	10N30	1N26

Day	⚷ Decl	⚷ Lat	♅ Decl	♅ Lat	♆ Decl	♆ Lat	♇ Decl	♇ Lat
1	10S50	6N59	6S19	0S49	15S14	0S17	16S48	6N36
6	10 54	6 57	6 23	0 48	15 16	0 17	16 50	6 34
11	10 57	6 54	6 26	0 48	15 17	0 17	16 51	6 33
16	11 00	6 52	6 30	0 48	15 18	0 17	16 53	6 31
21	11 02	6 49	6 33	0 48	15 19	0 17	16 54	6 30
26	11 05	6 47	6 36	0 48	15 19	0 17	16 56	6 28
31	11S06	6N44	6S38	0S48	15S19	0S17	16S57	6N27

Day	⚴ Decl	⚴ Lat	⚵ Decl	⚵ Lat	⚶ Decl	⚶ Lat	Eris Decl	Eris Lat
1	1S43	9N03	5S41	8N34	23S45	0S33	4S59	14S15
6	2 43	8 17	6 11	8 35	24 02	0 43	5 00	14 15
11	3 40	7 32	6 41	8 35	24 17	0 53	5 01	14 15
16	4 33	6 48	7 10	8 36	24 29	1 03	5 02	14 15
21	5 22	6 04	7 38	8 38	24 38	1 12	5 03	14 15
26	6 07	5 22	8 05	8 39	24 45	1 20	5 04	14 15
31	6S47	4N41	8S30	8N42	24S48	1S28	5S04	14S14

Moon Phenomena

Max/0 Decl
dy hr mn
2 10:19 28N17
9 10:06 0 S
16 23:24 28S12
23 18:46 0 N
29 18:20 28N07

Max/0 Lat
dy hr mn
1 1:28 5N12
7 20:05 0 S
15 7:03 5S08
22 9:00 0 N
28 8:23 5N04

Perigee/Apogee
dy hr m kilometers
13 9:53 a 406492
26 11:51 p 356758

PH dy hr mn
☾ 3 10:07 9♋49
● 11 5:02 17♎30
☽ 19 8:34 25♑35
○ 26 4:53 2♉23

Void of Course Moon

Last Aspect	☽ Ingress
2 10:53 ♇ ☍	♋ 2 16:58
3 20:42 ♅ △	♌ 4 22:28
7 5:29 ♀ ☌	♍ 7 7:04
9 11:09 ♇ □	♎ 9 17:59
11 23:24 ♇ ⚹	♏ 12 6:14
13 21:24 ♅ □	♐ 14 18:59
17 0:34 ♇ ☌	♑ 17 7:04
19 8:34 ☉ □	♒ 19 16:53
21 19:37 ☉ △	♓ 21 23:03
23 20:18 ♇ □	♈ 24 1:25
25 21:47 ☿ ☍	♉ 26 1:08
27 7:17 ♆ □	♊ 28 0:12
29 19:52 ♇ ☍	♋ 30 0:51

DAILY ASPECTARIAN

1 M
☉△☽ 3:02
☿⚹♄ 6:17
☽△⚷ 8:10
☽☍♃ 14:17
☽□♅ 16:53
☽⚼☿ 22:14
☽△♆ 22:59

2 Tu
☉⚼⚳ 2:11
☽⊻⚳ 5:48
☽⚼⚷ 9:27
☽⚹♀ 9:32
☽☍♇ 10:53
☽☌♂ 19:56
☽⚹♄ 23:18

3 W
☽⚼♆ 0:44
☽△☿ 1:39
☽∠⚳ 7:39
☉□☽ 10:07
☽⊼⚷ 11:31
☽∠♀ 13:02
♀△♇ 13:17
☽⊼♃ 18:40
☽△♅ 20:42

4 Th
☽∠♄ 2:04
☽⊼♆ 3:17
☉△⚷ 5:05
☽⚹⚳ 10:17
☽⊼♇ 16:03
☽⊻♀ 17:33
☽∥♂ 20:46
☽⚼♃ 22:08
☽⚼♅ 23:50

5 F
☽⊻♂ 3:26
☽#♃ 4:19
☽⊻♄ 5:40
☿∥♇ 6:27
☽□☿ 10:54
☽☍⚷ 18:06
☽⚼♇ 19:51
☉⚹☽ 21:14

6 Sa
☽△♃ 2:25
☽⊼♅ 3:45
☽#☿ 7:46
☽∠♂ 8:29
☽#♇ 9:03
☽☍♆ 10:48
☽#♆ 16:27
☽□⚳ 17:49

7 Su
☽△♇ 0:23
☉∠☽ 4:13
☽☌♀ 5:29
☽∥♄ 10:29
☽#⚷ 12:01
☽⚹♂ 14:14
☽☌♄ 15:08
☽∥♀ 18:39
☽∥⚳ 20:18
☽⚹☿ 22:46

8 M
☽⊼⚷ 3:33
♀ ♍ 6:54
☽#♅ 7:18
☉#☽ 9:49
☉⊻☽ 11:57
☽□♃ 13:04
☽☍♅ 13:32
☽⊼♆ 20:57

9 Tu
♂⚹♄ 3:45
☽△⚳ 3:45
☉⚹♃ 4:06
☽∠☿ 5:14
☉⊼♅ 6:50
♂⚼♆ 7:28
☽⚼⚷ 9:05
☽□♇ 11:09
♃□♅ 18:25
☽⊻♀ 20:27

10 W
☉∥♅ 0:59
☽⚼♆ 2:42
☽⊻♄ 2:48
☽□♂ 3:22
☉∠♀ 6:43
☽⚼⚳ 9:19
☽⊻☿ 11:47
☽∥♅ 13:21
☉∥☽ 14:14
☽△⚷ 14:59
♀∥⚳ 22:03

11 Th
☽#♀ 0:08
☽#⚳ 0:11
☽⊼♅ 1:05
☽⚹♃ 1:36
☽∠♀ 4:41
☉☌☽ 5:02
☽△♆ 8:46
☽∠♄ 9:10
☽∥⚷ 9:23
☽#♄ 10:08
☽⊼⚳ 15:09
☽⚹♇ 23:24

12 F
☿ R 4:00
☽∥♆ 5:58
☽⚼♅ 7:16
☽∠♃ 8:17
☽⚹♀ 13:14
☽∥♇ 13:58
☽⚹♄ 15:44
☽△♂ 17:44
☽∥☿ 18:25

13 Sa
☽☌☿ 0:32
☉△♆ 1:41
☽□⚷ 3:28
☽∠♇ 5:48
☉∠♄ 12:14
☽△♅ 13:33
☽⊻♃ 15:06
☽□♆ 21:24
☽∥♃ 22:20
☉⊻☽ 23:13

14 Su
☽⚼♂ 1:05
☽☍⚳ 3:09
♀☌♄ 4:29
☽#♂ 6:48
☽⊻♇ 12:14
☉#♀ 18:48

15 M
♄#⚷ 2:27
☽□♄ 5:00
☽□♀ 6:42
☉∠☽ 8:19
☽⊼♂ 8:20
☽⊻☿ 11:52
☽⚹⚷ 16:07
☉⊼⚳ 16:34

16 Tu
☽□♅ 1:59
♂∠⚳ 2:56
☽☌♃ 4:33
☉#⚳ 5:49
☽⚹♆ 9:50
☽⊼⚳ 14:47
☽∠☿ 16:39
☿∥♇ 17:06
☉⚹☽ 17:06
♀⚹♂ 17:38
☽∠⚷ 22:06

17 W
☽☌♇ 0:34
☿⚹♀ 3:19
☿△♂ 8:37
☽∠♆ 15:33
☽△♄ 17:18
☽⚼⚳ 20:02
☽⚹☿ 20:39
☽☍♂ 21:44
☽△♀ 23:08

18 Th
☽⊻⚷ 3:35
☽⚹♅ 12:59
☽⊻♃ 16:25
☽⊻♆ 20:37
☽⚼♄ 22:35

19 F
☽△⚳ 0:37
☽⚼♀ 6:16
⚶ ♑ 7:42
☉□☽ 8:34
☽⊻♇ 10:48
☽#♂ 12:43
☿⚹♄ 13:55
☽∠♅ 17:25
⚷ D 20:10
☽∥♃ 20:22
☽∠♃ 21:13

20 Sa
☿∥♆ 0:33
☽□☿ 1:57
☽⊼♄ 2:59
☽⊼♂ 8:08
♀⊼⚷ 10:57
☽☌⚷ 12:14
☽⊼♀ 12:19
☉⚹♇ 13:40
☽∠♇ 14:38
☽⊻♅ 20:56

21 Su
☽⚹♃ 1:02
☽∥♇ 1:58
☽☌♆ 4:09
☽□⚳ 7:12
☽∥♆ 9:05
☽⚼♂ 11:46
☽∥☿ 13:19
☽⚹♇ 17:29
☉#♄ 19:31
☉△☽ 19:37
☿∠♃ 23:33

22 M
♀#♅ 1:33
☽∥⚷ 2:38
☉∥☽ 3:17
☽△☿ 3:24
☽#♄ 3:46
☽☍♄ 8:48
☽#⚳ 12:10
☽△♂ 14:20
☉∥⚷ 14:39
☽⊻⚷ 17:01
☽∥♅ 19:32
☽#♀ 20:18
☽☍♀ 20:51
☉⚼☽ 23:17

23 Tu
☽☌♅ 1:00
☽⚼☿ 2:51
☽□♃ 5:34
☽⊻♆ 7:47
☽⚹⚳ 9:59
☽∠⚷ 18:01
☉ ♏ 19:16
☽□♇ 20:18
☉⚼♅ 23:32
☉☌☿ 23:56

24 W
☿⚼♅ 0:16
☽⊼☿ 1:35
☉⊼☽ 1:52
☿R♎ 3:38
☽∠♆ 8:19
☽∠⚳ 10:08
☽⊼♄ 10:51
☿∠♀ 14:59
☽∥♀ 15:02
☽□♂ 16:39
☽#♅ 17:27
☽⚹⚷ 18:17
☉∥☿ 21:37

25 Th
☽∥⚳ 0:05
☽⊼♀ 1:13
☽⊻♅ 1:44
☽△♃ 6:45
☽∥♄ 7:47
☽⚹♆ 8:14
♀☍♅ 9:09
☽#⚷ 9:15
☽⊻⚳ 9:43
☽#☿ 10:36
☽⚼♄ 10:52
☉#☽ 12:52
☽△♇ 20:17
☽☍☿ 21:47
☿∥⚷ 22:35

26 F
☽#♆ 1:03
☽∠♅ 1:20
☽⚼♀ 2:28
☉☍☽ 4:53
☽⚼♃ 6:37
☽#♇ 7:26
☽△♄ 10:33
☿#♄ 13:28
☽⚹♂ 16:43
☽□⚷ 17:33
☿⚹♇ 17:53
☽⚼♇ 19:48

27 Sa
☽⚹♅ 0:46
☽△♀ 3:33
☽⊼♃ 6:24
☽□♆ 7:17
☽☌⚳ 8:08
☽#♃ 9:41
☉∠♃ 13:33
☽∥♂ 16:18
☽∠♂ 16:36
☽⊼☿ 17:46
☽⊼♇ 19:23

28 Su
☉⊼☽ 7:20
☽□♄ 10:02
☽⚼☿ 16:18
☽⊻♂ 16:48
☽△⚷ 16:57

29 M
☽□♅ 0:18
♂⊼⚷ 3:15
☽□♀ 6:41
☽☍♃ 6:50
☽△♆ 7:06
☽⊻⚳ 7:20
♀□♃ 9:09
☉⚼☽ 9:15
♀⊼♆ 12:49
♀△⚳ 14:30
☽△☿ 15:34
☽⚼⚷ 17:24
☽☍♇ 19:52
⚳□♆ 22:28

30 Tu
⚳⊼♃ 1:06
☉⚹♄ 3:43
♃⚹♆ 4:00
☽∠⚳ 7:50
☽⚼♆ 7:58
☽⚹♄ 11:33
☿#⚳ 11:53
☉△☽ 12:05
☽⊼⚷ 18:39
☽☌♂ 19:12

31 W
☽△♅ 2:23
☽⚹⚳ 9:11
☽⊼♆ 9:44
☽⊼♃ 10:10
☽⚹♀ 13:20
☽∠♄ 13:36
⚴ D 13:58
☽□☿ 17:14
♆ D 20:07
☽∥♂ 22:37
☽⊼♇ 23:33

LONGITUDE

November 2007

Day	Sid.Time	☉	☽	☽ 12 hour	Mean ☊	True ☊	☿	♀	♂	⚳	♃	♄	⚷	♅	♆	♇
	h m s	° ' "	° ' "	° ' "	° '	° '	° '	° '	° '	° '	° '	° '	° '	° '	° '	° '
1 Th	2 39 37	8♏10 38	27♋18 41	3♌58 09	3♓34.2	4♓52.1	23♎26.8	21♍45.0	11♋05.0	18♉47.8	19♐36.4	6♍29.1	10♒32.7	15♓00.1	19♒14.9	27♐03.8
2 F	2 43 34	9 10 39	10♌31 09	16 58 08	3 31.1	4D 51.5	23D 21.5	22 46.6	11 15.7	18R 34.4	19 48.3	6 33.9	10 33.6	14R 59.0	19 14.9	27 05.4
3 Sa	2 47 31	10 10 43	23 19 39	29 36 16	3 27.9	4R 52.0	23 27.6	23 48.5	11 25.7	18 20.9	20 00.2	6 38.7	10 34.5	14 57.9	19 15.0	27 07.0
4 Su	2 51 27	11 10 48	5♍48 35	11♍57 09	3 24.7	4 52.3	23 44.3	24 50.8	11 35.0	18 07.3	20 12.2	6 43.3	10 35.5	14 56.9	19 15.0	27 08.7
5 M	2 55 24	12 10 55	18 02 33	24 05 18	3 21.5	4 51.4	24 11.0	25 53.5	11 43.6	17 53.6	20 24.2	6 47.9	10 36.5	14 55.9	19 15.2	27 10.3
6 Tu	2 59 20	13 11 05	0♎05 54	6♎04 46	3 18.4	4 48.4	24 47.0	26 56.6	11 51.5	17 39.7	20 36.3	6 52.4	10 37.6	14 55.0	19 15.3	27 12.0
7 W	3 03 17	14 11 17	12 02 20	17 58 56	3 15.2	4 42.6	25 31.2	28 00.0	11 58.6	17 25.9	20 48.5	6 56.8	10 38.8	14 54.1	19 15.5	27 13.8
8 Th	3 07 13	15 11 30	23 54 54	29 50 30	3 12.0	4 33.8	26 22.8	29 03.7	12 04.9	17 11.9	21 00.8	7 01.2	10 40.1	14 53.3	19 15.7	27 15.5
9 F	3 11 10	16 11 45	5♏45 58	11♏41 31	3 08.8	4 22.4	27 21.0	0♎07.8	12 10.4	16 58.0	21 13.1	7 05.4	10 41.4	14 52.5	19 16.0	27 17.3
10 Sa	3 15 06	17 12 03	17 37 19	23 33 31	3 05.6	4 09.1	28 25.0	1 12.1	12 15.2	16 44.0	21 25.4	7 09.5	10 42.8	14 51.7	19 16.3	27 19.0
11 Su	3 19 03	18 12 22	29 30 19	5♐27 50	3 02.5	3 54.8	29 33.9	2 16.8	12 19.2	16 30.0	21 37.9	7 13.6	10 44.3	14 51.0	19 16.6	27 20.8
12 M	3 23 00	19 12 42	11♐26 16	17 25 47	2 59.3	3 40.9	0♏47.2	3 21.7	12 22.4	16 16.1	21 50.4	7 17.6	10 45.8	14 50.4	19 17.0	27 22.7
13 Tu	3 26 56	20 13 05	23 26 36	29 28 58	2 56.1	3 28.3	2 04.0	4 27.0	12 24.7	16 02.2	22 03.0	7 21.5	10 47.4	14 49.8	19 17.4	27 24.5
14 W	3 30 53	21 13 29	5♑33 09	11♑39 30	2 52.9	3 18.1	3 24.1	5 32.5	12 26.3	15 48.3	22 15.6	7 25.3	10 49.0	14 49.2	19 17.8	27 26.4
15 Th	3 34 49	22 13 54	17 48 21	24 00 08	2 49.8	3 10.8	4 46.7	6 38.3	12R 27.0	15 34.5	22 28.2	7 29.0	10 50.8	14 48.7	19 18.3	27 28.3
16 F	3 38 46	23 14 21	0♒15 16	6♒34 14	2 46.6	3 06.5	6 11.5	7 44.4	12 26.9	15 20.8	22 41.0	7 32.6	10 52.5	14 48.3	19 18.8	27 30.2
17 Sa	3 42 42	24 14 49	12 57 32	19 25 41	2 43.4	3D 04.6	7 38.2	8 50.7	12 25.9	15 07.1	22 53.8	7 36.1	10 54.4	14 47.9	19 19.3	27 32.1
18 Su	3 46 39	25 15 18	25 59 10	2♓38 27	2 40.2	3R 04.3	9 06.5	9 57.2	12 24.1	14 53.6	23 06.6	7 39.5	10 56.3	14 47.5	19 19.9	27 34.0
19 M	3 50 35	26 15 49	9♓23 57	16 16 02	2 37.1	3 04.2	10 35.9	11 04.0	12 21.4	14 40.3	23 19.5	7 42.8	10 58.3	14 47.2	19 20.5	27 35.9
20 Tu	3 54 32	27 16 20	23 14 55	0♈20 41	2 33.9	3 03.2	12 06.4	12 11.0	12 17.9	14 27.0	23 32.4	7 46.0	11 00.3	14 47.0	19 21.1	27 37.9
21 W	3 58 29	28 16 53	7♈33 14	14 52 19	2 30.7	3 00.0	13 37.8	13 18.2	12 13.5	14 14.0	23 45.4	7 49.1	11 02.4	14 46.8	19 21.8	27 39.9
22 Th	4 02 25	29 17 28	22 17 23	29 47 41	2 27.5	2 54.1	15 09.8	14 25.7	12 08.3	14 01.1	23 58.4	7 52.2	11 04.5	14 46.6	19 22.5	27 41.9
23 F	4 06 22	0♐18 03	7♉22 16	14♉59 57	2 24.3	2 45.5	16 42.3	15 33.4	12 02.2	13 48.4	24 11.4	7 55.1	11 06.7	14 46.5	19 23.2	27 43.9
24 Sa	4 10 18	1 18 40	22 39 22	0♊19 05	2 21.2	2 34.7	18 15.3	16 41.3	11 55.2	13 35.9	24 24.5	7 57.9	11 09.0	14D 46.5	19 24.0	27 45.9
25 Su	4 14 15	2 19 19	7♊57 37	15 33 30	2 18.0	2 23.0	19 48.6	17 49.4	11 47.4	13 23.6	24 37.7	8 00.6	11 11.3	14 46.5	19 24.8	27 47.9
26 M	4 18 11	3 19 59	23 05 24	0♋32 07	2 14.8	2 11.7	21 22.1	18 57.7	11 38.7	13 11.6	24 50.9	8 03.3	11 13.7	14 46.5	19 25.6	27 50.0
27 Tu	4 22 08	4 20 40	7♋52 42	15 06 23	2 11.6	2 02.1	22 55.8	20 06.2	11 29.1	12 59.8	25 04.1	8 05.8	11 16.2	14 46.6	19 26.5	27 52.0
28 W	4 26 05	5 21 23	22 12 42	29 11 23	2 08.5	1 55.1	24 29.6	21 14.9	11 18.7	12 48.2	25 17.4	8 08.2	11 18.7	14 46.8	19 27.4	27 54.1
29 Th	4 30 01	6 22 07	6♌02 24	12♌45 53	2 05.3	1 50.8	26 03.6	22 23.8	11 07.5	12 36.9	25 30.7	8 10.5	11 21.2	14 47.0	19 28.3	27 56.2
30 F	4 33 58	7♐22 53	19 22 09	25 51 38	2♓02.1	1♓49.0	27♏37.5	23♎32.8	10♋55.4	12♉25.9	25♐44.0	8♍12.7	11♒23.8	14♓47.2	19♒29.3	27♐58.3

1st of Month

Julian Day # 2454405.5
Obliquity 23°26'26"
SVP 5♓08'55"
GC 26♐56.9
Eris 20♈50.0R

Day	⚴	Day	⚵	Day	⚶
1	0♓52.0	1	17♏08.2	1	5♑45.1
6	0 57.0	6	18 50.1	6	8 04.8
11	1 10.5	11	20 32.4	11	10 26.5
16	1 32.0	16	22 14.7	16	12 49.7
21	2 01.1	21	23 57.0	21	15 14.5
26	2 37.4	26	25 39.2	26	17 40.5

DECLINATION and LATITUDE

Day	☉ Decl	☽ Decl	☽ Lat	☽12h Decl	☿ Decl	☿ Lat	♀ Decl	♀ Lat	♂ Decl	♂ Lat	⚳ Decl	⚳ Lat	♃ Decl	♃ Lat	♄ Decl	♄ Lat
1 Th	14S14	23N44	3N06	21N48	7S49	1N23	3N41	0N27	23N57	0N58	8N18	9S28	22S46	0N16	10N28	1N27
2 F	14 33	19 37	2 06	17 15	7 36	1 36	3 22	0 33	23 58	1 01	8 16	9 26	22 47	0 16	10 27	1 27
3 Sa	14 52	14 42	1 01	12 03	7 28	1 46	3 02	0 38	24 00	1 03	8 15	9 24	22 48	0 16	10 25	1 27
4 Su	15 11	9 18	0S05	6 30	7 26	1 55	2 42	0 43	24 02	1 06	8 13	9 22	22 49	0 16	10 24	1 27
5 M	15 30	3 40	1 10	0 49	7 29	2 02	2 22	0 48	24 04	1 08	8 12	9 19	22 50	0 16	10 22	1 27
6 Tu	15 48	2S01	2 10	4S50	7 37	2 07	2 01	0 53	24 05	1 11	8 11	9 17	22 51	0 16	10 21	1 28
7 W	16 06	7 35	3 04	10 15	7 50	2 11	1 40	0 57	24 07	1 14	8 10	9 14	22 52	0 16	10 19	1 28
8 Th	16 24	12 50	3 49	15 17	8 06	2 14	1 19	1 02	24 10	1 16	8 08	9 11	22 53	0 16	10 18	1 28
9 F	16 41	17 36	4 24	19 44	8 25	2 15	0 58	1 06	24 12	1 19	8 07	9 09	22 54	0 16	10 16	1 28
10 Sa	16 58	21 41	4 48	23 25	8 48	2 16	0 36	1 11	24 14	1 22	8 06	9 06	22 54	0 15	10 15	1 28
11 Su	17 15	24 55	4 59	26 08	9 13	2 15	0 14	1 15	24 16	1 24	8 05	9 03	22 55	0 15	10 14	1 29
12 M	17 32	27 04	4 57	27 41	9 40	2 13	0S08	1 19	24 19	1 27	8 04	8 60	22 56	0 15	10 12	1 29
13 Tu	17 48	27 59	4 42	27 56	10 09	2 11	0 30	1 23	24 21	1 30	8 04	8 57	22 57	0 15	10 11	1 29
14 W	18 04	27 34	4 15	26 51	10 39	2 08	0 53	1 26	24 24	1 33	8 03	8 53	22 58	0 15	10 10	1 29
15 Th	18 20	25 48	3 35	24 26	11 10	2 04	1 16	1 30	24 27	1 36	8 02	8 50	22 59	0 15	10 09	1 30
16 F	18 35	22 46	2 44	20 49	11 42	1 60	1 38	1 33	24 30	1 39	8 02	8 47	22 60	0 15	10 08	1 30
17 Sa	18 50	18 35	1 44	16 08	12 15	1 55	2 02	1 37	24 33	1 41	8 01	8 43	23 00	0 15	10 07	1 30
18 Su	19 05	13 27	0 37	10 34	12 48	1 50	2 25	1 40	24 36	1 44	8 01	8 39	23 01	0 14	10 06	1 30
19 M	19 19	7 32	0N33	4 21	13 21	1 44	2 48	1 43	24 39	1 47	8 01	8 36	23 02	0 14	10 05	1 30
20 Tu	19 33	1 05	1 44	2N15	13 55	1 38	3 11	1 46	24 42	1 50	8 01	8 32	23 03	0 14	10 04	1 31
21 W	19 47	5N37	2 51	8 57	14 28	1 32	3 35	1 49	24 45	1 53	8 01	8 28	23 03	0 14	10 03	1 31
22 Th	19 60	12 13	3 48	15 20	15 01	1 26	3 59	1 51	24 49	1 56	8 01	8 24	23 04	0 14	10 02	1 31
23 F	20 13	18 15	4 31	20 53	15 34	1 19	4 22	1 54	24 52	1 59	8 01	8 20	23 05	0 14	10 01	1 31
24 Sa	20 25	23 12	4 55	25 06	16 06	1 13	4 46	1 56	24 56	2 02	8 01	8 16	23 06	0 14	9 60	1 32
25 Su	20 38	26 33	4 58	27 30	16 38	1 06	5 10	1 59	24 60	2 05	8 01	8 12	23 06	0 14	9 59	1 32
26 M	20 49	27 56	4 40	27 51	17 09	0 59	5 34	2 01	25 03	2 08	8 02	8 08	23 07	0 14	9 58	1 32
27 Tu	21 01	27 16	4 04	26 13	17 40	0 52	5 58	2 03	25 07	2 11	8 03	8 04	23 07	0 14	9 58	1 32
28 W	21 12	24 47	3 13	22 59	18 10	0 45	6 22	2 05	25 11	2 14	8 03	7 59	23 08	0 13	9 57	1 33
29 Th	21 22	20 53	2 12	18 34	18 39	0 38	6 46	2 06	25 15	2 17	8 04	7 55	23 09	0 13	9 56	1 33
30 F	21S33	16N03	1N05	13N24	19S08	0N31	7S10	2N08	25N19	2N20	8N05	7S51	23S09	0N13	9N56	1N33

Day	⚷ Decl	⚷ Lat	♅ Decl	♅ Lat	♆ Decl	♆ Lat	♇ Decl	♇ Lat
1	11S06	6N44	6S39	0S48	15S19	0S17	16S58	6N27
6	11 07	6 42	6 40	0 48	15 19	0 17	16 59	6 26
11	11 08	6 39	6 42	0 47	15 19	0 17	17 00	6 25
16	11 08	6 37	6 43	0 47	15 18	0 17	17 02	6 23
21	11 08	6 35	6 43	0 47	15 17	0 17	17 03	6 22
26	11 07	6 32	6 43	0 47	15 16	0 17	17 04	6 21

Day	⚴ Decl	⚴ Lat	⚵ Decl	⚵ Lat	⚶ Decl	⚶ Lat	Eris Decl	Eris Lat
1	6S54	4N33	8S35	8N42	24S49	1S30	5S05	14S14
6	7 29	3 54	9 00	8 45	24 49	1 38	5 05	14 14
11	7 60	3 17	9 23	8 48	24 47	1 45	5 06	14 13
16	8 25	2 41	9 45	8 52	24 41	1 52	5 06	14 13
21	8 47	2 07	10 06	8 56	24 33	1 59	5 06	14 12
26	9 05	1 34	10 25	8 60	24 21	2 06	5 07	14 11

Moon Phenomena

Max/0 Decl
dy hr mn
5 15:26 0 S
13 4:33 28S00
20 3:54 0 N
26 3:48 27N57

Perigee/Apogee
dy hr m kilometers
9 12:33 a 406672
24 0:14 p 357194

PH dy hr mn
☾ 1 21:19 9♌04
● 9 23:04 17♏10
☽ 17 22:34 25♒12
○ 24 14:31 1♊55

Max/0 Lat
dy hr mn
3 22:11 0 S
11 8:41 5S00
18 12:46 0 N
24 15:26 5N00
30 23:10 0 S

Void of Course Moon

Last Aspect	☽ Ingress
31 17:14 ☿ □	♌ 1 4:49
3 7:15 ♇ △	♍ 3 12:46
5 18:12 ♇ □	♎ 5 23:48
8 6:47 ♇ ⚹	♏ 8 12:19
10 3:20 ♆ □	♐ 11 1:00
13 7:54 ♇ ☌	♑ 13 13:02
15 9:20 ☉ ⚹	♒ 15 23:31
18 2:52 ♇ ⚹	♓ 18 7:16
20 7:27 ♇ □	♈ 20 11:25
22 8:41 ♇ △	♉ 22 12:20
23 18:54 ♆ □	♊ 24 11:30
26 7:39 ♇ ☍	♋ 26 11:08
28 4:24 ☿ △	♌ 28 13:24
30 17:26 ☿ □	♍ 30 19:45

DAILY ASPECTARIAN

1 Th ☽⚼♅ 4:49
☽⋕♃ 6:15
☽⚼♃ 13:22
☽⊻♄ 16:41
☽∠♀ 18:31
☉□☽ 21:19
☿ D 23:02

2 F ☽☍⚷ 0:04
☽⊻♂ 1:24
☽⚼♇ 2:55
☽⊼♅ 8:17
☽⋕♇ 13:20
☿⊻♀ 14:28
☽□⚳ 14:45
☽☍♆ 16:17
☽△♃ 17:36
☽⋕♆ 21:09
☉⋕☽ 23:17

3 Sa ☽⚹☿ 0:15
☽⊻♀ 1:00
☽∠♂ 5:59
☽△♇ 7:15
☉□⚷ 9:39
☽⋕⚷ 16:07
☽∥♄ 19:15

4 Su ☽☌♄ 1:47
☽∥⚳ 4:40
☽∠☿ 5:53
☽⋕☿ 8:00
☽⊼⚷ 9:21
☉∥♆ 10:39
☽⋕♅ 11:18
☉△♂ 11:20
☽⚹♂ 11:25
☉⚹☽ 11:25
♀⚼⚷ 17:24
☽☍♅ 17:52
☽△⚳ 23:43
☉∠♇ 23:45

5 M ☽⊼♆ 2:24
☽□♃ 4:45
☽∥♀ 5:49
☽⊻☿ 12:47
☽⚼⚷ 15:03
☽☌♀ 17:05
☽□♇ 18:12
☉∠☽ 19:49
☽⋕♀ 23:59

6 Tu ☽⚼⚳ 5:02
♀□♇ 6:02
☽⚼♆ 8:20
☽⊻♄ 13:41
☽∥♅ 20:03
☽△⚷ 21:11
☽□♂ 23:52

7 W ☽∥☿ 1:10
☽⋕⚳ 2:35
☉⊻☽ 4:44
☽⊼♅ 5:46
☽⊼⚳ 10:41
☽⋕♄ 12:16
☽△♆ 14:35
☽∥⚷ 16:02
☉△♅ 16:50
☽⚹♃ 18:01
☽∠♄ 20:08

8 Th ☿⋕⚳ 3:12
☽☌☿ 5:25
☽⚹♇ 6:47
☽⊻♀ 11:27
☽⚼♅ 12:05
☽∥♆ 12:11
☉∥☽ 18:51
☽∥♇ 20:49
♀ ♎ 21:06
☿⚹♇ 22:28

9 F ☽∠♃ 0:56
☽⚹♄ 2:42
☽□⚷ 9:59
☽△♂ 13:04
☽∠♇ 13:14
☉☍⚳ 14:56
☽△♅ 18:25
☽∠♀ 20:50
☽☍⚳ 22:14
☉☌☽ 23:04

10 Sa ☉∥♇ 2:44
☽□♆ 3:20
☽⊻♃ 7:49
☽∥♃ 8:17
♀⚼⚳ 9:45
☽⋕♂ 18:30
☽⚼♂ 19:34
☽⊻♇ 19:38

11 Su ☽⊻☿ 0:08
☿⚼♅ 5:40
☽⚹♀ 6:09
☿ ♏ 8:42
☽□♄ 15:38
☽⚹⚷ 22:39

12 M ☉□♆ 1:43
☽⊼♂ 1:53
☽□♅ 6:49
☽⊼⚳ 9:30
☽∠☿ 9:44
☽⚹♆ 15:43
☉⊻☽ 16:59
♀⚼♆ 20:27
☽☌♃ 21:10

13 Tu ☿⋕♄ 1:58
☽∠⚷ 4:41
☽☌♇ 7:54
☽⚼⚳ 14:48
☽⚹☿ 19:13
☽∠♆ 21:31
☽□♀ 23:59

14 W ☉∠☽ 1:27
☽△♄ 3:42
☽⊻⚷ 10:23
☽☍♂ 13:33
☽⚹♅ 18:10
☽△⚳ 19:44
☿∥⚷ 22:30

15 Th ☽⊻♆ 2:55
☉⊻♃ 7:13
♂ R 8:26
☽⚼♄ 9:07
☽⊻♃ 9:12
☉⚹☽ 9:20
☽⋕♂ 11:45
☽⊻♇ 18:43
♀⊻♄ 19:29
☽∥♃ 22:29
☽∠♅ 23:08

16 F ☽□☿ 12:44
☽⊼♄ 13:54
☽∠♃ 14:20
☽△♀ 15:33
☽☌⚷ 20:09
☉∥☽ 22:48
☽⊼♂ 23:01
☽∠♇ 23:12
☿⚹♄ 23:23

17 Sa ☽⊻♅ 3:25
☽□⚳ 3:57
☿∠♃ 4:58
☽∥♇ 7:42
☽☌♆ 11:49
☽∥♆ 15:48
☽⚹♃ 18:40
☽⚼♀ 21:57
☉□☽ 22:34

18 Su ☽∥☿ 2:30
☽⚼♂ 2:34
☽⚹♇ 2:52
☽∥⚷ 9:42
⚳⚹♅ 11:13
☽⋕♄ 13:58
☽☍♄ 21:01
♀△⚷ 21:53
☽⋕⚳ 22:08

19 M ☽△☿ 2:22
☽⊻⚷ 2:46
☽∥♅ 3:07
☽⊼♀ 3:11
☽△♂ 5:10
☿□⚷ 6:05
☽⚹⚳ 9:05
☽☌♅ 9:26
☽∥♀ 16:44
☽⊻♆ 17:19

20 Tu ☽□♃ 0:30
☉⚼♂ 0:35
♀□♂ 2:20
☿△♂ 2:54
☿⊻♀ 4:35
☽∠⚷ 4:42
☽⚼☿ 7:20
☉△☽ 7:21
☽□♇ 7:27
☿∠♇ 8:28
☉⊻♇ 8:50
☽∠⚳ 10:20
☽⋕♀ 16:17
☽∠♆ 18:42
☉∠♀ 19:14

21 W ☽⊼♄ 0:26
☽⋕♅ 3:56
☽⚹⚷ 5:45
☽□♂ 7:38
☿☍⚳ 8:18
☽∥⚳ 8:35
☉⚼☽ 10:06
☽☍♀ 10:13
☽⊻⚳ 10:48
☽⊼☿ 11:08
☽⊻♅ 11:51
☽∥♄ 15:56
♀⊼⚳ 16:39
☿△♅ 17:59
☽⚹♆ 19:18
☽⋕⚷ 19:58

22 Th ☽⚼♄ 0:56
☽△♃ 2:45
♀⊼♅ 7:24
☽△♇ 8:41
☿∥♆ 11:34
☽⋕♆ 11:49
☽⋕☿ 11:50
☽∠♅ 11:58
☉⊼☽ 12:00
☉ ♐ 16:51
☽⋕♇ 18:59

23 F ☽△♄ 0:52
☽⚼♃ 2:55
☽□⚷ 5:54
☽⚹♂ 7:18
☽⚼♇ 8:27
☉⋕☽ 9:12
☽☌⚳ 9:59
☽⚹♅ 11:39
☽⊼♀ 13:54
☽☍☿ 16:20
☽□♆ 18:54
☽⋕♃ 23:26

24 Sa ☽⊼♃ 2:47
☽∠♂ 6:37
☽⊼♇ 8:01
♅ D 10:16
☽∥♂ 11:05
☉☍☽ 14:31
☽⚼♀ 15:17
☿□♆ 17:50

25 Su ☽□♄ 0:05
☽△⚷ 5:06
☽⊻♂ 5:59
☽⊻⚳ 8:28
☽□♅ 10:46
☽△♀ 16:52
☽△♆ 18:09
☿∥♇ 19:46
☽⊼☿ 20:56

26 M ☽☍♃ 2:52
☽⚼⚷ 5:03
☽☍♇ 7:39
☽∠⚳ 8:06
♀△♆ 9:56
☉⊼☽ 17:47
☽⚼♆ 18:21

27 Tu ☽⚼☿ 0:06
☽⚹♄ 0:22
☽⊼⚷ 5:37
☽☌♂ 5:54
☽⚹⚳ 8:22
☽△♅ 11:27
⚳⚼♇ 13:33
☽⊼♆ 19:19
☉⚼☽ 20:36
☽∥♂ 20:58
☽□♀ 22:13

28 W ♂⊼⚷ 0:07
☽∠♄ 1:35
☽△☿ 4:24
☽⊼♃ 5:21
☽⊼♇ 9:48
☽⋕♃ 11:01
☽⚼♅ 13:02
☿⊻♃ 14:12
♀∥♅ 20:58
☉⋕☽ 21:27

29 Th ☉△☽ 0:38
☿⚼♂ 0:53
☽⊻♄ 3:48
☽⚼♃ 8:05
☽⊻♂ 8:55
☽☍⚷ 9:30
☽⋕☿ 10:30
☽□⚳ 11:34
☽⚼♇ 12:21
☽⊼♅ 15:39
♀∠♄ 16:48
☽⋕♇ 19:10

30 F ☽☍♆ 0:13
☽⋕♆ 3:41
☿⊻♇ 5:25
☽⚹♀ 8:27
☽∠♂ 11:55
☽△♃ 11:58
☽△♇ 15:59
☽□☿ 17:26
☉□♄ 20:24
☽⋕⚷ 22:03

December 2007

LONGITUDE

Day	Sid.Time	☉	☽	☽ 12 hour	Mean ☊	True ☊	☿	♀	♂	⚳	♃	♄	⚷	♅	♆	♇
	h m s	° ' "	° ' "	° ' "	° '	° '	° '	° '	° '	° '	° '	° '	° '	° '	° '	° '
1 Sa	4 37 54	8♐23 40	2♍14 53	8♍32 29	1♓58.9	1♓48.6	29♏11.6	24♎42.1	10♋42.5	12♉15.2	25♐57.4	8♍14.8	11♒26.5	14♓47.5	19♒30.3	28♐00.4
2 Su	4 41 51	9 24 29	14 45 04	20 53 18	1 55.8	1R 48.6	0♐45.6	25 51.5	10R 28.7	12R 04.7	26 10.8	8 16.8	11 29.2	14 47.9	19 31.3	28 02.5
3 M	4 45 47	10 25 19	26 57 51	2♎59 22	1 52.6	1 47.6	2 19.6	27 01.0	10 14.2	11 54.6	26 24.2	8 18.7	11 32.0	14 48.3	19 32.4	28 04.6
4 Tu	4 49 44	11 26 11	8♎58 27	14 55 43	1 49.4	1 44.7	3 53.6	28 10.8	9 58.8	11 44.8	26 37.6	8 20.5	11 34.8	14 48.8	19 33.5	28 06.8
5 W	4 53 40	12 27 03	20 51 42	26 46 54	1 46.2	1 39.0	5 27.7	29 20.6	9 42.7	11 35.3	26 51.1	8 22.2	11 37.7	14 49.3	19 34.6	28 08.9
6 Th	4 57 37	13 27 58	2♏41 46	8♏36 42	1 43.1	1 30.4	7 01.7	0♏30.7	9 25.9	11 26.2	27 04.6	8 23.7	11 40.7	14 49.9	19 35.7	28 11.1
7 F	5 01 34	14 28 53	14 32 04	20 28 08	1 39.9	1 19.1	8 35.7	1 40.8	9 08.3	11 17.4	27 18.2	8 25.2	11 43.6	14 50.5	19 36.9	28 13.2
8 Sa	5 05 30	15 29 50	26 25 10	2♐23 23	1 36.7	1 05.7	10 09.7	2 51.1	8 50.1	11 08.9	27 31.8	8 26.6	11 46.7	14 51.1	19 38.1	28 15.4
9 Su	5 09 27	16 30 48	8♐22 56	14 23 58	1 33.5	0 51.3	11 43.7	4 01.6	8 31.2	11 00.8	27 45.3	8 27.8	11 49.8	14 51.9	19 39.4	28 17.6
10 M	5 13 23	17 31 47	20 26 35	26 30 55	1 30.3	0 37.2	13 17.7	5 12.2	8 11.7	10 53.1	27 59.0	8 28.9	11 52.9	14 52.6	19 40.6	28 19.8
11 Tu	5 17 20	18 32 47	2♑37 02	8♑45 04	1 27.2	0 24.4	14 51.8	6 22.9	7 51.6	10 45.7	28 12.6	8 29.9	11 56.1	14 53.5	19 41.9	28 22.0
12 W	5 21 16	19 33 47	14 55 09	21 07 23	1 24.0	0 14.0	16 25.9	7 33.7	7 30.9	10 38.8	28 26.2	8 30.8	11 59.3	14 54.3	19 43.3	28 24.1
13 Th	5 25 13	20 34 48	27 21 58	3♒39 07	1 20.8	0 06.5	18 00.0	8 44.6	7 09.8	10 32.2	28 39.9	8 31.6	12 02.6	14 55.3	19 44.6	28 26.3
14 F	5 29 09	21 35 50	9♒59 03	16 22 04	1 17.6	0 02.0	19 34.2	9 55.7	6 48.1	10 26.0	28 53.6	8 32.3	12 06.0	14 56.2	19 46.0	28 28.5
15 Sa	5 33 06	22 36 53	22 48 27	29 19 40	1 14.5	0D 00.1	21 08.5	11 06.8	6 26.1	10 20.1	29 07.3	8 32.9	12 09.3	14 57.3	19 47.4	28 30.7
16 Su	5 37 03	23 37 56	5♓52 44	12♓31 19	1 11.3	0 00.0	22 42.9	12 18.1	6 03.6	10 14.7	29 21.0	8 33.3	12 12.8	14 58.3	19 48.9	28 33.0
17 M	5 40 59	24 38 59	19 14 39	26 03 03	1 08.1	0R 00.5	24 17.4	13 29.4	5 40.9	10 09.7	29 34.7	8 33.7	12 16.2	14 59.5	19 50.3	28 35.2
18 Tu	5 44 56	25 40 03	2♈56 43	9♈55 50	1 04.9	0 00.4	25 52.0	14 40.9	5 17.8	10 05.1	29 48.4	8 33.9	12 19.7	15 00.6	19 51.8	28 37.4
19 W	5 48 52	26 41 07	17 00 26	24 10 24	1 01.8	29♒58.6	27 26.8	15 52.4	4 54.6	10 00.9	0♑02.2	8R 34.0	12 23.3	15 01.8	19 53.3	28 39.6
20 Th	5 52 49	27 42 11	1♉25 29	8♉45 15	0 58.6	29 54.4	29 01.7	17 04.1	4 31.1	9 57.1	0 15.9	8 34.1	12 26.9	15 03.1	19 54.9	28 41.8
21 F	5 56 45	28 43 16	16 09 04	23 36 07	0 55.4	29 47.8	0♑36.7	18 15.8	4 07.5	9 53.7	0 29.7	8 34.0	12 30.5	15 04.4	19 56.5	28 44.0
22 Sa	6 00 42	29 44 21	1♊05 27	8♊35 57	0 52.2	29 39.2	2 12.0	19 27.7	3 43.9	9 50.7	0 43.4	8 33.7	12 34.2	15 05.8	19 58.1	28 46.2
23 Su	6 04 38	0♑45 27	16 06 26	23 35 39	0 49.1	29 29.7	3 47.5	20 39.6	3 20.1	9 48.1	0 57.2	8 33.4	12 37.9	15 07.2	19 59.7	28 48.4
24 M	6 08 35	1 46 32	1♋02 24	8♋25 34	0 45.9	29 20.3	5 23.1	21 51.6	2 56.4	9 45.9	1 10.9	8 33.0	12 41.7	15 08.7	20 01.3	28 50.7
25 Tu	6 12 32	2 47 39	15 44 06	22 57 10	0 42.7	29 12.3	6 59.0	23 03.7	2 32.8	9 44.1	1 24.7	8 32.5	12 45.5	15 10.2	20 03.0	28 52.9
26 W	6 16 28	3 48 45	0♌04 05	7♌04 23	0 39.5	29 06.5	8 35.1	24 15.9	2 09.3	9 42.7	1 38.5	8 31.8	12 49.3	15 11.7	20 04.7	28 55.1
27 Th	6 20 25	4 49 53	13 57 48	20 44 13	0 36.4	29 03.1	10 11.4	25 28.2	1 45.9	9 41.7	1 52.2	8 31.0	12 53.1	15 13.3	20 06.4	28 57.3
28 F	6 24 21	5 51 00	27 23 44	3♍56 34	0 33.2	29D 01.9	11 48.0	26 40.5	1 22.7	9D 41.1	2 06.0	8 30.2	12 57.0	15 15.0	20 08.2	28 59.5
29 Sa	6 28 18	6 52 08	10♍23 06	16 43 46	0 30.0	29 02.4	13 24.8	27 52.9	0 59.7	9 40.9	2 19.7	8 29.2	13 01.0	15 16.7	20 09.9	29 01.7
30 Su	6 32 14	7 53 17	22 59 06	29 09 42	0 26.8	29 03.6	15 01.8	29 05.4	0 37.0	9 41.1	2 33.5	8 28.1	13 04.9	15 18.4	20 11.7	29 03.9
31 M	6 36 11	8♑54 26	5♎16 11	11♎19 12	0♓23.7	29♒04.5	16♑39.0	0♐18.0	0♋14.7	9♉41.7	2♑47.2	8♍26.9	13♒08.9	15♓20.2	20♒13.5	29♐06.1

1st of Month

Julian Day # 2454435.5
Obliquity 23°26'25"
SVP 5♓08'50"
GC 26♐57.0
Eris 20♈35.1R

Day	⚴	Day	⚵	Day	⚶
1	3♓20.3	1	27♏21.1	1	20♑07.7
6	4 09.5	6	29 02.6	6	22 36.0
11	5 04.6	11	0♐43.6	11	25 05.2
16	6 05.2	16	2 23.8	16	27 35.3
21	7 10.8	21	4 03.1	21	0♒06.0
26	8 21.1	26	5 41.4	26	2 37.3
31	9 35.7	31	7 18.5	31	5 09.0

DECLINATION and LATITUDE

Day	☉ Decl	☽ Decl	☽ Lat	☽12h Decl	☿ Decl	☿ Lat	♀ Decl	♀ Lat	♂ Decl	♂ Lat	⚳ Decl	⚳ Lat	♃ Decl	♃ Lat	♄ Decl	♄ Lat
1 Sa	21S42	10N38	0S02	7N49	19S35	0N24	7S33	2N10	25N23	2N23	8N06	7S46	23S10	0N13	9N55	1N33
2 Su	21 52	4 58	1 08	2 06	20 02	0 17	7 57	2 11	25 27	2 26	8 07	7 42	23 10	0 13	9 55	1 34
3 M	22 01	0S46	2 09	3S35	20 28	0 10	8 21	2 12	25 31	2 29	8 09	7 37	23 11	0 13	9 54	1 34
4 Tu	22 09	6 21	3 03	9 03	20 53	0 03	8 45	2 13	25 35	2 32	8 10	7 33	23 11	0 13	9 54	1 34
5 W	22 17	11 40	3 48	14 10	21 17	0S04	9 09	2 14	25 39	2 35	8 12	7 28	23 11	0 13	9 54	1 34
6 Th	22 25	16 32	4 24	18 44	21 40	0 11	9 32	2 15	25 44	2 38	8 13	7 24	23 12	0 13	9 53	1 35
7 F	22 32	20 46	4 48	22 36	22 02	0 18	9 56	2 16	25 48	2 41	8 15	7 19	23 12	0 12	9 53	1 35
8 Sa	22 39	24 12	4 59	25 32	22 22	0 24	10 19	2 17	25 52	2 43	8 17	7 14	23 13	0 12	9 52	1 35
9 Su	22 45	26 36	4 58	27 21	22 42	0 31	10 42	2 17	25 56	2 46	8 19	7 09	23 13	0 12	9 52	1 35
10 M	22 51	27 48	4 43	27 54	23 01	0 37	11 05	2 18	25 60	2 49	8 21	7 05	23 13	0 12	9 52	1 36
11 Tu	22 57	27 40	4 15	27 05	23 18	0 43	11 28	2 18	26 04	2 51	8 24	7 00	23 14	0 12	9 52	1 36
12 W	23 02	26 10	3 35	24 55	23 34	0 50	11 51	2 18	26 07	2 54	8 26	6 55	23 14	0 12	9 52	1 36
13 Th	23 06	23 22	2 44	21 31	23 49	0 56	12 14	2 19	26 11	2 57	8 29	6 51	23 14	0 12	9 52	1 36
14 F	23 10	19 25	1 44	17 04	24 03	1 01	12 36	2 19	26 15	2 59	8 31	6 46	23 14	0 12	9 52	1 37
15 Sa	23 14	14 31	0 38	11 46	24 16	1 07	12 58	2 19	26 18	3 02	8 34	6 41	23 15	0 12	9 52	1 37
16 Su	23 17	8 52	0N31	5 51	24 27	1 13	13 20	2 18	26 22	3 04	8 37	6 36	23 15	0 12	9 52	1 37
17 M	23 20	2 43	1 41	0N29	24 37	1 18	13 42	2 18	26 25	3 06	8 40	6 31	23 15	0 12	9 52	1 37
18 Tu	23 22	3N42	2 46	6 56	24 46	1 23	14 03	2 18	26 28	3 08	8 43	6 27	23 15	0 11	9 52	1 38
19 W	23 24	10 07	3 43	13 12	24 53	1 28	14 24	2 17	26 31	3 11	8 46	6 22	23 15	0 11	9 52	1 38
20 Th	23 25	16 09	4 27	18 54	24 59	1 33	14 45	2 17	26 34	3 13	8 50	6 17	23 15	0 11	9 52	1 38
21 F	23 26	21 26	4 55	23 25	25 04	1 37	15 06	2 16	26 37	3 15	8 53	6 12	23 15	0 11	9 52	1 38
22 Sa	23 26	25 20	5 04	26 41	25 07	1 41	15 26	2 15	26 40	3 16	8 57	6 08	23 15	0 11	9 53	1 38
23 Su	23 26	27 33	4 51	27 54	25 09	1 45	15 46	2 14	26 42	3 18	9 00	6 03	23 15	0 11	9 53	1 39
24 M	23 26	27 45	4 19	27 06	25 09	1 49	16 05	2 13	26 44	3 20	9 04	5 58	23 15	0 11	9 54	1 39
25 Tu	23 25	25 59	3 30	24 27	25 08	1 53	16 24	2 12	26 46	3 22	9 08	5 53	23 15	0 11	9 54	1 39
26 W	23 22	22 33	2 29	20 21	25 05	1 56	16 43	2 11	26 48	3 23	9 12	5 49	23 15	0 11	9 55	1 39
27 Th	23 21	17 55	1 20	15 17	25 01	1 59	17 02	2 10	26 50	3 24	9 16	5 44	23 15	0 11	9 55	1 40
28 F	23 19	12 31	0 09	9 39	24 56	2 01	17 20	2 08	26 52	3 26	9 21	5 39	23 15	0 11	9 56	1 40
29 Sa	23 16	6 44	1S01	3 48	24 49	2 04	17 38	2 07	26 53	3 27	9 25	5 35	23 15	0 10	9 56	1 40
30 Su	23 12	0 52	2 05	2S02	24 40	2 06	17 55	2 05	26 54	3 28	9 29	5 30	23 15	0 10	9 57	1 40
31 M	23S08	4S53	3S02	7S39	24S30	2S07	18S12	2N04	26N56	3N29	9N34	5S26	23S14	0N10	9N58	1N41

Day	⚷ Decl	⚷ Lat	♅ Decl	♅ Lat	♆ Decl	♆ Lat	♇ Decl	♇ Lat
1	11S05	6N30	6S42	0S47	15S15	0S17	17S05	6N21
6	11 04	6 28	6 41	0 46	15 13	0 17	17 06	6 20
11	11 01	6 26	6 40	0 46	15 11	0 17	17 07	6 19
16	10 58	6 25	6 38	0 46	15 09	0 17	17 07	6 18
21	10 55	6 23	6 35	0 46	15 06	0 17	17 08	6 18
26	10 52	6 21	6 32	0 46	15 04	0 17	17 09	6 18
31	10S47	6N20	6S29	0S45	15S01	0S17	17S09	6N17

Day	⚴ Decl	⚴ Lat	⚵ Decl	⚵ Lat	⚶ Decl	⚶ Lat	Eris Decl	Eris Lat
1	9S19	1N02	10S43	9N05	24S07	2S12	5S07	14S11
6	9 29	0 33	10 59	9 10	23 49	2 18	5 07	14 10
11	9 35	0 04	11 14	9 16	23 29	2 24	5 07	14 09
16	9 39	0S24	11 26	9 23	23 06	2 30	5 06	14 08
21	9 39	0 50	11 38	9 29	22 40	2 36	5 06	14 08
26	9 37	1 16	11 47	9 37	22 12	2 42	5 06	14 07
31	9S32	1S41	11S54	9N45	21S41	2S47	5S05	14S06

Moon Phenomena

Max/0 Decl

dy	hr mn	
2	20:47	0 S
10	9:38	27S54
17	10:12	0 N
23	14:32	27N55
30	3:35	0 S

Max/0 Lat

dy	hr mn	
8	9:12	5S00
15	13:15	0 N
21	21:54	5N04
28	2:59	0 S

Perigee/Apogee

dy	hr m		kilometers
6	16:56	a	406235
22	10:12	p	360819

PH	dy	hr mn	
☾	1	12:45	8♍56
●	9	17:41	17♐16
☽	17	10:19	25♓05
○	24	1:17	1♋50
☾	31	7:52	9♎14

Void of Course Moon

Last Aspect			☽ Ingress		
3	2:13	♇ □	♎	3	6:02
5	14:49	♇ ⚹	♏	5	18:32
7	10:18	♆ □	♐	8	7:12
10	15:37	♇ ☌	♑	10	18:52
11	23:58	♅ ⚹	♒	13	5:02
15	11:52	♃ ⚹	♓	15	13:16
17	18:28	♃ □	♈	17	18:54
19	19:34	☿ △	♉	19	21:39
21	6:07	♆ □	♊	21	22:15
23	20:27	♇ ☍	♋	23	22:19
25	13:18	♀ △	♌	25	23:53
28	2:55	♇ △	♍	28	4:45
30	13:09	♀ ⚹	♎	30	13:38

DAILY ASPECTARIAN

1 Sa ☽∥♄ 3:05; ☽∥⚳ 10:46; ☽☌♄ 11:28; ☽⋕♀ 12:15; ☿ ♐ 12:22; ☉□☽ 12:45; ☽∠♀ 15:41; ☽⚹♂ 15:53; ☽⋕♅ 16:42; ☽⊼⚷ 17:39; ☽△⚳ 18:53

2 Su ☽☍♅ 0:06; ♀⚹♃ 8:15; ☽⊼♆ 9:20; ♀⋕⚳ 10:40; ☉⊼♂ 20:28; ☽□♃ 22:52; ☽⚼⚷ 23:09; ☽⚼⚳ 23:54

3 M ☽⊻♀ 0:07; ☽□♇ 2:13; ☽⚹☿ 12:17; ☽⚼♆ 15:07; ♃∠⚷ 17:39; ♀⚹♇ 22:35; ☽⊻♄ 22:44

4 Tu ☽∥♅ 1:29; ☽□♂ 1:59; ☉⚹⚷ 3:35; ☽△⚷ 5:16; ☉⚹☽ 5:25; ☽⊼⚳ 5:30; ☉⊼⚳ 6:20; ⚳⚼♃ 7:26; ☽⋕⚳ 8:03; ☽∥♀ 11:27; ☽⊼♅ 11:46; ☽⋕♄ 15:47; ⚳□⚷ 19:17; ☽∥⚷ 21:12; ☽△♆ 21:24; ☽∠☿ 23:04

5 W ☽∠♄ 5:06; ♀⚼♅ 9:54; ☽⚹♃ 12:23; ♀ ♏ 13:30; ☉∠☽ 14:37; ☽⚹♇ 14:49; ☽∥♆ 17:14; ☽⚼♅ 18:11; ☽☌♀ 19:05

6 Th ☽∥♇ 3:00; ☽⊻☿ 10:08; ☽⚹♄ 11:35; ☽△♂ 13:20; ☽☍⚳ 17:30; ☽□⚷ 18:17; ☽∠♃ 19:24; ♀⋕♄ 20:54; ☿□♄ 21:17; ☽∠♇ 21:20; ☉⊻☽ 23:53

7 F ☽△♅ 0:37; ☿⊼♂ 7:00; ☉□♅ 8:36; ☽∥☿ 8:58; ☽□♆ 10:18; ☉∥☽ 11:58; ☽∥♃ 16:22; ☽⚼♂ 18:55

8 Sa ☽⊻♃ 2:17; ☽⊻♇ 3:42; ☿⊼⚳ 13:55; ☽⊻♀ 14:20; ☽⋕♂ 15:50; ⚵ ♐ 20:07

9 Su ☽□♄ 0:10; ☽⊼♂ 0:16; ☿⚹⚷ 1:36; ♂⚹♄ 4:00; ☽⊼⚳ 5:12; ☉∥☿ 6:19; ☽⚹⚷ 6:55; ☽☌☿ 7:41; ☽□♅ 12:56; ☉☌☽ 17:41; ♀∥⚷ 20:19; ☽⚹♆ 22:29; ☽∠♀ 23:28

10 M ☽⚼⚳ 10:39; ☽∠⚷ 12:47; ☽☌♃ 15:10; ☽☌♇ 15:37; ☿∥♃ 17:41

11 Tu ☿□♅ 0:26; ☽∠♆ 4:05; ☽⚹♀ 8:09; ☽☍♂ 9:59; ☽△♄ 11:31; ☽△⚳ 15:46; ☽⊻⚷ 18:17; ♃☌♇ 19:37; ♀△♂ 23:17; ☽⚹♅ 23:58

12 W ☽⋕♂ 0:24; ☽⊻☿ 3:21; ☉⚹♆ 3:49; ☽⊻♆ 9:19; ☉⊻☽ 9:47; ☽⚼♄ 16:37; ♀⚹♄ 19:34; ☽∥☿ 20:56

13 Th ☽∥♃ 0:55; ☉∥☽ 1:46; ☽⊻♇ 2:04; ☽⊻♃ 2:32; ☽∠♅ 4:54; ☽∠☿ 12:17; ☉∠☽ 17:02; ☽⊼♂ 18:09; ☽⊼♄ 21:16; ☽□♀ 23:53

14 F ☽□⚳ 0:50; ☿⚹♆ 3:03; ☽☌⚷ 4:00; ☽∠♇ 6:36; ☽∠♃ 7:30; ☽⊻♅ 9:20; ♀☍⚳ 9:26; ☽∥♇ 11:46; ☽☌♆ 18:23; ☽⚹☿ 20:29; ☽∥♆ 21:05; ☽⚼♂ 21:31; ☉⚹☽ 23:37

15 Sa ☉∥♃ 3:28; ☊R♒ 6:02; ☽∥♀ 6:26; ☽⚹♇ 10:34; ☽⚹♃ 11:52; ☽∥⚷ 15:21; ☽⋕♄ 19:58; ☊ ♓ 21:29; ♀□⚷ 22:08

16 Su ☽△♂ 0:19; ☽⋕⚳ 1:02; ☽☍♄ 4:51; ☽⚹⚳ 7:51; ☽∥♅ 8:57; ☽⊻⚷ 11:30; ☽△♀ 12:44; ☽☌♅ 16:25

17 M ☽⊻♆ 1:03; ♀∠♇ 1:59; ☽□☿ 10:04; ☉□☽ 10:19; ☽∠⚳ 10:23; ☉⚼⚳ 11:13; ☿⚼⚳ 12:39; ☽∠⚷ 14:12; ☉☌☿ 15:28; ☽□♇ 16:28; ☽⚼♀ 17:48; ☽□♃ 18:28

18 Tu ♀∠♃ 3:08; ☽∠♆ 3:19; ☽□♂ 3:57; ♀△♅ 6:44; ☊R♒ 8:06; ☽⊼♄ 9:40; ☽⋕♅ 10:47; ☽⊻⚳ 12:12; ☽⚹⚷ 16:09; ☽∥⚳ 18:52; ♃ ♑ 20:12; ☽⊻♅ 20:40; ☽⊼♀ 21:55; ☽∥♄ 23:04; ☿∠⚷ 23:05

19 W ♂⚼♆ 1:11; ☽⋕⚷ 3:11; ☽⚹♆ 4:51; ☽⚼♄ 10:59; ♄R 14:11; ☉△☽ 17:24; ☉∠⚷ 17:37; ☽⋕♀ 17:52; ☿☌♇ 18:52; ☽△♇ 19:29; ☽△☿ 19:34; ☽⋕♆ 19:43; ☽∠♅ 21:44; ☽△♃ 22:04

20 Th ☽⋕♇ 4:12; ☽⚹♂ 4:57; ☽△♄ 11:42; ☽☌⚳ 13:54; ☿ ♑ 14:44; ☽□⚷ 18:05; ⚶ ♒ 19:15; ☉⚼☽ 19:47; ☽⚼♇ 20:05; ☿☌♃ 21:55; ☽⚹♅ 22:15; ☽⚼♃ 22:55; ☽⚼☿ 23:01

21 F ☉☌♇ 0:18; ♀∥♆ 0:59; ☽☍♀ 3:42; ☽∠♂ 4:40; ☽□♆ 6:07; ☽⋕♃ 10:16; ☉⋕☽ 11:22; ♀⚼♂ 13:00; ☽⊼♇ 20:17; ☉⊼☽ 21:41; ☽⋕☿ 22:22; ☽⊼♃ 23:24

22 Sa ☽⊼☿ 1:59; ☽⊻♂ 4:07; ☉ ♑ 6:09; ♀□♆ 10:23; ☽□♄ 11:56; ☽∥♂ 12:08; ☽⊻⚳ 13:57; ☽△⚷ 18:25; ☿☍♂ 18:30; ☽□♅ 22:25

23 Su ☉☌♃ 5:57; ☽△♆ 6:14; ☽⊼♀ 7:56; ☽∠⚳ 13:54; ☿∠♆ 18:26; ☽⚼⚷ 18:35; ☽☍♇ 20:27

24 M ☽☍♃ 0:14; ☉☍☽ 1:17; ☽☌♂ 3:00; ☽⚼♆ 6:28; ☽☍☿ 7:54; ☽⚼♀ 10:17; ☽⚹♄ 12:12; ☽⚹⚳ 14:10; ☽∥♂ 16:10; ☽⊼⚷ 19:04; ☉☍♂ 19:48; ☽△♅ 23:04

25 Tu ☽⋕☿ 7:08; ☽⊼♆ 7:10; ☽∠♄ 12:59; ☽△♀ 13:18; ☉⋕☽ 18:58; ☽⋕♃ 19:50; ☽⊼♇ 22:03; ☿△♄ 23:11

26 W ☽⚼♅ 0:13; ☽⊼♃ 2:43; ☽⊻♂ 3:27; ☉⊼☽ 6:54; ☽⊻♄ 14:31; ☽⊼☿ 16:32; ☽□⚳ 16:33; ☿△⚳ 16:40; ♂☍♃ 19:53; ☽☍⚷ 22:06; ☽⚼♇ 23:59

27 Th ☽⊼♅ 2:13; ☽⋕♇ 3:35; ☽⋕♀ 3:53; ☽∠♂ 4:48; ☽⚼♃ 5:13; ☉∠♆ 6:41; ♀∥♇ 9:08; ☽☍♆ 10:54; ☉⚼☽ 11:14; ☽⋕♆ 13:03; ☿∠♀ 16:36; ☽□♀ 22:34; ☽⚼☿ 22:46

28 F ☽△♇ 2:55; ☽⚹♂ 7:04; ☽⋕⚷ 7:07; ☽△♃ 8:45; ☽∥♄ 10:51; ☽∥⚳ 13:08; ☉△☽ 16:52; ☿⊻⚷ 17:51; ☽☌♄ 20:27; ☽△⚳ 22:41; ⚳ D 23:25

29 Sa ☽⋕♅ 0:58; ☽⊼⚷ 4:59; ☽△☿ 6:32; ☉∥♃ 7:28; ☽☍♅ 9:16; ☽⊼♆ 18:37; ♀⊻♇ 23:29

30 Su ☽⚼⚳ 3:18; ☿⚹♅ 4:11; ☽⚼⚷ 9:57; ☽□♇ 11:51; ☽⚹♀ 13:09; ☉△♄ 13:24; ☽□♂ 14:25; ♀ ♐ 18:03; ☽□♃ 19:01; ♀⊼♂ 23:10; ☽⚼♆ 23:55

31 M ☽⊻♄ 6:17; ☽∥♅ 6:50; ☉□☽ 7:52; ☽⊼⚳ 8:47; ☽△⚷ 15:44; ♂R♊ 16:01; ☉△⚳ 18:52; ☽⊼♅ 20:04; ☽⋕⚳ 20:47; ☽∠♀ 22:11; ☽⋕♄ 22:18

LONGITUDE

Day	Sid.Time	☉	☽	☽ 12 hour	Mean☊	True☊	☿	♀	♂	⚳	♃	♄	⚷	♅	♆	♇
	h m s	° ' "	° ' "	° ' "	° '	° '	° '	° '	° '	° '	° '	° '	° '	° '	° '	° '
1 Tu	6 40 08	9♑55 35	17♎19 24	23♎17 27	0♓20.5	29♒04.2	18♑16.4	1♐30.6	29♊52.7	9♉42.7	3♑00.9	8♍25.6	13♒13.0	15♓22.0	20♒15.3	29♐08.3
2 W	6 44 04	10 56 45	29 13 56	5♏09 30	0 17.3	29R 02.1	19 54.0	2 43.3	29R 31.2	9 44.1	3 14.7	8R 24.2	13 17.0	15 23.9	20 17.2	29 10.4
3 Th	6 48 01	11 57 55	11♏04 42	17 00 03	0 14.1	28 57.9	21 31.7	3 56.1	29 10.1	9 45.9	3 28.4	8 22.6	13 21.1	15 25.8	20 19.1	29 12.6
4 F	6 51 57	12 59 05	22 56 04	28 53 10	0 10.9	28 51.7	23 09.6	5 08.9	28 49.5	9 48.1	3 42.1	8 21.0	13 25.2	15 27.8	20 21.0	29 14.8
5 Sa	6 55 54	14 00 16	4♐51 44	10♐52 07	0 07.8	28 43.9	24 47.4	6 21.8	28 29.5	9 50.7	3 55.7	8 19.3	13 29.4	15 29.8	20 22.9	29 17.0
6 Su	6 59 50	15 01 27	16 54 36	22 59 25	0 04.6	28 35.3	26 25.3	7 34.8	28 10.0	9 53.6	4 09.4	8 17.4	13 33.6	15 31.8	20 24.8	29 19.1
7 M	7 03 47	16 02 38	29 06 44	5♑16 41	0 01.4	28 26.6	28 03.0	8 47.8	27 51.1	9 56.9	4 23.1	8 15.5	13 37.8	15 33.9	20 26.8	29 21.3
8 Tu	7 07 43	17 03 49	11♑29 22	17 44 52	29♒58.2	28 18.9	29 40.6	10 00.8	27 32.9	10 00.7	4 36.7	8 13.4	13 42.0	15 36.0	20 28.7	29 23.4
9 W	7 11 40	18 05 00	24 03 11	0♒24 21	29 55.1	28 12.7	1♒17.9	11 13.9	27 15.3	10 04.7	4 50.3	8 11.3	13 46.3	15 38.2	20 30.7	29 25.5
10 Th	7 15 37	19 06 10	6♒48 23	13 15 17	29 51.9	28 08.5	2 54.6	12 27.1	26 58.5	10 09.2	5 03.9	8 09.0	13 50.6	15 40.4	20 32.7	29 27.6
11 F	7 19 33	20 07 20	19 45 03	26 17 43	29 48.7	28D 06.4	4 30.8	13 40.3	26 42.3	10 14.0	5 17.5	8 06.7	13 54.9	15 42.6	20 34.7	29 29.7
12 Sa	7 23 30	21 08 30	2♓53 19	9♓31 54	29 45.5	28 06.1	6 06.2	14 53.5	26 26.9	10 19.2	5 31.1	8 04.2	13 59.2	15 44.9	20 36.8	29 31.8
13 Su	7 27 26	22 09 39	16 13 31	22 58 15	29 42.4	28 07.2	7 40.4	16 06.8	26 12.2	10 24.8	5 44.6	8 01.7	14 03.5	15 47.2	20 38.8	29 33.9
14 M	7 31 23	23 10 48	29 46 11	6♈37 23	29 39.2	28 08.8	9 13.4	17 20.1	25 58.3	10 30.7	5 58.1	7 59.1	14 07.9	15 49.6	20 40.9	29 36.0
15 Tu	7 35 19	24 11 55	13♈31 52	20 29 41	29 36.0	28R 10.1	10 44.7	18 33.4	25 45.1	10 36.9	6 11.5	7 56.3	14 12.3	15 52.0	20 43.0	29 38.1
16 W	7 39 16	25 13 03	27 30 46	4♉35 01	29 32.8	28 10.5	12 13.9	19 46.8	25 32.8	10 43.5	6 25.0	7 53.5	14 16.7	15 54.4	20 45.0	29 40.1
17 Th	7 43 12	26 14 09	11♉42 15	18 52 12	29 29.6	28 09.5	13 40.7	21 00.2	25 21.3	10 50.5	6 38.4	7 50.6	14 21.1	15 56.9	20 47.2	29 42.1
18 F	7 47 09	27 15 15	26 04 30	3♊18 39	29 26.5	28 07.1	15 04.5	22 13.7	25 10.6	10 57.8	6 51.7	7 47.6	14 25.5	15 59.4	20 49.3	29 44.2
19 Sa	7 51 06	28 16 20	10♊34 07	17 50 13	29 23.3	28 03.4	16 24.8	23 27.1	25 00.7	11 05.4	7 05.1	7 44.5	14 30.0	16 02.0	20 51.4	29 46.2
20 Su	7 55 02	29 17 24	25 06 14	2♋21 23	29 20.1	27 59.1	17 40.9	24 40.7	24 51.6	11 13.3	7 18.4	7 41.3	14 34.5	16 04.5	20 53.6	29 48.2
21 M	7 58 59	0♒18 28	9♋34 54	16 45 59	29 17.0	27 54.8	18 52.2	25 54.2	24 43.3	11 21.6	7 31.7	7 38.0	14 39.0	16 07.1	20 55.7	29 50.1
22 Tu	8 02 55	1 19 30	23 55 55	0♌57 59	29 13.8	27 51.1	19 57.9	27 07.8	24 35.9	11 30.2	7 44.9	7 34.7	14 43.5	16 09.8	20 57.9	29 52.1
23 W	8 06 52	2 20 32	7♌57 39	14 52 23	29 10.6	27 48.5	20 57.2	28 21.4	24 29.2	11 39.1	7 58.1	7 31.3	14 48.0	16 12.5	21 00.1	29 54.1
24 Th	8 10 48	3 21 33	21 41 52	28 25 52	29 07.4	27D 47.3	21 49.3	29 35.1	24 23.4	11 48.3	8 11.2	7 27.8	14 52.5	16 15.2	21 02.3	29 56.0
25 F	8 14 45	4 22 34	5♍04 15	11♍37 03	29 04.2	27 47.3	22 33.3	0♑48.8	24 18.3	11 57.9	8 24.3	7 24.2	14 57.0	16 17.9	21 04.5	29 57.9
26 Sa	8 18 41	5 23 33	18 04 23	24 26 29	29 01.1	27 48.4	23 08.4	2 02.5	24 14.1	12 07.7	8 37.4	7 20.5	15 01.5	16 20.7	21 06.7	29 59.8
27 Su	8 22 38	6 24 33	0♎43 41	6♎56 21	28 57.9	27 49.9	23 33.7	3 16.2	24 10.6	12 17.8	8 50.4	7 16.8	15 06.1	16 23.5	21 08.9	0♑01.7
28 M	8 26 35	7 25 31	13 04 58	19 10 02	28 54.7	27 51.6	23R 48.7	4 30.0	24 08.0	12 28.2	9 03.4	7 13.0	15 10.6	16 26.3	21 11.1	0 03.5
29 Tu	8 30 31	8 26 29	25 12 07	1♏11 46	28 51.5	27 52.9	23 52.6	5 43.8	24 06.1	12 38.9	9 16.3	7 09.1	15 15.2	16 29.1	21 13.3	0 05.4
30 W	8 34 28	9 27 26	7♏09 37	13 06 16	28 48.4	27R 53.5	23 45.3	6 57.6	24D 05.0	12 49.9	9 29.2	7 05.2	15 19.8	16 32.0	21 15.6	0 07.2
31 Th	8 38 24	10♒28 23	19 02 18	24 58 20	28♒45.2	27♒53.2	23♒06.2	8♑11.4	24♊04.7	13♉01.2	9♑42.0	7♍01.2	15♒24.3	16♓34.9	21♒17.8	0♑09.0

1st of Month

Julian Day # 2454466.5
Obliquity 23°26'25"
SVP 5♓08'44"
GC 26♐57.1
Eris 20♈27.5R

Day	⚴		Day	⚵		Day	⚶
1	9♓51.1		1	7♐37.7		1	5♒39.4
6	11 10.5		6	9 13.2		6	8 11.6
11	12 33.5		11	10 47.0		11	10 44.1
16	14 00.0		16	12 19.0		16	13 16.7
21	15 29.6		21	13 49.0		21	15 49.4
26	17 02.0		26	15 16.7		26	18 22.1
31	18 37.0		31	16 42.0		31	20 54.7

DECLINATION and LATITUDE

Day	☉ Decl	☽ Decl	☽ Lat	☽12h Decl	☿ Decl	☿ Lat	♀ Decl	♀ Lat	♂ Decl	♂ Lat	⚳ Decl	⚳ Lat	♃ Decl	♃ Lat	♄ Decl	♄ Lat
1 Tu	23S04	10S21	3S50	12S55	24S19	2S08	18S28	2N02	26N56	3N30	9N39	5S21	23S14	0N10	9N58	1N41
2 W	22 59	15 22	4 27	17 40	24 05	2 09	18 44	2 00	26 57	3 31	9 43	5 16	23 14	0 10	9 59	1 41
3 Th	22 54	19 47	4 53	21 43	23 51	2 09	18 60	1 59	26 58	3 32	9 48	5 12	23 14	0 10	9 60	1 41
4 F	22 48	23 26	5 06	24 55	23 34	2 09	19 15	1 57	26 58	3 32	9 53	5 07	23 13	0 10	10 01	1 42
5 Sa	22 42	26 07	5 06	27 02	23 17	2 08	19 29	1 55	26 59	3 33	9 58	5 03	23 13	0 10	10 02	1 42
6 Su	22 36	27 39	4 52	27 55	22 57	2 07	19 43	1 53	26 59	3 33	10 03	4 59	23 13	0 10	10 02	1 42
7 M	22 29	27 51	4 25	27 27	22 36	2 06	19 57	1 51	26 59	3 34	10 09	4 54	23 12	0 10	10 03	1 42
8 Tu	22 21	26 41	3 45	25 35	22 14	2 03	20 10	1 49	26 59	3 34	10 14	4 50	23 12	0 10	10 04	1 43
9 W	22 13	24 09	2 54	22 25	21 50	2 01	20 22	1 46	26 59	3 34	10 19	4 45	23 12	0 09	10 05	1 43
10 Th	22 05	20 24	1 53	18 07	21 25	1 57	20 34	1 44	26 59	3 34	10 25	4 41	23 11	0 09	10 06	1 43
11 F	21 56	15 37	0 45	12 54	20 58	1 53	20 45	1 42	26 58	3 34	10 30	4 37	23 11	0 09	10 08	1 43
12 Sa	21 47	10 02	0N26	7 02	20 30	1 48	20 56	1 40	26 58	3 34	10 36	4 33	23 10	0 09	10 09	1 44
13 Su	21 37	3 57	1 37	0 47	20 01	1 43	21 06	1 37	26 57	3 34	10 42	4 28	23 10	0 09	10 10	1 44
14 M	21 27	2N25	2 44	5N36	19 30	1 37	21 16	1 35	26 57	3 34	10 47	4 24	23 09	0 09	10 11	1 44
15 Tu	21 16	8 45	3 43	11 49	18 59	1 30	21 25	1 32	26 56	3 34	10 53	4 20	23 09	0 09	10 12	1 44
16 W	21 06	14 46	4 29	17 32	18 26	1 22	21 33	1 30	26 55	3 33	10 59	4 16	23 08	0 09	10 13	1 44
17 Th	20 54	20 05	4 60	22 22	17 53	1 13	21 41	1 27	26 54	3 33	11 05	4 12	23 08	0 09	10 15	1 45
18 F	20 43	24 19	5 12	25 54	17 19	1 03	21 49	1 24	26 54	3 33	11 11	4 08	23 07	0 09	10 16	1 45
19 Sa	20 30	27 04	5 05	27 46	16 45	0 53	21 55	1 22	26 53	3 32	11 17	4 04	23 06	0 09	10 17	1 45
20 Su	20 18	27 59	4 38	27 43	16 11	0 41	22 01	1 19	26 52	3 32	11 24	3 60	23 06	0 08	10 19	1 45
21 M	20 05	26 59	3 54	25 48	15 38	0 29	22 06	1 16	26 51	3 31	11 30	3 56	23 05	0 08	10 20	1 45
22 Tu	19 52	24 12	2 55	22 15	15 04	0 16	22 11	1 13	26 50	3 30	11 36	3 52	23 05	0 08	10 22	1 46
23 W	19 38	19 60	1 47	17 30	14 32	0 01	22 15	1 11	26 49	3 30	11 43	3 48	23 04	0 08	10 23	1 46
24 Th	19 24	14 48	0 33	11 58	14 01	0N14	22 19	1 08	26 48	3 29	11 49	3 44	23 03	0 08	10 25	1 46
25 F	19 10	9 02	0S40	6 03	13 32	0 30	22 21	1 05	26 47	3 28	11 55	3 41	23 02	0 08	10 26	1 46
26 Sa	18 55	3 02	1 49	0 03	13 05	0 46	22 24	1 02	26 46	3 27	12 02	3 37	23 02	0 08	10 28	1 46
27 Su	18 40	2S55	2 52	5S48	12 40	1 03	22 25	0 59	26 45	3 27	12 09	3 33	23 01	0 08	10 29	1 47
28 M	18 25	8 36	3 44	11 18	12 19	1 21	22 26	0 56	26 44	3 26	12 15	3 29	23 00	0 08	10 31	1 47
29 Tu	18 09	13 52	4 26	16 18	12 01	1 39	22 26	0 53	26 43	3 25	12 22	3 26	22 59	0 08	10 32	1 47
30 W	17 53	18 33	4 55	20 37	11 46	1 56	22 25	0 50	26 42	3 24	12 29	3 22	22 58	0 08	10 34	1 47
31 Th	17S37	22S28	5S12	24S06	11S36	2N13	22S24	0N47	26N41	3N23	12N35	3S18	22S58	0N08	10N36	1N47

Day	⚷ Decl	⚷ Lat	♅ Decl	♅ Lat	♆ Decl	♆ Lat	♇ Decl	♇ Lat
1	10S47	6N20	6S28	0S45	15S00	0S17	17S09	6N17
6	10 42	6 19	6 24	0 45	14 57	0 17	17 10	6 17
11	10 37	6 18	6 20	0 45	14 54	0 17	17 10	6 17
16	10 32	6 17	6 15	0 45	14 51	0 17	17 10	6 17
21	10 26	6 16	6 10	0 45	14 48	0 17	17 10	6 17
26	10 20	6 15	6 04	0 45	14 44	0 17	17 10	6 17
31	10S14	6N15	5S59	0S44	14S41	0S17	17S10	6N17

Day	⚴ Decl	⚴ Lat	⚵ Decl	⚵ Lat	⚶ Decl	⚶ Lat	Eris Decl	Eris Lat
1	9S30	1S45	11S56	9N47	21S35	2S48	5S05	14S06
6	9 22	2 09	12 01	9 55	21 01	2 54	5 04	14 05
11	9 12	2 33	12 05	10 05	20 25	2 59	5 03	14 04
16	8 59	2 55	12 06	10 15	19 47	3 04	5 02	14 03
21	8 45	3 17	12 06	10 26	19 06	3 09	5 01	14 02
26	8 29	3 39	12 04	10 37	18 24	3 15	5 00	14 01
31	8S12	4S01	12S00	10N49	17S41	3S20	4S59	14S00

Moon Phenomena

Max/0 Decl
dy hr mn
6 15:51 27S56
13 14:56 0 N
19 23:44 27N59
26 12:11 0 S

Perigee/Apogee
dy hr m kilometers
3 8:04 a 405330
19 8:30 p 366431
31 4:20 a 404532

PH dy hr mn
● 8 11:38 17♑33
☽ 15 19:47 25♈02
○ 22 13:36 1♌54
☾ 30 5:04 9♏40

Max/0 Lat
dy hr mn
4 11:49 5S08
11 15:17 0 N
18 3:14 5N12
24 10:51 0 S
31 17:53 5S15

Void of Course Moon

Last Aspect			☽ Ingress		
2 0:34	♂	△	♏	2	1:33
4 0:32	☿	✶	♐	4	14:14
7 0:28	♇	☌	♑	7	1:44
8 11:38	☉	☌	♒	9	11:14
11 17:53	♇	✶	♓	11	18:45
13 23:42	♇	□	♈	14	0:24
16 3:41	♇	△	♉	16	4:14
18 2:06	☉	△	♊	18	6:31
20 7:47	♇	☍	♋	20	8:06
21 10:57	♅	△	♌	22	10:21
24 14:44	♇	△	♍	24	14:49
26 11:33	♂	□	♎	26	22:36
28 21:49	♂	△	♏	29	9:36
31 8:36	☿	□	♐	31	22:09

DAILY ASPECTARIAN

1 Tu
☽∥⚷ 1:59
☽□☿ 2:12
☽△♆ 5:54
☽∠♄ 12:15
☽∥♆ 22:10
☽✶♇ 23:53

2 W
☽△♂ 0:34
☽⚼♅ 2:22
☿⊻♆ 5:49
☽⊻♀ 7:52
☽✶♃ 8:17
☽∥♇ 9:17
♀⊻♃ 12:44
☽✶♄ 18:32
☽∥♀ 19:06
☽☍⚳ 21:20
♂☍♇ 21:24

3 Th
☉✶☽ 1:58
☽□⚷ 4:38
☽⚼♂ 6:05
☽∠♇ 6:22
☽△♅ 8:51
☽∠♃ 15:16
☽□♆ 18:46
☉∥☽ 19:33
☽∥♃ 22:26

4 F
☽✶☿ 0:32
☽∥☿ 0:58
☿⚼♄ 2:46
☉⊻⚷ 11:00
☉∠☽ 11:08
☽⊼♂ 11:33
☽⊻♇ 12:46
☽⊻♃ 22:06

5 Sa
♂⚼⚷ 0:06
☽☌♀ 3:21
☿∥♃ 4:28
☽□♄ 6:54
☽⊼⚳ 10:00
☽#♂ 11:10
☽∠☿ 11:24
☽✶⚷ 17:19
⚳∥♄ 18:52
☉⊻☽ 19:55
☽□♅ 21:15

6 Su
☽✶♆ 6:57
☉✶♅ 12:20
♀□♄ 13:40
☽⚼⚳ 15:49
☿⊼♂ 21:33
☽☍♂ 21:36
☽⊻☿ 21:36
☽∠⚷ 23:03

7 M
☽☌♇ 0:28
☽☌♃ 10:28
☽∠♆ 12:21
☉∥☿ 12:33
☽△♄ 17:43
☿⊻♇ 19:40
☽#♂ 19:54
☽⊻♀ 20:51
☽△⚳ 21:08
♀⊼⚳ 23:57

8 Tu
☽⊻⚷ 4:16
☿ ♒ 4:47
☽✶♅ 7:55
☉☌☽ 11:38
☿∠♅ 13:58
☽⊻♆ 17:15
☽⚼♄ 22:22

9 W
☽∠♀ 4:34
☽⊼♂ 5:56
☽∥♃ 6:53
☽⊻♇ 10:11
☽∠♅ 12:28
☉∥☽ 13:44
☽☌☿ 15:39
☽∥☿ 17:29
☽⊻♃ 20:41
☽∥♀ 23:05

10 Th
☽⊼♄ 2:30
☽□⚳ 6:17
☽⚼♂ 9:26
☽✶♀ 11:36
☽☌⚷ 13:10
☽∠♇ 14:16
☽⊻♅ 16:32
☽∥♇ 16:41

11 F
☉⊻☽ 0:44
☽∠♃ 1:01
☽☌♆ 1:32
☽∥♆ 3:13
♀✶⚷ 5:05
☿∥♀ 7:46
☉⊻♆ 11:07
☽△♂ 12:30
☿⊻♃ 13:40
☽✶♇ 17:53
☽∥⚷ 21:41
☽#⚳ 21:45
☽#♄ 23:34

12 Sa
⚳#⚷ 0:44
☽✶♃ 4:51
☉∠☽ 6:23
☽⊻☿ 6:36
☽☍♄ 9:20
♃∠♆ 11:56
☽✶⚳ 13:31
☽∥♅ 14:54
♀□♅ 17:24
☽⊻⚷ 20:06
☽☌♅ 23:13
☽□♀ 23:47

13 Su
☿⊼♄ 5:18
☽⊻♆ 7:54
☉✶☽ 11:25
☽∠☿ 12:58
☽∠⚳ 16:26
☽□♂ 17:25
☉⚼♄ 19:35
☽∠⚷ 22:52
☽□♇ 23:42

14 M
☽∠♆ 10:23
☽□♃ 11:02
☉∥♀ 13:27
☽⊼♄ 14:19
☽#♅ 14:30
☽✶☿ 18:35
☽⊻⚳ 18:54
☿□⚳ 21:47

15 Tu
☿⚼♂ 0:07
☽✶⚷ 1:10
☽⊻♅ 4:03
☽∥♄ 5:38
☽#⚷ 6:56
☽∥⚳ 8:26
☽△♀ 9:30
♂∠⚳ 10:21
☽✶♆ 12:25
☽⚼♄ 16:08
☉□☽ 19:47
☽✶♂ 20:42

16 W
☽#♆ 0:21
☽△♇ 3:41
☽∠♅ 5:47
☉⊼♂ 6:30
☽#♇ 10:19
☽⚼♀ 13:30
☽#☿ 14:33
☽△♃ 15:20
☽△♄ 17:31
♀✶♆ 19:37
☽∠♂ 21:46
☽☌⚳ 22:32

17 Th
☽□☿ 3:41
☉#☽ 3:57
☽□⚷ 4:28
☽⚼♇ 5:02
☽✶♅ 7:08
☽#♀ 8:29
☿☌⚷ 12:06
☽□♆ 15:14
☽#♃ 16:23
☽⚼♃ 16:53
☽⊼♀ 17:00
☿∠♇ 17:57
☽⊻♂ 22:31

18 F
☉△☽ 2:06
☽⊼♇ 6:05
☿∥♇ 6:46
☿⊻♅ 16:50
☽⊼♃ 18:09
☽□♄ 19:21
☽∥♂ 21:49

19 Sa
☽⊻⚳ 0:52
☉⚼☽ 4:48
☽△⚷ 6:31
☽□♅ 9:03
☽△☿ 10:35
☽△♆ 17:02
☽☍♀ 23:14
☽☌♂ 23:36

20 Su
☽∠⚳ 1:52
♀☍♂ 3:11
☽⚼⚷ 7:26
☉⊼☽ 7:27
☽☍♇ 7:47
☉⊻♇ 12:30
☽⚼☿ 13:41
☉ ♒ 16:45
☽⚼♆ 17:55
☽☍♃ 20:32
☽✶♄ 20:46

21 M
☽∥♂ 1:36
☽✶⚳ 3:00
☽⊼⚷ 8:30
♃△♄ 9:15
♀⚼⚳ 10:06
☽△♅ 10:57
☽⊼☿ 16:50
☽⊼♆ 19:02
☉∠♅ 20:00
☽∠♄ 21:47

22 Tu
☽⊻♂ 1:10
☽⊼♀ 6:00
☽#♃ 7:11
☽⊼♇ 10:09
☽#♀ 12:10
☽⚼♅ 12:23
☿∥♆ 13:00
☉☍☽ 13:36
☽⊻♄ 23:15

23 W
☽⊼♃ 0:01
☿☌♆ 1:16
☉#☽ 1:52
☽∠♂ 2:37
☽□⚳ 6:28
♄#⚷ 7:12
☽⚼♀ 10:16
☽☍⚷ 11:56
☽⚼♇ 12:05
☽#♇ 13:31
☽⊼♅ 14:23
☽☍♆ 22:50

24 Th
☽#♆ 0:10
☽☍☿ 0:14
☽⚼♃ 2:41
☽#☿ 3:42
☽✶♂ 4:45
♀∠⚷ 6:02
♀☌♇ 7:00
♀ ♑ 8:07
☽∥⚳ 12:23
☽△♇ 14:44
☽△♀ 15:30
☽∥♄ 18:19
☽#⚷ 18:35
☉⊼☽ 22:38

25 F
☽☌♄ 4:14
☽△♃ 6:12
♇∠⚷ 8:10
☽#♅ 11:51
☽△⚳ 12:48
☽⊼⚷ 18:17
☽☍♅ 20:46

26 Sa
♇ ♑ 2:38
☉⚼☽ 4:44
☽⊼♆ 5:43
☽⊼☿ 9:54
☽□♂ 11:33
☽⚼⚳ 17:21
☽□♇ 22:39
☽⚼⚷ 22:47

27 Su
☽□♀ 5:26
☽⚼♆ 10:30
☉△☽ 11:57
☽⊻♄ 12:36
☽∥♅ 13:01
☽⚼☿ 15:31
☽□♃ 15:59
☉⊼♄ 19:22
☽⊼⚳ 22:47

28 M
☿#⚳ 3:06
☽△⚷ 4:09
☽⊼♅ 6:38
☽∥⚷ 7:27
☽#♄ 8:29
☽∥☿ 15:42
☽△♆ 16:03
☽#⚳ 16:44
☽∠♄ 17:57
☿ R 20:34
☽△☿ 21:22
☽△♂ 21:49

29 Tu
☽∥♆ 4:02
☽✶♇ 9:48
♀∠♆ 9:55
☽⚼♅ 12:38
☉⚼♂ 15:17
☽∥♇ 16:31
☉∥☽ 20:36
☽✶♀ 23:33
☽✶♄ 23:51

30 W
☉⊻♃ 0:53
♀△♄ 2:20
☽⚼♂ 3:53
☽✶♃ 4:47
☉□☽ 5:04
☽☍⚳ 11:38
☽∠♇ 16:07
☽□⚷ 16:36
☽△♅ 19:01
♂ D 22:35
☽∥♀ 23:31

31 Th
☽∥♃ 3:24
☿∠♀ 3:41
☽□♆ 4:35
☽□☿ 8:36
☽∠♀ 9:22
☽⊼♂ 10:12
☽∠♃ 11:40
☽⊻♇ 22:31

February 2008

LONGITUDE

Day	Sid.Time	☉	☽	☽ 12 hour	Mean☊	True☊	☿	♀	♂	⚳	♃	♄	⚷	♅	♆	♇
	h m s	° ' "	° ' "	° ' "	° '	° '	° '	° '	° '	° '	° '	° '	° '	° '	° '	° '
1 F	8 42 21	11♒29 19	0♐54 56	6♐52 41	28♒42.0	27♒52.2	22♒56.9	9♑25.3	24♊05.1	13♉12.7	9♑54.8	6♍57.1	15♒28.9	16♓37.9	21♒20.1	0♑10.8
2 Sa	8 46 17	12 30 14	12 52 05	18 53 39	28 38.8	27R 50.4	22R 16.6	10 39.2	24 06.3	13 24.6	10 07.5	6R 53.0	15 33.5	16 40.8	21 22.3	0 12.5
3 Su	8 50 14	13 31 08	24 57 48	1♑04 57	28 35.6	27 48.3	21 26.8	11 53.1	24 08.2	13 36.7	10 20.2	6 48.8	15 38.1	16 43.8	21 24.6	0 14.3
4 M	8 54 10	14 32 02	7♑15 27	13 29 34	28 32.5	27 46.2	20 28.8	13 07.1	24 10.8	13 49.0	10 32.8	6 44.5	15 42.7	16 46.9	21 26.9	0 16.0
5 Tu	8 58 07	15 32 55	19 47 31	26 09 28	28 29.3	27 44.3	19 24.2	14 21.0	24 14.2	14 01.7	10 45.4	6 40.2	15 47.2	16 49.9	21 29.1	0 17.7
6 W	9 02 04	16 33 46	2♒35 29	9♒05 37	28 26.1	27 42.9	18 15.0	15 35.0	24 18.3	14 14.5	10 57.9	6 35.9	15 51.8	16 53.0	21 31.4	0 19.4
7 Th	9 06 00	17 34 36	15 39 48	22 17 57	28 22.9	27D 42.1	17 03.1	16 49.0	24 23.0	14 27.7	11 10.3	6 31.5	15 56.4	16 56.0	21 33.7	0 21.0
8 F	9 09 57	18 35 26	28 59 53	5♓45 25	28 19.8	27 41.8	15 50.7	18 03.0	24 28.5	14 41.1	11 22.7	6 27.0	16 01.0	16 59.2	21 36.0	0 22.7
9 Sa	9 13 53	19 36 13	12♓34 18	19 26 16	28 16.6	27 42.1	14 39.6	19 17.0	24 34.7	14 54.7	11 35.0	6 22.5	16 05.6	17 02.3	21 38.2	0 24.3
10 Su	9 17 50	20 37 00	26 21 01	3♈18 14	28 13.4	27 42.7	13 31.7	20 31.0	24 41.5	15 08.6	11 47.2	6 18.0	16 10.1	17 05.4	21 40.5	0 25.9
11 M	9 21 46	21 37 45	10♈17 36	17 18 50	28 10.2	27 43.3	12 28.5	21 45.0	24 48.9	15 22.7	11 59.4	6 13.4	16 14.7	17 08.6	21 42.8	0 27.4
12 Tu	9 25 43	22 38 28	24 21 35	1♉25 33	28 07.1	27 43.8	11 31.1	22 59.1	24 57.0	15 37.0	12 11.5	6 08.8	16 19.3	17 11.8	21 45.1	0 28.9
13 W	9 29 39	23 39 10	8♉30 28	15 36 01	28 03.9	27 44.2	10 40.6	24 13.1	25 05.8	15 51.6	12 23.5	6 04.1	16 23.8	17 15.0	21 47.4	0 30.5
14 Th	9 33 36	24 39 50	22 41 55	29 47 54	28 00.7	27R 44.3	9 57.6	25 27.2	25 15.1	16 06.4	12 35.5	5 59.5	16 28.4	17 18.2	21 49.6	0 31.9
15 F	9 37 33	25 40 28	6♊53 40	13♊58 56	27 57.5	27 44.3	9 22.4	26 41.3	25 25.0	16 21.5	12 47.4	5 54.8	16 32.9	17 21.5	21 51.9	0 33.4
16 Sa	9 41 29	26 41 05	21 03 25	28 06 48	27 54.3	27 44.2	8 55.0	27 55.3	25 35.6	16 36.7	12 59.2	5 50.0	16 37.4	17 24.7	21 54.2	0 34.8
17 Su	9 45 26	27 41 40	5♋08 46	12♋09 00	27 51.2	27D 44.1	8 35.6	29 09.4	25 46.7	16 52.2	13 10.9	5 45.3	16 41.9	17 28.0	21 56.5	0 36.2
18 M	9 49 22	28 42 13	19 07 12	26 03 00	27 48.0	27 44.2	8 23.7	0♒23.5	25 58.3	17 07.9	13 22.6	5 40.5	16 46.4	17 31.3	21 58.7	0 37.6
19 Tu	9 53 19	29 42 45	2♌56 07	9♌46 14	27 44.8	27 44.3	8D 19.3	1 37.6	26 10.6	17 23.7	13 34.2	5 35.7	16 50.9	17 34.6	22 01.0	0 39.0
20 W	9 57 15	0♓43 14	16 33 04	23 16 21	27 41.6	27R 44.5	8 21.9	2 51.7	26 23.3	17 39.8	13 45.7	5 30.9	16 55.4	17 37.9	22 03.3	0 40.3
21 Th	10 01 12	1 43 43	29 55 54	6♍31 33	27 38.5	27 44.5	8 31.1	4 05.8	26 36.5	17 56.1	13 57.1	5 26.1	16 59.9	17 41.2	22 05.5	0 41.6
22 F	10 05 08	2 44 09	13♍03 09	19 30 41	27 35.3	27 44.4	8 46.5	5 19.9	26 50.3	18 12.5	14 08.4	5 21.3	17 04.3	17 44.6	22 07.8	0 42.9
23 Sa	10 09 05	3 44 34	25 54 08	2♎13 35	27 32.1	27 43.9	9 07.7	6 34.1	27 04.6	18 29.2	14 19.7	5 16.5	17 08.7	17 47.9	22 10.0	0 44.1
24 Su	10 13 02	4 44 57	8♎29 09	14 41 04	27 28.9	27 43.1	9 34.2	7 48.2	27 19.3	18 46.1	14 30.8	5 11.6	17 13.2	17 51.3	22 12.3	0 45.4
25 M	10 16 58	5 45 19	20 49 33	26 54 58	27 25.7	27 42.0	10 05.8	9 02.3	27 34.5	19 03.1	14 41.9	5 06.8	17 17.5	17 54.7	22 14.5	0 46.5
26 Tu	10 20 55	6 45 39	2♏57 39	8♏58 03	27 22.6	27 40.8	10 42.0	10 16.5	27 50.2	19 20.3	14 52.9	5 01.9	17 21.9	17 58.0	22 16.7	0 47.7
27 W	10 24 51	7 45 58	14 56 37	20 53 53	27 19.4	27 39.7	11 22.5	11 30.7	28 06.3	19 37.7	15 03.8	4 57.1	17 26.3	18 01.4	22 19.0	0 48.8
28 Th	10 28 48	8 46 15	26 50 21	2♐46 36	27 16.2	27 38.9	12 06.9	12 44.8	28 22.9	19 55.3	15 14.6	4 52.3	17 30.6	18 04.8	22 21.2	0 49.9
29 F	10 32 44	9♓46 32	8♐43 13	14 40 47	27♒13.0	27♒38.5	12♒55.0	13♒59.0	28♊39.9	20♉13.0	15♑25.3	4♍47.5	17♒34.9	18♓08.2	22♒23.4	0♑51.0

1st of Month

Julian Day # 2454497.5
Obliquity 23°26'25"
SVP 5♓08'39"
GC 26♐57.1
Eris 20♈30.2

Day	⚴	⚵	⚶
1	18♓56.3	16♐58.8	21♒25.2
6	20 34.3	18 20.8	23 57.6
11	22 14.6	19 39.8	26 29.7
16	23 56.9	20 55.4	29 01.4
21	25 41.0	22 07.4	1♓32.7
26	27 26.9	23 15.5	4 03.4

DECLINATION and LATITUDE

Day	☉ Decl	☽ Decl	☽ Lat	☽12h Decl	☿ Decl	☿ Lat	♀ Decl	♀ Lat	♂ Decl	♂ Lat	⚳ Decl	⚳ Lat	♃ Decl	♃ Lat	♄ Decl	♄ Lat
1 F	17S20	25S29	5S15	26S35	11S30	2N30	22S22	0N44	26N40	3N22	12N42	3S15	22S57	0N07	10N37	1N48
2 Sa	17 03	27 23	5 05	27 52	11 28	2 46	22 20	0 41	26 39	3 21	12 49	3 11	22 56	0 07	10 39	1 48
3 Su	16 46	28 01	4 41	27 50	11 31	2 60	22 16	0 38	26 38	3 20	12 56	3 08	22 55	0 07	10 41	1 48
4 M	16 28	27 18	4 04	26 25	11 37	3 12	22 13	0 35	26 37	3 19	13 03	3 04	22 54	0 07	10 43	1 48
5 Tu	16 11	25 11	3 15	23 38	11 48	3 23	22 08	0 32	26 37	3 18	13 10	3 01	22 53	0 07	10 44	1 48
6 W	15 52	21 46	2 14	19 37	12 01	3 31	22 03	0 29	26 36	3 17	13 17	2 58	22 52	0 07	10 46	1 48
7 Th	15 34	17 12	1 06	14 33	12 17	3 37	21 57	0 26	26 35	3 16	13 24	2 54	22 51	0 07	10 48	1 49
8 F	15 15	11 43	0N07	8 43	12 35	3 40	21 50	0 23	26 34	3 15	13 31	2 51	22 50	0 07	10 50	1 49
9 Sa	14 56	5 35	1 21	2 23	12 55	3 41	21 43	0 20	26 33	3 14	13 38	2 48	22 49	0 07	10 51	1 49
10 Su	14 37	0N53	2 32	4N08	13 15	3 40	21 35	0 17	26 32	3 12	13 45	2 44	22 48	0 07	10 53	1 49
11 M	14 18	7 22	3 35	10 31	13 36	3 36	21 27	0 14	26 31	3 11	13 53	2 41	22 47	0 07	10 55	1 49
12 Tu	13 58	13 33	4 25	16 25	13 57	3 30	21 18	0 11	26 31	3 10	13 60	2 38	22 46	0 06	10 57	1 49
13 W	13 38	19 04	4 59	21 27	14 18	3 23	21 08	0 08	26 30	3 09	14 07	2 35	22 45	0 06	10 59	1 49
14 Th	13 18	23 32	5 16	25 16	14 38	3 15	20 58	0 05	26 29	3 08	14 14	2 32	22 44	0 06	11 01	1 50
15 F	12 58	26 36	5 13	27 31	14 56	3 05	20 47	0 02	26 28	3 07	14 21	2 28	22 43	0 06	11 02	1 50
16 Sa	12 37	27 59	4 51	27 59	15 14	2 54	20 35	0S01	26 28	3 06	14 29	2 25	22 42	0 06	11 04	1 50
17 Su	12 16	27 32	4 12	26 39	15 30	2 42	20 23	0 03	26 27	3 04	14 36	2 22	22 41	0 06	11 06	1 50
18 M	11 56	25 21	3 18	23 40	15 45	2 30	20 10	0 06	26 26	3 03	14 43	2 19	22 40	0 06	11 08	1 50
19 Tu	11 34	21 40	2 13	19 23	15 58	2 18	19 57	0 09	26 25	3 02	14 51	2 16	22 39	0 06	11 10	1 50
20 W	11 13	16 51	1 02	14 09	16 10	2 05	19 43	0 12	26 24	3 01	14 58	2 13	22 38	0 06	11 12	1 50
21 Th	10 52	11 18	0S12	8 22	16 20	1 52	19 28	0 15	26 24	2 60	15 05	2 10	22 37	0 06	11 14	1 50
22 F	10 30	5 22	1 24	2 21	16 28	1 40	19 13	0 17	26 23	2 59	15 13	2 07	22 36	0 06	11 16	1 50
23 Sa	10 08	0S40	2 30	3S38	16 35	1 27	18 57	0 20	26 22	2 58	15 20	2 05	22 35	0 06	11 17	1 50
24 Su	9 46	6 32	3 27	9 21	16 40	1 14	18 41	0 23	26 21	2 56	15 27	2 02	22 34	0 05	11 19	1 51
25 M	9 24	12 02	4 13	14 36	16 43	1 02	18 24	0 26	26 20	2 55	15 35	1 59	22 32	0 05	11 21	1 51
26 Tu	9 02	16 60	4 48	19 13	16 45	0 50	18 07	0 28	26 19	2 54	15 42	1 56	22 31	0 05	11 23	1 51
27 W	8 39	21 14	5 09	23 01	16 46	0 38	17 49	0 31	26 19	2 53	15 49	1 53	22 30	0 05	11 25	1 51
28 Th	8 17	24 35	5 16	25 52	16 45	0 26	17 31	0 33	26 18	2 52	15 57	1 50	22 29	0 05	11 27	1 51
29 F	7S54	26S52	5S10	27S34	16S42	0N15	17S12	0S36	26N17	2N51	16N04	1S48	22S28	0N05	11N28	1N51

Day	⚷ Decl	⚷ Lat	♅ Decl	♅ Lat	♆ Decl	♆ Lat	♇ Decl	♇ Lat
1	10S13	6N15	5S58	0S44	14S40	0S17	17S10	6N17
6	10 07	6 15	5 52	0 44	14 36	0 18	17 09	6 17
11	10 00	6 15	5 45	0 44	14 33	0 18	17 09	6 17
16	9 53	6 15	5 39	0 44	14 29	0 18	17 09	6 18
21	9 47	6 15	5 33	0 44	14 26	0 18	17 08	6 18
26	9S40	6N15	5S26	0S44	14S22	0S18	17S08	6N18

Day	⚴ Decl	⚴ Lat	⚵ Decl	⚵ Lat	⚶ Decl	⚶ Lat	Eris Decl	Eris Lat
1	8S08	4S05	11S59	10N52	17S32	3S21	4S59	14S00
6	7 49	4 26	11 53	11 05	16 46	3 26	4 57	13 59
11	7 29	4 47	11 45	11 19	15 59	3 31	4 56	13 58
16	7 07	5 08	11 36	11 34	15 11	3 36	4 55	13 58
21	6 45	5 29	11 24	11 49	14 22	3 41	4 53	13 57
26	6S22	5S51	11S11	12N06	13S32	3S46	4S52	13S56

Moon Phenomena

Max/0 Decl
dy hr mn
2 23:37 28S01
9 20:47 0 N
16 6:02 28N02
22 21:21 0 S

Max/0 Lat
dy hr mn
7 21:40 0 N
14 8:28 5N17
20 20:02 0 S
28 1:36 5S16

Perigee/Apogee
dy hr m kilometers
14 1:08 p 370219
28 1:19 a 404443

PH dy hr mn
● 7 3:46 17♒44
● 7 3:56 A 02'12"
☽ 14 3:35 24♉49
○ 21 3:32 1♍53
● 21 3:27 T 1.106
☾ 29 2:19 9♐52

Void of Course Moon

Last Aspect	☽ Ingress
2 22:22 ♂ ☍	♑ 3 9:53
4 18:21 ♅ ⚹	♒ 5 19:11
7 15:51 ♂ △	♓ 8 1:47
9 21:06 ♂ □	♈ 10 6:18
12 1:01 ♂ ⚹	♉ 12 9:35
14 5:06 ♀ △	♊ 14 12:20
16 10:18 ☉ △	♋ 16 15:13
17 21:14 ♅ △	♌ 18 18:52
20 17:54 ♂ ⚹	♍ 21 0:07
23 2:16 ♂ □	♎ 23 7:46
25 13:36 ♂ △	♏ 25 18:07
27 14:55 ♆ □	♐ 28 6:23

DAILY ASPECTARIAN

1 F
♀☌♃ 11:35
☽□♄ 12:05
☽#♂ 13:07
☉∥♇ 15:02
☽⚺♃ 18:25
☽⚺♀ 19:04
☉⚹☽ 23:12

2 Sa
☽⚻⚳ 1:06
☽⚹⚷ 5:24
☽□♅ 7:38
☽⚹♆ 16:58
☽⚹☿ 17:32
☽☍♂ 22:22

3 Su
☿☌♆ 0:57
☉□⚳ 2:43
☽⚼⚳ 7:17
☉∠☽ 7:37
☽☌♇ 10:22
☽∠⚷ 11:12
☽∠☿ 20:49
☽∠♆ 22:26
☽△♄ 23:00

4 M
☽☌♃ 6:27
☽#♂ 9:36
☽☌♀ 12:31
☽△⚳ 12:50
☉⚺☽ 15:13
☽⚺⚷ 16:20
♀△⚳ 16:25
☉∠♇ 17:50
☽⚹♅ 18:21
☽⚺☿ 23:19

5 Tu
☽⚺♆ 3:13
☽⚼♄ 3:32
☉☌⚷ 6:07
☽⚻♂ 8:26
☽∥♃ 17:05
☽⚺♇ 19:46
☽∥♀ 22:15
☽∠♅ 22:41

6 W
♀⚺⚷ 5:49
☽⚻♄ 7:22
☉⚺♅ 7:58
☽⚼♂ 12:28
☽⚺♃ 15:41
☉☌☿ 18:20
☽□⚳ 21:47
☽∠♇ 23:26

7 Th
☽∥♇ 0:11
☽☌⚷ 0:30
☿⚺♅ 2:15
☽⚺♀ 2:18
☽☌☿ 2:19
☽⚺♅ 2:19
☿⚺♀ 2:19
♀⚹♅ 2:24
☉☌☽ 3:46
☉∥☽ 7:57
☽☌♆ 10:42
☽∥♆ 11:50
☽△♂ 15:51
☽#⚳ 16:36
☽∠♃ 19:15
☽∥☿ 20:34
☿☌⚷ 20:47

8 F
☽⚹♇ 2:28
☽#♄ 3:34
☽∥⚷ 6:40
☽∠♀ 7:56
☿∠♇ 9:10
☽☍♄ 13:09
☿□⚳ 19:41
☽⚹♃ 22:14
☽∥♅ 23:12

9 Sa
☽⚺☿ 3:22
☽⚹⚳ 4:10
☽⚺⚷ 6:12
☽☌♅ 7:51
☽⚹♀ 12:53
☉⚺☽ 13:16
☽⚺♆ 15:52
☽□♂ 21:06

10 Su
☽∠☿ 3:29
☉∥♆ 4:44
☽∠⚳ 6:40
☽□♇ 7:04
☽∠⚷ 8:22
☉⚺♀ 10:50
♀⚼♄ 14:20
☽⚻♄ 17:03
☉∠☽ 17:14
☽∠♆ 17:51
☽#♅ 18:01
♀⚺♆ 23:15

11 M
☉☌♆ 2:05
☽□♃ 2:57
☽⚹☿ 3:29
☽⚺⚳ 8:51
⚳⚼♇ 8:53
☿⚺♃ 9:46
☽#⚷ 9:58
☽⚹⚷ 10:14
☽⚺♅ 11:45
☽∥♄ 13:38
☽⚼♄ 18:34
☽⚹♆ 19:33
☉⚹☽ 20:51
☽□♀ 21:26
☉#⚳ 22:29

12 Tu
☉∥☿ 0:28
☽⚹♂ 1:01
☉#☽ 1:38
☽#☿ 1:46
☽∥⚳ 1:53
☽#♆ 4:03
☿#⚳ 4:24
☽△♇ 10:25
☽∠♅ 13:21
☽#♇ 15:15
☽△♄ 19:54

13 W
☽∠♂ 2:43
☽□☿ 3:29
☽△♃ 6:40
☽#♀ 9:59
☽⚼♇ 11:52
☽☌⚳ 12:40
☽□⚷ 13:25
☽⚹♅ 14:51
☿⚼♂ 15:37
☿∥♆ 15:40
☽#♃ 19:14
♀⚻♂ 19:30
☽□♆ 22:31

14 Th
☉□☽ 3:35
☽⚺♂ 4:22
☽△♀ 5:06
☽⚼♃ 8:23
☽⚻♇ 13:16
☉△♂ 16:40
☽□♄ 22:21
☽∥♂ 22:40

15 F
☽△☿ 4:03
☽⚼♀ 8:53
☽⚻♃ 10:07
☽⚺⚳ 16:19
☽△⚷ 16:26
☽□♅ 17:47

16 Sa
⚳#♆ 1:10
☽△♆ 1:26
⚳□⚷ 1:32
☽⚼☿ 4:44
☽☌♂ 7:49
☉△☽ 10:18
☽⚻♀ 12:48
☽☍♇ 16:14
☽⚼⚷ 18:05
☽∠⚳ 18:18

17 Su
☽⚹♄ 1:02
☽⚼♆ 3:05
☽⚻☿ 5:48
☉⚼☽ 13:57
☽☍♃ 13:58
☽∥♂ 14:10
☉∠♃ 14:22
♀ ♒ 16:23
☽⚻⚷ 19:56
☽⚹⚳ 20:30
☽△♅ 21:14
⚶ ♓ 22:25

18 M
☽∠♄ 2:40
♀⚺♇ 4:40
☽⚻♆ 4:57
☽⚺♂ 12:02
☉⚻☽ 17:56
☽#♃ 18:18
☽⚻♇ 20:00
☽☍♀ 21:29
☽⚼♅ 23:22

19 Tu
☿ D 2:58
☽⚺♄ 4:38
☉ ♓ 6:51
☽☍☿ 9:27
☽#♀ 9:36
☽∠♂ 14:42
☽⚻♃ 18:59
♀∠♅ 19:19
⚳⚹♅ 20:27
☽⚼♇ 22:26
☽#♇ 22:42
☉⚹♇ 22:49

20 W
☽☍⚷ 0:40
☉#♄ 1:21
☽⚻♅ 1:56
☽□⚳ 2:01
☽#☿ 3:04
☽∥⚳ 8:17
☽☍♆ 9:51
☽#♆ 10:47
☽⚹♂ 17:54
☽⚼♃ 22:12

21 Th
☽∥♄ 0:20
☽△♇ 1:23
☉#☽ 1:58
☉☍☽ 3:32
☽#⚷ 6:19
☽⚻♀ 8:21
☽☌♄ 9:57
☽⚻☿ 15:57
☽#♅ 23:23

22 F
♀⚻♄ 0:25
☽△♃ 2:03
☽⚻⚷ 7:30
☽☍♅ 8:44
☽△⚳ 9:47
☽⚼♀ 14:59
☽⚻♆ 16:57
☽⚼☿ 20:33

23 Sa
☽□♂ 2:16
☽□♇ 9:11
☽⚼⚷ 11:55
☽⚼⚳ 14:44
☉⚻☽ 16:12
☽⚺♄ 17:43
☽∥♅ 19:36
☽⚼♆ 21:32
☽△♀ 22:32

24 Su
☽△☿ 2:11
☉∥⚷ 4:24
☉☍♄ 9:49
☽□♃ 11:51
☉∥☽ 12:59
☽∥⚷ 13:31
☽△⚷ 17:03
☽⚻♅ 18:16
☽⚻⚳ 20:26
☽#♄ 20:52
☽∠♄ 22:37
☉⚼☽ 23:51

25 M
☽△♆ 2:47
☽∥♆ 10:55
☽△♂ 13:36
☽#⚳ 17:15
☽⚹♇ 19:41
☽∥☿ 22:45

26 Tu
☽⚼♅ 0:01
☽∥♇ 0:42
☽⚹♄ 4:06
☽∥♀ 5:35
☉△☽ 8:17
☽□♀ 16:18
☽□☿ 16:23
☿☌♀ 17:53
☽⚼♂ 20:13

27 W
☽⚹♃ 0:15
☽∠♇ 1:45
☽□⚷ 5:03
☽△♅ 6:14
☽∥♃ 8:19
☽☍⚳ 9:41
☽□♆ 14:55

28 Th
☽⚻♂ 3:12
☽∠♃ 6:59
☽⚺♇ 8:05
♀⚼♂ 15:58
☽□♄ 16:07
☽#♂ 16:38

29 F
☉□☽ 2:19
♀∥♇ 5:44
☽⚹☿ 9:06
☽⚹♀ 11:49
☽⚺♃ 13:42
☽⚹⚷ 17:56
☽□♅ 19:02
☽⚻⚳ 23:42

LONGITUDE — March 2008

Day	Sid.Time	☉	☽	☽ 12 hour	Mean ☊	True ☊	☿	♀	♂	⚳	♃	♄	⚷	♅	♆	♇
	h m s	° ' "	° ' "	° ' "	° '	° '	° '	° '	° '	° '	° '	° '	° '	° '	° '	° '
1 Sa	10 36 41	10♓46 46	20♐39 54	26♐41 09	27♒09.9	27♒38.8	13♒46.5	15♒13.2	28♊57.3	20♉30.9	15♑35.9	4♍42.7	17♒39.2	18♓11.6	22♒25.6	0♑52.1
2 Su	10 40 37	11 46 59	2♑45 07	8♑52 21	27 06.7	27 39.6	14 41.2	16 27.4	29 15.2	20 49.0	15 46.4	4R 37.9	17 43.5	18 15.1	22 27.7	0 53.1
3 M	10 44 34	12 47 11	15 03 22	21 18 39	27 03.5	27 40.8	15 38.8	17 41.6	29 33.4	21 07.3	15 56.8	4 33.1	17 47.8	18 18.5	22 29.9	0 54.1
4 Tu	10 48 31	13 47 21	27 38 36	4♒03 34	27 00.3	27 42.2	16 39.2	18 55.8	29 52.1	21 25.7	16 07.1	4 28.4	17 52.0	18 21.9	22 32.1	0 55.0
5 W	10 52 27	14 47 29	10♒33 50	17 09 33	26 57.2	27 43.4	17 42.1	20 10.0	0♋11.1	21 44.3	16 17.3	4 23.6	17 56.2	18 25.4	22 34.2	0 55.9
6 Th	10 56 24	15 47 35	23 50 48	0♓37 33	26 54.0	27R 44.0	18 47.4	21 24.2	0 30.5	22 03.0	16 27.4	4 18.9	18 00.4	18 28.8	22 36.4	0 56.8
7 F	11 00 20	16 47 40	7♓29 36	14 26 42	26 50.8	27 43.8	19 55.0	22 38.4	0 50.3	22 21.9	16 37.4	4 14.3	18 04.5	18 32.2	22 38.5	0 57.7
8 Sa	11 04 17	17 47 43	21 28 25	28 34 17	26 47.6	27 42.6	21 04.7	23 52.5	1 10.5	22 41.0	16 47.3	4 09.6	18 08.7	18 35.7	22 40.6	0 58.5
9 Su	11 08 13	18 47 44	5♈43 39	12♈55 51	26 44.4	27 40.4	22 16.5	25 06.7	1 31.0	23 00.2	16 57.1	4 05.0	18 12.7	18 39.1	22 42.7	0 59.3
10 M	11 12 10	19 47 43	20 10 08	27 25 45	26 41.3	27 37.4	23 30.1	26 20.9	1 51.9	23 19.5	17 06.7	4 00.4	18 16.8	18 42.5	22 44.8	1 00.1
11 Tu	11 16 06	20 47 40	4♉41 56	11♉57 56	26 38.1	27 34.1	24 45.6	27 35.1	2 13.1	23 39.0	17 16.3	3 55.9	18 20.8	18 46.0	22 46.9	1 00.8
12 W	11 20 03	21 47 35	19 13 04	26 26 43	26 34.9	27 31.1	26 02.8	28 49.3	2 34.6	23 58.6	17 25.7	3 51.4	18 24.8	18 49.4	22 49.0	1 01.5
13 Th	11 24 00	22 47 27	3♊38 20	10♊47 30	26 31.7	27 28.9	27 21.7	0♓03.5	2 56.4	24 18.4	17 35.0	3 46.9	18 28.8	18 52.8	22 51.0	1 02.2
14 F	11 27 56	23 47 18	17 53 51	24 57 07	26 28.6	27D 27.8	28 42.1	1 17.7	3 18.6	24 38.3	17 44.2	3 42.5	18 32.8	18 56.3	22 53.0	1 02.9
15 Sa	11 31 53	24 47 06	1♋57 09	8♋53 50	26 25.4	27 27.8	0♓04.2	2 31.8	3 41.1	24 58.4	17 53.3	3 38.2	18 36.7	18 59.7	22 55.0	1 03.5
16 Su	11 35 49	25 46 52	15 47 08	22 37 02	26 22.2	27 28.9	1 27.8	3 46.0	4 03.9	25 18.5	18 02.2	3 33.9	18 40.5	19 03.1	22 57.0	1 04.1
17 M	11 39 46	26 46 35	29 23 36	6♌06 52	26 19.0	27 30.4	2 52.8	5 00.2	4 26.9	25 38.8	18 11.1	3 29.6	18 44.4	19 06.5	22 59.0	1 04.6
18 Tu	11 43 42	27 46 17	12♌46 54	19 23 46	26 15.8	27 31.9	4 19.2	6 14.3	4 50.3	25 59.2	18 19.8	3 25.4	18 48.2	19 09.9	23 01.0	1 05.1
19 W	11 47 39	28 45 56	25 57 32	2♍28 16	26 12.7	27R 32.6	5 47.1	7 28.5	5 13.9	26 19.8	18 28.3	3 21.3	18 51.9	19 13.3	23 02.9	1 05.6
20 Th	11 51 35	29 45 33	8♍56 00	15 20 46	26 09.5	27 32.1	7 16.4	8 42.6	5 37.8	26 40.5	18 36.8	3 17.2	18 55.6	19 16.7	23 04.9	1 06.0
21 F	11 55 32	0♈45 07	21 42 38	28 01 37	26 06.3	27 29.9	8 47.0	9 56.8	6 01.9	27 01.2	18 45.1	3 13.2	18 59.3	19 20.1	23 06.8	1 06.5
22 Sa	11 59 29	1 44 40	4♎17 46	10♎31 08	26 03.1	27 25.9	10 19.0	11 10.9	6 26.3	27 22.1	18 53.3	3 09.3	19 03.0	19 23.5	23 08.7	1 06.8
23 Su	12 03 25	2 44 10	16 41 49	22 49 54	26 00.0	27 20.5	11 52.4	12 25.1	6 50.9	27 43.1	19 01.3	3 05.4	19 06.6	19 26.9	23 10.5	1 07.2
24 M	12 07 22	3 43 39	28 55 33	4♏58 54	25 56.8	27 13.9	13 27.0	13 39.2	7 15.8	28 04.3	19 09.3	3 01.6	19 10.2	19 30.2	23 12.4	1 07.5
25 Tu	12 11 18	4 43 06	11♏00 13	16 59 44	25 53.6	27 07.0	15 03.1	14 53.3	7 41.0	28 25.5	19 17.1	2 57.8	19 13.7	19 33.6	23 14.2	1 07.8
26 W	12 15 15	5 42 31	22 57 47	28 54 42	25 50.4	27 00.3	16 40.4	16 07.5	8 06.3	28 46.8	19 24.7	2 54.1	19 17.2	19 36.9	23 16.0	1 08.1
27 Th	12 19 11	6 41 54	4♐50 54	10♐46 50	25 47.2	26 54.7	18 19.1	17 21.6	8 31.9	29 08.3	19 32.2	2 50.5	19 20.6	19 40.2	23 17.8	1 08.3
28 F	12 23 08	7 41 15	16 43 00	22 39 55	25 44.1	26 50.6	19 59.2	18 35.7	8 57.7	29 29.8	19 39.6	2 47.0	19 24.0	19 43.6	23 19.6	1 08.5
29 Sa	12 27 04	8 40 35	28 38 09	4♑38 18	25 40.9	26D 48.2	21 40.6	19 49.8	9 23.7	29 51.5	19 46.8	2 43.5	19 27.4	19 46.9	23 21.3	1 08.6
30 Su	12 31 01	9 39 53	10♑40 58	16 46 46	25 37.7	26 47.6	23 23.4	21 04.0	9 50.0	0♊13.3	19 53.9	2 40.2	19 30.7	19 50.2	23 23.1	1 08.8
31 M	12 34 58	10♈39 09	22 56 20	29 10 15	25♒34.5	26♒48.3	25♓07.5	22♓18.1	10♋16.4	0♊35.1	20♑00.8	2♍36.9	19♒34.0	19♓53.4	23♒24.8	1♑08.9

1st of Month

Julian Day # 2454526.5
Obliquity 23°26'26"
SVP 5♓08'35"
GC 26♐57.2
Eris 20♈41.6

Day	⚴
1	28♓52.8
6	0♈41.5
11	2 31.6
16	4 22.9
21	6 15.4
26	8 08.9
31	10 03.5

Day	⚵
1	24♐07.0
6	25 07.2
11	26 02.4
16	26 52.3
21	27 36.6
26	28 14.7
31	28 46.3

Day	⚶
1	6♓03.6
6	8 33.3
11	11 02.3
16	13 30.4
21	15 57.7
26	18 23.9
31	20 49.2

DECLINATION and LATITUDE

Day	☉ Decl	☽ Decl	☽ Lat	☽ 12h Decl	☿ Decl	☿ Lat	♀ Decl	♀ Lat	♂ Decl	♂ Lat	⚳ Decl	⚳ Lat	♃ Decl	♃ Lat	♄ Decl	♄ Lat
1 Sa	7S32	27S57	4S51	28S01	16S38	0N04	16S53	0S38	26N16	2N50	16N12	1S45	22S27	0N05	11N30	1N51
2 Su	7 09	27 44	4 19	27 06	16 32	0S07	16 33	0 41	26 15	2 48	16 19	1 42	22 26	0 05	11 32	1 51
3 M	6 46	26 08	3 34	24 51	16 25	0 17	16 13	0 43	26 14	2 47	16 26	1 40	22 25	0 05	11 34	1 51
4 Tu	6 23	23 13	2 39	21 18	16 16	0 27	15 52	0 45	26 13	2 46	16 34	1 37	22 23	0 05	11 36	1 51
5 W	5 59	19 05	1 33	16 37	16 06	0 36	15 31	0 48	26 12	2 45	16 41	1 34	22 22	0 05	11 37	1 51
6 Th	5 36	13 55	0 21	11 00	15 54	0 45	15 09	0 50	26 10	2 44	16 48	1 32	22 21	0 04	11 39	1 51
7 F	5 13	7 56	0N54	4 44	15 41	0 54	14 47	0 52	26 09	2 43	16 56	1 29	22 20	0 04	11 41	1 51
8 Sa	4 49	1 26	2 07	1N54	15 27	1 02	14 25	0 54	26 08	2 42	17 03	1 27	22 19	0 04	11 43	1 51
9 Su	4 26	5N15	3 14	8 32	15 11	1 10	14 02	0 56	26 07	2 41	17 10	1 24	22 18	0 04	11 44	1 51
10 M	4 02	11 44	4 10	14 47	14 54	1 17	13 39	0 58	26 05	2 40	17 17	1 21	22 17	0 04	11 46	1 51
11 Tu	3 39	17 37	4 49	20 13	14 36	1 24	13 15	1 00	26 04	2 39	17 25	1 19	22 16	0 04	11 48	1 51
12 W	3 15	22 30	5 11	24 26	14 16	1 31	12 51	1 02	26 02	2 37	17 32	1 16	22 14	0 04	11 49	1 51
13 Th	2 52	25 59	5 12	27 06	13 55	1 37	12 27	1 04	26 01	2 36	17 39	1 14	22 13	0 04	11 51	1 51
14 F	2 28	27 46	4 54	27 59	13 32	1 43	12 02	1 06	25 59	2 35	17 46	1 12	22 12	0 04	11 53	1 51
15 Sa	2 04	27 44	4 19	27 04	13 09	1 49	11 37	1 07	25 58	2 34	17 54	1 09	22 11	0 04	11 54	1 51
16 Su	1 41	25 58	3 29	24 30	12 43	1 54	11 12	1 09	25 56	2 33	18 01	1 07	22 10	0 03	11 56	1 51
17 M	1 17	22 41	2 28	20 36	12 17	1 58	10 47	1 11	25 54	2 32	18 08	1 04	22 09	0 03	11 57	1 51
18 Tu	0 53	18 15	1 20	15 42	11 50	2 02	10 21	1 12	25 52	2 31	18 15	1 02	22 08	0 03	11 59	1 51
19 W	0 29	13 00	0 09	10 11	11 21	2 06	9 54	1 14	25 50	2 30	18 22	0 60	22 07	0 03	12 00	1 51
20 Th	0 06	7 16	1S02	4 18	10 51	2 10	9 28	1 15	25 48	2 29	18 29	0 57	22 06	0 03	12 02	1 51
21 F	0N18	1 20	2 08	1S38	10 19	2 12	9 01	1 17	25 46	2 28	18 36	0 55	22 05	0 03	12 03	1 51
22 Sa	0 42	4S34	3 07	7 25	9 47	2 15	8 34	1 18	25 44	2 27	18 43	0 53	22 04	0 03	12 05	1 51
23 Su	1 05	10 11	3 56	12 50	9 13	2 17	8 07	1 19	25 42	2 26	18 50	0 50	22 03	0 03	12 06	1 51
24 M	1 29	15 21	4 33	17 41	8 38	2 18	7 40	1 20	25 39	2 25	18 57	0 48	22 02	0 03	12 07	1 51
25 Tu	1 52	19 50	4 58	21 47	8 02	2 20	7 12	1 22	25 37	2 24	19 04	0 46	22 01	0 03	12 09	1 51
26 W	2 16	23 29	5 09	24 57	7 25	2 20	6 45	1 23	25 34	2 23	19 11	0 44	21 60	0 02	12 10	1 51
27 Th	2 40	26 08	5 07	27 01	6 46	2 20	6 17	1 24	25 32	2 22	19 18	0 41	21 59	0 02	12 11	1 51
28 F	3 03	27 37	4 51	27 53	6 07	2 20	5 48	1 24	25 29	2 21	19 24	0 39	21 58	0 02	12 12	1 51
29 Sa	3 26	27 49	4 23	27 26	5 26	2 19	5 20	1 25	25 26	2 20	19 31	0 37	21 57	0 02	12 14	1 51
30 Su	3 50	26 43	3 44	25 41	4 44	2 18	4 52	1 26	25 23	2 19	19 38	0 35	21 56	0 02	12 15	1 51
31 M	4N13	24S20	2S53	22S40	4S01	2S16	4S23	1S27	25N20	2N18	19N45	0S33	21S55	0N02	12N16	1N51

Day	⚷ Decl	⚷ Lat	♅ Decl	♅ Lat	♆ Decl	♆ Lat	♇ Decl	♇ Lat
1	9S34	6N16	5S21	0S44	14S19	0S18	17S08	6N19
6	9 27	6 17	5 14	0 44	14 16	0 18	17 07	6 19
11	9 20	6 17	5 07	0 44	14 12	0 18	17 07	6 20
16	9 13	6 18	5 00	0 44	14 09	0 18	17 06	6 20
21	9 07	6 20	4 54	0 44	14 06	0 18	17 05	6 21
26	9 00	6 21	4 47	0 44	14 03	0 18	17 05	6 21
31	8S54	6N22	4S41	0S44	14S00	0S18	17S04	6N22

Day	⚴ Decl	⚴ Lat	⚵ Decl	⚵ Lat	⚶ Decl	⚶ Lat	Eris Decl	Eris Lat
1	6S04	6S08	10S60	12N19	12S51	3S50	4S50	13S56
6	5 40	6 29	10 44	12 37	11 60	3 56	4 49	13 55
11	5 16	6 50	10 27	12 56	11 08	4 01	4 47	13 54
16	4 52	7 12	10 08	13 16	10 16	4 06	4 46	13 54
21	4 28	7 34	9 49	13 36	9 24	4 11	4 44	13 53
26	4 05	7 57	9 28	13 58	8 32	4 17	4 43	13 53
31	3S41	8S20	9S06	14N20	7S40	4S23	4S41	13S53

Moon Phenomena

Max/0 Decl

dy	hr mn	
1	7:58	28S02
8	5:10	0 N
14	11:32	27N59
21	5:21	0 S
28	16:01	27S54

Max/0 Lat

dy	hr mn	
6	6:54	0 N
12	13:46	5N14
19	2:55	0 S
26	8:04	5S10

Perigee/Apogee

dy	hr m		kilometers
10	21:50	p	366299
26	20:18	a	405092

PH	dy	hr mn	
●	7	17:15	17♓31
☽	14	10:47	24♊14
○	21	18:41	1♎31
☾	29	21:48	9♑34

Void of Course Moon

Last Aspect			☽ Ingress		
1 16:55	♂	☍	♑	1	18:34
3 6:17	♅	⚹	♒	4	4:26
5 21:47	♆	☌	♓	6	10:54
7 19:05	♅	☌	♈	8	14:24
10 11:10	♀	⚹	♉	10	16:15
12 17:27	♀	□	♊	12	17:55
14 20:25	☿	△	♋	14	20:39
16 18:59	☉	△	♌	17	1:05
18 18:39	♆	☍	♍	19	7:26
20 19:29	♅	☍	♎	21	15:46
23 12:42	♆	△	♏	24	2:07
26 0:37	♆	□	♐	26	14:12
28 13:22	♆	⚹	♑	29	2:44
31 4:55	☿	⚹	♒	31	13:35

DAILY ASPECTARIAN

1 Sa	☽⚹♆ 3:32; ☿⚼♂ 7:14; ♀⊻♃ 8:33; ♀∠♇ 12:45; ☽☍♂ 16:55; ☽∠☿ 17:27; ☽☌♇ 20:19; ☽∠♀ 21:09; ☽∠⚷ 23:57
2 Su	☿∥♀ 2:00; ☽△♄ 3:40; ☽⚼⚳ 6:11; ☽∠♆ 9:16; ♀⋕⚳ 12:23; ☉⚹☽ 19:13; ☿⋕⚳ 21:39; ☽⋕♂ 23:03
3 M	☽⊻☿ 1:14; ☽☌♃ 1:44; ♀☌⚷ 2:08; ☽⊻⚷ 5:18; ☽⊻♀ 5:38; ☿∠♇ 6:16; ☽⚹♅ 6:17; ☽⚼♄ 8:35; ☿⊻♃ 8:47; ☽△⚳ 11:56; ♀⊻♅ 12:31; ☽⊻♆ 14:18
4 Tu	☉∠☽ 2:20; ♀ ♈ 2:23; ☽⊼♂ 4:17; ☽∥♃ 5:26; ☽⊻♇ 6:09; ♂ ♋ 10:02; ☽∠♅ 10:45; ☽⊼♄ 12:41
5 W	☿☌⚷ 5:37; ☉⊻☽ 8:21; ☽⚼♂ 8:38; ☽∥♇ 9:39; ☽∠♇ 9:47; ☽⊻♃ 10:34; ☽⋕⚳ 11:25; ☽☌⚷ 13:28; ☽☌☿ 14:08; ☽⊻♅ 14:20; ☽∥☿ 14:53; ☿⊻♅ 16:52; ☽∥♀ 18:12; ☽☌♀ 19:11; ☽□⚳ 20:43; ☽☌♆ 21:47; ☽∥♆ 22:29
6 Th	☽⋕♄ 9:20; ☽△♂ 12:05; ☽⚹♇ 12:35; ☽∠♃ 13:38; ♀□⚳ 16:52; ☽∥⚷ 18:11; ☽☍♄ 18:22; ☉⚹♃ 19:05
7 F	♀☌♆ 0:03; ☉∥♅ 0:18; ♂☍♇ 9:13; ☽∥♅ 10:15; ☉∥☽ 10:51; ☽⚹♃ 15:55; ☉☌☽ 17:15; ☽⊻⚷ 18:18; ☽☌♅ 19:05; ☽⊻☿ 23:16; ⚳□♆ 23:30
8 Sa	☽⊻♆ 2:03; ☽⚹⚳ 2:06; ☽⊻♀ 4:28; ☉⊻⚷ 8:59; ♀∥♆ 11:28; ⚳⋕♇ 12:52; ☽□♇ 16:03; ☽□♂ 16:47; ☽∠⚷ 19:46; ☉☌♅ 20:20; ☉⋕☽ 21:14; ☽⊼♄ 21:16; ☽⋕♅ 23:43
9 Su	☽∠☿ 2:49; ☽∠♆ 3:19; ☽∠⚳ 3:53; ☽∠♀ 8:00; ☿☌♆ 8:53; ☽⋕⚷ 15:05; ☽□♃ 18:53; ☿□⚳ 19:23; ☽⚹⚷ 20:51; ☽⊻♅ 21:34; ☽⚼♄ 22:05; ☉⊻☽ 23:20
10 M	☽∥♄ 0:08; ☽⚹♆ 4:16; ☽⊻⚳ 5:20; ☽⚹☿ 6:02; ☽⋕♀ 7:00; ☽⋕♆ 9:43; ☽⚹♀ 11:10; ☽⋕☿ 11:54; ☽△♇ 17:55; ☽⚹♂ 19:48; ☽⋕♇ 21:45; ☽∠♅ 22:27; ☽△♄ 22:44; ☽∥⚳ 23:03
11 Tu	☉∠☽ 1:57; ☽⚼♇ 18:43; ☽△♃ 21:00; ☽∠♂ 21:13; ☽⋕♃ 22:32; ☽□⚷ 22:40; ☽⚹♅ 23:21
12 W	☉⚹☽ 4:35; ☿∥♆ 5:04; ☽□♆ 5:59; ☽☌⚳ 8:05; ☽□☿ 12:28; ☽□♀ 17:27; ☽⊼♇ 19:39; ☽⚼♃ 22:13; ☽⊻♂ 22:48; ♀ ♓ 22:52
13 Th	☽□♄ 0:14; ☽∥♂ 0:16; ☉⊻♆ 1:28; ♀⚹♇ 19:10; ☽⊼♃ 23:43
14 F	☽△⚷ 1:06; ☽□♅ 1:46; ☽△♆ 8:30; ♀⋕♄ 8:50; ☉□☽ 10:47; ☽⊻⚳ 11:45; ♂⚼⚷ 18:19; ☽△☿ 20:25; ♂⚹♄ 21:25; ☽☍♇ 22:28; ☿ ♓ 22:47
15 Sa	☽△♀ 1:06; ☽⚼⚷ 2:52; ☽⚹♄ 2:53; ☽☌♂ 3:04; ☉⚹⚳ 6:49; ♀∠♃ 7:53; ☽⚼♆ 10:20; ☽∠⚳ 14:13; ☿⚹♇ 17:11; ♀☍♄ 20:17
16 Su	☽∥♂ 0:19; ☽⚼☿ 1:19; ☽☍♃ 3:59; ☽∠♄ 4:51; ☽⊼⚷ 5:05; ☽⚼♀ 5:45; ☽△♅ 5:45; ♀△♂ 8:22; ☽⊼♆ 12:37; ☽⚹⚳ 17:11; ☉△☽ 18:59
17 M	☽⊼♇ 3:00; ☽⋕♃ 3:16; ☿∠♃ 5:41; ☽⊼☿ 6:57; ☽⊻♄ 7:16; ☽⚼♅ 8:27; ☽⊻♂ 9:17; ☿☍♄ 9:48; ☽⊼♀ 11:02; ☿⋕♄ 16:30; ☉⚼☽ 23:59
18 Tu	☽∥⚳ 0:01; ☽⋕♇ 5:34; ☽⚼♇ 5:59; ☽⊼♃ 10:10; ♃⚼♄ 10:43; ☽☍⚷ 10:58; ☽⊼♅ 11:38; ☿△♂ 11:38; ☽∠♂ 13:12; ☽☍♆ 18:39; ☽⋕♆ 19:07
19 W	☽□⚳ 0:42; ☽∥♄ 4:16; ☉⊼☽ 5:35; ☽⋕☿ 7:46; ☽△♇ 9:28; ☽☌♄ 13:34; ☽⚼♃ 14:00; ☽⋕♀ 14:12; ☽⋕⚷ 16:18; ☽⚹♂ 17:39; ☽☍☿ 20:30; ☽☍♀ 23:32
20 Th	☉ ♈ 5:49; ☽⋕♅ 9:33; ☽△♃ 18:21; ☽⊼⚷ 18:50; ♀∥⚷ 19:00; ☽☍♅ 19:29
21 F	☽⊼♆ 2:40; ☉∥☽ 3:53; ☉⋕☽ 7:02; ☉□♇ 8:39; ☽△⚳ 10:22; ☽□♇ 17:54; ☉☍☽ 18:41; ☽⊻♄ 21:49; ☽⚼⚷ 23:31
22 Sa	☽∥♅ 1:17; ☽□♂ 4:16; ☽⚼♆ 7:26; ☽⊼☿ 13:16; ☽⊼♀ 14:45; ☽∥♀ 15:40; ☽⚼⚳ 16:02; ☽∥⚷ 19:06; ☽∥☿ 20:08
23 Su	☽∠♄ 2:42; ☽□♃ 4:35; ☽△⚷ 4:44; ☽⊼♅ 5:24; ☿∥⚷ 6:35; ☉⊼♄ 8:02; ☽⋕♄ 8:38; ☽△♆ 12:42; ☽∥♆ 17:49; ☽⊼⚳ 22:16; ☽⚼☿ 22:55; ☽⚼♀ 23:24
24 M	☽⚹♇ 4:21; ♃⊻⚷ 4:59; ☽⚹♄ 8:05; ☽∥♇ 8:50; ☉⊼☽ 10:22; ☽⚼♅ 11:06; ☉∠⚷ 11:23; ☿☌♀ 13:30; ☽△♂ 17:08; ☽⋕⚳ 19:27
25 Tu	☽△♀ 8:40; ☽△☿ 9:22; ☽∠♇ 10:16; ☽∥♃ 13:28; ☽□⚷ 16:34; ☽⚹♃ 16:47; ☽△♅ 17:14; ☉⚼☽ 19:03
26 W	☽⚼♂ 0:18; ☽□♆ 0:37; ♂⚼♆ 9:50; ☽☍⚳ 12:06; ☽⊻♇ 16:30; ☽⋕♂ 17:42; ☽□♄ 19:58; ☽∠♃ 23:22
27 Th	☉△☽ 4:05; ☽⊼♂ 7:44; ☿⊻⚷ 15:18; ☿⚹♃ 18:57; ☿☌♅ 20:09
28 F	☽□♀ 4:14; ☽⚹⚷ 5:27; ☽⊻♃ 6:00; ☽□♅ 6:06; ☽□☿ 7:41; ☽⚹♆ 13:22; ☉∠♆ 15:58; ♀⊻⚷ 16:23; ♀⚹♃ 22:55; ♀☌♅ 22:59
29 Sa	♃⚹♅ 0:18; ☽⊼⚳ 2:32; ☽☌♇ 5:01; ☽△♄ 8:09; ⚳ ♊ 9:23; ☿∥♀ 11:06; ☽∠⚷ 11:41; ☽∠♆ 19:26; ☉□☽ 21:48; ☽☍♂ 22:15; ☿⊻♆ 23:55
30 Su	☿∥♅ 1:19; ☉□♂ 7:22; ♀∥♅ 8:23; ☽⚼⚳ 9:13; ☽⚼♄ 13:41; ☽⋕♂ 15:09; ☽⊻⚷ 17:25; ☽⚹♅ 18:03; ☽☌♃ 18:16; ☉⋕☿ 19:50; ☽⚹♀ 22:38
31 M	☽⊻♆ 0:55; ☉⋕♀ 4:38; ☽⚹☿ 4:55; ☽△⚳ 15:09; ☽⊻♇ 15:47; ☽∥♃ 16:56; ☽⊼♄ 18:29; ♀⊻♆ 22:05; ☽∠♅ 22:59

April 2008 — LONGITUDE

Day	Sid.Time	☉	☽	☽ 12 hour	Mean☊	True☊	☿	♀	♂	⚳	♃	♄	⚷	♅	♆	♇
	h m s	° ' "	° ' "	° ' "	° '	° '	° '	° '	° '	° '	° '	° '	° '	° '	° '	° '
1 Tu	12 38 54	11♈38 23	5♒29 07	11♒53 27	25♒31.4	26♒49.6	26♓53.1	23♓32.2	10♋43.1	0♊57.1	20♑07.6	2♍33.7	19♒37.2	19♓56.7	23♒26.4	1♑08.9
2 W	12 42 51	12 37 35	18 23 44	25 00 21	25 28.2	26R 50.8	28 40.0	24 46.3	11 09.9	1 19.1	20 14.3	2R 30.5	19 40.4	19 59.9	23 28.1	1R 08.9
3 Th	12 46 47	13 36 46	1♓43 34	8♓33 32	25 25.0	26 51.0	0♈28.3	26 00.4	11 37.0	1 41.3	20 20.8	2 27.5	19 43.5	20 03.2	23 29.7	1 08.9
4 F	12 50 44	14 35 54	15 30 15	22 33 33	25 21.8	26 49.4	2 18.0	27 14.5	12 04.2	2 03.6	20 27.1	2 24.5	19 46.6	20 06.4	23 31.3	1 08.9
5 Sa	12 54 40	15 35 01	29 43 04	6♈58 14	25 18.6	26 45.7	4 09.2	28 28.6	12 31.7	2 25.9	20 33.3	2 21.6	19 49.6	20 09.6	23 32.9	1 08.8
6 Su	12 58 37	16 34 06	14♈18 22	21 42 32	25 15.5	26 39.9	6 01.8	29 42.7	12 59.3	2 48.3	20 39.3	2 18.8	19 52.6	20 12.7	23 34.5	1 08.7
7 M	13 02 33	17 33 08	29 09 43	6♉38 47	25 12.3	26 32.5	7 55.8	0♈56.8	13 27.1	3 10.8	20 45.2	2 16.1	19 55.6	20 15.9	23 36.0	1 08.6
8 Tu	13 06 30	18 32 09	14♉08 33	21 37 51	25 09.1	26 24.4	9 51.2	2 10.8	13 55.1	3 33.5	20 50.9	2 13.5	19 58.4	20 19.0	23 37.5	1 08.4
9 W	13 10 26	19 31 08	29 05 33	6♊30 38	25 05.9	26 16.7	11 48.1	3 24.9	14 23.3	3 56.2	20 56.4	2 11.0	20 01.3	20 22.1	23 39.0	1 08.3
10 Th	13 14 23	20 30 04	13♊52 13	21 09 34	25 02.8	26 10.3	13 46.3	4 39.0	14 51.6	4 18.9	21 01.8	2 08.6	20 04.1	20 25.2	23 40.5	1 08.0
11 F	13 18 20	21 28 59	28 22 08	5♋29 33	24 59.6	26 05.9	15 45.9	5 53.0	15 20.1	4 41.8	21 07.0	2 06.3	20 06.8	20 28.3	23 41.9	1 07.8
12 Sa	13 22 16	22 27 50	12♋31 36	19 28 15	24 56.4	26D 03.6	17 46.8	7 07.0	15 48.8	5 04.7	21 12.1	2 04.1	20 09.5	20 31.3	23 43.3	1 07.5
13 Su	13 26 13	23 26 40	26 19 32	3♌05 38	24 53.2	26 03.2	19 49.0	8 21.1	16 17.6	5 27.8	21 17.0	2 02.0	20 12.1	20 34.4	23 44.7	1 07.2
14 M	13 30 09	24 25 27	9♌46 48	16 23 19	24 50.1	26 03.9	21 52.3	9 35.1	16 46.6	5 50.9	21 21.7	1 59.9	20 14.7	20 37.4	23 46.0	1 06.8
15 Tu	13 34 06	25 24 12	22 55 30	29 23 43	24 46.9	26R 04.5	23 56.7	10 49.1	17 15.7	6 14.0	21 26.3	1 58.0	20 17.2	20 40.3	23 47.3	1 06.4
16 W	13 38 02	26 22 55	5♍48 18	12♍09 33	24 43.7	26 04.1	26 02.1	12 03.1	17 45.0	6 37.3	21 30.6	1 56.2	20 19.7	20 43.3	23 48.6	1 06.0
17 Th	13 41 59	27 21 35	18 27 47	24 43 16	24 40.5	26 01.7	28 08.3	13 17.0	18 14.4	7 00.6	21 34.8	1 54.5	20 22.1	20 46.2	23 49.9	1 05.6
18 F	13 45 55	28 20 13	0♎56 14	7♎06 54	24 37.3	25 56.8	0♉15.2	14 31.0	18 44.0	7 23.9	21 38.9	1 52.8	20 24.4	20 49.1	23 51.1	1 05.1
19 Sa	13 49 52	29 18 50	13 15 28	19 22 04	24 34.2	25 49.2	2 22.5	15 45.0	19 13.6	7 47.4	21 42.8	1 51.3	20 26.7	20 52.0	23 52.3	1 04.6
20 Su	13 53 49	0♉17 24	25 26 51	1♏29 57	24 31.0	25 39.2	4 30.0	16 58.9	19 43.5	8 10.9	21 46.4	1 49.9	20 29.0	20 54.8	23 53.5	1 04.1
21 M	13 57 45	1 15 56	7♏31 29	13 31 36	24 27.8	25 27.5	6 37.5	18 12.9	20 13.4	8 34.5	21 50.0	1 48.5	20 31.1	20 57.6	23 54.7	1 03.5
22 Tu	14 01 42	2 14 27	19 30 27	25 28 12	24 24.6	25 15.0	8 44.6	19 26.8	20 43.5	8 58.1	21 53.3	1 47.3	20 33.3	21 00.4	23 55.8	1 02.9
23 W	14 05 38	3 12 55	1♐25 03	7♐21 14	24 21.4	25 02.8	10 51.2	20 40.8	21 13.7	9 21.9	21 56.5	1 46.2	20 35.3	21 03.2	23 56.9	1 02.3
24 Th	14 09 35	4 11 22	13 17 03	19 12 47	24 18.3	24 51.9	12 56.8	21 54.7	21 44.0	9 45.6	21 59.5	1 45.2	20 37.4	21 05.9	23 57.9	1 01.7
25 F	14 13 31	5 09 47	25 08 50	1♑05 36	24 15.1	24 43.1	15 01.3	23 08.6	22 14.5	10 09.5	22 02.3	1 44.3	20 39.3	21 08.6	23 59.0	1 01.0
26 Sa	14 17 28	6 08 11	7♑03 34	13 03 12	24 11.9	24 36.9	17 04.1	24 22.5	22 45.1	10 33.4	22 04.9	1 43.5	20 41.2	21 11.3	24 00.0	1 00.3
27 Su	14 21 24	7 06 33	19 05 05	25 09 47	24 08.7	24 33.3	19 05.2	25 36.5	23 15.8	10 57.4	22 07.3	1 42.8	20 43.0	21 13.9	24 00.9	0 59.6
28 M	14 25 21	8 04 53	1♒17 54	7♒30 05	24 05.6	24D 31.8	21 04.0	26 50.4	23 46.6	11 21.4	22 09.6	1 42.2	20 44.8	21 16.5	24 01.9	0 58.8
29 Tu	14 29 18	9 03 12	13 46 55	20 09 04	24 02.4	24R 31.7	23 00.4	28 04.3	24 17.5	11 45.5	22 11.7	1 41.7	20 46.5	21 19.1	24 02.8	0 58.1
30 W	14 33 14	10♉01 30	26 37 04	3♓11 29	23♒59.2	24♒31.8	24♉54.2	29♈18.2	24♋48.6	12♊09.6	22♑13.5	1♍41.3	20♒48.2	21♓21.7	24♒03.7	0♑57.2

1st of Month

Julian Day # 2454557.5
Obliquity 23°26'26"
SVP 5♓08'31"
GC 26♐57.3
Eris 21♈00.0

Day	⚴	⚵	⚶
1	10♈26.5	28♐51.8	21♓18.2
6	12 22.1	29 15.1	23 42.1
11	14 18.5	29 30.9	26 04.9
16	16 15.7	29 39.0	28 26.3
21	18 13.4	29 39.0R	0♈46.3
26	20 11.7	29 30.8R	3 04.9

DECLINATION and LATITUDE

Day	☉ Decl	☽ Decl	☽ Lat	☽12h Decl	☿ Decl	☿ Lat	♀ Decl	♀ Lat	♂ Decl	♂ Lat	⚳ Decl	⚳ Lat	♃ Decl	♃ Lat	♄ Decl	♄ Lat
1 Tu	4N36	20S43	1S53	18S30	3S17	2S14	3S54	1S27	25N17	2N17	19N51	0S30	21S54	0N02	12N17	1N51
2 W	4 59	16 02	0 46	13 10	2 32	2 12	3 25	1 28	25 14	2 16	19 58	0 28	21 53	0 02	12 18	1 51
3 Th	5 22	10 27	0N26	7 23	1 46	2 08	2 56	1 29	25 11	2 16	20 04	0 26	21 52	0 02	12 19	1 51
4 F	5 45	4 12	1 39	0 54	0 59	2 05	2 27	1 29	25 08	2 15	20 11	0 24	21 51	0 02	12 20	1 51
5 Sa	6 08	2N27	2 47	5N48	0 11	2 00	1 58	1 29	25 04	2 14	20 17	0 22	21 51	0 01	12 21	1 51
6 Su	6 31	9 07	3 47	12 21	0N37	1 56	1 29	1 30	25 00	2 13	20 24	0 20	21 50	0 01	12 22	1 50
7 M	6 53	15 25	4 32	18 16	1 27	1 50	0 60	1 30	24 57	2 12	20 30	0 18	21 49	0 01	12 23	1 50
8 Tu	7 16	20 50	4 59	23 04	2 18	1 45	0 31	1 30	24 53	2 11	20 37	0 16	21 48	0 01	12 24	1 50
9 W	7 38	24 55	5 05	26 20	3 09	1 38	0 01	1 30	24 49	2 10	20 43	0 14	21 48	0 01	12 25	1 50
10 Th	8 01	27 17	4 52	27 46	4 01	1 32	0N28	1 30	24 45	2 09	20 49	0 11	21 47	0 01	12 26	1 50
11 F	8 23	27 45	4 19	27 16	4 54	1 25	0 57	1 30	24 41	2 08	20 55	0 09	21 46	0 01	12 26	1 50
12 Sa	8 45	26 21	3 31	25 03	5 48	1 17	1 27	1 30	24 37	2 07	21 02	0 07	21 46	0 01	12 27	1 50
13 Su	9 06	23 23	2 32	21 25	6 41	1 09	1 56	1 30	24 32	2 06	21 08	0 05	21 45	0 01	12 28	1 50
14 M	9 28	19 11	1 26	16 45	7 36	1 00	2 25	1 30	24 28	2 06	21 14	0 03	21 44	0 00	12 28	1 50
15 Tu	9 50	14 08	0 17	11 24	8 30	0 51	2 55	1 29	24 23	2 05	21 20	0 01	21 44	0 00	12 29	1 50
16 W	10 11	8 35	0S52	5 42	9 25	0 42	3 24	1 29	24 19	2 04	21 26	0N01	21 43	0 00	12 29	1 50
17 Th	10 32	2 47	1 56	0S09	10 19	0 32	3 53	1 29	24 14	2 03	21 31	0 03	21 43	0 00	12 30	1 49
18 F	10 53	3S02	2 53	5 53	11 13	0 22	4 22	1 28	24 09	2 02	21 37	0 05	21 42	0S00	12 30	1 49
19 Sa	11 14	8 40	3 43	11 20	12 07	0 11	4 51	1 28	24 04	2 01	21 43	0 07	21 42	0 00	12 31	1 49
20 Su	11 34	13 54	4 21	16 18	13 01	0 01	5 20	1 27	23 59	2 00	21 49	0 08	21 41	0 00	12 31	1 49
21 M	11 55	18 33	4 47	20 35	13 53	0N10	5 49	1 26	23 53	1 60	21 54	0 10	21 41	0 00	12 32	1 49
22 Tu	12 15	22 25	5 00	24 00	14 45	0 21	6 17	1 26	23 48	1 59	21 60	0 12	21 40	0 01	12 32	1 49
23 W	12 35	25 20	4 60	26 23	15 35	0 32	6 46	1 25	23 42	1 58	22 05	0 14	21 40	0 01	12 32	1 49
24 Th	12 55	27 08	4 46	27 34	16 24	0 43	7 14	1 24	23 37	1 57	22 11	0 16	21 39	0 01	12 33	1 49
25 F	13 15	27 42	4 21	27 30	17 11	0 53	7 43	1 23	23 31	1 56	22 16	0 18	21 39	0 01	12 33	1 49
26 Sa	13 34	26 58	3 44	26 08	17 57	1 04	8 11	1 22	23 25	1 55	22 22	0 20	21 39	0 01	12 33	1 49
27 Su	13 53	24 59	2 56	23 33	18 41	1 14	8 39	1 21	23 19	1 55	22 27	0 22	21 39	0 01	12 33	1 48
28 M	14 12	21 49	1 60	19 50	19 22	1 23	9 06	1 20	23 13	1 54	22 32	0 24	21 38	0 01	12 33	1 48
29 Tu	14 31	17 36	0 57	15 08	20 01	1 33	9 34	1 19	23 07	1 53	22 37	0 26	21 38	0 01	12 33	1 48
30 W	14N49	12S28	0N11	9S37	20N38	1N42	10N01	1S18	23N00	1N52	22N42	0N28	21S38	0S02	12N33	1N48

Day	⚷ Decl	⚷ Lat	♅ Decl	♅ Lat	♆ Decl	♆ Lat	♇ Decl	♇ Lat
1	8S52	6N22	4S40	0S44	13S60	0S18	17S04	6N22
6	8 46	6 24	4 33	0 44	13 57	0 18	17 04	6 22
11	8 40	6 26	4 27	0 44	13 55	0 18	17 03	6 23
16	8 35	6 28	4 21	0 44	13 53	0 19	17 03	6 23
21	8 30	6 29	4 16	0 44	13 51	0 19	17 02	6 24
26	8 25	6 31	4 11	0 45	13 49	0 19	17 02	6 24

Day	⚴ Decl	⚴ Lat	⚵ Decl	⚵ Lat	⚶ Decl	⚶ Lat	Eris Decl	Eris Lat
1	3S36	8S25	9S02	14N24	7S29	4S24	4S41	13S53
6	3 14	8 48	8 39	14 47	6 37	4 29	4 40	13 52
11	2 51	9 13	8 16	15 10	5 46	4 35	4 38	13 52
16	2 30	9 38	7 53	15 34	4 55	4 41	4 37	13 52
21	2 10	10 03	7 29	15 57	4 05	4 47	4 36	13 52
26	1 50	10 30	7 06	16 20	3 16	4 53	4 34	13 52

Moon Phenomena

Max/0 Decl
dy hr mn
4 15:14 0 N
10 17:51 27N48
17 11:24 0 S
24 22:41 27S42

Perigee/Apogee
dy hr m kilometers
7 19:41 p 361082
23 9:34 a 405943

PH dy hr mn
● 6 3:56 16♈44
☽ 12 18:33 23♋13
○ 20 10:26 0♏43
☾ 28 14:13 8♒39

Max/0 Lat
dy hr mn
2 15:18 0 N
8 19:39 5N06
15 5:50 0 S
22 11:21 5S02
29 20:08 0 N

Void of Course Moon

Last Aspect			☽ Ingress		
2	9:15	♆ ☌	♓	2	20:56
4	21:44	♀ ☌	♈	5	0:28
6	15:02	♆ ⚹	♉	7	1:21
8	15:14	♆ □	♊	9	1:28
10	16:12	♆ △	♋	11	2:44
12	18:33	☉ □	♌	13	6:30
15	4:57	☉ △	♍	15	13:08
17	6:00	♃ △	♎	17	22:11
19	20:55	♆ △	♏	20	9:01
22	8:55	♆ □	♐	22	21:08
24	21:39	♆ ⚹	♑	25	9:48
27	14:19	♀ □	♒	27	21:28
30	5:26	♀ ⚹	♓	30	6:12

DAILY ASPECTARIAN

1 Tu
☉⋕♅ 3:17
☽⋕⚳ 4:45
☽∠♀ 6:21
☽⚻♂ 10:10
☉⚹☽ 12:29
⚳⚻♇ 12:55
☽∠☿ 13:54
☽∥♇ 19:07
☽∠♇ 19:53

2 W
☽☌⚷ 2:21
☽⚺♅ 2:56
☽⚺♃ 3:24
☽∥♆ 9:14
☽☌♆ 9:15
♇ R 9:24
☽⚺♀ 12:46
☽⚼♂ 14:34
☽⋕♄ 16:21
☿ ♈ 17:46
☉∠☽ 18:02
☽⚺☿ 21:26
☽⚹♇ 22:59
☽□⚳ 23:56

3 Th
☽☍♄ 1:17
☽∠♃ 6:26
☽∥⚷ 6:26
☿□♇ 8:56
☽△♂ 17:53
☉⋕☽ 18:31
☿⚹⚳ 20:03
☉⚺☽ 22:20
☽∥♅ 22:31

4 F
☿⚻♄ 1:22
☽∥♀ 6:52
☽⚺⚷ 7:19
☽☌♅ 7:53
☽⚹♃ 8:30
☽∥☿ 13:15
☽⚺♆ 13:39
☽⋕☿ 16:47
⚳□♄ 19:57
☽☌♀ 21:44
☽⋕♀ 22:25

5 Sa
☽□♇ 2:23
☽⚻♄ 4:22
☽⚹⚳ 4:38
☽⋕♅ 7:34
☽☌☿ 8:26
☽∠⚷ 8:30
☿∠⚷ 8:54
☉∥☽ 13:58
☽∠♆ 14:37
☽□♂ 21:47
☽⋕⚷ 22:43

6 Su
☉☌☽ 3:56
☽⚼♄ 4:52
♀ ♈ 5:36
☽∠⚳ 5:50
☽⚹⚷ 9:04
☽⚺♅ 9:37
☽□♃ 10:22
☽∥♄ 12:07
☽⚹♆ 15:02
☿⋕♀ 15:43
☉⚼♄ 17:23
☽⋕♆ 18:10

7 M
☽⚺♀ 3:07
☽△♇ 3:11
♀□♇ 3:50
☽△♄ 4:58
☽⚺⚳ 6:37
☽⋕♇ 6:49
☿∠♆ 8:30
☽∠♅ 9:49
☽⚺☿ 16:07
☽∥⚳ 22:52
☽⚹♂ 23:38

8 Tu
♀⚻♄ 0:51
☉∠⚳ 0:52
☽⚼♇ 3:12
☽⋕♃ 4:58
☽∠♀ 5:18
☉⚺☽ 7:32
☽□⚷ 9:22
☽⚹♅ 9:56
☽△♃ 10:49
☽□♆ 15:14
☽∠☿ 19:45
☽∥♂ 23:16

9 W
☽∠♂ 0:29
☽⚻♇ 3:18
☽□♄ 4:59
☽⚹♀ 7:37
☽☌⚳ 8:02
☉∠☽ 9:24
☽⚼♃ 11:09
☉⚹⚷ 12:53
♀⚹⚳ 14:37
☉⚺♅ 21:55
☽⚹☿ 23:49

10 Th
☽⚺♂ 1:41
♀∠⚷ 8:27
☽△⚷ 10:14
☽□♅ 10:49
☉⚹☽ 11:42
☽⚻♃ 11:52
☿⋕♅ 12:01
☉□♃ 14:12
☽△♆ 16:12
☿□♂ 17:14

11 F
☽☍♇ 4:38
☽⚹♄ 6:16
☽⚺⚳ 10:57
☽⚼⚷ 11:24
☽□♀ 13:53
☿⚼♄ 15:42
☽⚼♆ 17:29
☉⋕⚷ 18:28

12 Sa
☽☌♂ 5:52
☽∠♄ 7:49
☽□☿ 10:37
☽⚻⚷ 13:14
☽∠⚳ 13:26
☽△♅ 13:53
☽☍♃ 15:06
☽∥♂ 15:42
☉□☽ 18:33
☽⚻♆ 19:27

13 Su
☿⚹⚷ 4:37
☉⚹♆ 7:31
♀∠♆ 7:48
☽⚻♇ 8:29
☿⚺♅ 9:05
☿∠⚳ 9:19
☽⋕♃ 10:05
☽⚺♄ 10:05
☽∥⚳ 13:17
☽⚼♅ 16:30
☽⚹⚳ 16:43
☿□♃ 17:50
☽△♀ 23:37

14 M
♂∠♄ 10:19
☽⋕♇ 10:34
☽⚼♇ 11:30
☽⚺♂ 13:12
☽☍⚷ 19:08
☽⚻♅ 19:50
☽⚻♃ 21:15
☿⚹♆ 22:11

15 Tu
☽⋕♆ 1:09
☽☍♆ 1:36
☽△☿ 2:15
☿⋕⚷ 2:31
☉△☽ 4:57
☽⚼♀ 5:55
☽∥♄ 7:20
☽△♇ 15:11
⚳⚼♃ 15:36
☽☌♄ 16:46
☉∥☽ 17:39

16 W
☽⚼♃ 1:20
☽□⚳ 1:35
☉☌☿ 7:25
☉⚼☽ 11:24
☽⚼☿ 11:50
☽⚻♀ 13:04
☽⋕♅ 17:34
☽∥♀ 19:48
☽⚹♂ 23:33

17 Th
☽⚻⚷ 3:39
☽☍♅ 4:26
☽△♃ 6:00
☉∥☿ 9:17
☽⚻♆ 10:18
☉⚻☽ 18:33
☿ ♉ 21:08
♀⋕♅ 21:42
☽⚻☿ 22:24

18 F
☽□♇ 0:17
☽⚺♄ 1:49
☽∥♅ 5:20
☽⋕♀ 6:04
☽⚼⚷ 8:42
☿△♇ 9:23
⚵ R 12:50
☽△⚳ 12:58
☽⚼♆ 15:25
⚳⋕♃ 18:09
☿△♄ 18:12
☽∠♂ 18:02
☽∥☿ 21:00
☽⋕⚷ 24:00
☽∥⚷ 23:24

19 Sa
☽☍♀ 5:26
☽∠♄ 7:03
⚶ ♈ 8:09
☿∥♄ 10:41
☽□♂ 12:13
☉⋕☽ 12:18
☽△⚷ 14:10
☽⚻♅ 15:01
☽□♃ 16:42
☉ ♉ 16:52
☽⋕♄ 17:28
☽⋕☿ 18:53
☽⚼⚳ 19:22
☽△♆ 20:55
♀⚼♄ 21:07
☽∥♆ 23:47

20 Su
☉☍☽ 10:26
☽⚹♇ 11:08
☽⚹♄ 12:38
☽∥♇ 15:50
☿∠♅ 16:20
☉△♇ 18:58
☽⚼♅ 20:52
☽☍☿ 21:49
☿⋕♆ 22:52

21 M
☽⚻⚳ 2:10
☉△♄ 13:06
♂⚻⚷ 15:14
☽∠♇ 17:04
☽∥♃ 18:55
☽⋕⚳ 21:02
☽⚻♀ 23:52

22 Tu
☽□⚷ 2:07
☽△♂ 2:33
☽△♅ 3:02
☿⚺⚳ 3:09
☽⚹♃ 4:49
☽□♆ 8:55
☽⋕♂ 10:01
♂△♅ 14:49
☉∥♄ 20:37
♀⚹⚷ 22:11
☽⚺♇ 23:14

23 W
☽□♄ 0:43
☉⚻☽ 3:57
♀⚺♅ 7:34
☽⚼♀ 9:37
☽⚼♂ 10:09
☽∠♃ 11:13
☽☍⚳ 16:37
♀□♂ 18:08
☽⚻☿ 23:10

24 Th
♀□♃ 1:37
☉⚼☽ 13:01
♂☍♃ 13:24
☽⚹⚷ 14:54
☽□♅ 15:53
☽⚺♃ 17:41
☽⚻♂ 17:52
☿⋕♇ 19:11
☽△♀ 19:29
☽⚹♆ 21:39

25 F
☿⚼♇ 11:34
☽☌♇ 11:50
☽⚼☿ 11:54
☽△♄ 13:17
♀⚹♆ 16:35
☽∠⚷ 21:14
☉△☽ 21:59

26 Sa
☉∠♅ 1:20
☽∠♆ 3:54
☽⚻⚳ 7:15
♀⋕⚷ 11:41
☉⋕♆ 18:30
☽⚼♄ 19:18

27 Su
☽△☿ 0:00
☽⚺⚷ 3:14
☽⚹♅ 4:16
☽☌♃ 6:02
☽☍♂ 8:37
☽⚺♆ 9:45
♀∠⚳ 10:03
☽⚼⚳ 14:01
☽⋕♂ 14:07
☽□♀ 14:19
☽⋕⚳ 19:21
☿□⚷ 20:02
☽⚺♇ 23:23

28 M
☽⚻♄ 0:47
☽∥♃ 1:10
☿⚹♅ 2:37
☽∠♅ 9:40
♂⚻♆ 12:15
☽⋕☿ 12:38
☿△♃ 13:42
☉□☽ 14:13
☽△⚳ 20:01

29 Tu
☽∥♇ 2:51
☽∠♇ 4:08
☿□♆ 13:11
☽☌⚷ 13:12
☉⋕☽ 14:02
☽⚺♅ 14:14
☽⚺♃ 15:51
☽∥♆ 18:07
☽☌♆ 19:16
☽□☿ 20:18
☽⚻♂ 20:31
☿⚹♂ 22:20
☽⋕♄ 23:37

30 W
☽⚹♀ 5:26
☽⚹♇ 7:56
☽☍♄ 9:16
☽⋕♀ 9:38
♀ ♉ 13:35
☽∥⚷ 17:12
☽∠♃ 19:18

May 2008

LONGITUDE

Day	Sid.Time	☉	☽	☽ 12 hour	Mean☊	True☊	☿	♀	♂	⚳	♃	♄	⚷	♅	♆	♇
	h m s	° ' "	° ' "	° ' "	° '	° '	° '	° '	° '	° '	° '	° '	° '	° '	° '	° '
1 Th	14 37 11	10♉59 45	9♓52 44	16♓41 11	23♒56.0	24♒31.0	26♉45.0	0♉32.1	25♋19.7	12♊33.8	22♑15.3	1♍41.0	20♒49.8	21♓24.2	24♒04.5	0♑56.4
2 F	14 41 07	11 57 59	23 37 01	0♈40 15	23 52.9	24R 28.4	28 32.7	1 45.9	25 51.0	12 58.1	22 16.8	1R 40.9	20 51.3	21 26.7	24 05.3	0R 55.6
3 Sa	14 45 04	12 56 12	7♈50 44	15 08 04	23 49.7	24 23.2	0♊17.1	2 59.8	26 22.3	13 22.4	22 18.1	1D 40.8	20 52.8	21 29.1	24 06.1	0 54.7
4 Su	14 49 00	13 54 23	22 31 38	0♉00 34	23 46.5	24 15.4	1 58.0	4 13.7	26 53.8	13 46.8	22 19.2	1 40.8	20 54.2	21 31.5	24 06.9	0 53.8
5 M	14 52 57	14 52 33	7♉33 49	15 10 08	23 43.3	24 05.5	3 35.3	5 27.6	27 25.4	14 11.2	22 20.2	1 41.0	20 55.5	21 33.9	24 07.6	0 52.8
6 Tu	14 56 53	15 50 41	22 48 09	0♊26 26	23 40.1	23 54.6	5 09.0	6 41.4	27 57.1	14 35.6	22 20.9	1 41.2	20 56.8	21 36.2	24 08.3	0 51.9
7 W	15 00 50	16 48 47	8♊03 34	15 38 11	23 37.0	23 44.0	6 38.8	7 55.3	28 28.9	15 00.2	22 21.5	1 41.6	20 58.0	21 38.5	24 09.0	0 50.9
8 Th	15 04 47	17 46 52	23 09 05	0♋35 12	23 33.8	23 34.8	8 04.7	9 09.1	29 00.8	15 24.7	22 21.9	1 42.1	20 59.2	21 40.8	24 09.6	0 49.9
9 F	15 08 43	18 44 55	7♋55 44	15 10 03	23 30.6	23 28.1	9 26.7	10 23.0	29 32.8	15 49.4	22R 22.1	1 42.7	21 00.3	21 43.0	24 10.2	0 48.8
10 Sa	15 12 40	19 42 56	22 17 49	29 18 49	23 27.4	23 24.0	10 44.6	11 36.8	0♌04.9	16 14.0	22 22.1	1 43.3	21 01.3	21 45.2	24 10.7	0 47.8
11 Su	15 16 36	20 40 55	6♌13 05	13♌00 46	23 24.3	23 22.2	11 58.4	12 50.6	0 37.1	16 38.7	22 21.9	1 44.1	21 02.3	21 47.4	24 11.3	0 46.7
12 M	15 20 33	21 38 52	19 42 11	26 17 40	23 21.1	23 21.8	13 08.0	14 04.5	1 09.3	17 03.5	22 21.5	1 45.0	21 03.2	21 49.5	24 11.8	0 45.6
13 Tu	15 24 29	22 36 48	2♍47 42	9♍12 44	23 17.9	23 21.7	14 13.4	15 18.3	1 41.7	17 28.3	22 20.9	1 46.0	21 04.0	21 51.6	24 12.2	0 44.5
14 W	15 28 26	23 34 41	15 33 17	21 49 49	23 14.7	23 20.6	15 14.5	16 32.1	2 14.2	17 53.1	22 20.2	1 47.1	21 04.8	21 53.6	24 12.7	0 43.4
15 Th	15 32 23	24 32 33	28 02 51	4♎12 48	23 11.6	23 17.6	16 11.3	17 45.8	2 46.7	18 18.0	22 19.2	1 48.3	21 05.5	21 55.6	24 13.0	0 42.2
16 F	15 36 19	25 30 23	10♎20 07	16 25 09	23 08.4	23 11.9	17 03.6	18 59.6	3 19.3	18 42.9	22 18.1	1 49.6	21 06.1	21 57.5	24 13.4	0 41.0
17 Sa	15 40 16	26 28 11	22 28 16	28 29 46	23 05.2	23 03.3	17 51.4	20 13.4	3 52.0	19 07.9	22 16.8	1 51.0	21 06.7	21 59.4	24 13.7	0 39.8
18 Su	15 44 12	27 25 58	4♏29 54	10♏28 55	23 02.0	22 52.2	18 34.7	21 27.2	4 24.8	19 32.9	22 15.3	1 52.5	21 07.2	22 01.3	24 14.0	0 38.6
19 M	15 48 09	28 23 43	16 27 01	22 24 22	22 58.8	22 39.2	19 13.3	22 40.9	4 57.6	19 57.9	22 13.6	1 54.1	21 07.7	22 03.2	24 14.3	0 37.4
20 Tu	15 52 05	29 21 27	28 21 10	4♐17 33	22 55.7	22 25.3	19 47.3	23 54.7	5 30.6	20 23.0	22 11.7	1 55.9	21 08.1	22 04.9	24 14.5	0 36.1
21 W	15 56 02	0♊19 09	10♐13 43	16 09 50	22 52.5	22 11.7	20 16.6	25 08.4	6 03.6	20 48.1	22 09.7	1 57.7	21 08.4	22 06.7	24 14.7	0 34.8
22 Th	15 59 58	1 16 51	22 06 06	28 02 45	22 49.3	21 59.4	20 41.1	26 22.2	6 36.7	21 13.3	22 07.4	1 59.6	21 08.6	22 08.4	24 14.9	0 33.5
23 F	16 03 55	2 14 31	4♑00 01	9♑58 14	22 46.1	21 49.4	21 00.8	27 35.9	7 09.9	21 38.4	22 05.0	2 01.6	21 08.8	22 10.1	24 15.1	0 32.2
24 Sa	16 07 52	3 12 10	15 57 44	21 58 53	22 43.0	21 42.1	21 15.8	28 49.7	7 43.1	22 03.7	22 02.4	2 03.7	21 09.0	22 11.7	24 15.2	0 30.9
25 Su	16 11 48	4 09 47	28 02 07	4♒07 53	22 39.8	21 37.6	21 25.9	0♊03.4	8 16.4	22 28.9	21 59.6	2 06.0	21R 09.0	22 13.3	24 15.2	0 29.6
26 M	16 15 45	5 07 24	10♒16 42	16 29 07	22 36.6	21D 35.5	21R 31.3	1 17.2	8 49.8	22 54.2	21 56.6	2 08.3	21 09.0	22 14.8	24R 15.3	0 28.2
27 Tu	16 19 41	6 05 00	22 45 40	29 06 55	22 33.4	21 35.1	21 32.1	2 30.9	9 23.3	23 19.5	21 53.5	2 10.7	21 09.0	22 16.3	24 15.3	0 26.9
28 W	16 23 38	7 02 35	5♓33 26	12♓05 45	22 30.3	21R 35.3	21 28.2	3 44.6	9 56.8	23 44.9	21 50.2	2 13.2	21 08.8	22 17.7	24 15.2	0 25.5
29 Th	16 27 34	8 00 09	18 44 20	25 29 37	22 27.1	21 34.9	21 20.0	4 58.4	10 30.4	24 10.3	21 46.7	2 15.8	21 08.6	22 19.1	24 15.2	0 24.1
30 F	16 31 31	8 57 42	2♈21 55	9♈21 22	22 23.9	21 33.0	21 07.6	6 12.1	11 04.1	24 35.7	21 43.0	2 18.5	21 08.4	22 20.5	24 15.1	0 22.7
31 Sa	16 35 27	9♊55 14	16 27 59	23 41 35	22♒20.7	21♒28.8	20♊51.2	7♊25.9	11♌37.9	25♊01.1	21♑39.2	2♍21.3	21♒08.0	22♓21.8	24♒15.0	0♑21.2

1st of Month

Julian Day # 2454587.5
Obliquity 23°26'25"
SVP 5♓08'27"
GC 26♐57.3
Eris 21♈19.5

Day	⚴
1	22♈10.6
6	24 10.0
11	26 09.7
16	28 09.8
21	0♉10.1
26	2 10.6
31	4 11.3

Day	⚵
1	29♐14.3R
6	28 49.3R
11	28 16.1R
16	27 35.0R
21	26 46.8R
26	25 52.2R
31	24 52.0R

Day	⚶
1	5♈21.9
6	7 37.3
11	9 50.9
16	12 02.4
21	14 12.0
26	16 19.4
31	18 24.5

DECLINATION and LATITUDE

Day	☉ Decl	☽ Decl	☽ Lat	☽ 12h Decl	☿ Decl	☿ Lat	♀ Decl	♀ Lat	♂ Decl	♂ Lat	⚳ Decl	⚳ Lat	♃ Decl	♃ Lat	♄ Decl	♄ Lat
1 Th	15N08	6S37	1N20	3S30	21N13	1N50	10N28	1S16	22N54	1N51	22N47	0N29	21S38	0S02	12N33	1N48
2 F	15 26	0 17	2 27	2N60	21 45	1 57	10 55	1 15	22 47	1 51	22 52	0 31	21 38	0 02	12 33	1 48
3 Sa	15 43	6N17	3 28	9 33	22 14	2 04	11 22	1 14	22 41	1 50	22 57	0 33	21 38	0 02	12 33	1 48
4 Su	16 01	12 43	4 16	15 45	22 41	2 10	11 48	1 12	22 34	1 49	23 02	0 35	21 37	0 02	12 33	1 48
5 M	16 18	18 34	4 48	21 07	23 06	2 16	12 14	1 11	22 27	1 48	23 07	0 37	21 37	0 02	12 33	1 47
6 Tu	16 35	23 19	5 00	25 06	23 28	2 20	12 40	1 09	22 20	1 48	23 12	0 39	21 37	0 02	12 33	1 47
7 W	16 52	26 26	4 51	27 17	23 47	2 24	13 05	1 08	22 12	1 47	23 16	0 41	21 38	0 02	12 33	1 47
8 Th	17 08	27 37	4 22	27 27	24 04	2 27	13 30	1 06	22 05	1 46	23 21	0 42	21 38	0 03	12 32	1 47
9 F	17 24	26 47	3 35	25 40	24 19	2 29	13 55	1 04	21 58	1 45	23 25	0 44	21 38	0 03	12 32	1 47
10 Sa	17 40	24 10	2 36	22 18	24 32	2 30	14 20	1 03	21 50	1 44	23 30	0 46	21 38	0 03	12 32	1 47
11 Su	17 55	20 10	1 29	17 47	24 42	2 30	14 44	1 01	21 42	1 44	23 34	0 48	21 38	0 03	12 31	1 47
12 M	18 11	15 13	0 19	12 31	24 51	2 29	15 07	0 59	21 35	1 43	23 38	0 50	21 38	0 03	12 31	1 47
13 Tu	18 26	9 42	0S50	6 50	24 57	2 28	15 31	0 57	21 27	1 42	23 42	0 52	21 38	0 03	12 30	1 47
14 W	18 40	3 56	1 54	1 02	25 01	2 25	15 54	0 55	21 19	1 41	23 46	0 53	21 39	0 03	12 30	1 46
15 Th	18 54	1S51	2 52	4S42	25 04	2 21	16 16	0 53	21 10	1 41	23 50	0 55	21 39	0 04	12 29	1 46
16 F	19 08	7 28	3 41	10 10	25 04	2 16	16 39	0 51	21 02	1 40	23 54	0 57	21 39	0 04	12 29	1 46
17 Sa	19 22	12 45	4 19	15 11	25 03	2 11	17 00	0 50	20 54	1 39	23 58	0 59	21 40	0 04	12 28	1 46
18 Su	19 35	17 29	4 45	19 36	25 00	2 04	17 22	0 47	20 45	1 39	24 02	1 01	21 40	0 04	12 27	1 46
19 M	19 48	21 30	4 58	23 12	24 56	1 56	17 43	0 45	20 36	1 38	24 06	1 02	21 40	0 04	12 27	1 46
20 Tu	20 01	24 38	4 58	25 48	24 50	1 48	18 03	0 43	20 28	1 37	24 09	1 04	21 41	0 04	12 26	1 46
21 W	20 13	26 41	4 45	27 16	24 43	1 38	18 23	0 41	20 19	1 36	24 13	1 06	21 41	0 04	12 25	1 46
22 Th	20 25	27 32	4 20	27 28	24 34	1 27	18 43	0 39	20 10	1 36	24 16	1 08	21 42	0 04	12 24	1 45
23 F	20 37	27 06	3 43	26 24	24 24	1 16	19 02	0 37	20 01	1 35	24 20	1 09	21 42	0 05	12 24	1 45
24 Sa	20 48	25 24	2 56	24 07	24 12	1 03	19 20	0 35	19 51	1 34	24 23	1 11	21 43	0 05	12 23	1 45
25 Su	20 59	22 32	2 01	20 42	23 60	0 50	19 38	0 33	19 42	1 33	24 26	1 13	21 44	0 05	12 22	1 45
26 M	21 09	18 37	0 60	16 20	23 46	0 36	19 55	0 30	19 33	1 33	24 30	1 15	21 44	0 05	12 21	1 45
27 Tu	21 19	13 50	0N06	11 10	23 31	0 21	20 12	0 28	19 23	1 32	24 33	1 16	21 45	0 05	12 20	1 45
28 W	21 29	8 20	1 13	5 23	23 15	0 06	20 29	0 26	19 13	1 31	24 36	1 18	21 45	0 05	12 19	1 45
29 Th	21 39	2 20	2 19	0N48	22 59	0S11	20 45	0 23	19 03	1 31	24 39	1 20	21 46	0 06	12 18	1 45
30 F	21 48	3N58	3 18	7 09	22 41	0 27	20 60	0 21	18 54	1 30	24 42	1 22	21 47	0 06	12 17	1 44
31 Sa	21N56	10N17	4N08	13N21	22N23	0S44	21N14	0S19	18N44	1N29	24N44	1N24	21S48	0S06	12N16	1N44

Day	⚷ Decl	⚷ Lat	♅ Decl	♅ Lat	♆ Decl	♆ Lat	♇ Decl	♇ Lat
1	8S20	6N33	4S06	0S45	13S48	0S19	17S02	6N25
6	8 16	6 35	4 01	0 45	13 47	0 19	17 01	6 25
11	8 13	6 37	3 57	0 45	13 46	0 19	17 01	6 25
16	8 09	6 39	3 53	0 45	13 45	0 19	17 01	6 25
21	8 07	6 41	3 49	0 45	13 45	0 19	17 01	6 25
26	8 05	6 43	3 46	0 45	13 45	0 19	17 01	6 25
31	8S03	6N45	3S44	0S46	13S45	0S20	17S01	6N25

Day	⚴ Decl	⚴ Lat	⚵ Decl	⚵ Lat	⚶ Decl	⚶ Lat	Eris Decl	Eris Lat
1	1S32	10S57	6S43	16N43	2S27	4S60	4S33	13S52
6	1 16	11 25	6 21	17 05	1 40	5 07	4 32	13 52
11	1 01	11 54	5 60	17 26	0 54	5 13	4 31	13 52
16	0 47	12 24	5 40	17 45	0 09	5 20	4 31	13 52
21	0 36	12 56	5 22	18 02	0N34	5 28	4 30	13 53
26	0 26	13 28	5 07	18 16	1 16	5 35	4 29	13 53
31	0S19	14S02	4S54	18N28	1N56	5S43	4S29	13S53

Moon Phenomena

Max/0 Decl

dy	hr mn	
2	1:01	0 N
8	1:36	27N37
14	16:17	0 S
22	3:52	27S33
29	8:56	0 N

Max/0 Lat

dy	hr mn	
6	1:30	5N00
12	6:39	0 S
19	12:15	4S59
26	21:45	0 N

Perigee/Apogee

dy	hr m		kilometers
6	3:08	p	357773
20	14:27	a	406403

PH	dy	hr mn	
●	5	12:19	15♉22
☽	12	3:48	21♌48
○	20	2:12	29♏27
☾	28	2:58	7♓10

Void of Course Moon

Last Aspect				☽ Ingress		
2	9:36	☿	⚹	♈	2	10:52
4	7:17	♂	□	♉	4	11:59
6	8:23	♂	⚹	♊	6	11:18
8	1:37	♆	△	♋	8	11:03
10	0:07	♃	☍	♌	10	13:11
12	8:10	♆	☍	♍	12	18:49
14	16:39	☉	△	♎	15	3:47
17	3:30	♆	△	♏	17	15:00
20	2:12	☉	☍	♐	20	3:20
22	4:20	♆	⚹	♑	22	15:56
24	12:27	♅	⚹	♒	25	3:53
27	2:50	♆	☌	♓	27	13:39
29	6:24	♅	☌	♈	29	19:54
31	12:55	♆	⚹	♉	31	22:20

DAILY ASPECTARIAN

1 Th	☽⚼♂	0:50
	☉⚹☽	2:08
	☽□⚳	4:54
	♀△♇	7:49
	☽∥♅	9:46
	☽∠♀	10:58
	♂∥⚳	13:31
	☿⋕♃	18:37
	☽⚺⚷	19:14
	☽☌♅	20:15
	☽⚹♃	21:42
	♀△♄	22:21
2 F	☽⚺♆	0:49
	☽△♂	3:58
	☉∠☽	6:09
	☽⚹☿	9:36
	☽□♇	12:25
	☽⚻♄	13:42
	☽⚺♀	15:09
	☽⋕♅	15:53
	☿ ♊	20:01
	☽∠⚷	20:43
3 Sa	☽∠♆	2:05
	♄ D	3:08
	☽⋕⚷	7:23
	☿⚻♇	8:46
	☉⚺☽	9:00
	☽⚹⚳	9:22
	☽∠☿	13:50
	☽⚼♄	14:31
	☉⚺⚳	18:35
	☿∥♂	18:40
	☿□♄	19:51
	☽∥♀	20:11
	☽⚹⚷	21:22
	☽⚺♅	22:23
	☽∥♄	23:20
	☽□♃	23:40
4 Su	☽⚹♆	2:34
	☽⋕♆	4:07
	☽□♂	7:17
	☽∠⚳	10:19
	☽△♇	13:24
	☉∥☽	13:45
	☽△♄	14:40
	☽⚺☿	16:57
	☽⋕♇	17:17
	☽☌♀	20:22
	☽∠♅	22:25
5 M	☿∥⚳	1:41
	☽⚺⚳	10:44
	☉☌☽	12:19
	☽⚼♇	13:06
	☽⋕♃	14:38
	♀∥♄	17:37
	☽∥♂	18:33
	☽□⚷	21:05
	☽⚹♅	22:07
	♀∠♅	22:15
	☽△♃	23:17
	☽∥⚳	23:17
6 Tu	☉⚼♇	0:29
	☽∥☿	1:00
	☽□♆	2:06
	☽⚹♂	8:23
	☽⚻♇	12:39
	☽□♄	13:58
	☽☌☿	21:32
	☽⚼♃	22:54
	☽⚺♀	23:46
7 W	☽∠♂	8:54
	☽☌⚳	11:18
	☿⚼♃	11:51
	☉⋕♇	14:10
	☉⚺☽	14:50
	☽△⚷	20:32
	☽□♅	21:38
	☽⚻♃	22:44
8 Th	☽△♆	1:37
	☽∠♀	1:45
	☽⚺♂	9:48
	☽☍♇	12:23
	☽⚹♄	13:49
	♀⋕♆	15:13
	☉∠☽	16:40
	☽⚼⚷	20:50
9 F	☽⚼♆	2:03
	☽⚺☿	2:45
	☽⚹♀	4:26
	♃ R	12:12
	☽⚺⚳	13:29
	☽∠♄	14:36
	☉⚹☽	19:19
	♂ ♌	20:21
	☽∥☿	21:28
	☽⚻⚷	21:50
	☽△♅	23:05
10 Sa	☽☍♃	0:07
	☽⚻♆	3:12
	☽∥⚳	4:29
	☽∠☿	6:27
	☽☌♂	13:52
	☽⚻♇	14:33
	☽∥♂	15:14
	☽∠⚳	15:47
	☽⋕♃	15:56
	☽⚺♄	16:11
11 Su	☽⚼♅	1:00
	♂⚻♇	6:57
	☉□⚷	8:59
	☉∥☽	10:45
	☽⚹☿	11:07
	☽□♀	12:53
	♂⋕♃	13:19
	☽⋕♇	15:38
	☽⚼♇	16:55
	☽⚹⚳	19:05
12 M	☽∥♀	0:23
	☽☍⚷	2:27
	☉□☽	3:48
	☽⚻♅	3:51
	☉⚹♅	4:34
	☽⚻♃	4:49
	☽⋕♆	6:32
	☽☍♆	8:10
	☽∥♄	12:01
	☉△♃	17:30
	☽△♇	20:12
	☽⚺♂	21:52
	☽☌♄	22:05
13 Tu	♂⚺♄	3:17
	☽⋕⚷	6:24
	♀⚼♇	8:24
	☽⚼♃	8:30
	☽□☿	23:21
14 W	☽⋕♅	0:08
	☽△♀	2:04
	☽∠♂	3:21
	☽□⚳	4:36
	☽⚻⚷	10:34
	☽☍♅	12:09
	☽△♃	12:57
	☉□♆	15:51
	☽⚻♆	16:35
	☉△☽	16:39
15 Th	☽□♇	5:09
	☽⚺♄	7:19
	☽∥♅	8:34
	☽⚹♂	9:37
	☽⚼♀	10:11
	☽⚼⚷	15:41
	♀⚺⚳	15:48
	☽⚼♆	21:49
16 F	☉⚼☽	0:22
	☽∥⚷	3:00
	☽∠♄	12:50
	☽△☿	14:13
	☽△⚳	17:08
	☽⚻♀	19:02
	☽△⚷	21:18
	☽⋕♄	22:42
	☽⚻♅	23:03
	☽□♃	23:37
17 Sa	♀⋕♇	0:48
	☽△♆	3:30
	☽∥♆	4:51
	☉⚻☽	8:39
	☽⚹♇	16:18
	♀□⚷	17:28
	☽⚹♄	18:44
	☽∥♇	21:30
	☽⚼☿	22:03
	☽⋕♀	23:18
	☽□♂	23:49
18 Su	☽⚼⚳	0:06
	☽⚼♅	5:04
	♀⚹♅	11:24
	☉⋕☽	12:39
	♀△♃	15:19
	☽⋕♂	18:25
	☽∠♇	22:20
19 M	♂∠⚳	0:51
	☽∥♃	1:08
	☽⚻☿	5:53
	☽⚻⚳	7:20
	☽□⚷	9:26
	☽△♅	11:19
	☽⚹♃	11:36
	☽☍♀	14:00
	☽□♆	15:42
	☽⋕⚳	19:43
20 Tu	☽⋕☿	1:50
	☉☍☽	2:12
	☽⚺♇	4:32
	♀□♆	6:29
	☽□♄	7:15
	⚴ ♉	13:57
	☽△♂	15:10
	☉ ♊	16:02
	☽∠♃	17:49
21 W	☉⚻♇	6:23
	☉∥♂	6:30
	♃⚹♅	18:06
	⚳△⚷	19:33
	☽☍☿	21:03
	☽⚹⚷	22:04
	☽☍⚳	22:09
	☽⚼♂	22:58
22 Th	☽⚺♃	0:03
	☽□♅	0:05
	☽⚹♆	4:20
	☽⚻♀	9:37
	☽☌♇	17:02
	☉□♄	18:26
	☽△♄	20:01
	☉⚻☽	20:09
23 F	♂⚼♅	0:09
	☽∠⚷	4:19
	☿∥⚳	6:40
	☽⚻♂	6:40
	☽∠♆	10:33
	☿△⚷	11:59
	☽⚼♀	19:15
	⚳⚻♃	22:55
24 Sa	☽⚼♄	2:12
	☉⚼☽	4:52
	⚳□♅	8:09
	☽⋕⚳	9:27
	☽⚺⚷	10:21
	☽⚻☿	10:45
	☽⋕☿	12:02
	☽☌♃	12:04
	☽⚹♅	12:27
	☽⚻⚳	12:36
	☽⚺♆	16:31
	♀ ♊	22:53
25 Su	♀∥♂	3:36
	☽△♀	4:26
	☽⚺♇	4:50
	☽∥♃	5:29
	☽⚻♄	8:02
	♀⚻♇	8:22
	☉⋕☽	9:49
	⚷ R	11:43
	☉△☽	13:05
	☽⚼☿	16:39
	☽⋕♀	17:07
	☽∠♅	18:05
	☽⋕♂	18:38
	☽⚼⚳	19:13
	☽☍♂	21:03
26 M	☽∥♇	8:29
	☽∠♇	10:02
	☿ R	15:49
	♆ R	16:16
	♀□♄	17:11
	☽☌⚷	20:56
	☽△☿	21:40
	☽⚺♃	22:21
	☽⚺♅	23:04
27 Tu	☽∥♆	0:24
	☽△⚳	1:07
	☽☌♆	2:50
	☽⋕♄	6:51
	☽⚹♇	14:28
	☽☍♄	17:47
	☉⚼♃	19:07
	☽□♀	20:17
28 W	☽∥⚷	1:07
	☽∠♃	2:21
	☉□☽	2:58
	☽⚻♂	8:26
	☽∥♅	18:28
29 Th	☽⚺⚷	4:18
	☽□☿	4:34
	⚳△♆	4:39
	☽⚹♃	5:24
	☽☌♅	6:24
	☽⚺♆	9:49
	☽□⚳	9:59
	☽⚼♂	12:32
	☽□♇	20:33
	☉⋕♃	21:42
	☿△⚷	22:38
	☽⋕♅	23:07
	☽⚻♄	23:54
30 F	☽∠⚷	6:30
	☽⚹♀	7:15
	♀⚼♃	9:34
	☽∠♆	11:49
	☉⚹☽	12:09
	☽⋕⚷	15:26
	☽△♂	15:31
31 Sa	☽⚼♄	1:29
	☽⚹☿	7:09
	☽∥♄	7:39
	☽⚹⚷	7:46
	☽□♃	8:35
	☽⚺♅	9:49
	☽∠♀	10:50
	☽⚹♆	12:55
	☽⋕♆	13:37
	☽⚹⚳	14:36
	☉∠☽	15:00
	☽△♇	22:52

June 2008

LONGITUDE

Day	Sid.Time	☉	☽	☽ 12 hour	Mean ☊	True ☊	☿	♀	♂	⚳	♃	♄	⚷	♅	♆	♇
	h m s	° ' "	° ' "	° ' "	° '	° '	° '	° '	° '	° '	° '	° '	° '	° '	° '	° '
1 Su	16 39 24	10♊52 46	1♉01 45	8♉27 51	22♒17.5	21♒22.2	20♊31.1	8♊39.6	12♌11.7	25♊26.6	21♑35.2	2♍24.2	21♒07.7	22♓23.1	24♒14.8	0♑19.8
2 M	16 43 21	11 50 17	15 59 00	23 34 09	22 14.4	21R 13.6	20R 07.7	9 53.3	12 45.6	25 52.1	21R 31.0	2 27.2	21R 07.2	22 24.3	24R 14.6	0R 18.4
3 Tu	16 47 17	12 47 46	1♊12 00	8♊51 13	22 11.2	21 03.9	19 41.3	11 07.1	13 19.6	26 17.6	21 26.6	2 30.2	21 06.7	22 25.5	24 14.4	0 16.9
4 W	16 51 14	13 45 16	16 30 20	24 07 56	22 08.0	20 54.3	19 12.5	12 20.8	13 53.6	26 43.2	21 22.1	2 33.4	21 06.1	22 26.6	24 14.2	0 15.4
5 Th	16 55 10	14 42 44	1♋42 39	9♋13 15	22 04.8	20 46.0	18 41.7	13 34.6	14 27.7	27 08.8	21 17.5	2 36.7	21 05.5	22 27.7	24 13.9	0 14.0
6 F	16 59 07	15 40 11	16 38 42	23 58 09	22 01.7	20 39.8	18 09.4	14 48.3	15 01.9	27 34.4	21 12.7	2 40.0	21 04.8	22 28.7	24 13.6	0 12.5
7 Sa	17 03 03	16 37 37	1♌11 02	8♌16 56	21 58.5	20 36.1	17 36.2	16 02.0	15 36.2	28 00.1	21 07.7	2 43.5	21 04.0	22 29.7	24 13.2	0 11.0
8 Su	17 07 00	17 35 02	15 15 41	22 07 18	21 55.3	20D 34.6	17 02.7	17 15.7	16 10.5	28 25.7	21 02.6	2 47.0	21 03.2	22 30.6	24 12.8	0 09.5
9 M	17 10 56	18 32 26	28 51 58	5♍29 58	21 52.1	20 34.7	16 29.4	18 29.4	16 44.9	28 51.4	20 57.3	2 50.6	21 02.3	22 31.5	24 12.4	0 08.0
10 Tu	17 14 53	19 29 48	12♍01 43	18 27 42	21 49.0	20R 35.4	15 56.8	19 43.2	17 19.3	29 17.1	20 51.9	2 54.3	21 01.3	22 32.4	24 12.0	0 06.5
11 W	17 18 50	20 27 10	24 48 25	1♎04 26	21 45.8	20 35.5	15 25.7	20 56.9	17 53.8	29 42.9	20 46.3	2 58.1	21 00.3	22 33.2	24 11.5	0 04.9
12 Th	17 22 46	21 24 30	7♎16 18	13 24 35	21 42.6	20 34.1	14 56.4	22 10.6	18 28.3	0♋08.6	20 40.6	3 02.0	20 59.2	22 33.9	24 11.0	0 03.4
13 F	17 26 43	22 21 50	19 29 47	25 32 27	21 39.4	20 30.7	14 29.5	23 24.3	19 02.9	0 34.4	20 34.8	3 06.0	20 58.1	22 34.6	24 10.5	0 01.9
14 Sa	17 30 39	23 19 08	1♏33 02	7♏31 58	21 36.3	20 25.0	14 05.4	24 38.1	19 37.6	1 00.2	20 28.9	3 10.0	20 56.9	22 35.3	24 09.9	0 00.3
15 Su	17 34 36	24 16 26	13 29 41	19 26 31	21 33.1	20 17.2	13 44.5	25 51.8	20 12.3	1 26.0	20 22.8	3 14.2	20 55.7	22 35.9	24 09.3	29♐58.8
16 M	17 38 32	25 13 43	25 22 49	1♐18 51	21 29.9	20 07.8	13 27.2	27 05.5	20 47.1	1 51.8	20 16.6	3 18.4	20 54.4	22 36.4	24 08.7	29 57.2
17 Tu	17 42 29	26 10 59	7♐14 53	13 11 09	21 26.7	19 57.7	13 13.8	28 19.2	21 22.0	2 17.6	20 10.3	3 22.7	20 53.0	22 36.9	24 08.0	29 55.7
18 W	17 46 25	27 08 15	19 07 52	25 05 13	21 23.5	19 47.7	13 04.6	29 32.9	21 56.9	2 43.5	20 03.9	3 27.1	20 51.6	22 37.4	24 07.4	29 54.2
19 Th	17 50 22	28 05 30	1♑03 25	7♑02 38	21 20.4	19 38.8	12D 59.6	0♋46.6	22 31.8	3 09.4	19 57.3	3 31.5	20 50.1	22 37.8	24 06.7	29 52.6
20 F	17 54 19	29 02 45	13 03 05	19 04 58	21 17.2	19 31.7	12 59.1	2 00.3	23 06.8	3 35.3	19 50.7	3 36.0	20 48.6	22 38.2	24 05.9	29 51.1
21 Sa	17 58 15	29 59 59	25 08 30	1♒13 59	21 14.0	19 26.7	13 03.2	3 14.0	23 41.9	4 01.2	19 43.9	3 40.6	20 47.0	22 38.5	24 05.2	29 49.5
22 Su	18 02 12	0♋57 13	7♒21 40	13 31 52	21 10.8	19D 23.9	13 12.0	4 27.7	24 17.0	4 27.1	19 37.1	3 45.3	20 45.3	22 38.8	24 04.4	29 47.9
23 M	18 06 08	1 54 26	19 44 55	26 01 12	21 07.7	19 23.1	13 25.5	5 41.5	24 52.2	4 53.0	19 30.2	3 50.1	20 43.6	22 39.0	24 03.6	29 46.4
24 Tu	18 10 05	2 51 40	2♓21 07	8♓45 03	21 04.5	19 23.8	13 43.7	6 55.2	25 27.4	5 19.0	19 23.2	3 54.9	20 41.9	22 39.2	24 02.7	29 44.8
25 W	18 14 01	3 48 53	15 13 25	21 46 37	21 01.3	19 25.0	14 06.6	8 08.9	26 02.7	5 45.0	19 16.1	3 59.8	20 40.1	22 39.3	24 01.8	29 43.3
26 Th	18 17 58	4 46 06	28 25 02	5♈09 00	20 58.1	19R 26.0	14 34.1	9 22.6	26 38.1	6 11.0	19 08.9	4 04.8	20 38.2	22 39.4	24 00.9	29 41.7
27 F	18 21 54	5 43 19	11♈58 46	18 54 31	20 55.0	19 26.0	15 06.4	10 36.3	27 13.5	6 37.0	19 01.6	4 09.9	20 36.3	22R 39.4	24 00.0	29 40.2
28 Sa	18 25 51	6 40 33	25 56 17	3♉04 01	20 51.8	19 24.5	15 43.2	11 50.1	27 48.9	7 03.0	18 54.3	4 15.0	20 34.3	22 39.4	23 59.1	29 38.6
29 Su	18 29 48	7 37 46	10♉17 27	17 36 10	20 48.6	19 21.2	16 24.6	13 03.8	28 24.5	7 29.0	18 46.9	4 20.2	20 32.3	22 39.3	23 58.1	29 37.1
30 M	18 33 44	8♋35 00	24 59 35	2♊26 53	20♒45.4	19♒16.5	17♊10.4	14♋17.6	29♌00.0	7♋55.0	18♑39.5	4♍25.4	20♒30.3	22♓39.2	23♒57.1	29♐35.6

1st of Month
Julian Day # 2454618.5
Obliquity 23°26'24"
SVP 5♓08'23"
GC 26♐57.4
Eris 21♈36.5

Day	⚴	⚵	⚶
1	4♉35.5	24♐39.4R	18♈49.3
6	6 36.3	23 34.4R	20 51.4
11	8 37.1	22 26.9R	22 50.7
16	10 37.7	21 18.6R	24 47.1
21	12 38.2	20 11.0R	26 40.3
26	14 38.4	19 05.5R	28 30.3

DECLINATION and LATITUDE

Day	☉ Decl	☽ Decl	☽ Lat	☽ 12h Decl	☿ Decl	☿ Lat	♀ Decl	♀ Lat	♂ Decl	♂ Lat	⚳ Decl	⚳ Lat	♃ Decl	♃ Lat	♄ Decl	♄ Lat
1 Su	22N05	16N15	4N44	18N58	22N05	1S02	21N29	0S16	18N33	1N29	24N47	1N25	21S48	0S06	12N14	1N44
2 M	22 12	21 55	5 01	23 32	21 46	1 19	21 42	0 14	18 28	1 28	24 50	1 27	21 49	0 06	12 13	1 44
3 Tu	22 20	25 15	4 58	26 31	21 26	1 36	21 55	0 12	18 13	1 27	24 52	1 29	21 50	0 06	12 12	1 44
4 W	22 27	27 17	4 33	27 32	21 07	1 54	22 07	0 09	18 02	1 26	24 55	1 31	21 51	0 06	12 11	1 44
5 Th	22 34	27 15	3 49	26 28	20 47	2 11	22 19	0 07	17 52	1 26	24 57	1 32	21 52	0 07	12 09	1 44
6 F	22 40	25 13	2 50	23 33	20 28	2 27	22 30	0 05	17 41	1 25	24 59	1 34	21 53	0 07	12 08	1 44
7 Sa	22 46	21 33	1 41	19 15	20 10	2 43	22 40	0 02	17 30	1 24	25 01	1 36	21 54	0 07	12 07	1 44
8 Su	22 52	16 43	0 28	14 00	19 52	2 58	22 50	0N00	17 19	1 23	25 03	1 38	21 55	0 07	12 05	1 43
9 M	22 57	11 11	0S44	8 16	19 34	3 12	22 59	0 02	17 08	1 23	25 05	1 39	21 55	0 07	12 04	1 43
10 Tu	23 01	5 20	1 52	2 22	19 18	3 25	23 07	0 05	16 57	1 22	25 07	1 41	21 56	0 07	12 03	1 43
11 W	23 06	0S34	2 52	3S28	19 03	3 37	23 15	0 07	16 46	1 22	25 09	1 43	21 57	0 07	12 01	1 43
12 Th	23 10	6 17	3 43	9 02	18 49	3 48	23 22	0 10	16 34	1 21	25 11	1 45	21 58	0 08	11 60	1 43
13 F	23 13	11 40	4 22	14 10	18 37	3 57	23 28	0 12	16 23	1 20	25 13	1 46	21 60	0 08	11 58	1 43
14 Sa	23 16	16 31	4 49	18 42	18 26	4 05	23 34	0 14	16 11	1 20	25 14	1 48	22 01	0 08	11 56	1 43
15 Su	23 19	20 42	5 03	22 28	18 17	4 12	23 39	0 17	15 60	1 19	25 16	1 50	22 02	0 08	11 55	1 43
16 M	23 21	24 01	5 03	25 18	18 10	4 17	23 43	0 19	15 48	1 18	25 17	1 52	22 03	0 08	11 53	1 43
17 Tu	23 23	26 18	4 51	27 01	18 04	4 21	23 47	0 21	15 36	1 18	25 19	1 53	22 04	0 08	11 52	1 43
18 W	23 25	27 25	4 26	27 30	18 01	4 23	23 50	0 24	15 24	1 17	25 20	1 55	22 05	0 09	11 50	1 42
19 Th	23 26	27 16	3 50	26 42	17 59	4 25	23 52	0 26	15 12	1 16	25 21	1 57	22 06	0 09	11 48	1 42
20 F	23 26	25 50	3 03	24 39	17 59	4 25	23 54	0 28	15 00	1 16	25 22	1 59	22 07	0 09	11 47	1 42
21 Sa	23 26	23 11	2 07	21 27	18 00	4 24	23 54	0 30	14 48	1 15	25 23	2 00	22 08	0 09	11 45	1 42
22 Su	23 26	19 28	1 04	17 16	18 04	4 21	23 55	0 33	14 36	1 14	25 24	2 02	22 09	0 09	11 43	1 42
23 M	23 26	14 52	0N02	12 17	18 09	4 18	23 54	0 35	14 23	1 13	25 25	2 04	22 11	0 09	11 41	1 42
24 Tu	23 25	9 33	1 10	6 42	18 15	4 13	23 53	0 37	14 11	1 13	25 26	2 06	22 12	0 09	11 39	1 42
25 W	23 23	3 45	2 15	0 43	18 24	4 08	23 50	0 39	13 58	1 12	25 26	2 08	22 13	0 10	11 37	1 42
26 Th	23 21	2N21	3 15	5N27	18 33	4 01	23 48	0 41	13 46	1 12	25 27	2 09	22 14	0 10	11 36	1 42
27 F	23 19	8 31	4 06	11 31	18 44	3 54	23 44	0 43	13 33	1 11	25 27	2 11	22 15	0 10	11 34	1 42
28 Sa	23 16	14 26	4 44	17 11	18 56	3 46	23 40	0 45	13 20	1 10	25 28	2 13	22 16	0 10	11 32	1 42
29 Su	23 13	19 44	5 06	22 02	19 08	3 37	23 35	0 48	13 07	1 10	25 28	2 15	22 17	0 10	11 30	1 41
30 M	23N10	23N59	5N08	25N34	19N22	3S28	23N30	0N50	12N54	1N09	25N28	2N16	22S19	0S10	11N28	1N41

Day	⚷ Decl	⚷ Lat	♅ Decl	♅ Lat	♆ Decl	♆ Lat	♇ Decl	♇ Lat
1	8S03	6N45	3S43	0S46	13S45	0S20	17S01	6N25
6	8 02	6 47	3 41	0 46	13 45	0 20	17 01	6 25
11	8 02	6 49	3 40	0 46	13 46	0 20	17 02	6 25
16	8 02	6 51	3 39	0 46	13 47	0 20	17 02	6 24
21	8 02	6 53	3 38	0 46	13 48	0 20	17 03	6 24
26	8 04	6 54	3 38	0 47	13 50	0 20	17 03	6 23

Day	⚴ Decl	⚴ Lat	⚵ Decl	⚵ Lat	⚶ Decl	⚶ Lat	Eris Decl	Eris Lat
1	0S18	14S09	4S51	18N29	2N04	5S44	4S29	13S53
6	0 14	14 44	4 41	18 37	2 41	5 53	4 28	13 54
11	0 12	15 21	4 35	18 41	3 18	6 01	4 28	13 54
16	0 13	15 60	4 31	18 41	3 52	6 10	4 28	13 55
21	0 17	16 40	4 30	18 37	4 24	6 19	4 28	13 55
26	0 24	17 22	4 33	18 30	4 53	6 28	4 28	13 56

Moon Phenomena

Max/0 Decl
dy hr mn
4 11:34 27N31
10 21:40 0 S
18 9:05 27S31
25 14:49 0 N

Max/0 Lat
dy hr mn
2 8:07 5N02
8 9:17 0 S
15 13:32 5S05
22 23:18 0 N
29 14:49 5N09

Perigee/Apogee
dy hr m kilometers
3 13:14 p 357256
16 17:34 a 406228

PH dy hr mn
● 3 19:24 13♊34
☽ 10 15:05 20♍06
○ 18 17:32 27♐50
☾ 26 12:11 5♈15

Void of Course Moon

Last Aspect			☽ Ingress	
2 13:04	♆	□	♊	2 22:07
4 12:10	♆	△	♋	4 21:17
6 9:33	♅	△	♌	6 22:01
8 15:42	♆	☍	♍	9 2:02
10 19:43	♅	☍	♎	11 9:56
13 9:16	♆	△	♏	13 20:54
15 21:30	♆	□	♐	16 9:21
18 21:38	♇	☌	♑	18 21:53
20 19:03	♅	✶	♒	21 9:35
23 19:05	♇	✶	♓	23 19:33
26 2:17	♇	□	♈	26 2:50
28 6:15	♇	△	♉	28 6:51
30 6:44	♂	□	♊	30 8:04

DAILY ASPECTARIAN

1 Su ☉∥☿ 0:00; ☽△♄ 2:14; ☽#♇ 3:16; ☽∠☿ 7:05; ☽∥♂ 9:46; ☽∠♅ 10:17; ☽⊻♀ 13:25; ☽∠⚳ 15:37; ☉⊻☽ 16:57; ☽□♂ 18:40; ☿#♃ 19:35; ☽⚼♇ 22:56

2 M ☽∥♀ 1:34; ☽∥☿ 1:41; ☽#♃ 2:08; ☿∥♀ 2:35; ☉∥☽ 4:23; ☽⊻☿ 6:23; ☽□⚷ 8:08; ☽△♃ 8:43; ☽✶♅ 10:11; ☽□♆ 13:04; ♀#♃ 14:09; ☽⊻⚳ 16:04; ☽∥⚳ 21:01; ☽⊼♇ 22:34

3 Tu ☽□♄ 2:03; ☽⚼♃ 8:11; ☽☌♀ 16:54; ☉☌☽ 19:24; ☽✶♂ 19:45

4 W ☽☌☿ 4:07; ☽△⚷ 7:13; ☽⊼♃ 7:36; ☉✶♂ 8:36; ☽□♅ 9:21; ☽△♆ 12:10; ☽☌⚳ 16:33; ☽∠♂ 20:17; ☽☍♇ 21:39

5 Th ☽✶♄ 1:26; ☽⚼⚷ 6:59; ☽⚼♆ 12:01; ☽⊻♀ 20:45; ☽⊻♂ 21:17; ☉⊻☽ 22:18

6 F ☽∠♄ 1:40; ☽∥⚳ 1:50; ☽⊻☿ 2:23; ♂⚼♇ 7:06; ☽⊼⚷ 7:14; ☽☍♃ 7:25; ♀✶♂ 8:17; ☽△♅ 9:33; ☽⊼♆ 12:25; ☉∥☽ 17:06; ☽∥♀ 17:47; ☽⊻⚳ 18:31; ☽#♃ 22:03; ☽⊼♇ 22:20; ☽∠♀ 23:43

7 Sa ☉∠☽ 0:48; ☽∠☿ 2:18; ☽⊻♄ 2:36; ☽∥☿ 7:54; ☽⚼♅ 10:40; ☉☌☿ 15:28; ♃⊻⚷ 20:35; ☽∠⚳ 20:44; ☿☌♀ 21:04; ☽∥♂ 21:06; ☽#♇ 22:33; ☽⚼♇ 23:49

8 Su ☽☌♂ 1:39; ☽✶☿ 2:59; ☽✶♀ 3:49; ☉✶☽ 4:21; ☽⊼♃ 10:02; ☽☍⚷ 10:06; ☉∥♀ 10:18; ☽⊼♅ 12:42; ☽#♆ 13:04; ☽☍♆ 15:42; ☿✶♂ 18:29; ☽∥♄ 20:16; ☽✶⚳ 23:59

9 M ☽△♇ 2:16; ☉☌♀ 4:22; ☽☌♄ 7:12; ☽⚼♃ 12:45; ☽#⚷ 13:01; ♂#♇ 14:03

10 Tu ☽#♅ 6:44; ☽□☿ 7:00; ☽⊻♂ 10:19; ☉□☽ 15:05; ☽□♀ 15:54; ☽△♃ 16:24; ☽⊼⚷ 16:48; ☽☍♅ 19:43; ♀⊼♃ 20:48; ☽⊼♆ 22:50

11 W ♀△⚷ 1:05; ☉⊼♃ 7:18; ☽□⚳ 9:43; ☽□♇ 10:04; ☽∥♅ 12:49; ☉△⚷ 13:38; ☽⊻♄ 15:44; ⚳ ♋ 15:59; ☽∠♂ 16:16; ⚳☍♇ 19:26; ☽⚼⚷ 21:30

12 Th ☽⚼♆ 3:43; ☽∥⚷ 7:33; ♀□♅ 7:39; ☽△☿ 14:28; ☽∠♄ 21:13; ☽✶♂ 23:04

13 F ☽#♄ 1:25; ☽□♃ 2:08; ☽△⚷ 2:55; ☉□♅ 5:25; ☽⊼♅ 6:07; ☉△☽ 6:10; ☽△♀ 8:38; ☽△♆ 9:16; ☽∥♆ 10:06; ♀△♆ 14:54; ☽⚼☿ 19:14; ☽✶♇ 20:55; ☽#♂ 22:21; ☽△⚳ 22:52

14 Sa ☽∥♇ 2:44; ☽✶♄ 3:15; ♇R♐ 5:14; ☽#☿ 10:06; ☽⚼♅ 12:07; ☉⚼☽ 14:46; ☽⚼♀ 18:05; ☉△♆ 21:03

15 Su ☽⊼☿ 0:29; ☽∠♇ 2:59; ♂⊼♃ 6:08; ☽⚼⚳ 6:09; ☽∥♃ 8:53; ☽✶♃ 13:46; ☽□♂ 14:14; ☽□⚷ 14:58; ☽△♅ 18:23; ☉#☽ 18:34; ☽□♆ 21:30; ☽#♀ 21:32; ☉⊼☽ 23:40

16 M ☽⊼♀ 3:52; ♂☍⚷ 4:48; ☽⊻♇ 9:14; ☽#⚳ 12:01; ☽⊼⚳ 13:36; ☽□♄ 16:08; ☽∠♃ 19:50

17 ☽☍☿ 11:55

18 W ☽⊻♃ 1:52; ☽✶⚷ 3:29; ☽△♂ 5:58; ♀☍♇ 6:47; ☽□♅ 7:03; ♀ ♋ 8:50; ☽✶♆ 10:03; ☉☍☽ 17:32; ☽☌♇ 21:38; ☽☍♀ 23:22

19 Th ♂⊼♅ 4:09; ☽☍⚳ 4:22; ☽△♄ 4:59; ☽∠⚷ 9:34; ☽⚼♂ 13:38; ☿ D 14:32; ☽∠♆ 16:07; ☽⊼☿ 23:52

20 F ⚳✶♄ 0:52; ☽#⚳ 4:59; ☽⚼♄ 11:07; ☽☌♃ 13:23; ☽⊻⚷ 15:24; ☽#♀ 18:22; ☽✶♅ 19:03; ☉☍♇ 19:43; ☽⊼♂ 21:00; ☽⊻♆ 21:55; ☉#☽ 22:03

21 Sa ☉ ♋ 0:00; ☽⚼☿ 5:48; ☽∥♃ 7:24; ☽⊻♇ 9:13; ♀✶♄ 9:15; ☉⊼☽ 10:23; ♂☍♆ 15:33; ☽⊼♄ 16:54; ☽⊼♀ 17:42; ☽⊼⚳ 18:06; ♀☌⚳ 23:41

22 Su ☽∠♅ 0:33; ☽#☿ 7:39; ☽△☿ 11:33; ☽∥♇ 13:08; ☽∠♇ 14:26; ☉⚼☽ 18:04; ☽⊻♃ 23:32

23 M ☽⚼⚳ 0:16; ♀⚼⚷ 0:42; ☽☌⚷ 1:53; ☽⚼♀ 2:00; ☽#♂ 2:22; ☽∥♆ 4:57; ☽⊻♅ 5:34; ☽☌♆ 8:15; ☽☍♂ 10:17; ☽#♄ 14:46; ☽✶♇ 19:05

24 Tu ☉△☽ 1:02; ☽☍♄ 2:58; ☽∠♃ 3:48; ☽△⚳ 5:46; ☽∥⚷ 6:23; ☽△♀ 9:29; ⚳⚼⚷ 19:46; ☽□☿ 21:53

25 W ☽∥♅ 0:28; ☉✶♄ 5:02; ☽✶♃ 7:21; ☽⊻⚷ 9:57; ☽☌♅ 13:36; ♂#♆ 15:57; ☽⊻♆ 16:04; ♀⚼♆ 17:02; ☽⊼♂ 20:39

26 Th ☽□♇ 2:17; ☽#♅ 4:57; ♃⚼♄ 7:58; ☽⊼♄ 10:10; ☉□☽ 12:11; ☽∠⚷ 12:50; ☽□⚳ 14:17; ☽∠♆ 18:47; ☉⚼⚷ 21:09; ☽□♀ 21:22; ☽#⚷ 22:15

27 F ♅ R 0:02; ☽⚼♂ 0:27; ☽✶☿ 5:41; ☽∥♄ 12:06; ☽□♃ 12:06; ☽⚼♄ 12:31; ☽✶⚷ 14:53; ☽⊻♅ 18:25; ☽∥♂ 19:35; ☽✶♆ 20:41; ☽#♆ 21:33

28 Sa ☽△♂ 3:19; ☽△♇ 6:15; ☽∠☿ 8:28; ☽#♇ 11:25; ☽△♄ 14:03; ☉☌⚳ 17:15; ☽✶⚳ 19:13; ☉✶☽ 19:17; ☽∠♅ 19:38; ☽∥☿ 20:58

29 Su ☽✶♀ 4:59; ☽⚼♇ 7:06; ☽⊻☿ 10:35; ♀∠♂ 12:58; ☽#♃ 13:34; ☽△♃ 13:48; ☽□⚷ 16:44; ☉∥☽ 18:45; ☽✶♅ 20:13; ☽∠⚳ 20:32; ☽∥♀ 20:50; ☉∠☽ 21:34; ☽□♆ 22:19

30 M ⚶ ♉ 5:00; ☽□♂ 6:44; ☽⊼♇ 7:24; ☽∠♀ 7:33; ☉⚼♆ 9:06; ☽∥⚳ 11:12; ☽⚼♃ 13:49; ☽□♄ 15:15; ☽⊻⚳ 21:22; ♂△♇ 22:58; ☉⊻☽ 23:18

LONGITUDE

July 2008

Day	Sid.Time	☉	☽	☽ 12 hour	Mean ☊	True ☊	☿	♀	♂	⚳	♃	♄	⚷	♅	♆	♇
	h m s	° ' "	° ' "	° ' "	° '	° '	° '	° '	° '	° '	° '	° '	° '	° '	° '	° '
1 Tu	18 37 41	9♋32 13	9♊57 08	17♊29 17	20♒42.3	19♒10.9	18♊00.7	15♋31.3	29♌35.7	8♋21.1	18♑32.0	4♍30.8	20♒28.2	22♓39.0	23♒56.0	29♐34.0
2 W	18 41 37	10 29 27	25 02 08	2♋34 29	20 39.1	19R 05.3	18 55.4	16 45.1	0♍11.3	8 47.1	18R 24.4	4 36.2	20R 26.0	22R 38.8	23R 55.0	29R 32.5
3 Th	18 45 34	11 26 41	10♋05 07	17 32 52	20 35.9	19 00.4	19 54.4	17 58.8	0 47.1	9 13.2	18 16.8	4 41.6	20 23.8	22 38.5	23 53.9	29 31.0
4 F	18 49 30	12 23 55	24 56 43	2♌15 44	20 32.7	18 56.9	20 57.6	19 12.6	1 22.9	9 39.3	18 09.2	4 47.2	20 21.6	22 38.2	23 52.8	29 29.5
5 Sa	18 53 27	13 21 08	9♌29 12	16 36 32	20 29.6	18D 55.1	22 05.0	20 26.3	1 58.7	10 05.4	18 01.6	4 52.8	20 19.3	22 37.9	23 51.7	29 28.0
6 Su	18 57 24	14 18 22	23 37 22	0♍31 31	20 26.4	18 54.9	23 16.5	21 40.1	2 34.6	10 31.5	17 53.9	4 58.4	20 16.9	22 37.5	23 50.5	29 26.5
7 M	19 01 20	15 15 35	7♍18 57	13 59 46	20 23.2	18 55.8	24 32.2	22 53.9	3 10.6	10 57.6	17 46.2	5 04.2	20 14.5	22 37.0	23 49.4	29 25.0
8 Tu	19 05 17	16 12 48	20 34 13	27 02 39	20 20.0	18 57.3	25 51.8	24 07.6	3 46.6	11 23.7	17 38.5	5 09.9	20 12.1	22 36.5	23 48.2	29 23.6
9 W	19 09 13	17 10 00	3♎25 28	9♎43 11	20 16.8	18 58.7	27 15.4	25 21.4	4 22.7	11 49.8	17 30.8	5 15.8	20 09.7	22 35.9	23 47.0	29 22.1
10 Th	19 13 10	18 07 13	15 56 17	22 05 21	20 13.7	18R 59.4	28 43.0	26 35.1	4 58.8	12 15.9	17 23.0	5 21.7	20 07.2	22 35.3	23 45.7	29 20.6
11 F	19 17 06	19 04 26	28 10 56	4♏13 36	20 10.5	18 59.0	0♋14.3	27 48.9	5 34.9	12 42.0	17 15.3	5 27.6	20 04.6	22 34.7	23 44.5	29 19.2
12 Sa	19 21 03	20 01 38	10♏13 54	16 12 23	20 07.3	18 57.4	1 49.4	29 02.6	6 11.1	13 08.1	17 07.6	5 33.6	20 02.0	22 34.0	23 43.2	29 17.8
13 Su	19 24 59	20 58 51	22 09 32	28 05 52	20 04.1	18 54.5	3 28.2	0♌16.4	6 47.4	13 34.2	16 59.9	5 39.7	19 59.4	22 33.3	23 41.9	29 16.3
14 M	19 28 56	21 56 04	4♐01 50	9♐57 50	20 01.0	18 50.7	5 10.5	1 30.1	7 23.7	14 00.3	16 52.2	5 45.8	19 56.8	22 32.5	23 40.6	29 14.9
15 Tu	19 32 53	22 53 16	15 54 16	21 51 29	19 57.8	18 46.5	6 56.2	2 43.9	8 00.1	14 26.4	16 44.6	5 52.0	19 54.1	22 31.7	23 39.3	29 13.5
16 W	19 36 49	23 50 29	27 49 48	3♑49 29	19 54.6	18 42.3	8 45.1	3 57.7	8 36.5	14 52.6	16 37.0	5 58.2	19 51.4	22 30.8	23 37.9	29 12.2
17 Th	19 40 46	24 47 43	9♑50 48	15 53 59	19 51.4	18 38.5	10 37.0	5 11.4	9 12.9	15 18.7	16 29.4	6 04.5	19 48.6	22 29.9	23 36.6	29 10.8
18 F	19 44 42	25 44 56	21 59 13	28 06 41	19 48.3	18 35.6	12 31.8	6 25.2	9 49.4	15 44.8	16 21.9	6 10.9	19 45.8	22 29.0	23 35.2	29 09.4
19 Sa	19 48 39	26 42 10	4♒16 35	10♒29 03	19 45.1	18 33.9	14 29.1	7 38.9	10 26.0	16 10.9	16 14.4	6 17.2	19 43.0	22 28.0	23 33.8	29 08.1
20 Su	19 52 35	27 39 25	16 44 14	23 02 19	19 41.9	18D 33.2	16 28.7	8 52.7	11 02.6	16 37.0	16 06.9	6 23.7	19 40.2	22 26.9	23 32.4	29 06.8
21 M	19 56 32	28 36 39	29 23 27	5♓47 47	19 38.7	18 33.5	18 30.3	10 06.4	11 39.2	17 03.2	15 59.5	6 30.2	19 37.3	22 25.8	23 30.9	29 05.5
22 Tu	20 00 28	29 33 55	12♓15 29	18 46 43	19 35.6	18 34.5	20 33.6	11 20.2	12 15.9	17 29.3	15 52.2	6 36.7	19 34.4	22 24.7	23 29.5	29 04.2
23 W	20 04 25	0♌31 11	25 21 38	2♈00 24	19 32.4	18 35.8	22 38.3	12 33.9	12 52.7	17 55.4	15 45.0	6 43.2	19 31.5	22 23.5	23 28.0	29 02.9
24 Th	20 08 22	1 28 28	8♈43 10	15 30 03	19 29.2	18 37.1	24 44.1	13 47.7	13 29.5	18 21.5	15 37.8	6 49.9	19 28.5	22 22.3	23 26.5	29 01.7
25 F	20 12 18	2 25 46	22 21 06	29 16 23	19 26.0	18R 37.9	26 50.5	15 01.4	14 06.3	18 47.6	15 30.6	6 56.5	19 25.6	22 21.1	23 25.0	29 00.4
26 Sa	20 16 15	3 23 05	6♉15 51	13♉19 24	19 22.8	18 38.1	28 57.4	16 15.2	14 43.2	19 13.7	15 23.6	7 03.2	19 22.6	22 19.8	23 23.5	28 59.2
27 Su	20 20 11	4 20 25	20 26 50	27 37 53	19 19.7	18 37.6	1♌04.4	17 29.0	15 20.2	19 39.8	15 16.7	7 10.0	19 19.6	22 18.4	23 22.0	28 58.0
28 M	20 24 08	5 17 46	4♊52 07	12♊09 03	19 16.5	18 36.6	3 11.3	18 42.7	15 57.2	20 05.9	15 09.8	7 16.7	19 16.5	22 17.1	23 20.5	28 56.8
29 Tu	20 28 04	6 15 09	19 28 05	26 48 31	19 13.3	18 35.2	5 17.8	19 56.5	16 34.2	20 32.0	15 03.0	7 23.6	19 13.5	22 15.7	23 19.0	28 55.7
30 W	20 32 01	7 12 32	4♋09 35	11♋30 27	19 10.1	18 33.8	7 23.6	21 10.3	17 11.3	20 58.1	14 56.4	7 30.4	19 10.4	22 14.2	23 17.4	28 54.5
31 Th	20 35 57	8♌09 56	18 50 18	26 08 16	19♒07.0	18♒32.7	9♌28.7	22♌24.0	17♍48.5	21♋24.2	14♑49.8	7♍37.3	19♒07.4	22♓12.7	23♒15.9	28♐53.4

1st of Month

Julian Day # 2454648.5
Obliquity 23°26'24"
SVP 5♓08'17"
GC 26♐57.5
Eris 21♈46.1

Day	⚴
1	16♉38.3
6	18 37.7
11	20 36.5
16	22 34.4
21	24 31.5
26	26 27.5
31	28 22.2

Day	⚵
1	18♐03.8R
6	17 07.1R
11	16 16.7R
16	15 33.4R
21	14 57.9R
26	14 30.6R
31	14 11.8R

Day	⚶
1	0♉16.6
6	1 58.9
11	3 36.9
16	5 10.3
21	6 38.7
26	8 01.8
31	9 18.9

DECLINATION and LATITUDE

Day	☉ Decl	☽ Decl	☽ Lat	☽12h Decl	☿ Decl	☿ Lat	♀ Decl	♀ Lat	♂ Decl	♂ Lat	⚳ Decl	⚳ Lat	♃ Decl	♃ Lat	♄ Decl	♄ Lat
1 Tu	23N06	26N43	4N50	27N23	19N37	3S18	23N23	0N52	12N41	1N08	25N29	2N18	22S20	0S10	11N26	1N41
2 W	23 02	27 32	4 11	27 10	19 52	3 07	23 16	0 53	12 28	1 08	25 29	2 20	22 21	0 11	11 24	1 41
3 Th	22 57	26 18	3 15	24 58	20 08	2 56	23 09	0 55	12 15	1 07	25 29	2 22	22 21	0 11	11 22	1 41
4 F	22 52	23 13	2 07	21 06	20 23	2 45	23 00	0 57	12 01	1 06	25 29	2 24	22 23	0 11	11 19	1 41
5 Sa	22 46	18 42	0 51	16 04	20 40	2 33	22 51	0 59	11 48	1 06	25 28	2 25	22 25	0 11	11 17	1 41
6 Su	22 40	13 15	0S26	10 18	20 56	2 21	22 42	1 01	11 34	1 05	25 28	2 27	22 26	0 11	11 15	1 41
7 M	22 34	7 18	1 39	4 15	21 12	2 08	22 31	1 02	11 21	1 05	25 28	2 29	22 27	0 11	11 13	1 41
8 Tu	22 27	1 13	2 44	1S47	21 27	1 55	22 20	1 04	11 07	1 04	25 27	2 31	22 28	0 11	11 11	1 41
9 W	22 20	4S43	3 39	7 34	21 42	1 43	22 09	1 06	10 53	1 03	25 27	2 33	22 29	0 12	11 09	1 41
10 Th	22 13	10 18	4 22	12 55	21 57	1 30	21 56	1 07	10 39	1 03	25 26	2 35	22 30	0 12	11 06	1 41
11 F	22 05	15 23	4 53	17 40	22 10	1 16	21 44	1 09	10 26	1 02	25 26	2 36	22 31	0 12	11 04	1 41
12 Sa	21 57	19 46	5 09	21 40	22 22	1 03	21 30	1 10	10 12	1 01	25 25	2 38	22 33	0 12	11 02	1 41
13 Su	21 48	23 20	5 12	24 45	22 33	0 50	21 16	1 12	9 58	1 01	25 24	2 40	22 34	0 12	10 60	1 40
14 M	21 39	25 54	5 02	26 45	22 43	0 37	21 01	1 13	9 44	1 00	25 23	2 42	22 35	0 12	10 57	1 40
15 Tu	21 30	27 19	4 39	27 33	22 51	0 25	20 46	1 15	9 29	0 59	25 22	2 44	22 36	0 12	10 55	1 40
16 W	21 20	27 29	4 03	27 04	22 57	0 12	20 30	1 16	9 15	0 59	25 21	2 46	22 37	0 13	10 53	1 40
17 Th	21 10	26 21	3 17	25 18	23 01	0 00	20 13	1 17	9 01	0 58	25 20	2 47	22 38	0 13	10 50	1 40
18 F	20 60	23 58	2 21	22 20	23 02	0N11	19 56	1 18	8 46	0 58	25 19	2 49	22 39	0 13	10 48	1 40
19 Sa	20 49	20 27	1 18	18 19	23 02	0 23	19 38	1 19	8 32	0 57	25 17	2 51	22 40	0 13	10 45	1 40
20 Su	20 38	15 59	0 10	13 27	22 58	0 33	19 20	1 20	8 18	0 56	25 16	2 53	22 41	0 13	10 43	1 40
21 M	20 26	10 45	0N59	7 56	22 53	0 43	19 01	1 21	8 03	0 56	25 15	2 55	22 42	0 13	10 41	1 40
22 Tu	20 15	5 00	2 07	1 60	22 44	0 53	18 42	1 22	7 48	0 55	25 13	2 57	22 43	0 13	10 38	1 40
23 W	20 02	1N03	3 09	4N07	22 33	1 01	18 22	1 23	7 34	0 54	25 12	2 59	22 44	0 13	10 36	1 40
24 Th	19 50	7 10	4 03	10 10	22 19	1 09	18 02	1 24	7 19	0 54	25 10	3 01	22 45	0 14	10 33	1 40
25 F	19 37	13 05	4 43	15 51	22 02	1 17	17 41	1 25	7 04	0 53	25 08	3 03	22 46	0 14	10 31	1 40
26 Sa	19 24	18 27	5 09	20 50	21 43	1 23	17 20	1 26	6 50	0 53	25 06	3 04	22 47	0 14	10 28	1 40
27 Su	19 11	22 56	5 16	24 42	21 22	1 29	16 58	1 26	6 35	0 52	25 04	3 06	22 48	0 14	10 26	1 40
28 M	18 57	26 05	5 03	27 02	20 58	1 34	16 36	1 27	6 20	0 51	25 02	3 08	22 49	0 14	10 23	1 40
29 Tu	18 43	27 32	4 31	27 32	20 31	1 38	16 13	1 27	6 05	0 51	25 00	3 10	22 50	0 14	10 20	1 40
30 W	18 28	27 04	3 40	26 07	20 03	1 41	15 50	1 28	5 50	0 50	24 58	3 12	22 50	0 14	10 18	1 40
31 Th	18N14	24N42	2N37	22N54	19N32	1N43	15N26	1N28	5N35	0N49	24N56	3N14	22S51	0S14	10N15	1N40

Day	⚷ Decl	⚷ Lat	♅ Decl	♅ Lat	♆ Decl	♆ Lat	♇ Decl	♇ Lat
1	8S05	6N56	3S38	0S47	13S52	0S20	17S04	6N23
6	8 08	6 57	3 39	0 47	13 54	0 20	17 04	6 22
11	8 10	6 58	3 40	0 47	13 56	0 20	17 05	6 21
16	8 13	6 59	3 42	0 47	13 58	0 20	17 06	6 20
21	8 17	6 60	3 44	0 48	14 00	0 21	17 07	6 19
26	8 21	7 00	3 46	0 48	14 03	0 21	17 08	6 18
31	8S25	7N01	3S49	0S48	14S05	0S21	17S09	6N17

Day	⚴ Decl	⚴ Lat	⚵ Decl	⚵ Lat	⚶ Decl	⚶ Lat	Eris Decl	Eris Lat
1	0S34	18S05	4S40	18N19	5N21	6S38	4S28	13S56
6	0 48	18 51	4 49	18 05	5 46	6 48	4 28	13 57
11	1 05	19 39	5 01	17 48	6 09	6 59	4 28	13 57
16	1 27	20 29	5 16	17 29	6 29	7 10	4 29	13 58
21	1 52	21 21	5 33	17 08	6 46	7 22	4 29	13 59
26	2 21	22 16	5 53	16 46	7 01	7 34	4 30	13 59
31	2S54	23S14	6S14	16N22	7N13	7S46	4S31	13S60

Moon Phenomena

Max/0 Decl

dy	hr mn	
1	21:49	27N32
8	4:52	0 S
15	15:06	27S34
22	19:52	0 N
29	6:07	27N36

Perigee/Apogee

dy	hr m		kilometers
1	21:39	p	359515
14	4:12	a	405452
29	23:34	p	363883

Max/0 Lat

dy	hr mn	
5	15:55	0 S
12	17:29	5S13
20	3:28	0 N
26	21:03	5N16

PH	dy	hr mn	
●	3	2:20	11♋32
☽	10	4:36	18♎18
○	18	8:00	26♑04
☾	25	18:43	3♉10

Void of Course Moon

Last Aspect			☽ Ingress		
2 7:09	♇	☍	♋	2	7:54
3 20:15	♅	△	♌	4	8:16
6 10:05	♇	△	♍	6	11:05
8 16:22	♇	□	♎	8	17:32
11 2:15	♇	⚹	♏	11	3:36
13 3:06	♆	□	♐	13	15:51
16 2:45	♇	☌	♑	16	4:21
18 8:00	☉	☍	♒	18	15:41
20 23:26	♇	⚹	♓	21	1:09
23 6:40	♇	□	♈	23	8:23
25 11:31	♇	△	♉	25	13:15
27 4:53	♆	□	♊	27	15:56
29 15:26	♇	☍	♋	29	17:13
31 5:32	♅	△	♌	31	18:23

DAILY ASPECTARIAN

1 Tu
☽ ⊻ ♀ 9:40
☿ ⊼ ♃ 12:16
☽ ⊼ ♃ 13:33
☽ ☌ ☿ 13:39
♂ ♍ 16:22
☽ △ ⚷ 16:42
☽ □ ♅ 20:12
☽ △ ♆ 22:13

2 W
⚳ ⚼ ♆ 6:57
☽ ☍ ♇ 7:09
☽ ⚹ ♂ 8:32
☽ ⚹ ♄ 15:20
☽ ⚼ ⚷ 16:31
☽ ⚼ ♆ 22:06
☽ ☌ ⚳ 22:34

3 Th
☉ ☌ ☽ 2:20
♀ ☍ ♃ 5:19
☽ ∥ ⚳ 7:51
☽ ∠ ♂ 9:32
☿ △ ⚷ 10:59
☽ ☍ ♃ 13:04
☽ ☌ ♀ 13:51
☽ ∠ ♄ 15:34
☽ ⊼ ⚷ 16:34
☽ ⊻ ☿ 17:01
☽ △ ♅ 20:15
☽ ⊼ ♆ 22:16

4 F
☽ ∥ ♀ 1:21
☉ ∥ ☽ 2:13
☽ ⋕ ♃ 4:55
☽ ⊼ ♇ 7:26
☽ ⊻ ♂ 11:00
♀ ∠ ♄ 12:11
☽ ∥ ☿ 14:52
☽ ⊻ ♄ 16:17
☽ ∠ ☿ 19:39
☽ ⚼ ♅ 20:54
♀ ⊼ ⚷ 21:46

5 Sa
☽ ⊻ ⚳ 1:02
☉ ⊻ ☽ 6:58
☽ ⋕ ♇ 7:30
☽ ⚼ ♇ 8:22
☿ □ ♅ 11:08
☽ ⊼ ♃ 14:17
☽ ☍ ⚷ 18:17
☽ ⊻ ♀ 20:19
☽ ⋕ ♆ 21:17
☽ ⊼ ♅ 22:17
☽ ⚹ ☿ 23:21

6 Su
☽ ☍ ♆ 0:23
☽ ∠ ⚳ 3:24
☽ ∥ ♂ 7:10
☽ ∥ ♄ 8:14
☉ ∥ ♀ 8:40
☽ △ ♇ 10:05
♂ ⚼ ♃ 10:35
☉ ∠ ☽ 10:36
☿ △ ♆ 10:47
☽ ⚼ ♃ 16:01
☽ ☌ ♂ 16:20
♀ △ ♅ 18:33
☽ ☌ ♄ 19:59
☽ ⋕ ⚷ 20:41

7 M
☽ ∠ ♀ 1:09
☽ ⚹ ⚳ 6:44
♀ ⋕ ♃ 9:10
☽ ⋕ ♅ 14:23
☉ ⚹ ☽ 15:24
♂ ∥ ♄ 16:01
♀ ⊼ ♆ 17:47
☽ △ ♃ 18:41
☉ ⋕ ♃ 22:03
☽ ⊼ ⚷ 23:19

8 Tu
☽ ☍ ♅ 3:45
☽ ⊼ ♆ 5:58
☽ ⚹ ♀ 7:16
☽ □ ☿ 10:58
☽ □ ♇ 16:22
☽ ∥ ♅ 19:39

9 W
☽ ⊻ ♂ 1:54
☽ ⚼ ⚷ 3:17
☽ ⊻ ♄ 3:31
☉ ☍ ♃ 7:40
☽ ⚼ ♆ 10:11
☽ ∥ ⚷ 14:33
☽ □ ⚳ 16:38
☿ ∥ ♀ 23:56

10 Th
☽ ⋕ ♂ 1:31
☽ □ ♃ 2:47
☽ ⋕ ♄ 3:36
☉ □ ☽ 4:36
☽ △ ⚷ 8:07
☽ ∠ ♂ 8:17
☽ ∠ ♄ 8:41
☿ ☍ ♇ 9:51
☽ ⊼ ♅ 12:58
☽ △ ♆ 15:15
☽ ∥ ♆ 16:50
♂ ☌ ♄ 18:12
☉ ∥ ☿ 18:18
☿ ♋ 20:18
☽ □ ♀ 23:11

11 F
☽ ⚹ ♇ 2:15
☽ △ ☿ 4:41
☽ ∥ ♇ 8:52
☽ ⚹ ♄ 14:35
☽ ⚹ ♂ 15:29
☽ ⚼ ♅ 18:40

12 Sa
☉ ⊼ ⚷ 0:09
♀ ⊼ ♇ 4:50
☽ △ ⚳ 6:03
☽ ∠ ♇ 8:08
☽ ⋕ ♀ 10:13
☉ ⋕ ☽ 13:21
☽ ⚹ ♃ 13:42
☉ ∠ ♄ 15:01
☽ ⚼ ☿ 15:21
☽ ⋕ ☿ 17:52
☽ ∥ ♃ 18:11
♀ ♌ 18:40
☽ □ ⚷ 19:38
☉ △ ☽ 21:25

13 Su
☿ ⋕ ♃ 0:46
☽ △ ♅ 0:48
☽ □ ♆ 3:06
☽ ⚼ ⚳ 13:27
☽ ⊻ ♇ 14:21
☽ △ ♀ 18:18
☽ ⋕ ⚳ 18:22
☽ ∠ ♃ 19:41
☿ ⚼ ⚷ 20:54

14 M
☽ ⊼ ☿ 2:43
☽ □ ♄ 3:32
☉ ⚼ ☽ 6:23
☽ □ ♂ 7:10
☿ ⚹ ♄ 8:37
☉ △ ♅ 15:04
☽ ⊼ ⚳ 20:56

15 Tu
☽ ⊻ ♃ 1:40
☽ ⚼ ♀ 4:07
☉ ∠ ♂ 7:49
☽ ⚹ ⚷ 8:02
☽ □ ♅ 13:20
☉ ⊼ ☽ 15:18
☽ ⚹ ♆ 15:35
☉ ⊼ ♆ 18:51
☿ ⚹ ♂ 21:12
☿ ⚼ ♆ 22:28

16 W
☽ ☌ ♇ 2:45
☽ ⊼ ♀ 13:40
☽ ∠ ⚷ 14:00
☽ △ ♄ 16:26
☽ ∠ ♆ 21:33
☽ △ ♂ 22:41

17 Th
☽ ☍ ☿ 1:49
☽ ☍ ⚳ 11:14
☽ ⋕ ⚳ 11:47
☽ ☌ ♃ 13:02
♀ ⊻ ♄ 18:55
☽ ⊻ ⚷ 19:39
☽ ⚼ ♄ 22:24

18 F
☽ ⚹ ♅ 0:58
☽ ⊻ ♆ 3:08
☽ ⚼ ♂ 5:52
☽ ⋕ ☿ 7:04
☉ ☍ ☽ 8:00
☽ ∥ ♃ 9:47
☽ ⊻ ♇ 14:01
♀ ⚼ ♅ 20:29
☉ ⋕ ☽ 21:41

19 Sa
⚳ ☍ ♃ 2:28
☽ ⊼ ♄ 3:56
☽ ⋕ ♀ 5:05
☽ ∠ ♅ 6:10
☽ ☍ ♀ 7:15
☽ ⊼ ♂ 12:31
☽ ∥ ♇ 18:19
☽ ∠ ♇ 18:59
☿ ☍ ♃ 19:55
☽ ⊻ ♃ 22:49
☽ ⊼ ☿ 23:25
☽ ⊼ ⚳ 23:46

20 Su
☿ ☌ ⚳ 2:07
♂ ⋕ ⚷ 2:19
☽ ☌ ⚷ 5:34
☽ ∥ ♆ 9:27
☽ ⊻ ♅ 10:52
☽ ☌ ♆ 12:55
☉ ⊼ ☽ 22:25
☽ ⚹ ♇ 23:26

21 M
☽ ⋕ ♄ 0:22
☽ ∠ ♃ 2:59
☽ ⚼ ⚳ 5:10
☽ ⚼ ☿ 9:11
☽ ∥ ⚷ 10:31
☉ ⊼ ♇ 11:49
☽ ⋕ ♂ 12:01
☿ ⊼ ⚷ 12:47
☽ ☍ ♄ 13:26
☽ ⊼ ♀ 22:07

22 Tu
☽ ☍ ♂ 0:01
☿ ⋕ ♃ 2:06
☉ ⚼ ☽ 4:36
☽ ∥ ♅ 5:05
☽ ⚹ ♃ 6:36
☽ △ ⚳ 9:58
☉ ♌ 10:56
☿ ∠ ♄ 12:50
☽ ⊻ ⚷ 13:24
☽ △ ☿ 18:07
☽ ☌ ♅ 18:37
☽ ⊻ ♆ 20:34
☿ △ ♅ 21:11

23 W
☽ ⚼ ♀ 4:24
☽ □ ♇ 6:40
☿ ⊼ ♆ 9:24
☉ △ ☽ 10:03
☽ ⋕ ♅ 10:33
♀ ⊻ ♂ 12:10
☽ ∠ ⚷ 16:27
☽ ⊼ ♄ 20:36
☽ ∠ ♆ 23:30

24 Th
☽ ∥ ♂ 0:34
♀ ⚼ ♇ 4:28
☽ ⋕ ⚷ 4:34
☽ ⊼ ♂ 8:51
☽ △ ♀ 9:53
☽ □ ♃ 12:07
☽ ∥ ♄ 13:27
☽ □ ⚳ 17:35
☽ ⚹ ⚷ 18:55
☽ ⚼ ♄ 23:17
☽ ⊻ ♅ 24:00

25 F
☽ ⚹ ♆ 1:51
☽ ⋕ ♆ 4:04
♀ ⊼ ♃ 8:40
☽ □ ☿ 9:12
☽ △ ♇ 11:31
☽ ⚼ ♂ 12:15
☽ ⋕ ♇ 17:47
☉ □ ☽ 18:43
☽ ∥ ♀ 19:01

26 Sa
☿ ⊼ ♇ 0:20
☽ △ ♄ 1:21
☽ ∠ ♅ 1:49
☉ ∥ ☽ 4:25
⚳ ⊼ ⚷ 7:19
☿ ♌ 11:49
☿ ∠ ♂ 12:12
♀ ⋕ ♇ 12:34
☽ ⚼ ♇ 13:06
☽ △ ♂ 15:01
☽ △ ♃ 15:22
☽ ∥ ☿ 15:36
☽ □ ♀ 18:33
♂ △ ♃ 22:05
☽ □ ⚷ 22:07
☽ ⚹ ⚳ 22:39
☽ ⋕ ♃ 23:12

27 Su
☽ ⚹ ♅ 3:07
☽ □ ♆ 4:53
☽ ⊼ ♇ 14:12
☽ ∥ ⚳ 14:49
☽ ⚼ ♃ 16:16
☽ ⚹ ☿ 20:45

28 M
☽ ∠ ⚳ 0:23
☉ ⚹ ☽ 0:45
☽ □ ♄ 4:01
♀ ☍ ⚷ 10:34
☽ ⊼ ♃ 16:49
☽ □ ♂ 19:03
☽ △ ⚷ 23:36

29 Tu
☽ ⚹ ♀ 0:51
☽ ∠ ☿ 1:35
☽ ⊻ ⚳ 1:48
☉ ∠ ☽ 3:07
☽ □ ♅ 4:34
☽ △ ♆ 6:17
☽ ☍ ♇ 15:26
♀ ⊻ ⚳ 17:52
☉ ☌ ☿ 20:06
☿ ⚼ ♅ 22:13

30 W
☽ ⚼ ⚷ 0:01
☉ ⚼ ♅ 0:41
☿ ⊻ ♄ 1:23
☽ ∠ ♀ 3:35
☉ ⊻ ☽ 5:19
☽ ⚹ ♄ 5:30
☽ ⊻ ☿ 6:09
☽ ⚼ ♆ 6:44
☉ ⊻ ♄ 8:30
☽ ☍ ♃ 17:29
♀ ⊼ ♅ 20:24
☽ ⚹ ♂ 22:14
☽ ∥ ⚳ 22:16

31 Th
☽ ⊼ ⚷ 0:28
☽ ☌ ⚳ 4:20
☽ △ ♅ 5:32
☽ ∠ ♄ 6:16
☽ ⊻ ♀ 6:23
☽ ⊼ ♆ 7:15
☽ ⋕ ♃ 12:13
♀ ☍ ♆ 16:30
☽ ⊼ ♇ 16:31

LONGITUDE

Day	Sid.Time	☉	☽	☽ 12 hour	Mean ☊	True ☊	☿	♀	♂	⚳	♃	♄	⚷	♅	♆	♇
	h m s	° ' "	° ' "	° ' "	° '	° '	° '	° '	° '	° '	° '	° '	° '	° '	° '	° '
1 F	20 39 54	9♌07 21	3♌23 32	10♌35 22	19♒03.8	18♒31.9	11♌32.7	23♌37.8	18♍25.7	21♋50.2	14♑43.4	7♍44.3	19♒04.3	22♓11.2	23♒14.3	28♐52.3
2 Sa	20 43 51	10 04 47	17 43 03	24 46 03	19 00.6	18D 31.7	13 35.7	24 51.6	19 03.0	22 16.3	14R 37.1	7 51.2	19R 01.2	22R 09.7	23R 12.7	28R 51.2
3 Su	20 47 47	11 02 13	1♍43 53	8♍36 15	18 57.4	18 31.9	15 37.4	26 05.4	19 40.3	22 42.3	14 30.8	7 58.3	18 58.0	22 08.1	23 11.1	28 50.2
4 M	20 51 44	11 59 41	15 22 54	22 03 47	18 54.3	18 32.3	17 37.9	27 19.1	20 17.7	23 08.4	14 24.8	8 05.3	18 54.9	22 06.4	23 09.5	28 49.2
5 Tu	20 55 40	12 57 09	28 38 56	5♎08 29	18 51.1	18 32.9	19 36.9	28 32.9	20 55.1	23 34.4	14 18.8	8 12.4	18 51.8	22 04.7	23 07.9	28 48.2
6 W	20 59 37	13 54 38	11♎32 41	17 51 51	18 47.9	18 33.4	21 34.5	29 46.6	21 32.6	24 00.4	14 13.0	8 19.5	18 48.6	22 03.0	23 06.3	28 47.2
7 Th	21 03 33	14 52 07	24 06 23	0♏16 43	18 44.7	18 33.8	23 30.7	1♍00.4	22 10.1	24 26.4	14 07.3	8 26.6	18 45.5	22 01.3	23 04.7	28 46.2
8 F	21 07 30	15 49 38	6♏23 23	12 26 53	18 41.5	18R 33.9	25 25.3	2 14.1	22 47.6	24 52.4	14 01.7	8 33.8	18 42.3	21 59.5	23 03.1	28 45.3
9 Sa	21 11 26	16 47 09	18 27 47	24 26 40	18 38.4	18 34.0	27 18.4	3 27.9	23 25.2	25 18.3	13 56.3	8 41.0	18 39.2	21 57.7	23 01.5	28 44.4
10 Su	21 15 23	17 44 41	0♐24 04	6♐20 34	18 35.2	18D 33.9	29 10.0	4 41.6	24 02.9	25 44.3	13 51.0	8 48.2	18 36.0	21 55.9	22 59.9	28 43.5
11 M	21 19 20	18 42 14	12 16 44	18 13 06	18 32.0	18 33.9	1♍00.1	5 55.3	24 40.6	26 10.2	13 45.9	8 55.4	18 32.8	21 54.0	22 58.2	28 42.6
12 Tu	21 23 16	19 39 48	24 10 11	0♑08 28	18 28.8	18 34.0	2 48.6	7 09.1	25 18.4	26 36.1	13 40.9	9 02.7	18 29.7	21 52.1	22 56.6	28 41.8
13 W	21 27 13	20 37 23	6♑08 25	12 10 26	18 25.7	18 34.2	4 35.6	8 22.8	25 56.2	27 02.0	13 36.1	9 10.0	18 26.5	21 50.2	22 55.0	28 41.0
14 Th	21 31 09	21 34 59	18 14 54	24 22 09	18 22.5	18 34.5	6 21.2	9 36.5	26 34.0	27 27.9	13 31.5	9 17.3	18 23.4	21 48.3	22 53.3	28 40.2
15 F	21 35 06	22 32 36	0♒32 29	6♒46 37	18 19.3	18 34.8	8 05.2	10 50.2	27 11.9	27 53.8	13 27.0	9 24.7	18 20.2	21 46.3	22 51.7	28 39.4
16 Sa	21 39 02	23 30 14	13 03 14	19 24 00	18 16.1	18R 35.0	9 47.8	12 03.9	27 49.9	28 19.6	13 22.6	9 32.0	18 17.1	21 44.3	22 50.1	28 38.7
17 Su	21 42 59	24 27 54	25 48 28	2♓16 41	18 13.0	18 34.9	11 28.8	13 17.6	28 27.9	28 45.4	13 18.5	9 39.4	18 14.0	21 42.3	22 48.4	28 38.0
18 M	21 46 55	25 25 34	8♓48 40	15 24 20	18 09.8	18 34.6	13 08.5	14 31.2	29 05.9	29 11.2	13 14.5	9 46.8	18 10.8	21 40.2	22 46.8	28 37.3
19 Tu	21 50 52	26 23 16	22 03 37	28 46 23	18 06.6	18 33.9	14 46.7	15 44.9	29 44.0	29 37.0	13 10.6	9 54.2	18 07.7	21 38.1	22 45.2	28 36.7
20 W	21 54 49	27 20 59	5♈32 29	12♈21 45	18 03.4	18 32.9	16 23.4	16 58.6	0♎22.1	0♌02.7	13 07.0	10 01.6	18 04.6	21 36.0	22 43.5	28 36.0
21 Th	21 58 45	28 18 44	19 13 59	26 08 59	18 00.2	18 31.8	17 58.8	18 12.2	1 00.3	0 28.5	13 03.5	10 09.1	18 01.5	21 33.9	22 41.9	28 35.4
22 F	22 02 42	29 16 31	3♉06 31	10♉06 22	17 57.1	18 30.7	19 32.7	19 25.9	1 38.6	0 54.2	13 00.2	10 16.5	17 58.5	21 31.7	22 40.3	28 34.9
23 Sa	22 06 38	0♍14 19	17 08 17	24 12 02	17 53.9	18D 29.9	21 05.2	20 39.5	2 16.9	1 19.8	12 57.0	10 24.0	17 55.4	21 29.6	22 38.6	28 34.3
24 Su	22 10 35	1 12 09	1♊17 19	8♊23 54	17 50.7	18 29.7	22 36.3	21 53.2	2 55.2	1 45.5	12 54.1	10 31.5	17 52.4	21 27.4	22 37.0	28 33.8
25 M	22 14 31	2 10 01	15 31 28	22 39 43	17 47.5	18 30.0	24 05.9	23 06.8	3 33.6	2 11.1	12 51.3	10 39.0	17 49.3	21 25.2	22 35.4	28 33.3
26 Tu	22 18 28	3 07 55	29 48 19	6♋56 53	17 44.4	18 30.8	25 34.2	24 20.4	4 12.1	2 36.8	12 48.7	10 46.5	17 46.3	21 22.9	22 33.8	28 32.9
27 W	22 22 24	4 05 51	14♋05 04	21 12 26	17 41.2	18 31.9	27 01.0	25 34.1	4 50.6	3 02.3	12 46.3	10 54.1	17 43.3	21 20.7	22 32.2	28 32.5
28 Th	22 26 21	5 03 48	28 18 34	5♌23 01	17 38.0	18 33.0	28 26.3	26 47.7	5 29.2	3 27.9	12 44.0	11 01.6	17 40.4	21 18.4	22 30.6	28 32.1
29 F	22 30 18	6 01 47	12♌25 20	19 25 05	17 34.8	18R 33.7	29 50.1	28 01.3	6 07.8	3 53.4	12 42.0	11 09.1	17 37.4	21 16.1	22 29.0	28 31.7
30 Sa	22 34 14	6 59 48	26 21 49	3♍15 09	17 31.6	18 33.6	1♎12.5	29 14.9	6 46.4	4 18.9	12 40.1	11 16.7	17 34.5	21 13.8	22 27.5	28 31.4
31 Su	22 38 11	7♍57 50	10♍04 42	16 50 10	17♒28.5	18♒32.6	2♎33.3	0♎28.5	7♎25.2	4♌44.4	12♑38.5	11♍24.2	17♒31.6	21♓11.5	22♒25.9	28♐31.1

1st of Month

Julian Day # 2454679.5
Obliquity 23°26'24"
SVP 5♓08'11"
GC 26♐57.5
Eris 21♈46.6R

Day	⚴		Day	⚵		Day	⚶
1	28♉45.0		1	14♐09.1R		1	9♉33.6
6	0♊37.8		6	14 00.6R		6	10 42.9
11	2 28.7		11	14 00.8		11	11 45.2
16	4 17.5		16	14 09.3		16	12 39.8
21	6 03.7		21	14 25.8		21	13 26.3
26	7 47.1		26	14 50.1		26	14 04.0
31	9 27.1		31	15 21.8		31	14 32.3

DECLINATION and LATITUDE

Day	☉ Decl	☽ Decl	☽ Lat	☽ 12h Decl	☿ Decl	☿ Lat	♀ Decl	♀ Lat	♂ Decl	♂ Lat	⚳ Decl	⚳ Lat	♃ Decl	♃ Lat	♄ Decl	♄ Lat
1 F	17N59	20N44	1N23	18N17	19N00	1N45	15N02	1N28	5N20	0N49	24N54	3N16	22S52	0S15	10N13	1N40
2 Sa	17 43	15 36	0 04	12 43	18 26	1 46	14 38	1 29	5 04	0 48	24 51	3 18	22 53	0 15	10 10	1 40
3 Su	17 28	9 44	1S13	6 40	17 51	1 46	14 13	1 29	4 49	0 48	24 49	3 20	22 54	0 15	10 07	1 40
4 M	17 12	3 33	2 23	0 28	17 14	1 46	13 48	1 29	4 34	0 47	24 46	3 22	22 55	0 15	10 05	1 40
5 Tu	16 56	2S35	3 24	5S34	16 36	1 45	13 22	1 29	4 19	0 46	24 44	3 24	22 55	0 15	10 02	1 40
6 W	16 39	8 27	4 13	11 12	15 57	1 43	12 56	1 29	4 03	0 46	24 41	3 26	22 56	0 15	9 59	1 40
7 Th	16 22	13 49	4 49	16 16	15 17	1 41	12 30	1 29	3 48	0 45	24 39	3 28	22 57	0 15	9 57	1 40
8 F	16 06	18 31	5 10	20 34	14 36	1 39	12 04	1 29	3 33	0 45	24 36	3 30	22 57	0 15	9 54	1 40
9 Sa	15 48	22 24	5 17	23 58	13 54	1 35	11 37	1 28	3 17	0 44	24 33	3 32	22 58	0 16	9 51	1 40
10 Su	15 31	25 17	5 10	26 19	13 12	1 32	11 09	1 28	3 02	0 43	24 30	3 34	22 59	0 16	9 49	1 40
11 M	15 13	27 04	4 50	27 30	12 29	1 27	10 42	1 28	2 46	0 43	24 27	3 36	22 59	0 16	9 46	1 40
12 Tu	14 55	27 36	4 18	27 24	11 46	1 23	10 14	1 27	2 31	0 42	24 24	3 38	22 60	0 16	9 43	1 40
13 W	14 37	26 52	3 34	26 01	11 02	1 18	9 46	1 27	2 15	0 41	24 21	3 40	23 01	0 16	9 40	1 40
14 Th	14 19	24 51	2 40	23 23	10 18	1 12	9 18	1 26	1 59	0 41	24 18	3 42	23 01	0 16	9 38	1 40
15 F	13 60	21 38	1 38	19 38	9 34	1 07	8 49	1 26	1 44	0 40	24 15	3 44	23 02	0 16	9 35	1 40
16 Sa	13 41	17 23	0 31	14 56	8 50	1 01	8 21	1 25	1 28	0 40	24 12	3 47	23 02	0 16	9 32	1 40
17 Su	13 22	12 17	0N40	9 30	8 06	0 54	7 52	1 24	1 12	0 39	24 08	3 49	23 03	0 16	9 29	1 40
18 M	13 03	6 34	1 50	3 33	7 21	0 48	7 22	1 23	0 57	0 38	24 05	3 51	23 03	0 16	9 27	1 40
19 Tu	12 43	0 28	2 55	2N38	6 37	0 41	6 53	1 22	0 41	0 38	24 02	3 53	23 04	0 16	9 24	1 40
20 W	12 24	5N45	3 52	8 48	5 53	0 33	6 24	1 21	0 25	0 37	23 58	3 55	23 04	0 17	9 21	1 40
21 Th	12 04	11 47	4 36	14 36	5 09	0 26	5 54	1 20	0 10	0 37	23 55	3 57	23 05	0 17	9 18	1 40
22 F	11 44	17 19	5 05	19 47	4 25	0 18	5 24	1 19	0S06	0 36	23 51	3 59	23 05	0 17	9 15	1 40
23 Sa	11 23	21 60	5 16	23 54	3 42	0 11	4 54	1 18	0 22	0 35	23 47	4 02	23 05	0 17	9 13	1 40
24 Su	11 03	25 27	5 08	26 36	2 58	0 03	4 24	1 17	0 38	0 35	23 44	4 04	23 06	0 17	9 10	1 40
25 M	10 42	27 19	4 42	27 36	2 16	0S06	3 53	1 15	0 54	0 34	23 40	4 06	23 06	0 17	9 07	1 40
26 Tu	10 21	27 24	3 58	26 45	1 33	0 14	3 23	1 14	1 09	0 33	23 36	4 08	23 06	0 17	9 04	1 40
27 W	10 00	25 40	2 59	24 10	0 51	0 22	2 52	1 13	1 25	0 33	23 32	4 10	23 07	0 17	9 01	1 40
28 Th	9 39	22 17	1 49	20 05	0 09	0 31	2 22	1 11	1 41	0 32	23 28	4 13	23 07	0 17	8 58	1 40
29 F	9 18	17 37	0 34	14 55	0S32	0 39	1 51	1 10	1 57	0 32	23 24	4 15	23 07	0 17	8 56	1 40
30 Sa	8 57	12 03	0S43	9 04	1 13	0 48	1 20	1 08	2 13	0 31	23 20	4 17	23 07	0 17	8 53	1 40
31 Su	8N35	6N00	1S56	2N54	1S53	0S57	0N49	1N06	2S29	0N30	23N16	4N19	23S08	0S18	8N50	1N40

Day	⚷ Decl	⚷ Lat	♅ Decl	♅ Lat	♆ Decl	♆ Lat	♇ Decl	♇ Lat
1	8S26	7N01	3S50	0S48	14S06	0S21	17S09	6N17
6	8 31	7 01	3 53	0 48	14 09	0 21	17 11	6 15
11	8 35	7 01	3 57	0 48	14 11	0 21	17 12	6 14
16	8 40	7 00	4 01	0 48	14 14	0 21	17 12	6 13
21	8 46	6 60	4 05	0 48	14 17	0 21	17 14	6 12
26	8 51	6 59	4 09	0 48	14 19	0 21	17 16	6 10
31	8S56	6N58	4S14	0S48	14S22	0S21	17S17	6N09

Day	⚴ Decl	⚴ Lat	⚵ Decl	⚵ Lat	⚶ Decl	⚶ Lat	Eris Decl	Eris Lat
1	3S01	23S25	6S19	16N18	7N15	7S49	4S31	13S60
6	3 40	24 26	6 42	15 53	7 24	8 02	4 32	14 00
11	4 23	25 30	7 06	15 29	7 30	8 15	4 33	14 01
16	5 11	26 36	7 31	15 04	7 32	8 29	4 33	14 01
21	6 03	27 45	7 57	14 40	7 32	8 43	4 34	14 02
26	7 00	28 57	8 24	14 16	7 29	8 58	4 35	14 02
31	8S02	30S13	8S50	13N53	7N23	9S13	4S37	14S03

Moon Phenomena

Max/0 Decl

dy	hr mn	
4	13:49	0 S
11	22:19	27S37
19	1:49	0 N
25	13:06	27N35
31	23:14	0 S

Max/0 Lat

dy	hr mn	
2	1:22	0 S
9	0:10	5S17
16	10:27	0 N
23	2:11	5N16
29	10:32	0 S

Perigee/Apogee

dy	hr m		kilometers
10	20:26	a	404555
26	3:58	p	368696

PH	dy	hr mn	
●	1	10:14	9♌32
●	1	10:22	T 02'27"
☽	8	20:21	16♏38
○	16	21:18	24♒21
●	16	21:11	P 0.807
☾	23	23:51	1♊12
●	30	19:59	7♍48

Void of Course Moon

Last Aspect			☽ Ingress		
2 19:00	♇	△	♍	2	21:00
5 0:17	♇	□	♎	5	2:29
7 9:03	♇	✶	♏	7	11:27
9 21:03	☿	□	♐	9	23:11
12 9:05	♇	☌	♑	12	11:43
14 17:10	♂	△	♒	14	22:57
17 5:15	♇	✶	♓	17	7:47
19 11:42	♇	□	♈	19	14:11
21 16:54	☉	△	♉	21	18:39
23 9:20	♆	□	♊	23	21:49
25 21:53	♇	☍	♋	26	0:20
28 0:15	☿	✶	♌	28	2:52
30 3:45	♇	△	♍	30	6:19

DAILY ASPECTARIAN

1 F
☽∠♂ 0:04; ☽⚼♅ 6:18; ☽⚺♄ 7:18; ☽∥☿ 9:42; ☉☌☽ 10:14; ☉∥☽ 14:07; ☽☌☿ 15:53; ☽⋕♇ 17:08; ☽⚼♇ 17:29; ⚳△♅ 18:14; ☽⚻♃ 18:48; ♂⚻⚷ 22:55

2 Sa
☽☍⚷ 2:12; ☽⚺♂ 2:22; ☿⚼♇ 3:01; ☽∥♀ 4:26; ☽⋕♆ 6:17; ☽⚻♅ 7:32; ☽⚺⚳ 7:59; ☽☍♆ 9:19; ☿⚻♃ 11:28; ☽☌♀ 13:20; ☽△♇ 19:00; ☽⚼♃ 20:11; ☽∥♄ 22:26

3 Su
☽⋕⚷ 4:58; ♀⋕♆ 5:31; ☽∠⚳ 10:46; ☽☌♄ 10:59; ☉⚺☽ 17:32; ☽∥♂ 19:57; ⚳∠♄ 20:07; ☽△♃ 22:17; ☽⋕♅ 22:49

4 M
⚳⚻♆ 1:01; ☉⋕♇ 2:23; ☿⋕♇ 2:24; ☉∥☿ 2:24; ☽⚺☿ 4:44; ☽⚻⚷ 6:18; ♀ ♊ 7:34; ☽☌♂ 9:14; ☽☍♅ 12:03; ☽⚻♆ 13:57; ☽✶⚳ 14:25; ☿☍⚷ 15:06; ☉∠☽ 22:37; ☽⚺♀ 23:48

5 Tu
☽□♇ 0:17; ♀△♇ 4:54; ☽∥♅ 5:09; ☽⋕♂ 6:37; ☽⚼⚷ 9:35; ☽∠☿ 13:00; ♀⚼♃ 13:50; ☽⚼♆ 17:33; ☽⚺♄ 17:53; ☉⚼♇ 20:56; ☿⚺♂ 23:24

6 W
☽∥⚷ 0:15; ♀ ♍ 4:21; ☉✶☽ 4:50; ☽□♃ 5:01; ☿⚻♅ 5:47; ☽⋕♄ 6:35; ☽∠♀ 6:47; ☉⚻♃ 6:57; ☽△⚷ 13:45; ♂⋕♅ 14:55; ☽⋕♀ 18:20; ♂☍♅ 18:39; ☿☍♆ 18:41; ☽⚻♅ 19:59; ☽⚺♂ 20:04; ☽△♆ 22:01; ☽✶☿ 22:38; ☽∠♄ 22:42

7 Th
☽□⚳ 0:40; ☽∥♆ 1:36; ☽⋕☿ 6:12; ☽✶♇ 9:03; ☉⋕☽ 11:52; ☽✶♀ 14:55; ☿⚺⚳ 15:02; ☽∥♇ 16:47

8 F
☽⚼♅ 1:11; ☽∠♂ 2:55; ☽✶♄ 4:20; ♂⚻♆ 9:28; ⚵ D 9:41; ☽∠♇ 14:35; ☿⋕♆ 14:47; ☽✶♃ 15:02; ☉□☽ 20:21

9 Sa
☽□⚷ 0:23; ☽∥♃ 4:10; ☽△♅ 7:00; ☽□♆ 9:08; ☽✶♂ 10:30; ☽△⚳ 14:15; ☽⋕⚳ 16:41; ☿△♇ 18:19; ☿⚼♃ 20:05; ☽⚺♇ 20:37; ☽∠♃ 20:54; ☽□☿ 21:03

10 Su
☽□♀ 9:40; ☿ ♍ 10:52; ☽□♄ 17:09; ☉☍⚷ 20:17; ☽⚼⚳ 21:40

11 M
☽⚺♃ 2:59; ☽✶⚷ 12:36; ☉△☽ 14:07; ☽□♅ 19:23; ☽✶♆ 21:32

12 Tu
☽□♂ 2:25; ☽⚻⚳ 5:05; ☽☌♇ 9:05; ☽∠⚷ 18:38; ☽△☿ 20:23; ☉⚼☽ 22:53

13 W
☽∠♆ 3:32; ☽△♀ 4:58; ♀∥♄ 5:30; ☽△♄ 6:05; ☽☌♃ 14:44; ♀☌♄ 17:04

14 Th
☽⚺⚷ 0:17; ☽⋕⚳ 4:49; ☉⚻♅ 5:21; ☽✶♅ 6:58; ☉⋕♆ 7:06; ☉⚻☽ 7:06; ☽⚼☿ 7:07; ☽⚺♆ 9:05; ☽⚼♄ 11:58; ☽⚼♀ 13:51; ☽∥♃ 14:36; ☽△♂ 17:10; ☽☍⚳ 18:41; ☽⚺♇ 20:21; ☿∥♄ 23:34

15 F
☉☍♆ 7:44; ♀⋕⚷ 8:03; ☽∠♅ 11:58; ☽⚻☿ 16:49; ☽⚻♄ 17:14; ☿☌♄ 20:00; ☽⚻♀ 21:55; ☽⚼♂ 23:33

16 Sa
☽⚺♃ 0:37; ☽∥♇ 0:51; ☽∠♇ 1:07; ☿⋕⚷ 5:01; ☽☌⚷ 9:52; ☽∥♆ 15:13; ☽⚺♅ 16:21; ⚳⚻♇ 17:17; ☽☌♆ 18:24; ☉⋕☽ 18:53; ☉☍☽ 21:18

17 Su
♀△♃ 0:17; ☽∠♃ 4:38; ☽⚻♂ 5:12; ☽✶♇ 5:15; ☽⚻⚳ 5:40; ♂□♇ 6:16; ☽⋕♄ 12:07; ♀∠⚳ 13:57; ☽∥⚷ 15:18; ☽⋕☿ 20:22; ☽⋕♀ 20:27; ☿∥♀ 22:16

18 M
☿△♃ 1:24; ☽☍♄ 1:47; ☽✶♃ 8:02; ☽☍☿ 9:01; ☽∥♅ 10:03; ☽⚼⚳ 10:07; ♂✶⚳ 10:20; ☽☍♀ 11:28; ☽⚺⚷ 16:57; ☿∠⚳ 20:46; ☽⋕♂ 23:08; ☽☌♅ 23:14

19 Tu
☽⚺♆ 1:14; ☽∥♂ 4:17; ☉⚻☽ 8:21; ♂ ♎ 10:04; ☽□♇ 11:42; ☽△⚳ 13:57; ☽☍♂ 14:23; ☽⋕♅ 17:30; ☽∠⚷ 19:40; ⚳ ♌ 21:28

20 W
☽∥☿ 0:29; ☽∥♀ 2:20; ☽∠♆ 3:51; ☽⚻♄ 7:58; ☽⋕⚷ 11:47; ☉⚼☽ 12:53; ☽□♃ 13:16; ☽∥♄ 14:03; ☉⚼♃ 18:01; ♀⚻⚷ 20:39; ☽⚻☿ 21:32; ☽✶⚷ 21:54; ☽⚻♀ 22:02

21 Th
☿⚻⚷ 0:41; ☉∥☽ 1:05; ☽⚺♅ 4:03; ☽✶♆ 6:01; ☉△♇ 6:52; ☽⚼♄ 10:22; ☽⋕♆ 10:29; ☿☌♀ 15:45; ☽△♇ 16:12; ☉△☽ 16:54; ☽□⚳ 20:05; ☽⚻♂ 21:21; ☽⋕♇ 23:40

22 F
☽⚼♀ 2:30; ☽⚼☿ 2:47; ☽∠♅ 5:51; ☿⋕♅ 10:26; ☽△♄ 12:24; ☽△♃ 16:53; ☽⚼♇ 17:56; ☉ ♍ 18:03

23 Sa
☽⚼♂ 0:15; ☽□⚷ 1:20; ☿☍♅ 6:14; ☽△♀ 6:33; ☽⋕♃ 6:39; ☽✶♅ 7:23; ☽△☿ 7:32; ☽□♆ 9:20; ☽∥⚳ 11:03; ♀☍♅ 15:50; ☽⚼♃ 18:17; ☽⚻♇ 19:24; ♂⚼⚷ 22:20; ☉□☽ 23:51

24 Su
☿⚻♆ 0:12; ☽✶⚳ 0:49; ☽△♂ 2:53; ♀⋕♅ 12:16; ♀⚻♆ 13:59; ☽□♄ 15:43; ☽⚻♃ 19:31

25 M
☉⚺⚳ 0:50; ☽∠⚳ 2:53; ☽△⚷ 3:51; ☽□♅ 9:53; ☽△♆ 11:51; ☽□♀ 13:57; ☽□☿ 16:04; ☽☍♇ 21:53

26 Tu
☽⚺⚳ 4:52; ☽⚼⚷ 4:58; ☉✶☽ 6:00; ☽□♂ 7:44; ☿⋕♂ 9:42; ☽⚼♆ 13:01; ☽✶♄ 18:36; ☽☍♃ 21:48

27 W
☽⚻⚷ 6:06; ☉∠☽ 9:03; ☽△♅ 12:12; ☽⚻♆ 14:13; ☽∥⚳ 16:32; ☽⋕♃ 18:57; ☽∠♄ 20:06; ☽✶♀ 21:12

28 Th
☽✶☿ 0:15; ☽⚻♇ 0:23; ☿□♇ 1:38; ☽☌⚳ 9:01; ☉⚺☽ 12:18; ☽✶♂ 12:45; ☽⚼♅ 13:32; ♀⋕♂ 20:55; ☽⚺♄ 21:49

29 F
☽⚻♃ 0:28; ☽∠♀ 1:07; ☽⋕♇ 1:34; ☽⚼♇ 1:54; ☿ ♎ 2:51; ☽∠☿ 4:35; ☉⚺♂ 7:25; ☽☍⚷ 8:53; ♀□♇ 9:52; ♄⋕⚷ 9:53; ☽⋕♆ 14:26; ☽⚻♅ 15:09; ☽∠♂ 15:40; ☽☍♆ 17:15

30 Sa
☉⋕⚷ 1:38; ☽⚼♃ 2:16; ☿⋕♀ 2:27; ☽△♇ 3:45; ☉∥♄ 4:55; ☽⚺♀ 5:30; ☽⚺☿ 9:21; ☽⋕⚷ 12:34; ☽∥♄ 12:51; ☉∥☽ 13:17; ☽⚺⚳ 14:18; ♀ ♎ 14:42; ☽⚺♂ 19:05; ☉☌☽ 19:59; ☿⚼⚷ 23:31

31 Su
♂⚼♆ 0:26; ☽☌♄ 2:22; ☽△♃ 4:32; ☽⋕♅ 6:50; ☽⋕♂ 13:05; ☽⚻⚷ 13:11; ☽⋕☿ 14:24; ☽∠⚳ 17:45; ☽☍♅ 19:45; ☽∥♀ 21:52; ☽⚻♆ 21:59

LONGITUDE — September 2008

Day	Sid.Time	☉	☽	☽ 12 hour	Mean ☊	True ☊	☿	♀	♂	⚳	♃	♄	⚷	♅	♆	♇
	h m s	° ' "	° ' "	° ' "	° '	° '	° '	° '	° '	° '	° '	° '	° '	° '	° '	° '
1 M	22 42 07	8♍55 54	23♍31 18	0♎07 56	17♒25.3	18♒30.5	3♎52.5	1♎42.1	8♎03.9	5♌09.8	12♑37.0	11♍31.8	17♒28.8	21♓09.2	22♒24.3	28♐30.8
2 Tu	22 46 04	9 53 59	6♎39 57	13 07 21	17 22.1	18R 27.7	5 10.1	2 55.7	8 42.7	5 35.2	12R 35.7	11 39.4	17R 25.9	21R 06.9	22R 22.8	28R 30.6
3 W	22 50 00	10 52 06	19 30 10	25 48 35	17 18.9	18 24.3	6 26.1	4 09.2	9 21.6	6 00.5	12 34.6	11 46.9	17 23.1	21 04.5	22 21.2	28 30.4
4 Th	22 53 57	11 50 15	2♏02 47	8♏13 06	17 15.8	18 20.8	7 40.2	5 22.8	10 00.5	6 25.8	12 33.7	11 54.5	17 20.4	21 02.2	22 19.7	28 30.2
5 F	22 57 53	12 48 25	14 19 52	20 23 32	17 12.6	18 17.7	8 52.6	6 36.3	10 39.5	6 51.1	12 33.0	12 02.0	17 17.6	20 59.8	22 18.2	28 30.0
6 Sa	23 01 50	13 46 36	26 24 33	2♐23 27	17 09.4	18 15.4	10 03.1	7 49.9	11 18.5	7 16.3	12 32.5	12 09.6	17 14.9	20 57.4	22 16.7	28 29.9
7 Su	23 05 47	14 44 50	8♐20 46	14 17 06	17 06.2	18D 14.1	11 11.6	9 03.4	11 57.6	7 41.5	12 32.1	12 17.2	17 12.2	20 55.0	22 15.2	28 29.8
8 M	23 09 43	15 43 04	20 13 03	26 09 12	17 03.0	18 14.0	12 18.0	10 16.9	12 36.7	8 06.6	12D 32.0	12 24.7	17 09.6	20 52.7	22 13.8	28 29.8
9 Tu	23 13 40	16 41 20	2♑06 11	8♑04 35	16 59.9	18 14.9	13 22.2	11 30.4	13 15.9	8 31.7	12 32.1	12 32.3	17 07.0	20 50.3	22 12.3	28D 29.8
10 W	23 17 36	17 39 38	14 05 00	20 08 01	16 56.7	18 16.5	14 24.1	12 43.8	13 55.1	8 56.8	12 32.3	12 39.8	17 04.4	20 47.9	22 10.9	28 29.8
11 Th	23 21 33	18 37 57	26 14 08	2♒23 52	16 53.5	18 18.2	15 23.5	13 57.3	14 34.4	9 21.8	12 32.8	12 47.4	17 01.9	20 45.5	22 09.4	28 29.8
12 F	23 25 29	19 36 18	8♒37 38	14 55 50	16 50.3	18R 19.6	16 20.2	15 10.7	15 13.7	9 46.8	12 33.4	12 54.9	16 59.4	20 43.1	22 08.0	28 29.9
13 Sa	23 29 26	20 34 40	21 18 44	27 46 35	16 47.2	18 19.9	17 14.2	16 24.2	15 53.1	10 11.7	12 34.2	13 02.4	16 57.0	20 40.7	22 06.6	28 30.0
14 Su	23 33 22	21 33 04	4♓19 28	10♓57 26	16 44.0	18 18.8	18 05.1	17 37.6	16 32.5	10 36.6	12 35.3	13 09.9	16 54.6	20 38.3	22 05.2	28 30.1
15 M	23 37 19	22 31 30	17 40 24	24 28 10	16 40.8	18 16.1	18 52.8	18 51.0	17 12.0	11 01.4	12 36.5	13 17.4	16 52.2	20 35.9	22 03.9	28 30.3
16 Tu	23 41 16	23 29 58	1♈20 26	8♈16 51	16 37.6	18 11.9	19 37.1	20 04.3	17 51.5	11 26.2	12 37.9	13 24.9	16 49.9	20 33.5	22 02.5	28 30.5
17 W	23 45 12	24 28 27	15 16 55	22 20 06	16 34.4	18 06.6	20 17.6	21 17.7	18 31.1	11 50.9	12 39.4	13 32.4	16 47.6	20 31.1	22 01.2	28 30.7
18 Th	23 49 09	25 26 59	29 25 49	6♉33 28	16 31.3	18 00.8	20 54.1	22 31.0	19 10.7	12 15.6	12 41.2	13 39.9	16 45.4	20 28.7	21 59.9	28 31.0
19 F	23 53 05	26 25 32	13♉42 25	20 52 05	16 28.1	17 55.3	21 26.2	23 44.4	19 50.4	12 40.2	12 43.2	13 47.3	16 43.2	20 26.3	21 58.6	28 31.3
20 Sa	23 57 02	27 24 08	28 01 55	5♊11 23	16 24.9	17 50.9	21 53.7	24 57.7	20 30.2	13 04.8	12 45.3	13 54.8	16 41.1	20 23.9	21 57.4	28 31.6
21 Su	0 00 58	28 22 47	12♊20 05	19 27 36	16 21.7	17 48.0	22 16.2	26 11.0	21 10.0	13 29.3	12 47.7	14 02.2	16 39.0	20 21.6	21 56.1	28 32.0
22 M	0 04 55	29 21 27	26 33 40	3♋38 01	16 18.6	17D 46.9	22 33.3	27 24.3	21 49.8	13 53.7	12 50.2	14 09.6	16 37.0	20 19.2	21 54.9	28 32.4
23 Tu	0 08 51	0♎20 10	10♋40 30	17 40 57	16 15.4	17 47.2	22 44.7	28 37.6	22 29.7	14 18.1	12 52.9	14 17.0	16 35.0	20 16.8	21 53.7	28 32.8
24 W	0 12 48	1 18 55	24 39 17	1♌35 25	16 12.2	17 48.4	22R 49.9	29 50.8	23 09.7	14 42.5	12 55.8	14 24.3	16 33.1	20 14.5	21 52.5	28 33.2
25 Th	0 16 45	2 17 42	8♌29 16	15 20 47	16 09.0	17R 49.6	22 48.5	1♏04.1	23 49.7	15 06.7	12 58.9	14 31.7	16 31.2	20 12.2	21 51.4	28 33.7
26 F	0 20 41	3 16 32	22 09 51	28 56 24	16 05.8	17 49.8	22 40.4	2 17.3	24 29.8	15 31.0	13 02.1	14 39.0	16 29.4	20 09.8	21 50.2	28 34.2
27 Sa	0 24 38	4 15 23	5♍40 18	12♍21 25	16 02.7	17 48.3	22 25.0	3 30.6	25 09.9	15 55.1	13 05.6	14 46.3	16 27.6	20 07.5	21 49.1	28 34.8
28 Su	0 28 34	5 14 17	18 59 38	25 34 48	15 59.5	17 44.6	22 02.2	4 43.8	25 50.1	16 19.2	13 09.2	14 53.5	16 25.9	20 05.2	21 48.0	28 35.4
29 M	0 32 31	6 13 13	2♎06 45	8♎35 23	15 56.3	17 38.7	21 31.9	5 57.0	26 30.3	16 43.2	13 13.0	15 00.8	16 24.2	20 02.9	21 47.0	28 36.0
30 Tu	0 36 27	7♎12 10	15 00 36	21 22 19	15♒53.1	17♒30.7	20♎54.2	7♏10.1	27♎10.6	17♌07.1	13♑17.0	15♍08.0	16♒22.6	20♓00.7	21♒45.9	28♐36.6

1st of Month

Julian Day # 2454710.5
Obliquity 23°26'25"
SVP 5♓08'07"
GC 26♐57.6
Eris 21♈37.5R

Day	⚴	⚵	⚶
1	9♊46.6	15♐29.0	14♉36.7
6	11 21.8	16 09.1	14 52.7
11	12 52.4	16 55.7	14 58.2R
16	14 17.7	17 48.5	14 52.6R
21	15 37.0	18 46.9	14 35.8R
26	16 49.5	19 50.8	14 07.7R

DECLINATION and LATITUDE

Day	☉ Decl	☽ Decl	☽ Lat	☽ 12h Decl	☿ Decl	☿ Lat	♀ Decl	♀ Lat	♂ Decl	♂ Lat	⚳ Decl	⚳ Lat	♃ Decl	♃ Lat	♄ Decl	♄ Lat
1 M	8N13	0S12	3S01	3S15	2S33	1S06	0N19	1N04	2S45	0N30	23N12	4N22	23S08	0S18	8N47	1N40
2 Tu	7 51	6 14	3 55	9 07	3 12	1 15	0S12	1 03	3 00	0 29	23 08	4 24	23 08	0 18	8 44	1 40
3 W	7 29	11 52	4 35	14 28	3 50	1 23	0 43	1 01	3 16	0 29	23 04	4 26	23 08	0 18	8 41	1 40
4 Th	7 07	16 54	5 01	19 07	4 27	1 32	1 14	0 59	3 32	0 28	22 60	4 29	23 09	0 18	8 39	1 40
5 F	6 45	21 07	5 13	22 53	5 04	1 41	1 45	0 57	3 48	0 27	22 56	4 31	23 09	0 18	8 36	1 40
6 Sa	6 23	24 23	5 11	25 37	5 40	1 50	2 16	0 55	4 04	0 27	22 51	4 33	23 09	0 18	8 33	1 41
7 Su	6 00	26 33	4 55	27 11	6 15	1 59	2 47	0 53	4 20	0 26	22 47	4 36	23 09	0 18	8 30	1 41
8 M	5 38	27 30	4 26	27 31	6 49	2 07	3 18	0 51	4 35	0 26	22 43	4 38	23 09	0 18	8 27	1 41
9 Tu	5 15	27 12	3 47	26 34	7 22	2 16	3 49	0 48	4 51	0 25	22 38	4 41	23 09	0 18	8 24	1 41
10 W	4 53	25 37	2 57	24 22	7 54	2 24	4 19	0 46	5 07	0 24	22 34	4 43	23 09	0 18	8 22	1 41
11 Th	4 30	22 50	1 58	21 01	8 24	2 33	4 50	0 44	5 23	0 24	22 30	4 45	23 09	0 18	8 19	1 41
12 F	4 07	18 57	0 53	16 39	8 54	2 41	5 20	0 41	5 39	0 23	22 25	4 48	23 09	0 18	8 16	1 41
13 Sa	3 44	14 08	0N16	11 27	9 22	2 49	5 51	0 39	5 54	0 22	22 21	4 50	23 09	0 18	8 13	1 41
14 Su	3 21	8 35	1 26	5 36	9 49	2 56	6 21	0 37	6 10	0 22	22 16	4 53	23 09	0 19	8 10	1 41
15 M	2 58	2 31	2 33	0N37	10 14	3 04	6 51	0 34	6 26	0 21	22 12	4 55	23 09	0 19	8 07	1 41
16 Tu	2 35	3N47	3 33	6 56	10 37	3 11	7 21	0 32	6 41	0 21	22 07	4 58	23 09	0 19	8 05	1 41
17 W	2 12	10 02	4 21	13 01	10 59	3 18	7 51	0 29	6 57	0 20	22 03	5 01	23 09	0 19	8 02	1 41
18 Th	1 49	15 51	4 54	18 29	11 18	3 24	8 21	0 26	7 13	0 19	21 58	5 03	23 09	0 19	7 59	1 41
19 F	1 25	20 52	5 09	22 57	11 36	3 30	8 51	0 24	7 28	0 19	21 53	5 06	23 09	0 19	7 56	1 42
20 Sa	1 02	24 40	5 05	26 01	11 51	3 35	9 20	0 21	7 44	0 18	21 49	5 08	23 09	0 19	7 53	1 42
21 Su	0 39	26 56	4 42	27 24	12 04	3 39	9 49	0 18	7 59	0 18	21 44	5 11	23 08	0 19	7 51	1 42
22 M	0 15	27 26	4 02	26 60	12 14	3 43	10 18	0 16	8 15	0 17	21 39	5 14	23 08	0 19	7 48	1 42
23 Tu	0S08	26 07	3 07	24 51	12 21	3 46	10 47	0 13	8 30	0 16	21 35	5 16	23 08	0 19	7 45	1 42
24 W	0 31	23 12	2 02	21 13	12 24	3 48	11 16	0 10	8 45	0 16	21 30	5 19	23 08	0 19	7 42	1 42
25 Th	0 55	18 57	0 50	16 27	12 25	3 49	11 44	0 07	9 01	0 15	21 25	5 22	23 08	0 19	7 40	1 42
26 F	1 18	13 45	0S23	10 55	12 22	3 49	12 12	0 04	9 16	0 15	21 21	5 24	23 07	0 19	7 37	1 42
27 Sa	1 42	7 58	1 35	4 57	12 15	3 48	12 40	0 02	9 31	0 14	21 16	5 27	23 07	0 19	7 34	1 42
28 Su	2 05	1 54	2 40	1S08	12 03	3 45	13 07	0S01	9 46	0 13	21 11	5 30	23 07	0 19	7 32	1 42
29 M	2 28	4S08	3 35	7 03	11 48	3 40	13 34	0 04	10 02	0 13	21 06	5 33	23 06	0 19	7 29	1 43
30 Tu	2S52	9S53	4S19	12S35	11S28	3S34	14S01	0S07	10S17	0N12	21N02	5N35	23S06	0S20	7N26	1N43

Day	⚷ Decl	⚷ Lat	♅ Decl	♅ Lat	♆ Decl	♆ Lat	♇ Decl	♇ Lat
1	8S57	6N58	4S15	0S48	14S23	0S21	17S18	6N08
6	9 02	6 57	4 20	0 48	14 25	0 21	17 19	6 07
11	9 07	6 55	4 24	0 48	14 28	0 21	17 20	6 05
16	9 12	6 54	4 29	0 48	14 30	0 21	17 22	6 04
21	9 17	6 52	4 34	0 48	14 32	0 21	17 23	6 02
26	9 22	6 50	4 38	0 48	14 34	0 21	17 25	6 01

Day	⚴ Decl	⚴ Lat	⚵ Decl	⚵ Lat	⚶ Decl	⚶ Lat	Eris Decl	Eris Lat
1	8S15	30S28	8S55	13N48	7N21	9S16	4S37	14S03
6	9 23	31 47	9 22	13 25	7 12	9 31	4 38	14 03
11	10 35	33 09	9 48	13 03	6 59	9 45	4 39	14 03
16	11 51	34 34	10 14	12 42	6 44	9 59	4 40	14 03
21	13 11	36 02	10 38	12 22	6 27	10 12	4 41	14 04
26	14 35	37 32	11 03	12 02	6 07	10 25	4 42	14 04

Moon Phenomena

Max/0 Decl

dy	hr mn	
8	6:10	27S33
15	9:38	0 N
21	18:38	27N28
28	7:31	0 S

Max/0 Lat

dy	hr mn	
5	7:47	5S14
12	18:24	0 N
19	6:56	5N10
25	16:22	0 S

Perigee/Apogee

dy	hr m		kilometers
7	15:01	a	404212
20	3:29	p	368886

PH	dy	hr mn	
☽	7	14:05	15♐19
○	15	9:14	22♓54
☾	22	5:05	29♊34
●	29	8:13	6♎33

Void of Course Moon

Last Aspect				☽ Ingress		
1	9:03	♇	□	♎	1	11:46
3	17:10	♇	⚹	♏	3	20:03
5	15:46	♆	□	♐	6	7:12
8	16:44	♇	☌	♑	8	19:46
10	13:16	♅	⚹	♒	11	7:21
13	13:20	♇	⚹	♓	13	16:06
15	19:04	♇	□	♈	15	21:40
17	22:27	♇	△	♉	18	0:58
19	22:52	☉	△	♊	20	3:18
22	5:05	☉	□	♋	22	5:50
23	21:18	♂	□	♌	24	9:15
26	11:21	♇	△	♍	26	13:53
28	17:32	♇	□	♎	28	20:07

DAILY ASPECTARIAN

1 M
☽ ⋕ ♀ 0:25
☽ □ ♇ 9:03
☽ ∥ ☿ 10:19
☽ ∥ ♂ 10:27
☿ ∥ ♂ 12:15
♀ ⚼ ⚷ 14:40
☽ ∥ ♅ 16:01
☽ ⚼ ⚷ 16:14
☽ ☌ ♀ 16:24
☽ ☌ ☿ 20:56
☽ ⚹ ⚳ 21:56

2 Tu
⚳ ⋕ ♃ 0:14
☽ ⚼ ♆ 1:19
☽ ☌ ♂ 3:59
☉ ⋕ ☽ 6:18
☉ ⚺ ☽ 6:29
☽ ⚺ ♄ 9:21
☽ ⋕ ♄ 10:18
☽ □ ♃ 11:00
☽ ∥ ⚷ 11:25
☿ ⚹ ⚳ 11:46
☽ △ ⚷ 20:01

3 W
☽ ⚻ ♅ 2:58
⚳ ⚼ ♅ 3:29
☽ △ ♆ 5:24
☽ ∥ ♆ 11:40
☉ ∠ ☽ 13:08
☽ ∠ ♄ 14:00
☽ ⚹ ♇ 17:10
☿ ⚼ ♆ 17:26
☿ ∥ ♅ 17:38

4 Th
☉ ☌ ♄ 2:01
☽ ∥ ♇ 2:10
☽ ⚺ ♀ 7:11
☽ ⚼ ♅ 7:43
☽ □ ⚳ 8:49
☽ ⚺ ☿ 12:08
☽ ⚺ ♂ 16:22
☉ △ ♃ 17:42
☽ ⚹ ♄ 19:26
☽ ⚹ ♃ 20:30
☉ ⚹ ☽ 20:44
☽ ∠ ♇ 22:22

5 F
☽ □ ⚷ 5:50
♀ ⚹ ⚳ 7:20
☽ ⋕ ⚳ 12:07
☽ △ ♅ 13:10
♀ ⚼ ♆ 13:24
☽ ∥ ♃ 14:00
☽ □ ♆ 15:46
☽ ∠ ♀ 16:03
☽ ∠ ☿ 21:00
☽ ∠ ♂ 23:47

6 Sa
☽ ∠ ♃ 2:16
☽ ⚺ ♇ 4:11
☉ ⋕ ☿ 17:55
☽ △ ⚳ 22:38

7 Su
♂ ∥ ♅ 1:27
☽ ⚹ ♀ 1:36
☽ ⚹ ☿ 6:21
☽ ⚹ ♂ 7:43
☽ □ ♄ 8:03
☽ ⚺ ♃ 8:28
☉ □ ☽ 14:05
♂ ⚺ ♄ 14:53
☽ ⚹ ⚷ 17:50
♂ □ ♃ 21:06

8 M
☽ □ ♅ 1:20
☿ ⚺ ♄ 2:48
☽ ⚹ ♆ 4:04
♃ D 4:17
☿ □ ♃ 5:10
☽ ⚼ ⚳ 6:04
☽ ☌ ♇ 16:44
☿ ☌ ♂ 17:45
♃ △ ♄ 23:19

9 Tu
☽ ∠ ⚷ 0:02
♇ D 3:15
☉ ⚻ ⚷ 10:07
☽ ∠ ♆ 10:14
☽ ⚻ ⚳ 13:22
☉ ⋕ ♂ 15:00
♀ □ ♃ 20:13
☽ ☌ ♃ 20:55
☽ □ ♀ 21:00
☽ △ ♄ 21:08
♀ ⚺ ♄ 22:33
☽ □ ♂ 23:39

10 W
☽ □ ☿ 0:41
♀ ∥ ♅ 3:20
☽ ⚺ ⚷ 5:55
☉ △ ☽ 7:44
☽ ⚹ ♅ 13:16
☉ ⋕ ♀ 14:59
☽ ⚺ ♆ 16:00
☿ ⋕ ♄ 19:52
☽ ∥ ♃ 21:41
⚶ R 23:47

11 Th
☽ ⋕ ⚳ 2:27
☽ ⚼ ♄ 3:04
☽ ⚺ ♇ 4:25
☉ ⋕ ♅ 5:33
☉ ⚼ ☽ 15:37
☽ ∠ ♅ 18:26

12 F
♀ ☌ ♂ 2:07
☽ ☍ ⚳ 2:17
☽ ⚺ ♃ 7:30
☽ ⚻ ♄ 8:16
☽ ∥ ♇ 8:30
☽ ∠ ♇ 9:17
☿ ∥ ⚷ 12:51
☽ △ ♂ 13:15
☽ △ ♀ 13:48
☽ △ ☿ 15:47
☽ ☌ ⚷ 15:50
☿ △ ⚷ 16:33
☽ ∥ ♆ 22:28
☉ ⚻ ☽ 22:31
☽ ⚺ ♅ 22:49

13 Sa
☽ ☌ ♆ 1:29
☉ ☍ ♅ 2:23
♀ ∥ ♂ 5:35
♀ △ ⚷ 10:24
☽ ∠ ♃ 11:38
☽ ⚹ ♇ 13:20
☽ ⚼ ♂ 18:39
☽ ∥ ☿ 19:17
☽ ⚼ ♀ 20:35
☽ ∥ ⚷ 21:35
☽ ⚼ ☿ 21:35

14 Su
☽ ⋕ ♄ 1:43
☽ ∥ ♀ 8:19
☽ ∥ ♂ 9:21
☽ ⚻ ⚳ 11:44
♂ △ ⚷ 12:39
☉ ⚻ ♆ 12:55
☽ ⚹ ♃ 14:57
☽ ☍ ♄ 16:07
☽ ∥ ♅ 16:28
☉ ⋕ ☽ 22:10
☽ ⚺ ⚷ 22:35
☽ ⚻ ♂ 23:07

15 M
☿ ☌ ♀ 1:38
☽ ⚻ ☿ 2:16
☽ ⚻ ♀ 2:18
☽ ☌ ♅ 5:10
☽ ⚺ ♆ 7:45
☉ ☍ ☽ 9:14
☽ ⚼ ⚳ 15:11
☽ □ ♇ 19:04
☉ ∥ ☽ 19:42

16 Tu
☽ ∠ ⚷ 0:51
☽ ⋕ ♅ 2:39
♀ ⚻ ♅ 9:14
☽ ∠ ♆ 9:51
☽ ⋕ ♂ 11:32
☽ ⋕ ♀ 14:48
☽ ∥ ♄ 16:16
☽ △ ⚳ 17:57
☽ □ ♃ 19:30
☽ ⋕ ⚷ 20:51
☽ ⚻ ♄ 21:00

17 W
☽ ⚹ ⚷ 2:34
☽ ⋕ ☿ 3:59
☽ ☍ ♂ 5:47
♀ ⋕ ♄ 7:42
☿ ⚻ ♅ 8:04
☽ ⚺ ♅ 8:53
☽ ☍ ☿ 8:56
☽ ☍ ♀ 11:12
☽ ⚹ ♆ 11:27
♀ △ ♆ 13:59
☉ ⚻ ☽ 16:47
☽ ⋕ ♆ 18:14
☽ △ ♇ 22:27
☽ ⚼ ♄ 22:42

18 Th
☽ ⋕ ♇ 6:51
☽ ∠ ♅ 10:09
☉ ⚼ ☽ 19:54
☽ □ ⚳ 22:13
☽ △ ♃ 22:20
☽ ⚼ ♇ 23:41

19 F
☽ △ ♄ 0:08
⚳ ⚻ ♃ 3:11
☽ □ ⚷ 5:02
☽ ∥ ⚳ 5:36
☽ ⚻ ♂ 10:47
☽ ⚹ ♅ 11:15
☽ ⋕ ♃ 13:17
☽ ⚻ ☿ 13:24
☽ □ ♆ 13:50
☽ ⚻ ♀ 18:23
♂ ⚻ ♅ 20:27
♀ ∥ ⚷ 20:48
☉ △ ☽ 22:52
☽ ⚼ ♃ 23:32

20 Sa
☽ ⚻ ♇ 0:50
☿ △ ♆ 3:22
♂ ⋕ ♄ 12:56
☽ ⚼ ♂ 13:08
☽ ⚼ ☿ 15:17
☽ ⚼ ♀ 21:53

21 Su
☽ ⚻ ♃ 0:47
☽ ⚹ ⚳ 2:00
⚳ ⚼ ♇ 2:41
☽ □ ♄ 2:53
☉ □ ♇ 3:47
☉ ∠ ⚳ 4:34
☽ △ ⚷ 7:15
☽ □ ♅ 13:29
☽ △ ♂ 15:37
☽ △ ♆ 16:09
☽ △ ☿ 17:06

22 M
☽ △ ♀ 1:34
♂ △ ♆ 2:58
☽ ☍ ♇ 3:21
☽ ∠ ⚳ 4:04
☉ □ ☽ 5:05
☽ ⚼ ⚷ 8:33
☉ ♎ 15:46
☽ ⚼ ♆ 17:34
⚳ ⚺ ♄ 22:22
♀ ⚹ ♇ 22:25

23 Tu
☽ ☍ ♃ 3:47
☽ ⚹ ♄ 6:14
☽ ⚺ ⚳ 6:23
☽ ⚻ ⚷ 10:05
☿ ☌ ♂ 10:52
♀ ∠ ♄ 14:21
☽ △ ♅ 16:25
☽ ⚻ ♆ 19:13
☽ □ ☿ 20:51
☽ □ ♂ 21:18

24 W
☽ ⋕ ♃ 0:26
♀ ♏ 3:00
☉ ⚼ ⚷ 5:36
☽ ⚻ ♇ 6:45
☿ R 7:18
☽ ∠ ♄ 8:17
☽ □ ♀ 9:51
☽ ∥ ⚳ 10:35
☉ ⚹ ☽ 12:24
☽ ⚼ ♅ 18:18

25 Th
☽ ⋕ ♇ 7:30
☽ ⚻ ♃ 7:53
☽ ⚼ ♇ 8:53
☽ ⚺ ♄ 10:40
☽ ☌ ⚳ 11:57
☽ ☍ ⚷ 14:02
☉ ∠ ☽ 16:37
☽ ⋕ ♆ 20:29
☽ ⚻ ♅ 20:29
☽ ☍ ♆ 23:25

26 F
☽ ⚹ ☿ 0:53
☽ ⚹ ♂ 4:20
☽ ⋕ ☿ 6:03
☽ ⋕ ♀ 6:08
☿ ∥ ♀ 6:56
♂ ∥ ⚷ 9:44
☽ ⚼ ♃ 10:26
☽ △ ♇ 11:21
☽ ⋕ ♂ 17:58
☽ ⋕ ⚷ 18:17
☽ ⚹ ♀ 19:45
☉ ⚺ ☽ 21:16

27 Sa
☽ ∥ ♄ 1:35
☽ ∠ ☿ 3:03
☽ ∠ ♂ 8:29
☽ ⋕ ♅ 13:08
☽ △ ♃ 13:23
☽ ☌ ♄ 16:30
☽ ⚺ ⚳ 19:00
☽ ⚻ ⚷ 19:22
☉ ⋕ ☽ 23:20

28 Su
☽ ∠ ♀ 1:28
☽ ☍ ♅ 1:59
☽ ⚻ ♆ 5:06
☽ ⚺ ☿ 5:21
⚳ ☍ ⚷ 6:16
♀ ⚼ ♅ 6:49
☿ △ ♆ 12:26
☽ ⚺ ♂ 13:08
☉ ∥ ☽ 16:52
☽ □ ♇ 17:32
☽ ⚼ ⚷ 22:42
☽ ∠ ⚳ 23:15

29 M
☽ ∥ ♅ 2:14
☽ ⚺ ♀ 7:50
☉ ☌ ☽ 8:13
☽ ⚼ ♆ 8:38
☉ ⚼ ♆ 13:30
☽ ⋕ ♄ 13:40
☽ □ ♃ 20:45
☽ ∥ ⚷ 22:00

30 Tu
☽ ⚺ ♄ 0:14
☽ ∥ ♂ 1:48
☽ △ ⚷ 2:34
☉ ⚺ ♀ 3:26
☽ ⚹ ⚳ 4:06
☽ ∥ ☿ 6:29
☽ ⚻ ♅ 9:24
☽ ☌ ☿ 10:31
☽ △ ♆ 12:44
☽ ∥ ♀ 20:30
☽ ∥ ♆ 21:25

October 2008

LONGITUDE

Day	Sid.Time	☉	☽	☽ 12 hour	Mean ☊	True ☊	☿	♀	♂	⚳	♃	♄	⚷	♅	♆	♇
	h m s	° ' "	° ' "	° ' "	° '	° '	° '	° '	° '	° '	° '	° '	° '	° '	° '	° '
1 W	0 40 24	8♎11 10	27♎40 32	3♏55 16	15♒50.0	17♒21.5	20♎09.1	8♏23.3	27♎50.9	17♌31.0	13♑21.2	15♍15.2	16♒21.1	19♓58.4	21♒44.9	28♐37.3
2 Th	0 44 20	9 10 12	10♏06 37	16 14 43	15 46.8	17R 11.8	19R 17.2	9 36.5	28 31.3	17 54.8	13 25.5	15 22.3	16R 19.6	19R 56.2	21R 43.9	28 38.0
3 F	0 48 17	10 09 16	22 19 48	28 22 08	15 43.6	17 02.7	18 19.2	10 49.6	29 11.8	18 18.5	13 30.0	15 29.5	16 18.1	19 54.0	21 43.0	28 38.7
4 Sa	0 52 13	11 08 21	4♐22 05	10♐20 02	15 40.4	16 55.0	17 16.0	12 02.7	29 52.3	18 42.1	13 34.7	15 36.6	16 16.8	19 51.8	21 42.0	28 39.5
5 Su	0 56 10	12 07 29	16 16 28	22 11 53	15 37.2	16 49.3	16 08.8	13 15.8	0♏32.8	19 05.6	13 39.6	15 43.6	16 15.4	19 49.6	21 41.1	28 40.3
6 M	1 00 07	13 06 38	28 06 51	4♑01 56	15 34.1	16 45.9	14 59.3	14 28.9	1 13.4	19 29.1	13 44.6	15 50.7	16 14.2	19 47.5	21 40.3	28 41.1
7 Tu	1 04 03	14 05 49	9♑57 48	15 55 05	15 30.9	16D 44.4	13 49.1	15 41.9	1 54.1	19 52.5	13 49.8	15 57.7	16 13.0	19 45.3	21 39.4	28 42.0
8 W	1 08 00	15 05 02	21 54 27	27 56 34	15 27.7	16 44.6	12 40.2	16 54.9	2 34.8	20 15.8	13 55.2	16 04.6	16 11.9	19 43.2	21 38.6	28 42.9
9 Th	1 11 56	16 04 16	4♒02 04	10♒11 38	15 24.5	16 45.4	11 34.5	18 07.9	3 15.6	20 39.0	14 00.7	16 11.5	16 10.8	19 41.1	21 37.8	28 43.8
10 F	1 15 53	17 03 33	16 25 49	22 45 12	15 21.4	16R 45.9	10 33.8	19 20.9	3 56.4	21 02.1	14 06.4	16 18.4	16 09.8	19 39.1	21 37.0	28 44.7
11 Sa	1 19 49	18 02 51	29 10 15	5♓41 21	15 18.2	16 45.1	9 40.0	20 33.9	4 37.2	21 25.2	14 12.3	16 25.2	16 08.8	19 37.1	21 36.3	28 45.7
12 Su	1 23 46	19 02 11	12♓18 47	19 02 41	15 15.0	16 42.3	8 54.4	21 46.8	5 18.2	21 48.1	14 18.3	16 32.0	16 07.9	19 35.1	21 35.6	28 46.7
13 M	1 27 42	20 01 32	25 53 03	2♈49 42	15 11.8	16 37.0	8 18.4	22 59.7	5 59.1	22 11.0	14 24.5	16 38.8	16 07.1	19 33.1	21 34.9	28 47.8
14 Tu	1 31 39	21 00 56	9♈52 19	17 00 23	15 08.6	16 29.3	7 52.7	24 12.6	6 40.2	22 33.7	14 30.9	16 45.5	16 06.3	19 31.1	21 34.3	28 48.8
15 W	1 35 36	22 00 22	24 13 14	1♉30 02	15 05.5	16 19.7	7D 37.8	25 25.4	7 21.2	22 56.4	14 37.4	16 52.2	16 05.6	19 29.2	21 33.7	28 49.9
16 Th	1 39 32	22 59 49	8♉49 52	16 11 45	15 02.3	16 09.2	7 34.1	26 38.2	8 02.4	23 18.9	14 44.0	16 58.8	16 05.0	19 27.3	21 33.1	28 51.0
17 F	1 43 29	23 59 19	23 34 38	0♊57 30	14 59.1	15 59.1	7 41.3	27 51.0	8 43.6	23 41.4	14 50.8	17 05.4	16 04.4	19 25.5	21 32.5	28 52.2
18 Sa	1 47 25	24 58 51	8♊19 23	15 39 27	14 55.9	15 50.5	7 59.2	29 03.8	9 24.8	24 03.7	14 57.8	17 11.9	16 03.9	19 23.7	21 32.0	28 53.4
19 Su	1 51 22	25 58 26	22 56 56	0♋11 14	14 52.8	15 44.3	8 27.2	0♐16.6	10 06.1	24 26.0	15 04.9	17 18.4	16 03.5	19 21.9	21 31.5	28 54.6
20 M	1 55 18	26 58 03	7♋21 56	14 28 41	14 49.6	15 40.6	9 04.6	1 29.3	10 47.5	24 48.1	15 12.2	17 24.8	16 03.1	19 20.1	21 31.1	28 55.8
21 Tu	1 59 15	27 57 42	21 31 20	28 29 50	14 46.4	15D 39.2	9 50.6	2 42.0	11 28.9	25 10.2	15 19.6	17 31.2	16 02.8	19 18.4	21 30.7	28 57.1
22 W	2 03 11	28 57 23	5♌24 12	12♌14 34	14 43.2	15R 39.1	10 44.5	3 54.7	12 10.3	25 32.1	15 27.2	17 37.5	16 02.5	19 16.7	21 30.3	28 58.4
23 Th	2 07 08	29 57 06	19 01 04	25 43 54	14 40.1	15 39.2	11 45.4	5 07.4	12 51.9	25 53.9	15 34.9	17 43.8	16 02.3	19 15.1	21 29.9	28 59.7
24 F	2 11 05	0♏56 52	2♍23 17	8♍59 23	14 36.9	15 38.2	12 52.4	6 20.0	13 33.4	26 15.6	15 42.7	17 50.0	16 02.2	19 13.4	21 29.6	29 01.0
25 Sa	2 15 01	1 56 40	15 32 23	22 02 27	14 33.7	15 35.0	14 04.9	7 32.6	14 15.1	26 37.2	15 50.7	17 56.2	16D 02.2	19 11.9	21 29.3	29 02.4
26 Su	2 18 58	2 56 30	28 29 42	4♎54 13	14 30.5	15 28.9	15 22.0	8 45.2	14 56.8	26 58.6	15 58.8	18 02.3	16 02.2	19 10.3	21 29.0	29 03.8
27 M	2 22 54	3 56 22	11♎16 04	17 35 18	14 27.3	15 19.8	16 43.2	9 57.7	15 38.5	27 19.9	16 07.1	18 08.3	16 02.2	19 08.8	21 28.8	29 05.2
28 Tu	2 26 51	4 56 17	23 51 57	0♏06 01	14 24.2	15 08.0	18 07.7	11 10.2	16 20.3	27 41.1	16 15.5	18 14.3	16 02.4	19 07.3	21 28.6	29 06.6
29 W	2 30 47	5 56 13	6♏17 31	12 26 30	14 21.0	14 54.4	19 35.0	12 22.7	17 02.2	28 02.1	16 24.0	18 20.3	16 02.6	19 05.9	21 28.4	29 08.1
30 Th	2 34 44	6 56 11	18 33 01	24 37 08	14 17.8	14 40.0	21 04.7	13 35.2	17 44.1	28 23.1	16 32.7	18 26.1	16 02.9	19 04.5	21 28.3	29 09.6
31 F	2 38 40	7♏56 12	0♐39 01	6♐38 48	14♒14.6	14♒26.2	22♎36.3	14♐47.6	18♏26.1	28♌43.8	16♑41.5	18♍31.9	16♒03.2	19♓03.2	21♒28.2	29♐11.1

1st of Month

Julian Day # 2454740.5
Obliquity 23°26'25"
SVP 5♓08'04"
GC 26♐57.7
Eris 21♈22.0R

Day	⚴	⚵	⚶
1	17♊53.9	20♐59.7	13♉28.6R
6	18 49.4	22 13.3	12 39.1R
11	19 34.9	23 31.4	11 40.2R
16	20 09.1	24 53.4	10 33.6R
21	20 31.0	26 19.3	9 20.9R
26	20 39.0	27 48.7	8 04.1R
31	20 32.1R	29 21.4	6 45.8R

DECLINATION and LATITUDE

Day	☉ Decl	☽ Decl	☽ Lat	☽12h Decl	☿ Decl	☿ Lat	♀ Decl	♀ Lat	♂ Decl	♂ Lat	⚳ Decl	⚳ Lat	♃ Decl	♃ Lat	♄ Decl	♄ Lat
1 W	3S15	15S07	4S48	17S29	11S03	3S26	14S28	0S10	10S32	0N12	20N57	5N38	23S06	0S20	7N23	1N43
2 Th	3 38	19 39	5 03	21 34	10 35	3 16	14 54	0 13	10 47	0 11	20 52	5 41	23 05	0 20	7 21	1 43
3 F	4 01	23 15	5 04	24 40	10 02	3 05	15 20	0 16	11 02	0 10	20 47	5 44	23 05	0 20	7 18	1 43
4 Sa	4 24	25 48	4 52	26 38	9 25	2 51	15 45	0 19	11 17	0 10	20 43	5 47	23 04	0 20	7 16	1 43
5 Su	4 48	27 09	4 27	27 22	8 45	2 36	16 10	0 22	11 31	0 09	20 38	5 50	23 04	0 20	7 13	1 43
6 M	5 11	27 16	3 50	26 51	8 02	2 19	16 35	0 25	11 46	0 08	20 33	5 53	23 04	0 20	7 10	1 43
7 Tu	5 34	26 07	3 04	25 06	7 18	2 00	16 60	0 28	12 01	0 08	20 28	5 56	23 03	0 20	7 08	1 44
8 W	5 57	23 47	2 09	22 11	6 33	1 41	17 23	0 31	12 15	0 07	20 24	5 59	23 03	0 20	7 05	1 44
9 Th	6 19	20 20	1 08	18 15	5 49	1 21	17 47	0 34	12 30	0 07	20 19	6 02	23 02	0 20	7 03	1 44
10 F	6 42	15 56	0 02	13 26	5 06	1 00	18 10	0 37	12 44	0 06	20 14	6 05	23 01	0 20	7 00	1 44
11 Sa	7 05	10 44	1N06	7 53	4 26	0 39	18 33	0 41	12 59	0 05	20 10	6 08	23 01	0 20	6 57	1 44
12 Su	7 27	4 55	2 12	1 50	3 50	0 19	18 55	0 44	13 13	0 05	20 05	6 11	23 00	0 20	6 55	1 44
13 M	7 50	1N19	3 12	4N29	3 18	0N00	19 18	0 47	13 27	0 04	20 00	6 14	22 60	0 20	6 52	1 44
14 Tu	8 12	7 38	4 03	10 44	2 51	0 19	19 38	0 50	13 41	0 04	19 56	6 17	22 59	0 20	6 50	1 45
15 W	8 34	13 44	4 40	16 34	2 29	0 36	19 58	0 53	13 55	0 03	19 51	6 21	22 58	0 20	6 48	1 45
16 Th	8 56	19 10	4 60	21 30	2 13	0 51	20 18	0 56	14 09	0 02	19 47	6 24	22 58	0 20	6 45	1 45
17 F	9 18	23 30	4 60	25 07	2 03	1 06	20 38	0 59	14 23	0 02	19 42	6 27	22 57	0 20	6 43	1 45
18 Sa	9 40	26 18	4 40	27 01	1 58	1 18	20 57	1 02	14 37	0 01	19 38	6 30	22 56	0 20	6 40	1 45
19 Su	10 02	27 16	4 01	27 03	1 59	1 29	21 16	1 05	14 50	0 01	19 33	6 34	22 56	0 20	6 38	1 45
20 M	10 24	26 22	3 08	25 16	2 05	1 39	21 34	1 07	15 04	0 00	19 29	6 37	22 55	0 21	6 36	1 46
21 Tu	10 45	23 46	2 04	21 56	2 16	1 47	21 51	1 10	15 17	0S01	19 24	6 40	22 54	0 21	6 33	1 46
22 W	11 06	19 48	0 54	17 25	2 31	1 53	22 08	1 13	15 31	0 01	19 20	6 44	22 53	0 21	6 31	1 46
23 Th	11 27	14 50	0S18	12 07	2 50	1 58	22 24	1 16	15 44	0 02	19 15	6 47	22 52	0 21	6 29	1 46
24 F	11 48	9 16	1 27	6 21	3 13	2 02	22 40	1 19	15 57	0 02	19 11	6 50	22 51	0 21	6 26	1 46
25 Sa	12 09	3 23	2 31	0 24	3 38	2 05	22 55	1 22	16 10	0 03	19 07	6 54	22 51	0 21	6 24	1 46
26 Su	12 30	2S33	3 26	5S27	4 07	2 06	23 09	1 24	16 23	0 04	19 03	6 57	22 50	0 21	6 22	1 47
27 M	12 50	8 17	4 09	10 60	4 38	2 06	23 23	1 27	16 35	0 04	18 59	7 01	22 49	0 21	6 20	1 47
28 Tu	13 10	13 35	4 40	16 01	5 10	2 06	23 36	1 30	16 48	0 05	18 54	7 05	22 48	0 21	6 17	1 47
29 W	13 30	18 16	4 56	20 19	5 44	2 05	23 49	1 33	17 01	0 05	18 50	7 08	22 47	0 21	6 15	1 47
30 Th	13 50	22 08	4 59	23 41	6 20	2 03	24 00	1 35	17 13	0 06	18 46	7 12	22 46	0 21	6 13	1 47
31 F	14S09	24S59	4S48	25S59	6S56	1N60	24S11	1S38	17S25	0S07	18N42	7N15	22S45	0S21	6N11	1N48

Day	⚷ Decl	⚷ Lat	♅ Decl	♅ Lat	♆ Decl	♆ Lat	♇ Decl	♇ Lat
1	9S26	6N48	4S43	0S48	14S36	0S21	17S26	5N60
6	9 30	6 46	4 47	0 48	14 37	0 21	17 28	5 58
11	9 34	6 44	4 51	0 48	14 38	0 21	17 29	5 57
16	9 37	6 42	4 55	0 48	14 39	0 21	17 31	5 55
21	9 40	6 39	4 58	0 48	14 40	0 21	17 32	5 54
26	9 42	6 37	5 01	0 48	14 41	0 21	17 34	5 53
31	9S44	6N35	5S04	0S48	14S41	0S21	17S35	5N51

Day	⚴ Decl	⚴ Lat	⚵ Decl	⚵ Lat	⚶ Decl	⚶ Lat	Eris Decl	Eris Lat
1	16S03	39S04	11S26	11N44	5N46	10S35	4S43	14S04
6	17 33	40 38	11 48	11 26	5 23	10 44	4 44	14 04
11	19 04	42 13	12 09	11 09	4 60	10 51	4 45	14 04
16	20 37	43 48	12 29	10 52	4 37	10 54	4 46	14 03
21	22 10	45 23	12 47	10 37	4 14	10 55	4 47	14 03
26	23 42	46 55	13 03	10 22	3 53	10 53	4 48	14 03
31	25S12	48S24	13S18	10N08	3N34	10S47	4S49	14S03

Moon Phenomena

Max/0 Decl
dy hr mn
5 14:06 27S22
12 19:01 0 N
19 0:05 27N16
25 13:38 0 S

Max/0 Lat
dy hr mn
2 13:42 5S06
10 0:38 0 N
16 11:47 5N02
22 18:02 0 S
29 16:33 5S00

Perigee/Apogee
dy hr m kilometers
5 10:34 a 404719
17 6:04 p 363825

PH dy hr mn
☽ 7 9:05 14♑28
○ 14 20:03 21♈51
☾ 21 11:56 28♋27
● 28 23:15 5♏54

Void of Course Moon

Last Aspect	☽ Ingress
1 1:49 ♇ ⚹	♏ 1 4:27
2 22:47 ♆ □	♐ 3 15:15
6 1:10 ♇ ☌	♑ 6 3:50
7 19:38 ♅ ⚹	♒ 8 16:04
10 23:14 ♇ ⚹	♓ 11 1:32
13 5:04 ♇ □	♈ 13 7:08
15 7:37 ♇ △	♉ 15 9:32
17 7:34 ♀ ☍	♊ 17 10:26
19 9:53 ♇ ☍	♋ 19 11:41
21 11:56 ☉ □	♌ 21 14:36
23 17:54 ♇ △	♍ 23 19:41
26 1:04 ♇ □	♎ 26 2:49
28 10:07 ♇ ⚹	♏ 28 11:48
30 5:46 ♆ □	♐ 30 22:42

DAILY ASPECTARIAN

1 W	☽☌♂	0:21
	☽⚹♇	1:49
	☽∠♄	4:59
	☿⚻♅	5:27
	♀∥♆	7:07
	☽∥♇	11:47
	☽⚼♅	14:00
	☿∥♂	17:32
	☉⚺☽	22:01
	☽☌♀	22:55
2 Th	♂⚹♇	4:02
	☽⚹♃	6:31
	☽∠♇	6:53
	☽#⚳	7:18
	☽⚹♄	10:23
	☽□⚷	12:08
	☽□⚳	15:47
	☽⚺☿	16:41
	☽△♅	19:13
	☽∥♃	22:42
	☽□♆	22:47
3 F	☿⚹⚳	0:12
	☉∠☽	6:06
	☽∠♃	12:21
	☽⚺♇	12:34
	☽⚺♂	14:28
	☽∠☿	20:08
	☿∥⚷	21:36
4 Sa	♂ ♏	4:35
	☉⚹☽	14:51
	☽⚺♀	17:13
	☽⚺♃	18:41
	☿△⚷	21:38
	☉∥♅	22:24
	☽∠♂	22:26
	☽□♄	22:53
	☽⚹☿	23:46
	☽⚹⚷	23:58
5 Su	☽△⚳	5:54
	☽□♅	7:10
	♂∠♄	7:44
	☿⚺♄	7:57
	♀∠♇	8:08
	♀⚹♃	8:23
	☽⚹♆	10:57
6 M	☽☌♇	1:10
	☽∠♀	3:05
	☿⚺♀	5:06
	☽∠⚷	6:19
	☽⚹♂	6:41
	☽⚼⚳	13:21
	☉□♃	16:53
	⚳⚻♅	17:14
	☽∠♆	17:19
	☉☌☿	20:54
	☿□♃	23:47
7 Tu	♀⚹♄	5:43
	☿#♄	5:49
	☽□☿	7:05
	☽☌♃	7:51
	☉□☽	9:05
	♀□⚷	10:03
	☽△♄	12:12
	☽⚺⚷	12:35
	☽⚹♀	12:52
	☽⚹♅	19:38
	☽⚻⚳	20:36
	☽⚺♆	23:28
8 W	♀∥♇	5:11
	☽∥♃	5:49
	☉∥☿	13:03
	☽⚺♇	13:33
	☽⚼♄	18:22
	♄⚻⚷	21:44
	☽□♂	22:23
9 Th	☽#⚳	0:09
	☽∠♅	1:16
	☉△⚷	2:35
	☉⚺♄	3:19
	☽∥♀	13:23
	☽△☿	13:33
	☽∥♇	16:07
	☽∠♇	18:51
	☽⚺♃	19:31
	☽☌⚷	23:29
	☽⚻♄	23:46
10 F	☉△☽	1:18
	♀△♅	5:49
	☽⚺♅	6:07
	☽□♀	6:09
	☽∥♆	6:21
	☽☍⚳	9:02
	☿∥♅	9:12
	☽☌♆	9:51
	☽∥♂	14:30
	☽⚼☿	16:07
	☉#♄	17:05
	☽⚹♇	23:14
	♂⚼♅	23:54
11 Sa	☽∠♃	0:04
	☽∥⚷	5:00
	☉⚼☽	7:45
	☽△♂	10:36
	⚳☍♆	11:18
	☉∥☽	14:23
	☽#♄	15:54
	☽⚻☿	18:10
	♀□♆	20:21
12 Su	☽∥♅	0:12
	♀□⚳	0:38
	☽⚹♃	3:36
	☽∥☿	4:41
	☽⚺⚷	6:49
	☽☍♄	7:37
	☉⚻♅	12:52
	☽☌♅	12:55
	☉⚻☽	12:55
	☽⚼♂	14:58
	☽⚺♆	16:29
	☽⚻⚳	17:21
	☽△♀	18:28
13 M	☿∠♀	4:21
	☽□♇	5:04
	☽#☿	6:59
	☽∠⚷	9:03
	☽#♅	13:31
	☽⚻♂	18:17
	☽∠♆	18:24
	☽⚼⚳	19:58
	☽☍☿	20:42
	☽∥♄	20:57
	☽⚼♀	22:46
14 Tu	☉#☽	2:17
	☽#⚷	7:33
	☽□♃	7:53
	☽⚹⚷	10:29
	☿∠⚳	11:15
	☽⚻♄	11:40
	☉△♆	13:20
	☽⚺♅	16:09
	♀#⚳	17:16
	☽⚹♆	19:36
	☉☍☽	20:03
	☽△⚳	21:49
15 W	☽#♂	0:48
	☽⚻♀	2:10
	☽#♆	3:49
	☽△♇	7:37
	☿⚺♂	8:13
	☽⚼♄	12:42
	☽#♇	16:14
	☽∠♅	16:52
	☿ D	20:09
	☽⚻☿	21:56
	☽☍♂	22:39
16 Th	☽∥⚳	2:56
	☽#♀	6:05
	☽⚼♇	8:12
	☽△♃	9:42
	☽□⚷	11:49
	☉⚹⚳	12:23
	☽△♄	13:23
	☽⚹♅	17:16
	☽#♃	20:30
	☽□♆	20:42
	☽⚼☿	22:32
17 F	☽□⚳	0:11
	☉⚻☽	0:43
	☽☍♀	7:34
	☽⚻♇	8:37
	☽⚼♃	10:16
	♀⚺♇	20:30
	☉∥⚷	21:43
	☽△☿	23:26
18 Sa	☽⚻♂	1:52
	☉⚼☽	2:54
	♂∥♆	5:31
	☽⚻♃	10:57
	☽△⚷	12:40
	☽□♄	14:38
	☽□♅	18:06
	♀ ♐	18:32
	♀∠♃	19:44
	☽△♆	21:39
19 Su	☽⚹⚳	2:31
	☽⚼♂	3:44
	☉△☽	5:22
	☽☍♇	9:53
	☽⚻♀	13:16
	☽⚼⚷	13:27
	☽⚼♆	22:35
20 M	☽□☿	3:02
	☽∠⚳	4:12
	☽△♂	6:04
	☽☍♃	13:21
	☽⚻⚷	14:40
	☽⚼♀	16:52
	☽⚹♄	17:07
	☽△♅	20:13
	☽⚻♆	23:59
21 Tu	☽#♃	5:55
	☽⚺⚳	6:26
	☽#♀	11:37
	☉□☽	11:56
	☽⚻♇	12:48
	☿∠⚳	15:21
	☽∠♄	19:07
	☽△♀	21:09
	☽⚼♅	22:02
22 W	☉⚹♇	0:24
	☽∥⚳	2:28
	☽⚹☿	10:05
	☽#♇	11:23
	☽□♂	12:31
	☽⚼♇	15:05
	☽⚻♃	17:50
	☽☍⚷	18:43
	☽#♂	20:07
	☽⚺♄	21:42
23 Th	☽⚻♅	0:25
	☽#♆	0:45
	☉ ♏	1:10
	☽☍♆	4:25
	☽☌⚳	12:38
	☉#☽	13:56
	☽∠☿	15:05
	☽△♇	17:54
	☽⚼♃	20:56
	☉⚹☽	21:11
	☽#⚷	22:14
24 F	☽□♀	7:53
	☽∥♄	11:41
	♂∠♇	16:26
	☽#♅	17:26
	♀∥♃	17:37
	☽⚺☿	21:02
	☽⚹♂	21:30
	☽#☿	23:01
25 Sa	☽△♃	0:34
	☽⚻⚷	0:55
	☉∠☽	2:48
	☽☌♄	4:27
	☽☍♅	6:44
	☿⚺♂	7:12
	⚷ D	8:14
	☽⚻♆	10:58
	☽⚺⚳	21:05
26 Su	☽□♇	1:04
	☉∠♄	2:35
	☽∠♂	2:52
	☽⚼⚷	4:45
	⚴ R	5:54
	☽∥☿	7:03
	☉⚺☽	9:01
	♃⚺⚷	9:52
	☽∥♅	10:12
	☿△⚷	12:01
	☿□♃	12:15
	☽⚼♆	14:58
	☽#♄	15:44
	☽⚹♀	21:16
27 M	☽∠⚳	2:04
	☉⚼♅	4:52
	☽∥⚷	6:16
	☽⚺♂	8:47
	☽△⚷	9:03
	☽□♃	9:18
	☽☌☿	11:38
	☽⚺♄	13:09
	♂□⚷	13:40
	☽⚻♅	14:57
	☿∥♅	18:09
	☽△♆	19:25
	♂⚹♃	20:30
	☉∥☽	21:52
28 Tu	☿⚺♄	2:00
	☽∠♀	4:54
	☽∥♆	5:16
	☽⚹⚳	7:33
	☽⚹♇	10:07
	☿⚻♅	16:12
	☽∥♂	16:48
	☽∠♄	18:13
	☽⚼♅	19:45
	☽∥♇	20:08
	☉☌☽	23:15
29 W	☽#⚳	3:09
	☽⚺♀	13:11
	☽∠♇	15:21
	☽□⚷	19:04
	☿#♄	19:49
	☽⚹♃	20:00
	☽☌♂	22:18
	☽⚹♄	23:46
30 Th	☽△♅	1:02
	☽∥♃	4:36
	☽⚺☿	5:42
	☽□♆	5:46
	☿△♆	6:13
	☽∥♀	15:48
	☽□⚳	20:04
	☽⚺♇	21:04
31 F	☽∠♃	2:06
	♂⚹♄	3:53
	☉⚺☽	15:55
	☽∠☿	16:00
	♂∥♇	19:18
	♂△♅	20:33

LONGITUDE

Day	Sid.Time	☉	☽	☽ 12 hour	Mean ☊	True ☊	☿	♀	♂	⚳	♃	♄	⚷	♅	♆	♇
	h m s	° ′ ″	° ′ ″	° ′ ″	° ′	° ′	° ′	° ′	° ′	° ′	° ′	° ′	° ′	° ′	° ′	° ′
1 Sa	2 42 37	8♏56 14	12♐36 44	18♐33 05	14♒11.5	14♒14.1	24♎09.5	16♐00.0	19♏08.1	29♌04.5	16♑50.4	18♍37.7	16♒03.6	19♓01.9	21♒28.1	29♐12.7
2 Su	2 46 34	9 56 17	24 28 12	0♑22 28	14 08.3	14R 04.4	25 44.0	17 12.4	19 50.2	29 25.0	16 59.5	18 43.4	16 04.1	19R 00.6	21D 28.1	29 14.2
3 M	2 50 30	10 56 23	6♑16 21	12 10 20	14 05.1	13 57.7	27 19.4	18 24.7	20 32.3	29 45.3	17 08.7	18 49.0	16 04.7	18 59.4	21 28.1	29 15.8
4 Tu	2 54 27	11 56 30	18 04 59	24 00 54	14 01.9	13 53.8	28 55.5	19 37.0	21 14.5	0♍05.5	17 18.0	18 54.5	16 05.3	18 58.3	21 28.1	29 17.4
5 W	2 58 23	12 56 38	29 58 43	5♒59 05	13 58.7	13 52.1	0♏32.2	20 49.3	21 56.8	0 25.6	17 27.4	19 00.0	16 05.9	18 57.1	21 28.2	29 19.1
6 Th	3 02 20	13 56 49	12♒02 42	18 10 16	13 55.6	13 51.8	2 09.3	22 01.5	22 39.1	0 45.4	17 37.0	19 05.4	16 06.7	18 56.1	21 28.3	29 20.7
7 F	3 06 16	14 57 00	24 22 27	0♓39 55	13 52.4	13 51.7	3 46.7	23 13.7	23 21.4	1 05.2	17 46.7	19 10.7	16 07.5	18 55.0	21 28.5	29 22.4
8 Sa	3 10 13	15 57 13	7♓03 18	13 33 08	13 49.2	13 50.6	5 24.2	24 25.8	24 03.8	1 24.7	17 56.5	19 16.0	16 08.4	18 54.0	21 28.6	29 24.1
9 Su	3 14 09	16 57 28	20 09 55	26 53 56	13 46.0	13 47.4	7 01.7	25 37.9	24 46.2	1 44.1	18 06.4	19 21.1	16 09.3	18 53.1	21 28.9	29 25.8
10 M	3 18 06	17 57 44	3♈45 26	10♈44 23	13 42.9	13 41.7	8 39.3	26 49.9	25 28.7	2 03.4	18 16.4	19 26.3	16 10.3	18 52.2	21 29.1	29 27.6
11 Tu	3 22 03	18 58 02	17 50 38	25 03 46	13 39.7	13 33.3	10 16.8	28 01.9	26 11.3	2 22.4	18 26.5	19 31.3	16 11.3	18 51.3	21 29.4	29 29.3
12 W	3 25 59	19 58 21	2♉23 09	9♉47 57	13 36.5	13 22.7	11 54.1	29 13.8	26 53.9	2 41.3	18 36.8	19 36.3	16 12.5	18 50.5	21 29.7	29 31.1
13 Th	3 29 56	20 58 42	17 17 07	24 49 29	13 33.3	13 11.1	13 31.3	0♑25.7	27 36.6	3 00.0	18 47.1	19 41.1	16 13.7	18 49.8	21 30.0	29 32.9
14 F	3 33 52	21 59 04	2♊23 44	9♊58 31	13 30.1	12 59.6	15 08.3	1 37.5	28 19.3	3 18.6	18 57.6	19 45.9	16 14.9	18 49.1	21 30.4	29 34.7
15 Sa	3 37 49	22 59 28	17 32 32	25 04 31	13 27.0	12 49.8	16 45.1	2 49.2	29 02.1	3 36.9	19 08.2	19 50.7	16 16.2	18 48.4	21 30.8	29 36.6
16 Su	3 41 45	23 59 55	2♋33 23	9♋58 09	13 23.8	12 42.4	18 21.7	4 00.9	29 44.9	3 55.1	19 18.8	19 55.3	16 17.6	18 47.8	21 31.3	29 38.4
17 M	3 45 42	25 00 22	17 18 07	24 32 42	13 20.6	12 37.8	19 58.0	5 12.6	0♐27.8	4 13.1	19 29.6	19 59.9	16 19.1	18 47.2	21 31.8	29 40.3
18 Tu	3 49 38	26 00 52	1♌41 34	8♌44 34	13 17.4	12D 35.8	21 34.2	6 24.2	1 10.7	4 30.9	19 40.5	20 04.4	16 20.6	18 46.7	21 32.3	29 42.2
19 W	3 53 35	27 01 24	15 41 40	22 33 00	13 14.3	12R 35.5	23 10.1	7 35.7	1 53.7	4 48.4	19 51.5	20 08.8	16 22.2	18 46.3	21 32.9	29 44.1
20 Th	3 57 32	28 01 57	29 18 47	5♍59 20	13 11.1	12 35.6	24 45.8	8 47.2	2 36.7	5 05.8	20 02.5	20 13.1	16 23.8	18 45.8	21 33.4	29 46.0
21 F	4 01 28	29 02 32	12♍34 58	19 06 05	13 07.9	12 34.9	26 21.3	9 58.6	3 19.9	5 23.0	20 13.7	20 17.3	16 25.5	18 45.5	21 34.1	29 48.0
22 Sa	4 05 25	0♐03 08	25 33 03	1♎56 14	13 04.7	12 32.2	27 56.6	11 10.0	4 03.0	5 39.9	20 25.0	20 21.4	16 27.2	18 45.2	21 34.7	29 49.9
23 Su	4 09 21	1 03 47	8♎15 59	14 32 38	13 01.6	12 26.9	29 31.6	12 21.3	4 46.2	5 56.7	20 36.3	20 25.5	16 29.0	18 44.9	21 35.4	29 51.9
24 M	4 13 18	2 04 27	20 46 28	26 57 44	12 58.4	12 18.6	1♐06.6	13 32.5	5 29.5	6 13.2	20 47.8	20 29.5	16 30.9	18 44.7	21 36.1	29 53.9
25 Tu	4 17 14	3 05 09	3♏06 40	9♏13 27	12 55.2	12 07.7	2 41.3	14 43.7	6 12.8	6 29.5	20 59.3	20 33.3	16 32.9	18 44.5	21 36.9	29 55.9
26 W	4 21 11	4 05 52	15 18 15	21 21 13	12 52.0	11 55.1	4 15.9	15 54.7	6 56.2	6 45.6	21 10.9	20 37.1	16 34.8	18 44.4	21 37.6	29 57.9
27 Th	4 25 07	5 06 37	27 22 29	3♐22 11	12 48.9	11 41.8	5 50.3	17 05.8	7 39.6	7 01.4	21 22.7	20 40.8	16 36.9	18D 44.3	21 38.5	29 59.9
28 F	4 29 04	6 07 23	9♐20 27	15 17 26	12 45.7	11 28.9	7 24.7	18 16.7	8 23.1	7 17.0	21 34.5	20 44.4	16 39.0	18 44.3	21 39.3	0♑02.0
29 Sa	4 33 01	7 08 10	21 13 19	27 08 17	12 42.5	11 17.5	8 58.9	19 27.6	9 06.6	7 32.4	21 46.4	20 47.9	16 41.2	18 44.4	21 40.2	0 04.0
30 Su	4 36 57	8♐08 59	3♑02 36	8♑56 32	12♒39.3	11♒08.4	10♐33.0	20♑38.3	9♐50.2	7♍47.5	21♑58.3	20♍51.3	16♒43.4	18♓44.5	21♒41.1	0♑06.1

1st of Month

Julian Day # 2454771.5
Obliquity 23°26'24"
SVP 5♓08'00"
GC 26♐57.8
Eris 21♈03.6R

Day	⚴
1	20♊28.9R
6	20 03.1R
11	19 21.2R
16	18 23.6R
21	17 11.2R
26	15 45.8R

Day	⚵
1	29♐40.3
6	1♑16.7
11	2 55.9
16	4 37.6
21	6 21.8
26	8 08.2

Day	⚶
1	6♉30.2R
6	5 13.3R
11	4 00.3R
16	2 53.4R
21	1 54.2R
26	1 04.3R

DECLINATION and LATITUDE

Day	☉ Decl	☽ Decl	☽ Lat	☽ 12h Decl	☿ Decl	☿ Lat	♀ Decl	♀ Lat	♂ Decl	♂ Lat	⚳ Decl	⚳ Lat	♃ Decl	♃ Lat	♄ Decl	♄ Lat
1 Sa	14S29	26S41	4S24	27S04	7S34	1N57	24S22	1S40	17S37	0S07	18N38	7N19	22S44	0S21	6N09	1N48
2 Su	14 48	27 09	3 49	26 54	8 12	1 53	24 32	1 43	17 49	0 08	18 35	7 23	22 43	0 21	6 07	1 48
3 M	15 07	26 22	3 05	25 31	8 50	1 48	24 41	1 45	18 01	0 08	18 31	7 27	22 41	0 21	6 05	1 48
4 Tu	15 25	24 24	2 12	22 60	9 29	1 44	24 49	1 47	18 13	0 09	18 27	7 30	22 40	0 21	6 03	1 48
5 W	15 43	21 20	1 13	19 27	10 07	1 39	24 57	1 50	18 25	0 10	18 23	7 34	22 39	0 21	6 01	1 49
6 Th	16 02	17 20	0 10	15 01	10 46	1 33	25 04	1 52	18 36	0 10	18 20	7 38	22 38	0 21	5 59	1 49
7 F	16 19	12 32	0N55	9 52	11 24	1 28	25 10	1 54	18 47	0 11	18 16	7 42	22 37	0 21	5 57	1 49
8 Sa	16 37	7 04	1 59	4 19	12 02	1 22	25 16	1 56	18 58	0 11	18 13	7 46	22 36	0 21	5 55	1 49
9 Su	16 54	1 09	2 59	1N55	12 40	1 15	25 20	1 58	19 09	0 12	18 10	7 50	22 34	0 22	5 53	1 49
10 M	17 11	5N02	3 51	8 08	13 18	1 09	25 24	2 00	19 20	0 13	18 06	7 54	22 33	0 22	5 52	1 50
11 Tu	17 28	11 10	4 31	14 07	13 55	1 03	25 28	2 02	19 31	0 13	18 03	7 58	22 32	0 22	5 50	1 50
12 W	17 44	16 55	4 55	19 29	14 31	0 56	25 30	2 04	19 41	0 14	17 60	8 02	22 30	0 22	5 48	1 50
13 Th	18 00	21 47	4 60	23 44	15 07	0 50	25 32	2 06	19 52	0 14	17 57	8 06	22 29	0 22	5 46	1 50
14 F	18 16	25 16	4 44	26 22	15 42	0 43	25 33	2 08	20 02	0 15	17 54	8 11	22 27	0 22	5 45	1 50
15 Sa	18 31	26 58	4 08	27 04	16 16	0 36	25 34	2 09	20 12	0 16	17 51	8 15	22 26	0 22	5 43	1 51
16 Su	18 46	26 40	3 15	25 47	16 50	0 29	25 33	2 11	20 22	0 16	17 48	8 19	22 25	0 22	5 41	1 51
17 M	19 01	24 28	2 10	22 45	17 22	0 22	25 32	2 12	20 31	0 17	17 46	8 23	22 23	0 22	5 40	1 51
18 Tu	19 16	20 43	0 57	18 24	17 54	0 16	25 31	2 14	20 41	0 17	17 43	8 28	22 22	0 22	5 38	1 51
19 W	19 30	15 52	0S16	13 10	18 25	0 09	25 28	2 15	20 50	0 18	17 40	8 32	22 20	0 22	5 37	1 52
20 Th	19 43	10 21	1 27	7 27	18 56	0 02	25 25	2 16	20 59	0 19	17 38	8 36	22 18	0 22	5 35	1 52
21 F	19 57	4 30	2 32	1 33	19 25	0S05	25 21	2 17	21 08	0 19	17 36	8 41	22 17	0 22	5 34	1 52
22 Sa	20 10	1S24	3 27	4S17	19 53	0 12	25 16	2 18	21 17	0 20	17 34	8 45	22 15	0 22	5 32	1 52
23 Su	20 22	7 07	4 10	9 50	20 21	0 18	25 11	2 19	21 25	0 20	17 31	8 50	22 13	0 22	5 31	1 53
24 M	20 35	12 27	4 41	14 55	20 47	0 25	25 05	2 20	21 34	0 21	17 29	8 55	22 12	0 22	5 30	1 53
25 Tu	20 47	17 13	4 58	19 19	21 13	0 31	24 58	2 21	21 42	0 21	17 28	8 59	22 10	0 22	5 28	1 53
26 W	20 58	21 13	5 01	22 53	21 37	0 38	24 50	2 22	21 50	0 22	17 26	9 04	22 08	0 22	5 27	1 53
27 Th	21 09	24 17	4 51	25 25	22 00	0 44	24 42	2 22	21 58	0 23	17 24	9 09	22 07	0 22	5 26	1 54
28 F	21 20	26 15	4 27	26 47	22 22	0 50	24 33	2 23	22 05	0 23	17 22	9 13	22 05	0 22	5 25	1 54
29 Sa	21 30	27 01	3 53	26 56	22 43	0 56	24 23	2 23	22 13	0 24	17 21	9 18	22 03	0 23	5 24	1 54
30 Su	21S40	26S32	3S08	25S50	23S03	1S02	24S13	2S23	22S20	0S24	17N20	9N23	22S01	0S23	5N23	1N54

Day	⚷ Decl	⚷ Lat	♅ Decl	♅ Lat	♆ Decl	♆ Lat	♇ Decl	♇ Lat
1	9S45	6N34	5S04	0S48	14S41	0S21	17S35	5N51
6	9 46	6 32	5 06	0 47	14 41	0 21	17 36	5 50
11	9 47	6 30	5 08	0 47	14 41	0 21	17 37	5 49
16	9 47	6 27	5 09	0 47	14 40	0 21	17 39	5 48
21	9 47	6 25	5 10	0 47	14 39	0 21	17 40	5 47
26	9 46	6 23	5 10	0 47	14 38	0 21	17 40	5 46

Day	⚴ Decl	⚴ Lat	⚵ Decl	⚵ Lat	⚶ Decl	⚶ Lat	Eris Decl	Eris Lat
1	25S29	48S42	13S21	10N05	3N30	10S46	4S49	14S02
6	26 54	50 06	13 34	9 52	3 15	10 36	4 49	14 02
11	28 13	51 23	13 45	9 39	3 03	10 24	4 50	14 02
16	29 25	52 32	13 55	9 27	2 55	10 09	4 50	14 01
21	30 28	53 31	14 02	9 15	2 52	9 52	4 51	14 00
26	31 21	54 19	14 08	9 05	2 53	9 33	4 51	13 60

Moon Phenomena

Max/0 Decl
dy hr mn
1 21:01 27S09
9 4:30 0 N
15 8:12 27N05
21 18:17 0 S
29 2:33 27S01

Perigee/Apogee
dy hr m kilometers
2 4:52 a 405723
14 9:59 p 358976
29 16:54 a 406480

Max/0 Lat
dy hr mn
6 3:34 0 N
12 17:38 5N00
18 18:37 0 S
25 17:28 5S02

PH
☽ 6 4:04 14♒07
○ 13 6:18 21♉15
☾ 19 21:32 27♌56
● 27 16:56 5♐49

Void of Course Moon

Last Aspect	☽ Ingress
2 9:43 ♇ ☌	♑ 2 11:14
4 6:48 ♂ ⚹	♒ 5 0:03
7 9:34 ♇ ⚹	♓ 7 10:44
9 16:29 ♇ □	♈ 9 17:27
11 19:19 ♇ △	♉ 11 20:06
13 17:14 ♂ ☍	♊ 13 20:12
15 19:18 ♇ ☍	♋ 15 19:53
17 13:44 ☉ △	♌ 17 21:09
20 0:49 ♇ △	♍ 20 1:14
22 8:03 ♇ □	♎ 22 8:21
24 17:46 ♇ ⚹	♏ 24 17:55
26 12:34 ♆ □	♐ 27 5:15
29 0:55 ♆ ⚹	♑ 29 17:49

DAILY ASPECTARIAN

1 Sa
♀⚹⚷ 1:12
☽⚹⚷ 6:58
☽☌♀ 7:37
☽⚺♃ 8:39
⚳△♇ 10:21
☽□♄ 12:15
☽□♅ 12:57
☽⚺♂ 14:01
☉∥♆ 15:26
☽⚹♆ 17:55
♀⚺♃ 19:06

2 Su
⚵ ♑ 0:47
☉∠☽ 1:02
☽⚹☿ 2:58
♆ D 6:40
☽☌♇ 9:43
☽△⚳ 10:21
☽∠⚷ 13:25
☽∠♂ 22:25

3 M
☽∠♆ 0:24
♀□♄ 8:42
☉⚹☽ 10:23
♀□♅ 11:20
⚳ ♍ 17:26
☽⚼⚳ 17:45
☽⚺⚷ 19:57
☽∥♀ 20:03
☽☌♃ 22:23

4 Tu
☽△♄ 1:41
☽⚹♅ 1:48
☽⚺♀ 3:28
☿⚹♇ 5:33
☽⚹♂ 6:48
☽⚺♆ 6:51
♂□♆ 7:45
☿∥⚷ 10:31
♄☍♅ 13:37
☽∥♃ 14:35
☿ ♏ 16:01
☿⚹⚳ 21:55
♂∦⚳ 22:22
☽⚺♇ 22:40

5 W
☽⚻⚳ 0:55
☽□☿ 1:18
☽∠♅ 7:56
☽⚼♄ 8:06
♀⚹♆ 12:57
☽∠♀ 12:58
☽∥♂ 17:16
☽∦⚳ 18:25
☽∥♇ 22:32

6 Th
☉□☽ 4:04
☽∠♇ 4:32
☉∥☽ 6:30
☽☌⚷ 7:59
☉∠♇ 9:49
☽⚺♃ 11:04
☽⚺♅ 13:28
☽∥♆ 13:42
☽⚻♄ 13:53
☽☌♆ 18:25
☽⚹♀ 21:34
☽□♂ 21:56

7 F
☿⚼♅ 2:02
☽∥☿ 4:36
♀⚺♂ 6:14
☿∠♄ 6:15
☽⚹♇ 9:34
☽∥⚷ 12:26
☽☍⚳ 13:08
☽∠♃ 16:12
☽△☿ 20:28

8 Sa
☉□⚷ 4:30
☽∦♄ 4:49
☽∥♅ 8:05
☽⚺⚷ 16:44
☉△☽ 17:44
☽⚹♃ 20:14
☽☌♅ 21:42
☽☍♄ 22:32

9 Su
☽⚺♆ 2:22
☽⚼☿ 3:48
☽△♂ 8:41
☽□♀ 10:42
☽□♇ 16:29
☽∠⚷ 19:30
☽⚻⚳ 20:58
☉⚼☽ 22:31

10 M
☽∦♅ 0:23
☽∥♄ 3:12
☽∠♆ 4:43
☉⚹♃ 8:55
☽⚻☿ 9:33
☽⚼♂ 12:10
☽∦⚷ 18:28
☽⚹⚷ 21:13
☉△♅ 21:22
☽⚼⚳ 23:12

11 Tu
☽□♃ 1:01
☽⚺♅ 1:41
☉⚻☽ 2:01
☽⚻♄ 2:49
☽⚹♆ 6:05
☽∦☿ 12:25
☽∦♆ 14:19
☉⚹♄ 14:26
☉∥♇ 14:28
☽⚻♂ 14:34
☽△♀ 18:23
☽△♇ 19:19

12 W
☽△⚳ 0:30
☽∠♅ 2:22
☽∦♇ 3:14
☽⚼♄ 3:37
☉∦☽ 3:55
☽∥⚳ 4:53
♀☌♇ 5:56
☿∥♆ 6:21
☽∦♂ 13:29
♀ ♑ 15:26
☽☍☿ 17:15
☽⚼♇ 19:37
☉∦⚳ 19:58
☽⚼♀ 20:46
☽□⚷ 22:18

13 Th
☽△♃ 2:25
☽⚹♅ 2:28
☽△♄ 3:51
☽∦♃ 4:04
♃⚹♅ 5:41
☉☍☽ 6:18
☽□♆ 6:43
☉□♆ 12:32
☿∠♇ 15:32
♀∠⚷ 16:20
☽☍♂ 17:14
☽⚻♇ 19:32
☽⚻♀ 22:40

14 F
☽□⚳ 1:29
☽⚼♃ 2:30
☽∦♀ 2:43
☿□⚷ 16:45
☽△⚷ 21:59
☽⚻☿ 22:36

15 Sa
☽□♅ 2:01
☽⚻♃ 2:34
☽□♄ 3:41
☽△♆ 6:19
☉⚻☽ 9:18
☽⚻♂ 19:16
☽☍♇ 19:18
♂⚺♇ 20:13
♀△⚳ 21:23
☽⚼⚷ 21:58

16 Su
☽⚼☿ 1:27
☽⚹⚳ 2:15
☽☍♀ 2:34
☽⚼♆ 6:25
☿△♅ 6:28
♂ ♐ 8:28
☉⚼☽ 11:11
☽∦♀ 14:23
☿⚹♃ 16:01
☽⚼♂ 20:49
☽⚻⚷ 22:23

17 M
☿⚹♄ 0:29
☽△♅ 2:27
☽∠⚳ 3:14
☽☍♃ 3:40
☽⚹♄ 4:28
☽△☿ 4:57
☽⚻♆ 6:59
☿∥♇ 12:18
☉△☽ 13:44
☿∠♀ 14:13
☽∦♃ 14:25
☿∦⚳ 16:02
☽⚻♇ 20:38
☽△♂ 23:05
☿□♆ 23:32

18 Tu
☽∦♂ 0:12
♀∠♆ 2:44
☽⚼♅ 3:32
☽⚺⚳ 4:53
☽∠♄ 5:46
☉∦☽ 7:20
☽⚻♀ 8:45
☽∦☿ 13:03
☽∥⚳ 15:29
☽∦♇ 15:40
☽⚼♇ 22:20

19 W
☽☍⚷ 1:11
☽⚻♅ 5:22
☽∦♆ 5:29
☽⚻♃ 7:22
☽⚺♄ 7:49
☽☍♆ 10:15
⚳⚼♃ 11:22
⚳∦♇ 11:55
☽⚼♀ 13:14
☽□☿ 14:50
☉□☽ 21:32

20 Th
☽△♇ 0:49
☽∦⚷ 2:21
☽□♂ 6:15
☽⚼♃ 10:26
☽☌⚳ 10:37
☽△♀ 18:46
☽∥♄ 19:39
☽∦♅ 21:18

21 F
☽⚻⚷ 7:04
☽☍♅ 11:22
♃△♄ 12:14
☽☌♄ 14:17
☽△♃ 14:18
☽⚻♆ 16:35
☉⚺♇ 18:35
☉ ♐ 22:45

22 Sa
☽⚹☿ 5:07
☽□♇ 8:03
☉⚹☽ 9:10
☽⚼⚷ 11:07
☽∥♅ 15:42
☽⚹♂ 16:57
☽∦♄ 17:13
☽⚺⚳ 19:29
☽⚼♆ 20:48

23 Su
☉∥☿ 2:42
☿⚺♇ 5:13
☿ ♐ 7:10
☽□♀ 8:37
☽∥⚷ 11:44
☽∠☿ 13:42
☽△⚷ 15:46
☉∠☽ 16:14
☽⚻♅ 20:05
☽∠♂ 23:25
☽⚺♄ 23:27

24 M
☽□♃ 0:03
☽∠⚳ 0:53
☽△♆ 1:36
☽∥♆ 10:37
♂∠♃ 13:48
☽⚹♇ 17:46
☽⚺☿ 23:03
☉⚺☽ 23:57

25 Tu
☽⚼♅ 1:14
☽∦⚳ 1:21
☽∥♇ 2:31
☽∠♄ 4:49
☽⚺♂ 6:28
☽⚹⚳ 6:47
♂□⚳ 14:42
☉☌☿ 16:53
☉∥☽ 22:14
☽∠♇ 23:20

26 W
☽⚹♀ 1:20
☽□⚷ 2:32
☽∥☿ 3:03
☽∥♂ 4:23
☽∥♃ 6:23
☽△♅ 6:48
☽⚹♄ 10:36
☽⚹♃ 11:51
☽□♆ 12:34
♀⚺⚷ 13:57
☿∥♂ 20:02

27 Th
♇ ♑ 1:04
☽∥♀ 3:48
☽⚺♇ 5:16
☿∥♃ 6:27
☿∠♃ 9:24
☽∠♀ 10:29
♅ D 16:10
☉☌☽ 16:56
☽∠♃ 18:20
☽☌☿ 19:32
☽□⚳ 19:46
☿□⚳ 21:40
☽☌♂ 21:57
♂∥♃ 23:10

28 F
♀⚹♅ 9:21
♃⚺♆ 10:36
☉∠♃ 13:17
☽⚹⚷ 14:48
☽□♅ 18:58
☽⚺♀ 20:02
☽□♄ 23:08

29 Sa
☽⚹♆ 0:55
☽⚺♃ 1:08
☿☌♂ 3:40
☉□⚳ 12:43
☽☌♇ 18:00
☽∠⚷ 21:18

30 Su
♀△♄ 4:38
☽∠♆ 7:25
☽△⚳ 9:52
☉⚺☽ 11:22
☽⚺♂ 14:44
☽⚺☿ 17:37
♀⚺♆ 21:37

December 2008

LONGITUDE

Day	Sid.Time	☉	☽	☽ 12 hour	Mean ☊	True ☊	☿	♀	♂	⚳	♃	♄	⚷	♅	♆	♇
	h m s	° ' "	° ' "	° ' "	° '	° '	° '	° '	° '	° '	° '	° '	° '	° '	° '	° '
1 M	4 40 54	9♐09 48	14♑50 25	20♑44 35	12♒36.2	11♒02.1	12♐07.1	21♑49.0	10♐33.9	8♍02.3	22♑10.4	20♍54.6	16♒45.7	18♓44.6	21♒42.1	0♑08.1
2 Tu	4 44 50	10 10 39	26 39 30	2♒35 37	12 33.0	10R 58.5	13 41.1	22 59.6	11 17.6	8 16.9	22 22.5	20 57.8	16 48.0	18 44.8	21 43.1	0 10.2
3 W	4 48 47	11 11 31	8♒33 26	14 33 30	12 29.8	10D 57.3	15 15.0	24 10.1	12 01.3	8 31.2	22 34.7	21 01.0	16 50.4	18 45.0	21 44.1	0 12.3
4 Th	4 52 43	12 12 23	20 36 26	26 42 50	12 26.6	10 57.6	16 48.9	25 20.5	12 45.1	8 45.3	22 47.0	21 04.0	16 52.9	18 45.3	21 45.1	0 14.4
5 F	4 56 40	13 13 16	2♓53 20	9♓08 35	12 23.4	10R 58.5	18 22.8	26 30.8	13 28.9	8 59.1	22 59.4	21 06.9	16 55.4	18 45.7	21 46.2	0 16.6
6 Sa	5 00 37	14 14 10	15 29 12	21 55 48	12 20.3	10 58.9	19 56.6	27 41.0	14 12.8	9 12.6	23 11.8	21 09.7	16 58.0	18 46.1	21 47.3	0 18.7
7 Su	5 04 33	15 15 05	28 28 54	5♈09 00	12 17.1	10 57.9	21 30.5	28 51.1	14 56.7	9 25.9	23 24.3	21 12.4	17 00.6	18 46.6	21 48.4	0 20.8
8 M	5 08 30	16 16 01	11♈56 25	18 51 24	12 13.9	10 54.9	23 04.4	0♒01.1	15 40.7	9 38.8	23 36.8	21 15.0	17 03.2	18 47.1	21 49.6	0 22.9
9 Tu	5 12 26	17 16 57	25 53 59	3♉04 01	12 10.7	10 49.7	24 38.2	1 10.9	16 24.8	9 51.5	23 49.5	21 17.6	17 05.9	18 47.6	21 50.8	0 25.1
10 W	5 16 23	18 17 54	10♉21 08	17 44 44	12 07.6	10 42.6	26 12.1	2 20.7	17 08.9	10 03.9	24 02.2	21 20.0	17 08.7	18 48.2	21 52.0	0 27.2
11 Th	5 20 19	19 18 52	25 13 59	2♊47 50	12 04.4	10 34.5	27 46.0	3 30.3	17 53.0	10 16.0	24 14.9	21 22.3	17 11.5	18 48.9	21 53.3	0 29.4
12 F	5 24 16	20 19 50	10♊25 05	18 04 23	12 01.2	10 26.3	29 20.0	4 39.7	18 37.2	10 27.8	24 27.8	21 24.5	17 14.4	18 49.6	21 54.6	0 31.6
13 Sa	5 28 12	21 20 49	25 44 17	3♋23 24	11 58.0	10 19.2	0♑53.9	5 49.1	19 21.4	10 39.2	24 40.7	21 26.6	17 17.3	18 50.4	21 55.9	0 33.8
14 Su	5 32 09	22 21 49	11♋00 20	18 33 52	11 54.9	10 14.0	2 27.9	6 58.3	20 05.7	10 50.4	24 53.6	21 28.6	17 20.3	18 51.2	21 57.2	0 35.9
15 M	5 36 06	23 22 50	26 02 54	3♌26 34	11 51.7	10D 11.0	4 01.8	8 07.3	20 50.0	11 01.3	25 06.6	21 30.5	17 23.3	18 52.0	21 58.6	0 38.1
16 Tu	5 40 02	24 23 52	10♌44 11	17 55 18	11 48.5	10 10.2	5 35.7	9 16.2	21 34.4	11 11.8	25 19.7	21 32.3	17 26.4	18 53.0	22 00.0	0 40.3
17 W	5 43 59	25 24 55	24 59 40	1♍57 11	11 45.3	10 10.9	7 09.5	10 25.0	22 18.9	11 22.0	25 32.8	21 33.9	17 29.5	18 53.9	22 01.4	0 42.5
18 Th	5 47 55	26 25 58	8♍47 57	15 32 11	11 42.2	10 12.3	8 43.2	11 33.6	23 03.3	11 31.9	25 46.0	21 35.5	17 32.6	18 54.9	22 02.9	0 44.7
19 F	5 51 52	27 27 03	22 10 10	28 42 19	11 39.0	10R 13.3	10 16.8	12 42.0	23 47.9	11 41.4	25 59.2	21 37.0	17 35.8	18 56.0	22 04.4	0 46.9
20 Sa	5 55 48	28 28 08	5♎09 03	11♎30 52	11 35.8	10 13.2	11 50.2	13 50.3	24 32.4	11 50.6	26 12.5	21 38.3	17 39.0	18 57.1	22 05.9	0 49.1
21 Su	5 59 45	29 29 14	17 48 13	24 01 35	11 32.6	10 11.4	13 23.3	14 58.4	25 17.1	11 59.4	26 25.8	21 39.6	17 42.3	18 58.3	22 07.4	0 51.3
22 M	6 03 41	0♑30 21	0♏11 28	6♏18 16	11 29.4	10 07.6	14 56.1	16 06.3	26 01.8	12 07.9	26 39.2	21 40.7	17 45.7	18 59.5	22 09.0	0 53.5
23 Tu	6 07 38	1 31 29	12 22 27	18 24 23	11 26.3	10 02.2	16 28.4	17 14.1	26 46.5	12 16.1	26 52.6	21 41.7	17 49.0	19 00.7	22 10.6	0 55.7
24 W	6 11 35	2 32 37	24 24 25	0♐22 54	11 23.1	9 55.5	18 00.1	18 21.7	27 31.3	12 23.8	27 06.1	21 42.7	17 52.4	19 02.0	22 12.2	0 57.9
25 Th	6 15 31	3 33 46	6♐20 07	12 16 21	11 19.9	9 48.2	19 31.1	19 29.1	28 16.1	12 31.2	27 19.6	21 43.5	17 55.9	19 03.4	22 13.8	1 00.1
26 F	6 19 28	4 34 56	18 11 50	24 06 48	11 16.7	9 41.1	21 01.1	20 36.3	29 01.0	12 38.2	27 33.2	21 44.2	17 59.4	19 04.8	22 15.5	1 02.3
27 Sa	6 23 24	5 36 06	0♑01 30	5♑56 06	11 13.6	9 35.0	22 30.1	21 43.3	29 45.9	12 44.8	27 46.8	21 44.8	18 02.9	19 06.2	22 17.2	1 04.4
28 Su	6 27 21	6 37 16	11 50 52	17 46 00	11 10.4	9 30.2	23 57.7	22 50.0	0♑30.9	12 51.1	28 00.5	21 45.2	18 06.5	19 07.7	22 18.9	1 06.6
29 M	6 31 17	7 38 26	23 41 46	29 38 35	11 07.2	9 27.2	25 23.7	23 56.6	1 15.9	12 56.9	28 14.1	21 45.6	18 10.1	19 09.3	22 20.6	1 08.8
30 Tu	6 35 14	8 39 36	5♒36 10	11♒35 26	11 04.0	9D 25.9	26 47.8	25 02.9	2 00.9	13 02.4	28 27.9	21 45.8	18 13.7	19 10.9	22 22.4	1 11.0
31 W	6 39 10	9♑40 47	17 36 30	23 39 46	11♒00.9	9♒26.1	28♑09.5	26♒09.0	2♑46.0	13♍07.4	28♑41.6	21♍46.0	18♒17.4	19♓12.5	22♒24.1	1♑13.2

1st of Month

Julian Day #
2454801.5
Obliquity
23°26'23"
SVP 5♓07'55"
GC 26♐57.8
Eris 20♈48.9R

Day	⚴
1	14♊10.8R
6	12 30.1R
11	10 48.4R
16	9 10.5R
21	7 40.6R
26	6 22.9R
31	5 20.4R

Day	⚵
1	9♑56.7
6	11 47.1
11	13 39.3
16	15 33.0
21	17 28.2
26	19 24.8
31	21 22.6

Day	⚶
1	0♉24.7R
6	29♈56.2R
11	29 39.0R
16	29 33.1R
21	29 38.1
26	29 53.7
31	0♉19.5

DECLINATION and LATITUDE

Day	☉ Decl	☽ Decl	☽ Lat	☽12h Decl	☿ Decl	☿ Lat	♀ Decl	♀ Lat	♂ Decl	♂ Lat	⚳ Decl	⚳ Lat	♃ Decl	♃ Lat	♄ Decl	♄ Lat
1 M	21S49	24S51	2S15	23S35	23S22	1S08	24S02	2S23	22S27	0S25	17N19	9N28	21S59	0S23	5N21	1N55
2 Tu	21 59	22 04	1 16	20 18	23 39	1 13	23 50	2 23	22 33	0 26	17 18	9 33	21 57	0 23	5 20	1 55
3 W	22 07	18 20	0 13	16 09	23 56	1 19	23 38	2 23	22 40	0 26	17 17	9 38	21 55	0 23	5 19	1 55
4 Th	22 15	13 48	0N52	11 18	24 11	1 24	23 25	2 23	22 46	0 27	17 16	9 43	21 53	0 23	5 18	1 55
5 F	22 23	8 39	1 55	5 54	24 25	1 29	23 11	2 23	22 52	0 27	17 16	9 48	21 51	0 23	5 18	1 56
6 Sa	22 31	3 02	2 54	0 07	24 37	1 34	22 57	2 23	22 58	0 28	17 15	9 53	21 49	0 23	5 17	1 56
7 Su	22 37	2N52	3 47	5N51	24 49	1 39	22 42	2 22	23 04	0 28	17 15	9 58	21 47	0 23	5 16	1 56
8 M	22 44	8 50	4 29	11 46	24 59	1 43	22 27	2 21	23 09	0 29	17 15	10 03	21 45	0 23	5 15	1 56
9 Tu	22 50	14 36	4 56	17 25	25 07	1 47	22 11	2 21	23 14	0 30	17 15	10 09	21 43	0 23	5 14	1 57
10 W	22 55	19 46	5 07	21 59	25 15	1 51	21 54	2 20	23 19	0 30	17 15	10 14	21 41	0 23	5 14	1 57
11 Th	23 01	23 52	4 57	25 21	25 20	1 55	21 37	2 19	23 24	0 31	17 15	10 19	21 39	0 23	5 13	1 57
12 F	23 05	26 24	4 26	26 57	25 25	1 59	21 20	2 18	23 28	0 31	17 15	10 25	21 37	0 23	5 12	1 57
13 Sa	23 09	26 58	3 36	26 29	25 28	2 02	21 01	2 17	23 32	0 32	17 16	10 30	21 34	0 23	5 12	1 58
14 Su	23 13	25 29	2 31	24 02	25 30	2 05	20 43	2 15	23 36	0 32	17 16	10 35	21 32	0 23	5 11	1 58
15 M	23 16	22 11	1 16	19 58	25 30	2 07	20 23	2 14	23 40	0 33	17 17	10 41	21 30	0 23	5 11	1 58
16 Tu	23 19	17 30	0S03	14 48	25 28	2 09	20 04	2 12	23 44	0 33	17 18	10 46	21 27	0 24	5 10	1 59
17 W	23 22	11 57	1 19	8 59	25 26	2 11	19 43	2 11	23 47	0 34	17 20	10 52	21 25	0 24	5 10	1 59
18 Th	23 24	5 58	2 29	2 56	25 21	2 12	19 23	2 09	23 50	0 35	17 21	10 58	21 23	0 24	5 09	1 59
19 F	23 25	0S05	3 28	3S03	25 15	2 13	19 01	2 07	23 53	0 35	17 22	11 03	21 20	0 24	5 09	1 59
20 Sa	23 26	5 56	4 14	8 44	25 08	2 14	18 40	2 05	23 55	0 36	17 24	11 09	21 18	0 24	5 09	1 60
21 Su	23 26	11 24	4 47	13 56	24 59	2 14	18 18	2 02	23 57	0 36	17 26	11 15	21 15	0 24	5 09	1 60
22 M	23 26	16 18	5 05	18 29	24 49	2 13	17 55	1 60	23 59	0 37	17 28	11 20	21 13	0 24	5 08	2 00
23 Tu	23 26	20 28	5 10	22 13	24 37	2 13	17 32	1 57	24 01	0 37	17 30	11 26	21 10	0 24	5 08	2 00
24 W	23 25	23 43	5 00	24 58	24 24	2 11	17 09	1 55	24 03	0 38	17 32	11 32	21 08	0 24	5 08	2 01
25 Th	23 24	25 56	4 38	26 36	24 09	2 09	16 45	1 52	24 04	0 38	17 35	11 38	21 05	0 24	5 08	2 01
26 F	23 22	26 57	4 03	27 01	23 53	2 06	16 21	1 49	24 05	0 39	17 37	11 44	21 03	0 24	5 08	2 01
27 Sa	23 19	26 45	3 19	26 11	23 35	2 03	15 56	1 46	24 06	0 39	17 40	11 50	21 00	0 24	5 08	2 02
28 Su	23 16	25 19	2 25	24 10	23 16	1 59	15 32	1 43	24 06	0 40	17 43	11 56	20 57	0 24	5 08	2 02
29 M	23 13	22 46	1 25	21 06	22 56	1 54	15 06	1 40	24 06	0 40	17 47	12 02	20 55	0 24	5 08	2 02
30 Tu	23 09	19 13	0 21	17 07	22 34	1 48	14 41	1 36	24 06	0 41	17 50	12 08	20 52	0 24	5 08	2 02
31 W	23S05	14S51	0N45	12S25	22S12	1S42	14S15	1S33	24S06	0S41	17N53	12N14	20S49	0S25	5N09	2N03

Day	⚷ Decl	⚷ Lat	♅ Decl	♅ Lat	♆ Decl	♆ Lat	♇ Decl	♇ Lat
1	9S45	6N21	5S10	0S46	14S36	0S21	17S41	5N45
6	9 44	6 19	5 09	0 46	14 35	0 21	17 42	5 44
11	9 41	6 17	5 08	0 46	14 33	0 21	17 43	5 44
16	9 39	6 15	5 06	0 46	14 31	0 21	17 43	5 43
21	9 36	6 13	5 04	0 46	14 28	0 21	17 44	5 43
26	9 32	6 12	5 01	0 45	14 26	0 21	17 44	5 42
31	9S28	6N10	4S58	0S45	14S23	0S21	17S44	5N42

Day	⚴ Decl	⚴ Lat	⚵ Decl	⚵ Lat	⚶ Decl	⚶ Lat	Eris Decl	Eris Lat
1	32S03	54S55	14S11	8N54	2N59	9S13	4S51	13S59
6	32 33	55 17	14 13	8 44	3 09	8 52	4 51	13 58
11	32 50	55 25	14 12	8 35	3 23	8 30	4 51	13 58
16	32 53	55 19	14 10	8 26	3 41	8 09	4 51	13 57
21	32 43	55 00	14 05	8 17	4 02	7 48	4 50	13 56
26	32 20	54 29	13 58	8 09	4 27	7 27	4 50	13 55
31	31S45	53S46	13S49	8N01	4N55	7S07	4S49	13S54

Moon Phenomena

Max/0 Decl
dy hr mn
6 12:27 0 N
12 18:52 27N01
18 23:42 0 S
26 7:57 27S01

Perigee/Apogee
dy hr m kilometers
12 21:53 p 356567
26 17:45 a 406602

Max/0 Lat
dy hr mn
3 4:48 0 N
10 0:23 5N07
15 23:03 0 S
22 19:26 5S10
30 7:40 0 N

PH dy hr mn
☽ 5 21:27 14♓08
○ 12 16:38 21♊02
☾ 19 10:30 27♍54
● 27 12:23 6♑08

Void of Course Moon

Last Aspect	☽ Ingress
1 15:45 ♀ ☌	♒ 2 6:46
4 2:16 ♆ ☌	♓ 4 18:24
7 0:44 ♀ ✶	♈ 7 2:45
8 21:36 ♆ △	♉ 9 6:53
10 22:24 ♃ △	♊ 11 7:34
12 18:02 ♆ △	♋ 13 6:41
14 22:28 ♃ ☍	♌ 15 6:24
17 0:47 ☉ △	♍ 17 8:37
19 10:30 ☉ □	♎ 19 14:24
21 16:58 ♃ □	♏ 21 23:38
24 5:31 ♃ ✶	♐ 24 11:14
26 23:26 ♂ ☌	♑ 26 23:57
29 9:21 ♃ ☌	♒ 29 12:44

DAILY ASPECTARIAN

1 M ☽⊻⚷ 3:55
☽✶♅ 7:56
☽∥♀ 8:38
♀☌♃ 8:46
☽△♄ 12:24
☽∥☿ 12:31
☽⊻♆ 13:58
☽☌♃ 15:10
☽☌♀ 15:45
☽⚼⚳ 17:01
☽∥♂ 20:27
☉∠☽ 20:43
☉∥♃ 21:17
☽∠♂ 23:13

2 Tu ☉∥☽ 0:36
☽∥♃ 0:47
☽∠☿ 4:44
☽⊻♇ 7:08
♀⚼⚳ 7:24
☿∥♀ 8:57
☽∠♅ 14:20
☽⚼♄ 18:52
☽⊼⚳ 23:56

3 W ☽∥♇ 3:37
☉✶☽ 5:46
☽⋕⚳ 5:56
☽✶♂ 7:23
☽∠♇ 13:20
☽✶☿ 15:22
☽☌⚷ 16:36
☽∥♆ 20:05
☽⊻♅ 20:20

4 Th ☽⊼♄ 0:55
☿✶⚷ 1:03
☽☌♆ 2:16
☽⊻♃ 4:22
☽⊻♀ 10:18
☽✶♇ 18:56
☽∥⚷ 19:11

5 F ⚶R♈ 4:45
☿□♅ 5:53
☽∠♃ 9:58
☽☍⚳ 11:55
☽⋕♄ 14:36
☽∥♅ 15:10
☽∠♀ 18:11
☉□☽ 21:27
☽□♂ 21:28
☉☌♂ 22:05
♀∥♂ 23:07

6 Sa ☽⊻⚷ 2:47
☽☌♅ 6:08
☽□☿ 9:28
☽☍♄ 10:37
☽⊻♆ 11:45
☽✶♃ 14:34
☿□♄ 19:15

7 Su ☽✶♀ 0:44
☽□♇ 3:23
☿✶♆ 4:39
☉∥♀ 5:30
☽∠⚷ 6:24
☽⋕♅ 9:09
☽∥♄ 9:36
☽∠♆ 14:58
☽⊼⚳ 19:54
♀ ♒ 23:38

8 M ☽⋕⚷ 3:32
☽△♂ 6:53
♀⊻♇ 7:45
☉△☽ 8:08
☽✶⚷ 8:55
☿⊻♃ 9:36
☽⊻♅ 11:53
☽⊼♄ 16:09
☽✶♆ 17:07
☉✶⚷ 19:28
☽□♃ 20:26
☽△☿ 21:36
☽⚼⚳ 22:13
☽⋕♆ 23:49

9 Tu ☽△♇ 7:36
☽□♀ 9:38
☽⚼♂ 9:45
☉⚼☽ 11:30
☽∥⚳ 11:47
♀∠♂ 12:56
☽∠♅ 13:13
☽⋕♇ 13:57
☽⚼♄ 17:23
☽△⚳ 23:31
♂✶⚷ 23:55

10 W ☽⚼☿ 1:33
☽⚼♇ 8:19
☽⋕♃ 10:10
☽⋕♀ 10:49
☽□⚷ 11:04
☽⊼♂ 11:36
☉□♅ 12:04
☽✶♅ 13:43
☉⊼☽ 13:50
☽△♄ 17:49
☉⋕☽ 18:07
☽□♆ 18:39
☽⋕♂ 20:41
♀∥♃ 21:41
☽△♃ 22:24

11 Th ☽⊼☿ 4:30
♀∠♅ 6:30
☽⊼♇ 8:22
☽⋕☿ 12:16
☽△♀ 14:12
☽⚼♃ 22:29

12 F ☽□⚳ 0:04
♂□♅ 6:52
☿ ♑ 10:14
☽△⚷ 10:44
☽□♅ 13:11
☽☍♂ 13:30
☽⚼♀ 15:40
☉☍☽ 16:38
☽□♄ 17:16
☽△♆ 18:02
☿☌♇ 18:44
☽⊼♃ 22:19

13 Sa ☉□♄ 2:21
☽☍♇ 7:35
☽☍☿ 9:01
☽⚼⚷ 10:18
♀⚼♄ 13:24
☉✶♆ 14:06
☽⊼♀ 17:07
☽⚼♆ 17:36
☿∠⚷ 22:00
☽✶⚳ 23:44
☽⋕☿ 23:57

14 Su ☽⊼⚷ 10:05
☽△♅ 12:28
☽⋕♂ 14:43
☽⊼♂ 15:12
☽✶♄ 16:41
☉⋕☽ 17:17
☽⊼♆ 17:27
☉⊼☽ 19:24
☽☍♃ 22:28
☽∠⚳ 23:57

15 M ☽⋕♃ 3:56
☽⊼♇ 7:27
☽⋕♀ 10:37
☽⚼♅ 12:43
☽⊼☿ 14:31
☽⚼♂ 16:46
☽∠♄ 17:04
☽☍♀ 21:22
☉⚼☽ 21:37
♂□♄ 22:48
☽⋕♇ 22:56

16 Tu ☽⊻⚳ 0:46
☽∥⚳ 0:52
⚶ D 4:33
☽⚼♇ 8:15
☽☍⚷ 11:14
☽⋕♆ 13:15
☽⊼♅ 13:38
♂✶♆ 14:17
☽⊻♄ 18:09
☽⚼☿ 18:34
☽☍♆ 18:56
☽△♂ 19:11
☿∠♆ 21:54
☉∠♀ 23:49

17 W ☉△☽ 0:47
☽⊼♃ 0:58
☉⊻♃ 3:57
☽⋕⚷ 9:25
☽△♇ 9:52
♀⊼⚳ 23:19
☽△☿ 23:51

18 Th ☽∥♄ 3:14
☽⋕♅ 3:31
☽⚼♃ 3:33
☽☌⚳ 4:54
☽⊼♀ 5:21
☽⊼⚷ 15:41
☽☍♅ 18:07
☽☌♄ 22:59
☽⊼♆ 23:49

19 F ☽□♂ 3:09
☽△♃ 7:07
☉□☽ 10:30
☽⚼♀ 11:07
☽□♇ 15:54
☽⚼⚷ 19:18
☽∥♅ 20:23
☽⋕♄ 20:42

20 Sa ☿△⚳ 0:07
☽⚼♆ 3:40
☽⊻⚳ 12:46
☽□☿ 14:23
☽∥⚷ 15:50
☽△♀ 18:03
☽△⚷ 23:49

21 Su ☽⊼♅ 2:15
☽⊻♄ 7:26
☽△♆ 8:20
☉ ♑ 12:05
☽∥♆ 14:37
☽✶♂ 15:22
☽□♃ 16:58
☽∠⚳ 17:58
♀∠♇ 19:17

22 M ☉✶☽ 0:40
☽✶♇ 1:22
☽⋕⚳ 6:19
☽⚼♅ 7:28
☽∥♇ 7:45
☽∥♀ 8:04
☉☌♇ 9:25
♀∥♇ 11:41
☽∠♄ 12:45
☽∠♂ 22:44
☽✶⚳ 23:47

23 Tu ♀⋕⚳ 2:00
☽∥♃ 4:38
♂⊻♃ 4:42
☽∠♇ 7:05
☉∠☽ 9:01
☽✶☿ 9:20
☽□♀ 10:40
☽□⚷ 10:53
♀☌⚷ 13:03
☽△♅ 13:14
☽✶♄ 18:36
☽□♆ 19:35
☉∥☽ 21:25
☿⊻⚷ 21:55

24 W ☽∥♂ 2:55
☽✶♃ 5:31
☽∥☿ 5:38
☽⊻♂ 6:40
☉∠⚷ 8:14
☽⊻♇ 13:13
♀⊻♅ 14:39
☿✶♅ 16:34
☉⊻☽ 17:53
☽∠☿ 19:48
☿⊻♀ 21:58

25 Th ☿∥♂ 6:48
☽∠♃ 12:21
☽□⚳ 12:38
☽✶⚷ 23:35

26 F ☽□♅ 1:48
☽✶♀ 5:23
☽⊻☿ 6:33
☽□♄ 7:11
☽✶♆ 8:15
☿△♄ 11:39
⚳⚼♃ 17:23
☽⊻♃ 19:21
☿⊻♆ 20:25
☽☌♂ 23:26

27 Sa ♀⊼♄ 0:32
☽☌♇ 2:08
☽∠⚷ 6:10
♂ ♑ 7:31
⚶ ♉ 10:03
☉☌☽ 12:23
♀☌♆ 12:30
☽∠♆ 14:47
☽∠♀ 15:01
☉∥☿ 23:09

28 Su ☽△⚳ 2:03
⚳⋕♇ 7:26
☽∥♂ 12:37
☽⊻⚷ 12:45
☽✶♅ 14:47
☉∠♆ 16:48
♂☌♇ 20:03
☽△♄ 20:05
☉∥☽ 20:14
☽⊻♆ 21:15
☽∥☿ 22:30

29 M ☽⊻♀ 0:33
☽☌☿ 3:54
☽⚼⚳ 8:39
☽☌♃ 9:21
☽∥♃ 13:24
☽⊻♇ 15:05
☽⊻♂ 16:18
☽∠♅ 21:08

30 Tu ☽⚼♄ 2:20
☉⊻☽ 6:42
☽⋕⚳ 7:55
☽∥♇ 8:32
☽⊼⚳ 15:00
♀∥♆ 16:48
☽∠♇ 21:14
☿⚼⚳ 23:21

31 W ☽∠♂ 0:20
☽☌⚷ 1:22
☽∥♆ 2:22
☽⊻♅ 3:11
☽∥♀ 3:17
☽⊼♄ 8:15
☽☌♆ 9:32
☿☌♃ 11:41
☉∠☽ 15:17
♄ R 18:09
♂∠⚷ 18:10
☽☌♀ 18:35
☽⊻♃ 22:20
☽⊻☿ 23:22

LONGITUDE

Day	Sid.Time	☉	☽	☽ 12 hour	Mean ☊	True ☊	☿	♀	♂	⚳	♃	♄	⚷	♅	♆	♇
	h m s	° ' "	° ' "	° ' "	° '	° '	° '	° '	° '	° '	° '	° '	° '	° '	° '	° '
1 Th	6 43 07	10♑41 57	29♒45 37	5♓54 30	10♒57.7	9♒27.4	29♑28.4	27♒14.9	3♑31.2	13♍12.1	28♑55.4	21♍46.0	18♒21.1	19♓14.2	22♒25.9	1♑15.4
2 F	6 47 04	11 43 08	12♓06 52	18 23 11	10 54.5	9 29.2	0♒44.1	28 20.5	4 16.4	13 16.3	29 09.2	21R 45.9	18 24.9	19 15.9	22 27.8	1 17.5
3 Sa	6 51 00	12 44 18	24 43 56	1♈09 35	10 51.3	9 30.9	1 55.9	29 25.8	5 01.6	13 20.2	29 23.1	21 45.7	18 28.6	19 17.7	22 29.6	1 19.7
4 Su	6 54 57	13 45 27	7♈40 37	14 17 24	10 48.2	9R 31.9	3 03.3	0♓30.8	5 46.9	13 23.6	29 37.0	21 45.4	18 32.5	19 19.5	22 31.5	1 21.9
5 M	6 58 53	14 46 37	21 00 21	27 49 41	10 45.0	9 31.9	4 05.5	1 35.6	6 32.2	13 26.6	29 50.9	21 45.0	18 36.3	19 21.4	22 33.3	1 24.0
6 Tu	7 02 50	15 47 46	4♉45 36	11♉48 08	10 41.8	9 30.7	5 01.6	2 40.1	7 17.5	13 29.2	0♒04.8	21 44.5	18 40.2	19 23.3	22 35.3	1 26.2
7 W	7 06 46	16 48 55	18 57 10	26 12 24	10 38.6	9 28.6	5 51.0	3 44.2	8 02.9	13 31.4	0 18.8	21 43.9	18 44.1	19 25.3	22 37.2	1 28.3
8 Th	7 10 43	17 50 03	3♊33 22	10♊59 23	10 35.4	9 25.7	6 32.7	4 48.1	8 48.3	13 33.1	0 32.8	21 43.1	18 48.0	19 27.2	22 39.1	1 30.4
9 F	7 14 40	18 51 11	18 29 37	26 03 04	10 32.3	9 22.8	7 05.8	5 51.6	9 33.8	13 34.4	0 46.8	21 42.3	18 52.0	19 29.3	22 41.1	1 32.6
10 Sa	7 18 36	19 52 19	3♋38 35	11♋14 57	10 29.1	9 20.2	7 29.4	6 54.8	10 19.3	13 35.3	1 00.8	21 41.3	18 56.0	19 31.4	22 43.1	1 34.7
11 Su	7 22 33	20 53 26	18 50 53	26 25 10	10 25.9	9 18.4	7R 42.6	7 57.6	11 04.9	13R 35.8	1 14.9	21 40.3	19 00.0	19 33.5	22 45.1	1 36.8
12 M	7 26 29	21 54 33	3♌56 34	11♌24 03	10 22.7	9D 17.6	7 44.9	9 00.1	11 50.5	13 35.8	1 29.0	21 39.1	19 04.0	19 35.6	22 47.1	1 38.9
13 Tu	7 30 26	22 55 40	18 46 39	26 03 36	10 19.6	9 17.7	7 35.5	10 02.2	12 36.1	13 35.4	1 43.0	21 37.8	19 08.1	19 37.8	22 49.1	1 41.0
14 W	7 34 22	23 56 46	3♍14 19	10♍18 24	10 16.4	9 18.5	7 14.4	11 03.9	13 21.8	13 34.5	1 57.1	21 36.4	19 12.2	19 40.1	22 51.1	1 43.0
15 Th	7 38 19	24 57 53	17 15 38	24 05 58	10 13.2	9 19.7	6 41.6	12 05.2	14 07.5	13 33.2	2 11.3	21 35.0	19 16.3	19 42.3	22 53.2	1 45.1
16 F	7 42 15	25 58 58	0♎49 28	7♎26 22	10 10.0	9 20.9	5 57.6	13 06.0	14 53.2	13 31.5	2 25.4	21 33.4	19 20.4	19 44.7	22 55.3	1 47.1
17 Sa	7 46 12	27 00 04	13 57 00	20 21 44	10 06.9	9 21.8	5 03.4	14 06.5	15 39.0	13 29.3	2 39.5	21 31.7	19 24.6	19 47.0	22 57.3	1 49.2
18 Su	7 50 09	28 01 10	26 41 04	2♏55 30	10 03.7	9R 22.1	4 00.3	15 06.5	16 24.8	13 26.6	2 53.7	21 29.9	19 28.7	19 49.4	22 59.4	1 51.2
19 M	7 54 05	29 02 15	9♏05 34	15 11 49	10 00.5	9 21.9	2 50.3	16 06.1	17 10.7	13 23.6	3 07.9	21 28.0	19 32.9	19 51.8	23 01.6	1 53.2
20 Tu	7 58 02	0♒03 20	21 14 49	27 15 06	9 57.3	9 21.2	1 35.5	17 05.2	17 56.6	13 20.1	3 22.0	21 26.0	19 37.1	19 54.3	23 03.7	1 55.2
21 W	8 01 58	1 04 25	3♐13 11	9♐09 36	9 54.2	9 20.2	0 18.2	18 03.8	18 42.5	13 16.1	3 36.2	21 23.8	19 41.4	19 56.8	23 05.8	1 57.2
22 Th	8 05 55	2 05 29	15 04 50	20 59 18	9 51.0	9 19.2	29♑00.8	19 01.9	19 28.5	13 11.7	3 50.4	21 21.6	19 45.6	19 59.3	23 08.0	1 59.2
23 F	8 09 51	3 06 33	26 53 27	2♑47 40	9 47.8	9 18.1	27 45.7	19 59.5	20 14.5	13 06.9	4 04.6	21 19.3	19 49.9	20 01.9	23 10.2	2 01.1
24 Sa	8 13 48	4 07 36	8♑42 18	14 37 41	9 44.6	9 17.4	26 34.7	20 56.6	21 00.6	13 01.6	4 18.8	21 16.9	19 54.2	20 04.5	23 12.3	2 03.1
25 Su	8 17 44	5 08 38	20 34 07	26 31 51	9 41.5	9 16.9	25 29.7	21 53.1	21 46.7	12 55.9	4 33.0	21 14.5	19 58.5	20 07.1	23 14.5	2 05.0
26 M	8 21 41	6 09 40	2♒31 09	8♒32 15	9 38.3	9D 16.7	24 32.0	22 49.0	22 32.8	12 49.8	4 47.2	21 11.9	20 02.8	20 09.8	23 16.7	2 06.9
27 Tu	8 25 38	7 10 41	14 35 21	20 40 39	9 35.1	9 16.6	23 42.3	23 44.3	23 18.9	12 43.2	5 01.4	21 09.2	20 07.1	20 12.5	23 18.9	2 08.8
28 W	8 29 34	8 11 41	26 48 22	2♓58 40	9 31.9	9 16.7	23 01.3	24 38.9	24 05.1	12 36.2	5 15.6	21 06.4	20 11.4	20 15.2	23 21.1	2 10.6
29 Th	8 33 31	9 12 40	9♓11 47	15 27 53	9 28.7	9R 16.8	22 29.3	25 33.0	24 51.3	12 28.9	5 29.8	21 03.5	20 15.8	20 18.0	23 23.3	2 12.5
30 F	8 37 27	10 13 38	21 47 12	28 09 55	9 25.6	9 16.7	22 06.0	26 26.3	25 37.6	12 21.1	5 44.0	21 00.6	20 20.1	20 20.8	23 25.6	2 14.3
31 Sa	8 41 24	11♒14 34	4♈36 15	11♈06 26	9♒22.4	9♒16.5	21♑51.4	27♓18.9	26♑23.8	12♍12.9	5♒58.2	20♍57.5	20♒24.5	20♓23.6	23♒27.8	2♑16.1

1st of Month

Julian Day # 2454832.5
Obliquity 23°26'23"
SVP 5♓07'49"
GC 26♐57.9
Eris 20♈41.5R

Day	⚴	⚵	⚶
1	5♊09.9R	21♑46.3	0♉25.8
6	4 28.4R	23 45.4	1 02.9
11	4 05.3R	25 45.4	1 48.8
16	4 00.5	27 46.2	2 42.7
21	4 13.5	29 47.8	3 44.0
26	4 43.3	1♒50.1	4 52.2
31	5 28.9	3 52.8	6 06.7

DECLINATION and LATITUDE

Day	☉ Decl	☽ Decl	☽ Lat	☽ 12h Decl	☿ Decl	☿ Lat	♀ Decl	♀ Lat	♂ Decl	♂ Lat	⚳ Decl	⚳ Lat	♃ Decl	♃ Lat	♄ Decl	♄ Lat
1 Th	23S01	9S51	1N49	7S10	21S48	1S35	13S49	1S29	24S06	0S42	17N57	12N20	20S47	0S25	5N09	2N03
2 F	22 55	4 24	2 50	1 33	21 24	1 26	13 23	1 25	24 05	0 43	18 01	12 26	20 44	0 25	5 09	2 03
3 Sa	22 50	1N20	3 44	4N14	20 59	1 17	12 56	1 21	24 04	0 43	18 05	12 32	20 41	0 25	5 09	2 03
4 Su	22 44	7 09	4 28	10 01	20 33	1 07	12 29	1 17	24 02	0 44	18 09	12 38	20 38	0 25	5 10	2 04
5 M	22 37	12 49	4 59	15 30	20 08	0 55	12 02	1 13	24 01	0 44	18 14	12 44	20 35	0 25	5 10	2 04
6 Tu	22 30	18 02	5 14	20 22	19 42	0 43	11 35	1 08	23 59	0 45	18 19	12 50	20 32	0 25	5 11	2 04
7 W	22 23	22 26	5 11	24 11	19 17	0 30	11 08	1 04	23 57	0 45	18 23	12 57	20 29	0 25	5 11	2 05
8 Th	22 15	25 34	4 48	26 31	18 53	0 15	10 40	0 59	23 54	0 46	18 28	13 03	20 27	0 25	5 12	2 05
9 F	22 07	27 00	4 05	26 59	18 29	0N01	10 12	0 54	23 52	0 46	18 33	13 09	20 24	0 25	5 12	2 05
10 Sa	21 58	26 28	3 04	25 26	18 07	0 17	9 44	0 49	23 49	0 47	18 39	13 15	20 21	0 25	5 13	2 05
11 Su	21 49	23 56	1 51	22 01	17 47	0 34	9 16	0 44	23 46	0 47	18 44	13 21	20 18	0 25	5 14	2 06
12 M	21 39	19 45	0 30	17 10	17 29	0 52	8 48	0 39	23 42	0 48	18 50	13 27	20 15	0 25	5 14	2 06
13 Tu	21 29	14 22	0S52	11 24	17 14	1 11	8 19	0 33	23 38	0 48	18 55	13 33	20 12	0 25	5 15	2 06
14 W	21 19	8 19	2 09	5 11	17 01	1 30	7 51	0 28	23 34	0 48	19 01	13 39	20 08	0 25	5 16	2 06
15 Th	21 08	2 02	3 15	1S05	16 51	1 49	7 22	0 22	23 30	0 49	19 07	13 46	20 05	0 26	5 17	2 07
16 F	20 57	4S07	4 08	7 04	16 44	2 07	6 53	0 16	23 26	0 49	19 14	13 52	20 02	0 26	5 18	2 07
17 Sa	20 46	9 54	4 47	12 35	16 40	2 24	6 25	0 10	23 21	0 50	19 20	13 58	19 59	0 26	5 18	2 07
18 Su	20 34	15 06	5 09	17 25	16 39	2 40	5 56	0 04	23 16	0 50	19 27	14 04	19 56	0 26	5 19	2 07
19 M	20 21	19 32	5 17	21 25	16 41	2 55	5 27	0N02	23 11	0 51	19 33	14 10	19 53	0 26	5 20	2 08
20 Tu	20 08	23 03	5 10	24 26	16 46	3 07	4 58	0 09	23 05	0 51	19 40	14 16	19 50	0 26	5 21	2 08
21 W	19 55	25 33	4 50	26 21	16 53	3 17	4 29	0 15	22 59	0 52	19 47	14 22	19 46	0 26	5 23	2 08
22 Th	19 42	26 52	4 18	27 05	17 01	3 25	4 00	0 22	22 53	0 52	19 54	14 27	19 43	0 26	5 24	2 08
23 F	19 28	26 58	3 34	26 34	17 11	3 30	3 32	0 29	22 47	0 53	20 01	14 33	19 40	0 26	5 25	2 09
24 Sa	19 14	25 51	2 42	24 50	17 22	3 32	3 03	0 36	22 40	0 53	20 09	14 39	19 37	0 26	5 26	2 09
25 Su	18 59	23 33	1 42	21 60	17 34	3 32	2 34	0 43	22 34	0 54	20 16	14 45	19 33	0 27	5 27	2 09
26 M	18 44	20 12	0 37	18 12	17 46	3 30	2 05	0 50	22 26	0 54	20 24	14 50	19 30	0 27	5 28	2 09
27 Tu	18 29	15 59	0N30	13 36	17 58	3 26	1 37	0 57	22 19	0 54	20 31	14 56	19 27	0 27	5 30	2 10
28 W	18 13	11 05	1 36	8 25	18 11	3 21	1 08	1 05	22 12	0 55	20 39	15 01	19 23	0 27	5 31	2 10
29 Th	17 57	5 40	2 39	2 50	18 23	3 13	0 40	1 13	22 04	0 55	20 47	15 07	19 20	0 27	5 32	2 10
30 F	17 41	0N02	3 35	2N56	18 35	3 05	0 11	1 20	21 56	0 56	20 55	15 12	19 16	0 27	5 34	2 10
31 Sa	17S24	5N50	4N21	8N41	18S46	2N56	0N17	1N28	21S47	0S56	21N03	15N17	19S13	0S27	5N35	2N11

Day	⚷ Decl	⚷ Lat	♅ Decl	♅ Lat	♆ Decl	♆ Lat	♇ Decl	♇ Lat
1	9S27	6N10	4S57	0S45	14S22	0S21	17S45	5N42
6	9 23	6 09	4 53	0 45	14 19	0 21	17 45	5 41
11	9 18	6 08	4 49	0 45	14 16	0 21	17 45	5 41
16	9 13	6 07	4 45	0 45	14 13	0 21	17 45	5 41
21	9 07	6 06	4 40	0 44	14 09	0 21	17 45	5 41
26	9 01	6 05	4 35	0 44	14 06	0 21	17 45	5 41
31	8S55	6N04	4S29	0S44	14S02	0S21	17S44	5N41

Day	⚴ Decl	⚴ Lat	⚵ Decl	⚵ Lat	⚶ Decl	⚶ Lat	Eris Decl	Eris Lat
1	31S37	53S36	13S47	7N59	5N01	7S03	4S49	13S54
6	30 48	52 41	13 36	7 52	5 32	6 43	4 48	13 53
11	29 50	51 39	13 23	7 45	6 05	6 25	4 47	13 52
16	28 43	50 29	13 07	7 38	6 40	6 07	4 46	13 51
21	27 28	49 15	12 50	7 31	7 16	5 50	4 45	13 50
26	26 07	47 56	12 31	7 25	7 54	5 34	4 44	13 49
31	24S41	46S34	12S10	7N19	8N32	5S19	4S43	13S49

Moon Phenomena

Max/0 Decl
dy hr mn
2 18:29 0 N
9 5:23 27N03
15 7:50 0 S
22 14:01 27S05
29 23:51 0 N

Max/0 Lat
dy hr mn
6 8:02 5N15
12 8:36 0 S
19 0:30 5S17
26 13:28 0 N

Perigee/Apogee
dy hr m kilometers
10 10:50 p 357502
23 0:10 a 406118

PH dy hr mn
☽ 4 11:57 14♈16
○ 11 3:28 21♋02
☾ 18 2:47 28♎08
● 26 7:56 6♒30
• 26 8:00 A 07'54"

Void of Course Moon

Last Aspect			☽ Ingress		
31	18:35	♀ ☌	♓	1	0:28
3	8:52	♃ ⚹	♈	3	9:51
5	2:45	♆ ⚹	♉	5	15:47
7	6:06	♆ □	♊	7	18:13
9	6:41	♆ △	♋	9	18:15
11	4:28	♄ ⚹	♌	11	17:42
13	6:39	♆ ☍	♍	13	18:34
15	14:38	☉ △	♎	15	22:31
18	2:47	☉ □	♏	18	6:21
20	3:38	♆ □	♐	20	17:31
22	16:25	♆ ⚹	♑	23	6:19
25	9:09	☿ ☌	♒	25	18:58
27	17:14	♆ ☌	♓	28	6:13
30	9:25	♀ ☌	♈	30	15:26

DAILY ASPECTARIAN

1 Th ☽∥⚷ 1:48; ☽⚹♇ 2:56; ☽⚹♂ 7:50; ☿ ♒ 9:52; ☽#♄ 20:46; ☽∥♅ 21:40; ☉⚹☽ 23:10

2 F ☽☍⚳ 2:14; ☽∠♃ 3:59; ☽∠☿ 7:42; ☿⚺♇ 11:20; ☽⚺⚷ 12:07; ☽☌♅ 13:42; ☽☍♄ 18:24; ☽⚺♆ 19:46; ♀⚺♃ 22:44

3 Sa ☽⚹♃ 8:52; ☽⚺♀ 9:36; ☽□♇ 12:21; ♀ ♓ 12:37; ☽⚹☿ 14:43; ☽#♅ 14:48; ☉△⚳ 14:56; ☽∥♄ 15:48; ☽∠⚷ 16:22; ☿∥♃ 19:00; ☽□♂ 20:19; ☽∠♆ 23:43

4 Su ☽#⚷ 9:26; ☽⚻⚳ 10:25; ☉□☽ 11:57; ☽∠♀ 15:27; ♀⚹♇ 19:33; ☽⚹⚷ 19:43; ☽#♀ 20:54; ☽⚺♅ 21:04

5 M ☽⚻♄ 1:19; ☽⚹♆ 2:45; ☽#♆ 6:42; ☿∠♅ 6:46; ☽⚼⚳ 13:07; ♃ ♒ 15:42; ☽□♃ 15:47; ☽△♇ 18:15; ☽⚹♀ 20:06; ☽#♇ 22:36; ☽∠♅ 23:22

6 Tu ☽□☿ 0:29; ☽∥⚳ 1:24; ☽⚼♄ 3:24; ☽△♂ 4:35; ☽#☿ 7:47; ♂∠♆ 9:48; ☽#♃ 12:50; ☽△⚳ 14:53; ☽⚼♇ 19:51; ☉△☽ 20:09; ☽□⚷ 23:38; ☉#☽ 23:42

7 W ☽⚹♅ 0:47; ☽△♄ 4:37; ☽□♆ 6:06; ☽⚼♂ 7:10; ☽#♂ 10:05; ☽△♃ 19:01; ☽⚻♇ 20:40; ☉⚼☽ 22:44

8 Th ☽□♀ 2:10; ☽△☿ 5:03; ☿⚼♄ 6:44; ☽⚻♂ 8:56; ☽□⚳ 16:08; ☽⚼♃ 19:36; ☿#⚳ 20:36

9 F ☉⚺⚷ 0:20; ☽△⚷ 0:36; ☉⚻☽ 0:37; ☽□♅ 1:35; ☽□♄ 5:06; ☽⚼☿ 5:54; ☽△♆ 6:41; ☉⚹♅ 15:29; ☽⚻♃ 19:47; ☽☍♇ 20:44

10 Sa ☽⚼⚷ 0:28; ☽△♀ 5:33; ☽⚻☿ 6:11; ☽⚼♆ 6:27; ☽☍♂ 11:05; ☽⚹⚳ 15:42; ☿⚺♀ 17:15; ♀∥⚷ 22:15

11 Su ☽⚻⚷ 0:14; ☽△♅ 1:08; ☽#♂ 1:16; ☿∥♇ 3:00; ☉☍☽ 3:28; ☽⚹♄ 4:28; ☽⚻♆ 6:12; ☽⚼♀ 7:00; ⚳ R 13:05; ☉#☽ 13:40; ☽∠⚳ 15:28; ☿ R 16:46; ☉△♄ 18:03; ☽☍♃ 20:00; ☽⚻♇ 20:19; ☽#♃ 21:30

12 M ☽⚼♅ 1:03; ☽∠♄ 4:20; ☽∥⚳ 4:21; ☽☍☿ 6:04; ☽⚻♀ 8:44; ☽#♇ 9:26; ☽#☿ 11:10; ☽⚻♂ 13:24; ☽⚺⚳ 15:33; ♃⚺♇ 19:52; ☽⚼♇ 20:34; ☉⚺♆ 21:20

13 Tu ☽#♆ 0:31; ☽☍⚷ 0:35; ☽⚻♅ 1:24; ☽⚺♄ 4:41; ☽☍♆ 6:39; ☉⚻☽ 7:20; ☽⚼♂ 15:23; ☽#⚷ 20:24; ☽△♇ 21:26; ☽⚻♃ 21:48

14 W ☽#♀ 1:58; ♂△⚳ 6:32; ☽⚻☿ 6:33; ☉⚼☽ 10:26; ☽∥♄ 11:40; ☽#♅ 13:35; ☽☍♀ 14:21; ☽☌⚳ 17:35; ☽△♂ 18:15; ⚴ D 19:51; ☽⚼♃ 23:52

15 Th ☽⚻⚷ 3:32; ☿⚼♄ 4:13; ☽☍♅ 4:17; ☽⚼☿ 7:24; ☽☌♄ 7:33; ☽⚻♆ 9:53; ☉△☽ 14:38

16 F ☽□♇ 1:44; ☽∥♅ 2:29; ☽△♃ 2:56; ☽#♄ 4:43; ☽⚼⚷ 6:23; ☽△☿ 8:44; ♀☍⚳ 9:44; ☽∥♀ 10:23; ☽⚼♆ 12:55; ☽∥⚷ 20:57; ☽⚺⚳ 23:09

17 Sa ☽⚻♀ 0:19; ☽□♂ 3:22; ☿∠♅ 6:18; ☽△⚷ 10:16; ☽⚻♅ 10:57; ☽⚺♄ 14:10; ☽△♆ 16:57; ☽∥♆ 19:36

18 Su ☉□☽ 2:47; ☽∠⚳ 3:21; ☽⚼♀ 7:08; ☽∥☿ 8:01; ☉⚼⚳ 9:33; ☽⚹♇ 9:57; ☽□♃ 12:10; ☽□☿ 12:54; ☽∥♇ 13:49; ☽⚼♅ 15:44; ☽∠♄ 18:53; ☿☌♃ 19:08

19 M ☽#⚳ 0:10; ☽∥♃ 2:06; ☉∥☽ 4:48; ♀#♄ 5:18; ☽⚹⚳ 8:24; ☽△♀ 15:00; ☽∠♇ 15:23; ☽⚹♂ 16:59; ☿⚺♇ 17:57; ☿∠♀ 18:44; ☽□⚷ 20:45; ☽△♅ 21:19; ☉ ♒ 22:41

20 Tu ☽∥♂ 0:12; ☽⚹♄ 0:22; ☽□♆ 3:38; ♀∥♅ 14:54; ☉☌☿ 16:00; ☽⚹☿ 18:42; ☉⚹☽ 19:16; ☽⚺♇ 21:26; ⚳#♃ 22:19

21 W ☽⚹♃ 0:47; ☽∠♂ 1:03; ☿R♑ 5:37; ☉#⚳ 9:34; ⚵ ♒ 11:59; ♀∠♃ 17:42; ☽□⚳ 20:12; ☉∥♃ 20:46; ☉⚺♇ 21:26; ☽∠☿ 22:03

22 Th ☉∠☽ 4:28; ☽∠♃ 7:47; ☽□♀ 8:44; ☽⚺♂ 9:33; ☽⚹⚷ 9:34; ♂⚺⚷ 9:50; ☽□♅ 10:00; ☽□♄ 12:43; ☽⚹♆ 16:25; ☿⚼⚳ 16:38; ♂⚹♅ 17:01; ♀⚺⚷ 19:39

23 F ♀☌♅ 1:02; ☽⚺☿ 1:36; ☽☌♇ 10:27; ☉⚺☽ 13:50; ☽⚺♃ 14:54; ☽∠⚷ 16:14; ☽∠♆ 22:59

24 Sa ☉☌♃ 5:45; ♂△♄ 8:06; ♀☍♄ 8:16; ☽△⚳ 8:41; ♀⚹♂ 9:06; ☽⚺⚷ 22:48; ☽⚹♅ 23:05; ☉∠♅ 23:22

25 Su ☽△♄ 1:21; ☽☌♂ 2:36; ☽⚹♀ 2:53; ☽⚺♆ 5:24; ☽∥♂ 8:10; ☽☌☿ 9:09; ☽⚼⚳ 14:41; ☿∥♇ 21:36; ☽#⚳ 22:51; ☽⚺♇ 23:11

26 M ☉⚼♄ 0:50; ☽∥♃ 4:25; ☽☌♃ 4:37; ☽∠♅ 5:18; ☽⚼♄ 7:19; ☉☌☽ 7:56; ☉∥☽ 9:29; ☽∠♀ 11:27; ♀⚺♆ 12:30; ☽∥☿ 13:45; ☽∥♇ 14:32; ☽⚻⚳ 20:20; ☿⚹♀ 23:32; ♂⚺♆ 23:59

27 Tu ☽∠♇ 5:04; ☿☌♂ 6:12; ☽∥♆ 9:41; ☽☌⚷ 10:58; ☽⚺♅ 11:07; ☿⚺♆ 12:23; ☽⚻♄ 12:53; ☽⚺☿ 16:58; ☽☌♆ 17:14; ☽⚺♂ 18:20; ☽⚺♀ 19:27; ♃∠♅ 23:06

28 W ☉∥☿ 2:00; ☽∥⚷ 9:33; ☽⚹♇ 10:28; ☽⚺♃ 16:44; ☽∠☿ 20:50

29 Th ☉⚺☽ 0:02; ☽#♄ 0:33; ☽∠♂ 1:21; ☽∥♅ 4:55; ☽☍⚳ 6:14; ☉∥♇ 18:32; ☽⚺⚷ 21:14; ☽☌♅ 21:16; ☽∠♃ 21:58; ☽☍♄ 22:32; ☽∥♀ 23:00

30 F ☽⚹☿ 0:35; ☽#♀ 0:35; ☽⚺♆ 3:06; ☉∠☽ 7:03; ☽⚹♂ 7:42; ☽☌♀ 9:25; ♅⚺⚷ 9:57; ☽#♅ 18:26; ☽□♇ 19:39; ☽∥♄ 22:59; ♃⚼♄ 23:04

31 Sa ☽∠⚷ 1:30; ☽⚹♃ 2:35; ☽∠♆ 7:09; ☽#⚷ 12:55; ☉⚹☽ 13:17; ☽⚻⚳ 13:53; ☉⚻⚳ 20:09; ♂⚼⚳ 21:28

February 2009

LONGITUDE

Day	Sid.Time	☉	☽	☽ 12 hour	Mean☊	True☊	☿	♀	♂	⚳	♃	♄	⚷	♅	♆	♇
	h m s	° ' "	° ' "	° ' "	° '	° '	° '	° '	° '	° '	° '	° '	° '	° '	° '	° '
1 Su	8 45 20	12♒15 30	17♈40 40	24♈19 09	9♒19.2	9♒16.3	21♑45.1	28♓10.8	27♑10.1	12♍04.3	6♒12.4	20♍54.4	20♒28.8	20♓26.4	23♒30.1	2♑17.9
2 M	8 49 17	13 16 24	1♉02 04	7♉49 32	9 16.0	9D 16.0	21D 46.6	29 02.0	27 56.5	11R 55.4	6 26.5	20R 51.2	20 33.2	20 29.3	23 32.3	2 19.7
3 Tu	8 53 13	14 17 17	14 41 42	21 38 34	9 12.9	9 15.9	21 55.5	29 52.3	28 42.8	11 46.1	6 40.7	20 47.9	20 37.6	20 32.2	23 34.6	2 21.5
4 W	8 57 10	15 18 08	28 40 07	5♊46 14	9 09.7	9 16.1	22 11.1	0♈41.8	29 29.2	11 36.4	6 54.8	20 44.5	20 42.0	20 35.1	23 36.8	2 23.2
5 Th	9 01 07	16 18 58	12♊56 41	20 11 10	9 06.5	9 16.5	22 33.0	1 30.5	0♒15.6	11 26.4	7 09.0	20 41.1	20 46.4	20 38.1	23 39.1	2 24.9
6 F	9 05 03	17 19 47	27 29 12	4♋50 14	9 03.3	9 17.2	23 00.7	2 18.2	1 02.0	11 16.0	7 23.1	20 37.5	20 50.8	20 41.1	23 41.4	2 26.6
7 Sa	9 09 00	18 20 34	12♋13 36	19 38 30	9 00.2	9 18.0	23 33.7	3 05.0	1 48.5	11 05.4	7 37.2	20 33.9	20 55.2	20 44.1	23 43.6	2 28.3
8 Su	9 12 56	19 21 20	27 04 04	4♌29 23	8 57.0	9R 18.5	24 11.5	3 50.8	2 35.0	10 54.4	7 51.2	20 30.3	20 59.6	20 47.1	23 45.9	2 29.9
9 M	9 16 53	20 22 04	11♌53 31	19 15 30	8 53.8	9 18.7	24 53.8	4 35.7	3 21.5	10 43.1	8 05.3	20 26.5	21 04.0	20 50.2	23 48.2	2 31.6
10 Tu	9 20 49	21 22 47	26 34 26	3♍49 28	8 50.6	9 18.3	25 40.1	5 19.4	4 08.0	10 31.5	8 19.3	20 22.7	21 08.4	20 53.3	23 50.5	2 33.2
11 W	9 24 46	22 23 28	10♍59 53	18 05 01	8 47.4	9 17.2	26 30.2	6 02.1	4 54.6	10 19.7	8 33.4	20 18.8	21 12.8	20 56.4	23 52.7	2 34.7
12 Th	9 28 42	23 24 08	25 04 26	1♎57 45	8 44.3	9 15.5	27 23.6	6 43.6	5 41.1	10 07.6	8 47.4	20 14.9	21 17.1	20 59.5	23 55.0	2 36.3
13 F	9 32 39	24 24 47	8♎44 47	15 25 29	8 41.1	9 13.4	28 20.2	7 24.0	6 27.7	9 55.2	9 01.3	20 10.9	21 21.5	21 02.6	23 57.3	2 37.8
14 Sa	9 36 36	25 25 25	21 59 55	28 28 17	8 37.9	9 11.2	29 19.7	8 03.2	7 14.4	9 42.6	9 15.3	20 06.8	21 25.9	21 05.8	23 59.6	2 39.3
15 Su	9 40 32	26 26 02	4♏50 54	11♏08 09	8 34.7	9 09.4	0♒21.9	8 41.0	8 01.0	9 29.8	9 29.2	20 02.7	21 30.3	21 09.0	24 01.9	2 40.8
16 M	9 44 29	27 26 37	17 20 30	23 28 29	8 31.6	9D 08.2	1 26.5	9 17.6	8 47.7	9 16.8	9 43.1	19 58.5	21 34.7	21 12.2	24 04.1	2 42.3
17 Tu	9 48 25	28 27 12	29 32 39	5♐33 36	8 28.4	9 07.8	2 33.3	9 52.8	9 34.4	9 03.6	9 56.9	19 54.3	21 39.1	21 15.4	24 06.4	2 43.7
18 W	9 52 22	29 27 45	11♐31 57	17 28 19	8 25.2	9 08.3	3 42.3	10 26.6	10 21.1	8 50.2	10 10.8	19 50.0	21 43.4	21 18.6	24 08.7	2 45.1
19 Th	9 56 18	0♓28 17	23 23 19	29 17 32	8 22.0	9 09.6	4 53.3	10 59.0	11 07.8	8 36.7	10 24.6	19 45.6	21 47.8	21 21.9	24 11.0	2 46.5
20 F	10 00 15	1 28 47	5♑11 34	11♑05 57	8 18.8	9 11.3	6 06.1	11 29.8	11 54.6	8 23.0	10 38.4	19 41.2	21 52.1	21 25.1	24 13.2	2 47.8
21 Sa	10 04 11	2 29 17	17 01 14	22 57 14	8 15.7	9 13.1	7 20.7	11 59.0	12 41.4	8 09.3	10 52.1	19 36.8	21 56.5	21 28.4	24 15.5	2 49.2
22 Su	10 08 08	3 29 44	28 56 23	4♒57 06	8 12.5	9R 14.4	8 36.9	12 26.6	13 28.2	7 55.4	11 05.8	19 32.3	22 00.8	21 31.7	24 17.8	2 50.5
23 M	10 12 05	4 30 11	11♒00 23	17 06 33	8 09.3	9 14.8	9 54.7	12 52.5	14 15.0	7 41.5	11 19.5	19 27.8	22 05.1	21 35.0	24 20.0	2 51.8
24 Tu	10 16 01	5 30 35	23 15 51	29 28 27	8 06.1	9 13.9	11 14.0	13 16.7	15 01.8	7 27.5	11 33.1	19 23.3	22 09.4	21 38.4	24 22.3	2 53.0
25 W	10 19 58	6 30 58	5♓44 30	12♓04 07	8 03.0	9 11.7	12 34.7	13 39.0	15 48.7	7 13.5	11 46.7	19 18.7	22 13.7	21 41.7	24 24.5	2 54.2
26 Th	10 23 54	7 31 20	18 27 18	24 54 05	7 59.8	9 08.1	13 56.7	13 59.4	16 35.5	6 59.4	12 00.2	19 14.1	22 18.0	21 45.0	24 26.8	2 55.4
27 F	10 27 51	8 31 39	1♈24 24	7♈58 11	7 56.6	9 03.5	15 20.1	14 17.8	17 22.4	6 45.4	12 13.7	19 09.4	22 22.2	21 48.4	24 29.0	2 56.6
28 Sa	10 31 47	9♓31 57	14 35 20	21 15 45	7♒53.4	8♒58.3	16♒44.8	14♈34.3	18♒09.3	6♍31.4	12♒27.2	19♍04.8	22♒26.5	21♓51.8	24♒31.2	2♑57.7

1st of Month

Julian Day # 2454863.5
Obliquity 23°26'23"
SVP 5♓07'44"
GC 26♐58.0
Eris 20♈44.4

Day	⚴
1	5♊39.8
6	6 42.6
11	7 57.9
16	9 24.5
21	11 01.2
26	12 46.8

Day	⚵
1	4♒17.4
6	6 20.6
11	8 24.0
16	10 27.7
21	12 31.4
26	14 35.2

Day	⚶
1	6♉22.3
6	7 43.6
11	9 09.9
16	10 40.8
21	12 16.0
26	13 55.1

DECLINATION and LATITUDE

Day	☉ Decl	☽ Decl	☽ Lat	☽12h Decl	☿ Decl	☿ Lat	♀ Decl	♀ Lat	♂ Decl	♂ Lat	⚳ Decl	⚳ Lat	♃ Decl	♃ Lat	♄ Decl	♄ Lat
1 Su	17S07	11N29	4N55	14N11	18S57	2N46	0N45	1N36	21S39	0S56	21N11	15N22	19S10	0S27	5N37	2N11
2 M	16 50	16 44	5 14	19 07	19 07	2 35	1 13	1 45	21 30	0 57	21 19	15 27	19 06	0 27	5 38	2 11
3 Tu	16 33	21 17	5 16	23 10	19 17	2 24	1 41	1 53	21 21	0 57	21 27	15 32	19 03	0 27	5 39	2 11
4 W	16 15	24 44	4 60	25 56	19 25	2 13	2 08	2 01	21 12	0 58	21 35	15 37	18 59	0 27	5 41	2 11
5 Th	15 57	26 43	4 25	27 04	19 33	2 02	2 35	2 10	21 02	0 58	21 43	15 42	18 56	0 28	5 43	2 12
6 F	15 38	26 57	3 32	26 21	19 40	1 50	3 02	2 19	20 53	0 58	21 51	15 46	18 52	0 28	5 44	2 12
7 Sa	15 20	25 17	2 25	23 46	19 46	1 39	3 29	2 28	20 43	0 59	21 60	15 51	18 49	0 28	5 46	2 12
8 Su	15 01	21 51	1 07	19 34	19 50	1 27	3 55	2 37	20 33	0 59	22 08	15 55	18 45	0 28	5 47	2 12
9 M	14 42	16 60	0S14	14 11	19 54	1 16	4 22	2 46	20 22	0 60	22 16	15 59	18 42	0 28	5 49	2 12
10 Tu	14 23	11 11	1 34	8 03	19 57	1 05	4 47	2 55	20 12	0 60	22 24	16 03	18 38	0 28	5 51	2 13
11 W	14 03	4 52	2 47	1 40	19 58	0 54	5 13	3 04	20 01	1 00	22 32	16 07	18 35	0 28	5 52	2 13
12 Th	13 43	1S31	3 47	4S38	19 59	0 43	5 38	3 14	19 50	1 01	22 40	16 10	18 31	0 28	5 54	2 13
13 F	13 23	7 39	4 33	10 31	19 58	0 33	6 03	3 23	19 39	1 01	22 48	16 14	18 27	0 28	5 56	2 13
14 Sa	13 03	13 14	5 02	15 46	19 56	0 22	6 27	3 33	19 27	1 01	22 56	16 17	18 24	0 29	5 58	2 13
15 Su	12 42	18 05	5 15	20 10	19 52	0 12	6 51	3 43	19 15	1 02	23 04	16 21	18 20	0 29	5 59	2 14
16 M	12 22	22 00	5 13	23 35	19 48	0 02	7 15	3 52	19 03	1 02	23 12	16 24	18 17	0 29	6 01	2 14
17 Tu	12 01	24 52	4 56	25 53	19 42	0S07	7 38	4 02	18 51	1 02	23 20	16 26	18 13	0 29	6 03	2 14
18 W	11 40	26 35	4 27	26 58	19 35	0 16	8 00	4 12	18 39	1 03	23 27	16 29	18 09	0 29	6 05	2 14
19 Th	11 18	27 03	3 47	26 49	19 27	0 25	8 22	4 22	18 27	1 03	23 35	16 32	18 06	0 29	6 07	2 14
20 F	10 57	26 17	2 57	25 27	19 17	0 34	8 43	4 33	18 14	1 03	23 42	16 34	18 02	0 29	6 09	2 14
21 Sa	10 35	24 20	1 59	22 56	19 07	0 42	9 04	4 43	18 01	1 04	23 50	16 36	17 59	0 29	6 10	2 14
22 Su	10 14	21 18	0 56	19 25	18 55	0 50	9 25	4 53	17 48	1 04	23 57	16 38	17 55	0 29	6 12	2 15
23 M	9 52	17 19	0N10	15 01	18 41	0 57	9 44	5 03	17 35	1 04	24 04	16 40	17 51	0 30	6 14	2 15
24 Tu	9 29	12 34	1 16	9 57	18 27	1 05	10 03	5 14	17 21	1 04	24 11	16 41	17 48	0 30	6 16	2 15
25 W	9 07	7 14	2 20	4 24	18 11	1 12	10 21	5 24	17 08	1 05	24 17	16 43	17 44	0 30	6 18	2 15
26 Th	8 45	1 31	3 19	1N25	17 53	1 18	10 39	5 34	16 54	1 05	24 24	16 44	17 40	0 30	6 20	2 15
27 F	8 23	4N21	4 08	7 16	17 35	1 25	10 55	5 44	16 40	1 05	24 30	16 45	17 37	0 30	6 22	2 15
28 Sa	7S60	10N07	4N45	12N53	17S15	1S30	11N11	5N55	16S26	1S06	24N36	16N46	17S33	0S30	6N24	2N15

Day	⚷ Decl	⚷ Lat	♅ Decl	♅ Lat	♆ Decl	♆ Lat	♇ Decl	♇ Lat
1	8S54	6N04	4S28	0S44	14S01	0S21	17S44	5N41
6	8 47	6 04	4 22	0 44	13 58	0 21	17 44	5 41
11	8 41	6 04	4 16	0 44	13 54	0 21	17 44	5 41
16	8 34	6 04	4 10	0 44	13 50	0 22	17 43	5 41
21	8 27	6 04	4 03	0 44	13 47	0 22	17 43	5 42
26	8S20	6N04	3S57	0S44	13S43	0S22	17S43	5N42

Day	⚴ Decl	⚴ Lat	⚵ Decl	⚵ Lat	⚶ Decl	⚶ Lat	Eris Decl	Eris Lat
1	24S23	46S18	12S05	7N18	8N40	5S16	4S43	13S48
6	22 52	44 53	11 42	7 12	9 20	5 01	4 42	13 48
11	21 19	43 28	11 18	7 06	10 00	4 47	4 40	13 47
16	19 44	42 02	10 51	7 01	10 41	4 34	4 39	13 46
21	18 09	40 36	10 23	6 56	11 22	4 22	4 37	13 45
26	16S33	39S10	9S54	6N50	12N02	4S10	4S36	13S45

Moon Phenomena

Max/0 Decl

dy	hr mn	
5	14:59	27N05
11	18:15	0 S
18	21:12	27S03
26	6:14	0 N

Max/0 Lat

dy	hr mn	
2	14:33	5N18
8	19:48	0 S
15	8:10	5S16
22	20:31	0 N

Perigee/Apogee

dy	hr m		kilometers
7	20:18	p	361490
19	17:04	a	405128

PH	dy	hr mn	
☽	2	23:14	14♉15
○	9	14:50	21♌00
(eclipse)	9	14:39	A 0.900
☾	16	21:38	28♏21
●	25	1:36	6♓35

Void of Course Moon

Last Aspect			☽ Ingress		
1 18:09	♂	□	♉	1	22:10
4 1:28	♂	△	♊	4	2:16
5 17:45	♆	△	♋	6	4:07
7 19:08	☿	☍	♌	8	4:44
9 19:30	♆	☍	♍	10	5:39
12 4:19	☿	△	♎	12	8:34
14 14:47	☿	□	♏	14	14:52
16 21:38	☉	□	♐	17	0:54
19 1:37	♆	✶	♑	19	13:26
21 9:02	♅	✶	♒	22	2:07
24 2:09	♆	☌	♓	24	13:01
26 6:11	♅	☌	♈	26	21:25

DAILY ASPECTARIAN

1 Su
☽⊻♅ 5:02
☽✶⚷ 5:06
☽⊼♄ 5:50
☿ D 7:11
☽□☿ 7:22
☽✶♆ 10:33
☽⋕♆ 11:15
☽⚼⚳ 16:45
☽□♂ 18:09
☽⊻♀ 20:12
☿∥♃ 22:03

2 M
☉⋕☽ 0:27
☽△♇ 2:18
☽⋕♇ 4:56
☽∠♅ 7:55
☽⚼♄ 8:30
☽□♃ 9:44
☽⋕♃ 11:46
☽⋕☿ 12:27
♂⋕⚳ 16:01
☽△⚳ 18:58
☉□☽ 23:14

3 Tu
☽∠♀ 0:20
☽⋕♂ 0:26
☽∥⚳ 1:04
♀ ♈ 3:42
☽⚼♇ 4:37
☽✶♅ 10:08
☽□⚷ 10:18
☽△♄ 10:30
☽△☿ 12:42
☽□♆ 15:21

4 W
☽△♂ 1:28
☽✶♀ 3:39
☽⊼♇ 6:19
♄⊼⚷ 7:46
☽△♃ 14:09
☽⚼☿ 14:44
♂ ♒ 15:56
☽□⚳ 21:31

5 Th
☽⚼♂ 4:04
☉△☽ 6:01
♄☍♅ 10:57
☽□♄ 12:46
☽□♅ 12:47
☽△⚷ 13:02
☽⚼♃ 15:29
☽⊼☿ 16:24
☽△♆ 17:45
☉∠♀ 21:11

6 F
☉∠♇ 2:46
♀□♇ 4:26
☽⊼♂ 6:07
☽☍♇ 8:07
☽□♀ 8:19
☉⚼☽ 8:30
☽⚼⚷ 13:43
☽⊼♃ 16:24
☽⚼♆ 18:18
☽✶⚳ 22:11

7 Sa
☿⊻♆ 7:03
☉⊼☽ 10:37
☽✶♄ 13:26
☽△♅ 13:49
☽⊼⚷ 14:08
☽⊼♆ 18:39
☽☍☿ 19:08
♂⊻♇ 21:18
☽∠⚳ 22:09
☽∥⚳ 22:26

8 Su
☽⋕♂ 7:21
☽⊼♇ 8:48
☽☍♂ 9:24
☽⋕☿ 10:30
☽△♀ 11:33
☽∠♄ 13:35
☽⚼♅ 14:09
☽⋕♃ 16:08
☽☍♃ 17:44
☽⋕♇ 20:41
♀⋕♅ 21:13
☽⊻⚳ 22:07

9 M
☉⊼♄ 1:40
☽⚼♇ 9:11
☉⋕☽ 10:26
☉⊻♅ 11:43
☽⋕♆ 13:04
☽⚼♀ 13:13
☽⊻♄ 13:53
☽⊼♅ 14:38
☉☍☽ 14:50
☽☍⚷ 15:02
☉☌⚷ 17:51
☽☍♆ 19:30
☿⚼⚳ 20:32
☽⊼☿ 22:25

10 Tu
☽⋕⚷ 9:36
☽△♇ 9:54
☽⊼♂ 13:14
☽⊼♀ 15:15
☽⊼♃ 19:50
☽∥♄ 20:15
☽∥♀ 22:47
☽☌⚳ 22:53

11 W
☽⚼☿ 0:54
☽⋕♅ 2:16
☿∥♂ 5:05
♀∠⚷ 6:49
☉∥♆ 11:23
♂⚼♄ 11:32
☽☌♄ 15:44
☽⚼♂ 16:00
☽☍♅ 16:57
☽⊼⚷ 17:27
☉⊼☽ 20:53
☽⚼♃ 21:45
☽⊼♆ 22:00

12 Th
☽△☿ 4:19
♂∠♅ 10:08
☽∥♅ 10:27
☉☌♆ 12:42
☽□♇ 13:09
♀∥♄ 16:47
☽⋕♄ 17:05
☽⋕♀ 17:06
☽△♂ 19:42
☽⚼⚷ 19:44
☽☍♀ 21:29

13 F
☽⚼♆ 0:22
☽△♃ 0:30
☉⚼☽ 1:17
☽⊻⚳ 2:04
☽∥⚷ 4:03
☽⊻♄ 20:33
☽⊼♅ 22:20
☽△⚷ 22:57
☉∥☽ 23:11

14 Sa
☽∥♆ 2:53
☽△♆ 3:41
☽∠⚳ 4:55
☉△☽ 6:52
☽□☿ 14:47
☿ ♒ 15:40
☽✶♇ 19:54
☽∥♇ 22:05

15 Su
☽∠♄ 0:22
⚳⊼♃ 0:32
☽∥♃ 1:23
☽⚼♅ 2:29
☽∥♂ 6:17
☽□♂ 6:25
☽⊼♀ 7:41
☽✶⚳ 8:42
☽□♃ 9:00
☽∥☿ 10:03
♀∠♆ 14:27
♀⊼⚳ 23:35

16 M
☽∠♇ 0:42
☽✶♄ 5:06
☽△♅ 7:34
☽□⚷ 8:19
☽⋕⚳ 9:18
♂⊼⚳ 11:40
☽□♆ 13:13
☽⚼♀ 14:18
☉□☽ 21:38

17 Tu
☿⊻♇ 3:44
♀✶♃ 4:48
☽⊻♇ 6:21
☽✶☿ 6:37
♂☌♃ 16:28
☽□⚳ 18:40
☽✶♃ 21:13
☽✶♂ 21:27
☽△♀ 21:42

18 W
♀✶♂ 9:32
☉ ♓ 12:47
☽∠☿ 16:06
☽□♄ 16:41
☽□♅ 19:52
☽✶⚷ 20:45
☿⚼♄ 21:35

19 Th
☽✶♆ 1:37
☽∠♃ 4:11
☽∠♂ 5:58
♀⋕⚷ 8:03
☉✶☽ 15:45
☽☌♇ 19:07

20 F
☽⊻☿ 2:04
☽∠⚷ 3:26
☽△⚳ 6:22
☿∠♅ 6:28
☽∠♆ 8:13
☽⊻♃ 11:17
☽□♀ 13:22
☽⊻♂ 14:36

21 Sa
☉∠☽ 1:02
☽⋕⚳ 4:25
☽△♄ 5:12
♂∥♃ 6:17
☉✶♇ 8:04
☽✶♅ 9:02
☽⊻⚷ 10:00
☽⚼⚳ 12:09
☿⊼⚳ 13:00
☽⊻♆ 14:39

22 Su
☽⊻♇ 7:49
♂∥♇ 9:02
☉⊻☽ 9:56
☽⚼♄ 11:07
☽∠♅ 15:12
☽∥☿ 15:49
☽⊼⚳ 17:34
☽∥♃ 20:58
☽☌☿ 21:35
☽∥♇ 21:47
☽∥♂ 22:28

23 M
☽☌♃ 0:38
☽✶♀ 3:49
☉⋕♀ 4:17
☽☌♂ 6:50
☽∠♇ 13:30
☽⊼♄ 16:30
☽∥♆ 18:21
☽⊻♅ 20:50
☽☌⚷ 21:50

24 Tu
☽☌♆ 2:09
☿☌♃ 6:54
☽∠♀ 10:00
☽⋕♀ 10:56
☉∥☽ 15:07
☽✶♇ 18:34
☽∥⚷ 19:04

25 W
☉☌☽ 1:36
☽☍⚳ 2:46
☽⋕♄ 3:58
♃∥♇ 8:14
☽⊻♃ 11:40
☉☍⚳ 13:43
☽∥♅ 13:54
☽⊻☿ 14:31
☽⊻♀ 15:24
☽⊻♂ 20:17

26 Th
☿✶♀ 1:00
☽☍♄ 1:27
☽☌♅ 6:11
☽⊻⚷ 7:13
☽⊻♆ 11:11
☿∥♇ 14:21
☽∠♃ 16:10
☿∥♃ 21:28
☽∠☿ 21:48
☽⋕♅ 22:15

27 F
☽∠♂ 1:53
☽□♇ 2:49
☉∥⚷ 4:17
☽∥♄ 8:20
☽⊼⚳ 9:37
☽∠⚷ 10:58
☉⊻☽ 14:05
☽∠♆ 14:48
☉⋕☽ 15:36
☽⋕⚷ 16:17
♂∠♇ 17:55
☽✶♃ 20:04
☽☌♀ 23:58

28 Sa
☽✶☿ 4:21
☽∥♀ 4:48
☽✶♂ 6:49
☽⊼♄ 8:02
☽⚼⚳ 12:15
☽⊻♅ 13:08
☽✶⚷ 14:11
☽⋕♆ 15:32
☽✶♆ 17:52
☉∠☽ 19:17
☿∠♇ 20:40

LONGITUDE

Day	Sid.Time	☉	☽	☽ 12 hour	Mean ☊	True ☊	☿	♀	♂	⚳	♃	♄	⚷	♅	♆	♇
	h m s	° ' "	° ' "	° ' "	° '	° '	° '	° '	° '	° '	° '	° '	° '	° '	° '	° '
1 Su	10 35 44	10♓32 12	27♈59 17	4♉45 48	7♒50.2	8♒53.4	18♒10.7	14♈48.6	18♒56.2	6♍17.4	12♒40.6	19♍00.1	22♒30.7	21♓55.1	24♒33.4	2♑58.8
2 M	10 39 40	11 32 26	11♉35 12	18 27 20	7 47.1	8R 49.2	19 37.8	15 00.8	19 43.1	6R 03.5	12 54.0	18R 55.4	22 34.9	21 58.5	24 35.6	2 59.9
3 Tu	10 43 37	12 32 38	25 22 05	2♊19 20	7 43.9	8 46.4	21 06.1	15 10.8	20 30.0	5 49.7	13 07.3	18 50.6	22 39.1	22 01.9	24 37.8	3 00.9
4 W	10 47 34	13 32 48	9♊18 58	16 20 50	7 40.7	8D 45.2	22 35.6	15 18.5	21 16.9	5 36.0	13 20.5	18 45.9	22 43.3	22 05.3	24 40.0	3 01.9
5 Th	10 51 30	14 32 56	23 24 49	0♋30 43	7 37.5	8 45.4	24 06.2	15 23.8	22 03.8	5 22.4	13 33.8	18 41.1	22 47.5	22 08.7	24 42.2	3 02.9
6 F	10 55 27	15 33 01	7♋38 21	14 47 28	7 34.4	8 46.6	25 38.0	15R 26.8	22 50.8	5 08.9	13 46.9	18 36.4	22 51.6	22 12.2	24 44.4	3 03.9
7 Sa	10 59 23	16 33 05	21 57 46	29 08 52	7 31.2	8 48.1	27 10.9	15 27.4	23 37.7	4 55.6	14 00.0	18 31.6	22 55.7	22 15.6	24 46.5	3 04.8
8 Su	11 03 20	17 33 06	6♌20 21	13♌31 44	7 28.0	8R 48.9	28 44.9	15 25.4	24 24.7	4 42.5	14 13.1	18 26.8	22 59.8	22 19.0	24 48.7	3 05.7
9 M	11 07 16	18 33 05	20 42 29	27 51 59	7 24.8	8 48.4	0♓20.1	15 21.0	25 11.6	4 29.5	14 26.1	18 22.0	23 03.9	22 22.4	24 50.8	3 06.6
10 Tu	11 11 13	19 33 02	4♍59 38	12♍04 49	7 21.7	8 45.9	1 56.4	15 14.1	25 58.6	4 16.8	14 39.0	18 17.2	23 07.9	22 25.9	24 52.9	3 07.4
11 W	11 15 09	20 32 57	19 06 54	26 05 20	7 18.5	8 41.4	3 33.9	15 04.6	26 45.5	4 04.3	14 51.9	18 12.5	23 11.9	22 29.3	24 55.0	3 08.2
12 Th	11 19 06	21 32 49	2♎59 33	9♎49 09	7 15.3	8 35.1	5 12.5	14 52.6	27 32.5	3 52.0	15 04.7	18 07.7	23 15.9	22 32.7	24 57.1	3 09.0
13 F	11 23 03	22 32 41	16 33 46	23 13 10	7 12.1	8 27.6	6 52.3	14 38.1	28 19.5	3 39.9	15 17.4	18 02.9	23 19.9	22 36.1	24 59.2	3 09.7
14 Sa	11 26 59	23 32 30	29 47 12	6♏15 53	7 08.9	8 19.8	8 33.2	14 21.2	29 06.5	3 28.1	15 30.1	17 58.2	23 23.8	22 39.6	25 01.3	3 10.4
15 Su	11 30 56	24 32 17	12♏39 17	18 57 37	7 05.8	8 12.5	10 15.3	14 01.8	29 53.4	3 16.6	15 42.8	17 53.4	23 27.7	22 43.0	25 03.3	3 11.1
16 M	11 34 52	25 32 03	25 11 11	1♐20 24	7 02.6	8 06.5	11 58.6	13 40.2	0♓40.4	3 05.4	15 55.3	17 48.7	23 31.6	22 46.4	25 05.4	3 11.8
17 Tu	11 38 49	26 31 47	7♐25 41	13 27 36	6 59.4	8 02.4	13 43.2	13 16.3	1 27.4	2 54.5	16 07.8	17 44.0	23 35.4	22 49.9	25 07.4	3 12.4
18 W	11 42 45	27 31 30	19 26 42	25 23 38	6 56.2	8D 00.3	15 28.9	12 50.2	2 14.4	2 43.9	16 20.2	17 39.3	23 39.3	22 53.3	25 09.4	3 13.0
19 Th	11 46 42	28 31 10	1♑19 01	7♑13 31	6 53.0	7 59.9	17 15.9	12 22.1	3 01.4	2 33.6	16 32.6	17 34.7	23 43.1	22 56.7	25 11.4	3 13.5
20 F	11 50 38	29 30 49	13 07 48	19 02 33	6 49.9	8 00.7	19 04.1	11 52.2	3 48.4	2 23.7	16 44.9	17 30.0	23 46.8	23 00.1	25 13.4	3 14.1
21 Sa	11 54 35	0♈30 26	24 58 23	0♒55 58	6 46.7	8 01.9	20 53.5	11 20.6	4 35.4	2 14.1	16 57.1	17 25.4	23 50.6	23 03.6	25 15.3	3 14.6
22 Su	11 58 32	1 30 02	6♒55 53	12 58 42	6 43.5	8R 02.6	22 44.2	10 47.4	5 22.4	2 04.8	17 09.2	17 20.8	23 54.2	23 07.0	25 17.3	3 15.0
23 M	12 02 28	2 29 35	19 04 54	25 14 56	6 40.3	8 01.9	24 36.2	10 12.9	6 09.4	1 55.9	17 21.3	17 16.3	23 57.9	23 10.4	25 19.2	3 15.4
24 Tu	12 06 25	3 29 07	1♓29 11	7♓47 56	6 37.2	7 59.1	26 29.4	9 37.3	6 56.4	1 47.4	17 33.3	17 11.8	24 01.5	23 13.8	25 21.1	3 15.8
25 W	12 10 21	4 28 36	14 11 23	20 39 38	6 34.0	7 54.0	28 23.9	9 00.8	7 43.3	1 39.3	17 45.2	17 07.3	24 05.1	23 17.2	25 23.0	3 16.2
26 Th	12 14 18	5 28 04	27 12 42	3♈50 28	6 30.8	7 46.5	0♈19.7	8 23.6	8 30.3	1 31.6	17 57.0	17 02.9	24 08.7	23 20.5	25 24.8	3 16.5
27 F	12 18 14	6 27 30	10♈32 44	17 19 14	6 27.6	7 37.1	2 16.6	7 46.1	9 17.3	1 24.3	18 08.7	16 58.5	24 12.2	23 23.9	25 26.7	3 16.8
28 Sa	12 22 11	7 26 54	24 09 36	1♉03 23	6 24.4	7 26.9	4 14.8	7 08.3	10 04.2	1 17.3	18 20.4	16 54.2	24 15.7	23 27.3	25 28.5	3 17.1
29 Su	12 26 07	8 26 15	8♉00 07	14 59 19	6 21.3	7 16.8	6 14.0	6 30.7	10 51.2	1 10.8	18 31.9	16 49.9	24 19.1	23 30.6	25 30.3	3 17.3
30 M	12 30 04	9 25 35	22 00 28	29 03 05	6 18.1	7 07.9	8 14.4	5 53.4	11 38.1	1 04.7	18 43.4	16 45.7	24 22.5	23 34.0	25 32.1	3 17.5
31 Tu	12 34 00	10♈24 52	6♊06 44	13♊11 00	6♒14.9	7♒01.2	10♈15.7	5♈16.6	12♓25.0	0♍59.1	18♒54.8	16♍41.5	24♒25.9	23♓37.3	25♒33.8	3♑17.7

1st of Month

Julian Day # 2454891.5
Obliquity 23°26'23"
SVP 5♓07'40"
GC 26♐58.0
Eris 20♈55.3

Day	⚴	⚵	⚶
1	13♊53.9	15♒49.4	14♉56.2
6	15 51.6	17 52.8	16 40.7
11	17 55.6	19 56.0	18 28.1
16	20 04.9	21 58.8	20 18.1
21	22 18.8	24 01.1	22 10.6
26	24 36.9	26 02.9	24 05.3
31	26 58.4	28 03.9	26 02.0

DECLINATION and LATITUDE

Day	☉ Decl	☽ Decl	☽ Lat	☽ 12h Decl	☿ Decl	☿ Lat	♀ Decl	♀ Lat	♂ Decl	♂ Lat	⚳ Decl	⚳ Lat	♃ Decl	♃ Lat	♄ Decl	♄ Lat
1 Su	7S37	15N31	5N07	17N59	16S54	1S36	11N26	6N05	16S11	1S06	24N42	16N46	17S29	0S30	6N26	2N15
2 M	7 14	20 15	5 12	22 15	16 32	1 41	11 40	6 15	15 57	1 06	24 48	16 47	17 26	0 30	6 28	2 16
3 Tu	6 51	23 57	4 59	25 18	16 08	1 46	11 53	6 25	15 42	1 06	24 53	16 47	17 22	0 31	6 30	2 16
4 W	6 28	26 17	4 29	26 51	15 43	1 51	12 05	6 35	15 27	1 06	24 58	16 47	17 18	0 31	6 32	2 16
5 Th	6 05	26 59	3 42	26 40	15 17	1 55	12 16	6 44	15 12	1 07	25 04	16 47	17 15	0 31	6 34	2 16
6 F	5 42	25 55	2 42	24 44	14 50	1 58	12 26	6 54	14 57	1 07	25 08	16 46	17 11	0 31	6 35	2 16
7 Sa	5 18	23 08	1 31	21 11	14 21	2 02	12 35	7 03	14 42	1 07	25 13	16 46	17 07	0 31	6 37	2 16
8 Su	4 55	18 54	0 13	16 21	13 51	2 05	12 42	7 12	14 27	1 07	25 17	16 45	17 04	0 31	6 39	2 16
9 M	4 32	13 34	1S04	10 37	13 20	2 07	12 49	7 21	14 11	1 08	25 21	16 44	17 00	0 31	6 41	2 16
10 Tu	4 08	7 32	2 17	4 29	12 48	2 09	12 54	7 29	13 55	1 08	25 25	16 43	16 56	0 31	6 43	2 16
11 W	3 45	1 13	3 21	1S56	12 14	2 11	12 57	7 37	13 40	1 08	25 29	16 42	16 53	0 32	6 45	2 16
12 Th	3 21	5S02	4 12	8 02	11 39	2 12	12 59	7 44	13 24	1 08	25 32	16 40	16 49	0 32	6 47	2 16
13 F	2 58	10 55	4 46	13 58	11 03	2 13	13 00	7 51	13 07	1 08	25 35	16 39	16 46	0 32	6 49	2 16
14 Sa	2 34	16 09	5 05	18 27	10 26	2 14	12 59	7 58	12 51	1 08	25 38	16 37	16 42	0 32	6 51	2 16
15 Su	2 10	20 31	5 08	22 19	9 47	2 14	12 57	8 04	12 35	1 09	25 41	16 35	16 38	0 32	6 53	2 16
16 M	1 47	23 50	4 55	25 03	9 07	2 13	12 54	8 09	12 18	1 09	25 43	16 33	16 35	0 32	6 55	2 16
17 Tu	1 23	25 58	4 29	26 35	8 26	2 12	12 48	8 14	12 02	1 09	25 45	16 31	16 31	0 32	6 56	2 16
18 W	0 59	26 52	3 52	26 51	7 44	2 11	12 42	8 17	11 45	1 09	25 47	16 28	16 28	0 33	6 58	2 16
19 Th	0 35	26 31	3 05	25 53	7 01	2 09	12 33	8 20	11 28	1 09	25 48	16 26	16 24	0 33	7 00	2 16
20 F	0 12	24 57	2 10	23 45	6 16	2 07	12 24	8 23	11 11	1 09	25 50	16 23	16 20	0 33	7 02	2 16
21 Sa	0N12	22 17	1 10	20 34	5 31	2 04	12 13	8 24	10 54	1 09	25 51	16 20	16 17	0 33	7 04	2 16
22 Su	0 36	18 38	0 06	16 30	4 44	2 01	11 60	8 25	10 37	1 10	25 51	16 17	16 13	0 33	7 06	2 16
23 M	0 59	14 10	0N59	11 40	3 56	1 57	11 46	8 24	10 20	1 10	25 52	16 14	16 10	0 33	7 07	2 16
24 Tu	1 23	9 02	2 02	6 17	3 07	1 52	11 31	8 23	10 03	1 10	25 52	16 11	16 06	0 34	7 09	2 16
25 W	1 47	3 26	3 01	0 31	2 17	1 48	11 14	8 21	9 45	1 10	25 52	16 08	16 03	0 34	7 11	2 16
26 Th	2 10	2N26	3 52	5N24	1 26	1 42	10 57	8 18	9 28	1 10	25 52	16 04	15 59	0 34	7 13	2 16
27 F	2 34	8 20	4 31	11 12	0 34	1 36	10 38	8 14	9 10	1 10	25 51	16 01	15 56	0 34	7 14	2 16
28 Sa	2 57	13 57	4 56	16 33	0N19	1 30	10 19	8 09	8 52	1 10	25 50	15 57	15 52	0 34	7 16	2 16
29 Su	3 21	18 58	5 04	21 08	1 12	1 23	9 58	8 03	8 35	1 10	25 49	15 53	15 49	0 34	7 18	2 16
30 M	3 44	22 60	4 54	24 32	2 07	1 15	9 37	7 56	8 17	1 10	25 48	15 49	15 46	0 34	7 19	2 16
31 Tu	4N07	25N42	4N26	26N27	3N02	1S07	9N16	7N49	7S59	1S10	25N47	15N46	15S42	0S35	7N21	2N16

Day	⚷ Decl	⚷ Lat	♅ Decl	♅ Lat	♆ Decl	♆ Lat	♇ Decl	♇ Lat
1	8S16	6N04	3S53	0S44	13S41	0S22	17S42	5N42
6	8 09	6 05	3 46	0 44	13 37	0 22	17 42	5 42
11	8 02	6 05	3 39	0 44	13 34	0 22	17 41	5 43
16	7 55	6 06	3 32	0 44	13 30	0 22	17 41	5 43
21	7 48	6 07	3 25	0 44	13 27	0 22	17 40	5 44
26	7 41	6 08	3 19	0 44	13 24	0 22	17 40	5 44
31	7S34	6N09	3S12	0S44	13S21	0S22	17S39	5N45

Day	⚴ Decl	⚴ Lat	⚵ Decl	⚵ Lat	⚶ Decl	⚶ Lat	Eris Decl	Eris Lat
1	15S36	38S19	9S36	6N47	12N26	4S03	4S35	13S44
6	14 02	36 54	9 05	6 42	13 07	3 52	4 33	13 44
11	12 30	35 31	8 32	6 38	13 42	3 42	4 32	13 43
16	10 60	34 09	7 59	6 33	14 25	3 32	4 30	13 43
21	9 32	32 48	7 24	6 28	15 03	3 22	4 29	13 42
26	8 08	31 29	6 49	6 23	15 41	3 13	4 27	13 42
31	6S47	30S11	6S13	6N18	16N17	3S04	4S26	13S41

Moon Phenomena

Max/0 Decl
dy hr mn
4 21:47 26N59
11 4:38 0 S
18 5:02 26S54
25 14:06 0 N

Max/0 Lat
dy hr mn
1 19:14 5N12
8 4:08 0 S
14 15:44 5S08
22 2:12 0 N
28 22:54 5N04

Perigee/Apogee
dy hr m kilometers
7 15:10 p 367018
19 13:18 a 404297

PH dy hr mn
☽ 4 7:47 13♊52
○ 11 2:39 20♍40
☾ 18 17:48 28♐16
● 26 16:07 6♈08

Void of Course Moon

Last Aspect	☽ Ingress
28 17:52 ♆ ⚹	♉ 1 3:34
2 22:43 ♆ □	♊ 3 8:00
5 2:11 ♆ △	♋ 5 11:08
7 0:30 ♅ △	♌ 7 13:25
9 7:57 ♂ ☍	♍ 9 15:35
11 5:49 ♅ ☍	♎ 11 18:47
13 22:40 ♂ △	♏ 14 0:24
16 0:44 ☉ △	♐ 16 9:23
18 17:48 ☉ □	♑ 18 21:20
20 20:07 ♅ ⚹	♒ 21 10:08
23 12:10 ♆ ☌	♓ 23 21:09
25 16:54 ♅ ☌	♈ 26 5:04
28 2:18 ♆ ⚹	♉ 28 10:10
30 6:02 ♆ □	♊ 30 13:37

DAILY ASPECTARIAN

1 Su
♂⚻♄ 1:49
☽⫲♂ 3:00
☽⫲☿ 6:08
☽△♇ 8:52
☽⫲♃ 9:21
☽⫲♇ 10:33
☽⚼♄ 10:36
☿⚻♄ 12:57
☽△⚳ 14:27
☽∠♅ 15:52
☉⚹☽ 23:55

2 M
☽□♃ 2:20
☿☌♂ 3:06
☽⚺♀ 6:05
☽⚼♇ 11:13
☽△♄ 12:44
☽□♂ 15:03
☽□☿ 15:43
☽⚹♅ 18:12
☽□⚷ 19:16
☽□♆ 22:43

3 Tu
☽∥⚳ 8:17
☽∠♀ 8:24
☽⚻♇ 13:12
☿⚺♅ 15:36
☉⚺♃ 17:44
☽□⚳ 17:44
☉⫲♄ 20:41

4 W
☿☌⚷ 2:10
☽△♃ 6:59
☉□☽ 7:47
☽⚹♀ 10:18
☽□♄ 16:01
☽△♂ 21:35
☽□♅ 21:51
☽△⚷ 22:56

5 Th
☽△☿ 1:19
☽△♆ 2:11
♂⚺♅ 2:42
☽⚼♃ 8:51
☿☌♆ 9:41
☿∥♂ 9:51
☽☍♇ 16:18
☽⚹⚳ 19:53
☉⚺♀ 21:27

6 F
☽⚼♂ 0:22
☽⚼⚷ 0:22
♂☌⚷ 0:27
☽⚼♆ 3:32
☽⚼☿ 5:38
☽∥⚳ 7:59
☽⚻♃ 10:28
☽□♀ 13:07
☉△☽ 14:16
♀ R 17:18
☽⚹♄ 18:17
☽∠⚳ 20:39

7 Sa
☽△♅ 0:30
☽⚻⚷ 1:37
☽⚻♂ 2:57
☽⚻♆ 4:43
☽⚻☿ 9:47
☉⚼☽ 17:12
☽⚻♇ 18:35
☽∠♄ 19:12
☽⚺⚳ 21:19

8 Su
☽⚼♅ 1:38
☽⫲♇ 5:50
☽⫲♃ 8:53
☿∥♆ 12:31
♂☌♆ 12:51
☽☍♃ 13:21
☽△♀ 15:06
☿ ♓ 18:57
☽⚼♇ 19:39
☉☍♄ 19:54
☽⚺♄ 20:06
☉⚻☽ 20:07
☽⫲♂ 21:19
☽⫲♆ 23:58

9 M
☿∠♀ 0:12
☽⫲☿ 1:05
☽⚻♅ 2:48
☽∥♀ 3:07
☽☍⚷ 3:58
☽☍♆ 6:57
☽☍♂ 7:57
☽⚼♀ 16:03
☽☍☿ 18:12
☿⫲♀ 20:15
☽△♇ 20:51
☽⫲⚷ 22:03
☽☌⚳ 22:49

10 Tu
☽∥♄ 3:10
☉⫲☽ 13:51
☽⫲♅ 14:49
☽⚻♃ 16:38
☽⚻♀ 17:11
☿⚹♇ 17:39
☽☌♄ 22:27

11 W
☉☍☽ 2:39
☽☍♅ 5:49
☉∥♅ 6:13
☿☍⚳ 6:35
☽⚻⚷ 7:03
♂∥♆ 9:28
☽⚻♆ 10:00
♀⚹♃ 12:36
☽⚻♂ 13:57
☉∥☽ 17:51
☽∥♅ 18:32
☽⚼♃ 18:50

12 Th
☽□♇ 0:17
☽⚺⚳ 1:30
☽⚻☿ 4:25
☽⫲♄ 6:58
☽⚼⚷ 9:18
☽∥⚷ 11:48
☽⚼♆ 12:16
☽⚼♂ 17:52
☽☍♀ 20:37
☽△♃ 21:41

13 F
☽∥☿ 0:31
☉☌♅ 1:29
☽⚺♄ 2:39
☽∠⚳ 3:43
☽⫲♀ 9:09
☽∥♂ 9:15
☽⚻♅ 10:56
☽⚼☿ 10:57
♀⫲♂ 11:08
☽∥♆ 11:33
☉⚻☽ 11:39
☽△⚷ 12:16
☽△♆ 15:15
☉⚺⚷ 20:16
☽△♂ 22:40

14 Sa
☽∥♃ 2:44
♀∠♂ 5:24
☽∠♄ 5:50
☽⚹♇ 6:16
☽⚹⚳ 6:42
☽∥♇ 7:52
☽⚼♅ 14:40
☉⚼☽ 17:38
☽△☿ 18:47

15 Su
☽⚻♀ 2:32
♂ ♓ 3:21
☽□♃ 5:54
☽⚹♄ 9:54
☽∠♇ 10:32
⚳△♇ 11:04
☉⚺♆ 12:54
☽△♅ 19:19
☽□⚷ 20:46
☽□♆ 23:49

16 M
☉△☽ 0:44
☽⚼♀ 6:34
☽□♂ 11:26
☽□⚳ 15:13
☽⚺♇ 15:40
☿⚺♀ 19:02
☽⫲⚳ 20:37

17 Tu
☽△♀ 11:14
☽□☿ 14:40
☽⚹♃ 17:39
☿∥⚷ 19:29
☽□♄ 20:26

18 W
☽□♅ 6:58
☽⚹⚷ 8:32
☽⚹♆ 11:33
♂☍⚳ 12:20
☿⚺♃ 13:04
☉□☽ 17:48

19 Th
☿⫲♄ 0:18
☽∠♃ 0:28
☽△⚳ 2:29
☽⚹♂ 3:43
☽☌♇ 3:53
☿☍♄ 4:01
♂⚹♇ 6:16
☽⫲⚳ 12:54
☽∠⚷ 15:07
☽∠♆ 18:05
☽□♀ 21:33

20 F
☽⚺♃ 7:29
☽⚼⚳ 8:32
☽△♄ 8:49
☉ ♈ 11:45
☽∠♂ 12:20
☽⚹☿ 14:14
☽⚹♅ 20:07
☽⚺⚷ 21:42

21 Sa
☽⚺♆ 0:34
☉⚹☽ 12:09
☽⚻⚳ 14:25
☽⚼♄ 14:54
☽⚺♇ 16:38
☽⚺♂ 20:40

22 Su
☽∠☿ 1:54
☽∠♅ 2:22
☿☌♅ 5:03
☽∥♇ 5:32
☽⚹♀ 7:20
☉⚻⚳ 12:11
☽∥♃ 13:38
☿⚺⚷ 15:33
♃⚻♄ 16:47
☉∠♃ 19:48
♀∠♆ 19:55
☽⚻♄ 20:29
☽☌♃ 20:34
☉∠☽ 20:37
☽∠♇ 22:23

23 M
☽∥♆ 3:39
☽⚺♅ 8:01
☿⚺♆ 9:18
☽☌⚷ 9:34
☽∠♀ 11:24
☽⫲♀ 12:09
☽☌♆ 12:10
☽⚺☿ 12:40
☿∥♅ 16:44
☉□♇ 18:37
☽∥♂ 19:14

24 Tu
☽☍⚳ 0:35
☽⚹♇ 3:24
☉⚺☽ 4:08
☽∥⚷ 5:47
☽⫲♄ 8:13
☽☌♂ 11:03
☽⚺♀ 14:44
♀∠⚷ 21:26
☽∠⚷ 21:36
☽⚺♂ 21:37
☽∠♆ 23:49

25 W
☽∥♅ 0:25
☽☍♄ 5:25
☽∥☿ 5:34
☉⫲☽ 6:24
☽⚺♃ 6:44
☉⫲☿ 9:44
☽☌♅ 16:54
☽⚺⚷ 18:22
☿ ♈ 19:56
☽⫲☿ 20:26
☽⚺♆ 20:43
♀⚺♂ 22:06
☉∥☽ 22:51

26 Th
☽⫲♅ 3:31
☽☌☿ 6:38
☽⚻⚳ 7:45
☽∠♃ 10:33
☽□♇ 10:59
☿⚻⚳ 13:55
☉☌☽ 16:07
☽☌♀ 19:16
☽∥♄ 19:29
☽⫲⚷ 21:15

27 F
☽⫲♂ 3:18
☽∥♀ 9:06
☽⚼⚳ 10:18
☽⚻♄ 11:20
☿∠♃ 11:47
☿□♇ 12:17
☽⚹♃ 13:39
♃∠♇ 17:04
☉☌♀ 19:25
☽⫲♆ 21:27
☽⚺♅ 22:46

28 Sa
☽⚹⚷ 0:11
☽∠♂ 1:41
☽⚹♆ 2:18
☽⫲♃ 8:41
☽△⚳ 12:18
☽⚼♄ 13:24
☽△♇ 15:52
☽⫲♇ 17:23
☉⫲♅ 18:09
☽⚺☿ 20:27
☽⚺♀ 21:32

29 Su
☉⚺☽ 0:48
☽∠♅ 0:53
☿☌♀ 2:32
☽⚹♂ 5:12
☽△♄ 15:05
☽⚼♇ 17:39
☽□♃ 18:19
☽∠♀ 22:10
☉∠⚷ 22:41

30 M
☽∠☿ 2:27
☽⚹♅ 2:40
☽□⚷ 4:03
☉∠☽ 4:26
☽□♆ 6:02
☿∠⚷ 13:53
☽□⚳ 15:21
☽⚻♇ 19:13
☽⚹♀ 22:38

31 Tu
☽∥⚳ 1:04
☉☌☿ 3:30
☿∠♆ 3:37
☉∠♆ 3:44
☿⫲♅ 4:22
☉⚹☽ 7:51
☽⚹☿ 8:14
☽□♂ 11:20
☽□♄ 17:52
☽△♃ 22:01

April 2009

LONGITUDE

Day	Sid.Time	☉	☽	☽ 12 hour	Mean ☊	True ☊	☿	♀	♂	⚳	♃	♄	⚷	♅	♆	♇
	h m s	° ' "	° ' "	° ' "	° '	° '	° '	° '	° '	° '	° '	° '	° '	° '	° '	° '
1 W	12 37 57	11♈24 07	20♊15 32	27♊20 04	6♒11.7	6♒57.0	12♈17.9	4♈40.7	13♓12.0	0♍53.8	19♒06.1	16♍37.3	24♒29.2	23♓40.6	25♒35.5	3♑17.8
2 Th	12 41 54	12 23 20	4♋24 21	11♋28 13	6 08.6	6D 55.2	14 20.9	4R 05.8	13 58.9	0R 49.0	19 17.3	16R 33.3	24 32.5	23 43.9	25 37.3	3 17.9
3 F	12 45 50	13 22 30	18 31 31	25 34 09	6 05.4	6 55.0	16 24.6	3 32.1	14 45.7	0 44.6	19 28.4	16 29.3	24 35.7	23 47.2	25 39.0	3 18.0
4 Sa	12 49 47	14 21 38	2♌36 01	9♌36 59	6 02.2	6R 55.4	18 28.6	3 00.0	15 32.6	0 40.6	19 39.4	16 25.3	24 38.9	23 50.5	25 40.6	3R 18.0
5 Su	12 53 43	15 20 43	16 36 58	23 35 48	5 59.0	6 55.2	20 32.9	2 29.4	16 19.5	0 37.1	19 50.3	16 21.4	24 42.0	23 53.7	25 42.3	3 18.0
6 M	12 57 40	16 19 47	0♍33 18	7♍29 15	5 55.9	6 53.1	22 37.2	2 00.6	17 06.3	0 34.0	20 01.1	16 17.6	24 45.2	23 57.0	25 43.9	3 18.0
7 Tu	13 01 36	17 18 47	14 23 23	21 15 24	5 52.7	6 48.4	24 41.2	1 33.9	17 53.1	0 31.3	20 11.9	16 13.9	24 48.2	24 00.2	25 45.5	3 18.0
8 W	13 05 33	18 17 46	28 04 58	4♎51 45	5 49.5	6 40.9	26 44.6	1 09.1	18 39.9	0 29.1	20 22.5	16 10.2	24 51.2	24 03.4	25 47.0	3 17.9
9 Th	13 09 29	19 16 43	11♎35 24	18 15 38	5 46.3	6 30.9	28 47.2	0 46.6	19 26.7	0 27.3	20 33.0	16 06.6	24 54.2	24 06.6	25 48.6	3 17.7
10 F	13 13 26	20 15 37	24 52 07	1♏24 39	5 43.1	6 19.0	0♉48.5	0 26.4	20 13.5	0 25.9	20 43.4	16 03.0	24 57.1	24 09.8	25 50.1	3 17.6
11 Sa	13 17 23	21 14 30	7♏53 02	14 17 11	5 40.0	6 06.6	2 48.3	0 08.5	21 00.3	0 24.9	20 53.7	15 59.6	25 00.0	24 12.9	25 51.6	3 17.4
12 Su	13 21 19	22 13 20	20 37 05	26 52 48	5 36.8	5 54.6	4 46.1	29♓53.1	21 47.0	0D 24.4	21 03.9	15 56.2	25 02.8	24 16.0	25 53.1	3 17.2
13 M	13 25 16	23 12 09	3♐04 29	9♐12 24	5 33.6	5 44.2	6 41.7	29 40.1	22 33.7	0 24.3	21 14.0	15 52.9	25 05.6	24 19.2	25 54.5	3 17.0
14 Tu	13 29 12	24 10 56	15 16 51	21 18 15	5 30.4	5 36.1	8 34.6	29 29.6	23 20.4	0 24.6	21 24.0	15 49.6	25 08.3	24 22.3	25 55.9	3 16.7
15 W	13 33 09	25 09 41	27 17 03	3♑13 48	5 27.2	5 30.7	10 24.6	29 21.5	24 07.1	0 25.4	21 33.9	15 46.5	25 11.0	24 25.3	25 57.3	3 16.4
16 Th	13 37 05	26 08 25	9♑09 04	15 03 28	5 24.1	5 27.7	12 11.3	29 15.9	24 53.8	0 26.5	21 43.6	15 43.4	25 13.7	24 28.4	25 58.7	3 16.0
17 F	13 41 02	27 07 07	20 57 40	26 52 20	5 20.9	5D 26.6	13 54.5	29D 12.7	25 40.4	0 28.1	21 53.3	15 40.4	25 16.3	24 31.4	26 00.0	3 15.7
18 Sa	13 44 58	28 05 47	2♒48 10	8♒45 51	5 17.7	5R 26.6	15 33.8	29 12.0	26 27.1	0 30.1	22 02.8	15 37.5	25 18.8	24 34.4	26 01.3	3 15.3
19 Su	13 48 55	29 04 25	14 46 04	20 49 30	5 14.5	5 26.4	17 09.1	29 13.6	27 13.7	0 32.5	22 12.2	15 34.7	25 21.3	24 37.4	26 02.6	3 14.9
20 M	13 52 52	0♉03 02	26 56 45	3♓08 26	5 11.4	5 25.0	18 40.2	29 17.6	28 00.3	0 35.3	22 21.5	15 32.0	25 23.7	24 40.4	26 03.9	3 14.4
21 Tu	13 56 48	1 01 37	9♓25 03	15 47 02	5 08.2	5 21.5	20 06.8	29 23.8	28 46.8	0 38.5	22 30.7	15 29.3	25 26.1	24 43.3	26 05.1	3 13.9
22 W	14 00 45	2 00 10	22 14 44	28 48 21	5 05.0	5 15.4	21 28.9	29 32.3	29 33.3	0 42.1	22 39.7	15 26.8	25 28.4	24 46.2	26 06.3	3 13.4
23 Th	14 04 41	2 58 42	5♈28 01	12♈13 40	5 01.8	5 06.7	22 46.2	29 43.0	0♈19.8	0 46.2	22 48.6	15 24.3	25 30.7	24 49.1	26 07.4	3 12.9
24 F	14 08 38	3 57 11	19 05 06	26 01 58	4 58.6	4 55.8	23 58.6	29 55.7	1 06.3	0 50.6	22 57.4	15 21.9	25 32.9	24 51.9	26 08.6	3 12.3
25 Sa	14 12 34	4 55 39	3♉03 48	10♉09 57	4 55.5	4 43.8	25 06.1	0♈10.5	1 52.8	0 55.4	23 06.1	15 19.6	25 35.1	24 54.7	26 09.7	3 11.7
26 Su	14 16 31	5 54 06	17 19 43	24 32 19	4 52.3	4 31.9	26 08.5	0 27.2	2 39.2	1 00.6	23 14.6	15 17.5	25 37.2	24 57.5	26 10.8	3 11.1
27 M	14 20 27	6 52 30	1♊46 53	9♊02 35	4 49.1	4 21.3	27 05.8	0 45.9	3 25.6	1 06.1	23 23.0	15 15.4	25 39.2	25 00.3	26 11.8	3 10.4
28 Tu	14 24 24	7 50 53	16 18 37	23 34 14	4 45.9	4 13.1	27 57.9	1 06.4	4 11.9	1 12.1	23 31.3	15 13.4	25 41.2	25 03.0	26 12.8	3 09.7
29 W	14 28 21	8 49 13	0♋48 45	8♋01 38	4 42.8	4 07.6	28 44.6	1 28.7	4 58.3	1 18.4	23 39.4	15 11.5	25 43.2	25 05.8	26 13.8	3 09.0
30 Th	14 32 17	9♉47 31	15 12 26	22 20 48	4♒39.6	4♒04.9	29♉26.1	1♈52.7	5♈44.6	1♍25.1	23♒47.4	15♍09.7	25♒45.1	25♓08.4	26♒14.8	3♑08.3

1st of Month

Julian Day # 2454922.5
Obliquity 23°26'23"
SVP 5♓07'37"
GC 26♐58.1
Eris 21♈13.7

Day	⚴
1	27♊27.1
6	29 52.1
11	2♋19.3
16	4 48.5
21	7 19.3
26	9 51.5

Day	⚵
1	28♒28.0
6	0♓27.9
11	2 26.8
16	4 24.7
21	6 21.2
26	8 16.4

Day	⚶
1	26♉25.6
6	28 24.5
11	0♊24.8
16	2 26.6
21	4 29.7
26	6 33.9

DECLINATION and LATITUDE

Day	☉ Decl	☽ Decl	☽ Lat	☽ 12h Decl	☿ Decl	☿ Lat	♀ Decl	♀ Lat	♂ Decl	♂ Lat	⚳ Decl	⚳ Lat	♃ Decl	♃ Lat	♄ Decl	♄ Lat
1 W	4N31	26N46	3N42	26N39	3N57	0S59	8N54	7N40	7S41	1S10	25N45	15N42	15S39	0S35	7N22	2N16
2 Th	4 54	26 06	2 44	25 07	4 53	0 50	8 31	7 31	7 23	1 10	25 43	15 37	15 36	0 35	7 24	2 16
3 F	5 17	23 45	1 36	22 01	5 50	0 41	8 09	7 21	7 05	1 10	25 41	15 33	15 33	0 35	7 25	2 16
4 Sa	5 40	19 57	0 23	17 37	6 46	0 31	7 46	7 11	6 47	1 10	25 38	15 29	15 29	0 35	7 27	2 16
5 Su	6 03	15 02	0S51	12 17	7 42	0 21	7 24	6 60	6 29	1 10	25 36	15 25	15 26	0 36	7 28	2 16
6 M	6 25	9 22	2 02	6 22	8 39	0 10	7 02	6 48	6 10	1 10	25 33	15 20	15 22	0 36	7 30	2 16
7 Tu	6 48	3 18	3 05	0 13	9 34	0N01	6 40	6 36	5 52	1 10	25 30	15 16	15 19	0 36	7 31	2 16
8 W	7 10	2S51	3 56	5S52	10 30	0 12	6 19	6 23	5 34	1 10	25 26	15 12	15 16	0 36	7 32	2 16
9 Th	7 33	8 47	4 34	11 34	11 24	0 23	5 58	6 10	5 15	1 10	25 23	15 07	15 13	0 36	7 34	2 16
10 F	7 55	14 12	4 55	16 39	12 17	0 34	5 38	5 57	4 57	1 10	25 19	15 03	15 10	0 36	7 35	2 16
11 Sa	8 17	18 53	5 01	20 52	13 09	0 45	5 19	5 44	4 38	1 10	25 15	14 58	15 07	0 37	7 36	2 15
12 Su	8 39	22 35	4 52	24 01	14 00	0 57	5 00	5 30	4 20	1 10	25 11	14 53	15 03	0 37	7 38	2 15
13 M	9 01	25 09	4 28	25 59	14 49	1 08	4 43	5 17	4 01	1 10	25 07	14 49	15 00	0 37	7 39	2 15
14 Tu	9 23	26 29	3 53	26 40	15 36	1 19	4 26	5 03	3 43	1 10	25 02	14 44	14 57	0 37	7 40	2 15
15 W	9 44	26 32	3 08	26 06	16 21	1 29	4 10	4 49	3 24	1 10	24 58	14 39	14 54	0 37	7 41	2 15
16 Th	10 06	25 22	2 15	24 21	17 04	1 39	3 55	4 36	3 06	1 10	24 53	14 34	14 51	0 38	7 42	2 15
17 F	10 27	23 03	1 16	21 31	17 45	1 49	3 41	4 22	2 47	1 10	24 48	14 30	14 48	0 38	7 43	2 15
18 Sa	10 48	19 46	0 14	17 47	18 23	1 58	3 29	4 08	2 29	1 10	24 43	14 25	14 46	0 38	7 44	2 15
19 Su	11 09	15 37	0N49	13 17	18 59	2 06	3 17	3 55	2 10	1 10	24 38	14 20	14 43	0 38	7 45	2 15
20 M	11 29	10 47	1 51	8 10	19 32	2 14	3 06	3 41	1 51	1 09	24 32	14 15	14 40	0 38	7 46	2 15
21 Tu	11 50	5 25	2 49	2 35	20 02	2 21	2 57	3 28	1 33	1 09	24 26	14 11	14 37	0 39	7 47	2 14
22 W	12 10	0N18	3 41	3N14	20 30	2 28	2 48	3 15	1 14	1 09	24 21	14 06	14 34	0 39	7 48	2 14
23 Th	12 30	6 10	4 22	9 05	20 56	2 33	2 40	3 02	0 55	1 09	24 15	14 01	14 32	0 39	7 49	2 14
24 F	12 50	11 56	4 49	14 40	21 18	2 37	2 34	2 50	0 37	1 09	24 09	13 56	14 29	0 39	7 50	2 14
25 Sa	13 10	17 14	5 00	19 35	21 39	2 41	2 28	2 37	0 18	1 09	24 02	13 51	14 26	0 39	7 50	2 14
26 Su	13 29	21 41	4 53	23 28	21 56	2 43	2 24	2 25	0N00	1 09	23 56	13 46	14 24	0 40	7 51	2 14
27 M	13 49	24 53	4 27	25 53	22 11	2 45	2 20	2 13	0 19	1 08	23 49	13 42	14 21	0 40	7 52	2 14
28 Tu	14 08	26 27	3 44	26 33	22 24	2 45	2 18	2 02	0 38	1 08	23 43	13 37	14 18	0 40	7 52	2 13
29 W	14 26	26 12	2 46	25 25	22 34	2 45	2 16	1 50	0 56	1 08	23 36	13 32	14 16	0 40	7 53	2 13
30 Th	14N45	24N12	1N38	22N36	22N41	2N43	2N16	1N39	1N15	1S08	23N29	13N27	14S14	0S40	7N54	2N13

Day	⚷ Decl	⚷ Lat	♅ Decl	♅ Lat	♆ Decl	♆ Lat	♇ Decl	♇ Lat
1	7S33	6N09	3S11	0S44	13S20	0S22	17S39	5N45
6	7 27	6 10	3 04	0 44	13 18	0 22	17 39	5 45
11	7 21	6 12	2 58	0 44	13 15	0 22	17 39	5 45
16	7 15	6 13	2 52	0 44	13 13	0 22	17 38	5 46
21	7 09	6 15	2 46	0 44	13 11	0 23	17 38	5 46
26	7 04	6 16	2 41	0 44	13 09	0 23	17 38	5 46

Day	⚴ Decl	⚴ Lat	⚵ Decl	⚵ Lat	⚶ Decl	⚶ Lat	Eris Decl	Eris Lat
1	6S31	29S56	6S06	6N17	16N24	3S02	4S26	13S41
6	5 14	28 41	5 30	6 12	16 59	2 54	4 24	13 41
11	4 01	27 27	4 53	6 07	17 32	2 46	4 23	13 41
16	2 53	26 15	4 16	6 02	18 04	2 38	4 21	13 41
21	1 48	25 05	3 38	5 57	18 35	2 30	4 20	13 41
26	0 48	23 56	3 01	5 52	19 04	2 23	4 19	13 41

Moon Phenomena

Max/0 Decl

dy	hr mn	
1	2:39	26N47
7	12:50	0 S
14	13:01	26S40
21	22:45	0 N
28	8:45	26N34

Max/0 Lat

dy	hr mn	
4	7:23	0 S
10	20:50	5S01
18	5:19	0 N
25	2:38	5N00

Perigee/Apogee

dy	hr m		kilometers
2	2:26	p	370013
16	9:14	a	404229
28	6:22	p	366041

PH	dy	hr mn	
☽	2	14:35	12♋59
○	9	14:57	19♎53
☾	17	13:37	27♑40
●	25	3:24	5♉04

Void of Course Moon

Last Aspect				☽ Ingress		
1	9:04	♆	△	♋	1	16:31
3	9:00	♅	△	♌	3	19:34
5	15:40	♆	☍	♍	5	23:02
7	16:53	♅	☍	♎	8	3:23
10	1:46	♆	△	♏	10	9:24
12	17:30	♀	△	♐	12	18:02
15	4:08	♀	□	♑	15	5:28
17	16:43	♀	⚹	♒	17	18:20
19	22:17	♆	☌	♓	20	5:56
22	13:30	♀	☌	♈	22	14:10
24	12:12	♆	⚹	♉	24	18:47
26	15:43	☿	☌	♊	26	21:03
28	16:24	♆	△	♋	28	22:39

DAILY ASPECTARIAN

1 W
☽□♅ 5:49
☽△⚷ 7:12
☽△♆ 9:04
♂∥⚷ 11:31
☿⚺♂ 17:03
☽⚹⚳ 17:56
♀∠♃ 17:57
☽☍♇ 22:07
♂⋕♄ 22:59
☽□♀ 23:30
☽⚼♃ 23:48

2 Th
☉∥☿ 0:17
☽∥⚳ 5:25
☽⚼⚷ 8:45
☽⚼♆ 10:35
☉□☽ 14:35
☿⚼⚳ 16:30
☽△♂ 17:13
☽∠⚳ 19:17
☽□☿ 19:47
☽⚹♄ 20:33

3 F
☿⚻♄ 0:53
☽⚻♃ 1:38
☽△♅ 9:00
☽⚻⚷ 10:23
♀□♇ 10:24
☽⚻♆ 12:10
☽⚼♂ 20:17
☽⚺⚳ 20:44
☽∠♄ 22:00

4 Sa
☿⋕♂ 0:14
☽△♀ 0:39
☽⚻♇ 1:12
☽⚼♅ 10:43
☽⋕♇ 11:49
☿⚹♃ 15:00
♇ R 17:37
☿∥♄ 17:48
☿⋕⚷ 17:56
☿∥♀ 18:25
♀⋕⚷ 19:45
♀∥♄ 19:51
⚵ ♓ 19:58
♄⋕⚷ 20:40
☉△☽ 21:39
☽⋕♃ 22:14
☽⚻♂ 23:28
☽⚺♄ 23:33

5 Su
♂☍♄ 0:56
☽⚼♀ 1:27
☽⚼♇ 2:54
☽☍♃ 5:36
☉⚼⚳ 6:18
☽⋕♆ 7:39
☽△☿ 7:56
☽⚻♅ 12:34
☽☍⚷ 13:57
☉⋕♂ 15:15
☽☍♆ 15:40
☉⚻♄ 23:11

6 M
☽☌⚳ 0:01
☉⚼☽ 1:26
☽⚻♀ 2:26
☽∥☿ 2:32
☽△♇ 4:45
⚴ ♋ 6:30
☽∥♄ 7:30
☽⋕⚷ 7:45
☽∥♀ 9:57
☉∥☽ 11:05
☽⋕♂ 13:26
☽⚼☿ 14:23
☿⚺♅ 15:51
☉∥♀ 19:53

7 Tu
☽⋕♅ 0:58
☿⚹⚷ 1:24
☽☌♄ 3:12
☉⚻☽ 5:30
☽☍♂ 6:28
☽⚻♃ 10:17
☿⚹♆ 12:39
☽☍♅ 16:53
☽⚻⚷ 18:18
☽⚻♆ 19:57
☽⚻☿ 21:13

8 W
☽∥♅ 0:42
☽⚺⚳ 4:14
☽☍♀ 5:16
☽□♇ 9:13
☽∥♂ 10:16
☽⚼♃ 13:05
☽⋕♀ 13:05
☉⋕⚷ 13:58
☽∥⚷ 18:13
☉⋕☽ 18:32
☽⋕♄ 18:55
☽⚼⚷ 20:58
☽⚼♆ 22:36

9 Th
☉∥♄ 1:08
☽∠⚳ 6:56
☽⚺♄ 8:05
☽⋕☿ 13:28
☿ ♉ 14:22
☉☍☽ 14:57
☽⚻♂ 15:02
☽△♃ 16:22
☿△⚳ 19:33
☽∥♆ 19:36
☉⚺♂ 19:48
☿⚺♀ 20:13
☽⚻♅ 22:42
⚶ ♊ 23:22

10 F
☽△⚷ 0:09
♀⚻⚳ 0:42
☽△♆ 1:46
☿⚼♄ 2:49
☽∥♃ 4:32
☽⚻♀ 9:59
☽⚹⚳ 10:11
☽∠♄ 11:17
☽☍☿ 12:52
☉⚹♃ 13:44
☽⚹♇ 15:28
☽∥♇ 17:12
♂⚺♃ 19:42
☽⚼♂ 20:17

11 Sa
☽⚼♅ 2:30
☿⋕♆ 2:36
☿△♇ 5:53
♀R♓ 12:48
☽⚼♀ 13:20
☽⚹♄ 15:09
☽∠♇ 19:34

12 Su
☽□♃ 0:52
☽△♂ 2:22
☉⚻☽ 3:19
☽△♅ 7:00
☽□⚷ 8:30
☽□♆ 10:06
☽△♀ 17:30
⚳ D 17:41
☽□⚳ 18:49
☽⋕⚳ 23:32

13 M
☽⚺♇ 0:24
☿⋕♃ 5:21
☽⚻☿ 8:22
☉⚼☽ 10:54
☿∠♂ 18:47

14 Tu
☽□♄ 1:05
☉⚺♅ 4:53
☿∠♅ 10:37
☽⚹♃ 12:22
☽□♂ 17:12
☽□♅ 18:13
☉△☽ 19:21
☽⚼☿ 19:33
☽⚹⚷ 19:46
☽⚹♆ 21:19

15 W
☉⚹⚷ 0:35
☽□♀ 4:08
☽△⚳ 6:20
♂☌♅ 10:01
☽☌♇ 12:05
☽∠♃ 19:01
☉⚹♆ 19:56

16 Th
☽∠⚷ 2:12
☽∠♆ 3:43
☽⋕⚳ 6:16
☽△☿ 7:14
♂⚺⚷ 10:50
☽⚼⚳ 12:49
☽△♄ 13:18
♂∥♅ 18:56
☿⋕♇ 20:03

17 F
☽⚺♃ 1:55
☿∠♀ 4:16
☽⚹♅ 7:16
☽⚺⚷ 8:47
☽⚹♂ 10:15
☽⚺♆ 10:15
♂⚺♆ 10:22
☉□☽ 13:37
☽⚹♀ 16:43
☽⚻⚳ 19:20
♀ D 19:25
☽⚼♄ 19:37

18 Sa
☿△♄ 0:53
☽⚺♇ 0:55
☽⋕☿ 7:23
☽∥♇ 12:52
☽∠♅ 13:41
☽∠♂ 18:35
☽∠♀ 22:55

19 Su
☽⚻♄ 1:36
☉⚺♀ 3:58
☽∥♃ 4:48
☽□☿ 5:26
☽∠♇ 6:54
☽∥♆ 12:27
☽☌♃ 14:54
☿⚼♇ 17:07
☽⚺♅ 19:32
☉⋕☽ 20:53
☽☌⚷ 20:58
☽☌♆ 22:17
☉ ♉ 22:45

20 M
☽⚺♂ 2:12
☽⚺♀ 4:36
☉⚹☽ 6:33
☽☍⚳ 7:06
☉⚼♄ 11:20
☽⚹♇ 12:11
☽⋕♄ 13:42
☉△⚳ 13:58
☽∥⚷ 16:26

21 Tu
☽⋕♀ 10:48
☽∥♅ 11:17
☽☍♄ 11:24
☉∠☽ 13:29
☽∥♂ 17:17
☽⚹☿ 22:26
♀☌♂ 23:20

22 W
☽⚺♃ 0:47
☽⋕♂ 3:37
☽☌♅ 4:39
☽⚺⚷ 5:57
☽⚺♆ 7:05
☽⋕♅ 9:59
☽∥♀ 10:00
♀⋕♅ 10:31
☽☌♀ 13:30
♂ ♈ 13:45
☽☌♂ 14:11
☽⚻⚳ 15:31
☉⚺☽ 19:11
☽□♇ 19:58

23 Th
☿□♃ 0:54
☽⋕⚷ 3:51
☽∠♃ 4:13
☽∠☿ 4:31
☉△♇ 5:45
☽∥♄ 6:44
☽∠⚷ 9:00
☽∠♆ 10:04
♂⚻⚳ 14:59
☽⚻♄ 17:32
☽⚼⚳ 18:19

24 F
☉∥☽ 4:10
☽⋕♆ 5:20
☽⚹♃ 6:47
♀ ♈ 7:19
☽⚺☿ 9:13
☽⚺♅ 10:02
☽⋕♃ 11:06
☽⚹⚷ 11:12
☽⚹♆ 12:12
☽⚺♀ 19:00
☽⚼♄ 19:21
☿⚹♅ 19:39
☽△⚳ 20:20
☽⚺♂ 21:52
☉⋕♆ 23:11

25 Sa
☽△♇ 0:13
☽⋕♇ 1:57
☉☌☽ 3:24
☿□⚷ 11:17
☽∠♅ 11:37
☽△♄ 20:36
☽∠♀ 20:48

26 Su
☽∠♂ 0:34
☿□♆ 0:55
☽⚼♇ 1:26
☽∥☿ 1:41
☽□♃ 9:57
☽⚹♅ 12:44
☽□⚷ 13:50
☽□♆ 14:44
☽∥⚳ 15:07
☽☌☿ 15:43
♂□♇ 16:15
☽⚹♀ 22:17
☽□⚳ 22:52

27 M
☽⚻♇ 2:18
☽⚹♂ 2:52
☉⚺☽ 9:01
☽□♄ 22:13

28 Tu
♀⚻⚳ 8:46
☉∠☽ 11:35
☽△♃ 12:02
☉⋕♃ 12:15
☽□♅ 14:30
☽△⚷ 15:32
☽△♆ 16:24
☽⚺☿ 20:23

29 W
☽⚹⚳ 0:50
☽□♀ 1:08
☽☍♇ 3:53
☽□♂ 7:18
☽⚼♃ 13:10
☉⚹☽ 14:17
☽⚼⚷ 16:32
☽⚼♆ 17:22
☽∠☿ 22:39
☽⚹♄ 23:55

30 Th
☽∠⚳ 2:03
☽∥⚳ 5:53
☉∠♅ 9:02
☽∥☿ 11:07
☽⚻♃ 14:34
☽△♅ 16:46
☽⚻⚷ 17:47
☽⚻♆ 18:36
☿ ♊ 22:30

LONGITUDE

Day	Sid.Time	☉	☽	☽ 12 hour	Mean☊	True☊	☿	♀	♂	⚳	♃	♄	⚷	♅	♆	♇
	h m s	° ' "	° ' "	° ' "	° '	° '	° '	° '	° '	° '	° '	° '	° '	° '	° '	° '
1 F	14 36 14	10♉45 48	29♋26 30	6♌29 25	4♒36.4	4♒04.1	0♊02.1	2♈18.4	6♈30.8	1♍32.2	23♒55.2	15♍08.0	25♒46.9	25♓11.1	26♒15.7	3♑07.5
2 Sa	14 40 10	11 44 02	13♌29 27	20 26 36	4 33.2	4R 04.1	0 32.7	2 45.6	7 17.0	1 39.6	24 02.9	15R 06.4	25 48.7	25 13.7	26 16.6	3R 06.7
3 Su	14 44 07	12 42 14	27 20 53	4♍12 22	4 30.1	4 03.6	0 57.8	3 14.4	8 03.2	1 47.4	24 10.5	15 04.9	25 50.4	25 16.3	26 17.5	3 05.9
4 M	14 48 03	13 40 24	11♍01 04	17 47 02	4 26.9	4 01.3	1 17.5	3 44.7	8 49.4	1 55.5	24 17.9	15 03.5	25 52.0	25 18.8	26 18.3	3 05.0
5 Tu	14 52 00	14 38 32	24 30 17	1♎10 48	4 23.7	3 56.5	1 31.8	4 16.4	9 35.5	2 04.0	24 25.2	15 02.2	25 53.6	25 21.4	26 19.1	3 04.2
6 W	14 55 56	15 36 38	7♎48 34	14 23 32	4 20.5	3 49.0	1 40.8	4 49.5	10 21.5	2 12.8	24 32.3	15 01.0	25 55.1	25 23.8	26 19.9	3 03.3
7 Th	14 59 53	16 34 42	20 55 36	27 24 42	4 17.3	3 38.8	1R 44.4	5 23.9	11 07.6	2 21.9	24 39.3	14 59.9	25 56.6	25 26.3	26 20.6	3 02.4
8 F	15 03 50	17 32 45	3♏50 45	10♏13 39	4 14.2	3 27.0	1 42.9	5 59.6	11 53.6	2 31.4	24 46.2	14 59.0	25 58.0	25 28.7	26 21.3	3 01.4
9 Sa	15 07 46	18 30 46	16 33 22	22 49 50	4 11.0	3 14.3	1 36.5	6 36.6	12 39.5	2 41.2	24 52.8	14 58.1	25 59.4	25 31.1	26 22.0	3 00.4
10 Su	15 11 43	19 28 45	29 03 06	5♐13 12	4 07.8	3 02.2	1 25.4	7 14.7	13 25.5	2 51.3	24 59.4	14 57.3	26 00.7	25 33.4	26 22.6	2 59.5
11 M	15 15 39	20 26 43	11♐20 16	17 24 26	4 04.6	2 51.5	1 09.8	7 53.9	14 11.3	3 01.7	25 05.8	14 56.6	26 01.9	25 35.7	26 23.2	2 58.4
12 Tu	15 19 36	21 24 39	23 25 57	29 25 07	4 01.5	2 43.0	0 50.1	8 34.3	14 57.2	3 12.4	25 12.0	14 56.0	26 03.1	25 38.0	26 23.8	2 57.4
13 W	15 23 32	22 22 34	5♑22 16	11♑17 49	3 58.3	2 37.2	0 26.6	9 15.7	15 43.0	3 23.4	25 18.1	14 55.6	26 04.2	25 40.3	26 24.4	2 56.4
14 Th	15 27 29	23 20 27	17 12 15	23 06 04	3 55.1	2 34.0	29♉59.9	9 58.1	16 28.8	3 34.8	25 24.0	14 55.2	26 05.3	25 42.5	26 24.9	2 55.3
15 F	15 31 25	24 18 20	28 59 50	4♒54 09	3 51.9	2D 32.8	29 30.4	10 41.5	17 14.5	3 46.4	25 29.7	14 54.9	26 06.3	25 44.6	26 25.4	2 54.2
16 Sa	15 35 22	25 16 11	10♒49 40	16 47 01	3 48.8	2 33.0	28 58.6	11 25.8	18 00.2	3 58.3	25 35.3	14 54.7	26 07.2	25 46.8	26 25.8	2 53.0
17 Su	15 39 19	26 14 00	22 46 54	28 49 59	3 45.6	2R 33.4	28 25.2	12 11.0	18 45.8	4 10.5	25 40.7	14D 54.7	26 08.1	25 48.8	26 26.2	2 51.9
18 M	15 43 15	27 11 49	4♓56 56	11♓08 23	3 42.4	2 33.2	27 50.6	12 57.1	19 31.5	4 22.9	25 46.0	14 54.7	26 08.9	25 50.9	26 26.6	2 50.7
19 Tu	15 47 12	28 09 36	17 24 58	23 47 14	3 39.2	2 31.4	27 15.7	13 44.0	20 17.0	4 35.7	25 51.1	14 54.9	26 09.7	25 52.9	26 27.0	2 49.6
20 W	15 51 08	29 07 22	0♈15 37	6♈50 32	3 36.0	2 27.5	26 40.8	14 31.7	21 02.5	4 48.7	25 56.0	14 55.1	26 10.4	25 54.9	26 27.3	2 48.3
21 Th	15 55 05	0♊05 07	13 32 12	20 20 43	3 32.9	2 21.3	26 06.7	15 20.2	21 48.0	5 02.0	26 00.8	14 55.5	26 11.0	25 56.8	26 27.6	2 47.1
22 F	15 59 01	1 02 51	27 16 03	4♉17 56	3 29.7	2 13.3	25 34.0	16 09.3	22 33.4	5 15.5	26 05.4	14 55.9	26 11.5	25 58.7	26 27.8	2 45.9
23 Sa	16 02 58	2 00 34	11♉25 58	18 39 33	3 26.5	2 04.1	25 03.1	16 59.2	23 18.8	5 29.3	26 09.8	14 56.5	26 12.0	26 00.5	26 28.0	2 44.6
24 Su	16 06 54	2 58 16	25 57 54	3♊20 08	3 23.3	1 54.8	24 34.6	17 49.8	24 04.2	5 43.4	26 14.0	14 57.2	26 12.5	26 02.3	26 28.2	2 43.4
25 M	16 10 51	3 55 57	10♊45 14	18 12 07	3 20.2	1 46.5	24 08.9	18 41.0	24 49.5	5 57.7	26 18.1	14 58.0	26 12.9	26 04.1	26 28.4	2 42.1
26 Tu	16 14 48	4 53 36	25 39 41	3♋06 54	3 17.0	1 40.2	23 46.4	19 32.8	25 34.7	6 12.3	26 22.0	14 58.8	26 13.2	26 05.8	26 28.5	2 40.8
27 W	16 18 44	5 51 14	10♋32 46	17 56 23	3 13.8	1 36.2	23 27.5	20 25.3	26 19.9	6 27.1	26 25.7	14 59.8	26 13.4	26 07.5	26 28.6	2 39.4
28 Th	16 22 41	6 48 51	25 17 01	2♌34 02	3 10.6	1D 34.5	23 12.4	21 18.3	27 05.0	6 42.2	26 29.2	15 00.9	26 13.6	26 09.1	26 28.6	2 38.1
29 F	16 26 37	7 46 26	9♌46 59	16 55 32	3 07.5	1 34.6	23 01.4	22 11.8	27 50.1	6 57.4	26 32.5	15 02.1	26 13.7	26 10.7	26R 28.7	2 36.7
30 Sa	16 30 34	8 44 00	23 59 30	0♍58 47	3 04.3	1 35.4	22 54.6	23 05.9	28 35.1	7 13.0	26 35.7	15 03.4	26R 13.8	26 12.3	26 28.7	2 35.4
31 Su	16 34 30	9♊41 32	7♍53 25	14 43 28	3♒01.1	1♒36.1	22♉52.1	24♈00.5	29♈20.1	7♍28.7	26♒38.7	15♍04.8	26♒13.8	26♓13.8	26♒28.6	2♑34.0

1st of Month

Julian Day # 2454952.5
Obliquity 23°26'22"
SVP 5♓07'33"
GC 26♐58.2
Eris 21♈33.2

Day	⚴	⚵	⚶
1	12♋24.7	10♓09.8	8♊39.2
6	14 58.6	12 01.5	10 45.4
11	17 33.0	13 51.2	12 52.3
16	20 07.8	15 38.7	14 59.9
21	22 42.7	17 23.7	17 08.2
26	25 17.8	19 06.1	19 17.0
31	27 52.9	20 45.3	21 26.3

DECLINATION and LATITUDE

Day	☉ Decl	☽ Decl	☽ Lat	☽12h Decl	☿ Decl	☿ Lat	♀ Decl	♀ Lat	♂ Decl	♂ Lat	⚳ Decl	⚳ Lat	♃ Decl	♃ Lat	♄ Decl	♄ Lat
1 F	15N03	20N40	0N24	18N27	22N46	2N40	2N16	1N28	1N33	1S08	23N22	13N22	14S11	0S41	7N54	2N13
2 Sa	15 21	15 59	0S50	13 19	22 49	2 36	2 17	1 17	1 52	1 07	23 15	13 18	14 09	0 41	7 55	2 13
3 Su	15 39	10 31	1 60	7 36	22 49	2 31	2 19	1 07	2 10	1 07	23 08	13 13	14 07	0 41	7 55	2 13
4 M	15 57	4 37	3 02	1 37	22 47	2 25	2 22	0 57	2 28	1 07	23 00	13 08	14 04	0 41	7 55	2 13
5 Tu	16 14	1S23	3 53	4S21	22 42	2 17	2 25	0 47	2 47	1 07	22 53	13 03	14 02	0 41	7 56	2 12
6 W	16 31	7 15	4 31	10 02	22 36	2 08	2 29	0 37	3 05	1 06	22 45	12 59	13 60	0 42	7 56	2 12
7 Th	16 48	12 42	4 54	15 12	22 27	1 58	2 35	0 28	3 23	1 06	22 37	12 54	13 58	0 42	7 56	2 12
8 F	17 04	17 31	5 01	19 36	22 16	1 47	2 40	0 19	3 41	1 06	22 30	12 49	13 56	0 42	7 57	2 12
9 Sa	17 20	21 28	4 53	23 03	22 02	1 35	2 47	0 10	3 60	1 06	22 22	12 45	13 54	0 42	7 57	2 12
10 Su	17 36	24 21	4 31	25 21	21 47	1 22	2 54	0 02	4 18	1 05	22 14	12 40	13 52	0 43	7 57	2 12
11 M	17 52	26 03	3 57	26 25	21 30	1 08	3 02	0S07	4 36	1 05	22 05	12 35	13 50	0 43	7 57	2 11
12 Tu	18 07	26 28	3 12	26 13	21 11	0 53	3 11	0 15	4 54	1 05	21 57	12 31	13 48	0 43	7 57	2 11
13 W	18 22	25 39	2 19	24 48	20 51	0 37	3 20	0 22	5 12	1 05	21 49	12 26	13 46	0 43	7 57	2 11
14 Th	18 37	23 40	1 21	22 17	20 29	0 21	3 29	0 30	5 29	1 04	21 40	12 22	13 44	0 44	7 57	2 11
15 F	18 51	20 40	0 19	18 50	20 06	0 04	3 40	0 37	5 47	1 04	21 32	12 17	13 43	0 44	7 57	2 11
16 Sa	19 05	16 49	0N44	14 37	19 43	0S13	3 51	0 44	6 05	1 04	21 23	12 13	13 41	0 44	7 57	2 11
17 Su	19 19	12 15	1 46	9 46	19 18	0 31	4 02	0 51	6 23	1 03	21 15	12 08	13 39	0 44	7 57	2 10
18 M	19 32	7 09	2 44	4 27	18 53	0 49	4 14	0 58	6 40	1 03	21 06	12 04	13 38	0 44	7 57	2 10
19 Tu	19 45	1 40	3 36	1N11	18 29	1 06	4 26	1 04	6 58	1 03	20 57	11 60	13 36	0 45	7 56	2 10
20 W	19 58	4N03	4 18	6 56	18 04	1 23	4 39	1 10	7 15	1 02	20 48	11 55	13 35	0 45	7 56	2 10
21 Th	20 10	9 46	4 48	12 33	17 40	1 40	4 52	1 16	7 32	1 02	20 39	11 51	13 33	0 45	7 56	2 10
22 F	20 22	15 13	5 03	17 43	17 16	1 56	5 06	1 22	7 50	1 01	20 30	11 47	13 32	0 45	7 56	2 10
23 Sa	20 34	20 01	5 01	22 03	16 54	2 12	5 20	1 27	8 07	1 01	20 21	11 42	13 31	0 46	7 55	2 09
24 Su	20 45	23 45	4 38	25 05	16 33	2 26	5 34	1 32	8 24	1 01	20 12	11 38	13 30	0 46	7 55	2 09
25 M	20 56	25 59	3 58	26 25	16 13	2 40	5 49	1 37	8 41	1 00	20 02	11 34	13 28	0 46	7 54	2 09
26 Tu	21 07	26 22	3 00	25 51	15 56	2 53	6 04	1 42	8 58	0 60	19 53	11 30	13 27	0 46	7 54	2 09
27 W	21 17	24 51	1 50	23 26	15 40	3 04	6 20	1 47	9 14	0 60	19 44	11 26	13 26	0 47	7 53	2 09
28 Th	21 27	21 38	0 34	19 30	15 26	3 15	6 35	1 51	9 31	0 59	19 34	11 22	13 25	0 47	7 53	2 08
29 F	21 36	17 06	0S44	14 28	15 14	3 24	6 51	1 55	9 47	0 59	19 25	11 17	13 24	0 47	7 52	2 08
30 Sa	21 45	11 40	1 58	8 46	15 04	3 32	7 08	1 59	10 04	0 58	19 15	11 13	13 24	0 47	7 51	2 08
31 Su	21N54	5N47	3S03	2N46	14N57	3S40	7N24	2S03	10N20	0S58	19N05	11N09	13S23	0S48	7N51	2N08

Day	⚷ Decl	⚷ Lat	♅ Decl	♅ Lat	♆ Decl	♆ Lat	♇ Decl	♇ Lat
1	6S59	6N18	2S35	0S44	13S07	0S23	17S37	5N47
6	6 55	6 20	2 30	0 44	13 06	0 23	17 37	5 47
11	6 51	6 22	2 26	0 44	13 05	0 23	17 37	5 47
16	6 47	6 23	2 22	0 45	13 04	0 23	17 37	5 47
21	6 44	6 25	2 18	0 45	13 04	0 23	17 37	5 47
26	6 42	6 27	2 14	0 45	13 03	0 23	17 38	5 47
31	6S40	6N29	2S11	0S45	13S04	0S24	17S38	5N47

Day	⚴ Decl	⚴ Lat	⚵ Decl	⚵ Lat	⚶ Decl	⚶ Lat	Eris Decl	Eris Lat
1	0N07	22S50	2S24	5N46	19N31	2S16	4S18	13S41
6	0 58	21 45	1 48	5 41	19 56	2 09	4 17	13 41
11	1 45	20 42	1 12	5 35	20 20	2 02	4 16	13 41
16	2 27	19 41	0 37	5 28	20 41	1 55	4 15	13 41
21	3 05	18 41	0 03	5 22	21 01	1 49	4 14	13 41
26	3 38	17 43	0N31	5 14	21 18	1 42	4 14	13 42
31	4N07	16S46	1N02	5N07	21N34	1S36	4S13	13S42

Moon Phenomena

Max/0 Decl
dy hr mn
4 18:27 0 S
11 20:09 26S29
19 7:02 0 N
25 17:03 26N27
31 23:03 0 S

Max/0 Lat
dy hr mn
1 7:52 0 S
7 23:22 5S01
15 7:12 0 N
22 8:19 5N05
28 10:21 0 S

Perigee/Apogee
dy hr m kilometers
14 2:52 a 404915
26 3:36 p 361155

PH dy hr mn
☽ 1 20:45 11♌36
○ 9 4:03 18♏41
☾ 17 7:27 26♒32
● 24 12:12 3♊28
☽ 31 3:23 9♍50

Void of Course Moon

Last Aspect	☽ Ingress
30 16:46 ♅ △	♌ 1 0:57
2 22:09 ♆ ☍	♍ 3 4:38
5 1:32 ♅ ☍	♎ 5 9:52
7 10:02 ♅ △	♏ 7 16:49
9 18:49 ♆ □	♐ 10 1:50
12 5:56 ♆ ⚹	♑ 12 13:10
15 1:00 ♅ △	♒ 15 2:02
17 10:41 ☿ □	♓ 17 14:18
19 21:44 ☉ ⚹	♈ 19 23:31
21 22:37 ♆ ⚹	♉ 22 4:41
24 0:50 ♆ □	♊ 24 6:35
26 1:19 ♆ △	♋ 26 6:59
28 3:07 ♂ □	♌ 28 7:45
30 8:19 ♂ △	♍ 30 10:19

DAILY ASPECTARIAN

1 F: ☽⚹☿ 1:03; ☽∠♄ 1:10; ☽⊻⚳ 3:35; ☽△♀ 5:02; ☽⊼♇ 6:15; ☽△♂ 12:44; ☽#♇ 16:07; ☽⚼♅ 18:23; ☉□☽ 20:45

2 Sa: ☉∥☽ 2:44; ☽⊻♄ 2:47; ☽⚼♀ 7:37; ☽⚼♇ 7:58; ☽#♃ 8:25; ☽#♆ 12:55; ☽⚼♂ 16:05; ♀□♇ 17:12; ☽☍♃ 18:25; ☽⊼♅ 20:22; ☽☍⚷ 21:22; ☽☍♆ 22:09

3 Su: ☽□☿ 6:29; ☽☌⚳ 7:50; ☽△♇ 10:03; ☽⊼♀ 10:42; ☽∥♄ 10:43; ♀∥♂ 13:26; ☽#⚷ 14:40; ☽⊼♂ 19:53

4 M: ☉△☽ 5:04; ♂#♅ 5:05; ☽☌♄ 7:09; ☽∥♂ 8:10; ☽#♅ 8:20; ☽∥♀ 8:57; ♂∠♃ 17:40; ☽⊼♃ 23:51

5 Tu: ☽☍♅ 1:32; ☽⊼⚷ 2:30; ☽⊼♆ 3:15; ☽#♀ 4:12; ☽∥♅ 4:34; ☽#♂ 5:54; ☉△♄ 9:35; ☉⚼☽ 9:57; ☽△☿ 12:48; ☽⊻⚳ 13:45; ☽□♇ 15:24; ☽☍♀ 18:21; ☽∥⚷ 22:36

6 W: ☽#♄ 2:55; ☽⚼♃ 3:10; ♀#♅ 4:20; ☽☍♂ 4:55; ☽⚼⚷ 5:40; ☽⚼♆ 6:25; ☽⊻♄ 13:08; ☉⊼☽ 15:22; ☽⚼☿ 16:17; ☽∠⚳ 17:22; ♂∠⚷ 18:07

7 Th: ☽∥♆ 1:51; ☿ R 5:01; ☽∥♃ 5:55; ♂∠♆ 6:55; ☽△♃ 6:57; ☽⊼♅ 8:22; ☽△⚷ 9:18; ☽△♆ 10:02; ☽∠♄ 16:48; ☽⊼☿ 20:02; ☉#☽ 21:27; ☽⚹⚳ 21:30; ☽⚹♇ 22:28

8 F: ☽∥♇ 0:36; ☽⊼♀ 4:14; ☉⚼♇ 11:40; ☽⚼♅ 12:31; ☽⊼♂ 16:07; ☽⚹♄ 20:59

9 Sa: ☽∠♇ 2:46; ☽#☿ 3:51; ☉☍☽ 4:03; ☽#⚳ 6:17; ☽⚼♀ 10:10; ☽□♃ 16:05; ☽△♅ 17:14; ☽□⚷ 18:07; ☽□♆ 18:49; ☽⚼♂ 22:42

10 Su: ☉#♇ 1:58; ☽☍☿ 4:31; ☽□⚳ 7:29; ☽⊻♇ 7:39; ☽△♀ 16:51; ⚳△♇ 17:15

11 M: ☽△♂ 6:00; ☽□♄ 7:07; ☉⊼☽ 19:37; ♂⊼♄ 23:24

12 Tu: ☽⚹♃ 3:34; ☽□♅ 4:25; ☽⚹⚷ 5:15; ☽⚹♆ 5:56; ☽⊼☿ 14:23; ☿∠♂ 18:25; ☽☌♇ 19:06; ☽△⚳ 19:56

13 W: ☉⚼☽ 4:25; ☽□♀ 8:22; ☽∠♃ 10:04; ☽∠⚷ 11:34; ☽∠♆ 12:14; ☽△♄ 19:22; ☽⚼☿ 19:41; ☽□♂ 22:26; ☿R♉ 23:54

14 Th: ☽⚼⚳ 2:51; ☉△☽ 13:36; ♀∠♃ 16:35; ☽⊻♃ 16:49; ☽⚹♅ 17:22; ☽#⚳ 17:30; ☽⊻⚷ 18:06; ☽⊻♆ 18:45

15 F: ☽△☿ 1:00; ☽⚼♄ 1:52; ☽#☿ 4:17; ☽⊻♇ 7:56; ☽⊼⚳ 9:52; ☉#☽ 11:15; ♀∠⚷ 13:48; ☽∥♇ 19:19; ☽∠♅ 23:54

16 Sa: ♀∠♆ 0:00; ☽⚹♀ 1:18; ☽⊼♄ 8:14; ☉□♃ 8:46; ☉⚹♅ 13:10; ☽∠♇ 14:11; ☽⚹♂ 15:26; ☽∥♃ 16:55; ☽∥♆ 19:56; ☉□⚷ 21:31; ☉∥☿ 23:46

17 Su: ♄ D 2:08; ☉□♆ 5:07; ☽☌♃ 5:48; ☽⊻♅ 6:03; ☽☌⚷ 6:40; ☽☌♆ 7:16; ☉□☽ 7:27; ☽∠♀ 9:20; ☽□☿ 10:41; ♂⚼⚳ 17:49; ☽⚹♇ 19:54; ☽#♄ 20:24; ☿∠♀ 22:06; ☽☍⚳ 22:53; ☽∠♂ 23:07

18 M: ☽∥⚷ 1:43; ☽#♂ 2:03; ♂#⚷ 7:59; ☉☌☿ 10:03; ☽#♀ 12:28; ☽⊻♀ 16:31; ☽☍♄ 19:14; ☽∥♅ 21:10

19 Tu: ☽⊻♂ 5:46; ♃⊻♅ 14:26; ☽☌♅ 15:57; ☽⊻♃ 15:57; ☽⊻⚷ 16:26; ☽#♅ 16:44; ☽⊻♆ 16:58; ☽⚹☿ 17:40; ☉⚹☽ 21:44

20 W: ☽∥♀ 2:36; ☽□♇ 4:39; ☽⊼⚳ 8:28; ☿□♆ 9:22; ☽#⚷ 11:14; ♀⊼♄ 11:44; ☽∥♂ 14:04; ☽∥♄ 16:13; ☽∠♃ 19:28; ☽∠⚷ 19:48; ☽∠☿ 19:51; ☽∠♆ 20:18; ☿□⚷ 21:02; ☉ ♊ 21:52

21 Th: ☿#♇ 2:15; ☽⊼♄ 2:28; ☉∠☽ 2:57; ☽☌♀ 3:24; ☿□♃ 3:46; ☿⚹♅ 6:47; ☽⚼⚳ 11:39; ☽#♆ 14:16; ☽☌♂ 15:23; ☽#♃ 16:24; ☽⊻☿ 21:11; ☽⊻♅ 21:46; ☽⚹♃ 21:58; ☽⚹⚷ 22:09; ☽⚹♆ 22:37

22 F: ☽⚼♄ 4:34; ☉⊻☽ 6:57; ♂∥♄ 8:12; ☽∥☿ 9:04; ☉∥⚳ 9:09; ☽△♇ 9:23; ☽#♇ 11:31; ☽△⚳ 13:51; ☉∠♀ 19:45; ☽∠♅ 23:17

23 Sa: ☽∥⚳ 1:47; ☉∥☽ 3:12; ☽△♄ 5:51; ☽⊻♀ 9:48; ☽⚼♇ 10:28; ♃☌⚷ 14:13; ☉⊼♇ 17:56; ☽⊻♂ 20:44; ☽☌☿ 21:48

24 Su: ☽⚹♅ 0:07; ☽□⚷ 0:24; ☽□♃ 0:26; ☽□♆ 0:50; ☿⊻♂ 10:10; ☽⊼♇ 10:59; ☽∠♀ 11:52; ☉☌☽ 12:12; ☽□⚳ 16:08; ☽∠♂ 22:25

25 M: ☽□♄ 6:48; ☽⚹♀ 13:34; ☽⊻☿ 21:02; ☽⚹♂ 23:52

26 Tu: ☽□♅ 0:42; ☽△⚷ 0:54; ☽△♃ 1:08; ☽△♆ 1:19; ☽☍♇ 11:17; ☉⊻☽ 15:54; ♂⊻♅ 17:10; ☽⚹⚳ 17:16; ♂⚹⚷ 20:33; ☽∠☿ 20:41

27 W: ☽⚼⚷ 1:06; ☽⚼♃ 1:26; ☽⚼♆ 1:30; ♂⚹♃ 3:20; ♂⚹♆ 4:38; ☽⚹♄ 7:13; ☽□♀ 17:04; ☉∠☽ 17:55; ☽∠⚳ 18:02; ♃☌♆ 20:07; ☉□⚳ 20:13; ☽⚹☿ 20:39

28 Th: ☉∥☽ 1:04; ☽△♅ 1:26; ☽⊼⚷ 1:33; ☽⊼♆ 1:58; ☽⊼♃ 1:59; ☽□♂ 3:07; ☽∠♄ 7:48; ♀#⚷ 8:20; ☽∥⚳ 12:03; ☽⊼♇ 12:06; ♀⚼⚳ 15:00; ☽⊻⚳ 19:12; ☉⚹☽ 20:24; ☽#♇ 21:26

29 F: ☽⚼♅ 2:20; ♆ R 4:30; ☽⊻♄ 8:50; ☽∥☿ 8:53; ☽⚼♇ 13:08; ☽#♃ 16:40; ☽#♆ 18:08; ☿⊻♀ 19:24; ☽□☿ 22:10; ☽△♀ 22:22

30 Sa: ☽⊼♅ 3:48; ☽☍⚷ 3:50; ☽☍♆ 4:15; ☽☍♃ 4:28; ☽∥♂ 6:24; ☽△♂ 8:19; ⚷ R 11:13; ☽△♇ 14:46; ☽∥♄ 15:43; ☽∥♀ 17:48; ☽#⚷ 20:28; ☽☌⚳ 23:16

31 Su: ♅⊻⚷ 0:23; ☿ D 1:22; ☽⚼♀ 2:06; ☉□☽ 3:23; ☽⚼♂ 11:58; ☽☌♄ 12:39; ☽#♅ 14:21; ♂ ♉ 21:19

June 2009

LONGITUDE

Day	Sid.Time	☉	☽	☽ 12 hour	Mean ☊	True ☊	☿	♀	♂	⚳	♃	♄	⚷	♅	♆	♇
	h m s	° ' "	° ' "	° ' "	° '	° '	° '	° '	° '	° '	° '	° '	° '	° '	° '	° '
1 M	16 38 27	10♊39 03	21♍29 05	28♍10 25	2♒57.9	1♒35.5	22♉54.1	24♈55.6	0♉05.0	7♍44.6	26♒41.5	15♍06.3	26♒13.7	26♓15.2	26♒28.5	2♑32.6
2 Tu	16 42 23	11 36 32	4♎47 42	11♎21 05	2 54.8	1R 33.1	23 00.5	25 51.2	0 49.9	8 00.8	26 44.1	15 07.9	26R 13.6	26 16.6	26R 28.4	2R 31.2
3 W	16 46 20	12 34 01	17 50 48	24 17 01	2 51.6	1 28.7	23 11.5	26 47.3	1 34.7	8 17.2	26 46.5	15 09.5	26 13.4	26 18.0	26 28.3	2 29.8
4 Th	16 50 17	13 31 28	0♏39 56	6♏59 41	2 48.4	1 22.3	23 26.9	27 43.8	2 19.4	8 33.8	26 48.8	15 11.3	26 13.2	26 19.3	26 28.1	2 28.3
5 F	16 54 13	14 28 54	13 16 25	19 30 18	2 45.2	1 14.6	23 46.7	28 40.7	3 04.1	8 50.6	26 50.8	15 13.2	26 12.9	26 20.6	26 27.9	2 26.9
6 Sa	16 58 10	15 26 18	25 41 26	1♐49 58	2 42.0	1 06.4	24 10.9	29 38.1	3 48.8	9 07.6	26 52.7	15 15.2	26 12.5	26 21.8	26 27.7	2 25.4
7 Su	17 02 06	16 23 42	7♐56 02	13 59 46	2 38.9	0 58.4	24 39.5	0♉35.8	4 33.3	9 24.8	26 54.4	15 17.3	26 12.1	26 23.0	26 27.4	2 24.0
8 M	17 06 03	17 21 05	20 01 20	26 00 56	2 35.7	0 51.4	25 12.3	1 34.0	5 17.9	9 42.2	26 55.9	15 19.5	26 11.6	26 24.2	26 27.1	2 22.5
9 Tu	17 09 59	18 18 28	1♑58 47	7♑55 07	2 32.5	0 46.1	25 49.2	2 32.6	6 02.4	9 59.7	26 57.2	15 21.8	26 11.0	26 25.3	26 26.8	2 21.0
10 W	17 13 56	19 15 49	13 50 12	19 44 24	2 29.3	0 42.6	26 30.2	3 31.5	6 46.8	10 17.5	26 58.3	15 24.2	26 10.4	26 26.3	26 26.4	2 19.5
11 Th	17 17 53	20 13 10	25 38 03	1♒31 33	2 26.2	0D 41.1	27 15.2	4 30.8	7 31.1	10 35.5	26 59.2	15 26.6	26 09.7	26 27.3	26 26.0	2 18.0
12 F	17 21 49	21 10 30	7♒25 21	13 19 55	2 23.0	0 41.2	28 04.0	5 30.4	8 15.5	10 53.6	27 00.0	15 29.2	26 09.0	26 28.3	26 25.6	2 16.5
13 Sa	17 25 46	22 07 50	19 15 48	25 13 31	2 19.8	0 42.4	28 56.7	6 30.4	8 59.7	11 11.9	27 00.5	15 31.9	26 08.2	26 29.2	26 25.2	2 15.0
14 Su	17 29 42	23 05 09	1♓13 39	7♓16 48	2 16.6	0 44.0	29 53.2	7 30.7	9 43.9	11 30.3	27 00.9	15 34.6	26 07.3	26 30.1	26 24.7	2 13.5
15 M	17 33 39	24 02 27	13 23 35	19 34 34	2 13.5	0R 45.3	0♊53.2	8 31.4	10 28.0	11 49.0	27R 01.0	15 37.5	26 06.4	26 30.9	26 24.2	2 12.0
16 Tu	17 37 35	24 59 46	25 50 22	2♈11 33	2 10.3	0 45.9	1 56.9	9 32.3	11 12.1	12 07.8	27 01.0	15 40.4	26 05.4	26 31.6	26 23.6	2 10.4
17 W	17 41 32	25 57 03	8♈38 37	15 12 02	2 07.1	0 45.1	3 04.2	10 33.5	11 56.1	12 26.8	27 00.8	15 43.4	26 04.4	26 32.3	26 23.0	2 08.9
18 Th	17 45 28	26 54 21	21 52 08	28 39 11	2 03.9	0 42.9	4 14.9	11 35.1	12 40.1	12 45.9	27 00.4	15 46.5	26 03.3	26 33.0	26 22.4	2 07.4
19 F	17 49 25	27 51 39	5♉33 17	12♉34 24	2 00.7	0 39.4	5 29.0	12 36.9	13 24.0	13 05.2	26 59.7	15 49.8	26 02.2	26 33.6	26 21.8	2 05.8
20 Sa	17 53 22	28 48 56	19 42 17	26 56 33	1 57.6	0 35.2	6 46.5	13 38.9	14 07.8	13 24.7	26 58.9	15 53.1	26 01.0	26 34.2	26 21.1	2 04.3
21 Su	17 57 18	29 46 13	4♊16 36	11♊41 38	1 54.4	0 30.7	8 07.4	14 41.3	14 51.6	13 44.3	26 57.9	15 56.5	25 59.7	26 34.7	26 20.4	2 02.8
22 M	18 01 15	0♋43 29	19 10 45	26 42 52	1 51.2	0 26.7	9 31.6	15 43.8	15 35.3	14 04.1	26 56.8	15 59.9	25 58.4	26 35.2	26 19.7	2 01.2
23 Tu	18 05 11	1 40 46	4♋16 49	11♋51 24	1 48.0	0 23.7	10 59.1	16 46.7	16 18.9	14 24.0	26 55.4	16 03.5	25 57.0	26 35.7	26 19.0	1 59.7
24 W	18 09 08	2 38 02	19 25 27	26 57 47	1 44.9	0D 22.1	12 29.8	17 49.7	17 02.5	14 44.1	26 53.8	16 07.2	25 55.6	26 36.0	26 18.2	1 58.1
25 Th	18 13 04	3 35 17	4♌27 23	11♌53 19	1 41.7	0 21.8	14 03.7	18 53.0	17 46.0	15 04.3	26 52.0	16 10.9	25 54.1	26 36.4	26 17.4	1 56.6
26 F	18 17 01	4 32 32	19 14 48	26 31 13	1 38.5	0 22.6	15 40.8	19 56.5	18 29.4	15 24.6	26 50.1	16 14.8	25 52.6	26 36.7	26 16.6	1 55.0
27 Sa	18 20 57	5 29 47	3♍42 08	10♍47 15	1 35.3	0 23.9	17 21.0	21 00.2	19 12.8	15 45.1	26 47.9	16 18.7	25 51.0	26 36.9	26 15.7	1 53.5
28 Su	18 24 54	6 27 01	17 46 24	24 39 36	1 32.2	0 25.3	19 04.3	22 04.2	19 56.1	16 05.8	26 45.6	16 22.7	25 49.4	26 37.1	26 14.8	1 51.9
29 M	18 28 51	7 24 14	1♎26 55	8♎08 31	1 29.0	0R 26.1	20 50.5	23 08.3	20 39.3	16 26.5	26 43.1	16 26.7	25 47.7	26 37.2	26 13.9	1 50.4
30 Tu	18 32 47	8♋21 27	14 44 40	21 15 40	1♒25.8	0♒26.0	22♊39.7	24♉12.6	21♉22.5	16♍47.4	26♒40.4	16♍30.9	25♒45.9	26♓37.3	26♒13.0	1♑48.9

1st of Month

Julian Day # 2454983.5
Obliquity 23°26'22"
SVP 5♓07'28"
GC 26♐58.2
Eris 21♈50.3

Day	⚴		Day	⚵		Day	⚶
1	28♋23.9		1	21♓04.8		1	21♊52.2
6	0♌58.7		6	22 40.0		6	24 01.8
11	3 33.3		11	24 11.6		11	26 11.8
16	6 07.5		16	25 39.0		16	28 22.0
21	8 41.3		21	27 01.9		21	0♋32.3
26	11 14.8		26	28 19.7		26	2 42.8

DECLINATION and LATITUDE

Day	☉ Decl	☽ Decl	☽ Lat	☽12h Decl	☿ Decl	☿ Lat	♀ Decl	♀ Lat	♂ Decl	♂ Lat	⚳ Decl	⚳ Lat	♃ Decl	♃ Lat	♄ Decl	♄ Lat
1 M	22N03	0S14	3S56	3S12	14N52	3S45	7N41	2S07	10N36	0S57	18N55	11N05	13S22	0S48	7N50	2N08
2 Tu	22 11	6 07	4 35	8 55	14 49	3 50	7 58	2 10	10 52	0 57	18 46	11 01	13 21	0 48	7 49	2 08
3 W	22 18	11 36	4 59	14 08	14 48	3 54	8 15	2 14	11 08	0 56	18 36	10 57	13 21	0 48	7 48	2 07
4 Th	22 25	16 30	5 08	18 40	14 49	3 56	8 32	2 17	11 24	0 56	18 26	10 54	13 20	0 49	7 47	2 07
5 F	22 32	20 36	5 01	22 17	14 53	3 58	8 50	2 20	11 40	0 56	18 16	10 50	13 20	0 49	7 47	2 07
6 Sa	22 39	23 43	4 40	24 51	14 58	3 58	9 07	2 23	11 56	0 55	18 06	10 46	13 20	0 49	7 46	2 07
7 Su	22 45	25 41	4 07	26 13	15 06	3 57	9 25	2 25	12 11	0 55	17 56	10 42	13 19	0 50	7 45	2 07
8 M	22 50	26 26	3 22	26 19	15 15	3 56	9 43	2 28	12 26	0 54	17 45	10 38	13 19	0 50	7 44	2 07
9 Tu	22 55	25 55	2 29	25 12	15 26	3 54	10 01	2 30	12 42	0 54	17 35	10 35	13 19	0 50	7 43	2 06
10 W	23 00	24 13	1 30	22 58	15 38	3 50	10 19	2 32	12 57	0 53	17 25	10 31	13 19	0 50	7 42	2 06
11 Th	23 05	21 28	0 27	19 45	15 52	3 46	10 37	2 34	13 12	0 52	17 15	10 27	13 19	0 51	7 40	2 06
12 F	23 09	17 49	0N37	15 43	16 08	3 41	10 55	2 36	13 26	0 52	17 04	10 24	13 19	0 51	7 39	2 06
13 Sa	23 12	13 28	1 40	11 04	16 25	3 36	11 13	2 37	13 41	0 51	16 54	10 20	13 19	0 51	7 38	2 06
14 Su	23 16	8 34	2 39	5 57	16 43	3 30	11 31	2 39	13 55	0 51	16 43	10 16	13 19	0 51	7 37	2 06
15 M	23 18	3 16	3 32	0 31	17 02	3 23	11 49	2 40	14 10	0 50	16 33	10 13	13 19	0 52	7 36	2 05
16 Tu	23 21	2N16	4 17	5N04	17 22	3 15	12 07	2 41	14 24	0 50	16 22	10 09	13 19	0 52	7 34	2 05
17 W	23 23	7 52	4 50	10 37	17 43	3 07	12 25	2 42	14 38	0 49	16 12	10 06	13 19	0 52	7 33	2 05
18 Th	23 24	13 17	5 09	15 51	18 04	2 58	12 43	2 43	14 52	0 49	16 01	10 02	13 20	0 52	7 32	2 05
19 F	23 25	18 16	5 11	20 28	18 27	2 49	13 01	2 44	15 06	0 48	15 51	9 59	13 20	0 53	7 30	2 05
20 Sa	23 26	22 24	4 56	24 01	18 49	2 40	13 19	2 44	15 19	0 48	15 40	9 55	13 21	0 53	7 29	2 05
21 Su	23 26	25 16	4 20	26 05	19 12	2 29	13 37	2 45	15 33	0 47	15 29	9 52	13 21	0 53	7 27	2 04
22 M	23 26	26 26	3 27	26 18	19 35	2 19	13 55	2 45	15 46	0 46	15 18	9 49	13 22	0 54	7 26	2 04
23 Tu	23 26	25 40	2 18	24 34	19 59	2 08	14 12	2 46	15 59	0 46	15 07	9 45	13 23	0 54	7 24	2 04
24 W	23 25	23 01	0 60	21 04	20 22	1 57	14 30	2 46	16 12	0 45	14 57	9 42	13 24	0 54	7 23	2 04
25 Th	23 24	18 47	0S23	16 13	20 44	1 46	14 47	2 46	16 25	0 45	14 46	9 39	13 24	0 54	7 21	2 04
26 F	23 22	13 26	1 42	10 30	21 07	1 34	15 04	2 45	16 38	0 44	14 35	9 36	13 25	0 55	7 19	2 04
27 Sa	23 20	7 27	2 57	4 22	21 29	1 22	15 21	2 45	16 50	0 43	14 24	9 33	13 26	0 55	7 18	2 03
28 Su	23 17	1 16	3 52	1S48	21 49	1 10	15 38	2 45	17 02	0 43	14 13	9 29	13 27	0 55	7 16	2 03
29 M	23 14	4S48	4 36	7 42	22 09	0 58	15 54	2 44	17 14	0 42	14 02	9 26	13 29	0 55	7 14	2 03
30 Tu	23N11	10S28	5S04	13S06	22N28	0S46	16N11	2S44	17N26	0S41	13N50	9N23	13S30	0S56	7N13	2N03

Day	⚷ Decl	⚷ Lat	♅ Decl	♅ Lat	♆ Decl	♆ Lat	♇ Decl	♇ Lat
1	6S40	6N29	2S11	0S45	13S04	0S24	17S38	5N47
6	6 38	6 31	2 08	0 45	13 04	0 24	17 38	5 47
11	6 38	6 33	2 06	0 45	13 05	0 24	17 39	5 47
16	6 37	6 35	2 05	0 46	13 06	0 24	17 39	5 46
21	6 38	6 36	2 04	0 46	13 07	0 24	17 40	5 46
26	6 39	6 38	2 03	0 46	13 08	0 24	17 40	5 45

Day	⚴ Decl	⚴ Lat	⚵ Decl	⚵ Lat	⚶ Decl	⚶ Lat	Eris Decl	Eris Lat
1	4N13	16S35	1N08	5N05	21N37	1S35	4S13	13S42
6	4 37	15 41	1 38	4 57	21 50	1 29	4 13	13 42
11	4 57	14 47	2 06	4 48	22 01	1 22	4 12	13 43
16	5 13	13 56	2 31	4 38	22 09	1 16	4 12	13 43
21	5 26	13 05	2 55	4 27	22 16	1 10	4 12	13 44
26	5 35	12 16	3 15	4 16	22 20	1 04	4 12	13 44

Moon Phenomena

Max/0 Decl
dy hr mn
8 1:58 26S26
15 14:13 0 N
22 2:29 26N27
28 4:57 0 S

Perigee/Apogee
dy hr m kilometers
10 16:05 a 405787
23 10:38 p 358020

Max/0 Lat
dy hr mn
4 1:15 5S08
11 10:17 0 N
18 15:34 5N13
24 17:26 0 S

PH dy hr mn
○ 7 18:13 17♐07
☾ 15 22:16 24♓56
● 22 19:36 1♋30
☽ 29 11:30 7♎52

Void of Course Moon

Last Aspect		☽ Ingress
1 8:33	♅ ☍	♎ 1 15:18
3 18:01	♀ ☍	♏ 3 22:45
6 2:19	♃ □	♐ 6 8:25
8 13:52	♃ ⚹	♑ 8 20:01
11 3:32	☿ △	♒ 11 8:54
13 21:06	☿ □	♓ 13 21:33
16 1:19	♅ ☌	♈ 16 7:53
18 9:36	☉ ⚹	♉ 18 14:21
20 12:03	♃ □	♊ 20 17:01
22 12:21	♃ △	♋ 22 17:13
24 11:26	♅ △	♌ 24 16:51
26 12:30	♃ ☍	♍ 26 17:48
28 15:27	♅ ☍	♎ 28 21:26

DAILY ASPECTARIAN

1 M	♂ ⚼ ♄	0:42
	☽ △ ☿	2:33
	☽ ⚻ ♀	6:37
	☽ ∥ ♅	7:49
	☽ ⚻ ⚷	8:30
	☽ ☍ ♅	8:33
	☽ ⚻ ♆	8:56
	☽ ⚻ ♃	9:22
	♀ ∥ ♄	12:21
	☽ ⚻ ♂	16:22
	☽ □ ♇	19:52
2 Tu	☽ ∥ ⚷	2:17
	☽ ⚼ ☿	5:56
	☽ ⚺ ⚳	6:00
	☽ ⋕ ♄	7:13
	☽ ⋕ ♀	8:17
	♀ ⚹ ⚷	9:35
	♀ ⚺ ♅	11:11
	☽ ⚼ ⚷	11:46
	☽ ⚼ ♆	12:13
	☽ ⚼ ♃	12:45
	☉ △ ☽	13:28
	♀ ⚹ ♆	15:55
	☽ ⚺ ♄	19:01
	☽ ⋕ ♂	21:46
	♀ ⚹ ♃	23:41
3 W	☽ ∥ ♆	6:48
	☽ ∥ ♃	8:09
	☽ ⚻ ☿	10:08
	☽ ∠ ⚳	10:21
	☽ ⋕ ☿	15:18
	☽ △ ⚷	15:38
	☽ ⚻ ♅	15:48
	☽ △ ♆	16:06
	☽ △ ♃	16:43
	☽ ☍ ♀	18:01
	☉ ⚼ ☽	19:38
	☽ ∠ ♄	23:06
4 Th	⚴ ♌	2:27
	☽ ☍ ♂	3:20
	☽ ⚹ ♇	3:25
	♂ △ ♇	4:38
	☽ ∥ ♇	6:08
	☽ ⋕ ⚳	10:14
	☽ ⚹ ⚳	15:20
	☽ ⚼ ♅	20:18
5 F	☉ ⚻ ☽	2:31
	☽ ⚹ ♄	3:45
	☽ ∠ ♇	8:01
	☉ ⋕ ☽	14:27
	☉ □ ♄	19:12
	☽ ☍ ☿	20:58
6 Sa	☽ □ ⚷	1:00
	☽ △ ♅	1:19
	☽ □ ♆	1:30
	☽ □ ♃	2:19
	☽ ⚻ ♀	8:21
	♀ ♉	9:08
	☽ ⚺ ♇	13:08
	♀ ⚼ ♄	16:02
	☽ ⚻ ♂	16:55
7 Su	☽ □ ⚳	3:00
	☽ □ ♄	14:37
	☽ ⚼ ♀	16:30
	☉ ☍ ☽	18:13
8 M	☽ ⚼ ♂	0:35
	☽ ⚻ ☿	10:55
	☽ ⚹ ⚷	12:21
	☽ □ ♅	12:48
	☽ ⚹ ♆	12:52
	☽ ⚹ ♃	13:52
	⚳ ⋕ ♇	16:48
	♀ △ ♇	19:24
9 Tu	☽ ☌ ♇	0:45
	☽ △ ♀	1:14
	☽ △ ♂	8:45
	☿ □ ⚷	12:52
	☽ △ ⚳	16:37
	☽ ∠ ⚷	18:36
	☽ ⚼ ☿	18:58
	☽ ∠ ♆	19:08
	☽ ∠ ♃	20:13
	☿ ⚹ ♅	21:47
	☿ □ ♆	21:54
10 W	♅ ⚺ ♆	1:45
	☽ △ ♄	3:11
	☉ ⋕ ☽	11:19
	☉ ⚻ ☽	12:00
	♂ ⋕ ♆	12:50
	☿ □ ♃	15:35
	☽ ⚼ ⚳	23:55
11 Th	☽ ⚺ ⚷	1:04
	☽ ⚺ ♆	1:38
	☽ ⚹ ♅	1:41
	☽ ⚺ ♃	2:46
	☽ △ ☿	3:32
	☽ ⚼ ♄	9:50
	♂ ⋕ ♃	11:16
	☽ ⚺ ♇	13:33
	☽ □ ♀	19:45
	☉ ⚼ ☽	21:14
12 F	☽ ∥ ♇	1:04
	☽ □ ♂	1:49
	☽ ⋕ ⚳	4:36
	☽ ⚻ ⚳	7:14
	☽ ∠ ♅	8:14
	☽ ⋕ ☿	9:10
	☽ ⚻ ♄	16:26
	☽ ∠ ♇	19:57
	☽ ⋕ ♂	22:57
13 Sa	☽ ∥ ♃	0:49
	☽ ∥ ♆	1:58
	☉ △ ☽	6:17
	☽ ⋕ ♀	10:40
	☽ ☌ ⚷	13:49
	☽ ☌ ♆	14:23
	☽ ⚺ ♅	14:33
	☽ ☌ ♃	15:35
	☽ □ ☿	21:06
14 Su	☿ ∥ ⚳	0:41
	☽ ⚹ ♇	1:59
	☿ ♊	2:48
	☽ ⋕ ♄	4:25
	☽ ∥ ⚷	8:57
	☽ ⚹ ♀	13:35
	☽ ⚹ ♂	17:54
	☽ ☍ ⚳	20:50
15 M	☽ ☍ ♄	4:22
	☽ ∥ ♅	5:10
	♃ R	7:51
	☽ ∠ ♀	21:18
	☉ □ ☽	22:16
	☽ ⋕ ♅	23:10
16 Tu	☽ ⚺ ⚷	0:29
	☽ ∠ ♂	0:44
	☽ ⚺ ♆	1:03
	☽ ☌ ♅	1:19
	☽ ⚺ ♃	2:14
	☿ ⚻ ♇	4:49
	♂ ∠ ♅	10:49
	☽ □ ♇	11:56
	☽ ⚹ ☿	12:38
	☽ ⋕ ⚷	18:39
	☿ ⋕ ♇	19:54
	☽ ∥ ♄	22:39
17 W	☉ △ ⚷	3:02
	☽ ⚺ ♀	3:49
	☽ ∠ ⚷	4:28
	☽ ∠ ♆	5:02
	☽ ∠ ♃	6:11
	☽ ⚺ ♂	6:24
	☽ ⚻ ⚳	7:09
	☉ △ ♆	10:46
	☽ ⚻ ♄	13:00
	☉ □ ♅	14:58
	☽ ∠ ☿	18:51
	☽ ∥ ♀	21:15
	☽ ⋕ ♆	23:08
	♀ ∠ ♅	23:12
18 Th	☽ ⋕ ♃	0:11
	☉ △ ♃	2:30
	♂ △ ⚳	5:41
	☽ ⚹ ⚷	7:25
	☽ ∥ ♂	7:38
	☽ ⚹ ♆	7:59
	☽ ⚺ ♅	8:18
	☽ ⚹ ♃	9:06
	☉ ⚹ ☽	9:36
	☽ ⚼ ⚳	10:41
	☽ ∥ ⚳	12:21
	☽ ⚼ ♄	15:46
	☽ △ ♇	18:01
	☽ ⋕ ♇	20:53
	☽ ⚺ ☿	23:52
19 F	☽ ∥ ☿	1:01
	♀ ⋕ ♆	6:53
	☽ ∠ ♅	10:17
	☽ ☌ ♀	13:01
	☽ △ ⚳	13:10
	☉ ∠ ☽	13:23
	☽ ☌ ♂	14:08
	♀ △ ⚳	15:59
	☽ △ ♄	17:34
	⚶ ♋	18:14
	☽ ⚼ ♇	19:36
20 Sa	♀ ⋕ ♃	2:25
	☉ ∥ ☽	7:24
	☽ □ ⚷	10:27
	☽ □ ♆	11:01
	☽ ⚹ ♅	11:24
	☽ □ ♃	12:03
	☉ ⚺ ☽	16:08
	♂ ∥ ⚳	20:15
	☽ ⚻ ♇	20:22
21 Su	☉ ♋	5:47
	☽ ☌ ☿	6:53
	☉ ∠ ♂	9:31
	♀ ☌ ♂	13:11
	☽ □ ⚳	15:38
	☽ ⚺ ♂	17:58
	☽ ⚺ ♀	18:04
	☽ □ ♄	18:54
	☉ ∠ ♀	22:26
22 M	♀ △ ♄	6:32
	☽ △ ⚷	10:48
	☽ △ ♆	11:23
	☽ □ ♅	11:48
	☽ △ ♃	12:21
	♂ △ ♄	14:45
	☽ ∠ ♂	19:04
	☉ ☌ ☽	19:36
	☽ ∠ ♀	19:44
	☽ ☍ ♇	20:23
23 Tu	♀ ⚼ ♇	4:50
	☉ ☍ ♇	7:43
	☽ ⚼ ⚷	10:33
	☽ ⚼ ♆	11:08
	☽ ⚺ ☿	11:47
	☽ ⚼ ♃	12:05
	☽ ⚹ ⚳	16:24
	☽ ⚹ ♄	18:44
	☽ ⚹ ♂	20:02
	☉ ∥ ☽	21:12
	☽ ⚹ ♀	21:17
	♂ ⚼ ♇	21:40
24 W	☽ ⚻ ⚷	10:20
	☽ ⚻ ♆	10:56
	☽ △ ♅	11:26
	☽ ⚻ ♃	11:52
	☽ ∠ ☿	14:20
	☽ ∥ ☿	14:38
	☽ ∠ ⚳	16:48
	☽ ∠ ♄	18:43
	☽ ⚻ ♇	19:58
	☉ ⚺ ☽	22:31
	♀ ∥ ⚳	22:50
25 Th	☽ ⋕ ♇	5:21
	☽ ∥ ♂	10:41
	☽ ⚼ ♅	11:33
	☽ ∥ ♀	17:23
	☽ ⚹ ☿	17:26
	☽ ⚺ ⚳	17:35
	☽ ∥ ⚳	19:00
	☿ □ ⚳	19:02
	☽ ⚺ ♄	19:04
	☽ ⚼ ♇	20:12
	☽ □ ♂	22:42
26 F	☽ ⋕ ♃	0:03
	☉ ∠ ☽	0:31
	☽ □ ♀	1:14
	☽ ⋕ ♆	1:14
	☿ □ ♄	8:33
	☽ ☍ ⚷	10:55
	☽ ☍ ♆	11:35
	☽ ⚻ ♅	12:09
	☽ ☍ ♃	12:30
	☽ △ ♇	20:58
27 Sa	☽ ∥ ♄	0:37
	☽ ⋕ ⚷	3:09
	☉ ⚹ ☽	3:14
	☽ ⋕ ♅	20:58
	☽ ☌ ⚳	21:02
	☽ ☌ ♄	21:35
28 Su	☽ □ ☿	2:34
	☽ △ ♂	3:57
	☽ △ ♀	8:06
	☽ ∥ ♅	13:00
	☽ ⚻ ⚷	14:01
	☽ ⚻ ♆	14:46
	☽ ☍ ♅	15:27
	☽ ⚻ ♃	15:39
	☿ ⚺ ♂	19:49
29 M	⚳ ☌ ♄	0:18
	☽ □ ♇	0:42
	☽ ∥ ⚷	7:39
	☽ ⚼ ♂	7:57
	☽ ⋕ ♄	10:02
	☉ □ ☽	11:30
	☽ ⚼ ♀	13:03
	☽ ⚼ ⚷	16:46
	☽ ⚼ ♆	17:34
	☽ ⚼ ♃	18:25
30 Tu	☽ ⚺ ♄	3:16
	☽ ⚺ ⚳	3:51
	☽ ∥ ♆	12:18
	☽ ⚻ ♂	12:56
	☽ ∥ ♃	13:57
	☽ ⋕ ⚳	15:00
	☽ △ ☿	17:04
	☽ ⚻ ♀	19:04
	☽ △ ⚷	20:20
	☽ △ ♆	21:12
	☽ ⚻ ♅	21:59
	☽ △ ♃	22:00

LONGITUDE — July 2009

Day	Sid.Time	☉	☽	☽ 12 hour	Mean ☊	True ☊	☿	♀	♂	⚳	♃	♄	⚷	♅	♆	♇
	h m s	° ' "	° ' "	° ' "	° '	° '	° '	° '	° '	° '	° '	° '	° '	° '	° '	° '
1 W	18 36 44	9♋18 39	27♎41 51	4♏03 34	1♒22.6	0♒25.0	24♊31.8	25♉17.1	22♉05.6	17♍08.4	26♒37.5	16♍35.1	25♒44.1	26♓37.3	26♒12.0	1♑47.3
2 Th	18 40 40	10 15 51	10♏21 11	16 35 04	1 19.5	0R 23.2	26 26.5	26 21.9	22 48.6	17 29.6	26R 34.4	16 39.4	25R 42.3	26R 37.3	26R 11.0	1R 45.8
3 F	18 44 37	11 13 03	22 45 34	28 53 04	1 16.3	0 20.6	28 23.7	27 26.8	23 31.5	17 50.8	26 31.1	16 43.8	25 40.4	26 37.3	26 10.0	1 44.3
4 Sa	18 48 33	12 10 14	4♐57 51	11♐00 17	1 13.1	0 17.9	0♋23.4	28 31.9	24 14.4	18 12.2	26 27.7	16 48.3	25 38.4	26 37.2	26 08.9	1 42.8
5 Su	18 52 30	13 07 26	17 00 40	22 59 16	1 09.9	0 15.2	2 25.2	29 37.1	24 57.2	18 33.7	26 24.1	16 52.9	25 36.4	26 37.0	26 07.9	1 41.3
6 M	18 56 26	14 04 37	28 56 23	4♑52 18	1 06.8	0 13.0	4 28.9	0♊42.6	25 39.9	18 55.3	26 20.3	16 57.5	25 34.4	26 36.8	26 06.8	1 39.8
7 Tu	19 00 23	15 01 48	10♑47 17	16 41 36	1 03.6	0 11.4	6 34.3	1 48.2	26 22.6	19 17.1	26 16.4	17 02.2	25 32.3	26 36.6	26 05.7	1 38.3
8 W	19 04 20	15 58 59	22 35 31	28 29 20	1 00.4	0D 10.6	8 41.2	2 54.0	27 05.2	19 38.9	26 12.3	17 07.0	25 30.2	26 36.3	26 04.5	1 36.8
9 Th	19 08 16	16 56 11	4♒23 21	10♒17 51	0 57.2	0 10.5	10 49.1	3 59.9	27 47.7	20 00.8	26 08.0	17 11.8	25 28.0	26 35.9	26 03.4	1 35.3
10 F	19 12 13	17 53 22	16 13 12	22 09 44	0 54.0	0 11.0	12 57.9	5 06.1	28 30.1	20 22.9	26 03.5	17 16.7	25 25.8	26 35.5	26 02.2	1 33.8
11 Sa	19 16 09	18 50 34	28 07 49	4♓07 52	0 50.9	0 11.8	15 07.2	6 12.3	29 12.5	20 45.1	25 58.9	17 21.7	25 23.5	26 35.1	26 01.0	1 32.4
12 Su	19 20 06	19 47 46	10♓10 17	16 15 32	0 47.7	0 12.9	17 16.7	7 18.8	29 54.8	21 07.3	25 54.1	17 26.8	25 21.2	26 34.6	25 59.8	1 30.9
13 M	19 24 02	20 44 59	22 24 02	28 36 17	0 44.5	0 13.8	19 26.2	8 25.4	0♊37.0	21 29.7	25 49.2	17 31.9	25 18.9	26 34.1	25 58.5	1 29.5
14 Tu	19 27 59	21 42 12	4♈52 44	11♈13 52	0 41.3	0 14.5	21 35.4	9 32.1	1 19.2	21 52.2	25 44.1	17 37.1	25 16.5	26 33.5	25 57.3	1 28.0
15 W	19 31 55	22 39 25	17 40 06	24 11 53	0 38.2	0R 14.8	23 44.0	10 39.0	2 01.3	22 14.7	25 38.8	17 42.4	25 14.1	26 32.9	25 56.0	1 26.6
16 Th	19 35 52	23 36 39	0♉49 32	7♉33 23	0 35.0	0 14.8	25 51.9	11 46.0	2 43.3	22 37.4	25 33.4	17 47.7	25 11.6	26 32.2	25 54.7	1 25.2
17 F	19 39 49	24 33 54	14 23 38	21 20 23	0 31.8	0 14.5	27 58.7	12 53.2	3 25.2	23 00.1	25 27.8	17 53.1	25 09.1	26 31.5	25 53.4	1 23.8
18 Sa	19 43 45	25 31 10	28 23 37	5♊33 09	0 28.6	0 14.1	0♌04.5	14 00.5	4 07.0	23 23.0	25 22.1	17 58.5	25 06.6	26 30.7	25 52.0	1 22.4
19 Su	19 47 42	26 28 26	12♊48 38	20 09 36	0 25.5	0 13.6	2 08.9	15 08.0	4 48.8	23 46.0	25 16.3	18 04.1	25 04.0	26 29.9	25 50.7	1 21.1
20 M	19 51 38	27 25 44	27 35 23	5♋05 07	0 22.3	0 13.3	4 12.0	16 15.6	5 30.5	24 09.0	25 10.3	18 09.7	25 01.4	26 29.1	25 49.3	1 19.7
21 Tu	19 55 35	28 23 01	12♋37 53	20 12 34	0 19.1	0 13.1	6 13.6	17 23.3	6 12.1	24 32.1	25 04.2	18 15.3	24 58.8	26 28.2	25 47.9	1 18.4
22 W	19 59 31	29 20 20	27 48 02	5♌23 06	0 15.9	0 13.1	8 13.7	18 31.1	6 53.7	24 55.4	24 58.0	18 21.0	24 56.1	26 27.3	25 46.5	1 17.1
23 Th	20 03 28	0♌17 38	12♌56 34	20 27 20	0 12.8	0 13.1	10 12.1	19 39.1	7 35.1	25 18.7	24 51.6	18 26.8	24 53.4	26 26.3	25 45.1	1 15.8
24 F	20 07 25	1 14 58	27 54 22	5♍16 46	0 09.6	0 13.1	12 08.9	20 47.1	8 16.5	25 42.1	24 45.2	18 32.6	24 50.7	26 25.2	25 43.6	1 14.5
25 Sa	20 11 21	2 12 17	12♍33 47	19 44 50	0 06.4	0 12.9	14 04.0	21 55.3	8 57.7	26 05.5	24 38.6	18 38.5	24 47.9	26 24.2	25 42.2	1 13.2
26 Su	20 15 18	3 09 37	26 49 32	3♎47 37	0 03.2	0 12.6	15 57.4	23 03.6	9 38.9	26 29.1	24 31.8	18 44.5	24 45.2	26 23.0	25 40.7	1 11.9
27 M	20 19 14	4 06 58	10♎39 00	17 23 45	0 00.0	0 12.3	17 49.2	24 12.0	10 20.0	26 52.7	24 25.0	18 50.5	24 42.3	26 21.9	25 39.2	1 10.7
28 Tu	20 23 11	5 04 19	24 02 02	0♏34 09	29♑56.9	0D 12.1	19 39.2	25 20.6	11 01.1	27 16.4	24 18.1	18 56.5	24 39.5	26 20.7	25 37.7	1 09.5
29 W	20 27 07	6 01 40	7♏00 27	13 21 21	29 53.7	0 12.0	21 27.5	26 29.2	11 42.0	27 40.2	24 11.1	19 02.6	24 36.6	26 19.4	25 36.2	1 08.3
30 Th	20 31 04	6 59 02	19 37 19	25 48 52	29 50.5	0 12.1	23 14.1	27 37.9	12 22.8	28 04.1	24 04.0	19 08.8	24 33.8	26 18.2	25 34.7	1 07.1
31 F	20 35 00	7♌56 24	1♐56 31	8♐00 45	29♑47.3	0♒12.6	24♌59.0	28♊46.8	13♊03.6	28♍28.0	23♒56.8	19♍15.0	24♒30.9	26♓16.8	25♒33.2	1♑05.9

1st of Month

Julian Day # 2455013.5
Obliquity 23°26'21"
SVP 5♓07'23"
GC 26♐58.3
Eris 22♈00.0

Day	⚴
1	13♌47.7
6	16 20.1
11	18 51.9
16	21 23.2
21	23 53.9
26	26 24.0
31	28 53.5

Day	⚵
1	29♓31.8
6	0♈37.9
11	1 37.4
16	2 29.5
21	3 13.6
26	3 48.9
31	4 14.9

Day	⚶
1	4♋53.3
6	7 03.7
11	9 14.1
16	11 24.2
21	13 34.2
26	15 43.9
31	17 53.2

DECLINATION and LATITUDE

Day	☉ Decl	☽ Decl	☽ Lat	☽12h Decl	☿ Decl	☿ Lat	♀ Decl	♀ Lat	♂ Decl	♂ Lat	⚳ Decl	⚳ Lat	♃ Decl	♃ Lat	♄ Decl	♄ Lat
1 W	23N07	15S33	5S15	17S48	22N46	0S34	16N27	2S43	17N38	0S41	13N39	9N20	13S31	0S56	7N11	2N03
2 Th	23 03	19 50	5 11	21 37	23 01	0 22	16 43	2 42	17 50	0 40	13 28	9 17	13 32	0 56	7 09	2 03
3 F	22 58	23 09	4 52	24 25	23 15	0 10	16 58	2 41	18 01	0 39	13 17	9 14	13 34	0 56	7 07	2 03
4 Sa	22 53	25 23	4 20	26 03	23 27	0N01	17 14	2 40	18 12	0 39	13 06	9 11	13 35	0 57	7 05	2 02
5 Su	22 48	26 24	3 37	26 26	23 37	0 12	17 29	2 39	18 23	0 38	12 55	9 08	13 36	0 57	7 03	2 02
6 M	22 42	26 10	2 44	25 36	23 45	0 23	17 44	2 38	18 34	0 37	12 43	9 05	13 38	0 57	7 01	2 02
7 Tu	22 36	24 45	1 45	23 37	23 50	0 33	17 58	2 36	18 45	0 37	12 32	9 02	13 40	0 57	6 60	2 02
8 W	22 29	22 14	0 42	20 37	23 52	0 43	18 12	2 35	18 55	0 36	12 21	8 59	13 41	0 58	6 58	2 02
9 Th	22 22	18 47	0N23	16 46	23 52	0 52	18 26	2 33	19 06	0 35	12 09	8 56	13 43	0 58	6 56	2 02
10 F	22 15	14 35	1 28	12 15	23 49	1 01	18 40	2 32	19 16	0 35	11 58	8 53	13 45	0 58	6 53	2 02
11 Sa	22 07	9 48	2 29	7 14	23 44	1 09	18 53	2 30	19 26	0 34	11 47	8 50	13 46	0 58	6 51	2 01
12 Su	21 59	4 36	3 24	1 54	23 35	1 16	19 06	2 28	19 36	0 33	11 35	8 47	13 48	0 59	6 49	2 01
13 M	21 50	0N50	4 11	3N35	23 24	1 23	19 18	2 26	19 45	0 32	11 24	8 44	13 50	0 59	6 47	2 01
14 Tu	21 41	6 20	4 47	9 03	23 10	1 29	19 30	2 24	19 55	0 32	11 12	8 42	13 52	0 59	6 45	2 01
15 W	21 32	11 42	5 10	14 16	22 54	1 34	19 42	2 22	20 04	0 31	11 01	8 39	13 54	0 59	6 43	2 01
16 Th	21 23	16 43	5 18	18 59	22 35	1 38	19 53	2 20	20 13	0 30	10 49	8 36	13 56	0 60	6 41	2 01
17 F	21 13	21 03	5 08	22 52	22 14	1 42	20 04	2 18	20 21	0 29	10 38	8 33	13 58	0 60	6 38	2 01
18 Sa	21 02	24 21	4 40	25 29	21 50	1 44	20 14	2 16	20 30	0 29	10 26	8 31	14 00	1 00	6 36	2 01
19 Su	20 52	26 12	3 54	26 29	21 25	1 46	20 24	2 13	20 38	0 28	10 15	8 28	14 03	1 00	6 34	2 01
20 M	20 40	26 17	2 52	25 36	20 57	1 48	20 33	2 11	20 47	0 27	10 03	8 25	14 05	1 01	6 32	2 00
21 Tu	20 29	24 26	1 36	22 50	20 28	1 48	20 42	2 09	20 55	0 26	9 51	8 23	14 07	1 01	6 29	2 00
22 W	20 17	20 49	0 13	18 28	19 57	1 48	20 51	2 06	21 02	0 26	9 40	8 20	14 09	1 01	6 27	2 00
23 Th	20 05	15 48	1S10	12 56	19 25	1 47	20 59	2 04	21 10	0 25	9 28	8 18	14 12	1 01	6 25	2 00
24 F	19 53	9 53	2 28	6 44	18 51	1 46	21 07	2 01	21 18	0 24	9 16	8 15	14 14	1 01	6 22	2 00
25 Sa	19 40	3 33	3 34	0 21	18 16	1 44	21 14	1 58	21 25	0 23	9 05	8 12	14 16	1 02	6 20	1 60
26 Su	19 27	2S48	4 26	5S52	17 40	1 41	21 20	1 55	21 32	0 22	8 53	8 10	14 19	1 02	6 17	1 60
27 M	19 14	8 48	4 59	11 36	17 03	1 38	21 26	1 53	21 39	0 22	8 41	8 07	14 21	1 02	6 15	1 60
28 Tu	18 60	14 13	5 16	16 37	16 25	1 35	21 32	1 50	21 45	0 21	8 30	8 05	14 24	1 02	6 13	1 60
29 W	18 46	18 49	5 15	20 46	15 47	1 31	21 37	1 47	21 52	0 20	8 18	8 02	14 26	1 02	6 10	1 60
30 Th	18 32	22 27	4 60	23 51	15 08	1 26	21 41	1 44	21 58	0 19	8 06	7 60	14 29	1 02	6 08	1 59
31 F	18N17	24S58	4S30	25S47	14N28	1N21	21N45	1S41	22N04	0S18	7N54	7N58	14S31	1S03	6N05	1N59

Day	⚷ Decl	⚷ Lat	♅ Decl	♅ Lat	♆ Decl	♆ Lat	♇ Decl	♇ Lat
1	6S40	6N39	2S03	0S46	13S10	0S24	17S41	5N45
6	6 42	6 41	2 03	0 46	13 12	0 24	17 42	5 44
11	6 44	6 42	2 04	0 47	13 14	0 24	17 43	5 43
16	6 47	6 43	2 06	0 47	13 16	0 25	17 43	5 42
21	6 51	6 44	2 07	0 47	13 18	0 25	17 44	5 42
26	6 55	6 44	2 09	0 47	13 21	0 25	17 45	5 41
31	6S59	6N45	2S12	0S47	13S24	0S25	17S47	5N40

Day	⚴ Decl	⚴ Lat	⚵ Decl	⚵ Lat	⚶ Decl	⚶ Lat	Eris Decl	Eris Lat
1	5N40	11S29	3N32	4N03	22N23	0S58	4S12	13S45
6	5 43	10 42	3 46	3 50	22 23	0 52	4 12	13 45
11	5 42	9 56	3 56	3 34	22 21	0 46	4 13	13 46
16	5 39	9 12	4 01	3 18	22 17	0 40	4 13	13 46
21	5 33	8 28	4 02	2 60	22 11	0 34	4 14	13 47
26	5 24	7 46	3 58	2 40	22 03	0 28	4 14	13 48
31	5N13	7S04	3N48	2N18	21N53	0S22	4S15	13S48

Moon Phenomena

Max/0 Decl — dy hr mn
5 7:36 26S28
12 20:22 0 N
19 13:01 26N28
25 13:20 0 S

Max/0 Lat — dy hr mn
1 5:03 5S15
8 15:25 0 N
15 23:01 5N18
22 3:49 0 S
28 11:18 5S18

Perigee/Apogee — dy hr m kilometers
7 21:36 a 406232
21 20:26 p 357465

PH dy hr mn
○ 7 9:23 15♑24
7 9:40 A 0.156
◐ 15 9:54 23♈03
● 22 2:36 29♋27
22 2:36 T 06'39"
☽ 28 22:01 5♏57

Void of Course Moon

Last Aspect				☽ Ingress		
30	22:00	♃	△	♏	1	4:20
3	10:04	♀	☍	♐	3	14:12
5	19:18	♅	□	♑	6	2:09
8	9:44	♂	△	♒	8	15:04
11	2:18	♂	□	♓	11	3:45
13	8:04	♅	☌	♈	13	14:41
15	15:08	♆	✶	♉	15	22:31
17	20:49	♅	✶	♊	18	2:42
19	22:13	♅	□	♋	20	3:52
22	2:36	☉	☌	♌	22	3:29
23	20:29	♆	☍	♍	24	3:24
25	23:15	♅	☍	♎	26	5:27
28	2:54	♆	△	♏	28	10:57
30	12:56	♅	△	♐	30	20:11

DAILY ASPECTARIAN

1 W: ♃ ⚺ ♅ 1:05; ☽ ⋕ ♀ 4:58; ♂ ⋕ ♇ 5:42; ☽ ∠ ♄ 7:22; ♅ R 7:39; ☽ ✶ ♇ 7:41; ☽ ∠ ⚳ 8:36; ♀ □ ⚷ 9:44; ☽ ∥ ♇ 11:21; ☽ ⋕ ♂ 11:37; ☿ △ ⚷ 14:58; ⚳ ⋕ ♃ 16:16; ♀ □ ♆ 20:02; ☿ △ ♆ 20:49; ☿ ⚺ ♀ 21:50; ☉ △ ☽ 23:49

2 Th: ☉ ∥ ☿ 1:27; ☿ △ ♃ 1:36; ☿ □ ♅ 2:14; ☽ ⚼ ♅ 2:26; ☽ ⚼ ☿ 2:28; ♀ □ ♃ 4:25; ♀ ✶ ♅ 5:43; ☉ ⚼ ⚷ 10:44; ☽ ✶ ♄ 12:13; ☽ ∠ ♇ 12:19; ☽ ✶ ⚳ 14:10; ☉ ⋕ ☽ 22:25; ☉ ⚼ ♆ 22:44

3 F: ☽ ⋕ ☿ 0:55; ☽ ☍ ♂ 1:35; ⚵ ♈ 1:43; ☽ □ ⚷ 5:41; ☽ □ ♆ 6:39; ☉ ⚼ ♃ 7:10; ☽ □ ♃ 7:19; ☉ ⚼ ☽ 7:20; ☽ △ ♅ 7:33; ☽ ☍ ♀ 10:04; ☽ ⚻ ☿ 13:11; ⚳ ⋕ ♆ 13:18; ☽ ⚺ ♇ 17:35; ☿ ♋ 19:21

4 Sa: ☿ ☍ ♇ 15:30; ☉ ⚻ ☽ 15:33; ☽ □ ♄ 23:44

5 Su: ☽ □ ⚳ 3:12; ♀ ♊ 8:24; ☽ ⚻ ♂ 16:58; ☽ ✶ ⚷ 17:14; ☽ ✶ ♆ 18:18; ☽ ✶ ♃ 18:47; ☽ □ ♅ 19:18; ♀ ⋕ ♇ 20:40; ♂ □ ⚷ 21:02

6 M: ☽ ⚻ ♀ 3:56; ☽ ☌ ♇ 5:30; ☽ ☍ ☿ 13:36; ♂ □ ♆ 14:44; ♀ ⚻ ♇ 20:27; ♂ □ ♃ 20:49; ☽ ∠ ⚷ 23:30

7 Tu: ☽ ∠ ♆ 0:37; ☽ ∠ ♃ 0:59; ☽ ⚼ ♂ 1:16; ♂ ✶ ♅ 7:50; ☉ ☍ ☽ 9:23; ☽ ⋕ ☿ 9:43; ☽ △ ♄ 12:47; ☽ ⚼ ♀ 13:28; ☽ △ ⚳ 17:49; ☉ ⋕ ☽ 21:55

8 W: ☽ ⚺ ⚷ 5:54; ☽ ⚺ ♆ 7:05; ☽ ⚺ ♃ 7:18; ☽ ✶ ♅ 8:10; ☽ △ ♂ 9:44; ☽ ⚺ ♇ 18:19; ☽ ⚼ ♄ 19:31; ☿ ⚼ ⚷ 20:07; ☽ ⋕ ♂ 22:08; ☽ △ ♀ 23:08

9 Th: ☽ ⚼ ⚳ 1:19; ☽ ⋕ ♀ 2:02; ☿ ⚼ ♆ 2:39; ☿ ⚼ ♃ 3:24; ☽ ∥ ♇ 6:33; ☉ ✶ ♄ 7:10; ☽ ∠ ♅ 14:38; ☽ ⚻ ☿ 15:57

10 F: ☽ ∠ ♇ 0:42; ☽ ⚻ ♄ 2:09; ☉ ⚻ ☽ 3:40; ☽ ∥ ♃ 4:21; ☽ ∥ ♆ 7:03; ☽ ⚻ ⚳ 8:41; ☿ ∠ ♂ 8:55; ♃ ☌ ♆ 9:14; ☽ ⋕ ⚳ 13:57; ☽ ☌ ⚷ 18:31; ☽ ☌ ♃ 19:43; ☽ ☌ ♆ 19:46; ☽ ⚺ ♅ 20:54

11 Sa: ☽ □ ♂ 2:18; ☽ ⚼ ☿ 4:52; ☽ ✶ ♇ 6:49; ☉ ⚼ ☽ 12:24; ☽ ⋕ ♄ 13:51; ☽ ∥ ⚷ 14:15; ☽ □ ♀ 17:46

12 Su: ☿ ✶ ♄ 1:56; ♂ ♊ 2:57; ☽ ∥ ♅ 11:15; ☽ ☍ ♄ 14:26; ☽ △ ☿ 17:00; ☉ △ ☽ 20:31; ☽ ☍ ⚳ 22:11

13 M: ☽ ⋕ ♅ 5:27; ☽ ⚺ ⚷ 5:38; ☽ ⚺ ♃ 6:35; ☽ ⚺ ♆ 6:55; ☽ ☌ ♅ 8:04; ♄ ⋕ ⚷ 14:22; ☽ ✶ ♂ 16:48; ☽ □ ♇ 17:30

14 Tu: ☽ ∥ ♄ 1:50; ☽ ⋕ ⚷ 1:56; ☉ ☌ ☿ 2:17; ☿ ✶ ⚳ 3:47; ♂ ⚻ ♇ 4:53; ☉ ✶ ⚳ 6:53; ☽ ✶ ♀ 9:39; ☽ ∠ ⚷ 10:10; ☽ ∠ ♃ 11:00; ☽ ∠ ♆ 11:28; ☽ ∥ ⚳ 20:57; ☽ ∠ ♂ 22:44

15 W: ☽ ⚻ ♄ 0:04; ☽ ⋕ ♆ 7:13; ☽ ⚻ ⚳ 8:41; ☉ □ ☽ 9:54; ☽ ⋕ ♃ 10:18; ☽ □ ☿ 13:19; ☽ ✶ ⚷ 13:51; ☽ ✶ ♃ 14:32; ☽ ✶ ♆ 15:08; ☽ ∠ ♀ 16:00; ☽ ⚺ ♅ 16:16; ☿ ⚻ ⚷ 16:34; ☿ ⚻ ♃ 20:40

16 Th: ☿ ⚻ ♆ 0:32; ☽ △ ♇ 1:04; ☽ ⚼ ♄ 3:33; ☽ ⚺ ♂ 3:35; ☽ ⋕ ♇ 5:12; ☿ △ ♅ 7:34; ☽ ⚼ ⚳ 12:28; ☽ ∥ ♀ 17:47; ☽ ∠ ♅ 18:59; ☽ ∥ ♂ 19:38; ☽ ⚺ ♀ 21:08; ☿ ∠ ♀ 21:46

17 F: ☉ ∥ ☽ 0:55; ☽ ⚼ ♇ 3:28; ☽ △ ♄ 6:06; ☽ ∥ ☿ 6:50; ☉ ⚻ ⚷ 14:08; ☽ △ ⚳ 15:15; ☽ □ ⚷ 18:27; ☉ ✶ ☽ 18:47; ☽ □ ♃ 18:55; ☽ □ ♆ 19:44; ☉ ⚻ ♃ 20:34; ☽ ✶ ♅ 20:49; ☿ ♌ 23:09

18 Sa: ☽ ✶ ☿ 3:19; ☽ ⚻ ♇ 5:00; ☉ ⚻ ♆ 8:33; ☽ ☌ ♂ 10:06; ☿ ⚻ ♇ 14:50; ☉ ∠ ☽ 21:39

19 Su: ☉ △ ♅ 0:37; ☽ ☌ ♀ 4:07; ☽ ∠ ☿ 8:15; ☽ □ ♄ 8:39; ☿ ∠ ♄ 11:13; ☉ ∥ ♂ 16:19; ☽ □ ⚳ 18:19; ☽ △ ⚷ 19:53; ☽ △ ♃ 20:08; ☽ △ ♆ 21:10; ☽ □ ♅ 22:13; ☉ ⚺ ☽ 23:43

20 M: ☽ ☍ ♇ 5:59; ☿ ∥ ♂ 6:48; ☉ ∥ ♀ 8:16; ☽ ⚺ ☿ 12:14; ☽ ⚺ ♂ 13:17; ☿ ∥ ♀ 14:55; ☽ ⚼ ⚷ 19:48; ☽ ⚼ ♃ 19:58; ☽ ⚼ ♆ 21:06; ☉ ∥ ☿ 22:20; ☿ ✶ ♂ 23:33

21 Tu: ☽ ⚺ ♀ 8:09; ☽ ✶ ♄ 8:58; ☽ ∠ ♂ 14:13; ☽ ✶ ⚳ 19:20; ☽ ⚻ ⚷ 19:29; ☽ ⚻ ♃ 19:33; ♀ □ ♄ 20:06; ☽ ⚻ ♆ 20:48; ☽ △ ♅ 21:52; ☽ ∥ ♂ 22:49; ☽ ∥ ♀ 23:51

22 W: ⚳ ⚻ ⚷ 0:42; ⚳ ⚻ ♃ 2:08; ☉ ☌ ☽ 2:36; ☉ ∥ ☽ 2:59; ☽ ∥ ☿ 5:13; ☽ ⚻ ♇ 5:30; ☽ ∠ ♄ 8:50; ☽ ∠ ♀ 9:46; ♃ ☌ ⚷ 12:20; ☽ ✶ ♂ 15:05; ☽ ⋕ ♇ 15:21; ☉ ♌ 16:37; ☽ ☌ ☿ 18:59; ☽ ∠ ⚳ 19:42; ☽ ⚼ ♅ 21:37

23 Th: ☿ ∠ ⚳ 1:40; ☽ ⚼ ♇ 5:17; ☽ ⋕ ♃ 6:46; ☽ ⚺ ♄ 8:50; ☽ ⋕ ♆ 10:23; ☽ ✶ ♀ 11:35; ☿ ⚼ ♅ 15:04; ☽ ☍ ♃ 18:57; ☽ ☍ ⚷ 19:04; ☽ ⚺ ⚳ 20:20; ☽ ☍ ♆ 20:29; ☽ ⚻ ♅ 21:36; ☉ ⚻ ♇ 23:48

24 F: ⚳ ⚻ ♆ 1:31; ☽ ∥ ⚳ 2:26; ☽ △ ♇ 5:24; ☉ ⚺ ☽ 5:48; ☽ ⋕ ⚷ 11:26; ☽ ∥ ♄ 13:28; ☽ □ ♂ 17:45

25 Sa: ☽ ⚺ ☿ 2:53; ☽ ⋕ ♅ 5:13; ☉ ∠ ☽ 8:17; ☽ ☌ ♄ 10:13; ☽ □ ♀ 17:02; ⚳ ☍ ♅ 18:08; ☽ ⚻ ♃ 20:07; ☿ ⋕ ♇ 20:27; ☽ ⚻ ⚷ 20:29; ☽ ∥ ♅ 21:32; ☽ ⚻ ♆ 22:03; ☽ ☍ ♅ 23:15; ☽ ☌ ⚳ 23:24

26 Su: ☿ ⚼ ♇ 3:04; ☽ □ ♇ 7:30; ☽ ∠ ☿ 8:12; ☉ ✶ ☽ 11:43; ☽ ⋕ ♄ 13:38; ☽ ∥ ⚷ 16:15; ☉ ∠ ♄ 16:17; ☽ ⚼ ♃ 21:51; ☽ ⚼ ⚷ 22:20; ☽ △ ♂ 23:25; ☽ ⋕ ⚳ 23:32

27 M: ☽ ⚼ ♆ 0:00; ♀ △ ♃ 4:08; ♀ △ ⚷ 10:12; ☿ ⚺ ♄ 14:06; ☽ ⚺ ♄ 14:43; ☽ ✶ ☿ 14:48; ☽ ∥ ♆ 20:01

28 Tu: ☽ △ ♃ 0:29; ☽ ∥ ♃ 0:54; ☽ △ ⚷ 1:08; ☽ △ ♀ 2:37; ☽ △ ♆ 2:54; ☽ ⚼ ♂ 3:49; ☽ ⚻ ♅ 4:13; ♀ △ ♆ 5:53; ☽ ⚺ ⚳ 6:07; ☽ ⋕ ☿ 9:38; ☽ ✶ ♇ 13:04; ☽ ∥ ♇ 18:06; ☽ ∠ ♄ 18:25; ♀ □ ♅ 20:39; ☉ □ ☽ 22:01; ☉ ⋕ ☽ 23:44

29 W: ☽ ⚼ ♅ 8:08; ☽ ⚼ ♀ 9:17; ☽ ⚻ ♂ 9:21; ☽ ∠ ⚳ 11:03; ☽ ∠ ♇ 17:17; ☽ ⋕ ♀ 18:14; ☽ ⋕ ♂ 20:16; ☽ ✶ ♄ 23:05

30 Th: ☽ □ ☿ 8:08; ☽ □ ♃ 8:31; ☽ □ ⚷ 9:32; ☿ ☍ ♃ 10:39; ☽ □ ♆ 11:31; ☽ △ ♅ 12:56; ♀ □ ⚳ 13:59; ☽ ✶ ⚳ 16:57; ☽ ⚻ ♀ 17:09; ☿ ☍ ⚷ 17:43; ☿ ⋕ ♃ 21:56; ☽ ⚺ ♇ 22:21

31 F: ☿ ☍ ♆ 7:48; ☉ △ ☽ 12:52; ☿ ⚻ ♅ 17:50; ☽ ☍ ♂ 23:22

August 2009

LONGITUDE

Day	Sid.Time	☉	☽	☽ 12 hour	Mean☊	True☊	☿	♀	♂	⚳	♃	♄	⚷	♅	♆	♇
	h m s	° ' "	° ' "	° ' "	° '	° '	° '	° '	° '	° '	° '	° '	° '	° '	° '	° '
1 Sa	20 38 57	8♌53 48	14♐02 06	20♐01 04	29♑44.2	0♒13.4	26♌42.2	29♊55.7	13♊44.2	28♍52.0	23♒49.5	19♍21.3	24♒27.9	26♓15.5	25♒31.6	1♑04.8
2 Su	20 42 54	9 51 11	25 58 08	1♑53 45	29 41.0	0 14.3	28 23.7	1♋04.8	14 24.8	29 16.1	23R 42.2	19 27.6	24R 25.0	26R 14.1	25R 30.1	1R 03.7
3 M	20 46 50	10 48 36	7♑48 20	13 42 19	29 37.8	0 15.2	0♍03.6	2 14.0	15 05.3	29 40.3	23 34.8	19 33.9	24 22.0	26 12.7	25 28.5	1 02.6
4 Tu	20 50 47	11 46 01	19 36 03	25 29 55	29 34.6	0R 15.9	1 41.8	3 23.2	15 45.7	0♎04.5	23 27.3	19 40.3	24 19.1	26 11.2	25 26.9	1 01.5
5 W	20 54 43	12 43 27	1♒24 14	7♒19 17	29 31.5	0 16.1	3 18.3	4 32.6	16 26.0	0 28.7	23 19.8	19 46.8	24 16.1	26 09.7	25 25.4	1 00.4
6 Th	20 58 40	13 40 54	13 15 24	19 12 48	29 28.3	0 15.8	4 53.2	5 42.1	17 06.3	0 53.1	23 12.2	19 53.3	24 13.1	26 08.1	25 23.8	0 59.4
7 F	21 02 36	14 38 21	25 11 47	1♓12 35	29 25.1	0 14.7	6 26.4	6 51.7	17 46.4	1 17.5	23 04.5	19 59.8	24 10.0	26 06.5	25 22.2	0 58.4
8 Sa	21 06 33	15 35 50	7♓15 25	13 20 34	29 21.9	0 12.9	7 58.0	8 01.4	18 26.4	1 42.0	22 56.8	20 06.4	24 07.0	26 04.9	25 20.6	0 57.4
9 Su	21 10 29	16 33 20	19 28 15	25 38 44	29 18.7	0 10.7	9 27.9	9 11.2	19 06.4	2 06.5	22 49.1	20 13.0	24 04.0	26 03.2	25 19.0	0 56.4
10 M	21 14 26	17 30 51	1♈52 15	8♈09 04	29 15.6	0 08.1	10 56.1	10 21.0	19 46.2	2 31.1	22 41.3	20 19.7	24 00.9	26 01.6	25 17.3	0 55.5
11 Tu	21 18 22	18 28 24	14 29 26	20 53 40	29 12.4	0 05.7	12 22.6	11 31.0	20 26.0	2 55.7	22 33.5	20 26.4	23 57.9	25 59.8	25 15.7	0 54.5
12 W	21 22 19	19 25 58	27 21 59	3♉54 41	29 09.2	0 03.8	13 47.5	12 41.1	21 05.7	3 20.4	22 25.7	20 33.2	23 54.8	25 58.1	25 14.1	0 53.7
13 Th	21 26 16	20 23 33	10♉32 01	17 14 11	29 06.0	0D 02.6	15 10.5	13 51.3	21 45.3	3 45.2	22 17.9	20 39.9	23 51.7	25 56.3	25 12.5	0 52.8
14 F	21 30 12	21 21 10	24 01 24	0♊53 48	29 02.8	0 02.3	16 31.8	15 01.6	22 24.8	4 10.0	22 10.0	20 46.8	23 48.6	25 54.5	25 10.8	0 51.9
15 Sa	21 34 09	22 18 48	7♊51 26	14 54 19	28 59.7	0 02.9	17 51.4	16 11.9	23 04.2	4 34.9	22 02.2	20 53.6	23 45.6	25 52.6	25 09.2	0 51.1
16 Su	21 38 05	23 16 28	22 02 20	29 15 14	28 56.5	0 04.1	19 09.0	17 22.4	23 43.5	4 59.8	21 54.3	21 00.5	23 42.5	25 50.7	25 07.6	0 50.3
17 M	21 42 02	24 14 10	6♋32 41	13♋54 11	28 53.3	0 05.5	20 24.8	18 33.0	24 22.7	5 24.8	21 46.5	21 07.5	23 39.4	25 48.8	25 05.9	0 49.6
18 Tu	21 45 58	25 11 53	21 19 05	28 46 39	28 50.1	0R 06.5	21 38.6	19 43.6	25 01.8	5 49.8	21 38.6	21 14.4	23 36.3	25 46.9	25 04.3	0 48.8
19 W	21 49 55	26 09 37	6♌16 00	13♌46 07	28 47.0	0 06.6	22 50.3	20 54.4	25 40.8	6 14.9	21 30.8	21 21.4	23 33.3	25 44.9	25 02.7	0 48.1
20 Th	21 53 52	27 07 23	21 15 59	28 44 31	28 43.8	0 05.4	24 00.0	22 05.2	26 19.7	6 40.1	21 23.0	21 28.5	23 30.2	25 42.9	25 01.0	0 47.4
21 F	21 57 48	28 05 11	6♍10 38	13♍33 20	28 40.6	0 02.9	25 07.5	23 16.1	26 58.4	7 05.2	21 15.2	21 35.5	23 27.1	25 40.9	24 59.4	0 46.7
22 Sa	22 01 45	29 02 59	20 51 42	28 04 54	28 37.4	29♑59.2	26 12.7	24 27.1	27 37.1	7 30.5	21 07.5	21 42.6	23 24.1	25 38.8	24 57.7	0 46.1
23 Su	22 05 41	0♍00 49	5♎12 18	12♎13 24	28 34.3	29 54.9	27 15.5	25 38.1	28 15.7	7 55.8	20 59.8	21 49.8	23 21.0	25 36.7	24 56.1	0 45.5
24 M	22 09 38	0 58 40	19 07 54	25 55 38	28 31.1	29 50.5	28 15.8	26 49.3	28 54.1	8 21.1	20 52.2	21 56.9	23 18.0	25 34.6	24 54.5	0 44.9
25 Tu	22 13 34	1 56 33	2♏36 37	9♏10 59	28 27.9	29 46.7	29 13.4	28 00.5	29 32.5	8 46.5	20 44.6	22 04.1	23 14.9	25 32.5	24 52.8	0 44.4
26 W	22 17 31	2 54 26	15 39 01	22 01 06	28 24.7	29 44.0	0♎08.2	29 11.8	0♋10.7	9 11.9	20 37.0	22 11.3	23 11.9	25 30.4	24 51.2	0 43.8
27 Th	22 21 27	3 52 21	28 17 41	4♐29 19	28 21.5	29D 42.7	1 00.1	0♌23.2	0 48.8	9 37.4	20 29.6	22 18.5	23 08.9	25 28.2	24 49.6	0 43.4
28 F	22 25 24	4 50 17	10♐36 34	16 40 02	28 18.4	29 42.7	1 48.8	1 34.6	1 26.8	10 02.9	20 22.2	22 25.7	23 05.9	25 26.0	24 48.0	0 42.9
29 Sa	22 29 20	5 48 15	22 40 20	28 38 06	28 15.2	29 43.8	2 34.2	2 46.2	2 04.7	10 28.4	20 14.9	22 33.0	23 02.9	25 23.8	24 46.4	0 42.5
30 Su	22 33 17	6 46 14	4♑33 57	10♑28 29	28 12.0	29 45.4	3 16.1	3 57.8	2 42.5	10 54.0	20 07.6	22 40.3	23 00.0	25 21.6	24 44.8	0 42.1
31 M	22 37 14	7♍44 14	16 22 17	22 15 53	28♑08.8	29♑47.0	3♎54.2	5♌09.5	3♋20.2	11♎19.6	20♒00.5	22♍47.6	22♒57.0	25♓19.3	24♒43.2	0♑41.7

1st of Month

Julian Day # 2455044.5
Obliquity 23°26'21"
SVP 5♓07'17"
GC 26♐58.4
Eris 22♈00.6R

Day	⚴
1	29♌23.4
6	1♍52.1
11	4 20.1
16	6 47.5
21	9 14.3
26	11 40.4
31	14 05.8

Day	⚵
1	4♈18.9
6	4 32.8
11	4 36.1R
16	4 28.2R
21	4 09.0R
26	3 38.5R
31	2 57.2R

Day	⚶
1	18♋19.0
6	20 27.8
11	22 35.9
16	24 43.5
21	26 50.4
26	28 56.5
31	1♌01.6

DECLINATION and LATITUDE

Day	☉ Decl	☽ Decl	☽ Lat	☽ 12h Decl	☿ Decl	☿ Lat	♀ Decl	♀ Lat	♂ Decl	♂ Lat	⚳ Decl	⚳ Lat	♃ Decl	♃ Lat	♄ Decl	♄ Lat
1 Sa	18N02	26S17	3S49	26S29	13N48	1N15	21N48	1S38	22N10	0S17	7N43	7N55	14S34	1S03	6N03	1N59
2 Su	17 47	26 22	2 59	25 57	13 07	1 09	21 51	1 35	22 15	0 17	7 31	7 53	14 37	1 03	6 00	1 59
3 M	17 31	25 14	2 01	24 14	12 26	1 03	21 53	1 32	22 21	0 16	7 19	7 50	14 39	1 03	5 57	1 59
4 Tu	17 16	22 59	0 59	21 28	11 45	0 57	21 55	1 29	22 26	0 15	7 07	7 48	14 42	1 03	5 55	1 59
5 W	16 59	19 45	0N06	17 49	11 04	0 50	21 56	1 26	22 31	0 14	6 56	7 46	14 45	1 04	5 52	1 59
6 Th	16 43	15 42	1 11	13 26	10 22	0 42	21 56	1 23	22 36	0 13	6 44	7 43	14 47	1 04	5 50	1 59
7 F	16 26	11 01	2 14	8 30	9 41	0 35	21 56	1 19	22 40	0 12	6 32	7 41	14 50	1 04	5 47	1 59
8 Sa	16 10	5 54	3 11	3 13	8 60	0 27	21 56	1 16	22 45	0 11	6 20	7 39	14 52	1 04	5 44	1 59
9 Su	15 52	0 30	3 60	2N15	8 19	0 19	21 54	1 13	22 49	0 10	6 08	7 36	14 55	1 04	5 42	1 59
10 M	15 35	4N60	4 38	7 43	7 37	0 10	21 53	1 10	22 53	0 10	5 57	7 34	14 58	1 04	5 39	1 59
11 Tu	15 17	10 23	5 04	12 58	6 57	0 02	21 50	1 06	22 57	0 09	5 45	7 32	15 01	1 04	5 36	1 59
12 W	14 60	15 26	5 15	17 45	6 16	0S07	21 47	1 03	23 01	0 08	5 33	7 30	15 03	1 04	5 34	1 59
13 Th	14 41	19 53	5 10	21 48	5 36	0 16	21 44	0 60	23 04	0 07	5 21	7 28	15 06	1 05	5 31	1 58
14 F	14 23	23 26	4 48	24 45	4 56	0 25	21 39	0 57	23 07	0 06	5 09	7 25	15 09	1 05	5 28	1 58
15 Sa	14 04	25 43	4 10	26 18	4 16	0 35	21 35	0 53	23 10	0 05	4 58	7 23	15 11	1 05	5 25	1 58
16 Su	13 46	26 26	3 15	26 08	3 37	0 44	21 29	0 50	23 13	0 04	4 46	7 21	15 14	1 05	5 23	1 58
17 M	13 27	25 23	2 06	24 10	2 59	0 54	21 23	0 47	23 16	0 03	4 34	7 19	15 16	1 05	5 20	1 58
18 Tu	13 07	22 33	0 48	20 31	2 21	1 03	21 16	0 43	23 18	0 02	4 22	7 17	15 19	1 05	5 17	1 58
19 W	12 48	18 10	0S34	15 30	1 43	1 13	21 09	0 40	23 21	0 01	4 10	7 15	15 22	1 05	5 14	1 58
20 Th	12 28	12 37	1 54	9 33	1 07	1 23	21 01	0 37	23 23	0 00	3 59	7 13	15 24	1 05	5 11	1 58
21 F	12 08	6 22	3 05	3 08	0 31	1 33	20 53	0 33	23 25	0N01	3 47	7 11	15 27	1 05	5 09	1 58
22 Sa	11 48	0S06	4 03	3S18	0S04	1 43	20 44	0 30	23 27	0 02	3 35	7 09	15 29	1 05	5 06	1 58
23 Su	11 28	6 25	4 45	9 24	0 38	1 53	20 35	0 27	23 28	0 03	3 23	7 06	15 32	1 06	5 03	1 58
24 M	11 08	12 14	5 07	14 51	1 11	2 03	20 24	0 24	23 30	0 03	3 11	7 04	15 35	1 06	5 00	1 58
25 Tu	10 47	17 16	5 13	19 26	1 43	2 13	20 14	0 20	23 31	0 04	2 60	7 02	15 37	1 06	4 57	1 58
26 W	10 26	21 19	5 01	22 56	2 14	2 23	20 02	0 17	23 32	0 05	2 48	7 00	15 39	1 06	4 54	1 58
27 Th	10 05	24 15	4 35	25 15	2 44	2 32	19 51	0 14	23 33	0 06	2 36	6 58	15 42	1 06	4 52	1 58
28 F	9 44	25 57	3 57	26 19	3 12	2 42	19 38	0 11	23 33	0 07	2 24	6 56	15 44	1 06	4 49	1 58
29 Sa	9 23	26 23	3 09	26 08	3 39	2 52	19 25	0 07	23 34	0 08	2 13	6 55	15 47	1 06	4 46	1 58
30 Su	9 02	25 35	2 13	24 45	4 04	3 01	19 12	0 04	23 34	0 09	2 01	6 53	15 49	1 06	4 43	1 58
31 M	8N40	23S38	1S13	22S16	4S27	3S10	18N58	0S01	23N34	0N11	1N49	6N51	15S51	1S06	4N40	1N58

Day	⚷ Decl	⚷ Lat	♅ Decl	♅ Lat	♆ Decl	♆ Lat	♇ Decl	♇ Lat
1	6S60	6N45	2S13	0S47	13S24	0S25	17S47	5N39
6	7 04	6 45	2 16	0 47	13 27	0 25	17 48	5 38
11	7 09	6 45	2 19	0 48	13 30	0 25	17 49	5 37
16	7 14	6 45	2 23	0 48	13 32	0 25	17 50	5 36
21	7 19	6 45	2 27	0 48	13 35	0 25	17 52	5 35
26	7 25	6 44	2 31	0 48	13 38	0 25	17 53	5 33
31	7S30	6N44	2S35	0S48	13S41	0S25	17S54	5N32

Day	⚴ Decl	⚴ Lat	⚵ Decl	⚵ Lat	⚶ Decl	⚶ Lat	Eris Decl	Eris Lat
1	5N11	6S56	3N45	2N13	21N51	0S21	4S15	13S48
6	4 58	6 15	3 29	1 49	21 38	0 15	4 16	13 49
11	4 43	5 35	3 05	1 22	21 25	0 08	4 17	13 49
16	4 26	4 56	2 36	0 54	21 09	0 02	4 18	13 50
21	4 08	4 17	1 60	0 22	20 52	0N05	4 19	13 50
26	3 49	3 39	1 17	0S11	20 34	0 12	4 20	13 51
31	3N28	3S01	0N28	0S47	20N14	0N19	4S21	13S51

Moon Phenomena

Max/0 Decl

dy hr mn	
1 13:33	26S29
9 2:09	0 N
15 22:07	26N27
21 23:36	0 S
28 20:24	26S24

Max/0 Lat

dy hr mn	
4 21:41	0 N
12 4:53	5N16
18 14:08	0 S
24 18:58	5S13

Perigee/Apogee

dy hr m		kilometers
4 0:45	a	406028
19 4:49	p	359642
31 11:03	a	405268

PH	dy hr mn	
○	6 0:56	13♒43
☍	6 0:40	A 0.402
☾	13 18:56	21♉09
●	20 10:03	27♌32
☽	27 11:43	4♐21

Void of Course Moon

Last Aspect			☽ Ingress	
2 5:43	☿	△	♑	2 8:09
4 13:22	♅	⚹	♒	4 21:09
7 0:21	♆	☌	♓	7 9:35
9 12:46	♅	☌	♈	9 20:24
11 20:04	♆	⚹	♉	12 4:51
14 3:18	♅	⚹	♊	14 10:27
16 6:20	♅	□	♋	16 13:14
18 7:10	♅	△	♌	18 13:58
20 10:03	☉	☌	♍	20 14:02
22 11:45	♂	□	♎	22 15:13
24 18:11	♂	△	♏	24 19:17
26 18:36	♅	△	♐	27 3:17
29 5:27	♅	□	♑	29 14:45

DAILY ASPECTARIAN

1 Sa ♀ ♋ 1:29; ☽□♄ 10:46; ☿∦♆ 13:46; ☽⚹♃ 19:28; ☽⚹⚷ 20:53; ☉⚼☽ 21:33; ☽⚹♆ 23:03; ♀☍♇ 23:37; ☉∦♇ 23:45

2 Su ☽□♅ 0:32; ⚴ ♍ 5:31; ☽△☿ 5:43; ☽□⚳ 6:55; ☽☌♇ 10:17; ☽☍♀ 11:28; ☿⊻⚳ 16:33; ☿ ♍ 23:08

3 M ☽∠♃ 1:33; ☽∠⚷ 3:10; ☽∠♆ 5:25; ☉⚻☽ 6:39; ☉⚼♅ 9:48; ☿△♇ 14:13; ☽⚻♂ 15:43; ☽⚼☿ 17:08; ⚳ ♎ 19:34

4 Tu ☽△♄ 0:09; ☽∦♂ 4:27; ☽⊻♃ 7:46; ☽∦♀ 8:36; ☽⊻⚷ 9:33; ⚳∦⚷ 9:40; ☽⊻♆ 11:52; ☽⚹♅ 13:22; ☽△⚳ 22:03; ☽⊻♇ 23:12

5 W ☽⚼♂ 0:04; ☽⚻☿ 4:28; ☽⚼♄ 6:55; ☽⚻♀ 7:04; ☽∥♇ 12:05; ☉∦☽ 17:56; ☽∠♅ 19:43

6 Th ☉☍☽ 0:56; ☽∥♃ 4:52; ☽⚼⚳ 5:29; ☽∠♇ 5:30; ⚳□♇ 5:58; ☽△♂ 8:13; ☽∥♆ 11:53; ☽⚻♄ 13:29; ☽⚼♀ 16:36; ☽☌♃ 19:48; ☽☌⚷ 21:57

7 F ☽☌♆ 0:21; ☽⊻♅ 1:49; ☽∦☿ 7:26; ☽⚹♇ 11:31; ☽⚻⚳ 12:35; ☽∥⚷ 18:30; ☽∦⚳ 21:54; ♀⚼♃ 22:35

8 Sa ☽∦♄ 0:42; ☽☍☿ 1:36; ☽△♀ 1:40; ☿⚹♀ 3:53; ☉⚼♇ 8:51; ☽∥♅ 16:05; ☉⚻☽ 17:49; ♀⚼⚷ 21:38; ☽□♂ 23:15

9 Su ⚵ R 0:00; ☽☍♄ 1:28; ☽⊻♃ 6:27; ☽⊻⚷ 8:54; ☽⊻♆ 11:20; ☽∦♅ 12:12; ☽☌♅ 12:46; ☽□♇ 22:11; ♀⚼♆ 22:45

10 M ☉∠⚳ 0:09; ☽☍⚳ 1:17; ☉⚼☽ 1:20; ☽∥♄ 2:50; ☽∥⚳ 4:01; ☽∦⚷ 9:26; ☽∥☿ 10:18; ☽∠♃ 11:00; ☽∠⚷ 13:35; ☽∠♆ 16:02; ☿∦⚷ 16:53; ☽□♀ 17:49; ☽⚻☿ 19:30

11 Tu ♂□♄ 0:17; ☉△☽ 8:05; ☽⚻♄ 11:15; ☽⚹♂ 11:45; ☽∦♆ 14:33; ☽⚹♃ 14:57; ☽⚹⚷ 17:38; ☉∦♃ 19:47; ☽⚹♆ 20:04; ☽⊻♅ 21:25; ☉∥☽ 21:57; ☽∦♃ 22:06; ⚳∥♄ 22:32

12 W ☽⚼☿ 2:56; ☽△♇ 6:29; ☽⚻⚳ 11:19; ☽∦♇ 12:23; ☽⚼♄ 15:07; ☽∠♂ 16:49

13 Th ☽∠♅ 0:44; ☿∥♄ 3:04; ☽⚹♀ 6:32; ☉⊻♄ 7:45; ☽△☿ 9:16; ☽⚼♇ 9:34; ☽∥♀ 11:19; ☿∥⚳ 12:15; ☽⚼⚳ 15:09; ♂△♃ 16:31; ☽△♄ 18:14; ☉□☽ 18:56; ☽□♃ 20:46; ☽⊻♂ 21:01; ☽∥♂ 21:31; ☽□⚷ 23:38

14 F ☽□♆ 2:02; ☽⚹♅ 3:18; ☽∠♀ 11:28; ☽⚻♇ 11:56; ☉☍♃ 17:54; ☽△⚳ 18:12

15 Sa ☽⊻♀ 15:28; ☽□☿ 18:41; ☽□♄ 22:16; ♂△⚷ 23:27; ☽△♃ 23:47

16 Su ☉⚹☽ 2:13; ☽△⚷ 2:47; ☽☌♂ 2:57; ☽△♆ 5:08; ☽□♅ 6:20; ☉☍⚷ 10:17; ☽☍♇ 14:36; ☉∦♆ 16:17; ☽□⚳ 22:05

17 M ☽⚼♃ 0:22; ☽⚼⚷ 3:27; ☉∠☽ 4:43; ☽⚼♆ 5:48; ☉⚹♂ 10:59; ☿☌♄ 15:15; ☽∥♂ 18:47; ☉☍♆ 20:56; ☽☌♀ 21:13; ☿∦♅ 21:38; ☽⚹♄ 23:52

18 Tu ☿⚻♃ 0:01; ☽⚻♃ 0:31; ☽⚹☿ 0:34; ♂△♆ 1:29; ☽⚻⚷ 3:40; ☽⚻♆ 6:02; ☽⊻♂ 6:15; ☉⊻☽ 6:41; ☽△♅ 7:10; ☽∥♀ 8:00; ☉⚻♅ 14:04; ☽⚻♇ 15:15; ☽⚹⚳ 23:58

19 W ☽∠♄ 0:09; ☽∦♇ 1:27; ♂□♅ 2:25; ☽∠☿ 2:44; ☽⚼♅ 7:09; ☽∠♂ 7:23; ♀⚹♄ 10:12; ♀⚻♃ 11:08; ⚳⚼♃ 11:35; ☽∦♃ 12:31; ☿⚻⚷ 14:04; ♃⚻♄ 15:08; ☽⚼♇ 15:14; ☽∦♆ 20:06

20 Th ☽☍♃ 0:11; ☽⊻♄ 0:20; ☉∥☽ 0:37; ☽∠⚳ 0:40; ☽⊻♀ 1:26; ☽☍⚷ 3:34; ☽⊻☿ 4:45; ☽☍♆ 6:00; ☽⚻♅ 7:07; ☽⚹♂ 8:29; ☉☌☽ 10:03; ☽△♇ 15:17; ☽∦⚷ 20:28; ☿⚻♆ 21:08

21 F ☽⊻⚳ 1:31; ♀⚻⚷ 3:35; ☽∠♀ 3:41; ☽∥♄ 4:37; ☽∥⚳ 9:56; ☿☍♅ 11:48; ☽∦♅ 14:31; ☊R♑ 19:27; ☽∦☿ 23:24; ☽∥☿ 23:51

22 Sa ☽⚻♃ 0:26; ☽☌♄ 1:25; ☽⚻⚷ 4:11; ☽⚹♀ 6:29; ☽⚻♆ 6:47; ☽☍♅ 7:55; ☽∥♅ 8:50; ☽☌☿ 9:35; ♀⚻♆ 10:08; ☽□♂ 11:45; ☽∦⚳ 12:40; ☉⊻☽ 14:36; ☽□♇ 16:30; ☽∦♄ 18:43; ♀△♅ 23:33; ☉ ♍ 23:40

23 Su ☽⚼♃ 1:20; ☽∥⚷ 3:43; ☽☌⚳ 4:47; ☽⚼⚷ 5:20; ☽⚼♆ 8:03; ☉∠☽ 18:05; ☉△♇ 18:21; ☉∦☽ 19:30; ⚳⚼⚷ 21:21

24 M ☽△♃ 3:01; ☽⊻♄ 5:00; ☽∥♆ 6:13; ☽△⚷ 7:19; ☽△♆ 10:10; ☽⚻♅ 11:21; ☽□♀ 14:55; ☽∥♃ 15:36; ☽⊻☿ 17:26; ☽△♂ 18:11; ☽⚹♇ 20:37; ☉⚹☽ 22:42

25 Tu ☽∥♇ 3:17; ☽∠♄ 8:12; ☽⊻⚳ 11:38; ☽⚼♅ 14:28; ☽∦♀ 16:06; ♂ ♋ 17:17; ☿ ♎ 20:19; ☽∠☿ 22:58; ☽⚼♂ 23:04

26 W ☽∠♇ 0:09; ☿□♂ 3:58; ☽□♃ 9:15; ☽⚹♄ 12:26; ☿∥♅ 13:57; ☽□⚷ 14:11; ☿□♇ 16:10; ♀ ♌ 16:13; ☽∠⚳ 16:43; ☽∦♂ 17:14; ☽□♆ 17:22; ☽△♅ 18:36; ☿∦⚳ 19:29; ♂☍♇ 20:36

27 Th ☽△♀ 4:28; ☽⊻♇ 4:41; ☽⚻♂ 5:07; ☽⚹☿ 5:36; ♀⚻♇ 6:44; ⚳∦♅ 8:00; ⚳⚼♆ 10:51; ☉□☽ 11:43; ♀⊻♂ 18:25; ☽⚹⚳ 22:51

28 F ⚶ ♌ 12:48; ☽⚼♀ 13:07; ☿⚹♀ 13:27; ☽⚹♃ 19:12; ☽□♄ 23:45

29 Sa ☽⚹⚷ 0:45; ☽⚹♆ 4:13; ☽□♅ 5:27; ☽☌♇ 16:11; ☽☍♂ 20:02; ☽□☿ 21:13; ☽⚻♀ 22:38

30 Su ☽∠♃ 1:08; ☉△☽ 4:52; ☽∠⚷ 6:56; ☽∠♆ 10:30; ☽□⚳ 13:21

31 M ☽∦♂ 0:37; ☽⊻♃ 7:20; ☿∦♄ 12:06; ☽△♄ 13:13; ☽⊻⚷ 13:20; ☉⚼☽ 14:07; ☽⊻♆ 16:58; ☽⚹♅ 18:10; ♄⚻⚷ 22:06

LONGITUDE

September 2009

Day	Sid.Time	☉	☽	☽ 12 hour	Mean ☊	True ☊	☿	♀	♂	⚳	♃	♄	⚷	♅	♆	♇
	h m s	° ' "	° ' "	° ' "	° '	° '	° '	° '	° '	° '	° '	° '	° '	° '	° '	° '
1 Tu	22 41 10	8♍42 15	28♑09 48	4♒04 32	28♑05.7	29♑47.7	4♎28.3	6♌21.2	3♋57.7	11♎45.2	19♒53.4	22♍54.9	22♒54.1	25♓17.1	24♒41.6	0♑41.3
2 W	22 45 07	9 40 18	10♒00 29	15 58 03	28 02.5	29R 47.2	4 58.1	7 33.1	4 35.2	12 10.9	19R 46.5	23 02.3	22R 51.2	25R 14.8	24R 40.1	0R 41.0
3 Th	22 49 03	10 38 23	21 57 34	27 59 20	27 59.3	29 44.8	5 23.4	8 45.0	5 12.5	12 36.7	19 39.6	23 09.6	22 48.3	25 12.5	24 38.5	0 40.7
4 F	22 53 00	11 36 29	4♓03 35	10♓10 32	27 56.1	29 40.6	5 43.8	9 57.0	5 49.7	13 02.4	19 32.9	23 17.0	22 45.5	25 10.2	24 37.0	0 40.5
5 Sa	22 56 56	12 34 36	16 20 20	22 33 07	27 52.9	29 34.5	5 59.1	11 09.0	6 26.8	13 28.2	19 26.2	23 24.4	22 42.6	25 07.9	24 35.4	0 40.3
6 Su	23 00 53	13 32 46	28 48 56	5♈07 53	27 49.8	29 27.1	6 09.0	12 21.2	7 03.7	13 54.0	19 19.7	23 31.8	22 39.8	25 05.5	24 33.9	0 40.1
7 M	23 04 49	14 30 57	11♈29 58	17 55 13	27 46.6	29 19.2	6R 13.1	13 33.4	7 40.6	14 19.9	19 13.3	23 39.2	22 37.0	25 03.2	24 32.4	0 39.9
8 Tu	23 08 46	15 29 10	24 23 40	0♉55 18	27 43.4	29 11.4	6 11.3	14 45.7	8 17.3	14 45.8	19 07.0	23 46.6	22 34.3	25 00.8	24 30.8	0 39.8
9 W	23 12 43	16 27 25	7♉30 09	14 08 15	27 40.2	29 04.7	6 03.2	15 58.1	8 53.9	15 11.7	19 00.8	23 54.1	22 31.6	24 58.5	24 29.3	0 39.7
10 Th	23 16 39	17 25 42	20 49 37	27 34 17	27 37.1	28 59.8	5 48.7	17 10.5	9 30.4	15 37.6	18 54.8	24 01.5	22 28.9	24 56.1	24 27.9	0 39.6
11 F	23 20 36	18 24 01	4♊22 20	11♊13 47	27 33.9	28 56.8	5 27.5	18 23.0	10 06.7	16 03.6	18 48.9	24 09.0	22 26.2	24 53.7	24 26.4	0D 39.5
12 Sa	23 24 32	19 22 23	18 08 41	25 07 03	27 30.7	28D 55.9	4 59.8	19 35.6	10 42.9	16 29.6	18 43.1	24 16.4	22 23.6	24 51.3	24 24.9	0 39.5
13 Su	23 28 29	20 20 46	2♋08 52	9♋14 03	27 27.5	28 56.3	4 25.5	20 48.2	11 19.0	16 55.7	18 37.5	24 23.9	22 21.0	24 48.9	24 23.5	0 39.6
14 M	23 32 25	21 19 12	16 22 29	23 33 57	27 24.4	28R 57.3	3 44.8	22 01.0	11 54.9	17 21.8	18 32.0	24 31.4	22 18.4	24 46.5	24 22.1	0 39.6
15 Tu	23 36 22	22 17 39	0♌48 07	8♌04 34	27 21.2	28 57.7	2 58.1	23 13.8	12 30.7	17 47.9	18 26.7	24 38.8	22 15.9	24 44.1	24 20.7	0 39.7
16 W	23 40 18	23 16 09	15 22 47	22 42 07	27 18.0	28 56.6	2 06.1	24 26.6	13 06.4	18 14.0	18 21.6	24 46.3	22 13.4	24 41.7	24 19.3	0 39.8
17 Th	23 44 15	24 14 41	0♍01 50	7♍21 07	27 14.8	28 53.3	1 09.3	25 39.5	13 41.9	18 40.1	18 16.5	24 53.8	22 11.0	24 39.3	24 17.9	0 40.0
18 F	23 48 12	25 13 15	14 39 07	21 54 56	27 11.6	28 47.5	0 08.9	26 52.5	14 17.3	19 06.3	18 11.7	25 01.3	22 08.5	24 36.9	24 16.6	0 40.2
19 Sa	23 52 08	26 11 51	29 07 42	6♎16 36	27 08.5	28 39.5	29♍06.0	28 05.6	14 52.6	19 32.5	18 07.0	25 08.8	22 06.2	24 34.5	24 15.2	0 40.4
20 Su	23 56 05	27 10 28	13♎20 55	20 20 01	27 05.3	28 30.1	28 02.0	29 18.7	15 27.6	19 58.7	18 02.5	25 16.3	22 03.8	24 32.1	24 13.9	0 40.6
21 M	0 00 01	28 09 08	27 13 25	4♏00 47	27 02.1	28 20.3	26 58.4	0♍31.9	16 02.6	20 25.0	17 58.2	25 23.7	22 01.5	24 29.7	24 12.6	0 40.9
22 Tu	0 03 58	29 07 49	10♏41 56	17 16 50	26 58.9	28 11.3	25 56.7	1 45.1	16 37.3	20 51.2	17 54.0	25 31.2	21 59.3	24 27.3	24 11.3	0 41.2
23 W	0 07 54	0♎06 32	23 45 36	0♐08 29	26 55.7	28 03.9	24 58.6	2 58.4	17 12.0	21 17.5	17 50.0	25 38.7	21 57.1	24 24.9	24 10.1	0 41.5
24 Th	0 11 51	1 05 17	6♐25 50	12 38 06	26 52.6	27 58.7	24 05.5	4 11.7	17 46.4	21 43.8	17 46.2	25 46.2	21 54.9	24 22.5	24 08.9	0 41.9
25 F	0 15 47	2 04 04	18 45 49	24 49 34	26 49.4	27 55.8	23 18.9	5 25.1	18 20.7	22 10.1	17 42.6	25 53.6	21 52.8	24 20.2	24 07.6	0 42.3
26 Sa	0 19 44	3 02 52	0♑49 59	6♑47 44	26 46.2	27D 54.8	22 39.9	6 38.5	18 54.9	22 36.5	17 39.1	26 01.1	21 50.7	24 17.8	24 06.5	0 42.7
27 Su	0 23 41	4 01 42	12 43 30	18 37 58	26 43.0	27 55.0	22 09.7	7 52.0	19 28.9	23 02.8	17 35.9	26 08.5	21 48.7	24 15.4	24 05.3	0 43.2
28 M	0 27 37	5 00 34	24 31 50	0♒25 43	26 39.9	27R 55.5	21 49.0	9 05.6	20 02.7	23 29.2	17 32.8	26 16.0	21 46.8	24 13.1	24 04.1	0 43.7
29 Tu	0 31 34	5 59 28	6♒20 18	12 16 10	26 36.7	27 55.2	21D 38.2	10 19.2	20 36.3	23 55.6	17 29.9	26 23.4	21 44.8	24 10.7	24 03.0	0 44.2
30 W	0 35 30	6♎58 23	18 13 52	24 13 56	26♑33.5	27♑53.2	21♍37.7	11♍32.9	21♋09.8	24♎22.0	17♒27.2	26♍30.8	21♒43.0	24♓08.4	24♒01.9	0♑44.8

1st of Month

Julian Day # 2455075.5
Obliquity 23°26'22"
SVP 5♓07'13"
GC 26♐58.5
Eris 21♈51.6R

Day	⚴
1	14♍34.7
6	16 59.2
11	19 23.0
16	21 46.0
21	24 08.3
26	26 29.8

Day	⚵
1	2♈47.7R
6	1 54.7R
11	0 53.3R
16	29♓45.4R
21	28 33.3R
26	27 19.7R

Day	⚶
1	1♌26.5
6	3 30.3
11	5 32.9
16	7 34.2
21	9 33.9
26	11 32.0

DECLINATION and LATITUDE

Day	☉ Decl	☽ Decl	☽ Lat	☽ 12h Decl	☿ Decl	☿ Lat	♀ Decl	♀ Lat	♂ Decl	♂ Lat	⚳ Decl	⚳ Lat	♃ Decl	♃ Lat	♄ Decl	♄ Lat
1 Tu	8N18	20S40	0S09	18S52	4S49	3S19	18N43	0N02	23N34	0N12	1N38	6N49	15S54	1S06	4N37	1N58
2 W	7 57	16 51	0N55	14 40	5 08	3 27	18 28	0 05	23 34	0 13	1 26	6 47	15 56	1 06	4 34	1 58
3 Th	7 35	12 20	1 58	9 52	5 26	3 35	18 12	0 08	23 34	0 14	1 14	6 45	15 58	1 06	4 31	1 58
4 F	7 13	7 18	2 55	4 39	5 41	3 42	17 56	0 11	23 33	0 15	1 03	6 43	16 00	1 06	4 28	1 58
5 Sa	6 50	1 56	3 45	0N49	5 53	3 49	17 39	0 14	23 33	0 16	0 51	6 41	16 02	1 06	4 25	1 58
6 Su	6 28	3N35	4 26	6 20	6 03	3 56	17 22	0 17	23 32	0 17	0 39	6 39	16 04	1 06	4 22	1 58
7 M	6 06	9 03	4 53	11 41	6 09	4 01	17 04	0 20	23 31	0 18	0 28	6 38	16 06	1 06	4 20	1 58
8 Tu	5 43	14 12	5 07	16 36	6 13	4 06	16 46	0 23	23 30	0 19	0 16	6 36	16 08	1 06	4 17	1 58
9 W	5 21	18 49	5 05	20 49	6 13	4 09	16 28	0 26	23 28	0 20	0 05	6 34	16 10	1 06	4 14	1 58
10 Th	4 58	22 33	4 46	24 01	6 09	4 12	16 08	0 29	23 27	0 21	0S07	6 32	16 12	1 06	4 11	1 58
11 F	4 35	25 08	4 11	25 54	6 02	4 13	15 49	0 31	23 25	0 22	0 19	6 30	16 14	1 06	4 08	1 58
12 Sa	4 12	26 16	3 22	26 13	5 51	4 12	15 29	0 34	23 24	0 23	0 30	6 29	16 16	1 06	4 05	1 58
13 Su	3 49	25 45	2 19	24 51	5 35	4 11	15 08	0 37	23 22	0 24	0 42	6 27	16 17	1 06	4 02	1 58
14 M	3 27	23 33	1 07	21 52	5 16	4 07	14 47	0 39	23 20	0 26	0 53	6 25	16 19	1 06	3 59	1 58
15 Tu	3 03	19 49	0S10	17 28	4 53	4 02	14 26	0 42	23 18	0 27	1 04	6 23	16 21	1 06	3 56	1 58
16 W	2 40	14 50	1 27	11 60	4 25	3 55	14 04	0 44	23 15	0 28	1 16	6 22	16 22	1 06	3 53	1 58
17 Th	2 17	8 59	2 39	5 51	3 54	3 46	13 42	0 47	23 13	0 29	1 27	6 20	16 24	1 06	3 50	1 58
18 F	1 54	2 40	3 40	0S33	3 20	3 35	13 19	0 49	23 10	0 30	1 39	6 18	16 25	1 06	3 47	1 58
19 Sa	1 31	3S43	4 26	6 49	2 44	3 22	12 57	0 52	23 08	0 31	1 50	6 16	16 27	1 06	3 44	1 58
20 Su	1 07	9 47	4 54	12 36	2 05	3 07	12 33	0 54	23 05	0 32	2 01	6 15	16 28	1 06	3 41	1 58
21 M	0 44	15 13	5 05	17 36	1 24	2 51	12 10	0 56	23 02	0 34	2 13	6 13	16 29	1 06	3 38	1 58
22 Tu	0 21	19 44	4 58	21 36	0 44	2 33	11 46	0 58	22 59	0 35	2 24	6 11	16 30	1 06	3 36	1 58
23 W	0S03	23 09	4 35	24 23	0 02	2 14	11 21	1 00	22 56	0 36	2 35	6 10	16 31	1 06	3 33	1 59
24 Th	0 26	25 19	3 59	25 46	0N36	1 55	10 56	1 02	22 52	0 37	2 46	6 08	16 33	1 05	3 30	1 59
25 F	0 49	26 10	3 13	26 07	1 12	1 35	10 31	1 04	22 49	0 38	2 58	6 06	16 34	1 05	3 27	1 59
26 Sa	1 13	25 46	2 19	25 06	1 46	1 14	10 06	1 06	22 45	0 40	3 09	6 05	16 35	1 05	3 24	1 59
27 Su	1 36	24 10	1 20	22 58	2 17	0 54	9 40	1 08	22 42	0 41	3 20	6 03	16 36	1 05	3 21	1 59
28 M	1 59	21 31	0 18	19 50	2 43	0 35	9 15	1 10	22 38	0 42	3 31	6 02	16 37	1 05	3 18	1 59
29 Tu	2 23	17 58	0N45	15 54	3 05	0 16	8 48	1 12	22 34	0 43	3 42	5 60	16 37	1 05	3 15	1 59
30 W	2S46	13S41	1N46	11S19	3N21	0N02	8N22	1N13	22N30	0N45	3S53	5N58	16S38	1S05	3N12	1N59

Day	⚷ Decl	⚷ Lat	♅ Decl	♅ Lat	♆ Decl	♆ Lat	♇ Decl	♇ Lat
1	7S31	6N43	2S36	0S48	13S41	0S25	17S55	5N32
6	7 37	6 42	2 41	0 48	13 44	0 25	17 56	5 30
11	7 42	6 41	2 46	0 48	13 46	0 25	17 57	5 29
16	7 47	6 40	2 50	0 48	13 49	0 25	17 59	5 28
21	7 52	6 39	2 55	0 48	13 51	0 25	18 00	5 26
26	7 57	6 37	2 60	0 48	13 53	0 25	18 01	5 25

Day	⚴ Decl	⚴ Lat	⚵ Decl	⚵ Lat	⚶ Decl	⚶ Lat	Eris Decl	Eris Lat
1	3N24	2S54	0N17	0S54	20N10	0N20	4S21	13S51
6	3 03	2 16	0S38	1 31	19 49	0 27	4 22	13 51
11	2 41	1 39	1 38	2 10	19 26	0 34	4 23	13 52
16	2 18	1 03	2 42	2 50	19 03	0 42	4 24	13 52
21	1 56	0 26	3 47	3 30	18 40	0 50	4 25	13 52
26	1 33	0N11	4 52	4 09	18 15	0 58	4 26	13 52

Moon Phenomena

Max/0 Decl

dy	hr mn	
5	8:25	0 N
12	4:32	26N17
18	9:58	0 S
25	3:58	26S11

Perigee/Apogee

dy	hr m		kilometers
16	7:52	p	364056
28	3:27	a	404431

Max/0 Lat

dy	hr mn	
1	3:18	0 N
8	8:42	5N08
14	20:57	0 S
21	1:50	5S05
28	6:54	0 N

PH	dy	hr mn	
○	4	16:04	12♓15
☾	12	2:17	19♊28
●	18	18:45	25♍59
☽	26	4:51	3♑15

Void of Course Moon

Last Aspect			☽ Ingress		
31 18:10	♅	⚹	♒	1	3:44
3 5:20	♆	☌	♓	3	15:59
5 16:54	♅	☌	♈	6	2:15
8 0:13	♅	⚹	♉	8	10:19
10 7:18	♅	⚹	♊	10	16:18
12 11:31	♅	□	♋	12	20:21
14 13:58	♅	△	♌	14	22:40
16 16:12	♀	☌	♍	16	23:57
18 23:57	☿	☌	♎	19	1:27
20 18:44	♆	△	♏	21	4:53
23 3:34	♄	⚹	♐	23	11:44
25 14:16	♄	□	♑	25	22:20
28 3:34	♄	△	♒	28	11:08
30 11:35	♆	☌	♓	30	23:27

DAILY ASPECTARIAN

1 Tu
☽⚺♇ 5:08
☽⚻♂ 12:26
☽△☿ 13:23
☽#♀ 13:47
☿⚼♃ 16:05
☽∥♇ 17:47
☽☍♀ 18:29
☽⚼♄ 19:59
☉⚻☽ 23:16

2 W
☽∠♅ 0:29
☽△⚳ 4:33
☽∥♃ 5:08
♂⚼♃ 6:08
♀∠♄ 10:51
☽∠♇ 11:25
☽∥♆ 17:03
☽☌♃ 19:27
☽⚼♂ 20:19
☽⚼☿ 20:46

3 Th
☉#⚷ 1:23
☽☌⚷ 1:41
☽⚻♄ 2:25
☽☌♆ 5:20
☽⚺♅ 6:27
☽⚼⚳ 11:40
☿□♂ 16:21
☽⚹♇ 17:19
☽∥⚷ 22:45

4 F
☉#☽ 0:26
♀#♇ 0:56
☽⚻☿ 3:22
☽△♂ 3:40
♀⚼♅ 4:16
☽∥☿ 7:04
☽⚻♀ 12:49
☽#♄ 12:53
☉☍☽ 16:04
☽⚻⚳ 18:13
☽∥♅ 20:46

5 Sa
☽#⚳ 4:53
☽⚺♃ 5:57
☽∥⚳ 11:41
☽⚺⚷ 12:16
☽☍♄ 13:47
☽⚺♆ 15:53
☽☌♅ 16:54
☽#♅ 20:03
☽⚼♀ 20:55

6 Su
☽∥♄ 3:23
☽□♇ 3:32
☽∠♃ 10:23
☽#☿ 10:58
☉∥☽ 11:46
☽☍☿ 14:01
☉⚺⚳ 15:47
☽□♂ 16:27
☽∠⚷ 16:43
☽#⚷ 17:40
☽∠♆ 20:19
☉#☿ 20:53
♂⚼⚷ 21:52

7 M
☽△♀ 4:15
☿ R 4:45
☽☍⚳ 5:29
☉⚻☽ 6:07
☽⚹♃ 14:18
☽⚹⚷ 20:39
☽#♆ 21:46
☽⚻♄ 22:51

8 Tu
♀⚹⚳ 0:03
☽⚹♆ 0:13
☽⚺♅ 1:08
☽#♃ 9:42
☽△♇ 11:31
☽∥♀ 12:06
☉⚼☽ 12:06
♀⚼♇ 17:54
☽#♇ 19:11
☽⚻☿ 21:24

9 W
☽⚼♄ 2:34
☽⚹♂ 2:39
☽∠♅ 4:28
☽⚻⚳ 14:22
☽⚼♇ 14:44
☽□♀ 16:49
☉△☽ 17:26
♀#♃ 19:57
☽□♃ 20:36
♂⚼♆ 22:26
☽⚼☿ 23:58

10 Th
☽□⚷ 2:57
☽△♄ 5:45
☽□♆ 6:28
☽∠♂ 6:52
☽∥♂ 7:01
☽⚹♅ 7:18
☽⚻♇ 17:28
☽⚼⚳ 17:59

11 F
☉⚺♀ 1:43
☽△☿ 1:51
♀☍♃ 7:55
☉⚻♃ 9:18
☽⚺♂ 10:31
♇ D 16:59
☽△⚳ 21:03

12 Sa
☽△♃ 0:59
☉□☽ 2:17
☽⚹♀ 2:44
☿∠♀ 5:34
☽△⚷ 7:18
☉∥♄ 9:04
☽□♄ 10:39
☽△♆ 10:47
☽□♅ 11:31
☽☍♇ 21:28
♄⚻♆ 22:59

13 Su
☽⚼♃ 2:30
☽□☿ 3:42
☽∠♀ 6:47
☽⚼⚷ 8:47
☽⚼♆ 12:15
☽☌♂ 16:11

14 M
☽□⚳ 1:42
☽∥♂ 1:44
☽⚻♃ 3:35
♀☍⚷ 5:34
☿⚼♃ 7:47
☉⚹☽ 8:52
☽⚻⚷ 9:53
☽⚺♀ 10:17
☽⚻♆ 13:19
☽⚹♄ 13:43
☽△♅ 13:58
⚵R♓ 23:03
☉⚻⚷ 23:18
☽⚻♇ 23:46

15 Tu
☽⚹☿ 3:23
☽#♇ 9:30
☉∠☽ 11:29
♄☍♅ 12:52
☉#♅ 13:54
☽⚼♅ 14:41
☽∠♄ 14:43
☽#♃ 17:09
☽⚺♂ 20:07
♀☍♆ 21:38

16 W
☽⚼♇ 0:28
☽∠☿ 2:39
☽∥♀ 3:33
☽#♆ 4:25
♀⚻♅ 4:49
☽⚹⚳ 4:49
☽☍♃ 4:51
⚳△♃ 5:50
♀⚺♄ 7:14
☽☍⚷ 11:11
☉⚺☽ 13:51
☽☍♆ 14:38
☽⚻♅ 15:13
☽⚺♄ 15:31
☽☌♀ 16:12
♀#♆ 16:31
☽∠♂ 21:44

17 Th
☽△♇ 1:02
☉⚻♆ 1:18
☽⚺☿ 1:44
☿#♄ 3:26
☽#⚷ 4:33
☽∠⚳ 6:09
☉☍♅ 9:42
☿□♇ 11:47
☉☌♄ 18:23
☽∥♄ 19:46
☽#☿ 21:13
☽#♅ 23:13
☽⚹♂ 23:23

18 F
☉∥☽ 3:03
☿R♍ 3:27
☽#⚳ 3:42
☽⚻♃ 5:49
☽⚺⚳ 7:35
☉#⚳ 10:34
☽⚻⚷ 12:21
☽⚻♆ 15:54
☉#☽ 16:08
☽☍♅ 16:26
☽∥⚳ 16:39
☽☌♄ 17:18
☿∥♅ 17:55
☉☌☽ 18:45
☽∥☿ 20:34
☽∥♅ 20:51
☽⚺♀ 22:07
☽☌☿ 23:57

19 Sa
☽#♄ 0:05
☽□♇ 2:35
☽⚼♃ 6:39
☿⚺♀ 10:36
☽⚼⚷ 13:22
☽∥⚷ 16:08
☽⚼♆ 17:01

20 Su
☿∥⚳ 1:31
☽∠♀ 1:48
☽□♂ 3:46
☽△♃ 8:00
☉☌☿ 10:06
☽#♀ 11:01
☽☌⚳ 11:45
♀ ♍ 13:33
☽△⚷ 14:57
☽∥♆ 17:37
☽△♆ 18:44
☽⚻♅ 19:15
☽⚺♄ 20:46
☽⚺☿ 23:36

21 M
☉⚺☽ 1:45
♀△♇ 2:58
☽⚹♇ 6:06
☽∥♃ 6:16
☽⚹♀ 6:24
☽∥♇ 14:09
♀∠♂ 19:11
☽⚼♅ 21:46
☽∠♄ 23:40

22 Tu
☽∠☿ 0:25
☉∠☽ 6:44
☽∠♇ 9:05
☿☌♄ 9:09
☽△♂ 11:18
☽□♃ 13:04
☽⚺⚳ 19:15
☽□⚷ 20:38
☉ ♎ 21:20
☽#♂ 22:11

23 W
☉∥☿ 0:18
☽□♆ 0:46
☽△♅ 1:13
☽⚹☿ 2:07
☽⚹♄ 3:34
☉#☿ 8:56
☉⚹☽ 12:56
☽⚺♇ 13:03
☉□♇ 14:23
☿☍♅ 15:37
☽⚼♂ 16:40
☽□♀ 19:15
☿⚻♆ 22:22
♂⚻♃ 23:51

24 Th
☽∠⚳ 0:36
⚳△⚷ 9:23
☽⚹♃ 21:56
☽⚻♂ 23:08

25 F
⚳∥♅ 3:13
☽⚹⚷ 6:08
☽⚹⚳ 6:59
☽□☿ 8:31
☽⚹♆ 10:36
☽□♅ 10:59
☽□♄ 14:16
☉⚼♃ 14:51
☽☌♇ 23:45

26 Sa
☿⚺⚳ 1:23
☽∠♃ 3:38
☉□☽ 4:51
☽∠⚷ 12:04
☽△♀ 13:02
☽∠♆ 16:39

27 Su
⚳#♄ 1:56
♀∠⚳ 5:29
☽⚺♃ 9:51
☽☍♂ 14:25
☽#♂ 14:39
☽⚺⚷ 18:25
☽△☿ 18:36
☽□⚳ 21:48
☽⚼♀ 23:00
☽⚺♆ 23:04
☽⚹♅ 23:22

28 M
☽△♄ 3:34
☿⚻⚷ 4:05
☽⚺♇ 12:37
☿#♅ 21:33
☉△☽ 23:14
☽∥♇ 23:34

29 Tu
☽⚼☿ 0:36
☽∠♅ 5:44
⚳△♆ 6:30
☽∥♃ 7:55
☽⚻♀ 8:59
☽⚼♄ 10:20
☿∥♄ 12:19
⚳⚻♅ 12:41
☿ D 13:15
☉⚼⚷ 17:55
☽∠♇ 19:00
☽☌♃ 22:27
☽∥♆ 22:49

30 W
☽⚻♂ 6:10
☽⚻☿ 6:52
☽☌⚷ 6:58
☉⚼☽ 8:10
☽☌♆ 11:35
☽⚺♅ 11:47
☽△⚳ 12:44
☿⚻⚷ 13:35
☽⚻♄ 16:42
♀#⚷ 18:08
☉∥♅ 18:47
♂⚻⚷ 22:38

October 2009

LONGITUDE

Day	Sid.Time	☉	☽	☽ 12 hour	Mean ☊	True ☊	☿	♀	♂	⚳	♃	♄	⚷	♅	♆	♇
	h m s	° ' "	° ' "	° ' "	° '	° '	° '	° '	° '	° '	° '	° '	° '	° '	° '	° '
1 Th	0 39 27	7♎57 20	0♓16 48	6♓22 52	26♑30.3	27♑48.8	21♍47.4	12♍46.6	21♋43.1	24♎48.4	17♒24.7	26♍38.2	21♒41.1	24♓06.1	24♒00.8	0♑45.4
2 F	0 43 23	8 56 19	12 32 26	18 45 45	26 27.1	27R 41.8	22 07.3	14 00.3	22 16.3	25 14.8	17R 22.4	26 45.6	21R 39.4	24R 03.8	23R 59.8	0 46.0
3 Sa	0 47 20	9 55 20	25 02 59	1♈24 12	26 24.0	27 32.2	22 36.9	15 14.1	22 49.2	25 41.2	17 20.3	26 52.9	21 37.7	24 01.5	23 58.8	0 46.7
4 Su	0 51 16	10 54 23	7♈49 25	14 18 34	26 20.8	27 20.7	23 15.8	16 28.0	23 22.0	26 07.7	17 18.4	27 00.3	21 36.0	23 59.2	23 57.8	0 47.3
5 M	0 55 13	11 53 27	20 51 30	27 28 02	26 17.6	27 08.2	24 03.4	17 41.9	23 54.6	26 34.1	17 16.7	27 07.6	21 34.4	23 57.0	23 56.8	0 48.1
6 Tu	0 59 09	12 52 34	4♉07 55	10♉50 55	26 14.4	26 56.0	24 59.0	18 55.9	24 27.0	27 00.6	17 15.1	27 14.9	21 32.8	23 54.7	23 55.9	0 48.8
7 W	1 03 06	13 51 43	17 36 43	24 25 04	26 11.3	26 45.2	26 01.9	20 09.9	24 59.3	27 27.0	17 13.8	27 22.2	21 31.3	23 52.5	23 54.9	0 49.6
8 Th	1 07 03	14 50 54	1♊15 42	8♊08 21	26 08.1	26 36.8	27 11.4	21 24.0	25 31.3	27 53.5	17 12.7	27 29.5	21 29.9	23 50.3	23 54.0	0 50.4
9 F	1 10 59	15 50 08	15 02 51	21 59 01	26 04.9	26 31.2	28 26.6	22 38.1	26 03.2	28 20.0	17 11.7	27 36.7	21 28.5	23 48.1	23 53.2	0 51.2
10 Sa	1 14 56	16 49 24	28 56 44	5♋55 52	26 01.7	26 28.2	29 46.9	23 52.2	26 34.8	28 46.5	17 11.0	27 44.0	21 27.1	23 46.0	23 52.4	0 52.1
11 Su	1 18 52	17 48 42	12♋56 23	19 58 12	25 58.5	26 27.3	1♎11.7	25 06.5	27 06.3	29 13.0	17 10.5	27 51.2	21 25.9	23 43.8	23 51.5	0 53.0
12 M	1 22 49	18 48 03	27 01 16	4♌05 28	25 55.4	26 27.3	2 40.1	26 20.7	27 37.6	29 39.5	17 10.1	27 58.3	21 24.7	23 41.7	23 50.8	0 53.9
13 Tu	1 26 45	19 47 26	11♌10 42	18 16 46	25 52.2	26 26.8	4 11.7	27 35.0	28 08.6	0♏06.1	17D 10.0	28 05.5	21 23.5	23 39.6	23 50.0	0 54.9
14 W	1 30 42	20 46 51	25 23 28	2♍30 27	25 49.0	26 24.7	5 46.0	28 49.4	28 39.4	0 32.6	17 10.0	28 12.6	21 22.4	23 37.6	23 49.3	0 55.9
15 Th	1 34 39	21 46 18	9♍37 20	16 43 41	25 45.8	26 19.8	7 22.3	0♎03.8	29 10.0	0 59.1	17 10.3	28 19.7	21 21.3	23 35.5	23 48.6	0 56.9
16 F	1 38 35	22 45 48	23 48 56	0♎52 33	25 42.7	26 12.0	9 00.4	1 18.2	29 40.4	1 25.6	17 10.8	28 26.8	21 20.4	23 33.5	23 47.9	0 57.9
17 Sa	1 42 32	23 45 20	7♎53 53	14 52 22	25 39.5	26 01.6	10 39.8	2 32.6	0♌10.6	1 52.2	17 11.4	28 33.8	21 19.4	23 31.5	23 47.3	0 59.0
18 Su	1 46 28	24 44 54	21 47 24	28 38 28	25 36.3	25 49.2	12 20.3	3 47.1	0 40.5	2 18.7	17 12.3	28 40.8	21 18.6	23 29.6	23 46.7	1 00.1
19 M	1 50 25	25 44 30	5♏25 04	12♏06 52	25 33.1	25 36.3	14 01.4	5 01.7	1 10.2	2 45.3	17 13.4	28 47.8	21 17.8	23 27.6	23 46.1	1 01.2
20 Tu	1 54 21	26 44 08	18 43 36	25 15 07	25 29.9	25 24.0	15 43.1	6 16.3	1 39.6	3 11.8	17 14.6	28 54.7	21 17.0	23 25.7	23 45.6	1 02.4
21 W	1 58 18	27 43 47	1♐41 23	8♐02 29	25 26.8	25 13.6	17 25.1	7 30.9	2 08.9	3 38.4	17 16.1	29 01.6	21 16.3	23 23.9	23 45.1	1 03.6
22 Th	2 02 14	28 43 29	14 18 39	20 30 11	25 23.6	25 05.7	19 07.3	8 45.5	2 37.8	4 04.9	17 17.8	29 08.5	21 15.7	23 22.0	23 44.6	1 04.8
23 F	2 06 11	29 43 13	26 37 29	2♑41 01	25 20.4	25 00.6	20 49.5	10 00.2	3 06.5	4 31.4	17 19.6	29 15.3	21 15.2	23 20.2	23 44.2	1 06.0
24 Sa	2 10 07	0♏42 58	8♑41 20	14 39 02	25 17.2	24 58.0	22 31.6	11 14.9	3 34.9	4 58.0	17 21.7	29 22.1	21 14.7	23 18.5	23 43.8	1 07.3
25 Su	2 14 04	1 42 45	20 34 47	26 29 14	25 14.1	24D 57.2	24 13.5	12 29.6	4 03.1	5 24.5	17 24.0	29 28.8	21 14.3	23 16.7	23 43.4	1 08.6
26 M	2 18 01	2 42 34	2♒23 05	8♒17 02	25 10.9	24R 57.1	25 55.1	13 44.4	4 31.0	5 51.0	17 26.4	29 35.5	21 13.9	23 15.0	23 43.1	1 09.9
27 Tu	2 21 57	3 42 24	14 11 47	20 08 01	25 07.7	24 56.8	27 36.4	14 59.2	4 58.7	6 17.5	17 29.1	29 42.2	21 13.6	23 13.4	23 42.8	1 11.2
28 W	2 25 54	4 42 16	26 06 25	2♓07 35	25 04.5	24 55.0	29 17.4	16 14.0	5 26.0	6 44.0	17 31.9	29 48.8	21 13.4	23 11.8	23 42.5	1 12.6
29 Th	2 29 50	5 42 10	8♓12 07	14 20 32	25 01.4	24 51.0	0♏57.9	17 28.9	5 53.1	7 10.5	17 35.0	29 55.3	21 13.2	23 10.2	23 42.2	1 14.0
30 F	2 33 47	6 42 05	20 33 17	26 50 45	24 58.2	24 44.4	2 38.1	18 43.7	6 19.9	7 37.0	17 38.2	0♎01.9	21 13.1	23 08.6	23 42.0	1 15.4
31 Sa	2 37 43	7♏42 02	3♈13 11	9♈40 45	24♑55.0	24♑35.2	4♏17.8	19♎58.6	6♌46.4	8♏03.5	17♒41.6	0♎08.3	21♒13.0	23♓07.1	23♒41.8	1♑16.9

1st of Month

Julian Day # 2455105.5
Obliquity 23°26'22"
SVP 5♓07'10"
GC 26♐58.5
Eris 21♈36.2R

Day	⚴	⚵	⚶
1	28♍50.3	26♓07.6R	13♌28.1
6	1♎10.0	24 59.5R	15 22.1
11	3 28.7	23 57.9R	17 13.9
16	5 46.4	23 05.2R	19 03.0
21	8 03.1	22 23.2R	20 49.3
26	10 18.6	21 53.3R	22 32.4
31	12 32.9	21 36.3R	24 11.9

DECLINATION and LATITUDE

Day	☉ Decl	☽ Decl	☽ Lat	☽ 12h Decl	☿ Decl	☿ Lat	♀ Decl	♀ Lat	♂ Decl	♂ Lat	⚳ Decl	⚳ Lat	♃ Decl	♃ Lat	♄ Decl	♄ Lat
1 Th	3S09	8S50	2N43	6S14	3N33	0N19	7N55	1N15	22N26	0N46	4S04	5N57	16S39	1S05	3N09	1N59
2 F	3 33	3 34	3 34	0 50	3 39	0 35	7 28	1 17	22 22	0 47	4 15	5 55	16 39	1 05	3 07	1 59
3 Sa	3 56	1N56	4 15	4N42	3 41	0 49	7 01	1 18	22 18	0 48	4 26	5 54	16 40	1 05	3 04	1 59
4 Su	4 19	7 27	4 44	10 09	3 37	1 02	6 34	1 20	22 14	0 50	4 37	5 52	16 40	1 05	3 01	1 59
5 M	4 42	12 46	4 59	15 15	3 29	1 14	6 06	1 21	22 10	0 51	4 48	5 51	16 41	1 05	2 58	1 59
6 Tu	5 05	17 35	4 59	19 42	3 16	1 24	5 38	1 22	22 05	0 52	4 58	5 49	16 41	1 04	2 55	1 59
7 W	5 28	21 35	4 42	23 11	2 59	1 32	5 10	1 23	22 01	0 54	5 09	5 48	16 42	1 04	2 52	1 60
8 Th	5 51	24 28	4 08	25 23	2 39	1 40	4 42	1 24	21 56	0 55	5 20	5 46	16 42	1 04	2 50	1 60
9 F	6 14	25 55	3 20	26 03	2 14	1 46	4 14	1 26	21 52	0 56	5 31	5 45	16 42	1 04	2 47	1 60
10 Sa	6 37	25 46	2 20	25 05	1 47	1 51	3 46	1 27	21 47	0 58	5 41	5 43	16 42	1 04	2 44	1 60
11 Su	6 59	23 59	1 11	22 31	1 16	1 54	3 17	1 27	21 42	0 59	5 52	5 42	16 42	1 04	2 41	1 60
12 M	7 22	20 42	0S03	18 35	0 44	1 57	2 48	1 28	21 37	1 00	6 03	5 40	16 42	1 04	2 39	2 00
13 Tu	7 44	16 11	1 17	13 34	0 09	1 58	2 19	1 29	21 32	1 02	6 13	5 39	16 42	1 04	2 36	2 00
14 W	8 07	10 45	2 27	7 48	0S28	1 59	1 50	1 30	21 28	1 03	6 24	5 37	16 42	1 04	2 33	2 00
15 Th	8 29	4 46	3 27	1 40	1 06	1 59	1 21	1 30	21 23	1 05	6 34	5 36	16 42	1 04	2 30	2 00
16 F	8 51	1S26	4 14	4S30	1 46	1 58	0 52	1 31	21 18	1 06	6 44	5 34	16 42	1 03	2 28	2 01
17 Sa	9 13	7 30	4 46	10 23	2 26	1 56	0 23	1 31	21 13	1 07	6 55	5 33	16 41	1 03	2 25	2 01
18 Su	9 35	13 07	4 59	15 39	3 08	1 54	0S06	1 32	21 08	1 09	7 05	5 31	16 41	1 03	2 22	2 01
19 M	9 57	17 58	4 56	20 02	3 50	1 51	0 35	1 32	21 03	1 10	7 15	5 30	16 41	1 03	2 20	2 01
20 Tu	10 19	21 49	4 36	23 18	4 32	1 47	1 05	1 32	20 57	1 12	7 26	5 29	16 40	1 03	2 17	2 01
21 W	10 40	24 27	4 02	25 17	5 15	1 44	1 34	1 33	20 52	1 13	7 36	5 27	16 39	1 03	2 14	2 01
22 Th	11 01	25 47	3 17	25 57	5 57	1 39	2 03	1 33	20 47	1 15	7 46	5 26	16 39	1 03	2 12	2 01
23 F	11 22	25 48	2 24	25 20	6 40	1 35	2 32	1 33	20 42	1 16	7 56	5 24	16 38	1 03	2 09	2 01
24 Sa	11 43	24 34	1 25	23 32	7 23	1 30	3 02	1 33	20 37	1 18	8 06	5 23	16 37	1 03	2 07	2 02
25 Su	12 04	22 15	0 23	20 43	8 05	1 24	3 31	1 33	20 32	1 19	8 16	5 22	16 37	1 02	2 04	2 02
26 M	12 25	18 59	0N39	17 04	8 48	1 19	3 60	1 33	20 27	1 21	8 26	5 20	16 36	1 02	2 02	2 02
27 Tu	12 45	14 58	1 40	12 44	9 29	1 13	4 29	1 32	20 21	1 23	8 36	5 19	16 35	1 02	1 59	2 02
28 W	13 05	10 21	2 37	7 52	10 11	1 07	4 58	1 32	20 16	1 24	8 46	5 17	16 34	1 02	1 57	2 02
29 Th	13 25	5 17	3 28	2 37	10 52	1 01	5 27	1 31	20 11	1 26	8 55	5 16	16 33	1 02	1 54	2 02
30 F	13 45	0N05	4 10	2N50	11 32	0 54	5 56	1 31	20 06	1 27	9 05	5 15	16 32	1 02	1 52	2 03
31 Sa	14S05	5N35	4N41	8N18	12S12	0N48	6S25	1N31	20N01	1N29	9S15	5N13	16S31	1S02	1N49	2N03

Day	⚷ Decl	⚷ Lat	♅ Decl	♅ Lat	♆ Decl	♆ Lat	♇ Decl	♇ Lat
1	8S02	6N35	3S04	0S48	13S55	0S25	18S03	5N23
6	8 06	6 33	3 09	0 48	13 57	0 25	18 04	5 22
11	8 10	6 31	3 13	0 48	13 58	0 25	18 05	5 21
16	8 14	6 29	3 17	0 48	13 59	0 25	18 07	5 20
21	8 17	6 27	3 21	0 47	14 00	0 25	18 08	5 18
26	8 20	6 25	3 24	0 47	14 01	0 25	18 09	5 17
31	8S23	6N23	3S27	0S47	14S01	0S25	18S10	5N16

Day	⚴ Decl	⚴ Lat	⚵ Decl	⚵ Lat	⚶ Decl	⚶ Lat	Eris Decl	Eris Lat
1	1N11	0N47	5S56	4S47	17N51	1N07	4S27	13S52
6	0 49	1 24	6 56	5 23	17 26	1 15	4 28	13 52
11	0 28	2 01	7 52	5 57	17 01	1 25	4 29	13 52
16	0 07	2 37	8 41	6 29	16 36	1 34	4 30	13 52
21	0S13	3 15	9 24	6 57	16 12	1 44	4 31	13 52
26	0 31	3 52	9 59	7 23	15 48	1 55	4 32	13 52
31	0S48	4N31	10S27	7S45	15N26	2N06	4S33	13S51

Moon Phenomena

Max/0 Decl
dy hr mn
2 15:37 0 N
9 9:48 26N03
15 18:27 0 S
22 12:10 25S57
29 23:36 0 N

Max/0 Lat
dy hr mn
5 11:13 5N01
11 23:02 0 S
18 6:52 5S00
25 8:52 0 N

Perigee/Apogee
dy hr m kilometers
13 12:25 p 369067
25 23:28 a 404166

PH dy hr mn
○ 4 6:11 11♈10
☾ 11 8:57 18♋11
● 18 5:34 24♎59
☽ 26 0:43 2♒44

Void of Course Moon

Last Aspect	☽ Ingress
3 3:30 ♄ ☍	♈ 3 9:22
5 5:47 ♂ □	♉ 5 16:34
7 17:20 ♄ △	♊ 7 21:48
10 1:36 ♀ □	♋ 10 1:49
12 1:38 ♄ ✶	♌ 12 5:04
13 21:21 ♆ ☍	♍ 14 7:46
16 10:19 ♂ ✶	♎ 16 10:31
18 5:34 ☉ ☌	♏ 18 14:24
20 18:58 ♄ ✶	♐ 20 20:50
23 6:40 ☉ ✶	♑ 23 6:40
25 18:16 ♄ △	♒ 25 19:09
28 7:23 ♆ ☌	♓ 28 7:46
30 4:57 ♅ ☌	♈ 30 17:57

DAILY ASPECTARIAN

1 Th
☉#♄ 0:08
☽✶♇ 0:57
☽∥⚷ 3:43
☽#♀ 4:39
☿✶♂ 6:01
☽⚼♂ 13:15
☉⊼☽ 16:23
☽⚼⚳ 19:23
☽∥⚳ 21:02
☽#☿ 23:35

2 F
☉∥☽ 0:05
☉⚼♆ 1:23
☽#♄ 2:01
☽∥♅ 2:05
☽☍♀ 3:09
♄#♅ 7:58
☉#☿ 8:13
☽⊻♃ 9:18
☽⊻⚷ 17:30
☽☍☿ 19:09
☽△♂ 19:34
☽⊻♆ 21:58
☽☌♅ 22:04

3 Sa
☽⊼⚳ 1:15
☽☍♄ 3:30
☽∥♄ 4:51
☽#♅ 5:05
☽∥☿ 7:32
☉#☽ 9:17
☽□♇ 10:50
☽#⚳ 11:11
♀ ♎ 11:47
☽∠♃ 13:43
☽∥♀ 20:24
☽∠⚷ 21:44

4 Su
☽∠♆ 2:07
☽#⚷ 2:46
☉☍☽ 6:11
☿✶♂ 11:38
♀⊼♃ 15:59
☽✶♃ 17:28
☽⊼♀ 17:37
☿⊼♆ 20:58
☿☍♅ 21:07

5 M
☽✶⚷ 1:18
♂⊼♆ 1:34
♂△♅ 1:38
♅⊻♆ 3:09
☽#♆ 5:35
☽⊻♅ 5:37
☽✶♆ 5:37
☽□♂ 5:47
☽⊼☿ 6:14
☽☍⚳ 10:44
☉∥⚳ 10:57
☽⊼♄ 11:29
☽△♇ 18:02
☽#♃ 19:18
☽⚼♀ 23:36

6 Tu
☽#♇ 2:40
☽∠♅ 8:32
☿#♅ 10:40
☽⚼☿ 11:19
☽⚼♄ 14:37
☉#♀ 15:40
☉⊼☽ 16:50
⚳⊻♄ 17:58
☽⚼♇ 20:50
☽□♃ 23:20

7 W
♀#⚳ 0:43
☽∥♂ 2:55
☽△♀ 4:58
☽□⚷ 6:53
☿∥♄ 9:47
☽✶♅ 11:01
☽□♆ 11:06
☽✶♂ 13:32
☽△☿ 16:11
☽△♄ 17:20
☽⊼⚳ 17:54
☉⚼☽ 21:20
☽⊼♇ 23:16

8 Th
♀⊼⚷ 1:52
☿☌♄ 6:35
☽∠♂ 16:47
☿⊻⚳ 20:54
☽⚼⚳ 20:56

9 F
☉△☽ 1:28
☽△♃ 3:43
☽△⚷ 11:06
☽□♀ 14:24
☽□♅ 15:06
☽△♆ 15:16
☽⊻♂ 19:46
☽□♄ 21:54
♀☍♅ 22:02
☽△⚳ 23:42

10 Sa
♀⊼♆ 0:02
☽□☿ 1:36
☽☍♇ 3:19
☿ ♎ 3:47
☽⚼♃ 5:34
☉△♃ 8:39
☽⚼⚷ 12:52
☽⚼♆ 17:01
☿□♇ 18:45

11 Su
♀#♅ 3:04
☽⊼♃ 7:14
☉□☽ 8:57
☽⊼⚷ 14:28
☿⚼♃ 15:59
☽∥♂ 18:04
☽△♅ 18:21
☽⊼♆ 18:36
☽✶♀ 22:44

12 M
☽☌♂ 1:04
☽✶♄ 1:38
☽□⚳ 4:38
☽⊼♇ 6:36
♀∥♄ 8:53
☽✶☿ 10:44
☽#♇ 14:31
⚳ ♏ 18:31
☽⚼♅ 19:45
♂✶♄ 20:52
☽#♃ 21:30

13 Tu
☽∠♀ 2:36
☽∠♄ 3:16
♃ D 4:36
☽⚼♇ 8:01
☽☍♃ 10:07
☽#♆ 10:10
♀☌♄ 10:53
☽∠☿ 15:13
☉✶☽ 15:38
☽☍⚷ 17:14
♀✶♂ 18:32
☽⊼♅ 21:02
☽☍♆ 21:21

14 W
☽⊻♄ 4:48
☽⊻♂ 5:43
☽⊻♀ 6:20
☉∥⚷ 6:33
☽✶⚳ 8:58
☿⚼⚷ 9:02
☽△♇ 9:21
☉#☽ 10:09
☽#⚷ 10:22
☉△⚷ 14:06
☽#⚳ 17:07
☉∠☽ 18:50
☽⊻☿ 19:43
⚳✶♇ 21:54
♀ ♎ 22:47

15 Th
☿#♀ 5:20
☽#♅ 5:47
☽∠♂ 7:57
☽∥♄ 8:50
☽∠⚳ 11:05
☽⊼♃ 12:45
☽#☿ 12:50
☽∥♀ 14:19
♀□♇ 17:22
☽⊼⚷ 19:48
☿⚼♆ 20:59
☽#♀ 21:59
☉⊻☽ 22:05
☽☍♅ 23:34
☽⊼♆ 23:58

16 F
☽∥☿ 1:26
♀⊻⚳ 3:44
☽#♄ 3:57
☽∥♅ 7:13
☽☌♄ 7:56
☽✶♂ 10:19
☽□♇ 12:10
☽⊻⚳ 13:22
☽☌♀ 13:58
☽⚼♃ 14:14
♂ ♌ 15:33
♀⚼♃ 17:06
☉⊼♅ 18:37
☽⚼⚷ 21:18
☽∥⚳ 21:32
☿#♄ 23:15

17 Sa
☉△♆ 0:48
☽⚼♆ 1:32
☽∥⚷ 3:03
☽☌☿ 5:24
☉∥☽ 7:34
☽△♃ 16:02
☽△⚷ 23:10

18 Su
☽⊼♅ 2:58
☽△♆ 3:28
☽∥♆ 4:02
☉☌☽ 5:34
☿∥♅ 6:26
☽⊻♄ 12:10
☽□♂ 16:11
☽✶♇ 16:11
♂⊼♇ 16:25
☽∥♃ 17:09
☽☌⚳ 19:06
☽⊻♀ 23:14

19 M
☽∥♇ 0:50
☽⚼♅ 5:25
☽∠♄ 15:10
☽⊻☿ 17:43
☽#♂ 18:08
☽∠♇ 19:06
☽□♃ 21:17

20 Tu
♀⚼⚷ 0:14
☽□⚷ 4:41
☽∠♀ 5:09
☽△♅ 8:37
☽□♆ 9:14
☉⊻☽ 15:59
☽✶♄ 18:58
☿△♃ 21:51
☽⊻♇ 22:49

21 W
☽△♂ 0:54
☽∠☿ 1:35
☽⊻⚳ 3:48
☽✶♀ 12:12
☉∠☽ 22:46
♀⚼♆ 23:43

22 Th
☽✶♃ 5:47
♀#♄ 6:36
☽⚼♂ 6:40
☽∠⚳ 9:35
☽✶☿ 10:48
☉⊻♄ 11:20
☽✶⚷ 13:28
☽□♅ 17:33
☽✶♆ 18:20

23 F
☽□♄ 5:15
☿△⚷ 6:01
☉✶☽ 6:40
☉ ♏ 6:45
☽☌♇ 8:52
☽∠♃ 11:19
☽⊼♂ 13:22
☽✶⚳ 16:16
☽∠⚷ 19:06

24 Sa
☽∠♆ 0:05
☽□♀ 5:45
☉✶♇ 9:58
☿⊼♅ 10:51
☿△♆ 16:57
☽⊻♃ 17:32
♀∥♅ 17:56

25 Su
☽⊻⚷ 1:20
☽✶♅ 5:28
☽⊻♆ 6:23
☿∥⚳ 7:54
☿∥⚷ 8:16
☽□☿ 8:38
⚳∥⚷ 9:31
☽#♂ 13:46
☽△♄ 18:16
☽⊻♇ 21:31

26 M
☉□☽ 0:43
☽☍♂ 4:31
☽∥♇ 5:22
☽□⚳ 7:20
☽∠♅ 11:54
☽∥♃ 14:49

27 Tu
☽⚼♄ 1:02
☽△♀ 1:47
☽∠♇ 4:02
☽∥♆ 5:12
☽☌♃ 6:41
☉∥☽ 11:03
☽☌⚷ 14:12
☽⊻♅ 18:11
☽☌♆ 19:12

28 W
☽∥☿ 0:44
☽△☿ 7:23
☽⊼♄ 7:28
☽∥⚳ 7:28
☿⊻♄ 8:00
☽∥⚷ 9:38
☿ ♏ 10:10
☽✶♇ 10:12
☽⚼♀ 11:24
☉△☽ 18:38
☽⊼♂ 19:16
☽△⚳ 21:54
☽∥♀ 23:16

29 Th
♀△♃ 2:03
☿✶♇ 3:54
☉□♂ 7:57
☽∥♅ 8:20
☽#♄ 15:18
♄ ♎ 17:10
☽⚼☿ 17:30
☽⊻♃ 18:21
☽⊼♀ 20:06

30 F
☽⊻⚷ 1:16
☽⚼♂ 1:33
☉⚼☽ 2:23
☽⚼⚳ 4:06
☽☌♅ 4:57
☽⊻♆ 6:01
☽∥♄ 7:42
☽#♅ 14:42
☽☍♄ 18:10
☉∥♆ 19:33
☽□♇ 20:22
☽∠♃ 23:01

31 Sa
☽⊼☿ 2:19
⚳⚼♅ 3:06
☽#♀ 4:00
☽∠⚷ 5:35
⚷ D 5:48
☽△♂ 6:51
☉⊼☽ 9:02
☽⊼⚳ 9:19
☉⚼♅ 9:47
☽∠♆ 10:11
☽#⚷ 12:21
☉☌⚳ 15:23
☽#⚳ 16:43
♀△⚷ 23:50

LONGITUDE — November 2009

Day	Sid.Time	☉	☽	☽ 12 hour	Mean☊	True☊	☿	♀	♂	⚳	♃	♄	⚷	♅	♆	♇
	h m s	° ' "	° ' "	° ' "	° '	° '	° '	° '	° '	° '	° '	° '	° '	° '	° '	° '
1 Su	2 41 40	8♏42 01	16♈13 31	22♈51 26	24♑51.8	24♑23.9	5♏57.1	21♎13.5	7♌12.6	8♏30.0	17♒45.2	0♎14.7	21♒13.1	23♓05.6	23♒41.7	1♑18.3
2 M	2 45 36	9 42 02	29 34 18	6♉21 51	24 48.6	24R 11.6	7 35.9	22 28.5	7 38.5	8 56.4	17 49.0	0 21.1	21 13.1	23R 04.2	23R 41.6	1 19.8
3 Tu	2 49 33	10 42 04	13♉13 41	20 09 19	24 45.5	23 59.4	9 14.3	23 43.5	8 04.1	9 22.9	17 53.0	0 27.4	21 13.3	23 02.8	23 41.5	1 21.4
4 W	2 53 30	11 42 08	27 08 15	4♊09 53	24 42.3	23 48.7	10 52.3	24 58.5	8 29.4	9 49.3	17 57.2	0 33.7	21 13.5	23 01.5	23D 41.5	1 22.9
5 Th	2 57 26	12 42 15	11♊13 38	18 18 56	24 39.1	23 40.2	12 29.8	26 13.5	8 54.4	10 15.8	18 01.6	0 39.9	21 13.8	23 00.2	23 41.4	1 24.5
6 F	3 01 23	13 42 23	25 25 14	2♋32 02	24 35.9	23 34.6	14 06.9	27 28.6	9 19.0	10 42.2	18 06.1	0 46.1	21 14.1	22 58.9	23 41.5	1 26.1
7 Sa	3 05 19	14 42 33	9♋38 54	16 45 29	24 32.8	23D 31.8	15 43.6	28 43.6	9 43.3	11 08.6	18 10.8	0 52.2	21 14.5	22 57.7	23 41.5	1 27.7
8 Su	3 09 16	15 42 46	23 51 30	0♌56 42	24 29.6	23 31.1	17 19.9	29 58.7	10 07.3	11 35.0	18 15.7	0 58.2	21 15.0	22 56.5	23 41.6	1 29.3
9 M	3 13 12	16 43 00	8♌00 56	15 04 05	24 26.4	23R 31.4	18 55.8	1♏13.9	10 30.9	12 01.3	18 20.8	1 04.2	21 15.5	22 55.3	23 41.7	1 31.0
10 Tu	3 17 09	17 43 16	22 06 01	29 06 40	24 23.2	23 31.5	20 31.4	2 29.0	10 54.1	12 27.7	18 26.0	1 10.2	21 16.1	22 54.3	23 41.9	1 32.6
11 W	3 21 05	18 43 35	6♍05 58	13♍03 47	24 20.1	23 30.2	22 06.6	3 44.2	11 17.0	12 54.0	18 31.5	1 16.0	21 16.7	22 53.2	23 42.1	1 34.3
12 Th	3 25 02	19 43 55	20 00 01	26 54 29	24 16.9	23 26.6	23 41.5	4 59.4	11 39.5	13 20.4	18 37.1	1 21.9	21 17.5	22 52.2	23 42.3	1 36.1
13 F	3 28 59	20 44 17	3♎47 01	10♎37 23	24 13.7	23 20.4	25 16.1	6 14.6	12 01.6	13 46.7	18 42.9	1 27.6	21 18.2	22 51.2	23 42.6	1 37.8
14 Sa	3 32 55	21 44 41	17 25 20	24 10 36	24 10.5	23 11.7	26 50.4	7 29.8	12 23.4	14 13.0	18 48.8	1 33.3	21 19.1	22 50.3	23 42.9	1 39.6
15 Su	3 36 52	22 45 07	0♏52 53	7♏31 56	24 07.3	23 01.4	28 24.4	8 45.0	12 44.7	14 39.2	18 54.9	1 38.9	21 20.0	22 49.5	23 43.2	1 41.3
16 M	3 40 48	23 45 35	14 07 29	20 39 19	24 04.2	22 50.4	29 58.1	10 00.3	13 05.6	15 05.5	19 01.2	1 44.5	21 21.0	22 48.6	23 43.6	1 43.1
17 Tu	3 44 45	24 46 05	27 07 17	3♐31 16	24 01.0	22 40.0	1♐31.6	11 15.6	13 26.1	15 31.7	19 07.7	1 50.0	21 22.0	22 47.9	23 44.0	1 44.9
18 W	3 48 41	25 46 36	9♐51 13	16 07 10	23 57.8	22 31.0	3 04.8	12 30.9	13 46.1	15 57.9	19 14.3	1 55.4	21 23.1	22 47.2	23 44.4	1 46.8
19 Th	3 52 38	26 47 08	22 19 14	28 27 36	23 54.6	22 24.3	4 37.8	13 46.2	14 05.8	16 24.1	19 21.1	2 00.7	21 24.3	22 46.5	23 44.9	1 48.6
20 F	3 56 34	27 47 42	4♑32 32	10♑33 42	23 51.5	22 20.0	6 10.6	15 01.5	14 24.9	16 50.3	19 28.0	2 06.0	21 25.5	22 45.9	23 45.4	1 50.5
21 Sa	4 00 31	28 48 17	16 33 31	22 30 25	23 48.3	22D 18.2	7 43.2	16 16.8	14 43.7	17 16.4	19 35.1	2 11.2	21 26.8	22 45.3	23 45.9	1 52.4
22 Su	4 04 28	29 48 54	28 25 35	4♒19 37	23 45.1	22 18.2	9 15.6	17 32.2	15 01.9	17 42.5	19 42.4	2 16.4	21 28.1	22 44.8	23 46.5	1 54.3
23 M	4 08 24	0♐49 32	10♒13 06	16 06 41	23 41.9	22 19.2	10 47.8	18 47.5	15 19.7	18 08.6	19 49.8	2 21.4	21 29.5	22 44.3	23 47.1	1 56.2
24 Tu	4 12 21	1 50 11	22 01 00	27 56 44	23 38.8	22R 20.5	12 19.7	20 02.9	15 37.0	18 34.6	19 57.4	2 26.4	21 31.0	22 43.9	23 47.7	1 58.2
25 W	4 16 17	2 50 51	3♓54 34	9♓55 10	23 35.6	22 20.9	13 51.5	21 18.3	15 53.8	19 00.7	20 05.1	2 31.3	21 32.5	22 43.5	23 48.4	2 00.1
26 Th	4 20 14	3 51 32	15 59 12	22 07 16	23 32.4	22 20.0	15 23.1	22 33.6	16 10.1	19 26.6	20 13.0	2 36.1	21 34.1	22 43.2	23 49.1	2 02.1
27 F	4 24 10	4 52 14	28 19 58	4♈37 47	23 29.2	22 17.1	16 54.5	23 49.0	16 25.8	19 52.6	20 21.0	2 40.9	21 35.8	22 42.9	23 49.9	2 04.0
28 Sa	4 28 07	5 52 57	11♈01 11	17 30 30	23 26.0	22 12.2	18 25.7	25 04.4	16 41.1	20 18.5	20 29.2	2 45.6	21 37.5	22 42.7	23 50.6	2 06.0
29 Su	4 32 03	6 53 41	24 05 58	0♉47 41	23 22.9	22 05.7	19 56.6	26 19.8	16 55.8	20 44.4	20 37.5	2 50.1	21 39.2	22 42.5	23 51.4	2 08.0
30 M	4 36 00	7♐54 27	7♉35 36	14 29 34	23♑19.7	21♑58.3	21♐27.3	27♏35.2	17♌10.0	21♏10.2	20♒46.0	2♎54.7	21♒41.1	22♓42.4	23♒52.3	2♑10.1

1st of Month

Julian Day # 2455136.5
Obliquity 23°26'21"
SVP 5♓07'07"
GC 26♐58.6
Eris 21♈17.9R

Day	⚴	Day	⚵	Day	⚶
1	12♎59.6	1	21♓34.5R	1	24♌31.4
6	15 12.3	6	21 33.4	6	26 06.2
11	17 23.6	11	21 45.6	11	27 36.6
16	19 33.4	16	22 10.8	16	29 02.2
21	21 41.5	21	22 48.7	21	0♍22.3
26	23 47.8	26	23 38.6	26	1 36.5

DECLINATION and LATITUDE

Day	☉ Decl	☽ Decl	☽ Lat	☽ 12h Decl	☿ Decl	☿ Lat	♀ Decl	♀ Lat	♂ Decl	♂ Lat	⚳ Decl	⚳ Lat	♃ Decl	♃ Lat	♄ Decl	♄ Lat
1 Su	14S24	10N58	4N58	13N33	12S51	0N41	6S53	1N30	19N56	1N31	9S24	5N12	16S29	1S02	1N47	2N03
2 M	14 43	15 60	5 00	18 16	13 30	0 35	7 22	1 30	19 51	1 32	9 34	5 11	16 28	1 01	1 44	2 03
3 Tu	15 02	20 20	4 45	22 08	14 08	0 28	7 50	1 29	19 46	1 34	9 43	5 09	16 27	1 01	1 42	2 03
4 W	15 21	23 37	4 13	24 45	14 45	0 21	8 18	1 28	19 41	1 36	9 53	5 08	16 25	1 01	1 40	2 03
5 Th	15 39	25 30	3 25	25 50	15 21	0 15	8 46	1 27	19 36	1 38	10 02	5 07	16 24	1 01	1 37	2 04
6 F	15 57	25 45	2 23	25 14	15 57	0 08	9 14	1 26	19 31	1 39	10 11	5 06	16 22	1 01	1 35	2 04
7 Sa	16 15	24 18	1 13	22 59	16 32	0 01	9 42	1 25	19 26	1 41	10 21	5 04	16 21	1 01	1 33	2 04
8 Su	16 33	21 18	0S02	19 18	17 06	0S06	10 09	1 24	19 21	1 43	10 30	5 03	16 19	1 01	1 31	2 04
9 M	16 50	17 02	1 16	14 32	17 39	0 12	10 36	1 23	19 17	1 45	10 39	5 02	16 17	1 01	1 28	2 04
10 Tu	17 07	11 50	2 26	9 00	18 11	0 19	11 03	1 22	19 12	1 46	10 48	5 00	16 16	1 01	1 26	2 04
11 W	17 24	6 04	3 27	3 05	18 42	0 26	11 30	1 21	19 08	1 48	10 57	4 59	16 14	1 00	1 24	2 05
12 Th	17 40	0 04	4 14	2S56	19 13	0 32	11 56	1 20	19 03	1 50	11 06	4 58	16 12	1 00	1 22	2 05
13 F	17 56	5S53	4 47	8 45	19 42	0 39	12 22	1 18	18 59	1 52	11 15	4 57	16 10	1 00	1 20	2 05
14 Sa	18 12	11 30	5 02	14 05	20 11	0 45	12 48	1 17	18 54	1 54	11 24	4 55	16 08	1 00	1 18	2 05
15 Su	18 28	16 29	5 01	18 39	20 38	0 51	13 13	1 15	18 50	1 56	11 33	4 54	16 06	1 00	1 16	2 05
16 M	18 43	20 35	4 44	22 14	21 05	0 57	13 39	1 14	18 46	1 58	11 41	4 53	16 04	0 60	1 14	2 06
17 Tu	18 58	23 35	4 11	24 38	21 30	1 04	14 04	1 12	18 42	1 60	11 50	4 52	16 02	0 60	1 12	2 06
18 W	19 12	25 21	3 27	25 43	21 55	1 09	14 28	1 11	18 38	2 02	11 59	4 50	15 60	0 60	1 10	2 06
19 Th	19 26	25 46	2 34	25 30	22 18	1 15	14 52	1 09	18 34	2 04	12 07	4 49	15 58	0 60	1 08	2 06
20 F	19 40	24 56	1 34	24 04	22 40	1 21	15 16	1 08	18 30	2 06	12 16	4 48	15 55	0 59	1 06	2 06
21 Sa	19 54	22 55	0 31	21 32	23 01	1 26	15 39	1 06	18 27	2 08	12 24	4 47	15 53	0 59	1 04	2 07
22 Su	20 07	19 56	0N33	18 08	23 21	1 32	16 02	1 04	18 23	2 10	12 32	4 45	15 51	0 59	1 02	2 07
23 M	20 19	16 09	1 35	14 01	23 40	1 37	16 25	1 02	18 20	2 12	12 41	4 44	15 48	0 59	1 00	2 07
24 Tu	20 32	11 45	2 33	9 22	23 57	1 42	16 47	1 00	18 17	2 14	12 49	4 43	15 46	0 59	0 59	2 07
25 W	20 44	6 53	3 26	4 19	24 13	1 46	17 09	0 59	18 14	2 16	12 57	4 42	15 43	0 59	0 57	2 08
26 Th	20 55	1 42	4 09	0N58	24 28	1 51	17 30	0 57	18 11	2 18	13 05	4 41	15 41	0 59	0 55	2 08
27 F	21 06	3N39	4 43	6 21	24 42	1 55	17 51	0 55	18 08	2 20	13 13	4 39	15 38	0 59	0 54	2 08
28 Sa	21 17	9 00	5 03	11 37	24 55	1 59	18 11	0 53	18 06	2 22	13 21	4 38	15 35	0 59	0 52	2 08
29 Su	21 28	14 07	5 09	16 31	25 06	2 03	18 31	0 51	18 03	2 25	13 29	4 37	15 32	0 59	0 50	2 09
30 M	21S38	18N44	4N58	20N44	25S16	2S06	18S50	0N48	18N01	2N27	13S37	4N36	15S30	0S58	0N49	2N09

Day	⚷ Decl	⚷ Lat	♅ Decl	♅ Lat	♆ Decl	♆ Lat	♇ Decl	♇ Lat
1	8S23	6N22	3S28	0S47	14S01	0S25	18S10	5N16
6	8 25	6 20	3 30	0 47	14 01	0 25	18 11	5 14
11	8 26	6 18	3 32	0 47	14 01	0 25	18 12	5 13
16	8 27	6 16	3 34	0 47	14 00	0 25	18 13	5 12
21	8 27	6 13	3 35	0 46	13 60	0 25	18 14	5 11
26	8 27	6 11	3 36	0 46	13 59	0 25	18 15	5 10

Day	⚴ Decl	⚴ Lat	⚵ Decl	⚵ Lat	⚶ Decl	⚶ Lat	Eris Decl	Eris Lat
1	0S51	4N38	10S31	7S49	15N22	2N08	4S33	13S51
6	1 06	5 17	10 50	8 09	15 01	2 20	4 34	13 50
11	1 20	5 57	11 00	8 26	14 41	2 32	4 34	13 50
16	1 31	6 37	11 04	8 41	14 24	2 46	4 35	13 49
21	1 40	7 19	11 00	8 53	14 08	2 59	4 35	13 49
26	1 47	8 01	10 50	9 04	13 55	3 14	4 35	13 48

Moon Phenomena

Max/0 Decl

dy	hr mn	
5	15:37	25N51
12	0:15	0 S
18	19:59	25S48
26	7:39	0 N

Max/0 Lat

dy	hr mn	
1	14:34	5N01
7	23:25	0 S
14	10:06	5S04
21	11:34	0 N
28	20:27	5N09

Perigee/Apogee

dy	hr m		kilometers
7	7:25	p	368903
22	20:13	a	404732

PH	dy	hr mn	
○	2	19:15	10♉30
☾	9	15:57	17♌23
●	16	19:15	24♏34
☽	24	21:40	2♓45

Void of Course Moon

Last Aspect				☽ Ingress		
1	13:30	♆	⚹	♉	2	0:46
3	18:05	♆	□	♊	4	4:54
6	3:48	♀	△	♋	6	7:44
7	22:27	♅	△	♌	8	10:24
10	2:44	♆	☍	♍	10	13:31
12	7:14	☿	⚹	♎	12	17:23
14	11:11	♆	△	♏	14	22:25
16	19:15	☉	☌	♐	17	5:23
19	2:47	♆	⚹	♑	19	15:02
22	3:05	☉	⚹	♒	22	3:12
24	3:37	♆	☌	♓	24	16:09
26	14:18	♀	△	♈	27	3:12
28	23:34	♆	⚹	♉	29	10:35

DAILY ASPECTARIAN

1 Su ☽⚹♃ 2:48 · ☽⚹⚷ 9:03 · ☽#☿ 10:00 · ☽☍♀ 10:00 · ☽⚺♅ 12:24 · ☽⚹♆ 13:30 · ☽#♆ 14:16 · ☉#☽ 17:13

2 M ☿□♂ 0:52 · ☽⚻♄ 1:24 · ☽#♃ 2:24 · ☽△♇ 3:08 · ☿⚼♅ 6:48 · ♀⚻♅ 11:13 · ☽#♇ 11:29 · ☽□♂ 14:42 · ☽∠♅ 14:58 · ☽☍☿ 16:06 · ☽☍⚳ 17:04 · ☉☍☽ 19:15 · ☿∥♆ 19:49 · ☽∥♂ 20:38 · ♂⚼♅ 22:50 · ♀△♆ 23:22

3 Tu ☿☌⚳ 2:52 · ☽⚼♄ 3:54 · ☽⚼♇ 5:26 · ☽□♃ 8:07 · ☽□⚷ 13:50 · ☽⚹♅ 16:57 · ☽□♆ 18:05 · ☽⚻♀ 19:56 · ⚵ D 21:19

4 W ♀∥⚷ 5:11 · ☽△♄ 5:54 · ☽⚻♇ 7:16 · ♆ D 18:11 · ☽⚹♂ 19:57 · ☽⚻⚳ 22:19 · ☽⚼♀ 24:00

5 Th ☽⚻☿ 2:26 · ☉⚻☽ 2:42 · ☉☌☿ 8:04 · ☽△♃ 11:34 · ☽△⚷ 16:56 · ☽□♅ 19:53 · ☽△♆ 21:05 · ☽∠♂ 22:05

6 F ☉∥☿ 0:17 · ☽⚼⚳ 0:30 · ☽△♀ 3:48 · ☉⚼☽ 5:58 · ☽⚼☿ 7:02 · ☽□♄ 9:05 · ☽☍♇ 10:10 · ☽⚼♃ 13:02 · ☿∥♃ 16:42 · ☽⚼⚷ 18:15 · ☽⚼♆ 22:23

7 Sa ☽⚺♂ 0:08 · ☿∠♄ 2:17 · ☽△⚳ 2:36 · ☉∥♃ 7:11 · ☉△☽ 9:11 · ☿∠♇ 11:10 · ☽△☿ 11:34 · ☽⚻♃ 14:29 · ☽⚻⚷ 19:35 · ☽△♅ 22:27 · ☽⚻♆ 23:43

8 Su ♀ ♏ 0:24 · ☉∠♄ 6:51 · ☽□♀ 11:22 · ☽∥♂ 11:55 · ☽⚹♄ 12:08 · ☽⚻♇ 12:57 · ☿□♃ 14:44 · ☽#♇ 18:00 · ☉∠♇ 19:04 · ♀⚺♄ 20:40 · ☽#☿ 21:12 · ☽⚼♅ 23:51

9 M ☉#☽ 0:56 · ☽#♃ 3:41 · ♀∥⚳ 4:06 · ☽☌♂ 4:22 · ♀⚹♇ 5:35 · ☽□⚳ 7:02 · ☽∠♄ 13:48 · ☽#♆ 14:20 · ☽⚼♇ 14:30 · ☉□☽ 15:57 · ☽☍♃ 17:42 · ☽□☿ 20:58 · ☽☍⚷ 22:35

10 Tu ☿∥♇ 0:50 · ☽⚻♅ 1:22 · ☽☍♆ 2:44 · ☽#♀ 3:09 · ☽#⚳ 4:20 · ☿□⚷ 11:20 · ☽#⚷ 14:22 · ☽⚺♄ 15:38 · ☽△♇ 16:12 · ☉□♃ 18:42 · ☽⚹♀ 19:32

11 W ☽⚺♂ 9:11 · ☽#♅ 10:09 · ☿△♅ 11:39 · ☽⚹⚳ 12:06 · ☿#♂ 17:10 · ☽∥♄ 18:47 · ☽⚻♃ 21:35 · ☉⚹☽ 23:30 · ☽∠♀ 23:59

12 Th ☿□♆ 0:12 · ☽⚻⚷ 2:14 · ☽☍♅ 4:58 · ☽#♄ 5:40 · ☽⚻♆ 6:26 · ☽⚹☿ 7:14 · ☽∠♂ 11:53 · ☽∥♅ 14:28 · ☽∠⚳ 14:58 · ☽☌♄ 19:55 · ☽□♇ 20:14 · ☽⚼♃ 23:53

13 F ☉∠☽ 3:42 · ☽⚼⚷ 4:25 · ☽⚺♀ 4:44 · ☽⚼♆ 8:38 · ☽∥⚷ 10:41 · ☽∠☿ 12:51 · ☉□⚷ 13:41 · ☽⚹♂ 14:52 · ☽⚺⚳ 18:09 · ☽∥⚳ 23:34

14 Sa ☉∥♇ 1:23 · ☽△♃ 2:29 · ♀⚼♅ 6:28 · ☽∥♀ 6:30 · ☽△⚷ 6:55 · ☉⚺☽ 8:17 · ☽⚻♅ 9:36 · ☽△♆ 11:11 · ☽∥♆ 11:40 · ☽⚺☿ 18:58 · ☽∥♃ 22:04

15 Su ☽⚺♄ 1:23 · ☽⚹♇ 1:27 · ☉△♅ 1:42 · ☽∥♇ 9:30 · ☉∥☽ 11:35 · ☽⚼♅ 12:31 · ☽#♂ 12:50 · ♄□♇ 15:21 · ☽☌♀ 15:42 · ☽□♂ 22:04 · ☉□♆ 23:12

16 M ☿ ♐ 0:29 · ☽☌⚳ 1:50 · ☽∥☿ 3:52 · ☉#♂ 3:59 · ☽∠♇ 4:46 · ☽∠♄ 4:50 · ☽□♃ 9:04 · ☽□⚷ 13:18 · ☽△♅ 15:58 · ☽□♆ 17:42 · ☉☌☽ 19:15 · ♀∥♆ 20:55

17 Tu ☿⚺♇ 3:30 · ☿⚹♄ 5:01 · ☽⚺♇ 8:41 · ☽⚹♄ 8:53 · ☽☌☿ 9:23

18 W ☽⚺♀ 5:39 · ☽△♂ 7:41 · ☽⚺⚳ 12:08 · ☽⚹♃ 18:11 · ☽⚹⚷ 22:13

19 Th ☽□♅ 0:53 · ☽⚹♆ 2:47 · ♀□♂ 8:24 · ☉⚺☽ 9:30 · ☽⚼♂ 13:37 · ⚶ ♍ 13:43 · ☽∠♀ 14:03 · ☽∠⚳ 18:27 · ☽☌♇ 18:39 · ☽□♄ 19:08 · ☽∠♃ 23:51

20 F ⚳∠♇ 0:14 · ☽⚺☿ 3:43 · ☽∠⚷ 3:45 · ☽∠♆ 8:23 · ☉∠☽ 17:58 · ⚳∠♄ 18:03 · ☽⚻♂ 20:13 · ☽∥☿ 23:13 · ☽⚹♀ 23:23

21 Sa ☽⚹⚳ 1:30 · ☽⚺♃ 6:10 · ☽⚺⚷ 9:53 · ♀∠♇ 11:37 · ☽⚹♅ 12:30 · ♀∥♃ 12:55 · ☽∠☿ 14:17 · ☽⚺♆ 14:34 · ♀∠♄ 18:36 · ☉∥☽ 22:51

22 Su ☉⚹☽ 3:05 · ☉ ♐ 4:24 · ♀☌⚳ 5:02 · ☽⚺♇ 7:05 · ☽△♄ 7:53 · ☽#♂ 10:31 · ☽∥♇ 11:20 · ☽∠♅ 18:57 · ☽∥♀ 22:36

23 M ☽⚹☿ 1:21 · ☽∥♃ 2:03 · ☽☍♂ 10:40 · ☽∥♆ 12:11 · ☽∠♇ 13:43 · ☽⚼♄ 14:38 · ☽□⚳ 16:45 · ☽∥⚳ 18:36 · ☽□♀ 19:32 · ☽☌♃ 19:46 · ♀□♃ 22:03 · ☽☌⚷ 22:59

24 Tu ☽⚺♅ 1:27 · ☉⚺♇ 3:16 · ☽☌♆ 3:37 · ☉⚹♄ 15:36 · ☽∥⚷ 16:28 · ♂#♇ 17:55 · ☽⚹♇ 20:10 · ☽⚻♄ 21:12 · ☉□☽ 21:40

25 W ♀□⚷ 4:39 · ☽∥♅ 15:20 · ☽□☿ 22:39

26 Th ☽⚻♂ 0:22 · ♀△♅ 3:01 · ☽#♄ 3:32 · ☽△⚳ 7:02 · ☽⚺♃ 8:23 · ☽⚺⚷ 10:57 · ☽∥♄ 11:43 · ☽☌♅ 13:09 · ☽△♀ 14:18 · ☿△♂ 14:54 · ☽⚺♆ 15:19 · ☽#♅ 23:44

27 F ♀□♆ 0:16 · ☽⚼♂ 6:03 · ☽□♇ 7:09 · ☽☍♄ 8:21 · ☽⚼⚳ 12:54 · ☽∠♃ 13:30 · ☉△☽ 13:32 · ☽∠⚷ 15:45 · ♀#♂ 18:33 · ☽∠♆ 19:56 · ☽#⚷ 21:27 · ☽⚼♀ 22:03

28 Sa ♀∥♇ 5:08 · ☽△♂ 10:41 · ⚳□♃ 14:35 · ☽△☿ 15:28 · ☽⚹♃ 17:38 · ☽⚻⚳ 17:42 · ☽⚹⚷ 19:34 · ☉⚼☽ 19:40 · ☽#⚳ 20:47 · ☽⚺♅ 21:29 · ☽#♆ 23:13 · ☽⚹♆ 23:34

29 Su ☽⚻♀ 4:26 · ☽#♃ 6:57 · ☿⚹♃ 11:55 · ☽△♇ 14:25 · ☽⚻♄ 15:42 · ☿⚺⚳ 17:40 · ☽∥♂ 20:05 · ☽#♇ 21:21 · ☽⚼☿ 21:45

30 M ♂⚼♇ 0:06 · ☽∠♅ 0:12 · ☉⚻☽ 0:36 · ☽#♀ 0:39 · ☿⚹⚷ 3:43 · ☽⚼♇ 16:39 · ☽□♂ 16:53 · ☽⚼♄ 17:59 · ☉#☽ 18:52 · ☿□♅ 19:54 · ☽□♃ 23:00

December 2009

LONGITUDE

Day	Sid.Time	☉	☽	☽ 12 hour	Mean ☊	True ☊	☿	♀	♂	⚳	♃	♄	⚷	♅	♆	♇
	h m s	° ' "	° ' "	° ' "	° '	° '	° '	° '	° '	° '	° '	° '	° '	° '	° '	° '
1 Tu	4 39 57	8♐55 13	21♉29 14	28♉34 08	23♑16.5	21♑50.7	22♐57.8	28♏50.6	17♌23.7	21♏36.0	20♒54.6	2♎59.1	21♒43.0	22♓42.3	23♒53.1	2♑12.1
2 W	4 43 53	9 56 01	5♊43 40	12♊57 05	23 13.3	21R 44.0	24 27.9	0♐06.0	17 36.7	22 01.8	21 03.3	3 03.4	21 44.9	22D 42.3	23 54.0	2 14.1
3 Th	4 47 50	10 56 50	20 13 37	27 32 23	23 10.2	21 38.9	25 57.6	1 21.5	17 49.2	22 27.6	21 12.2	3 07.7	21 46.9	22 42.3	23 55.0	2 16.2
4 F	4 51 46	11 57 40	4♋52 31	12♋13 09	23 07.0	21 35.7	27 27.0	2 36.9	18 01.1	22 53.3	21 21.2	3 11.9	21 48.9	22 42.4	23 56.0	2 18.3
5 Sa	4 55 43	12 58 31	19 33 28	26 52 42	23 03.8	21D 34.6	28 55.8	3 52.4	18 12.5	23 19.0	21 30.3	3 16.0	21 51.1	22 42.5	23 57.0	2 20.3
6 Su	4 59 39	13 59 23	4♌10 13	11♌25 25	23 00.6	21 35.1	0♑24.1	5 07.8	18 23.2	23 44.6	21 39.6	3 20.0	21 53.2	22 42.7	23 58.0	2 22.4
7 M	5 03 36	15 00 17	18 37 52	25 47 12	22 57.5	21 36.5	1 51.8	6 23.3	18 33.2	24 10.2	21 49.0	3 23.9	21 55.4	22 42.9	23 59.0	2 24.5
8 Tu	5 07 33	16 01 12	2♍53 11	9♍55 36	22 54.3	21 37.9	3 18.8	7 38.7	18 42.7	24 35.7	21 58.6	3 27.7	21 57.7	22 43.2	24 00.1	2 26.6
9 W	5 11 29	17 02 08	16 54 23	23 49 29	22 51.1	21R 38.5	4 44.8	8 54.2	18 51.5	25 01.2	22 08.2	3 31.4	22 00.0	22 43.6	24 01.3	2 28.7
10 Th	5 15 26	18 03 05	0♎40 54	7♎28 40	22 47.9	21 37.8	6 09.8	10 09.7	18 59.6	25 26.7	22 18.0	3 35.1	22 02.4	22 44.0	24 02.4	2 30.9
11 F	5 19 22	19 04 04	14 12 49	20 53 26	22 44.7	21 35.5	7 33.6	11 25.2	19 07.0	25 52.1	22 27.9	3 38.6	22 04.8	22 44.4	24 03.6	2 33.0
12 Sa	5 23 19	20 05 04	27 30 35	4♏04 19	22 41.6	21 31.7	8 56.0	12 40.7	19 13.8	26 17.5	22 38.0	3 42.1	22 07.3	22 44.9	24 04.8	2 35.1
13 Su	5 27 15	21 06 05	10♏34 42	17 01 46	22 38.4	21 26.9	10 16.7	13 56.2	19 19.8	26 42.8	22 48.1	3 45.5	22 09.8	22 45.4	24 06.0	2 37.3
14 M	5 31 12	22 07 07	23 25 36	29 46 15	22 35.2	21 21.7	11 35.4	15 11.7	19 25.2	27 08.1	22 58.4	3 48.7	22 12.4	22 46.0	24 07.3	2 39.4
15 Tu	5 35 08	23 08 10	6♐03 45	12♐18 12	22 32.0	21 16.6	12 51.8	16 27.2	19 29.8	27 33.4	23 08.8	3 51.9	22 15.1	22 46.7	24 08.6	2 41.6
16 W	5 39 05	24 09 13	18 29 40	24 38 16	22 28.9	21 12.4	14 05.6	17 42.7	19 33.7	27 58.5	23 19.3	3 55.0	22 17.8	22 47.4	24 10.0	2 43.7
17 Th	5 43 02	25 10 18	0♑44 08	6♑47 25	22 25.7	21 09.4	15 16.2	18 58.3	19 36.8	28 23.7	23 29.9	3 58.0	22 20.5	22 48.1	24 11.3	2 45.9
18 F	5 46 58	26 11 23	12 48 21	18 47 10	22 22.5	21D 07.8	16 23.2	20 13.8	19 39.2	28 48.8	23 40.6	4 00.8	22 23.3	22 48.9	24 12.7	2 48.1
19 Sa	5 50 55	27 12 28	24 44 07	0♒39 34	22 19.3	21 07.6	17 26.0	21 29.3	19 40.8	29 13.8	23 51.5	4 03.6	22 26.1	22 49.8	24 14.1	2 50.2
20 Su	5 54 51	28 13 34	6♒33 52	12 27 25	22 16.2	21 08.4	18 24.0	22 44.8	19R 41.6	29 38.8	24 02.4	4 06.3	22 29.0	22 50.7	24 15.6	2 52.4
21 M	5 58 48	29 14 41	18 20 40	24 14 07	22 13.0	21 10.0	19 16.4	24 00.3	19 41.6	0♐03.7	24 13.5	4 08.9	22 31.9	22 51.7	24 17.0	2 54.6
22 Tu	6 02 44	0♑15 48	0♓08 17	6♓03 43	22 09.8	21 11.8	20 02.4	25 15.9	19 40.9	0 28.5	24 24.6	4 11.3	22 34.9	22 52.7	24 18.5	2 56.8
23 W	6 06 41	1 16 54	12 01 00	18 00 43	22 06.6	21 13.4	20 41.3	26 31.4	19 39.4	0 53.3	24 35.9	4 13.7	22 37.9	22 53.7	24 20.1	2 58.9
24 Th	6 10 37	2 18 01	24 03 30	0♈09 55	22 03.5	21R 14.4	21 12.0	27 46.9	19 37.0	1 18.1	24 47.3	4 16.0	22 40.9	22 54.8	24 21.6	3 01.1
25 F	6 14 34	3 19 09	6♈20 37	12 36 08	22 00.3	21 14.5	21 33.8	29 02.4	19 33.9	1 42.7	24 58.7	4 18.2	22 44.0	22 56.0	24 23.2	3 03.3
26 Sa	6 18 31	4 20 16	18 57 02	25 23 48	21 57.1	21 13.9	21R 45.7	0♑17.9	19 29.9	2 07.3	25 10.3	4 20.2	22 47.2	22 57.2	24 24.8	3 05.5
27 Su	6 22 27	5 21 23	1♉56 50	8♉36 27	21 53.9	21 12.5	21 46.9	1 33.4	19 25.1	2 31.9	25 21.9	4 22.2	22 50.4	22 58.4	24 26.4	3 07.7
28 M	6 26 24	6 22 31	15 22 52	22 16 09	21 50.7	21 10.7	21 36.7	2 48.9	19 19.6	2 56.4	25 33.7	4 24.0	22 53.6	22 59.7	24 28.1	3 09.8
29 Tu	6 30 20	7 23 38	29 16 14	6♊22 51	21 47.6	21 08.7	21 14.8	4 04.4	19 13.2	3 20.8	25 45.5	4 25.8	22 56.9	23 01.2	24 29.8	3 12.0
30 W	6 34 17	8 24 46	13♊35 36	20 53 54	21 44.4	21 07.0	20 41.1	5 19.9	19 05.9	3 45.1	25 57.4	4 27.4	23 00.2	23 02.5	24 31.5	3 14.2
31 Th	6 38 13	9♑25 54	28 17 01	5♋44 02	21♑41.2	21♑05.7	19♑55.8	6♑35.4	18♌57.9	4♐09.4	26♒09.4	4♎29.0	23♒03.5	23♓03.9	24♒33.2	3♑16.4

1st of Month

Julian Day # 2455166.5
Obliquity 23°26'20"
SVP 5♓07'02"
GC 26♐58.7
Eris 21♈03.1R

Day	⚴
1	25♎52.1
6	27 54.2
11	29 54.1
16	1♏51.4
21	3 46.0
26	5 37.5
31	7 25.7

Day	⚵
1	24♓39.7
6	25 51.3
11	27 12.7
16	28 43.1
21	0♈22.0
26	2 08.6
31	4 02.2

Day	⚶
1	2♍44.1
6	3 44.7
11	4 37.4
16	5 21.6
21	5 56.6
26	6 21.6
31	6 36.0

DECLINATION and LATITUDE

Day	☉ Decl	☽ Decl	☽ Lat	☽ 12h Decl	☿ Decl	☿ Lat	♀ Decl	♀ Lat	♂ Decl	♂ Lat	⚳ Decl	⚳ Lat	♃ Decl	♃ Lat	♄ Decl	♄ Lat
1 Tu	21S47	22N27	4N29	23N52	25S24	2S09	19S09	0N46	17N59	2N29	13S44	4N35	15S27	0S58	0N47	2N09
2 W	21 56	24 55	3 43	25 34	25 31	2 12	19 27	0 44	17 57	2 31	13 52	4 33	15 24	0 58	0 46	2 09
3 Th	22 05	25 46	2 42	25 32	25 37	2 15	19 45	0 42	17 56	2 34	13 60	4 32	15 21	0 58	0 44	2 09
4 F	22 13	24 51	1 30	23 43	25 41	2 17	20 02	0 40	17 54	2 36	14 07	4 31	15 18	0 58	0 43	2 10
5 Sa	22 21	22 12	0 11	20 19	25 44	2 18	20 18	0 38	17 53	2 38	14 15	4 30	15 15	0 58	0 41	2 10
6 Su	22 29	18 07	1S08	15 39	25 46	2 20	20 34	0 35	17 52	2 41	14 22	4 29	15 12	0 58	0 40	2 10
7 M	22 36	12 59	2 22	10 10	25 46	2 20	20 50	0 33	17 51	2 43	14 29	4 28	15 09	0 58	0 39	2 10
8 Tu	22 42	7 14	3 26	4 14	25 44	2 21	21 05	0 31	17 50	2 45	14 36	4 26	15 06	0 58	0 37	2 11
9 W	22 48	1 13	4 17	1S47	25 42	2 20	21 19	0 28	17 50	2 48	14 44	4 25	15 02	0 58	0 36	2 11
10 Th	22 54	4S44	4 52	7 36	25 37	2 20	21 33	0 26	17 49	2 50	14 51	4 24	14 59	0 58	0 35	2 11
11 F	22 59	10 22	5 10	12 59	25 31	2 18	21 45	0 24	17 49	2 53	14 58	4 23	14 56	0 57	0 34	2 11
12 Sa	23 04	15 25	5 11	17 39	25 24	2 16	21 58	0 21	17 49	2 55	15 05	4 22	14 52	0 57	0 33	2 12
13 Su	23 08	19 40	4 55	21 25	25 16	2 14	22 09	0 19	17 50	2 57	15 12	4 21	14 49	0 57	0 32	2 12
14 M	23 12	22 54	4 25	24 06	25 06	2 10	22 20	0 17	17 51	2 60	15 18	4 20	14 46	0 57	0 30	2 12
15 Tu	23 16	24 58	3 43	25 32	24 55	2 06	22 31	0 14	17 51	3 02	15 25	4 18	14 42	0 57	0 29	2 13
16 W	23 19	25 46	2 50	25 40	24 42	2 01	22 40	0 12	17 53	3 05	15 32	4 17	14 39	0 57	0 28	2 13
17 Th	23 21	25 16	1 50	24 29	24 29	1 55	22 49	0 09	17 54	3 07	15 38	4 16	14 35	0 57	0 28	2 13
18 F	23 23	23 35	0 46	22 20	24 14	1 49	22 58	0 07	17 56	3 10	15 45	4 15	14 31	0 57	0 27	2 13
19 Sa	23 25	20 51	0N20	19 09	23 58	1 41	23 05	0 05	17 58	3 13	15 51	4 14	14 28	0 57	0 26	2 14
20 Su	23 26	17 16	1 24	15 13	23 42	1 32	23 12	0 02	17 60	3 15	15 58	4 13	14 24	0 57	0 25	2 14
21 M	23 26	13 02	2 25	10 43	23 24	1 22	23 18	0S00	18 02	3 18	16 04	4 12	14 20	0 57	0 24	2 14
22 Tu	23 26	8 19	3 19	5 49	23 07	1 11	23 24	0 03	18 05	3 20	16 10	4 10	14 17	0 57	0 24	2 14
23 W	23 26	3 16	4 06	0 40	22 49	0 59	23 29	0 05	18 08	3 23	16 16	4 09	14 13	0 57	0 23	2 15
24 Th	23 25	1N57	4 42	4N35	22 31	0 45	23 33	0 07	18 11	3 25	16 22	4 08	14 09	0 57	0 22	2 15
25 F	23 24	7 12	5 06	9 47	22 13	0 30	23 36	0 10	18 14	3 28	16 28	4 07	14 05	0 56	0 22	2 15
26 Sa	23 22	12 18	5 16	14 43	21 55	0 14	23 38	0 12	18 18	3 30	16 34	4 06	14 01	0 56	0 21	2 16
27 Su	23 20	17 01	5 11	19 08	21 38	0N03	23 40	0 15	18 22	3 33	16 40	4 05	13 57	0 56	0 21	2 16
28 M	23 17	21 03	4 49	22 42	21 22	0 21	23 41	0 17	18 26	3 35	16 46	4 04	13 53	0 56	0 20	2 16
29 Tu	23 14	24 03	4 09	25 02	21 06	0 40	23 42	0 19	18 30	3 38	16 51	4 03	13 49	0 56	0 20	2 16
30 W	23 10	25 38	3 13	25 47	20 52	0 59	23 41	0 22	18 35	3 40	16 57	4 01	13 45	0 56	0 19	2 17
31 Th	23S06	25N29	2N03	24N43	20S40	1N19	23S40	0S24	18N40	3N43	17S02	4N00	13S41	0S56	0N19	2N17

Day	⚷ Decl	⚷ Lat	♅ Decl	♅ Lat	♆ Decl	♆ Lat	♇ Decl	♇ Lat
1	8S26	6N09	3S36	0S46	13S57	0S25	18S16	5N10
6	8 25	6 07	3 36	0 46	13 56	0 25	18 16	5 09
11	8 23	6 05	3 35	0 46	13 54	0 25	18 17	5 08
16	8 21	6 03	3 33	0 45	13 52	0 25	18 17	5 08
21	8 18	6 02	3 32	0 45	13 49	0 25	18 18	5 07
26	8 14	6 00	3 29	0 45	13 47	0 25	18 18	5 06
31	8S11	5N59	3S26	0S45	13S44	0S25	18S18	5N06

Day	⚴ Decl	⚴ Lat	⚵ Decl	⚵ Lat	⚶ Decl	⚶ Lat	Eris Decl	Eris Lat
1	1S50	8N44	10S35	9S13	13N45	3N30	4S35	13S48
6	1 51	9 29	10 14	9 21	13 38	3 46	4 35	13 47
11	1 49	10 15	9 47	9 28	13 35	4 03	4 35	13 46
16	1 44	11 03	9 17	9 34	13 36	4 21	4 35	13 45
21	1 35	11 53	8 42	9 39	13 40	4 40	4 34	13 44
26	1 22	12 44	8 03	9 43	13 50	5 00	4 34	13 44
31	1S05	13N37	7S21	9S46	14N03	5N21	4S33	13S43

Moon Phenomena

Max/0 Decl
dy hr mn
2 23:52 25N46
9 4:52 0 S
16 2:31 25S46
23 15:04 0 N
30 10:03 25N47

Max/0 Lat
dy hr mn
5 3:18 0 S
11 13:13 5S13
18 16:42 0 N
26 4:12 5N17

Perigee/Apogee
dy hr m kilometers
4 14:22 p 363483
20 14:56 a 405730

PH dy hr mn
○ 2 7:32 10♊15
☾ 9 0:14 17♍03
● 16 12:03 24♐40
☽ 24 17:37 3♈03
○ 31 19:14 10♋15
• 31 19:24 P 0.076

Void of Course Moon

Last Aspect	☽ Ingress
1 13:40 ♀ ☍	♊ 1 14:25
3 10:29 ☿ ☍	♋ 3 16:02
5 5:10 ♅ △	♌ 5 17:08
7 8:59 ♅ ☍	♍ 7 19:07
9 10:06 ♅ ☍	♎ 9 22:48
11 17:46 ♆ △	♏ 12 4:33
14 1:19 ♆ □	♐ 14 12:26
16 12:03 ☉ ☌	♑ 16 22:33
18 20:09 ♅ ✶	♒ 19 10:40
21 12:55 ☉ ✶	♓ 21 23:43
24 8:10 ♀ □	♈ 24 11:41
26 11:45 ♃ ✶	♉ 26 20:27
28 17:55 ♃ □	♊ 29 1:14
30 20:31 ♃ △	♋ 31 2:46

DAILY ASPECTARIAN

1 Tu
☽☍⚳ 0:12
☽□⚷ 0:23
☽✶♅ 2:04
☽⚻☿ 2:49
☽□♆ 4:05
⚳□⚷ 6:57
☽☍♀ 13:40
☿✶♆ 14:53
☽⚻♇ 18:09
☽△♄ 19:31
♅ D 20:29
♀ ♐ 22:05

2 W
☉☍☽ 7:32
☽#☿ 12:30
⚳∥♆ 14:56
☽✶♂ 19:59

3 Th
☽△♃ 1:37
☽△⚷ 2:34
☽⚻⚳ 3:47
☽□♅ 4:04
☽△♆ 6:04
☽#☿ 8:24
☽☍☿ 10:29
⚳△♅ 13:47
♀⊻♇ 17:54
☽☍♇ 19:47
☽⚻♀ 19:58
☽∠♂ 20:56
☽□♄ 21:15

4 F
☽⚼♃ 2:26
☽⚼⚷ 3:11
☽⚼⚳ 5:04
☽⚼♆ 6:38
♀✶♄ 11:46
☉⚻☽ 12:26
☽⊻♂ 21:46
☽⚼♀ 22:46
☉#☽ 22:54

5 Sa
☽⚻♃ 3:13
☽⚻⚷ 3:46
☽△♅ 5:10
☽△⚳ 6:20
☽⚻♆ 7:12
☽#♀ 11:15
♂∠♄ 12:20
☉⚼☽ 14:50
☽⚻☿ 17:06
☿ ♑ 17:25
☽⚻♇ 21:02
☽✶♄ 22:37
☽#♇ 23:10

6 Su
☽∥♂ 1:17
☽△♀ 1:44
☽⚼♅ 5:51
⚳□♆ 13:06
☽#♃ 14:15
☽#⚳ 17:30
☉△☽ 17:30
☽#♆ 19:53
☽⚼☿ 20:43
☽⚼♇ 21:57
☽∠♄ 23:37
☽☌♂ 23:52

7 M
☽☍♃ 5:24
☽☍⚷ 5:32
☽⚻♅ 6:50
☽☍♆ 8:59
☿☌♇ 9:13
☽□⚳ 9:34
☽#⚷ 19:15
♃☌⚷ 21:10
☽△♇ 23:15

8 Tu
☽△☿ 0:48
☽⊻♄ 0:59
☿□♄ 2:36
☿⚼♂ 7:25
☽□♀ 8:54
☽#♅ 14:36

9 W
☉□☽ 0:14
☽∥♄ 2:28
☽⊻♂ 3:25
☽#♄ 7:15
☽⚻⚷ 8:51
☽⚻♃ 9:10
☽☍♅ 10:06
☽⚻♆ 12:22
☽✶⚳ 14:32
☽∥♅ 19:17

10 Th
☽□♇ 3:14
☽☌♄ 5:08
☽∠♂ 5:53
☽□☿ 10:47
☽⚼⚷ 11:15
☽⚼♃ 11:50
☽⚼♆ 14:48
☽∥⚷ 15:20
☿∠⚷ 15:28
☽∠⚳ 17:50
☽✶♀ 18:30
⚳∥♃ 19:34
☿∠♃ 22:08

11 F
☉△♂ 1:19
♀ ♏ 5:59
☽✶♂ 8:53
☉✶☽ 9:26
☽△⚷ 14:12
☽△♃ 15:02
☽⚻♅ 15:21
☽∥♆ 16:24
☽△♆ 17:46
☽∥♃ 21:17
☽⊻⚳ 21:43
☽∥⚳ 22:14

12 Sa
☽∠♀ 0:20
☿∠♆ 2:39
☽✶♇ 9:18
☽⊻♄ 11:22
☽#♂ 12:59
☉∠☽ 15:02
☽∥♇ 15:36
♃⊻♅ 17:21
☽⚼♅ 18:47
☽✶☿ 23:23

13 Su
☽⊻♀ 6:54
☽∠♇ 13:09
☽∠♄ 15:18
☽□♂ 16:25
☽∥♀ 18:50
☉⊻☽ 21:19
☽□⚷ 21:42
☽△♅ 22:45
☽□♃ 23:08

14 M
☽□♆ 1:19
☉✶⚷ 2:11
☉∥☽ 2:49
☽∠☿ 6:39
☽☌⚳ 7:15
☿∠⚳ 15:13
☉□♅ 15:28
☽⊻♇ 17:33
☽✶♄ 19:47
☽∥☿ 23:08

15 Tu
☉✶♃ 0:18
☽⊻☿ 14:32
☽☌♀ 22:18

16 W
☉✶♆ 0:18
☽△♂ 2:05
☽✶⚷ 7:27
☽□♅ 8:23
☽✶♃ 9:34
☽✶♆ 11:06
☉☌☽ 12:03
☽⊻⚳ 19:13

17 Th
☽☌♇ 4:02
☽□♄ 6:25
☽⚼♂ 7:42
♀△♂ 12:40
☽∠⚷ 13:09
☽∥☿ 15:17
☽∠♃ 15:38
☽∠♆ 16:48

18 F
☉∥☽ 2:02
☽∠⚳ 2:05
☽∥♀ 5:56
☽☌☿ 7:53
☽⚻♂ 13:47
☽⊻♀ 16:40
☽⊻⚷ 19:20
☽✶♅ 20:09
☽⊻♃ 22:12
☽⊻♆ 22:59

19 Sa
☉⊻☽ 5:28
☽✶⚳ 9:26
☽⊻♇ 16:28
☽∥♇ 17:39
♀✶⚷ 18:46
☽△♄ 18:59
☽#♂ 19:34
⚵ ♈ 22:10

20 Su
♀□♅ 1:53
☽∠♅ 2:37
☽∠♀ 2:42
☽∥⚳ 7:36
♂ R 13:27
☉∠☽ 14:51
☽∥♃ 16:50
☽∥♆ 19:45
⚳ ♐ 20:27
☉∥☿ 21:36
☽∠♇ 23:07

21 M
☽⚼♄ 1:39
☽⊻☿ 2:02
☽☍♂ 2:45
♀✶♃ 4:54
♀✶♆ 5:25
☿∥♀ 6:13
☽☌⚷ 8:34
♃☌♆ 8:52
☽⊻♅ 9:13
☽☌♆ 12:08
☽☌♃ 12:10
☿⚻♂ 12:34
☽✶♀ 12:55
☉ ♑ 17:48

22 Tu
☽∥⚷ 0:08
☉✶☽ 0:17
☽□⚳ 0:43
☽✶♇ 5:43
☽⚻♄ 8:14
☉⊻⚳ 8:25
☽∠☿ 10:32
☉∥♀ 11:24
☽∥♅ 22:52

23 W
☽#♄ 13:21
☽⚻♂ 15:14
☽∥♄ 16:47
☽✶☿ 18:07
☽⊻⚷ 21:16
☽☌♅ 21:44

24 Th
☽⊻♆ 0:36
☽⊻♃ 1:28
☽#♅ 7:03
☽□♀ 8:10
☽△⚳ 14:42
☉☌♇ 17:33
☽□♇ 17:37
☉□☽ 17:37
☽☍♄ 20:02
☽⚼♂ 20:35

25 F
☽∠⚷ 2:41
☽#⚷ 4:51
☽∠♆ 5:52
☽∠♃ 7:06
♀ ♑ 18:18
☽⚼⚳ 20:27
♂#♇ 23:06
☉□♄ 23:59

26 Sa
☽△♂ 1:01
☉⚼♂ 3:32
☽□☿ 5:18
☽✶⚷ 7:12
☽#♆ 7:16
☽⊻♅ 7:29
☽#♃ 8:21
☽✶♆ 10:12
☽✶♃ 11:45
☿ R 14:40
☽#⚳ 22:06
☽△♀ 23:13

27 Su
☽⚻⚳ 1:06
☽△♇ 2:09
☽⚻♄ 4:24
☉△☽ 6:41
☽#♇ 7:08
☽∥♂ 7:38
♂∠♄ 9:52
☽∠♅ 10:53

28 M
☽#☿ 1:58
♀⊻⚳ 3:30
☽⚼♀ 4:42
☽⚼♇ 4:53
♀☌♇ 6:50
☽□♂ 6:51
☽⚼♄ 7:02
☽△☿ 10:37
☉⚼☽ 11:17
☽□⚷ 13:08
☽✶♅ 13:16
⚳⊻♇ 14:31
☽□♆ 15:49
☉#☽ 16:31
☽□♃ 17:55
☽#♀ 20:33

29 Tu
♀⚼♂ 2:32
☽⚻♇ 6:40
♀□♄ 6:56
☽☍⚳ 7:06
☽△♄ 8:44
☽⚻♀ 8:55
☽⚼☿ 11:22
☉∠⚷ 13:48
☉⚻☽ 14:44

30 W
♃∥♆ 2:24
☽✶♂ 8:59
☽⚻☿ 11:07
☽△⚷ 15:29
☽□♅ 15:31
☽△♆ 17:56
☽△♃ 20:31

31 Th
☉∠♆ 2:57
♅⊻⚷ 4:56
☽☍♇ 8:04
☽∠♂ 9:04
☽⚻⚳ 9:44
☽□♄ 10:00
☿∠⚳ 14:14
☽☍♀ 14:36
☽⚼⚷ 15:47
☽⚼♆ 18:09
☉☍☽ 19:14
⚳✶♄ 20:36
☽⚼♃ 20:58
☽#♀ 22:47

LONGITUDE — January 2010

Day	Sid.Time	☉	☽	☽ 12 hour	Mean ☊	True ☊	☿	♀	♂	⚳	♃	♄	⚷	♅	♆	♇
	h m s	° ' "	° ' "	° ' "	° '	° '	° '	° '	° '	° '	° '	° '	° '	° '	° '	° '
1 F	6 42 10	10♑27 01	13♋13 58	20♋45 44	21♑38.0	21♑05.1	18♑59.8	7♑50.9	18♌49.1	4♐33.6	26♒21.5	4♎30.4	23♒06.9	23♓05.4	24♒34.9	3♑18.5
2 Sa	6 46 07	11 28 09	28 18 12	5♌50 14	21 34.9	21D 05.1	17R 54.4	9 06.4	18R 39.4	4 57.8	26 33.7	4 31.7	23 10.3	23 06.9	24 36.7	3 20.7
3 Su	6 50 03	12 29 17	13♌20 46	20 48 48	21 31.7	21 05.5	16 41.6	10 21.9	18 28.9	5 21.8	26 46.0	4 32.9	23 13.8	23 08.5	24 38.5	3 22.9
4 M	6 54 00	13 30 25	28 13 26	5♍33 54	21 28.5	21 06.2	15 23.4	11 37.4	18 17.6	5 45.8	26 58.3	4 34.0	23 17.3	23 10.2	24 40.3	3 25.0
5 Tu	6 57 56	14 31 33	12♍49 37	20 00 07	21 25.3	21 06.9	14 02.6	12 52.9	18 05.5	6 09.8	27 10.7	4 35.0	23 20.8	23 11.8	24 42.1	3 27.2
6 W	7 01 53	15 32 42	27 05 06	4♎04 22	21 22.2	21 07.4	12 41.7	14 08.4	17 52.6	6 33.6	27 23.2	4 35.9	23 24.4	23 13.5	24 44.0	3 29.3
7 Th	7 05 49	16 33 51	10♎57 54	17 45 46	21 19.0	21R 07.6	11 23.4	15 23.9	17 38.9	6 57.4	27 35.8	4 36.7	23 28.0	23 15.3	24 45.8	3 31.4
8 F	7 09 46	17 34 59	24 28 06	1♏05 08	21 15.8	21 07.6	10 10.0	16 39.4	17 24.5	7 21.1	27 48.4	4 37.4	23 31.6	23 17.1	24 47.7	3 33.6
9 Sa	7 13 42	18 36 08	7♏37 08	14 04 25	21 12.6	21 07.4	9 03.3	17 54.9	17 09.2	7 44.7	28 01.2	4 38.0	23 35.2	23 19.0	24 49.7	3 35.7
10 Su	7 17 39	19 37 18	20 27 20	26 46 12	21 09.5	21 07.3	8 04.8	19 10.4	16 53.3	8 08.2	28 14.0	4 38.4	23 38.9	23 20.9	24 51.6	3 37.8
11 M	7 21 36	20 38 27	3♐01 22	9♐13 11	21 06.3	21D 07.1	7 15.4	20 25.8	16 36.6	8 31.7	28 26.8	4 38.8	23 42.7	23 22.8	24 53.5	3 39.9
12 Tu	7 25 32	21 39 36	15 21 58	21 28 03	21 03.1	21 07.2	6 35.8	21 41.3	16 19.2	8 55.0	28 39.8	4 39.0	23 46.4	23 24.8	24 55.5	3 42.0
13 W	7 29 29	22 40 45	27 31 42	3♑33 14	20 59.9	21 07.3	6 06.1	22 56.8	16 01.1	9 18.3	28 52.8	4R 39.1	23 50.2	23 26.8	24 57.5	3 44.1
14 Th	7 33 25	23 41 54	9♑32 54	15 30 58	20 56.8	21R 07.4	5 46.0	24 12.3	15 42.4	9 41.5	29 05.9	4 39.1	23 54.0	23 28.9	24 59.5	3 46.2
15 F	7 37 22	24 43 02	21 27 41	27 23 18	20 53.6	21 07.5	5D 35.4	25 27.8	15 23.1	10 04.6	29 19.0	4 39.1	23 57.8	23 31.0	25 01.5	3 48.3
16 Sa	7 41 18	25 44 10	3♒18 03	9♒12 13	20 50.4	21 07.4	5 33.6	26 43.2	15 03.1	10 27.6	29 32.2	4 38.9	24 01.7	23 33.1	25 03.6	3 50.3
17 Su	7 45 15	26 45 18	15 06 03	20 59 49	20 47.2	21 07.0	5 40.2	27 58.7	14 42.6	10 50.5	29 45.5	4 38.5	24 05.6	23 35.3	25 05.6	3 52.4
18 M	7 49 11	27 46 24	26 53 51	2♓48 27	20 44.0	21 06.2	5 54.4	29 14.1	14 21.6	11 13.4	29 58.8	4 38.1	24 09.5	23 37.6	25 07.7	3 54.4
19 Tu	7 53 08	28 47 31	8♓43 58	14 40 46	20 40.9	21 05.1	6 15.6	0♒29.6	14 00.1	11 36.1	0♓12.2	4 37.6	24 13.4	23 39.8	25 09.8	3 56.5
20 W	7 57 05	29 48 36	20 39 16	26 39 53	20 37.7	21 03.9	6 43.2	1 45.0	13 38.1	11 58.7	0 25.6	4 36.9	24 17.4	23 42.1	25 11.9	3 58.5
21 Th	8 01 01	0♒49 40	2♈43 04	8♈49 18	20 34.5	21 02.7	7 16.7	3 00.4	13 15.8	12 21.2	0 39.1	4 36.2	24 21.3	23 44.5	25 14.0	4 00.5
22 F	8 04 58	1 50 44	14 59 04	21 12 53	20 31.3	21 01.7	7 55.5	4 15.8	12 53.0	12 43.6	0 52.6	4 35.3	24 25.3	23 46.9	25 16.1	4 02.4
23 Sa	8 08 54	2 51 47	27 31 14	3♉54 38	20 28.2	21D 01.1	8 39.0	5 31.2	12 30.0	13 05.9	1 06.2	4 34.4	24 29.4	23 49.3	25 18.2	4 04.4
24 Su	8 12 51	3 52 49	10♉23 31	16 58 20	20 25.0	21 01.2	9 26.8	6 46.6	12 06.7	13 28.1	1 19.8	4 33.3	24 33.4	23 51.7	25 20.4	4 06.4
25 M	8 16 47	4 53 49	23 39 37	0♊27 09	20 21.8	21 01.8	10 18.5	8 02.0	11 43.1	13 50.2	1 33.5	4 32.1	24 37.4	23 54.2	25 22.5	4 08.3
26 Tu	8 20 44	5 54 49	7♊21 37	14 22 54	20 18.6	21 02.9	11 13.7	9 17.4	11 19.4	14 12.2	1 47.3	4 30.9	24 41.5	23 56.8	25 24.7	4 10.2
27 W	8 24 40	6 55 48	21 30 56	28 45 28	20 15.5	21 04.1	12 12.1	10 32.7	10 55.5	14 34.1	2 01.0	4 29.5	24 45.6	23 59.3	25 26.9	4 12.2
28 Th	8 28 37	7 56 45	6♋06 02	13♋32 03	20 12.3	21 05.1	13 13.4	11 48.1	10 31.6	14 55.9	2 14.9	4 28.0	24 49.7	24 01.9	25 29.1	4 14.0
29 F	8 32 34	8 57 42	21 02 41	28 36 58	20 09.1	21R 05.6	14 17.4	13 03.4	10 07.5	15 17.5	2 28.7	4 26.4	24 53.8	24 04.5	25 31.3	4 15.9
30 Sa	8 36 30	9 58 37	6♌13 47	13♌51 53	20 05.9	21 05.1	15 23.7	14 18.8	9 43.5	15 39.1	2 42.6	4 24.7	24 58.0	24 07.2	25 33.5	4 17.8
31 Su	8 40 27	10♒59 32	21 30 01	29 06 50	20♑02.8	21♑03.6	16♑32.3	15♒34.1	9♌19.6	16♐00.5	2♓56.6	4♎22.9	25♒02.1	24♓09.9	25♒35.7	4♑19.6

1st of Month

Julian Day # 2455197.5
Obliquity 23°26'20"
SVP 5♓06'56"
GC 26♐58.7
Eris 20♈55.5R

Day	⚴
1	7♏46.9
6	9 30.8
11	11 10.6
16	12 46.1
21	14 16.8
26	15 42.1
31	17 01.8

Day	⚵
1	4♈25.7
6	6 27.0
11	8 34.1
16	10 46.5
21	13 03.9
26	15 25.7
31	17 51.5

Day	⚶
1	6♍37.6
6	6 38.8R
11	6 28.3R
16	6 05.9R
21	5 31.8R
26	4 46.6R
31	3 51.1R

DECLINATION and LATITUDE

Day	☉ Decl	☽ Decl	☽ Lat	☽ 12h Decl	☿ Decl	☿ Lat	♀ Decl	♀ Lat	♂ Decl	♂ Lat	⚳ Decl	⚳ Lat	♃ Decl	♃ Lat	♄ Decl	♄ Lat
1 F	23S02	23N30	0N43	21N52	20S28	1N38	23S39	0S26	18N45	3N45	17S08	3N59	13S37	0S56	0N19	2N17
2 Sa	22 57	19 51	0 14	17 30	20 19	1 57	23 36	0 28	18 50	3 48	17 14	3 58	13 32	0 56	0 18	2 18
3 Su	22 51	14 53	2 01	12 04	20 10	2 15	23 33	0 31	18 56	3 50	17 19	3 57	13 28	0 56	0 18	2 18
4 M	22 45	9 05	3 12	6 01	20 03	2 31	23 29	0 33	19 02	3 53	17 24	3 56	13 24	0 56	0 18	2 18
5 Tu	22 39	2 54	4 10	0S13	19 58	2 45	23 24	0 35	19 08	3 55	17 29	3 55	13 20	0 56	0 18	2 18
6 W	22 32	3S17	4 51	6 16	19 54	2 57	23 18	0 37	19 14	3 57	17 34	3 53	13 15	0 56	0 18	2 19
7 Th	22 25	9 08	5 13	11 51	19 51	3 06	23 12	0 39	19 21	3 60	17 39	3 52	13 11	0 56	0 18	2 19
8 F	22 17	14 24	5 17	16 44	19 50	3 13	23 05	0 42	19 27	4 02	17 44	3 51	13 06	0 56	0 18	2 19
9 Sa	22 09	18 51	5 05	20 43	19 51	3 18	22 58	0 44	19 34	4 04	17 49	3 50	13 02	0 56	0 18	2 20
10 Su	22 00	22 19	4 37	23 37	19 52	3 20	22 49	0 46	19 41	4 06	17 54	3 49	12 58	0 56	0 18	2 20
11 M	21 51	24 38	3 57	25 20	19 55	3 20	22 40	0 48	19 48	4 08	17 58	3 48	12 53	0 56	0 18	2 20
12 Tu	21 42	25 43	3 06	25 47	19 59	3 17	22 31	0 50	19 55	4 10	18 03	3 47	12 48	0 56	0 18	2 20
13 W	21 32	25 32	2 08	24 60	20 04	3 14	22 20	0 52	20 03	4 12	18 08	3 46	12 44	0 56	0 18	2 21
14 Th	21 22	24 09	1 04	23 03	20 10	3 08	22 09	0 54	20 10	4 14	18 12	3 44	12 39	0 56	0 19	2 21
15 F	21 11	21 42	0N02	20 07	20 17	3 02	21 57	0 55	20 18	4 16	18 17	3 43	12 35	0 56	0 19	2 21
16 Sa	20 60	18 20	1 07	16 22	20 25	2 55	21 45	0 57	20 25	4 18	18 21	3 42	12 30	0 56	0 19	2 22
17 Su	20 48	14 15	2 09	11 59	20 33	2 46	21 32	0 59	20 33	4 19	18 25	3 41	12 25	0 55	0 20	2 22
18 M	20 36	9 38	3 06	7 11	20 41	2 37	21 18	1 01	20 41	4 21	18 30	3 40	12 21	0 55	0 20	2 22
19 Tu	20 24	4 40	3 55	2 06	20 49	2 28	21 04	1 02	20 48	4 22	18 34	3 39	12 16	0 55	0 20	2 22
20 W	20 11	0N30	4 34	3N06	20 58	2 18	20 49	1 04	20 56	4 24	18 38	3 37	12 11	0 55	0 21	2 23
21 Th	19 58	5 41	5 01	8 15	21 06	2 08	20 33	1 05	21 04	4 25	18 42	3 36	12 06	0 55	0 21	2 23
22 F	19 45	10 45	5 15	13 10	21 14	1 58	20 17	1 07	21 12	4 26	18 46	3 35	12 02	0 55	0 22	2 23
23 Sa	19 31	15 29	5 15	17 40	21 21	1 48	19 60	1 09	21 19	4 27	18 50	3 34	11 57	0 55	0 23	2 24
24 Su	19 17	19 40	4 59	21 28	21 29	1 38	19 43	1 10	21 27	4 28	18 54	3 33	11 52	0 55	0 23	2 24
25 M	19 02	22 60	4 27	24 14	21 35	1 28	19 25	1 12	21 34	4 29	18 57	3 32	11 47	0 55	0 24	2 24
26 Tu	18 48	25 09	3 39	25 40	21 41	1 17	19 06	1 13	21 42	4 30	19 01	3 30	11 42	0 55	0 25	2 24
27 W	18 32	25 46	2 37	25 27	21 46	1 07	18 47	1 14	21 49	4 30	19 05	3 29	11 37	0 55	0 26	2 25
28 Th	18 17	24 40	1 22	23 22	21 50	0 57	18 27	1 15	21 56	4 31	19 08	3 28	11 32	0 55	0 27	2 25
29 F	18 01	21 48	0 00	19 46	21 53	0 48	18 07	1 17	22 03	4 31	19 12	3 27	11 27	0 55	0 27	2 25
30 Sa	17 45	17 23	1S23	14 42	21 55	0 38	17 47	1 18	22 10	4 32	19 15	3 26	11 22	0 55	0 28	2 25
31 Su	17S28	11N48	2S40	8N44	21S57	0N28	17S25	1S19	22N17	4N32	19S19	3N25	11S17	0S55	0N29	2N26

Day	⚷ Decl	⚷ Lat	♅ Decl	♅ Lat	♆ Decl	♆ Lat	♇ Decl	♇ Lat
1	8S10	5N58	3S26	0S45	13S43	0S25	18S18	5N06
6	8 06	5 57	3 22	0 45	13 40	0 25	18 18	5 06
11	8 01	5 56	3 18	0 44	13 37	0 25	18 18	5 05
16	7 56	5 55	3 14	0 44	13 34	0 25	18 18	5 05
21	7 50	5 54	3 10	0 44	13 30	0 25	18 18	5 05
26	7 45	5 53	3 05	0 44	13 27	0 25	18 18	5 05
31	7S39	5N52	2S59	0S44	13S23	0S25	18S17	5N05

Day	⚴ Decl	⚴ Lat	⚵ Decl	⚵ Lat	⚶ Decl	⚶ Lat	Eris Decl	Eris Lat
1	1S02	13N48	7S13	9S47	14N07	5N26	4S33	13S43
6	0 40	14 43	6 27	9 49	14 26	5 47	4 33	13 42
11	0 14	15 41	5 40	9 51	14 51	6 09	4 32	13 41
16	0N16	16 41	4 50	9 53	15 20	6 32	4 31	13 40
21	0 51	17 44	3 58	9 54	15 53	6 54	4 30	13 39
26	1 31	18 49	3 04	9 54	16 31	7 16	4 29	13 38
31	2N16	19N57	2S10	9S55	17N11	7N37	4S27	13S37

Moon Phenomena

Max/0 Decl
dy hr mn
5 11:10 0 S
12 8:31 25S48
19 21:43 0 N
26 21:12 25N47

Max/0 Lat
dy hr mn
1 12:30 0 S
7 18:03 5S18
14 23:19 0 N
22 11:37 5N17
29 0:04 0 S

Perigee/Apogee
dy hr m kilometers
1 20:46 p 358685
17 1:43 a 406435
30 9:02 p 356598

PH dy hr mn
☾ 7 10:41 17♎01
● 15 7:12 25♑01
● 15 7:08 A 11'07"
☽ 23 10:54 3♉20
○ 30 6:19 10♌15

Void of Course Moon

Last Aspect	☽ Ingress
1 15:44 ♅ △	♌ 2 2:42
3 21:56 ♃ ☍	♍ 4 2:54
5 17:26 ♅ ☍	♎ 6 4:59
8 6:08 ♃ △	♏ 8 10:01
10 15:03 ♃ □	♐ 10 18:11
13 2:44 ♃ ✶	♑ 13 4:55
15 9:04 ♀ ☌	♒ 15 17:18
17 20:24 ♆ ☌	♓ 18 6:18
20 6:07 ♅ ☌	♈ 20 18:37
22 19:47 ♆ ✶	♉ 23 4:41
25 3:04 ♆ □	♊ 25 11:12
27 6:33 ♆ △	♋ 27 14:02
29 4:50 ♅ △	♌ 29 14:11
31 6:28 ♆ ☍	♍ 31 13:24

DAILY ASPECTARIAN

1 F ☉#☽ 3:53 · ☿⚻♂ 4:54 · ♀∠⚷ 5:19 · ☽☍☿ 8:36 · ☽⚺♂ 8:49 · ☽⚼⚳ 10:22 · ☽△♅ 15:44 · ☽⚻⚷ 15:48 · ☽⚻♆ 18:07 · ☽⚻♃ 21:11 · ☽#☿ 21:19

2 Sa ☉∠♃ 2:43 · ☽∥♂ 5:14 · ☽⚻♇ 8:03 · ☽#♇ 8:04 · ♀∠♆ 9:51 · ☽✶♄ 9:56 · ☽△⚳ 10:54 · ☽#⚳ 13:06 · ☽⚼♅ 15:40 · ☽⚻♀ 18:48 · ☉⚻☽ 22:32

3 Su ⚶ R 0:00 · ☽⚻☿ 4:57 · ☽#♆ 5:08 · ☽#♃ 6:12 · ☽⚼♇ 8:06 · ☽☌♂ 8:09 · ☽∠♄ 9:59 · ♂⚼♇ 10:58 · ☽⚻♅ 15:47 · ☽☍⚷ 15:58 · ☽☍♆ 18:13 · ☽⚼♀ 21:10 · ☽☍♃ 21:56

4 M ☉⚼☽ 0:30 · ☽⚼☿ 3:14 · ☽#⚷ 3:48 · ♀∠♃ 7:57 · ☽△♇ 8:30 · ☽⚺♄ 10:23 · ☽□⚳ 12:40 · ☉☌☿ 19:07 · ☽#♅ 22:07

5 Tu ☽△♀ 0:06 · ☽△☿ 1:51 · ☉△☽ 3:03 · ☽⚺♂ 8:40 · ☽∥♄ 10:01 · ☿☌♀ 10:41 · ☽#♄ 12:19 · ☽☍♅ 17:26 · ☽⚻⚷ 17:43 · ☽⚻♆ 19:59

6 W ☽∥♅ 0:21 · ☽⚻♃ 0:31 · ☿∠♃ 4:49 · ☽∠♂ 9:47 · ☽□♇ 11:01 · ☽☌♄ 12:55 · ☽✶⚳ 16:48 · ☽∥⚷ 19:31 · ☽⚼⚷ 19:37 · ☽⚼♆ 21:54

7 Th ☽□☿ 0:41 · ☽⚼♃ 2:55 · ☽□♀ 8:36 · ☉□☽ 10:41 · ☽✶♂ 11:36 · ☽∥♃ 17:54 · ☽∠⚳ 20:05 · ☽∥♆ 20:24 · ☉⚻♂ 20:40 · ☽⚻♅ 21:52 · ☽△⚷ 22:18

8 F ☽△♆ 0:35 · ☽△♃ 6:08 · ☿∠♆ 7:30 · ♀⚻♂ 11:57 · ☽✶♇ 16:34 · ☽∥⚳ 17:50 · ☽⚺♄ 18:30 · ☽∥♇ 20:45

9 Sa ☽⚺⚳ 0:14 · ☽⚼♅ 1:18 · ☽✶☿ 2:28 · ☽#♂ 4:32 · ☽∥☿ 6:12 · ☿∠⚷ 10:25 · ☽□♂ 17:25 · ☽∠♇ 20:33 · ☽✶♀ 21:19 · ☉∥☽ 21:37 · ☉✶☽ 22:17 · ☽∠♄ 22:28 · ☿⚺⚳ 22:56

10 Su ☽∥♀ 4:08 · ☽∠☿ 4:39 · ☽△♅ 5:30 · ☽□⚷ 6:05 · ☽□♆ 8:23 · ☽□♃ 15:03

11 M ☽⚺♇ 1:15 · ☽✶♄ 3:08 · ☽∠♀ 5:11 · ☉∠☽ 5:31 · ☽⚺☿ 7:44 · ☽☌⚳ 11:00 · ☉☌♀ 21:07

12 Tu ☽△♂ 1:50 · ☉⚺☽ 13:31 · ☽⚺♀ 13:52 · ☽□♅ 15:53 · ☽✶⚷ 16:39 · ☽✶♆ 18:53

13 W ☽✶♃ 2:44 · ☽⚼♂ 6:46 · ♀✶♅ 9:49 · ☽☌♇ 12:24 · ☽□♄ 14:12 · ♄ R 15:58 · ☽☌☿ 16:36 · ♀⚺⚷ 17:52 · ☉✶♅ 18:43 · ☽∠⚷ 22:42

14 Th ☽⚺⚳ 0:18 · ☽∠♆ 0:54 · ☉⚺⚷ 5:04 · ☽∠♃ 9:19 · ☽⚻♂ 12:04 · ♀∠⚳ 13:24 · ☿#♂ 14:43 · ♀⚺♆ 15:26 · ☽∥♀ 21:42

15 F ☽✶♅ 4:10 · ☉∥☽ 4:20 · ☽⚺⚷ 5:05 · ⚳∥♇ 7:10 · ☉☌☽ 7:12 · ☽⚺♆ 7:14 · ☉⚺♆ 7:30 · ☽∠⚳ 7:34 · ☽☌♀ 9:04 · ☽#♂ 10:19 · ☽∥☿ 10:21 · ☉∠⚳ 13:35 · ☽⚺♃ 16:13 · ☿ D 16:53 · ☽∥⚳ 23:51

16 Sa ☽∥♇ 0:10 · ☽⚺♇ 1:06 · ☽△♄ 2:44 · ☽⚺☿ 4:37 · ☽∠♅ 10:43 · ☽✶⚳ 15:03 · ☽☍♂ 23:14

17 Su ☿#♂ 1:51 · ☽∥♆ 3:46 · ☽∠♇ 7:42 · ☽⚼♄ 9:14 · ☽∥♃ 9:55 · ☽∠☿ 11:32 · ☽⚺♅ 17:20 · ☽☌⚷ 18:24 · ☉∥☿ 18:28 · ☉#♂ 18:53 · ☽☌♆ 20:24

18 M ☉⚺☽ 1:57 · ♃ ♓ 2:11 · ☽⚺♀ 5:19 · ☽☌♃ 6:23 · ☽∥⚷ 8:35 · ☽✶♇ 14:16 · ♀ ♒ 14:36 · ☽⚻♄ 15:42 · ♀⚺♃ 17:16 · ☽✶☿ 18:49

19 Tu ☽□⚳ 5:59 · ☽∥♅ 6:56 · ☽⚻♂ 10:19 · ☉∠☽ 11:10 · ☿∥♀ 14:37 · ☽∠♀ 15:15 · ♀#♂ 16:12 · ☽#♄ 20:07 · ☽∥♄ 23:20

20 W ☉ ♒ 4:29 · ☽☌♅ 6:07 · ☽⚺⚷ 7:18 · ☽⚺♆ 9:06 · ☽#♅ 12:20 · ☽⚼♂ 15:27 · ☉⚺♃ 18:39 · ☽⚺♃ 19:50 · ☉✶☽ 19:55

21 Th ☽✶♀ 0:38 · ☽□♇ 2:33 · ☽☍♄ 3:43 · ☽□☿ 9:27 · ☽#⚷ 10:03 · ☽∠⚷ 13:07 · ☽∠♆ 14:48 · ☽△⚳ 19:29 · ♀⚺♇ 19:37 · ☽△♂ 20:03

22 F ☽∠♃ 1:46 · ♂△⚳ 5:00 · ♀△♄ 6:08 · ☽#♃ 6:10 · ☽#♆ 13:35 · ☽⚺♅ 16:57 · ☽✶⚷ 18:13 · ☽✶♆ 19:47

23 Sa ☽⚼⚳ 1:08 · ☽✶♃ 6:52 · ☉□☽ 10:54 · ☽△♇ 12:20 · ☽⚻♄ 13:13 · ☽#♇ 15:40 · ☽□♀ 16:37 · ☽#⚳ 19:09 · ☽∠♅ 21:10 · ☉#☽ 21:44 · ☽△☿ 22:09

24 Su ☽#♀ 0:15 · ☽□♂ 3:04 · ☿∠⚷ 3:27 · ☉⚺♇ 5:31 · ☽⚻⚳ 5:48 · ☽∥♂ 12:22 · ☽#☿ 12:31 · ☉△♄ 15:38 · ☽⚼♇ 15:53 · ☽⚼♄ 16:38

25 M ☽✶♅ 0:26 · ☽□⚷ 1:44 · ☿∠♆ 1:53 · ☽□♆ 3:04 · ☽⚼☿ 3:08 · ☉∥⚳ 6:29 · ☿#♂ 9:04 · ☽□♃ 14:10 · ♀∠♅ 17:12 · ☽⚻♇ 18:28 · ☽△♄ 19:05 · ☉△☽ 21:18

26 Tu ☿⚻♂ 1:41 · ☽△♀ 3:39 · ♀∥⚳ 5:13 · ☽✶♂ 6:37 · ☽⚻☿ 7:07 · ☽☍⚳ 12:00

27 W ☉⚼☽ 0:45 · ☽□♅ 4:08 · ☽△⚷ 5:25 · ♀☍♂ 5:30 · ☽△♆ 6:33 · ☽∠♂ 7:08 · ☽⚼♀ 7:20 · ☽△♃ 17:37 · ☽☍♇ 20:57 · ☽□♄ 21:21 · ☉∥♇ 22:51

28 Th ☉⚻☽ 3:13 · ☽⚼⚷ 6:04 · ☽⚺♂ 6:58 · ☽⚼♆ 7:07 · ☽⚻♀ 10:04 · ♀∥♇ 11:44 · ☽☍☿ 12:22 · ☽⚻⚳ 14:35 · ☽⚼♃ 18:14 · ☽∥♂ 22:20 · ☽#☿ 23:26

29 F ☉∠♅ 2:49 · ☽△♅ 4:50 · ☽⚻⚷ 6:09 · ☽⚻♆ 7:07 · ☽#⚳ 14:46 · ☽⚼⚳ 15:00 · ☽⚻♃ 18:22 · ☽#♇ 19:34 · ☉☍♂ 19:44 · ☽⚻♇ 20:57 · ☽✶♄ 21:09 · ☽#♀ 21:57 · ☉#☽ 22:08

30 Sa ☽⚼♅ 4:33 · ☽☌♂ 5:21 · ☉☍☽ 6:19 · ☿⚺⚳ 7:57 · ☉∥♀ 9:02 · ☽☍♀ 13:50 · ☽△⚳ 15:10 · ☽⚻☿ 15:34 · ☽#♆ 17:33 · ☽⚼♇ 20:35 · ☽∠♄ 20:41

31 Su ☽#♃ 2:06 · ☽⚻♅ 4:12 · ☽☍⚷ 5:35 · ☽☍♆ 6:28 · ♂⚼♅ 8:42 · ♀✶⚳ 11:45 · ☽#⚷ 16:13 · ☽⚼☿ 17:10 · ☽☍♃ 18:20 · ☽△♇ 20:18 · ☽⚺♄ 20:18 · ♄□♇ 21:28

February 2010

LONGITUDE

Day	Sid.Time	☉	☽	☽ 12 hour	Mean☊	True☊	☿	♀	♂	⚳	♃	♄	⚷	♅	♆	♇
	h m s	° ' "	° ' "	° ' "	° '	° '	° '	° '	° '	° '	° '	° '	° '	° '	° '	° '
1 M	8 44 23	12♒00 25	6♍41 06	14♍11 38	19♑59.6	21♑01.1	17♑42.8	16♒49.4	8♌55.7	16♐21.8	3♓10.6	4♎21.1	25♒06.3	24♓12.6	25♒37.9	4♑21.5
2 Tu	8 48 20	13 01 18	21 37 26	28 57 37	19 56.4	20R 58.1	18 55.2	18 04.7	8R 31.9	16 43.0	3 24.6	4R 19.1	25 10.4	24 15.4	25 40.2	4 23.3
3 W	8 52 16	14 02 09	6♎11 32	13♎18 42	19 53.2	20 55.0	20 09.4	19 20.0	8 08.3	17 04.1	3 38.6	4 17.0	25 14.6	24 18.1	25 42.4	4 25.0
4 Th	8 56 13	15 03 00	20 18 52	27 11 55	19 50.0	20 52.3	21 25.1	20 35.2	7 44.9	17 25.0	3 52.7	4 14.8	25 18.8	24 21.0	25 44.6	4 26.8
5 F	9 00 09	16 03 50	3♏57 57	10♏37 42	19 46.9	20D 50.6	22 42.3	21 50.5	7 21.8	17 45.8	4 06.8	4 12.5	25 23.0	24 23.8	25 46.9	4 28.6
6 Sa	9 04 06	17 04 39	17 09 53	23 36 31	19 43.7	20 50.0	24 00.9	23 05.7	6 59.0	18 06.5	4 21.0	4 10.1	25 27.2	24 26.7	25 49.2	4 30.3
7 Su	9 08 03	18 05 28	29 57 34	6♐13 32	19 40.5	20 50.6	25 20.9	24 21.0	6 36.6	18 27.0	4 35.2	4 07.7	25 31.4	24 29.6	25 51.4	4 32.0
8 M	9 11 59	19 06 15	12♐24 59	18 32 28	19 37.3	20 52.0	26 42.1	25 36.2	6 14.5	18 47.5	4 49.4	4 05.1	25 35.6	24 32.5	25 53.7	4 33.7
9 Tu	9 15 56	20 07 02	24 36 31	0♑37 42	19 34.2	20 53.8	28 04.5	26 51.4	5 52.9	19 07.8	5 03.6	4 02.5	25 39.9	24 35.4	25 56.0	4 35.3
10 W	9 19 52	21 07 47	6♑36 31	12 33 27	19 31.0	20 55.5	29 28.0	28 06.6	5 31.7	19 27.9	5 17.9	3 59.7	25 44.1	24 38.4	25 58.2	4 37.0
11 Th	9 23 49	22 08 31	18 28 57	24 23 26	19 27.8	20R 56.3	0♒52.6	29 21.8	5 11.0	19 47.9	5 32.2	3 56.9	25 48.3	24 41.4	26 00.5	4 38.6
12 F	9 27 45	23 09 14	0♒17 17	6♒10 52	19 24.6	20 55.9	2 18.3	0♓37.0	4 50.9	20 07.8	5 46.5	3 53.9	25 52.6	24 44.5	26 02.8	4 40.2
13 Sa	9 31 42	24 09 56	12 04 28	17 58 23	19 21.4	20 53.8	3 45.0	1 52.2	4 31.3	20 27.5	6 00.9	3 50.9	25 56.8	24 47.5	26 05.1	4 41.8
14 Su	9 35 38	25 10 36	23 52 52	29 48 10	19 18.3	20 49.9	5 12.6	3 07.3	4 12.3	20 47.0	6 15.2	3 47.8	26 01.1	24 50.6	26 07.4	4 43.3
15 M	9 39 35	26 11 15	5♓44 29	11♓42 02	19 15.1	20 44.4	6 41.3	4 22.5	3 54.0	21 06.5	6 29.6	3 44.7	26 05.3	24 53.7	26 09.6	4 44.9
16 Tu	9 43 32	27 11 53	17 41 02	23 41 40	19 11.9	20 37.7	8 10.9	5 37.6	3 36.3	21 25.7	6 44.0	3 41.4	26 09.5	24 56.8	26 11.9	4 46.4
17 W	9 47 28	28 12 29	29 44 10	5♈48 46	19 08.7	20 30.4	9 41.5	6 52.7	3 19.3	21 44.8	6 58.4	3 38.1	26 13.8	24 59.9	26 14.2	4 47.8
18 Th	9 51 25	29 13 03	11♈55 43	18 05 17	19 05.6	20 23.3	11 13.0	8 07.8	3 03.0	22 03.8	7 12.8	3 34.7	26 18.0	25 03.1	26 16.5	4 49.3
19 F	9 55 21	0♓13 35	24 17 45	0♉33 27	19 02.4	20 17.1	12 45.5	9 22.8	2 47.4	22 22.6	7 27.3	3 31.2	26 22.2	25 06.3	26 18.7	4 50.7
20 Sa	9 59 18	1 14 06	6♉52 42	13 15 53	18 59.2	20 12.5	14 18.8	10 37.9	2 32.5	22 41.2	7 41.7	3 27.6	26 26.5	25 09.4	26 21.0	4 52.1
21 Su	10 03 14	2 14 35	19 42 33	26 15 32	18 56.0	20 09.8	15 53.2	11 52.9	2 18.4	22 59.6	7 56.2	3 24.0	26 30.7	25 12.7	26 23.3	4 53.5
22 M	10 07 11	3 15 02	2♊52 43	9♊35 16	18 52.8	20D 08.9	17 28.4	13 07.9	2 05.0	23 17.9	8 10.6	3 20.3	26 34.9	25 15.9	26 25.6	4 54.9
23 Tu	10 11 07	4 15 28	16 23 29	23 17 37	18 49.7	20 09.5	19 04.6	14 22.9	1 52.5	23 36.0	8 25.1	3 16.5	26 39.1	25 19.1	26 27.8	4 56.2
24 W	10 15 04	5 15 51	0♋17 46	7♋23 58	18 46.5	20 10.8	20 41.8	15 37.9	1 40.7	23 54.0	8 39.6	3 12.7	26 43.3	25 22.4	26 30.1	4 57.5
25 Th	10 19 01	6 16 13	14 36 08	21 53 59	18 43.3	20R 11.8	22 19.9	16 52.8	1 29.7	24 11.7	8 54.1	3 08.8	26 47.5	25 25.7	26 32.4	4 58.8
26 F	10 22 57	7 16 32	29 17 03	6♌44 43	18 40.1	20 11.6	23 59.0	18 07.7	1 19.4	24 29.3	9 08.6	3 04.8	26 51.7	25 29.0	26 34.6	5 00.0
27 Sa	10 26 54	8 16 50	14♌16 08	21 50 19	18 37.0	20 09.4	25 39.1	19 22.6	1 10.0	24 46.7	9 23.1	3 00.8	26 55.9	25 32.3	26 36.9	5 01.2
28 Su	10 30 50	9♓17 05	29 26 08	7♍02 18	18♑33.8	20♑05.0	27♒20.1	20♓37.5	1♌01.4	25♐04.0	9♓37.6	2♎56.7	27♒00.0	25♓35.6	26♒39.1	5♑02.4

1st of Month

Julian Day # 2455228.5
Obliquity 23°26'20"
SVP 5♓06'50"
GC 26♐58.8
Eris 20♈58.2

Day	⚴	Day	⚵	Day	⚶
1	17♏17.0	1	18♈21.1	1	3♍38.9R
6	18 29.1	6	20 51.2	6	2 32.8R
11	19 34.2	11	23 24.5	11	1 19.9R
16	20 31.7	16	26 00.9	16	0 02.5R
21	21 20.9	21	28 39.9	21	28♌43.2R
26	22 01.1	26	1♉21.2	26	27 24.8R

DECLINATION and LATITUDE

Day	☉ Decl	☽ Decl	☽ Lat	☽12h Decl	☿ Decl	☿ Lat	♀ Decl	♀ Lat	♂ Decl	♂ Lat	⚳ Decl	⚳ Lat	♃ Decl	♃ Lat	♄ Decl	♄ Lat
1 M	17S12	5N33	3S46	2N20	21S57	0N19	17S04	1S20	22N24	4N32	19S22	3N23	11S12	0S55	0N30	2N26
2 Tu	16 54	0S53	4 35	4S03	21 56	0 10	16 42	1 21	22 30	4 32	19 25	3 22	11 07	0 55	0 31	2 26
3 W	16 37	7 07	5 05	10 03	21 54	0 01	16 19	1 22	22 36	4 32	19 29	3 21	11 02	0 55	0 32	2 26
4 Th	16 19	12 48	5 15	15 20	21 51	0S07	15 56	1 23	22 42	4 31	19 32	3 20	10 57	0 55	0 33	2 27
5 F	16 01	17 39	5 07	19 42	21 47	0 16	15 32	1 23	22 48	4 31	19 35	3 18	10 52	0 55	0 35	2 27
6 Sa	15 43	21 28	4 43	22 57	21 42	0 24	15 08	1 24	22 53	4 31	19 38	3 17	10 46	0 55	0 36	2 27
7 Su	15 24	24 07	4 05	24 59	21 35	0 32	14 44	1 25	22 58	4 30	19 41	3 16	10 41	0 55	0 37	2 27
8 M	15 06	25 31	3 16	25 45	21 28	0 40	14 19	1 25	23 03	4 29	19 44	3 15	10 36	0 55	0 38	2 28
9 Tu	14 47	25 39	2 20	25 16	21 19	0 47	13 54	1 26	23 08	4 29	19 47	3 14	10 31	0 55	0 39	2 28
10 W	14 27	24 34	1 18	23 36	21 09	0 54	13 29	1 26	23 13	4 28	19 50	3 12	10 26	0 55	0 41	2 28
11 Th	14 08	22 23	0 13	20 56	20 57	1 01	13 03	1 27	23 17	4 27	19 52	3 11	10 20	0 55	0 42	2 28
12 F	13 48	19 15	0N51	17 24	20 44	1 07	12 37	1 27	23 21	4 26	19 55	3 10	10 15	0 55	0 43	2 29
13 Sa	13 28	15 22	1 53	13 11	20 30	1 14	12 10	1 27	23 25	4 25	19 58	3 08	10 10	0 55	0 45	2 29
14 Su	13 08	10 53	2 50	8 28	20 15	1 20	11 43	1 27	23 28	4 24	20 00	3 07	10 05	0 55	0 46	2 29
15 M	12 47	5 59	3 40	3 27	19 59	1 25	11 16	1 28	23 31	4 22	20 03	3 06	9 59	0 56	0 48	2 29
16 Tu	12 27	0 52	4 21	1N44	19 41	1 31	10 48	1 28	23 34	4 21	20 06	3 05	9 54	0 56	0 49	2 30
17 W	12 06	4N20	4 50	6 54	19 22	1 36	10 21	1 28	23 37	4 19	20 08	3 03	9 49	0 56	0 51	2 30
18 Th	11 45	9 25	5 07	11 52	19 01	1 40	9 53	1 28	23 39	4 18	20 10	3 02	9 43	0 56	0 52	2 30
19 F	11 24	14 12	5 09	16 25	18 39	1 45	9 24	1 27	23 42	4 16	20 13	3 01	9 38	0 56	0 54	2 30
20 Sa	11 02	18 29	4 57	20 21	18 16	1 49	8 56	1 27	23 43	4 15	20 15	2 59	9 33	0 56	0 55	2 30
21 Su	10 41	21 60	4 30	23 23	17 52	1 53	8 27	1 27	23 45	4 13	20 18	2 58	9 27	0 56	0 57	2 31
22 M	10 19	24 28	3 48	25 13	17 26	1 56	7 58	1 27	23 47	4 11	20 20	2 57	9 22	0 56	0 59	2 31
23 Tu	9 57	25 36	2 53	25 36	16 59	1 59	7 29	1 26	23 48	4 08	20 22	2 55	9 16	0 56	1 00	2 31
24 W	9 35	25 12	1 46	24 23	16 31	2 02	6 59	1 26	23 49	4 06	20 24	2 54	9 11	0 56	1 02	2 31
25 Th	9 13	23 08	0 30	21 30	16 01	2 04	6 29	1 25	23 49	4 06	20 26	2 52	9 06	0 56	1 04	2 31
26 F	8 50	19 30	0S49	17 10	15 30	2 06	5 60	1 25	23 50	4 04	20 29	2 51	9 00	0 56	1 06	2 31
27 Sa	8 28	14 32	2 06	11 40	14 58	2 07	5 30	1 25	23 50	4 02	20 31	2 50	8 55	0 56	1 07	2 32
28 Su	8S05	8N37	3S15	5N26	14S24	2S08	4S60	1S24	23N50	4N00	20S33	2N48	8S49	0S56	1N09	2N32

Day	⚷ Decl	⚷ Lat	♅ Decl	♅ Lat	♆ Decl	♆ Lat	♇ Decl	♇ Lat
1	7S37	5N52	2S58	0S44	13S22	0S25	18S17	5N05
6	7 31	5 51	2 52	0 44	13 19	0 25	18 17	5 05
11	7 24	5 51	2 47	0 44	13 15	0 25	18 17	5 05
16	7 18	5 51	2 40	0 43	13 11	0 25	18 16	5 05
21	7 11	5 51	2 34	0 43	13 07	0 25	18 16	5 05
26	7S04	5N51	2S27	0S43	13S03	0S25	18S15	5N05

Day	⚴ Decl	⚴ Lat	⚵ Decl	⚵ Lat	⚶ Decl	⚶ Lat	Eris Decl	Eris Lat
1	2N25	20N11	1S59	9S55	17N19	7N41	4S27	13S37
6	3 16	21 22	1 03	9 55	18 01	8 00	4 26	13 36
11	4 11	22 36	0 07	9 54	18 44	8 18	4 25	13 35
16	5 12	23 52	0N49	9 53	19 26	8 33	4 23	13 35
21	6 17	25 11	1 46	9 52	20 07	8 46	4 22	13 34
26	7N26	26N32	2N42	9S51	20N44	8N55	4S20	13S33

Moon Phenomena

Max/0 Decl (dy hr mn)
1 20:40 0 S
8 14:29 25S45
16 3:59 0 N
23 5:55 25N39

Perigee/Apogee (dy hr m kilometers)
13 2:12 a 406541
27 21:52 p 357830

Max/0 Lat (dy hr mn)
4 0:53 5S15
11 4:59 0 N
18 16:20 5N10
25 9:12 0 S

PH (dy hr mn)
☾ 5 23:50 17♏04
● 14 2:52 25♒18
☽ 22 0:43 3♊17
○ 28 16:39 9♍59

Void of Course Moon

Last Aspect				☽ Ingress		
2	4:18	♅	☍	♎	2	13:43
4	9:28	♆	△	♏	4	16:57
6	16:12	♆	□	♐	7	0:05
9	4:59	♀	⚹	♑	9	10:45
11	12:40	♅	⚹	♒	11	23:25
14	4:34	♆	☌	♓	14	12:24
16	14:33	♅	☌	♈	17	0:31
19	3:53	♆	⚹	♉	19	10:56
21	12:16	♆	□	♊	21	18:48
23	17:30	♆	△	♋	23	23:30
25	17:49	♅	△	♌	26	1:09
27	20:16	☿	☍	♍	28	0:53

DAILY ASPECTARIAN

1 M
☽⚺♂ 3:29
☉⚻☽ 9:07
☽#♅ 9:40
☿∠♃ 11:30
☽□⚳ 15:52
☽⚻♀ 17:44
☽∥♄ 18:45
☽△☿ 19:14
☽#♄ 22:37

2 Tu
☽∠♂ 3:01
☽☍♅ 4:18
☽⚻⚷ 5:49
☽⚻♆ 6:37
☽∥♅ 7:45
☉⚼☽ 11:14
☽⚻♃ 19:41
☽⚼♀ 20:36
☽☌♄ 20:49
☽□♇ 21:02
♀⚼♄ 23:05

3 W
♀∠♇ 1:40
☽∥⚷ 1:50
☽⚹♂ 3:11
☽⚼⚷ 6:50
☽⚼♆ 7:36
☉△☽ 14:16
☽∥♃ 15:58
☽⚹⚳ 18:53
☽⚼♃ 21:29

4 Th
☽△♀ 0:31
☽□☿ 2:06
☽∥♆ 2:27
☽⚻♅ 7:02
☽△⚷ 8:44
☽△♆ 9:28
☽∥♀ 13:50
☉∥☽ 15:56
☽∠⚳ 21:48

5 F
☽△♃ 0:16
☽⚺♄ 0:26
☽⚹♇ 0:55
☽∥♇ 3:35
☽□♂ 5:56
♃⚻♄ 8:15
☽⚼♅ 9:49
☽∥⚳ 11:26
☉□☽ 23:50

6 Sa
☽∥☿ 1:39
☽⚺⚳ 1:48
☽∠♄ 3:42
☽∠♇ 4:21
☿⚹♅ 8:03
☽#♂ 11:50
☽□♀ 12:14
☽△♅ 13:37
☽⚹☿ 14:15
☽□⚷ 15:33
☽□♆ 16:12
♃⚹♇ 17:52

7 Su
♀⚺♅ 2:51
☿⚺⚷ 3:18
☽⚹♄ 7:56
☽⚺♇ 8:46
☽□♃ 9:01
☿⚺♆ 9:20
☽△♂ 12:22
☉⚹⚳ 12:50
☽∠☿ 22:26
☉⚼♄ 23:34
♀☌⚷ 23:48

8 M
♀☌♆ 5:45
☉∠♇ 11:08
☽☌⚳ 12:51
☉⚹☽ 14:18
☽⚼♂ 16:50
☽□♅ 23:58

9 Tu
☽⚹⚷ 2:07
☽⚹♆ 2:38
☽⚹♀ 4:59
☽⚺☿ 7:48
☽□♄ 18:46
☽☌♇ 19:59
☽⚹♃ 21:19
☽⚻♂ 21:53
☉∠☽ 22:57

10 W
☽∠⚷ 8:22
☽∠♆ 8:49
☿ ♒ 9:07
♂⚻♃ 9:25
♀∥♆ 12:39
☽∠♀ 14:40
☽#♂ 15:40

11 Th
☽⚺⚳ 2:45
☽∠♃ 4:15
☉⚺☽ 8:08
♀ ♓ 12:11
☽∥☿ 12:39
☽⚹♅ 12:40
♂⚼⚳ 13:49
☽⚺⚷ 14:58
☽⚺♆ 15:20
☽∥⚳ 19:29

12 F
☽⚺♀ 0:45
☽☌☿ 4:41
☽∥♇ 6:27
☽△♄ 7:19
☽⚺♇ 8:57
☽☍♂ 9:02
☽∠⚳ 10:08
☽⚺♃ 11:24
♂⚻♇ 12:01
☽∠♅ 19:20

13 Sa
☿△♄ 1:35
☿☍♂ 10:26
☉∥☽ 11:20
☽∥♆ 11:50
☽⚼♄ 13:43
☽∠♇ 15:32
☉⚺♅ 15:39
☿⚺♇ 15:52
☽⚹⚳ 17:32
☉∥♆ 18:14
☽∥♀ 19:14

14 Su
☽⚺♅ 1:58
☉☌☽ 2:52
☽∥♃ 4:08
☽☌⚷ 4:22
☽☌♆ 4:34
☿∠⚳ 11:58
♀⚻♄ 12:25
♀⚻♂ 16:40
☽∥⚷ 17:37
☿∥⚳ 18:35
☽⚻♄ 19:59
☿⚺♃ 20:14
☽⚻♂ 20:22
☽☌♀ 20:55
☉☌⚷ 21:28
☽⚹♇ 21:59
☉☌♆ 23:20

15 M
☽☌♃ 1:33
☽⚺☿ 2:11
♀⚹♇ 7:18
♂⚹♄ 15:21
☽∥♅ 15:34

16 Tu
☽#♄ 0:11
☽⚼♂ 1:48
⚶R♌ 3:47
☽□⚳ 7:41
☽∥♄ 7:48
☽∠☿ 12:33
☽☌♅ 14:33
☽#♅ 16:15
☽⚺⚷ 17:00
☽⚺♆ 17:02
☉⚺☽ 20:42

17 W
♀☌♃ 2:15
☿∠♅ 5:01
♆☌⚷ 5:08
☽△♂ 6:56
☽☍♄ 7:40
☽□♇ 10:01
☽#⚷ 13:41
☽⚺♃ 14:34
☽⚺♀ 15:42
☽⚹☿ 22:25
☽∠♆ 22:43
☽∠⚷ 22:46

18 Th
☽#♃ 1:26
☽#♀ 2:01
☉∠☽ 4:52
♀∥♃ 9:37
☉#☽ 10:38
☽#♆ 18:30
☉ ♓ 18:37
☽△⚳ 20:12
☽∠♃ 20:23

19 F
☽∠♀ 0:11
☽⚺♅ 1:34
☽⚹♆ 3:53
☽⚹⚷ 4:01
☉⚹☽ 12:22
☽□♂ 15:56
☽⚻♄ 17:33
☽△♇ 20:11
☽#♇ 22:41
☽#☿ 22:49

20 Sa
☿∥♇ 0:13
☽⚼⚳ 1:34
☽⚹♃ 1:34
☽∠♅ 6:12
☽⚹♀ 7:50
☽#⚳ 11:27
☽□☿ 15:54
☽⚼♄ 21:34

21 Su
☽⚼♇ 0:19
☉⚻♂ 1:14
☽⚻⚳ 6:10
☽⚹♅ 10:08
☽□♆ 12:16
☽□⚷ 12:32
☽∥♂ 15:56
☽⚹♂ 22:35

22 M
☉□☽ 0:43
☽△♄ 0:49
☉⚻♄ 1:57
☽⚻♇ 3:40
☽□♃ 9:40
☿⚼♄ 12:29
☽□♀ 20:07

23 Tu
☽∠♂ 0:50
☽△☿ 5:19
⚵ ♉ 11:48
☽☍⚳ 12:48
☿∠♇ 12:56
☽□♅ 15:33
☉⚹♇ 16:32
☽△♆ 17:30
♀∥⚷ 17:46
☽△⚷ 17:52

24 W
☽⚺♂ 2:19
☽□♄ 4:55
☽☍♇ 7:54
☉△☽ 9:03
☽⚼☿ 10:19
☽△♃ 14:21
♀⚼♂ 17:31
☽∥♂ 17:52
☽⚼♆ 18:54
☽⚼⚷ 19:19

25 Th
☽△♀ 4:07
☉∥♃ 9:54
☉⚼☽ 11:47
☽⚻☿ 14:18
☽⚼♃ 15:31
☽⚻⚳ 16:04
☽△♅ 17:49
☽#⚳ 18:28
☽⚻♆ 19:36
☽⚻⚷ 20:03

26 F
☽☌♂ 3:15
☽⚹♄ 6:05
☽#♇ 6:34
☽⚼♀ 6:46
☿⚹⚳ 8:51
☽⚻♇ 9:13
☉⚻☽ 13:46
☽⚻♃ 16:06
☽⚼⚳ 16:42
☽⚼♅ 18:02
☽#☿ 21:54
☿⚺♅ 22:20

27 Sa
☽∠♄ 5:55
☽#♆ 6:22
☽⚻♀ 8:50
☽⚼♇ 9:08
☿☌♆ 14:04
☽△⚳ 16:58
☽⚻♅ 17:55
☿☌⚷ 19:02
☽☍♆ 19:36
☽☍⚷ 20:08
☽☍☿ 20:16
☽#♃ 23:11

28 Su
☉#☽ 2:09
☽⚺♂ 2:29
☽⚺♄ 5:31
☽#⚷ 6:07
☽△♇ 8:51
☉☌♃ 10:45
☽#♀ 14:49
☽☍♃ 16:21
☉☍☽ 16:39
☽#♅ 23:17

LONGITUDE

March 2010

Day	Sid.Time	☉	☽	☽ 12 hour	Mean ☊	True ☊	☿	♀	♂	⚳	♃	♄	⚷	♅	♆	♇
	h m s	° ' "	° ' "	° ' "	° '	° '	° '	° '	° '	° '	° '	° '	° '	° '	° '	° '
1 M	10 34 47	10♓17 19	14♍37 32	22♍10 30	18♑30.6	19♑58.4	29♒02.2	21♓52.3	0♌53.5	25♐21.0	9♓52.1	2♎52.6	27♒04.2	25♓38.9	26♒41.3	5♑03.6
2 Tu	10 38 43	11 17 31	29 39 58	7♎04 47	18 27.4	19R 50.5	0♓45.3	23 07.1	0R 46.5	25 37.9	10 06.6	2R 48.4	27 08.3	25 42.3	26 43.6	5 04.7
3 W	10 42 40	12 17 41	14♎23 59	21 36 47	18 24.2	19 42.1	2 29.5	24 21.9	0 40.2	25 54.5	10 21.1	2 44.2	27 12.4	25 45.6	26 45.8	5 05.8
4 Th	10 46 36	13 17 50	28 42 37	5♏41 07	18 21.1	19 34.3	4 14.7	25 36.7	0 34.7	26 11.0	10 35.6	2 39.9	27 16.5	25 49.0	26 48.0	5 06.9
5 F	10 50 33	14 17 57	12♏32 08	19 15 43	18 17.9	19 28.1	6 01.0	26 51.4	0 30.0	26 27.3	10 50.0	2 35.5	27 20.6	25 52.4	26 50.2	5 07.9
6 Sa	10 54 30	15 18 03	25 52 04	2♐21 32	18 14.7	19 24.0	7 48.4	28 06.2	0 26.0	26 43.4	11 04.5	2 31.2	27 24.7	25 55.7	26 52.4	5 08.9
7 Su	10 58 26	16 18 07	8♐44 35	15 01 46	18 11.5	19D 22.0	9 36.8	29 20.9	0 22.8	26 59.2	11 19.0	2 26.8	27 28.8	25 59.1	26 54.6	5 09.9
8 M	11 02 23	17 18 10	21 13 41	27 20 59	18 08.4	19 21.7	11 26.4	0♈35.6	0 20.4	27 14.9	11 33.5	2 22.3	27 32.8	26 02.5	26 56.7	5 10.9
9 Tu	11 06 19	18 18 11	3♑24 20	9♑24 25	18 05.2	19 22.4	13 17.0	1 50.2	0 18.8	27 30.3	11 47.9	2 17.8	27 36.8	26 05.9	26 58.9	5 11.8
10 W	11 10 16	19 18 10	15 21 52	21 17 20	18 02.0	19R 23.2	15 08.8	3 04.9	0D 17.9	27 45.6	12 02.4	2 13.3	27 40.8	26 09.3	27 01.1	5 12.7
11 Th	11 14 12	20 18 08	27 11 26	3♒04 45	17 58.8	19 22.9	17 01.6	4 19.5	0 17.7	28 00.6	12 16.8	2 08.8	27 44.8	26 12.8	27 03.2	5 13.6
12 F	11 18 09	21 18 04	8♒57 47	14 51 03	17 55.7	19 20.8	18 55.5	5 34.1	0 18.3	28 15.4	12 31.2	2 04.2	27 48.8	26 16.2	27 05.3	5 14.4
13 Sa	11 22 05	22 17 58	20 44 58	26 39 56	17 52.5	19 16.1	20 50.4	6 48.6	0 19.6	28 30.0	12 45.6	1 59.6	27 52.7	26 19.6	27 07.4	5 15.2
14 Su	11 26 02	23 17 50	2♓36 16	8♓34 15	17 49.3	19 08.8	22 46.4	8 03.2	0 21.6	28 44.3	13 00.0	1 54.9	27 56.7	26 23.0	27 09.5	5 16.0
15 M	11 29 59	24 17 40	14 34 07	20 36 04	17 46.1	18 58.9	24 43.2	9 17.7	0 24.3	28 58.5	13 14.4	1 50.3	28 00.6	26 26.5	27 11.6	5 16.8
16 Tu	11 33 55	25 17 29	26 40 15	2♈46 46	17 42.9	18 47.1	26 41.0	10 32.2	0 27.8	29 12.3	13 28.8	1 45.6	28 04.4	26 29.9	27 13.7	5 17.5
17 W	11 37 52	26 17 15	8♈55 43	15 07 10	17 39.8	18 34.3	28 39.5	11 46.6	0 31.9	29 26.0	13 43.1	1 40.9	28 08.3	26 33.3	27 15.8	5 18.2
18 Th	11 41 48	27 17 00	21 21 12	27 37 51	17 36.6	18 21.7	0♈38.7	13 01.1	0 36.7	29 39.4	13 57.4	1 36.2	28 12.1	26 36.7	27 17.8	5 18.8
19 F	11 45 45	28 16 42	3♉57 14	10♉19 24	17 33.4	18 10.4	2 38.5	14 15.5	0 42.2	29 52.5	14 11.7	1 31.5	28 15.9	26 40.2	27 19.8	5 19.4
20 Sa	11 49 41	29 16 23	16 44 29	23 12 37	17 30.2	18 01.3	4 38.7	15 29.8	0 48.3	0♑05.5	14 26.0	1 26.8	28 19.7	26 43.6	27 21.9	5 20.0
21 Su	11 53 38	0♈16 01	29 43 59	6♊18 44	17 27.0	17 55.0	6 39.0	16 44.2	0 55.0	0 18.1	14 40.2	1 22.0	28 23.4	26 47.0	27 23.9	5 20.6
22 M	11 57 34	1 15 37	12♊57 07	19 39 21	17 23.9	17 51.5	8 39.3	17 58.5	1 02.4	0 30.5	14 54.5	1 17.3	28 27.1	26 50.5	27 25.8	5 21.1
23 Tu	12 01 31	2 15 10	26 25 39	3♋16 13	17 20.7	17D 50.2	10 39.4	19 12.8	1 10.5	0 42.7	15 08.6	1 12.6	28 30.8	26 53.9	27 27.8	5 21.6
24 W	12 05 27	3 14 42	10♋11 14	17 10 49	17 17.5	17R 50.2	12 38.9	20 27.0	1 19.1	0 54.5	15 22.8	1 07.9	28 34.5	26 57.3	27 29.7	5 22.1
25 Th	12 09 24	4 14 11	24 15 01	1♌23 45	17 14.3	17 50.2	14 37.4	21 41.2	1 28.3	1 06.2	15 36.9	1 03.2	28 38.1	27 00.7	27 31.7	5 22.5
26 F	12 13 21	5 13 37	8♌36 51	15 53 59	17 11.2	17 48.9	16 34.8	22 55.4	1 38.1	1 17.5	15 51.0	0 58.4	28 41.7	27 04.1	27 33.6	5 22.9
27 Sa	12 17 17	6 13 01	23 14 38	0♍38 11	17 08.0	17 45.3	18 30.5	24 09.6	1 48.5	1 28.6	16 05.1	0 53.7	28 45.3	27 07.5	27 35.5	5 23.3
28 Su	12 21 14	7 12 23	8♍03 49	15 30 36	17 04.8	17 38.9	20 24.3	25 23.7	1 59.4	1 39.4	16 19.1	0 49.1	28 48.8	27 10.9	27 37.3	5 23.6
29 M	12 25 10	8 11 43	22 57 29	0♎23 21	17 01.6	17 29.8	22 15.6	26 37.7	2 10.9	1 49.9	16 33.1	0 44.4	28 52.3	27 14.3	27 39.2	5 23.9
30 Tu	12 29 07	9 11 00	7♎47 06	15 07 37	16 58.4	17 18.9	24 04.1	27 51.8	2 22.9	2 00.2	16 47.1	0 39.7	28 55.7	27 17.7	27 41.0	5 24.2
31 W	12 33 03	10♈10 16	22 23 53	29 35 03	16♑55.3	17♑07.1	25♈49.3	29♈05.8	2♌35.4	2♑10.1	17♓01.0	0♎35.1	28♒59.2	27♓21.1	27♒42.8	5♑24.4

1st of Month

Julian Day # 2455256.5
Obliquity 23°26'20"
SVP 5♓06'47"
GC 26♐58.9
Eris 21♈09.1

Day	⚴
1	22♏20.7
6	22 45.2
11	22 59.1
16	23 01.5R
21	22 51.9R
26	22 30.2R
31	21 56.2R

Day	⚵
1	2♉59.0
6	5 43.6
11	8 29.9
16	11 17.7
21	14 06.9
26	16 57.2
31	19 48.4

Day	⚶
1	26♌39.2R
6	25 27.5R
11	24 22.9R
16	23 27.3R
21	22 42.2R
26	22 08.6R
31	21 47.0R

DECLINATION and LATITUDE

Day	☉ Decl	☽ Decl	☽ Lat	☽ 12h Decl	☿ Decl	☿ Lat	♀ Decl	♀ Lat	♂ Decl	♂ Lat	⚳ Decl	⚳ Lat	♃ Decl	♃ Lat	♄ Decl	♄ Lat
1 M	7S43	2N12	4S11	1S04	13S49	2S09	4S29	1S23	23N50	3N58	20S35	2N47	8S44	0S56	1N11	2N32
2 Tu	7 20	4S16	4 48	7 23	13 13	2 09	3 59	1 22	23 49	3 56	20 37	2 45	8 39	0 56	1 13	2 32
3 W	6 57	10 22	5 05	13 09	12 35	2 09	3 29	1 21	23 49	3 54	20 39	2 44	8 33	0 56	1 14	2 32
4 Th	6 34	15 44	5 03	18 03	11 57	2 08	2 58	1 20	23 48	3 52	20 41	2 42	8 28	0 56	1 16	2 32
5 F	6 11	20 05	4 42	21 49	11 16	2 07	2 27	1 19	23 47	3 50	20 43	2 41	8 22	0 56	1 18	2 33
6 Sa	5 48	23 13	4 07	24 18	10 35	2 06	1 57	1 18	23 46	3 48	20 45	2 39	8 17	0 56	1 20	2 33
7 Su	5 24	25 03	3 20	25 28	9 52	2 04	1 26	1 17	23 45	3 46	20 46	2 38	8 11	0 56	1 22	2 33
8 M	5 01	25 34	2 25	25 30	9 08	2 01	0 55	1 16	23 43	3 44	20 48	2 36	8 06	0 56	1 24	2 33
9 Tu	4 38	24 48	1 25	23 59	8 23	1 58	0 24	1 14	23 41	3 42	20 50	2 35	8 00	0 57	1 26	2 33
10 W	4 14	22 55	0 22	21 35	7 37	1 55	0N06	1 13	23 39	3 39	20 52	2 33	7 55	0 57	1 28	2 33
11 Th	3 51	20 02	0N42	18 17	6 49	1 50	0 37	1 12	23 37	3 37	20 54	2 32	7 50	0 57	1 29	2 33
12 F	3 27	16 22	1 43	14 17	6 00	1 46	1 08	1 10	23 35	3 35	20 56	2 30	7 44	0 57	1 31	2 33
13 Sa	3 03	12 03	2 39	9 43	5 10	1 41	1 39	1 09	23 33	3 33	20 57	2 28	7 39	0 57	1 33	2 33
14 Su	2 40	7 17	3 29	4 47	4 19	1 35	2 10	1 07	23 30	3 31	20 59	2 27	7 33	0 57	1 35	2 34
15 M	2 16	2 14	4 10	0N22	3 27	1 29	2 41	1 06	23 28	3 29	21 01	2 25	7 28	0 57	1 37	2 34
16 Tu	1 52	2N58	4 40	5 33	2 34	1 22	3 12	1 04	23 25	3 27	21 03	2 24	7 22	0 57	1 39	2 34
17 W	1 29	8 06	4 58	10 35	1 41	1 15	3 42	1 02	23 22	3 25	21 04	2 22	7 17	0 57	1 41	2 34
18 Th	1 05	12 59	5 02	15 16	0 46	1 07	4 13	1 00	23 19	3 23	21 06	2 20	7 11	0 57	1 43	2 34
19 F	0 41	17 23	4 51	19 20	0N09	0 59	4 43	0 59	23 16	3 20	21 08	2 18	7 06	0 57	1 45	2 34
20 Sa	0 17	21 04	4 25	22 30	1 05	0 50	5 14	0 57	23 12	3 18	21 10	2 17	7 01	0 57	1 47	2 34
21 Su	0N06	23 46	3 46	24 40	2 02	0 40	5 44	0 55	23 09	3 16	21 11	2 15	6 55	0 57	1 49	2 34
22 M	0 30	25 13	2 54	25 25	2 58	0 30	6 14	0 53	23 05	3 14	21 13	2 13	6 50	0 58	1 51	2 34
23 Tu	0 54	25 14	1 51	24 40	3 55	0 20	6 44	0 51	23 01	3 12	21 15	2 11	6 44	0 58	1 53	2 34
24 W	1 17	23 43	0 40	22 24	4 51	0 09	7 14	0 49	22 57	3 10	21 16	2 10	6 39	0 58	1 54	2 34
25 Th	1 41	20 42	0S34	18 41	5 48	0N02	7 44	0 47	22 53	3 08	21 18	2 08	6 34	0 58	1 56	2 34
26 F	2 05	16 22	1 48	13 48	6 44	0 14	8 13	0 45	22 49	3 06	21 20	2 06	6 28	0 58	1 58	2 34
27 Sa	2 28	11 00	2 56	8 02	7 39	0 25	8 43	0 42	22 45	3 04	21 22	2 04	6 23	0 58	2 00	2 34
28 Su	2 52	4 57	3 53	1 47	8 33	0 37	9 12	0 40	22 40	3 02	21 23	2 02	6 17	0 58	2 02	2 34
29 M	3 15	1S24	4 34	4S33	9 26	0 49	9 41	0 38	22 36	3 00	21 25	2 00	6 12	0 58	2 04	2 34
30 Tu	3 38	7 38	4 57	10 34	10 17	1 01	10 10	0 36	22 31	2 58	21 27	1 58	6 07	0 58	2 06	2 34
31 W	4N02	13S21	4S59	15S54	11N07	1N13	10N38	0S33	22N26	2N56	21S29	1N56	6S01	0S58	2N08	2N34

Day	⚷ Decl	⚷ Lat	♅ Decl	♅ Lat	♆ Decl	♆ Lat	♇ Decl	♇ Lat
1	6S59	5N51	2S23	0S43	13S01	0S25	18S15	5N06
6	6 52	5 51	2 17	0 43	12 57	0 26	18 15	5 06
11	6 45	5 51	2 10	0 43	12 54	0 26	18 14	5 06
16	6 38	5 52	2 03	0 43	12 50	0 26	18 14	5 06
21	6 31	5 52	1 56	0 43	12 47	0 26	18 13	5 06
26	6 24	5 53	1 49	0 43	12 44	0 26	18 13	5 07
31	6S17	5N54	1S43	0S43	12S40	0S26	18S13	5N07

Day	⚴ Decl	⚴ Lat	⚵ Decl	⚵ Lat	⚶ Decl	⚶ Lat	Eris Decl	Eris Lat
1	8N10	27N22	3N15	9S50	21N04	8N60	4S19	13S33
6	9 26	28 45	4 10	9 48	21 34	9 05	4 18	13 32
11	10 45	30 10	5 04	9 46	21 58	9 07	4 16	13 32
16	12 07	31 35	5 57	9 44	22 17	9 07	4 15	13 31
21	13 31	33 00	6 49	9 41	22 30	9 05	4 13	13 31
26	14 56	34 23	7 39	9 38	22 37	9 00	4 12	13 30
31	16N21	35N44	8N27	9S35	22N39	8N54	4S10	13S30

Moon Phenomena

Max/0 Decl

dy	hr mn	
1	8:05	0 S
7	21:25	25S34
15	10:20	0 N
22	12:19	25N25
28	18:43	0 S

Max/0 Lat

dy	hr mn	
3	8:40	5S07
10	8:08	0 N
17	18:23	5N02
24	13:06	0 S
30	15:27	5S01

Perigee/Apogee

dy	hr m		kilometers
12	10:06	a	406008
28	4:51	p	361879

PH	dy	hr mn	
☾	7	15:43	16♐57
●	15	21:02	25♓10
☽	23	11:01	2♋43
○	30	2:27	9♎17

Void of Course Moon

Last Aspect		☽ Ingress
1 17:37	♅ ☍	♎ 2 0:32
3 20:45	♆ △	♏ 4 2:12
6 4:33	♀ △	♐ 6 7:37
8 11:14	♆ ⚹	♑ 8 17:14
10 22:00	♅ ⚹	♒ 11 5:43
13 12:58	♆ ☌	♓ 13 18:45
16 0:02	☿ ☌	♈ 16 6:33
18 11:24	♆ ⚹	♉ 18 16:30
20 19:42	♆ □	♊ 21 0:29
23 1:50	♆ △	♋ 23 6:17
25 4:40	♅ △	♌ 25 9:40
27 7:05	♆ ☍	♍ 27 10:58
29 6:56	♅ ☍	♎ 29 11:22
31 12:14	♀ ☍	♏ 31 12:42

DAILY ASPECTARIAN

1 M ☽∠♂ 2:00 · ☽∥♄ 3:43 · ☽#♄ 12:30 · ☽☍♀ 12:33 · ☿ ♓ 13:29 · ☽∥♅ 16:53 · ☽□⚳ 17:24 · ☽☍♅ 17:37 · ☽⚻♆ 19:16 · ☽⚻⚷ 19:55 · ☽∥♀ 23:00

2 Tu ☿⚻♂ 0:15 · ☽⚹♂ 1:46 · ☽⚻☿ 1:59 · ☽☌♄ 5:03 · ⚳□♅ 7:54 · ☿∥♆ 8:23 · ☽□♇ 8:46 · ☽∥⚷ 10:18 · ☉∥☽ 11:05 · ☽∥♃ 16:44 · ☽⚻♃ 17:14 · ☽⚼♆ 19:39 · ☉⚻☽ 20:17 · ☽⚼⚷ 20:22

3 W ☉∥⚷ 0:27 · ☿⚻♄ 3:14 · ☽⚼☿ 5:50 · ☽∥☿ 8:31 · ☽∥♆ 11:15 · ☽⚻♀ 18:14 · ☽⚼♃ 18:37 · ☽⚻♅ 19:04 · ☽⚹⚳ 19:37 · ☽△♆ 20:45 · ☽△⚷ 21:33 · ☉⚼☽ 23:15

4 Th ☽□♂ 3:10 · ♀☌♅ 4:08 · ☽⚺♄ 6:45 · ☽△☿ 10:54 · ☽⚹♇ 11:02 · ☿⚹♇ 11:56 · ☽∥♇ 13:09 · ♀□⚳ 14:06 · ☽△♃ 20:57 · ☽⚼♅ 21:03 · ☽∠⚳ 22:03 · ☽⚼♀ 22:41 · ♀⚺♆ 23:35

5 F ☉△☽ 3:23 · ☽∥⚳ 4:12 · ♀∥♅ 7:43 · ☽∠♄ 8:57 · ♀⚺⚷ 9:55 · ☽∠♇ 13:35

6 Sa ☽△♅ 0:07 · ☽⚺⚳ 1:36 · ☽□♆ 1:51 · ☽□⚷ 2:51 · ☉⚼♂ 3:00 · ☽△♀ 4:33 · ☽#♂ 5:31 · ☽△♂ 8:23 · ☽⚹♄ 12:14 · ⚳⚹♆ 15:48 · ☽⚺♇ 17:15

7 Su ☽□☿ 1:56 · ♀#♄ 3:05 · ☽□♃ 4:59 · ♀ ♈ 12:34 · ☽⚼♂ 12:38 · ☉□☽ 15:43 · ♀△♂ 19:16

8 M ☿☌♃ 1:47 · ☽□♅ 9:28 · ☽⚹♆ 11:14 · ☽☌⚳ 12:03 · ☽⚹⚷ 12:27 · ☽⚻♂ 17:52 · ☽□♀ 20:31 · ☽□♄ 21:48

9 Tu ☽☌♇ 3:35 · ♀☍♄ 8:22 · ☿∥♃ 13:23 · ⚳⚹⚷ 13:49 · ☽#♂ 15:53 · ☽⚹♃ 17:09 · ☽∠♆ 17:14 · ☽∠⚷ 18:33 · ☽⚹☿ 23:29

10 W ☿⚼♂ 1:56 · ☉⚹☽ 8:42 · ♂ D 17:10 · ☽∥⚳ 17:37 · ☽⚹♅ 22:00 · ☽⚺♆ 23:43

11 Th ☽∠♃ 0:11 · ☽⚺⚷ 1:08 · ☽⚺⚳ 1:42 · ☿∥⚷ 2:04 · ☽☍♂ 6:20 · ☽△♄ 10:02 · ☽∠☿ 11:45 · ☽∥♇ 12:21 · ☽⚹♀ 16:15 · ☽⚺♇ 16:24 · ♀□♇ 17:37 · ☉∠☽ 18:04

12 F ☽∠♅ 4:44 · ☽⚺♃ 7:24 · ☽∠⚳ 8:56 · ☽⚼♄ 16:25 · ♀∥♄ 19:08 · ☽∥♆ 19:40 · ☽∠♇ 23:00

13 Sa ☽⚺☿ 0:13 · ☽∠♀ 2:24 · ☉⚺☽ 3:26 · ☽⚺♅ 11:22 · ☽☌♆ 12:58 · ☽☌⚷ 14:32 · ☽⚹⚳ 16:02 · ☽⚻♂ 19:27 · ♀#♅ 20:55 · ☽⚻♄ 22:37 · ☽∥♃ 22:42

14 Su ☽∥⚷ 2:58 · ☽⚹♇ 5:22 · ☽⚺♀ 12:14 · ⚴ R 12:39 · ☉#♀ 13:05 · ☉☌☿ 13:17 · ☽∥☿ 17:05 · ☽☌♃ 21:18 · ☽#♀ 22:05 · ☉∥☽ 23:48

15 M ☽∥♅ 0:43 · ☽⚼♂ 1:41 · ☽#♄ 2:49 · ☉∥♅ 12:23 · ☿#♀ 13:25 · ☽∥♄ 17:54 · ☉#☽ 19:19 · ☽#♅ 19:49 · ☉☌☽ 21:02 · ☿☌♅ 21:41 · ☽#☿ 22:28 · ☽☌♅ 23:39

16 Tu ☽☌☿ 0:02 · ☽⚺♆ 1:06 · ☽∥♀ 1:11 · ☽⚺⚷ 2:47 · ☽□⚳ 5:05 · ☿⚺♆ 6:45 · ☽△♂ 7:30 · ☽☍♄ 9:56 · ☉#♄ 12:23 · ☿∥♅ 14:23 · ☽□♇ 16:56 · ☽#⚷ 17:00 · ☿⚺⚷ 17:29 · ☽#♃ 20:12 · ☿#♄ 23:51

17 W ☽☌♀ 6:09 · ☽∠♆ 6:29 · ☉☌♅ 6:51 · ☽∠⚷ 8:13 · ☉∥☿ 9:27 · ☽⚺♃ 9:28 · ♀∠♆ 9:39 · ☿□⚳ 10:34 · ☿ ♈ 16:13 · ☽#♆ 23:08 · ☿△♂ 23:34

18 Th ☉⚺♆ 0:20 · ♀∠⚷ 3:45 · ☽⚺♅ 10:06 · ☿☍♄ 11:05 · ☽⚹♆ 11:24 · ☉⚺☽ 12:19 · ☽⚹⚷ 13:09 · ☽∠♃ 14:48 · ☽△⚳ 16:08 · ☽□♂ 17:48 · ☽⚻♄ 19:26 · ☽⚺☿ 21:03 · ♀⚺♃ 22:30 · ☉⚺⚷ 23:40

19 F ☽△♇ 2:35 · ☽#♇ 5:00 · ☉#☿ 9:35 · ⚳ ♑ 13:48 · ☽∠♅ 14:35 · ☉∠☽ 19:01 · ☽⚹♃ 19:37 · ☽⚼⚳ 20:52 · ☽⚺♀ 21:26 · ☽⚼♄ 23:27

20 Sa ☽#⚳ 0:39 · ☽∠☿ 6:23 · ☽⚼♇ 6:41 · ☿□♇ 8:17 · ☉ ♈ 17:33 · ☽∥♂ 17:35 · ☿∥♄ 18:20 · ☽⚹♅ 18:34 · ☽□♆ 19:42 · ☽□⚷ 21:32 · ☿#♅ 21:48

21 Su ☉⚹☽ 1:03 · ☽⚻⚳ 1:04 · ☉□⚳ 1:04 · ☽⚹♂ 2:11 · ☽△♄ 2:58 · ☽∠♀ 4:03 · ☽⚻♇ 10:15 · ☽⚹☿ 14:52 · ☉△♂ 17:55

22 M ☉☍♄ 0:38 · ☽□♃ 3:35 · ☽∠♂ 5:36 · ☽⚹♀ 9:55 · ♀#⚷ 11:42

23 Tu ♀#♃ 0:03 · ☽□♅ 0:50 · ☽△♆ 1:50 · ☽△⚷ 3:41 · ♂⚹♄ 3:54 · ♄#♅ 7:33 · ☽☍⚳ 7:38 · ☽□♄ 8:21 · ☽⚺♂ 8:25 · ☉□☽ 11:01 · ☽☍♇ 15:39 · ☿∠♆ 22:08

24 W ☽⚼♆ 3:59 · ☽□☿ 4:56 · ☽⚼⚷ 5:51 · ☽∥♂ 7:29 · ☽△♃ 9:04 · ☿∠⚷ 11:35 · ☽□♀ 19:15 · ⚳□♄ 19:33 · ☽#⚳ 20:03

25 Th ☽△♅ 4:40 · ☽⚻♆ 5:32 · ☽⚻⚷ 7:25 · ☉#♅ 9:26 · ☽⚼♃ 10:52 · ☽⚹♄ 11:22 · ☽⚻⚳ 11:40 · ☽☌♂ 12:16 · ☿⚺♃ 13:47 · ☽#♇ 14:34 · ☿#⚷ 15:45 · ☉∥♄ 16:56 · ☿#♃ 17:56 · ☉△☽ 17:58 · ☽⚻♇ 18:38

26 F ☉□♇ 3:47 · ☽⚼♅ 5:43 · ☽∠♄ 12:03 · ☽⚻♃ 12:07 · ☽⚼⚳ 12:48 · ☽△☿ 15:07 · ☽#♆ 16:44 · ☽⚼♇ 19:20 · ☉⚼☽ 20:27

27 Sa ♃∥⚷ 0:56 · ☽△♀ 1:38 · ☽⚻♅ 6:20 · ☽☍♆ 7:05 · ☽∥♀ 8:37 · ☽☍⚷ 8:59 · ☽∥☿ 11:47 · ☽⚺♄ 12:21 · ☽△⚳ 13:31 · ☽⚺♂ 14:04 · ☽#⚷ 18:33 · ☽#♃ 18:45 · ☽⚼☿ 19:05 · ☽△♇ 19:41 · ☉⚻☽ 22:31

28 Su ☽⚼♀ 4:06 · ☉∥☽ 7:29 · ☽∥♄ 11:01 · ☽#♅ 12:04 · ☽☍♃ 13:31 · ☽∠♂ 14:34 · ☽⚻☿ 22:43

29 M ☽∥♅ 1:21 · ☽#♄ 2:32 · ☽⚻♀ 6:28 · ☽☍♅ 6:56 · ☉#☽ 7:29 · ☽⚻♆ 7:36 · ☽⚻⚷ 9:35 · ♀⚺♅ 12:25 · ☽☌♄ 12:30 · ☽□⚳ 14:30 · ☽⚹♂ 15:06 · ☿∥♀ 16:06 · ☽∥♃ 18:07 · ☽∥⚷ 18:50 · ☽□♇ 20:08 · ♀⚹♆ 20:26

30 Tu ☉☍☽ 2:27 · ☽⚼♆ 8:01 · ☽⚼⚷ 10:05 · ☽#♀ 11:13 · ☽#☿ 12:38 · ☽⚻♃ 14:58 · ☽∥♆ 21:02 · ♀⚹⚷ 21:45

31 W ☽☍☿ 6:28 · ☽⚻♅ 8:17 · ☽△♆ 8:53 · ☽△⚷ 11:02 · ☽☍♀ 12:14 · ☽⚺♄ 13:37 · ☽⚼♃ 16:22 · ☽⚹⚳ 16:33 · ☽□♂ 17:20 · ♀ ♉ 17:36 · ☽⚹♇ 21:51 · ☿⚺♅ 22:23

April 2010

LONGITUDE

Day	Sid.Time	☉	☽	☽ 12 hour	Mean☊	True☊	☿	♀	♂	⚳	♃	♄	⚷	♅	♆	♇
	h m s	° ' "	° ' "	° ' "	° '	° '	° '	° '	° '	° '	° '	° '	° '	° '	° '	° '
1 Th	12 37 00	11♈09 29	6♏40 22	13♏39 17	16♑52.1	16♑56.0	27♓30.9	0♉19.7	2♌48.4	2♑19.8	17♓14.9	0♎30.5	29♒02.6	27♓24.4	27♒44.6	5♑24.6
2 F	12 40 56	12 08 41	20 31 28	27 16 44	16 48.9	16R 46.5	29 08.5	1 33.7	3 01.9	2 29.2	17 28.7	0R 25.9	29 05.9	27 27.8	27 46.4	5 24.8
3 Sa	12 44 53	13 07 51	3♐55 07	10♐26 46	16 45.7	16 39.5	0♈41.7	2 47.6	3 15.9	2 38.3	17 42.5	0 21.4	29 09.2	27 31.1	27 48.1	5 25.0
4 Su	12 48 50	14 06 59	16 52 00	23 11 16	16 42.6	16 35.1	2 10.2	4 01.4	3 30.4	2 47.0	17 56.3	0 16.8	29 12.5	27 34.4	27 49.9	5 25.1
5 M	12 52 46	15 06 05	29 25 04	5♑34 00	16 39.4	16 33.0	3 33.7	5 15.3	3 45.3	2 55.5	18 10.0	0 12.3	29 15.7	27 37.8	27 51.6	5 25.2
6 Tu	12 56 43	16 05 10	11♑38 43	17 39 54	16 36.2	16 32.5	4 51.9	6 29.1	4 00.8	3 03.7	18 23.7	0 07.9	29 18.9	27 41.1	27 53.2	5 25.2
7 W	13 00 39	17 04 13	23 38 13	29 34 24	16 33.0	16 32.5	6 04.5	7 42.8	4 16.6	3 11.5	18 37.3	0 03.4	29 22.1	27 44.3	27 54.9	5R 25.2
8 Th	13 04 36	18 03 14	5♒29 07	11♒23 03	16 29.9	16 31.7	7 11.4	8 56.6	4 32.9	3 19.1	18 50.9	29♍59.1	29 25.2	27 47.6	27 56.5	5 25.2
9 F	13 08 32	19 02 13	17 16 49	23 11 01	16 26.7	16 29.3	8 12.3	10 10.3	4 49.6	3 26.3	19 04.4	29 54.7	29 28.3	27 50.9	27 58.1	5 25.2
10 Sa	13 12 29	20 01 10	29 06 14	5♓02 57	16 23.5	16 24.4	9 07.2	11 23.9	5 06.8	3 33.2	19 17.9	29 50.4	29 31.3	27 54.1	27 59.7	5 25.1
11 Su	13 16 25	21 00 06	11♓01 37	17 02 38	16 20.3	16 16.7	9 55.9	12 37.6	5 24.3	3 39.8	19 31.3	29 46.2	29 34.3	27 57.4	28 01.3	5 25.0
12 M	13 20 22	21 58 59	23 06 19	29 12 55	16 17.1	16 06.4	10 38.2	13 51.2	5 42.3	3 46.0	19 44.7	29 42.0	29 37.3	28 00.6	28 02.8	5 24.8
13 Tu	13 24 19	22 57 51	5♈22 38	11♈35 36	16 14.0	15 54.0	11 14.1	15 04.7	6 00.7	3 51.9	19 58.1	29 37.8	29 40.2	28 03.8	28 04.3	5 24.7
14 W	13 28 15	23 56 41	17 51 51	24 11 25	16 10.8	15 40.6	11 43.7	16 18.3	6 19.4	3 57.4	20 11.3	29 33.7	29 43.1	28 06.9	28 05.8	5 24.5
15 Th	13 32 12	24 55 29	0♉34 16	7♉00 18	16 07.6	15 27.2	12 06.7	17 31.8	6 38.6	4 02.7	20 24.5	29 29.7	29 45.9	28 10.1	28 07.2	5 24.2
16 F	13 36 08	25 54 15	13 29 26	20 01 34	16 04.4	15 15.2	12 23.4	18 45.2	6 58.1	4 07.5	20 37.7	29 25.7	29 48.7	28 13.2	28 08.7	5 24.0
17 Sa	13 40 05	26 52 59	26 36 33	3♊14 18	16 01.2	15 05.5	12 33.7	19 58.6	7 18.0	4 12.0	20 50.8	29 21.7	29 51.4	28 16.4	28 10.1	5 23.7
18 Su	13 44 01	27 51 41	9♊54 42	16 37 43	15 58.1	14 58.6	12R 37.8	21 12.0	7 38.2	4 16.2	21 03.8	29 17.9	29 54.1	28 19.5	28 11.5	5 23.4
19 M	13 47 58	28 50 21	23 23 17	0♋11 25	15 54.9	14 54.6	12 35.9	22 25.3	7 58.8	4 20.0	21 16.8	29 14.1	29 56.7	28 22.5	28 12.8	5 23.0
20 Tu	13 51 54	29 48 59	7♋02 06	13 55 23	15 51.7	14D 53.1	12 28.1	23 38.6	8 19.7	4 23.5	21 29.7	29 10.3	29 59.3	28 25.6	28 14.1	5 22.6
21 W	13 55 51	0♉47 34	20 51 17	27 49 51	15 48.5	14R 53.0	12 14.8	24 51.9	8 41.0	4 26.6	21 42.5	29 06.7	0♓01.8	28 28.6	28 15.4	5 22.2
22 Th	13 59 48	1 46 07	4♌51 04	11♌54 52	15 45.4	14 53.1	11 56.2	26 05.1	9 02.6	4 29.3	21 55.3	29 03.1	0 04.3	28 31.6	28 16.7	5 21.8
23 F	14 03 44	2 44 38	19 01 11	26 09 47	15 42.2	14 52.1	11 33.0	27 18.3	9 24.5	4 31.7	22 08.0	28 59.5	0 06.8	28 34.6	28 17.9	5 21.3
24 Sa	14 07 41	3 43 07	3♍20 25	10♍32 42	15 39.0	14 49.2	11 05.5	28 31.4	9 46.7	4 33.7	22 20.6	28 56.1	0 09.1	28 37.6	28 19.1	5 20.8
25 Su	14 11 37	4 41 33	17 46 07	25 00 07	15 35.8	14 43.7	10 34.3	29 44.5	10 09.2	4 35.4	22 33.2	28 52.7	0 11.5	28 40.5	28 20.3	5 20.3
26 M	14 15 34	5 39 57	2♎14 00	9♎27 03	15 32.6	14 35.8	10 00.0	0♊57.5	10 32.0	4 36.7	22 45.7	28 49.4	0 13.8	28 43.4	28 21.5	5 19.7
27 Tu	14 19 30	6 38 20	16 38 28	23 47 27	15 29.5	14 26.0	9 23.2	2 10.5	10 55.1	4 37.6	22 58.1	28 46.2	0 16.0	28 46.3	28 22.6	5 19.1
28 W	14 23 27	7 36 40	0♏53 17	7♏55 13	15 26.3	14 15.4	8 44.8	3 23.4	11 18.4	4R 38.1	23 10.4	28 43.0	0 18.2	28 49.2	28 23.7	5 18.5
29 Th	14 27 23	8 34 59	14 52 39	21 45 04	15 23.1	14 05.3	8 05.4	4 36.3	11 42.1	4 38.3	23 22.7	28 39.9	0 20.3	28 52.0	28 24.7	5 17.8
30 F	14 31 20	9♉33 16	28 32 06	5♐13 29	15♑19.9	13♑56.6	7♉25.7	5♊49.2	12♌06.0	4♑38.1	23♓34.9	28♍36.9	0♓22.4	28♓54.8	28♒25.8	5♑17.2

1st of Month

Julian Day # 2455287.5
Obliquity 23°26'20"
SVP 5♓06'44"
GC 26♐58.9
Eris 21♈27.3

Day	⚴
1	21♍48.0R
6	20 59.6R
11	19 59.7R
16	18 49.4R
21	17 30.4R
26	16 04.8R

Day	⚵
1	20♉22.7
6	23 14.8
11	26 07.5
16	29 00.6
21	1♊54.1
26	4 47.6

Day	⚶
1	21♌44.1R
6	21 36.9R
11	21 41.5
16	21 57.7
21	22 25.0
26	23 02.6

DECLINATION and LATITUDE

Day	☉ Decl	☽ Decl	☽ Lat	☽ 12h Decl	☿ Decl	☿ Lat	♀ Decl	♀ Lat	♂ Decl	♂ Lat	⚳ Decl	⚳ Lat	♃ Decl	♃ Lat	♄ Decl	♄ Lat
1 Th	4N25	18S12	4S43	20S12	11N54	1N25	11N06	0S31	22N21	2N54	21S31	1N54	5S56	0S59	2N09	2N34
2 F	4 48	21 54	4 11	23 16	12 40	1 36	11 34	0 28	22 16	2 52	21 32	1 52	5 51	0 59	2 11	2 34
3 Sa	5 11	24 17	3 25	24 57	13 23	1 47	12 02	0 26	22 11	2 50	21 34	1 50	5 46	0 59	2 13	2 34
4 Su	5 34	25 17	2 30	25 16	14 04	1 58	12 29	0 24	22 06	2 49	21 36	1 48	5 40	0 59	2 15	2 34
5 M	5 57	24 56	1 29	24 17	14 43	2 08	12 57	0 21	22 01	2 47	21 38	1 46	5 35	0 59	2 16	2 34
6 Tu	6 20	23 22	0 26	22 10	15 18	2 18	13 23	0 18	21 55	2 45	21 40	1 44	5 30	0 59	2 18	2 34
7 W	6 42	20 45	0N38	19 07	15 51	2 27	13 50	0 16	21 50	2 43	21 42	1 42	5 25	0 59	2 20	2 34
8 Th	7 05	17 18	1 39	15 19	16 21	2 35	14 16	0 13	21 44	2 41	21 44	1 40	5 19	0 59	2 22	2 34
9 F	7 27	13 12	2 35	10 56	16 47	2 42	14 42	0 11	21 38	2 39	21 46	1 38	5 14	0 59	2 23	2 34
10 Sa	7 50	8 35	3 25	6 08	17 11	2 48	15 07	0 08	21 32	2 38	21 48	1 36	5 09	0 60	2 25	2 34
11 Su	8 12	3 38	4 06	1 05	17 32	2 53	15 32	0 05	21 26	2 36	21 50	1 33	5 04	0 60	2 27	2 34
12 M	8 34	1N30	4 37	4N05	17 49	2 57	15 57	0 03	21 20	2 34	21 52	1 31	4 59	0 60	2 28	2 34
13 Tu	8 56	6 39	4 55	9 10	18 03	3 00	16 21	0 00	21 14	2 32	21 54	1 29	4 54	0 60	2 30	2 34
14 W	9 17	11 37	4 60	13 59	18 14	3 02	16 45	0N03	21 07	2 31	21 56	1 26	4 48	1 00	2 31	2 34
15 Th	9 39	16 12	4 50	18 15	18 22	3 03	17 09	0 05	21 01	2 29	21 59	1 24	4 43	1 00	2 33	2 33
16 F	10 00	20 06	4 25	21 43	18 27	3 02	17 32	0 08	20 54	2 27	22 01	1 22	4 38	1 00	2 34	2 33
17 Sa	10 22	23 03	3 46	24 06	18 28	2 60	17 54	0 11	20 48	2 26	22 03	1 19	4 33	1 01	2 36	2 33
18 Su	10 43	24 48	2 54	25 09	18 26	2 57	18 16	0 13	20 41	2 24	22 05	1 17	4 28	1 01	2 37	2 33
19 M	11 04	25 08	1 51	24 43	18 21	2 52	18 38	0 16	20 34	2 22	22 08	1 14	4 23	1 01	2 39	2 33
20 Tu	11 24	23 57	0 41	22 48	18 12	2 45	18 59	0 19	20 27	2 21	22 10	1 12	4 18	1 01	2 40	2 33
21 W	11 45	21 18	0S32	19 29	18 01	2 38	19 20	0 22	20 20	2 19	22 12	1 09	4 13	1 01	2 41	2 33
22 Th	12 05	17 22	1 44	15 00	17 46	2 29	19 40	0 24	20 13	2 17	22 15	1 07	4 09	1 01	2 43	2 33
23 F	12 25	12 25	2 51	9 39	17 29	2 18	19 60	0 27	20 05	2 16	22 17	1 04	4 04	1 01	2 44	2 33
24 Sa	12 45	6 45	3 47	3 45	17 10	2 07	20 19	0 30	19 57	2 14	22 20	1 02	3 59	1 02	2 45	2 33
25 Su	13 05	0 41	4 30	2S23	16 48	1 54	20 37	0 32	19 50	2 13	22 23	0 59	3 54	1 02	2 47	2 32
26 M	13 25	5S24	4 55	8 21	16 24	1 40	20 55	0 35	19 42	2 11	22 25	0 56	3 49	1 02	2 48	2 32
27 Tu	13 44	11 11	5 02	13 51	15 58	1 25	21 13	0 38	19 34	2 10	22 28	0 54	3 44	1 02	2 49	2 32
28 W	14 03	16 18	4 50	18 31	15 31	1 09	21 30	0 41	19 26	2 08	22 31	0 51	3 40	1 02	2 50	2 32
29 Th	14 22	20 27	4 20	22 04	15 02	0 53	21 46	0 43	19 18	2 07	22 33	0 48	3 35	1 02	2 51	2 32
30 F	14N40	23S21	3S36	24S17	14N34	0N36	22N02	0N46	19N10	2N05	22S36	0N45	3S30	1S03	2N52	2N32

Day	⚷ Decl	⚷ Lat	♅ Decl	♅ Lat	♆ Decl	♆ Lat	♇ Decl	♇ Lat
1	6S16	5N54	1S41	0S43	12S40	0S26	18S13	5N07
6	6 09	5 55	1 35	0 43	12 37	0 26	18 12	5 08
11	6 03	5 56	1 28	0 43	12 34	0 26	18 12	5 08
16	5 57	5 58	1 22	0 43	12 32	0 26	18 12	5 08
21	5 51	5 59	1 16	0 43	12 30	0 26	18 11	5 09
26	5 46	6 00	1 10	0 43	12 28	0 27	18 11	5 09

Day	⚴ Decl	⚴ Lat	⚵ Decl	⚵ Lat	⚶ Decl	⚶ Lat	Eris Decl	Eris Lat
1	16N38	35N59	8N36	9S34	22N39	8N53	4S10	13S30
6	18 01	37 15	9 22	9 31	22 34	8 46	4 09	13 30
11	19 22	38 26	10 05	9 27	22 25	8 37	4 07	13 29
16	20 38	39 30	10 46	9 23	22 11	8 29	4 06	13 29
21	21 50	40 26	11 24	9 19	21 54	8 20	4 05	13 29
26	22 54	41 13	11 60	9 15	21 32	8 10	4 03	13 29

Moon Phenomena

Max/0 Decl (dy hr mn)
4 5:22 25S19
11 17:02 0 N
18 17:22 25N11
25 2:42 0 S

Max/0 Lat (dy hr mn)
6 9:45 0 N
13 19:57 5N00
20 13:39 0 S
26 20:29 5S02

Perigee/Apogee (dy hr m kilometers)
9 2:39 a 405001
24 21:05 p 367141

PH dy hr mn
☾ 6 9:38 16♑29
● 14 12:30 24♈27
☽ 21 18:21 1♌32
○ 28 12:20 8♏07

Void of Course Moon

Last Aspect	☽ Ingress
2 12:55 ♆ □	♐ 2 16:54
4 20:59 ♆ ✶	♑ 5 1:08
7 8:19 ♅ ✶	♒ 7 12:52
9 21:45 ♆ ☌	♓ 10 1:49
12 12:52 ♄ ☍	♈ 12 13:32
14 19:24 ♆ ✶	♉ 14 22:56
17 4:58 ♄ △	♊ 17 6:09
19 10:22 ☉ ✶	♋ 19 11:40
21 14:08 ♄ ✶	♌ 21 15:43
23 15:36 ♆ ☍	♍ 23 18:25
25 18:22 ♄ ☌	♎ 25 20:18
27 19:46 ♅ ☍	♏ 27 22:30
30 0:41 ♅ △	♐ 30 2:37

DAILY ASPECTARIAN

1 Th	☽∥♇ 0:04; ♀⊼♄ 3:17; ☿✶♆ 3:22; ☉⊼☽ 8:17; ☽⚼♅ 9:53; ☽∠♄ 15:08; ☽△♃ 18:34; ☽∠⚳ 18:37; ☽∥⚳ 21:12; ☿✶⚷ 23:20; ☿#♆ 23:34; ☽∠♇ 23:48
2 F	☽#♂ 2:53; ☽△♅ 12:23; ☉⚼☽ 12:42; ☽□♆ 12:55; ☿ ♉ 13:07; ☽□⚷ 15:20; ☉∠♆ 15:45; ☽⊼☿ 17:23; ☽✶♄ 17:34; ☿⊼♄ 18:54; ♀△⚳ 20:33; ☽⊻⚳ 21:39; ☽⊼♀ 21:44; ♀∠♃ 21:59; ☽△♂ 22:47
3 Sa	☽⊻♇ 2:44; ♀□♂ 11:26; ☉△☽ 18:24
4 Su	☽⚼☿ 0:39; ☽□♃ 2:04; ☉∠⚷ 2:22; ☽⚼♂ 3:09; ☽⚼♀ 4:31; ☉#♃ 5:19; ♀#♆ 7:27; ☿△⚳ 11:36; ☿∠♃ 15:40; ☽□♅ 20:31; ☽✶♆ 20:59; ☽✶⚷ 23:42
5 M	☽□♄ 1:31; ♀△♇ 3:13; ☿□♂ 4:18; ☽☌⚳ 6:54; ☽⊼♂ 8:38; ☽△☿ 9:03; ☽☌♇ 11:43; ☽△♀ 12:40; ☉#⚷ 13:41
6 Tu	☽∠♆ 2:28; ☽∠⚷ 5:20; ☉□☽ 9:38; ☿△♇ 10:48; ⚶ D 12:37; ☽✶♃ 13:43; ☽#♂ 14:48; ☽∥⚳ 16:19
7 W	♇ R 2:35; ☽✶♅ 8:19; ☽⊻♆ 8:40; ☽⊻⚷ 11:38; ☽△♄ 12:54; ☽∥♇ 18:14; ♄R♍ 18:52; ☽⊻⚳ 19:33; ☽∠♃ 20:37; ☽☍♂ 22:03; ☽⊻♇ 23:52; ♂#⚳ 23:59
8 Th	☽□☿ 3:48; ☽#☿ 5:18; ☽□♀ 7:51; ☽∠♅ 14:56; ☽#♀ 16:22; ☽⚼♄ 19:13
9 F	☉⊻♃ 1:10; ☽∠⚳ 2:23; ☽∥♆ 3:17; ☽⊻♃ 3:43; ☉✶☽ 3:54; ☽∠♇ 6:23; ☽⊻♅ 21:33; ☽☌♆ 21:45
10 Sa	☽☌⚷ 0:51; ☽⊼♄ 1:29; ☉#☽ 3:30; ☽✶⚳ 9:04; ☽∥⚷ 12:24; ☽⊼♂ 12:26; ☽✶♇ 12:44; ☉∠☽ 13:01; ☽∥♃ 17:04; ☽✶☿ 21:39
11 Su	♂⊼♇ 0:52; ☽✶♀ 3:34; ☽#♄ 5:35; ♀∠♅ 6:45; ☽∥♅ 10:12; ☽☌♃ 17:14; ☽⚼♂ 19:08; ☉⊻☽ 21:35; ☽#♅ 23:47
12 M	☽∥♄ 4:31; ☽∠☿ 5:16; ☽☌♅ 9:41; ☽⊻♆ 9:44; ☽∠♀ 12:33; ☽⊻⚷ 12:51; ☽☍♄ 12:52; ♀⚼♄ 15:41; ♄⊼⚷ 15:49; ☽#♃ 15:53; ☽#⚷ 21:00; ☽□⚳ 21:02
13 Tu	☽□♇ 0:04; ☽△♂ 1:16; ♅⊻♆ 7:44; ☉∥☽ 11:40; ☽⊻☿ 11:48; ☽∠♆ 14:52; ☿#♇ 17:38; ☽∠⚷ 17:58; ☽⊻♀ 20:42
14 W	☽⊻♃ 4:30; ☽#♆ 4:38; ☉☌☽ 12:30; ☽✶♆ 19:24; ☽⊻♅ 19:28; ☽⊼♄ 22:00; ☽✶⚷ 22:29
15 Th	☽∥♀ 6:00; ☽△⚳ 6:32; ☽△♇ 9:01; ☽∠♃ 9:11; ☽□♂ 11:37; ☽#♇ 11:41; ☽∥☿ 13:03; ☽☌☿ 21:56; ☽∠♅ 23:30
16 F	☽⚼♄ 1:43; ☽∥♂ 5:34; ♀⚼⚳ 7:47; ☽⚼⚳ 10:25; ☽☌♀ 10:40; ☽⚼♇ 12:41; ☽✶♃ 13:19; ☽#⚳ 14:40
17 Sa	☉⊻☽ 0:32; ☽□♆ 2:50; ☽✶♅ 3:02; ☽△♄ 4:58; ☽□⚷ 5:55; ♀⚼♇ 8:09; ☽⊼⚳ 13:49; ☽⊼♇ 15:53; ⚵ ♊ 17:06; ♀#♇ 18:41; ☽✶♂ 19:49; ♀✶♃ 20:44
18 Su	☿ R 4:06; ☽⊻☿ 4:52; ☉∠☽ 5:42; ☉✶♆ 8:17; ☿∥♀ 8:36; ☉⊻♅ 11:59; ☽□♃ 20:12; ☽⊻♀ 22:07; ☽∠♂ 23:15
19 M	☽∠☿ 7:23; ☽△♆ 8:32; ☽□♅ 8:50; ☉⊼♄ 9:08; ☽□♄ 10:16; ☉✶☽ 10:22; ☽△⚷ 11:36; ☽☍⚳ 19:21; ☽☍♇ 21:06
20 Tu	☿#♇ 1:40; ☽⊻♂ 2:19; ☽∠♀ 3:05; ☉✶⚷ 4:25; ☉ ♉ 4:31; ⚷ ♓ 6:38; ☽✶☿ 9:20; ☽⚼♆ 10:49; ☽⚼⚷ 13:53; ☽#⚳ 17:08
21 W	☽△♃ 1:30; ☽∥♂ 6:54; ☽✶♀ 7:34; ☽∥♀ 11:53; ☽⊼♆ 12:45; ☽△♅ 13:09; ☽✶♄ 14:08; ☽⊼⚷ 15:49; ☉□☽ 18:21; ☽#♇ 19:31; ☽∥☿ 21:41; ☽⊼⚳ 23:23
22 Th	☽⊼♇ 0:52; ☽⚼♃ 3:35; ☽☌♂ 7:19; ☽□☿ 11:44; ☽⚼♅ 14:47; ☽∠♄ 15:33; ☽#♆ 23:43; ☉∥☽ 23:58
23 F	☽⚼⚳ 0:52; ☽⚼♇ 2:15; ☉#♆ 3:55; ♀∥♂ 4:39; ☽⊼♃ 5:19; ☽□♀ 15:12; ☽☍♆ 15:36; ☽⊼♅ 16:06; ☽⊻♄ 16:40; ☽☍⚷ 18:40; ♀□♆ 19:55
24 Sa	☉△☽ 0:41; ☽△⚳ 2:03; ♀✶♅ 2:07; ☽△♇ 3:21; ☽#⚷ 3:50; ♀△♄ 7:45; ☽⊻♂ 11:01; ☽#♃ 11:13; ☽△☿ 12:28; ☽∥♄ 15:51; ☉△⚳ 21:24; ☽#♅ 22:02
25 Su	☉⚼☽ 3:25; ♀ ♊ 5:06; ☽∥♅ 7:20; ☽☍♃ 8:03; ♀□⚷ 9:10; ☿□♂ 10:42; ☽⚼☿ 12:28; ☽∠♂ 12:35; ☽#♄ 13:37; ☉△♇ 15:45; ☽⊼♆ 17:33; ☽∥♃ 17:47; ☽☍♅ 18:09; ☽☌♄ 18:22; ☽⊼⚷ 20:40; ☽△♀ 21:41
26 M	☽∥⚷ 1:25; ☽□⚳ 3:57; ☽□♇ 5:08; ☉⊼☽ 6:07; ☽⊼☿ 12:24; ☽✶♂ 14:11; ☽⚼♆ 18:32; ☽⚼⚷ 21:42; ♄☍♅ 23:24
27 Tu	☽⚼♀ 0:59; ☽∥♆ 5:36; ☽⊼♃ 10:46; ☉#☽ 12:12; ☽△♆ 19:46; ☽⊻♄ 20:20; ☽#☿ 20:20; ☽⊼♅ 20:29; ☽△⚷ 23:00
28 W	☽⊼♀ 4:40; ☽✶⚳ 6:23; ☽✶♇ 7:31; ☽∥♇ 10:08; ☉☍☽ 12:20; ☽⚼♃ 12:37; ☽☍☿ 12:49; ☿∠♃ 15:59; ☉☌☿ 16:45; ☽#♂ 16:57; ☉∠♃ 17:36; ☽□♂ 18:21; ☽∠♄ 21:54; ☽⚼♅ 22:15; ⚳ R 23:02
29 Th	♀⊼⚳ 0:39; ☽∠⚳ 8:18; ☽∠♇ 9:27; ☽#♀ 10:35; ♀⊼♇ 13:33; ☽△♃ 15:05; ☽∥⚳ 16:32; ☉∥☿ 20:33; ☽□♆ 23:49
30 F	☽✶♄ 0:09; ☽△♅ 0:41; ☽□⚷ 3:17; ☽⊻⚳ 10:56; ☽⊻♇ 12:06; ☽☍♀ 14:24; ☽⊼☿ 15:14; ☿⊻♀ 20:40; ☉⊼☽ 21:27

LONGITUDE — May 2010

Day	Sid.Time	☉	☽	☽ 12 hour	Mean ☊	True ☊	☿	♀	♂	⚳	♃	♄	⚷	♅	♆	♇
	h m s	° ' "	° ' "	° ' "	° '	° '	° '	° '	° '	° '	° '	° '	° '	° '	° '	° '
1 Sa	14 35 17	10♉31 31	11♐49 07	18♐19 01	15♑16.8	13♑50.1	6♉46.4	7♊02.0	12♌30.2	4♑37.5	23♓47.0	28♍34.0	0♓24.4	28♓57.6	28♒26.8	5♑16.5
2 Su	14 39 13	11 29 44	24 43 21	1♑02 22	15 13.6	13R 46.1	6R 08.3	8 14.7	12 54.6	4R 36.6	23 59.0	28R 31.2	0 26.4	29 00.3	28 27.8	5R 15.8
3 M	14 43 10	12 27 57	7♑16 27	13 26 03	15 10.4	13D 44.3	5 32.0	9 27.5	13 19.3	4 35.2	24 11.0	28 28.5	0 28.3	29 03.0	28 28.7	5 15.0
4 Tu	14 47 06	13 26 07	19 31 39	25 33 53	15 07.2	13 44.3	4 58.0	10 40.1	13 44.2	4 33.5	24 22.8	28 25.8	0 30.2	29 05.7	28 29.6	5 14.2
5 W	14 51 03	14 24 16	1♒33 19	7♒30 37	15 04.1	13 45.0	4 26.9	11 52.8	14 09.4	4 31.4	24 34.6	28 23.2	0 32.0	29 08.4	28 30.5	5 13.4
6 Th	14 54 59	15 22 24	13 26 26	19 21 27	15 00.9	13R 45.6	3 59.2	13 05.4	14 34.8	4 29.0	24 46.3	28 20.7	0 33.8	29 11.0	28 31.3	5 12.6
7 F	14 58 56	16 20 30	25 16 19	1♓11 41	14 57.7	13 45.2	3 35.2	14 17.9	15 00.5	4 26.1	24 57.9	28 18.4	0 35.5	29 13.6	28 32.2	5 11.7
8 Sa	15 02 52	17 18 35	7♓08 10	13 06 22	14 54.5	13 43.0	3 15.2	15 30.4	15 26.4	4 22.9	25 09.5	28 16.1	0 37.1	29 16.2	28 32.9	5 10.9
9 Su	15 06 49	18 16 38	19 06 51	25 10 05	14 51.3	13 38.7	2 59.5	16 42.8	15 52.5	4 19.3	25 20.9	28 13.8	0 38.7	29 18.7	28 33.7	5 10.0
10 M	15 10 46	19 14 40	1♈16 32	7♈26 34	14 48.2	13 32.2	2 48.3	17 55.3	16 18.8	4 15.3	25 32.2	28 11.7	0 40.2	29 21.2	28 34.4	5 09.0
11 Tu	15 14 42	20 12 40	13 40 30	19 58 33	14 45.0	13 24.1	2D 41.6	19 07.6	16 45.4	4 10.9	25 43.5	28 09.7	0 41.7	29 23.6	28 35.1	5 08.1
12 W	15 18 39	21 10 39	26 20 51	2♉47 29	14 41.8	13 15.0	2 39.6	20 19.9	17 12.2	4 06.2	25 54.6	28 07.8	0 43.1	29 26.1	28 35.8	5 07.1
13 Th	15 22 35	22 08 37	9♉18 24	15 53 32	14 38.6	13 05.9	2 42.2	21 32.2	17 39.1	4 01.1	26 05.7	28 05.9	0 44.5	29 28.5	28 36.4	5 06.1
14 F	15 26 32	23 06 33	22 32 41	29 15 38	14 35.5	12 57.7	2 49.5	22 44.4	18 06.3	3 55.6	26 16.6	28 04.2	0 45.8	29 30.8	28 37.0	5 05.1
15 Sa	15 30 28	24 04 28	6♊02 06	12♊51 47	14 32.3	12 51.1	3 01.3	23 56.6	18 33.7	3 49.8	26 27.5	28 02.6	0 47.1	29 33.1	28 37.6	5 04.0
16 Su	15 34 25	25 02 21	19 44 19	26 39 23	14 29.1	12 46.8	3 17.7	25 08.7	19 01.4	3 43.6	26 38.2	28 01.0	0 48.2	29 35.4	28 38.1	5 03.0
17 M	15 38 21	26 00 13	3♋36 38	10♋35 46	14 25.9	12D 44.6	3 38.5	26 20.8	19 29.2	3 37.0	26 48.9	27 59.6	0 49.4	29 37.7	28 38.6	5 01.9
18 Tu	15 42 18	26 58 03	17 36 28	24 38 28	14 22.8	12 44.3	4 03.6	27 32.8	19 57.2	3 30.1	26 59.4	27 58.2	0 50.4	29 39.9	28 39.1	5 00.8
19 W	15 46 15	27 55 51	1♌41 33	8♌45 28	14 19.6	12 45.3	4 32.9	28 44.8	20 25.3	3 22.9	27 09.9	27 57.0	0 51.4	29 42.1	28 39.5	4 59.6
20 Th	15 50 11	28 53 38	15 50 02	22 55 03	14 16.4	12R 46.5	5 06.3	29 56.7	20 53.7	3 15.3	27 20.2	27 55.9	0 52.4	29 44.2	28 39.9	4 58.5
21 F	15 54 08	29 51 23	0♍00 19	7♍05 39	14 13.2	12 47.0	5 43.7	1♋08.6	21 22.2	3 07.4	27 30.4	27 54.8	0 53.3	29 46.3	28 40.3	4 57.3
22 Sa	15 58 04	0♊49 06	14 10 49	21 15 33	14 10.0	12 46.2	6 24.9	2 20.4	21 51.0	2 59.1	27 40.5	27 53.9	0 54.1	29 48.4	28 40.6	4 56.1
23 Su	16 02 01	1 46 48	28 19 34	5♎22 33	14 06.9	12 43.7	7 09.8	3 32.1	22 19.9	2 50.6	27 50.5	27 53.0	0 54.9	29 50.4	28 40.9	4 54.9
24 M	16 05 57	2 44 27	12♎24 10	19 24 00	14 03.7	12 39.5	7 58.3	4 43.8	22 48.9	2 41.7	28 00.4	27 52.3	0 55.6	29 52.4	28 41.2	4 53.7
25 Tu	16 09 54	3 42 06	26 21 41	3♏16 48	14 00.5	12 34.1	8 50.3	5 55.4	23 18.1	2 32.5	28 10.2	27 51.6	0 56.2	29 54.3	28 41.4	4 52.4
26 W	16 13 50	4 39 43	10♏08 57	16 57 46	13 57.3	12 28.1	9 45.7	7 06.9	23 47.5	2 23.1	28 19.8	27 51.1	0 56.8	29 56.2	28 41.6	4 51.2
27 Th	16 17 47	5 37 19	23 42 55	0♐24 07	13 54.2	12 22.3	10 44.4	8 18.4	24 17.1	2 13.3	28 29.3	27 50.7	0 57.4	29 58.1	28 41.8	4 49.9
28 F	16 21 44	6 34 53	7♐01 08	13 33 48	13 51.0	12 17.4	11 46.3	9 29.8	24 46.8	2 03.3	28 38.7	27 50.3	0 57.8	29 59.9	28 41.9	4 48.6
29 Sa	16 25 40	7 32 27	20 02 04	26 25 55	13 47.8	12 13.9	12 51.3	10 41.2	25 16.6	1 53.0	28 48.0	27 50.1	0 58.3	0♈01.6	28 42.0	4 47.3
30 Su	16 29 37	8 29 59	2♑45 26	9♑00 47	13 44.6	12D 11.9	13 59.4	11 52.5	25 46.6	1 42.4	28 57.2	27D 50.0	0 58.6	0 03.4	28 42.1	4 46.0
31 M	16 33 33	9♊27 31	15 12 12	21 19 59	13♑41.5	12♑11.6	15♉10.5	13♋03.7	26♌16.8	1♑31.6	29♓06.2	27♍50.0	0♓58.9	0♈05.1	28♒42.1	4♑44.6

1st of Month

Julian Day # 2455317.5
Obliquity 23°26'19"
SVP 5♓06'40"
GC 26♐59.0
Eris 21♈46.9

Day	⚴	Day	⚵	Day	⚶
1	14♏34.9R	1	7♊41.2	1	23♌49.9
6	13 03.3R	6	10 34.6	6	24 46.2
11	11 32.7R	11	13 27.9	11	25 50.9
16	10 05.8R	16	16 20.9	16	27 03.3
21	8 45.1R	21	19 13.6	21	28 22.8
26	7 32.7R	26	22 05.6	26	29 48.9
31	6 30.0R	31	24 57.1	31	1♍21.0

DECLINATION and LATITUDE

Day	☉ Decl	☽ Decl	☽ Lat	☽ 12h Decl	☿ Decl	☿ Lat	♀ Decl	♀ Lat	♂ Decl	♂ Lat	⚳ Decl	⚳ Lat	♃ Decl	♃ Lat	♄ Decl	♄ Lat
1 Sa	14N59	24S52	2S42	25S06	14N05	0N19	22N17	0N49	19N02	2N04	22S39	0N43	3S26	1S03	2N53	2N32
2 Su	15 17	24 60	1 40	24 33	13 36	0 02	22 31	0 51	18 54	2 02	22 42	0 40	3 21	1 03	2 54	2 31
3 M	15 35	23 49	0 34	22 47	13 07	0S16	22 45	0 54	18 45	2 01	22 45	0 37	3 17	1 03	2 55	2 31
4 Tu	15 52	21 30	0N31	19 60	12 40	0 33	22 59	0 56	18 37	1 60	22 48	0 34	3 12	1 03	2 56	2 31
5 W	16 10	18 17	1 34	16 24	12 14	0 49	23 11	0 59	18 28	1 58	22 51	0 31	3 07	1 03	2 57	2 31
6 Th	16 27	14 21	2 32	12 11	11 49	1 06	23 23	1 01	18 19	1 57	22 54	0 28	3 03	1 04	2 58	2 31
7 F	16 43	9 54	3 24	7 31	11 26	1 21	23 34	1 04	18 10	1 55	22 57	0 25	2 59	1 04	2 59	2 31
8 Sa	16 60	5 05	4 06	2 34	11 05	1 36	23 45	1 06	18 01	1 54	23 00	0 22	2 54	1 04	2 59	2 30
9 Su	17 16	0 02	4 39	2N31	10 47	1 50	23 55	1 09	17 52	1 53	23 03	0 19	2 50	1 04	3 00	2 30
10 M	17 32	5N05	4 59	7 37	10 30	2 04	24 04	1 11	17 43	1 51	23 07	0 16	2 45	1 04	3 01	2 30
11 Tu	17 48	10 05	5 06	12 30	10 16	2 16	24 13	1 14	17 34	1 50	23 10	0 13	2 41	1 05	3 01	2 30
12 W	18 03	14 48	4 58	16 57	10 05	2 28	24 21	1 16	17 24	1 49	23 13	0 09	2 37	1 05	3 02	2 30
13 Th	18 18	18 56	4 35	20 42	9 56	2 38	24 28	1 18	17 15	1 47	23 16	0 06	2 33	1 05	3 02	2 29
14 F	18 33	22 13	3 57	23 27	9 49	2 48	24 35	1 21	17 05	1 46	23 20	0 03	2 29	1 05	3 03	2 29
15 Sa	18 47	24 20	3 05	24 53	9 45	2 56	24 41	1 23	16 55	1 45	23 23	0S00	2 24	1 05	3 03	2 29
16 Su	19 02	25 03	2 01	24 49	9 44	3 04	24 46	1 25	16 46	1 44	23 27	0 04	2 20	1 06	3 04	2 29
17 M	19 15	24 12	0 49	23 12	9 45	3 10	24 50	1 27	16 36	1 42	23 30	0 07	2 16	1 06	3 04	2 29
18 Tu	19 29	21 51	0S26	20 09	9 48	3 16	24 54	1 29	16 26	1 41	23 34	0 10	2 12	1 06	3 05	2 28
19 W	19 42	18 09	1 41	15 53	9 53	3 21	24 57	1 31	16 16	1 40	23 37	0 14	2 08	1 06	3 05	2 28
20 Th	19 55	13 24	2 49	10 43	10 00	3 25	24 59	1 33	16 05	1 39	23 41	0 17	2 04	1 06	3 05	2 28
21 F	20 07	7 55	3 48	5 00	10 10	3 28	25 01	1 35	15 55	1 37	23 44	0 20	2 01	1 07	3 05	2 28
22 Sa	20 19	2 02	4 32	0S57	10 21	3 30	25 02	1 37	15 44	1 36	23 48	0 24	1 57	1 07	3 06	2 28
23 Su	20 31	3S55	5 00	6 50	10 35	3 31	25 02	1 39	15 34	1 35	23 52	0 27	1 53	1 07	3 06	2 27
24 M	20 42	9 39	5 10	12 20	10 50	3 31	25 02	1 40	15 23	1 34	23 55	0 31	1 49	1 07	3 06	2 27
25 Tu	20 53	14 51	5 01	17 09	11 07	3 31	25 00	1 42	15 12	1 33	23 59	0 34	1 46	1 07	3 06	2 27
26 W	21 04	19 12	4 35	20 59	11 25	3 30	24 58	1 44	15 02	1 31	24 03	0 38	1 42	1 08	3 06	2 27
27 Th	21 14	22 28	3 53	23 37	11 45	3 28	24 56	1 45	14 51	1 30	24 06	0 41	1 38	1 08	3 06	2 27
28 F	21 24	24 26	2 60	24 54	12 06	3 26	24 52	1 47	14 40	1 29	24 10	0 45	1 35	1 08	3 06	2 26
29 Sa	21 34	25 01	1 58	24 48	12 29	3 22	24 48	1 48	14 28	1 28	24 14	0 48	1 31	1 08	3 06	2 26
30 Su	21 43	24 16	0 51	23 25	12 53	3 18	24 43	1 49	14 17	1 27	24 17	0 52	1 28	1 09	3 06	2 26
31 M	21N52	22S18	0N16	20S56	13N18	3S14	24N38	1N51	14N06	1N26	24S21	0S55	1S24	1S09	3N05	2N26

Day	⚷ Decl	⚷ Lat	♅ Decl	♅ Lat	♆ Decl	♆ Lat	♇ Decl	♇ Lat
1	5S41	6N02	1S05	0S44	12S26	0S27	18S11	5N09
6	5 36	6 03	0 60	0 44	12 24	0 27	18 11	5 09
11	5 32	6 05	0 55	0 44	12 23	0 27	18 11	5 09
16	5 28	6 07	0 50	0 44	12 22	0 27	18 11	5 09
21	5 25	6 08	0 46	0 44	12 22	0 27	18 12	5 09
26	5 22	6 10	0 42	0 44	12 21	0 27	18 12	5 09
31	5S20	6N12	0S39	0S44	12S21	0S27	18S12	5N09

Day	⚴ Decl	⚴ Lat	⚵ Decl	⚵ Lat	⚶ Decl	⚶ Lat	Eris Decl	Eris Lat
1	23N51	41N52	12N32	9S10	21N07	8N01	4S02	13S29
6	24 39	42 20	13 02	9 06	20 39	7 51	4 01	13 29
11	25 19	42 39	13 28	9 01	20 08	7 42	4 00	13 29
16	25 49	42 49	13 51	8 56	19 34	7 33	3 60	13 30
21	26 10	42 49	14 11	8 51	18 58	7 24	3 59	13 30
26	26 21	42 42	14 28	8 45	18 19	7 16	3 58	13 30
31	26N24	42N27	14N41	8S40	17N38	7N07	3S58	13S30

Moon Phenomena

Max/0 Decl

dy	hr mn	
1	14:06	25S06
9	0:09	0 N
15	23:19	25N03
22	8:10	0 S
28	22:23	25S02

Max/0 Lat

dy	hr mn	
3	12:35	0 N
10	23:32	5N06
17	15:40	0 S
24	0:18	5S10
30	18:09	0 N

Perigee/Apogee

dy	hr m		kilometers
6	22:02	a	404235
20	8:49	p	369733

PH	dy	hr mn	
☾	6	4:16	15♒33
●	14	1:05	23♉09
☽	20	23:44	29♌51
○	27	23:08	6♐33

Void of Course Moon

Last Aspect			☽ Ingress	
2 8:09	♅	□	♑	2 10:01
4 19:08	♅	✶	♒	4 20:53
7 6:37	♆	☌	♓	7 9:35
9 20:13	♅	☌	♈	9 21:30
12 4:12	♆	✶	♉	12 6:49
14 12:29	♅	✶	♊	14 13:19
16 17:07	♅	□	♋	16 17:47
18 20:36	♅	△	♌	18 21:07
20 23:44	☉	□	♍	20 23:59
23 2:35	♅	☍	♎	23 2:51
25 4:02	♆	△	♏	25 6:18
27 11:15	♅	△	♐	27 11:17
29 16:41	♃	□	♑	29 18:45

DAILY ASPECTARIAN

1 Sa ☽△♂ 1:18
☽⚼♅ 17:35
☽□♃ 22:35

2 Su ☉⚼☽ 3:38
☽⚼♂ 6:14
☽✶♆ 7:06
☽□♄ 7:10
☽□♅ 8:09
☽✶⚷ 10:53
☽☌⚳ 18:49
☽☌♇ 20:06
☽△☿ 20:47
♄⚻♆ 22:23
♀∦⚳ 22:47

3 M ☽⚻♀ 4:42
♂∠♄ 7:58
☉△☽ 10:58
☽∦♀ 11:14
☿△♇ 12:02
☽∠♆ 12:06
☽∥⚳ 12:10
☽⚻♂ 12:12
☽∠⚷ 16:03
☉⚼♄ 23:52

4 Tu ☽✶♃ 9:48
☉□♂ 13:10
☽⚼♀ 13:35
☿∦♆ 13:40
☉∠♅ 17:08
☽△♄ 17:40
☽⚺♆ 17:53
☽✶♅ 19:08
☿△⚳ 20:05
☽⚺⚷ 21:57
☽∦♂ 22:44
♂⚼♅ 22:54

5 W ☽∥♇ 0:39
☽□☿ 5:36
☽⚺⚳ 5:57
☽⚺♇ 7:23
☉∦☽ 12:32
☽∠♃ 16:27
☽△♀ 23:12
☽⚼♄ 23:49

6 Th ☽∠♅ 1:31
☽☍♂ 2:24
☉□☽ 4:16
☽∥♆ 10:48
☽∠⚳ 12:12
☽∠♇ 13:43
☽∦☿ 15:16
♂∦♇ 21:29
☽⚺♃ 23:22

7 F ♃∦♄ 0:00
☽⚻♄ 6:08
☽☌♆ 6:37
☽⚺♅ 8:03
☽☌⚷ 10:48
☽✶☿ 16:22
☽✶⚳ 18:28
☽✶♇ 20:04
☽∥⚷ 21:36
♀✶♂ 21:56

8 Sa ☽∦♄ 10:00
☽∥♃ 10:35
☽⚻♂ 17:18
☽□♀ 18:41
☽∥♅ 19:42
☽∠☿ 21:48
☉✶☽ 22:11

9 Su ☽∦♅ 4:34
☽☌♃ 12:33
☽∦♃ 13:14
☽∥♄ 14:16
☽☍♄ 17:59
☽⚺♆ 18:42
☽☌♅ 20:13
☿∠♀ 21:57
☽⚺⚷ 22:49

10 M ☽⚼♂ 0:05
☉⚼⚳ 0:14
☽∦⚷ 2:11
☽⚺☿ 2:57
☽□⚳ 5:47
☉∠☽ 6:17
☽□♇ 7:33
☉∥♂ 10:24
☉⚼♇ 22:08
☽∠♆ 23:50

11 Tu ☽∥☿ 0:52
☽∠⚷ 3:52
☽△♂ 6:06
☽∦♆ 11:26
☽✶♀ 11:29
☉⚺☽ 13:28
☿ D 22:29
☽⚺♃ 23:10

12 W ☽⚻♄ 3:19
☽✶♆ 4:12
☽⚺♅ 5:47
☽✶⚷ 8:10
☽☌☿ 11:47
☉∦♇ 12:54
☽∥♂ 14:06
☽△⚳ 14:20
☽△♇ 16:17
☽∠♀ 18:24
☽∦♇ 19:21
☉∥☽ 19:47

13 Th ☽∠♃ 3:19
☽⚼♄ 6:55
☽∠♅ 9:27
☽□♂ 15:43
☽⚼⚳ 17:32
☽⚼♇ 19:35

14 F ☽⚺♀ 0:23
☉☌☽ 1:05
☽✶♃ 6:46
☽△♄ 9:52
☽□♆ 10:52
☽∦⚳ 11:04
☽✶♅ 12:29
☽□⚷ 14:42
☽⚺☿ 18:35
☽⚻⚳ 20:08
☽⚻♇ 22:18

15 Sa ☽∥♀ 7:06
♂⚼⚳ 11:26
☉⚺♀ 13:14
☽∠☿ 21:26
☽✶♂ 22:43

16 Su ☉⚺☽ 9:53
☽☌♀ 10:17
☽□♃ 12:07
☽∥♀ 12:28
☽□♄ 14:20
☽△♆ 15:26
☽□♅ 17:07
☽△⚷ 19:11
☿△⚳ 22:48

17 M ☽☍⚳ 0:01
☽✶☿ 0:03
☽∠♂ 1:34
☽☍♇ 2:26
☽∦⚳ 8:37
♀□♃ 10:58
☉∠☽ 13:38
☽⚼♆ 17:14
☽⚼⚷ 20:59

18 Tu ☉✶♃ 0:42
♂⚼♇ 2:58
☽⚺♂ 4:09
♀□♄ 8:19
☉∥☽ 15:19
☽△♃ 16:12
☉✶☽ 17:08
☽✶♄ 17:39
☽⚺♀ 18:31
☽⚻♆ 18:50
☽△♅ 20:36
♀△♆ 22:13
☽⚻⚷ 22:35
☽∦♇ 23:44

19 W ☉△♄ 0:28
☽⚻⚳ 2:51
☽□☿ 5:03
☽⚻♇ 5:36
☽∥♂ 10:28
☽⚼♃ 18:00
☉□♆ 18:15
☿△♇ 18:48
☽∠♄ 19:05
♀□♅ 19:42
☽⚼♅ 22:08
☽∠♀ 22:21

20 Th ♀ ♋ 1:06
☽⚼⚳ 4:04
☽∦♆ 4:43
☽⚼♇ 7:00
☽☌♂ 8:52
☽∥☿ 14:43
♀△⚷ 18:50
☽⚻♃ 19:43
☽⚺♄ 20:28
☽☍♆ 21:44
☉✶♅ 21:49
☽⚻♅ 23:36
☉□☽ 23:44

21 F ☽☍⚷ 1:30
☽✶♀ 2:06
☉ ♊ 3:35
☽△⚳ 5:14
☽△♇ 8:22
☽△☿ 10:10
☽∦⚷ 10:21
☽∥♄ 19:44

22 Sa ☽∦♃ 0:22
☉□⚷ 2:07
☽∦♅ 5:10
☽∥♅ 11:09
♀☍⚳ 11:36
☽⚼☿ 12:56
☽⚺♂ 13:28
☽∥♃ 15:49
☽∦♄ 20:38
☽☍♃ 23:10
☽☌♄ 23:15

23 Su ☽⚻♆ 0:36
☽☍♅ 2:35
☽⚻⚷ 4:24
♃☍♄ 5:38
☽∥⚷ 6:00
☉△☽ 6:18
☽□⚳ 7:36
☽□♀ 9:41
☽□♇ 11:12
☽∠♂ 15:53
☽⚻☿ 15:57
☉⚻⚳ 23:01

24 M ☽⚼♆ 2:12
♀☍♇ 3:16
☽∦☿ 5:27
☽⚼⚷ 6:02
☉⚼☽ 9:50
☽∥♆ 12:07
☽✶♂ 18:32

25 Tu ☽∦♂ 1:46
☽⚺♄ 2:36
☽⚻♃ 3:10
☽△♆ 4:02
☽⚻♅ 6:09
☽△⚷ 7:56
☽✶⚳ 10:36
☉⚻☽ 13:41
☽✶♇ 14:45
☽∥♇ 17:58
☽△♀ 18:11
☽☍☿ 23:16

26 W ☉⚻♇ 4:40
☽∠♄ 4:45
☽⚼♃ 5:39
☽⚼♅ 8:26
☽∠⚳ 12:36
☉∦☽ 13:21
⚶ ♍ 14:51
☽∠♇ 17:06
☽⚼♀ 23:12

27 Th ☽□♂ 1:03
☽✶♄ 7:24
☽△♃ 8:39
☽□♆ 8:56
☽△♅ 11:15
☽□⚷ 13:01
☽⚺⚳ 15:06
☽∥⚳ 19:16
☽⚺♇ 19:59
☉☍☽ 23:08

28 F ♅ ♈ 1:45
☽⚻♀ 4:59
♃⚺♆ 8:15
☽⚻☿ 9:29
♀∠♂ 9:47
☽∦♀ 9:55
☿∦♆ 16:04
☿⚼♄ 23:33

29 Sa ☽△♂ 10:14
☽∦♀ 13:18
☽□♄ 14:39
☽⚼☿ 16:07
☽✶♆ 16:17
☽□♃ 16:41
☽□♅ 18:51
☽✶⚷ 20:36
☽☌⚳ 22:02
☿∠♃ 23:07
☽∥⚳ 23:36

30 Su ☽☌♇ 3:50
☉⚻☽ 11:56
☽⚼♂ 16:04
♄ D 18:09
☽☍♀ 19:24
☽∠♆ 21:05
☿∠♅ 22:09
☽△☿ 23:56

31 M ☽∠⚷ 1:31
☉∦☽ 3:48
♀⚼♆ 12:57
♆ R 18:49
☉⚼☽ 19:43
☽⚻♂ 22:43
☿⚼⚳ 22:53

June 2010

LONGITUDE

Day	Sid.Time	☉	☽	☽ 12 hour	Mean ☊	True ☊	☿	♀	♂	⚳	♃	♄	⚷	♅	♆	♇
	h m s	° ' "	° ' "	° ' "	° '	° '	° '	° '	° '	° '	° '	° '	° '	° '	° '	° '
1 Tu	16 37 30	10♊25 01	27♑24 31	3♒26 13	13♑38.3	12♑12.4	16♉24.5	14♋14.9	26♌47.1	1♑20.5	29♓15.2	27♍50.0	0♓59.1	0♈06.7	28♒42.1	4♑43.3
2 W	16 41 26	11 22 31	9♒25 34	15 23 05	13 35.1	12 14.0	17 41.4	15 26.0	27 17.6	1R 09.2	29 24.0	27 50.2	0 59.3	0 08.3	28R 42.1	4R 41.9
3 Th	16 45 23	12 19 59	21 19 19	27 14 50	13 31.9	12 15.7	19 01.2	16 37.1	27 48.2	0 57.7	29 32.6	27 50.5	0 59.4	0 09.9	28 42.1	4 40.5
4 F	16 49 19	13 17 27	3♓10 16	9♓06 11	13 28.8	12R 17.0	20 23.7	17 48.1	28 18.9	0 45.9	29 41.1	27 50.9	0R 59.5	0 11.4	28 42.0	4 39.1
5 Sa	16 53 16	14 14 54	15 03 14	21 02 00	13 25.6	12 17.5	21 49.0	18 59.0	28 49.8	0 34.0	29 49.5	27 51.3	0 59.4	0 12.9	28 41.9	4 37.7
6 Su	16 57 13	15 12 21	27 03 05	3♈07 04	13 22.4	12 16.8	23 17.0	20 09.8	29 20.8	0 21.9	29 57.8	27 51.9	0 59.4	0 14.3	28 41.7	4 36.3
7 M	17 01 09	16 09 47	9♈14 27	15 25 45	13 19.2	12 15.0	24 47.7	21 20.6	29 51.9	0 09.6	0♈05.9	27 52.6	0 59.2	0 15.7	28 41.5	4 34.9
8 Tu	17 05 06	17 07 12	21 41 25	28 01 47	13 16.0	12 12.3	26 21.2	22 31.3	0♍23.2	29♐57.1	0 13.9	27 53.4	0 59.0	0 17.0	28 41.3	4 33.4
9 W	17 09 02	18 04 36	4♉27 10	10♉57 45	13 12.9	12 08.9	27 57.3	23 42.0	0 54.6	29 44.5	0 21.7	27 54.3	0 58.8	0 18.3	28 41.0	4 32.0
10 Th	17 12 59	19 02 00	17 33 41	24 14 56	13 09.7	12 05.4	29 36.1	24 52.5	1 26.2	29 31.7	0 29.4	27 55.3	0 58.5	0 19.6	28 40.8	4 30.5
11 F	17 16 55	19 59 24	1♊01 25	7♊52 55	13 06.5	12 02.2	1♊17.6	26 03.0	1 57.9	29 18.9	0 37.0	27 56.4	0 58.1	0 20.8	28 40.4	4 29.1
12 Sa	17 20 52	20 56 46	14 49 09	21 49 42	13 03.3	11 58.7	3 01.7	27 13.5	2 29.7	29 05.9	0 44.4	27 57.6	0 57.7	0 22.0	28 40.1	4 27.6
13 Su	17 24 48	21 54 09	28 54 04	6♋01 43	13 00.2	11D 58.3	4 48.4	28 23.8	3 01.6	28 52.8	0 51.7	27 58.9	0 57.2	0 23.1	28 39.7	4 26.1
14 M	17 28 45	22 51 30	13♋12 02	20 24 24	12 57.0	11 57.9	6 37.7	29 34.1	3 33.7	28 39.7	0 58.8	28 00.3	0 56.6	0 24.1	28 39.3	4 24.6
15 Tu	17 32 42	23 48 51	27 38 09	4♌52 40	12 53.8	11 58.4	8 29.5	0♌44.3	4 05.9	28 26.5	1 05.8	28 01.8	0 56.0	0 25.2	28 38.9	4 23.1
16 W	17 36 38	24 46 10	12♌07 19	19 21 32	12 50.6	11 59.4	10 23.7	1 54.4	4 38.2	28 13.2	1 12.6	28 03.4	0 55.4	0 26.1	28 38.4	4 21.6
17 Th	17 40 35	25 43 29	26 34 47	3♍46 37	12 47.5	12 00.6	12 20.4	3 04.5	5 10.6	27 59.9	1 19.2	28 05.1	0 54.6	0 27.0	28 37.9	4 20.1
18 F	17 44 31	26 40 47	10♍56 36	18 04 13	12 44.3	12 01.5	14 19.3	4 14.4	5 43.2	27 46.6	1 25.7	28 06.9	0 53.8	0 27.9	28 37.4	4 18.6
19 Sa	17 48 28	27 38 04	25 09 41	2♎12 15	12 41.1	12R 02.0	16 20.4	5 24.3	6 15.9	27 33.3	1 32.1	28 08.7	0 53.0	0 28.7	28 36.8	4 17.0
20 Su	17 52 24	28 35 20	9♎11 52	16 08 24	12 37.9	12 01.8	18 23.5	6 34.0	6 48.6	27 20.0	1 38.2	28 10.7	0 52.1	0 29.5	28 36.2	4 15.5
21 M	17 56 21	29 32 35	23 01 42	29 51 41	12 34.7	12 01.0	20 28.5	7 43.7	7 21.5	27 06.8	1 44.3	28 12.8	0 51.1	0 30.3	28 35.6	4 14.0
22 Tu	18 00 17	0♋29 50	6♏38 17	13♏21 25	12 31.6	11 59.8	22 35.1	8 53.3	7 54.5	26 53.5	1 50.1	28 15.0	0 50.1	0 30.9	28 35.0	4 12.5
23 W	18 04 14	1 27 04	20 01 05	26 37 13	12 28.4	11 58.4	24 43.2	10 02.8	8 27.6	26 40.4	1 55.8	28 17.3	0 49.1	0 31.6	28 34.3	4 10.9
24 Th	18 08 11	2 24 18	3♐09 50	9♐38 56	12 25.2	11 57.2	26 52.4	11 12.2	9 00.8	26 27.3	2 01.4	28 19.6	0 47.9	0 32.2	28 33.6	4 09.4
25 F	18 12 07	3 21 31	16 04 32	22 26 42	12 22.0	11 56.2	29 02.6	12 21.4	9 34.2	26 14.3	2 06.7	28 22.1	0 46.8	0 32.7	28 32.9	4 07.9
26 Sa	18 16 04	4 18 43	28 45 30	5♑01 01	12 18.9	11 55.6	1♋13.4	13 30.6	10 07.6	26 01.4	2 11.9	28 24.7	0 45.5	0 33.2	28 32.1	4 06.3
27 Su	18 20 00	5 15 56	11♑13 23	17 22 45	12 15.7	11D 55.4	3 24.5	14 39.7	10 41.1	25 48.6	2 17.0	28 27.3	0 44.2	0 33.7	28 31.3	4 04.8
28 M	18 23 57	6 13 08	23 29 18	29 33 18	12 12.5	11 55.5	5 35.8	15 48.7	11 14.7	25 35.9	2 21.8	28 30.1	0 42.9	0 34.1	28 30.5	4 03.2
29 Tu	18 27 53	7 10 20	5♒34 58	11♒34 38	12 09.3	11 55.9	7 46.8	16 57.5	11 48.4	25 23.3	2 26.5	28 32.9	0 41.5	0 34.4	28 29.6	4 01.7
30 W	18 31 50	8♋07 31	17 32 37	23 29 19	12♑06.2	11♑56.3	9♋57.4	18♌06.3	12♍22.3	25♐10.9	2♈31.1	28♍35.8	0♓40.1	0♈34.7	28♒28.8	4♑00.2

1st of Month

Julian Day #
2455348.5
Obliquity
23°26'18"
SVP 5♓06'35"
GC 26♐59.1
Eris 22♈04.0

Day	⚴
1	6♏18.8R
6	5 29.2R
11	4 51.4R
16	4 25.4R
21	4 11.4R
26	4 08.9

Day	⚵
1	25♊31.3
6	28 22.0
11	1♋11.9
16	4 01.1
21	6 49.3
26	9 36.5

Day	⚶
1	1♍40.1
6	3 18.6
11	5 02.2
16	6 50.5
21	8 43.0
26	10 39.4

DECLINATION and LATITUDE

Day	☉ Decl	☽ Decl	☽ Lat	☽ 12h Decl	☿ Decl	☿ Lat	♀ Decl	♀ Lat	♂ Decl	♂ Lat	⚳ Decl	⚳ Lat	♃ Decl	♃ Lat	♄ Decl	♄ Lat
1 Tu	22N01	19S20	1N22	17S33	13N44	3S09	24N32	1N52	13N55	1N25	24S25	0S59	1S21	1S09	3N05	2N26
2 W	22 09	15 35	2 24	13 29	14 11	3 03	24 25	1 53	13 43	1 23	24 28	1 02	1 18	1 09	3 05	2 25
3 Th	22 16	11 16	3 18	8 57	14 39	2 56	24 17	1 54	13 31	1 22	24 32	1 06	1 15	1 09	3 05	2 25
4 F	22 24	6 33	4 04	4 05	15 07	2 49	24 09	1 55	13 20	1 21	24 36	1 10	1 11	1 10	3 04	2 25
5 Sa	22 31	1 36	4 39	0N56	15 37	2 42	24 00	1 56	13 08	1 20	24 39	1 13	1 08	1 10	3 04	2 25
6 Su	22 37	3N28	5 03	5 59	16 06	2 34	23 51	1 57	12 56	1 19	24 43	1 17	1 05	1 10	3 03	2 24
7 M	22 43	8 28	5 13	10 53	16 37	2 26	23 41	1 57	12 44	1 18	24 47	1 20	1 02	1 10	3 03	2 24
8 Tu	22 49	13 14	5 10	15 28	17 07	2 17	23 30	1 58	12 32	1 17	24 50	1 24	0 59	1 11	3 03	2 24
9 W	22 54	17 34	4 51	19 28	17 38	2 08	23 18	1 59	12 20	1 16	24 54	1 27	0 56	1 11	3 02	2 24
10 Th	22 59	21 10	4 16	22 36	18 09	1 58	23 06	1 59	12 08	1 15	24 57	1 31	0 54	1 11	3 01	2 24
11 F	23 04	23 44	3 27	24 32	18 40	1 48	22 54	1 60	11 55	1 14	25 01	1 35	0 51	1 11	3 01	2 23
12 Sa	23 08	24 58	2 24	24 60	19 10	1 38	22 40	1 60	11 43	1 13	25 04	1 38	0 48	1 12	3 00	2 23
13 Su	23 11	24 37	1 11	23 51	19 40	1 27	22 26	2 00	11 30	1 12	25 08	1 42	0 46	1 12	2 59	2 23
14 M	23 15	22 40	0S07	21 07	20 10	1 16	22 12	2 00	11 18	1 11	25 11	1 45	0 43	1 12	2 59	2 23
15 Tu	23 18	19 14	1 25	17 03	20 39	1 05	21 57	2 00	11 05	1 10	25 14	1 49	0 40	1 13	2 58	2 23
16 W	23 20	14 37	2 39	11 58	21 07	0 54	21 41	2 00	10 52	1 09	25 18	1 52	0 38	1 13	2 57	2 22
17 Th	23 22	9 10	3 42	6 15	21 34	0 42	21 25	2 00	10 40	1 08	25 21	1 56	0 36	1 13	2 56	2 22
18 F	23 24	3 17	4 31	0 17	22 00	0 31	21 08	1 60	10 27	1 07	25 24	1 59	0 33	1 13	2 55	2 22
19 Sa	23 25	2S43	5 03	5S38	22 24	0 20	20 51	1 59	10 14	1 06	25 28	2 03	0 31	1 14	2 54	2 22
20 Su	23 26	8 29	5 16	11 12	22 47	0 09	20 33	1 59	10 01	1 05	25 31	2 06	0 29	1 14	2 53	2 21
21 M	23 26	13 45	5 10	16 07	23 08	0N02	20 15	1 58	9 48	1 04	25 34	2 09	0 27	1 14	2 52	2 21
22 Tu	23 26	18 15	4 48	20 08	23 27	0 13	19 56	1 58	9 34	1 03	25 37	2 13	0 25	1 14	2 51	2 21
23 W	23 26	21 45	4 09	23 03	23 44	0 24	19 36	1 57	9 21	1 02	25 40	2 16	0 22	1 15	2 50	2 21
24 Th	23 25	24 02	3 19	24 41	23 58	0 34	19 17	1 56	9 08	1 01	25 43	2 19	0 21	1 15	2 49	2 21
25 F	23 24	25 00	2 18	24 59	24 10	0 44	18 56	1 55	8 54	0 60	25 46	2 23	0 19	1 15	2 48	2 20
26 Sa	23 22	24 38	1 12	23 59	24 19	0 53	18 36	1 54	8 41	0 59	25 49	2 26	0 17	1 16	2 47	2 20
27 Su	23 20	23 02	0 04	21 49	24 25	1 02	18 14	1 53	8 27	0 58	25 51	2 29	0 15	1 16	2 45	2 20
28 M	23 18	20 21	1N04	18 40	24 29	1 10	17 53	1 52	8 14	0 57	25 54	2 32	0 13	1 16	2 44	2 20
29 Tu	23 15	16 49	2 08	14 47	24 30	1 17	17 31	1 51	7 60	0 56	25 57	2 36	0 12	1 16	2 43	2 20
30 W	23N11	12S38	3N05	10S22	24N27	1N24	17N08	1N49	7N46	0N55	25S60	2S39	0S10	1S17	2N41	2N19

Day	⚷ Decl	⚷ Lat	♅ Decl	♅ Lat	♆ Decl	♆ Lat	♇ Decl	♇ Lat
1	5S19	6N12	0S38	0S44	12S21	0S28	18S12	5N0[illegible]
6	5 17	6 14	0 35	0 45	12 22	0 28	18 13	5 0[illegible]
11	5 16	6 15	0 33	0 45	12 22	0 28	18 13	5 0[illegible]
16	5 16	6 17	0 31	0 45	12 23	0 28	18 14	5 0[illegible]
21	5 16	6 19	0 29	0 45	12 24	0 28	18 14	5 0[illegible]
26	5 16	6 20	0 28	0 45	12 25	0 28	18 15	5 0[illegible]

Day	⚴ Decl	⚴ Lat	⚵ Decl	⚵ Lat	⚶ Decl	⚶ Lat	Eris Decl	Eris Lat
1	26N24	42N23	14N43	8S39	17N30	7N05	3S57	13S3[illegible]
6	26 16	42 01	14 53	8 33	16 46	6 57	3 57	13 3[illegible]
11	26 02	41 35	14 59	8 27	16 00	6 50	3 57	13 3[illegible]
16	25 40	41 04	15 02	8 21	15 13	6 42	3 56	13 3[illegible]
21	25 13	40 31	15 01	8 15	14 23	6 35	3 56	13 3[illegible]
26	24 40	39 55	14 57	8 09	13 33	6 28	3 56	13 3[illegible]

Moon Phenomena

Max/0 Decl

dy	hr mn	
5	7:35	0 N
12	6:57	25N02
18	13:07	0 S
25	5:11	25S02

Max/0 Lat

dy	hr mn	
7	5:47	5N14
13	21:56	0 S
20	4:48	5S16
27	1:21	0 N

Perigee/Apogee

dy	hr m		kilometers
3	16:56	a	404264
15	15:04	p	365934

PH	dy	hr mn	
☾	4	22:14	14♓11
●	12	11:16	21♊24
☽	19	4:31	27♍49
○	26	11:31	4♑46
☍	26	11:40	P 0.537

Void of Course Moon

Last Aspect				☽ Ingress		
1	3:42	♃	⚹	♒	1	5:09
3	14:57	♆	☌	♓	3	17:35
6	5:50	♃	☌	♈	6	5:51
8	13:14	♆	⚹	♉	8	15:42
10	19:51	♆	□	♊	10	22:12
12	23:36	♆	△	♋	13	1:51
15	0:39	♄	⚹	♌	15	3:55
17	3:25	♆	☍	♍	17	5:42
19	5:05	♄	☌	♎	19	8:14
21	9:46	♆	△	♏	21	12:15
23	15:33	♆	□	♐	23	18:11
25	23:34	♆	⚹	♑	26	2:22
28	9:57	♄	△	♒	28	12:53

DAILY ASPECTARIAN

1 Tu
☽△♄ 0:51
☽⊻♆ 2:34
☽⚹♃ 3:42
☽⚹♅ 5:23
☿∥♂ 6:42
☽⊻⚷ 7:07
☽∥♇ 7:42
☽⊻⚳ 7:42
☽⊻♇ 14:32
♀#⚳ 16:23

2 W
☉△☽ 4:16
☽⚼♄ 6:52
☽#☿ 7:19
☽∠♃ 10:08
☽#♂ 11:13
♀⚼⚷ 11:15
☽∠♅ 11:32
☽∠⚳ 13:20
☽⊼♀ 13:26
☽∥♆ 18:10
☽□☿ 18:45
⚳⚹⚷ 20:25
☽∠♇ 20:41

3 Th
♂⊻♄ 1:51
☿⚼♇ 11:22
☽⊼♄ 13:13
☽☍♂ 13:43
☽☌♆ 14:57
☽⊻♃ 16:51
☽⊻♅ 17:57
☽⚹⚳ 19:12
☽☌⚷ 19:35
☽⚼♀ 23:10

4 F
☽⚹♇ 3:00
☽∥⚷ 6:08
⚷ R 7:05
☽#♄ 16:56
♂☍♆ 17:53
☉□☽ 22:14

5 Sa
☽∥♃ 2:11
☽∥♅ 4:46
☽△♀ 8:45
☽#♅ 10:23
☽#♃ 12:51
☽⚹☿ 15:26
☽∥♄ 22:05

6 Su
☽☍♄ 1:37
☽⊻♆ 3:16
☽⊼♂ 4:45
☽☌♃ 5:50
☽☌♅ 6:20
☽□⚳ 6:27
♃ ♈ 6:29
☽⊻⚷ 7:48
☽#⚷ 8:42
⚳□♅ 13:15
☽□♇ 14:54

7 M
☽∠☿ 1:14
⚳□♃ 4:16
♂ ♍ 6:12
☽∠♆ 8:38
♂△⚳ 9:41
☽⚼♂ 11:23
☽∠⚷ 13:04
♂⊼♃ 14:27
☉⚹☽ 14:32
⚳R♐ 18:25
♂⊼♅ 19:04
☽#♆ 19:28
☽∥♂ 20:31

8 Tu
☽□♀ 1:45
☽⊻☿ 10:06
♃☌♅ 11:28
☽⊼♄ 11:45
☽⚹♆ 13:14
☽△⚳ 15:21
☽⊻♅ 16:15
☽⊻♃ 16:18
☽△♂ 17:07
☽⚹⚷ 17:32
♂#♆ 20:10
⚵ ♋ 21:09
☉∠☽ 21:14
☿△♄ 23:15

9 W
☽△♇ 0:09
☽∥☿ 0:30
♂☍⚷ 3:09
☽#♇ 4:00
☿□♆ 10:40
☽⚼♄ 15:34
☽⚼⚳ 18:36
☽∠♅ 19:57
☽∠♃ 20:13
☿⊼⚳ 23:04

10 Th
☉⊻☽ 2:52
☿#♇ 3:25
☽⚼♇ 3:30
☿ ♊ 5:42
☉∥♀ 10:06
☿⚹♅ 10:29
☿⚹♃ 13:43
☽⚹♀ 14:22
☽∥♀ 15:36
☉∥☽ 16:17
☽△♄ 18:33
☿□⚷ 19:27
☽□♆ 19:51
☽⊼⚳ 21:02
☽⚹♅ 22:48
☽⚹♃ 23:17
☽□⚷ 23:54

11 F
☽☌☿ 0:33
☽□♂ 1:43
☽⊼♇ 6:04
☿□♂ 13:29
☽∠♀ 19:07

12 Sa
☉☌☽ 11:16
♀⚹♄ 15:19
☿⊼♇ 19:06
☽□♄ 22:27
☽⊻♀ 23:04
☽△♆ 23:36
☽☍⚳ 23:58

13 Su
☽□♅ 2:30
☽□♃ 3:20
☽△⚷ 3:28
♀⊼♆ 5:24
☽⚹♂ 7:14
♀⊼⚳ 8:20
☽☍♇ 9:18
☽⊻☿ 11:23
♃⊻⚷ 17:13
☉∥☽ 18:42

14 M
⚳⚹♆ 0:39
☽⚼♆ 0:46
☽∥♀ 4:19
☽⚼⚷ 4:34
♀ ♌ 8:51
☽∠♂ 9:17
☽∠☿ 16:06
☽∥☿ 16:13
☉⊻☽ 17:13
♀△♅ 17:21

15 Tu
☽⚹♄ 0:39
☽⊼⚳ 1:19
☽⊼♆ 1:41
♀⊼⚷ 3:58
☽△♅ 4:37
☽⊼⚷ 5:28
☽☌♀ 5:36
☽#♇ 5:43
☽△♃ 5:47
♀△♃ 8:08
☽⊻♂ 11:07
☽⊼♇ 11:10
♂△♇ 12:13
☉∠☽ 19:50
☽⚹☿ 20:42

16 W
☽∠♄ 1:33
☽⚼⚳ 1:48
☽⚼♅ 5:30
☽⚼♃ 6:50
☽#♆ 10:11
☽⚼♇ 11:59
⚳□♄ 15:48
☽∥♂ 17:26
☿∥♀ 18:49
☉⚹☽ 22:29

17 Th
☽△⚳ 2:20
☽⊻♄ 2:31
☽☍♆ 3:25
☽⊼♅ 6:27
☽☍⚷ 7:13
☽⊼♃ 7:58
☽⊻♀ 11:47
☽△♇ 12:55
☽☌♂ 14:54
☽#⚷ 16:02

18 F
♀⊼♇ 1:24
☽∥♄ 1:27
☽□☿ 6:36
☽#♃ 10:58
☽#♅ 11:07
☽∥♅ 15:07
☽∠♀ 15:13
☽∥♃ 15:14
☉☍⚳ 22:23

19 Sa
☽#♄ 0:47
☽□⚳ 4:00
☉□☽ 4:31
☽☌♄ 5:05
☽⊼♆ 5:52
☽☍♅ 9:04
☽⊼⚷ 9:44
☽∥⚷ 10:26
☽☍♃ 10:56
☉□♄ 13:19
♃∥♅ 13:24
☽□♇ 15:32
☽⚹♀ 19:04
☽⊻♂ 19:44

20 Su
☉△♆ 0:23
☽#♂ 6:26
☽⚼♆ 7:36
♀⊻♂ 9:31
☽⚼⚷ 11:31
☽∥♆ 17:33
☽△☿ 18:44
☽∠♂ 22:47

21 M
☽⚹⚳ 7:03
☽⊻♄ 9:07
☽△♆ 9:46
☉ ♋ 11:30
☉△☽ 12:18
☽⊼♅ 13:09
☽△⚷ 13:44
☽⊼♃ 15:25
☽⚹♇ 19:42
☉∥☿ 22:56
☽∥♇ 23:57

22 Tu
☉□♅ 0:28
☽⚼☿ 2:00
☽⚹♂ 2:21
☽□♀ 4:23
☉△⚷ 8:21
☽∠⚳ 9:13
☽#♀ 9:44
☽∠♄ 11:50
☽⚼♅ 15:53
☉⚼☽ 17:04
☽⚼♃ 18:23
☽∠♇ 22:29

23 W
☿∠♀ 7:55
☽⊼☿ 10:12
☽⊻⚳ 11:54
☉□♃ 13:22
☽⚹♄ 15:06
☽□♆ 15:33
☉#☽ 16:06
☽△♅ 19:10
☽□⚷ 19:39
☿☍⚳ 19:46
☽△♃ 21:53
☉⊼☽ 22:30
☽#☿ 22:52

24 Th
☽⊻♇ 1:50
♀⚼⚳ 4:24
☽□♂ 11:18
⚴ D 14:30
☽△♀ 16:22
☿□♄ 16:25
☿△♆ 18:34

25 F
☿ ♋ 10:33
☿□♅ 16:37
☽☌⚳ 18:52
☉☍♇ 18:56
☿△⚷ 18:57
♀∠♄ 21:51
☽□♄ 23:20
☽⚼♀ 23:29
☽⚹♆ 23:34

26 Sa
☽□♅ 3:26
☽⚹⚷ 3:49
☽☍☿ 5:43
☽#☿ 6:01
☽□♃ 6:38
☽☌♇ 10:14
☿□♃ 11:09
☉☍☽ 11:31
☉#☽ 20:26
☽△♂ 22:54
♀#♇ 22:56

27 Su
☽∠♆ 4:28
☿☍♇ 7:17
☽⊼♀ 7:23
☽∠⚷ 8:47
♀⚼♅ 18:53

28 M
♄⊼♆ 2:47
☽⊻⚳ 4:06
☽⚼♂ 5:42
☽⊻♆ 9:55
☽△♄ 9:57
☉☌☿ 12:08
☽⚹♅ 14:01
☽⊻⚷ 14:17
☽∥♇ 14:46
☽⚹♃ 17:42
☽#♀ 19:09
☽⊻♇ 20:54

29 Tu
☉⊼☽ 3:27
☽⊼☿ 5:22
☽∠⚳ 9:27
♀⚼♃ 10:50
☽⊼♂ 13:05
☽⚼♄ 16:01
☽∠♅ 20:02
☽∠♃ 23:57

30 W
☽∥♆ 1:02
☽☍♀ 1:15
☽∠♇ 2:56
☉⚼☽ 12:15
☽⚹⚳ 15:10
☽⚼☿ 18:19
♀⚼♇ 18:25
☽☌♆ 22:04
☽⊼♄ 22:26

LONGITUDE

July 2010

Day	Sid.Time	☉	☽	☽ 12 hour	Mean☊	True☊	☿	♀	♂	⚳	♃	♄	⚷	♅	♆	♇
	h m s	° ' "	° ' "	° ' "	° '	° '	° '	° '	° '	° '	° '	° '	° '	° '	° '	° '
1 Th	18 35 47	9♋04 43	29♒25 07	5♓20 30	12♑03.0	11♑56.7	12♋07.3	19♌14.9	12♍56.2	24♐58.7	2♈35.4	28♍38.8	0♓38.6	0♈35.0	28♒27.9	3♑58.7
2 F	18 39 43	10 01 55	11♓15 54	17 11 51	11 59.8	11 56.9	14 16.2	20 23.5	13 30.2	24R 46.6	2 39.6	28 41.9	0R 37.0	0 35.2	28R 26.9	3R 57.1
3 Sa	18 43 40	10 59 07	23 08 51	29 07 29	11 56.6	11 57.1	16 24.0	21 31.9	14 04.3	24 34.7	2 43.6	28 45.1	0 35.4	0 35.3	28 26.0	3 55.6
4 Su	18 47 36	11 56 19	5♈08 16	11♈11 47	11 53.5	11 57.1	18 30.6	22 40.2	14 38.5	24 23.1	2 47.4	28 48.4	0 33.7	0 35.4	28 25.0	3 54.1
5 M	18 51 33	12 53 31	17 18 35	23 29 13	11 50.3	11 57.1	20 35.7	23 48.4	15 12.9	24 11.6	2 51.0	28 51.8	0 32.0	0R 35.5	28 24.0	3 52.6
6 Tu	18 55 29	13 50 44	29 44 13	6♉04 04	11 47.1	11 57.2	22 39.2	24 56.5	15 47.3	24 00.3	2 54.5	28 55.2	0 30.3	0 35.5	28 23.0	3 51.0
7 W	18 59 26	14 47 56	12♉29 11	18 59 58	11 43.9	11 57.4	24 41.1	26 04.4	16 21.8	23 49.3	2 57.7	28 58.8	0 28.5	0 35.5	28 21.9	3 49.5
8 Th	19 03 22	15 45 10	25 36 43	2♊19 36	11 40.7	11 57.7	26 41.3	27 12.3	16 56.4	23 38.5	3 00.8	29 02.4	0 26.6	0 35.4	28 20.9	3 48.0
9 F	19 07 19	16 42 23	9♊08 44	16 04 03	11 37.6	11 58.1	28 39.7	28 20.0	17 31.1	23 28.0	3 03.7	29 06.1	0 24.7	0 35.2	28 19.8	3 46.5
10 Sa	19 11 16	17 39 37	23 05 24	0♋12 27	11 34.4	11 58.5	0♌36.2	29 27.5	18 05.9	23 17.7	3 06.4	29 09.9	0 22.8	0 35.1	28 18.6	3 45.1
11 Su	19 15 12	18 36 52	7♋24 44	14 41 39	11 31.2	11R 58.7	2 30.9	0♍35.0	18 40.8	23 07.7	3 08.9	29 13.8	0 20.8	0 34.8	28 17.5	3 43.6
12 M	19 19 09	19 34 06	22 02 27	29 26 18	11 28.0	11 58.7	4 23.6	1 42.3	19 15.8	22 58.0	3 11.3	29 17.8	0 18.8	0 34.5	28 16.3	3 42.1
13 Tu	19 23 05	20 31 21	6♌52 16	14♌19 22	11 24.9	11 58.2	6 14.5	2 49.5	19 50.9	22 48.5	3 13.4	29 21.8	0 16.7	0 34.2	28 15.1	3 40.7
14 W	19 27 02	21 28 35	21 46 36	29 12 59	11 21.7	11 57.4	8 03.5	3 56.5	20 26.0	22 39.4	3 15.3	29 26.0	0 14.6	0 33.8	28 13.9	3 39.2
15 Th	19 30 58	22 25 50	6♍37 36	13♍59 35	11 18.5	11 56.2	9 50.5	5 03.4	21 01.3	22 30.5	3 17.1	29 30.2	0 12.4	0 33.4	28 12.7	3 37.8
16 F	19 34 55	23 23 05	21 18 13	28 32 53	11 15.3	11 55.0	11 35.7	6 10.1	21 36.6	22 22.0	3 18.6	29 34.4	0 10.2	0 33.0	28 11.4	3 36.3
17 Sa	19 38 51	24 20 20	5♎43 05	12♎48 28	11 12.2	11 54.1	13 18.9	7 16.7	22 12.1	22 13.8	3 20.0	29 38.8	0 07.9	0 32.4	28 10.2	3 34.9
18 Su	19 42 48	25 17 35	19 48 50	26 44 03	11 09.0	11D 53.5	15 00.2	8 23.1	22 47.6	22 05.9	3 21.2	29 43.2	0 05.6	0 31.9	28 08.9	3 33.5
19 M	19 46 45	26 14 50	3♏34 08	10♏19 10	11 05.8	11 53.6	16 39.6	9 29.4	23 23.2	21 58.4	3 22.1	29 47.8	0 03.3	0 31.3	28 07.6	3 32.1
20 Tu	19 50 41	27 12 05	16 59 17	23 34 42	11 02.6	11 54.2	18 17.1	10 35.4	23 58.9	21 51.2	3 22.9	29 52.3	0 01.0	0 30.6	28 06.2	3 30.8
21 W	19 54 38	28 09 21	0♐05 40	6♐32 27	10 59.4	11 55.3	19 52.7	11 41.3	24 34.7	21 44.3	3 23.5	29 57.0	29♒58.6	0 29.9	28 04.9	3 29.4
22 Th	19 58 34	29 06 37	12 55 20	19 14 35	10 56.3	11 56.7	21 26.4	12 47.0	25 10.5	21 37.7	3 23.9	0♎01.7	29 56.1	0 29.2	28 03.5	3 28.0
23 F	20 02 31	0♌03 53	25 30 31	1♑43 23	10 53.1	11 57.8	22 58.2	13 52.6	25 46.5	21 31.5	3R 24.1	0 06.6	29 53.7	0 28.4	28 02.1	3 26.7
24 Sa	20 06 27	1 01 10	7♑53 27	14 00 59	10 49.9	11R 58.5	24 28.0	14 57.9	26 22.5	21 25.7	3 24.1	0 11.4	29 51.1	0 27.5	28 00.7	3 25.4
25 Su	20 10 24	1 58 27	20 06 14	26 09 24	10 46.7	11 58.3	25 55.9	16 03.1	26 58.6	21 20.2	3 23.9	0 16.4	29 48.6	0 26.6	27 59.3	3 24.1
26 M	20 14 20	2 55 45	2♒10 45	8♒10 29	10 43.6	11 57.1	27 21.8	17 08.0	27 34.8	21 15.1	3 23.5	0 21.4	29 46.0	0 25.7	27 57.9	3 22.8
27 Tu	20 18 17	3 53 03	14 08 51	20 06 05	10 40.4	11 54.9	28 45.8	18 12.8	28 11.1	21 10.3	3 22.9	0 26.5	29 43.4	0 24.8	27 56.4	3 21.5
28 W	20 22 14	4 50 22	26 02 25	1♓58 07	10 37.2	11 51.8	0♍07.7	19 17.3	28 47.4	21 05.9	3 22.1	0 31.6	29 40.8	0 23.7	27 55.0	3 20.3
29 Th	20 26 10	5 47 41	7♓53 29	13 48 49	10 34.0	11 47.9	1 27.5	20 21.6	29 23.8	21 01.8	3 21.1	0 36.9	29 38.1	0 22.7	27 53.5	3 19.0
30 F	20 30 07	6 45 02	19 44 26	25 40 43	10 30.9	11 43.9	2 45.3	21 25.7	0♎00.3	20 58.1	3 20.0	0 42.1	29 35.5	0 21.6	27 52.0	3 17.8
31 Sa	20 34 03	7♌42 24	1♈38 04	7♈36 53	10♑27.7	11♑40.0	4♍00.9	22♍29.6	0♎36.9	20♐54.7	3♈18.6	0♎47.5	29♒32.7	0♈20.4	27♒50.5	3♑16.6

1st of Month

Julian Day # 2455378.5
Obliquity 23°26'18"
SVP 5♓06'30"
GC 26♐59.2
Eris 22♈13.9

Day	⚴
1	4♏17.4
6	4 36.2
11	5 04.8
16	5 42.4
21	6 28.6
26	7 22.4
31	8 23.2

Day	⚵
1	12♋22.6
6	15 07.7
11	17 51.7
16	20 34.4
21	23 15.8
26	25 55.9
31	28 34.6

Day	⚶
1	12♍39.3
6	14 42.5
11	16 48.9
16	18 58.2
21	21 10.2
26	23 24.6
31	25 41.3

DECLINATION and LATITUDE

Day	☉ Decl	☽ Decl	☽ Lat	☽ 12h Decl	☿ Decl	☿ Lat	♀ Decl	♀ Lat	♂ Decl	♂ Lat	⚳ Decl	⚳ Lat	♃ Decl	♃ Lat	♄ Decl	♄ Lat
1 Th	23N08	8S01	3N54	5S36	24N23	1N30	16N45	1N48	7N32	0N54	26S02	2S42	0S09	1S17	2N40	2N19
2 F	23 04	3 08	4 33	0 38	24 15	1 35	16 22	1 46	7 18	0 53	26 05	2 45	0 07	1 17	2 39	2 19
3 Sa	22 59	1N53	5 00	4N23	24 05	1 40	15 58	1 44	7 04	0 52	26 07	2 48	0 06	1 18	2 37	2 19
4 Su	22 54	6 52	5 15	9 17	23 52	1 44	15 34	1 43	6 50	0 51	26 10	2 51	0 05	1 18	2 36	2 19
5 M	22 49	11 39	5 16	13 56	23 37	1 47	15 10	1 41	6 36	0 50	26 12	2 54	0 04	1 18	2 34	2 18
6 Tu	22 43	16 05	5 02	18 06	23 20	1 49	14 45	1 38	6 22	0 50	26 14	2 57	0 03	1 18	2 32	2 18
7 W	22 37	19 55	4 33	21 32	22 60	1 51	14 20	1 36	6 08	0 49	26 17	2 59	0 02	1 19	2 31	2 18
8 Th	22 31	22 53	3 50	23 56	22 38	1 51	13 55	1 34	5 53	0 48	26 19	3 02	0 01	1 19	2 29	2 18
9 F	22 24	24 39	2 52	25 01	22 15	1 52	13 29	1 32	5 39	0 47	26 21	3 05	0N00	1 19	2 28	2 18
10 Sa	22 16	24 58	1 43	24 31	21 50	1 51	13 03	1 29	5 25	0 46	26 23	3 08	0 01	1 20	2 26	2 17
11 Su	22 09	23 39	0 25	22 23	21 23	1 50	12 37	1 27	5 10	0 45	26 26	3 10	0 02	1 20	2 24	2 17
12 M	22 01	20 43	0S56	18 43	20 55	1 48	12 10	1 24	4 56	0 44	26 28	3 13	0 02	1 20	2 22	2 17
13 Tu	21 52	16 24	2 14	13 49	20 25	1 46	11 44	1 21	4 41	0 43	26 30	3 15	0 03	1 21	2 21	2 17
14 W	21 43	11 02	3 23	8 06	19 54	1 43	11 17	1 18	4 26	0 43	26 32	3 18	0 03	1 21	2 19	2 17
15 Th	21 34	5 04	4 19	1 59	19 22	1 39	10 49	1 15	4 12	0 42	26 34	3 20	0 04	1 21	2 17	2 16
16 F	21 25	1S06	4 56	4S08	18 49	1 35	10 22	1 12	3 57	0 41	26 36	3 23	0 04	1 21	2 15	2 16
17 Sa	21 15	7 05	5 15	9 55	18 16	1 30	9 54	1 09	3 42	0 40	26 38	3 25	0 04	1 22	2 13	2 16
18 Su	21 05	12 35	5 13	15 03	17 41	1 25	9 26	1 05	3 28	0 39	26 39	3 28	0 05	1 22	2 11	2 16
19 M	20 54	17 19	4 54	19 19	17 06	1 19	8 58	1 02	3 13	0 38	26 41	3 30	0 05	1 22	2 09	2 16
20 Tu	20 43	21 03	4 19	22 29	16 31	1 13	8 30	0 58	2 58	0 37	26 43	3 32	0 05	1 23	2 07	2 16
21 W	20 32	23 37	3 31	24 25	15 54	1 07	8 01	0 55	2 43	0 37	26 45	3 34	0 05	1 23	2 05	2 15
22 Th	20 20	24 53	2 34	25 02	15 18	0 60	7 33	0 51	2 28	0 36	26 47	3 37	0 05	1 23	2 03	2 15
23 F	20 08	24 51	1 30	24 22	14 41	0 52	7 04	0 47	2 13	0 35	26 48	3 39	0 04	1 24	2 01	2 15
24 Sa	19 56	23 35	0 23	22 31	14 04	0 45	6 35	0 43	1 58	0 34	26 50	3 41	0 04	1 24	1 59	2 15
25 Su	19 43	21 12	0N45	19 39	13 27	0 36	6 06	0 39	1 43	0 33	26 52	3 43	0 04	1 24	1 57	2 15
26 M	19 30	17 54	1 49	15 59	12 49	0 28	5 37	0 35	1 27	0 32	26 53	3 45	0 03	1 24	1 55	2 15
27 Tu	19 17	13 54	2 48	11 42	12 12	0 19	5 08	0 31	1 12	0 32	26 55	3 47	0 03	1 25	1 53	2 14
28 W	19 03	9 24	3 39	7 01	11 35	0 10	4 39	0 26	0 57	0 31	26 57	3 49	0 02	1 25	1 51	2 14
29 Th	18 49	4 35	4 21	2 06	10 58	0 01	4 09	0 22	0 42	0 30	26 58	3 51	0 02	1 25	1 48	2 14
30 F	18 35	0N24	4 51	2N54	10 21	0S09	3 40	0 17	0 27	0 29	26 60	3 52	0 01	1 26	1 46	2 14
31 Sa	18N21	5N22	5N09	7N48	9N45	0S19	3N10	0N13	0N11	0N28	27S01	3S54	0N00	1S26	1N44	2N14

Day	⚷ Decl	⚷ Lat	♅ Decl	♅ Lat	♆ Decl	♆ Lat	♇ Decl	♇ Lat
1	5S17	6N21	0S28	0S45	12S27	0S28	18S16	5N07
6	5 19	6 23	0 28	0 46	12 29	0 28	18 17	5 06
11	5 21	6 24	0 28	0 46	12 31	0 28	18 18	5 06
16	5 24	6 25	0 29	0 46	12 33	0 29	18 19	5 05
21	5 27	6 26	0 30	0 46	12 35	0 29	18 20	5 04
26	5 31	6 27	0 32	0 46	12 38	0 29	18 21	5 03
31	5S35	6N27	0S34	0S46	12S40	0S29	18S22	5N02

Day	⚴ Decl	⚴ Lat	⚵ Decl	⚵ Lat	⚶ Decl	⚶ Lat	Eris Decl	Eris Lat
1	24N03	39N18	14N51	8S03	12N40	6N21	3S56	13S33
6	23 23	38 40	14 41	7 57	11 46	6 14	3 57	13 34
11	22 39	38 01	14 28	7 50	10 51	6 08	3 57	13 34
16	21 53	37 23	14 13	7 44	9 54	6 02	3 57	13 35
21	21 04	36 45	13 55	7 38	8 57	5 56	3 58	13 35
26	20 15	36 08	13 34	7 31	7 58	5 50	3 58	13 36
31	19N24	35N32	13N11	7S25	6N58	5N44	3S59	13S36

Moon Phenomena

Max/0 Decl
dy hr mn
2 15:01 0 N
9 16:54 25N02
15 19:44 0 S
22 11:21 25S02
29 22:06 0 N

Perigee/Apogee
dy hr m kilometers
1 10:12 a 405034
13 11:23 p 361119
28 23:50 a 405955

Max/0 Lat
dy hr mn
4 13:29 5N17
11 7:32 0 S
17 10:25 5S16
24 7:59 0 N
31 20:02 5N13

PH dy hr mn
☾ 4 14:36 12♈31
● 11 19:42 19♋24
• 11 19:35 T 05'20"
☽ 18 10:12 25♎42
○ 26 1:38 3♒00

Void of Course Moon

Last Aspect	☽ Ingress
30 22:04 ♆ ☌	♓ 1 1:11
3 11:18 ♄ ☍	♈ 3 13:45
5 21:25 ♆ ✶	♉ 6 0:30
8 6:11 ♄ △	♊ 8 7:52
10 10:18 ♄ □	♋ 10 11:39
12 11:49 ♄ ✶	♌ 12 12:55
14 10:24 ♆ ☍	♍ 14 13:16
16 13:47 ♄ ☌	♎ 16 14:25
18 14:27 ♆ △	♏ 18 17:43
20 23:44 ♄ ✶	♐ 20 23:50
23 4:52 ♆ ✶	♑ 23 8:40
25 14:21 ♂ △	♒ 25 19:39
28 3:47 ♆ ☌	♓ 28 8:01
30 3:45 ♀ ☍	♈ 30 20:43

DAILY ASPECTARIAN

1 Th
☽⚺♅ 2:22
☽☌⚷ 2:28
☽⋕♂ 2:32
☽⚺♃ 6:28
☽✶♇ 9:13
☿✶♂ 12:20
☽∥⚷ 13:29
☿⚼♆ 14:53
☉△☽ 21:17

2 F
☽⋕♄ 2:21
☽☍♂ 4:46
☽△☿ 7:25
☽∥♅ 12:48
☽∥♃ 14:29
☿⚼⚷ 14:57
☽⋕♃ 15:32
☽⋕♅ 17:13
☽⚻♀ 20:24

3 Sa
♅⚺⚷ 1:01
☽□⚳ 2:50
☽∥♄ 3:31
☽⚺♆ 10:36
☽☍♄ 11:18
☽⚺⚷ 14:54
☽☌♅ 14:56
☽⋕⚷ 16:27
☽☌♃ 19:18
☽□♇ 21:33
☽∥♂ 23:54

4 Su
☽⚼♀ 5:33
☉□☽ 14:36
☽∠♆ 16:21
☽⚻♂ 19:42
☽∠⚷ 20:32

5 M
☽⋕♆ 4:15
♀△⚳ 7:00
☽□☿ 7:41
☉⚼♆ 12:34
☽△⚳ 13:10
☽△♀ 13:53
♅ R 16:50
☽∥♀ 17:09
☽✶♆ 21:25
☽⚻♄ 22:26

6 Tu
☽✶⚷ 1:28
☽⚺♅ 1:38
☽⚼♂ 2:06
☽⚺♃ 6:03
☽△♇ 7:48
☽⋕♇ 13:10
☿⚻⚳ 14:36
☽⚼⚳ 17:16

7 W
☽⚼♄ 2:47
☉✶☽ 4:37
☽∠♅ 5:44
☽△♂ 7:30
☽∠♃ 10:08
☽⚼♇ 11:40
☉⚼⚷ 16:28
☽⚻⚳ 20:29
☉∥☽ 20:35
☽∥☿ 21:58

8 Th
☽✶☿ 2:16
☽□♀ 3:08
☽□♆ 4:54
☽△♄ 6:11
☽□⚷ 8:38
☽✶♅ 8:55
☉∠☽ 9:54
☉∥☿ 11:32
☽✶♃ 13:16
☿⚺♀ 14:34
☽⚻♇ 14:35
☿⚻♆ 19:59
♀☍♆ 23:56

9 F
☿✶♄ 5:36
☽∠☿ 9:08
☉⚺☽ 14:03
☽□♂ 15:07
☿ ♌ 16:30
♀⚺♄ 17:22
☿⚻⚷ 21:16
☿△♅ 23:46

10 Sa
☽☍⚳ 0:21
♂⋕⚷ 6:16
☽△♆ 8:48
☽□♄ 10:18
♀ ♍ 11:33
☽✶♀ 11:40
☽△⚷ 12:16
☽□♅ 12:38
☽⚺☿ 14:37
☽□♃ 16:54
☽☍♇ 17:53
♀☍⚷ 19:06
♀⚻♅ 23:57

11 Su
☉✶♂ 4:14
♀⋕♆ 5:31
☿△♃ 8:14
☽⚼♆ 9:41
☽⚼⚷ 13:02
☉∥☽ 14:28
☽∠♀ 14:34
☿⚻♇ 15:14
☽✶♂ 19:17
☉☌☽ 19:42
☿∠♂ 21:33
☽∥☿ 22:34

12 M
☽⚻⚳ 1:29
☽⚻♆ 10:06
☽✶♄ 11:49
☽⚻⚷ 13:23
☽△♅ 13:50
☽⋕♇ 14:15
☽⚺♀ 16:56
☽△♃ 18:06
☽⚻♇ 18:51
☽∠♂ 20:36
☽☌☿ 22:51

13 Tu
☽⚼⚳ 1:30
♀⚻♃ 8:49
☽∠♄ 12:07
☽⚼♅ 14:00
☽⋕♆ 17:40
♀△♇ 17:56
☽⚼♃ 18:19
☽⚼♇ 18:59
☿⚼⚳ 19:04
☽⚺♂ 21:45
☽∥♀ 22:55
☉⚺☽ 23:29

14 W
☽△⚳ 1:24
☽☍♆ 10:24
☽⚺♄ 12:25
☽☍⚷ 13:38
☽⚻♅ 14:10
☽⚻♃ 18:34
☽△♇ 19:09
☽☌♀ 21:15
☽⋕⚷ 22:46

15 Th
☉∠☽ 1:24
☉⚻⚳ 1:43
☽∥♂ 3:34
☽⚺☿ 5:56
☽∥♄ 10:55
☽⋕♅ 17:52
☽∥♃ 19:28
☽⋕♃ 20:01
☽∥♅ 21:37

16 F
☽☌♂ 0:32
☽□⚳ 1:44
☉✶☽ 3:41
☽⋕♄ 4:32
☽∠☿ 9:57
☽⋕♂ 10:51
☽⚻♆ 11:23
☽☌♄ 13:47
☽⚻⚷ 14:40
☽☍♅ 15:20
☽∥⚷ 17:08
☽☍♃ 19:59
☽□♇ 20:25
☿⋕♇ 21:50

17 Sa
♂□⚳ 0:57
☽⚺♀ 2:51
☽⋕♀ 11:02
☽⚼♆ 12:36
☽✶☿ 14:38
☽⚼⚷ 15:55
☿∠♄ 19:46
☽∥♆ 23:56

18 Su
☽✶⚳ 3:55
☽⚺♂ 5:23
☽∠♀ 6:43
☿⚼♅ 7:33
☉□☽ 10:12
☽△♆ 14:27
☽⚺♄ 17:19
☽△⚷ 17:50
☽⚻♅ 18:38
☽⋕☿ 22:59
☽⚻♃ 23:39
☽✶♇ 23:56

19 M
☽∥♇ 5:52
☽∠⚳ 5:59
☽∠♂ 8:57
☽✶♀ 11:27
☽∠♄ 20:09
☽⚼♅ 21:20
☉⋕☽ 21:42

20 Tu
☿⚼♃ 1:27
☽⚼♃ 2:32
☽□☿ 2:41
☽∠♇ 2:46
☿⚼♇ 3:21
☽⚺⚳ 8:46
⚷R♒ 9:37
☽✶♂ 13:21
☉△☽ 20:08
☽□♆ 20:17
☉⚻♆ 22:10
☽✶♄ 23:44
☽□⚷ 23:47

21 W
☽△♅ 0:45
♄⚻⚷ 5:13
☽△♃ 6:08
☽⚺♇ 6:18
♄ ♎ 15:11
☽□♀ 23:43

22 Th
☉⚼☽ 2:26
☿△⚳ 2:45
☽☌⚳ 16:25
☽△☿ 18:27
☉⚻⚷ 19:53
☉ ♌ 22:22

23 F
☽□♂ 0:32
☉✶♄ 1:13
☽✶♆ 4:52
☽✶⚷ 8:26
☽□♄ 8:56
☉⚻☽ 9:31
☽□♅ 9:34
☉△♅ 10:07
♃ R 12:04
☽□♃ 15:15
☽☌♇ 15:19
♂∥♄ 21:14

24 Sa
☽⚼☿ 3:30
☽∠♆ 10:00
☽∠⚷ 13:36
☽△♀ 15:13

25 Su
☽⚺⚳ 2:25
♃□♇ 4:21
☉⋕☽ 12:17
☽⚻☿ 13:07
☽△♂ 14:21
☽⚺♆ 15:37
☽⚺⚷ 19:12
☽△♄ 20:20
☽✶♅ 20:31
☽∥♇ 21:04
☽⚼♀ 23:54

26 M
☉☍☽ 1:38
☽⚺♇ 2:24
☽✶♃ 2:25
♀⋕⚷ 5:14
☿⚺♂ 6:26
☿⋕♆ 7:24
☽∠⚳ 8:05
☿☍♆ 10:04
☉⚻♇ 11:05
☉△♃ 11:31
♂⚻♆ 14:42
♄☍♅ 17:08
☽⚼♂ 21:57

27 Tu
☽∠♅ 2:33
☽⚼♄ 2:37
☽∥♆ 6:57
☽∠♇ 8:28
☽∠♃ 8:31
☽⚻♀ 9:00
☽⋕☿ 10:49
☽✶⚳ 14:04
☿☍⚷ 16:19
☿ ♍ 21:44

28 W
☽☌♆ 3:47
☿⚻♅ 4:43
☽⚻♂ 5:52
☽☌⚷ 7:20
☿⚺♄ 7:38
☽⚺♅ 8:48
☽⚻♄ 9:09
☽☍☿ 9:20
☽✶♇ 14:45
☽⚺♃ 14:49
☽∥⚷ 19:16
☉⚻☽ 19:23

29 Th
☽⋕♀ 2:17
☉⚼⚳ 5:32
♂⚻⚷ 8:47
♂⋕♅ 12:47
☽⋕♄ 13:31
♀□⚳ 14:11
☽∥♅ 19:23
☽⋕♂ 19:45
☽⋕♃ 22:01
☽∥♃ 22:10
♂ ♎ 23:47

30 F
☽∥♂ 0:13
☽⋕♅ 0:49
☽□⚳ 2:28
☽☍♀ 3:45
☉⚼☽ 4:25
☽∥♄ 6:33
☿△♇ 10:05
☿⚻♃ 10:45
♂☍♅ 13:32
☽∥♀ 14:19
☽⚺♆ 16:23
☽⚺⚷ 19:49
☽☌♅ 21:24
☽☍♂ 21:50
☉⋕♇ 21:58
☽☍♄ 22:18

31 Sa
☽⋕⚷ 1:01
☽□♇ 3:18
☽☌♃ 3:22
☽⚻☿ 5:20
♂☌♄ 8:08
☉△☽ 13:14
♂⋕♃ 16:56
♂∥♃ 18:43
☽∥☿ 19:17
☽∠♆ 22:23

August 2010

LONGITUDE

Day	Sid.Time	☉	☽	☽ 12 hour	Mean ☊	True ☊	☿	♀	♂	⚳	♃	♄	⚷	♅	♆	♇
	h m s	° ' "	° ' "	° ' "	° '	° '	° '	° '	° '	° '	° '	° '	° '	° '	° '	° '
1 Su	20 38 00	8♌39 46	13♈37 38	19♈40 47	10♑24.5	11♑36.9	5♍14.2	23♍33.3	1♎13.6	20♐51.7	3♈17.0	0♎52.9	29♒30.0	0♈19.2	27♒49.0	3♑15.4
2 M	20 41 56	9 37 10	25 46 51	1♉56 20	10 21.3	11R 34.8	6 25.4	24 36.7	1 50.3	20R 49.1	3R 15.3	0 58.4	29R 27.2	0R 18.0	27R 47.4	3R 14.2
3 Tu	20 45 53	10 34 35	8♉09 47	14 27 42	10 18.1	11D 33.9	7 34.1	25 39.9	2 27.1	20 46.8	3 13.3	1 03.9	29 24.4	0 16.8	27 45.9	3 13.1
4 W	20 49 49	11 32 01	20 50 37	27 19 00	10 15.0	11 34.2	8 40.5	26 42.8	3 04.0	20 44.9	3 11.1	1 09.5	29 21.6	0 15.4	27 44.4	3 12.0
5 Th	20 53 46	12 29 28	3♊53 19	10♊33 55	10 11.8	11 35.4	9 44.3	27 45.5	3 41.0	20 43.4	3 08.8	1 15.2	29 18.8	0 14.1	27 42.8	3 10.8
6 F	20 57 43	13 26 57	17 21 06	24 15 04	10 08.6	11 36.9	10 45.5	28 48.0	4 18.1	20 42.2	3 06.3	1 20.9	29 15.9	0 12.7	27 41.2	3 09.8
7 Sa	21 01 39	14 24 27	1♋15 50	8♋23 20	10 05.4	11R 38.1	11 44.0	29 50.2	4 55.2	20 41.4	3 03.5	1 26.7	29 13.1	0 11.3	27 39.7	3 08.7
8 Su	21 05 36	15 21 58	15 37 15	22 57 09	10 02.3	11 38.4	12 39.6	0♎52.1	5 32.5	20D 40.9	3 00.6	1 32.5	29 10.2	0 09.8	27 38.1	3 07.7
9 M	21 09 32	16 19 30	0♌22 21	7♌52 00	9 59.1	11 37.3	13 32.2	1 53.7	6 09.8	20 40.8	2 57.5	1 38.4	29 07.3	0 08.3	27 36.5	3 06.6
10 Tu	21 13 29	17 17 03	15 25 06	23 00 28	9 55.9	11 34.4	14 21.6	2 55.0	6 47.2	20 41.1	2 54.2	1 44.4	29 04.4	0 06.8	27 34.9	3 05.6
11 W	21 17 25	18 14 38	0♍36 52	8♍13 00	9 52.7	11 30.1	15 07.7	3 56.1	7 24.6	20 41.7	2 50.7	1 50.4	29 01.4	0 05.2	27 33.3	3 04.7
12 Th	21 21 22	19 12 13	15 47 35	23 19 23	9 49.6	11 24.9	15 50.4	4 56.8	8 02.2	20 42.7	2 47.0	1 56.4	28 58.5	0 03.6	27 31.6	3 03.7
13 F	21 25 18	20 09 50	0♎47 17	8♎10 22	9 46.4	11 19.4	16 29.4	5 57.2	8 39.8	20 44.0	2 43.2	2 02.5	28 55.5	0 01.9	27 30.0	3 02.8
14 Sa	21 29 15	21 07 27	15 27 51	22 39 10	9 43.2	11 14.5	17 04.5	6 57.3	9 17.5	20 45.7	2 39.1	2 08.7	28 52.5	0 00.3	27 28.4	3 01.9
15 Su	21 33 12	22 05 05	29 43 57	6♏42 02	9 40.0	11 10.9	17 35.5	7 57.0	9 55.2	20 47.7	2 34.9	2 14.9	28 49.5	29♓58.5	27 26.8	3 01.0
16 M	21 37 08	23 02 45	13♏33 25	20 18 13	9 36.8	11D 08.9	18 02.3	8 56.4	10 33.1	20 50.1	2 30.6	2 21.2	28 46.6	29 56.8	27 25.1	3 00.1
17 Tu	21 41 05	24 00 25	26 56 42	3♐29 14	9 33.7	11 08.5	18 24.5	9 55.4	11 11.0	20 52.8	2 26.0	2 27.5	28 43.6	29 55.0	27 23.5	2 59.3
18 W	21 45 01	24 58 06	9♐56 13	16 18 09	9 30.5	11 09.4	18 41.9	10 54.0	11 49.0	20 55.9	2 21.3	2 33.8	28 40.6	29 53.2	27 21.9	2 58.5
19 Th	21 48 58	25 55 49	22 35 31	28 48 48	9 27.3	11 10.7	18 54.4	11 52.3	12 27.1	20 59.3	2 16.4	2 40.2	28 37.6	29 51.3	27 20.2	2 57.7
20 F	21 52 54	26 53 32	4♑58 31	11♑05 08	9 24.1	11R 11.8	19R 01.6	12 50.1	13 05.2	21 03.0	2 11.3	2 46.7	28 34.6	29 49.5	27 18.6	2 57.0
21 Sa	21 56 51	27 51 17	17 09 08	23 10 55	9 21.0	11 11.8	19 03.5	13 47.5	13 43.4	21 07.1	2 06.1	2 53.2	28 31.6	29 47.6	27 17.0	2 56.3
22 Su	22 00 47	28 49 03	29 10 53	5♒09 23	9 17.8	11 10.0	18 59.7	14 44.5	14 21.7	21 11.5	2 00.8	2 59.7	28 28.5	29 45.6	27 15.3	2 55.6
23 M	22 04 44	29 46 50	11♒06 46	17 03 18	9 14.6	11 06.1	18 50.2	15 41.0	15 00.1	21 16.2	1 55.2	3 06.3	28 25.5	29 43.7	27 13.7	2 54.9
24 Tu	22 08 41	0♍44 38	22 59 16	28 54 54	9 11.4	11 00.0	18 34.8	16 37.1	15 38.5	21 21.2	1 49.6	3 12.9	28 22.5	29 41.7	27 12.0	2 54.2
25 W	22 12 37	1 42 28	4♓50 24	10♓46 01	9 08.2	10 51.9	18 13.6	17 32.6	16 17.0	21 26.6	1 43.8	3 19.5	28 19.5	29 39.6	27 10.4	2 53.6
26 Th	22 16 34	2 40 19	16 41 55	22 38 19	9 05.1	10 42.4	17 46.5	18 27.7	16 55.5	21 32.3	1 37.8	3 26.2	28 16.5	29 37.6	27 08.8	2 53.0
27 F	22 20 30	3 38 12	28 35 26	4♈33 29	9 01.9	10 32.4	17 13.8	19 22.3	17 34.2	21 38.2	1 31.7	3 32.9	28 13.5	29 35.5	27 07.2	2 52.5
28 Sa	22 24 27	4 36 07	10♈32 43	16 33 26	8 58.7	10 22.7	16 35.6	20 16.3	18 12.9	21 44.5	1 25.4	3 39.7	28 10.6	29 33.4	27 05.5	2 51.9
29 Su	22 28 23	5 34 03	22 35 54	28 40 30	8 55.5	10 14.1	15 52.3	21 09.7	18 51.7	21 51.1	1 19.1	3 46.5	28 07.6	29 31.3	27 03.9	2 51.4
30 M	22 32 20	6 32 01	4♉47 34	10♉57 31	8 52.4	10 07.5	15 04.6	22 02.7	19 30.5	21 58.0	1 12.6	3 53.3	28 04.6	29 29.2	27 02.3	2 51.0
31 Tu	22 36 16	7♍30 00	17 10 48	23 27 51	8♑49.2	10♑03.2	14♍13.1	22♎55.0	20♎09.5	22♐05.2	1♈06.0	4♎00.2	28♒01.7	29♓27.0	27♒00.7	2♑50.5

1st of Month

Julian Day #
2455409.5
Obliquity
23°26'18"
SVP 5♓06'25"
GC 26♐59.2
Eris 22♈14.6R

Day	⚴	⚵	⚶
1	8♏36.2	29♋06.2	26♍08.9
6	9 44.7	1♌43.2	28 28.1
11	10 59.1	4 18.7	0♎49.5
16	12 18.8	6 52.5	3 12.6
21	13 43.3	9 24.7	5 37.5
26	15 12.2	11 55.1	8 04.0
31	16 45.1	14 23.7	10 32.0

DECLINATION and LATITUDE

Day	☉ Decl	☽ Decl	☽ Lat	☽ 12h Decl	☿ Decl	☿ Lat	♀ Decl	♀ Lat	♂ Decl	♂ Lat	⚳ Decl	⚳ Lat	♃ Decl	♃ Lat	♄ Decl	♄ Lat
1 Su	18N06	10N11	5N13	12N29	9N08	0S29	2N41	0N08	0S04	0N28	27S03	3S56	0S01	1S26	1N42	2N14
2 M	17 51	14 40	5 04	16 44	8 33	0 39	2 11	0 03	0 19	0 27	27 04	3 58	0 02	1 27	1 39	2 14
3 Tu	17 35	18 39	4 40	20 22	7 57	0 50	1 42	0S02	0 35	0 26	27 06	3 59	0 03	1 27	1 37	2 13
4 W	17 19	21 52	4 03	23 07	7 23	1 01	1 12	0 07	0 50	0 25	27 07	4 01	0 04	1 27	1 35	2 13
5 Th	17 03	24 04	3 12	24 42	6 49	1 12	0 42	0 12	1 05	0 24	27 09	4 03	0 05	1 27	1 32	2 13
6 F	16 47	24 59	2 09	24 52	6 15	1 23	0 13	0 17	1 21	0 24	27 10	4 04	0 06	1 28	1 30	2 13
7 Sa	16 31	24 22	0 56	23 28	5 43	1 34	0S17	0 23	1 36	0 23	27 12	4 06	0 08	1 28	1 27	2 13
8 Su	16 14	22 10	0S22	20 29	5 11	1 45	0 47	0 28	1 52	0 22	27 13	4 07	0 09	1 28	1 25	2 13
9 M	15 57	18 26	1 40	16 05	4 41	1 57	1 16	0 34	2 07	0 21	27 15	4 09	0 11	1 28	1 23	2 13
10 Tu	15 39	13 27	2 54	10 36	4 11	2 08	1 46	0 39	2 23	0 20	27 16	4 10	0 12	1 29	1 20	2 12
11 W	15 22	7 35	3 55	4 28	3 43	2 19	2 15	0 45	2 38	0 20	27 18	4 11	0 14	1 29	1 18	2 12
12 Th	15 04	1 18	4 40	1S52	3 16	2 31	2 45	0 51	2 54	0 19	27 19	4 13	0 16	1 29	1 15	2 12
13 F	14 46	4S59	5 05	7 59	2 51	2 42	3 14	0 57	3 09	0 18	27 20	4 14	0 17	1 30	1 12	2 12
14 Sa	14 27	10 50	5 09	13 31	2 27	2 53	3 43	1 03	3 25	0 17	27 22	4 15	0 19	1 30	1 10	2 12
15 Su	14 09	15 58	4 54	18 09	2 05	3 04	4 12	1 09	3 40	0 17	27 23	4 17	0 21	1 30	1 07	2 12
16 M	13 50	20 04	4 22	21 41	1 44	3 15	4 41	1 15	3 56	0 16	27 25	4 18	0 23	1 30	1 05	2 12
17 Tu	13 31	22 59	3 37	23 57	1 26	3 25	5 10	1 21	4 12	0 15	27 26	4 19	0 25	1 31	1 02	2 12
18 W	13 12	24 36	2 41	24 54	1 10	3 36	5 39	1 27	4 27	0 14	27 27	4 20	0 27	1 31	0 60	2 12
19 Th	12 53	24 53	1 39	24 33	0 56	3 45	6 08	1 34	4 43	0 14	27 29	4 22	0 29	1 31	0 57	2 11
20 F	12 33	23 54	0 34	22 59	0 45	3 54	6 36	1 40	4 58	0 13	27 30	4 23	0 32	1 31	0 54	2 11
21 Sa	12 13	21 48	0N32	20 23	0 36	4 03	7 05	1 47	5 14	0 12	27 32	4 24	0 34	1 32	0 52	2 11
22 Su	11 53	18 46	1 36	16 57	0 31	4 11	7 33	1 53	5 29	0 11	27 33	4 25	0 36	1 32	0 49	2 11
23 M	11 33	14 58	2 34	12 51	0 28	4 17	8 01	1 60	5 45	0 11	27 34	4 26	0 39	1 32	0 46	2 11
24 Tu	11 13	10 37	3 26	8 17	0 29	4 23	8 29	2 07	6 00	0 10	27 36	4 27	0 41	1 32	0 44	2 11
25 W	10 52	5 53	4 08	3 26	0 32	4 28	8 56	2 13	6 16	0 09	27 37	4 28	0 44	1 32	0 41	2 11
26 Th	10 31	0 58	4 39	1N32	0 40	4 32	9 24	2 20	6 31	0 09	27 38	4 29	0 46	1 33	0 38	2 11
27 F	10 10	4N00	4 59	6 27	0 50	4 34	9 51	2 27	6 47	0 08	27 40	4 30	0 49	1 33	0 35	2 11
28 Sa	9 49	8 51	5 05	11 10	1 05	4 34	10 18	2 34	7 02	0 07	27 41	4 31	0 51	1 33	0 33	2 11
29 Su	9 28	13 24	4 58	15 31	1 22	4 33	10 45	2 41	7 17	0 06	27 43	4 32	0 54	1 33	0 30	2 11
30 M	9 07	17 28	4 38	19 16	1 43	4 30	11 11	2 48	7 33	0 06	27 44	4 33	0 57	1 33	0 27	2 11
31 Tu	8N45	20N52	4N04	22N13	2N08	4S25	11S37	2S55	7S48	0N05	27S45	4S34	0S60	1S34	0N24	2N10

Day	⚷ Decl	⚷ Lat	♅ Decl	♅ Lat	♆ Decl	♆ Lat	♇ Decl	♇ Lat
1	5S35	6N27	0S35	0S46	12S41	0S29	18S22	5N02
6	5 40	6 28	0 38	0 47	12 44	0 29	18 23	5 01
11	5 45	6 28	0 41	0 47	12 47	0 29	18 24	4 60
16	5 50	6 28	0 44	0 47	12 49	0 29	18 26	4 59
21	5 55	6 28	0 48	0 47	12 52	0 29	18 27	4 58
26	6 00	6 28	0 52	0 47	12 55	0 29	18 28	4 56
31	6S06	6N27	0S56	0S47	12S58	0S29	18S29	4N55

Day	⚴ Decl	⚴ Lat	⚵ Decl	⚵ Lat	⚶ Decl	⚶ Lat	Eris Decl	Eris Lat
1	19N14	35N25	13N06	7S24	6N46	5N43	3S59	13S37
6	18 22	34 49	12 40	7 17	5 46	5 37	4 00	13 37
11	17 31	34 15	12 12	7 11	4 45	5 32	4 01	13 38
16	16 39	33 43	11 42	7 04	3 43	5 27	4 02	13 38
21	15 48	33 11	11 11	6 57	2 41	5 21	4 03	13 38
26	14 57	32 41	10 38	6 51	1 39	5 16	4 04	13 39
31	14N07	32N12	10N03	6S44	0N36	5N11	4S05	13S39

Moon Phenomena

Max/0 Decl
dy hr mn
6 2:40 24N59
12 4:54 0 S
18 17:15 24S56
26 4:38 0 N

Max/0 Lat
dy hr mn
7 17:24 0 S
13 17:09 5S10
20 12:13 0 N
27 23:43 5N05

Perigee/Apogee
dy hr m kilometers
10 18:07 p 357861
25 5:55 a 406389

PH dy hr mn
☾ 3 5:00 10♉47
● 10 3:09 17♌25
☽ 16 18:15 23♏47
○ 24 17:06 1♓26

Void of Course Moon

Last Aspect			☽ Ingress		
2 3:55	♆	⚹	♉	2	8:14
4 12:45	♆	□	♊	4	16:55
6 21:23	♀	□	♋	6	21:51
7 18:47	☿	⚹	♌	8	23:24
10 19:11	♆	☍	♍	10	23:02
12 0:05	☿	☌	♎	12	22:44
14 20:07	♆	△	♏	15	0:27
17 5:25	♅	△	♐	17	5:35
19 13:59	♅	□	♑	19	14:18
22 1:09	♅	⚹	♒	22	1:38
24 8:31	♆	☌	♓	24	14:12
27 2:01	♅	☌	♈	27	2:50
29 8:49	♆	⚹	♉	29	14:36

DAILY ASPECTARIAN

1 Su	☽∠⚷	1:44
	☽#♆	13:07
	☽△⚳	14:17
	☽⚼☿	14:32
	☽⊼♀	21:30
2 M	☉∠♀	1:50
	☽⚹♆	3:55
	☽⚹⚷	7:09
	☽⊻♅	8:48
	☽⊼♄	10:12
	☽⊼♂	12:25
	☽△♇	14:29
	☽⊻♃	14:31
	⚵ ♌	17:01
	☉∥☽	17:37
	☽⚼⚳	19:26
	☽#♇	22:14
	☽△☿	22:45
3 Tu	♂∥♅	2:08
	♀∥♄	4:05
	☉□☽	5:00
	☽⚼♀	5:13
	♃□♇	5:34
	☽∠♅	13:31
	☽⚼♄	15:08
	☽⚼♂	18:32
	☽∠♃	19:02
	☽⚼♇	19:03
	☽⊼⚳	23:49
4 W	♂☍♃	4:21
	♂□♇	4:59
	♀#♂	11:40
	☽△♀	11:50
	☽□♆	12:45
	☽□⚷	15:42
	☽⚹♅	17:22
	☽△♄	19:10
	☽⚹♃	22:40
	☽⊼♇	22:43
	♀⊼♆	22:58
	☽△♂	23:37
5 Th	♀#♅	4:08
	☽□☿	11:24
	☉⚹☽	16:36
6 F	♀#♃	4:52
	☽☍⚳	5:51
	♀⊼⚷	10:18
	♂#♄	11:59
	♀∥♃	16:10
	☽△♆	17:52
	☽△⚷	20:32
	☉∠☽	20:37
	☽□♀	21:23
	☽□♅	22:10
7 Sa	☽□♄	0:19
	☿#⚷	1:27
	☽□♃	3:02
	☽☍♇	3:11
	♀ ♎	3:49
	☽□♂	6:28
	♀☍♅	8:00
	♀∥♅	17:38
	☽⚹☿	18:47
	☉⚼♅	19:04
	☽⚼♆	19:04
	☽⚼⚷	21:37
	☉⊻☽	23:33
8 Su	☽⊼⚳	8:18
	♀☌♄	17:25
	⚳ D	18:32
	☽⊼♆	19:33
	☽∠☿	20:52
	☽⊼⚷	22:00
	☽△♅	23:37
9 M	☽#♇	0:12
	☽⚹♄	2:03
	☽⚹♀	2:38
	☽△♃	4:08
	☽⊼♇	4:23
	♀#♄	4:46
	⚶ ♎	6:11
	☽⚼⚳	8:31
	☉∠♄	8:48
	☽⚹♂	9:41
	☉∥☽	13:23
	☽⊻☿	22:14
	☽⚼♅	23:31
	♀☍♃	23:41
10 Tu	☽∠♄	2:06
	☽#♆	2:56
	☉☌☽	3:09
	☽⚼♃	3:55
	♀□♇	4:06
	☽⚼♇	4:14
	☽∠♀	4:14
	☽△⚳	8:20
	☽∠♂	10:30
	☉⚼♃	14:36
	☽☍♆	19:11
	☉⚼♇	19:55
	☽☍⚷	21:30
	☽⊼♅	23:10
11 W	☽⊻♄	1:57
	☽⊼♃	3:30
	☽△♇	3:53
	☽⊻♀	5:37
	☽#⚷	7:06
	☽⊻♂	11:11
	☽∥☿	16:00
	☽#♂	18:11
	☽#♀	18:56
12 Th	☽☌☿	0:05
	☽∥♄	0:11
	☽#♅	2:17
	☽#♃	3:55
	☉⊻☽	5:48
	☽∥♃	5:55
	☽∥♅	7:32
	☽□⚳	7:50
	☽#♄	9:35
	☿#♂	12:53
	☿#♀	13:41
	♀∥♂	16:03
	☽#☿	16:15
	☽∥♂	16:38
	☽∥♀	16:39
	☽⊼♆	18:43
	☽⊼⚷	21:00
	☽☍♅	22:47
13 F	☽☌♄	2:03
	☽☍♃	3:07
	☽∥⚷	3:09
	☽□♇	3:39
	☉∠☽	7:35
	☽☌♀	9:00
	☽☌♂	13:23
	☉△⚳	14:38
	☽⚼♆	19:04
	☽⚼⚷	21:23
14 Sa	☽⊻☿	2:47
	♅R♓	3:37
	☽∥♆	8:45
	☽⚹⚳	8:51
	☉⚹☽	10:07
	☉#☽	15:32
	☽△♆	20:07
	☽△⚷	22:28
15 Su	☽⊼♅	0:25
	☽⊻♄	4:21
	☽⊼♃	4:52
	☽∠☿	5:04
	☽⚹♇	5:38
	☽∠⚳	10:28
	☽∥♇	13:35
	☽⊻♀	15:16
	☽⊻♂	18:28
16 M	☽⚼♅	2:27
	☽∠♄	6:47
	☽⚼♃	6:58
	☽∠♇	7:53
	☽⚹☿	8:11
	☽⊻⚳	13:00
	☉□☽	18:15
	☽∠♀	20:02
	♃☍♄	20:46
	☽∠♂	22:33
17 Tu	☽□♆	0:49
	☽□⚷	3:14
	☽△♅	5:25
	☽△♃	10:00
	☽⚹♄	10:11
	☽⊻♇	11:04
18 W	☽⚹♀	1:57
	☽⚹♂	3:43
	♀∥⚷	10:53
	☽□☿	16:51
	♂⚼♆	19:52
	☽☌⚳	20:55
	☿∥♄	22:00
19 Th	☉#♆	1:39
	☉△☽	6:58
	☽⚹♆	9:07
	♀⚼♆	11:16
	☽⚹⚷	11:35
	☽□♅	13:59
	☽□♃	18:36
	☿#♅	18:49
	☽□♄	19:40
	☽☌♇	20:03
20 F	☉☍♆	10:08
	☽∠♆	14:23
	☉⚼☽	14:46
	☽□♀	16:47
	☽□♂	16:50
	☽∠⚷	16:51
	♂⚼⚷	17:06
	♀⚼⚷	17:39
	♀☌♂	18:50
	☿ R	20:00
21 Sa	☽△☿	3:47
	☿#♃	6:35
	☽⊻⚳	7:56
	♄□♇	10:17
	☉☍⚷	15:54
	☽⊻♆	20:09
	☽⊻⚷	22:36
	☉⊼☽	23:12
22 Su	♄#♅	1:01
	☽⚹♅	1:09
	☽∥♇	2:08
	☽⚹♃	5:38
	☽⊻♇	7:30
	☽△♄	7:43
	☽⚼☿	9:34
	☽∠⚳	14:10
	☉⊼♅	22:43
23 M	☉ ♍	5:28
	☽∠♅	7:17
	☽△♂	8:18
	☽△♀	10:01
	☽∠♃	11:38
	☽∥♆	11:45
	☽∠♇	13:44
	☽⚼♄	14:15
	☽⊼☿	15:18
	☉∠♂	16:22
	♂∥⚷	20:31
	☉#☽	20:36
	☽⚹⚳	20:40
24 Tu	☽☌♆	8:31
	☽∥♀	10:03
	☽☌⚷	10:52
	♃#♄	11:40
	☽⊻♅	13:32
	☽⚼♂	16:23
	☉☍☽	17:06
	☽⊻♃	17:45
	☽⚼♀	18:57
	☽⚹♇	20:04
	☽⊼♄	20:54
	☽∥♂	22:15
	☽∥⚷	23:31
25 W	☉⊼♃	0:29
	☿⊻♀	12:10
	☿∥♄	20:46
26 Th	☽∥♅	0:27
	☽⊼♂	0:29
	☽∥♃	0:55
	☽#☿	1:24
	☽#♄	1:35
	☽☍☿	2:05
	☽⊼♀	3:52
	☉△♇	5:13
	☽∥♄	7:37
	☽∥☿	8:05
	☽#♃	8:24
	☽#♅	8:50
	☽□⚳	9:52
	☿⊻♂	17:19
	☿#♃	19:42
	☽⊻♆	21:03
	☉⊻♄	21:32
	☽⊻⚷	23:16
27 F	☽☌♅	2:01
	☿#♅	4:57
	☽☌♃	5:52
	☽□♇	8:37
	☉#♀	9:45
	☽#⚷	9:54
	☽☍♄	10:04
	☉⊼☽	11:03
	☽#♂	14:21
28 Sa	☽∠♆	3:05
	☉∥☽	4:37
	☽∠⚷	5:14
	☽#♀	8:13
	☽⊼☿	11:25
	☽☍♂	16:10
	☉⚼☽	19:37
	☽☍♀	20:56
	☽#♆	21:30
	☽△⚳	22:30
29 Su	♃∥♅	6:41
	☽⚹♆	8:49
	☽⚹⚷	10:53
	☽⊻♅	13:38
	☽⚼☿	15:20
	☽⊻♃	17:03
	☽△♇	20:12
	♀⚹⚳	21:33
	☽⊼♄	22:13
30 M	☉△☽	3:41
	☽⚼⚳	4:17
	☽#♇	6:37
	☽△☿	18:41
	☽∠♅	18:46
	☽∠♃	21:57
31 Tu	☽⚼♇	1:16
	☽⚼♄	3:32
	☽⊼♂	6:01
	☽⊼⚳	9:28
	☽⊼♀	11:46
	☽□♆	18:41
	☽□⚷	20:33
	☽⚹♅	23:14

LONGITUDE

Day	Sid.Time	☉	☽	☽ 12 hour	Mean ☊	True ☊	☿	♀	♂	⚳	♃	♄	⚷	♅	♆	♇
	h m s	° ' "	° ' "	° ' "	° '	° '	° '	° '	° '	° '	° '	° '	° '	° '	° '	° '
1 W	22 40 13	8♍28 02	29♉49 11	6♊15 16	8♑46.0	10♑01.1	13♍18.6	23♎46.7	20♎48.5	22♐12.6	0♈59.2	4♎07.1	27♒58.7	29♓24.8	26♒59.1	2♑50.1
2 Th	22 44 10	9 26 06	12♊46 35	19 23 36	8 42.8	10D 00.8	12R 22.1	24 37.8	21 27.6	22 20.4	0R 52.4	4 14.1	27R 55.8	29R 22.6	26R 57.5	2R 49.7
3 F	22 48 06	10 24 11	26 06 42	2♋56 14	8 39.6	10 01.3	11 24.7	25 28.2	22 06.7	22 28.5	0 45.4	4 21.0	27 52.9	29 20.4	26 55.9	2 49.3
4 Sa	22 52 03	11 22 19	9♋52 27	16 55 28	8 36.5	10R 01.8	10 27.7	26 18.0	22 45.9	22 36.8	0 38.3	4 28.0	27 50.0	29 18.2	26 54.3	2 49.0
5 Su	22 55 59	12 20 29	24 05 14	1♌21 31	8 33.3	10 01.0	9 32.3	27 07.0	23 25.2	22 45.4	0 31.1	4 35.1	27 47.1	29 15.9	26 52.8	2 48.7
6 M	22 59 56	13 18 40	8♌43 54	16 11 45	8 30.1	9 58.2	8 39.7	27 55.3	24 04.6	22 54.3	0 23.9	4 42.1	27 44.2	29 13.6	26 51.2	2 48.4
7 Tu	23 03 52	14 16 53	23 44 10	1♍20 07	8 26.9	9 52.8	7 51.2	28 42.9	24 44.1	23 03.5	0 16.5	4 49.2	27 41.4	29 11.3	26 49.6	2 48.2
8 W	23 07 49	15 15 08	8♍58 20	16 37 29	8 23.8	9 45.1	7 07.9	29 29.7	25 23.6	23 12.9	0 09.1	4 56.3	27 38.6	29 09.0	26 48.1	2 48.0
9 Th	23 11 45	16 13 25	24 16 06	1♎52 47	8 20.6	9 35.7	6 31.0	0♏15.7	26 03.2	23 22.6	0 01.5	5 03.4	27 35.8	29 06.7	26 46.6	2 47.8
10 F	23 15 42	17 11 44	9♎26 10	16 55 02	8 17.4	9 25.7	6 01.2	1 00.8	26 42.9	23 32.6	29♓53.9	5 10.6	27 33.0	29 04.4	26 45.1	2 47.7
11 Sa	23 19 39	18 10 04	24 18 20	1♏35 14	8 14.2	9 16.5	5 39.4	1 45.1	27 22.6	23 42.8	29 46.3	5 17.8	27 30.2	29 02.0	26 43.5	2 47.5
12 Su	23 23 35	19 08 26	8♏45 09	15 47 43	8 11.0	9 09.0	5D 26.2	2 28.4	28 02.4	23 53.3	29 38.5	5 25.0	27 27.5	28 59.7	26 42.1	2 47.5
13 M	23 27 32	20 06 50	22 42 47	29 30 24	8 07.9	9 03.8	5 22.0	3 10.7	28 42.3	24 04.0	29 30.7	5 32.2	27 24.8	28 57.3	26 40.6	2 47.4
14 Tu	23 31 28	21 05 15	6♐10 48	12♐44 20	8 04.7	9 01.0	5 26.9	3 52.1	29 22.2	24 15.0	29 22.9	5 39.4	27 22.1	28 54.9	26 39.1	2D 47.4
15 W	23 35 25	22 03 42	19 11 27	25 32 43	8 01.5	9D 00.1	5 41.2	4 32.4	0♏02.3	24 26.2	29 15.0	5 46.7	27 19.5	28 52.5	26 37.7	2 47.4
16 Th	23 39 21	23 02 10	1♑48 44	8♑00 06	7 58.3	9R 00.3	6 04.7	5 11.6	0 42.4	24 37.7	29 07.1	5 54.0	27 16.9	28 50.2	26 36.2	2 47.4
17 F	23 43 18	24 00 40	14 07 27	20 11 24	7 55.2	9 00.3	6 37.2	5 49.7	1 22.5	24 49.4	28 59.2	6 01.3	27 14.3	28 47.8	26 34.8	2 47.5
18 Sa	23 47 14	24 59 12	26 12 35	2♒11 33	7 52.0	8 59.1	7 18.4	6 26.5	2 02.7	25 01.3	28 51.2	6 08.6	27 11.7	28 45.4	26 33.4	2 47.6
19 Su	23 51 11	25 57 45	8♒08 51	14 04 58	7 48.8	8 55.7	8 08.0	7 02.2	2 43.0	25 13.5	28 43.2	6 15.9	27 09.2	28 43.0	26 32.1	2 47.7
20 M	23 55 08	26 56 20	20 00 22	25 55 26	7 45.6	8 49.7	9 05.4	7 36.6	3 23.4	25 25.9	28 35.2	6 23.2	27 06.7	28 40.6	26 30.7	2 47.9
21 Tu	23 59 04	27 54 56	1♓50 31	7♓45 57	7 42.4	8 40.8	10 10.0	8 09.6	4 03.8	25 38.5	28 27.2	6 30.6	27 04.3	28 38.1	26 29.3	2 48.1
22 W	0 03 01	28 53 35	13 41 59	19 38 50	7 39.3	8 29.4	11 21.4	8 41.3	4 44.3	25 51.3	28 19.2	6 37.9	27 01.9	28 35.7	26 28.0	2 48.3
23 Th	0 06 57	29 52 15	25 36 42	1♈35 45	7 36.1	8 16.1	12 38.8	9 11.5	5 24.9	26 04.3	28 11.2	6 45.3	26 59.5	28 33.3	26 26.7	2 48.6
24 F	0 10 54	0♎50 57	7♈36 07	13 37 57	7 32.9	8 02.0	14 01.5	9 40.3	6 05.5	26 17.6	28 03.2	6 52.7	26 57.2	28 30.9	26 25.4	2 48.9
25 Sa	0 14 50	1 49 42	19 41 22	25 46 30	7 29.7	7 48.3	15 29.1	10 07.4	6 46.2	26 31.0	27 55.2	7 00.0	26 54.9	28 28.5	26 24.1	2 49.2
26 Su	0 18 47	2 48 28	1♉53 32	8♉02 38	7 26.6	7 36.0	17 00.7	10 33.0	7 27.0	26 44.7	27 47.2	7 07.4	26 52.6	28 26.1	26 22.9	2 49.5
27 M	0 22 43	3 47 16	14 13 59	20 27 50	7 23.4	7 26.2	18 35.9	10 57.0	8 07.8	26 58.6	27 39.3	7 14.8	26 50.4	28 23.7	26 21.7	2 49.9
28 Tu	0 26 40	4 46 07	26 44 27	3♊04 09	7 20.2	7 19.2	20 14.1	11 19.2	8 48.7	27 12.6	27 31.4	7 22.2	26 48.2	28 21.3	26 20.5	2 50.3
29 W	0 30 36	5 45 00	9♊27 17	15 54 12	7 17.0	7 15.1	21 54.7	11 39.6	9 29.7	27 26.9	27 23.5	7 29.6	26 46.1	28 19.0	26 19.3	2 50.8
30 Th	0 34 33	6♎43 55	22 25 17	29 00 57	7♑13.8	7♑13.3	23♍37.3	11♏58.2	10♏10.8	27♐41.4	27♓15.7	7♎37.0	26♒44.0	28♓16.6	26♒18.1	2♑51.3

1st of Month

Julian Day #
2455440.5
Obliquity
23°26'18"
SVP 5♓06'21"
GC 26♐59.3
Eris 22♈05.8R

Day	⚴
1	17♏04.2
6	18 41.4
11	20 21.9
16	22 05.5
21	23 51.6
26	25 40.2

Day	⚵
1	14♌53.2
6	17 19.6
11	19 44.0
16	22 06.3
21	24 26.3
26	26 43.9

Day	⚶
1	11♎01.8
6	13 31.5
11	16 02.6
16	18 34.9
21	21 08.3
26	23 42.8

DECLINATION and LATITUDE

Day	☉ Decl	☽ Decl	☽ Lat	☽ 12h Decl	☿ Decl	☿ Lat	♀ Decl	♀ Lat	♂ Decl	♂ Lat	⚳ Decl	⚳ Lat	♃ Decl	♃ Lat	♄ Decl	♄ Lat
1 W	8N24	23N20	3N18	24N09	2N35	4S19	12S03	3S02	8S03	0N04	27S46	4S34	1S02	1S34	0N21	2N10
2 Th	8 02	24 39	2 20	24 48	3 04	4 10	12 29	3 10	8 19	0 03	27 48	4 35	1 05	1 34	0 19	2 10
3 F	7 40	24 37	1 14	24 02	3 35	3 60	12 54	3 17	8 34	0 03	27 49	4 36	1 08	1 34	0 16	2 10
4 Sa	7 18	23 05	0 01	21 46	4 08	3 47	13 19	3 24	8 49	0 02	27 50	4 37	1 11	1 34	0 13	2 10
5 Su	6 56	20 04	1S14	18 03	4 42	3 33	13 44	3 31	9 05	0 01	27 52	4 38	1 14	1 34	0 10	2 10
6 M	6 34	15 43	2 27	13 07	5 16	3 18	14 08	3 39	9 20	0 01	27 53	4 38	1 17	1 35	0 07	2 10
7 Tu	6 11	10 17	3 31	7 18	5 50	3 01	14 32	3 46	9 35	0S00	27 54	4 39	1 20	1 35	0 05	2 10
8 W	5 49	4 11	4 21	0 60	6 22	2 43	14 56	3 54	9 50	0 01	27 55	4 40	1 23	1 35	0 02	2 10
9 Th	5 26	2S12	4 52	5S20	6 53	2 24	15 19	4 01	10 05	0 01	27 57	4 41	1 26	1 35	0S01	2 10
10 F	5 03	8 22	5 03	11 16	7 22	2 05	15 42	4 08	10 20	0 02	27 58	4 41	1 30	1 35	0 04	2 10
11 Sa	4 41	13 57	4 52	16 24	7 48	1 45	16 05	4 16	10 35	0 03	27 59	4 42	1 33	1 35	0 07	2 10
12 Su	4 18	18 34	4 24	20 27	8 11	1 26	16 27	4 23	10 50	0 03	28 00	4 43	1 36	1 35	0 10	2 10
13 M	3 55	21 59	3 40	23 11	8 31	1 07	16 49	4 31	11 05	0 04	28 02	4 44	1 39	1 35	0 13	2 10
14 Tu	3 32	24 03	2 45	24 33	8 46	0 48	17 10	4 38	11 19	0 05	28 03	4 44	1 42	1 35	0 16	2 10
15 W	3 09	24 43	1 43	24 33	8 58	0 30	17 31	4 46	11 34	0 06	28 04	4 45	1 46	1 36	0 18	2 10
16 Th	2 46	24 04	0 38	23 17	9 05	0 12	17 51	4 53	11 49	0 06	28 05	4 46	1 49	1 36	0 21	2 10
17 F	2 23	22 14	0N27	20 57	9 09	0N04	18 11	5 00	12 04	0 07	28 06	4 46	1 52	1 36	0 24	2 10
18 Sa	1 60	19 26	1 30	17 44	9 08	0 19	18 30	5 08	12 18	0 08	28 07	4 47	1 55	1 36	0 27	2 10
19 Su	1 36	15 51	2 28	13 49	9 02	0 34	18 49	5 15	12 33	0 08	28 08	4 47	1 58	1 36	0 30	2 10
20 M	1 13	11 40	3 19	9 24	8 53	0 47	19 07	5 22	12 47	0 09	28 09	4 48	2 02	1 36	0 33	2 10
21 Tu	0 50	7 04	4 01	4 40	8 40	0 59	19 25	5 29	13 01	0 10	28 10	4 49	2 05	1 36	0 36	2 10
22 W	0 26	2 13	4 33	0N15	8 22	1 09	19 42	5 36	13 16	0 10	28 11	4 49	2 08	1 36	0 39	2 10
23 Th	0 03	2N44	4 53	5 11	8 02	1 19	19 58	5 43	13 30	0 11	28 12	4 50	2 11	1 36	0 42	2 10
24 F	0S20	7 36	4 60	9 57	7 37	1 27	20 14	5 50	13 44	0 11	28 13	4 50	2 14	1 36	0 45	2 10
25 Sa	0 44	12 13	4 53	14 23	7 10	1 34	20 30	5 57	13 58	0 12	28 14	4 51	2 18	1 36	0 48	2 10
26 Su	1 07	16 24	4 34	18 16	6 40	1 40	20 44	6 04	14 12	0 13	28 15	4 51	2 21	1 36	0 50	2 10
27 M	1 30	19 56	4 01	21 24	6 07	1 45	20 58	6 10	14 26	0 13	28 16	4 52	2 24	1 36	0 53	2 10
28 Tu	1 54	22 36	3 16	23 33	5 32	1 48	21 11	6 17	14 39	0 14	28 17	4 53	2 27	1 36	0 56	2 10
29 W	2 17	24 11	2 21	24 31	4 54	1 51	21 23	6 23	14 53	0 15	28 18	4 53	2 30	1 36	0 59	2 10
30 Th	2S40	24N30	1N17	24N09	4N15	1N53	21S35	6S29	15S07	0S15	28S19	4S54	2S33	1S36	1S02	2N10

Day	⚷ Decl	⚷ Lat	♅ Decl	♅ Lat	♆ Decl	♆ Lat	♇ Decl	♇ Lat
1	6S07	6N27	0S57	0S47	12S59	0S29	18S30	4N55
6	6 12	6 26	1 02	0 47	13 01	0 29	18 31	4 54
11	6 18	6 25	1 06	0 47	13 04	0 29	18 32	4 52
16	6 24	6 24	1 11	0 47	13 06	0 29	18 33	4 51
21	6 29	6 23	1 16	0 47	13 09	0 29	18 35	4 50
26	6 34	6 22	1 21	0 47	13 11	0 29	18 36	4 49

Day	⚴ Decl	⚴ Lat	⚵ Decl	⚵ Lat	⚶ Decl	⚶ Lat	Eris Decl	Eris Lat
1	13N57	32N07	9N56	6S43	0N24	5N10	4S05	13S39
6	13 08	31 39	9 20	6 36	0S39	5 05	4 06	13 40
11	12 20	31 14	8 43	6 30	1 41	5 01	4 07	13 40
16	11 34	30 49	8 05	6 23	2 43	4 56	4 08	13 40
21	10 49	30 26	7 27	6 17	3 45	4 51	4 09	13 40
26	10 06	30 04	6 48	6 10	4 46	4 46	4 10	13 40

Moon Phenomena

Max/0 Decl
dy hr mn
2 11:26 24N48
8 15:45 0 S
14 23:55 24S43
22 10:45 0 N
29 17:49 24N33

Max/0 Lat
dy hr mn
4 0:16 0 S
9 23:58 5S03
16 13:57 0 N
24 0:46 5N00

Perigee/Apogee
dy hr m kilometers
8 3:48 p 357193
21 8:05 a 406166

PH dy hr mn
☾ 1 17:23 9♊10
● 8 10:31 15♍41
☽ 15 5:51 22♐18
○ 23 9:18 0♈15

Void of Course Moon

Last Aspect			☽ Ingress		
31 23:14	♅	⚹	♊	1	0:20
3 5:41	♅	□	♋	3	6:52
5 8:32	♅	△	♌	5	9:46
7 8:18	♀	⚹	♍	7	9:54
9 9:00	♃	☍	♎	9	9:02
11 5:17	♂	☌	♏	11	9:22
13 11:54	♃	△	♐	13	12:53
15 18:53	♃	□	♑	15	20:31
18 5:14	♃	⚹	♒	18	7:36
20 13:10	♆	☌	♓	20	20:16
23 5:53	♅	☌	♈	23	8:48
25 13:13	♆	⚹	♉	25	20:18
28 3:04	♅	⚹	♊	28	6:12
30 10:38	♅	□	♋	30	13:47

DAILY ASPECTARIAN

1 W
☽⚹♃ 2:10
☽⚻♇ 5:38
☽△♄ 8:06
☽⚼♂ 11:46
☉#♂ 13:05
☉□☽ 17:23
☽⚼♀ 17:50
☽□☿ 23:18

2 Th
☽△♂ 16:31
☽☍⚳ 17:28
☽△♀ 22:47

3 F
☽△♆ 1:27
☽△⚷ 3:07
♀∥♆ 5:23
☽□♅ 5:41
☽□♃ 8:07
☉∠♀ 11:46
☽☍♇ 11:48
☉☌☿ 12:36
☿∠♀ 12:40
☽□♄ 14:35
♂⚹⚳ 16:53

4 Sa
☽⚹☿ 0:57
☉⚹☽ 2:45
☽⚼♆ 3:28
☽⚼⚷ 5:02
♀△♆ 17:12
☽⚻⚳ 21:46
☽□♂ 22:50

5 Su
☽∠☿ 0:42
☽⚻♆ 4:37
☽□♀ 5:19
☉∠☽ 5:47
☽⚻⚷ 6:06
☽△♅ 8:32
☽#♇ 9:24
☽△♃ 10:32
☽⚻♇ 14:22
☽⚹♄ 17:24
☿∠♂ 17:25
♀△⚷ 18:45
☽⚼⚳ 22:39
☽⚺☿ 23:54

6 M
☽#♀ 6:53
☉⚺☽ 7:53
☽⚼♅ 8:49
☽⚼♃ 10:38
☽#♆ 12:23
☽⚼♇ 14:34
☽∠♄ 17:44
☉#⚷ 21:32
☽△⚳ 22:55

7 Tu
☽⚹♂ 1:39
☽#♂ 2:47
☽☍♆ 4:53
☽☍⚷ 6:14
☽⚹♀ 8:18
☽⚻♅ 8:36
☉∥☿ 9:19
☽⚻♃ 10:15
♀⚻♅ 13:50
☽△♇ 14:18
☽#⚷ 16:06
☽∥☿ 16:16
☉∥☽ 17:21
☽⚺♄ 17:37
☿#⚷ 18:09
☽☌☿ 21:14

8 W
☽∠♂ 2:20
☽∠♀ 9:07
☽#♃ 10:26
☉☌☽ 10:31
☽#♅ 11:44
☽#♄ 15:44
☽∥♄ 15:45
♀ ♏ 15:46
♀⚻♃ 17:37
☽∥♅ 19:46
☽∥♃ 21:09
☽□⚳ 22:35

9 Th
☽⚺♂ 2:56
☽⚻♆ 3:56
♃R♓ 4:51
☽⚻⚷ 5:13
☽☍♅ 7:37
☽☍♃ 9:00
☽⚺♀ 9:56
☉#☽ 11:41
☽□♇ 13:27
☽∥⚷ 15:40
☽☌♄ 17:10
☽⚺☿ 18:43
☽#☿ 19:38

10 F
♂△♆ 1:17
☽⚼♆ 3:42
☽⚼⚷ 4:58
☽∥♂ 8:26
☉⚺☽ 13:19
☽∠☿ 18:11
☽∥♆ 19:56
☽⚹⚳ 23:01

11 Sa
☽△♆ 3:58
♂△⚷ 4:18
☽△⚷ 5:14
☽☌♂ 5:17
☽⚻♅ 7:45
☽⚻♃ 8:55
☽∥♀ 11:15
☽☌♀ 12:55
☽⚹♇ 14:00
☉∠☽ 15:42
☽⚺♄ 18:21
☽⚹☿ 18:29
☽∥♇ 23:48

12 Su
☽∠⚳ 0:14
☿⚺♄ 1:55
☽⚼♅ 8:53
☽⚼♃ 9:56
♀⚹♇ 10:44
☽∠♇ 15:26
☉⚹☽ 19:07
☽∠♄ 20:10
☿ D 23:12

13 M
☽⚺⚳ 2:24
☽□♆ 6:58
☽□⚷ 8:15
♂⚻♅ 8:31
☽△♅ 10:59
☽⚺♂ 11:07
☽△♃ 11:54
☽⚺♇ 17:53
☽⚺♀ 19:36
☽□☿ 22:40
☽⚹♄ 23:03

14 Tu
♂⚻♃ 0:20
♇ D 4:37
☽∠♂ 15:50
♂ ♏ 22:39

15 W
☽∠♀ 0:41
☉□☽ 5:51
☿⚺♄ 9:49
☽☌⚳ 10:03
☽⚹♆ 14:02
☽⚹⚷ 15:20
☽□♅ 18:18
☽□♃ 18:53
☽⚹♂ 21:45

16 Th
☽☌♇ 1:53
☽⚹♀ 6:54
☽□♄ 7:59
☽△☿ 8:36
☽∠♆ 19:01
☽∠⚷ 20:18

17 F
♀⚺♄ 9:18
☽⚼☿ 15:42
☉△☽ 21:20
☽⚺⚳ 21:35

18 Sa
☽⚺♆ 0:42
☉□⚳ 1:05
☽⚺⚷ 1:58
☉#♃ 3:58
♀∥♇ 4:58
☽⚹♅ 5:05
☽⚹♃ 5:14
☽∥♀ 6:09
☽∥♇ 6:16
☽□♂ 12:24
☽⚺♇ 13:13
☽△♄ 20:10
☽□♀ 21:39
☽⚻☿ 23:58

19 Su
♃☌♅ 1:04
♂⚹♇ 2:49
☽∠⚳ 4:16
☉⚼☽ 6:12
☽∠♃ 11:08
☽∠♅ 11:13
☉⚻♆ 13:44
☽∥♆ 15:53
☽∥♂ 18:11
☽∠♇ 19:31
☉#♅ 22:08

20 M
☽⚼♄ 2:50
☉⚻⚷ 4:05
☽⚹⚳ 11:12
☽☌♆ 13:10
☽☌⚷ 14:22
☉⚻☽ 15:19
☽#☿ 15:25
☽⚺♃ 17:12
☽⚺♅ 17:31

21 Tu
☽⚹♇ 1:57
☽∥⚷ 2:55
☽△♂ 4:46
☽⚻♄ 9:33
☉☍♃ 11:37
☉#♄ 12:41
♂∥♆ 12:52
☽△♀ 13:24
☉☍♅ 16:59
☽☍☿ 18:43

22 W
☽∥♃ 0:23
☽∥♅ 4:31
☽∥♄ 7:32
☉#☽ 9:21
☉∥☽ 11:57
☽⚼♂ 12:55
☽#♄ 14:01
☽#♅ 17:01
☽⚼♀ 21:01
☽#♃ 21:20

23 Th
☽□⚳ 0:57
☽⚺♆ 1:40
☽⚺⚷ 2:46
☉ ♎ 3:10
☽☌♃ 5:07
☽☌♅ 5:53
☉☍☽ 9:18
☽□♇ 14:26
☽#⚷ 18:39
☽⚻♂ 20:48
☽☍♄ 22:32

24 F
☽∥☿ 0:06
☽⚻♀ 4:17
☽∠♆ 7:36
☽∠⚷ 8:38
⚳⚹♆ 12:49
☽⚻☿ 14:31

25 Sa
☉∥♄ 4:35
☽#♆ 5:13
♂⚺♄ 9:56
☽#♂ 10:11
☽⚹♆ 13:13
☽△⚳ 13:43
☽⚹⚷ 14:12
☽⚺♃ 16:02
☽⚺♅ 17:15

26 Su
☽⚼☿ 0:16
☉□♇ 0:27
☽△♇ 1:50
☉⚻☽ 1:57
☿#⚷ 4:02
☽⚻♄ 10:19
☽☍♂ 11:29
⚳⚹⚷ 11:49
☽#♇ 14:17
☉∥♅ 14:38
☽☍♀ 17:26
☽⚼⚳ 19:33
☽∠♃ 20:59
☽∠♅ 22:23

27 M
☽⚼♇ 6:57
☽#♀ 8:58
☉⚼☽ 9:32
☽△☿ 9:40
☽⚼♄ 15:34
☽□♆ 23:14

28 Tu
☽□⚷ 0:07
☽⚻⚳ 0:55
☽⚹♃ 1:28
☽⚹♅ 3:04
☽⚻♇ 11:34
☉△☽ 16:28
☽△♄ 20:17
⚳□♃ 20:20

29 W
☽⚻♂ 0:05
☽⚻♀ 4:13
☉∥♃ 15:34

30 Th
☽□☿ 2:32
☽⚼♂ 5:19
☽△♆ 7:04
☽△⚷ 7:51
☽⚼♀ 8:29
☽□♃ 8:44
☽☍⚳ 9:47
☽□♅ 10:38
♀⚼♃ 16:59
☽☍♇ 18:56

October 2010

LONGITUDE

Day	Sid.Time	☉	☽	☽ 12 hour	Mean ☊	True ☊	☿	♀	♂	⚳	♃	♄	⚷	♅	♆	♇
	h m s	° ' "	° ' "	° ' "	° '	° '	° '	° '	° '	° '	° '	° '	° '	° '	° '	° '
1 F	0 38 30	7♎42 53	5♋41 33	12♋27 27	7♑10.7	7♑13.0	25♍21.4	12♏14.9	10♏51.9	27♐56.0	27♓07.9	7♎44.4	26♒42.0	28♓14.2	26♒17.0	2♑51.8
2 Sa	0 42 26	8 41 53	19 18 56	26 16 14	7 07.5	7R 12.9	27 06.8	12 29.6	11 33.1	28 10.9	27R 00.2	7 51.8	26R 40.0	28R 11.9	26R 15.9	2 52.3
3 Su	0 46 23	9 40 55	3♌19 27	10♌28 32	7 04.3	7 11.6	28 53.0	12 42.4	12 14.3	28 25.9	26 52.6	7 59.2	26 38.0	28 09.5	26 14.8	2 52.9
4 M	0 50 19	10 39 59	17 43 18	25 03 22	7 01.1	7 08.3	0♎39.7	12 53.0	12 55.7	28 41.1	26 45.0	8 06.6	26 36.1	28 07.2	26 13.7	2 53.5
5 Tu	0 54 16	11 39 06	2♍28 08	9♍56 50	6 58.0	7 02.2	2 26.8	13 01.5	13 37.1	28 56.5	26 37.5	8 14.0	26 34.3	28 04.8	26 12.7	2 54.1
6 W	0 58 12	12 38 15	17 28 29	25 01 57	6 54.8	6 53.4	4 14.0	13 07.9	14 18.5	29 12.0	26 30.1	8 21.4	26 32.5	28 02.5	26 11.7	2 54.8
7 Th	1 02 09	13 37 26	2♎35 58	10♎09 14	6 51.6	6 42.7	6 01.2	13 12.0	15 00.1	29 27.8	26 22.7	8 28.8	26 30.7	28 00.2	26 10.7	2 55.5
8 F	1 06 05	14 36 39	17 40 24	25 08 14	6 48.4	6 31.3	7 48.2	13R 13.9	15 41.7	29 43.7	26 15.5	8 36.2	26 29.0	27 57.9	26 09.7	2 56.2
9 Sa	1 10 02	15 35 54	2♏31 34	9♏49 25	6 45.2	6 20.4	9 34.8	13 13.4	16 23.4	29 59.8	26 08.4	8 43.6	26 27.3	27 55.7	26 08.8	2 57.0
10 Su	1 13 59	16 35 11	17 01 02	24 05 49	6 42.1	6 11.3	11 21.1	13 10.6	17 05.1	0♑16.1	26 01.3	8 50.9	26 25.7	27 53.4	26 07.9	2 57.8
11 M	1 17 55	17 34 31	1♐03 25	7♐53 43	6 38.9	6 04.7	13 06.9	13 05.3	17 47.0	0 32.5	25 54.4	8 58.3	26 24.2	27 51.2	26 07.0	2 58.6
12 Tu	1 21 52	18 33 52	14 36 46	21 12 46	6 35.7	6 00.8	14 52.1	12 57.7	18 28.8	0 49.1	25 47.6	9 05.7	26 22.7	27 49.0	26 06.2	2 59.4
13 W	1 25 48	19 33 14	27 42 05	4♑05 10	6 32.5	5D 59.2	16 36.8	12 47.6	19 10.8	1 05.8	25 40.9	9 13.0	26 21.3	27 46.8	26 05.4	3 00.3
14 Th	1 29 45	20 32 39	10♑22 36	16 34 58	6 29.4	5R 59.1	18 20.8	12 35.1	19 52.8	1 22.7	25 34.3	9 20.3	26 19.9	27 44.6	26 04.6	3 01.2
15 F	1 33 41	21 32 05	22 42 55	28 47 08	6 26.2	5 59.2	20 04.2	12 20.3	20 34.9	1 39.8	25 27.9	9 27.6	26 18.6	27 42.5	26 03.8	3 02.1
16 Sa	1 37 38	22 31 33	4♒48 16	10♒47 00	6 23.0	5 58.5	21 47.0	12 03.0	21 17.0	1 57.0	25 21.6	9 34.9	26 17.3	27 40.4	26 03.1	3 03.1
17 Su	1 41 34	23 31 03	16 43 56	22 39 42	6 19.8	5 56.0	23 29.1	11 43.5	21 59.2	2 14.3	25 15.4	9 42.2	26 16.1	27 38.3	26 02.4	3 04.1
18 M	1 45 31	24 30 34	28 34 51	4♓29 54	6 16.6	5 51.1	25 10.6	11 21.7	22 41.5	2 31.8	25 09.4	9 49.4	26 14.9	27 36.2	26 01.7	3 05.1
19 Tu	1 49 28	25 30 08	10♓25 21	16 21 37	6 13.5	5 43.4	26 51.4	10 57.7	23 23.9	2 49.4	25 03.5	9 56.7	26 13.8	27 34.1	26 01.0	3 06.2
20 W	1 53 24	26 29 43	22 19 03	28 17 58	6 10.3	5 33.4	28 31.5	10 31.7	24 06.3	3 07.2	24 57.7	10 03.9	26 12.8	27 32.1	26 00.4	3 07.3
21 Th	1 57 21	27 29 19	4♈18 39	10♈21 17	6 07.1	5 21.5	0♏11.0	10 03.7	24 48.7	3 25.1	24 52.2	10 11.1	26 11.8	27 30.1	25 59.8	3 08.4
22 F	2 01 17	28 28 58	16 26 03	22 33 04	6 03.9	5 08.8	1 49.9	9 34.0	25 31.3	3 43.1	24 46.7	10 18.3	26 10.8	27 28.2	25 59.3	3 09.5
23 Sa	2 05 14	29 28 39	28 42 26	4♉54 11	6 00.8	4 56.4	3 28.2	9 02.7	26 13.9	4 01.3	24 41.5	10 25.4	26 10.0	27 26.2	25 58.8	3 10.7
24 Su	2 09 10	0♏28 22	11♉08 24	17 25 05	5 57.6	4 45.3	5 05.9	8 29.9	26 56.5	4 19.6	24 36.4	10 32.5	26 09.1	27 24.3	25 58.3	3 11.8
25 M	2 13 07	1 28 07	23 44 19	0♊06 07	5 54.4	4 36.5	6 43.0	7 55.9	27 39.2	4 38.1	24 31.4	10 39.6	26 08.4	27 22.4	25 57.8	3 13.1
26 Tu	2 17 03	2 27 53	6♊30 33	12 57 44	5 51.2	4 30.4	8 19.5	7 20.9	28 22.0	4 56.6	24 26.7	10 46.7	26 07.7	27 20.6	25 57.4	3 14.3
27 W	2 21 00	3 27 43	19 27 46	26 00 48	5 48.0	4 27.0	9 55.6	6 45.1	29 04.9	5 15.3	24 22.1	10 53.8	26 07.1	27 18.8	25 57.0	3 15.6
28 Th	2 24 57	4 27 34	2♋37 00	9♋16 33	5 44.9	4D 25.9	11 31.0	6 08.8	29 47.8	5 34.1	24 17.7	11 00.8	26 06.5	27 17.0	25 56.6	3 16.9
29 F	2 28 53	5 27 27	15 59 39	22 46 30	5 41.7	4 26.3	13 06.0	5 32.2	0♐30.8	5 53.0	24 13.5	11 07.8	26 06.0	27 15.3	25 56.3	3 18.2
30 Sa	2 32 50	6 27 23	29 37 16	6♌32 06	5 38.5	4R 27.0	14 40.5	4 55.6	1 13.9	6 12.1	24 09.4	11 14.7	26 05.5	27 13.6	25 56.0	3 19.6
31 Su	2 36 46	7♏27 21	13♌31 05	20 34 12	5♑35.3	4♑27.0	16♏14.5	4♏19.2	1♐57.0	6♑31.3	24♓05.5	11♎21.6	26♒05.1	27♓11.9	25♒55.8	3♑20.9

1st of Month

Julian Day # 2455470.5
Obliquity 23°26'18"
SVP 5♓06'18"
GC 26♐59.4
Eris 21♈50.5R

Day	⚴	Day	⚵	Day	⚶
1	27♏31.0	1	28♌59.1	1	26♎18.2
6	29 23.7	6	1♍11.8	6	28 54.6
11	1♐18.3	11	3 21.7	11	1♏31.9
16	3 14.4	16	5 28.5	16	4 09.8
21	5 12.0	21	7 32.2	21	6 48.5
26	7 10.7	26	9 32.6	26	9 27.7
31	9 10.5	31	11 29.5	31	12 07.5

DECLINATION and LATITUDE

Day	☉ Decl	☽ Decl	☽ Lat	☽ 12h Decl	☿ Decl	☿ Lat	♀ Decl	♀ Lat	♂ Decl	♂ Lat	⚳ Decl	⚳ Lat	♃ Decl	♃ Lat	♄ Decl	♄ Lat
1 F	3S04	23N27	0N08	22N24	3N35	1N53	21S46	6S35	15S20	0S16	28S19	4S54	2S36	1S36	1S05	2N10
2 Sa	3 27	20 60	1S04	19 17	2 53	1 54	21 56	6 40	15 34	0 17	28 20	4 55	2 39	1 36	1 08	2 10
3 Su	3 50	17 15	2 13	14 57	2 10	1 53	22 05	6 46	15 47	0 17	28 21	4 55	2 42	1 36	1 11	2 10
4 M	4 13	12 24	3 16	9 39	1 26	1 51	22 13	6 51	16 00	0 18	28 22	4 56	2 45	1 36	1 14	2 10
5 Tu	4 36	6 44	4 08	3 42	0 42	1 49	22 20	6 55	16 13	0 18	28 22	4 56	2 48	1 36	1 16	2 10
6 W	4 60	0 36	4 44	2S32	0S03	1 47	22 26	6 60	16 26	0 19	28 23	4 57	2 51	1 35	1 19	2 10
7 Th	5 23	5S37	4 60	8 37	0 48	1 44	22 31	7 04	16 39	0 20	28 23	4 57	2 54	1 35	1 22	2 10
8 F	5 46	11 28	4 55	14 08	1 34	1 40	22 35	7 07	16 52	0 20	28 24	4 58	2 57	1 35	1 25	2 10
9 Sa	6 08	16 34	4 30	18 43	2 19	1 36	22 38	7 11	17 04	0 21	28 24	4 58	2 59	1 35	1 28	2 10
10 Su	6 31	20 34	3 48	22 04	3 05	1 32	22 40	7 13	17 17	0 22	28 25	4 59	3 02	1 35	1 31	2 10
11 M	6 54	23 12	2 54	23 58	3 51	1 27	22 40	7 16	17 29	0 22	28 25	4 59	3 05	1 35	1 34	2 10
12 Tu	7 17	24 23	1 51	24 26	4 36	1 22	22 40	7 17	17 41	0 23	28 26	4 60	3 07	1 35	1 36	2 10
13 W	7 39	24 09	0 44	23 33	5 21	1 17	22 38	7 18	17 54	0 23	28 26	5 00	3 10	1 35	1 39	2 10
14 Th	8 01	22 39	0N23	21 29	6 06	1 11	22 34	7 19	18 06	0 24	28 26	5 01	3 12	1 35	1 42	2 10
15 F	8 24	20 05	1 28	18 29	6 50	1 05	22 30	7 18	18 17	0 25	28 27	5 01	3 15	1 34	1 45	2 10
16 Sa	8 46	16 41	2 27	14 45	7 34	0 59	22 23	7 18	18 29	0 25	28 27	5 01	3 17	1 34	1 48	2 11
17 Su	9 08	12 40	3 18	10 29	8 18	0 53	22 16	7 17	18 41	0 26	28 27	5 02	3 20	1 34	1 50	2 11
18 M	9 30	8 12	4 01	5 51	9 01	0 47	22 07	7 15	18 52	0 26	28 27	5 02	3 22	1 34	1 53	2 11
19 Tu	9 52	3 26	4 33	1 00	9 43	0 40	21 57	7 12	19 03	0 27	28 27	5 03	3 24	1 34	1 56	2 11
20 W	10 13	1N27	4 54	3N54	10 25	0 34	21 45	7 08	19 14	0 27	28 27	5 03	3 26	1 34	1 59	2 11
21 Th	10 35	6 20	5 02	8 42	11 07	0 27	21 31	7 04	19 25	0 28	28 27	5 04	3 28	1 34	2 02	2 11
22 F	10 56	11 01	4 56	13 14	11 47	0 21	21 17	6 59	19 36	0 28	28 27	5 04	3 30	1 33	2 04	2 11
23 Sa	11 17	15 19	4 37	17 16	12 27	0 14	21 01	6 53	19 47	0 29	28 27	5 05	3 32	1 33	2 07	2 11
24 Su	11 38	19 02	4 04	20 35	13 07	0 07	20 44	6 46	19 57	0 30	28 27	5 05	3 34	1 33	2 10	2 11
25 M	11 59	21 55	3 19	22 58	13 45	0 00	20 25	6 38	20 08	0 30	28 27	5 06	3 36	1 33	2 12	2 11
26 Tu	12 20	23 45	2 23	24 12	14 23	0S06	20 06	6 29	20 18	0 31	28 27	5 06	3 37	1 33	2 15	2 11
27 W	12 40	24 20	1 19	24 07	15 00	0 13	19 45	6 20	20 28	0 31	28 26	5 07	3 39	1 32	2 18	2 12
28 Th	13 00	23 34	0 10	22 41	15 36	0 20	19 23	6 10	20 38	0 32	28 26	5 07	3 41	1 32	2 20	2 12
29 F	13 20	21 28	1S01	19 56	16 12	0 27	19 00	5 59	20 47	0 33	28 26	5 07	3 42	1 32	2 23	2 12
30 Sa	13 40	18 06	2 11	16 00	16 46	0 33	18 37	5 48	20 57	0 33	28 25	5 08	3 43	1 32	2 26	2 12
31 Su	13S60	13N40	3S13	11N08	17S20	0S40	18S13	5S36	21S06	0S34	28S25	5S08	3S45	1S32	2S28	2N12

Day	⚷ Decl	⚷ Lat	♅ Decl	♅ Lat	♆ Decl	♆ Lat	♇ Decl	♇ Lat
1	6S39	6N20	1S25	0S47	13S13	0S29	18S37	4N47
6	6 44	6 18	1 30	0 47	13 15	0 29	18 38	4 46
11	6 48	6 17	1 34	0 47	13 16	0 29	18 40	4 45
16	6 52	6 15	1 39	0 47	13 18	0 29	18 41	4 44
21	6 56	6 13	1 43	0 47	13 19	0 29	18 42	4 42
26	6 59	6 11	1 46	0 47	13 20	0 29	18 43	4 41
31	7S02	6N09	1S50	0S47	13S20	0S29	18S44	4N40

Day	⚴ Decl	⚴ Lat	⚵ Decl	⚵ Lat	⚶ Decl	⚶ Lat	Eris Decl	Eris Lat
1	9N24	29N43	6N08	6S04	5S46	4N42	4S12	13S40
6	8 44	29 23	5 29	5 57	6 46	4 37	4 13	13 40
11	8 07	29 05	4 49	5 50	7 44	4 33	4 14	13 40
16	7 31	28 48	4 10	5 44	8 42	4 28	4 14	13 40
21	6 57	28 32	3 32	5 37	9 38	4 24	4 15	13 40
26	6 26	28 17	2 54	5 30	10 33	4 19	4 16	13 40
31	5N56	28N04	2N16	5S23	11S26	4N15	4S17	13S39

Moon Phenomena

Max/0 Decl

dy	hr mn	
6	2:17	0 S
12	7:44	24S27
19	16:54	0 N
26	22:48	24N20

Max/0 Lat

dy	hr mn	
1	2:42	0 S
7	6:19	5S00
13	15:36	0 N
21	1:58	5N02
28	3:16	0 S

Perigee/Apogee

dy	hr m		kilometers
6	13:42	p	359459
18	18:22	a	405427

PH	dy	hr mn	
☾	1	3:53	7♋52
●	7	18:46	14♎24
☽	14	21:29	21♑26
○	23	1:38	29♈33
☾	30	12:47	6♌59

Void of Course Moon

Last Aspect		☽ Ingress	
2 15:23	☿ ⚹	♌	2 18:22
4 13:53	♀ ☍	♍	4 20:01
6 16:44	♅ ☍	♎	6 19:53
8 13:39	♅ ☍	♏	8 19:53
10 18:28	♅ △	♐	10 22:10
13 0:09	♅ □	♑	13 4:18
15 9:50	♅ ⚹	♒	15 14:25
17 18:50	♀ □	♓	18 2:53
20 10:26	♅ ☌	♈	20 15:24
23 1:38	☉ ☍	♉	23 2:31
25 7:50	♂ ☍	♊	25 11:49
27 14:20	♅ □	♋	27 19:15
29 19:49	♅ △	♌	30 0:40

DAILY ASPECTARIAN

1 F: ☉☌♄ 0:43; ☽□♄ 3:41; ☉□☽ 3:53; ☽△♂ 9:41; ☽⚼♆ 9:55; ☽⚼⚷ 10:38; ☿∠♂ 11:26; ☉#☿ 11:34; ☽△♀ 11:51; ☿⚻♆ 12:33; ☽#♀ 16:45; ☿⚻⚷ 18:02; ☿☍♃ 22:37

2 Sa: ⚳□♅ 1:23; ☿∠♀ 5:56; ☿#♃ 7:15; ☽⚻♆ 11:58; ☽⚻⚷ 12:39; ☽△♃ 13:08; ♂⚼♃ 13:19; ☿☍♅ 14:24; ☽△♅ 15:15; ☽⚹☿ 15:23; ☽⚻⚳ 15:32; ☽#♇ 16:02; ☿□⚳ 16:53; ☽⚻♇ 23:15

3 Su: ⚵ ♍ 6:45; ☽#♂ 7:27; ☽⚹♄ 7:55; ☉⚹☽ 11:28; ☽⚼♃ 14:12; ☿ ♎ 15:05; ☽□♂ 15:41; ☽□♀ 15:55; ☽⚼♅ 16:25; ☽⚼⚳ 17:13; ☽∠☿ 20:08; ☽#♆ 20:12; ♀☌♂ 21:59; ☿#♅ 23:07

4 M: ☽⚼♇ 0:17; ♂⚼♅ 6:19; ☿#♄ 6:33; ☽∠♄ 8:54; ☉⚼♆ 13:28; ☽☍♆ 13:53; ☉∠☽ 13:55; ☽☍⚷ 14:29; ☽⚻♃ 14:38; ☽⚻♅ 16:56; ☽△⚳ 18:12; ☉⚼⚷ 22:06; ☽⚺☿ 23:58

5 Tu: ☽#⚷ 0:04; ☽△♇ 0:42; ☿□♇ 6:09; ☉#☽ 7:56; ♀⚼♅ 8:25; ☽⚺♄ 9:20; ♃⚺⚷ 13:49; ☽#♃ 15:22; ☉⚺☽ 15:45; ☽⚹♀ 17:02; ♂∠⚳ 17:58; ☽⚹♂ 18:43; ☽#♅ 20:32; ☽#♄ 21:13

6 W: ☽#☿ 1:52; ☽∥☿ 2:49; ☽∥♄ 7:25; ☽∥♅ 8:04; ☉⚺♀ 13:03; ☽∥♃ 13:21; ☽⚻♆ 13:50; ☽☍♃ 14:13; ☽⚻⚷ 14:22; ☽☍♅ 16:44; ☽∠♀ 17:00; ☽□⚳ 18:56; ☽∠♂ 19:41; ☉∥☽ 23:00

7 Th: ☽□♇ 0:31; ☽∥⚷ 4:29; ☽☌☿ 6:09; ☽☌♄ 9:25; ☽⚼♆ 13:37; ☽⚼⚷ 14:08; ⚴ ♐ 14:12; ☽⚺♀ 16:54; ☉☌☽ 18:46; ☿∥♄ 19:09; ☽⚺♂ 20:41; ☿∥♅ 22:56

8 F: ⚶ ♏ 1:58; ♀ R 7:06; ☽∥♆ 7:56; ☿☌♄ 11:36; ☽△♆ 13:39; ☽⚻♃ 13:42; ☽△⚷ 14:09; ☽⚻♅ 16:32; ☽⚹⚳ 19:48; ♃⚺♆ 22:15

9 Sa: ⚳ ♑ 0:18; ☽⚹♇ 0:42; ☽∥♂ 2:48; ☽⚺♄ 10:16; ☽∥♇ 11:36; ☽⚺☿ 13:13; ☽⚼♃ 14:04; ☽⚼♅ 17:07; ☽☌♀ 17:36; ☽∠⚳ 21:01; ☿⚼♆ 21:03; ☿∥♃ 22:24; ☉⚺☽ 23:13

10 Su: ☽☌♂ 0:07; ☿⚼⚷ 1:03; ☽∠♇ 1:36; ☽∠♄ 11:41; ☽△♃ 15:10; ☽□♆ 15:28; ☽□⚷ 15:58; ☉∥⚷ 17:49; ☽∥♀ 18:01; ☽∠☿ 18:10; ☽△♅ 18:28; ☽⚺⚳ 23:05; ☿⚺♀ 23:40

11 M: ☉∠☽ 2:51; ☽⚺♇ 3:21; ♂∠♇ 6:48; ♄∥♅ 8:59; ☽⚹♄ 14:02; ☉⚺♂ 17:06; ☽⚺♀ 21:04

12 Tu: ☽⚹☿ 0:32; ☽⚺♂ 7:24; ☉⚹☽ 7:45; ☽□♃ 20:17; ☽⚹♆ 21:00; ☽⚹⚷ 21:30

13 W: ☽□♅ 0:09; ☽∠♀ 0:10; ♀⚼♅ 2:10; ☽☌⚳ 6:30; ☽☌♇ 9:58; ☽∠♂ 12:53; ☽□♄ 21:59

14 Th: ☽∥♀ 0:53; ☽∠♆ 1:21; ☽∠⚷ 1:50; ☽⚹♀ 4:11; ☽□☿ 17:58; ☽⚹♂ 19:33; ☉□☽ 21:29

15 F: ☿∥⚷ 0:41; ☽⚹♃ 5:22; ☽⚺♆ 6:36; ☽⚺⚷ 7:05; ☽⚹♅ 9:50; ☽∥♇ 10:37; ☿⚺♂ 12:06; ☽∥♂ 12:37; ☽⚺⚳ 18:09; ☽⚺♇ 20:29

16 Sa: ☽△♄ 9:41; ☽∠♃ 11:03; ☽□♀ 14:10; ☽∠♅ 15:46; ☽∥♆ 20:26

17 Su: ♂∥♇ 0:23; ☽∠⚳ 1:03; ☉☌☿ 1:06; ☽∠♇ 2:42; ☽□♂ 11:18; ☉△☽ 14:59; ☽△☿ 15:57; ☽⚼♄ 16:18; ☽⚺♃ 17:07; ☉∥☽ 17:43; ☽☌♆ 18:50; ☽☌⚷ 19:17; ☽∥☿ 20:19; ☽⚺♅ 22:01; ☿⚻♃ 23:44

18 M: ☽∥⚷ 6:39; ☽⚹⚳ 8:13; ☽⚹♇ 9:09; ☿△♆ 12:04; ☉⚻♃ 14:13; ☿△⚷ 15:08; ☽⚻♄ 23:01

19 Tu: ☉⚼☽ 0:11; ☽∥♃ 0:12; ☽△♀ 1:03; ☽⚼☿ 3:23; ☽∥♄ 7:21; ☽∥♅ 8:38; ☉∥☿ 9:36; ☿⚻♅ 10:02; ☉△♆ 12:19; ☉△⚷ 17:17

20 W: ⚳☌♇ 0:06; ☽#♅ 1:11; ☽#♄ 2:36; ☽△♂ 3:49; ☽☌♃ 5:16; ☽⚼♀ 6:13; ☽⚺♆ 7:24; ☽⚺⚷ 7:48; ☉⚻☽ 9:09; ☽#♃ 9:46; ☽☌♅ 10:26; ☽⚻☿ 14:27; ♀⚺♄ 19:04; ☿ ♏ 21:20; ☽□♇ 21:40; ☽□⚳ 22:11

21 Th: ☉⚻♅ 0:19; ♂△♃ 1:43; ☽#⚷ 3:02; ☽⚻♀ 10:59; ☽⚼♂ 11:36; ♀⚼♃ 11:39; ☽☍♄ 11:47; ☽∠♆ 13:16; ☽∠⚷ 13:39; ♂∠♄ 15:11; ☉#☽ 23:33

22 F: ☽#☿ 4:52; ☽#♆ 12:30; ♂□♆ 15:36; ☽⚺♃ 16:14; ☽⚹♆ 18:42; ☽⚻♂ 18:53; ☽⚹⚷ 19:04; ☿⚹♇ 19:39; ☽⚺♅ 21:32; ♂□⚷ 21:51

23 Sa: ☉☍☽ 1:38; ☽△♇ 8:41; ☿⚹⚳ 9:59; ☽△⚳ 10:33; ☽☍☿ 10:38; ☉ ♏ 12:36; ☽☍♀ 19:09; ☽∠♃ 21:05; ☽#♇ 21:41; ☽⚻♄ 22:51

24 Su: ☽∠♅ 2:25; ☽#♂ 7:19; ☿∥♆ 7:52; ☽#♀ 11:53; ☽⚼♇ 13:30; ♂△♅ 14:58; ☽⚼⚳ 16:01

25 M: ☽⚹♃ 1:29; ☽⚼♄ 3:40; ☽□♆ 4:12; ☽□⚷ 4:32; ☽⚹♅ 6:51; ☽☍♂ 7:50; ☿☌♀ 13:18; ♀∥♂ 14:02; ☉⚻☽ 15:48; ☽⚻♇ 17:53; ☽⚻⚳ 21:00

26 Tu: ☽⚻♀ 1:30; ☽⚻☿ 3:52; ☽△♄ 8:01; ☿⚼♃ 16:00; ☉⚹♇ 19:02; ☉⚼☽ 22:00

27 W: ☽⚼♀ 4:01; ☽□♃ 8:57; ♄⚼♆ 10:31; ☽⚼☿ 11:24; ☽△♆ 11:53; ☽△⚷ 12:11; ☽□♅ 14:20; ☿⚺♄ 15:46; ☽⚻♂ 18:36

28 Th: ☽☍♇ 1:12; ☉△☽ 3:36; ☽☍⚳ 5:28; ☽△♀ 6:06; ♂ ♐ 6:49; ☿⚼♅ 11:23; ☽⚼♆ 14:59; ♀⚹⚳ 15:01; ☽□♄ 15:15; ☽⚼⚷ 15:16; ☽△☿ 18:09; ♄⚼⚷ 18:18; ☽⚼♂ 23:06; ☉∥♆ 23:20

29 F: ☉☌♀ 1:11; ☽#♂ 5:17; ☽△♃ 14:29; ☉⚹⚳ 15:01; ♀∥♇ 17:30; ☽⚻♆ 17:33; ☽⚻⚷ 17:50; ☽△♅ 19:49; ☽#♇ 20:06; ☽#♀ 20:24

30 Sa: ☽△♂ 2:57; ☽⚻♇ 6:27; ☽#☿ 6:51; ☽□♀ 8:50; ☽⚻⚳ 11:41; ☉□☽ 12:47; ☽⚼♃ 16:27; ☽⚹♄ 20:16; ☽⚼♅ 21:45; ☉#☽ 22:30

31 Su: ☽#♆ 1:40; ☽□☿ 5:14; ☽⚼♇ 8:15; ☽⚼⚳ 13:55; ☽⚻♃ 17:52; ☽☍♆ 21:02; ☽☍⚷ 21:18; ☽∠♄ 21:57; ☿∥♀ 22:16; ☽⚻♅ 23:08

LONGITUDE

November 2010

Day	Sid.Time	☉	☽	☽ 12 hour	Mean☊	True☊	☿	♀	♂	⚳	♃	♄	⚷	♅	♆	♇
	h m s	° ' "	° ' "	° ' "	° '	° '	° '	° '	° '	° '	° '	° '	° '	° '	° '	° '
1 M	2 40 43	8♏27 21	27♌41 22	4♍52 21	5♑32.2	4♑25.4	17♏48.0	3♏43.3	2♐40.2	6♑50.6	24♓01.9	11♎28.5	26♒04.8	27♓10.2	25♒55.5	3♑22.3
2 Tu	2 44 39	9 27 23	12♍06 49	19 24 16	5 29.0	4R 21.5	19 21.1	3R 08.0	3 23.4	7 09.9	23R 58.4	11 35.4	26R 04.6	27R 08.6	25R 55.3	3 23.8
3 W	2 48 36	10 27 27	26 44 05	4♎05 30	5 25.8	4 15.4	20 53.8	2 33.7	4 06.7	7 29.5	23 55.1	11 42.2	26 04.3	27 07.1	25 55.2	3 25.2
4 Th	2 52 32	11 27 33	11♎27 39	18 49 34	5 22.6	4 07.6	22 26.0	2 00.6	4 50.1	7 49.1	23 52.0	11 49.0	26 04.2	27 05.5	25 55.0	3 26.7
5 F	2 56 29	12 27 41	26 10 17	3♏28 47	5 19.4	3 59.1	23 57.8	1 28.8	5 33.5	8 08.8	23 49.1	11 55.7	26D 04.1	27 04.1	25 54.9	3 28.2
6 Sa	3 00 25	13 27 52	10♏44 07	17 55 26	5 16.3	3 50.9	25 29.2	0 58.5	6 17.0	8 28.6	23 46.3	12 02.4	26 04.1	27 02.6	25 54.9	3 29.7
7 Su	3 04 22	14 28 04	25 01 57	2♐03 04	5 13.1	3 44.0	27 00.2	0 30.0	7 00.6	8 48.6	23 43.8	12 09.1	26 04.1	27 01.2	25D 54.8	3 31.2
8 M	3 08 19	15 28 18	8♐58 19	15 47 25	5 09.9	3 39.2	28 30.8	0 03.3	7 44.3	9 08.6	23 41.5	12 15.7	26 04.3	26 59.8	25 54.8	3 32.8
9 Tu	3 12 15	16 28 33	22 30 13	29 06 44	5 06.7	3D 36.5	0♐01.0	29♎38.6	8 28.0	9 28.8	23 39.4	12 22.3	26 04.4	26 58.5	25 54.9	3 34.4
10 W	3 16 12	17 28 51	5♑37 08	12♑01 41	5 03.6	3 35.9	1 30.8	29 16.1	9 11.7	9 49.0	23 37.5	12 28.9	26 04.7	26 57.2	25 55.0	3 36.0
11 Th	3 20 08	18 29 09	18 20 47	24 34 53	5 00.4	3 36.8	3 00.1	28 55.8	9 55.5	10 09.4	23 35.8	12 35.3	26 05.0	26 56.0	25 55.1	3 37.7
12 F	3 24 05	19 29 29	0♒44 30	6♒50 15	4 57.2	3 38.2	4 29.1	28 37.7	10 39.4	10 29.8	23 34.3	12 41.8	26 05.3	26 54.8	25 55.2	3 39.3
13 Sa	3 28 01	20 29 51	12 52 43	18 52 34	4 54.0	3R 39.5	5 57.5	28 22.1	11 23.4	10 50.3	23 33.1	12 48.2	26 05.7	26 53.7	25 55.4	3 41.0
14 Su	3 31 58	21 30 14	24 50 24	0♓46 54	4 50.9	3 39.7	7 25.5	28 08.8	12 07.3	11 11.0	23 32.0	12 54.5	26 06.2	26 52.6	25 55.6	3 42.7
15 M	3 35 55	22 30 38	6♓42 40	12 38 19	4 47.7	3 38.4	8 53.1	27 58.0	12 51.4	11 31.7	23 31.1	13 00.8	26 06.8	26 51.5	25 55.9	3 44.4
16 Tu	3 39 51	23 31 03	18 34 25	24 31 31	4 44.5	3 35.3	10 20.0	27 49.7	13 35.5	11 52.5	23 30.4	13 07.1	26 07.4	26 50.5	25 56.1	3 46.1
17 W	3 43 48	24 31 30	0♈30 07	6♈30 39	4 41.3	3 30.5	11 46.5	27 43.8	14 19.7	12 13.3	23 30.0	13 13.3	26 08.0	26 49.5	25 56.5	3 47.9
18 Th	3 47 44	25 31 59	12 33 33	18 39 07	4 38.1	3 24.4	13 12.2	27D 40.4	15 03.9	12 34.3	23D 29.7	13 19.4	26 08.8	26 48.6	25 56.8	3 49.7
19 F	3 51 41	26 32 28	24 47 40	0♉59 24	4 35.0	3 17.5	14 37.3	27 39.5	15 48.2	12 55.4	23 29.7	13 25.5	26 09.6	26 47.7	25 57.2	3 51.5
20 Sa	3 55 37	27 32 59	7♉14 29	13 33 02	4 31.8	3 10.8	16 01.7	27 40.9	16 32.5	13 16.5	23 29.9	13 31.5	26 10.4	26 46.9	25 57.6	3 53.3
21 Su	3 59 34	28 33 32	19 55 04	26 20 36	4 28.6	3 04.8	17 25.1	27 44.8	17 16.9	13 37.7	23 30.2	13 37.5	26 11.3	26 46.1	25 58.1	3 55.1
22 M	4 03 30	29 34 06	2♊49 35	9♊21 56	4 25.4	3 00.1	18 47.7	27 51.0	18 01.4	13 59.0	23 30.8	13 43.4	26 12.3	26 45.4	25 58.6	3 57.0
23 Tu	4 07 27	0♐34 41	15 57 32	22 36 15	4 22.3	2 57.2	20 09.1	27 59.6	18 45.9	14 20.3	23 31.6	13 49.2	26 13.4	26 44.7	25 59.1	3 58.8
24 W	4 11 24	1 35 18	29 17 56	6♋02 28	4 19.1	2D 56.0	21 29.4	28 10.4	19 30.5	14 41.8	23 32.6	13 55.0	26 14.5	26 44.1	25 59.6	4 00.7
25 Th	4 15 20	2 35 57	12♋49 42	19 39 30	4 15.9	2 56.3	22 48.3	28 23.4	20 15.1	15 03.3	23 33.8	14 00.8	26 15.6	26 43.5	26 00.2	4 02.6
26 F	4 19 17	3 36 37	26 31 44	3♌26 17	4 12.7	2 57.6	24 05.6	28 38.6	20 59.8	15 24.8	23 35.2	14 06.4	26 16.8	26 42.9	26 00.8	4 04.5
27 Sa	4 23 13	4 37 19	10♌23 03	17 21 55	4 09.6	2 59.2	25 21.1	28 55.8	21 44.5	15 46.5	23 36.8	14 12.0	26 18.1	26 42.3	26 01.5	4 06.5
28 Su	4 27 10	5 38 02	24 22 44	1♍25 24	4 06.4	3R 00.5	26 34.6	29 15.1	22 29.3	16 08.2	23 38.6	14 17.6	26 19.4	26 42.0	26 02.2	4 08.4
29 M	4 31 06	6 38 47	8♍29 43	15 35 29	4 03.2	3 00.9	27 45.7	29 36.3	23 14.1	16 30.0	23 40.6	14 23.1	26 20.8	26 41.6	26 02.9	4 10.4
30 Tu	4 35 03	7♐39 33	22 42 26	29 50 17	4♑00.0	3♑00.1	28♐54.1	29♎59.4	23♐59.1	16♑51.9	23♓42.8	14♎28.5	26♒22.3	26♓41.3	26♒03.7	4♑12.3

1st of Month

Julian Day # 2455501.5
Obliquity 23°26'18"
SVP 5♓06'15"
GC 26♐59.4
Eris 21♈32.2R

Day	⚴		Day	⚵		Day	⚶
1	9♐34.6		1	11♍52.4		1	12♏39.5
6	11 35.5		6	13 44.6		6	15 19.8
11	13 37.3		11	15 32.7		11	18 00.6
16	15 39.6		16	17 16.2		16	20 41.5
21	17 42.3		21	18 54.8		21	23 22.7
26	19 45.4		26	20 28.4		26	26 04.0

DECLINATION and LATITUDE

Day	☉ Decl	☽ Decl	☽ Lat	☽ 12h Decl	☿ Decl	☿ Lat	♀ Decl	♀ Lat	♂ Decl	♂ Lat	⚳ Decl	⚳ Lat	♃ Decl	♃ Lat	♄ Decl	♄ Lat
1 M	14S19	8N26	4S06	5N35	17S53	0S47	17S49	5S23	21S15	0S34	28S24	5S09	3S46	1S31	2S31	2N12
2 Tu	14 38	2 39	4 43	0S20	18 25	0 53	17 24	5 10	21 24	0 35	28 23	5 09	3 47	1 31	2 33	2 12
3 W	14 57	3S20	5 03	6 18	18 56	0 59	16 59	4 56	21 33	0 35	28 23	5 10	3 48	1 31	2 36	2 12
4 Th	15 16	9 11	5 03	11 56	19 26	1 06	16 35	4 42	21 41	0 36	28 22	5 10	3 49	1 31	2 38	2 12
5 F	15 35	14 30	4 43	16 51	19 55	1 12	16 10	4 27	21 50	0 36	28 21	5 11	3 50	1 30	2 41	2 13
6 Sa	15 53	18 55	4 05	20 42	20 24	1 18	15 45	4 13	21 58	0 37	28 20	5 11	3 51	1 30	2 43	2 13
7 Su	16 11	22 08	3 12	23 12	20 51	1 24	15 21	3 58	22 06	0 37	28 20	5 12	3 52	1 30	2 46	2 13
8 M	16 28	23 55	2 09	24 15	21 17	1 30	14 58	3 43	22 13	0 38	28 19	5 12	3 53	1 30	2 48	2 13
9 Tu	16 46	24 13	0 60	23 50	21 42	1 35	14 35	3 27	22 21	0 38	28 18	5 13	3 53	1 29	2 51	2 13
10 W	17 03	23 08	0N11	22 08	22 06	1 41	14 12	3 12	22 28	0 39	28 17	5 13	3 54	1 29	2 53	2 13
11 Th	17 20	20 53	1 19	19 23	22 29	1 46	13 51	2 57	22 35	0 39	28 15	5 13	3 54	1 29	2 55	2 13
12 F	17 36	17 41	2 22	15 49	22 51	1 51	13 30	2 41	22 42	0 40	28 14	5 14	3 55	1 29	2 58	2 14
13 Sa	17 52	13 48	3 16	11 40	23 12	1 56	13 10	2 26	22 49	0 40	28 13	5 14	3 55	1 28	3 00	2 14
14 Su	18 08	9 26	4 02	7 08	23 32	2 00	12 52	2 11	22 55	0 41	28 12	5 15	3 55	1 28	3 03	2 14
15 M	18 24	4 46	4 37	2 21	23 50	2 05	12 34	1 57	23 01	0 41	28 10	5 15	3 55	1 28	3 05	2 14
16 Tu	18 39	0N05	4 60	2N31	24 07	2 09	12 17	1 42	23 07	0 42	28 09	5 16	3 55	1 28	3 07	2 14
17 W	18 54	4 56	5 10	7 19	24 23	2 13	12 02	1 28	23 13	0 42	28 08	5 16	3 55	1 27	3 09	2 14
18 Th	19 09	9 39	5 06	11 55	24 38	2 16	11 48	1 14	23 19	0 43	28 06	5 17	3 55	1 27	3 12	2 15
19 F	19 23	14 04	4 49	16 06	24 51	2 19	11 35	1 00	23 24	0 43	28 04	5 17	3 55	1 27	3 14	2 15
20 Sa	19 37	17 59	4 17	19 40	25 03	2 22	11 23	0 47	23 29	0 44	28 03	5 18	3 54	1 27	3 16	2 15
21 Su	19 50	21 08	3 33	22 21	25 14	2 24	11 12	0 34	23 34	0 44	28 01	5 18	3 54	1 26	3 18	2 15
22 M	20 03	23 17	2 37	23 55	25 24	2 26	11 02	0 21	23 38	0 45	27 59	5 19	3 54	1 26	3 20	2 15
23 Tu	20 16	24 13	1 31	24 10	25 32	2 28	10 54	0 09	23 43	0 45	27 57	5 19	3 53	1 26	3 22	2 15
24 W	20 29	23 46	0 20	23 01	25 39	2 29	10 47	0N03	23 47	0 46	27 56	5 20	3 52	1 26	3 24	2 16
25 Th	20 41	21 55	0S54	20 30	25 44	2 30	10 41	0 14	23 51	0 46	27 54	5 20	3 52	1 25	3 26	2 16
26 F	20 52	18 47	2 06	16 48	25 48	2 30	10 36	0 26	23 54	0 47	27 52	5 21	3 51	1 25	3 28	2 16
27 Sa	21 04	14 34	3 11	12 08	25 50	2 29	10 32	0 36	23 58	0 47	27 49	5 21	3 50	1 25	3 30	2 16
28 Su	21 15	9 32	4 06	6 48	25 51	2 28	10 29	0 47	24 01	0 47	27 47	5 22	3 49	1 25	3 32	2 16
29 M	21 25	3 58	4 46	1 04	25 51	2 26	10 27	0 57	24 04	0 48	27 45	5 23	3 48	1 24	3 34	2 17
30 Tu	21S35	1S50	5S09	4S44	25S49	2S23	10S26	1N06	24S06	0S48	27S43	5S23	3S47	1S24	3S36	2N17

Day	⚷ Decl	⚷ Lat	♅ Decl	♅ Lat	♆ Decl	♆ Lat	♇ Decl	♇ Lat
1	7S03	6N08	1S50	0S47	13S20	0S29	18S44	4N40
6	7 05	6 06	1 53	0 46	13 20	0 29	18 45	4 39
11	7 06	6 04	1 56	0 46	13 20	0 29	18 46	4 38
16	7 08	6 02	1 58	0 46	13 20	0 29	18 46	4 37
21	7 08	5 60	1 59	0 46	13 19	0 29	18 47	4 36
26	7 08	5 58	2 00	0 46	13 18	0 29	18 48	4 35

Day	⚴ Decl	⚴ Lat	⚵ Decl	⚵ Lat	⚶ Decl	⚶ Lat	Eris Decl	Eris Lat
1	5N51	28N01	2N09	5S22	11S36	4N14	4S17	13S39
6	5 25	27 49	1 33	5 14	12 27	4 09	4 18	13 39
11	5 01	27 38	0 58	5 07	13 16	4 05	4 18	13 38
16	4 39	27 27	0 25	4 60	14 04	4 00	4 19	13 38
21	4 20	27 18	0S06	4 52	14 49	3 56	4 19	13 37
26	4 04	27 10	0 35	4 44	15 31	3 51	4 19	13 37

Moon Phenomena

Max/0 Decl (dy hr mn):
2 10:38 0 S
8 17:03 24S17
15 23:37 0 N
23 4:16 24N14
29 16:25 0 S

Max/0 Lat (dy hr mn):
3 12:10 5S06
9 20:15 0 N
17 5:55 5N10
24 6:28 0 S
30 17:21 5S14

Perigee/Apogee (dy hr m kilometers):
3 17:32 p 364193
15 11:46 a 404629
30 18:55 p 369430

PH dy hr mn:
● 6 4:53 13♏40
☽ 13 16:40 21♒12
○ 21 17:28 29♉18
☾ 28 20:38 6♍30

Void of Course Moon

Last Aspect			☽ Ingress		
31	21:02	♆ ☍	♍	1	3:52
3	0:37	♅ ☍	♎	3	5:20
4	23:35	♆ △	♏	5	6:17
7	3:45	☿ ☌	♐	7	8:29
9	12:36	♀ ✶	♑	9	13:38
11	19:58	♀ □	♒	11	22:33
14	6:34	♀ △	♓	14	10:25
16	16:38	♅ ☌	♈	16	23:00
19	5:34	♀ ☍	♉	19	10:05
21	17:28	☉ ☍	♊	21	18:47
23	21:58	♀ △	♋	24	1:15
26	3:45	♀ □	♌	26	6:02
28	8:31	♀ ✶	♍	28	9:35
30	11:18	☿ □	♎	30	12:16

DAILY ASPECTARIAN

1 M: ☽⋕⚷ 5:54; ☽□♂ 8:46; ☿∠♇ 8:58; ☽△♇ 9:31; ☽✶♀ 9:41; ☉⚼♃ 13:02; ♀✶♇ 13:38; ☽△⚳ 15:37; ♀⚺♂ 19:17; ☉✶☽ 19:17; ☽⋕♃ 19:24; ☽⚺♄ 23:08

2 Tu: ♂⚺♇ 0:12; ☽⋕♄ 0:23; ☽⋕♅ 3:14; ☽∠♀ 9:32; ☽✶☿ 13:19; ☿∥♇ 14:43; ☽∥♅ 18:03; ☽☍♃ 19:25; ☽∥♄ 21:00; ☉∠☽ 21:46; ☽⚻♆ 22:40; ☽⚻⚷ 22:55

3 W: ☽☍♅ 0:37; ☽∥♃ 1:53; ☽⚺♀ 9:10; ☽□♇ 10:55; ☽✶♂ 12:39; ☽∥⚷ 15:07; ☽∠☿ 16:41; ☽□⚳ 17:56; ☽⚼♆ 23:07; ☽⚼⚷ 23:22; ☉⚺☽ 24:00

4 Th: ☽☌♄ 0:35; ☿∠⚳ 7:40; ☉⚺♄ 9:39; ☽∠♂ 14:21; ☉⚼♅ 14:48; ☽∥♆ 18:27; ☽⚺☿ 19:58; ☽⚻♃ 20:10; ☿△♃ 21:47; ☽△♆ 23:35; ☽△⚷ 23:50

5 F: ☽⚻♅ 1:28; ☉∥☽ 5:43; ☽∥♀ 7:42; ☽☌♀ 8:25; ☽✶♇ 12:00; ☽⚺♂ 16:14; ⚷ D 18:44; ☉∥♀ 19:47; ☽✶⚳ 20:10; ☽⚼♃ 20:45; ☽∥♇ 22:54

6 Sa: ☽⚼♅ 2:10; ☽⚺♄ 2:11; ☉☌☽ 4:53; ☿□♆ 6:45; ☿□⚷ 9:12; ☽∥☿ 11:24; ☽∠♇ 12:59; ☽△♃ 21:48; ☽∠⚳ 21:53; ☽∥♂ 23:37

7 Su: ☿△♅ 0:16; ☽□♆ 1:30; ☽□⚷ 1:46; ☿∠♄ 2:33; ☽△♅ 3:23; ☽∠♄ 3:38; ☽☌☿ 3:45; ♆ D 6:05; ☽⚺♀ 9:02; ☽⚺♇ 14:34; ☽☌♂ 21:44

8 M: ☽⚺⚳ 0:18; ♀R♎ 3:07; ☽✶♄ 5:49; ☽∠♀ 10:23; ☉⚺☽ 12:21; ☿⚺♀ 19:17; ☿ ♐ 23:44

9 Tu: ☽□♃ 2:05; ☽✶♆ 6:10; ☽✶⚷ 6:28; ☽□♅ 8:05; ☽✶♀ 12:36; ☽⚺☿ 15:26; ☉∠☽ 17:42; ☽☌♇ 20:15

10 W: ☽⚺♂ 7:05; ☽∥♂ 7:55; ☽☌⚳ 8:03; ☽∠♆ 9:54; ☽∠⚷ 10:13; ☽∥☿ 10:32; ☽□♄ 12:58; ☽∠☿ 23:15

11 Th: ☉✶☽ 0:17; ☉∠♇ 3:29; ☿∥♂ 9:18; ☽✶♃ 10:05; ☿⚺♇ 10:18; ☽∠♂ 13:28; ♂⚺⚳ 14:10; ☽⚺♆ 14:36; ☽⚺⚷ 14:55; ☽✶♅ 16:32; ☽∥♇ 16:33; ☽□♀ 19:58

12 F: ☉∥☽ 0:31; ☽⚺♇ 5:44; ☽✶☿ 8:22; ♀∥♆ 11:49; ☽∠♃ 15:24; ☽⚺⚳ 19:49; ☽✶♂ 20:50; ☽∠♅ 22:02; ☽△♄ 23:51

13 Sa: ☽∥♆ 2:41; ☽∥♀ 3:55; ⚳∠♆ 5:57; ☽∠♇ 11:38; ☉□☽ 16:40; ⚳∠⚷ 18:21; ☽⚺♃ 21:22

14 Su: ☽☌♆ 2:12; ☽☌⚷ 2:33; ☽∠⚳ 2:47; ☽⚺♅ 4:06; ☽⚼♄ 6:15; ☽△♀ 6:34; ☽∥⚷ 12:02; ☽✶♇ 17:58

15 M: ♀∠♂ 2:58; ☽∥♃ 4:13; ☽□☿ 5:01; ♂✶♄ 5:59; ☽∥♄ 8:20; ☽✶⚳ 10:03; ☽⚼♀ 12:30; ☽⚻♄ 12:52; ☽□♂ 13:16; ☽∥♅ 13:58; ☉△♃ 23:45

16 Tu: ☽⋕♅ 9:17; ☽☌♃ 9:57; ☉△☽ 10:53; ☉∥♇ 11:41; ☽⚺♆ 14:51; ☽⋕♄ 15:07; ☽⚺⚷ 15:14; ☽☌♅ 16:38; ☽⚻♀ 18:29; ☽⋕♃ 18:58

17 W: ☽□♇ 6:36; ☿⚺⚳ 9:55; ☽⋕⚷ 11:02; ☿∠♀ 15:20; ☉⚼☽ 19:37; ☽∠♆ 20:48; ☽∠⚷ 21:12

18 Th: ☽□⚳ 0:02; ☽△☿ 1:27; ☽☍♄ 1:31; ☿✶♄ 2:10; ☽△♂ 5:16; ☉□♆ 9:55; ☽⋕♀ 10:48; ☉□⚷ 14:48; ♃ D 16:55; ☽⋕♆ 19:46; ♀ D 21:19; ☽⚺♃ 21:28

19 F: ☽✶♆ 2:15; ☽✶⚷ 2:39; ☉⚻☽ 3:42; ☽⚺♅ 3:53; ☽☍♀ 5:34; ☉△♅ 5:58; ☽⚼☿ 10:33; ☽⚼♂ 12:22; ☽△♇ 17:34

20 Sa: ☽∠♃ 2:24; ☉⚺♀ 3:18; ☽⋕♇ 5:31; ☽∠♅ 8:38; ☽△⚳ 11:48; ☽⚻♄ 12:03; ☉⋕☽ 12:29; ☽⚻☿ 18:44; ☽⚻♂ 18:44; ☿☌♂ 18:54; ☽⚼♇ 22:07; ⚳□♄ 23:40

21 Su: ☉∠♄ 1:44; ☉∠⚳ 2:32; ☽✶♃ 6:43; ☽□♆ 11:18; ☽□⚷ 11:44; ☽✶♅ 12:47; ☽⚻♀ 14:43; ☽⚼♄ 16:22; ☽⚼⚳ 16:42; ☉☍☽ 17:28

22 M: ☽⚻♇ 2:04; ☽⋕♂ 6:25; ☉ ♐ 10:16; ☽⚼♀ 18:33; ☽△♄ 20:05; ☽⚻⚳ 20:59

23 Tu: ☽☍♂ 5:23; ☽☍☿ 8:26; ☽□♃ 13:40; ☽△♆ 18:05; ☽△⚷ 18:31; ☽□♅ 19:25; ☽△♀ 21:58; ☽⋕♂ 23:42

24 W: ☉⚻☽ 4:25; ☽☍♇ 8:25; ☽⚼♆ 20:47; ☽⚼⚷ 21:14

25 Th: ☽□♄ 2:06; ☽☍⚳ 4:02; ☉⚼☽ 9:04; ☉⋕☽ 10:01; ☽⚻♂ 13:47; ☿□♃ 14:19; ☽△♃ 18:52; ☽⚻☿ 19:19; ☽⚻♆ 23:06; ☽⚻⚷ 23:34; ☽⋕♇ 23:59

26 F: ☽△♅ 0:20; ☽□♀ 3:45; ☉⚺♇ 11:24; ☽⚻♇ 13:08; ☉△☽ 13:16; ☽⚼♂ 17:21; ☽⚼♃ 20:56; ☽⚼☿ 23:56

27 Sa: ☽⚼♅ 2:17; ☽⋕♆ 6:23; ☽✶♄ 6:37; ☽⚻⚳ 9:31; ☿✶♆ 13:14; ☽⚼♇ 15:01; ☿✶⚷ 18:55; ☽⋕♀ 19:41; ☽△♂ 20:35; ☽⚻♃ 22:44

28 Su: ☿□♅ 2:28; ☽☍♆ 2:50; ☽☍⚷ 3:19; ☽⚻♅ 3:57; ☽△☿ 4:06; ☽∠♄ 8:26; ☽✶♀ 8:31; ☽⋕⚷ 10:31; ☽⚼⚳ 11:49; ☽△♇ 16:39; ☉□☽ 20:38

29 M: ☽⋕♃ 0:41; ☽⋕♄ 1:38; ☽⋕♅ 8:07; ☽⚺♄ 10:01; ☽∠♀ 10:37; ☽△⚳ 13:53; ♂□♃ 14:52

30 Tu: ♀ ♏ 0:34; ☽∥♅ 0:43; ☽☍♃ 1:42; ☽□♂ 2:16; ☽⚻♆ 5:39; ☽⚻⚷ 6:11; ☽☍♅ 6:42; ☽∥♄ 7:21; ☽∥♃ 8:01; ☽□☿ 11:18; ☽⚺♀ 12:37; ☽□♇ 19:23; ☽∥⚷ 22:10

December 2010

LONGITUDE

Day	Sid.Time	☉	☽	☽ 12 hour	Mean ☊	True ☊	☿	♀	♂	⚳	♃	♄	⚷	♅	♆	♇
	h m s	° ' "	° ' "	° ' "	° '	° '	° '	° '	° '	° '	° '	° '	° '	° '	° '	° '
1 W	4 38 59	8♐40 21	6♎58 39	14♎07 08	3♑56.8	2♑58.1	29♐59.5	0♏24.4	24♐44.0	17♑13.8	23♓45.2	14♎33.8	26♒23.8	26♓41.0	26♒04.5	4♑14.3
2 Th	4 42 56	9 41 11	21 15 15	28 22 29	3 53.7	2R 55.3	1♑01.3	0 51.1	25 29.0	17 35.8	23 47.9	14 39.1	26 25.4	26R 40.8	26 05.3	4 16.3
3 F	4 46 53	10 42 02	5♏28 20	12♏32 13	3 50.5	2 51.9	1 59.2	1 19.5	26 14.1	17 57.8	23 50.7	14 44.3	26 27.0	26 40.6	26 06.1	4 18.3
4 Sa	4 50 49	11 42 54	19 33 37	26 31 58	3 47.3	2 48.7	2 52.4	1 49.5	26 59.2	18 19.9	23 53.7	14 49.4	26 28.7	26 40.4	26 07.0	4 20.3
5 Su	4 54 46	12 43 48	3♐26 49	10♐17 44	3 44.1	2 46.1	3 40.3	2 21.1	27 44.4	18 42.1	23 56.9	14 54.5	26 30.4	26 40.4	26 07.9	4 22.4
6 M	4 58 42	13 44 42	17 04 21	23 46 24	3 41.0	2 44.4	4 22.4	2 54.2	28 29.7	19 04.4	24 00.3	14 59.5	26 32.2	26D 40.3	26 08.9	4 24.4
7 Tu	5 02 39	14 45 38	0♑23 42	6♑56 09	3 37.8	2D 43.7	4 57.7	3 28.8	29 15.0	19 26.7	24 03.9	15 04.4	26 34.1	26 40.3	26 09.9	4 26.5
8 W	5 06 35	15 46 35	13 23 47	19 46 39	3 34.6	2 44.0	5 25.4	4 04.7	0♑00.3	19 49.0	24 07.7	15 09.2	26 36.0	26 40.4	26 10.9	4 28.6
9 Th	5 10 32	16 47 32	26 04 58	2♒18 59	3 31.4	2 45.0	5 44.8	4 42.0	0 45.7	20 11.4	24 11.7	15 14.0	26 38.0	26 40.5	26 11.9	4 30.6
10 F	5 14 28	17 48 30	8♒29 03	14 35 32	3 28.3	2 46.4	5R 54.8	5 20.6	1 31.2	20 33.9	24 15.9	15 18.6	26 40.0	26 40.7	26 13.0	4 32.7
11 Sa	5 18 25	18 49 29	20 38 55	26 39 41	3 25.1	2 47.8	5 54.9	6 00.4	2 16.6	20 56.4	24 20.3	15 23.2	26 42.1	26 40.9	26 14.1	4 34.8
12 Su	5 22 22	19 50 29	2♓38 23	8♓35 35	3 21.9	2 48.9	5 44.1	6 41.4	3 02.2	21 19.0	24 24.9	15 27.7	26 44.2	26 41.2	26 15.3	4 36.9
13 M	5 26 18	20 51 29	14 31 51	20 27 49	3 18.7	2R 49.5	5 22.0	7 23.6	3 47.8	21 41.6	24 29.6	15 32.2	26 46.4	26 41.6	26 16.4	4 39.0
14 Tu	5 30 15	21 52 29	26 24 04	2♈21 11	3 15.6	2 49.5	4 48.4	8 06.8	4 33.4	22 04.2	24 34.6	15 36.5	26 48.6	26 41.9	26 17.6	4 41.1
15 W	5 34 11	22 53 30	8♈19 47	14 20 26	3 12.4	2 49.0	4 03.4	8 51.1	5 19.1	22 26.9	24 39.7	15 40.8	26 50.9	26 42.4	26 18.9	4 43.3
16 Th	5 38 08	23 54 32	20 23 39	26 29 57	3 09.2	2 48.2	3 07.6	9 36.5	6 04.8	22 49.7	24 45.0	15 44.9	26 53.3	26 42.9	26 20.1	4 45.4
17 F	5 42 04	24 55 34	2♉39 47	8♉53 33	3 06.0	2 47.1	2 02.1	10 22.8	6 50.6	23 12.5	24 50.5	15 49.0	26 55.6	26 43.4	26 21.4	4 47.5
18 Sa	5 46 01	25 56 37	15 11 36	21 34 12	3 02.8	2 46.1	0 48.7	11 10.0	7 36.4	23 35.3	24 56.1	15 53.1	26 58.1	26 44.0	26 22.7	4 49.7
19 Su	5 49 57	26 57 40	28 01 32	4♊33 42	2 59.7	2 45.3	29♐29.5	11 58.2	8 22.2	23 58.2	25 02.0	15 57.0	27 00.6	26 44.6	26 24.1	4 51.8
20 M	5 53 54	27 58 43	11♊10 44	17 52 34	2 56.5	2 44.7	28 07.1	12 47.3	9 08.1	24 21.1	25 08.0	16 00.8	27 03.1	26 45.3	26 25.5	4 54.0
21 Tu	5 57 51	28 59 47	24 39 01	1♋29 51	2 53.3	2D 44.5	26 44.4	13 37.2	9 54.1	24 44.0	25 14.2	16 04.6	27 05.7	26 46.1	26 26.9	4 56.1
22 W	6 01 47	0♑00 52	8♋24 45	15 23 17	2 50.1	2 44.4	25 24.1	14 27.9	10 40.1	25 07.0	25 20.5	16 08.2	27 08.3	26 46.9	26 28.3	4 58.3
23 Th	6 05 44	1 01 57	22 25 02	29 29 28	2 47.0	2 44.6	24 08.7	15 19.4	11 26.1	25 30.1	25 27.1	16 11.8	27 11.0	26 47.7	26 29.8	5 00.4
24 F	6 09 40	2 03 03	6♌36 05	13♌44 19	2 43.8	2R 44.7	23 00.4	16 11.7	12 12.2	25 53.1	25 33.8	16 15.2	27 13.7	26 48.6	26 31.3	5 02.6
25 Sa	6 13 37	3 04 09	20 53 38	28 03 31	2 40.6	2 44.7	22 00.8	17 04.7	12 58.3	26 16.2	25 40.6	16 18.6	27 16.5	26 49.5	26 32.8	5 04.7
26 Su	6 17 33	4 05 16	5♍13 28	12♍23 01	2 37.4	2 44.6	21 11.2	17 58.4	13 44.4	26 39.4	25 47.6	16 21.9	27 19.3	26 50.5	26 34.3	5 06.9
27 M	6 21 30	5 06 23	19 31 45	26 39 19	2 34.3	2 44.5	20 32.0	18 52.8	14 30.6	27 02.6	25 54.8	16 25.1	27 22.2	26 51.6	26 35.9	5 09.1
28 Tu	6 25 26	6 07 31	3♎45 22	10♎49 39	2 31.1	2D 44.4	20 03.6	19 47.8	15 16.9	27 25.8	26 02.2	16 28.2	27 25.1	26 52.7	26 37.5	5 11.2
29 W	6 29 23	7 08 39	17 51 56	24 51 59	2 27.9	2 44.4	19 45.7	20 43.4	16 03.2	27 49.0	26 09.7	16 31.2	27 28.0	26 53.8	26 39.1	5 13.4
30 Th	6 33 20	8 09 49	1♏49 40	8♏44 49	2 24.7	2 44.7	19D 37.9	21 39.6	16 49.5	28 12.3	26 17.3	16 34.1	27 31.0	26 55.0	26 40.7	5 15.6
31 F	6 37 16	9♑10 58	15 37 18	22 27 00	2♑21.6	2♑45.3	19♐39.7	22♏36.6	17♑35.9	28♑35.6	26♓25.1	16♎36.9	27♒34.1	26♓56.2	26♒42.4	5♑17.7

1st of Month

Julian Day # 2455531.5
Obliquity 23°26'17"
SVP 5♓06'10"
GC 26♐59.5
Eris 21♈17.2R

Day	⚴	Day	⚵	Day	⚶
1	21♐48.7	1	21♏56.4	1	28♏45.4
6	23 52.2	6	23 18.3	6	1♐26.7
11	25 55.5	11	24 33.7	11	4 08.0
16	27 58.7	16	25 42.1	16	6 48.9
21	0♑01.5	21	26 43.1	21	9 29.6
26	2 04.0	26	27 36.0	26	12 09.8
31	4 05.8	31	28 20.5	31	14 49.6

DECLINATION and LATITUDE

Day	☉ Decl	☽ Decl	☽ Lat	☽ 12h Decl	☿ Decl	☿ Lat	♀ Decl	♀ Lat	♂ Decl	♂ Lat	⚳ Decl	⚳ Lat	♃ Decl	♃ Lat	♄ Decl	♄ Lat
1 W	21S45	7S34	5S13	10S18	25S46	2S20	10S26	1N16	24S09	0S49	27S41	5S24	3S46	1S24	3S38	2N17
2 Th	21 54	12 54	4 58	15 18	25 42	2 16	10 27	1 24	24 11	0 49	27 38	5 24	3 44	1 23	3 40	2 17
3 F	22 03	17 30	4 25	19 26	25 36	2 11	10 29	1 33	24 13	0 50	27 36	5 25	3 43	1 23	3 42	2 17
4 Sa	22 11	21 05	3 36	22 26	25 29	2 04	10 32	1 41	24 14	0 50	27 33	5 25	3 42	1 23	3 43	2 18
5 Su	22 19	23 22	2 34	23 59	25 20	1 57	10 35	1 49	24 15	0 50	27 31	5 26	3 40	1 23	3 45	2 18
6 M	22 27	24 13	1 25	24 07	25 10	1 49	10 39	1 56	24 17	0 51	27 28	5 26	3 38	1 23	3 47	2 18
7 Tu	22 34	23 39	0 15	22 52	24 60	1 39	10 44	2 03	24 17	0 51	27 25	5 27	3 37	1 22	3 49	2 18
8 W	22 41	21 47	0N59	20 27	24 48	1 28	10 50	2 10	24 18	0 52	27 22	5 28	3 35	1 22	3 50	2 19
9 Th	22 47	18 53	2 06	17 06	24 34	1 16	10 56	2 17	24 18	0 52	27 20	5 28	3 33	1 22	3 52	2 19
10 F	22 53	15 10	3 05	13 05	24 20	1 02	11 03	2 23	24 18	0 52	27 17	5 29	3 31	1 21	3 53	2 19
11 Sa	22 58	10 53	3 55	8 37	24 05	0 47	11 11	2 29	24 18	0 53	27 14	5 29	3 29	1 21	3 55	2 19
12 Su	23 03	6 16	4 34	3 53	23 50	0 31	11 19	2 34	24 17	0 53	27 11	5 30	3 27	1 21	3 57	2 19
13 M	23 07	1 28	5 01	0N58	23 33	0 13	11 28	2 39	24 16	0 53	27 08	5 30	3 25	1 21	3 58	2 20
14 Tu	23 11	3N23	5 15	5 47	23 16	0N05	11 37	2 44	24 15	0 54	27 04	5 31	3 23	1 20	3 59	2 20
15 W	23 15	8 08	5 15	10 25	22 58	0 25	11 47	2 49	24 14	0 54	27 01	5 32	3 21	1 20	4 01	2 20
16 Th	23 18	12 37	5 02	14 43	22 39	0 45	11 57	2 53	24 12	0 55	26 58	5 32	3 18	1 20	4 02	2 20
17 F	23 20	16 42	4 35	18 30	22 20	1 05	12 07	2 57	24 10	0 55	26 55	5 33	3 16	1 20	4 04	2 21
18 Sa	23 23	20 07	3 54	21 31	22 01	1 25	12 18	3 01	24 08	0 55	26 51	5 34	3 14	1 19	4 05	2 21
19 Su	23 24	22 39	3 01	23 30	21 43	1 44	12 30	3 05	24 06	0 56	26 48	5 34	3 11	1 19	4 06	2 21
20 M	23 25	24 03	1 57	24 14	21 24	2 01	12 41	3 08	24 03	0 56	26 44	5 35	3 08	1 19	4 07	2 21
21 Tu	23 26	24 04	0 45	23 33	21 07	2 17	12 53	3 11	24 00	0 56	26 41	5 35	3 06	1 19	4 09	2 22
22 W	23 26	22 39	0S31	21 24	20 51	2 31	13 05	3 14	23 57	0 57	26 37	5 36	3 03	1 18	4 10	2 22
23 Th	23 26	19 49	1 47	17 55	20 36	2 43	13 18	3 16	23 53	0 57	26 33	5 37	3 00	1 18	4 11	2 22
24 F	23 25	15 46	2 57	13 22	20 24	2 52	13 30	3 19	23 50	0 57	26 29	5 37	2 57	1 18	4 12	2 22
25 Sa	23 24	10 47	3 57	8 04	20 14	2 58	13 43	3 21	23 46	0 57	26 26	5 38	2 54	1 18	4 13	2 23
26 Su	23 22	5 14	4 41	2 20	20 07	3 03	13 56	3 23	23 41	0 58	26 22	5 39	2 51	1 17	4 14	2 23
27 M	23 20	0S35	5 09	3S30	20 02	3 05	14 09	3 24	23 37	0 58	26 18	5 40	2 48	1 17	4 15	2 23
28 Tu	23 18	6 21	5 17	9 06	19 60	3 05	14 23	3 26	23 32	0 58	26 14	5 40	2 45	1 17	4 16	2 23
29 W	23 15	11 43	5 06	14 11	19 60	3 03	14 36	3 27	23 27	0 59	26 10	5 41	2 42	1 17	4 17	2 24
30 Th	23 11	16 26	4 37	18 28	20 02	3 00	14 49	3 28	23 21	0 59	26 06	5 42	2 39	1 16	4 18	2 24
31 F	23S07	20S13	3S53	21S41	20S07	2N56	15S03	3N29	23S15	0S59	26S01	5S42	2S35	1S16	4S19	2N24

Day	⚷ Decl	⚷ Lat	♅ Decl	♅ Lat	♆ Decl	♆ Lat	♇ Decl	♇ Lat
1	7S08	5N56	2S01	0S45	13S17	0S29	18S48	4N34
6	7 07	5 54	2 01	0 45	13 15	0 29	18 49	4 33
11	7 06	5 52	2 00	0 45	13 14	0 29	18 49	4 33
16	7 04	5 50	1 60	0 45	13 12	0 29	18 49	4 32
21	7 01	5 48	1 58	0 45	13 09	0 29	18 49	4 32
26	6 58	5 47	1 56	0 44	13 07	0 29	18 50	4 31
31	6S55	5N45	1S54	0S44	13S04	0S29	18S50	4N31

Day	⚴ Decl	⚴ Lat	⚵ Decl	⚵ Lat	⚶ Decl	⚶ Lat	Eris Decl	Eris Lat
1	3N50	27N04	1S02	4S36	16S12	3N47	4S19	13S36
6	3 38	26 58	1 27	4 28	16 49	3 42	4 19	13 35
11	3 30	26 53	1 48	4 19	17 25	3 37	4 19	13 35
16	3 24	26 49	2 07	4 10	17 57	3 33	4 19	13 34
21	3 20	26 47	2 22	4 00	18 27	3 28	4 19	13 33
26	3 20	26 45	2 34	3 50	18 54	3 23	4 18	13 32
31	3N21	26N45	2S41	3S39	19S18	3N18	4S18	13S31

Moon Phenomena

Max/0 Decl (dy hr mn)
6 1:59 24S14
13 7:14 0 N
20 12:36 24N14
26 21:34 0 S

Perigee/Apogee (dy hr m kilometers)
13 8:32 a 404404
25 12:17 p 368466

Max/0 Lat (dy hr mn)
7 4:16 0 N
14 12:56 5N17
21 14:09 0 S
27 22:24 5S17

PH (dy hr mn)
● 5 17:37 13♐28
☽ 13 14:00 21♓27
○ 21 8:15 29♊21
☍ 21 8:18 T 1.256
☾ 28 4:20 6♎19

Void of Course Moon

Last Aspect	☽ Ingress
2 8:09 ♆ △	♏ 2 14:45
4 12:15 ♅ △	♐ 4 18:00
6 21:47 ♂ ☌	♑ 6 23:17
9 1:08 ♅ ⚹	♒ 9 7:32
11 11:10 ♆ ☌	♓ 11 18:42
14 0:36 ♅ ☌	♈ 14 7:16
16 11:42 ♆ ⚹	♉ 16 18:50
18 21:38 ♅ ⚹	♊ 19 3:38
21 8:15 ☉ ☍	♋ 21 9:23
23 7:27 ♅ △	♌ 23 12:52
25 9:29 ♆ ☍	♍ 25 15:15
27 12:22 ♅ ☍	♎ 27 17:39
29 15:06 ♆ △	♏ 29 20:51

DAILY ASPECTARIAN

1 W
☿ ♑ 0:12
☉⚹☽ 3:04
☽⚼♆ 6:53
☽⚼⚷ 7:26
☽∥♀ 12:39
☽☌♄ 12:50
☿⚹♀ 16:35
☽□⚳ 17:41

2 Th
☽∥♆ 1:51
☽⚻♃ 4:18
☉∠☽ 6:13
☽⚹♂ 7:31
☽△♆ 8:09
☽△⚷ 8:43
☽⚻♅ 9:08
☽☌♀ 16:44
☽⚹☿ 17:41
♂⚹♆ 19:40
☽⚹♇ 22:01

3 F
☽⚼♃ 5:44
♂⚹⚷ 7:07
⚶ ♐ 7:30
☽∥♇ 7:53
☉⚺☽ 9:34
♃∥♄ 10:13
☽∠♂ 10:20
☽⚼♅ 10:32
♂□♅ 14:02
☽⚺♄ 15:51
☽∠☿ 20:55
☽⚹⚳ 21:50
☽∠♇ 23:37

4 Sa
☽△♃ 7:29
☉∥☽ 10:30
☽□♆ 11:18
☽□⚷ 11:56
☽△♅ 12:15
☽⚺♂ 13:31
☽∠♄ 17:48
☽⚺♀ 22:01

5 Su
☽⚺☿ 0:25
☽∠⚳ 0:27
☽⚺♇ 1:37
☉☌☽ 17:37
☽⚹♄ 20:17

6 M
☿☌♇ 1:21
☽∠♀ 1:33
♅ D 1:51
☽⚺⚳ 3:40
☽□♃ 12:28
☽⚹♆ 16:18
☽⚹⚷ 17:02
☽□♅ 17:14
☽☌♂ 21:47

7 Tu
☽⚹♀ 5:54
☽☌♇ 7:26
☉⚹♄ 8:01
☽☌☿ 8:42
☉∥☽ 14:52
☽∠♆ 19:52
☽∠⚷ 20:38
♂ ♑ 23:50

8 W
☽□♄ 3:19
☉⚺☽ 4:51
☽☌⚳ 12:26
♀⚹♇ 16:21
☽⚹♃ 20:22

9 Th
☽⚺♆ 0:13
☽∥♇ 0:27
☽⚺⚷ 1:03
☽⚹♅ 1:08
☽⚺♂ 9:35
☉∠☽ 11:58
☽⚺♇ 16:18
☽□♀ 17:32
☽⚺☿ 18:57

10 F
☽∠♃ 1:32
☿∥♂ 3:52
☽∠♅ 6:16
♅⚺⚷ 9:18
☽∥♆ 11:11
☿ R 12:06
☽△♄ 13:30
☽∠♂ 16:52
☉⚹☽ 20:03
☿⚹♀ 21:02
☽∠♇ 21:52
☽∥♀ 22:29

11 Sa
☽∠☿ 0:31
☽⚺⚳ 0:36
☽⚺♃ 7:24
☽☌♆ 11:10
☽⚺♅ 12:03
☽☌⚷ 12:07
☽⚼♄ 19:36
☽∥⚷ 19:50

12 Su
☽⚹♂ 0:51
☽⚹♇ 3:59
☽⚹☿ 6:05
☽∠⚳ 7:39
☽△♀ 8:40
☽∥♄ 11:38
☽∥♃ 14:13
☽∥♅ 21:20

13 M
☽⚻♄ 2:03
☉□☽ 14:00
☽⚹⚳ 14:58
☽⚼♀ 16:55
☽⋕♅ 17:08
☽☌♃ 20:17
☽⚺♆ 23:47

14 Tu
☽⋕♃ 0:00
☽☌♅ 0:36
☽⚺⚷ 0:50
☽⋕♄ 3:03
☿☌♇ 4:06
☿☌♂ 4:11
♂☌♇ 4:16
☉∥☿ 4:53
☉⚺⚳ 7:21
☽□☿ 15:58
☽□♇ 16:44
☽□♂ 17:33
☽⋕⚷ 18:34

15 W
☽⚻♀ 1:07
☽∠♆ 5:59
☽∠⚷ 7:03
☽☍♄ 14:45
☽⋕♀ 20:07

16 Th
☽⋕♆ 3:10
☽□⚳ 4:57
♀⚼♃ 5:03
☉△☽ 7:33
☽⚺♃ 8:38
☽⚹♆ 11:42
☽⚺♅ 12:26
☽⚹⚷ 12:48
☉□♃ 21:48
☽△☿ 22:53

17 F
☽△♇ 4:08
☽△♂ 8:35
☽∠♃ 13:55
☽⋕♇ 14:15
☉⚼☽ 15:13
☽☍♀ 15:50
☽∠♅ 17:25

18 Sa
☽⚼☿ 1:04
☽⚻♄ 1:19
☽⚼♇ 8:46
☉⚹♆ 10:30
☽⚼♂ 14:49
☿R♐ 14:54
☽⋕☿ 15:01
☽△⚳ 16:15
♀⚼♅ 17:10
☽⚹♃ 18:25
☉□♅ 18:49
☽□♆ 20:59
☽⚹♅ 21:38
☉⚻☽ 21:52
☽□⚷ 22:07

19 Su
☉∠♀ 1:06
☉⚹⚷ 1:12
☽⚻☿ 2:27
☽⚼♄ 5:25
☉⋕☽ 10:26
☽⚻♇ 12:35
☽⚻♂ 20:05
☽⚼⚳ 20:36

20 M
☽⋕♂ 0:17
☉☌☿ 1:24
☽⚻♀ 3:05
☿∠♀ 3:36
☽△♄ 8:43
☿⚹⚷ 17:59
♀ ♑ 22:29
☿□♅ 23:31

21 Tu
☽⚻⚳ 0:09
☽□♃ 1:02
☽⋕♂ 2:22
☽△♆ 3:10
☽☍☿ 3:21
☽□♅ 3:44
☽△⚷ 4:19
☿⚹♆ 5:04
☽⚼♀ 7:26
☉☍☽ 8:15
☉⋕☽ 13:40
☽☍♇ 18:02
☉ ♑ 23:40

22 W
☿□♃ 1:00
☿⚺⚳ 4:03
☽☍♂ 4:07
☽⚼♆ 5:17
♀∥♆ 6:23
☽⚼⚷ 6:27
☽△♀ 11:06
☽□♄ 13:20
☽⋕☿ 17:52
⚳⚹♃ 19:37

23 Th
♂∠♆ 1:59
☽⚻☿ 2:42
☽△♃ 5:12
☽☍⚳ 5:23
☽⋕♇ 6:30
☽⚻♆ 6:56
☽△♅ 7:27
☽⚻⚷ 8:07
☉⚻☽ 15:44
☽⚻♇ 21:22

24 F
♂∠⚷ 0:52
♀⚺♄ 1:44
☽⚼☿ 2:12
☽⚼♃ 6:43
☽⚼♅ 8:46
☽⚻♂ 9:57
☽⋕♀ 10:53
☽⋕♆ 13:11
☽⚹♄ 16:17
☽□♀ 17:11
☉⚼☽ 18:54
☽⚼♇ 22:38

25 Sa
☽△☿ 1:46
☽⚻♃ 8:05
☽⚻⚳ 9:15
☽☍♆ 9:29
☽⚻♅ 9:57
☽☍⚷ 10:43
☽⚼♂ 12:32
☽⋕⚷ 16:39
☽∠♄ 17:31
⚳⚺♆ 18:22
☉△☽ 21:57
☽△♇ 23:49

26 Su
☽⋕♄ 4:07
☽⋕♃ 9:55
☽⚼⚳ 11:05
⚳⚹♅ 12:05
☽⋕♅ 13:38
☽△♂ 15:05
☽⚺♄ 18:45
☽⚹♀ 22:50

27 M
☉☌♇ 1:06
☽□☿ 1:38
☽∥♅ 5:30
☽∥♃ 9:03
☽☍♃ 10:51
☽⚻♆ 11:56
☽☍♅ 12:22
☽△⚳ 13:00
☽⚻⚷ 13:15
☽∥♄ 15:12
⚳⚺⚷ 23:12

28 Tu
☽∠♀ 1:53
☽□♇ 2:26
☽∥⚷ 2:35
☉□☽ 4:20
☿⚺♀ 4:54
♀∠♇ 10:34
☽⚼♆ 13:23
☽⚼⚷ 14:46
☽□♂ 20:43
☽☌♄ 21:42

29 W
☽⚹☿ 3:12
☽⚺♀ 5:14
☽∥♆ 6:31
☽⚻♃ 14:21
☽∥♀ 14:52
☽△♆ 15:06
♂□♄ 15:30
☽⚻♅ 15:31
☽△⚷ 16:32
☽□⚳ 17:34

30 Th
☽∠☿ 4:51
☽⚹♇ 5:57
☿ D 7:21
☉⚹☽ 11:52
☽∥♇ 14:20
☽⚼♃ 16:35
☽⚼♅ 17:33
☽∥☿ 23:10

31 F
☽⚺♄ 1:45
☽⚹♂ 3:40
☽⚺☿ 7:09
☽∠♇ 8:14
☽☌♀ 13:12
☉∠☽ 16:17
☽△♃ 19:12
☽□♆ 19:34
☽△♅ 19:58
☽□⚷ 21:08
☽⚹⚳ 23:33

LONGITUDE

January 2011

Day	Sid.Time	☉	☽	☽ 12 hour	Mean ☊	True ☊	☿	♀	♂	⚳	♃	♄	⚷	♅	♆	♇
	h m s	° ' "	° ' "	° ' "	° '	° '	° '	° '	° '	° '	° '	° '	° '	° '	° '	° '
1 Sa	6 41 13	10♑12 08	29♏13 48	5♐57 36	2♑18.4	2♑46.0	19♐50.3	23♏33.8	18♑22.3	28♑58.9	26♓33.1	16♎39.6	27♒37.1	26♓57.5	26♒44.1	5♑19.9
2 Su	6 45 09	11 13 19	12♐38 18	19 15 48	2 15.2	2 46.7	20 09.0	24 31.7	19 08.7	29 22.3	26 41.2	16 42.2	27 40.2	26 58.9	26 45.8	5 22.0
3 M	6 49 06	12 14 29	25 50 02	2♑20 55	2 12.0	2R 47.2	20 35.0	25 30.1	19 55.2	29 45.6	26 49.5	16 44.7	27 43.4	27 00.2	26 47.5	5 24.2
4 Tu	6 53 02	13 15 40	8♑48 25	15 12 29	2 08.9	2 47.2	21 07.7	26 29.0	20 41.7	0♒09.1	26 57.9	16 47.1	27 46.6	27 01.7	26 49.3	5 26.3
5 W	6 56 59	14 16 51	21 33 09	27 50 27	2 05.7	2 46.6	21 46.4	27 28.4	21 28.3	0 32.5	27 06.5	16 49.5	27 49.8	27 03.2	26 51.1	5 28.5
6 Th	7 00 56	15 18 01	4♒04 28	10♒15 18	2 02.5	2 45.3	22 30.4	28 28.2	22 14.9	0 55.9	27 15.2	16 51.7	27 53.1	27 04.7	26 52.9	5 30.6
7 F	7 04 52	16 19 12	16 23 10	22 28 14	1 59.3	2 43.5	23 19.2	29 28.4	23 01.5	1 19.4	27 24.0	16 53.8	27 56.4	27 06.3	26 54.7	5 32.8
8 Sa	7 08 49	17 20 22	28 30 49	4♓31 12	1 56.1	2 41.2	24 12.2	0♐29.0	23 48.2	1 42.9	27 33.0	16 55.8	27 59.7	27 07.9	26 56.5	5 34.9
9 Su	7 12 45	18 21 32	10♓29 47	16 26 56	1 53.0	2 38.8	25 09.0	1 30.1	24 34.9	2 06.4	27 42.1	16 57.6	28 03.1	27 09.6	26 58.4	5 37.0
10 M	7 16 42	19 22 41	22 23 09	28 18 53	1 49.8	2 36.5	26 09.2	2 31.5	25 21.6	2 30.0	27 51.4	16 59.4	28 06.5	27 11.3	27 00.3	5 39.1
11 Tu	7 20 38	20 23 50	4♈14 41	10♈11 06	1 46.6	2 34.9	27 12.4	3 33.4	26 08.3	2 53.5	28 00.7	17 01.1	28 10.0	27 13.0	27 02.2	5 41.2
12 W	7 24 35	21 24 58	16 08 43	22 08 08	1 43.4	2D 34.0	28 18.3	4 35.5	26 55.1	3 17.1	28 10.3	17 02.7	28 13.4	27 14.8	27 04.1	5 43.3
13 Th	7 28 31	22 26 06	28 09 55	4♉14 42	1 40.3	2 34.0	29 26.7	5 38.1	27 41.9	3 40.7	28 19.9	17 04.2	28 17.0	27 16.7	27 06.1	5 45.4
14 F	7 32 28	23 27 14	10♉23 04	16 35 34	1 37.1	2 34.9	0♑37.2	6 40.9	28 28.8	4 04.2	28 29.7	17 05.5	28 20.5	27 18.6	27 08.0	5 47.5
15 Sa	7 36 25	24 28 20	22 52 45	29 15 06	1 33.9	2 36.4	1 49.7	7 44.1	29 15.6	4 27.8	28 39.6	17 06.8	28 24.1	27 20.5	27 10.0	5 49.6
16 Su	7 40 21	25 29 26	5♊43 01	12♊16 50	1 30.7	2 38.0	3 03.9	8 47.7	0♒02.5	4 51.5	28 49.6	17 07.9	28 27.7	27 22.5	27 12.0	5 51.7
17 M	7 44 18	26 30 32	18 56 49	25 43 02	1 27.6	2 39.4	4 19.8	9 51.5	0 49.4	5 15.1	28 59.8	17 09.0	28 31.3	27 24.5	27 14.0	5 53.7
18 Tu	7 48 14	27 31 36	2♋35 31	9♋34 05	1 24.4	2R 39.9	5 37.2	10 55.6	1 36.4	5 38.7	29 10.0	17 09.9	28 34.9	27 26.6	27 16.0	5 55.8
19 W	7 52 11	28 32 40	16 38 26	23 48 05	1 21.2	2 39.3	6 55.9	12 00.2	2 23.4	6 02.4	29 20.4	17 10.8	28 38.6	27 28.7	27 18.1	5 57.8
20 Th	7 56 07	29 33 44	1♌02 25	8♌20 42	1 18.0	2 37.3	8 15.9	13 04.7	3 10.3	6 26.0	29 30.9	17 11.5	28 42.3	27 30.8	27 20.1	5 59.8
21 F	8 00 04	0♒34 47	15 42 03	23 05 31	1 14.9	2 34.0	9 37.0	14 09.6	3 57.4	6 49.7	29 41.5	17 12.1	28 46.1	27 33.0	27 22.2	6 01.8
22 Sa	8 04 00	1 35 49	0♍30 06	7♍54 47	1 11.7	2 29.8	10 59.2	15 14.9	4 44.4	7 13.3	29 52.2	17 12.6	28 49.8	27 35.2	27 24.3	6 03.8
23 Su	8 07 57	2 36 50	15 18 36	22 40 38	1 08.5	2 25.3	12 22.4	16 20.4	5 31.5	7 37.0	0♈03.1	17 13.0	28 53.6	27 37.5	27 26.4	6 05.8
24 M	8 11 54	3 37 51	0♎00 04	7♎16 14	1 05.3	2 21.3	13 46.6	17 26.1	6 18.5	8 00.7	0 14.0	17 13.3	28 57.4	27 39.8	27 28.5	6 07.8
25 Tu	8 15 50	4 38 52	14 28 33	21 36 38	1 02.1	2 18.3	15 11.7	18 32.0	7 05.6	8 24.4	0 25.1	17 13.5	29 01.2	27 42.1	27 30.7	6 09.8
26 W	8 19 47	5 39 52	28 40 12	5♏39 06	0 59.0	2D 16.7	16 37.6	19 38.2	7 52.8	8 48.1	0 36.2	17R 13.6	29 05.1	27 44.5	27 32.8	6 11.7
27 Th	8 23 43	6 40 52	12♏33 19	19 22 54	0 55.8	2 16.7	18 04.4	20 44.7	8 39.9	9 11.7	0 47.5	17 13.6	29 08.9	27 46.9	27 34.9	6 13.6
28 F	8 27 40	7 41 51	26 07 58	2♐48 44	0 52.6	2 17.7	19 32.0	21 51.3	9 27.1	9 35.4	0 58.8	17 13.4	29 12.8	27 49.3	27 37.1	6 15.6
29 Sa	8 31 36	8 42 50	9♐25 24	15 58 14	0 49.4	2 19.4	21 00.4	22 58.1	10 14.3	9 59.1	1 10.3	17 13.2	29 16.7	27 51.8	27 39.3	6 17.5
30 Su	8 35 33	9 43 48	22 27 27	28 53 19	0 46.3	2R 20.7	22 29.5	24 05.2	11 01.5	10 22.8	1 21.8	17 12.8	29 20.6	27 54.3	27 41.5	6 19.3
31 M	8 39 29	10♒44 45	5♑16 02	11♑35 49	0♑43.1	2♑21.1	23♑59.4	25♐12.4	11♒48.8	10♒46.5	1♈33.5	17♎12.4	29♒24.6	27♓56.9	27♒43.7	6♑21.2

1st of Month

Julian Day # 2455562.5
Obliquity 23°26'16"
SVP 5♓06'04"
GC 26♐59.6
Eris 21♈09.5R

Day	⚴
1	4♑30.1
6	6 31.2
11	8 31.4
16	10 30.5
21	12 28.5
26	14 25.3
31	16 20.6

Day	⚵
1	28♍28.3
6	29 01.6
11	29 25.2
16	29 38.6
21	29 41.5R
26	29 33.6R
31	29 14.9R

Day	⚶
1	15♐21.5
6	18 00.6
11	20 38.9
16	23 16.3
21	25 52.8
26	28 28.2
31	1♑02.5

DECLINATION and LATITUDE

Day	☉ Decl	☽ Decl	☽ Lat	☽ 12h Decl	☿ Decl	☿ Lat	♀ Decl	♀ Lat	♂ Decl	♂ Lat	⚳ Decl	⚳ Lat	♃ Decl	♃ Lat	♄ Decl	♄ Lat
1 Sa	23S03	22S50	2S55	23S39	20S13	2N50	15S16	3N30	23S10	0S59	25S57	5S43	2S32	1S16	4S19	2N25
2 Su	22 58	24 07	1 49	24 14	20 21	2 44	15 30	3 30	23 03	0 60	25 53	5 44	2 29	1 16	4 20	2 25
3 M	22 52	24 01	0 38	23 27	20 30	2 37	15 43	3 31	22 57	0 60	25 48	5 45	2 25	1 16	4 21	2 25
4 Tu	22 47	22 35	0N33	21 26	20 39	2 29	15 57	3 31	22 50	1 00	25 44	5 45	2 22	1 15	4 21	2 25
5 W	22 40	20 02	1 42	18 24	20 50	2 21	16 10	3 31	22 43	1 00	25 40	5 46	2 18	1 15	4 22	2 26
6 Th	22 34	16 34	2 45	14 35	21 01	2 13	16 24	3 31	22 36	1 01	25 35	5 47	2 14	1 15	4 23	2 26
7 F	22 26	12 27	3 38	10 13	21 12	2 04	16 37	3 30	22 28	1 01	25 30	5 48	2 11	1 15	4 23	2 26
8 Sa	22 19	7 54	4 21	5 32	21 23	1 55	16 50	3 30	22 21	1 01	25 26	5 48	2 07	1 14	4 24	2 26
9 Su	22 11	3 07	4 52	0 41	21 35	1 46	17 03	3 29	22 13	1 01	25 21	5 49	2 03	1 14	4 24	2 27
10 M	22 02	1N44	5 10	4N08	21 46	1 37	17 16	3 28	22 04	1 02	25 16	5 50	1 59	1 14	4 25	2 27
11 Tu	21 53	6 30	5 15	8 49	21 57	1 28	17 28	3 27	21 56	1 02	25 12	5 51	1 55	1 14	4 25	2 27
12 W	21 44	11 04	5 07	13 13	22 07	1 19	17 41	3 26	21 47	1 02	25 07	5 51	1 51	1 14	4 25	2 28
13 Th	21 34	15 15	4 45	17 09	22 17	1 10	17 53	3 25	21 38	1 02	25 02	5 52	1 47	1 13	4 26	2 28
14 F	21 24	18 53	4 09	20 25	22 26	1 00	18 05	3 23	21 29	1 02	24 57	5 53	1 43	1 13	4 26	2 28
15 Sa	21 13	21 45	3 22	22 49	22 34	0 51	18 17	3 22	21 19	1 03	24 52	5 54	1 39	1 13	4 26	2 28
16 Su	21 02	23 36	2 23	24 05	22 42	0 43	18 28	3 20	21 10	1 03	24 47	5 55	1 35	1 13	4 26	2 29
17 M	20 51	24 13	1 15	24 00	22 48	0 34	18 39	3 19	20 60	1 03	24 42	5 56	1 31	1 13	4 26	2 29
18 Tu	20 39	23 25	0 00	22 28	22 54	0 25	18 50	3 17	20 49	1 03	24 37	5 56	1 26	1 12	4 27	2 29
19 W	20 27	21 09	1S16	19 29	22 59	0 17	19 01	3 15	20 39	1 03	24 32	5 57	1 22	1 12	4 27	2 30
20 Th	20 14	17 30	2 29	15 14	23 03	0 08	19 11	3 12	20 28	1 03	24 26	5 58	1 18	1 12	4 27	2 30
21 F	20 02	12 43	3 34	10 01	23 05	0 00	19 21	3 10	20 18	1 03	24 21	5 59	1 13	1 12	4 27	2 30
22 Sa	19 48	7 09	4 25	4 12	23 07	0S08	19 30	3 08	20 06	1 04	24 16	6 00	1 09	1 12	4 27	2 30
23 Su	19 34	1 12	4 59	1S49	23 07	0 16	19 40	3 06	19 55	1 04	24 10	6 01	1 04	1 12	4 26	2 31
24 M	19 20	4S46	5 12	7 39	23 07	0 23	19 48	3 03	19 44	1 04	24 05	6 02	0 60	1 11	4 26	2 31
25 Tu	19 06	10 24	5 05	12 59	23 05	0 31	19 57	3 00	19 32	1 04	23 59	6 03	0 55	1 11	4 26	2 31
26 W	18 51	15 21	4 40	17 30	23 02	0 38	20 05	2 58	19 20	1 04	23 54	6 04	0 51	1 11	4 26	2 31
27 Th	18 36	19 23	3 59	20 59	22 58	0 45	20 12	2 55	19 08	1 04	23 48	6 05	0 46	1 11	4 26	2 32
28 F	18 21	22 16	3 05	23 14	22 52	0 52	20 20	2 52	18 55	1 04	23 43	6 06	0 41	1 11	4 25	2 32
29 Sa	18 05	23 52	2 02	24 10	22 45	0 58	20 26	2 49	18 42	1 04	23 37	6 07	0 37	1 11	4 25	2 32
30 Su	17 49	24 07	0 54	23 45	22 37	1 04	20 33	2 46	18 30	1 04	23 32	6 07	0 32	1 10	4 25	2 33
31 M	17S32	23S04	0N16	22S06	22S28	1S10	20S38	2N43	18S17	1S04	23S26	6S08	0S27	1S10	4S24	2N33

Day	⚷ Decl	⚷ Lat	♅ Decl	♅ Lat	♆ Decl	♆ Lat	♇ Decl	♇ Lat
1	6S54	5N45	1S53	0S44	13S03	0S29	18S50	4N30
6	6 50	5 43	1 50	0 44	13 00	0 29	18 50	4 30
11	6 45	5 42	1 47	0 44	12 57	0 29	18 49	4 30
16	6 40	5 41	1 43	0 44	12 54	0 29	18 49	4 29
21	6 35	5 40	1 38	0 43	12 50	0 29	18 49	4 29
26	6 30	5 39	1 34	0 43	12 47	0 29	18 49	4 29
31	6S24	5N38	1S29	0S43	12S43	0S29	18S49	4N29

Day	⚴ Decl	⚴ Lat	⚵ Decl	⚵ Lat	⚶ Decl	⚶ Lat	Eris Decl	Eris Lat
1	3N22	26N45	2S42	3S37	19S22	3N17	4S18	13S31
6	3 27	26 45	2 45	3 25	19 43	3 12	4 17	13 30
11	3 34	26 47	2 42	3 12	20 00	3 07	4 16	13 29
16	3 44	26 50	2 35	2 59	20 15	3 01	4 15	13 28
21	3 57	26 54	2 23	2 44	20 27	2 56	4 14	13 28
26	4 12	26 59	2 06	2 29	20 36	2 50	4 13	13 27
31	4N29	27N06	1S43	2S12	20S42	2N44	4S12	13S26

Moon Phenomena

Max/0 Decl

dy	hr mn	
2	10:04	24S14
9	15:25	0 N
16	22:57	24N13
23	4:46	0 S
29	16:30	24S11

Max/0 Lat

dy	hr mn	
3	12:48	0 N
10	20:40	5N15
18	0:07	0 S
24	3:44	5S12
30	18:30	0 N

Perigee/Apogee

dy	hr m		kilometers
10	5:33	a	404975
22	0:11	p	362792

PH	dy	hr mn	
●	4	9:04	13♑39
●	4	8:52	P 0.858
☽	12	11:33	21♈54
○	19	21:22	29♋27
☾	26	12:58	6♏13

Void of Course Moon

Last Aspect				☽ Ingress		
31	19:58	♅	△	♐	1	1:22
3	2:09	♅	□	♑	3	7:40
5	12:16	♀	✶	♒	5	16:09
7	20:52	♆	☌	♓	8	2:58
10	11:13	♃	☌	♈	10	15:25
13	2:48	☿	△	♉	13	3:38
15	12:48	♂	△	♊	15	13:24
17	17:58	♃	□	♋	17	19:30
19	21:27	♃	△	♌	19	22:17
21	18:59	♆	☍	♍	21	23:11
23	20:09	♅	☍	♎	23	24:00
25	22:05	♆	△	♏	26	2:17
28	3:02	♅	△	♐	28	6:56
30	10:12	♅	□	♑	30	14:05

DAILY ASPECTARIAN

1 Sa
☉∥☽ 2:32
☽∥♂ 3:58
☽∠♄ 4:20
☽∠♂ 7:49
☽⊻♇ 10:54
☉⊻☽ 21:14

2 Su
☽∠⚳ 3:13
☽✶♄ 7:23
☽⊻♂ 12:31
☉∠♆ 13:07
☽☌☿ 14:03
♃⊻♆ 16:52
☽⊻♀ 23:21

3 M
☽✶♆ 1:46
☽□♃ 1:50
☽□♅ 2:09
☽✶⚷ 3:29
☽⊻⚳ 7:27
☉∠⚷ 11:58
⚳ ♒ 14:43
☽☌♇ 17:43
☽∥♂ 20:47
☉∥☽ 21:36

4 Tu
☽∠♀ 5:25
☽∠♆ 5:39
☽∠⚷ 7:28
♀□♆ 8:29
☉☌☽ 9:04
♃☌♅ 12:54
♀△♅ 13:35
♀△♃ 13:40
☽□♄ 15:01
☽∥☿ 17:50
☽☌♂ 23:50

5 W
☽⊻☿ 0:27
☽∥♇ 9:00
♀□⚷ 9:08
☽⊻♆ 10:08
☽✶♅ 10:31
☽✶♃ 10:43
☽⊻⚷ 12:02
☽✶♀ 12:16
☽☌⚳ 17:45

6 Th
☽∥♀ 1:02
☽⊻♇ 2:47
☽∠☿ 7:06
☽∠♅ 15:36
☽∠♃ 16:06
☽∥♆ 20:59
☉⊻☽ 23:52

7 F
☽△♄ 1:00
☽∠♇ 8:13
♀ ♐ 12:32
☽⊻♂ 14:00
☉□♄ 14:01
☽✶☿ 14:45
☽☌♆ 20:52
☽⊻♅ 21:15
☽⊻♃ 22:03
☽☌⚷ 22:58

8 Sa
☽□♀ 4:18
☽∥⚷ 5:36
☽⊻⚳ 6:36
☽⚼♄ 6:50
☉∠☽ 8:21
☽✶♇ 14:10
☽∥♄ 17:38
☽∠♂ 22:02

9 Su
☽∥♃ 5:22
☽∥♅ 6:32
♀∠♄ 11:06
☽⊼♄ 13:04
☽∠⚳ 13:47
☉✶☽ 17:21
♀✶⚳ 23:00

10 M
☽#♅ 0:16
☽#♃ 1:14
☽✶♂ 6:27
☽□☿ 8:21
☽⊻♆ 9:22
☽☌♅ 9:45
☽☌♃ 11:13
☽⊻⚷ 11:38
☽#♄ 13:23
☉∥☿ 20:01
☿✶♆ 20:04
☽✶⚳ 21:10
☽△♀ 22:28
☿∥♂ 23:06

11 Tu
☿□♅ 0:14
☽#⚷ 1:16
☽□♇ 2:56
☽∠♆ 15:47
☽∠⚷ 18:06
☿□♃ 20:38
☿✶⚷ 22:09

12 W
☽☍♄ 1:49
♂⊻♆ 4:49
☽⚼♀ 7:34
☽#♆ 10:25
♂✶♅ 10:31
☉□☽ 11:33
♃⊻⚷ 12:27
☽✶♆ 21:53
☽⊻♅ 22:14
☽□♂ 23:01

13 Th
☽✶⚷ 0:14
☽⊻♃ 0:20
☽△☿ 2:48
♀⊻♇ 2:55
☽□⚳ 11:15
☿ ♑ 11:26
☽△♇ 15:01
♃∥♅ 15:23
☽⊼♀ 16:06
☽#♀ 17:59
♂⊻⚷ 19:25
☽#♇ 23:36

14 F
♂✶♃ 0:36
☽∠♅ 3:45
☽∠♃ 6:07
☽⚼☿ 11:12
☽⊼♄ 12:59
☉#☽ 19:21
☽⚼♇ 20:05
☽#♂ 20:11

15 Sa
☉△☽ 3:17
☽□♆ 8:07
☽✶♅ 8:27
☽#☿ 9:35
☽□⚷ 10:27
☽✶♃ 11:02
☽△♂ 12:48
☽⚼♄ 17:21
☽⊼☿ 18:35
☽△⚳ 22:22
♂ ♒ 22:42

16 Su
☽⊼♇ 0:16
☽☍♀ 6:09
☉⚼☽ 9:29
☽⚼♂ 18:03
☽△♄ 20:47

17 M
☽⚼⚳ 2:24
☉⊼☽ 14:28
☽△♆ 14:42
☽□♅ 15:00
☽△⚷ 16:59
☉⊻♆ 17:40
☽□♃ 17:58
☉✶♅ 21:57
♀∥♇ 22:00
☽⊼♂ 22:11

18 Tu
☿⊻⚳ 0:41
☽⊼⚳ 5:26
☽☍☿ 5:46
☽☍♇ 5:47
☿☌♇ 5:52
☽#☿ 6:44
☽⊼♀ 15:30
☽⚼♆ 16:38
☽⚼⚷ 18:55
⚳⊻♇ 18:56

19 W
☽□♄ 0:55
☉⊻⚷ 2:29
☽#♂ 4:01
☉#☽ 5:38
☽#♀ 14:19
☽#♇ 16:11
☽⊼♆ 17:52
☽△♅ 18:09
☽⚼♀ 18:43
☽⊼⚷ 20:08
⚵ R 20:42
☉☍☽ 21:22
☽△♃ 21:27
☉✶♃ 22:40

20 Th
☽☍♂ 3:43
☽⊼♇ 8:10
☽☍⚳ 9:07
☉ ♒ 10:20
☽⊼☿ 13:04
☽⚼♅ 18:51
☽△♀ 21:18
☽⚼♃ 22:20
☽#♆ 23:26

21 F
☽✶♄ 2:27
☽⚼♇ 8:41
☽⚼☿ 15:56
☽☍♆ 18:59
☽⊼♅ 19:16
☽☍⚷ 21:17
☽⊼♃ 22:58

22 Sa
☉⊼☽ 1:54
☽#⚷ 2:25
☽∠♄ 2:46
☽⊼♂ 7:15
☽△♇ 9:02
☽#♄ 11:02
☽⊼⚳ 11:11
♃ ♈ 17:12
☉∥♀ 18:35
☽△☿ 18:44
☽#♅ 22:21

23 Su
☽#♃ 0:30
☿∠♆ 1:11
☽□♀ 1:48
☽⊻♄ 3:06
☉⚼☽ 4:01
☽∥♃ 8:57
☽⚼♂ 8:58
☽∥♅ 11:10
☽⚼⚳ 12:14
♀∥♂ 18:09
♂⊻♇ 18:17
♀✶♄ 19:20
☽⊼♆ 19:51
☽☍♅ 20:09
☽⊼⚷ 22:17
☽∥♄ 22:38

24 M
☽☍♃ 0:23
☿∠⚷ 3:13
☉△☽ 6:26
☽∥⚷ 7:16
☽□♇ 10:08
☽△♂ 11:00
☽△⚳ 13:36
☽⚼♆ 20:43
☽⚼⚷ 23:14

25 Tu
☽□☿ 1:20
☽☌♄ 4:37
☽✶♀ 7:23
☽∥♆ 11:05
☽△♆ 22:05
☽⊼♅ 22:25

26 W
☽△⚷ 0:43
☽⊼♃ 3:21
☉∥♇ 3:50
♄ R 6:11
☿□♄ 9:59
☽∠♀ 11:08
☉⊻♇ 12:56
☽✶♇ 12:58
☉□☽ 12:58
☽□♂ 16:49
☽□⚳ 17:58
☉∥☽ 19:07
☽∥♇ 20:09
☽∥♂ 22:19

27 Th
☽⚼♅ 0:24
☽⚼♃ 5:45
☽∥♀ 6:07
☽⊻♄ 8:12
☽✶☿ 10:51
☽∠♇ 15:18
☽⊻♀ 15:42

28 F
☽□♆ 2:40
☽△♅ 3:02
☽□⚷ 5:33
☽∥☿ 6:32
♂☌⚳ 8:30
☽△♃ 8:49
☽∠♄ 10:56
♂∥♇ 12:16
☽∠☿ 17:00
☽⊻♇ 18:17
☽∥⚳ 18:55
☉✶☽ 22:36
⚶ ♑ 23:17

29 Sa
☽✶⚳ 1:03
☽✶♂ 1:35
☽✶♄ 14:18

30 Su
☽⊻☿ 0:04
☽☌♀ 3:19
☉∠☽ 4:35
☽∠⚳ 5:37
☽∠♂ 7:05
☽✶♆ 9:47
☽□♅ 10:12
☽✶⚷ 12:55
☽□♃ 16:54
☽∥⚳ 17:49

31 M
☉☌⚳ 1:08
☽☌♇ 2:03
☽∥☿ 8:36
☽⊻⚳ 10:46
☉⊻☽ 11:17
☽⊻♂ 13:14
☽∠♆ 14:12
☽∠⚷ 17:27
♀∠⚳ 18:45
☽□♄ 22:41

February 2011

LONGITUDE

Day	Sid.Time	☉	☽	☽ 12 hour	Mean☊	True☊	☿	♀	♂	⚳	♃	♄	⚷	♅	♆	♇
	h m s	° ' "	° ' "	° ' "	° '	° '	° '	° '	° '	° '	° '	° '	° '	° '	° '	° '
1 Tu	8 43 26	11♒45 42	17♑52 53	24♑07 21	0♑39.9	2♑19.8	25♑30.1	26♐19.8	12♒36.0	11♒10.2	1♈45.2	17♎11.8	29♒28.5	27♓59.5	27♒45.9	6♑23.1
2 W	8 47 23	12 46 37	0♒19 24	6♒29 09	0 36.7	2R 16.5	27 01.5	27 27.4	13 23.3	11 33.9	1 57.1	17R 11.2	29 32.5	28 02.1	27 48.1	6 24.9
3 Th	8 51 19	13 47 32	12 36 44	18 42 15	0 33.6	2 11.0	28 33.6	28 35.1	14 10.6	11 57.6	2 09.0	17 10.4	29 36.5	28 04.7	27 50.3	6 26.7
4 F	8 55 16	14 48 25	24 45 51	0♓47 39	0 30.4	2 03.7	0♒06.5	29 43.0	14 57.8	12 21.2	2 21.0	17 09.5	29 40.5	28 07.4	27 52.6	6 28.5
5 Sa	8 59 12	15 49 17	6♓47 48	12 46 31	0 27.2	1 55.1	1 40.1	0♑51.1	15 45.2	12 44.9	2 33.1	17 08.5	29 44.5	28 10.1	27 54.8	6 30.3
6 Su	9 03 09	16 50 08	18 43 59	24 40 28	0 24.0	1 46.0	3 14.4	1 59.3	16 32.5	13 08.6	2 45.3	17 07.4	29 48.5	28 12.9	27 57.0	6 32.0
7 M	9 07 05	17 50 58	0♈36 16	6♈31 42	0 20.8	1 37.4	4 49.5	3 07.7	17 19.8	13 32.2	2 57.6	17 06.2	29 52.6	28 15.7	27 59.3	6 33.8
8 Tu	9 11 02	18 51 46	12 27 09	18 23 04	0 17.7	1 29.9	6 25.3	4 16.2	18 07.1	13 55.8	3 09.9	17 04.9	29 56.6	28 18.5	28 01.5	6 35.5
9 W	9 14 58	19 52 32	24 19 55	0♉18 12	0 14.5	1 24.3	8 02.0	5 24.8	18 54.5	14 19.5	3 22.3	17 03.5	0♓00.7	28 21.3	28 03.8	6 37.2
10 Th	9 18 55	20 53 18	6♉18 28	12 21 20	0 11.3	1 20.9	9 39.4	6 33.6	19 41.8	14 43.1	3 34.9	17 02.0	0 04.7	28 24.2	28 06.1	6 38.9
11 F	9 22 52	21 54 02	18 27 21	24 37 11	0 08.1	1D 19.5	11 17.6	7 42.5	20 29.2	15 06.7	3 47.4	17 00.4	0 08.8	28 27.1	28 08.3	6 40.5
12 Sa	9 26 48	22 54 44	0♊51 27	7♊10 45	0 04.9	1 19.7	12 56.6	8 51.5	21 16.6	15 30.2	4 00.1	16 58.7	0 12.9	28 30.0	28 10.6	6 42.2
13 Su	9 30 45	23 55 24	13 35 39	20 06 43	0 01.8	1 20.8	14 36.4	10 00.7	22 03.9	15 53.8	4 12.8	16 56.9	0 17.0	28 32.9	28 12.9	6 43.8
14 M	9 34 41	24 56 03	26 44 24	3♋29 04	29♐58.6	1R 21.7	16 17.0	11 09.9	22 51.3	16 17.4	4 25.7	16 55.0	0 21.1	28 35.9	28 15.2	6 45.4
15 Tu	9 38 38	25 56 41	10♋20 56	17 20 06	29 55.4	1 21.4	17 58.5	12 19.3	23 38.7	16 40.9	4 38.5	16 53.0	0 25.2	28 38.9	28 17.4	6 46.9
16 W	9 42 34	26 57 16	24 26 29	1♌39 46	29 52.2	1 19.1	19 40.9	13 28.8	24 26.1	17 04.4	4 51.5	16 50.9	0 29.3	28 41.9	28 19.7	6 48.5
17 Th	9 46 31	27 57 50	8♌59 26	16 24 46	29 49.1	1 14.5	21 24.1	14 38.4	25 13.5	17 27.9	5 04.5	16 48.7	0 33.4	28 45.0	28 22.0	6 50.0
18 F	9 50 27	28 58 23	23 54 48	1♍28 26	29 45.9	1 07.4	23 08.3	15 48.1	26 00.8	17 51.4	5 17.6	16 46.4	0 37.5	28 48.0	28 24.3	6 51.5
19 Sa	9 54 24	29 58 53	9♍04 22	16 41 15	29 42.7	0 58.7	24 53.6	16 58.0	26 48.2	18 14.8	5 30.7	16 44.0	0 41.6	28 51.1	28 26.6	6 53.0
20 Su	9 58 21	0♓59 23	24 17 41	1♎52 21	29 39.5	0 49.2	26 39.3	18 07.9	27 35.6	18 38.3	5 43.9	16 41.5	0 45.7	28 54.2	28 28.8	6 54.4
21 M	10 02 17	1 59 50	9♎23 58	16 51 27	29 36.4	0 40.3	28 26.1	19 17.9	28 23.0	19 01.7	5 57.1	16 39.0	0 49.7	28 57.3	28 31.1	6 55.8
22 Tu	10 06 14	3 00 17	24 13 55	1♏30 38	29 33.2	0 33.0	0♓13.9	20 28.0	29 10.4	19 25.1	6 10.5	16 36.3	0 53.8	29 00.5	28 33.4	6 57.2
23 W	10 10 10	4 00 42	8♏41 08	15 45 09	29 30.0	0 27.9	2 02.7	21 38.2	29 57.8	19 48.4	6 23.8	16 33.6	0 57.9	29 03.7	28 35.7	6 58.6
24 Th	10 14 07	5 01 06	22 42 36	29 33 34	29 26.8	0D 25.3	3 52.3	22 48.5	0♓45.2	20 11.8	6 37.3	16 30.8	1 02.0	29 06.9	28 37.9	7 00.0
25 F	10 18 03	6 01 28	6♐18 16	12♐57 02	29 23.6	0 24.6	5 42.8	23 58.9	1 32.6	20 35.1	6 50.7	16 27.9	1 06.1	29 10.1	28 40.2	7 01.3
26 Sa	10 22 00	7 01 49	19 30 15	25 58 22	29 20.5	0R 24.9	7 34.2	25 09.4	2 20.0	20 58.4	7 04.3	16 24.9	1 10.2	29 13.3	28 42.5	7 02.6
27 Su	10 25 56	8 02 09	2♑21 51	8♑41 12	29 17.3	0 25.2	9 26.5	26 20.0	3 07.4	21 21.7	7 17.9	16 21.8	1 14.3	29 16.5	28 44.7	7 03.9
28 M	10 29 53	9♓02 28	14 56 51	21 09 17	29♐14.1	0♑24.2	11♓19.5	27♑30.6	3♓54.8	21♒44.9	7♈31.5	16♎18.6	1♓18.4	29♓19.8	28♒47.0	7♑05.1

1st of Month

Julian Day # 2455593.5
Obliquity 23°26'16"
SVP 5♓05'59"
GC 26♐59.6
Eris 21♈12.1

Day	⚴	Day	⚵	Day	⚶
1	16♑43.5	1	29♍09.8R	1	1♑33.2
6	18 37.0	6	28 38.2R	6	4 05.8
11	20 28.6	11	27 56.4R	11	6 36.9
16	22 18.3	16	27 05.3R	16	9 06.3
21	24 05.8	21	26 06.0R	21	11 33.9
26	25 51.1	26	25 00.0R	26	13 59.6

DECLINATION and LATITUDE

Day	☉ Decl	☽ Decl	☽ Lat	☽ 12h Decl	☿ Decl	☿ Lat	♀ Decl	♀ Lat	♂ Decl	♂ Lat	⚳ Decl	⚳ Lat	♃ Decl	♃ Lat	♄ Decl	♄ Lat
1 Tu	17S16	20S52	1N23	19S23	22S17	1S16	20S44	2N40	18S03	1S05	23S20	6S09	0S22	1S10	4S24	2N33
2 W	16 58	17 42	2 26	15 50	22 05	1 22	20 48	2 36	17 50	1 05	23 14	6 10	0 18	1 10	4 23	2 33
3 Th	16 41	13 49	3 21	11 40	21 52	1 27	20 53	2 33	17 36	1 05	23 08	6 11	0 13	1 10	4 23	2 34
4 F	16 23	9 24	4 05	7 05	21 37	1 32	20 56	2 30	17 23	1 05	23 03	6 12	0 08	1 10	4 22	2 34
5 Sa	16 06	4 42	4 39	2 17	21 21	1 36	20 60	2 26	17 09	1 05	22 57	6 13	0 03	1 09	4 21	2 34
6 Su	15 47	0N08	4 60	2N33	21 04	1 41	21 03	2 23	16 54	1 05	22 51	6 15	0N02	1 09	4 21	2 35
7 M	15 29	4 56	5 07	7 17	20 45	1 45	21 05	2 19	16 40	1 05	22 45	6 16	0 07	1 09	4 20	2 35
8 Tu	15 10	9 33	5 02	11 44	20 25	1 48	21 06	2 16	16 26	1 05	22 39	6 17	0 12	1 09	4 19	2 35
9 W	14 51	13 49	4 43	15 47	20 03	1 52	21 08	2 12	16 11	1 05	22 33	6 18	0 17	1 09	4 18	2 35
10 Th	14 32	17 35	4 12	19 14	19 41	1 55	21 08	2 08	15 56	1 05	22 27	6 19	0 22	1 09	4 18	2 36
11 F	14 12	20 41	3 30	21 54	19 16	1 58	21 08	2 05	15 41	1 05	22 21	6 20	0 27	1 09	4 17	2 36
12 Sa	13 53	22 53	2 36	23 35	18 51	1 60	21 08	2 01	15 26	1 05	22 15	6 21	0 33	1 08	4 16	2 36
13 Su	13 33	23 59	1 34	24 04	18 24	2 02	21 07	1 57	15 11	1 05	22 08	6 22	0 38	1 08	4 15	2 36
14 M	13 13	23 49	0 25	23 12	17 55	2 04	21 05	1 53	14 55	1 05	22 02	6 23	0 43	1 08	4 14	2 37
15 Tu	12 52	22 14	0S48	20 55	17 25	2 05	21 03	1 50	14 39	1 05	21 56	6 24	0 48	1 08	4 13	2 37
16 W	12 32	19 15	2 00	17 16	16 54	2 06	21 00	1 46	14 24	1 05	21 50	6 25	0 53	1 08	4 12	2 37
17 Th	12 11	14 60	3 07	12 28	16 22	2 06	20 57	1 42	14 08	1 05	21 44	6 27	0 59	1 08	4 11	2 37
18 F	11 50	9 44	4 03	6 49	15 47	2 06	20 53	1 38	13 52	1 05	21 37	6 28	1 04	1 08	4 10	2 38
19 Sa	11 29	3 48	4 42	0 44	15 12	2 06	20 49	1 34	13 35	1 05	21 31	6 29	1 09	1 08	4 09	2 38
20 Su	11 07	2S21	5 02	5S23	14 35	2 05	20 43	1 30	13 19	1 05	21 25	6 30	1 15	1 08	4 08	2 38
21 M	10 46	8 20	5 00	11 07	13 57	2 04	20 38	1 26	13 02	1 04	21 18	6 31	1 20	1 07	4 06	2 38
22 Tu	10 24	13 43	4 39	16 04	13 17	2 02	20 32	1 22	12 46	1 04	21 12	6 33	1 25	1 07	4 05	2 39
23 W	10 02	18 10	3 59	19 58	12 36	1 60	20 25	1 18	12 29	1 04	21 06	6 34	1 31	1 07	4 04	2 39
24 Th	9 40	21 27	3 07	22 36	11 54	1 57	20 17	1 14	12 12	1 04	20 59	6 35	1 36	1 07	4 03	2 39
25 F	9 18	23 24	2 05	23 52	11 11	1 54	20 10	1 10	11 55	1 04	20 53	6 36	1 41	1 07	4 01	2 39
26 Sa	8 56	23 59	0 58	23 46	10 26	1 50	20 01	1 06	11 38	1 04	20 46	6 38	1 47	1 07	3 60	2 39
27 Su	8 33	23 15	0N10	22 25	9 39	1 45	19 52	1 02	11 21	1 04	20 40	6 39	1 52	1 07	3 59	2 40
28 M	8S11	21S20	1N16	19S60	8S52	1S40	19S42	0N58	11S04	1S04	20S33	6S40	1N58	1S07	3S57	2N40

Day	⚷ Decl	⚷ Lat	♅ Decl	♅ Lat	♆ Decl	♆ Lat	♇ Decl	♇ Lat
1	6S23	5N38	1S28	0S43	12S42	0S29	18S48	4N29
6	6 16	5 37	1 22	0 43	12 38	0 29	18 48	4 29
11	6 10	5 37	1 16	0 43	12 34	0 29	18 48	4 29
16	6 03	5 36	1 10	0 43	12 31	0 29	18 47	4 29
21	5 56	5 36	1 04	0 43	12 27	0 29	18 47	4 29
26	5S49	5N36	0S58	0S43	12S23	0S29	18S46	4N29

Day	⚴ Decl	⚴ Lat	⚵ Decl	⚵ Lat	⚶ Decl	⚶ Lat	Eris Decl	Eris Lat
1	4N32	27N07	1S38	2S09	20S42	2N43	4S12	13S26
6	4 52	27 15	1 09	1 51	20 45	2 37	4 10	13 25
11	5 14	27 23	0 36	1 32	20 45	2 31	4 09	13 24
16	5 38	27 33	0N03	1 13	20 43	2 25	4 08	13 23
21	6 04	27 45	0 45	0 52	20 38	2 18	4 06	13 23
26	6N32	27N57	1N30	0S31	20S32	2N11	4S05	13S22

Moon Phenomena

Max/0 Decl
dy hr mn
5 23:19 0 N
13 8:57 24N05
19 14:49 0 S
25 22:20 23S59

Perigee/Apogee
dy hr m kilometers
6 23:16 a 405924
19 7:19 p 358251

PH dy hr mn
● 3 2:32 13♒54
☽ 11 7:19 22♉13
○ 18 8:37 29♌20
☾ 24 23:27 6♐00

Max/0 Lat
dy hr mn
7 1:59 5N07
14 8:14 0 S
20 10:11 5S04
26 20:20 0 N

Void of Course Moon

Last Aspect	☽ Ingress
1 19:33 ♅ ✶	♒ 1 23:22
4 6:12 ♆ ☌	♓ 4 10:25
6 19:14 ♅ ☌	♈ 6 22:47
9 7:32 ♆ ✶	♉ 9 11:24
11 19:28 ♅ ✶	♊ 11 22:22
14 3:20 ♅ □	♋ 14 5:50
16 7:07 ♅ △	♌ 16 9:15
18 8:37 ☉ ☍	♍ 18 9:40
20 7:19 ♅ ☍	♎ 20 9:02
22 8:36 ♂ △	♏ 22 9:30
24 11:16 ♅ △	♐ 24 12:47
26 18:10 ♅ □	♑ 26 19:33

DAILY ASPECTARIAN

1 Tu
☽∥♀ 1:11
♂∠♅ 12:36
☽∥♇ 16:19
☽☌☿ 16:43
☽⚺♀ 17:53
☽⚺♆ 19:06
☽✶♅ 19:33
☽⚺⚷ 22:29
☽∥♂ 23:04

2 W
☽✶♃ 3:13
☉∥☽ 5:13
☉∠♅ 6:22
♀✶♆ 7:36
☽⚺♇ 11:53
☿⚺♆ 12:28
♀□♅ 12:48
☿✶♅ 16:16
☽☌⚳ 22:41

3 Th
☽∠♅ 0:55
☿⚺♀ 1:28
☽∠♀ 2:06
☉☌☽ 2:32
☽☌♂ 3:17
☽∥♆ 6:25
☽△♄ 8:58
☽∠♃ 9:05
☿⚺⚷ 17:00
☽∠♇ 17:28
☿ ♒ 22:20
♀✶⚷ 23:03

4 F
♀ ♑ 5:59
☽☌♆ 6:12
☽⚺♅ 6:42
☽☌⚷ 9:49
☽✶♀ 10:53
☽⚺☿ 12:13
☽⚼♄ 14:42
☽⚺♃ 15:22
☽∥⚷ 15:57
☉☌♂ 16:41
♀∠♂ 17:08
☉∠♀ 18:00
☽✶♇ 23:25

5 Sa
☽∥♄ 1:42
☽⚺⚳ 12:21
☿✶♃ 15:31
☽∥♅ 16:31
☽⚺♂ 19:16
☉⚺☽ 19:49
☽⚻♄ 20:46
☽∠☿ 22:51
☽⋕♃ 23:09
☽∥♃ 23:28

6 Su
☿∥♀ 1:24
⚳∠♅ 4:59
☽⋕♅ 6:04
☉△♄ 6:41
♂△♄ 17:17
☽⚺♆ 18:41
☽☌♅ 19:14
☽∠⚳ 19:40
♀□♃ 19:40
☽⋕♄ 20:56
☽⚺⚷ 22:31

7 M
☉∠♃ 3:16
☽∠♂ 3:45
☽☌♃ 4:51
☉∠☽ 4:58
☽□♀ 5:39
☽⋕⚷ 6:40
☽✶☿ 9:53
☽□♇ 12:06

8 Tu
☽∠♆ 1:10
♂∠♃ 1:54
☿⚺♇ 2:35
☽✶⚳ 3:06
☽∠⚷ 5:04
☽☍♄ 9:21
☽✶♂ 12:17
☉✶☽ 14:11
☽⋕♆ 16:55
⚷ ♓ 20:01

9 W
☉⋕☽ 5:45
☽✶♆ 7:32
☽⚺♅ 8:07
☽✶⚷ 11:29
☽⋕♂ 13:41
☽⚺♃ 18:28

10 Th
☽△♀ 0:33
☽△♇ 0:41
♀☌♇ 1:53
☽□☿ 7:42
☽⋕♇ 8:41
☽⋕☿ 13:42
☽∠♅ 14:07
☽□⚳ 17:13
☉∠♇ 18:31
☽⚻♄ 21:10

11 F
☽∠♃ 0:40
☽□♂ 4:14
☽⋕♀ 4:16
☽⚼♇ 6:18
☉□☽ 7:19
☽⚼♀ 9:09
☽⋕⚳ 16:14
☽□♆ 18:51
☽✶♅ 19:28
☽□⚷ 22:46

12 Sa
☽⚼♄ 2:08
☿∥♇ 2:47
☽✶♃ 6:05
☿∠♅ 8:18
☽⚻♇ 11:07
♂∠♇ 13:26
☽⚻♀ 16:40

13 Su
☽△☿ 2:09
☽△⚳ 4:24
☽△♄ 6:11
☽△♂ 16:33
☉△☽ 20:29

14 M
☿☌⚳ 0:06
☽△♆ 2:43
☽□♅ 3:20
☽△⚷ 6:29
☽⚼⚳ 8:22
☿△♄ 8:49
☽⚼☿ 9:16
☽□♃ 13:53
☽☍♇ 17:47
☽⚼♂ 20:52

15 Tu
☉⚼☽ 1:07
☽⋕⚳ 3:10
☽☍♀ 3:43
☽⚼♆ 5:05
☽⚼⚷ 8:46
☽⋕♀ 11:03
☽⚻⚳ 11:12
☽□♄ 11:12
⚳△♄ 11:19
☽⚻☿ 14:53
♀∠♆ 20:45
☽⚻♂ 23:59

16 W
☉∥♆ 1:14
☿∠♃ 2:50
☽⋕♇ 2:59
☉⚻☽ 4:31
☽⚻♆ 6:30
☽△♅ 7:07
☽⚻⚷ 10:06
☽⋕☿ 16:00
☽△♃ 17:31
☽⚻♇ 20:29

17 Th
☽⋕♂ 4:29
☿∠♇ 6:04
☽⚼♅ 7:44
☽⚻♀ 9:55
☉☌♆ 9:57
☽⋕♆ 11:53
☽✶♄ 12:36
☽☍⚳ 14:03
☉⋕☽ 14:13
☽⚼♃ 18:08
☉⚺♅ 19:41
♀∠⚷ 20:06
☽⚼♇ 20:43
☽☍☿ 22:36

18 F
☽☍♂ 3:32
☽☍♆ 7:09
☽⚻♅ 7:47
☉☍☽ 8:37
☽☍⚷ 10:42
☽⚼♀ 11:51
☽∠♄ 12:26
♃⋕♅ 14:10
☽⋕⚷ 15:20
☽⚻♃ 18:18
♀□♄ 19:22
☽△♇ 20:32
☽⋕♄ 22:39

19 Sa
☉ ♓ 0:26
☽∥♃ 10:12
☽⋕♅ 10:33
☽⚺♄ 12:02
☽△♀ 13:28
☽⚻⚳ 14:50
☉☌⚷ 18:09
☽∥♅ 19:04
☽⋕♃ 19:36

20 Su
☽⚻☿ 4:14
☽⚻♂ 5:30
☽⚻♆ 6:38
☽∥♄ 6:57
☽☍♅ 7:19
☽⚻⚷ 10:17
☉⚻☽ 11:21
☽∥⚷ 14:15
☽⚼⚳ 15:12
♀⚺⚳ 15:40
☉⚼♄ 16:04
☽☍♃ 18:25
☽□♇ 20:03
☿☌♂ 22:45

21 M
☿☌♆ 1:08
♂☌♆ 4:18
☽⚼♆ 6:38
☽⚼♂ 6:45
☿⚺♅ 7:11
☽⚼☿ 7:22
☉∥☽ 9:49
☽⚼⚷ 10:23
☽☌♄ 11:38
☉⚼☽ 13:07
☽△⚳ 15:56
☽□♀ 17:20
☽∥♆ 18:00
♂⚺♅ 18:38
☽∥♂ 19:45
☿ ♓ 20:54
☽∥☿ 22:14

22 Tu
☽△♆ 7:08
☽⚻♅ 7:53
☽△♂ 8:36
☿☌⚷ 9:11
☽△⚷ 11:02
☽△☿ 11:18
☉△☽ 15:35
☿⚼♄ 17:46
☽⚻♃ 20:06
☽✶♇ 21:07

23 W
♂ ♓ 1:07
☽∥♇ 3:50
♂∥♆ 6:07
☿∥♆ 6:38
☿∥♂ 6:58
☽⚼♅ 9:09
☽⚺♄ 13:20
☽∥♀ 14:46
☽□⚳ 19:31
☽∥⚳ 20:04
☽⚼♃ 22:05
☽∠♇ 22:46

24 Th
☽✶♀ 0:11
♂☌⚷ 9:20
☽□♆ 10:24
☽△♅ 11:16
☽□⚷ 14:41
☽□♂ 14:59
☽∠♄ 15:24
♂⚼♄ 21:45
☽□☿ 22:46
☉□☽ 23:27

25 F
☽△♃ 0:59
☽⚺♇ 1:17
☽∠♀ 5:17
☉☌☿ 8:49
☿⚺♃ 16:41
☿✶♇ 17:07
☽✶♄ 18:21
♃□♇ 20:41

26 Sa
☉✶♇ 0:19
☉⚺♃ 1:16
☽✶⚳ 2:48
☽⚺♀ 11:32
☽✶♆ 17:10
☽□♅ 18:10
☽✶⚷ 21:52

27 Su
☽✶♂ 1:32
☽∠⚳ 7:49
☽☌♇ 8:55
☽□♃ 9:32
☉✶☽ 11:42
☽✶☿ 15:49
☽∠♆ 21:45

28 M
♄⚼⚷ 0:53
☽□♄ 2:37
☽∠⚷ 2:38
☽∥⚳ 7:32
☽∠♂ 8:10
☽⚺⚳ 13:35
☽∥♀ 15:15
☉∠☽ 19:11
☽∥♇ 21:37
⚳∠♇ 22:01

LONGITUDE

March 2011

Day	Sid.Time	☉	☽	☽ 12 hour	Mean☊	True☊	☿	♀	♂	⚳	♃	♄	⚷	♅	♆	♇
	h m s	° ' "	° ' "	° ' "	° '	° '	° '	° '	° '	° '	° '	° '	° '	° '	° '	° '
1 Tu	10 33 50	10♓02 44	27♑18 53	3♒26 02	29♐10.9	0♑21.0	13♓13.3	28♑41.3	4♓42.1	22♒08.1	7♈45.2	16♎15.4	1♓22.4	29♓23.1	28♒49.2	7♑06.3
2 W	10 37 46	11 02 59	9♒31 05	15 34 19	29 07.8	0R 14.9	15 07.7	29 52.1	5 29.5	22 31.3	7 58.9	16R 12.1	1 26.5	29 26.4	28 51.5	7 07.5
3 Th	10 41 43	12 03 13	21 36 00	27 36 21	29 04.6	0 05.9	17 02.7	1♒03.0	6 16.9	22 54.5	8 12.7	16 08.7	1 30.5	29 29.7	28 53.7	7 08.7
4 F	10 45 39	13 03 25	3♓35 34	9♓33 50	29 01.4	29♐54.2	18 58.1	2 13.9	7 04.2	23 17.6	8 26.6	16 05.2	1 34.6	29 33.0	28 56.0	7 09.8
5 Sa	10 49 36	14 03 35	15 31 16	21 28 04	28 58.2	29 40.6	20 53.8	3 24.9	7 51.6	23 40.7	8 40.4	16 01.7	1 38.6	29 36.3	28 58.2	7 10.9
6 Su	10 53 32	15 03 43	27 24 20	3♈20 17	28 55.0	29 26.3	22 49.6	4 36.0	8 38.9	24 03.7	8 54.3	15 58.1	1 42.6	29 39.6	29 00.4	7 12.0
7 M	10 57 29	16 03 49	9♈16 04	15 11 54	28 51.9	29 12.3	24 45.3	5 47.1	9 26.3	24 26.7	9 08.3	15 54.4	1 46.6	29 43.0	29 02.6	7 13.0
8 Tu	11 01 25	17 03 53	21 08 03	27 04 46	28 48.7	28 59.9	26 40.7	6 58.2	10 13.6	24 49.7	9 22.3	15 50.7	1 50.6	29 46.3	29 04.8	7 14.0
9 W	11 05 22	18 03 56	3♉02 24	9♉01 20	28 45.5	28 49.9	28 35.5	8 09.4	11 00.9	25 12.6	9 36.3	15 46.9	1 54.6	29 49.7	29 07.0	7 15.0
10 Th	11 09 18	19 03 56	15 01 59	21 04 48	28 42.3	28 42.7	0♈29.3	9 20.7	11 48.2	25 35.5	9 50.4	15 43.0	1 58.5	29 53.1	29 09.2	7 16.0
11 F	11 13 15	20 03 54	27 10 19	3♊19 04	28 39.2	28 38.5	2 21.8	10 32.0	12 35.4	25 58.4	10 04.5	15 39.1	2 02.5	29 56.5	29 11.3	7 16.9
12 Sa	11 17 12	21 03 50	9♊31 38	15 48 36	28 36.0	28D 36.6	4 12.7	11 43.4	13 22.7	26 21.2	10 18.6	15 35.1	2 06.4	29 59.9	29 13.5	7 17.8
13 Su	11 21 08	22 03 44	22 10 36	28 38 11	28 32.8	28R 36.3	6 01.4	12 54.8	14 10.0	26 44.0	10 32.7	15 31.0	2 10.3	0♈03.3	29 15.6	7 18.7
14 M	11 25 05	23 03 36	5♋11 56	11♋52 20	28 29.6	28 36.2	7 47.6	14 06.3	14 57.2	27 06.7	10 46.9	15 26.9	2 14.2	0 06.7	29 17.8	7 19.5
15 Tu	11 29 01	24 03 25	18 39 47	25 34 35	28 26.4	28 35.2	9 30.7	15 17.8	15 44.4	27 29.4	11 01.2	15 22.8	2 18.1	0 10.1	29 19.9	7 20.3
16 W	11 32 58	25 03 12	2♌36 53	9♌46 36	28 23.3	28 32.2	11 10.3	16 29.4	16 31.6	27 52.0	11 15.4	15 18.6	2 22.0	0 13.5	29 22.0	7 21.1
17 Th	11 36 54	26 02 57	17 03 30	24 27 04	28 20.1	28 26.6	12 45.9	17 41.0	17 18.7	28 14.6	11 29.7	15 14.4	2 25.8	0 16.9	29 24.1	7 21.9
18 F	11 40 51	27 02 40	1♍56 33	9♍30 59	28 16.9	28 18.3	14 17.0	18 52.6	18 05.9	28 37.1	11 43.9	15 10.1	2 29.6	0 20.4	29 26.2	7 22.6
19 Sa	11 44 47	28 02 20	17 09 09	24 49 41	28 13.7	28 07.9	15 43.1	20 04.3	18 53.0	28 59.6	11 58.3	15 05.8	2 33.4	0 23.8	29 28.2	7 23.3
20 Su	11 48 44	29 01 58	2♎31 06	10♎11 52	28 10.6	27 56.5	17 03.7	21 16.0	19 40.1	29 22.1	12 12.6	15 01.4	2 37.2	0 27.2	29 30.3	7 23.9
21 M	11 52 41	0♈01 35	17 50 29	25 25 35	28 07.4	27 45.5	18 18.5	22 27.8	20 27.2	29 44.4	12 26.9	14 57.0	2 40.9	0 30.6	29 32.3	7 24.5
22 Tu	11 56 37	1 01 09	2♏55 56	10♏20 32	28 04.2	27 36.2	19 27.1	23 39.6	21 14.3	0♓06.8	12 41.3	14 52.6	2 44.6	0 34.1	29 34.3	7 25.1
23 W	12 00 34	2 00 42	17 38 37	24 49 38	28 01.0	27 29.4	20 29.0	24 51.5	22 01.3	0 29.1	12 55.7	14 48.1	2 48.3	0 37.5	29 36.3	7 25.7
24 Th	12 04 30	3 00 13	1♐53 18	8♐49 33	27 57.8	27 25.3	21 24.0	26 03.4	22 48.3	0 51.3	13 10.1	14 43.6	2 52.0	0 40.9	29 38.3	7 26.2
25 F	12 08 27	3 59 42	15 38 30	22 20 24	27 54.7	27D 23.6	22 11.9	27 15.3	23 35.3	1 13.5	13 24.5	14 39.1	2 55.6	0 44.4	29 40.3	7 26.7
26 Sa	12 12 23	4 59 10	28 55 39	5♑24 42	27 51.5	27R 23.3	22 52.4	28 27.3	24 22.3	1 35.6	13 39.0	14 34.5	2 59.3	0 47.8	29 42.3	7 27.2
27 Su	12 16 20	5 58 36	11♑48 08	18 06 29	27 48.3	27 23.2	23 25.3	29 39.3	25 09.3	1 57.7	13 53.4	14 30.0	3 02.8	0 51.2	29 44.2	7 27.7
28 M	12 20 16	6 58 00	24 20 21	0♒30 19	27 45.1	27 22.2	23 50.7	0♓51.4	25 56.2	2 19.7	14 07.9	14 25.4	3 06.4	0 54.6	29 46.1	7 28.1
29 Tu	12 24 13	7 57 22	6♒36 56	12 40 45	27 42.0	27 19.2	24 08.5	2 03.4	26 43.1	2 41.7	14 22.4	14 20.7	3 09.9	0 58.0	29 48.0	7 28.4
30 W	12 28 10	8 56 43	18 42 16	24 41 57	27 38.8	27 13.4	24R 18.6	3 15.5	27 30.0	3 03.6	14 36.9	14 16.1	3 13.4	1 01.4	29 49.9	7 28.8
31 Th	12 32 06	9♈56 01	0♓40 11	6♓37 22	27♐35.6	27♐04.8	24♈21.3	4♓27.7	28♓16.9	3♓25.4	14♈51.4	14♎11.5	3♓16.9	1♈04.8	29♒51.8	7♑29.1

1st of Month

Julian Day # 2455621.5
Obliquity 23°26'17"
SVP 5♓05'55"
GC 26♐59.7
Eris 21♈22.8

Day	⚴	⚵	⚶
1	26♑53.1	24♍17.8R	15♑26.0
6	28 34.2	23 04.6R	17 48.2
11	0♒12.5	21 49.7R	20 07.8
16	1 47.7	20 35.1R	22 24.8
21	3 19.5	19 23.0R	24 38.9
26	4 47.7	18 15.2R	26 49.8
31	6 12.1	17 13.4R	28 57.4

DECLINATION and LATITUDE

Day	☉ Decl	☽ Decl	☽ Lat	☽12h Decl	☿ Decl	☿ Lat	♀ Decl	♀ Lat	♂ Decl	♂ Lat	⚳ Decl	⚳ Lat	♃ Decl	♃ Lat	♄ Decl	♄ Lat
1 Tu	7S48	18S27	2N18	16S42	8S03	1S35	19S32	0N54	10S46	1S04	20S27	6S41	2N03	1S07	3S56	2N40
2 W	7 25	14 47	3 12	12 44	7 14	1 29	19 21	0 50	10 29	1 03	20 20	6 43	2 09	1 07	3 54	2 40
3 Th	7 02	10 35	3 56	8 19	6 23	1 22	19 10	0 46	10 11	1 03	20 14	6 44	2 14	1 06	3 53	2 40
4 F	6 39	5 60	4 30	3 38	5 31	1 15	18 58	0 42	9 54	1 03	20 07	6 45	2 20	1 06	3 51	2 41
5 Sa	6 16	1 14	4 51	1N10	4 38	1 07	18 46	0 39	9 36	1 03	20 01	6 47	2 25	1 06	3 50	2 41
6 Su	5 53	3N33	4 60	5 54	3 45	0 59	18 33	0 35	9 18	1 03	19 54	6 48	2 31	1 06	3 48	2 41
7 M	5 30	8 12	4 56	10 25	2 51	0 50	18 20	0 31	8 60	1 03	19 48	6 50	2 37	1 06	3 47	2 41
8 Tu	5 06	12 33	4 38	14 33	1 56	0 40	18 06	0 27	8 42	1 03	19 41	6 51	2 42	1 06	3 45	2 41
9 W	4 43	16 25	4 09	18 08	1 01	0 30	17 51	0 23	8 24	1 02	19 35	6 52	2 48	1 06	3 43	2 42
10 Th	4 20	19 40	3 28	20 59	0 06	0 19	17 36	0 19	8 06	1 02	19 28	6 54	2 53	1 06	3 42	2 42
11 F	3 56	22 05	2 38	22 56	0N49	0 08	17 21	0 16	7 47	1 02	19 22	6 55	2 59	1 06	3 40	2 42
12 Sa	3 33	23 31	1 39	23 48	1 44	0N04	17 05	0 12	7 29	1 02	19 15	6 57	3 04	1 06	3 38	2 42
13 Su	3 09	23 46	0 34	23 26	2 38	0 16	16 48	0 08	7 11	1 02	19 08	6 58	3 10	1 06	3 37	2 42
14 M	2 45	22 45	0S35	21 45	3 31	0 28	16 31	0 05	6 52	1 01	19 02	6 60	3 16	1 06	3 35	2 42
15 Tu	2 22	20 25	1 44	18 47	4 24	0 41	16 14	0 01	6 34	1 01	18 55	7 01	3 21	1 06	3 33	2 42
16 W	1 58	16 50	2 49	14 36	5 14	0 54	15 56	0S02	6 15	1 01	18 49	7 03	3 27	1 05	3 32	2 43
17 Th	1 34	12 08	3 46	9 27	6 04	1 07	15 38	0 06	5 57	1 01	18 42	7 04	3 33	1 05	3 30	2 43
18 F	1 11	6 35	4 29	3 36	6 51	1 19	15 19	0 09	5 38	1 00	18 36	7 06	3 38	1 05	3 28	2 43
19 Sa	0 47	0 33	4 55	2S32	7 36	1 32	14 60	0 13	5 19	1 00	18 29	7 07	3 44	1 05	3 26	2 43
20 Su	0 23	5S34	4 59	8 32	8 19	1 45	14 40	0 16	5 00	0 60	18 22	7 09	3 49	1 05	3 25	2 43
21 M	0N01	11 20	4 42	13 57	8 59	1 57	14 20	0 20	4 42	0 60	18 16	7 10	3 55	1 05	3 23	2 43
22 Tu	0 24	16 20	4 05	18 25	9 36	2 09	13 60	0 23	4 23	0 59	18 09	7 12	4 01	1 05	3 21	2 43
23 W	0 48	20 11	3 13	21 36	10 10	2 20	13 39	0 26	4 04	0 59	18 03	7 14	4 06	1 05	3 19	2 43
24 Th	1 12	22 40	2 10	23 21	10 41	2 31	13 17	0 29	3 45	0 59	17 56	7 15	4 12	1 05	3 17	2 43
25 F	1 35	23 41	1 02	23 40	11 08	2 41	12 56	0 32	3 26	0 58	17 50	7 17	4 18	1 05	3 16	2 44
26 Sa	1 59	23 18	0N08	22 37	11 31	2 50	12 34	0 35	3 08	0 58	17 43	7 19	4 23	1 05	3 14	2 44
27 Su	2 22	21 40	1 15	20 26	11 51	2 58	12 11	0 38	2 49	0 58	17 37	7 20	4 29	1 05	3 12	2 44
28 M	2 46	18 60	2 17	17 21	12 07	3 05	11 49	0 41	2 30	0 58	17 30	7 22	4 35	1 05	3 10	2 44
29 Tu	3 09	15 32	3 11	13 34	12 19	3 11	11 26	0 44	2 11	0 57	17 24	7 24	4 40	1 05	3 08	2 44
30 W	3 33	11 29	3 56	9 17	12 27	3 15	11 02	0 47	1 52	0 57	17 17	7 25	4 46	1 05	3 06	2 44
31 Th	3N56	7S02	4N30	4S43	12N31	3N18	10S39	0S50	1S33	0S57	17S11	7S27	4N51	1S05	3S05	2N44

Day	⚷ Decl	⚷ Lat	♅ Decl	♅ Lat	♆ Decl	♆ Lat	♇ Decl	♇ Lat
1	5S45	5N36	0S54	0S43	12S20	0S29	18S46	4N29
6	5 38	5 36	0 47	0 42	12 17	0 29	18 46	4 29
11	5 31	5 36	0 40	0 42	12 13	0 29	18 45	4 29
16	5 24	5 36	0 33	0 42	12 09	0 30	18 45	4 30
21	5 16	5 37	0 27	0 42	12 06	0 30	18 44	4 30
26	5 09	5 37	0 20	0 42	12 02	0 30	18 44	4 30
31	5S02	5N38	0S13	0S42	11S59	0S30	18S44	4N30

Day	⚴ Decl	⚴ Lat	⚵ Decl	⚵ Lat	⚶ Decl	⚶ Lat	Eris Decl	Eris Lat
1	6N50	28N05	1N59	0S19	20S26	2N07	4S04	13S21
6	7 20	28 19	2 47	0N03	20 16	1 60	4 02	13 21
11	7 53	28 35	3 37	0 24	20 05	1 52	4 01	13 20
16	8 26	28 52	4 25	0 45	19 52	1 44	3 59	13 20
21	9 01	29 10	5 13	1 06	19 37	1 36	3 58	13 19
26	9 38	29 29	5 57	1 25	19 22	1 27	3 56	13 19
31	10N15	29N50	6N38	1N44	19S06	1N18	3S55	13S19

Moon Phenomena

Max/0 Decl
dy hr mn
5 6:09 0 N
12 17:11 23N49
19 2:09 0 S
25 4:59 23S43

Perigee/Apogee
dy hr m kilometers
6 7:51 a 406583
19 19:20 p 356578

PH dy hr mn
● 4 20:47 13♓56
☽ 12 23:46 22♊03
○ 19 18:11 28♍48
☾ 26 12:08 5♑29

Max/0 Lat
dy hr mn
6 3:58 5N00
13 11:56 0 S
19 17:04 5S00
25 21:10 0 N

Void of Course Moon

Last Aspect	☽ Ingress
1 4:04 ♅ ⚹	♒ 1 5:15
3 14:38 ♆ ☌	♓ 3 16:48
6 4:35 ♅ ☌	♈ 6 5:15
8 16:05 ♆ ⚹	♉ 8 17:53
11 5:27 ♅ ⚹	♊ 11 5:32
13 13:11 ♆ △	♋ 13 14:31
15 10:06 ☉ △	♌ 15 19:34
17 19:59 ♆ ☍	♍ 17 20:54
19 18:11 ☉ ☍	♎ 19 20:04
21 18:36 ♆ △	♏ 21 19:18
23 20:09 ♆ □	♐ 23 20:46
26 1:26 ♆ ⚹	♑ 26 1:58
28 3:18 ♂ ⚹	♒ 28 11:01
30 22:22 ♆ ☌	♓ 30 22:39

DAILY ASPECTARIAN

1 Tu
☽ ∠ ☿ 2:06
♀ ⚺ ♆ 2:46
☽ ⚺ ♆ 2:57
☽ ☌ ♀ 2:58
☽ ⚹ ♅ 4:04
☽ ⚺ ⚷ 8:00
☉ ∥ ☿ 13:39
♀ ⚹ ♅ 14:50
☿ ∠ ♀ 15:28
☽ ⚺ ♂ 15:30
☽ ⚺ ♇ 19:16
☽ ⚹ ♃ 20:54

2 W
♀ ♒ 2:40
☉ ⚺ ☽ 3:18
☽ ∠ ♅ 9:48
☿ ⚻ ♄ 13:04
☽ △ ♄ 13:11
☽ ⚺ ☿ 13:13
☽ ∥ ♆ 14:22

3 Th
☽ ∠ ♇ 1:05
☽ ∥ ♂ 2:15
☽ ☌ ⚳ 2:42
☽ ∠ ♃ 3:17
♀ ⚺ ⚷ 9:53
☊R ♐ 12:38
☽ ☌ ♆ 14:38
☽ ⚺ ♅ 15:51
☽ ⚼ ♄ 19:00
☿ ∥ ⚷ 19:22
☽ ☌ ⚷ 19:56
☉ ∥ ☽ 20:19
☽ ⚺ ♀ 20:58

4 F
☽ ∥ ⚷ 1:38
♂ ⚹ ♇ 2:53
☽ ∥ ☿ 3:00
☽ ⚹ ♇ 7:11
☽ ☌ ♂ 7:29
☽ ⚺ ♃ 9:56
☽ ∥ ♄ 10:54
☽ ⋕ ♃ 18:09
☉ ☌ ☽ 20:47
⚳ ∠ ♃ 23:22

5 Sa
♀ ∥ ♇ 0:14
☽ ⚻ ♄ 1:01
☽ ∥ ♅ 2:08
☽ ∠ ♀ 6:29
☽ ⋕ ♅ 10:08
☽ ☌ ☿ 12:57
☽ ⚺ ⚳ 17:01
☽ ∥ ♃ 18:39
☿ ∥ ♄ 22:24

6 Su
☽ ⋕ ☿ 0:49
☽ ⋕ ♄ 1:15
☽ ⚺ ♆ 3:15
☽ ☌ ♅ 4:35
☽ ⚺ ⚷ 8:45
☽ ⋕ ⚷ 10:32
☉ ⋕ ☽ 10:59
♂ ⚺ ♃ 11:04
☽ ⚹ ♀ 16:10
☉ ∥ ⚷ 16:46
☿ ⚺ ⚳ 19:11
☽ □ ♇ 19:51
☉ ⚻ ♄ 20:28
☽ ☌ ♃ 23:44

7 M
☽ ⚺ ♂ 0:22
☽ ∠ ⚳ 0:22
☽ ⋕ ♂ 4:00
☿ ⋕ ♃ 5:38
☽ ∠ ♆ 9:42
☽ ☍ ♄ 13:22
☉ ⚺ ☽ 15:01
☽ ∠ ⚷ 15:17
☽ ⋕ ♆ 22:20

8 Tu
♀ ⚺ ♇ 5:24
☽ ⚹ ⚳ 7:42
☽ ∠ ♂ 8:51
☽ ⚺ ☿ 13:20
☽ ⚹ ♆ 16:05
☽ ⚺ ♅ 17:31
☽ ⚹ ⚷ 21:43

9 W
☉ ∠ ☽ 0:03
☿ ⚺ ♆ 6:45
☿ ∥ ♅ 8:03
☽ △ ♇ 8:28
☽ ⋕ ♀ 9:15
☽ □ ♀ 11:24
☽ ⚺ ♃ 13:26
☿ ☌ ♅ 16:07
☽ ⋕ ♇ 16:42
☽ ⚹ ♂ 17:06
☿ ♈ 17:48
☽ ⋕ ⚳ 22:26
☽ ∠ ♅ 23:42

10 Th
☽ ∠ ☿ 1:04
☽ ⚻ ♄ 1:21
♀ ♒ 8:32
☉ ⚹ ☽ 8:44
♀ ⚹ ♃ 12:26
☽ ⚼ ♇ 14:22
☿ ⚺ ⚷ 19:42
☽ ∠ ♃ 19:48
☿ ⋕ ♅ 20:16
☽ □ ⚳ 21:34

11 F
☽ □ ♆ 3:58
☽ ⚹ ♅ 5:27
☽ ⚼ ♄ 6:46
☽ □ ⚷ 9:34
☽ ⚹ ☿ 11:56
☉ ∥ ♄ 17:29
☽ ⚻ ♇ 19:42

12 Sa
♅ ♈ 0:50
☽ ⚹ ♃ 1:32
☽ △ ♀ 4:39
☽ □ ♂ 7:52
☽ △ ♄ 11:31
☉ ⋕ ♃ 23:05
☉ □ ☽ 23:46

13 Su
☽ △ ⚳ 8:44
☉ ⋕ ☿ 9:37
☽ ⚼ ♀ 11:44
☽ △ ♆ 13:11
☽ □ ♅ 14:40
☿ ∥ ♃ 16:05
☿ □ ♇ 17:33
☽ △ ⚷ 18:35

14 M
☿ ⋕ ♄ 1:40
☽ ☍ ♇ 3:51
☽ □ ☿ 5:24
☽ □ ♃ 10:14
☽ ⚼ ⚳ 12:47
♂ ⚻ ♄ 13:55
☽ ⚼ ♆ 16:21
☽ ⚻ ♀ 17:30
☽ □ ♄ 18:15
☽ △ ♂ 18:33
♀ ∠ ♅ 21:17
☽ ⚼ ⚷ 21:36

15 Tu
♀ △ ♄ 1:35
☉ △ ☽ 10:06
☽ ⋕ ⚳ 11:21
☽ ⋕ ♇ 12:10
☽ ⚻ ⚳ 15:42
☽ ⚻ ♆ 18:28
☽ △ ♅ 19:56
☽ ⚼ ♂ 22:03
☽ ⚻ ⚷ 23:35

16 W
☿ ☌ ♃ 1:28
♀ ⚺ ♂ 2:11
☿ ⋕ ⚷ 4:13
☽ ⋕ ♀ 5:22
☽ ⚻ ♇ 7:58
☉ ⚼ ☽ 13:23
⚳ ∥ ♇ 14:26
☽ △ ♃ 14:42
♃ ⋕ ♄ 15:27
☽ △ ☿ 16:06
☽ ⚹ ♄ 21:02
☽ ⚼ ♅ 21:05
☿ ⋕ ♂ 21:24
☽ ⋕ ♆ 23:56

17 Th
☽ ⚻ ♂ 0:26
☽ ☍ ♀ 1:07
☽ ⚼ ♇ 8:38
☿ ∠ ⚳ 9:50
☽ ⚼ ♃ 15:32
☉ ⚻ ☽ 15:37
☽ ☍ ⚳ 18:33
☽ ⚼ ☿ 19:17
☽ ☍ ♆ 19:59
☽ ∠ ♄ 21:11
☽ ⚻ ♅ 21:26
☽ ∥ ☿ 23:02

18 F
☽ ☍ ⚷ 0:53
☿ ∠ ♆ 2:33
☽ ⋕ ♂ 4:06
☽ ⋕ ⚷ 5:04
☽ △ ♇ 8:38
☽ ∥ ♃ 11:42
☽ ⋕ ♄ 12:36
☿ ☍ ♄ 13:56
☽ ⚻ ♃ 15:44
☽ ⚺ ♄ 20:47
☽ ⚻ ☿ 21:32
☉ ⋕ ☽ 23:02
♂ ∥ ⚷ 23:55

19 Sa
☽ ⋕ ♅ 0:14
☽ ☍ ♂ 2:51
☽ ∥ ♅ 4:02
☉ ∥ ☽ 4:52
☽ ⚻ ♀ 4:57
☽ ∥ ♄ 15:29
☽ ⋕ ♃ 16:58
☉ ☍ ☽ 18:11
☉ ∥ ♅ 18:42
☽ ⚻ ⚳ 18:58
☽ ⚻ ♆ 19:17
☽ ☍ ♅ 20:46
☽ ∥ ♂ 21:52
☽ ∥ ⚷ 22:54

20 Su
☽ ⚻ ⚷ 0:10
☽ ⚼ ♀ 6:21
☽ □ ♇ 7:38
⚳ ☌ ♆ 9:41
☿ ∠ ⚷ 11:02
☉ ⚺ ♆ 11:48
☽ ⋕ ☿ 12:36
☉ ⚺ ⚳ 12:57
☽ ☍ ♃ 15:24
☽ ⚼ ♆ 18:48
☽ ⚼ ⚳ 19:00
☽ ☌ ♄ 19:28
♀ ∠ ♇ 22:54
☉ ♈ 23:22
☽ ⚼ ⚷ 23:45

21 M
☽ ☍ ☿ 0:48
☽ ∥ ♆ 3:21
☽ ⚻ ♂ 4:21
☽ △ ♀ 7:56
⚳ ⚼ ♄ 11:15
☉ ☌ ♅ 12:25
☽ ∥ ♀ 12:56
⚳ ♓ 16:42
☽ △ ♆ 18:36
☽ △ ⚳ 19:22
☽ ⚻ ♅ 20:11
☉ ⚻ ☽ 20:43
☽ △ ⚷ 23:42

22 Tu
☉ ⋕ ♅ 0:57
☽ ⚼ ♂ 5:38
☽ ⚹ ♇ 7:15
☽ ∥ ⚳ 10:09
☽ ∥ ♇ 14:03
☽ ⚻ ♃ 16:06
☽ ⚺ ♄ 19:20
☽ ⚼ ♅ 20:39
♂ ⋕ ♃ 21:49
☉ ⚼ ☽ 22:53

23 W
☽ ⚻ ☿ 5:04
☽ △ ♂ 7:43
☽ ∠ ♇ 7:59
⚳ ⚺ ♅ 10:44
☽ □ ♀ 13:10
☽ ⚼ ♃ 17:33
☽ □ ♆ 20:09
☽ ∠ ♄ 20:19
☉ ⚺ ⚷ 20:28
☽ △ ♅ 21:56
☽ □ ⚳ 22:11

24 Th
☽ □ ⚷ 1:41
☉ △ ☽ 2:04
☽ ⚼ ☿ 8:17
☽ ⚺ ♇ 9:35
♄ ⚼ ♆ 19:31
☽ △ ♃ 19:59
☽ ⚹ ♄ 22:15

25 F
☽ △ ☿ 12:24
☽ □ ♂ 15:10
♂ ∥ ♄ 15:13
☽ ⚹ ♀ 23:03

26 Sa
☽ ⚹ ♆ 1:26
☽ □ ♅ 3:27
♀ ∠ ♃ 4:53
☽ ⚹ ⚳ 5:03
☽ ⚹ ⚷ 7:32
☉ □ ☽ 12:08
☽ ☌ ♇ 15:50
♀ ⚼ ♄ 21:04

27 Su
♀ ☌ ♆ 1:40
☽ □ ♃ 4:02
☽ □ ♄ 5:05
☽ ∠ ♆ 5:35
☽ ∠ ♀ 5:59
♀ ♓ 6:54
☽ ∠ ⚳ 10:06
♀ ∥ ♆ 10:44
☽ ∠ ⚷ 11:56
☿ ⋕ ♀ 12:20
☿ ⋕ ♆ 14:30
☉ ⋕ ♂ 14:49
☽ □ ☿ 23:01

28 M
♀ ⚺ ♅ 1:09
☽ ∥ ♇ 2:00
☽ ⚹ ♂ 3:18
☽ ⚺ ♆ 10:35
☽ ∥ ⚳ 11:15
☉ □ ♇ 12:14
☽ ⚹ ♅ 12:51
☽ ⚺ ♀ 14:04
☽ ⚺ ⚳ 16:03
☽ ⚺ ⚷ 17:11
♃ ☍ ♄ 21:56
☉ ⋕ ♄ 22:56

29 Tu
☽ ⚺ ♇ 1:42
☉ ⚹ ☽ 2:53
☽ ∠ ♂ 10:47
☽ △ ♄ 15:13
☽ ⚹ ♃ 15:41
♀ ☌ ⚳ 18:18
☽ ⋕ ☿ 18:37
☽ ∠ ♅ 18:38
☽ ∥ ♆ 21:04
♀ ☌ ⚷ 23:16

30 W
☽ ∥ ♀ 2:40
☽ ∠ ♇ 7:33
☽ ⚹ ☿ 11:18
☉ ∠ ☽ 11:26
⚳ ☌ ⚷ 12:52
☽ ⚺ ♂ 18:51
☿ R 20:50
☽ ⚼ ♄ 21:03
☽ ∠ ♃ 22:20
☽ ☌ ♆ 22:22

31 Th
♃ ∠ ♆ 0:42
☽ ⚺ ♅ 0:50
☽ ☌ ⚷ 5:17
☽ ☌ ⚳ 5:43
☽ ☌ ♀ 8:30
☽ ∥ ⚷ 10:21
☽ ⋕ ♃ 11:02
☽ ⚹ ♇ 13:45
☉ ⋕ ☽ 14:45
☽ ∠ ☿ 17:26
☉ ⚺ ☽ 20:23
☽ ∥ ♄ 20:29

April 2011

LONGITUDE

Day	Sid.Time	☉	☽	☽ 12 hour	Mean☊	True☊	☿	♀	♂	⚳	♃	♄	⚷	♅	♆	♇
	h m s	° ' "	° ' "	° ' "	° '	° '	° '	° '	° '	° '	° '	° '	° '	° '	° '	° '
1 F	12 36 03	10♈55 18	12♓33 48	18♓29 47	27♐32.4	26♐53.6	24♈16.8	5♓39.9	29♓03.7	3♓47.2	15♈05.9	14♎06.8	3♓20.4	1♈08.2	29♒53.6	7♑29.4
2 Sa	12 39 59	11 54 32	24 25 34	0♈21 20	27 29.2	26R 40.6	24R 05.2	6 52.0	29 50.5	4 08.9	15 20.4	14R 02.2	3 23.8	1 11.6	29 55.4	7 29.6
3 Su	12 43 56	12 53 45	6♈17 19	12 13 39	27 26.1	26 26.7	23 47.2	8 04.3	0♈37.3	4 30.6	15 34.9	13 57.5	3 27.1	1 15.0	29 57.2	7 29.8
4 M	12 47 52	13 52 56	18 10 31	24 08 05	27 22.9	26 13.1	23 23.0	9 16.5	1 24.0	4 52.1	15 49.4	13 52.8	3 30.5	1 18.4	29 59.0	7 30.0
5 Tu	12 51 49	14 52 04	0♉06 30	6♉05 59	27 19.7	26 01.0	22 53.3	10 28.8	2 10.7	5 13.6	16 03.9	13 48.1	3 33.8	1 21.7	0♓00.7	7 30.2
6 W	12 55 45	15 51 11	12 06 43	18 08 57	27 16.5	25 51.2	22 18.7	11 41.1	2 57.4	5 35.1	16 18.5	13 43.5	3 37.1	1 25.1	0 02.5	7 30.3
7 Th	12 59 42	16 50 15	24 12 58	0♊19 04	27 13.3	25 44.2	21 40.1	12 53.4	3 44.0	5 56.5	16 33.0	13 38.8	3 40.3	1 28.4	0 04.2	7 30.4
8 F	13 03 39	17 49 18	6♊27 37	12 39 00	27 10.2	25 40.0	20 58.2	14 05.7	4 30.7	6 17.8	16 47.5	13 34.2	3 43.5	1 31.8	0 05.9	7 30.4
9 Sa	13 07 35	18 48 18	18 53 39	25 12 01	27 07.0	25D 38.2	20 13.9	15 18.1	5 17.2	6 39.0	17 02.0	13 29.5	3 46.7	1 35.1	0 07.5	7R 30.5
10 Su	13 11 32	19 47 16	1♋34 35	8♋01 50	27 03.8	25 38.2	19 28.1	16 30.4	6 03.8	7 00.1	17 16.5	13 24.9	3 49.8	1 38.4	0 09.2	7 30.5
11 M	13 15 28	20 46 11	14 34 15	21 12 17	27 00.6	25R 38.7	18 41.7	17 42.8	6 50.3	7 21.2	17 31.0	13 20.3	3 52.9	1 41.7	0 10.8	7 30.4
12 Tu	13 19 25	21 45 05	27 56 20	4♌46 43	26 57.5	25 38.6	17 55.5	18 55.2	7 36.7	7 42.2	17 45.5	13 15.7	3 55.9	1 45.0	0 12.4	7 30.4
13 W	13 23 21	22 43 56	11♌43 40	18 47 15	26 54.3	25 37.1	17 10.6	20 07.6	8 23.2	8 03.1	18 00.0	13 11.1	3 58.9	1 48.2	0 14.0	7 30.3
14 Th	13 27 18	23 42 44	25 57 24	3♍13 51	26 51.1	25 33.3	16 27.5	21 20.0	9 09.6	8 23.9	18 14.5	13 06.5	4 01.9	1 51.5	0 15.5	7 30.1
15 F	13 31 14	24 41 30	10♍36 06	18 03 29	26 47.9	25 27.3	15 47.0	22 32.5	9 55.9	8 44.7	18 28.9	13 02.0	4 04.8	1 54.7	0 17.0	7 30.0
16 Sa	13 35 11	25 40 14	25 35 06	3♎09 49	26 44.7	25 19.4	15 09.9	23 45.0	10 42.2	9 05.3	18 43.4	12 57.5	4 07.7	1 57.9	0 18.5	7 29.8
17 Su	13 39 08	26 38 56	10♎46 27	18 23 37	26 41.6	25 10.6	14 36.5	24 57.4	11 28.5	9 25.9	18 57.8	12 53.0	4 10.6	2 01.1	0 20.0	7 29.5
18 M	13 43 04	27 37 36	25 59 57	3♏34 06	26 38.4	25 02.0	14 07.3	26 09.9	12 14.7	9 46.4	19 12.3	12 48.6	4 13.4	2 04.3	0 21.4	7 29.3
19 Tu	13 47 01	28 36 14	11♏04 48	18 30 54	26 35.2	24 54.6	13 42.7	27 22.4	13 00.9	10 06.8	19 26.7	12 44.2	4 16.1	2 07.5	0 22.9	7 29.0
20 W	13 50 57	29 34 50	25 51 29	3♐05 47	26 32.0	24 49.2	13 22.9	28 35.0	13 47.1	10 27.1	19 41.1	12 39.8	4 18.8	2 10.6	0 24.2	7 28.7
21 Th	13 54 54	0♉33 25	10♐13 18	17 13 42	26 28.9	24 46.2	13 08.1	29 47.5	14 33.2	10 47.4	19 55.4	12 35.5	4 21.5	2 13.7	0 25.6	7 28.4
22 F	13 58 50	1 31 57	24 06 54	0♑52 56	26 25.7	24D 45.3	12 58.3	1♈00.1	15 19.3	11 07.5	20 09.8	12 31.2	4 24.1	2 16.8	0 26.9	7 28.0
23 Sa	14 02 47	2 30 28	7♑32 02	14 04 33	26 22.5	24 45.8	12D 53.6	2 12.7	16 05.3	11 27.6	20 24.1	12 27.0	4 26.7	2 19.9	0 28.3	7 27.6
24 Su	14 06 43	3 28 58	20 30 55	26 51 38	26 19.3	24 46.9	12 54.0	3 25.3	16 51.3	11 47.6	20 38.5	12 22.8	4 29.3	2 23.0	0 29.5	7 27.2
25 M	14 10 40	4 27 26	3♒07 16	9♒18 25	26 16.2	24R 47.5	12 59.4	4 37.9	17 37.3	12 07.4	20 52.8	12 18.6	4 31.8	2 26.0	0 30.8	7 26.7
26 Tu	14 14 37	5 25 52	15 25 40	21 29 37	26 13.0	24 47.0	13 09.7	5 50.6	18 23.2	12 27.2	21 07.0	12 14.5	4 34.2	2 29.0	0 32.0	7 26.2
27 W	14 18 33	6 24 16	27 30 51	3♓29 56	26 09.8	24 44.6	13 24.8	7 03.2	19 09.1	12 46.9	21 21.3	12 10.4	4 36.6	2 32.0	0 33.2	7 25.7
28 Th	14 22 30	7 22 39	9♓27 25	15 23 45	26 06.6	24 40.1	13 44.6	8 15.9	19 54.9	13 06.4	21 35.5	12 06.4	4 38.9	2 35.0	0 34.4	7 25.1
29 F	14 26 26	8 21 00	21 19 27	27 14 53	26 03.4	24 33.8	14 08.8	9 28.5	20 40.7	13 25.9	21 49.7	12 02.5	4 41.2	2 37.9	0 35.5	7 24.6
30 Sa	14 30 23	9♉19 20	3♈10 27	9♈06 29	26♐00.3	24♐26.1	14♈37.3	10♈41.2	21♈26.5	13♓45.3	22♈03.9	11♎58.6	4♓43.5	2♈40.8	0♓36.6	7♑24.0

1st of Month

Julian Day # 2455652.5
Obliquity 23°26'16"
SVP 5♓05'53"
GC 26♐59.8
Eris 21♈41.0

Day	⚴	⚵	⚶
1	6♒28.5	17♍01.8R	29♑22.5
6	7 47.8	16 08.8R	1♒25.5
11	9 02.5	15 24.4R	3 24.4
16	10 12.2	14 49.2R	5 18.9
21	11 16.7	14 23.4R	7 08.5
26	12 15.5	14 07.2R	8 53.0

DECLINATION and LATITUDE

Day	☉ Decl	☽ Decl	☽ Lat	☽12h Decl	☿ Decl	☿ Lat	♀ Decl	♀ Lat	♂ Decl	♂ Lat	⚳ Decl	⚳ Lat	♃ Decl	♃ Lat	♄ Decl	♄ Lat
1 F	4N19	2S21	4N51	0N01	12N30	3N20	10S15	0S52	1S14	0S56	17S05	7S29	4N57	1S05	3S03	2N44
2 Sa	4 42	2N23	5 00	4 43	12 26	3 20	9 51	0 55	0 55	0 56	16 58	7 31	5 03	1 05	3 01	2 44
3 Su	5 06	7 02	4 56	9 16	12 18	3 18	9 26	0 58	0 36	0 56	16 52	7 32	5 08	1 05	2 59	2 44
4 M	5 29	11 25	4 39	13 29	12 06	3 15	9 01	1 00	0 17	0 55	16 46	7 34	5 14	1 05	2 57	2 44
5 Tu	5 51	15 28	4 10	17 11	11 50	3 10	8 36	1 03	0N02	0 55	16 39	7 36	5 19	1 05	2 55	2 44
6 W	6 14	18 47	3 29	20 12	11 31	3 03	8 11	1 05	0 21	0 54	16 33	7 38	5 25	1 05	2 54	2 44
7 Th	6 37	21 23	2 39	22 20	11 09	2 55	7 45	1 07	0 39	0 54	16 27	7 40	5 31	1 05	2 52	2 44
8 F	6 60	23 02	1 40	23 27	10 44	2 45	7 19	1 09	0 58	0 54	16 20	7 42	5 36	1 05	2 50	2 44
9 Sa	7 22	23 34	0 36	23 23	10 17	2 34	6 53	1 11	1 17	0 53	16 14	7 44	5 42	1 05	2 48	2 44
10 Su	7 44	22 54	0S32	22 06	9 48	2 22	6 27	1 14	1 36	0 53	16 08	7 46	5 47	1 05	2 46	2 44
11 M	8 07	20 60	1 39	19 36	9 18	2 08	6 01	1 16	1 55	0 52	16 02	7 48	5 53	1 05	2 45	2 44
12 Tu	8 29	17 54	2 43	15 57	8 47	1 54	5 34	1 17	2 13	0 52	15 56	7 50	5 58	1 05	2 43	2 44
13 W	8 50	13 45	3 40	11 19	8 15	1 38	5 08	1 19	2 32	0 52	15 50	7 52	6 04	1 05	2 41	2 44
14 Th	9 12	8 42	4 25	5 56	7 44	1 22	4 41	1 21	2 51	0 51	15 43	7 54	6 09	1 05	2 39	2 44
15 F	9 34	3 03	4 54	0 05	7 13	1 06	4 14	1 23	3 09	0 51	15 37	7 56	6 15	1 05	2 38	2 44
16 Sa	9 55	2S54	5 04	5S52	6 44	0 49	3 46	1 24	3 28	0 50	15 31	7 58	6 20	1 05	2 36	2 44
17 Su	10 17	8 45	4 53	11 31	6 15	0 33	3 19	1 26	3 46	0 50	15 26	7 60	6 26	1 05	2 34	2 44
18 M	10 38	14 06	4 21	16 26	5 49	0 16	2 52	1 27	4 05	0 50	15 20	8 02	6 31	1 05	2 33	2 44
19 Tu	10 59	18 30	3 32	20 14	5 24	0S00	2 24	1 29	4 23	0 49	15 14	8 04	6 37	1 05	2 31	2 44
20 W	11 19	21 37	2 28	22 38	5 02	0 16	1 56	1 30	4 41	0 49	15 08	8 06	6 42	1 05	2 29	2 44
21 Th	11 40	23 15	1 17	23 30	4 42	0 32	1 29	1 31	4 60	0 48	15 02	8 08	6 47	1 05	2 28	2 44
22 F	12 00	23 22	0 03	22 53	4 24	0 47	1 01	1 32	5 18	0 48	14 56	8 10	6 53	1 05	2 26	2 44
23 Sa	12 21	22 05	1N08	21 00	4 09	1 01	0 33	1 34	5 36	0 47	14 51	8 12	6 58	1 05	2 25	2 43
24 Su	12 41	19 40	2 14	18 06	3 57	1 15	0 05	1 35	5 54	0 47	14 45	8 15	7 04	1 05	2 23	2 43
25 M	13 00	16 21	3 11	14 27	3 47	1 28	0N23	1 35	6 12	0 46	14 39	8 17	7 09	1 05	2 22	2 43
26 Tu	13 20	12 25	3 58	10 16	3 40	1 40	0 51	1 36	6 30	0 46	14 34	8 19	7 14	1 05	2 20	2 43
27 W	13 39	8 03	4 34	5 46	3 35	1 51	1 19	1 37	6 48	0 45	14 28	8 21	7 20	1 05	2 19	2 43
28 Th	13 58	3 26	4 57	1 05	3 33	2 02	1 47	1 38	7 06	0 45	14 23	8 24	7 25	1 05	2 17	2 43
29 F	14 17	1N16	5 07	3N36	3 33	2 12	2 15	1 38	7 23	0 45	14 17	8 26	7 30	1 05	2 16	2 43
30 Sa	14N36	5N55	5N04	8N10	3N36	2S21	2N43	1S39	7N41	0S44	14S12	8S28	7N35	1S05	2S14	2N43

Day	⚷ Decl	⚷ Lat	♅ Decl	♅ Lat	♆ Decl	♆ Lat	♇ Decl	♇ Lat
1	5S01	5N38	0S12	0S42	11S58	0S30	18S44	4N30
6	4 54	5 39	0 05	0 42	11 55	0 30	18 43	4 31
11	4 48	5 40	0N02	0 42	11 53	0 30	18 43	4 31
16	4 42	5 41	0 08	0 42	11 50	0 30	18 43	4 31
21	4 36	5 42	0 14	0 42	11 48	0 30	18 43	4 31
26	4 30	5 43	0 20	0 43	11 45	0 30	18 43	4 31

Day	⚴ Decl	⚴ Lat	⚵ Decl	⚵ Lat	⚶ Decl	⚶ Lat	Eris Decl	Eris Lat
1	10N22	29N54	6N46	1N48	19S02	1N16	3S55	13S18
6	11 01	30 16	7 23	2 05	18 46	1 07	3 53	13 18
11	11 40	30 39	7 55	2 21	18 29	0 56	3 52	13 18
16	12 19	31 04	8 22	2 36	18 12	0 46	3 50	13 18
21	12 58	31 30	8 45	2 49	17 56	0 34	3 49	13 18
26	13 38	31 57	9 03	3 02	17 41	0 22	3 48	13 18

Moon Phenomena

Max/0 Decl
dy hr mn
1 11:56 0 N
8 23:03 23N34
15 12:21 0 S
21 13:45 23S30
28 17:33 0 N

Max/0 Lat
dy hr mn
2 4:25 5N00
9 12:49 0 S
15 23:46 5S04
22 1:07 0 N
29 6:27 5N07

Perigee/Apogee
dy hr m kilometers
2 9:03 a 406657
17 5:52 p 358093
29 18:04 a 406039

PH dy hr mn
● 3 14:33 13♈30
☽ 11 12:06 21♋16
○ 18 2:45 27♎44
☾ 25 2:48 4♒34

Void of Course Moon

Last Aspect	☽ Ingress
31 13:45 ♇ ⚹	♈ 2 11:17
4 10:05 ☿ ☌	♉ 4 23:47
5 23:03 ♀ ⚹	♊ 7 11:23
9 2:25 ☿ ⚹	♋ 9 21:03
11 12:06 ☉ □	♌ 12 3:38
13 19:59 ☉ △	♍ 14 6:41
15 20:50 ♀ ☍	♎ 16 7:00
18 2:45 ☉ ☍	♏ 18 6:20
20 4:54 ☉ △	♐ 20 6:51
21 16:58 ♃ △	♑ 22 10:25
24 0:14 ♃ □	♒ 24 18:00
26 11:29 ♃ ⚹	♓ 27 4:59
27 19:54 ♇ ⚹	♈ 29 17:34

DAILY ASPECTARIAN

1 F
☽⊼♄ 3:07
☽⊻♃ 5:14
☽∥♂ 6:07
☽∥♅ 11:00
☽#♅ 12:52
♃#⚷ 14:12
☽#♂ 17:03
☽⊻☿ 23:20

2 Sa
♂⊻♆ 2:37
☽#♄ 3:13
♂ ♈ 4:52
☽⊻♆ 11:09
☽☌♂ 11:44
⚶ ♒ 12:11
♀⚹♇ 12:31
☉∥☽ 13:00
☽#⚷ 13:21
☽☌♅ 13:46
☽∥♃ 13:56
☉#⚷ 16:58
☽⊻⚷ 18:14
☽⊻⚳ 20:17

3 Su
☽□♇ 2:27
☉∥♃ 3:38
☽⊻♀ 4:01
☿∠♀ 10:51
☽#♀ 11:48
☉☌☽ 14:33
☽☍♄ 15:24
☽∠♆ 17:33
☽☌♃ 19:10
♂☌♅ 20:53
☉☍♄ 23:57

4 M
☽∠⚷ 0:40
☽#♆ 2:59
☽∠⚳ 3:31
☽∥☿ 3:40
☽☌☿ 10:05
♂∥♅ 12:59
☽∠♀ 13:40
♆ ♓ 13:52
☿#♆ 15:19
☽⚹♆ 23:48

5 Tu
☽⊻♅ 2:32
☉∠♆ 3:37
☽⊻♂ 4:26
♂#♅ 5:30
☽⚹⚷ 6:57
☽#⚳ 8:05
☽⚹⚳ 10:34
☽△♇ 14:48
☽⚹♀ 23:03
☽#♇ 23:31

6 W
☽⊼♄ 3:11
☉⊻☽ 8:06
☽⊻♃ 8:31
☽∠♅ 8:36
☽∠♂ 12:25
☉☌♃ 14:41
☽⊻☿ 19:14
☽⚼♇ 20:37
♂⊻⚷ 21:56

7 Th
☽⚼♄ 8:40
☽□♆ 11:32
♀⊼♄ 14:10
☽⚹♅ 14:20
☽∠♃ 14:42
☉∠☽ 16:17
☿∠⚳ 16:41
☽□⚷ 18:39
☽⚹♂ 19:57
☽∠☿ 23:06
☽□⚳ 23:40

8 F
☽⊼♇ 2:02
☉#♀ 9:53
☽△♄ 13:41
☽□♀ 16:22
☽⚹♃ 20:22
☉∠⚷ 23:18
☉⚹☽ 23:49

9 Sa
☽⚹☿ 2:25
♇ R 8:52
☉☌☿ 19:37
☽△♆ 21:20

10 Su
☽□♅ 0:07
☽△⚷ 4:13
☽□♂ 8:53
☽△⚳ 10:23
☽☍♇ 11:02
☿∠⚷ 18:34
♀⊻♃ 19:07
☽□♄ 21:46

11 M
☽⚼♆ 1:07
☽□♃ 5:27
♀#♃ 6:04
☽△♀ 6:17
☽□☿ 7:04
☽⚼⚷ 7:51
⚳⚹♇ 10:31
☿⊻♀ 11:54
☉□☽ 12:06
☽⚼⚳ 14:26
☽#♇ 18:27
♂□♇ 20:42

12 Tu
☿☌♃ 4:00
☽⊼♆ 4:00
♂⊻⚳ 5:07
☽△♅ 6:44
☉∥☿ 8:16
☽⊼⚷ 10:34
☽⚼♀ 11:31
☽#⚳ 12:25
☽⊼♇ 16:44
☽⊼⚳ 17:31
☽△♂ 17:55

13 W
☽⚹♄ 2:29
☽⚼♅ 8:41
☽△☿ 8:49
☽#♆ 9:26
♂#♄ 10:44
☽△♃ 10:51
☉∠⚳ 12:07
☽⊼♀ 15:34
☽⚼♇ 18:14
☉△☽ 19:59
♀∥⚷ 20:45
☽⚼♂ 20:50
☉∥☽ 21:55

14 Th
☽∠♄ 3:33
☽∥☿ 4:43
☽☍♆ 7:08
☽⚼☿ 8:41
☽⊼♅ 9:47
☽∥♃ 10:53
☽⚼♃ 12:13
☽☍⚷ 13:21
☽#⚷ 17:06
☽#♀ 18:45
☽△♇ 18:58
☽☍⚳ 20:55
☉⚼☽ 22:25
☽⊼♂ 22:51
☽∥♂ 23:36

15 F
☽#♄ 1:44
☽⊻♄ 3:54
☽⊼☿ 8:01
☽∥♅ 11:52
☽#♅ 12:51
☽⊼♃ 12:53
☿∠♆ 18:25
☽☍♀ 20:50
☽∥♄ 22:48

16 Sa
☉⊼☽ 0:09
☽#♂ 2:24
☽∥♀ 3:16
☽∥⚷ 7:13
☽⊼♆ 7:30
♀#♂ 9:45
☽☍♅ 10:08
☽⊼⚷ 13:34
☽#♃ 14:09
☽#☿ 14:22
☿∥♃ 16:34
☽□♇ 18:50
☽⊼⚳ 21:50

17 Su
☽☍♂ 1:10
☽☌♄ 3:18
☽☍☿ 5:50
☉#☽ 6:58
☽⚼♆ 7:11
☽☍♃ 13:06
☽⚼⚷ 13:16
☽∥♆ 13:22
☽⚼⚳ 22:01

18 M
☽⊼♀ 0:17
♃∠⚷ 2:17
☉☍☽ 2:45
☽∥⚳ 6:01
☽△♆ 6:55
☽⊼♅ 9:39
☽△⚷ 13:05
♂☍♄ 16:03
♀∥♄ 17:37
☽⚹♇ 18:15
☽△⚳ 22:25

19 Tu
☽∥♇ 1:23
☽⚼♀ 2:16
☽⊻♄ 2:39
☽⊼♂ 3:17
☽⊼☿ 4:08
☽⚼♅ 9:47
☽⊼♃ 13:44
☿☌♂ 14:59
♂#⚷ 18:21
☽∠♇ 18:28

20 W
☽∠♄ 2:58
☽⚼☿ 4:05
☽△♀ 4:54
☽⚼♂ 5:06
☉⊼☽ 6:36
☽□♆ 7:32
☉ ♉ 10:19
☽△♅ 10:30
☿∥♂ 12:31
☽□⚷ 14:05
☽⚼♃ 14:55
☽⊻♇ 19:21
☉⚹♆ 20:44

21 Th
☽□⚳ 0:59
☽⚹♄ 4:01
♀ ♈ 4:07
☽△☿ 4:54
☽△♂ 7:50
☿#⚷ 8:21
☉#♆ 8:44
☉⚼☽ 9:48
♀⊻♆ 12:50
☽△♃ 16:58

22 F
♂∠♆ 4:06
☽⚹♆ 11:15
☽□♀ 13:26
☉△☽ 14:12
☽□♅ 14:34
☽⚹⚷ 18:23
☉⊻♅ 19:25
☽☌♇ 23:52

23 Sa
♀☌♅ 2:29
☽⚹⚳ 7:22
☽□♄ 8:57
☽□☿ 9:48
☿ D 10:05
♀#♅ 13:34
☽∠♆ 14:37
☽□♂ 16:44
☽∠⚷ 22:04

24 Su
☽□♃ 0:14
☉⊻♀ 6:14
☽∥♇ 7:29
☽∠⚳ 12:12
☽⊻♆ 18:58
♀∥♅ 20:36
♀⊻⚷ 21:54
☽⚹♅ 22:40

25 M
☉⚹⚷ 1:51
☽⊻⚷ 2:44
☉□☽ 2:48
☽⚹♀ 3:14
☽⊻♇ 8:22
☽∥⚳ 11:01
⚳⊼♄ 11:12
☽△♄ 17:46
☽⊻⚳ 18:00
☉#☽ 19:03
☽⚹☿ 19:28

26 Tu
☽∥♆ 3:44
☽∠♅ 4:04
☽⚹♂ 6:14
☽⚹♃ 11:29
☽∠♀ 11:54
☽∠♇ 13:52
☽⚼♄ 23:19

27 W
☽∠☿ 1:51
☽#♃ 3:44
☽☌♆ 6:06
☽#♂ 6:11
♀□♇ 7:22
☽⊻♅ 10:06
☽∠♂ 14:13
☽☌⚷ 14:17
♂∠⚷ 15:10
☽∠♃ 18:06
☽∥⚷ 18:41
☉⚹☽ 19:26
☽⚹♇ 19:54
☽⊻♀ 21:19
☽#☿ 23:25

28 Th
☉△♇ 1:01
☽⊼♄ 5:19
☽∥♄ 5:55
☽☌⚳ 7:35
☽#♀ 7:42
☽⊻☿ 8:57
☽#♅ 15:34
☽∥♅ 19:33
☽⊻♂ 22:36
☉#⚳ 23:56

29 F
♀#♄ 0:40
☽⊻♃ 1:03
☉∠☽ 4:28
☽#♄ 5:04
☽∥♀ 5:35
☽∥☿ 11:50
♂∥♃ 13:02
☽#⚷ 16:18
☽⊻♆ 18:48
☽☌♅ 23:00

30 Sa
☽⊻⚷ 3:09
☽□♇ 8:32
☽∥♃ 9:05
☽∥♂ 10:04
☉⊻☽ 13:32
☽☌♀ 16:55
☽☍♄ 17:42
☽⊻⚳ 21:58

LONGITUDE

Day	Sid.Time	☉	☽	☽ 12 hour	Mean☊	True☊	☿	♀	♂	⚳	♃	♄	⚷	♅	♆	♇
	h m s	° ' "	° ' "	° ' "	° '	° '	° '	° '	° '	° '	° '	° '	° '	° '	° '	° '
1 Su	14 34 19	10♉17 38	15♈03 17	21♈01 07	25♐57.1	24♐17.7	15♈10.0	11♈53.9	22♈12.2	14♓04.5	22♈18.0	11♎54.7	4♓45.7	2♈43.7	0♓37.7	7♑23.3
2 M	14 38 16	11 15 54	27 00 11	3♉00 42	25 53.9	24R 09.4	16 46.6	13 06.6	22 57.9	14 23.7	22 32.2	11R 51.0	4 47.8	2 46.6	0 38.7	7R 22.7
3 Tu	14 42 12	12 14 09	9♉02 52	15 06 49	25 50.7	24 02.1	16 27.1	14 19.4	23 43.5	14 42.7	22 46.2	11 47.3	4 49.9	2 49.4	0 39.8	7 22.0
4 W	14 46 09	13 12 22	21 12 44	27 20 46	25 47.6	23 56.2	17 11.3	15 32.1	24 29.0	15 01.6	23 00.3	11 43.6	4 52.0	2 52.2	0 40.8	7 21.3
5 Th	14 50 05	14 10 33	3♊31 04	9♊43 50	25 44.4	23 52.3	17 59.0	16 44.8	25 14.6	15 20.5	23 14.3	11 40.1	4 54.0	2 55.0	0 41.7	7 20.5
6 F	14 54 02	15 08 43	15 59 13	22 17 27	25 41.2	23D 50.4	18 50.1	17 57.6	26 00.0	15 39.2	23 28.3	11 36.6	4 55.9	2 57.8	0 42.6	7 19.8
7 Sa	14 57 59	16 06 50	28 38 45	5♋03 22	25 38.0	23 50.2	19 44.4	19 10.3	26 45.5	15 57.7	23 42.2	11 33.1	4 57.8	3 00.5	0 43.5	7 19.0
8 Su	15 01 55	17 04 56	11♋31 33	18 03 35	25 34.8	23 51.2	20 41.9	20 23.1	27 30.8	16 16.2	23 56.1	11 29.8	4 59.7	3 03.2	0 44.4	7 18.2
9 M	15 05 52	18 03 00	24 39 43	1♌20 12	25 31.7	23 52.7	21 42.3	21 35.9	28 16.2	16 34.5	24 10.0	11 26.5	5 01.5	3 05.9	0 45.2	7 17.3
0 Tu	15 09 48	19 01 02	8♌05 17	14 55 09	25 28.5	23R 54.0	22 45.7	22 48.6	29 01.5	16 52.7	24 23.8	11 23.3	5 03.2	3 08.5	0 46.0	7 16.5
1 W	15 13 45	19 59 02	21 49 54	28 49 37	25 25.3	23 54.5	23 51.9	24 01.4	29 46.7	17 10.8	24 37.6	11 20.1	5 04.9	3 11.1	0 46.8	7 15.6
2 Th	15 17 41	20 57 00	5♍54 12	13♍03 30	25 22.1	23 53.6	25 00.8	25 14.2	0♉31.8	17 28.8	24 51.4	11 17.1	5 06.5	3 13.7	0 47.5	7 14.6
3 F	15 21 38	21 54 56	20 17 12	27 34 51	25 19.0	23 51.3	26 12.4	26 27.0	1 17.0	17 46.6	25 05.0	11 14.1	5 08.1	3 16.2	0 48.3	7 13.7
4 Sa	15 25 34	22 52 51	4♎55 51	12♎19 28	25 15.8	23 47.8	27 26.5	27 39.8	2 02.0	18 04.3	25 18.7	11 11.2	5 09.6	3 18.7	0 48.9	7 12.7
5 Su	15 29 31	23 50 43	19 44 51	27 11 03	25 12.6	23 43.8	28 43.2	28 52.6	2 47.0	18 21.9	25 32.3	11 08.4	5 11.1	3 21.2	0 49.6	7 11.8
6 M	15 33 28	24 48 34	4♏37 04	12♏01 52	25 09.4	23 39.7	0♉02.3	0♉05.4	3 32.0	18 39.3	25 45.9	11 05.6	5 12.5	3 23.6	0 50.2	7 10.7
7 Tu	15 37 24	25 46 24	19 24 26	26 43 49	25 06.2	23 36.2	1 23.8	1 18.2	4 16.9	18 56.6	25 59.4	11 03.0	5 13.8	3 26.0	0 50.8	7 09.7
8 W	15 41 21	26 44 12	3♐59 10	11♐09 43	25 03.1	23 33.8	2 47.7	2 31.1	5 01.8	19 13.8	26 12.8	11 00.4	5 15.1	3 28.4	0 51.3	7 08.7
9 Th	15 45 17	27 41 58	18 14 54	25 14 14	24 59.9	23D 32.7	4 14.0	3 43.9	5 46.6	19 30.8	26 26.2	10 58.0	5 16.4	3 30.7	0 51.8	7 07.6
0 F	15 49 14	28 39 44	2♑07 27	8♑54 24	24 56.7	23 32.8	5 42.5	4 56.8	6 31.4	19 47.6	26 39.6	10 55.6	5 17.5	3 33.0	0 52.3	7 06.5
1 Sa	15 53 10	29 37 28	15 35 06	22 09 39	24 53.5	23 33.9	7 13.4	6 09.6	7 16.1	20 04.4	26 52.9	10 53.3	5 18.7	3 35.3	0 52.8	7 05.4
2 Su	15 57 07	0♊35 11	28 38 20	5♒01 27	24 50.4	23 35.4	8 46.6	7 22.5	8 00.8	20 21.0	27 06.1	10 51.1	5 19.7	3 37.5	0 53.2	7 04.2
3 M	16 01 04	1 32 52	11♒19 26	17 32 45	24 47.2	23 36.8	10 22.1	8 35.4	8 45.4	20 37.4	27 19.3	10 49.0	5 20.8	3 39.7	0 53.6	7 03.1
4 Tu	16 05 00	2 30 33	23 41 55	29 47 30	24 44.0	23R 37.9	11 59.8	9 48.3	9 29.9	20 53.7	27 32.5	10 46.9	5 21.7	3 41.9	0 53.9	7 01.9
5 W	16 08 57	3 28 13	5♓50 03	11♓50 09	24 40.8	23 38.1	13 39.7	11 01.2	10 14.4	21 09.8	27 45.5	10 45.0	5 22.6	3 44.0	0 54.2	7 00.7
6 Th	16 12 53	4 25 51	17 48 23	23 45 19	24 37.7	23 37.5	15 22.0	12 14.1	10 58.9	21 25.8	27 58.6	10 43.1	5 23.5	3 46.0	0 54.5	6 59.5
7 F	16 16 50	5 23 29	29 41 30	5♈37 27	24 34.5	23 36.0	17 06.5	13 27.1	11 43.3	21 41.6	28 11.5	10 41.4	5 24.2	3 48.1	0 54.8	6 58.3
8 Sa	16 20 46	6 21 06	11♈33 40	17 30 38	24 31.3	23 34.0	18 53.2	14 40.0	12 27.6	21 57.2	28 24.4	10 39.7	5 25.0	3 50.1	0 55.0	6 57.0
9 Su	16 24 43	7 18 41	23 28 46	29 28 29	24 28.1	23 31.6	20 42.2	15 53.0	13 11.9	22 12.7	28 37.2	10 38.2	5 25.6	3 52.0	0 55.2	6 55.8
0 M	16 28 39	8 16 16	5♉30 06	11♉33 58	24 24.9	23 29.2	22 33.4	17 05.9	13 56.2	22 28.0	28 50.0	10 36.7	5 26.2	3 53.9	0 55.3	6 54.5
1 Tu	16 32 36	9♊13 50	17 40 19	23 49 25	24♐21.8	23♐27.1	24♉26.8	18♉18.9	14♉40.4	22♓43.1	29♈02.7	10♎35.4	5♓26.8	3♈55.8	0♓55.5	6♑53.2

1st of Month

Julian Day # 2455682.5
Obliquity 23°26'16"
SVP 5♓05'50"
GC 26♐59.9
Eris 22♈00.5

Day	⚴	Day	⚵	Day	⚶
1	13♒08.1	1	14♍00.3R	1	10♒31.7
6	13 54.1	6	14 02.5	6	12 04.2
11	14 33.1	11	14 13.7	11	13 29.9
16	15 04.5	16	14 33.1	16	14 48.3
21	15 28.1	21	15 00.3	21	15 58.8
26	15 43.3	26	15 34.7	26	17 00.9
31	15 49.6	31	16 15.9	31	17 53.7

DECLINATION and LATITUDE

Day	☉ Decl	☽ Decl	☽ Lat	☽ 12h Decl	☿ Decl	☿ Lat	♀ Decl	♀ Lat	♂ Decl	♂ Lat	⚳ Decl	⚳ Lat	♃ Decl	♃ Lat	♄ Decl	♄ Lat
1 Su	14N54	10N21	4N48	12N27	3N41	2S29	3N11	1S39	7N58	0S43	14S06	8S31	7N41	1S05	2S13	2N43
2 M	15 13	14 26	4 19	16 16	3 48	2 36	3 39	1 40	8 16	0 43	14 01	8 33	7 46	1 05	2 12	2 42
3 Tu	15 30	17 58	3 38	19 28	3 58	2 43	4 07	1 40	8 33	0 42	13 56	8 36	7 51	1 05	2 10	2 42
4 W	15 48	20 45	2 47	21 49	4 09	2 49	4 34	1 40	8 50	0 42	13 51	8 38	7 56	1 05	2 09	2 42
5 Th	16 06	22 37	1 48	23 10	4 23	2 54	5 02	1 40	9 08	0 41	13 46	8 41	8 01	1 05	2 08	2 42
6 F	16 23	23 24	0 43	23 21	4 38	2 58	5 30	1 40	9 25	0 41	13 41	8 43	8 06	1 05	2 06	2 42
7 Sa	16 40	22 60	0S26	22 20	4 55	3 01	5 57	1 40	9 41	0 40	13 36	8 46	8 11	1 05	2 05	2 42
8 Su	16 56	21 22	1 35	20 06	5 14	3 04	6 25	1 40	9 58	0 40	13 31	8 48	8 16	1 05	2 04	2 42
9 M	17 12	18 34	2 40	16 46	5 35	3 06	6 52	1 40	10 15	0 39	13 26	8 51	8 22	1 05	2 03	2 41
0 Tu	17 28	14 44	3 38	12 29	5 57	3 08	7 19	1 40	10 32	0 39	13 21	8 53	8 27	1 05	2 02	2 41
1 W	17 44	10 03	4 25	7 27	6 20	3 09	7 46	1 40	10 48	0 38	13 16	8 56	8 32	1 05	2 01	2 41
2 Th	17 60	4 44	4 57	1 56	6 45	3 09	8 13	1 39	11 04	0 37	13 12	8 58	8 37	1 05	1 60	2 41
3 F	18 15	0S56	5 12	3S48	7 12	3 08	8 40	1 39	11 21	0 37	13 07	9 01	8 41	1 06	1 59	2 41
4 Sa	18 29	6 39	5 06	9 25	7 39	3 07	9 07	1 38	11 37	0 36	13 03	9 04	8 46	1 06	1 58	2 41
5 Su	18 44	12 03	4 41	14 31	8 08	3 05	9 33	1 38	11 53	0 36	12 58	9 06	8 51	1 06	1 57	2 40
6 M	18 58	16 46	3 56	18 44	8 38	3 02	9 59	1 37	12 08	0 35	12 54	9 09	8 56	1 06	1 56	2 40
7 Tu	19 12	20 24	2 56	21 43	9 09	2 59	10 25	1 37	12 24	0 35	12 50	9 12	9 01	1 06	1 55	2 40
8 W	19 26	22 40	1 45	23 14	9 41	2 56	10 51	1 36	12 40	0 34	12 45	9 15	9 06	1 06	1 54	2 40
9 Th	19 39	23 24	0 29	23 12	10 14	2 51	11 16	1 35	12 55	0 33	12 41	9 18	9 11	1 06	1 53	2 40
0 F	19 52	22 38	0N47	21 45	10 48	2 47	11 42	1 34	13 11	0 33	12 37	9 20	9 15	1 06	1 53	2 39
1 Sa	20 04	20 34	1 58	19 08	11 23	2 41	12 07	1 33	13 26	0 32	12 33	9 23	9 20	1 06	1 52	2 39
2 Su	20 16	17 28	3 01	15 38	11 58	2 35	12 31	1 32	13 41	0 32	12 29	9 26	9 25	1 06	1 51	2 39
3 M	20 28	13 38	3 53	11 31	12 34	2 29	12 56	1 31	13 56	0 31	12 25	9 29	9 29	1 06	1 51	2 39
4 Tu	20 40	9 19	4 33	7 02	13 11	2 22	13 20	1 30	14 10	0 30	12 22	9 32	9 34	1 06	1 50	2 39
5 W	20 51	4 43	5 00	2 22	13 48	2 15	13 44	1 28	14 25	0 30	12 18	9 35	9 39	1 06	1 50	2 38
6 Th	21 02	0 00	5 13	2N21	14 25	2 07	14 07	1 27	14 39	0 29	12 14	9 38	9 43	1 06	1 49	2 38
7 F	21 12	4N40	5 13	6 57	15 03	1 58	14 31	1 26	14 54	0 29	12 11	9 41	9 48	1 07	1 49	2 38
8 Sa	21 22	9 10	4 60	11 18	15 41	1 50	14 54	1 24	15 08	0 28	12 07	9 44	9 52	1 07	1 48	2 38
9 Su	21 32	13 21	4 33	15 16	16 19	1 41	15 16	1 23	15 22	0 27	12 04	9 47	9 57	1 07	1 48	2 37
0 M	21 41	17 02	3 55	18 39	16 56	1 31	15 38	1 21	15 36	0 27	12 01	9 50	10 01	1 07	1 47	2 37
1 Tu	21N50	20N03	3N05	21N15	17N34	1S21	15N60	1S20	15N49	0S26	11S58	9S53	10N05	1S07	1S47	2N37

Day	⚷ Decl	⚷ Lat	♅ Decl	♅ Lat	♆ Decl	♆ Lat	♇ Decl	♇ Lat
1	4S25	5N45	0N26	0S43	11S44	0S31	18S43	4N31
6	4 20	5 46	0 31	0 43	11 42	0 31	18 43	4 31
11	4 15	5 47	0 37	0 43	11 41	0 31	18 43	4 32
16	4 11	5 49	0 42	0 43	11 40	0 31	18 43	4 32
21	4 08	5 50	0 46	0 43	11 39	0 31	18 44	4 32
26	4 04	5 52	0 50	0 43	11 38	0 31	18 44	4 31
31	4S02	5N53	0N54	0S43	11S38	0S31	18S45	4N31

Day	⚴ Decl	⚴ Lat	⚵ Decl	⚵ Lat	⚶ Decl	⚶ Lat	Eris Decl	Eris Lat
1	14N17	32N25	9N16	3N13	17S27	0N09	3S47	13S18
6	14 56	32 53	9 25	3 24	17 14	0S04	3 46	13 18
11	15 33	33 23	9 29	3 33	17 04	0 18	3 45	13 18
16	16 09	33 53	9 29	3 42	16 56	0 33	3 44	13 18
21	16 44	34 23	9 26	3 50	16 50	0 50	3 43	13 18
26	17 17	34 53	9 19	3 57	16 48	1 07	3 43	13 19
31	17N47	35N23	9N09	4N04	16S49	1S25	3S42	13S19

Moon Phenomena

Max/0 Decl
dy hr mn
6 3:49 23N25
12 20:07 0 S
18 23:41 23S24
26 0:02 0 N

Perigee/Apogee
dy hr m kilometers
15 11:25 p 362139
27 9:57 a 405002

Max/0 Lat
dy hr mn
6 14:55 0 S
13 5:45 5S12
19 9:05 0 N
26 11:42 5N15

PH dy hr mn
● 3 6:52 12♉31
☽ 10 20:34 19♌51
○ 17 11:10 26♏13
☾ 24 18:53 3♓16

Void of Course Moon

Last Aspect	☽ Ingress
1 15:21 ♂ ☌	♉ 2 5:59
3 6:52 ☉ ☌	♊ 4 17:10
6 20:13 ♂ ✶	♋ 7 2:33
9 6:54 ♂ □	♌ 9 9:36
11 4:53 ♃ △	♍ 11 14:00
13 2:53 ☉ △	♎ 13 15:58
15 16:02 ♀ ☍	♏ 15 16:33
17 11:10 ☉ ☍	♐ 17 17:24
19 14:19 ♃ △	♑ 19 20:17
21 21:05 ♃ □	♒ 22 2:33
24 7:42 ♃ ✶	♓ 24 12:25
25 18:16 ☿ ✶	♈ 27 0:37
29 10:29 ♃ ☌	♉ 29 13:03
31 15:38 ☿ ☌	♊ 31 23:57

DAILY ASPECTARIAN

☽☌☿ 0:14
♀☍♄ 0:16
☽∠♆ 1:09
♂☌♃ 4:27
☽#♆ 7:48
☽∠⚷ 9:30
☽☌♃ 14:52
☽☌♂ 15:21
☿∠♆ 18:55
☽#⚳ 21:32

☽∠⚳ 4:55
☉∥☽ 5:24
⚵ D 5:34
☽✶♆ 7:17
☽⊻♅ 11:35
☿∥♀ 12:06
☉⊼♄ 13:35
☽✶⚷ 15:36
☽△♇ 20:40

☽⊼♄ 5:24
☽#♇ 5:51
☉☌☽ 6:52
♀⊻⚳ 10:26
☽✶⚳ 11:30
☽⊻♀ 11:36
♀#⚷ 13:27
☽⊻☿ 15:34
☽∠♅ 17:24

☽⚼♇ 2:14
♀∠♆ 2:54
☽⊻♃ 3:35
☽⊻♂ 6:50
☽⚼♄ 10:44
☽□♆ 18:31
☽∠♀ 20:11
☿#⚷ 21:03
☽✶♅ 22:50
☽∠☿ 22:53

5 Th
☽□⚷ 2:41
☽⊼♇ 7:23
☽∠♃ 9:18
☽∠♂ 13:50
☽△♄ 15:39
☉⊻☽ 22:15
☽□⚳ 23:21

6 F
☽✶♀ 4:10
☽✶☿ 5:51
☽✶♃ 14:30
☉✶⚳ 18:29
☽✶♂ 20:13

7 Sa
☽△♆ 3:55
☉∠☽ 5:01
☿∠⚷ 5:55
☽□♅ 8:12
☽△⚷ 11:51
♀∠⚷ 16:05
☽☍♇ 16:11
☽□♄ 23:57

8 Su
☽⚼♆ 7:46
☽△⚳ 8:56
☉✶☽ 11:02
☽⚼⚷ 15:34
☽□♀ 17:53
☽□☿ 18:11
☽#♇ 22:53
☽□♃ 23:05

9 M
☉∠♅ 1:15
☽□♂ 6:54
☉∥☽ 8:35
☽⊼♆ 10:58
☽⚼⚳ 12:43
☽△♅ 15:12
☿☌♀ 15:45
☽⊼⚷ 18:37
☽⊼♇ 22:34

10 Tu
☽✶♄ 5:47
☽#⚳ 7:37
☽⊼⚳ 15:46
☽#♆ 16:04
☽⚼♅ 17:40
☉□☽ 20:34
☽∥♂ 20:34

11 W
☽⚼♇ 0:44
☽△☿ 3:49
☽△♀ 4:08
☽△♃ 4:53
☽∥♃ 7:01
♂ ♉ 7:05
☽∠♄ 7:43
☽∥♀ 9:44
☽△♂ 14:23
♀☌♃ 14:43
☽☍♆ 15:20
☽∥☿ 15:47
☽⊼♅ 19:28
☿☌♃ 19:58
☽☍⚷ 22:39

12 Th
☽#⚷ 2:10
☽△♇ 2:15
☽⚼♃ 6:45
☽⚼☿ 7:32
☽⚼♀ 7:57
♂✶♆ 8:29
☽⊻♄ 9:00
☽#♄ 11:46
☽⚼♂ 17:00
☽∥♅ 17:26
☽☍⚳ 19:46
☽#♅ 22:48

13 F
♀∥♃ 1:37
☉△☽ 2:53
☽∥♄ 4:22
☉⚼♇ 7:39
☽⊼♃ 8:02
☽⊼☿ 10:38
☽⊼♀ 11:04
☽∥⚷ 13:45
☽⊼♆ 17:17
☽⊼♂ 19:02
☽☍♅ 21:21

14 Sa
☽⊼⚷ 0:22
☽□♇ 3:42
☽#☿ 4:45
♂#♆ 4:48
☉⚼☽ 5:08
☽#♃ 9:20
☽☌♄ 10:07
☽#♀ 11:37
☽⚼♆ 17:40
☽⊼⚳ 21:43
☽∥♆ 22:11
☉#♇ 23:00
☽#♂ 23:08

15 Su
☽⚼⚷ 0:42
☽∥⚳ 4:18
☉⊼☽ 7:04
☽☍♃ 9:29
☽☍☿ 15:53
☽☍♀ 16:02
☽△♆ 17:53
♂⊻♅ 19:16
☽⊼♅ 22:01
☽☍♂ 22:09
♀ ♉ 22:13
☽⚼⚳ 22:25
☿ ♉ 23:19

16 M
☽△⚷ 0:57
☽✶♇ 4:08
♂∠⚳ 6:20
☿☌♀ 9:26
☽⊻♄ 10:27
☽∥♇ 11:55
☿✶♆ 14:18
☉#☽ 14:29
♀✶♆ 14:53
☿∥♃ 16:27
☽⚼♅ 22:24
☽△⚳ 23:14

17 Tu
☽∠♇ 4:30
☉⚼♄ 6:36
☉⊻♃ 7:01
☽∠♄ 10:51
☽⊼♃ 10:57
☉☍☽ 11:10
☽□♆ 18:48
☽⊼♀ 21:20
☽⊼☿ 21:48
☽△♅ 23:09

18 W
☽⊼♂ 1:50
☽□⚷ 2:07
☽⊻♇ 5:16
♂#⚳ 6:46
♂✶⚷ 7:20
☽✶♄ 11:42
☿⊻♅ 11:43
☽⚼♃ 12:17
♀⊻♅ 19:31

19 Th
☽⚼♀ 0:54
☽⚼☿ 1:53
☽□⚳ 2:12
☽⚼♂ 4:34
☿∠⚳ 5:42
☽△♃ 14:19
☿✶⚷ 17:12
☉⊼☽ 17:30
♀∠⚳ 20:06
♀#♆ 21:24
☽✶♆ 21:48

20 F
☽□♅ 2:31
☽△♀ 5:28
☽✶⚷ 5:35
♀✶⚷ 6:57
☽△☿ 7:06
☽△♂ 8:13
☽☌♇ 8:47
☽□♄ 15:34
♂△♇ 18:24
☿△♇ 21:55
☉⚼☽ 22:08

21 Sa
☽∠♆ 0:32
☿☌♂ 1:21
☉#☽ 4:07
☽✶⚳ 8:21
☽∠⚷ 8:37
☉ ♊ 9:22
☿#♆ 10:43
☽∥♇ 15:04
♀△♇ 18:05
☽□♃ 21:05
♀#⚳ 22:10

22 Su
☉△☽ 3:56
☽⊻♆ 4:12
☉□♆ 7:33
☽✶♅ 9:23
☽⊻⚷ 12:36
☽∠⚳ 12:54
☽⊻♇ 15:51
☽□♀ 18:13
☿#⚳ 18:37
☽□♂ 18:47
☽□☿ 21:54
☽#♂ 22:25
☽△♄ 23:02

23 M
☽#♀ 3:44
☽#☿ 5:22
☿⊼♄ 6:32
☽∥⚳ 7:05
♀☌♂ 8:27
☽∥♆ 11:22
☽∠♅ 14:13
☽⊻⚳ 18:24
☽∠♇ 20:45
☽#♃ 22:42

24 Tu
☽⚼♄ 4:05
☽✶♃ 7:42
☽☌♆ 14:12
☿∥♀ 16:45
♀⊼♄ 18:48
☉□☽ 18:53
☽⊻♅ 19:48
☽☌⚷ 23:05

25 W
☽✶♇ 2:21
☽∥⚷ 3:15
☉✶♅ 6:48
☽✶♂ 9:23
☽⊼♄ 9:48
☽✶♀ 11:32
☽∠♃ 14:06
☽∥♄ 14:47
♂⊼♄ 15:50
☽✶☿ 18:16
☽#♅ 19:48

26 Th
☽∥♅ 4:19
☽☌⚳ 7:28
☽#♄ 9:18
☿∥♂ 14:35
☽∠♂ 17:36
☽#⚷ 20:53
☽⊻♃ 20:55
☽∠♀ 21:12

27 F
☉□⚷ 0:19
☽⊻♆ 2:28
☽∠☿ 5:44
☽☌♅ 8:20
☽⊻⚷ 11:34
☉✶☽ 12:33
☽□♇ 14:42
☽☍♄ 22:11
☿∠♅ 23:17

28 Sa
☽⊻♂ 1:56
☽∥♃ 3:57
☽⊻♀ 6:59
☽∠♆ 8:47
☽#♆ 13:53
☉⊼♇ 14:39
☽#⚳ 16:31
☽⊻☿ 17:25
☽∠⚷ 17:52
☽⊻⚳ 21:24
☉∠☽ 21:27

29 Su
☽☌♃ 10:29
☽∥♀ 13:22
☽∥♂ 13:30
☽✶♆ 14:53
☿⚼♇ 15:45
♀∥♂ 16:41
☽⊻♅ 20:48
☿✶⚳ 22:40
☽∥☿ 23:10
☽✶⚷ 23:52

30 M
☽△♇ 2:47
☽∠⚳ 3:59
☉⊻☽ 5:58
☽⊼♄ 10:06
☽#♇ 12:47
☽☌♂ 17:44

31 Tu
☽☌♀ 1:24
☽∠♅ 2:28
☽⚼♇ 8:13
☽✶⚳ 10:03
♀∠♅ 12:26
☿⚼♄ 14:08
☽⚼♄ 15:24
☽☌☿ 15:38
☉∥☽ 20:35
☽⊻♃ 22:30
⚴ R 23:09

June 2011

LONGITUDE

Day	Sid.Time	☉	☽	☽ 12 hour	Mean ☊	True ☊	☿	♀	♂	⚳	♃	♄	⚷	♅	♆	♇
	h m s	° ' "	° ' "	° ' "	° '	° '	° '	° '	° '	° '	° '	° '	° '	° '	° '	° '
1 W	16 36 33	10♊11 23	0♊01 25	6♊16 31	24♐18.6	23♐25.6	26♉22.3	19♉31.9	15♉24.5	22♓58.1	29♈15.3	10♎34.1	5♓27.3	3♈57.6	0♓55.6	6♑51.9
2 Th	16 40 29	11 08 55	12 34 48	18 56 21	24 15.4	23D 24.7	28 20.0	20 44.9	16 08.6	23 12.9	29 27.9	10R 32.9	5 27.7	3 59.4	0 55.6	6R 50.5
3 F	16 44 26	12 06 26	25 21 16	1♋49 33	24 12.2	23 24.5	0♊19.8	21 57.9	16 52.6	23 27.5	29 40.4	10 31.8	5 28.1	4 01.2	0R 55.6	6 49.2
4 Sa	16 48 22	13 03 56	8♋21 14	14 56 19	24 09.1	23 24.8	2 21.5	23 10.9	17 36.6	23 41.9	29 52.8	10 30.9	5 28.4	4 02.9	0 55.6	6 47.8
5 Su	16 52 19	14 01 24	21 34 48	28 16 38	24 05.9	23 25.5	4 25.1	24 24.0	18 20.5	23 56.1	0♉05.2	10 30.0	5 28.7	4 04.5	0 55.6	6 46.5
6 M	16 56 15	14 58 52	5♌01 49	11♌50 16	24 02.7	23 26.3	6 30.5	25 37.0	19 04.3	24 10.1	0 17.4	10 29.2	5 28.8	4 06.2	0 55.5	6 45.1
7 Tu	17 00 12	15 56 18	18 41 56	25 36 44	23 59.5	23 27.0	8 37.5	26 50.0	19 48.1	24 24.0	0 29.6	10 28.6	5 29.0	4 07.7	0 55.4	6 43.7
8 W	17 04 08	16 53 43	2♍34 34	9♍35 16	23 56.4	23 27.4	10 45.9	28 03.1	20 31.8	24 37.6	0 41.7	10 28.0	5R 29.1	4 09.3	0 55.3	6 42.3
9 Th	17 08 05	17 51 07	16 38 40	23 44 32	23 53.2	23R 27.6	12 55.5	29 16.1	21 15.5	24 51.1	0 53.8	10 27.5	5 29.1	4 10.8	0 55.1	6 40.9
10 F	17 12 02	18 48 30	0♎52 36	8♎02 32	23 50.0	23 27.5	15 06.1	0♊29.2	21 59.1	25 04.3	1 05.7	10 27.2	5 29.0	4 12.2	0 54.9	6 39.4
11 Sa	17 15 58	19 45 52	15 13 57	22 26 23	23 46.8	23 27.3	17 17.4	1 42.3	22 42.6	25 17.4	1 17.6	10 26.9	5 28.9	4 13.6	0 54.7	6 38.0
12 Su	17 19 55	20 43 12	29 39 21	6♏52 19	23 43.7	23 27.0	19 29.2	2 55.4	23 26.1	25 30.2	1 29.4	10 26.7	5 28.8	4 15.0	0 54.4	6 36.6
13 M	17 23 51	21 40 32	14♏04 41	21 15 52	23 40.5	23 26.7	21 41.3	4 08.4	24 09.5	25 42.8	1 41.1	10D 26.6	5 28.6	4 16.3	0 54.1	6 35.1
14 Tu	17 27 48	22 37 51	28 25 15	5♐32 14	23 37.3	23D 26.6	23 53.3	5 21.6	24 52.9	25 55.3	1 52.7	10 26.7	5 28.3	4 17.5	0 53.8	6 33.6
15 W	17 31 44	23 35 09	12♐36 16	19 36 48	23 34.1	23R 26.6	26 04.9	6 34.7	25 36.2	26 07.5	2 04.2	10 26.8	5 28.0	4 18.7	0 53.4	6 32.2
16 Th	17 35 41	24 32 26	26 33 23	3♑25 38	23 31.0	23 26.6	28 16.0	7 47.8	26 19.5	26 19.5	2 15.6	10 27.1	5 27.6	4 19.9	0 53.0	6 30.7
17 F	17 39 37	25 29 43	10♑13 13	16 55 56	23 27.8	23 26.6	0♋26.2	9 00.9	27 02.7	26 31.2	2 27.0	10 27.4	5 27.1	4 21.1	0 52.6	6 29.2
18 Sa	17 43 34	26 26 59	23 33 39	0♒06 20	23 24.6	23 26.4	2 35.3	10 14.1	27 45.8	26 42.8	2 38.2	10 27.8	5 26.6	4 22.1	0 52.2	6 27.7
19 Su	17 47 31	27 24 15	6♒34 02	12 56 54	23 21.4	23 26.0	4 43.1	11 27.3	28 28.9	26 54.1	2 49.4	10 28.4	5 26.1	4 23.2	0 51.7	6 26.2
20 M	17 51 27	28 21 30	19 15 11	25 29 10	23 18.2	23 25.4	6 49.5	12 40.5	29 11.9	27 05.2	3 00.5	10 29.0	5 25.5	4 24.2	0 51.2	6 24.7
21 Tu	17 55 24	29 18 45	1♓39 12	7♓45 44	23 15.1	23 24.8	8 54.3	13 53.7	29 54.9	27 16.0	3 11.4	10 29.7	5 24.8	4 25.1	0 50.6	6 23.2
22 W	17 59 20	0♋16 00	13 49 14	19 50 12	23 11.9	23 24.3	10 57.3	15 06.9	0♊37.8	27 26.6	3 22.3	10 30.6	5 24.1	4 26.0	0 50.1	6 21.7
23 Th	18 03 17	1 13 14	25 49 10	1♈46 43	23 08.7	23D 24.0	12 58.4	16 20.1	1 20.7	27 37.0	3 33.1	10 31.5	5 23.3	4 26.8	0 49.5	6 20.1
24 F	18 07 13	2 10 29	7♈43 27	13 39 47	23 05.5	23 24.0	14 57.7	17 33.4	2 03.5	27 47.1	3 43.8	10 32.5	5 22.4	4 27.6	0 48.8	6 18.6
25 Sa	18 11 10	3 07 43	19 36 29	25 34 03	23 02.4	23 24.4	16 54.9	18 46.6	2 46.2	27 57.0	3 54.3	10 33.7	5 21.5	4 28.4	0 48.2	6 17.1
26 Su	18 15 06	4 04 57	1♉33 01	7♉33 56	22 59.2	23 25.1	18 50.0	19 59.9	3 28.9	28 06.6	4 04.8	10 34.9	5 20.6	4 29.1	0 47.5	6 15.6
27 M	18 19 03	5 02 11	13 37 18	19 43 33	22 56.0	23 26.2	20 43.1	21 13.2	4 11.5	28 16.0	4 15.2	10 36.2	5 19.6	4 29.7	0 46.7	6 14.0
28 Tu	18 23 00	5 59 25	25 53 08	2♊06 23	22 52.8	23 27.3	22 34.0	22 26.6	4 54.0	28 25.1	4 25.4	10 37.6	5 18.5	4 30.4	0 46.0	6 12.5
29 W	18 26 56	6 56 40	8♊23 37	14 45 05	22 49.7	23 28.2	24 22.8	23 39.9	5 36.5	28 33.9	4 35.6	10 39.2	5 17.4	4 30.9	0 45.2	6 11.0
30 Th	18 30 53	7♋53 54	21 10 56	27 41 16	22♐46.5	23♐28.6	26♋09.5	24♊53.3	6♊19.0	28♓42.5	4♉45.6	10♎40.8	5♓16.2	4♈31.4	0♓44.4	6♑09.5

1st of Month

Julian Day # 2455713.5
Obliquity 23°26'15"
SVP 5♓05'45"
GC 26♐59.9
Eris 22♈17.8

Day	⚴
1	15♒49.8R
6	15 45.0R
11	15 30.8R
16	15 06.9R
21	14 33.6R
26	13 50.9R

Day	⚵
1	16♍24.9
6	17 13.6
11	18 07.9
16	19 07.4
21	20 11.7
26	21 20.3

Day	⚶
1	18♒03.0
6	18 43.8
11	19 13.9
16	19 32.9
21	19 40.2
26	19 35.5R

DECLINATION and LATITUDE

Day	☉ Decl	☽ Decl	☽ Lat	☽ 12h Decl	☿ Decl	☿ Lat	♀ Decl	♀ Lat	♂ Decl	♂ Lat	⚳ Decl	⚳ Lat	♃ Decl	♃ Lat	♄ Decl	♄ Lat
1 W	21N59	22N12	2N06	22N53	18N11	1S11	16N21	1S18	16N03	0S26	11S55	9S57	10N10	1S07	1S47	2N37
2 Th	22 07	23 17	0 60	23 23	18 48	1 01	16 42	1 17	16 16	0 25	11 52	9 60	10 14	1 07	1 46	2 37
3 F	22 14	23 11	0S11	22 39	19 24	0 50	17 03	1 15	16 29	0 24	11 49	10 03	10 18	1 07	1 46	2 36
4 Sa	22 22	21 49	1 22	20 40	19 59	0 40	17 23	1 13	16 42	0 24	11 46	10 06	10 23	1 07	1 46	2 36
5 Su	22 29	19 15	2 30	17 33	20 33	0 29	17 43	1 11	16 55	0 23	11 44	10 10	10 27	1 07	1 46	2 36
6 M	22 35	15 36	3 31	13 26	21 06	0 18	18 02	1 10	17 08	0 22	11 41	10 13	10 31	1 08	1 46	2 36
7 Tu	22 42	11 05	4 21	8 35	21 37	0 07	18 21	1 08	17 20	0 22	11 39	10 16	10 35	1 08	1 46	2 35
8 W	22 48	5 57	4 56	3 13	22 07	0N04	18 39	1 06	17 33	0 21	11 36	10 20	10 39	1 08	1 46	2 35
9 Th	22 53	0 26	5 15	2S22	22 35	0 14	18 57	1 04	17 45	0 20	11 34	10 23	10 43	1 08	1 46	2 35
10 F	22 58	5S09	5 14	7 53	23 01	0 25	19 15	1 02	17 57	0 20	11 32	10 27	10 48	1 08	1 46	2 35
11 Sa	23 03	10 31	4 54	13 01	23 24	0 35	19 32	0 60	18 08	0 19	11 30	10 30	10 52	1 08	1 46	2 34
12 Su	23 07	15 20	4 16	17 26	23 46	0 44	19 48	0 58	18 20	0 18	11 28	10 34	10 55	1 08	1 46	2 34
13 M	23 11	19 16	3 21	20 48	24 04	0 54	20 04	0 56	18 31	0 18	11 26	10 37	10 59	1 08	1 46	2 34
14 Tu	23 14	21 59	2 14	22 50	24 20	1 03	20 19	0 53	18 43	0 17	11 24	10 41	11 03	1 08	1 47	2 34
15 W	23 17	23 18	0 60	23 23	24 34	1 11	20 34	0 51	18 54	0 16	11 23	10 44	11 07	1 09	1 47	2 33
16 Th	23 19	23 06	0N17	22 28	24 44	1 19	20 48	0 49	19 05	0 16	11 21	10 48	11 11	1 09	1 47	2 33
17 F	23 22	21 31	1 32	20 16	24 52	1 26	21 02	0 47	19 15	0 15	11 20	10 51	11 15	1 09	1 48	2 33
18 Sa	23 23	18 46	2 39	17 02	24 57	1 32	21 15	0 44	19 26	0 14	11 19	10 55	11 18	1 09	1 48	2 33
19 Su	23 25	15 08	3 37	13 04	24 59	1 38	21 27	0 42	19 36	0 14	11 18	10 59	11 22	1 09	1 48	2 32
20 M	23 26	10 53	4 22	8 38	24 58	1 42	21 39	0 40	19 46	0 13	11 17	11 02	11 26	1 09	1 49	2 32
21 Tu	23 26	6 18	4 54	3 56	24 55	1 47	21 51	0 38	19 56	0 12	11 16	11 06	11 29	1 09	1 49	2 32
22 W	23 26	1 33	5 12	0N49	24 49	1 50	22 01	0 35	20 06	0 12	11 15	11 10	11 33	1 09	1 50	2 32
23 Th	23 26	3N11	5 16	5 30	24 40	1 53	22 12	0 33	20 15	0 11	11 14	11 14	11 36	1 10	1 51	2 31
24 F	23 25	7 46	5 07	9 57	24 30	1 55	22 21	0 30	20 24	0 10	11 14	11 18	11 40	1 10	1 51	2 31
25 Sa	23 24	12 03	4 44	14 03	24 17	1 56	22 30	0 28	20 33	0 09	11 13	11 21	11 43	1 10	1 52	2 31
26 Su	23 22	15 54	4 09	17 37	24 02	1 56	22 38	0 26	20 42	0 09	11 13	11 25	11 47	1 10	1 53	2 31
27 M	23 20	19 09	3 23	20 29	23 45	1 56	22 46	0 23	20 51	0 08	11 13	11 29	11 50	1 10	1 53	2 30
28 Tu	23 18	21 36	2 27	22 28	23 26	1 55	22 53	0 21	20 59	0 07	11 13	11 33	11 53	1 10	1 54	2 30
29 W	23 15	23 04	1 22	23 22	23 06	1 54	22 59	0 18	21 08	0 07	11 13	11 37	11 57	1 10	1 55	2 30
30 Th	23N12	23N21	0N13	23N02	22N44	1N51	23N04	0S16	21N16	0S06	11S13	11S41	11N60	1S11	1S56	2N30

Day	⚷ Decl	⚷ Lat	♅ Decl	♅ Lat	♆ Decl	♆ Lat	♇ Decl	♇ Lat
1	4S01	5N54	0N55	0S43	11S38	0S31	18S45	4N31
6	3 59	5 55	0 58	0 44	11 38	0 32	18 45	4 31
11	3 58	5 57	1 01	0 44	11 39	0 32	18 46	4 31
16	3 57	5 58	1 03	0 44	11 39	0 32	18 46	4 30
21	3 57	5 60	1 05	0 44	11 40	0 32	18 47	4 30
26	3 57	6 01	1 06	0 44	11 42	0 32	18 48	4 30

Day	⚴ Decl	⚴ Lat	⚵ Decl	⚵ Lat	⚶ Decl	⚶ Lat	Eris Decl	Eris Lat
1	17N52	35N29	9N07	4N05	16S49	1S28	3S42	13S19
6	18 19	35 58	8 54	4 11	16 55	1 48	3 41	13 19
11	18 41	36 25	8 38	4 17	17 05	2 08	3 41	13 20
16	18 60	36 50	8 19	4 22	17 19	2 29	3 41	13 20
21	19 13	37 13	7 58	4 27	17 38	2 52	3 41	13 21
26	19 22	37 32	7 36	4 32	18 01	3 15	3 41	13 21

Moon Phenomena

Max/0 Decl
dy hr mn
2 9:52 23N23
9 1:53 0 S
15 8:49 23S24
22 7:51 0 N
29 17:51 23N24

Max/0 Lat
dy hr mn
2 20:22 0 S
9 11:30 5S17
15 18:36 0 N
22 19:09 5N17
30 4:14 0 S

Perigee/Apogee
dy hr m kilometers
12 1:34 p 367190
24 4:07 a 404270

PH dy hr mn
● 1 21:04 11♊02
◐ 1 21:17 P 0.601
☽ 9 2:12 17♍56
○ 15 20:15 24♐23
◐ 15 20:14 T 1.700
☾ 23 11:49 1♈41

Void of Course Moon

Last Aspect			☽ Ingress	
3 8:09	♃	⚹	♋	3 8:37
5 5:34	♀	⚹	♌	5 15:04
7 15:28	♀	□	♍	7 19:34
9 8:14	♂	△	♎	9 22:32
11 8:05	☉	△	♏	12 0:34
13 17:45	♂	☍	♐	14 2:39
16 3:32	♀	☍	♑	16 6:00
18 8:08	♂	△	♒	18 11:48
20 20:24	♂	□	♓	20 20:46
22 2:52	♀	□	♈	23 8:25
24 22:08	♀	⚹	♉	25 20:54
27 16:25	☿	⚹	♊	28 7:57
30 7:34	♀	☌	♋	30 16:14

DAILY ASPECTARIAN

1 W ☽□♆ 1:44 · ☽⚹♅ 7:35 · ☉△♄ 9:17 · ☽□⚷ 10:26 · ☽⚻♇ 13:06 · ☽△♄ 20:09 · ☉☌☽ 21:04 · ☿#♇ 21:56

2 Th ☽∠♃ 3:38 · ☽⚺♂ 7:09 · ☿⚺♃ 15:14 · ☽⚺♀ 17:01 · ☿ ♊ 20:04 · ☽□⚳ 20:24 · ♀⚼♇ 21:11

3 F ☿□♆ 7:06 · ♆ R 7:29 · ☽⚹♃ 8:09 · ☽△♆ 10:20 · ☽⚺☿ 10:56 · ☽∠♂ 12:49 · ☽□♅ 16:05 · ☉∥☽ 17:07 · ☽△⚷ 18:43 · ☽☍♇ 21:09 · ☽∠♀ 23:39

4 Sa ☽□♄ 3:57 · ☉⚺☽ 9:16 · ♀⚹⚳ 12:38 · ☽⚼♆ 13:48 · ♃ ♉ 13:57 · ☽∥☿ 14:59 · ☽⚹♂ 17:49 · ☽∠☿ 19:23 · ☿⚹♅ 19:58 · ☽⚼⚷ 22:01

5 Su ☽#♇ 3:39 · ☽△⚳ 4:18 · ☽⚹♀ 5:34 · ☽∥♀ 9:57 · ☿□⚷ 12:13 · ☉∠☽ 14:21 · ☽∥♂ 15:10 · ☽□♃ 15:27 · ☽⚻♆ 16:43 · ♀⚼♄ 21:28 · ☽△♅ 22:21

6 M ☽⚻⚷ 0:48 · ♂∠♅ 1:03 · ☿⚻♇ 2:45 · ☽⚻♇ 3:02 · ☽⚹☿ 3:06 · ☽⚼⚳ 7:26 · ☽⚹♄ 9:37 · ☉∠♃ 9:51 · ☉⚹☽ 18:49 · ☽#⚳ 21:13 · ☽#♆ 21:16

7 Tu ☽⚼♅ 0:45 · ☽□♂ 2:02 · ☽∥♃ 2:25 · ⚳∥♆ 3:14 · ☽⚼♇ 5:16 · ☽⚻⚳ 10:04 · ☽∠♄ 11:45 · ☽□♀ 15:28 · ☿△♄ 20:41 · ☽△♃ 20:43 · ☽☍♆ 21:09

8 W ☽⚻♅ 2:43 · ☽☍⚷ 4:59 · ☽△♇ 7:04 · ♀#♇ 8:07 · ☽#⚷ 8:42 · ☽⚺♄ 13:29 · ☽□☿ 16:32 · ☽#♄ 18:18 · ⚷ R 19:08 · ☽∥♅ 21:37 · ☽⚼♃ 22:43

9 Th ☉□☽ 2:12 · ♃⚹♆ 2:40 · ☽#♅ 6:08 · ☽△♂ 8:14 · ☽∥♄ 9:26 · ♂⚼♇ 13:32 · ☽☍⚳ 14:05 · ♀ ♊ 14:24 · ☽∥⚷ 18:53 · ☉∥☿ 20:36 · ☽△♀ 23:17

10 F ☽⚻♆ 0:04 · ☽⚻♃ 0:22 · ☽☍♅ 5:35 · ☽⚻⚷ 7:43 · ♀□♆ 8:25 · ☽□♇ 9:40 · ☽⚼♂ 10:47 · ☿∠♃ 12:00 · ♀⚺♃ 14:19 · ☽☌♄ 16:01

11 Sa ☽⚼♆ 1:08 · ☽#♃ 1:36 · ☽⚼♀ 2:41 · ☽△☿ 4:03 · ☽∥⚳ 4:35 · ☽∥♆ 5:18 · ☉△☽ 8:05 · ☽⚼⚷ 8:44 · ☽⚻♂ 13:07 · ☽⚻⚳ 17:00

12 Su ☽△♆ 2:05 · ☽☍♃ 3:05 · ☽⚻♀ 5:56 · ☽⚻♅ 7:39 · ☽⚼☿ 9:29 · ☽△⚷ 9:41 · ☉⚼☽ 10:48 · ☽⚹♇ 11:33 · ☽⚺♄ 17:57 · ☽⚼⚳ 18:19 · ☽#♂ 18:39 · ☽∥♇ 20:34 · ☉☌☿ 23:45

13 M ♀⚹♅ 2:37 · ♄ D 3:52 · ☽#♀ 6:32 · ☽⚼♅ 8:41 · ☽∠♇ 12:31 · ☉⚻☽ 13:36 · ☽⚻☿ 15:01 · ☽☍♂ 17:45 · ☽∠♄ 19:00 · ☽△⚳ 19:44

14 Tu ♀□⚷ 2:12 · ☽□♆ 4:10 · ☽⚻♃ 5:54 · ♂#♇ 7:46 · ☽△♅ 9:55 · ☽□⚷ 11:53 · ☽☍♀ 12:48 · ☽⚺♇ 13:43 · ☿⚺♂ 16:12 · ♂⚼♄ 18:46 · ☽⚹♄ 20:20 · ♀⚻♇ 23:12 · ☉#☽ 23:28 · ☉#☽ 23:30

15 W ☿□⚳ 0:31 · ☽⚼♃ 7:44 · ☉☍☽ 20:15 · ☽⚻♂ 23:35 · ☽□⚳ 23:35 · ♂⚹⚳ 23:59

16 Th ☽☍☿ 3:32 · ☽⚹♆ 7:32 · ☽△♃ 10:06 · ☽□♅ 13:37 · ☽⚹⚷ 15:34 · ☽☌♇ 17:24 · ☿ ♋ 19:10 · ☽⚻♀ 21:39

17 F ☽□♄ 0:25 · ☽⚼♂ 3:26 · ☽#♀ 4:36 · ☿△♆ 4:53 · ☽∠♆ 10:06 · ☽∠⚷ 18:21 · ☽#♂ 19:13 · ☽∥♇ 23:53

18 Sa ☿⚹♃ 0:36 · ⚳#♃ 1:36 · ☽⚼♀ 3:22 · ♀△♄ 4:32 · ☉⚻☽ 5:42 · ☽⚹⚳ 5:51 · ☽△♂ 8:08 · ☉□⚳ 8:16 · ☽⚺♆ 13:24 · ☽□♃ 16:56 · ☽⚻☿ 19:52 · ☽⚹♅ 19:56 · ☿□♅ 20:12 · ☽⚺⚷ 21:53 · ☽⚺♇ 23:45

19 Su ☽△♄ 7:20 · ☿△⚷ 8:05 · ☽△♀ 10:09 · ☽∠⚳ 10:10 · ☉⚼☽ 11:52 · ☿☍♇ 19:19 · ☽∥♆ 19:47 · ☽#♃ 21:07 · ☽∥⚳ 21:54

20 M ☽∠♅ 0:17 · ☽∠♇ 4:08 · ☽⚼☿ 5:56 · ☽⚼♄ 12:00 · ☽⚺⚳ 15:20 · ☉△☽ 19:03 · ☽□♂ 20:24 · ☽☌♆ 22:25

21 Tu ♂ ♊ 2:51 · ☽⚹♃ 3:03 · ☽⚺♅ 5:26 · ☽☌⚷ 7:22 · ☽⚹♇ 9:16 · ☽∥⚷ 11:58 · ⚶ R 13:27 · ☽△☿ 17:10 · ☉ ♋ 17:18 · ☽⚻♄ 17:25 · ☿□♄ 18:43 · ☽∥♄ 22:36

22 W ☽#♅ 2:21 · ☽□♀ 2:52 · ♂□♆ 6:46 · ☽∠♃ 9:13 · ☽∥♅ 13:22 · ☉△♆ 14:08 · ☽#♄ 17:10

23 Th ☽☌⚳ 3:40 · ☽#⚷ 3:56 · ☽⚺♆ 10:04 · ☉□☽ 11:49 · ☽⚹♂ 11:50 · ☉⚺♂ 12:20 · ☽⚺♃ 15:49 · ☽☌♅ 17:24 · ☽⚺⚷ 19:16 · ☽□♇ 21:09

24 F ☽☍♄ 5:42 · ♃#♆ 8:09 · ☿⚼♆ 10:22 · ☽∠♆ 16:20 · ☽□☿ 17:30 · ☽#⚳ 19:12 · ☽∠♂ 20:03 · ☽#♆ 21:52 · ☽∥♃ 22:03 · ☽⚹♀ 22:08

25 Sa ☽∠⚷ 1:31 · ♀∠♃ 2:56 · ☿∠♂ 16:55 · ☽⚺⚳ 17:01 · ☽⚹♆ 22:29 · ☉⚹♃ 23:55

26 Su ☽⚺♂ 4:06 · ☽☌♃ 5:08 · ☉⚹☽ 5:30 · ☽⚺♅ 5:52 · ☽⚹⚷ 7:34 · ☽∠♀ 7:40 · ☽△♇ 9:23 · ☉□♅ 10:15 · ☽⚻♄ 18:01 · ☿⚼⚷ 19:01 · ☽#♇ 21:09 · ☽∠⚳ 23:17

27 M ♂⚺♃ 2:45 · ☉△⚷ 7:09 · ♂⚹♅ 10:27 · ☽∠♅ 11:34 · ☉∠☽ 13:40 · ☽⚼♇ 14:55 · ☽⚹☿ 16:25 · ☽⚺♀ 16:34 · ☽∥♂ 16:39 · ☿⚺♀ 19:08 · ☽⚼♄ 23:30

28 Tu ☽⚹⚳ 4:58 · ☉☍♇ 5:21 · ☽□♆ 9:25 · ☉∥☿ 11:39 · ♃⚺♅ 12:21 · ♂□⚷ 13:28 · ☽⚹♅ 16:36 · ☽⚺♃ 16:40 · ☽□⚷ 18:06 · ☽☌♂ 18:23 · ☽⚻♇ 19:48 · ☉⚺☽ 21:01 · ☽∥♀ 21:48

29 W ☽∥☿ 0:50 · ☽∠☿ 2:11 · ☽△♄ 4:17 · ☉∥☽ 5:51 · ☿∥♀ 6:25 · ♂⚻♇ 18:48 · ☽∠♃ 21:19

30 Th ☽☌♀ 7:34 · ☉∥☽ 7:36 · ☽∥♀ 9:49 · ☽⚺☿ 10:37 · ☽□⚳ 14:01 · ☽△♆ 17:34 · ☉∥♀ 21:24

LONGITUDE

July 2011

Day	Sid.Time	☉	☽	☽ 12 hour	Mean☊	True☊	☿	♀	♂	⚳	♃	♄	⚷	♅	♆	♇
	h m s	° ' "	° ' "	° ' "	° '	° '	° '	° '	° '	° '	° '	° '	° '	° '	° '	° '
1 F	18 34 49	8♋51 08	4♋16 06	10♋55 23	22♐43.3	23♐28.4	27♋53.9	26♊06.6	7♊01.3	28♓50.8	4♉55.5	10♎42.5	5♓15.0	4♈31.9	0♓43.6	6♑07.9
2 Sa	18 38 46	9 48 21	17 38 59	24 26 40	22 40.1	23R 27.3	29 36.2	27 20.0	7 43.7	28 58.8	5 05.3	10 44.4	5R 13.7	4 32.3	0R 42.7	6R 06.4
3 Su	18 42 42	10 45 35	1♌18 10	8♌13 10	22 37.0	23 25.6	1♌16.4	28 33.4	8 25.9	29 06.5	5 15.0	10 46.3	5 12.4	4 32.7	0 41.8	6 04.9
4 M	18 46 39	11 42 49	15 11 15	22 12 02	22 33.8	23 23.3	2 54.3	29 46.8	9 08.1	29 14.0	5 24.6	10 48.3	5 11.0	4 33.0	0 40.9	6 03.4
5 Tu	18 50 35	12 40 02	29 15 02	6♍19 51	22 30.6	23 20.8	4 30.1	1♋00.3	9 50.2	29 21.1	5 34.0	10 50.4	5 09.6	4 33.3	0 40.0	6 01.8
6 W	18 54 32	13 37 15	13♍25 59	20 33 02	22 27.4	23 18.5	6 03.7	2 13.7	10 32.3	29 28.0	5 43.4	10 52.6	5 08.1	4 33.5	0 39.0	6 00.3
7 Th	18 58 29	14 34 27	27 40 34	4♎48 12	22 24.2	23 16.9	7 35.0	3 27.2	11 14.3	29 34.6	5 52.6	10 54.9	5 06.5	4 33.6	0 38.0	5 58.8
8 F	19 02 25	15 31 39	11♎55 35	19 02 25	22 21.1	23D 16.2	9 04.2	4 40.6	11 56.2	29 40.8	6 01.6	10 57.3	5 04.9	4 33.8	0 37.0	5 57.3
9 Sa	19 06 22	16 28 52	26 08 23	3♏13 13	22 17.9	23 16.4	10 31.0	5 54.1	12 38.1	29 46.8	6 10.6	10 59.8	5 03.3	4 33.8	0 36.0	5 55.8
10 Su	19 10 18	17 26 03	10♏16 41	17 18 33	22 14.7	23 17.4	11 55.6	7 07.6	13 19.9	29 52.5	6 19.4	11 02.4	5 01.6	4R 33.9	0 34.9	5 54.3
11 M	19 14 15	18 23 15	24 18 36	1♐16 37	22 11.5	23 18.8	13 17.9	8 21.2	14 01.6	29 57.8	6 28.1	11 05.0	4 59.9	4 33.8	0 33.8	5 52.8
12 Tu	19 18 11	19 20 27	8♐12 23	15 05 42	22 08.4	23 20.1	14 37.9	9 34.7	14 43.3	0♈02.9	6 36.7	11 07.8	4 58.1	4 33.8	0 32.7	5 51.3
13 W	19 22 08	20 17 39	21 56 20	28 44 06	22 05.2	23R 20.7	15 55.5	10 48.2	15 24.9	0 07.7	6 45.1	11 10.6	4 56.3	4 33.7	0 31.6	5 49.9
14 Th	19 26 04	21 14 51	5♑28 46	12♑10 08	22 02.0	23 20.2	17 10.6	12 01.8	16 06.4	0 12.1	6 53.4	11 13.6	4 54.4	4 33.5	0 30.4	5 48.4
15 F	19 30 01	22 12 03	18 48 04	25 22 23	21 58.8	23 18.3	18 23.3	13 15.4	16 47.9	0 16.2	7 01.6	11 16.6	4 52.5	4 33.3	0 29.3	5 47.0
16 Sa	19 33 58	23 09 16	1♒52 58	8♒19 46	21 55.7	23 15.0	19 33.4	14 29.0	17 29.4	0 20.0	7 09.6	11 19.7	4 50.6	4 33.0	0 28.1	5 45.5
17 Su	19 37 54	24 06 28	14 42 45	21 01 58	21 52.5	23 10.6	20 40.8	15 42.6	18 10.7	0 23.5	7 17.5	11 22.9	4 48.6	4 32.7	0 26.8	5 44.1
18 M	19 41 51	25 03 41	27 17 28	3♓29 27	21 49.3	23 05.4	21 45.6	16 56.3	18 52.0	0 26.6	7 25.2	11 26.2	4 46.5	4 32.3	0 25.6	5 42.7
19 Tu	19 45 47	26 00 55	9♓38 05	15 43 41	21 46.1	23 00.0	22 47.5	18 09.9	19 33.3	0 29.4	7 32.8	11 29.6	4 44.4	4 31.9	0 24.3	5 41.2
20 W	19 49 44	26 58 09	21 46 34	27 47 07	21 42.9	22 55.1	23 46.5	19 23.6	20 14.4	0 31.9	7 40.3	11 33.1	4 42.3	4 31.5	0 23.0	5 39.8
21 Th	19 53 40	27 55 24	3♈45 47	9♈43 02	21 39.8	22 51.3	24 42.6	20 37.3	20 55.6	0 34.0	7 47.6	11 36.6	4 40.1	4 31.0	0 21.7	5 38.4
22 F	19 57 37	28 52 40	15 39 25	21 35 28	21 36.6	22 48.8	25 35.5	21 51.0	21 36.6	0 35.8	7 54.8	11 40.3	4 37.9	4 30.4	0 20.4	5 37.1
23 Sa	20 01 33	29 49 56	27 31 47	3♉28 59	21 33.4	22D 47.8	26 25.1	23 04.8	22 17.6	0 37.2	8 01.8	11 44.0	4 35.7	4 29.8	0 19.1	5 35.7
24 Su	20 05 30	0♌47 14	9♉27 40	15 28 26	21 30.2	22 48.1	27 11.4	24 18.6	22 58.5	0 38.3	8 08.7	11 47.8	4 33.4	4 29.2	0 17.7	5 34.4
25 M	20 09 27	1 44 32	21 31 56	27 38 44	21 27.1	22 49.4	27 54.1	25 32.3	23 39.4	0 39.1	8 15.4	11 51.6	4 31.1	4 28.5	0 16.3	5 33.0
26 Tu	20 13 23	2 41 51	3♊49 24	10♊04 28	21 23.9	22 50.9	28 33.1	26 46.2	24 20.2	0R 39.5	8 21.9	11 55.6	4 28.7	4 27.8	0 14.9	5 31.7
27 W	20 17 20	3 39 11	16 24 24	22 49 34	21 20.7	22R 52.0	29 08.3	28 00.0	25 00.9	0 39.5	8 28.3	11 59.6	4 26.3	4 27.0	0 13.5	5 30.4
28 Th	20 21 16	4 36 32	29 20 19	5♋56 50	21 17.5	22 52.0	29 39.4	29 13.8	25 41.6	0 39.2	8 34.6	12 03.8	4 23.9	4 26.2	0 12.1	5 29.1
29 F	20 25 13	5 33 54	12♋39 12	19 27 24	21 14.4	22 50.3	0♍06.3	0♌27.7	26 22.2	0 38.6	8 40.7	12 08.0	4 21.4	4 25.3	0 10.7	5 27.8
30 Sa	20 29 09	6 31 16	26 21 14	3♌20 24	21 11.2	22 46.7	0 28.9	1 41.6	27 02.8	0 37.5	8 46.6	12 12.2	4 18.9	4 24.4	0 09.2	5 26.6
31 Su	20 33 06	7♌28 40	10♌24 26	17 32 46	21♐08.0	22♐41.3	0♍46.9	2♌55.5	27♊43.3	0♈36.1	8♉52.3	12♎16.6	4♓16.4	4♈23.5	0♓07.7	5♑25.3

1st of Month

Julian Day # 2455743.5
Obliquity 23°26'14"
SVP 5♓05'40"
GC 27♐00.0
Eris 22♈27.7

Day	⚴	⚵	⚶
1	12♒59.3R	22♒32.9	19♒18.6R
6	11 59.6R	23 49.1	18 49.7R
11	10 52.8R	25 08.7	18 09.4R
16	9 40.3R	26 31.3	17 18.9R
21	8 23.6R	27 56.7	16 19.4R
26	7 04.2R	29 24.5	15 12.8R
31	5 44.2R	0♓54.7	14 01.1R

DECLINATION and LATITUDE

Day	☉ Decl	☽ Decl	☽ Lat	☽12h Decl	☿ Decl	☿ Lat	♀ Decl	♀ Lat	♂ Decl	♂ Lat	⚳ Decl	⚳ Lat	♃ Decl	♃ Lat	♄ Decl	♄ Lat
1 F	23N08	22N23	0S59	21N25	22N21	1N48	23N09	0S13	21N24	0S05	11S14	11S45	12N03	1S11	1S57	2N29
2 Sa	23 04	20 08	2 10	18 34	21 56	1 45	23 14	0 11	21 31	0 05	11 14	11 49	12 06	1 11	1 58	2 29
3 Su	23 00	16 43	3 14	14 38	21 31	1 41	23 17	0 08	21 39	0 04	11 15	11 53	12 09	1 11	1 59	2 29
4 M	22 55	12 20	4 08	9 51	21 04	1 36	23 20	0 06	21 46	0 03	11 16	11 57	12 12	1 11	1 60	2 29
5 Tu	22 50	7 14	4 47	4 31	20 36	1 31	23 22	0 04	21 53	0 02	11 17	12 01	12 15	1 11	2 01	2 28
6 W	22 44	1 44	5 10	1S04	20 07	1 25	23 24	0 02	21 60	0 02	11 18	12 06	12 18	1 12	2 02	2 28
7 Th	22 38	3S52	5 14	6 37	19 38	1 18	23 25	0N01	22 06	0 01	11 19	12 10	12 21	1 12	2 03	2 28
8 F	22 32	9 17	4 58	11 49	19 08	1 11	23 25	0 04	22 13	0 00	11 20	12 14	12 24	1 12	2 04	2 28
9 Sa	22 25	14 12	4 24	16 22	18 37	1 04	23 25	0 06	22 19	0N00	11 22	12 18	12 27	1 12	2 05	2 28
10 Su	22 18	18 18	3 35	19 57	18 07	0 56	23 23	0 09	22 25	0 01	11 23	12 22	12 29	1 12	2 07	2 27
11 M	22 10	21 19	2 33	22 21	17 35	0 48	23 21	0 11	22 31	0 02	11 25	12 26	12 32	1 12	2 08	2 27
12 Tu	22 03	23 02	1 22	23 21	17 04	0 39	23 19	0 13	22 36	0 03	11 27	12 31	12 35	1 13	2 09	2 27
13 W	21 54	23 19	0 08	22 56	16 32	0 30	23 16	0 16	22 42	0 03	11 29	12 35	12 37	1 13	2 10	2 27
14 Th	21 46	22 13	1N06	21 12	16 00	0 20	23 12	0 18	22 47	0 04	11 31	12 39	12 40	1 13	2 12	2 26
15 F	21 36	19 53	2 15	18 20	15 28	0 10	23 07	0 20	22 52	0 05	11 33	12 43	12 42	1 13	2 13	2 26
16 Sa	21 27	16 34	3 15	14 37	14 57	0S01	23 02	0 23	22 56	0 06	11 36	12 48	12 45	1 13	2 15	2 26
17 Su	21 17	12 31	4 04	10 18	14 25	0 11	22 56	0 25	23 01	0 06	11 38	12 52	12 47	1 14	2 16	2 26
18 M	21 07	8 01	4 41	5 40	13 54	0 22	22 49	0 27	23 05	0 07	11 41	12 56	12 49	1 14	2 18	2 25
19 Tu	20 57	3 16	5 03	0 53	13 23	0 34	22 42	0 30	23 09	0 08	11 44	13 01	12 52	1 14	2 19	2 25
20 W	20 46	1N30	5 11	3N52	12 53	0 46	22 34	0 32	23 13	0 09	11 47	13 05	12 54	1 14	2 21	2 25
21 Th	20 35	6 10	5 06	8 25	12 23	0 58	22 25	0 34	23 17	0 09	11 50	13 09	12 56	1 14	2 22	2 25
22 F	20 23	10 34	4 47	12 38	11 54	1 10	22 16	0 36	23 20	0 10	11 53	13 14	12 58	1 14	2 24	2 25
23 Sa	20 11	14 34	4 16	16 23	11 25	1 22	22 06	0 38	23 24	0 11	11 56	13 18	13 00	1 15	2 25	2 24
24 Su	19 59	18 01	3 34	19 29	10 58	1 35	21 55	0 40	23 27	0 12	11 60	13 22	13 02	1 15	2 27	2 24
25 M	19 46	20 45	2 42	21 47	10 31	1 48	21 44	0 43	23 29	0 12	12 03	13 26	13 04	1 15	2 29	2 24
26 Tu	19 33	22 35	1 42	23 06	10 05	2 01	21 32	0 45	23 32	0 13	12 07	13 31	13 06	1 15	2 31	2 24
27 W	19 20	23 19	0 35	23 15	9 41	2 14	21 19	0 47	23 34	0 14	12 11	13 35	13 08	1 15	2 32	2 23
28 Th	19 07	22 51	0S35	22 08	9 18	2 27	21 06	0 49	23 37	0 15	12 15	13 39	13 10	1 16	2 34	2 23
29 F	18 53	21 05	1 45	19 44	8 57	2 40	20 52	0 50	23 39	0 15	12 19	13 44	13 12	1 16	2 36	2 23
30 Sa	18 38	18 05	2 51	16 09	8 37	2 52	20 38	0 52	23 40	0 16	12 24	13 48	13 13	1 16	2 38	2 23
31 Su	18N24	13N58	3S48	11N34	8N18	3S05	20N23	0N54	23N42	0N17	12S28	13S52	13N15	1S16	2S40	2N23

Day	⚷ Decl	⚷ Lat	♅ Decl	♅ Lat	♆ Decl	♆ Lat	♇ Decl	♇ Lat
1	3S58	6N02	1N07	0S44	11S43	0S32	18S49	4N29
6	3 59	6 04	1 08	0 45	11 45	0 32	18 50	4 29
11	4 01	6 05	1 08	0 45	11 47	0 32	18 51	4 28
16	4 03	6 06	1 07	0 45	11 49	0 33	18 52	4 27
21	4 06	6 07	1 06	0 45	11 51	0 33	18 53	4 26
26	4 09	6 08	1 05	0 45	11 54	0 33	18 54	4 26
31	4S13	6N08	1N03	0S45	11S56	0S33	18S55	4N25

Day	⚴ Decl	⚴ Lat	⚵ Decl	⚵ Lat	⚶ Decl	⚶ Lat	Eris Decl	Eris Lat
1	19N25	37N48	7N11	4N36	18S29	3S38	3S41	13S22
6	19 22	37 58	6 45	4 41	19 01	4 02	3 41	13 22
11	19 12	38 04	6 17	4 45	19 37	4 27	3 41	13 23
16	18 56	38 03	5 48	4 49	20 15	4 50	3 42	13 23
21	18 33	37 56	5 18	4 53	20 55	5 13	3 42	13 24
26	18 04	37 43	4 46	4 57	21 36	5 35	3 43	13 24
31	17N29	37N23	4N14	5N01	22S17	5S56	3S43	13S25

Moon Phenomena

Max/0 Decl

dy	hr mn	
6	7:25	0 S
12	17:02	23S23
19	16:25	0 N
27	2:55	23N20

Perigee/Apogee

dy	hr m		kilometers
7	13:53	p	369569
21	22:55	a	404355

Max/0 Lat

dy	hr mn	
6	16:40	5S15
13	2:28	0 N
20	2:13	5N11
27	12:04	0 S

PH	dy	hr mn	
●	1	8:55	9♋12
☀	1	8:40	P 0.097
☽	8	6:31	15♎47
○	15	6:41	22♑28
☾	23	5:03	0♉02
●	30	18:41	7♌16

Void of Course Moon

Last Aspect			☽ Ingress		
1 11:38	♄	□	♌	2	21:44
3 16:27	♄	⚹	♍	5	1:16
6 0:20	☉	⚹	♎	7	3:55
8 6:31	☉	□	♏	9	6:32
10 13:06	☉	△	♐	11	9:48
12 12:22	☿	△	♑	13	14:15
15 6:41	☉	☍	♒	15	20:31
17 12:24	☿	☍	♓	18	5:14
20 11:16	☉	△	♈	20	16:26
22 21:36	☿	△	♉	23	4:59
25 13:13	☿	□	♊	25	16:35
28 0:36	☿	⚹	♋	28	1:13
28 23:04	♄	□	♌	30	6:17

DAILY ASPECTARIAN

1 F: ☽□♅ 0:29; ☽∥☿ 0:37; ☽⚹♃ 1:12; ☽△⚷ 1:46; ☽☍♇ 3:22; ☽⚺♂ 5:16; ☉☌☽ 8:55; ☽∥♂ 11:30; ☽□♄ 11:38; ☿△⚳ 14:24; ☽⚼♆ 20:34

2 Sa: ☽⚼⚷ 4:34; ☿ ♌ 5:39; ☽∠♂ 9:28; ☽#♇ 10:09; ☿⚻♆ 15:44; ☿∥♂ 18:08; ♃⚹⚷ 18:14; ☽⚺♀ 18:44; ☽△⚳ 20:08; ☽⚻♆ 22:57; ☽☌☿ 23:56

3 Su: ☉□♄ 0:18; ☽△♅ 5:38; ☽⚻⚷ 6:46; ☽□♃ 6:56; ☽⚻♇ 8:17; ♀□⚳ 12:03; ☽⚹♂ 13:02; ☽⚹♄ 16:27; ☉⚺☽ 17:35; ☽⚼⚳ 22:21; ☽∠♀ 23:14

4 M: ☽∥♃ 0:38; ☽#♆ 2:58; ♀ ♋ 4:18; ☽#⚳ 5:16; ☽⚼♅ 7:29; ☽⚼♇ 10:02; ♀△♆ 17:28; ☽∠♄ 18:11; ☉∠☽ 21:07

5 Tu: ☽⚻⚳ 0:10; ☿△♅ 0:48; ☽☍♆ 2:24; ☽⚹♀ 3:16; ☽⚻♅ 9:00; ☿⚻⚷ 9:54; ☽☍⚷ 10:00; ☽⚺☿ 10:01; ☽△♃ 10:50; ☽△♇ 11:28; ☽#⚷ 14:21; ☿□♃ 18:10; ☽□♂ 18:52; ☽⚺♄ 19:40; ☽#♄ 22:45; ☿⚻♇ 23:09

6 W: ☉⚹☽ 0:20; ☽∥♅ 2:36; ☽#♅ 12:15; ♂△♄ 12:17; ☽⚼♃ 12:25; ☽∠☿ 14:24; ☽∥♄ 16:09

7 Th: ☽∥⚷ 0:30; ☽☍⚳ 3:13; ☽⚻♆ 4:58; ☽□♀ 10:38; ☽☍♅ 11:36; ☽⚻⚷ 12:30; ☽⚻♃ 13:57; ☽□♇ 13:57; ♃△♇ 14:08; ☽⚹☿ 18:38; ♀□♅ 21:45; ☽☌♄ 22:21

8 F: ☽△♂ 0:01; ☉⚼♆ 2:13; ☽⚼♆ 6:13; ☉□☽ 6:31; ♀△⚷ 7:46; ☽∥⚳ 9:41; ☽∥♆ 11:42; ☽⚼⚷ 13:44; ☿#♇ 13:57; ☽#♃ 14:58

9 Sa: ♀☍♇ 0:32; ☽⚼♂ 2:40; ♀⚹♃ 6:07; ☽⚻⚳ 6:12; ☽△♆ 7:33; ☿⚹♄ 8:20; ☉∥♂ 11:19; ☽⚻♅ 14:17; ☽△⚷ 15:05; ☽⚹♇ 16:34; ☽☍♃ 17:12; ☽△♀ 18:08; ☽#☿ 22:54

10 Su: ♅ R 0:36; ☽⚺♄ 1:18; ☽□☿ 3:07; ☽∥♇ 3:44; ☽⚻♂ 5:29; ☽⚼⚳ 7:53; ☉△☽ 13:06; ☽⚼♅ 15:52; ☽∠♇ 18:08; ☽⚼♀ 22:12

11 M: ☽∠♄ 3:04; ☉#☽ 9:08; ☽△⚳ 9:48; ⚳ ♈ 10:01; ☽□♆ 10:45; ☽#♂ 15:28; ☉⚼☽ 16:48; ☽△♅ 17:41; ☽□⚷ 18:24; ☽⚺♇ 19:56; ☽⚻♃ 21:12

12 Tu: ☽⚻♀ 2:37; ☿⚹♂ 3:29; ☽⚹♄ 5:06; ☿⚼⚳ 8:10; ☽#♀ 8:46; ☽☍♂ 11:57; ☽△☿ 12:22; ☉⚼⚷ 15:19; ☉⚻☽ 20:54; ☽⚼♃ 23:40

13 W: ☽#♀ 3:09; ♀□♄ 7:37; ☽□⚳ 14:33; ☽⚹♆ 15:09; ☽#♂ 15:41; ☽⚼☿ 17:31; ☽□♅ 22:21; ☽⚹⚷ 22:59

14 Th: ☽☌♇ 0:35; ☽△♃ 2:33; ☉#☽ 6:19; ☽□♄ 10:21; ☽☍♀ 12:57; ☽∠♆ 18:00; ☽⚻♂ 20:10; ☽⚻☿ 23:10

15 F: ☽∠⚷ 1:57; ☉☍☽ 6:41; ☽∥♇ 8:08; ☽⚹⚳ 21:07; ☽⚺♆ 21:23; ☿⚼♅ 23:53

16 Sa: ☽⚼♂ 1:11; ☽⚹♅ 4:57; ☽⚺⚷ 5:29; ☽⚺♇ 7:11; ☽□♃ 9:55; ☽#☿ 11:33; ♀∥♂ 12:04; ☽△♄ 17:42; ♀⚼♆ 18:56; ☽#♃ 22:32

17 Su: ☿⚼♇ 1:10; ☽∠⚳ 1:17; ☽⚻♀ 2:05; ☽∥♆ 3:50; ☽∥⚳ 4:49; ☽△♂ 6:57; ☽∠♅ 9:10; ☽∠♇ 11:25; ☽☍☿ 12:24; ⚳⚺♆ 18:17; ☉⚻☽ 19:21; ☽⚼♄ 22:21

18 M: ☽☌♆ 6:03; ☽⚺⚳ 6:07; ☽⚼♀ 9:58; ☽⚺♅ 14:02; ☽☌⚷ 14:28; ☽⚹♇ 16:18; ☽⚹♃ 19:52; ☽∥⚷ 19:58

19 Tu: ☉⚼☽ 2:56; ☽⚻♄ 3:40; ☽∥♄ 4:46; ☽#♅ 10:50; ☽△♀ 18:44; ☽□♂ 20:46; ☽∥♅ 22:00; ☿∥♃ 22:59

20 W: ☽∠♃ 1:48; ☽#♄ 4:16; ☽⚻☿ 4:20; ♀⚼⚷ 5:55; ☉△☽ 11:16; ☽#⚷ 13:12; ☽⚺♆ 17:11; ☽☌⚳ 17:34

21 Th: ☽☌♅ 1:31; ☽⚺⚷ 1:49; ☽□♇ 3:46; ☽⚺♃ 8:12; ☽⚼☿ 12:58; ♀⚺♂ 13:24; ⚳∥♆ 13:37; ☽☍♄ 15:54; ☽∠♆ 23:22

22 F: ☿#⚳ 0:32; ☿#♆ 1:34; ☽∥☿ 6:49; ☽#♆ 7:26; ☽#⚳ 7:39; ☽∠⚷ 8:01; ☽⚹♂ 12:46; ☽□♀ 13:58; ☽∥♃ 14:10; ☽△☿ 21:36

23 Sa: ☉ ♌ 4:13; ☉□☽ 5:03; ☽⚹♆ 5:37; ☽⚺⚳ 6:15; ☿∠♄ 10:25; ☉⚻♆ 11:56; ☽⚺♅ 14:02; ☽⚹⚷ 14:11; ☽△♇ 16:13; ☉△⚳ 20:13; ☽∠♂ 20:51; ☽☌♃ 21:20

24 Su: ☽⚻♄ 4:42; ☽#♇ 6:56; ♂∠♃ 7:08; ☽∠⚳ 12:21; ☉∥☽ 15:14; ☽∠♅ 19:56; ☽⚼♇ 22:04

25 M: ☽⚺♂ 4:26; ☽⚹♀ 8:45; ☽∥♀ 10:12; ☽⚼♄ 10:31; ☽□☿ 13:13; ☽□♆ 17:05; ☽⚹⚳ 17:52; ☉⚹☽ 21:38

26 Tu: ☽⚹♅ 1:14; ☽□⚷ 1:16; ☽⚻♇ 3:17; ☽⚺♃ 8:49; ♅⚺⚷ 13:37; ⚳ R 14:55; ☽△♄ 15:37; ☽∠♀ 16:52

27 W: ☉∠☽ 4:33; ☽∠♃ 13:18; ☽☌♂ 16:56; ☉⚻⚷ 18:56; ☉△♅ 19:44; ⚵ ♎ 23:34; ☽⚺♀ 23:47

28 Th: ☽⚹☿ 0:36; ☽△♆ 1:34; ☽□⚳ 2:24; ☽△⚷ 9:10; ☽□♅ 9:16; ☉⚺☽ 10:20; ☽☍♇ 11:09; ☿⚺♀ 13:20; ♀ ♌ 15:00; ☽⚹♃ 16:51; ☿ ♍ 18:00; ♀⚻♆ 18:34; ☉#♇ 20:42; ☉⚻♇ 21:31; ☽□♄ 23:04

29 F: ☽∥♀ 2:21; ♀△⚳ 3:29; ☿☍♆ 4:01; ☽⚼♆ 4:28; ☽∠☿ 4:29; ☽⚼⚷ 11:47; ☽#♇ 18:12; ☉∥☽ 19:51

30 Sa: ☽⚺♂ 1:15; ☽⚻♆ 6:32; ☽⚺☿ 7:17; ☽△⚳ 7:21; ☿⚻⚳ 10:01; ☽☌♀ 10:04; ☽⚻⚷ 13:37; ☽△♅ 13:48; ☽⚻♇ 15:34; ☉☌☽ 18:41; ☽□♃ 21:23

31 Su: ☽⚹♄ 3:10; ☽∥♃ 3:40; ☽∠♂ 4:06; ☽#⚳ 7:30; ☽⚼⚳ 8:44; ☽#♆ 10:11; ☽⚼♅ 15:04; ☽⚼♇ 16:47

August 2011

LONGITUDE

Day	Sid.Time	☉	☽	☽ 12 hour	Mean☊	True☊	☿	♀	♂	⚳	♃	♄	⚷	♅	♆	♇
	h m s	° ' "	° ' "	° ' "	° '	° '	° '	° '	° '	° '	° '	° '	° '	° '	° '	° '
1 M	20 37 03	8♌26 04	24♌44 41	1♍59 26	21♐04.8	22♐34.7	1♍00.2	4♌09.4	28♊23.7	0♈34.4	8♉57.9	12♎21.0	4♓13.9	4♈22.5	0♓06.3	5♑24.1
2 Tu	20 40 59	9 23 29	9♍16 08	16 33 58	21 01.6	22R 27.5	1 08.6	5 23.4	29 04.0	0R 32.2	9 03.3	12 25.5	4R 11.3	4R 21.4	0R 04.8	5R 22.9
3 W	20 44 56	10 20 54	23 52 03	1♎09 36	20 58.5	22 20.8	1R 12.0	6 37.3	29 44.3	0 29.8	9 08.6	12 30.1	4 08.7	4 20.3	0 03.2	5 21.7
4 Th	20 48 52	11 18 20	8♎25 51	15 40 12	20 55.3	22 15.3	1 10.2	7 51.3	0♋24.5	0 26.9	9 13.6	12 34.8	4 06.0	4 19.2	0 01.7	5 20.5
5 F	20 52 49	12 15 47	22 52 07	0♏01 09	20 52.1	22 11.8	1 03.2	9 05.3	1 04.6	0 23.7	9 18.5	12 39.5	4 03.4	4 18.0	0 00.2	5 19.4
6 Sa	20 56 45	13 13 15	7♏07 02	14 09 32	20 48.9	22D 10.2	0 51.0	10 19.3	1 44.7	0 20.1	9 23.3	12 44.3	4 00.7	4 16.8	29♒58.6	5 18.2
7 Su	21 00 42	14 10 43	21 08 35	28 04 07	20 45.8	22 10.2	0 33.4	11 33.3	2 24.7	0 16.2	9 27.8	12 49.2	3 57.9	4 15.5	29 57.1	5 17.1
8 M	21 04 38	15 08 12	4♐56 10	11♐44 49	20 42.6	22 11.1	0 10.7	12 47.4	3 04.6	0 11.9	9 32.2	12 54.1	3 55.2	4 14.2	29 55.5	5 16.0
9 Tu	21 08 35	16 05 42	18 30 09	25 12 16	20 39.4	22R 11.9	29♌43.0	14 01.4	3 44.5	0 07.3	9 36.4	12 59.1	3 52.5	4 12.9	29 53.9	5 15.0
10 W	21 12 32	17 03 13	1♑51 17	8♑27 15	20 36.2	22 11.5	29 10.4	15 15.5	4 24.3	0 02.3	9 40.4	13 04.2	3 49.7	4 11.5	29 52.4	5 13.9
11 Th	21 16 28	18 00 44	15 00 17	21 30 24	20 33.0	22 09.2	28 33.5	16 29.6	5 04.0	29♓57.0	9 44.3	13 09.3	3 46.9	4 10.1	29 50.8	5 12.9
12 F	21 20 25	18 58 17	27 57 40	4♒22 05	20 29.9	22 04.5	27 52.5	17 43.7	5 43.7	29 51.3	9 47.9	13 14.5	3 44.1	4 08.7	29 49.2	5 11.9
13 Sa	21 24 21	19 55 50	10♒43 40	17 02 26	20 26.7	21 57.3	27 08.1	18 57.8	6 23.2	29 45.3	9 51.4	13 19.8	3 41.2	4 07.2	29 47.6	5 10.9
14 Su	21 28 18	20 53 24	23 18 23	29 31 33	20 23.5	21 48.1	26 20.9	20 11.9	7 02.8	29 38.9	9 54.7	13 25.1	3 38.4	4 05.7	29 46.0	5 10.0
15 M	21 32 14	21 51 00	5♓42 00	11♓49 47	20 20.3	21 37.4	25 31.8	21 26.1	7 42.2	29 32.2	9 57.8	13 30.5	3 35.5	4 04.1	29 44.3	5 09.0
16 Tu	21 36 11	22 48 37	17 55 03	23 57 58	20 17.2	21 26.4	24 41.6	22 40.2	8 21.6	29 25.1	10 00.7	13 36.0	3 32.6	4 02.5	29 42.7	5 08.1
17 W	21 40 07	23 46 15	29 58 43	5♈57 36	20 14.0	21 15.8	23 51.1	23 54.4	9 00.9	29 17.7	10 03.5	13 41.5	3 29.8	4 00.8	29 41.1	5 07.2
18 Th	21 44 04	24 43 55	11♈54 56	17 51 04	20 10.8	21 06.8	23 01.5	25 08.6	9 40.2	29 10.0	10 06.0	13 47.1	3 26.9	3 59.2	29 39.5	5 06.4
19 F	21 48 00	25 41 36	23 46 28	29 41 34	20 07.6	20 59.9	22 13.6	26 22.8	10 19.4	29 01.9	10 08.4	13 52.7	3 23.9	3 57.5	29 37.8	5 05.5
20 Sa	21 51 57	26 39 19	5♉36 56	11♉33 06	20 04.4	20 55.4	21 28.6	27 37.1	10 58.5	28 53.5	10 10.5	13 58.4	3 21.0	3 55.7	29 36.2	5 04.7
21 Su	21 55 54	27 37 04	17 30 42	23 30 20	20 01.3	20D 53.2	20 47.3	28 51.3	11 37.5	28 44.8	10 12.5	14 04.2	3 18.1	3 53.9	29 34.5	5 03.9
22 M	21 59 50	28 34 50	29 32 40	5♊38 22	19 58.1	20 52.6	20 10.6	0♍05.6	12 16.5	28 35.8	10 14.3	14 10.0	3 15.2	3 52.1	29 32.9	5 03.2
23 Tu	22 03 47	29 32 38	11♊48 04	18 02 26	19 54.9	20R 53.0	19 39.4	1 19.9	12 55.4	28 26.5	10 15.8	14 15.8	3 12.2	3 50.3	29 31.3	5 02.4
24 W	22 07 43	0♍30 27	24 22 03	0♋47 29	19 51.7	20 53.1	19 14.3	2 34.2	13 34.2	28 16.9	10 17.2	14 21.7	3 09.3	3 48.4	29 29.6	5 01.7
25 Th	22 11 40	1 28 18	7♋19 12	13 57 35	19 48.6	20 52.0	18 56.1	3 48.5	14 13.0	28 07.0	10 18.4	14 27.7	3 06.3	3 46.5	29 28.0	5 01.1
26 F	22 15 36	2 26 11	20 42 54	27 35 13	19 45.4	20 48.9	18D 45.1	5 02.8	14 51.7	27 56.9	10 19.4	14 33.7	3 03.4	3 44.6	29 26.3	5 00.4
27 Sa	22 19 33	3 24 06	4♌34 30	11♌40 28	19 42.2	20 43.2	18 41.8	6 17.2	15 30.3	27 46.4	10 20.2	14 39.8	3 00.4	3 42.6	29 24.7	4 59.8
28 Su	22 23 29	4 22 02	18 52 41	26 10 28	19 39.0	20 35.0	18 46.5	7 31.5	16 08.9	27 35.7	10 20.8	14 46.0	2 57.5	3 40.6	29 23.1	4 59.2
29 M	22 27 26	5 20 00	3♍32 59	10♍59 14	19 35.9	20 25.0	18 59.2	8 45.9	16 47.4	27 24.8	10 21.1	14 52.1	2 54.5	3 38.6	29 21.4	4 58.6
30 Tu	22 31 23	6 18 00	18 28 04	25 58 17	19 32.7	20 14.2	19 20.1	10 00.3	17 25.8	27 13.5	10R 21.3	14 58.4	2 51.6	3 36.6	29 19.8	4 58.1
31 W	22 35 19	7♍16 01	3♎28 40	10♎58 02	19♐29.5	20♐03.8	19♌49.2	11♍14.7	18♋04.1	27♓02.1	10♉21.3	15♎04.6	2♓48.7	3♈34.5	29♒18.2	4♑57.5

1st of Month

Julian Day # 2455774.5
Obliquity 23°26'15"
SVP 5♓05'34"
GC 27♐00.1
Eris 22♈28.7R

Day	⚴
1	5♒28.3R
6	4 09.9R
11	2 54.8R
16	1 44.8R
21	0 41.0R
26	29♑44.5R
31	28 56.4R

Day	⚵
1	1♎13.0
6	2 45.6
11	4 20.1
16	5 56.3
21	7 33.9
26	9 12.9
31	10 53.1

Day	⚶
1	13♒46.4R
6	12 32.3R
11	11 19.2R
16	10 09.5R
21	9 05.6R
26	8 09.6R
31	7 23.0R

DECLINATION and LATITUDE

Day	☉ Decl	☽ Decl	☽ Lat	☽12h Decl	☿ Decl	☿ Lat	♀ Decl	♀ Lat	♂ Decl	♂ Lat	⚳ Decl	⚳ Lat	♃ Decl	♃ Lat	♄ Decl	♄ Lat
1 M	18N09	8N59	4S32	6N17	8N02	3S18	20N07	0N56	23N43	0N18	12S33	13S56	13N17	1S16	2S42	2N22
2 Tu	17 54	3 28	4 59	0 36	7 48	3 30	19 51	0 58	23 44	0 18	12 37	14 01	13 18	1 17	2 44	2 22
3 W	17 39	2S16	5 07	5S06	7 35	3 42	19 35	0 59	23 45	0 19	12 42	14 05	13 18	1 17	2 45	2 22
4 Th	17 23	7 52	4 55	10 30	7 25	3 53	19 17	1 01	23 46	0 20	12 47	14 09	13 21	1 17	2 47	2 22
5 F	17 07	12 59	4 25	15 16	7 18	4 04	18 59	1 03	23 47	0 21	12 52	14 13	13 22	1 17	2 49	2 22
6 Sa	16 51	17 19	3 38	19 06	7 13	4 14	18 41	1 04	23 47	0 21	12 57	14 17	13 24	1 17	2 52	2 22
7 Su	16 34	20 36	2 39	21 46	7 11	4 23	18 22	1 06	23 47	0 22	13 02	14 21	13 25	1 18	2 54	2 21
8 M	16 18	22 37	1 31	23 07	7 11	4 31	18 03	1 07	23 47	0 23	13 08	14 25	13 26	1 18	2 56	2 21
9 Tu	16 01	23 16	0 20	23 05	7 14	4 38	17 43	1 09	23 47	0 24	13 13	14 29	13 27	1 18	2 58	2 21
10 W	15 43	22 34	0N52	21 44	7 20	4 43	17 22	1 10	23 46	0 24	13 19	14 33	13 28	1 18	2 60	2 21
11 Th	15 26	20 37	1 59	19 15	7 29	4 47	17 02	1 11	23 46	0 25	13 24	14 37	13 29	1 18	3 02	2 21
12 F	15 08	17 38	2 59	15 50	7 40	4 50	16 40	1 13	23 45	0 26	13 30	14 40	13 30	1 19	3 04	2 20
13 Sa	14 50	13 52	3 49	11 45	7 54	4 51	16 18	1 14	23 44	0 27	13 36	14 44	13 31	1 19	3 06	2 20
14 Su	14 32	9 32	4 27	7 14	8 11	4 50	15 56	1 15	23 43	0 28	13 42	14 48	13 31	1 19	3 09	2 20
15 M	14 13	4 54	4 52	2 31	8 30	4 47	15 33	1 16	23 41	0 28	13 47	14 51	13 33	1 19	3 11	2 20
16 Tu	13 55	0 08	5 03	2N15	8 51	4 42	15 10	1 17	23 40	0 29	13 54	14 55	13 33	1 20	3 13	2 20
17 W	13 36	4N35	4 60	6 51	9 13	4 36	14 47	1 18	23 38	0 30	13 60	14 59	13 34	1 20	3 15	2 20
18 Th	13 17	9 04	4 44	11 11	9 37	4 28	14 23	1 19	23 36	0 31	14 06	15 02	13 35	1 20	3 18	2 19
19 F	12 57	13 11	4 16	15 04	10 02	4 18	13 58	1 20	23 34	0 31	14 12	15 05	13 35	1 20	3 20	2 19
20 Sa	12 38	16 48	3 37	18 21	10 28	4 06	13 34	1 21	23 31	0 32	14 18	15 08	13 36	1 20	3 22	2 19
21 Su	12 18	19 44	2 48	20 55	10 53	3 52	13 08	1 21	23 29	0 33	14 25	15 12	13 36	1 21	3 25	2 19
22 M	11 58	21 51	1 51	22 34	11 19	3 38	12 43	1 22	23 26	0 34	14 31	15 15	13 36	1 21	3 27	2 19
23 Tu	11 38	22 60	0 48	23 09	11 43	3 22	12 17	1 23	23 23	0 35	14 37	15 18	13 37	1 21	3 30	2 19
24 W	11 18	23 01	0S19	22 34	12 07	3 05	11 51	1 23	23 20	0 35	14 44	15 20	13 37	1 21	3 32	2 19
25 Th	10 57	21 48	1 26	20 44	12 29	2 48	11 24	1 24	23 17	0 36	14 50	15 23	13 37	1 22	3 34	2 18
26 F	10 36	19 21	2 31	17 40	12 49	2 30	10 58	1 24	23 13	0 37	14 57	15 26	13 37	1 22	3 37	2 18
27 Sa	10 15	15 43	3 30	13 08	13 08	2 12	10 31	1 24	23 10	0 38	15 03	15 29	13 37	1 22	3 39	2 18
28 Su	9 54	11 05	4 17	8 29	13 24	1 53	10 03	1 25	23 06	0 39	15 10	15 31	13 37	1 22	3 42	2 18
29 M	9 33	5 43	4 48	2 52	13 37	1 35	9 36	1 25	23 02	0 39	15 16	15 34	13 37	1 22	3 44	2 18
30 Tu	9 12	0S03	5 01	2S59	13 48	1 17	9 08	1 25	22 58	0 40	15 23	15 36	13 37	1 22	3 47	2 18
31 W	8N50	5S52	4S53	8S39	13N56	0S59	8N39	1N25	22N54	0N41	15S29	15S38	13N37	1S23	3S49	2N18

Day	⚷ Decl	⚷ Lat	♅ Decl	♅ Lat	♆ Decl	♆ Lat	♇ Decl	♇ Lat
1	4S14	6N08	1N03	0S45	11S57	0S33	18S55	4N25
6	4 18	6 09	1 00	0 46	11 60	0 33	18 56	4 24
11	4 23	6 09	0 57	0 46	12 02	0 33	18 58	4 23
16	4 28	6 09	0 54	0 46	12 05	0 33	18 59	4 22
21	4 33	6 09	0 51	0 46	12 08	0 33	19 00	4 21
26	4 38	6 09	0 47	0 46	12 11	0 33	19 01	4 19
31	4S44	6N09	0N43	0S46	12S14	0S33	19S02	4N18

Day	⚴ Decl	⚴ Lat	⚵ Decl	⚵ Lat	⚶ Decl	⚶ Lat	Eris Decl	Eris Lat
1	17N21	37N18	4N08	5N02	22S25	5S60	3S43	13S25
6	16 39	36 50	3 35	5 06	23 04	6 18	3 44	13 25
11	15 52	36 15	3 01	5 10	23 40	6 33	3 45	13 26
16	15 00	35 35	2 26	5 14	24 12	6 46	3 46	13 26
21	14 05	34 50	1 52	5 18	24 40	6 57	3 47	13 27
26	13 07	34 01	1 17	5 22	25 03	7 05	3 48	13 27
31	12N07	33N08	0N42	5N26	25S21	7S11	3S49	13S28

Moon Phenomena

Max/0 Decl

dy	hr mn	
2	14:31	0 S
8	23:31	23S16
16	0:39	0 N
23	12:21	23N09
29	23:46	0 S

Max/0 Lat

dy	hr mn	
2	21:40	5S07
9	6:36	0 N
16	6:50	5N03
23	17:24	0 S
30	2:36	5S01

Perigee/Apogee

dy	hr m		kilometers
2	21:15	p	365762
18	16:25	a	405160
30	17:45	p	360861

PH	dy	hr mn	
☽	6	11:09	13♏40
○	13	18:59	20♒41
☾	21	21:56	28♉30
●	29	3:05	5♍27

Void of Course Moon

Last Aspect			☽ Ingress		
1 6:21	♂	⚹	♍	1	8:43
1 23:39	♃	△	♎	3	10:05
5 11:57	♆	△	♏	5	11:58
7 15:15	♆	□	♐	7	15:22
9 20:25	♆	⚹	♑	9	20:39
10 20:35	♄	□	♒	12	3:49
14 12:26	♆	☌	♓	14	12:55
15 8:22	♃	⚹	♈	17	0:03
19 11:51	♆	⚹	♉	19	12:37
22 0:00	♆	□	♊	22	0:54
24 9:34	♆	△	♋	24	10:32
25 13:05	♂	☌	♌	26	16:10
28 17:12	♆	☍	♍	28	18:14
29 22:16	♂	⚹	♎	30	18:26

DAILY ASPECTARIAN

1 M
♀⚻⚷ 1:23
♀△♅ 4:10
☽∠♄ 4:21
☽∥☿ 4:30
☽⚹♂ 6:21
☽☍♆ 8:52
☽⚻⚳ 9:38
☽☌☿ 10:29
☉□♃ 14:42
☽☍⚷ 15:39
☽⚻♅ 15:55
☽⚺♀ 17:01
☽△♇ 17:36
☽#⚷ 20:43
☽△♃ 23:39
♀⚻♇ 23:50

2 Tu
☉⚺☽ 0:13
☽#♄ 3:06
☽⚺♄ 5:13
☽∥♅ 10:12
☽#♅ 18:49
☽∠♀ 19:58

3 W
☽⚼♃ 0:27
☽∥♄ 2:04
☉∠☽ 2:36
☿ R 3:50
☽∥⚷ 8:25
♂ ♋ 9:23
☽□♂ 10:07
☽⚻♆ 10:10
☽☍⚳ 10:52
♂△♆ 10:54
☽⚺☿ 12:04
☽⚻⚷ 16:52
☽☍♅ 17:13
☽□♇ 18:54
☽#☿ 22:07
☽⚹♀ 22:58

4 Th
☽⚻♃ 1:20
♂□⚳ 1:21
☉⚹☽ 5:06
☽☌♄ 6:54
☽⚼♆ 10:55
☽∠☿ 12:45
☽⚼⚷ 17:39
☽∥♆ 19:03
☿⚹♂ 23:20
☽∥⚳ 23:23

5 F
☽#♃ 1:58
♆R♒ 2:55
♀#♇ 4:11
♀□♃ 4:35
☉⚹♄ 10:48
☽△♆ 11:57
☽⚻⚳ 12:35
☽⚹☿ 13:34
☽△♂ 14:28
☽△⚷ 18:45
☽⚻♅ 19:12
☽⚹♇ 20:56
☉#☽ 21:18

6 Sa
☽☍♃ 3:53
☽□♀ 5:58
☽#♀ 8:16
☽⚺♄ 9:38
☽∥♇ 10:51
☉□☽ 11:09
☽⚼⚳ 13:57
☽⚼♂ 17:15
☽⚼♅ 20:46
☽∠♇ 22:31

7 Su
☽∠♄ 11:38
☽□♆ 15:15
☽△⚳ 15:45
☽□☿ 15:55
☽⚻♂ 20:35
☽□⚷ 22:13
☿⚻⚳ 22:35
☽△♅ 22:47

8 M
☽⚺♇ 0:35
☉⚼⚳ 1:27
♀⚹♄ 2:20
☽⚻♃ 8:08
☿R♌ 9:47
☽⚹♄ 14:08
☿☍♆ 14:28
☽△♀ 15:14
☉△☽ 19:23

9 Tu
♂△⚷ 4:30
☽⚼♃ 10:59
♂□♅ 16:35
☽△☿ 19:21
♀⚼⚳ 20:00
☽⚹♆ 20:25
☽□⚳ 20:44
☽⚼♀ 20:49

10 W
☉⚼☽ 0:23
☽⚹⚷ 3:34
☽□♅ 4:14
☽☍♂ 4:52
☽☌♇ 6:07
⚳R♓ 10:39
☽△♃ 14:18
☽□♄ 20:35
☽⚼☿ 21:28
☽∠♆ 23:43

11 Th
☽⚻♀ 3:02
♂☍♇ 5:16
☉⚻☽ 5:59
☽∠⚷ 6:56
☿∠♄ 12:47
☽∥♇ 14:14
☽⚻☿ 23:51

12 F
⚳#♃ 1:58
☽⚺♆ 3:28
☽⚹⚳ 3:31
☉⚼♅ 4:14
☽#♀ 7:20
☽⚺⚷ 10:46
☽⚹♅ 11:33
⚳⚺♆ 11:43
☽⚺♇ 13:33
☽⚻♂ 15:21
☉#☽ 17:44
☽□♃ 22:21

13 Sa
☽∥⚳ 1:32
☽#♃ 2:00
♀⚼♅ 2:58
☽△♄ 4:58
☉⚼♇ 6:11
☽∠⚳ 7:35
☽∥♆ 10:17
☽∠♅ 15:56
☽☍♀ 17:23
☽∠♇ 17:59
☉☍☽ 18:59
☽⚼♂ 21:27
♀⚼♇ 23:22

14 Su
☽☍☿ 5:30
☽#☿ 6:41
☽⚼♄ 9:56
☽⚺⚳ 12:08
☽☌♆ 12:26
☽☌⚷ 19:55
☽⚺♅ 20:50
☽⚹♇ 22:56

15 M
☽∥⚷ 2:16
☽△♂ 4:08
☽⚹♃ 8:22
☽∥♄ 8:34
☽⚻♄ 15:25
☽#♅ 20:05

16 Tu
☉#⚳ 1:09
☽∥♅ 5:12
☽⚻♀ 10:30
☉⚻☽ 10:32
☉☌♀ 12:09
☽⚻☿ 12:34
☽∠♃ 14:08
☽#♄ 17:08
☿∠♂ 21:23
☽☌⚳ 22:39
☿☌♀ 23:22
☽⚺♆ 23:25
☽#⚷ 23:29

17 W
☉☌☿ 1:05
☉∥♃ 2:03
♀∠♂ 4:28
☽⚺⚷ 7:01
☽☌♅ 8:04
☽□♇ 10:18
☽⚼☿ 16:40
☉∠♂ 19:08
☽□♂ 19:12
☉⚼☽ 19:13
☽⚼♀ 20:01
☽⚺♃ 20:19

18 Th
☽∥☿ 3:27
☽☍♄ 3:48
☽∠♆ 5:32
☽∠⚷ 13:09
♀#⚳ 13:20
♂⚹♃ 16:51
☽#♆ 17:31
☽△☿ 21:03
☉∥☽ 22:42

19 F
☽∥♃ 2:30
☉△☽ 4:14
☽∥♀ 4:27
☽△♀ 5:54
☽#⚳ 6:34
☽⚺⚳ 10:32
☽⚹♆ 11:51
☽⚹⚷ 19:26
☽⚺♅ 20:36
♀∥♃ 22:01
☽△♇ 22:55

20 Sa
☽☌♃ 9:15
☽⚹♂ 11:28
☽∠⚳ 16:31
☽⚻♄ 17:01
☽#♇ 17:22
♀⚻⚳ 22:08

21 Su
☽∠♅ 2:47
♀∠♄ 4:30
☽⚼♇ 5:07
☽□☿ 6:14
☉#♆ 11:21
♀☍♆ 13:40
☽∠♂ 19:15
☉□☽ 21:56
☽⚹⚳ 22:09
♀ ♍ 22:12
☽⚼♄ 23:15

22 M
☽□♆ 0:00
☉⚻⚳ 0:22
☽□♀ 1:12
☿⚼♇ 5:26
☽□⚷ 7:17
☽⚹♅ 8:30
☽⚻♇ 10:50
☉∠♄ 16:14
☽⚺♃ 21:01
☉∥☿ 21:08
☉☍♆ 23:27

23 Tu
☽⚺♂ 2:17
☽△♄ 4:48
♀#♆ 6:56
☉ ♍ 11:22
☽⚹☿ 14:34
☿∥♀ 16:20

24 W
☽∠♃ 1:44
☿#♆ 3:31
☽□⚳ 7:15
☽△♆ 9:34
♀☍⚷ 10:54
☉⚹☽ 12:24
⚴R♑ 13:24
☽△⚷ 16:18
☽⚹♀ 16:54
☽□♅ 17:31
☽∠☿ 17:55
☽☍♇ 19:48
♀⚻♅ 23:23

25 Th
♄⚼♆ 0:50
☽⚹♃ 5:26
♂⚼♆ 8:54
♂□♄ 10:47
☽⚼♆ 12:53
☽□♄ 13:00
☽☌♂ 13:05
☉∠☽ 17:45
☽⚼⚷ 19:19
☽⚺☿ 20:34
☽∠♀ 22:42
♀△♇ 23:14

26 F
☽#♇ 2:30
☿⚼♅ 2:39
☽△⚳ 12:28
☉☍⚷ 14:40
☽⚻♆ 15:10
☽⚻⚷ 21:20
☉⚺☽ 21:51
☿ D 22:06
☽△♅ 22:32

27 Sa
☽⚻♇ 0:43
☽⚺♀ 3:11
☽#⚳ 3:40
☿⚼♅ 5:28
☉⚻♅ 7:25
☽□♃ 9:45
☽∥♃ 11:27
☽∥☿ 13:12
☽⚼⚳ 13:40
☽⚹♄ 17:07
☽#♆ 18:37
☽⚺♂ 19:16
☽⚼♅ 23:40
☽☌☿ 23:50

28 Su
☽⚼♇ 1:50
☽∥♀ 5:20
☉∥☽ 5:56
☽⚻⚳ 14:09
☉△♇ 15:14
☽☍♆ 17:12
☽∠♄ 17:59
☽∠♂ 21:01
☽☍⚷ 22:58
☿∥♃ 23:33

29 M
☽⚻♅ 0:09
☽△♇ 2:18
☉☌☽ 3:05
☽#⚷ 4:21
☽#♄ 8:17
☉∥♀ 8:19
☽☌♀ 9:11
☽△♃ 10:59
☽⚺♄ 18:22
☽∥♅ 20:46
☽⚹♂ 22:16

30 Tu
☽⚺☿ 1:26
☽#♅ 2:45
♀△♃ 6:47
♃ R 9:18
☽⚼♃ 11:01
☽☍⚳ 13:50
♂⚼⚷ 15:01
☽∥♄ 15:25
☽⚻♆ 17:20
☽∥⚷ 19:13
☽⚻⚷ 22:56

31 W
☽☍♅ 0:09
☽∠☿ 2:14
☽□♇ 2:22
☿⚼♇ 5:47
☉⚺☽ 6:29
☽⚻♃ 11:01
☽#♀ 11:04
☉#☽ 12:03
☽⚺♀ 13:34
☽⚼♆ 17:20
☽☌♄ 18:44
☽⚼⚷ 22:56

LONGITUDE

September 2011

Day	Sid.Time	☉	☽	☽ 12 hour	Mean☊	True☊	☿	♀	♂	⚳	♃	♄	⚷	♅	♆	♇
	h m s	° ' "	° ' "	° ' "	° '	° '	° '	° '	° '	° '	° '	° '	° '	° '	° '	° '
1 Th	22 39 16	8♍14 03	18♎25 16	25♎49 24	19♐26.3	19♐55.2	20♌26.3	12♍29.1	18♋42.3	26♓50.4	10♉21.1	15♎11.0	2♓45.7	3♈32.4	29♒16.6	4♑57.1
2 F	22 43 12	9 12 07	3♏09 39	10♏25 23	19 23.1	19R 48.9	21 11.3	13 43.5	19 20.5	26R 38.6	10R 20.6	15 17.3	2R 42.8	3R 30.3	29R 14.9	4R 56.6
3 Sa	22 47 09	10 10 12	17 36 09	24 41 42	19 20.0	19 45.3	22 03.8	14 57.9	19 58.6	26 26.5	10 20.0	15 23.7	2 39.9	3 28.2	29 13.3	4 56.2
4 Su	22 51 05	11 08 19	1♐41 54	8♐36 47	19 16.8	19D 43.9	23 03.6	16 12.4	20 36.6	26 14.3	10 19.2	15 30.2	2 37.0	3 26.0	29 11.7	4 55.8
5 M	22 55 02	12 06 27	15 26 29	22 11 13	19 13.6	19R 43.7	24 10.3	17 26.8	21 14.5	26 01.8	10 18.2	15 36.7	2 34.1	3 23.8	29 10.1	4 55.4
6 Tu	22 58 58	13 04 37	28 51 16	5♑26 56	19 10.4	19 43.6	25 23.5	18 41.3	21 52.4	25 49.3	10 16.9	15 43.2	2 31.2	3 21.6	29 08.6	4 55.1
7 W	23 02 55	14 02 47	11♑58 33	18 26 25	19 07.3	19 42.2	26 42.7	19 55.7	22 30.1	25 36.5	10 15.5	15 49.8	2 28.3	3 19.4	29 07.0	4 54.7
8 Th	23 06 52	15 01 00	24 50 52	1♒12 11	19 04.1	19 38.6	28 07.3	21 10.2	23 07.8	25 23.7	10 13.9	15 56.4	2 25.5	3 17.2	29 05.4	4 54.5
9 F	23 10 48	15 59 14	7♒30 35	13 46 20	19 00.9	19 32.3	29 36.9	22 24.7	23 45.4	25 10.7	10 12.1	16 03.1	2 22.6	3 14.9	29 03.9	4 54.2
10 Sa	23 14 45	16 57 29	19 59 36	26 10 33	18 57.7	19 23.0	1♍10.9	23 39.2	24 23.0	24 57.6	10 10.1	16 09.8	2 19.8	3 12.6	29 02.3	4 54.0
11 Su	23 18 41	17 55 46	2♓19 19	8♓26 01	18 54.5	19 11.2	2 48.9	24 53.6	25 00.4	24 44.4	10 07.8	16 16.5	2 17.0	3 10.3	29 00.8	4 53.8
12 M	23 22 38	18 54 05	14 30 46	20 33 40	18 51.4	18 57.7	4 30.1	26 08.1	25 37.8	24 31.1	10 05.4	16 23.2	2 14.2	3 08.0	28 59.3	4 53.6
13 Tu	23 26 34	19 52 26	26 34 50	2♈34 25	18 48.2	18 43.6	6 14.2	27 22.6	26 15.1	24 17.8	10 02.8	16 30.0	2 11.4	3 05.7	28 57.7	4 53.5
14 W	23 30 31	20 50 48	8♈32 32	14 29 25	18 45.0	18 30.1	8 00.6	28 37.1	26 52.3	24 04.4	10 00.0	16 36.9	2 08.7	3 03.4	28 56.2	4 53.4
15 Th	23 34 27	21 49 13	20 25 16	26 20 21	18 41.8	18 18.3	9 48.9	29 51.7	27 29.4	23 51.0	9 57.0	16 43.7	2 06.0	3 01.0	28 54.8	4 53.4
16 F	23 38 24	22 47 39	2♉15 01	8♉09 35	18 38.6	18 08.9	11 38.7	1♎06.2	28 06.5	23 37.5	9 53.8	16 50.6	2 03.3	2 58.7	28 53.3	4D 53.3
17 Sa	23 42 21	23 46 08	14 04 31	20 00 15	18 35.5	18 02.3	13 29.5	2 20.7	28 43.4	23 24.0	9 50.5	16 57.5	2 00.6	2 56.3	28 51.8	4 53.3
18 Su	23 46 17	24 44 38	25 57 19	1♊56 15	18 32.3	17 58.5	15 21.1	3 35.3	29 20.3	23 10.6	9 46.9	17 04.5	1 57.9	2 53.9	28 50.4	4 53.3
19 M	23 50 14	25 43 11	7♊57 40	14 02 12	18 29.1	17D 56.9	17 13.1	4 49.8	29 57.1	22 57.1	9 43.2	17 11.4	1 55.3	2 51.6	28 49.0	4 53.4
20 Tu	23 54 10	26 41 46	20 10 28	26 23 09	18 25.9	17R 56.6	19 05.4	6 04.4	0♌33.9	22 43.7	9 39.2	17 18.5	1 52.7	2 49.2	28 47.6	4 53.4
21 W	23 58 07	27 40 24	2♋40 53	9♋04 18	18 22.8	17 56.6	20 57.6	7 18.9	1 10.5	22 30.4	9 35.1	17 25.5	1 50.2	2 46.8	28 46.2	4 53.6
22 Th	0 02 03	28 39 03	15 33 59	22 10 26	18 19.6	17 55.7	22 49.6	8 33.5	1 47.0	22 17.0	9 30.8	17 32.5	1 47.6	2 44.4	28 44.8	4 53.7
23 F	0 06 00	29 37 45	28 54 03	5♌45 07	18 16.4	17 52.9	24 41.3	9 48.1	2 23.5	22 03.8	9 26.3	17 39.6	1 45.1	2 42.0	28 43.4	4 53.9
24 Sa	0 09 56	0♎36 29	12♌43 46	19 49 55	18 13.2	17 47.6	26 32.5	11 02.7	2 59.9	21 50.7	9 21.7	17 46.7	1 42.7	2 39.6	28 42.1	4 54.1
25 Su	0 13 53	1 35 15	27 03 16	4♍23 19	18 10.0	17 39.8	28 23.0	12 17.3	3 36.2	21 37.6	9 16.8	17 53.9	1 40.2	2 37.1	28 40.8	4 54.3
26 M	0 17 50	2 34 03	11♍49 17	19 20 14	18 06.9	17 30.0	0♎13.0	13 31.9	4 12.3	21 24.7	9 11.8	18 01.0	1 37.8	2 34.7	28 39.5	4 54.6
27 Tu	0 21 46	3 32 53	26 54 59	4♎32 12	18 03.7	17 19.2	2 02.1	14 46.5	4 48.4	21 11.9	9 06.6	18 08.2	1 35.4	2 32.3	28 38.2	4 54.9
28 W	0 25 43	4 31 45	12♎10 31	19 48 28	18 00.5	17 08.8	3 50.6	16 01.1	5 24.4	20 59.3	9 01.3	18 15.3	1 33.1	2 29.9	28 36.9	4 55.3
29 Th	0 29 39	5 30 40	27 24 42	4♏57 57	17 57.3	17 00.0	5 38.2	17 15.7	6 00.3	20 46.8	8 55.8	18 22.5	1 30.8	2 27.5	28 35.7	4 55.6
30 F	0 33 36	6♎29 36	12♏27 05	19 51 11	17♐54.2	16♐53.6	7♎24.9	18♎30.3	6♌36.1	20♓34.5	8♉50.1	18♎29.8	1♓28.6	2♈25.1	28♒34.5	4♑56.0

1st of Month

Julian Day # 2455805.5
Obliquity 23°26'15"
SVP 5♓05'31"
GC 27♐00.1
Eris 22♈20.0R

Day	⚴
1	28♑47.8R
6	28 10.3R
11	27 42.0R
16	27 22.9R
21	27 12.9R
26	27 11.8

Day	⚵
1	11♎13.3
6	12 54.7
11	14 37.1
16	16 20.2
21	18 04.0
26	19 48.3

Day	⚶
1	7♒14.9R
6	6 41.3R
11	6 19.3R
16	6 09.0R
21	6 10.3
26	6 23.1

DECLINATION and LATITUDE

Day	☉ Decl	☽ Decl	☽ Lat	☽12h Decl	☿ Decl	☿ Lat	♀ Decl	♀ Lat	♂ Decl	♂ Lat	⚳ Decl	⚳ Lat	♃ Decl	♃ Lat	♄ Decl	♄ Lat
1 Th	8N29	11S18	4S25	13S46	14N01	0S42	8N11	1N25	22N49	0N42	15S36	15S40	13N37	1S23	3S52	2N17
2 F	8 07	16 00	3 40	17 59	14 02	0 25	7 42	1 25	22 45	0 43	15 42	15 42	13 36	1 23	3 54	2 17
3 Sa	7 45	19 39	2 41	21 01	14 00	0 10	7 14	1 25	22 40	0 44	15 49	15 44	13 36	1 23	3 57	2 17
4 Su	7 23	22 02	1 34	22 42	13 55	0N06	6 45	1 25	22 35	0 44	15 55	15 45	13 35	1 24	3 60	2 17
5 M	7 01	23 01	0 23	22 59	13 46	0 20	6 15	1 24	22 30	0 45	16 01	15 47	13 35	1 24	4 02	2 17
6 Tu	6 39	22 38	0N48	21 57	13 34	0 33	5 46	1 24	22 25	0 46	16 07	15 48	13 34	1 24	4 05	2 17
7 W	6 17	20 60	1 55	19 46	13 19	0 45	5 16	1 24	22 20	0 47	16 14	15 49	13 34	1 24	4 07	2 17
8 Th	5 54	18 18	2 54	16 38	13 00	0 56	4 47	1 23	22 14	0 48	16 20	15 50	13 33	1 24	4 10	2 17
9 F	5 32	14 47	3 44	12 47	12 38	1 06	4 17	1 23	22 09	0 48	16 26	15 51	13 32	1 25	4 13	2 17
10 Sa	5 09	10 40	4 22	8 28	12 13	1 15	3 47	1 22	22 03	0 49	16 32	15 52	13 31	1 25	4 15	2 16
11 Su	4 46	6 11	4 47	3 51	11 45	1 23	3 17	1 22	21 57	0 50	16 37	15 53	13 31	1 25	4 18	2 16
12 M	4 23	1 30	4 59	0N51	11 15	1 30	2 47	1 21	21 51	0 51	16 43	15 53	13 30	1 25	4 21	2 16
13 Tu	4 01	3N11	4 57	5 28	10 42	1 35	2 16	1 20	21 45	0 52	16 49	15 54	13 29	1 25	4 23	2 16
14 W	3 38	7 42	4 42	9 51	10 07	1 40	1 46	1 19	21 38	0 53	16 54	15 54	13 28	1 26	4 26	2 16
15 Th	3 15	11 54	4 15	13 50	9 29	1 44	1 15	1 19	21 32	0 53	16 60	15 54	13 26	1 26	4 29	2 16
16 F	2 52	15 38	3 36	17 17	8 50	1 46	0 45	1 18	21 25	0 54	17 05	15 54	13 25	1 26	4 31	2 16
17 Sa	2 28	18 45	2 49	20 01	8 09	1 48	0 14	1 17	21 19	0 55	17 10	15 54	13 24	1 26	4 34	2 16
18 Su	2 05	21 05	1 54	21 55	7 27	1 49	0S16	1 16	21 12	0 56	17 15	15 53	13 23	1 26	4 37	2 16
19 M	1 42	22 30	0 53	22 50	6 44	1 50	0 47	1 14	21 05	0 57	17 20	15 53	13 21	1 26	4 40	2 16
20 Tu	1 19	22 53	0S12	22 39	5 60	1 49	1 17	1 13	20 58	0 58	17 25	15 52	13 20	1 27	4 42	2 16
21 W	0 56	22 07	1 17	21 18	5 14	1 48	1 48	1 12	20 51	0 59	17 30	15 51	13 19	1 27	4 45	2 16
22 Th	0 32	20 12	2 21	18 48	4 29	1 46	2 19	1 11	20 44	0 59	17 34	15 50	13 17	1 27	4 48	2 16
23 F	0 09	17 08	3 19	15 12	3 42	1 44	2 49	1 09	20 36	1 00	17 38	15 49	13 16	1 27	4 51	2 16
24 Sa	0S15	13 03	4 07	10 38	2 55	1 41	3 20	1 08	20 29	1 01	17 42	15 48	13 14	1 27	4 53	2 15
25 Su	0 38	8 04	4 43	5 20	2 08	1 38	3 50	1 07	20 21	1 02	17 46	15 47	13 12	1 28	4 56	2 15
26 M	1 01	2 30	5 00	0S24	1 21	1 34	4 20	1 05	20 13	1 03	17 50	15 45	13 11	1 28	4 59	2 15
27 Tu	1 25	3S19	4 57	6 13	0 34	1 30	4 51	1 03	20 06	1 04	17 54	15 44	13 09	1 28	5 02	2 15
28 W	1 48	9 00	4 34	11 40	0S13	1 26	5 21	1 02	19 58	1 05	17 57	15 42	13 07	1 28	5 04	2 15
29 Th	2 11	14 08	3 50	16 21	1 00	1 21	5 51	1 00	19 50	1 05	18 00	15 40	13 05	1 28	5 07	2 15
30 F	2S35	18S18	2S52	19S55	1S47	1N15	6S21	0N58	19N41	1N06	18S03	15S38	13N03	1S28	5S10	2N15

Day	⚷ Decl	⚷ Lat	♅ Decl	♅ Lat	♆ Decl	♆ Lat	♇ Decl	♇ Lat
1	4S45	6N09	0N42	0S46	12S15	0S33	19S03	4N18
6	4 50	6 08	0 38	0 46	12 18	0 33	19 04	4 17
11	4 56	6 08	0 33	0 46	12 20	0 33	19 05	4 16
16	5 02	6 07	0 29	0 46	12 23	0 33	19 06	4 15
21	5 07	6 06	0 24	0 46	12 25	0 33	19 07	4 14
26	5 13	6 04	0 19	0 46	12 28	0 33	19 09	4 12

Day	⚴ Decl	⚴ Lat	⚵ Decl	⚵ Lat	⚶ Decl	⚶ Lat	Eris Decl	Eris Lat
1	11N55	32N57	0N34	5N27	25S24	7S12	3S49	13S28
6	10 54	32 01	0S01	5 31	25 36	7 15	3 50	13 28
11	9 53	31 03	0 36	5 36	25 43	7 16	3 51	13 28
16	8 52	30 04	1 11	5 40	25 46	7 16	3 52	13 28
21	7 52	29 05	1 46	5 45	25 44	7 14	3 53	13 29
26	6 54	28 06	2 21	5 50	25 38	7 12	3 55	13 29

Moon Phenomena

Max/0 Decl
dy hr mn
5 4:55 23S03
12 7:40 0 N
19 20:17 22N53
26 10:21 0 S

Perigee/Apogee
dy hr m kilometers
15 6:24 a 406065
28 0:51 p 357558

Max/0 Lat
dy hr mn
5 7:36 0 N
12 8:37 5N00
19 19:39 0 S
26 8:53 5S01

PH dy hr mn
☽ 4 17:40 11♐51
○ 12 9:28 19♓17
☾ 20 13:40 27♊15
● 27 11:10 4♎00

Void of Course Moon

Last Aspect	☽ Ingress
1 17:36 ♆ △	♏ 1 18:49
3 19:42 ♆ □	♐ 3 21:05
6 0:31 ♆ ✱	♑ 6 2:05
7 20:36 ♂ ☍	♒ 8 9:43
10 17:33 ♆ ☌	♓ 10 19:28
13 1:47 ♀ ☍	♈ 13 6:50
15 17:11 ♆ ✱	♉ 15 19:26
18 7:10 ♂ ✱	♊ 18 8:07
20 16:35 ♆ △	♋ 20 18:55
23 1:23 ☉ ✱	♌ 23 1:56
25 2:40 ♆ ☍	♍ 25 4:50
25 19:48 ♃ △	♎ 27 4:52
29 1:52 ♆ △	♏ 29 4:06

DAILY ASPECTARIAN

1 Th ☽□♂ 0:29; ☽✱☿ 3:25; ☽∥♆ 4:29; ☉∠☽ 8:20; ☽#♃ 11:11; ☽#☿ 13:21; ☽⚻⚳ 13:29; ☽∠♀ 16:04; ☽△♆ 17:36; ☽∥⚳ 22:15; ☽△⚷ 23:16

2 F ☽⚻♅ 0:34; ☽✱♇ 2:56; ☉✱☽ 10:41; ☽☍♃ 11:52; ☽⚼⚳ 13:50; ☽✱♀ 19:09; ☽∥♇ 19:25; ☽⚺♄ 20:16

3 Sa ☽⚼♅ 1:27; ☽∠♇ 3:56; ☉△♃ 4:00; ☽△♂ 4:11; ☽□☿ 8:05; ♀⚺♄ 9:06; ☽△⚳ 14:46; ☽□♆ 19:42; ☽∠♄ 21:56

4 Su ☽□⚷ 1:35; ☽△♅ 2:59; ☽⚺♇ 5:35; ☽⚼♂ 7:06; ☽#♂ 8:52; ☽⚻♃ 14:58; ☉□☽ 17:40

5 M ☽✱♄ 0:18; ☽□♀ 3:55; ☽⚻♂ 10:49; ☽△☿ 17:06; ☽⚼♃ 17:34; ☽□⚳ 18:37; ☿∥♃ 23:58

6 Tu ☽✱♆ 0:31; ☽#♂ 4:45; ☽✱⚷ 6:38; ☿⚻⚳ 6:53; ☽□♅ 8:10; ☽☌♇ 11:01; ☽△♃ 20:50; ☽⚼☿ 23:27

7 W ☽∠♆ 3:57; ☉△☽ 4:09; ☽□♄ 7:12; ☽∠⚷ 10:09; ☽△♀ 16:22; ☽∥♇ 17:55; ♀#⚷ 19:19; ☽☍♂ 20:36

8 Th ☽✱⚳ 1:01; ☽⚻☿ 6:58; ☽⚺♆ 7:59; ☉⚼☽ 10:34; ☽∥⚳ 13:40; ☽⚺⚷ 14:16; ☿☍♆ 15:26; ☽✱♅ 15:54; ☽⚺♇ 19:02; ⚳∠♃ 20:59; ☽⚼♀ 23:47

9 F ☉⚺♄ 1:47; ♀#♄ 3:01; ☽∠⚳ 5:01; ☽□♃ 5:08; ☿ ♍ 6:00; ☽#♃ 7:37; ☽#☿ 14:17; ☽∥♆ 14:41; ☽△♄ 16:32; ☉⚻☽ 17:38; ☿#♆ 18:09; ☽∠♅ 20:34; ☿∠♄ 23:41; ☽∠♇ 23:49

10 Sa ☽⚻♀ 7:53; ☽⚻♂ 8:58; ☽⚺⚳ 9:28; ☉#⚷ 14:07; ♂△⚳ 16:25; ☿☍⚷ 16:30; ☽☌♆ 17:33; ♀☍⚳ 21:28; ☽⚼♄ 21:56; ☽☌⚷ 23:55

11 Su ☽☍☿ 1:07; ☽⚺♅ 1:40; ♀✱♂ 4:23; ♀⚼♃ 4:26; ☿⚻♅ 5:02; ☽✱♇ 5:03; ☽∥⚷ 6:25; ☉#☽ 7:55; ☽∥♄ 9:36; ☽✱♃ 15:18; ☽⚼♂ 15:55; ☽#♀ 16:43

12 M ☉#♄ 2:37; ☽⚻♄ 3:45; ☽#♅ 4:56; ☿△♇ 5:28; ☉☍☽ 9:28; ☽∥♅ 10:23; ☽☌⚳ 19:31; ☽∥♀ 19:46; ☽∠♃ 20:57; ☽△♂ 23:18

13 Tu ☽☍♀ 1:47; ☉∥☽ 3:59; ☽⚺♆ 4:45; ☽#♄ 6:22; ☽#⚷ 9:24; ☽⚺⚷ 11:11; ☽☌♅ 13:00; ☽□♇ 16:39; ☽⚻☿ 22:44

14 W ☽⚺♃ 2:56; ♀⚻♆ 6:02; ☽∠♆ 10:52; ☽∥☿ 11:45; ☽☍♄ 16:27; ☽∠⚷ 17:18

15 Th ☿△♃ 1:44; ♀ ♎ 2:41; ☽#♆ 2:50; ☉⚻☽ 3:05; ☽⚺⚳ 6:49; ☽∥♃ 9:25; ☽⚼☿ 10:32; ☽□♂ 15:08; ☽✱♆ 17:11; ☽⚻♀ 21:24; ☽✱⚷ 23:36

16 F ☽⚺♅ 1:28; ☽△♇ 5:21; ☽#⚳ 10:49; ☉⚼☽ 12:16; ☽∠⚳ 12:42; ♀∥♅ 13:13; ☽☌♃ 15:27; ☉☍⚳ 16:38; ♀⚻⚷ 17:45; ♇ D 18:26; ☽△☿ 22:36

17 Sa ☽#♇ 3:14; ☿∠♂ 4:30; ♂⚻♆ 5:15; ☽⚻♄ 5:54; ☽⚼♀ 7:24; ♄⚼⚷ 7:41; ☽∠♅ 7:48; ♀☍♅ 11:06; ☽⚼♇ 11:46; ☽✱⚳ 18:30; ☉△☽ 21:21; ⚶ D 21:56

18 Su ☉⚼♃ 0:52; ☽∥♂ 1:26; ☽□♆ 5:47; ☽✱♂ 7:10; ♀#♅ 7:59; ☽□⚷ 12:01; ☽⚼♄ 12:24; ☽✱♅ 13:53; ☽△♀ 17:03; ☽⚻♇ 17:53; ☿⚺♄ 23:37

19 M ♀□♇ 1:09; ♂ ♌ 1:52; ☽⚺♃ 3:28; ☽∠♂ 14:32; ☽△♄ 18:21; ☽□☿ 21:31

20 Tu ☉#♀ 0:37; ☽□⚳ 4:52; ☽∠♃ 8:37; ☉□☽ 13:40; ☽△♆ 16:35; ☽⚺♂ 21:00; ☽△⚷ 22:24

21 W ☽□♅ 0:11; ☿#⚷ 3:37; ☽☍♇ 4:10; ☽□♀ 9:39; ☽✱♃ 12:53; ☿#♄ 14:31; ☿☍⚳ 17:45; ☽∥♂ 18:21; ☽⚼♆ 20:40

22 Th ♂⚻⚷ 0:22; ☽⚼⚷ 2:14; ☉⚻♆ 2:18; ☽□♄ 3:39; ☽#♇ 9:23; ☉∥♅ 9:57; ☽△⚳ 12:00; ☽✱☿ 15:18; ♀⚻♃ 17:24; ☽#⚳ 20:38; ☿⚼♃ 20:54; ☽⚻♆ 23:41

23 F ☉✱☽ 1:23; ☽⚻⚷ 5:00; ☽☌♂ 6:25; ☽△♅ 6:40; ☉ ♎ 9:06; ☽⚻♇ 10:31; ♂△♅ 11:25; ☽⚼⚳ 14:03; ☿#♀ 16:29; ☽□♃ 18:16; ☽✱♀ 20:50; ☽∠☿ 21:40; ☽∥♃ 22:55

24 Sa ☽#♆ 3:00; ⚴ D 3:39; ☉∠☽ 5:15; ☉#♅ 6:24; ☽⚼♅ 8:20; ☽✱♄ 8:37; ☽⚼♇ 12:07; ☽⚻⚳ 15:08

25 Su ☽∠♀ 0:25; ☉⚻⚷ 1:57; ☽⚺☿ 2:30; ☽☍♆ 2:40; ☿⚻♆ 3:49; ☽☍⚷ 7:33; ☉⚺☽ 7:58; ☽⚻♅ 9:06; ☽∠♄ 9:39; ☽⚺♂ 11:11; ☽#⚷ 12:34; ☽△♇ 12:50; ☽#♄ 13:37; ☽#♀ 16:53; ☽△♃ 19:48; ☿ ♎ 21:10

26 M ☉☍♅ 0:16; ♀⚼♆ 2:25; ☽⚺♀ 2:59; ☽∥☿ 5:30; ☉#☽ 5:45; ☉#☿ 6:48; ☽∥♅ 9:04; ☽⚺♄ 9:59; ☽#♅ 11:37; ☽∠♂ 12:17; ☽#☿ 14:01; ☽☍⚳ 15:05; ☉∥☽ 15:35; ☿⚻⚷ 18:14; ☽⚼♃ 19:36

27 Tu ☽⚻♆ 2:43; ♂⚻♇ 4:22; ☿☍♅ 6:31; ☽∥♀ 6:55; ☽∥♄ 7:07; ☽⚻⚷ 7:21; ☽∥⚷ 7:56; ☿∥♅ 8:15; ☽☍♅ 8:50; ☽☌☿ 9:09; ♀∥♄ 9:24; ☉☌☽ 11:10; ☽□♇ 12:36; ☽✱♂ 12:56; ♀∥⚷ 18:57; ☽⚻♃ 19:05

28 W ☿#♅ 2:00; ☽⚼♆ 2:16; ☽☌♀ 6:34; ☽⚼⚷ 6:52; ☉□♇ 9:38; ☽☌♄ 9:38; ♀⚼⚷ 10:00; ☽⚻⚳ 13:40; ☿□♇ 14:27; ☽∥♆ 15:51; ♂⚼⚳ 17:16; ☽#♃ 18:48; ☉☌☿ 20:17

29 Th ☽△♆ 1:52; ☽△⚷ 6:29; ☿✱♂ 7:28; ☽⚻♅ 7:59; ☽✱♇ 11:57; ☽⚼⚳ 13:07; ☉⚺☽ 13:46; ☽□♂ 14:14; ☽⚺☿ 14:50; ☽☍♃ 18:14; ☽∥⚳ 22:23; ♀☌♄ 23:49

30 F ☽∥♇ 6:07; ☉✱♂ 6:45; ☽⚼♅ 8:01; ☽#♂ 9:47; ☽⚺♄ 9:52; ☽⚺♀ 10:43; ☽∠♇ 12:08; ☽△⚳ 13:00; ☉∠☽ 15:44; ☿⚻♃ 18:17; ☽∠☿ 18:25

October 2011

LONGITUDE

Day	Sid.Time	☉	☽	☽ 12 hour	Mean ☊	True ☊	☿	♀	♂	⚳	♃	♄	⚷	♅	♆	♇
	h m s	° ' "	° ' "	° ' "	° '	° '	° '	° '	° '	° '	° '	° '	° '	° '	° '	° '
1 Sa	0 37 32	7♎28 34	27♏09 33	4♐21 43	17♐51.0	16♐49.9	9♎10.8	19♎44.9	7♌11.8	20♓22.3	8♉44.3	18♎37.0	1♓26.3	2♈22.7	28♒33.3	4♑56.4
2 Su	0 41 29	8 27 34	11♐27 24	18 26 29	17 47.8	16D 48.5	10 55.9	20 59.5	7 47.4	20R 10.4	8R 38.3	18 44.2	1R 24.2	2R 20.3	28R 32.1	4 56.9
3 M	0 45 25	9 26 36	25 19 04	2♑05 21	17 44.6	16 48.6	12 40.0	22 14.2	8 22.9	19 58.7	8 32.2	18 51.5	1 22.0	2 17.9	28 31.0	4 57.4
4 Tu	0 49 22	10 25 39	8♑45 37	15 20 16	17 41.4	16R 49.0	14 23.4	23 28.8	8 58.3	19 47.2	8 26.0	18 58.8	1 20.0	2 15.5	28 29.8	4 57.9
5 W	0 53 18	11 24 44	21 49 43	28 14 25	17 38.3	16 48.5	16 05.8	24 43.4	9 33.6	19 36.0	8 19.6	19 06.1	1 17.9	2 13.1	28 28.7	4 58.5
6 Th	0 57 15	12 23 51	4♒34 49	10♒51 23	17 35.1	16 46.1	17 47.5	25 58.0	10 08.8	19 25.0	8 13.1	19 13.4	1 15.9	2 10.8	28 27.7	4 59.1
7 F	1 01 12	13 23 00	17 04 32	23 14 41	17 31.9	16 41.3	19 28.3	27 12.6	10 43.9	19 14.3	8 06.4	19 20.7	1 13.9	2 08.4	28 26.6	4 59.7
8 Sa	1 05 08	14 22 10	29 22 13	5♓27 27	17 28.7	16 34.0	21 08.3	28 27.2	11 18.9	19 03.8	7 59.6	19 28.0	1 12.0	2 06.1	28 25.6	5 00.3
9 Su	1 09 05	15 21 23	11♓30 42	17 32 13	17 25.6	16 24.4	22 47.5	29 41.8	11 53.8	18 53.6	7 52.7	19 35.3	1 10.2	2 03.7	28 24.6	5 01.0
10 M	1 13 01	16 20 37	23 32 16	29 31 03	17 22.4	16 13.3	24 25.9	0♏56.4	12 28.5	18 43.7	7 45.7	19 42.6	1 08.3	2 01.4	28 23.6	5 01.7
11 Tu	1 16 58	17 19 53	5♈28 46	11♈25 36	17 19.2	16 01.7	26 03.5	2 11.0	13 03.2	18 34.0	7 38.6	19 49.9	1 06.6	1 59.1	28 22.7	5 02.4
12 W	1 20 54	18 19 11	17 21 44	23 17 20	17 16.0	15 50.5	27 40.4	3 25.6	13 37.7	18 24.7	7 31.4	19 57.2	1 04.8	1 56.8	28 21.7	5 03.2
13 Th	1 24 51	19 18 31	29 12 36	5♉07 46	17 12.8	15 40.8	29 16.6	4 40.2	14 12.2	18 15.7	7 24.1	20 04.6	1 03.2	1 54.5	28 20.9	5 04.0
14 F	1 28 47	20 17 53	11♉03 02	16 58 41	17 09.7	15 33.1	0♏52.1	5 54.9	14 46.5	18 07.0	7 16.6	20 11.9	1 01.5	1 52.3	28 20.0	5 04.8
15 Sa	1 32 44	21 17 17	22 55 01	28 52 22	17 06.5	15 28.0	2 26.9	7 09.5	15 20.7	17 58.6	7 09.1	20 19.2	1 00.0	1 50.0	28 19.1	5 05.7
16 Su	1 36 41	22 16 44	4♊51 07	10♊51 40	17 03.3	15D 25.3	4 01.0	8 24.1	15 54.9	17 50.5	7 01.5	20 26.5	0 58.4	1 47.8	28 18.3	5 06.6
17 M	1 40 37	23 16 13	16 54 31	23 00 07	17 00.1	15 24.6	5 34.5	9 38.7	16 28.9	17 42.8	6 53.9	20 33.9	0 57.0	1 45.6	28 17.6	5 07.5
18 Tu	1 44 34	24 15 44	29 09 01	5♋21 46	16 57.0	15 25.3	7 07.3	10 53.3	17 02.7	17 35.4	6 46.1	20 41.2	0 55.6	1 43.5	28 16.8	5 08.4
19 W	1 48 30	25 15 17	11♋38 54	18 01 01	16 53.8	15 26.6	8 39.5	12 07.9	17 36.5	17 28.3	6 38.3	20 48.5	0 54.2	1 41.3	28 16.1	5 09.4
20 Th	1 52 27	26 14 53	24 28 39	1♌02 18	16 50.6	15R 27.3	10 11.0	13 22.5	18 10.1	17 21.6	6 30.4	20 55.8	0 52.9	1 39.2	28 15.4	5 10.4
21 F	1 56 23	27 14 31	7♌42 24	14 29 19	16 47.4	15 26.7	11 41.9	14 37.1	18 43.6	17 15.3	6 22.5	21 03.1	0 51.6	1 37.1	28 14.7	5 11.5
22 Sa	2 00 20	28 14 11	21 23 19	28 24 27	16 44.2	15 24.4	13 12.2	15 51.7	19 17.0	17 09.3	6 14.5	21 10.4	0 50.4	1 35.0	28 14.1	5 12.5
23 Su	2 04 16	29 13 54	5♍32 41	12♍47 44	16 41.1	15 20.1	14 41.9	17 06.3	19 50.3	17 03.7	6 06.5	21 17.7	0 49.3	1 32.9	28 13.5	5 13.6
24 M	2 08 13	0♏13 38	20 09 05	27 36 04	16 37.9	15 14.2	16 10.9	18 20.9	20 23.4	16 58.4	5 58.4	21 25.0	0 48.2	1 30.9	28 12.9	5 14.7
25 Tu	2 12 10	1 13 25	5♎07 45	12♎43 02	16 34.7	15 07.4	17 39.4	19 35.6	20 56.4	16 53.5	5 50.3	21 32.3	0 47.1	1 28.9	28 12.4	5 15.9
26 W	2 16 06	2 13 14	20 20 41	27 59 19	16 31.5	15 00.7	19 07.2	20 50.2	21 29.3	16 49.0	5 42.2	21 39.5	0 46.2	1 26.9	28 11.9	5 17.0
27 Th	2 20 03	3 13 05	5♏37 35	13♏14 06	16 28.3	14 55.0	20 34.3	22 04.8	22 02.0	16 44.8	5 34.1	21 46.8	0 45.2	1 24.9	28 11.4	5 18.2
28 F	2 23 59	4 12 58	20 47 36	28 16 58	16 25.2	14 51.0	22 00.8	23 19.4	22 34.6	16 41.1	5 25.9	21 54.0	0 44.4	1 23.0	28 11.0	5 19.4
29 Sa	2 27 56	5 12 53	5♐41 12	12♐59 33	16 22.0	14D 49.0	23 26.6	24 34.0	23 07.0	16 37.7	5 17.8	22 01.2	0 43.6	1 21.1	28 10.6	5 20.7
30 Su	2 31 52	6 12 50	20 11 28	27 16 36	16 18.8	14 48.8	24 51.7	25 48.6	23 39.3	16 34.6	5 09.6	22 08.4	0 42.8	1 19.3	28 10.2	5 22.0
31 M	2 35 49	7♏12 48	4♑14 46	11♑06 00	16♐15.6	14♐49.8	26♏16.0	27♏03.2	24♌11.4	16♓32.0	5♉01.5	22♎15.6	0♓42.1	1♈17.4	28♒09.8	5♑23.3

1st of Month

Julian Day # 2455835.5
Obliquity 23°26'15"
SVP 5♓05'28"
GC 27♐00.2
Eris 22♈04.7R

Day	⚴	⚵	⚶
1	27♑19.2	21♎33.1	6♒46.9
6	27 34.8	23 18.2	7 21.2
11	27 58.1	25 03.5	8 05.3
16	28 28.6	26 48.8	8 58.5
21	29 05.7	28 34.1	10 00.1
26	29 49.2	0♏19.3	11 09.5
31	0♒38.5	2 04.2	12 26.1

DECLINATION and LATITUDE

Day	☉ Decl	☽ Decl	☽ Lat	☽ 12h Decl	☿ Decl	☿ Lat	♀ Decl	♀ Lat	♂ Decl	♂ Lat	⚳ Decl	⚳ Lat	♃ Decl	♃ Lat	♄ Decl	♄ Lat
1 Sa	2S58	21S11	1S42	22S05	2S34	1N10	6S51	0N57	19N33	1N07	18S06	15S36	13N01	1S28	5S13	2N15
2 Su	3 21	22 37	0 28	22 47	3 20	1 04	7 21	0 55	19 25	1 08	18 09	15 33	12 59	1 28	5 15	2 15
3 M	3 45	22 36	0N45	22 05	4 06	0 59	7 50	0 53	19 17	1 09	18 11	15 31	12 57	1 28	5 18	2 15
4 Tu	4 08	21 15	1 54	20 08	4 52	0 52	8 20	0 51	19 08	1 10	18 13	15 28	12 55	1 28	5 21	2 15
5 W	4 31	18 47	2 55	17 13	5 37	0 46	8 49	0 49	18 60	1 11	18 15	15 26	12 53	1 29	5 24	2 15
6 Th	4 54	15 28	3 46	13 33	6 22	0 40	9 18	0 47	18 51	1 12	18 17	15 23	12 51	1 29	5 26	2 15
7 F	5 17	11 31	4 25	9 22	7 06	0 33	9 47	0 45	18 42	1 13	18 19	15 20	12 49	1 29	5 29	2 15
8 Sa	5 40	7 09	4 50	4 53	7 50	0 27	10 15	0 43	18 34	1 14	18 20	15 17	12 46	1 29	5 32	2 15
9 Su	6 03	2 35	5 02	0 16	8 33	0 20	10 44	0 41	18 25	1 14	18 22	15 14	12 44	1 29	5 35	2 15
10 M	6 26	2N03	5 01	4N20	9 16	0 13	11 12	0 39	18 16	1 15	18 23	15 11	12 42	1 29	5 38	2 15
11 Tu	6 48	6 34	4 47	8 44	9 58	0 06	11 40	0 36	18 07	1 16	18 23	15 07	12 39	1 29	5 40	2 15
12 W	7 11	10 49	4 20	12 47	10 39	0S01	12 07	0 34	17 58	1 17	18 24	15 04	12 37	1 29	5 43	2 15
13 Th	7 33	14 38	3 41	16 21	11 20	0 07	12 35	0 32	17 49	1 18	18 24	15 01	12 35	1 29	5 46	2 15
14 F	7 56	17 53	2 53	19 15	12 00	0 14	13 02	0 30	17 40	1 19	18 25	14 57	12 32	1 29	5 48	2 15
15 Sa	8 18	20 24	1 58	21 20	12 39	0 21	13 28	0 27	17 30	1 20	18 25	14 53	12 30	1 29	5 51	2 15
16 Su	8 40	22 02	0 57	22 28	13 18	0 28	13 55	0 25	17 21	1 21	18 24	14 50	12 27	1 29	5 54	2 15
17 M	9 02	22 40	0S08	22 34	13 56	0 35	14 21	0 23	17 12	1 22	18 24	14 46	12 25	1 29	5 57	2 15
18 Tu	9 24	22 13	1 13	21 34	14 33	0 42	14 46	0 20	17 02	1 23	18 23	14 42	12 22	1 29	5 59	2 15
19 W	9 46	20 39	2 17	19 28	15 09	0 49	15 12	0 18	16 53	1 24	18 22	14 38	12 20	1 29	6 02	2 15
20 Th	10 08	18 01	3 15	16 20	15 45	0 56	15 37	0 15	16 44	1 25	18 21	14 34	12 17	1 29	6 05	2 15
21 F	10 29	14 24	4 05	12 15	16 20	1 02	16 01	0 13	16 34	1 26	18 20	14 30	12 14	1 29	6 08	2 15
22 Sa	10 51	9 55	4 42	7 24	16 54	1 09	16 25	0 10	16 25	1 27	18 19	14 26	12 12	1 29	6 10	2 15
23 Su	11 12	4 45	5 04	2 00	17 27	1 15	16 49	0 08	16 15	1 28	18 17	14 21	12 09	1 29	6 13	2 15
24 M	11 33	0S49	5 08	3S39	17 59	1 22	17 12	0 05	16 05	1 29	18 15	14 17	12 07	1 29	6 16	2 15
25 Tu	11 54	6 29	4 50	9 13	18 30	1 28	17 35	0 03	15 56	1 30	18 13	14 13	12 04	1 29	6 18	2 15
26 W	12 15	11 51	4 12	14 17	19 01	1 34	17 58	0 00	15 46	1 31	18 11	14 09	12 01	1 29	6 21	2 15
27 Th	12 35	16 29	3 16	18 24	19 30	1 40	18 20	0S03	15 37	1 32	18 09	14 04	11 59	1 29	6 24	2 15
28 F	12 55	19 59	2 07	21 13	19 59	1 46	18 41	0 05	15 27	1 33	18 06	13 60	11 56	1 29	6 26	2 15
29 Sa	13 16	22 04	0 49	22 31	20 26	1 52	19 02	0 08	15 17	1 34	18 04	13 55	11 53	1 29	6 29	2 15
30 Su	13 35	22 35	0N29	22 17	20 53	1 57	19 23	0 10	15 07	1 35	18 01	13 51	11 51	1 29	6 31	2 16
31 M	13S55	21S38	1N44	20S41	21S18	2S02	19S42	0S13	14N58	1N36	17S58	13S46	11N48	1S29	6S34	2N16

Day	⚷ Decl	⚷ Lat	♅ Decl	♅ Lat	♆ Decl	♆ Lat	♇ Decl	♇ Lat
1	5S18	6N03	0N14	0S46	12S30	0S33	19S10	4N1
6	5 23	6 02	0 10	0 46	12 32	0 33	19 11	4 1
11	5 28	6 00	0 05	0 46	12 34	0 33	19 12	4 09
16	5 32	5 58	0 01	0 46	12 35	0 33	19 13	4 08
21	5 36	5 57	0S04	0 46	12 36	0 33	19 14	4 07
26	5 40	5 55	0 07	0 46	12 37	0 33	19 15	4 0
31	5S43	5N53	0S11	0S46	12S38	0S33	19S15	4N0

Day	⚴ Decl	⚴ Lat	⚵ Decl	⚵ Lat	⚶ Decl	⚶ Lat	Eris Decl	Eris Lat
1	5N57	27N07	2S55	5N55	25S28	7S08	3S56	13S29
6	5 04	26 10	3 28	6 00	25 15	7 04	3 57	13 29
11	4 12	25 14	4 01	6 06	24 59	6 60	3 58	13 29
16	3 24	24 19	4 33	6 12	24 40	6 55	3 59	13 29
21	2 39	23 27	5 05	6 18	24 18	6 50	3 59	13 28
26	1 57	22 37	5 35	6 25	23 54	6 45	4 00	13 28
31	1N18	21N47	6S04	6N31	23S27	6S39	4S01	13S28

Moon Phenomena

Max/0 Decl
dy hr mn
2 11:32 22S47
9 13:22 0 N
17 2:07 22N40
23 20:33 0 S
29 20:21 22S36

Max/0 Lat
dy hr mn
2 9:10 0 N
9 9:35 5N04
16 21:02 0 S
23 16:07 5S09
29 15:01 0 N

Perigee/Apogee
dy hr m kilometers
12 11:44 a 406434
26 12:27 p 357057

PH dy hr mn
☽ 4 3:16 10♑34
○ 12 2:07 18♈24
☾ 20 3:31 26♋24
● 26 19:57 3♏03

Void of Course Moon

Last Aspect	☽ Ingress
1 2:19 ♆ □	♐ 1 4:43
3 5:38 ♆ ⚹	♑ 3 8:17
5 5:59 ♀ □	♒ 5 15:19
7 22:09 ♆ ☌	♓ 8 1:14
8 16:52 ♃ ⚹	♈ 10 12:58
13 0:09 ☿ ☍	♉ 13 1:36
15 10:52 ♆ □	♊ 15 14:16
17 22:19 ♆ △	♋ 18 1:39
20 3:31 ☉ □	♌ 20 10:07
22 12:36 ☉ ⚹	♍ 22 14:42
23 20:48 ♀ ⚹	♎ 24 15:50
26 12:19 ♆ △	♏ 26 15:09
28 11:50 ♆ □	♐ 28 14:46
30 13:31 ♆ ⚹	♑ 30 16:40

DAILY ASPECTARIAN

1 Sa ☽□♆ 2:19; ☽□⚷ 7:06; ☽△♅ 8:39; ♀⚻⚳ 10:22; ☽∠♄ 10:51; ☽⚺♇ 12:59; ☽∠♀ 13:51; ☽△♂ 17:30; ☉⚹☽ 18:32; ☽⚻♃ 19:15; ☽⚹☿ 22:59

2 Su ☉∥☿ 1:03; ☉⚻♃ 3:58; ☽⚹♄ 12:37; ☽□⚳ 14:48; ☽⚹♀ 18:04; ☽⚼♂ 20:27; ☽⚼♃ 20:54

3 M ♂□♃ 5:22; ☽⚹♆ 5:38; ☽⚹⚷ 10:41; ☿⚼♆ 11:40; ☽□♅ 12:20; ☽☌♇ 17:09; ♂⫲♇ 18:04; ☽△♃ 23:25

4 Tu ☽⚻♂ 0:24; ♄∥⚷ 1:37; ☉□☽ 3:16; ☽∠♆ 8:37; ☽□☿ 11:48; ☽∠⚷ 13:48; ☿∥⚷ 15:44; ☿∥♄ 16:20; ☽□♄ 18:53; ☽⚹⚳ 19:55; ☽∥♇ 20:45; ☽⫲♂ 22:11

5 W ☿⚼⚷ 2:47; ☽∥⚳ 4:10; ☽□♀ 5:59; ☽⚺♆ 12:26; ☽⚺⚷ 17:44; ☽⚹♅ 19:27; ☽∠⚳ 23:42

6 Th ☽⚺♇ 0:46; ☽□♃ 6:53; ☽☍♂ 11:10; ⚳⚻♄ 15:27; ☉△☽ 16:15; ☽⫲♃ 16:22; ☽∥♆ 18:04; ☿⚻⚳ 20:58; ☿☌♄ 22:02

7 F ☽∠♅ 0:07; ☉⚼♆ 1:27; ☽⚺⚳ 4:08; ☽△♄ 4:27; ☽△☿ 5:23; ☽∠♇ 5:40; ☉∥⚷ 7:42; ☽∥♀ 8:47; ☉∥♄ 14:37; ☽∥☿ 20:52; ☽△♀ 22:00; ☽☌♆ 22:09; ♀△♆ 23:29; ☉⚼☽ 24:00

8 Sa ☽☌⚷ 3:35; ☽⚺♅ 5:21; ☉∥☽ 7:17; ☽∥♄ 8:30; ☽∥⚷ 9:11; ☽⚼♄ 10:09; ☽⚹♇ 11:07; ☽⚼☿ 15:27; ☽⚹♃ 16:52

9 Su ☽⚻♂ 0:48; ♀ ♏ 5:51; ☽⚼♀ 7:04; ♂⫲⚳ 7:42; ☉⚻☽ 8:20; ☽⫲♅ 12:49; ☽∥♅ 13:55; ☽☌⚳ 14:30; ☽⚻♄ 16:16; ☉⚼⚷ 19:11; ☽∠♃ 22:28

10 M ☽⚻☿ 2:04; ♀△⚷ 3:44; ☽⚼♂ 8:18; ☽⚺♆ 9:44; ☽⚺⚷ 15:13; ☽⚻♀ 16:35; ☽☌♅ 16:59; ☽⫲⚷ 18:03; ☽⫲♄ 19:08; ♀⚻♅ 20:17; ☽□♇ 23:07

11 Tu ☉⫲☽ 1:27; ☽⚺♃ 4:19; ☽∠♆ 15:55; ☽△♂ 16:04; ☽∠⚷ 21:25; ☽⫲☿ 22:53; ♀⚼⚳ 23:44

12 W ☉⚻⚳ 1:56; ☽⚺⚳ 2:06; ☉☍☽ 2:07; ☽☍♄ 5:18; ☽⫲♀ 8:55; ☿△♆ 10:11; ☽⫲♆ 10:37; ☽∥♃ 10:49; ☽⚹♆ 22:15; ♀∥♆ 23:37; ♀⫲♃ 24:00

13 Th ☽☍☿ 0:09; ♃⫲♆ 3:43; ☽⚹⚷ 3:44; ☽⚺♅ 5:27; ♀⚹♇ 7:44; ☽∠⚳ 8:07; ☿ ♏ 10:53; ☽△♇ 11:53; ☽☍♀ 12:22; ☽☌♃ 16:26; ☉☌♄ 21:14; ☽∥♂ 22:14

14 F ☿△⚷ 2:20; ☽⫲⚳ 4:25; ☽□♂ 7:55; ☽⫲♇ 11:39; ☽∠♅ 11:45; ☽⚹⚳ 14:08; ☿⚻♅ 14:52; ☽⚼♇ 18:18; ☿⫲♃ 18:23; ☽⚻♄ 18:42; ☉⚻☽ 20:25; ☿∥♆ 21:07; ♀☍♃ 23:54

15 Sa ☿⚼⚳ 7:25; ☽□♆ 10:52; ☽□⚷ 16:14; ☽⚹♅ 17:54; ☽⚻☿ 22:05

16 Su ☽⚻♇ 0:31; ☽⚼♄ 1:12; ☽⚺♃ 4:18; ☉⚼☽ 5:17; ☽⚻♀ 7:55; ☿⚹♇ 16:59; ☽⚹♂ 23:07

17 M ☽□⚳ 1:34; ☽△♄ 7:17; ☽⚼☿ 8:17; ☽∠♃ 9:44; ♂⚼♅ 11:09; ☉△☽ 13:38; ☽⚼♀ 16:56; ☿☍♃ 18:56; ☽△♆ 22:19

18 Tu ☽△⚷ 3:26; ☽□♅ 4:58; ☽∠♂ 5:53; ☽☍♇ 11:35; ☽⚹♃ 14:33; ☽△☿ 17:31; ♂⚻⚳ 19:11

19 W ☽△♀ 1:01; ☽⚼♆ 3:04; ☿∥♀ 4:57; ☽⚼⚷ 8:01; ☽△⚳ 10:53; ☽⚺♂ 11:45; ☽⫲♇ 14:12; ☽□♄ 17:22; ☽⫲⚳ 21:24

20 Th ☉□☽ 3:31; ☽⚻♆ 6:56; ☽∥♂ 9:45; ☽⚻⚷ 11:42; ☽△♅ 13:05; ☽⫲☿ 13:37; ☽⚼⚳ 14:17; ☽⫲♀ 14:59; ☽⚻♇ 19:29; ☽□♃ 21:39

21 F ☿⫲♂ 7:51; ☽□☿ 7:58; ☽⫲♆ 10:05; ☽∥♃ 12:10; ☽□♀ 13:27; ☽⚼♅ 15:41; ☽⚻⚳ 16:43; ☉⫲☽ 19:38; ☽☌♂ 20:13; ☽⚼♇ 21:58; ♀⫲♂ 23:28; ☽⚹♄ 23:38; ☉△♆ 23:58

22 Sa ☽☍♆ 11:42; ☉⚹☽ 12:36; ♀⚼♅ 13:32; ☽☍⚷ 16:05; ☽⚻♅ 17:19; ☽⫲♄ 17:30; ☽⫲⚷ 20:07; ♀△⚳ 23:12; ☽△♇ 23:28

23 Su ☽△♃ 0:56; ☽∠♄ 1:16; ☉∠☽ 15:24; ☽⚹☿ 16:49; ♂⚼♇ 17:27; ☉ ♏ 18:31; ☽☍⚳ 18:52; ☽⫲♅ 20:08; ☽⚹♀ 20:48; ☽∥♅ 20:58

24 M ☽⚺♂ 0:24; ☽⚼♃ 1:19; ☽⚺♄ 2:04; ☿⚼♅ 5:16; ☿∥⚳ 11:45; ☿△⚳ 12:10; ☽⚻♆ 12:58; ☉△⚷ 13:38; ☽⚻⚷ 17:06; ☉⚺☽ 17:21; ☽☍♅ 18:13; ☽∠☿ 19:39; ☽∥⚷ 20:27; ☽∠♀ 23:04; ☽∥♄ 23:15

25 Tu ☽□♇ 0:13; ☽⚻♃ 1:07; ☽∠♂ 1:20; ⚵ ♏ 1:59; ☉⚻♅ 6:00; ☉⫲♃ 10:16; ☽⚼♆ 12:46; ♀∠♇ 13:10; ☉⚼⚳ 14:56; ☽⚼⚷ 16:49; ☽⚻⚳ 18:29; ☽⚺☿ 21:52

26 W ☽⚺♀ 0:50; ☽⫲♃ 0:51; ☽⚹♂ 1:52; ☉∥☽ 2:03; ☽☌♄ 2:05; ☽∥♆ 3:43; ♂⚹♄ 9:39; ☿∥♇ 11:15; ☽△♆ 12:19; ♀∥⚳ 13:21; ☽△⚷ 16:21; ☽⚻♅ 17:24; ♀⚺♄ 17:35; ☽⚼⚳ 17:56; ☽⫲♂ 19:15; ☿∠♇ 19:29; ☉☌☽ 19:57; ♀□♂ 22:24; ☽⚹♇ 23:30; ☽☍♃ 23:55

27 Th ☉∥♆ 2:36; ⚴ ♒ 3:34; ☽∥⚳ 10:14; ☽∥♀ 12:52; ☽⚼♅ 17:00; ☽△⚳ 17:29; ☽∥♇ 18:06; ☿⚺♄ 21:56; ☽∠♇ 23:15; ☽∥☿ 23:54

28 F ☽⚺♄ 1:47; ☽☌☿ 2:09; ☽□♂ 2:57; ☽☌♀ 4:24; ☽□♆ 11:50; ☿□♂ 15:09; ☽□⚷ 15:57; ♃△♇ 16:30; ☽△♅ 16:58; ☉⚺☽ 23:10; ☽⚻♃ 23:22; ☽⚺♇ 23:27

29 Sa ☉☍♃ 1:43; ☽∠♄ 2:12; ☉⚹♇ 3:12; ♀∥♇ 15:16; ☽□⚳ 17:58; ☽⚼♃ 23:57

30 Su ☉∠☽ 1:51; ☽⚹♄ 3:19; ☽△♂ 6:04; ☽⚺☿ 8:46; ☽⚺♀ 10:25; ☽⚹♆ 13:31; ☽⚹⚷ 17:53; ☽□♅ 18:54

31 M ☽△♃ 1:20; ☽☌♇ 1:59; ☽∥☿ 3:48; ☉⚹☽ 5:35; ☽⚼♂ 8:59; ☽∠☿ 13:42; ☽∠♀ 15:04; ☽∠♆ 15:39; ☽∥♀ 19:09; ☽∠⚷ 20:09; ♀□♆ 21:21; ☽⚹⚳ 21:36

LONGITUDE

November 2011

Day	Sid.Time	☉	☽	☽ 12 hour	Mean ☊	True ☊	☿	♀	♂	⚳	♃	♄	⚷	♅	♆	♇
	h m s	° ' "	° ' "	° ' "	° '	° '	° '	° '	° '	° '	° '	° '	° '	° '	° '	° '
1 Tu	2 39 45	8♏12 48	17♑50 26	24♑28 22	16♐12.5	14♐51.4	27♏39.6	28♏17.8	24♌43.4	16♓29.8	4♉53.3	22♎22.8	0♓41.5	1♈15.7	28♒09.5	5♑24.6
2 W	2 43 42	9 12 50	1♒00 08	7♒26 12	16 09.3	14R 52.6	29 02.2	29 32.4	25 15.3	16R 27.9	4R 45.2	22 29.9	0R 40.9	1R 13.9	28R 09.3	5 26.0
3 Th	2 47 39	10 12 53	13 47 02	20 03 10	16 06.1	14 52.8	0♐24.0	0♐47.0	25 47.0	16 26.4	4 37.1	22 37.0	0 40.4	1 12.2	28 09.0	5 27.4
4 F	2 51 35	11 12 58	26 15 07	2♓23 24	16 02.9	14 51.6	1 44.8	2 01.6	26 18.5	16 25.3	4 29.1	22 44.1	0 40.0	1 10.5	28 08.8	5 28.8
5 Sa	2 55 32	12 13 04	8♓28 33	14 31 02	15 59.8	14 48.9	3 04.5	3 16.2	26 49.8	16 24.5	4 21.1	22 51.2	0 39.6	1 08.8	28 08.6	5 30.2
6 Su	2 59 28	13 13 12	20 31 21	26 29 55	15 56.6	14 44.7	4 23.0	4 30.7	27 21.1	16D 24.1	4 13.1	22 58.2	0 39.2	1 07.2	28 08.5	5 31.6
7 M	3 03 25	14 13 22	2♈27 09	8♈23 25	15 53.4	14 39.6	5 40.3	5 45.3	27 52.1	16 24.1	4 05.2	23 05.2	0 39.0	1 05.7	28 08.4	5 33.1
8 Tu	3 07 21	15 13 33	14 19 04	20 14 25	15 50.2	14 34.1	6 56.1	6 59.8	28 23.0	16 24.5	3 57.4	23 12.2	0 38.8	1 04.1	28 08.3	5 34.6
9 W	3 11 18	16 13 45	26 09 44	2♉05 17	15 47.0	14 28.8	8 10.4	8 14.4	28 53.7	16 25.3	3 49.6	23 19.2	0 38.6	1 02.6	28D 08.2	5 36.1
10 Th	3 15 14	17 14 00	8♉01 19	13 58 03	15 43.9	14 24.2	9 22.9	9 28.9	29 24.2	16 26.4	3 41.9	23 26.1	0D 38.5	1 01.2	28 08.2	5 37.7
11 F	3 19 11	18 14 16	19 55 43	25 54 32	15 40.7	14 20.8	10 33.4	10 43.5	29 54.6	16 27.9	3 34.2	23 33.0	0 38.5	0 59.7	28 08.2	5 39.3
12 Sa	3 23 08	19 14 34	1♊54 42	7♊56 29	15 37.5	14 18.8	11 41.8	11 58.0	0♍24.8	16 29.7	3 26.7	23 39.9	0 38.5	0 58.4	28 08.3	5 40.8
13 Su	3 27 04	20 14 53	14 00 05	20 05 47	15 34.3	14D 18.2	12 47.7	13 12.5	0 54.8	16 31.9	3 19.2	23 46.7	0 38.6	0 57.0	28 08.4	5 42.5
14 M	3 31 01	21 15 15	26 13 52	2♋24 37	15 31.2	14 18.7	13 50.9	14 27.0	1 24.7	16 34.5	3 11.8	23 53.5	0 38.8	0 55.8	28 08.5	5 44.1
15 Tu	3 34 57	22 15 38	8♋38 22	14 55 26	15 28.0	14 20.0	14 50.9	15 41.5	1 54.3	16 37.4	3 04.5	24 00.3	0 39.0	0 54.5	28 08.7	5 45.8
16 W	3 38 54	23 16 03	21 16 12	27 41 00	15 24.8	14 21.6	15 47.4	16 56.0	2 23.8	16 40.7	2 57.3	24 07.0	0 39.3	0 53.3	28 08.9	5 47.4
17 Th	3 42 50	24 16 30	4♌10 12	10♌44 09	15 21.6	14 23.1	16 39.9	18 10.6	2 53.1	16 44.3	2 50.3	24 13.7	0 39.6	0 52.1	28 09.1	5 49.1
18 F	3 46 47	25 16 59	17 23 10	24 07 31	15 18.5	14R 24.0	17 28.0	19 25.0	3 22.1	16 48.3	2 43.3	24 20.4	0 40.0	0 51.0	28 09.4	5 50.8
19 Sa	3 50 43	26 17 30	0♍57 24	7♍52 58	15 15.3	14 24.1	18 11.0	20 39.5	3 51.0	16 52.6	2 36.5	24 27.0	0 40.5	0 49.9	28 09.7	5 52.6
20 Su	3 54 40	27 18 02	14 54 14	22 01 05	15 12.1	14 23.4	18 48.4	21 54.0	4 19.7	16 57.2	2 29.8	24 33.6	0 41.0	0 48.9	28 10.0	5 54.3
21 M	3 58 37	28 18 36	29 13 18	6♎30 29	15 08.9	14 21.9	19 19.4	23 08.5	4 48.1	17 02.2	2 23.2	24 40.1	0 41.5	0 47.9	28 10.4	5 56.1
22 Tu	4 02 33	29 19 12	13♎52 04	21 17 22	15 05.7	14 20.1	19 43.3	24 23.0	5 16.4	17 07.6	2 16.7	24 46.6	0 42.2	0 47.0	28 10.8	5 57.9
23 W	4 06 30	0♐19 50	28 45 32	6♏15 35	15 02.6	14 18.2	19 59.4	25 37.5	5 44.4	17 13.2	2 10.4	24 53.1	0 42.9	0 46.1	28 11.2	5 59.7
24 Th	4 10 26	1 20 30	13♏46 29	21 17 07	14 59.4	14 16.6	20R 06.8	26 51.9	6 12.2	17 19.2	2 04.2	24 59.5	0 43.6	0 45.3	28 11.7	6 01.5
25 F	4 14 23	2 21 11	28 46 21	6♐13 07	14 56.2	14 15.6	20 04.9	28 06.4	6 39.8	17 25.5	1 58.2	25 05.8	0 44.5	0 44.5	28 12.2	6 03.4
26 Sa	4 18 19	3 21 53	13♐36 25	20 55 19	14 53.0	14D 15.3	19 53.0	29 20.8	7 07.1	17 32.2	1 52.4	25 12.1	0 45.4	0 43.7	28 12.7	6 05.3
27 Su	4 22 16	4 22 37	28 09 06	5♑17 07	14 49.9	14 15.5	19 30.5	0♑35.3	7 34.2	17 39.2	1 46.6	25 18.4	0 46.3	0 43.0	28 13.3	6 07.1
28 M	4 26 12	5 23 22	12♑18 57	19 14 19	14 46.7	14 16.2	18 57.1	1 49.7	8 01.0	17 46.4	1 41.1	25 24.6	0 47.3	0 42.4	28 13.9	6 09.0
29 Tu	4 30 09	6 24 08	26 03 06	2♒45 19	14 43.5	14 17.0	18 12.8	3 04.2	8 27.6	17 54.0	1 35.7	25 30.7	0 48.4	0 41.8	28 14.6	6 10.9
30 W	4 34 06	7♐24 55	9♒21 07	15 50 47	14♐40.3	14♐17.7	17♐18.1	4♑18.6	8♍53.9	18♓01.9	1♉30.5	25♎36.8	0♓49.5	0♈41.2	28♒15.2	6♑12.9

1st of Month

Julian Day #
2455866.5
Obliquity
23°26'14"
SVP 5♓05'25"
GC 27♐00.3
Eris 21♈46.4R

Day	⚴	⚵	⚶
1	0♒49.0	2♏25.1	12♒42.2
6	1 44.7	4 09.5	14 06.7
11	2 45.2	5 53.3	15 37.0
16	3 50.2	7 36.5	17 12.6
21	4 59.3	9 18.8	18 53.1
26	6 12.2	11 00.2	20 38.0

DECLINATION and LATITUDE

Day	☉ Decl	☽ Decl	☽ Lat	☽ 12h Decl	☿ Decl	☿ Lat	♀ Decl	♀ Lat	♂ Decl	♂ Lat	⚳ Decl	⚳ Lat	♃ Decl	♃ Lat	♄ Decl	♄ Lat
1 Tu	14S15	19S26	2N50	17S57	21S42	2S07	20S02	0S16	14N48	1N37	17S54	13S42	11N45	1S29	6S37	2N16
2 W	14 34	16 16	3 45	14 24	22 06	2 12	20 18	0 18	14 38	1 38	17 50	13 37	11 43	1 29	6 39	2 16
3 Th	14 53	12 25	4 28	10 18	22 28	2 17	20 39	0 21	14 28	1 39	17 47	13 32	11 40	1 28	6 42	2 16
4 F	15 12	8 07	4 56	5 52	22 49	2 21	20 57	0 23	14 19	1 40	17 44	13 28	11 38	1 28	6 44	2 16
5 Sa	15 30	3 35	5 10	1 17	23 08	2 25	21 15	0 26	14 09	1 41	17 40	13 23	11 35	1 28	6 47	2 16
6 Su	15 48	1N00	5 11	3N17	23 27	2 28	21 30	0 29	13 59	1 42	17 36	13 19	11 33	1 28	6 49	2 16
7 M	16 06	5 31	4 57	7 42	23 44	2 32	21 46	0 31	13 49	1 43	17 31	13 14	11 30	1 28	6 52	2 16
8 Tu	16 24	9 49	4 31	11 50	24 00	2 35	22 02	0 34	13 40	1 44	17 27	13 09	11 28	1 28	6 54	2 16
9 W	16 41	13 44	3 54	15 30	24 15	2 37	22 16	0 36	13 30	1 45	17 22	13 05	11 25	1 28	6 57	2 16
10 Th	16 59	17 07	3 06	18 33	24 28	2 39	22 30	0 39	13 20	1 46	17 18	13 00	11 23	1 28	6 59	2 16
11 F	17 15	19 48	2 10	20 51	24 40	2 40	22 44	0 41	13 11	1 47	17 13	12 55	11 20	1 27	7 02	2 16
12 Sa	17 32	21 39	1 08	22 12	24 51	2 41	22 57	0 44	13 01	1 49	17 08	12 51	11 18	1 27	7 04	2 17
13 Su	17 48	22 30	0 02	22 32	24 60	2 41	23 09	0 46	12 51	1 50	17 03	12 46	11 15	1 27	7 07	2 17
14 M	18 04	22 18	1S05	21 47	25 08	2 41	23 20	0 49	12 42	1 51	16 57	12 41	11 13	1 27	7 09	2 17
15 Tu	18 20	20 59	2 10	19 56	25 14	2 40	23 31	0 51	12 32	1 52	16 52	12 37	11 11	1 27	7 11	2 17
16 W	18 35	18 37	3 10	17 04	25 18	2 38	23 41	0 54	12 23	1 53	16 46	12 32	11 08	1 26	7 14	2 17
17 Th	18 50	15 18	4 02	13 19	25 21	2 36	23 50	0 56	12 13	1 54	16 41	12 28	11 06	1 26	7 16	2 17
18 F	19 05	11 09	4 42	8 48	25 22	2 32	23 59	0 58	12 04	1 55	16 35	12 23	11 04	1 26	7 18	2 17
19 Sa	19 19	6 20	5 08	3 45	25 22	2 27	24 07	1 01	11 54	1 56	16 29	12 18	11 02	1 26	7 21	2 17
20 Su	19 33	1 05	5 16	1S38	25 19	2 22	24 14	1 03	11 45	1 58	16 23	12 14	10 60	1 26	7 23	2 17
21 M	19 47	4S22	5 06	7 04	25 15	2 15	24 21	1 05	11 36	1 59	16 17	12 09	10 58	1 25	7 25	2 18
22 Tu	20 00	9 42	4 35	12 13	25 09	2 07	24 27	1 08	11 26	1 60	16 11	12 05	10 56	1 25	7 27	2 18
23 W	20 13	14 33	3 46	16 41	25 01	1 58	24 32	1 10	11 17	2 01	16 04	12 00	10 54	1 25	7 30	2 18
24 Th	20 26	18 32	2 41	20 04	24 51	1 47	24 36	1 12	11 08	2 02	15 58	11 56	10 52	1 25	7 32	2 18
25 F	20 38	21 16	1 25	22 04	24 38	1 35	24 39	1 14	10 59	2 04	15 51	11 51	10 50	1 25	7 34	2 18
26 Sa	20 50	22 29	0 04	22 31	24 24	1 21	24 42	1 16	10 50	2 05	15 45	11 47	10 48	1 24	7 36	2 18
27 Su	21 01	22 09	1N16	21 26	24 07	1 06	24 44	1 18	10 41	2 06	15 38	11 42	10 47	1 24	7 38	2 18
28 M	21 12	20 23	2 30	19 03	23 47	0 49	24 46	1 20	10 32	2 07	15 31	11 38	10 45	1 24	7 40	2 19
29 Tu	21 23	17 28	3 32	15 41	23 26	0 31	24 46	1 22	10 23	2 09	15 24	11 33	10 43	1 24	7 43	2 19
30 W	21S33	13S43	4N21	11S38	23S02	0S12	24S46	1S24	10N14	2N10	15S17	11S29	10N42	1S23	7S45	2N19

Day	⚷ Decl	⚷ Lat	♅ Decl	♅ Lat	♆ Decl	♆ Lat	♇ Decl	♇ Lat
1	5S44	5N52	0S12	0S46	12S38	0S33	19S16	4N04
6	5 46	5 50	0 15	0 46	12 38	0 33	19 16	4 03
11	5 48	5 48	0 18	0 45	12 38	0 33	19 17	4 02
16	5 50	5 47	0 20	0 45	12 38	0 33	19 17	4 01
21	5 51	5 45	0 22	0 45	12 37	0 33	19 18	4 00
26	5 52	5 43	0 24	0 45	12 37	0 33	19 18	3 60

Day	⚴ Decl	⚴ Lat	⚵ Decl	⚵ Lat	⚶ Decl	⚶ Lat	Eris Decl	Eris Lat
1	1N10	21N37	6S10	6N32	23S21	6S38	4S01	13S28
6	0 35	20 50	6 38	6 39	22 51	6 33	4 02	13 27
11	0 04	20 06	7 05	6 46	22 19	6 28	4 02	13 27
16	0S25	19 23	7 31	6 54	21 45	6 23	4 03	13 26
21	0 50	18 42	7 55	7 02	21 08	6 18	4 03	13 26
26	1 12	18 03	8 18	7 11	20 30	6 13	4 03	13 25

Moon Phenomena

Max/0 Decl

dy	hr mn	
5	18:44	0 N
13	7:20	22N33
20	4:48	0 S
26	6:32	22S33

Perigee/Apogee

dy	hr m		kilometers
8	13:21	a	406177
23	23:34	p	359691

Max/0 Lat

dy	hr mn	
5	12:31	5N12
13	0:35	0 S
19	23:13	5S16
26	1:03	0 N

PH	dy	hr mn	
☽	2	16:39	9♒55
○	10	20:17	18♉05
☾	18	15:10	25♌55
●	25	6:11	2♐37
●	25	6:21	P 0.905

Void of Course Moon

Last Aspect				☽ Ingress		
1	21:01	♀	✶	♒	1	22:09
4	3:41	♆	☌	♓	4	7:19
5	8:06	☉	△	♈	6	19:03
9	5:47	♂	△	♉	9	7:46
11	16:28	♆	□	♊	11	20:11
14	3:43	♆	△	♋	14	7:20
16	5:23	♄	□	♌	16	16:18
18	19:06	♆	☍	♍	18	22:20
20	22:23	☉	✶	♎	21	1:17
22	23:05	♆	△	♏	23	1:59
24	23:05	♆	□	♐	25	1:58
27	0:07	♆	✶	♑	27	3:06
28	23:02	♄	□	♒	29	7:03

DAILY ASPECTARIAN

1 Tu	☽∥♇	1:32
	☽□♄	8:16
	☿□♆	8:38
	☽∥⚳	12:35
	☽⚻♂	12:59
	☽⚺♆	18:45
	☽✶☿	19:57
	☽✶♀	21:01
	☽⚺⚷	23:24
2 W	☽✶♅	0:25
	☽∠⚳	0:51
	☉#♂	3:38
	☽□♃	6:54
	☽⚺♇	8:16
	♀ ♐	8:52
	☉∥☽	10:11
	☽#♂	11:03
	☉□☽	16:39
	☿ ♐	16:55
	♀□⚷	21:54
	☽∥♆	22:41
3 Th	☽#♃	4:20
	☽∠♅	4:36
	☿□⚷	4:49
	☽⚺⚳	5:03
	♀△♅	7:55
	☽∠♇	12:48
	☿△♅	13:59
	☽△♄	17:07
4 F	☽☍♂	0:07
	☽☌♆	3:41
	☽∥♄	7:21
	☽☌⚷	8:37
	☽⚺♅	9:36
	☽□☿	12:03
	☽□♀	12:34
	☽∥⚷	12:37
	☽✶♃	15:57
	☽✶♇	18:07
	☽⚼♄	22:45
5 Sa	☉△☽	8:06
	☽☌⚳	15:46
	☽∥♅	17:27
	♀⚻♃	18:53
	☽#♅	20:02
	☿⚻♃	21:14
	☽∠♃	21:25
6 Su	☽⚻♄	4:57
	⚳ D	11:40
	☽⚻♂	14:20
	☽⚺♆	15:18
	☉⚼☽	16:53
	♀⚺♇	20:00
	☽⚺⚷	20:22
	☽☌♅	21:16
	☿⚺♇	21:43
7 M	☽#⚷	1:23
	☽⚺♃	3:16
	☽□♇	6:16
	☽△☿	7:17
	☽#♄	7:24
	☽△♀	7:27
	♂☍♆	12:35
	☽∠♆	21:37
	☽⚼♂	22:01
8 Tu	☉⚻☽	2:01
	☽∠⚷	2:41
	☽⚺⚳	4:14
	☽∥♃	9:39
	☽#♆	17:01
	☽⚼☿	17:15
	☽⚼♀	17:23
	☽☍♄	18:11
	☉⚼♅	19:40
	☽∥♂	22:34
9 W	♀∠♄	1:42
	☿∠♄	3:11
	☽✶♆	4:00
	☉△⚳	4:40
	☽△♂	5:47
	☽✶⚷	9:04
	☽⚺♅	9:52
	☽∠⚳	10:40
	☽☌♃	15:21
	♆ D	18:55
	☽△♇	19:09
	☉#☽	22:49
10 Th	☽#⚳	1:22
	☽⚻☿	3:03
	☽⚻♀	3:18
	☽∠♅	16:06
	☽✶⚳	17:01
	☽#♇	18:43
	☉☍☽	20:17
	☉∥⚳	20:59
	⚷ D	23:15
11 F	☽⚼♇	1:28
	♂ ♍	4:16
	☽⚻♄	7:21
	☽□♆	16:28
	☽□♂	20:53
	☽□⚷	21:28
	☽✶♅	22:08
12 Sa	☽⚺♃	3:01
	☽⚻♇	7:31
	♂☍⚷	10:58
	☽⚼♄	13:34
	☽☍☿	21:23
	☽☍♀	22:15
13 Su	♂⚻♅	1:42
	☽□⚳	5:00
	☽∠♃	8:25
	☉∠♇	11:16
	☉⚻☽	13:24
	☽△♄	19:24
14 M	☽△♆	3:43
	☽△⚷	8:35
	♂#♆	8:59
	☽□♅	9:07
	☽✶♂	10:29
	☽✶♃	13:23
	☽☍♇	18:28
	☉⚼☽	21:07
15 Tu	☽⚼♆	8:37
	☽⚻☿	12:50
	☽⚼⚷	13:23
	☽⚻♀	14:55
	☽△⚳	15:17
	☽∠♂	16:24
	☽#♇	18:10
	♀□⚳	18:49
16 W	☉#☽	0:17
	☉△☽	4:04
	☽□♄	5:23
	☽⚻♆	12:52
	☽#⚳	14:31
	☽⚻⚷	17:31
	☽△♅	17:55
	♀⚼♃	18:02
	☽⚼☿	19:04
	☽⚼⚳	19:30
	☽⚺♂	21:32
	☽□♃	21:34
	☽⚼♀	21:59
	♂△♃	22:09
	☉⚺♄	22:46
17 Th	☿□⚳	2:16
	☽⚻♇	3:02
	☽#♆	15:52
	☽∥♂	18:51
	☽⚼♅	21:15
	☽⚻⚳	22:57
18 F	☽△☿	0:09
	☽∥♃	0:24
	☽△♀	4:00
	☽⚼♇	6:12
	☿⚼♃	7:07
	☽✶♄	12:29
	☉□☽	15:10
	☽☍♆	19:06
	☽#♄	19:12
	☉∥♇	21:26
	☽☍⚷	23:30
	☽⚻♅	23:47
19 Sa	☽#⚷	2:19
	☽△♃	2:51
	☽☌♂	5:13
	☽△♇	8:33
	☽∠♄	14:48
20 Su	☽#♅	3:11
	☽☍⚳	3:30
	☽⚼♃	4:21
	☽∥♅	6:25
	☽□☿	6:52
	☽□♀	12:55
	☽⚺♄	16:22
	☉□♆	20:43
	☽⚻♆	22:16
	☉✶☽	22:23
21 M	☽⚻⚷	2:26
	☽☍♅	2:36
	☽⚻♃	5:11
	☽∥⚷	6:34
	☽⚺♂	9:30
	☽□♇	11:05
	☽∥♄	13:41
	☽⚼♆	22:53
22 Tu	☉∠☽	0:47
	☽⚼⚷	2:59
	☽⚻⚳	5:19
	☽#♃	5:46
	☽#♂	7:59
	♀✶♄	8:20
	☽✶☿	9:40
	☽∠♂	10:42
	☽∥♆	14:02
	☉ ♐	16:09
	☽☌♄	17:44
	⚳∠♃	18:24
	☽✶♀	18:31
	☽△♆	23:05
23 W	☉⚺☽	2:42
	☽△⚷	3:08
	☽⚻♅	3:13
	☽☍♃	5:26
	☽⚼⚳	5:35
	☽∥⚳	8:14
	☉□⚷	9:14
	☽∠☿	10:05
	☉△♅	10:15
	☽✶♂	11:32
	☽✶♇	11:36
	♂△♇	14:08
	☽∠♀	20:41
24 Th	☽⚼♅	3:10
	☽△⚳	5:42
	☽∥♇	5:43
	☿ R	7:20
	☽⚺☿	10:08
	☽∠♇	11:37
	☉⚻♃	15:44
	☉∥☽	16:35
	☽⚺♄	18:04
	☿∥♀	22:26
	☽⚺♀	22:50
	☽□♆	23:05
	♅⚺⚷	24:00
25 F	♀✶♆	1:53
	☽△♅	3:10
	☽□⚷	3:10
	☽⚻♃	5:07
	☉☌☽	6:11
	☽⚺♇	11:46
	☽□♂	13:07
	☽∠♄	18:25
26 Sa	♂∥♃	4:42
	☽⚼♃	5:18
	☽□⚳	6:29
	☽☌☿	10:04
	♀ ♑	12:37
	☽✶♄	19:14
27 Su	☽✶♆	0:07
	♀□♅	2:28
	♀✶⚷	3:36
	☽□♅	4:18
	☽✶⚷	4:24
	☽☌♀	4:28
	☽△♃	6:02
	☉⚺☽	11:16
	☽☌♇	13:27
	☉∥☽	15:44
	☽△♂	16:24
	♀△♃	21:24
28 M	☽∠♆	1:35
	☽∠⚷	6:00
	☽✶⚳	9:32
	☽∥♇	9:50
	☽⚺☿	10:57
	☉∠☽	15:08
	☉⚺♇	18:37
	☽⚼♂	19:16
	☽□♄	23:02
29 Tu	☽⚺♆	3:54
	☿□⚳	7:37
	☽✶♅	8:17
	☽⚺⚷	8:30
	☽□♃	9:51
	☽∠☿	12:02
	☽∠⚳	12:23
	☽⚺♀	13:52
	☽∥⚳	14:14
	☽⚺♇	18:15
	☉✶☽	20:10
	☽⚻♂	23:08
30 W	☽∥♆	6:34
	☽∠♅	11:42
	☽✶☿	13:37
	☽⚺⚳	16:15
	☽#♃	17:19
	☿⚼♃	19:35
	☽#♂	20:23
	☽∠♀	20:28
	☽∠♇	22:07

December 2011

LONGITUDE

Day	Sid.Time	☉	☽	☽ 12 hour	Mean☊	True☊	☿	♀	♂	⚳	♃	♄	⚷	♅	♆	♇
	h m s	° ' "	° ' "	° ' "	° '	° '	° '	° '	° '	° '	° '	° '	° '	° '	° '	° '
1 Th	4 38 02	8♐25 43	22♒14 40	28♒33 13	14♐37.2	14♐18.2	16♐13.9	5♑33.0	9♍20.0	18♓10.2	1♉25.5	25♎42.9	0♓50.7	0♈40.7	28♒15.9	6♑14.8
2 F	4 41 59	9 26 32	4♓46 54	10♓56 16	14 34.0	14R 18.5	15R 01.7	6 47.4	9 45.8	18 18.7	1R 20.6	25 48.9	0 51.9	0R 40.3	28 16.7	6 16.8
3 Sa	4 45 55	10 27 21	17 01 53	23 04 18	14 30.8	14 18.5	13 43.4	8 01.7	10 11.4	18 27.5	1 15.9	25 54.8	0 53.2	0 39.9	28 17.5	6 18.7
4 Su	4 49 52	11 28 12	29 04 06	5♈01 52	14 27.6	14 18.3	12 21.5	9 16.1	10 36.6	18 36.5	1 11.4	26 00.7	0 54.6	0 39.5	28 18.3	6 20.7
5 M	4 53 48	12 29 03	10♈58 09	16 53 28	14 24.4	14 18.1	10 58.6	10 30.4	11 01.6	18 45.9	1 07.1	26 06.5	0 56.0	0 39.2	28 19.1	6 22.7
6 Tu	4 57 45	13 29 56	22 48 20	28 43 15	14 21.3	14D 17.9	9 37.7	11 44.7	11 26.4	18 55.6	1 02.9	26 12.2	0 57.4	0 39.0	28 20.0	6 24.7
7 W	5 01 41	14 30 49	4♉38 39	10♉34 56	14 18.1	14 17.9	8 21.4	12 59.0	11 50.8	19 05.5	0 59.0	26 17.9	0 59.0	0 38.8	28 20.9	6 26.7
8 Th	5 05 38	15 31 43	16 32 29	22 31 39	14 14.9	14 17.9	7 12.1	14 13.3	12 14.9	19 15.7	0 55.2	26 23.6	1 00.5	0 38.7	28 21.8	6 28.7
9 F	5 09 35	16 32 38	28 32 43	4♊35 57	14 11.7	14 18.1	6 11.6	15 27.6	12 38.7	19 26.2	0 51.6	26 29.1	1 02.2	0 38.6	28 22.8	6 30.8
10 Sa	5 13 31	17 33 34	10♊41 34	16 49 48	14 08.6	14R 18.2	5 21.3	16 41.8	13 02.3	19 37.0	0 48.3	26 34.7	1 03.9	0D 38.5	28 23.8	6 32.8
11 Su	5 17 28	18 34 31	23 00 47	29 14 40	14 05.4	14 18.2	4 42.0	17 56.0	13 25.5	19 48.0	0 45.1	26 40.1	1 05.6	0 38.5	28 24.8	6 34.9
12 M	5 21 24	19 35 28	5♋31 34	11♋51 35	14 02.2	14 17.9	4 14.1	19 10.2	13 48.4	19 59.3	0 42.1	26 45.5	1 07.4	0 38.6	28 25.9	6 36.9
13 Tu	5 25 21	20 36 27	18 14 48	24 41 17	13 59.0	14 17.2	3 57.3	20 24.4	14 11.0	20 10.8	0 39.3	26 50.8	1 09.3	0 38.7	28 27.0	6 39.0
14 W	5 29 17	21 37 27	1♌11 07	7♌44 21	13 55.9	14 16.4	3D 51.4	21 38.6	14 33.2	20 22.6	0 36.8	26 56.0	1 11.2	0 38.9	28 28.1	6 41.1
15 Th	5 33 14	22 38 27	14 21 01	21 01 11	13 52.7	14 15.3	3 55.6	22 52.7	14 55.1	20 34.6	0 34.4	27 01.2	1 13.1	0 39.1	28 29.3	6 43.2
16 F	5 37 10	23 39 28	27 44 53	4♍32 08	13 49.5	14 14.3	4 09.3	24 06.8	15 16.7	20 46.9	0 32.2	27 06.3	1 15.2	0 39.4	28 30.5	6 45.3
17 Sa	5 41 07	24 40 31	11♍22 58	18 17 20	13 46.3	14 13.5	4 31.6	25 20.9	15 37.9	20 59.4	0 30.2	27 11.3	1 17.2	0 39.7	28 31.7	6 47.4
18 Su	5 45 04	25 41 34	25 15 12	2♎16 29	13 43.2	14D 13.2	5 01.7	26 35.0	15 58.7	21 12.1	0 28.5	27 16.3	1 19.3	0 40.0	28 32.9	6 49.5
19 M	5 49 00	26 42 38	9♎21 02	16 28 39	13 40.0	14 13.5	5 38.8	27 49.1	16 19.1	21 25.1	0 26.9	27 21.2	1 21.5	0 40.5	28 34.2	6 51.6
20 Tu	5 52 57	27 43 44	23 39 03	0♏51 53	13 36.8	14 14.3	6 22.1	29 03.1	16 39.2	21 38.3	0 25.6	27 26.0	1 23.7	0 40.9	28 35.5	6 53.7
21 W	5 56 53	28 44 50	8♏06 43	15 23 02	13 33.6	14 15.4	7 10.9	0♒17.1	16 58.9	21 51.7	0 24.4	27 30.7	1 26.0	0 41.5	28 36.8	6 55.9
22 Th	6 00 50	29 45 57	22 40 16	29 57 44	13 30.4	14 16.5	8 04.6	1 31.1	17 18.2	22 05.4	0 23.5	27 35.3	1 28.3	0 42.0	28 38.2	6 58.0
23 F	6 04 46	0♑47 04	7♐14 45	14♐30 34	13 27.3	14R 17.3	9 02.6	2 45.1	17 37.0	22 19.3	0 22.8	27 39.9	1 30.7	0 42.7	28 39.6	7 00.1
24 Sa	6 08 43	1 48 13	21 44 25	28 55 35	13 24.1	14 17.3	10 04.3	3 59.0	17 55.5	22 33.4	0 22.3	27 44.4	1 33.1	0 43.3	28 41.0	7 02.3
25 Su	6 12 40	2 49 22	6♑03 21	13♑07 05	13 20.9	14 16.2	11 09.4	5 12.9	18 13.5	22 47.7	0D 22.0	27 48.8	1 35.6	0 44.1	28 42.5	7 04.4
26 M	6 16 36	3 50 31	20 06 14	27 00 19	13 17.7	14 14.2	12 17.4	6 26.8	18 31.1	23 02.2	0 21.9	27 53.2	1 38.1	0 44.9	28 43.9	7 06.5
27 Tu	6 20 33	4 51 40	3♒49 01	10♒32 07	13 14.6	14 11.3	13 28.0	7 40.6	18 48.2	23 17.0	0 22.0	27 57.4	1 40.7	0 45.7	28 45.4	7 08.7
28 W	6 24 29	5 52 49	17 09 29	23 41 10	13 11.4	14 08.0	14 40.8	8 54.4	19 04.9	23 31.9	0 22.3	28 01.6	1 43.3	0 46.6	28 47.0	7 10.8
29 Th	6 28 26	6 53 59	0♓07 16	6♓28 04	13 08.2	14 04.6	15 55.6	10 08.2	19 21.1	23 47.1	0 22.9	28 05.6	1 45.9	0 47.5	28 48.5	7 13.0
30 F	6 32 22	7 55 08	12 43 52	18 55 05	13 05.0	14 01.6	17 12.2	11 22.0	19 36.8	24 02.4	0 23.6	28 09.6	1 48.6	0 48.5	28 50.1	7 15.1
31 Sa	6 36 19	8♑56 18	25 02 11	1♈05 44	13♐01.9	13♐59.6	18♐30.4	12♒35.6	19♍52.0	24♓17.9	0♉24.6	28♎13.5	1♓51.3	0♈49.5	28♒51.7	7♑17.3

1st of Month

Julian Day # 2455896.5
Obliquity 23°26'13"
SVP 5♓05'20"
GC 27♐00.3
Eris 21♈31.4R

Day	⚴	⚵	⚶
1	7♒28.5	12♏40.4	22♒27.1
6	8 48.0	14 19.4	24 19.8
11	10 10.2	15 56.8	26 15.9
16	11 35.0	17 32.7	28 14.9
21	13 02.2	19 06.7	0♓16.6
26	14 31.4	20 38.7	2 20.9
31	16 02.6	22 08.4	4 27.4

DECLINATION and LATITUDE

Day	☉ Decl	☽ Decl	☽ Lat	☽12h Decl	☿ Decl	☿ Lat	♀ Decl	♀ Lat	♂ Decl	♂ Lat	⚳ Decl	⚳ Lat	♃ Decl	♃ Lat	♄ Decl	♄ Lat
1 Th	21S42	9S27	4N54	7S12	22S35	0N08	24S45	1S26	10N06	2N11	15S09	11S25	10N40	1S23	7S47	2N19
2 F	21 52	4 54	5 13	2 34	22 07	0 29	24 43	1 28	9 57	2 12	15 02	11 20	10 39	1 23	7 49	2 19
3 Sa	22 01	0 15	5 17	2N03	21 38	0 49	24 41	1 29	9 49	2 14	14 55	11 16	10 37	1 22	7 51	2 19
4 Su	22 09	4N20	5 07	6 33	21 08	1 09	24 37	1 31	9 40	2 15	14 47	11 12	10 36	1 22	7 53	2 20
5 M	22 17	8 42	4 44	10 45	20 38	1 28	24 34	1 33	9 32	2 16	14 40	11 08	10 35	1 22	7 55	2 20
6 Tu	22 25	12 43	4 09	14 33	20 10	1 45	24 29	1 34	9 24	2 18	14 32	11 03	10 34	1 22	7 57	2 20
7 W	22 32	16 15	3 23	17 47	19 43	2 01	24 23	1 36	9 16	2 19	14 24	10 59	10 33	1 21	7 58	2 20
8 Th	22 39	19 09	2 28	20 18	19 18	2 14	24 17	1 37	9 08	2 20	14 16	10 55	10 32	1 21	8 00	2 20
9 F	22 45	21 14	1 26	21 56	18 57	2 26	24 10	1 38	8 60	2 22	14 09	10 51	10 31	1 21	8 02	2 20
10 Sa	22 51	22 23	0 20	22 33	18 39	2 35	24 03	1 40	8 52	2 23	14 01	10 47	10 30	1 21	8 04	2 21
11 Su	22 57	22 27	0S48	22 04	18 26	2 41	23 54	1 41	8 44	2 24	13 52	10 43	10 29	1 21	8 06	2 21
12 M	23 02	21 24	1 55	20 28	18 16	2 46	23 45	1 42	8 37	2 26	13 44	10 39	10 28	1 20	8 07	2 21
13 Tu	23 06	19 16	2 58	17 48	18 11	2 49	23 35	1 43	8 29	2 27	13 36	10 35	10 28	1 20	8 09	2 21
14 W	23 10	16 07	3 52	14 13	18 09	2 49	23 25	1 44	8 22	2 29	13 28	10 31	10 27	1 19	8 11	2 21
15 Th	23 14	12 08	4 35	9 53	18 10	2 49	23 14	1 45	8 15	2 30	13 19	10 27	10 26	1 19	8 13	2 22
16 F	23 17	7 30	5 04	4 60	18 15	2 47	23 02	1 46	8 08	2 32	13 11	10 23	10 26	1 19	8 13	2 22
17 Sa	23 20	2 25	5 17	0S13	18 22	2 44	22 49	1 47	8 01	2 33	13 03	10 19	10 25	1 18	8 16	2 22
18 Su	23 22	2S52	5 11	5 31	18 31	2 39	22 36	1 48	7 54	2 35	12 54	10 15	10 25	1 18	8 17	2 22
19 M	23 24	8 06	4 47	10 36	18 43	2 34	22 22	1 48	7 48	2 36	12 45	10 12	10 25	1 18	8 19	2 22
20 Tu	23 25	12 58	4 05	15 10	18 56	2 28	22 07	1 49	7 41	2 38	12 37	10 08	10 25	1 18	8 20	2 23
21 W	23 26	17 10	3 07	18 53	19 10	2 22	21 52	1 50	7 35	2 39	12 28	10 04	10 24	1 17	8 22	2 23
22 Th	23 26	20 19	1 57	21 25	19 26	2 15	21 36	1 50	7 29	2 41	12 19	10 01	10 24	1 17	8 23	2 23
23 F	23 26	22 09	0 39	22 31	19 42	2 08	21 20	1 50	7 23	2 42	12 10	9 57	10 24	1 17	8 25	2 23
24 Sa	23 25	22 30	0N41	22 06	19 58	2 00	21 03	1 51	7 17	2 44	12 01	9 53	10 25	1 16	8 26	2 23
25 Su	23 24	21 21	1 57	20 15	20 15	1 53	20 45	1 51	7 11	2 45	11 52	9 50	10 25	1 16	8 28	2 24
26 M	23 23	18 53	3 05	17 15	20 32	1 45	20 27	1 51	7 06	2 47	11 43	9 46	10 25	1 16	8 29	2 24
27 Tu	23 21	15 24	4 00	13 23	20 49	1 37	20 08	1 51	7 01	2 48	11 34	9 43	10 25	1 15	8 30	2 24
28 W	23 18	11 14	4 41	8 59	21 06	1 28	19 49	1 51	6 56	2 50	11 25	9 39	10 26	1 15	8 31	2 24
29 Th	23 15	6 39	5 06	4 18	21 22	1 20	19 29	1 51	6 51	2 52	11 16	9 36	10 26	1 15	8 33	2 25
30 F	23 12	1 56	5 15	0N26	21 38	1 12	19 08	1 51	6 46	2 53	11 07	9 32	10 27	1 14	8 34	2 25
31 Sa	23S08	2N45	5N09	5N02	21S53	1N03	18S47	1S50	6N41	2N55	10S57	9S29	10N27	1S14	8S35	2N25

Day	⚷ Decl	⚷ Lat	♅ Decl	♅ Lat	♆ Decl	♆ Lat	♇ Decl	♇ Lat
1	5S52	5N41	0S25	0S45	12S35	0S33	19S19	3N59
6	5 51	5 39	0 25	0 44	12 34	0 33	19 19	3 58
11	5 50	5 37	0 25	0 44	12 32	0 33	19 19	3 57
16	5 48	5 35	0 24	0 44	12 30	0 33	19 19	3 57
21	5 46	5 33	0 24	0 44	12 28	0 33	19 20	3 56
26	5 43	5 32	0 22	0 44	12 26	0 33	19 20	3 56
31	5S40	5N30	0S20	0S43	12S23	0S33	19S19	3N55

Day	⚴ Decl	⚴ Lat	⚵ Decl	⚵ Lat	⚶ Decl	⚶ Lat	Eris Decl	Eris Lat
1	1S31	17N26	8S39	7N20	19S49	6S08	4S04	13S24
6	1 46	16 50	8 59	7 29	19 07	6 04	4 04	13 24
11	1 59	16 16	9 16	7 39	18 23	5 60	4 04	13 23
16	2 10	15 44	9 33	7 49	17 38	5 55	4 03	13 22
21	2 17	15 13	9 47	8 00	16 51	5 51	4 03	13 21
26	2 22	14 43	9 60	8 12	16 02	5 48	4 03	13 21
31	2S24	14N15	10S10	8N24	15S12	5S44	4S02	13S20

Moon Phenomena

Max/0 Decl
dy hr mn
3 1:17 0 N
10 13:38 22N33
17 10:59 0 S
23 17:27 22S33
30 9:50 0 N

Max/0 Lat
dy hr mn
2 18:38 5N18
10 7:04 0 S
17 4:51 5S17
23 11:38 0 N
30 2:27 5N15

Perigee/Apogee
dy hr m kilometers
6 1:10 a 405414
22 2:50 p 364801

PH dy hr mn
☽ 2 9:53 9♓52
○ 10 14:37 18♊11
◐ 10 14:33 T 1.106
☾ 18 0:49 25♍44
● 24 18:08 2♑34

Void of Course Moon

Last Aspect	☽ Ingress
1 11:28 ♆ ☌	♓ 1 14:46
2 18:07 ☿ □	♈ 4 1:52
6 11:14 ♆ ⚹	♉ 6 14:36
8 23:40 ♆ □	♊ 9 2:53
11 10:25 ♆ △	♋ 11 13:27
13 16:06 ♄ □	♌ 13 21:49
16 1:21 ♆ ☍	♍ 16 4:00
18 2:30 ♀ △	♎ 18 8:07
20 9:50 ♀ □	♏ 20 10:34
22 9:50 ♆ □	♐ 22 12:04
24 11:37 ♆ ⚹	♑ 24 13:48
26 13:37 ♄ □	♒ 26 17:15
28 21:32 ♆ ☌	♓ 28 23:46
30 13:39 ♂ ☍	♈ 31 9:49

DAILY ASPECTARIAN

1 Th: ☽△♄ 6:38; ☽∥♄ 8:51; ☽☌♆ 11:28; ♀☌♇ 13:52; ☽⚺♅ 16:04; ☽☌⚷ 16:25; ☽⚹♃ 17:24; ☽∥⚷ 18:59

2 F: ☽⚹♇ 2:55; ☽⚹♀ 4:20; ☉∥☿ 9:49; ☉□☽ 9:53; ☽☍♂ 10:03; ☽⚼♄ 11:51; ☉□♂ 13:09; ☽□☿ 18:07; ☽∠♃ 22:30; ☽∥♅ 23:08

3 Sa: ☽☌⚳ 2:52; ☽#♅ 3:27; ☉∠♄ 11:59; ☽⚻♄ 17:49; ☽⚺♆ 22:28

4 Su: ☽☌♅ 3:12; ☽⚺⚷ 3:42; ☽⚺♃ 4:14; ☽#⚷ 8:14; ☉☌☿ 8:53; ☽□♇ 14:42; ☽#♄ 19:33; ☿∠♄ 21:52; ☽□♀ 22:57; ☿□♂ 23:20

5 M: ☽△☿ 0:01; ☽⚻♂ 0:07; ☉△☽ 3:21; ☿⚺♀ 4:20; ☽∥♂ 4:40; ☽∠♆ 4:46; ♂∠♄ 6:07; ☽∠⚷ 10:05; ☽∥♃ 10:55; ♀△♂ 15:08; ☽⚺⚳ 16:01; ☽#♆ 23:04

6 Tu: ☽⚼☿ 3:20; ☽☍♄ 6:57; ☽⚼♂ 7:38; ☽⚹♆ 11:14; ☽#⚳ 11:27; ☉⚼☽ 12:38; ☽⚺♅ 15:54; ☽⚹⚷ 16:34; ☽☌♃ 16:38; ☽∠⚳ 22:52

7 W: ♃⚹⚷ 0:04; ☽△♇ 3:39; ☽⚻☿ 6:49; ♀∠♆ 7:09; ☽△♂ 15:04; ☽△♀ 18:48; ☉⚻☽ 21:46; ☽∠♅ 22:12; ☿∥♇ 22:53

8 Th: ☽#☿ 1:18; ☽#♇ 1:40; ☽⚹⚳ 5:32; ☉⚼♃ 8:44; ☽⚼♇ 9:56; ☿⚺♇ 16:15; ☽⚻♄ 19:52; ☽□♆ 23:40

9 F: ☽⚹♅ 4:10; ☽⚼♀ 4:14; ☽⚺♃ 4:35; ☽□⚷ 4:57; ♀∠⚷ 11:27; ☽☍☿ 14:08; ☽⚻♇ 15:49

10 Sa: ☽⚼♄ 1:45; ☽□♂ 4:45; ♅D 7:05; ☽∠♃ 9:57; ☽⚻♀ 13:03; ☉☍☽ 14:37; ☽□⚳ 17:41

11 Su: ☽△♄ 7:06; ☽△♆ 10:25; ☽□♅ 14:41; ☽⚹♃ 14:50; ☽△⚷ 15:35; ☽⚻☿ 21:37

12 M: ☿∠♀ 0:57; ☽☍♇ 2:05; ☉□⚳ 11:32; ☽⚼♆ 14:59; ☽⚹♂ 16:09; ♀⚹⚳ 18:46; ☽⚼⚷ 20:04; ☽#♇ 23:26

13 Tu: ☽⚼☿ 1:18; ☽△⚳ 3:40; ☽☍♀ 4:28; ☉⚻☽ 4:47; ♃⚺♅ 5:24; ☽#☿ 9:17; ☽□♄ 16:06; ☽⚻♆ 18:59; ☽∠♂ 20:55; ☉⚺♀ 21:56; ☽□♃ 22:57; ☽△♅ 23:01

14 W: ☽⚻⚷ 0:00; ☿D 1:43; ☽△☿ 4:54; ☽⚼⚳ 7:48; ☽⚻♇ 10:06; ☉⚼☽ 10:48; ☽#⚳ 17:02; ☽#♆ 21:53; ☉∥♀ 23:27

15 Th: ☽⚺♂ 1:03; ☽⚼♅ 2:21; ♂#♄ 6:27; ☽∥♃ 9:07; ☽⚻⚳ 11:23; ☽⚼♇ 13:17; ☉△☽ 16:07; ☽⚻♀ 16:53; ☽#♄ 20:21; ☽∥♂ 20:46; ☽⚹♄ 22:51

16 F: ☽☍♆ 1:21; ☽△♃ 4:56; ☽⚻♅ 5:09; ☽☍⚷ 6:13; ☽#⚷ 8:10; ☽□☿ 11:37; ☽△♇ 15:56; ♂⚼♃ 16:02; ☽⚼♀ 22:01

17 Sa: ☽∠♄ 1:25; ☽⚼♃ 7:09; ☽☌♂ 7:35; ☽#♅ 9:08; ☽∥♅ 12:50; ☽☍⚳ 16:55

18 Su: ☉□☽ 0:49; ☽△♀ 2:30; ☽⚺♄ 3:29; ☽⚻♆ 5:39; ☽⚻♃ 8:55; ☽☍♅ 9:16; ☽⚻⚷ 10:24; ☽∥⚷ 13:15; ♀□♄ 14:19; ☽⚹☿ 17:25; ☽□♇ 19:47; ☽#♂ 22:35

19 M: ☽∥♄ 1:00; ☽⚼♆ 7:07; ☽#♃ 11:04; ☽⚼⚷ 11:50; ☽⚺♂ 12:01; ♀⚺♆ 14:54; ☉⚹♄ 16:26; ☽∠☿ 19:58; ☽⚻⚳ 20:35; ☽∥♆ 21:25; ☽∥⚳ 22:10

20 Tu: ☽☌♄ 6:20; ☉⚹☽ 7:18; ⚶ ♓ 7:46; ☽△♆ 8:14; ☽□♀ 9:50; ☽☍♃ 11:15; ☽⚻♅ 11:42; ☽△⚷ 12:55; ☽∠♂ 13:37; ☿⚺♇ 16:33; ♀ ♒ 18:27; ☉⚹♆ 20:47; ☽⚼⚳ 21:54; ☽⚹♇ 22:03; ☽⚺☿ 22:22; ⚳∥♆ 23:37

21 W: ♀□♃ 2:20; ♀⚹♅ 7:58; ☉∠☽ 10:00; ☽⚼♅ 12:31; ☿∥♇ 14:38; ☽⚹♂ 14:58; ☽∥♇ 15:24; ☽∥☿ 15:29; ☽∠♇ 22:50; ☽△⚳ 23:02; ♀⚺⚷ 23:04

22 Th: ☉ ♑ 5:31; ☽⚺♄ 8:08; ☽□♆ 9:50; ☉⚺☽ 12:33; ☽∥♀ 12:39; ☽⚻♃ 12:42; ☽△♅ 13:13; ☽□⚷ 14:31; ☉△♃ 14:34; ☽⚹♀ 15:54; ♀⚼♂ 20:31; ☉□♅ 22:15; ☽⚺♇ 23:36

23 F: ☽☌☿ 3:11; ☽∠♄ 9:00; ☽⚼♃ 13:26; ☽□♂ 17:31; ☉⚹⚷ 17:49; ☽∠♀ 18:59

24 Sa: ☽□⚳ 1:23; ☽⚹♄ 10:04; ☽⚹♆ 11:37; ☽△♃ 14:25; ☽□♅ 15:02; ☽⚹⚷ 16:27; ☉☌☽ 18:08; ☽⚺♀ 22:27

25 Su: ☽☌♇ 1:44; ☽∥♀ 7:59; ☽⚺☿ 9:24; ☽∥☿ 10:48; ☽∠♆ 13:02; ☽∠⚷ 18:00; ☽∥♇ 20:22; ☿∥♀ 20:33; ☽△♂ 21:12; ♃D 22:09

26 M: ☽⚹⚳ 5:10; ☿∠♄ 13:03; ♀⚺♇ 13:19; ☽□♄ 13:37; ☽∠☿ 13:40; ☽⚺♆ 15:03; ☽□♃ 17:54; ☽⚹♅ 18:36; ☽⚺⚷ 20:12; ☽⚼♂ 23:59

27 Tu: ☉⚺☽ 2:00; ☽⚺♇ 5:56; ☽☌♀ 7:34; ☽∠⚳ 8:07; ♀∠⚳ 14:49; ☽∥♆ 17:29; ☽⚹☿ 19:02; ☽∠♅ 21:29; ☽∥⚳ 22:55

28 W: ☽⚻♂ 3:36; ☽#♃ 4:18; ☉∠☽ 7:24; ☽∠♇ 9:15; ☽⚺⚳ 11:57; ☿⚼♃ 13:29; ☽∥♄ 14:18; ☽△♄ 20:11; ☽☌♆ 21:32; ☽#♂ 23:01

29 Th: ☽⚹♃ 0:29; ☽⚺♅ 1:16; ☽☌⚷ 3:06; ☽∥⚷ 4:57; ☉☌♇ 7:44; ♀∥♇ 11:06; ☽⚹♇ 13:28; ☉⚹☽ 13:57; ☽⚺♀ 21:05

30 F: ☽⚼♄ 0:50; ☽∠♃ 5:09; ☽∥♅ 8:05; ☽□☿ 9:41; ☽#♅ 11:34; ☽☍♂ 13:39; ☽☌⚳ 22:31

31 Sa: ☽∠♀ 5:37; ☽⚻♄ 6:20; ☽⚺♆ 7:35; ☽⚺♃ 10:39; ☽☌♅ 11:29; ☽⚺⚷ 13:34; ☽#⚷ 15:22; ☽∥♂ 20:36

LONGITUDE

January 2012

Day	Sid.Time	☉	☽	☽ 12 hour	Mean ☊	True ☊	☿	♀	♂	⚳	♃	♄	⚷	♅	♆	♇
	h m s	° ' "	° ' "	° ' "	° '	° '	° '	° '	° '	° '	° '	° '	° '	° '	° '	° '
1 Su	6 40 15	9♑57 27	7♈06 16	13♈04 25	12♐58.7	13♐58.7	19♐50.0	13♒49.3	20♍06.8	24♓33.7	0♉25.7	28♎17.4	1♓54.1	0♈50.6	28♒53.3	7♑19.4
2 M	6 44 12	10 58 36	19 00 47	24 56 01	12 55.5	13D 59.0	21 10.8	15 02.9	20 21.0	24 49.6	0 27.1	28 21.1	1 57.0	0 51.8	28 55.0	7 21.6
3 Tu	6 48 09	11 59 45	0♉50 43	6♉45 33	12 52.3	14 00.2	22 32.8	16 16.5	20 34.8	25 05.6	0 28.7	28 24.7	1 59.8	0 52.9	28 56.7	7 23.7
4 W	6 52 05	13 00 54	12 41 04	18 37 54	12 49.1	14 02.0	23 55.8	17 30.0	20 48.0	25 21.9	0 30.5	28 28.3	2 02.7	0 54.2	28 58.4	7 25.8
5 Th	6 56 02	14 02 03	24 36 33	0♊37 33	12 46.0	14 03.9	25 19.7	18 43.5	21 00.7	25 38.4	0 32.5	28 31.7	2 05.7	0 55.5	29 00.1	7 28.0
6 F	6 59 58	15 03 11	6♊41 21	12 48 22	12 42.8	14R 05.1	26 44.4	19 56.9	21 12.8	25 55.0	0 34.7	28 35.1	2 08.7	0 56.8	29 01.8	7 30.1
7 Sa	7 03 55	16 04 19	18 58 55	25 13 19	12 39.6	14 05.3	28 10.0	21 10.3	21 24.4	26 11.8	0 37.1	28 38.4	2 11.7	0 58.2	29 03.6	7 32.2
8 Su	7 07 51	17 05 27	1♋31 44	7♋54 20	12 36.4	14 03.9	29 36.2	22 23.6	21 35.4	26 28.7	0 39.7	28 41.6	2 14.8	0 59.6	29 05.4	7 34.4
9 M	7 11 48	18 06 35	14 21 10	20 52 13	12 33.3	14 00.7	1♑03.2	23 36.9	21 45.9	26 45.8	0 42.5	28 44.7	2 17.9	1 01.1	29 07.2	7 36.5
10 Tu	7 15 44	19 07 42	27 27 22	4♌06 29	12 30.1	13 56.0	2 30.8	24 50.1	21 55.7	27 03.1	0 45.4	28 47.6	2 21.0	1 02.6	29 09.1	7 38.6
11 W	7 19 41	20 08 50	10♌49 19	17 35 38	12 26.9	13 50.1	3 59.0	26 03.2	22 05.0	27 20.6	0 48.6	28 50.5	2 24.2	1 04.1	29 10.9	7 40.7
12 Th	7 23 38	21 09 57	24 25 05	1♍17 22	12 23.7	13 43.6	5 27.8	27 16.3	22 13.7	27 38.1	0 52.0	28 53.4	2 27.4	1 05.8	29 12.8	7 42.8
13 F	7 27 34	22 11 04	8♍12 07	15 08 59	12 20.6	13 37.5	6 57.1	28 29.4	22 21.7	27 55.9	0 55.6	28 56.1	2 30.6	1 07.4	29 14.7	7 44.9
14 Sa	7 31 31	23 12 10	22 07 40	29 07 50	12 17.4	13 32.5	8 27.1	29 42.4	22 29.1	28 13.8	0 59.4	28 58.7	2 33.9	1 09.1	29 16.6	7 47.0
15 Su	7 35 27	24 13 17	6♎09 14	13♎11 35	12 14.2	13 29.1	9 57.5	0♓55.3	22 35.9	28 31.8	1 03.3	29 01.2	2 37.2	1 10.9	29 18.5	7 49.1
16 M	7 39 24	25 14 24	20 14 41	27 18 20	12 11.0	13D 27.6	11 28.5	2 08.1	22 42.0	28 50.0	1 07.5	29 03.6	2 40.6	1 12.7	29 20.5	7 51.1
17 Tu	7 43 20	26 15 30	4♏22 23	11♏26 38	12 07.9	13 27.7	13 00.1	3 20.9	22 47.4	29 08.4	1 11.8	29 05.9	2 44.0	1 14.5	29 22.5	7 53.2
18 W	7 47 17	27 16 36	18 30 57	25 35 08	12 04.7	13 28.9	14 32.2	4 33.7	22 52.1	29 26.8	1 16.3	29 08.1	2 47.4	1 16.4	29 24.4	7 55.3
19 Th	7 51 13	28 17 42	2♐38 59	9♐42 16	12 01.5	13R 30.2	16 04.8	5 46.3	22 56.2	29 45.4	1 21.1	29 10.2	2 50.8	1 18.3	29 26.4	7 57.3
20 F	7 55 10	29 18 48	16 44 42	23 45 58	11 58.3	13 30.5	17 37.9	6 58.9	22 59.5	0♈04.2	1 26.0	29 12.2	2 54.3	1 20.3	29 28.5	7 59.3
21 Sa	7 59 07	0♒19 54	0♑45 43	7♑43 34	11 55.2	13 29.1	19 11.6	8 11.5	23 02.1	0 23.1	1 31.0	29 14.1	2 57.8	1 22.3	29 30.5	8 01.4
22 Su	8 03 03	1 20 59	14 39 05	21 31 52	11 52.0	13 25.4	20 45.9	9 23.9	23 04.0	0 42.1	1 36.3	29 15.9	3 01.3	1 24.3	29 32.6	8 03.4
23 M	8 07 00	2 22 03	28 21 30	5♒07 34	11 48.8	13 19.3	22 20.7	10 36.3	23 05.2	1 01.3	1 41.7	29 17.6	3 04.9	1 26.4	29 34.6	8 05.4
24 Tu	8 10 56	3 23 07	11♒49 44	18 27 43	11 45.6	13 11.2	23 56.1	11 48.7	23R 05.6	1 20.6	1 47.4	29 19.2	3 08.4	1 28.6	29 36.7	8 07.4
25 W	8 14 53	4 24 10	25 01 16	1♓30 16	11 42.4	13 01.7	25 32.1	13 00.9	23 05.2	1 40.0	1 53.2	29 20.7	3 12.1	1 30.7	29 38.8	8 09.3
26 Th	8 18 49	5 25 12	7♓54 40	14 14 29	11 39.3	12 51.9	27 08.6	14 13.1	23 04.1	1 59.5	1 59.1	29 22.1	3 15.7	1 32.9	29 40.9	8 11.3
27 F	8 22 46	6 26 13	20 29 53	26 41 06	11 36.1	12 42.8	28 45.8	15 25.1	23 02.2	2 19.2	2 05.3	29 23.4	3 19.3	1 35.2	29 43.1	8 13.2
28 Sa	8 26 42	7 27 13	2♈48 26	8♈52 16	11 32.9	12 35.2	0♒23.6	16 37.1	22 59.6	2 38.9	2 11.6	29 24.5	3 23.0	1 37.5	29 45.2	8 15.2
29 Su	8 30 39	8 28 12	14 53 05	20 51 24	11 29.7	12 29.8	2 02.1	17 49.0	22 56.2	2 58.8	2 18.0	29 25.6	3 26.7	1 39.8	29 47.3	8 17.1
30 M	8 34 36	9 29 09	26 47 48	2♉42 53	11 26.6	12 26.6	3 41.2	19 00.8	22 51.9	3 18.8	2 24.7	29 26.6	3 30.4	1 42.2	29 49.5	8 19.0
31 Tu	8 38 32	10♒30 06	8♉37 18	14 31 44	11♐23.4	12♐25.6	5♒21.0	20♓12.5	22♍47.0	3♈38.9	2♉31.5	29♎27.4	3♓34.2	1♈44.6	29♒51.7	8♑20.9

1st of Month

Julian Day # 2455927.5
Obliquity 23°26'13"
SVP 5♓05'15"
GC 27♐00.4
Eris 21♈23.5R

Day	⚴	Day	⚵	Day	⚶
1	16♒21.0	1	22♏26.1	1	4♓52.9
6	17 54.1	6	23 52.7	6	7 01.7
11	19 28.6	11	25 16.7	11	9 12.3
16	21 04.3	16	26 37.6	16	11 24.3
21	22 41.1	21	27 55.2	21	13 37.8
26	24 18.9	26	29 09.2	26	15 52.5
31	25 57.4	31	0♐19.3	31	18 08.2

DECLINATION and LATITUDE

Day	☉ Decl	☽ Decl	☽ Lat	☽ 12h Decl	☿ Decl	☿ Lat	♀ Decl	♀ Lat	♂ Decl	♂ Lat	⚳ Decl	⚳ Lat	♃ Decl	♃ Lat	♄ Decl	♄ Lat
1 Su	23S04	7N15	4N50	9N23	22S08	0N55	18S26	1S50	6N37	2N56	10S48	9S25	10N28	1S14	8S36	2N25
2 M	22 59	11 25	4 18	13 20	22 22	0 47	18 04	1 49	6 33	2 58	10 39	9 22	10 29	1 13	8 37	2 25
3 Tu	22 54	15 08	3 36	16 46	22 35	0 39	17 41	1 49	6 29	2 60	10 29	9 19	10 30	1 13	8 38	2 26
4 W	22 48	18 15	2 44	19 32	22 47	0 31	17 18	1 48	6 26	3 01	10 20	9 15	10 31	1 13	8 39	2 26
5 Th	22 42	20 37	1 45	21 28	22 59	0 22	16 55	1 48	6 22	3 03	10 10	9 12	10 31	1 13	8 40	2 26
6 F	22 35	22 05	0 40	22 27	23 09	0 15	16 31	1 47	6 19	3 05	10 01	9 09	10 33	1 12	8 41	2 26
7 Sa	22 28	22 32	0S27	22 20	23 19	0 07	16 07	1 46	6 16	3 07	9 51	9 06	10 34	1 12	8 42	2 27
8 Su	22 21	21 52	1 34	21 06	23 27	0S01	15 42	1 45	6 13	3 08	9 42	9 03	10 35	1 12	8 43	2 27
9 M	22 13	20 03	2 38	18 44	23 34	0 08	15 17	1 44	6 10	3 10	9 32	8 60	10 36	1 11	8 44	2 27
10 Tu	22 04	17 10	3 35	15 21	23 40	0 16	14 51	1 43	6 08	3 12	9 22	8 56	10 38	1 11	8 45	2 27
11 W	21 56	13 20	4 21	11 08	23 46	0 23	14 25	1 41	6 06	3 13	9 12	8 53	10 39	1 11	8 46	2 28
12 Th	21 46	8 46	4 53	6 17	23 49	0 30	13 59	1 40	6 04	3 15	9 03	8 50	10 40	1 10	8 46	2 28
13 F	21 37	3 43	5 09	1 05	23 52	0 37	13 32	1 39	6 03	3 17	8 53	8 47	10 42	1 10	8 47	2 28
14 Sa	21 27	1S35	5 07	4S13	23 53	0 43	13 05	1 37	6 01	3 19	8 43	8 44	10 44	1 10	8 48	2 28
15 Su	21 16	6 50	4 46	9 21	23 54	0 50	12 38	1 35	6 00	3 20	8 33	8 41	10 45	1 09	8 48	2 29
16 M	21 05	11 45	4 09	13 60	23 52	0 56	12 10	1 34	5 60	3 22	8 23	8 39	10 47	1 09	8 49	2 29
17 Tu	20 54	16 03	3 16	17 53	23 50	1 02	11 42	1 32	5 59	3 24	8 13	8 36	10 49	1 09	8 50	2 29
18 W	20 42	19 26	2 11	20 42	23 46	1 08	11 14	1 30	5 59	3 26	8 03	8 33	10 51	1 09	8 50	2 29
19 Th	20 30	21 39	0 58	22 15	23 41	1 14	10 46	1 28	5 59	3 27	7 53	8 30	10 52	1 08	8 51	2 30
20 F	20 18	22 29	0N18	22 22	23 35	1 19	10 17	1 26	5 59	3 29	7 43	8 27	10 54	1 08	8 51	2 30
21 Sa	20 05	21 54	1 32	21 06	23 27	1 24	9 48	1 24	5 60	3 31	7 33	8 24	10 56	1 08	8 51	2 30
22 Su	19 51	19 59	2 40	18 35	23 18	1 29	9 18	1 22	6 00	3 33	7 23	8 22	10 59	1 07	8 52	2 31
23 M	19 38	16 56	3 38	15 04	23 07	1 34	8 49	1 19	6 02	3 35	7 13	8 19	11 01	1 07	8 52	2 31
24 Tu	19 24	13 02	4 22	10 52	22 55	1 38	8 19	1 17	6 03	3 36	7 03	8 16	11 03	1 07	8 52	2 31
25 W	19 09	8 36	4 51	6 16	22 42	1 42	7 49	1 15	6 05	3 38	6 53	8 13	11 05	1 07	8 53	2 31
26 Th	18 55	3 53	5 05	1 30	22 27	1 46	7 19	1 12	6 07	3 40	6 43	8 11	11 08	1 06	8 53	2 32
27 F	18 40	0N53	5 03	3N14	22 11	1 49	6 49	1 09	6 09	3 41	6 33	8 08	11 10	1 06	8 53	2 32
28 Sa	18 24	5 31	4 47	7 43	21 54	1 52	6 18	1 07	6 12	3 43	6 22	8 06	11 12	1 06	8 53	2 32
29 Su	18 09	9 51	4 19	11 51	21 34	1 55	5 48	1 04	6 15	3 45	6 12	8 03	11 15	1 05	8 53	2 32
30 M	17 53	13 44	3 40	15 29	21 14	1 58	5 17	1 01	6 18	3 46	6 02	8 01	11 17	1 05	8 54	2 33
31 Tu	17S36	17N04	2N51	18N29	20S52	1S60	4S46	0S58	6N21	3N48	5S52	7S58	11N20	1S05	8S54	2N33

Day	⚷ Decl	⚷ Lat	♅ Decl	♅ Lat	♆ Decl	♆ Lat	♇ Decl	♇ Lat
1	5S40	5N30	0S20	0S43	12S22	0S33	19S19	3N55
6	5 36	5 28	0 17	0 43	12 19	0 33	19 19	3 55
11	5 32	5 27	0 14	0 43	12 16	0 33	19 19	3 54
16	5 27	5 26	0 10	0 43	12 13	0 33	19 19	3 54
21	5 22	5 25	0 06	0 43	12 09	0 33	19 18	3 54
26	5 17	5 23	0 02	0 42	12 06	0 33	19 18	3 53
31	5S11	5N23	0N03	0S42	12S02	0S33	19S18	3N53

Day	⚴ Decl	⚴ Lat	⚵ Decl	⚵ Lat	⚶ Decl	⚶ Lat	Eris Decl	Eris Lat
1	2S24	14N09	10S12	8N27	15S02	5S43	4S02	13S20
6	2 23	13 42	10 20	8 40	14 11	5 40	4 01	13 19
11	2 20	13 17	10 26	8 54	13 19	5 37	4 00	13 18
16	2 15	12 52	10 30	9 08	12 25	5 33	3 60	13 17
21	2 08	12 28	10 32	9 23	11 31	5 30	3 59	13 16
26	1 59	12 06	10 32	9 39	10 36	5 28	3 57	13 15
31	1S48	11N44	10S30	9N56	9S40	5S25	3S56	13S14

Moon Phenomena

Max/0 Decl
dy hr mn
6 21:53 22N32
13 16:53 0 S
20 1:57 22S29
26 19:31 0 N

Perigee/Apogee
dy hr m kilometers
2 20:27 a 404577
17 21:19 p 369886
30 17:48 a 404321

Max/0 Lat
dy hr mn
6 14:29 0 S
13 9:16 5S10
19 18:28 0 N
26 9:14 5N06

PH dy hr mn
☽ 1 6:16 10♈13
○ 9 7:31 18♋26
☾ 16 9:09 25♎38
● 23 7:40 2♒42
☽ 31 4:11 10♉41

Void of Course Moon

Last Aspect	☽ Ingress
2 20:08 ♆ ⚹	♉ 2 22:17
5 8:47 ♆ □	♊ 5 10:45
7 19:53 ☿ ☍	♋ 7 21:06
10 2:26 ♄ □	♌ 10 4:36
12 8:24 ♆ ☍	♍ 12 9:45
14 1:59 ☉ △	♎ 14 13:29
16 15:30 ♆ △	♏ 16 16:35
18 18:32 ♆ □	♐ 18 19:30
20 21:50 ♆ ⚹	♑ 20 22:41
23 1:39 ♄ □	♒ 23 2:54
25 8:34 ♆ ☌	♓ 25 9:12
27 4:54 ♂ ☍	♈ 27 18:29
30 6:09 ♆ ⚹	♉ 30 6:29

DAILY ASPECTARIAN

1 Su
☽ □ ♇ 0:26
☿ □ ♂ 6:07
☉ □ ☽ 6:16
☽ ⋕ ♄ 7:35
☽ ∠ ♆ 13:41
☽ ⚹ ♀ 15:04
☽ ∥ ♃ 18:23
☽ ⋕ ⚳ 19:32
☽ ∠ ⚷ 19:48

2 M
☽ ⚻ ♂ 2:46
☽ △ ☿ 4:57
☽ ⋕ ♆ 5:47
☽ ⚺ ⚳ 12:03
♀ ∠ ♅ 16:11
☽ ☍ ♄ 19:02
☽ ⚹ ♆ 20:08
⚳ ⋕ ♃ 22:50
☽ ☌ ♃ 23:15

3 Tu
☽ ⚺ ♅ 0:05
☽ ⚹ ⚷ 2:21
☽ ⚼ ♂ 9:48
☽ △ ♇ 13:20
☽ ⚼ ☿ 15:23
☽ ⋕ ♀ 17:05
☽ ∠ ⚳ 19:12

4 W
☉ △ ☽ 0:44
☉ ∥ ☿ 0:51
☽ ∠ ♅ 6:31
☽ ⋕ ♇ 9:55
☽ □ ♀ 10:50
☽ △ ♂ 16:39
☽ ⚼ ♇ 19:42
☉ ∠ ♆ 23:13

5 Th
☽ ⚻ ☿ 1:38
☽ ⚹ ⚳ 2:07
☿ □ ⚳ 6:37
☽ ⚻ ♄ 7:52
☽ □ ♆ 8:47
☉ ⚼ ☽ 9:39
☽ ⚺ ♃ 11:52
☽ ⚹ ♅ 12:37
☽ □ ⚷ 14:59

6 F
☽ ⚻ ♇ 1:36
☽ ⚼ ♄ 13:35
☉ ⋕ ☽ 16:14
☽ ∠ ♃ 17:27
☉ ⚻ ☽ 17:51

7 Sa
☽ △ ♀ 4:41
☽ □ ♂ 4:45
♀ ⚻ ♂ 5:28
☿ ⚹ ♄ 8:14
☉ ⋕ ☽ 8:27
☽ □ ⚳ 14:11
☿ ⚹ ♆ 15:16
☽ △ ♄ 18:36
☽ △ ♆ 19:22
☽ ☍ ☿ 19:53
☽ ⚹ ♃ 22:21
☽ □ ♅ 22:59

8 Su
☽ △ ⚷ 1:22
♀ ∠ ♇ 3:38
☉ ∠ ⚷ 3:51
☿ ♑ 6:35
☽ ☍ ♇ 11:24
☽ ⚼ ♀ 12:12
☿ △ ♃ 18:06
☿ □ ♅ 23:24
☽ ⚼ ♆ 23:34

9 M
☽ ⚼ ⚷ 5:28
☽ ⋕ ♇ 6:56
☉ ☍ ☽ 7:31
☽ ⚹ ♂ 13:49
☽ ⚻ ♀ 18:45
☿ ⚹ ⚷ 21:14
☽ △ ⚳ 23:15

10 Tu
☽ □ ♄ 2:26
☽ ⚻ ♆ 3:05
☽ □ ♃ 6:00
☽ △ ♅ 6:30
☽ ⚻ ⚷ 8:52
☽ ⚻ ☿ 10:16
☽ ⋕ ♀ 16:54
☽ ∠ ♂ 17:15
☽ ⚻ ♇ 18:23

11 W
☽ ⚼ ⚳ 2:46
☽ ⋕ ♆ 5:55
☽ ⚼ ♅ 9:19
☽ ∥ ♃ 14:25
☽ ⚼ ☿ 16:13
☉ ⚻ ☽ 17:50
☽ ⚺ ♂ 20:07
☽ ⚼ ♇ 21:00
☽ ⋕ ⚳ 22:36
☽ ⋕ ♄ 24:00

12 Th
☽ ☍ ♀ 5:29
☽ ⚻ ⚳ 5:45
☽ ⚹ ♄ 7:51
☽ ☍ ♆ 8:24
♀ ⚺ ⚳ 9:27
☽ △ ♃ 11:19
☽ ⚻ ♅ 11:41
☽ ∥ ♂ 13:06
☽ ☍ ⚷ 14:05
☽ ⋕ ⚷ 15:42
☽ △ ☿ 21:34
☉ ⚼ ☽ 22:06
☽ △ ♇ 23:13

13 F
☉ △ ♂ 4:47
♀ △ ♄ 9:06
☽ ∠ ♄ 9:56
☿ ☌ ♇ 13:04
⚳ ∥ ♄ 13:13
☽ ⚼ ♃ 13:24
♀ ☌ ♆ 15:18
☽ ⋕ ♅ 15:58
☽ ∥ ♅ 17:47

14 Sa
☽ ☌ ♂ 0:37
☉ △ ☽ 1:59
♀ ♓ 5:48
☽ ☍ ⚳ 10:41
☽ ⚺ ♄ 11:46
☽ ⚻ ♆ 12:17
☽ ⚻ ♀ 14:13
☽ ⚻ ♃ 15:15
☽ ☍ ♅ 15:29
☽ ∥ ⚷ 17:42
☽ ⚻ ⚷ 17:57
☽ ⋕ ♂ 20:11

15 Su
♀ ⚹ ♃ 2:49
☽ □ ♇ 2:51
♀ ⚺ ♅ 5:16
☽ □ ☿ 7:16
☽ ∥ ⚳ 7:54
☽ ∥ ♄ 9:24
☽ ⚼ ♆ 13:56
☽ ⚼ ♀ 18:13
☽ ⋕ ♃ 19:04
☽ ⚼ ⚷ 19:37
♀ ∥ ♆ 21:50

16 M
☽ ∥ ♀ 2:00
☽ ∥ ♆ 2:24
☽ ⚺ ♂ 4:12
☉ □ ☽ 9:09
♀ ☌ ⚷ 11:13
☽ ⚻ ⚳ 14:55
☽ ☌ ♄ 15:01
☽ △ ♆ 15:30
☽ ☍ ♃ 18:35
☽ ⚻ ♅ 18:40
⚳ ⚻ ♄ 20:20
☽ △ ⚷ 21:12
☽ △ ♀ 22:06

17 Tu
☽ ∠ ♂ 5:50
☽ ⚹ ♇ 5:59
☽ ⚹ ☿ 16:25
☽ ⚼ ⚳ 16:56
☽ ⚼ ♅ 20:11
⚳ ⚺ ♆ 20:32
☿ ∠ ♆ 21:57
☽ ∥ ♇ 22:57

18 W
♃ ⚺ ♅ 0:14
☽ ⚹ ♂ 7:25
☽ ∠ ♇ 7:30
☉ ∥ ☽ 11:03
☉ ⚹ ☽ 16:02
☽ ⚺ ♄ 18:04
☽ □ ♆ 18:32
♀ ⋕ ♃ 18:34
☽ △ ⚳ 18:58
☽ ∠ ☿ 21:00
☽ △ ♅ 21:43
☽ ⚻ ♃ 21:47

19 Th
☽ □ ⚷ 0:20
☽ □ ♀ 5:48
☽ ⚺ ♇ 9:03
⚳ ♈ 18:38
☉ ∠ ☽ 19:32
☽ ∠ ♄ 19:39
☉ □ ♄ 21:20
☽ ⚼ ♃ 23:28

20 F
☽ ⚺ ☿ 1:42
☉ ⚺ ♆ 3:56
☿ ∠ ⚷ 4:22
☽ □ ♂ 10:43
☉ ♒ 16:11
♀ ⚹ ♇ 20:33
☽ ⚹ ♄ 21:22
☽ ⚹ ♆ 21:50
☉ ⚺ ☽ 23:12
☽ □ ⚳ 23:20

21 Sa
☽ □ ♅ 1:03
☽ △ ♃ 1:18
☉ ⚹ ⚳ 1:49
☽ ⚹ ⚷ 3:48
☽ ☌ ♇ 12:33
☽ ⚹ ♀ 14:01
☽ ∠ ♆ 23:49

22 Su
☉ ∥ ☽ 1:17
☉ ⚹ ♅ 1:22
☽ ∠ ⚷ 5:54
☽ ∥ ♇ 6:04
☉ □ ♃ 6:36
☽ ☌ ☿ 12:03
☽ △ ♂ 14:43
☽ ∠ ♀ 18:41
♀ ∥ ♄ 21:21

23 M
☽ □ ♄ 1:39
☽ ⚺ ♆ 2:10
☽ ⚹ ⚳ 4:49
☽ ⚹ ♅ 5:28
☽ □ ♃ 5:57
☉ ☌ ☽ 7:40
☽ ⚺ ⚷ 8:24
☿ △ ♂ 11:17
☽ ⚼ ♂ 17:18
☽ ⚺ ♇ 17:20
☉ ⚺ ⚷ 17:52
☽ ⚺ ♀ 23:58

24 Tu
♂ R 0:55
☽ ∥ ♆ 5:12
☽ ∠ ⚳ 8:21
☽ ∠ ♅ 8:25
☉ ∥ ♇ 9:22
☽ ⋕ ♃ 10:57
⚳ ☌ ♅ 11:08
☽ ⚻ ♂ 20:27
☽ ∠ ♇ 20:34
☽ ∥ ♄ 22:33

25 W
☽ ⚺ ☿ 1:05
☽ ∥ ♀ 4:31
☽ △ ♄ 8:00
☽ ☌ ♆ 8:34
☽ ∥ ⚳ 9:10
☽ ⚺ ♅ 12:03
☽ ⚺ ⚳ 12:37
☽ ⚹ ♃ 12:49
☽ ⋕ ♂ 12:50
☽ ☌ ⚷ 15:14
☽ ∥ ⚷ 16:57
☉ ⚺ ☽ 18:55
⚳ ⚺ ♃ 23:20

26 Th
☽ ⚹ ♇ 0:31
♀ ⚼ ♄ 3:04
☽ ∠ ☿ 9:11
☽ ⚼ ♄ 12:16
☽ ☌ ♀ 13:13
☽ ∠ ♃ 17:23
☽ ∥ ♅ 19:25
☽ ⋕ ♅ 19:37

27 F
☉ ∠ ☽ 1:58
☽ ☍ ♂ 4:54
☿ □ ♄ 9:21
☿ ⚺ ♆ 14:22
☽ ⚻ ♄ 17:19
☽ ⚺ ♆ 17:59
☿ ♒ 18:13
☽ ⚹ ☿ 18:32
♀ ∥ ⚳ 19:15
☽ ☌ ♅ 21:40
☽ ⋕ ⚷ 22:33
☽ ⚺ ♃ 22:47
☽ ☌ ⚳ 23:41

28 Sa
☽ ⚺ ⚷ 1:09
☽ ∥ ♂ 3:42
☽ ⋕ ♀ 3:49
☽ ⋕ ⚳ 4:27
♀ ⋕ ♂ 4:42
☉ ⚹ ☽ 10:02
☽ □ ♇ 10:48
☉ ⚼ ♂ 12:06
♀ ∠ ♃ 12:38
☿ ⚹ ♅ 18:27
☽ ⋕ ♄ 18:32
♂ ⋕ ⚳ 19:22
☉ ⚺ ♇ 19:29
☽ ∠ ♆ 23:48

29 Su
☿ □ ♃ 4:09
☽ ⚺ ♀ 6:32
☽ ∠ ⚷ 7:11
☽ ∥ ♃ 8:23
☽ ⋕ ♆ 13:12
⚵ ♐ 14:14
☽ ⚻ ♂ 16:06
☿ ⚹ ⚳ 17:13
☿ ⚺ ⚷ 21:18

30 M
♀ ∥ ⚷ 3:59
☽ ☍ ♄ 5:22
☽ ⚹ ♆ 6:09
☽ ⚺ ♅ 9:59
☽ ☌ ♃ 11:30
☽ ⚺ ⚳ 13:36
☽ ⚹ ⚷ 13:41
☽ □ ☿ 16:16
☽ ∠ ♀ 16:17
☿ ∠ ♀ 16:48
⚳ ⚺ ⚷ 17:04
☽ ⚼ ♂ 22:18
☽ △ ♇ 23:27

31 Tu
☉ ⋕ ☽ 3:58
☉ □ ☽ 4:11
☽ ∠ ♅ 16:33
☽ ⋕ ♇ 19:43
☽ ∠ ⚳ 20:57

February 2012

LONGITUDE

Day	Sid.Time	☉	☽	☽ 12 hour	Mean ☊	True ☊	☿	♀	♂	⚳	♃	♄	⚷	♅	♆	♇
	h m s	° ' "	° ' "	° ' "	° '	° '	° '	° '	° '	° '	° '	° '	° '	° '	° '	° '
1 W	8 42 29	11♒31 01	20♉26 52	26♉23 22	11♐20.2	12♐25.9	7♒01.5	21♓24.1	22♍41.2	3♈59.1	2♉38.5	29♎28.2	3♓37.9	1♈47.0	29♒53.9	8♑22.8
2 Th	8 46 25	12 31 55	2♊21 56	8♊23 11	11 17.0	12R 26.8	8 42.6	22 35.6	22R 34.6	4 19.4	2 45.6	29 28.8	3 41.7	1 49.5	29 56.0	8 24.6
3 F	8 50 22	13 32 48	14 27 46	20 36 16	11 13.8	12 27.1	10 24.5	23 47.0	22 27.3	4 39.9	2 52.9	29 29.4	3 45.5	1 52.0	29 58.2	8 26.5
4 Sa	8 54 18	14 33 39	26 49 11	3♋06 59	11 10.7	12 26.0	12 07.1	24 58.2	22 19.1	5 00.4	3 00.3	29 29.8	3 49.3	1 54.6	0♓00.5	8 28.3
5 Su	8 58 15	15 34 30	9♋30 01	15 58 32	11 07.5	12 22.7	13 50.4	26 09.4	22 10.2	5 21.0	3 07.9	29 30.1	3 53.2	1 57.1	0 02.7	8 30.1
6 M	9 02 11	16 35 18	22 32 43	29 12 32	11 04.3	12 16.7	15 34.5	27 20.5	22 00.5	5 41.7	3 15.7	29 30.3	3 57.0	1 59.8	0 04.9	8 31.9
7 Tu	9 06 08	17 36 06	5♌57 55	12♌48 35	11 01.1	12 08.2	17 19.3	28 31.4	21 50.0	6 02.6	3 23.6	29R 30.5	4 00.9	2 02.4	0 07.1	8 33.6
8 W	9 10 05	18 36 52	19 44 09	26 44 09	10 58.0	11 57.8	19 04.8	29 42.2	21 38.7	6 23.5	3 31.6	29 30.5	4 04.7	2 05.1	0 09.4	8 35.4
9 Th	9 14 01	19 37 37	3♍47 56	10♍54 51	10 54.8	11 46.5	20 51.1	0♈52.9	21 26.7	6 44.5	3 39.8	29 30.4	4 08.6	2 07.8	0 11.6	8 37.1
10 F	9 17 58	20 38 21	18 04 08	25 15 03	10 51.6	11 35.5	22 38.0	2 03.5	21 13.9	7 05.6	3 48.1	29 30.2	4 12.5	2 10.5	0 13.9	8 38.8
11 Sa	9 21 54	21 39 03	2♎26 51	9♎38 49	10 48.4	11 26.0	24 25.7	3 13.9	21 00.4	7 26.8	3 56.6	29 29.9	4 16.4	2 13.3	0 16.1	8 40.5
12 Su	9 25 51	22 39 45	16 50 22	24 00 54	10 45.2	11 18.9	26 14.0	4 24.2	20 46.1	7 48.0	4 05.2	29 29.4	4 20.3	2 16.1	0 18.4	8 42.2
13 M	9 29 47	23 40 25	1♏10 01	8♏17 20	10 42.1	11 14.6	28 03.0	5 34.4	20 31.1	8 09.4	4 13.9	29 28.9	4 24.3	2 18.9	0 20.6	8 43.8
14 Tu	9 33 44	24 41 04	15 22 37	22 25 43	10 38.9	11D 12.7	29 52.5	6 44.4	20 15.3	8 30.8	4 22.8	29 28.3	4 28.2	2 21.8	0 22.9	8 45.5
15 W	9 37 40	25 41 43	29 26 31	6♐25 01	10 35.7	11R 12.5	1♓42.4	7 54.3	19 58.9	8 52.4	4 31.8	29 27.6	4 32.2	2 24.7	0 25.2	8 47.1
16 Th	9 41 37	26 42 20	13♐21 11	20 15 04	10 32.5	11 12.6	3 32.8	9 04.1	19 41.8	9 14.0	4 41.0	29 26.7	4 36.1	2 27.6	0 27.5	8 48.6
17 F	9 45 34	27 42 56	27 06 41	3♑56 02	10 29.4	11 11.8	5 23.5	10 13.7	19 24.0	9 35.7	4 50.2	29 25.8	4 40.1	2 30.5	0 29.8	8 50.2
18 Sa	9 49 30	28 43 31	10♑43 07	17 27 54	10 26.2	11 08.8	7 14.3	11 23.2	19 05.6	9 57.4	4 59.6	29 24.8	4 44.1	2 33.5	0 32.0	8 51.7
19 Su	9 53 27	29 44 05	24 10 17	0♒50 10	10 23.0	11 03.0	9 05.1	12 32.5	18 46.5	10 19.3	5 09.2	29 23.6	4 48.0	2 36.5	0 34.3	8 53.3
20 M	9 57 23	0♓44 37	7♒27 26	14 01 54	10 19.8	10 54.0	10 55.6	13 41.7	18 26.9	10 41.2	5 18.8	29 22.4	4 52.0	2 39.5	0 36.6	8 54.8
21 Tu	10 01 20	1 45 07	20 33 26	27 01 50	10 16.7	10 42.4	12 45.7	14 50.7	18 06.8	11 03.2	5 28.6	29 21.1	4 56.0	2 42.5	0 38.9	8 56.2
22 W	10 05 16	2 45 37	3♓26 59	9♓48 46	10 13.5	10 29.0	14 35.1	15 59.6	17 46.1	11 25.3	5 38.5	29 19.6	5 00.0	2 45.6	0 41.2	8 57.7
23 Th	10 09 13	3 46 04	16 07 06	22 21 58	10 10.3	10 14.9	16 23.5	17 08.3	17 24.9	11 47.4	5 48.5	29 18.1	5 04.0	2 48.7	0 43.4	8 59.1
24 F	10 13 09	4 46 30	28 33 25	4♈41 33	10 07.1	10 01.4	18 10.4	18 16.8	17 03.3	12 09.6	5 58.7	29 16.4	5 07.9	2 51.8	0 45.7	9 00.5
25 Sa	10 17 06	5 46 54	10♈46 32	16 48 38	10 03.9	9 49.8	19 55.6	19 25.1	16 41.3	12 31.9	6 08.9	29 14.7	5 11.9	2 54.9	0 48.0	9 01.8
26 Su	10 21 03	6 47 16	22 48 10	28 45 32	10 00.8	9 40.7	21 38.5	20 33.3	16 18.9	12 54.3	6 19.3	29 12.8	5 15.9	2 58.0	0 50.3	9 03.2
27 M	10 24 59	7 47 36	4♉41 10	10♉35 35	9 57.6	9 34.5	23 18.7	21 41.2	15 56.2	13 16.7	6 29.8	29 10.9	5 19.9	3 01.2	0 52.5	9 04.5
28 Tu	10 28 56	8 47 55	16 29 22	22 23 06	9 54.4	9 31.0	24 55.6	22 49.0	15 33.2	13 39.1	6 40.3	29 08.8	5 23.9	3 04.4	0 54.8	9 05.8
29 W	10 32 52	9♓48 11	28 17 27	4♊13 05	9♐51.2	9♐29.7	26♓28.7	23♈56.6	15♍10.0	14♈01.7	6♉51.0	29♎06.7	5♓27.8	3♈07.6	0♓57.1	9♑07.1

1st of Month

Julian Day # 2455958.5
Obliquity 23°26'13"
SVP 5♓05'10
GC 27♐00.5
Eris 21♈25.9

Day	⚴
1	26♒17.1
6	27 56.3
11	29 35.8
16	1♓15.6
21	2 55.6
26	4 35.6

Day	⚵
1	0♐32.8
6	1 37.7
11	2 37.9
16	3 33.2
21	4 23.0
26	5 06.9

Day	⚶
1	18♓35.5
6	20 52.3
11	23 09.8
16	25 27.9
21	27 46.6
26	0♈05.7

DECLINATION and LATITUDE

Day	☉ Decl	☽ Decl	☽ Lat	☽ 12h Decl	☿ Decl	☿ Lat	♀ Decl	♀ Lat	♂ Decl	♂ Lat	⚳ Decl	⚳ Lat	♃ Decl	♃ Lat	♄ Decl	♄ Lat
1 W	17S20	19N42	1N55	20N43	20S29	2S02	4S15	0S55	6N25	3N50	5S41	7S55	11N23	1S05	8S54	2N33
2 Th	17 03	21 31	0 54	22 04	20 04	2 03	3 44	0 52	6 29	3 51	5 31	7 53	11 25	1 04	8 54	2 33
3 F	16 45	22 21	0S11	22 23	19 37	2 04	3 13	0 49	6 33	3 53	5 21	7 51	11 28	1 04	8 54	2 34
4 Sa	16 28	22 08	1 16	21 36	19 09	2 05	2 42	0 45	6 38	3 54	5 10	7 48	11 31	1 04	8 53	2 34
5 Su	16 10	20 47	2 19	19 41	18 40	2 05	2 10	0 42	6 43	3 56	5 00	7 46	11 34	1 04	8 53	2 34
6 M	15 52	18 19	3 17	16 41	18 09	2 05	1 39	0 39	6 48	3 57	4 50	7 43	11 36	1 03	8 53	2 35
7 Tu	15 33	14 49	4 05	12 44	17 37	2 04	1 07	0 35	6 54	3 59	4 39	7 41	11 39	1 03	8 53	2 35
8 W	15 15	10 27	4 40	8 01	17 03	2 03	0 36	0 32	6 59	3 60	4 29	7 39	11 42	1 03	8 53	2 35
9 Th	14 56	5 28	4 59	2 48	16 28	2 02	0 05	0 28	7 05	4 01	4 19	7 36	11 45	1 03	8 52	2 35
10 F	14 37	0 06	5 00	2S36	15 51	1 60	0N27	0 24	7 11	4 03	4 08	7 34	11 48	1 02	8 52	2 36
11 Sa	14 17	5S17	4 42	7 54	15 13	1 57	0 58	0 20	7 18	4 04	3 58	7 32	11 51	1 02	8 52	2 36
12 Su	13 58	10 25	4 07	12 46	14 33	1 54	1 30	0 17	7 25	4 05	3 47	7 30	11 55	1 02	8 51	2 36
13 M	13 38	14 56	3 15	16 52	13 53	1 50	2 01	0 13	7 31	4 06	3 37	7 27	11 58	1 02	8 51	2 36
14 Tu	13 18	18 33	2 12	19 57	13 10	1 46	2 33	0 09	7 39	4 07	3 27	7 25	12 01	1 01	8 50	2 37
15 W	12 57	21 02	1 02	21 48	12 27	1 41	3 04	0 05	7 46	4 08	3 16	7 23	12 04	1 01	8 50	2 37
16 Th	12 37	22 13	0N11	22 17	11 42	1 36	3 35	0 01	7 54	4 09	3 06	7 21	12 08	1 01	8 49	2 37
17 F	12 16	22 01	1 23	21 25	10 56	1 30	4 06	0N04	8 01	4 10	2 55	7 19	12 11	1 01	8 49	2 37
18 Sa	11 55	20 31	2 29	19 20	10 08	1 23	4 37	0 08	8 09	4 10	2 45	7 17	12 14	1 00	8 48	2 38
19 Su	11 34	17 53	3 26	16 13	9 20	1 16	5 08	0 12	8 17	4 11	2 35	7 14	12 18	1 00	8 48	2 38
20 M	11 13	14 21	4 11	12 20	8 31	1 08	5 39	0 16	8 26	4 12	2 24	7 12	12 21	0 60	8 47	2 38
21 Tu	10 51	10 10	4 42	7 55	7 41	0 60	6 10	0 21	8 34	4 12	2 14	7 10	12 24	0 60	8 46	2 38
22 W	10 29	5 36	4 58	3 15	6 50	0 50	6 41	0 25	8 42	4 13	2 03	7 08	12 28	0 59	8 46	2 39
23 Th	10 08	0 53	4 59	1N28	5 59	0 40	7 11	0 29	8 51	4 13	1 53	7 06	12 32	0 59	8 45	2 39
24 F	9 46	3N47	4 45	6 02	5 08	0 30	7 41	0 34	8 60	4 13	1 42	7 04	12 35	0 59	8 44	2 39
25 Sa	9 23	8 13	4 18	10 18	4 17	0 19	8 11	0 38	9 08	4 13	1 32	7 02	12 39	0 59	8 43	2 39
26 Su	9 01	12 16	3 40	14 07	3 25	0 07	8 41	0 43	9 17	4 13	1 22	7 00	12 42	0 59	8 42	2 40
27 M	8 39	15 48	2 53	17 19	2 34	0N05	9 11	0 48	9 26	4 13	1 11	6 58	12 46	0 58	8 41	2 40
28 Tu	8 16	18 40	1 59	19 48	1 44	0 18	9 41	0 52	9 35	4 13	1 01	6 56	12 50	0 58	8 40	2 40
29 W	7S54	20N44	0N59	21N27	0S55	0N31	10N10	0N57	9N43	4N13	0S50	6S54	12N53	0S58	8S39	2N40

Day	⚷ Decl	⚷ Lat	♅ Decl	♅ Lat	♆ Decl	♆ Lat	♇ Decl	♇ Lat
1	5S10	5N22	0N04	0S42	12S01	0S33	19S18	3N5
6	5 04	5 22	0 09	0 42	11 57	0 33	19 17	3 5
11	4 57	5 21	0 14	0 42	11 53	0 33	19 17	3 5
16	4 51	5 21	0 20	0 42	11 49	0 33	19 16	3 5
21	4 44	5 20	0 26	0 42	11 45	0 33	19 16	3 5
26	4S37	5N20	0N33	0S42	11S41	0S33	19S15	3N5

Day	⚴ Decl	⚴ Lat	⚵ Decl	⚵ Lat	⚶ Decl	⚶ Lat	Eris Decl	Eris Lat
1	1S46	11N39	10S29	9N59	9S29	5S25	3S56	13S1
6	1 33	11 18	10 24	10 17	8 33	5 22	3 55	13 1
11	1 19	10 58	10 17	10 36	7 36	5 20	3 53	13 1
16	1 04	10 39	10 07	10 56	6 40	5 18	3 52	13 1
21	0 47	10 20	9 56	11 16	5 43	5 16	3 51	13 1
26	0S29	10N01	9S42	11N37	4S46	5S14	3S49	13S1

Moon Phenomena

Max/0 Decl
dy hr mn
3 7:09 22N24
10 0:28 0 S
16 8:29 22S18
23 4:31 0 N

Max/0 Lat
dy hr mn
2 20:02 0 S
9 13:17 5S02
15 20:17 0 N
22 13:02 5N00
29 22:37 0 S

Perigee/Apogee
dy hr m kilometers
11 18:41 p 367922
27 14:04 a 404861

PH dy hr mn
○ 7 21:55 18♌32
☾ 14 17:05 25♏24
● 21 22:36 2♓42

Void of Course Moon

Last Aspect			☽ Ingress		
1 19:07	♆	□	♊	1	19:1
4 5:07	♄	△	♋	4	6:0
6 12:32	♄	□	♌	6	13:2
8 16:43	♄	⚹	♍	8	17:3
10 5:13	♂	☌	♎	10	19:5
12 21:10	♄	☌	♏	12	22:0
14 17:05	☉	□	♐	15	0:5
17 4:04	♄	⚹	♑	17	5:0
19 9:23	♄	□	♒	19	10:2
21 16:18	♄	△	♓	21	17:3
23 2:25	♂	☍	♈	24	2:4
26 12:53	♄	☍	♉	26	14:3
28 19:47	☿	⚹	♊	29	3:2

DAILY ASPECTARIAN

1 W
☽⚹♀ 2:09
☽△♂ 4:29
☽⚼♇ 5:57
☽⋕☿ 7:19
☿⚼♂ 8:53
☽⚻♄ 18:13
☽□♆ 19:07
☿⚺♇ 19:40
☽⚹♅ 22:55
♀☍♂ 23:42

2 Th
☽⚺♃ 0:48
☽□⚷ 2:40
☽⚹⚳ 4:02
☽⚻♇ 12:05
☽△☿ 14:42
☉△☽ 22:02

3 F
☽⚼♄ 0:03
☽∠♃ 6:46
☽□♂ 15:25
☿∥♇ 17:11
♆ ♓ 19:04
☽□♀ 20:04

4 Sa
☽⚼☿ 0:40
☽△♄ 5:07
☉⚼☽ 5:42
☽△♆ 6:07
☽□♅ 9:45
⚳∥⚷ 11:36
☽⚹♃ 11:54
☽△⚷ 13:24
☽□⚳ 16:00
☽☍♇ 22:08

5 Su
☽⚻☿ 9:18
☽⚼♆ 10:19
☉⚻☽ 12:13
☽⋕♇ 15:44
☽⚼⚷ 17:25
☽⚹♂ 23:02

6 M
☽⋕☿ 1:34
☽△♀ 9:29
☉∠♅ 10:05
☽□♄ 12:32
☽⚻♆ 13:36
☽△♅ 17:01
☉⋕☽ 19:02
☽□♃ 19:24
☿∠♅ 20:03
☽⚻⚷ 20:32

7 Tu
☽△⚳ 0:08
☽∠♂ 1:31
☽⚻♇ 4:35
☉☌☿ 9:04
♄ R 14:04
☽⚼♀ 14:29
☽⋕♆ 16:20
☽∥♃ 17:36
☽⚼♅ 19:24
♀⚻♄ 20:01
☉☍☽ 21:55
☽☍☿ 22:42

8 W
☽⚼⚳ 2:55
☽⚺♂ 3:14
♀ ♈ 6:02
☽⚼♇ 6:38
☽⋕♄ 7:52
♀⚺♆ 9:31
☽∥♂ 16:35
☽⚹♄ 16:43
☽☍♆ 17:52
♀⋕♅ 18:20
☽⚻♀ 18:36
☽⚻♅ 21:10
☽△♃ 23:46

9 Th
☽☍⚷ 0:35
☽⋕⚷ 2:08
☽⚻⚳ 5:06
☽⋕⚳ 5:25
☿⚻♂ 7:10
☽△♇ 8:09
♀∥♅ 13:16
☿∠⚳ 14:57
☽∠♄ 18:02
☽∥♀ 22:37
☽∥♅ 23:29

10 F
☽⚼♃ 1:14
☽⋕♅ 1:27
♀☌♅ 2:30
☽⋕♀ 2:43
☉⚻☽ 4:37
☽☌♂ 5:13
☽⚻☿ 8:43
☉⚻♂ 11:32
☿∠♇ 13:47
☽∥⚳ 18:14
☽⚺♄ 19:05
☽⚻♆ 20:22
☽∥⚷ 22:29
☽☍♅ 23:37

11 Sa
☽☍♀ 1:25
☽⚻♃ 2:31
☽⚻⚷ 3:03
☉⚼☽ 7:32
☽☍⚳ 8:33
☽⋕♂ 9:22
☽□♇ 10:24
♃⋕♆ 11:17
☽⚼☿ 13:18
☽∥♄ 16:29
♀⚺♃ 16:35
☽⚼♆ 21:26
♀⚺⚷ 22:36

12 Su
☽⚼⚷ 4:12
☉∠⚳ 5:03
⚴ ♓ 5:07
☽⚺♂ 6:27
☽∥♆ 7:21
☽⋕♃ 7:38
☉△☽ 10:29
☉∥☽ 17:10
☽△☿ 18:00
☽∥☿ 18:50
☽☌♄ 21:10
☽△♆ 22:37

13 M
☉∠♇ 1:23
☽⚻♅ 1:56
☽☍♃ 5:13
☽△⚷ 5:28
☽∠♂ 7:12
☽⚻♀ 8:05
☽⚻⚳ 12:05
☽⚹♇ 12:46
☉∥☿ 16:11
☿△♄ 18:45

14 Tu
☿ ♓ 1:39
☽⚼♅ 3:23
☽∥♇ 5:52
☿☌♆ 6:48
☽⚹♂ 8:08
☽⚼♀ 11:48
☽⚼⚳ 14:13
☽∠♇ 14:18
☉□☽ 17:05
⚳□♇ 17:37

15 W
☽⚺♄ 0:02
♃⚹⚷ 1:38
☽□♆ 1:41
☽□☿ 4:29
☽△♅ 5:07
♀⋕⚳ 7:10
☽□⚷ 8:48
☽⚻♃ 8:51
☿⚺♅ 9:26
☿⋕♃ 11:14
☽△♀ 15:54
☽⚺♇ 16:07
☽△⚳ 16:40
♀□♇ 18:34
☿∥♆ 19:54

16 Th
♂⚼♃ 0:43
☽∠♄ 1:54
♀☌⚳ 4:56
☽□♂ 10:48
☽⚼♃ 11:08
☿☌⚷ 14:15
☿⚹♃ 16:08

17 F
☉⚹☽ 1:09
☽⚹♄ 4:04
☉⋕♃ 5:02
☽⚹♆ 5:58
☽□♅ 9:31
☽⚹⚷ 13:22
☽△♃ 13:45
☽⚹☿ 16:52
☽☌♇ 20:42
☽□⚳ 22:37

18 Sa
☽□♀ 1:18
☉∠☽ 5:46
♀⋕⚷ 7:52
☉∥♆ 8:33
☽∠♆ 8:35
☽∥♇ 12:35
☽△♂ 14:34
☉△♄ 16:03
☽∠⚷ 16:08
☿⚹♇ 21:24
☽∠☿ 23:49

19 Su
☉ ♓ 6:19
☽□♄ 9:23
☉⚺☽ 10:50
☽⚺♆ 11:33
☽⚹♅ 15:16
☿∥♄ 16:11
☽⚼♂ 16:54
☽⚺⚷ 19:16
☽□♃ 20:03
☿⚺⚳ 20:05
☉☌♆ 20:42

20 M
☿⋕♂ 2:17
☽⚺♇ 2:39
☽⚹⚳ 6:03
☽⚺☿ 7:21
☽⋕♃ 11:42
☽⚹♀ 12:29
☽∥♆ 15:13
☽∠♅ 18:44
☽⚻♂ 19:36
☉∥☽ 19:58

21 Tu
☽∠♇ 6:16
☽∥♄ 7:33
☽⋕♂ 8:22
☽∠⚳ 10:29
☽∥☿ 16:13
☽△♄ 16:18
♀∠♆ 17:21
☽☌♆ 18:48
☽∠♀ 18:57
☽⋕♀ 19:03
☿⚼♄ 20:38
☉☌☽ 22:36
☽⚺♅ 22:42
☉⚺♅ 23:59

22 W
☽☌⚷ 2:56
☿⋕♀ 2:56
☽⚹♃ 4:11
☽∥⚷ 4:38
♂⋕♄ 8:01
☽⚹♇ 10:24
☽⚺⚳ 15:30
☽∥⚳ 18:46
☽⚼♄ 20:32

23 Th
☽☌☿ 0:37
☽⋕♅ 2:04
☽⚺♀ 2:09
☽☍♂ 2:25
♀⚻♂ 4:26
☽∥♅ 7:00
☽∠♃ 9:07
☿☍♂ 11:26
☽⋕⚳ 13:38

24 F
☽⚻♄ 1:24
☿⚺♀ 4:02
☽⚺♆ 4:19
☽⋕⚷ 4:37
☽⋕☿ 6:00
☽☌♅ 8:27
☉☌⚷ 9:07
☽⚺⚷ 12:56
☉⚺☽ 13:15
☿∥⚷ 13:33
☽⚺♃ 14:44
☽□♇ 20:33
☽∥♀ 23:49

25 Sa
☽⋕♄ 2:48
☽☌⚳ 3:36
☽∥♂ 5:24
☉⋕☽ 6:07
☽∠♆ 10:01
☉⚹♃ 10:34
☽⚻♂ 11:24
☉⋕♂ 11:40
♀∠⚷ 17:30
☽∠⚷ 18:53
☿∠♃ 18:57
☽☌♀ 19:01
⚶ ♈ 19:06
☽⋕♆ 20:23
☽⚺☿ 21:17
☉∠☽ 21:47

26 Su
♀⋕♄ 0:37
☽∥♃ 2:47
☉⋕♀ 9:03
☽☍♄ 12:53
☽⚹♆ 16:15
☽⚼♂ 16:38
☽⚺♅ 20:36
☉∥♄ 21:07

27 M
☽⚹⚷ 1:19
☽☌♃ 3:44
☉⚹☽ 6:54
☽∠☿ 8:33
☽△♇ 8:56
♀∥♂ 16:54
☽⚺⚳ 18:02
☽△♂ 22:09

28 Tu
☽∠♅ 3:14
☽⋕♇ 5:58
☉⚹♇ 7:16
☽⚺♀ 14:14
☽⚼♇ 15:31
☽⚹☿ 19:47

29 W
☽∠⚳ 1:33
☽⚻♄ 1:40
☿∥⚳ 3:00
☽□♆ 5:25
☿⋕♅ 9:04
☽⚹♅ 9:50
☽□⚷ 14:36
☽⚺♃ 17:34
☽⚻♇ 21:55
☽∠♀ 23:45

LONGITUDE

March 2012

Day	Sid.Time	☉	☽	☽ 12 hour	Mean ☊	True ☊	☿	♀	♂	⚳	♃	♄	⚷	♅	♆	♇
	h m s	° ' "	° ' "	° ' "	° '	° '	° '	° '	° '	° '	° '	° '	° '	° '	° '	° '
1 Th	10 36 49	10♓48 26	10♊10 42	16♊11 01	9♐48.1	9♐29.5	27♓57.5	25♈03.9	14♍46.6	14♈24.3	7♉01.8	29♎04.5	5♓31.8	3♈10.8	0♓59.3	9♑08.3
2 F	10 40 45	11 48 39	22 14 42	28 22 28	9 44.9	9R 29.3	29 21.2	26 11.1	14R 23.0	14 46.9	7 12.7	29R 02.2	5 35.8	3 14.1	1 01.6	9 09.5
3 Sa	10 44 42	12 48 49	4♋34 58	10♋52 47	9 41.7	9 28.0	0♈39.3	27 18.0	13 59.4	15 09.6	7 23.7	28 59.8	5 39.7	3 17.3	1 03.8	9 10.7
4 Su	10 48 38	13 48 57	17 16 27	23 46 24	9 38.5	9 24.5	1 51.3	28 24.7	13 35.6	15 32.4	7 34.8	28 57.3	5 43.7	3 20.6	1 06.1	9 11.9
5 M	10 52 35	14 49 04	0♌22 59	7♌06 22	9 35.3	9 18.5	2 56.5	29 31.2	13 11.9	15 55.2	7 46.0	28 54.7	5 47.6	3 23.9	1 08.3	9 13.0
6 Tu	10 56 32	15 49 08	13 56 34	20 53 27	9 32.2	9 09.8	3 54.5	0♉37.4	12 48.2	16 18.1	7 57.3	28 52.1	5 51.6	3 27.2	1 10.5	9 14.1
7 W	11 00 28	16 49 10	27 56 42	5♍05 47	9 29.0	8 59.0	4 44.7	1 43.4	12 24.6	16 41.0	8 08.7	28 49.3	5 55.5	3 30.5	1 12.7	9 15.2
8 Th	11 04 25	17 49 10	12♍20 01	19 38 34	9 25.8	8 47.1	5 26.9	2 49.2	12 01.0	17 04.0	8 20.1	28 46.5	5 59.4	3 33.8	1 14.9	9 16.2
9 F	11 08 21	18 49 08	27 00 26	4♎24 34	9 22.6	8 35.5	6 00.5	3 54.6	11 37.7	17 27.0	8 31.7	28 43.5	6 03.3	3 37.1	1 17.1	9 17.2
10 Sa	11 12 18	19 49 05	11♎49 54	19 15 20	9 19.4	8 25.3	6 25.5	4 59.9	11 14.5	17 50.0	8 43.4	28 40.5	6 07.2	3 40.5	1 19.3	9 18.2
11 Su	11 16 14	20 48 59	26 39 51	4♏02 33	9 16.3	8 17.6	6 41.6	6 04.8	10 51.6	18 13.1	8 55.1	28 37.5	6 11.1	3 43.8	1 21.5	9 19.2
12 M	11 20 11	21 48 52	11♏22 37	18 39 26	9 13.1	8 12.7	6R 48.9	7 09.5	10 28.9	18 36.3	9 06.9	28 34.3	6 15.0	3 47.2	1 23.7	9 20.1
13 Tu	11 24 07	22 48 44	25 52 30	3♐01 28	9 09.9	8D 10.4	6 47.4	8 13.9	10 06.6	18 59.5	9 18.8	28 31.1	6 18.8	3 50.6	1 25.8	9 21.0
14 W	11 28 04	23 48 33	10♐06 09	17 06 27	9 06.7	8 10.0	6 37.4	9 18.0	9 44.7	19 22.8	9 30.8	28 27.8	6 22.7	3 54.0	1 28.0	9 21.9
15 Th	11 32 00	24 48 21	24 02 24	0♑54 06	9 03.6	8R 10.2	6 19.2	10 21.8	9 23.1	19 46.0	9 42.9	28 24.4	6 26.5	3 57.4	1 30.1	9 22.7
16 F	11 35 57	25 48 08	7♑41 42	14 22 22	9 00.4	8 09.7	5 53.3	11 25.3	9 02.0	20 09.4	9 55.0	28 20.9	6 30.3	4 00.8	1 32.3	9 23.5
17 Sa	11 39 54	26 47 53	21 05 19	27 41 45	8 57.2	8 07.4	5 20.5	12 28.5	8 41.3	20 32.8	10 07.2	28 17.4	6 34.1	4 04.2	1 34.4	9 24.3
18 Su	11 43 50	27 47 36	4♒14 50	10♒44 45	8 54.0	8 02.4	4 41.6	13 31.4	8 21.2	20 56.2	10 19.5	28 13.8	6 37.9	4 07.6	1 36.5	9 25.1
19 M	11 47 47	28 47 17	17 11 37	23 35 34	8 50.9	7 54.7	3 57.4	14 33.9	8 01.5	21 19.6	10 31.9	28 10.2	6 41.6	4 11.0	1 38.6	9 25.8
20 Tu	11 51 43	29 46 56	29 56 42	6♓15 04	8 47.7	7 44.6	3 09.0	15 36.2	7 42.5	21 43.1	10 44.4	28 06.5	6 45.4	4 14.4	1 40.6	9 26.5
21 W	11 55 40	0♈46 33	12♓30 43	18 43 43	8 44.5	7 32.7	2 17.6	16 38.0	7 24.0	22 06.7	10 56.9	28 02.7	6 49.1	4 17.8	1 42.7	9 27.1
22 Th	11 59 36	1 46 09	24 54 07	1♈01 58	8 41.3	7 20.2	1 24.2	17 39.5	7 06.2	22 30.2	11 09.5	27 58.8	6 52.8	4 21.3	1 44.7	9 27.8
23 F	12 03 33	2 45 42	7♈07 22	13 10 24	8 38.1	7 08.2	0 30.1	18 40.6	6 49.0	22 53.8	11 22.1	27 54.9	6 56.5	4 24.7	1 46.8	9 28.4
24 Sa	12 07 29	3 45 14	19 11 14	25 10 03	8 35.0	6 57.7	29♓36.4	19 41.4	6 32.6	23 17.5	11 34.8	27 51.0	7 00.1	4 28.1	1 48.8	9 28.9
25 Su	12 11 26	4 44 43	1♉07 05	7♉02 37	8 31.8	6 49.5	28 44.1	20 41.7	6 16.8	23 41.1	11 47.6	27 46.9	7 03.7	4 31.5	1 50.8	9 29.5
26 M	12 15 23	5 44 10	12 56 59	18 50 34	8 28.6	6 44.0	27 54.2	21 41.7	6 01.7	24 04.8	12 00.5	27 42.9	7 07.4	4 35.0	1 52.8	9 30.0
27 Tu	12 19 19	6 43 35	24 43 48	0♊37 10	8 25.4	6 41.0	27 07.5	22 41.2	5 47.3	24 28.6	12 13.4	27 38.8	7 10.9	4 38.4	1 54.7	9 30.4
28 W	12 23 16	7 42 58	6♊31 14	12 26 32	8 22.2	6D 40.2	26 24.9	23 40.2	5 33.7	24 52.3	12 26.3	27 34.6	7 14.5	4 41.8	1 56.7	9 30.9
29 Th	12 27 12	8 42 19	18 23 42	24 23 21	8 19.1	6 40.7	25 46.8	24 38.9	5 20.8	25 16.1	12 39.4	27 30.4	7 18.0	4 45.2	1 58.6	9 31.3
30 F	12 31 09	9 41 37	0♋26 10	6♋32 48	8 15.9	6R 41.6	25 13.7	25 37.0	5 08.8	25 39.9	12 52.4	27 26.2	7 21.5	4 48.7	2 00.5	9 31.7
31 Sa	12 35 05	10♈40 53	12 43 55	19 00 10	8♐12.7	6♐41.9	24♓46.0	26♉34.7	4♍57.4	26♈03.8	13♉05.6	27♎21.9	7♓25.0	4♈52.1	2♓02.4	9♑32.0

1st of Month

Julian Day # 2455987.5
Obliquity 23°26'13"
SVP 5♓05'06"
GC 27♐00.6
Eris 21♈37.0

Day	⚴		Day	⚵		Day	⚶
1	5♓55.5		1	5♐37.5		1	1♈57.2
6	7 35.1		6	6 09.9		6	4 16.7
11	9 14.4		11	6 35.4		11	6 36.2
16	10 53.2		16	6 53.5		16	8 55.9
21	12 31.3		21	7 04.0		21	11 15.5
26	14 08.8		26	7 06.4R		26	13 34.9
31	15 45.3		31	7 00.6R		31	15 54.2

DECLINATION and LATITUDE

Day	☉ Decl	☽ Decl	☽ Lat	☽12h Decl	☿ Decl	☿ Lat	♀ Decl	♀ Lat	♂ Decl	♂ Lat	⚳ Decl	⚳ Lat	♃ Decl	♃ Lat	♄ Decl	♄ Lat
1 Th	7S31	21N55	0S04	22N08	0S07	0N45	10N39	1N02	9N52	4N12	0S40	6S53	12N57	0S58	8S38	2N41
2 F	7 08	22 06	1 07	21 47	0N39	0 59	11 08	1 06	10 01	4 12	0 30	6 51	13 01	0 58	8 37	2 41
3 Sa	6 45	21 13	2 09	20 22	1 23	1 13	11 37	1 11	10 10	4 11	0 19	6 49	13 04	0 57	8 36	2 41
4 Su	6 22	19 15	3 06	17 52	2 04	1 27	12 05	1 16	10 18	4 10	0 09	6 47	13 08	0 57	8 35	2 41
5 M	5 59	16 14	3 55	14 22	2 43	1 41	12 33	1 21	10 27	4 10	0N02	6 45	13 12	0 57	8 34	2 41
6 Tu	5 36	12 17	4 33	10 00	3 19	1 55	13 01	1 25	10 35	4 09	0 12	6 43	13 16	0 57	8 33	2 42
7 W	5 12	7 34	4 55	4 59	3 51	2 09	13 29	1 30	10 43	4 08	0 22	6 42	13 20	0 57	8 32	2 42
8 Th	4 49	2 18	5 00	0S26	4 20	2 22	13 56	1 35	10 51	4 07	0 33	6 40	13 24	0 56	8 31	2 42
9 F	4 25	3S11	4 46	5 54	4 45	2 35	14 23	1 40	10 59	4 06	0 43	6 38	13 27	0 56	8 29	2 42
10 Sa	4 02	8 32	4 12	11 03	5 06	2 46	14 50	1 45	11 07	4 04	0 53	6 36	13 31	0 56	8 28	2 42
11 Su	3 38	13 24	3 21	15 32	5 22	2 57	15 16	1 50	11 14	4 03	1 04	6 35	13 35	0 56	8 27	2 43
12 M	3 15	17 25	2 17	18 60	5 34	3 07	15 42	1 55	11 21	4 01	1 14	6 33	13 39	0 56	8 26	2 43
13 Tu	2 51	20 16	1 05	21 12	5 41	3 15	16 08	1 59	11 29	3 60	1 24	6 31	13 43	0 55	8 24	2 43
14 W	2 27	21 48	0N10	22 02	5 44	3 22	16 33	2 04	11 35	3 58	1 34	6 29	13 47	0 55	8 23	2 43
15 Th	2 04	21 55	1 23	21 28	5 41	3 28	16 58	2 09	11 42	3 57	1 45	6 28	13 51	0 55	8 22	2 43
16 F	1 40	20 43	2 30	19 41	5 35	3 32	17 23	2 14	11 48	3 55	1 55	6 26	13 55	0 55	8 20	2 44
17 Sa	1 16	18 22	3 27	16 51	5 23	3 34	17 47	2 19	11 55	3 53	2 05	6 24	13 59	0 55	8 19	2 44
18 Su	0 53	15 07	4 12	13 13	5 08	3 34	18 11	2 24	12 00	3 51	2 15	6 23	14 03	0 55	8 18	2 44
19 M	0 29	11 11	4 43	9 02	4 49	3 32	18 34	2 28	12 06	3 49	2 25	6 21	14 07	0 54	8 16	2 44
20 Tu	0 05	6 49	4 60	4 32	4 26	3 28	18 57	2 33	12 11	3 47	2 35	6 19	14 11	0 54	8 15	2 44
21 W	0N19	2 13	5 01	0N05	4 00	3 22	19 20	2 38	12 16	3 45	2 46	6 18	14 15	0 54	8 13	2 44
22 Th	0 42	2N23	4 48	4 39	3 32	3 15	19 42	2 43	12 21	3 43	2 56	6 16	14 19	0 54	8 12	2 44
23 F	1 06	6 51	4 23	8 58	3 03	3 06	20 04	2 47	12 25	3 41	3 06	6 15	14 23	0 54	8 10	2 45
24 Sa	1 30	10 59	3 45	12 53	2 31	2 55	20 25	2 52	12 29	3 38	3 16	6 13	14 27	0 54	8 09	2 45
25 Su	1 53	14 38	2 58	16 15	1 60	2 43	20 46	2 57	12 33	3 36	3 26	6 12	14 31	0 53	8 07	2 45
26 M	2 17	17 41	2 03	18 56	1 28	2 30	21 06	3 01	12 36	3 34	3 36	6 10	14 36	0 53	8 05	2 45
27 Tu	2 40	19 59	1 04	20 48	0 56	2 16	21 26	3 06	12 39	3 31	3 46	6 09	14 40	0 53	8 04	2 45
28 W	3 04	21 25	0 01	21 46	0 26	2 01	21 46	3 10	12 42	3 29	3 56	6 07	14 44	0 53	8 02	2 45
29 Th	3 27	21 53	1S03	21 45	0S03	1 46	22 05	3 15	12 45	3 26	4 06	6 06	14 48	0 53	8 01	2 45
30 F	3 50	21 22	2 04	20 43	0 31	1 31	22 23	3 19	12 47	3 24	4 16	6 04	14 52	0 53	7 59	2 45
31 Sa	4N14	19N49	3S01	18N40	0S56	1N15	22N41	3N24	12N49	3N21	4N26	6S03	14N56	0S53	7S58	2N45

Day	⚷ Decl	⚷ Lat	♅ Decl	♅ Lat	♆ Decl	♆ Lat	♇ Decl	♇ Lat
1	4S31	5N20	0N38	0S42	11S38	0S33	19S15	3N53
6	4 24	5 20	0 44	0 42	11 34	0 33	19 15	3 53
11	4 17	5 20	0 51	0 41	11 30	0 33	19 14	3 53
16	4 10	5 20	0 58	0 41	11 27	0 33	19 14	3 53
21	4 03	5 20	1 04	0 41	11 23	0 33	19 13	3 53
26	3 56	5 21	1 11	0 41	11 20	0 33	19 13	3 53
31	3S49	5N21	1N18	0S41	11S16	0S34	19S13	3N53

Day	⚴ Decl	⚴ Lat	⚵ Decl	⚵ Lat	⚶ Decl	⚶ Lat	Eris Decl	Eris Lat
1	0S14	9N47	9S30	11N55	4S00	5S12	3S48	13S10
6	0N05	9 29	9 13	12 18	3 03	5 11	3 47	13 09
11	0 26	9 12	8 54	12 41	2 07	5 09	3 45	13 09
16	0 46	8 55	8 33	13 05	1 11	5 08	3 44	13 08
21	1 08	8 38	8 10	13 30	0 15	5 07	3 42	13 08
26	1 29	8 22	7 46	13 55	0N40	5 05	3 41	13 07
31	1N51	8N05	7S20	14N20	1N34	5S04	3S39	13S07

Moon Phenomena

Max/0 Decl
dy hr mn
1 16:16 22N09
8 10:07 0 S
14 14:09 22S02
21 11:32 0 N
28 23:44 21N53

Max/0 Lat
dy hr mn
7 18:18 5S01
13 20:42 0 N
20 14:38 5N02
28 0:18 0 S

Perigee/Apogee
dy hr m kilometers
10 9:59 p 362404
26 6:02 a 405776

PH dy hr mn
☽ 1 1:23 10♊52
○ 8 9:41 18♍13
☾ 15 1:26 24♐52
● 22 14:38 2♈22
☽ 30 19:42 10♋30

Void of Course Moon

Last Aspect	☽ Ingress
2 13:15 ♄ △	♋ 2 15:09
4 22:18 ♀ □	♌ 4 23:19
7 1:28 ♄ ✶	♍ 7 3:28
8 9:41 ☉ ☍	♎ 9 4:51
11 3:10 ♄ ☌	♏ 11 5:25
12 18:31 ☉ △	♐ 13 6:55
15 7:35 ♄ ✶	♑ 15 10:25
17 13:02 ♄ □	♒ 17 16:13
19 20:32 ♄ △	♓ 20 0:06
21 8:40 ♀ ✶	♈ 22 9:58
24 17:18 ♄ ☍	♉ 24 21:44
27 4:36 ☿ ✶	♊ 27 10:44
29 18:06 ♄ △	♋ 29 23:08

DAILY ASPECTARIAN

1 Th
☉□☽ 1:23
⚳#♅ 4:38
☽⚼♄ 7:46
☽✶⚳ 8:44
☽□♂ 8:54
♂⊼⚳ 11:36
☿⊼♄ 18:34
☿#⚳ 20:03
☽∠♃ 23:56

2 F
☿∥♅ 0:09
☽✶♀ 8:30
☿ ♈ 11:42
☽△♄ 13:15
☽□☿ 15:34
☽△♆ 17:12
☽□♅ 21:30
♂∠♄ 23:32
♀#♆ 23:46

3 Sa
☽△⚷ 2:05
☽✶♃ 5:28
☿⊻♆ 8:11
☽☍♇ 8:47
☉△☽ 16:59
☽✶♂ 17:19
☉☍♂ 20:11
☽□⚳ 20:40
☽⚼♆ 21:48

4 Su
☽#♇ 0:02
♀⚼♂ 2:54
☉⚼♄ 3:12
☽⚼⚷ 6:26
♀☍♄ 11:19
☽∠♂ 20:10
☽□♄ 21:21
☽□♀ 22:18
☉⚼☽ 22:54

5 M
☽⊼♆ 1:22
☽△☿ 4:58
☽△♅ 5:26
☽⊼⚷ 9:43
♀ ♉ 10:26
☿☌♅ 11:36
☽□♃ 13:21
⚳∠♆ 15:13
☽⊼♇ 15:45
☽∥♃ 18:36
☽∥♀ 20:18
☽⊻♂ 22:04

6 Tu
☉⊼☽ 3:31
☽#♆ 3:53
☽△⚳ 4:13
☽⚼♅ 7:50
☽∥♂ 8:48
☽⚼☿ 9:10
♀✶♆ 12:26
♀∥♃ 14:39
☽⚼♇ 17:44
☉⊻⚳ 18:42
☽#♄ 19:18

7 W
☽✶♄ 1:28
☽☍♆ 5:31
☽⚼⚳ 6:28
☽△♀ 6:53
☽⊼♅ 9:23
☉#☽ 11:52
☽⊼☿ 12:02
☽☍⚷ 13:26
☽#⚷ 14:48
☽∥☿ 15:38
☽△♃ 17:18
☽△♇ 18:56
☽☌♂ 23:29

8 Th
☉∠♀ 0:03
☿#⚷ 0:53
☽∠♄ 2:22
☽∥♅ 6:41
☽∥⚳ 7:31
☽⊼⚳ 7:59
☉☍☽ 9:41
☽⚼♀ 9:44
☽#⚳ 12:54
☽#♅ 13:35
☉#☿ 13:57
♀⊻♅ 17:14
☽⚼♃ 18:16

9 F
☿⊻⚷ 2:41
☽⊻♄ 2:47
☽∥⚷ 5:02
☉∥☽ 5:06
☉∥⚷ 6:01
☽⊼♆ 6:58
☽#☿ 7:25
☽☍♅ 10:46
☽⊼♀ 12:05
⚳∥♅ 14:13
☽⊼⚷ 14:44
☽☍☿ 15:02
☽⊼♃ 18:55
☽□♇ 19:55
☽⊻♂ 23:04
☽∥♄ 23:41

10 Sa
☽⚼♆ 7:17
☽☍⚳ 9:58
☽#♂ 12:37
☉⊼☽ 13:51
☽∥♆ 14:16
☽⚼⚷ 15:05
☽∠♂ 22:44

11 Su
☽#♃ 1:01
♀✶⚷ 2:29
☽☌♄ 3:10
☽△♆ 7:39
☽⊼♅ 11:32
☽#♀ 11:43
☽△⚷ 15:34
☿⊻♀ 15:47
☉⚼☽ 15:59
☽⊼☿ 16:29
☽☍♀ 16:33
☽☍♃ 20:14
☽✶♇ 20:39
☽✶♂ 22:34

12 M
☿ R 7:49
☽⊼⚳ 12:14
☽⚼♅ 12:16
☽∥♇ 14:01
☽⚼☿ 17:14
☉△☽ 18:31
☽∠♇ 21:27

13 Tu
♂#♆ 1:04
☽⊻♄ 4:24
♃△♇ 4:45
☽□♆ 9:20
☽△♅ 13:26
☽⚼⚳ 14:01
☽□⚷ 17:39
☽△☿ 18:11
☽⊼♀ 22:31
☽⊻♇ 22:45
☽⊼♃ 22:59
☽□♂ 23:24

14 W
♀△♇ 1:29
☽∠♄ 5:43
♀☌♃ 5:55
♀△♂ 7:29
♂△♃ 9:52
☽△⚳ 16:23
☿⊻⚷ 16:54
☉∠♃ 21:14

15 Th
♂△♇ 0:25
☽⚼♃ 1:11
☉□☽ 1:26
☽⚼♀ 2:30
☽✶♄ 7:35
☽✶♆ 13:05
☉#⚳ 13:37
☽□♅ 17:27
☽□☿ 20:55
☽✶⚷ 21:53

16 F
☽△♂ 2:19
☽☌♇ 3:01
☽△♃ 4:01
☽△♀ 7:12
☽∠♆ 15:50
☽∥♇ 16:23
☽□⚳ 22:59

17 Sa
☽∠⚷ 0:52
☽#♀ 4:16
☽⚼♂ 4:35
☉✶☽ 11:13
☽□♄ 13:02
☉#♅ 16:35
☽⊻♆ 19:08
☽✶♅ 23:47

18 Su
☽✶☿ 0:47
☽⊻⚷ 4:25
☽#♃ 6:43
☽⊼♂ 7:23
☽⊻♇ 9:33
☉⊼♄ 9:57
☽□♃ 11:24
☉∠☽ 17:07
☿☌♅ 17:23
☽□♀ 18:40
☽#♂ 18:47
☽∥♆ 22:41

19 M
☽∠☿ 3:06
☽∠♅ 3:44
☽✶⚳ 7:59
☽∠♇ 13:35
☽∥♄ 16:17
☽△♄ 20:32
☉⊻☽ 23:40

20 Tu
⚳∠⚷ 2:43
☽☌♆ 3:18
☉ ♈ 5:16
☽⊻☿ 5:43
☽⊻♅ 8:12
☽☌⚷ 13:02
☽∠⚳ 13:19
☽#☿ 13:45
☽☍♂ 14:26
☽∥⚷ 14:29
♀#♇ 17:15
☽✶♇ 18:07
☽✶♃ 20:57
☽#⚳ 21:19
☿#⚷ 21:52

21 W
☽⚼♄ 1:01
☽#♅ 5:55
☿∠♀ 8:18
☽✶♀ 8:40
☉#☽ 9:09
♂⚼⚳ 10:02
☉∥☽ 14:22
☿⊻♆ 15:11
☽∥♅ 17:12
☽⊻⚳ 19:10
☉☌☿ 19:22
☉⊻♆ 23:25

22 Th
☽∠♃ 2:30
☽∥⚳ 2:57
☽∥☿ 5:30
☽⊼♄ 5:59
☽#⚷ 8:36
☽☌☿ 11:51
☽⊻♆ 13:26
☉☌☽ 14:38
♂☍⚷ 15:22
☽∠♀ 16:35
☽☌♅ 18:37
☿∥⚳ 22:07
☽⊼♂ 23:25
☽⊻⚷ 23:38

23 F
☉∥♅ 1:25
☽□♇ 4:39
☽#♄ 7:24
☽⊻♃ 8:34
☿R♓ 13:23
♀∠♅ 18:26
☽∠♆ 19:14

24 Sa
☽⊻♀ 1:06
☽#♆ 2:16
☽⚼♂ 4:37
☽∠⚷ 5:40
☽☌⚳ 8:31
☽∥♂ 9:37
☽☍♄ 17:18
☉☌♅ 18:21
☽⊻☿ 19:31
☽∥♃ 23:09
⚵ R 23:33

25 Su
☽✶♆ 1:29
☉∥☿ 2:51
☽⊻♅ 6:56
☉⊻☽ 8:01
☽△♂ 10:14
☽✶⚷ 12:06
☽△♇ 16:59
☽☌♃ 22:03
☽∠☿ 23:55

26 M
☉⊼♂ 5:40
☿⊼♄ 6:10
☿∥♅ 12:06
☽∠♅ 13:34
☽#♇ 15:04
☉∠☽ 17:19
☽☌♀ 19:27
☿∠♃ 21:35
☽⊻⚳ 23:28
☽⚼♇ 23:33

27 Tu
☽✶☿ 4:36
☽⊼♄ 5:55
☉⊻⚷ 11:45
☽□♆ 14:40
⚳#⚷ 17:39
☽✶♅ 20:17
☽□♂ 22:05

28 W
☽□⚷ 1:28
☉✶☽ 2:39
☽⊼♇ 6:05
☽∠⚳ 7:02
☽⚼♄ 12:12
☽⊻♃ 12:13
♀⚼♇ 20:52

29 Th
☿⊻⚳ 12:40
☽⊻♀ 13:37
☽□☿ 14:06
☽✶⚳ 14:13
☿✶♀ 17:44
☽△♄ 18:06
☽∠♃ 18:50
☉□♇ 19:57
☉#⚷ 23:42

30 F
♀⊻⚳ 2:04
☽△♆ 3:06
☽□♅ 8:39
☽✶♂ 9:07
☽△⚷ 13:39
☽☍♇ 17:49
☉□☽ 19:42
☽∠♀ 21:35

31 Sa
☽✶♃ 0:42
☽#♇ 6:37
☽⚼♆ 8:17
♂⊼♅ 9:04
☽∠♂ 13:37
♀⊼♄ 18:25
☽⚼⚷ 18:33
☉∥⚳ 21:33
☽△☿ 22:14
☿#♅ 23:57

April 2012

LONGITUDE

Day	Sid.Time	☉	☽	☽ 12 hour	Mean ☊	True ☊	☿	♀	♂	⚳	♃	♄	⚷	♅	♆	♇
	h m s	° ' "	° ' "	° ' "	° '	° '	° '	° '	° '	° '	° '	° '	° '	° '	° '	° '
1 Su	12 39 02	11♈40 07	25♋22 07	1♌50 21	8♐09.5	6♐40.9	24♓23.8	27♉31.8	4♍46.9	26♈27.6	13♉18.8	27♎17.5	7♓28.4	4♈55.5	2♓04.3	9♑32.3
2 M	12 42 58	12 39 18	8♌25 19	15 07 21	8 06.4	6R 37.8	24R 07.3	28 28.4	4R 37.2	26 51.5	13 32.0	27R 13.2	7 31.9	4 58.9	2 06.1	9 32.6
3 Tu	12 46 55	13 38 27	21 56 40	28 53 21	8 03.2	6 32.7	23 56.5	29 24.5	4 28.2	27 15.4	13 45.3	27 08.8	7 35.3	5 02.3	2 07.9	9 32.9
4 W	12 50 52	14 37 34	5♍57 14	13♍08 01	8 00.0	6 25.9	23D 51.4	0♊20.0	4 20.0	27 39.3	13 58.6	27 04.4	7 38.6	5 05.7	2 09.7	9 33.1
5 Th	12 54 48	15 36 39	20 25 09	27 47 54	7 56.8	6 18.0	23 51.8	1 15.0	4 12.6	28 03.3	14 12.0	26 59.9	7 41.9	5 09.1	2 11.5	9 33.3
6 F	12 58 45	16 35 41	5♎15 21	12♎46 25	7 53.6	6 10.1	23 57.6	2 09.3	4 06.0	28 27.3	14 25.4	26 55.4	7 45.2	5 12.5	2 13.3	9 33.4
7 Sa	13 02 41	17 34 41	20 19 54	27 54 34	7 50.5	6 03.2	24 08.7	3 03.0	4 00.2	28 51.3	14 38.9	26 50.9	7 48.5	5 15.8	2 15.0	9 33.6
8 Su	13 06 38	18 33 39	5♏29 07	13♏02 22	7 47.3	5 58.1	24 24.8	3 56.1	3 55.2	29 15.3	14 52.4	26 46.4	7 51.7	5 19.2	2 16.8	9 33.7
9 M	13 10 34	19 32 35	20 33 10	28 00 34	7 44.1	5 55.1	24 45.7	4 48.5	3 50.9	29 39.3	15 06.0	26 41.9	7 54.9	5 22.6	2 18.5	9 33.7
10 Tu	13 14 31	20 31 30	5♐23 43	12♐41 58	7 40.9	5D 54.2	25 11.3	5 40.2	3 47.4	0♉03.3	15 19.6	26 37.3	7 58.1	5 25.9	2 20.1	9R 33.8
11 W	13 18 27	21 30 23	19 54 52	27 02 06	7 37.8	5 54.7	25 41.3	6 31.2	3 44.6	0 27.4	15 33.2	26 32.7	8 01.2	5 29.2	2 21.8	9 33.8
12 Th	13 22 24	22 29 14	4♑03 31	10♑59 06	7 34.6	5 56.0	26 15.6	7 21.5	3 42.7	0 51.5	15 46.9	26 28.1	8 04.3	5 32.6	2 23.4	9 33.7
13 F	13 26 21	23 28 03	17 48 58	24 33 18	7 31.4	5R 57.0	26 53.8	8 11.0	3 41.4	1 15.6	16 00.6	26 23.5	8 07.4	5 35.9	2 25.0	9 33.7
14 Sa	13 30 17	24 26 51	1♒12 20	7♒46 24	7 28.2	5 56.9	27 35.8	8 59.7	3D 40.9	1 39.7	16 14.3	26 18.9	8 10.4	5 39.2	2 26.6	9 33.6
15 Su	13 34 14	25 25 37	14 15 47	20 40 51	7 25.0	5 55.2	28 21.4	9 47.6	3 41.2	2 03.8	16 28.1	26 14.3	8 13.4	5 42.4	2 28.2	9 33.5
16 M	13 38 10	26 24 21	27 01 56	3♓19 22	7 21.9	5 51.7	29 10.5	10 34.7	3 42.2	2 27.9	16 41.9	26 09.7	8 16.3	5 45.7	2 29.7	9 33.3
17 Tu	13 42 07	27 23 03	9♓33 28	15 44 31	7 18.7	5 46.6	0♈02.9	11 20.9	3 43.9	2 52.1	16 55.8	26 05.1	8 19.2	5 49.0	2 31.2	9 33.1
18 W	13 46 03	28 21 44	21 52 49	27 58 38	7 15.5	5 40.3	0 58.3	12 06.2	3 46.3	3 16.3	17 09.7	26 00.5	8 22.1	5 52.2	2 32.7	9 32.9
19 Th	13 50 00	29 20 23	4♈02 11	10♈03 42	7 12.3	5 33.6	1 56.8	12 50.6	3 49.4	3 40.4	17 23.6	25 55.9	8 24.9	5 55.4	2 34.1	9 32.7
20 F	13 53 56	0♉19 00	16 03 25	22 01 32	7 09.2	5 27.1	2 58.1	13 33.9	3 53.2	4 04.6	17 37.5	25 51.3	8 27.7	5 58.6	2 35.6	9 32.4
21 Sa	13 57 53	1 17 35	27 58 17	3♉53 52	7 06.0	5 21.5	4 02.1	14 16.3	3 57.7	4 28.8	17 51.5	25 46.7	8 30.4	6 01.8	2 37.0	9 32.1
22 Su	14 01 49	2 16 09	9♉48 31	15 42 31	7 02.8	5 17.3	5 08.7	14 57.6	4 02.9	4 53.0	18 05.5	25 42.1	8 33.1	6 05.0	2 38.4	9 31.8
23 M	14 05 46	3 14 40	21 36 06	27 29 35	6 59.6	5 14.7	6 17.9	15 37.8	4 08.8	5 17.2	18 19.5	25 37.6	8 35.8	6 08.1	2 39.7	9 31.4
24 Tu	14 09 43	4 13 09	3♊23 18	9♊17 37	6 56.4	5D 13.8	7 29.5	16 16.9	4 15.3	5 41.4	18 33.5	25 33.0	8 38.4	6 11.2	2 41.0	9 31.0
25 W	14 13 39	5 11 37	15 12 56	21 09 39	6 53.3	5 14.2	8 43.4	16 54.7	4 22.5	6 05.7	18 47.6	25 28.5	8 41.0	6 14.4	2 42.3	9 30.6
26 Th	14 17 36	6 10 03	27 08 16	3♋09 15	6 50.1	5 15.5	9 59.6	17 31.4	4 30.3	6 29.9	19 01.7	25 24.0	8 43.5	6 17.4	2 43.6	9 30.1
27 F	14 21 32	7 08 26	9♋13 08	15 20 26	6 46.9	5 17.3	11 18.0	18 06.7	4 38.7	6 54.1	19 15.7	25 19.5	8 46.0	6 20.5	2 44.8	9 29.7
28 Sa	14 25 29	8 06 47	21 31 44	27 47 33	6 43.7	5 18.8	12 38.5	18 40.7	4 47.8	7 18.3	19 29.9	25 15.1	8 48.5	6 23.6	2 46.0	9 29.2
29 Su	14 29 25	9 05 07	4♌08 27	10♌34 55	6 40.6	5R 19.7	14 01.2	19 13.3	4 57.4	7 42.6	19 44.0	25 10.7	8 50.9	6 26.6	2 47.2	9 28.6
30 M	14 33 22	10♉03 24	17 07 27	23 46 25	6♐37.4	5♐19.6	15♈25.9	19♊44.5	5♍07.6	8♉06.8	19♉58.1	25♎06.3	8♓53.2	6♈29.6	2♓48.4	9♑28.1

1st of Month

Julian Day # 2456018.5
Obliquity 23°26'13"
SVP 5♓05'03"
GC 27♐00.6
Eris 21♈55.3

Day	⚴		Day	⚵		Day	⚶
1	16♓04.4		1	6♐58.4R		1	16♉22.0
6	17 39.7		6	6 42.6R		6	18 40.9
11	19 13.7		11	6 18.6R		11	20 59.3
16	20 46.5		16	5 46.3R		16	23 17.4
21	22 17.7		21	5 06.3R		21	25 34.9
26	23 47.3		26	4 19.0R		26	27 51.9

DECLINATION and LATITUDE

Day	☉ Decl	☽ Decl	☽ Lat	☽ 12h Decl	☿ Decl	☿ Lat	♀ Decl	♀ Lat	♂ Decl	♂ Lat	⚳ Decl	⚳ Lat	♃ Decl	♃ Lat	♄ Decl	♄ Lat
1 Su	4N37	17N16	3S51	15N39	1S19	0N59	22N59	3N28	12N50	3N19	4N35	6S01	15N00	0S52	7S56	2N46
2 M	4 60	13 48	4 31	11 44	1 40	0 43	23 16	3 32	12 52	3 16	4 45	5 60	15 04	0 52	7 54	2 46
3 Tu	5 23	9 30	4 57	7 06	1 59	0 28	23 32	3 36	12 52	3 14	4 55	5 58	15 08	0 52	7 53	2 46
4 W	5 46	4 34	5 07	1 56	2 15	0 13	23 48	3 40	12 53	3 11	5 05	5 57	15 12	0 52	7 51	2 46
5 Th	6 09	0S46	4 58	3S30	2 28	0S02	24 04	3 44	12 53	3 09	5 15	5 55	15 16	0 52	7 49	2 46
6 F	6 31	6 12	4 29	8 50	2 39	0 16	24 19	3 48	12 53	3 06	5 24	5 54	15 21	0 52	7 48	2 46
7 Sa	6 54	11 21	3 41	13 41	2 47	0 30	24 33	3 52	12 53	3 03	5 34	5 53	15 25	0 52	7 46	2 46
8 Su	7 16	15 49	2 37	17 40	2 53	0 43	24 47	3 56	12 53	3 01	5 44	5 51	15 29	0 51	7 44	2 46
9 M	7 39	19 12	1 22	20 24	2 56	0 56	25 01	3 59	12 52	2 58	5 53	5 50	15 33	0 51	7 43	2 46
10 Tu	8 01	21 15	0 03	21 43	2 57	1 07	25 14	4 03	12 51	2 56	6 03	5 48	15 37	0 51	7 41	2 46
11 W	8 23	21 48	1N15	21 32	2 55	1 19	25 26	4 06	12 49	2 53	6 12	5 47	15 41	0 51	7 39	2 46
12 Th	8 45	20 56	2 27	20 01	2 51	1 29	25 38	4 10	12 48	2 51	6 22	5 46	15 45	0 51	7 38	2 46
13 F	9 07	18 49	3 28	17 23	2 45	1 39	25 50	4 13	12 46	2 48	6 31	5 44	15 49	0 51	7 36	2 46
14 Sa	9 28	15 44	4 15	13 54	2 37	1 48	26 00	4 16	12 43	2 45	6 41	5 43	15 53	0 51	7 34	2 46
15 Su	9 50	11 56	4 49	9 51	2 26	1 57	26 11	4 19	12 41	2 43	6 50	5 42	15 57	0 51	7 33	2 46
16 M	10 11	7 41	5 07	5 28	2 14	2 05	26 21	4 22	12 38	2 40	6 60	5 40	16 01	0 50	7 31	2 46
17 Tu	10 32	3 12	5 10	0 55	1 60	2 12	26 30	4 24	12 35	2 38	7 09	5 39	16 05	0 50	7 29	2 46
18 W	10 53	1N21	4 58	3N35	1 44	2 19	26 39	4 27	12 32	2 35	7 18	5 38	16 09	0 50	7 28	2 46
19 Th	11 14	5 47	4 33	7 55	1 26	2 25	26 47	4 29	12 29	2 33	7 28	5 36	16 13	0 50	7 26	2 46
20 F	11 35	9 57	3 56	11 53	1 07	2 30	26 55	4 31	12 25	2 30	7 37	5 35	16 17	0 50	7 24	2 46
21 Sa	11 55	13 42	3 10	15 22	0 46	2 35	27 02	4 33	12 21	2 28	7 46	5 34	16 21	0 50	7 23	2 46
22 Su	12 16	16 53	2 15	18 13	0 23	2 39	27 09	4 35	12 17	2 26	7 55	5 33	16 25	0 50	7 21	2 46
23 M	12 36	19 21	1 14	20 17	0N01	2 42	27 15	4 37	12 13	2 23	8 04	5 31	16 29	0 50	7 20	2 46
24 Tu	12 55	20 60	0 10	21 28	0 27	2 45	27 20	4 38	12 08	2 21	8 13	5 30	16 33	0 50	7 18	2 46
25 W	13 15	21 43	0S55	21 42	0 54	2 47	27 26	4 39	12 03	2 18	8 22	5 29	16 37	0 49	7 16	2 46
26 Th	13 35	21 27	1 58	20 56	1 22	2 49	27 30	4 40	11 58	2 16	8 31	5 28	16 41	0 49	7 15	2 46
27 F	13 54	20 11	2 56	19 12	1 52	2 50	27 34	4 41	11 53	2 14	8 40	5 26	16 45	0 49	7 13	2 46
28 Sa	14 13	17 58	3 48	16 31	2 23	2 50	27 38	4 42	11 47	2 11	8 49	5 25	16 49	0 49	7 12	2 46
29 Su	14 31	14 51	4 30	12 59	2 55	2 50	27 41	4 42	11 42	2 09	8 58	5 24	16 53	0 49	7 10	2 46
30 M	14N50	10N56	4S59	8N44	3N28	2S49	27N44	4N42	11N36	2N07	9N07	5S23	16N57	0S49	7S09	2N46

Day	⚷ Decl	⚷ Lat	♅ Decl	♅ Lat	♆ Decl	♆ Lat	♇ Decl	♇ Lat
1	3S47	5N21	1N19	0S41	11S16	0S34	19S13	3N53
6	3 41	5 22	1 26	0 41	11 12	0 34	19 13	3 54
11	3 34	5 23	1 33	0 41	11 09	0 34	19 12	3 54
16	3 28	5 24	1 39	0 41	11 07	0 34	19 12	3 54
21	3 22	5 24	1 46	0 41	11 04	0 34	19 12	3 54
26	3 16	5 26	1 52	0 42	11 02	0 34	19 12	3 54

Day	⚴ Decl	⚴ Lat	⚵ Decl	⚵ Lat	⚶ Decl	⚶ Lat	Eris Decl	Eris Lat
1	1N55	8N02	7S15	14N25	1N45	5S04	3S39	13S07
6	2 17	7 46	6 48	14 49	2 38	5 03	3 37	13 07
11	2 38	7 30	6 21	15 13	3 31	5 03	3 36	13 07
16	2 60	7 14	5 53	15 37	4 22	5 02	3 35	13 06
21	3 20	6 58	5 25	15 58	5 12	5 01	3 33	13 06
26	3 40	6 41	4 57	16 19	6 01	5 01	3 32	13 06

Moon Phenomena

Max/0 Decl (dy hr mn)
4 20:35 0 S
10 21:14 21S49
17 16:52 0 N
25 5:34 21N44

Perigee/Apogee (dy hr m kilometers)
7 17:08 p 358319
22 13:48 a 406419

Max/0 Lat (dy hr mn)
4 0:37 5S07
10 0:49 0 N
16 16:47 5N10
24 3:44 0 S

PH	dy	hr mn	
○	6	19:20	17♎23
☾	13	10:51	23♑55
●	21	7:20	1♉35
☽	29	9:59	9♌29

Void of Course Moon

Last Aspect	☽ Ingress
1 4:21 ♀ ✱	♌ 1 8:37
3 13:48 ♀ □	♍ 3 13:54
5 5:38 ☿ ☍	♎ 5 15:33
7 10:16 ♄ ☌	♏ 7 15:19
9 6:57 ☿ △	♐ 9 15:13
11 11:07 ♄ ✱	♑ 11 17:03
13 17:06 ☿ ✱	♒ 13 21:49
15 22:43 ☉ ✱	♓ 16 5:39
17 14:35 ♃ ✱	♈ 18 16:00
20 19:36 ♄ ☍	♉ 21 4:06
22 17:11 ♃ ☌	♊ 23 17:06
25 20:32 ♄ △	♋ 26 5:43
28 7:07 ♄ □	♌ 28 16:12
30 14:18 ♄ ✱	♍ 30 23:03

DAILY ASPECTARIAN

1 Su ☽□⚳ 2:06, ☽□♄ 3:34, ☽✱♀ 4:21, ☽⊼♆ 12:27, ☽∥♃ 16:01, ☽⚺♂ 17:10, ☽△♅ 17:44, ☽⊼⚷ 22:23

2 M ☽⚼☿ 1:15, ☽⊼♇ 2:01, ☽∥♂ 5:34, ☉△☽ 8:12, ☽□♃ 9:20, ☽#♆ 14:44, ⚳☍♄ 18:23, ☽⚼♅ 20:39

3 Tu ☽⊼☿ 3:26, ☉⚺♃ 3:35, ☽⚼♇ 4:31, ☽#♄ 8:13, ☽✱♄ 8:58, ☽△⚳ 9:28, ☉⚼☽ 12:27, ☽□♀ 13:48, ♀ ♊ 15:19, ☽☍♆ 17:34, ☉∥☽ 18:47, ☽☌♂ 21:17, ☽∥⚳ 21:40, ☽⊼♅ 22:33

4 W ☽☍⚷ 2:51, ☽#⚷ 3:54, ☽△♇ 6:02, ☽#☿ 10:07, ☽∠♄ 10:11, ☿ D 10:12, ☽⚼⚳ 11:31, ☽△♃ 13:36, ☽∥♅ 14:20, ☉⊼☽ 15:31

5 Th ☽#♅ 2:51, ☽☍☿ 5:38, ☽∥☿ 7:45, ☽⚺♄ 10:39, ☽⊼⚳ 12:45, ☽∥⚷ 12:50, ☽⚼♃ 14:29, ☽△♀ 18:42, ☽⊼♆ 19:07, ☽#⚳ 20:21, ☽⚺♂ 22:10, ☽☍♅ 23:55

6 F ☉#☽ 1:34, ♀□♆ 1:50, ☽⊼⚷ 4:01, ☽□♇ 6:53, ☽∥♄ 7:10, ☽⊼♃ 14:51, ☉∠♆ 15:46, ☽⚼♆ 19:06, ☉☍☽ 19:20, ☽⚼♀ 20:09, ☽∠♂ 21:54, ☽∥♆ 23:15

7 Sa ☽⚼⚷ 3:56, ☽⊼☿ 6:08, ☽#♂ 7:45, ☽☌♄ 10:16, ☽☍⚳ 13:52, ☽△♆ 18:55, ☽⊼♀ 21:23, ☽✱♂ 21:32, ☽#♃ 21:59, ♀□♂ 23:37, ☽⊼♅ 23:44

8 Su ☽△⚷ 3:47, ☽⚼☿ 6:22, ☽✱♇ 6:28, ☉⚼♂ 8:08, ☽☍♃ 15:09, ☉⊼☽ 22:16, ☽⚼♅ 23:43

9 M ☽∥♇ 0:01, ☉#♄ 3:56, ☽∠♇ 6:26, ☽△☿ 6:57, ☽⚺♄ 9:50, ☽⊼⚳ 15:04, ♀✱♅ 16:53, ☽□♆ 19:00, ⚳ ♉ 20:41, ☽□♂ 21:23

10 Tu ☽△♅ 0:04, ☉⚼☽ 0:14, ☽☍♀ 0:29, ☽□⚷ 4:14, ☽⚺♇ 6:50, ☽∠♄ 10:10, ☽⚼⚳ 16:21, ♇ R 16:25, ☽⊼♃ 16:37

11 W ☉∠♀ 2:22, ☉△☽ 2:52, ☽□☿ 10:07, ☽✱♄ 11:07, ☽⚼♃ 18:17, ☽△⚳ 18:21, ☽✱♆ 21:08, ☽△♂ 23:24

12 Th ☽□♅ 2:34, ☽⊼♀ 6:04, ☽✱⚷ 6:58, ☿⊼♄ 7:17, ☽☌♇ 9:31, ☉∠⚷ 15:06, ☽∥♇ 20:23, ☽△♃ 20:45, ♀□⚷ 22:07, ☽∠♆ 23:18

13 F ☽⚼♂ 1:33, ☽∠⚷ 9:28, ☽⚼♀ 10:10, ☉□☽ 10:51, ☽□♄ 15:13, ☽✱☿ 17:06, ☽#♃ 22:58

14 Sa ☽□⚳ 0:51, ☽⚺♆ 2:15, ♂ D 3:54, ☽⊼♂ 4:30, ☽✱♅ 8:09, ☽⚺⚷ 12:47, ☽△♀ 15:11, ☽⚺♇ 15:17, ♀⊼♇ 16:53, ☽#♂ 19:30, ☽∠☿ 22:12

15 Su ☽□♃ 4:11, ☽∥♆ 4:48, ☉#☽ 11:12, ☽∠♅ 12:06, ☉☍♄ 18:27, ☽∠♇ 19:18, ☽△♄ 22:22, ☉✱☽ 22:43

16 M ☽∥♄ 0:57, ⚳✱♆ 1:52, ☽#⚳ 3:39, ☽⚺☿ 4:22, ☽☌♆ 10:26, ☽✱⚳ 10:42, ☽☍♂ 12:45, ♀⚼♄ 16:29, ☽⚺♅ 16:45, ☽☌⚷ 21:36, ☿ ♈ 22:43, ☽∥⚷ 22:43, ☽✱♇ 23:59

17 Tu ☽⚼♄ 2:56, ☽□♀ 3:42, ☉∠☽ 5:57, ☽∥☿ 6:42, ☽#♅ 7:59, ☽✱♃ 14:35, ☽∠⚳ 16:42

18 W ☽∥♅ 1:52, ☽#☿ 1:56, ☿#♅ 2:49, ☽⊼♄ 8:04, ☽#⚷ 11:02, ☉#♆ 13:45, ☉⚺☽ 13:53, ☽☌☿ 19:29, ⚳#♄ 20:36, ☽∠♃ 20:40, ☽⚺♆ 21:05, ☽⚺⚳ 23:15, ☽⊼♂ 23:35

19 Th ☽☌♅ 3:46, ☽⚺⚷ 8:45, ☽#♄ 9:13, ☽∥⚳ 9:47, ♂△⚳ 10:29, ☽□♇ 10:58, ☿∠♃ 13:45, ☿⚺♆ 15:06, ☉ ♉ 16:13, ☽✱♀ 18:41

20 F ☽∠♆ 3:05, ☽⚺♃ 3:13, ☽⚼♂ 5:43, ☽#♆ 6:53, ☉∥☽ 11:03, ☽∠⚷ 14:57, ☽∥♂ 15:09, ☽☍♄ 19:36, ☿⊼♂ 22:16

21 Sa ☽∠♀ 2:48, ☉☌☽ 7:20, ☽✱♆ 9:25, ☽△♂ 12:13, ☽⚺☿ 13:32, ☽☌⚳ 13:39, ☿⚺⚳ 15:16, ☽⚺♅ 16:24, ☽∥♃ 20:07, ☽✱⚷ 21:26, ☽△♇ 23:26

22 Su ☉∥♂ 1:20, ☉✱♆ 9:19, ☽⚺♀ 11:07, ☽☌♃ 17:11, ☿☌♅ 20:30, ☽#♇ 22:20, ☽∠♅ 23:03, ☽∠☿ 23:19

23 M ☽⚼♇ 5:57, ☽⊼♄ 8:09, ☽□♆ 22:34

24 Tu ☉△♂ 1:00, ☽□♂ 1:47, ☉⚺☽ 1:51, ☽⚺⚳ 4:51, ☽✱♅ 5:43, ☽✱☿ 9:18, ☽□⚷ 10:43, ☽⊼♇ 12:27, ☽⚼♄ 14:27, ☿⚺⚷ 23:13

25 W ☽☌♀ 3:37, ☽⚺♃ 7:22, ⚳⚺♅ 9:52, ☉∠☽ 10:57, ☽∠⚳ 12:17, ☿□♇ 14:52, ☽△♄ 20:32

26 Th ☉⚺♅ 3:13, ☽△♆ 11:10, ☉☌⚳ 13:56, ☽∠♃ 14:00, ☽✱♂ 14:51, ☽□♅ 18:18, ☽✱⚳ 19:16, ☉✱☽ 19:33, ☽△⚷ 23:06

27 F ☽☍♇ 0:33, ☿∥♅ 0:54, ☽□☿ 4:35, ☽#♇ 11:50, ☽⚼♆ 16:43, ☽⚺♀ 18:14, ☽✱♃ 20:00, ☽∠♂ 20:37

28 Sa ☽⚼⚷ 4:24, ☽□♄ 7:07, ☽∥♃ 9:26, ☉✱⚷ 17:53, ☽⊼♆ 21:27

29 Su ☽∠♀ 0:10, ☽⚺♂ 1:33, ☉∥☽ 2:01, ☽△♅ 4:20, ☽□⚳ 6:53, ☽⊼⚷ 8:49, ☉△♇ 9:35, ☽⊼♇ 9:57, ☉□☽ 9:59, ☿#⚷ 12:26, ☽∥♂ 20:09, ☽△☿ 20:32, ☽#♆ 23:38

30 M ☽✱♀ 4:56, ☽□♃ 5:15, ☽⚼♅ 7:56, ☽∥⚳ 9:40, ☽⚼♇ 13:14, ☽✱♄ 14:18, ⚶ ♉ 16:49, ☽#♄ 20:17, ♀⚺♃ 20:56

LONGITUDE

Day	Sid.Time	☉	☽	☽ 12 hour	Mean ☊	True ☊	☿	♀	♂	⚳	♃	♄	⚷	♅	♆	♇
	h m s	° ' "	° ' "	° ' "	° '	° '	° '	° '	° '	° '	° '	° '	° '	° '	° '	° '
1 Tu	14 37 18	11♉01 39	0♍32 08	7♍24 48	6♐34.2	5♐18.4	16♈52.6	20♊14.2	5♍18.4	8♉31.0	20♉12.3	25♎01.9	8♓55.5	6♈32.6	2♓49.5	9♑27.5
2 W	14 41 15	11 59 52	14 24 28	21 31 02	6 31.0	5R 16.3	18 21.3	20 42.3	5 29.8	8 55.3	20 26.4	24R 57.6	8 57.8	6 35.5	2 50.6	9R 26.8
3 Th	14 45 12	12 58 03	28 44 14	6♎03 35	6 27.8	5 13.5	19 52.1	21 08.8	5 41.7	9 19.5	20 40.6	24 53.4	9 00.0	6 38.4	2 51.6	9 26.2
4 F	14 49 08	13 56 12	13♎28 26	20 57 57	6 24.7	5 10.6	21 24.7	21 33.6	5 54.2	9 43.7	20 54.8	24 49.1	9 02.1	6 41.3	2 52.7	9 25.5
5 Sa	14 53 05	14 54 19	28 31 07	6♏06 49	6 21.5	5 08.1	22 59.4	21 56.6	6 07.2	10 07.9	21 09.0	24 44.9	9 04.2	6 44.2	2 53.7	9 24.8
6 Su	14 57 01	15 52 25	13♏43 50	21 20 55	6 18.3	5 06.3	24 35.9	22 17.9	6 20.7	10 32.2	21 23.2	24 40.8	9 06.3	6 47.0	2 54.7	9 24.1
7 M	15 00 58	16 50 28	28 56 48	6♐30 19	6 15.1	5D 05.5	26 14.5	22 37.3	6 34.7	10 56.4	21 37.4	24 36.7	9 08.3	6 49.9	2 55.6	9 23.3
8 Tu	15 04 54	17 48 31	14♐00 22	21 26 02	6 12.0	5 05.5	27 54.9	22 54.8	6 49.2	11 20.6	21 51.6	24 32.6	9 10.3	6 52.6	2 56.5	9 22.6
9 W	15 08 51	18 46 32	28 46 29	6♑01 09	6 08.8	5 06.3	29 37.3	23 10.4	7 04.2	11 44.8	22 05.8	24 28.6	9 12.2	6 55.4	2 57.4	9 21.8
10 Th	15 12 47	19 44 31	13♑09 34	20 11 29	6 05.6	5 07.4	1♉21.6	23 23.9	7 19.7	12 09.0	22 20.1	24 24.7	9 14.1	6 58.1	2 58.2	9 20.9
11 F	15 16 44	20 42 29	27 06 47	3♒55 31	6 02.4	5 08.5	3 07.9	23 35.3	7 35.7	12 33.2	22 34.3	24 20.8	9 15.9	7 00.9	2 59.1	9 20.1
12 Sa	15 20 41	21 40 26	10♒37 50	17 13 58	5 59.3	5R 09.3	4 56.2	23 44.6	7 52.1	12 57.4	22 48.5	24 17.0	9 17.7	7 03.5	2 59.9	9 19.2
13 Su	15 24 37	22 38 21	23 44 16	0♓09 07	5 56.1	5 09.5	6 46.3	23 51.7	8 08.9	13 21.6	23 02.7	24 13.2	9 19.4	7 06.2	3 00.6	9 18.3
14 M	15 28 34	23 36 15	6♓28 56	12 44 12	5 52.9	5 09.2	8 38.5	23 56.5	8 26.2	13 45.8	23 17.0	24 09.5	9 21.0	7 08.8	3 01.3	9 17.4
15 Tu	15 32 30	24 34 08	18 55 23	25 02 55	5 49.7	5 08.4	10 32.5	23R 59.1	8 43.9	14 10.0	23 31.2	24 05.8	9 22.6	7 11.4	3 02.0	9 16.4
16 W	15 36 27	25 32 00	1♈07 19	7♈08 59	5 46.5	5 07.3	12 28.5	23 59.3	9 02.1	14 34.1	23 45.4	24 02.2	9 24.2	7 13.9	3 02.7	9 15.5
17 Th	15 40 23	26 29 50	13 08 23	19 05 54	5 43.4	5 06.0	14 26.4	23 57.2	9 20.7	14 58.3	23 59.6	23 58.7	9 25.7	7 16.4	3 03.3	9 14.5
18 F	15 44 20	27 27 39	25 01 57	0♉56 53	5 40.2	5 04.9	16 26.1	23 52.7	9 39.6	15 22.4	24 13.8	23 55.2	9 27.1	7 18.9	3 03.9	9 13.4
19 Sa	15 48 16	28 25 27	6♉51 04	12 44 47	5 37.0	5 04.0	18 27.7	23 45.8	9 59.0	15 46.6	24 28.0	23 51.8	9 28.5	7 21.4	3 04.5	9 12.4
20 Su	15 52 13	29 23 14	18 38 23	24 32 09	5 33.8	5 03.5	20 31.0	23 36.5	10 18.8	16 10.7	24 42.2	23 48.5	9 29.9	7 23.8	3 05.0	9 11.3
21 M	15 56 10	0♊20 59	0♊26 21	6♊21 17	5 30.7	5D 03.2	22 35.9	23 24.8	10 39.0	16 34.8	24 56.4	23 45.2	9 31.2	7 26.2	3 05.5	9 10.3
22 Tu	16 00 06	1 18 43	12 17 14	18 14 27	5 27.5	5 03.2	24 42.4	23 10.6	10 59.5	16 58.9	25 10.6	23 42.1	9 32.4	7 28.5	3 06.0	9 09.2
23 W	16 04 03	2 16 26	24 13 14	0♋13 53	5 24.3	5 03.4	26 50.2	22 54.1	11 20.5	17 23.0	25 24.8	23 39.0	9 33.6	7 30.8	3 06.4	9 08.0
24 Th	16 07 59	3 14 07	6♋16 43	12 22 01	5 21.1	5 03.6	28 59.3	22 35.3	11 41.8	17 47.1	25 38.9	23 35.9	9 34.7	7 33.1	3 06.8	9 06.9
25 F	16 11 56	4 11 47	18 30 08	24 41 35	5 17.9	5R 03.8	1♊09.5	22 14.1	12 03.4	18 11.1	25 53.1	23 33.0	9 35.7	7 35.3	3 07.2	9 05.7
26 Sa	16 15 52	5 09 26	0♌56 13	7♌14 54	5 14.8	5 03.8	3 20.4	21 50.7	12 25.4	18 35.1	26 07.2	23 30.1	9 36.8	7 37.5	3 07.5	9 04.5
27 Su	16 19 49	6 07 03	13 37 49	20 05 21	5 11.6	5 03.8	5 32.0	21 25.2	12 47.8	18 59.1	26 21.3	23 27.3	9 37.7	7 39.7	3 07.8	9 03.3
28 M	16 23 45	7 04 38	26 37 48	3♍15 31	5 08.4	5D 03.7	7 43.9	20 57.7	13 10.4	19 23.1	26 35.4	23 24.6	9 38.6	7 41.8	3 08.1	9 02.1
29 Tu	16 27 42	8 02 12	9♍58 43	16 47 38	5 05.2	5 03.7	9 55.8	20 28.3	13 33.5	19 47.1	26 49.4	23 22.0	9 39.4	7 43.9	3 08.3	9 00.9
30 W	16 31 39	8 59 45	23 42 23	0♎42 59	5 02.1	5 03.8	12 07.6	19 57.2	13 56.8	20 11.0	27 03.5	23 19.5	9 40.2	7 45.9	3 08.5	8 59.6
31 Th	16 35 35	9♊57 16	7♎49 21	15 01 16	4♐58.9	5♐04.1	14♊18.9	19♊24.5	14♍20.4	20♉35.0	27♉17.5	23♎17.0	9♓40.9	7♈47.9	3♓08.7	8♑58.4

1st of Month

Julian Day # 2456048.5
Obliquity 23°26'12"
SVP 5♓05'00"
GC 27♐00.7
Eris 22♈14.8

Day	⚴
1	25♓15.1
6	26 40.8
11	28 04.3
16	29 25.4
21	0♈43.9
26	1 59.6
31	3 12.0

Day	⚵
1	3♐25.3R
6	2 26.3R
11	1 23.1R
16	0 17.0R
21	29♏09.5R
26	28 02.2R
31	26 56.6R

Day	⚶
1	0♉08.1
6	2 23.6
11	4 38.4
16	6 52.2
21	9 05.2
26	11 17.1
31	13 27.9

DECLINATION and LATITUDE

Day	☉ Decl	☽ Decl	☽ Lat	☽ 12h Decl	☿ Decl	☿ Lat	♀ Decl	♀ Lat	♂ Decl	♂ Lat	⚳ Decl	⚳ Lat	♃ Decl	♃ Lat	♄ Decl	♄ Lat
1 Tu	15N08	6N23	5S14	3N55	4N02	2S48	27N46	4N42	11N30	2N05	9N16	5S22	17N00	0S49	7S07	2N46
2 W	15 26	1 21	5 11	1S16	4 38	2 46	27 48	4 42	11 24	2 02	9 24	5 20	17 04	0 49	7 06	2 45
3 Th	15 44	3S55	4 49	6 33	5 14	2 44	27 49	4 41	11 17	2 00	9 33	5 19	17 08	0 49	7 04	2 45
4 F	16 01	9 07	4 08	11 35	5 52	2 41	27 49	4 40	11 11	1 58	9 42	5 18	17 12	0 49	7 03	2 45
5 Sa	16 18	13 53	3 09	15 58	6 30	2 38	27 49	4 38	11 04	1 56	9 50	5 17	17 16	0 49	7 01	2 45
6 Su	16 35	17 48	1 55	19 18	7 09	2 34	27 49	4 37	10 57	1 54	9 59	5 16	17 20	0 48	6 60	2 45
7 M	16 52	20 28	0 34	21 16	7 49	2 29	27 48	4 35	10 50	1 52	10 07	5 14	17 23	0 48	6 59	2 45
8 Tu	17 08	21 40	0N49	21 40	8 29	2 24	27 47	4 32	10 42	1 50	10 16	5 13	17 27	0 48	6 57	2 45
9 W	17 24	21 18	2 07	20 35	9 11	2 18	27 45	4 30	10 35	1 48	10 24	5 12	17 31	0 48	6 56	2 45
10 Th	17 40	19 32	3 16	18 13	9 53	2 12	27 42	4 27	10 27	1 46	10 32	5 11	17 34	0 48	6 55	2 45
11 F	17 56	16 39	4 10	14 52	10 35	2 06	27 40	4 23	10 19	1 44	10 41	5 10	17 38	0 48	6 53	2 44
12 Sa	18 11	12 56	4 49	10 52	11 18	1 59	27 36	4 19	10 11	1 42	10 49	5 09	17 42	0 48	6 52	2 44
13 Su	18 26	8 43	5 11	6 29	12 01	1 51	27 32	4 15	10 03	1 40	10 57	5 08	17 46	0 48	6 51	2 44
14 M	18 40	4 13	5 17	1 56	12 45	1 43	27 27	4 10	9 55	1 38	11 05	5 06	17 49	0 48	6 49	2 44
15 Tu	18 55	0N21	5 08	2N36	13 29	1 35	27 22	4 05	9 46	1 36	11 13	5 05	17 53	0 48	6 48	2 44
16 W	19 09	4 48	4 45	6 57	14 13	1 26	27 16	3 59	9 38	1 34	11 21	5 04	17 56	0 48	6 47	2 44
17 Th	19 22	9 01	4 10	10 60	14 57	1 17	27 10	3 53	9 29	1 32	11 29	5 03	17 60	0 48	6 46	2 44
18 F	19 35	12 51	3 24	14 35	15 40	1 07	27 03	3 46	9 20	1 30	11 37	5 02	18 03	0 48	6 45	2 43
19 Sa	19 48	16 10	2 30	17 35	16 24	0 58	26 56	3 39	9 11	1 28	11 45	5 01	18 07	0 48	6 44	2 43
20 Su	20 01	18 49	1 30	19 50	17 07	0 48	26 48	3 31	9 02	1 26	11 53	4 60	18 10	0 47	6 43	2 43
21 M	20 13	20 39	0 26	21 15	17 49	0 37	26 39	3 23	8 53	1 25	12 01	4 59	18 14	0 47	6 42	2 43
22 Tu	20 25	21 36	0S40	21 43	18 31	0 27	26 29	3 14	8 43	1 23	12 09	4 58	18 17	0 47	6 41	2 43
23 W	20 37	21 34	1 45	21 11	19 11	0 16	26 19	3 05	8 34	1 21	12 16	4 57	18 21	0 47	6 40	2 42
24 Th	20 48	20 32	2 45	19 39	19 50	0 06	26 08	2 55	8 24	1 19	12 24	4 55	18 24	0 47	6 39	2 42
25 F	20 59	18 33	3 39	17 12	20 28	0N05	25 57	2 44	8 14	1 18	12 31	4 54	18 28	0 47	6 38	2 42
26 Sa	21 09	15 40	4 23	13 55	21 04	0 15	25 44	2 34	8 04	1 16	12 39	4 53	18 31	0 47	6 37	2 42
27 Su	21 20	12 00	4 56	9 55	21 39	0 26	25 32	2 22	7 54	1 14	12 46	4 52	18 34	0 47	6 36	2 42
28 M	21 29	7 42	5 14	5 22	22 11	0 36	25 18	2 11	7 44	1 13	12 54	4 51	18 38	0 47	6 35	2 41
29 Tu	21 39	2 56	5 17	0 26	22 41	0 46	25 04	1 58	7 33	1 11	13 01	4 50	18 41	0 47	6 35	2 41
30 W	21 48	2S07	5 01	4S40	23 09	0 55	24 49	1 46	7 23	1 09	13 08	4 49	18 44	0 47	6 34	2 41
31 Th	21N56	7S12	4S28	9S40	23N35	1N04	24N33	1N33	7N12	1N08	13N16	4S48	18N47	0S47	6S33	2N41

Day	⚷ Decl	⚷ Lat	♅ Decl	♅ Lat	♆ Decl	♆ Lat	♇ Decl	♇ Lat
1	3S10	5N27	1N58	0S42	10S60	0S34	19S13	3N54
6	3 05	5 28	2 03	0 42	10 58	0 34	19 13	3 54
11	3 01	5 29	2 09	0 42	10 57	0 35	19 13	3 54
16	2 56	5 30	2 14	0 42	10 56	0 35	19 13	3 54
21	2 52	5 32	2 18	0 42	10 55	0 35	19 14	3 54
26	2 49	5 33	2 23	0 42	10 54	0 35	19 14	3 54
31	2S46	5N34	2N27	0S42	10S54	0S35	19S15	3N54

Day	⚴ Decl	⚴ Lat	⚵ Decl	⚵ Lat	⚶ Decl	⚶ Lat	Eris Decl	Eris Lat
1	3N60	6N25	4S30	16N37	6N49	5S01	3S31	13S06
6	4 18	6 08	4 05	16 52	7 36	5 01	3 30	13 06
11	4 36	5 51	3 41	17 05	8 21	5 00	3 29	13 06
16	4 52	5 33	3 20	17 14	9 04	5 00	3 28	13 07
21	5 07	5 15	3 01	17 20	9 46	5 01	3 27	13 07
26	5 20	4 57	2 45	17 23	10 26	5 01	3 27	13 07
31	5N31	4N38	2S32	17N22	11N05	5S01	3S26	13S07

Moon Phenomena

Max/0 Decl
dy hr mn
2 6:12 0 S
8 6:10 21S43
14 22:12 0 N
22 11:14 21N43
29 14:02 0 S

Max/0 Lat
dy hr mn
1 8:17 5S15
7 9:45 0 N
13 21:31 5N17
21 9:21 0 S
28 15:15 5S18

Perigee/Apogee
dy hr m kilometers
6 3:23 p 356958
19 16:13 a 406449

PH dy hr mn
○ 6 3:36 16♏01
☾ 12 21:48 22♒33
● 20 23:48 0♊21
● 20 23:54 A 05'36"
☽ 28 20:17 7♍53

Void of Course Moon

Last Aspect			☽ Ingress		
2 10:59	♀	□	♎	3	2:05
4 18:03	♄	☌	♏	5	2:21
6 12:15	♃	☍	♐	7	1:40
9 1:35	♀	☍	♑	9	2:01
10 19:12	♄	□	♒	11	5:04
13 0:53	♄	△	♓	13	11:43
15 12:00	☉	⚹	♈	15	21:47
17 21:45	♄	☍	♉	18	10:04
20 12:36	♃	☌	♊	20	23:06
22 22:52	♄	△	♋	23	11:32
25 14:35	♃	⚹	♌	25	22:12
27 23:55	♃	□	♍	28	6:07
30 5:51	♃	△	♎	30	10:47

DAILY ASPECTARIAN

1 Tu ☽⚼☿ 2:38 · ☽☍♆ 4:01 · ☽☌♂ 8:28 · ☽∥☿ 10:11 · ☽⊼♅ 10:32 · ☽△⚳ 14:19 · ☽☍⚷ 14:39 · ☽△♇ 15:31 · ☽#⚷ 15:33 · ☿∠♆ 15:38 · ☽∠♄ 16:26 · ☉△☽ 19:35 · ☽∥♅ 21:05

2 W ⚳⚹⚷ 2:43 · ☽⊼☿ 7:28 · ☽△♃ 10:22 · ☽□♀ 10:59 · ☽#♅ 15:16 · ☽⚼⚳ 16:29 · ☽⊻♄ 17:39 · ☽∥⚷ 20:28 · ☉⚼☽ 22:38

3 Th ⚳△♇ 6:28 · ☽#☿ 6:47 · ☽⊼♆ 6:47 · ☽⚼♃ 11:34 · ☽⊻♂ 11:34 · ☽☍♅ 12:59 · ☽∥♄ 14:20 · ☿⚼♂ 14:55 · ☿⊻♃ 14:55 · ☽⊼⚷ 16:49 · ☽□♇ 17:28 · ☽⊼⚳ 17:47

4 F ☉⊼☽ 0:48 · ☽#⚳ 2:50 · ☿⚹♀ 3:02 · ☽⚼♆ 7:04 · ☽∥♆ 9:00 · ☽#♂ 9:45 · ☽∠♂ 12:04 · ☽⊼♃ 12:06 · ☽△♀ 13:17 · ☽☍☿ 14:11 · ☽⚼⚷ 16:56 · ☽☌♄ 18:03

5 Sa ☽△♆ 6:56 · ☽⚹♂ 12:11 · ☽⊼♅ 13:01 · ☽⚼♀ 13:38 · ☉#☽ 15:14 · ☿∠⚷ 16:32 · ☽△⚷ 16:42 · ☽⚹♇ 17:11 · ♂#♆ 18:29 · ☿#♄ 18:44 · ☽☍⚳ 18:50 · ☽#♃ 20:41

6 Su ☿☍♄ 1:09 · ☉☍☽ 3:36 · ☽∥♇ 11:12 · ☽☍♃ 12:15 · ☽⚼♅ 12:44 · ☽⊼♀ 13:48 · ☽∠♇ 16:48 · ☽⊻♄ 17:11 · ☽⊼☿ 19:12

7 M ☽□♆ 6:19 · ☽□♂ 12:19 · ☽△♅ 12:34 · ☽□⚷ 16:14 · ☽⊻♇ 16:35 · ☽∠♄ 16:53 · ☽⊼⚳ 19:37 · ☽⚼☿ 22:01

8 Tu ♃∠♅ 2:10 · ☉⊼☽ 6:33 · ♂⊼♅ 6:46 · ☽⊼♃ 12:54 · ☽☍♀ 14:40 · ☽⚹♄ 16:59 · ☽⚼⚳ 20:35

9 W ☽△☿ 1:35 · ☿ ♉ 5:16 · ☽⚹♆ 6:55 · ☉⚼☽ 8:52 · ☉∥♃ 12:39 · ☽□♅ 13:33 · ☽△♂ 14:00 · ☽⚼♃ 14:02 · ♂∥⚳ 16:03 · ☽⚹⚷ 17:22 · ☽☌♇ 17:35 · ☽△⚳ 22:15

10 Th ☽∥♇ 3:10 · ☽∠♆ 8:12 · ☉△☽ 12:04 · ☉#☽ 15:05 · ☽△♃ 15:58 · ☽⚼♂ 15:59 · ☿∥♂ 16:29 · ☽#♃ 16:46 · ☽⊼♀ 17:47 · ☽∠⚷ 19:02 · ☽□♄ 19:12 · ☿⚹♆ 22:00

11 F ☿∥⚳ 3:53 · ☽⊻♆ 10:21 · ☿#♆ 12:04 · ☽□☿ 12:13 · ☽⚹♅ 17:34 · ☽⊼♂ 18:56 · ☽⚼♀ 20:34 · ♄⚼⚷ 20:59 · ☽⊻⚷ 21:35 · ☽⊻♇ 21:39

12 Sa ☽□⚳ 4:20 · ☽#☿ 8:09 · ☉∠♅ 10:02 · ☽∥♆ 11:37 · ☽#⚳ 11:56 · ♇⚹⚷ 14:15 · ☽#♂ 16:22 · ☽∠♅ 20:57 · ⚳#♆ 21:31 · ☉□☽ 21:48 · ☽□♃ 22:41

13 Su ☽△♀ 0:14 · ☽△♄ 0:53 · ☽∠♇ 1:03 · ☿⊻♅ 4:23 · ☽∥♄ 10:08 · ☉☌♃ 13:24 · ☽☌♆ 17:25 · ☿△♂ 20:55

14 M ☽⊻♅ 1:16 · ☽☍♂ 3:49 · ☿∠♀ 3:57 · ☽⚹☿ 4:52 · ☽⚼♄ 5:05 · ☽⚹♇ 5:22 · ☽☌⚷ 5:30 · ☽∥⚷ 6:37 · ☿△♇ 8:10 · ☉⊻♀ 8:55 · ☿⚹⚷ 9:08 · ☽#♅ 10:36 · ☉⊼♄ 12:57 · ☽⚹⚳ 14:27 · ☉⚼♇ 16:47

15 Tu ☽⚹♃ 9:10 · ☽□♀ 9:55 · ☽∥♅ 9:59 · ☽⊼♄ 10:05 · ☉⚹☽ 12:00 · ☽#⚷ 13:53 · ♀ R 14:34 · ☽∠☿ 15:25 · ☽∠⚳ 20:49

16 W ♂∠♄ 0:07 · ☽⊻♆ 3:49 · ☉#♇ 8:35 · ☽#♄ 11:00 · ☽☌♅ 12:12 · ☽∠♃ 15:31 · ☽⊼♂ 16:11 · ☽□♇ 16:12 · ♂△♇ 16:27 · ☽⊻⚷ 16:32 · ☉∠☽ 20:25 · ♀⊻♃ 20:42 · ♃⊼♄ 22:43

17 Th ☽∥♂ 2:39 · ☽⊻☿ 3:08 · ☽⊻⚳ 3:49 · ⚵ R♏ 6:16 · ♂☍⚷ 6:57 · ☿☌⚳ 8:04 · ☽∠♆ 9:54 · ☽#♆ 11:32 · ☽∥⚳ 15:39 · ☽⚹♀ 21:41 · ☽☍♄ 21:45 · ☽⊻♃ 22:21 · ☽∠⚷ 22:49 · ☽⚼♂ 23:14 · ♃⚼♇ 23:23

18 F ⚴ ♈ 4:19 · ☉⊻☽ 5:21 · ☽⚹♆ 16:19

19 Sa ☽⊻♅ 1:02 · ☽∥☿ 2:28 · ☽∠♀ 3:51 · ☽△♇ 4:47 · ☽⚹⚷ 5:21 · ☽△♂ 6:33 · ☽∥♃ 17:25 · ☽☌⚳ 18:49

20 Su ☽#♇ 4:36 · ☽☌☿ 4:38 · ☽∠♅ 7:40 · ☽⊻♀ 9:58 · ☽⊼♄ 10:28 · ☽⚼♇ 11:17 · ☽☌♃ 12:36 · ☉ ♊ 15:17 · ☉∥☽ 16:17 · ☿∠♅ 22:06 · ☉☌☽ 23:48

21 M ☽□♆ 5:23 · ☿⊻♀ 8:25 · ☿⊼♄ 12:52 · ☽⚹♅ 14:14 · ☿∥♃ 15:39 · ☽⚼♄ 16:47 · ☽⊼♇ 17:40 · ☿⚼♇ 17:47 · ☽□⚷ 18:26 · ☽□♂ 21:18

22 Tu ☿☌♃ 5:59 · ☽⊻⚳ 9:48 · ☽☌♀ 21:25 · ☽△♄ 22:52

23 W ☿#♇ 1:50 · ☽⊻♃ 2:26 · ☽⊻☿ 6:22 · ☽∠⚳ 16:50 · ☉⊻☽ 17:27 · ☽△♆ 17:44 · ☉∥☽ 20:08 · ☉□♆ 20:56

24 Th ☽□♅ 2:31 · ☽☍♇ 5:36 · ☽△⚷ 6:31 · ☽∥☿ 7:17 · ☽∠♃ 8:48 · ☽⚹♂ 11:00 · ☿ ♊ 11:13 · ☽#♇ 16:49 · ☽∠☿ 18:26 · ☽⚼♆ 23:15 · ☽⚹⚳ 23:22

25 F ☽∥♃ 0:47 · ☉∠☽ 1:28 · ☽⊻♀ 7:02 · ☽□♄ 9:46 · ☽⚼⚷ 11:50 · ☽⚹♃ 14:35 · ☽∠♂ 17:04 · ☿□♆ 21:38

26 Sa ☽⊼♆ 4:11 · ☉∥☿ 4:52 · ☽⚹☿ 5:33 · ☉⚹☽ 8:42 · ☽∠♀ 10:53 · ☽△♅ 12:45 · ☽⊼♇ 15:26 · ☽⊼⚷ 16:29 · ☽∥⚳ 19:26 · ☽⊻♂ 22:24

27 Su ☽#♆ 6:27 · ☽□⚳ 10:17 · ☉☌☿ 11:20 · ☽⚹♀ 13:58 · ☽⚼♅ 16:47 · ☽⚹♄ 18:08 · ☽⚼♇ 19:16 · ☿⚹♅ 23:37 · ☽∥♂ 23:52 · ☽□♃ 23:55

28 M ☽#♄ 5:48 · ☿⚼♄ 7:16 · ☽☍♆ 11:47 · ☿⊼♇ 14:06 · ☉⚹♅ 16:05 · ☽⊼♅ 20:00 · ☉□☽ 20:17 · ☿□⚷ 21:00 · ☽∠♄ 21:09 · ☽△♇ 22:18 · ☽☍⚷ 23:26 · ☽□☿ 23:54

29 Tu ☽#⚷ 0:42 · ☽∥♅ 2:29 · ☽☌♂ 6:30 · ☉⚼♄ 7:54 · ☽△⚳ 17:43 · ☽□♀ 17:45 · ♀⊻⚳ 18:02 · ☽⊻♄ 23:21 · ☉⊼♇ 23:57

30 W ☽#♅ 1:31 · ☽∥⚷ 3:08 · ☽△♃ 5:51 · ☽⊼♆ 16:07 · ☉□⚷ 17:06 · ☽⚼⚳ 20:08 · ☽∥♄ 20:56 · ☽☍♅ 23:58

31 Th ☽#♂ 0:02 · ☿□♂ 0:21 · ☽□♇ 1:55 · ☽⊼⚷ 3:07 · ☉△☽ 3:49 · ☽⚼♃ 7:35 · ☽⊻♂ 11:11 · ☽△☿ 12:45 · ☽⚼♆ 17:10 · ☽∥♆ 18:11 · ☽△♀ 18:31 · ☽⊼⚳ 21:46

June 2012

LONGITUDE

Day	Sid.Time	☉	☽	☽ 12 hour	Mean ☊	True ☊	☿	♀	♂	⚳	♃	♄	⚷	♅	♆	♇
	h m s	° ' "	° ' "	° ' "	° '	° '	° '	° '	° '	° '	° '	° '	° '	° '	° '	° '
1 F	16 39 32	10♊54 46	22♎18 22	29♎40 09	4♐55.7	5♐04.5	16♊29.4	18♊50.4	14♍44.4	20♉58.9	27♉31.5	23♎14.7	9♓41.6	7♈49.9	3♓08.8	8♑57.1
2 Sa	16 43 28	11 52 15	7♏05 58	14♏35 00	4 52.5	5 05.1	18 38.9	18R 15.1	15 08.6	21 22.8	27 45.5	23R 12.4	9 42.2	7 51.8	3 09.0	8R 55.8
3 Su	16 47 25	12 49 42	22 06 19	29 38 56	4 49.4	5R 05.5	20 47.2	17 38.8	15 33.2	21 46.6	27 59.4	23 10.2	9 42.8	7 53.7	3 09.0	8 54.5
4 M	16 51 21	13 47 09	7♐11 45	14♐43 38	4 46.2	5 05.7	22 54.0	17 01.8	15 58.0	22 10.4	28 13.4	23 08.1	9 43.3	7 55.6	3R 09.1	8 53.1
5 Tu	16 55 18	14 44 34	22 13 29	29 40 15	4 43.0	5 05.4	24 59.1	16 24.3	16 23.1	22 34.3	28 27.3	23 06.1	9 43.7	7 57.4	3 09.1	8 51.8
6 W	16 59 14	15 41 59	7♑02 59	14♑20 49	4 39.8	5 04.6	27 02.4	15 46.6	16 48.5	22 58.0	28 41.1	23 04.2	9 44.1	7 59.1	3 09.1	8 50.5
7 Th	17 03 11	16 39 23	21 33 05	28 39 13	4 36.7	5 03.3	29 03.7	15 08.9	17 14.1	23 21.8	28 55.0	23 02.4	9 44.4	8 00.9	3 09.0	8 49.1
8 F	17 07 08	17 36 46	5♒38 51	12♒31 48	4 33.5	5 01.9	1♋02.9	14 31.4	17 40.0	23 45.5	29 08.8	23 00.6	9 44.7	8 02.5	3 08.9	8 47.7
9 Sa	17 11 04	18 34 08	19 17 59	25 57 31	4 30.3	5 00.4	2 59.9	13 54.4	18 06.2	24 09.3	29 22.6	22 59.0	9 44.9	8 04.2	3 08.8	8 46.3
10 Su	17 15 01	19 31 30	2♓30 35	8♓57 32	4 27.1	4 59.2	4 54.6	13 18.1	18 32.7	24 32.9	29 36.4	22 57.4	9 45.1	8 05.8	3 08.7	8 44.9
11 M	17 18 57	20 28 51	15 18 44	21 34 41	4 23.9	4D 58.6	6 47.0	12 42.8	18 59.4	24 56.6	29 50.1	22 56.0	9 45.2	8 07.3	3 08.5	8 43.5
12 Tu	17 22 54	21 26 12	27 45 53	3♈52 54	4 20.8	4 58.6	8 37.0	12 08.7	19 26.3	25 20.2	0♊03.8	22 54.6	9R 45.2	8 08.8	3 08.3	8 42.1
13 W	17 26 50	22 23 32	9♈56 17	15 56 37	4 17.6	4 59.3	10 24.6	11 36.0	19 53.5	25 43.8	0 17.4	22 53.3	9 45.2	8 10.3	3 08.0	8 40.6
14 Th	17 30 47	23 20 52	21 54 30	27 50 28	4 14.4	5 00.6	12 09.7	11 04.7	20 20.9	26 07.4	0 31.0	22 52.2	9 45.1	8 11.7	3 07.7	8 39.2
15 F	17 34 43	24 18 11	3♉45 04	9♉38 50	4 11.2	5 02.1	13 52.4	10 35.2	20 48.6	26 30.9	0 44.6	22 51.1	9 45.0	8 13.1	3 07.4	8 37.7
16 Sa	17 38 40	25 15 31	15 32 15	21 25 47	4 08.1	5 03.6	15 32.5	10 07.6	21 16.5	26 54.4	0 58.2	22 50.1	9 44.8	8 14.4	3 07.1	8 36.2
17 Su	17 42 37	26 12 49	27 19 51	3♊14 51	4 04.9	5R 04.5	17 10.2	9 41.9	21 44.6	27 17.9	1 11.7	22 49.3	9 44.6	8 15.7	3 06.7	8 34.8
18 M	17 46 33	27 10 07	9♊11 09	15 09 04	4 01.7	5 04.7	18 45.3	9 18.4	22 13.0	27 41.3	1 25.1	22 48.5	9 44.3	8 16.9	3 06.3	8 33.3
19 Tu	17 50 30	28 07 25	21 08 53	27 10 52	3 58.5	5 03.7	20 17.9	8 57.0	22 41.6	28 04.7	1 38.5	22 47.8	9 43.9	8 18.1	3 05.9	8 31.8
20 W	17 54 26	29 04 43	3♋15 14	9♋22 11	3 55.4	5 01.7	21 47.9	8 37.8	23 10.4	28 28.0	1 51.9	22 47.2	9 43.5	8 19.3	3 05.4	8 30.3
21 Th	17 58 23	0♋02 00	15 31 54	21 44 32	3 52.2	4 58.5	23 15.4	8 21.0	23 39.5	28 51.4	2 05.2	22 46.7	9 43.0	8 20.4	3 04.9	8 28.8
22 F	18 02 19	0 59 16	28 00 14	4♌19 07	3 49.0	4 54.6	24 40.2	8 06.5	24 08.7	29 14.6	2 18.5	22 46.4	9 42.5	8 21.4	3 04.4	8 27.3
23 Sa	18 06 16	1 56 32	10♌41 20	17 06 58	3 45.8	4 50.4	26 02.4	7 54.4	24 38.2	29 37.9	2 31.7	22 46.1	9 41.9	8 22.4	3 03.8	8 25.8
24 Su	18 10 13	2 53 47	23 36 09	0♍09 00	3 42.6	4 46.4	27 21.9	7 44.7	25 07.8	0♊01.1	2 44.9	22 45.9	9 41.3	8 23.4	3 03.2	8 24.3
25 M	18 14 09	3 51 01	6♍45 38	13 26 09	3 39.5	4 43.1	28 38.7	7 37.3	25 37.7	0 24.2	2 58.1	22D 45.8	9 40.6	8 24.3	3 02.6	8 22.8
26 Tu	18 18 06	4 48 15	20 10 39	26 59 12	3 36.3	4 40.9	29 52.7	7 32.4	26 07.8	0 47.3	3 11.1	22 45.8	9 39.8	8 25.1	3 02.0	8 21.3
27 W	18 22 02	5 45 29	3♎51 53	10♎48 42	3 33.1	4D 40.1	1♌03.9	7D 29.7	26 38.1	1 10.4	3 24.1	22 45.9	9 39.0	8 26.0	3 01.3	8 19.8
28 Th	18 25 59	6 42 42	17 49 38	24 54 35	3 29.9	4 40.5	2 12.2	7 29.4	27 08.5	1 33.4	3 37.1	22 46.2	9 38.2	8 26.7	3 00.6	8 18.2
29 F	18 29 55	7 39 54	2♏03 23	9♏15 49	3 26.8	4 41.7	3 17.5	7 31.4	27 39.2	1 56.4	3 50.0	22 46.5	9 37.3	8 27.4	2 59.8	8 16.7
30 Sa	18 33 52	8♋37 06	16 31 30	23 49 59	3♐23.6	4♐43.1	4♌19.7	7♊35.7	28♍10.0	2♊19.3	4♊02.9	22♎46.9	9♓36.3	8♈28.1	2♓59.1	8♑15.2

1st of Month

Julian Day # 2456079.5
Obliquity 23°26'11"
SVP 5♓04'56
GC 27♐00.8
Eris 22♈32.0

Day	⚴
1	3♈26.1
6	4 34.4
11	5 38.9
16	6 39.3
21	7 35.3
26	8 26.3

Day	⚵
1	26♏43.8R
6	25 42.3R
11	24 45.4R
16	23 54.3R
21	23 09.9R
26	22 32.9R

Day	⚶
1	13♉53.9
6	16 03.2
11	18 11.2
16	20 17.9
21	22 23.0
26	24 26.5

DECLINATION and LATITUDE

Day	☉ Decl	☽ Decl	☽ Lat	☽ 12h Decl	☿ Decl	☿ Lat	♀ Decl	♀ Lat	♂ Decl	♂ Lat	⚳ Decl	⚳ Lat	♃ Decl	♃ Lat	♄ Decl	♄ Lat
1 F	22N05	12S01	3S36	14S14	23N57	1N13	24N17	1N20	7N02	1N06	13N23	4S47	18N51	0S47	6S33	2N41
2 Sa	22 13	16 14	2 29	17 59	24 18	1 21	24 01	1 06	6 51	1 05	13 30	4 46	18 54	0 47	6 32	2 40
3 Su	22 20	19 27	1 12	20 34	24 35	1 28	23 44	0 52	6 40	1 03	13 37	4 45	18 57	0 47	6 31	2 40
4 M	22 27	21 19	0N12	21 41	24 50	1 35	23 26	0 38	6 29	1 02	13 44	4 44	19 00	0 47	6 31	2 40
5 Tu	22 34	21 39	1 34	21 14	25 01	1 41	23 09	0 24	6 18	0 60	13 51	4 43	19 03	0 47	6 30	2 40
6 W	22 40	20 27	2 48	19 20	25 11	1 46	22 51	0 10	6 06	0 58	13 58	4 42	19 06	0 47	6 30	2 39
7 Th	22 46	17 55	3 50	16 15	25 17	1 51	22 32	0S04	5 55	0 57	14 05	4 41	19 09	0 47	6 29	2 39
8 F	22 52	14 23	4 36	12 21	25 21	1 55	22 14	0 18	5 44	0 56	14 11	4 40	19 12	0 47	6 29	2 39
9 Sa	22 57	10 12	5 05	7 57	25 22	1 58	21 56	0 32	5 32	0 54	14 18	4 39	19 15	0 47	6 29	2 39
10 Su	23 01	5 39	5 17	3 19	25 21	2 00	21 38	0 46	5 20	0 53	14 25	4 38	19 18	0 47	6 28	2 39
11 M	23 06	0 60	5 12	1N19	25 17	2 02	21 20	1 00	5 08	0 51	14 31	4 37	19 21	0 46	6 28	2 38
12 Tu	23 10	3N35	4 52	5 47	25 12	2 03	21 02	1 14	4 57	0 50	14 38	4 36	19 24	0 46	6 28	2 38
13 W	23 13	7 55	4 20	9 57	25 04	2 03	20 44	1 27	4 45	0 48	14 44	4 35	19 27	0 46	6 27	2 38
14 Th	23 16	11 53	3 37	13 41	24 54	2 02	20 28	1 40	4 33	0 47	14 51	4 34	19 30	0 46	6 27	2 38
15 F	23 19	15 21	2 45	16 51	24 43	2 01	20 11	1 52	4 20	0 46	14 57	4 33	19 33	0 46	6 27	2 37
16 Sa	23 21	18 11	1 46	19 19	24 30	1 59	19 55	2 04	4 08	0 44	15 03	4 32	19 36	0 46	6 27	2 37
17 Su	23 23	20 15	0 43	20 58	24 15	1 56	19 40	2 16	3 56	0 43	15 10	4 31	19 38	0 46	6 27	2 37
18 M	23 24	21 27	0S23	21 42	23 59	1 52	19 25	2 27	3 43	0 42	15 16	4 30	19 41	0 46	6 27	2 37
19 Tu	23 25	21 41	1 28	21 26	23 41	1 48	19 12	2 38	3 31	0 40	15 22	4 29	19 44	0 46	6 27	2 36
20 W	23 26	20 55	2 29	20 09	23 22	1 43	18 59	2 48	3 18	0 39	15 28	4 27	19 47	0 46	6 27	2 36
21 Th	23 26	19 09	3 25	17 55	23 02	1 38	18 46	2 57	3 06	0 38	15 34	4 26	19 49	0 46	6 27	2 36
22 F	23 26	16 27	4 11	14 48	22 41	1 31	18 35	3 07	2 53	0 36	15 40	4 25	19 52	0 46	6 27	2 35
23 Sa	23 25	12 57	4 46	10 57	22 19	1 25	18 25	3 15	2 40	0 35	15 46	4 24	19 55	0 46	6 27	2 35
24 Su	23 24	8 48	5 08	6 32	21 57	1 17	18 15	3 24	2 27	0 34	15 51	4 23	19 57	0 46	6 27	2 35
25 M	23 23	4 11	5 15	1 44	21 34	1 09	18 06	3 31	2 14	0 33	15 57	4 22	19 60	0 46	6 27	2 35
26 Tu	23 21	0S44	5 02	3S14	21 10	1 01	17 58	3 38	2 01	0 31	16 03	4 21	20 02	0 46	6 28	2 34
27 W	23 19	5 43	4 34	8 10	20 45	0 52	17 51	3 45	1 48	0 30	16 08	4 20	20 05	0 46	6 28	2 34
28 Th	23 16	10 31	3 49	12 45	20 21	0 42	17 45	3 51	1 35	0 29	16 14	4 19	20 07	0 46	6 28	2 34
29 F	23 13	14 50	2 49	16 42	19 56	0 32	17 40	3 57	1 21	0 28	16 19	4 18	20 10	0 46	6 29	2 34
30 Sa	23N09	18S20	1S38	19S41	19N31	0N21	17N35	4S03	1N08	0N27	16N25	4S17	20N12	0S46	6S29	2N33

Day	⚷ Decl	⚷ Lat	♅ Decl	♅ Lat	♆ Decl	♆ Lat	♇ Decl	♇ Lat
1	2S46	5N35	2N28	0S42	10S54	0S35	19S15	3N5
6	2 44	5 36	2 31	0 42	10 54	0 35	19 16	3 5
11	2 42	5 37	2 34	0 43	10 54	0 36	19 16	3 5
16	2 41	5 39	2 37	0 43	10 55	0 36	19 17	3 5
21	2 40	5 40	2 39	0 43	10 56	0 36	19 18	3 5
26	2 40	5 41	2 41	0 43	10 57	0 36	19 19	3 5

Day	⚴ Decl	⚴ Lat	⚵ Decl	⚵ Lat	⚶ Decl	⚶ Lat	Eris Decl	Eris Lat
1	5N33	4N34	2S30	17N22	11N13	5S01	3S26	13S0
6	5 42	4 14	2 21	17 17	11 49	5 02	3 26	13 0
11	5 48	3 53	2 16	17 10	12 24	5 02	3 25	13 0
16	5 52	3 31	2 15	16 60	12 57	5 03	3 25	13 0
21	5 53	3 08	2 17	16 47	13 28	5 04	3 25	13 0
26	5 51	2 43	2 22	16 33	13 57	5 05	3 25	13

Moon Phenomena

Max/0 Decl
dy hr mn
4 17:11 21S43
11 5:09 0 N
18 17:43 21N43
25 20:26 0 S

Perigee/Apogee
dy hr m kilometers
3 13:19 p 358489
16 1:23 a 405787

Max/0 Lat
dy hr mn
3 20:39 0 N
10 4:32 5N17
17 15:42 0 S
24 20:23 5S13

PH dy hr mn
○ 4 11:13 14♐14
● 4 11:04 P 0.370
☾ 11 10:42 20♓54
● 19 15:03 28♊43
☽ 27 3:31 5♎54

Void of Course Moon

Last Aspect	☽ Ingress
1 1:32 ♄ ☌	♏ 1 12:32
3 9:31 ♃ ☍	♐ 3 12:3
5 5:09 ☿ ☍	♑ 5 12:3
7 12:39 ♃ △	♒ 7 14:1
9 18:34 ♃ □	♓ 9 19:2
11 10:42 ☉ □	♈ 12 4:2
14 3:10 ☉ ⚹	♉ 14 16:2
16 12:10 ♂ △	♊ 17 5:2
19 15:03 ☉ ☌	♋ 19 17:3
21 16:49 ☿ ☌	♌ 22 3:4
23 22:27 ♄ ⚹	♍ 24 11:4
26 10:54 ♂ ☌	♎ 26 17:1
28 8:23 ♄ ☌	♏ 28 20:3
30 19:47 ♂ ⚹	♐ 30 22:0

DAILY ASPECTARIAN

1 F
☽☌♄ 1:32
☽⚼⚷ 3:54
☉⚼☽ 6:18
☽⋕⚳ 7:29
☽⚻♃ 8:39
☽∠♂ 12:27
☿∥♀ 12:51
☽⚼☿ 17:30
☽△♆ 17:38
☽⚼♀ 18:02
☿☌♀ 20:32

2 Sa
☽⚻♅ 1:14
☽⚹♇ 2:56
☽△⚷ 4:11
☉⚻☽ 8:11
☽⚹♂ 13:15
☽⚻♀ 17:10
☽⋕♃ 19:33
☽⚻☿ 21:33
☽∥♇ 22:17
☽☍⚳ 23:28

3 Su
☽⚼♅ 1:16
☽⚺♄ 1:41
☽∠♇ 2:52
☽☍♃ 9:31
☿⚺⚳ 13:49
☽□♆ 17:34
♂⋕♄ 19:25

4 M
☽△♅ 1:10
☽∠♄ 1:29
☿△♄ 2:39
☽⚺♇ 2:41
☽□⚷ 4:01
☉☍☽ 11:13
☽□♂ 14:23
☽☍♀ 15:03
♆R 21:05

5 Tu
♀□♂ 0:29
☽⚻⚳ 0:34
☽⚹♄ 1:24
☽☍☿ 5:09
☽⚻♃ 10:12
☽⚹♆ 17:39

6 W
☉☌♀ 1:10
⚳∠♅ 1:11
☽□♅ 1:32
☽⚼⚳ 1:33
☽☌♇ 2:56
☽⚹⚷ 4:24
⚳⚻♄ 5:45
☉∥♀ 10:23
☽⚼♃ 11:05
☽∥♇ 12:37
☽⚻♀ 13:46
☽⋕♃ 13:48
☉⚻☽ 15:15
☽△♂ 16:34
☽∠♆ 18:19
☿⚺♃ 22:02

7 Th
☽□♄ 2:30
☽△⚳ 3:08
☽∠⚷ 5:22
☿ ♋ 11:17
☽△♃ 12:39
☽⚼♀ 13:56
☽⚻☿ 14:48
☉⚼☽ 18:23
☽⚼♂ 18:42
☽⚺♆ 19:42

8 F
☽⋕⚳ 1:10
⚳⚼♇ 2:04
☉□♂ 2:31
☽⚹♅ 4:10
☽⚺♇ 5:27
☽⚺⚷ 7:07
☽△♀ 14:50
☽∥♆ 20:09
☽⚼☿ 21:17
☽⚻♂ 21:48
☉△☽ 22:36

9 Sa
☿△♆ 1:50
♃⋕♇ 6:21
☽△♄ 6:36
☽∠♅ 6:47
☽∠♇ 8:01
☽□⚳ 9:00
☽□♃ 18:34
☽∥♄ 19:45

10 Su
☽☌♆ 1:10
☽⋕♂ 1:41
☽△☿ 5:12
☽⚼♄ 10:06
☽⚺♅ 10:24
☽⚹♇ 11:35
☽☌⚷ 13:29
☽∥⚷ 15:13
☽⋕♅ 15:54
☽□♀ 19:17

11 M
☽☍♂ 7:17
☉□☽ 10:42
☽⚻♄ 14:35
♃ ♊ 17:23
☿□♅ 17:42
☽∥♅ 18:39
☽⚹⚳ 19:07
☽⋕⚷ 19:17

12 Tu
☿☍♇ 1:06
☽⚹♃ 4:35
⚷R 5:13
☽∥♂ 7:03
☽⚺♆ 10:32
☿△⚷ 15:09
☽⋕♄ 15:44
☽☌♅ 20:29
☽□♇ 21:30
☽⚺⚷ 23:38

13 W
☽□☿ 1:06
☽∠⚳ 1:38
☽⚹♀ 3:10
☿∠⚳ 5:35
☽∠♃ 10:54
☉△♄ 12:14
☿⚺♀ 12:28
☽∠♆ 16:23
☽⋕♆ 17:51
☽⚻♂ 20:44

14 Th
☽☍♄ 1:56
☉⚹☽ 3:10
☽∠⚷ 5:45
☽∠♀ 8:05
☽⚺⚳ 8:49
☽⚺♃ 17:46
☽∥⚳ 20:57
☽⚹♆ 22:43

15 F
☽⚼♂ 4:22
☽⚺♅ 9:06
☽△♇ 9:54
☽⚹⚷ 12:12
☉∠☽ 12:18
☽⚺♀ 13:23

16 Sa
☽⚹☿ 0:01
☿∠♃ 7:14
☽⋕♇ 11:40
☽△♂ 12:10
☽⚻♄ 14:51
☽∥♃ 15:39
☽∠♅ 15:43
☽⚼♇ 16:23
☽∥♀ 17:03
♀□⚷ 21:24
☉⚺☽ 21:32
☽☌⚳ 23:56

17 Su
♀∥♃ 2:03
☽☌♃ 7:59
☽∠☿ 11:21
☽□♆ 11:43
☿⚼♆ 14:07
☽⚼♄ 21:13
☽⚹♅ 22:10
☽⚻♇ 22:44

18 M
☽☌♀ 0:14
☽□⚷ 1:07
♀⋕♇ 13:17
☽⚺☿ 22:03
☉⚺⚳ 22:04

19 Tu
☽□♂ 3:12
☽△♄ 3:17
♂⚺♄ 5:04
☽⚺⚳ 14:14
☉☌☽ 15:03
☉∥☿ 19:22
☽⚺♃ 21:13
☽△♆ 23:41

20 W
☽□♅ 9:58
☽☍♇ 10:17
☽⚺♀ 10:19
♀⚻♇ 11:19
☽△⚷ 12:41
☿□♄ 16:06
☽∥♃ 16:25
☽∠⚳ 20:38
☽⋕♇ 22:18
☉ ♋ 23:10

21 Th
♀⚹♅ 0:56
☿∠♀ 1:20
☽∠♃ 3:04
☽∥♀ 4:11
☽⚼♆ 4:56
☿⚹♂ 10:16
☽□♄ 13:59
☽∠♀ 14:48
☽⚹♂ 16:19
☽☌☿ 16:49
☽⚼⚷ 17:42

22 F
☿⚼⚷ 0:40
☽⚹⚳ 2:26
☽∥⚳ 5:44
☉⚺☽ 6:09
☽⚹♃ 8:20
☽⚻♆ 9:38
☽⚹♀ 18:51
☽△♅ 19:39
☽⚻♇ 19:46
☽∠♂ 21:57
☽⚻⚷ 22:09
♂⋕⚷ 23:54

23 Sa
♂∥♅ 0:30
☽⋕♆ 12:05
☉∠☽ 12:36
☉⚺♃ 19:11
♀⚼♄ 20:36
☽⚹♄ 22:27
♅⋕⚷ 22:39
⚳ ♊ 22:53
☽⚼♅ 23:36
☽⚼♇ 23:38

24 Su
☽⚺♂ 2:55
☉△♆ 3:55
☽⚺☿ 7:40
♅□♇ 9:13
☽□⚳ 12:07
☽⋕♄ 12:26
☽□♃ 17:01
☽☍♆ 17:16
☉⚹☽ 18:19

25 M
☽□♀ 1:33
☽∠♄ 1:49
☽△♇ 2:55
☽⚻♅ 2:58
☽☍⚷ 5:15
☽∥♅ 7:25
☽⋕⚷ 7:27
♃□♆ 7:57
♄D 8:01
☽∥♂ 10:01
☽∠☿ 13:38

26 Tu
☿ ♌ 2:25
☽⚺♄ 4:34
☽⋕♂ 5:53
☽∥⚷ 9:16
☽⋕♅ 9:19
☽☌♂ 10:54
☽⚹☿ 18:41
☽△⚳ 19:11
☽⚻♆ 22:32
☽△♃ 23:11

27 W
☿⚹⚳ 3:22
☉□☽ 3:31
☽∥♄ 3:38
☽△♀ 6:17
☽□♇ 7:43
☽☍♅ 7:55
☽⚻⚷ 10:00
♀D 15:08
☽⚼⚳ 21:47

28 Th
☽⚼♆ 0:19
☽⚼♃ 1:22
☽∥♆ 2:19
☽⚼♀ 7:55
☽☌♄ 8:23
☽⚼⚷ 11:32
☿∥♃ 11:59
☽⚺♂ 16:21
☿⚻♆ 17:29
☉⚺♀ 20:15
☽⚻⚳ 23:48

29 F
☽△♆ 1:34
☽□☿ 2:14
☽⚻♃ 3:01
☽⚻♀ 9:09
☽⋕⚳ 9:40
☉△☽ 10:00
☽⚹♇ 10:21
☽⚻♅ 10:40
☽△⚷ 12:35
☉☍♇ 15:03
☿⚹♃ 15:39
☽∠♂ 18:15
☽⋕♀ 18:20
☉□♅ 20:11

30 Sa
☽∥♇ 8:35
☽⋕☿ 8:50
☽⚺♄ 10:17
☿⋕♇ 10:21
☽∠♇ 11:02
☽⚼♅ 11:25
☉⚼☽ 12:27
☽⋕♃ 17:54
☽⚹♂ 19:47

July 2012

LONGITUDE

Day	Sid.Time	☉	☽	☽ 12 hour	Mean ☊	True ☊	☿	♀	♂	⚳	♃	♄	⚷	♅	♆	♇
	h m s	° ' "	° ' "	° ' "	° '	° '	° '	° '	° '	° '	° '	° '	° '	° '	° '	° '
1 Su	18 37 48	9♋34 18	1♐10 44	8♐33 04	3♐20.4	4♐43.9	5♌18.9	7♊42.1	28♍41.0	2♊42.2	4♊15.7	22♎47.4	9♓35.3	8♈28.7	2♓58.3	8♑13.7
2 M	18 41 45	10 31 29	15 56 14	23 19 24	3 17.2	4R 43.5	6 14.7	7 50.7	29 12.2	3 05.0	4 28.4	22 48.0	9R 34.2	8 29.3	2R 57.5	8R 12.2
3 Tu	18 45 42	11 28 40	0♑41 41	8♑02 10	3 14.1	4 41.5	7 07.3	8 01.5	29 43.5	3 27.8	4 41.1	22 48.7	9 33.1	8 29.8	2 56.6	8 10.6
4 W	18 49 38	12 25 51	15 19 57	22 34 11	3 10.9	4 37.7	7 56.4	8 14.3	0♎15.1	3 50.5	4 53.7	22 49.6	9 31.9	8 30.3	2 55.8	8 09.1
5 Th	18 53 35	13 23 02	29 44 05	6♒48 59	3 07.7	4 32.5	8 41.9	8 29.1	0 46.8	4 13.2	5 06.3	22 50.5	9 30.7	8 30.8	2 54.9	8 07.6
6 F	18 57 31	14 20 13	13♒48 19	20 41 42	3 04.5	4 26.5	9 23.7	8 45.8	1 18.6	4 35.8	5 18.8	22 51.5	9 29.4	8 31.1	2 53.9	8 06.1
7 Sa	19 01 28	15 17 24	27 28 52	4♓09 42	3 01.4	4 20.3	10 01.7	9 04.5	1 50.7	4 58.4	5 31.2	22 52.6	9 28.1	8 31.5	2 53.0	8 04.6
8 Su	19 05 24	16 14 35	10♓44 14	17 12 39	2 58.2	4 14.9	10 35.8	9 24.9	2 22.9	5 20.9	5 43.5	22 53.8	9 26.7	8 31.8	2 52.0	8 03.1
9 M	19 09 21	17 11 47	23 35 12	29 52 18	2 55.0	4 10.7	11 05.7	9 47.1	2 55.2	5 43.4	5 55.8	22 55.1	9 25.2	8 32.0	2 51.0	8 01.6
10 Tu	19 13 17	18 08 59	6♈04 24	12♈12 01	2 51.8	4 08.1	11 31.4	10 11.1	3 27.8	6 05.8	6 08.0	22 56.5	9 23.8	8 32.2	2 50.0	8 00.1
11 W	19 17 14	19 06 12	18 15 46	24 16 15	2 48.6	4D 07.3	11 52.8	10 36.7	4 00.4	6 28.2	6 20.2	22 58.0	9 22.2	8 32.3	2 48.9	7 58.6
12 Th	19 21 11	20 03 25	0♉14 06	6♉09 58	2 45.5	4 07.8	12 09.7	11 03.8	4 33.3	6 50.4	6 32.3	22 59.6	9 20.7	8 32.4	2 47.9	7 57.1
13 F	19 25 07	21 00 38	12 04 30	17 58 21	2 42.3	4 09.0	12 22.0	11 32.5	5 06.3	7 12.7	6 44.3	23 01.3	9 19.0	8R 32.5	2 46.8	7 55.7
14 Sa	19 29 04	21 57 52	23 52 07	29 46 25	2 39.1	4R 10.3	12 29.7	12 02.7	5 39.4	7 34.9	6 56.2	23 03.0	9 17.4	8 32.5	2 45.6	7 54.2
15 Su	19 33 00	22 55 07	5♊41 47	11♊38 44	2 35.9	4 10.7	12R 32.5	12 34.2	6 12.8	7 57.0	7 08.0	23 04.9	9 15.6	8 32.4	2 44.5	7 52.7
16 M	19 36 57	23 52 22	17 37 45	23 39 16	2 32.8	4 09.7	12 30.6	13 07.2	6 46.2	8 19.0	7 19.8	23 06.9	9 13.9	8 32.3	2 43.3	7 51.3
17 Tu	19 40 53	24 49 38	29 43 36	5♋51 06	2 29.6	4 06.6	12 23.8	13 41.4	7 19.8	8 41.0	7 31.5	23 09.0	9 12.1	8 32.2	2 42.1	7 49.8
18 W	19 44 50	25 46 54	12♋01 59	18 16 26	2 26.4	4 01.4	12 12.2	14 16.9	7 53.6	9 02.9	7 43.1	23 11.1	9 10.2	8 32.0	2 40.9	7 48.4
19 Th	19 48 46	26 44 10	24 34 32	0♌56 22	2 23.2	3 54.1	11 55.9	14 53.6	8 27.5	9 24.7	7 54.6	23 13.4	9 08.3	8 31.7	2 39.7	7 47.0
20 F	19 52 43	27 41 27	7♌21 55	13 51 07	2 20.1	3 45.3	11 35.0	15 31.5	9 01.6	9 46.5	8 06.1	23 15.7	9 06.4	8 31.4	2 38.4	7 45.6
21 Sa	19 56 40	28 38 45	20 23 52	27 00 02	2 16.9	3 35.9	11 09.8	16 10.4	9 35.8	10 08.2	8 17.4	23 18.2	9 04.4	8 31.1	2 37.2	7 44.2
22 Su	20 00 36	29 36 03	3♍39 26	10♍21 56	2 13.7	3 26.8	10 40.5	16 50.5	10 10.1	10 29.8	8 28.7	23 20.7	9 02.3	8 30.7	2 35.9	7 42.8
23 M	20 04 33	0♌33 21	17 07 19	23 55 26	2 10.5	3 19.0	10 07.4	17 31.6	10 44.6	10 51.4	8 39.9	23 23.3	9 00.3	8 30.2	2 34.5	7 41.4
24 Tu	20 08 29	1 30 40	0♎46 07	7♎39 15	2 07.3	3 13.1	9 31.0	18 13.7	11 19.2	11 12.8	8 51.0	23 26.1	8 58.2	8 29.8	2 33.2	7 40.0
25 W	20 12 26	2 27 58	14 34 42	21 32 21	2 04.2	3 09.6	8 51.9	18 56.7	11 54.0	11 34.2	9 02.0	23 28.9	8 56.0	8 29.2	2 31.9	7 38.7
26 Th	20 16 22	3 25 18	28 32 07	5♏33 54	2 01.0	3D 08.2	8 10.5	19 40.6	12 28.9	11 55.5	9 12.8	23 31.8	8 53.8	8 28.6	2 30.5	7 37.4
27 F	20 20 19	4 22 37	12♏37 38	19 43 09	1 57.8	3 08.4	7 27.7	20 25.5	13 03.9	12 16.8	9 23.6	23 34.7	8 51.6	8 28.0	2 29.1	7 36.0
28 Sa	20 24 15	5 19 58	26 50 20	3♐58 56	1 54.6	3R 08.9	6 44.1	21 11.2	13 39.1	12 37.9	9 34.4	23 37.8	8 49.3	8 27.3	2 27.7	7 34.7
29 Su	20 28 12	6 17 18	11♐08 43	18 19 19	1 51.5	3 08.8	6 00.4	21 57.7	14 14.4	12 59.0	9 45.0	23 41.0	8 47.1	8 26.6	2 26.3	7 33.4
30 M	20 32 09	7 14 39	25 30 20	2♑41 16	1 48.3	3 07.0	5 17.5	22 45.0	14 49.8	13 19.9	9 55.5	23 44.2	8 44.7	8 25.9	2 24.8	7 32.2
31 Tu	20 36 05	8♌12 01	9♑51 33	17 00 36	1♐45.1	3♐02.7	4♌36.1	23♊33.1	15♎25.3	13♊40.8	10♊05.9	23♎47.6	8♓42.4	8♈25.1	2♓23.4	7♑30.9

1st of Month

Julian Day #
2456109.5
Obliquity
23°26'11"
SVP 5♓04'51"
GC 27♐00.8
Eris 22♈41.8

Day	⚴
1	9♈12.0
6	9 52.0
11	10 25.8
16	10 53.0
21	11 12.9
26	11 25.1
31	11 29.2R

Day	⚵
1	22♏03.8R
6	21 42.7R
11	21 29.8R
16	21 25.0R
21	21 28.3
26	21 39.3
31	21 57.9

Day	⚶
1	26♉28.2
6	28 28.1
11	0♊25.9
16	2 21.6
21	4 14.8
26	6 05.5
31	7 53.3

DECLINATION and LATITUDE

Day	☉ Decl	☽ Decl	☽ Lat	☽ 12h Decl	☿ Decl	☿ Lat	♀ Decl	♀ Lat	♂ Decl	♂ Lat	⚳ Decl	⚳ Lat	♃ Decl	♃ Lat	♄ Decl	♄ Lat
1 Su	23N05	20S43	0S19	21S23	19N06	0N10	17N31	4S07	0N55	0N25	16N30	4S16	20N14	0S46	6S29	2N33
2 M	23 01	21 41	1N01	21 36	18 40	0S02	17 28	4 12	0 41	0 24	16 36	4 15	20 17	0 46	6 30	2 33
3 Tu	22 56	21 09	2 17	20 20	18 16	0 14	17 26	4 16	0 28	0 23	16 41	4 14	20 19	0 46	6 30	2 33
4 W	22 51	19 11	3 23	17 45	17 51	0 27	17 24	4 20	0 14	0 22	16 46	4 13	20 21	0 46	6 31	2 32
5 Th	22 46	16 02	4 15	14 07	17 27	0 40	17 23	4 23	0 00	0 21	16 51	4 12	20 24	0 46	6 32	2 32
6 F	22 40	12 02	4 51	9 49	17 03	0 53	17 23	4 26	0S13	0 20	16 56	4 11	20 26	0 46	6 32	2 32
7 Sa	22 34	7 31	5 08	5 10	16 39	1 07	17 23	4 28	0 27	0 18	17 01	4 10	20 28	0 46	6 33	2 32
8 Su	22 27	2 47	5 08	0 24	16 17	1 21	17 24	4 30	0 41	0 17	17 06	4 09	20 30	0 46	6 34	2 31
9 M	22 20	1N56	4 53	4N14	15 55	1 35	17 26	4 32	0 55	0 16	17 11	4 08	20 32	0 46	6 34	2 31
10 Tu	22 12	6 27	4 24	8 34	15 34	1 50	17 27	4 34	1 09	0 15	17 16	4 07	20 34	0 46	6 35	2 31
11 W	22 05	10 36	3 43	12 30	15 14	2 04	17 30	4 35	1 23	0 14	17 20	4 06	20 36	0 46	6 36	2 30
12 Th	21 56	14 15	2 53	15 52	14 55	2 19	17 33	4 36	1 37	0 13	17 25	4 05	20 38	0 46	6 37	2 30
13 F	21 48	17 19	1 57	18 34	14 38	2 33	17 36	4 37	1 51	0 12	17 30	4 04	20 40	0 46	6 38	2 30
14 Sa	21 39	19 38	0 56	20 29	14 22	2 48	17 39	4 37	2 05	0 11	17 34	4 03	20 42	0 46	6 38	2 30
15 Su	21 29	21 07	0S08	21 31	14 07	3 02	17 43	4 37	2 19	0 10	17 39	4 02	20 44	0 46	6 39	2 29
16 M	21 20	21 40	1 12	21 34	13 54	3 17	17 47	4 37	2 33	0 09	17 43	4 01	20 46	0 46	6 40	2 29
17 Tu	21 10	21 13	2 13	20 36	13 43	3 30	17 52	4 37	2 47	0 08	17 48	4 00	20 48	0 46	6 41	2 29
18 W	20 59	19 45	3 09	18 39	13 33	3 44	17 56	4 36	3 02	0 07	17 52	3 59	20 50	0 46	6 42	2 28
19 Th	20 48	17 19	3 57	15 13	13 26	3 56	18 01	4 35	3 16	0 06	17 56	3 58	20 52	0 46	6 43	2 28
20 F	20 37	14 00	4 34	12 04	13 20	4 08	18 06	4 34	3 30	0 05	18 00	3 57	20 54	0 46	6 45	2 28
21 Sa	20 26	9 59	4 58	7 45	13 16	4 19	18 11	4 33	3 45	0 04	18 05	3 56	20 56	0 46	6 46	2 28
22 Su	20 14	5 25	5 05	2 60	13 15	4 29	18 17	4 32	3 59	0 03	18 09	3 55	20 57	0 46	6 47	2 28
23 M	20 02	0 32	4 57	1S58	13 15	4 37	18 22	4 30	4 13	0 02	18 13	3 54	20 59	0 46	6 48	2 27
24 Tu	19 49	4S27	4 31	6 54	13 17	4 45	18 28	4 28	4 28	0 01	18 17	3 53	21 01	0 46	6 49	2 27
25 W	19 36	9 16	3 50	11 32	13 22	4 51	18 33	4 26	4 42	0S00	18 20	3 52	21 02	0 46	6 51	2 27
26 Th	19 23	13 40	2 54	15 36	13 28	4 55	18 38	4 24	4 57	0 01	18 24	3 51	21 04	0 46	6 52	2 27
27 F	19 10	17 20	1 47	18 48	13 36	4 57	18 44	4 22	5 11	0 02	18 28	3 50	21 06	0 46	6 53	2 26
28 Sa	18 56	19 60	0 34	20 52	13 46	4 58	18 49	4 20	5 26	0 03	18 32	3 49	21 07	0 46	6 55	2 26
29 Su	18 42	21 24	0N43	21 36	13 58	4 57	18 55	4 17	5 40	0 04	18 35	3 47	21 09	0 46	6 56	2 26
30 M	18 28	21 25	1 56	20 54	14 11	4 55	19 00	4 15	5 55	0 05	18 39	3 46	21 10	0 46	6 57	2 26
31 Tu	18N13	20S02	3N03	18S51	14N25	4S50	19N05	4S12	6S10	0S06	18N43	3S45	21N12	0S46	6S59	2N25

Day	⚷ Decl	⚷ Lat	♅ Decl	♅ Lat	♆ Decl	♆ Lat	♇ Decl	♇ Lat
1	2S41	5N43	2N42	0S43	10S58	0S36	19S20	3N51
6	2 42	5 44	2 43	0 43	11 00	0 36	19 21	3 51
11	2 43	5 45	2 43	0 44	11 02	0 36	19 22	3 50
16	2 46	5 46	2 43	0 44	11 04	0 37	19 23	3 49
21	2 48	5 47	2 42	0 44	11 06	0 37	19 24	3 49
26	2 51	5 48	2 41	0 44	11 09	0 37	19 25	3 48
31	2S55	5N48	2N40	0S44	11S12	0S37	19S27	3N47

Day	⚴ Decl	⚴ Lat	⚵ Decl	⚵ Lat	⚶ Decl	⚶ Lat	Eris Decl	Eris Lat
1	5N45	2N18	2S31	16N17	14N24	5S06	3S25	13S10
6	5 36	1 51	2 42	16 00	14 49	5 07	3 25	13 11
11	5 23	1 22	2 56	15 42	15 12	5 08	3 26	13 11
16	5 06	0 52	3 13	15 24	15 34	5 10	3 26	13 12
21	4 44	0 19	3 32	15 05	15 53	5 12	3 26	13 12
26	4 17	0S15	3 53	14 47	16 11	5 13	3 27	13 13
31	3N46	0S51	4S15	14N28	16N26	5S15	3S28	13S13

Moon Phenomena

Max/0 Decl

dy	hr mn	
2	3:20	21S42
8	14:05	0 N
16	1:12	21N40
23	2:33	0 S
29	12:16	21S35

Max/0 Lat

dy	hr mn	
1	5:47	0 N
7	12:14	5N10
14	20:55	0 S
21	23:44	5S05
28	10:36	0 N

Perigee/Apogee

dy	hr m		kilometers
1	18:11	p	362368
13	16:51	a	404778
29	8:27	p	367316

PH	dy	hr mn	
○	3	18:53	12♑14
☾	11	1:49	19♈11
●	19	4:25	26♋55
☽	26	8:57	3♏47

Void of Course Moon

Last Aspect			☽ Ingress		
2 22:22	♂	□	♑	2	22:52
4 12:26	♄	□	♒	5	0:27
6 15:50	♄	△	♓	7	4:30
8 11:01	☉	△	♈	9	12:15
11 9:24	♄	☍	♉	11	23:32
13 19:47	☉	⚹	♊	14	12:28
16 10:58	♄	△	♋	17	0:32
19 4:25	☉	☌	♌	19	10:14
21 5:19	♄	⚹	♍	21	17:25
23 0:45	♀	□	♎	23	22:39
25 15:23	♄	☌	♏	26	2:30
26 15:39	☿	□	♐	28	5:19
29 21:02	♄	⚹	♑	30	7:30

DAILY ASPECTARIAN

1 Su
☉△⚷ 0:24
☽☍⚳ 2:33
☽□♆ 2:55
☽☍♃ 5:06
☽△☿ 7:12
☽☍♀ 10:43
☽∠♄ 10:46
☽⊻♇ 11:27
☽△♅ 11:53
☽□⚷ 13:40
☉⊼☽ 14:36
⚳□♆ 16:20
♀⚼♄ 16:32

2 M
☽⚼☿ 9:11
☽⚹♄ 11:10
☽□♂ 22:22

3 Tu
☽⚹♆ 3:40
☽⊼⚳ 4:38
☽⊼♃ 6:37
☽⊼☿ 11:08
☽⋕♃ 12:00
☽⊼♀ 12:09
☽☌♇ 12:13
♂ ♎ 12:33
☽□♅ 12:46
☽⚹⚷ 14:28
♀⊼♇ 15:46
☉☍☽ 18:53
☽∥♇ 22:34

4 W
☽∠♆ 4:17
☽⚼⚳ 5:58
☿⊼♇ 6:20
☽⚼♃ 7:40
☽□♄ 12:26
☽⋕☿ 12:51
☽⚼♀ 13:20
☿⚹♀ 13:27
☽⋕♀ 14:36
☽∠⚷ 15:15
☿△♅ 17:54
☽⋕⚳ 18:38

5 Th
☽△♂ 1:50
♀⚹♅ 2:37
☿∥♀ 3:14
☽⊻♆ 5:22
☽△⚳ 7:48
☽△♃ 9:13
☽⊻♇ 14:13
☽⚹♅ 14:54
☽△♀ 15:09
☽☍☿ 16:01
☽⊻⚷ 16:35

6 F
☉⊼☽ 0:59
☿⊼⚷ 3:20
☽⚼♂ 4:31
☿∥⚳ 5:30
☽∥♆ 5:41
☽△♄ 15:50
☽∠♇ 16:12
☽∠♅ 16:59

7 Sa
☽∥♄ 4:58
☉⚼☽ 5:25
☽⊼♂ 8:09
☽☌♆ 9:41
☽□⚳ 13:52
☽□♃ 14:42
☽⚼♄ 18:47
☽⚹♇ 19:05
☽⊻♅ 19:57
☽□♀ 21:30
☽☌⚷ 21:38
☽⊼☿ 23:44

8 Su
☽⋕♅ 0:20
☽∥⚷ 0:23
♀□⚷ 1:51
☽∥♂ 10:07
☉△☽ 11:01
☽⋕♂ 18:28
♂⊼♆ 20:58
☽⊼♄ 22:44

9 M
☽⋕⚷ 4:02
☽∥♅ 4:04
☽⚼☿ 4:57
☉⚼♆ 16:10
☽⊻♆ 17:43
☽☍♂ 18:42
⚶ ♊ 21:26

10 Tu
☽⚹⚳ 0:03
☽⚹♃ 0:07
☽⋕♄ 0:46
☽□♇ 3:45
☽☌♅ 4:49
⚳☌♃ 5:14
☽⊻⚷ 6:29
♅⋕⚷ 7:07
☽⚹♀ 8:19
☽△☿ 11:01
☽∠♆ 23:07

11 W
☉□☽ 1:49
☽⋕♆ 2:43
☽∠♃ 6:14
☽∠⚳ 6:36
☽☍♄ 9:24
☽∠⚷ 12:10
☽∠♀ 15:16

12 Th
☽∥☿ 4:25
☽⚹♆ 5:10
☽⊼♂ 9:10
☽⊻♃ 12:58
☽⊻⚳ 13:48
☽△♇ 15:35
☽⊻♅ 16:49
☽⚹⚷ 18:24
☽⊻♀ 22:52

13 F
☽□☿ 0:36
☽∥⚳ 1:43
☽∥♀ 2:38
♅ R 9:50
☽⚼♂ 17:09
☉⚹☽ 19:47
☽⋕♇ 20:53
☽⚼♇ 22:02
☽⊼♄ 22:20
☉∠♃ 23:07
☽∠♅ 23:20

14 Sa
☽∥♃ 16:08
☽□♆ 18:02
⚳⊼♇ 19:41
☿⚹♀ 22:43

15 Su
☽△♂ 1:06
☉∠⚳ 1:16
☿ R 2:16
☽☌♃ 2:57
☉□♄ 4:15
☽⊼♇ 4:24
☽☌⚳ 4:42
☽⚼♄ 4:50
☉∠☽ 4:53
☽⚹♅ 5:45
☽□⚷ 7:11
☉∥☽ 8:49
⚳⚼♄ 9:29
☽⚹☿ 13:47
☽☌♀ 14:31

16 M
☉⚼⚷ 8:44
☽△♄ 10:58
⚵ D 10:58
☉⊻☽ 13:30
⚳⚹♅ 14:25
♂⋕♅ 16:30
☽∠☿ 19:28
♂∥⚷ 21:38

17 Tu
☉∥☽ 1:33
☽△♆ 5:50
☽∥♃ 8:23
♂△♃ 12:40
☽⊻♃ 15:30
☽□♂ 15:35
☽☍♇ 15:49
☽□♅ 17:13
☽⊻⚳ 18:03
☽△⚷ 18:28
♂□♇ 20:28

18 W
☽⊻☿ 0:19
☽⋕♇ 4:09
☽⊻♀ 4:33
⚳□⚷ 7:23
♃⊼♇ 9:48
☽⚼♆ 10:51
☉∥♃ 17:16
☽∥♀ 18:03
☽∥⚳ 18:46
☽∠♃ 20:48
☽□♄ 21:26
☽⚼⚷ 23:10
☽∠⚳ 23:41

19 Th
♂☍♅ 2:56
☉☌☽ 4:25
☽∠♀ 10:33
☽⊼♆ 15:12

20 F
☽⊼♇ 0:44
☽⚹♃ 1:23
☽△♅ 2:09
♂⊼⚷ 3:10
☽⊼⚷ 3:13
☽⚹♂ 3:14
☽∥☿ 4:23
☽⚹⚳ 4:36
☽☌☿ 7:35
☽⚹♀ 15:52
☽⋕♆ 17:38

21 Sa
♃⚼♄ 2:01
☽⚼♇ 4:15
☽⚹♄ 5:19
☽⚼♅ 5:41
☽∠♂ 7:59
☉⊻☽ 16:08
☽⋕♄ 17:04
☽☍♆ 22:06

22 Su
♃⚹♅ 4:05
☿⚹⚳ 4:47
☽⋕♂ 6:49
☽△♇ 7:15
☽∠♄ 8:25
☽⊼♅ 8:41
☽□♃ 8:45
☽☍⚷ 9:37
☉ ♌ 10:02
☿⚹♂ 10:56
☽⊻☿ 12:04
☽⊻♂ 12:10
☽□⚳ 12:34
☽⋕⚷ 12:53
☽∥♅ 13:27
☉∠☽ 21:01

23 M
☽□♀ 0:45
☽⊻♄ 11:06
♂△⚳ 12:21
☽∠☿ 13:31
☽⋕♅ 15:31
☽∥⚷ 16:09

24 Tu
☽∥♂ 0:04
☉⚹☽ 1:24
☽⊼♆ 3:07
☽∥♄ 11:40
☽□♇ 12:00
♃□⚷ 13:09
☽☍♅ 13:27
☽⊼⚷ 14:15
☽△♃ 14:16
☽⚹☿ 14:33
☽△⚳ 18:39
☽☌♂ 19:10
☿⚹♃ 19:15
☿⊼⚷ 21:23

25 W
☉⊼♆ 1:35
☽⚼♆ 5:05
☽△♀ 7:57
☽∥♆ 9:52
☿△♅ 13:28
☽☌♄ 15:23
☽⚼⚷ 16:04
☽⚼♃ 16:30
☉⋕♇ 20:14
☽⚼⚳ 21:10
☽⋕☿ 22:50

26 Th
☽△♆ 6:47
☉□☽ 8:57
☽⚼♀ 11:04
☽⚹♇ 15:29
☽□☿ 15:39
☽⊼♅ 16:57
☽△⚷ 17:37
☽⊼♃ 18:27
☿⊼♇ 19:14
☽⊼⚳ 23:24

27 F
☽⊻♂ 0:47
☽⋕⚳ 9:16
☽⋕♀ 11:46
☽⊼♀ 13:56
☉⋕☽ 14:04
☽∠♇ 16:50
☽∥♇ 17:56
☽⚼♅ 18:18
☽⊻♄ 18:35

28 Sa
☽∠♂ 3:11
☉∥♀ 8:09
☿∠♀ 8:46
☽□♆ 9:26
☉△☽ 15:17
☽△☿ 15:49
☽⋕♃ 17:07
☽⊻♇ 18:00
☽△♅ 19:29
☽∠♄ 19:52
☉☌☿ 19:58
☽□⚷ 20:03
☽☍♃ 21:38

29 Su
☽☍⚳ 3:09
☽⚹♂ 5:24
☉∥⚳ 8:36
☽⚼☿ 15:42
☉⚼☽ 18:10
☽☍♀ 19:08
☽⚹♄ 21:02

30 M
♄⚼⚷ 2:05
☽⋕♃ 6:31
☉⊼♇ 7:10
☽⚹♆ 11:31
☽⊼☿ 15:36
☽☌♇ 20:05
☉⊼☽ 21:01
☽□♅ 21:35
☽⚹⚷ 22:04
⚴ R 22:32

31 Tu
☽⊼♃ 0:24
☉△♅ 5:23
☽∥♇ 6:24
☽⊼⚳ 6:34
♀△♄ 7:40
☽⋕♀ 9:32
☽□♂ 9:44
☉⊼⚷ 12:11
☽∠♆ 12:37
☽⋕⚳ 13:01
☉⋕☽ 19:11
☽∠⚷ 23:13
☽□♄ 23:32

August 2012

LONGITUDE

Day	Sid.Time	☉	☽	☽ 12 hour	Mean ☊	True ☊	☿	♀	♂	⚳	♃	♄	⚷	♅	♆	♇
	h m s	° ' "	° ' "	° ' "	° '	° '	° '	° '	° '	° '	° '	° '	° '	° '	° '	° '
1 W	20 40 02	9♌09 24	24♑07 44	1♒12 20	1♐41.9	2♐55.9	3♌57.1	24♊22.0	16♎01.0	14♊01.6	10♊16.2	23♎51.0	8♓40.0	8♈24.2	2♓21.9	7♑29.7
2 Th	20 43 58	10 06 47	8♒13 43	15 11 17	1 38.8	2R 46.8	3R 21.2	25 11.6	16 36.8	14 22.4	10 26.4	23 54.5	8R 37.5	8R 23.3	2R 20.5	7R 28.4
3 F	20 47 55	11 04 11	22 04 30	28 52 56	1 35.6	2 36.3	2 49.1	26 01.8	17 12.7	14 43.0	10 36.5	23 58.1	8 35.1	8 22.4	2 19.0	7 27.2
4 Sa	20 51 51	12 01 36	5♓36 12	12♓14 06	1 32.4	2 25.3	2 21.5	26 52.8	17 48.7	15 03.5	10 46.5	24 01.7	8 32.6	8 21.4	2 17.5	7 26.0
5 Su	20 55 48	12 59 02	18 46 32	25 13 29	1 29.2	2 15.2	1 58.8	27 44.4	18 24.9	15 23.9	10 56.3	24 05.5	8 30.1	8 20.3	2 15.9	7 24.9
6 M	20 59 44	13 56 29	1♈35 08	7♈51 42	1 26.0	2 06.7	1 41.7	28 36.6	19 01.1	15 44.3	11 06.1	24 09.3	8 27.5	8 19.3	2 14.4	7 23.7
7 Tu	21 03 41	14 53 57	14 03 32	20 11 04	1 22.9	2 00.6	1 30.6	29 29.5	19 37.5	16 04.5	11 15.7	24 13.2	8 25.0	8 18.2	2 12.9	7 22.6
8 W	21 07 38	15 51 26	26 14 49	2♉15 21	1 19.7	1 56.8	1D 25.8	0♋22.9	20 14.0	16 24.7	11 25.3	24 17.2	8 22.4	8 17.0	2 11.3	7 21.5
9 Th	21 11 34	16 48 57	8♉13 17	14 09 15	1 16.5	1D 55.2	1 27.6	1 16.9	20 50.6	16 44.7	11 34.7	24 21.3	8 19.7	8 15.8	2 09.8	7 20.4
10 F	21 15 31	17 46 29	20 03 56	25 58 02	1 13.3	1 54.9	1 36.1	2 11.5	21 27.4	17 04.6	11 44.0	24 25.4	8 17.1	8 14.5	2 08.2	7 19.3
11 Sa	21 19 27	18 44 03	1♊52 13	7♊47 10	1 10.1	1R 55.0	1 51.6	3 06.6	22 04.2	17 24.5	11 53.2	24 29.6	8 14.4	8 13.3	2 06.6	7 18.3
12 Su	21 23 24	19 41 38	13 43 32	19 41 58	1 07.0	1 54.5	2 14.0	4 02.2	22 41.2	17 44.2	12 02.3	24 34.0	8 11.7	8 11.9	2 05.0	7 17.2
13 M	21 27 20	20 39 15	25 43 03	1♋47 18	1 03.8	1 52.4	2 43.5	4 58.3	23 18.3	18 03.8	12 11.2	24 38.3	8 09.0	8 10.6	2 03.4	7 16.2
14 Tu	21 31 17	21 36 53	7♋55 14	14 07 13	1 00.6	1 48.0	3 20.0	5 54.9	23 55.5	18 23.3	12 20.0	24 42.8	8 06.3	8 09.2	2 01.8	7 15.2
15 W	21 35 13	22 34 32	20 23 37	26 44 39	0 57.4	1 40.9	4 03.3	6 51.9	24 32.8	18 42.7	12 28.7	24 47.3	8 03.5	8 07.7	2 00.2	7 14.3
16 Th	21 39 10	23 32 12	3♌10 28	9♌41 05	0 54.3	1 31.3	4 53.5	7 49.4	25 10.2	19 01.9	12 37.3	24 51.9	8 00.7	8 06.2	1 58.6	7 13.3
17 F	21 43 07	24 29 55	16 16 27	22 56 25	0 51.1	1 19.9	5 50.4	8 47.3	25 47.8	19 21.1	12 45.7	24 56.6	7 57.9	8 04.7	1 57.0	7 12.4
18 Sa	21 47 03	25 27 38	29 40 41	6♍28 56	0 47.9	1 07.5	6 53.6	9 45.7	26 25.4	19 40.1	12 54.0	25 01.3	7 55.1	8 03.2	1 55.3	7 11.5
19 Su	21 51 00	26 25 22	13♍20 46	20 15 42	0 44.7	0 55.5	8 03.1	10 44.2	27 03.2	19 59.0	13 02.2	25 06.1	7 52.3	8 01.6	1 53.7	7 10.7
20 M	21 54 56	27 23 08	27 13 16	4♎12 59	0 41.6	0 45.0	9 18.5	11 43.6	27 41.1	20 17.7	13 10.2	25 11.0	7 49.5	7 59.9	1 52.1	7 09.8
21 Tu	21 58 53	28 20 55	11♎14 21	18 16 58	0 38.4	0 36.9	10 39.6	12 43.1	28 19.1	20 36.4	13 18.1	25 16.0	7 46.6	7 58.3	1 50.4	7 09.0
22 W	22 02 49	29 18 43	25 20 25	2♏24 23	0 35.2	0 31.6	12 05.9	13 43.0	28 57.2	20 54.9	13 25.8	25 21.0	7 43.8	7 56.6	1 48.8	7 08.2
23 Th	22 06 46	0♍16 33	9♏28 34	16 32 45	0 32.0	0 29.0	13 37.2	14 43.2	29 35.4	21 13.2	13 33.4	25 26.1	7 40.9	7 54.8	1 47.1	7 07.4
24 F	22 10 42	1 14 24	23 36 46	0♐40 29	0 28.8	0 28.2	15 12.9	15 43.8	0♏13.7	21 31.4	13 40.9	25 31.2	7 38.0	7 53.1	1 45.5	7 06.7
25 Sa	22 14 39	2 12 15	7♐43 47	14 46 34	0 25.7	0 28.2	16 52.8	16 44.8	0 52.1	21 49.5	13 48.2	25 36.4	7 35.2	7 51.3	1 43.9	7 06.0
26 Su	22 18 36	3 10 09	21 48 43	28 50 07	0 22.5	0 27.5	18 36.2	17 46.1	1 30.6	22 07.5	13 55.4	25 41.7	7 32.3	7 49.4	1 42.2	7 05.3
27 M	22 22 32	4 08 03	5♑50 36	12♑49 59	0 19.3	0 25.0	20 22.8	18 47.7	2 09.3	22 25.2	14 02.4	25 47.1	7 29.4	7 47.6	1 40.6	7 04.6
28 Tu	22 26 29	5 05 58	19 47 59	26 44 20	0 16.1	0 20.0	22 12.1	19 49.6	2 48.0	22 42.9	14 09.3	25 52.5	7 26.5	7 45.7	1 38.9	7 04.0
29 W	22 30 25	6 03 55	3♒38 43	10♒30 44	0 13.0	0 12.1	24 03.6	20 51.8	3 26.8	23 00.4	14 16.0	25 57.9	7 23.6	7 43.7	1 37.3	7 03.4
30 Th	22 34 22	7 01 53	17 20 03	24 06 15	0 09.8	0 01.8	25 57.0	21 54.3	4 05.7	23 17.7	14 22.5	26 03.5	7 20.7	7 41.8	1 35.7	7 02.8
31 F	22 38 18	7♍59 53	0♓49 01	7♓28 01	0♐06.6	29♏49.8	27♌51.8	22♋57.2	4♏44.7	23♊34.9	14♊29.0	26♎09.0	7♓17.8	7♈39.8	1♓34.0	7♑02.3

1st of Month

Julian Day # 2456140.5
Obliquity 23°26'11"
SVP 5♓04'46"
GC 27♐00.9
Eris 22♈42.5R

Day	⚴
1	11♈29.0R
6	11 22.8R
11	11 07.6R
16	10 43.0R
21	10 09.0R
26	9 25.7R
31	8 33.4R

Day	⚵
1	22♏02.4
6	22 29.4
11	23 03.1
16	23 43.0
21	24 28.9
26	25 20.4
31	26 17.1

Day	⚶
1	8♊14.5
6	9 58.7
11	11 39.6
16	13 16.8
21	14 50.1
26	16 18.9
31	17 43.1

DECLINATION and LATITUDE

Day	☉ Decl	☽ Decl	☽ Lat	☽ 12h Decl	☿ Decl	☿ Lat	♀ Decl	♀ Lat	♂ Decl	♂ Lat	⚳ Decl	⚳ Lat	♃ Decl	♃ Lat	♄ Decl	♄ Lat
1 W	17N58	17S24	3N57	15S41	14N40	4S44	19N10	4S09	6S24	0S07	18N46	3S44	21N13	0S46	7S00	2N25
2 Th	17 43	13 46	4 36	11 40	14 55	4 36	19 15	4 06	6 39	0 07	18 50	3 43	21 15	0 46	7 02	2 25
3 F	17 27	9 27	4 58	7 08	15 12	4 27	19 20	4 03	6 53	0 08	18 53	3 42	21 16	0 47	7 03	2 25
4 Sa	17 11	4 46	5 02	2 22	15 28	4 16	19 25	3 59	7 08	0 09	18 56	3 41	21 17	0 47	7 05	2 24
5 Su	16 55	0N01	4 50	2N22	15 45	4 04	19 29	3 56	7 22	0 10	18 60	3 40	21 19	0 47	7 06	2 24
6 M	16 39	4 40	4 24	6 53	16 02	3 51	19 33	3 53	7 37	0 11	19 03	3 39	21 20	0 47	7 08	2 24
7 Tu	16 22	9 01	3 46	11 01	16 18	3 36	19 37	3 49	7 52	0 12	19 06	3 38	21 20	0 47	7 10	2 24
8 W	16 05	12 53	2 58	14 37	16 34	3 21	19 41	3 45	8 06	0 13	19 09	3 36	21 21	0 47	7 11	2 24
9 Th	15 48	16 11	2 02	17 34	16 49	3 06	19 44	3 42	8 21	0 14	19 12	3 35	21 23	0 47	7 13	2 23
10 F	15 30	18 46	1 03	19 45	17 03	2 49	19 47	3 38	8 35	0 14	19 15	3 34	21 25	0 47	7 15	2 23
11 Sa	15 12	20 32	0 00	21 06	17 16	2 33	19 50	3 34	8 50	0 15	19 18	3 33	21 26	0 47	7 16	2 23
12 Su	14 55	21 25	1S02	21 29	17 27	2 16	19 53	3 30	9 04	0 16	19 21	3 32	21 27	0 47	7 18	2 23
13 M	14 36	21 19	2 03	20 54	17 37	1 59	19 55	3 26	9 19	0 17	19 24	3 31	21 29	0 47	7 20	2 22
14 Tu	14 18	20 14	2 59	19 18	17 45	1 42	19 57	3 22	9 33	0 18	19 27	3 30	21 30	0 47	7 22	2 22
15 W	13 59	18 09	3 47	16 45	17 52	1 25	19 58	3 18	9 48	0 19	19 30	3 28	21 31	0 47	7 24	2 22
16 Th	13 40	15 08	4 25	13 18	17 56	1 09	19 59	3 13	10 02	0 19	19 33	3 27	21 32	0 47	7 26	2 22
17 F	13 21	11 20	4 51	9 11	17 58	0 53	20 00	3 09	10 17	0 20	19 35	3 26	21 33	0 47	7 27	2 22
18 Sa	13 02	6 53	5 01	4 32	17 57	0 37	20 00	3 05	10 31	0 21	19 38	3 25	21 34	0 47	7 29	2 21
19 Su	12 42	2 01	4 54	0S30	17 54	0 22	20 00	3 00	10 46	0 22	19 41	3 24	21 35	0 47	7 31	2 21
20 M	12 23	3S01	4 30	5 31	17 49	0 07	19 60	2 56	10 60	0 22	19 43	3 22	21 36	0 47	7 33	2 21
21 Tu	12 03	7 57	3 49	10 18	17 40	0N07	19 59	2 51	11 14	0 23	19 46	3 21	21 37	0 47	7 35	2 21
22 W	11 43	12 30	2 54	14 32	17 29	0 20	19 58	2 47	11 28	0 24	19 48	3 20	21 38	0 47	7 37	2 21
23 Th	11 23	16 22	1 49	17 57	17 15	0 32	19 56	2 42	11 43	0 25	19 51	3 19	21 39	0 47	7 39	2 20
24 F	11 02	19 16	0 36	20 11	16 58	0 43	19 54	2 38	11 57	0 25	19 53	3 17	21 39	0 47	7 41	2 20
25 Sa	10 41	20 58	0N38	21 20	16 38	0 54	19 51	2 33	12 11	0 26	19 55	3 16	21 40	0 47	7 43	2 20
26 Su	10 21	21 21	1 50	21 02	16 15	1 03	19 48	2 29	12 25	0 27	19 58	3 15	21 41	0 47	7 45	2 20
27 M	9 60	20 23	2 55	19 26	15 50	1 12	19 44	2 24	12 39	0 28	20 00	3 13	21 42	0 47	7 48	2 20
28 Tu	9 38	18 11	3 50	16 41	15 22	1 20	19 40	2 19	12 53	0 28	20 02	3 12	21 43	0 48	7 50	2 20
29 W	9 17	14 58	4 30	13 03	14 51	1 26	19 36	2 15	13 07	0 29	20 05	3 11	21 43	0 48	7 52	2 19
30 Th	8 56	10 58	4 54	8 47	14 18	1 32	19 31	2 10	13 21	0 30	20 07	3 10	21 44	0 48	7 54	2 19
31 F	8N34	6S29	5N01	4S09	13N43	1N37	19N25	2S05	13S35	0S31	20N09	3S08	21N45	0S48	7S56	2N19

Day	⚷ Decl	⚷ Lat	♅ Decl	♅ Lat	♆ Decl	♆ Lat	♇ Decl	♇ Lat
1	2S56	5N49	2N39	0S44	11S12	0S37	19S27	3N47
6	2 60	5 49	2 37	0 44	11 15	0 37	19 28	3 46
11	3 04	5 50	2 35	0 44	11 18	0 37	19 29	3 45
16	3 09	5 50	2 32	0 45	11 21	0 37	19 30	3 44
21	3 14	5 50	2 29	0 45	11 24	0 37	19 32	3 43
26	3 19	5 50	2 25	0 45	11 27	0 37	19 33	3 42
31	3S25	5N50	2N21	0S45	11S30	0S37	19S34	3N41

Day	⚴ Decl	⚴ Lat	⚵ Decl	⚵ Lat	⚶ Decl	⚶ Lat	Eris Decl	Eris Lat
1	3N39	0S59	4S20	14N24	16N29	5S16	3S28	13S13
6	3 00	1 38	4 44	14 06	16 42	5 18	3 29	13 14
11	2 17	2 19	5 09	13 48	16 54	5 20	3 29	13 14
16	1 27	3 02	5 35	13 31	17 04	5 22	3 30	13 15
21	0 32	3 47	6 01	13 15	17 12	5 24	3 31	13 15
26	0S28	4 34	6 29	12 59	17 19	5 27	3 32	13 16
31	1S33	5S23	6S56	12N43	17N24	5S30	3S33	13S16

Moon Phenomena

Max/0 Decl (dy hr mn)
4 23:55 0 N
12 9:48 21N30
19 9:39 0 S
25 18:52 21S23

Perigee/Apogee (dy hr m kilometers)
10 10:52 a 404121
23 19:25 p 369728

PH (dy hr mn)
○ 2 3:29 10♒15
☾ 9 18:56 17♉34
● 17 15:55 25♌08
☽ 24 13:55 1♐48
○ 31 13:59 8♓34

Max/0 Lat (dy hr mn)
3 18:27 5N03
11 0:05 0 S
18 2:23 5S01
24 11:39 0 N
30 22:22 5N01

Void of Course Moon

Last Aspect	☽ Ingress
31 23:32 ♄ □	♒ 1 9:57
3 7:25 ♀ △	♓ 3 13:59
5 17:57 ♀ □	♈ 5 21:00
7 20:05 ♄ ☍	♉ 8 7:29
9 18:56 ☉ □	♊ 10 20:12
12 21:51 ♄ △	♋ 13 8:29
15 8:22 ♄ □	♌ 15 18:06
17 17:56 ♂ ⚹	♍ 18 0:34
18 23:27 ♃ □	♎ 20 4:46
22 7:14 ☉ ⚹	♏ 22 7:55
23 9:35 ♀ △	♐ 24 10:51
26 6:40 ♄ ⚹	♑ 26 14:00
28 10:34 ♄ □	♒ 28 17:40
30 17:49 ☿ ☍	♓ 30 22:32

DAILY ASPECTARIAN

1 W: ☽⚻♀ 0:26, ☽⚼♃ 1:57, ☽⚼⚳ 8:30, ☽⚺♆ 13:57, ☽☍☿ 15:59, ☽⋕☿ 17:22, ☽⚺♇ 22:42
2 Th: ☽⚹♅ 0:16, ☽⚺⚷ 0:41, ☉☍☽ 3:29, ☽⚼♀ 3:35, ☽△♃ 3:51, ☉⚹♃ 9:57, ☽△⚳ 10:51, ☽∥♆ 14:30, ☽△♂ 15:08, ☉∠♀ 15:54
3 F: ☽∠♇ 0:40, ☽∠♅ 2:16, ☽△♄ 3:20, ♂⚼♆ 4:01, ☽△♀ 7:25, ☽∥♄ 12:21, ☽∥♂ 12:38, ☽☌♆ 18:05, ☽⚻☿ 18:22, ♂∥♄ 18:29, ☽⚼♂ 18:46
4 Sa: ☽⚹♇ 3:18, ☿⚻♆ 4:07, ☽⚺♅ 4:57, ☽☌⚷ 5:17, ☽⚼♄ 6:12, ☽∥⚷ 9:00, ☽□♃ 9:28, ☽⋕♅ 10:42, ☉⚻☽ 12:32, ♀⋕♇ 15:59, ☽□⚳ 17:37, ☽⚼☿ 20:46, ☽⚻♂ 23:18
5 Su: ☽⚻♄ 9:56, ☽∥♅ 13:19, ☽⋕⚷ 15:13, ☽□♀ 17:57, ☉⚼☽ 18:35
6 M: ☽△☿ 0:12, ☽⚺♆ 1:15, ☽□♇ 11:05, ☽☌♅ 12:52, ☽⚺⚷ 13:06, ☽⋕♄ 13:27, ☽⋕♂ 17:02, ☽⚹♃ 18:30
7 Tu: ☉△☽ 1:47, ☉∥☿ 2:42, ☽⚹⚳ 4:03, ☽∠♆ 6:09, ☽☍♂ 11:28, ☽⋕♆ 13:34, ♀ ♋ 13:44, ☽∠⚷ 18:19, ☽☍♄ 20:05
8 W: ☽∠♃ 0:21, ☿∠⚳ 1:17, ☿ D 5:40, ☽⚹♀ 8:55, ☽□☿ 10:21, ☽∠⚳ 10:36, ☽⚹♆ 11:50, ☉∥☽ 21:12, ☉⚹⚳ 21:16, ☽△♇ 22:13
9 Th: ☽⚺♅ 0:05, ☽⚹⚷ 0:13, ☿⚺♀ 5:15, ☽∥☿ 5:49, ☽⚺♃ 6:52, ☽∠♀ 17:40, ☽⚺⚳ 17:45, ☉□☽ 18:56, ♀△♆ 22:35
10 F: ☽⚻♂ 2:59, ☽⚼♇ 4:35, ☽∥⚳ 5:48, ☽∠♅ 6:27, ☽⋕♇ 8:27, ☽⚻♄ 8:55, ☽∥♀ 12:48, ☽⚹☿ 23:59
11 Sa: ☽□♆ 0:29, ☽⚺♀ 2:44, ☽⚻♇ 11:00, ☽⚼♂ 11:08, ☽⚹♅ 12:51, ☽□⚷ 12:52, ☽⚼♄ 15:33, ☿⚻♆ 15:48, ♅⚺⚷ 19:57, ☽☌♃ 20:33
12 Su: ☽∥♃ 3:30, ☽∠☿ 7:20, ☽☌⚳ 8:17, ☉⚹☽ 13:02, ☽∥♃ 15:08, ♂⚼⚷ 18:25, ☽△♂ 18:56, ☽△♄ 21:51
13 M: ☽△♆ 12:30, ☽⚺☿ 14:32, ☽☌♀ 19:46, ☉∠☽ 21:14, ☽☍♇ 22:42
14 Tu: ☽△⚷ 0:21, ☽□♅ 0:27, ☿∠⚳ 3:47, ☽∥♀ 3:59, ☽⚺♃ 8:39, ☽⋕♇ 9:44, ☽∥⚳ 10:05, ☉⚼♇ 15:42, ☽⚼♆ 17:33, ☽⚺⚳ 20:43
15 W: ☽∥☿ 2:33, ⚳⋕♇ 2:58, ☉⚺☽ 4:29, ☽⚼⚷ 5:02, ☽□♂ 8:16, ☽□♄ 8:22, ♀☍♇ 9:12, ♂☌♄ 10:36, ☉⚼♅ 13:28, ☽∠♃ 13:32, ☽⚻♆ 21:47
16 Th: ☽∠⚳ 1:38, ☽☌☿ 3:25, ♀△⚷ 4:29, ♀□♅ 6:49, ☽⚻♇ 7:28, ☽⚻⚷ 8:54, ☽△♅ 9:05, ☽⚺♀ 9:16, ☉∥☽ 10:42, ☽⚹♃ 17:33, ☽⋕♆ 23:51
17 F: ☽⋕♂ 5:39, ☽⚹⚳ 5:41, ☽⚼♇ 10:40, ☉⚹♄ 12:05, ☽⚼♅ 12:13, ☽∠♀ 14:34, ☽⚹♄ 15:40, ☉☌☽ 15:55, ☽⚹♂ 17:56, ☽⋕♄ 20:55
18 Sa: ☽☍♆ 3:58, ☿⚻♇ 6:18, ☽△♇ 13:14, ☽⚺☿ 13:52, ☽☍⚷ 14:28, ☽⚻♅ 14:44, ☽∠♄ 18:18, ☽⋕⚷ 18:19, ☽⚹♀ 19:06, ☿⚻⚷ 20:32, ☽∠♂ 21:38, ☽∥♅ 21:42, ☽□♃ 23:27, ☿△♅ 23:30
19 Su: ☽□⚳ 11:47, ☽∠☿ 18:28, ☽⚺♄ 20:28, ☽⋕♅ 21:29
20 M: ☉⚺☽ 0:18, ☽⚺♂ 0:50, ☽∥⚷ 0:57, ☽⚻♆ 7:58, ☽□♇ 17:01, ☽⚻⚷ 18:07, ☽☍♅ 18:26, ☉⚹♂ 21:47, ☽∥♄ 22:08, ☽⚹☿ 22:54, ♂⚼♃ 23:12
21 Tu: ☽□♀ 2:43, ☽△♃ 3:33, ☉∠☽ 3:52, ☽⚼♆ 9:32, ♀⚺♃ 16:07, ☽△⚳ 16:19, ♂∥♆ 16:54, ☽∥♆ 17:55, ☽∥♂ 17:58, ☽⚼⚷ 19:35, ☉⋕☽ 19:54
22 W: ☽☌♄ 0:01, ☽⚼♃ 5:18, ☽☌♂ 6:26, ☉⚹☽ 7:14, ☉⋕♂ 9:53, ☽△♆ 10:58, ☉ ♍ 17:08, ☽⚼⚳ 18:21, ☽⚹♇ 20:01, ☽△⚷ 20:58, ☉⋕♆ 20:59, ☽⚻♅ 21:21, ☿⚹♃ 22:57
23 Th: ☽⋕☿ 5:57, ☽⚻♃ 6:59, ☽□☿ 7:55, ☽△♀ 9:35, ♂ ♏ 15:25, ☽⚻⚳ 20:22, ☽∠♇ 21:27, ☽⚼♅ 22:46
24 F: ☽∥♇ 2:59, ☽⚺♄ 3:16, ♀∥⚳ 3:43, ☽⋕♀ 6:59, ☽⋕⚳ 7:07, ☽⚺♂ 11:47, ☉☍♆ 12:33, ☽⚼♀ 13:02, ☽□♆ 13:49, ☉□☽ 13:55, ☿⚺♀ 19:15, ☽⚺♇ 22:56, ♀⚼♆ 23:39, ☽□⚷ 23:45
25 Sa: ☽△♅ 0:13, ☽∠♄ 4:56, ☽☍♃ 10:26, ☽∠♂ 14:31, ☽⚻♀ 16:34, ☽△☿ 17:45
26 Su: ☽☍⚳ 0:33, ☽⚹♄ 6:40, ♂△♆ 6:54, ☽⚹♆ 16:52, ☽⚹♂ 17:22, ☉△☽ 20:51, ☽⚼☿ 23:05
27 M: ☽☌♇ 2:07, ☽⚹⚷ 2:49, ☽□♅ 3:20, ☽⋕⚳ 5:12, ☽⋕♀ 8:46, ☽∥♇ 10:40, ☽⚻♃ 14:12, ☽∠♆ 18:35, ☿⚼♇ 22:15
28 Tu: ☽☍♀ 0:03, ☉⚼☽ 0:33, ☽∠⚷ 4:33, ☽⚻☿ 4:47, ☽⚻⚳ 5:09, ☿⚼♅ 7:09, ☿⚹⚳ 7:56, ☽□♄ 10:34, ☽⚼♃ 16:19, ☽⚺♆ 20:29, ☽□♂ 23:38
29 W: ☽⋕☿ 0:51, ☉⚻☽ 4:32, ☽⚺♇ 5:57, ☽⚺⚷ 6:31, ☽⚹♅ 7:07, ☽⚼⚳ 7:47, ☽∥♂ 10:56, ♀⋕♇ 11:52, ☽△♃ 18:45, ☽∥♆ 21:06
30 Th: ☉△♇ 0:23, ☿⚹♄ 1:26, ☊R♏ 3:41, ☉☍⚷ 7:25, ☽∠♇ 8:20, ☽⚻♀ 8:46, ☽∠♅ 9:28, ♀⚼⚷ 9:38, ☽△⚳ 10:47, ☉⋕☽ 12:09, ☽△♄ 15:35, ☉⚻♅ 15:58, ☽∥♄ 16:31, ☽☍☿ 17:49
31 F: ☽☌♆ 1:21, ☿⋕♂ 4:06, ☽△♂ 7:26, ☽⚹♇ 11:13, ☽☌⚷ 11:39, ☽⚺♅ 12:20, ☉∠♀ 12:53, ☉☍☽ 13:59, ☽⚼♀ 14:00, ☽∥⚷ 15:41, ☽⚼♄ 18:50, ♀⚺⚳ 19:40, ☽⋕♅ 21:12

LONGITUDE

Day	Sid.Time	☉	☽	☽ 12 hour	Mean☊	True☊	☿	♀	♂	⚳	♃	♄	⚷	♅	♆	♇
	h m s	° ' "	° ' "	° ' "	° '	° '	° '	° '	° '	° '	° '	° '	° '	° '	° '	° '
1 Sa	22 42 15	8♍57 54	14♓02 57	20♓33 40	0♐03.4	29♏37.3	29♌47.6	24♋00.3	5♏23.8	23♊52.0	14♊35.2	26♎14.7	7♓14.9	7♈37.8	1♓32.4	7♑01.7
2 Su	22 46 11	9 55 57	27 00 00	3♈21 55	0 00.2	29R 25.6	1♍44.2	25 03.7	6 03.0	24 08.8	14 41.3	26 20.4	7R 12.0	7R 35.8	1R 30.8	7R 01.2
3 M	22 50 08	10 54 02	9♈39 29	15 52 49	29♏57.1	29 15.5	3 41.1	26 07.4	6 42.3	24 25.5	14 47.2	26 26.1	7 09.1	7 33.7	1 29.2	7 00.8
4 Tu	22 54 04	11 52 08	22 02 10	28 07 50	29 53.9	29 08.0	5 38.2	27 11.4	7 21.7	24 42.1	14 53.0	26 31.9	7 06.3	7 31.6	1 27.5	7 00.3
5 W	22 58 01	12 50 17	4♉10 12	10♉09 45	29 50.7	29 03.1	7 35.1	28 15.6	8 01.2	24 58.5	14 58.6	26 37.8	7 03.4	7 29.5	1 25.9	6 59.9
6 Th	23 01 58	13 48 27	16 06 57	22 02 25	29 47.5	29 00.6	9 31.8	29 20.1	8 40.8	25 14.7	15 04.1	26 43.7	7 00.5	7 27.4	1 24.3	6 59.5
7 F	23 05 54	14 46 39	27 56 45	3♊50 36	29 44.3	28D 59.9	11 27.9	0♌24.8	9 20.5	25 30.7	15 09.4	26 49.7	6 57.6	7 25.2	1 22.7	6 59.2
8 Sa	23 09 51	15 44 53	9♊44 37	15 39 30	29 41.2	29R 00.1	13 23.5	1 29.8	10 00.3	25 46.5	15 14.5	26 55.7	6 54.8	7 23.0	1 21.2	6 58.8
9 Su	23 13 47	16 43 10	21 35 56	27 34 37	29 38.0	29 00.1	15 18.3	2 35.0	10 40.2	26 02.2	15 19.4	27 01.8	6 51.9	7 20.8	1 19.6	6 58.6
10 M	23 17 44	17 41 28	3♋36 12	9♋41 19	29 34.8	28 58.9	17 12.3	3 40.5	11 20.2	26 17.7	15 24.2	27 07.9	6 49.1	7 18.6	1 18.0	6 58.3
11 Tu	23 21 40	18 39 49	15 50 34	22 04 29	29 31.6	28 55.7	19 05.4	4 46.2	12 00.3	26 32.9	15 28.8	27 14.1	6 46.3	7 16.4	1 16.5	6 58.1
12 W	23 25 37	19 38 11	28 23 32	4♌48 04	29 28.5	28 50.2	20 57.5	5 52.1	12 40.5	26 48.0	15 33.2	27 20.3	6 43.5	7 14.1	1 14.9	6 57.9
13 Th	23 29 33	20 36 36	11♌18 22	17 54 33	29 25.3	28 42.2	22 48.6	6 58.2	13 20.7	27 02.9	15 37.4	27 26.6	6 40.7	7 11.8	1 13.4	6 57.7
14 F	23 33 30	21 35 02	24 36 39	1♍24 32	29 22.1	28 32.4	24 38.7	8 04.6	14 01.1	27 17.6	15 41.5	27 32.9	6 37.9	7 09.5	1 11.9	6 57.5
15 Sa	23 37 27	22 33 31	8♍17 56	15 16 26	29 18.9	28 21.7	26 27.8	9 11.1	14 41.6	27 32.1	15 45.4	27 39.2	6 35.2	7 07.2	1 10.4	6 57.4
16 Su	23 41 23	23 32 01	22 19 31	29 26 32	29 15.7	28 11.1	28 15.8	10 17.9	15 22.1	27 46.3	15 49.0	27 45.6	6 32.4	7 04.9	1 08.9	6 57.3
17 M	23 45 20	24 30 34	6♎36 46	13♎49 27	29 12.6	28 01.9	0♎02.7	11 24.8	16 02.8	28 00.4	15 52.5	27 52.0	6 29.7	7 02.6	1 07.4	6 57.3
18 Tu	23 49 16	25 29 08	21 03 48	28 19 03	29 09.4	27 54.9	1 48.6	12 32.0	16 43.5	28 14.2	15 55.9	27 58.5	6 27.0	7 00.2	1 05.9	6D 57.3
19 W	23 53 13	26 27 44	5♏34 27	12♏49 20	29 06.2	27 50.5	3 33.5	13 39.3	17 24.3	28 27.8	15 59.0	28 05.0	6 24.3	6 57.9	1 04.5	6 57.3
20 Th	23 57 09	27 26 22	20 03 08	27 15 22	29 03.0	27D 48.6	5 17.3	14 46.8	18 05.3	28 41.2	16 01.9	28 11.6	6 21.7	6 55.5	1 03.0	6 57.3
21 F	0 01 06	28 25 01	4♐25 37	11♐33 37	28 59.9	27 48.5	7 00.1	15 54.5	18 46.3	28 54.4	16 04.7	28 18.2	6 19.1	6 53.1	1 01.6	6 57.4
22 Sa	0 05 02	29 23 43	18 39 08	25 42 01	28 56.7	27R 49.2	8 41.9	17 02.3	19 27.4	29 07.3	16 07.3	28 24.8	6 16.5	6 50.7	1 00.2	6 57.5
23 Su	0 08 59	0♎22 26	2♑42 11	9♑39 35	28 53.5	27 49.5	10 22.7	18 10.4	20 08.6	29 20.0	16 09.6	28 31.5	6 13.9	6 48.3	0 58.8	6 57.6
24 M	0 12 56	1 21 10	16 34 12	23 25 59	28 50.3	27 48.4	12 02.5	19 18.6	20 49.9	29 32.4	16 11.8	28 38.2	6 11.4	6 45.9	0 57.5	6 57.8
25 Tu	0 16 52	2 19 56	0♒14 58	7♒01 05	28 47.1	27 45.2	13 41.3	20 27.0	21 31.2	29 44.6	16 13.8	28 45.0	6 08.9	6 43.5	0 56.1	6 58.0
26 W	0 20 49	3 18 44	13 44 19	20 24 37	28 44.0	27 39.7	15 19.2	21 35.5	22 12.7	29 56.6	16 15.6	28 51.7	6 06.4	6 41.1	0 54.8	6 58.2
27 Th	0 24 45	4 17 34	27 01 54	3♓36 05	28 40.8	27 32.2	16 56.2	22 44.2	22 54.2	0♋08.3	16 17.2	28 58.5	6 03.9	6 38.7	0 53.5	6 58.5
28 F	0 28 42	5 16 25	10♓07 07	16 34 54	28 37.6	27 23.3	18 32.3	23 53.1	23 35.8	0 19.7	16 18.6	29 05.4	6 01.5	6 36.3	0 52.2	6 58.8
29 Sa	0 32 38	6 15 18	22 59 22	29 20 28	28 34.4	27 13.9	20 07.5	25 02.1	24 17.5	0 30.9	16 19.8	29 12.2	5 59.1	6 33.9	0 50.9	6 59.1
30 Su	0 36 35	7♎14 14	5♈38 13	11♈52 35	28♏31.3	27♏05.1	21♎41.8	26♌11.2	24♏59.3	0♋41.8	16♊20.8	29♎19.1	5♓56.8	6♈31.5	0♓49.7	6♑59.4

1st of Month

Julian Day # 2456171.5
Obliquity 23°26'11"
SVP 5♓04'42"
GC 27♐01.0
Eris 22♈33.7R

Day	⚴
1	8♈22.0R
6	7 19.7R
11	6 10.2R
16	4 54.5R
21	3 34.4R
26	2 11.7R

Day	⚵
1	26♏29.0
6	27 31.3
11	28 38.1
16	29 49.1
21	1♐03.9
26	2 22.4

Day	⚶
1	17♊59.3
6	19 17.3
11	20 29.6
16	21 35.6
21	22 34.8
26	23 26.6

DECLINATION and LATITUDE

Day	☉ Decl	☽ Decl	☽ Lat	☽12h Decl	☿ Decl	☿ Lat	♀ Decl	♀ Lat	♂ Decl	♂ Lat	⚳ Decl	⚳ Lat	♃ Decl	♃ Lat	♄ Decl	♄ Lat
1 Sa	8N12	1S47	4N51	0N34	13N06	1N40	19N20	2S01	13S49	0S31	20N11	3S07	21N45	0S48	7S58	2N19
2 Su	7 51	2N54	4 27	5 10	12 28	1 43	19 13	1 56	14 02	0 32	20 13	3 05	21 46	0 48	8 01	2 19
3 M	7 29	7 21	3 50	9 26	11 47	1 45	19 06	1 51	14 16	0 33	20 15	3 04	21 47	0 48	8 03	2 18
4 Tu	7 07	11 24	3 03	13 14	11 06	1 47	18 59	1 46	14 30	0 33	20 17	3 03	21 47	0 48	8 05	2 18
5 W	6 44	14 55	2 08	16 25	10 23	1 47	18 51	1 42	14 43	0 34	20 19	3 01	21 48	0 48	8 07	2 18
6 Th	6 22	17 45	1 08	18 52	9 39	1 47	18 42	1 37	14 56	0 35	20 21	2 60	21 48	0 48	8 10	2 18
7 F	5 60	19 47	0 06	20 30	8 54	1 46	18 33	1 32	15 10	0 35	20 23	2 58	21 49	0 48	8 12	2 18
8 Sa	5 37	20 58	0S57	21 13	8 08	1 45	18 24	1 28	15 23	0 36	20 25	2 57	21 49	0 48	8 14	2 18
9 Su	5 15	21 13	1 57	20 59	7 22	1 43	18 14	1 23	15 36	0 37	20 27	2 55	21 50	0 48	8 16	2 18
10 M	4 52	20 30	2 53	19 47	6 35	1 40	18 04	1 18	15 49	0 37	20 29	2 54	21 50	0 48	8 19	2 17
11 Tu	4 29	18 49	3 42	17 37	5 48	1 37	17 53	1 14	16 02	0 38	20 31	2 53	21 51	0 48	8 21	2 17
12 W	4 06	16 12	4 22	14 34	5 01	1 33	17 41	1 09	16 15	0 39	20 33	2 51	21 51	0 48	8 23	2 17
13 Th	3 43	12 44	4 50	10 44	4 13	1 29	17 29	1 04	16 28	0 39	20 35	2 49	21 52	0 48	8 26	2 17
14 F	3 20	8 33	5 03	6 15	3 26	1 25	17 17	0 60	16 41	0 40	20 37	2 48	21 52	0 48	8 28	2 17
15 Sa	2 57	3 50	4 59	1 20	2 38	1 20	17 04	0 55	16 53	0 40	20 39	2 46	21 52	0 48	8 31	2 17
16 Su	2 34	1S12	4 37	3S45	1 50	1 15	16 51	0 51	17 06	0 41	20 40	2 45	21 53	0 48	8 33	2 17
17 M	2 11	6 16	3 58	8 43	1 03	1 10	16 37	0 46	17 18	0 42	20 42	2 43	21 53	0 49	8 35	2 16
18 Tu	1 48	11 03	3 03	13 13	0 16	1 04	16 22	0 42	17 31	0 42	20 44	2 42	21 53	0 49	8 38	2 16
19 W	1 24	15 12	1 56	16 57	0S31	0 58	16 08	0 37	17 43	0 43	20 46	2 40	21 54	0 49	8 40	2 16
20 Th	1 01	18 25	0 41	19 35	1 18	0 52	15 52	0 33	17 55	0 43	20 48	2 38	21 54	0 49	8 43	2 16
21 F	0 38	20 27	0N35	20 58	2 04	0 46	15 37	0 29	18 07	0 44	20 49	2 37	21 54	0 49	8 45	2 16
22 Sa	0 14	21 08	1 49	20 58	2 50	0 40	15 20	0 24	18 18	0 45	20 51	2 35	21 54	0 49	8 48	2 16
23 Su	0S09	20 29	2 56	19 41	3 36	0 33	15 04	0 20	18 30	0 45	20 53	2 33	21 55	0 49	8 50	2 16
24 M	0 32	18 35	3 51	17 14	4 21	0 26	14 47	0 16	18 42	0 46	20 55	2 31	21 55	0 49	8 52	2 16
25 Tu	0 56	15 40	4 32	13 53	5 06	0 20	14 29	0 12	18 53	0 46	20 57	2 30	21 55	0 49	8 55	2 16
26 W	1 19	11 57	4 57	9 52	5 50	0 13	14 11	0 08	19 04	0 47	20 58	2 28	21 55	0 49	8 57	2 15
27 Th	1 42	7 42	5 06	5 27	6 34	0 06	13 53	0 03	19 16	0 47	21 00	2 26	21 55	0 49	8 60	2 15
28 F	2 06	3 09	4 59	0 51	7 17	0S01	13 34	0N01	19 27	0 48	21 02	2 24	21 55	0 49	9 02	2 15
29 Sa	2 29	1N27	4 36	3N43	7 60	0 09	13 15	0 05	19 38	0 48	21 04	2 22	21 55	0 49	9 05	2 15
30 Su	2S52	5N55	4N00	8N03	8S42	0S16	12N55	0N08	19S48	0S49	21N06	2S20	21N55	0S49	9S07	2N15

Day	⚷ Decl	⚷ Lat	♅ Decl	♅ Lat	♆ Decl	♆ Lat	♇ Decl	♇ Lat
1	3S26	5N49	2N20	0S45	11S30	0S37	19S34	3N41
6	3 32	5 49	2 16	0 45	11 33	0 37	19 35	3 40
11	3 38	5 48	2 12	0 45	11 36	0 37	19 36	3 39
16	3 43	5 48	2 07	0 45	11 39	0 37	19 37	3 38
21	3 49	5 47	2 03	0 45	11 41	0 37	19 39	3 37
26	3 55	5 46	1 58	0 45	11 44	0 37	19 40	3 36

Day	⚴ Decl	⚴ Lat	⚵ Decl	⚵ Lat	⚶ Decl	⚶ Lat	Eris Decl	Eris Lat
1	1S47	5S33	7S01	12N40	17N25	5S30	3S33	13S16
6	2 57	6 22	7 29	12 26	17 28	5 33	3 34	13 16
11	4 10	7 13	7 56	12 12	17 31	5 36	3 36	13 17
16	5 26	8 03	8 23	11 59	17 32	5 39	3 37	13 17
21	6 43	8 52	8 50	11 46	17 33	5 41	3 38	13 17
26	7 59	9 40	9 16	11 35	17 33	5 44	3 39	13 17

Moon Phenomena

Max/0 Decl
dy hr mn
1 9:06 0 N
8 18:17 21N15
15 18:20 0 S
22 0:09 21S08
28 16:25 0 N

Max/0 Lat
dy hr mn
7 2:08 0 S
14 6:47 5S03
20 12:55 0 N
27 0:48 5N06

Perigee/Apogee
dy hr m kilometers
7 5:56 a 404293
19 2:44 p 365752

PH dy hr mn
☾ 8 13:16 16♊17
● 16 2:12 23♍37
☽ 22 19:42 0♑12
○ 30 3:20 7♈22

Void of Course Moon

Last Aspect	☽ Ingress
1 20:03 ♀ △	♈ 2 5:38
4 11:07 ♀ □	♉ 4 15:42
5 18:56 ☉ △	♊ 7 4:11
9 11:00 ♄ △	♋ 9 16:50
11 22:00 ♄ □	♌ 12 3:02
14 5:15 ♄ ✶	♍ 14 9:32
16 11:27 ☿ ☌	♎ 16 12:56
18 11:31 ♆ ☍	♏ 18 14:47
20 13:12 ☉ ✶	♐ 20 16:35
22 16:46 ♄ ✶	♑ 22 19:22
24 21:20 ♄ □	♒ 24 23:34
27 3:34 ♄ △	♓ 27 5:25
29 2:36 ♂ △	♈ 29 13:15

DAILY ASPECTARIAN

1 Sa
☽□♃ 1:00
☿ ♍ 2:33
☽⚼♂ 12:19
☉#♄ 14:07
☽□⚳ 18:33
☽△♀ 20:03
☽∥♅ 21:03
☿☍♆ 21:17
☽⊼♄ 22:45

2 Su
☽#⚷ 2:57
☽⊻♆ 8:29
☽⊼☿ 10:32
☽⊼♂ 18:03
☽□♇ 18:57
☽⊻⚷ 19:13
☽☌♅ 20:00

3 M
☉∥☽ 0:39
☉⊼☽ 2:35
☽#♄ 3:58
♀□♄ 7:45
☿#♆ 9:06
☽✶♃ 9:58
♂✶♇ 11:06
☽∠♆ 13:09
☉∠♄ 14:44
♂△⚷ 15:13
☽⚼☿ 20:45
☽∥☿ 22:21

4 Tu
☽∠⚷ 0:08
☽#♆ 0:49
☽✶⚳ 5:21
♂⊼♅ 5:42
☽☍♄ 8:55
☉⚼☽ 10:20
☽□♀ 11:07
☽∠♃ 15:36
☿△♇ 16:48
☿☍⚷ 17:38
☽✶♆ 18:34
☽#♂ 22:26
☿⊼♅ 22:52

5 W
☽△♇ 5:39
☽✶⚷ 5:45
☽⊻♅ 6:37
☿✶♂ 8:07
☽☍♂ 8:09
☽△☿ 8:09
☽∠⚳ 11:54
☉△☽ 18:56
☽⊻♃ 21:52

6 Th
♇✶⚷ 9:25
☽∥♀ 9:28
☽⚼♇ 11:54
☽∠♅ 12:48
♀ ♌ 14:49
♀∠♃ 17:47
☽⊻⚳ 18:56
☽#♇ 21:09
☽⊼♄ 21:42

7 F
☿∠♄ 4:45
☽✶♀ 5:32
☽□♆ 6:58
☽∥⚳ 10:13
☉□♃ 10:16
☽□⚷ 18:16
☽⊼♇ 18:23
☽✶♅ 19:13
♀⊼♆ 20:54
☿#♄ 21:05

8 Sa
☽⊼♂ 0:34
☽⚼♄ 4:29
☽□☿ 8:50
☽☌♃ 11:14
☉□☽ 13:16
☽∠♀ 15:05

9 Su
☿□♃ 0:15
☽⚼♂ 8:40
☽☌⚳ 9:07
☽△♄ 11:00
☽△♆ 19:26
♂⚼⚳ 21:32

10 M
☽⊻♀ 0:09
☽∥⚳ 0:17
☽△⚷ 6:20
☽☍♇ 6:39
☽□♅ 7:18
☉☌☿ 12:45
☽#♇ 14:22
☽△♂ 16:06
☽⊻♃ 23:17

11 Tu
☽⚼♆ 0:50
☉✶☽ 5:55
☽✶☿ 7:23
☽∥♀ 10:21
☽⚼⚷ 11:23
☽⊻⚳ 20:56
☿∠♀ 21:10
☽□♄ 22:00
☽#♂ 23:37

12 W
☽∠♃ 4:05
☽⊼♆ 5:22
☉∠☽ 12:39
☽☌♀ 15:17
☽⊼⚷ 15:31
☽⊼♇ 16:00
☽△♅ 16:28
☽∠☿ 16:30
♀⊼⚷ 17:54
♀⊼♇ 23:48

13 Th
☽∠⚳ 1:23
☉#⚷ 3:24
☽□♂ 3:56
♀△♅ 4:46
☽#♆ 6:47
☽✶♃ 7:54
☿#⚷ 16:29
☉⊻☽ 18:11
☽⚼♇ 19:16
☽⚼♅ 19:38

14 F
☽⊻☿ 0:04
☽#♄ 0:28
☽✶⚳ 4:50
☽✶♄ 5:15
☉∥☿ 5:19
☽☍♆ 11:36
☽☍⚷ 21:02
☽△♇ 21:40
☽⊼♅ 21:58

15 Sa
☽#⚷ 0:38
☽⊻♀ 1:40
☉∥☽ 4:38
☽∥☿ 6:54
☽∠♄ 7:34
☽∥♅ 8:13
♀#♂ 10:01
☽✶♂ 11:34
☽□♃ 12:53
☿∥♅ 15:23
☿□⚳ 16:26
☿⊻♄ 16:51
⚳△♄ 21:44

16 Su
☉☌☽ 2:12
☽#☿ 2:37
☽#♅ 4:19
☽∠♀ 5:27
☉#☽ 5:58
☽⊻♄ 9:14
☽□⚳ 9:21
☽☌☿ 11:27
☽∥⚷ 11:55
☽∠♂ 14:14
☽⊼♆ 14:50
♂⊼♃ 17:25
⚵ ♐ 17:51
☿ ♎ 23:23
☽⊼⚷ 23:48

17 M
☽□♇ 0:34
☽☍♅ 0:43
☉∥♅ 4:53
☽✶♀ 8:40
☽∥♄ 11:29
☿⊼♆ 14:26
☽△♃ 15:28
☽⚼♆ 15:47
☽⊻♂ 16:28
☿∠♂ 22:06

18 Tu
☽⚼⚷ 0:38
☽∥♆ 3:20
♇ D 5:08
☉⊻☽ 7:51
☽☌♄ 11:31
☽△⚳ 12:03
☽⚼♃ 16:23
☽△♆ 16:34
♀∠⚳ 18:54
☽⊻☿ 20:13

19 W
☽△⚷ 1:22
☽✶♇ 2:17
☽⊼♅ 2:18
☽#♀ 5:46
♅□♇ 5:58
☉∠☽ 10:27
☽⚼⚳ 13:16
☽□♀ 14:30
☽⊼♃ 17:18
☉#☿ 18:14
☽∥♂ 19:18
☽☌♂ 20:34

20 Th
☽∠☿ 0:27
☽⚼♅ 3:06
☽∠♇ 3:10
☽∥♇ 12:37
☉✶☽ 13:12
☽⊻♄ 13:40
☽⊼⚳ 14:37
☿⊼⚷ 14:38
☽□♆ 18:19
☉⊻♄ 20:51
☿☍♅ 22:24
☿#♅ 23:07
☿□♇ 23:22

21 F
☽□⚷ 3:10
♀✶♃ 3:46
☽△♅ 4:07
☽⊻♇ 4:15
☽✶☿ 4:55
☽#⚳ 8:16
☽∠♄ 15:04
☉□⚳ 15:24
☽☍♃ 19:42
☽△♀ 21:02

22 Sa
☽⊻♂ 1:26
☉ ♎ 14:50
☽#⚳ 15:07
☽✶♄ 16:46
☽☍⚳ 18:08
☉□☽ 19:42
☽✶♆ 21:03

23 Su
☽⚼♀ 0:53
☽∠♂ 4:25
☽✶⚷ 6:04
☽□♅ 7:03
☽☌♇ 7:20
☿∥⚷ 8:14
☽∥♇ 12:19
☉⊼♆ 14:32
☽□☿ 15:03
☽∠♆ 22:56
☽∥♂ 23:01
☽⊼♃ 23:21

24 M
☽⊼♀ 5:13
☽✶♂ 7:50
☽∠⚷ 8:03
☽□♄ 21:20
☽⊼⚳ 23:06

25 Tu
☽⊻♆ 1:13
☽⚼♃ 1:44
☉△☽ 3:58
♂⚼♅ 6:44
☽#♀ 8:48
☽⊻⚷ 10:25
☽✶♅ 11:27
☽⊻♇ 11:55
♂∠♇ 15:35

26 W
☽∥♆ 1:17
♀⚼♅ 1:54
☽⚼⚳ 2:11
☽△☿ 3:14
☽△♃ 4:32
⚳ ♋ 7:01
♀⚼♇ 7:58
☿⚼♆ 8:39
☉⚼☽ 8:52
☿△♃ 14:10
☽∠♅ 14:16
☽∠♇ 14:49
☽☍♀ 15:28
☽□♂ 16:06
☽∥♄ 16:57

27 Th
☽△♄ 3:34
☽∥☿ 5:14
☽△⚳ 5:45
☽☌♆ 7:02
♀□♂ 8:50
☽⚼☿ 10:12
☉⊼☽ 14:21
☉#♅ 14:21
☽☌⚷ 16:28
☽⊻♅ 17:32
☽✶♇ 18:12
☽∥⚷ 19:55

28 F
☉∥☽ 5:06
☽#♅ 6:24
☽⚼♄ 7:26
☽□♃ 11:31
☉⊼⚷ 17:40
☽⊼☿ 17:52

29 Sa
☽∥♅ 2:27
☽△♂ 2:36
☽⊼♀ 4:14
☉#☽ 5:58
♂∥♇ 6:01
☉☍♅ 7:16
☽⊼♄ 11:51
☿⚼⚷ 12:48
☽#⚷ 13:24
☽□⚳ 14:26
☽⊻♆ 14:50
☉□♇ 17:56

30 Su
☽⊻⚷ 0:35
☽☌♅ 1:42
☽□♇ 2:36
☉☍☽ 3:20
☽⚼♂ 8:51
☽⚼♀ 11:46
☿∥♄ 15:37
⚳△♆ 15:50
☽#♄ 18:32
☽#☿ 19:05
☽∠♆ 19:37
☽✶♃ 20:41

October 2012

LONGITUDE

Day	Sid.Time	☉	☽	☽ 12 hour	Mean☊	True☊	☿	♀	♂	⚳	♃	♄	⚷	♅	♆	♇
	h m s	° ' "	° ' "	° ' "	° '	° '	° '	° '	° '	° '	° '	° '	° '	° '	° '	° '
1 M	0 40 31	8♎13 11	18♈03 41	24♈11 37	28♏28.1	26♏57.6	23♎15.2	27♌20.6	25♏41.1	0♋52.4	16♊21.6	29♎26.0	5♓54.4	6♈29.0	0♓48.4	6♑59.8
2 Tu	0 44 28	9 12 10	0♉16 33	6♉18 42	28 24.9	26R 52.1	24 47.8	28 30.0	26 23.1	1 02.8	16 22.2	29 33.0	5R 52.2	6R 26.6	0R 47.2	7 00.2
3 W	0 48 25	10 11 12	12 18 22	18 15 53	28 21.7	26 48.8	26 19.5	29 39.7	27 05.1	1 12.9	16 22.6	29 39.9	5 49.9	6 24.2	0 46.0	7 00.7
4 Th	0 52 21	11 10 15	24 11 38	0♊06 04	28 18.5	26D 47.6	27 50.4	0♍49.4	27 47.2	1 22.7	16R 22.9	29 46.9	5 47.7	6 21.8	0 44.9	7 01.1
5 F	0 56 18	12 09 21	5♊59 40	11 52 59	28 15.4	26 47.9	29 20.5	1 59.4	28 29.4	1 32.2	16 22.9	29 54.0	5 45.5	6 19.4	0 43.7	7 01.6
6 Sa	1 00 14	13 08 29	17 46 34	23 41 02	28 12.2	26 49.3	0♏49.7	3 09.4	29 11.7	1 41.5	16 22.7	0♏01.0	5 43.4	6 17.0	0 42.6	7 02.2
7 Su	1 04 11	14 07 40	29 37 00	5♋35 08	28 09.0	26 50.8	2 18.1	4 19.6	29 54.1	1 50.4	16 22.3	0 08.1	5 41.3	6 14.6	0 41.5	7 02.7
8 M	1 08 07	15 06 53	11♋36 03	17 40 26	28 05.8	26R 51.8	3 45.6	5 29.9	0♐36.5	1 59.0	16 21.7	0 15.2	5 39.3	6 12.2	0 40.5	7 03.3
9 Tu	1 12 04	16 06 08	23 48 54	0♌02 03	28 02.7	26 51.5	5 12.3	6 40.4	1 19.0	2 07.3	16 20.9	0 22.3	5 37.3	6 09.9	0 39.4	7 04.0
10 W	1 16 00	17 05 25	6♌20 27	12 44 36	27 59.5	26 49.6	6 38.1	7 51.0	2 01.6	2 15.4	16 19.9	0 29.4	5 35.3	6 07.5	0 38.4	7 04.6
11 Th	1 19 57	18 04 45	19 14 54	25 51 41	27 56.3	26 46.1	8 03.0	9 01.7	2 44.3	2 23.1	16 18.7	0 36.5	5 33.4	6 05.1	0 37.4	7 05.3
12 F	1 23 53	19 04 07	2♍35 08	9♍25 19	27 53.1	26 41.2	9 27.0	10 12.6	3 27.1	2 30.4	16 17.3	0 43.7	5 31.5	6 02.8	0 36.5	7 06.0
13 Sa	1 27 50	20 03 31	16 22 06	23 25 13	27 49.9	26 35.5	10 50.0	11 23.5	4 09.9	2 37.5	16 15.7	0 50.8	5 29.7	6 00.5	0 35.5	7 06.8
14 Su	1 31 47	21 02 57	0♎34 15	7♎48 36	27 46.8	26 29.7	12 12.1	12 34.6	4 52.8	2 44.2	16 13.9	0 58.0	5 27.9	5 58.1	0 34.6	7 07.6
15 M	1 35 43	22 02 26	15 07 30	22 30 05	27 43.6	26 24.6	13 33.1	13 45.8	5 35.9	2 50.5	16 11.9	1 05.2	5 26.2	5 55.8	0 33.7	7 08.4
16 Tu	1 39 40	23 01 56	29 55 24	7♏22 24	27 40.4	26 20.9	14 53.1	14 57.1	6 18.9	2 56.6	16 09.6	1 12.4	5 24.5	5 53.6	0 32.9	7 09.2
17 W	1 43 36	24 01 29	14♏50 04	22 17 22	27 37.2	26D 18.9	16 11.9	16 08.5	7 02.1	3 02.2	16 07.2	1 19.6	5 22.8	5 51.3	0 32.0	7 10.1
18 Th	1 47 33	25 01 04	29 43 23	7♐07 13	27 34.0	26 18.5	17 29.5	17 20.0	7 45.4	3 07.6	16 04.6	1 26.9	5 21.2	5 49.0	0 31.2	7 11.0
19 F	1 51 29	26 00 40	14♐28 09	21 45 32	27 30.9	26 19.3	18 45.8	18 31.6	8 28.7	3 12.6	16 01.8	1 34.1	5 19.7	5 46.8	0 30.5	7 11.9
20 Sa	1 55 26	27 00 18	28 58 54	6♑07 53	27 27.7	26 20.8	20 00.6	19 43.3	9 12.1	3 17.2	15 58.8	1 41.4	5 18.2	5 44.6	0 29.7	7 12.9
21 Su	1 59 22	27 59 59	13♑12 14	20 11 51	27 24.5	26 22.2	21 14.0	20 55.2	9 55.5	3 21.4	15 55.6	1 48.6	5 16.8	5 42.4	0 29.0	7 13.9
22 M	2 03 19	28 59 40	27 06 39	3♒56 43	27 21.3	26R 22.9	22 25.7	22 07.1	10 39.1	3 25.3	15 52.2	1 55.9	5 15.4	5 40.2	0 28.4	7 14.9
23 Tu	2 07 16	29 59 23	10♒42 07	17 23 00	27 18.2	26 22.4	23 35.7	23 19.1	11 22.7	3 28.9	15 48.7	2 03.1	5 14.1	5 38.1	0 27.7	7 15.9
24 W	2 11 12	0♏59 08	23 59 34	0♓31 59	27 15.0	26 20.8	24 43.6	24 31.2	12 06.4	3 32.0	15 44.9	2 10.4	5 12.8	5 36.0	0 27.1	7 17.0
25 Th	2 15 09	1 58 55	7♓00 27	13 25 12	27 11.8	26 18.0	25 49.4	25 43.4	12 50.1	3 34.8	15 40.9	2 17.6	5 11.5	5 33.9	0 26.5	7 18.1
26 F	2 19 05	2 58 43	19 46 26	26 04 20	27 08.6	26 14.5	26 52.9	26 55.6	13 34.0	3 37.2	15 36.8	2 24.9	5 10.4	5 31.8	0 26.0	7 19.2
27 Sa	2 23 02	3 58 33	2♈19 06	8♈30 55	27 05.5	26 10.8	27 53.7	28 08.0	14 17.8	3 39.2	15 32.5	2 32.2	5 09.3	5 29.8	0 25.4	7 20.3
28 Su	2 26 58	4 58 25	14 39 59	20 46 28	27 02.3	26 07.3	28 51.5	29 20.5	15 01.8	3 40.8	15 28.0	2 39.4	5 08.2	5 27.7	0 24.9	7 21.5
29 M	2 30 55	5 58 19	26 50 33	2♉52 26	26 59.1	26 04.4	29 46.2	0♎33.0	15 45.8	3 42.1	15 23.3	2 46.7	5 07.2	5 25.8	0 24.5	7 22.7
30 Tu	2 34 51	6 58 15	8♉52 20	14 50 27	26 55.9	26 02.5	0♐37.2	1 45.6	16 29.9	3 42.9	15 18.5	2 53.9	5 06.2	5 23.8	0 24.1	7 24.0
31 W	2 38 48	7♏58 12	20 47 03	26 42 22	26♏52.7	26♏01.5	1♐24.3	2♎58.4	17♐14.1	3♋43.4	15♊13.5	3♏01.2	5♓05.3	5♈21.9	0♓23.7	7♑25.2

1st of Month

Julian Day # 2456201.5
Obliquity 23°26'11"
SVP 5♓04'40"
GC 27♐01.0
Eris 22♈18.4R

Day	⚴
1	0♈48.3R
6	29♓26.3R
11	28 07.6R
16	26 54.0R
21	25 47.4R
26	24 49.1R
31	24 00.0R

Day	✱
1	3♐44.0
6	5 08.8
11	6 36.3
16	8 06.6
21	9 39.3
26	11 14.2
31	12 51.1

Day	⚶
1	24♊10.5
6	24 45.9
11	25 12.1
16	25 28.4
21	25 34.3
26	25 29.4R
31	25 13.6R

DECLINATION and LATITUDE

Day	☉ Decl	☽ Decl	☽ Lat	☽ 12h Decl	☿ Decl	☿ Lat	♀ Decl	♀ Lat	♂ Decl	♂ Lat	⚳ Decl	⚳ Lat	♃ Decl	♃ Lat	♄ Decl	♄ Lat
1 M	3S16	10N04	3N14	11N58	9S23	0S23	12N35	0N12	19S59	0S50	21N08	2S18	21N55	0S49	9S10	2N15
2 Tu	3 39	13 44	2 18	15 20	10 04	0 30	12 15	0 16	20 09	0 50	21 09	2 17	21 55	0 49	9 12	2 15
3 W	4 02	16 46	1 18	18 00	10 44	0 37	11 54	0 20	20 20	0 51	21 11	2 15	21 55	0 49	9 15	2 15
4 Th	4 25	19 03	0 14	19 53	11 24	0 45	11 33	0 23	20 30	0 51	21 13	2 13	21 55	0 49	9 17	2 15
5 F	4 48	20 29	0S50	20 52	12 03	0 52	11 11	0 27	20 40	0 52	21 15	2 11	21 55	0 49	9 20	2 15
6 Sa	5 11	21 01	1 52	20 56	12 41	0 59	10 49	0 31	20 49	0 52	21 17	2 08	21 55	0 49	9 22	2 15
7 Su	5 34	20 37	2 49	20 04	13 18	1 06	10 27	0 34	20 59	0 53	21 19	2 06	21 55	0 49	9 25	2 15
8 M	5 57	19 17	3 40	18 16	13 55	1 13	10 04	0 37	21 08	0 53	21 21	2 04	21 55	0 50	9 28	2 15
9 Tu	6 20	17 03	4 21	15 36	14 31	1 20	9 42	0 41	21 18	0 53	21 23	2 02	21 55	0 50	9 30	2 14
10 W	6 43	13 58	4 52	12 09	15 06	1 27	9 18	0 44	21 27	0 54	21 25	2 00	21 55	0 50	9 33	2 14
11 Th	7 05	10 09	5 09	8 00	15 40	1 34	8 55	0 47	21 36	0 54	21 27	1 58	21 55	0 50	9 35	2 14
12 F	7 28	5 44	5 10	3 20	16 13	1 40	8 31	0 50	21 44	0 55	21 29	1 56	21 54	0 50	9 38	2 14
13 Sa	7 50	0 52	4 53	1S39	16 46	1 47	8 07	0 53	21 53	0 55	21 31	1 53	21 54	0 50	9 40	2 14
14 Su	8 13	4S11	4 18	6 41	17 18	1 53	7 42	0 56	22 01	0 56	21 33	1 51	21 54	0 50	9 43	2 14
15 M	8 35	9 08	3 26	11 27	17 48	1 59	7 18	0 59	22 09	0 56	21 36	1 49	21 54	0 50	9 45	2 14
16 Tu	8 57	13 37	2 19	15 35	18 18	2 05	6 53	1 02	22 17	0 57	21 38	1 46	21 54	0 50	9 48	2 14
17 W	9 19	17 17	1 02	18 42	18 47	2 11	6 28	1 05	22 25	0 57	21 40	1 44	21 53	0 50	9 50	2 14
18 Th	9 41	19 47	0N19	20 32	19 14	2 17	6 02	1 07	22 33	0 57	21 42	1 42	21 53	0 50	9 53	2 14
19 F	10 03	20 54	1 38	20 56	19 41	2 22	5 37	1 10	22 40	0 58	21 45	1 39	21 53	0 50	9 55	2 14
20 Sa	10 24	20 36	2 50	19 56	20 06	2 27	5 11	1 12	22 47	0 58	21 47	1 37	21 52	0 50	9 58	2 14
21 Su	10 46	18 58	3 50	17 44	20 31	2 32	4 45	1 15	22 54	0 59	21 50	1 34	21 52	0 50	10 00	2 14
22 M	11 07	16 14	4 35	14 33	20 54	2 36	4 19	1 17	23 01	0 59	21 52	1 32	21 52	0 50	10 03	2 14
23 Tu	11 28	12 41	5 03	10 41	21 16	2 41	3 52	1 19	23 07	0 59	21 55	1 29	21 51	0 50	10 05	2 14
24 W	11 49	8 34	5 14	6 23	21 36	2 44	3 26	1 22	23 14	0 60	21 57	1 26	21 51	0 50	10 08	2 14
25 Th	12 10	4 09	5 09	1 53	21 55	2 48	2 59	1 24	23 20	1 00	21 60	1 24	21 50	0 50	10 10	2 14
26 F	12 30	0N23	4 49	2N37	22 13	2 51	2 32	1 26	23 26	1 01	22 02	1 21	21 50	0 50	10 13	2 14
27 Sa	12 51	4 49	4 15	6 57	22 30	2 53	2 05	1 28	23 31	1 01	22 05	1 18	21 49	0 50	10 15	2 14
28 Su	13 11	8 59	3 29	10 56	22 44	2 55	1 38	1 29	23 37	1 01	22 08	1 15	21 49	0 50	10 18	2 14
29 M	13 31	12 45	2 34	14 25	22 58	2 56	1 10	1 31	23 42	1 02	22 11	1 13	21 49	0 50	10 20	2 14
30 Tu	13 50	15 56	1 33	17 16	23 09	2 56	0 43	1 33	23 47	1 02	22 13	1 10	21 48	0 50	10 23	2 14
31 W	14S10	18N25	0N29	19N21	23S19	2S56	0N16	1N34	23S51	1S02	22N16	1S07	21N47	0S50	10S25	2N14

Day	⚷ Decl	⚷ Lat	♅ Decl	♅ Lat	♆ Decl	♆ Lat	♇ Decl	♇ Lat
1	3S60	5N45	1N53	0S45	11S46	0S37	19S41	3N3
6	4 05	5 43	1 48	0 45	11 48	0 37	19 41	3 3
11	4 10	5 42	1 44	0 45	11 50	0 37	19 42	3 3
16	4 15	5 40	1 39	0 45	11 52	0 37	19 43	3 3
21	4 19	5 39	1 35	0 45	11 53	0 37	19 44	3 3
26	4 23	5 37	1 31	0 45	11 54	0 37	19 45	3 3
31	4S26	5N35	1N27	0S45	11S55	0S37	19S45	3N2

Day	⚴ Decl	⚴ Lat	✱ Decl	✱ Lat	⚶ Decl	⚶ Lat	Eris Decl	Eris Lat
1	9S14	10S26	9S42	11N24	17N32	5S47	3S40	13S1
6	10 26	11 09	10 06	11 13	17 31	5 50	3 41	13 1
11	11 34	11 49	10 30	11 03	17 29	5 52	3 42	13 1
16	12 37	12 25	10 53	10 54	17 28	5 54	3 43	13 1
21	13 34	12 59	11 15	10 46	17 26	5 56	3 44	13 1
26	14 24	13 28	11 35	10 38	17 25	5 56	3 45	13 1
31	15S07	13S55	11S55	10N30	17N25	5S56	3S45	13S1

Moon Phenomena

Max/0 Decl

dy	hr mn	
6	1:42	21N01
13	4:10	0 S
19	6:37	20S58
25	22:00	0 N

Perigee/Apogee

dy	hr m		kilometers
5	0:37	a	405160
17	0:50	p	360673

Max/0 Lat

dy	hr mn	
4	5:16	0 S
11	13:33	5S11
17	18:29	0 N
24	4:14	5N15
31	10:37	0 S

PH	dy	hr mn	
☾	8	7:34	15♋26
●	15	12:04	22♎32
☽	22	3:33	29♑09
○	29	19:51	6♉48

Void of Course Moon

Last Aspect		☽ Ingress
1 22:33	♄ ☍	♉ 1 23:2
4 7:45	♂ ☍	♊ 4 11:4
5 21:09	♃ ☌	♋ 7 0:4
8 7:34	☉ □	♌ 9 11:5
10 21:41	☉ ✶	♍ 11 19:2
12 23:49	♃ □	♎ 13 23:0
15 12:04	☉ ☌	♏ 16 0:0
17 2:24	☿ ☌	♐ 18 0:2
19 20:28	☉ ✶	♑ 20 1:4
22 3:33	☉ □	♒ 22 5:0
24 1:28	☿ □	♓ 24 11:0
26 15:05	♀ ☍	♈ 26 19:3
28 1:33	♃ ✶	♉ 29 6:1
29 21:03	♇ △	♊ 31 18:4

DAILY ASPECTARIAN

1 M
☽∠⚷ 5:32
☽⋕♆ 10:44
☽☍☿ 11:38
☽∥♀ 14:43
☽⚻♂ 15:51
☽△♀ 20:07
☽☍♄ 22:33

2 Tu
☽✶♆ 1:01
☽✶⚳ 1:33
☽∠♃ 2:10
☽✶⚷ 11:05
☽⚺♅ 12:13
☽△♇ 13:23
☉⚻☽ 19:22

3 W
☉∥⚷ 0:02
♀✶♄ 0:06
♀ ♍ 7:00
♀⋕♆ 7:49
☽∠⚳ 7:59
☽⚺♃ 8:12
☽∠♅ 18:17
☽⚼♇ 19:35
⚴R♓ 22:18
☿⚺♂ 22:25
♀☍♆ 22:27

4 Th
☿⋕♀ 3:28
☉⚼☽ 4:23
☽☍♂ 7:45
☽⚻☿ 8:29
☽⋕♇ 8:58
☽⚻♄ 11:28
♀✶⚳ 13:14
☽□♆ 13:18
♃R 13:19
☿∥♆ 14:32
☽⚺⚳ 14:48
☽□♀ 14:57
☽□⚷ 23:31

5 F
☽✶♅ 0:40
☽⚻♇ 2:06
☽⋕♂ 5:44
☿☌♄ 9:45
☿ ♏ 10:36
☉△☽ 13:42
☽⚼♄ 18:20
☽⚼☿ 19:28
♄ ♏ 20:35
☽☌♃ 21:09
☿△♆ 22:07

6 Sa
☿⚼♃ 8:54
☽⋕♂ 13:27
☿△⚳ 15:37

7 Su
☽⚻♂ 0:37
☽△♄ 1:03
☽△♆ 2:10
♂ ♐ 3:22
☽☌⚳ 4:32
☽△☿ 6:10
♂⚺♄ 9:31
☽✶♀ 10:30
☽△⚷ 12:10
☽□♅ 13:16
☽☍♇ 14:56
☽⋕♇ 18:06

8 M
♂□♆ 2:11
♀☍⚷ 3:05
☉□☽ 7:34
☽⚼♆ 8:03
☽⚼♂ 8:25
☽⚺♃ 9:24
☉⚼♆ 13:22
♀⚻♅ 13:56
☽⚼⚷ 17:48
☽∠♀ 19:23

9 Tu
☉△♃ 5:53
☿△⚷ 6:49
♀△♇ 8:05
♀⋕♄ 10:46
☽□♄ 12:46
☽⚻♆ 13:10
☽∠♃ 14:30
☽△♂ 15:19
☿⚻♅ 15:39
☽⚺⚳ 16:10
☽⋕☿ 17:07
♂⋕⚳ 18:06
☉∠♂ 18:32
☽⚻⚷ 22:35
☽△♅ 23:36

10 W
☽□☿ 0:37
☽⚻♇ 1:23
☽⚺♀ 3:08
☿✶♇ 7:33
♂⚻⚳ 9:27
☽⋕♆ 13:58
☽✶♃ 18:37
☽∠⚳ 20:33
☉✶☽ 21:41

11 Th
♄△♆ 2:40
☽⋕♄ 3:14
☽⚼♅ 3:21
☽⚼♇ 5:11
☽∥♀ 7:44
☉⋕☽ 15:36
☽☍♆ 20:30
☽✶♄ 20:40
☽✶⚳ 23:52

12 F
☽□♂ 1:37
☉∠☽ 2:49
☽☍⚷ 5:10
☽⚻♅ 6:05
☽⋕⚷ 7:47
☽△♇ 7:57
☽✶☿ 13:24
☽☌♀ 14:37
☽∥♅ 20:01
☽∠♄ 23:06
☽□♃ 23:49

13 Sa
♂⋕♃ 3:36
☉⚺☽ 6:47
☉⋕♀ 8:26
☉⚼⚷ 10:15
☽⋕♅ 12:12
☽∠☿ 17:46

14 Su
☽⚻♆ 0:01
☽∥⚷ 0:10
☽⚺♄ 0:40
☽□⚳ 3:38
☽✶♂ 7:32
☽⚻⚷ 8:07
☽☍♅ 8:56
☽□♇ 10:53
☽⋕♀ 15:39
♂□⚷ 18:48
☉∥☽ 21:04
☽⚺☿ 21:10
☽⚺♀ 21:35

15 M
☽⚼♆ 0:43
☽△♃ 1:45
☽∥♄ 3:12
☽⚼⚷ 8:38
☽∠♂ 9:22
♂△♅ 10:35
☉☌☽ 12:04
☽∥♆ 14:10
♃⚼♄ 16:57

16 Tu
☽∠♀ 0:03
☽△♆ 1:00
☽⚼♃ 1:59
☽☌♄ 2:05
☽△⚳ 4:54
☽△⚷ 8:49
☽⚻♅ 9:36
☽⚺♂ 10:49
☽✶♇ 11:39
☿✶♀ 12:32
☿⚻♃ 22:37
♀□♃ 23:35

17 W
☽⚻♃ 2:04
☽✶♀ 2:17
☽☌☿ 2:24
♀∠♄ 4:10
♂⚺♇ 4:31
☽⚼⚳ 5:11
☽⚼♅ 9:40
☽∠♇ 11:49
☉⚺☽ 15:51
☽∥☿ 15:55
☽∥♇ 23:15

18 Th
☽□♆ 1:17
☽⚺♄ 2:49
☽⚻⚳ 5:33
☽□⚷ 9:07
☽△♅ 9:51
☽⚺♇ 12:07
☿⚼⚳ 12:47
☽☌♂ 13:42
☉∥♄ 14:43
☉∠☽ 17:56

19 F
☽☍♃ 2:33
☿∥♇ 2:41
☽∠♄ 3:28
☽□♀ 7:16
☽⚺☿ 7:43
☉✶☽ 20:28

20 Sa
☽✶♆ 2:32
☽✶♄ 4:34
☽☍⚳ 7:15
☽∥☿ 7:22
☽✶⚷ 10:35
☽∠☿ 11:04
☽□♅ 11:19
☽☌♇ 13:51
☿⚼♅ 13:54
☽∥♇ 14:52
☽⚺♂ 18:07

21 Su
☽∠♆ 3:54
☽⚻♃ 4:38
⚶R 6:35
☽∠⚷ 12:07
☽△♀ 14:30
☽✶☿ 15:06
☿∠♇ 20:16
⚳∥♃ 20:20
☽∠♂ 21:19
♀⋕⚷ 22:52

22 M
☉□☽ 3:33
☽⚺♆ 5:53
☽⚼♃ 6:33
☽□♄ 8:32
☽⚻⚳ 11:08
☽⚺⚷ 14:18
☽✶♅ 15:01
☽⚺♇ 17:52
☽⚼♀ 19:20

23 Tu
☉ ♏ 0:15
☽✶♂ 1:17
☽∥♆ 4:52
☉∥☽ 6:48
☽△♃ 9:07
☉△♆ 11:16
☽⚼⚳ 14:02
☽∥♄ 15:17
☽∠♅ 17:50
☉⚼♃ 18:37
☽∠♇ 20:53

24 W
☽⚻♀ 1:04
☽□☿ 1:28
☉∥♆ 5:21
☽☌♆ 11:50
☉△☽ 13:54
☽△♄ 15:10
☽△⚳ 17:37
☿⋕♃ 17:39
☽☌⚷ 20:38
☽⚺♅ 21:19
☽∥⚷ 22:50

25 Th
☽✶♇ 0:33
☿⋕⚳ 6:28
☽⋕♀ 6:53
☉☌♄ 8:33
☽□♂ 11:34
☽⋕♅ 13:57
☽□♃ 16:10
☿✶♀ 17:11
☽⚼♄ 19:29
☉⚼☽ 20:19

26 F
☽∥♅ 6:03
☽∥♀ 10:29
☽△☿ 14:45
☽☍♀ 15:05
☉△⚳ 15:59
☽⚺♆ 20:21
☽⋕⚷ 21:40

27 Sa
☽⚻♄ 0:25
☽□⚳ 2:35
☉⚻☽ 3:29
☽⚺⚷ 5:28
☽☌♅ 6:08
☽□♇ 9:44
☽⚼☿ 22:17

28 Su
☽△♂ 0:45
☽∠♆ 1:28
☽✶♃ 1:33
☉△⚷ 3:51
♀∥♅ 7:45
☽⋕♄ 8:05
☽∠⚷ 10:44
☉⚻♅ 11:22
♂☍♃ 12:56
♀ ♎ 13:05
☽⋕♆ 18:21
♀⚻♆ 21:12

29 M
☉⋕☽ 5:57
☽⚻☿ 6:16
☿ ♐ 6:19
☽∠♃ 7:00
☽✶♆ 7:05
☽⚻♀ 8:11
☽⚼♂ 8:18
☽☍♄ 11:56
☽✶⚳ 13:40
☽✶⚷ 16:28
☽⚺♅ 17:03
☿□♆ 17:41
☉☍☽ 19:51
☽△♇ 21:03

30 Tu
☉✶♇ 10:31
☽⚺♃ 12:51
☽⚻♂ 16:21
☽⚼♀ 17:40
☽∠⚳ 19:50
☽∠♅ 23:09

31 W
♀⚺♄ 1:02
☽⚼♇ 3:19
♀□⚳ 14:53
⚳R 15:47
☽⋕♇ 18:10
☽□♆ 19:29
☽☍☿ 22:56

LONGITUDE

Day	Sid.Time	☉	☽	☽ 12 hour	Mean☊	True☊	☿	♀	♂	⚳	♃	♄	⚷	♅	♆	♇
	h m s	° ' "	° ' "	° ' "	° '	° '	° '	° '	° '	° '	° '	° '	° '	° '	° '	° '
1 Th	2 42 45	8♏58 12	2♊36 43	8♊30 24	26♏49.6	26♏01.6	2♐06.9	4♎11.1	17♐58.3	3♋43.5	15♊08.3	3♏08.4	5♓04.5	5♈20.0	0♓23.3	7♑26.5
2 F	2 46 41	9 58 14	14 23 48	20 17 17	26 46.4	26 02.4	2 44.6	5 24.0	18 42.6	3R 43.1	15R 02.9	3 15.6	5R 03.7	5R 18.1	0R 23.0	7 27.8
3 Sa	2 50 38	10 58 17	26 11 16	2♋06 13	26 43.2	26 03.7	3 16.7	6 37.0	19 27.0	3 42.4	14 57.4	3 22.9	5 03.0	5 16.3	0 22.7	7 29.1
4 Su	2 54 34	11 58 23	8♋02 36	14 00 56	26 40.0	26 05.1	3 42.8	7 50.0	20 11.4	3 41.2	14 51.8	3 30.1	5 02.3	5 14.5	0 22.4	7 30.5
5 M	2 58 31	12 58 31	20 01 46	26 05 37	26 36.9	26 06.3	4 02.2	9 03.1	20 55.9	3 39.7	14 45.9	3 37.3	5 01.7	5 12.7	0 22.2	7 31.9
6 Tu	3 02 27	13 58 40	2♌13 05	8♌24 42	26 33.7	26 07.1	4R 14.1	10 16.3	21 40.5	3 37.7	14 40.0	3 44.5	5 01.1	5 11.0	0 22.0	7 33.3
7 W	3 06 24	14 58 52	14 41 03	21 02 38	26 30.5	26R 07.4	4 18.0	11 29.6	22 25.1	3 35.4	14 33.8	3 51.7	5 00.6	5 09.3	0 21.8	7 34.7
8 Th	3 10 20	15 59 06	27 29 57	4♍03 27	26 27.3	26 07.2	4 13.3	12 42.9	23 09.8	3 32.6	14 27.6	3 58.8	5 00.2	5 07.6	0 21.7	7 36.2
9 F	3 14 17	16 59 22	10♍43 28	17 30 16	26 24.1	26 06.5	3 59.2	13 56.3	23 54.6	3 29.4	14 21.1	4 06.0	4 59.8	5 06.0	0 21.6	7 37.7
10 Sa	3 18 14	17 59 40	24 23 59	1♎24 36	26 21.0	26 05.6	3 35.4	15 09.8	24 39.4	3 25.8	14 14.6	4 13.1	4 59.5	5 04.4	0 21.5	7 39.2
11 Su	3 22 10	18 59 59	8♎31 58	15 45 45	26 17.8	26 04.7	3 01.6	16 23.3	25 24.3	3 21.7	14 07.9	4 20.2	4 59.2	5 02.8	0D 21.5	7 40.7
12 M	3 26 07	20 00 21	23 05 24	0♏30 15	26 14.6	26 03.9	2 17.7	17 36.9	26 09.3	3 17.3	14 01.1	4 27.3	4 59.0	5 01.3	0 21.5	7 42.3
13 Tu	3 30 03	21 00 45	7♏59 26	15 31 56	26 11.4	26 03.5	1 24.2	18 50.6	26 54.3	3 12.5	13 54.2	4 34.4	4 58.9	4 59.8	0 21.6	7 43.8
14 W	3 34 00	22 01 10	23 06 38	0♐42 22	26 08.3	26D 03.3	0 21.8	20 04.3	27 39.4	3 07.2	13 47.1	4 41.5	4D 58.8	4 58.4	0 21.6	7 45.4
15 Th	3 37 56	23 01 37	8♐17 54	15 52 03	26 05.1	26 03.4	29♎11.7	21 18.1	28 24.6	3 01.6	13 40.0	4 48.5	4 58.8	4 57.0	0 21.8	7 47.0
16 F	3 41 53	24 02 06	23 23 40	0♑51 45	26 01.9	26 03.5	27 55.7	22 31.9	29 09.8	2 55.5	13 32.7	4 55.5	4 58.8	4 55.7	0 21.9	7 48.7
17 Sa	3 45 49	25 02 36	8♑15 25	15 33 55	25 58.7	26 03.7	26 35.8	23 45.8	29 55.1	2 49.1	13 25.3	5 02.5	4 58.9	4 54.4	0 22.1	7 50.3
18 Su	3 49 46	26 03 08	22 46 42	29 53 22	25 55.6	26R 03.7	25 14.7	24 59.7	0♑40.4	2 42.2	13 17.9	5 09.5	4 59.1	4 53.1	0 22.3	7 52.0
19 M	3 53 43	27 03 40	6♒53 43	13♒47 39	25 52.4	26 03.7	23 55.0	26 13.7	1 25.8	2 35.0	13 10.3	5 16.4	4 59.3	4 51.9	0 22.6	7 53.7
20 Tu	3 57 39	28 04 14	20 35 15	27 16 40	25 49.2	26D 03.6	22 39.4	27 27.7	2 11.2	2 27.4	13 02.7	5 23.3	4 59.6	4 50.7	0 22.8	7 55.4
21 W	4 01 36	29 04 49	3♓52 10	10♓22 05	25 46.0	26 03.6	21 30.2	28 41.7	2 56.7	2 19.4	12 55.0	5 30.2	4 59.9	4 49.6	0 23.2	7 57.2
22 Th	4 05 32	0♐05 25	16 46 48	23 06 44	25 42.8	26 03.8	20 29.6	29 55.8	3 42.2	2 11.0	12 47.2	5 37.0	5 00.3	4 48.5	0 23.5	7 58.9
23 F	4 09 29	1 06 02	29 22 19	5♈34 01	25 39.7	26 04.2	19 39.0	1♏10.0	4 27.8	2 02.3	12 39.3	5 43.8	5 00.7	4 47.5	0 23.9	8 00.7
24 Sa	4 13 25	2 06 41	11♈42 14	17 47 26	25 36.5	26 04.8	18 59.4	2 24.2	5 13.5	1 53.2	12 31.4	5 50.6	5 01.3	4 46.5	0 24.3	8 02.5
25 Su	4 17 22	3 07 21	23 50 00	29 50 20	25 33.3	26 05.5	18 31.5	3 38.4	5 59.2	1 43.8	12 23.4	5 57.4	5 01.8	4 45.5	0 24.8	8 04.3
26 M	4 21 18	4 08 01	5♉48 49	11♉45 48	25 30.1	26 06.3	18D 15.2	4 52.7	6 45.0	1 34.0	12 15.4	6 04.1	5 02.5	4 44.6	0 25.3	8 06.1
27 Tu	4 25 15	5 08 44	17 41 35	23 36 28	25 27.0	26R 06.8	18 10.2	6 07.0	7 30.8	1 23.9	12 07.4	6 10.8	5 03.2	4 43.8	0 25.8	8 08.0
28 W	4 29 12	6 09 27	29 30 47	5♊24 45	25 23.8	26 06.9	18 16.1	7 21.3	8 16.6	1 13.5	11 59.3	6 17.4	5 03.9	4 43.0	0 26.3	8 09.8
29 Th	4 33 08	7 10 12	11♊18 41	17 12 48	25 20.6	26 06.4	18 31.9	8 35.7	9 02.5	1 02.7	11 51.1	6 24.0	5 04.7	4 42.2	0 26.9	8 11.7
30 F	4 37 05	8♐10 58	23 07 23	29 02 42	25♏17.4	26♏05.3	18♏56.9	9♏50.2	9♑48.5	0♋51.7	11♊43.0	6♏30.6	5♓05.6	4♈41.5	0♓27.6	8♑13.6

1st of Month

Julian Day # 2456232.5
Obliquity 23°26'10"
SVP 5♓04'37"
GC 27♐01.1
Eris 22♈00.0R

Day	⚴
1	23♓51.3R
6	23 14.2R
11	22 47.6R
16	22 31.6R
21	22 26.3R
26	22 31.3

Day	⚵
1	13♐10.7
6	14 49.8
11	16 30.7
16	18 13.1
21	19 56.9
26	21 41.9

Day	⚶
1	25♊09.1R
6	24 40.0R
11	23 59.9R
16	23 09.6R
21	22 10.0R
26	21 02.6R

DECLINATION and LATITUDE

Day	☉ Decl	☽ Decl	☽ Lat	☽12h Decl	☿ Decl	☿ Lat	♀ Decl	♀ Lat	♂ Decl	♂ Lat	⚳ Decl	⚳ Lat	♃ Decl	♃ Lat	♄ Decl	♄ Lat
1 Th	14S29	20N05	0S36	20N35	23S27	2S55	0S12	1N36	23S56	1S03	22N19	1S04	21N47	0S50	10S28	2N14
2 F	14 48	20 52	1 40	20 55	23 32	2 53	0 40	1 37	24 00	1 03	22 22	1 01	21 46	0 50	10 30	2 14
3 Sa	15 07	20 43	2 40	20 18	23 36	2 50	1 07	1 38	24 04	1 03	22 25	0 58	21 46	0 50	10 32	2 14
4 Su	15 26	19 39	3 33	18 47	23 37	2 46	1 35	1 40	24 08	1 04	22 28	0 55	21 45	0 50	10 35	2 14
5 M	15 44	17 42	4 17	16 25	23 36	2 41	2 03	1 41	24 11	1 04	22 32	0 52	21 44	0 50	10 37	2 14
6 Tu	16 02	14 56	4 51	13 17	23 32	2 35	2 30	1 42	24 14	1 04	22 35	0 49	21 44	0 50	10 40	2 14
7 W	16 20	11 27	5 11	9 29	23 25	2 27	2 58	1 43	24 17	1 04	22 38	0 45	21 43	0 50	10 42	2 14
8 Th	16 37	7 22	5 18	5 08	23 15	2 18	3 26	1 44	24 20	1 05	22 41	0 42	21 42	0 50	10 44	2 14
9 F	16 54	2 48	5 07	0 24	23 02	2 07	3 54	1 44	24 23	1 05	22 45	0 39	21 42	0 50	10 47	2 14
10 Sa	17 11	2S04	4 40	4S32	22 45	1 55	4 21	1 45	24 25	1 05	22 48	0 36	21 41	0 50	10 49	2 14
11 Su	17 28	6 59	3 55	9 22	22 25	1 41	4 49	1 46	24 27	1 05	22 51	0 32	21 40	0 50	10 51	2 14
12 M	17 44	11 39	2 53	13 48	22 01	1 25	5 17	1 46	24 28	1 06	22 55	0 29	21 40	0 50	10 54	2 14
13 Tu	18 00	15 44	1 39	17 25	21 33	1 08	5 44	1 47	24 30	1 06	22 58	0 25	21 39	0 49	10 56	2 14
14 W	18 16	18 49	0 16	19 52	21 02	0 50	6 12	1 47	24 31	1 06	23 02	0 22	21 38	0 49	10 58	2 14
15 Th	18 32	20 34	1N08	20 54	20 28	0 30	6 39	1 47	24 32	1 06	23 06	0 18	21 37	0 49	11 01	2 14
16 F	18 47	20 50	2 26	20 24	19 51	0 10	7 06	1 47	24 33	1 07	23 09	0 15	21 36	0 49	11 03	2 14
17 Sa	19 01	19 37	3 34	18 31	19 13	0N11	7 33	1 47	24 33	1 07	23 13	0 11	21 36	0 49	11 05	2 15
18 Su	19 16	17 08	4 26	15 31	18 34	0 31	8 00	1 47	24 33	1 07	23 17	0 08	21 35	0 49	11 07	2 15
19 M	19 30	13 42	5 01	11 43	17 55	0 51	8 27	1 47	24 33	1 07	23 21	0 04	21 34	0 49	11 10	2 15
20 Tu	19 44	9 37	5 17	7 26	17 18	1 10	8 54	1 47	24 33	1 07	23 24	0 00	21 33	0 49	11 12	2 15
21 W	19 57	5 11	5 15	2 55	16 44	1 27	9 21	1 47	24 32	1 08	23 28	0N03	21 32	0 49	11 14	2 15
22 Th	20 10	0 39	4 58	1N36	16 13	1 43	9 47	1 47	24 31	1 08	23 32	0 07	21 31	0 49	11 16	2 15
23 F	20 23	3N49	4 26	5 58	15 47	1 56	10 13	1 46	24 30	1 08	23 36	0 11	21 30	0 49	11 18	2 15
24 Sa	20 35	8 03	3 43	10 01	15 25	2 07	10 39	1 46	24 28	1 08	23 40	0 15	21 29	0 49	11 21	2 15
25 Su	20 47	11 53	2 50	13 37	15 09	2 17	11 05	1 45	24 26	1 08	23 44	0 18	21 29	0 49	11 23	2 15
26 M	20 58	15 12	1 51	16 37	14 57	2 24	11 30	1 45	24 24	1 08	23 48	0 22	21 28	0 48	11 25	2 15
27 Tu	21 09	17 51	0 47	18 54	14 51	2 29	11 55	1 44	24 22	1 09	23 52	0 26	21 27	0 48	11 27	2 15
28 W	21 20	19 44	0S19	20 21	14 49	2 33	12 20	1 43	24 19	1 09	23 56	0 30	21 26	0 48	11 29	2 15
29 Th	21 30	20 45	1 23	20 55	14 52	2 34	12 45	1 42	24 16	1 09	23 60	0 34	21 25	0 48	11 31	2 16
30 F	21S40	20N51	2S24	20N33	14S58	2N35	13S10	1N41	24S13	1S09	24N04	0N38	21N24	0S48	11S33	2N16

Day	⚷ Decl	⚷ Lat	♅ Decl	♅ Lat	♆ Decl	♆ Lat	♇ Decl	♇ Lat
1	4S27	5N35	1N26	0S45	11S55	0S37	19S45	3N29
6	4 30	5 33	1 23	0 44	11 55	0 37	19 46	3 28
11	4 32	5 31	1 20	0 44	11 55	0 37	19 46	3 27
16	4 34	5 29	1 17	0 44	11 55	0 37	19 47	3 26
21	4 36	5 27	1 15	0 44	11 55	0 37	19 47	3 25
26	4 36	5 26	1 13	0 44	11 54	0 37	19 48	3 24

Day	⚴ Decl	⚴ Lat	⚵ Decl	⚵ Lat	⚶ Decl	⚶ Lat	Eris Decl	Eris Lat
1	15S15	13S59	11S58	10N29	17N25	5S56	3S45	13S16
6	15 51	14 22	12 16	10 22	17 25	5 55	3 46	13 16
11	16 19	14 42	12 32	10 16	17 26	5 53	3 47	13 15
16	16 42	14 59	12 47	10 10	17 27	5 49	3 47	13 15
21	16 58	15 14	12 60	10 05	17 29	5 44	3 47	13 14
26	17 08	15 28	13 11	10 01	17 32	5 37	3 48	13 13

Moon Phenomena

Max/0 Decl

dy	hr mn	
2	8:15	20N55
9	13:56	0 S
15	16:11	20S55
22	3:25	0 N
29	14:34	20N56

Max/0 Lat

dy	hr mn	
7	21:29	5S18
14	4:39	0 N
20	9:47	5N18
27	17:05	0 S

Perigee/Apogee

dy	hr m		kilometers
1	15:30	a	406050
14	10:20	p	357366
28	19:33	a	406362

PH	dy	hr mn	
☾	7	0:37	15♌00
●	13	22:09	21♏57
●	13	22:13	T 04'02"
☽	20	14:33	28♒41
○	28	14:47	6♊47
○	28	14:34	A 0.915

Void of Course Moon

Last Aspect				☽ Ingress		
2	9:23	♂	☍	♋	3	7:44
4	8:38	☉	△	♌	5	19:40
7	15:28	♂	△	♍	8	4:36
10	0:28	♂	□	♎	10	9:36
12	5:14	♂	✶	♏	12	11:11
14	10:40	☿	☌	♐	14	10:53
16	9:45	♂	☌	♑	16	10:37
18	5:55	☉	✶	♒	18	12:11
20	14:33	☉	□	♓	20	16:56
22	6:33	☿	△	♈	23	1:13
24	1:36	♃	✶	♉	25	12:19
27	0:58	☿	☍	♊	28	0:59
29	1:05	♃	☌	♋	30	13:56

DAILY ASPECTARIAN

1 Th	☽ ⚻ ♄	1:05
	☽ ⚺ ⚳	2:16
	☽ △ ♀	3:34
	☽ □ ⚷	5:00
	☽ ✶ ♅	5:31
	♂ ∠ ♄	6:32
	☽ ⚻ ♇	9:51
	☉ ⚻ ☽	14:09
	♀ ⚻ ⚷	17:23
	♀ ☍ ♅	22:06
2 F	☽ ☌ ♃	1:19
	☽ ⚼ ♄	7:57
	☽ ☍ ♂	9:23
	☉ ⚼ ☽	23:31
3 Sa	☿ ⚺ ♄	6:57
	☽ △ ♆	8:30
	☽ △ ♄	14:44
	♀ ⋕ ♅	14:52
	☽ ⚻ ☿	14:57
	☽ ☌ ⚳	15:13
	♀ □ ♇	17:28
	☽ △ ⚷	17:57
	☽ □ ♅	18:22
	☽ ⋕ ♇	22:14
	☿ ⚻ ⚳	22:27
	☽ ☍ ♇	22:55
	☽ □ ♀	23:32
4 Su	☉ △ ☽	8:38
	☽ ⚺ ♃	13:35
	☽ ⚼ ♆	14:43
	☽ ⚼ ☿	21:59
	☽ ⚼ ⚷	24:00
5 M	☽ ⚻ ♂	1:55
	⚳ △ ♄	6:24
	☉ ⋕ ☽	16:06
	☽ ∠ ♃	19:03
	☽ ⚻ ♆	20:23
6 Tu	☽ ⚺ ⚳	2:44
	☽ □ ♄	3:00
	☽ △ ☿	3:58
	☽ ⚻ ⚷	5:26
	☽ △ ♅	5:45
	☽ ⚼ ♂	9:12
	☽ ⚻ ♇	10:22
	☉ ⚻ ♃	14:57
	☽ ✶ ♀	17:16
	☽ ⋕ ♆	21:02
	☿ R	23:05
	☽ ✶ ♃	23:46
7 W	☉ □ ☽	0:37
	☽ ⋕ ♄	4:38
	☽ ∠ ⚳	7:22
	☽ ⚼ ♅	10:19
	☽ ⚼ ♇	14:54
	☽ △ ♂	15:28
8 Th	☽ ∠ ♀	0:26
	☽ ☍ ♆	5:16
	☽ ✶ ⚳	11:01
	☽ ✶ ♄	11:58
	☽ □ ☿	12:07
	☽ ☍ ⚷	13:42
	☽ ⚻ ♅	13:54
	☽ ⋕ ⚷	15:10
	☿ ⚺ ♄	17:24
	☽ △ ♇	18:26
	☽ ⋕ ♀	18:55
9 F	☽ ⚺ ♀	6:17
	☽ □ ♃	6:24
	☽ ∥ ♅	7:17
	♀ △ ♃	7:27
	☉ ✶ ☽	11:58
	☽ ∠ ♄	14:55
	☽ ⋕ ♅	20:29
	☿ ⋕ ⚳	20:32
10 Sa	☽ □ ♂	0:28
	♀ ⚼ ♆	3:50
	☿ ⚻ ⚳	8:39
	♀ ∥ ⚷	9:14
	☉ ⚼ ⚳	9:45
	☽ ⚻ ♆	10:13
	☽ ∥ ⚷	12:01
	☽ ∥ ♀	12:18
	☽ ✶ ☿	15:07
	☽ □ ⚳	15:21
	☉ ∠ ☽	15:48
	☽ ⚺ ♄	16:54
	☽ ⚻ ⚷	18:03
	☽ ☍ ♅	18:10
	☽ □ ♇	22:34
11 Su	♆ D	7:53
	☽ △ ♃	9:14
	☽ ⚼ ♆	11:20
	☽ ☌ ♀	14:14
	☽ ∠ ☿	15:00
	☉ ⚺ ☽	18:36
	☽ ⚼ ⚷	18:56
	☽ ∥ ♄	19:54
	☿ ∠ ♀	20:13
12 M	☉ ⚼ ♅	0:22
	☽ ∥ ♆	1:27
	☽ ✶ ♂	5:14
	☽ ⚼ ♃	9:32
	☽ △ ♆	11:46
	☽ ⚺ ☿	14:04
	☽ △ ⚳	16:23
	☽ ☌ ♄	18:29
	☿ ⋕ ♃	19:02
	☽ △ ⚷	19:11
	☽ ⚻ ♅	19:13
	☽ ✶ ♇	23:35
13 Tu	☽ ∠ ♂	6:34
	☽ ⚻ ♃	9:20
	☽ ⚼ ⚳	16:09
	♅ ⚺ ⚷	17:24
	☉ ∥ ☽	18:30
	☽ ⚺ ♀	18:46
	☽ ⚼ ♅	19:03
	☉ ☌ ☽	22:09
	♀ ⚼ ⚷	22:12
	☽ ∠ ♇	23:26
14 W	☿ □ ♆	0:04
	☽ ⚺ ♂	7:33
	☿ R ♏	7:43
	☽ ☌ ☿	10:40
	☽ ∥ ♇	10:49
	☽ □ ♆	11:27
	☽ ⚻ ⚳	15:43
	☉ ∠ ♇	18:03
	☽ ⚺ ♄	18:26
	☽ △ ♅	18:43
	☽ □ ⚷	18:45
	☽ ∠ ♀	20:34
	⚷ D	20:39
	☽ ∥ ☿	22:26
	☽ ⚺ ♇	23:11
15 Th	☽ ☍ ♃	8:26
	☿ ⚺ ♂	9:27
	☽ ∠ ♄	18:25
	☽ ✶ ♀	22:30
16 F	♄ ⚻ ♅	0:28
	☉ ⚺ ☽	1:06
	☿ ∥ ♇	2:44
	☽ ⚺ ☿	6:41
	☽ ☌ ♂	9:45
	☽ ✶ ♆	11:12
	♄ △ ⚷	11:24
	☽ ☍ ⚳	15:14
	☽ □ ♅	18:33
	☽ ✶ ⚷	18:40
	☽ ✶ ♄	18:44
	☽ ∥ ♇	21:50
	☽ ☌ ♇	23:19
17 Sa	♂ ♑	2:37
	☉ ∠ ☽	3:08
	☽ ∠ ☿	5:00
	☉ ∥ ☿	5:08
	☉ ∥ ☽	6:11
	☽ ∥ ☿	6:46
	☽ ⚻ ♃	8:24
	☽ ∠ ♆	11:41
	♂ ✶ ♆	14:23
	☉ ☌ ☿	15:48
	☽ ∠ ⚷	19:20
18 Su	☿ ⚺ ♀	2:20
	☽ ✶ ☿	3:47
	☽ □ ♀	4:04
	☉ ✶ ☽	5:55
	☽ ⚼ ♃	9:13
	☽ ⚺ ♆	12:50
	☽ ⚺ ♂	14:05
	☽ ⚻ ⚳	16:40
	☽ ✶ ♅	20:31
	☽ ⚺ ⚷	20:43
	☽ □ ♄	21:11
19 M	☽ ⚺ ♇	1:44
	☽ △ ♃	10:49
	☽ ∥ ♆	10:50
	☽ ∥ ♄	15:06
	☽ ∠ ♂	17:37
	☽ ⚼ ⚳	18:30
	☿ ∠ ♇	18:53
	☽ ∠ ♅	22:41
20 Tu	☽ □ ☿	3:23
	☽ ∥ ♀	3:36
	☽ ∠ ♇	4:11
	☉ ∥ ♇	6:20
	♂ ☍ ⚳	7:17
	♀ ⚼ ♃	10:17
	☽ △ ♀	13:36
	☉ □ ☽	14:33
	☽ ☌ ♆	17:38
	☽ △ ⚳	21:12
	☽ ✶ ♂	22:12
21 W	⚴ D	1:25
	☽ ⚺ ♅	1:45
	☽ ☌ ⚷	2:04
	☽ △ ♄	3:02
	☽ ∥ ⚷	3:09
	☽ ✶ ♇	7:32
	☽ □ ♃	16:35
	☽ ⚼ ♀	20:09
	☽ ⋕ ♅	20:51
	☉ ♐	21:51
22 Th	♀ ♏	1:21
	☽ △ ☿	6:33
	☉ □ ♆	7:12
	☽ ⚼ ♄	7:19
	♀ △ ♆	9:00
	☽ ∥ ♅	10:01
	☉ ⚺ ♀	17:01
	☿ ⚼ ♅	19:29
23 F	☽ ⚺ ♆	1:59
	☿ ∠ ♂	2:58
	☉ △ ☽	3:38
	☽ ⚻ ♀	3:51
	☽ ⋕ ⚷	4:19
	☽ □ ⚳	5:05
	☽ ⚼ ☿	9:39
	♂ □ ♅	10:06
	☽ ☌ ♅	10:29
	☽ □ ♂	10:30
	☽ ⚺ ⚷	10:56
	☽ ⚻ ♄	12:26
	♀ △ ⚳	15:06
	☽ □ ♇	16:49
	♂ ✶ ⚷	17:29
	☉ ⚻ ⚳	19:23
24 Sa	☽ ✶ ♃	1:36
	☽ ∠ ♆	7:17
	☉ ⚼ ☽	11:37
	☽ ⚻ ☿	13:48
	☽ ∠ ⚷	16:26
	☽ ⋕ ♀	18:03
	☽ ⋕ ♄	20:39
	♂ ✶ ♄	22:52
25 Su	☽ ⋕ ♆	0:08
	☽ ∠ ♃	7:01
	☽ ✶ ♆	13:09
	☽ ✶ ⚳	15:35
	♀ ∥ ♄	18:27
	☉ ⚻ ☽	20:18
	♀ ⚻ ♅	21:26
	☽ ⚺ ♅	21:51
	☽ ☍ ♀	21:54
	☽ ⋕ ☿	22:13
	☽ ✶ ⚷	22:27
26 M	☽ ☍ ♄	0:31
	☽ △ ♂	2:01
	♀ △ ⚷	3:11
	☽ △ ♇	4:37
	☽ ⚺ ♃	12:51
	☉ △ ♅	14:16
	☽ ∠ ⚳	21:25
	☉ □ ⚷	21:46
	♀ ∥ ♆	22:18
	☿ D	22:51
27 Tu	☽ ☍ ☿	0:58
	♀ ☌ ♄	1:20
	☽ ∠ ♅	4:07
	☽ ⚼ ♂	10:27
	☽ ⚼ ♇	11:04
	♂ ☌ ♇	20:18
28 W	☽ ⋕ ♇	0:57
	☽ □ ♆	1:53
	☽ ⚺ ⚳	3:26
	☉ ⚺ ♄	3:31
	☽ ✶ ♅	10:34
	☽ □ ⚷	11:18
	☉ ⋕ ♃	12:04
	☽ ⚻ ♄	13:55
	☉ ☍ ☽	14:47
	♀ ✶ ♇	16:03
	☽ ⚻ ♇	17:39
	☽ ⚻ ♀	17:50
	☽ ⚻ ♂	19:04
29 Th	☽ ☌ ♃	1:05
	☽ ⚻ ☿	15:11
	☽ ⚼ ♄	20:42
	♀ ✶ ♂	22:34
30 F	☉ ⚺ ♇	1:04
	☽ ⚼ ♀	3:53
	☽ △ ♆	14:53
	☽ ☌ ⚳	15:26
	☽ ⚼ ☿	22:59
	☽ □ ♅	23:23

December 2012

LONGITUDE

Day	Sid.Time	☉	☽	☽ 12 hour	Mean ☊	True ☊	☿	♀	♂	⚳	♃	♄	⚷	♅	♆	♇
	h m s	° ' "	° ' "	° ' "	° '	° '	° '	° '	° '	° '	° '	° '	° '	° '	° '	° '
1 Sa	4 41 01	9♐11 45	4♋59 00	10♋56 35	25♏14.3	26♏03.6	19♏30.3	11♏04.6	10♑34.5	0♋40.4	11♊34.8	6♏37.1	5♓06.5	4♈40.9	0♓28.2	8♑15.5
2 Su	4 44 58	10 12 33	16 55 46	22 56 50	25 11.1	26R 01.5	20 11.0	12 19.1	11 20.5	0R 28.7	11R 26.7	6 43.6	5 07.5	4R 40.3	0 28.9	8 17.4
3 M	4 48 54	11 13 23	29 00 10	5♌06 06	25 07.9	25 59.1	20 58.4	13 33.7	12 06.6	0 16.8	11 18.5	6 50.0	5 08.5	4 39.7	0 29.6	8 19.3
4 Tu	4 52 51	12 14 14	11♌15 03	17 27 24	25 04.7	25 56.9	21 51.5	14 48.3	12 52.8	0 04.7	11 10.3	6 56.4	5 09.6	4 39.2	0 30.4	8 21.3
5 W	4 56 47	13 15 07	23 43 33	0♍03 58	25 01.5	25 55.1	22 49.8	16 02.9	13 38.9	29♊52.3	11 02.1	7 02.7	5 10.8	4 38.7	0 31.2	8 23.2
6 Th	5 00 44	14 16 00	6♍29 04	12 59 14	24 58.4	25D 54.1	23 52.5	17 17.5	14 25.2	29 39.6	10 54.0	7 09.0	5 12.0	4 38.3	0 32.0	8 25.2
7 F	5 04 41	15 16 55	19 34 53	26 16 21	24 55.2	25 53.9	24 59.0	18 32.2	15 11.5	29 26.8	10 45.8	7 15.3	5 13.3	4 37.9	0 32.9	8 27.2
8 Sa	5 08 37	16 17 52	3♎03 55	9♎57 47	24 52.0	25 54.6	26 08.9	19 46.9	15 57.8	29 13.7	10 37.7	7 21.5	5 14.6	4 37.6	0 33.7	8 29.2
9 Su	5 12 34	17 18 49	16 58 04	24 04 42	24 48.8	25 56.0	27 21.7	21 01.6	16 44.2	29 00.5	10 29.6	7 27.6	5 16.0	4 37.4	0 34.7	8 31.2
10 M	5 16 30	18 19 48	1♏17 32	8♏36 13	24 45.7	25 57.4	28 37.0	22 16.4	17 30.6	28 47.0	10 21.6	7 33.7	5 17.4	4 37.2	0 35.6	8 33.2
11 Tu	5 20 27	19 20 48	16 00 15	23 28 54	24 42.5	25R 58.5	29 54.5	23 31.2	18 17.0	28 33.4	10 13.5	7 39.8	5 18.9	4 37.0	0 36.6	8 35.2
12 W	5 24 23	20 21 49	1♐01 19	8♐36 27	24 39.3	25 58.7	1♐13.9	24 46.0	19 03.5	28 19.7	10 05.6	7 45.8	5 20.5	4 36.9	0 37.6	8 37.3
13 Th	5 28 20	21 22 51	16 13 10	23 30 11	24 36.1	25 57.6	2 34.8	26 00.8	19 50.1	28 05.8	9 57.7	7 51.7	5 22.1	4D 36.8	0 38.7	8 39.3
14 F	5 32 16	22 23 54	1♑26 15	9♑00 05	24 33.0	25 55.1	3 57.2	27 15.7	20 36.7	27 51.9	9 49.9	7 57.6	5 23.8	4 36.8	0 39.8	8 41.4
15 Sa	5 36 13	23 24 57	16 30 29	23 56 21	24 29.8	25 51.5	5 20.8	28 30.6	21 23.3	27 37.8	9 42.1	8 03.4	5 25.5	4 36.9	0 40.9	8 43.5
16 Su	5 40 10	24 26 02	1♒16 45	8♒30 58	24 26.6	25 47.2	6 45.5	29 45.5	22 10.0	27 23.7	9 34.4	8 09.2	5 27.2	4 37.0	0 42.0	8 45.5
17 M	5 44 06	25 27 06	15 38 25	22 38 47	24 23.4	25 43.0	8 11.0	1♐00.4	22 56.7	27 09.5	9 26.8	8 14.9	5 29.1	4 37.1	0 43.2	8 47.6
18 Tu	5 48 03	26 28 11	29 31 52	6♓17 44	24 20.3	25 39.3	9 37.4	2 15.3	23 43.4	26 55.3	9 19.3	8 20.6	5 30.9	4 37.4	0 44.4	8 49.7
19 W	5 51 59	27 29 16	12♓56 32	19 28 36	24 17.1	25 36.9	11 04.5	3 30.3	24 30.2	26 41.1	9 11.9	8 26.2	5 32.9	4 37.6	0 45.6	8 51.8
20 Th	5 55 56	28 30 22	25 54 19	2♈14 13	24 13.9	25D 35.9	12 32.2	4 45.2	25 17.0	26 26.9	9 04.6	8 31.7	5 34.8	4 37.9	0 46.9	8 53.9
21 F	5 59 52	29 31 27	8♈28 49	14 38 43	24 10.7	25 36.2	14 00.5	6 00.2	26 03.8	26 12.7	8 57.4	8 37.1	5 36.9	4 38.3	0 48.2	8 56.0
22 Sa	6 03 49	0♑32 33	20 44 32	26 46 53	24 07.5	25 37.6	15 29.3	7 15.2	26 50.7	25 58.5	8 50.3	8 42.5	5 39.0	4 38.7	0 49.5	8 58.1
23 Su	6 07 45	1 33 40	2♉46 21	8♉43 32	24 04.4	25 39.4	16 58.5	8 30.1	27 37.5	25 44.4	8 43.3	8 47.9	5 41.1	4 39.2	0 50.9	9 00.2
24 M	6 11 42	2 34 46	14 39 00	20 33 15	24 01.2	25R 41.0	18 28.2	9 45.2	28 24.5	25 30.4	8 36.4	8 53.1	5 43.3	4 39.7	0 52.2	9 02.3
25 Tu	6 15 39	3 35 53	26 26 48	2♊20 06	23 58.0	25 41.6	19 58.3	11 00.2	29 11.4	25 16.5	8 29.7	8 58.3	5 45.5	4 40.2	0 53.7	9 04.4
26 W	6 19 35	4 36 59	8♊13 32	14 07 30	23 54.8	25 40.6	21 28.7	12 15.2	29 58.4	25 02.6	8 23.1	9 03.4	5 47.8	4 40.9	0 55.1	9 06.6
27 Th	6 23 32	5 38 07	20 02 18	25 58 14	23 51.7	25 37.7	22 59.5	13 30.3	0♒45.4	24 48.9	8 16.6	9 08.5	5 50.1	4 41.5	0 56.6	9 08.7
28 F	6 27 28	6 39 14	1♋55 33	7♋54 27	23 48.5	25 32.7	24 30.6	14 45.3	1 32.4	24 35.4	8 10.3	9 13.5	5 52.5	4 42.3	0 58.0	9 10.8
29 Sa	6 31 25	7 40 21	13 55 08	19 57 47	23 45.3	25 25.9	26 02.0	16 00.4	2 19.5	24 22.0	8 04.1	9 18.4	5 54.9	4 43.0	0 59.6	9 12.9
30 Su	6 35 21	8 41 29	26 02 44	2♌09 32	23 42.1	25 17.8	27 33.8	17 15.5	3 06.5	24 08.7	7 58.0	9 23.2	5 57.3	4 43.9	1 01.1	9 15.1
31 M	6 39 18	9♑42 37	8♌18 55	14 30 50	23♏39.0	25♏09.1	29♐05.9	18♐30.6	3♒53.6	23♊55.7	7♊52.1	9♏28.0	5♓59.9	4♈44.7	1♓02.7	9♑17.2

1st of Month

Julian Day # 2456262.5
Obliquity 23°26'10"
SVP 5♓04'32"
GC 27♐01.2
Eris 21♈45.1R

Day	⚴
1	22♓46.2
6	23 10.7
11	23 44.2
16	24 26.4
21	25 16.7
26	26 14.5
31	27 19.4

Day	⚵
1	23♐27.9
6	25 15.0
11	27 02.8
16	28 51.4
21	0♑40.6
26	2 30.1
31	4 20.0

Day	⚶
1	19♊49.2R
6	18 31.8R
11	17 12.8R
16	15 54.6R
21	14 39.8R
26	13 30.6R
31	12 28.9R

DECLINATION and LATITUDE

Day	☉ Decl	☽ Decl	☽ Lat	☽ 12h Decl	☿ Decl	☿ Lat	♀ Decl	♀ Lat	♂ Decl	♂ Lat	⚳ Decl	⚳ Lat	♃ Decl	♃ Lat	♄ Decl	♄ Lat
1 Sa	21S50	20N01	3S19	19N16	15S08	2N34	13S34	1N40	24S10	1S09	24N08	0N42	21N23	0S48	11S35	2N16
2 Su	21 59	18 18	4 06	17 07	15 21	2 32	13 57	1 39	24 06	1 09	24 12	0 46	21 22	0 48	11 37	2 16
3 M	22 07	15 45	4 42	14 12	15 36	2 29	14 21	1 38	24 02	1 09	24 16	0 50	21 21	0 48	11 39	2 16
4 Tu	22 15	12 29	5 06	10 38	15 53	2 25	14 44	1 37	23 58	1 09	24 20	0 54	21 20	0 47	11 41	2 16
5 W	22 23	8 38	5 16	6 31	16 12	2 21	15 07	1 36	23 53	1 09	24 24	0 58	21 19	0 47	11 43	2 16
6 Th	22 31	4 19	5 11	2 01	16 33	2 16	15 29	1 34	23 49	1 10	24 28	1 02	21 18	0 47	11 45	2 16
7 F	22 37	0S19	4 50	2S42	16 54	2 10	15 51	1 33	23 43	1 10	24 32	1 06	21 17	0 47	11 47	2 16
8 Sa	22 44	5 05	4 12	7 26	17 17	2 04	16 13	1 31	23 38	1 10	24 36	1 10	21 16	0 47	11 49	2 17
9 Su	22 50	9 44	3 19	11 56	17 40	1 57	16 34	1 30	23 33	1 10	24 40	1 14	21 15	0 47	11 51	2 17
10 M	22 55	13 59	2 12	15 52	18 03	1 51	16 55	1 28	23 27	1 10	24 44	1 18	21 14	0 47	11 52	2 17
11 Tu	23 01	17 30	0 55	18 52	18 27	1 44	17 15	1 27	23 20	1 10	24 48	1 22	21 13	0 46	11 54	2 17
12 W	23 05	19 54	0N28	20 36	18 50	1 36	17 35	1 25	23 14	1 10	24 52	1 27	21 12	0 46	11 56	2 17
13 Th	23 09	20 55	1 49	20 50	19 13	1 29	17 54	1 23	23 07	1 10	24 56	1 31	21 11	0 46	11 58	2 17
14 F	23 13	20 23	3 03	19 33	19 36	1 21	18 13	1 21	23 00	1 10	24 60	1 35	21 10	0 46	11 60	2 17
15 Sa	23 16	18 24	4 03	16 56	19 59	1 14	18 32	1 20	22 53	1 10	25 04	1 39	21 09	0 46	12 01	2 17
16 Su	23 19	15 13	4 46	13 18	20 21	1 06	18 50	1 18	22 46	1 10	25 07	1 43	21 08	0 46	12 03	2 18
17 M	23 21	11 13	5 09	9 01	20 42	0 59	19 07	1 16	22 38	1 10	25 11	1 47	21 07	0 45	12 05	2 18
18 Tu	23 23	6 45	5 13	4 25	21 03	0 51	19 24	1 14	22 30	1 10	25 15	1 51	21 06	0 45	12 06	2 18
19 W	23 25	2 05	4 59	0N14	21 23	0 43	19 41	1 12	22 22	1 10	25 18	1 55	21 05	0 45	12 08	2 18
20 Th	23 26	2N31	4 31	4 44	21 43	0 36	19 57	1 10	22 13	1 10	25 22	1 59	21 04	0 45	12 10	2 18
21 F	23 26	6 53	3 50	8 56	22 01	0 28	20 12	1 08	22 05	1 10	25 26	2 03	21 03	0 45	12 11	2 18
22 Sa	23 26	10 50	2 60	12 41	22 18	0 20	20 27	1 05	21 56	1 10	25 29	2 07	21 02	0 44	12 13	2 19
23 Su	23 26	14 21	2 02	15 51	22 35	0 13	20 41	1 03	21 46	1 10	25 33	2 11	21 01	0 44	12 14	2 19
24 M	23 25	17 11	0 60	18 20	22 51	0 06	20 54	1 01	21 37	1 10	25 36	2 14	21 01	0 44	12 16	2 19
25 Tu	23 23	19 17	0S04	20 02	23 05	0S02	21 07	0 59	21 27	1 10	25 39	2 18	20 60	0 44	12 17	2 19
26 W	23 21	20 34	1 08	20 51	23 19	0 09	21 20	0 56	21 17	1 10	25 43	2 22	20 59	0 44	12 19	2 19
27 Th	23 19	20 55	2 09	20 45	23 31	0 16	21 31	0 54	21 07	1 10	25 46	2 26	20 58	0 43	12 20	2 19
28 F	23 16	20 21	3 04	19 43	23 42	0 23	21 43	0 52	20 57	1 09	25 49	2 30	20 57	0 43	12 22	2 20
29 Sa	23 13	18 52	3 52	17 48	23 52	0 30	21 53	0 49	20 46	1 09	25 52	2 33	20 57	0 43	12 23	2 20
30 Su	23 09	16 31	4 29	15 04	24 01	0 36	22 03	0 47	20 35	1 09	25 55	2 37	20 56	0 43	12 24	2 20
31 M	23S05	13N26	4S55	11N38	24S09	0S43	22S12	0N44	20S24	1S09	25N58	2N41	20N55	0S43	12S26	2N20

Day	⚷ Decl	⚷ Lat	♅ Decl	♅ Lat	♆ Decl	♆ Lat	♇ Decl	♇ Lat
1	4S37	5N24	1N12	0S44	11S53	0S37	19S48	3N23
6	4 36	5 22	1 11	0 43	11 51	0 37	19 48	3 23
11	4 36	5 20	1 10	0 43	11 50	0 37	19 48	3 22
16	4 34	5 18	1 11	0 43	11 48	0 37	19 48	3 21
21	4 32	5 17	1 11	0 43	11 45	0 37	19 48	3 21
26	4 30	5 15	1 13	0 43	11 43	0 37	19 48	3 20
31	4S27	5N13	1N14	0S42	11S40	0S37	19S47	3N20

Day	⚴ Decl	⚴ Lat	⚵ Decl	⚵ Lat	⚶ Decl	⚶ Lat	Eris Decl	Eris Lat
1	17S13	15S40	13S21	9N57	17N36	5S28	3S48	13S13
6	17 13	15 50	13 28	9 53	17 40	5 17	3 48	13 12
11	17 08	15 60	13 34	9 50	17 45	5 05	3 48	13 11
16	16 59	16 09	13 39	9 47	17 51	4 52	3 47	13 10
21	16 47	16 17	13 41	9 45	17 58	4 37	3 47	13 10
26	16 31	16 25	13 43	9 43	18 06	4 21	3 47	13 09
31	16S13	16S33	13S40	9N42	18N15	4S04	3S46	13S08

Moon Phenomena

Max/0 Decl
dy hr mn
6 22:22 0 S
13 3:29 20S56
19 10:47 0 N
26 21:30 20N56

Perigee/Apogee
dy hr m kilometers
12 23:28 p 357075
25 21:20 a 406098

Max/0 Lat
dy hr mn
5 4:06 5S16
11 15:58 0 N
17 17:18 5N14
24 22:27 0 S

PH dy hr mn
☾ 6 15:33 14♍55
● 13 8:43 21♐45
☽ 20 5:20 28♓44
○ 28 10:22 7♋06

Void of Course Moon

Last Aspect	☽ Ingress
2 6:56 ☿ △	♌ 3 1:58
4 22:09 ☿ □	♍ 5 11:53
7 10:37 ☿ ✶	♎ 7 18:36
9 0:38 ☉ ✶	♏ 9 21:52
11 13:09 ♀ ☌	♐ 11 22:23
13 8:43 ☉ ☌	♑ 13 21:44
15 21:16 ♀ ✶	♒ 15 21:54
17 18:13 ☉ ✶	♓ 18 0:49
20 5:20 ☉ □	♈ 20 7:44
22 12:58 ♂ □	♉ 22 18:26
25 5:59 ♂ △	♊ 25 7:14
27 6:51 ☿ ☍	♋ 27 20:08
28 14:44 ♄ △	♌ 30 7:46

DAILY ASPECTARIAN

1 Sa
☽ △ ⚷ 0:15
☽ △ ♄ 3:20
☽ # ♇ 3:59
♂ # ⚳ 5:28
☿ ⚼ ♅ 6:34
☽ ☍ ♇ 6:37
♀ ⚻ ♃ 8:46
☉ ⚻ ☽ 9:16
☽ ☍ ♂ 12:02
☽ ⚺ ♃ 13:08
☽ △ ♀ 13:42
☽ ⚼ ♆ 21:06
⚳ △ ♆ 23:41

2 Su
♂ ⚻ ♃ 2:43
☽ ⚼ ⚷ 6:23
☽ △ ☿ 6:56
☉ ⚼ ☽ 18:00
☽ ∠ ♃ 18:44

3 M
☽ # ☿ 1:08
☉ ☍ ♃ 1:46
☽ ⚺ ⚳ 2:29
☽ ⚻ ♆ 2:57
☽ # ♀ 9:45
☽ △ ♅ 11:08
☽ ⚻ ⚷ 12:06
☽ □ ♄ 15:31
☽ ⚻ ♇ 18:21
☽ ✶ ♃ 23:51

4 Tu
☉ △ ☽ 2:05
☽ ⚻ ♂ 3:22
☽ # ♆ 4:08
♀ ⚼ ⚳ 4:32
☽ # ♄ 5:15
☽ ∠ ⚳ 7:18
☽ □ ♀ 7:39
⚳ R ♊ 9:07
☽ ⚼ ♅ 16:13
☽ □ ☿ 22:09
☽ ⚼ ♇ 23:21

5 W
☽ ⚼ ♂ 9:56
☽ ✶ ⚳ 11:27
☽ ☍ ♆ 12:52
☿ ∠ ♇ 13:26
☽ ⚻ ♅ 20:34
☽ ☍ ⚷ 21:36
☽ # ⚷ 22:25

6 Th
☽ ✶ ♄ 1:15
☽ △ ♇ 3:36
☽ □ ♃ 8:05
☉ ⚺ ♂ 15:02
☽ △ ♂ 15:32
☉ □ ☽ 15:33
☽ ∥ ♅ 16:21
☽ ✶ ♀ 21:55

7 F
☽ # ♅ 4:20
☽ ∠ ♄ 4:51
☽ ✶ ☿ 10:37
♂ ∠ ♆ 11:18
☽ □ ⚳ 17:21
☽ ⚻ ♆ 19:36
♀ ⚼ ♅ 21:02
☽ ∥ ⚷ 21:36

8 Sa
☽ ☍ ♅ 2:44
☽ ∠ ♀ 3:18
☽ ⚻ ⚷ 3:49
☽ ⚺ ♄ 7:33
☽ □ ♇ 9:28
☽ △ ♃ 13:01
☽ ∠ ☿ 15:22
♄ ∥ ♆ 21:17
☽ ⚼ ♆ 21:38
☽ □ ♂ 23:35

9 Su
☉ ✶ ☽ 0:38
☽ ⚼ ⚷ 5:36
☽ ⚺ ♀ 7:32
☽ ∥ ♆ 11:29
☽ ∥ ♄ 11:37
☽ ⚼ ♃ 14:14
☽ ⚺ ☿ 19:08
☽ △ ⚳ 19:55
☽ △ ♆ 22:51

10 M
☿ ⚻ ⚳ 2:40
☉ ∠ ☽ 3:37
☽ ⚻ ♅ 5:29
☽ △ ⚷ 6:35
☽ ☌ ♄ 10:22
☽ ✶ ♇ 11:57
☽ ⚻ ♃ 14:43
☽ ⚼ ⚳ 20:06
☽ ∥ ♀ 21:49

11 Tu
♀ ∠ ♇ 1:20
☿ ♐ 1:41
☽ ✶ ♂ 3:52
☉ ⚺ ☽ 5:46
☽ ⚼ ♅ 5:49
☽ ∥ ☿ 9:27
☽ ∠ ♇ 12:12
☿ □ ♆ 12:58
☽ ☌ ♀ 13:09
☽ ⚻ ⚳ 19:47
☽ ∥ ♇ 22:33
☽ □ ♆ 23:22

12 W
☽ ☌ ☿ 0:22
☽ ∠ ♂ 5:04
☽ △ ♅ 5:41
☽ □ ⚷ 6:51
☽ ⚺ ♄ 10:44
☽ ⚺ ♇ 12:03
☽ ☍ ♃ 14:13
☉ ∥ ♂ 19:40

13 Th
☽ ⚺ ♂ 6:00
☉ ☌ ☽ 8:43
☽ ∠ ♄ 10:32
♅ D 12:03
☽ ⚺ ♀ 16:49
♂ ∠ ⚷ 17:06
☽ ☍ ⚳ 18:26
☽ ✶ ♆ 22:46

14 F
☽ ⚺ ☿ 4:23
☽ □ ♅ 5:02
☽ ✶ ⚷ 6:17
☽ ∥ ♇ 8:54
☽ ∥ ☿ 9:29
♀ ⚻ ⚳ 9:46
☽ ✶ ♄ 10:25
☿ △ ♅ 11:25
☽ ☌ ♇ 11:32
☿ ∥ ♇ 12:22
☽ ⚻ ♃ 13:13
☉ ∠ ♄ 14:39
☽ ∠ ♀ 18:46
☽ ∠ ♆ 22:40
☽ ∥ ♀ 22:52

15 Sa
☿ □ ⚷ 1:21
☽ ∠ ⚷ 6:19
☽ ∠ ☿ 6:50
☽ ☌ ♂ 8:18
☉ ⚺ ☽ 11:59
☽ ⚼ ♃ 13:08
☽ ⚻ ⚳ 17:44
☽ ✶ ♀ 21:16
☽ ⚺ ♆ 23:03

16 Su
♀ ♐ 4:39
☽ ✶ ♅ 5:31
☽ ⚺ ⚷ 6:55
☽ ✶ ☿ 10:04
☽ □ ♄ 11:28
☽ ⚺ ♇ 12:26
☽ △ ♃ 13:39
☉ ∠ ☽ 14:34
☿ ∠ ♂ 15:11
☽ ⚼ ⚳ 18:13
♀ □ ♆ 18:24
☽ ∥ ♄ 19:12
☽ ∥ ♆ 20:49

17 M
☿ ⚺ ♄ 1:10
☽ ∠ ♅ 6:48
☿ ⚺ ♇ 10:26
☽ ⚺ ♂ 13:16
☽ ∠ ♇ 14:01
☉ ✶ ☽ 18:13
☿ ☍ ♃ 19:23
☽ △ ⚳ 19:30

18 Tu
☽ ☌ ♆ 2:08
☿ # ♃ 3:12
☽ □ ♀ 5:18
☉ ☍ ⚳ 8:39
☽ ⚺ ♅ 9:01
☽ ☌ ⚷ 10:38
☽ ∥ ⚷ 11:19
☽ △ ♄ 15:47
♂ ⚼ ♃ 15:54
☽ ✶ ♇ 16:36
☽ □ ♃ 17:17
☽ ∠ ♂ 17:23
☽ □ ☿ 20:11

19 W
⚵ ♑ 3:27
☽ # ♅ 4:39
♀ ∥ ♇ 10:40
☽ ∥ ♅ 16:58
☽ ⚼ ♄ 19:31
♀ △ ♅ 21:39
☽ ✶ ♂ 22:45

20 Th
☽ □ ⚳ 1:00
☉ □ ☽ 5:20
☽ ⚺ ♆ 9:15
☽ # ⚷ 10:55
♀ □ ⚷ 16:20
☽ ☌ ♅ 16:36
☽ ⚺ ⚷ 18:27
☽ △ ♀ 18:41

21 F
☽ ⚻ ♄ 0:16
☽ □ ♇ 0:53
☽ ✶ ♃ 0:55
☿ ∥ ♂ 3:17
♂ ⚻ ⚳ 3:30
♃ ⚻ ♇ 3:37
☉ ♑ 11:13
☽ △ ☿ 12:14
☽ ∠ ♆ 14:18
☽ ∠ ⚷ 23:49

22 Sa
☽ ⚼ ♀ 3:20
☽ # ♆ 5:43
☽ ∠ ♃ 6:05
☉ ✶ ♆ 6:49
☽ # ♄ 8:53
☽ ✶ ⚳ 10:12
☽ □ ♂ 12:58
♃ ⚻ ♄ 15:04
☽ ✶ ♆ 20:08
☉ △ ☽ 21:20
☽ ⚼ ☿ 22:10

23 Su
☽ ⚺ ♅ 3:47
♀ ☍ ♃ 3:51
☽ ✶ ⚷ 5:53
♀ ⚺ ♄ 6:06
♀ ⚺ ♇ 9:54
☽ ⚺ ♃ 11:53
☽ ☍ ♄ 12:14
☽ △ ♇ 12:36
☽ ⚻ ♀ 12:54
☽ ∠ ⚳ 15:46

24 M
☉ ⚼ ☽ 6:31
☽ ⚻ ☿ 8:53
☽ ∠ ♅ 10:11
♀ # ♃ 10:40
☽ ⚼ ♇ 19:09
☽ ⚺ ⚳ 21:39

25 Tu
☽ △ ♂ 5:59
☽ # ♇ 7:45
☽ □ ♆ 9:05
☉ ⚻ ☽ 15:57
☽ ✶ ♅ 16:46
☽ □ ⚷ 19:02
♀ ∥ ♂ 21:18

26 W
☽ ☌ ♃ 0:19
♂ ♒ 0:50
☉ □ ♅ 1:32
☽ ⚻ ♄ 1:42
☽ ⚻ ♇ 1:48
☉ ∥ ☿ 4:25
☽ ☍ ♀ 9:10
☽ ⚼ ♂ 14:42

27 Th
♄ ✶ ♇ 1:42
☉ ✶ ⚷ 4:54
♂ ⚺ ♆ 5:53
☽ ☍ ☿ 6:51
☽ ⚼ ♄ 8:22
☽ ☌ ⚳ 9:29
☿ ∠ ♄ 19:14
☽ △ ♆ 22:04
♂ # ♃ 22:14
☽ ⚻ ♂ 23:10

28 F
☿ ☍ ⚳ 1:06
☽ □ ♅ 5:35
☽ △ ⚷ 7:57
☉ ☍ ☽ 10:22
☽ # ♇ 10:50
☽ ⚺ ♃ 12:25
☽ ☍ ♇ 14:35
☽ △ ♄ 14:44

29 Sa
☽ ⚼ ♆ 4:08
☽ ⚻ ♀ 4:38
⚳ ⚼ ♄ 4:45
☉ ⚻ ♃ 8:28
☽ ⚼ ⚷ 13:56
☽ ∠ ♃ 17:59
☽ ⚺ ⚳ 20:20

30 Su
☽ ⚻ ☿ 3:25
☽ ⚻ ♆ 9:47
☽ ⚼ ♀ 13:35
☉ ☌ ♇ 13:40
☽ ☍ ♂ 14:48
☽ △ ♅ 17:03
☉ ✶ ♄ 17:46
☽ ⚻ ⚷ 19:29
☽ ✶ ♃ 23:08

31 M
☽ ∠ ⚳ 1:10
☽ ⚻ ♇ 1:53
☽ □ ♄ 2:15
☉ ⚻ ☽ 2:57
☽ # ♄ 6:47
☽ # ♆ 11:49
☽ ⚼ ☿ 12:47
☿ ♑ 14:04
♀ ∠ ♂ 19:47
☽ △ ♀ 21:53
☽ ⚼ ♅ 22:05

LONGITUDE

Day	Sid.Time	☉	☽	☽ 12 hour	Mean☊	True☊	☿	♀	♂	⚳	♃	♄	⚷	♅	♆	♇
	h m s	° ' "	° ' "	° ' "	° '	° '	° '	° '	° '	° '	° '	° '	° '	° '	° '	° '
1 Tu	6 43 15	10♑43 45	20♌45 26	27♌02 54	23♏35.8	25♏00.6	0♑38.3	19♐45.7	4♒40.8	23♊42.8	7♊46.4	9♏32.7	6♓02.4	4♈45.6	1♓04.3	9♑19.3
2 W	6 47 11	11 44 53	3♍23 24	9♍47 10	23 32.6	24R 53.3	2 11.1	21 00.8	5 27.9	23R 30.2	7R 40.8	9 37.3	6 05.0	4 46.6	1 05.9	9 21.5
3 Th	6 51 08	12 46 02	16 14 26	22 45 25	23 29.4	24 47.9	3 44.1	22 15.9	6 15.1	23 17.8	7 35.4	9 41.8	6 07.6	4 47.6	1 07.5	9 23.6
4 F	6 55 04	13 47 11	29 20 25	5♎59 41	23 26.2	24 44.6	5 17.6	23 31.0	7 02.3	23 05.7	7 30.1	9 46.2	6 10.3	4 48.7	1 09.2	9 25.7
5 Sa	6 59 01	14 48 20	12♎43 28	19 32 01	23 23.1	24D 43.5	6 51.4	24 46.2	7 49.5	22 53.8	7 25.0	9 50.6	6 13.0	4 49.8	1 10.9	9 27.8
6 Su	7 02 57	15 49 29	26 25 31	3♏24 07	23 19.9	24 43.9	8 25.5	26 01.3	8 36.7	22 42.2	7 20.1	9 54.9	6 15.8	4 51.0	1 12.6	9 29.9
7 M	7 06 54	16 50 39	10♏27 52	17 36 42	23 16.7	24R 44.9	10 00.2	27 16.5	9 24.0	22 30.8	7 15.4	9 59.1	6 18.6	4 52.2	1 14.3	9 32.1
8 Tu	7 10 50	17 51 49	24 50 26	2♐08 45	23 13.5	24 45.5	11 35.0	28 31.7	10 11.2	22 19.8	7 10.8	10 03.2	6 21.5	4 53.5	1 16.1	9 34.2
9 W	7 14 47	18 52 59	9♐31 08	16 56 58	23 10.4	24 44.6	13 10.3	29 46.8	10 58.5	22 09.1	7 06.4	10 07.3	6 24.3	4 54.8	1 17.9	9 36.3
10 Th	7 18 44	19 54 09	24 25 23	1♑55 27	23 07.2	24 41.3	14 46.0	1♑02.0	11 45.8	21 58.7	7 02.2	10 11.3	6 27.3	4 56.2	1 19.7	9 38.4
11 F	7 22 40	20 55 19	9♑26 04	16 56 03	23 04.0	24 35.5	16 22.2	2 17.2	12 33.2	21 48.6	6 58.2	10 15.1	6 30.2	4 57.6	1 21.5	9 40.5
12 Sa	7 26 37	21 56 28	24 24 15	1♒49 28	23 00.8	24 27.4	17 58.9	3 32.4	13 20.5	21 38.9	6 54.4	10 18.9	6 33.2	4 59.1	1 23.4	9 42.6
13 Su	7 30 33	22 57 37	9♒10 36	16 26 43	22 57.7	24 17.8	19 35.9	4 47.6	14 07.9	21 29.5	6 50.8	10 22.6	6 36.3	5 00.6	1 25.2	9 44.7
14 M	7 34 30	23 58 46	23 36 57	0♓40 43	22 54.5	24 07.8	21 13.5	6 02.8	14 55.3	21 20.5	6 47.3	10 26.2	6 39.4	5 02.2	1 27.1	9 46.8
15 Tu	7 38 26	24 59 54	7♓37 35	14 27 17	22 51.3	23 58.7	22 51.5	7 18.0	15 42.6	21 11.9	6 44.1	10 29.8	6 42.5	5 03.8	1 29.0	9 48.8
16 W	7 42 23	26 01 02	21 09 49	27 45 18	22 48.1	23 51.4	24 30.1	8 33.2	16 30.0	21 03.6	6 41.0	10 33.2	6 45.6	5 05.4	1 30.9	9 50.9
17 Th	7 46 19	27 02 08	4♈14 01	10♈36 23	22 44.9	23 46.4	26 09.2	9 48.4	17 17.4	20 55.8	6 38.2	10 36.5	6 48.8	5 07.1	1 32.9	9 52.9
18 F	7 50 16	28 03 14	16 52 53	23 04 08	22 41.8	23D 43.8	27 48.7	11 03.6	18 04.8	20 48.3	6 35.5	10 39.8	6 52.0	5 08.8	1 34.9	9 55.0
19 Sa	7 54 13	29 04 19	29 10 45	5♉13 25	22 38.6	23 43.1	29 28.9	12 18.8	18 52.2	20 41.2	6 33.1	10 42.9	6 55.3	5 10.6	1 36.8	9 57.0
20 Su	7 58 09	0♒05 24	11♉12 49	17 09 41	22 35.4	23 43.5	1♒09.5	13 34.0	19 39.7	20 34.6	6 30.9	10 46.0	6 58.5	5 12.5	1 38.8	9 59.1
21 M	8 02 06	1 06 27	23 04 39	28 58 25	22 32.2	23R 43.9	2 50.7	14 49.1	20 27.1	20 28.3	6 28.8	10 48.9	7 01.8	5 14.3	1 40.8	10 01.1
22 Tu	8 06 02	2 07 29	4♊51 38	10♊45 42	22 29.1	23 43.3	4 32.5	16 04.3	21 14.5	20 22.5	6 27.0	10 51.8	7 05.2	5 16.2	1 42.9	10 03.1
23 W	8 09 59	3 08 31	16 38 41	22 33 36	22 25.9	23 40.6	6 14.7	17 19.5	22 01.9	20 17.0	6 25.4	10 54.6	7 08.5	5 18.2	1 44.9	10 05.1
24 Th	8 13 55	4 09 32	28 30 04	4♋28 28	22 22.7	23 35.3	7 57.5	18 34.7	22 49.4	20 12.0	6 23.9	10 57.3	7 11.9	5 20.2	1 47.0	10 07.1
25 F	8 17 52	5 10 31	10♋29 09	16 32 22	22 19.5	23 27.2	9 40.9	19 49.9	23 36.8	20 07.4	6 22.7	10 59.9	7 15.3	5 22.3	1 49.1	10 09.0
26 Sa	8 21 48	6 11 30	22 38 21	28 47 14	22 16.4	23 16.4	11 24.7	21 05.1	24 24.2	20 03.2	6 21.7	11 02.3	7 18.8	5 24.3	1 51.2	10 11.0
27 Su	8 25 45	7 12 28	4♌59 07	11♌14 03	22 13.2	23 03.7	13 09.0	22 20.2	25 11.7	19 59.5	6 20.9	11 04.7	7 22.3	5 26.5	1 53.3	10 13.0
28 M	8 29 42	8 13 25	17 32 01	23 53 01	22 10.0	22 50.0	14 53.6	23 35.4	25 59.1	19 56.2	6 20.3	11 07.0	7 25.8	5 28.6	1 55.4	10 14.9
29 Tu	8 33 38	9 14 21	0♍16 58	6♍43 48	22 06.8	22 36.7	16 38.7	24 50.6	26 46.5	19 53.3	6 19.9	11 09.2	7 29.3	5 30.8	1 57.5	10 16.8
30 W	8 37 35	10 15 16	13 13 28	19 45 55	22 03.6	22 24.9	18 24.0	26 05.7	27 34.0	19 50.8	6D 19.7	11 11.3	7 32.8	5 33.1	1 59.6	10 18.7
31 Th	8 41 31	11♒16 11	26 21 05	2♎58 59	22♏00.5	22♏15.5	20♒09.5	27♑20.9	28♒21.4	19♊48.7	6♊19.7	11♏13.3	7♓36.4	5♈35.4	2♓01.8	10♑20.6

1st of Month

Julian Day # 2456293.5
Obliquity 23°26'09"
SVP 5♓04'27"
GC 27♐01.3
Eris 21♈37.4R

Day	⚴
1	27♓33.1
6	28 45.8
11	0♈04.7
16	1 29.2
21	2 59.0
26	4 33.8
31	6 13.1

Day	⚵
1	4♑41.9
6	6 32.0
11	8 22.1
16	10 12.1
21	12 01.8
26	13 51.1
31	15 40.0

Day	⚶
1	12♊17.6R
6	11 26.7R
11	10 46.0R
16	10 16.4R
21	9 58.0R
26	9 50.9R
31	9 54.8

DECLINATION and LATITUDE

Day	☉ Decl	☽ Decl	☽ Lat	☽12h Decl	☿ Decl	☿ Lat	♀ Decl	♀ Lat	♂ Decl	♂ Lat	⚳ Decl	⚳ Lat	♃ Decl	♃ Lat	♄ Decl	♄ Lat
1 Tu	23S00	9N43	5S07	7N40	24S15	0S49	22S21	0N42	20S12	1S09	26N01	2N44	20N54	0S42	12S27	2N20
2 W	22 55	5 31	5 05	3 18	24 20	0 55	22 29	0 39	20 01	1 09	26 04	2 48	20 54	0 42	12 28	2 21
3 Th	22 49	1 01	4 47	1S18	24 24	1 01	22 36	0 37	19 49	1 09	26 07	2 51	20 53	0 42	12 29	2 21
4 F	22 43	3S37	4 14	5 56	24 26	1 07	22 42	0 34	19 37	1 09	26 10	2 55	20 52	0 42	12 31	2 21
5 Sa	22 37	8 12	3 27	10 23	24 28	1 12	22 48	0 32	19 25	1 09	26 13	2 58	20 52	0 42	12 32	2 21
6 Su	22 30	12 28	2 27	14 25	24 27	1 17	22 53	0 29	19 12	1 08	26 15	3 02	20 51	0 41	12 33	2 21
7 M	22 22	16 10	1 16	17 42	24 26	1 23	22 58	0 27	18 60	1 08	26 18	3 05	20 51	0 41	12 34	2 22
8 Tu	22 15	18 58	0N00	19 56	24 23	1 27	23 01	0 24	18 47	1 08	26 20	3 08	20 50	0 41	12 35	2 22
9 W	22 06	20 35	1 19	20 52	24 19	1 32	23 04	0 22	18 34	1 08	26 23	3 11	20 50	0 41	12 36	2 22
10 Th	21 58	20 47	2 32	20 20	24 13	1 36	23 07	0 19	18 20	1 08	26 26	3 15	20 49	0 40	12 37	2 22
11 F	21 48	19 31	3 36	18 21	24 06	1 41	23 08	0 17	18 07	1 08	26 28	3 18	20 49	0 40	12 38	2 22
12 Sa	21 39	16 54	4 24	15 10	23 57	1 44	23 09	0 14	17 53	1 07	26 31	3 21	20 48	0 40	12 39	2 23
13 Su	21 29	13 13	4 54	11 06	23 47	1 48	23 10	0 11	17 39	1 07	26 33	3 24	20 48	0 40	12 40	2 23
14 M	21 19	8 51	5 05	6 30	23 36	1 51	23 09	0 09	17 25	1 07	26 35	3 27	20 48	0 39	12 41	2 23
15 Tu	21 08	4 07	4 56	1 43	23 23	1 54	23 08	0 06	17 11	1 07	26 38	3 30	20 47	0 39	12 42	2 23
16 W	20 56	0N39	4 31	2N59	23 08	1 57	23 06	0 04	16 57	1 07	26 40	3 32	20 47	0 39	12 43	2 23
17 Th	20 45	5 14	3 53	7 24	22 52	1 59	23 03	0 01	16 42	1 06	26 42	3 35	20 47	0 39	12 44	2 24
18 F	20 33	9 27	3 04	11 23	22 34	2 01	23 00	0S01	16 27	1 06	26 44	3 38	20 46	0 39	12 44	2 24
19 Sa	20 20	13 10	2 07	14 47	22 15	2 03	22 56	0 04	16 12	1 06	26 47	3 41	20 46	0 38	12 45	2 24
20 Su	20 08	16 15	1 06	17 31	21 55	2 04	22 51	0 07	15 57	1 06	26 49	3 43	20 46	0 38	12 46	2 24
21 M	19 55	18 36	0 03	19 28	21 33	2 05	22 46	0 09	15 42	1 05	26 51	3 46	20 46	0 38	12 47	2 25
22 Tu	19 41	20 08	0S59	20 35	21 09	2 05	22 40	0 12	15 27	1 05	26 53	3 48	20 46	0 38	12 47	2 25
23 W	19 27	20 48	1 59	20 47	20 44	2 05	22 33	0 14	15 11	1 05	26 55	3 51	20 46	0 37	12 48	2 25
24 Th	19 13	20 32	2 54	20 03	20 17	2 05	22 25	0 17	14 55	1 05	26 57	3 53	20 46	0 37	12 49	2 25
25 F	18 58	19 21	3 41	18 25	19 49	2 04	22 17	0 19	14 40	1 04	26 59	3 56	20 46	0 37	12 49	2 25
26 Sa	18 43	17 16	4 20	15 55	19 19	2 03	22 08	0 21	14 24	1 04	27 01	3 58	20 46	0 37	12 50	2 26
27 Su	18 28	14 23	4 46	12 41	18 48	2 01	21 59	0 24	14 07	1 04	27 03	4 00	20 46	0 36	12 50	2 26
28 M	18 12	10 49	4 60	8 49	18 15	1 59	21 48	0 26	13 51	1 03	27 05	4 03	20 46	0 36	12 51	2 26
29 Tu	17 56	6 43	4 58	4 31	17 41	1 56	21 37	0 29	13 35	1 03	27 07	4 05	20 46	0 36	12 51	2 26
30 W	17 40	2 15	4 42	0S03	17 05	1 52	21 26	0 31	13 18	1 03	27 09	4 07	20 47	0 36	12 52	2 27
31 Th	17S24	2S22	4S10	4S41	16S28	1S48	21S14	0S33	13S01	1S03	27N11	4N09	20N47	0S35	12S52	2N27

Day	⚷ Decl	⚷ Lat	♅ Decl	♅ Lat	♆ Decl	♆ Lat	♇ Decl	♇ Lat
1	4S26	5N13	1N15	0S42	11S40	0S37	19S47	3N20
6	4 23	5 12	1 17	0 42	11 37	0 37	19 47	3 19
11	4 19	5 10	1 20	0 42	11 34	0 37	19 47	3 19
16	4 14	5 09	1 23	0 42	11 30	0 37	19 46	3 18
21	4 09	5 08	1 27	0 42	11 27	0 37	19 46	3 18
26	4 04	5 07	1 31	0 41	11 23	0 37	19 45	3 18
31	3S59	5N06	1N35	0S41	11S19	0S37	19S45	3N18

Day	⚴ Decl	⚴ Lat	⚵ Decl	⚵ Lat	⚶ Decl	⚶ Lat	Eris Decl	Eris Lat
1	16S09	16S34	13S40	9N42	18N17	4S01	3S46	13S08
6	15 47	16 42	13 36	9 41	18 27	3 44	3 45	13 07
11	15 22	16 50	13 31	9 40	18 39	3 27	3 45	13 06
16	14 56	16 57	13 24	9 41	18 52	3 10	3 44	13 05
21	14 26	17 05	13 15	9 41	19 05	2 53	3 43	13 04
26	13 58	17 13	13 04	9 42	19 20	2 37	3 42	13 04
31	13S27	17S21	12S51	9N43	19N36	2S21	3S40	13S03

Moon Phenomena

Max/0 Decl

dy	hr mn	
3	5:17	0 S
9	15:23	20S53
15	20:41	0 N
23	5:10	20N49
30	11:44	0 S

Max/0 Lat

dy	hr mn	
1	8:00	5S08
7	23:51	0 N
14	0:44	5N05
21	1:19	0 S
28	9:49	5S01

Perigee/Apogee

dy	hr m		kilometers
10	10:26	p	360053
22	10:52	a	405309

PH	dy	hr mn	
☾	5	3:59	14♎58
●	11	19:45	21♑46
☽	18	23:46	29♈04
○	27	4:39	7♌24

Void of Course Moon

Last Aspect			☽ Ingress	
31 21:53	♀	△	♍	1 17:36
3 12:16	♀	□	♎	4 1:12
5 23:14	♀	✶	♏	6 6:10
7 11:32	☉	✶	♐	8 8:29
9 2:29	♂	✶	♑	10 8:55
11 19:45	☉	☌	♒	12 9:02
13 8:38	♂	☌	♓	14 10:50
16 9:34	☉	✶	♈	16 16:08
19 0:41	☿	□	♉	19 1:37
20 18:17	♂	□	♊	21 14:05
23 11:43	♂	△	♋	24 3:01
25 20:36	♀	☍	♌	26 14:21
28 17:00	♂	☍	♍	28 23:28
31 2:00	♀	△	♎	31 6:37

DAILY ASPECTARIAN

1 Tu
♂✶♅ 2:33
☽✶⚳ 5:34
☽⚼♇ 6:50
☿✶♆ 6:51
☉⚼☽ 10:20
☽☍♆ 19:40
☽△☿ 21:25

2 W
☽⚻♅ 2:37
☽⚻♂ 4:10
☽☍⚷ 5:05
☽⋕⚷ 5:58
☽□♃ 8:00
☽△♇ 11:14
☽✶♄ 11:46
☉△☽ 17:00
♂⊻⚷ 20:00
☽∥♅ 22:44

3 Th
♂∥♇ 3:47
☽⚼♂ 9:50
☽⋕♅ 11:49
☽□♀ 12:16
☽□⚳ 12:47
☽∠♄ 15:38
☿□♅ 16:31
♀☍⚳ 17:01

4 F
☉∥♀ 2:05
☽⚻♆ 3:17
☽∥⚷ 4:01
☽☍♅ 9:53
☽□☿ 12:10
☽⚻⚷ 12:22
♂△♃ 12:47
☿✶⚷ 13:55
☽△♃ 14:36
☽△♂ 14:44
☽□♇ 18:11
☽⊻♄ 18:51

5 Sa
♀∠♄ 1:30
♂⚼⚳ 1:45
☉□☽ 3:59
☽⚼♆ 6:07
☿⚻♃ 8:10
☽⚼⚷ 15:00
☽⚼♃ 16:56
☽△⚳ 17:37
☽∥♆ 18:58
☽✶♀ 23:14

6 Su
☽∥♄ 0:28
☿⊻♂ 5:42
☽△♆ 8:16
☉∠♆ 9:20
☽⚻♅ 14:30
☿☌♇ 16:45
☽△⚷ 16:56
☽⚻♃ 18:36
☽⚼⚳ 19:04
☽□♂ 22:06
☽✶♇ 22:25
☽✶☿ 23:07
☽☌♄ 23:11
☿✶♄ 23:45

7 M
☽∠♀ 3:21
♂⊻♇ 4:18
☉✶☽ 11:32
☽⚼♅ 15:47
♂□♄ 19:34
☽⚻⚳ 19:54
☽∥♂ 22:13
☽∠♇ 23:33

8 Tu
☽∠☿ 3:13
☽⊻♀ 6:38
☽∥♇ 9:47
☽□♆ 10:35
☉∠☽ 14:09
☽△♅ 16:30
☽□⚷ 18:56
☽☍♃ 20:06

9 W
☽⊻♇ 0:08
☽⊻♄ 0:59
☽✶♂ 2:29
♀ ♑ 4:12
☽⊻☿ 6:37
☉⊻☽ 16:13
☽☍⚳ 20:07
☽⋕♃ 22:06
☽⋕♃ 22:06

10 Th
☽∠♄ 1:14
☽∠♂ 3:57
♀✶♆ 5:46
☽✶♆ 11:04
☽☌♀ 11:32
☽□♅ 16:50
⚴ ♈ 17:09
☽✶⚷ 19:18
☽⚻♃ 20:05
☽∥♇ 20:33
☿∠♆ 23:49

11 F
☽☌♇ 0:23
☽✶♄ 1:19
☽⊻♂ 5:16
☽∠♆ 11:06
☽☌☿ 12:26
☉∠⚷ 14:25
☽∥♂ 15:23
☉⚻⚳ 18:02
☽∠⚷ 19:24
☽⚻⚳ 19:37
☉☌☽ 19:45
☽⚼♃ 20:00
☉⚼♃ 23:14

12 Sa
☽⊻♆ 11:19
☽⊻♀ 16:10
☽✶♅ 17:10
☽⚼⚳ 19:39
☽⊻⚷ 19:46
☽△♃ 20:12

13 Su
☽⊻♇ 0:56
☽□♄ 1:59
☽∥♄ 3:11
♀□♅ 4:14
☽☌♂ 8:38
☽∥♆ 9:37
☽∠♅ 17:59
☽∠♀ 19:16
☽⊻☿ 19:28
☽△⚳ 20:13

14 M
☉⊻☽ 0:40
☿⚻⚳ 1:35
☽∠♇ 1:58
☿∠⚷ 6:33
☿⚼♃ 8:01
♀✶⚷ 12:10
☽☌♆ 13:21
♀⚻♃ 13:37
☽⊻♅ 19:32
☽☌⚷ 22:24
☽□♃ 22:27
☽∥⚷ 23:20
☽✶♀ 23:23

15 Tu
☽∠☿ 0:28
☽✶♇ 3:50
☉∠☽ 4:29
☽△♄ 5:02
♃□⚷ 6:11
☽⋕♅ 13:44
☽⊻♂ 15:07
☽□⚳ 23:49

16 W
☽∥♅ 3:44
☿∥♀ 3:45
☽✶☿ 6:55
☽⚼♄ 8:00
☉✶☽ 9:34
☽⋕⚷ 18:34
☽⊻♆ 18:59
☽∠♂ 20:09
☉⋕♃ 20:18

17 Th
♀☌♇ 1:30
☽☌♅ 1:39
☽✶♃ 4:29
☽⊻⚷ 4:51
☽□♇ 10:39
☽□♀ 11:38
☽⚻♄ 12:03
♀✶♄ 16:03
☽∠♆ 23:25

18 F
☽✶♂ 2:28
☽✶⚳ 7:31
☉☌☿ 8:57
☽∠♃ 9:06
☽∠⚷ 9:42
☽⋕♆ 12:36
☽⋕♄ 21:09
☉□☽ 23:46

19 Sa
☽□☿ 0:41
☽✶♆ 4:50
☿ ♒ 7:26
☽⊻♅ 11:56
☽∠⚳ 12:48
☽⊻♃ 14:36
☽✶⚷ 15:28
☽△♇ 21:31
☽⋕♂ 21:44
☉ ♒ 21:53
☽☍♄ 23:06

20 Su
☽△♀ 5:18
☿⊻♆ 7:06
♂∠♅ 17:16
☽∠♅ 18:13
☽□♂ 18:17
☽⊻⚳ 18:45

21 M
♂△⚳ 0:33
☽⚼♇ 3:57
☉⊻♆ 13:59
☽⚼♀ 15:21
☉∥♇ 15:29
☉⋕☽ 16:38
☽⋕♇ 16:49
☽□♆ 17:34
☉△☽ 17:54
☽△☿ 23:14

22 Tu
☽✶♅ 0:50
☽☌♃ 3:14
☽□⚷ 4:34
☿✶♅ 10:29
☽⚻♇ 10:37
☿⚼⚳ 11:09
☽⚻♄ 12:17
♀∠♆ 12:39
☽∥♃ 21:11
☽∥♃ 21:14
☽⋕☿ 21:48
☿⋕♃ 22:13

23 W
☽⚻♀ 1:33
☿△♃ 2:27
☉⚼☽ 3:20
☽☌⚳ 7:20
☽⚼☿ 10:55
☽△♂ 11:43
☿⊻⚷ 13:00
☽⚼♄ 18:51

24 Th
☽△♆ 6:37
☽⋕☿ 11:49
☉⚻☽ 12:25
☽□♅ 13:46
☽⊻♃ 15:49
☽⋕♇ 17:23
☽△⚷ 17:32
☽⚼♂ 20:01
☽⚻☿ 22:08
☉⚼⚳ 22:52
☽☍♇ 23:20

25 F
☽△♄ 1:01
☿∥♇ 2:50
☉✶♅ 4:47
♀⚻⚳ 5:18
☉⋕☽ 5:54
☿⊻♇ 6:39
☽⚼♆ 12:35
☿□♄ 18:43
☽⊻⚳ 18:57
☽☍♀ 20:36
☽∠♃ 21:30
☽⚼⚷ 23:21

26 Sa
☽⚻♂ 3:42
☉△♃ 3:57
♀⚼♃ 5:15
⚶ D 16:51
☽⚻♆ 18:00

27 Su
☽∠⚳ 0:01
♂∠♇ 0:41
♀∠⚷ 0:41
☽△♅ 0:53
☽⋕♂ 2:05
☽✶♃ 2:37
☉⊻⚷ 4:06
☽⚻⚷ 4:37
☉☍☽ 4:39
☽⚻♇ 10:05
☽⋕♄ 10:53
☽□♄ 11:44
☽☍☿ 18:11
☽⋕♆ 20:35

28 M
☉∥☿ 3:43
☽✶⚳ 4:32
☽⚼♅ 5:35
☽⚻♀ 12:42
☽⚼♇ 14:36
☽☍♂ 17:00

29 Tu
☽☍♆ 3:08
☽⚻♅ 9:46
☽□♃ 11:15
☽☍⚷ 13:28
☽⋕⚷ 14:45
☉⚻☽ 18:04
☽△♇ 18:37
☽⚼♀ 19:39
☽✶♄ 20:14

30 W
☉⊻♇ 1:24
☽∥♅ 3:33
☽⚻☿ 10:58
♃ D 11:38
☽□⚳ 12:07
☿△⚳ 19:21
☽⋕♅ 19:56
☉□♄ 22:50
☽∠♄ 23:46
☉⚼☽ 23:50

31 Th
☽△♀ 2:00
☽⚻♂ 3:52
☿∠♅ 6:00
☽∥⚷ 8:17
☽⚻♆ 10:19
♂∥♄ 13:03
☽☍♅ 16:45
☽△♃ 18:02
☽⚼☿ 18:20
☽⚻⚷ 20:25

February 2013

LONGITUDE

Day	Sid.Time	☉	☽	☽ 12 hour	Mean ☊	True ☊	☿	♀	♂	⚳	♃	♄	⚷	♅	♆	♇
	h m s	° ' "	° ' "	° ' "	° '	° '	° '	° '	° '	° '	° '	° '	° '	° '	° '	° '
1 F	8 45 28	12♒17 04	9♎39 36	16♎23 01	21♏57.3	22♏09.1	21♒55.1	28♑36.1	29♒08.8	19♊47.1	6♊19.9	11♏15.2	7♓40.0	5♈37.7	2♓04.0	10♑22.5
2 Sa	8 49 24	13 17 57	23 09 17	29 58 29	21 54.1	22R 05.6	23 40.7	29 51.2	29 56.2	19R 45.9	6 20.3	11 17.0	7 43.6	5 40.0	2 06.1	10 24.3
3 Su	8 53 21	14 18 49	6♏50 45	13♏46 09	21 50.9	22D 04.4	25 26.1	1♒06.4	0♓43.6	19 45.1	6 20.9	11 18.7	7 47.2	5 42.4	2 08.3	10 26.2
4 M	8 57 17	15 19 40	20 44 47	27 46 40	21 47.8	22R 04.3	27 11.1	2 21.6	1 31.0	19D 44.7	6 21.7	11 20.3	7 50.9	5 44.9	2 10.5	10 28.0
5 Tu	9 01 14	16 20 31	4♐51 46	11♐59 59	21 44.6	22 04.0	28 55.4	3 36.7	2 18.5	19 44.8	6 22.7	11 21.7	7 54.6	5 47.3	2 12.7	10 29.8
6 W	9 05 11	17 21 20	19 11 05	26 24 46	21 41.4	22 02.1	0♓38.9	4 51.9	3 05.9	19 45.3	6 24.0	11 23.1	7 58.3	5 49.8	2 14.9	10 31.6
7 Th	9 09 07	18 22 09	3♑40 32	10♑57 50	21 38.2	21 57.7	2 21.2	6 07.1	3 53.3	19 46.2	6 25.4	11 24.4	8 02.0	5 52.4	2 17.2	10 33.4
8 F	9 13 04	19 22 57	18 15 57	25 34 04	21 35.1	21 50.2	4 02.0	7 22.2	4 40.7	19 47.5	6 27.0	11 25.6	8 05.7	5 55.0	2 19.4	10 35.2
9 Sa	9 17 00	20 23 43	2♒51 20	10♒06 48	21 31.9	21 40.1	5 40.8	8 37.4	5 28.0	19 49.2	6 28.9	11 26.7	8 09.4	5 57.6	2 21.6	10 36.9
10 Su	9 20 57	21 24 29	17 19 35	24 28 48	21 28.7	21 28.0	7 17.1	9 52.5	6 15.4	19 51.3	6 30.9	11 27.6	8 13.2	6 00.2	2 23.9	10 38.6
11 M	9 24 53	22 25 13	1♓33 38	8♓33 26	21 25.5	21 15.2	8 50.6	11 07.7	7 02.8	19 53.9	6 33.1	11 28.5	8 17.0	6 02.9	2 26.1	10 40.3
12 Tu	9 28 50	23 25 55	15 27 37	22 15 50	21 22.3	21 03.2	10 20.5	12 22.8	7 50.1	19 56.8	6 35.5	11 29.2	8 20.7	6 05.6	2 28.4	10 42.0
13 W	9 32 46	24 26 37	28 57 49	5♈33 32	21 19.2	20 53.1	11 46.3	13 37.9	8 37.4	20 00.2	6 38.1	11 29.9	8 24.5	6 08.3	2 30.6	10 43.7
14 Th	9 36 43	25 27 16	12♈03 03	18 26 35	21 16.0	20 45.6	13 07.4	14 53.0	9 24.8	20 03.9	6 41.0	11 30.4	8 28.3	6 11.1	2 32.9	10 45.3
15 F	9 40 40	26 27 54	24 44 29	0♉57 13	21 12.8	20 40.9	14 23.0	16 08.1	10 12.1	20 08.1	6 44.0	11 30.9	8 32.2	6 13.9	2 35.2	10 46.9
16 Sa	9 44 36	27 28 30	7♉05 17	13 09 18	21 09.6	20 38.7	15 32.4	17 23.2	10 59.4	20 12.6	6 47.2	11 31.2	8 36.0	6 16.7	2 37.4	10 48.5
17 Su	9 48 33	28 29 05	19 09 55	25 07 48	21 06.4	20 38.2	16 35.0	18 38.3	11 46.6	20 17.5	6 50.6	11 31.4	8 39.8	6 19.6	2 39.7	10 50.1
18 M	9 52 29	29 29 37	1♊03 39	6♊58 10	21 03.3	20 38.2	17 30.0	19 53.4	12 33.9	20 22.9	6 54.1	11R 31.6	8 43.7	6 22.4	2 42.0	10 51.6
19 Tu	9 56 26	0♓30 08	12 52 04	18 46 02	21 00.1	20 37.7	18 16.8	21 08.4	13 21.1	20 28.5	6 57.9	11 31.6	8 47.5	6 25.3	2 44.3	10 53.2
20 W	10 00 22	1 30 38	24 40 42	0♋36 43	20 56.9	20 35.5	18 54.9	22 23.5	14 08.3	20 34.6	7 01.9	11 31.5	8 51.4	6 28.3	2 46.6	10 54.7
21 Th	10 04 19	2 31 05	6♋34 39	12 35 02	20 53.7	20 30.9	19 23.6	23 38.5	14 55.5	20 41.0	7 06.0	11 31.3	8 55.3	6 31.2	2 48.8	10 56.2
22 F	10 08 15	3 31 31	18 38 21	24 44 58	20 50.6	20 23.5	19 42.6	24 53.5	15 42.7	20 47.8	7 10.3	11 31.0	8 59.1	6 34.2	2 51.1	10 57.6
23 Sa	10 12 12	4 31 54	0♌55 13	7♌09 21	20 47.4	20 13.6	19R 51.6	26 08.6	16 29.8	20 55.0	7 14.8	11 30.6	9 03.0	6 37.2	2 53.4	10 59.1
24 Su	10 16 09	5 32 16	13 27 32	19 49 49	20 44.2	20 01.7	19 50.7	27 23.6	17 16.9	21 02.5	7 19.5	11 30.1	9 06.9	6 40.3	2 55.7	11 00.5
25 M	10 20 05	6 32 36	26 16 13	2♍46 39	20 41.0	19 48.9	19 39.8	28 38.6	18 04.0	21 10.3	7 24.3	11 29.5	9 10.7	6 43.3	2 58.0	11 01.9
26 Tu	10 24 02	7 32 54	9♍20 56	15 58 52	20 37.9	19 36.2	19 19.4	29 53.5	18 51.1	21 18.5	7 29.4	11 28.8	9 14.6	6 46.4	3 00.2	11 03.2
27 W	10 27 58	8 33 11	22 40 11	29 24 36	20 34.7	19 25.0	18 49.8	1♓08.5	19 38.2	21 27.1	7 34.5	11 28.0	9 18.5	6 49.5	3 02.5	11 04.6
28 Th	10 31 55	9♓33 26	6♎11 48	13♎01 28	20♏31.5	19♏16.0	18♓12.0	2♓23.5	20♓25.2	21♊35.9	7♊39.9	11♏27.1	9♓22.4	6♈52.6	3♓04.8	11♑05.9

1st of Month

Julian Day #
2456324.5
Obliquity
23°26'10"
SVP 5♓04'22
GC 27♐01.3
Eris 21♈40.0

Day	⚴
1	6♈33.5
6	8 18.1
11	10 06.6
16	11 59.0
21	13 55.0
26	15 54.2

Day	⚵
1	16♑01.7
6	17 49.7
11	19 37.0
16	21 23.2
21	23 08.3
26	24 52.1

Day	⚶
1	9♊56.8
6	10 13.3
11	10 39.8
16	11 15.8
21	12 00.5
26	12 53.3

DECLINATION and LATITUDE

Day	☉ Decl	☽ Decl	☽ Lat	☽ 12h Decl	☿ Decl	☿ Lat	♀ Decl	♀ Lat	♂ Decl	♂ Lat	⚳ Decl	⚳ Lat	♃ Decl	♃ Lat	♄ Decl	♄ Lat
1 F	17S07	6S57	3S24	9S10	15S50	1S43	21S01	0S35	12S44	1S02	27N13	4N11	20N47	0S35	12S52	2N27
2 Sa	16 50	11 16	2 27	13 14	15 10	1 38	20 47	0 38	12 27	1 02	27 15	4 13	20 47	0 35	12 53	2 27
3 Su	16 32	15 03	1 20	16 40	14 29	1 32	20 33	0 40	12 10	1 02	27 17	4 15	20 48	0 35	12 53	2 28
4 M	16 14	18 03	0 07	19 10	13 47	1 25	20 19	0 42	11 53	1 01	27 19	4 17	20 48	0 35	12 53	2 28
5 Tu	15 56	20 00	1N07	20 31	13 04	1 18	20 03	0 44	11 36	1 01	27 21	4 19	20 48	0 34	12 53	2 28
6 W	15 38	20 42	2 18	20 32	12 20	1 10	19 48	0 46	11 18	1 01	27 23	4 21	20 49	0 34	12 54	2 28
7 Th	15 19	20 02	3 21	19 12	11 35	1 01	19 31	0 48	11 01	1 00	27 24	4 23	20 49	0 34	12 54	2 29
8 F	15 00	18 03	4 11	16 36	10 50	0 51	19 14	0 50	10 43	0 60	27 26	4 25	20 50	0 34	12 54	2 29
9 Sa	14 41	14 54	4 45	12 59	10 04	0 41	18 56	0 52	10 26	0 59	27 28	4 26	20 50	0 33	12 54	2 29
10 Su	14 22	10 53	4 59	8 39	9 18	0 30	18 38	0 54	10 08	0 59	27 30	4 28	20 51	0 33	12 54	2 29
11 M	14 02	6 19	4 56	3 55	8 32	0 18	18 20	0 56	9 50	0 59	27 32	4 30	20 52	0 33	12 54	2 30
12 Tu	13 42	1 31	4 34	0N52	7 47	0 06	18 00	0 58	9 32	0 58	27 34	4 31	20 52	0 33	12 54	2 30
13 W	13 22	3N13	3 57	5 29	7 02	0N07	17 41	0 59	9 14	0 58	27 36	4 33	20 53	0 33	12 54	2 30
14 Th	13 02	7 40	3 09	9 43	6 18	0 21	17 21	1 01	8 56	0 57	27 37	4 34	20 53	0 32	12 54	2 30
15 F	12 42	11 38	2 13	13 24	5 36	0 36	16 60	1 03	8 37	0 57	27 39	4 36	20 54	0 32	12 54	2 30
16 Sa	12 21	14 60	1 11	16 25	4 56	0 50	16 39	1 04	8 19	0 57	27 41	4 37	20 55	0 32	12 54	2 31
17 Su	11 60	17 38	0 08	18 40	4 17	1 06	16 17	1 06	8 01	0 56	27 43	4 39	20 56	0 32	12 54	2 31
18 M	11 39	19 28	0S55	20 04	3 42	1 21	15 55	1 08	7 42	0 56	27 45	4 40	20 57	0 31	12 53	2 31
19 Tu	11 18	20 26	1 55	20 35	3 09	1 37	15 32	1 09	7 24	0 55	27 47	4 42	20 57	0 31	12 53	2 31
20 W	10 56	20 30	2 50	20 11	2 40	1 52	15 09	1 10	7 05	0 55	27 48	4 43	20 58	0 31	12 53	2 32
21 Th	10 35	19 39	3 38	18 53	2 15	2 07	14 46	1 12	6 47	0 55	27 50	4 44	20 59	0 31	12 53	2 32
22 F	10 13	17 54	4 17	16 42	1 54	2 22	14 22	1 13	6 28	0 54	27 52	4 46	21 00	0 31	12 52	2 32
23 Sa	9 51	15 19	4 45	13 44	1 37	2 36	13 58	1 14	6 09	0 54	27 54	4 47	21 01	0 30	12 52	2 32
24 Su	9 29	11 60	4 59	10 06	1 25	2 50	13 33	1 15	5 50	0 53	27 56	4 48	21 02	0 30	12 52	2 33
25 M	9 07	8 04	4 59	5 55	1 18	3 02	13 08	1 17	5 32	0 53	27 57	4 50	21 03	0 30	12 51	2 33
26 Tu	8 44	3 41	4 44	1 22	1 16	3 13	12 43	1 18	5 13	0 52	27 59	4 51	21 04	0 30	12 51	2 33
27 W	8 22	0S58	4 13	3S18	1 19	3 23	12 18	1 19	4 54	0 52	28 01	4 52	21 05	0 30	12 50	2 33
28 Th	7S59	5S38	3S27	7S54	1S26	3N31	11S52	1S20	4S35	0S51	28N03	4N53	21N06	0S29	12S50	2N34

Day	⚷ Decl	⚷ Lat	♅ Decl	♅ Lat	♆ Decl	♆ Lat	♇ Decl	♇ Lat
1	3S57	5N06	1N36	0S41	11S18	0S37	19S45	3N1
6	3 52	5 05	1 41	0 41	11 14	0 37	19 44	3 1
11	3 45	5 04	1 47	0 41	11 10	0 37	19 44	3 1
16	3 39	5 04	1 52	0 41	11 06	0 37	19 43	3 1
21	3 32	5 03	1 58	0 41	11 02	0 37	19 43	3 1
26	3S25	5N03	2N04	0S41	10S58	0S37	19S42	3N1

Day	⚴ Decl	⚴ Lat	⚵ Decl	⚵ Lat	⚶ Decl	⚶ Lat	Eris Decl	Eris Lat
1	13S21	17S23	12S49	9N44	19N40	2S18	3S40	13S0
6	12 48	17 32	12 34	9 46	19 57	2 03	3 39	13 0
11	12 15	17 41	12 18	9 48	20 14	1 49	3 38	13 0
16	11 41	17 50	12 00	9 51	20 32	1 36	3 36	13 0
21	11 06	17 60	11 41	9 54	20 51	1 23	3 35	12 6
26	10S31	18S10	11S20	9N58	21N10	1S11	3S33	12S5

Moon Phenomena

Max/0 Decl
dy hr mn
6 0:13 20S42
12 7:37 0 N
19 13:36 20N35
26 19:04 0 S

Max/0 Lat
dy hr mn
4 2:16 0 N
10 6:44 5N00
17 2:57 0 S
24 12:10 5S01

Perigee/Apogee
dy hr m kilometers
7 12:15 p 365320
19 6:26 a 404470

PH dy hr mn
☾ 3 13:57 14♏54
● 10 7:21 21♒43
☽ 17 20:32 29♉21
○ 25 20:27 7♍24

Void of Course Moon

Last Aspect			☽ Ingress		
2 1:04	☿	△	♏	2	12:03
4 12:32	☿	□	♐	4	15:46
5 20:43	☉	⚹	♑	6	17:56
7 12:45	♄	⚹	♒	8	19:18
10 7:21	☉	☌	♓	10	21:21
11 17:04	♄	△	♈	13	1:52
15 3:36	☉	⚹	♉	15	10:09
17 20:32	☉	□	♊	17	21:51
19 18:49	♀	△	♋	20	10:46
22 2:09	☿	△	♌	22	22:13
25 4:51	♀	☍	♍	25	6:54
26 18:14	♂	☍	♎	27	13:03

DAILY ASPECTARIAN

1 F
☽□♇ 1:17
☽⊻♄ 2:51
☉△☽ 5:05
☽⚼♂ 8:31
☽⚼♆ 13:15
☽△⚳ 18:01
☽⚼♃ 20:47
☽⚼⚷ 23:14

2 Sa
☽∥♆ 0:10
♀⋕♃ 0:13
☽△☿ 1:04
♂ ♓ 1:55
♀ ♒ 2:48
♀⊻♂ 4:18
☽∥♂ 6:39
☽∥♄ 9:44
☽△♂ 12:40
☽□♀ 12:59
☽△♆ 15:46
☽⚼⚳ 20:21
☽∥☿ 20:44
☽⚻♅ 22:01
☽⚻♃ 23:08

3 Su
☿∠♇ 0:01
☽△⚷ 1:39
☽⚹♇ 6:15
☽☌♄ 7:46
☉∥☽ 10:00
☉□☽ 13:57
♀⊻♆ 20:22
☽⚻⚳ 22:17

4 M
☽⚼♅ 0:00
☽∠♇ 8:05
⚳ D 8:50
☽□☿ 12:32
☽□♂ 19:26
☽□♆ 19:31
☽∥♇ 19:45
♂☌♆ 20:57
☽⚹♀ 21:41

5 Tu
☽∥♀ 0:49
☽△♅ 1:34
☽☍♃ 2:34
☽□⚷ 5:09
☿∥♄ 5:43
☽⊻♇ 9:30
☽⊻♄ 10:57
☿ ♓ 14:57
☉⚹☽ 20:43
♀⚼⚳ 21:51

6 W
☽☍⚳ 0:57
☽∠♀ 1:14
♀∥♇ 4:39
♂∥♆ 5:47
☽∠♄ 11:58
♀⚹♅ 19:09
☽⚹☿ 21:32
☽⚹♆ 21:42
☿☌♆ 23:01
☉∠☽ 23:27

7 Th
☽⚹♂ 0:22
☽□♅ 3:38
☽⊻♀ 4:24
☽⚻♃ 4:32
☽∥♇ 4:50
♀△♃ 5:59
☽⚹⚷ 7:12
☽∥♀ 9:22
☽☌♇ 11:21
☿∥♆ 11:33
☽⚹♄ 12:45
☽∠♆ 22:27

8 F
☽∠☿ 1:25
☉⊻☽ 1:58
☽∠♂ 2:27
☽⚻⚳ 2:31
☽⚼♃ 5:15
☿∥♂ 5:26
☽∠⚷ 7:58
☉△⚳ 9:56
♀⊻⚷ 14:37
☿☌♂ 17:58
☽⊻♆ 23:11

9 Sa
☉∥☽ 1:31
☽⚼⚳ 3:15
☿⊻♅ 4:15
☽⊻♂ 4:34
☽⚹♅ 5:08
☽⊻☿ 5:15
☽△♃ 6:00
☽⊻⚷ 8:48
☽☌♀ 10:26
☿□♃ 12:09
☽∥♄ 12:28
☽⊻♇ 12:51
☉∠♅ 13:58
☽□♄ 14:13
♂⊻♅ 15:50
☽∥♆ 22:17

10 Su
☽△⚳ 4:15
☽∥♂ 4:23
☽∠♅ 6:10
☉☌☽ 7:21
♂□♃ 8:13
☽∥☿ 10:16
☽∠♇ 14:00
☿☌⚷ 14:54
♀⊻♇ 15:04

11 M
☽☌♆ 1:30
♀□♄ 6:43
☽⊻♅ 7:42
☽□♃ 8:34
☽☌♂ 9:58
☽☌⚷ 11:35
☽∥⚷ 12:55
☽☌☿ 14:01
☽⚹♇ 15:42
☽△♄ 17:04
☽⊻♀ 18:05
☽⋕♅ 22:38

12 Tu
☿⚹♇ 6:01
☽□⚳ 7:56
☉⊻☽ 15:14
☽∥♅ 16:45
♂☌⚷ 16:53
☿△♄ 19:16
☽⚼♄ 19:34
☽∠♀ 23:20

13 W
☽⋕⚷ 2:34
☽⊻♆ 6:27
☽☌♅ 13:07
☽⚹♃ 14:02
☽⊻⚷ 17:20
☽⋕☿ 17:31
☽⊻♂ 18:47
☉∠☽ 20:47
☽□♇ 21:35
☽⚻♄ 22:59

14 Th
☽⊻☿ 2:14
☽⚹♀ 5:52
☽⋕♂ 6:48
☉∠♇ 7:20
☉∥♄ 9:31
☽∠♆ 10:20
☽⚹⚳ 15:09
☽∠♃ 18:13
☽⋕♆ 20:42
☽∠⚷ 21:41

15 F
☽∠♂ 0:57
☉⚹☽ 3:36
☉⋕☽ 6:25
☽⋕♄ 8:28
☽∠☿ 9:54
☽⚹♆ 15:14
♂⚹♇ 18:18
☽∠⚳ 20:17
☽⊻♅ 22:24
☽⊻♃ 23:24

16 Sa
☽⚹⚷ 3:00
☽△♇ 7:22
☽⚹♂ 8:14
☽☍♄ 8:45
☽⋕♀ 12:24
♂△♄ 16:15
☽⚹☿ 18:22
☽□♀ 22:49

17 Su
☽⊻⚳ 2:17
☽∠♅ 4:21
☽⚼♇ 13:27
☉□☽ 20:32

18 M
☽□♆ 3:20
☿∥⚷ 4:04
☽⋕♇ 4:30
♀△⚳ 10:11
☽⚹♅ 10:50
☽☌♃ 11:56
☉ ♓ 12:03
☽□⚷ 15:40
♄ R 17:03
☽⚻♇ 19:58
☽⚻♄ 21:16

19 Tu
☽□♂ 1:03
♀∠♅ 5:38
☽□☿ 11:41
☽☌⚳ 15:36
☉∥♆ 15:52
☽△♀ 18:49

20 W
☽⚼♄ 3:44
☉△☽ 15:05
☽△♆ 16:25
☽⋕♇ 22:39
☽□♅ 23:53

21 Th
☽⊻♃ 1:03
☽⚼♀ 4:37
☽△⚷ 4:43
☉☌♆ 7:20
☽☍♇ 8:44
☽△♄ 9:53
☿⋕♅ 17:34
☽△♂ 17:48
☽⚼♆ 22:26
☉⚼☽ 23:45

22 F
☽△☿ 2:09
☽⊻⚳ 4:18
☽∠♃ 7:00
☽⚼⚷ 10:34
☽⚻♀ 13:40
♀∠♇ 20:54

23 Sa
☽⚼♂ 1:11
☽⚻♆ 3:49
☉⚻☽ 7:35
☽⚼☿ 7:37
☿ R 9:42
☽∠⚳ 9:43
☽△♅ 11:01
☽⋕♀ 11:49
☽⚹♃ 12:15
☽⚻⚷ 15:42
☽⋕♄ 18:10
☽⚻♇ 19:20
☽□♄ 20:17

24 Su
☽⋕♆ 6:25
☽⚻♂ 7:41
☽⚻☿ 11:54
☽⚹⚳ 14:25
☽⚼♅ 15:30
☉⋕☽ 17:17
☽⚼♇ 23:33

25 M
☉⊻♅ 4:30
☽☍♀ 4:51
☽☍♆ 12:23
☽⋕♂ 15:10
♀∥♄ 16:40
☽⚻♅ 19:17
☉☍☽ 20:27
☽□♃ 20:36
☉□♃ 22:27
☽☍⚷ 23:48

26 Tu
☽⋕⚷ 1:21
♀ ♓ 2:04
☽△♇ 3:06
☽⚹♄ 3:52
☽∥♅ 8:22
☿☌♂ 9:10
☽⋕☿ 12:30
☽☍☿ 17:24
☽☍♂ 18:14
☽□⚳ 21:48

27 W
☽∥☿ 1:48
☽⋕♅ 5:47
☽∠♄ 6:46
☽∥⚷ 12:24
☽⚻♀ 16:36
☽⚻♆ 18:29
☽∥♂ 18:55
☉☌⚷ 19:18

28 Th
☽☍♅ 1:12
☽△♃ 2:36
☽⚻⚷ 5:37
☉⚻☽ 6:23
☽□♇ 8:38
☽⊻♄ 9:14
☉∥☽ 11:31
♀☌♆ 13:38
☽⚻☿ 19:58
☽⚼♆ 20:54
☽⚼♀ 21:36

LONGITUDE — March 2013

Day	Sid.Time	☉	☽	☽ 12 hour	Mean ☊	True ☊	☿	♀	♂	⚳	♃	♄	⚷	♅	♆	♇
	h m s	° ' "	° ' "	° ' "	° '	° '	° '	° '	° '	° '	° '	° '	° '	° '	° '	° '
1 F	10 35 51	10♓33 39	19♎53 21	26♎47 09	20♏28.3	19♏10.0	17♓26.8	3♓38.4	21♓12.2	21♊45.1	7♊45.4	11♏26.1	9♓26.3	6♈55.8	3♓07.0	11♑07.2
2 Sa	10 39 48	11 33 51	3♏42 39	10♏39 40	20 25.1	19R 06.8	16R 35.5	4 53.4	21 59.2	21 54.7	7 51.1	11R 25.0	9 30.2	6 58.9	3 09.3	11 08.4
3 Su	10 43 44	12 34 01	17 38 03	24 37 41	20 22.0	19D 05.8	15 39.4	6 08.3	22 46.1	22 04.5	7 57.0	11 23.8	9 34.0	7 02.1	3 11.6	11 09.7
4 M	10 47 41	13 34 10	1♐38 28	8♐40 18	20 18.8	19R 06.1	14 39.8	7 23.2	23 33.0	22 14.7	8 03.0	11 22.5	9 37.9	7 05.3	3 13.8	11 10.9
5 Tu	10 51 37	14 34 17	15 43 08	22 46 52	20 15.6	19 06.4	13 38.4	8 38.2	24 19.9	22 25.1	8 09.2	11 21.1	9 41.8	7 08.5	3 16.1	11 12.1
6 W	10 55 34	15 34 23	29 51 20	6♑56 23	20 12.4	19 05.6	12 36.5	9 53.1	25 06.8	22 35.9	8 15.6	11 19.6	9 45.7	7 11.7	3 18.3	11 13.2
7 Th	10 59 31	16 34 28	14♑01 46	21 07 11	20 09.3	19 02.6	11 35.6	11 08.0	25 53.7	22 47.0	8 22.1	11 18.0	9 49.5	7 15.0	3 20.5	11 14.3
8 F	11 03 27	17 34 30	28 12 17	5♒16 38	20 06.1	18 57.1	10 37.0	12 22.9	26 40.5	22 58.4	8 28.8	11 16.3	9 53.4	7 18.3	3 22.8	11 15.4
9 Sa	11 07 24	18 34 31	12♒19 44	19 21 05	20 02.9	18 49.2	9 41.8	13 37.7	27 27.3	23 10.1	8 35.6	11 14.5	9 57.2	7 21.5	3 25.0	11 16.5
10 Su	11 11 20	19 34 30	26 20 07	3♓16 19	19 59.7	18 39.7	8 50.9	14 52.6	28 14.0	23 22.1	8 42.6	11 12.6	10 01.1	7 24.8	3 27.2	11 17.6
11 M	11 15 17	20 34 28	10♓09 09	16 58 10	19 56.5	18 29.5	8 05.3	16 07.5	29 00.8	23 34.3	8 49.7	11 10.6	10 04.9	7 28.1	3 29.4	11 18.6
12 Tu	11 19 13	21 34 23	23 42 55	0♈23 07	19 53.4	18 19.8	7 25.3	17 22.3	29 47.5	23 46.9	8 57.0	11 08.5	10 08.7	7 31.5	3 31.6	11 19.6
13 W	11 23 10	22 34 17	6♈58 31	13 29 00	19 50.2	18 11.6	6 51.4	18 37.1	0♈34.1	23 59.7	9 04.4	11 06.4	10 12.5	7 34.8	3 33.8	11 20.5
14 Th	11 27 06	23 34 08	19 54 32	26 15 14	19 47.0	18 05.6	6 24.0	19 51.9	1 20.8	24 12.8	9 12.0	11 04.1	10 16.3	7 38.1	3 36.0	11 21.4
15 F	11 31 03	24 33 58	2♉31 15	8♉42 54	19 43.8	18 01.9	6 02.9	21 06.7	2 07.4	24 26.1	9 19.7	11 01.7	10 20.1	7 41.5	3 38.1	11 22.3
16 Sa	11 35 00	25 33 45	14 50 31	20 54 33	19 40.6	18D 00.6	5 48.3	22 21.5	2 53.9	24 39.8	9 27.6	10 59.3	10 23.9	7 44.9	3 40.3	11 23.2
17 Su	11 38 56	26 33 31	26 55 30	2♊53 56	19 37.5	18 00.9	5D 40.1	23 36.3	3 40.4	24 53.7	9 35.6	10 56.8	10 27.7	7 48.2	3 42.4	11 24.0
18 M	11 42 53	27 33 14	8♊50 26	14 45 38	19 34.3	18 02.0	5 38.1	24 51.0	4 26.9	25 07.8	9 43.7	10 54.2	10 31.4	7 51.6	3 44.6	11 24.9
19 Tu	11 46 49	28 32 54	20 40 11	26 34 45	19 31.1	18R 03.2	5 42.0	26 05.7	5 13.4	25 22.2	9 52.0	10 51.5	10 35.2	7 55.0	3 46.7	11 25.6
20 W	11 50 46	29 32 33	2♋29 59	8♋26 34	19 27.9	18 03.5	5 51.7	27 20.5	5 59.8	25 36.9	10 00.4	10 48.7	10 38.9	7 58.4	3 48.8	11 26.4
21 Th	11 54 42	0♈32 09	14 25 06	20 26 14	19 24.8	18 02.2	6 06.8	28 35.1	6 46.2	25 51.7	10 08.9	10 45.8	10 42.6	8 01.8	3 50.9	11 27.1
22 F	11 58 39	1 31 43	26 30 31	2♌38 30	19 21.6	17 59.1	6 27.0	29 49.8	7 32.5	26 06.9	10 17.6	10 42.9	10 46.3	8 05.2	3 53.0	11 27.8
23 Sa	12 02 35	2 31 15	8♌50 37	15 07 16	19 18.4	17 54.0	6 52.2	1♈04.5	8 18.8	26 22.2	10 26.4	10 39.9	10 49.9	8 08.6	3 55.0	11 28.5
24 Su	12 06 32	3 30 45	21 28 46	27 55 21	19 15.2	17 47.5	7 22.0	2 19.1	9 05.0	26 37.8	10 35.3	10 36.8	10 53.6	8 12.0	3 57.1	11 29.1
25 M	12 10 29	4 30 12	4♍27 06	11♍04 03	19 12.0	17 40.1	7 56.2	3 33.7	9 51.3	26 53.6	10 44.4	10 33.6	10 57.2	8 15.5	3 59.1	11 29.7
26 Tu	12 14 25	5 29 37	17 46 06	24 33 02	19 08.9	17 32.6	8 34.5	4 48.3	10 37.4	27 09.6	10 53.5	10 30.3	11 00.8	8 18.9	4 01.1	11 30.3
27 W	12 18 22	6 29 00	1♎24 33	8♎20 16	19 05.7	17 26.0	9 16.7	6 02.9	11 23.6	27 25.9	11 02.8	10 27.0	11 04.4	8 22.3	4 03.1	11 30.8
28 Th	12 22 18	7 28 20	15 19 43	22 22 21	19 02.5	17 20.9	10 02.5	7 17.5	12 09.6	27 42.3	11 12.2	10 23.6	11 08.0	8 25.7	4 05.1	11 31.3
29 F	12 26 15	8 27 39	29 27 39	6♏35 00	18 59.3	17 17.7	10 51.7	8 32.0	12 55.7	27 59.0	11 21.7	10 20.2	11 11.5	8 29.2	4 07.1	11 31.8
30 Sa	12 30 11	9 26 56	13♏43 52	20 53 40	18 56.1	17D 16.4	11 44.2	9 46.6	13 41.7	28 15.9	11 31.3	10 16.7	11 15.1	8 32.6	4 09.0	11 32.2
31 Su	12 34 08	10♈26 11	28 03 54	5♐14 06	18♏53.0	17♏16.7	12♓39.8	11♈01.1	14♈27.7	28♊33.0	11♊41.1	10♏13.1	11♓18.6	8♈36.0	4♓11.0	11♑32.6

1st of Month

Julian Day # 2456352.5
Obliquity 23°26'10"
SVP 5♓04'19"
GC 27♐01.4
Eris 21♈50.7

Day	⚴
1	17♈07.3
6	19 11.5
11	21 18.7
16	23 28.8
21	25 41.5
26	27 56.6
31	0♉14.2

Day	⚵
1	25♑53.7
6	27 35.1
11	29 14.8
16	0♒52.5
21	2 27.9
26	4 01.0
31	5 31.5

Day	⚶
1	13♊28.6
6	14 33.0
11	15 44.0
16	17 01.0
21	18 23.5
26	19 51.0
31	21 23.1

DECLINATION and LATITUDE

Day	☉ Decl	☽ Decl	☽ Lat	☽ 12h Decl	☿ Decl	☿ Lat	♀ Decl	♀ Lat	♂ Decl	♂ Lat	⚳ Decl	⚳ Lat	♃ Decl	♃ Lat	♄ Decl	♄ Lat
1 F	7S36	10S04	2S29	12S07	1S38	3N36	11S25	1S20	4S16	0S51	28N04	4N54	21N07	0S29	12S49	2N34
2 Sa	7 14	14 01	1 21	15 44	1 55	3 40	10 59	1 21	3 57	0 50	28 06	4 55	21 08	0 29	12 49	2 34
3 Su	6 51	17 13	0 08	18 27	2 15	3 42	10 32	1 22	3 38	0 50	28 08	4 56	21 10	0 29	12 48	2 34
4 M	6 28	19 24	1N06	20 04	2 38	3 41	10 05	1 23	3 19	0 49	28 10	4 57	21 11	0 29	12 48	2 34
5 Tu	6 04	20 24	2 17	20 25	3 04	3 39	9 37	1 23	3 00	0 49	28 11	4 59	21 12	0 28	12 47	2 35
6 W	5 41	20 07	3 19	19 29	3 32	3 34	9 09	1 24	2 41	0 48	28 13	4 60	21 13	0 28	12 46	2 35
7 Th	5 18	18 33	4 10	17 20	4 01	3 27	8 41	1 24	2 22	0 48	28 14	5 01	21 14	0 28	12 46	2 35
8 F	4 55	15 52	4 45	14 10	4 31	3 19	8 13	1 25	2 03	0 47	28 16	5 02	21 16	0 28	12 45	2 35
9 Sa	4 31	12 15	5 02	10 12	5 01	3 09	7 45	1 25	1 44	0 47	28 18	5 03	21 17	0 28	12 44	2 36
10 Su	4 08	8 00	5 02	5 43	5 30	2 58	7 16	1 26	1 25	0 46	28 19	5 04	21 18	0 27	12 43	2 36
11 M	3 44	3 23	4 43	1 02	5 59	2 46	6 48	1 26	1 06	0 46	28 21	5 04	21 19	0 27	12 43	2 36
12 Tu	3 20	1N19	4 09	3N37	6 26	2 32	6 19	1 26	0 47	0 45	28 22	5 05	21 21	0 27	12 42	2 36
13 W	2 57	5 51	3 22	7 60	6 51	2 18	5 49	1 26	0 28	0 45	28 24	5 06	21 22	0 27	12 41	2 36
14 Th	2 33	10 01	2 25	11 54	7 14	2 04	5 20	1 26	0 09	0 44	28 25	5 07	21 23	0 27	12 40	2 37
15 F	2 10	13 38	1 22	15 11	7 36	1 49	4 51	1 26	0N10	0 44	28 27	5 08	21 25	0 26	12 39	2 37
16 Sa	1 46	16 34	0 17	17 44	7 55	1 35	4 21	1 26	0 29	0 43	28 28	5 09	21 26	0 26	12 38	2 37
17 Su	1 22	18 41	0S48	19 26	8 12	1 20	3 51	1 26	0 48	0 43	28 30	5 10	21 27	0 26	12 37	2 37
18 M	0 58	19 58	1 50	20 16	8 26	1 05	3 22	1 26	1 07	0 42	28 31	5 11	21 29	0 26	12 36	2 37
19 Tu	0 35	20 20	2 47	20 11	8 38	0 51	2 52	1 26	1 26	0 42	28 33	5 12	21 30	0 26	12 35	2 37
20 W	0 11	19 48	3 37	19 12	8 48	0 37	2 22	1 25	1 45	0 41	28 34	5 12	21 32	0 26	12 34	2 38
21 Th	0N13	18 23	4 18	17 22	8 55	0 23	1 52	1 25	2 04	0 41	28 35	5 13	21 33	0 25	12 33	2 38
22 F	0 36	16 08	4 48	14 44	8 60	0 09	1 22	1 24	2 23	0 40	28 37	5 14	21 34	0 25	12 32	2 38
23 Sa	1 00	13 08	5 05	11 23	9 03	0S03	0 51	1 24	2 42	0 39	28 38	5 15	21 36	0 25	12 31	2 38
24 Su	1 24	9 28	5 08	7 26	9 03	0 16	0 21	1 23	3 00	0 39	28 39	5 16	21 37	0 25	12 30	2 38
25 M	1 47	5 17	4 56	3 02	9 01	0 28	0N09	1 23	3 19	0 38	28 40	5 16	21 39	0 25	12 29	2 38
26 Tu	2 11	0 44	4 27	1S37	8 58	0 39	0 39	1 22	3 38	0 38	28 41	5 17	21 40	0 24	12 28	2 39
27 W	2 34	3S58	3 43	6 18	8 52	0 50	1 09	1 21	3 56	0 37	28 42	5 18	21 42	0 24	12 26	2 39
28 Th	2 58	8 34	2 45	10 44	8 44	1 01	1 40	1 20	4 15	0 37	28 43	5 19	21 43	0 24	12 25	2 39
29 F	3 21	12 46	1 35	14 37	8 35	1 10	2 10	1 20	4 33	0 36	28 44	5 19	21 45	0 24	12 24	2 39
30 Sa	3 45	16 16	0 19	17 40	8 23	1 20	2 40	1 19	4 52	0 35	28 45	5 20	21 46	0 24	12 23	2 39
31 Su	4N08	18S46	0N59	19S35	8S10	1S29	3N10	1S18	5N10	0S35	28N46	5N21	21N48	0S24	12S22	2N39

Day	⚷ Decl	⚷ Lat	♅ Decl	♅ Lat	♆ Decl	♆ Lat	♇ Decl	♇ Lat
1	3S21	5N03	2N08	0S41	10S56	0S37	19S42	3N17
6	3 14	5 03	2 14	0 40	10 52	0 37	19 42	3 17
11	3 07	5 02	2 21	0 40	10 48	0 37	19 41	3 17
16	2 60	5 03	2 27	0 40	10 44	0 37	19 41	3 17
21	2 53	5 03	2 34	0 40	10 40	0 37	19 40	3 17
26	2 46	5 03	2 41	0 40	10 37	0 37	19 40	3 17
31	2S39	5N03	2N48	0S40	10S33	0S37	19S40	3N17

Day	⚴ Decl	⚴ Lat	⚵ Decl	⚵ Lat	⚶ Decl	⚶ Lat	Eris Decl	Eris Lat
1	10S10	18S16	11S08	10N00	21N21	1S04	3S33	12S58
6	9 35	18 27	10 45	10 05	21 40	0 53	3 31	12 58
11	8 60	18 39	10 21	10 10	21 58	0 43	3 30	12 57
16	8 25	18 50	9 57	10 15	22 15	0 33	3 28	12 57
21	7 50	19 02	9 31	10 21	22 32	0 23	3 27	12 56
26	7 16	19 15	9 05	10 27	22 48	0 14	3 25	12 56
31	6S43	19S28	8S38	10N34	23N03	0S06	3S24	12S56

Moon Phenomena

Max/0 Decl
dy hr mn
5 6:34 20S27
11 17:16 0 N
18 21:54 20N20
26 3:44 0 S

Perigee/Apogee
dy hr m kilometers
5 23:12 p 369957
19 3:06 a 404260
31 3:49 p 367504

Max/0 Lat
dy hr mn
3 2:30 0 N
9 10:57 5N04
16 6:15 0 S
23 17:09 5S09
30 5:56 0 N

PH	dy	hr mn	
☾	4	21:54	14♐29
●	11	19:52	21♓24
☽	19	17:28	29♊16
○	27	9:28	6♎52

Void of Course Moon

Last Aspect				☽ Ingress		
28	8:38	♇	□	♏	1	17:35
3	9:20	♂	△	♐	3	21:12
5	15:29	♂	□	♑	6	0:15
7	21:15	♂	⚹	♒	8	3:03
8	22:09	♄	□	♓	10	6:20
11	19:52	☉	☌	♈	12	11:18
13	8:03	♇	□	♉	14	19:09
16	23:12	☉	⚹	♊	17	6:10
19	17:28	☉	□	♋	19	18:56
20	18:03	♇	☍	♌	22	6:51
23	3:29	♄	□	♍	24	15:50
25	12:47	♇	△	♎	26	21:33
27	18:16	♂	☍	♏	29	0:55
29	20:26	☿	△	♐	31	3:14

DAILY ASPECTARIAN

1 F
☽⚻♂ 2:26
☽△⚳ 3:17
☽∥♆ 4:55
☽⚼♃ 5:02
☽∥♀ 7:02
☽⚼⚷ 7:57
☉⚼☽ 10:39
☉⚹♇ 13:39
☽∥♄ 16:15
☉△♄ 20:32
☽⚼☿ 20:33
♂□⚳ 21:06
☽△♆ 23:02

2 Sa
☽△♀ 2:14
♀∥♆ 3:19
☽⚼⚳ 5:36
☽⚻♅ 5:40
☽⚼♂ 6:00
☽⚻♃ 7:12
☽△⚷ 10:03
☽⚹♇ 12:51
☽☌♄ 13:17
☉△☽ 14:36
☿#♅ 18:52
☽△☿ 20:49

3 Su
☽⚼♅ 7:35
☽⚻⚳ 7:43
☽△♂ 9:20
☽∠♇ 14:39
♀⚺♅ 18:00

4 M
☽□♆ 2:43
♂∥⚷ 2:58
☽∥♇ 4:43
☽△♅ 9:20
☽□♀ 10:46
☽☍♃ 11:01
☉☌☿ 12:59
☽□⚷ 13:42
♀□♃ 13:54
☽⚺♇ 16:18
☽⚺♄ 16:35
☽□☿ 20:42
☉□☽ 21:54
☿∥♂ 21:59

5 Tu
☿∥⚷ 9:40
☽☍⚳ 11:32
☽□♂ 15:29
☽∠♄ 18:02
♀☌⚷ 21:30

6 W
☽⚹♆ 5:52
☽∥♇ 8:36
☽□♅ 12:29
☽⚻♃ 14:21
☽⚹⚷ 16:51
☽⚹♀ 18:37
☽☌♇ 19:16
☽⚹♄ 19:23
☽⚹☿ 20:09

7 Th
♀⚹♇ 2:04
♀△♄ 3:08
☉⚹☽ 4:38
☿☌♀ 4:55
☿△♄ 7:18
☽∠♆ 7:19
♂#♅ 7:36
☿⚹♇ 8:25
♂⚼♄ 12:02
☽⚻⚳ 15:01
☽⚼♃ 15:56
☽∠⚷ 18:21
☽∠☿ 19:53
☽⚹♂ 21:15
☽∠♀ 22:28

8 F
♄⚹♇ 7:07
☉∠☽ 7:59
☽⚺♆ 8:48
☉∥☿ 10:41
☽⚹♅ 15:30
☽⚼⚳ 16:49
☿☌⚷ 17:34
☽△♃ 17:35
☽⚺☿ 19:47
☽⚺⚷ 19:56
☽∥♄ 21:05
☽□♄ 22:09
☽⚺♇ 22:12

9 Sa
☽∠♂ 0:14
☽⚺♀ 2:26
☽∥♆ 8:27
☉⚺☽ 11:29
☽∠♅ 17:14
☽△⚳ 18:49
☽∠♇ 23:56

10 Su
☽⚺♂ 3:28
☿□♃ 3:39
☽∥♀ 4:21
☽∥☿ 11:55
☽☌♆ 12:21
☽⚺♅ 19:17
☽☌☿ 20:34
☽□♃ 21:40
☉∥☽ 22:04
☽☌⚷ 23:53

11 M
☽∥⚷ 1:24
☽△♄ 1:47
☽⚹♇ 2:02
☽#♅ 5:17
☽☌♀ 11:34
☽∥♂ 12:31
☉☌☽ 19:52
☿⚺♅ 20:22
☿∥♀ 20:57
☽#♂ 21:25

12 Tu
☽□⚳ 0:07
☽⚼♄ 4:20
☽∥♅ 5:29
♂ ♈ 6:27
☽#⚷ 9:11
☉#☽ 9:42
☽☌♂ 11:36
☉∥⚷ 16:10
☽⚺♆ 17:45
☽⚺☿ 23:48
☽#♀ 23:51

13 W
☽☌♅ 1:07
☽⚹♃ 3:53
☽⚺⚷ 5:58
☽#☿ 6:05
⚵ ♒ 7:13
☽⚻♄ 7:35
☽□♇ 8:03
☽∠♆ 21:32
☽⚺♀ 23:55

14 Th
☽∠☿ 2:43
☽#♆ 4:35
☉⚺☽ 7:30
☉#♅ 8:07
☽∠♃ 8:11
☽⚹⚳ 8:16
☽∠⚷ 10:11
☽#♄ 17:04
☉□⚳ 19:57
☽⚺♂ 23:11

15 F
☽⚹♆ 2:09
☽⚹☿ 6:40
☽∠♀ 7:43
☽⚺♅ 10:03
☽⚺♃ 13:20
☽∠⚳ 13:39
☉∠☽ 14:52
☽⚹⚷ 15:14
☽☍♄ 16:28
☽△♇ 17:13

16 Sa
☽∠♂ 6:27
☉⚼♄ 9:51
☽∠♅ 15:44
☽⚹♀ 16:36
☽⚺⚳ 19:52
☽⚼♇ 22:57
☉⚹☽ 23:12

17 Su
♂⚺♆ 1:05
☽□♆ 13:40
☽⚹♂ 14:30
☽#♇ 16:57
☽□☿ 17:31
☉#♂ 18:57
☿ D 20:05
☽⚹♅ 22:00

18 M
☽☌♃ 1:49
☽□⚷ 3:26
☽⚻♄ 4:10
☽⚻♇ 5:13
♀□⚳ 6:40
♀⚼♄ 19:34
♀∥⚷ 20:46

19 Tu
☽☌⚳ 9:45
☽⚼♄ 10:30
☽□♀ 12:19
♀#♅ 15:32
☉□☽ 17:28
☿⚺♂ 18:21

20 W
☽△♆ 2:40
☽#♇ 2:53
☽△☿ 6:55
☽□♂ 7:34
☉ ♈ 11:03
☽□♅ 11:06
☽⚺♃ 15:20
⚳⚼♄ 16:02
☽△⚷ 16:31
☽△♄ 16:42
♀#♂ 17:57
☽☍♇ 18:03

21 Th
☽⚼♆ 8:52
♄△⚷ 11:43
☽⚼☿ 13:42
☽∠♃ 21:35
☽⚼⚷ 22:32
☽⚺⚳ 23:12

22 F
♀ ♈ 3:16
☽△♀ 7:15
☉△☽ 10:42
☽⚻♆ 14:27
♂∥♅ 17:29
♂☌♅ 18:18
☽⚻☿ 20:03
☉#♀ 20:06
☽△♅ 22:39
☽△♂ 22:55

23 Sa
☽⚹♃ 3:06
☽□♄ 3:29
☽⚻⚷ 3:50
☽#♄ 4:23
☽∠⚳ 4:57
☽⚻♇ 5:03
♂#⚷ 9:51
☽⚼♀ 15:19
☽#♆ 16:46
☉⚼☽ 17:57

24 Su
☽#☿ 2:33
♃⚻♄ 2:52
☽⚼♅ 3:14
☽⚼♂ 5:11
☽⚼♇ 9:21
☽⚹⚳ 9:48
☉⚺♆ 11:00
☽⚻♀ 22:12
☽☍♆ 23:09

25 M
☉⚻☽ 0:06
☽☍☿ 6:39
☽⚻♅ 6:57
♀⚺♆ 8:23
☽∥♂ 9:51
☽⚻♂ 10:25
☽⚹♄ 11:02
☽□♃ 11:32
☽☍⚷ 11:51
☽△♇ 12:47
☽#⚷ 13:24
☿⚺♅ 13:35
☽∥♅ 13:55
☉∥☽ 17:04
♂⚻♄ 20:33

26 Tu
☽∥♀ 0:21
☽#♀ 7:56
♂⚹♃ 10:28
♂⚺⚷ 13:12
☽∠♄ 13:37
☉#☽ 16:13
☽□⚳ 16:55
☽#♅ 17:30
☽∥⚷ 17:43
☽#♂ 23:48

27 W
♂□♇ 3:48
☽⚻♆ 4:36
♃□⚷ 6:47
☉∥♅ 8:28
☽☍♀ 8:50
☉#⚷ 9:24
☉☍☽ 9:28
☽☍♅ 12:06
☽⚻☿ 14:24
☽⚺♄ 15:34
☽⚻⚷ 16:47
☽△♃ 16:51
♅#⚷ 16:53
☽□♇ 17:28
☽☍♂ 18:16

28 Th
☽∥☿ 0:53
☽⚼♆ 6:25
☿△♄ 9:49
☽∥♆ 11:07
☉☌♀ 17:06
☽⚼☿ 17:32
☽⚼⚷ 18:27
☽⚼♃ 18:42
☽△⚳ 21:27
☽∥♄ 21:46
♀☌♅ 23:02

29 F
☉☌♅ 0:39
☽△♆ 7:52
☿☌⚷ 9:53
☽⚻♅ 15:16
☉⚻☽ 16:17
☽⚻♀ 16:44
☿□♃ 16:57
☽☌♄ 18:14
☿⚹♇ 18:35
☽△⚷ 19:49
☽⚻♃ 20:15
☽⚹♇ 20:19
☽△☿ 20:26
☽⚼⚳ 23:12
☽⚻♂ 23:56

30 Sa
♀#⚷ 0:00
♃⚻♇ 2:20
♀∥♅ 5:16
♀⚻♄ 9:15
⚴ ♉ 11:41
☽⚼♅ 16:30
☉⚻♄ 18:59
☉⚼☽ 19:17
☽⚼♀ 20:15
☽∠♇ 21:27

31 Su
☽⚻⚳ 0:50
☽⚼♂ 2:28
♀⚺⚷ 5:54
♀□♇ 10:13
☽□♆ 10:16
☽∥♇ 13:31
♀⚹♃ 14:50
☽△♅ 17:42
☽⚺♄ 20:16
☉△☽ 22:15
☽□⚷ 22:16
☉⚺⚷ 22:33
☽⚺♇ 22:35
☽☍♃ 23:04
☽△♀ 23:45

April 2013

LONGITUDE

Day	Sid.Time	☉	☽	☽ 12 hour	Mean ☊	True ☊	☿	♀	♂	⚳	♃	♄	⚷	♅	♆	♇
	h m s	° ' "	° ' "	° ' "	° '	° '	° '	° '	° '	° '	° '	° '	° '	° '	° '	° '
1 M	12 38 04	11♈25 25	12♐23 51	19♐32 47	18♏49.8	17♏18.0	13♓38.3	12♈15.6	15♈13.6	28♊50.2	11♊50.9	10♏09.4	11♓22.0	8♈39.4	4♓12.9	11♑33.0
2 Tu	12 42 01	12 24 36	26 40 35	3♑47 01	18 46.6	17 19.4	14 39.5	13 30.1	15 59.5	29 07.7	12 00.9	10R 05.7	11 25.5	8 42.9	4 14.8	11 33.4
3 W	12 45 58	13 23 46	10♑51 49	17 54 49	18 43.4	17R 20.2	15 43.4	14 44.6	16 45.3	29 25.4	12 10.9	10 01.9	11 28.9	8 46.3	4 16.7	11 33.7
4 Th	12 49 54	14 22 55	24 55 49	1♒54 40	18 40.3	17 19.8	16 49.7	15 59.0	17 31.1	29 43.2	12 21.1	9 58.1	11 32.3	8 49.7	4 18.5	11 34.0
5 F	12 53 51	15 22 01	8♒51 12	15 45 16	18 37.1	17 17.9	17 58.5	17 13.5	18 16.9	0♋01.3	12 31.4	9 54.2	11 35.7	8 53.1	4 20.4	11 34.2
6 Sa	12 57 47	16 21 06	22 36 43	29 25 22	18 33.9	17 14.6	19 09.5	18 27.9	19 02.6	0 19.5	12 41.8	9 50.3	11 39.0	8 56.5	4 22.2	11 34.5
7 Su	13 01 44	17 20 08	6♓11 04	12♓53 38	18 30.7	17 10.4	20 22.7	19 42.3	19 48.3	0 37.9	12 52.2	9 46.3	11 42.3	8 59.9	4 24.0	11 34.7
8 M	13 05 40	18 19 09	19 32 57	26 08 51	18 27.6	17 05.6	21 38.0	20 56.7	20 33.9	0 56.5	13 02.8	9 42.2	11 45.6	9 03.3	4 25.8	11 34.8
9 Tu	13 09 37	19 18 08	2♈41 13	9♈09 58	18 24.4	17 01.2	22 55.3	22 11.1	21 19.5	1 15.3	13 13.5	9 38.1	11 48.9	9 06.7	4 27.5	11 35.0
10 W	13 13 33	20 17 05	15 35 03	21 56 27	18 21.2	16 57.4	24 14.6	23 25.5	22 05.0	1 34.2	13 24.2	9 34.0	11 52.1	9 10.1	4 29.2	11 35.1
11 Th	13 17 30	21 16 01	28 14 11	4♉28 22	18 18.0	16 54.9	25 35.8	24 39.8	22 50.5	1 53.3	13 35.1	9 29.8	11 55.3	9 13.5	4 31.0	11 35.1
12 F	13 21 26	22 14 54	10♉39 08	16 46 39	18 14.8	16D 53.6	26 58.8	25 54.1	23 36.0	2 12.6	13 46.1	9 25.6	11 58.5	9 16.9	4 32.6	11R 35.2
13 Sa	13 25 23	23 13 45	22 51 12	28 53 04	18 11.7	16 53.6	28 23.7	27 08.4	24 21.4	2 32.0	13 57.1	9 21.3	12 01.6	9 20.2	4 34.3	11 35.2
14 Su	13 29 20	24 12 34	4♊52 36	10♊50 12	18 08.5	16 54.6	29 50.4	28 22.7	25 06.7	2 51.6	14 08.2	9 17.0	12 04.7	9 23.6	4 36.0	11 35.2
15 M	13 33 16	25 11 21	16 46 19	22 41 26	18 05.3	16 56.1	1♈18.8	29 37.0	25 52.1	3 11.4	14 19.5	9 12.7	12 07.8	9 26.9	4 37.6	11 35.1
16 Tu	13 37 13	26 10 05	28 36 05	4♋30 47	18 02.1	16 57.8	2 48.9	0♉51.3	26 37.3	3 31.3	14 30.8	9 08.3	12 10.8	9 30.2	4 39.2	11 35.0
17 W	13 41 09	27 08 48	10♋26 08	16 22 43	17 58.9	16 59.2	4 20.8	2 05.5	27 22.5	3 51.4	14 42.1	9 03.9	12 13.8	9 33.5	4 40.7	11 34.9
18 Th	13 45 06	28 07 28	22 21 08	28 22 00	17 55.8	17R 00.0	5 54.3	3 19.7	28 07.7	4 11.6	14 53.6	8 59.5	12 16.7	9 36.8	4 42.3	11 34.8
19 F	13 49 02	29 06 06	4♌25 53	10♌33 24	17 52.6	17 00.0	7 29.5	4 33.9	28 52.8	4 31.9	15 05.2	8 55.1	12 19.7	9 40.1	4 43.8	11 34.6
20 Sa	13 52 59	0♉04 42	16 45 04	23 01 24	17 49.4	16 59.2	9 06.4	5 48.1	29 37.8	4 52.4	15 16.8	8 50.6	12 22.5	9 43.4	4 45.3	11 34.4
21 Su	13 56 55	1 03 16	29 22 52	5♍49 50	17 46.2	16 57.7	10 45.0	7 02.2	0♉22.8	5 13.0	15 28.5	8 46.1	12 25.4	9 46.6	4 46.8	11 34.2
22 M	14 00 52	2 01 47	12♍22 37	19 01 24	17 43.1	16 55.9	12 25.2	8 16.3	1 07.8	5 33.8	15 40.2	8 41.6	12 28.2	9 49.9	4 48.2	11 33.9
23 Tu	14 04 49	3 00 17	25 46 18	2♎37 15	17 39.9	16 53.9	14 07.2	9 30.4	1 52.7	5 54.7	15 52.1	8 37.1	12 31.0	9 53.1	4 49.6	11 33.6
24 W	14 08 45	3 58 44	9♎34 07	16 36 34	17 36.7	16 52.2	15 50.8	10 44.5	2 37.5	6 15.8	16 04.0	8 32.6	12 33.7	9 56.3	4 51.0	11 33.3
25 Th	14 12 42	4 57 09	23 44 12	0♏56 26	17 33.5	16 51.0	17 36.1	11 58.6	3 22.3	6 36.9	16 16.0	8 28.1	12 36.4	9 59.5	4 52.4	11 32.9
26 F	14 16 38	5 55 32	8♏12 36	15 31 55	17 30.3	16D 50.4	19 23.1	13 12.6	4 07.1	6 58.2	16 28.0	8 23.5	12 39.0	10 02.7	4 53.7	11 32.5
27 Sa	14 20 35	6 53 54	22 53 35	0♐16 43	17 27.2	16 50.3	21 11.8	14 26.6	4 51.8	7 19.6	16 40.2	8 19.0	12 41.6	10 05.8	4 55.0	11 32.1
28 Su	14 24 31	7 52 14	7♐40 24	15 03 47	17 24.0	16 50.7	23 02.2	15 40.6	5 36.4	7 41.2	16 52.3	8 14.4	12 44.2	10 09.0	4 56.3	11 31.7
29 M	14 28 28	8 50 32	22 26 02	29 46 24	17 20.8	16 51.3	24 54.3	16 54.6	6 21.0	8 02.9	17 04.6	8 09.8	12 46.7	10 12.1	4 57.5	11 31.2
30 Tu	14 32 24	9♉48 49	7♑04 12	14♑18 53	17♏17.6	16♏52.0	26♈48.2	18♉08.6	7♉05.6	8♋24.6	17♊16.9	8♏05.3	12♓49.2	10♈15.2	4♓58.8	11♑30.7

1st of Month

Julian Day # 2456383.5
Obliquity 23°26'10"
SVP 5♓04'16"
GC 27♐01.5
Eris 22♈08.9

Day	⚴
1	0♉42.0
6	3 02.5
11	5 25.2
16	7 50.1
21	10 17.1
26	12 46.0

Day	⚵
1	5♒49.2
6	7 16.2
11	8 39.9
16	10 00.1
21	11 16.3
26	12 28.3

Day	⚶
1	21♊42.0
6	23 19.0
11	24 59.7
16	26 44.0
21	28 31.3
26	0♋21.5

DECLINATION and LATITUDE

Day	☉ Decl	☽ Decl	☽ Lat	☽ 12h Decl	☿ Decl	☿ Lat	♀ Decl	♀ Lat	♂ Decl	♂ Lat	⚳ Decl	⚳ Lat	♃ Decl	♃ Lat	♄ Decl	♄ Lat
1 M	4N31	20S05	2N13	20S15	7S55	1S37	3N40	1S17	5N28	0S34	28N47	5N21	21N49	0S23	12S20	2N39
2 Tu	4 54	20 05	3 19	19 36	7 39	1 44	4 10	1 16	5 46	0 34	28 48	5 22	21 51	0 23	12 19	2 40
3 W	5 17	18 49	4 12	17 44	7 21	1 52	4 40	1 14	6 04	0 33	28 49	5 23	21 52	0 23	12 18	2 40
4 Th	5 40	16 24	4 49	14 50	7 01	1 58	5 10	1 13	6 23	0 32	28 50	5 24	21 54	0 23	12 16	2 40
5 F	6 03	13 04	5 09	11 08	6 40	2 04	5 39	1 12	6 41	0 32	28 50	5 24	21 55	0 23	12 15	2 40
6 Sa	6 26	9 04	5 11	6 54	6 17	2 10	6 09	1 11	6 58	0 31	28 51	5 25	21 56	0 23	12 14	2 40
7 Su	6 48	4 39	4 56	2 23	5 53	2 15	6 38	1 09	7 16	0 31	28 52	5 26	21 58	0 23	12 12	2 40
8 M	7 11	0 05	4 24	2N11	5 27	2 19	7 08	1 08	7 34	0 30	28 52	5 26	21 59	0 22	12 11	2 40
9 Tu	7 33	4N25	3 39	6 35	5 00	2 23	7 37	1 06	7 52	0 29	28 53	5 27	22 01	0 22	12 10	2 40
10 W	7 56	8 39	2 44	10 36	4 32	2 27	8 06	1 05	8 09	0 29	28 53	5 27	22 02	0 22	12 08	2 40
11 Th	8 18	12 25	1 41	14 04	4 02	2 30	8 34	1 03	8 27	0 28	28 53	5 28	22 04	0 22	12 07	2 40
12 F	8 40	15 34	0 34	16 51	3 31	2 32	9 03	1 01	8 44	0 28	28 54	5 29	22 05	0 22	12 06	2 41
13 Sa	9 02	17 57	0S33	18 50	2 59	2 34	9 31	0 60	9 01	0 27	28 54	5 29	22 07	0 22	12 04	2 41
14 Su	9 23	19 30	1 38	19 57	2 26	2 35	9 60	0 58	9 18	0 26	28 54	5 30	22 08	0 21	12 03	2 41
15 M	9 45	20 10	2 37	20 09	1 52	2 36	10 27	0 56	9 36	0 26	28 54	5 31	22 10	0 21	12 01	2 41
16 Tu	10 06	19 55	3 30	19 28	1 16	2 36	10 55	0 55	9 52	0 25	28 55	5 31	22 11	0 21	11 60	2 41
17 W	10 27	18 48	4 14	17 56	0 39	2 36	11 22	0 53	10 09	0 25	28 55	5 32	22 13	0 21	11 58	2 41
18 Th	10 48	16 51	4 48	15 35	0 02	2 35	11 50	0 51	10 26	0 24	28 55	5 33	22 14	0 21	11 57	2 41
19 F	11 09	14 09	5 09	12 33	0N37	2 34	12 16	0 49	10 43	0 23	28 54	5 33	22 15	0 21	11 56	2 41
20 Sa	11 30	10 47	5 16	8 53	1 17	2 32	12 43	0 47	10 59	0 23	28 54	5 34	22 17	0 21	11 54	2 41
21 Su	11 50	6 52	5 09	4 44	1 58	2 30	13 09	0 45	11 16	0 22	28 54	5 34	22 18	0 20	11 53	2 41
22 M	12 11	2 31	4 46	0 14	2 39	2 27	13 35	0 43	11 32	0 21	28 54	5 35	22 20	0 20	11 51	2 41
23 Tu	12 31	2S06	4 07	4S25	3 22	2 23	14 01	0 41	11 48	0 21	28 53	5 36	22 21	0 20	11 50	2 41
24 W	12 51	6 44	3 12	8 59	4 05	2 19	14 26	0 39	12 04	0 20	28 53	5 36	22 22	0 20	11 48	2 41
25 Th	13 10	11 09	2 05	13 10	4 50	2 15	14 51	0 36	12 20	0 20	28 53	5 37	22 24	0 20	11 47	2 41
26 F	13 30	14 60	0 48	16 36	5 35	2 10	15 15	0 34	12 36	0 19	28 52	5 37	22 25	0 20	11 45	2 41
27 Sa	13 49	17 57	0N34	19 00	6 20	2 05	15 40	0 32	12 51	0 18	28 51	5 38	22 27	0 20	11 44	2 41
28 Su	14 08	19 44	1 53	20 06	7 07	1 59	16 03	0 30	13 07	0 18	28 51	5 39	22 28	0 20	11 43	2 41
29 M	14 27	20 08	3 05	19 50	7 54	1 52	16 27	0 28	13 22	0 17	28 50	5 39	22 29	0 19	11 41	2 41
30 Tu	14N45	19S11	4N04	18S14	8N41	1S46	16N50	0S25	13N37	0S16	28N49	5N40	22N30	0S19	11S40	2N41

Day	⚷ Decl	⚷ Lat	♅ Decl	♅ Lat	♆ Decl	♆ Lat	♇ Decl	♇ Lat
1	2S37	5N03	2N49	0S40	10S32	0S37	19S40	3N17
6	2 30	5 04	2 56	0 40	10 29	0 37	19 40	3 17
11	2 24	5 04	3 02	0 40	10 26	0 38	19 40	3 17
16	2 17	5 05	3 09	0 40	10 23	0 38	19 40	3 17
21	2 11	5 06	3 15	0 40	10 21	0 38	19 40	3 17
26	2 05	5 07	3 22	0 40	10 18	0 38	19 40	3 17

Day	⚴ Decl	⚴ Lat	⚵ Decl	⚵ Lat	⚶ Decl	⚶ Lat	Eris Decl	Eris Lat
1	6S36	19S31	8S32	10N35	23N06	0S04	3S23	12S56
6	6 04	19 44	8 05	10 43	23 20	0N04	3 22	12 55
11	5 33	19 58	7 37	10 50	23 32	0 12	3 20	12 55
16	5 03	20 12	7 09	10 59	23 43	0 19	3 19	12 55
21	4 34	20 27	6 41	11 07	23 52	0 26	3 18	12 55
26	4 06	20 42	6 13	11 17	23 59	0 33	3 17	12 55

Moon Phenomena

Max/0 Decl
dy hr mn
1 12:02 20S15
8 0:27 0 N
15 5:27 20N11
22 13:11 0 S
28 19:17 20S10

Max/0 Lat
dy hr mn
5 14:40 5N12
12 12:13 0 S
20 0:23 5S16
26 14:07 0 N

Perigee/Apogee
dy hr m kilometers
15 22:28 a 404862
27 20:03 p 362270

PH dy hr mn
☾ 3 4:38 13♑35
● 10 9:36 20♈41
☽ 18 12:32 28♋38
○ 25 19:58 5♏46
• 25 20:09 P 0.015

Void of Course Moon

Last Aspect			☽ Ingress		
1 5:01	♂	△	♑	2	5:36
3 10:36	♂	□	♒	4	8:43
5 17:23	♂	✶	♓	6	13:01
8 4:11	☿	☌	♈	8	19:03
10 16:26	♀	☌	♉	11	3:23
13 12:31	☿	✶	♊	13	14:14
15 19:42	♂	✶	♋	16	2:50
18 12:32	☉	□	♌	18	15:15
19 21:07	♃	✶	♍	21	1:10
22 6:04	♃	□	♎	23	7:26
24 12:13	☿	☍	♏	25	10:26
26 8:57	♀	☍	♐	27	11:33
29 4:38	☿	△	♑	29	12:22

DAILY ASPECTARIAN

1 M
☽□☿ 2:14
☉□♇ 3:06
☽△♂ 5:01
☉✶♃ 12:25
☽∠♄ 21:21

2 Tu
☽☍⚳ 4:13
☽∥♇ 10:45
☽✶♆ 12:49
☽□♅ 20:26
☽✶♄ 22:36

3 W
☽✶⚷ 1:03
☽☌♇ 1:11
☽⚻♃ 2:16
☉□☽ 4:38
☽□♀ 7:14
☽✶☿ 8:58
☽□♂ 10:36
☽∠♆ 14:22

4 Th
☽∠⚷ 2:46
☽⚼♃ 4:12
☽⚻⚳ 8:25
♇✶⚷ 12:54
☽∠☿ 12:55
☽⚺♆ 16:10
⚳ ♋ 22:18
☿∦♂ 23:26

5 F
☽✶♅ 0:03
☽□♄ 1:49
☽⚺♇ 4:43
☽⚺⚷ 4:47
☽∥♄ 5:12
☽△♃ 6:27
☽⚼⚳ 10:58
☉✶☽ 12:12
☽∥♆ 15:49
☽✶♀ 16:01
☽⚺☿ 17:22
☽✶♂ 17:23
☿⚺♂ 17:42
☉∦☿ 19:21

6 Sa
☽∠♅ 2:21
☿∦♀ 3:34
☽∠♇ 6:58
♂∠♆ 10:42
☽∦♂ 10:51
☉∦☽ 13:24
☽△⚳ 13:55
☽∦♀ 14:27
☉∠☽ 16:37
☽∥☿ 16:51
♀∠♆ 17:56
☽☌♆ 20:49
☽∠♀ 21:06
☽∠♂ 21:24

7 Su
♀☌♂ 4:59
☽⚺♅ 5:03
☽△♄ 6:22
☽∦♅ 8:57
☽✶♇ 9:38
☽☌⚷ 9:55
☽∥⚷ 11:30
☽□♃ 12:07
☉⚺☽ 21:36

8 M
☽⚺♂ 1:57
☽⚺♀ 2:48
☽☌☿ 4:11
☽⚼♄ 9:19
☉∥♀ 11:34
☽∦⚷ 13:23
☽∥♅ 16:16
☽□⚳ 21:18

9 Tu
☽∦☿ 2:53
☽⚺♆ 3:17
☉∠♆ 3:56
☽☌♅ 11:57
☽⚻♄ 12:48
☽□♇ 16:30
☽⚺⚷ 17:01
☉∥☽ 19:19
☽✶♃ 19:51
☽∥♀ 20:18
☽∥♂ 20:51

10 W
☿⚼♄ 5:30
☽∠♆ 7:22
♀∥♂ 7:25
☉☌☽ 9:36
☽∦♆ 11:00
☽☌♂ 13:03
☽☌♀ 16:26
☽⚺☿ 18:20
☽∠⚷ 21:28
☽∦♄ 21:58

11 Th
☽∠♃ 0:41
☽✶⚳ 7:12
☽✶♆ 12:07
☽⚺♅ 21:19
☽☍♄ 21:37

12 F
☽△♇ 1:49
☽✶⚷ 2:36
☽∠☿ 2:56
☽⚺♃ 6:11
☽∠⚳ 13:12
♇ R 19:35
☿∦♅ 19:59
♀∠⚷ 21:42
☉∥♂ 22:56

13 Sa
☉⚺☽ 0:49
☽∠♅ 2:57
☽⚺♂ 3:11
♄⚻♅ 3:30
☽⚼♇ 7:25
☽⚺♀ 9:30
☽✶☿ 12:31
☽⚺⚳ 19:50
☽□♆ 23:27

14 Su
☿ ♈ 2:38
☽∦♇ 3:35
☿∥⚷ 4:39
☽⚻♄ 8:49
☽✶♅ 9:08
☉∠☽ 9:30
☽∠♂ 11:15
☽⚻♇ 13:31
☽□⚷ 14:34
♀∠♃ 17:19
☽☌♃ 18:58
☽∠♀ 19:08
♀∦♆ 20:56

15 M
♀ ♉ 7:26
☽⚼♄ 15:00
☉✶☽ 18:37
☽✶♂ 19:42

16 Tu
☽✶♀ 5:07
☽∦♇ 7:34
☽□☿ 9:49
☽☌⚳ 10:17
☽△♆ 12:19
☿□⚳ 14:14
☉∦♆ 18:53
♂∠⚷ 19:02
☽△♄ 21:15
☽□♅ 22:13

17 W
☉∠⚷ 2:09
☽☍♇ 2:19
☽△⚷ 3:39
☿⚺♆ 5:15
☽⚺♃ 8:46
♂∦♆ 18:33
☽⚼♆ 18:41

18 Th
☉☌♂ 0:21
♀∦♄ 6:15
☽⚼⚷ 9:53
☽□♂ 12:17
☉□☽ 12:32
☽∠♃ 15:16
♀✶⚳ 23:07

19 F
☽⚺⚳ 0:12
☽□♀ 0:18
☽⚻♆ 0:35
♀✶♆ 3:16
☽△☿ 6:55
☽□♄ 8:45
☽△♅ 10:19
☽∥♀ 12:17
☽⚻♇ 13:59
⚳△♆ 15:02
☽⚻⚷ 15:30
☽∦♄ 16:26
☉∥☽ 19:40
☿⚻♄ 20:17
☽✶♃ 21:07
☉ ♉ 22:04
☽∥♂ 22:45

20 Sa
☽∦♆ 2:48
☽∠⚳ 6:10
☉∠♃ 6:11
☿☌♅ 9:21
♂ ♉ 11:49
☽⚼♅ 15:17
☽⚼☿ 16:09
☽⚼♇ 18:43

21 Su
☽△♂ 1:59
☉∦♄ 2:34
☉△☽ 3:23
♂∠♃ 4:05
☿∦⚷ 7:34
☽☍♆ 10:04
☽✶⚳ 11:10
☿□♇ 11:48
☽△♀ 15:43
☽✶♄ 17:19
☽⚻♅ 19:20
☽∥♅ 19:55
☽△♇ 22:31
☽∥☿ 23:21

22 M
☽⚻☿ 0:05
☽☍⚷ 0:10
☿⚺⚷ 0:43
☽∦⚷ 1:52
☽□♃ 6:04
☽⚼♂ 7:12
♀☍♄ 7:44
☉⚼☽ 9:05
☽∠♄ 20:13
☽⚼♀ 21:32
☿∥♅ 21:44

23 Tu
☽∥⚷ 0:16
♂∦♄ 2:29
☽∦♅ 6:14
♀⚺♅ 7:41
☽∦☿ 7:44
☽⚻♂ 11:19
☉⚻☽ 13:38
☽⚻♆ 15:51
☽□⚳ 18:10
☽⚺♄ 22:15

24 W
☽☍♅ 0:38
☽⚻♀ 2:12
☽□♇ 3:24
☿✶♃ 3:26
☽⚻⚷ 5:08
☽△♃ 11:14
☽☍☿ 12:13
♀△♇ 15:44
☽⚼♆ 17:30
☽∥♆ 19:18
☉✶♆ 21:59

25 Th
⚶ ♋ 0:49
☽∥♄ 3:41
☽⚼⚷ 6:29
☽∦♂ 7:27
♀✶⚷ 12:43
☽⚼♃ 12:43
☉∦☽ 13:12
☽☍♂ 16:54
☽△♆ 18:32
☉☍☽ 19:58
☽△⚳ 21:55

26 F
☽☌♄ 0:18
☽∦♀ 2:06
☽⚻♅ 3:01
☽✶♇ 5:28
☿∠♆ 6:53
☽△⚷ 7:18
☽☍♀ 8:57
☽⚻♃ 13:43
☽⚻☿ 20:51
☽⚼⚳ 23:03

27 Sa
♂✶♆ 1:47
☽⚼♅ 3:36
☽∠♇ 5:55
☉✶⚳ 16:47
☽□♆ 19:33
☽⚻♂ 20:28
☽∥♇ 22:47

28 Su
☽⚻⚳ 0:01
☉⚻☽ 0:21
☽⚼☿ 0:40
☽⚺♄ 0:55
☽△♅ 4:02
☽⚺♇ 6:15
☽□⚷ 8:15
☉☍♄ 8:28
☽⚻♀ 14:11
☽☍♃ 15:09
☽⚼♂ 22:08

29 M
☽∠♄ 1:11
☉⚼☽ 2:28
♀⚺♃ 3:52
☽△☿ 4:38
⚳△♄ 6:23
☽∥♇ 15:32
☽⚼♀ 16:56
☽✶♆ 20:33

30 Tu
☽△♂ 0:02
☽✶♄ 1:40
☽☍⚳ 2:16
☉△☽ 4:52
☽□♅ 5:17
☽☌♇ 7:21
☽✶⚷ 9:33
☉⚺♅ 11:28
☿∠⚷ 12:59
☽⚻♃ 17:11
☽△♀ 20:07
☽∠♆ 21:29
☽∦♀ 22:21

LONGITUDE

Day	Sid.Time	☉	☽	☽ 12 hour	Mean ☊	True ☊	☿	♀	♂	⚳	♃	♄	⚷	♅	♆	♇
	h m s	° ' "	° ' "	° ' "	° '	° '	° '	° '	° '	° '	° '	° '	° '	° '	° '	° '
W	14 36 21	10♉47 04	21♑29 58	28♑37 04	17♏14.5	16♏52.5	28♈43.8	19♉22.6	7♉50.1	8♋46.5	17♊29.3	8♏00.7	12♓51.7	10♈18.2	5♓00.0	11♑30.2
Th	14 40 18	11 45 18	5♒39 58	12♒38 27	17 11.3	16R 52.8	0♉41.1	20 36.5	8 34.5	9 08.6	17 41.7	7R 56.2	12 54.1	10 21.3	5 01.1	11R 29.7
F	14 44 14	12 43 30	19 32 29	26 22 01	17 08.1	16 52.8	2 40.0	21 50.4	9 18.9	9 30.7	17 54.2	7 51.7	12 56.4	10 24.3	5 02.3	11 29.1
Sa	14 48 11	13 41 41	3♓07 07	9♓47 52	17 04.9	16 52.6	4 40.6	23 04.3	10 03.3	9 52.9	18 06.7	7 47.1	12 58.7	10 27.3	5 03.4	11 28.5
Su	14 52 07	14 39 51	16 24 24	22 56 52	17 01.8	16 52.4	6 42.8	24 18.2	10 47.6	10 15.3	18 19.3	7 42.6	13 01.0	10 30.3	5 04.5	11 27.8
M	14 56 04	15 37 58	29 25 28	5♈50 20	16 58.6	16 52.2	8 46.5	25 32.1	11 31.9	10 37.7	18 32.0	7 38.1	13 03.2	10 33.3	5 05.5	11 27.2
Tu	15 00 00	16 36 05	12♈11 42	18 29 43	16 55.4	16D 52.1	10 51.7	26 46.0	12 16.1	11 00.3	18 44.7	7 33.6	13 05.4	10 36.2	5 06.5	11 26.5
W	15 03 57	17 34 10	24 44 36	0♉56 32	16 52.2	16 52.1	12 58.2	27 59.8	13 00.2	11 23.0	18 57.5	7 29.2	13 07.5	10 39.1	5 07.5	11 25.8
Th	15 07 53	18 32 13	7♉05 42	13 12 19	16 49.0	16R 52.2	15 06.0	29 13.6	13 44.3	11 45.8	19 10.3	7 24.7	13 09.6	10 42.0	5 08.5	11 25.0
F	15 11 50	19 30 15	19 16 34	25 18 39	16 45.9	16 52.2	17 14.8	0♊27.5	14 28.4	12 08.7	19 23.2	7 20.3	13 11.6	10 44.9	5 09.4	11 24.3
Sa	15 15 47	20 28 15	1♊18 50	7♊17 20	16 42.7	16 52.1	19 24.4	1 41.3	15 12.4	12 31.7	19 36.1	7 15.9	13 13.6	10 47.7	5 10.3	11 23.5
Su	15 19 43	21 26 14	13 14 25	19 10 23	16 39.5	16 51.7	21 34.8	2 55.0	15 56.3	12 54.7	19 49.0	7 11.6	13 15.5	10 50.5	5 11.2	11 22.7
M	15 23 40	22 24 11	25 05 31	1♋00 12	16 36.3	16 51.1	23 45.5	4 08.8	16 40.2	13 17.9	20 02.0	7 07.2	13 17.4	10 53.3	5 12.0	11 21.8
Tu	15 27 36	23 22 07	6♋54 47	12 49 40	16 33.2	16 50.3	25 56.5	5 22.5	17 24.0	13 41.2	20 15.1	7 02.9	13 19.2	10 56.0	5 12.8	11 20.9
W	15 31 33	24 20 01	18 45 17	24 42 06	16 30.0	16 49.4	28 07.4	6 36.2	18 07.8	14 04.6	20 28.2	6 58.7	13 21.0	10 58.7	5 13.6	11 20.1
Th	15 35 29	25 17 53	0♌40 35	6♌41 15	16 26.8	16 48.5	0♊17.9	7 49.9	18 51.5	14 28.0	20 41.3	6 54.5	13 22.7	11 01.4	5 14.3	11 19.1
F	15 39 26	26 15 43	12 44 38	18 51 16	16 23.6	16 47.8	2 27.8	9 03.6	19 35.2	14 51.6	20 54.5	6 50.3	13 24.4	11 04.1	5 15.0	11 18.2
Sa	15 43 22	27 13 32	25 01 40	1♍16 24	16 20.4	16D 47.5	4 36.7	10 17.3	20 18.8	15 15.2	21 07.7	6 46.2	13 26.1	11 06.7	5 15.7	11 17.2
Su	15 47 19	28 11 19	7♍35 57	14 00 50	16 17.3	16 47.6	6 44.4	11 30.9	21 02.4	15 38.9	21 20.9	6 42.1	13 27.6	11 09.3	5 16.4	11 16.3
M	15 51 16	29 09 04	20 31 28	27 08 14	16 14.1	16 48.3	8 50.7	12 44.5	21 45.9	16 02.7	21 34.2	6 38.0	13 29.2	11 11.8	5 17.0	11 15.2
Tu	15 55 12	0♊06 47	3♎51 25	10♎41 13	16 10.9	16 49.2	10 55.3	13 58.1	22 29.3	16 26.6	21 47.5	6 34.0	13 30.6	11 14.4	5 17.5	11 14.2
W	15 59 09	1 04 29	17 37 41	24 40 46	16 07.7	16 50.3	12 57.9	15 11.7	23 12.7	16 50.5	22 00.8	6 30.1	13 32.1	11 16.9	5 18.1	11 13.2
Th	16 03 05	2 02 10	1♏50 13	9♏05 40	16 04.6	16 51.2	14 58.4	16 25.3	23 56.1	17 14.6	22 14.2	6 26.2	13 33.4	11 19.3	5 18.6	11 12.1
F	16 07 02	2 59 49	16 26 30	23 52 01	16 01.4	16R 51.6	16 56.7	17 38.8	24 39.4	17 38.7	22 27.6	6 22.4	13 34.7	11 21.7	5 19.1	11 11.0
Sa	16 10 58	3 57 27	1♐21 19	8♐53 22	15 58.2	16 51.2	18 52.5	18 52.3	25 22.6	18 02.9	22 41.0	6 18.6	13 36.0	11 24.1	5 19.5	11 09.9
Su	16 14 55	4 55 03	16 27 04	24 01 13	15 55.0	16 50.0	20 45.7	20 05.8	26 05.8	18 27.1	22 54.5	6 14.9	13 37.2	11 26.5	5 20.0	11 08.8
M	16 18 51	5 52 39	1♑34 39	9♑06 13	15 51.9	16 48.0	22 36.4	21 19.3	26 48.9	18 51.5	23 07.9	6 11.2	13 38.4	11 28.8	5 20.4	11 07.6
Tu	16 22 48	6 50 13	16 34 49	23 59 32	15 48.7	16 45.5	24 24.3	22 32.8	27 32.0	19 15.9	23 21.4	6 07.6	13 39.5	11 31.1	5 20.7	11 06.5
W	16 26 45	7 47 47	1♒19 32	8♒34 10	15 45.5	16 43.0	26 09.4	23 46.2	28 15.0	19 40.4	23 35.0	6 04.1	13 40.6	11 33.4	5 21.0	11 05.3
Th	16 30 41	8 45 19	15 43 00	22 45 42	15 42.3	16 40.9	27 51.6	24 59.6	28 58.0	20 04.9	23 48.5	6 00.6	13 41.6	11 35.6	5 21.3	11 04.1
F	16 34 38	9♊42 51	29 42 09	6♓32 20	15♏39.1	16♏39.6	29♊31.0	26♊13.0	29♉40.9	20♋29.6	24♊02.1	5♏57.2	13♓42.5	11♈37.7	5♓21.6	11♑02.9

1st of Month

Julian Day # 2456413.5
Obliquity 23°26'09"
SVP 5♓04'13"
GC 27♐01.5
Eris 22♈28.4

Day	⚴
1	15♉16.9
6	17 49.8
11	20 24.5
16	23 01.0
21	25 39.2
26	28 19.1
31	1♊00.5

Day	⚵
1	13♒35.8
6	14 38.2
11	15 35.2
16	16 26.2
21	17 10.8
26	17 48.5
31	18 18.9

Day	⚶
1	2♋14.3
6	4 09.5
11	6 06.9
16	8 06.4
21	10 07.7
26	12 10.7
31	14 15.3

DECLINATION and LATITUDE

Day	☉ Decl	☽ Decl	☽ Lat	☽ 12h Decl	☿ Decl	☿ Lat	♀ Decl	♀ Lat	♂ Decl	♂ Lat	⚳ Decl	⚳ Lat	♃ Decl	♃ Lat	♄ Decl	♄ Lat
W	15N03	16S60	4N47	15S31	9N29	1S38	17N12	0S23	13N52	0S16	28N48	5N40	22N32	0S19	11S38	2N41
Th	15 22	13 49	5 11	11 57	10 18	1 30	17 34	0 21	14 07	0 15	28 47	5 41	22 33	0 19	11 37	2 41
F	15 39	9 56	5 17	7 49	11 07	1 22	17 56	0 18	14 22	0 14	28 46	5 42	22 35	0 19	11 35	2 41
Sa	15 57	5 37	5 05	3 22	11 55	1 14	18 17	0 16	14 37	0 14	28 45	5 42	22 36	0 19	11 34	2 41
Su	16 14	1 07	4 36	1N08	12 44	1 04	18 38	0 13	14 51	0 13	28 44	5 43	22 37	0 19	11 33	2 41
M	16 31	3N21	3 54	5 31	13 33	0 55	18 58	0 11	15 05	0 12	28 43	5 43	22 38	0 19	11 31	2 41
Tu	16 48	7 36	3 01	9 35	14 22	0 45	19 17	0 09	15 20	0 12	28 41	5 44	22 39	0 18	11 30	2 41
W	17 04	11 26	1 60	13 10	15 10	0 35	19 37	0 06	15 34	0 11	28 40	5 44	22 40	0 18	11 29	2 41
Th	17 20	14 44	0 54	16 07	15 58	0 25	19 55	0 04	15 48	0 11	28 39	5 45	22 42	0 18	11 27	2 40
F	17 36	17 20	0S13	18 20	16 45	0 15	20 13	0 01	16 01	0 10	28 37	5 46	22 43	0 18	11 26	2 40
Sa	17 52	19 07	1 19	19 42	17 30	0 04	20 31	0N01	16 15	0 09	28 35	5 46	22 44	0 18	11 24	2 40
Su	18 07	20 03	2 21	20 10	18 15	0N06	20 48	0 04	16 28	0 09	28 34	5 47	22 45	0 18	11 23	2 40
M	18 22	20 04	3 17	19 45	18 59	0 17	21 04	0 06	16 41	0 08	28 32	5 47	22 46	0 18	11 22	2 40
Tu	18 37	19 12	4 04	18 27	19 41	0 27	21 20	0 08	16 54	0 07	28 30	5 48	22 47	0 18	11 21	2 40
W	18 51	17 30	4 40	16 22	20 21	0 37	21 35	0 11	17 07	0 07	28 28	5 48	22 48	0 17	11 19	2 40
Th	19 05	15 03	5 05	13 33	20 59	0 48	21 50	0 13	17 20	0 06	28 26	5 49	22 49	0 17	11 18	2 40
F	19 19	11 55	5 16	10 09	21 35	0 57	22 04	0 16	17 32	0 05	28 24	5 50	22 50	0 17	11 17	2 40
Sa	19 32	8 15	5 14	6 14	22 09	1 07	22 17	0 18	17 45	0 05	28 22	5 50	22 51	0 17	11 16	2 40
Su	19 45	4 08	4 56	1 57	22 40	1 16	22 30	0 21	17 57	0 04	28 19	5 51	22 52	0 17	11 14	2 39
M	19 58	0S17	4 24	2S34	23 09	1 24	22 42	0 23	18 09	0 03	28 17	5 51	22 53	0 17	11 13	2 39
Tu	20 10	4 50	3 36	7 06	23 36	1 32	22 54	0 26	18 21	0 03	28 15	5 52	22 54	0 17	11 12	2 39
W	20 22	9 18	2 35	11 25	23 59	1 39	23 05	0 28	18 32	0 02	28 12	5 53	22 55	0 17	11 11	2 39
Th	20 34	13 24	1 22	15 12	24 20	1 46	23 15	0 30	18 44	0 02	28 10	5 53	22 56	0 17	11 10	2 39
F	20 45	16 47	0 02	18 07	24 39	1 52	23 24	0 33	18 55	0 01	28 07	5 54	22 57	0 16	11 09	2 39
Sa	20 56	19 08	1N19	19 49	24 55	1 57	23 33	0 35	19 06	0 00	28 04	5 54	22 58	0 16	11 08	2 39
Su	21 07	20 09	2 36	20 07	25 08	2 01	23 41	0 38	19 17	0N00	28 01	5 55	22 59	0 16	11 06	2 38
M	21 17	19 43	3 43	18 58	25 18	2 05	23 49	0 40	19 28	0 01	27 58	5 55	22 59	0 16	11 05	2 38
Tu	21 27	17 54	4 33	16 32	25 27	2 08	23 56	0 42	19 38	0 02	27 55	5 56	23 00	0 16	11 04	2 38
W	21 36	14 55	5 04	13 05	25 32	2 10	24 02	0 45	19 48	0 02	27 52	5 57	23 01	0 16	11 03	2 38
Th	21 46	11 06	5 15	8 59	25 36	2 11	24 07	0 47	19 58	0 03	27 49	5 57	23 02	0 16	11 02	2 38
F	21N54	6S47	5N07	4S31	25N38	2N11	24N12	0N49	20N08	0N04	27N46	5N58	23N02	0S16	11S01	2N38

Day	⚷ Decl	⚷ Lat	♅ Decl	♅ Lat	♆ Decl	♆ Lat	♇ Decl	♇ Lat
1	1S59	5N08	3N28	0S40	10S16	0S38	19S40	3N17
6	1 54	5 09	3 33	0 40	10 14	0 38	19 40	3 17
11	1 49	5 10	3 39	0 40	10 13	0 38	19 41	3 17
16	1 45	5 11	3 44	0 41	10 11	0 39	19 41	3 17
21	1 41	5 12	3 49	0 41	10 10	0 39	19 42	3 16
26	1 37	5 13	3 54	0 41	10 09	0 39	19 42	3 16
31	1S34	5N14	3N58	0S41	10S09	0S39	19S43	3N16

Day	⚴ Decl	⚴ Lat	⚵ Decl	⚵ Lat	⚶ Decl	⚶ Lat	Eris Decl	Eris Lat
1	3S41	20S57	5S46	11N26	24N05	0N40	3S16	12S55
6	3 17	21 13	5 19	11 36	24 09	0 47	3 15	12 55
11	2 54	21 29	4 53	11 47	24 11	0 53	3 14	12 55
16	2 34	21 45	4 29	11 57	24 10	0 59	3 13	12 55
21	2 16	22 01	4 06	12 08	24 08	1 05	3 12	12 55
26	2 00	22 18	3 44	12 19	24 03	1 11	3 11	12 56
31	1S47	22S35	3S25	12N30	23N57	1N17	3S11	12S56

Moon Phenomena

Max/0 Decl
dy hr mn
5 5:56 0 N
12 12:33 20N10
19 22:27 0 S
26 4:39 20S11

Perigee/Apogee
dy hr m kilometers
13 13:33 a 405825
26 1:32 p 358378

PH dy hr mn
☾ 2 11:15 12♒13
● 10 0:30 19♉31
● 10 0:26 A 06'03"
☽ 18 4:36 27♌25
○ 25 4:26 4♐08
● 25 4:11 A 0.015
☾ 31 18:59 10♓28

Max/0 Lat
dy hr mn
2 19:26 5N17
9 19:14 0 S
17 7:57 5S17
24 0:40 0 N
30 1:32 5N15

Void of Course Moon

Last Aspect	☽ Ingress
1 14:08 ♀ □	♒ 1 14:21
3 4:26 ♀ □	♓ 3 18:26
5 16:01 ♀ ✶	♈ 6 1:04
7 12:42 ♃ ✶	♉ 8 10:10
10 0:30 ☉ ☌	♊ 10 21:22
12 13:33 ♃ ☌	♋ 13 9:58
15 12:15 ☉ ✶	♌ 15 22:39
18 4:36 ☉ □	♍ 18 9:34
20 16:49 ☉ △	♎ 20 17:08
22 7:36 ♃ △	♏ 22 20:56
24 13:56 ♂ ☍	♐ 24 21:50
26 10:23 ♃ ☍	♑ 26 21:30
28 18:42 ♂ △	♒ 28 21:49
30 23:58 ♂ □	♓ 31 0:31

DAILY ASPECTARIAN

♂☍♄ 5:13
☽∠⚷ 10:45
☉#☽ 14:03
☽□☿ 14:08
☿ ♉ 15:38
☉△♇ 17:37
☽⚼♃ 18:51
☽#♂ 22:04
☿#♆ 22:53
☽⚺♆ 22:54

☽□♄ 3:52
☽□♂ 5:16
☽⚻⚳ 6:08
☽✶♅ 8:05
☽⚺♇ 10:01
☉□☽ 11:15
☽⚺⚷ 12:29
☽∥♄ 14:06
☽#☿ 18:14
☽△♃ 21:06
☽∥♆ 22:07

☿∠♃ 3:10
☽□♀ 4:26
☉✶⚷ 5:33
☽⚼⚳ 8:58
☽∠♅ 10:20
☽∠♇ 12:12
♂✶⚳ 12:43
☿#♄ 13:48

☽✶☿ 3:17
☽☌♆ 3:28
☿✶♆ 4:32
☽△♄ 8:19
☽#♅ 11:11
☽△⚳ 12:30
☽✶♂ 13:12
☽⚺♅ 13:14
♂⚺♅ 13:57
☽✶♇ 15:01
☽☌⚷ 17:49
☽∥⚷ 19:43
☉✶☽ 20:34

5 Su ☽□♃ 3:34
☿☍♄ 11:14
☽⚼♄ 11:30
☽∠☿ 11:33
☽✶♀ 16:01
☽#⚷ 16:10
☽∠♂ 18:18
⚳□♅ 18:31
♂△♇ 21:30

6 M ♀∠♅ 0:24
☽∥♅ 1:08
☉∠☽ 2:26
♀∠⚳ 2:38
☽⚺♆ 10:37
☽⚻♄ 15:17
♀⚼♇ 17:44
☿⚺♅ 20:58
☽☌♅ 20:58
☽⚺☿ 20:58
☽□⚳ 21:41
☽□♇ 22:34
☽∠♀ 23:06

7 Tu ☽⚺♂ 0:09
☽⚺⚷ 1:42
☿✶⚳ 2:00
☿△♇ 6:35
☉⚺☽ 9:05
☽✶♃ 12:42
☽∠♆ 15:07
☽#♆ 16:05

8 W ☽#♄ 0:14
☿☌♂ 0:34
☿✶⚷ 1:47
⚳☍♇ 2:50
♂✶⚷ 4:09
♀#♇ 5:11
☽∠⚷ 6:33
☽⚺♀ 6:59
☿∥♂ 16:48
☽∠♃ 18:11
☽✶♆ 20:11

9 Th ☽☍♄ 0:37
☽⚺♅ 7:06
☽△♇ 8:28
☽✶⚳ 9:27
☽∥♂ 9:51
☽✶⚷ 11:57
☽☌♂ 13:53
♀ ♊ 15:04
☽∥☿ 15:07
☽☌☿ 19:07
☉⚺♃ 20:14

10 F ☽⚺♃ 0:13
☉☌☽ 0:30
☉∥☽ 3:31
☽∠♅ 12:55
☽⚼♇ 14:10
☽∠⚳ 16:10

11 Sa ☽☌♀ 0:50
☿⚺♃ 2:23
☽□♆ 7:45
☽#♇ 11:36
☽⚻♄ 11:53
☉∥☿ 17:16
☽✶♅ 19:08
☽⚻♇ 20:15
☉☌☿ 21:11
☽⚺⚳ 23:19

12 Su ☽□⚷ 0:02
☽⚺♂ 5:49
☽☌♃ 13:33
☽⚼♄ 18:01
☉⚺☽ 18:04
☽⚺☿ 20:41
⚳△⚷ 23:24

13 M ☽#♇ 13:34
☽∠♂ 14:14
☽∥☿ 17:54
☽⚺♀ 20:31
☽△♆ 20:33
♀□♆ 20:48
☿∠♅ 23:55

14 Tu ☿#♇ 0:15
☽△♄ 0:16
☉∠☽ 3:13
☿⚼♇ 4:27
☽□♅ 8:11
☉∥☽ 8:25
☽☍♇ 8:59
☽∠☿ 10:01
☽△⚷ 13:02
☽☌⚳ 14:12
☽✶♂ 22:39

15 W ☽⚼♆ 2:59
☽⚺♃ 3:32
☽∥♂ 3:51
☽∠♀ 6:25
♀⚻♄ 6:55
☉✶☽ 12:15
☿∠⚳ 12:48
☽⚼⚷ 19:23
☿ ♊ 20:42
☽✶☿ 23:04

16 Th ☽⚻♆ 9:07
☽∠♃ 10:12
☽□♄ 12:22
☽✶♀ 15:53
☉∠♅ 18:56
☽△♅ 20:41
☽⚻♇ 21:10

17 F ☉⚼♇ 1:01
☽⚻⚷ 1:19
☽⚺⚳ 4:18
☽#♄ 4:28
☽#♆ 11:46
☽□♂ 14:16
☽✶♃ 16:18

18 ☽⚼♅ 2:06

Sa ☽⚼♇ 2:26
☉□☽ 4:36
☿□♆ 7:21
☽∠⚳ 10:23
☿∥♀ 10:32
♀✶♅ 16:41
☉#♇ 17:19
♀⚻♇ 19:17
☽☍♆ 19:36
☽□☿ 22:03
☽✶♄ 22:19
☿⚻♄ 23:34

19 Su ☽∥♅ 1:53
☽⚻♅ 6:42
☽△♇ 6:53
☽□♀ 8:07
☿∥♃ 9:55
☽☍⚷ 11:00
☽#⚷ 13:21
♂⚺♃ 14:41
☽✶⚳ 15:30

20 M ☽□♃ 1:56
☽∠♄ 2:01
☽△♂ 2:24
♃⚼♄ 5:22
☽∥⚷ 7:23
♀□⚷ 14:51
☉△☽ 16:49
☽#♅ 18:36
☉ ♊ 21:11
♅□♇ 23:03

21 ♀∥♃ 0:48

Tu ☽⚻♆ 2:32
☿⚻♇ 3:39
☿✶♅ 3:47
☽⚺♄ 4:46
☽⚼♂ 6:46
☽□♇ 12:56
☽☍♅ 13:00
☽△☿ 14:34
☽⚻⚷ 16:56
☽△♀ 19:25
☉⚼☽ 21:08
☽□⚳ 22:37

22 W ☽⚼♆ 4:34
☽∥♆ 4:49
☿□⚷ 6:50
☽△♃ 7:36
☽⚻♂ 10:02
☽∥♄ 10:35
☽⚼⚷ 18:31
☽⚼☿ 20:23
☽⚼♀ 23:15

23 Th ☉⚻☽ 0:21
☽△♆ 5:46
☽☌♄ 7:35
☉∠⚳ 8:52
☽⚼♃ 9:05
☽✶♇ 15:26
☽⚻♅ 15:42
☽△⚷ 19:20
♀⚺⚳ 23:57

24 F ☽⚻☿ 0:56
☽△⚳ 2:00
☽⚻♀ 2:08
☽⚻♃ 9:53
☿⚺⚳ 10:56
☽☍♂ 13:56
☽∠♇ 15:42
☽⚼♅ 16:03
☽#♂ 23:30
☿☌♀ 23:55

25 Sa ☽⚼⚳ 2:47
☉☍☽ 4:26
☽□♆ 6:20
☽⚺♄ 7:52
☽∥♇ 9:35
☽⚺♇ 15:36
☽△♅ 16:02
☽□⚷ 19:30

26 Su ♂⚼♇ 1:37
☽⚻⚳ 3:16
☿⚼♄ 6:04
☽☍♀ 6:17
☽∠♄ 7:34
☽☍☿ 7:47
☽☍♃ 10:23
☉□♆ 10:27
♂∠♅ 12:10
☽⚻♂ 16:03
♀⚼♄ 21:29

27 M ☽∥♇ 0:08
☽#♂ 4:13
☽✶♆ 6:00
☉⚻♄ 7:17
☽✶♄ 7:19
☉⚻☽ 7:19
☿☌♃ 7:57
☽☌♇ 15:13
☽□♅ 15:51
☽⚼♂ 17:10
☽✶⚷ 19:18

28 Tu ☽☍⚳ 4:27
☽∠♆ 6:05
☉⚼☽ 9:05
☽⚻♀ 10:31
♂#♇ 11:01
☽⚻♃ 11:08
☽⚻☿ 14:24
☽△♂ 18:42
♀☌♃ 19:30
☽∠⚷ 19:39

29 W ♀ ♋ 3:10
☽⚺♆ 6:39
☽□♄ 7:49
☉△☽ 11:29
☽⚼♃ 12:13
☽⚼♀ 13:29
☽⚺♇ 16:11
☽✶♅ 17:02
☽⚼☿ 18:32
☽⚺⚷ 20:35

30 Th ☽∥♄ 0:21
☽∥♆ 5:28
☽⚻⚳ 7:38
☽△♃ 14:02
⚳⚼♆ 16:09
☽△♀ 17:22
☽∠♇ 17:40
☽∠♅ 18:39
☽△⚳ 23:38
☽□♂ 23:58

31 F ☿⚺♂ 4:21
☿ ♋ 7:08
☽☌♆ 9:55
☽⚼⚳ 10:28
♂ ♊ 10:40
☽△♄ 10:55
☽#♅ 14:49
☉⚼☽ 18:59
☽✶♇ 19:59
☽⚺♅ 21:07

June 2013

LONGITUDE

Day	Sid.Time	☉	☽	☽ 12 hour	Mean ☊	True ☊	☿	♀	♂	⚳	♃	♄	⚷	♅	♆	♇
	h m s	° ' "	° ' "	° ' "	° '	° '	° '	° '	° '	° '	° '	° '	° '	° '	° '	° '
1 Sa	16 38 34	10♊40 22	13♓16 24	19♓54 34	15♏36.0	16♏39.3	1♋07.5	27♊26.4	0♊23.8	20♋54.3	24♊15.7	5♏53.9	13♓43.4	11♈39.9	5♓21.8	11♑01.6
2 Su	16 42 31	11 37 52	26 27 08	2♈54 29	15 32.8	16 40.0	2 41.0	28 39.8	1 06.6	21 19.0	24 29.3	5R 50.6	13 44.2	11 42.0	5 22.0	11R 00.4
3 M	16 46 27	12 35 21	9♈17 01	15 35 09	15 29.6	16 41.3	4 11.6	29 53.2	1 49.4	21 43.8	24 43.0	5 47.4	13 45.0	11 44.0	5 22.1	10 59.1
4 Tu	16 50 24	13 32 50	21 49 19	27 59 58	15 26.4	16 43.0	5 39.1	1♋06.5	2 32.1	22 08.7	24 56.6	5 44.3	13 45.7	11 46.1	5 22.3	10 57.8
5 W	16 54 20	14 30 18	4♉07 29	10♉12 18	15 23.3	16 44.3	7 03.6	2 19.9	3 14.8	22 33.7	25 10.3	5 41.2	13 46.4	11 48.0	5 22.4	10 56.5
6 Th	16 58 17	15 27 45	16 14 47	22 15 16	15 20.1	16R 44.9	8 25.1	3 33.2	3 57.4	22 58.7	25 24.0	5 38.2	13 47.0	11 50.0	5 22.4	10 55.2
7 F	17 02 14	16 25 11	28 14 07	4♊11 36	15 16.9	16 44.3	9 43.4	4 46.5	4 40.0	23 23.8	25 37.7	5 35.3	13 47.6	11 51.9	5R 22.5	10 53.8
8 Sa	17 06 10	17 22 37	10♊08 01	16 03 38	15 13.7	16 42.3	10 58.5	5 59.8	5 22.5	23 49.0	25 51.4	5 32.5	13 48.1	11 53.8	5 22.4	10 52.5
9 Su	17 10 07	18 20 02	21 58 43	27 53 29	15 10.6	16 38.7	12 10.5	7 13.0	6 04.9	24 14.2	26 05.1	5 29.8	13 48.5	11 55.6	5 22.4	10 51.1
10 M	17 14 03	19 17 26	3♋48 11	9♋43 05	15 07.4	16 33.7	13 19.2	8 26.3	6 47.4	24 39.4	26 18.9	5 27.1	13 48.9	11 57.4	5 22.3	10 49.8
11 Tu	17 18 00	20 14 49	15 38 25	21 34 27	15 04.2	16 27.9	14 24.5	9 39.5	7 29.7	25 04.8	26 32.6	5 24.5	13 49.2	11 59.1	5 22.2	10 48.4
12 W	17 21 56	21 12 12	27 31 28	3♌29 47	15 01.0	16 21.8	15 26.5	10 52.7	8 12.0	25 30.2	26 46.4	5 22.0	13 49.5	12 00.8	5 22.1	10 47.0
13 Th	17 25 53	22 09 33	9♌29 45	15 31 41	14 57.8	16 15.9	16 25.0	12 05.9	8 54.2	25 55.6	27 00.1	5 19.6	13 49.7	12 02.4	5 21.9	10 45.6
14 F	17 29 49	23 06 53	21 36 01	27 43 09	14 54.7	16 11.0	17 19.9	13 19.1	9 36.4	26 21.1	27 13.9	5 17.3	13 49.9	12 04.0	5 21.7	10 44.2
15 Sa	17 33 46	24 04 13	3♍53 31	10♍07 35	14 51.5	16 07.5	18 11.2	14 32.2	10 18.6	26 46.6	27 27.6	5 15.1	13 50.0	12 05.6	5 21.5	10 42.7
16 Su	17 37 43	25 01 32	16 25 49	22 48 43	14 48.3	16D 05.6	18 58.7	15 45.4	11 00.7	27 12.2	27 41.4	5 12.9	13R 50.1	12 07.1	5 21.2	10 41.3
17 M	17 41 39	25 58 49	29 16 44	5♎50 19	14 45.1	16 05.3	19 42.4	16 58.5	11 42.7	27 37.9	27 55.2	5 10.9	13 50.1	12 08.6	5 20.9	10 39.9
18 Tu	17 45 36	26 56 06	12♎29 52	19 15 44	14 42.0	16 06.1	20 22.1	18 11.5	12 24.6	28 03.6	28 09.0	5 08.9	13 50.0	12 10.0	5 20.6	10 38.4
19 W	17 49 32	27 53 22	26 08 11	3♏07 21	14 38.8	16 07.4	20 57.8	19 24.6	13 06.6	28 29.3	28 22.7	5 07.0	13 49.9	12 11.4	5 20.3	10 36.9
20 Th	17 53 29	28 50 38	10♏13 15	17 25 45	14 35.6	16R 08.4	21 29.3	20 37.6	13 48.4	28 55.1	28 36.5	5 05.2	13 49.7	12 12.8	5 19.9	10 35.5
21 F	17 57 25	29 47 52	24 44 30	2♐08 59	14 32.4	16 08.3	21 56.6	21 50.6	14 30.2	29 20.9	28 50.3	5 03.5	13 49.5	12 14.1	5 19.4	10 34.0
22 Sa	18 01 22	0♋45 07	9♐38 28	17 12 02	14 29.3	16 06.4	22 19.5	23 03.6	15 12.0	29 46.8	29 04.0	5 01.9	13 49.2	12 15.3	5 19.0	10 32.5
23 Su	18 05 18	1 42 20	24 48 34	2♑26 51	14 26.1	16 02.5	22 38.0	24 16.6	15 53.7	0♌12.7	29 17.8	5 00.4	13 48.9	12 16.5	5 18.5	10 31.0
24 M	18 09 15	2 39 33	10♑05 32	17 43 15	14 22.9	15 56.9	22 51.9	25 29.5	16 35.4	0 38.7	29 31.5	4 59.0	13 48.5	12 17.7	5 18.0	10 29.6
25 Tu	18 13 12	3 36 46	25 18 39	2♒50 28	14 19.7	15 50.1	23 01.3	26 42.4	17 17.0	1 04.7	29 45.3	4 57.6	13 48.0	12 18.8	5 17.5	10 28.1
26 W	18 17 08	4 33 59	10♒17 36	17 39 05	14 16.6	15 43.1	23R 06.2	27 55.3	17 58.5	1 30.8	29 59.0	4 56.4	13 47.5	12 19.9	5 16.9	10 26.6
27 Th	18 21 05	5 31 11	24 54 10	2♓02 22	14 13.4	15 36.8	23 06.4	29 08.2	18 40.0	1 56.9	0♋12.8	4 55.3	13 47.0	12 20.9	5 16.3	10 25.1
28 F	18 25 01	6 28 24	9♓03 21	15 57 01	14 10.2	15 31.9	23 02.0	0♌21.0	19 21.5	2 23.0	0 26.5	4 54.2	13 46.3	12 21.9	5 15.7	10 23.6
29 Sa	18 28 58	7 25 36	22 43 26	29 22 51	14 07.0	15 29.0	22 53.2	1 33.8	20 02.9	2 49.2	0 40.2	4 53.3	13 45.7	12 22.8	5 15.0	10 22.0
30 Su	18 32 54	8♋22 49	5♈55 36	12♈22 09	14♏03.8	15♏27.9	22♋40.0	2♌46.6	20♊44.2	3♌15.4	0♋53.9	4♏52.4	13♓45.0	12♈23.7	5♓14.3	10♑20.5

1st of Month

Julian Day
2456444.5
Obliquity
23°26'08"
SVP 5♓04'0
GC 27♐01.
Eris 22♈45.

Day	⚴
1	1♊33.0
6	4 16.3
11	7 01.1
16	9 47.3
21	12 34.7
26	15 23.3

Day	⚵
1	18♒24.0
6	18 44.8
11	18 57.0
16	19 00.3
21	18 54.3
26	18 38.9

Day	⚶
1	14♋40.3
6	16 46.7
11	18 54.3
16	21 03.2
21	23 13.2
26	25 24.1

DECLINATION and LATITUDE

Day	☉	☽		☽ 12h	☿		♀		♂		⚳		♃		♄	
	Decl	Decl	Lat	Decl	Decl	Lat	Decl	Lat	Decl	Lat	Decl	Lat	Decl	Lat	Decl	Lat
1 Sa	22N03	2S14	4N42	0N03	25N37	2N11	24N16	0N51	20N18	0N04	27N43	5N58	23N03	0S16	11S01	2N37
2 Su	22 11	2N18	4 02	4 30	25 34	2 10	24 19	0 53	20 28	0 05	27 39	5 59	23 04	0 15	10 60	2 37
3 M	22 18	6 37	3 12	8 38	25 30	2 08	24 22	0 56	20 37	0 06	27 36	5 60	23 04	0 15	10 59	2 37
4 Tu	22 25	10 33	2 13	12 20	25 24	2 05	24 24	0 58	20 46	0 06	27 32	6 00	23 05	0 15	10 58	2 37
5 W	22 32	13 58	1 09	15 27	25 17	2 02	24 25	0 60	20 55	0 07	27 29	6 01	23 06	0 15	10 57	2 37
6 Th	22 39	16 44	0 03	17 51	25 07	1 58	24 25	1 02	21 04	0 08	27 25	6 01	23 06	0 15	10 56	2 36
7 F	22 45	18 45	1S03	19 26	24 57	1 53	24 25	1 04	21 12	0 08	27 21	6 02	23 07	0 15	10 56	2 36
8 Sa	22 50	19 55	2 05	20 10	24 45	1 47	24 24	1 06	21 20	0 09	27 17	6 03	23 07	0 15	10 55	2 36
9 Su	22 55	20 11	3 01	19 59	24 32	1 40	24 22	1 08	21 28	0 09	27 13	6 03	23 08	0 15	10 54	2 36
10 M	23 00	19 34	3 49	18 56	24 19	1 33	24 19	1 10	21 36	0 10	27 09	6 04	23 08	0 15	10 53	2 36
11 Tu	23 05	18 05	4 28	17 03	24 04	1 25	24 16	1 11	21 44	0 11	27 05	6 04	23 09	0 15	10 53	2 35
12 W	23 09	15 50	4 54	14 27	23 48	1 16	24 12	1 13	21 51	0 11	27 01	6 05	23 09	0 14	10 52	2 35
13 Th	23 12	12 54	5 09	11 13	23 32	1 07	24 08	1 15	21 59	0 12	26 56	6 06	23 10	0 14	10 52	2 35
14 F	23 15	9 25	5 10	7 29	23 15	0 56	24 02	1 17	22 06	0 13	26 52	6 06	23 10	0 14	10 51	2 35
15 Sa	23 18	5 28	4 56	3 23	22 57	0 46	23 56	1 18	22 13	0 13	26 48	6 07	23 11	0 14	10 51	2 34
16 Su	23 21	1 14	4 29	0S58	22 39	0 34	23 50	1 20	22 19	0 14	26 43	6 07	23 11	0 14	10 50	2 34
17 M	23 22	3S11	3 47	5 24	22 21	0 22	23 42	1 21	22 26	0 15	26 38	6 08	23 11	0 14	10 50	2 34
18 Tu	23 24	7 35	2 52	9 43	22 03	0 09	23 34	1 23	22 32	0 15	26 34	6 09	23 11	0 14	10 49	2 34
19 W	23 25	11 45	1 46	13 39	21 44	0S04	23 25	1 24	22 38	0 16	26 29	6 09	23 12	0 14	10 49	2 33
20 Th	23 26	15 23	0 32	16 55	21 25	0 18	23 15	1 26	22 44	0 16	26 24	6 10	23 12	0 14	10 48	2 33
21 F	23 26	18 12	0N46	19 11	21 07	0 32	23 06	1 27	22 49	0 17	26 19	6 11	23 12	0 14	10 48	2 33
22 Sa	23 26	19 51	2 04	20 10	20 49	0 47	22 55	1 28	22 54	0 18	26 14	6 11	23 12	0 14	10 48	2 33
23 Su	23 25	20 07	3 14	19 41	20 31	1 02	22 43	1 29	22 60	0 18	26 09	6 12	23 13	0 13	10 48	2 33
24 M	23 25	18 54	4 10	17 46	20 13	1 17	22 31	1 31	23 04	0 19	26 04	6 13	23 13	0 13	10 47	2 32
25 Tu	23 23	16 21	4 48	14 39	19 56	1 34	22 19	1 32	23 09	0 20	25 59	6 13	23 13	0 13	10 47	2 32
26 W	23 21	12 44	5 06	10 39	19 39	1 50	22 05	1 33	23 14	0 20	25 53	6 14	23 13	0 13	10 47	2 32
27 Th	23 19	8 27	5 04	6 09	19 23	2 06	21 51	1 34	23 18	0 21	25 48	6 14	23 13	0 13	10 47	2 32
28 F	23 17	3 48	4 42	1 27	19 08	2 22	21 37	1 35	23 22	0 21	25 42	6 15	23 13	0 13	10 47	2 31
29 Sa	23 14	0N52	4 05	3N09	18 54	2 38	21 21	1 35	23 26	0 22	25 37	6 16	23 13	0 13	10 47	2 31
30 Su	23N10	5N22	3N16	7N28	18N41	2S54	21N06	1N36	23N29	0N23	25N31	6N16	23N13	0S13	10S47	2N31

Day	⚷		♅		♆		♇	
	Decl	Lat	Decl	Lat	Decl	Lat	Decl	Lat
1	1S33	5N15	3N59	0S41	10S09	0S39	19S43	3N
6	1 31	5 16	4 03	0 41	10 09	0 39	19 44	3
11	1 29	5 17	4 06	0 41	10 09	0 39	19 45	3
16	1 27	5 18	4 09	0 41	10 10	0 40	19 46	3
21	1 26	5 20	4 12	0 41	10 10	0 40	19 47	3
26	1 26	5 21	4 14	0 42	10 11	0 40	19 48	3

Day	⚴		⚵		⚶		Eris	
	Decl	Lat	Decl	Lat	Decl	Lat	Decl	Lat
1	1S45	22S38	3S21	12N32	23N55	1N18	3S11	12S
6	1 34	22 55	3 05	12 43	23 46	1 24	3 10	12
11	1 26	23 13	2 52	12 53	23 35	1 29	3 10	12
16	1 21	23 30	2 41	13 03	23 21	1 35	3 09	12
21	1 18	23 47	2 35	13 12	23 05	1 41	3 09	12
26	1 19	24 04	2 32	13 20	22 48	1 46	3 09	12

Moon Phenomena

Max/0 Decl

dy	hr mn	
1	11:45	0 N
8	19:22	20N12
16	6:43	0 S
22	16:20	20S11
28	19:30	0 N

Max/0 Lat

dy	hr mn	
6	1:00	0 S
13	13:22	5S11
20	9:51	0 N
26	8:43	5N08

Perigee/Apogee

dy	hr m		kilometers
9	21:38	a	406486
23	11:12	p	356997

PH	dy	hr mn	
●	8	15:57	18♊01
☽	16	17:25	25♍43
○	23	11:33	2♑10
☾	30	4:55	8♈35

Void of Course Moon

Last Aspect				☽ Ingres		
2	4:31	♀	□	♈	2	6:3
4	6:10	♃	✱	♉	4	15:5
5	13:26	♇	△	♊	7	3:3
9	8:30	♃	☌	♋	9	16:1
10	21:16	☿	☌	♌	12	4:5
14	11:15	♃	✱	♍	14	16:2
16	21:27	♃	□	♎	17	1:2
19	3:56	♃	△	♏	19	6:4
20	19:17	☿	△	♐	21	8:3
23	7:10	♃	☍	♑	23	8:0
25	2:25	♀	☍	♒	25	7:2
26	13:09	♂	△	♓	27	8:3
29	0:17	☿	△	♈	29	13:0

DAILY ASPECTARIAN

1 Sa ☽☌⚷ 0:49 · ☽∥⚷ 3:33 · ☉⊼♇ 8:41 · ☽⚼♄ 13:45 · ☽△⚳ 14:16 · ☽#⚷ 19:58 · ☽□♃ 20:19

2 Su ☉✱♅ 1:47 · ☽□♀ 4:31 · ☽✱♂ 9:09 · ☽∥♅ 9:17 · ☽□☿ 13:08 · ☽⊻♆ 16:37 · ☽⊼♄ 17:26

3 M ♀ ♋ 2:14 · ☽□♇ 3:13 · ☽☌♅ 4:40 · ☉✱☽ 6:48 · ☽⊻⚷ 8:30 · ☽∠♂ 15:14 · ☿△♆ 19:19 · ☽∠♆ 21:12 · ☽#♆ 21:23

4 Tu ☽□⚳ 0:39 · ☿△♄ 1:23 · ☽#♄ 2:41 · ☉□⚷ 5:27 · ☽✱♃ 6:10 · ☽∠⚷ 13:30 · ☉∠☽ 14:10 · ☽✱♀ 20:05 · ☽⊻♂ 22:10

5 W ☽✱♆ 2:27 · ☽☍♄ 3:04 · ☽✱☿ 6:31 · ☽∠♃ 12:10 · ☽△♇ 13:26 · ☽⊻♅ 15:12 · ☽✱⚷ 19:06 · ☉⊻☽ 22:18

6 Th ☽∠♀ 5:07 · ☽✱⚳ 13:56 · ☽∠☿ 16:06 · ☽⊻♃ 18:40 · ♀⊻♂ 18:55 · ☽⚼♇ 19:19 · ☽∠♅ 21:14

7 F ♆ R 8:26 · ♀△♆ 11:47 · ☽☌♂ 13:46 · ☽□♆ 14:23 · ☽⊻♀ 14:41 · ☽⊼♄ 14:45 · ♀△♄ 15:24 · ☽#♇ 19:02 · ☽∠⚳ 21:14 · ☿☍♇ 22:04 · ♂□♆ 23:59

8 Sa ☽⊼♇ 1:30 · ☽⊻☿ 1:54 · ☽✱♅ 3:34 · ♂⊼♄ 5:19 · ☽□⚷ 7:26 · ☉☌☽ 15:57 · ☿□♅ 18:48 · ☽⚼♄ 21:00

9 Su ☽⊻⚳ 4:45 · ☽☌♃ 8:30 · ☽#♇ 19:30 · ☿∥♀ 22:08

10 M ☽△♆ 3:11 · ☽△♄ 3:20 · ☽⊻♂ 6:27 · ☽☌♀ 10:29 · ☿△⚷ 10:49 · ☽☍♇ 14:14 · ☽□♅ 16:35 · ☽△⚷ 20:19 · ☽☌☿ 21:16

11 Tu ☉⚼♄ 3:54 · ☽⚼♆ 9:34 · ☉⊻☽ 10:08 · ☽∠♂ 14:44 · ☽☌⚳ 19:47 · ♀☍♇ 22:09 · ☽⊻♃ 22:27 · ♄△♆ 23:27

12 W ☽⚼⚷ 2:37 · ☉∥♃ 5:22 · ☽□♄ 15:42 · ☽⊼♆ 15:45 · ☉∠☽ 18:56 · ☽✱♂ 22:45 · ♀□♅ 22:50

13 Th ☽⊼♇ 2:31 · ☽△♅ 5:05 · ☽∠♃ 5:05 · ☽⊻♀ 5:46 · ☽⊼⚷ 8:38 · ☽#♄ 14:30 · ☽⊻☿ 14:54 · ☽#♆ 19:10 · ☉∥☿ 23:11

14 F ☉✱☽ 3:14 · ☿∥♃ 6:08 · ☽⚼♇ 8:06 · ☽⊻⚳ 9:40 · ♀△⚷ 10:08 · ☽⚼♅ 10:45 · ☽✱♃ 11:15 · ☽∠♀ 14:37 · ☽∠☿ 22:32

15 Sa ☽✱♄ 2:37 · ☽☍♆ 2:50 · ⚵ R 6:43 · ☽∥♅ 7:39 · ☽□♂ 13:05 · ☽△♇ 13:06 · ♂⊼♇ 13:20 · ☽∠⚳ 15:41 · ☽⊼♅ 15:47 · ☽☍⚷ 19:05 · ☽✱♀ 22:35 · ☽#⚷ 22:44

16 Su ☽✱☿ 5:07 · ☽∠♄ 7:07 · ⚷ R 9:18 · ☽∥⚷ 14:37 · ☉□☽ 17:25 · ☿∥♂ 19:33 · ☽✱⚳ 20:51 · ☽□♃ 21:27

17 M ☽#♅ 5:18 · ☽⊻♄ 10:47 · ☽⊼♆ 11:06 · ♂✱♅ 15:21 · ☽□♇ 20:41 · ☿⚼♆ 23:04 · ☽☍♅ 23:24 · ☽△♂ 23:50

18 Tu ☽⊼⚷ 2:23 · ⚳⊻♃ 10:52 · ☽□♀ 11:06 · ☽⚼♆ 13:54 · ☽□☿ 14:36 · ☽∥♆ 14:38 · ☽∥♄ 18:26

19 W ☉∥♀ 0:29 · ☉△☽ 3:15 · ☽⚼♂ 3:35 · ☽△♃ 3:56 · ☽□⚳ 4:11 · ☽⚼⚷ 4:39 · ☽☌♄ 15:21 · ☽△♆ 15:45 · ☉☌♃ 16:12 · ♀⚼♆ 18:12 · ⚳⚼⚷ 19:02

20 Th ☽✱♇ 0:37 · ♂□⚷ 0:44 · ☽⊼♅ 3:20 · ☉⊻⚳ 3:24 · ☽⚼♃ 5:45 · ☽△⚷ 6:02 · ☽⊼♂ 6:18 · ☉⚼☽ 6:29 · ♀∥♃ 9:00 · ♂∠⚳ 9:59 · ☽△♀ 18:50 · ☽△☿ 19:17

21 F ☽∠♇ 1:20 · ☿☌♀ 2:58 · ☽⚼♅ 4:04 · ☉ ♋ 5:05 · ☽⊼♃ 6:45 · ☽△⚳ 7:42 · ☉⊼☽ 8:46 · ☽⊻♄ 16:39 · ☽□♆ 17:05 · ☽⚼☿ 20:13 · ☽⚼♀ 21:15 · ☽∥♇ 22:24

22 Sa ♀∥♂ 0:40 · ☽⊻♇ 1:26 · ☽△♅ 4:10 · ☽□⚷ 6:38 · ☽⚼⚳ 8:24 · ☽☍♂ 9:15 · ⚳ ♌ 12:14 · ☽∠♄ 16:27 · ☽⊼☿ 20:31 · ☽⊼♀ 23:05

23 Su ☽☍♃ 7:10 · ☽⊼⚳ 8:44 · ☽∥♇ 9:43 · ☉☍☽ 11:33 · ☽✱♄ 15:59 · ☽✱♆ 16:29

24 M ☽☌♇ 0:38 · ☽□♅ 3:28 · ☽✱⚷ 5:50 · ☽⊼♂ 10:42 · ☽∠♆ 16:04 · ☽☍☿ 20:21

25 Tu ☽☍♀ 2:25 · ☽∠⚷ 5:33 · ☽⊼♃ 7:11 · ☽☍⚳ 9:27 · ☽⚼♂ 11:39 · ☿#♇ 11:47 · ☉⊼☽ 14:08 · ☽□♄ 15:23 · ☽⊻♆ 15:55 · ♂∥♃ 20:37

26 W ☽⊻♇ 0:15 · ♃ ♋ 1:41 · ☽✱♅ 3:19 · ☽⊻⚷ 5:41 · ☽⚼♃ 7:45 · ☉△♄ 9:13 · ☽∥♄ 11:18 · ☿ R 13:09 · ☽△♂ 13:09 · ☽∥♆ 14:33 · ☉⚼☽ 16:13 · ♀⚼⚷ 17:04 · ☉△♆ 17:49 · ☽⊼☿ 21:01

27 Th ☽∠♇ 0:51 · ☽∠♅ 4:06 · ☉∥♂ 4:48 · ☽⊼♀ 7:45 · ☽△♃ 9:03 · ☽⊼⚳ 12:13 · ☽△♄ 16:53 · ♀ ♌ 17:04 · ☽☌♆ 17:29 · ☉△☽ 19:14 · ☽#♅ 21:46 · ☽⚼☿ 22:15

28 F ♀⊻♃ 2:13 · ☽✱♇ 2:18 · ☽⊻♅ 5:44 · ☽☌⚷ 8:11 · ☽⚼♀ 12:01 · ☽∥⚷ 12:08 · ☽⚼⚳ 15:00 · ♂⚼♄ 18:33 · ☽⚼♄ 18:57 · ☽□♂ 18:59

29 Sa ☽△☿ 0:17 · ☽#⚷ 2:56 · ☉∥♃ 3:04 · ☽□♃ 14:36 · ☽△♀ 17:37 · ☽∥♅ 17:57 · ☽△⚳ 18:55 · ☽⊼♄ 22:04 · ☽⊻♆ 22:44

30 Su ☉□☽ 4:55 · ☽□♇ 8:11 · ☽☌♅ 12:04 · ☽⊻⚷ 14:35 · ♀☌⚳ 14:50

LONGITUDE

Day	Sid.Time	☉	☽	☽ 12 hour	Mean☊	True☊	☿	♀	♂	⚳	♃	♄	⚷	♅	♆	♇
	h m s	° ' "	° ' "	° ' "	° '	° '	° '	° '	° '	° '	° '	° '	° '	° '	° '	° '
1 M	18 36 51	9♋20 01	18♈43 00	24♈58 43	14♏00.7	15♏28.2	22♋22.6	3♌59.4	21♊25.5	3♌41.7	1♋07.6	4♏51.7	13♓44.2	12♈24.5	5♓13.6	10♑19.0
2 Tu	18 40 47	10 17 14	1♉09 53	7♉17 07	13 57.5	15 29.2	22R 01.2	5 12.2	22 06.8	4 08.0	1 21.3	4R 51.0	13R 43.4	12 25.3	5R 12.8	10R 17.5
3 W	18 44 44	11 14 27	13 20 59	19 22 03	13 54.3	15R 29.8	21 36.2	6 24.9	22 48.0	4 34.3	1 34.9	4 50.4	13 42.5	12 26.0	5 12.1	10 16.0
4 Th	18 48 41	12 11 40	25 20 51	1♊17 55	13 51.1	15 29.3	21 07.8	7 37.6	23 29.2	5 00.7	1 48.6	4 50.0	13 41.5	12 26.7	5 11.3	10 14.5
5 F	18 52 37	13 08 54	7♊13 41	13 08 30	13 48.0	15 26.9	20 36.4	8 50.3	24 10.3	5 27.1	2 02.2	4 49.6	13 40.6	12 27.4	5 10.4	10 13.0
6 Sa	18 56 34	14 06 07	19 03 03	24 57 23	13 44.8	15 22.1	20 02.6	10 03.0	24 51.3	5 53.5	2 15.8	4 49.3	13 39.5	12 28.0	5 09.6	10 11.5
7 Su	19 00 30	15 03 21	0♋51 52	6♋46 48	13 41.6	15 14.8	19 26.9	11 15.6	25 32.3	6 20.0	2 29.4	4 49.2	13 38.4	12 28.5	5 08.7	10 10.0
8 M	19 04 27	16 00 35	12 42 25	18 38 55	13 38.4	15 05.3	18 49.8	12 28.3	26 13.3	6 46.6	2 42.9	4D 49.1	13 37.3	12 29.0	5 07.8	10 08.5
9 Tu	19 08 23	16 57 49	24 36 30	0♌35 21	13 35.3	14 54.3	18 12.0	13 40.9	26 54.2	7 13.1	2 56.5	4 49.1	13 36.1	12 29.5	5 06.8	10 07.0
10 W	19 12 20	17 55 03	6♌35 38	12 37 32	13 32.1	14 42.6	17 34.1	14 53.4	27 35.1	7 39.7	3 10.0	4 49.2	13 34.8	12 29.9	5 05.9	10 05.5
11 Th	19 16 16	18 52 17	18 41 14	24 46 56	13 28.9	14 31.4	16 56.7	16 06.0	28 15.9	8 06.3	3 23.5	4 49.5	13 33.5	12 30.2	5 04.9	10 04.0
12 F	19 20 13	19 49 31	0♍54 53	7♍05 19	13 25.7	14 21.5	16 20.5	17 18.5	28 56.6	8 33.0	3 37.0	4 49.8	13 32.2	12 30.5	5 03.9	10 02.5
13 Sa	19 24 10	20 46 45	13 18 31	19 34 49	13 22.5	14 13.8	15 46.2	18 31.0	29 37.3	8 59.7	3 50.4	4 50.2	13 30.8	12 30.8	5 02.8	10 01.0
14 Su	19 28 06	21 43 59	25 54 33	2♎18 05	13 19.4	14 08.5	15 14.3	19 43.4	0♋18.0	9 26.4	4 03.8	4 50.7	13 29.4	12 31.0	5 01.8	9 59.5
15 M	19 32 03	22 41 13	8♎45 48	15 18 07	13 16.2	14 05.8	14 45.4	20 55.8	0 58.6	9 53.1	4 17.2	4 51.4	13 27.9	12 31.1	5 00.7	9 58.0
16 Tu	19 35 59	23 38 27	21 55 25	28 38 03	13 13.0	14D 05.0	14 20.1	22 08.2	1 39.1	10 19.9	4 30.5	4 52.1	13 26.3	12 31.2	4 59.6	9 56.6
17 W	19 39 56	24 35 42	5♏26 21	12♏20 35	13 09.8	14R 05.2	13 58.9	23 20.6	2 19.6	10 46.7	4 43.8	4 52.9	13 24.7	12R 31.3	4 58.4	9 55.1
18 Th	19 43 52	25 32 56	19 20 54	26 27 20	13 06.7	14 05.2	13 42.1	24 32.9	3 00.0	11 13.5	4 57.1	4 53.8	13 23.1	12 31.3	4 57.3	9 53.7
19 F	19 47 49	26 30 11	3♐39 48	10♐57 59	13 03.5	14 04.0	13 30.1	25 45.2	3 40.4	11 40.3	5 10.4	4 54.8	13 21.4	12 31.3	4 56.1	9 52.2
20 Sa	19 51 45	27 27 26	18 21 27	25 49 29	13 00.3	14 00.6	13D 23.3	26 57.4	4 20.8	12 07.2	5 23.6	4 55.9	13 19.7	12 31.2	4 54.9	9 50.8
21 Su	19 55 42	28 24 41	3♑21 13	10♑55 37	12 57.1	13 54.6	13 21.9	28 09.6	5 01.1	12 34.1	5 36.8	4 57.1	13 17.9	12 31.1	4 53.7	9 49.4
22 M	19 59 39	29 21 56	18 31 27	26 07 25	12 54.0	13 46.2	13 26.0	29 21.8	5 41.3	13 01.0	5 49.9	4 58.4	13 16.1	12 30.9	4 52.4	9 48.0
23 Tu	20 03 35	0♌19 12	3♒42 10	11♒14 22	12 50.8	13 36.2	13 35.8	0♍34.0	6 21.5	13 27.9	6 03.0	4 59.8	13 14.3	12 30.6	4 51.2	9 46.6
24 W	20 07 32	1 16 29	18 42 46	26 06 15	12 47.6	13 25.6	13 51.4	1 46.1	7 01.7	13 54.9	6 16.0	5 01.3	13 12.4	12 30.4	4 49.9	9 45.2
25 Th	20 11 28	2 13 46	3♓23 53	10♓34 55	12 44.4	13 15.8	14 13.0	2 58.1	7 41.8	14 21.9	6 29.1	5 02.9	13 10.5	12 30.0	4 48.6	9 43.9
26 F	20 15 25	3 11 04	17 38 53	24 35 28	12 41.2	13 07.8	14 40.4	4 10.1	8 21.8	14 48.9	6 42.0	5 04.6	13 08.5	12 29.7	4 47.3	9 42.5
27 Sa	20 19 21	4 08 23	1♈24 36	8♈06 23	12 38.1	13 02.2	15 13.8	5 22.1	9 01.8	15 15.9	6 55.0	5 06.4	13 06.5	12 29.2	4 45.9	9 41.1
28 Su	20 23 18	5 05 42	14 41 06	21 09 09	12 34.9	12 59.0	15 53.1	6 34.1	9 41.8	15 42.9	7 07.9	5 08.3	13 04.4	12 28.8	4 44.6	9 39.8
29 M	20 27 14	6 03 03	27 31 00	3♉47 15	12 31.7	12D 57.7	16 38.2	7 46.0	10 21.7	16 10.0	7 20.7	5 10.2	13 02.3	12 28.3	4 43.2	9 38.5
30 Tu	20 31 11	7 00 25	9♉58 30	16 05 27	12 28.5	12R 57.6	17 29.1	8 57.9	11 01.5	16 37.1	7 33.5	5 12.3	13 00.2	12 27.7	4 41.8	9 37.2
31 W	20 35 08	7♌57 48	22 08 43	28 08 59	12♏25.4	12♏57.4	18♋25.8	10♍09.7	11♋41.4	17♌04.2	7♋46.2	5♏14.4	12♓58.0	12♈27.1	4♓40.4	9♑35.9

1st of Month

Julian Day # 2456474.5
Obliquity 23°26'08"
SVP 5♓04'04"
GC 27♐01.7
Eris 22♈55.5

Day	⚴	Day	⚵	Day	⚶
1	18♊13.0	1	18♒13.9R	1	27♋36.1
6	21 03.9	6	17 39.4R	6	29 48.9
11	23 55.6	11	16 55.7R	11	2♌02.6
16	26 48.1	16	16 03.7R	16	4 16.9
21	29 41.2	21	15 04.4R	21	6 32.0
26	2♋34.8	26	13 59.0R	26	8 47.6
31	5 28.8	31	12 49.2R	31	11 03.8

DECLINATION and LATITUDE

Day	☉ Decl	☽ Decl	☽ Lat	☽12h Decl	☿ Decl	☿ Lat	♀ Decl	♀ Lat	♂ Decl	♂ Lat	⚳ Decl	⚳ Lat	♃ Decl	♃ Lat	♄ Decl	♄ Lat
1 M	23N06	9N28	2N19	11N21	18N28	3S09	20N49	1N37	23N33	0N23	25N26	6N17	23N13	0S13	10S47	2N30
2 Tu	23 02	13 04	1 16	14 38	18 17	3 24	20 32	1 37	23 36	0 24	25 20	6 18	23 13	0 13	10 47	2 30
3 W	22 58	16 02	0 12	17 14	18 07	3 38	20 15	1 38	23 39	0 25	25 14	6 18	23 13	0 12	10 47	2 30
4 Th	22 53	18 15	0S53	19 03	17 58	3 51	19 57	1 38	23 42	0 25	25 08	6 19	23 13	0 12	10 47	2 30
5 F	22 47	19 39	1 54	20 01	17 50	4 04	19 38	1 39	23 44	0 26	25 02	6 20	23 13	0 12	10 47	2 29
6 Sa	22 41	20 10	2 50	20 06	17 44	4 15	19 19	1 39	23 47	0 26	24 56	6 20	23 13	0 12	10 47	2 29
7 Su	22 35	19 48	3 38	19 17	17 39	4 25	18 59	1 39	23 49	0 27	24 50	6 21	23 13	0 12	10 47	2 29
8 M	22 29	18 34	4 17	17 39	17 36	4 34	18 39	1 39	23 51	0 28	24 44	6 22	23 12	0 12	10 47	2 29
9 Tu	22 22	16 32	4 45	15 14	17 33	4 41	18 18	1 40	23 52	0 28	24 37	6 22	23 12	0 12	10 48	2 28
10 W	22 14	13 47	5 00	12 10	17 32	4 47	17 57	1 40	23 54	0 29	24 31	6 23	23 12	0 12	10 48	2 28
11 Th	22 06	10 26	5 02	8 34	17 33	4 51	17 35	1 39	23 55	0 30	24 24	6 24	23 12	0 12	10 48	2 28
12 F	21 58	6 37	4 51	4 34	17 35	4 53	17 13	1 39	23 56	0 30	24 18	6 24	23 12	0 12	10 49	2 28
13 Sa	21 50	2 28	4 25	0 20	17 38	4 54	16 51	1 39	23 57	0 31	24 11	6 25	23 11	0 12	10 49	2 27
14 Su	21 41	1S51	3 47	4S01	17 42	4 53	16 28	1 39	23 57	0 31	24 05	6 26	23 11	0 11	10 50	2 27
15 M	21 32	6 10	2 56	8 17	17 48	4 51	16 04	1 38	23 58	0 32	23 58	6 27	23 11	0 11	10 50	2 27
16 Tu	21 22	10 19	1 55	12 15	17 54	4 47	15 40	1 38	23 58	0 33	23 51	6 27	23 10	0 11	10 50	2 26
17 W	21 12	14 03	0 46	15 41	18 02	4 42	15 16	1 38	23 58	0 33	23 44	6 28	23 10	0 11	10 51	2 26
18 Th	21 02	17 07	0N28	18 18	18 10	4 35	14 52	1 37	23 58	0 34	23 38	6 29	23 09	0 11	10 52	2 26
19 F	20 51	19 13	1 42	19 49	18 20	4 27	14 27	1 36	23 57	0 34	23 30	6 29	23 09	0 11	10 52	2 26
20 Sa	20 40	20 05	2 51	20 00	18 30	4 17	14 01	1 35	23 57	0 35	23 23	6 30	23 09	0 11	10 53	2 25
21 Su	20 29	19 34	3 50	18 46	18 40	4 07	13 35	1 35	23 56	0 36	23 16	6 31	23 08	0 11	10 53	2 25
22 M	20 17	17 39	4 33	16 13	18 51	3 55	13 09	1 34	23 55	0 36	23 09	6 32	23 08	0 11	10 54	2 25
23 Tu	20 05	14 30	4 57	12 34	19 02	3 43	12 43	1 33	23 54	0 37	23 02	6 32	23 07	0 11	10 55	2 25
24 W	19 52	10 27	5 00	8 12	19 14	3 30	12 16	1 32	23 52	0 37	22 55	6 33	23 07	0 11	10 56	2 24
25 Th	19 40	5 51	4 43	3 28	19 25	3 16	11 49	1 31	23 51	0 38	22 47	6 34	23 06	0 10	10 56	2 24
26 F	19 27	1 04	4 09	1N19	19 36	3 02	11 22	1 29	23 49	0 39	22 40	6 35	23 06	0 10	10 57	2 24
27 Sa	19 13	3N38	3 21	5 52	19 47	2 48	10 54	1 28	23 47	0 39	22 32	6 35	23 05	0 10	10 58	2 24
28 Su	18 59	7 60	2 24	9 60	19 58	2 33	10 26	1 27	23 45	0 40	22 25	6 36	23 04	0 10	10 59	2 23
29 M	18 45	11 51	1 21	13 32	20 07	2 18	9 58	1 25	23 42	0 40	22 17	6 37	23 04	0 10	10 60	2 23
30 Tu	18 31	15 03	0 16	16 23	20 16	2 02	9 30	1 24	23 39	0 41	22 10	6 38	23 03	0 10	11 01	2 23
31 W	18N16	17N31	0S48	18N27	20N24	1S47	9N01	1N22	23N37	0N42	22N02	6N38	23N02	0S10	11S02	2N22

Day	⚷ Decl	⚷ Lat	♅ Decl	♅ Lat	♆ Decl	♆ Lat	♇ Decl	♇ Lat
1	1S26	5N22	4N16	0S42	10S13	0S40	19S49	3N14
6	1 27	5 23	4 17	0 42	10 14	0 40	19 50	3 13
11	1 28	5 24	4 18	0 42	10 16	0 40	19 51	3 13
16	1 30	5 25	4 18	0 42	10 18	0 40	19 52	3 12
21	1 32	5 26	4 18	0 42	10 21	0 41	19 53	3 11
26	1 35	5 27	4 17	0 43	10 23	0 41	19 55	3 11
31	1S39	5N28	4N16	0S43	10S26	0S41	19S56	3N10

Day	⚴ Decl	⚴ Lat	⚵ Decl	⚵ Lat	⚶ Decl	⚶ Lat	Eris Decl	Eris Lat
1	1S22	24S22	2S33	13N26	22N28	1N51	3S09	12S59
6	1 28	24 39	2 39	13 30	22 05	1 57	3 10	12 59
11	1 37	24 56	2 50	13 32	21 41	2 02	3 10	12 60
16	1 49	25 13	3 05	13 31	21 15	2 08	3 10	13 00
21	2 03	25 30	3 26	13 27	20 47	2 13	3 11	13 01
26	2 21	25 46	3 51	13 19	20 18	2 19	3 11	13 01
31	2S42	26S02	4S20	13N08	19N46	2N25	3S12	13S02

Moon Phenomena

Max/0 Decl

dy	hr mn	
6	2:03	20N10
13	13:49	0 S
20	3:03	20S06
26	5:20	0 N

Max/0 Lat

dy	hr mn	
3	4:16	0 S
10	15:54	5S03
17	15:00	0 N
23	15:41	5N01
30	5:50	0 S

Perigee/Apogee

dy	hr m		kilometers
7	0:40	a	406490
21	20:34	p	358403

PH	dy	hr mn	
●	8	7:15	16♋18
☽	16	3:19	23♎46
○	22	18:17	0♒06
☾	29	17:44	6♉45

Void of Course Moon

Last Aspect				☽ Ingress		
1	6:49	☿	□	♉	1	21:44
3	15:52	☿	⚹	♊	4	9:23
6	12:31	♂	☌	♋	6	22:15
8	11:45	☿	☌	♌	9	10:49
11	19:56	♂	⚹	♍	11	22:13
13	15:27	☉	⚹	♎	14	7:42
16	3:19	☉	□	♏	16	14:25
18	11:14	☉	△	♐	18	17:55
20	15:01	♀	△	♑	20	18:40
21	15:54	☿	☍	♒	22	18:08
23	14:02	♅	⚹	♓	24	18:23
25	18:44	☿	△	♈	26	21:30
28	2:20	☿	□	♉	29	4:44
30	15:59	☿	⚹	♊	31	15:43

DAILY ASPECTARIAN

1 M	☽∠♆	2:53
	☽#♆	4:39
	☽⚹♂	5:28
	☽□☿	6:49
	☽#♄	8:16
	♀□♄	17:04
	☽∠⚷	19:15
	☿⚺♂	21:55
2 Tu	☉☍♇	0:07
	♀⚻♆	0:13
	☽⚹♃	0:23
	☽□⚳	6:01
	☽☍♄	7:12
	☽⚹♆	7:55
	☽□♀	8:46
	☽∠♂	12:21
	☽△♇	17:54
	☉⚹☽	19:27
	☽⚺♅	22:11
3 W	☽⚹⚷	0:43
	☽∠♃	6:34
	⚳□♄	14:26
	☽⚹☿	15:52
	☽⚺♂	20:02
	☽∥☿	20:42
	☽⚼♇	23:47
4 Th	☉∠☽	4:03
	☽∠♅	4:14
	☉□♅	6:23
	♀#♇	9:10
	⚳⚻♆	9:20
	☽⚺♃	13:17
	☽⚻♄	19:08
	☽□♆	19:51
	☽⚹⚳	20:16
	☽∠☿	20:52
	☽∥♀	23:50
5 F	☽⚹♀	3:38
	☽#♇	5:10
	☽⚻♇	6:03
	☽⚹♅	10:37
	☉△⚷	13:03
	☽□⚷	13:04
	☉⚺☽	13:04
	♀∠♂	15:09
	☿⚼♆	19:04
6 Sa	☽⚼♄	1:34
	☽⚺☿	1:55
	♀⚻♇	2:44
	☽∠⚳	3:53
	⚶ ♌	10:00
	☽☌♂	12:31
	☽∠♀	13:35
	☽#♇	22:57
7 Su	☽☌♃	3:22
	☽△♄	8:01
	☽△♆	8:40
	☽⚺⚳	11:32
	☽☍♇	18:49
	☽∥♀	22:29
	☽⚺♀	23:28
	☽□♅	23:33
8 M	♀△♅	0:15
	☽△⚷	1:51
	♄ D	5:13
	☉☌☽	7:15
	☽☌☿	11:45
	☽∥☿	12:52
	☽⚼♆	14:58
	♀⚻⚷	22:27
9 Tu	☽⚺♂	4:53
	☽⚼⚷	8:00
	☽⚺♃	17:02
	☉☌☿	18:42
	☽□♄	20:28
	☽⚻♆	21:01
10 W	☽☌⚳	2:13
	☽⚻♇	6:57
	☽△♅	11:45
	☽∠♂	12:38
	☽⚻⚷	13:52
	☽☌♀	18:19
	☽⚺☿	20:43
	☽#♄	21:28
	☽∠♃	23:24
11 Th	☉⚺☽	0:24
	☽#♆	1:02
	☿∥♀	2:32
	☿⚺♀	11:09
	☽⚼♇	12:32
	☽⚼♅	17:21
	☽⚹♂	19:56
12 F	☽∠☿	0:48
	☽⚹♃	5:22
	☉⚼♆	5:55
	☽⚹♄	7:37
	☽☍♆	8:04
	☉∠☽	8:15
	☽∥♅	13:37
	☽⚺⚳	15:23
	☽△♇	17:40
	☽⚻♅	22:28
13 Sa	☽☍⚷	0:24
	☽⚹☿	4:31
	☽#⚷	5:33
	♀∠♃	7:54
	☽⚺♀	11:02
	☽∠♄	12:30
	♂ ♋	13:23
	☉⚹☽	15:27
	☽∠⚳	21:07
	☽∥⚷	22:02
14 Su	☽□♂	8:43
	☽#♅	13:33
	☽□♃	15:33
	☽⚺♄	16:45
	☽⚻♆	17:04
	☽∠♀	18:13
15 M	♂∥⚳	0:30
	☽⚹⚳	2:09
	☽□♇	2:13
	⚳⚻♇	4:12
	☽☍♅	6:55
	☽⚻⚷	8:38
	☽□☿	10:39
	☽⚼♆	20:31
	☽∥♆	23:56
16 Tu	☽⚹♀	0:25
	☽∥♄	3:11
	☉□☽	3:19
	☽⚼⚷	11:38
	☽△♂	18:15
	☽△♃	22:44
	☽☌♄	23:01
	☽△♆	23:11
17 W	☽⚹♇	7:47
	☽#♀	7:49
	☽□⚳	9:36
	☽⚻♅	12:18
	☽△⚷	13:49
	☽△☿	14:31
	♅ R	17:21
	♃△♄	17:33
	☽⚼♂	21:35
18 Th	♃△♆	0:15
	☽⚼♃	1:03
	♀⚼♇	6:46
	☽∠♇	9:22
	☽□♀	9:36
	☉△☽	11:14
	☽#☿	11:24
	☽⚼♅	13:47
	☽⚼☿	15:31
19 F	☽⚻♂	0:01
	☽⚺♄	2:04
	☽□♆	2:06
	☽⚻♃	2:32
	☽⚺♇	10:11
	♄△♆	13:21
	☽△⚳	13:34
	☉⚼☽	13:46
	☽∥♇	14:07
	☽△♅	14:32
	☽□⚷	15:52
	☽⚻☿	15:59
20 Sa	☽∠♄	2:33
	♀⚼♅	11:12
	☽⚼⚳	14:30
	☽△♀	15:01
	☉⚻☽	15:36
	☽∥♇	16:08
	☿ D	18:24
	♂△♆	19:43
	☉⚼⚷	21:16
	⚳△♅	21:20
	♂△♄	21:35
21 Su	☽⚹♆	2:27
	☽⚹♄	2:32
	☽☍♂	2:46
	☽☍♃	3:38
	☿∠♀	4:10
	☽☌♇	10:14
	☽#☿	12:05
	⚴ ♋	13:02
	☽□♅	14:31
	☽⚻⚳	15:02
	☽⚹⚷	15:43
	☽☍☿	15:54
	☽⚼♀	16:52
22 M	☉⚺♀	0:12
	☽∠♆	2:08
	⚳∥♃	5:34
	♂☌♃	7:36
	⚳⚻⚷	12:38
	♀ ♍	12:42
	☽∠⚷	15:22
	☉ ♌	15:57
	☉☍☽	18:17
	☽⚻♀	18:36
23 Tu	☽⚺♆	1:49
	☽□♄	2:04
	☽⚻♃	3:47
	☽⚻♂	4:25
	☽⚺♇	9:39
	☽#♀	12:31
	☽⚹♅	14:02
	☽⚺⚷	15:10
	☿⚺⚳	15:17
	☽⚻☿	16:02
	☽☍⚳	16:03
	☉#♇	20:42
	☽∥♄	21:24
24 W	☽∥♆	0:28
	☽⚼♃	4:12
	☽⚼♂	5:37
	☽∠♇	9:47
	☽∠♅	14:17
	☽⚼☿	16:55
	☉⚻☽	21:56
	☽☍♀	23:13
25 Th	☽☌♆	2:20
	☽△♄	2:45
	☽△♃	5:13
	☽△♂	7:30
	☽#♅	7:53
	☽⚹♇	10:33
	☉∥☿	14:14
	☽⚺♅	15:14
	☽☌⚷	16:21
	☽△☿	18:44
	☽⚻⚳	19:00
	☽∥⚷	21:22
26 F	☉⚼☽	0:59
	☽⚼♄	4:11
	♀☍♆	12:09
	☽#⚷	13:25
	♀⚹♄	18:37
	♀#♄	20:52
	☽⚼⚳	21:54
27 Sa	☽∥♅	3:25
	☿⚺⚳	5:03
	☉△☽	5:14
	☽⚺♆	5:59
	☽⚻♄	6:37
	☽⚻♀	7:46
	☽□♃	10:01
	☽□♂	14:24
	☽□♇	14:50
	☉⚻♆	15:21
	☿#♇	17:39
	☽☌♅	19:57
	☽⚺⚷	21:03
	♂☍♇	22:52
28 Su	☉□♄	1:07
	♀#♆	1:56
	☽△⚳	1:58
	☽□☿	2:20
	☽∠♆	9:21
	☽∥♀	13:11
	♀⚹♃	13:43
	☽⚼♀	14:06
	☽#♆	14:36
	☽#♄	18:21
29 M	☽∠⚷	0:59
	☽⚹♆	13:46
	☽☍♄	14:43
	☉□☽	17:44
	☽⚹♃	19:13
	☽△♀	21:49
	☽△♇	23:18
30 Tu	☽⚹♂	2:10
	☽⚺♅	4:52
	☽⚹⚷	5:54
	♀△♇	12:53
	☽□⚳	13:33
	☽⚹☿	15:59
	☉⚺♃	17:47
31 W	☽∠♃	1:16
	☽⚼♇	4:53
	☉∥☽	8:19
	☽∠♂	9:36
	☽∠♅	10:35

August 2013

LONGITUDE

Day	Sid.Time	☉	☽	☽ 12 hour	Mean ☊	True ☊	☿	♀	♂	⚳	♃	♄	⚷	♅	♆	♇
	h m s	° ' "	° ' "	° ' "	° '	° '	° '	° '	° '	° '	° '	° '	° '	° '	° '	° '
1 Th	20 39 04	8♌55 12	4♊06 54	10♊03 04	12♏22.2	12♏56.2	19♋28.1	11♍21.6	12♋21.1	17♌31.3	7♋58.9	5♏16.7	12♓55.8	12♈26.4	4♓38.9	9♑34.6
2 F	20 43 01	9 52 37	15 58 05	21 52 29	12 19.0	12R 52.9	20 35.9	12 33.3	13 00.9	17 58.5	8 11.6	5 19.0	12R 53.5	12R 25.7	4R 37.5	9R 33.4
3 Sa	20 46 57	10 50 03	27 46 46	3♋41 24	12 15.8	12 46.9	21 49.0	13 45.1	13 40.5	18 25.6	8 24.2	5 21.5	12 51.3	12 25.0	4 36.0	9 32.1
4 Su	20 50 54	11 47 30	9♋36 45	15 33 10	12 12.6	12 38.2	23 07.4	14 56.8	14 20.2	18 52.8	8 36.7	5 24.0	12 48.9	12 24.2	4 34.6	9 30.9
5 M	20 54 50	12 44 59	21 30 57	27 30 21	12 09.5	12 27.0	24 30.8	16 08.4	14 59.7	19 20.0	8 49.2	5 26.6	12 46.6	12 23.4	4 33.1	9 29.7
6 Tu	20 58 47	13 42 28	3♌31 34	9♌34 45	12 06.3	12 14.0	25 59.0	17 20.0	15 39.3	19 47.2	9 01.6	5 29.3	12 44.2	12 22.5	4 31.6	9 28.5
7 W	21 02 43	14 39 58	15 40 02	21 47 31	12 03.1	12 00.3	27 31.8	18 31.6	16 18.8	20 14.4	9 14.0	5 32.1	12 41.8	12 21.5	4 30.1	9 27.3
8 Th	21 06 40	15 37 30	27 57 17	4♍09 24	11 59.9	11 46.9	29 08.9	19 43.2	16 58.2	20 41.7	9 26.3	5 35.0	12 39.4	12 20.6	4 28.5	9 26.2
9 F	21 10 37	16 35 02	10♍23 58	16 41 02	11 56.8	11 35.1	0♌50.1	20 54.6	17 37.6	21 08.9	9 38.5	5 38.0	12 36.9	12 19.5	4 27.0	9 25.0
10 Sa	21 14 33	17 32 35	23 00 44	29 23 11	11 53.6	11 25.7	2 34.9	22 06.1	18 16.9	21 36.2	9 50.7	5 41.0	12 34.4	12 18.5	4 25.5	9 23.9
11 Su	21 18 30	18 30 09	5♎48 32	12♎16 59	11 50.4	11 19.1	4 23.1	23 17.5	18 56.2	22 03.5	10 02.8	5 44.2	12 31.9	12 17.4	4 23.9	9 22.8
12 M	21 22 26	19 27 44	18 48 43	25 24 00	11 47.2	11 15.3	6 14.2	24 28.8	19 35.4	22 30.7	10 14.9	5 47.4	12 29.3	12 16.2	4 22.3	9 21.7
13 Tu	21 26 23	20 25 21	2♏03 04	8♏46 09	11 44.0	11D 13.9	8 07.9	25 40.1	20 14.6	22 58.0	10 26.9	5 50.7	12 26.7	12 15.0	4 20.7	9 20.7
14 W	21 30 19	21 22 58	15 33 32	22 25 24	11 40.9	11R 13.7	10 03.8	26 51.4	20 53.8	23 25.3	10 38.8	5 54.1	12 24.1	12 13.8	4 19.2	9 19.7
15 Th	21 34 16	22 20 36	29 21 55	6♐23 11	11 37.7	11 13.6	12 01.6	28 02.6	21 32.9	23 52.7	10 50.6	5 57.6	12 21.5	12 12.5	4 17.6	9 18.6
16 F	21 38 12	23 18 14	13♐29 10	20 39 45	11 34.5	11 12.4	14 00.7	29 13.7	22 11.9	24 20.0	11 02.4	6 01.2	12 18.9	12 11.2	4 16.0	9 17.7
17 Sa	21 42 09	24 15 54	27 54 39	5♑13 26	11 31.3	11 09.2	16 00.9	0♎24.8	22 50.9	24 47.3	11 14.1	6 04.8	12 16.2	12 09.8	4 14.4	9 16.7
18 Su	21 46 06	25 13 35	12♑35 30	20 00 06	11 28.2	11 03.3	18 01.8	1 35.8	23 29.8	25 14.6	11 25.7	6 08.6	12 13.5	12 08.5	4 12.7	9 15.8
19 M	21 50 02	26 11 17	27 26 20	4♒53 10	11 25.0	10 55.1	20 03.2	2 46.8	24 08.7	25 42.0	11 37.3	6 12.4	12 10.8	12 07.0	4 11.1	9 14.8
20 Tu	21 53 59	27 09 01	12♒19 32	19 44 18	11 21.8	10 45.1	22 04.6	3 57.7	24 47.6	26 09.3	11 48.7	6 16.3	12 08.1	12 05.6	4 09.5	9 13.9
21 W	21 57 55	28 06 45	27 06 22	4♓24 41	11 18.6	10 34.5	24 05.9	5 08.5	25 26.4	26 36.7	12 00.1	6 20.2	12 05.4	12 04.0	4 07.9	9 13.1
22 Th	22 01 52	29 04 31	11♓38 19	18 46 31	11 15.5	10 24.6	26 06.8	6 19.3	26 05.1	27 04.0	12 11.5	6 24.3	12 02.6	12 02.5	4 06.2	9 12.2
23 F	22 05 48	0♍02 18	25 48 40	2♈44 21	11 12.3	10 16.3	28 07.2	7 30.1	26 43.8	27 31.4	12 22.7	6 28.4	11 59.9	12 00.9	4 04.6	9 11.4
24 Sa	22 09 45	1 00 06	9♈33 20	16 15 33	11 09.1	10 10.4	0♍06.8	8 40.7	27 22.5	27 58.7	12 33.8	6 32.6	11 57.1	11 59.3	4 02.9	9 10.6
25 Su	22 13 41	1 57 57	22 51 07	29 20 15	11 05.9	10 07.0	2 05.6	9 51.3	28 01.1	28 26.1	12 44.9	6 36.9	11 54.3	11 57.6	4 01.3	9 09.8
26 M	22 17 38	2 55 49	5♉43 22	12♉00 53	11 02.7	10D 05.7	4 03.5	11 01.9	28 39.6	28 53.4	12 55.9	6 41.2	11 51.5	11 55.9	3 59.7	9 09.1
27 Tu	22 21 35	3 53 43	18 13 23	24 21 26	10 59.6	10 05.8	6 00.3	12 12.4	29 18.2	29 20.8	13 06.8	6 45.7	11 48.7	11 54.2	3 58.0	9 08.3
28 W	22 25 31	4 51 39	0♊25 41	6♊26 48	10 56.4	10R 06.3	7 56.0	13 22.8	29 56.6	29 48.2	13 17.6	6 50.2	11 45.8	11 52.4	3 56.4	9 07.7
29 Th	22 29 28	5 49 36	12 25 25	18 22 14	10 53.2	10 06.2	9 50.6	14 33.2	0♌35.1	0♍15.6	13 28.3	6 54.7	11 43.0	11 50.6	3 54.7	9 07.0
30 F	22 33 24	6 47 36	24 17 52	0♋12 56	10 50.0	10 04.5	11 43.9	15 43.5	1 13.4	0 42.9	13 39.0	6 59.4	11 40.2	11 48.8	3 53.1	9 06.3
31 Sa	22 37 21	7♍45 37	6♋08 03	12 03 45	10♏46.8	10♏00.7	13♌36.1	16♎53.7	1♌51.8	1♍10.3	13♋49.5	7♏04.1	11♓37.3	11♈47.0	3♓51.4	9♑05.7

1st of Month

Julian Day # 2456505.5
Obliquity 23°26'08"
SVP 5♓03'59"
GC 27♐01.7
Eris 22♈56.4R

Day	⚴
1	6♋03.7
6	8 58.0
11	11 52.3
16	14 46.3
21	17 40.0
26	20 33.0
31	23 25.4

Day	⚵
1	12♒34.8R
6	11 22.0R
11	10 09.0R
16	8 57.9R
21	7 50.9R
26	6 49.6R
31	5 55.6R

Day	⚶
1	11♌31.1
6	13 47.9
11	16 05.2
16	18 22.7
21	20 40.6
26	22 58.7
31	25 17.0

DECLINATION and LATITUDE

Day	☉ Decl	☽ Decl	☽ Lat	☽ 12h Decl	☿ Decl	☿ Lat	♀ Decl	♀ Lat	♂ Decl	♂ Lat	⚳ Decl	⚳ Lat	♃ Decl	♃ Lat	♄ Decl	♄ Lat
1 Th	18N02	19N10	1S50	19N41	20N31	1S32	8N32	1N20	23N34	0N42	21N54	6N39	23N02	0S10	11S03	2N22
2 F	17 46	19 58	2 45	20 01	20 36	1 16	8 03	1 18	23 30	0 43	21 46	6 40	23 01	0 10	11 04	2 22
3 Sa	17 31	19 52	3 33	19 29	20 39	1 01	7 34	1 17	23 27	0 43	21 39	6 41	23 00	0 10	11 05	2 22
4 Su	17 15	18 54	4 12	18 06	20 41	0 47	7 05	1 15	23 23	0 44	21 31	6 41	22 60	0 10	11 06	2 21
5 M	16 59	17 06	4 40	15 55	20 41	0 32	6 35	1 13	23 20	0 44	21 23	6 42	22 59	0 10	11 07	2 21
6 Tu	16 42	14 33	4 56	13 02	20 39	0 18	6 05	1 11	23 16	0 45	21 15	6 43	22 58	0 09	11 08	2 21
7 W	16 26	11 22	4 59	9 34	20 34	0 05	5 35	1 08	23 12	0 46	21 07	6 44	22 57	0 09	11 09	2 21
8 Th	16 09	7 40	4 48	5 40	20 27	0N08	5 05	1 06	23 07	0 46	20 58	6 45	22 57	0 09	11 10	2 20
9 F	15 52	3 36	4 23	1 29	20 18	0 20	4 35	1 04	23 03	0 47	20 50	6 45	22 56	0 09	11 12	2 20
10 Sa	15 34	0S41	3 45	2S51	20 06	0 32	4 04	1 01	22 58	0 47	20 42	6 46	22 55	0 09	11 12	2 20
11 Su	15 17	4 60	2 55	7 06	19 51	0 42	3 34	0 59	22 53	0 48	20 34	6 47	22 54	0 09	11 14	2 20
12 M	14 59	9 09	1 56	11 06	19 33	0 52	3 03	0 56	22 48	0 49	20 25	6 48	22 53	0 09	11 15	2 19
13 Tu	14 41	12 56	0 48	14 38	19 13	1 02	2 33	0 54	22 43	0 49	20 17	6 49	22 53	0 09	11 17	2 19
14 W	14 22	16 08	0N23	17 25	18 51	1 10	2 02	0 51	22 38	0 50	20 09	6 50	22 52	0 09	11 18	2 19
15 Th	14 04	18 28	1 35	19 15	18 25	1 17	1 31	0 48	22 32	0 50	20 00	6 50	22 51	0 09	11 19	2 19
16 F	13 45	19 44	2 42	19 54	17 57	1 24	1 00	0 46	22 27	0 51	19 52	6 51	22 50	0 09	11 21	2 18
17 Sa	13 26	19 45	3 41	19 15	17 27	1 29	0 29	0 43	22 21	0 51	19 43	6 52	22 49	0 09	11 22	2 18
18 Su	13 07	18 26	4 26	17 18	16 55	1 34	0S01	0 40	22 15	0 52	19 35	6 53	22 48	0 08	11 24	2 18
19 M	12 47	15 52	4 53	14 11	16 21	1 38	0 32	0 37	22 09	0 53	19 26	6 54	22 47	0 08	11 25	2 18
20 Tu	12 28	12 16	5 01	10 11	15 45	1 41	1 03	0 34	22 02	0 53	19 17	6 55	22 46	0 08	11 27	2 17
21 W	12 08	7 56	4 49	5 36	15 07	1 44	1 34	0 31	21 56	0 54	19 09	6 56	22 45	0 08	11 28	2 17
22 Th	11 48	3 13	4 19	0 48	14 27	1 45	2 05	0 28	21 49	0 54	18 60	6 56	22 45	0 08	11 30	2 17
23 F	11 27	1N35	3 32	3N55	13 47	1 46	2 36	0 24	21 42	0 55	18 51	6 57	22 44	0 08	11 31	2 17
24 Sa	11 07	6 09	2 35	8 17	13 05	1 46	3 07	0 21	21 35	0 55	18 42	6 58	22 43	0 08	11 33	2 17
25 Su	10 46	10 17	1 30	12 07	12 22	1 45	3 38	0 18	21 28	0 56	18 33	6 59	22 42	0 08	11 34	2 16
26 M	10 26	13 48	0 23	15 17	11 38	1 44	4 09	0 14	21 21	0 56	18 25	7 00	22 41	0 08	11 36	2 16
27 Tu	10 05	16 34	0S43	17 38	10 53	1 42	4 39	0 11	21 13	0 57	18 16	7 01	22 40	0 08	11 38	2 16
28 W	9 44	18 30	1 46	19 09	10 08	1 40	5 10	0 07	21 06	0 58	18 07	7 02	22 39	0 08	11 39	2 16
29 Th	9 22	19 35	2 43	19 47	9 22	1 37	5 40	0 04	20 58	0 58	17 58	7 03	22 38	0 08	11 41	2 15
30 F	9 01	19 46	3 33	19 32	8 36	1 33	6 11	0 00	20 50	0 59	17 49	7 04	22 37	0 07	11 43	2 15
31 Sa	8N39	19N05	4S13	18N25	7N50	1N30	6S41	0S03	20N42	0N59	17N40	7N05	22N36	0S07	11S45	2N15

Day	⚷ Decl	⚷ Lat	♅ Decl	♅ Lat	♆ Decl	♆ Lat	♇ Decl	♇ Lat
1	1S39	5N28	4N16	0S43	10S26	0S41	19S56	3N10
6	1 43	5 28	4 14	0 43	10 29	0 41	19 57	3 09
11	1 47	5 29	4 12	0 43	10 32	0 41	19 58	3 08
16	1 52	5 29	4 09	0 43	10 35	0 41	19 60	3 07
21	1 57	5 29	4 06	0 43	10 38	0 41	20 01	3 07
26	2 02	5 29	4 03	0 43	10 41	0 41	20 02	3 06
31	2S08	5N29	3N60	0S43	10S44	0S41	20S03	3N05

Day	⚴ Decl	⚴ Lat	⚵ Decl	⚵ Lat	⚶ Decl	⚶ Lat	Eris Decl	Eris Lat
1	2S46	26S06	4S26	13N06	19N39	2N26	3S12	13S02
6	3 11	26 22	5 00	12 50	19 06	2 31	3 13	13 02
11	3 37	26 37	5 37	12 31	18 31	2 37	3 14	13 03
16	4 07	26 53	6 17	12 08	17 54	2 43	3 14	13 03
21	4 39	27 08	6 58	11 43	17 16	2 49	3 15	13 04
26	5 14	27 23	7 40	11 15	16 36	2 55	3 16	13 04
31	5S51	27S37	8S21	10N45	15N56	3N01	3S17	13S04

Moon Phenomena

Max/0 Decl
dy hr mn
2 9:20 20N02
9 20:14 0 S
16 12:13 19S54
22 16:01 0 N
29 17:05 19N48

Max/0 Lat
dy hr mn
6 16:57 5S00
13 16:21 0 N
19 21:40 5N02
26 8:19 0 S

Perigee/Apogee
dy hr m kilometers
3 8:54 a 405832
19 1:15 p 362264
30 23:55 a 404881

PH dy hr mn
● 6 21:52 14♌35
☽ 14 10:57 21♏49
○ 21 1:46 28♒11
☾ 28 9:36 5♊15

Void of Course Moon

Last Aspect	☽ Ingress
1 16:50 ♅ ✱	♋ 3 4:31
5 6:50 ☿ ☌	♌ 5 16:59
6 21:52 ☉ ☌	♍ 8 3:58
9 22:06 ♀ ☌	♎ 10 13:09
12 1:30 ♂ □	♏ 12 20:19
14 21:31 ♀ ✱	♐ 15 1:05
16 17:33 ☉ △	♑ 17 3:26
18 18:27 ♂ ☍	♒ 19 4:08
21 1:46 ☉ ☍	♓ 21 4:44
23 1:39 ♂ △	♈ 23 7:14
25 10:03 ♂ □	♉ 25 13:14
27 22:59 ♂ ✱	♊ 27 23:09
29 4:46 ♀ △	♋ 30 11:34

DAILY ASPECTARIAN

1 Th ☽ ∠ ☿ 0:47; ☽ □ ♆ 1:05; ☽ ⚻ ♄ 2:21; ♂ □ ♅ 3:09; ☿ ⚼ ♆ 3:54; ☽ ⚺ ♃ 7:57; ☉ ✱ ☽ 10:34; ☽ ⚻ ♇ 11:01; ☉ ⚻ ♇ 16:07; ☽ □ ♀ 16:18; ☽ ✱ ♅ 16:50; ☽ ⚺ ♂ 17:39; ☽ □ ⚷ 17:47; ♂ △ ⚷ 19:49; ♀ ⚻ ♅ 21:29; ☽ ⋕ ♇ 22:35; ☽ ⋕ ♇ 22:36

2 F ☽ ✱ ⚳ 4:14; ♀ ☍ ⚷ 6:33; ☽ ⚼ ♄ 8:52; ☽ ⚺ ☿ 10:28; ☉ ∠ ☽ 19:42; ♀ ✱ ♂ 20:36

3 Sa ☽ ∠ ⚳ 11:55; ☽ △ ♆ 13:49; ☽ △ ♄ 15:26; ☽ ☌ ♃ 21:56; ☽ ☍ ♇ 23:48

4 Su ☉ ⚺ ☽ 4:48; ☽ □ ♅ 5:38; ☽ △ ⚷ 6:27; ☽ ☌ ♂ 10:06; ☽ ✱ ♀ 11:59; ☉ △ ♅ 15:06; ☽ ⚺ ⚳ 19:26; ☽ ⚼ ♆ 20:04

5 M ☉ ⚻ ⚷ 0:39; ☉ ∥ ☽ 1:27; ☽ ☌ ☿ 6:50; ☽ ⚼ ⚷ 12:30; ☽ ∠ ♀ 21:22

6 Tu ☽ ⚻ ♆ 1:59; ☽ □ ♄ 3:55; ☽ ⚺ ♃ 11:06; ☽ ⚻ ♇ 11:46; ☽ △ ♅ 17:30; ☽ ⚻ ⚷ 18:10; ☉ ☌ ☽ 21:52

7 W ☽ ⚺ ♂ 1:20; ☽ ⋕ ♄ 1:29; ☿ ⚼ ⚷ 2:27; ☽ ⋕ ♆ 5:57; ☽ ⚺ ♀ 6:13; ☽ ☌ ⚳ 9:19; ☽ ∠ ♃ 17:03; ☽ ⚼ ♇ 17:10; ☽ ⚼ ♅ 22:49; ♃ ☍ ♇ 23:47

8 Th ☽ ⚺ ☿ 2:40; ☽ ∠ ♂ 8:13; ☿ ♌ 12:14; ☽ ☍ ♆ 12:35; ☽ ✱ ♄ 14:48; ☽ ∥ ♀ 17:35; ♀ ∠ ♄ 18:09; ☽ ∥ ♅ 20:30; ☽ △ ♇ 22:07; ☽ ✱ ♃ 22:31

9 F ☽ ⚻ ♅ 3:41; ☽ ☍ ⚷ 4:14; ♀ ⚺ ⚳ 7:45; ☽ ⋕ ⚷ 10:23; ☽ ∠ ☿ 12:02; ☉ ⚺ ☽ 12:47; ☽ ✱ ♂ 14:33; ♀ ∥ ♅ 17:45; ☽ ∠ ♄ 19:35; ☽ ⚺ ⚳ 21:14; ☽ ☌ ♀ 22:06

10 Sa ☽ ∥ ⚷ 6:06; ☿ ⋕ ♇ 12:26; ☽ ⋕ ♀ 16:52; ♂ ∥ ♃ 18:30; ☉ ∠ ☽ 19:21; ☽ ⋕ ♅ 19:33; ☽ ✱ ☿ 20:54; ☽ ⚻ ♆ 21:23; ☽ ⚺ ♄ 23:52

11 Su ☿ ⚻ ♆ 0:11; ☽ ∠ ⚳ 2:24; ☽ □ ♇ 6:37; ☽ □ ♃ 7:59; ☽ ☍ ♅ 12:00; ☽ ⚻ ⚷ 12:25; ♂ ⚼ ♆ 16:17; ☿ □ ♄ 18:06

12 M ☽ ⚼ ♆ 1:01; ☉ ✱ ☽ 1:17; ☽ □ ♂ 1:30; ☽ ✱ ⚳ 7:00; ☽ ∥ ♆ 8:29; ☉ ⚺ ♂ 10:03; ☽ ⚺ ♀ 11:21; ☽ ∥ ♄ 13:02; ☽ ⚼ ⚷ 15:44

13 Tu ☽ △ ♆ 4:06; ☽ ☌ ♄ 6:49; ☉ ⋕ ☽ 11:19; ☽ □ ☿ 12:40; ☽ ✱ ♇ 13:00; ☿ ⚻ ♇ 14:59; ☽ △ ♃ 15:12; ☽ ∠ ♀ 16:51; ☽ ⚻ ♅ 18:08; ☽ △ ⚷ 18:27

14 W ☿ ⚺ ♃ 7:58; ♀ ⋕ ⚷ 9:00; ☽ △ ♂ 9:48; ☉ □ ☽ 10:57; ☽ □ ⚳ 14:12; ☽ ∠ ♇ 15:17; ☽ ⚼ ♃ 17:50; ☽ ⚼ ♅ 20:18; ☽ ✱ ♀ 21:31; ☽ ⋕ ☿ 23:27

15 Th ☿ △ ♅ 2:12; ⚳ ⋕ ♇ 2:16; ☿ ⚻ ⚷ 3:57; ☽ □ ♆ 8:25; ☽ ⚺ ♄ 11:19; ☽ ⚼ ♂ 12:52; ☽ ⚺ ♇ 16:56; ☽ ⚻ ♃ 19:49; ☽ △ ♅ 21:49; ☽ □ ⚷ 22:02; ⚳ ⚼ ♇ 22:02

16 F ☽ △ ☿ 1:02; ☽ ⋕ ⚳ 4:30; ☿ ∠ ♀ 6:24; ☽ ∠ ♄ 12:39; ☽ ⚻ ♂ 15:14; ♀ ♎ 15:38; ☉ △ ☽ 17:33; ☽ △ ⚳ 18:41

17 Sa ☉ ⚼ ♇ 0:19; ☽ ⋕ ⚳ 1:05; ☽ □ ♀ 4:29; ☽ ⚼ ☿ 5:55; ☽ ✱ ♆ 10:22; ☽ ✱ ♄ 13:27; ☽ ☌ ♇ 18:36; ☉ ⚼ ☽ 19:53; ☽ ⚼ ⚳ 20:04; ☽ ☍ ♃ 22:05; ☽ □ ♅ 23:16; ☽ ✱ ⚷ 23:24

18 Su ☉ ☌ ⚳ 0:49; ☽ ⚻ ☿ 10:12; ☽ ∠ ♆ 10:42; ☽ ☍ ♂ 18:27; ☽ ⋕ ☿ 19:17; ☽ ⚻ ⚳ 21:06; ☉ ⚻ ☽ 21:51; ☽ ∠ ⚷ 23:35

19 M ☽ △ ♀ 9:21; ☽ ⚺ ♆ 10:51; ☉ ∠ ♃ 13:29; ☽ □ ♄ 14:11; ☽ ⚺ ♇ 19:01; ☉ ⚼ ♅ 22:36; ☉ ⋕ ☽ 22:47; ☽ ⚻ ♃ 23:10; ☽ ✱ ♅ 23:37; ☽ ⚺ ⚷ 23:42

20 Tu ♀ ⚻ ♆ 3:54; ☽ ∥ ♄ 4:49; ☽ ∥ ♆ 9:30; ☽ ⚼ ♀ 11:40; ☽ ☍ ☿ 18:19; ☽ ∠ ♇ 19:17; ☽ ⚻ ♂ 21:09; ☽ ☍ ⚳ 23:10; ☽ ⚼ ♃ 23:50; ☽ ∠ ♅ 23:56

21 W ☿ ⚼ ♇ 1:25; ☉ ☍ ☽ 1:46; ♃ □ ♅ 7:17; ♃ △ ⚷ 8:56; ☽ ☌ ♆ 11:31; ☽ ⚻ ♀ 14:23; ☽ △ ♄ 15:15; ♀ ∥ ⚷ 18:09; ☽ ⋕ ♅ 19:34; ☽ ✱ ♇ 19:57; ⚳ ⚼ ♅ 22:44; ☽ ⚼ ♂ 23:02; ☿ ⚺ ♂ 23:30

22 Th ☽ ⚺ ♅ 0:40; ☽ ☌ ⚷ 0:40; ☽ △ ♃ 0:56; ♀ ⚺ ♄ 1:47; ♅ ⚺ ⚷ 2:42; ☽ ∥ ♀ 5:04; ☽ ∥ ⚷ 6:11; ☿ ⚼ ♅ 10:57; ⚳ ∠ ♃ 11:06; ☿ ∠ ♃ 14:12; ☿ ☌ ⚳ 14:45; ☽ ⚼ ♄ 16:33; ☉ ⋕ ♄ 19:45; ☉ ♍ 23:03

23 F ☽ △ ♂ 1:39; ☽ ⋕ ⚷ 2:03; ☽ ⚻ ⚳ 3:03; ☽ ⚻ ☿ 4:39; ☽ ⋕ ♀ 5:51; ☉ ⚻ ☽ 7:51; ♂ ⚼ ⚷ 9:18; ☽ ∥ ♅ 12:53; ☽ ⚺ ♆ 14:19; ☽ ⚻ ♄ 18:39; ☽ ☍ ♀ 22:18; ☿ ♍ 22:38; ☽ □ ♇ 23:20

24 Sa ☽ ⚺ ⚷ 4:15; ☽ ☌ ♅ 4:19; ☽ □ ♃ 5:26; ☽ ⚼ ⚳ 6:19; ♀ □ ♇ 10:02; ☽ ⚼ ☿ 11:41; ☉ ⚼ ☽ 12:26; ☽ ∠ ♆ 17:01; ☉ ☌ ☿ 20:57

25 Su ☽ ⋕ ♆ 2:27; ☉ ∥ ☽ 2:50; ☉ ⋕ ♆ 6:52; ☽ ∠ ⚷ 7:27; ☽ ⋕ ♄ 8:22; ☽ □ ♂ 10:03; ☽ △ ⚳ 10:42; ☽ ∥ ☿ 11:18; ☉ △ ☽ 18:18; ♀ ⋕ ♅ 19:47; ☽ △ ☿ 20:17; ☽ ✱ ♆ 20:44; ☿ ☍ ♆ 23:14

26 M ☿ ⋕ ♄ 1:00; ☽ ☍ ♄ 1:50; ☽ △ ♇ 6:31; ☽ ⚻ ♀ 11:10; ☽ ✱ ⚷ 11:39; ☽ ⚺ ♅ 11:49; ☽ ✱ ♃ 13:58; ♀ ⚻ ⚷ 16:14; ♀ ☍ ♅ 17:57

27 Tu ☉ ☍ ♆ 1:44; ♂ ⚺ ⚳ 5:45; ☿ ⋕ ♆ 6:14; ☿ ✱ ♄ 9:45; ☽ ⚼ ♇ 11:34; ☽ ∠ ♅ 16:59; ☽ ∥ ⚳ 18:38; ☽ ⚼ ♀ 19:30; ☽ ∠ ♃ 19:42; ♀ □ ♃ 21:54; ☽ □ ⚳ 22:43; ☽ ✱ ♂ 22:59

28 W ♂ ♌ 2:06; ☽ □ ♆ 6:58; ☉ □ ☽ 9:36; ⚳ ♍ 10:21; ☽ ⚻ ♄ 12:52; ☿ △ ♇ 14:53; ☽ ⚻ ♇ 17:21; ☽ □ ☿ 17:50; ☽ □ ⚷ 22:35; ☽ ✱ ♅ 22:50; ☉ ∥ ☿ 23:57

29 Th ☽ ⚺ ♃ 2:09; ☽ △ ♀ 4:46; ☽ ∠ ♂ 6:44; ☽ ⚼ ♄ 19:18; ☿ ☍ ⚷ 23:13; ♀ ∠ ⚳ 23:42

30 F ☿ ⚻ ♅ 1:01; ☉ ✱ ♄ 5:19; ☽ ✱ ⚳ 13:32; ☽ ⚺ ♂ 14:51; ☽ △ ♆ 19:24

31 Sa ☽ △ ♄ 1:54; ♀ ✱ ♃ 3:11; ☉ ✱ ☽ 3:35; ☽ ☍ ♇ 6:00; ☽ △ ⚷ 11:04; ☽ □ ♅ 11:24; ☽ ☌ ♃ 15:48; ☽ ✱ ♀ 17:54; ☽ ∠ ⚳ 21:06; ☿ ⋕ ♀ 21:19

LONGITUDE

Day	Sid.Time	☉	☽	☽ 12 hour	Mean☊	True☊	☿	♀	♂	⚳	♃	♄	⚷	♅	♆	♇
	h m s	° ' "	° ' "	° ' "	° '	° '	° '	° '	° '	° '	° '	° '	° '	° '	° '	° '
1 Su	22 41 17	8♍43 40	18♋00 32	23♋58 51	10♏43.7	9♏54.5	15♍27.0	18♎03.9	2♌30.1	1♏37.7	13♋59.9	7♏08.9	11♓34.5	11♈45.1	3♓49.8	9♑05.1
2 M	22 45 14	9 41 45	29 59 06	6♌01 38	10 40.5	9R 46.1	17 16.7	19 14.0	3 08.3	2 05.1	14 10.3	7 13.8	11R 31.6	11R 43.2	3R 48.2	9R 04.6
3 Tu	22 49 10	10 39 52	12♌06 44	18 14 37	10 37.3	9 36.1	19 05.1	20 24.1	3 46.5	2 32.4	14 20.5	7 18.7	11 28.8	11 41.2	3 46.5	9 04.0
4 W	22 53 07	11 38 00	24 25 26	0♍39 18	10 34.1	9 25.4	20 52.3	21 34.1	4 24.6	2 59.8	14 30.7	7 23.7	11 25.9	11 39.2	3 44.9	9 03.5
5 Th	22 57 04	12 36 10	6♍56 17	13 16 24	10 31.0	9 14.9	22 38.3	22 44.0	5 02.7	3 27.2	14 40.7	7 28.7	11 23.1	11 37.2	3 43.3	9 03.1
6 F	23 01 00	13 34 22	19 39 38	26 05 55	10 27.8	9 05.7	24 23.0	23 53.8	5 40.8	3 54.5	14 50.6	7 33.9	11 20.2	11 35.2	3 41.7	9 02.6
7 Sa	23 04 57	14 32 36	2♎35 13	9♎07 28	10 24.6	8 58.5	26 06.6	25 03.6	6 18.8	4 21.9	15 00.5	7 39.1	11 17.4	11 33.1	3 40.0	9 02.2
8 Su	23 08 53	15 30 51	15 42 35	22 20 32	10 21.4	8 53.7	27 48.9	26 13.3	6 56.7	4 49.2	15 10.2	7 44.3	11 14.5	11 31.0	3 38.4	9 01.8
9 M	23 12 50	16 29 08	29 01 15	5♏44 45	10 18.2	8D 51.3	29 30.1	27 22.9	7 34.6	5 16.6	15 19.8	7 49.6	11 11.7	11 28.9	3 36.8	9 01.4
10 Tu	23 16 46	17 27 27	12♏31 01	19 20 04	10 15.1	8 50.9	1♎10.2	28 32.4	8 12.4	5 43.9	15 29.3	7 55.0	11 08.8	11 26.8	3 35.2	9 01.1
11 W	23 20 43	18 25 47	26 11 55	3♐06 35	10 11.9	8 51.7	2 49.1	29 41.8	8 50.2	6 11.2	15 38.7	8 00.4	11 06.0	11 24.6	3 33.7	9 00.8
12 Th	23 24 39	19 24 09	10♐04 04	17 04 22	10 08.7	8R 52.7	4 26.9	0♏51.2	9 27.9	6 38.5	15 48.0	8 05.9	11 03.2	11 22.4	3 32.1	9 00.5
13 F	23 28 36	20 22 32	24 07 23	1♑13 00	10 05.5	8 53.0	6 03.5	2 00.5	10 05.6	7 05.8	15 57.1	8 11.5	11 00.4	11 20.2	3 30.5	9 00.3
14 Sa	23 32 33	21 20 57	8♑21 02	15 31 10	10 02.4	8 51.7	7 39.1	3 09.7	10 43.2	7 33.1	16 06.2	8 17.1	10 57.6	11 18.0	3 29.0	9 00.1
15 Su	23 36 29	22 19 23	22 43 01	29 56 09	9 59.2	8 48.4	9 13.6	4 18.8	11 20.8	8 00.4	16 15.1	8 22.8	10 54.8	11 15.8	3 27.4	8 59.9
16 M	23 40 26	23 17 51	7♒09 57	14♒23 48	9 56.0	8 43.4	10 47.0	5 27.7	11 58.3	8 27.7	16 23.9	8 28.5	10 52.1	11 13.5	3 25.9	8 59.7
17 Tu	23 44 22	24 16 21	21 37 00	28 48 47	9 52.8	8 37.0	12 19.3	6 36.6	12 35.8	8 54.9	16 32.6	8 34.3	10 49.3	11 11.3	3 24.4	8 59.6
18 W	23 48 19	25 14 52	5♓58 26	13♓05 13	9 49.6	8 30.0	13 50.6	7 45.4	13 13.2	9 22.1	16 41.1	8 40.1	10 46.6	11 09.0	3 22.9	8 59.5
19 Th	23 52 15	26 13 25	20 08 26	27 07 29	9 46.5	8 23.5	15 20.8	8 54.1	13 50.6	9 49.3	16 49.5	8 46.0	10 43.8	11 06.7	3 21.4	8 59.4
20 F	23 56 12	27 12 00	4♈01 52	10♈51 11	9 43.3	8 18.1	16 49.9	10 02.7	14 27.9	10 16.5	16 57.8	8 52.0	10 41.1	11 04.3	3 19.9	8D 59.4
21 Sa	0 00 08	28 10 36	17 35 09	24 13 36	9 40.1	8 14.4	18 18.0	11 11.2	15 05.2	10 43.7	17 06.0	8 58.0	10 38.5	11 02.0	3 18.5	8 59.4
22 Su	0 04 05	29 09 15	0♉46 33	7♉14 03	9 36.9	8D 12.6	19 45.0	12 19.5	15 42.4	11 10.9	17 14.0	9 04.0	10 35.8	10 59.6	3 17.0	8 59.4
23 M	0 08 01	0♎07 56	13 36 20	19 53 39	9 33.7	8 12.5	21 10.9	13 27.8	16 19.6	11 38.0	17 21.9	9 10.1	10 33.1	10 57.3	3 15.6	8 59.5
24 Tu	0 11 58	1 06 40	26 06 25	2♊15 04	9 30.6	8 13.5	22 35.7	14 35.9	16 56.7	12 05.2	17 29.7	9 16.2	10 30.5	10 54.9	3 14.2	8 59.6
25 W	0 15 55	2 05 25	8♊20 07	14 22 07	9 27.4	8 15.2	23 59.4	15 43.9	17 33.8	12 32.3	17 37.3	9 22.4	10 27.9	10 52.5	3 12.8	8 59.7
26 Th	0 19 51	3 04 13	20 21 39	26 19 19	9 24.2	8 16.7	25 21.9	16 51.9	18 10.8	12 59.4	17 44.8	9 28.6	10 25.4	10 50.1	3 11.4	8 59.8
27 F	0 23 48	4 03 03	2♋15 45	8♋11 35	9 21.0	8R 17.5	26 43.2	17 59.7	18 47.8	13 26.5	17 52.2	9 34.9	10 22.8	10 47.8	3 10.0	9 00.0
28 Sa	0 27 44	5 01 55	14 07 25	20 03 52	9 17.9	8 17.1	28 03.4	19 07.3	19 24.7	13 53.5	17 59.4	9 41.2	10 20.3	10 45.3	3 08.7	9 00.2
29 Su	0 31 41	6 00 49	26 01 31	2♌00 55	9 14.7	8 15.2	29 22.2	20 14.9	20 01.5	14 20.6	18 06.5	9 47.6	10 17.8	10 42.9	3 07.4	9 00.5
30 M	0 35 37	6♎59 46	8♌02 34	14 06 58	9♏11.5	8♏11.9	0♏39.7	21♏22.3	20♌38.4	14♏47.6	18♋13.4	9♏54.0	10♓15.3	10♈40.5	3♓06.1	9♑00.8

1st of Month

Julian Day # 2456536.5
Obliquity 23°26'08"
SVP 5♓03'56"
GC 27♐01.8
Eris 22♈47.8R

Day	⚴
1	23♋59.7
6	26 50.8
11	29 40.5
16	2♌28.5
21	5 14.7
26	7 58.7

Day	⚵
1	5♒45.8R
6	5 02.3R
11	4 28.7R
16	4 05.5R
21	3 53.1R
26	3 51.3

Day	⚶
1	25♌44.7
6	28 03.2
11	0♍21.7
16	2 40.2
21	4 58.5
26	7 16.7

DECLINATION and LATITUDE

Day	☉ Decl	☽ Decl	☽ Lat	☽12h Decl	☿ Decl	☿ Lat	♀ Decl	♀ Lat	♂ Decl	♂ Lat	⚳ Decl	⚳ Lat	♃ Decl	♃ Lat	♄ Decl	♄ Lat
1 Su	8N18	17N33	4S43	16N30	7N03	1N25	7S11	0S07	20N34	0N60	17N31	7N06	22N35	0S07	11S46	2N15
2 M	7 56	15 16	4 60	13 51	6 16	1 21	7 42	0 11	20 26	1 00	17 21	7 07	22 34	0 07	11 48	2 15
3 Tu	7 34	12 18	5 04	10 35	5 29	1 16	8 11	0 14	20 18	1 01	17 12	7 08	22 33	0 07	11 50	2 14
4 W	7 12	8 45	4 54	6 49	4 42	1 11	8 41	0 18	20 09	1 02	17 03	7 09	22 32	0 07	11 52	2 14
5 Th	6 50	4 47	4 30	2 41	3 55	1 05	9 11	0 22	20 00	1 02	16 54	7 09	22 31	0 07	11 53	2 14
6 F	6 27	0 32	3 52	1S38	3 08	0 59	9 40	0 26	19 52	1 03	16 45	7 10	22 30	0 07	11 55	2 14
7 Sa	6 05	3S49	3 02	5 57	2 21	0 53	10 10	0 30	19 43	1 03	16 36	7 11	22 29	0 07	11 57	2 14
8 Su	5 43	8 03	2 01	10 03	1 35	0 47	10 39	0 34	19 34	1 04	16 26	7 12	22 28	0 07	11 59	2 13
9 M	5 20	11 57	0 53	13 42	0 49	0 40	11 07	0 38	19 25	1 04	16 17	7 13	22 27	0 07	12 01	2 13
10 Tu	4 57	15 17	0N20	16 39	0 03	0 33	11 36	0 42	19 15	1 05	16 08	7 14	22 26	0 06	12 03	2 13
11 W	4 35	17 48	1 32	18 42	0S43	0 26	12 04	0 45	19 06	1 05	15 58	7 15	22 25	0 06	12 05	2 13
12 Th	4 12	19 19	2 40	19 38	1 28	0 19	12 33	0 49	18 56	1 06	15 49	7 16	22 24	0 06	12 07	2 13
13 F	3 49	19 39	3 39	19 21	2 13	0 12	13 00	0 54	18 47	1 07	15 40	7 18	22 23	0 06	12 09	2 13
14 Sa	3 26	18 45	4 26	17 50	2 58	0 05	13 28	0 58	18 37	1 07	15 30	7 19	22 22	0 06	12 11	2 12
15 Su	3 03	16 39	4 56	15 12	3 42	0S02	13 55	1 02	18 27	1 08	15 21	7 20	22 21	0 06	12 13	2 12
16 M	2 40	13 30	5 08	11 37	4 25	0 10	14 22	1 06	18 17	1 08	15 12	7 21	22 20	0 06	12 15	2 12
17 Tu	2 16	9 33	5 01	7 21	5 08	0 17	14 49	1 10	18 07	1 09	15 02	7 22	22 19	0 06	12 17	2 12
18 W	1 53	5 04	4 34	2 44	5 51	0 25	15 16	1 14	17 57	1 09	14 53	7 23	22 18	0 06	12 19	2 12
19 Th	1 30	0 22	3 51	1N59	6 33	0 33	15 42	1 18	17 47	1 10	14 43	7 24	22 17	0 06	12 21	2 12
20 F	1 07	4N16	2 55	6 29	7 14	0 40	16 07	1 22	17 37	1 10	14 34	7 25	22 16	0 06	12 23	2 11
21 Sa	0 43	8 35	1 50	10 34	7 55	0 48	16 33	1 26	17 26	1 11	14 25	7 26	22 15	0 05	12 25	2 11
22 Su	0 20	12 22	0 40	14 00	8 35	0 56	16 58	1 30	17 16	1 11	14 15	7 27	22 14	0 05	12 27	2 11
23 M	0S03	15 27	0S29	16 42	9 15	1 03	17 23	1 34	17 05	1 12	14 06	7 28	22 13	0 05	12 29	2 11
24 Tu	0 27	17 43	1 36	18 32	9 53	1 11	17 47	1 38	16 54	1 13	13 56	7 29	22 12	0 05	12 31	2 11
25 W	0 50	19 07	2 37	19 28	10 32	1 19	18 11	1 42	16 44	1 13	13 47	7 30	22 12	0 05	12 33	2 11
26 Th	1 13	19 36	3 30	19 30	11 09	1 26	18 34	1 46	16 33	1 14	13 37	7 32	22 11	0 05	12 35	2 10
27 F	1 37	19 12	4 13	18 41	11 45	1 34	18 57	1 51	16 22	1 14	13 28	7 33	22 10	0 05	12 37	2 10
28 Sa	1 60	17 57	4 45	17 02	12 21	1 41	19 20	1 55	16 11	1 15	13 18	7 34	22 09	0 05	12 39	2 10
29 Su	2 23	15 56	5 05	14 40	12 56	1 48	19 42	1 59	15 60	1 15	13 09	7 35	22 08	0 05	12 41	2 10
30 M	2S47	13N13	5S12	11N38	13S30	1S56	20S04	2S02	15N48	1N16	12N60	7N36	22N07	0S05	12S43	2N10

Day	⚷ Decl	⚷ Lat	♅ Decl	♅ Lat	♆ Decl	♆ Lat	♇ Decl	♇ Lat
1	2S09	5N29	3N59	0S43	10S45	0S41	20S03	3N05
6	2 14	5 29	3 55	0 44	10 48	0 41	20 04	3 04
11	2 20	5 28	3 51	0 44	10 50	0 41	20 05	3 03
16	2 26	5 28	3 46	0 44	10 53	0 41	20 07	3 02
21	2 32	5 27	3 42	0 44	10 56	0 41	20 08	3 01
26	2 37	5 26	3 37	0 44	10 59	0 41	20 08	2 60

Day	⚴ Decl	⚴ Lat	⚵ Decl	⚵ Lat	⚶ Decl	⚶ Lat	Eris Decl	Eris Lat
1	5S59	27S40	8S30	10N38	15N47	3N02	3S18	13S04
6	6 38	27 54	9 11	10 07	15 05	3 08	3 19	13 05
11	7 20	28 07	9 50	9 34	14 23	3 15	3 20	13 05
16	8 04	28 21	10 28	9 00	13 39	3 21	3 21	13 05
21	8 49	28 33	11 03	8 27	12 55	3 28	3 22	13 05
26	9 36	28 46	11 36	7 54	12 10	3 35	3 23	13 05

Moon Phenomena

Max/0 Decl (dy hr mn)	
6 2:57	0 S
12 18:41	19S41
19 1:52	0 N
26 1:01	19N36

Perigee/Apogee (dy hr m)		kilometers
15 16:34	p	367392
27 18:23	a	404306

PH	dy hr mn	
●	5 11:37	13♍04
☽	12 17:09	20♐06
○	19 11:14	26♓41
☾	27 3:57	4♋13

Max/0 Lat (dy hr mn)	
2 19:10	5S04
9 17:30	0 N
16 2:25	5N08
22 13:49	0 S
30 0:15	5S12

Void of Course Moon

Last Aspect		☽ Ingress	
1 0:08	♀ □	♌	2 0:02
3 17:53	♀ ⚹	♍	4 10:45
6 10:11	☿ ☌	♎	6 19:14
8 20:47	♀ ☌	♏	9 1:45
10 9:22	☉ ⚹	♐	11 6:37
12 17:09	☉ □	♑	13 9:57
14 23:18	☉ △	♒	15 12:06
16 8:20	♂ ☍	♓	17 13:59
19 11:14	☉ ☍	♈	19 16:59
21 1:26	☿ ☍	♉	21 22:34
23 7:14	♃ ⚹	♊	24 7:35
26 11:22	☿ △	♋	26 19:26
29 7:31	☿ □	♌	29 7:58

DAILY ASPECTARIAN

☽□♀ 0:08; ☽∥⚳ 0:37; ☽⚼♆ 1:39; ☉△♇ 8:47; ☉∠☽ 12:30; ♀⚼♆ 15:21; ☽⚼⚷ 17:07

☽⚺⚳ 4:21; ☽∠☿ 5:22; ☽☌♂ 6:37; ☉⋕♀ 6:40; ☽⚻♆ 7:34; ☽□♄ 14:28; ☿∠♂ 17:36; ☽⚻♇ 18:01; ☉⚺☽ 20:54; ☽⚻⚷ 22:46; ☽△♅ 23:10

♂⚻♆ 0:01; ☽⋕♄ 3:19; ☽⚺♃ 4:26; ☽⋕♆ 10:46; ☽⚺☿ 15:57; ☽⚹♀ 17:53; ☉☍⚷ 19:15; ☽⚼♇ 23:18

☽⋕♀ 0:22; ☉⚻♅ 0:29; ☽⚼♅ 4:18; ☽∠♃ 9:56; ☉∥☽ 10:39; ♂⋕♇ 13:41; ☽☌⚳ 17:06; ☽☍♆ 17:53; ☽⚺♂ 20:12; ☿∠♄ 21:43; ☿∥♅ 23:39

5 Th ☽⚹♄ 1:02; ☽∠♀ 1:40; ☿⚺♀ 3:53; ☽△♇ 4:01; ☽∥♅ 4:56; ☽∥☿ 6:07; ☽☍⚷ 8:24; ☽⚻♅ 8:51; ☉☌☽ 11:37; ⚳☍♆ 13:20; ☽⋕⚷ 14:32; ☽⚹♃ 14:50

6 F ☽∠♂ 2:00; ☽∠♄ 5:28; ☽⚺♀ 8:41; ☽☌☿ 10:11; ☽∥⚷ 15:23; ☽⋕☿ 17:11

7 Sa ☽⋕♅ 0:30; ☽⚻♆ 1:59; ☿⋕⚷ 3:00; ☽⚺⚳ 3:23; ☽⚹♂ 7:12; ☽⚺♄ 9:22; ☉⋕☽ 11:43; ☽□♇ 11:50; ☉⚹♃ 13:48; ☽⚻⚷ 15:54; ☽☍♅ 16:23; ☽□♃ 23:00; ☉⚺☽ 23:37

8 Su ♀⚼⚷ 0:25; ☽⚼♆ 5:18; ☽∠⚳ 7:43; ♀∥♆ 8:37; ☽∥♆ 16:47; ☽∥♀ 17:56; ☽⚼⚷ 18:57; ☽☌♀ 20:47

9 M ☽∥♄ 0:28; ☽⚺☿ 0:59; ☉∠☽ 4:45; ☿ ♎ 7:08; ☽△♆ 8:11; ♂□♄ 11:07; ☽⚹⚳ 11:33; ☽☌♄ 15:48; ☽□♂ 16:00; ☽⚹♇ 17:49; ☽△⚷ 21:35; ☽⚻♅ 22:07

10 Tu ⚶ ♍ 5:10; ☽△♃ 5:18; ☽⋕⚳ 6:48; ☽∠☿ 7:20; ☉⚹☽ 9:22; ☽∠♇ 20:11

11 W ♀∥♄ 0:17; ☽⚼♅ 0:22; ♀ ♏ 6:17; ☽⚺♀ 6:38; ♂⚻♇ 6:41; ☽⚼♃ 7:49; ☿⚻♆ 10:44; ☽□♆ 12:45; ☽⚹☿ 13:02; ⚴ ♌ 13:53; ☽⋕♂ 16:57; ☽□⚳ 17:54; ☽⚺♄ 20:35; ☽⚺♇ 22:11; ☽△♂ 22:55

12 Th ☽□⚷ 1:41; ☽△♅ 2:14; ☽⚻♃ 9:56; ☽∠♀ 10:48; ☉□☽ 17:09; ☽∠♄ 22:25; ☉∥♅ 23:50

13 F ☽⚼♂ 1:43; ☿∥⚷ 5:06; ☽⚹♀ 14:31; ☽⚹♆ 15:50; ☿⚺⚳ 21:53; ☽△⚳ 22:37; ☽□☿ 22:41; ☽⚹♄ 23:53

14 Sa ☽☌♇ 1:05; ☽⋕♂ 2:11; ☽⚻♂ 4:09; ☽⚹⚷ 4:22; ☽□♅ 4:56; ♀△♆ 6:34; ♂⚻⚷ 8:32; ☉⋕☿ 10:04; ☿⚺♄ 10:14; ☽☍♃ 13:07; ☽∠♆ 16:55; ☿□♇ 20:30; ♂△♅ 20:58; ☉△☽ 23:18

15 Su ☽⚼⚳ 0:30; ☿⋕♅ 2:59; ☽∠⚷ 5:18; ☽⋕⚳ 11:21; ☽⚺♆ 17:49; ☽∥♀ 18:43; ☽□♀ 20:56

16 M ⚳⚹♄ 0:59; ☿⚻⚷ 1:16; ☉⚼☽ 2:01; ☽□♄ 2:11; ☽⚻⚳ 2:13; ☽⚺♇ 3:02; ☉∠♄ 4:52; ☽⚺⚷ 6:07; ☿☍♅ 6:42; ☽⚹♅ 6:43; ☽△☿ 6:43; ☽∥♄ 8:03; ☽☍♂ 8:20; ☉⋕⚷ 13:39; ☽⚻♃ 15:29; ☽∥♆ 16:16

17 Tu ☽∠♇ 3:57; ⚳△♇ 4:07; ☉⚻☽ 4:45; ☿⚹♂ 7:18; ☽∠♅ 7:36; ♀⋕⚳ 8:49; ☽⚼☿ 10:38; ☽⚼♃ 16:44; ☽☌♆ 19:39; ☽∥☿ 20:30

18 W ☽△♀ 3:16; ☽△♄ 4:34; ☽⚹♇ 5:05; ☽☍⚳ 5:54; ☽⋕♅ 6:51; ☽☌⚷ 8:04; ☽⚺♅ 8:42; ☽⚻♂ 12:47; ☽∥⚷ 13:16; ☽⚻☿ 14:52; ☉⋕☽ 17:43; ☽△♃ 18:17; ♀☌♄ 20:55

19 Th ♀⚹♇ 1:52; ☽⚼♄ 6:16; ☽⚼♀ 7:01; ☉∥☽ 8:49; ☉☍☽ 11:14; ☽⋕⚷ 14:42; ☽⚼♂ 15:41; ☽∥♅ 21:02; ☽⚺♆ 22:47

20 F ☿□♃ 2:22; ♀⚹⚳ 8:03; ☽⚻♄ 8:33; ☽□♇ 8:43; ☽⚻⚳ 11:22; ☽⚻♀ 11:33; ☽⚺⚷ 11:40; ☽☌♅ 12:21; ♀△⚷ 12:58; ♇ D 15:30; ☽△♂ 19:19; ☽⋕☿ 19:19; ⚳☍⚷ 19:46; ♀⚻♅ 20:54; ☽□♃ 23:07

21 Sa ☿⚼♆ 0:08; ☽∠♆ 1:18; ☽☍☿ 1:26; ♄⚹♇ 5:46; ☽⋕♆ 14:26; ☽∠⚷ 14:32; ⚳⚻♅ 14:52; ☽⚼⚳ 15:16; ☉⚻☽ 20:46

22 Su ☽⋕♄ 0:31; ☽⚹♆ 4:38; ♀⋕♂ 12:06; ☽∥⚳ 13:15; ☽△♇ 15:18; ☽☍♄ 15:34; ☽⚹⚷ 18:15; ☽⚺♅ 19:00; ☽△⚳ 20:08; ☉ ♎ 20:45; ☽☍♀ 23:42

23 M ☉⚼☽ 3:09; ☽□♂ 5:27; ☽⚹♃ 7:14; ☽∥♂ 15:02; ☽⚻☿ 16:20; ☽⚼♇ 19:54; ☽∠♅ 23:38

24 Tu ☽⋕♀ 1:02; ⚵ D 7:18; ☉△☽ 10:37; ☽∠♃ 12:37; ☽□♆ 13:55

25 W ☽⚻♇ 1:18; ☽⚼☿ 1:28; ☽⚻♄ 2:05; ♂⚺♃ 2:53; ☽□⚷ 4:13; ☽⚹♅ 5:02; ☽□⚳ 8:41; ☽⚻♀ 16:16; ☿∥♆ 17:13; ☽⚺♃ 18:42; ☽⚹♂ 19:23

26 Th ☿⚼⚷ 0:59; ☉⚻♆ 2:52; ☉∠♂ 7:15; ☽⚼♄ 8:21; ☽△☿ 11:22; ♀△♃ 21:02

27 F ☽⚼♀ 1:38; ☽△♆ 1:50; ☽∠♂ 3:16; ☉□☽ 3:57; ☽⋕♀ 4:30; ☽☍♇ 13:38; ☽△♄ 14:57; ☽△⚷ 16:22; ☽□♅ 17:13; ☽⚹⚳ 23:31

28 Sa ☽☌♃ 7:54; ☽⚼♆ 8:07; ☽△♀ 11:09; ☽⚺♂ 11:16; ☿∥♄ 13:01; ♀□♂ 13:33; ☽⚼⚷ 22:32; ☿∠⚳ 23:14; ☽∥♂ 23:23

29 Su ♃⚼♆ 2:39; ☽∠⚳ 6:55; ☿⋕⚳ 6:58; ☽□☿ 7:31; ☿ ♏ 11:39; ☽⚻♆ 14:11; ☉∥⚷ 18:46; ☉⚹☽ 21:44; ☽⋕☿ 22:04

30 M ☽∥⚳ 1:52; ☽⚻♇ 1:55; ☽□♄ 3:43; ☽⋕♄ 3:48; ☽⚻⚷ 4:22; ☽△♅ 5:12; ♀∥♇ 5:28; ☽⚺⚳ 13:50; ☽⋕♆ 16:22; ☽⚺♃ 20:15

October 2013

LONGITUDE

Day	Sid.Time	☉	☽	☽ 12 hour	Mean☊	True☊	☿	♀	♂	⚳	♃	♄	⚷	♅	♆	♇
	h m s	° ' "	° ' "	° ' "	° '	° '	° '	° '	° '	° '	° '	° '	° '	° '	° '	° '
1 Tu	0 39 34	7♎58 45	20♌14 31	26♌25 34	9♏08.3	8♏07.6	1♏55.8	22♏29.6	21♌15.1	15♍14.6	18♋20.2	10♏00.4	10♓12.9	10♈38.1	3♓04.8	9♑01.1
2 W	0 43 30	8 57 46	2♍40 25	8♍59 17	9 05.1	8R 02.8	3 10.5	23 36.8	21 51.8	15 41.5	18 26.8	10 06.9	10R 10.5	10R 35.7	3R 03.5	9 01.4
3 Th	0 47 27	9 56 49	15 22 19	21 49 37	9 02.0	7 57.9	4 23.6	24 43.8	22 28.4	16 08.5	18 33.2	10 13.4	10 08.1	10 33.3	3 02.3	9 01.8
4 F	0 51 24	10 55 55	28 21 09	4♎56 51	8 58.8	7 53.7	5 35.0	25 50.7	23 05.0	16 35.4	18 39.5	10 20.0	10 05.8	10 30.8	3 01.1	9 02.2
5 Sa	0 55 20	11 55 02	11♎36 36	18 20 12	8 55.6	7 50.5	6 44.7	26 57.5	23 41.5	17 02.3	18 45.7	10 26.6	10 03.5	10 28.4	2 59.9	9 02.6
6 Su	0 59 17	12 54 12	25 07 24	1♏57 56	8 52.4	7D 48.7	7 52.5	28 04.1	24 18.0	17 29.1	18 51.7	10 33.2	10 01.2	10 26.0	2 58.7	9 03.0
7 M	1 03 13	13 53 23	8♏51 27	15 47 40	8 49.3	7 48.1	8 58.3	29 10.5	24 54.4	17 56.0	18 57.5	10 39.9	9 59.0	10 23.6	2 57.5	9 03.5
8 Tu	1 07 10	14 52 37	22 46 14	29 46 47	8 46.1	7 48.7	10 01.8	0♐16.8	25 30.8	18 22.7	19 03.2	10 46.6	9 56.8	10 21.1	2 56.4	9 04.1
9 W	1 11 06	15 51 52	6♐49 02	13♐52 39	8 42.9	7 50.0	11 03.0	1 22.9	26 07.0	18 49.5	19 08.7	10 53.3	9 54.6	10 18.7	2 55.3	9 04.6
10 Th	1 15 03	16 51 09	20 57 19	28 02 45	8 39.7	7 51.4	12 01.5	2 28.8	26 43.3	19 16.2	19 14.1	11 00.1	9 52.5	10 16.3	2 54.2	9 05.2
11 F	1 18 59	17 50 28	5♑08 41	12♑14 51	8 36.5	7R 52.5	12 57.3	3 34.6	27 19.4	19 42.9	19 19.2	11 06.9	9 50.4	10 13.9	2 53.2	9 05.8
12 Sa	1 22 56	18 49 49	19 20 57	26 26 45	8 33.4	7 52.9	13 49.9	4 40.2	27 55.5	20 09.6	19 24.2	11 13.7	9 48.4	10 11.5	2 52.1	9 06.4
13 Su	1 26 53	19 49 12	3♒31 57	10♒36 16	8 30.2	7 52.4	14 39.1	5 45.6	28 31.5	20 36.2	19 29.1	11 20.6	9 46.4	10 09.1	2 51.1	9 07.1
14 M	1 30 49	20 48 36	17 39 24	24 41 03	8 27.0	7 51.1	15 24.6	6 50.8	29 07.5	21 02.8	19 33.7	11 27.5	9 44.4	10 06.8	2 50.2	9 07.8
15 Tu	1 34 46	21 48 01	1♓40 52	8♓38 33	8 23.8	7 49.2	16 05.9	7 55.7	29 43.4	21 29.3	19 38.2	11 34.4	9 42.5	10 04.4	2 49.2	9 08.6
16 W	1 38 42	22 47 29	15 33 46	22 26 11	8 20.7	7 47.2	16 42.8	9 00.5	0♍19.3	21 55.8	19 42.6	11 41.3	9 40.6	10 02.1	2 48.3	9 09.3
17 Th	1 42 39	23 46 58	29 15 30	6♈01 26	8 17.5	7 45.2	17 14.7	10 05.0	0 55.0	22 22.2	19 46.7	11 48.3	9 38.8	9 59.7	2 47.4	9 10.1
18 F	1 46 35	24 46 30	12♈43 45	19 22 14	8 14.3	7 43.7	17 41.2	11 09.4	1 30.8	22 48.7	19 50.7	11 55.2	9 37.0	9 57.4	2 46.5	9 10.9
19 Sa	1 50 32	25 46 03	25 56 44	2♉27 10	8 11.1	7D 42.8	18 01.8	12 13.4	2 06.4	23 15.0	19 54.5	12 02.2	9 35.3	9 55.1	2 45.7	9 11.8
20 Su	1 54 28	26 45 38	8♉53 28	15 15 40	8 07.9	7 42.5	18 15.9	13 17.3	2 42.0	23 41.4	19 58.1	12 09.2	9 33.6	9 52.8	2 44.9	9 12.7
21 M	1 58 25	27 45 16	21 33 53	27 48 15	8 04.8	7 42.9	18R 22.9	14 20.8	3 17.5	24 07.6	20 01.5	12 16.3	9 31.9	9 50.5	2 44.1	9 13.6
22 Tu	2 02 21	28 44 55	3♊58 59	10♊06 23	8 01.6	7 43.5	18 22.4	15 24.2	3 53.0	24 33.9	20 04.7	12 23.3	9 30.4	9 48.3	2 43.3	9 14.5
23 W	2 06 18	29 44 37	16 10 46	22 12 31	7 58.4	7 44.4	18 13.8	16 27.2	4 28.4	25 00.1	20 07.8	12 30.4	9 28.8	9 46.0	2 42.6	9 15.5
24 Th	2 10 15	0♏44 21	28 12 05	4♋09 56	7 55.2	7 45.2	17 56.7	17 30.0	5 03.7	25 26.2	20 10.7	12 37.5	9 27.3	9 43.8	2 41.9	9 16.5
25 F	2 14 11	1 44 07	10♋06 34	16 02 32	7 52.1	7 45.9	17 30.6	18 32.6	5 39.0	25 52.3	20 13.4	12 44.6	9 25.9	9 41.6	2 41.3	9 17.5
26 Sa	2 18 08	2 43 55	21 58 24	27 54 45	7 48.9	7 46.3	16 55.5	19 34.8	6 14.2	26 18.4	20 15.9	12 51.7	9 24.5	9 39.4	2 40.6	9 18.5
27 Su	2 22 04	3 43 46	3♌52 09	9♌51 12	7 45.7	7R 46.4	16 11.4	20 36.7	6 49.3	26 44.4	20 18.2	12 58.9	9 23.1	9 37.3	2 40.0	9 19.6
28 M	2 26 01	4 43 39	15 52 30	21 56 36	7 42.5	7 46.3	15 18.6	21 38.3	7 24.3	27 10.3	20 20.3	13 06.0	9 21.8	9 35.1	2 39.5	9 20.7
29 Tu	2 29 57	5 43 33	28 04 03	4♍15 22	7 39.3	7 46.1	14 17.7	22 39.6	7 59.3	27 36.2	20 22.2	13 13.2	9 20.6	9 33.0	2 38.9	9 21.9
30 W	2 33 54	6 43 30	10♍31 00	16 51 22	7 36.2	7 46.0	13 10.0	23 40.6	8 34.2	28 02.0	20 23.9	13 20.3	9 19.4	9 30.9	2 38.4	9 23.0
31 Th	2 37 50	7♏43 30	23 16 49	29 47 35	7♏33.0	7♏45.9	11♏57.0	24♐41.2	9♍09.0	28♍27.8	20♋25.5	13♏27.5	9♓18.2	9♈28.9	2♓37.9	9♑24.2

1st of Month

Julian Day # 2456566.5
Obliquity 23°26'08"
SVP 5♓03'5
GC 27♐01.
Eris 22♈32.5

Day	⚴
1	10♌40.3
6	13 19.1
11	15 54.7
16	18 26.8
21	20 54.9
26	23 18.8
31	25 37.9

Day	⚵
1	4♒00.2
6	4 19.6
11	4 49.0
16	5 28.0
21	6 16.0
26	7 12.6
31	8 17.2

Day	⚶
1	9♍34.6
6	11 52.2
11	14 09.3
16	16 25.7
21	18 41.5
26	20 56.5
31	23 10.5

DECLINATION and LATITUDE

Day	☉ Decl	☽ Decl	☽ Lat	☽ 12h Decl	☿ Decl	☿ Lat	♀ Decl	♀ Lat	♂ Decl	♂ Lat	⚳ Decl	⚳ Lat	♃ Decl	♃ Lat	♄ Decl	♄ Lat
1 Tu	3S10	9N54	5S06	8N03	14S04	2S03	20S26	2S06	15N37	1N16	12N50	7N37	22N06	0S04	12S46	2N10
2 W	3 33	6 06	4 48	4 03	14 36	2 09	20 47	2 10	15 26	1 17	12 41	7 39	22 06	0 04	12 48	2 10
3 Th	3 56	1 56	4 09	0S13	15 07	2 16	21 07	2 14	15 14	1 17	12 31	7 40	22 05	0 04	12 50	2 10
4 F	4 20	2S24	3 20	4 35	15 37	2 23	21 27	2 18	15 03	1 18	12 22	7 41	22 04	0 04	12 52	2 09
5 Sa	4 43	6 43	2 19	8 48	16 07	2 29	21 46	2 22	14 51	1 19	12 12	7 42	22 03	0 04	12 54	2 09
6 Su	5 06	10 48	1 09	12 39	16 35	2 35	22 05	2 26	14 40	1 19	12 03	7 44	22 03	0 04	12 56	2 09
7 M	5 29	14 21	0N06	15 52	17 01	2 41	22 24	2 29	14 28	1 20	11 53	7 45	22 02	0 04	12 59	2 09
8 Tu	5 52	17 09	1 22	18 11	17 27	2 46	22 42	2 33	14 16	1 20	11 44	7 46	22 01	0 04	13 01	2 09
9 W	6 14	18 56	2 33	19 23	17 51	2 51	22 59	2 37	14 05	1 21	11 35	7 47	22 01	0 04	13 03	2 09
10 Th	6 37	19 32	3 36	19 23	18 14	2 56	23 16	2 40	13 53	1 21	11 25	7 49	21 60	0 04	13 05	2 09
11 F	6 60	18 55	4 26	18 09	18 35	3 00	23 33	2 44	13 41	1 22	11 16	7 50	21 59	0 03	13 07	2 09
12 Sa	7 23	17 06	4 59	15 48	18 55	3 04	23 48	2 47	13 29	1 22	11 07	7 51	21 59	0 03	13 09	2 09
13 Su	7 45	14 15	5 15	12 31	19 13	3 08	24 04	2 50	13 17	1 23	10 57	7 52	21 58	0 03	13 12	2 08
14 M	8 07	10 36	5 11	8 32	19 29	3 10	24 18	2 54	13 05	1 23	10 48	7 54	21 58	0 03	13 14	2 08
15 Tu	8 30	6 22	4 49	4 08	19 43	3 13	24 32	2 57	12 53	1 24	10 39	7 55	21 57	0 03	13 16	2 08
16 W	8 52	1 51	4 10	0N27	19 56	3 14	24 46	3 00	12 41	1 25	10 29	7 56	21 56	0 03	13 18	2 08
17 Th	9 14	2N43	3 17	4 56	20 05	3 15	24 59	3 03	12 28	1 25	10 20	7 58	21 56	0 03	13 20	2 08
18 F	9 36	7 05	2 14	9 07	20 13	3 14	25 11	3 06	12 16	1 26	10 11	7 59	21 56	0 03	13 23	2 08
19 Sa	9 57	11 02	1 05	12 47	20 17	3 13	25 23	3 09	12 04	1 26	10 02	8 01	21 55	0 03	13 25	2 08
20 Su	10 19	14 21	0S07	15 45	20 19	3 11	25 34	3 12	11 52	1 27	9 52	8 02	21 55	0 02	13 27	2 08
21 M	10 40	16 56	1 16	17 54	20 18	3 08	25 45	3 15	11 39	1 27	9 43	8 03	21 54	0 02	13 29	2 08
22 Tu	11 02	18 38	2 21	19 09	20 13	3 03	25 54	3 17	11 27	1 28	9 34	8 05	21 54	0 02	13 31	2 08
23 W	11 23	19 27	3 18	19 30	20 05	2 57	26 04	3 20	11 14	1 28	9 25	8 06	21 54	0 02	13 34	2 08
24 Th	11 44	19 21	4 05	18 58	19 53	2 49	26 12	3 23	11 02	1 29	9 16	8 08	21 53	0 02	13 36	2 08
25 F	12 05	18 23	4 41	17 35	19 36	2 40	26 21	3 25	10 49	1 29	9 07	8 09	21 53	0 02	13 38	2 08
26 Sa	12 25	16 37	5 05	15 28	19 16	2 29	26 28	3 27	10 37	1 30	8 58	8 11	21 53	0 02	13 40	2 07
27 Su	12 46	14 09	5 17	12 41	18 51	2 16	26 35	3 29	10 24	1 31	8 49	8 12	21 52	0 02	13 42	2 07
28 M	13 06	11 04	5 14	9 20	18 21	2 01	26 41	3 31	10 12	1 31	8 40	8 13	21 52	0 02	13 45	2 07
29 Tu	13 26	7 29	4 58	5 32	17 48	1 45	26 47	3 33	9 59	1 32	8 31	8 15	21 52	0 01	13 47	2 07
30 W	13 46	3 30	4 27	1 24	17 11	1 27	26 52	3 35	9 47	1 32	8 22	8 16	21 52	0 01	13 49	2 07
31 Th	14S05	0S44	3S43	2S54	16S30	1S08	26S56	3S37	9N34	1N33	8N13	8N18	21N52	0S01	13S51	2N07

Day	⚷ Decl	⚷ Lat	♅ Decl	♅ Lat	♆ Decl	♆ Lat	♇ Decl	♇ Lat
1	2S43	5N25	3N32	0S44	11S01	0S41	20S09	2N5
6	2 48	5 24	3 28	0 44	11 03	0 41	20 10	2 5
11	2 53	5 23	3 23	0 44	11 05	0 41	20 11	2 5
16	2 58	5 21	3 18	0 44	11 07	0 41	20 12	2 5
21	3 03	5 20	3 14	0 43	11 08	0 41	20 12	2 5
26	3 07	5 18	3 10	0 43	11 09	0 41	20 13	2 5
31	3S11	5N17	3N06	0S43	11S10	0S41	20S13	2N5

Day	⚴ Decl	⚴ Lat	⚵ Decl	⚵ Lat	⚶ Decl	⚶ Lat	Eris Decl	Eris Lat
1	10S24	28S58	12S05	7N22	11N24	3N42	3S24	13S
6	11 13	29 10	12 32	6 50	10 38	3 49	3 25	13
11	12 03	29 22	12 55	6 19	9 53	3 57	3 26	13
16	12 53	29 33	13 15	5 50	9 07	4 05	3 27	13
21	13 44	29 44	13 31	5 21	8 21	4 13	3 28	13
26	14 35	29 55	13 44	4 54	7 35	4 21	3 29	13
31	15S25	30S06	13S53	4N27	6N50	4N30	3S29	13S

Moon Phenomena

Max/0 Decl
dy hr mn
3 10:47 0 S
9 23:50 19S32
16 9:41 0 N
23 9:13 19N31
30 19:52 0 S

Max/0 Lat
dy hr mn
6 22:10 0 N
13 7:17 5N16
19 21:47 0 S
27 7:49 5S17

Perigee/Apogee
dy hr m kilometers
10 23:10 p 369814
25 14:27 a 404555

PH dy hr mn
● 5 0:36 11♎56
☽ 11 23:03 18♑47
○ 18 23:39 25♈45
18 23:51 A 0.765
☾ 26 23:42 3♌43

Void of Course Moon

Last Aspect			☽ Ingress		
1 4:49	♀	□	♍	1	18:5
3 18:59	♀	⚹	♎	4	3:0
5 22:29	♂	⚹	♏	6	8:3
8 4:55	♂	□	♐	8	12:2
10 10:12	♂	△	♑	10	15:1
12 0:06	♃	☍	♒	12	18:0
14 20:29	♂	☍	♓	14	21:0
16 7:16	♃	△	♈	17	1:1
18 23:39	☉	☍	♉	19	7:2
20 21:03	♃	⚹	♊	21	16:1
23 0:36	♀	☍	♋	24	3:3
25 20:32	♃	☌	♌	26	16:1
28 12:27	♀	△	♍	29	3:4
31 2:49	♀	□	♎	31	12:2

DAILY ASPECTARIAN

1 Tu ☽☌♂ 2:04; ☽□♀ 4:49; ☉∠☽ 5:47; ☽⚼♇ 7:21; ⚳⋕♄ 9:16; ☽⚼♅ 10:26; ☿△♆ 21:47; ☉⋕♅ 22:17

2 W ☽☍♆ 0:44; ☽⚹☿ 1:04; ☉□♇ 1:29; ☽∠♃ 1:29; ♀∠♇ 8:51; ♄△⚷ 9:38; ☽△♇ 12:04; ☉⚺☽ 12:57; ☉⋕☽ 13:36; ☽☍⚷ 14:12; ☽⚹♄ 14:15; ☽⚻♅ 14:59; ☽∥♅ 15:05; ☽⋕⚷ 19:26

3 Th ☽☌⚳ 1:29; ☿⋕♂ 4:08; ☉⚻⚷ 4:25; ☽⚹♃ 5:59; ☉⚺♄ 7:36; ☽∠☿ 8:15; ☽⚺♂ 13:51; ☉☍♅ 14:13; ♀⚼♅ 17:06; ☽∠♄ 18:25; ☽⚹♀ 18:59

4 F ☽∥⚷ 2:02; ☽⋕♅ 5:59; ☽⚻♆ 8:29; ☉∥☽ 11:39; ☽⚺☿ 14:25; ☉∠♀ 16:18; ☽∠♂ 18:30; ☽□♇ 19:23; ☽⚻⚷ 21:13; ☽⚺♄ 21:53; ☽☍♅ 21:58

5 Sa ☉☌☽ 0:36; ☽∠♀ 0:41; ♄⚻♅ 4:47; ☽⚺⚳ 10:01; ☽⚼♆ 11:23; ☽□♃ 12:51; ♂⚼♇ 14:01; ♀⋕♃ 20:31; ☽⚹♂ 22:29; ☽⚼⚷ 23:49

6 Su ☽∥♆ 1:37; ☽⚺♀ 5:38; ☽⋕⚳ 7:39; ☽∠⚳ 13:21; ☽△♆ 13:45; ☽∥♄ 14:04

7 M ☽☌☿ 0:13; ☽⚹♇ 0:21; ☽⋕♂ 0:47; ☽△⚷ 1:57; ☿⚹♇ 1:58; ☽⚻♅ 2:39; ☽☌♄ 3:10; ☉⚺☽ 9:23; ☽⚹⚳ 16:12; ☽△♃ 17:34; ♀ ♐ 17:55; ♂⚼♅ 18:03; ☿△⚷ 22:08

8 Tu ☽∠♇ 2:14; ☽∥☿ 4:00; ☽⚼♅ 4:25; ☽□♂ 4:55; ☿⚻♅ 7:12; ☉∠☽ 13:05; ☽☌♀ 13:57; ☽□♆ 17:22; ☽⚼♃ 19:25; ☿☌♄ 19:40

9 W ☽⚺♇ 3:51; ☽□⚷ 5:15; ☽△♅ 5:56; ☽⚺♄ 6:59; ☽⚺☿ 7:44; ☉⚹☽ 16:32; ☽□⚳ 21:03; ☽⚻♃ 21:04; ⚳⚹♃ 21:34

10 Th ☽∠♄ 8:37; ♀□♆ 9:06; ☽△♂ 10:12; ☽∠☿ 11:00; ☽⚹♆ 20:11; ☽⚺♀ 21:08

11 F ☉⚼♆ 1:04; ☽∥☿ 4:34; ☽☌♇ 6:41; ☽⚹⚷ 7:55; ☽□♅ 8:34; ☽⚹♄ 10:10; ☽⚼♂ 12:40; ☽⚹☿ 14:04; ♀⚼♃ 17:41; ☽∠♆ 21:30; ☉□☽ 23:03

12 Sa ☽☍♃ 0:06; ☽∠♀ 0:35; ☽△⚳ 1:25; ⚳⋕♆ 2:49; ☽∠⚷ 9:12; ☽⚻♂ 15:09; ☉□♃ 15:10; ☽⚺♆ 22:51

13 Su ☽⚼⚳ 3:37; ☽⚹♀ 4:05; ☽⋕♂ 7:18; ☽∥♄ 7:23; ♂⋕♄ 8:40; ☽⚺♇ 9:29; ☽⚺⚷ 10:34; ☽⚹♅ 11:12; ☽□♄ 13:22; ☽□☿ 19:58; ☽∥♆ 20:56; ☽⋕⚳ 22:44

14 M ☽⚻♃ 3:16; ☉△☽ 5:47; ☽⚻⚳ 5:58; ☉⚺⚳ 10:21; ☽∠♇ 11:04; ☽∠♅ 12:42; ☉∥☽ 13:12; ☽☍♂ 20:29

15 Tu ☽☌♆ 1:57; ☽⚼♃ 5:07; ☉⚼☽ 9:30; ♂ ♍ 11:06; ☽□♀ 11:41; ☽⚹♇ 12:53; ☽☌⚷ 13:49; ☽⚺♅ 14:26; ☽⋕♅ 16:20; ☽△♄ 17:13; ☽∥⚷ 18:08

16 W ☽△☿ 2:05; ♀⚺♇ 3:19; ☽△♃ 7:16; ☽☍⚳ 11:29; ☉⚻☽ 13:36; ♀□⚷ 14:30; ☽⚼♄ 19:38; ♀△♅ 22:05

17 Th ☽⋕⚷ 1:27; ☽∥♅ 3:03; ☽⚻♂ 3:04; ☽⚼☿ 5:29; ☽⚺♆ 6:15; ☽□♇ 17:38; ☽⚺⚷ 18:26; ☽☌♅ 19:02; ☉⚼⚷ 20:17; ☿∥♇ 20:36; ☽△♀ 20:56; ☽⚻♄ 22:32

18 F ☽⚼♂ 7:09; ☽∠♆ 9:06; ☽⚻☿ 9:12; ☽□♃ 12:55; ☉⋕☽ 16:27; ☽∥⚳ 17:51; ☽⚻⚳ 18:54; ♀⚺♄ 19:17; ☽∠⚷ 21:31; ☉☍☽ 23:39

19 Sa ☽⋕♆ 0:41; ☽⚼♀ 2:33; ☉⋕⚳ 3:20; ☽∥♂ 6:36; ☽△♂ 11:54; ☽⚹♆ 12:34; ☽⋕♄ 16:53; ☽⚼⚳ 23:37

20 Su ☽△♇ 0:36; ☽⚹⚷ 1:15; ☽⚺♅ 1:51; ♂☍♆ 1:54; ☽☍♄ 6:11; ☽⚻♀ 9:01; ☽☍☿ 17:53; ☽⚹♃ 21:03

21 M ☽△⚳ 5:06; ☽⚼♇ 5:07; ☽∠♅ 6:16; ☿ R 10:30; ☉⚻☽ 12:56; ☽□♆ 21:33; ☽□♂ 23:48

22 Tu ☽∠♃ 2:09; ☿∥♇ 3:05; ☉∥♆ 7:51; ☽⚻♇ 10:19; ☽□⚷ 10:48; ☽⚹♅ 11:22; ☽⚻♄ 16:40; ☉⋕♂ 17:58; ☉⚼☽ 20:54

23 W ☽☍♀ 0:36; ☽⚻☿ 4:00; ☉ ♏ 6:11; ☽⚺♃ 7:53; ♂⋕♆ 10:37; ☽□⚳ 18:15; ☽⚼♄ 22:50

24 Th ♂∠♃ 5:09; ☉△☽ 5:34; ☿⚺♀ 7:28; ☽△♆ 9:02; ☽⚼☿ 9:14; ☽⚹♂ 14:32; ☽☍♇ 22:21; ☽△⚷ 22:38; ☽□♅ 23:10

25 F ☽△♄ 5:23; ☽△☿ 14:18; ☽⚼♆ 15:19; ☽⚻♀ 18:42; ☽☌♃ 20:32; ☽∠♂ 22:26; ☉△♆ 22:42

26 Sa ☽⚼⚷ 4:55; ☽⚹⚳ 9:05; ♀⚻♃ 16:32; ☽⚻♆ 21:35; ☉□☽ 23:42

27 Su ☽⋕♄ 3:42; ☽⚼♀ 3:50; ☽⚺♂ 6:14; ☉⋕☽ 10:15; ☽⚻♇ 10:58; ☽⚻⚷ 11:03; ☽△♅ 11:30; ♅⋕⚷ 13:08; ☽∠⚳ 16:21; ☽□♄ 18:26; ☽□☿ 22:57; ☽⋕♆ 23:20

28 M ☽∥♂ 6:31; ☽⚺♃ 8:52; ♇⚹⚷ 10:57; ☽△♀ 12:27; ☽⚼♇ 16:45; ☽∥⚳ 17:06; ☽⚼♅ 17:09; ☽⚺⚳ 23:04

29 Tu ☽☍♆ 8:53; ☽∠♃ 14:11; ☉⚹☽ 16:07; ☽☌♂ 20:06; ☿☌♄ 20:49; ☽☍⚷ 21:44; ☽△♇ 21:50; ☽⚻♅ 22:06

30 W ☽⋕⚷ 1:54; ☿∠⚳ 1:59; ☽∥♅ 2:17; ☽⚹☿ 4:36; ☉∥♄ 4:46; ☽⚹♄ 5:25; ☽⚹♃ 18:40; ☉∠☽ 22:53; ⚳∠♄ 23:34

31 Th ☽□♀ 2:49; ♂☍⚷ 6:09; ☽∠☿ 6:11; ☽∠♄ 9:38; ☽☌⚳ 9:53; ♂△♇ 10:51; ♂⚻♅ 12:56; ☽⋕♅ 12:59; ☽∥⚷ 13:33; ☽⚻♆ 17:10; ☿∠♀ 23:49

LONGITUDE

November 2013

Day	Sid.Time	☉	☽	☽ 12 hour	Mean☊	True☊	☿	♀	♂	⚳	♃	♄	⚷	♅	♆	♇
	h m s	° ' "	° ' "	° ' "	° '	° '	° '	° '	° '	° '	° '	° '	° '	° '	° '	° '
1 F	2 41 47	8♏43 31	6♎23 50	13♎05 39	7♏29.8	7♏46.0	10♏40.4	25♐41.5	9♍43.8	28♍53.5	20♋26.8	13♏34.7	9♓17.2	9♈26.8	2♓37.5	9♑25.4
2 Sa	2 45 44	9 43 34	19 52 58	26 45 37	7 26.6	7 46.1	9R 22.6	26 41.4	10 18.5	29 19.2	20 27.9	13 41.9	9R 16.1	9R 24.8	2R 37.1	9 26.7
3 Su	2 49 40	10 43 39	3♏43 20	10♏45 43	7 23.5	7R 46.2	8 05.9	27 40.9	10 53.1	29 44.8	20 28.9	13 49.1	9 15.1	9 22.9	2 36.7	9 27.9
4 M	2 53 37	11 43 47	17 52 16	25 02 24	7 20.3	7 46.1	6 52.7	28 40.0	11 27.6	0♎10.3	20 29.6	13 56.3	9 14.2	9 20.9	2 36.3	9 29.2
5 Tu	2 57 33	12 43 56	2♐15 27	9♐30 41	7 17.1	7 45.8	5 45.5	29 38.7	12 02.0	0 35.8	20 30.2	14 03.5	9 13.4	9 19.0	2 36.0	9 30.5
6 W	3 01 30	13 44 07	16 47 21	24 04 42	7 13.9	7 45.3	4 46.2	0♑37.0	12 36.4	1 01.2	20 30.5	14 10.7	9 12.6	9 17.1	2 35.8	9 31.9
7 Th	3 05 26	14 44 19	1♑21 59	8♑38 30	7 10.7	7 44.5	3 56.5	1 34.9	13 10.6	1 26.5	20R 30.6	14 17.9	9 11.8	9 15.3	2 35.5	9 33.3
8 F	3 09 23	15 44 33	15 53 37	23 06 45	7 07.6	7 43.7	3 17.4	2 32.2	13 44.8	1 51.8	20 30.6	14 25.1	9 11.1	9 13.5	2 35.3	9 34.6
9 Sa	3 13 19	16 44 49	0♒17 27	7♒25 18	7 04.4	7 43.0	2 49.8	3 29.1	14 18.9	2 17.0	20 30.3	14 32.3	9 10.5	9 11.7	2 35.1	9 36.1
10 Su	3 17 16	17 45 05	14 30 00	21 31 19	7 01.2	7D 42.7	2D 33.9	4 25.5	14 52.9	2 42.1	20 29.9	14 39.5	9 09.9	9 09.9	2 35.0	9 37.5
11 M	3 21 13	18 45 24	28 29 06	5♓23 17	6 58.0	7 42.8	2 29.6	5 21.3	15 26.8	3 07.2	20 29.2	14 46.7	9 09.4	9 08.2	2 34.9	9 39.0
12 Tu	3 25 09	19 45 43	12♓13 50	19 00 44	6 54.9	7 43.5	2 36.3	6 16.6	16 00.6	3 32.1	20 28.4	14 53.9	9 08.9	9 06.6	2 34.8	9 40.5
13 W	3 29 06	20 46 04	25 44 02	2♈23 48	6 51.7	7 44.5	2 53.6	7 11.3	16 34.4	3 57.0	20 27.3	15 01.0	9 08.5	9 04.9	2D 34.8	9 42.0
14 Th	3 33 02	21 46 27	9♈00 07	15 33 03	6 48.5	7 45.7	3 20.5	8 05.5	17 08.0	4 21.8	20 26.0	15 08.2	9 08.1	9 03.3	2 34.7	9 43.5
15 F	3 36 59	22 46 50	22 02 41	28 29 06	6 45.3	7 46.7	3 56.3	8 58.9	17 41.6	4 46.5	20 24.6	15 15.4	9 07.8	9 01.8	2 34.8	9 45.0
16 Sa	3 40 55	23 47 16	4♉52 24	11♉12 38	6 42.1	7R 47.3	4 40.0	9 51.8	18 15.0	5 11.2	20 22.9	15 22.5	9 07.6	9 00.2	2 34.8	9 46.6
17 Su	3 44 52	24 47 43	17 29 55	23 44 20	6 39.0	7 47.0	5 30.8	10 43.9	18 48.4	5 35.8	20 21.1	15 29.7	9 07.4	8 58.8	2 34.9	9 48.2
18 M	3 48 48	25 48 11	29 55 59	6♊05 00	6 35.8	7 45.8	6 27.8	11 35.4	19 21.7	6 00.2	20 19.0	15 36.8	9 07.3	8 57.3	2 35.1	9 49.8
19 Tu	3 52 45	26 48 41	12♊11 31	18 15 43	6 32.6	7 43.6	7 30.1	12 26.1	19 54.8	6 24.6	20 16.8	15 43.9	9D 07.2	8 55.9	2 35.2	9 51.5
20 W	3 56 42	27 49 13	24 17 47	0♋17 57	6 29.4	7 40.6	8 37.2	13 16.1	20 27.9	6 48.9	20 14.3	15 51.0	9 07.2	8 54.6	2 35.4	9 53.1
21 Th	4 00 38	28 49 46	6♋16 29	12 13 43	6 26.3	7 37.0	9 48.4	14 05.3	21 00.9	7 13.1	20 11.7	15 58.1	9 07.3	8 53.2	2 35.6	9 54.8
22 F	4 04 35	29 50 21	18 09 59	24 05 40	6 23.1	7 33.3	11 03.0	14 53.7	21 33.8	7 37.3	20 08.9	16 05.2	9 07.4	8 52.0	2 35.9	9 56.5
23 Sa	4 08 31	0♐50 58	0♌01 12	5♌57 03	6 19.9	7 30.0	12 20.6	15 41.2	22 06.5	8 01.3	20 05.8	16 12.3	9 07.6	8 50.7	2 36.2	9 58.2
24 Su	4 12 28	1 51 36	11 53 43	17 51 44	6 16.7	7 27.3	13 40.7	16 27.8	22 39.2	8 25.2	20 02.6	16 19.3	9 07.8	8 49.5	2 36.5	10 00.0
25 M	4 16 24	2 52 16	23 51 40	29 54 05	6 13.6	7D 25.7	15 03.0	17 13.6	23 11.8	8 49.1	19 59.2	16 26.3	9 08.1	8 48.4	2 36.9	10 01.7
26 Tu	4 20 21	3 52 57	5♍59 34	12♍08 44	6 10.4	7 25.4	16 27.1	17 58.3	23 44.2	9 12.8	19 55.6	16 33.3	9 08.4	8 47.3	2 37.3	10 03.5
27 W	4 24 17	4 53 40	18 22 09	24 40 23	6 07.2	7 26.1	17 52.7	18 42.1	24 16.6	9 36.5	19 51.8	16 40.3	9 08.8	8 46.2	2 37.8	10 05.3
28 Th	4 28 14	5 54 25	1♎03 58	7♎33 22	6 04.0	7 27.6	19 19.6	19 24.8	24 48.8	10 00.0	19 47.9	16 47.3	9 09.3	8 45.2	2 38.2	10 07.1
29 F	4 32 11	6 55 11	14 08 59	20 51 06	6 00.8	7 29.3	20 47.5	20 06.5	25 20.9	10 23.4	19 43.7	16 54.2	9 09.8	8 44.3	2 38.7	10 08.9
30 Sa	4 36 07	7♐55 59	27 39 56	4♏35 32	5♏57.7	7♏30.6	22♏16.4	20♑47.0	25♍52.9	10♎46.7	19♋39.4	17♏01.1	9♓10.4	8♈43.4	2♓39.3	10♑10.7

1st of Month

Julian Day #
2456597.5
Obliquity
23°26'08"
SVP 5♓03'50"
GC 27♐01.9
Eris 22♈14.1R

Day	⚴	⚵	⚶
1	26♌05.1	8♒31.1	23♍37.2
6	28 17.8	9 44.7	25 49.9
11	0♍24.5	11 05.4	28 01.2
16	2 24.7	12 32.6	0♎11.0
21	4 17.8	14 05.7	2 19.1
26	6 03.2	15 44.5	4 25.4

DECLINATION and LATITUDE

Day	☉ Decl	☽ Decl	☽ Lat	☽ 12h Decl	☿ Decl	☿ Lat	♀ Decl	♀ Lat	♂ Decl	♂ Lat	⚳ Decl	⚳ Lat	♃ Decl	♃ Lat	♄ Decl	♄ Lat
1 F	14S24	5S04	2S45	7S12	15S47	0S48	26S60	3S38	9N22	1N33	8N04	8N20	21N52	0S01	13S53	2N07
2 Sa	14 44	9 17	1 38	11 16	15 03	0 28	27 03	3 39	9 09	1 34	7 56	8 21	21 52	0 01	13 55	2 07
3 Su	15 02	13 06	0 22	14 47	14 19	0 07	27 05	3 41	8 56	1 34	7 47	8 23	21 52	0 01	13 58	2 07
4 M	15 21	16 16	0N56	17 30	13 36	0N13	27 07	3 42	8 44	1 35	7 38	8 24	21 52	0 01	13 60	2 07
5 Tu	15 39	18 27	2 12	19 07	12 55	0 33	27 09	3 43	8 31	1 36	7 30	8 26	21 52	0 01	14 02	2 07
6 W	15 58	19 28	3 20	19 29	12 18	0 51	27 09	3 43	8 19	1 36	7 21	8 28	21 52	0 00	14 04	2 07
7 Th	16 15	19 10	4 15	18 33	11 45	1 08	27 10	3 44	8 06	1 37	7 13	8 29	21 52	0 00	14 06	2 07
8 F	16 33	17 37	4 54	16 25	11 18	1 24	27 09	3 44	7 53	1 37	7 04	8 31	21 52	0 00	14 08	2 07
9 Sa	16 50	14 58	5 14	13 18	10 56	1 37	27 08	3 45	7 41	1 38	6 56	8 32	21 52	0 00	14 10	2 07
10 Su	17 07	11 27	5 15	9 28	10 39	1 49	27 06	3 45	7 28	1 38	6 47	8 34	21 52	0N00	14 13	2 07
11 M	17 24	7 22	4 56	5 11	10 29	1 59	27 04	3 45	7 15	1 39	6 39	8 36	21 53	0 00	14 15	2 07
12 Tu	17 40	2 57	4 21	0 41	10 24	2 07	27 02	3 45	7 03	1 40	6 31	8 38	21 53	0 00	14 17	2 07
13 W	17 57	1N33	3 32	3N46	10 24	2 13	26 58	3 44	6 50	1 40	6 22	8 39	21 53	0 00	14 19	2 07
14 Th	18 12	5 54	2 33	7 58	10 29	2 17	26 54	3 44	6 38	1 41	6 14	8 41	21 54	0 01	14 21	2 07
15 F	18 28	9 55	1 26	11 44	10 38	2 20	26 50	3 43	6 25	1 41	6 06	8 43	21 54	0 01	14 23	2 07
16 Sa	18 43	13 24	0 16	14 53	10 51	2 22	26 45	3 42	6 12	1 42	5 58	8 44	21 54	0 01	14 25	2 07
17 Su	18 58	16 12	0S53	17 18	11 07	2 22	26 40	3 40	5 60	1 42	5 50	8 46	21 55	0 01	14 27	2 07
18 M	19 12	18 11	1 59	18 51	11 27	2 21	26 34	3 39	5 47	1 43	5 42	8 48	21 55	0 01	14 29	2 07
19 Tu	19 26	19 18	2 59	19 31	11 49	2 20	26 28	3 37	5 35	1 44	5 34	8 50	21 56	0 01	14 31	2 07
20 W	19 40	19 30	3 49	19 16	12 13	2 17	26 21	3 35	5 22	1 44	5 26	8 52	21 56	0 01	14 33	2 07
21 Th	19 54	18 49	4 29	18 09	12 38	2 14	26 13	3 33	5 10	1 45	5 18	8 54	21 57	0 02	14 35	2 07
22 F	20 07	17 18	4 56	16 16	13 05	2 10	26 06	3 31	4 57	1 45	5 11	8 55	21 57	0 02	14 37	2 07
23 Sa	20 19	15 04	5 11	13 42	13 33	2 05	25 58	3 28	4 45	1 46	5 03	8 57	21 58	0 02	14 39	2 07
24 Su	20 32	12 12	5 13	10 34	14 02	2 00	25 49	3 25	4 33	1 46	4 55	8 59	21 58	0 02	14 41	2 07
25 M	20 44	8 49	5 01	6 58	14 31	1 55	25 40	3 22	4 20	1 47	4 48	9 01	21 59	0 02	14 43	2 07
26 Tu	20 55	5 02	4 36	3 01	15 01	1 49	25 31	3 19	4 08	1 48	4 40	9 03	21 60	0 02	14 45	2 07
27 W	21 07	0 57	3 58	1S09	15 31	1 43	25 21	3 15	3 56	1 48	4 33	9 05	22 00	0 02	14 47	2 07
28 Th	21 17	3S17	3 07	5 24	16 01	1 36	25 11	3 11	3 44	1 49	4 26	9 07	22 01	0 03	14 49	2 07
29 F	21 28	7 30	2 05	9 32	16 30	1 30	25 00	3 07	3 31	1 49	4 18	9 09	22 02	0 03	14 51	2 07
30 Sa	21S38	11S29	0S54	13S18	16S60	1N23	24S50	3S02	3N19	1N50	4N11	9N11	22N03	0N03	14S53	2N07

Day	⚷ Decl	⚷ Lat	♅ Decl	♅ Lat	♆ Decl	♆ Lat	♇ Decl	♇ Lat
1	3S12	5N17	3N05	0S43	11S11	0S41	20S13	2N53
6	3 15	5 15	3 01	0 43	11 11	0 41	20 14	2 52
11	3 18	5 13	2 58	0 43	11 11	0 41	20 14	2 51
16	3 20	5 11	2 55	0 43	11 11	0 41	20 14	2 51
21	3 22	5 10	2 52	0 43	11 11	0 41	20 15	2 50
26	3 23	5 08	2 50	0 43	11 10	0 41	20 15	2 49

Day	⚴ Decl	⚴ Lat	⚵ Decl	⚵ Lat	⚶ Decl	⚶ Lat	Eris Decl	Eris Lat
1	15S35	30S08	13S55	4N22	6N41	4N32	3S30	13S04
6	16 25	30 18	13 60	3 57	5 57	4 41	3 30	13 04
11	17 13	30 28	14 02	3 33	5 14	4 50	3 31	13 03
16	17 60	30 38	13 60	3 10	4 31	5 00	3 31	13 03
21	18 45	30 47	13 55	2 48	3 50	5 11	3 32	13 02
26	19 28	30 56	13 47	2 27	3 09	5 21	3 32	13 02

Moon Phenomena

Max/0 Decl
dy hr mn
6 6:32 19S31
12 15:41 0 N
19 17:20 19N32
27 5:27 0 S

Max/0 Lat
dy hr mn
3 6:54 0 N
9 12:30 5N17
16 5:30 0 S
23 15:05 5S14
30 17:00 0 N

Perigee/Apogee
dy hr m kilometers
6 9:21 p 365363
22 9:49 a 405442

PH dy hr mn
● 3 12:51 11♏16
• 3 12:48 AT01'40"
☽ 10 5:58 18♒00
○ 17 15:17 25♉26
☾ 25 19:29 3♍42

Void of Course Moon

Last Aspect	☽ Ingress
2 12:48 ♀ ✶	♏ 2 17:36
4 4:24 ♃ △	♐ 4 20:15
5 16:49 ♂ □	♑ 6 21:45
8 7:40 ♃ ☍	♒ 8 23:31
10 5:58 ☉ □	♓ 11 2:37
12 14:35 ♃ △	♈ 13 7:40
14 20:58 ♃ □	♉ 15 14:50
17 15:17 ☉ ☍	♊ 18 0:08
19 16:01 ♂ □	♋ 20 11:24
22 7:12 ♂ ✶	♌ 22 23:58
24 9:00 ♄ □	♍ 25 12:12
27 11:45 ♂ ☌	♎ 27 22:01
29 11:15 ♀ □	♏ 30 4:04

DAILY ASPECTARIAN

1 F: ☉⊻☽ 4:32; ☽⊼⚷ 5:11; ☽□♇ 5:27; ☽☍♅ 5:28; ☽⊻♂ 6:16; ☽⊻☿ 7:00; ♅□♇ 10:31; ☿✶♂ 12:04; ☽⊻♄ 12:58; ☉△⚷ 13:13; ☽#⚳ 16:23; ☉⊼♅ 16:45; ☉✶♇ 17:06; ☽⚼♆ 20:01; ☉☌☿ 20:20; ☿✶♇ 22:45; ☽#♂ 23:16; ☿⊼♅ 23:16

2 Sa: ☽□♃ 1:01; ☿△⚷ 2:01; ☉∥☿ 7:30; ☽⚼⚷ 7:40; ☽∠♂ 9:53; ☽∥♆ 11:30; ☽✶♀ 12:48; ☽⊻⚳ 16:57; ☽△♆ 22:06

3 Su: ☽∥♄ 6:00; ☽☌☿ 6:52; ☽∥☿ 6:59; ☉✶♂ 8:50; ☽△⚷ 9:26; ☽⊼♅ 9:38; ☽✶♇ 9:49; ☿∥♄ 11:16; ☽✶♂ 12:43; ☉☌☽ 12:51; ⚳ ♎ 14:16; ☉∥☽ 15:31; ☽∠♀ 16:23; ☽☌♄ 17:19; ☽∠⚳ 19:19

4 M: ☽△♃ 4:24; ♀∠♄ 7:32; ☽⚼♅ 10:49; ☽∠♇ 11:06; ☽⊻♀ 19:21; ☽✶⚳ 21:10

5 Tu: ☽□♆ 0:34; ☽⚼♃ 5:23; ☽⊻☿ 5:25; ♀ ♑ 8:44; ☽□⚷ 11:31; ☽△♅ 11:39; ☽⊻♇ 12:01; ☽□♂ 16:49; ☉⊻☽ 18:36; ☽⊻♄ 19:40

6 W: ☽∠☿ 4:37; ☽⊼♃ 6:08; ☉☌♄ 12:02; ♀□⚳ 17:49; ☽∠♄ 20:34; ☉∠☽ 21:07

7 Th: ☽□⚳ 0:08; ☽☌♀ 0:23; ☽✶♆ 2:01; ☽✶☿ 4:03; ♃ R 5:04; ☽✶⚷ 12:54; ☽□♅ 12:59; ☽☌♇ 13:32; ☽△♂ 20:18; ☽✶♄ 21:32; ☉✶☽ 23:44

8 F: ♀✶♆ 1:17; ☽∠♆ 2:49; ☿∥♆ 6:22; ☽☍♃ 7:40; ☉∥☽ 9:41; ☿✶♀ 12:25; ☽∠⚷ 13:47; ☽⚼♂ 22:18

9 Sa: ☽△⚳ 3:27; ☽⊻♆ 3:51; ☽□☿ 4:10; ☽⊻♀ 5:45; ☽∥♄ 5:49; ♂✶♄ 11:58; ☽⊻⚷ 14:57; ☽✶♅ 14:58; ☽⊻♇ 15:43; ⚳⊼♆ 17:13; ☿⊻⚳ 18:37; ☿△♆ 21:36; ☉∠⚳ 21:59

10 Su: ☽□♄ 0:16; ⚴ ♍ 0:18; ☽⊼♂ 0:41; ♅⊻⚷ 1:14; ☽∥♆ 1:40; ☽∥☿ 5:13; ☽⚼⚳ 5:38; ☉□☽ 5:58; ☽∠♀ 9:00; ☽⊼♃ 10:14; ☽∠♅ 16:31; ☽∠♇ 17:22; ☿ D 21:15

11 M: ☽#♂ 0:37; ☽#⚳ 4:06; ☽△☿ 6:59; ☽☌♆ 7:06; ☽⊼⚳ 8:18; ☽⚼♃ 12:10; ☽✶♀ 12:48; ☽⊻♅ 18:31; ☽☌⚷ 18:35; ☽✶♇ 19:30; ☿△♆ 20:47; ☽∥⚷ 22:05; ☽#♅ 23:57

12 Tu: ☽△♄ 4:45; ☽☍♂ 6:58; ☽⚼☿ 9:40; ☉△☽ 14:25; ☽△♃ 14:35; ☉△♃ 16:40

13 W: ☽∥♅ 7:30; ☽⚼♄ 7:46; ☽#⚷ 9:33; ☽⊻♆ 12:20; ☽⊼☿ 13:19; ☽☍⚳ 15:17; ♆ D 18:43; ☉⚼☽ 19:36; ☽□♀ 22:13

14 Th: ☽☌♅ 0:06; ☽⊻⚷ 0:15; ☽□♇ 1:19; ☽∥⚳ 1:49; ☽∥♂ 3:56; ☽⊼♄ 11:21; ☽⊼♂ 15:35; ☽∠♆ 15:44; ☽□♃ 20:58

15 F: ♀□♅ 1:14; ☉⊼☽ 1:29; ☽∠⚷ 3:52; ♀✶⚷ 4:00; ☽#☿ 4:53; ☽#♆ 8:19; ⚶ ♎ 13:46; ☽✶♆ 19:41; ☽⚼♂ 20:48; ♀☌♇ 21:34; ☽☍☿ 23:35

16 Sa: ☽⊼⚳ 0:37; ☉⚼♅ 5:02; ☽⊻♅ 7:48; ☽✶⚷ 8:02; ☽#♄ 8:09; ☽△♇ 9:18; ☽△♀ 10:08; ☽☍♄ 20:08

17 Su: ☉∠♇ 0:12; ☽△♂ 2:37; ☿⊻⚳ 3:58; ☿∥♆ 5:04; ☽✶♃ 5:28; ☽⚼⚳ 6:09; ☽∠♅ 12:26; ☽⚼♇ 14:05; ☉☍☽ 15:17; ☽⚼♀ 17:02

18 M: ☽□♆ 5:10; ☽∠♃ 10:28; ☽△⚳ 12:15; ☽⊼☿ 13:54; ☽✶♅ 17:36; ☽□⚷ 17:57; ☽⊼♇ 19:24

19 Tu: ☽⊼♀ 0:31; ♂∥⚳ 4:46; ☽⊼♄ 7:04; ⚷ D 13:09; ♂✶♃ 14:50; ☽⊻♃ 15:57; ☽□♂ 16:01; ☽⚼☿ 22:31

20 W: ☿⊼♅ 5:51; ☉⊼☽ 7:41; ☿△⚷ 10:17; ☽⚼♄ 13:14; ☽△♆ 16:36

21 Th: ☽□⚳ 1:58; ☿✶♇ 2:10; ☽□♅ 5:15; ☽△⚷ 5:44; ☽☍♇ 7:21; ☽△☿ 7:56; ☉⚼☽ 16:39; ☽☍♀ 16:54; ☽△♄ 19:45; ☽⚼♆ 22:51

22 F: ☉ ♐ 3:49; ☽☌♃ 4:00; ☉∠♀ 6:17; ☽✶♂ 7:12; ☽⚼⚷ 12:04; ☉∥♇ 14:48

23 Sa: ☉△☽ 1:50; ☽#♄ 3:44; ☽⊼♆ 5:14; ☽#☿ 11:24; ☽∠♂ 15:02; ☽✶⚳ 16:45; ☽△♅ 17:49; ☽⊼⚷ 18:25; ♀✶♄ 18:47; ☽⊼♇ 20:10

24 Su: ☽□☿ 4:03; ☽#♆ 7:38; ☽□♄ 9:00; ☽⊼♀ 9:49; ☽⊻♃ 16:18; ☉□♆ 17:54; ☽⊻♂ 22:37; ⚳☍♅ 23:21; ☽⚼♅ 23:54; ☽∠⚳ 23:55

25 M: ☽⚼♇ 2:20; ☿∥♄ 10:26; ♀∠♆ 12:34; ☽☍♆ 17:22; ☽⚼♀ 17:41; ☉□☽ 19:29; ⚳⊼⚷ 19:29; ☽∠♃ 21:55

26 Tu: ☿☌♄ 1:55; ☽∥⚳ 2:14; ☽⊼♅ 5:28; ☽∥♂ 5:41; ☽☍⚷ 6:09; ☽⊻⚳ 6:30; ☽△♇ 7:58; ☽#⚷ 9:51; ☽∥♅ 13:07; ☽✶♄ 20:43; ☽✶☿ 22:56; ☉⚼♃ 23:19

27 W: ☽△♀ 0:41; ☽✶♃ 2:51; ☽☌♂ 11:45; ☽#♅ 21:25

28 Th: ☽∥⚷ 0:37; ☽∠♄ 1:21; ☽#♂ 2:25; ☿✶♀ 2:46; ☽⊼♆ 2:55; ☽#⚳ 6:18; ☽∠☿ 6:49; ☿△♃ 7:24; ⚳□♇ 7:51; ☉✶☽ 9:43; ♀☍♃ 12:02; ☽☍♅ 14:11; ☽⊼⚷ 14:56; ☽□♇ 16:43; ☽☌⚳ 16:58

29 F: ☽⊻♄ 5:00; ☽⚼♆ 6:17; ☽□♃ 9:57; ☽□♀ 11:15; ☽⊻☿ 13:21; ☉∠☽ 15:01; ♂#⚷ 15:34; ☽⚼⚷ 17:52; ☽⊻♂ 20:45; ☽∥♆ 22:00

30 Sa: ☽△♆ 8:40; ☉△♅ 18:26; ☽⊼♅ 19:03; ☉⊻☽ 19:06; ☽△⚷ 19:51; ☽✶♇ 21:35; ☿⚼♅ 23:05; ☽⊻⚳ 23:12; ☽∥♄ 23:36; ☽∠♂ 23:37

December 2013

LONGITUDE

Day	Sid.Time	☉	☽	☽ 12 hour	Mean☊	True☊	☿	♀	♂	⚳	♃	♄	⚷	♅	♆	♇
	h m s	° ' "	° ' "	° ' "	° '	° '	° '	° '	° '	° '	° '	° '	° '	° '	° '	° '
1 Su	4 40 04	8♐56 48	11♏37 47	18♏46 23	5♏54.5	7♏30.8	23♏46.0	21♑26.3	26♍24.8	11♎09.9	19♋34.9	17♏08.0	9♓11.0	8♈42.5	2♓39.8	10♑12.6
2 M	4 44 00	9 57 38	26 00 55	3♐20 42	5 51.3	7R 29.6	25 16.2	22 04.5	26 56.5	11 33.0	19R 30.2	17 14.8	9 11.7	8R 41.7	2 40.5	10 14.5
3 Tu	4 47 57	10 58 30	10♐44 56	18 12 39	5 48.1	7 26.7	26 46.9	22 41.4	27 28.1	11 56.0	19 25.3	17 21.6	9 12.5	8 40.9	2 41.1	10 16.3
4 W	4 51 53	11 59 23	25 42 46	3♑14 05	5 45.0	7 22.3	28 18.1	23 16.9	27 59.6	12 18.9	19 20.3	17 28.4	9 13.3	8 40.2	2 41.8	10 18.2
5 Th	4 55 50	13 00 17	10♑45 26	18 15 38	5 41.8	7 16.9	29 49.6	23 51.1	28 31.0	12 41.6	19 15.1	17 35.2	9 14.2	8 39.5	2 42.5	10 20.2
6 F	4 59 46	14 01 12	25 43 34	3♒08 16	5 38.6	7 11.3	1♐21.4	24 23.8	29 02.2	13 04.2	19 09.8	17 41.9	9 15.1	8 38.9	2 43.2	10 22.1
7 Sa	5 03 43	15 02 08	10♒28 51	17 44 41	5 35.4	7 06.3	2 53.4	24 55.0	29 33.3	13 26.7	19 04.2	17 48.6	9 16.1	8 38.3	2 44.0	10 24.0
8 Su	5 07 40	16 03 04	24 55 14	2♓00 13	5 32.3	7 02.8	4 25.7	25 24.7	0♎04.2	13 49.1	18 58.6	17 55.3	9 17.2	8 37.8	2 44.8	10 26.0
9 M	5 11 36	17 04 01	8♓59 26	15 52 53	5 29.1	7D 00.9	5 58.1	25 52.7	0 35.0	14 11.3	18 52.7	18 01.9	9 18.3	8 37.3	2 45.7	10 28.0
10 Tu	5 15 33	18 04 59	22 40 41	29 23 03	5 25.9	7 00.7	7 30.6	26 19.0	1 05.7	14 33.4	18 46.8	18 08.5	9 19.4	8 36.9	2 46.5	10 29.9
11 W	5 19 29	19 05 57	6♈00 15	12♈32 38	5 22.7	7 01.7	9 03.3	26 43.6	1 36.2	14 55.3	18 40.6	18 15.0	9 20.6	8 36.5	2 47.5	10 31.9
12 Th	5 23 26	20 06 56	19 00 34	25 24 26	5 19.5	7 03.2	10 36.1	27 06.3	2 06.6	15 17.1	18 34.4	18 21.5	9 21.9	8 36.2	2 48.4	10 33.9
13 F	5 27 22	21 07 55	1♉44 35	8♉01 25	5 16.4	7R 04.3	12 09.0	27 27.1	2 36.8	15 38.8	18 28.0	18 28.0	9 23.2	8 35.9	2 49.4	10 35.9
14 Sa	5 31 19	22 08 55	14 15 15	20 26 26	5 13.2	7 04.1	13 42.1	27 46.0	3 06.9	16 00.4	18 21.5	18 34.4	9 24.6	8 35.7	2 50.4	10 37.9
15 Su	5 35 15	23 09 56	26 35 13	2♊41 53	5 10.0	7 02.1	15 15.2	28 02.9	3 36.8	16 21.7	18 14.8	18 40.8	9 26.0	8 35.6	2 51.4	10 40.0
16 M	5 39 12	24 10 57	8♊46 39	14 49 42	5 06.8	6 57.6	16 48.5	28 17.6	4 06.5	16 43.0	18 08.0	18 47.1	9 27.5	8 35.4	2 52.5	10 42.0
17 Tu	5 43 09	25 11 59	20 51 15	26 51 27	5 03.7	6 50.9	18 21.8	28 30.2	4 36.1	17 04.1	18 01.1	18 53.4	9 29.1	8D 35.4	2 53.6	10 44.1
18 W	5 47 05	26 13 02	2♋50 28	8♋48 27	5 00.5	6 42.1	19 55.3	28 40.6	5 05.6	17 25.0	17 54.1	18 59.6	9 30.7	8 35.4	2 54.7	10 46.1
19 Th	5 51 02	27 14 05	14 45 34	20 42 01	4 57.3	6 32.0	21 29.0	28 48.7	5 34.9	17 45.8	17 47.0	19 05.8	9 32.3	8 35.4	2 55.9	10 48.2
20 F	5 54 58	28 15 09	26 38 00	2♌33 46	4 54.1	6 21.4	23 02.8	28 54.5	6 04.0	18 06.4	17 39.8	19 12.0	9 34.0	8 35.5	2 57.1	10 50.2
21 Sa	5 58 55	29 16 13	8♌29 34	14 25 43	4 51.0	6 11.3	24 36.7	28R 57.9	6 32.9	18 26.9	17 32.5	19 18.0	9 35.8	8 35.6	2 58.3	10 52.3
22 Su	6 02 51	0♑17 18	20 22 34	26 20 32	4 47.8	6 02.6	26 10.8	28 58.9	7 01.6	18 47.2	17 25.1	19 24.1	9 37.6	8 35.8	2 59.5	10 54.4
23 M	6 06 48	1 18 24	2♍20 01	8♍21 33	4 44.6	5 55.9	27 45.2	28 57.5	7 30.2	19 07.3	17 17.6	19 30.1	9 39.4	8 36.1	3 00.8	10 56.5
24 Tu	6 10 45	2 19 30	14 25 37	20 32 46	4 41.4	5 51.7	29 19.7	28 53.6	7 58.6	19 27.3	17 10.0	19 36.0	9 41.3	8 36.4	3 02.1	10 58.6
25 W	6 14 41	3 20 38	26 43 36	2♎58 43	4 38.3	5D 49.8	0♑54.4	28 47.2	8 26.8	19 47.1	17 02.3	19 41.9	9 43.3	8 36.7	3 03.5	11 00.7
26 Th	6 18 38	4 21 45	9♎18 42	15 44 09	4 35.1	5 49.6	2 29.4	28 38.3	8 54.8	20 06.7	16 54.6	19 47.7	9 45.3	8 37.1	3 04.8	11 02.7
27 F	6 22 34	5 22 54	22 15 36	28 53 34	4 31.9	5 50.4	4 04.6	28 26.9	9 22.7	20 26.2	16 46.8	19 53.5	9 47.3	8 37.6	3 06.2	11 04.9
28 Sa	6 26 31	6 24 03	5♏38 28	12♏30 36	4 28.7	5R 50.9	5 40.1	28 13.0	9 50.3	20 45.4	16 39.0	19 59.2	9 49.4	8 38.1	3 07.6	11 07.0
29 Su	6 30 27	7 25 12	19 30 07	26 37 03	4 25.5	5 50.1	7 15.8	27 56.8	10 17.7	21 04.5	16 31.0	20 04.9	9 51.6	8 38.6	3 09.1	11 09.1
30 M	6 34 24	8 26 22	3♐51 09	11♐11 59	4 22.4	5 47.0	8 51.9	27 38.1	10 44.9	21 23.3	16 23.1	20 10.5	9 53.8	8 39.2	3 10.6	11 11.2
31 Tu	6 38 20	9♑27 33	18 38 54	26 10 59	4♏19.2	5♏41.3	10♑28.2	27♑17.1	11♎11.9	21♎42.0	16♋15.1	20♏16.0	9♓56.0	8♈39.9	3♓12.1	11♑13.3

1st of Month

Julian Day # 2456627.5
Obliquity 23°26'07"
SVP 5♓03'46"
GC 27♐02.0
Eris 21♈59.1R

Day	⚴	Day	⚵	Day	⚶
1	7♍40.0	1	17♒28.6	1	6♎29.5
6	9 07.3	6	19 17.6	6	8 31.2
11	10 24.4	11	21 11.3	11	10 30.1
16	11 30.3	16	23 09.2	16	12 26.0
21	12 24.3	21	25 11.0	21	14 18.6
26	13 05.3	26	27 16.7	26	16 07.5
31	13 32.3	31	29 25.8	31	17 52.2

DECLINATION and LATITUDE

Day	☉ Decl	☽ Decl	☽ Lat	☽12h Decl	☿ Decl	☿ Lat	♀ Decl	♀ Lat	♂ Decl	♂ Lat	⚳ Decl	⚳ Lat	♃ Decl	♃ Lat	♄ Decl	♄ Lat
1 Su	21S47	14S58	0N23	16S25	17S29	1N16	24S39	2S57	3N07	1N51	4N04	9N13	22N03	0N03	14S55	2N07
2 M	21 56	17 39	1 39	18 35	17 58	1 09	24 27	2 52	2 55	1 51	3 57	9 15	22 04	0 03	14 57	2 07
3 Tu	22 05	19 13	2 51	19 32	18 26	1 02	24 16	2 47	2 43	1 52	3 50	9 17	22 05	0 03	14 58	2 07
4 W	22 13	19 29	3 53	19 06	18 53	0 55	24 04	2 41	2 31	1 52	3 43	9 19	22 06	0 03	15 00	2 07
5 Th	22 21	18 23	4 38	17 20	19 20	0 48	23 52	2 35	2 19	1 53	3 37	9 21	22 07	0 04	15 02	2 08
6 F	22 29	16 00	5 05	14 25	19 46	0 40	23 40	2 28	2 07	1 54	3 30	9 24	22 08	0 04	15 04	2 08
7 Sa	22 36	12 38	5 10	10 40	20 12	0 33	23 27	2 21	1 55	1 54	3 23	9 26	22 08	0 04	15 06	2 08
8 Su	22 42	8 34	4 56	6 22	20 36	0 26	23 15	2 14	1 44	1 55	3 17	9 28	22 09	0 04	15 07	2 08
9 M	22 48	4 07	4 24	1 51	20 60	0 19	23 02	2 06	1 32	1 56	3 10	9 30	22 10	0 04	15 09	2 08
10 Tu	22 54	0N26	3 38	2N40	21 22	0 12	22 49	1 58	1 20	1 56	3 04	9 32	22 11	0 04	15 11	2 08
11 W	22 59	4 50	2 40	6 56	21 44	0 04	22 36	1 50	1 09	1 57	2 58	9 34	22 12	0 04	15 13	2 08
12 Th	23 04	8 56	1 36	10 48	22 04	0S03	22 23	1 41	0 57	1 57	2 51	9 37	22 13	0 05	15 14	2 08
13 F	23 08	12 32	0 29	14 06	22 24	0 09	22 10	1 32	0 46	1 58	2 45	9 39	22 14	0 05	15 16	2 08
14 Sa	23 12	15 30	0S39	16 42	22 43	0 16	21 57	1 22	0 35	1 59	2 39	9 41	22 15	0 05	15 18	2 08
15 Su	23 16	17 43	1 43	18 30	22 60	0 23	21 44	1 12	0 23	1 59	2 33	9 44	22 16	0 05	15 19	2 08
16 M	23 18	19 05	2 43	19 26	23 16	0 30	21 30	1 02	0 12	1 60	2 27	9 46	22 17	0 05	15 21	2 08
17 Tu	23 21	19 34	3 34	19 29	23 31	0 36	21 17	0 51	0 01	2 01	2 22	9 48	22 19	0 05	15 23	2 08
18 W	23 22	19 10	4 15	18 38	23 45	0 42	21 04	0 40	0S10	2 01	2 16	9 51	22 20	0 05	15 24	2 09
19 Th	23 24	17 55	4 44	16 60	23 58	0 49	20 51	0 28	0 21	2 02	2 11	9 53	22 21	0 06	15 26	2 09
20 F	23 25	15 54	5 01	14 38	24 10	0 55	20 38	0 16	0 32	2 02	2 05	9 55	22 22	0 06	15 27	2 09
21 Sa	23 26	13 13	5 05	11 40	24 20	1 00	20 25	0 03	0 43	2 03	1 60	9 58	22 23	0 06	15 29	2 09
22 Su	23 26	10 00	4 56	8 14	24 29	1 06	20 12	0N10	0 54	2 04	1 54	10 00	22 24	0 06	15 30	2 09
23 M	23 26	6 22	4 34	4 26	24 37	1 12	19 59	0 23	1 04	2 04	1 49	10 03	22 25	0 06	15 32	2 09
24 Tu	23 25	2 27	3 59	0 24	24 43	1 17	19 47	0 37	1 15	2 05	1 44	10 05	22 26	0 06	15 33	2 09
25 W	23 24	1S39	3 13	3S44	24 48	1 22	19 34	0 51	1 25	2 06	1 39	10 08	22 27	0 06	15 35	2 09
26 Th	23 22	5 47	2 17	7 49	24 52	1 27	19 22	1 05	1 36	2 06	1 34	10 10	22 28	0 07	15 36	2 09
27 F	23 20	9 47	1 12	11 39	24 54	1 32	19 10	1 20	1 46	2 07	1 30	10 13	22 30	0 07	15 38	2 10
28 Sa	23 17	13 25	0 01	15 02	24 55	1 36	18 58	1 35	1 56	2 08	1 25	10 16	22 31	0 07	15 39	2 10
29 Su	23 14	16 27	1N12	17 38	24 54	1 40	18 46	1 50	2 06	2 08	1 20	10 18	22 32	0 07	15 40	2 10
30 M	23 10	18 34	2 23	19 12	24 52	1 44	18 35	2 05	2 17	2 09	1 16	10 21	22 33	0 07	15 42	2 10
31 Tu	23S06	19S31	3N27	19S28	24S49	1S48	18S24	2N21	2S26	2N10	1N12	10N24	22N34	0N07	15S43	2N10

Day	⚷ Decl	⚷ Lat	♅ Decl	♅ Lat	♆ Decl	♆ Lat	♇ Decl	♇ Lat
1	3S24	5N06	2N48	0S42	11S09	0S41	20S15	2N48
6	3 24	5 04	2 47	0 42	11 08	0 41	20 15	2 48
11	3 23	5 03	2 46	0 42	11 06	0 41	20 15	2 47
16	3 22	5 01	2 46	0 42	11 05	0 40	20 14	2 46
21	3 21	4 59	2 46	0 42	11 02	0 40	20 14	2 46
26	3 19	4 58	2 47	0 41	11 00	0 40	20 14	2 45
31	3S16	4N56	2N48	0S41	10S57	0S40	20S14	2N45

Day	⚴ Decl	⚴ Lat	⚵ Decl	⚵ Lat	⚶ Decl	⚶ Lat	Eris Decl	Eris Lat
1	20S08	31S04	13S35	2N06	2N31	5N33	3S32	13S01
6	20 44	31 12	13 21	1 46	1 54	5 44	3 32	13 00
11	21 16	31 18	13 03	1 27	1 19	5 57	3 32	12 60
16	21 43	31 23	12 43	1 09	0 46	6 10	3 32	12 59
21	22 05	31 26	12 19	0 51	0 15	6 23	3 31	12 58
26	22 20	31 27	11 53	0 34	0S13	6 38	3 31	12 57
31	22S28	31S25	11S24	0N17	0S39	6N52	3S30	12S56

Moon Phenomena

Max/0 Decl
dy hr mn
3 16:44 19S33
9 21:45 0 N
17 0:52 19N34
24 14:22 0 S
31 4:37 19S32

Max/0 Lat
dy hr mn
6 18:37 5N11
13 10:11 0 S
20 19:26 5S05
28 0:22 0 N

Perigee/Apogee
dy hr m kilometers
4 10:08 p 360071
19 23:48 a 406269

PH dy hr mn
● 3 0:23 10♐59
☽ 9 15:13 17♓43
○ 17 9:29 25♊36
☾ 25 13:49 3♎56

Void of Course Moon

Last Aspect		☽ Ingress	
2 1:35	♂ ✶	♐	2 6:32
4 3:46	♂ □	♑	4 6:50
6 5:33	♂ △	♒	6 6:54
7 12:12	♄ □	♓	8 8:35
10 6:42	♀ ✶	♈	10 13:07
12 15:38	♀ □	♉	12 20:41
15 2:55	♀ △	♊	15 6:42
17 9:29	☉ ☍	♋	17 18:18
20 4:38	♀ ☍	♌	20 6:49
22 13:27	☿ △	♍	22 19:20
25 3:56	♀ △	♎	25 6:18
27 11:01	♀ □	♏	27 13:59
29 13:55	♀ ✶	♐	29 17:38
30 11:37	♂ ✶	♑	31 18:02

DAILY ASPECTARIAN

1 Su ☉□⚷ 5:41; ☽☌♄ 9:20; ☽△♃ 13:16; ☽✶♀ 17:12; ☽⚼♅ 20:10; ☽☌☿ 22:38; ☽∠♇ 22:43; ☿∠♇ 23:32

2 M ☽∠⚳ 0:54; ☽✶♂ 1:35; ☽∥☿ 4:48; ☉⚺♇ 6:51; ☽□♆ 10:55; ☽⚼♃ 13:48; ♂∥♅ 14:28; ☽∠♀ 18:51; ☽△♅ 20:40; ☽□⚷ 21:31; ☽⚺♇ 23:14; ☉⋕♃ 23:26

3 Tu ☉☌☽ 0:23; ☽✶⚳ 1:58; ☿∠⚳ 3:12; ☽⚺♄ 10:43; ☽⚻♃ 13:52; ☿✶♂ 16:36; ☽⚺♀ 19:58

4 W ☽□♂ 3:46; ☽⚺☿ 4:36; ☽∠♄ 10:52; ☽✶♆ 11:09; ☽∥☿ 11:44; ☉✶⚳ 12:16; ☽□♅ 20:39; ☽✶⚷ 21:34; ☽☌♇ 23:20

5 Th ☿ ♐ 2:43; ☽□⚳ 3:10; ☉⚺☽ 3:51; ☽∠☿ 7:14; ☽✶♄ 11:00; ☽∠♆ 11:08; ☽☍♃ 13:31; ♀∠⚷ 17:21; ☽∠⚷ 21:37; ☽☌♀ 21:47

6 F ☽△♂ 5:33; ☉∠☽ 5:43; ☽∥♄ 7:16; ☽✶☿ 10:10; ☽⚺♆ 11:20; ☽✶♅ 20:59; ☿□♆ 21:32; ☽⚺⚷ 22:01; ⚳⋕⚷ 22:20; ☽⚺♇ 23:52

7 Sa ☿∥♇ 3:05; ☽△⚳ 5:01; ☽⚼♂ 6:58; ☉✶☽ 8:04; ☽∥♆ 9:14; ☽□♄ 12:12; ☽⚻♃ 14:07; ☿⚼♃ 17:22; ♂ ♎ 20:42; ☽∠♅ 21:50

8 Su ☽⚺♀ 0:51; ☽∠♇ 0:52; ☽⚼⚳ 6:46; ☽⚻♂ 9:02; ☽☌♆ 13:17; ☽⚼♃ 15:16; ☽□☿ 18:09; ☽⚺♅ 23:22

9 M ☽☌⚷ 0:33; ☽✶♇ 2:34; ☽∠♀ 3:23; ☽∥⚷ 3:51; ☽⋕⚳ 5:08; ☽⋕♅ 7:06; ☽⚻⚳ 9:17; ☽⋕♂ 14:15; ☉□☽ 15:13; ☽△♄ 15:54; ☽△♃ 17:09; ☉∥♀ 17:29

10 Tu ☉⚺♄ 1:32; ☽∥♂ 4:41; ☽✶♀ 6:42; ☽∥♅ 12:36; ☽∥⚳ 13:52; ☉⚻♃ 14:57; ☽☍♂ 15:41; ☽⋕⚷ 15:58; ☿△♅ 17:06; ☽⚺♆ 18:09; ☽⚼♄ 18:57

11 W ☿□⚷ 4:33; ☽☌♅ 4:46; ☽⚺⚷ 6:07; ☽△☿ 6:20; ☽□♇ 8:19; ☽☍⚳ 16:52; ☽∠♆ 21:45; ☽⚻♄ 22:47; ☽□♃ 23:12; ☿⚺♇ 23:25

12 Th ☉△☽ 2:15; ☽∠⚷ 10:03; ☿⋕♃ 11:19; ☿∥♀ 13:32; ☽⋕♆ 14:00; ☽⚼☿ 14:05; ☽□♀ 15:38; ♀⋕♃ 16:26; ⚳∥♅ 20:47

13 F ♃△♄ 0:02; ☽⚻♂ 1:44; ☽✶♆ 2:04; ☿∠♀ 5:56; ☉⚼☽ 9:07; ♂⚻♆ 10:22; ☽⚺♅ 13:06; ☽✶⚷ 14:39; ☽△♇ 17:00; ☽⋕♄ 22:09; ☽⚻☿ 22:47

14 Sa ☽⚻⚳ 3:29; ☽⚼♂ 7:48; ☽✶♃ 7:53; ☽☍♄ 8:26; ☉⚻☽ 16:42; ☽∠♅ 18:09; ☽⚼♇ 22:12

15 Su ☽△♀ 2:55; ♂∠♄ 4:04; ☽⚼⚳ 9:39; ☽□♆ 12:20; ☽∠♃ 12:58; ☽△♂ 14:23; ☿✶⚳ 22:11; ☽✶♅ 23:38

16 M ☽□⚷ 1:21; ☽⚻♇ 3:49; ☉∥☿ 3:59; ☽⚼♀ 9:07; ☽△⚳ 16:14; ☽☍☿ 18:18; ☽⚺♃ 18:24; ☿⚻♃ 19:03; ☽⚻♄ 20:03

17 Tu ☿⚺♄ 8:41; ☉☍☽ 9:29; ☽⚻♀ 15:32; ♅ D 17:40; ♃⚼♆ 22:20

18 W ☽△♆ 0:09; ☽⚼♄ 2:20; ☽□♂ 4:43; ☽□♅ 11:34; ☽△⚷ 13:27; ☽☍♇ 16:00

19 Th ⚳□♃ 1:03; ☽☌♃ 6:03; ☽□⚳ 6:15; ☽⚼♆ 6:25; ☽△♄ 8:50; ⚳⚼♆ 12:23; ☽⚻☿ 15:39; ☽⚼⚷ 19:49

20 F ☉⚻☽ 3:35; ☽⋕♄ 4:19; ☽☍♀ 4:38; ☽⚻♆ 12:48; ☉⚺♀ 16:30; ☽✶♂ 19:54

21 Sa ☽△♅ 0:12; ☽⚻⚷ 2:14; ☽⚼☿ 2:37; ☽⚻♇ 4:50; ☉⚼☽ 12:47; ☽⋕♆ 16:42; ☉ ♑ 17:12; ☽⚺♃ 18:06; ♀∥♇ 19:59; ☽✶⚳ 20:42; ♀ R 21:55; ☽□♄ 22:01

22 Su ☽∠♂ 3:28; ☽⚼♅ 6:29; ☽⚼♇ 11:09; ☽△☿ 13:27; ☽⚻♀ 17:16; ☉△☽ 21:45; ☽∠♃ 23:55

23 M ☽☍♆ 1:22; ☽∠⚳ 3:40; ☽⚺♂ 10:43; ☽⚻♅ 12:29; ☽☍⚷ 14:37; ☽△♇ 17:10; ☿⚺♀ 17:42; ☽⋕⚷ 18:44; ☽∥♅ 22:01; ☽⚼♀ 22:57

24 Tu ☽∥⚳ 4:16; ☽✶♃ 5:20; ☽⋕♂ 6:46; ☽⚺⚳ 10:09; ☿ ♑ 10:13; ☽✶♄ 10:14; ⚳⚺♄ 14:59; ☉✶♆ 17:06; ☽∥♂ 22:35; ☽⋕⚳ 23:59

25 W ☽△♀ 3:56; ☽⋕♅ 6:30; ♂☍♅ 8:34; ☽□☿ 9:12; ☽∥⚷ 9:36; ☽⚻♆ 12:10; ☉□☽ 13:49; ☽∠♄ 15:24; ♂⋕⚳ 21:46; ☽☍♅ 22:42; ☽☌♂ 23:13

26 Th ☽⚻⚷ 0:50; ☽□♇ 3:16; ☿✶♆ 9:04; ☉∠♄ 11:16; ☽□♃ 14:02; ☽⚼♆ 16:22; ☽⚺♄ 19:38; ☽☌⚳ 20:35

27 F ☽⚼⚷ 4:37; ☽∥♆ 7:39; ☽□♀ 11:01; ☿∠♄ 13:05; ☽△♆ 19:33; ♂⚻⚷ 23:13

28 Sa ☽✶☿ 0:03; ☉✶☽ 1:27; ☽⚻♅ 5:15; ☽△⚷ 7:21; ☽⚺♂ 7:37; ☽✶♇ 9:36; ☽∥♄ 17:13; ☽△♃ 18:57

29 Su ☽☌♄ 0:59; ☽⚺⚳ 2:44; ☽∠☿ 5:16; ☉∠☽ 5:20; ☉☌☿ 6:29; ☽⚼♅ 7:01; ☽∠♂ 10:06; ☽∠♇ 11:15; ☽✶♀ 13:55; ☽⚼♃ 19:58; ☿□♅ 20:50; ☽□♆ 22:53

30 M ☽∥♀ 0:14; ☽∠⚳ 4:15; ☉□♅ 5:06; ☽△♅ 7:52; ☉⚺☽ 8:04; ☽⚺☿ 9:12; ☽□⚷ 9:54; ☽✶♂ 11:37; ☽⚺♇ 12:00; ☽∠♀ 14:00; ☿✶⚷ 15:48; ☽⚻♃ 20:11

31 Tu ♂□♇ 1:23; ☽⚺♄ 2:36; ☽✶⚳ 4:59; ☿☌♇ 11:27; ☉✶⚷ 11:37; ☽⚺♀ 13:25; ☿□♂ 15:00; ☽✶♆ 23:07

LONGITUDE

Day	Sid.Time	☉	☽	☽ 12 hour	Mean☊	True☊	☿	♀	♂	⚳	♃	♄	⚷	♅	♆	♇
	h m s	° ' "	° ' "	° ' "	° '	° '	° '	° '	° '	° '	° '	° '	° '	° '	° '	° '
W	6 42 17	10♑28 43	3♑47 06	11♑25 58	4♏16.0	5♏33.1	12♑04.9	26♑53.9	11♎38.6	22♎00.5	16♋07.0	20♏21.5	9♓58.3	8♈40.6	3♓13.6	11♑15.4
Th	6 46 14	11 29 54	19 06 09	26 46 09	4 12.8	5R 23.1	13 41.9	26R 28.6	12 05.2	22 18.8	15R 59.0	20 26.9	10 00.7	8 41.4	3 15.2	11 17.5
F	6 50 10	12 31 05	4♒24 31	11♒59 50	4 09.7	5 12.6	15 19.2	26 01.2	12 31.5	22 36.8	15 50.9	20 32.2	10 03.1	8 42.2	3 16.7	11 19.6
Sa	6 54 07	13 32 16	19 30 52	26 56 33	4 06.5	5 02.8	16 56.9	25 32.0	12 57.5	22 54.7	15 42.8	20 37.5	10 05.5	8 43.1	3 18.3	11 21.7
Su	6 58 03	14 33 26	4♓16 03	11♓28 48	4 03.3	4 54.9	18 34.9	25 01.1	13 23.3	23 12.3	15 34.7	20 42.7	10 08.0	8 44.0	3 20.0	11 23.8
M	7 02 00	15 34 36	18 34 26	25 32 49	4 00.1	4 49.6	20 13.3	24 28.7	13 48.9	23 29.7	15 26.5	20 47.8	10 10.5	8 44.9	3 21.6	11 26.0
Tu	7 05 56	16 35 46	2♈24 00	9♈08 13	3 57.0	4 46.8	21 51.9	23 54.9	14 14.2	23 46.9	15 18.4	20 52.9	10 13.1	8 46.0	3 23.3	11 28.1
W	7 09 53	17 36 55	15 45 50	22 17 15	3 53.8	4D 45.9	23 31.0	23 20.0	14 39.3	24 03.9	15 10.3	20 57.9	10 15.7	8 47.0	3 25.0	11 30.2
Th	7 13 49	18 38 04	28 43 01	5♉03 40	3 50.6	4R 46.1	25 10.3	22 44.2	15 04.1	24 20.6	15 02.2	21 02.8	10 18.3	8 48.1	3 26.7	11 32.3
F	7 17 46	19 39 12	11♉19 46	17 31 54	3 47.4	4 46.0	26 50.0	22 07.9	15 28.7	24 37.1	14 54.2	21 07.7	10 21.0	8 49.3	3 28.5	11 34.4
Sa	7 21 43	20 40 20	23 40 35	29 46 23	3 44.2	4 44.5	28 29.9	21 31.1	15 53.0	24 53.4	14 46.1	21 12.4	10 23.7	8 50.5	3 30.3	11 36.5
Su	7 25 39	21 41 28	5♊49 45	11♊51 08	3 41.1	4 40.6	0♒10.0	20 54.2	16 17.0	25 09.5	14 38.1	21 17.2	10 26.5	8 51.8	3 32.1	11 38.5
M	7 29 36	22 42 35	17 50 56	23 49 30	3 37.9	4 33.8	1 50.4	20 17.5	16 40.7	25 25.3	14 30.1	21 21.8	10 29.3	8 53.1	3 33.9	11 40.6
Tu	7 33 32	23 43 41	29 47 08	5♋44 07	3 34.7	4 23.8	3 30.9	19 41.1	17 04.1	25 40.8	14 22.2	21 26.3	10 32.2	8 54.5	3 35.7	11 42.7
W	7 37 29	24 44 47	11♋40 39	17 36 57	3 31.5	4 11.3	5 11.4	19 05.4	17 27.3	25 56.1	14 14.4	21 30.8	10 35.0	8 55.9	3 37.6	11 44.8
Th	7 41 25	25 45 52	23 33 11	29 29 30	3 28.4	3 56.9	6 52.0	18 30.7	17 50.2	26 11.1	14 06.5	21 35.2	10 38.0	8 57.3	3 39.5	11 46.8
F	7 45 22	26 46 57	5♌26 03	11♌22 59	3 25.2	3 41.8	8 32.4	17 57.0	18 12.7	26 25.9	13 58.8	21 39.5	10 40.9	8 58.8	3 41.4	11 48.9
Sa	7 49 18	27 48 02	17 20 28	23 18 39	3 22.0	3 27.2	10 12.5	17 24.8	18 35.0	26 40.5	13 51.1	21 43.8	10 43.9	9 00.4	3 43.3	11 50.9
Su	7 53 15	28 49 05	29 17 47	5♍18 04	3 18.8	3 14.2	11 52.2	16 54.1	18 56.9	26 54.7	13 43.5	21 47.9	10 46.9	9 02.0	3 45.2	11 53.0
M	7 57 12	29 50 09	11♍19 49	17 23 20	3 15.7	3 03.9	13 31.3	16 25.1	19 18.5	27 08.7	13 36.0	21 52.0	10 50.0	9 03.6	3 47.2	11 55.0
Tu	8 01 08	0♒51 12	23 28 59	29 37 11	3 12.5	2 56.5	15 09.5	15 58.1	19 39.8	27 22.4	13 28.5	21 56.0	10 53.1	9 05.3	3 49.1	11 57.0
W	8 05 05	1 52 14	5♎48 24	12♎03 06	3 09.3	2 52.2	16 46.7	15 33.1	20 00.7	27 35.8	13 21.2	21 59.9	10 56.2	9 07.0	3 51.1	11 59.1
Th	8 09 01	2 53 17	18 21 49	24 45 05	3 06.1	2 50.4	18 22.4	15 10.3	20 21.3	27 49.0	13 13.9	22 03.7	10 59.4	9 08.8	3 53.1	12 01.1
F	8 12 58	3 54 18	1♏13 27	7♏47 25	3 02.9	2 50.0	19 56.4	14 49.7	20 41.5	28 01.8	13 06.7	22 07.5	11 02.5	9 10.6	3 55.2	12 03.1
Sa	8 16 54	4 55 20	14 27 30	21 14 06	2 59.8	2 49.9	21 28.2	14 31.6	21 01.3	28 14.4	12 59.7	22 11.1	11 05.8	9 12.5	3 57.2	12 05.0
Su	8 20 51	5 56 20	28 07 33	5♐08 02	2 56.6	2 48.7	22 57.3	14 15.8	21 20.8	28 26.6	12 52.7	22 14.7	11 09.0	9 14.4	3 59.2	12 07.0
M	8 24 47	6 57 21	12♐15 36	19 30 05	2 53.4	2 45.3	24 23.3	14 02.5	21 39.9	28 38.5	12 45.9	22 18.2	11 12.3	9 16.3	4 01.3	12 09.0
Tu	8 28 44	7 58 20	26 51 07	4♑18 04	2 50.2	2 39.2	25 45.6	13 51.7	21 58.6	28 50.2	12 39.2	22 21.6	11 15.6	9 18.3	4 03.4	12 10.9
W	8 32 41	8 59 20	11♑50 06	19 26 08	2 47.1	2 30.4	27 03.4	13 43.4	22 16.9	29 01.5	12 32.6	22 24.9	11 18.9	9 20.4	4 05.5	12 12.9
Th	8 36 37	10 00 18	27 04 54	4♒44 58	2 43.9	2 19.5	28 16.0	13 37.6	22 34.8	29 12.5	12 26.2	22 28.1	11 22.3	9 22.4	4 07.6	12 14.8
F	8 40 34	11♒01 15	12♒24 53	20 03 06	2♏40.7	2♏07.8	29♒22.8	13♑34.3	22♎52.3	29♎23.2	12♋19.8	22♏31.2	11♓25.7	9♈24.6	4♓09.7	12♑16.7

1st of Month

Julian Day # 2456658.5
Obliquity 23°26'07"
SVP 5♓03'41"
GC 27♐02.1
Eris 21♈51.3R

Day	⚴	⚵	⚶
1	13♍36.0	29♒52.1	18♎12.6
6	13 45.1	2♓05.2	19 51.7
11	13 38.5R	4 21.3	21 25.5
16	13 16.2R	6 40.3	22 53.6
21	12 38.0R	9 02.0	24 15.5
26	11 44.3R	11 26.1	25 30.3
31	10 36.3R	13 52.7	26 37.5

DECLINATION and LATITUDE

Day	☉ Decl	☽ Decl	☽ Lat	☽12h Decl	☿ Decl	☿ Lat	♀ Decl	♀ Lat	♂ Decl	♂ Lat	⚳ Decl	⚳ Lat	♃ Decl	♃ Lat	♄ Decl	♄ Lat
W	23S01	19S05	4N18	18S21	24S44	1S51	18S13	2N36	2S36	2N10	1N08	10N26	22N35	0N07	15S44	2N10
Th	22 56	17 17	4 51	15 54	24 38	1 55	18 02	2 52	2 46	2 11	1 03	10 29	22 36	0 08	15 46	2 10
F	22 51	14 15	5 02	12 23	24 30	1 57	17 52	3 08	2 56	2 12	0 59	10 32	22 37	0 08	15 47	2 10
Sa	22 45	10 19	4 53	8 08	24 21	1 60	17 42	3 23	3 05	2 12	0 56	10 34	22 38	0 08	15 48	2 11
Su	22 38	5 50	4 24	3 30	24 10	2 02	17 32	3 39	3 14	2 13	0 52	10 37	22 39	0 08	15 50	2 11
M	22 32	1 09	3 39	1N10	23 57	2 04	17 23	3 54	3 24	2 14	0 48	10 40	22 41	0 08	15 51	2 11
Tu	22 24	3N27	2 43	5 38	23 43	2 05	17 14	4 09	3 33	2 14	0 45	10 43	22 42	0 08	15 52	2 11
W	22 17	7 44	1 39	9 42	23 28	2 06	17 05	4 23	3 42	2 15	0 41	10 46	22 43	0 08	15 53	2 11
Th	22 08	11 31	0 32	13 11	23 11	2 07	16 57	4 38	3 51	2 16	0 38	10 49	22 44	0 09	15 54	2 11
F	21 60	14 41	0S35	15 59	22 52	2 07	16 49	4 51	3 60	2 17	0 35	10 51	22 45	0 09	15 55	2 11
Sa	21 51	17 06	1 38	18 01	22 32	2 07	16 42	5 05	4 08	2 17	0 32	10 54	22 46	0 09	15 56	2 12
Su	21 41	18 42	2 36	19 11	22 10	2 07	16 35	5 17	4 17	2 18	0 29	10 57	22 47	0 09	15 57	2 12
M	21 31	19 27	3 27	19 29	21 47	2 05	16 28	5 29	4 25	2 18	0 26	11 00	22 48	0 09	15 59	2 12
Tu	21 21	19 19	4 07	18 55	21 22	2 04	16 22	5 41	4 34	2 19	0 23	11 03	22 49	0 09	15 60	2 12
W	21 10	18 19	4 37	17 32	20 56	2 01	16 17	5 51	4 42	2 20	0 21	11 06	22 50	0 09	16 01	2 12
Th	20 59	16 33	4 55	15 23	20 28	1 59	16 12	6 01	4 50	2 21	0 18	11 09	22 51	0 09	16 02	2 12
F	20 48	14 04	4 59	12 36	19 59	1 55	16 07	6 10	4 58	2 21	0 16	11 12	22 52	0 10	16 02	2 13
Sa	20 36	11 01	4 51	9 18	19 28	1 51	16 03	6 18	5 05	2 22	0 14	11 15	22 53	0 10	16 03	2 13
Su	20 24	7 30	4 30	5 37	18 56	1 47	15 59	6 26	5 13	2 23	0 11	11 18	22 53	0 10	16 04	2 13
M	20 11	3 40	3 56	1 41	18 23	1 41	15 56	6 32	5 20	2 24	0 09	11 21	22 54	0 10	16 05	2 13
Tu	19 58	0S21	3 12	2S23	17 48	1 35	15 53	6 38	5 28	2 24	0 08	11 24	22 55	0 10	16 06	2 13
W	19 44	4 25	2 18	6 25	17 13	1 28	15 51	6 43	5 35	2 25	0 06	11 28	22 56	0 10	16 07	2 13
Th	19 31	8 22	1 16	10 15	16 36	1 21	15 49	6 48	5 42	2 26	0 04	11 31	22 57	0 10	16 08	2 14
F	19 16	12 02	0 08	13 42	15 59	1 12	15 48	6 51	5 49	2 26	0 03	11 34	22 58	0 10	16 08	2 14
Sa	19 02	15 12	1N01	16 32	15 21	1 03	15 47	6 54	5 56	2 27	0 02	11 37	22 59	0 11	16 09	2 14
Su	18 47	17 38	2 09	18 30	14 42	0 53	15 46	6 56	6 02	2 28	0 00	11 40	22 59	0 11	16 10	2 14
M	18 32	19 05	3 12	19 22	14 03	0 42	15 46	6 58	6 09	2 29	0S01	11 43	23 00	0 11	16 11	2 14
Tu	18 16	19 20	4 04	18 57	13 25	0 31	15 47	6 58	6 15	2 29	0 02	11 47	23 01	0 11	16 11	2 15
W	18 00	18 14	4 41	17 12	12 46	0 18	15 47	6 59	6 21	2 30	0 03	11 50	23 02	0 11	16 12	2 15
Th	17 44	15 51	4 59	14 13	12 09	0 04	15 48	6 58	6 27	2 31	0 03	11 53	23 02	0 11	16 13	2 15
F	17S28	12S21	4N56	10S16	11S32	0N10	15S49	6N57	6S33	2N31	0S04	11N56	23N03	0N11	16S13	2N15

Day	⚷ Decl	⚷ Lat	♅ Decl	♅ Lat	♆ Decl	♆ Lat	♇ Decl	♇ Lat
1	3S15	4N56	2N49	0S41	10S57	0S40	20S14	2N45
6	3 12	4 54	2 50	0 41	10 54	0 40	20 13	2 44
11	3 09	4 53	2 53	0 41	10 51	0 40	20 13	2 44
16	3 04	4 52	2 56	0 41	10 47	0 40	20 12	2 43
21	2 60	4 51	2 59	0 40	10 44	0 40	20 12	2 43
26	2 55	4 50	3 03	0 40	10 40	0 40	20 11	2 43
31	2S50	4N49	3N07	0S40	10S36	0S40	20S11	2N42

Day	⚴ Decl	⚴ Lat	⚵ Decl	⚵ Lat	⚶ Decl	⚶ Lat	Eris Decl	Eris Lat
1	22S28	31S24	11S18	0N14	0S44	6N56	3S30	12S56
6	22 25	31 17	10 46	0S03	1 06	7 11	3 30	12 55
11	22 12	31 06	10 12	0 19	1 25	7 28	3 29	12 55
16	21 49	30 48	9 36	0 34	1 41	7 45	3 28	12 54
21	21 19	30 23	8 57	0 50	1 54	8 04	3 27	12 53
26	20 23	29 50	8 16	1 05	2 03	8 23	3 26	12 52
31	19S20	29S07	7S34	1S20	2S08	8N42	3S25	12S51

Moon Phenomena

Max/0 Decl
dy hr mn
6 5:56 0 N
13 8:11 19N30
20 21:57 0 S
27 16:38 19S23

Max/0 Lat
dy hr mn
3 1:03 5N02
9 11:27 0 S
16 20:37 4S59
24 2:57 0 N
30 8:00 5N00

Perigee/Apogee
dy hr m kilometers
1 21:12 p 356925
16 1:59 a 406532
30 9:57 p 357085

PH dy hr mn
● 1 11:15 10♑57
☽ 8 3:40 17♈46
○ 16 4:53 25♋58
☾ 24 5:20 4♏08
● 30 21:40 10♒55

Void of Course Moon

Last Aspect	☽ Ingress
2 11:13 ♀ ☌	♒ 2 17:04
4 1:48 ♄ □	♓ 4 16:59
6 9:45 ♀ ⚹	♈ 6 19:46
8 16:23 ☿ □	♉ 9 2:25
11 10:59 ☿ △	♊ 11 12:27
12 21:34 ♂ △	♋ 14 0:26
16 4:53 ☉ ☍	♌ 16 13:02
18 8:53 ♄ □	♍ 19 1:25
20 20:56 ♄ ⚹	♎ 21 12:44
23 3:52 ♂ ☌	♏ 23 21:45
25 13:56 ☿ □	♐ 26 3:14
27 22:03 ☿ ⚹	♑ 28 5:05
29 16:48 ♂ □	♒ 30 4:34

DAILY ASPECTARIAN

☽∠♄ 2:29
⚵ ♓ 7:15
☽□♅ 7:41
☽⚹⚷ 9:44
☉☌☽ 11:15
☽☌♇ 11:45
☽□♂ 12:42
☽☌☿ 14:33
☽∥♀ 15:03
☉☌♇ 18:58
☽☍♃ 19:10
☽∠♆ 22:40

☽⚹♄ 2:07
☽□⚳ 5:07
♂#♅ 7:43
☽∠⚷ 9:16
☽☌♀ 11:13
☽∥♄ 12:59
☽⚺♆ 22:13

☉□♂ 0:15
☽⚹♅ 6:47
☿☍♃ 7:12
☽⚺⚷ 8:56
☽⚺♇ 10:58
☽△♂ 13:13
☉⚺☽ 13:46
☽⚻♃ 17:58
☽⚺☿ 19:23
☽∥♆ 20:36

☽□♄ 1:48
☽△⚳ 5:35
☽∠♅ 6:47
☽⚺♀ 9:24
☽∠♇ 11:05
☽⚼♂ 14:04
☉∠☽ 15:41
☽⚼♃ 17:59
♀∠⚷ 19:09
☿∠♆ 20:17
♂∥⚷ 20:24
☉#♃ 20:37
☽☌♆ 22:27
☽∠☿ 22:44

5 Su
☽⚼⚳ 6:40
☽⚺♅ 7:25
☽∠♀ 9:13
☽☌⚷ 9:46
☽⚹♇ 11:54
☽∥♂ 12:55
☽∥⚷ 13:31
☽#♅ 15:24
☽⚻♂ 15:41
☉⚹☽ 18:31
☽△♃ 18:44
☉☍♃ 21:12

6 M
☽#⚳ 1:50
☽⚹☿ 3:11
☽△♄ 3:50
☽⚻⚳ 8:38
☿⚹♄ 8:52
☽⚹♀ 9:45
☽∥⚳ 9:58
♀ R 10:21
☽∥♅ 20:49
☽#⚷ 22:39

7 Tu
☽#♂ 0:34
☽⚺♆ 1:45
♀□⚳ 3:43
☽⚼♄ 6:13
☽☌♅ 11:21
☽⚺⚷ 13:59
☽□♇ 16:15
☽☍♂ 21:55
☿☌♀ 22:03
☽□♃ 22:56

8 W
☉□☽ 3:40
☽∠♆ 4:52
☿□⚳ 9:35
☽⚻♄ 9:37
☽□♀ 13:20
☽☍⚳ 15:38
☽□☿ 16:23
☽∠⚷ 17:35
☉∠♆ 19:26
☽#♆ 19:38
♂□♃ 22:37

9 Th
☿∠⚷ 1:59
☽⚹♆ 8:57
☽⚺♅ 19:11
☽⚹⚷ 22:07

10 F
☽△♇ 0:28
☽⚹♃ 6:49
☽⚻♂ 8:17
☿#♃ 8:35
☽#♄ 11:28
☉△☽ 17:35
☽☍♄ 19:08
☽#♀ 19:40
☽△♀ 19:58

11 Sa
☽∠♅ 0:19
☽⚻⚳ 2:26
☽⚼♇ 5:46
♀⚹♄ 10:45
☽△☿ 10:59
☽∠♃ 11:52
☉☌♀ 12:26
☉⚹♄ 13:40
☽⚼♂ 14:41
☽□♆ 19:26
☿ ♒ 21:36

12 Su
☽⚼♀ 0:08
☉⚼☽ 1:52
☽⚹♅ 6:03
☽⚼⚳ 8:49
☽□⚷ 9:13
☽⚻♇ 11:37
☽⚺♃ 17:22
☽△♂ 21:34
☽⚼☿ 21:39

13 M
☽⚻♀ 4:40
☽⚻♄ 7:06
⚳⚼⚷ 7:36
☉⚻☽ 10:40
☽△⚳ 15:33

14 Tu
☿⚺♆ 1:11
☉∥☿ 1:40
☽△♆ 7:42
☽⚻☿ 8:45
☽⚼♄ 13:30
☽□♅ 18:26
☽△⚷ 21:47

15 W
☽☍♇ 0:08
☽☌♃ 5:07
☽□♂ 12:04
☽⚼♆ 14:05
☽☍♀ 14:17
♀∠♆ 18:11
☽△♄ 20:00
☉∠⚷ 20:44

16 Th
☽#♀ 3:57
☽⚼⚷ 4:13
☉☍☽ 4:53
☽□⚳ 5:26
☽#♄ 5:33
☉□⚳ 13:07
☿∥♇ 13:12
♀□♂ 17:14
☽⚻♆ 20:28

17 F
☿⚹♅ 6:26
☽△♅ 7:10
☽☍☿ 7:17
☽⚻⚷ 10:38
☽⚻♇ 12:54
☽⚺♃ 17:03
♀∥♄ 21:04

18 Sa
☽⚻♀ 0:08
☽#♆ 1:47
☽⚹♂ 2:35
☿⚺⚷ 7:47
☽□♄ 8:53
♂⚼♆ 9:57
☽⚼♅ 13:26
☽⚹⚳ 19:08
☽⚼♇ 19:09
☽∠♃ 22:52
☉⚻☽ 22:57

19 Su
☿⚺♇ 0:12
☽⚼♀ 5:00
☽☍♆ 8:56
☽∠♂ 9:35
☽#♂ 14:03
☽⚻♅ 19:29
☉∥♇ 22:27
☽☍⚷ 23:01

20 M
☿⚻♃ 1:04
☽△♇ 1:10
☽∠⚳ 1:39
☉ ♒ 3:52
☽#⚷ 4:00
☽∥♅ 4:14
☽⚹♃ 4:27
☽⚻☿ 5:02
☉⚼☽ 7:35
☽△♀ 9:43
☽⚺♂ 16:16
☽⚹♄ 20:56
☽∥⚳ 21:11
☽#⚳ 22:43

21 Tu
☽⚺⚳ 7:46
☿⚺♀ 9:28
♅#⚷ 11:56
☽⚼☿ 15:02
☽∥⚷ 15:34
☽#♅ 15:35
☉△☽ 15:42
☽⚻♆ 20:13

22 W
☽∠♄ 2:19
☽☍♅ 6:23
☽∥♂ 7:13
☽⚻⚷ 9:54
☽□♇ 11:54
☽□♃ 14:21
☽□♀ 18:07

23 Th
☽△☿ 0:01
☽⚼♆ 0:59
☽☌♂ 3:52
☽⚺♄ 7:00
☽⚼⚷ 14:22
☽∥♆ 14:58
☿∥♄ 17:53
☽☌⚳ 18:00

24 F
☉⚺♆ 0:21
☽△♆ 4:58
☉□☽ 5:20
☿∥♀ 7:05
☽⚻♅ 14:33
☿△♂ 14:58
☽△⚷ 17:57
☽⚹♇ 19:44
☽△♃ 21:24

25 Sa
☽⚹♀ 0:07
☽∥☿ 0:59
☽∥♀ 5:00
☽∥♄ 8:28
☽⚺♂ 11:55
☿□♄ 11:57
☽☌♄ 13:44
☽□☿ 13:56
☽⚼♅ 17:14
☽∠♇ 22:15
☽⚼♃ 23:35

26 Su
☽⚺⚳ 0:33
☽∠♀ 1:56
☽□♆ 10:04
☉∥☽ 14:19
☽∠♂ 14:23
☉⚹☽ 14:24
☽△♅ 18:59
☿∠♅ 21:58
☽□⚷ 22:14
☽⚺♇ 23:49

27 M
☽⚻♃ 0:50
☽∠⚳ 2:20
☽⚺♀ 2:56
☽⚹♂ 15:53
☽⚺♄ 16:39
☉∠☽ 17:13
☽⚹☿ 22:03

28 Tu
☽⚹⚳ 3:15
☽⚹♆ 11:38
☽∠♄ 16:57
☉⚺☽ 19:09
☽□♅ 20:02
☽⚹⚷ 23:10

29 W
☽∠☿ 0:23
☽☌♇ 0:36
☽☍♃ 1:07
☽☌♀ 2:58
☿∠♇ 3:07
☉∥☽ 3:29
☉⚹♅ 8:34
☿⚼♃ 8:41
☽∠♆ 11:29
♂⚺♄ 12:56
☽⚹♄ 16:44
☽□♂ 16:48
☽∥♄ 21:01
☽∠⚷ 22:53

30 Th
☽∥♀ 0:21
☽⚺☿ 2:01
☽□⚳ 3:22
☿∠♀ 7:05
☽⚺♆ 11:03
☽⚹♅ 19:17
☉☌☽ 21:40
☽⚺⚷ 22:27
☽⚻♃ 23:52

31 F
☿△⚳ 0:09
☽⚺♀ 1:49
☽∥☿ 5:37
♃☍♇ 9:17
☽∥♆ 10:09
☉⚺⚷ 10:11
☿ ♓ 14:30
☽□♄ 15:57
☽△♂ 16:46
☽∠♅ 18:56
♀ D 20:50
☽⚼♃ 23:21
☽∠♇ 23:29

February 2014

LONGITUDE

Day	Sid.Time	☉	☽	☽ 12 hour	Mean ☊	True ☊	☿	♀	♂	⚳	♃	♄	⚷	♅	♆	♇
	h m s	° ' "	° ' "	° ' "	° '	° '	° '	° '	° '	° '	° '	° '	° '	° '	° '	° '
1 Sa	8 44 30	12♒02 12	27♒38 13	5♓08 57	2♏37.5	1♏56.7	0♓22.9	13♑33.4	23♎09.3	29♎33.5	12♋13.7	22♏34.2	11♓29.1	9♈26.7	4♓11.9	12♑18.6
2 Su	8 48 27	13 03 07	12♓34 10	19 53 00	2 34.4	1R 47.4	1 15.5	13 34.9	23 25.9	29 43.5	12R 07.6	22 37.1	11 32.5	9 28.9	4 14.0	12 20.5
3 M	8 52 23	14 04 01	27 04 49	4♈09 12	2 31.2	1 40.8	1 59.9	13 38.8	23 42.0	29 53.2	12 01.7	22 40.0	11 36.0	9 31.2	4 16.2	12 22.3
4 Tu	8 56 20	15 04 53	11♈06 00	17 55 16	2 28.0	1 36.9	2 35.1	13 45.0	23 57.7	0♏02.5	11 56.0	22 42.7	11 39.5	9 33.4	4 18.4	12 24.2
5 W	9 00 16	16 05 44	24 37 11	1♉12 07	2 24.8	1D 35.5	3 00.6	13 53.5	24 12.9	0 11.5	11 50.4	22 45.4	11 43.0	9 35.8	4 20.5	12 26.0
6 Th	9 04 13	17 06 34	7♉40 32	14 02 59	2 21.6	1R 35.4	3R 15.8	14 04.2	24 27.7	0 20.1	11 45.0	22 47.9	11 46.5	9 38.1	4 22.7	12 27.8
7 F	9 08 10	18 07 23	20 20 04	26 32 25	2 18.5	1 35.5	3 20.2	14 17.1	24 41.9	0 28.3	11 39.7	22 50.4	11 50.1	9 40.5	4 24.9	12 29.6
8 Sa	9 12 06	19 08 09	2♊40 39	8♊45 25	2 15.3	1 34.6	3 13.7	14 32.0	24 55.7	0 36.3	11 34.6	22 52.7	11 53.6	9 42.9	4 27.1	12 31.4
9 Su	9 16 03	20 08 55	14 47 19	20 46 56	2 12.1	1 31.8	2 56.2	14 49.0	25 08.9	0 43.8	11 29.7	22 55.0	11 57.2	9 45.4	4 29.4	12 33.2
10 M	9 19 59	21 09 39	26 44 49	2♋41 28	2 08.9	1 26.3	2 28.2	15 08.0	25 21.7	0 51.0	11 24.9	22 57.1	12 00.8	9 47.9	4 31.6	12 34.9
11 Tu	9 23 56	22 10 21	8♋37 20	14 32 51	2 05.8	1 18.1	1 50.3	15 28.9	25 33.9	0 57.8	11 20.4	22 59.2	12 04.4	9 50.4	4 33.8	12 36.7
12 W	9 27 52	23 11 02	20 28 20	26 24 08	2 02.6	1 07.4	1 03.3	15 51.7	25 45.6	1 04.2	11 16.0	23 01.2	12 08.1	9 53.0	4 36.1	12 38.4
13 Th	9 31 49	24 11 41	2♌20 29	8♌17 38	1 59.4	0 55.0	0 08.6	16 16.2	25 56.8	1 10.3	11 11.7	23 03.0	12 11.7	9 55.6	4 38.3	12 40.1
14 F	9 35 45	25 12 19	14 15 46	20 15 03	1 56.2	0 41.9	29♒07.6	16 42.5	26 07.4	1 15.9	11 07.7	23 04.8	12 15.4	9 58.2	4 40.6	12 41.7
15 Sa	9 39 42	26 12 55	26 15 37	2♍17 36	1 53.0	0 29.1	28 02.1	17 10.5	26 17.4	1 21.2	11 03.8	23 06.4	12 19.1	10 00.9	4 42.8	12 43.4
16 Su	9 43 39	27 13 30	8♍21 09	14 26 22	1 49.9	0 17.9	26 54.0	17 40.0	26 26.8	1 26.1	11 00.1	23 08.0	12 22.8	10 03.6	4 45.1	12 45.0
17 M	9 47 35	28 14 03	20 33 26	26 42 29	1 46.7	0 08.9	25 45.0	18 11.1	26 35.7	1 30.6	10 56.6	23 09.5	12 26.5	10 06.3	4 47.3	12 46.6
18 Tu	9 51 32	29 14 35	2♎53 44	9♎07 23	1 43.5	0 02.6	24 36.9	18 43.7	26 44.0	1 34.7	10 53.3	23 10.8	12 30.2	10 09.1	4 49.6	12 48.2
19 W	9 55 28	0♓15 06	15 23 43	21 43 02	1 40.3	29♎59.2	23 31.4	19 17.8	26 51.6	1 38.4	10 50.2	23 12.1	12 33.9	10 11.9	4 51.9	12 49.8
20 Th	9 59 25	1 15 35	28 05 38	4♏31 53	1 37.2	29D 58.0	22 29.9	19 53.2	26 58.6	1 41.7	10 47.2	23 13.2	12 37.6	10 14.7	4 54.2	12 51.3
21 F	10 03 21	2 16 03	11♏02 08	17 36 46	1 34.0	29 58.4	21 33.5	20 29.9	27 05.0	1 44.6	10 44.5	23 14.3	12 41.4	10 17.5	4 56.4	12 52.8
22 Sa	10 07 18	3 16 30	24 16 08	1♐00 36	1 30.8	29R 59.3	20 43.2	21 07.9	27 10.8	1 47.1	10 41.9	23 15.2	12 45.1	10 20.4	4 58.7	12 54.3
23 Su	10 11 14	4 16 55	7♐50 24	14 45 46	1 27.6	29 59.5	19 59.7	21 47.2	27 15.9	1 49.1	10 39.5	23 16.1	12 48.9	10 23.3	5 01.0	12 55.8
24 M	10 15 11	5 17 20	21 46 47	28 53 27	1 24.4	29 58.2	19 23.3	22 27.6	27 20.3	1 50.7	10 37.4	23 16.8	12 52.7	10 26.2	5 03.3	12 57.3
25 Tu	10 19 08	6 17 42	6♑05 33	13♑22 46	1 21.3	29 54.8	18 54.3	23 09.1	27 24.0	1 52.0	10 35.4	23 17.5	12 56.5	10 29.2	5 05.6	12 58.7
26 W	10 23 04	7 18 04	20 44 33	28 10 12	1 18.1	29 49.2	18 32.6	23 51.7	27 27.0	1 52.7	10 33.6	23 18.0	13 00.3	10 32.2	5 07.8	13 00.1
27 Th	10 27 01	8 18 24	5♒38 48	13♒09 20	1 14.9	29 41.9	18 18.2	24 35.3	27 29.3	1R 53.1	10 32.0	23 18.5	13 04.0	10 35.2	5 10.1	13 01.5
28 F	10 30 57	9♓18 42	20 40 37	28 11 29	1♏11.7	29♎33.8	18♒10.8	25♑19.9	27♎30.9	1♏53.0	10♋30.7	23♏18.8	13♓07.8	10♈38.2	5♓12.4	13♑02.9

1st of Month

Julian Day
2456689.5
Obliquity
23°26'07"
SVP 5♓03'3
GC 27♐02.
Eris 21♈53.

Day	⚴
1	10♍21.1
6	8 58.3
11	7 26.3
16	5 48.2
21	4 07.5
26	2 27.8

Day	⚵
1	14♓22.3
6	16 51.6
11	19 23.0
16	21 56.2
21	24 31.3
26	27 08.2

Day	⚶
1	26♎50.0
6	27 47.0
11	28 34.7
16	29 12.5
21	29 39.7
26	29 55.6

DECLINATION and LATITUDE

Day	☉ Decl	☽ Decl	☽ Lat	☽ 12h Decl	☿ Decl	☿ Lat	♀ Decl	♀ Lat	♂ Decl	♂ Lat	⚳ Decl	⚳ Lat	♃ Decl	♃ Lat	♄ Decl	♄ Lat
1 Sa	17S11	8S03	4N31	5S43	10S57	0N25	15S51	6N56	6S38	2N32	0S04	11N60	23N04	0N11	16S14	2N15
2 Su	16 54	3 19	3 48	0 55	10 24	0 40	15 53	6 54	6 44	2 33	0 05	12 03	23 04	0 12	16 14	2 16
3 M	16 36	1N28	2 52	3N47	9 53	0 57	15 55	6 51	6 49	2 34	0 05	12 06	23 05	0 12	16 15	2 16
4 Tu	16 19	6 01	1 46	8 08	9 25	1 13	15 57	6 49	6 54	2 34	0 05	12 10	23 06	0 12	16 15	2 16
5 W	16 01	10 07	0 37	11 55	8 60	1 30	15 59	6 45	6 59	2 35	0 05	12 13	23 06	0 12	16 16	2 16
6 Th	15 42	13 34	0S32	15 01	8 39	1 47	16 02	6 42	7 04	2 36	0 04	12 16	23 07	0 12	16 16	2 16
7 F	15 24	16 15	1 38	17 18	8 21	2 04	16 04	6 38	7 08	2 36	0 04	12 20	23 07	0 12	16 17	2 17
8 Sa	15 05	18 08	2 37	18 44	8 08	2 20	16 07	6 34	7 13	2 37	0 04	12 23	23 08	0 12	16 17	2 17
9 Su	14 46	19 08	3 28	19 18	7 60	2 36	16 10	6 29	7 17	2 38	0 03	12 26	23 09	0 12	16 17	2 17
10 M	14 27	19 15	4 09	18 59	7 56	2 51	16 13	6 24	7 21	2 38	0 02	12 29	23 09	0 12	16 18	2 17
11 Tu	14 07	18 31	4 39	17 51	7 57	3 04	16 15	6 19	7 25	2 39	0 01	12 33	23 10	0 13	16 18	2 17
12 W	13 47	16 59	4 57	15 57	8 03	3 16	16 18	6 14	7 28	2 40	0 00	12 36	23 10	0 13	16 18	2 18
13 Th	13 27	14 44	5 02	13 22	8 12	3 26	16 21	6 09	7 32	2 40	0N01	12 39	23 11	0 13	16 19	2 18
14 F	13 07	11 52	4 54	10 14	8 26	3 34	16 23	6 03	7 35	2 41	0 02	12 43	23 11	0 13	16 19	2 18
15 Sa	12 47	8 29	4 32	6 39	8 43	3 39	16 26	5 57	7 38	2 42	0 03	12 46	23 11	0 13	16 19	2 18
16 Su	12 26	4 45	3 59	2 47	9 04	3 42	16 28	5 51	7 41	2 42	0 05	12 49	23 12	0 13	16 19	2 18
17 M	12 05	0 46	3 14	1S15	9 26	3 43	16 30	5 45	7 43	2 43	0 06	12 53	23 12	0 13	16 19	2 19
18 Tu	11 44	3S17	2 19	5 17	9 50	3 42	16 32	5 39	7 46	2 43	0 08	12 56	23 13	0 13	16 20	2 19
19 W	11 23	7 15	1 17	9 09	10 15	3 38	16 34	5 32	7 48	2 44	0 10	12 59	23 13	0 13	16 20	2 19
20 Th	11 01	10 57	0 10	12 39	10 40	3 32	16 35	5 26	7 50	2 45	0 12	13 02	23 13	0 13	16 20	2 19
21 F	10 40	14 12	0N59	15 36	11 05	3 25	16 36	5 19	7 52	2 45	0 14	13 06	23 14	0 14	16 20	2 19
22 Sa	10 18	16 48	2 06	17 46	11 29	3 16	16 37	5 13	7 53	2 46	0 16	13 09	23 14	0 14	16 20	2 20
23 Su	9 56	18 31	3 09	18 59	11 52	3 06	16 38	5 06	7 55	2 46	0 18	13 12	23 14	0 14	16 20	2 20
24 M	9 34	19 10	4 01	19 03	12 14	2 54	16 38	4 59	7 56	2 47	0 21	13 15	23 14	0 14	16 20	2 20
25 Tu	9 12	18 38	4 40	17 53	12 35	2 42	16 39	4 52	7 56	2 47	0 23	13 18	23 15	0 14	16 20	2 20
26 W	8 50	16 51	5 02	15 31	12 54	2 30	16 38	4 46	7 57	2 48	0 26	13 21	23 15	0 14	16 20	2 20
27 Th	8 27	13 56	5 05	12 06	13 11	2 16	16 38	4 39	7 58	2 48	0 29	13 24	23 15	0 14	16 20	2 21
28 F	8S05	10S04	4N46	7S53	13S26	2N03	16S37	4N32	7S58	2N49	0N31	13N27	23N15	0N14	16S20	2N21

Day	⚷ Decl	⚷ Lat	♅ Decl	♅ Lat	♆ Decl	♆ Lat	♇ Decl	♇ Lat
1	2S48	4N48	3N08	0S40	10S36	0S40	20S10	2N
6	2 43	4 48	3 12	0 40	10 32	0 40	20 10	2
11	2 37	4 47	3 17	0 40	10 28	0 40	20 09	2
16	2 30	4 46	3 23	0 40	10 24	0 40	20 09	2
21	2 24	4 46	3 28	0 39	10 19	0 40	20 08	2
26	2S17	4N45	3N34	0S39	10S15	0S40	20S08	2N

Day	⚴ Decl	⚴ Lat	⚵ Decl	⚵ Lat	⚶ Decl	⚶ Lat	Eris Decl	Eris Lat
1	19S06	28S58	7S25	1S23	2S09	8N46	3S25	12S
6	17 47	28 02	6 41	1 37	2 09	9 07	3 23	12
11	16 13	26 55	5 55	1 52	2 06	9 28	3 22	12
16	14 28	25 37	5 08	2 06	1 59	9 50	3 21	12
21	12 32	24 09	4 19	2 20	1 47	10 12	3 19	12
26	10S27	22S31	3S30	2S34	1S32	10N35	3S18	12S

Moon Phenomena

Max/0 Decl

dy	hr mn	
2	16:36	0 N
9	15:23	19N18
17	4:34	0 S
24	1:16	19S10

Max/0 Lat

dy	hr mn	
5	12:43	0 S
12	21:13	5S02
20	3:30	0 N
26	14:35	5N06

Perigee/Apogee

dy	hr m		kilometers
12	5:11	a	406231
27	20:02	p	360442

PH	dy	hr mn	
☽	6	19:23	17♉56
○	14	23:54	26♌13
☾	22	17:16	4♐00

Void of Course Moon

Last Aspect			☽ Ingres		
31 16:46	♂	△	♓	1	3:4
2 16:36	♄	△	♈	3	4:5
4 23:15	♂	☍	♉	5	9:4
7 4:51	♄	☍	♊	7	18:4
9 21:10	♂	△	♋	10	6:3
12 10:52	♂	□	♌	12	19:1
15 3:14	☿	☍	♍	15	7:2
17 5:06	♄	⚹	♎	17	18:2
19 21:53	♂	☌	♏	20	3:3
21 22:11	♄	☌	♐	22	10:1
24 9:26	♂	⚹	♑	24	13:5
26 10:52	♂	□	♒	26	14:5
28 10:56	♂	△	♓	28	14:5

DAILY ASPECTARIAN

1 Sa	☽∠♀	1:28
	☽△⚳	3:06
	☉⊼♃	4:06
	☽☌☿	4:40
	☉⊻♇	6:40
	☽∥♂	7:09
	☽☌♆	10:30
	☿∥♆	15:39
	☽⚼♂	17:10
	☽⊻♅	18:59
	☽☌⚷	22:19
	☽△♃	23:17
	☽⚹♇	23:38
2 Su	☉⊻☽	0:51
	☽⋕♅	0:54
	☽⚹♀	1:39
	☽∥⚷	2:41
	☽⚼⚳	3:34
	☉⊻♀	13:16
	☽∥⚳	16:13
	☽△♄	16:36
	☽⋕⚳	17:00
	☽⊼♂	18:14
3 M	☉∠☽	3:36
	☽⊼⚳	4:47
	☽⋕⚷	6:40
	☽⊻☿	8:43
	☽∥♅	8:45
	☽⊻♆	12:14
	⚳ ♏	17:30
	☽⚼♄	18:06
	☽☌♅	21:19
4 Tu	☽⊻⚷	0:59
	☽□♃	1:27
	☽□♇	2:17
	☉∥♄	4:17
	☽□♀	4:41
	☽⋕♂	5:02
	☉⚹☽	7:32
	☽∠☿	11:49
	☽∠♆	14:30
	☽⋕☿	17:45
	☽⊼♄	20:38
	☽☍♂	23:15
5 W	☉∥♀	1:30
	☽⋕♆	2:45
	☽∠⚷	3:49
	☽☍⚳	10:16
	☽⚹☿	15:40
	☽⚹♆	17:51
	♃△⚷	19:54
6 Th	☽⊻♅	3:41
	☽⚹♃	7:36
	☽⚹⚷	7:44
	☽△♇	9:01
	☽△♀	12:14
	☉⋕☽	16:27
	☉□☽	19:23
	☿ R	21:47
	☽⋕♀	22:04
7 F	☽⋕♄	0:12
	☽☍♄	4:51
	☽∠♅	8:24
	☽⊼♂	8:35
	☽∠♃	12:09
	☽⚼♇	13:53
	☽⚼♀	17:42
	☽⊼⚳	19:53
8 Sa	☽□☿	1:04
	☽□♆	3:30
	☽⚹♅	13:57
	☽⚼♂	14:36
	☽⊻♃	17:29
	☽□⚷	18:19
	☽⊼♇	19:32
9 Su	☽⊼♀	0:04
	☽⚼⚳	1:54
	☉△☽	11:43
	☽⊼♄	16:20
	☽△♂	21:10
10 M	☽△⚳	8:22
	☽△☿	11:00
	☽△♆	15:46
	☉⚼☽	20:47
	☽⚼♄	22:43
11 Tu	☽□♅	2:29
	☽☌♃	5:28
	☽△⚷	7:02
	☽☍♇	8:06
	☽☍♀	14:21
	☽⚼☿	15:38
	☉□♄	19:58
	☽⚼♆	22:14
	☿△⚳	23:37
12 W	☿∠♀	3:42
	♀∥♄	3:57
	☽△♄	5:10
	☉⊼☽	6:00
	☽⋕♀	7:57
	☽⋕♄	8:02
	☽□♂	10:52
	☽⚼⚷	13:33
	☽⊼☿	19:54
	☽□⚳	21:37
13 Th	☿R♒	3:31
	☽⊼♆	4:39
	☉⋕☽	12:46
	☽△♅	15:21
	☽⊻♃	17:44
	☉∠♅	18:10
	☽⊼⚷	19:57
	☽⊼♇	20:51
14 F	☽⊼♀	5:06
	☽⋕♆	10:41
	☽□♄	17:42
	☉⚼♃	20:36
	☽⚼♅	21:30
	☽⋕☿	22:32
	☽∠♃	23:37
	☉☍☽	23:54
15 Sa	☽⚹♂	0:04
	☉△♂	2:07
	☽⚼♇	2:55
	☽☍☿	3:14
	☽⋕♂	5:35
	☿∠♇	6:31
	☽⚹⚳	10:12
	☽⚼♀	12:15
	☽☍♆	16:51
	☉☌☿	20:23
16 Su	☽⊼♅	3:23
	☽⚹♃	5:12
	☽∠♂	6:11
	☽☍⚷	7:59
	☽∥♅	8:19
	☿△♂	8:20
	☽△♇	8:42
	☉∠♇	12:50
	☽⋕⚷	13:43
	☽∠⚳	16:01
	☽△♀	19:09
	☿⚼♃	19:44
17 M	☽∥⚳	3:56
	☽⚹♄	5:06
	☽⋕⚳	5:14
	☽⊼☿	9:16
	☽⊻♂	11:55
	☿∠♅	13:01
	☉⊼☽	16:18
	☽∥⚷	19:10
	☽⊻⚳	21:26
18 Tu	☽⋕♅	0:48
	☽⊼♆	3:45
	☽∠♄	10:12
	☽⚼☿	11:54
	☽☍♅	14:02
	☽□♃	15:19
	☊R♎	16:20
	☉ ♓	18:01
	☽⊼⚷	18:34
	☽□♇	19:06
	☉⚼☽	23:42
19 W	☽∥♂	3:29
	☿∥♆	6:01
	☿□♄	7:12
	☽□♀	7:46
	☽⚼♆	8:31
	☽△☿	14:15
	☽⊻♄	14:50
	☽∥♆	19:52
	☽∥☿	21:46
	☽☌♂	21:53
	☽⚼⚷	23:07
20 Th	☉∥☽	0:28
	♀∠♆	0:42
	☉△☽	6:25
	☽☌⚳	6:45
	☉△⚳	10:54
	☉∥☿	11:13
	☽△♆	12:44
	☽⊼♅	22:38
	☽△♃	23:28
21 F	☽△⚷	3:03
	☽⚹♇	3:23
	☿⊻♀	17:09
	☽□☿	17:59
	☽⚹♀	18:05
	☽∥♄	19:08
	☽∥♀	22:09
	☽☌♄	22:11
	☉∥♆	23:34
22 Sa	☽⚼♅	1:55
	☽⚼♃	2:33
	☽⊻♂	5:14
	☽∠♇	6:30
	☽⊻⚳	13:24
	☉□☽	17:16
	☽□♆	19:03
	☽∠♀	22:04
23 Su	☽△♅	4:27
	☽⊼♃	4:54
	☽∠♂	7:44
	☽□⚷	8:41
	☽⊻♇	8:51
	☽∠⚳	15:34
	☉☌♆	18:12
	☽⚹☿	20:05
24 M	☽⊻♀	1:13
	☽⊻♄	2:33
	☽⚹♂	9:26
	☽⚹⚳	16:58
	☽∠☿	20:28
	☽⚹♆	22:20
25 Tu	☉⚹☽	0:22
	☽∠♄	3:38
	♀⚹♄	4:51
	☽□♅	7:16
	☽☍♃	7:24
	☽⚹⚷	11:20
	☽☌♇	11:22
	☽⊻☿	20:30
	♇⚹⚷	22:36
	☽∠♆	23:00
26 W	☽∥♀	2:05
	☉∠☽	2:43
	☽⚹♄	4:09
	☽∥♄	5:00
	☽☌♀	5:18
	♃□♅	7:30
	☽□♂	10:52
	☽∠⚷	11:47
	☽□⚳	17:58
	☽⊻♆	23:14
27 Th	☉⊻☽	4:34
	☽∥☿	4:46
	☽⊼♃	7:48
	☽⚹♅	7:55
	⚳ R	8:09
	☽⊻♇	11:49
	☽⊻⚷	11:55
	☽☌☿	20:02
	☽∥♆	23:08
28 F	☽□♄	4:12
	☉∥♂	7:21
	☽⚼♃	7:42
	☽⊻♀	7:49
	☽∠♅	7:57
	☽△♂	10:56
	☽∥♂	11:36
	☽∠♇	11:47
	☉∥☽	12:00
	☿ D	14:01
	☽△⚳	17:54
	☽☌♆	23:18

LONGITUDE — March 2014

Day	Sid.Time	☉	☽	☽ 12 hour	Mean ☊	True ☊	☿	♀	♂	⚳	♃	♄	⚷	♅	♆	♇
	h m s	° ' "	° ' "	° ' "	° '	° '	° '	° '	° '	° '	° '	° '	° '	° '	° '	° '
1 Sa	10 34 54	10♓18 59	5♓40 40	13♓07 00	1♏08.6	29♎25.9	18♒10.3	26♑05.5	27♎31.8	1♏52.5	10♋29.5	23♏19.0	13♓11.6	10♈41.3	5♓14.7	13♑04.2
2 Su	10 38 50	11 19 13	20 29 24	27 46 55	1 05.4	29R 19.4	18 16.2	26 51.9	27R 31.9	1R 51.6	10R 28.5	23R 19.1	13 15.4	10 44.3	5 16.9	13 05.5
3 M	10 42 47	12 19 26	4♈58 46	12♈04 22	1 02.2	29 14.8	18 28.1	27 39.3	27 31.3	1 50.2	10 27.7	23 19.2	13 19.2	10 47.4	5 19.2	13 06.8
4 Tu	10 46 43	13 19 37	19 03 18	25 55 24	0 59.0	29D 12.4	18 45.9	28 27.4	27 30.0	1 48.5	10 27.1	23 19.1	13 23.0	10 50.5	5 21.5	13 08.0
5 W	10 50 40	14 19 47	2♉40 36	9♉19 03	0 55.8	29 12.0	19 09.0	29 16.4	27 27.9	1 46.2	10 26.7	23 18.9	13 26.8	10 53.7	5 23.7	13 09.3
6 Th	10 54 36	15 19 54	15 51 00	22 16 51	0 52.7	29 12.9	19 37.1	0♒06.1	27 25.0	1 43.6	10D 26.5	23 18.6	13 30.6	10 56.8	5 26.0	13 10.5
7 F	10 58 33	16 19 59	28 37 02	4♊52 06	0 49.5	29 14.4	20 10.0	0 56.6	27 21.4	1 40.5	10 26.5	23 18.2	13 34.4	11 00.0	5 28.2	13 11.6
8 Sa	11 02 30	17 20 02	11♊02 37	17 09 12	0 46.3	29R 15.5	20 47.2	1 47.7	27 17.0	1 37.0	10 26.8	23 17.7	13 38.2	11 03.2	5 30.5	13 12.8
9 Su	11 06 26	18 20 02	23 12 28	29 13 02	0 43.1	29 15.6	21 28.5	2 39.6	27 11.8	1 33.1	10 27.2	23 17.1	13 42.0	11 06.4	5 32.7	13 13.9
10 M	11 10 23	19 20 01	5♋11 30	11♋08 29	0 40.0	29 14.0	22 13.6	3 32.1	27 05.9	1 28.8	10 27.8	23 16.4	13 45.8	11 09.7	5 35.0	13 15.0
11 Tu	11 14 19	20 19 58	17 04 31	23 00 09	0 36.8	29 10.8	23 02.2	4 25.2	26 59.2	1 24.0	10 28.6	23 15.6	13 49.6	11 12.9	5 37.2	13 16.1
12 W	11 18 16	21 19 52	28 55 53	4♌52 09	0 33.6	29 05.8	23 54.1	5 19.0	26 51.8	1 18.9	10 29.6	23 14.7	13 53.3	11 16.2	5 39.4	13 17.1
13 Th	11 22 12	22 19 44	10♌49 21	16 47 53	0 30.4	28 59.7	24 49.2	6 13.3	26 43.5	1 13.3	10 30.7	23 13.7	13 57.1	11 19.4	5 41.6	13 18.1
14 F	11 26 09	23 19 34	22 48 02	28 50 06	0 27.2	28 53.1	25 47.1	7 08.2	26 34.5	1 07.4	10 32.1	23 12.6	14 00.9	11 22.7	5 43.8	13 19.1
15 Sa	11 30 05	24 19 22	4♍54 16	11♍00 46	0 24.1	28 46.5	26 47.7	8 03.7	26 24.8	1 01.0	10 33.7	23 11.5	14 04.6	11 26.0	5 46.0	13 20.1
16 Su	11 34 02	25 19 08	17 09 45	23 21 18	0 20.9	28 40.7	27 51.0	8 59.7	26 14.3	0 54.2	10 35.4	23 10.2	14 08.3	11 29.4	5 48.2	13 21.0
17 M	11 37 59	26 18 51	29 35 34	5♎52 35	0 17.7	28 36.3	28 56.6	9 56.2	26 03.0	0 47.1	10 37.4	23 08.8	14 12.1	11 32.7	5 50.3	13 21.9
18 Tu	11 41 55	27 18 33	12♎12 27	18 35 13	0 14.5	28 33.5	0♓04.6	10 53.2	25 50.9	0 39.5	10 39.5	23 07.3	14 15.8	11 36.0	5 52.5	13 22.8
19 W	11 45 52	28 18 13	25 00 56	1♏29 41	0 11.3	28D 32.3	1 14.7	11 50.6	25 38.2	0 31.6	10 41.9	23 05.7	14 19.5	11 39.4	5 54.6	13 23.6
20 Th	11 49 48	29 17 51	8♏01 33	14 36 35	0 08.2	28 32.6	2 26.9	12 48.6	25 24.7	0 23.3	10 44.4	23 04.0	14 23.2	11 42.7	5 56.8	13 24.4
21 F	11 53 45	0♈17 27	21 14 54	27 56 34	0 05.0	28 33.8	3 41.0	13 46.9	25 10.5	0 14.7	10 47.1	23 02.3	14 26.9	11 46.1	5 58.9	13 25.2
22 Sa	11 57 41	1 17 02	4♐41 41	11♐30 20	0 01.8	28 35.4	4 57.1	14 45.7	24 55.5	0 05.7	10 49.9	23 00.4	14 30.6	11 49.5	6 01.0	13 25.9
23 Su	12 01 38	2 16 35	18 22 33	25 18 23	29♎58.6	28 36.8	6 15.0	15 44.9	24 39.9	29♎56.3	10 53.0	22 58.5	14 34.2	11 52.9	6 03.1	13 26.7
24 M	12 05 34	3 16 06	2♑17 47	9♑20 40	29 55.5	28R 37.4	7 34.6	16 44.5	24 23.6	29 46.7	10 56.3	22 56.4	14 37.9	11 56.3	6 05.2	13 27.4
25 Tu	12 09 31	4 15 35	16 26 52	23 36 08	29 52.3	28 36.9	8 56.0	17 44.5	24 06.7	29 36.6	10 59.7	22 54.3	14 41.5	11 59.7	6 07.3	13 28.0
26 W	12 13 28	5 15 03	0♒48 07	8♒02 23	29 49.1	28 35.4	10 19.0	18 44.9	23 49.1	29 26.3	11 03.3	22 52.1	14 45.1	12 03.1	6 09.3	13 28.6
27 Th	12 17 24	6 14 29	15 18 24	22 35 30	29 45.9	28 32.9	11 43.6	19 45.6	23 30.9	29 15.7	11 07.1	22 49.7	14 48.7	12 06.5	6 11.4	13 29.3
28 F	12 21 21	7 13 53	29 53 01	7♓10 10	29 42.7	28 30.0	13 09.8	20 46.6	23 12.1	29 04.7	11 11.0	22 47.3	14 52.3	12 09.9	6 13.4	13 29.8
29 Sa	12 25 17	8 13 15	14♓26 10	21 40 14	29 39.6	28 27.1	14 37.5	21 48.0	22 52.8	28 53.5	11 15.2	22 44.9	14 55.8	12 13.3	6 15.4	13 30.4
30 Su	12 29 14	9 12 35	28 51 35	5♈59 31	29 36.4	28 24.8	16 06.8	22 49.7	22 32.9	28 42.0	11 19.5	22 42.3	14 59.4	12 16.8	6 17.4	13 30.9
31 M	12 33 10	10♈11 54	13♈03 24	20 02 40	29♎33.2	28♎23.3	17♓37.5	23♒51.6	22♎12.6	28♎30.3	11♋23.9	22♏39.6	15♓02.9	12♈20.2	6♓19.4	13♑31.3

1st of Month

Julian Day # 2456717.5
Obliquity 23°26'07"
SVP 5♓03'33"
GC 27♐02.2
Eris 22♈04.3

Day	⚴	Day	⚵	Day	⚶
1	1♍30.0R	1	28♓43.1	1	29♎59.4
6	29♌59.2R	6	1♈22.6	6	29 55.9R
11	28 37.9R	11	4 03.5	11	29 40.2R
16	27 28.1R	16	6 45.9	16	29 12.2R
21	26 31.1R	21	9 29.5	21	28 32.6R
26	25 47.5R	26	12 14.4	26	27 42.1R
31	25 17.7R	31	15 00.4	31	26 42.0R

DECLINATION and LATITUDE

Day	☉ Decl	☽ Decl	☽ Lat	☽ 12h Decl	☿ Decl	☿ Lat	♀ Decl	♀ Lat	♂ Decl	♂ Lat	⚳ Decl	⚳ Lat	♃ Decl	♃ Lat	♄ Decl	♄ Lat
1 Sa	7S42	5S35	4N08	3S13	13S39	1N50	16S36	4N25	7S58	2N49	0N34	13N30	23N15	0N14	16S19	2N21
2 Su	7 19	0 49	3 13	1N35	13 50	1 36	16 34	4 18	7 57	2 50	0 37	13 33	23 16	0 14	16 19	2 21
3 M	6 56	3N55	2 07	6 10	13 59	1 22	16 32	4 11	7 57	2 50	0 41	13 36	23 16	0 14	16 19	2 21
4 Tu	6 33	8 18	0 55	10 17	14 06	1 09	16 29	4 04	7 56	2 50	0 44	13 39	23 16	0 14	16 19	2 22
5 W	6 10	12 06	0S19	13 44	14 11	0 56	16 26	3 57	7 55	2 50	0 47	13 41	23 16	0 15	16 19	2 22
6 Th	5 47	15 10	1 29	16 23	14 15	0 43	16 23	3 50	7 54	2 51	0 51	13 44	23 16	0 15	16 19	2 22
7 F	5 24	17 22	2 32	18 08	14 16	0 31	16 19	3 42	7 52	2 51	0 54	13 47	23 16	0 15	16 18	2 22
8 Sa	5 00	18 41	3 27	18 59	14 16	0 19	16 15	3 35	7 50	2 51	0 58	13 49	23 16	0 15	16 18	2 22
9 Su	4 37	19 05	4 11	18 57	14 14	0 07	16 11	3 28	7 48	2 51	1 01	13 52	23 16	0 15	16 17	2 23
10 M	4 13	18 37	4 43	18 04	14 10	0S04	16 06	3 21	7 46	2 51	1 05	13 54	23 16	0 15	16 17	2 23
11 Tu	3 50	17 20	5 03	16 24	14 05	0 15	16 00	3 14	7 44	2 51	1 09	13 57	23 16	0 15	16 17	2 23
12 W	3 26	15 18	5 10	14 03	13 58	0 26	15 54	3 07	7 41	2 52	1 12	13 59	23 16	0 15	16 16	2 23
13 Th	3 03	12 39	5 04	11 06	13 49	0 36	15 48	3 01	7 38	2 52	1 16	14 01	23 16	0 15	16 16	2 23
14 F	2 39	9 26	4 44	7 40	13 38	0 46	15 41	2 54	7 35	2 51	1 20	14 03	23 16	0 15	16 15	2 24
15 Sa	2 15	5 49	4 11	3 53	13 27	0 55	15 34	2 47	7 32	2 51	1 24	14 05	23 16	0 15	16 15	2 24
16 Su	1 52	1 54	3 27	0S07	13 13	1 04	15 26	2 40	7 28	2 51	1 28	14 07	23 16	0 15	16 14	2 24
17 M	1 28	2S09	2 32	4 11	12 58	1 12	15 18	2 33	7 24	2 51	1 32	14 09	23 16	0 15	16 14	2 24
18 Tu	1 04	6 11	1 28	8 07	12 42	1 20	15 09	2 26	7 20	2 51	1 36	14 11	23 16	0 15	16 13	2 24
19 W	0 40	9 59	0 19	11 44	12 24	1 28	14 60	2 20	7 16	2 50	1 41	14 12	23 16	0 16	16 13	2 24
20 Th	0 17	13 22	0N52	14 50	12 04	1 35	14 50	2 13	7 11	2 50	1 45	14 14	23 16	0 16	16 13	2 25
21 F	0N07	16 07	2 01	17 11	11 44	1 41	14 40	2 07	7 06	2 50	1 49	14 15	23 15	0 16	16 12	2 25
22 Sa	0 31	18 02	3 05	18 37	11 22	1 47	14 29	2 00	7 02	2 49	1 53	14 16	23 15	0 16	16 11	2 25
23 Su	0 54	18 56	4 00	18 58	10 58	1 53	14 18	1 54	6 56	2 48	1 57	14 17	23 15	0 16	16 11	2 25
24 M	1 18	18 43	4 42	18 10	10 33	1 58	14 07	1 47	6 51	2 48	2 02	14 18	23 15	0 16	16 10	2 25
25 Tu	1 42	17 20	5 07	16 14	10 07	2 03	13 55	1 41	6 46	2 47	2 06	14 19	23 15	0 16	16 09	2 26
26 W	2 05	14 52	5 14	13 15	9 40	2 07	13 42	1 35	6 40	2 46	2 10	14 20	23 15	0 16	16 08	2 26
27 Th	2 29	11 27	5 01	9 27	9 11	2 11	13 29	1 28	6 34	2 46	2 14	14 21	23 14	0 16	16 07	2 26
28 F	2 52	7 19	4 29	5 04	8 41	2 15	13 16	1 22	6 28	2 45	2 18	14 21	23 14	0 16	16 07	2 26
29 Sa	3 16	2 45	3 39	0 25	8 10	2 18	13 02	1 16	6 22	2 44	2 22	14 22	23 14	0 16	16 06	2 26
30 Su	3 39	1N56	2 36	4N13	7 38	2 20	12 48	1 10	6 15	2 43	2 27	14 22	23 13	0 16	16 05	2 26
31 M	4N02	6N26	1N24	8N33	7S04	2S22	12S33	1N04	6S09	2N41	2N31	14N22	23N13	0N16	16S04	2N26

Day	⚷ Decl	⚷ Lat	♅ Decl	♅ Lat	♆ Decl	♆ Lat	♇ Decl	♇ Lat
1	2S13	4N45	3N38	0S39	10S13	0S40	20S07	2N41
6	2 06	4 45	3 44	0 39	10 09	0 40	20 07	2 41
11	1 59	4 44	3 50	0 39	10 05	0 41	20 06	2 41
16	1 52	4 44	3 57	0 39	10 01	0 41	20 06	2 41
21	1 45	4 44	4 03	0 39	9 57	0 41	20 06	2 41
26	1 38	4 45	4 10	0 39	9 53	0 41	20 05	2 41
31	1S31	4N45	4N17	0S39	9S49	0S41	20S05	2N41

Day	⚴ Decl	⚴ Lat	⚵ Decl	⚵ Lat	⚶ Decl	⚶ Lat	Eris Decl	Eris Lat
1	9S10	21S28	2S60	2S42	1S20	10N48	3S17	12S47
6	6 57	19 39	2 09	2 56	0 59	11 10	3 16	12 46
11	4 44	17 45	1 18	3 10	0 34	11 30	3 14	12 46
16	2 33	15 50	0 26	3 24	0 06	11 50	3 13	12 45
21	0 27	13 55	0N25	3 38	0N24	12 07	3 11	12 45
26	1N33	12 03	1 17	3 51	0 55	12 22	3 10	12 45
31	3N25	10S15	2N09	4S05	1N27	12N34	3S08	12S44

Moon Phenomena

Max/0 Decl

dy	hr mn	
2	4:03	0 N
8	22:59	19N05
16	11:17	0 S
23	7:24	19S00
29	14:06	0 N

Max/0 Lat

dy	hr mn	
4	17:48	0 S
12	0:17	5S10
19	6:32	0 N
25	20:26	5N14

Perigee/Apogee

dy	hr m		kilometers
11	19:53	a	405363
27	18:41	p	365705

PH	dy	hr mn	
●	1	8:01	10♓39
☽	8	13:28	17♊54
○	16	17:09	26♍02
☾	24	1:47	3♑21
●	30	18:46	9♈59

Void of Course Moon

Last Aspect			☽ Ingress		
2 11:05	♀	✶	♈	2	15:41
4 17:32	♀	□	♉	4	19:13
6 13:56	♄	☍	♊	7	2:38
9 7:54	♂	△	♋	9	13:34
11 19:52	♂	□	♌	12	2:10
14 7:25	♂	✶	♍	14	14:19
16 17:09	☉	☍	♎	17	0:47
19 1:08	♂	☌	♏	19	9:14
21 3:13	♄	☌	♐	21	15:40
23 10:41	♂	✶	♑	23	20:04
25 12:36	♂	□	♒	25	22:40
27 13:14	♂	△	♓	28	0:12
29 13:45	♄	△	♈	30	1:55

DAILY ASPECTARIAN

1 Sa
☉△♃ 4:06
☽△♃ 7:45
☉☌☽ 8:01
☽⊻♅ 8:06
☽∠♀ 9:12
☉⊻♅ 9:21
☽#♅ 9:52
☽⚼♂ 11:03
☽✶♇ 11:57
☽☌⚷ 12:11
♂ R 16:25
☽∥⚷ 17:04
☽⚼⚳ 18:05
☽⊻☿ 20:20

2 Su
☽#⚳ 0:55
⚶ R 2:11
☽△♄ 4:38
☽∥⚳ 7:15
☽✶♀ 11:05
☽⊼♂ 11:35
☽#⚷ 15:02
♄ R 16:20
☽⊼⚳ 18:45
♀□♂ 20:05
☽∠☿ 21:25
☽∥♅ 22:42

3 M
☽⊻♆ 0:34
☉⚼♂ 4:39
☽⚼♄ 5:38
☽□♃ 9:15
☽☌♅ 9:51
⚵ ♈ 10:00
☉⊻☽ 13:23
☽□♇ 13:48
☽⊻⚷ 14:12
☉#☽ 14:55
☉✶♇ 19:17
♀∠⚷ 21:38
☽#♂ 21:53
☽✶☿ 23:29

4 Tu
☉☌⚷ 1:27
☽∠♆ 2:16
☽⊼♄ 7:25
☽#♆ 11:15
☽☍♂ 14:45
☽∠⚷ 16:26
☉∠♀ 16:32
☽□♀ 17:32
☉∠☽ 17:33
☽☍⚳ 22:23

5 W
☽✶♆ 4:54
☽✶♃ 14:03
☽⊻♅ 14:56
☽#☿ 15:59
☽△♇ 19:03
☽✶⚷ 19:40
♀ ♒ 21:04
⚴ R ♌ 22:57
☉✶☽ 22:58

6 Th
☽□☿ 7:18
♃ D 10:43
☽#♄ 11:14
☽#♀ 11:48
☽☍♄ 13:56
☽∠♃ 17:58
☽∠♅ 19:00
☽⊼♂ 21:37
☽⚼♇ 23:12

7 F
☽△♀ 4:46
☽⊼⚳ 5:50
☉⚼⚳ 7:47
♀∥♄ 9:09
☽□♆ 13:12
♀□⚳ 19:20
☽⊻♃ 22:50

8 Sa
☽✶♅ 0:01
☽⚼♂ 2:25
☽⊼♇ 4:15
☽□⚷ 5:06
☽⚼⚳ 10:53
☽⚼♀ 12:09
☉□☽ 13:28
☽△☿ 20:20

9 Su
☽⊼♄ 0:09
☽△♂ 7:54
☽△⚳ 16:35
☽⊼♀ 20:24

10 M
☽△♆ 0:47
☽⚼☿ 4:23
☽⚼♄ 6:12
☽☌♃ 10:38
☽□♅ 12:06
☽☍♇ 16:17
☽△⚷ 17:23
☉#♅ 23:33

11 Tu
☿□♄ 6:15
☽⚼♆ 7:12
☉△☽ 7:12
☽△♄ 12:30
☽⊼☿ 13:00
☽#♄ 13:33
☽#♀ 17:24
☽□♂ 19:52
☽⚼⚷ 23:55

12 W
☽□⚳ 4:47
♀⊻♆ 9:26
☽#☿ 13:30
☽⊼♆ 13:38
☽☍♀ 13:58
☉⚼☽ 16:19
☽⊻♃ 23:22

13 Th
☽△♅ 1:01
☽⊼♇ 5:00
☽⊼⚷ 6:19
☿⚼♃ 17:45
☽#♆ 19:45
☉△♄ 21:17

14 F
☽□♄ 0:49
☉⊼☽ 1:09
☽∠♃ 5:27
☽☍☿ 6:29
☽⚼♅ 7:09
☽✶♂ 7:25
☽⚼♇ 10:59
☽#♂ 12:45
☿∠♅ 15:03
☿△♂ 16:18
☽✶⚳ 16:23

15 Sa
☽☍♆ 1:42
☽⊼♀ 6:43
☽✶♃ 11:08
☽∥♅ 11:40
☽∠♂ 12:36
☽⊼♅ 12:53
☽△♇ 16:34
☽☍⚷ 18:05
☽∠⚳ 21:34
☉∥⚷ 23:47

16 Su
☽#⚷ 0:12
☉#☽ 0:15
☽∥⚳ 2:30
☿∠♇ 11:14
☽✶♄ 11:37
☽⚼♀ 14:19
☉☍☽ 17:09
☽⊻♂ 17:18
☉⊼♂ 18:39
☉#⚳ 20:08
☉∥☽ 20:17
☽#⚳ 20:19
☽∥⚷ 22:09
☽⊼☿ 22:38

17 M
☽⊻⚳ 2:16
☽#♅ 10:47
☽⊼♆ 11:58
☽∠♄ 16:17
♀⊼♃ 18:03
☽□♃ 21:04
☽△♀ 21:18
☿ ♓ 22:25
☽☍♅ 22:51

18 Tu
☽□♇ 2:13
☽⊼⚷ 3:54
☽⚼☿ 5:57
☽∥♂ 6:59
☿△⚳ 10:51
☽⚼♆ 16:20
♀✶♅ 19:01
☽⊻♄ 20:26
☽∥♆ 23:56

19 W
☽☌♂ 1:08
☉⊼☽ 6:37
☽⚼⚷ 8:02
☽☌⚳ 10:06
☽△☿ 12:42
☽∥☿ 15:15
☽△♆ 20:11

20 Th
☽△♃ 4:58
⚳#⚷ 5:45
☽⊼♅ 6:46
☽□♀ 9:25
☽✶♇ 9:49
☽∥♀ 11:20
☽△⚷ 11:39
☉⚼☽ 12:22
♀⊻♇ 14:57
☉ ♈ 16:58
☉⊼⚳ 23:02

21 F
☽∥♄ 0:46
☽☌♄ 3:13
☽⊻♂ 6:55
☽⚼♃ 8:10
☽⚼♅ 9:57
☽∠♇ 12:52
☽⊻⚳ 15:56
♀⊻⚷ 17:25
☉△☽ 17:28

22 Sa
☽□☿ 0:30
☽□♆ 2:21
☽∠♂ 9:03
☽⊼♃ 10:52
☽△♅ 12:37
⚳ R ♎ 14:43
☽⊻♇ 15:23
☽□⚷ 17:20
☽∠⚳ 18:05
☽✶♀ 19:04
☿☌♆ 20:17

23 Su
☽⊻♄ 7:57
☽✶♂ 10:41
☽✶⚳ 19:44
☽∠♀ 22:59

24 M
☉□☽ 1:47
☽✶♆ 6:29
☽∠♄ 9:36
☽✶☿ 9:57
☽☍♃ 14:45
⚳⚼⚷ 15:32
☽□♅ 16:27
☽☌♇ 18:58
☽✶⚷ 21:02
☉#⚷ 21:33

25 Tu
☽⊻♀ 2:20
☿⚼♂ 2:34
☽∠♆ 7:52
☽✶♄ 10:48
☿∥♆ 12:15
☽□♂ 12:36
☽∥♄ 12:50
☽∠☿ 13:53
☽□⚳ 21:46
☽∠⚷ 22:15

26 W
☉∥⚳ 5:57
☉✶☽ 7:55
☽⊻♆ 8:54
☽∥♀ 9:25
☿△♃ 13:12
☽⊼♃ 17:03
☽⊻☿ 17:27
☽✶♅ 18:42
☽⊻♇ 21:00
☉⊻♆ 22:42
☽⊻⚷ 23:11

27 Th
☿⊻♅ 6:41
☽☌♀ 7:53
☽∥♆ 9:34
☉∠☽ 10:29
☽□♄ 12:21
☽△♂ 13:14
☽∥☿ 15:20
☽⚼♃ 17:53
☽∠♅ 19:31
☽∠♇ 21:43
☽△⚳ 22:42

28 F
☽∥♂ 4:43
☿✶♇ 5:33
☽☌♆ 10:28
☉⚼♄ 12:59
☉⊻☽ 12:59
☿⚼⚳ 13:22
☽⚼♂ 13:24
☽#♅ 16:25
☽△♃ 18:43
☽⊻♅ 20:20
☉#☽ 21:37
☽✶♇ 22:28
☽⚼⚳ 23:07

29 Sa
☽☌☿ 0:21
☽☌⚷ 0:49
☽#⚳ 1:56
☿☌⚷ 5:10
☽∥⚷ 6:11
♂⊻♄ 11:05
☽⊻♀ 13:09
☽⊼♂ 13:42
☽△♄ 13:45
♀△♂ 19:06
♀□♄ 21:15
☽#⚷ 21:59
☽⊼⚳ 23:44

30 Su
☽∥⚳ 2:43
☉∥☽ 9:49
☽∥♅ 12:15
☽⊻♆ 12:32
☽⚼♄ 14:51
☽∠♀ 16:18
☉☌☽ 18:46
☽□♃ 21:10
☽#♂ 22:27
☽☌♅ 22:46

31 M
☽□♇ 0:48
☽#☿ 3:07
☽⊻⚷ 3:25
☽⊻☿ 8:48
☽∠♆ 14:15
☽☍♂ 15:22
☉∥♅ 15:49
☽⊼♄ 16:29
☽#♆ 19:40
☽✶♀ 20:08

April 2014

LONGITUDE

Day	Sid.Time	☉	☽	☽ 12 hour	Mean☊	True☊	☿	♀	♂	⚳	♃	♄	⚷	♅	♆	♇
	h m s	° ' "	° ' "	° ' "	° '	° '	° '	° '	° '	° '	° '	° '	° '	° '	° '	° '
1 Tu	12 37 07	11♈11 10	26♈56 53	3♉45 47	29♎30.0	28♎22.7	19♓09.7	24♒53.9	21♎51.8	28♎18.3	11♋28.6	22♏36.9	15♓06.4	12♈23.6	6♓21.4	13♑31.8
2 W	12 41 03	12 10 24	10♉29 08	17 06 53	29 26.9	28D 23.0	20 43.4	25 56.4	21R 30.6	28R 06.1	11 33.4	22R 34.1	15 09.9	12 27.0	6 23.3	13 32.2
3 Th	12 45 00	13 09 36	23 39 05	0♊05 53	29 23.7	28 24.0	22 18.5	26 59.2	21 09.0	27 53.6	11 38.4	22 31.2	15 13.3	12 30.5	6 25.2	13 32.6
4 F	12 48 56	14 08 46	6♊27 33	12 44 23	29 20.5	28 25.2	23 55.1	28 02.3	20 47.1	27 41.0	11 43.5	22 28.2	15 16.7	12 33.9	6 27.1	13 33.0
5 Sa	12 52 53	15 07 53	18 56 49	25 05 19	29 17.3	28 26.4	25 33.2	29 05.6	20 24.9	27 28.2	11 48.9	22 25.1	15 20.2	12 37.3	6 29.0	13 33.3
6 Su	12 56 50	16 06 59	1♋10 22	7♋12 31	29 14.1	28 27.4	27 12.7	0♓09.2	20 02.4	27 15.3	11 54.3	22 22.0	15 23.5	12 40.8	6 30.9	13 33.6
7 M	13 00 46	17 06 02	13 12 21	19 10 26	29 11.0	28R 27.8	28 53.6	1 13.0	19 39.8	27 02.1	12 00.0	22 18.8	15 26.9	12 44.2	6 32.7	13 33.8
8 Tu	13 04 43	18 05 02	25 07 21	1♌03 42	29 07.8	28 27.7	0♈36.0	2 17.0	19 17.0	26 48.9	12 05.8	22 15.5	15 30.2	12 47.6	6 34.6	13 34.1
9 W	13 08 39	19 04 01	7♌00 02	12 56 55	29 04.6	28 27.2	2 19.9	3 21.3	18 54.0	26 35.6	12 11.7	22 12.2	15 33.5	12 51.0	6 36.4	13 34.3
10 Th	13 12 36	20 02 57	18 54 54	24 54 27	29 01.4	28 26.3	4 05.3	4 25.8	18 31.0	26 22.1	12 17.8	22 08.8	15 36.8	12 54.4	6 38.2	13 34.4
11 F	13 16 32	21 01 51	0♍56 04	7♍00 09	28 58.3	28 25.3	5 52.1	5 30.4	18 08.0	26 08.6	12 24.0	22 05.3	15 40.1	12 57.8	6 39.9	13 34.6
12 Sa	13 20 29	22 00 42	13 07 06	19 17 15	28 55.1	28 24.4	7 40.5	6 35.3	17 45.0	25 55.0	12 30.4	22 01.8	15 43.3	13 01.2	6 41.7	13 34.7
13 Su	13 24 25	22 59 32	25 30 51	1♎48 09	28 51.9	28 23.6	9 30.4	7 40.4	17 22.0	25 41.4	12 37.0	21 58.2	15 46.5	13 04.6	6 43.4	13 34.8
14 M	13 28 22	23 58 19	8♎09 17	14 34 22	28 48.7	28 23.2	11 21.8	8 45.7	16 59.2	25 27.7	12 43.7	21 54.5	15 49.6	13 08.0	6 45.1	13R 34.8
15 Tu	13 32 19	24 57 04	21 03 26	27 36 29	28 45.5	28D 22.9	13 14.7	9 51.1	16 36.5	25 14.0	12 50.5	21 50.8	15 52.7	13 11.4	6 46.7	13 34.8
16 W	13 36 15	25 55 47	4♏13 27	10♏54 12	28 42.4	28 22.9	15 09.2	10 56.8	16 13.9	25 00.4	12 57.5	21 47.0	15 55.8	13 14.8	6 48.4	13 34.8
17 Th	13 40 12	26 54 29	17 38 35	24 26 23	28 39.2	28 23.0	17 05.1	12 02.6	15 51.6	24 46.7	13 04.6	21 43.2	15 58.9	13 18.1	6 50.0	13 34.8
18 F	13 44 08	27 53 08	1♐17 23	8♐07 12	28 36.0	28R 23.1	19 02.6	13 08.6	15 29.6	24 33.1	13 11.9	21 39.3	16 01.9	13 21.5	6 51.6	13 34.7
19 Sa	13 48 05	28 51 46	15 07 54	22 06 51	28 32.8	28 23.1	21 01.6	14 14.8	15 07.9	24 19.6	13 19.3	21 35.3	16 05.0	13 24.8	6 53.2	13 34.6
20 Su	13 52 01	29 50 22	29 07 51	6♑10 38	28 29.7	28 23.0	23 02.0	15 21.1	14 46.5	24 06.1	13 26.8	21 31.3	16 07.9	13 28.1	6 54.8	13 34.4
21 M	13 55 58	0♉48 57	13♑14 52	20 20 15	28 26.5	28 22.9	25 03.9	16 27.6	14 25.6	23 52.7	13 34.5	21 27.3	16 10.9	13 31.5	6 56.3	13 34.3
22 Tu	13 59 54	1 47 30	27 26 29	4♒33 16	28 23.3	28D 22.8	27 07.1	17 34.2	14 05.0	23 39.4	13 42.3	21 23.2	16 13.8	13 34.8	6 57.8	13 34.1
23 W	14 03 51	2 46 01	11♒40 17	18 47 13	28 20.1	28 22.8	29 11.5	18 41.0	13 44.9	23 26.2	13 50.2	21 19.1	16 16.6	13 38.1	6 59.3	13 33.9
24 Th	14 07 48	3 44 30	25 53 46	2♓59 34	28 16.9	28 23.1	1♉17.1	19 48.0	13 25.3	23 13.2	13 58.2	21 14.9	16 19.5	13 41.3	7 00.8	13 33.6
25 F	14 11 44	4 42 58	10♓04 19	17 07 40	28 13.8	28 23.5	3 23.8	20 55.1	13 06.3	23 00.3	14 06.4	21 10.7	16 22.3	13 44.6	7 02.2	13 33.3
26 Sa	14 15 41	5 41 25	24 09 15	1♈08 43	28 10.6	28 24.2	5 31.3	22 02.3	12 47.7	22 47.6	14 14.7	21 06.5	16 25.0	13 47.8	7 03.6	13 33.0
27 Su	14 19 37	6 39 50	8♈05 43	14 59 55	28 07.4	28 24.8	7 39.6	23 09.6	12 29.8	22 35.0	14 23.1	21 02.2	16 27.7	13 51.1	7 05.0	13 32.7
28 M	14 23 34	7 38 13	21 51 00	28 38 39	28 04.2	28R 25.2	9 48.3	24 17.1	12 12.5	22 22.7	14 31.7	20 57.9	16 30.4	13 54.3	7 06.3	13 32.3
29 Tu	14 27 30	8 36 34	5♉22 38	12♉02 44	28 01.0	28 25.2	11 57.4	25 24.7	11 55.9	22 10.6	14 40.4	20 53.6	16 33.0	13 57.5	7 07.6	13 31.9
30 W	14 31 27	9♉34 54	18 38 46	25 10 38	27♎57.9	28♎24.6	14♉06.4	26♓32.4	11♎39.9	21♎58.7	14♋49.1	20♏49.2	16♓35.6	14♈00.7	7♓08.9	13♑31.4

1st of Month

Julian Day # 2456748.5
Obliquity 23°26'07"
SVP 5♓03'31"
GC 27♐02.3
Eris 22♈22.4

Day	⚴	⚵	⚶
1	25♌13.4R	15♈33.8	26♎29.0R
6	24 59.9R	18 21.2	25 20.0R
11	24 59.5	21 09.5	24 06.4R
16	25 11.1	23 58.7	22 50.7R
21	25 34.1	26 48.8	21 35.9R
26	26 07.4	29 39.7	20 24.5R

DECLINATION and LATITUDE

Day	☉ Decl	☽ Decl	☽ Lat	☽12h Decl	☿ Decl	☿ Lat	♀ Decl	♀ Lat	♂ Decl	♂ Lat	⚳ Decl	⚳ Lat	♃ Decl	♃ Lat	♄ Decl	♄ Lat
1 Tu	4N26	10N30	0N08	12N18	6S29	2S24	12S18	0N58	6S02	2N40	2N35	14N22	23N13	0N16	16S03	2N27
2 W	4 49	13 55	1S06	15 19	5 54	2 25	12 03	0 52	5 56	2 39	2 39	14 22	23 12	0 16	16 03	2 27
3 Th	5 12	16 30	2 15	17 27	5 16	2 25	11 47	0 47	5 49	2 38	2 42	14 21	23 12	0 17	16 02	2 27
4 F	5 35	18 11	3 15	18 40	4 38	2 25	11 31	0 41	5 42	2 36	2 46	14 21	23 12	0 17	16 01	2 27
5 Sa	5 58	18 55	4 04	18 56	3 59	2 25	11 14	0 36	5 35	2 35	2 50	14 20	23 11	0 17	15 60	2 27
6 Su	6 20	18 44	4 41	18 20	3 19	2 24	10 57	0 30	5 28	2 33	2 54	14 19	23 11	0 17	15 59	2 27
7 M	6 43	17 43	5 05	16 54	2 37	2 23	10 39	0 25	5 21	2 31	2 57	14 18	23 10	0 17	15 58	2 27
8 Tu	7 05	15 55	5 16	14 46	1 55	2 21	10 21	0 19	5 14	2 30	3 01	14 17	23 10	0 17	15 57	2 28
9 W	7 28	13 28	5 13	12 01	1 11	2 18	10 03	0 14	5 07	2 28	3 04	14 16	23 09	0 17	15 56	2 28
10 Th	7 50	10 27	4 57	8 46	0 27	2 16	9 45	0 09	5 00	2 26	3 07	14 14	23 09	0 17	15 55	2 28
11 F	8 12	6 58	4 27	5 06	0N18	2 12	9 26	0 04	4 53	2 24	3 11	14 13	23 08	0 17	15 54	2 28
12 Sa	8 34	3 10	3 45	1 05	1 05	2 08	9 06	0S01	4 46	2 22	3 14	14 11	23 08	0 17	15 53	2 28
13 Su	8 56	0S51	2 52	2S53	1 52	2 04	8 47	0 06	4 39	2 20	3 17	14 09	23 07	0 17	15 52	2 28
14 M	9 18	4 55	1 50	6 55	2 40	1 59	8 27	0 11	4 33	2 18	3 19	14 07	23 07	0 17	15 51	2 28
15 Tu	9 40	8 50	0 41	10 41	3 29	1 54	8 07	0 15	4 26	2 16	3 22	14 05	23 06	0 17	15 50	2 28
16 W	10 01	12 25	0N32	14 00	4 19	1 48	7 46	0 20	4 19	2 14	3 25	14 02	23 05	0 17	15 49	2 28
17 Th	10 22	15 25	1 45	16 37	5 09	1 41	7 25	0 24	4 13	2 11	3 27	13 60	23 05	0 17	15 48	2 28
18 F	10 43	17 36	2 53	18 19	5 60	1 34	7 04	0 29	4 07	2 09	3 29	13 57	23 04	0 17	15 47	2 29
19 Sa	11 04	18 47	3 51	18 57	6 51	1 27	6 42	0 33	4 01	2 07	3 32	13 54	23 03	0 18	15 46	2 29
20 Su	11 25	18 49	4 37	18 24	7 43	1 19	6 21	0 37	3 54	2 04	3 34	13 51	23 03	0 18	15 45	2 29
21 M	11 45	17 42	5 06	16 43	8 36	1 11	5 58	0 41	3 49	2 02	3 35	13 48	23 02	0 18	15 44	2 29
22 Tu	12 06	15 29	5 17	14 01	9 29	1 02	5 36	0 45	3 43	1 60	3 37	13 45	23 01	0 18	15 43	2 29
23 W	12 26	12 20	5 09	10 29	10 21	0 53	5 14	0 49	3 38	1 57	3 39	13 42	23 01	0 18	15 42	2 29
24 Th	12 46	8 28	4 41	6 20	11 14	0 44	4 51	0 53	3 32	1 55	3 40	13 38	22 60	0 18	15 40	2 29
25 F	13 05	4 08	3 57	1 52	12 07	0 34	4 28	0 56	3 27	1 52	3 41	13 35	22 59	0 18	15 39	2 29
26 Sa	13 25	0N25	2 59	2N41	12 59	0 24	4 05	1 00	3 22	1 49	3 42	13 31	22 58	0 18	15 38	2 29
27 Su	13 44	4 54	1 50	7 02	13 51	0 14	3 41	1 04	3 18	1 47	3 43	13 27	22 57	0 18	15 37	2 29
28 M	14 03	9 04	0 36	10 58	14 42	0 03	3 18	1 07	3 14	1 44	3 44	13 23	22 56	0 18	15 36	2 29
29 Tu	14 22	12 42	0S38	14 16	15 32	0N08	2 54	1 10	3 09	1 42	3 44	13 18	22 56	0 18	15 35	2 29
30 W	14N41	15N37	1S50	16N45	16N22	0N18	2S30	1S13	3S06	1N39	3N44	13N14	22N55	0N18	15S34	2N29

Day	⚷ Decl	⚷ Lat	♅ Decl	♅ Lat	♆ Decl	♆ Lat	♇ Decl	♇ Lat
1	1S29	4N45	4N18	0S39	9S49	0S41	20S05	2N41
6	1 22	4 45	4 25	0 39	9 45	0 41	20 05	2 40
11	1 16	4 46	4 31	0 39	9 42	0 41	20 05	2 40
16	1 09	4 46	4 38	0 39	9 39	0 41	20 05	2 40
21	1 03	4 47	4 44	0 39	9 36	0 41	20 05	2 40
26	0 57	4 47	4 51	0 39	9 34	0 42	20 05	2 40

Day	⚴ Decl	⚴ Lat	⚵ Decl	⚵ Lat	⚶ Decl	⚶ Lat	Eris Decl	Eris Lat
1	3N46	9S54	2N19	4S08	1N33	12N36	3S08	12S44
6	5 27	8 12	3 10	4 21	2 04	12 43	3 06	12 44
11	6 58	6 35	4 00	4 35	2 33	12 46	3 05	12 44
16	8 20	5 05	4 50	4 49	2 58	12 45	3 04	12 43
21	9 32	3 41	5 38	5 02	3 20	12 39	3 02	12 43
26	10 35	2 22	6 25	5 16	3 36	12 29	3 01	12 43

Moon Phenomena

Max/0 Decl
dy hr mn
5 7:12 18N57
12 18:57 0 S
19 12:56 18S57
25 21:49 0 N

Perigee/Apogee
dy hr m kilometers
8 14:56 a 404498
23 0:31 p 369765

Max/0 Lat
dy hr mn
1 2:30 0 S
8 6:43 5S17
15 13:24 0 N
22 1:27 5N17
28 11:36 0 S

PH dy hr mn
☽ 7 8:32 17♋27
○ 15 7:43 25♎16
● 15 7:47 T 1.290
☾ 22 7:53 2♒07
● 29 6:15 8♉52
● 29 6:05 A non-C

Void of Course Moon

Last Aspect			☽ Ingress	
31 20:08	♀	✶	♉	1 5:21
3 6:44	♀	□	♊	3 11:49
5 14:56	☿	□	♋	5 21:41
7 18:15	♄	△	♌	8 9:51
10 6:27	♄	□	♍	10 22:09
12 17:13	♄	✶	♎	13 8:34
15 7:43	☉	☍	♏	15 16:21
17 7:10	♄	☌	♐	17 21:45
20 1:18	☉	△	♑	20 1:29
21 23:22	☿	□	♒	22 4:19
23 16:12	♄	□	♓	24 6:56
25 20:04	♀	☌	♈	26 10:02
27 11:03	♃	□	♉	28 14:24
30 15:54	♀	✶	♊	30 20:57

DAILY ASPECTARIAN

1 Tu
☽☍⚳ 2:20
☽∠⚷ 5:34
☉□♃ 7:40
☽⋕♀ 11:11
☽∠☿ 14:22
☽✶♆ 16:39
☿∥♂ 22:16

2 W
☽✶♃ 1:56
☉⚺☽ 3:17
☽⚺♅ 3:33
☽△♇ 5:30
☉☌♅ 7:10
♂⚼♆ 7:29
☽✶⚷ 8:29
☿⚻♂ 9:45
♀⚼♃ 15:21
☽⋕♄ 19:00
☽⚻♂ 19:31
☽✶☿ 21:11
☽☍♄ 21:55

3 Th
☉⋕☿ 1:53
☿△♄ 3:04
☽∠♃ 5:35
☽□♀ 6:44
☽∠♅ 7:11
☽⚻⚳ 7:45
☉∠☽ 9:04
☽⚼♇ 9:06
☉□♇ 9:23
♀∠♅ 12:35
♀△⚳ 17:16
☽⚼♂ 22:45
☽□♆ 23:59

4 F
☉⋕♂ 5:56
☿⋕♅ 9:41
☽⚺♃ 10:07
♀∠♇ 11:41
☽⚼⚳ 11:42
☽✶♅ 11:43
☽⚻♇ 13:34
☉✶☽ 15:58
☽□⚷ 16:58

5 Sa
☽△♂ 2:46
☉⚺⚷ 5:17
☽⚻♄ 6:44
☽□☿ 14:56
☽△⚳ 16:24
♀ ♓ 20:32
☽△♀ 21:47

6 Su
☿⚻⚳ 0:33
☽△♆ 10:39
☽⚼♄ 12:16
☿⋕⚳ 13:26
☽☌♃ 21:34
☽□♅ 23:03

7 M
☽☍♇ 0:43
☽△⚷ 4:31
☽⚼♀ 6:38
☉□☽ 8:32
☽□♂ 12:35
☿ ♈ 15:36
☽⚼♆ 16:49
☽△♄ 18:15
☽⋕♄ 23:40

8 Tu
☽□⚳ 3:21
☽⚼⚷ 10:55
☽△☿ 12:57
☽⚻♀ 15:54
♀ D 16:15
☿∥⚷ 20:08
☉☍♂ 21:05
☽⚻♆ 23:12

9 W
♀⚼♂ 9:00
☽⚺♃ 10:34
☽△♅ 11:51
☽⚻♇ 13:15
☽⚻⚷ 17:20
☽✶♂ 23:14

10 Th
☽⚼☿ 0:24
☉△☽ 2:29
♀∥♆ 2:36
☽⋕♆ 5:20
☽⋕♀ 5:37
☽□♄ 6:27
☿⚺♀ 11:44
☽✶⚳ 14:38
☉∥☽ 16:33
☽∠♃ 16:55
☽⚼♅ 18:04
☽⚼♇ 19:19

11 F
☽∠♂ 4:13
☽☍♀ 9:56
☿⚺♆ 10:48
☉⚼☽ 10:58
☽☍♆ 11:22
☽⚻☿ 11:28
☽⋕♂ 13:45
☽∥♅ 15:31
☿⚼♄ 15:44
☉∠♆ 16:00
☽∠⚳ 19:46
☽✶♃ 22:48
☽∥⚳ 23:36
☽⚻♅ 23:48

12 Sa
☉⚻♄ 0:24
☽△♇ 0:54
♀☌♆ 2:25
☿⋕⚷ 4:43
☽☍⚷ 5:06
☽⚺♂ 8:45
☽∥☿ 10:29
☽⋕⚷ 11:39
☽✶♄ 17:13
☉⋕♀ 18:33
☉⚻☽ 18:44

13 Su
☽⚺⚳ 0:20
☽∥⚷ 2:07
☽⋕☿ 7:25
☽⋕⚳ 14:27
♂⋕♅ 16:13
☽⚻♆ 21:21
☽∠♄ 21:40
☽∥♂ 21:51
☽⋕♅ 22:03

14 M
☽⚻♀ 1:15
☽☍☿ 7:02
☽□♃ 8:38
☽☍♅ 9:22
☽□♇ 10:09
☽⚻⚷ 14:23
☽☌♂ 16:01
☿□♃ 18:33
☽∥♀ 19:46
☿∥⚳ 20:28
☿☌♅ 23:17
♇ R 23:48

15 Tu
☉⋕♆ 0:08
☽⚼♆ 1:20
☽⚺♄ 1:27
☿□♇ 4:14
☽∥♆ 5:14
☉☍⚳ 5:38
☉⋕☽ 5:47
♀⚼⚳ 6:56
☽☌⚳ 7:32
☽⚼♀ 7:36
☉☍☽ 7:43
☽⚼⚷ 18:01
☉∠♀ 20:39

16 W
☿⋕♂ 0:22
☽△♆ 4:40
☿∥♅ 9:30
☿⚺⚷ 9:58
☿☍♂ 11:16
☽△♀ 13:09
☽△♃ 15:49
☽⚻♅ 16:15
☽✶♇ 16:47
♂⚻⚷ 17:05
☽⚺♂ 20:55
☽△⚷ 21:02
☽⚻☿ 22:51

17 Th
☽∥♄ 3:37
☽☌♄ 7:10
☽⚺⚳ 12:23
☉⚻☽ 17:35
☽⚼♃ 18:33
☽⚼♅ 18:51
☽∠♇ 19:16
☽∠♂ 22:39

18 F
♀△♃ 1:20
♀⚺♅ 4:55
☽⚼☿ 5:36
♀✶♇ 9:27
☽□♆ 9:43
☽∠⚳ 14:08
☽⚻♃ 20:51
☿⋕♀ 21:00
☽△♅ 21:02
☽⚺♇ 21:19
☉⚼☽ 21:39
☽□♀ 22:21

19 Sa
☽✶♂ 0:00
☽□⚷ 1:39
☿⚻♄ 6:32
☿∠♆ 10:27
☽⚺♄ 11:03
☽△☿ 11:50
♀⚻♂ 14:32
☽✶⚳ 15:32

20 Su
☉△☽ 1:18
☉ ♉ 3:57
♃□♅ 7:30
☿☍⚳ 11:24
☽∠♄ 12:32
☽✶♆ 13:16
♀☌⚷ 17:41
♃☍♇ 23:27

21 M
☽□♅ 0:28
☽☌♇ 0:33
☽☍♃ 0:34
☽□♂ 1:57
☽✶⚷ 4:59
☽✶♀ 5:54
☉∠⚷ 9:27
☽✶♄ 13:49
☽∠♆ 14:44
☽□⚳ 17:42
♅□♇ 19:22
☽∥♄ 21:57
☽□☿ 23:22

22 Tu
☿⋕♆ 3:14
☽∠⚷ 6:25
☉□☽ 7:53
☽∠♀ 9:23
☽⚺♆ 16:05
♂□♃ 19:29
♂⋕⚳ 20:26
☉⋕☽ 23:25

23 W
☽⚺♇ 3:11
☽✶♅ 3:19
☽△♂ 3:25
☽⚻♃ 3:41
♂☍♅ 7:09
☽⚺⚷ 7:48
☿ ♉ 9:17
☽⋕☿ 10:23
☽⚺♀ 12:50
♂□♇ 13:39
☽□♄ 16:12
☽∥♆ 17:27
☽△⚳ 19:33

24 Th
☿∠⚷ 0:27
♀⋕♅ 2:38
☽⚼♂ 4:10
☽∠♇ 4:30
☽∠♅ 4:44
☽⚼♃ 5:15
☽✶☿ 10:42
☉✶☽ 14:15
☽☌♆ 18:50
☽⋕♅ 20:17
☽⚼⚳ 20:33
☽∥♀ 22:02

25 F
☽⋕⚳ 2:22
☽∥♂ 3:40
☽⚻♂ 5:02
♀△♄ 5:16
☽✶♇ 5:55
☽⚺♅ 6:16
☽△♃ 6:55
☽☌⚷ 10:45
☽∠☿ 16:41
☽∥⚷ 16:50
☉∠☽ 17:38
☽△♄ 18:49
☽☌♀ 20:04
☽⚻⚳ 21:42

26 Sa
☽⋕⚷ 2:47
☉☌☿ 3:28
♀⚻⚳ 13:37
⚵ ♉ 14:15
☽⋕♂ 15:27
☿✶♆ 17:28
☽∥⚳ 17:32
☽⋕♀ 17:57
☉∥☿ 19:04
☽⚼♄ 20:27
☉⚺☽ 21:20
☽⚺♆ 22:15
♀⋕⚳ 22:24
☽⚺☿ 23:07
☽∥♅ 23:49

27 Su
☽☍♂ 7:29
☽□♇ 9:28
☽☌♅ 10:02
☉✶♆ 10:35
☽□♃ 11:03
☿∠♀ 11:46
☽⚺⚷ 14:36
☽⚻♄ 22:27

28 M
☽∠♆ 0:27
☽☍⚳ 0:55
☽⋕♆ 2:54
☽⚺♀ 4:41
♀∥♂ 5:02
☽∠⚷ 17:09
☿⚻♂ 23:45

29 Tu
☿⋕♄ 1:05
☽✶♆ 3:09
⚳⚼♆ 5:17
☉☌☽ 6:15
☽∠♀ 9:53
☽⚻♂ 11:34
☽☌☿ 14:08
☉∥☽ 14:29
☽△♇ 14:41
☽⚺♅ 15:32
☽✶♃ 16:57
☿△♇ 17:31
☽✶⚷ 20:15
☿⚺♅ 22:54
☽⋕♄ 23:29

30 W
☽☍♄ 3:58
☽⚻⚳ 6:01
☿✶♃ 8:33
☽∥☿ 12:21
☽⚼♂ 14:28
☽✶♀ 15:54
☽⚼♇ 18:11
☽∠♅ 19:11
☽∠♃ 20:51

LONGITUDE

Day	Sid.Time	☉	☽	☽ 12 hour	Mean☊	True☊	☿	♀	♂	⚳	♃	♄	⚷	♅	♆	♇
	h m s	° ' "	° ' "	° ' "	° '	° '	° '	° '	° '	° '	° '	° '	° '	° '	° '	° '
Th	14 35 23	10♉33 11	1♊38 17	8♊01 46	27♎54.7	28♎23.4	16♉15.2	27♓40.2	11♎24.6	21♎47.0	14♋58.1	20♏44.8	16♓38.2	14♈03.8	7♓10.2	13♑31.0
F	14 39 20	11 31 27	14 21 08	20 36 34	27 51.5	28R 21.8	18 23.4	28 48.1	11R 10.1	21R 35.6	15 07.1	20R 40.4	16 40.7	14 07.0	7 11.4	13R 30.5
Sa	14 43 17	12 29 41	26 48 17	2♋56 33	27 48.3	28 19.8	20 30.7	29 56.1	10 56.3	21 24.5	15 16.2	20 36.0	16 43.2	14 10.1	7 12.7	13 30.0
Su	14 47 13	13 27 53	9♋01 45	15 04 14	27 45.2	28 17.7	22 36.9	1♈04.2	10 43.2	21 13.6	15 25.4	20 31.5	16 45.6	14 13.2	7 13.8	13 29.4
M	14 51 10	14 26 04	21 04 28	27 02 57	27 42.0	28 16.0	24 41.7	2 12.5	10 30.9	21 03.1	15 34.8	20 27.0	16 48.0	14 16.3	7 15.0	13 28.9
Tu	14 55 06	15 24 12	3♌00 11	8♌56 43	27 38.8	28 14.7	26 44.7	3 20.8	10 19.4	20 52.8	15 44.3	20 22.6	16 50.4	14 19.3	7 16.1	13 28.3
W	14 59 03	16 22 18	14 53 08	20 50 00	27 35.6	28D 14.2	28 45.7	4 29.2	10 08.6	20 42.8	15 53.8	20 18.1	16 52.7	14 22.4	7 17.2	13 27.7
Th	15 02 59	17 20 22	26 47 56	2♍47 29	27 32.5	28 14.5	0♊44.4	5 37.7	9 58.7	20 33.2	16 03.5	20 13.6	16 55.0	14 25.4	7 18.3	13 27.0
F	15 06 56	18 18 25	8♍49 16	14 53 50	27 29.3	28 15.5	2 40.7	6 46.3	9 49.5	20 23.9	16 13.3	20 09.1	16 57.2	14 28.4	7 19.3	13 26.3
Sa	15 10 52	19 16 25	21 01 43	27 13 24	27 26.1	28 17.0	4 34.2	7 55.0	9 41.2	20 14.9	16 23.1	20 04.6	16 59.4	14 31.3	7 20.3	13 25.6
Su	15 14 49	20 14 24	3♎29 21	9♎49 56	27 22.9	28 18.5	6 24.9	9 03.7	9 33.6	20 06.3	16 33.1	20 00.0	17 01.5	14 34.3	7 21.3	13 24.9
M	15 18 45	21 12 21	16 15 29	22 46 14	27 19.7	28R 19.7	8 12.6	10 12.6	9 26.9	19 58.0	16 43.1	19 55.5	17 03.6	14 37.2	7 22.2	13 24.1
Tu	15 22 42	22 10 16	29 22 18	6♏03 44	27 16.6	28 20.1	9 57.1	11 21.5	9 20.9	19 50.1	16 53.3	19 51.0	17 05.6	14 40.1	7 23.1	13 23.3
W	15 26 39	23 08 10	12♏50 28	19 42 19	27 13.4	28 19.5	11 38.4	12 30.5	9 15.8	19 42.6	17 03.6	19 46.5	17 07.6	14 43.0	7 24.0	13 22.5
Th	15 30 35	24 06 02	26 38 57	3♐39 59	27 10.2	28 17.6	13 16.3	13 39.6	9 11.5	19 35.4	17 13.9	19 42.0	17 09.5	14 45.8	7 24.9	13 21.7
F	15 34 32	25 03 52	10♐44 54	17 53 06	27 07.0	28 14.6	14 50.9	14 48.8	9 07.9	19 28.6	17 24.3	19 37.5	17 11.4	14 48.6	7 25.7	13 20.9
Sa	15 38 28	26 01 42	25 03 56	2♑16 41	27 03.9	28 10.8	16 21.9	15 58.1	9 05.1	19 22.1	17 34.8	19 33.1	17 13.3	14 51.4	7 26.5	13 20.0
Su	15 42 25	26 59 30	9♑30 38	16 45 05	27 00.7	28 06.8	17 49.5	17 07.4	9 03.2	19 16.1	17 45.4	19 28.6	17 15.1	14 54.1	7 27.2	13 19.1
M	15 46 21	27 57 17	23 59 20	1♒12 47	26 57.5	28 03.1	19 13.4	18 16.9	9 02.0	19 10.4	17 56.1	19 24.2	17 16.9	14 56.9	7 28.0	13 18.2
Tu	15 50 18	28 55 02	8♒24 52	15 35 06	26 54.3	28 00.5	20 37.1	19 26.4	9D 01.5	19 05.1	18 06.9	19 19.8	17 18.6	14 59.6	7 28.7	13 17.2
W	15 54 15	29 52 47	22 43 06	29 48 33	26 51.2	27D 59.1	21 50.3	20 35.9	9 01.9	19 00.2	18 17.8	19 15.3	17 20.2	15 02.2	7 29.3	13 16.2
Th	15 58 11	0♊50 30	6♓51 14	13♓51 00	26 48.0	27 59.0	23 03.2	21 45.6	9 02.9	18 55.7	18 28.7	19 11.0	17 21.8	15 04.9	7 29.9	13 15.2
F	16 02 08	1 48 12	20 47 45	27 41 26	26 44.8	28 00.0	24 12.3	22 55.3	9 04.8	18 51.6	18 39.7	19 06.6	17 23.4	15 07.5	7 30.5	13 14.2
Sa	16 06 04	2 45 54	4♈31 59	11♈19 27	26 41.6	28 01.4	25 17.5	24 05.0	9 07.4	18 47.8	18 50.8	19 02.3	17 24.9	15 10.1	7 31.1	13 13.2
Su	16 10 01	3 43 34	18 03 51	24 45 11	26 38.4	28R 02.7	26 18.9	25 14.9	9 10.7	18 44.5	19 02.0	18 58.0	17 26.3	15 12.6	7 31.6	13 12.1
M	16 13 57	4 41 13	1♉23 28	7♉58 43	26 35.3	28 03.0	27 16.3	26 24.8	9 14.8	18 41.6	19 13.2	18 53.7	17 27.7	15 15.1	7 32.1	13 11.1
Tu	16 17 54	5 38 52	14 30 54	21 00 03	26 32.1	28 01.8	28 09.6	27 34.7	9 19.6	18 39.1	19 24.6	18 49.5	17 29.1	15 17.6	7 32.6	13 10.0
W	16 21 50	6 36 29	27 26 08	3♊49 10	26 28.9	27 58.7	28 58.8	28 44.7	9 25.1	18 36.9	19 35.9	18 45.3	17 30.4	15 20.0	7 33.1	13 08.8
Th	16 25 47	7 34 05	10♊09 08	16 26 04	26 25.7	27 53.8	29 43.8	29 54.8	9 31.3	18 35.2	19 47.4	18 41.1	17 31.6	15 22.4	7 33.5	13 07.7
F	16 29 44	8 31 40	22 40 00	28 51 02	26 22.6	27 47.4	0♋24.6	1♉04.9	9 38.2	18 33.9	19 59.0	18 37.0	17 32.8	15 24.8	7 33.8	13 06.5
Sa	16 33 40	9♊29 14	4♋59 16	11♋04 52	26♎19.4	27♎40.0	1♋01.0	2♉15.1	9♎45.8	18♎32.9	20♋10.6	18♏32.9	17♓34.0	15♈27.1	7♓34.2	13♑05.4

1st of Month

Julian Day # 2456778.5
Obliquity 23°26'07"
SVP 5♓03'28"
GC 27♐02.4
Eris 22♈41.9

Day	⚴	Day	⚵	Day	⚶
1	26♌50.3	1	2♉31.3	1	19♎19.2R
6	27 41.9	6	5 23.5	6	18 22.3R
11	28 41.4	11	8 16.2	11	17 35.5R
16	29 48.1	16	11 09.4	16	17 00.1R
21	1♍01.1	21	14 03.0	21	16 36.7R
26	2 19.9	26	16 57.0	26	16 25.7R
31	3 44.0	31	19 51.2	31	16 27.2

DECLINATION and LATITUDE

Day	☉ Decl	☽ Decl	☽ Lat	☽12h Decl	☿ Decl	☿ Lat	♀ Decl	♀ Lat	♂ Decl	♂ Lat	⚳ Decl	⚳ Lat	♃ Decl	♃ Lat	♄ Decl	♄ Lat
Th	14N59	17N39	2S54	18N19	17N09	0N29	2S06	1S16	3S02	1N36	3N44	13N10	22N54	0N18	15S32	2N29
F	15 17	18 45	3 47	18 57	17 56	0 39	1 41	1 19	2 59	1 34	3 44	13 05	22 53	0 18	15 31	2 29
Sa	15 35	18 55	4 29	18 39	18 41	0 50	1 17	1 22	2 56	1 31	3 44	13 01	22 52	0 18	15 30	2 29
Su	15 53	18 10	4 58	17 30	19 23	1 00	0 52	1 25	2 53	1 28	3 44	12 56	22 51	0 18	15 29	2 29
M	16 10	16 38	5 13	15 35	20 04	1 10	0 28	1 28	2 51	1 26	3 43	12 51	22 50	0 18	15 28	2 29
Tu	16 27	14 23	5 14	13 02	20 43	1 19	0 03	1 30	2 49	1 23	3 42	12 46	22 49	0 18	15 27	2 29
W	16 44	11 33	5 02	9 56	21 19	1 28	0N22	1 33	2 47	1 20	3 41	12 41	22 48	0 18	15 26	2 29
Th	17 00	8 14	4 37	6 26	21 53	1 37	0 47	1 35	2 46	1 18	3 40	12 36	22 47	0 19	15 24	2 29
F	17 17	4 33	3 60	2 37	22 24	1 45	1 12	1 37	2 44	1 15	3 39	12 31	22 45	0 19	15 23	2 29
Sa	17 32	0 38	3 11	1S23	22 53	1 52	1 37	1 39	2 44	1 12	3 37	12 26	22 44	0 19	15 22	2 29
Su	17 48	3S25	2 13	5 26	23 19	1 58	2 02	1 41	2 43	1 10	3 35	12 21	22 43	0 19	15 21	2 29
M	18 03	7 24	1 06	9 20	23 43	2 04	2 27	1 43	2 43	1 07	3 33	12 15	22 42	0 19	15 20	2 29
Tu	18 18	11 10	0N06	12 52	24 04	2 09	2 53	1 45	2 43	1 05	3 31	12 10	22 41	0 19	15 18	2 29
W	18 33	14 26	1 19	15 49	24 23	2 14	3 18	1 47	2 43	1 02	3 29	12 04	22 40	0 19	15 17	2 29
Th	18 48	16 59	2 29	17 54	24 39	2 17	3 43	1 49	2 44	0 60	3 27	11 59	22 38	0 19	15 16	2 29
F	19 02	18 33	3 32	18 55	24 53	2 20	4 09	1 50	2 45	0 57	3 24	11 53	22 37	0 19	15 15	2 29
Sa	19 15	18 59	4 22	18 43	25 05	2 21	4 34	1 51	2 46	0 55	3 21	11 48	22 36	0 19	15 14	2 29
Su	19 29	18 10	4 56	17 19	25 14	2 22	4 59	1 53	2 47	0 52	3 18	11 42	22 34	0 19	15 13	2 29
M	19 42	16 11	5 12	14 48	25 22	2 22	5 25	1 54	2 49	0 50	3 15	11 37	22 33	0 19	15 12	2 29
Tu	19 55	13 12	5 07	11 25	25 27	2 22	5 50	1 55	2 51	0 47	3 12	11 31	22 32	0 19	15 10	2 28
W	20 07	9 28	4 44	7 23	25 31	2 20	6 15	1 56	2 53	0 45	3 08	11 25	22 30	0 19	15 09	2 28
Th	20 19	5 13	4 04	2 60	25 32	2 17	6 40	1 57	2 56	0 43	3 04	11 19	22 29	0 19	15 08	2 28
F	20 31	0 45	3 09	1N30	25 32	2 14	7 05	1 58	2 59	0 40	3 01	11 14	22 27	0 19	15 07	2 28
Sa	20 43	3N43	2 05	5 52	25 30	2 09	7 30	1 59	3 02	0 38	2 57	11 08	22 26	0 19	15 06	2 28
Su	20 54	7 55	0 54	9 52	25 27	2 04	7 55	1 59	3 05	0 36	2 53	11 02	22 24	0 19	15 05	2 28
M	21 04	11 40	0S18	13 19	25 22	1 58	8 20	1 60	3 09	0 34	2 48	10 56	22 23	0 20	15 04	2 28
Tu	21 15	14 47	1 28	16 03	25 16	1 51	8 44	2 00	3 13	0 31	2 44	10 50	22 21	0 20	15 03	2 28
W	21 25	17 06	2 33	17 56	25 09	1 43	9 09	2 01	3 17	0 29	2 39	10 45	22 20	0 20	15 02	2 28
Th	21 34	18 32	3 28	18 54	24 60	1 34	9 33	2 01	3 21	0 27	2 34	10 39	22 18	0 20	15 01	2 28
F	21 43	19 01	4 13	18 55	24 50	1 24	9 57	2 01	3 26	0 25	2 30	10 33	22 16	0 20	14 60	2 27
Sa	21N52	18N36	4S45	18N03	24N39	1N14	10N22	2S01	3S31	0N23	2N24	10N27	22N15	0N20	14S59	2N27

Day	⚷ Decl	⚷ Lat	♅ Decl	♅ Lat	♆ Decl	♆ Lat	♇ Decl	♇ Lat
1	0S51	4N48	4N57	0S39	9S31	0S42	20S06	2N40
6	0 45	4 49	5 03	0 39	9 29	0 42	20 06	2 40
11	0 40	4 50	5 09	0 39	9 28	0 42	20 07	2 40
16	0 36	4 51	5 14	0 39	9 26	0 42	20 07	2 40
21	0 31	4 52	5 19	0 39	9 25	0 42	20 08	2 39
26	0 27	4 53	5 24	0 39	9 24	0 43	20 09	2 39
31	0S24	4N54	5N29	0S39	9S23	0S43	20S09	2N39

Day	⚴ Decl	⚴ Lat	⚵ Decl	⚵ Lat	⚶ Decl	⚶ Lat	Eris Decl	Eris Lat
1	11N29	1S09	7N11	5S29	3N47	12N15	3S00	12S43
6	12 14	0 02	7 55	5 43	3 52	11 57	2 59	12 43
11	12 53	1N01	8 38	5 57	3 51	11 37	2 58	12 43
16	13 24	1 59	9 18	6 10	3 43	11 15	2 57	12 44
21	13 48	2 53	9 56	6 24	3 30	10 51	2 56	12 44
26	14 06	3 43	10 32	6 37	3 11	10 26	2 56	12 44
31	14N19	4N30	11N06	6S51	2N46	9N60	2S55	12S44

Moon Phenomena

Max/0 Decl
dy hr mn
2 16:05 18N58
10 3:44 0 S
16 20:24 18S59
23 3:59 0 N
30 0:34 19N01

Max/0 Lat
dy hr mn
5 14:26 5S16
12 22:07 0 N
19 6:38 5N13
25 17:57 0 S

Perigee/Apogee
dy hr m kilometers
6 10:22 a 404316
18 11:58 p 367103

PH dy hr mn
☽ 7 3:16 16♌30
○ 14 19:17 23♏55
☾ 21 13:00 0♓24
● 28 18:41 7♊21

Void of Course Moon

Last Aspect			☽ Ingress		
1 23:33	♅	⚹	♋	3	6:14
5 8:47	☿	⚹	♌	5	17:57
7 10:52	♄	□	♍	8	6:25
9 22:09	♄	⚹	♎	10	17:20
12 0:52	♃	□	♏	13	1:08
14 19:17	☉	☍	♐	15	5:45
16 7:44	☿	☍	♑	17	8:13
19 7:03	☉	△	♒	19	9:59
20 22:22	☿	△	♓	21	12:19
23 6:27	☿	□	♈	23	16:02
25 15:59	☿	⚹	♉	25	21:29
27 9:11	♃	⚹	♊	28	4:49
29 10:00	♅	⚹	♋	30	14:14

DAILY ASPECTARIAN

1 Th
☿⚹⚷ 4:23
☽⚼⚳ 9:31
☽□♆ 10:24
☉⚻♂ 16:56
☽△♂ 18:03
☉⚺☽ 18:10
☽⚻♇ 22:24
☽⚹♅ 23:33

2 F
☽⚺♃ 1:29
☽□⚷ 4:28
☽⚺☿ 9:19
☽⚻♄ 12:03
☽△⚳ 13:42
☉⋕♄ 17:36

3 Sa
☿☍♄ 0:57
♀ ♈ 1:22
☉∠☽ 1:28
☽∥☿ 4:59
☽□♀ 6:44
☿⚻⚳ 9:23
☽⚼♄ 17:07
☽△♆ 20:26
☽∠☿ 20:37

4 Su
☉△♇ 0:38
☽□♂ 3:18
♀∥⚷ 5:05
☽☍♇ 8:51
☉⚹☽ 9:34
☽□♅ 10:21
☽☌♃ 12:52
☽△⚷ 15:25
☉⚺♅ 19:44
☽△♄ 22:45
☽□⚳ 23:57

5 M
☿⋕♇ 1:11
☽⚼♆ 2:22
☉∥☽ 4:51
☿⚼♂ 8:43
☽⚹☿ 8:47
☽⋕♄ 13:24
☽⚼⚷ 21:39

6 Tu
☽△♀ 0:46
☽⚻♆ 8:38
☉⚹♃ 9:55
☽⚹♂ 14:34
☿⚼♇ 20:25
☽⚻♇ 21:08
☽△♅ 22:58

7 W
☽⚺♃ 2:04
☉□☽ 3:16
☽⚻⚷ 4:02
☿∠♅ 7:33
☽⚼♀ 10:16
☽□♄ 10:52
☽⚹⚳ 11:36
☉⚹⚷ 13:04
☿ ♊ 14:58
☽⋕♆ 15:18
♀⚼♄ 16:05
☽∠♂ 20:23
♀⋕⚷ 20:41

8 Th
☽⚼♇ 3:19
☿∠♃ 4:15
☽⚼♅ 5:17
☽∠♃ 8:39
☽□☿ 9:26
☽∠⚳ 17:17
☽⚻♀ 19:30
☽∥♅ 20:31
☽☍♆ 21:01

9 F
☽⚺♂ 1:58
☽∥⚳ 5:41
☽△♇ 9:07
☽⚻♅ 11:13
☽⋕♂ 11:15
♀⚺♆ 11:43
☽⚹♃ 14:48
☽☍⚷ 16:05
☿∥♃ 16:51
☽∥♀ 18:36
☉△☽ 20:17
☽⚹♄ 22:09
☽⚺⚳ 22:30
☽⋕⚷ 23:38

10 Sa
☽∥⚷ 7:48
☿⚼⚳ 8:07
☽⋕♀ 14:53
☉☍♄ 18:29
☽∥♂ 19:52
☉⚻⚳ 21:05

11 Su
☽⋕⚳ 1:01
☽∠♄ 2:51
☉⚼☽ 3:36
☽△☿ 6:29
☽⚻♆ 7:20
♀☍♂ 9:28

12 M
☽□♃ 0:52
☽⚻⚷ 1:29
☽⚺♄ 6:44
☽☌⚳ 6:47
☉⚻☽ 9:52
☽⚼♆ 11:17
☽∥♆ 12:47
♀⋕♂ 14:28
☽⚼☿ 14:46
☿△♂ 16:03
⚳⚺♄ 17:28

13 Tu
☽⚼⚷ 4:55
☽△♆ 14:22
☽⚺♂ 17:43
☽⚻☿ 21:35
☽⚻♀ 23:22

14 W
☽⚹♇ 0:56
☽⚻♅ 3:18
☽∥♄ 7:09
☽△♃ 7:29
☽△⚷ 7:32
♀∥⚳ 9:29
♃△⚷ 11:37
☽⚺⚳ 11:54
☽☌♄ 12:03
♀□♇ 17:51
☽⋕♅ 10:20
☽☌♂ 11:23
☽☍♀ 11:36
☿□♆ 12:35
☽□♇ 18:41
☽☍♅ 20:57
☉☍☽ 19:17
☽∠♂ 19:47

15 Th
☿⚻♇ 1:20
☉⚼♂ 2:07
☽∠♇ 2:56
☽⚼♀ 3:46
☽⚼♅ 5:21
☽⚼♃ 9:40
☽∠⚳ 13:28
☽□♆ 18:23
☽⚹♂ 21:17
☿⚹♀ 21:55
☿⚹♅ 23:24
♀☌♅ 23:55

16 F
☽⚺♇ 4:23
☽△♅ 6:52
☽△♀ 7:27
☽☍☿ 7:44
☽□⚷ 10:52
☽⚻♃ 11:20
☽⚹⚳ 14:33
☽⚺♄ 14:50
⚴ ♍ 20:20

17 Sa
☉⚻☽ 1:43
☿□⚷ 14:15
☽∠♄ 15:42
☽⚹♆ 20:35
☿⚺♃ 22:43
☽□♂ 23:15

18 Su
♀⚺⚷ 2:43
☉⚼☽ 4:24
☽☌♇ 6:18
☽□♅ 8:58
☽⚹⚷ 12:51
☽□♀ 13:43
☽☍♃ 13:50
☽⚻☿ 15:16
♀□♃ 15:32
☽□⚳ 16:04
☽⚹♄ 16:26
♀∥♅ 16:42
☽∠♆ 21:28
☿△⚳ 23:11

19 M
☿⚻♄ 3:00
☉△☽ 7:03
☉⚼♇ 8:32
☽∥♄ 8:53
☽∠⚷ 13:48
♀☍⚳ 17:10
☽⚼☿ 18:46
♀⚻♄ 21:52
☽⚺♆ 22:26

20 Tu
☽△♂ 1:01
♂ D 1:32
☽⚺♇ 8:08
☽⚹♅ 11:03
☽⚺⚷ 14:55
☽⚻♃ 16:27
☽△⚳ 17:47
☽□♄ 18:12
☽⚹♀ 20:07
☽△☿ 22:22

21 W
☽∥♆ 0:16
☉⋕♇ 1:07
☽⚼♂ 2:13
☉ ♊ 3:00
☉∠♅ 4:07
☽∠♇ 9:23
☽∠♅ 12:26
☉□☽ 13:00
☽⋕♀ 16:43
☽⚼♃ 18:10
☽⚼⚳ 19:02
☽⋕♅ 23:21
☽∠♀ 23:49

22 Th
☽☌♆ 1:06
☽⚻♂ 3:46
☽⚹♇ 10:58
☽⋕⚳ 11:45
☽∥♂ 12:13
☽⚺♅ 14:10
♀∠♆ 15:25
☽☌⚷ 18:06
☽△♃ 20:15
☽⚻⚳ 20:40
☽△♄ 21:06

23 F
☽∥⚷ 1:21
☽⚺♀ 4:02
♂⋕⚳ 6:24
☽□☿ 6:27
☽⋕⚷ 6:36
⚳□♃ 19:09
☽∥⚳ 19:53
☽⋕♂ 20:15
☉⚹☽ 20:39
☽⚼♄ 23:08

24 Sa
☽⚺♆ 5:16
☽☍♂ 8:08
☽∥♅ 9:16
☽□♇ 15:21
♃△♄ 17:48
☽☌♅ 18:53
☽⚺⚷ 22:53
☽∥♀ 23:59

25 Su
☉⚼⚳ 0:22
☽☍⚳ 1:12
☉∠☽ 1:16
☽⚻♄ 1:36
☽□♃ 1:45
☽∠♆ 8:00
☽⋕♆ 9:04
☉∠♃ 9:31
☽☌♀ 14:08
☽⚹☿ 15:59

26 M
☽∠⚷ 1:57
☉⚺☽ 6:28
☽⚹♆ 11:12
☽⚻♂ 14:24
☽∠☿ 21:20
☽△♇ 21:31

27 Tu
☽⚺♅ 1:26
☽⋕♄ 2:22
☽⚹⚷ 5:30
☽⚻⚳ 7:37
☽☍♄ 7:55
☽⚹♃ 9:11
☽⚼♂ 18:19
⚶ D 22:01

28 W
☽⚼♇ 1:20
☽⚺♀ 2:42
☽⚺☿ 3:05
☽∠♅ 5:27
☽⚼⚳ 11:35
☽∠♃ 13:41
☿⚹♀ 13:59
♀⋕♆ 14:27
☉☌☽ 18:41
☽□♆ 19:04
☽△♂ 22:47
☉□♆ 23:44

29 Th
♀ ♉ 1:47
☽⚻♇ 5:40
☿ ♋ 9:13
☽⚹♅ 10:00
☽∠♀ 10:01
☽□⚷ 14:07
☽△⚳ 16:06
☽⚻♄ 16:14
☽⚺♃ 18:44

30 F
☽☌☿ 15:50
☽⚹♀ 18:05
☽⚼♄ 21:12

31 Sa
⚳⚺♄ 0:02
☽△♆ 5:05
♀∠⚷ 6:33
☉△♂ 8:02
☽□♂ 9:30
☉⚺☽ 9:37
☽☍♇ 15:57
☽□♅ 20:43

June 2014

LONGITUDE

Day	Sid.Time	☉	☽	☽ 12 hour	Mean ☊	True ☊	☿	♀	♂	⚳	♃	♄	⚷	♅	♆	♇
	h m s	° ' "	° ' "	° ' "	° '	° '	° '	° '	° '	° '	° '	° '	° '	° '	° '	° '
1 Su	16 37 37	10♊26 47	17♋08 03	23♋09 04	26♎16.2	27♎32.4	1♋33.0	3♉25.4	9♎54.1	18♎32.4	20♋22.2	18♏28.9	17♓35.1	15♈29.4	7♓34.5	13♑04.2
2 M	16 41 33	11 24 18	29 08 12	5♌05 51	26 13.0	27R 25.3	2 00.6	4 35.6	10 03.0	18D 32.3	20 34.0	18R 24.9	17 36.1	15 31.7	7 34.7	13R 03.0
3 Tu	16 45 30	12 21 48	11♌02 23	16 58 17	26 09.8	27 19.5	2 23.6	5 46.0	10 12.6	18 32.5	20 45.8	18 21.0	17 37.1	15 33.9	7 35.0	13 01.7
4 W	16 49 26	13 19 17	22 54 02	28 50 10	26 06.7	27 15.3	2 42.0	6 56.4	10 22.8	18 33.2	20 57.6	18 17.1	17 38.0	15 36.1	7 35.2	13 00.5
5 Th	16 53 23	14 16 45	4♍47 16	10♍45 55	26 03.5	27D 13.1	2 55.8	8 06.8	10 33.7	18 34.2	21 09.5	18 13.3	17 38.9	15 38.3	7 35.4	12 59.2
6 F	16 57 19	15 14 12	16 46 45	22 50 22	26 00.3	27 12.5	3 04.9	9 17.3	10 45.2	18 35.6	21 21.5	18 09.5	17 39.7	15 40.4	7 35.5	12 58.0
7 Sa	17 01 16	16 11 37	28 57 25	5♎08 30	25 57.1	27 13.2	3R 09.5	10 27.8	10 57.3	18 37.4	21 33.5	18 05.8	17 40.5	15 42.5	7 35.6	12 56.7
8 Su	17 05 13	17 09 01	11♎24 14	17 45 08	25 54.0	27 14.4	3 09.5	11 38.4	11 09.9	18 39.6	21 45.6	18 02.1	17 41.2	15 44.5	7 35.7	12 55.4
9 M	17 09 09	18 06 24	24 11 43	0♏44 22	25 50.8	27R 15.2	3 05.0	12 49.0	11 23.2	18 42.2	21 57.8	17 58.5	17 41.9	15 46.5	7R 35.7	12 54.0
10 Tu	17 13 06	19 03 46	7♏23 25	14 09 03	25 47.6	27 14.8	2 56.2	13 59.6	11 37.0	18 45.1	22 10.0	17 55.0	17 42.5	15 48.4	7 35.7	12 52.7
11 W	17 17 02	20 01 07	21 01 18	28 00 05	25 44.4	27 12.5	2 43.2	15 10.4	11 51.4	18 48.4	22 22.2	17 51.5	17 43.0	15 50.4	7 35.7	12 51.4
12 Th	17 20 59	20 58 27	5♐05 07	12♐15 54	25 41.3	27 08.0	2 26.2	16 21.1	12 06.3	18 52.1	22 34.5	17 48.1	17 43.5	15 52.2	7 35.7	12 50.0
13 F	17 24 55	21 55 47	19 31 49	26 52 04	25 38.1	27 01.5	2 05.6	17 31.9	12 21.8	18 56.1	22 46.9	17 44.8	17 44.0	15 54.1	7 35.6	12 48.6
14 Sa	17 28 52	22 53 05	4♑15 42	11♑41 41	25 34.9	26 53.5	1 41.6	18 42.8	12 37.8	19 00.5	22 59.3	17 41.5	17 44.3	15 55.9	7 35.5	12 47.3
15 Su	17 32 48	23 50 23	19 08 53	26 36 13	25 31.7	26 45.1	1 14.7	19 53.7	12 54.3	19 05.3	23 11.7	17 38.3	17 44.7	15 57.6	7 35.3	12 45.9
16 M	17 36 45	24 47 41	4♒02 34	11♒26 58	25 28.6	26 37.1	0 45.2	21 04.6	13 11.3	19 10.4	23 24.2	17 35.2	17 45.0	15 59.3	7 35.1	12 44.5
17 Tu	17 40 42	25 44 58	18 48 31	26 06 28	25 25.4	26 30.7	0 13.7	22 15.6	13 28.8	19 15.8	23 36.7	17 32.1	17 45.2	16 01.0	7 34.9	12 43.0
18 W	17 44 38	26 42 15	3♓16 00	10♓29 29	25 22.2	26 26.4	29♊40.7	23 26.7	13 46.8	19 21.6	23 49.3	17 29.1	17 45.3	16 02.6	7 34.7	12 41.6
19 Th	17 48 35	27 39 31	17 33 51	24 33 16	25 19.0	26D 24.3	29 06.8	24 37.8	14 05.3	19 27.7	24 01.9	17 26.2	17 45.5	16 04.2	7 34.4	12 40.2
20 F	17 52 31	28 36 47	1♈27 45	8♈17 22	25 15.8	26 23.9	28 32.4	25 48.9	14 24.2	19 34.1	24 14.6	17 23.4	17R 45.5	16 05.8	7 34.1	12 38.7
21 Sa	17 56 28	29 34 03	15 02 20	21 42 52	25 12.7	26R 24.4	27 58.3	27 00.1	14 43.6	19 40.9	24 27.3	17 20.6	17 45.5	16 07.2	7 33.7	12 37.3
22 Su	18 00 24	0♋31 19	28 19 14	4♉51 42	25 09.5	26 24.7	27 25.0	28 11.4	15 03.5	19 48.0	24 40.0	17 17.9	17 45.5	16 08.7	7 33.4	12 35.8
23 M	18 04 21	1 28 35	11♉20 34	17 46 06	25 06.3	26 23.7	26 53.0	29 22.6	15 23.8	19 55.4	24 52.8	17 15.3	17 45.4	16 10.1	7 33.0	12 34.4
24 Tu	18 08 17	2 25 51	24 08 31	0♊28 03	25 03.1	26 20.6	26 22.9	0♊34.0	15 44.5	20 03.2	25 05.6	17 12.8	17 45.2	16 11.5	7 32.5	12 32.9
25 W	18 12 14	3 23 06	6♊44 54	12 59 14	25 00.0	26 14.8	25 55.3	1 45.3	16 05.7	20 11.2	25 18.5	17 10.4	17 45.0	16 12.8	7 32.1	12 31.4
26 Th	18 16 11	4 20 21	19 11 10	25 20 50	24 56.8	26 06.3	25 30.6	2 56.7	16 27.3	20 19.6	25 31.4	17 08.0	17 44.7	16 14.1	7 31.6	12 29.9
27 F	18 20 07	5 17 36	1♋28 21	7♋33 48	24 53.6	25 55.6	25 09.2	4 08.2	16 49.3	20 28.3	25 44.3	17 05.7	17 44.4	16 15.3	7 31.0	12 28.5
28 Sa	18 24 04	6 14 51	13 37 20	19 39 02	24 50.4	25 43.4	24 51.5	5 19.7	17 11.7	20 37.2	25 57.2	17 03.5	17 44.0	16 16.5	7 30.5	12 27.0
29 Su	18 28 00	7 12 06	25 39 04	1♌37 36	24 47.3	25 30.7	24 37.8	6 31.2	17 34.5	20 46.5	26 10.2	17 01.4	17 43.6	16 17.6	7 29.9	12 25.5
30 M	18 31 57	8♋09 20	7♌34 51	13 31 03	24♎44.1	25♎18.6	24♊28.4	7♊42.7	17♎57.8	20♎56.1	26♋23.2	16♏59.4	17♓43.1	16♈18.7	7♓29.3	12♑25.0

1st of Month

Julian Day # 2456809.5
Obliquity 23°26'06"
SVP 5♓03'23"
GC 27♐02.4
Eris 22♈59.2

Day	⚴
1	4♍01.4
6	5 31.3
11	7 05.3
16	8 43.1
21	10 24.3
26	12 08.7

Day	⚵
1	20♉26.1
6	23 20.4
11	26 14.8
16	29 09.1
21	2♊03.3
26	4 57.2

Day	⚶
1	16♎28.9
6	16 45.0
11	17 12.7
16	17 51.4
21	18 40.2
26	19 38.6

DECLINATION and LATITUDE

Day	☉ Decl	☽ Decl	☽ Lat	☽ 12h Decl	☿ Decl	☿ Lat	♀ Decl	♀ Lat	♂ Decl	♂ Lat	⚳ Decl	⚳ Lat	♃ Decl	♃ Lat	♄ Decl	♄ Lat
1 Su	22N01	17N19	5S03	16N24	24N28	1N02	10N45	2S01	3S36	0N21	2N19	10N21	22N13	0N20	14S58	2N27
2 M	22 09	15 18	5 08	14 03	24 15	0 50	11 09	2 01	3 42	0 19	2 14	10 15	22 11	0 20	14 57	2 27
3 Tu	22 16	12 39	4 60	11 07	24 02	0 37	11 33	2 01	3 47	0 17	2 09	10 10	22 10	0 20	14 56	2 27
4 W	22 24	9 29	4 38	7 46	23 47	0 23	11 56	2 00	3 53	0 15	2 03	10 04	22 08	0 20	14 55	2 27
5 Th	22 31	5 57	4 06	4 04	23 33	0 09	12 19	2 00	3 59	0 13	1 57	9 58	22 06	0 20	14 54	2 27
6 F	22 37	2 08	3 21	0 10	23 17	0S07	12 42	1 60	4 05	0 11	1 51	9 52	22 04	0 20	14 53	2 26
7 Sa	22 43	1S50	2 26	3S49	23 02	0 22	13 04	1 59	4 12	0 09	1 45	9 47	22 03	0 20	14 53	2 26
8 Su	22 49	5 48	1 24	7 45	22 45	0 38	13 27	1 58	4 19	0 07	1 39	9 41	22 01	0 20	14 52	2 26
9 M	22 54	9 38	0 16	11 26	22 29	0 55	13 49	1 58	4 25	0 05	1 33	9 35	21 59	0 20	14 51	2 26
10 Tu	22 59	13 07	0N54	14 39	22 12	1 12	14 11	1 57	4 32	0 03	1 27	9 30	21 57	0 20	14 50	2 26
11 W	23 04	16 01	2 04	17 09	21 56	1 29	14 32	1 56	4 40	0 02	1 20	9 24	21 55	0 21	14 49	2 26
12 Th	23 08	18 03	3 09	18 40	21 39	1 46	14 53	1 55	4 47	0S00	1 14	9 18	21 53	0 21	14 49	2 25
13 F	23 11	18 59	4 03	18 60	21 22	2 03	15 14	1 54	4 55	0 02	1 07	9 13	21 51	0 21	14 48	2 25
14 Sa	23 15	18 40	4 42	18 02	21 06	2 20	15 35	1 53	5 03	0 04	1 00	9 07	21 49	0 21	14 47	2 25
15 Su	23 18	17 05	5 02	15 50	20 49	2 36	15 55	1 52	5 11	0 05	0 53	9 02	21 47	0 21	14 46	2 25
16 M	23 20	14 20	5 02	12 37	20 34	2 52	16 15	1 51	5 19	0 07	0 47	8 56	21 45	0 21	14 46	2 25
17 Tu	23 22	10 42	4 42	8 39	20 19	3 07	16 34	1 49	5 27	0 09	0 39	8 51	21 43	0 21	14 45	2 24
18 W	23 24	6 29	4 04	4 14	20 04	3 22	16 53	1 48	5 36	0 10	0 32	8 45	21 41	0 21	14 44	2 24
19 Th	23 25	1 58	3 12	0N18	19 50	3 35	17 12	1 46	5 44	0 12	0 25	8 40	21 39	0 21	14 44	2 24
20 F	23 26	2N33	2 09	4 45	19 38	3 48	17 30	1 45	5 53	0 13	0 18	8 35	21 36	0 21	14 43	2 24
21 Sa	23 26	6 51	1 00	8 51	19 26	3 59	17 48	1 43	6 02	0 15	0 10	8 29	21 34	0 21	14 43	2 24
22 Su	23 26	10 43	0S10	12 26	19 16	4 09	18 06	1 42	6 11	0 16	0 03	8 24	21 32	0 21	14 42	2 23
23 M	23 26	13 59	1 19	15 21	19 06	4 17	18 23	1 40	6 20	0 18	0S05	8 19	21 30	0 21	14 42	2 23
24 Tu	23 25	16 31	2 22	17 28	18 59	4 25	18 40	1 38	6 30	0 19	0 12	8 14	21 28	0 21	14 41	2 23
25 W	23 23	18 12	3 17	18 42	18 52	4 30	18 56	1 37	6 39	0 21	0 20	8 09	21 25	0 21	14 41	2 23
26 Th	23 22	18 59	4 02	19 01	18 47	4 34	19 12	1 35	6 49	0 22	0 28	8 04	21 23	0 22	14 40	2 22
27 F	23 20	18 51	4 35	18 27	18 44	4 37	19 27	1 33	6 58	0 24	0 36	7 58	21 21	0 22	14 40	2 22
28 Sa	23 17	17 51	4 55	17 03	18 42	4 38	19 42	1 31	7 08	0 25	0 44	7 53	21 18	0 22	14 39	2 22
29 Su	23 14	16 04	5 01	14 55	18 42	4 38	19 56	1 29	7 18	0 26	0 52	7 48	21 16	0 22	14 39	2 22
30 M	23N11	13N37	4S55	12N11	18N43	4S36	20N10	1S27	7S28	0S28	1S00	7N44	21N14	0N22	14S39	2N22

Day	⚷ Decl	⚷ Lat	♅ Decl	♅ Lat	♆ Decl	♆ Lat	♇ Decl	♇ Lat
1	0S23	4N54	5N29	0S39	9S23	0S43	20S10	2N3
6	0 20	4 55	5 34	0 40	9 23	0 43	20 10	2
11	0 18	4 56	5 37	0 40	9 23	0 43	20 11	2
16	0 16	4 58	5 41	0 40	9 23	0 43	20 12	2
21	0 15	4 59	5 44	0 40	9 24	0 43	20 13	2
26	0 14	4 60	5 46	0 40	9 25	0 44	20 15	2

Day	⚴ Decl	⚴ Lat	⚵ Decl	⚵ Lat	⚶ Decl	⚶ Lat	Eris Decl	Eris Lat
1	14N21	4N39	11N12	6S53	2N41	9N55	2S55	12S4
6	14 28	5 22	11 43	7 07	2 11	9 29	2 54	12 4
11	14 30	6 02	12 10	7 20	1 37	9 03	2 54	12 4
16	14 28	6 40	12 35	7 34	0 59	8 38	2 54	12 4
21	14 23	7 16	12 56	7 47	0 18	8 14	2 54	12 4
26	14 14	7 50	13 14	8 00	0S25	7 50	2 54	12 4

Moon Phenomena

Max/0 Decl
dy hr mn
6 13:01 0 S
13 6:00 19S02
19 10:22 0 N
26 8:30 19N02

Perigee/Apogee
dy hr m kilometers
3 4:21 a 404953
15 3:21 p 362066
30 19:12 a 405930

PH dy hr mn
☽ 5 20:40 15♍06
○ 13 4:13 22♐06
☾ 19 18:40 28♓24
● 27 8:10 5♋37

Max/0 Lat
dy hr mn
1 20:38 5S08
9 5:38 0 N
15 12:08 5N05
21 20:31 0 S
28 23:48 5S01

Void of Course Moon

Last Aspect	☽ Ingress
1 6:33 ♃ ☌	♌ 2 1:4
3 14:43 ♄ □	♍ 4 14:2
6 9:14 ♃ ✶	♎ 7 2:0
8 19:48 ♃ □	♏ 9 10:3
11 2:22 ♃ △	♐ 11 15:2
13 4:13 ☉ ☍	♑ 13 17:0
15 6:36 ♃ ☍	♒ 15 17:2
17 18:08 ☿ △	♓ 17 18:2
19 19:07 ☿ □	♈ 19 21:2
21 22:25 ☿ ✶	♉ 22 3:0
24 1:50 ♃ ✶	♊ 24 11:0
26 11:57 ☿ ☌	♋ 26 21:0
29 1:04 ♃ ☌	♌ 29 8:4

DAILY ASPECTARIAN

1 Su: ☽△⚷ 0:54; ☽△♄ 2:40; ☽□⚳ 2:48; ☽☌♃ 6:33; ☽⚼♆ 10:51; ☉∠☽ 18:02; ⚳ D 20:16

2 M: ☽#♄ 3:29; ☽⚺☿ 5:59; ☉∥♃ 6:52; ☽⚼⚷ 6:59; ☽□♀ 12:11; ☽⚻♆ 17:01; ☽✶♂ 22:18

3 Tu: ☉✶☽ 2:55; ☽⚻♇ 4:01; ☽∥♀ 7:48; ☽△♅ 9:11; ☽∠☿ 13:13; ☽⚻⚷ 13:20; ☽□♄ 14:43; ☽✶⚳ 15:12; ☉⚻♇ 16:19; ☽⚺♃ 20:00

4 W: ☽#♆ 0:46; ☽∠♂ 5:06; ☽⚼♇ 10:19; ♀✶♆ 13:16; ☽⚼♅ 15:37; ☽✶☿ 20:12; ☽∠⚳ 21:33

5 Th: ☽∥♅ 2:36; ☽∠♃ 2:48; ☽☍♆ 5:38; ☽△♀ 7:25; ☽⚺♂ 11:47; ☽#♂ 12:12; ☽△♇ 16:25; ☉□☽ 20:40; ☽⚻♅ 21:48

6 F: ☽☍⚷ 1:45; ☽∥⚳ 1:46; ☽✶♄ 2:44; ☽⚺⚳ 3:37; ☽✶♃ 9:14; ☽#⚷ 10:58; ☉✶♅ 11:21; ☿⚼♄ 11:37; ☽∥⚷ 15:02; ☽⚼♀ 16:26; ☽#⚳ 23:36

7 Sa: ☽∠♄ 8:00; ☽□☿ 8:11; ☿ R 11:58; ♀⚻♂ 12:11; ☽∥♂ 14:40; ☽⚻♆ 16:43; ☉∥☿ 20:18; ☽#♅ 22:40; ☽☌♂ 23:32

8 Su: ☽⚻♀ 0:30; ☽□♇ 2:53; ☽☍♅ 8:14; ☉△☽ 11:45; ☽⚻⚷ 11:53; ☽⚺♄ 12:28; ☉□⚷ 13:37; ☽☌⚳ 13:45; ☽□♃ 19:48; ☉⚻♄ 20:54; ☽⚼♆ 21:02; ☽∥♆ 22:22

9 M: ♀△♇ 1:41; ☽⚼⚷ 15:34; ☉△⚳ 15:46; ☽△☿ 16:05; ☉⚼☽ 17:33; ♆ R 19:51

10 Tu: ☽△♆ 0:22; ☿⚼♄ 3:37; ☽⚺♂ 7:39; ☽#♀ 9:12; ☽✶♇ 9:44; ☽☍♀ 12:50; ☽∥♄ 13:25; ☽⚻♅ 14:57; ☽△⚷ 18:15; ☽⚼☿ 18:21; ☽☌♄ 18:31; ☽⚺⚳ 20:08; ☉⚻☽ 22:08

11 W: ☿∥♃ 1:05; ☽△♃ 2:22; ☽∠♂ 10:13; ☽∠♇ 11:44; ♀⚺♅ 13:56; ☽⚼♅ 16:52; ♀#♄ 18:53; ☽⚻☿ 19:38; ☽∠⚳ 21:56

12 Th: ♃⚼♆ 2:13; ☽□♆ 4:13; ☽⚼♃ 4:14; ☽✶♂ 11:57; ☽⚺♇ 12:55; ☿∠♀ 17:11; ☽△♅ 18:01; ☽⚻♀ 20:25; ☽□⚷ 21:02; ☽⚺♄ 21:05; ☽✶⚳ 23:01

13 F: ♀✶⚷ 4:06; ♀☍♄ 4:10; ☉☍☽ 4:13; ☽⚻♃ 5:24; ♄△⚷ 5:25; ☽☍☿ 19:57; ☽∠♄ 21:28; ☽⚼♀ 23:02

14 Sa: ☉⚺♃ 3:18; ☽✶♆ 5:23; ♀⚻⚳ 6:26; ♂□♇ 12:45; ☽☌♇ 13:44; ☽□♂ 13:46; ☽□♅ 18:52; ☽✶♄ 21:35; ☽✶⚷ 21:44; ☽□⚳ 23:54

15 Su: ☽△♀ 1:18; ☽∠♆ 5:32; ☽☍♃ 6:36; ☉⚻☽ 8:04; ☽#♀ 10:05; ☽⚻☿ 18:52; ☽∥♄ 20:48; ☽∠⚷ 21:55

16 M: ☽⚺♆ 5:44; ☉⚼☽ 9:57; ☽⚺♇ 14:05; ☽△♂ 15:08; ☽⚼☿ 18:21; ☽✶♅ 19:26; ☽□♄ 21:55; ☽⚺⚷ 22:16

17 Tu: ☽△⚳ 0:45; ☽□♀ 6:10; ☽∥♆ 7:44; ☽⚻♃ 8:00; ☿#♇ 9:44; ☿R♊ 10:06; ⚵ ♊ 11:04; ☉△☽ 12:13; ☽∠♇ 14:38; ☽⚼♂ 16:16; ☽△☿ 18:08; ☽∠♅ 20:10

18 W: ☽⚼⚳ 1:43; ☽#♅ 4:13; ☽∥♂ 4:39; ☽☌♆ 7:06; ♀✶♃ 9:17; ☽⚼♃ 9:20; ☽✶♇ 15:42; ☽⚻♂ 17:57; ♂#♅ 18:53; ☽⚺♅ 21:27; ☽△♄ 23:47

19 Th: ☽☌⚷ 0:20; ☽⚻⚳ 3:16; ☽#⚳ 8:23; ☽∥⚷ 9:01; ☽△♃ 11:16; ☽#⚷ 11:44; ☽∥⚳ 12:15; ☽✶♀ 13:16; ☉□☽ 18:40; ☽□☿ 19:07; ☉☌☿ 22:51

20 F: ☽⚼♄ 1:37; ⚳#⚷ 7:58; ☽⚺♆ 10:43; ⚷ R 12:45; ☽∥♅ 17:31; ☽∠♀ 18:04; ☽#♂ 19:06; ☽□♇ 19:42; ☽☍♂ 23:26

21 Sa: ☽☌♅ 1:56; ☽⚻♄ 4:07; ☽⚺⚷ 4:52; ☽☍⚳ 8:24; ☉ ♋ 10:52; ♀⚼♇ 12:17; ☿⚺♀ 13:19; ☽∠♆ 13:32; ☽#♆ 15:29; ☽□♃ 17:14; ☽✶☿ 22:25; ☽⚺♀ 23:44

22 Su: ☉✶☽ 4:21; ☽∠⚷ 8:08; ☽✶♆ 16:58

23 M: ☽∠☿ 0:58; ☽△♇ 2:17; ☽#♄ 6:01; ☽⚻♂ 7:46; ☽⚺♅ 9:01; ☉∠☽ 10:21; ☽☍♄ 11:00; ☽✶⚷ 11:58; ♀ ♊ 12:35; ☽⚻⚳ 16:13; ☉⚼♄ 18:45

24 Tu: ☽✶♃ 1:50; ☽⚺☿ 4:05; ♀⚼♂ 5:02; ☽⚼♇ 6:26; ⚳∥⚷ 6:47; ♀∠♅ 12:51; ☽⚼♂ 12:53; ☽∠♅ 13:24; ☽☌♀ 13:27; ☉⚺☽ 17:02; ☿∥♀ 19:55; ☽⚼⚳ 20:59

25 W: ☽□♆ 1:30; ☽∠♃ 6:57; ♂☍♅ 8:27; ☽⚻♇ 11:05; ☽∥☿ 15:53; ☽✶♅ 18:16; ☽△♂ 18:33; ☽⚻♄ 20:02; ☽□⚷ 21:12; ☿⚺♃ 23:29

26 Th: ☽△⚳ 2:14; ☽☌☿ 11:57; ☽⚺♃ 12:34

27 F: ☽⚼♄ 1:13; ☽∥☿ 4:31; ☽⚺♀ 5:48; ☉☌☽ 8:10; ☽△♆ 11:54; ♂⚺♄ 16:04; ☽☍♇ 21:41

28 Sa: ☽□♅ 5:17; ♀⚼⚳ 6:46; ☽△♄ 6:49; ☽□♂ 7:20; ☽△⚷ 8:10; ☽□⚳ 14:07; ☽∠♀ 14:49; ☽⚼♆ 17:42; ☽⚺☿ 21:59

29 Su: ☽☌♃ 1:04; ☉△♆ 7:23; ♂⚻⚷ 9:11; ☽⚼⚷ 14:12; ☽#♄ 14:40; ♀□♆ 19:32; ☽⚻♆ 23:49

30 M: ☽✶♀ 0:18; ☉⚺☽ 1:16; ☽∠☿ 3:47; ☽⚻♇ 9:43; ♀#♇ 9:56; ☽△♅ 17:41; ☽□♄ 18:59; ☽⚻⚷ 20:29; ☽✶♂ 21:43

LONGITUDE

July 2014

Day	Sid.Time	☉	☽	☽ 12 hour	Mean☊	True☊	☿	♀	♂	⚳	♃	♄	⚷	♅	♆	♇
	h m s	° ' "	° ' "	° ' "	° '	° '	° '	° '	° '	° '	° '	° '	° '	° '	° '	° '
1 Tu	18 35 53	9♋06 34	19♌26 31	25♌21 35	24♎40.9	25♎08.1	24♊23.6	8♊54.3	18♎21.4	21♎06.0	26♋36.2	16♏57.5	17♓42.5	16♈19.7	7♓28.6	12♑22.5
2 W	18 39 50	10 03 47	1♍16 38	7♍12 07	24 37.7	25R 00.0	24D 23.4	10 06.0	18 45.3	21 16.1	26 49.3	16R 55.7	17R 41.9	16 20.7	7R 28.0	12R 21.0
3 Th	18 43 46	11 01 00	13 08 30	19 06 21	24 34.5	24 54.4	24 28.1	11 17.7	19 09.7	21 26.5	27 02.4	16 53.9	17 41.3	16 21.7	7 27.3	12 19.5
4 F	18 47 43	11 58 13	25 06 13	1♎08 42	24 31.4	24 51.4	24 37.7	12 29.4	19 34.4	21 37.2	27 15.5	16 52.3	17 40.6	16 22.6	7 26.5	12 18.0
5 Sa	18 51 40	12 55 26	7♎14 26	13 24 04	24 28.2	24D 50.3	24 52.2	13 41.1	19 59.5	21 48.2	27 28.6	16 50.7	17 39.8	16 23.4	7 25.8	12 16.5
6 Su	18 55 36	13 52 38	19 38 14	25 57 34	24 25.0	24R 50.2	25 11.8	14 52.9	20 24.9	21 59.5	27 41.8	16 49.3	17 39.0	16 24.2	7 25.0	12 15.0
7 M	18 59 33	14 49 50	2♏22 41	8♏54 07	24 21.8	24 50.1	25 36.4	16 04.7	20 50.6	22 11.0	27 54.9	16 47.9	17 38.1	16 25.0	7 24.2	12 13.5
8 Tu	19 03 29	15 47 02	15 32 20	22 17 42	24 18.7	24 48.9	26 06.1	17 16.6	21 16.7	22 22.7	28 08.1	16 46.6	17 37.2	16 25.7	7 23.3	12 12.0
9 W	19 07 26	16 44 14	29 10 26	6♐10 35	24 15.5	24 45.6	26 40.8	18 28.5	21 43.2	22 34.8	28 21.3	16 45.4	17 36.3	16 26.3	7 22.4	12 10.5
10 Th	19 11 22	17 41 25	13♐18 01	20 32 23	24 12.3	24 39.8	27 20.4	19 40.4	22 09.9	22 47.0	28 34.5	16 44.3	17 35.2	16 26.9	7 21.5	12 09.0
11 F	19 15 19	18 38 37	27 53 08	5♑19 26	24 09.1	24 31.5	28 04.9	20 52.4	22 36.9	22 59.5	28 47.8	16 43.3	17 34.2	16 27.5	7 20.6	12 07.5
12 Sa	19 19 15	19 35 49	12♑50 18	20 24 33	24 06.0	24 21.5	28 54.4	22 04.4	23 04.3	23 12.3	29 01.0	16 42.4	17 33.1	16 28.0	7 19.7	12 06.0
13 Su	19 23 12	20 33 01	28 00 52	5♒37 51	24 02.8	24 10.7	29 48.7	23 16.5	23 32.0	23 25.3	29 14.3	16 41.6	17 31.9	16 28.5	7 18.7	12 04.5
14 M	19 27 09	21 30 13	13♒14 09	20 48 25	23 59.6	24 00.4	0♋47.7	24 28.6	23 59.9	23 38.5	29 27.6	16 40.9	17 30.7	16 28.9	7 17.7	12 03.0
15 Tu	19 31 05	22 27 25	28 19 27	5♓46 13	23 56.4	23 51.9	1 51.5	25 40.8	24 28.1	23 52.0	29 40.9	16 40.3	17 29.4	16 29.3	7 16.7	12 01.6
16 W	19 35 02	23 24 38	13♓07 52	20 33 35	23 53.2	23 45.8	2 59.9	26 52.9	24 56.7	24 05.6	29 54.2	16 39.8	17 28.1	16 29.6	7 15.6	12 00.1
17 Th	19 38 58	24 21 52	27 33 34	4♈36 59	23 50.1	23 42.3	4 12.9	28 05.2	25 25.5	24 19.5	0♌07.5	16 39.4	17 26.7	16 29.9	7 14.5	11 58.6
18 F	19 42 55	25 19 06	11♈33 59	18 24 42	23 46.9	23D 40.9	5 30.3	29 17.5	25 54.6	24 33.6	0 20.8	16 39.0	17 25.3	16 30.1	7 13.4	11 57.2
19 Sa	19 46 51	26 16 21	25 09 21	1♉48 16	23 43.7	23R 40.7	6 52.2	0♋29.8	26 23.9	24 48.0	0 34.1	16 38.8	17 23.8	16 30.3	7 12.3	11 55.7
20 Su	19 50 48	27 13 37	8♉21 50	14 50 28	23 40.5	23 40.5	8 18.5	1 42.1	26 53.5	25 02.5	0 47.4	16D 38.7	17 22.3	16 30.4	7 11.2	11 54.3
21 M	19 54 44	28 10 53	21 14 37	27 34 44	23 37.4	23 39.1	9 48.9	2 54.5	27 23.4	25 17.3	1 00.8	16 38.6	17 20.8	16 30.5	7 10.0	11 52.8
22 Tu	19 58 41	29 08 10	3♊51 14	10♊04 31	23 34.2	23 35.5	11 23.4	4 07.0	27 53.6	25 32.2	1 14.1	16 38.7	17 19.2	16R 30.5	7 08.8	11 51.4
23 W	20 02 38	0♌05 28	16 14 58	22 22 55	23 31.0	23 29.2	13 01.8	5 19.5	28 24.0	25 47.4	1 27.5	16 38.9	17 17.5	16 30.5	7 07.6	11 50.0
24 Th	20 06 34	1 02 47	28 28 40	4♋32 30	23 27.8	23 20.1	14 44.0	6 32.0	28 54.7	26 02.8	1 40.8	16 39.1	17 15.9	16 30.4	7 06.4	11 48.6
25 F	20 10 31	2 00 07	10♋34 37	16 35 14	23 24.7	23 08.5	16 29.7	7 44.6	29 25.6	26 18.3	1 54.1	16 39.5	17 14.1	16 30.3	7 05.1	11 47.2
26 Sa	20 14 27	2 57 27	22 34 33	28 32 44	23 21.5	22 55.4	18 18.7	8 57.2	29 56.8	26 34.1	2 07.5	16 39.9	17 12.4	16 30.1	7 03.8	11 45.8
27 Su	20 18 24	3 54 48	4♌29 56	10♌26 20	23 18.3	22 41.8	20 10.8	10 09.8	0♏28.3	26 50.1	2 20.8	16 40.5	17 10.5	16 29.9	7 02.5	11 44.5
28 M	20 22 20	4 52 09	16 22 05	22 17 25	23 15.1	22 28.7	22 05.6	11 22.5	0 59.9	27 06.2	2 34.2	16 41.1	17 08.7	16 29.7	7 01.2	11 43.1
29 Tu	20 26 17	5 49 31	28 12 31	4♍07 39	23 11.9	22 17.3	24 02.9	12 35.3	1 31.8	27 22.5	2 47.5	16 41.9	17 06.8	16 29.4	6 59.9	11 41.8
30 W	20 30 13	6 46 54	10♍03 06	15 59 13	23 08.8	22 08.3	26 02.3	13 48.0	2 04.0	27 39.0	3 00.8	16 42.7	17 04.8	16 29.0	6 58.5	11 40.4
31 Th	20 34 10	7♌44 18	21 56 21	27 54 55	23♎05.6	22♎02.0	28♋03.6	15♋00.8	2♏36.3	27♎55.7	3♌14.1	16♏43.7	17♓02.8	16♈28.6	6♓57.2	11♑39.1

1st of Month

Julian Day # 2456839.5
Obliquity 23°26'06"
SVP 5♓03'18"
GC 27♐02.5
Eris 23♈09.2

Day	⚴
1	13♍56.0
6	15 45.9
11	17 38.2
16	19 32.6
21	21 29.0
26	23 27.3
31	25 27.2

Day	⚵
1	7♊50.8
6	10 43.9
11	13 36.3
16	16 28.0
21	19 18.9
26	22 08.9
31	24 57.6

Day	⚶
1	20♎46.0
6	22 01.5
11	23 24.6
16	24 54.6
21	26 30.8
26	28 12.8
31	0♏00.3

DECLINATION and LATITUDE

Day	☉ Decl	☽ Decl	☽ Lat	☽12h Decl	☿ Decl	☿ Lat	♀ Decl	♀ Lat	♂ Decl	♂ Lat	⚳ Decl	⚳ Lat	♃ Decl	♃ Lat	♄ Decl	♄ Lat
1 Tu	23N07	10N38	4S35	8N58	18N46	4S34	20N23	1S25	7S39	0S29	1S08	7N39	21N11	0N22	14S38	2N21
2 W	23 03	7 13	4 04	5 24	18 50	4 29	20 36	1 22	7 49	0 30	1 16	7 34	21 09	0 22	14 38	2 21
3 Th	22 59	3 31	3 22	1 36	18 55	4 24	20 48	1 20	7 59	0 32	1 25	7 29	21 06	0 22	14 38	2 21
4 F	22 54	0S22	2 31	2S19	19 02	4 18	21 00	1 18	8 10	0 33	1 33	7 24	21 04	0 22	14 38	2 21
5 Sa	22 48	4 17	1 32	6 13	19 10	4 10	21 11	1 16	8 21	0 34	1 42	7 19	21 01	0 22	14 37	2 20
6 Su	22 43	8 06	0 28	9 56	19 19	4 02	21 22	1 13	8 31	0 35	1 50	7 15	20 59	0 22	14 37	2 20
7 M	22 37	11 40	0N40	13 18	19 29	3 53	21 32	1 11	8 42	0 37	1 59	7 10	20 56	0 22	14 37	2 20
8 Tu	22 30	14 47	1 47	16 05	19 40	3 43	21 41	1 09	8 53	0 38	2 07	7 05	20 54	0 22	14 37	2 20
9 W	22 23	17 11	2 51	18 03	19 51	3 32	21 50	1 06	9 04	0 39	2 16	7 01	20 51	0 22	14 37	2 19
10 Th	22 16	18 39	3 46	18 57	20 03	3 21	21 59	1 04	9 15	0 40	2 25	6 56	20 49	0 23	14 37	2 19
11 F	22 08	18 56	4 29	18 36	20 16	3 09	22 06	1 01	9 26	0 41	2 33	6 52	20 46	0 23	14 37	2 19
12 Sa	22 00	17 56	4 55	16 57	20 29	2 57	22 13	0 59	9 37	0 42	2 42	6 47	20 43	0 23	14 37	2 19
13 Su	21 52	15 39	4 60	14 06	20 42	2 44	22 20	0 56	9 49	0 43	2 51	6 43	20 41	0 23	14 37	2 18
14 M	21 43	12 18	4 44	10 19	20 55	2 31	22 26	0 54	9 60	0 45	2 60	6 39	20 38	0 23	14 37	2 18
15 Tu	21 34	8 10	4 08	5 55	21 08	2 18	22 31	0 51	10 11	0 46	3 09	6 34	20 35	0 23	14 37	2 18
16 W	21 24	3 36	3 17	1 16	21 20	2 04	22 36	0 48	10 23	0 47	3 18	6 30	20 33	0 23	14 37	2 18
17 Th	21 14	1N04	2 13	3N21	21 32	1 51	22 40	0 46	10 34	0 48	3 26	6 26	20 30	0 23	14 37	2 17
18 F	21 04	5 33	1 04	7 39	21 42	1 37	22 43	0 43	10 46	0 49	3 36	6 22	20 27	0 23	14 37	2 17
19 Sa	20 54	9 37	0S08	11 26	21 53	1 23	22 46	0 40	10 57	0 50	3 45	6 17	20 24	0 23	14 37	2 17
20 Su	20 43	13 05	1 17	14 33	22 02	1 09	22 48	0 38	11 09	0 51	3 54	6 13	20 21	0 23	14 38	2 17
21 M	20 31	15 49	2 20	16 52	22 09	0 55	22 49	0 35	11 21	0 52	4 03	6 09	20 19	0 23	14 38	2 16
22 Tu	20 20	17 43	3 15	18 21	22 15	0 42	22 50	0 32	11 33	0 53	4 12	6 05	20 16	0 24	14 38	2 16
23 W	20 08	18 45	3 60	18 55	22 19	0 29	22 50	0 30	11 44	0 54	4 21	6 01	20 13	0 24	14 38	2 16
24 Th	19 55	18 53	4 33	18 37	22 22	0 16	22 50	0 27	11 56	0 55	4 30	5 57	20 10	0 24	14 39	2 15
25 F	19 43	18 09	4 53	17 28	22 22	0 03	22 48	0 24	12 08	0 55	4 39	5 53	20 07	0 24	14 39	2 15
26 Sa	19 30	16 37	5 00	15 34	22 20	0N09	22 47	0 21	12 20	0 56	4 49	5 49	20 04	0 24	14 39	2 15
27 Su	19 16	14 22	4 54	13 02	22 15	0 22	22 44	0 19	12 32	0 57	4 58	5 45	20 01	0 24	14 40	2 15
28 M	19 03	11 33	4 35	9 58	22 08	0 31	22 41	0 16	12 44	0 58	5 07	5 42	19 58	0 24	14 40	2 14
29 Tu	18 49	8 16	4 04	6 30	21 59	0 42	22 37	0 13	12 56	0 59	5 17	5 38	19 55	0 24	14 41	2 14
30 W	18 34	4 40	3 23	2 47	21 47	0 51	22 33	0 11	13 07	0 60	5 26	5 34	19 52	0 24	14 41	2 14
31 Th	18N20	0N52	2S32	1S04	21N32	1N00	22N28	0S08	13S19	1S01	5S35	5N30	19N49	0N24	14S42	2N14

Day	⚷ Decl	⚷ Lat	♅ Decl	♅ Lat	♆ Decl	♆ Lat	♇ Decl	♇ Lat
1	0S14	5N01	5N48	0S40	9S26	0S44	20S16	2N37
6	0 15	5 02	5 50	0 40	9 28	0 44	20 17	2 36
11	0 16	5 03	5 51	0 40	9 30	0 44	20 18	2 36
16	0 17	5 04	5 51	0 41	9 32	0 44	20 19	2 35
21	0 19	5 05	5 52	0 41	9 34	0 44	20 21	2 34
26	0 22	5 05	5 51	0 41	9 36	0 44	20 22	2 34
31	0S25	5N06	5N51	0S41	9S39	0S45	20S23	2N33

Day	⚴ Decl	⚴ Lat	⚵ Decl	⚵ Lat	⚶ Decl	⚶ Lat	Eris Decl	Eris Lat
1	14N01	8N22	13N29	8S14	1S12	7N27	2S54	12S47
6	13 46	8 52	13 41	8 27	1 60	7 05	2 54	12 47
11	13 29	9 21	13 49	8 40	2 50	6 44	2 54	12 48
16	13 09	9 49	13 54	8 53	3 41	6 23	2 54	12 48
21	12 48	10 16	13 55	9 06	4 34	6 04	2 55	12 49
26	12 24	10 42	13 53	9 20	5 28	5 45	2 55	12 49
31	11N60	11N07	13N48	9S33	6S22	5N27	2S56	12S50

Moon Phenomena

Max/0 Decl
dy hr mn
3 21:48 0 S
10 17:39 18S59
16 18:28 0 N
23 15:34 18N56
31 5:24 0 S

Max/0 Lat
dy hr mn
6 9:52 0 N
12 18:09 5N00
18 21:21 0 S
26 0:37 5S00

Perigee/Apogee
dy hr m kilometers
13 8:23 p 358264
28 3:31 a 406567

PH dy hr mn
◑ 5 12:00 13♎24
○ 12 11:26 20♑03
◐ 19 2:09 26♈21
● 26 22:43 3♌52

Void of Course Moon

Last Aspect	☽ Ingress
1 10:01 ☿ ✶	♍ 1 21:25
4 4:22 ♃ ✶	♎ 4 9:44
6 15:32 ♄ □	♏ 6 19:35
8 22:34 ♄ △	♐ 9 1:26
11 0:20 ☿ ☍	♑ 11 3:26
13 1:57 ♃ ☍	♒ 13 3:08
14 19:24 ♀ △	♓ 15 2:41
17 0:58 ♀ □	♈ 17 4:08
19 2:19 ♂ ☍	♉ 19 8:44
21 14:14 ☉ ✶	♊ 21 16:37
24 0:54 ♂ △	♋ 24 3:00
25 13:54 ♀ ☌	♌ 26 14:56
28 0:39 ♄ □	♍ 29 3:38
31 14:49 ☿ ✶	♎ 31 16:10

DAILY ASPECTARIAN

1 Tu ☽✶⚳ 3:25 · ☽⋕♆ 8:39 · ☽✶☿ 10:01 · ☉∠☽ 10:18 · ☿ D 12:51 · ☽⊻♃ 14:48 · ☽⚼♇ 16:03 · ☽⋕♂ 20:09 · ☉⊻♀ 20:21

2 W ☽⚼♅ 0:08 · ☽∠♂ 5:12 · ☽∥♅ 9:19 · ☽∠⚳ 10:16 · ☽☍♆ 12:31 · ☉✶☽ 19:20 · ☽□♀ 19:51 · ☽∠♃ 21:44 · ☽△♇ 22:21

3 Th ☽⊼♅ 6:30 · ☽✶♄ 7:33 · ☽☍⚷ 9:09 · ☽⊻♂ 12:33 · ☽⋕⚳ 12:39 · ☽⊻⚳ 16:56 · ♀∠♃ 18:19 · ♀⊼♇ 20:16 · ☽⋕⚷ 20:19 · ☽□☿ 23:02 · ☽∥⚷ 23:17

4 F ☽✶♃ 4:22 · ♀∥♃ 6:43 · ☽∥⚳ 7:34 · ☉☍♇ 8:04 · ☽∠♄ 13:24

5 Sa ☽⊼♆ 0:22 · ☽⋕♅ 9:34 · ☽□♇ 9:48 · ☉□☽ 12:00 · ☽△♀ 13:53 · ☽☍♅ 17:47 · ☽⊻♄ 18:37 · ☽⊼⚷ 20:12

6 Su ☽☌♂ 1:32 · ☽∥♂ 2:49 · ☽☌⚳ 4:33 · ☽⚼♆ 5:17 · ☽∥♆ 8:53 · ☽△☿ 10:54 · ☽□♃ 15:32 · ☽⚼♀ 21:20

7 M ☽⚼⚷ 0:29 · ♀✶♅ 6:50 · ☽△♆ 9:15 · ♀⊼♄ 14:10 · ☽⚼☿ 15:40 · ☽✶♇ 18:00 · ☽∥♄ 22:36

8 Tu ☉△☽ 0:28 · ⚳⚼♆ 1:05 · ☽⊼♅ 1:36 · ☽☌♄ 2:13 · ☽⊼♀ 3:25 · ☽△⚷ 3:43 · ♀□⚷ 6:48 · ☽⊻♂ 10:33 · ☽⊻⚳ 12:20 · ☉□♅ 16:24 · ☽⊼☿ 19:28 · ☽∠♇ 20:32 · ☽△♃ 22:34

9 W ☉△♄ 0:29 · ☽⚼♅ 3:54 · ☉⚼☽ 4:44 · ☽∠♂ 13:20 · ☽□♆ 14:01 · ☽∠⚳ 14:35 · ☉△⚷ 21:27 · ☽⊻♇ 22:05

10 Th ☽⚼♃ 0:28 · ☽△♅ 5:15 · ☽⊻♄ 5:43 · ☽□⚷ 7:07 · ☉⊼☽ 7:49 · ♂⚼♆ 10:02 · ☽☍♀ 11:31 · ☽✶♂ 15:08 · ☽✶⚳ 15:54

11 F ☽☍☿ 0:20 · ☽⊼♃ 1:30 · ☉∥♀ 3:14 · ☿⋕♇ 3:52 · ☽∠♄ 6:12 · ♂∥♆ 7:50 · ☽✶♆ 15:13 · ☽☌♇ 22:50

12 Sa ☿⊻♃ 4:05 · ☽□♅ 5:46 · ☽✶♄ 6:08 · ☽✶⚷ 7:28 · ☉☍☽ 11:26 · ♂☌⚳ 13:06 · ☽∠♆ 15:01 · ☽⊼♀ 15:53 · ☽□⚳ 16:39 · ☽□♂ 16:43 · ☿∥♃ 22:08

13 Su ☽☍♃ 1:57 · ☽⊼☿ 3:01 · ♀△⚳ 3:35 · ☿ ♋ 4:46 · ☽∠⚷ 7:06 · ☽∥♄ 8:14 · ♀△♂ 8:23 · ☽⊻♆ 14:38 · ☽⚼♀ 17:33 · ☽⊻♇ 22:08

14 M ☽⚼☿ 4:21 · ☽✶♅ 5:08 · ☽□♄ 5:27 · ☽⊻⚷ 6:46 · ☽∥♂ 13:12 · ☉⊼☽ 14:00 · ☽∥♆ 16:31 · ☽△⚳ 16:46 · ☽△♂ 17:38 · ☽△♀ 19:24 · ☉⚼♆ 19:34 · ☿⚼♄ 19:58 · ☽∠♇ 21:55

15 Tu ☽⊼♃ 2:13 · ☽∠♅ 5:05 · ☽△☿ 6:08 · ☽⋕♅ 12:19 · ☽☌♆ 14:26 · ☉⚼☽ 15:45 · ☽⚼⚳ 17:18 · ☽⚼♂ 18:37 · ☽✶♇ 22:09

16 W ☽∥⚳ 1:32 · ☽⚼♃ 2:57 · ☉∥☿ 4:57 · ☽⊻♅ 5:32 · ☽△♄ 5:49 · ☽☌⚷ 7:08 · ♃ ♌ 10:32 · ☽∥⚷ 16:59 · ☉△☽ 18:15 · ☽⊼⚳ 18:28 · ☽⋕⚷ 19:58 · ☽⊼♂ 20:17 · ☉□⚳ 22:42

17 Th ☽□♀ 0:58 · ☽△♃ 4:25 · ☽⚼♄ 6:57 · ☽□☿ 12:27 · ☽⋕⚳ 12:56 · ☽⊻♆ 16:30

18 F ☽□♇ 0:40 · ☽∥♅ 1:45 · ☽☌♅ 8:38 · ☽⊼♄ 8:54 · ☽⊻⚷ 10:14 · ♀ ♋ 14:07 · ☽∠♆ 18:44 · ☽☍⚳ 23:21 · ☽⋕♆ 23:36

19 Sa ♀⊻♃ 1:46 · ☉□☽ 2:09 · ☽☍♂ 2:19 · ☿△♆ 5:37 · ☉□♂ 6:33 · ☽⋕♂ 9:18 · ☽□♃ 9:55 · ☽✶♀ 10:35 · ☽∠⚷ 13:03 · ☽✶♆ 21:50 · ♀⚼♄ 22:51 · ☽✶☿ 23:53

20 Su ☽△♇ 6:32 · ♃⋕♇ 9:02 · ☽⋕♄ 12:46 · ☽⊻♅ 15:07 · ☽☍♄ 15:22 · ☽✶⚷ 16:42 · ☽∠♀ 17:05 · ♄ D 20:37

21 M ☽∠☿ 7:42 · ☽⊼⚳ 7:48 · ☽⚼♇ 10:39 · ☽⊼♂ 12:07 · ☉✶☽ 14:14 · ☽✶♃ 18:53 · ☽∠♅ 19:30 · ☉⋕♇ 21:46

22 Tu ☽⊻♀ 0:34 · ♅ R 2:54 · ☽□♆ 6:20 · ☿☍♇ 6:50 · ☉∥♃ 10:18 · ☽⚼⚳ 13:10 · ☽⊼♇ 15:25 · ☽⊻☿ 16:45 · ☽⚼♂ 18:13 · ☉∠☽ 21:33 · ☉ ♌ 21:42

23 W ☽∠♃ 0:25 · ☽✶♅ 0:30 · ☽⊼♄ 0:47 · ☽□⚷ 2:02 · ☽△⚳ 19:06

24 Th ☽△♂ 0:54 · ☉⊻☽ 5:31 · ☽⚼♄ 6:17 · ☽⊻♃ 6:27 · ♀△♆ 11:10 · ☽△♆ 17:04 · ☽☌♀ 17:44 · ☉☌♃ 20:45

25 F ☿□♅ 0:09 · ☿△♄ 2:12 · ☽☍♇ 2:24 · ☉⚼⚷ 5:42 · ☿△⚷ 9:43 · ☽□♅ 11:50 · ☽△♄ 12:09 · ☽△⚷ 13:16 · ☽☌☿ 13:54 · ☽⚼♆ 22:58

26 Sa ♂ ♏ 2:26 · ♃⚼⚷ 7:42 · ☽□⚳ 8:12 · ☽□♂ 15:30 · ☽⚼⚷ 19:20 · ☽☌♃ 19:35 · ☽⋕♄ 21:13 · ☉☌☽ 22:43

27 Su ☽⊼♆ 5:08 · ☽⊻♀ 12:45 · ☽⊼♇ 14:36 · ☽⋕♂ 15:08 · ☿⚼♆ 23:06

28 M ☽△♅ 0:15 · ☽□♄ 0:39 · ☽⊼⚷ 1:34 · ♀☍♇ 6:40 · ☽⊻☿ 13:53 · ☽⋕♆ 14:26 · ☽⚼♇ 20:56 · ☽✶⚳ 22:16 · ☽∠♀ 22:36

29 Tu ☽⚼♅ 6:39 · ☽✶♂ 7:03 · ☽⊻♃ 9:28 · ☽∥♅ 16:20 · ☉⊻☽ 16:48 · ☽☍♆ 17:47 · ☽⋕⚳ 19:16

30 W ♂⚼⚷ 0:36 · ☽∠☿ 2:24 · ☽△♇ 3:17 · ☉⊼♆ 4:45 · ☽∠⚳ 5:23 · ☽✶♀ 8:27 · ☽⊼♅ 13:00 · ☽✶♄ 13:29 · ☽☍⚷ 14:10 · ☽∠♂ 14:51 · ☽∠♃ 16:24 · ☿□⚳ 22:12 · ⚶ ♏ 23:43

31 Th ☉∠☽ 1:45 · ☽⋕⚷ 2:50 · ☽∥⚷ 7:58 · ☽⊻⚳ 12:19 · ☽✶☿ 14:49 · ☽∠♄ 19:39 · ☽⊻♂ 22:23 · ☿ ♌ 22:47 · ☽✶♃ 23:03

August 2014

LONGITUDE

Day	Sid.Time	☉	☽	☽ 12 hour	Mean☊	True☊	☿	♀	♂	⚳	♃	♄	⚷	♅	♆	♇
	h m s	° ' "	° ' "	° ' "	° '	° '	° '	° '	° '	° '	° '	° '	° '	° '	° '	° '
1 F	20 38 07	8♌41 42	3♎55 24	9♎58 18	23♎02.4	21♎58.4	0♌06.3	16♋13.7	3♏08.9	28♎12.5	3♌27.5	16♏44.7	17♓00.8	16♈28.1	6♓55.8	11♑37.8
2 Sa	20 42 03	9 39 06	16 04 09	22 13 31	22 59.2	21D 57.1	2 10.1	17 26.5	3 41.7	28 29.6	3 40.8	16 45.8	16R 58.7	16R 27.6	6R 54.4	11R 36.5
3 Su	20 46 00	10 36 32	28 27 00	4♏45 12	22 56.0	21 57.0	4 14.6	18 39.5	4 14.8	28 46.8	3 54.0	16 47.1	16 56.6	16 27.1	6 53.0	11 35.2
4 M	20 49 56	11 33 58	11♏08 43	17 38 06	22 52.9	21R 57.3	6 19.7	19 52.4	4 48.0	29 04.1	4 07.3	16 48.4	16 54.5	16 26.5	6 51.5	11 34.0
5 Tu	20 53 53	12 31 24	24 13 52	0♐56 28	22 49.7	21 56.7	8 24.8	21 05.4	5 21.5	29 21.6	4 20.6	16 49.8	16 52.3	16 25.8	6 50.1	11 32.7
6 W	20 57 49	13 28 52	7♐46 15	14 43 23	22 46.5	21 54.5	10 29.9	22 18.4	5 55.2	29 39.3	4 33.8	16 51.4	16 50.1	16 25.1	6 48.6	11 31.5
7 Th	21 01 46	14 26 20	21 47 56	28 59 44	22 43.3	21 50.0	12 34.6	23 31.5	6 29.0	29 57.2	4 47.1	16 53.0	16 47.9	16 24.4	6 47.1	11 30.3
8 F	21 05 42	15 23 49	6♑18 24	13♑43 18	22 40.2	21 43.2	14 38.8	24 44.6	7 03.1	0♏15.1	5 00.3	16 54.7	16 45.6	16 23.6	6 45.6	11 29.1
9 Sa	21 09 39	16 21 18	21 13 38	28 48 19	22 37.0	21 34.7	16 42.2	25 57.7	7 37.4	0 33.3	5 13.5	16 56.5	16 43.3	16 22.8	6 44.1	11 28.0
10 Su	21 13 36	17 18 49	6♒26 07	14♒05 41	22 33.8	21 25.4	18 44.6	27 10.9	8 11.8	0 51.6	5 26.7	16 58.4	16 41.0	16 21.9	6 42.6	11 26.8
11 M	21 17 32	18 16 20	21 45 33	29 24 18	22 30.6	21 16.5	20 46.1	28 24.1	8 46.5	1 10.0	5 39.8	17 00.4	16 38.6	16 21.0	6 41.1	11 25.7
12 Tu	21 21 29	19 13 53	7♓00 33	14♓33 03	22 27.5	21 09.0	22 46.3	29 37.4	9 21.3	1 28.6	5 53.0	17 02.5	16 36.2	16 20.1	6 39.5	11 24.6
13 W	21 25 25	20 11 27	22 00 44	29 22 44	22 24.3	21 03.7	24 45.4	0♌50.7	9 56.3	1 47.3	6 06.1	17 04.7	16 33.8	16 19.1	6 38.0	11 23.5
14 Th	21 29 22	21 09 02	6♈38 21	13♈47 13	22 21.1	21 00.8	26 43.2	2 04.0	10 31.5	2 06.1	6 19.2	17 06.9	16 31.3	16 18.0	6 36.4	11 22.4
15 F	21 33 18	22 06 38	20 49 05	27 43 56	22 17.9	21D 00.0	28 39.6	3 17.4	11 06.9	2 25.1	6 32.3	17 09.3	16 28.9	16 16.9	6 34.8	11 21.3
16 Sa	21 37 15	23 04 17	4♉31 53	11♉13 12	22 14.7	21 00.5	0♍34.6	4 30.8	11 42.4	2 44.2	6 45.3	17 11.7	16 26.3	16 15.8	6 33.2	11 20.3
17 Su	21 41 11	24 01 56	17 48 14	24 17 25	22 11.6	21R 01.2	2 28.2	5 44.3	12 18.1	3 03.4	6 58.3	17 14.3	16 23.8	16 14.6	6 31.7	11 19.3
18 M	21 45 08	24 59 38	0♊41 15	7♊00 14	22 08.4	21 01.2	4 20.5	6 57.8	12 54.1	3 22.8	7 11.3	17 16.9	16 21.3	16 13.4	6 30.1	11 18.3
19 Tu	21 49 05	25 57 21	13 14 54	19 25 45	22 05.2	20 59.6	6 11.3	8 11.3	13 30.1	3 42.3	7 24.3	17 19.6	16 18.7	16 12.1	6 28.5	11 17.3
20 W	21 53 01	26 55 05	25 33 19	1♋38 03	22 02.0	20 55.9	8 00.7	9 24.9	14 06.4	4 01.9	7 37.2	17 22.4	16 16.1	16 10.8	6 26.8	11 16.4
21 Th	21 56 58	27 52 51	7♋40 25	13 40 49	21 58.9	20 50.0	9 48.7	10 38.5	14 42.8	4 21.7	7 50.1	17 25.3	16 13.5	16 09.5	6 25.2	11 15.5
22 F	22 00 54	28 50 39	19 39 39	25 37 14	21 55.7	20 42.1	11 35.2	11 52.2	15 19.4	4 41.6	8 03.0	17 28.3	16 10.8	16 08.1	6 23.6	11 14.6
23 Sa	22 04 51	29 48 28	1♌33 54	7♌29 56	21 52.5	20 32.9	13 20.4	13 05.9	15 56.2	5 01.6	8 15.9	17 31.4	16 08.1	16 06.7	6 22.0	11 13.7
24 Su	22 08 47	0♍46 19	13 25 33	19 21 01	21 49.3	20 23.3	15 04.2	14 19.6	16 33.1	5 21.7	8 28.7	17 34.6	16 05.5	16 05.2	6 20.3	11 12.8
25 M	22 12 44	1 44 11	25 16 32	1♍12 19	21 46.1	20 14.0	16 46.7	15 33.4	17 10.2	5 41.9	8 41.4	17 37.8	16 02.8	16 03.7	6 18.7	11 12.0
26 Tu	22 16 40	2 42 05	7♍08 33	13 05 27	21 43.0	20 06.0	18 27.8	16 47.2	17 47.5	6 02.3	8 54.2	17 41.1	16 00.1	16 02.2	6 17.0	11 11.2
27 W	22 20 37	3 40 00	19 03 16	25 02 12	21 39.8	19 59.9	20 07.5	18 01.0	18 24.9	6 22.7	9 06.8	17 44.6	15 57.3	16 00.6	6 15.4	11 10.4
28 Th	22 24 34	4 37 57	1♎02 33	7♎04 35	21 36.6	19 55.9	21 46.0	19 14.9	19 02.5	6 43.3	9 19.5	17 48.1	15 54.6	15 59.0	6 13.7	11 09.7
29 F	22 28 30	5 35 55	13 08 38	19 15 02	21 33.4	19D 54.0	23 23.1	20 28.8	19 40.2	7 03.9	9 32.1	17 51.6	15 51.8	15 57.3	6 12.1	11 08.9
30 Sa	22 32 27	6 33 54	25 24 12	1♏36 32	21 30.3	19 53.9	24 58.9	21 42.8	20 18.1	7 24.7	9 44.7	17 55.3	15 49.1	15 55.6	6 10.5	11 08.2
31 Su	22 36 23	7♍31 55	7♏52 27	14 12 26	21♎27.1	19♎54.9	26♍33.4	22♌56.7	20♏56.2	7♏45.6	9♌57.2	17♏59.0	15♓46.3	15♈53.9	6♓08.8	11♑07.5

1st of Month

Julian Day # 2456870.5
Obliquity 23°26'06"
SVP 5♓03'14"
GC 27♐02.6
Eris 23♈10.3R

Day	⚴	⚵	⚶
1	25♍51.4	25♊31.2	0♏22.3
6	27 53.2	28 18.4	2 15.6
11	29 56.3	1♋04.0	4 13.2
16	2♎00.7	3 47.9	6 14.7
21	4 06.3	6 30.1	8 20.0
26	6 12.9	9 10.1	10 28.7
31	8 20.6	11 47.8	12 40.5

DECLINATION and LATITUDE

Day	☉ Decl	☽ Decl	☽ Lat	☽12h Decl	☿ Decl	☿ Lat	♀ Decl	♀ Lat	♂ Decl	♂ Lat	⚳ Decl	⚳ Lat	♃ Decl	♃ Lat	♄ Decl	♄ Lat
1 F	18N05	3S00	1S34	4S55	21N14	1N09	22N22	0S05	13S31	1S01	5S45	5N27	19N46	0N24	14S42	2N13
2 Sa	17 50	6 48	0 31	8 38	20 54	1 16	22 15	0 03	13 43	1 02	5 54	5 23	19 43	0 24	14 43	2 13
3 Su	17 34	10 23	0N35	12 03	20 32	1 22	22 08	0N00	13 55	1 03	6 03	5 19	19 40	0 25	14 44	2 13
4 M	17 19	13 35	1 40	14 58	20 07	1 28	22 01	0 03	14 07	1 04	6 13	5 16	19 37	0 25	14 44	2 13
5 Tu	17 03	16 12	2 43	17 13	19 39	1 33	21 52	0 05	14 19	1 05	6 22	5 12	19 34	0 25	14 45	2 12
6 W	16 46	18 00	3 38	18 33	19 10	1 37	21 43	0 08	14 31	1 05	6 32	5 09	19 31	0 25	14 45	2 12
7 Th	16 30	18 48	4 23	18 46	18 38	1 40	21 34	0 11	14 43	1 06	6 41	5 05	19 28	0 25	14 46	2 12
8 F	16 13	18 25	4 53	17 45	18 05	1 43	21 23	0 13	14 55	1 07	6 51	5 02	19 25	0 25	14 47	2 12
9 Sa	15 56	16 46	5 03	15 29	17 29	1 45	21 13	0 16	15 07	1 08	6 60	4 58	19 22	0 25	14 48	2 11
10 Su	15 39	13 56	4 53	12 07	16 53	1 46	21 01	0 18	15 19	1 08	7 09	4 55	19 19	0 25	14 48	2 11
11 M	15 21	10 07	4 22	7 56	16 14	1 46	20 49	0 21	15 31	1 09	7 19	4 52	19 16	0 25	14 49	2 11
12 Tu	15 03	5 39	3 32	3 17	15 35	1 45	20 36	0 23	15 42	1 10	7 28	4 48	19 13	0 25	14 50	2 11
13 W	14 45	0 54	2 28	1N29	14 54	1 44	20 23	0 26	15 54	1 10	7 38	4 45	19 09	0 26	14 51	2 10
14 Th	14 27	3N48	1 16	6 02	14 13	1 43	20 09	0 28	16 06	1 11	7 47	4 42	19 06	0 26	14 52	2 10
15 F	14 08	8 08	0 01	10 06	13 31	1 41	19 55	0 31	16 18	1 12	7 57	4 39	19 03	0 26	14 53	2 10
16 Sa	13 49	11 54	1S12	13 31	12 48	1 38	19 40	0 33	16 29	1 12	8 06	4 35	18 60	0 26	14 54	2 09
17 Su	13 30	14 55	2 18	16 07	12 04	1 35	19 24	0 35	16 41	1 13	8 16	4 32	18 57	0 26	14 55	2 09
18 M	13 11	17 06	3 16	17 51	11 20	1 31	19 08	0 37	16 52	1 13	8 25	4 29	18 54	0 26	14 56	2 09
19 Tu	12 52	18 22	4 03	18 40	10 35	1 27	18 51	0 40	17 04	1 14	8 35	4 26	18 50	0 26	14 57	2 09
20 W	12 32	18 45	4 37	18 36	9 50	1 22	18 34	0 42	17 15	1 15	8 44	4 23	18 47	0 26	14 58	2 09
21 Th	12 12	18 15	4 58	17 42	9 05	1 17	18 16	0 44	17 27	1 15	8 54	4 20	18 44	0 26	14 59	2 08
22 F	11 52	16 57	5 06	16 01	8 20	1 12	17 58	0 46	17 38	1 16	9 03	4 17	18 41	0 27	14 60	2 08
23 Sa	11 32	14 55	5 01	13 40	7 34	1 06	17 39	0 48	17 49	1 16	9 12	4 14	18 37	0 27	15 01	2 08
24 Su	11 12	12 17	4 42	10 46	6 49	1 00	17 20	0 50	18 01	1 17	9 22	4 11	18 34	0 27	15 02	2 08
25 M	10 51	9 09	4 11	7 26	6 03	0 54	17 00	0 52	18 12	1 17	9 31	4 08	18 31	0 27	15 03	2 07
26 Tu	10 31	5 38	3 30	3 47	5 18	0 48	16 40	0 54	18 23	1 18	9 41	4 05	18 28	0 27	15 04	2 07
27 W	10 10	1 54	2 39	0S01	4 32	0 41	16 19	0 56	18 34	1 18	9 50	4 02	18 25	0 27	15 05	2 07
28 Th	9 49	1S57	1 40	3 52	3 47	0 34	15 58	0 58	18 45	1 19	9 59	3 59	18 21	0 27	15 07	2 07
29 F	9 27	5 45	0 37	7 35	3 02	0 27	15 36	0 60	18 55	1 19	10 09	3 56	18 18	0 27	15 08	2 06
30 Sa	9 06	9 22	0N30	11 03	2 17	0 19	15 14	1 02	19 06	1 20	10 18	3 53	18 15	0 27	15 09	2 06
31 Su	8N45	12S37	1N36	14S04	1N33	0N12	14N52	1N03	19S17	1S20	10S27	3N51	18N12	0N28	15S10	2N06

Day	⚷ Decl	⚷ Lat	♅ Decl	♅ Lat	♆ Decl	♆ Lat	♇ Decl	♇ Lat
1	0S25	5N06	5N50	0S41	9S39	0S45	20S23	2N33
6	0 29	5 07	5 49	0 41	9 42	0 45	20 24	2 32
11	0 33	5 07	5 48	0 41	9 45	0 45	20 26	2 31
16	0 37	5 08	5 45	0 41	9 48	0 45	20 27	2 31
21	0 42	5 08	5 43	0 42	9 51	0 45	20 28	2 30
26	0 47	5 08	5 40	0 42	9 54	0 45	20 29	2 29
31	0S52	5N08	5N37	0S42	9S57	0S45	20S30	2N28

Day	⚴ Decl	⚴ Lat	⚵ Decl	⚵ Lat	⚶ Decl	⚶ Lat	Eris Decl	Eris Lat
1	11N54	11N12	13N47	9S35	6S33	5N23	2S56	12S50
6	11 28	11 36	13 37	9 48	7 28	5 06	2 57	12 51
11	11 01	11 59	13 24	10 01	8 22	4 50	2 58	12 51
16	10 32	12 22	13 09	10 14	9 17	4 34	2 59	12 51
21	10 04	12 45	12 50	10 28	10 12	4 19	2 59	12 52
26	9 34	13 07	12 28	10 41	11 06	4 04	3 00	12 52
31	9N05	13N29	12N03	10S54	11S59	3N50	3S01	12S53

Moon Phenomena

Max/0 Decl
dy hr mn
7 4:19 18S49
13 4:31 0 N
19 22:12 18N45
27 11:52 0 S

Max/0 Lat
dy hr mn
2 11:27 0 N
9 0:20 5N03
15 0:19 0 S
22 2:01 5S06
29 13:15 0 N

Perigee/Apogee
dy hr m kilometers
10 17:52 p 356900
24 6:12 a 406524

PH dy hr mn
☽ 4 0:51 11♏36
○ 10 18:10 18♒02
☾ 17 12:27 24♉32
● 25 14:14 2♍19

Void of Course Moon

Last Aspect	☽ Ingress
2 2:59 ♀ □	♏ 3 2:58
4 17:44 ♀ △	♐ 5 10:20
6 14:53 ♅ △	♑ 7 13:40
9 8:10 ♀ ☍	♒ 9 13:53
10 22:13 ☿ ☍	♓ 11 12:56
12 16:02 ♄ △	♈ 13 13:01
15 15:51 ☿ △	♉ 15 15:59
17 12:27 ☉ □	♊ 17 22:42
20 2:55 ☉ ⚹	♋ 20 8:46
21 19:35 ♄ △	♌ 22 20:50
24 8:27 ♄ □	♍ 25 9:34
27 2:30 ☿ ☌	♎ 27 21:55
29 16:01 ♀ ⚹	♏ 30 8:54

DAILY ASPECTARIAN

1 F
♀ □ ♅ 4:44
☽ ⚻ ♆ 5:58
☉ ⚹ ☽ 10:17
♀ △ ♄ 10:23
⚳ # ♅ 14:41
♀ △ ⚷ 15:06
☽ □ ♇ 15:15
☽ # ♅ 17:50
☽ ∥ ⚳ 17:58
☿ ⚼ ⚷ 21:51
♂ □ ♃ 22:47

2 Sa
☽ ☍ ♅ 0:46
☽ ⚺ ♄ 1:22
☽ ⚻ ⚷ 1:47
☽ □ ♀ 2:59
☽ ⚼ ♆ 11:22
☽ ∥ ♆ 19:04
☿ ☌ ♃ 19:34

3 Su
☿ □ ♂ 0:02
☽ ☌ ⚳ 0:39
☽ ⚼ ⚷ 6:39
☿ # ♇ 7:47
☽ □ ♃ 10:34
☽ ☌ ♂ 11:33
☽ □ ☿ 13:12
☽ △ ♆ 15:59

4 M
☉ ⚻ ♇ 0:00
☽ ⚹ ♇ 0:47
☉ □ ☽ 0:51
☽ ∥ ♂ 4:50
☿ ⚻ ♆ 6:02
☽ ⚻ ♅ 9:48
☽ ∥ ♄ 9:53
☽ ☌ ♄ 10:30
☽ △ ⚷ 10:38
☽ △ ♀ 17:44

5 Tu
☽ ∠ ♇ 4:09
☿ ∥ ♃ 4:38
☉ # ☽ 8:36
☽ ⚺ ⚳ 9:24
☽ ⚼ ♅ 12:51
♀ ⚼ ♆ 14:24
♄ △ ⚷ 16:10
☽ △ ♃ 18:18
☽ ⚺ ♂ 20:38
☽ □ ♆ 22:20
☽ ⚼ ♀ 23:07

6 W
☽ △ ☿ 5:34
☽ ⚺ ♇ 6:30
☉ △ ☽ 10:36
☿ ⚻ ♇ 11:44
☽ ∠ ⚳ 12:08
☽ △ ♅ 14:53
☽ □ ⚷ 15:34
☽ ⚺ ♄ 15:40
☽ # ☿ 19:23
☽ ⚼ ♃ 20:33
☽ ∠ ♂ 23:27

7 Th
☽ ⚻ ♀ 3:10
⚳ ♏ 3:49
♂ ∥ ♄ 6:33
☽ ⚼ ☿ 11:16
♂ △ ♆ 12:14
☉ ⚼ ☽ 13:38
☽ ⚹ ⚳ 13:52
☽ ∠ ♄ 16:48
☽ ⚻ ♃ 21:51

8 F
☽ ⚹ ♆ 0:44
☽ ⚹ ♂ 1:16
☽ ☌ ♇ 8:23
☽ # ☿ 10:59
☽ ⚻ ☿ 15:38
☉ ⚻ ☽ 15:42
☽ □ ♅ 16:16
☉ ☌ ☿ 16:22
☽ ⚹ ⚷ 16:50
☽ ⚹ ♄ 17:09
☿ △ ♅ 20:15

9 Sa
☿ ⚻ ⚷ 0:13
☉ △ ♅ 0:37
☽ ∠ ♆ 0:48
⚵ ♋ 1:30
☿ □ ♄ 2:51
☽ ☍ ♀ 8:10
☉ ⚻ ⚷ 8:50
☉ # ☽ 9:02
☽ ∥ ♂ 14:04
☽ □ ⚳ 15:03
☉ □ ♄ 15:11
☽ ∠ ⚷ 16:33
☽ ∥ ♄ 17:28
☽ ☍ ♃ 22:25

10 Su
☽ ⚺ ♆ 0:26
☽ □ ♂ 2:52
☽ ⚺ ♇ 7:51
☽ ⚹ ♅ 15:32
☽ ⚺ ⚷ 16:01
☉ # ♂ 16:10
☽ □ ♄ 16:33
☉ ☍ ☽ 18:10
☽ ☍ ☿ 22:13

11 M
☽ ∥ ♆ 2:04
♀ ♎ 3:33
☽ ∠ ♇ 7:19
☽ ⚻ ♀ 11:20
☽ ∥ ⚳ 14:49
☽ ∠ ♅ 15:03
☽ △ ⚳ 15:05
☿ # ♂ 20:33
☽ ⚻ ♃ 22:11
☽ # ♅ 23:18
☽ ☌ ♆ 23:27

12 Tu
☽ △ ♂ 3:52
☽ ⚹ ♇ 6:59
♀ ♌ 7:25
⚳ ⚼ ⚷ 8:44
☽ ⚼ ♀ 13:11
☽ ⚺ ♅ 14:50
☽ ☌ ⚷ 15:15
☽ ⚼ ⚳ 15:24
☽ △ ♄ 16:02
☉ # ♄ 16:38
♀ # ♇ 18:31
☉ ⚻ ☽ 20:51
☽ ⚼ ♃ 22:30

13 W
☽ ∥ ⚷ 1:36
☿ # ♄ 2:02
☽ ⚼ ♂ 4:57
☽ ⚻ ☿ 5:08
☽ # ⚷ 7:27
☉ ∥ ☿ 9:48
♀ ⚼ ⚷ 13:40
☽ △ ♀ 15:44
☽ ⚻ ⚳ 16:19
☽ ⚼ ♄ 16:29
☿ ⚼ ♇ 19:47
☉ ⚼ ☽ 23:08
☽ △ ♃ 23:28
☽ ⚺ ♆ 23:57

14 Th
♀ □ ⚳ 0:55
☽ ⚻ ♂ 6:47
☽ □ ♇ 7:55
☽ ⚼ ☿ 9:52
☽ ∥ ♅ 10:34
☽ ☌ ♅ 16:15
☽ ⚺ ⚷ 16:36
☽ ⚻ ♄ 17:42
☽ # ⚳ 22:49

15 F
☽ ∠ ♆ 1:19
☉ △ ☽ 2:24
♃ ⚻ ♆ 4:13
♂ ⚹ ♇ 9:30
☽ # ♆ 10:03
☽ △ ☿ 15:51
☿ ♍ 16:45
☽ ∠ ⚷ 18:32
☽ ☍ ⚳ 20:44
☽ □ ♀ 23:58

16 Sa
☽ ⚹ ♆ 3:36
☽ □ ♃ 4:02
☽ ∥ ☿ 5:17
☿ ⚼ ♅ 8:34
☽ △ ♇ 12:12
☉ ∥ ☽ 13:09
☽ ☍ ♂ 13:29
☽ ⚺ ♅ 21:09
☽ ⚹ ⚷ 21:26
☽ ☍ ♄ 22:57
☽ # ♄ 23:55

17 Su
☿ ⚹ ⚳ 9:03
☉ □ ☽ 12:27
♀ ⚻ ♆ 15:09
☽ ⚼ ♇ 15:46
☽ # ♂ 20:44

18 M
☽ ∠ ♅ 1:01
☽ ⚻ ⚳ 5:14
♀ ☌ ♃ 5:22
☽ □ ☿ 8:07
☽ □ ♆ 11:01
☽ ⚹ ♃ 12:34
☽ ⚹ ♀ 13:13
☽ ⚻ ♇ 20:13

19 Tu
☽ ⚻ ♂ 0:31
♀ ∥ ♃ 1:43
☿ ☍ ♆ 3:41
☽ ⚹ ♅ 5:43
☽ □ ⚷ 5:55
☽ ⚻ ♄ 7:56
☉ ⚼ ♇ 8:10
☽ ⚼ ⚳ 10:53
☽ ∥ ♀ 13:36
☿ ⚺ ♃ 18:08
☽ ∠ ♃ 18:08
☽ ∠ ♀ 21:31
☿ # ♆ 23:51

20 W
☉ ⚹ ☽ 2:55
☽ ⚼ ♂ 7:22
☽ ⚼ ♄ 13:31
☽ △ ⚳ 17:14
☽ △ ♆ 21:31
☽ ∥ ♀ 23:11

21 Th
☽ ⚺ ♃ 0:20
☽ ⚹ ☿ 5:00
☿ # ⚳ 5:01
☽ ⚺ ♀ 6:36
☽ ☍ ♇ 7:09
☉ ∠ ☽ 11:18
♀ ⚻ ♇ 11:53
☽ # ♂ 14:23
☽ △ ♂ 14:49
☽ □ ♅ 16:56
☽ △ ⚷ 17:02
☿ △ ♇ 19:21
☽ △ ♄ 19:35

22 F
☽ ⚼ ♆ 3:29
☿ ⚺ ♀ 12:47
♀ # ♂ 15:53
☽ ∠ ☿ 16:22
☉ ⚺ ☽ 20:08
☽ # ♄ 23:03
☽ ⚼ ⚷ 23:08

23 Sa
☉ ♍ 4:47
♂ ⚻ ♅ 6:33
☽ □ ⚳ 7:12
♂ △ ⚷ 7:15
☽ ⚻ ♆ 9:41
☽ ☌ ♃ 13:48
☽ ⚻ ♇ 19:32

24 Su
☽ ☌ ♀ 2:02
☽ ⚺ ☿ 3:54
♅ ⚺ ⚷ 5:18
☽ ⚻ ⚷ 5:23
☽ △ ♅ 5:23
☽ □ ♂ 6:41
☉ ⚼ ♅ 7:38
☽ □ ♄ 8:27
☉ ∥ ☽ 9:44
☿ ☍ ⚷ 13:56
☿ ⚻ ♅ 14:02
☽ # ♆ 18:34
☽ # ⚳ 21:24

25 M
☽ ⚼ ♇ 1:52
☿ ⚹ ♂ 8:47
♀ ⚻ ⚷ 9:13
♀ △ ♅ 9:39
☽ ⚼ ♅ 11:41
☿ ∥ ♅ 12:03
☿ ⚹ ♄ 12:30
☉ ☌ ☽ 14:14
♂ ☌ ♄ 19:31
☽ ⚹ ⚳ 21:42
☽ ☍ ♆ 22:16
☽ ∥ ♅ 23:49

26 Tu
☽ ∥ ☿ 2:50
☽ ⚺ ♃ 3:37
☽ △ ♇ 8:09
♂ # ♃ 8:22
⚳ △ ♆ 16:05
☽ ☍ ⚷ 17:48
☽ ⚻ ♅ 17:53
♀ □ ♄ 18:23
☽ ⚹ ♄ 21:21
☽ ⚺ ♀ 21:41
☽ ⚹ ♂ 22:39

27 W
☽ ☌ ☿ 2:30
☽ ∠ ⚳ 4:48
☽ # ⚷ 6:49
☽ ∠ ♃ 10:20
⚳ ∥ ♆ 12:59
☉ # ⚳ 15:31
♀ □ ♂ 15:47
☉ # ♆ 16:33
☽ ∥ ⚷ 16:57
☿ ∠ ⚳ 23:10

28 Th
☽ ∠ ♄ 3:31
☽ ∠ ♂ 6:18
☽ ∠ ♀ 7:07
☉ ⚺ ☽ 7:46
☽ # ☿ 9:37
☽ ⚻ ♆ 10:18
☽ ⚺ ⚳ 11:38
☽ ⚹ ♃ 16:45
☽ □ ♇ 20:04
☽ # ♅ 23:16

29 F
☽ ⚻ ⚷ 5:20
☽ ☍ ♅ 5:31
☽ ⚺ ♄ 9:19
☽ ⚺ ♂ 13:31
☉ ☍ ♆ 14:34
☽ ⚼ ♆ 15:47
☉ ∠ ☽ 15:53
☽ ⚹ ♀ 16:01
☿ ∠ ♃ 19:52
☉ # ☽ 22:23
☽ ⚺ ☿ 23:04

30 Sa
☽ ∥ ♆ 4:06
♀ # ♄ 5:18
☽ ∥ ⚳ 6:57
☽ ⚼ ⚷ 10:26
☽ △ ♆ 20:43
☉ ⚹ ☽ 23:18
☽ ☌ ⚳ 23:47

31 Su
☽ □ ♃ 4:01
☽ ⚹ ♇ 6:10
☽ ∠ ☿ 7:59
☉ ⚹ ⚳ 8:51
☽ △ ⚷ 14:53
☽ ⚻ ♅ 15:09
☽ # ♀ 16:49
☽ ☌ ♄ 19:11
☿ # ⚷ 21:34
☽ ∥ ♄ 22:28

LONGITUDE

Day	Sid.Time	☉	☽	☽ 12 hour	Mean☊	True☊	☿	♀	♂	⚳	♃	♄	⚷	♅	♆	♇
	h m s	° ' "	° ' "	° ' "	° '	° '	° '	° '	° '	° '	° '	° '	° '	° '	° '	° '
M	22 40 20	8♍29 57	20♏36 56	27♏06 23	21♎23.9	19♎56.4	28♍06.6	24♌10.7	21♏34.4	8♏06.6	10♌09.6	18♏02.9	15♓43.5	15♈52.1	6♓07.2	11♑06.9
Tu	22 44 16	9 28 01	3♐41 14	10♐21 52	21 20.7	19R 57.4	29 38.6	25 24.8	22 12.7	8 27.7	10 22.1	18 06.8	15R 40.7	15R 50.3	6R 05.5	11R 06.3
W	22 48 13	10 26 06	17 08 35	24 01 37	21 17.5	19 57.3	1♎09.2	26 38.8	22 51.2	8 48.8	10 34.4	18 10.8	15 37.9	15 48.5	6 03.9	11 05.7
Th	22 52 09	11 24 13	1♑01 05	8♑06 57	21 14.4	19 55.8	2 38.5	27 52.9	23 29.8	9 10.1	10 46.8	18 14.8	15 35.1	15 46.7	6 02.2	11 05.1
F	22 56 06	12 22 20	15 19 01	22 36 56	21 11.2	19 52.6	4 06.6	29 07.1	24 08.6	9 31.5	10 59.0	18 19.0	15 32.3	15 44.8	6 00.6	11 04.6
Sa	23 00 02	13 20 30	0♒00 05	7♒27 45	21 08.0	19 48.2	5 33.3	0♍21.2	24 47.5	9 52.9	11 11.3	18 23.2	15 29.5	15 42.9	5 59.0	11 04.1
Su	23 03 59	14 18 40	14 59 00	22 32 44	21 04.8	19 43.1	6 58.7	1 35.4	25 26.5	10 14.5	11 23.4	18 27.5	15 26.7	15 40.9	5 57.3	11 03.6
M	23 07 56	15 16 53	0♓07 46	7♓42 50	21 01.7	19 38.2	8 22.8	2 49.6	26 05.7	10 36.1	11 35.5	18 31.8	15 23.9	15 39.0	5 55.7	11 03.1
Tu	23 11 52	16 15 06	15 16 42	22 48 06	20 58.5	19 34.0	9 45.5	4 03.9	26 45.0	10 57.8	11 47.6	18 36.3	15 21.0	15 37.0	5 54.1	11 02.7
W	23 15 49	17 13 22	0♈15 57	7♈39 15	20 55.3	19 31.3	11 06.7	5 18.1	27 24.4	11 19.6	11 59.6	18 40.8	15 18.2	15 34.9	5 52.5	11 02.3
Th	23 19 45	18 11 39	14 57 09	22 09 02	20 52.1	19D 30.1	12 26.6	6 32.4	28 03.9	11 41.5	12 11.5	18 45.4	15 15.4	15 32.9	5 50.9	11 01.9
F	23 23 42	19 09 59	29 14 26	6♉13 06	20 48.9	19 30.3	13 44.9	7 46.8	28 43.6	12 03.5	12 23.4	18 50.0	15 12.6	15 30.8	5 49.3	11 01.6
Sa	23 27 38	20 08 20	13♉04 55	19 49 56	20 45.8	19 31.5	15 01.8	9 01.2	29 23.4	12 25.6	12 35.2	18 54.7	15 09.8	15 28.7	5 47.7	11 01.3
Su	23 31 35	21 06 44	26 28 22	3♊00 31	20 42.6	19 33.1	16 17.0	10 15.6	0♐03.4	12 47.7	12 47.0	18 59.5	15 07.0	15 26.5	5 46.1	11 01.0
M	23 35 31	22 05 10	9♊26 46	15 47 34	20 39.4	19 34.4	17 30.6	11 30.0	0 43.5	13 09.9	12 58.7	19 04.4	15 04.2	15 24.4	5 44.6	11 00.7
Tu	23 39 28	23 03 38	22 03 26	28 14 53	20 36.2	19R 35.0	18 42.4	12 44.5	1 23.6	13 32.2	13 10.3	19 09.3	15 01.4	15 22.2	5 43.0	11 00.5
W	23 43 25	24 02 08	4♋22 29	10♋26 48	20 33.1	19 34.6	19 52.5	13 59.0	2 04.0	13 54.6	13 21.8	19 14.3	14 58.7	15 20.0	5 41.4	11 00.3
Th	23 47 21	25 00 40	16 28 21	22 27 41	20 29.9	19 33.0	21 00.6	15 13.5	2 44.4	14 17.0	13 33.3	19 19.4	14 55.9	15 17.8	5 39.9	11 00.1
F	23 51 18	25 59 14	28 25 19	4♌21 44	20 26.7	19 30.3	22 06.6	16 28.0	3 25.0	14 39.5	13 44.7	19 24.5	14 53.2	15 15.6	5 38.4	11 00.0
Sa	23 55 14	26 57 51	10♌17 22	16 12 40	20 23.5	19 27.0	23 10.5	17 42.6	4 05.7	15 02.1	13 56.1	19 29.7	14 50.4	15 13.3	5 36.9	10 59.9
Su	23 59 11	27 56 29	22 08 00	28 03 44	20 20.3	19 23.3	24 12.1	18 57.2	4 46.5	15 24.8	14 07.3	19 35.0	14 47.7	15 11.0	5 35.4	10 59.8
M	0 03 07	28 55 10	4♍00 11	9♍57 39	20 17.2	19 19.8	25 11.2	20 11.8	5 27.4	15 47.5	14 18.5	19 40.3	14 45.0	15 08.7	5 33.9	10 59.8
Tu	0 07 04	29 53 52	15 56 24	21 56 40	20 14.0	19 16.9	26 07.7	21 26.5	6 08.4	16 10.3	14 29.7	19 45.7	14 42.3	15 06.4	5 32.4	10D 59.8
W	0 11 00	0♎52 37	27 58 40	4♎02 37	20 10.8	19 14.7	27 01.2	22 41.2	6 49.6	16 33.2	14 40.7	19 51.1	14 39.6	15 04.1	5 31.0	10 59.8
Th	0 14 57	1 51 24	10♎08 42	16 17 07	20 07.6	19D 13.6	27 51.7	23 55.9	7 30.9	16 56.1	14 51.6	19 56.6	14 36.9	15 01.7	5 29.5	10 59.8
F	0 18 54	2 50 12	22 28 03	28 41 41	20 04.4	19 13.4	28 38.9	25 10.6	8 12.3	17 19.1	15 02.5	20 02.2	14 34.3	14 59.4	5 28.1	10 59.9
Sa	0 22 50	3 49 03	4♏58 13	11♏17 50	20 01.3	19 13.9	29 22.5	26 25.3	8 53.8	17 42.2	15 13.3	20 07.8	14 31.7	14 57.0	5 26.7	11 00.0
Su	0 26 47	4 47 55	17 40 46	24 07 12	19 58.1	19 15.0	0♏02.1	27 40.1	9 35.4	18 05.3	15 24.0	20 13.4	14 29.1	14 54.7	5 25.3	11 00.1
M	0 30 43	5 46 49	0♐37 23	7♐11 30	19 54.9	19 16.2	0 37.5	28 54.9	10 17.2	18 28.5	15 34.6	20 19.2	14 26.5	14 52.3	5 23.9	11 00.3
Tu	0 34 40	6♎45 46	13 49 46	20 32 21	19♎51.7	19♎17.2	1♏08.2	0♎09.7	10♐59.0	18♏51.7	15♌45.1	20♏24.9	14♓24.0	14♈49.9	5♓22.6	11♑00.5

1st of Month

Julian Day # 2456901.5
Obliquity 23°26'06"
SVP 5♓03'11"
GC 27♐02.6
Eris 23♈01.7R

Day	⚴
1	8♎46.2
6	10 54.9
11	13 04.3
16	15 14.5
21	17 25.2
26	19 36.6

Day	⚵
1	12♋19.1
6	14 53.7
11	17 25.4
16	19 54.1
21	22 19.4
26	24 41.0

Day	⚶
1	13♏07.3
6	15 22.6
11	17 40.4
16	20 00.6
21	22 23.0
26	24 47.5

DECLINATION and LATITUDE

Day	☉ Decl	☽ Decl	☽ Lat	☽12h Decl	☿ Decl	☿ Lat	♀ Decl	♀ Lat	♂ Decl	♂ Lat	⚳ Decl	⚳ Lat	♃ Decl	♃ Lat	♄ Decl	♄ Lat
M	8N23	15S21	2N39	16S27	0N49	0N04	14N29	1N05	19S27	1S21	10S37	3N48	18N08	0N28	15S12	2N06
Tu	8 01	17 21	3 35	18 02	0 05	0S04	14 05	1 06	19 38	1 21	10 46	3 45	18 05	0 28	15 13	2 05
W	7 39	18 28	4 22	18 38	0S38	0 12	13 42	1 08	19 48	1 22	10 55	3 42	18 02	0 28	15 14	2 05
Th	7 17	18 31	4 54	18 07	1 21	0 20	13 18	1 09	19 58	1 22	11 05	3 40	17 59	0 28	15 15	2 05
F	6 55	17 25	5 10	16 26	2 03	0 28	12 53	1 11	20 08	1 23	11 14	3 37	17 55	0 28	15 17	2 05
Sa	6 33	15 09	5 06	13 37	2 45	0 36	12 28	1 12	20 18	1 23	11 23	3 34	17 52	0 28	15 18	2 05
Su	6 10	11 51	4 42	9 52	3 27	0 44	12 03	1 13	20 28	1 23	11 32	3 32	17 49	0 28	15 20	2 04
M	5 48	7 43	3 57	5 27	4 08	0 52	11 38	1 15	20 38	1 24	11 41	3 29	17 46	0 29	15 21	2 04
Tu	5 25	3 06	2 56	0 42	4 48	1 01	11 12	1 16	20 47	1 24	11 51	3 26	17 42	0 29	15 22	2 04
W	5 03	1N41	1 43	4N01	5 27	1 09	10 46	1 17	20 57	1 25	11 60	3 24	17 39	0 29	15 24	2 04
Th	4 40	6 16	0 25	8 24	6 06	1 18	10 19	1 18	21 06	1 25	12 09	3 21	17 36	0 29	15 25	2 03
F	4 17	10 22	0S53	12 10	6 45	1 26	9 52	1 19	21 16	1 25	12 18	3 19	17 33	0 29	15 27	2 03
Sa	3 54	13 46	2 06	15 09	7 22	1 34	9 25	1 20	21 25	1 26	12 27	3 16	17 30	0 29	15 28	2 03
Su	3 31	16 18	3 09	17 13	7 59	1 42	8 58	1 21	21 34	1 26	12 36	3 14	17 26	0 29	15 30	2 03
M	3 08	17 54	4 01	18 21	8 35	1 51	8 30	1 22	21 42	1 26	12 45	3 11	17 23	0 29	15 31	2 03
Tu	2 45	18 33	4 39	18 33	9 10	1 59	8 03	1 22	21 51	1 27	12 54	3 09	17 20	0 30	15 33	2 02
W	2 22	18 19	5 03	17 52	9 44	2 07	7 35	1 23	21 59	1 27	13 03	3 06	17 17	0 30	15 34	2 02
Th	1 59	17 14	5 14	16 24	10 17	2 15	7 06	1 24	22 08	1 27	13 12	3 04	17 14	0 30	15 36	2 02
F	1 36	15 24	5 10	14 15	10 49	2 22	6 38	1 24	22 16	1 27	13 21	3 01	17 11	0 30	15 37	2 02
Sa	1 12	12 56	4 54	11 30	11 20	2 30	6 09	1 25	22 24	1 28	13 29	2 59	17 07	0 30	15 39	2 02
Su	0 49	9 57	4 25	8 18	11 49	2 37	5 40	1 25	22 32	1 28	13 38	2 57	17 04	0 30	15 41	2 02
M	0 26	6 33	3 44	4 45	12 18	2 44	5 11	1 25	22 39	1 28	13 47	2 54	17 01	0 30	15 42	2 01
Tu	0 02	2 53	2 53	0 58	12 45	2 51	4 42	1 26	22 47	1 28	13 56	2 52	16 58	0 31	15 44	2 01
W	0S21	0S57	1 55	2S53	13 10	2 58	4 13	1 26	22 54	1 29	14 04	2 49	16 55	0 31	15 45	2 01
Th	0 44	4 47	0 50	6 39	13 35	3 04	3 44	1 26	23 01	1 29	14 13	2 47	16 52	0 31	15 47	2 01
F	1 08	8 28	0N18	10 12	13 57	3 10	3 14	1 26	23 08	1 29	14 22	2 45	16 49	0 31	15 49	2 01
Sa	1 31	11 49	1 26	13 20	14 18	3 16	2 44	1 26	23 15	1 29	14 30	2 43	16 46	0 31	15 50	2 00
Su	1 54	14 41	2 31	15 52	14 36	3 20	2 15	1 26	23 22	1 29	14 39	2 40	16 43	0 31	15 52	2 00
M	2 18	16 51	3 30	17 38	14 53	3 25	1 45	1 26	23 28	1 30	14 47	2 38	16 40	0 31	15 54	2 00
Tu	2S41	18S11	4N18	18S28	15S08	3S29	1N15	1N26	23S34	1S30	14S56	2N36	16N37	0N32	15S55	1N60

Day	⚷ Decl	⚷ Lat	♅ Decl	♅ Lat	♆ Decl	♆ Lat	♇ Decl	♇ Lat
1	0S54	5N08	5N36	0S42	9S58	0S45	20S31	2N28
6	0 59	5 08	5 32	0 42	10 01	0 45	20 32	2 27
11	1 05	5 07	5 28	0 42	10 04	0 45	20 33	2 26
16	1 11	5 07	5 24	0 42	10 07	0 45	20 34	2 26
21	1 16	5 06	5 20	0 42	10 10	0 45	20 35	2 25
26	1 22	5 06	5 15	0 42	10 12	0 45	20 35	2 24

Day	⚴ Decl	⚴ Lat	⚵ Decl	⚵ Lat	⚶ Decl	⚶ Lat	Eris Decl	Eris Lat
1	8N59	13N33	11N58	10S56	12S10	3N47	3S02	12S53
6	8 29	13 55	11 30	11 10	13 02	3 34	3 03	12 53
11	7 59	14 16	11 00	11 23	13 53	3 21	3 04	12 53
16	7 30	14 38	10 28	11 36	14 43	3 08	3 05	12 53
21	7 01	14 59	9 54	11 50	15 32	2 56	3 06	12 54
26	6 33	15 20	9 18	12 04	16 18	2 44	3 07	12 54

Moon Phenomena

Max/0 Decl

dy	hr mn	
3	13:15	18S38
9	15:31	0 N
16	5:11	18N35
23	18:05	0 S
30	19:35	18S32

Perigee/Apogee

dy	hr m		kilometers
8	3:21	p	358391
20	14:24	a	405844

PH	dy	hr mn	
☽	2	11:12	9♐55
○	9	1:39	16♓19
☾	16	2:06	23♊09
●	24	6:15	1♎08

Max/0 Lat

dy	hr mn	
5	7:24	5N11
11	7:34	0 S
18	6:07	5S14
25	17:42	0 N

Void of Course Moon

Last Aspect				☽ Ingress		
1	15:41	☿	⚹	♐	1	17:18
3	18:07	♀	△	♑	3	22:16
5	15:09	♂	⚹	♒	5	24:00
7	17:20	♂	□	♓	7	23:48
9	19:11	♂	△	♈	9	23:34
11	0:59	♅	☌	♉	12	1:18
13	13:32	☉	△	♊	14	6:27
16	2:06	☉	□	♋	16	15:25
18	18:39	☉	⚹	♌	19	3:11
21	4:34	☿	⚹	♍	21	15:55
23	12:16	♀	☌	♎	24	4:00
26	12:40	☿	☌	♏	26	14:30
28	20:32	♀	⚹	♐	28	22:51

DAILY ASPECTARIAN

☽☌♂ 1:52
☽□♀ 7:18
☽∠♇ 10:10
☽⚹☿ 15:41
☽⚼♅ 18:50

☽□♆ 4:20
☿ ♎ 5:39
☽⚺⚳ 8:50
☉□☽ 11:12
☽△♃ 12:12
☽#♃ 12:27
☽⚺♇ 13:19
♀⚼♇ 13:21
☽□⚷ 21:21
☽△♅ 21:39

☽⚺♄ 1:50
☉⚺♃ 4:23
☿∥⚷ 10:08
☽⚺♂ 10:27
☽∠⚳ 11:56
☽⚼♃ 14:53
☉△♇ 16:11
☽△♀ 18:07

☽□☿ 3:05
☽∠♄ 3:48
☽⚹♆ 8:29
☿∠♄ 10:20
☽∠♂ 13:14
☽⚹⚳ 14:07
☽#♃ 15:31
☽⚻♃ 16:42
☽☌♇ 16:57
☉△☽ 18:46
☽⚼♀ 21:50

5 F
☽⚹⚷ 0:22
☽□♅ 0:43
☽⚹♄ 4:58
☽∠♆ 9:21
♃⚻♇ 10:24
☽⚹♂ 15:09
♀ ♍ 17:08
☉⚼☽ 21:08
☽∥♄ 22:44

6 Sa
☽⚻♀ 0:37
☽∠⚷ 0:47
♀⚼♅ 6:50
☿⚻♆ 7:02
☽⚺♆ 9:37
☽△☿ 9:53
☽□⚳ 16:15
☽⚺♇ 17:45
☽☍♃ 18:12
☽#♀ 22:30
☉⚻☽ 22:51

7 Su
☽⚺⚷ 0:44
☽⚹♅ 1:07
☽∥⚳ 1:52
☽□♄ 5:33
♂∥♇ 9:21
☽∥♆ 11:03
☽⚼☿ 12:14
☽□♂ 17:20
☽∠♇ 17:33
♀#⚳ 21:19
♂∠♇ 22:28

8 M
☽∠♅ 0:49
☉☍⚷ 2:45
☽☍♀ 4:39
☉⚻♅ 8:48
☽☌♆ 9:09
☉#☽ 11:05
☽#♅ 11:41
☽⚻☿ 14:22
☽∥☿ 16:26
☽△⚳ 16:59
☽⚹♇ 17:17
☽⚻♃ 18:23
☉∥♅ 18:54

9 Tu
☽☌⚷ 0:07
☽⚺♅ 0:32
☉☍☽ 1:39
⚳⚹♇ 5:15
☽△♄ 5:19
☽∥⚷ 10:15
☉#☿ 14:28
☽⚼⚳ 17:30
☽⚼♃ 18:39
☽△♂ 19:11
☽#⚷ 20:50
☿□♇ 22:41

10 W
☿#♅ 1:06
☿⚺⚳ 5:17
☽⚼♄ 5:33
☽⚻♀ 8:55
☽⚺♆ 9:05
♀☍♆ 10:52
☉∥☽ 16:03
☽□♇ 17:32
☽⚻⚳ 18:29
☿⚹♃ 18:38
☽△♃ 19:23
☽☍☿ 19:27
☽∥♅ 19:42
☽⚼♂ 20:44
☽#☿ 22:56

11 Th
☽⚺⚷ 0:30
☽☌♅ 0:59
☉⚻☽ 5:46
☽⚻♄ 6:21
☽∠♆ 9:48
☽⚼♀ 12:01
♀#♆ 13:21
☉⚹♄ 15:04
☽∥♀ 21:11
☽#♆ 22:07
☽⚻♂ 23:05
☿∠♂ 23:10

12 F
☽∠⚷ 1:39
☉⚼☽ 9:05
☽⚹♆ 11:18
☽#⚳ 13:33
☽△♀ 16:10
☽△♇ 20:23
☽☍⚳ 22:49
☽□♃ 23:07

13 Sa
☿⚻⚷ 2:27
☽⚹⚷ 3:40
☽⚻☿ 3:48
☽⚺♅ 4:14
☿☍♅ 8:17
☽☍♄ 10:25
☉△☽ 13:32
☽#♄ 15:20
♂ ♐ 21:58
⚳□♃ 22:21
☽⚼♇ 23:10

14 Su
☽☍♂ 6:55
☽∠♅ 7:15
☽⚼☿ 9:44
♂⚼♅ 13:10
♀△♇ 14:36
☽∥♃ 14:59
☽□♆ 17:05
☿#♀ 22:26

15 M
☽⚻♇ 2:57
☽□♀ 4:17
☽⚹♃ 6:46
☽⚻⚳ 7:13
☽□⚷ 10:35
☽⚹♅ 11:14
☽△☿ 16:54
☽⚻♄ 18:23

16 Tu
☉□☽ 2:06
☿⚺♄ 9:50
♀⚺♃ 9:51
☽∠♃ 12:02
☽⚼⚳ 12:57
☽⚻♂ 19:12
♀⚹⚳ 21:59
☽⚼♄ 23:44

17 W
☽△♆ 2:35
☽☍♇ 13:06
☿⚼♆ 16:49
☿∥♆ 17:32
☽⚺♃ 18:05
♀☍⚷ 18:33
☽△⚳ 19:29
☽△⚷ 20:56
☽⚹♀ 21:13
☽□♅ 21:40
☽∥♃ 23:59

18 Th
♀⚻♅ 1:21
☽⚼♂ 2:41
☽△♄ 5:45
☽⚼♆ 8:23
☽□☿ 10:01
☉⚹☽ 18:39
☽#♄ 21:33

19 F
☽⚼⚷ 2:57
☽∠♀ 6:52
☽△♂ 10:42
⚳△⚷ 12:56
☽⚻♆ 14:33
☽#⚳ 19:21
☉#⚷ 21:14

20 Sa
☽⚻♇ 1:26
☉∠☽ 3:42
☽☌♃ 7:30
☽⚻⚷ 9:11
☽□⚳ 9:56
☽△♅ 9:58
⚳⚻♅ 10:47
☽#☿ 11:31
☽⚺♀ 16:48
☽□♄ 18:48
☽#♆ 22:26

21 Su
☽⚹☿ 4:34
☽⚼♇ 7:49
☉⚺☽ 12:49
♀⚹♄ 13:04
☽⚼♅ 16:14
♀∥♅ 17:30

22 M
☽□♂ 3:07
☽☍♆ 3:09
♂□♆ 3:40
☽∥♅ 8:17
☽∥♀ 10:28
☉∠♃ 11:48
☽∠☿ 13:32
☽△♇ 14:05
☽⚺♃ 21:03
☽☍⚷ 21:32
☽⚻♅ 22:20

23 Tu
☽⚹⚳ 0:29
♇ D 0:37
☉ ♎ 2:30
☽⚹♄ 7:42
☽#⚷ 9:50
☽☌♀ 12:16
☉#☽ 16:39
☉∥☽ 19:50
☽⚺☿ 21:57
♃⚻⚷ 22:06

24 W
☽∥⚷ 2:23
☽∠♃ 3:25
☉☌☽ 6:15
☽∠⚳ 7:19
☽∠♄ 13:42
☽⚻♆ 14:52
☽#♀ 18:05
☽⚹♂ 18:32

25 Th
☽□♇ 1:40
☽#♅ 3:06
☉∠⚳ 3:09
☽⚻⚷ 8:43
☽⚹♃ 9:22
☽☍♅ 9:31
☽⚺⚳ 13:41
♃△♅ 18:20
☽⚺♄ 19:15
☽⚼♆ 20:08

26 F
☽∠♂ 1:31
☽⚺♀ 5:49
☽∥♆ 12:06
☽☌☿ 12:40
☽⚼⚷ 13:38
☉∥⚷ 15:40
☉⚺☽ 21:37

27 Sa
☽△♆ 0:54
☿⚼⚷ 5:03
☽⚺♂ 7:53
☽⚹♇ 11:26
☽∠♀ 13:34
☽△⚷ 18:02
☽⚻♅ 18:49
☽□♃ 19:40
☿ ♏ 22:40
☽∥☿ 23:13
☽∥⚳ 23:39

28 Su
☽☌⚳ 0:47
☉∠☽ 4:17
☽☌♄ 4:47
☿∥⚳ 6:19
☉#♀ 9:06
☉∠♄ 11:31
☽∥♄ 12:09
☉⚻♆ 14:53
☽∠♇ 15:29
☽⚹♀ 20:32
☽#♃ 21:32
☽⚼♅ 22:37

29 M
☽⚺☿ 0:00
☽□♆ 8:43
☉⚹☽ 10:11
♀#⚷ 14:46
☽☌♂ 18:35
☽⚺♇ 18:55
♀ ♎ 20:53

30 Tu
♂⚺♇ 0:53
☽□⚷ 1:01
☽△♅ 1:48
☽△♃ 3:30
☽∠☿ 4:17
☽⚺⚳ 9:17
☽⚺♄ 11:52
♀∠♃ 13:13

October 2014

LONGITUDE

Day	Sid.Time	☉	☽	☽ 12 hour	Mean☊	True☊	☿	♀	♂	⚳	♃	♄	⚷	♅	♆	♇
	h m s	° ' "	° ' "	° ' "	°	°	° '	° '	° '	° '	° '	° '	° '	° '	° '	° '
1 W	0 38 36	7♎44 43	27♐19 24	4♑11 03	19♎48.6	19♎17.9	1♏34.0	1♎24.5	11♐40.9	19♏15.0	15♌55.6	20♏30.8	14♓21.4	14♈47.5	5♓21.2	11♑00.7
2 Th	0 42 33	8 43 43	11♑07 18	18 08 09	19 45.4	19R 18.1	1 54.3	2 39.4	12 23.0	19 38.4	16 05.9	20 36.7	14R 18.9	14R 45.1	5R 19.9	11 01.0
3 F	0 46 29	9 42 44	25 13 27	2♒23 00	19 42.2	19 17.8	2 08.8	3 54.2	13 05.1	20 01.8	16 16.2	20 42.6	14 16.5	14 42.6	5 18.6	11 01.3
4 Sa	0 50 26	10 41 47	9♒36 28	16 53 23	19 39.0	19 17.1	2R 17.0	5 09.1	13 47.4	20 25.3	16 26.3	20 48.6	14 14.0	14 40.2	5 17.4	11 01.6
5 Su	0 54 23	11 40 52	24 13 10	1♓35 11	19 35.8	19 16.2	2 18.5	6 24.0	14 29.7	20 48.8	16 36.4	20 54.6	14 11.6	14 37.8	5 16.1	11 02.0
6 M	0 58 19	12 39 58	8♓58 37	16 22 37	19 32.7	19 15.4	2 12.8	7 38.9	15 12.2	21 12.3	16 46.3	21 00.7	14 09.2	14 35.4	5 14.9	11 02.4
7 Tu	1 02 16	13 39 06	23 46 19	1♈08 46	19 29.5	19 14.8	1 59.5	8 53.8	15 54.7	21 36.0	16 56.2	21 06.8	14 06.9	14 32.9	5 13.7	11 02.8
8 W	1 06 12	14 38 16	8♈29 05	15 46 23	19 26.3	19D 14.5	1 38.4	10 08.7	16 37.4	21 59.6	17 05.9	21 13.0	14 04.6	14 30.5	5 12.5	11 03.2
9 Th	1 10 09	15 37 28	22 59 52	0♉08 52	19 23.1	19 14.4	1 09.3	11 23.7	17 20.1	22 23.3	17 15.6	21 19.2	14 02.3	14 28.1	5 11.3	11 03.7
10 F	1 14 05	16 36 43	7♉12 47	14 11 10	19 19.9	19 14.5	0 32.1	12 38.6	18 02.9	22 47.1	17 25.1	21 25.5	14 00.0	14 25.7	5 10.2	11 04.2
11 Sa	1 18 02	17 35 59	21 03 43	27 50 14	19 16.8	19 14.7	29♎46.9	13 53.6	18 45.8	23 10.9	17 34.5	21 31.8	13 57.8	14 23.2	5 09.0	11 04.7
12 Su	1 21 58	18 35 18	4♊30 42	11♊05 11	19 13.6	19R 14.8	28 54.3	15 08.6	19 28.8	23 34.7	17 43.9	21 38.2	13 55.6	14 20.8	5 08.0	11 05.3
13 M	1 25 55	19 34 39	17 33 51	23 57 01	19 10.4	19 14.9	27 54.8	16 23.6	20 11.9	23 58.6	17 53.1	21 44.6	13 53.5	14 18.4	5 06.9	11 05.9
14 Tu	1 29 51	20 34 02	0♋15 02	6♋28 20	19 07.2	19 14.8	26 49.5	17 38.6	20 55.1	24 22.6	18 02.2	21 51.0	13 51.4	14 16.0	5 05.8	11 06.5
15 W	1 33 48	21 33 27	12 37 24	18 42 48	19 04.1	19D 14.7	25 39.8	18 53.7	21 38.4	24 46.6	18 11.2	21 57.5	13 49.3	14 13.6	5 04.8	11 07.2
16 Th	1 37 45	22 32 55	24 45 03	0♌44 45	19 00.9	19 14.7	24 27.4	20 08.8	22 21.8	25 10.6	18 20.1	22 04.0	13 47.3	14 11.2	5 03.8	11 07.9
17 F	1 41 41	23 32 25	6♌42 29	12 38 50	18 57.7	19 14.8	23 14.1	21 23.8	23 05.2	25 34.7	18 28.9	22 10.5	13 45.3	14 08.8	5 02.9	11 08.6
18 Sa	1 45 38	24 31 58	18 34 22	24 29 39	18 54.5	19 15.2	22 02.0	22 38.9	23 48.8	25 58.8	18 37.5	22 17.1	13 43.3	14 06.4	5 01.9	11 09.4
19 Su	1 49 34	25 31 32	0♍25 13	6♍21 35	18 51.3	19 15.8	20 53.4	23 54.0	24 32.4	26 22.9	18 46.0	22 23.7	13 41.4	14 04.0	5 01.0	11 10.1
20 M	1 53 31	26 31 09	12 19 13	18 18 34	18 48.2	19 16.5	19 50.1	25 09.2	25 16.1	26 47.1	18 54.4	22 30.4	13 39.6	14 01.7	5 00.1	11 10.9
21 Tu	1 57 27	27 30 48	24 20 01	0♎23 57	18 45.0	19 17.3	18 54.2	26 24.3	25 59.9	27 11.4	19 02.7	22 37.0	13 37.7	13 59.3	4 59.3	11 11.8
22 W	2 01 24	28 30 29	6♎30 38	12 40 22	18 41.8	19 17.9	18 07.2	27 39.4	26 43.8	27 35.6	19 10.8	22 43.8	13 36.0	13 57.0	4 58.5	11 12.6
23 Th	2 05 20	29 30 12	18 53 20	25 09 43	18 38.6	19R 18.2	17 30.2	28 54.6	27 27.8	27 59.9	19 18.8	22 50.5	13 34.2	13 54.6	4 57.7	11 13.5
24 F	2 09 17	0♏29 57	1♏29 37	7♏53 07	18 35.5	19 17.9	17 04.1	0♏09.7	28 11.8	28 24.3	19 26.7	22 57.3	13 32.5	13 52.3	4 56.9	11 14.4
25 Sa	2 13 14	1 29 45	14 20 13	20 50 55	18 32.3	19 17.0	16D 49.3	1 24.9	28 56.0	28 48.6	19 34.5	23 04.1	13 30.9	13 50.0	4 56.1	11 15.4
26 Su	2 17 10	2 29 34	27 25 09	4♐02 52	18 29.1	19 15.6	16 45.8	2 40.1	29 40.2	29 13.0	19 42.1	23 10.9	13 29.3	13 47.8	4 55.4	11 16.4
27 M	2 21 07	3 29 25	10♐43 56	17 28 15	18 25.9	19 13.6	16 53.5	3 55.3	0♑24.5	29 37.5	19 49.6	23 17.8	13 27.7	13 45.5	4 54.8	11 17.4
28 Tu	2 25 03	4 29 18	24 15 40	1♑06 02	18 22.7	19 11.6	17 11.9	5 10.5	1 08.9	0♐01.9	19 56.9	23 24.7	13 26.3	13 43.3	4 54.1	11 18.4
29 W	2 29 00	5 29 12	7♑59 11	14 54 59	18 19.6	19 09.7	17 40.2	6 25.7	1 53.3	0 26.4	20 04.1	23 31.6	13 24.8	13 41.1	4 53.5	11 19.5
30 Th	2 32 56	6 29 09	21 53 14	28 53 47	18 16.4	19 08.4	18 17.8	7 40.9	2 37.9	0 50.9	20 11.2	23 38.5	13 23.4	13 38.9	4 52.9	11 20.6
31 F	2 36 53	7♏29 06	5♒56 25	13♒00 57	18♎13.2	19♎07.9	19♎03.7	8♏56.1	3♑22.5	1♐15.5	20♌18.1	23♏45.5	13♓22.1	13♈36.7	4♓52.4	11♑21.7

1st of Month

Julian Day
2456931.5
Obliquity
23°26'06"
SVP 5♓03'0
GC 27♐02.
Eris 22♈46.5

Day	⚴
1	21♎48.4
6	24 00.6
11	26 13.0
16	28 25.7
21	0♏38.5
26	2 51.5
31	5 04.4

Day	⚵
1	26♋58.4
6	29 11.3
11	1♌19.3
16	3 22.0
21	5 18.9
26	7 09.4
31	8 52.9

Day	⚶
1	27♏13.9
6	29 41.9
11	2♐11.5
16	4 42.6
21	7 15.0
26	9 48.6
31	12 23.3

DECLINATION and LATITUDE

Day	☉ Decl	☽ Decl	☽ Lat	☽ 12h Decl	☿ Decl	☿ Lat	♀ Decl	♀ Lat	♂ Decl	♂ Lat	⚳ Decl	⚳ Lat	♃ Decl	♃ Lat	♄ Decl	♄ Lat
1 W	3S04	18S30	4N54	18S16	15S20	3S32	0N45	1N25	23S40	1S30	15S04	2N34	16N34	0N32	15S57	1N60
2 Th	3 28	17 45	5 14	16 58	15 29	3 34	0 15	1 25	23 46	1 30	15 13	2 31	16 31	0 32	15 59	1 60
3 F	3 51	15 55	5 15	14 36	15 35	3 36	0S15	1 25	23 51	1 30	15 21	2 29	16 28	0 32	16 00	1 59
4 Sa	4 14	13 04	4 57	11 18	15 38	3 36	0 45	1 24	23 57	1 30	15 29	2 27	16 25	0 32	16 02	1 59
5 Su	4 37	9 21	4 20	7 15	15 38	3 35	1 15	1 24	24 02	1 31	15 37	2 25	16 22	0 32	16 04	1 59
6 M	5 00	5 02	3 25	2 43	15 35	3 34	1 46	1 23	24 07	1 31	15 46	2 23	16 19	0 33	16 06	1 59
7 Tu	5 23	0 23	2 17	1N58	15 27	3 30	2 16	1 23	24 12	1 31	15 54	2 21	16 17	0 33	16 07	1 59
8 W	5 46	4N16	0 59	6 30	15 15	3 26	2 46	1 22	24 16	1 31	16 02	2 18	16 14	0 33	16 09	1 59
9 Th	6 09	8 37	0S21	10 35	14 59	3 19	3 16	1 21	24 20	1 31	16 10	2 16	16 11	0 33	16 11	1 59
10 F	6 32	12 22	1 38	13 57	14 38	3 11	3 46	1 20	24 25	1 31	16 18	2 14	16 08	0 33	16 13	1 58
11 Sa	6 54	15 19	2 48	16 27	14 13	3 01	4 16	1 19	24 28	1 31	16 26	2 12	16 06	0 33	16 14	1 58
12 Su	7 17	17 20	3 46	17 58	13 44	2 50	4 45	1 18	24 32	1 31	16 34	2 10	16 03	0 34	16 16	1 58
13 M	7 40	18 22	4 30	18 31	13 10	2 36	5 15	1 17	24 35	1 31	16 42	2 08	16 00	0 34	16 18	1 58
14 Tu	8 02	18 26	5 00	18 07	12 32	2 21	5 45	1 16	24 38	1 31	16 49	2 06	15 58	0 34	16 20	1 58
15 W	8 24	17 36	5 15	16 53	11 51	2 04	6 14	1 15	24 41	1 31	16 57	2 04	15 55	0 34	16 21	1 58
16 Th	8 46	15 59	5 16	14 55	11 07	1 46	6 44	1 14	24 44	1 31	17 05	2 02	15 52	0 34	16 23	1 58
17 F	9 08	13 42	5 03	12 21	10 22	1 26	7 13	1 13	24 46	1 31	17 13	1 60	15 50	0 34	16 25	1 57
18 Sa	9 30	10 52	4 37	9 16	9 36	1 06	7 42	1 12	24 49	1 31	17 20	1 58	15 47	0 35	16 27	1 57
19 Su	9 52	7 35	3 59	5 49	8 51	0 45	8 11	1 10	24 51	1 31	17 28	1 56	15 45	0 35	16 29	1 57
20 M	10 14	3 59	3 11	2 07	8 08	0 25	8 40	1 09	24 52	1 31	17 35	1 54	15 43	0 35	16 30	1 57
21 Tu	10 35	0 12	2 14	1S44	7 28	0 04	9 08	1 07	24 54	1 31	17 43	1 52	15 40	0 35	16 32	1 57
22 W	10 57	3S40	1 10	5 34	6 52	0N15	9 37	1 06	24 55	1 31	17 50	1 50	15 38	0 35	16 34	1 57
23 Th	11 18	7 26	0 02	9 14	6 21	0 33	10 05	1 04	24 56	1 31	17 57	1 48	15 35	0 36	16 36	1 57
24 F	11 39	10 57	1N07	12 32	5 56	0 50	10 33	1 03	24 56	1 31	18 05	1 46	15 33	0 36	16 38	1 57
25 Sa	11 60	13 60	2 14	15 18	5 36	1 06	11 00	1 01	24 57	1 31	18 12	1 44	15 30	0 36	16 39	1 57
26 Su	12 20	16 24	3 16	17 18	5 22	1 19	11 28	0 59	24 57	1 31	18 19	1 42	15 29	0 36	16 41	1 56
27 M	12 41	17 58	4 08	18 26	5 14	1 31	11 55	0 58	24 57	1 31	18 26	1 40	15 27	0 36	16 43	1 56
28 Tu	13 01	18 32	4 47	18 26	5 11	1 42	12 22	0 56	24 57	1 31	18 33	1 38	15 24	0 37	16 45	1 56
29 W	13 21	18 02	5 10	17 23	5 14	1 50	12 48	0 54	24 56	1 31	18 40	1 37	15 22	0 37	16 47	1 56
30 Th	13 41	16 28	5 15	15 18	5 22	1 57	13 15	0 52	24 55	1 31	18 47	1 35	15 20	0 37	16 48	1 56
31 F	14S00	13S54	5N02	12S17	5S34	2N03	13S41	0N50	24S54	1S31	18S54	1N33	15N18	0N37	16S50	1N56

Day	⚷ Decl	⚷ Lat	♅ Decl	♅ Lat	♆ Decl	♆ Lat	♇ Decl	♇ Lat
1	1S28	5N05	5N11	0S42	10S15	0S45	20S36	2N
6	1 33	5 04	5 06	0 42	10 17	0 45	20 37	2
11	1 39	5 03	5 02	0 42	10 19	0 45	20 38	2
16	1 44	5 02	4 57	0 42	10 21	0 45	20 38	2
21	1 49	5 00	4 52	0 42	10 23	0 45	20 39	2
26	1 53	4 59	4 48	0 42	10 24	0 45	20 39	2
31	1S57	4N57	4N44	0S42	10S25	0S45	20S40	2N

Day	⚴ Decl	⚴ Lat	⚵ Decl	⚵ Lat	⚶ Decl	⚶ Lat	Eris Decl	Eris Lat
1	6N05	15N42	8N41	12S18	17S03	2N33	3S08	12S
6	5 39	16 04	8 03	12 32	17 47	2 22	3 09	12
11	5 13	16 26	7 23	12 46	18 27	2 11	3 10	12
16	4 49	16 48	6 43	13 01	19 06	2 00	3 11	12
21	4 26	17 10	6 03	13 15	19 42	1 50	3 12	12
26	4 04	17 33	5 24	13 30	20 16	1 40	3 13	12
31	3N44	17N57	4N44	13S45	20S47	1N30	3S13	12S

Moon Phenomena

Max/0 Decl

dy	hr mn	
7	1:56	0 N
13	13:35	18N31
21	1:14	0 S
28	0:50	18S32

Max/0 Lat

dy	hr mn	
2	14:00	5N17
8	17:45	0 S
15	13:03	5S17
23	0:48	0 N
29	19:22	5N16

Perigee/Apogee

dy	hr m		kilometers
6	9:37	p	362480
18	6:03	a	404895

PH	dy	hr mn	
☽	1	19:34	8♑33
○	8	10:52	15♈05
●	8	10:56	T 1.166
☾	15	19:13	22♋21
●	23	21:58	0♏25
●	23	21:46	P 0.811
☽	31	2:49	7♒36

Void of Course Moon

Last Aspect				☽ Ingress
30	3:30	♃	△	♑ 1 4:4
2	16:19	♄	✶	♒ 3 8:
4	18:33	♄	□	♓ 5 9:
6	19:39	♄	△	♈ 7 10:
8	14:21	♃	△	♉ 9 11:
11	0:50	♄	☍	♊ 11 15:5
13	17:59	☿	△	♋ 13 23:
15	23:28	☿	□	♌ 16 10:
18	13:11	☉	✶	♍ 18 23:
21	3:31	♂	□	♎ 21 11:
23	17:23	♂	✶	♏ 23 21:
25	16:12	♄	☌	♐ 26 4:
27	16:19	♃	△	♑ 28 10:
30	3:02	♄	✶	♒ 30 13:

DAILY ASPECTARIAN

1 W	☿⊻♀	4:21
	☽⚼♃	6:24
	☽✶☿	7:39
	☽□♀	7:53
	☽∠⚳	12:28
	☽✶♆	14:01
	☽∠♄	14:25
	☉□☽	19:34
	☽☌♇	23:49
2 Th	☽⊻♂	2:17
	☽✶⚷	5:28
	☽□♅	6:12
	☽⊼♃	8:38
	☽✶⚳	14:58
	☽∠♆	15:42
	☽✶♄	16:19
	☽#♃	17:56
	☽∥♄	23:05
3 F	☽∥☿	3:08
	☽∠♂	5:03
	☽∥⚳	5:12
	☽∠⚷	6:47
	☽□☿	11:44
	☽△♀	15:55
	☽⊻♆	16:51
4 Sa	☉△☽	1:56
	☽⊻♇	2:21
	♀⊼♆	2:37
	☽✶♂	7:15
	♀∠⚳	7:33
	☽⊻⚷	7:37
	☉□♇	8:07
	☽✶♅	8:20
	☽☍♃	11:23
	♀∠♄	13:46
	♂□⚷	14:18
	☿ R	17:04
	☽□⚳	18:17
	☽∥♆	18:26
	☽□♄	18:33
	☽⚼♀	18:58
5 Su	☿∥⚳	2:13
	☽∠♇	2:58
	☉⚼☽	4:18
	♂△♅	4:19
	⚳☌♄	8:03
	☽∠♅	8:48
	☽△☿	13:07
	♀∥⚷	13:58
	☽☌♆	17:57
	☽⊼♀	21:39
	☽#♅	23:36
6 M	☉∥☽	0:07
	☽✶♇	3:21
	☉#♅	6:02
	☉⊼☽	6:25
	☽☌⚷	8:22
	☽⊻♅	9:05
	☽□♂	10:36
	☽⊼♃	12:47
	☽⚼☿	13:11
	⚶ ♐	14:33
	☽∥♀	15:19
	☽∥⚷	17:55
	☽△♄	19:39
	☽△⚳	20:23
7 Tu	☽#⚷	10:02
	☉⊼⚷	10:51
	☽⊼☿	13:06
	☽⚼♃	13:26
	☽#♀	15:09
	☽⊻♆	18:38
	☽⚼♄	20:15
	☉☍♅	20:59
	⚵ ♌	21:08
	☽⚼⚳	21:29
8 W	☿∠♂	0:23
	☽☍♀	2:59
	☽□♇	4:13
	☽∥♅	4:14
	☉#☽	8:45
	☽⊻⚷	9:10
	☽☌♅	9:53
	☉☍☽	10:52
	☽△♂	14:06
	☽△♃	14:21
	♀□♇	17:34
	☽∠♆	19:20
	♂△♃	20:44
	☽⊼♄	21:11
	☽⊼⚳	22:57
9 Th	♃#♄	1:32
	⚳#♃	2:35
	⚳∥♄	3:21
	☽∠⚷	10:06
	☽#♆	10:17
	☽☍☿	13:09
	☽⚼♂	16:32
	☽✶♆	20:31
10 F	☽△♇	6:37
	☽⊼♀	10:15
	☽✶⚷	11:39
	☽⊻♅	12:23
	☽#☿	15:31
	☿R♎	17:28
	☉⊼☽	17:28
	☽□♃	17:50
	☽⊼♂	19:45
	☉✶♃	23:19
11 Sa	☽☍♄	0:50
	♀⊼⚷	1:19
	☽☍⚳	3:51
	☽∥♃	7:47
	☽⚼♇	8:53
	♀☍♅	9:11
	☽#♄	9:42
	☽#⚳	12:37
	☽⊼☿	14:33
	☽∠♅	14:44
	☽⚼♀	15:19
	☉⚼☽	22:12
	☿⚼⚷	23:24
12 Su	☽□♆	1:07
	♀#♅	11:53
	☽⊼♇	12:01
	☽⚼☿	16:00
	☽□⚷	17:12
	☽✶♅	17:58
	☽△♀	21:35
13 M	☽✶♃	0:36
	☉△☽	4:05
	☽☍♂	5:13
	☽⊼♄	7:54
	☽⊼⚳	12:27
	☉⚼♆	12:48
	☽△☿	17:59
14 Tu	☽∠♃	5:25
	♀✶♃	8:34
	☽△♆	9:19
	☽⚼♄	12:51
	☽⚼⚳	18:15
	☽☍♇	21:03
15 W	☽△⚷	2:21
	☽□♅	3:08
	☉✶♂	7:20
	☽#⚳	10:09
	☉⊻♄	10:53
	☽⊻♃	11:06
	♂⊻♄	12:25
	☿⊻⚳	13:18
	☽□♀	13:47
	☽⚼♆	14:41
	☽△♄	18:36
	☽⊼♂	18:56
	☽#♄	19:02
	☉□☽	19:13
	♀⚼♆	22:27
	☽□☿	23:28
16 Th	☽△⚳	0:53
	☽∥♃	1:23
	☽⚼⚷	8:03
	☽⊼♆	20:39
	☉☌☿	20:41
17 F	☿∥♆	0:07
	☿✶♂	1:50
	☽⚼♂	2:58
	☽⊼♇	8:58
	☽⊼⚷	14:12
	☽△♅	14:59
	♀⊻♄	16:21
	☿☌♀	17:57
	☿⊻♄	19:21
18 Sa	☽☌♃	0:06
	☉∥☿	2:02
	☽#♆	3:51
	☽✶☿	6:23
	☽□♄	7:36
	☽✶♀	9:14
	☉#☽	9:15
	⚳∠♇	10:51
	☽△♂	11:19
	☽#☿	12:28
	☉✶☽	13:11
	☽⚼♇	15:23
	☽□⚳	15:32
	☽#♀	20:20
	☽⚼♅	21:16
19 Su	☽☍♆	9:17
	☽∠☿	10:08
	⚴ ♏	13:12
	☿∥♀	13:19
	☽∥♅	18:09
	☽∠♀	19:08
	☿⚼♆	19:59
	☽△♇	21:43
	☉∠☽	22:15
20 M	☽☍⚷	2:41
	☽⊼♅	3:25
	♀✶♂	5:20
	☉∥♆	9:50
	☉⊻⚳	10:49
	☽⊻♃	13:21
	☽#⚷	13:56
	☽⊻☿	13:56
	☽✶♄	20:33
	☿✶♃	20:39
21 Tu	☽□♂	3:31
	☽⊻♀	4:35
	☽✶⚳	5:51
	☉⊻☽	6:52
	☽∥⚷	12:32
	☽∠♃	19:23
	☽⊼♆	21:00
	♀⊻⚳	22:12
22 W	☉⚼⚷	2:08
	☽∠♄	2:24
	☽#♅	7:28
	☽□♇	9:10
	☽∠⚳	12:15
	☽⊼⚷	13:46
	☽☍♅	14:26
	♀⚼⚷	17:39
	☽∥☿	17:50
	☽☌☿	21:27
23 Th	☽✶♃	0:50
	☽⚼♆	2:03
	☽⊻♄	7:39
	☉ ♏	11:58
	♀∥♆	15:59
	☽✶♂	17:23
	☽⊻⚳	17:58
	☽⚼⚷	18:26
	☽∥♆	20:03
	☽∥♀	20:42
	♀ ♏	20:53
	☽☌♀	21:13
	☉☌☽	21:58
24 F	☉∥☽	5:47
	☽△♆	6:30
	♂⊻⚳	15:04
	☽✶♇	18:17
	☽△⚷	22:29
	☽⊼♅	23:04
	☽∠♂	23:12
25 Sa	⚳⚼♅	1:17
	☽⊻☿	4:33
	☉☌♀	7:32
	☽□♃	9:45
	☽#♃	14:01
	☽☌♄	16:12
	☿ D	19:20
	☽∠♇	21:55
26 Su	☽⚼♅	2:30
	☽☌⚳	3:22
	☽∥♄	3:33
	☽⊻♂	4:20
	☽∠☿	7:55
	☉⊻☽	9:56
	☽⊻♀	10:30
	♂ ♑	10:44
	☽□♆	13:34
27 M	☽⊻♇	1:00
	☽□⚷	4:52
	☽△♅	5:23
	☽✶☿	11:11
	☉∠☽	14:54
	☽∠♀	16:03
	☽△♃	16:19
	♀△♆	18:49
	⚳ ♐	22:07
	☽⊻♄	22:29
28 Tu	☉△♆	9:50
	☽⊻⚳	10:26
	☽☌♂	12:46
	☽✶♆	18:37
	☽⚼♃	18:53
	☉✶☽	19:19
	☽✶♀	21:01
29 W	☽∠♄	0:57
	☽☌♇	5:48
	☽✶⚷	9:23
	☽□♅	9:51
	☽∠⚳	13:18
	☽□☿	17:31
	☽∥♄	19:58
	☽∠♆	20:33
	☽⊼♃	21:03
30 Th	☽✶♄	3:02
	☽∠⚷	11:07
	☽#♃	11:45
	☽✶⚳	15:47
	☽⊻♂	19:23
	☽⊻♆	22:11
	☉∥☽	23:12
31 F	☽∥♀	1:30
	☉□☽	2:49
	☽□♀	5:35
	☽⊻♇	9:13
	☽⊻⚷	12:35
	☽✶♅	12:59
	☿⚼♆	21:45
	☽∠♂	22:13
	☽△☿	23:42

LONGITUDE

Day	Sid.Time	☉	☽	☽ 12 hour	Mean ☊	True ☊	☿	♀	♂	⚳	♃	♄	⚷	♅	♆	♇
	h m s	° ' "	° ' "	° ' "	° '	° '	° '	° '	° '	° '	° '	° '	° '	° '	° '	° '
1 Sa	2 40 49	8♏29 06	20♒07 09	27♒14 45	18♎10.0	19♎08.2	19♎57.2	10♏11.3	4♑07.1	1♐40.0	20♌24.8	23♏52.4	13♓20.8	13♈34.6	4♓51.8	11♑22.8
2 Su	2 44 46	9 29 07	4♓23 27	11♓32 57	18 06.9	19 09.3	20 57.3	11 26.6	4 51.8	2 04.6	20 31.4	23 59.4	13R 19.5	13R 32.5	4R 51.3	11 24.0
3 M	2 48 43	10 29 09	18 42 52	25 52 46	18 03.7	19 10.7	22 03.2	12 41.8	5 36.6	2 29.3	20 37.9	24 06.4	13 18.3	13 30.4	4 50.9	11 25.2
4 Tu	2 52 39	11 29 13	3♈02 14	10♈10 44	18 00.5	19 11.9	23 14.3	13 57.0	6 21.5	2 53.9	20 44.2	24 13.5	13 17.2	13 28.3	4 50.5	11 26.4
5 W	2 56 36	12 29 19	17 17 47	24 22 51	17 57.3	19R 12.6	24 29.6	15 12.2	7 06.4	3 18.5	20 50.4	24 20.5	13 16.1	13 26.3	4 50.1	11 27.7
6 Th	3 00 32	13 29 26	1♉25 23	8♉24 53	17 54.1	19 12.1	25 48.7	16 27.5	7 51.4	3 43.2	20 56.4	24 27.6	13 15.0	13 24.2	4 49.7	11 28.9
7 F	3 04 29	14 29 35	15 20 51	22 12 51	17 51.0	19 10.3	27 11.0	17 42.7	8 36.5	4 07.9	21 02.3	24 34.6	13 14.1	13 22.3	4 49.4	11 30.2
8 Sa	3 08 25	15 29 46	29 00 31	5♊43 32	17 47.8	19 07.3	28 35.9	18 58.0	9 21.6	4 32.7	21 08.0	24 41.7	13 13.1	13 20.3	4 49.1	11 31.6
9 Su	3 12 22	16 29 59	12♊21 43	18 54 56	17 44.6	19 03.1	0♏03.1	20 13.2	10 06.8	4 57.4	21 13.5	24 48.8	13 12.2	13 18.4	4 48.8	11 32.9
10 M	3 16 18	17 30 14	25 23 10	1♋46 29	17 41.4	18 58.4	1 32.0	21 28.5	10 52.0	5 22.2	21 18.9	24 55.9	13 11.4	13 16.5	4 48.6	11 34.3
11 Tu	3 20 15	18 30 30	8♋05 04	14 19 10	17 38.3	18 53.7	3 02.5	22 43.7	11 37.3	5 46.9	21 24.1	25 03.0	13 10.7	13 14.6	4 48.4	11 35.7
12 W	3 24 12	19 30 49	20 29 06	26 35 19	17 35.1	18 49.6	4 34.2	23 59.0	12 22.7	6 11.7	21 29.1	25 10.2	13 09.9	13 12.8	4 48.2	11 37.1
13 Th	3 28 08	20 31 10	2♌38 15	8♌38 26	17 31.9	18 46.6	6 06.8	25 14.3	13 08.1	6 36.5	21 34.0	25 17.3	13 09.3	13 11.0	4 48.1	11 38.6
14 F	3 32 05	21 31 32	14 36 25	20 32 50	17 28.7	18D 45.0	7 40.3	26 29.6	13 53.5	7 01.4	21 38.7	25 24.4	13 08.7	13 09.3	4 48.0	11 40.0
15 Sa	3 36 01	22 31 56	26 28 17	2♍23 23	17 25.6	18 44.8	9 14.3	27 44.9	14 39.1	7 26.2	21 43.3	25 31.6	13 08.1	13 07.5	4 48.0	11 41.5
16 Su	3 39 58	23 32 22	8♍18 47	14 15 08	17 22.4	18 45.8	10 48.8	29 00.2	15 24.7	7 51.1	21 47.7	25 38.7	13 07.6	13 05.8	4D 47.9	11 43.0
17 M	3 43 54	24 32 50	20 13 03	26 13 06	17 19.2	18 47.4	12 23.6	0♐15.4	16 10.3	8 15.9	21 51.9	25 45.9	13 07.2	13 04.2	4 47.9	11 44.6
18 Tu	3 47 51	25 33 20	2♎15 54	8♎21 56	17 16.0	18 49.2	13 58.7	1 30.7	16 56.0	8 40.8	21 55.9	25 53.0	13 06.8	13 02.6	4 48.0	11 46.1
19 W	3 51 47	26 33 52	14 31 42	20 45 35	17 12.8	18R 50.2	15 33.9	2 46.1	17 41.7	9 05.7	21 59.7	26 00.2	13 06.5	13 01.0	4 48.0	11 47.7
20 Th	3 55 44	27 34 25	27 03 58	3♏27 04	17 09.7	18 50.0	17 09.2	4 01.4	18 27.5	9 30.6	22 03.4	26 07.3	13 06.3	12 59.5	4 48.2	11 49.3
21 F	3 59 40	28 35 00	9♏55 03	16 28 01	17 06.5	18 47.9	18 44.5	5 16.7	19 13.4	9 55.5	22 06.9	26 14.5	13 06.0	12 58.0	4 48.3	11 50.9
22 Sa	4 03 37	29 35 37	23 05 53	29 48 33	17 03.3	18 43.9	20 19.8	6 32.0	19 59.3	10 20.4	22 10.2	26 21.6	13 05.9	12 56.5	4 48.5	11 52.6
23 Su	4 07 34	0♐36 15	6♐35 45	13♐27 10	17 00.1	18 38.0	21 55.1	7 47.3	20 45.3	10 45.4	22 13.3	26 28.8	13D 05.8	12 55.1	4 48.7	11 54.2
24 M	4 11 30	1 36 54	20 22 21	27 20 51	16 57.0	18 30.9	23 30.4	9 02.6	21 31.3	11 10.3	22 16.3	26 35.9	13 05.8	12 53.7	4 49.0	11 55.9
25 Tu	4 15 27	2 37 35	4♑22 06	11♑25 34	16 53.8	18 23.4	25 05.5	10 18.0	22 17.3	11 35.3	22 19.0	26 43.1	13 05.8	12 52.4	4 49.2	11 57.6
26 W	4 19 23	3 38 17	18 30 41	25 36 53	16 50.6	18 16.3	26 40.6	11 33.3	23 03.4	12 00.2	22 21.6	26 50.2	13 05.9	12 51.1	4 49.6	11 59.3
27 Th	4 23 20	4 39 01	2♒43 40	9♒50 34	16 47.4	18 10.7	28 15.5	12 48.6	23 49.6	12 25.2	22 24.0	26 57.3	13 06.1	12 49.9	4 49.9	12 01.1
28 F	4 27 16	5 39 45	16 57 12	24 03 12	16 44.3	18 07.0	29 50.3	14 03.9	24 35.8	12 50.1	22 26.2	27 04.4	13 06.3	12 48.7	4 50.3	12 02.8
29 Sa	4 31 13	6 40 30	1♓08 20	8♓12 21	16 41.1	18D 05.3	1♐25.1	15 19.2	25 22.0	13 15.1	22 28.2	27 11.5	13 06.5	12 47.5	4 50.7	12 04.6
30 Su	4 35 10	7♐41 16	15 15 07	22 16 29	16♎37.9	18♎05.4	2♐59.7	16♐34.6	26♑08.2	13♐40.0	22♌30.0	27♏18.6	13♓06.8	12♈46.4	4♓51.2	12♑06.4

1st of Month

Julian Day # 2456962.5
Obliquity 23°26'06"
SVP 5♓03'05"
GC 27♐02.8
Eris 22♈28.2R

Day	⚴	Day	⚵	Day	⚶
1	5♏30.9	1	9♌12.7	1	12♐54.4
6	7 43.6	6	10 46.9	6	15 30.2
11	9 56.1	11	12 12.9	11	18 06.9
16	12 08.2	16	13 29.7	16	20 44.4
21	14 20.0	21	14 36.7	21	23 22.5
26	16 31.2	26	15 32.9	26	26 01.3

DECLINATION and LATITUDE

Day	☉ Decl	☽ Decl	☽ Lat	☽12h Decl	☿ Decl	☿ Lat	♀ Decl	♀ Lat	♂ Decl	♂ Lat	⚳ Decl	⚳ Lat	♃ Decl	♃ Lat	♄ Decl	♄ Lat
1 Sa	14S20	10S29	4N31	8S32	5S51	2N07	14S06	0N48	24S53	1S30	19S00	1N31	15N16	0N37	16S52	1N56
2 Su	14 39	6 26	3 43	4 15	6 11	2 09	14 32	0 46	24 51	1 30	19 07	1 29	15 14	0 38	16 54	1 56
3 M	14 58	2 00	2 40	0N17	6 34	2 11	14 56	0 44	24 49	1 30	19 14	1 27	15 12	0 38	16 55	1 56
4 Tu	15 17	2N33	1 28	4 47	6 59	2 12	15 21	0 42	24 47	1 30	19 20	1 25	15 11	0 38	16 57	1 56
5 W	15 35	6 57	0 11	9 00	7 28	2 11	15 45	0 40	24 44	1 30	19 27	1 24	15 09	0 38	16 59	1 56
6 Th	15 53	10 55	1S07	12 40	7 58	2 10	16 09	0 38	24 42	1 30	19 33	1 22	15 07	0 38	17 01	1 56
7 F	16 11	14 13	2 19	15 33	8 29	2 07	16 32	0 36	24 39	1 29	19 40	1 20	15 06	0 39	17 03	1 55
8 Sa	16 29	16 39	3 21	17 31	9 02	2 05	16 55	0 34	24 35	1 29	19 46	1 18	15 04	0 39	17 04	1 55
9 Su	16 46	18 07	4 11	18 28	9 36	2 01	17 17	0 32	24 32	1 29	19 52	1 16	15 02	0 39	17 06	1 55
10 M	17 03	18 34	4 47	18 26	10 10	1 57	17 39	0 29	24 28	1 29	19 58	1 14	15 01	0 39	17 08	1 55
11 Tu	17 20	18 05	5 07	17 30	10 46	1 53	18 01	0 27	24 24	1 29	20 04	1 13	14 59	0 39	17 10	1 55
12 W	17 36	16 43	5 13	15 46	11 21	1 48	18 22	0 25	24 20	1 28	20 10	1 11	14 58	0 40	17 11	1 55
13 Th	17 53	14 38	5 04	13 15	11 57	1 42	18 42	0 23	24 15	1 28	20 16	1 09	14 57	0 40	17 13	1 55
14 F	18 08	11 57	4 42	10 26	12 32	1 37	19 02	0 20	24 10	1 28	20 22	1 07	14 55	0 40	17 15	1 55
15 Sa	18 24	8 48	4 08	7 05	13 08	1 31	19 22	0 18	24 05	1 28	20 28	1 06	14 54	0 40	17 17	1 55
16 Su	18 39	5 18	3 23	3 28	13 43	1 25	19 41	0 16	23 60	1 28	20 34	1 04	14 53	0 41	17 18	1 55
17 M	18 54	1 35	2 30	0S20	14 18	1 18	19 59	0 13	23 54	1 27	20 40	1 02	14 52	0 41	17 20	1 55
18 Tu	19 09	2S16	1 29	4 11	14 53	1 12	20 17	0 11	23 48	1 27	20 45	1 00	14 50	0 41	17 22	1 55
19 W	19 23	6 05	0 23	7 57	15 27	1 05	20 34	0 08	23 42	1 27	20 51	0 58	14 49	0 41	17 23	1 55
20 Th	19 37	9 44	0N45	11 26	16 01	0 59	20 51	0 06	23 35	1 26	20 56	0 57	14 48	0 41	17 25	1 55
21 F	19 50	13 01	1 52	14 27	16 34	0 52	21 07	0 04	23 29	1 26	21 02	0 55	14 48	0 42	17 27	1 55
22 Sa	20 04	15 43	2 55	16 47	17 06	0 45	21 23	0 01	23 22	1 26	21 07	0 53	14 47	0 42	17 29	1 55
23 Su	20 16	17 38	3 50	18 14	17 38	0 38	21 37	0S01	23 14	1 26	21 12	0 52	14 46	0 42	17 30	1 55
24 M	20 29	18 34	4 32	18 37	18 09	0 31	21 52	0 04	23 07	1 25	21 17	0 50	14 45	0 42	17 32	1 55
25 Tu	20 41	18 23	4 59	17 52	18 39	0 24	22 05	0 06	22 59	1 25	21 23	0 48	14 44	0 43	17 34	1 55
26 W	20 53	17 04	5 08	16 00	19 08	0 17	22 18	0 08	22 51	1 25	21 28	0 46	14 44	0 43	17 35	1 55
27 Th	21 04	14 42	4 58	13 10	19 36	0 10	22 31	0 11	22 43	1 24	21 33	0 45	14 43	0 43	17 37	1 55
28 F	21 15	11 27	4 30	9 34	20 03	0 04	22 42	0 13	22 35	1 24	21 37	0 43	14 43	0 43	17 38	1 55
29 Sa	21 25	7 33	3 46	5 26	20 30	0S03	22 53	0 16	22 26	1 24	21 42	0 41	14 42	0 43	17 40	1 55
30 Su	21S35	3S14	2N48	1S00	20S55	0S10	23S03	0S18	22S17	1S23	21S47	0N39	14N42	0N44	17S42	1N55

Day	⚷ Decl	⚷ Lat	♅ Decl	♅ Lat	♆ Decl	♆ Lat	♇ Decl	♇ Lat
1	1S58	4N57	4N43	0S42	10S25	0S45	20S40	2N18
6	2 02	4 56	4 39	0 42	10 26	0 45	20 40	2 17
11	2 05	4 54	4 35	0 41	10 26	0 45	20 40	2 16
16	2 07	4 52	4 32	0 41	10 27	0 45	20 40	2 15
21	2 10	4 51	4 29	0 41	10 26	0 45	20 40	2 15
26	2 11	4 49	4 27	0 41	10 26	0 45	20 40	2 14

Day	⚴ Decl	⚴ Lat	⚵ Decl	⚵ Lat	⚶ Decl	⚶ Lat	Eris Decl	Eris Lat
1	3N41	18N01	4N36	13S48	20S53	1N28	3S14	12S53
6	3 23	18 25	3 58	14 04	21 20	1 19	3 14	12 52
11	3 08	18 50	3 21	14 19	21 45	1 10	3 15	12 52
16	2 54	19 15	2 46	14 34	22 06	1 00	3 15	12 51
21	2 43	19 41	2 14	14 49	22 25	0 52	3 16	12 51
26	2 34	20 08	1 44	15 04	22 43	0 43	3 16	12 50

Moon Phenomena

Max/0 Decl
dy hr mn
3 10:33 0 N
9 23:17 18N35
17 9:54 0 S
24 8:09 18S37
30 17:22 0 N

Max/0 Lat
dy hr mn
5 3:14 0 S
11 20:49 5S13
19 8:19 0 N
25 23:45 5N08

Perigee/Apogee
dy hr m kilometers
3 0:22 p 367879
15 1:49 a 404336
27 23:11 p 369827

PH dy hr mn
○ 6 22:24 14♉26
☾ 14 15:17 22♌10
● 22 12:33 0♐07
☽ 29 10:07 7♓06

Void of Course Moon

Last Aspect	☽ Ingress
1 6:23 ♄ □	♓ 1 16:38
3 9:06 ♄ △	♈ 3 18:54
5 13:26 ♄ ☍	♉ 5 21:34
7 16:18 ♄ ☍	♊ 8 1:46
9 16:23 ♃ ⚹	♋ 10 8:39
12 9:17 ♄ △	♌ 12 18:45
15 2:54 ♀ □	♍ 15 7:09
17 11:12 ♄ ⚹	♎ 17 19:31
19 14:26 ♃ ⚹	♏ 20 5:32
22 5:54 ♄ ☌	♐ 22 12:20
24 3:17 ♃ △	♑ 24 16:33
26 15:31 ♄ ⚹	♒ 26 19:24
28 17:15 ♄ □	♓ 28 22:04

DAILY ASPECTARIAN

1 Sa ☽∥♆ 0:24 · ☽☍♃ 0:30 · ☽□♄ 6:23 · ☽∠♇ 10:34 · ☿⚹♃ 12:45 · ☽∠♅ 14:12 · ☽□⚳ 20:00 · ♀⚹♇ 23:10 · ♂⚹♆ 23:44

2 Su ☽☌♆ 0:47 · ☽⚹♂ 0:50 · ☽∥☿ 1:22 · ☽⚼☿ 2:50 · ☉△☽ 9:11 · ☽#♅ 9:36 · ☽⚹♇ 11:46 · ☽△♀ 12:57 · ☽☌⚷ 14:57 · ☽⚺♅ 15:18

3 M ☽∥⚷ 0:04 · ♂⚼♃ 0:47 · ☽⚻♃ 3:14 · ☉∥♀ 5:54 · ☽⚻☿ 6:05 · ☽△♄ 9:06 · ♀△⚷ 11:29 · ☉⚼☽ 12:12 · ♀#♃ 14:37 · ♀⚻♅ 15:05 · ☽⚼♀ 16:29 · ☉#♃ 17:07 · ☽#⚷ 21:05 · ☉⚹♇ 22:52 · ☽△⚳ 23:46

4 Tu ☽⚺♆ 3:02 · ☽⚼♃ 4:34 · ☽□♂ 5:53 · ☽⚼♄ 10:29 · ☽∥♅ 11:21 · ☽□♇ 14:09 · ☉⚻☽ 15:17 · ☽⚺⚷ 17:13 · ☽☌♅ 17:30 · ☽⚻♀ 20:08 · ☿⚺♄ 20:52

5 W ☽⚼⚳ 1:46 · ☽#☿ 3:16 · ☽∠♆ 4:17 · ☽△♃ 6:02 · ☽⚻♄ 12:02 · ☽☍☿ 13:26 · ☉△⚷ 18:21 · ☽∠⚷ 18:35 · ☽#♆ 20:50 · ☉⚻♅ 22:00

6 Th ☽⚻⚳ 4:03 · ☽⚹♆ 5:50 · ☽△♂ 11:40 · ☽△♇ 17:19 · ☽⚹⚷ 20:20 · ☽⚺♅ 20:35 · ☉☍☽ 22:24

7 F ☽☍♀ 4:32 · ☽∥♃ 7:32 · ☽□♃ 10:00 · ☽⚼♂ 15:18 · ☽☍♄ 16:18 · ☿⚼⚷ 17:41 · ☽⚼♇ 19:36 · ☉#☽ 21:32 · ☽∠♅ 22:49 · ☽⚻☿ 23:11

8 Sa ☽#♀ 4:10 · ☽#♄ 5:32 · ☽☍⚳ 10:12 · ☽□♆ 10:22 · ♀∥♄ 10:57 · ♂∠♄ 12:41 · ⚳□♆ 15:46 · ☽⚻♂ 19:40 · ☽⚻♇ 22:31 · ☿ ♏ 23:10

9 Su ☽□⚷ 1:32 · ☽⚹♅ 1:43 · ☽⚼☿ 5:32 · ☉⚻☽ 8:11 · ☽⚻♀ 15:57 · ☽⚹♃ 16:23 · ♀□♃ 20:42 · ☽⚻♄ 23:09

10 M ☉∥♄ 7:33 · ☿∥♆ 10:58 · ☽△☿ 13:06 · ☉⚼☽ 14:32 · ☽△♆ 17:45 · ☽⚻⚳ 19:27 · ☽∠♃ 20:46 · ♂☌♇ 23:07 · ☽⚼♀ 23:15

11 Tu ☽#♀ 1:08 · ☽⚼♄ 3:48 · ☽☍♇ 6:45 · ☽☍♂ 7:14 · ☽△⚷ 9:47 · ☽□♅ 9:54 · ☉#☽ 12:23 · ☽#♄ 17:13 · ☉△☽ 21:56 · ☽⚼♆ 22:40

12 W ☽⚼⚳ 1:26 · ☽⚺♃ 1:58 · ☿△♆ 3:39 · ☽△♀ 7:39 · ☽△♄ 9:17 · ☽⚼⚷ 15:06 · ☽∥♃ 20:50

13 Th ♂⚹⚷ 0:38 · ♀☌♄ 1:03 · ♂□♅ 1:30 · ☽⚻♆ 4:19 · ☽□☿ 7:58 · ☽△⚳ 8:13 · ☿⚺⚳ 10:25 · ☽⚻♇ 18:04 · ☽#☿ 19:57 · ☽⚻⚷ 21:03 · ☽△♅ 21:05 · ☽⚻♂ 22:28

14 F ☉□♃ 3:06 · ♀∠♇ 3:24 · ♅⚺⚷ 11:40 · ☽#♆ 11:53 · ☽☌♃ 14:19 · ☉□☽ 15:17 · ☽□♄ 22:04

15 Sa ☽⚼♇ 0:27 · ☽□♀ 2:54 · ☽⚼♅ 3:21 · ☽⚼♂ 6:53 · ♀⚼♅ 7:04 · ☽☍♆ 16:53 · ☽□⚳ 23:02

16 Su ☽∥♅ 5:05 · ☽⚹☿ 5:50 · ☽△♇ 6:54 · ♆ D 7:07 · ☽⚻♅ 9:39 · ☽☍⚷ 9:43 · ☿⚹♇ 13:58 · ☽△♂ 15:19 · ♀ ♐ 19:05 · ☽#⚷ 20:31

17 M ⚳∥♇ 2:22 · ☽⚺♃ 3:19 · ☉⚹☽ 9:28 · ☿⚻♅ 10:05 · ☿△⚷ 10:58 · ☽⚹♄ 11:12 · ☽∠☿ 16:30 · ☿#♃ 22:14 · ☽⚹♀ 22:20 · ☽∥⚷ 23:13

18 Tu ☽⚻♆ 5:00 · ☉☌♄ 8:51 · ☽∠♃ 9:14 · ☽⚹⚳ 13:03 · ☽#♅ 14:01 · ☽∠♄ 17:05 · ☉∠☽ 17:44 · ☽□♇ 18:41 · ♀∠♂ 20:30 · ☽☍♅ 21:04 · ☽⚻⚷ 21:15

19 W ☽⚺☿ 2:18 · ☉∠♇ 5:38 · ☽□♂ 6:31 · ☽∠♀ 6:57 · ♀∥♇ 8:28 · ☽⚼♆ 10:10 · ☽⚹♃ 14:26 · ☽∠⚳ 18:59 · ☽⚺♄ 22:12

20 Th ☉⚺☽ 1:03 · ☽⚼⚷ 1:58 · ☽∥♆ 4:55 · ☉⚼♅ 9:41 · ♀∥⚳ 11:48 · ☽⚺♀ 14:29 · ☽△♆ 14:31 · ♀□♆ 14:56

21 F ☽⚺⚳ 0:01 · ☽⚹♇ 3:34 · ☽⚻♅ 5:36 · ☽△⚷ 5:51 · ☿⚹♂ 14:02 · ☽#♃ 14:59 · ☽⚹♂ 18:03 · ♂∠♆ 18:19 · ☽☌☿ 18:20 · ☽□♃ 22:19

22 Sa ☽☌♄ 5:54 · ☽∠♇ 6:47 · ☽⚼♅ 8:40 · ☉ ♐ 9:39 · ☉☌☽ 12:33 · ☿∥♄ 17:53 · ☽□♆ 20:51 · ☽∥♄ 21:55 · ☽∠♂ 22:26 · ☽∥☿ 23:58

23 Su ☽☌♀ 2:18 · ☿□♃ 4:44 · ☽☌⚳ 7:31 · ☽⚺♇ 9:19 · ☽△♅ 11:03 · ☽□⚷ 11:23 · ⚷ D 23:46

24 M ☽⚺♂ 2:06 · ☽△♃ 3:17 · ☽⚺☿ 6:06 · ☽⚺♄ 10:48 · ☽∥☿ 18:15 · ☉⚺☽ 20:48 · ☉∥♇ 22:35

25 Tu ☽⚹♆ 0:46 · ♂⚻♃ 0:56 · ☽⚼♃ 5:02 · ☽∠☿ 10:58 · ☽⚺♀ 11:04 · ☽∠♄ 12:36 · ☽⚺⚳ 12:39 · ☽☌♇ 12:56 · ☽□♅ 14:26 · ☽⚹⚷ 14:50 · ☽∥♄ 16:44 · ⚳⚺♇ 23:05

26 W ☉∠☽ 0:14 · ☽∠♆ 2:13 · ☿☌♄ 2:38 · ☿∠♇ 4:50 · ☽⚻♃ 6:31 · ☽☌♂ 8:07 · ♀⚺♇ 8:29 · ♀☌⚳ 12:50 · ☽⚹♄ 14:11 · ☽∠⚳ 14:47 · ☽∠♀ 14:54 · ☽⚹☿ 15:31 · ☽∠⚷ 16:12 · ☿⚼♅ 17:36 · ☽#♃ 23:49

27 Th ♀△♅ 0:24 · ☉⚹☽ 3:29 · ☽⚺♆ 3:33 · ☉□♆ 4:20 · ♀□⚷ 5:34 · ♀∥♂ 14:47 · ☽⚺♇ 15:42 · ♄∠♇ 16:48 · ☽⚹⚳ 16:50 · ☽⚹♅ 17:01 · ☽⚺⚷ 17:30 · ☽⚹♀ 18:39 · ⚳△♅ 22:40

28 F ☿ ♐ 2:27 · ☽∥♆ 6:39 · ☽☍♃ 9:17 · ☽⚺♂ 13:40 · ⚳□⚷ 15:41 · ☽∠♇ 17:06 · ☽□♄ 17:15 · ☽∠♅ 18:20

29 Sa ☽□☿ 0:32 · ☽☌♆ 6:18 · ☿∥♇ 9:45 · ☉□☽ 10:07 · ☽∠♂ 16:35 · ☽#♅ 17:33 · ☽⚹♇ 18:38 · ☽⚺♅ 19:47 · ☽☌⚷ 20:21 · ☽□⚳ 21:13

30 Su ☽□♀ 2:29 · ☽∥⚷ 5:34 · ☽⚻♃ 12:25 · ☽⚹♂ 19:42 · ☽△♄ 20:48

December 2014

LONGITUDE

Day	Sid.Time	☉	☽	☽ 12 hour	Mean ☊	True ☊	☿	♀	♂	⚳	♃	♄	⚷	♅	♆	♇
	h m s	° ' "	° ' "	° ' "	° '	° '	° '	° '	° '	° '	° '	° '	° '	° '	° '	° '
1 M	4 39 06	8♐42 03	29♓16 23	6♈14 43	16♎34.7	18♎06.4	4♐34.2	17♐49.9	26♑54.5	14♐05.0	22♌31.6	27♏25.7	13♓07.2	12♈45.3	4♓51.7	12♑08.2
2 Tu	4 43 03	9 42 51	13♈11 24	20 06 19	16 31.5	18R 07.3	6 08.7	19 05.2	27 40.9	14 29.9	22 33.0	27 32.7	13 07.6	12R 44.3	4 52.2	12 10.0
3 W	4 46 59	10 43 40	26 59 22	3♉50 23	16 28.4	18 07.1	7 43.1	20 20.5	28 27.2	14 54.8	22 34.3	27 39.8	13 08.1	12 43.3	4 52.8	12 11.8
4 Th	4 50 56	11 44 30	10♉39 12	17 25 37	16 25.2	18 04.8	9 17.4	21 35.8	29 13.6	15 19.8	22 35.3	27 46.8	13 08.7	12 42.4	4 53.4	12 13.7
5 F	4 54 52	12 45 21	24 09 24	0♊50 19	16 22.0	17 59.9	10 51.6	22 51.1	0♒00.1	15 44.7	22 36.2	27 53.8	13 09.3	12 41.5	4 54.0	12 15.6
6 Sa	4 58 49	13 46 13	7♊28 08	14 02 38	16 18.8	17 52.5	12 25.9	24 06.4	0 46.5	16 09.7	22 36.8	28 00.8	13 09.9	12 40.7	4 54.6	12 17.4
7 Su	5 02 45	14 47 06	20 33 36	27 00 54	16 15.7	17 42.9	14 00.1	25 21.7	1 33.0	16 34.6	22 37.3	28 07.7	13 10.7	12 39.9	4 55.3	12 19.3
8 M	5 06 42	15 48 00	3♋24 24	9♋44 04	16 12.5	17 32.0	15 34.3	26 37.0	2 19.6	16 59.5	22R 37.5	28 14.7	13 11.4	12 39.2	4 56.1	12 21.2
9 Tu	5 10 39	16 48 55	15 59 56	22 12 04	16 09.3	17 20.8	17 08.5	27 52.3	3 06.1	17 24.4	22 37.6	28 21.6	13 12.3	12 38.5	4 56.8	12 23.2
10 W	5 14 35	17 49 51	28 20 39	4♌25 56	16 06.1	17 10.3	18 42.8	29 07.6	3 52.7	17 49.3	22 37.5	28 28.5	13 13.2	12 37.9	4 57.6	12 25.1
11 Th	5 18 32	18 50 48	10♌28 14	16 27 56	16 03.0	17 01.6	20 17.1	0♑22.8	4 39.3	18 14.2	22 37.2	28 35.4	13 14.1	12 37.3	4 58.5	12 27.0
12 F	5 22 28	19 51 46	22 25 30	28 21 26	15 59.8	16 55.2	21 51.4	1 38.1	5 25.9	18 39.1	22 36.7	28 42.2	13 15.1	12 36.8	4 59.3	12 29.0
13 Sa	5 26 25	20 52 45	4♍16 18	10♍10 42	15 56.6	16 51.3	23 25.9	2 53.4	6 12.6	19 04.0	22 35.9	28 49.1	13 16.2	12 36.3	5 00.2	12 31.0
14 Su	5 30 21	21 53 46	16 05 17	22 00 43	15 53.4	16D 49.7	25 00.4	4 08.7	6 59.3	19 28.9	22 35.0	28 55.8	13 17.3	12 35.8	5 01.1	12 32.9
15 M	5 34 18	22 54 47	27 57 41	3♎56 53	15 50.2	16 49.6	26 35.0	5 24.0	7 46.0	19 53.7	22 33.9	29 02.6	13 18.4	12 35.4	5 02.1	12 34.9
16 Tu	5 38 14	23 55 49	9♎58 59	16 04 40	15 47.1	16R 50.1	28 09.7	6 39.3	8 32.7	20 18.6	22 32.6	29 09.3	13 19.7	12 35.1	5 03.1	12 36.9
17 W	5 42 11	24 56 53	22 14 35	28 29 17	15 43.9	16 50.1	29 44.6	7 54.6	9 19.5	20 43.4	22 31.1	29 16.0	13 20.9	12 34.8	5 04.1	12 38.9
18 Th	5 46 08	25 57 57	4♏49 20	11♏15 10	15 40.7	16 48.6	1♑19.6	9 09.8	10 06.3	21 08.2	22 29.4	29 22.7	13 22.3	12 34.6	5 05.2	12 41.0
19 F	5 50 04	26 59 02	17 47 06	24 25 22	15 37.5	16 44.7	2 54.7	10 25.1	10 53.1	21 33.1	22 27.5	29 29.4	13 23.7	12 34.4	5 06.2	12 43.0
20 Sa	5 54 01	28 00 08	1♐10 02	8♐01 01	15 34.4	16 38.0	4 29.9	11 40.4	11 39.9	21 57.8	22 25.4	29 36.0	13 25.1	12 34.3	5 07.4	12 45.0
21 Su	5 57 57	29 01 15	14 58 04	22 00 46	15 31.2	16 28.8	6 05.4	12 55.7	12 26.8	22 22.6	22 23.1	29 42.5	13 26.6	12D 34.2	5 08.5	12 47.1
22 M	6 01 54	0♑02 22	29 08 31	6♑20 38	15 28.0	16 17.6	7 40.9	14 11.0	13 13.6	22 47.4	22 20.6	29 49.0	13 28.1	12 34.2	5 09.7	12 49.1
23 Tu	6 05 50	1 03 30	13♑36 13	20 54 23	15 24.8	16 05.6	9 16.6	15 26.2	14 00.5	23 12.1	22 18.0	29 55.5	13 29.7	12 34.2	5 10.9	12 51.2
24 W	6 09 47	2 04 38	28 14 07	5♒34 27	15 21.7	15 54.2	10 52.4	16 41.5	14 47.4	23 36.8	22 15.1	0♐02.0	13 31.4	12 34.3	5 12.1	12 53.2
25 Th	6 13 43	3 05 47	12♒54 28	20 13 16	15 18.5	15 44.6	12 28.3	17 56.8	15 34.4	24 01.5	22 12.0	0 08.4	13 33.1	12 34.4	5 13.4	12 55.3
26 F	6 17 40	4 06 56	27 30 09	4♓44 29	15 15.3	15 37.6	14 04.3	19 12.0	16 21.3	24 26.2	22 08.8	0 14.8	13 34.9	12 34.6	5 14.7	12 57.4
27 Sa	6 21 37	5 08 04	11♓55 46	19 03 41	15 12.1	15 33.5	15 40.3	20 27.2	17 08.2	24 50.9	22 05.4	0 21.1	13 36.7	12 34.8	5 16.0	12 59.5
28 Su	6 25 33	6 09 13	26 08 01	3♈08 41	15 08.9	15D 31.8	17 16.3	21 42.5	17 55.2	25 15.5	22 01.8	0 27.4	13 38.5	12 35.1	5 17.4	13 01.5
29 M	6 29 30	7 10 21	10♈05 39	16 59 00	15 05.8	15R 31.6	18 52.3	22 57.7	18 42.1	25 40.1	21 58.0	0 33.6	13 40.4	12 35.5	5 18.8	13 03.6
30 Tu	6 33 26	8 11 30	23 48 52	0♉35 23	15 02.6	15 31.5	20 28.2	24 12.9	19 29.1	26 04.6	21 54.0	0 39.8	13 42.4	12 35.9	5 20.2	13 05.7
31 W	6 37 23	9♑12 38	7♉18 43	13 59 01	14♎59.4	15♎30.1	22♑03.9	25♑28.1	20♒16.0	26♐29.2	21♌49.9	0♐45.9	13♓44.4	12♈36.3	5♓21.6	13♑07.8

1st of Month

Julian Day # 2456992.5
Obliquity 23°26'05"
SVP 5♓03'01"
GC 27♐02.9
Eris 22♈13.1R

Day	⚴
1	18♏41.6
6	20 51.3
11	23 00.0
16	25 07.7
21	27 14.2
26	29 19.3
31	1♐22.8

Day	⚵
1	16♌17.7
6	16 50.4
11	17 10.5
16	17 17.3
21	17 10.5R
26	16 50.2R
31	16 16.7R

Day	⚶
1	28♐40.5
6	1♑20.1
11	3 59.9
16	6 40.0
21	9 20.3
26	12 00.6
31	14 40.9

DECLINATION and LATITUDE

Day	☉ Decl	☽ Decl	☽ Lat	☽12h Decl	☿ Decl	☿ Lat	♀ Decl	♀ Lat	♂ Decl	♂ Lat	⚳ Decl	⚳ Lat	♃ Decl	♃ Lat	♄ Decl	♄ Lat
1 M	21S45	1N14	1N40	3N27	21S19	0S17	23S13	0S20	22S08	1S23	21S52	0N38	14N42	0N44	17S43	1N55
2 Tu	21 54	5 37	0 27	7 42	21 43	0 23	23 22	0 23	21 58	1 22	21 56	0 36	14 41	0 44	17 45	1 55
3 W	22 03	9 40	0S48	11 29	22 05	0 30	23 30	0 25	21 48	1 22	22 01	0 34	14 41	0 44	17 46	1 55
4 Th	22 11	13 09	1 58	14 37	22 26	0 36	23 38	0 28	21 38	1 22	22 05	0 33	14 41	0 45	17 48	1 55
5 F	22 19	15 53	3 01	16 55	22 46	0 43	23 44	0 30	21 28	1 21	22 10	0 31	14 41	0 45	17 50	1 55
6 Sa	22 27	17 44	3 53	18 17	23 05	0 49	23 50	0 32	21 18	1 21	22 14	0 29	14 41	0 45	17 51	1 55
7 Su	22 34	18 35	4 31	18 39	23 23	0 55	23 56	0 35	21 07	1 20	22 18	0 28	14 41	0 45	17 53	1 55
8 M	22 41	18 28	4 55	18 04	23 40	1 01	24 00	0 37	20 56	1 20	22 22	0 26	14 41	0 46	17 54	1 55
9 Tu	22 47	17 27	5 04	16 37	23 55	1 06	24 04	0 39	20 45	1 20	22 26	0 24	14 42	0 46	17 56	1 55
10 W	22 53	15 37	4 58	14 27	24 09	1 12	24 07	0 41	20 34	1 19	22 30	0 22	14 42	0 46	17 57	1 55
11 Th	22 58	13 07	4 39	11 41	24 22	1 17	24 10	0 44	20 22	1 19	22 34	0 21	14 42	0 46	17 59	1 55
12 F	23 03	10 07	4 08	8 28	24 34	1 23	24 11	0 46	20 10	1 18	22 38	0 19	14 43	0 47	18 00	1 55
13 Sa	23 07	6 44	3 27	4 56	24 44	1 28	24 12	0 48	19 58	1 18	22 42	0 17	14 43	0 47	18 01	1 55
14 Su	23 11	3 05	2 36	1 12	24 53	1 32	24 12	0 50	19 46	1 17	22 45	0 16	14 44	0 47	18 03	1 55
15 M	23 15	0S42	1 39	2S37	25 00	1 37	24 12	0 52	19 34	1 17	22 49	0 14	14 44	0 47	18 04	1 55
16 Tu	23 18	4 31	0 36	6 23	25 07	1 41	24 10	0 54	19 21	1 16	22 53	0 12	14 45	0 48	18 06	1 55
17 W	23 20	8 13	0N29	9 58	25 12	1 46	24 08	0 56	19 08	1 16	22 56	0 11	14 45	0 48	18 07	1 55
18 Th	23 22	11 39	1 34	13 12	25 15	1 49	24 05	0 58	18 55	1 16	22 59	0 09	14 46	0 48	18 09	1 55
19 F	23 24	14 37	2 37	15 52	25 17	1 53	24 02	1 00	18 42	1 15	23 03	0 07	14 47	0 48	18 10	1 55
20 Sa	23 25	16 55	3 32	17 45	25 18	1 56	23 57	1 02	18 29	1 15	23 06	0 06	14 48	0 48	18 11	1 55
21 Su	23 26	18 19	4 17	18 37	25 17	1 59	23 52	1 04	18 15	1 14	23 09	0 04	14 49	0 49	18 13	1 55
22 M	23 26	18 38	4 48	18 21	25 15	2 02	23 46	1 06	18 01	1 14	23 12	0 02	14 50	0 49	18 14	1 55
23 Tu	23 26	17 45	5 01	16 52	25 11	2 05	23 40	1 08	17 47	1 13	23 15	0 00	14 51	0 49	18 15	1 55
24 W	23 25	15 42	4 54	14 17	25 06	2 07	23 32	1 09	17 33	1 12	23 18	0S01	14 52	0 49	18 17	1 55
25 Th	23 24	12 38	4 28	10 48	24 59	2 08	23 24	1 11	17 19	1 12	23 21	0 03	14 53	0 50	18 18	1 55
26 F	23 22	8 49	3 45	6 42	24 50	2 10	23 16	1 13	17 04	1 11	23 24	0 05	14 55	0 50	18 19	1 55
27 Sa	23 20	4 30	2 48	2 15	24 40	2 10	23 06	1 14	16 49	1 11	23 26	0 06	14 56	0 50	18 20	1 55
28 Su	23 18	0N00	1 41	2N15	24 29	2 11	22 56	1 16	16 34	1 10	23 29	0 08	14 57	0 50	18 22	1 56
29 M	23 14	4 26	0 29	6 33	24 16	2 11	22 45	1 17	16 19	1 10	23 32	0 10	14 59	0 51	18 23	1 56
30 Tu	23 11	8 34	0S44	10 27	24 02	2 10	22 34	1 19	16 04	1 09	23 34	0 11	15 00	0 51	18 24	1 56
31 W	23S07	12N11	1S52	13N44	23S45	2S10	22S21	1S20	15S49	1S09	23S36	0S13	15N02	0N51	18S25	1N56

Day	⚷ Decl	⚷ Lat	♅ Decl	♅ Lat	♆ Decl	♆ Lat	♇ Decl	♇ Lat
1	2S12	4N47	4N25	0S41	10S25	0S44	20S40	2N13
6	2 13	4 46	4 23	0 41	10 24	0 44	20 40	2 13
11	2 13	4 44	4 22	0 41	10 22	0 44	20 40	2 12
16	2 12	4 43	4 21	0 40	10 21	0 44	20 39	2 11
21	2 11	4 41	4 21	0 40	10 19	0 44	20 39	2 11
26	2 09	4 39	4 21	0 40	10 16	0 44	20 38	2 10
31	2S07	4N38	4N22	0S40	10S14	0S44	20S38	2N10

Day	⚴ Decl	⚴ Lat	⚵ Decl	⚵ Lat	⚶ Decl	⚶ Lat	Eris Decl	Eris Lat
1	2N28	20N35	1N18	15S19	22S52	0N34	3S16	12S49
6	2 24	21 03	0 56	15 32	23 00	0 25	3 16	12 49
11	2 23	21 33	0 39	15 44	23 06	0 17	3 16	12 48
16	2 25	22 03	0 27	15 54	23 07	0 09	3 16	12 47
21	2 29	22 34	0 21	16 03	23 06	0 00	3 16	12 47
26	2 37	23 07	0 22	16 08	23 01	0S08	3 15	12 46
31	2N48	23N41	0N29	16S10	22S54	0S16	3S15	12S45

Moon Phenomena

Max/0 Decl (dy hr mn)

dy	hr mn	
7	9:00	18N40
14	19:35	0 S
21	18:31	18S40
27	23:59	0 N

Max/0 Lat (dy hr mn)

dy	hr mn	
2	8:33	0 S
9	2:30	5S04
16	13:29	0 N
23	3:53	5N01
29	9:27	0 S

Perigee/Apogee (dy hr m kilometers)

dy	hr m		kilometers
12	23:12	a	404581
24	16:49	p	364800

PH	dy	hr mn	
○	6	12:28	14♊18
☾	14	12:52	22♍26
●	22	1:37	0♑06
☽	28	18:33	6♈56

Void of Course Moon

Last Aspect				☽ Ingress		
30	20:48	♄	△	♈	1	1:15
3	2:43	♂	□	♉	3	5:16
5	6:46	♄	☍	♊	5	10:29
7	9:53	♀	☍	♋	7	17:35
10	0:16	♄	△	♌	10	3:15
12	12:50	♄	□	♍	12	15:20
15	2:12	♄	✱	♎	15	4:06
17	5:41	☉	✱	♏	17	14:53
19	21:12	♄	☌	♐	19	21:56
21	12:36	♃	△	♑	22	1:26
23	3:18	♀	☌	♒	24	2:53
25	15:12	♃	☍	♓	26	4:08
27	15:45	♀	✱	♈	28	6:36
30	0:47	♀	□	♉	30	10:57

DAILY ASPECTARIAN

1 M	☿ □ ♆	4:27
	☽ # ⚷	5:13
	☽ ⚺ ♆	9:37
	☽ △ ☿	10:16
	☽ ⚼ ♃	14:14
	☽ ∥ ♅	17:15
	☉ △ ☽	17:31
	♂ ✱ ♄	19:01
	☽ □ ♇	22:13
	☽ ⚼ ♄	22:52
	☽ ☌ ♅	23:13
	☽ ⚺ ⚷	23:53
2 Tu	☽ △ ⚳	2:20
	♂ ∥ ⚳	3:03
	☉ ∥ ♂	5:00
	☽ △ ♀	11:15
	☉ ∥ ⚳	11:21
	☿ ∥ ♂	11:23
	☽ ∠ ♆	11:36
	♂ ∠ ⚷	14:00
	☽ ⚼ ☿	15:35
	☽ △ ♃	16:17
	☿ ∥ ⚳	18:06
	☉ ∥ ☿	20:17
	☉ ⚼ ☽	21:37
3 W	☽ ⚻ ♄	1:11
	☽ ∠ ⚷	2:00
	☽ □ ♂	2:43
	☽ # ♆	4:48
	☽ ⚼ ⚳	5:17
	♄ ⚼ ♅	10:47
	⚶ ♑	11:49
	☽ ✱ ♆	13:50
	☽ ⚼ ♀	16:07
	☽ ⚻ ☿	21:17
4 Th	☉ ⚻ ☽	2:05
	☽ △ ♇	2:47
	☽ ⚺ ♅	3:38
	☽ ✱ ⚷	4:24
	☽ ⚻ ⚳	8:32
	☉ ⚺ ♇	11:53
	☽ ∥ ♃	12:35
	♀ △ ♃	19:12
	☽ □ ♃	21:13
	☽ ⚻ ♀	21:26
	☉ △ ♅	22:31
	♂ ♒	23:58
5 F	☽ ⚼ ♇	5:34
	☽ ∠ ♅	6:20
	☽ ☍ ♄	6:46
	☉ □ ⚷	9:32
	☽ △ ♂	11:08
	☽ □ ♆	19:21
	☿ ⚺ ♇	21:48
6 Sa	☽ # ♄	2:20
	☿ △ ♅	3:45
	☽ ⚻ ♇	8:49
	☽ ✱ ♅	9:29
	☽ ☍ ☿	10:17
	☽ □ ⚷	10:24
	☿ □ ⚷	11:19
	☉ ☍ ☽	12:28
	☽ ⚼ ♂	16:08
	☽ ☍ ⚳	16:25
7 Su	♂ ∠ ⚳	1:43
	☽ ✱ ♃	3:49
	☽ ☍ ♀	9:53
	☽ ⚻ ♄	14:13
	☽ ⚻ ♂	21:50
8 M	☽ △ ♆	2:53
	☽ ∠ ♃	7:59
	☉ ☌ ☿	9:52
	☽ # ♄	15:17
	☽ ☍ ♇	17:03
	☽ □ ♅	17:34
	☽ △ ⚷	18:38
	☽ ⚼ ♄	18:53
	♃ R	20:42
9 Tu	☉ ⚻ ☽	1:43
	☽ ⚻ ☿	2:31
	☽ ⚻ ⚳	2:49
	☿ ☌ ⚳	5:30
	☽ ⚼ ♆	7:38
	♀ ⚺ ♄	10:18
	♂ ∥ ♇	11:29
	☽ ⚺ ♃	12:50
	☿ ∥ ♀	20:00
	☉ ☌ ⚳	23:40
	☽ ⚼ ⚷	23:45
10 W	☽ △ ♄	0:16
	☽ ⚻ ♀	1:43
	☿ ∠ ♂	5:00
	☽ ⚼ ⚳	9:08
	☽ ∥ ♃	9:31
	☉ ⚼ ☽	9:38
	☽ ☍ ♂	11:39
	☽ ⚼ ☿	12:09
	☽ ⚻ ♆	13:04
	♀ ♑	16:43
11 Th	☽ ⚻ ♇	3:58
	☽ △ ♅	4:18
	☽ ⚻ ⚷	5:32
	♂ ⚺ ♆	10:03
	☽ ⚼ ♀	10:58
	☽ △ ⚳	16:07
	☉ △ ☽	18:21
	☽ # ♆	22:08
	☽ △ ☿	22:41
12 F	☽ ☌ ♃	0:23
	☽ ⚼ ♇	10:16
	☽ ⚼ ♅	10:29
	☿ △ ♃	11:25
	☽ □ ♄	12:50
	☽ △ ♀	20:52
13 Sa	☽ ☍ ♆	1:29
	☽ ⚻ ♂	4:13
	☽ ∥ ♅	15:46
	☽ △ ♇	16:48
	☽ ⚻ ♅	16:55
	☽ ☍ ⚷	18:18
14 Su	☽ # ⚷	5:38
	☽ □ ⚳	7:08
	☉ ∠ ♂	9:16
	☽ ⚼ ♂	12:47
	☉ □ ☽	12:52
	☽ ⚺ ♃	13:08
	☉ △ ♃	15:57
	♀ ✱ ♆	16:56
	☽ □ ☿	20:48
15 M	☽ ✱ ♄	2:12
	♅ □ ♇	5:15
	☽ ∥ ⚷	9:25
	☽ ⚻ ♆	14:11
	☽ □ ♀	16:38
	☽ ∠ ♃	19:10
	☽ △ ♂	20:57
	☽ # ♅	22:59
16 Tu	⚵ R	0:30
	☽ ☍ ♅	5:08
	☽ □ ♇	5:13
	☽ ⚻ ⚷	6:37
	☽ ∠ ♄	8:18
	☿ ⚺ ♄	16:14
	♀ ⚼ ♃	16:40
	☽ ⚼ ♆	19:47
	☽ ✱ ⚳	20:57
17 W	☽ ✱ ♃	0:32
	☿ ♑	3:54
	☉ ✱ ☽	5:41
	☽ ⚼ ⚷	11:45
	☽ ⚺ ♄	13:36
	☽ ∥ ♆	14:30
	☽ ✱ ☿	16:27
18 Th	☽ △ ♆	0:30
	☽ ∠ ⚳	2:33
	☽ ✱ ♀	9:00
	☽ □ ♂	10:30
	☉ ∠ ☽	12:27
	☽ ⚻ ♅	14:27
	☽ ✱ ♇	14:41
	☽ △ ⚷	15:56
19 F	☽ ∠ ☿	0:16
	☽ # ♃	1:28
	☽ ⚺ ⚳	7:03
	☽ □ ♃	8:27
	☽ ∠ ♀	15:12
	☽ ⚼ ♅	17:38
	☽ ∠ ♇	17:56
	☉ ⚺ ☽	17:56
	☽ ☌ ♄	21:12
	♀ ⚺ ♂	23:35
20 Sa	☽ ⚺ ☿	6:38
	☽ □ ♆	6:58
	☿ ✱ ♆	9:32
	♀ □ ♅	17:09
	☽ ✱ ♂	19:24
	☽ △ ♅	19:53
	☽ ⚺ ♀	20:09
	☽ ⚺ ♇	20:14
	☽ ∥ ♄	21:05
	♀ ☌ ♇	21:11
	☽ □ ⚷	21:23
	☽ ∥ ♂	22:28
21 Su	⚳ △ ♃	0:26
	♂ ∥ ♄	3:48
	♂ ✱ ♅	3:48
	♀ ✱ ⚷	10:04
	♂ ⚺ ♇	10:52
	☽ △ ♃	12:36
	☽ ☌ ⚳	13:00
	☉ ⚺ ♄	18:09
	☿ ⚼ ♃	19:03
	☽ ∠ ♂	22:23
	♅ D	22:46
	☉ ♑	23:04
22 M	☽ ⚺ ♄	1:08
	☉ ☌ ☽	1:37
	♂ ⚺ ⚷	7:41
	☽ ✱ ♆	10:03
	♀ ∠ ♄	13:18
	☽ ⚼ ♃	13:37
	☽ ∥ ♄	14:23
	☽ ☌ ☿	15:58
	☽ □ ♅	22:18
	☽ ☌ ♇	22:46
	☽ ∥ ♂	23:18
	☽ ✱ ⚷	23:49
23 Tu	☽ ⚺ ♂	0:42
	☽ ∠ ♄	2:12
	☽ ☌ ♀	3:18
	☽ ∠ ♆	10:50
	☽ ⚻ ♃	14:14
	☽ ⚺ ⚳	16:13
	♄ ♐	16:35
24 W	☽ ∠ ⚷	0:28
	☽ ✱ ♄	2:58
	☉ ⚺ ☽	6:45
	☽ # ♃	7:13
	☽ ⚺ ♆	11:25
	☽ ∠ ⚳	17:28
	☽ ⚺ ☿	23:12
	☽ ✱ ♅	23:27
25 Th	☽ ⚺ ♇	0:01
	☽ ⚺ ⚷	1:03
	☉ ∥ ♀	1:15
	☿ □ ♅	1:32
	☽ ☌ ♂	4:37
	☿ ☌ ♇	6:55
	♀ ∥ ⚳	7:11
	☽ ⚺ ♀	9:02
	☉ ∠ ☽	9:09
	☽ ☍ ♃	15:12
	☽ ∥ ♆	15:17
	☿ ✱ ⚷	16:31
	☉ ∥ ⚳	16:35
	☽ ✱ ⚳	18:48
26 F	☽ ∠ ♅	0:07
	☽ ∠ ♇	0:45
	☽ ∠ ☿	2:55
	☽ □ ♄	4:34
	☉ ✱ ☽	11:48
	☽ ∠ ♀	12:09
	☽ ☌ ♆	12:52
	☿ ∠ ♄	18:52
	♀ ∠ ♆	20:22
27 Sa	☽ # ♅	0:46
	☽ ⚺ ♅	1:06
	☽ ✱ ♇	1:47
	☽ ☌ ⚷	2:50
	☉ ✱ ♆	3:11
	☽ ✱ ☿	7:05
	☽ ⚺ ♂	9:16
	☽ ∥ ⚷	12:37
	⚴ ♐	15:24
	☽ ✱ ♀	15:45
	☽ ⚻ ♃	17:03
	☽ □ ⚳	22:28
28 Su	♀ ⚻ ♃	5:52
	☽ △ ♄	7:26
	☽ # ⚷	11:24
	☽ ∠ ♂	12:18
	☽ ⚺ ♆	15:43
	☉ □ ☽	18:33
	☽ ⚼ ♃	18:37
	☿ ⚺ ♂	19:01
	☉ ⚼ ♃	19:26
	☽ ∥ ♅	23:35
29 M	☽ ☌ ♅	4:20
	☽ □ ♇	5:10
	☽ ⚺ ⚷	6:14
	☽ ⚼ ♄	9:35
	☽ ✱ ♂	15:55
	☽ □ ☿	17:20
	☽ ∠ ♆	17:52
	☽ △ ♃	20:39
	☿ ∠ ♆	21:58
30 Tu	☽ □ ♀	0:47
	☽ △ ⚳	4:07
	☽ ∠ ⚷	8:41
	☽ # ♆	10:36
	☽ ⚻ ♄	12:13
	☽ ✱ ♆	20:30
	☿ ⚻ ♃	20:38
31 W	☉ △ ☽	3:41
	☽ ⚼ ⚳	7:44
	☽ ⚺ ♅	9:31
	☽ △ ♇	10:29
	☿ ∥ ⚳	11:14
	☽ ✱ ⚷	11:35
	☽ ∥ ♃	23:36

LONGITUDE

Day	Sid.Time	☉	☽	☽ 12 hour	Mean☊	True☊	☿	♀	♂	⚳	♃	♄	⚷	♅	♆	♇
	h m s	° ' "	° ' "	° ' "	° '	° '	° '	° '	° '	° '	° '	° '	° '	° '	° '	° '
Th	6 41 19	10♑13 47	20♉36 24	27♉11 01	14♎56.2	15♎26.4	23♑39.3	26♑43.3	21♒03.0	26♐53.7	21♌45.5	0♐52.0	13♓46.4	12♈36.8	5♓23.1	13♑09.9
F	6 45 16	11 14 55	3♊42 54	10♊12 08	14 53.1	15R 19.7	25 14.3	27 58.4	21 50.0	27 18.2	21R 41.0	0 58.0	13 48.5	12 37.4	5 24.6	13 12.0
Sa	6 49 12	12 16 03	16 38 41	23 02 35	14 49.9	15 09.9	26 48.8	29 13.6	22 37.0	27 42.6	21 36.4	1 04.0	13 50.7	12 38.0	5 26.1	13 14.1
Su	6 53 09	13 17 11	29 23 48	5♋42 17	14 46.7	14 57.4	28 22.6	0♒28.7	23 23.9	28 07.1	21 31.6	1 09.9	13 52.9	12 38.6	5 27.6	13 16.2
M	6 57 06	14 18 19	11♋58 00	18 10 57	14 43.5	14 43.2	29 55.6	1 43.9	24 10.9	28 31.4	21 26.6	1 15.8	13 55.1	12 39.3	5 29.2	13 18.3
Tu	7 01 02	15 19 27	24 21 08	0♌28 36	14 40.4	14 28.6	1♒27.4	2 59.0	24 57.9	28 55.8	21 21.4	1 21.6	13 57.4	12 40.1	5 30.8	13 20.4
W	7 04 59	16 20 35	6♌33 26	12 35 47	14 37.2	14 14.7	2 57.9	4 14.1	25 44.9	29 20.1	21 16.1	1 27.4	13 59.7	12 40.9	5 32.4	13 22.5
Th	7 08 55	17 21 43	18 35 51	24 33 52	14 34.0	14 02.7	4 26.7	5 29.2	26 31.9	29 44.4	21 10.7	1 33.1	14 02.1	12 41.7	5 34.1	13 24.6
F	7 12 52	18 22 51	0♍30 11	6♍25 09	14 30.8	13 53.4	5 53.5	6 44.3	27 18.8	0♑08.7	21 05.0	1 38.7	14 04.5	12 42.6	5 35.7	13 26.6
Sa	7 16 48	19 23 59	12 19 12	18 12 51	14 27.7	13 47.0	7 17.8	7 59.4	28 05.8	0 32.9	20 59.3	1 44.3	14 06.9	12 43.6	5 37.4	13 28.7
Su	7 20 45	20 25 07	24 06 38	0♎01 09	14 24.5	13 43.5	8 39.2	9 14.4	28 52.8	0 57.1	20 53.4	1 49.9	14 09.4	12 44.6	5 39.1	13 30.8
M	7 24 41	21 26 14	5♎57 01	11 54 55	14 21.3	13D 42.1	9 57.1	10 29.5	29 39.7	1 21.2	20 47.3	1 55.3	14 12.0	12 45.6	5 40.9	13 32.9
Tu	7 28 38	22 27 22	17 55 32	23 59 33	14 18.1	13R 42.0	11 10.9	11 44.5	0♓26.7	1 45.3	20 41.1	2 00.7	14 14.6	12 46.7	5 42.6	13 35.0
W	7 32 35	23 28 30	0♏07 41	6♏20 37	14 14.9	13 41.9	12 20.0	12 59.5	1 13.7	2 09.4	20 34.8	2 06.1	14 17.2	12 47.9	5 44.4	13 37.0
Th	7 36 31	24 29 37	12 39 00	19 03 25	14 11.8	13 40.7	13 23.6	14 14.5	2 00.6	2 33.4	20 28.4	2 11.4	14 19.8	12 49.1	5 46.2	13 39.1
F	7 40 28	25 30 45	25 34 24	2♐12 22	14 08.6	13 37.4	14 20.9	15 29.5	2 47.6	2 57.4	20 21.8	2 16.6	14 22.5	12 50.4	5 48.1	13 41.2
Sa	7 44 24	26 31 52	8♐57 34	15 50 08	14 05.4	13 31.4	15 11.1	16 44.5	3 34.5	3 21.3	20 15.1	2 21.7	14 25.3	12 51.7	5 49.9	13 43.2
Su	7 48 21	27 32 59	22 50 00	29 56 54	14 02.2	13 22.9	15 53.2	17 59.5	4 21.4	3 45.2	20 08.3	2 26.8	14 28.1	12 53.0	5 51.8	13 45.3
M	7 52 17	28 34 06	7♑10 22	14♑29 41	13 59.1	13 12.3	16 26.4	19 14.4	5 08.4	4 09.1	20 01.4	2 31.8	14 30.9	12 54.4	5 53.7	13 47.3
Tu	7 56 14	29 35 12	21 53 59	29 22 10	13 55.9	13 00.7	16 49.8	20 29.3	5 55.3	4 32.9	19 54.3	2 36.8	14 33.7	12 55.9	5 55.6	13 49.4
W	8 00 10	0♒36 18	6♒53 05	14♒25 27	13 52.7	12 49.5	17R 02.8	21 44.3	6 42.2	4 56.6	19 47.2	2 41.6	14 36.6	12 57.3	5 57.5	13 51.4
Th	8 04 07	1 37 23	21 57 59	29 29 27	13 49.5	12 39.9	17 04.6	22 59.1	7 29.1	5 20.3	19 40.0	2 46.4	14 39.6	12 58.9	5 59.5	13 53.4
F	8 08 04	2 38 27	6♓58 43	14♓24 48	13 46.4	12 32.9	16 55.0	24 14.0	8 16.0	5 44.0	19 32.7	2 51.2	14 42.5	13 00.5	6 01.4	13 55.4
Sa	8 12 00	3 39 30	21 46 51	29 04 14	13 43.2	12 28.8	16 33.7	25 28.9	9 02.8	6 07.6	19 25.3	2 55.8	14 45.5	13 02.1	6 03.4	13 57.4
Su	8 15 57	4 40 33	6♈16 31	13♈23 24	13 40.0	12D 27.2	16 01.1	26 43.7	9 49.7	6 31.1	19 17.8	3 00.4	14 48.5	13 03.8	6 05.4	13 59.4
M	8 19 53	5 41 34	20 24 47	27 20 40	13 36.8	12 27.2	15 17.8	27 58.5	10 36.5	6 54.6	19 10.3	3 04.9	14 51.6	13 05.5	6 07.4	14 01.4
Tu	8 23 50	6 42 34	4♉11 13	10♉56 37	13 33.6	12R 27.6	14 24.7	29 13.2	11 23.3	7 18.0	19 02.7	3 09.3	14 54.7	13 07.3	6 09.5	14 03.4
W	8 27 46	7 43 33	17 37 09	24 13 07	13 30.5	12 27.2	13 23.3	0♓28.0	12 10.1	7 41.4	18 55.0	3 13.6	14 57.8	13 09.1	6 11.5	14 05.3
Th	8 31 43	8 44 31	0♊44 52	7♊12 42	13 27.3	12 24.9	12 15.4	1 42.7	12 56.9	8 04.7	18 47.3	3 17.9	15 01.0	13 11.0	6 13.6	14 07.3
F	8 35 39	9 45 27	13 36 57	19 57 54	13 24.1	12 20.0	11 03.1	2 57.4	13 43.7	8 28.0	18 39.5	3 22.1	15 04.1	13 12.9	6 15.6	14 09.2
Sa	8 39 36	10♒46 23	26 15 48	2♋30 54	13♎20.9	12♎12.5	9♒48.5	4♓12.0	14♓30.4	8♑51.2	18♌31.7	3♐26.2	15♓07.4	13♈14.8	6♓17.7	14♑11.1

1st of Month

Julian Day # 2457023.5
Obliquity 23°26'05"
SVP 5♓02'56"
GC 27♐02.9
Eris 22♈05.1R

Day	⚴	⚵	⚶
1	1♐47.2	16♌08.5R	15♑12.9
6	3 48.6	15 20.5R	17 53.0
11	5 48.0	14 22.0R	20 32.9
16	7 45.3	13 14.7R	23 12.5
21	9 40.1	12 01.0R	25 51.8
26	11 32.3	10 43.8R	28 30.6
31	13 21.4	9 26.0R	1♒08.8

DECLINATION and LATITUDE

Day	☉ Decl	☽ Decl	☽ Lat	☽12h Decl	☿ Decl	☿ Lat	♀ Decl	♀ Lat	♂ Decl	♂ Lat	⚳ Decl	⚳ Lat	♃ Decl	♃ Lat	♄ Decl	♄ Lat
Th	23S02	15N06	2S54	16N16	23S28	2S08	22S08	1S21	15S33	1S08	23S39	0S15	15N04	0N51	18S26	1N56
F	22 58	17 12	3 45	17 55	23 09	2 06	21 55	1 23	15 18	1 08	23 41	0 17	15 05	0 52	18 27	1 56
Sa	22 52	18 23	4 24	18 37	22 48	2 03	21 41	1 24	15 02	1 07	23 43	0 18	15 07	0 52	18 29	1 56
Su	22 46	18 37	4 49	18 23	22 26	1 60	21 26	1 25	14 46	1 06	23 45	0 20	15 09	0 52	18 30	1 56
M	22 40	17 56	4 59	17 16	22 03	1 56	21 10	1 26	14 30	1 06	23 47	0 22	15 11	0 52	18 31	1 56
Tu	22 33	16 24	4 55	15 21	21 38	1 51	20 54	1 27	14 13	1 05	23 49	0 23	15 12	0 52	18 32	1 56
W	22 26	14 09	4 38	12 48	21 13	1 46	20 37	1 28	13 57	1 05	23 51	0 25	15 14	0 53	18 33	1 56
Th	22 18	11 19	4 08	9 44	20 46	1 40	20 20	1 29	13 40	1 04	23 53	0 27	15 16	0 53	18 34	1 56
F	22 10	8 04	3 27	6 19	20 18	1 33	20 02	1 30	13 24	1 04	23 55	0 29	15 18	0 53	18 35	1 56
Sa	22 02	4 30	2 38	2 39	19 49	1 25	19 44	1 31	13 07	1 03	23 56	0 30	15 20	0 53	18 36	1 57
Su	21 53	0 47	1 42	1S06	19 19	1 16	19 25	1 32	12 50	1 02	23 58	0 32	15 22	0 53	18 37	1 57
M	21 44	2S59	0 41	4 51	18 49	1 06	19 05	1 32	12 33	1 02	23 59	0 34	15 25	0 54	18 38	1 57
Tu	21 34	6 41	0N22	8 28	18 18	0 56	18 45	1 33	12 16	1 01	24 01	0 36	15 27	0 54	18 39	1 57
W	21 24	10 10	1 26	11 47	17 48	0 44	18 24	1 33	11 59	1 00	24 02	0 37	15 29	0 54	18 40	1 57
Th	21 13	13 18	2 27	14 40	17 18	0 31	18 03	1 34	11 41	0 60	24 04	0 39	15 31	0 54	18 41	1 57
F	21 02	15 52	3 23	16 53	16 48	0 18	17 41	1 34	11 24	0 59	24 05	0 41	15 33	0 54	18 42	1 57
Sa	20 51	17 41	4 09	18 15	16 20	0 03	17 19	1 35	11 06	0 59	24 06	0 43	15 36	0 55	18 43	1 57
Su	20 39	18 32	4 43	18 32	15 52	0N13	16 56	1 35	10 49	0 58	24 07	0 44	15 38	0 55	18 44	1 57
M	20 27	18 15	4 60	17 39	15 27	0 29	16 33	1 35	10 31	0 57	24 08	0 46	15 40	0 55	18 45	1 58
Tu	20 14	16 45	4 58	15 33	15 03	0 46	16 10	1 35	10 13	0 57	24 09	0 48	15 43	0 55	18 45	1 58
W	20 01	14 06	4 36	12 24	14 43	1 04	15 46	1 35	9 55	0 56	24 10	0 50	15 45	0 55	18 46	1 58
Th	19 48	10 29	3 54	8 25	14 25	1 22	15 21	1 35	9 37	0 55	24 11	0 52	15 48	0 56	18 47	1 58
F	19 34	6 13	2 57	3 56	14 10	1 40	14 56	1 35	9 19	0 55	24 12	0 53	15 50	0 56	18 48	1 58
Sa	19 20	1 37	1 48	0N43	13 59	1 58	14 31	1 35	9 01	0 54	24 13	0 55	15 53	0 56	18 49	1 58
Su	19 05	2N60	0 33	5 12	13 52	2 16	14 05	1 35	8 42	0 53	24 13	0 57	15 55	0 56	18 49	1 58
M	18 51	7 19	0S42	9 18	13 49	2 32	13 39	1 34	8 24	0 53	24 14	0 59	15 58	0 56	18 50	1 58
Tu	18 36	11 08	1 53	12 48	13 50	2 48	13 13	1 34	8 06	0 52	24 15	1 01	16 00	0 56	18 51	1 58
W	18 20	14 16	2 56	15 32	13 54	3 02	12 46	1 33	7 47	0 51	24 15	1 02	16 03	0 56	18 51	1 59
Th	18 04	16 35	3 48	17 25	14 01	3 14	12 19	1 33	7 29	0 51	24 16	1 04	16 05	0 57	18 52	1 59
F	17 48	18 01	4 27	18 23	14 12	3 23	11 51	1 32	7 10	0 50	24 16	1 06	16 08	0 57	18 53	1 59
Sa	17S32	18N31	4S52	18N25	14S24	3N31	11S23	1S32	6S52	0S49	24S16	1S08	16N10	0N57	18S53	1N59

Day	⚷ Decl	⚷ Lat	♅ Decl	♅ Lat	♆ Decl	♆ Lat	♇ Decl	♇ Lat
1	2S06	4N38	4N22	0S40	10S13	0S44	20S38	2N10
6	2 03	4 36	4 24	0 40	10 10	0 44	20 37	2 09
11	2 00	4 35	4 26	0 39	10 07	0 44	20 37	2 09
16	1 56	4 34	4 28	0 39	10 04	0 44	20 36	2 08
21	1 52	4 33	4 31	0 39	10 00	0 44	20 36	2 08
26	1 47	4 31	4 34	0 39	9 57	0 44	20 35	2 08
31	1S42	4N30	4N38	0S39	9S53	0S44	20S34	2N07

Day	⚴ Decl	⚴ Lat	⚵ Decl	⚵ Lat	⚶ Decl	⚶ Lat	Eris Decl	Eris Lat
1	2N50	23N47	0N32	16S10	22S52	0S18	3S15	12S45
6	3 04	24 23	0 47	16 07	22 40	0 26	3 14	12 44
11	3 22	24 59	1 10	15 60	22 25	0 34	3 13	12 43
16	3 43	25 37	1 40	15 47	22 08	0 42	3 12	12 42
21	4 07	26 17	2 16	15 30	21 47	0 50	3 11	12 41
26	4 34	26 58	2 58	15 07	21 24	0 58	3 10	12 41
31	5N05	27N40	3N44	14S39	20S59	1S06	3S09	12S40

Moon Phenomena

Max/0 Decl (dy hr mn)
3 17:56 18N39
11 4:58 0 S
18 6:09 18S34
24 8:19 0 N
31 0:55 18N31

Max/0 Lat (dy hr mn)
5 5:09 5S00
12 15:34 0 N
19 9:43 5N02
25 10:25 0 S

Perigee/Apogee (dy hr m kilometers)
9 18:22 a 405407
21 20:19 p 359647

PH dy hr mn
○ 5 4:54 14♋31
☾ 13 9:48 22♎52
● 20 13:15 0♒09
☽ 27 4:50 6♉55

Void of Course Moon

Last Aspect	☽ Ingress
1 12:20 ♀ △	♊ 1 17:10
3 11:56 ♂ △	♋ 4 1:09
5 4:54 ☉ ☍	♌ 6 11:04
8 17:06 ♂ ☍	♍ 8 22:59
10 15:47 ☉ △	♎ 11 11:58
13 9:48 ☉ □	♏ 13 23:45
15 23:53 ☉ ✱	♐ 16 8:02
17 19:26 ♃ △	♑ 18 12:05
19 10:52 ♇ ☌	♒ 20 13:01
22 1:46 ♀ ☌	♓ 22 12:49
23 11:14 ♇ ✱	♈ 24 13:32
26 14:24 ♀ ✱	♉ 26 16:38
28 2:20 ♃ □	♊ 28 22:37
30 9:25 ♃ ✱	♋ 31 7:10

DAILY ASPECTARIAN

☽□♂ 0:51
☽□♃ 2:05
☽#♂ 3:59
♀⚺⚳ 4:56
☽△☿ 6:19
☉⚼☽ 9:08
☽⚻⚳ 11:50
☽△♀ 12:20
☽∠♅ 12:48
☽⚼♇ 13:50
☽☍♄ 18:54
♂☍♃ 19:50

☽□♆ 3:08
☽⚼☿ 13:45
☉⚻☽ 15:08
♀∠⚷ 16:28
☽✱♅ 16:31
♂#♃ 16:53
☽⚻♇ 17:37
☉∥☿ 18:09
☽□⚷ 18:46
☽⚼♀ 19:00

☽#♄ 3:32
☉□♅ 8:41
☽✱♃ 9:14
☽△♂ 11:56
♀ ♒ 14:49
☿⚺⚳ 18:35
☽☍⚳ 21:30
☽⚻☿ 21:48
☉☌♇ 23:35

☽⚻♀ 2:17
Su ☽⚻♄ 3:23
☽#♄ 7:21
☿∠⚷ 7:58
☽△♆ 11:33
☽∠♃ 13:29
♀✱♄ 14:16
☉✱⚷ 14:32
☽⚼♂ 18:18

5 M ☿ ♒ 1:09
☽□♅ 1:20
☽☍♇ 2:35
☽△⚷ 3:46
☉☍☽ 4:54
☽⚼♄ 8:21
☽⚼♆ 16:30
☽⚺♃ 18:12
☿✱♄ 22:22

6 Tu ☽⚻♂ 1:17
☽⚼⚷ 9:03
☽⚻⚳ 9:16
☽∥♃ 13:21
☽△♄ 13:51
☽☍☿ 15:54
☽☍♀ 18:53
☽⚻♆ 21:59

7 W ♀∥♇ 0:19
☽#♂ 2:02
☉∠♄ 2:57
☽△♅ 12:11
☽⚻♇ 13:35
☽⚻⚷ 14:50
☽⚼⚳ 16:01
☉⚻☽ 21:18

8 Th ♀⚺♆ 1:35
☽☌♃ 5:08
☿∥♇ 7:22
☽#♆ 8:57
⚳ ♑ 15:25
☽☍♂ 17:06
☽⚼♅ 18:21
☿⚺♆ 18:57
☽⚼♇ 19:49
☽△⚳ 23:15

9 F ☽□♄ 2:20
☉⚼☽ 6:23
☽☍♆ 10:21
♂∠♅ 12:24
☽⚻☿ 12:25
☽⚻♀ 14:09

10 Sa ☽∥♅ 0:32
☽⚻♅ 0:50
☽△♇ 2:22
☽☍⚷ 3:40
☿∥♀ 11:10
♂∠♇ 12:15
☉△☽ 15:47
☽#⚷ 16:11
☽⚺♃ 17:30
☽⚼☿ 22:57

11 Su ☽⚼♀ 0:18
☉∠♆ 5:40
☉⚻♃ 10:06
☽⚻♂ 10:23
☽□⚳ 14:23
☽✱♄ 15:48
☽∥⚷ 17:38
☽⚻♆ 23:27
☽∠♃ 23:41

12 M ☿∥♄ 8:15
☽△☿ 9:00
☽#♅ 9:18
☽△♀ 10:13
♂ ♓ 10:21
☽☍♅ 13:43
☽□♇ 15:19
☽⚻⚷ 16:38
☽⚼♂ 18:43
☽∠♄ 22:10

13 Tu ☽✱♃ 5:26
☽⚼♆ 5:32
♀∥♄ 6:31
☉□☽ 9:48
⚳⚺♄ 19:47
♀✱♅ 20:13
☽⚼⚷ 22:21
☽∥♆ 23:22

14 W ☽△♂ 2:17
☽⚺♄ 3:51
☽✱⚳ 4:04
☿✱♅ 10:26
☽△♆ 10:52
☽∥♂ 12:18
♀⚺♇ 12:21

15 Th ☽⚻♅ 0:19
☽□☿ 1:31
♀⚺⚷ 1:46
☽✱♇ 1:54
☽△⚷ 3:11
☽□♀ 3:20
♂□♄ 6:11
☿⚺♇ 6:26
☽∠⚳ 9:30
☽□♃ 14:30
☽#♃ 20:40
☉✱☽ 23:53

16 F ☿⚺⚷ 0:45
☽⚼♅ 4:08
☽∠♇ 5:40
☽∥☿ 8:44
♂✱⚳ 10:15
☽☌♄ 12:12
☽⚺⚳ 13:45
☽□♂ 13:51
☽□♆ 18:27
☽∥♀ 19:12

17 Sa ☉∠☽ 4:52
☽△♅ 6:51
☽⚺♇ 8:21
☽□⚷ 9:35
☽✱☿ 11:29
☽✱♀ 14:54
☽△♃ 19:26

18 Su ☉∥♇ 5:50
☉⚺☽ 8:35
☿#♃ 12:00
☽∠☿ 14:09
☽⚺♄ 16:16
☽∠♀ 18:41
☽☌⚳ 18:52
☽✱♂ 20:27
☽⚼♃ 20:28
♀∠⚳ 21:29
☽✱♆ 21:53

19 M ☽□♅ 9:25
☽☌♇ 10:52
☽✱⚷ 12:04
♀☍♃ 13:45
☽⚺☿ 15:36
☽∠♄ 17:02
☽⚻♃ 20:48
☽⚺♀ 21:31
☽∠♂ 22:20
☽∠♆ 22:26
☉∠⚷ 23:24

20 Tu ♂☌♆ 0:10
☽∥♀ 7:30
☉ ♒ 9:44
☽#♃ 10:23
☽∠⚷ 12:21
☉☌☽ 13:15
⚳⚼♃ 16:42
♂∥♆ 16:45
☽✱♄ 17:17
☽∥☿ 18:35
☽⚺⚳ 20:49
☽⚺♆ 22:31
☽⚺♂ 23:42

21 W ♀#♃ 0:14
☽✱♅ 9:41
☽⚺♇ 11:07
☽⚺⚷ 12:20
☿R 15:56
☽☌☿ 16:14
☽☍♃ 20:22
☽∠⚳ 21:20

22 Th ☽☌♀ 1:46
☽∥♆ 2:57
☽∥♂ 5:32
☽∠♅ 9:36
☽∠♇ 11:04
☉⚺☽ 16:32
☽□♄ 17:21
☽✱⚳ 21:57
☽☌♆ 22:28

23 F ☽☌♂ 2:11
☉✱♄ 5:25
☽#♅ 8:49
☽⚺♅ 9:45
☽✱♇ 11:14
☽☌⚷ 12:31
☽⚺☿ 15:43
☉∠☽ 18:31
⚳✱♆ 19:23
☽⚻♃ 20:11
☽∥⚷ 22:55

24 Sa ☽⚺♀ 6:39
☽∠☿ 15:35
☽#⚷ 17:44
☽△♄ 18:31
☽⚼♃ 20:43
☉✱☽ 21:07
☽⚺♆ 23:41

25 Su ☽□⚳ 0:25
☽⚺♂ 6:19
☽∥♅ 8:29
☽∠♀ 10:04
☽☌♅ 11:28
☽□♇ 13:03
☿∥♀ 13:54
☽⚺⚷ 14:28
☽✱☿ 15:42
☽⚼♄ 19:59
☽△♃ 21:53

26 M ☉∥♄ 1:00
☽∠♆ 1:14
♀∠♅ 2:19
☽#♂ 5:59
☽∠♂ 9:31
☉⚺♆ 10:31
☿⚺⚷ 11:40
☽✱♀ 14:24
☽#♆ 16:01
☽∠⚷ 16:27
♀∠♇ 20:44
☽⚻♄ 22:10

27 Tu ☽✱♆ 3:30
☉□☽ 4:50
☽△⚳ 5:41
☿⚺♇ 8:24
☽#♀ 13:17
☽✱♂ 13:35
♀ ♓ 15:01
☽⚺♅ 15:56
☽□☿ 16:57
☽△♇ 17:37
☽✱⚷ 19:11
☽#☿ 20:42
☉⚺⚳ 22:38

28 W ☽□♃ 2:20
☿✱♅ 5:03
☽⚼⚳ 9:29
☿⚺♂ 15:27
☽∥♃ 17:52
☽∠♅ 19:16
⚶ ♒ 19:45
☽⚼♇ 20:59

29 Th ☽□♀ 1:58
☽☍♄ 4:45
♂⚺♅ 7:31
☽□♆ 10:11
☽⚻⚳ 14:02
☉△☽ 16:08
☽△☿ 19:36
☉#☽ 20:11
☽✱♅ 23:15

30 F ☽□♂ 0:13
☽⚻♇ 1:01
☽□⚷ 2:45
♀□♄ 8:24
☽✱♃ 9:25
♂✱♇ 13:41
☉☌☿ 13:46
☽⚼☿ 21:28
☉⚼☽ 22:59

31 Sa ☽∠♃ 13:48
☽⚻♄ 13:51
☿⚺⚳ 14:02
☽△♀ 16:57
☽△♆ 19:21
♂☌⚷ 20:24
☽⚻☿ 23:43

February 2015

LONGITUDE

Day	Sid.Time	☉	☽	☽ 12 hour	Mean☊	True☊	☿	♀	♂	⚳	♃	♄	⚷	♅	♆	♇
	h m s	° ' "	° ' "	° ' "	° '	° '	° '	° '	° '	° '	° '	° '	° '	° '	° '	° '
1 Su	8 43 33	11♒47 17	8♋43 24	14♋53 30	13♎17.8	12♎02.7	8♒33.8	5♓26.7	15♓17.1	9♑14.3	18♌23.8	3♐30.2	15♓10.6	13♈16.8	6♓19.8	14♑13.0
2 M	8 47 29	12 48 10	21 01 19	27 07 01	13 14.6	11R 51.5	7R 21.1	6 41.3	16 03.8	9 37.4	18R 15.9	3 34.1	15 13.9	13 18.8	6 22.0	14 14.9
3 Tu	8 51 26	13 49 02	3♌10 44	9♌12 35	13 11.4	11 39.7	6 12.3	7 55.8	16 50.4	10 00.4	18 08.0	3 38.0	15 17.2	13 20.9	6 24.1	14 16.8
4 W	8 55 22	14 49 53	15 12 42	21 11 14	13 08.2	11 28.5	5 08.9	9 10.3	17 37.1	10 23.3	18 00.0	3 41.8	15 20.5	13 23.0	6 26.2	14 18.7
5 Th	8 59 19	15 50 42	27 08 21	3♍04 15	13 05.0	11 18.9	4 12.1	10 24.8	18 23.7	10 46.2	17 52.1	3 45.4	15 23.8	13 25.2	6 28.4	14 20.5
6 F	9 03 15	16 51 31	8♍59 11	14 53 23	13 01.9	11 11.5	3 22.9	11 39.3	19 10.3	11 09.0	17 44.1	3 49.0	15 27.2	13 27.3	6 30.6	14 22.4
7 Sa	9 07 12	17 52 18	20 47 12	26 40 59	12 58.7	11 06.6	2 41.7	12 53.7	19 56.8	11 31.7	17 36.1	3 52.6	15 30.6	13 29.6	6 32.7	14 24.2
8 Su	9 11 08	18 53 05	2♎35 08	8♎30 06	12 55.5	11D 04.2	2 08.8	14 08.1	20 43.4	11 54.4	17 28.1	3 56.0	15 34.0	13 31.8	6 34.9	14 26.0
9 M	9 15 05	19 53 50	14 26 23	20 24 31	12 52.3	11 03.8	1 44.3	15 22.5	21 29.9	12 17.0	17 20.2	3 59.3	15 37.4	13 34.2	6 37.1	14 27.8
10 Tu	9 19 02	20 54 34	26 25 05	2♏28 40	12 49.2	11 04.8	1 27.9	16 36.8	22 16.3	12 39.5	17 12.2	4 02.6	15 40.8	13 36.5	6 39.3	14 29.5
11 W	9 22 58	21 55 17	8♏35 54	14 47 25	12 46.0	11 06.1	1D 19.4	17 51.1	23 02.8	13 02.0	17 04.3	4 05.7	15 44.3	13 38.9	6 41.5	14 31.3
12 Th	9 26 55	22 55 59	21 03 50	27 25 46	12 42.8	11R 06.9	1 18.5	19 05.4	23 49.2	13 24.4	16 56.4	4 08.8	15 47.8	13 41.3	6 43.8	14 33.0
13 F	9 30 51	23 56 41	3♐53 47	10♐28 23	12 39.6	11 06.3	1 24.7	20 19.6	24 35.6	13 46.7	16 48.5	4 11.8	15 51.3	13 43.8	6 46.0	14 34.8
14 Sa	9 34 48	24 57 21	17 09 58	23 58 50	12 36.4	11 04.0	1 37.5	21 33.8	25 22.0	14 08.9	16 40.7	4 14.7	15 54.9	13 46.2	6 48.2	14 36.5
15 Su	9 38 44	25 58 00	0♑55 09	7♑58 51	12 33.3	10 59.7	1 56.6	22 47.9	26 08.3	14 31.0	16 32.8	4 17.5	15 58.4	13 48.8	6 50.5	14 38.1
16 M	9 42 41	26 58 37	15 09 46	22 27 25	12 30.1	10 53.8	2 21.3	24 02.0	26 54.7	14 53.1	16 25.1	4 20.1	16 02.0	13 51.3	6 52.7	14 39.8
17 Tu	9 46 37	27 59 14	29 51 10	7♒20 09	12 26.9	10 47.0	2 51.3	25 16.1	27 40.9	15 15.1	16 17.4	4 22.8	16 05.6	13 53.9	6 55.0	14 41.4
18 W	9 50 34	28 59 49	14♒53 19	22 29 28	12 23.7	10 40.3	3 26.2	26 30.1	28 27.2	15 37.0	16 09.8	4 25.3	16 09.2	13 56.6	6 57.2	14 43.1
19 Th	9 54 31	0♓00 23	0♓07 17	7♓45 25	12 20.6	10 34.5	4 05.7	27 44.1	29 13.4	15 58.8	16 02.2	4 27.7	16 12.8	13 59.2	6 59.5	14 44.7
20 F	9 58 27	1 00 55	15 22 30	22 57 18	12 17.4	10 30.4	4 49.2	28 58.1	29 59.6	16 20.6	15 54.7	4 30.0	16 16.4	14 01.9	7 01.8	14 46.2
21 Sa	10 02 24	2 01 25	0♈28 39	7♈55 34	12 14.2	10D 28.3	5 36.5	0♈12.0	0♈45.8	16 42.2	15 47.2	4 32.2	16 20.0	14 04.6	7 04.0	14 47.8
22 Su	10 06 20	3 01 54	15 17 15	22 33 05	12 11.0	10 28.0	6 27.4	1 25.8	1 31.9	17 03.7	15 39.9	4 34.3	16 23.7	14 07.4	7 06.3	14 49.3
23 M	10 10 17	4 02 21	29 42 41	6♉45 48	12 07.8	10 29.0	7 21.5	2 39.6	2 18.0	17 25.2	15 32.6	4 36.3	16 27.3	14 10.2	7 08.6	14 50.9
24 Tu	10 14 13	5 02 46	13♉42 22	20 32 29	12 04.7	10 30.5	8 18.6	3 53.4	3 04.0	17 46.5	15 25.5	4 38.3	16 31.0	14 13.0	7 10.9	14 52.3
25 W	10 18 10	6 03 09	27 16 20	3♊54 12	12 01.5	10R 31.8	9 18.5	5 07.1	3 50.0	18 07.8	15 18.4	4 40.1	16 34.7	14 15.8	7 13.2	14 53.8
26 Th	10 22 06	7 03 30	10♊26 26	16 53 27	11 58.3	10 32.0	10 21.0	6 20.8	4 36.0	18 29.0	15 11.4	4 41.8	16 38.3	14 18.7	7 15.4	14 55.3
27 F	10 26 03	8 03 49	23 15 40	29 33 32	11 55.1	10 30.9	11 25.9	7 34.4	5 21.9	18 50.0	15 04.6	4 43.4	16 42.0	14 21.6	7 17.7	14 56.7
28 Sa	10 30 00	9♓04 07	5♋47 29	11♋57 56	11♎52.0	10♎28.2	12♒33.1	8♈47.9	6♈07.8	19♑11.0	14♌57.8	4♐45.0	16♓45.7	14♈24.5	7♓20.0	14♑58.1

1st of Month

Julian Day 2457054.5
Obliquity 23°26'05"
SVP 5♓02'5
GC 27♐03.
Eris 22♈07.

Day	⚴
1	13♐42.9
6	15 28.1
11	17 09.8
16	18 47.6
21	20 21.0
26	21 49.7

Day	⚵
1	9♌10.7
6	7 56.0
11	6 46.7
16	5 44.9
21	4 52.4
26	4 10.5

Day	⚶
1	1♒40.4
6	4 17.8
11	6 54.6
16	9 30.5
21	12 05.6
26	14 39.7

DECLINATION and LATITUDE

Day	☉ Decl	☽ Decl	☽ Lat	☽12h Decl	☿ Decl	☿ Lat	♀ Decl	♀ Lat	♂ Decl	♂ Lat	⚳ Decl	⚳ Lat	♃ Decl	♃ Lat	♄ Decl	♄ Lat
1 Su	17S15	18N06	5S03	17N34	14S39	3N35	10S55	1S31	6S33	0S49	24S17	1S10	16N13	0N57	18S54	1N59
2 M	16 58	16 51	5 00	15 56	14 55	3 38	10 27	1 30	6 14	0 48	24 17	1 12	16 15	0 57	18 55	1 59
3 Tu	16 41	14 51	4 43	13 36	15 12	3 38	9 58	1 29	5 55	0 47	24 17	1 14	16 18	0 57	18 55	1 59
4 W	16 23	12 14	4 14	10 44	15 30	3 35	9 30	1 28	5 37	0 47	24 17	1 16	16 18	0 57	18 56	1 60
5 Th	16 05	9 07	3 33	7 26	15 47	3 31	9 00	1 27	5 18	0 46	24 17	1 18	16 23	0 58	18 56	1 60
6 F	15 47	5 40	2 44	3 52	16 04	3 25	8 31	1 26	4 59	0 45	24 17	1 19	16 26	0 58	18 57	1 60
7 Sa	15 28	2 01	1 47	0 09	16 21	3 17	8 02	1 25	4 40	0 45	24 17	1 21	16 28	0 58	18 57	2 00
8 Su	15 10	1S43	0 46	3S35	16 37	3 08	7 32	1 24	4 21	0 44	24 17	1 23	16 31	0 58	18 58	2 00
9 M	14 51	5 25	0N18	7 12	16 52	2 58	7 02	1 22	4 02	0 43	24 17	1 25	16 33	0 58	18 58	2 00
10 Tu	14 31	8 55	1 22	10 34	17 06	2 48	6 32	1 21	3 43	0 43	24 17	1 27	16 36	0 58	18 59	2 00
11 W	14 12	12 06	2 23	13 32	17 19	2 36	6 01	1 20	3 24	0 42	24 17	1 29	16 38	0 58	18 59	2 01
12 Th	13 52	14 49	3 19	15 56	17 31	2 25	5 31	1 18	3 05	0 41	24 16	1 31	16 41	0 58	18 60	2 01
13 F	13 32	16 53	4 07	17 37	17 41	2 13	5 00	1 16	2 46	0 41	24 16	1 33	16 43	0 58	18 60	2 01
14 Sa	13 12	18 07	4 43	18 22	17 50	2 00	4 29	1 15	2 27	0 40	24 16	1 35	16 46	0 58	19 00	2 01
15 Su	12 52	18 21	5 05	18 03	17 58	1 48	3 59	1 13	2 08	0 39	24 15	1 37	16 48	0 58	19 01	2 01
16 M	12 31	17 28	5 08	16 35	18 04	1 36	3 28	1 11	1 49	0 38	24 15	1 39	16 51	0 59	19 01	2 01
17 Tu	12 10	15 25	4 53	13 58	18 09	1 24	2 57	1 09	1 30	0 38	24 14	1 41	16 53	0 59	19 01	2 02
18 W	11 49	12 17	4 14	10 22	18 13	1 12	2 25	1 08	1 11	0 37	24 14	1 43	16 55	0 59	19 02	2 02
19 Th	11 28	8 17	3 12	6 03	18 15	1 00	1 54	1 06	0 52	0 36	24 13	1 45	16 58	0 59	19 02	2 02
20 F	11 07	3 44	2 12	1 21	18 16	0 48	1 23	1 04	0 33	0 36	24 13	1 47	16 60	0 59	19 02	2 02
21 Sa	10 45	1N01	0 54	3N21	18 16	0 37	0 52	1 01	0 14	0 35	24 12	1 50	17 02	0 59	19 02	2 02
22 Su	10 23	5 37	0S26	7 46	18 14	0 26	0 20	0 59	0N05	0 34	24 11	1 52	17 04	0 59	19 03	2 02
23 M	10 02	9 46	1 43	11 35	18 11	0 15	0N11	0 57	0 24	0 34	24 11	1 54	17 07	0 59	19 03	2 02
24 Tu	9 40	13 13	2 52	14 39	18 06	0 05	0 43	0 55	0 43	0 33	24 10	1 56	17 09	0 59	19 03	2 03
25 W	9 17	15 51	3 48	16 49	18 00	0S05	1 14	0 52	1 02	0 32	24 09	1 58	17 11	0 59	19 03	2 03
26 Th	8 55	17 32	4 31	18 02	17 53	0 15	1 45	0 50	1 21	0 31	24 09	2 00	17 13	0 59	19 03	2 03
27 F	8 33	18 17	4 59	18 19	17 44	0 24	2 17	0 48	1 40	0 31	24 08	2 02	17 15	0 59	19 04	2 03
28 Sa	8S10	18N07	5S12	17N42	17S34	0S34	2N48	0S45	1N59	0S30	24S07	2S05	17N17	0N59	19S04	2N03

Day	⚷ Decl	⚷ Lat	♅ Decl	♅ Lat	♆ Decl	♆ Lat	♇ Decl	♇ Lat
1	1S41	4N30	4N39	0S39	9S52	0S44	20S34	2N
6	1 36	4 29	4 43	0 38	9 48	0 44	20 33	2
11	1 30	4 29	4 48	0 38	9 44	0 44	20 33	2
16	1 24	4 28	4 53	0 38	9 40	0 44	20 32	2
21	1 17	4 27	4 58	0 38	9 36	0 44	20 32	2
26	1S11	4N27	5N04	0S38	9S31	0S44	20S31	2N

Day	⚴ Decl	⚴ Lat	⚵ Decl	⚵ Lat	⚶ Decl	⚶ Lat	Eris Decl	Eris Lat
1	5N12	27N49	3N54	14S33	20S53	1S08	3S09	12S
6	5 46	28 34	4 44	13 60	20 25	1 16	3 08	12
11	6 24	29 20	5 35	13 23	19 54	1 24	3 07	12
16	7 05	30 08	6 28	12 44	19 21	1 33	3 05	12
21	7 48	30 58	7 20	12 03	18 47	1 41	3 04	12
26	8N35	31N49	8N10	11S21	18S10	1S49	3S02	12S

Moon Phenomena

Max/0 Decl
dy hr mn
7 12:56 0 S
14 17:22 18S24
20 18:51 0 N
27 7:19 18N20

Perigee/Apogee
dy hr m kilometers
6 6:28 a 406150
19 7:23 p 357000

PH dy hr mn
○ 3 23:10 14♌48
☾ 12 3:51 23♏06
● 18 23:48 0♓00
☽ 25 17:15 6♊47

Max/0 Lat
dy hr mn
1 6:19 5S04
8 17:11 0 N
15 17:00 5N09
21 16:08 0 S
28 9:01 5S13

Void of Course Moon

Last Aspect	☽ Ingress
1 13:38 ♂ △	♌ 2 17:4
4 5:32 ♃ ☌	♍ 5 5:4
6 22:10 ♂ ☍	♎ 7 18:4
9 11:59 ☉ △	♏ 10 7:0
12 5:33 ♂ △	♐ 12 16:4
14 15:16 ♂ □	♑ 14 22:2
16 20:18 ♂ ⚹	♒ 17 0:1
18 23:48 ☉ ☌	♓ 18 23:4
19 23:03 ♇ ⚹	♈ 20 23:1
22 0:37 ♃ △	♉ 23 0:2
24 2:58 ♃ □	♊ 25 4:5
26 8:45 ♃ ⚹	♋ 27 12:5

DAILY ASPECTARIAN

1 Su ☽☍⚳ 1:02 · ☉⚻☽ 6:29 · ☽□♅ 8:53 · ☽☍♇ 10:43 · ☽△⚷ 12:37 · ☽△♂ 13:38 · ♀☌♆ 17:37 · ☽⚺♃ 18:39 · ☽⚼♄ 19:10 · ☉#☽ 21:52

2 M ☽⚼♆ 0:41 · ☽⚼♀ 1:27 · ☿⚺♀ 6:36 · ☽∥♃ 7:49 · ☉⚹♅ 12:31 · ☽⚼⚷ 18:14 · ☿⚺♆ 19:53 · ☽#☿ 20:42 · ☽⚼♂ 21:10

3 Tu ☽△♄ 0:54 · ☽☍☿ 5:31 · ☽⚻♆ 6:25 · ♀∥♆ 6:54 · ☽⚻♀ 10:32 · ☉⚺♇ 11:18 · ☽⚻⚳ 14:02 · ☽△♅ 20:20 · ☽⚻♇ 22:12 · ☉☍☽ 23:10

4 W ☽⚻⚷ 0:16 · ☉#♃ 2:45 · ☽⚻♂ 5:10 · ☽☌♃ 5:32 · ♂⚻♃ 10:06 · ☉⚺⚷ 12:46 · ☽#♆ 18:53 · ☽⚼⚳ 21:09

5 Th ☽#♀ 0:58 · ☽⚼♅ 2:36 · ☽⚼♇ 4:28 · ♀⚹⚳ 9:55 · ☿⚹♄ 11:40 · ☿∠♂ 11:53 · ☉∥☿ 12:07 · ☽⚻☿ 13:20 · ☽□♄ 13:28 · ☽☍♆ 18:57

6 F ☽△⚳ 4:32 · ☽#♂ 5:03 · ☽☍♀ 6:04 · ☽∥♅ 6:19 · ☽⚻♅ 9:07 · ☽△♇ 10:59 · ☽☍⚷ 13:13 · ☉⚻☽ 17:31 · ☽⚺♃ 17:35 · ☽⚼☿ 18:02 · ☉☍♃ 18:21 · ♂#♅ 18:57 · ☽☍♂ 22:10

7 Sa ☽#⚷ 2:51 · ♀⚺♅ 11:56 · ☿#♃ 12:38 · ☽∥⚷ 22:54 · ☽△☿ 23:09 · ☽∠♃ 23:46

8 Su ☽⚹♄ 2:45 · ☉⚼☽ 2:53 · ♀⚹♇ 5:55 · ☽⚻♆ 8:08 · ☽∥♂ 15:40 · ☽□⚳ 19:30 · ☽#♅ 19:43 · ☽☍♅ 22:14

9 M ☽□♇ 0:03 · ☽⚻♀ 2:06 · ☽⚻⚷ 2:24 · ♀☌⚷ 5:03 · ☽⚹♃ 5:46 · ☽∠♄ 9:12 · ☽∥♀ 9:31 · ☉△☽ 11:59 · ☽⚼♆ 14:28 · ☽⚻♂ 15:10 · ☿∠♀ 21:33

10 Tu ☽∥♆ 5:57 · ☽⚼⚷ 8:30 · ☽□☿ 9:51 · ♀⚻♃ 10:20 · ☽⚼♀ 11:28 · ☽⚺♄ 15:09 · ☽△♆ 20:16 · ☽⚼♂ 22:51

11 W ☽⚹⚳ 8:53 · ☽⚻♅ 9:50 · ☽⚹♇ 11:31 · ☽△⚷ 13:53 · ☿ D 14:58 · ☉∥☽ 16:02 · ☽□♃ 16:13 · ☽△♀ 19:50

12 Th ☉□☽ 3:51 · ☽△♂ 5:33 · ☽∠⚳ 14:14 · ☽⚼♅ 14:24 · ☽∠♇ 16:00 · ☽⚹☿ 19:22 · ⚳□♅ 20:28 · ☽#♃ 21:43

13 F ☽☌♄ 0:33 · ☽□♆ 5:17 · ♀#♅ 7:55 · ☽∥☿ 15:28 · ☽△♅ 17:55 · ☽⚺⚳ 18:28 · ☽⚺♇ 19:26 · ☽□⚷ 21:46 · ☽∠☿ 23:01 · ☽△♃ 23:08

14 Sa ☽□♀ 8:32 · ☉⚹☽ 14:47 · ☽□♂ 15:16

15 Su ☽⚼♃ 1:04 · ☽⚺☿ 1:48 · ☽⚺♄ 5:46 · ⚳☌♇ 8:20 · ☽⚹♆ 10:06 · ☽∥☿ 12:43 · ☉⚺♂ 17:21 · ☉∠☽ 18:18 · ☽□♅ 21:49 · ☽☌♇ 23:10 · ☽☌⚳ 23:32

16 M ☽⚹⚷ 1:27 · ☽⚻♃ 2:04 · ☽∠♄ 6:54 · ☽#♃ 8:35 · ☽∠♆ 11:05 · ☽⚹♀ 15:54 · ☽⚹♂ 20:18 · ☉⚺☽ 20:46

17 Tu ☽∠⚷ 2:00 · ☽☌☿ 5:01 · ☽⚹♄ 7:18 · ♂∥⚷ 10:17 · ☽⚺♆ 11:21 · ☽∠♀ 18:09 · ☽∠♂ 21:36 · ☽⚹♅ 22:30 · ☉∠♅ 22:39 · ☽⚺♇ 23:44

18 W ☽⚺⚳ 1:11 · ♃⚻⚷ 1:17 · ☽☍♃ 2:00 · ☽⚺⚷ 2:00 · ☉∥☽ 3:17 · ☽∥♆ 16:22 · ☉∠♇ 17:36 · ☽⚺♀ 19:55 · ☽∠♅ 22:13 · ☽⚺♂ 22:31 · ☽∠♇ 23:24 · ☉☌☽ 23:48 · ☉ ♓ 23:51

19 Th ☽∠⚳ 1:23 · ⚳⚻♃ 2:44 · ☽⚺☿ 6:33 · ☽□♄ 6:50 · ☽☌♆ 10:49 · ☿⚹♄ 13:07 · ☽#♅ 17:46 · ⚳⚹⚷ 18:27 · ☽⚺♅ 21:52 · ☽⚹♇ 23:03

20 F ♂ ♈ 0:12 · ☽⚻♃ 0:50 · ☽☌⚷ 1:25 · ☽⚹⚳ 1:34 · ♀∥⚷ 3:33 · ☽∠☿ 7:24 · ☉∠⚳ 12:08 · ☽∥⚷ 12:19 · ☽∥♀ 13:21 · ☽∥♂ 17:14 · ♀ ♈ 20:07 · ☽#♂ 20:16 · ☽#♀ 23:17 · ☽☌♀ 23:31

21 Sa ☽☌♂ 0:29 · ☽⚼♃ 0:30 · ♂⚼♃ 0:40 · ☽#⚷ 1:21 · ☉⚺☽ 2:40 · ☽△♄ 6:32 · ☽⚹☿ 8:45 · ♀⚼♃ 10:25 · ☽⚺♆ 10:38 · ☽∥♅ 20:36 · ☽☌♅ 22:05 · ☽□♇ 23:14

22 Su ☽△♃ 0:37 · ☽⚺⚷ 1:50 · ☽□⚳ 2:59 · ☉∠☽ 4:51 · ♀☌♂ 5:14 · ☽⚼♄ 7:05 · ♀#♂ 7:12 · ☽∠♆ 11:17 · ☿⚺♆ 18:09 · ☽#♆ 22:48

23 M ☉#☽ 1:32 · ☽∠⚷ 2:58 · ☽⚺♂ 4:38 · ☽⚺♀ 5:28 · ☉⚹☽ 7:55 · ☽⚻♄ 8:20 · ☽⚹♆ 12:41 · ☉□♄ 13:57 · ☽□☿ 13:58

24 Tu ☽⚺♅ 0:54 · ♀∥♂ 1:03 · ☽△♇ 2:02 · ☽□♃ 2:58 · ☽⚹⚷ 4:56 · ☉∥♆ 7:15 · ☽△⚳ 7:19 · ☽∠♂ 8:05 · ☽∠♀ 9:59 · ♀△♄ 14:59 · ♀#⚷ 22:34

25 W ☽∠♅ 3:36 · ☽⚼♇ 4:44 · ☽⚼⚳ 10:53 · ♂#⚷ 11:50 · ☽⚹♂ 12:36 · ☽☍♄ 13:26 · ☽⚹♀ 15:41 · ☉□☽ 17:15 · ☽∥♃ 18:04 · ☽□♆ 18:07 · ☽△☿ 23:49

26 Th ♂△♄ 3:09 · ☉☌♆ 4:56 · ☽#☿ 6:45 · ☽⚹♅ 7:13 · ☽⚻♇ 8:20 · ☽⚹♃ 8:45 · ☽□⚷ 11:35 · ☽⚻⚳ 15:25 · ♀⚺♆ 18:23

27 F ☽⚼☿ 6:36 · ☽∠♃ 12:52 · ☽⚻♄ 21:59 · ♃⚻♇ 23:12

28 Sa ☽□♂ 0:42 · ☽△♆ 3:00 · ☽□♀ 6:28 · ☉△☽ 6:55 · ☽⚻☿ 14:30 · ☽□♅ 16:51 · ☽⚺♃ 17:42 · ☽#☿ 17:46 · ☽☍♇ 17:54 · ☽∥♃ 20:07 · ☽△⚷ 21:30

LONGITUDE

Day	Sid.Time	☉	☽	☽ 12 hour	Mean☊	True☊	☿	♀	♂	⚳	♃	♄	⚷	♅	♆	♇
	h m s	° ' "	° ' "	° ' "	° '	° '	° '	° '	° '	° '	° '	° '	° '	° '	° '	° '
1 Su	10 33 56	10♓04 22	18♋05 19	24♋10 01	11♎48.8	10♎24.2	13♒42.3	10♈01.4	6♈53.7	19♑31.9	14♌51.2	4♐46.4	16♓49.4	14♈27.5	7♓22.3	14♑59.5
2 M	10 37 53	11 04 35	0♌12 24	6♌12 49	11 45.6	10R 19.3	14 53.6	11 14.9	7 39.5	19 52.6	14R 44.7	4 47.7	16 53.2	14 30.5	7 24.5	15 00.8
3 Tu	10 41 49	12 04 46	12 11 34	18 08 56	11 42.4	10 14.1	16 06.8	12 28.2	8 25.3	20 13.3	14 38.3	4 49.0	16 56.9	14 33.5	7 26.8	15 02.1
4 W	10 45 46	13 04 56	24 05 13	0♍00 39	11 39.2	10 09.1	17 21.7	13 41.5	9 11.0	20 33.8	14 32.0	4 50.1	17 00.6	14 36.5	7 29.1	15 03.4
5 Th	10 49 42	14 05 03	5♍55 30	11 50 00	11 36.1	10 04.9	18 38.4	14 54.8	9 56.7	20 54.3	14 25.9	4 51.1	17 04.3	14 39.5	7 31.4	15 04.7
6 F	10 53 39	15 05 08	17 44 22	23 38 53	11 32.9	10 01.9	19 56.6	16 08.0	10 42.3	21 14.6	14 19.9	4 52.0	17 08.0	14 42.6	7 33.6	15 06.0
7 Sa	10 57 35	16 05 12	29 33 47	5♎29 20	11 29.7	10D 00.1	21 16.5	17 21.1	11 27.9	21 34.8	14 14.1	4 52.9	17 11.8	14 45.7	7 35.9	15 07.2
8 Su	11 01 32	17 05 14	11♎25 50	17 23 36	11 26.5	9 59.7	22 37.8	18 34.2	12 13.5	21 55.0	14 08.3	4 53.6	17 15.5	14 48.8	7 38.1	15 08.4
9 M	11 05 28	18 05 14	23 22 58	29 24 18	11 23.3	10 00.3	24 00.6	19 47.2	12 59.0	22 15.0	14 02.8	4 54.2	17 19.2	14 51.9	7 40.4	15 09.6
10 Tu	11 09 25	19 05 12	5♏28 00	11♏34 28	11 20.2	10 01.6	25 24.8	21 00.2	13 44.5	22 34.8	13 57.4	4 54.7	17 22.9	14 55.1	7 42.6	15 10.7
11 W	11 13 22	20 05 09	17 44 09	23 57 31	11 17.0	10 03.2	26 50.4	22 13.0	14 29.9	22 54.6	13 52.1	4 55.1	17 26.6	14 58.3	7 44.9	15 11.8
12 Th	11 17 18	21 05 04	0♐15 02	6♐37 08	11 13.8	10 04.7	28 17.3	23 25.9	15 15.3	23 14.3	13 47.0	4 55.5	17 30.4	15 01.5	7 47.1	15 12.9
13 F	11 21 15	22 04 58	13 04 19	19 36 58	11 10.6	10R 05.6	29 45.6	24 38.6	16 00.7	23 33.8	13 42.0	4 55.7	17 34.1	15 04.7	7 49.3	15 14.0
14 Sa	11 25 11	23 04 49	26 15 29	3♑00 09	11 07.5	10 05.9	1♓15.1	25 51.3	16 46.0	23 53.2	13 37.2	4R 55.8	17 37.8	15 07.9	7 51.6	15 15.0
15 Su	11 29 08	24 04 39	9♑51 14	16 48 48	11 04.3	10 05.3	2 46.0	27 04.0	17 31.3	24 12.5	13 32.6	4 55.8	17 41.5	15 11.1	7 53.8	15 16.0
16 M	11 33 04	25 04 28	23 52 52	1♒03 15	11 01.1	10 04.0	4 18.1	28 16.5	18 16.5	24 31.6	13 28.1	4 55.7	17 45.2	15 14.4	7 56.0	15 17.0
17 Tu	11 37 01	26 04 15	8♒19 35	15 41 22	10 57.9	10 02.4	5 51.4	29 29.0	19 01.7	24 50.6	13 23.9	4 55.5	17 48.9	15 17.7	7 58.2	15 18.0
18 W	11 40 57	27 04 00	23 07 55	0♓38 21	10 54.8	10 00.7	7 26.0	0♉41.5	19 46.8	25 09.5	13 19.7	4 55.2	17 52.6	15 21.0	8 00.4	15 18.9
19 Th	11 44 54	28 03 43	8♓11 40	15 46 45	10 51.6	9 59.2	9 01.9	1 53.8	20 31.9	25 28.3	13 15.8	4 54.8	17 56.3	15 24.3	8 02.5	15 19.8
20 F	11 48 51	29 03 24	23 22 23	0♈57 23	10 48.4	9 58.3	10 39.0	3 06.1	21 17.0	25 46.9	13 12.0	4 54.3	18 00.0	15 27.6	8 04.7	15 20.6
21 Sa	11 52 47	0♈03 03	8♈30 31	16 00 40	10 45.2	9D 58.0	12 17.4	4 18.3	22 02.0	26 05.3	13 08.4	4 53.7	18 03.6	15 30.9	8 06.9	15 21.5
22 Su	11 56 44	1 02 40	23 26 48	0♉48 02	10 42.0	9 58.2	13 57.0	5 30.5	22 46.9	26 23.7	13 05.0	4 53.0	18 07.3	15 34.3	8 09.0	15 22.3
23 M	12 00 40	2 02 16	8♉03 39	15 13 05	10 38.9	9 58.7	15 37.9	6 42.5	23 31.9	26 41.8	13 01.8	4 52.2	18 10.9	15 37.6	8 11.1	15 23.1
24 Tu	12 04 37	3 01 48	22 15 59	29 12 09	10 35.7	9 59.4	17 20.1	7 54.5	24 16.7	26 59.9	12 58.7	4 51.3	18 14.5	15 41.0	8 13.2	15 23.8
25 W	12 08 33	4 01 19	6♊01 31	12♊44 11	10 32.5	10 00.0	19 03.5	9 06.4	25 01.6	27 17.7	12 55.9	4 50.3	18 18.2	15 44.3	8 15.4	15 24.5
26 Th	12 12 30	5 00 47	19 20 23	25 50 26	10 29.3	10 00.4	20 48.3	10 18.2	25 46.3	27 35.5	12 53.2	4 49.3	18 21.8	15 47.7	8 17.4	15 25.2
27 F	12 16 26	6 00 14	2♋14 42	8♋33 40	10 26.1	10R 00.6	22 34.3	11 30.0	26 31.1	27 53.1	12 50.7	4 48.1	18 25.4	15 51.1	8 19.5	15 25.9
28 Sa	12 20 23	6 59 37	14 47 49	20 57 40	10 23.0	10 00.6	24 21.7	12 41.6	27 15.8	28 10.5	12 48.4	4 46.8	18 28.9	15 54.5	8 21.6	15 26.5
29 Su	12 24 20	7 58 59	27 03 45	3♌06 38	10 19.8	10 00.4	26 10.4	13 53.2	28 00.4	28 27.7	12 46.3	4 45.4	18 32.5	15 57.9	8 23.6	15 27.1
30 M	12 28 16	8 58 18	9♌06 48	15 04 48	10 16.6	10 00.3	28 00.4	15 04.7	28 45.0	28 44.8	12 44.3	4 43.9	18 36.0	16 01.3	8 25.7	15 27.7
31 Tu	12 32 13	9♈57 35	21 01 07	26 56 14	10♎13.4	10♎00.2	29♓51.8	16♉16.0	29♈29.5	29♑01.8	12♌42.6	4♐42.3	18♓39.6	16♈04.7	8♓27.7	15♑28.2

1st of Month

Julian Day #
2457082.5
Obliquity
23°26'06"
SVP 5♓02'48"
GC 27♐03.1
Eris 22♈17.8

Day	⚴
1	22♐40.4
6	24 00.6
11	25 14.8
16	26 22.7
21	27 23.4
26	28 16.6
31	29 01.4

Day	⚵
1	3♌50.8R
6	3 27.3R
11	3 15.2R
16	3 14.5
21	3 24.7
26	3 45.3
31	4 15.6

Day	⚶
1	16♒11.6
6	18 43.9
11	21 15.0
16	23 44.8
21	26 13.2
26	28 40.0
31	1♓05.2

DECLINATION and LATITUDE

Day	☉ Decl	☽ Decl	☽ Lat	☽12h Decl	☿ Decl	☿ Lat	♀ Decl	♀ Lat	♂ Decl	♂ Lat	⚳ Decl	⚳ Lat	♃ Decl	♃ Lat	♄ Decl	♄ Lat
1 Su	7S47	17N06	5S10	16N17	17S23	0S42	3N19	0S43	2N17	0S29	24S06	2S07	17N19	0N59	19S04	2N03
2 M	7 25	15 18	4 54	14 10	17 10	0 51	3 50	0 40	2 36	0 29	24 05	2 09	17 21	0 59	19 04	2 04
3 Tu	7 02	12 53	4 26	11 28	16 56	0 59	4 21	0 37	2 55	0 28	24 04	2 11	17 23	0 59	19 04	2 04
4 W	6 39	9 56	3 46	8 18	16 41	1 06	4 52	0 35	3 13	0 27	24 04	2 13	17 25	0 59	19 04	2 04
5 Th	6 16	6 36	2 57	4 50	16 24	1 14	5 23	0 32	3 32	0 26	24 03	2 16	17 26	0 59	19 04	2 04
6 F	5 53	3 01	1 60	1 10	16 06	1 21	5 54	0 29	3 51	0 26	24 02	2 18	17 28	0 59	19 04	2 04
7 Sa	5 29	0S42	0 57	2S34	15 47	1 27	6 25	0 26	4 09	0 25	24 01	2 20	17 30	0 59	19 04	2 04
8 Su	5 06	4 24	0N08	6 12	15 26	1 33	6 55	0 23	4 27	0 24	23 60	2 23	17 32	0 59	19 04	2 05
9 M	4 43	7 57	1 13	9 37	15 04	1 39	7 25	0 20	4 46	0 24	23 59	2 25	17 33	0 59	19 04	2 05
10 Tu	4 19	11 12	2 16	12 40	14 41	1 44	7 56	0 17	5 04	0 23	23 58	2 27	17 35	0 59	19 04	2 05
11 W	3 56	14 01	3 14	15 12	14 17	1 49	8 26	0 14	5 22	0 22	23 57	2 30	17 36	0 59	19 04	2 05
12 Th	3 32	16 14	4 03	17 04	13 51	1 54	8 55	0 11	5 41	0 21	23 56	2 32	17 38	0 59	19 04	2 05
13 F	3 08	17 42	4 42	18 06	13 24	1 58	9 25	0 08	5 59	0 21	23 55	2 34	17 39	0 59	19 03	2 05
14 Sa	2 45	18 15	5 08	18 10	12 56	2 02	9 54	0 05	6 17	0 20	23 54	2 37	17 40	0 59	19 03	2 06
15 Su	2 21	17 48	5 17	17 10	12 26	2 05	10 24	0 02	6 35	0 19	23 53	2 39	17 42	0 59	19 03	2 06
16 M	1 57	16 16	5 08	15 06	11 55	2 08	10 53	0N01	6 53	0 19	23 52	2 42	17 43	0 59	19 03	2 06
17 Tu	1 34	13 41	4 39	12 01	11 23	2 11	11 21	0 04	7 10	0 18	23 51	2 44	17 44	0 59	19 03	2 06
18 W	1 10	10 09	3 52	8 06	10 50	2 13	11 50	0 08	7 28	0 17	23 50	2 47	17 45	0 59	19 03	2 06
19 Th	0 46	5 54	2 47	3 36	10 16	2 15	12 18	0 11	7 46	0 17	23 49	2 49	17 46	0 59	19 02	2 06
20 F	0 23	1 14	1 31	1N09	9 40	2 16	12 46	0 14	8 03	0 16	23 48	2 52	17 47	0 59	19 02	2 07
21 Sa	0N01	3N30	0 08	5 47	9 03	2 17	13 13	0 17	8 21	0 15	23 47	2 54	17 48	0 59	19 02	2 07
22 Su	0 25	7 57	1S14	9 59	8 25	2 17	13 41	0 21	8 38	0 14	23 46	2 57	17 49	0 59	19 02	2 07
23 M	0 49	11 50	2 30	13 28	7 46	2 17	14 08	0 24	8 55	0 14	23 45	2 60	17 50	0 58	19 01	2 07
24 Tu	1 12	14 53	3 34	16 03	7 06	2 17	14 34	0 27	9 13	0 13	23 44	3 02	17 51	0 58	19 01	2 07
25 W	1 36	16 59	4 24	17 39	6 25	2 16	15 01	0 31	9 30	0 12	23 43	3 05	17 52	0 58	19 01	2 07
26 Th	1 59	18 04	4 58	18 14	5 42	2 14	15 27	0 34	9 47	0 12	23 42	3 07	17 52	0 58	19 00	2 07
27 F	2 23	18 10	5 15	17 52	4 58	2 12	15 52	0 37	10 03	0 11	23 41	3 10	17 53	0 58	18 60	2 08
28 Sa	2 47	17 22	5 17	16 40	4 13	2 10	16 17	0 41	10 20	0 10	23 40	3 13	17 54	0 58	18 60	2 08
29 Su	3 10	15 46	5 04	14 43	3 28	2 07	16 42	0 44	10 37	0 10	23 39	3 16	17 54	0 58	18 59	2 08
30 M	3 33	13 30	4 38	12 09	2 41	2 03	17 07	0 47	10 53	0 09	23 39	3 18	17 55	0 58	18 59	2 08
31 Tu	3N57	10N42	4S00	9N07	1S53	1S59	17N31	0N51	11N10	0S08	23S38	3S21	17N55	0N58	18S58	2N08

Day	⚷ Decl	⚷ Lat	♅ Decl	♅ Lat	♆ Decl	♆ Lat	♇ Decl	♇ Lat
1	1S07	4N26	5N07	0S38	9S29	0S44	20S31	2N06
6	0 60	4 26	5 13	0 38	9 25	0 44	20 30	2 05
11	0 53	4 26	5 19	0 38	9 21	0 44	20 30	2 05
16	0 46	4 26	5 25	0 37	9 17	0 44	20 29	2 05
21	0 39	4 25	5 32	0 37	9 13	0 44	20 29	2 05
26	0 32	4 25	5 38	0 37	9 09	0 44	20 29	2 05
31	0S25	4N26	5N45	0S37	9S05	0S44	20S29	2N05

Day	⚴ Decl	⚴ Lat	⚵ Decl	⚵ Lat	⚶ Decl	⚶ Lat	Eris Decl	Eris Lat
1	9N05	32N21	8N39	10S56	17S48	1S54	3S01	12S36
6	9 56	33 15	9 25	10 14	17 09	2 03	3 00	12 35
11	10 49	34 11	10 08	9 33	16 30	2 12	2 59	12 34
16	11 45	35 09	10 47	8 52	15 49	2 21	2 57	12 34
21	12 43	36 08	11 22	8 14	15 07	2 30	2 56	12 33
26	13 43	37 08	11 54	7 37	14 25	2 39	2 54	12 33
31	14N43	38N09	12N21	7S02	13S43	2S48	2S53	12S33

Moon Phenomena

Max/0 Decl
dy hr mn
6 19:29 0 S
14 1:33 18S16
20 6:15 0 N
26 14:33 18N14

Max/0 Lat
dy hr mn
7 21:06 0 N
15 0:17 5N17
21 2:19 0 S
27 14:47 5S18

Perigee/Apogee
dy hr m kilometers
5 7:37 a 406385
19 19:50 p 357586

PH dy hr mn
○ 5 18:07 14♍50
☾ 13 17:49 22♐49
● 20 9:37 29♓27
• 20 9:47 T 02'47"
☽ 27 7:44 6♋19

Void of Course Moon

Last Aspect			☽ Ingress		
28 17:54	♇	☍	♌	1	23:35
3 8:49	☿	☍	♍	4	11:59
5 18:38	♇	△	♎	7	0:53
9 1:25	☿	△	♏	9	13:11
11 19:47	☿	□	♐	11	23:32
13 23:12	♀	△	♑	14	6:41
16 8:03	♀	□	♒	16	10:15
17 18:19	♂	✶	♓	18	10:59
20 9:37	☉	☌	♈	20	10:29
21 22:52	♂	☌	♉	22	10:41
23 14:26	☿	✶	♊	24	13:24
26 12:36	♂	✶	♋	26	19:46
29 1:59	♂	□	♌	29	5:49
30 13:58	♅	△	♍	31	18:13

DAILY ASPECTARIAN

1 Su
☽☍⚳ 2:55
☽⚼♄ 3:19
☉⚺♀ 5:21
☿#♃ 6:46
☽⚼♆ 8:28
☉⚼☽ 15:03
♂⚺♆ 15:46
☿✶♅ 15:56
⚳∠♄ 17:56
☿☍♃ 21:16

2 M
☿⚺♇ 2:26
☽⚼⚷ 3:22
☽△♄ 9:11
☽⚻♆ 14:26
☽△♂ 15:54
☉⚻☽ 23:45

3 Tu
☽△♀ 0:37
☽△♅ 4:47
☽☌♃ 4:53
☽⚻♇ 5:44
☽☍☿ 8:49
☽⚻⚷ 9:38
♃△♅ 12:26
☽⚻⚳ 16:40
☿⚺⚷ 16:57

4 W
☽⚼♂ 0:12
☽#♆ 3:43
☽⚼♀ 10:24
☽⚼♅ 11:14
☽⚼♇ 12:07
♀∥♅ 14:50
♀△♃ 15:15
♀☌♅ 18:47
☽□♄ 21:49
☽⚼⚳ 23:57

5 Th
☉#☽ 2:36
☽☍♆ 3:15
♀□♇ 3:18
☽∥♀ 7:13
☉⚻♃ 7:34
☽⚻♂ 8:44
☽∥♅ 9:28
☉⚺♅ 14:31
☽⚺♃ 17:08
☽⚻♅ 17:49
☉☍☽ 18:07
☽△♇ 18:38
☽∥♂ 18:58
☽⚻♀ 20:22
☽☍⚷ 22:46
☉#♀ 23:23

6 F
☉✶♇ 0:20
☽⚻☿ 5:02
☽△⚳ 7:20
☽#⚷ 13:09
♀⚺⚷ 20:45
☽∠♃ 23:20

7 Sa
☽∥⚷ 1:44
☿⚺⚳ 7:16
☽✶♄ 10:47
☉#♅ 14:41
☽⚼☿ 15:20
☽⚻♆ 16:19

8 Su
☽#♂ 0:25
☽☍♂ 1:43
☉∥☽ 4:11
☉☌⚷ 4:22
☽✶♃ 5:25
☽#♅ 5:43
☽☍♅ 6:51
☽□♇ 7:29
☽⚻⚷ 11:47
☉⚻☽ 12:26
☽☍♀ 15:59
☽∠♄ 17:02
☽#♀ 19:44
☽□⚳ 21:40
☉#♂ 22:07
☽⚼♆ 22:35

9 M
☽△☿ 1:25
♀⚼♄ 2:19
☽∥♆ 10:08
☽⚼⚷ 17:52
☉⚼☽ 21:02
☽⚺♄ 22:54

10 Tu
☽△♆ 4:26
♂△♃ 6:05
⚳∠♆ 10:39
☽□♃ 16:32
☽⚻♂ 17:18
☽⚻♅ 18:36
☽✶♇ 19:04
♂∥♅ 19:26
☽△⚷ 23:26

11 W
☽∥☿ 2:10
☉△☽ 4:57
☽⚻♀ 9:35
☽✶⚳ 10:15
♀∠♆ 10:49
♂☌♅ 16:07
♀□⚳ 18:46
☽□☿ 19:47
♂□♇ 22:42
☽⚼♅ 23:34
☽∠♇ 23:56

12 Th
☽⚼♂ 0:01
☽☌♄ 8:49
☽□♆ 14:13
☽∠⚳ 15:25
☽⚼♀ 16:59
♀#♆ 19:13
☽#♃ 22:59

13 F
☽△♃ 1:09
☽△♅ 3:43
☿ ♓ 3:53
☽⚺♇ 3:59
☿∠♅ 5:20
☽△♂ 5:45
☿∠♇ 7:44
☽□⚷ 8:18
☉□☽ 17:49
☽⚺⚳ 19:38
⚵ D 19:43
☽△♀ 23:12

14 Sa
☽⚼♃ 4:12
☽✶☿ 10:01
♄ R 15:03
☽⚺♄ 15:24
☿∠♂ 16:19
☽✶♆ 20:35

15 Su
☽#♃ 2:28
☉✶⚳ 4:37
♂⚺⚷ 5:56
☽⚻♃ 6:21
☽□♅ 9:15
☽☌♇ 9:22
☽✶⚷ 13:34
☽□♂ 13:57
☽∠☿ 15:17
☽∠♄ 17:19
☽∠♆ 22:24

16 M
☽☌⚳ 1:07
☉✶☽ 2:10
☽□♀ 8:03
☿□♄ 9:42
☽∠⚷ 14:53
☽✶♄ 18:24
☽⚺☿ 19:27
☽⚺♆ 23:25

17 Tu
☿#♀ 0:50
♅□♇ 2:55
☉∠☽ 4:49
☽☍♃ 8:14
♀ ♉ 10:16
☽⚺♇ 11:23
☽✶♅ 11:24
☽#♀ 14:33
☽⚺⚷ 15:30
☽✶♂ 18:19
☽∥☿ 19:01

18 W
☽⚺⚳ 3:19
♂⚼♄ 4:26
☽∥♆ 5:26
☉⚺☽ 6:45
☿☌♆ 8:50
☽∠♇ 11:30
☽∠♅ 11:35
☽✶♀ 13:08
☽#♂ 14:33
☽□♄ 18:48
☽∠♂ 19:33
☽☌♆ 23:45

19 Th
☽☌☿ 1:29
☽#♅ 2:12
☽∠⚳ 3:41
☉⚼♃ 4:34
☉∥⚷ 5:05
☽⚻♃ 7:59
☽✶♇ 11:18
☽⚺♅ 11:27
☽∠♀ 14:57
☽☌⚷ 15:28
☽⚺♂ 20:31
♀∠⚷ 21:51

20 F
☿∠⚳ 2:23
☽∥⚷ 2:54
☽✶⚳ 3:53
☉∥☽ 4:45
☉#☽ 7:31
☽⚼♃ 7:36
☽#⚷ 9:34
☉☌☽ 9:37
☽⚺♀ 16:44
☿∥♆ 17:59
☽△♄ 18:15
☉ ♈ 22:46
☽⚺♆ 23:22

21 Sa
☽⚺☿ 6:47
☽△♃ 7:22
☽∥♅ 10:43
☽□♇ 10:58
☽☌♅ 11:15
♀⚻♄ 11:40
☿⚻♃ 11:55
☽⚺⚷ 15:22
☽⚼♄ 18:14
☿#♂ 18:33
☽☌♂ 22:52
☽∠♆ 23:31

22 Su
☽#☿ 2:20
☽∥♂ 4:13
☽□⚳ 4:54
☽#♆ 7:13
☽∠☿ 10:08
☉#⚷ 11:48
♂∠♆ 12:22
☉⚺☽ 13:18
☽∠⚷ 15:53
☽⚻♄ 18:43
☿✶♇ 20:28
☽☌♀ 21:33
☿⚺♅ 23:56

23 M
☽✶♆ 0:12
☽□♃ 8:17
☽△♇ 12:18
☽⚺♅ 12:45
☽✶☿ 14:26
☉∠☽ 16:13
☽✶⚷ 17:06
☽∥♀ 20:40
♂#♆ 20:55

24 Tu
☽⚺♂ 3:40
♀✶♆ 6:26
☽△⚳ 8:21
☿☌⚷ 13:08
☽⚼♇ 14:06
☽∠♅ 14:39
☉✶☽ 20:11
☽☍♄ 21:54

25 W
☽□♆ 3:59
☽⚺♀ 6:01
☽∠♂ 7:33
☽⚼⚳ 11:28
☽✶♃ 12:19
☽⚻♇ 16:51
☽✶♅ 17:30
☽∥♃ 17:37
☉△♄ 19:26
☽□⚷ 22:12

26 Th
☿#♅ 1:55
☽□☿ 3:06
☽∠♀ 12:08
☽✶♂ 12:36
☽⚻⚳ 15:37
☽∠♃ 15:46

27 F
☽⚻♄ 4:50
☉□☽ 7:44
☽∥♃ 11:28
☽△♆ 11:35
☽✶♀ 19:30
☽⚺♃ 20:10

28 Sa
☽☍♇ 1:15
☽□♅ 2:10
♀□♃ 2:12
☽△⚷ 7:12
☽⚼♄ 9:40
☽∥♀ 13:54
☽⚼♆ 16:45
⚶ ♓ 17:54
☽△☿ 21:56

29 Su
☽□♂ 1:59
☽☍⚳ 2:50
☉#☿ 6:03
☉⚺♆ 10:20
☽⚼⚷ 12:55
☽△♄ 15:15
☿⚼♃ 20:34
☽⚻♆ 22:37
☉△☽ 23:41
♂□⚳ 23:54

30 M
☽☌♃ 7:16
♀△♇ 7:48
☽⚼☿ 9:16
☿✶⚳ 11:20
☽⚻♇ 12:47
☽□♀ 13:20
☽△♅ 13:58
☿⚺♂ 16:02
☽⚻⚷ 19:12
♀⚺♅ 20:00
☽∥♂ 20:34

31 Tu
☿ ♈ 1:45
☉⚼☽ 8:43
☽#♆ 12:21
♂ ♉ 16:28
☽⚻⚳ 16:39
☽△♂ 18:20
☽⚼♇ 19:11
☽⚼♅ 20:31
☽⚻☿ 21:20

April 2015

LONGITUDE

Day	Sid.Time	☉	☽	☽ 12 hour	Mean ☊	True ☊	☿	♀	♂	⚳	♃	♄	⚷	♅	♆	♇
	h m s	° ' "	° ' "	° ' "	° '	° '	° '	° '	° '	° '	° '	° '	° '	° '	° '	° '
1 W	12 36 09	10♈56 49	2♍50 34	8♍44 34	10♎10.3	10♎00.3	1♈44.6	17♉27.3	0♉14.0	29♑18.6	12♌41.0	4♐40.7	18♓43.1	16♈08.1	8♓29.7	15♑28.7
2 Th	12 40 06	11 56 01	14 38 35	20 33 00	10 07.1	10 00.4	3 38.7	18 38.5	0 58.4	29 35.2	12R 39.7	4R 38.9	18 46.6	16 11.6	8 31.7	15 29.2
3 F	12 44 02	12 55 12	26 28 08	2♎24 18	10 03.9	10 00.6	5 34.2	19 49.6	1 42.8	29 51.6	12 38.5	4 37.1	18 50.0	16 15.0	8 33.6	15 29.7
4 Sa	12 47 59	13 54 20	8♎21 46	14 20 49	10 00.7	10R 00.7	7 30.9	21 00.6	2 27.1	0♒07.9	12 37.5	4 35.1	18 53.5	16 18.4	8 35.6	15 30.1
5 Su	12 51 55	14 53 26	20 21 40	26 24 33	9 57.5	10 00.6	9 29.0	22 11.5	3 11.4	0 24.0	12 36.7	4 33.1	18 56.9	16 21.8	8 37.5	15 30.5
6 M	12 55 52	15 52 30	2♏29 43	8♏37 21	9 54.4	10 00.3	11 28.4	23 22.3	3 55.6	0 39.9	12 36.1	4 31.0	19 00.3	16 25.3	8 39.4	15 30.8
7 Tu	12 59 48	16 51 32	14 47 41	21 00 56	9 51.2	9 59.6	13 29.0	24 33.0	4 39.8	0 55.6	12 35.7	4 28.8	19 03.7	16 28.7	8 41.3	15 31.2
8 W	13 03 45	17 50 32	27 17 18	3♐37 00	9 48.0	9 58.6	15 30.8	25 43.6	5 23.9	1 11.2	12D 35.5	4 26.5	19 07.1	16 32.1	8 43.2	15 31.5
9 Th	13 07 42	18 49 30	10♐00 15	16 27 18	9 44.8	9 57.5	17 33.6	26 54.0	6 08.0	1 26.5	12 35.4	4 24.1	19 10.4	16 35.6	8 45.1	15 31.7
10 F	13 11 38	19 48 27	22 58 20	29 33 35	9 41.6	9 56.4	19 37.5	28 04.4	6 52.1	1 41.7	12 35.6	4 21.7	19 13.8	16 39.0	8 46.9	15 32.0
11 Sa	13 15 35	20 47 21	6♑13 14	12♑57 27	9 38.5	9 55.6	21 42.2	29 14.7	7 36.0	1 56.7	12 35.9	4 19.1	19 17.1	16 42.4	8 48.7	15 32.2
12 Su	13 19 31	21 46 15	19 46 22	26 40 04	9 35.3	9D 55.3	23 47.5	0♊24.9	8 20.0	2 11.5	12 36.5	4 16.5	19 20.3	16 45.8	8 50.5	15 32.4
13 M	13 23 28	22 45 06	3♒38 34	10♒41 49	9 32.1	9 55.5	25 53.4	1 34.9	9 03.9	2 26.1	12 37.2	4 13.8	19 23.6	16 49.3	8 52.3	15 32.5
14 Tu	13 27 24	23 43 56	17 49 39	25 01 51	9 28.9	9 56.2	27 59.6	2 44.9	9 47.7	2 40.5	12 38.1	4 11.0	19 26.8	16 52.7	8 54.1	15 32.6
15 W	13 31 21	24 42 43	2♓18 01	9♓37 40	9 25.8	9 57.2	0♉05.9	3 54.7	10 31.5	2 54.7	12 39.1	4 08.1	19 30.0	16 56.1	8 55.8	15 32.7
16 Th	13 35 17	25 41 30	17 00 14	24 24 57	9 22.6	9 58.3	2 12.0	5 04.4	11 15.3	3 08.7	12 40.4	4 05.2	19 33.2	16 59.5	8 57.5	15 32.7
17 F	13 39 14	26 40 14	1♈51 02	9♈17 35	9 19.4	9R 59.0	4 17.6	6 14.0	11 59.0	3 22.5	12 41.9	4 02.2	19 36.3	17 02.9	8 59.2	15R 32.8
18 Sa	13 43 11	27 38 57	16 43 39	24 08 16	9 16.2	9 59.1	6 22.4	7 23.5	12 42.6	3 36.1	12 43.5	3 59.1	19 39.4	17 06.3	9 00.8	15 32.8
19 Su	13 47 07	28 37 37	1♉30 27	8♉49 19	9 13.0	9 58.2	8 26.0	8 32.9	13 26.3	3 49.4	12 45.3	3 55.9	19 42.5	17 09.7	9 02.5	15 32.7
20 M	13 51 04	29 36 16	16 04 01	23 13 50	9 09.9	9 56.3	10 28.3	9 42.1	14 09.8	4 02.5	12 47.3	3 52.7	19 45.5	17 13.0	9 04.1	15 32.6
21 Tu	13 55 00	0♉34 53	0♊18 10	7♊16 34	9 06.7	9 53.7	12 28.7	10 51.2	14 53.3	4 15.5	12 49.5	3 49.3	19 48.5	17 16.4	9 05.7	15 32.5
22 W	13 58 57	1 33 28	14 08 42	20 54 26	9 03.5	9 50.6	14 27.0	12 00.2	15 36.8	4 28.1	12 51.9	3 46.0	19 51.5	17 19.8	9 07.3	15 32.4
23 Th	14 02 53	2 32 00	27 33 46	4♋06 48	9 00.3	9 47.6	16 22.9	13 09.1	16 20.2	4 40.6	12 54.4	3 42.5	19 54.5	17 23.1	9 08.8	15 32.3
24 F	14 06 50	3 30 31	10♋33 47	16 55 03	8 57.2	9 45.1	18 16.1	14 17.8	17 03.5	4 52.8	12 57.2	3 39.0	19 57.4	17 26.4	9 10.3	15 32.1
25 Sa	14 10 46	4 28 59	23 11 02	29 22 13	8 54.0	9D 43.5	20 06.3	15 26.3	17 46.8	5 04.8	13 00.1	3 35.5	20 00.3	17 29.8	9 11.8	15 31.8
26 Su	14 14 43	5 27 25	5♌29 09	11♌32 25	8 50.8	9 43.0	21 53.3	16 34.8	18 30.1	5 16.5	13 03.2	3 31.8	20 03.1	17 33.1	9 13.3	15 31.6
27 M	14 18 40	6 25 49	17 32 37	23 30 22	8 47.6	9 43.5	23 36.8	17 43.0	19 13.3	5 28.0	13 06.4	3 28.2	20 05.9	17 36.4	9 14.7	15 31.3
28 Tu	14 22 36	7 24 11	29 26 16	5♍20 56	8 44.5	9 44.9	25 16.7	18 51.2	19 56.4	5 39.3	13 09.8	3 24.4	20 08.7	17 39.7	9 16.2	15 31.0
29 W	14 26 33	8 22 31	11♍14 58	17 08 54	8 41.3	9 46.6	26 52.7	19 59.1	20 39.5	5 50.3	13 13.4	3 20.6	20 11.5	17 42.9	9 17.5	15 30.7
30 Th	14 30 29	9♉20 49	23 03 19	28 58 40	8♎38.1	9♎48.3	28♉24.8	21♊06.9	21♉22.6	6♒01.0	13♌17.2	3♐16.8	20♓14.2	17♈46.2	9♓18.9	15♑30.3

1st of Month

Julian Day # 2457113.5
Obliquity 23°26'06"
SVP 5♓02'46"
GC 27♐03.1
Eris 22♈35.8

Day	⚴
1	29♐09.3
6	29 43.5
11	0♑08.1
16	0 22.4
21	0 25.9R
26	0 18.1R

Day	⚵
1	4♌22.7
6	5 03.6
11	5 52.6
16	6 48.8
21	7 51.8
26	9 00.9

Day	⚶
1	1♓34.1
6	3 57.1
11	6 18.3
16	8 37.6
21	10 54.6
26	13 09.3

DECLINATION and LATITUDE

Day	☉ Decl	☽ Decl	☽ Lat	☽12h Decl	☿ Decl	☿ Lat	♀ Decl	♀ Lat	♂ Decl	♂ Lat	⚳ Decl	⚳ Lat	♃ Decl	♃ Lat	♄ Decl	♄ Lat
1 W	4N20	7N28	3S12	5N44	1S04	1S55	17N54	0N54	11N26	0S08	23S37	3S24	17N55	0N58	18S58	2N08
2 Th	4 43	3 57	2 16	2 07	0 14	1 50	18 17	0 57	11 42	0 07	23 36	3 27	17 56	0 58	18 58	2 08
3 F	5 06	0 16	1 15	1S36	0N37	1 44	18 40	1 01	11 58	0 06	23 35	3 30	17 56	0 58	18 57	2 09
4 Sa	5 29	3S27	0 09	5 17	1 28	1 38	19 02	1 04	12 14	0 06	23 35	3 32	17 56	0 58	18 57	2 09
5 Su	5 52	7 04	0N57	8 47	2 21	1 32	19 24	1 07	12 30	0 05	23 34	3 35	17 56	0 58	18 56	2 09
6 M	6 15	10 26	2 02	11 58	3 14	1 25	19 45	1 11	12 46	0 04	23 33	3 38	17 57	0 58	18 56	2 09
7 Tu	6 37	13 23	3 02	14 39	4 08	1 17	20 06	1 14	13 01	0 04	23 33	3 41	17 57	0 57	18 55	2 09
8 W	6 60	15 45	3 54	16 41	5 02	1 09	20 26	1 17	13 16	0 03	23 32	3 44	17 57	0 57	18 55	2 09
9 Th	7 22	17 25	4 35	17 55	5 57	1 01	20 46	1 20	13 32	0 02	23 32	3 47	17 56	0 57	18 54	2 09
10 F	7 45	18 12	5 03	18 14	6 52	0 52	21 05	1 24	13 47	0 01	23 31	3 50	17 56	0 57	18 53	2 09
11 Sa	8 07	18 01	5 17	17 33	7 48	0 43	21 24	1 27	14 02	0 01	23 31	3 53	17 56	0 57	18 53	2 10
12 Su	8 29	16 49	5 13	15 51	8 43	0 33	21 42	1 30	14 17	0 00	23 30	3 56	17 56	0 57	18 52	2 10
13 M	8 51	14 37	4 51	13 10	9 39	0 23	21 60	1 33	14 31	0N01	23 30	3 60	17 56	0 57	18 52	2 10
14 Tu	9 13	11 30	4 11	9 39	10 34	0 12	22 17	1 36	14 46	0 01	23 30	4 03	17 55	0 57	18 51	2 10
15 W	9 34	7 38	3 14	5 29	11 29	0 02	22 33	1 39	15 00	0 02	23 29	4 06	17 55	0 57	18 50	2 10
16 Th	9 56	3 14	2 04	0 55	12 23	0N09	22 49	1 42	15 15	0 02	23 29	4 09	17 55	0 57	18 50	2 10
17 F	10 17	1N25	0 45	3N44	13 16	0 20	23 04	1 45	15 29	0 03	23 29	4 12	17 54	0 57	18 49	2 10
18 Sa	10 38	5 60	0S37	8 09	14 08	0 31	23 19	1 48	15 43	0 04	23 29	4 16	17 53	0 57	18 48	2 10
19 Su	10 59	10 11	1 56	12 01	14 59	0 42	23 33	1 51	15 56	0 04	23 29	4 19	17 53	0 56	18 48	2 10
20 M	11 20	13 40	3 06	15 05	15 48	0 53	23 47	1 54	16 10	0 05	23 29	4 22	17 52	0 56	18 47	2 10
21 Tu	11 40	16 15	4 03	17 09	16 35	1 04	23 60	1 57	16 23	0 06	23 29	4 26	17 52	0 56	18 46	2 11
22 W	12 01	17 47	4 44	18 10	17 21	1 14	24 12	1 60	16 37	0 06	23 29	4 29	17 51	0 56	18 46	2 11
23 Th	12 21	18 17	5 08	18 09	18 05	1 24	24 24	2 02	16 50	0 07	23 30	4 32	17 50	0 56	18 45	2 11
24 F	12 41	17 47	5 15	17 12	18 46	1 34	24 35	2 05	17 03	0 08	23 30	4 36	17 49	0 56	18 44	2 11
25 Sa	13 01	16 24	5 07	15 26	19 25	1 43	24 45	2 08	17 16	0 08	23 30	4 39	17 48	0 56	18 44	2 11
26 Su	13 20	14 18	4 44	13 01	20 02	1 52	24 55	2 10	17 28	0 09	23 31	4 43	17 47	0 56	18 43	2 11
27 M	13 40	11 37	4 09	10 06	20 36	1 60	25 04	2 12	17 41	0 10	23 31	4 46	17 46	0 56	18 42	2 11
28 Tu	13 59	8 29	3 24	6 47	21 08	2 07	25 12	2 15	17 53	0 10	23 32	4 50	17 45	0 56	18 41	2 11
29 W	14 18	5 01	2 31	3 13	21 37	2 14	25 20	2 17	18 05	0 11	23 33	4 53	17 44	0 56	18 41	2 11
30 Th	14N36	1N22	1S31	0S30	22N04	2N20	25N27	2N19	18N17	0N11	23S33	4S57	17N43	0N55	18S40	2N11

Day	⚷ Decl	⚷ Lat	♅ Decl	♅ Lat	♆ Decl	♆ Lat	♇ Decl	♇ Lat
1	0S23	4N26	5N46	0S37	9S04	0S44	20S28	2N05
6	0 16	4 26	5 53	0 37	9 01	0 45	20 28	2 04
11	0 10	4 26	5 60	0 37	8 57	0 45	20 28	2 04
16	0 03	4 27	6 06	0 37	8 54	0 45	20 29	2 04
21	0N04	4 27	6 13	0 37	8 51	0 45	20 29	2 04
26	0 10	4 28	6 19	0 37	8 48	0 45	20 29	2 04

Day	⚴ Decl	⚴ Lat	⚵ Decl	⚵ Lat	⚶ Decl	⚶ Lat	Eris Decl	Eris Lat
1	14N56	38N22	12N26	6S55	13S34	2S50	2S52	12S33
6	15 57	39 23	12 48	6 22	12 51	3 00	2 51	12 32
11	16 59	40 25	13 07	5 51	12 08	3 10	2 49	12 32
16	18 01	41 27	13 22	5 22	11 26	3 20	2 48	12 32
21	19 01	42 27	13 33	4 55	10 43	3 31	2 47	12 32
26	20 00	43 26	13 40	4 29	10 01	3 41	2 46	12 32

Moon Phenomena

Max/0 Decl

dy	hr mn	
3	1:41	0 S
10	7:43	18S15
16	16:42	0 N
22	23:38	18N17
30	8:48	0 S

Max/0 Lat

dy	hr mn	
4	3:19	0 N
11	6:34	5N17
17	13:07	0 S
23	22:33	5S15

Perigee/Apogee

dy	hr m		kilometers
1	13:02	a	406012
17	3:38	p	361025
29	3:52	a	405082

PH	dy	hr mn	
○	4	12:07	14♎24
(eclipse)	4	12:01	T 1.001
☾	12	3:46	21♑55
●	18	18:58	28♈25
☽	25	23:56	5♌27

Void of Course Moon

Last Aspect				☽ Ingress		
2	9:02	♀	△	♎	3	7:09
4	16:00	♅	☍	♏	5	19:05
7	20:43	♀	☍	♐	8	5:09
9	17:43	☉	△	♑	10	12:48
12	8:16	☿	□	♒	12	17:45
14	19:46	☿	⚹	♓	14	20:13
15	21:38	♇	⚹	♈	16	21:01
18	18:58	☉	☌	♉	18	21:32
19	23:08	♇	△	♊	20	23:29
22	5:39	♅	⚹	♋	23	4:27
24	17:05	☿	⚹	♌	25	13:14
27	14:13	☿	□	♍	28	1:08
30	12:25	☿	△	♎	30	14:04

DAILY ASPECTARIAN

1 W
♀∥♃ 1:26
☽□♄ 3:43
☽☍♆ 11:32
☽∥♅ 11:40
☉⚻☽ 17:59
☉∥☽ 19:22
☽⚺♃ 19:59
☿∥⚷ 20:08
☽⚼⚳ 23:53
☿∠♀ 23:53

2 Th
☽△♇ 1:43
♀⚹⚷ 2:52
☽⚼♂ 2:53
☽⚻♅ 3:10
☽☍⚷ 8:26
☽△♀ 9:02
☿△♄ 12:21
☿⋕⚷ 16:30
☉△♃ 17:21
☽∥☿ 22:09
☽⋕⚷ 23:29

3 F
☽∠♃ 2:22
☽∥⚷ 3:52
☽△⚳ 7:01
☽⋕☿ 7:19
☽⚻♂ 11:18
⚳ ♒ 12:22
☽⚹♄ 16:25
♀⋕♄ 18:03
☽⚼♀ 18:45
☽☍☿ 21:58

4 Sa
☽⚻♆ 0:28
☽⚹♃ 8:33
☉☍☽ 12:07
☿⚺♆ 13:23
☽□♇ 14:19
☉⋕☽ 14:54
☽⋕♅ 15:46
☽☍♅ 16:00
☽⚻⚷ 21:10
☽∠♄ 22:24
☉∥♅ 23:36

5 Su
☽⚻♀ 4:02
☽⚼♆ 6:30
☽∥♆ 13:37
☉□♇ 15:09
☽□⚳ 20:19

6 M
♂∠⚷ 2:47
☽⚼⚷ 2:59
☽☍♂ 2:59
☽⚺♄ 3:57
☽△♆ 12:06
☿△♃ 13:27
☉☌♅ 14:09
♂⚻♄ 18:18
☽□♃ 19:44
☽⋕♂ 20:30
☽⚻☿ 20:58

7 Tu
☽⚹♇ 1:24
☽⚻♅ 3:16
☉⚻☽ 4:20
☽△⚷ 8:17
☽☍♀ 20:43

8 W
☿□♇ 0:08
♀⋕♇ 2:38
☽∠♇ 6:09
☽⚼☿ 7:18
☽⚹⚳ 7:33
☽⚼♅ 8:06
☉⚼☽ 11:25
☿☌♅ 12:21
☽☌♄ 13:31
☽⚻♂ 16:18
♃ D 16:58
☽□♆ 21:39
☿∥♅ 23:50

9 Th
⚴ ♑ 2:49
☽△♃ 4:50
☉⚺⚷ 9:02
☽⚺♇ 10:17
☽∠⚳ 12:13
☽△♅ 12:19
☽⋕♃ 12:42
☉⚼♄ 13:32
☽△☿ 16:41
☽□⚷ 17:06
☉△☽ 17:43
☿⚺⚷ 19:17
☿⚼♄ 21:00
☽⚼♂ 21:51

10 F
☉☌☿ 4:01
☽⚼♃ 8:26
☽⚻♀ 10:13
☽⚺⚳ 16:10
☽⚺♄ 20:36

11 Sa
☽△♂ 2:37
☽⋕♃ 2:39
☽⚹♆ 4:39
☽⚻♃ 11:22
☉∥☿ 13:39
♀ ♊ 15:30
☽⚼♀ 15:37
☽☌♇ 16:34
☽□♅ 18:42
☽∠♄ 23:08
☽⚹⚷ 23:14

12 Su
☿∠♆ 0:35
♀⚼♇ 2:34
☉□☽ 3:46
☿⋕♆ 5:41
☽∠♆ 7:07
☽□☿ 8:16
♂⚹♆ 17:24
☽△♀ 20:09
☽☌⚳ 21:54

13 M
☽⋕♂ 0:49
☽⚹♄ 1:00
☽∠⚷ 1:17
♀∠♅ 5:10
☉⋕♆ 5:31
☽⚺♆ 8:56
☽□♂ 9:44
☽☍♃ 15:16
☽⚺♇ 20:10
♀△⚳ 22:08
☽⚹♅ 22:24

14 Tu
☽⚺⚷ 2:43
☉∠♆ 4:15
☽⋕☿ 5:00
☉⚹☽ 10:34
☉⋕☽ 13:28
☽∥♆ 16:28
☽⚹☿ 19:46
☽∠♇ 21:07
☿ ♉ 22:53
☽∠♅ 23:24

15 W
☽⚺⚳ 1:01
☽□♀ 2:52
☽□♄ 3:00
♀☍♄ 4:26
☽⋕♅ 8:40
☽☌♆ 10:53
☉∠☽ 13:00
☽⚹♂ 14:10
☽⚻♃ 16:57
☽⚹♇ 21:38
☽⚺♅ 23:59

16 Th
☽∠☿ 0:22
☽∠⚳ 1:53
☽☌⚷ 4:09
☿□⚳ 12:10
☉⚺☽ 15:03
☽∠♂ 15:44
☽∥⚷ 16:31
☽⋕⚷ 16:52
☽⚼♃ 17:17
☿⚻♄ 21:07

17 F
☽⚹⚳ 2:30
☽△♄ 3:31
☿∠⚷ 3:41
♇ R 3:56
☽⚺☿ 4:35
☽⚹♀ 7:40
☽⚺♆ 11:32
☽⚺♂ 17:11
☽△♃ 17:31
☽□♇ 22:05

18 Sa
♂□♃ 0:30
☽☌♅ 0:37
☽∥♅ 0:47
☽⚼♄ 3:38
☽⚺⚷ 4:45
☽∠♀ 9:57
☽∠♆ 11:49
☽⋕♆ 16:10
♀⋕⚳ 16:34
☉☌☽ 18:58

19 Su
☿⚺♀ 3:04
☽□⚳ 3:51
☽⚻♄ 3:57
☽∠⚷ 5:15
☉∥☽ 5:38
☿⚹♆ 7:13
⚳⚹♄ 9:28
♀□♆ 10:30
☽⚹♆ 12:23
☽⚺♀ 12:33
☽☌☿ 13:13
☽□♃ 18:33
☽☌♂ 20:40
☽△♇ 23:08

20 M
⚴ R 1:30
☽⚺♅ 1:56
☽⚹⚷ 6:11
☉ ♉ 9:43
☿∥♂ 15:32

21 Tu
☽⚼♇ 0:25
☉⚺☽ 0:31
☽∥♂ 1:59
☽∠♅ 3:23
☿□♃ 4:17
☽☍♄ 6:01
☽△⚳ 6:53
☽∥☿ 7:19
☽□♆ 15:11
☽☌♀ 19:54
♂△♇ 21:36
☽⚹♃ 21:45

22 W
☽⚺☿ 0:38
☽∥♃ 1:24
☽⚻♇ 2:28
☽⚺♂ 2:44
☉∠☽ 4:35
☽⚹♅ 5:39
☽⚼⚳ 9:35
☽□⚷ 10:10
☿△♇ 13:27
☿∥♃ 15:57
♀⚹♃ 18:42
☿☌♂ 23:04

23 Th
☽∠♃ 0:38
☽∥☿ 5:44
☽∠♂ 7:18
☽∠☿ 8:10
☉⚹☽ 9:49
☽⚻♄ 11:12
☿⚺♅ 13:04
☽⚻⚳ 13:15
☽△♆ 21:24
☿⋕♄ 22:57
☽∥♃ 22:58

24 F
☉⚻♄ 3:18
☽⚺♃ 4:31
☽⚺♀ 7:44
☽☍♇ 9:22
⚳∠⚷ 12:04
☽∥♂ 12:33
☽⚹♂ 13:01
☽□♅ 13:03
♂⚺♅ 13:45
☽⚼♄ 15:14
☽⚹☿ 17:05
☽△⚷ 17:52
☿⚹⚷ 22:38

25 Sa
♀⚻♇ 1:55
☽⚼♆ 1:58
☉∠⚷ 13:31
☽∠♀ 15:32
☉□⚳ 18:24
☽△♄ 20:10
☽⚼⚷ 23:08
☽☍⚳ 23:35
☉□☽ 23:56

26 Su
☽⚻♆ 7:24
☉∥☽ 8:08
☽☌♃ 15:05
☿⋕♇ 18:46
☽⚻♇ 19:57
♀⚹♅ 21:32

27 M
☽△♅ 0:08
☽⚹♀ 0:23
☽□♂ 3:35
☽⚻⚷ 5:09
♂∥♃ 9:38
☽□☿ 14:13
☽⋕♆ 21:43

28 Tu
☽⚼♇ 2:11
☽⚼♅ 6:34
♂⚹⚷ 7:18
☽□♄ 8:01
☽⚻⚳ 12:49
☽∥♅ 14:51
☉△☽ 17:38
☽☍♆ 20:01

29 W
☽⚺♃ 4:02
♀□⚷ 4:33
☽△♇ 8:40
☽⚻♅ 13:13
☽☍⚷ 18:15
☽□♀ 19:39
☽⚼⚳ 19:48
☽△♂ 20:22
♀⚼⚳ 21:31
☉⚹♆ 23:12

30 Th
☉⚼☽ 2:51
☽∥⚷ 7:12
☽⋕⚷ 10:24
☽∠♃ 10:40
☽△☿ 12:25
♀⚺♂ 15:15
⚴ R♐ 18:00
☽⚹♄ 20:34

LONGITUDE

Day	Sid.Time	☉	☽	☽ 12 hour	Mean☊	True☊	☿	♀	♂	⚳	♃	♄	⚷	♅	♆	♇
	h m s	° ' "	° ' "	° ' "	° '	° '	° '	° '	° '	° '	° '	° '	° '	° '	° '	° '
F	14 34 26	10♉19 05	4♎55 28	10♎54 07	8♎34.9	9♎49.3	29♉52.8	22♊14.5	22♉05.6	6♒11.5	13♌21.1	3♐12.9	20♓16.8	17♈49.4	9♓20.2	15♑29.9
Sa	14 38 22	11 17 19	16 54 59	22 58 24	8 31.7	9R 49.1	1♊16.6	23 22.0	22 48.5	6 21.8	13 25.2	3R 08.9	20 19.5	17 52.6	9 21.5	15R 29.5
Su	14 42 19	12 15 31	29 04 39	5♏13 58	8 28.6	9 47.5	2 36.1	24 29.3	23 31.4	6 31.7	13 29.5	3 04.9	20 22.1	17 55.8	9 22.8	15 29.0
M	14 46 15	13 13 41	11♏26 31	17 42 27	8 25.4	9 44.4	3 51.2	25 36.4	24 14.3	6 41.5	13 33.9	3 00.9	20 24.6	17 59.0	9 24.1	15 28.6
Tu	14 50 12	14 11 49	24 01 49	0♐24 41	8 22.2	9 39.7	5 01.8	26 43.4	24 57.0	6 50.9	13 38.5	2 56.8	20 27.1	18 02.2	9 25.3	15 28.1
W	14 54 09	15 09 56	6♐51 04	13 20 54	8 19.0	9 34.1	6 07.9	27 50.1	25 39.8	7 00.1	13 43.2	2 52.7	20 29.6	18 05.3	9 26.5	15 27.5
Th	14 58 05	16 08 02	19 54 10	26 30 46	8 15.8	9 28.0	7 09.4	28 56.7	26 22.5	7 09.0	13 48.1	2 48.5	20 32.0	18 08.5	9 27.7	15 27.0
F	15 02 02	17 06 06	3♑10 40	9♑53 44	8 12.7	9 22.3	8 06.2	0♋03.1	27 05.1	7 17.6	13 53.2	2 44.3	20 34.4	18 11.6	9 28.8	15 26.4
Sa	15 05 58	18 04 08	16 39 54	23 29 04	8 09.5	9 17.6	8 58.3	1 09.3	27 47.7	7 26.0	13 58.4	2 40.1	20 36.8	18 14.7	9 29.9	15 25.8
Su	15 09 55	19 02 09	0♒21 11	7♒16 08	8 06.3	9 14.4	9 45.6	2 15.3	28 30.3	7 34.0	14 03.8	2 35.9	20 39.1	18 17.7	9 31.0	15 25.1
M	15 13 51	20 00 09	14 13 51	21 14 15	8 03.1	9D 12.9	10 28.0	3 21.1	29 12.8	7 41.8	14 09.3	2 31.6	20 41.4	18 20.8	9 32.1	15 24.5
Tu	15 17 48	20 58 07	28 17 12	5♓22 33	8 00.0	9 12.9	11 05.5	4 26.7	29 55.2	7 49.3	14 15.0	2 27.2	20 43.6	18 23.8	9 33.1	15 23.8
W	15 21 44	21 56 04	12♓30 10	19 39 46	7 56.8	9 13.9	11 38.1	5 32.0	0♊37.7	7 56.5	14 20.8	2 22.9	20 45.8	18 26.8	9 34.1	15 23.0
Th	15 25 41	22 54 00	26 51 06	4♈03 47	7 53.6	9R 15.1	12 05.7	6 37.2	1 20.0	8 03.4	14 26.7	2 18.5	20 47.9	18 29.8	9 35.0	15 22.3
F	15 29 38	23 51 55	11♈17 23	18 31 24	7 50.4	9 15.6	12 28.3	7 42.2	2 02.3	8 09.9	14 32.9	2 14.1	20 50.0	18 32.7	9 35.9	15 21.5
Sa	15 33 34	24 49 48	25 45 15	2♉58 18	7 47.3	9 14.5	12 45.9	8 46.9	2 44.6	8 16.2	14 39.1	2 09.7	20 52.1	18 35.7	9 36.8	15 20.7
Su	15 37 31	25 47 40	10♉09 53	17 19 18	7 44.1	9 11.3	12 58.5	9 51.4	3 26.8	8 22.2	14 45.5	2 05.3	20 54.1	18 38.6	9 37.7	15 19.9
M	15 41 27	26 45 31	24 25 51	1♊28 52	7 40.9	9 06.0	13 06.1	10 55.7	4 09.0	8 27.8	14 52.0	2 00.9	20 56.0	18 41.5	9 38.6	15 19.1
Tu	15 45 24	27 43 20	8♊27 47	15 22 02	7 37.7	8 58.9	13R 08.9	11 59.7	4 51.1	8 33.1	14 58.7	1 56.4	20 57.9	18 44.3	9 39.4	15 18.2
W	15 49 20	28 41 08	22 11 14	28 55 02	7 34.5	8 50.8	13 06.9	13 03.5	5 33.2	8 38.1	15 05.6	1 51.9	20 59.8	18 47.1	9 40.1	15 17.3
Th	15 53 17	29 38 54	5♋33 17	12♋05 53	7 31.4	8 42.5	13 00.3	14 07.0	6 15.3	8 42.8	15 12.5	1 47.5	21 01.6	18 49.9	9 40.9	15 16.4
F	15 57 13	0♊36 39	18 32 56	24 54 35	7 28.2	8 34.9	12 49.2	15 10.2	6 57.2	8 47.1	15 19.6	1 43.0	21 03.4	18 52.7	9 41.6	15 15.5
Sa	16 01 10	1 34 23	1♌11 08	7♌22 57	7 25.0	8 28.9	12 34.0	16 13.2	7 39.2	8 51.2	15 26.8	1 38.5	21 05.1	18 55.4	9 42.3	15 14.5
Su	16 05 07	2 32 04	13 30 29	19 34 16	7 21.8	8 24.9	12 14.9	17 15.9	8 21.1	8 54.8	15 34.2	1 34.0	21 06.8	18 58.2	9 42.9	15 13.5
M	16 09 03	3 29 44	25 34 52	1♍32 54	7 18.7	8D 22.9	11 52.3	18 18.3	9 02.9	8 58.2	15 41.7	1 29.6	21 08.4	19 00.8	9 43.5	15 12.5
Tu	16 13 00	4 27 23	7♍29 02	13 23 54	7 15.5	8 22.6	11 26.6	19 20.4	9 44.7	9 01.2	15 49.3	1 25.1	21 10.0	19 03.5	9 44.1	15 11.5
W	16 16 56	5 25 00	19 18 10	25 12 30	7 12.3	8 23.3	10 58.2	20 22.1	10 26.4	9 03.9	15 57.0	1 20.6	21 11.5	19 06.1	9 44.7	15 10.4
Th	16 20 53	6 22 36	1♎07 34	7♎03 59	7 09.1	8R 24.2	10 27.7	21 23.6	11 08.1	9 06.2	16 04.9	1 16.2	21 13.0	19 08.7	9 45.2	15 09.4
F	16 24 49	7 20 10	13 02 20	19 03 11	7 05.9	8 24.3	9 55.5	22 24.7	11 49.8	9 08.2	16 12.8	1 11.7	21 14.4	19 11.2	9 45.7	15 08.3
Sa	16 28 46	8 17 43	25 07 02	1♏14 20	7 02.8	8 22.8	9 22.2	23 25.5	12 31.4	9 09.8	16 20.9	1 07.3	21 15.8	19 13.8	9 46.1	15 07.2
Su	16 32 42	9♊15 15	7♏25 28	13 40 43	6♎59.6	8♎19.2	8♊48.4	24♋25.9	13♊12.9	9♒11.1	16♌29.1	1♐02.9	21♓17.1	19♈16.2	9♓46.5	15♑06.0

1st of Month

Julian Day # 2457143.5
Obliquity 23°26'05"
SVP 5♓02'43"
GC 27♐03.2
Eris 22♈55.3

Day	⚴	⚵	⚶
1	29♐58.8R	10♌15.4	15♓21.5
6	29 27.8R	11 34.8	17 31.0
11	28 45.4R	12 58.6	19 37.7
16	27 51.9R	14 26.4	21 41.4
21	26 48.3R	15 57.7	23 41.7
26	25 35.7R	17 32.3	25 38.5
31	24 16.0R	19 09.7	27 31.4

DECLINATION and LATITUDE

Day	☉ Decl	☽ Decl	☽ Lat	☽12h Decl	☿ Decl	☿ Lat	♀ Decl	♀ Lat	♂ Decl	♂ Lat	⚳ Decl	⚳ Lat	♃ Decl	♃ Lat	♄ Decl	♄ Lat
F	14N55	2S22	0S27	4S13	22N29	2N25	25N34	2N22	18N29	0N12	23S34	5S01	17N42	0N55	18S39	2N11
Sa	15 13	6 03	0N39	7 49	22 50	2 29	25 40	2 24	18 41	0 13	23 35	5 04	17 40	0 55	18 38	2 11
Su	15 31	9 32	1 44	11 09	23 10	2 32	25 45	2 26	18 52	0 13	23 36	5 08	17 39	0 55	18 37	2 11
M	15 48	12 39	2 44	14 02	23 27	2 34	25 49	2 28	19 03	0 14	23 37	5 12	17 38	0 55	18 37	2 11
Tu	16 06	15 15	3 38	16 18	23 41	2 36	25 53	2 29	19 14	0 15	23 39	5 16	17 36	0 55	18 36	2 11
W	16 23	17 09	4 22	17 47	23 54	2 36	25 56	2 31	19 25	0 15	23 40	5 19	17 35	0 55	18 35	2 11
Th	16 40	18 11	4 53	18 20	24 04	2 36	25 59	2 33	19 36	0 16	23 41	5 23	17 33	0 55	18 34	2 11
F	16 56	18 15	5 09	17 54	24 12	2 34	26 01	2 35	19 46	0 16	23 43	5 27	17 32	0 55	18 33	2 11
Sa	17 13	17 18	5 08	16 26	24 17	2 32	26 02	2 36	19 56	0 17	23 44	5 31	17 30	0 55	18 32	2 11
Su	17 29	15 21	4 50	14 01	24 21	2 28	26 02	2 37	20 06	0 18	23 46	5 35	17 29	0 55	18 32	2 11
M	17 44	12 29	4 15	10 46	24 23	2 23	26 02	2 39	20 16	0 18	23 48	5 39	17 27	0 55	18 31	2 11
Tu	17 60	8 52	3 24	6 51	24 22	2 18	26 01	2 40	20 26	0 19	23 50	5 43	17 25	0 54	18 30	2 11
W	18 15	4 43	2 20	2 30	24 20	2 11	25 60	2 41	20 36	0 19	23 51	5 47	17 23	0 54	18 29	2 11
Th	18 30	0 14	1 07	2N03	24 16	2 03	25 58	2 42	20 45	0 20	23 54	5 51	17 22	0 54	18 28	2 11
F	18 44	4N18	0S11	6 29	24 10	1 54	25 55	2 43	20 54	0 21	23 56	5 55	17 20	0 54	18 27	2 11
Sa	18 58	8 35	1 28	10 33	24 02	1 44	25 52	2 44	21 03	0 21	23 58	5 59	17 18	0 54	18 27	2 11
Su	19 12	12 21	2 39	13 57	23 53	1 33	25 48	2 44	21 12	0 22	24 00	6 03	17 16	0 54	18 26	2 11
M	19 26	15 20	3 39	16 28	23 42	1 21	25 43	2 45	21 20	0 22	24 03	6 07	17 14	0 54	18 25	2 11
Tu	19 39	17 21	4 25	17 57	23 30	1 08	25 38	2 45	21 29	0 23	24 06	6 12	17 12	0 54	18 24	2 11
W	19 52	18 18	4 55	18 23	23 15	0 54	25 32	2 45	21 37	0 23	24 08	6 16	17 10	0 54	18 23	2 11
Th	20 04	18 13	5 07	17 48	23 00	0 39	25 26	2 46	21 44	0 24	24 11	6 20	17 08	0 54	18 22	2 11
F	20 16	17 09	5 03	16 18	22 43	0 24	25 19	2 46	21 52	0 25	24 14	6 24	17 06	0 54	18 22	2 11
Sa	20 28	15 16	4 44	14 05	22 25	0 07	25 11	2 46	21 60	0 25	24 17	6 29	17 03	0 54	18 21	2 11
Su	20 40	12 44	4 12	11 16	22 06	0S09	25 03	2 45	22 07	0 26	24 20	6 33	17 01	0 54	18 20	2 11
M	20 51	9 42	3 29	8 03	21 46	0 26	24 55	2 45	22 14	0 26	24 24	6 37	16 59	0 53	18 19	2 11
Tu	21 02	6 19	2 38	4 31	21 26	0 44	24 45	2 45	22 21	0 27	24 27	6 42	16 56	0 53	18 18	2 11
W	21 12	2 41	1 41	0 50	21 04	1 01	24 35	2 44	22 28	0 27	24 30	6 46	16 54	0 53	18 17	2 11
Th	21 22	1S03	0 39	2S55	20 43	1 19	24 25	2 43	22 34	0 28	24 34	6 51	16 52	0 53	18 17	2 11
F	21 32	4 46	0N25	6 35	20 21	1 36	24 14	2 42	22 40	0 28	24 38	6 55	16 49	0 53	18 16	2 11
Sa	21 41	8 21	1 28	10 02	19 59	1 53	24 03	2 41	22 46	0 29	24 42	6 60	16 47	0 53	18 15	2 11
Su	21N50	11S38	2N29	13S08	19N38	2S10	23N51	2N40	22N52	0N30	24S46	7S04	16N44	0N53	18S14	2N11

Day	⚷ Decl	⚷ Lat	♅ Decl	♅ Lat	♆ Decl	♆ Lat	♇ Decl	♇ Lat
1	0N16	4N28	6N25	0S37	8S46	0S45	20S29	2N04
6	0 21	4 29	6 31	0 37	8 44	0 45	20 30	2 03
11	0 27	4 30	6 37	0 37	8 42	0 46	20 30	2 03
16	0 31	4 30	6 43	0 37	8 40	0 46	20 31	2 03
21	0 36	4 31	6 48	0 37	8 39	0 46	20 32	2 03
26	0 40	4 32	6 53	0 38	8 38	0 46	20 33	2 02
31	0N44	4N33	6N58	0S38	8S37	0S46	20S34	2N02

Day	⚴ Decl	⚴ Lat	⚵ Decl	⚵ Lat	⚶ Decl	⚶ Lat	Eris Decl	Eris Lat
1	20N57	44N23	13N44	4S05	9S21	3S53	2S45	12S32
6	21 50	45 16	13 45	3 42	8 41	4 04	2 43	12 32
11	22 40	46 05	13 43	3 20	8 02	4 16	2 42	12 32
16	23 24	46 49	13 38	2 60	7 24	4 28	2 42	12 32
21	24 03	47 28	13 30	2 41	6 48	4 41	2 41	12 32
26	24 36	47 59	13 19	2 22	6 14	4 54	2 40	12 33
31	25N01	48N22	13N05	2S05	5S42	5S08	2S39	12S33

Moon Phenomena

Max/0 Decl

dy	hr mn	
7	13:42	18S20
14	1:12	0 N
20	9:41	18N23
27	17:18	0 S

Max/0 Lat

dy	hr mn	
1	9:50	0 N
8	10:59	5N11
14	20:38	0 S
21	5:39	5S07
28	14:42	0 N

Perigee/Apogee

dy	hr m		kilometers
15	0:09	p	366024
26	22:22	a	404244

PH	dy	hr mn	
○	4	3:43	13♏23
☾	11	10:37	20♒26
●	18	4:14	26♉56
☽	25	17:20	4♍11

Void of Course Moon

Last Aspect	☽ Ingress
2 14:04 ♀ △	♏ 3 1:48
5 1:50 ♂ ☍	♐ 5 11:14
7 17:53 ♂ △	♑ 7 18:17
9 20:36 ♂ △	♒ 9 23:23
11 10:37 ☉ □	♓ 12 2:54
13 16:56 ☉ ✶	♈ 14 5:15
15 12:05 ♅ ☌	♉ 16 7:03
18 4:14 ☉ ☌	♊ 18 9:28
19 17:59 ♅ ✶	♋ 20 13:57
22 0:37 ♀ ☌	♌ 22 21:43
24 10:51 ♅ △	♍ 25 8:53
27 2:22 ♀ ✶	♎ 27 21:43
29 20:21 ♀ □	♏ 30 9:35

DAILY ASPECTARIAN

☿ ♊ 2:01
☽ △ ⚳ 2:35
☽ ⚼ ♂ 4:38
☽ ⚻ ♆ 8:53
☿ ⚼ ♇ 10:26
☉ ⚻ ☽ 11:47
☽ ✶ ♃ 17:00
♂ # ♄ 19:26
☽ □ ♇ 21:10
☽ ⚼ ☿ 22:34

☽ ☍ ♅ 1:55
☽ ∠ ♄ 2:26
☽ # ♅ 2:37
☽ ⚻ ⚷ 6:47
☽ ⚻ ♂ 12:24
☽ △ ♀ 14:04
☽ ⚼ ♆ 14:45
☽ ∥ ♆ 18:28

☿ ∠ ♅ 6:27
☽ ⚻ ☿ 7:41
☽ ⚺ ♄ 7:47
☿ ☍ ♄ 8:36
☽ ⚼ ⚷ 12:18
☽ □ ⚳ 14:42
☽ △ ♆ 20:04
☽ ⚼ ♀ 22:14

☉ ☍ ☽ 3:43
☽ □ ♃ 4:06
♄ ⚼ ♅ 6:13
☽ ✶ ♇ 7:44
☉ □ ♃ 9:03
☽ ⚻ ♅ 12:35
☽ △ ⚷ 17:12
☿ # ⚳ 18:39

5 Tu
☽ ☍ ♂ 1:50
☽ ⚻ ♀ 5:34
☉ # ☽ 11:12
☽ ∠ ♇ 12:06
☽ ☌ ♄ 16:39
☽ ⚼ ♅ 16:58
☽ ☍ ☿ 22:33

6 W
☽ ✶ ⚳ 0:17
☽ □ ♆ 4:48
☉ △ ♇ 7:12
☽ # ♃ 7:41
☽ △ ♃ 12:46
☽ ⚺ ♇ 15:52
☉ ⚻ ☽ 16:34
♀ ∠ ♃ 20:40
☽ △ ♅ 20:46
☿ △ ⚳ 23:49

7 Th
☽ □ ⚷ 1:09
☽ ∠ ⚳ 4:08
☽ ⚻ ♂ 12:25
☽ ⚼ ♃ 16:14
☽ ☍ ♀ 17:53
☉ ⚼ ☽ 21:55
♀ ♋ 22:53
☽ ⚺ ♄ 23:13

8 F
☽ ⚺ ⚳ 7:27
☽ ⚻ ☿ 9:26
☽ ✶ ♆ 11:17
☽ ⚼ ♂ 16:46
☽ ⚻ ♃ 19:13
☽ # ♃ 20:18
☽ ☌ ♇ 21:49

9 Sa
☉ # ☽ 1:10
☽ ∠ ♄ 1:46
☉ △ ☽ 2:40
☽ □ ♅ 2:48
☉ ⚺ ♅ 4:36
☽ ✶ ⚷ 6:59
☽ ⚼ ☿ 13:39
☽ ∠ ♆ 13:48
☿ □ ♆ 16:10
☽ △ ♂ 20:36

10 Su
☉ ∥ ♃ 0:03
☽ ⚻ ♀ 3:36
☽ ✶ ♄ 3:53
♀ ⚻ ♄ 7:03
☽ ∠ ⚷ 9:14
☽ ☌ ⚳ 12:38
☽ ⚺ ♆ 15:54
☽ △ ☿ 17:11
☽ ☍ ♃ 23:52

11 M
☽ ⚺ ♇ 2:01
☽ ✶ ♅ 7:05
☽ ⚼ ♀ 7:40
☉ □ ☽ 10:37
☽ ⚺ ⚷ 11:06
☉ ✶ ⚷ 17:45

12 Tu
☽ ∥ ♆ 1:07
♂ ♊ 2:41
☽ □ ♂ 2:55
☽ ∠ ♇ 3:34
☽ □ ♄ 7:02
☽ ∠ ♅ 8:41
☽ △ ♀ 11:18
♂ # ♇ 11:19
☽ # ♅ 13:09
♂ ⚼ ♇ 15:52
☽ ⚺ ⚳ 16:16
☽ ☌ ♆ 19:04
☽ □ ☿ 22:29

13 W
☽ ⚻ ♃ 3:07
☽ ✶ ♇ 4:50
☽ ⚺ ♅ 10:00
☽ ☌ ⚷ 13:52
☉ ✶ ☽ 16:56
☽ ∠ ⚳ 17:37
☉ # ♄ 21:58
☽ # ⚷ 22:37

14 Th
☽ ∥ ⚷ 3:49
☽ ⚼ ♃ 4:21
☽ ✶ ♂ 7:51
☽ △ ♄ 9:02
☽ □ ♀ 17:34
☽ ✶ ⚳ 18:47
☉ ∠ ☽ 19:41
☽ ⚺ ♆ 21:11

15 F
☽ ✶ ☿ 2:00
☽ △ ♃ 5:27
♂ ☍ ♄ 6:04
☽ □ ♇ 6:45
☽ ⚼ ♄ 9:49
☽ ∠ ♂ 10:02
♀ ⚻ ⚳ 11:24
☽ ☌ ♅ 12:05
☽ ∥ ♅ 13:12
☽ ⚺ ⚷ 15:52
☽ ∠ ♆ 22:06
☉ ⚺ ☽ 22:21

16 Sa
☽ # ♆ 0:31
☽ ∠ ☿ 3:24
☿ # ⚳ 9:24
☽ ⚻ ♄ 10:36
☽ ⚺ ♂ 12:13
☽ ∠ ⚷ 16:52
♀ △ ♆ 18:50
☽ □ ⚳ 20:59
☽ ✶ ♆ 23:06
☽ ✶ ♀ 23:27

17 Su
☽ ⚺ ☿ 4:45
♂ ∠ ♅ 7:10
☽ □ ♃ 7:45
☽ △ ♇ 8:39
☽ ⚺ ♅ 14:16
☽ ✶ ⚷ 18:04

18 M
☽ ∠ ♀ 2:45
☉ ☌ ☽ 4:14
☽ ⚼ ♇ 10:00
☽ ☍ ♄ 12:51
☽ ∠ ♅ 15:50
☽ ☌ ♂ 17:27
☽ ∥ ♃ 21:47

19 Tu
☽ △ ⚳ 0:09
☿ R 1:49
☽ □ ♆ 2:04
☽ ⚺ ♀ 6:38
☽ ☌ ☿ 8:07
☽ ✶ ♃ 11:25
☽ ⚻ ♇ 11:53
☽ ✶ ♅ 17:59
☽ □ ⚷ 21:53

20 W
☿ ⚺ ♀ 1:12
☽ ⚼ ⚳ 2:35
☽ # ♄ 7:29
☉ ⚺ ☽ 12:29
☽ # ♄ 12:33
☽ ∠ ♃ 14:14
☽ ⚻ ♄ 17:13

21 Th
☽ ⚺ ♂ 1:21
☽ ⚻ ⚳ 5:48
☽ △ ♆ 7:33
☉ ♊ 8:46
♃ ⚻ ♇ 11:40
☽ ⚺ ☿ 13:30
☉ ⚼ ♇ 15:20
☽ ☌ ♀ 17:08
☽ ☍ ♇ 17:52
☽ ⚺ ♃ 17:56
☉ ∠ ☽ 18:04
☽ ⚼ ♄ 20:36

22 F
☽ □ ♅ 0:37
☽ ∥ ♃ 0:59
♀ ☍ ♇ 1:58
♀ ⚺ ♃ 4:02
☽ △ ⚷ 4:43
☽ ∠ ♂ 6:47
☽ ⚼ ♆ 11:36
☽ ∠ ☿ 17:13

23 Sa
☉ ✶ ☽ 0:49
☽ △ ♄ 0:52
☉ ☍ ♄ 1:36
☉ # ♇ 8:00
♀ ⚼ ♄ 9:02
☽ ⚼ ⚷ 9:30
☽ ✶ ♂ 13:17
☽ ☍ ⚳ 14:57
☽ ⚻ ♆ 16:33
☽ ✶ ☿ 21:35
☿ ∥ ♂ 23:21

24 Su
☽ ⚻ ♇ 3:23
☽ ☌ ♃ 4:07
☽ ⚺ ♀ 8:07
☽ △ ♅ 10:51
☽ ⚻ ⚷ 15:06
♂ △ ⚳ 21:04

25 M
☽ # ♆ 7:48
☽ ⚼ ♇ 9:17
☽ □ ♄ 11:49
☉ ∠ ♅ 13:34
☽ ∠ ♀ 17:02
☽ ⚼ ♅ 17:02
♀ □ ♅ 17:11
☉ □ ☽ 17:20
☽ ∥ ♅ 20:06
♂ □ ♆ 23:39

26 Tu
☽ ⚻ ⚳ 3:08
☽ ☍ ♆ 4:34
☽ □ ♂ 4:52
☽ □ ☿ 7:44
☽ △ ♇ 15:37
☽ ⚺ ♃ 17:07
☉ ∥ ☿ 18:06
☽ ⚻ ♅ 23:35

27 W
☽ ✶ ♀ 2:22
☽ ☍ ⚷ 3:51
♀ # ⚳ 8:50
☽ ⚼ ⚳ 9:43
☿ ☌ ♂ 10:38
☽ ∥ ⚷ 12:54
☉ ∠ ♀ 17:45
♀ △ ⚷ 19:46
☽ # ⚷ 21:45
☽ ∠ ♃ 23:54

28 Th
☽ ✶ ♄ 0:17
☿ # ♇ 10:32
☉ △ ☽ 11:32
☽ △ ⚳ 16:09
☽ ⚻ ♆ 17:25
☽ △ ☿ 18:01
☽ △ ♂ 21:26

29 F
☽ □ ♇ 4:12
☽ ∠ ♄ 6:16
☽ ✶ ♃ 6:25
☿ □ ♆ 7:02
☽ ☍ ♅ 12:19
☽ # ♅ 14:23
☽ ⚻ ⚷ 16:22
☉ ⚼ ☽ 20:06
☽ □ ♀ 20:21
☽ ⚼ ☿ 22:35
☽ ⚼ ♆ 23:19

30 Sa
☽ ∥ ♆ 1:53
☽ ⚼ ♂ 5:01
☿ △ ⚳ 8:27
☽ ⚺ ♄ 11:42
☿ ∠ ♀ 14:27
☉ ☌ ☿ 16:57
☽ ⚼ ⚷ 21:48
☉ △ ⚳ 22:14

31 Su
☽ ⚻ ☿ 2:33
☽ □ ⚳ 3:24
☉ ⚻ ☽ 3:49
☽ △ ♆ 4:32
♀ ⚼ ♆ 8:17
☽ ⚻ ♂ 11:46
☉ □ ♆ 13:09
☽ ✶ ♇ 14:41
☽ □ ♃ 17:32
☽ ⚻ ♅ 22:41

June 2015

LONGITUDE

Day	Sid.Time	☉	☽	☽ 12 hour	Mean ☊	True ☊	☿	♀	♂	⚳	♃	♄	⚷	♅	♆	♇
	h m s	° ' "	° ' "	° ' "	° '	° '	° '	° '	° '	° '	° '	° '	° '	° '	° '	° '
1 M	16 36 39	10♊12 45	20♏00 20	26♏24 27	6♎56.4	8♎13.1	8♊14.7	25♋25.9	13♊54.4	9♒12.0	16♌37.5	0♐58.5	21♓18.4	19♈18.7	9♓46.9	15♑04.9
2 Tu	16 40 36	11 10 14	2♐53 06	9♐26 14	6 53.2	8R 04.8	7R 41.7	26 25.6	14 35.9	9 12.6	16 45.9	0R 54.1	21 19.7	19 21.1	9 47.3	15R 03.7
3 W	16 44 32	12 07 42	16 03 43	22 45 21	6 50.1	7 54.9	7 10.0	27 24.9	15 17.3	9R 12.9	16 54.5	0 49.8	21 20.8	19 23.5	9 47.6	15 02.6
4 Th	16 48 29	13 05 10	29 30 50	6♑19 49	6 46.9	7 44.3	6 40.0	28 23.8	15 58.7	9 12.8	17 03.2	0 45.5	21 22.0	19 25.9	9 47.9	15 01.4
5 F	16 52 25	14 02 36	13♑11 56	20 06 45	6 43.7	7 34.1	6 12.3	29 22.3	16 40.0	9 12.3	17 11.9	0 41.2	21 23.0	19 28.2	9 48.1	15 00.2
6 Sa	16 56 22	15 00 02	27 03 53	4♒02 54	6 40.5	7 25.4	5 47.3	0♌20.4	17 21.3	9 11.5	17 20.8	0 36.9	21 24.1	19 30.4	9 48.4	14 58.9
7 Su	17 00 18	15 57 27	11♒03 27	18 05 10	6 37.4	7 18.8	5 25.5	1 18.0	18 02.5	9 10.3	17 29.8	0 32.7	21 25.0	19 32.7	9 48.6	14 57.7
8 M	17 04 15	16 54 51	25 07 46	2♓10 59	6 34.2	7 14.8	5 07.2	2 15.2	18 43.7	9 08.7	17 38.9	0 28.5	21 25.9	19 34.9	9 48.7	14 56.4
9 Tu	17 08 11	17 52 14	9♓14 39	16 18 33	6 31.0	7D 13.1	4 52.6	3 11.9	19 24.9	9 06.8	17 48.1	0 24.3	21 26.8	19 37.1	9 48.9	14 55.1
10 W	17 12 08	18 49 37	23 22 34	0♈26 35	6 27.8	7R 12.9	4 42.1	4 08.1	20 06.0	9 04.6	17 57.4	0 20.2	21 27.6	19 39.2	9 48.9	14 53.8
11 Th	17 16 05	19 47 00	7♈30 26	14 34 01	6 24.6	7 13.1	4D 35.7	5 03.9	20 47.0	9 01.9	18 06.8	0 16.1	21 28.4	19 41.3	9 49.0	14 52.5
12 F	17 20 01	20 44 22	21 37 08	28 39 35	6 21.5	7 12.5	4 33.8	5 59.2	21 28.1	8 58.9	18 16.3	0 12.0	21 29.1	19 43.3	9R 49.0	14 51.2
13 Sa	17 23 58	21 41 43	5♉41 08	12♉41 28	6 18.3	7 09.9	4 36.3	6 53.9	22 09.1	8 55.6	18 25.9	0 08.0	21 29.7	19 45.4	9 49.0	14 49.9
14 Su	17 27 54	22 39 04	19 40 14	26 37 05	6 15.1	7 04.7	4 43.3	7 48.1	22 50.0	8 51.8	18 35.6	0 04.0	21 30.3	19 47.3	9 49.0	14 48.5
15 M	17 31 51	23 36 25	3♊31 34	10♊23 16	6 11.9	6 56.7	4 54.9	8 41.7	23 30.9	8 47.7	18 45.4	0 00.1	21 30.9	19 49.3	9 48.9	14 47.2
16 Tu	17 35 47	24 33 45	17 11 47	23 56 43	6 08.8	6 46.4	5 11.1	9 34.8	24 11.8	8 43.3	18 55.3	29♏56.2	21 31.4	19 51.2	9 48.8	14 45.8
17 W	17 39 44	25 31 04	0♋37 43	7♋14 29	6 05.6	6 34.5	5 31.8	10 27.3	24 52.6	8 38.5	19 05.3	29 52.4	21 31.8	19 53.0	9 48.7	14 44.4
18 Th	17 43 40	26 28 23	13 46 48	20 14 33	6 02.4	6 22.3	5 57.0	11 19.1	25 33.4	8 33.4	19 15.4	29 48.6	21 32.2	19 54.8	9 48.5	14 43.0
19 F	17 47 37	27 25 42	26 37 42	2♌56 19	5 59.2	6 10.9	6 26.7	12 10.3	26 14.1	8 27.8	19 25.6	29 44.9	21 32.5	19 56.6	9 48.3	14 41.6
20 Sa	17 51 34	28 22 59	9♌10 32	15 20 36	5 56.1	6 01.3	7 00.8	13 00.9	26 54.8	8 22.0	19 35.8	29 41.3	21 32.8	19 58.3	9 48.1	14 40.2
21 Su	17 55 30	29 20 16	21 26 52	27 29 44	5 52.9	5 54.1	7 39.2	13 50.7	27 35.4	8 15.8	19 46.1	29 37.7	21 33.0	20 00.0	9 47.8	14 38.8
22 M	17 59 27	0♋17 32	3♍29 41	9♍27 16	5 49.7	5 49.5	8 21.9	14 39.8	28 16.0	8 09.3	19 56.6	29 34.2	21 33.2	20 01.7	9 47.6	14 37.4
23 Tu	18 03 23	1 14 48	15 23 04	21 17 42	5 46.5	5 47.2	9 08.7	15 28.2	28 56.6	8 02.4	20 07.1	29 30.7	21 33.3	20 03.3	9 47.2	14 35.9
24 W	18 07 20	2 12 02	27 11 50	3♎06 10	5 43.4	5 46.6	9 59.8	16 15.8	29 37.1	7 55.2	20 17.6	29 27.3	21R 33.3	20 04.8	9 46.9	14 34.5
25 Th	18 11 16	3 09 17	9♎01 21	14 58 05	5 40.2	5 46.5	10 54.8	17 02.5	0♋17.6	7 47.6	20 28.3	29 23.9	21 33.3	20 06.3	9 46.5	14 33.0
26 F	18 15 13	4 06 30	20 57 03	26 58 55	5 37.0	5 46.0	11 53.9	17 48.5	0 58.0	7 39.8	20 39.0	29 20.7	21 33.3	20 07.8	9 46.1	14 31.6
27 Sa	18 19 09	5 03 43	3♏04 16	9♏13 41	5 33.8	5 44.1	12 57.0	18 33.5	1 38.4	7 31.6	20 49.9	29 17.4	21 33.2	20 09.2	9 45.6	14 30.1
28 Su	18 23 06	6 00 56	15 27 41	21 46 41	5 30.6	5 40.0	14 03.9	19 17.6	2 18.8	7 23.1	21 00.7	29 14.3	21 33.0	20 10.6	9 45.1	14 28.6
29 M	18 27 03	6 58 08	28 11 02	4♐40 56	5 27.5	5 33.3	15 14.7	20 00.8	2 59.1	7 14.4	21 11.7	29 11.2	21 32.8	20 11.9	9 44.6	14 27.1
30 Tu	18 30 59	7♋55 19	11♐16 31	17 57 46	5♎24.3	5♎24.2	16♊29.2	20♌43.0	3♋39.4	7♒05.3	21♌22.7	29♏08.2	21♓32.5	20♈13.2	9♓44.1	14♑25.7

1st of Month

Julian Day #
2457174.5
Obliquity
23°26'05"
SVP 5♓02'3
GC 27♐03.
Eris 23♈12.

Day	⚴
1	23♐59.4
6	22 33.8
11	21 05.8
16	19 37.9
21	18 12.4
26	16 51.9

Day	⚵
1	19♌29.5
6	21 09.9
11	22 52.5
16	24 37.1
21	26 23.6
26	28 11.6

Day	⚶
1	27♓53.5
6	29 41.5
11	1♈25.0
16	3 03.5
21	4 36.8
26	6 04.2

DECLINATION and LATITUDE

Day	☉ Decl	☽ Decl	☽ Lat	☽ 12h Decl	☿ Decl	☿ Lat	♀ Decl	♀ Lat	♂ Decl	♂ Lat	⚳ Decl	⚳ Lat	♃ Decl	♃ Lat	♄ Decl	♄ Lat
1 M	21N59	14S28	3N23	15S40	19N17	2S26	23N39	2N39	22N58	0N30	24S50	7S09	16N42	0N53	18S13	2N10
2 Tu	22 07	16 40	4 09	17 28	18 57	2 41	23 26	2 37	23 03	0 31	24 54	7 13	16 39	0 53	18 13	2 10
3 W	22 15	18 02	4 42	18 22	18 37	2 55	23 13	2 35	23 08	0 31	24 58	7 18	16 36	0 53	18 12	2 10
4 Th	22 22	18 26	5 00	18 14	18 19	3 08	22 59	2 34	23 13	0 32	25 03	7 22	16 34	0 53	18 11	2 10
5 F	22 29	17 46	5 02	17 03	18 03	3 21	22 45	2 32	23 18	0 32	25 07	7 27	16 31	0 53	18 10	2 10
6 Sa	22 35	16 04	4 46	14 51	17 48	3 31	22 30	2 30	23 23	0 33	25 12	7 31	16 28	0 53	18 09	2 10
7 Su	22 42	13 24	4 13	11 45	17 34	3 41	22 16	2 27	23 27	0 33	25 16	7 36	16 25	0 53	18 09	2 10
8 M	22 47	9 56	3 24	7 58	17 23	3 50	22 00	2 25	23 31	0 34	25 21	7 41	16 23	0 53	18 08	2 10
9 Tu	22 53	5 54	2 23	3 44	17 13	3 57	21 44	2 22	23 35	0 34	25 26	7 45	16 20	0 53	18 07	2 10
10 W	22 58	1 31	1 13	0N44	17 06	4 03	21 28	2 19	23 39	0 35	25 31	7 50	16 17	0 52	18 06	2 09
11 Th	23 02	2N57	0S02	5 08	16 60	4 07	21 12	2 16	23 42	0 35	25 37	7 54	16 14	0 52	18 06	2 09
12 F	23 07	7 15	1 16	9 16	16 56	4 11	20 55	2 13	23 45	0 36	25 42	7 59	16 11	0 52	18 05	2 09
13 Sa	23 10	11 08	2 25	12 50	16 55	4 13	20 38	2 10	23 48	0 36	25 47	8 04	16 08	0 52	18 04	2 09
14 Su	23 14	14 21	3 25	15 40	16 55	4 14	20 21	2 06	23 51	0 37	25 53	8 08	16 05	0 52	18 04	2 09
15 M	23 17	16 44	4 12	17 33	16 57	4 14	20 03	2 02	23 54	0 37	25 58	8 13	16 02	0 52	18 03	2 09
16 Tu	23 19	18 06	4 44	18 24	17 01	4 12	19 45	1 58	23 56	0 38	26 04	8 18	15 59	0 52	18 02	2 09
17 W	23 22	18 26	4 60	18 14	17 07	4 10	19 27	1 54	23 58	0 38	26 10	8 22	15 55	0 52	18 02	2 08
18 Th	23 23	17 46	4 59	17 05	17 15	4 07	19 08	1 50	24 00	0 39	26 15	8 27	15 52	0 52	18 01	2 08
19 F	23 25	16 12	4 42	15 08	17 24	4 02	18 50	1 45	24 02	0 39	26 21	8 31	15 49	0 52	18 00	2 08
20 Sa	23 25	13 53	4 13	12 30	17 35	3 57	18 31	1 40	24 04	0 40	26 27	8 36	15 46	0 52	17 60	2 08
21 Su	23 26	11 00	3 32	9 24	17 47	3 51	18 11	1 35	24 05	0 40	26 33	8 40	15 42	0 52	17 59	2 08
22 M	23 26	7 42	2 42	5 56	17 60	3 45	17 52	1 30	24 06	0 41	26 39	8 45	15 39	0 52	17 59	2 08
23 Tu	23 26	4 08	1 46	2 17	18 14	3 37	17 33	1 25	24 07	0 41	26 46	8 49	15 36	0 52	17 58	2 07
24 W	23 25	0 25	0 45	1S27	18 30	3 29	17 13	1 19	24 08	0 42	26 52	8 54	15 32	0 52	17 57	2 07
25 Th	23 24	3S19	0N17	5 09	18 46	3 20	16 53	1 13	24 08	0 42	26 58	8 58	15 29	0 52	17 57	2 07
26 F	23 22	6 57	1 20	8 41	19 04	3 11	16 34	1 07	24 09	0 43	27 05	9 03	15 25	0 52	17 56	2 07
27 Sa	23 20	10 21	2 19	11 55	19 21	3 01	16 14	1 01	24 09	0 43	27 11	9 07	15 22	0 52	17 56	2 07
28 Su	23 18	13 23	3 14	14 42	19 40	2 51	15 54	0 54	24 08	0 44	27 17	9 12	15 18	0 52	17 55	2 07
29 M	23 15	15 51	3 60	16 49	19 58	2 40	15 34	0 48	24 08	0 44	27 24	9 16	15 15	0 52	17 55	2 06
30 Tu	23N12	17S35	4N35	18S07	20N17	2S28	15N14	0N41	24N08	0N45	27S30	9S20	15N11	0N52	17S54	2N06

Day	⚷ Decl	⚷ Lat	♅ Decl	♅ Lat	♆ Decl	♆ Lat	♇ Decl	♇ Lat
1	0N44	4N33	6N59	0S38	8S37	0S46	20S34	2N
6	0 48	4 34	7 03	0 38	8 37	0 47	20 35	2
11	0 50	4 35	7 07	0 38	8 36	0 47	20 36	2
16	0 52	4 36	7 11	0 38	8 37	0 47	20 37	2
21	0 54	4 37	7 14	0 38	8 37	0 47	20 38	2
26	0 55	4 38	7 17	0 38	8 38	0 47	20 39	2

Day	⚴ Decl	⚴ Lat	⚵ Decl	⚵ Lat	⚶ Decl	⚶ Lat	Eris Decl	Eris Lat
1	25N06	48N26	13N02	2S02	5S35	5S11	2S39	12S
6	25 22	48 40	12 46	1 46	5 06	5 25	2 39	12
11	25 31	48 46	12 28	1 31	4 38	5 40	2 38	12
16	25 33	48 42	12 07	1 16	4 14	5 56	2 38	12
21	25 26	48 31	11 45	1 02	3 52	6 12	2 38	12
26	25 11	48 11	11 20	0 49	3 33	6 29	2 38	12

Moon Phenomena

Max/0 Decl
dy hr mn
3 21:22 18S26
10 8:07 0 N
16 19:52 18N27
24 2:42 0 S

Max/0 Lat
dy hr mn
4 14:19 5N03
10 23:31 0 S
17 10:36 5S01
24 17:25 0 N

Perigee/Apogee
dy hr m kilometers
10 4:50 p 369711
23 17:06 a 404130

PH dy hr mn
○ 2 16:20 11♐49
☾ 9 15:43 18♓30
● 16 14:07 25♊07
☽ 24 11:04 2♎38

Void of Course Moon

Last Aspect			☽ Ingres		
1 11:02	♀	△	♐	1	18:4
3 6:00	♅	△	♑	4	0:5
5 10:55	♅	□	♒	6	5:0
7 14:32	♅	⚹	♓	8	8:1
9 18:09	♂	□	♈	10	11:1
11 23:44	♂	⚹	♉	12	14:1
13 22:07	♃	□	♊	14	17:5
16 14:07	☉	☌	♋	16	22:5
19 5:53	♄	△	♌	19	6:2
21 16:11	♄	□	♍	21	17:0
24 5:13	♂	□	♎	24	5:4
25 23:23	♃	⚹	♏	26	17:5
29 1:51	♄	☌	♐	29	3:2

DAILY ASPECTARIAN

1 M
☽ △ ⚷ 2:27
☽ △ ♀ 11:02
☽ ∠ ♇ 18:48
☽ ☌ ♄ 20:22
☽ # ♃ 23:48

2 Tu
☽ ⚼ ♅ 2:42
☽ ☍ ☿ 8:29
☽ ⚹ ⚳ 11:35
☽ □ ♆ 12:39
♂ ⊼ ♇ 15:41
☉ ☍ ☽ 16:20
☽ ⚼ ♀ 16:53
☽ ⊻ ♇ 22:10
☽ ☍ ♂ 22:32

3 W
☽ △ ♃ 1:32
⚳ R 4:21
☽ ∥ ♄ 4:46
♀ ∥ ♂ 5:49
☽ △ ♅ 6:00
☽ □ ⚷ 9:30
☽ ∠ ⚳ 14:36
☽ # ☿ 16:23
☽ ⊼ ♀ 21:52

4 Th
☽ ⊻ ♄ 2:11
☽ ⚼ ♃ 4:32
☽ ⊼ ☿ 12:10
☿ # ♄ 12:34
☽ ∥ ♄ 14:04
☽ # ☿ 14:52
☽ ⊻ ⚳ 17:02
☽ ⚹ ♆ 18:04

5 F
☉ ⊼ ☽ 1:35
☽ ☌ ♇ 3:08
☽ ∠ ♄ 4:18
☽ ⊼ ♂ 6:21
☽ ⊼ ♃ 7:02
☽ □ ♅ 10:55
☽ ⚼ ☿ 13:29
☽ ⚹ ⚷ 14:13
♀ ♌ 15:34
☉ ∥ ♀ 18:19
☽ # ♃ 19:18
☽ ∠ ♆ 20:06
☉ ⊼ ♇ 23:33
♂ ⚹ ♃ 23:39

6 Sa
☉ ⚼ ☽ 5:25
☽ ☍ ♀ 6:03
☽ ⚹ ♄ 6:05
♀ △ ♄ 6:24
☽ ⚼ ♂ 9:34
☽ △ ☿ 14:36
☽ ∠ ⚷ 16:03
☽ ☌ ⚳ 20:47
⚶ ♈ 21:06
☽ ⊻ ♆ 21:52

7 Su
☽ ⊻ ♇ 6:40
☉ △ ☽ 8:59
☽ ☍ ♃ 11:07
☽ △ ♂ 12:32
☽ ⚹ ♅ 14:32
☽ ⊻ ⚷ 17:42

8 M
☽ ∠ ♇ 8:10
☽ ∥ ♆ 8:12
☽ □ ♄ 9:03
☽ ⊼ ♀ 12:59
☽ ∠ ♅ 16:07
☽ □ ☿ 16:42
☽ # ♅ 17:11
☉ ⚹ ♃ 21:57
☽ ⊻ ⚳ 23:47

9 Tu
☽ ☌ ♆ 0:58
♂ ⚹ ♅ 7:31
☽ ⚹ ♇ 9:37
☽ ⊼ ♃ 14:42
☉ □ ☽ 15:43
☽ ⚼ ♀ 16:17
☽ ⊻ ♅ 17:40
☽ □ ♂ 18:09
☽ ☌ ⚷ 20:45

10 W
☽ ∠ ⚳ 1:11
☽ # ⚷ 3:40
☿ ∠ ♅ 6:53
☽ △ ♄ 11:46
☽ ∥ ⚷ 12:34
☿ ⚹ ♀ 12:53
☽ ⚼ ♃ 16:27
☽ ⚹ ☿ 19:05
☽ △ ♀ 19:34
☉ ⚹ ♅ 21:32

11 Th
☽ ⚹ ⚳ 2:35
☽ ⊻ ♆ 3:55
☽ □ ♇ 12:30
☽ ⚼ ♄ 13:08
☽ △ ♃ 18:14
☽ ∠ ☿ 20:30
☽ ☌ ♅ 20:46
☉ ⚹ ☽ 22:24
☿ D 22:35
☽ ∥ ♅ 23:16
☽ ⚹ ♂ 23:44
☽ ⊻ ⚷ 23:46

12 F
♂ □ ⚷ 0:36
☽ ∠ ♆ 5:27
☽ # ♆ 8:01
♆ R 9:09
♀ ⚼ ⚷ 13:15
☽ ⊼ ♄ 14:33
☉ □ ⚷ 18:56
☽ ⊻ ☿ 22:09

13 Sa
☽ ∠ ⚷ 1:23
☉ ∠ ☽ 1:51
☽ □ ♀ 2:13
♀ # ♇ 2:33
☽ ∠ ♂ 2:38
☽ □ ⚳ 5:31
☽ ⚹ ♆ 7:04
☽ △ ♇ 15:39
☽ □ ♃ 22:07

14 Su
☽ ⊻ ♅ 0:12
☽ ⚹ ⚷ 3:10
♀ ∠ ♂ 3:31
☉ ⊻ ☽ 5:31
☽ ⊻ ♂ 5:44
☿ ∠ ♅ 11:21
☉ ☌ ♂ 15:57
☽ ∥ ♃ 16:02
☽ ⚼ ♇ 17:30
☽ ☍ ♄ 17:54

15 M
♄ R♏ 0:37
☽ ∠ ♅ 2:16
☽ ☌ ☿ 2:28
♀ ☍ ⚳ 2:30
☽ ∥ ☿ 3:05
☉ ⚼ ⚳ 4:25
♂ ⚼ ⚳ 8:57
☽ △ ⚳ 9:10
☽ ⚹ ♀ 9:40
☽ □ ♆ 11:00
☽ ⊼ ♇ 19:42
☽ # ♄ 22:12

16 Tu
☽ ⚹ ♃ 3:06
☽ ⚹ ♅ 4:43
☉ ∠ ♀ 5:33
♀ ⊼ ♆ 6:22
☽ □ ⚷ 7:41
☽ ⚼ ⚳ 11:32
☽ ☌ ♂ 13:07
☽ ∠ ♀ 14:03
☉ ☌ ☽ 14:07
☽ ⊼ ♄ 22:39

17 W
☽ ∠ ♃ 6:21
☽ ⊻ ☿ 9:10
☽ ⊼ ⚳ 14:28
☽ △ ♆ 16:42
☽ # ♄ 18:12
☽ ⊻ ♀ 19:09

18 Th
☽ ☍ ♇ 1:44
☽ ⚼ ♄ 1:54
☽ ∥ ☿ 8:40
☽ ⊻ ♃ 10:18
☽ □ ♅ 11:25
☽ ∠ ☿ 13:50
☽ △ ⚷ 14:26
☽ ⚼ ♆ 20:34
☽ ⊻ ♂ 23:13

19 F
☉ ⊻ ☽ 1:38
☽ ∥ ♃ 4:40
☽ △ ♄ 5:53
☽ ⚼ ⚷ 18:55
☽ ⚹ ☿ 19:37
☽ ☍ ⚳ 22:27

20 Sa
☽ ⊼ ♆ 1:13
☽ ∠ ♂ 5:37
☽ ☌ ♀ 8:00
☉ ∠ ☽ 8:52
☽ ⊼ ♇ 10:40
♄ ∠ ♇ 11:46
☽ ☌ ♃ 20:38
☽ △ ♅ 21:08

21 Su
☽ ⊼ ⚷ 0:12
☉ ⊼ ♄ 6:52
☽ ⚹ ♂ 12:55
♀ # ♄ 15:53
☽ □ ♄ 16:11
☽ ⚼ ♇ 16:16
☉ ♋ 16:39
☉ ⚹ ☽ 17:02
☽ # ♆ 17:32
☿ △ ⚳ 18:04
☿ ∥ ♀ 18:22
☿ # ♄ 21:37
♀ ⊼ ♇ 22:49

22 M
☽ ⚼ ♅ 3:05
☽ ∥ ♅ 3:11
☽ ⊼ ⚳ 9:17
☽ □ ☿ 10:28
☽ ☍ ♆ 12:41
♃ △ ♅ 13:48
☽ △ ♇ 22:25

23 Tu
☽ ⊻ ♀ 0:11
☽ ⊼ ♅ 9:30
☽ ⊻ ♃ 9:45
☽ ☍ ⚷ 12:32
☽ ⚼ ⚳ 15:23
☿ □ ♆ 18:09
♂ ⊼ ♄ 18:37
☽ ∥ ⚷ 20:53

24 W
☽ ⚹ ♄ 4:34
☽ □ ♂ 5:13
☽ # ⚷ 8:31
☽ ∠ ♀ 8:51
☉ □ ☽ 11:04
⚷ R 11:37
♂ ♋ 13:34
☽ ∠ ♃ 16:42
☽ △ ⚳ 21:32

25 Th
☽ ⊼ ♆ 1:31
☽ △ ☿ 4:10
☽ ∠ ♄ 10:48
☽ □ ♇ 11:08
☽ ⚹ ♀ 17:17
☽ ☍ ♅ 22:21
☽ ⚹ ♃ 23:23

26 F
☽ ⊼ ⚷ 1:12
☽ # ♅ 2:15
☽ ⚼ ♆ 7:36
☽ ∥ ♆ 11:39
☽ ⚼ ☿ 12:56
☽ ⊻ ♄ 16:36
☽ △ ♂ 21:02

27 Sa
☉ △ ☽ 4:13
☽ ⚼ ⚷ 6:48
☽ □ ⚳ 8:36
☽ △ ♆ 13:01
☽ ⊼ ☿ 21:03
☽ ⚹ ♇ 22:07
☉ ∠ ♃ 23:54

28 Su
☽ ⚼ ♂ 3:44
☽ □ ♀ 7:45
☿ ⊼ ♇ 8:22
☽ ⊼ ♅ 8:59
☽ □ ♃ 10:42
☉ ⚼ ☽ 11:25
☽ △ ⚷ 11:34
☽ # ♃ 17:41
☽ # ♀ 21:14

29 M
☽ ☌ ♄ 1:51
☽ ∠ ♇ 2:21
☉ ⊼ ⚳ 5:54
♀ △ ♅ 6:27
☽ ⊼ ♂ 9:22
☽ ⚼ ♅ 12:58
☽ ⚹ ⚳ 16:29
☉ ⊼ ☽ 17:27
☽ □ ♆ 21:13

30 Tu
♀ ∥ ♃ 3:20
☽ ⊻ ♇ 5:40
☽ ∥ ♄ 6:33
☽ ☍ ☿ 10:21
☽ △ ♅ 16:02
☽ △ ♀ 17:48
☽ △ ♃ 18:19
☽ □ ⚷ 18:21
☽ ∠ ⚳ 19:06
♃ ⊼ ⚷ 20:32
⚵ ♍ 23:00

LONGITUDE

July 2015

Day	Sid.Time	☉	☽	☽ 12 hour	Mean☊	True☊	☿	♀	♂	⚳	♃	♄	⚷	♅	♆	♇
	h m s	° ' "	° ' "	° ' "	° '	° '	° '	° '	° '	° '	° '	° '	° '	° '	° '	° '
1 W	18 34 56	8♋52 31	24♐44 31	1♑36 30	5♎21.1	5♎13.3	17♊47.5	21♌24.2	4♋19.6	6♒55.9	21♌33.8	29♏05.3	21♓32.2	20♈14.5	9♓43.5	14♑24.2
2 Th	18 38 52	9 49 42	8♑33 19	15 34 24	5 17.9	5R 01.5	19 09.6	22 04.4	4 59.8	6R 46.3	21 45.0	29R 02.5	21R 31.8	20 15.7	9R 42.9	14R 22.7
3 F	18 42 49	10 46 53	22 39 11	29 46 57	5 14.8	4 50.1	20 35.3	22 43.4	5 39.9	6 36.4	21 56.3	28 59.7	21 31.4	20 16.8	9 42.3	14 21.2
4 Sa	18 46 45	11 44 04	6♒56 58	14♒08 32	5 11.6	4 40.3	22 04.5	23 21.3	6 20.0	6 26.2	22 07.6	28 57.0	21 30.9	20 17.9	9 41.6	14 19.7
5 Su	18 50 42	12 41 16	21 20 56	28 33 29	5 08.4	4 32.8	23 37.4	23 58.0	7 00.1	6 15.8	22 18.9	28 54.4	21 30.4	20 19.0	9 40.9	14 18.2
6 M	18 54 38	13 38 27	5♓45 37	12♓56 49	5 05.2	4 28.1	25 13.7	24 33.5	7 40.2	6 05.1	22 30.4	28 51.9	21 29.8	20 20.0	9 40.2	14 16.7
7 Tu	18 58 35	14 35 38	20 06 40	27 14 50	5 02.1	4 25.9	26 53.5	25 07.7	8 20.2	5 54.2	22 41.9	28 49.4	21 29.1	20 21.0	9 39.5	14 15.2
8 W	19 02 32	15 32 50	4♈21 05	11♈25 15	4 58.9	4 25.4	28 36.6	25 40.6	9 00.1	5 43.0	22 53.4	28 47.1	21 28.5	20 21.9	9 38.7	14 13.7
9 Th	19 06 28	16 30 02	18 27 13	25 26 56	4 55.7	4 25.5	0♋23.0	26 12.1	9 40.1	5 31.6	23 05.0	28 44.8	21 27.7	20 22.8	9 37.9	14 12.2
10 F	19 10 25	17 27 15	2♉24 20	9♉19 25	4 52.5	4 24.8	2 12.4	26 42.3	10 20.0	5 20.0	23 16.7	28 42.6	21 26.9	20 23.6	9 37.1	14 10.8
11 Sa	19 14 21	18 24 28	16 12 07	23 02 25	4 49.3	4 22.4	4 04.8	27 10.9	10 59.8	5 08.3	23 28.5	28 40.4	21 26.1	20 24.4	9 36.2	14 09.3
12 Su	19 18 18	19 21 42	29 50 14	6♊35 29	4 46.2	4 17.4	5 59.9	27 38.1	11 39.7	4 56.3	23 40.3	28 38.4	21 25.2	20 25.1	9 35.3	14 07.8
13 M	19 22 14	20 18 56	13♊18 02	19 57 46	4 43.0	4 09.7	7 57.6	28 03.7	12 19.5	4 44.1	23 52.1	28 36.5	21 24.2	20 25.8	9 34.4	14 06.3
14 Tu	19 26 11	21 16 10	26 34 30	3♋08 07	4 39.8	3 59.7	9 57.6	28 27.6	12 59.2	4 31.8	24 04.0	28 34.6	21 23.2	20 26.4	9 33.5	14 04.8
15 W	19 30 07	22 13 25	9♋38 27	16 05 23	4 36.6	3 48.2	11 59.7	28 49.9	13 38.9	4 19.3	24 16.0	28 32.8	21 22.2	20 27.0	9 32.5	14 03.3
16 Th	19 34 04	23 10 40	22 28 47	28 48 38	4 33.5	3 36.3	14 03.5	29 10.4	14 18.6	4 06.7	24 28.0	28 31.2	21 21.1	20 27.5	9 31.5	14 01.9
17 F	19 38 01	24 07 56	5♌04 53	11♌17 36	4 30.3	3 25.1	16 08.9	29 29.1	14 58.3	3 54.0	24 40.0	28 29.6	21 19.9	20 28.0	9 30.5	14 00.4
18 Sa	19 41 57	25 05 12	17 26 53	23 32 56	4 27.1	3 15.6	18 15.4	29 45.9	15 37.9	3 41.2	24 52.1	28 28.1	21 18.7	20 28.4	9 29.5	13 58.9
19 Su	19 45 54	26 02 28	29 35 58	5♍36 17	4 23.9	3 08.5	20 22.8	0♍00.8	16 17.5	3 28.2	25 04.3	28 26.7	21 17.5	20 28.8	9 28.4	13 57.5
20 M	19 49 50	26 59 44	11♍34 17	17 30 22	4 20.8	3 03.9	22 30.7	0 13.7	16 57.0	3 15.2	25 16.5	28 25.4	21 16.2	20 29.2	9 27.3	13 56.0
21 Tu	19 53 47	27 57 01	23 25 02	29 18 50	4 17.6	3D 01.6	24 38.9	0 24.5	17 36.5	3 02.1	25 28.7	28 24.1	21 14.8	20 29.4	9 26.2	13 54.6
22 W	19 57 43	28 54 18	5♎12 19	11♎06 07	4 14.4	3 01.2	26 47.0	0 33.2	18 16.0	2 49.0	25 41.0	28 23.0	21 13.4	20 29.7	9 25.1	13 53.1
23 Th	20 01 40	29 51 35	17 00 52	22 57 14	4 11.2	3 01.7	28 54.9	0 39.8	18 55.4	2 35.8	25 53.4	28 22.0	21 12.0	20 29.9	9 23.9	13 51.7
24 F	20 05 36	0♌48 52	28 55 53	4♏57 30	4 08.0	3R 02.2	1♌02.2	0 44.1	19 34.8	2 22.6	26 05.7	28 21.0	21 10.5	20 30.0	9 22.7	13 50.3
25 Sa	20 09 33	1 46 10	11♏02 45	17 12 16	4 04.9	3 01.8	3 08.8	0R 46.2	20 14.2	2 09.4	26 18.1	28 20.2	21 09.0	20 30.1	9 21.5	13 48.9
26 Su	20 13 30	2 43 29	23 26 39	29 46 26	4 01.7	2 59.6	5 14.4	0 46.0	20 53.5	1 56.1	26 30.6	28 19.5	21 07.4	20R 30.2	9 20.3	13 47.5
27 M	20 17 26	3 40 47	6♐12 05	12♐43 57	3 58.5	2 55.4	7 19.0	0 43.4	21 32.8	1 42.9	26 43.1	28 18.8	21 05.8	20 30.2	9 19.1	13 46.1
28 Tu	20 21 23	4 38 06	19 22 19	26 07 16	3 55.3	2 49.1	9 22.4	0 38.4	22 12.1	1 29.8	26 55.6	28 18.3	21 04.1	20 30.1	9 17.8	13 44.7
29 W	20 25 19	5 35 26	2♑58 47	9♑56 40	3 52.2	2 41.2	11 24.4	0 31.0	22 51.3	1 16.7	27 08.1	28 17.8	21 02.4	20 30.0	9 16.5	13 43.4
30 Th	20 29 16	6 32 46	17 00 32	24 09 53	3 49.0	2 32.4	13 25.0	0 21.3	23 30.5	1 03.6	27 20.7	28 17.5	21 00.6	20 29.9	9 15.2	13 42.0
31 F	20 33 12	7♌30 07	1♒24 02	8♒42 09	3♎45.8	2♎23.8	15♌24.2	0♍09.1	24♋09.7	0♒50.6	27♌33.4	28♏17.2	20♓58.8	20♈29.7	9♓13.9	13♑40.7

1st of Month

Julian Day # 2457204.5
Obliquity 23°26'04"
SVP 5♓02'34"
GC 27♐03.3
Eris 23♈22.9

Day	⚴	Day	⚵	Day	⚶
1	15♐38.2R	1	0♍00.9	1	7♈25.4
6	14 32.9R	6	1 51.5	6	8 39.9
11	13 37.1R	11	3 43.1	11	9 47.2
16	12 51.7R	16	5 35.7	16	10 46.6
21	12 17.3R	21	7 29.2	21	11 37.4
26	11 53.9R	26	9 23.3	26	12 19.0
31	11 41.4R	31	11 18.0	31	12 50.9

DECLINATION and LATITUDE

Day	☉ Decl	☽ Decl	☽ Lat	☽12h Decl	☿ Decl	☿ Lat	♀ Decl	♀ Lat	♂ Decl	♂ Lat	⚳ Decl	⚳ Lat	♃ Decl	♃ Lat	♄ Decl	♄ Lat
1 W	23N08	18S24	4N56	18S25	20N36	2S17	14N53	0N33	24N07	0N45	27S37	9S24	15N08	0N52	17S54	2N06
2 Th	23 04	18 10	5 00	17 38	20 55	2 05	14 33	0 26	24 06	0 45	27 44	9 29	15 04	0 52	17 54	2 06
3 F	22 60	16 49	4 47	15 44	21 13	1 53	14 13	0 18	24 05	0 46	27 50	9 33	15 00	0 52	17 53	2 06
4 Sa	22 55	14 25	4 15	12 52	21 31	1 41	13 53	0 10	24 03	0 46	27 57	9 37	14 57	0 52	17 53	2 05
5 Su	22 50	11 07	3 27	9 12	21 49	1 28	13 33	0 02	24 02	0 47	28 03	9 41	14 53	0 52	17 52	2 05
6 M	22 44	7 08	2 26	4 59	22 05	1 16	13 14	0S07	23 60	0 47	28 10	9 45	14 49	0 52	17 52	2 05
7 Tu	22 38	2 46	1 15	0 31	22 21	1 03	12 54	0 16	23 58	0 48	28 17	9 49	14 45	0 51	17 52	2 05
8 W	22 32	1N44	0 00	3N57	22 35	0 50	12 34	0 25	23 56	0 48	28 23	9 52	14 42	0 51	17 52	2 05
9 Th	22 25	6 06	1S14	8 09	22 48	0 38	12 15	0 34	23 53	0 49	28 30	9 56	14 38	0 51	17 51	2 04
10 F	22 18	10 04	2 23	11 51	22 59	0 26	11 56	0 44	23 51	0 49	28 36	9 60	14 34	0 51	17 51	2 04
11 Sa	22 10	13 27	3 22	14 51	23 09	0 13	11 37	0 54	23 48	0 49	28 43	10 03	14 30	0 51	17 51	2 04
12 Su	22 02	16 03	4 10	17 00	23 16	0 02	11 18	1 04	23 45	0 50	28 49	10 07	14 26	0 51	17 50	2 04
13 M	21 54	17 43	4 42	18 11	23 22	0N10	10 59	1 14	23 42	0 50	28 56	10 10	14 22	0 51	17 50	2 03
14 Tu	21 45	18 24	4 59	18 22	23 25	0 21	10 41	1 25	23 38	0 51	29 02	10 14	14 18	0 51	17 50	2 03
15 W	21 36	18 05	5 00	17 35	23 25	0 32	10 23	1 36	23 35	0 51	29 09	10 17	14 14	0 51	17 50	2 03
16 Th	21 27	16 51	4 46	15 56	23 23	0 42	10 05	1 47	23 31	0 51	29 15	10 20	14 10	0 51	17 50	2 03
17 F	21 17	14 49	4 18	13 33	23 18	0 51	9 48	1 58	23 27	0 52	29 21	10 24	14 06	0 51	17 50	2 03
18 Sa	21 07	12 08	3 38	10 37	23 11	0 60	9 31	2 10	23 23	0 52	29 27	10 27	14 02	0 51	17 50	2 02
19 Su	20 56	8 59	2 48	7 16	23 01	1 08	9 15	2 22	23 19	0 53	29 33	10 30	13 58	0 51	17 49	2 02
20 M	20 45	5 30	1 52	3 41	22 48	1 15	8 59	2 34	23 14	0 53	29 39	10 32	13 54	0 51	17 49	2 02
21 Tu	20 34	1 50	0 51	0S02	22 32	1 22	8 44	2 47	23 10	0 54	29 45	10 35	13 50	0 51	17 49	2 02
22 W	20 22	1S53	0N12	3 44	22 14	1 28	8 29	2 59	23 05	0 54	29 51	10 38	13 46	0 51	17 49	2 01
23 Th	20 11	5 32	1 14	7 18	21 53	1 33	8 14	3 12	22 60	0 54	29 57	10 40	13 42	0 51	17 49	2 01
24 F	19 58	9 00	2 14	10 37	21 30	1 37	8 01	3 25	22 55	0 55	30 02	10 43	13 37	0 51	17 49	2 01
25 Sa	19 46	12 08	3 09	13 33	21 05	1 41	7 48	3 38	22 49	0 55	30 08	10 45	13 33	0 51	17 49	2 01
26 Su	19 33	14 49	3 56	15 55	20 37	1 43	7 35	3 52	22 44	0 56	30 13	10 47	13 29	0 51	17 50	2 00
27 M	19 20	16 51	4 34	17 34	20 08	1 45	7 24	4 05	22 38	0 56	30 18	10 50	13 25	0 51	17 50	2 00
28 Tu	19 06	18 04	4 58	18 19	19 37	1 46	7 13	4 19	22 32	0 56	30 24	10 52	13 20	0 51	17 50	1 60
29 W	18 52	18 18	5 06	18 01	19 04	1 47	7 02	4 32	22 26	0 57	30 29	10 54	13 16	0 51	17 50	1 60
30 Th	18 38	17 27	4 56	16 36	18 30	1 47	6 53	4 46	22 20	0 57	30 33	10 55	13 12	0 51	17 50	1 59
31 F	18N24	15S29	4N28	14S06	17N54	1N46	6N45	4S59	22N13	0N57	30S38	10S57	13N07	0N51	17S50	1N59

Day	⚷ Decl	⚷ Lat	♅ Decl	♅ Lat	♆ Decl	♆ Lat	♇ Decl	♇ Lat
1	0N55	4N39	7N19	0S38	8S39	0S47	20S40	1N60
6	0 55	4 40	7 21	0 39	8 41	0 48	20 42	1 59
11	0 55	4 41	7 22	0 39	8 42	0 48	20 43	1 59
16	0 53	4 42	7 23	0 39	8 44	0 48	20 44	1 58
21	0 52	4 43	7 24	0 39	8 46	0 48	20 46	1 58
26	0 49	4 43	7 24	0 39	8 49	0 48	20 47	1 57
31	0N47	4N44	7N24	0S39	8S51	0S48	20S48	1N56

Day	⚴ Decl	⚴ Lat	⚵ Decl	⚵ Lat	⚶ Decl	⚶ Lat	Eris Decl	Eris Lat
1	24N50	47N44	10N54	0S36	3S17	6S47	2S38	12S35
6	24 21	47 11	10 26	0 24	3 05	7 05	2 38	12 36
11	23 47	46 31	9 57	0 12	2 56	7 24	2 38	12 36
16	23 07	45 47	9 27	0 01	2 51	7 44	2 39	12 37
21	22 22	44 59	8 55	0N10	2 50	8 04	2 39	12 37
26	21 34	44 08	8 22	0 21	2 53	8 25	2 40	12 38
31	20N42	43N14	7N48	0N31	3S01	8S47	2S40	12S38

Moon Phenomena

Max/0 Decl
dy hr mn
1 6:44 18S27
7 14:44 0 N
14 4:14 18N25
21 11:48 0 S
28 17:36 18S21

Perigee/Apogee
dy hr m kilometers
5 18:59 p 367094
21 11:03 a 404834

PH dy hr mn
○ 2 2:21 9♑55
☾ 8 20:25 16♈22
● 16 1:25 23♋14
☽ 24 4:05 0♏59
○ 31 10:44 7♒56

Max/0 Lat
dy hr mn
1 18:05 5N01
8 0:07 0 S
14 13:24 5S02
21 19:33 0 N
28 23:36 5N06

Void of Course Moon

Last Aspect		☽ Ingress	
30 18:19	♄ △	♑	1 9:12
3 10:39	♄ ✶	♒	3 12:22
5 12:33	♄ □	♓	5 14:24
7 14:37	♄ △	♈	7 16:39
9 13:48	♀ △	♉	9 19:51
11 21:53	♄ ☍	♊	12 0:17
14 3:32	♀ ✶	♋	14 6:15
16 11:25	♄ ✶	♌	16 14:16
18 21:42	♄ □	♍	19 0:48
21 10:08	♄ ✶	♎	21 13:24
23 18:13	♃ ✶	♏	24 2:08
26 9:16	♄ ☌	♐	26 12:26
28 13:38	♃ △	♑	28 18:49
30 18:51	♄ ✶	♒	30 21:41

DAILY ASPECTARIAN

1 W
♀ ⊼ ⚷ 4:40
☿ ⋕ ♇ 5:36
☽ ⊻ ♄ 7:35
♀ ☌ ♃ 7:52
☽ ☍ ♂ 17:33
☽ ⚼ ♃ 20:51
☽ ⊻ ⚳ 20:58
☉ △ ♆ 21:11
☽ ⚼ ♀ 21:19

2 Th
☽ ✶ ♆ 1:59
☉ ☍ ☽ 2:21
☽ ∥ ♄ 6:50
☽ ∠ ♄ 9:22
☽ ☌ ♇ 9:57
☿ ✶ ♅ 18:51
☽ □ ♅ 19:59
☽ ⊼ ☿ 20:07
☽ ✶ ⚷ 22:06
☽ ⊼ ♃ 22:47

3 F
☽ ⊼ ♀ 0:07
☽ ∠ ♆ 3:28
☽ ✶ ♄ 10:39
⚳ ∠ ⚷ 12:28
☿ ⚼ ⚳ 14:52
☿ □ ⚷ 15:07
☽ ⋕ ♃ 19:21
☽ ⊼ ♂ 22:55
☽ ☌ ⚳ 23:09
☽ ∠ ⚷ 23:16

4 Sa
☽ ⚼ ☿ 0:14
☿ ✶ ♃ 0:54
♂ ⊼ ⚳ 2:56
☽ ⊻ ♆ 4:35
☽ ⋕ ♀ 4:46
☉ ⊼ ☽ 8:33
☽ ⊻ ♇ 12:17
☽ ✶ ♅ 22:17

5 Su
☽ ⊻ ⚷ 0:16
☽ ⚼ ♂ 1:08
☽ ☍ ♃ 1:38
☽ △ ☿ 4:15
☽ ☍ ♀ 4:33
☿ ✶ ♀ 8:20
☉ ⚼ ☽ 11:18
☽ □ ♄ 12:33
☽ ∠ ♇ 13:13
☽ ∥ ♆ 15:06
♂ ∠ ♃ 15:47
☽ ⋕ ♅ 22:49
☽ ∠ ♅ 23:17

6 M
☽ ⊻ ⚳ 0:32
☽ △ ♂ 3:20
☉ ⚼ ♄ 5:24
☽ ☌ ♆ 6:31
☉ △ ☽ 14:06
☽ ✶ ♇ 14:12
☉ ☍ ♇ 15:39

7 Tu
☽ ⊻ ♅ 0:24
☽ ∠ ⚳ 1:19
☽ ☌ ⚷ 2:18
☽ ⊼ ♃ 4:24
☽ ⊼ ♀ 8:46
☽ ⋕ ⚷ 9:51
☽ □ ☿ 12:57
☽ △ ♄ 14:37
☽ ∥ ⚷ 19:37
☉ ∥ ☿ 19:51

8 W
☽ ✶ ⚳ 2:17
☿ ⊼ ♄ 2:20
☽ ⚼ ♃ 6:05
☽ □ ♂ 8:17
☽ ⊻ ♆ 8:58
☽ ⚼ ♀ 11:09
☽ ⚼ ♄ 15:59
☽ □ ♇ 16:45
☿ ♋ 18:53
☉ □ ☽ 20:25
♂ △ ♆ 22:43

9 Th
☽ ☌ ♅ 3:18
☽ ⊻ ⚷ 5:09
☽ ∥ ♅ 7:22
☽ △ ♃ 8:03
☽ ∠ ♆ 10:35
☽ △ ♀ 13:48
☽ ⋕ ♆ 15:21
☽ ⊼ ♄ 17:38
☽ ✶ ☿ 23:36

10 F
☽ □ ⚳ 5:00
☽ ∠ ⚷ 7:00
☽ ∥ ♀ 11:29
☽ ✶ ♆ 12:30
☽ ✶ ♂ 14:27
☽ △ ♇ 20:26

11 Sa
☉ ✶ ☽ 4:09
☽ ∠ ☿ 5:51
☽ ⊻ ♅ 7:22
☽ ∥ ♃ 8:37
☽ ✶ ⚷ 9:10
☿ ⊼ ⚳ 12:03
☽ □ ♃ 12:57
☽ ∠ ♂ 18:06
☽ □ ♀ 19:58
☽ ☍ ♄ 21:53
☽ ⚼ ♇ 22:45

12 Su
☉ ∠ ☽ 8:38
☽ △ ⚳ 8:55
☽ ∠ ♅ 9:55
☽ ⊻ ☿ 12:48
☽ □ ♆ 17:20
☽ ⊻ ♂ 22:09

13 M
☽ ⊼ ♇ 1:26
☽ ⋕ ♄ 2:33
☉ □ ♅ 2:54
☽ ⚼ ⚳ 11:25
☿ ∠ ♃ 12:10
☽ ✶ ♅ 12:51
☉ ⊻ ☽ 13:37
☽ □ ⚷ 14:35
☿ △ ♆ 19:15
☽ ✶ ♃ 19:22

14 Tu
☉ △ ⚷ 2:54
☽ ✶ ♀ 3:32
☽ ⊼ ♄ 3:39
♀ □ ♄ 6:49
☽ ⊼ ⚳ 14:20
♂ ⚼ ♄ 20:28
☽ ∠ ♃ 23:18
☽ △ ♆ 23:49

15 W
☽ ☌ ☿ 5:12
☽ ⋕ ♄ 6:44
☽ ⚼ ♄ 7:14
☽ ☌ ♂ 7:51
☽ ∠ ♀ 8:00
☽ ☍ ♇ 8:11
♀ ∠ ♂ 13:56
♂ ☍ ♇ 14:13
♀ ⚼ ♇ 14:29
☿ ⚼ ♄ 17:50
☽ □ ♅ 20:11
☽ △ ⚷ 21:53
☿ ☍ ♇ 23:41

16 Th
☉ ☌ ☽ 1:25
☿ ∠ ♀ 1:34
☽ ⊻ ♃ 3:49
☽ ⚼ ♆ 3:52
☿ ☌ ♂ 4:15
☽ △ ♄ 11:25
☽ ⊻ ♀ 13:01
☽ ☍ ⚳ 21:46

17 F
☽ ⚼ ⚷ 2:24
☽ ∥ ♃ 7:08
☽ ⊼ ♆ 8:32
☉ ⚼ ♆ 9:18
☉ ⊻ ♃ 17:04
☽ ⊼ ♇ 17:15
☽ ⊻ ♂ 20:15

18 Sa
☽ ⊻ ☿ 1:55
☽ △ ♅ 5:57
☽ ⊼ ⚷ 7:35
☽ ☌ ♃ 14:52
☉ ⊻ ☽ 16:20
☽ □ ♄ 21:42
☽ ∥ ♀ 21:55
♀ ♍ 22:39
☽ ⚼ ♇ 22:44

19 Su
☽ ☌ ♀ 0:50
☿ □ ♅ 1:08
☽ ⋕ ♆ 1:36
☽ ∠ ♂ 3:34
☽ ⊼ ⚳ 7:35
☿ △ ⚷ 10:10
☽ ∥ ♅ 11:07
☽ ⚼ ♅ 11:45
☽ ∠ ☿ 14:03
☽ ☍ ♆ 19:45
☉ ⋕ ♇ 23:52

20 M
☉ ∠ ☽ 0:56
☽ △ ♇ 4:46
☽ ✶ ♂ 11:31
☽ ⚼ ⚳ 13:16
☽ ⊼ ♅ 18:03
☽ ☍ ⚷ 19:36
♀ ⋕ ♆ 19:43
☿ ⚼ ♆ 21:39

21 Tu
☽ ✶ ☿ 3:03
☽ ⊻ ♃ 4:16
☽ ∥ ⚷ 6:16
☉ ✶ ☽ 10:02
☽ ✶ ♄ 10:08
☿ ⊻ ♃ 10:19
☉ △ ♄ 11:08
☽ ⊻ ♀ 14:25
☽ ⋕ ⚷ 17:20
☽ △ ⚳ 19:13

22 W
☽ ⊼ ♆ 8:34
☽ ∠ ♃ 11:21
☽ ∠ ♄ 16:37
☽ □ ♇ 17:37
☿ △ ♄ 17:52
☽ ∠ ♀ 21:14

23 Th
☉ ♌ 3:32
☽ □ ♂ 4:05
☽ ☍ ♅ 7:03
☽ ⊼ ⚷ 8:27
☿ ♌ 12:15
☽ ⋕ ♅ 12:42
☽ ⚼ ♆ 14:53
☽ ⋕ ♀ 17:23
☽ ✶ ♃ 18:13
☉ ☌ ☿ 19:25
☿ ⊻ ♀ 20:30
☉ ⊻ ♀ 21:54
☽ ∥ ♆ 22:31
☽ ⊻ ♄ 22:50

24 F
☽ ✶ ♀ 3:37
☉ □ ☽ 4:05
☽ □ ☿ 5:06
☽ □ ⚳ 6:45
☿ ☍ ⚳ 13:47
☽ ⚼ ⚷ 14:23
☽ △ ♆ 20:42

25 Sa
☽ ✶ ♇ 5:24
☉ ☍ ⚳ 7:53
♀ R 9:30
♂ □ ♅ 9:44
☽ ⋕ ♃ 11:45
☿ ⋕ ♇ 15:57
☽ ⊼ ♅ 18:22
☽ △ ♂ 18:50
☽ △ ⚷ 19:34

26 Su
☽ □ ♃ 5:56
♂ △ ⚷ 8:08
☽ ☌ ♄ 9:16
☿ ⚼ ⚷ 10:03
☽ ∠ ♇ 10:08
♅ R 10:39
☽ □ ♀ 13:50
☽ ✶ ⚳ 15:47
☉ △ ☽ 18:56
♀ ∥ ♅ 22:31
☽ ⚼ ♅ 22:42

27 M
☽ ⚼ ♂ 0:40
☽ △ ☿ 2:27
☽ □ ♆ 5:44
☽ ⊻ ♇ 13:52
☽ ∥ ♄ 17:35
☽ ∠ ⚳ 18:55
☿ ⊼ ♆ 23:07

28 Tu
☉ ⚼ ☽ 0:30
☽ △ ♅ 2:01
☽ □ ⚷ 3:02
☽ ⊼ ♂ 5:19
☽ ⚼ ☿ 10:29
☽ △ ♃ 13:38
☽ ⊻ ♄ 15:50
☽ △ ♀ 19:45
☽ ⊻ ⚳ 21:05

29 W
☉ ⊼ ☽ 4:51
☽ ✶ ♆ 10:50
☉ ⚼ ⚷ 10:57
☉ ∥ ☿ 14:27
☽ ⚼ ♃ 15:59
☽ ∥ ♄ 16:37
☽ ⊼ ☿ 16:55
☽ ∠ ♄ 17:42
☽ ☌ ♇ 18:24
☽ ⚼ ♀ 21:14

30 Th
☿ ⊼ ♇ 3:22
☽ □ ♅ 5:52
☽ ✶ ⚷ 6:43
☽ ☍ ♂ 11:25
☽ ∠ ♆ 12:08
☽ ⊼ ♃ 17:33
☽ ✶ ♄ 18:51
☽ ⊼ ♀ 21:58
☽ ☌ ⚳ 23:06

31 F
♂ ⚼ ♆ 2:31
☿ ⋕ ♄ 2:37
☽ ∠ ⚷ 7:31
☉ ☍ ☽ 10:44
☽ ⊻ ♆ 12:51
♀ R ♌ 15:28
☽ ⋕ ♃ 19:55
☽ ⊻ ♇ 20:06

August 2015

LONGITUDE

Day	Sid.Time	☉	☽	☽ 12 hour	Mean☊	True☊	☿	♀	♂	⚳	♃	♄	⚷	♅	♆	♇
	h m s	° ' "	° ' "	° ' "	° '	° '	° '	° '	° '	° '	° '	° '	° '	° '	° '	° '
1 Sa	20 37 09	8♌27 29	16♒03 21	23♒26 39	3♎42.6	2♎16.5	17♌21.8	29♌54.6	24♋48.8	0♒37.7	27♌46.0	28♏17.0	20♓57.0	20♈29.4	9♓12.5	13♑39.4
2 Su	20 41 05	9 24 51	0♓51 03	8♓15 36	3 39.4	2R 11.0	19 17.8	29R 37.7	25 27.9	0R 24.9	27 58.7	28D 17.0	20R 55.1	20R 29.1	9R 11.2	13R 38.0
3 M	20 45 02	10 22 15	15 39 21	23 01 29	3 36.3	2 07.8	21 12.3	29 18.5	26 06.9	0 12.1	28 11.4	28 17.0	20 53.2	20 28.8	9 09.8	13 36.7
4 Tu	20 48 59	11 19 39	0♈21 16	7♈38 07	3 33.1	2D 06.8	23 05.2	28 57.0	26 46.0	29♑59.6	28 24.1	28 17.1	20 51.3	20 28.4	9 08.4	13 35.5
5 W	20 52 55	12 17 05	14 51 32	22 01 10	3 29.9	2 07.2	24 56.5	28 33.5	27 25.0	29 47.1	28 36.9	28 17.3	20 49.3	20 28.0	9 07.0	13 34.2
6 Th	20 56 52	13 14 31	29 06 48	6♉08 18	3 26.7	2 08.2	26 46.2	28 07.8	28 04.0	29 34.8	28 49.7	28 17.6	20 47.2	20 27.5	9 05.6	13 32.9
7 F	21 00 48	14 12 00	13♉05 35	19 58 42	3 23.6	2R 08.9	28 34.4	27 40.3	28 42.9	29 22.6	29 02.5	28 18.0	20 45.2	20 26.9	9 04.1	13 31.7
8 Sa	21 04 45	15 09 29	26 47 42	3♊32 40	3 20.4	2 08.2	0♍20.9	27 10.9	29 21.8	29 10.7	29 15.3	28 18.6	20 43.1	20 26.4	9 02.7	13 30.5
9 Su	21 08 41	16 07 00	10♊13 45	16 51 04	3 17.2	2 05.8	2 05.9	26 39.8	0♌00.7	28 58.9	29 28.2	28 19.2	20 40.9	20 25.7	9 01.2	13 29.3
10 M	21 12 38	17 04 32	23 24 44	29 54 53	3 14.0	2 01.4	3 49.3	26 07.3	0 39.6	28 47.3	29 41.1	28 19.9	20 38.7	20 25.1	8 59.7	13 28.1
11 Tu	21 16 34	18 02 06	6♋21 39	12♋45 07	3 10.9	1 55.3	5 31.1	25 33.5	1 18.4	28 35.9	29 54.0	28 20.7	20 36.5	20 24.3	8 58.2	13 26.9
12 W	21 20 31	18 59 40	19 05 24	25 22 34	3 07.7	1 48.1	7 11.4	24 58.5	1 57.2	28 24.7	0♍06.9	28 21.6	20 34.3	20 23.6	8 56.7	13 25.7
13 Th	21 24 28	19 57 17	1♌36 45	7♌48 03	3 04.5	1 40.6	8 50.2	24 22.7	2 36.0	28 13.7	0 19.8	28 22.6	20 32.0	20 22.8	8 55.2	13 24.6
14 F	21 28 24	20 54 54	13 56 33	20 02 24	3 01.3	1 33.5	10 27.4	23 46.2	3 14.7	28 03.0	0 32.8	28 23.7	20 29.7	20 21.9	8 53.6	13 23.5
15 Sa	21 32 21	21 52 32	26 05 45	2♍06 48	2 58.1	1 27.6	12 03.1	23 09.2	3 53.5	27 52.5	0 45.8	28 24.8	20 27.4	20 21.0	8 52.1	13 22.4
16 Su	21 36 17	22 50 12	8♍05 44	14 02 50	2 55.0	1 23.3	13 37.3	22 31.9	4 32.1	27 42.3	0 58.7	28 26.1	20 25.0	20 20.1	8 50.5	13 21.3
17 M	21 40 14	23 47 53	19 58 22	25 52 42	2 51.8	1D 20.9	15 10.0	21 54.7	5 10.8	27 32.4	1 11.7	28 27.5	20 22.6	20 19.1	8 48.9	13 20.3
18 Tu	21 44 10	24 45 35	1♎46 10	7♎39 12	2 48.6	1 20.1	16 41.2	21 17.7	5 49.4	27 22.7	1 24.7	28 29.0	20 20.2	20 18.0	8 47.3	13 19.2
19 W	21 48 07	25 43 18	13 32 16	19 25 51	2 45.4	1 20.8	18 10.8	20 41.2	6 28.0	27 13.4	1 37.8	28 30.6	20 17.7	20 16.9	8 45.8	13 18.2
20 Th	21 52 03	26 41 02	25 20 29	1♏16 44	2 42.2	1 22.3	19 38.9	20 05.4	7 06.6	27 04.3	1 50.8	28 32.2	20 15.3	20 15.8	8 44.2	13 17.2
21 F	21 56 00	27 38 48	7♏15 10	13 16 25	2 39.1	1 24.0	21 05.4	19 30.6	7 45.1	26 55.5	2 03.8	28 34.0	20 12.7	20 14.6	8 42.6	13 16.3
22 Sa	21 59 57	28 36 34	19 21 04	25 30 05	2 35.9	1R 25.3	22 30.4	18 56.8	8 23.6	26 47.0	2 16.9	28 35.9	20 10.2	20 13.4	8 40.9	13 15.3
23 Su	22 03 53	29 34 22	1♐43 05	8♐01 36	2 32.7	1 25.7	23 53.8	18 24.4	9 02.1	26 38.9	2 29.9	28 37.8	20 07.7	20 12.2	8 39.3	13 14.4
24 M	22 07 50	0♍32 11	14 25 51	20 56 17	2 29.5	1 24.8	25 15.5	17 53.6	9 40.5	26 31.0	2 43.0	28 39.8	20 05.1	20 10.9	8 37.7	13 13.5
25 Tu	22 11 46	1 30 01	27 33 18	4♑17 10	2 26.4	1 22.6	26 35.6	17 24.4	10 18.9	26 23.5	2 56.0	28 42.0	20 02.5	20 09.6	8 36.1	13 12.6
26 W	22 15 43	2 27 53	11♑08 01	18 05 52	2 23.2	1 19.4	27 54.0	16 57.0	10 57.3	26 16.4	3 09.1	28 44.2	19 59.9	20 08.2	8 34.4	13 11.7
27 Th	22 19 39	3 25 45	25 10 31	2♒21 38	2 20.0	1 15.5	29 10.7	16 31.6	11 35.6	26 09.5	3 22.1	28 46.5	19 57.3	20 06.8	8 32.8	13 10.9
28 F	22 23 36	4 23 39	9♒38 42	17 01 00	2 16.8	1 11.7	0♎25.5	16 08.3	12 14.0	26 03.0	3 35.2	28 48.9	19 54.6	20 05.3	8 31.2	13 10.1
29 Sa	22 27 32	5 21 35	24 27 40	1♓57 43	2 13.7	1 08.3	1 38.4	15 47.2	12 52.3	25 56.8	3 48.2	28 51.5	19 52.0	20 03.8	8 29.5	13 09.3
30 Su	22 31 29	6 19 31	9♓30 03	17 03 30	2 10.5	1 06.0	2 49.4	15 28.4	13 30.5	25 51.0	4 01.3	28 54.0	19 49.3	20 02.3	8 27.9	13 08.6
31 M	22 35 26	7♍17 30	24 36 56	2♈09 12	2♎07.3	1♎04.9	3♎58.4	15♌11.9	14♌08.8	25♑45.5	4♍14.3	28♏56.7	19♓46.6	20♈00.7	8♓26.2	13♑07.8

1st of Month

Julian Day # 2457235.5
Obliquity 23°26'05"
SVP 5♓02'29"
GC 27♐03.4
Eris 23♈24.1R

Day	⚴	Day	⚵	Day	⚶
1	11♐40.2R	1	11♍41.0	1	12♈56.1
6	11 40.3	6	13 36.2	6	13 15.6
11	11 50.3	11	15 31.9	11	13 24.2
16	12 09.7	16	17 27.8	16	13 21.3R
21	12 38.0	21	19 23.9	21	13 06.7R
26	13 14.5	26	21 20.1	26	12 40.6R
31	13 58.6	31	23 16.3	31	12 03.3R

DECLINATION and LATITUDE

Day	☉ Decl	☽ Decl	☽ Lat	☽12h Decl	☿ Decl	☿ Lat	♀ Decl	♀ Lat	♂ Decl	♂ Lat	⚳ Decl	⚳ Lat	♃ Decl	♃ Lat	♄ Decl	♄ Lat
1 Sa	18N09	12S29	3N42	10S40	17N17	1N45	6N37	5S13	22N07	0N58	30S43	10S59	13N03	0N51	17S50	1N59
2 Su	17 54	8 40	2 40	6 32	16 39	1 43	6 30	5 26	21 60	0 58	30 47	11 00	12 59	0 51	17 51	1 59
3 M	17 38	4 19	1 28	2 01	16 01	1 40	6 24	5 39	21 53	0 59	30 51	11 02	12 54	0 51	17 51	1 58
4 Tu	17 23	0N17	0 09	2N34	15 21	1 37	6 19	5 52	21 46	0 59	30 56	11 03	12 50	0 52	17 51	1 58
5 W	17 07	4 48	1S08	6 57	14 40	1 33	6 16	6 05	21 38	0 59	30 60	11 04	12 46	0 52	17 51	1 58
6 Th	16 50	8 58	2 21	10 50	13 59	1 29	6 13	6 18	21 31	0 60	31 04	11 06	12 41	0 52	17 52	1 58
7 F	16 34	12 32	3 23	14 03	13 18	1 25	6 10	6 30	21 24	0 60	31 07	11 07	12 37	0 52	17 52	1 57
8 Sa	16 17	15 20	4 12	16 25	12 35	1 20	6 09	6 41	21 16	1 00	31 11	11 07	12 32	0 52	17 52	1 57
9 Su	16 00	17 15	4 47	17 50	11 53	1 14	6 09	6 52	21 08	1 01	31 14	11 08	12 28	0 52	17 53	1 57
10 M	15 43	18 11	5 06	18 17	11 10	1 09	6 10	7 03	20 60	1 01	31 18	11 09	12 23	0 52	17 53	1 57
11 Tu	15 25	18 09	5 08	17 47	10 27	1 03	6 12	7 13	20 52	1 01	31 21	11 10	12 19	0 52	17 54	1 56
12 W	15 08	17 12	4 55	16 25	9 44	0 56	6 15	7 22	20 43	1 02	31 24	11 10	12 14	0 52	17 54	1 56
13 Th	14 50	15 26	4 28	14 17	9 01	0 49	6 18	7 31	20 35	1 02	31 26	11 11	12 10	0 52	17 55	1 56
14 F	14 31	12 59	3 49	11 33	8 18	0 42	6 22	7 38	20 26	1 02	31 29	11 11	12 05	0 52	17 55	1 56
15 Sa	14 13	9 60	3 00	8 21	7 35	0 35	6 28	7 45	20 18	1 03	31 31	11 11	12 01	0 52	17 55	1 56
16 Su	13 54	6 37	2 03	4 51	6 52	0 27	6 33	7 52	20 09	1 03	31 34	11 11	11 56	0 52	17 56	1 55
17 M	13 35	3 02	1 02	1 11	6 09	0 20	6 40	7 57	19 60	1 03	31 36	11 11	11 51	0 52	17 57	1 55
18 Tu	13 16	0S40	0N02	2S30	5 26	0 12	6 47	8 01	19 51	1 04	31 38	11 11	11 47	0 52	17 57	1 55
19 W	12 57	4 19	1 06	6 06	4 44	0 04	6 55	8 05	19 41	1 04	31 40	11 11	11 42	0 52	17 58	1 55
20 Th	12 37	7 49	2 08	9 29	4 01	0S05	7 03	8 08	19 32	1 04	31 42	11 11	11 38	0 52	17 58	1 54
21 F	12 17	11 02	3 04	12 29	3 20	0 13	7 12	8 10	19 22	1 05	31 43	11 11	11 33	0 52	17 59	1 54
22 Sa	11 57	13 49	3 53	15 01	2 38	0 22	7 21	8 11	19 13	1 05	31 44	11 10	11 28	0 52	17 60	1 54
23 Su	11 37	16 03	4 33	16 54	1 57	0 31	7 31	8 11	19 03	1 05	31 46	11 10	11 24	0 52	18 00	1 54
24 M	11 17	17 33	5 00	17 59	1 16	0 40	7 41	8 10	18 53	1 06	31 47	11 09	11 19	0 52	18 01	1 53
25 Tu	10 56	18 12	5 13	18 09	0 36	0 49	7 51	8 08	18 43	1 06	31 48	11 09	11 14	0 52	18 02	1 53
26 W	10 36	17 50	5 09	17 15	0S03	0 58	8 01	8 06	18 33	1 06	31 49	11 08	11 10	0 52	18 02	1 53
27 Th	10 15	16 23	4 47	15 16	0 42	1 07	8 11	8 03	18 22	1 07	31 49	11 07	11 05	0 52	18 03	1 53
28 F	9 54	13 52	4 06	12 15	1 20	1 16	8 21	7 60	18 12	1 07	31 50	11 07	11 00	0 52	18 04	1 52
29 Sa	9 33	10 24	3 08	8 23	1 58	1 26	8 32	7 55	18 01	1 07	31 50	11 06	10 56	0 53	18 05	1 52
30 Su	9 11	6 13	1 56	3 56	2 35	1 35	8 42	7 50	17 51	1 08	31 51	11 05	10 51	0 53	18 05	1 52
31 M	8N50	1S36	0N36	0N46	3S11	1S44	8N52	7S45	17N40	1N08	31S51	11S04	10N46	0N53	18S06	1N52

Day	⚷ Decl	⚷ Lat	♅ Decl	♅ Lat	♆ Decl	♆ Lat	♇ Decl	♇ Lat
1	0N46	4N44	7N24	0S39	8S52	0S48	20S48	1N56
6	0 43	4 45	7 23	0 39	8 54	0 48	20 50	1 56
11	0 39	4 45	7 22	0 39	8 57	0 49	20 51	1 55
16	0 35	4 46	7 20	0 40	9 00	0 49	20 52	1 54
21	0 30	4 46	7 18	0 40	9 03	0 49	20 53	1 53
26	0 26	4 46	7 15	0 40	9 06	0 49	20 55	1 53
31	0N20	4N46	7N12	0S40	9S10	0S49	20S56	1N52

Day	⚴ Decl	⚴ Lat	⚵ Decl	⚵ Lat	⚶ Decl	⚶ Lat	Eris Decl	Eris Lat
1	20N31	43N03	7N42	0N33	3S03	8S51	2S40	12S38
6	19 36	42 08	7 07	0 43	3 16	9 13	2 41	12 39
11	18 40	41 12	6 31	0 53	3 33	9 35	2 42	12 39
16	17 42	40 16	5 55	1 03	3 54	9 57	2 43	12 40
21	16 44	39 20	5 18	1 12	4 20	10 19	2 44	12 40
26	15 46	38 25	4 41	1 21	4 49	10 39	2 45	12 40
31	14N48	37N30	4N03	1N31	5S21	10S59	2S46	12S41

Moon Phenomena

Max/0 Decl dy hr mn	Perigee/Apogee dy hr m kilometers
3 22:31 0 N	2 10:02 p 362142
10 11:09 18N17	18 2:30 a 405848
17 19:40 0 S	30 15:28 p 358294
25 3:36 18S12	
31 8:06 0 N	

Max/0 Lat dy hr mn	PH dy hr mn
4 2:53 0 S	☾ 7 2:04 14♉17
10 15:50 5S09	● 14 14:55 21♌31
17 23:07 0 N	☽ 22 19:32 29♏24
25 6:45 5N14	○ 29 18:36 6♓06
31 10:17 0 S	

Void of Course Moon

Last Aspect	☽ Ingress
1 22:04 ♀ ☍	♓ 1 22:37
3 20:36 ♄ △	♈ 3 23:25
5 23:30 ♃ △	♉ 6 1:30
8 4:47 ♂ ✶	♊ 8 5:41
10 11:46 ♃ ✶	♋ 10 12:09
12 17:45 ♄ △	♌ 12 20:53
15 4:37 ♄ □	♍ 15 7:47
17 17:17 ♄ ✶	♎ 17 20:24
20 2:58 ☉ ✶	♏ 20 9:25
22 19:32 ☉ □	♐ 22 20:42
24 22:05 ☿ □	♑ 25 4:23
27 7:21 ☿ △	♒ 27 8:05
29 7:04 ♄ □	♓ 29 8:52
31 6:55 ♄ △	♈ 31 8:34

DAILY ASPECTARIAN

1 Sa: ☽☍☿ 2:27, ☽✶♅ 7:12, ☽⊻⚷ 7:56, ☽⊼♂ 14:52, ☉⊼♆ 18:25, ☽☍♃ 19:17, ☽□♄ 19:50, ☽∠♇ 20:25, ☽☍♀ 22:04, ☽∥♆ 22:51, ☽⊻⚳ 23:18

2 Su: ☉#♄ 4:39, ♄ D 5:54, ☽#♅ 7:16, ☽∠♅ 7:30, ☽#♀ 12:29, ☽☌♆ 13:29, ☉⊼☽ 14:50, ☿△♅ 14:52, ☽⚼♂ 16:17, ☿⊼⚷ 20:02, ☽✶♇ 20:41, ☽∠⚳ 23:16

3 M: ☽⊻♅ 7:51, ☽☌⚷ 8:30, ☽⊼☿ 10:22, ♃□♄ 10:37, ⚴ D 11:15, ☉⚼☽ 16:56, ☽△♂ 17:51, ☽#⚷ 18:40, ☽△♄ 20:36, ☽⊼♃ 20:45, ☽⊼♀ 21:45, ⚳ R♑ 23:09, ☽✶⚳ 23:25

4 Tu: ☽∥⚷ 2:21, ☽⊻♆ 14:28, ☽⚼☿ 14:38, ♃⚼♇ 19:23, ☉△☽ 19:24, ☽⚼♄ 21:23, ♀☌♃ 21:48, ☽□♇ 21:51, ☽⚼♀ 21:53, ☽⚼♃ 21:54, ♀⚼♇ 23:15

5 W: ☽∥♀ 8:00, ☽☌♅ 9:23, ☽⊻⚷ 9:58, ☽∥♅ 14:33, ♀□♄ 15:09, ☽∠♆ 15:31, ☽△☿ 19:26, ☽□♂ 22:08, ☽△♀ 22:23, ☽⊼♄ 22:36, ☽△♃ 23:30, ☽#♆ 23:39

6 Th: ☽□⚳ 0:47, ♀⊻♂ 1:25, ☉⊼♇ 7:31, ♂△♄ 8:30, ☽∠⚷ 11:22, ☿☌♀ 14:26, ☽✶♆ 17:03, ☿□♄ 20:20, ☿⚼♇ 23:25

7 F: ☽∥♃ 0:32, ☽△♇ 0:45, ☉□☽ 2:04, ☿⊻♂ 3:00, ☽∥☿ 4:44, ☿☌♃ 7:10, ☿⊼⚳ 9:44, ☽⊻♅ 12:49, ☽✶⚷ 13:19, ♂⊻♃ 18:00, ♂☍⚳ 18:43, ☿ ♍ 19:16, ⚳⊼♃ 19:29

8 Sa: ☽□♀ 0:40, ☿∥♃ 2:05, ☽☍♄ 2:41, ☽⚼♇ 3:02, ☽△⚳ 4:10, ☽□♃ 4:26, ☽✶♂ 4:47, ☽□☿ 7:15, ☉∥☽ 9:11, ☽∠♅ 15:23, ☽□♆ 21:49, ♂ ♌ 23:33

9 Su: ☽⊼♇ 5:53, ☽⚼⚳ 6:41, ☽∠♂ 9:06, ☉✶☽ 11:30, ☽#♄ 13:17, ☽✶♅ 18:31, ☽□⚷ 18:56

10 M: ☽✶♀ 4:47, ☽⊼♄ 9:05, ☽⊼⚳ 9:46, ☽✶♃ 11:46, ☽⊻♂ 14:05, ☉∠☽ 17:18, ☽✶☿ 22:11, ☿⚼♅ 22:25

11 Tu: ♂#♇ 2:05, ☽△♆ 4:53, ☽∠♀ 7:32, ☽#♄ 9:04, ♃ ♍ 11:12, ☽⚼♄ 13:08, ☽☍♇ 13:18, ☽∠♃ 16:20, ☉⊻☽ 23:48

12 W: ☽□♅ 2:29, ☽△⚷ 2:49, ⚶ R 6:03, ⚳✶♄ 6:13, ☽∠☿ 6:48, ☽⚼♆ 9:14, ☽⊻♀ 10:43, ☽☍⚳ 17:34, ☽△♄ 17:45, ☽⊻♃ 21:29

13 Th: ☿☍♆ 1:12, ☿#♆ 1:25, ☽☌♂ 2:01, ☉∥☽ 7:31, ☽⚼⚷ 7:34, ☉△♅ 10:28, ☉⊼⚷ 13:55, ☽⊼♆ 14:09, ☽⊻☿ 16:09, ♄∠♇ 22:18, ☽⊼♇ 22:55

14 F: ☽∥♃ 7:48, ☽△♅ 12:38, ☽⊼⚷ 12:52, ☉☌☽ 14:55, ☽☌♀ 18:27

15 Sa: ☽⊼⚳ 3:30, ☽⚼♇ 4:32, ☽□♄ 4:37, ☽#♆ 7:19, ☿∥♅ 8:07, ☽☌♃ 9:28, ☿⚼⚳ 11:19, ☽⊻♂ 16:27, ☽⚼♅ 18:28, ☽∥♅ 19:07, ☉☌♀ 19:23, ☿△♇ 19:57, ☽∥☿ 21:57

16 Su: ☽∥♀ 0:27, ☽☍♆ 1:30, ☿∥♀ 8:53, ☽⚼⚳ 9:10, ☽△♇ 10:35, ☽☌☿ 12:49

17 M: ☽∠♂ 0:27, ☽⊼♅ 0:42, ☽☍⚷ 0:49, ☽⊻♀ 3:44, ♂⚼⚷ 6:55, ☉⊻☽ 8:28, ☽△⚳ 15:10, ☽∥⚷ 16:03, ☽✶♄ 17:17, ☽⊻♃ 23:16, ☽#⚷ 23:16

18 Tu: ☽✶♂ 8:45, ☽∠♀ 8:46, ☽⊼♆ 14:17, ☉∠☽ 17:45, ☽□♇ 23:31, ☽∠♄ 23:57

19 W: ☽#☿ 2:15, ☽∠♃ 6:25, ☽⊻☿ 10:48, ☽☍♅ 13:43, ☽⊼⚷ 13:43, ☽✶♀ 13:51, ♅⊻⚷ 13:54, ♀△♅ 16:45, ♀⊼⚷ 16:52, ☽#♀ 18:24, ☽#♅ 20:22, ☽⚼♆ 20:45

20 Th: ☉✶☽ 2:58, ☽□⚳ 3:28, ☿⊻♀ 5:12, ☽⊻♄ 6:29, ☉⊼⚳ 8:22, ☽∥♆ 8:54, ☿☍⚷ 9:45, ☿⊼♅ 10:03, ☽✶♃ 13:23, ☽⚼⚷ 19:56, ☽∠☿ 21:21

21 F: ☽□♂ 1:03, ☽△♆ 2:54, ☽#♃ 4:05, ☉#☽ 9:15, ☽✶♇ 11:59, ♀∥♅ 13:48, ☉⚼♇ 15:18, ☽□♀ 23:14, ☉□♄ 23:41

22 Sa: ☽△⚷ 1:36, ☽⊼♅ 1:43, ☽✶☿ 6:58, ♂⊼♆ 10:23, ☽✶⚳ 14:20, ☽∠♇ 17:19, ☽☌♄ 18:03, ☉□☽ 19:32

23 Su: ☽□♃ 1:31, ☿∠♂ 4:31, ☽⚼♅ 6:38, ☉ ♍ 10:38, ☽□♆ 13:09, ☽△♂ 14:38, ☽∠⚳ 18:37, ☉∥♃ 20:46, ☽⊻♇ 21:45

24 M: ☽△♀ 6:10, ☽□⚷ 10:24, ☽△♅ 10:36, ☽∥♄ 13:12, ☽⚼♂ 19:45, ☿△⚳ 20:39, ☽⊻⚳ 21:55, ☽□☿ 22:05

25 Tu: ☽⊻♄ 2:04, ☿∥⚷ 6:03, ☉△☽ 7:36, ☽⚼♀ 8:23, ☽△♃ 9:46, ☽∥♄ 17:21, ☽✶♆ 19:33, ☽⊼♂ 23:40

26 W: ☽☌♇ 3:34, ☽∠♄ 4:31, ☽⊼♀ 9:44, ☉⚼☽ 11:43, ☽⚼♃ 12:17, ☿#⚷ 13:27, ☽✶⚷ 15:12, ☽□♅ 15:27, ☿✶♄ 16:09, ☽∠♆ 21:16, ☉☌♃ 22:03

27 Th: ☽☌⚳ 1:38, ☽✶♄ 6:03, ☽△☿ 7:21, ☽⊼♃ 13:53, ☉⊼☽ 14:45, ☿ ♎ 15:46, ☽∠⚷ 16:14, ☽⊻♆ 22:10

28 F: ☽☍♂ 4:25, ☽⊻♇ 5:45, ☽⚼☿ 10:16, ☽☍♀ 10:19, ☿∠♀ 10:48, ☽⊻⚷ 16:38, ☉⚼♅ 16:50, ☽✶♅ 16:56, ♂#♄ 17:12, ☽#♃ 20:39

29 Sa: ☽⊻⚳ 2:22, ☉#☽ 5:43, ☽∠♇ 5:55, ☽□♄ 7:04, ☽∥♆ 7:35, ♂⊼♇ 10:29, ☽#♀ 10:44, ☽⊼☿ 12:28, ☽☍♃ 15:09, ☽∠♅ 16:55, ☽#♅ 18:31, ☉☍☽ 18:36, ☽☌♆ 22:21

30 Su: ☽∠⚳ 2:08, ☉#♆ 2:34, ☽✶♇ 5:47, ☽⊼♂ 6:39, ☽⊼♀ 9:18, ☽☌⚷ 16:20, ☽⊻♅ 16:42, ☽∥☿ 16:50, ☉∥♀ 22:40

31 M: ☽✶⚳ 1:48, ☽#⚷ 6:24, ☽△♄ 6:55, ☿⊻♃ 7:00, ☽⚼♂ 7:32, ☽⚼♀ 8:44, ☽∥⚷ 9:48, ☽⊼♃ 15:33, ☽☍☿ 16:06, ☉⊼☽ 21:36, ☽⊻♆ 22:00

LONGITUDE — September 2015

Day	Sid.Time	☉	☽	☽ 12 hour	Mean☊	True☊	☿	♀	♂	⚳	♃	♄	⚷	♅	♆	♇
	h m s	° ' "	° ' "	° ' "	° '	° '	° '	° '	° '	° '	° '	° '	° '	° '	° '	° '
Tu	22 39 22	8♍15 30	9♈39 15	17♈06 10	2♎04.1	1♎05.0	5♎05.3	14♌57.8	14♌47.0	25♑40.4	4♍27.4	28♏59.5	19♓43.9	19♈59.1	8♓24.6	13♑07.1
W	22 43 19	9 13 31	24 29 06	1♉47 24	2 00.9	1 05.9	6 09.9	14R 46.0	15 25.2	25R 35.6	4 40.4	29 02.3	19R 41.2	19R 57.5	8R 22.9	13R 06.5
Th	22 47 15	10 11 35	9♉00 35	16 08 15	1 57.8	1 07.2	7 12.2	14 36.8	16 03.3	25 31.2	4 53.4	29 05.3	19 38.4	19 55.8	8 21.3	13 05.8
F	22 51 12	11 09 41	23 10 14	0♊06 25	1 54.6	1 08.4	8 12.0	14 29.9	16 41.5	25 27.1	5 06.4	29 08.3	19 35.7	19 54.1	8 19.6	13 05.2
Sa	22 55 08	12 07 49	6♊56 50	13 41 38	1 51.4	1R 09.1	9 09.2	14 25.5	17 19.6	25 23.4	5 19.5	29 11.4	19 32.9	19 52.3	8 18.0	13 04.6
Su	22 59 05	13 05 58	20 20 58	26 55 08	1 48.2	1 09.1	10 03.6	14D 23.5	17 57.7	25 20.0	5 32.5	29 14.6	19 30.2	19 50.6	8 16.3	13 04.0
M	23 03 01	14 04 10	3♋24 24	9♋49 06	1 45.0	1 08.2	10 55.0	14 23.8	18 35.8	25 17.0	5 45.5	29 17.9	19 27.4	19 48.7	8 14.7	13 03.4
Tu	23 06 58	15 02 24	16 09 33	22 26 07	1 41.9	1 06.6	11 43.3	14 26.5	19 13.8	25 14.4	5 58.4	29 21.3	19 24.6	19 46.9	8 13.1	13 02.9
W	23 10 55	16 00 40	28 39 07	4♌48 53	1 38.7	1 04.5	12 28.3	14 31.4	19 51.8	25 12.1	6 11.4	29 24.7	19 21.9	19 45.0	8 11.4	13 02.4
Th	23 14 51	16 58 57	10♌55 45	17 00 00	1 35.5	1 02.4	13 09.6	14 38.6	20 29.8	25 10.2	6 24.3	29 28.3	19 19.1	19 43.1	8 09.8	13 02.0
F	23 18 48	17 57 17	23 01 57	29 01 52	1 32.3	1 00.4	13 47.0	14 48.0	21 07.8	25 08.6	6 37.3	29 31.9	19 16.3	19 41.2	8 08.2	13 01.5
Sa	23 22 44	18 55 39	5♍00 00	10♍56 42	1 29.2	0 58.8	14 20.3	14 59.5	21 45.7	25 07.4	6 50.2	29 35.6	19 13.5	19 39.2	8 06.6	13 01.1
Su	23 26 41	19 54 02	16 52 08	22 46 37	1 26.0	0 57.9	14 49.1	15 13.1	22 23.6	25 06.6	7 03.1	29 39.4	19 10.7	19 37.2	8 05.0	13 00.7
M	23 30 37	20 52 27	28 40 24	4♎33 47	1 22.8	0D 57.5	15 13.2	15 28.8	23 01.5	25D 06.1	7 16.0	29 43.3	19 07.9	19 35.2	8 03.4	13 00.4
Tu	23 34 34	21 50 54	10♎27 04	16 20 32	1 19.6	0 57.6	15 32.2	15 46.3	23 39.4	25 06.0	7 28.8	29 47.2	19 05.2	19 33.1	8 01.8	13 00.1
W	23 38 30	22 49 23	22 14 32	28 09 25	1 16.4	0 58.1	15 45.7	16 05.8	24 17.2	25 06.3	7 41.6	29 51.2	19 02.4	19 31.0	8 00.2	12 59.8
Th	23 42 27	23 47 53	4♏05 35	10♏03 25	1 13.3	0 58.8	15R 53.5	16 27.1	24 55.0	25 06.9	7 54.5	29 55.3	18 59.6	19 28.9	7 58.6	12 59.5
F	23 46 23	24 46 26	16 03 21	22 05 51	1 10.1	0 59.6	15 55.1	16 50.1	25 32.8	25 07.8	8 07.2	29 59.5	18 56.8	19 26.8	7 57.0	12 59.3
Sa	23 50 20	25 45 00	28 11 23	4♐20 26	1 06.9	1 00.2	15 50.2	17 14.9	26 10.5	25 09.2	8 20.0	0♐03.8	18 54.1	19 24.6	7 55.5	12 59.1
Su	23 54 17	26 43 36	10♐33 30	16 51 04	1 03.7	1 00.6	15 38.7	17 41.4	26 48.2	25 10.8	8 32.7	0 08.1	18 51.3	19 22.5	7 53.9	12 58.9
M	23 58 13	27 42 13	23 13 38	29 41 38	1 00.5	1R 00.7	15 20.1	18 09.4	27 25.9	25 12.9	8 45.4	0 12.5	18 48.6	19 20.3	7 52.4	12 58.8
Tu	0 02 10	28 40 52	6♑15 31	12♑55 36	0 57.4	1 00.7	14 54.5	18 39.0	28 03.6	25 15.2	8 58.1	0 17.0	18 45.8	19 18.0	7 50.9	12 58.7
W	0 06 06	29 39 33	19 42 10	26 35 24	0 54.2	1 00.6	14 21.7	19 10.1	28 41.2	25 17.9	9 10.7	0 21.5	18 43.1	19 15.8	7 49.4	12 58.6
Th	0 10 03	0♎38 16	3♒35 22	10♒41 57	0 51.0	1D 00.6	13 41.9	19 42.6	29 18.8	25 21.0	9 23.3	0 26.1	18 40.4	19 13.5	7 47.9	12 58.5
F	0 13 59	1 37 00	17 54 55	25 13 50	0 47.8	1 00.6	12 55.3	20 16.5	29 56.4	25 24.4	9 35.8	0 30.8	18 37.7	19 11.3	7 46.4	12D 58.5
Sa	0 17 56	2 35 45	2♓38 08	10♓07 01	0 44.7	1 00.7	12 02.6	20 51.8	0♍33.9	25 28.1	9 48.4	0 35.6	18 35.0	19 09.0	7 44.9	12 58.5
Su	0 21 52	3 34 33	17 39 36	25 14 47	0 41.5	1R 00.8	11 04.4	21 28.3	1 11.5	25 32.2	10 00.9	0 40.4	18 32.4	19 06.7	7 43.5	12 58.5
M	0 25 49	4 33 23	2♈51 27	10♈28 21	0 38.3	1 00.9	10 01.7	22 06.2	1 48.9	25 36.6	10 13.3	0 45.3	18 29.7	19 04.3	7 42.1	12 58.6
Tu	0 29 46	5 32 14	18 04 16	25 38 00	0 35.1	1 00.7	8 55.9	22 45.2	2 26.4	25 41.3	10 25.7	0 50.3	18 27.1	19 02.0	7 40.6	12 58.7
W	0 33 42	6♎31 08	3♉08 26	10♉34 34	0♎31.9	1♎00.3	7♎48.4	23♌25.4	3♍03.9	25♑46.3	10♍38.1	0♐55.3	18♓24.5	18♈59.6	7♓39.2	12♑58.8

1st of Month

Julian Day # 2457266.5
Obliquity 23°26'05"
SVP 5♓02'26"
GC 27♐03.5
Eris 23♈15.7R

Day	⚴
1	14♐08.2
6	15 00.6
11	15 59.1
16	17 03.5
21	18 13.2
26	19 27.7

Day	⚵
1	23♍39.5
6	25 35.6
11	27 31.6
16	29 27.3
21	1♎22.7
26	3 17.6

Day	⚶
1	11♈54.5R
6	11 04.6R
11	10 05.3R
16	8 58.2R
21	7 45.4R
26	6 29.2R

DECLINATION and LATITUDE

Day	☉ Decl	☽ Decl	☽ Lat	☽12h Decl	☿ Decl	☿ Lat	♀ Decl	♀ Lat	♂ Decl	♂ Lat	⚳ Decl	⚳ Lat	♃ Decl	♃ Lat	♄ Decl	♄ Lat
Tu	8N28	3N06	0S47	5N22	3S46	1S54	9N01	7S39	17N29	1N08	31S51	11S03	10N42	0N53	18S07	1N51
W	8 07	7 32	2 06	9 34	4 20	2 03	9 11	7 32	17 18	1 09	31 51	11 02	10 37	0 53	18 08	1 51
Th	7 45	11 25	3 15	13 05	4 53	2 12	9 20	7 25	17 07	1 09	31 51	11 01	10 32	0 53	18 09	1 51
F	7 23	14 32	4 10	15 45	5 25	2 21	9 29	7 18	16 56	1 09	31 50	10 59	10 27	0 53	18 10	1 51
Sa	7 01	16 43	4 49	17 27	5 56	2 30	9 38	7 10	16 44	1 09	31 50	10 58	10 23	0 53	18 10	1 51
Su	6 38	17 55	5 11	18 09	6 25	2 39	9 46	7 02	16 33	1 10	31 49	10 57	10 18	0 53	18 11	1 50
M	6 16	18 07	5 16	17 52	6 53	2 47	9 54	6 54	16 22	1 10	31 48	10 56	10 13	0 53	18 12	1 50
Tu	5 54	17 24	5 06	16 43	7 20	2 56	10 01	6 45	16 10	1 10	31 47	10 54	10 09	0 53	18 13	1 50
W	5 31	15 51	4 41	14 48	7 45	3 04	10 08	6 37	15 58	1 11	31 46	10 53	10 04	0 53	18 14	1 50
Th	5 08	13 35	4 03	12 14	8 08	3 12	10 15	6 28	15 46	1 11	31 45	10 51	9 59	0 53	18 15	1 49
F	4 46	10 46	3 15	9 11	8 30	3 19	10 21	6 19	15 35	1 11	31 44	10 50	9 54	0 53	18 16	1 49
Sa	4 23	7 31	2 19	5 47	8 49	3 27	10 27	6 09	15 23	1 11	31 43	10 48	9 50	0 53	18 17	1 49
Su	3 60	3 60	1 17	2 10	9 07	3 33	10 32	5 60	15 11	1 12	31 42	10 47	9 45	0 54	18 18	1 49
M	3 37	0 20	0 13	1S30	9 22	3 39	10 36	5 51	14 58	1 12	31 40	10 45	9 40	0 54	18 19	1 49
Tu	3 14	3S20	0N53	5 07	9 34	3 45	10 40	5 41	14 46	1 12	31 39	10 44	9 36	0 54	18 20	1 48
W	2 51	6 52	1 56	8 33	9 44	3 49	10 44	5 31	14 34	1 13	31 37	10 42	9 31	0 54	18 21	1 48
Th	2 28	10 09	2 54	11 39	9 50	3 53	10 47	5 22	14 21	1 13	31 35	10 40	9 26	0 54	18 22	1 48
F	2 05	13 02	3 45	14 18	9 54	3 56	10 49	5 12	14 09	1 13	31 33	10 39	9 21	0 54	18 23	1 48
Sa	1 41	15 24	4 28	16 21	9 54	3 58	10 51	5 03	13 56	1 13	31 32	10 37	9 17	0 54	18 24	1 48
Su	1 18	17 06	4 58	17 40	9 50	3 59	10 52	4 53	13 44	1 14	31 30	10 35	9 12	0 54	18 26	1 47
M	0 55	18 01	5 15	18 08	9 42	3 59	10 53	4 43	13 31	1 14	31 27	10 34	9 07	0 54	18 27	1 47
Tu	0 31	18 01	5 17	17 38	9 31	3 57	10 53	4 34	13 18	1 14	31 25	10 32	9 03	0 54	18 28	1 47
W	0 08	17 01	5 01	16 08	9 15	3 53	10 53	4 24	13 06	1 14	31 23	10 30	8 58	0 55	18 29	1 47
Th	0S15	14 60	4 28	13 37	8 54	3 48	10 52	4 15	12 53	1 15	31 21	10 28	8 53	0 55	18 30	1 47
F	0 39	12 00	3 38	10 11	8 30	3 41	10 50	4 05	12 40	1 15	31 18	10 26	8 49	0 55	18 31	1 46
Sa	1 02	8 10	2 32	6 01	8 01	3 32	10 48	3 56	12 27	1 15	31 16	10 25	8 44	0 55	18 32	1 46
Su	1 25	3 45	1 14	1 24	7 28	3 21	10 46	3 47	12 13	1 15	31 13	10 23	8 40	0 55	18 34	1 46
M	1 49	0N59	0S10	3N21	6 52	3 09	10 42	3 38	12 00	1 16	31 10	10 21	8 35	0 55	18 35	1 46
Tu	2 12	5 39	1 34	7 51	6 13	2 54	10 38	3 29	11 47	1 16	31 08	10 19	8 30	0 55	18 36	1 46
W	2S35	9N54	2S49	11N47	5S31	2S38	10N34	3S19	11N34	1N16	31S05	10S17	8N26	0N55	18S37	1N45

Day	⚷ Decl	⚷ Lat	♅ Decl	♅ Lat	♆ Decl	♆ Lat	♇ Decl	♇ Lat
1	0N19	4N46	7N12	0S40	9S10	0S49	20S56	1N52
6	0 14	4 46	7 08	0 40	9 13	0 49	20 57	1 51
11	0 08	4 46	7 05	0 40	9 16	0 49	20 58	1 50
16	0 03	4 45	7 01	0 40	9 19	0 49	20 59	1 50
21	0S03	4 45	6 57	0 40	9 22	0 49	21 00	1 49
26	0 09	4 44	6 53	0 40	9 25	0 49	21 01	1 48

Day	⚴ Decl	⚴ Lat	⚵ Decl	⚵ Lat	⚶ Decl	⚶ Lat	Eris Decl	Eris Lat
1	14N36	37N20	3N56	1N32	5S27	11S02	2S46	12S41
6	13 39	36 27	3 18	1 41	6 02	11 19	2 47	12 41
11	12 43	35 36	2 40	1 50	6 39	11 34	2 48	12 41
16	11 49	34 46	2 03	1 59	7 16	11 46	2 49	12 42
21	10 56	33 58	1 25	2 08	7 52	11 54	2 50	12 42
26	10 05	33 12	0 48	2 17	8 26	11 59	2 51	12 42

Moon Phenomena

Max/0 Decl
dy hr mn
6 17:09 18N10
14 2:10 0 S
21 12:02 18S08
27 19:04 0 N

Max/0 Lat
dy hr mn
6 19:51 5S16
14 4:39 0 N
21 14:26 5N18
27 21:06 0 S

Perigee/Apogee
dy hr m kilometers
14 11:28 a 406464
28 1:34 p 356878

PH dy hr mn
☾ 5 9:55 12♊32
● 13 6:42 20♍10
◑ 13 6:55 P 0.788
☽ 21 9:00 28♐04
○ 28 2:52 4♈40
◑ 28 2:48 T 1.276

Void of Course Moon

Last Aspect	☽ Ingress
1 16:39 ♄ ☍	♉ 2 9:03
4 10:21 ♄ ☍	♊ 4 11:49
5 23:05 ♅ ⚹	♋ 6 17:41
9 1:29 ♄ △	♌ 9 2:37
11 13:04 ♄ □	♍ 11 13:57
14 2:09 ♄ ⚹	♎ 14 2:42
16 4:23 ♂ ⚹	♏ 16 15:44
18 19:50 ♂ □	♐ 19 3:33
21 9:00 ☉ □	♑ 21 12:34
22 23:14 ♅ □	♒ 23 17:52
25 4:03 ♀ ☍	♓ 25 19:45
26 16:33 ♇ ⚹	♈ 27 19:30
29 7:46 ♀ △	♉ 29 18:58

DAILY ASPECTARIAN

☉☍♆ 3:39
☽⋕☿ 3:56
♀☌♂ 5:05
☽□♇ 5:34
☽⚼♄ 7:00
☽△♀ 8:26
☽△♂ 8:37
☽⚼♃ 16:03
☽⚺⚷ 16:13
☽☌♅ 16:39
☽∥♅ 22:00
☽∠♆ 22:12
☉⚼☽ 23:33
♀⋕♆ 23:50

☽□⚳ 1:48
☉∥☽ 3:02
☽⚻♄ 7:29
☽⋕♆ 9:42
☽∥♀ 10:04
☽∠⚷ 16:45
☽△♃ 17:02
☽∥♃ 18:15
☽⚻☿ 20:45
☽⚹♆ 22:54

☉△☽ 2:08
♃⚼♅ 3:53
☽△♇ 6:51
☉⚼⚳ 7:33
☽□♀ 9:20
☽□♂ 12:25
☽⚹⚷ 17:54
☽⚺♅ 18:25

4 F ☽⚼☿ 0:03
☿⚻♆ 3:04
☽△⚳ 3:55
☽⚼♇ 8:29
☽☍♄ 10:21
☉∥♅ 14:27
☽∠♅ 20:21
☽□♃ 21:06

5 Sa ☽∥♂ 0:16
☽□♆ 2:23
☽△☿ 4:12
☽⚼⚳ 6:05
☉□☽ 9:55
☽⚻♇ 10:53
☽⚹♀ 13:16
☽⚹♂ 19:28
☽□⚷ 22:28
☽⚹♅ 23:05
☉△♇ 23:12

6 Su ☉⋕☿ 6:15
♀ D 8:30
☽⚻⚳ 9:03
☽⚻♄ 16:21
☽∠♀ 16:33

7 M ☽∠♂ 0:22
☽⚹♃ 4:28
☉⚺♀ 8:22
☽△♆ 9:01
☿⋕♅ 12:33
☽□☿ 15:02
☽☍♇ 18:06
☽⚼♄ 20:33
☽⚺♀ 20:43
☉⚹☽ 21:42

8 Tu ☽⚺♂ 6:10
☽△⚷ 6:11
♂⚻⚷ 6:23
☽□♅ 6:54
☽∠♃ 9:21
☽⚼♆ 13:28
♀∥♃ 14:37
☽☍⚳ 17:21
♂△♅ 19:55
☽∥♂ 22:13

9 W ☽△♄ 1:29
☉∠☽ 4:58
☽⚼⚷ 11:05
☽⚺♃ 14:57
☽⚻♆ 18:34
☿□♇ 19:29

10 Th ☽⚻♇ 4:09
☽⚹☿ 4:39
☽☌♀ 7:25
☉⚺☽ 13:01
☽⚻⚷ 16:32
☽△♅ 17:21
☽☌♂ 20:00

11 F ☽∥♀ 3:06
☽⚻⚳ 4:12
☽∥♃ 6:45
☽⚼♇ 9:59
☽⋕♆ 11:17
☽∠☿ 12:05
☽□♄ 13:04
☽⋕☿ 15:26
☽⚼♅ 23:18

12 Sa ☽∥♅ 3:09
☽☌♃ 3:46
☽☍♆ 6:15
☉☍⚷ 7:01
☽⚼⚳ 10:20
☿∠♄ 14:08
☽△♇ 16:11
☉⚻♅ 17:19
☽⚺☿ 19:41
☽⚺♀ 20:35
☉∥☽ 23:58

13 Su ☽☍⚷ 4:40
☽⚻♅ 5:34
☉☌☽ 6:42
☽⚺♂ 11:51
☽△⚳ 16:44
☿∥♆ 17:51

14 M ☽∥⚷ 1:39
☽⚹♄ 2:09
☽⋕⚷ 2:41
☽∠♀ 3:46
☽⚺♃ 17:50
☽⚻♆ 19:05
⚳ D 19:15
☽∠♂ 20:08
☉⋕☽ 23:25

15 Tu ☿⋕♃ 2:14
☽□♇ 5:12
☽∠♄ 8:53
☽☌☿ 10:35
☽⚹♀ 11:08
☽⚻⚷ 17:31
☽☍♅ 18:29

16 W ☽∠♃ 0:56
☽⋕♅ 1:01
☉⚺☽ 1:17
☽⚼♆ 1:33
☽⚹♂ 4:23
☽□⚳ 5:49
☽⚺♄ 15:31
☽∥♆ 17:47
☽⋕♃ 18:42
☽∥☿ 21:34
☽⚼⚷ 23:48

17 Th ☽⋕♀ 5:01
♃☍♆ 6:55
♂⚻⚳ 7:44
☽△♆ 7:48
☽⚹♃ 7:49
⚵ ♎ 9:59
☉∠☽ 10:19
☽⚹♇ 17:53
☿ R 18:11
☽⚺☿ 23:44

18 F ☽□♀ 1:36
♄ ♐ 2:50
♃⋕♆ 3:50
☽△⚷ 5:44
☽⚻♅ 6:44
☉△⚳ 8:58
☽⋕♂ 9:43
☽⚹⚳ 18:01
☉⚹☽ 18:47
☽□♂ 19:50
☽∠♇ 23:36

19 Sa ☽☌♄ 3:41
☽∠☿ 5:07
☽⚼♅ 12:06
☽□♆ 18:54
☽□♃ 20:04
☽∠⚳ 23:16

20 Su ☽⚺♇ 4:38
☉⚺♂ 5:18
☽⚹☿ 9:30
☽△♀ 14:06
☽□⚷ 15:44
☽△♅ 16:43

21 M ☽⚺⚳ 3:43
☿∠♄ 6:40
☽△♂ 8:13
☉□☽ 9:00
☽⚺♄ 13:01
☽⚼♀ 19:04
♂⚼♇ 20:53

22 Tu ☽⚹♆ 2:52
♀⚻⚷ 4:57
☽△♃ 4:59
☿∥♆ 11:58
☽☌♇ 12:05
☽⚼♂ 12:50
☽□☿ 14:57
☽∠♄ 16:17
☽⚹⚷ 22:16
☽⚻♀ 23:01
☽□♅ 23:14

23 W ☉⋕⚷ 2:33
♀△♅ 4:01
☽∠♆ 5:27
☽⚼♃ 7:56
☉ ♎ 8:22
☽☌⚳ 9:48
☿∠♂ 12:49
☉∥⚷ 14:49
☽⚻♂ 16:21
☉△☽ 18:35
☽⚹♄ 18:35
☉⚹♄ 18:37

24 Th ☽∠⚷ 0:09
☿⋕♃ 1:11
☽⚺♆ 7:07
☽⚻♃ 9:57
☽⚺♇ 15:48
☽△☿ 16:09
☽⋕♂ 18:57
☉⚼☽ 21:42
☿□♇ 22:27

25 F ☽⚺⚷ 1:10
☽⚹♅ 2:06
♂ ♍ 2:19
☽☍♀ 4:03
♇ D 6:59
☽⋕♀ 7:52
☽⚺⚳ 12:20
☽⚼☿ 15:28
☽∠♇ 16:28
☽∥♆ 16:41
☽☍♂ 20:31
☽⋕♃ 20:40
☽□♄ 20:41
☉⚻☽ 23:56

26 Sa ☽∥☿ 1:02
♂□♄ 1:13
☽∠♅ 2:26
☽⋕♅ 7:20
☽☌♆ 8:12
☽☍♃ 11:40
☽∠⚳ 12:37
☽⚻☿ 14:10
☽⚹♇ 16:33

27 Su ☽☌⚷ 1:23
☽⚺♅ 2:18
☽⚻♀ 6:18
☉∥☽ 10:59
☽⚹⚳ 12:31
☽∥⚷ 18:08
☽⋕⚷ 20:00
☿⚺♃ 20:23
☽△♄ 20:40
☽⚻♂ 22:17

28 M ☿⋕♅ 0:42
☉☍☽ 2:52
☉⋕☽ 4:35
☽⚼♀ 6:59
☽⚺♆ 7:37
☽☍☿ 10:33
☽⚻♃ 11:46
☽□♇ 15:57
☽⚼♄ 20:27
☽⚼♂ 22:58

29 Tu ☽⚺⚷ 0:36
☽☌♅ 1:31
☽⋕☿ 2:37
☽∥♅ 6:22
☽∠♆ 7:17
☽△♀ 7:46
☽⚼♃ 11:50
☽□⚳ 12:09
☽∥♃ 15:29
☿∠♀ 15:49
☽⚻♄ 20:25
☽⋕♆ 21:18
☽△♂ 23:52

30 W ☽∠⚷ 0:26
☿⚻♆ 3:20
☽∥♀ 4:02
☉⚻☽ 5:49
☽⚻☿ 6:59
☽⚹♆ 7:16
☽∥♂ 9:57
☽△♃ 12:16
☉☌☿ 14:39
☽△♇ 15:55

October 2015

LONGITUDE

Day	Sid.Time	☉	☽	☽ 12 hour	Mean☊	True☊	☿	♀	♂	⚳	♃	♄	⚷	♅	♆	♇
	h m s	° ' "	° ' "	° ' "	° '	° '	° '	° '	° '	° '	° '	° '	° '	° '	° '	° '
1 Th	0 37 39	7♎30 03	17♉55 33	25♉10 42	0♎28.8	0♎59.7	6♎40.9	24♌06.7	3♍41.3	25♑51.6	10♍50.4	1♐00.4	18♓21.9	18♈57.3	7♓37.9	12♑59.0
2 F	0 41 35	8 29 02	2♊19 30	9♊21 39	0 25.6	0R 58.9	5R 35.1	24 49.1	4 18.7	25 57.3	11 02.7	1 05.5	18R 19.3	18R 54.9	7R 36.5	12 59.2
3 Sa	0 45 32	9 28 02	16 16 59	23 05 29	0 22.4	0 58.1	4 32.8	25 32.6	4 56.1	26 03.3	11 14.9	1 10.8	18 16.8	18 52.5	7 35.1	12 59.4
4 Su	0 49 28	10 27 05	29 47 18	6♋22 41	0 19.2	0D 57.5	3 35.8	26 17.1	5 33.4	26 09.5	11 27.1	1 16.0	18 14.2	18 50.1	7 33.8	12 59.6
5 M	0 53 25	11 26 10	12♋51 58	19 15 34	0 16.1	0 57.4	2 45.6	27 02.5	6 10.7	26 16.1	11 39.3	1 21.4	18 11.7	18 47.7	7 32.5	12 59.9
6 Tu	0 57 21	12 25 17	25 33 57	1♌47 36	0 12.9	0 57.7	2 03.6	27 48.9	6 48.0	26 23.0	11 51.3	1 26.8	18 09.3	18 45.3	7 31.2	13 00.2
7 W	1 01 18	13 24 27	7♌57 04	14 02 51	0 09.7	0 58.5	1 30.8	28 36.2	7 25.3	26 30.2	12 03.4	1 32.3	18 06.8	18 42.9	7 30.0	13 00.6
8 Th	1 05 15	14 23 39	20 05 29	26 05 27	0 06.5	0 59.7	1 08.2	29 24.4	8 02.6	26 37.7	12 15.4	1 37.8	18 04.4	18 40.4	7 28.7	13 00.9
9 F	1 09 11	15 22 53	2♍03 15	7♍59 21	0 03.3	1 01.0	0D 56.1	0♍13.3	8 39.8	26 45.5	12 27.3	1 43.4	18 02.0	18 38.0	7 27.5	13 01.3
10 Sa	1 13 08	16 22 09	13 54 10	19 48 07	0 00.2	1 02.1	0 54.7	1 03.1	9 17.0	26 53.5	12 39.2	1 49.0	17 59.6	18 35.6	7 26.3	13 01.8
11 Su	1 17 04	17 21 27	25 41 35	1♎34 54	29♍57.0	1R 02.8	1 04.1	1 53.7	9 54.1	27 01.9	12 51.0	1 54.7	17 57.3	18 33.1	7 25.1	13 02.2
12 M	1 21 01	18 20 48	7♎28 24	13 22 12	29 53.8	1 02.8	1 23.9	2 45.0	10 31.3	27 10.5	13 02.8	2 00.4	17 55.0	18 30.7	7 23.9	13 02.7
13 Tu	1 24 57	19 20 11	19 17 05	25 12 49	29 50.6	1 01.8	1 53.6	3 37.0	11 08.4	27 19.4	13 14.5	2 06.2	17 52.7	18 28.3	7 22.8	13 03.3
14 W	1 28 54	20 19 36	1♏09 49	7♏08 19	29 47.4	0 59.9	2 32.6	4 29.7	11 45.5	27 28.6	13 26.1	2 12.1	17 50.5	18 25.8	7 21.7	13 03.8
15 Th	1 32 50	21 19 02	13 08 34	19 10 47	29 44.3	0 57.0	3 20.3	5 23.1	12 22.5	27 38.1	13 37.7	2 18.0	17 48.3	18 23.4	7 20.6	13 04.4
16 F	1 36 47	22 18 31	25 15 14	1♐22 10	29 41.1	0 53.6	4 15.8	6 17.1	12 59.5	27 47.8	13 49.2	2 24.0	17 46.1	18 20.9	7 19.6	13 05.0
17 Sa	1 40 43	23 18 02	7♐31 51	13 44 34	29 37.9	0 49.9	5 18.4	7 11.8	13 36.5	27 57.8	14 00.7	2 30.0	17 44.0	18 18.5	7 18.5	13 05.7
18 Su	1 44 40	24 17 34	20 00 37	26 20 18	29 34.7	0 46.6	6 27.3	8 07.0	14 13.5	28 08.1	14 12.1	2 36.0	17 41.9	18 16.1	7 17.5	13 06.3
19 M	1 48 37	25 17 09	2♑43 56	9♑11 51	29 31.6	0 43.9	7 41.6	9 02.8	14 50.4	28 18.6	14 23.4	2 42.1	17 39.8	18 13.7	7 16.6	13 07.0
20 Tu	1 52 33	26 16 45	15 44 22	22 21 47	29 28.4	0D 42.3	9 00.7	9 59.2	15 27.3	28 29.4	14 34.6	2 48.3	17 37.8	18 11.3	7 15.6	13 07.8
21 W	1 56 30	27 16 23	29 04 22	5♒52 21	29 25.2	0 41.9	10 23.8	10 56.2	16 04.2	28 40.4	14 45.8	2 54.5	17 35.8	18 08.9	7 14.7	13 08.5
22 Th	2 00 26	28 16 02	12♒45 56	19 45 12	29 22.0	0 42.5	11 50.4	11 53.7	16 41.0	28 51.7	14 56.9	3 00.7	17 33.9	18 06.5	7 13.8	13 09.3
23 F	2 04 23	29 15 43	26 50 07	4♓00 36	29 18.9	0 43.9	13 19.9	12 51.6	17 17.8	29 03.2	15 07.9	3 07.0	17 32.0	18 04.1	7 12.9	13 10.1
24 Sa	2 08 19	0♏15 26	11♓16 22	18 37 01	29 15.7	0 45.4	14 51.8	13 50.1	17 54.6	29 15.0	15 18.8	3 13.3	17 30.2	18 01.7	7 12.1	13 11.0
25 Su	2 12 16	1 15 11	26 01 58	3♈30 30	29 12.5	0R 46.3	16 25.7	14 49.1	18 31.3	29 26.9	15 29.7	3 19.7	17 28.3	17 59.4	7 11.3	13 11.9
26 M	2 16 12	2 14 57	11♈01 43	18 34 38	29 09.3	0 46.0	18 01.1	15 48.5	19 08.0	29 39.2	15 40.5	3 26.1	17 26.6	17 57.0	7 10.5	13 12.8
27 Tu	2 20 09	3 14 45	26 08 07	3♉41 00	29 06.1	0 44.2	19 37.6	16 48.4	19 44.7	29 51.6	15 51.2	3 32.5	17 24.8	17 54.7	7 09.7	13 13.7
28 W	2 24 06	4 14 35	11♉12 05	18 40 13	29 03.0	0 40.7	21 15.4	17 48.7	20 21.4	0♒04.3	16 01.8	3 39.0	17 23.2	17 52.4	7 09.0	13 14.7
29 Th	2 28 02	5 14 27	26 04 19	3♊23 25	28 59.8	0 35.9	22 53.7	18 49.5	20 58.0	0 17.2	16 12.3	3 45.5	17 21.5	17 50.1	7 08.3	13 15.7
30 F	2 31 59	6 14 21	10♊36 45	17 43 39	28 56.6	0 30.4	24 32.5	19 50.7	21 34.6	0 30.3	16 22.8	3 52.1	17 19.9	17 47.8	7 07.6	13 16.7
31 Sa	2 35 55	7♏14 18	24 43 44	1♋36 42	28♍53.4	0♎24.9	26♎11.7	20♍52.2	22♍11.1	0♒43.6	16♍33.1	3♐58.6	17♓18.4	17♈45.5	7♓07.0	13♑17.7

1st of Mont

Julian Day
2457296.5
Obliquity
23°26'05"
SVP 5♓02'2
GC 27♐03.
Eris 23♈00.

Day	⚴	⚵	⚶
1	20♐46.5	5♎11.9	5♈12.1
6	22 09.2	7 05.7	3 56.6
11	23 35.6	8 58.8	2 45.0
16	25 05.2	10 51.0	1 39.6
21	26 37.9	12 42.4	0 42.5
26	28 13.2	14 32.6	29♓55.0
31	29 50.8	16 21.6	29 18.1

DECLINATION and LATITUDE

Day	☉ Decl	☽ Decl	☽ Lat	☽12h Decl	☿ Decl	☿ Lat	♀ Decl	♀ Lat	♂ Decl	♂ Lat	⚳ Decl	⚳ Lat	♃ Decl	♃ Lat	♄ Decl	♄ Lat
1 Th	2S59	13N27	3S52	14N53	4S48	2S20	10N29	3S10	11N20	1N16	31S02	10S16	8N21	0N55	18S38	1N45
2 F	3 22	16 04	4 39	16 59	4 05	2 01	10 23	3 02	11 07	1 17	30 59	10 14	8 17	0 56	18 40	1 45
3 Sa	3 45	17 38	5 07	18 01	3 22	1 42	10 17	2 53	10 54	1 17	30 56	10 12	8 12	0 56	18 41	1 45
4 Su	4 08	18 08	5 18	18 01	2 40	1 21	10 11	2 44	10 40	1 17	30 53	10 10	8 08	0 56	18 42	1 45
5 M	4 31	17 39	5 11	17 04	2 02	1 01	10 03	2 36	10 27	1 17	30 50	10 08	8 03	0 56	18 43	1 45
6 Tu	4 54	16 17	4 49	15 19	1 26	0 41	9 56	2 27	10 13	1 18	30 47	10 06	7 59	0 56	18 45	1 44
7 W	5 17	14 11	4 14	12 54	0 55	0 21	9 47	2 19	9 59	1 18	30 43	10 04	7 54	0 56	18 46	1 44
8 Th	5 40	11 29	3 28	9 58	0 29	0 02	9 38	2 10	9 46	1 18	30 40	10 03	7 50	0 56	18 47	1 44
9 F	6 03	8 21	2 34	6 39	0 08	0N16	9 29	2 02	9 32	1 18	30 37	10 01	7 45	0 56	18 48	1 44
10 Sa	6 26	4 53	1 34	3 05	0N08	0 33	9 19	1 54	9 18	1 19	30 33	9 59	7 41	0 57	18 50	1 44
11 Su	6 49	1 15	0 30	0S35	0 19	0 48	9 09	1 46	9 04	1 19	30 30	9 57	7 36	0 57	18 51	1 43
12 M	7 11	2S25	0N36	4 14	0 24	1 02	8 58	1 39	8 50	1 19	30 26	9 55	7 32	0 57	18 52	1 43
13 Tu	7 34	6 01	1 39	7 44	0 23	1 14	8 46	1 31	8 36	1 19	30 23	9 53	7 28	0 57	18 54	1 43
14 W	7 56	9 23	2 39	10 57	0 18	1 25	8 34	1 23	8 23	1 19	30 19	9 52	7 23	0 57	18 55	1 43
15 Th	8 19	12 24	3 32	13 44	0 07	1 35	8 22	1 16	8 09	1 20	30 15	9 50	7 19	0 57	18 56	1 43
16 F	8 41	14 55	4 16	15 57	0S08	1 42	8 09	1 08	7 55	1 20	30 11	9 48	7 15	0 57	18 57	1 43
17 Sa	9 03	16 48	4 49	17 28	0 26	1 49	7 55	1 01	7 41	1 20	30 07	9 46	7 10	0 58	18 59	1 43
18 Su	9 25	17 55	5 09	18 09	0 49	1 54	7 41	0 54	7 27	1 20	30 03	9 44	7 06	0 58	19 00	1 42
19 M	9 47	18 10	5 15	17 56	1 15	1 58	7 27	0 47	7 12	1 20	29 59	9 43	7 02	0 58	19 01	1 42
20 Tu	10 08	17 28	5 04	16 46	1 43	2 01	7 12	0 40	6 58	1 21	29 55	9 41	6 58	0 58	19 03	1 42
21 W	10 30	15 49	4 37	14 38	2 14	2 02	6 57	0 34	6 44	1 21	29 51	9 39	6 54	0 58	19 04	1 42
22 Th	10 51	13 14	3 54	11 37	2 48	2 03	6 41	0 27	6 30	1 21	29 47	9 37	6 49	0 58	19 05	1 42
23 F	11 13	9 49	2 56	7 50	3 23	2 03	6 25	0 21	6 16	1 21	29 43	9 36	6 45	0 58	19 07	1 42
24 Sa	11 34	5 43	1 45	3 29	3 59	2 02	6 08	0 14	6 02	1 21	29 39	9 34	6 41	0 59	19 08	1 42
25 Su	11 54	1 11	0 26	1N10	4 37	1 60	5 51	0 08	5 48	1 22	29 34	9 32	6 37	0 59	19 09	1 41
26 M	12 15	3N30	0S56	5 48	5 15	1 58	5 34	0 02	5 33	1 22	29 30	9 30	6 33	0 59	19 11	1 41
27 Tu	12 36	7 60	2 15	10 04	5 55	1 54	5 16	0N04	5 19	1 22	29 26	9 29	6 29	0 59	19 12	1 41
28 W	12 56	11 58	3 23	13 39	6 35	1 51	4 58	0 10	5 05	1 22	29 21	9 27	6 25	0 59	19 13	1 41
29 Th	13 16	15 06	4 17	16 17	7 15	1 47	4 39	0 15	4 51	1 22	29 17	9 25	6 21	0 59	19 15	1 41
30 F	13 36	17 12	4 53	17 49	7 55	1 42	4 20	0 21	4 36	1 23	29 12	9 24	6 17	0 60	19 16	1 41
31 Sa	13S56	18N10	5S10	18N14	8S36	1N37	4N01	0N26	4N22	1N23	29S07	9S22	6N13	0N60	19S17	1N41

Day	⚷ Decl	⚷ Lat	♅ Decl	♅ Lat	♆ Decl	♆ Lat	♇ Decl	♇ Lat
1	0S15	4N44	6N48	0S40	9S28	0S49	21S01	1N
6	0 20	4 43	6 44	0 40	9 30	0 49	21 02	1
11	0 26	4 42	6 39	0 40	9 32	0 49	21 02	1
16	0 31	4 41	6 34	0 40	9 34	0 49	21 03	1
21	0 36	4 40	6 30	0 40	9 36	0 49	21 03	1
26	0 41	4 39	6 25	0 40	9 37	0 49	21 04	1
31	0S45	4N37	6N21	0S40	9S39	0S49	21S04	1N

Day	⚴ Decl	⚴ Lat	⚵ Decl	⚵ Lat	⚶ Decl	⚶ Lat	Eris Decl	Eris Lat
1	9N17	32N28	0N10	2N26	8S57	12S00	2S52	12S
6	8 30	31 45	0S26	2 35	9 24	11 58	2 53	12
11	7 46	31 04	1 02	2 45	9 47	11 52	2 54	12
16	7 04	30 25	1 37	2 54	10 04	11 42	2 55	12
21	6 24	29 48	2 12	3 04	10 16	11 30	2 56	12
26	5 48	29 13	2 46	3 13	10 21	11 15	2 57	12
31	5N13	28N39	3S18	3N23	10S21	10S59	2S58	12S

Moon Phenomena

Max/0 Decl
dy hr mn
3 23:53 18N08
11 8:12 0 S
18 18:33 18S11
25 6:03 0 N
31 8:57 18N14

Max/0 Lat
dy hr mn
4 2:04 5S18
11 10:55 0 N
18 20:19 5N15
25 7:37 0 S
31 9:49 5S12

Perigee/Apogee
dy hr m kilometers
11 13:19 a 406388
26 13:04 p 358468

PH dy hr mn
☾ 4 21:07 11♋19
● 13 0:07 19♎20
☽ 20 20:32 27♑08
○ 27 12:06 3♉45

Void of Course Moon

Last Aspect	☽ Ingres
1 10:45 ♀ □	♊ 1 20:
3 17:20 ♀ ⚹	♋ 4 0:
5 11:05 ♅ □	♌ 6 8:
7 21:11 ♅ △	♍ 8 19:
9 22:13 ♇ △	♎ 11 8:
13 0:07 ☉ ☌	♏ 13 21:
15 0:59 ♃ ⚹	♐ 16 9:
18 8:50 ☉ ⚹	♑ 18 18:
20 20:32 ☉ □	♒ 21 1:
23 4:23 ☉ △	♓ 23 5:
24 11:19 ♂ ☍	♈ 25 6:
26 12:26 ☿ ☍	♉ 27 6:
28 15:21 ♂ △	♊ 29 6:
31 2:53 ☿ △	♋ 31 9:

DAILY ASPECTARIAN

1 Th
☽⚹⚷ 0:43
☽⚺♅ 1:41
☉⚻♆ 3:06
⚳⚼♃ 4:23
☽⚼☿ 5:45
☉⚼☽ 8:06
♂⚼♅ 9:39
☽□♀ 10:45
☽△⚳ 13:14
☽⚼♇ 16:42
☽☍♄ 21:54

2 F
☽∠♅ 2:41
☽□♂ 3:31
☽△☿ 5:09
☽□♆ 8:59
☉△☽ 11:17
☽⚼⚳ 14:51
☽□♃ 15:07
☉‖☿ 15:30
☽⚻♇ 18:16
☿⚺♂ 18:18

3 Sa
☽□⚷ 3:29
☽⚹♅ 4:32
☽⚹♀ 17:20
☽⚻⚳ 17:25
♀⚻⚳ 19:17

4 Su
☽⚻♄ 2:42
☽□☿ 6:29
☽⚹♂ 11:01
☽△♆ 14:09
☉□☽ 21:07
☽⚹♃ 21:43
☽∠♀ 22:22

5 M
☽☍♇ 0:15
☽⚼♄ 6:35
☉⚺♃ 6:41
☽△⚷ 9:58
☽□♅ 11:05
☽∠♂ 16:27
☽⚼♆ 18:12

6 Tu
☽☍⚳ 1:35
☽∠♃ 2:31
☽⚺♀ 4:36
♀⚼♇ 5:49
☽△♄ 11:25
☽⚹☿ 11:57
☉□♇ 14:16
☽⚼⚷ 14:36
☽⚺♂ 22:54
☿⚹♄ 22:59
☽⚻♆ 23:07

7 W
♂☍♆ 2:54
☽⚺♃ 8:12
☽⚻♇ 9:57
☉⚹☽ 11:41
☽∠☿ 16:20
☽⚻⚷ 20:00
☽△♅ 21:11

8 Th
☉∠♀ 1:37
☿‖⚷ 6:03
☽⚻⚳ 13:13
☽‖♂ 14:35
☽‖♀ 15:10
☽#♆ 15:18
☽⚼♇ 15:52
♀ ♍ 17:30
♀#♆ 17:45
☽☌♀ 20:02
☉∠☽ 20:19
☽⚺☿ 21:46
☽□♄ 23:20

9 F
♂#♆ 0:20
☽⚼♅ 3:11
☽‖♃ 4:19
☽☍♆ 10:54
☽‖♅ 11:49
☽☌♂ 14:06
☉#☽ 14:30
☿ D 14:59
♀‖♂ 17:24
☿⚺♀ 19:43
☽⚼⚳ 19:52
☽☌♃ 21:25
☽△♇ 22:13

10 Sa
☉⚺☽ 5:28
☽☍⚷ 8:18
☽⚻♅ 9:30
☉∠♄ 12:01
☉#♅ 13:57

11 Su
♀□♄ 0:32
☽△⚳ 2:46
☽#⚷ 5:21
☽‖☿ 5:59
☽#☿ 10:32
☽‖⚷ 11:04
☽☌☿ 11:13
☽⚹♄ 12:47
☽⚺♀ 13:37
☉⚻⚷ 13:57
☽⚻♆ 23:51
♃△♇ 23:52

12 M
☉☍♅ 3:51
☽⚺♂ 6:33
☽□♇ 11:21
☽⚺♃ 11:32
☉#♃ 18:19
☽∠♄ 19:32
♀⚼♅ 20:10
☽⚻⚷ 21:09
☽☍♅ 22:21
☽∠♀ 22:32

13 Tu
☉☌☽ 0:07
☽#♅ 4:08
☽⚼♆ 6:16
☽#♃ 9:49
☿⚹♄ 9:56
☉‖☽ 12:07
☽∠♂ 14:38
☽□⚳ 16:28
☽#♂ 17:02
☽#♀ 18:18
☽∠♃ 18:25

14 W
☽‖♆ 1:17
☽⚺♄ 2:06
☽⚺☿ 2:58
☽⚼⚷ 3:22
☽⚹♀ 7:14
☽△♆ 12:26
☉#♂ 17:15
☽⚹♂ 22:23
☽⚹♇ 23:52

15 Th
☽⚹♃ 0:59
☉#♀ 1:55
☽△⚷ 9:15
☽⚻♅ 10:24
☽∠☿ 11:09
♂⚼⚳ 13:40
☉⚺☽ 17:41

16 F
☉⚼♆ 0:25
♂△♇ 3:37
☽⚹⚳ 5:04
☽∠♇ 5:34
☽☌♄ 14:08
☽⚼♅ 15:49
☽⚹☿ 19:16
☽□♀ 23:18
☽□♆ 23:34

17 Sa
☉∠☽ 1:37
♀☍♆ 2:54
☿‖⚷ 6:57
☽∠⚳ 10:39
☽⚺♇ 10:46
☽□♂ 12:21
☽□♃ 12:43
☽□⚷ 19:36
☽△♅ 20:41
♂☌♃ 22:41

18 Su
☉⚹☽ 8:50
☉‖♆ 11:26
☽⚺⚳ 15:36
☿⚻♆ 16:12
☽⚺♄ 23:57

19 M
☽⚹♆ 8:26
☽□☿ 10:15
☽△♀ 12:38
☽☌♇ 19:14
☽△♃ 21:51
☽△♂ 23:27

20 Tu
♂‖♃ 1:26
☽⚹⚷ 3:26
☽∠♄ 3:47
☽□♅ 4:26
☽∠♆ 11:48
☽⚼♀ 17:59
☉□☽ 20:32
☽☌⚳ 23:17

21 W
☽⚼♃ 1:15
☽⚼♂ 3:42
☽∠⚷ 6:13
♀‖♃ 6:28
☽⚹♄ 6:50
☽⚺♆ 14:23
☽△☿ 22:13
☽⚻♀ 22:23

22 Th
☽⚺♇ 0:40
♂‖♅ 2:05
☿⚺♀ 2:32
☽⚻♃ 3:49
☽⚻♂ 7:03
☽⚺⚷ 8:14
☽⚹♅ 9:10
☉‖☽ 15:39
♄⚼♅ 16:00
☉□⚳ 17:45
♀‖♅ 18:56
☿□♇ 21:23

23 F
☽‖♆ 1:14
☽∠♇ 2:15
☽⚼☿ 2:49
☽⚺⚳ 3:47
☉△☽ 4:23
♀△♇ 7:44
♂☍⚷ 8:49
☽∠♅ 10:24
☽□♄ 10:35
☽☌♆ 17:18
☉ ♏ 17:48
☽#♃ 18:30
☽#♅ 19:53
☽#♀ 21:30
☽#♂ 22:10

24 Sa
☉∠♃ 1:41
☽⚹♇ 3:08
♂⚻♅ 4:23
☽☍♀ 4:30
☽∠⚳ 4:57
☽⚻☿ 6:35
☽☍♃ 6:42
☉⚼☽ 7:00
☿⚺♃ 7:52
☽‖☿ 8:13
☽☌⚷ 10:10
☽⚺♅ 11:01
☽☍♂ 11:19
♀⚼⚳ 12:43

25 Su
☽‖⚷ 2:37
☽⚹⚳ 5:34
☉⚻☽ 8:59
☽#⚷ 9:30
⚶R♓ 10:02
☽△♄ 11:48
☿⚻⚷ 15:31
☽⚺♆ 17:52
♀☌♃ 20:04
☿☍♅ 23:01

26 M
☽□♇ 3:29
♀‖♂ 3:32
☉⚼⚷ 4:32
☿∠♄ 6:41
☽⚻♃ 7:29
☿#♀ 7:50
☿#♂ 8:07
☽⚻♀ 8:08
☽‖♀ 10:06
☽⚺⚷ 10:11
☽‖♂ 10:11
☽#☿ 10:40
☽☌♅ 10:59
☽⚼♄ 11:51
☽☍☿ 12:26
☽⚻♂ 13:26
☽‖♅ 15:18
☽‖♃ 15:49
☽∠♆ 17:42

27 Tu
☿⚺♂ 2:46
☽□⚳ 6:00
☽⚼♃ 7:35
☉⚺♄ 7:59
☽#♆ 9:25
☽⚼♀ 9:39
☽∠⚷ 9:58
☽⚻♄ 11:52
☉☍☽ 12:06
♀☍⚷ 14:08
☽⚼♂ 14:16
⚳ ♒ 15:57
☽⚹♆ 17:32
☿#♅ 17:36
☿#♃ 18:54

28 W
♀⚻♅ 1:24
☽△♇ 3:17
☉#☽ 7:28
☽△♃ 7:50
☽⚹⚷ 9:55
☽⚺♅ 10:41
☽△♀ 11:23
♃‖♅ 12:02
☿⚼♆ 13:01
☽△♂ 15:21
☽⚻☿ 18:11

29 Th
☽⚼♇ 3:35
☽△⚳ 7:00
☽∠♅ 11:03
☽☍♄ 12:42
☉⚻☽ 16:11
☽□♆ 18:12
☽⚼☿ 21:59

30 F
☽⚻♇ 4:29
☽⚼⚳ 8:22
☽□♃ 9:50
☽□⚷ 11:19
☽⚹♅ 12:05
☽□♀ 16:50
☉⚼☽ 19:23
☽□♂ 19:25
☉∠♂ 20:46
☉△♆ 21:07

31 Sa
☽△☿ 2:53
☽⚻⚳ 10:37
⚴ ♑ 11:08
☽⚻♄ 16:18
☽△♆ 21:44
☉△☽ 23:44

LONGITUDE

November 2015

Day	Sid.Time	☉	☽	☽ 12 hour	Mean☊	True ☊	☿	♀	♂	⚳	♃	♄	⚷	♅	♆	♇
	h m s	° ' "	° ' "	° ' "	° '	° '	° '	° '	° '	° '	° '	° '	° '	° '	° '	° '
1 Su	2 39 52	8♏14 16	8♋22 32	15♋01 19	28♍50.3	0♎20.3	27♎51.0	21♍54.2	22♍47.7	0♒57.1	16♍43.4	4♐05.3	17♓16.9	17♈43.3	7♓06.4	13♑18.8
2 M	2 43 48	9 14 17	21 33 17	27 58 49	28 47.1	0R 17.0	29 30.5	22 56.6	23 24.2	1 10.9	16 53.6	4 11.9	17R 15.5	17R 41.1	7R 05.8	13 19.9
3 Tu	2 47 45	10 14 19	4♌18 23	10♌32 30	28 43.9	0D 15.4	1♏09.9	23 59.3	24 00.6	1 24.8	17 03.7	4 18.6	17 14.1	17 38.9	7 05.3	13 21.0
4 W	2 51 41	11 14 24	16 41 47	22 46 50	28 40.7	0 15.4	2 49.3	25 02.4	24 37.1	1 39.0	17 13.7	4 25.3	17 12.7	17 36.7	7 04.8	13 22.2
5 Th	2 55 38	12 14 31	28 48 19	4♍46 52	28 37.5	0 16.5	4 28.4	26 05.9	25 13.5	1 53.3	17 23.6	4 32.1	17 11.4	17 34.5	7 04.3	13 23.4
6 F	2 59 35	13 14 40	10♍43 08	16 37 44	28 34.4	0 18.1	6 07.4	27 09.6	25 49.9	2 07.8	17 33.4	4 38.8	17 10.2	17 32.4	7 03.9	13 24.6
7 Sa	3 03 31	14 14 51	22 31 16	28 24 17	28 31.2	0R 19.4	7 46.1	28 13.7	26 26.2	2 22.6	17 43.1	4 45.6	17 09.0	17 30.3	7 03.5	13 25.8
8 Su	3 07 28	15 15 04	4♎17 20	10♎10 52	28 28.0	0 19.6	9 24.5	29 18.1	27 02.5	2 37.5	17 52.7	4 52.5	17 07.8	17 28.2	7 03.1	13 27.1
9 M	3 11 24	16 15 19	16 05 21	22 01 10	28 24.8	0 18.1	11 02.7	0♎22.9	27 38.8	2 52.6	18 02.2	4 59.3	17 06.7	17 26.2	7 02.7	13 28.3
10 Tu	3 15 21	17 15 36	27 58 38	3♏58 03	28 21.6	0 14.3	12 40.5	1 27.9	28 15.0	3 07.9	18 11.5	5 06.2	17 05.7	17 24.1	7 02.4	13 29.7
11 W	3 19 17	18 15 54	9♏59 40	16 03 41	28 18.5	0 08.4	14 18.1	2 33.2	28 51.2	3 23.4	18 20.8	5 13.1	17 04.7	17 22.1	7 02.1	13 31.0
12 Th	3 23 14	19 16 15	22 10 15	28 19 29	28 15.3	0 00.4	15 55.3	3 38.7	29 27.3	3 39.1	18 30.0	5 20.0	17 03.8	17 20.2	7 01.9	13 32.3
13 F	3 27 10	20 16 37	4♐31 28	10♐46 17	28 12.1	29♍51.0	17 32.1	4 44.6	0♎03.5	3 55.0	18 39.0	5 27.0	17 02.9	17 18.2	7 01.7	13 33.7
14 Sa	3 31 07	21 17 01	17 03 58	23 24 34	28 08.9	29 41.0	19 08.7	5 50.7	0 39.5	4 11.0	18 48.0	5 33.9	17 02.0	17 16.3	7 01.5	13 35.1
15 Su	3 35 04	22 17 26	29 48 08	6♑14 43	28 05.8	29 31.6	20 45.0	6 57.0	1 15.6	4 27.2	18 56.8	5 40.9	17 01.3	17 14.4	7 01.4	13 36.6
16 M	3 39 00	23 17 53	12♑49 22	19 17 11	28 02.6	29 23.5	22 21.0	8 03.6	1 51.6	4 43.5	19 05.5	5 47.9	17 00.6	17 12.6	7 01.3	13 38.0
17 Tu	3 42 57	24 18 21	25 53 15	2♒32 42	27 59.4	29 17.5	23 56.6	9 10.4	2 27.5	5 00.1	19 14.1	5 54.9	16 59.9	17 10.8	7 01.2	13 39.5
18 W	3 46 53	25 18 51	9♒15 40	16 02 16	27 56.2	29 14.0	25 32.1	10 17.5	3 03.4	5 16.8	19 22.6	6 02.0	16 59.3	17 09.0	7D 01.2	13 41.0
19 Th	3 50 50	26 19 22	22 52 39	29 46 56	27 53.1	29D 12.7	27 07.2	11 24.8	3 39.3	5 33.6	19 30.9	6 09.0	16 58.7	17 07.3	7 01.1	13 42.5
20 F	3 54 46	27 19 54	6♓45 11	13♓47 28	27 49.9	29 12.9	28 42.1	12 32.3	4 15.1	5 50.6	19 39.1	6 16.0	16 58.2	17 05.6	7 01.2	13 44.1
21 Sa	3 58 43	28 20 27	20 53 43	28 03 48	27 46.7	29R 13.7	0♐16.8	13 40.0	4 50.9	6 07.8	19 47.2	6 23.1	16 57.8	17 03.9	7 01.2	13 45.6
22 Su	4 02 39	29 21 01	5♈17 30	12♈34 24	27 43.5	29 13.8	1 51.2	14 47.9	5 26.7	6 25.1	19 55.2	6 30.2	16 57.4	17 02.3	7 01.3	13 47.2
23 M	4 06 36	0♐21 37	19 54 03	27 15 47	27 40.3	29 12.0	3 25.5	15 56.0	6 02.4	6 42.6	20 03.0	6 37.3	16 57.1	17 00.7	7 01.5	13 48.8
24 Tu	4 10 33	1 22 14	4♉38 50	12♉02 20	27 37.2	29 07.8	4 59.6	17 04.3	6 38.0	7 00.2	20 10.7	6 44.4	16 56.8	16 59.2	7 01.6	13 50.4
25 W	4 14 29	2 22 52	19 25 19	26 46 47	27 34.0	29 00.8	6 33.5	18 12.8	7 13.6	7 17.9	20 18.3	6 51.5	16 56.6	16 57.7	7 01.8	13 52.1
26 Th	4 18 26	3 23 31	4♊05 43	11♊21 09	27 30.8	28 51.6	8 07.3	19 21.5	7 49.2	7 35.8	20 25.7	6 58.6	16 56.4	16 56.2	7 02.1	13 53.7
27 F	4 22 22	4 24 12	18 32 12	25 38 04	27 27.6	28 40.9	9 40.9	20 30.4	8 24.7	7 53.8	20 33.1	7 05.7	16 56.3	16 54.8	7 02.3	13 55.4
28 Sa	4 26 19	5 24 54	2♋38 09	9♋31 58	27 24.5	28 29.9	11 14.4	21 39.4	9 00.2	8 12.0	20 40.2	7 12.8	16D 56.3	16 53.4	7 02.6	13 57.1
29 Su	4 30 15	6 25 38	16 19 15	22 59 51	27 21.3	28 20.0	12 47.8	22 48.7	9 35.7	8 30.3	20 47.3	7 19.9	16 56.3	16 52.0	7 03.0	13 58.8
30 M	4 34 12	7♐26 23	29 33 51	6♌01 25	27♍18.1	28♍12.0	14♐21.1	23♎58.1	10♎11.1	8♒48.7	20♍54.1	7♐27.0	16♓56.4	16♈50.7	7♓03.3	14♑00.6

1st of Month

Julian Day # 2457327.5
Obliquity 23°26'05"
SVP 5♓02'21"
GC 27♐03.6
Eris 22♈42.2R

Day	⚴
1	0♑10.6
6	1 50.8
11	3 33.0
16	5 16.8
21	7 02.1
26	8 48.6

Day	⚵
1	16♎43.3
6	18 30.8
11	20 16.8
16	22 01.3
21	23 43.8
26	25 24.4

Day	⚶
1	29♓12.0R
6	28 48.5R
11	28 36.4R
16	28 35.8
21	28 46.4
26	29 07.6

DECLINATION and LATITUDE

Day	☉ Decl	☽ Decl	☽ Lat	☽12h Decl	☿ Decl	☿ Lat	♀ Decl	♀ Lat	♂ Decl	♂ Lat	⚳ Decl	⚳ Lat	♃ Decl	♃ Lat	♄ Decl	♄ Lat
1 Su	14S15	18N02	5S09	17N36	9S16	1N32	3N42	0N32	4N08	1N23	29S03	9S20	6N10	0N60	19S19	1N41
2 M	14 34	16 55	4 51	16 03	9 57	1 27	3 22	0 37	3 54	1 23	28 58	9 19	6 06	1 00	19 20	1 40
3 Tu	14 53	14 59	4 19	13 46	10 37	1 21	3 02	0 42	3 39	1 23	28 53	9 17	6 02	1 00	19 21	1 40
4 W	15 12	12 24	3 35	10 55	11 16	1 15	2 41	0 47	3 25	1 24	28 48	9 16	5 58	1 00	19 23	1 40
5 Th	15 30	9 20	2 43	7 40	11 56	1 09	2 20	0 51	3 11	1 24	28 43	9 14	5 55	1 01	19 24	1 40
6 F	15 49	5 56	1 45	4 09	12 34	1 03	1 59	0 56	2 56	1 24	28 38	9 13	5 51	1 01	19 25	1 40
7 Sa	16 07	2 19	0 42	0 28	13 13	0 56	1 38	1 01	2 42	1 24	28 33	9 11	5 47	1 01	19 27	1 40
8 Su	16 24	1S23	0N21	3S13	13 50	0 50	1 16	1 05	2 28	1 24	28 28	9 09	5 44	1 01	19 28	1 40
9 M	16 42	5 02	1 24	6 48	14 27	0 43	0 54	1 09	2 14	1 24	28 23	9 08	5 40	1 01	19 29	1 40
10 Tu	16 59	8 31	2 24	10 09	15 04	0 36	0 32	1 13	1 59	1 25	28 18	9 06	5 37	1 02	19 31	1 40
11 W	17 16	11 41	3 18	13 06	15 39	0 30	0 10	1 17	1 45	1 25	28 13	9 05	5 33	1 02	19 32	1 40
12 Th	17 32	14 24	4 03	15 32	16 14	0 23	0S13	1 21	1 31	1 25	28 07	9 03	5 30	1 02	19 33	1 39
13 F	17 49	16 30	4 37	17 16	16 48	0 16	0 35	1 25	1 17	1 25	28 02	9 02	5 27	1 02	19 35	1 39
14 Sa	18 05	17 51	4 59	18 12	17 21	0 09	0 58	1 28	1 02	1 25	27 57	9 01	5 23	1 02	19 36	1 39
15 Su	18 20	18 20	5 06	18 13	17 54	0 03	1 21	1 32	0 48	1 25	27 51	8 59	5 20	1 03	19 37	1 39
16 M	18 36	17 53	4 58	17 18	18 25	0S04	1 44	1 35	0 34	1 26	27 46	8 58	5 17	1 03	19 39	1 39
17 Tu	18 51	16 28	4 34	15 25	18 56	0 11	2 08	1 38	0 20	1 26	27 40	8 56	5 14	1 03	19 40	1 39
18 W	19 05	14 09	3 55	12 41	19 25	0 17	2 31	1 41	0 06	1 26	27 35	8 55	5 10	1 03	19 41	1 39
19 Th	19 20	11 01	3 02	9 11	19 54	0 24	2 55	1 44	0S08	1 26	27 29	8 54	5 07	1 03	19 42	1 39
20 F	19 34	7 13	1 57	5 07	20 22	0 31	3 19	1 47	0 22	1 26	27 23	8 52	5 04	1 04	19 44	1 39
21 Sa	19 47	2 56	0 45	0 40	20 48	0 37	3 42	1 50	0 36	1 26	27 18	8 51	5 01	1 04	19 45	1 39
22 Su	20 00	1N36	0S32	3N53	21 14	0 43	4 06	1 52	0 50	1 26	27 12	8 50	4 58	1 04	19 46	1 39
23 M	20 13	6 07	1 48	8 15	21 39	0 50	4 30	1 55	1 04	1 27	27 06	8 48	4 56	1 04	19 47	1 39
24 Tu	20 26	10 17	2 57	12 09	22 02	0 56	4 54	1 57	1 18	1 27	27 00	8 47	4 53	1 05	19 49	1 38
25 W	20 38	13 49	3 55	15 15	22 25	1 02	5 18	1 59	1 32	1 27	26 54	8 46	4 50	1 05	19 50	1 38
26 Th	20 50	16 27	4 36	17 21	22 46	1 08	5 42	2 01	1 46	1 27	26 48	8 45	4 47	1 05	19 51	1 38
27 F	21 01	17 59	4 59	18 23	23 06	1 13	6 07	2 03	2 00	1 27	26 42	8 43	4 45	1 05	19 52	1 38
28 Sa	21 12	18 22	5 02	18 09	23 25	1 19	6 31	2 05	2 14	1 27	26 36	8 42	4 42	1 06	19 54	1 38
29 Su	21 23	17 40	4 49	16 56	23 43	1 24	6 55	2 06	2 28	1 27	26 30	8 41	4 39	1 06	19 55	1 38
30 M	21S33	16N00	4S19	14N53	23S60	1S29	7S19	2N08	2S41	1N27	26S24	8S40	4N37	1N06	19S56	1N38

Day	⚷ Decl	⚷ Lat	♅ Decl	♅ Lat	♆ Decl	♆ Lat	♇ Decl	♇ Lat
1	0S46	4N37	6N20	0S40	9S39	0S49	21S04	1N43
6	0 50	4 36	6 16	0 40	9 40	0 49	21 04	1 42
11	0 54	4 34	6 12	0 40	9 41	0 49	21 04	1 41
16	0 57	4 33	6 09	0 40	9 41	0 48	21 04	1 41
21	0 59	4 31	6 06	0 40	9 41	0 48	21 04	1 40
26	1 01	4 30	6 03	0 39	9 40	0 48	21 04	1 39

Day	⚴ Decl	⚴ Lat	⚵ Decl	⚵ Lat	⚶ Decl	⚶ Lat	Eris Decl	Eris Lat
1	5N07	28N33	3S25	3N25	10S20	10S56	2S58	12S41
6	4 36	28 01	3 56	3 35	10 13	10 37	2 58	12 40
11	4 08	27 31	4 26	3 46	10 00	10 19	2 59	12 40
16	3 42	27 03	4 55	3 56	9 43	9 59	2 59	12 40
21	3 19	26 36	5 23	4 07	9 21	9 40	2 60	12 39
26	2 59	26 11	5 48	4 19	8 55	9 20	3 00	12 38

Moon Phenomena

Max/0 Decl
dy hr mn
7 15:05 0 S
15 0:29 18S20
21 15:33 0 N
27 20:17 18N23

Perigee/Apogee
dy hr m kilometers
7 21:55 a 405721
23 20:17 p 362819

PH dy hr mn
☾ 3 12:25 10♌45
● 11 17:48 19♏01
☽ 19 6:28 26♒36
○ 25 22:45 3♊20

Max/0 Lat
dy hr mn
7 15:55 0 N
14 23:34 5N06
21 13:57 0 S
27 17:04 5S03

Void of Course Moon

Last Aspect	☽ Ingress
2 3:36 ♂ ⚹	♌ 2 15:49
4 1:47 ♅ △	♍ 5 2:24
7 12:48 ♀ ☌	♎ 7 15:15
9 2:43 ♅ ☍	♏ 10 4:04
12 14:55 ♂ ⚹	♐ 12 15:15
14 3:20 ♃ □	♑ 15 0:22
16 20:54 ☉ ⚹	♒ 17 7:25
19 8:20 ☿ □	♓ 19 12:23
21 13:24 ☉ △	♈ 21 15:13
22 19:17 ♅ ☌	♉ 23 16:27
25 1:27 ♃ △	♊ 25 17:16
27 3:36 ♀ △	♋ 27 19:28
29 12:47 ♀ □	♌ 30 0:48

DAILY ASPECTARIAN

1 Su	☽ ☍ ♇	8:55
	☿ ∥ ♆	13:44
	☽ ⚹ ♃	15:18
	☽ △ ⚷	16:06
	☽ □ ♅	16:53
	☽ ⚼ ♄	19:37
2 M	☽ ⚼ ♆	1:00
	☽ ⚹ ♀	2:48
	☽ ⚹ ♂	3:36
	☿ ♏	7:07
	☽ □ ☿	17:07
	☽ ☍ ⚳	18:23
	☽ ∠ ♃	19:40
	☽ ⚼ ⚷	20:03
3 Tu	☽ △ ♄	0:00
	☉ ⋕ ☽	0:57
	♀ ☌ ♂	1:11
	☿ □ ⚳	4:11
	☽ ⚻ ♆	5:20
	☽ ∠ ♂	9:30
	☽ ∠ ♀	9:50
	☉ □ ☽	12:25
	☿ ∠ ♃	14:27
	☿ ⚼ ⚷	15:17
	☽ ⚻ ♇	17:29
	♃ ☍ ⚷	21:57
4 W	☽ ⚻ ⚷	1:01
	☽ ⚺ ♃	1:03
	☽ △ ♅	1:47
	☽ ⋕ ☿	7:36
	☽ ⚺ ♂	16:29
	☽ ⚺ ♀	18:04
	☽ ⋕ ♆	21:35
	☽ ⚼ ♇	23:10
5 Th	☿ ⚺ ♄	0:57
	☽ ⚻ ⚳	6:18
	☽ ⚼ ♅	7:32
	☽ □ ♄	11:37
	☽ ⚹ ☿	13:13
	☽ ☍ ♆	16:37
	☽ ∥ ♅	21:41
	♃ ⚻ ♅	22:03
6 F	☽ ∥ ♃	0:34
	⚳ ∠ ⚷	3:31
	☉ ⚹ ♇	4:02
	☽ △ ♇	5:28
	☉ ⚹ ☽	5:36
	☽ ☍ ⚷	13:05
	☽ ⚼ ⚳	13:18
	☿ △ ♆	13:40
	☽ ⚻ ♅	13:49
	☽ ☌ ♃	14:05
	☽ ∥ ♂	21:19
7 Sa	☽ ∠ ☿	0:35
	☽ ∥ ♀	4:58
	☽ ☌ ♂	8:25
	☽ ⋕ ⚷	9:33
	☽ ☌ ♀	12:48
	☉ ∠ ☽	15:00
	☽ △ ⚳	20:32
	☽ ∥ ⚷	20:38
	☽ ⋕ ♀	23:23
8 Su	☽ ⚹ ♄	1:12
	☽ ⚻ ♆	5:38
	☽ ⋕ ♂	6:40
	☽ ⚺ ☿	12:07
	♀ ♎	15:32
	☽ □ ♇	18:41
9 M	☉ ⚺ ☽	0:22
	☽ ⚻ ⚷	2:04
	♀ ⋕ ⚷	2:16
	☽ ☍ ♅	2:43
	☽ ⚺ ♃	4:00
	☽ ⋕ ♃	4:15
	☽ ∠ ♄	7:58
	☽ ⋕ ♅	8:04
	☽ ⚼ ♆	12:03
	☉ △ ⚷	20:07
10 Tu	☽ ⚺ ♂	0:35
	☉ ⚻ ♅	3:17
	☽ ⚺ ♀	7:41
	☽ ⚼ ⚷	8:15
	☽ ∥ ♆	8:29
	☽ □ ⚳	10:33
	☽ ∠ ♃	10:35
	☿ ⚹ ♇	12:15
	☿ ∠ ♂	13:28
	⚳ ⚼ ♃	14:00
	☽ ⚺ ♄	14:24
	☽ △ ♆	18:07
11 W	☉ ⚹ ♃	2:18
	☽ ⚹ ♇	6:59
	☽ ∠ ♂	8:02
	☽ ☌ ☿	9:50
	☽ △ ⚷	13:59
	☽ ⚻ ♅	14:32
	☽ ∠ ♀	16:24
	☽ ⚹ ♃	16:42
	☉ ☌ ☽	17:48
12 Th	♀ △ ⚳	0:11
	☊ R ♍	0:58
	☽ ∠ ♇	12:26
	☽ ⚹ ♂	14:55
	☿ △ ⚷	16:48
	☽ ⚼ ♅	19:43
	☿ ⚻ ♅	20:37
	♂ ♎	21:42
	☽ ⚹ ⚳	22:48
13 F	☽ ⚹ ♀	0:28
	☽ ☌ ♄	1:48
	☽ □ ♆	4:49
	☽ ∥ ☿	6:48
	♀ ⚹ ♄	17:13
	☽ ⚺ ♇	17:22
	⚶ D	18:10
	☿ ⚹ ♃	18:19
	♀ ∥ ⚷	21:03
	☽ □ ⚷	23:56
14 Sa	☽ △ ♅	0:23
	♀ ⋕ ♂	2:49
	☽ □ ♃	3:20
	☽ ∠ ⚳	4:06
	☽ ⚺ ☿	4:31
	☉ ⚺ ☽	8:41
	♂ ⋕ ⚷	11:33
	☉ ∥ ☽	23:13
	☉ ∥ ☽	23:13
15 Su	♀ ⚻ ♆	1:34
	☽ □ ♂	2:51
	☽ ⚺ ⚳	8:51
	☽ ⚺ ♄	11:03
	☽ ∠ ☿	12:39
	☽ ⚹ ♆	13:26
	☽ ∥ ☿	13:32
	☽ □ ♀	14:33
	☉ ∠ ☽	15:07
16 M	☽ ☌ ♇	1:39
	☽ ⚹ ⚷	7:50
	☽ □ ♅	8:11
	☽ △ ♃	11:46
	☽ ∠ ♄	14:53
	☉ ∥ ☿	16:01
	☽ ∠ ♆	16:59
	☽ ⚹ ☿	20:00
	☉ ⚹ ☽	20:54
17 Tu	☽ ∠ ⚷	11:01
	☿ ∠ ♀	11:37
	☽ △ ♂	12:24
	☉ ☌ ☿	14:54
	☽ ⚼ ♃	15:11
	☽ ☌ ⚳	16:45
	☽ ⚹ ♄	18:12
	☽ ⚺ ♆	20:00
18 W	☽ △ ♀	2:00
	☉ ∠ ♀	4:54
	☽ ⚺ ♇	7:51
	☿ ∥ ♄	13:39
	☽ ⚺ ⚷	13:40
	☽ ⚹ ♅	13:56
	☽ ⚼ ♂	16:16
	♆ D	16:32
	☽ ⚻ ♃	18:03
19 Th	☉ □ ☽	6:28
	☽ ⚼ ♀	6:42
	☽ □ ☿	8:20
	☽ ∥ ♆	8:51
	☽ ∠ ♇	10:10
	☽ ∠ ♅	16:00
	☽ ⚻ ♂	19:31
	☽ ⚺ ⚳	22:25
	☽ □ ♄	23:10
20 F	☽ ☌ ♆	0:27
	☿ ∠ ♇	0:30
	☽ ⋕ ♅	6:26
	☽ ⚻ ♀	10:44
	☽ ⚹ ♇	11:55
	☽ ⋕ ♃	12:22
	☽ ☌ ⚷	17:22
	☽ ⚺ ♅	17:33
	☉ ∥ ♄	19:32
	☿ ♐	19:44
	☽ ∥ ♀	20:07
	☽ ☍ ♃	22:07
21 Sa	☽ ∠ ⚳	0:24
	♀ □ ♇	2:03
	☉ ∠ ♇	10:14
	☽ ∥ ⚷	10:21
	☽ ∥ ♂	11:45
	☉ △ ☽	13:24
	☿ ∥ ♇	14:22
	☽ △ ☿	17:37
	☽ ⋕ ♂	19:45
	☽ ⋕ ⚷	20:45
22 Su	☽ ☍ ♂	0:16
	☽ ⚹ ⚳	1:54
	☽ △ ♄	2:01
	☿ ⚼ ♅	2:46
	☽ ⚺ ♆	2:52
	⚳ ⚹ ♄	11:48
	☽ □ ♇	14:01
	☽ ⋕ ♀	14:29
	☉ ♐	15:26
	♂ ∥ ⚷	15:56
	☉ ⚼ ☽	16:01
	☽ ☍ ♀	16:58
	☽ ∥ ♃	17:39
	☽ ⚺ ⚷	19:11
	☽ ☌ ♅	19:17
	☽ ⚼ ☿	21:18
	☽ ∥ ♅	23:48
23 M	☽ ⚻ ♃	0:15
	☽ ⚼ ♄	2:50
	☽ ∠ ♆	3:28
	☉ ⚻ ☽	18:17
	☽ ∠ ⚷	19:37
	☽ ⋕ ♆	20:20
	♀ ⚻ ⚷	21:23
	♀ ☍ ♅	22:14
	♀ ⋕ ♃	22:41
24 Tu	☽ ⚻ ☿	0:38
	☽ ⚼ ♃	0:52
	⚳ ⚺ ♆	2:00
	☽ ⚻ ♂	3:22
	☽ ⚻ ♄	3:25
	☽ ⚹ ♆	3:52
	☽ □ ⚳	3:54
	♂ ⚹ ♄	5:20
	☉ ⚼ ♅	14:16
	☽ △ ♇	14:57
	♂ ⚻ ♆	15:59
	☽ ⚹ ⚷	19:58
	☽ ⚺ ♅	20:00
	☽ ⚻ ♀	21:52
25 W	☽ △ ♃	1:27
	☽ ⚼ ♂	4:46
	☿ ☌ ♄	4:58
	♂ △ ⚳	5:47
	☿ □ ♆	7:16
	☿ ⚹ ⚳	14:02
	☽ ⚼ ♇	15:27
	☿ ⚹ ♂	16:33
	♅ ⚺ ⚷	19:30
	☽ ∠ ♅	20:27
	☉ ☍ ☽	22:45
26 Th	☽ ⚼ ♀	0:28
	☽ ☍ ♄	4:47
	☽ □ ♆	4:51
	☽ △ ⚳	5:54
	☽ △ ♂	6:24
	☽ ☍ ☿	7:27
	♄ □ ♆	12:16
	☽ ⚻ ♇	16:16
	♀ ⋕ ♅	19:53
	☽ ⚹ ♅	21:17
	☽ □ ⚷	21:19
27 F	♀ ⚺ ♃	1:03
	☽ □ ♃	3:25
	☽ △ ♀	3:36
	☉ ∥ ♇	5:42
	☽ ⚼ ⚳	7:31
28 Sa	☉ ⚻ ☽	5:12
	⚷ D	6:44
	☽ △ ♆	7:39
	☽ ⚻ ♄	8:01
	♀ ⚼ ♆	8:05
	☽ ⚻ ⚳	9:53
	☽ □ ♂	11:34
	♀ ∠ ♄	12:54
	☽ ⚻ ☿	16:56
	☽ ☍ ♇	19:50
29 Su	☽ □ ♅	0:58
	☽ △ ⚷	1:06
	☽ ⚹ ♃	8:05
	☉ ⚼ ☽	9:55
	☽ ⚼ ♆	10:17
	☽ ⚼ ♄	10:54
	☽ □ ♀	12:47
	☉ □ ♆	14:51
	☿ ⚺ ♇	18:36
	☽ ⚼ ☿	23:33
30 M	☉ ☌ ♄	0:17
	☽ ⚼ ⚷	4:23
	☽ ∠ ♃	11:53
	☽ ⚻ ♆	13:57
	☽ △ ♄	14:49
	☉ △ ☽	15:55
	☽ ☍ ⚳	17:40
	☽ ⚹ ♂	20:48

December 2015

LONGITUDE

Day	Sid.Time	☉	☽	☽ 12 hour	Mean ☊	True ☊	☿	♀	♂	⚳	♃	♄	⚷	♅	♆	♇
	h m s	° ' "	° ' "	° ' "	° '	° '	° '	° '	° '	° '	° '	° '	° '	° '	° '	° '
1 Tu	4 38 08	8♐27 10	12♌22 53	18♌38 42	27♍14.9	28♍06.4	15♐54.4	25♎07.7	10♎46.4	9♒07.3	21♍00.9	7♐34.1	16♓56.5	16♈49.5	7♓03.8	14♑02.3
2 W	4 42 05	9 27 58	24 49 23	0♍55 33	27 11.8	28R 03.3	17 27.5	26 17.4	11 21.7	9 26.0	21 07.5	7 41.2	16 56.7	16R 48.3	7 04.2	14 04.1
3 Th	4 46 02	10 28 47	6♍57 49	12 56 53	27 08.6	28D 02.2	19 00.6	27 27.3	11 57.0	9 44.8	21 13.9	7 48.4	16 56.9	16 47.1	7 04.7	14 05.9
4 F	4 49 58	11 29 38	18 53 27	24 48 13	27 05.4	28R 02.3	20 33.6	28 37.3	12 32.2	10 03.7	21 20.2	7 55.5	16 57.2	16 46.0	7 05.2	14 07.7
5 Sa	4 53 55	12 30 30	0♎41 53	6♎35 08	27 02.2	28 02.5	22 06.6	29 47.5	13 07.3	10 22.8	21 26.4	8 02.6	16 57.6	16 44.9	7 05.7	14 09.5
6 Su	4 57 51	13 31 24	12 28 38	18 23 00	26 59.0	28 01.5	23 39.4	0♏57.8	13 42.4	10 41.9	21 32.4	8 09.7	16 58.0	16 43.9	7 06.3	14 11.3
7 M	5 01 48	14 32 18	24 18 48	0♏16 34	26 55.9	27 58.5	25 12.2	2 08.3	14 17.5	11 01.2	21 38.2	8 16.8	16 58.4	16 42.9	7 06.9	14 13.2
8 Tu	5 05 44	15 33 15	6♏16 46	12 19 48	26 52.7	27 52.9	26 44.9	3 18.9	14 52.5	11 20.6	21 43.9	8 23.9	16 59.0	16 41.9	7 07.6	14 15.0
9 W	5 09 41	16 34 12	18 26 00	24 35 37	26 49.5	27 44.3	28 17.5	4 29.6	15 27.4	11 40.2	21 49.4	8 30.9	16 59.5	16 41.0	7 08.2	14 16.9
10 Th	5 13 37	17 35 10	0♐48 51	7♐05 47	26 46.3	27 33.0	29 50.0	5 40.5	16 02.3	11 59.8	21 54.8	8 38.0	17 00.2	16 40.2	7 08.9	14 18.8
11 F	5 17 34	18 36 10	13 26 27	19 50 50	26 43.2	27 19.8	1♑22.4	6 51.4	16 37.1	12 19.6	22 00.0	8 45.1	17 00.9	16 39.4	7 09.7	14 20.7
12 Sa	5 21 31	19 37 10	26 18 49	2♑50 14	26 40.0	27 05.8	2 54.5	8 02.5	17 11.9	12 39.4	22 05.1	8 52.1	17 01.6	16 38.7	7 10.5	14 22.6
13 Su	5 25 27	20 38 11	9♑24 56	16 02 40	26 36.8	26 52.4	4 26.4	9 13.7	17 46.6	12 59.4	22 09.9	8 59.2	17 02.4	16 38.0	7 11.3	14 24.6
14 M	5 29 24	21 39 13	22 43 13	29 26 23	26 33.6	26 40.6	5 58.0	10 25.0	18 21.3	13 19.5	22 14.6	9 06.2	17 03.3	16 37.3	7 12.1	14 26.5
15 Tu	5 33 20	22 40 16	6♒11 58	12♒59 45	26 30.5	26 31.6	7 29.2	11 36.4	18 55.8	13 39.6	22 19.2	9 13.2	17 04.2	16 36.7	7 13.0	14 28.5
16 W	5 37 17	23 41 19	19 49 39	26 41 32	26 27.3	26 25.6	9 00.0	12 47.9	19 30.4	13 59.9	22 23.5	9 20.2	17 05.2	16 36.2	7 13.9	14 30.4
17 Th	5 41 13	24 42 22	3♓35 20	10♓31 02	26 24.1	26 22.5	10 30.2	13 59.5	20 04.8	14 20.3	22 27.7	9 27.1	17 06.2	16 35.7	7 14.9	14 32.4
18 F	5 45 10	25 43 26	17 28 37	24 28 04	26 20.9	26 21.5	11 59.8	15 11.2	20 39.2	14 40.7	22 31.8	9 34.1	17 07.3	16 35.2	7 15.9	14 34.4
19 Sa	5 49 06	26 44 30	1♈29 23	8♈32 32	26 17.8	26 21.5	13 28.6	16 22.9	21 13.5	15 01.3	22 35.6	9 41.0	17 08.4	16 34.8	7 16.9	14 36.4
20 Su	5 53 03	27 45 35	15 37 25	22 43 54	26 14.6	26 20.9	14 56.3	17 34.8	21 47.8	15 21.9	22 39.3	9 47.9	17 09.6	16 34.5	7 17.9	14 38.4
21 M	5 57 00	28 46 39	29 51 46	7♉00 42	26 11.4	26 18.4	16 22.9	18 46.7	22 22.0	15 42.7	22 42.8	9 54.8	17 10.9	16 34.2	7 19.0	14 40.4
22 Tu	6 00 56	29 47 44	14♉10 18	21 20 05	26 08.2	26 13.3	17 48.1	19 58.8	22 56.1	16 03.5	22 46.1	10 01.6	17 12.2	16 34.0	7 20.1	14 42.4
23 W	6 04 53	0♑48 50	28 29 28	5♊37 48	26 05.0	26 05.2	19 11.6	21 10.9	23 30.1	16 24.4	22 49.2	10 08.4	17 13.5	16 33.8	7 21.2	14 44.4
24 Th	6 08 49	1 49 55	12♊44 25	19 48 35	26 01.9	25 54.5	20 33.1	22 23.1	24 04.1	16 45.4	22 52.2	10 15.2	17 14.9	16 33.6	7 22.4	14 46.5
25 F	6 12 46	2 51 01	26 49 38	3♋46 54	25 58.7	25 42.0	21 52.3	23 35.4	24 38.0	17 06.5	22 55.0	10 22.0	17 16.4	16 33.5	7 23.6	14 48.5
26 Sa	6 16 42	3 52 07	10♋39 49	17 27 54	25 55.5	25 29.1	23 08.7	24 47.7	25 11.9	17 27.6	22 57.6	10 28.8	17 17.9	16D 33.5	7 24.8	14 50.5
27 Su	6 20 39	4 53 14	24 10 47	0♌48 13	25 52.3	25 17.1	24 21.8	26 00.2	25 45.6	17 48.9	23 00.0	10 35.5	17 19.5	16 33.5	7 26.0	14 52.6
28 M	6 24 35	5 54 21	7♌20 06	13 46 28	25 49.2	25 07.1	25 31.1	27 12.7	26 19.3	18 10.2	23 02.2	10 42.2	17 21.1	16 33.6	7 27.3	14 54.6
29 Tu	6 28 32	6 55 29	20 07 27	26 23 19	25 46.0	24 59.7	26 36.0	28 25.3	26 53.0	18 31.6	23 04.3	10 48.8	17 22.8	16 33.7	7 28.6	14 56.7
30 W	6 32 29	7 56 37	2♍34 26	8♍41 15	25 42.8	24 55.2	27 35.8	29 37.9	27 26.5	18 53.0	23 06.1	10 55.4	17 24.5	16 33.9	7 30.0	14 58.8
31 Th	6 36 25	8♑57 45	14 44 18	20 44 10	25♍39.6	24♍53.1	28♑29.7	0♐50.6	28♎00.0	19♒14.6	23♍07.8	11♐02.0	17♓26.2	16♈34.1	7♓31.3	15♑00.8

1st of Month

Julian Day # 2457357.5
Obliquity 23°26'04"
SVP 5♓02'16"
GC 27♐03.7
Eris 22♈27.0R

Day	⚴	⚵	⚶
1	10♑36.2	27♎02.8	29♓38.8
6	12 24.8	28 38.9	0♈19.4
11	14 14.1	0♏12.4	1 08.8
16	16 04.1	1 43.1	2 06.3
21	17 54.5	3 10.7	3 11.4
26	19 45.2	4 34.9	4 23.3
31	21 36.1	5 55.5	5 41.4

DECLINATION and LATITUDE

Day	☉ Decl	☽ Decl	☽ Lat	☽ 12h Decl	☿ Decl	☿ Lat	♀ Decl	♀ Lat	♂ Decl	♂ Lat	⚳ Decl	⚳ Lat	♃ Decl	♃ Lat	♄ Decl	♄ Lat
1 Tu	21S43	13N36	3S38	12N10	24S15	1S34	7S43	2N09	2S55	1N28	26S17	8S39	4N35	1N06	19S57	1N38
2 W	21 52	10 37	2 47	8 58	24 29	1 39	8 07	2 11	3 09	1 28	26 11	8 37	4 32	1 06	19 58	1 38
3 Th	22 01	7 15	1 50	5 28	24 42	1 44	8 31	2 12	3 23	1 28	26 05	8 36	4 30	1 07	19 60	1 38
4 F	22 09	3 39	0 49	1 48	24 54	1 48	8 55	2 13	3 36	1 28	25 58	8 35	4 28	1 07	20 01	1 38
5 Sa	22 17	0S04	0N14	1S55	25 04	1 52	9 19	2 14	3 50	1 28	25 52	8 34	4 25	1 07	20 02	1 38
6 Su	22 25	3 46	1 16	5 34	25 13	1 56	9 42	2 15	4 03	1 28	25 45	8 33	4 23	1 07	20 03	1 38
7 M	22 32	7 20	2 15	9 02	25 20	1 60	10 06	2 15	4 17	1 28	25 39	8 32	4 21	1 08	20 04	1 38
8 Tu	22 39	10 39	3 08	12 10	25 27	2 03	10 29	2 16	4 30	1 28	25 32	8 31	4 19	1 08	20 05	1 38
9 W	22 45	13 34	3 54	14 50	25 31	2 06	10 52	2 16	4 43	1 28	25 26	8 30	4 17	1 08	20 07	1 38
10 Th	22 51	15 56	4 29	16 51	25 35	2 09	11 16	2 17	4 57	1 29	25 19	8 29	4 15	1 08	20 08	1 38
11 F	22 57	17 35	4 52	18 06	25 37	2 11	11 39	2 17	5 10	1 29	25 12	8 28	4 14	1 09	20 09	1 38
12 Sa	23 02	18 23	5 00	18 26	25 37	2 13	12 01	2 17	5 23	1 29	25 05	8 27	4 12	1 09	20 10	1 38
13 Su	23 06	18 14	4 53	17 46	25 36	2 14	12 24	2 17	5 36	1 29	24 59	8 26	4 10	1 09	20 11	1 38
14 M	23 10	17 05	4 30	16 08	25 33	2 16	12 46	2 17	5 49	1 29	24 52	8 25	4 08	1 09	20 12	1 38
15 Tu	23 14	14 58	3 52	13 35	25 29	2 16	13 08	2 17	6 02	1 29	24 45	8 24	4 07	1 10	20 13	1 38
16 W	23 17	12 01	3 00	10 16	25 24	2 17	13 30	2 17	6 15	1 29	24 38	8 23	4 05	1 10	20 14	1 38
17 Th	23 20	8 22	1 57	6 21	25 17	2 16	13 52	2 16	6 28	1 29	24 31	8 22	4 04	1 10	20 15	1 38
18 F	23 22	4 14	0 47	2 03	25 09	2 15	14 13	2 16	6 41	1 29	24 24	8 21	4 03	1 11	20 16	1 38
19 Sa	23 24	0N11	0S27	2N24	24 59	2 14	14 34	2 15	6 54	1 29	24 17	8 20	4 01	1 11	20 17	1 38
20 Su	23 25	4 37	1 40	6 45	24 47	2 12	14 55	2 15	7 07	1 29	24 10	8 19	4 00	1 11	20 18	1 38
21 M	23 26	8 49	2 47	10 45	24 34	2 10	15 16	2 14	7 19	1 29	24 02	8 18	3 59	1 11	20 19	1 38
22 Tu	23 26	12 31	3 44	14 06	24 20	2 06	15 36	2 13	7 32	1 29	23 55	8 18	3 58	1 12	20 20	1 38
23 W	23 26	15 29	4 27	16 37	24 05	2 02	15 56	2 12	7 44	1 30	23 48	8 17	3 57	1 12	20 21	1 38
24 Th	23 25	17 29	4 53	18 05	23 48	1 58	16 15	2 11	7 57	1 30	23 41	8 16	3 56	1 12	20 22	1 38
25 F	23 24	18 23	5 00	18 25	23 30	1 52	16 34	2 10	8 09	1 30	23 33	8 15	3 55	1 12	20 23	1 38
26 Sa	23 23	18 11	4 50	17 41	23 11	1 46	16 53	2 09	8 21	1 30	23 26	8 14	3 54	1 13	20 24	1 38
27 Su	23 21	16 57	4 24	15 59	22 51	1 38	17 11	2 07	8 34	1 30	23 18	8 14	3 54	1 13	20 25	1 38
28 M	23 18	14 50	3 44	13 30	22 30	1 30	17 29	2 06	8 46	1 30	23 11	8 13	3 53	1 13	20 26	1 38
29 Tu	23 15	12 02	2 53	10 27	22 09	1 21	17 47	2 04	8 58	1 30	23 03	8 12	3 53	1 14	20 27	1 38
30 W	23 12	8 45	1 55	6 60	21 47	1 10	18 04	2 03	9 10	1 30	22 56	8 11	3 52	1 14	20 28	1 38
31 Th	23S08	5N11	0S54	3N20	21S25	0S59	18S21	2N01	9S22	1N30	22S48	8S11	3N52	1N14	20S29	1N38

Day	⚷ Decl	⚷ Lat	♅ Decl	♅ Lat	♆ Decl	♆ Lat	♇ Decl	♇ Lat
1	1S02	4N28	6N00	0S39	9S40	0S48	21S04	1N39
6	1 03	4 26	5 58	0 39	9 39	0 48	21 03	1 38
11	1 03	4 25	5 57	0 39	9 37	0 48	21 03	1 37
16	1 03	4 23	5 56	0 39	9 36	0 48	21 02	1 37
21	1 02	4 22	5 55	0 38	9 34	0 48	21 02	1 36
26	1 01	4 20	5 55	0 38	9 31	0 48	21 01	1 36
31	0S59	4N19	5N56	0S38	9S29	0S48	21S01	1N35

Day	⚴ Decl	⚴ Lat	⚵ Decl	⚵ Lat	⚶ Decl	⚶ Lat	Eris Decl	Eris Lat
1	2N42	25N47	6S13	4N31	8S25	9S01	3S00	12S38
6	2 28	25 25	6 35	4 43	7 52	8 43	3 00	12 37
11	2 16	25 04	6 55	4 56	7 16	8 25	3 00	12 36
16	2 07	24 44	7 14	5 09	6 37	8 07	3 00	12 36
21	2 00	24 26	7 31	5 23	5 56	7 51	2 60	12 35
26	1 56	24 09	7 45	5 37	5 13	7 35	2 60	12 34
31	1N55	23N53	7S57	5N52	4S28	7S20	2S59	12S33

Moon Phenomena

Max/0 Decl

dy	hr mn	
4	23:36	0 S
12	8:10	18S26
18	23:03	0 N
25	7:21	18N27

Max/0 Lat

dy	hr mn	
4	18:35	0 N
12	1:19	5N00
18	15:14	0 S
24	22:15	5S00
31	20:21	0 N

Perigee/Apogee

dy	hr m		kilometers
5	15:00	a	404798
21	8:59	p	368417

PH	dy	hr mn	
☾	3	7:41	10♍48
●	11	10:30	19♐03
☽	18	15:15	26♓22
○	25	11:13	3♋20

Void of Course Moon

Last Aspect				☽ Ingress		
2	3:10	♀	⚹	♍	2	10:10
4	5:00	♃	☌	♎	4	22:35
7	2:04	☿	⚹	♏	7	11:27
9	6:40	♃	⚹	♐	9	22:26
11	16:07	♃	□	♑	12	6:48
13	23:08	♃	△	♒	14	13:00
16	7:18	☉	⚹	♓	16	17:46
18	15:15	☉	□	♈	18	21:27
20	22:02	☉	△	♉	21	0:14
22	14:27	♃	△	♊	23	2:32
24	20:05	♂	△	♋	25	5:28
27	3:37	♀	△	♌	27	10:32
29	17:39	♀	□	♍	29	18:59

DAILY ASPECTARIAN

1 Tu ☽⚻♇ 3:10; ☽△☿ 7:41; ☽△♅ 8:29; ☽⚻⚷ 8:43; ☿△♅ 14:01; ☿□⚷ 16:02; ☽⚺♃ 16:44; ☉⚹⚳ 22:51

2 W ☽∠♂ 3:10; ☽⚹♀ 3:10; ☽#♆ 7:05; ☽⚼♇ 8:21; ☽⚼♅ 13:43; ☽#♀ 16:10

3 Th ☽☍♆ 0:14; ☽□♄ 1:42; ☽⚻⚳ 5:43; ☉□☽ 7:41; ☽∥♅ 8:33; ☽⚺♂ 10:30; ☽∠♀ 12:12; ☽△♇ 14:21; ⚶ ♈ 17:59; ☽∥♃ 18:39; ☽⚻♅ 19:43; ☽☍⚷ 20:05

4 F ☽#♂ 0:18; ☽□☿ 3:54; ☽☌♃ 5:00; ☽⚼⚳ 12:52; ☿□♃ 12:54; ☽#⚷ 16:50; ☽⚺♀ 21:57

5 Sa ♀ ♏ 4:16; ☽∥⚷ 6:23; ☽⚻♆ 13:03; ☽⚹♄ 15:07; ☽△⚳ 20:17; ♀∥♆ 20:29

6 Su ☽∥♂ 2:02; ☉⚹☽ 2:20; ☽☌♂ 2:38; ☽□♇ 3:29; ☽#♃ 4:04; ☽☍♅ 8:38; ☽⚻⚷ 9:08; ☉⚹♂ 10:15; ☽#♅ 14:40; ☉⚺♇ 16:14; ☽⚺♃ 18:33; ☽⚼♆ 19:33; ♀⚼⚷ 20:37; ♂□♇ 20:53; ☽∠♄ 21:53

7 M ☽⚹☿ 2:04; ♂#♃ 7:01; ☉∠☽ 11:30; ☽⚼⚷ 15:25; ☿∠⚳ 16:02; ☽∥♆ 16:24; ☽☌♀ 17:26; ☽∥♀ 22:34

8 Tu ☽∠♃ 0:54; ☽△♆ 1:41; ☽⚺♄ 4:15; ☽□⚳ 10:20; ☿∥⚳ 11:45; ☽∠☿ 12:26; ☽⚹♇ 15:50; ☽⚺♂ 17:52; ☉⚺☽ 20:01; ☽⚻♅ 20:35; ☽△⚷ 21:10

9 W ☉△♅ 2:39; ☽⚹♃ 6:40; ☉□⚷ 10:05; ☽∠♇ 21:06; ☽⚺☿ 21:51

10 Th ☽∠♂ 0:27; ☽⚼♅ 1:38; ☿ ♑ 2:35; ⚵ ♏ 7:51; ☽⚺♀ 10:15; ☽□♆ 12:07; ☽☌♄ 15:03; ☽⚹⚳ 21:51

11 F ♂☍♅ 1:32; ☽⚺♇ 1:42; ♀∠♃ 3:08; ☽△♅ 6:02; ♀△♆ 6:14; ☽⚹♂ 6:15; ☽□⚷ 6:43; ☉☌☽ 10:30; ☽□♃ 16:07; ♂⚻⚷ 16:44; ☽∠♀ 17:20

12 Sa ☽∠⚳ 2:33; ☽☌☿ 13:44; ♀⚺♄ 18:34; ☽⚹♆ 19:57; ☽⚺♄ 23:13; ☽⚹♀ 23:38

13 Su ☽⚺⚳ 6:39; ☽☌♇ 9:04; ☽□♅ 13:03; ☽⚹⚷ 13:49; ☽□♂ 15:48; ☉⚺☽ 21:56; ☽∠♆ 23:04; ☽△♃ 23:08

14 M ☽∠♄ 2:30; ♂#♅ 12:15; ☉□♃ 15:03; ☽∠⚷ 16:40; ☿⚹♆ 19:41

15 Tu ☽⚺♆ 1:48; ☽⚼♃ 2:00; ☽⚺☿ 2:34; ☉∠☽ 2:49; ☽⚹♄ 5:23; ☽□♀ 10:28; ☽☌⚳ 13:30; ☽∥♀ 13:53; ☽⚺♇ 14:38; ☽⚹♅ 18:21; ☽⚺⚷ 19:11; ☽△♂ 23:25

16 W ☽⚻♃ 4:31; ☿⚺♄ 5:47; ☉⚹☽ 7:18; ☽∠☿ 8:12; ☽∥♆ 16:21; ☽∠♇ 16:57; ☽∠♅ 20:32

17 Th ☽⚼♂ 2:42; ☽☌♆ 6:21; ♀□⚳ 9:45; ☽□♄ 10:15; ☽∥♂ 10:43; ♀⚹♇ 11:20; ☽⚹☿ 13:25; ☽#♅ 14:25; ⚳⚺♇ 15:46; ☽⚹♇ 18:59; ☽⚺⚳ 19:04; ☽△♀ 19:41; ☽⚺♅ 22:28; ☽☌⚷ 23:23

18 F ☽#♃ 1:02; ☽⚻♂ 5:42; ☽☍♃ 8:43; ☉□☽ 15:15; ☽∥⚷ 17:24; ☽∠⚳ 21:26; ☽⚼♀ 23:48

19 Sa ♀⚻♅ 3:57; ☽#⚷ 4:40; ☽⚺♆ 9:52; ☽△♄ 14:03; ♀△⚷ 15:28; ☿☌♇ 18:57; ☽∥♃ 20:41; ☽□♇ 22:20; ☽□☿ 22:43; ☽⚹⚳ 23:33

20 Su ☽☌♅ 1:36; ☽⚺⚷ 2:36; ☽⚻♀ 3:37; ☽∥♅ 7:17; ☿⚺⚳ 9:16; ☽☍♂ 10:51; ☽∠♆ 11:17; ☽⚻♃ 11:55; ☽#♂ 14:46; ☽⚼♄ 15:36; ♂⚼♆ 21:50; ☉△☽ 22:02

21 M ☿□♅ 3:09; ☽∠⚷ 3:54; ☽#♆ 4:33; ☽⚹♆ 12:32; ☽⚼♃ 13:14; ☿⚹⚷ 13:40; ♂⚺♃ 16:14; ☽⚻♄ 17:00

22 Tu ☽△♇ 0:54; ☉⚼☽ 1:08; ☽□⚳ 3:14; ☽⚺♅ 4:01; ☉ ♑ 4:49; ☽⚹⚷ 5:05; ☽△☿ 6:44; ☽☍♀ 10:37; ☽△♃ 14:27; ☽⚻♂ 15:17

23 W ☽⚼♇ 2:06; ☉⚻☽ 4:12; ☽∠♅ 5:09; ☽#♀ 5:11; ☽⚼☿ 10:36; ⚳⚹♅ 10:38; ☽□♆ 14:55; ☽⚼♂ 17:32; ☽☍♄ 19:46; ☉∠⚳ 21:17

24 Th ☽⚻♇ 3:27; ☽⚹♅ 6:28; ☽△⚳ 6:59; ☽□⚷ 7:39; ♀⚹♃ 10:04; ☽⚻☿ 14:39; ☽□♃ 17:17; ☿∥⚳ 17:28; ☽⚻♀ 17:56; ☽△♂ 20:05

25 F ☉∥☿ 8:13; ☽⚼⚳ 9:20; ☿∠♆ 9:52; ☉☍☽ 11:13; ⚳⚺⚷ 12:09; ☽△♆ 18:18; ☿△♃ 20:20; ☽⚼♀ 22:20; ☽⚻♄ 23:40

26 Sa ♅ D 3:54; ☽☍♇ 7:22; ☽□♅ 10:24; ☽△⚷ 11:44; ☽⚻⚳ 12:19; ☉∥⚳ 13:11; ♂∠♄ 14:59; ♀⚺♂ 14:59; ☽⚼♆ 20:52; ☽#♀ 20:59; ☽⚹♃ 21:52

27 Su ☽☍☿ 0:22; ☽⚼♄ 2:34; ☽□♂ 2:59; ☽△♀ 3:37; ☽⚼⚷ 14:49; ☉⚻☽ 21:08

28 M ☽⚻♆ 0:13; ☽∠♃ 1:18; ☿∠♄ 4:24; ☽△♄ 6:19; ☽⚻♇ 14:10; ☽△♅ 17:15; ☽⚻⚷ 18:47; ☽☍⚳ 20:53

29 Tu ☉⚼☽ 3:44; ☽⚺♃ 5:38; ☉⚹♆ 13:19; ☽⚻☿ 13:31; ☽⚹♂ 13:34; ☿□♂ 14:54; ☽□♀ 17:39; ☽#♆ 18:50; ☽⚼♇ 18:56; ☽#♂ 21:19; ☽⚼♅ 22:02

30 W ♀∠♇ 7:05; ♀ ♐ 7:18; ☽☍♆ 9:41; ☉△☽ 11:30; ☽□♄ 16:34; ☽∥♅ 19:08; ☽∠♂ 20:22; ☽⚼☿ 21:20

31 Th ☽△♇ 0:33; ☽⚻♅ 3:39; ☽☍⚷ 5:24; ☽∥♃ 8:37; ☽⚻⚳ 9:17; ♂∥♆ 14:09; ♀⚼♅ 14:23; ☽☌♃ 16:51

LONGITUDE

January 2016

ay	Sid.Time	☉	☽	☽ 12 hour	Mean☊	True☊	☿	♀	♂	⚳	♃	♄	⚷	♅	♆	♇
	h m s	° ' "	° ' "	° ' "	° '	° '	° '	° '	° '	° '	° '	° '	° '	° '	° '	° '
F	6 40 22	9♑58 53	26♍41 29	2♎36 55	25♍36.5	24♍52.7	29♑16.9	2♐03.4	28♎33.4	19♒36.2	23♍09.3	11♐08.6	17♓28.0	16♈34.4	7♓32.7	15♑02.9
Sa	6 44 18	11 00 02	8♎31 11	14 24 58	25 33.3	24R 53.0	29 56.6	3 16.3	29 06.7	19 57.9	23 10.6	11 15.1	17 29.9	16 34.7	7 34.2	15 05.0
Su	6 48 15	12 01 12	20 18 58	26 13 54	25 30.1	24 52.7	0♒27.7	4 29.2	29 39.9	20 19.6	23 11.7	11 21.5	17 31.8	16 35.1	7 35.6	15 07.1
M	6 52 11	13 02 21	2♏10 24	8♏09 08	25 26.9	24 50.8	0 49.4	5 42.1	0♏13.0	20 41.4	23 12.6	11 28.0	17 33.8	16 35.5	7 37.1	15 09.1
Tu	6 56 08	14 03 31	14 10 42	20 15 38	25 23.7	24 46.7	1R 00.9	6 55.2	0 46.1	21 03.3	23 13.3	11 34.4	17 35.8	16 36.0	7 38.6	15 11.2
W	7 00 04	15 04 42	26 24 24	2♐37 25	25 20.6	24 39.9	1 01.4	8 08.3	1 19.0	21 25.3	23 13.8	11 40.7	17 37.8	16 36.5	7 40.1	15 13.3
Th	7 04 01	16 05 52	8♐55 00	15 17 22	25 17.4	24 30.6	0 50.4	9 21.4	1 51.9	21 47.3	23 14.1	11 47.0	17 39.9	16 37.1	7 41.7	15 15.4
F	7 07 58	17 07 03	21 44 38	28 16 48	25 14.2	24 19.4	0 27.5	10 34.6	2 24.7	22 09.4	23R 14.3	11 53.3	17 42.1	16 37.8	7 43.3	15 17.4
Sa	7 11 54	18 08 13	4♑53 48	11♑35 23	25 11.0	24 07.3	29♑52.8	11 47.8	2 57.4	22 31.5	23 14.2	11 59.5	17 44.3	16 38.5	7 44.9	15 19.5
Su	7 15 51	19 09 23	18 21 19	25 11 10	25 07.9	23 55.6	29 06.8	13 01.1	3 29.9	22 53.7	23 14.0	12 05.7	17 46.5	16 39.2	7 46.5	15 21.6
M	7 19 47	20 10 33	2♒04 33	9♒00 56	25 04.7	23 45.3	28 10.5	14 14.4	4 02.4	23 16.0	23 13.5	12 11.8	17 48.8	16 40.0	7 48.2	15 23.7
Tu	7 23 44	21 11 43	15 59 50	23 00 46	25 01.5	23 37.5	27 05.3	15 27.7	4 34.8	23 38.3	23 12.9	12 17.9	17 51.1	16 40.8	7 49.9	15 25.7
W	7 27 40	22 12 53	0♓03 12	7♓06 44	24 58.3	23 32.4	25 53.2	16 41.1	5 07.1	24 00.7	23 12.0	12 24.0	17 53.5	16 41.7	7 51.6	15 27.8
Th	7 31 37	23 14 01	14 10 56	21 15 29	24 55.2	23D 30.1	24 36.3	17 54.6	5 39.2	24 23.1	23 11.0	12 29.9	17 55.9	16 42.7	7 53.3	15 29.9
F	7 35 33	24 15 09	28 20 05	5♈24 30	24 52.0	23 29.8	23 17.2	19 08.0	6 11.3	24 45.6	23 09.8	12 35.9	17 58.4	16 43.7	7 55.1	15 31.9
Sa	7 39 30	25 16 17	12♈28 34	19 32 08	24 48.8	23R 30.5	21 58.3	20 21.5	6 43.2	25 08.2	23 08.4	12 41.7	18 00.9	16 44.7	7 56.9	15 34.0
Su	7 43 27	26 17 23	26 35 06	3♉37 19	24 45.6	23 31.0	20 42.1	21 35.1	7 15.0	25 30.7	23 06.7	12 47.5	18 03.4	16 45.8	7 58.6	15 36.0
M	7 47 23	27 18 29	10♉38 41	17 39 05	24 42.4	23 30.1	19 30.6	22 48.6	7 46.8	25 53.4	23 04.9	12 53.3	18 06.0	16 47.0	8 00.5	15 38.1
Tu	7 51 20	28 19 34	24 38 21	1♊36 16	24 39.3	23 27.1	18 25.6	24 02.2	8 18.4	26 16.0	23 03.0	12 59.0	18 08.6	16 48.2	8 02.3	15 40.1
W	7 55 16	29 20 38	8♊32 38	15 27 09	24 36.1	23 21.7	17 28.5	25 15.8	8 49.8	26 38.8	23 00.8	13 04.7	18 11.3	16 49.4	8 04.2	15 42.2
Th	7 59 13	0♒21 42	22 19 32	29 09 29	24 32.9	23 14.2	16 40.0	26 29.5	9 21.2	27 01.5	22 58.4	13 10.3	18 14.0	16 50.7	8 06.1	15 44.2
F	8 03 09	1 22 45	5♋56 38	12♋40 41	24 29.7	23 05.3	16 00.7	27 43.2	9 52.5	27 24.3	22 55.9	13 15.8	18 16.7	16 52.1	8 08.0	15 46.2
Sa	8 07 06	2 23 46	19 21 20	25 58 17	24 26.6	22 55.9	15 30.7	28 56.9	10 23.6	27 47.2	22 53.1	13 21.3	18 19.5	16 53.4	8 09.9	15 48.2
Su	8 11 03	3 24 47	2♌31 19	9♌00 17	24 23.4	22 47.2	15 09.9	0♑10.6	10 54.6	28 10.1	22 50.2	13 26.7	18 22.3	16 54.9	8 11.8	15 50.2
M	8 14 59	4 25 48	15 25 05	21 45 42	24 20.2	22 39.9	14D 58.1	1 24.4	11 25.5	28 33.0	22 47.1	13 32.0	18 25.1	16 56.4	8 13.8	15 52.2
Tu	8 18 56	5 26 47	28 02 12	4♍14 42	24 17.0	22 34.6	14 54.7	2 38.2	11 56.2	28 56.0	22 43.8	13 37.3	18 28.0	16 57.9	8 15.7	15 54.2
W	8 22 52	6 27 46	10♍23 26	16 28 42	24 13.9	22D 31.6	14 59.3	3 52.0	12 26.8	29 19.0	22 40.4	13 42.5	18 30.9	16 59.5	8 17.7	15 56.2
Th	8 26 49	7 28 44	22 30 51	28 30 20	24 10.7	22 30.8	15 11.4	5 05.9	12 57.3	29 42.0	22 36.7	13 47.7	18 33.8	17 01.1	8 19.7	15 58.2
F	8 30 45	8 29 41	4♎27 37	10♎23 14	24 07.5	22 31.4	15 30.2	6 19.7	13 27.6	0♓05.1	22 32.9	13 52.8	18 36.8	17 02.8	8 21.8	16 00.1
Sa	8 34 42	9 30 38	16 17 45	22 11 48	24 04.3	22 33.0	15 55.4	7 33.6	13 57.8	0 28.2	22 28.9	13 57.8	18 39.8	17 04.5	8 23.8	16 02.1
Su	8 38 38	10♒31 34	28 06 01	4♏01 01	24♍01.1	22♍34.5	16♑26.2	8♑47.5	14♏27.9	0♓51.3	22♍24.8	14♐02.7	18♓42.8	17♈06.2	8♓25.9	16♑04.0

1st of Month

Julian Day # 2457388.5
Obliquity 23°26'04"
SVP 5♓02'11"
GC 27♐03.8
Eris 22♈18.8R

Day	⚴
1	21♑58.3
6	23 49.2
11	25 40.0
16	27 30.5
21	29 20.6
26	1♒10.2
31	2 59.0

Day	⚵
1	6♏11.2
6	7 27.0
11	8 38.6
16	9 45.4
21	10 47.1
26	11 43.4
31	12 33.8

Day	⚶
1	5♈57.7
6	7 22.6
11	8 52.7
16	10 27.4
21	12 06.3
26	13 49.0
31	15 35.1

DECLINATION and LATITUDE

ay	☉ Decl	☽ Decl	☽ Lat	☽ 12h Decl	☿ Decl	☿ Lat	♀ Decl	♀ Lat	♂ Decl	♂ Lat	⚳ Decl	⚳ Lat	♃ Decl	♃ Lat	♄ Decl	♄ Lat
F	23S04	1N28	0N10	0S25	21S03	0S46	18S37	1N60	9S34	1N30	22S40	8S10	3N51	1N14	20S30	1N38
Sa	22 59	2S17	1 12	4 07	20 41	0 32	18 53	1 58	9 45	1 30	22 33	8 09	3 51	1 15	20 30	1 38
Su	22 53	5 55	2 11	7 40	20 20	0 17	19 08	1 56	9 57	1 30	22 25	8 09	3 51	1 15	20 31	1 38
M	22 48	9 20	3 05	10 56	19 59	0 01	19 23	1 54	10 09	1 30	22 17	8 08	3 51	1 15	20 32	1 38
Tu	22 42	12 25	3 51	13 47	19 40	0N16	19 37	1 52	10 20	1 30	22 09	8 07	3 51	1 16	20 33	1 38
W	22 35	15 01	4 27	16 05	19 23	0 34	19 51	1 50	10 31	1 30	22 01	8 07	3 51	1 16	20 34	1 38
Th	22 28	16 59	4 52	17 40	19 07	0 52	20 04	1 48	10 43	1 30	21 54	8 06	3 51	1 16	20 35	1 38
F	22 20	18 09	5 02	18 23	18 53	1 11	20 17	1 46	10 54	1 30	21 46	8 06	3 51	1 16	20 35	1 38
Sa	22 12	18 23	4 57	18 08	18 42	1 31	20 29	1 44	11 05	1 30	21 38	8 05	3 51	1 17	20 36	1 38
Su	22 04	17 37	4 36	16 51	18 33	1 49	20 41	1 41	11 16	1 30	21 30	8 04	3 52	1 17	20 37	1 38
M	21 55	15 49	3 58	14 33	18 26	2 08	20 52	1 39	11 27	1 30	21 22	8 04	3 52	1 17	20 38	1 38
Tu	21 46	13 04	3 06	11 24	18 22	2 25	21 02	1 37	11 38	1 30	21 13	8 03	3 53	1 17	20 38	1 38
W	21 36	9 33	2 02	7 34	18 20	2 41	21 12	1 34	11 49	1 30	21 05	8 03	3 53	1 18	20 39	1 38
Th	21 26	5 28	0 50	3 17	18 20	2 54	21 22	1 32	11 60	1 30	20 57	8 02	3 54	1 18	20 40	1 38
F	21 16	1 04	0S26	1N11	18 22	3 06	21 31	1 29	12 10	1 30	20 49	8 02	3 55	1 18	20 41	1 38
Sa	21 05	3N24	1 40	5 34	18 26	3 15	21 39	1 27	12 21	1 30	20 41	8 01	3 56	1 19	20 41	1 38
Su	20 53	7 39	2 48	9 37	18 31	3 22	21 46	1 24	12 31	1 30	20 33	8 01	3 56	1 19	20 42	1 38
M	20 42	11 27	3 45	13 07	18 37	3 26	21 53	1 21	12 41	1 30	20 24	8 00	3 57	1 19	20 43	1 39
Tu	20 30	14 35	4 29	15 50	18 44	3 28	21 60	1 19	12 52	1 29	20 16	7 60	3 58	1 19	20 43	1 39
W	20 17	16 51	4 56	17 37	18 52	3 27	22 05	1 16	13 02	1 29	20 08	7 60	3 60	1 20	20 44	1 39
Th	20 04	18 07	5 06	18 21	19 01	3 24	22 10	1 13	13 12	1 29	19 59	7 59	4 01	1 20	20 45	1 39
F	19 51	18 20	4 59	18 02	19 10	3 20	22 15	1 10	13 22	1 29	19 51	7 59	4 02	1 20	20 45	1 39
Sa	19 37	17 30	4 35	16 44	19 19	3 14	22 18	1 08	13 31	1 29	19 42	7 58	4 03	1 20	20 46	1 39
Su	19 23	15 45	3 56	14 35	19 29	3 07	22 21	1 05	13 41	1 29	19 34	7 58	4 05	1 21	20 46	1 39
M	19 09	13 14	3 07	11 45	19 38	2 58	22 24	1 02	13 51	1 29	19 25	7 58	4 06	1 21	20 47	1 39
Tu	18 54	10 09	2 08	8 26	19 48	2 49	22 26	0 59	14 00	1 29	19 17	7 57	4 08	1 21	20 48	1 39
W	18 39	6 40	1 05	4 50	19 57	2 40	22 27	0 56	14 10	1 29	19 08	7 57	4 09	1 22	20 48	1 39
Th	18 24	2 58	0N00	1 05	20 06	2 30	22 27	0 53	14 19	1 29	18 60	7 57	4 11	1 22	20 49	1 39
F	18 08	0S47	1 04	2S39	20 14	2 19	22 27	0 50	14 28	1 28	18 51	7 56	4 13	1 22	20 49	1 39
Sa	17 52	4 28	2 06	6 15	20 22	2 08	22 26	0 47	14 37	1 28	18 43	7 56	4 15	1 22	20 50	1 39
Su	17S36	7S58	3N01	9S37	20S29	1N57	22S24	0N44	14S46	1N28	18S34	7S56	4N16	1N23	20S50	1N39

Day	⚷ Decl	⚷ Lat	♅ Decl	♅ Lat	♆ Decl	♆ Lat	♇ Decl	♇ Lat
1	0S59	4N19	5N56	0S38	9S28	0S48	21S01	1N35
6	0 56	4 17	5 57	0 38	9 26	0 48	20 60	1 35
11	0 53	4 16	5 58	0 38	9 23	0 48	20 59	1 34
16	0 50	4 15	6 00	0 38	9 19	0 47	20 58	1 34
21	0 46	4 14	6 03	0 37	9 16	0 47	20 58	1 33
26	0 41	4 13	6 06	0 37	9 12	0 47	20 57	1 33
31	0S36	4N12	6N09	0S37	9S08	0S47	20S56	1N33

Day	⚴ Decl	⚴ Lat	⚵ Decl	⚵ Lat	⚶ Decl	⚶ Lat	Eris Decl	Eris Lat
1	1N55	23N50	7S59	5N55	4S19	7S17	2S59	12S33
6	1 56	23 36	8 08	6 11	3 33	7 02	2 58	12 32
11	2 00	23 22	8 15	6 28	2 45	6 49	2 58	12 31
16	2 06	23 10	8 19	6 45	1 56	6 36	2 57	12 31
21	2 15	22 59	8 21	7 03	1 06	6 23	2 56	12 30
26	2 25	22 49	8 20	7 22	0 16	6 12	2 55	12 29
31	2N38	22N40	8S16	7N42	0N35	6S00	2S54	12S28

Moon Phenomena

Max/0 Decl

dy	hr mn	
1	9:22	0 S
8	18:01	18S25
15	5:41	0 N
21	16:49	18N22
28	18:58	0 S

Max/0 Lat

dy	hr mn	
8	4:36	5N03
14	15:48	0 S
21	1:28	5S06
27	24:00	0 N

Perigee/Apogee

dy	hr m		kilometers
2	11:54	a	404274
15	2:18	p	369619
30	9:08	a	404551

PH	dy	hr mn	
☾	2	5:32	11♎14
●	10	1:32	19♑13
☽	16	23:27	26♈16
○	24	1:47	3♌29

Void of Course Moon

Last Aspect				☽ Ingress		
1	5:35	☿	△	♎	1	6:42
2	16:25	♅	☍	♏	3	19:37
5	17:49	♃	⚹	♐	6	6:57
8	2:45	♃	□	♑	8	15:08
10	17:41	☿	☌	♒	10	20:24
12	1:10	♅	⚹	♓	12	23:55
14	16:32	☉	⚹	♈	15	2:49
16	23:27	☉	□	♉	17	5:49
19	6:51	☉	△	♊	19	9:14
21	8:02	♀	☍	♋	21	13:29
23	6:22	♃	⚹	♌	23	19:22
25	2:52	♅	△	♍	26	3:47
28	0:12	♃	☌	♎	28	15:00
30	1:35	♅	☍	♏	31	3:51

DAILY ASPECTARIAN

☿∥♇ 2:27
☽⋕⚷ 3:06
☽⚺♂ 3:57
☽△☿ 5:35
☽⚹♀ 12:07
☽∥⚷ 15:36
☽⚼⚳ 16:33
☽⚻♆ 22:04

☿ ♒ 2:21
☉□☽ 5:32
☽⚹♄ 5:37
☉⚺♄ 6:36
☽⋕♃ 10:16
☿∥♄ 11:15
☽□♇ 13:24
☽☍♅ 16:25
☽⚻⚷ 18:19
☽∠♀ 22:07

☽△⚳ 0:01
☽⋕♅ 0:08
☽⚼♆ 4:38
☽⚺♃ 5:51
☽∠♄ 12:22
♂ ♏ 14:34
☽☌♂ 19:52
☽□☿ 21:13

☽⚼⚷ 0:47
☽∥♆ 0:49
☽∥♂ 6:23
☽⚺♀ 7:54
☽△♆ 10:57
☽∠♃ 12:08
☽⚺♄ 18:47
☉⚹☽ 23:44

5 Tu ☽⚹♇ 2:00
☿∥♀ 2:17
☽⚻♅ 4:48
☽△⚷ 6:47
☿□♂ 12:01
☿ R 13:07
☽□⚳ 13:59
♀□♆ 14:34
☽⚹♃ 17:49

6 W ☉☌♇ 3:29
☽∠♇ 7:24
☉∠☽ 7:44
☽⚹☿ 8:50
☽⚺♂ 9:56
☽⚼♅ 10:03
☽□♆ 21:41

7 Th ☽☌♀ 0:55
☽☌♄ 5:28
☽⚺♇ 11:58
☉□♅ 12:23
☽∠☿ 12:42
☽△♅ 14:30
☉⚺☽ 14:40
☽∠♂ 15:36
☽□⚷ 16:29

8 F ☽⚹⚳ 0:47
☽□♃ 2:45
♃ R 4:41
♂⚼⚷ 13:41
☉⚹⚷ 14:16
☽⚺☿ 15:20
☿R♑ 19:37
☽⚹♂ 20:21

9 Sa ♀☌♄ 4:12
☽∠⚳ 4:52
☽⚹♆ 5:08
☽⚺♄ 12:49
☽⚺♀ 13:36
♀∥♄ 15:17
☽☌♇ 18:41
☽□♅ 20:59
☽⚹⚷ 22:58

10 Su ☉☌☽ 1:32
☽∠♆ 7:48
☽⚺⚳ 8:13
☽△♃ 8:34
☿∠♀ 12:24
☽∠♄ 15:27
☽☌☿ 17:41
☽∠♀ 18:36
⚳⚻♃ 21:22

11 M ☽∠⚷ 1:17
☽□♂ 3:33
☽⚺♆ 9:56
☽⚼♃ 10:38
♀∥♇ 15:58
☽⚹♄ 17:36
☿∠♄ 19:57
☽⚹♀ 23:00
☽⚺♇ 23:01
♀⚺♇ 23:20

12 ☽⚹♅ 1:10
Tu ☽⚺⚷ 3:11
☉⚺☽ 9:36
☽∥♂ 9:52
☽⚻♃ 12:20
☽☌⚳ 13:26
♀∥⚳ 14:31
☽⚺☿ 17:29

13 W ♀△♅ 0:12
☽∠♇ 0:42
☽∥♆ 1:12
☽∠♅ 2:48
☽△♂ 8:57
☉∠☽ 13:07
☽☌♆ 13:18
☉∠♆ 15:38
☽∠☿ 16:53
⚳∥♇ 19:36
☽⋕♅ 21:02
☽□♄ 21:07
☉△♃ 22:50

14 Th ♀□⚷ 0:27
☽⚹♇ 2:14
☿⚺⚳ 3:07
☽⚺♅ 4:18
☉∥♀ 5:21
☽☌⚷ 6:23
☽□♀ 6:55
☽⋕♃ 8:36
☽⚼♂ 11:24
☉☌☿ 14:06
☽☍♃ 15:15
☽⚹☿ 16:10
☉⚹☽ 16:32
☽⚺⚳ 17:46

15 F ☽∥⚷ 1:11
☿△♃ 2:16
☿∠♆ 6:32
☽⋕⚷ 10:09
☽⚻♂ 13:51
☽⚺♆ 16:18
☉⚺⚳ 18:57
☽∠⚳ 19:55
⚳∥♄ 22:39

16 Sa ☽△♄ 0:23
☽∥♃ 2:55
☽□♇ 5:16
☽☌♅ 7:16
☽⚺⚷ 9:26
☉∥♇ 13:38
☽∥♅ 14:31
☽△♀ 14:41
☽□☿ 14:48
☿⚺♀ 15:26
☽∠♆ 17:51
☽⚻♃ 18:06
☽⚹⚳ 22:07
☉□☽ 23:27

17 Su ☽⚼♄ 2:04
☽⋕♆ 10:04
☽∠⚷ 11:04
☽⚼♀ 18:41
☽☍♂ 18:55
☽⚹♆ 19:29
☽⚼♃ 19:38
☉∥♄ 22:05
♀∠♂ 22:56

18 M ☽⚻♄ 3:52
♀□♃ 5:11
☽△♇ 8:34
☽⋕♂ 9:20
☽⚺♅ 10:32
♂△♆ 11:02
☽⚹⚷ 12:48
♂∠♃ 13:00
☽△☿ 14:04
☉∠♄ 15:06
☽△♃ 21:16
☽⚻♀ 22:52

19 Tu ☽□⚳ 2:53
☿⚹⚷ 6:31
☉△☽ 6:51
☽⚼♇ 10:25
☽∠♅ 12:22
☽⚼☿ 14:09
☽□♆ 23:11

20 W ☽⚻♂ 0:31
☽☍♄ 7:55
☉⚼☽ 10:52
☽⚻♇ 12:28
☽⚹♅ 14:25
☽⚻☿ 14:38
☉ ♒ 15:28
☽□⚷ 16:49
☿□♅ 18:27

21 Th ☽□♃ 1:08
☽⚼♂ 3:42
☽☍♀ 8:02
☽△⚳ 8:29
♀⚹⚳ 15:07
☉⚻☽ 15:16

22 F ☉∥⚳ 0:24
☽△♆ 3:54
☽△♂ 7:16
☿☌♇ 10:00
☽⚼⚳ 11:51
☽⚻♄ 13:08
☽☍☿ 17:18
☽☍♇ 17:35
⚴ ♒ 19:04
☽□♅ 19:33
☽△⚷ 22:08

23 Sa ☽⚹♃ 6:22
☽⚼♆ 6:55
☽⚻⚳ 15:46
☽⚼♄ 16:28
☉∥☿ 18:24
☽⚻♀ 19:15
♀ ♑ 20:33
☉∠⚷ 22:57

24 Su ☽⚼⚷ 1:34
☉☍☽ 1:47
☿∥⚳ 6:49
☽∠♃ 9:47
☽⚻♆ 10:31
☽□♂ 16:12
☽⋕♂ 19:01
☽△♄ 20:26
☽⚻☿ 23:10

25 M ☽⚻♇ 0:51
☽⚼♀ 2:04
☽△♅ 2:52
☽⚻⚷ 5:41
☽⚺♃ 13:53
☿ D 21:52

26 Tu ☽☍⚳ 1:47
☽⚼☿ 3:37
☽⚼♇ 5:32
☽⋕♆ 6:44
☽⚼♅ 7:36
☽△♀ 9:52
☉⚻☽ 15:38
☽☍♆ 19:53

27 W ☽∥♅ 3:42
☽⚹♂ 4:13
☽□♄ 6:34
☽△☿ 9:11
☽△♇ 10:57
☽⚻♅ 13:03
☽☍⚷ 16:06
☽∥♃ 16:16
☉⚼☽ 23:55

28 Th ☽☌♃ 0:12
☉⚼♃ 2:58
☽∠♂ 11:23
☽⋕⚷ 14:51
☽⚻⚳ 14:53
⚳ ♓ 18:43
☉⚺♆ 20:46
☽∥⚷ 23:03

29 ☽□♀ 4:13
F ☽⚻♆ 7:55
☉△☽ 8:56
☽⚺♂ 19:03
☽⚹♄ 19:14
☽⚼⚳ 22:16
☽⋕♃ 22:27
☽□☿ 23:13
☽□♇ 23:28
♂⚺♄ 23:57

30 Sa ☽☍♅ 1:35
☽⚻⚷ 4:50
☿☌♇ 6:00
☽⋕♅ 11:14
☽⚺♃ 12:30
☽⚼♆ 14:29
♀⚹♆ 16:45

31 Su ☽∠♄ 1:56
☽△⚳ 5:47
☽∥♆ 8:26
☽⚼⚷ 11:26
⚳∠♇ 14:18
☽∠♃ 18:45
☽△♆ 20:59

February 2016

LONGITUDE

Day	Sid.Time	☉	☽	☽ 12 hour	Mean ☊	True ☊	☿	♀	♂	⚳	♃	♄	⚷	♅	♆	♇
	h m s	° ' "	° ' "	° ' "	° '	° '	° '	° '	° '	° '	° '	° '	° '	° '	° '	° '
1 M	8 42 35	11♒32 29	9♏57 30	15♏56 06	23♍58.0	22♍35.3	17♑02.3	10♑01.5	14♏57.8	1♓14.5	22♍20.4	14♐07.6	18♓45.9	17♈08.1	8♓27.9	16♑05.9
2 Tu	8 46 31	12 33 24	21 57 29	28 02 14	23 54.8	22R 34.8	17 43.2	11 15.5	15 27.6	1 37.7	22R 15.9	14 12.4	18 49.0	17 09.9	8 30.0	16 07.8
3 W	8 50 28	13 34 18	4♐10 59	10♐24 15	23 51.6	22 32.6	18 28.4	12 29.5	15 57.2	2 01.0	22 11.3	14 17.2	18 52.1	17 11.8	8 32.1	16 09.7
4 Th	8 54 25	14 35 11	16 42 29	23 06 07	23 48.4	22 28.7	19 17.5	13 43.5	16 26.6	2 24.2	22 06.4	14 21.8	18 55.3	17 13.7	8 34.2	16 11.6
5 F	8 58 21	15 36 03	29 35 27	6♑10 38	23 45.3	22 23.4	20 10.3	14 57.5	16 55.9	2 47.5	22 01.4	14 26.4	18 58.4	17 15.7	8 36.4	16 13.5
6 Sa	9 02 18	16 36 54	12♑51 47	19 38 50	23 42.1	22 17.4	21 06.3	16 11.5	17 25.0	3 10.9	21 56.3	14 31.0	19 01.7	17 17.7	8 38.5	16 15.3
7 Su	9 06 14	17 37 44	26 31 35	3♒29 42	23 38.9	22 11.3	22 05.3	17 25.6	17 53.9	3 34.2	21 51.0	14 35.4	19 04.9	17 19.8	8 40.6	16 17.2
8 M	9 10 11	18 38 34	10♒32 46	17 40 11	23 35.7	22 06.1	23 07.0	18 39.7	18 22.7	3 57.6	21 45.6	14 39.8	19 08.2	17 21.9	8 42.8	16 19.0
9 Tu	9 14 07	19 39 21	24 51 17	2♓05 22	23 32.6	22 02.2	24 11.3	19 53.7	18 51.3	4 21.0	21 40.0	14 44.1	19 11.4	17 24.1	8 45.0	16 20.8
10 W	9 18 04	20 40 08	9♓21 37	16 39 15	23 29.4	21D 59.9	25 17.8	21 07.8	19 19.7	4 44.4	21 34.2	14 48.3	19 14.7	17 26.2	8 47.2	16 22.6
11 Th	9 22 00	21 40 53	23 57 30	1♈15 36	23 26.2	21 59.4	26 26.5	22 21.9	19 47.9	5 07.9	21 28.3	14 52.4	19 18.1	17 28.5	8 49.4	16 24.4
12 F	9 25 57	22 41 37	8♈32 52	15 48 41	23 23.0	22 00.1	27 37.2	23 36.0	20 15.9	5 31.3	21 22.3	14 56.4	19 21.4	17 30.7	8 51.6	16 26.1
13 Sa	9 29 54	23 42 19	23 02 32	0♉13 59	23 19.8	22 01.6	28 49.7	24 50.2	20 43.7	5 54.8	21 16.2	15 00.4	19 24.8	17 33.0	8 53.8	16 27.9
14 Su	9 33 50	24 42 59	7♉22 40	14 28 20	23 16.7	22 03.0	0♒04.0	26 04.3	21 11.3	6 18.3	21 09.9	15 04.3	19 28.2	17 35.4	8 56.0	16 29.6
15 M	9 37 47	25 43 38	21 30 46	28 29 50	23 13.5	22R 03.9	1 19.8	27 18.4	21 38.8	6 41.8	21 03.5	15 08.1	19 31.6	17 37.8	8 58.2	16 31.3
16 Tu	9 41 43	26 44 15	5♊25 28	12♊17 37	23 10.3	22 03.7	2 37.2	28 32.6	22 06.0	7 05.4	20 57.0	15 11.8	19 35.1	17 40.2	9 00.4	16 33.0
17 W	9 45 40	27 44 50	19 06 16	25 51 26	23 07.1	22 02.2	3 56.1	29 46.7	22 33.0	7 28.9	20 50.4	15 15.4	19 38.5	17 42.6	9 02.7	16 34.7
18 Th	9 49 36	28 45 24	2♋33 07	9♋11 22	23 03.9	21 59.8	5 16.3	1♒00.9	22 59.8	7 52.5	20 43.7	15 19.0	19 42.0	17 45.1	9 04.9	16 36.3
19 F	9 53 33	29 45 56	15 46 12	22 17 38	23 00.8	21 56.5	6 37.8	2 15.0	23 26.3	8 16.0	20 36.9	15 22.4	19 45.5	17 47.6	9 07.2	16 37.9
20 Sa	9 57 29	0♓46 26	28 45 44	5♌10 32	22 57.6	21 53.1	8 00.6	3 29.2	23 52.7	8 39.6	20 29.9	15 25.8	19 49.0	17 50.2	9 09.4	16 39.6
21 Su	10 01 26	1 46 54	11♌32 04	17 50 24	22 54.4	21 49.9	9 24.6	4 43.4	24 18.8	9 03.2	20 22.9	15 29.1	19 52.5	17 52.8	9 11.7	16 41.2
22 M	10 05 23	2 47 21	24 05 36	0♍17 47	22 51.2	21 47.3	10 49.8	5 57.5	24 44.7	9 26.8	20 15.8	15 32.3	19 56.0	17 55.4	9 14.0	16 42.7
23 Tu	10 09 19	3 47 46	6♍27 03	12 33 34	22 48.1	21 45.6	12 16.1	7 11.7	25 10.4	9 50.4	20 08.6	15 35.4	19 59.6	17 58.1	9 16.2	16 44.3
24 W	10 13 16	4 48 09	18 37 30	24 39 05	22 44.9	21D 44.9	13 43.6	8 25.9	25 35.8	10 14.0	20 01.3	15 38.4	20 03.1	18 00.7	9 18.5	16 45.8
25 Th	10 17 12	5 48 30	0♎38 33	6♎36 13	22 41.7	21 45.1	15 12.1	9 40.1	26 01.0	10 37.7	19 54.0	15 41.3	20 06.7	18 03.5	9 20.8	16 47.3
26 F	10 21 09	6 48 51	12 32 25	18 27 31	22 38.5	21 46.0	16 41.8	10 54.3	26 25.9	11 01.3	19 46.6	15 44.2	20 10.3	18 06.2	9 23.1	16 48.8
27 Sa	10 25 05	7 49 09	24 21 56	0♏16 07	22 35.3	21 47.2	18 12.5	12 08.5	26 50.5	11 24.9	19 39.1	15 46.9	20 13.9	18 09.0	9 25.3	16 50.2
28 Su	10 29 02	8 49 26	6♏10 33	12 05 45	22 32.2	21 48.6	19 44.2	13 22.7	27 14.9	11 48.6	19 31.5	15 49.5	20 17.5	18 11.8	9 27.6	16 51.7
29 M	10 32 58	9♓49 42	18 02 16	24 00 39	22♍29.0	21♍49.7	21♒17.1	14♒36.9	27♏39.1	12♓12.2	19♍23.9	15♐52.1	20♓21.1	18♈14.6	9♓29.9	16♑53.1

1st of Month

Julian Day 2457419.5
Obliquity 23°26'05"
SVP 5♓02'0
GC 27♐03.
Eris 22♈20.

Day	⚴
1	3♒20.7
6	5 08.7
11	6 55.6
16	8 41.5
21	10 26.0
26	12 09.2

Day	⚵
1	12♏43.2
6	13 26.1
11	14 02.1
16	14 30.9
21	14 52.2
26	15 05.4

Day	⚶
1	15♈56.7
6	17 46.5
11	19 39.1
16	21 34.2
21	23 31.5
26	25 30.7

DECLINATION and LATITUDE

Day	☉ Decl	☽ Decl	☽ Lat	☽ 12h Decl	☿ Decl	☿ Lat	♀ Decl	♀ Lat	♂ Decl	♂ Lat	⚳ Decl	⚳ Lat	♃ Decl	♃ Lat	♄ Decl	♄ Lat
1 M	17S19	11S10	3N49	12S37	20S35	1N46	22S22	0N41	14S55	1N28	18S25	7S55	4N18	1N23	20S51	1N39
2 Tu	17 02	13 56	4 28	15 07	20 41	1 35	22 19	0 38	15 04	1 28	18 17	7 55	4 20	1 23	20 51	1 40
3 W	16 45	16 08	4 56	16 59	20 46	1 25	22 16	0 35	15 13	1 28	18 08	7 55	4 22	1 23	20 52	1 40
4 Th	16 27	17 38	5 10	18 04	20 50	1 14	22 12	0 32	15 21	1 28	17 59	7 55	4 25	1 23	20 52	1 40
5 F	16 09	18 17	5 09	18 15	20 53	1 03	22 07	0 29	15 30	1 27	17 50	7 54	4 27	1 24	20 53	1 40
6 Sa	15 51	17 58	4 52	17 26	20 55	0 53	22 01	0 26	15 38	1 27	17 42	7 54	4 29	1 24	20 53	1 40
7 Su	15 33	16 38	4 18	15 34	20 56	0 42	21 55	0 23	15 46	1 27	17 33	7 54	4 31	1 24	20 53	1 40
8 M	15 14	14 16	3 27	12 44	20 56	0 32	21 48	0 20	15 54	1 27	17 24	7 54	4 34	1 24	20 54	1 40
9 Tu	14 55	10 59	2 23	9 04	20 54	0 22	21 40	0 17	16 02	1 26	17 15	7 54	4 36	1 25	20 54	1 40
10 W	14 36	6 60	1 09	4 49	20 52	0 13	21 32	0 14	16 10	1 26	17 06	7 54	4 38	1 25	20 55	1 40
11 Th	14 17	2 34	0S11	0 16	20 48	0 03	21 23	0 11	16 18	1 26	16 57	7 53	4 41	1 25	20 55	1 40
12 F	13 57	2N01	1 30	4N16	20 44	0S06	21 14	0 08	16 26	1 26	16 48	7 53	4 44	1 25	20 55	1 40
13 Sa	13 37	6 26	2 42	8 31	20 38	0 15	21 04	0 06	16 33	1 25	16 40	7 53	4 46	1 25	20 56	1 41
14 Su	13 17	10 26	3 44	12 12	20 31	0 23	20 53	0 03	16 41	1 25	16 31	7 53	4 49	1 26	20 56	1 41
15 M	12 57	13 46	4 31	15 08	20 22	0 32	20 42	0S00	16 48	1 25	16 22	7 53	4 51	1 26	20 56	1 41
16 Tu	12 36	16 15	5 02	17 08	20 13	0 40	20 30	0 03	16 56	1 25	16 13	7 53	4 54	1 26	20 57	1 41
17 W	12 15	17 46	5 14	18 08	20 02	0 47	20 17	0 06	17 03	1 24	16 04	7 53	4 57	1 26	20 57	1 41
18 Th	11 54	18 15	5 09	18 07	19 50	0 55	20 04	0 09	17 10	1 24	15 55	7 53	4 60	1 26	20 57	1 41
19 F	11 33	17 44	4 48	17 07	19 37	1 02	19 51	0 12	17 17	1 24	15 46	7 53	5 03	1 26	20 57	1 41
20 Sa	11 12	16 17	4 12	15 15	19 22	1 09	19 36	0 14	17 24	1 23	15 37	7 53	5 05	1 27	20 58	1 41
21 Su	10 50	14 03	3 24	12 41	19 06	1 15	19 21	0 17	17 30	1 23	15 28	7 53	5 08	1 27	20 58	1 41
22 M	10 29	11 11	2 27	9 33	18 49	1 21	19 06	0 20	17 37	1 23	15 19	7 53	5 11	1 27	20 58	1 41
23 Tu	10 07	7 51	1 24	6 04	18 31	1 27	18 50	0 23	17 43	1 22	15 10	7 53	5 14	1 27	20 58	1 42
24 W	9 45	4 14	0 17	2 22	18 11	1 33	18 33	0 25	17 50	1 22	15 01	7 53	5 17	1 27	20 59	1 42
25 Th	9 23	0 30	0N49	1S23	17 50	1 38	18 16	0 28	17 56	1 21	14 52	7 53	5 20	1 27	20 59	1 42
26 F	9 01	3S13	1 53	5 02	17 28	1 43	17 59	0 30	18 02	1 21	14 43	7 53	5 23	1 27	20 59	1 42
27 Sa	8 38	6 47	2 51	8 29	17 04	1 47	17 41	0 33	18 09	1 20	14 34	7 53	5 26	1 28	20 59	1 42
28 Su	8 16	10 05	3 42	11 35	16 39	1 51	17 22	0 35	18 15	1 20	14 25	7 53	5 29	1 28	20 59	1 42
29 M	7S53	12S58	4N24	14S14	16S13	1S55	17S03	0S38	18S20	1N20	14S16	7S53	5N33	1N28	20S59	1N42

Day	⚷ Decl	⚷ Lat	♅ Decl	♅ Lat	♆ Decl	♆ Lat	♇ Decl	♇ Lat
1	0S35	4N11	6N10	0S37	9S08	0S47	20S56	1N
6	0 30	4 10	6 13	0 37	9 04	0 47	20 55	1
11	0 24	4 10	6 18	0 37	8 60	0 47	20 54	1
16	0 18	4 09	6 22	0 36	8 55	0 47	20 54	1
21	0 12	4 08	6 27	0 36	8 51	0 47	20 53	1
26	0S06	4N08	6N32	0S36	8S47	0S47	20S52	1N

Day	⚴ Decl	⚴ Lat	⚵ Decl	⚵ Lat	⚶ Decl	⚶ Lat	Eris Decl	Eris Lat
1	2N41	22N39	8S15	7N46	0N45	5S58	2S53	12S
6	2 55	22 31	8 08	8 06	1 37	5 48	2 52	12
11	3 12	22 25	7 57	8 28	2 28	5 38	2 51	12
16	3 31	22 19	7 44	8 50	3 20	5 28	2 50	12
21	3 51	22 15	7 28	9 13	4 11	5 19	2 48	12
26	4N13	22N11	7S09	9N37	5N03	5S10	2S47	12S

Moon Phenomena

Max/0 Decl

dy	hr mn	
5	4:28	18S18
11	13:26	0 N
17	23:32	18N15
25	3:10	0 S

Max/0 Lat

dy	hr mn	
4	10:45	5N11
10	20:46	0 S
17	5:07	5S15
24	6:13	0 N

Perigee/Apogee

dy	hr m		kilometers
11	2:34	p	364361
27	3:24	a	405383

PH	dy	hr mn	
☾	1	3:29	11♏41
●	8	14:40	19♒16
☽	15	7:48	26♉03
○	22	18:21	3♍34

Void of Course Moon

Last Aspect			☽ Ingress	
2 0:36	♃	⚹	♐	2 15:
4 10:05	♃	□	♑	5 0:
6 15:55	♃	△	♒	7 6:
8 14:40	☉	☌	♓	9 8:
11 4:26	☿	⚹	♈	11 9:
13 10:33	☿	□	♉	13 11:
15 10:55	♀	△	♊	15 14:
17 16:38	☉	△	♋	17 19:
19 14:37	♂	△	♌	20 2:
22 1:18	♂	□	♍	22 11:
24 14:24	♂	⚹	♎	24 22:
26 11:19	♅	☍	♏	27 11:
29 19:56	♂	☌	♐	29 23:

DAILY ASPECTARIAN

1 M
☽⚹♀ 0:09
☉□☽ 3:29
☿□♅ 3:43
☽⚺♄ 8:26
☽☌♂ 10:29
☽⚹♇ 12:22
☽⚻♅ 14:26
☽⚹☿ 15:02
☽△⚷ 17:44

2 Tu
☽⚹♃ 0:36
☽∠♀ 9:27
☽∥♂ 12:18
☽∠♇ 18:06
☽□⚳ 19:39
☽⚼♅ 20:08
☽∠☿ 22:32

3 W
☉∥☽ 7:08
☽□♆ 8:26
♂⚹♇ 10:54
⚳∠♅ 12:11
☿⚹⚷ 12:37
☽⚺♀ 17:44
☉⚹♄ 18:19
☽☌♄ 19:32
☉⚹☽ 19:38
☽⚺♇ 23:01
☽⚺♂ 23:29

4 Th
☽△♅ 0:59
☽□⚷ 4:11
☽⚺☿ 5:13
☽∥⚳ 7:38
☽□♃ 10:05
♀⚺♄ 13:16
☿∥♄ 21:13

5 F
☉∠☽ 2:00
☽∠♂ 4:27
☽⚹⚳ 6:02
☉⚺♇ 15:13
☽⚹♆ 16:25
♂⚻♅ 17:32

6 Sa
♀☌♇ 1:16
☽⚺♄ 2:57
☽☌♇ 6:02
☽☌♀ 6:30
☉⚺☽ 7:12
☽□♅ 7:53
☽∥⚳ 7:53
☿∥♇ 7:57
☽⚹♂ 8:22
☽∠⚳ 9:42
☽⚹⚷ 10:57
☉∥♂ 11:55
☽☌☿ 15:40
☽△♃ 15:55
☉⚹♅ 16:40
☿△♃ 18:46
☽∠♆ 19:02
♀□♅ 22:04

7 Su
☽∠♄ 5:19
☽∥♂ 9:19
☉□♂ 12:09
☽⚺⚳ 12:28
☽∠⚷ 13:03
☉∥☽ 13:59
♀⚹♂ 15:02
☽⚼♃ 17:37
☽⚺♆ 20:53
☉⚺♀ 22:01

8 M
☽⚹♄ 6:59
♀∠⚳ 8:30
♀⚹⚷ 9:39
☽⚺♇ 9:45
☽⚹♅ 11:31
☉⚺⚷ 12:21
☽□♂ 13:38
☿∠♆ 13:57
☽⚺⚷ 14:31
☉☌☽ 14:40
☽⚺♀ 14:57
☿∥♇ 16:21
☽⚻♃ 18:43
☽⚺☿ 22:48

9 Tu
☿∥♄ 1:33
☽∠♇ 10:48
☽∥♆ 12:18
☽∠♅ 12:33
☽☌⚳ 16:10
☽∠♀ 18:11
♂△⚷ 19:16
☽☌♆ 23:03

10 W
☽∠☿ 1:40
☽⋕♅ 4:00
♄∥♇ 4:07
♀△♃ 7:55
☽□♄ 9:00
☽⚹♇ 11:34
☽⋕♃ 12:50
☽⚺♅ 13:19
☽☌⚷ 16:19
☽△♂ 16:56
☉⚻♃ 19:29
☽☍♃ 19:57
☉⚺☽ 19:59
☽⚹♀ 21:09

11 Th
☽⚹☿ 4:26
☽∥⚷ 11:21
☽⋕⚷ 15:30
☽⚼♂ 18:25
☽⚺⚳ 18:53
☉∠☽ 22:29

12 F
☽⚺♆ 0:31
♀∠♆ 5:11
☽△♄ 10:36
☽□♇ 13:04
☽∥♃ 14:39
☽☌♅ 14:51
☽⚺⚷ 17:57
☽⚻♂ 20:02
☽∠⚳ 20:22
☽⚻♃ 21:04
☽∥♅ 23:21

13 Sa
☉⚹☽ 1:11
☽∠♆ 1:25
☽□♀ 3:16
♂∥⚳ 8:56
☽□☿ 10:33
☽⚼♄ 11:40
☽⋕♆ 14:43
♀∥♄ 18:20
☽∠⚷ 19:05
☽⚼♃ 21:58
☽⚹⚳ 22:09
♀∥♇ 22:15
☿ ♒ 22:44
♂⚹♃ 23:00

14 Su
☿∠♄ 0:06
☽⚹♆ 2:38
☽⚻♄ 13:05
☽△♇ 15:28
☽⚺♅ 17:21
☉⋕☽ 18:07
☽⚹⚷ 20:36
☽△♃ 23:14

15 M
☽☍♂ 0:14
☉□☽ 7:48
☽△♀ 10:55
☽⚼♇ 17:16
☽△☿ 18:38
☽∠♅ 19:12
☽⋕⚳ 23:32

16 Tu
☽□⚳ 2:59
☽□♆ 6:16
☽⋕♂ 9:32
☽⚼♀ 15:36
☽☍♄ 17:11
☽⚻♇ 19:32
☽⚹♅ 21:32
☽⚼☿ 23:40

17 W
☽□⚷ 0:57
☽□♃ 3:03
♀ ♒ 4:18
☽⚻♂ 6:19
♀∠♄ 9:46
☿∠⚷ 13:20
☉△☽ 16:38
☽⚻♀ 20:57

18 Th
☽⚻☿ 5:28
☿⚼♃ 7:29
☽△⚳ 9:54
☽⚼♂ 10:11
☽△♆ 11:50
☉⚼☽ 22:01
☽⚻♄ 23:16

19 F
☽☍♇ 1:35
☽□♅ 3:43
☉ ♓ 5:35
☽△⚷ 7:21
☽⋕♂ 8:31
☽⚹♃ 8:49
☽⚼⚳ 14:14
☽△♂ 14:37
☽⚼♆ 15:25

20 Sa
☽⚼♄ 3:07
☉⚻☽ 4:04
☽⋕⚳ 8:41
☽☍♀ 9:46
☽⚼⚷ 11:23
☽∠♃ 12:30
☿⚺⚳ 15:33
☽⚻⚳ 19:09
☽☍☿ 19:29
☽⚻♆ 19:34
☿⚺♆ 20:14
☉∠♇ 21:39

21 Su
♀∠⚷ 3:07
☽△♄ 7:32
⚳☌♆ 9:34
☽⚻♇ 9:49
♀⚼♃ 11:41
☽△♅ 12:07
☽⚻⚷ 15:58
☽⚺♃ 16:43

22 M
☽□♂ 1:18
☉∠♅ 3:21
☉⋕☽ 5:56
☽⚼♇ 14:47
☽⚼♅ 17:10
☽⋕♆ 17:11
☉☍☽ 18:21

23 Tu
☽⚻♀ 1:37
☽☍♆ 5:33
☽☍⚳ 6:52
☽∥♅ 9:09
☽⚻☿ 12:59
☽∥♃ 17:13
☽□♄ 18:04
♃☍⚷ 20:02
☽△♇ 20:18
☽⚻♅ 22:47

24 W
☽☌♃ 2:45
☽☍⚷ 2:51
☽⚼♀ 10:40
☽⚹♂ 14:24
♀⚺♆ 17:33
☿∥♂ 18:34
☽⚼☿ 22:59

25 Th
☽⋕⚷ 2:25
☽∥⚷ 3:55
☿⚹♄ 8:06
☉⚻☽ 11:21
☽⚻♆ 17:36
☽△♀ 20:18
♀∥♂ 20:20
☽⚻⚳ 20:49
☽∠♂ 21:40

26 F
☿⚺♇ 1:54
♀⚺⚳ 3:19
☽⚹♄ 6:30
☽□♇ 8:41
☽△☿ 9:39
☽☍♅ 11:19
☽⚺♃ 14:31
☽⋕♃ 14:37
☉∥♆ 15:08
☽⚻⚷ 15:33
☉⚼☽ 20:34
☽⋕♅ 22:24
☿⚹♅ 23:03

27 Sa
☽⚼♆ 0:07
☽⚼⚳ 4:19
☽⚺♂ 5:13
☉∥☽ 11:49
☽∠♄ 13:06
☽∥♆ 14:05
☽∠♃ 20:41
☿⚻♃ 20:57
☽⚼⚷ 22:12

28 Su
☉△☽ 5:52
☽△♆ 6:41
☿⚺⚷ 8:59
☽△⚳ 11:49
☉☌♆ 15:48
☽□♀ 16:18
☽⚺♄ 19:37
☽⚹♇ 21:40

29 M
☽⚻♅ 0:25
☽⚹♃ 2:43
☽△⚷ 4:41
☽□☿ 7:31
☽∥⚳ 11:33
☽☌♂ 19:56

LONGITUDE

March 2016

Day	Sid.Time	☉	☽	☽ 12 hour	Mean☊	True☊	☿	♀	♂	⚳	♃	♄	⚷	♅	♆	♇
	h m s	° ' "	° ' "	° ' "	° '	° '	° '	° '	° '	° '	° '	° '	° '	° '	° '	° '
1 Tu	10 36 55	10♓49 56	0♐01 29	6♐05 21	22♍25.8	21♍50.5	22♒51.0	15♒51.2	28♏02.9	12♓35.9	19♍16.3	15♐54.6	20♓24.7	18♈17.5	9♓32.2	16♑54.5
2 W	10 40 52	11 50 08	12 12 51	18 24 32	22 22.6	21R 50.7	24 25.9	17 05.4	28 26.5	12 59.5	19R 08.6	15 56.9	20 28.4	18 20.4	9 34.4	16 55.9
3 Th	10 44 48	12 50 20	24 40 58	1♑02 39	22 19.5	21 50.5	26 01.9	18 19.6	28 49.7	13 23.2	19 00.9	15 59.2	20 32.0	18 23.3	9 36.7	16 57.2
4 F	10 48 45	13 50 29	7♑30 03	14 03 31	22 16.3	21 49.9	27 39.0	19 33.9	29 12.7	13 46.8	18 53.1	16 01.4	20 35.7	18 26.2	9 39.0	16 58.5
5 Sa	10 52 41	14 50 37	20 43 23	27 29 47	22 13.1	21 49.1	29 17.1	20 48.1	29 35.4	14 10.5	18 45.3	16 03.5	20 39.3	18 29.2	9 41.3	16 59.8
6 Su	10 56 38	15 50 44	4♒22 49	11♒22 21	22 09.9	21 48.3	0♓56.3	22 02.3	29 57.7	14 34.2	18 37.5	16 05.5	20 43.0	18 32.2	9 43.6	17 01.1
7 M	11 00 34	16 50 48	18 28 11	25 39 53	22 06.7	21 47.7	2 36.6	23 16.6	0♐19.7	14 57.8	18 29.7	16 07.3	20 46.6	18 35.2	9 45.8	17 02.3
8 Tu	11 04 31	17 50 51	2♓56 54	10♓18 31	22 03.6	21 47.3	4 18.0	24 30.8	0 41.4	15 21.5	18 21.9	16 09.1	20 50.3	18 38.3	9 48.1	17 03.6
9 W	11 08 27	18 50 53	17 43 53	25 12 03	22 00.4	21D 47.1	6 00.5	25 45.1	1 02.7	15 45.1	18 14.0	16 10.8	20 54.0	18 41.4	9 50.3	17 04.7
10 Th	11 12 24	19 50 52	2♈41 58	10♈12 34	21 57.2	21 47.1	7 44.1	26 59.3	1 23.7	16 08.8	18 06.2	16 12.4	20 57.6	18 44.4	9 52.6	17 05.9
11 F	11 16 21	20 50 49	17 42 46	25 11 32	21 54.0	21R 47.2	9 28.9	28 13.6	1 44.3	16 32.4	17 58.4	16 13.9	21 01.3	18 47.6	9 54.8	17 07.0
12 Sa	11 20 17	21 50 44	2♉37 54	10♉01 01	21 50.9	21 47.3	11 14.8	29 27.8	2 04.6	16 56.0	17 50.6	16 15.3	21 04.9	18 50.7	9 57.1	17 08.2
13 Su	11 24 14	22 50 37	17 20 08	24 34 40	21 47.7	21 47.2	13 01.9	0♓42.0	2 24.5	17 19.6	17 42.8	16 16.6	21 08.6	18 53.8	9 59.3	17 09.2
14 M	11 28 10	23 50 28	1♊44 09	8♊48 19	21 44.5	21 47.1	14 50.1	1 56.2	2 44.0	17 43.3	17 35.0	16 17.8	21 12.3	18 57.0	10 01.6	17 10.3
15 Tu	11 32 07	24 50 17	15 46 57	22 40 01	21 41.3	21D 46.9	16 39.5	3 10.5	3 03.1	18 06.9	17 27.3	16 18.9	21 15.9	19 00.2	10 03.8	17 11.3
16 W	11 36 03	25 50 03	29 27 35	6♋09 46	21 38.1	21 46.9	18 30.1	4 24.7	3 21.9	18 30.4	17 19.6	16 19.9	21 19.6	19 03.4	10 06.0	17 12.3
17 Th	11 40 00	26 49 48	12♋46 48	19 18 55	21 35.0	21 47.1	20 21.9	5 38.9	3 40.2	18 54.0	17 11.9	16 20.8	21 23.3	19 06.6	10 08.2	17 13.3
18 F	11 43 56	27 49 29	25 46 26	2♌09 40	21 31.8	21 47.5	22 14.9	6 53.1	3 58.1	19 17.6	17 04.3	16 21.6	21 26.9	19 09.9	10 10.4	17 14.3
19 Sa	11 47 53	28 49 09	8♌28 57	14 44 37	21 28.6	21 48.2	24 09.1	8 07.3	4 15.6	19 41.1	16 56.8	16 22.3	21 30.5	19 13.1	10 12.6	17 15.2
20 Su	11 51 49	29 48 46	20 56 58	27 06 21	21 25.4	21 49.0	26 04.4	9 21.5	4 32.7	20 04.7	16 49.3	16 22.8	21 34.2	19 16.4	10 14.8	17 16.1
21 M	11 55 46	0♈48 21	3♍13 04	9♍17 24	21 22.3	21 49.7	28 00.8	10 35.6	4 49.4	20 28.2	16 41.9	16 23.3	21 37.8	19 19.7	10 16.9	17 17.0
22 Tu	11 59 43	1 47 54	15 19 37	21 20 00	21 19.1	21R 50.2	29 58.3	11 49.8	5 05.6	20 51.7	16 34.5	16 23.7	21 41.4	19 23.0	10 19.1	17 17.8
23 W	12 03 39	2 47 25	27 18 48	3♎16 16	21 15.9	21 50.2	1♈56.9	13 04.0	5 21.3	21 15.1	16 27.2	16 24.0	21 45.0	19 26.3	10 21.2	17 18.6
24 Th	12 07 36	3 46 54	9♎12 38	15 08 11	21 12.7	21 49.6	3 56.5	14 18.2	5 36.6	21 38.6	16 20.0	16 24.2	21 48.6	19 29.6	10 23.4	17 19.4
25 F	12 11 32	4 46 21	21 03 08	26 57 47	21 09.5	21 48.4	5 56.9	15 32.3	5 51.4	22 02.0	16 12.9	16R 24.3	21 52.2	19 33.0	10 25.5	17 20.1
26 Sa	12 15 29	5 45 45	2♏52 23	8♏47 16	21 06.4	21 46.5	7 58.1	16 46.5	6 05.7	22 25.5	16 05.8	16 24.3	21 55.8	19 36.3	10 27.6	17 20.8
27 Su	12 19 25	6 45 08	14 42 45	20 39 11	21 03.2	21 44.2	10 00.0	18 00.7	6 19.6	22 48.9	15 58.9	16 24.2	21 59.4	19 39.7	10 29.7	17 21.5
28 M	12 23 22	7 44 29	26 36 55	2♐36 24	21 00.0	21 41.8	12 02.3	19 14.8	6 32.9	23 12.3	15 52.0	16 24.0	22 03.0	19 43.1	10 31.8	17 22.2
29 Tu	12 27 18	8 43 49	8♐38 01	14 42 15	20 56.8	21 39.5	14 04.9	20 29.0	6 45.7	23 35.6	15 45.3	16 23.7	22 06.5	19 46.4	10 33.9	17 22.8
30 W	12 31 15	9 43 06	20 49 34	27 00 27	20 53.6	21 37.7	16 07.6	21 43.1	6 57.9	23 59.0	15 38.6	16 23.3	22 10.0	19 49.8	10 35.9	17 23.4
31 Th	12 35 12	10♈42 22	3♑15 23	9♑34 54	20♍50.5	21♍36.7	18♈10.1	22♓57.3	7♐09.7	24♓22.3	15♍32.1	16♐22.8	22♓13.6	19♈53.2	10♓38.0	17♑24.0

1st of Month

Julian Day # 2457448.5
Obliquity 23°26'05"
SVP 5♓02'04"
GC 27♐03.9
Eris 22♈31.8

Day	⚴
1	13♒30.6
6	15 10.9
11	16 49.4
16	18 25.8
21	20 00.0
26	21 31.9
31	23 01.2

Day	⚵
1	15♏10.1
6	15 08.3R
11	14 57.7R
16	14 38.4R
21	14 10.5R
26	13 34.3R
31	12 50.3R

Day	⚶
1	27♈07.4
6	29 09.7
11	1♉13.5
16	3 18.6
21	5 24.8
26	7 32.0
31	9 40.0

DECLINATION and LATITUDE

Day	☉	☽		☽12h	☿		♀		♂		⚳		♃		♄	
	Decl	Decl	Lat	Decl	Decl	Lat	Decl	Lat	Decl	Lat	Decl	Lat	Decl	Lat	Decl	Lat
1 Tu	7S30	15S21	4N55	16S18	15S46	1S58	16S43	0S40	18S26	1N19	14S06	7S53	5N36	1N28	20S60	1N42
2 W	7 07	17 05	5 13	17 40	15 17	2 02	16 23	0 43	18 32	1 19	13 57	7 53	5 39	1 28	20 60	1 42
3 Th	6 44	18 03	5 17	18 12	14 47	2 04	16 03	0 45	18 38	1 18	13 48	7 54	5 42	1 28	20 60	1 43
4 F	6 21	18 08	5 06	17 49	14 16	2 06	15 42	0 47	18 43	1 17	13 39	7 54	5 45	1 28	20 60	1 43
5 Sa	5 58	17 15	4 38	16 26	13 43	2 08	15 20	0 49	18 48	1 17	13 30	7 54	5 48	1 28	21 00	1 43
6 Su	5 35	15 22	3 54	14 03	13 10	2 10	14 58	0 52	18 54	1 16	13 21	7 54	5 51	1 28	21 00	1 43
7 M	5 12	12 31	2 55	10 46	12 35	2 11	14 36	0 54	18 59	1 16	13 12	7 54	5 54	1 28	21 00	1 43
8 Tu	4 48	8 49	1 43	6 43	11 58	2 11	14 14	0 56	19 04	1 15	13 03	7 54	5 57	1 28	21 00	1 43
9 W	4 25	4 30	0 23	2 12	11 21	2 12	13 50	0 58	19 09	1 14	12 54	7 55	6 01	1 29	21 00	1 43
10 Th	4 01	0N09	1S00	2N30	10 42	2 11	13 27	0 60	19 14	1 14	12 45	7 55	6 04	1 29	21 00	1 43
11 F	3 38	4 48	2 19	7 01	10 02	2 11	13 03	1 02	19 19	1 13	12 36	7 55	6 07	1 29	21 00	1 43
12 Sa	3 14	9 07	3 28	11 03	9 20	2 09	12 39	1 04	19 23	1 12	12 27	7 55	6 10	1 29	21 00	1 44
13 Su	2 50	12 48	4 22	14 20	8 38	2 08	12 15	1 05	19 28	1 12	12 18	7 55	6 13	1 29	21 00	1 44
14 M	2 27	15 37	4 59	16 40	7 54	2 06	11 50	1 07	19 33	1 11	12 09	7 56	6 16	1 29	21 00	1 44
15 Tu	2 03	17 26	5 16	17 56	7 09	2 03	11 24	1 09	19 37	1 10	11 60	7 56	6 19	1 29	21 00	1 44
16 W	1 39	18 11	5 15	18 10	6 23	1 60	10 59	1 10	19 41	1 09	11 50	7 56	6 22	1 29	21 00	1 44
17 Th	1 16	17 54	4 57	17 23	5 36	1 56	10 33	1 12	19 46	1 09	11 41	7 57	6 25	1 29	21 00	1 44
18 F	0 52	16 40	4 24	15 44	4 48	1 52	10 07	1 13	19 50	1 08	11 32	7 57	6 28	1 29	21 00	1 44
19 Sa	0 28	14 37	3 38	13 21	3 58	1 47	9 41	1 15	19 54	1 07	11 23	7 57	6 31	1 29	21 00	1 44
20 Su	0 04	11 56	2 43	10 23	3 08	1 42	9 14	1 16	19 58	1 06	11 14	7 58	6 34	1 29	21 00	1 45
21 M	0N19	8 45	1 42	7 01	2 16	1 37	8 47	1 18	20 02	1 05	11 05	7 58	6 37	1 29	21 00	1 45
22 Tu	0 43	5 14	0 36	3 24	1 24	1 30	8 20	1 19	20 06	1 04	10 56	7 58	6 40	1 29	21 00	1 45
23 W	1 07	1 32	0N30	0S20	0 30	1 24	7 53	1 20	20 09	1 03	10 48	7 59	6 42	1 29	21 00	1 45
24 Th	1 30	2S12	1 35	4 02	0N24	1 16	7 25	1 21	20 13	1 02	10 39	7 59	6 45	1 29	20 60	1 45
25 F	1 54	5 49	2 35	7 33	1 19	1 08	6 58	1 22	20 17	1 01	10 30	7 59	6 48	1 29	20 60	1 45
26 Sa	2 17	9 12	3 28	10 46	2 14	1 00	6 30	1 23	20 20	0 60	10 21	7 60	6 51	1 28	20 60	1 45
27 Su	2 41	12 13	4 13	13 33	3 10	0 51	6 02	1 24	20 24	0 59	10 12	8 00	6 53	1 28	20 60	1 45
28 M	3 04	14 45	4 46	15 47	4 07	0 42	5 33	1 25	20 27	0 58	10 03	8 01	6 56	1 28	20 59	1 45
29 Tu	3 28	16 40	5 08	17 22	5 04	0 32	5 05	1 26	20 30	0 56	9 54	8 01	6 58	1 28	20 59	1 46
30 W	3 51	17 52	5 16	18 10	6 00	0 22	4 36	1 26	20 34	0 55	9 45	8 02	7 01	1 28	20 59	1 46
31 Th	4N14	18S14	5N10	18S05	6N57	0S11	4S08	1S27	20S37	0N54	9S36	8S02	7N03	1N28	20S59	1N46

Day	⚷		♅		♆		♇	
	Decl	Lat	Decl	Lat	Decl	Lat	Decl	Lat
1	0S01	4N07	6N37	0S36	8S44	0S48	20S52	1N31
6	0N06	4 07	6 43	0 36	8 39	0 48	20 51	1 30
11	0 13	4 06	6 48	0 36	8 35	0 48	20 51	1 30
16	0 20	4 06	6 55	0 36	8 31	0 48	20 51	1 30
21	0 27	4 06	7 01	0 36	8 27	0 48	20 50	1 30
26	0 34	4 06	7 07	0 36	8 23	0 48	20 50	1 29
31	0N41	4N06	7N14	0S36	8S19	0S48	20S50	1N29

Day	⚴		⚵		⚶		Eris	
	Decl	Lat	Decl	Lat	Decl	Lat	Decl	Lat
1	4N31	22N09	6S52	9N56	5N43	5S04	2S46	12S24
6	4 55	22 07	6 28	10 20	6 34	4 56	2 44	12 23
11	5 20	22 06	6 02	10 45	7 24	4 48	2 43	12 23
16	5 47	22 06	5 33	11 09	8 13	4 40	2 41	12 22
21	6 14	22 07	5 02	11 34	9 01	4 33	2 40	12 22
26	6 42	22 09	4 29	11 57	9 49	4 27	2 38	12 21
31	7N11	22N12	3S55	12N19	10N35	4S20	2S37	12S21

Moon Phenomena

Max/0 Decl
dy hr mn
3 14:21 18S13
9 23:14 0 N
16 5:01 18N12
23 9:50 0 S
30 22:18 18S14

Perigee/Apogee
dy hr m kilometers
10 6:58 p 359514
25 14:17 a 406125

Max/0 Lat
dy hr mn
2 18:37 5N18
9 6:31 0 S
15 10:26 5S18
22 13:01 0 N
30 1:31 5N16

PH dy hr mn
☾ 1 23:12 11♐48
● 9 1:56 18♓56
● 9 1:58 T 04'10"
☽ 15 17:04 25♊33
○ 23 12:02 3♎17
○ 23 11:48 A 0.775
☾ 31 15:18 11♑20

Void of Course Moon

Last Aspect	☽ Ingress
3 2:56 ☿ ✶	♑ 3 10:03
5 16:06 ♂ ✶	♒ 5 16:23
7 8:47 ♀ ☌	♓ 7 19:10
9 1:56 ☉ ☌	♈ 9 19:41
11 18:25 ♀ ✶	♉ 11 19:45
13 9:48 ☉ ✶	♊ 13 21:05
15 17:04 ☉ □	♋ 16 0:58
18 4:10 ☉ △	♌ 18 7:56
19 20:44 ♅ △	♍ 20 17:40
22 3:56 ♇ △	♎ 23 5:24
24 20:56 ♅ ☍	♏ 25 18:10
27 7:27 ♀ △	♐ 28 6:47
30 1:56 ♀ □	♑ 30 17:46

DAILY ASPECTARIAN

1 Tu ♀✶♄ 1:08; ☽∠♇ 3:45; ☽∥☿ 4:02; ☽⚼♅ 6:30; ☽∥♀ 15:02; ☽□♆ 18:50; ♀⚺♇ 20:52; ☉□☽ 23:12

2 W ☽□⚳ 1:34; ☽☌♄ 7:16; ☽⚺♇ 9:10; ☽✶♀ 10:30; ⚵ R 10:41; ☽△♅ 11:55; ☽□♃ 13:17; ☽□⚷ 16:03

3 Th ♀✶♅ 1:14; ☽✶☿ 2:56; ☉⋕♅ 5:13; ☽⚺♂ 8:05; ♀⚻♃ 12:05; ☽∠♀ 17:59; ☉☌⚳ 21:36

4 F ☽✶♆ 3:58; ☽∠☿ 10:46; ☽✶⚳ 11:51; ☉✶☽ 12:33; ☽∠♂ 12:38; ☽⚺♄ 15:36; ☽☌♇ 17:18; ☽□♅ 19:59; ☽△♃ 20:31; ♀⚺⚷ 21:01; ☽✶⚷ 23:53

5 Sa ☽⚺♀ 0:09; ☿□♂ 5:44; ☽∠♆ 7:04; ☉⋕♃ 9:07; ☿ ♓ 10:25; ☿∥⚳ 12:59; ☽∠⚳ 15:23; ☽✶♂ 16:06; ☽⚺☿ 17:12; ☉∠☽ 17:23; ☽∠♄ 18:17; ☽⚼♃ 22:42

6 Su ☽∠⚷ 2:19; ♂ ♐ 2:30; ☽∥♀ 4:28; ☉□♄ 6:05; ☽⚺♆ 9:13; ♃⚻♅ 11:46; ☿∠♇ 15:44; ☽⚺⚳ 17:55; ☽∥⚳ 18:36; ☽✶♄ 20:02; ☉⚺☽ 21:04; ☽⚺♇ 21:35; ☽∥☿ 23:28

7 M ☽⚻♃ 0:03; ☽✶♅ 0:12; ☽⚺⚷ 3:53; ☉✶♇ 4:42; ☽☌♀ 8:47; ☿∠♅ 14:20; ☽□♂ 20:12; ☽∠♇ 22:32

8 Tu ⚶ ♉ 0:54; ☽∠♅ 1:08; ☽∥♆ 1:09; ☽☌☿ 2:30; ☉☍♃ 10:58; ☽☌♆ 11:12; ☽⋕♅ 11:48; ☽⋕♃ 16:00; ☉⚺♅ 19:59; ☽☌⚳ 20:43; ☽□♄ 21:30; ☽✶♇ 22:57

9 W ☉∥☽ 0:31; ☽☍♃ 0:48; ☽⚺♅ 1:33; ☉☌☽ 1:56; ☽☌⚷ 5:07; ☽⚺♀ 14:03; ☽△♂ 21:52; ☽⋕⚷ 22:15

10 Th ☽∥⚷ 0:13; ⚳□♄ 3:58; ☽⚺☿ 9:06; ☽⚺♆ 11:30; ☽∠♀ 16:11; ☉⋕☽ 18:19; ☽△♄ 21:38; ☽⚺⚳ 22:04; ☽⚼♂ 22:24; ☽□♇ 23:03

11 F ☽⚻♃ 0:25; ☽☌♅ 1:44; ☉☌⚷ 4:28; ☽⚺⚷ 5:19; ☉⚺☽ 5:23; ☿☌♆ 6:02; ☽∥♃ 7:06; ☽∥♅ 10:52; ☽∠♆ 11:35; ☽∠☿ 12:19; ☽✶♀ 18:25; ☽⋕♆ 20:47; ☽⚼♄ 21:46; ☽∠⚳ 22:50; ☽⚻♂ 23:05

12 Sa ☽⚼♃ 0:20; ☽⋕☿ 1:07; ♂∠♇ 4:31; ☽∠⚷ 5:37; ☉∠☽ 7:20; ♀ ♓ 10:25; ☽✶♆ 11:56; ⚳✶♇ 12:56; ☽✶☿ 15:57; ♀∥⚳ 19:15; ☽⋕♀ 20:25; ☽⋕⚳ 20:30; ☽⚻♄ 22:15; ☽△♇ 23:42; ☽✶⚳ 23:59

13 Su ☽△♃ 0:37; ☿∥♆ 2:31; ☽⚺♅ 2:35; ☽✶⚷ 6:19; ☉✶☽ 9:48; ⚳☍♃ 17:41

14 M ☽□♀ 0:22; ☽⚼♇ 0:44; ☽☍♂ 1:43; ☽∠♅ 3:45; ♀∠♇ 4:37; ☽□♆ 14:08; ☿□♄ 19:27; ♀□♂ 20:49

15 Tu ☽☍♄ 0:55; ☽□☿ 1:45; ☽⚻♇ 2:27; ☽□♃ 2:52; ☽□⚳ 4:10; ☽✶♅ 5:37; ☿✶♇ 7:00; ☿⋕♅ 8:08; ☽□⚷ 9:35; ☿☍♃ 9:43; ♀∠♅ 16:49; ☉□☽ 17:04

16 W ☿☌⚳ 0:05; ☿⋕♃ 0:32; ☽⚻♂ 7:08; ☿⚺♅ 7:23; ☽△♀ 9:45; ☽△♆ 19:11; ♃△♇ 20:07

17 Th ☽⚻♄ 6:32; ☽✶♃ 8:01; ☽☍♇ 8:09; ☽⚼♂ 11:04; ☽△⚳ 11:35; ☽□♅ 11:40; ☿☌⚷ 13:30; ⚳⚺♅ 14:55; ☽△⚷ 15:55; ☽⚼♀ 16:00; ☽△☿ 16:19; ☽⚼♆ 22:53

18 F ☉△☽ 4:10; ☽⚼♄ 10:30; ☽∠♃ 11:43; ☽△♂ 15:47; ☽⚼⚳ 16:33; ♂⚼♅ 19:44; ☽⚼⚷ 20:13; ☽⚻♀ 23:14

19 Sa ☽⚼☿ 1:30; ☽⚻♆ 3:19; ☉⋕⚷ 3:51; ☉⚼☽ 11:06; ☽△♄ 15:09; ☽⚺♃ 16:05; ☽⚻♇ 16:52; ☽△♅ 20:44; ☽⚻⚳ 22:15

20 Su ☽⚻⚷ 1:13; ☉ ♈ 4:31; ☽⋕⚳ 5:45; ☽⚻☿ 11:51; ♀☌♆ 17:46; ☉⚻☽ 18:50; ☽⚼♇ 22:09; ☽⋕♀ 23:37

21 M ☽⋕♆ 2:06; ☽⚼♅ 2:12; ☽□♂ 3:14; ☉∥⚷ 8:20; ☽∥♅ 11:57; ☽☍♆ 14:01; ☽∥♃ 14:33; ☽☍♀ 16:15; ♀∥♆ 18:45

22 Tu ☿ ♈ 0:20; ☽□♄ 2:08; ☽☌♃ 2:28; ☽△♇ 3:56; ☽⚻♅ 8:08; ☽☍⚳ 11:26; ☉⋕☿ 12:42; ☽☍⚷ 12:47

23 W ☿⋕⚷ 0:11; ☉∥☽ 2:28; ☽∥⚷ 6:37; ☽⋕☿ 8:42; ♃□♄ 10:17; ☽∥☿ 10:32; ☽☍☿ 11:12; ☉☍☽ 12:02; ☽⋕⚷ 13:07; ☽✶♂ 16:34; ☉⋕☽ 18:59; ☉☌☿ 20:12

24 Th ☽⚻♆ 2:24; ☿∥⚷ 3:14; ☽⚻♀ 11:31; ⚳☌⚷ 12:09; ☽⚺♃ 14:17; ☽✶♄ 14:34; ☽□♇ 16:27; ♀⋕♅ 17:20; ☽☍♅ 20:56; ☿△♂ 22:46; ☽∠♂ 23:36

25 F ☽⚻⚷ 1:40; ☽⚻⚳ 2:04; ☽⋕♃ 6:50; ☽∥♀ 6:57; ♀⋕♃ 7:48; ☽⋕♅ 8:53; ☽⚼♆ 8:54; ♄ R 10:02; ♀☍♃ 11:59; ♀□♄ 16:49; ☽∥♆ 18:00; ☽∠♃ 20:26; ☽∠♄ 21:01; ☽⚼♀ 21:31

26 Sa ☉∥☿ 2:08; ☉⚻☽ 6:24; ☽⚺♂ 6:40; ☽⚼⚷ 8:17; ☽∥⚳ 8:19; ☽⚼⚳ 9:33; ☉△♂ 10:34; ♀✶♇ 11:13; ☽⚻☿ 12:29; ☽△♆ 15:26

27 Su ☽✶♃ 2:33; ☽⚺♄ 3:25; ☽✶♇ 5:21; ☿⚺♆ 5:57; ☽△♀ 7:27; ☽⚻♅ 10:03; ☽△⚷ 14:46; ☉⚼☽ 15:30; ☽△⚳ 16:55

28 M ☽⚼☿ 1:01; ♀⚺♅ 9:35; ☽∠♇ 11:32; ☽⚼♅ 16:17; ☽☌♂ 20:13

29 Tu ☉△☽ 0:13; ☿⋕♀ 0:25; ☽□♆ 3:50; ☽△☿ 12:57; ☽□♃ 13:56; ☽☌♄ 15:19; ☽⚺♇ 17:16; ☿⚻♃ 18:37; ☽△♅ 22:03

30 W ☽□♀ 1:56; ☽□⚷ 2:38; ☿△♄ 3:03; ☽□⚳ 6:21; ♀☌⚷ 9:09; ☿□♇ 14:55; ☉⋕♀ 21:02; ☉⚺♆ 22:09

31 Th ☿∥♃ 2:50; ☿∥♅ 7:14; ☽⚺♂ 7:32; ☽✶♆ 14:01; ☉□☽ 15:18; ☿☌♅ 20:51; ☽△♃ 22:58

April 2016

LONGITUDE

Day	Sid.Time	☉	☽	☽ 12 hour	Mean ☊	True ☊	☿	♀	♂	⚳	♃	♄	⚷	♅	♆	♇
	h m s	° ' "	° ' "	° ' "	° '	° '	° '	° '	° '	° '	° '	° '	° '	° '	° '	° '
1 F	12 39 08	11♈41 36	15♑59 28	22♑29 32	20♍47.3	21♍36.6	20♈12.2	24♓11.4	7♐20.8	24♓45.6	15♍25.7	16♐22.2	22♓17.1	19♈56.6	10♓40.0	17♑24.5
2 Sa	12 43 05	12 40 48	29 05 31	5♒47 47	20 44.1	21 37.3	22 13.5	25 25.5	7 31.4	25 08.9	15R 19.4	16R 21.5	22 20.6	20 00.0	10 42.0	17 25.0
3 Su	12 47 01	13 39 58	12♒36 35	19 32 05	20 40.9	21 38.6	24 13.7	26 39.7	7 41.4	25 32.1	15 13.2	16 20.7	22 24.0	20 03.5	10 44.0	17 25.5
4 M	12 50 58	14 39 07	26 34 20	3♓43 12	20 37.8	21 40.1	26 12.4	27 53.8	7 50.8	25 55.3	15 07.2	16 19.8	22 27.5	20 06.9	10 46.0	17 26.0
5 Tu	12 54 54	15 38 14	10♓58 24	18 19 28	20 34.6	21R 41.2	28 09.2	29 07.9	7 59.6	26 18.5	15 01.2	16 18.8	22 30.9	20 10.3	10 47.9	17 26.4
6 W	12 58 51	16 37 19	25 45 46	3♈16 26	20 31.4	21 41.4	0♉03.9	0♈22.0	8 07.8	26 41.7	14 55.4	16 17.7	22 34.3	20 13.7	10 49.9	17 26.8
7 Th	13 02 47	17 36 21	10♈50 29	18 26 46	20 28.2	21 40.4	1 56.0	1 36.2	8 15.3	27 04.8	14 49.8	16 16.5	22 37.7	20 17.2	10 51.8	17 27.1
8 F	13 06 44	18 35 22	26 04 03	3♉41 02	20 25.0	21 38.1	3 45.1	2 50.3	8 22.2	27 27.9	14 44.3	16 15.2	22 41.1	20 20.6	10 53.7	17 27.5
9 Sa	13 10 40	19 34 21	11♉16 26	18 49 01	20 21.9	21 34.7	5 30.9	4 04.4	8 28.4	27 51.0	14 38.9	16 13.8	22 44.5	20 24.0	10 55.6	17 27.8
10 Su	13 14 37	20 33 18	26 17 39	3♊41 23	20 18.7	21 30.6	7 13.1	5 18.4	8 34.0	28 14.0	14 33.7	16 12.3	22 47.8	20 27.4	10 57.5	17 28.0
11 M	13 18 34	21 32 13	10♊59 24	18 11 07	20 15.5	21 26.6	8 51.3	6 32.5	8 39.0	28 37.0	14 28.6	16 10.8	22 51.1	20 30.9	10 59.3	17 28.3
12 Tu	13 22 30	22 31 05	25 16 06	2♋14 09	20 12.3	21 23.2	10 25.2	7 46.6	8 43.2	29 00.0	14 23.7	16 09.1	22 54.4	20 34.3	11 01.1	17 28.5
13 W	13 26 27	23 29 55	9♋05 15	15 49 30	20 09.2	21 20.9	11 54.7	9 00.6	8 46.7	29 22.9	14 18.9	16 07.4	22 57.7	20 37.7	11 02.9	17 28.7
14 Th	13 30 23	24 28 43	22 27 09	28 58 33	20 06.0	21D 20.0	13 19.4	10 14.7	8 49.6	29 45.8	14 14.3	16 05.5	23 00.9	20 41.2	11 04.7	17 28.8
15 F	13 34 20	25 27 29	5♌24 08	11♌44 23	20 02.8	21 20.4	14 39.2	11 28.7	8 51.8	0♈08.7	14 09.9	16 03.6	23 04.2	20 44.6	11 06.5	17 28.9
16 Sa	13 38 16	26 26 12	17 59 49	24 10 59	19 59.6	21 21.7	15 53.9	12 42.7	8 53.2	0 31.5	14 05.6	16 01.6	23 07.4	20 48.0	11 08.2	17 29.0
17 Su	13 42 13	27 24 53	0♍18 25	6♍22 39	19 56.4	21 23.4	17 03.3	13 56.7	8R 53.9	0 54.3	14 01.5	15 59.4	23 10.5	20 51.4	11 10.0	17 29.1
18 M	13 46 09	28 23 32	12 24 11	18 23 31	19 53.3	21R 24.7	18 07.4	15 10.7	8 54.0	1 17.0	13 57.5	15 57.3	23 13.7	20 54.9	11 11.7	17R 29.1
19 Tu	13 50 06	29 22 09	24 21 05	0♎17 20	19 50.1	21 25.1	19 05.9	16 24.7	8 53.2	1 39.7	13 53.7	15 55.0	23 16.8	20 58.3	11 13.3	17 29.1
20 W	13 54 03	0♉20 43	6♎12 37	12 07 18	19 46.9	21 23.8	19 58.9	17 38.7	8 51.8	2 02.3	13 50.1	15 52.6	23 19.9	21 01.7	11 15.0	17 29.1
21 Th	13 57 59	1 19 16	18 01 43	23 56 08	19 43.7	21 20.7	20 46.1	18 52.7	8 49.6	2 24.9	13 46.7	15 50.2	23 22.9	21 05.1	11 16.6	17 29.0
22 F	14 01 56	2 17 46	29 50 50	5♏46 02	19 40.5	21 15.7	21 27.6	20 06.6	8 46.6	2 47.5	13 43.4	15 47.6	23 25.9	21 08.4	11 18.2	17 28.9
23 Sa	14 05 52	3 16 15	11♏41 59	17 38 52	19 37.4	21 09.0	22 03.3	21 20.6	8 42.9	3 10.0	13 40.3	15 45.0	23 28.9	21 11.8	11 19.8	17 28.8
24 Su	14 09 49	4 14 42	23 36 55	29 36 20	19 34.2	21 01.2	22 33.2	22 34.5	8 38.4	3 32.5	13 37.4	15 42.3	23 31.9	21 15.2	11 21.3	17 28.6
25 M	14 13 45	5 13 07	5♐37 21	11♐40 11	19 31.0	20 52.9	22 57.2	23 48.5	8 33.2	3 54.9	13 34.7	15 39.6	23 34.8	21 18.6	11 22.9	17 28.4
26 Tu	14 17 42	6 11 30	17 45 06	23 52 23	19 27.8	20 45.0	23 15.5	25 02.4	8 27.2	4 17.2	13 32.1	15 36.7	23 37.7	21 21.9	11 24.4	17 28.2
27 W	14 21 38	7 09 52	0♑02 19	6♑15 14	19 24.7	20 38.2	23 27.9	26 16.4	8 20.5	4 39.6	13 29.7	15 33.8	23 40.6	21 25.2	11 25.9	17 28.0
28 Th	14 25 35	8 08 12	12 31 29	18 51 28	19 21.5	20 33.2	23R 34.7	27 30.3	8 12.9	5 01.8	13 27.5	15 30.8	23 43.5	21 28.6	11 27.3	17 27.7
29 F	14 29 32	9 06 31	25 15 33	1♒44 08	19 18.3	20 30.2	23 35.9	28 44.2	8 04.7	5 24.1	13 25.5	15 27.7	23 46.3	21 31.9	11 28.8	17 27.4
30 Sa	14 33 28	10♉04 48	8♒17 37	14 56 23	19♍15.1	20♍29.2	23♉31.8	29♈58.1	7♐55.6	5♈46.3	13♍23.7	15♐24.6	23♓49.0	21♈35.2	11♓30.2	17♑27.1

1st of Month

Julian Day # 2457479.5
Obliquity 23°26'05"
SVP 5♓02'01"
GC 27♐04.0
Eris 22♈49.9

Day	⚴
1	23♒18.7
6	24 44.7
11	26 07.6
16	27 27.2
21	28 43.2
26	29 55.4

Day	⚵
1	12♏40.6R
6	11 48.1R
11	10 49.7R
16	9 46.5R
21	8 40.1R
26	7 31.8R

Day	⚶
1	10♉05.7
6	12 14.6
11	14 24.2
16	16 34.2
21	18 44.6
26	20 55.3

DECLINATION and LATITUDE

Day	☉ Decl	☽ Decl	☽ Lat	☽12h Decl	☿ Decl	☿ Lat	♀ Decl	♀ Lat	♂ Decl	♂ Lat	⚳ Decl	⚳ Lat	♃ Decl	♃ Lat	♄ Decl	♄ Lat
1 F	4N37	17S43	4N48	17S06	7N53	0S00	3S39	1S28	20S40	0N53	9S28	8S03	7N06	1N28	20S59	1N46
2 Sa	5 00	16 14	4 11	15 09	8 49	0N11	3 10	1 28	20 43	0 51	9 19	8 03	7 08	1 28	20 59	1 46
3 Su	5 24	13 50	3 19	12 18	9 44	0 22	2 41	1 29	20 46	0 50	9 10	8 04	7 10	1 28	20 59	1 46
4 M	5 46	10 33	2 14	8 38	10 38	0 34	2 12	1 29	20 49	0 49	9 01	8 04	7 13	1 28	20 58	1 46
5 Tu	6 09	6 33	0 59	4 20	11 31	0 45	1 43	1 29	20 52	0 47	8 53	8 05	7 15	1 28	20 58	1 46
6 W	6 32	2 02	0S22	0N20	12 23	0 57	1 13	1 30	20 54	0 46	8 44	8 05	7 17	1 28	20 58	1 46
7 Th	6 55	2N42	1 44	5 02	13 12	1 08	0 44	1 30	20 57	0 44	8 35	8 06	7 19	1 27	20 58	1 47
8 F	7 17	7 18	2 58	9 26	14 00	1 19	0 15	1 30	20 60	0 43	8 27	8 06	7 21	1 27	20 57	1 47
9 Sa	7 39	11 25	3 60	13 11	14 47	1 30	0N14	1 30	21 02	0 41	8 18	8 07	7 23	1 27	20 57	1 47
10 Su	8 02	14 43	4 44	15 60	15 30	1 41	0 44	1 30	21 05	0 39	8 09	8 08	7 25	1 27	20 57	1 47
11 M	8 24	16 60	5 08	17 43	16 12	1 51	1 13	1 30	21 07	0 38	8 01	8 08	7 27	1 27	20 57	1 47
12 Tu	8 46	18 09	5 13	18 17	16 51	2 01	1 43	1 30	21 09	0 36	7 52	8 09	7 29	1 27	20 56	1 47
13 W	9 07	18 10	4 59	17 46	17 28	2 10	2 12	1 30	21 12	0 34	7 44	8 10	7 30	1 27	20 56	1 47
14 Th	9 29	17 09	4 29	16 18	18 02	2 18	2 41	1 29	21 14	0 33	7 35	8 10	7 32	1 26	20 56	1 47
15 F	9 51	15 16	3 45	14 03	18 33	2 25	3 11	1 29	21 16	0 31	7 27	8 11	7 33	1 26	20 56	1 47
16 Sa	10 12	12 42	2 53	11 12	19 01	2 32	3 40	1 28	21 18	0 29	7 18	8 12	7 35	1 26	20 55	1 47
17 Su	10 33	9 36	1 53	7 55	19 27	2 38	4 09	1 28	21 20	0 27	7 10	8 12	7 36	1 26	20 55	1 47
18 M	10 54	6 09	0 49	4 20	19 50	2 43	4 38	1 27	21 22	0 25	7 02	8 13	7 38	1 26	20 55	1 48
19 Tu	11 15	2 29	0N16	0 37	20 10	2 47	5 07	1 27	21 24	0 23	6 53	8 14	7 39	1 26	20 54	1 48
20 W	11 35	1S15	1 20	3S06	20 28	2 50	5 36	1 26	21 26	0 21	6 45	8 14	7 40	1 26	20 54	1 48
21 Th	11 56	4 55	2 20	6 41	20 42	2 52	6 04	1 25	21 28	0 19	6 37	8 15	7 42	1 25	20 54	1 48
22 F	12 16	8 24	3 13	10 01	20 54	2 53	6 33	1 25	21 30	0 16	6 28	8 16	7 43	1 25	20 53	1 48
23 Sa	12 36	11 33	3 59	12 58	21 03	2 52	7 02	1 24	21 31	0 14	6 20	8 17	7 44	1 25	20 53	1 48
24 Su	12 56	14 15	4 34	15 23	21 09	2 51	7 30	1 23	21 33	0 12	6 12	8 18	7 45	1 25	20 53	1 48
25 M	13 16	16 21	4 58	17 09	21 13	2 48	7 58	1 22	21 34	0 09	6 04	8 18	7 46	1 25	20 52	1 48
26 Tu	13 35	17 46	5 08	18 10	21 13	2 44	8 26	1 21	21 36	0 07	5 56	8 19	7 46	1 24	20 52	1 48
27 W	13 54	18 22	5 04	18 21	21 11	2 38	8 54	1 20	21 37	0 05	5 48	8 20	7 47	1 24	20 51	1 48
28 Th	14 13	18 06	4 46	17 37	21 07	2 32	9 22	1 19	21 38	0 02	5 40	8 21	7 48	1 24	20 51	1 48
29 F	14 32	16 55	4 14	15 60	20 59	2 24	9 49	1 17	21 39	0S00	5 32	8 22	7 48	1 24	20 51	1 48
30 Sa	14N50	14S51	3N28	13S29	20N49	2N15	10N16	1S16	21S41	0S03	5S24	8S23	7N49	1N24	20S50	1N48

Day	⚷ Decl	⚷ Lat	♅ Decl	♅ Lat	♆ Decl	♆ Lat	♇ Decl	♇ Lat
1	0N42	4N06	7N15	0S36	8S18	0S48	20S50	1N29
6	0 49	4 06	7 21	0 36	8 15	0 48	20 50	1 29
11	0 56	4 06	7 28	0 36	8 11	0 48	20 50	1 28
16	1 03	4 06	7 34	0 35	8 08	0 48	20 50	1 28
21	1 09	4 07	7 41	0 35	8 05	0 49	20 50	1 28
26	1 15	4 07	7 47	0 35	8 02	0 49	20 51	1 28

Day	⚴ Decl	⚴ Lat	⚵ Decl	⚵ Lat	⚶ Decl	⚶ Lat	Eris Decl	Eris Lat
1	7N17	22N12	3S48	12N24	10N45	4S19	2S36	12S21
6	7 46	22 16	3 13	12 45	11 30	4 13	2 35	12 21
11	8 16	22 21	2 38	13 03	12 14	4 07	2 34	12 21
16	8 46	22 26	2 04	13 20	12 56	4 01	2 32	12 20
21	9 16	22 33	1 30	13 34	13 37	3 55	2 31	12 20
26	9 46	22 40	0 59	13 46	14 17	3 50	2 30	12 20

Moon Phenomena

Max/0 Decl
dy hr mn
6 10:19 0 N
12 12:15 18N17
19 16:00 0 S
27 4:45 18S23

Perigee/Apogee
dy hr m kilometers
7 17:45 p 357167
21 16:04 a 406351

Max/0 Lat
dy hr mn
5 17:27 0 S
11 17:30 5S13
18 18:05 0 N
26 5:48 5N08

PH dy hr mn
● 7 11:25 18♈04
☽ 14 4:00 24♋39
○ 22 5:25 2♏31
☾ 30 3:30 10♒13

Void of Course Moon

Last Aspect	☽ Ingress
1 16:40 ♀ ✶	♒ 2 1:38
3 23:17 ☿ ✶	♓ 4 5:47
5 10:34 ♇ ✶	♈ 6 6:47
7 14:57 ♅ ☌	♉ 8 6:12
9 9:51 ♇ △	♊ 10 6:00
11 18:58 ☉ ✶	♋ 12 8:08
14 4:00 ☉ □	♌ 14 13:54
16 17:50 ☉ △	♍ 16 23:24
18 12:30 ☿ △	♎ 19 11:25
21 6:14 ♅ ☍	♏ 22 0:19
23 21:47 ☿ ☍	♐ 24 12:47
26 15:52 ♀ △	♑ 26 23:56
29 7:08 ♀ □	♒ 29 8:48

DAILY ASPECTARIAN

1 F
☽ ⚺ ♄ 0:42
☽ ☌ ♇ 2:38
☽ □ ♅ 7:21
☽ □ ☿ 9:14
☿ # ♆ 10:39
☽ ✶ ⚷ 11:40
☽ ∠ ♂ 11:54
♀ ☌ ⚳ 16:08
☽ ✶ ⚳ 16:38
☽ ✶ ♀ 16:40
☽ ∠ ♆ 17:50

2 Sa
☿ ⚺ ⚷ 1:27
☽ ⚼ ♃ 2:12
☿ ⚼ ♂ 3:54
☽ ∠ ♄ 4:04
☿ # ⚳ 11:10
☽ ∠ ⚷ 14:48
☽ ✶ ♂ 15:15
☽ ∠ ⚳ 20:16
☽ ⚺ ♆ 20:42
☽ ∠ ♀ 22:11

3 Su
☉ ✶ ☽ 1:59
☽ ⚻ ♃ 4:31
☽ ✶ ♄ 6:29
☽ ⚺ ♇ 8:22
☽ ✶ ♅ 12:57
☽ ⚺ ⚷ 16:59
☿ ∠ ♆ 18:33
☿ ⚺ ⚳ 19:41
☽ ⚺ ⚳ 22:52
☽ ✶ ☿ 23:17
☽ # ☿ 23:33

4 M
☽ ⚺ ♀ 2:27
☉ ∠ ☽ 5:35
♂ ∥ ♇ 9:00
☽ ∠ ♇ 9:51
☽ ∥ ⚳ 9:59
☉ ⚻ ♃ 10:20
☽ ∥ ♆ 14:09
☽ ∠ ♅ 14:23
☽ □ ♂ 19:02
☽ # ♅ 19:34
☽ # ♃ 20:04
☽ ☌ ♆ 23:43

5 Tu
☉ # ☽ 1:59
☽ ∠ ☿ 4:07
☽ ☍ ♃ 6:35
☉ ⚺ ☽ 8:11
☽ □ ♄ 8:43
☽ ✶ ♇ 10:34
☽ ⚺ ♅ 15:03
☉ △ ♄ 16:10
♀ ♈ 16:52
☽ ☌ ⚷ 18:51
☿ ⚼ ♃ 22:18
☿ ♉ 23:10

6 W
☽ ☌ ⚳ 1:32
☽ ∥ ♀ 4:34
☽ # ⚷ 6:07
☽ ⚺ ☿ 7:52
☽ ☌ ♀ 8:02
☿ ⚺ ♀ 11:15
☽ ∥ ⚷ 14:32
☽ # ♀ 14:58
☿ ⚼ ♄ 15:34
♀ # ⚷ 18:59
☽ △ ♂ 19:52
☉ □ ♇ 20:14

7 Th
☽ ⚺ ♆ 0:02
♂ ∥ ♄ 5:29
☽ ⚻ ♃ 6:16
☽ △ ♄ 8:34
☽ □ ♇ 10:26
☉ ☌ ☽ 11:25
☽ ☌ ♅ 14:57
☽ ⚺ ⚷ 18:39
☽ ⚼ ♂ 19:43
☽ ∠ ♆ 23:44
☉ ∥ ☽ 23:54

8 F
☽ ∥ ♃ 0:17
☽ ∥ ♅ 0:32
☽ ⚺ ⚳ 2:15
☉ ∥ ♃ 4:46
☽ # ♆ 5:04
☽ ⚼ ♃ 5:45
☽ # ⚳ 6:07
☉ ∥ ♅ 7:50
☽ ⚼ ♄ 8:09
☽ ⚺ ♀ 11:36
☽ ☌ ☿ 13:42
☽ ∠ ⚷ 18:23
☽ ⚻ ♂ 19:32
☽ ✶ ♆ 23:27

9 Sa
☽ ∠ ⚳ 2:34
☽ △ ♃ 5:20
☽ ⚻ ♄ 7:52
☽ △ ♇ 9:51
☽ ∠ ♀ 13:31
☉ ⚺ ☽ 14:08
☽ ⚺ ♅ 14:35
⚳ ∥ ♆ 15:57
☽ ✶ ⚷ 18:21
☉ ☌ ♅ 21:28

10 Su
☽ ✶ ⚳ 3:13
☉ # ⚳ 6:01
☿ ∠ ⚷ 8:40
♀ ∥ ⚷ 9:16
☽ ∥ ☿ 10:00
☽ ⚼ ♇ 10:01
☉ # ♆ 10:54
☽ ∠ ♅ 14:57
☽ ✶ ♀ 16:00
☉ ∠ ☽ 16:08
☽ ⚺ ☿ 20:02
☽ ☍ ♂ 20:07
☿ ⚻ ♂ 20:47
☽ □ ♆ 24:00

11 M
☽ □ ♃ 5:46
☽ ☍ ♄ 8:37
☽ ⚻ ♇ 10:48
☽ ✶ ♅ 15:59
☉ ✶ ☽ 18:58
☽ □ ⚷ 19:58

12 Tu
☽ ∠ ☿ 0:17
☽ □ ⚳ 6:35
☿ ✶ ♆ 9:41
☉ ⚺ ⚷ 10:05
♀ △ ♂ 19:18
☽ ⚻ ♂ 23:27
☽ □ ♀ 23:51

13 W
☽ △ ♆ 3:29
☽ ✶ ☿ 5:36
☉ ⚼ ♂ 7:15
♃ ∥ ♅ 7:59
☽ ✶ ♃ 9:14
☽ ∥ ☿ 12:22
☽ ⚻ ♄ 12:30
☽ ☍ ♇ 14:59
☽ □ ♅ 20:46

14 Th
☽ △ ⚷ 1:02
☽ ⚼ ♂ 2:31
☉ □ ☽ 4:00
☽ ⚼ ♆ 6:40
⚳ # ♃ 7:51
⚳ # ♅ 8:39
☽ ∠ ♃ 12:25
☽ △ ⚳ 13:52
⚳ ♈ 14:53
☿ △ ♃ 15:28
☽ ⚼ ♄ 15:54
♀ ⚺ ♆ 16:37

15 F
☽ ⚼ ⚷ 5:03
☽ △ ♂ 6:33
☽ ⚻ ♆ 10:49
☽ △ ♀ 12:45
☿ ∠ ⚳ 13:20
☉ ∠ ♆ 16:26
☽ ⚺ ♃ 16:32
☽ ⚼ ⚳ 19:06
☽ □ ☿ 19:32
☽ △ ♄ 20:13
☽ ⚻ ♇ 23:01

16 Sa
☿ ⚻ ♄ 2:29
☽ △ ♅ 5:27
☽ ⚻ ⚷ 9:59
☉ ∥ ☽ 17:40
☉ △ ☽ 17:50
☽ ⚼ ♀ 21:01

17 Su
☽ ⚻ ⚳ 1:13
♀ ⚻ ♃ 1:27
☽ ⚼ ♇ 4:18
☿ △ ♇ 9:24
☽ # ♆ 10:33
☽ ⚼ ♅ 11:01
♂ R 12:15
☽ ∥ ♃ 14:00
☽ ∥ ♅ 14:07
☽ □ ♂ 17:01
☽ # ⚳ 17:50
☽ ☍ ♆ 21:35

18 M
☉ ⚼ ☽ 2:09
☽ ☌ ♃ 3:06
☽ ⚻ ♀ 6:11
☽ □ ♄ 7:05
♇ R 7:27
☽ ∥ ♀ 8:53
☽ △ ♇ 10:11
☽ △ ☿ 12:30
☉ ⚼ ♃ 13:04
♀ △ ♄ 14:38
☽ ⚻ ♅ 17:09
☽ ☍ ⚷ 21:50

19 Tu
☽ ∥ ⚷ 8:49
☉ ⚻ ☽ 11:03
☽ ☍ ⚳ 15:16
☉ ♉ 15:31
♀ □ ♇ 20:52
☽ ⚼ ☿ 21:19
☽ # ⚷ 23:16

20 W
☽ ✶ ♂ 5:22
☽ ⚻ ♆ 10:15
☉ ⚼ ♄ 12:33
☽ ⚺ ♃ 15:24
☽ ✶ ♄ 19:34
☽ □ ♇ 22:54

21 Th
☽ ☍ ♀ 1:56
☽ ⚻ ☿ 5:56
☽ ☍ ♅ 6:14
☽ # ♀ 9:01
☽ ⚻ ⚷ 10:55
☽ ∥ ⚳ 11:02
☿ ⚺ ♅ 11:28
☽ ∠ ♂ 11:44
☿ # ♇ 15:53
☽ ⚼ ♆ 16:48
☽ # ♅ 19:00
☽ # ♃ 19:06
♀ # ⚳ 20:57
☽ ∥ ♆ 21:42
☽ ∠ ♃ 21:44
☿ # ♄ 22:37

22 F
☽ ∠ ♄ 1:55
☉ ☍ ☽ 5:25
☽ ⚻ ⚳ 6:10
☽ ⚼ ⚷ 17:28
☽ ⚺ ♂ 18:00
☉ ⚺ ⚳ 19:49
♀ ☌ ♅ 21:01
☽ △ ♆ 23:15

23 Sa
☽ ✶ ♃ 3:58
☽ ⚺ ♄ 8:09
☉ # ☽ 10:03
☽ ✶ ♇ 11:40
☽ ⚼ ⚳ 13:28
☽ ⚻ ♅ 19:14
☽ ⚻ ♀ 21:40
☽ ☍ ☿ 21:47
☿ ⚺ ♀ 23:19
☽ △ ⚷ 23:50

24 Su
♀ ∥ ♅ 12:54
♀ ∥ ♃ 12:54
♃ ∥ ♅ 13:05
☽ ∠ ♇ 17:44
♀ ⚼ ♂ 19:23
♀ ⚺ ⚷ 19:23
☽ △ ⚳ 20:29
☉ ⚻ ☽ 23:08

25 M
☽ ⚼ ♅ 1:22
♀ # ♆ 3:50
☽ ☌ ♂ 5:47
☽ ⚼ ♀ 7:03
☽ □ ♆ 11:27
☽ □ ♃ 15:43
☽ ☌ ♄ 19:48
☽ ⚺ ♇ 23:27

26 Tu
☽ △ ♅ 7:08
☉ ⚼ ☽ 7:20
⚴ ♓ 7:56
☽ ⚻ ☿ 11:00
☽ □ ⚷ 11:34
☽ △ ♀ 15:52

27 W
♀ ∠ ♆ 3:09
☽ □ ⚳ 9:12
☉ △ ☽ 14:55
☽ ⚺ ♂ 15:51
☽ ⚼ ☿ 16:25
☽ ✶ ♆ 21:57

28 Th
☉ ⚻ ♂ 1:43
☽ △ ♃ 1:46
☽ ⚺ ♄ 5:39
☽ ☌ ♇ 9:22
☉ ∠ ⚷ 15:15
☽ □ ♅ 17:00
☿ R 17:21
♀ ⚼ ♃ 18:05
☽ ∠ ♂ 19:58
♄ ∥ ♇ 20:30
☽ △ ☿ 20:54
☽ ✶ ⚷ 21:13

29 F
☽ ∠ ♆ 2:17
☽ ⚼ ♃ 5:52
☽ □ ♀ 7:08
☽ ∠ ♄ 9:37
☽ ✶ ⚳ 19:16
☿ # ♇ 20:37
☿ # ♄ 21:43
☽ ✶ ♂ 23:20

30 Sa
☉ # ☽ 0:04
♀ ♉ 0:37
☽ ∠ ⚷ 0:57
☉ □ ☽ 3:30
☽ ⚺ ♆ 5:49
♀ ⚼ ♄ 8:14
☽ ⚻ ♃ 9:12
☽ ✶ ♄ 12:47
☽ ⚺ ♇ 16:29
☽ ∠ ⚳ 23:01
☽ ✶ ♅ 23:56

LONGITUDE — May 2016

Day	Sid.Time	☉	☽	☽ 12 hour	Mean☊	True☊	☿	♀	♂	⚳	♃	♄	⚷	♅	♆	♇
	h m s	° ' "	° ' "	° ' "	° '	° '	° '	° '	° '	° '	° '	° '	° '	° '	° '	° '
Su	14 37 25	11♉03 03	21♒40 47	28♒31 06	19♍12.0	20♍29.6	23♉22.4	1♉12.0	7♐45.8	6♈08.4	13♍22.0	15♐21.4	23♓51.8	21♈38.5	11♓31.5	17♑26.7
M	14 41 21	12 01 17	5♓27 32	12♓30 11	19 08.8	20 30.6	23R 08.3	2 25.9	7R 35.3	6 30.4	13R 20.5	15R 18.1	23 54.5	21 41.8	11 32.9	17R 26.4
Tu	14 45 18	12 59 30	19 39 02	26 53 53	19 05.6	20R 31.2	22 49.6	3 39.8	7 24.0	6 52.5	13 19.2	15 14.7	23 57.1	21 45.0	11 34.2	17 25.9
W	14 49 14	13 57 41	4♈14 22	11♈39 57	19 02.4	20 30.4	22 26.7	4 53.7	7 11.9	7 14.4	13 18.1	15 11.3	23 59.8	21 48.3	11 35.5	17 25.5
Th	14 53 11	14 55 50	19 09 53	26 43 12	18 59.2	20 27.6	22 00.2	6 07.6	6 59.2	7 36.3	13 17.2	15 07.8	24 02.4	21 51.5	11 36.8	17 25.0
F	14 57 07	15 53 58	4♉18 48	11♉55 27	18 56.1	20 22.4	21 30.5	7 21.5	6 45.7	7 58.1	13 16.5	15 04.3	24 04.9	21 54.7	11 38.0	17 24.5
Sa	15 01 04	16 52 05	19 31 50	27 06 37	18 52.9	20 15.2	20 58.2	8 35.4	6 31.6	8 19.9	13 15.9	15 00.7	24 07.4	21 57.9	11 39.2	17 24.0
Su	15 05 01	17 50 10	4♊38 29	12♊06 13	18 49.7	20 06.6	20 23.8	9 49.2	6 16.8	8 41.6	13 15.5	14 57.1	24 09.9	22 01.1	11 40.4	17 23.4
M	15 08 57	18 48 13	19 28 46	26 45 16	18 46.5	19 57.8	19 48.1	11 03.1	6 01.4	9 03.3	13D 15.3	14 53.3	24 12.3	22 04.3	11 41.6	17 22.9
Tu	15 12 54	19 46 14	3♋55 03	10♋57 40	18 43.4	19 49.9	19 11.6	12 16.9	5 45.4	9 24.9	13 15.3	14 49.6	24 14.7	22 07.4	11 42.7	17 22.3
W	15 16 50	20 44 14	17 52 52	24 40 40	18 40.2	19 43.6	18 35.1	13 30.8	5 28.8	9 46.4	13 15.5	14 45.8	24 17.1	22 10.5	11 43.8	17 21.6
Th	15 20 47	21 42 12	1♌21 10	7♌54 41	18 37.0	19 39.6	17 59.0	14 44.6	5 11.6	10 07.9	13 15.9	14 41.9	24 19.4	22 13.6	11 44.9	17 21.0
F	15 24 43	22 40 08	14 21 38	20 42 31	18 33.8	19D 37.7	17 24.1	15 58.4	4 54.0	10 29.2	13 16.4	14 38.0	24 21.7	22 16.7	11 45.9	17 20.3
Sa	15 28 40	23 38 02	26 57 55	3♍08 28	18 30.6	19 37.4	16 51.0	17 12.3	4 35.8	10 50.6	13 17.2	14 34.0	24 23.9	22 19.8	11 46.9	17 19.6
Su	15 32 36	24 35 54	9♍14 47	15 17 32	18 27.5	19R 37.9	16 20.1	18 26.1	4 17.2	11 11.8	13 18.1	14 30.0	24 26.1	22 22.8	11 47.9	17 18.8
M	15 36 33	25 33 44	21 17 22	27 14 54	18 24.3	19 38.2	15 52.0	19 39.9	3 58.1	11 33.0	13 19.2	14 25.9	24 28.3	22 25.8	11 48.8	17 18.1
Tu	15 40 30	26 31 33	3♎10 44	9♎05 25	18 21.1	19 37.3	15 27.1	20 53.6	3 38.7	11 54.1	13 20.4	14 21.9	24 30.4	22 28.8	11 49.7	17 17.3
W	15 44 26	27 29 20	14 59 29	20 53 24	18 17.9	19 34.3	15 05.8	22 07.4	3 18.9	12 15.1	13 21.9	14 17.7	24 32.4	22 31.8	11 50.6	17 16.5
Th	15 48 23	28 27 06	26 47 35	2♏42 26	18 14.8	19 28.8	14 48.3	23 21.2	2 58.9	12 36.0	13 23.5	14 13.6	24 34.4	22 34.7	11 51.5	17 15.6
F	15 52 19	29 24 50	8♏38 17	14 35 23	18 11.6	19 20.6	14 34.8	24 35.0	2 38.5	12 56.9	13 25.3	14 09.4	24 36.4	22 37.6	11 52.3	17 14.8
Sa	15 56 16	0♊22 32	20 34 00	26 34 20	18 08.4	19 10.1	14 25.7	25 48.7	2 18.0	13 17.7	13 27.3	14 05.1	24 38.3	22 40.5	11 53.1	17 13.9
Su	16 00 12	1 20 13	2♐36 32	8♐40 45	18 05.2	18 58.0	14D 21.0	27 02.5	1 57.2	13 38.4	13 29.4	14 00.9	24 40.2	22 43.4	11 53.8	17 13.0
M	16 04 09	2 17 53	14 47 06	20 55 42	18 02.0	18 45.2	14 20.7	28 16.3	1 36.3	13 59.0	13 31.8	13 56.6	24 42.1	22 46.2	11 54.6	17 12.1
Tu	16 08 05	3 15 32	27 06 37	3♑20 00	17 58.9	18 32.8	14 25.0	29 30.0	1 15.3	14 19.6	13 34.3	13 52.3	24 43.8	22 49.0	11 55.3	17 11.1
W	16 12 02	4 13 10	9♑35 56	15 54 34	17 55.7	18 21.9	14 33.8	0♊43.8	0 54.2	14 40.1	13 36.9	13 47.9	24 45.6	22 51.8	11 55.9	17 10.2
Th	16 15 59	5 10 46	22 16 04	28 40 37	17 52.5	18 13.4	14 47.1	1 57.5	0 33.2	15 00.5	13 39.8	13 43.6	24 47.3	22 54.5	11 56.6	17 09.2
F	16 19 55	6 08 22	5♒08 25	11♒39 44	17 49.3	18 07.6	15 04.9	3 11.2	0 12.1	15 20.8	13 42.8	13 39.2	24 48.9	22 57.3	11 57.2	17 08.2
Sa	16 23 52	7 05 56	18 14 49	24 53 55	17 46.2	18 04.4	15 27.0	4 25.0	29♏51.2	15 41.0	13 46.0	13 34.8	24 50.5	23 00.0	11 57.7	17 07.1
Su	16 27 48	8 03 30	1♓37 20	8♓25 19	17 43.0	18D 03.3	15 53.4	5 38.7	29 30.3	16 01.1	13 49.3	13 30.4	24 52.1	23 02.6	11 58.3	17 06.1
M	16 31 45	9 01 03	15 18 04	22 15 46	17 39.8	18R 03.2	16 24.1	6 52.5	29 09.6	16 21.1	13 52.8	13 26.0	24 53.6	23 05.3	11 58.8	17 05.0
Tu	16 35 41	9♊58 35	29 18 29	6♈26 10	17♍36.6	18♍03.0	16♉58.9	8♊06.2	28♏49.2	16♈41.1	13♍56.5	13♐21.6	24♓55.1	23♈07.9	11♓59.2	17♑03.9

1st of Month

Julian Day # 2457509.5
Obliquity 23°26'05"
SVP 5♓01'58"
GC 27♐04.0
Eris 23♈09.4

Day	⚴	⚵	⚶
1	1♓03.5	6♏23.4R	23♉06.2
6	2 07.1	5 16.2R	25 17.4
11	3 06.0	4 12.0R	27 28.6
16	3 59.7	3 12.1R	29 39.8
21	4 47.9	2 17.7R	1♊50.9
26	5 30.2	1 29.7R	4 01.8
31	6 06.2	0 48.9R	6 12.6

DECLINATION and LATITUDE

Day	☉ Decl	☽ Decl	☽ Lat	☽12h Decl	☿ Decl	☿ Lat	♀ Decl	♀ Lat	♂ Decl	♂ Lat	⚳ Decl	⚳ Lat	♃ Decl	♃ Lat	♄ Decl	♄ Lat
Su	15N08	11S55	2N29	10S11	20N37	2N04	10N43	1S15	21S42	0S06	5S16	8S24	7N49	1N24	20S50	1N48
M	15 26	8 16	1 20	6 12	20 22	1 53	11 10	1 14	21 42	0 08	5 08	8 24	7 50	1 23	20 50	1 48
Tu	15 44	4 02	0 05	1 45	20 05	1 40	11 36	1 12	21 43	0 11	5 01	8 25	7 50	1 23	20 49	1 48
W	16 02	0N34	1S13	2N54	19 46	1 26	12 02	1 11	21 44	0 14	4 53	8 26	7 50	1 23	20 49	1 49
Th	16 19	5 13	2 28	7 29	19 25	1 11	12 28	1 09	21 45	0 17	4 45	8 27	7 50	1 23	20 48	1 49
F	16 36	9 37	3 33	11 36	19 02	0 56	12 54	1 08	21 45	0 19	4 37	8 28	7 51	1 23	20 48	1 49
Sa	16 52	13 23	4 23	14 57	18 38	0 40	13 19	1 06	21 46	0 22	4 30	8 29	7 51	1 22	20 48	1 49
Su	17 09	16 14	4 54	17 15	18 13	0 23	13 44	1 04	21 46	0 25	4 22	8 30	7 51	1 22	20 47	1 49
M	17 25	17 57	5 05	18 21	17 46	0 06	14 09	1 03	21 46	0 28	4 15	8 31	7 50	1 22	20 47	1 49
Tu	17 41	18 27	4 56	18 15	17 20	0S12	14 33	1 01	21 46	0 31	4 07	8 32	7 50	1 22	20 46	1 49
W	17 56	17 47	4 29	17 04	16 53	0 29	14 57	0 59	21 46	0 34	3 60	8 33	7 50	1 22	20 46	1 49
Th	18 11	16 08	3 49	15 00	16 26	0 47	15 21	0 57	21 46	0 37	3 53	8 34	7 50	1 21	20 45	1 49
F	18 26	13 42	2 57	12 15	16 00	1 04	15 44	0 55	21 46	0 40	3 45	8 35	7 49	1 21	20 45	1 49
Sa	18 41	10 40	1 58	8 60	15 35	1 21	16 07	0 54	21 46	0 43	3 38	8 37	7 49	1 21	20 44	1 49
Su	18 55	7 15	0 55	5 26	15 10	1 37	16 29	0 52	21 45	0 46	3 31	8 38	7 48	1 21	20 44	1 49
M	19 09	3 35	0N09	1 43	14 48	1 52	16 51	0 50	21 45	0 49	3 24	8 39	7 48	1 21	20 44	1 49
Tu	19 22	0S10	1 12	2S03	14 26	2 07	17 13	0 48	21 44	0 53	3 17	8 40	7 47	1 20	20 43	1 49
W	19 36	3 54	2 11	5 42	14 07	2 21	17 34	0 46	21 43	0 56	3 10	8 41	7 46	1 20	20 43	1 49
Th	19 49	7 28	3 04	9 09	13 50	2 34	17 54	0 44	21 43	0 59	3 03	8 42	7 45	1 20	20 42	1 49
F	20 01	10 45	3 50	12 15	13 34	2 46	18 15	0 41	21 42	1 02	2 56	8 43	7 45	1 20	20 42	1 49
Sa	20 14	13 37	4 25	14 52	13 21	2 56	18 34	0 39	21 41	1 05	2 49	8 45	7 44	1 20	20 41	1 49
Su	20 25	15 57	4 49	16 52	13 11	3 06	18 53	0 37	21 40	1 08	2 42	8 46	7 43	1 19	20 41	1 49
M	20 37	17 35	5 00	18 07	13 02	3 15	19 12	0 35	21 38	1 11	2 35	8 47	7 42	1 19	20 40	1 49
Tu	20 48	18 26	4 58	18 32	12 56	3 22	19 30	0 33	21 37	1 14	2 28	8 48	7 40	1 19	20 40	1 49
W	20 59	18 25	4 41	18 04	12 53	3 29	19 48	0 30	21 36	1 17	2 22	8 49	7 39	1 19	20 39	1 49
Th	21 10	17 29	4 10	16 40	12 51	3 34	20 05	0 28	21 34	1 20	2 15	8 51	7 38	1 19	20 39	1 49
F	21 20	15 38	3 26	14 24	12 52	3 39	20 22	0 26	21 33	1 23	2 09	8 52	7 37	1 18	20 38	1 49
Sa	21 29	12 58	2 31	11 21	12 55	3 42	20 38	0 24	21 31	1 26	2 02	8 53	7 35	1 18	20 38	1 49
Su	21 39	9 33	1 26	7 37	13 00	3 44	20 54	0 21	21 30	1 29	1 56	8 55	7 34	1 18	20 37	1 48
M	21 48	5 34	0 15	3 25	13 08	3 46	21 08	0 19	21 28	1 32	1 50	8 56	7 32	1 18	20 37	1 48
Tu	21N56	1S11	0S59	1N05	13N17	3S46	21N23	0S17	21S26	1S35	1S43	8S57	7N31	1N18	20S36	1N48

Day	⚷ Decl	⚷ Lat	♅ Decl	♅ Lat	♆ Decl	♆ Lat	♇ Decl	♇ Lat
1	1N21	4N08	7N53	0S36	7S60	0S49	20S51	1N27
6	1 27	4 08	7 59	0 36	7 57	0 49	20 52	1 27
11	1 32	4 09	8 05	0 36	7 55	0 49	20 52	1 27
16	1 37	4 10	8 11	0 36	7 53	0 49	20 53	1 27
21	1 42	4 10	8 16	0 36	7 52	0 50	20 54	1 26
26	1 46	4 11	8 21	0 36	7 51	0 50	20 55	1 26
31	1N50	4N12	8N26	0S36	7S50	0S50	20S56	1N26

Day	⚴ Decl	⚴ Lat	⚵ Decl	⚵ Lat	⚶ Decl	⚶ Lat	Eris Decl	Eris Lat
1	10N16	22N48	0S30	13N54	14N55	3S44	2S29	12S20
6	10 45	22 57	0 03	13 60	15 32	3 39	2 28	12 20
11	11 13	23 06	0N20	14 03	16 07	3 34	2 27	12 20
16	11 40	23 16	0 39	14 03	16 40	3 29	2 26	12 21
21	12 07	23 27	0 55	14 00	17 11	3 25	2 25	12 21
26	12 31	23 38	1 06	13 56	17 40	3 20	2 24	12 21
31	12N54	23N50	1N14	13N49	18N08	3S15	2S24	12S21

Moon Phenomena

Max/0 Decl (dy hr mn)
3 21:05 0 N
9 22:08 18N27
16 22:56 0 S
24 11:22 18S32
31 6:15 0 N

Max/0 Lat (dy hr mn)
3 1:27 0 S
9 0:39 5S05
15 20:41 0 N
23 7:36 5N01
30 4:46 0 S

Perigee/Apogee (dy hr m kilometers)
6 4:04 p 357830
18 22:10 a 405933

PH (dy hr mn)
● 6 19:31 16♉41
☽ 13 17:03 23♌21
○ 21 21:16 1♐14
☾ 29 12:13 8♓33

Void of Course Moon

Last Aspect			☽ Ingress	
1 2:57	☿	□	♓	1 14:35
3 5:09	☿	⚹	♈	3 17:05
5 4:18	♅	☌	♉	5 17:11
7 2:12	☿	☌	♊	7 16:36
9 4:16	☿	⚹	♋	9 17:25
11 7:35	☿	□	♌	11 21:33
13 17:03	☉	□	♍	14 5:53
16 9:21	☉	△	♎	16 17:34
18 15:24	♅	☍	♏	19 6:31
21 11:41	♀	☍	♐	21 18:49
23 15:39	♅	△	♑	24 5:35
26 1:13	♅	□	♒	26 14:28
28 20:20	♂	□	♓	28 21:07
30 23:11	♂	△	♈	31 1:10

DAILY ASPECTARIAN

☽□☿ 2:57
☽⊻⚷ 3:52
☽⋕♀ 7:28
☉⚹♆ 12:01
☽⚹♀ 18:17
☽∠♇ 18:48

☽∥♆ 1:40
☽⊻⚳ 1:51
☽⋕♅ 2:08
☽∠♅ 2:08
☽⋕♃ 2:35
☽□♂ 3:36
☽☌♆ 10:24
☉⚹☽ 12:00
☽☍♃ 13:24
☽□♄ 16:39
☽∥⚳ 18:29
☽⚹♇ 20:18
☽∠♀ 22:12

☽⊻♅ 3:30
☽⚹☿ 5:09
☽☌⚷ 7:10
☉△♃ 7:59
☽⋕⚷ 13:50
☉∠☽ 14:46
♂△⚳ 22:16

☽⊻♀ 1:10
☽∥⚷ 4:21
☽△♂ 4:44
☽☌⚳ 4:59
☽∠☿ 5:03
☿∠⚳ 6:16
☽⊻♆ 11:54
☽⊼♃ 14:37
☉⊻☽ 16:46
☽△♄ 17:35
♅⋕♆ 20:22
☽□♇ 21:13
☽⋕⚳ 21:36

5 Th
☽☌♅ 4:18
☽⊻☿ 4:23
☽⚼♂ 4:26
☉⊼♄ 4:40
☿⊻♅ 6:32
☽⊻⚷ 7:46
♂⚼♅ 11:11
☽∠♆ 11:51
☽∥♃ 14:01
♀⊼♂ 14:12
☽⚼♃ 14:28
☽⋕♆ 14:38
☽∥♅ 14:45
☽⚼♄ 17:20

6 F
☽⊼♂ 3:48
☽☌♀ 5:13
☽⊻⚳ 5:54
☽∠⚷ 7:32
☽⚹♆ 11:33
☽△♃ 14:07
♀⊻⚳ 16:54
☽⊼♄ 16:54
☉☌☽ 19:31
☽△♇ 20:38
☽∥♀ 23:26

7 Sa
☽☌☿ 2:12
☽⊻♅ 3:52
☽∠⚳ 6:10
☽⚹⚷ 7:17
♀∠⚷ 10:47
☉△♇ 13:04
☽⚼♇ 20:24

8 Su
☽☍♂ 2:35
☽∠♅ 3:49
☽⚹⚳ 6:40
☽⊻♀ 9:04
☽□♆ 11:19
☉∥☽ 12:40
☽□♃ 13:52
☽☍♄ 16:33
☽⊼♇ 20:34
☽∥☿ 21:27
☉⊻☽ 22:49

9 M
☽⊻☿ 0:30
☽⚹♅ 4:16
☽□⚷ 7:48
☽∠♀ 11:51
♃ D 12:15
☉∥☿ 12:17
♀⚹♆ 12:42
☉☌☿ 15:13

10 Tu
☽∠☿ 0:27
☉∠☽ 1:33
☽⊼♂ 3:03
☽□⚳ 9:36
☽△♆ 13:19
☽⚹♀ 15:40
☽⚹♃ 15:58
☽⊼♄ 18:36
♀△♃ 19:01
☉∥☽ 21:27
☽☍♇ 23:05

11 W
☽⚹☿ 1:11
☽⚼♂ 4:28
☉⚹☽ 5:24
☽□♅ 7:35
☽△⚷ 11:20
☽⚼♆ 15:41
☽∠♃ 18:25
☽∥☿ 19:22
☽⚼♄ 21:01
♀⊼♄ 23:09

12 Th
☽△♂ 6:51
☽∥♀ 7:21
☉⊻♅ 13:45
☽⚼⚷ 14:39
☽△⚳ 16:34
☽⊼♆ 19:08
☽⊻♃ 21:58

13 F
☽△♄ 0:31
☿△♇ 2:46
☽□♀ 3:21
☽□☿ 5:29
☽⊼♇ 5:36
☿∥♀ 8:01
☽△♅ 15:03
☉□☽ 17:03
☽⊼⚷ 19:03
☿☌♀ 19:12
☽⚼⚳ 21:46

14 Sa
♀△♇ 2:21
☽⚼♇ 10:24
☽□♂ 14:29
☽∥♅ 17:51
☽⋕♆ 19:36
☉⚹⚷ 19:47
☽∥♃ 20:13
☽⚼♅ 20:18

15 Su
☽⊼⚳ 3:58
☽☍♆ 5:03
☽☌♃ 8:03
☽□♄ 10:22
☽△☿ 13:32
☽△♇ 16:01
☽△♀ 20:22

16 M
☽⋕⚳ 1:17
☽⊼♅ 2:18
☽☍⚷ 6:25
☉△☽ 9:21
☽∥⚷ 12:31
⚶ ♊ 18:30
☽⚼☿ 18:39
⚳⊻♆ 18:50

17 Tu
☽⚹♂ 0:55
☽⚼♀ 6:09
☽⋕⚷ 9:27
☉∠⚳ 14:42
☽⊼♆ 17:35
☽☍⚳ 18:15
☉⚼☽ 18:27
☽∥⚳ 19:21
☽⊻♃ 20:41
☽⚹♄ 22:36

18 W
☽⊼☿ 0:12
☽□♇ 4:38
☽∠♂ 6:35
♀⊻♅ 8:15
☽☍♅ 15:24
☽⊼♀ 16:12
☽⊼⚷ 19:29

19 Th
☽⚼♆ 0:08
☽⋕♃ 2:02
☽∥♆ 2:53
☽∠♃ 3:15
☉⊼☽ 3:40
☽∠♄ 4:55
☽⋕♅ 5:25
☽⊻♂ 12:12

20 F
♀⚹⚷ 0:29
☽⚼⚷ 1:58
☽△♆ 6:32
☽⊼⚳ 8:57
☽⚹♃ 9:40
☽⊻♄ 11:04
☽☍☿ 11:49
☉ ♊ 14:38
☽⚹♇ 17:19
☽⋕☿ 21:43

21 Sa
☽⊼♅ 4:14
♂∠♇ 4:54
☽△⚷ 8:10
☽☍♀ 11:41
⚳⊼♃ 12:22
☽⚼⚳ 15:53
☉☍☽ 21:16
☽☌♂ 22:44
☽∠♇ 23:13

22 Su
☽⚼♅ 10:09
☉☍♂ 11:18
☿ D 13:21
☽□♆ 18:21
☽□♃ 21:32
☉⚼♇ 21:37
⚳△♄ 21:38
☽☌♄ 22:22
☽△⚳ 22:23
☽⊼☿ 23:08

23 M
☽⊻♇ 4:43
☉⋕♄ 6:33
☽△♅ 15:39
♀∠⚳ 19:18
☽□⚷ 19:23

24 Tu
☽⚼☿ 4:30
☽⊼♀ 5:07
☽⊻♂ 7:47
♀ ♊ 9:46
☿⊻⚳ 9:56
☉⊼☽ 12:51
☉⋕♇ 14:01

25 W
♀☍♂ 2:39
☽⚹♆ 4:27
☽△♃ 7:41
☽⊻♄ 7:57
☽△☿ 9:36
☽□⚳ 9:55
☽∠♂ 11:40
☽⚼♀ 12:55
☽☌♇ 14:22
☉⚼☽ 19:45

26 Th
☽□♅ 1:13
♀⚼♇ 3:45
☽⚹⚷ 4:44
☽∠♆ 8:46
☽⚼♃ 12:01
☽∠♄ 12:01
♃□♄ 12:29
☽⚹♂ 15:05
♂⚼⚳ 18:59
☽△♀ 20:00

27 F
☉△☽ 2:00
☽∠⚷ 8:38
☽⊻♆ 12:32
♂R♏ 13:52
☽⚹♄ 15:33
☽⊼♃ 15:49
☽□☿ 18:46
☽⚹⚳ 19:13
☽⊻♇ 21:57
♀⋕♄ 23:44

28 Sa
☽⋕☿ 0:20
☉⋕♂ 4:05
☽⚹♅ 8:37
☽⊻⚷ 11:55
☽□♂ 20:20
☽∠⚳ 22:54
☉∠♅ 23:37

29 Su
☽∠♇ 0:51
♀⋕♇ 3:09
☽⋕♅ 7:14
☽□♀ 7:49
☽∥♆ 10:43
☽∠♅ 11:22
☉□☽ 12:13
☽⋕♃ 12:27
☿⊻⚳ 18:13
☽☌♆ 18:13
☽□♄ 20:46
☽☍♃ 21:31

30 M
⚳⋕⚷ 0:45
☽⊻⚳ 1:52
☽⚹☿ 1:59
☽⚹♇ 3:05
☽⊻♅ 13:27
☽☌⚷ 16:32
☽⋕⚷ 20:31
☽∥⚳ 21:03
☽△♂ 23:11

31 Tu
♀∠♅ 0:33
☿△♇ 3:10
☽∠☿ 4:43
♀⋕♂ 5:33
☽⋕⚳ 14:59
☽∥⚷ 15:57
☽⚹♀ 16:10
☉⚹☽ 19:11
☽⊻♆ 21:16
☽△♄ 23:24
☽⚼♂ 23:44

June 2016

LONGITUDE

Day	Sid.Time	☉	☽	☽ 12 hour	Mean☊	True☊	☿	♀	♂	⚳	♃	♄	⚷	♅	♆	♇
	h m s	° ' "	° ' "	° ' "	° '	° '	° '	° '	° '	° '	° '	° '	° '	° '	° '	° '
1 W	16 39 38	10♊56 06	13♈38 42	20♈55 45	17♍33.5	18♍01.3	17♉37.6	9♊20.0	28♏28.9	17♈00.9	14♍00.3	13♐17.1	24♓56.5	23♈10.4	11♓59.7	17♑02.8
2 Th	16 43 34	11 53 36	28 16 49	5♉41 18	17 30.3	17R 57.4	18 20.3	10 33.7	28R 09.0	17 20.7	14 04.3	13R 12.7	24 57.8	23 13.0	12 00.1	17R 01.7
3 F	16 47 31	12 51 06	13♉08 21	20 37 01	17 27.1	17 50.7	19 06.8	11 47.4	27 49.5	17 40.4	14 08.5	13 08.2	24 59.1	23 15.5	12 00.4	17 00.5
4 Sa	16 51 28	13 48 35	28 06 13	5♊34 47	17 23.9	17 41.5	19 57.0	13 01.2	27 30.3	17 59.9	14 12.8	13 03.8	25 00.4	23 17.9	12 00.8	16 59.3
5 Su	16 55 24	14 46 03	13♊01 32	20 25 20	17 20.7	17 30.7	20 50.8	14 14.9	27 11.5	18 19.4	14 17.3	12 59.3	25 01.6	23 20.4	12 01.1	16 58.1
6 M	16 59 21	15 43 30	27 45 05	4♋59 51	17 17.6	17 19.5	21 48.1	15 28.7	26 53.3	18 38.7	14 21.9	12 54.9	25 02.8	23 22.8	12 01.4	16 56.9
7 Tu	17 03 17	16 40 56	12♋08 51	19 11 28	17 14.4	17 09.0	22 48.9	16 42.5	26 35.5	18 58.0	14 26.7	12 50.5	25 03.9	23 25.2	12 01.6	16 55.7
8 W	17 07 14	17 38 22	26 07 19	2♌56 11	17 11.2	17 00.4	23 53.0	17 56.2	26 18.3	19 17.1	14 31.7	12 46.0	25 04.9	23 27.5	12 01.8	16 54.5
9 Th	17 11 10	18 35 46	9♌38 04	16 13 05	17 08.0	16 54.3	25 00.4	19 09.9	26 01.7	19 36.1	14 36.8	12 41.6	25 05.9	23 29.8	12 02.0	16 53.2
10 F	17 15 07	19 33 09	22 41 33	29 03 51	17 04.9	16 50.7	26 11.1	20 23.6	25 45.7	19 55.1	14 42.1	12 37.2	25 06.9	23 32.0	12 02.2	16 52.0
11 Sa	17 19 03	20 30 31	5♍20 31	11♍32 06	17 01.7	16D 49.3	27 24.9	21 37.3	25 30.3	20 13.9	14 47.5	12 32.8	25 07.8	23 34.3	12 02.3	16 50.7
12 Su	17 23 00	21 27 52	17 39 16	23 42 39	16 58.5	16R 49.0	28 42.0	22 51.0	25 15.6	20 32.5	14 53.0	12 28.5	25 08.6	23 36.5	12 02.3	16 49.4
13 M	17 26 57	22 25 12	29 42 55	5♎40 47	16 55.3	16 48.9	0♊02.1	24 04.8	25 01.6	20 51.1	14 58.7	12 24.1	25 09.4	23 38.6	12R 02.4	16 48.1
14 Tu	17 30 53	23 22 31	11♎36 53	17 31 53	16 52.2	16 47.9	1 25.3	25 18.5	24 48.3	21 09.6	15 04.6	12 19.8	25 10.2	23 40.7	12 02.4	16 46.8
15 W	17 34 50	24 19 49	23 26 23	29 20 57	16 49.0	16 45.0	2 51.5	26 32.2	24 35.8	21 27.9	15 10.6	12 15.5	25 10.8	23 42.8	12 02.4	16 45.4
16 Th	17 38 46	25 17 06	5♏16 09	11♏12 27	16 45.8	16 39.6	4 20.7	27 45.9	24 24.0	21 46.1	15 16.7	12 11.2	25 11.5	23 44.8	12 02.3	16 44.1
17 F	17 42 43	26 14 22	17 10 17	23 10 01	16 42.6	16 31.6	5 53.0	28 59.6	24 13.0	22 04.2	15 22.9	12 06.9	25 12.1	23 46.8	12 02.2	16 42.7
18 Sa	17 46 39	27 11 38	29 11 59	5♐16 25	16 39.4	16 21.2	7 28.2	0♋13.3	24 02.8	22 22.2	15 29.3	12 02.7	25 12.6	23 48.7	12 02.1	16 41.3
19 Su	17 50 36	28 08 53	11♐23 32	17 33 28	16 36.3	16 09.2	9 06.3	1 27.0	23 53.3	22 40.0	15 35.9	11 58.5	25 13.1	23 50.7	12 02.0	16 40.0
20 M	17 54 32	29 06 08	23 46 19	0♑02 07	16 33.1	15 56.4	10 47.4	2 40.7	23 44.7	22 57.7	15 42.6	11 54.4	25 13.5	23 52.5	12 01.8	16 38.6
21 Tu	17 58 29	0♋03 22	6♑20 54	12 42 39	16 29.9	15 44.1	12 31.4	3 54.4	23 36.9	23 15.3	15 49.4	11 50.3	25 13.9	23 54.4	12 01.6	16 37.2
22 W	18 02 26	1 00 36	19 07 19	25 34 52	16 26.7	15 33.2	14 18.2	5 08.1	23 29.9	23 32.7	15 56.3	11 46.2	25 14.2	23 56.2	12 01.3	16 35.8
23 Th	18 06 22	1 57 49	2♒05 16	8♒38 29	16 23.6	15 24.6	16 07.7	6 21.9	23 23.7	23 50.0	16 03.4	11 42.2	25 14.5	23 57.9	12 01.1	16 34.3
24 F	18 10 19	2 55 02	15 14 31	21 53 22	16 20.4	15 18.8	18 00.0	7 35.6	23 18.3	24 07.2	16 10.6	11 38.2	25 14.7	23 59.6	12 00.8	16 32.9
25 Sa	18 14 15	3 52 15	28 35 05	5♓19 44	16 17.2	15 15.7	19 54.8	8 49.3	23 13.8	24 24.2	16 17.9	11 34.2	25 14.8	24 01.3	12 00.4	16 31.5
26 Su	18 18 12	4 49 28	12♓07 22	18 58 05	16 14.0	15D 14.7	21 52.2	10 03.0	23 10.1	24 41.1	16 25.3	11 30.3	25 14.9	24 02.9	12 00.1	16 30.0
27 M	18 22 08	5 46 41	25 51 57	2♈49 03	16 10.9	15R 14.8	23 51.8	11 16.7	23 07.2	24 57.9	16 32.9	11 26.4	25R 15.0	24 04.5	11 59.7	16 28.6
28 Tu	18 26 05	6 43 53	9♈49 24	16 52 57	16 07.7	15 15.0	25 53.7	12 30.4	23 05.1	25 14.5	16 40.6	11 22.6	25 15.0	24 06.0	11 59.2	16 27.1
29 W	18 30 01	7 41 06	23 59 37	1♉09 12	16 04.5	15 14.0	27 57.5	13 44.2	23D 03.9	25 30.9	16 48.4	11 18.9	25 14.9	24 07.5	11 58.8	16 25.7
30 Th	18 33 58	8♋38 19	8♉21 22	15 35 45	16♍01.3	15♍11.0	0♋03.0	14♋57.9	23♏03.5	25♈47.2	16♍56.4	11♐15.2	25♓14.8	24♈08.9	11♓58.3	16♑24.2

1st of Mon

Julian Day
2457540.5
Obliquity
23°26'04"
SVP 5♓01'5
GC 27♐04.
Eris 23♈26

Day	⚴
1	6♓12.7
6	6 40.5
11	7 01.2
16	7 14.2
21	7 19.2
26	7 15.9

Day	⚵
1	0♏41.6
6	0 10.1
11	29♎46.8
16	29 31.7
21	29 24.8
26	29 25.8

Day	⚶
1	6♊38.7
6	8 49.2
11	10 59.4
16	13 09.0
21	15 18.2
26	17 26.8

DECLINATION and LATITUDE

Day	☉ Decl	☽ Decl	☽ Lat	☽12h Decl	☿ Decl	☿ Lat	♀ Decl	♀ Lat	♂ Decl	♂ Lat	⚳ Decl	⚳ Lat	♃ Decl	♃ Lat	♄ Decl	♄ Lat
1 W	22N05	3N22	2S11	5N37	13N28	3S46	21N37	0S14	21S25	1S38	1S37	8S59	7N29	1N17	20S36	1N48
2 Th	22 13	7 49	3 16	9 54	13 41	3 45	21 50	0 12	21 23	1 41	1 31	9 00	7 27	1 17	20 35	1 48
3 F	22 20	11 50	4 08	13 36	13 55	3 43	22 02	0 10	21 21	1 44	1 25	9 02	7 25	1 17	20 35	1 48
4 Sa	22 27	15 08	4 43	16 24	14 12	3 40	22 14	0 07	21 20	1 46	1 19	9 03	7 23	1 17	20 34	1 48
5 Su	22 34	17 24	4 60	18 06	14 29	3 36	22 25	0 05	21 18	1 49	1 13	9 04	7 22	1 17	20 34	1 48
6 M	22 40	18 29	4 56	18 34	14 48	3 32	22 36	0 03	21 16	1 52	1 07	9 06	7 20	1 16	20 33	1 48
7 Tu	22 46	18 21	4 33	17 51	15 08	3 27	22 46	0 00	21 14	1 54	1 01	9 07	7 18	1 16	20 33	1 48
8 W	22 52	17 05	3 54	16 05	15 29	3 21	22 55	0N02	21 13	1 57	0 56	9 09	7 15	1 16	20 32	1 48
9 Th	22 57	14 53	3 03	13 31	15 52	3 15	23 04	0 05	21 11	1 59	0 50	9 10	7 13	1 16	20 32	1 48
10 F	23 01	11 60	2 04	10 21	16 15	3 08	23 12	0 07	21 10	2 02	0 44	9 12	7 11	1 16	20 32	1 48
11 Sa	23 06	8 37	1 00	6 48	16 39	3 00	23 20	0 09	21 08	2 04	0 39	9 13	7 09	1 15	20 31	1 48
12 Su	23 10	4 57	0N04	3 03	17 04	2 52	23 26	0 12	21 07	2 06	0 34	9 15	7 07	1 15	20 31	1 47
13 M	23 13	1 09	1 08	0S45	17 29	2 44	23 32	0 14	21 06	2 08	0 28	9 17	7 04	1 15	20 30	1 47
14 Tu	23 16	2S38	2 07	4 30	17 55	2 35	23 38	0 16	21 04	2 10	0 23	9 18	7 02	1 15	20 30	1 47
15 W	23 19	6 18	3 01	8 03	18 21	2 25	23 42	0 19	21 03	2 12	0 18	9 20	6 59	1 15	20 29	1 47
16 Th	23 21	9 43	3 47	11 17	18 47	2 15	23 46	0 21	21 02	2 14	0 13	9 21	6 57	1 14	20 29	1 47
17 F	23 23	12 45	4 23	14 06	19 14	2 05	23 49	0 23	21 01	2 16	0 08	9 23	6 54	1 14	20 28	1 47
18 Sa	23 24	15 17	4 48	16 20	19 40	1 55	23 52	0 26	21 01	2 18	0 03	9 25	6 51	1 14	20 28	1 47
19 Su	23 25	17 12	4 60	17 52	20 06	1 44	23 54	0 28	21 00	2 20	0N02	9 26	6 49	1 14	20 27	1 47
20 M	23 26	18 20	4 58	18 34	20 32	1 33	23 55	0 30	20 60	2 22	0 07	9 28	6 46	1 14	20 27	1 47
21 Tu	23 26	18 35	4 42	18 22	20 57	1 21	23 55	0 32	20 59	2 24	0 12	9 30	6 43	1 14	20 27	1 46
22 W	23 26	17 55	4 11	17 14	21 22	1 10	23 55	0 35	20 59	2 25	0 17	9 32	6 40	1 13	20 26	1 46
23 Th	23 25	16 19	3 28	15 11	21 45	0 58	23 54	0 37	20 59	2 27	0 21	9 33	6 37	1 13	20 26	1 46
24 F	23 24	13 50	2 32	12 18	22 07	0 46	23 52	0 39	20 59	2 28	0 26	9 35	6 34	1 13	20 25	1 46
25 Sa	23 23	10 36	1 27	8 45	22 29	0 35	23 50	0 41	20 59	2 30	0 30	9 37	6 31	1 13	20 25	1 46
26 Su	23 21	6 45	0 17	4 40	22 48	0 23	23 46	0 43	20 60	2 31	0 34	9 39	6 28	1 13	20 25	1 46
27 M	23 19	2 30	0S56	0 17	23 03	0 11	23 43	0 45	21 00	2 32	0 39	9 41	6 25	1 13	20 24	1 46
28 Tu	23 16	1N57	2 07	4N10	23 22	0 00	23 38	0 47	21 01	2 34	0 43	9 43	6 22	1 12	20 24	1 46
29 W	23 13	6 21	3 11	8 27	23 36	0N11	23 33	0 49	21 02	2 35	0 47	9 44	6 19	1 12	20 24	1 45
30 Th	23N09	10N27	4S04	12N17	23N48	0N22	23N27	0N51	21S03	2S36	0N51	9S46	6N16	1N12	20S23	1N45

Day	⚷ Decl	⚷ Lat	♅ Decl	♅ Lat	♆ Decl	♆ Lat	♇ Decl	♇ Lat
1	1N51	4N12	8N27	0S36	7S50	0S50	20S56	1N
6	1 54	4 13	8 31	0 36	7 49	0 50	20 57	1
11	1 57	4 14	8 36	0 36	7 49	0 50	20 58	1
16	1 59	4 15	8 39	0 36	7 49	0 51	20 60	1
21	2 01	4 15	8 43	0 36	7 50	0 51	21 01	1
26	2 02	4 16	8 46	0 36	7 51	0 51	21 02	1

Day	⚴ Decl	⚴ Lat	⚵ Decl	⚵ Lat	⚶ Decl	⚶ Lat	Eris Decl	Eris Lat
1	12N58	23N52	1N15	13N48	18N13	3S15	2S24	12S
6	13 19	24 04	1 17	13 39	18 38	3 10	2 23	12
11	13 37	24 15	1 16	13 30	19 01	3 06	2 23	12
16	13 52	24 27	1 11	13 19	19 22	3 01	2 22	12
21	14 03	24 37	1 03	13 08	19 42	2 57	2 22	12
26	14 11	24 47	0 52	12 56	19 59	2 53	2 22	12

Moon Phenomena

Max/0 Decl

dy	hr mn	
6	9:07	18N34
13	7:15	0 S
20	19:00	18S37
27	13:33	0 N

Perigee/Apogee

dy	hr m		kilometers
3	10:54	p	361143
15	12:02	a	405023

Max/0 Lat

dy	hr mn	
5	7:05	5S01
11	22:21	0 N
19	9:06	5N01
26	5:29	0 S

PH	dy	hr mn	
●	5	3:01	14♊53
☽	12	8:11	21♍47
○	20	11:03	29♐33
☾	27	18:20	6♈30

Void of Course Moon

Last Aspect			☽ Ingress		
1	15:43	♅ ☌	♉	2	2:
3	23:04	♂ ☍	♊	4	3:
5	16:49	♅ ⚹	♋	6	3:
8	0:19	♂ △	♌	8	6:
10	7:15	☿ □	♍	10	13:
12	14:48	♂ ⚹	♎	13	0:
15	7:01	♀ △	♏	15	13:
17	13:54	♂ ☌	♐	18	1:
20	11:03	☉ ☍	♑	20	11:
22	8:58	♅ □	♒	22	20:
24	15:49	♅ ⚹	♓	25	2:
26	19:56	☿ □	♈	27	7:
29	7:47	☿ ⚹	♉	29	10:

DAILY ASPECTARIAN

1 W	☽⚻♃	0:36
	⚳□♇	2:07
	☽□♇	5:37
	☽☌⚳	5:42
	☽⚺☿	6:54
	☽☌♅	15:43
	☽⚺⚷	18:35
	☽∠♀	19:10
	☉∠☽	21:35
	☽∠♆	21:55
	☽∥♃	22:00
	☽⚻♂	23:48
	☽⚼♄	23:53
2 Th	☽#♆	0:05
	☽⚼♃	1:18
	☉□♆	2:43
	☽∥♅	3:41
	☽∠⚷	18:55
	☽⚺♀	21:38
	☽⚹♆	22:11
	☉⚺☽	23:30
	☽⚻♄	24:00
3 F	☽△♃	1:37
	♀□♆	4:15
	☽△♇	6:12
	☉☍♄	6:38
	☽⚺⚳	7:26
	☽☌☿	10:09
	☽∥☿	15:46
	☽⚺♅	16:17
	☽⚹⚷	19:02
	☽☍♂	23:04
4 Sa	♀☍♄	0:48
	☽⚼♇	6:13
	☽∠⚳	8:02
	☉□♃	10:58
	☽∠♅	16:25
	☽□♆	22:22
	☽☍♄	23:56
5 Su	♀□♃	0:50
	☽□♃	2:03
	☽☌♀	2:09
	☉☌☽	3:01
	☽⚻♇	6:23
	☽⚹⚳	8:47
	☽⚺☿	13:34
	☽⚹♅	16:49
	☽□⚷	19:33
	☽⚻♂	22:36
6 M	☽∠☿	16:09
	☉☌♀	21:40
	☽⚼♂	23:05
	☉∥♀	23:48
	☽△♆	23:48
7 Tu	☽⚻♄	1:10
	☽⚹♃	3:55
	♀⚻♇	4:14
	☉⚻♇	6:03
	☽☍♇	8:07
	☉⚺☽	8:16
	☽⚺♀	8:30
	☽□⚳	11:53
	☿⚺♅	14:15
	☽□♅	19:21
	☽⚹☿	19:46
	☽△⚷	22:11
	⚵R♎	23:04
8 W	☽△♂	0:19
	☽⚼♆	1:35
	☽⚼♄	2:52
	☽∠♃	6:01
	☉∠☽	12:21
	☽∠♀	13:12
	☽∥☿	15:48
9 Th	☽⚼⚷	0:50
	☿⚹⚷	1:56
	☽⚻♆	4:21
	☽△♄	5:31
	☽⚺♃	9:07
	♀⚹⚳	11:30
	☽⚻♇	13:13
	☿☍♂	17:02
	☉⚹☽	17:41
	☽△⚳	18:42
	☽⚹♀	19:16
10 F	☽△♅	1:35
	☽⚻⚷	4:33
	☽□♂	5:38
	☽□☿	7:15
	☉⚹⚳	13:39
	☽⚼♇	17:18
	☽⚼⚳	23:47
11 Sa	☽∥♅	0:08
	☽#♆	5:19
	☽⚼♅	6:15
	☽∥♃	9:52
	☽☍♆	12:59
	☽□♄	13:54
	☽☌♃	18:31
	☽△♇	22:22
12 Su	☽⚻⚳	5:51
	☉□☽	8:11
	♂△⚷	11:11
	☽□♀	11:27
	☽⚻♅	11:50
	☽⚹♂	14:48
	☽☍⚷	14:52
	♀⚹♅	15:14
	☽∥⚷	18:54
	☿ ♊	23:24
13 M	☽△☿	0:43
	☽#⚳	4:23
	☽∥⚳	9:59
	♀⚻♂	15:40
	☽#⚷	19:43
	☽∠♂	20:24
	♆ R	20:43
	♀□⚷	21:16
14 Tu	☽⚻♆	0:52
	☽⚹♄	1:26
	☿⚼♇	5:58
	☽⚺♃	7:05
	☉⚹♅	7:55
	☽□♇	10:27
	☽⚼☿	11:05
	☽☍⚳	19:53
15 W	☽☍♅	0:33
	☉△☽	1:58
	☽⚺♂	2:19
	☽⚻⚷	3:32
	☽#♃	4:38
	☉⚻♂	5:32
	☽△♀	7:01
	☽⚼♆	7:19
	☽∠♄	7:42
	☽∥♆	10:27
	☽∠♃	13:48
	☽#♅	16:19
	☉□⚷	21:37
	☽⚻☿	21:51
16 Th	☽⚼⚷	9:57
	☉⚼☽	11:01
	☽△♆	13:40
	☽⚺♄	13:53
	☽⚼♀	16:53
	☽⚹♃	20:22
	☽⚹♇	23:05
17 F	☽⚻⚳	10:04
	☽⚻♅	13:15
	☽☌♂	13:54
	☽△⚷	16:04
	♀ ♋	19:40
	☉⚻☽	19:41
	☿∠⚳	22:10
18 Sa	☽⚻♀	2:15
	♄□♆	3:30
	☽∠♇	4:55
	☽⚼⚳	16:31
	♂∥♇	18:39
	☽☍☿	18:50
	☽⚼♅	19:00
	☿∠♅	20:08
19 Su	☽☌♄	1:08
	☽□♆	1:15
	♂⚻♅	5:56
	☽□♃	8:16
	☽⚺♇	10:15
	☿#♄	19:31
	☽△⚳	22:24
	☽⚺♂	23:57
20 M	☽△♅	0:12
	☽□⚷	2:48
	☉☍☽	11:03
	☿☍♄	14:57
	☿□♆	17:12
	☽☍♀	18:52
	☉ ♋	22:35
21 Tu	☿#♂	2:09
	☿#♇	3:40
	☽∠♂	4:15
	☽⚺♄	10:18
	☽⚹♆	10:43
	⚴ R	13:22
	☽⚻☿	13:31
	☽△♃	18:00
	☽☌♇	19:17
	♂⚻⚳	21:09
22 W	☽⚹♂	8:04
	☽□⚳	8:25
	☽□♅	8:58
	☽⚹⚷	11:22
	☽∠♄	14:08
	☽∠♆	14:40
	⚵ D	20:02
	☽⚼☿	21:57
	☽⚼♃	22:05
	☿□♃	23:00
	☉⚻☽	23:45
23 Th	☿⚻♇	5:40
	☽⚻♀	8:39
	⚳☌♅	12:12
	☽∠⚷	14:55
	☽⚹♄	17:29
	☽⚺♆	18:09
24 F	☽⚻♃	1:42
	☽⚺♇	2:22
	☉⚼☽	5:13
	☽△☿	5:49
	♀⚼♂	13:05
	☽□♂	14:28
	☽⚼♀	14:36
	☽⚹♅	15:49
	☽⚹⚳	16:21
	☽⚺⚷	18:02
25 Sa	☽∠♇	5:14
	☉△☽	10:08
	☽#♅	11:53
	☽∥♆	17:31
	☽∠♅	18:34
	☽∠⚳	19:37
	☽△♀	19:59
	☽□♄	22:55
	☽☌♆	23:47
26 Su	☽#♃	1:41
	☽☍♃	7:37
	☽⚹♇	7:40
	♃△♇	12:31
	☿⚻♂	15:17
	☽△♂	19:15
	☽□☿	19:56
	☽⚺♅	20:53
	☽⚺⚳	22:24
	☽☌⚷	22:56
27 M	☽#⚷	2:32
	☿⚹♅	2:33
	♀⚻♄	3:01
	☽#⚳	9:56
	⚷ R	11:11
	♀△♆	13:54
	☿⚹⚳	15:07
	☉∥☿	15:41
	☿□⚷	16:26
	☽∥⚳	17:16
	☉□☽	18:20
	☽⚼♂	21:02
28 Tu	☽∥⚷	0:30
	⚳⚺⚷	0:47
	☽△♄	2:38
	☽⚺♆	3:41
	☽□♀	5:01
	☽□♇	11:15
	☽⚻♃	11:45
	☿∥♀	19:43
	☽⚻♂	22:26
	☽∥♃	23:49
29 W	☽☌♅	0:13
	☽⚺⚷	2:07
	☽☌⚳	2:36
	☽⚼♄	3:53
	☽∠♆	5:01
	☽⚹☿	7:47
	☽#♆	8:32
	☉⚼♂	9:27
	☽⚼♃	13:13
	☽∥♅	14:01
	☿ ♋	23:25
	♂ D	23:40
30 Th	☉⚹☽	0:30
	☽∠⚷	3:08
	♂∥♇	3:43
	☽⚻♄	4:47
	☽⚹♆	6:00
	☽⚹♀	11:58
	☽∠☿	12:59
	☽△♇	13:19
	☽△♃	14:21

LONGITUDE

Day	Sid.Time	☉	☽	☽ 12 hour	Mean☊	True☊	☿	♀	♂	⚳	♃	♄	⚷	♅	♆	♇
	h m s	° ' "	° ' "	° ' "	° '	° '	° '	° '	° '	° '	° '	° '	° '	° '	° '	° '
1 F	18 37 55	9♋35 33	22♉51 47	0♊08 49	15♍58.1	15♍05.6	2♋10.1	16♋11.6	23♏03.9	26♈03.3	17♍04.4	11♐11.5	25♓14.7	24♈10.3	11♓57.7	16♑22.7
2 Sa	18 41 51	10 32 46	7♊26 08	14 42 55	15 55.0	14R 57.9	4 18.4	17 25.4	23 05.1	26 19.3	17 12.6	11R 07.9	25R 14.5	24 11.7	11R 57.2	16R 21.3
3 Su	18 45 48	11 30 00	21 58 18	29 11 26	15 51.8	14 48.7	6 27.7	18 39.1	23 07.2	26 35.1	17 20.9	11 04.4	25 14.2	24 13.0	11 56.6	16 19.8
4 M	18 49 44	12 27 13	6♋21 28	13♋27 37	15 48.6	14 39.0	8 37.6	19 52.9	23 10.1	26 50.7	17 29.3	11 00.9	25 13.9	24 14.3	11 56.0	16 18.3
5 Tu	18 53 41	13 24 27	20 29 13	27 25 43	15 45.4	14 30.0	10 47.9	21 06.6	23 13.8	27 06.2	17 37.8	10 57.5	25 13.5	24 15.5	11 55.3	16 16.8
6 W	18 57 37	14 21 40	4♌16 40	11♌01 48	15 42.3	14 22.5	12 58.3	22 20.4	23 18.3	27 21.5	17 46.4	10 54.2	25 13.1	24 16.7	11 54.7	16 15.3
7 Th	19 01 34	15 18 54	17 41 00	24 14 14	15 39.1	14 17.2	15 08.5	23 34.1	23 23.6	27 36.7	17 55.2	10 50.9	25 12.6	24 17.8	11 54.0	16 13.9
8 F	19 05 31	16 16 07	0♍41 41	7♍03 35	15 35.9	14 14.3	17 18.3	24 47.9	23 29.7	27 51.6	18 04.0	10 47.7	25 12.1	24 18.9	11 53.2	16 12.4
9 Sa	19 09 27	17 13 20	13 20 18	19 32 17	15 32.7	14D 13.4	19 27.4	26 01.6	23 36.5	28 06.4	18 12.9	10 44.6	25 11.5	24 19.9	11 52.5	16 10.9
10 Su	19 13 24	18 10 33	25 40 03	1♎44 11	15 29.6	14 13.8	21 35.6	27 15.3	23 44.2	28 21.0	18 22.0	10 41.5	25 10.8	24 20.9	11 51.7	16 09.4
11 M	19 17 20	19 07 46	7♎45 16	13 43 57	15 26.4	14 14.8	23 42.6	28 29.1	23 52.6	28 35.4	18 31.1	10 38.5	25 10.1	24 21.8	11 50.9	16 07.9
12 Tu	19 21 17	20 04 59	19 40 53	25 36 44	15 23.2	14R 15.3	25 48.5	29 42.8	24 01.7	28 49.6	18 40.4	10 35.6	25 09.4	24 22.7	11 50.0	16 06.4
13 W	19 25 13	21 02 12	1♏32 06	7♏27 39	15 20.0	14 14.6	27 53.0	0♌56.6	24 11.5	29 03.6	18 49.7	10 32.7	25 08.6	24 23.5	11 49.2	16 04.9
14 Th	19 29 10	21 59 25	13 23 59	19 21 38	15 16.8	14 12.1	29 55.9	2 10.3	24 22.1	29 17.4	18 59.2	10 29.9	25 07.8	24 24.3	11 48.3	16 03.5
15 F	19 33 06	22 56 38	25 21 11	1♐23 04	15 13.7	14 07.7	1♌57.3	3 24.1	24 33.4	29 31.0	19 08.7	10 27.2	25 06.9	24 25.1	11 47.3	16 02.0
16 Sa	19 37 03	23 53 51	7♐27 44	13 35 33	15 10.5	14 01.3	3 57.1	4 37.8	24 45.4	29 44.5	19 18.4	10 24.6	25 05.9	24 25.8	11 46.4	16 00.5
17 Su	19 40 59	24 51 05	19 46 48	26 01 43	15 07.3	13 53.6	5 55.2	5 51.5	24 58.0	29 57.7	19 28.1	10 22.1	25 04.9	24 26.4	11 45.4	15 59.1
18 M	19 44 56	25 48 18	2♑20 29	8♑43 09	15 04.1	13 45.2	7 51.5	7 05.3	25 11.3	0♉10.7	19 37.9	10 19.6	25 03.9	24 27.0	11 44.4	15 57.6
19 Tu	19 48 53	26 45 32	15 09 46	21 40 16	15 01.0	13 37.0	9 46.0	8 19.0	25 25.3	0 23.6	19 47.8	10 17.3	25 02.8	24 27.6	11 43.4	15 56.2
20 W	19 52 49	27 42 47	28 14 33	4♒52 29	14 57.8	13 29.9	11 38.8	9 32.7	25 39.9	0 36.2	19 57.8	10 15.0	25 01.7	24 28.1	11 42.3	15 54.7
21 Th	19 56 46	28 40 01	11♒33 51	18 18 26	14 54.6	13 24.4	13 29.8	10 46.5	25 55.2	0 48.5	20 07.9	10 12.8	25 00.5	24 28.6	11 41.3	15 53.3
22 F	20 00 42	29 37 17	25 06 00	1♓56 18	14 51.4	13 21.0	15 19.0	12 00.2	26 11.0	1 00.7	20 18.1	10 10.6	24 59.2	24 29.0	11 40.2	15 51.8
23 Sa	20 04 39	0♌34 33	8♓49 06	15 44 10	14 48.3	13D 19.6	17 06.4	13 13.9	26 27.5	1 12.7	20 28.4	10 08.6	24 58.0	24 29.3	11 39.0	15 50.4
24 Su	20 08 35	1 31 50	22 41 16	29 40 14	14 45.1	13 19.8	18 52.0	14 27.7	26 44.6	1 24.4	20 38.7	10 06.6	24 56.6	24 29.6	11 37.9	15 49.0
25 M	20 12 32	2 29 07	6♈40 51	13♈42 58	14 41.9	13 21.0	20 35.8	15 41.4	27 02.2	1 35.9	20 49.1	10 04.8	24 55.2	24 29.9	11 36.7	15 47.6
26 Tu	20 16 28	3 26 26	20 46 23	27 50 56	14 38.7	13R 22.2	22 17.9	16 55.1	27 20.4	1 47.1	20 59.6	10 03.0	24 53.8	24 30.1	11 35.5	15 46.2
27 W	20 20 25	4 23 45	4♉56 24	12♉02 36	14 35.5	13 22.7	23 58.2	18 08.9	27 39.2	1 58.1	21 10.2	10 01.3	24 52.3	24 30.3	11 34.3	15 44.8
28 Th	20 24 22	5 21 06	19 09 15	26 16 05	14 32.4	13 22.0	25 36.8	19 22.6	27 58.6	2 08.9	21 20.9	9 59.7	24 50.8	24 30.4	11 33.1	15 43.4
29 F	20 28 18	6 18 27	3♊22 45	10♊28 51	14 29.2	13 19.6	27 13.6	20 36.3	28 18.5	2 19.5	21 31.6	9 58.2	24 49.3	24R 30.5	11 31.8	15 42.0
30 Sa	20 32 15	7 15 50	17 34 00	24 37 44	14 26.0	13 15.7	28 48.6	21 50.1	28 38.9	2 29.7	21 42.4	9 56.8	24 47.7	24 30.5	11 30.6	15 40.7
31 Su	20 36 11	8♌13 14	1♋39 35	8♋39 03	14♍22.8	13♍10.8	0♍21.9	23♌03.8	28♏59.8	2♉39.8	21♍53.3	9♐55.4	24♓46.0	24♈30.4	11♓29.3	15♑39.3

1st of Month

Julian Day # 2457570.5
Obliquity 23°26'04"
SVP 5♓01'50"
GC 27♐04.2
Eris 23♈36.7

Day	⚴	⚵	⚶
1	7♓04.0R	29♎34.5	19♊34.9
6	6 43.3R	29 50.8	21 42.2
11	6 13.8R	0♏14.1	23 48.8
16	5 35.6R	0 44.2	25 54.4
21	4 49.2R	1 20.6	27 59.1
26	3 54.9R	2 02.8	0♋02.7
31	2 53.6R	2 50.6	2 05.2

DECLINATION and LATITUDE

Day	☉ Decl	☽ Decl	☽ Lat	☽12h Decl	☿ Decl	☿ Lat	♀ Decl	♀ Lat	♂ Decl	♂ Lat	⚳ Decl	⚳ Lat	♃ Decl	♃ Lat	♄ Decl	♄ Lat
1 F	23N05	13N57	4S41	15N24	23N57	0N32	23N20	0N53	21S04	2S37	0N55	9S48	6N12	1N12	20S23	1N45
2 Sa	23 01	16 36	5 01	17 32	24 04	0 42	23 13	0 55	21 06	2 38	0 58	9 50	6 09	1 12	20 23	1 45
3 Su	22 56	18 11	5 01	18 32	24 08	0 51	23 05	0 57	21 07	2 39	1 02	9 52	6 06	1 12	20 22	1 45
4 M	22 51	18 35	4 42	18 20	24 09	0 60	22 56	0 59	21 09	2 40	1 06	9 54	6 02	1 11	20 22	1 45
5 Tu	22 46	17 49	4 06	17 02	24 08	1 08	22 47	1 01	21 11	2 41	1 09	9 56	5 59	1 11	20 22	1 44
6 W	22 40	16 00	3 17	14 46	24 03	1 15	22 37	1 02	21 13	2 42	1 13	9 58	5 55	1 11	20 22	1 44
7 Th	22 33	13 21	2 17	11 47	23 56	1 22	22 26	1 04	21 15	2 43	1 16	10 00	5 52	1 11	20 21	1 44
8 F	22 27	10 06	1 12	8 19	23 46	1 28	22 15	1 06	21 17	2 44	1 19	10 02	5 48	1 11	20 21	1 44
9 Sa	22 20	6 28	0 05	4 35	23 34	1 34	22 02	1 07	21 20	2 45	1 23	10 04	5 45	1 11	20 20	1 44
10 Su	22 12	2 39	1N01	0 44	23 19	1 38	21 50	1 09	21 22	2 45	1 26	10 06	5 41	1 11	20 20	1 44
11 M	22 04	1S12	2 03	3S05	23 01	1 42	21 37	1 10	21 25	2 46	1 29	10 08	5 37	1 10	20 20	1 43
12 Tu	21 56	4 56	2 59	6 44	22 42	1 45	21 23	1 12	21 28	2 46	1 32	10 11	5 33	1 10	20 20	1 43
13 W	21 47	8 28	3 46	10 07	22 20	1 47	21 08	1 13	21 31	2 47	1 34	10 13	5 30	1 10	20 19	1 43
14 Th	21 38	11 39	4 24	13 05	21 56	1 49	20 53	1 15	21 34	2 48	1 37	10 15	5 26	1 10	20 19	1 43
15 F	21 29	14 23	4 51	15 32	21 30	1 49	20 37	1 16	21 37	2 48	1 40	10 17	5 22	1 10	20 19	1 43
16 Sa	21 19	16 32	5 05	17 21	21 02	1 49	20 21	1 17	21 41	2 49	1 42	10 19	5 18	1 10	20 19	1 42
17 Su	21 09	17 58	5 05	18 22	20 33	1 49	20 04	1 18	21 44	2 49	1 45	10 21	5 14	1 10	20 19	1 42
18 M	20 59	18 34	4 51	18 31	20 02	1 48	19 47	1 19	21 48	2 49	1 47	10 24	5 10	1 10	20 19	1 42
19 Tu	20 48	18 14	4 22	17 42	19 30	1 46	19 29	1 21	21 52	2 50	1 49	10 26	5 06	1 09	20 18	1 42
20 W	20 37	16 56	3 39	15 56	18 57	1 43	19 10	1 22	21 56	2 50	1 51	10 28	5 02	1 09	20 18	1 42
21 Th	20 25	14 42	2 43	13 15	18 22	1 40	18 51	1 23	21 59	2 50	1 53	10 30	4 58	1 09	20 18	1 41
22 F	20 14	11 38	1 37	9 50	17 47	1 37	18 31	1 23	22 04	2 51	1 55	10 33	4 54	1 09	20 18	1 41
23 Sa	20 01	7 53	0 24	5 49	17 11	1 33	18 11	1 24	22 08	2 51	1 57	10 35	4 50	1 09	20 18	1 41
24 Su	19 49	3 41	0S51	1 28	16 34	1 28	17 51	1 25	22 12	2 51	1 59	10 37	4 46	1 09	20 18	1 41
25 M	19 36	0N46	2 03	2N59	15 56	1 23	17 30	1 26	22 16	2 51	2 00	10 40	4 41	1 09	20 18	1 41
26 Tu	19 23	5 11	3 09	7 18	15 18	1 18	17 08	1 26	22 20	2 52	2 02	10 42	4 37	1 09	20 18	1 40
27 W	19 09	9 20	4 04	11 13	14 40	1 12	16 46	1 27	22 25	2 52	2 03	10 45	4 33	1 08	20 18	1 40
28 Th	18 56	12 57	4 44	14 30	14 01	1 06	16 23	1 27	22 30	2 52	2 05	10 47	4 29	1 08	20 18	1 40
29 F	18 42	15 49	5 06	16 53	13 21	0 59	16 01	1 28	22 34	2 52	2 06	10 49	4 24	1 08	20 18	1 40
30 Sa	18 27	17 42	5 10	18 15	12 42	0 52	15 37	1 28	22 39	2 52	2 07	10 52	4 20	1 08	20 18	1 40
31 Su	18N12	18N30	4S55	18N29	12N02	0N44	15N13	1N29	22S44	2S52	2N08	10S54	4N16	1N08	20S18	1N39

Day	⚷ Decl	⚷ Lat	♅ Decl	♅ Lat	♆ Decl	♆ Lat	♇ Decl	♇ Lat
1	2N03	4N17	8N48	0S36	7S52	0S51	21S03	1N23
6	2 03	4 18	8 51	0 37	7 53	0 51	21 05	1 22
11	2 02	4 19	8 52	0 37	7 55	0 51	21 06	1 22
16	2 02	4 20	8 54	0 37	7 56	0 52	21 08	1 21
21	2 00	4 20	8 55	0 37	7 59	0 52	21 09	1 21
26	1 58	4 21	8 55	0 37	8 01	0 52	21 10	1 20
31	1N56	4N22	8N55	0S37	8S03	0S52	21S12	1N20

Day	⚴ Decl	⚴ Lat	⚵ Decl	⚵ Lat	⚶ Decl	⚶ Lat	Eris Decl	Eris Lat
1	14N15	24N56	0N37	12N44	20N14	2S48	2S22	12S24
6	14 15	25 03	0 21	12 33	20 27	2 44	2 22	12 24
11	14 09	25 08	0 02	12 21	20 37	2 40	2 23	12 25
16	13 59	25 10	0S19	12 09	20 46	2 36	2 23	12 25
21	13 42	25 10	0 42	11 57	20 54	2 32	2 23	12 26
26	13 20	25 05	1 07	11 46	20 59	2 27	2 24	12 26
31	12N52	24N57	1S32	11N36	21N02	2S23	2S25	12S27

Moon Phenomena

Max/0 Decl

dy	hr mn	
3	20:11	18N36
10	16:32	0 S
18	3:34	18S34
24	19:54	0 N
31	4:44	18N32

Max/0 Lat

dy	hr mn	
2	12:18	5S03
9	1:42	0 N
16	12:43	5N07
23	7:50	0 S
29	16:49	5S11

Perigee/Apogee

dy	hr m		kilometers
1	6:36	p	365985
13	5:20	a	404268
27	11:38	p	369662

PH	dy	hr mn	
●	4	11:02	12♋54
☽	12	0:53	20♎07
○	19	22:58	27♑40
☾	26	23:01	4♉21

Void of Course Moon

Last Aspect				☽ Ingress		
1	0:20	♂	☍	♊	1	11:45
3	3:44	♅	⚹	♋	3	13:21
5	6:31	♅	□	♌	5	16:29
7	12:08	♅	△	♍	7	22:42
10	3:29	♀	⚹	♎	10	8:33
12	15:02	☿	□	♏	12	20:53
14	22:23	♂	☌	♐	15	9:15
17	8:58	♅	△	♑	17	19:34
19	22:58	☉	☍	♒	20	3:11
22	1:57	♂	□	♓	22	8:36
24	7:07	♂	△	♈	24	12:34
26	6:20	♅	☌	♉	26	15:39
28	15:14	♂	☍	♊	28	18:18
30	11:48	♅	⚹	♋	30	21:10

DAILY ASPECTARIAN

1 F	☽☍♂ 0:20; ☽⚺♅ 2:10; ☉∠☽ 3:03; ♀☍♇ 3:33; ☽⚹⚷ 3:55; ☽⚺⚳ 5:22; ⚳⚼♄ 10:02; ☽⚼♇ 14:00; ☽∠♀ 14:59; ☽⚺☿ 17:58; ♀⚹♃ 19:19
2 Sa	☽∠♅ 2:54; ☉⚺☽ 5:29; ☽☍♄ 6:04; ☽∠⚳ 6:31; ☽□♆ 7:26; ☉⚻♄ 13:53; ☽⚻♇ 14:41; ☽□♃ 16:16; ☽⚺♀ 18:00
3 Su	☽⚻♂ 1:55; ☽⚹♅ 3:44; ☽□⚷ 5:25; ☽⚹⚳ 7:48; ☉△♆ 11:03; ☿⚼♂ 18:48
4 M	☽⚼♂ 3:04; ☽☌☿ 4:31; ⚳∠♆ 7:47; ☽⚻♄ 7:50; ☽△♆ 9:24; ☉☌☽ 11:02; ☽☍♇ 16:49; ☽⚹♃ 19:03
5 Tu	☽☌♀ 1:10; ☿⚻♄ 1:43; ☽△♂ 4:45; ☉∥♀ 6:24; ☽□♅ 6:31; ☽△⚷ 8:10; ☽⚼♄ 9:25; ☽⚼♆ 11:07; ☽□⚳ 11:39; ☿△♆ 12:21; ☽∠♃ 21:19
6 W	☽⚼⚷ 10:33; ☽△♄ 11:44; ☽⚻♆ 13:34; ☽⚺☿ 18:30; ☉⚺☽ 19:23; ♀△♂ 20:18; ☽⚻♇ 21:22
7 Th	☽⚺♃ 0:26; ☉☌☿ 3:25; ☽□♂ 10:32; ☽⚺♀ 11:53; ☿☍♇ 11:56; ☽△♅ 12:08; ☽⚻⚷ 13:47; ♀□♅ 14:26; ☽△⚳ 18:36; ☉☍♇ 22:28
8 F	☽⚼♇ 0:57; ☉∠☽ 1:10; ☽∠☿ 3:38; ⚵ ♏ 3:46; ♀△⚷ 7:49; ☽∥♅ 8:27; ☿⚹♃ 9:07; ☽⋕♆ 14:49; ☽⚼♅ 16:19; ♀⚼♄ 18:41; ☽□♄ 19:02; ☽∠♀ 19:05; ☽☍♆ 21:12; ☽⚼⚳ 23:33
9 Sa	☽∥♃ 4:44; ☽△♇ 5:28; ☉⚹☽ 8:08; ☽☌♃ 9:33; ☽⚹☿ 14:20; ♀⚼♆ 16:23; ☽⚹♂ 20:10; ☽⚻♅ 21:24; ☽☍⚷ 23:03
10 Su	☽⚹♀ 3:29; ☽∥⚷ 3:49; ☽⚻⚳ 5:24; ☉⚹♃ 5:42; ☽∥⚳ 7:32
11 M	☽⋕⚳ 1:49; ☿△♂ 2:01; ☽∠♂ 2:16; ♀□⚳ 2:32; ☽⋕⚷ 5:21; ☽⚹♄ 5:46; ☿□♅ 7:30; ☽⚻♆ 8:12; ☿△⚷ 16:34; ☽□♇ 16:48; ♀⋕♂ 16:49; ☿⚼♄ 21:35; ☽⚺♃ 21:56
12 Tu	☉□☽ 0:53; ☽⋕♃ 4:01; ♀ ♌ 5:35; ☽⚺♂ 8:55; ☽☍♅ 9:31; ☽⚻⚷ 11:04; ☿⚼♆ 11:45; ☽∠♄ 11:55; ☽⚼♆ 14:27; ☽□☿ 15:02; ☽☍⚳ 18:53; ☽∥♆ 20:10; ☽□♀ 22:40
13 W	♀⋕♇ 2:11; ☽⋕♅ 3:00; ☽∠♃ 4:43; ☿□⚳ 15:30; ☽⚼⚷ 17:24; ☽⚺♄ 18:10; ☽△♆ 20:47
14 Th	☿ ♌ 0:48; ♂⚻♅ 5:14; ☽⚹♇ 5:21; ☉⋕♂ 8:30; ☽⚹♃ 11:24; ☿⋕♂ 18:01; ☉△☽ 18:46; ☽⚻♅ 22:08; ☽☌♂ 22:23; ☽△⚷ 23:31
15 F	☉∥☿ 1:03; ☽⚻⚳ 8:27; ☽∠♇ 11:17; ☽△☿ 15:44; ♀∠♃ 16:43; ☽△♀ 17:48; ☿⋕♇ 19:25
16 Sa	☉⚼☽ 3:03; ♀⋕♄ 3:05; ☽⚼♅ 3:52; ☿∠♃ 4:41; ☽☌♄ 5:46; ☽□♆ 8:26; ☉□♅ 13:33; ☽⚼⚳ 14:30; ☽⚺♇ 16:40; ☿☌♀ 22:00; ☽□♃ 23:23
17 Su	☽⚼♀ 2:18; ☽⚼☿ 2:36; ☉⋕♇ 3:06; ☉△♂ 3:46; ⚳ ♉ 4:11; ☉△⚷ 5:43; ☽△♅ 8:58; ☽⚺♂ 10:09; ☽□⚷ 10:11; ☉⚻☽ 10:33; ☿⋕♄ 11:13; ♂△⚷ 11:43; ☉⚼♄ 12:28; ☽△⚳ 19:50
18 M	☽⚻♀ 9:54; ☽⚻☿ 12:13; ☽⚺♄ 14:58; ☽∠♂ 15:01; ☽⚹♆ 17:37; ☉⚼♆ 23:07
19 Tu	☽☌♇ 1:26; ☿∥♀ 2:11; ☿⚼⚷ 3:31; ☿△♄ 6:29; ☽△♃ 8:40; ☽□♅ 17:07; ☽⚹⚷ 18:09; ☽∠♄ 18:34; ☽⚹♂ 19:13; ☽∠♆ 21:12; ☉☍☽ 22:58
20 W	☿⚻♆ 0:45; ☽□⚳ 4:21; ♀⚼⚷ 9:16; ☽⚼♃ 12:19; ♀△♄ 13:21; ☽∠⚷ 21:13; ☽⚹♄ 21:35; ☽☍♀ 22:27
21 Th	☽⚺♆ 0:13; ☽☍☿ 3:59; ☽⚺♇ 7:41; ☉⋕♄ 14:54; ☽⚻♃ 15:25; ♀⚻♆ 17:35; ☽⚹♅ 22:55; ☽⚺⚷ 23:48
22 F	☽□♂ 1:57; ☿⚻♇ 7:12; ☉⚻☽ 8:32; ☉ ♌ 9:31; ☽∠♇ 10:06; ☽⚹⚳ 10:32; ☽⋕♅ 17:44; ☽∥♆ 23:22
23 Sa	☽∠♅ 1:10; ☽□♄ 2:18; ☽☌♆ 4:55; ☽⚻♀ 8:25; ☽⚹♇ 12:10; ☉⚼☽ 12:35; ☽∠⚳ 13:00; ☽⚻☿ 16:28; ☽⋕♃ 17:53; ☉□⚳ 20:05; ☽☍♃ 20:26
24 Su	⚳∥⚷ 1:56; ☽⚺♅ 3:07; ☽☌⚷ 3:53; ☽△♂ 7:07; ☽⋕⚳ 9:12; ☽⋕⚷ 9:15; ☽⚼♀ 12:46; ☽⚺⚳ 15:11; ☉△☽ 16:18; ☽⚼☿ 21:53
25 M	♀⚻♇ 1:58; ☿⚺♃ 3:27; ☽△♄ 5:47; ☽∥⚷ 6:30; ☽∥⚳ 6:43; ☽⚺♆ 8:24; ☽⚼♂ 9:20; ☽□♇ 15:31; ☽△♀ 16:50; ☽∥♃ 20:56; ⚶ ♋ 21:22
26 Tu	☽⚻♃ 0:23; ☽△☿ 2:56; ☽☌♅ 6:20; ☽⚺⚷ 6:59; ☽⚼♄ 7:14; ☽∠♆ 9:51; ☽⚻♂ 11:23; ☽⋕♆ 16:09; ☽☌⚳ 18:55; ☽∥♅ 21:30; ☉□☽ 23:01
27 W	☽⚼♃ 2:06; ☿△♅ 7:46; ☽∠⚷ 8:19; ☽⚻♄ 8:34; ☽⚹♆ 11:11; ☿⚻⚷ 12:56; ☽△♇ 18:13
28 Th	☽□♀ 0:25; ☽△♃ 3:45; ☽∥☿ 6:38; ☽⚺♅ 9:02; ☽⚹⚷ 9:35; ☽□☿ 12:18; ☽☍♂ 15:14; ☽⚼♇ 19:29; ☽⚺⚳ 22:12
29 F	☽∥♀ 1:43; ☉⚹☽ 5:18; ☉∠♃ 6:46; ☽∠♅ 10:21; ☽☍♄ 11:07; ☽□♆ 13:45; ☽⚻♇ 20:48; ☿□♂ 20:50; ♀⚺♃ 21:04; ♅ R 21:07; ☽∠⚳ 23:53
30 Sa	☽□♃ 7:07; ☽⚹♀ 7:56; ☉∠☽ 8:33; ☽⚹♅ 11:48; ☽□⚷ 12:15; ☉∥☽ 14:02; ☿ ♍ 18:19; ☽⚻♂ 19:20; ☽⚹☿ 21:31
31 Su	☽⚹⚳ 1:44; ☿⚼♇ 4:28; ☽∠♀ 12:03; ☉⚺☽ 12:05; ☽⚻♄ 14:10; ☽△♆ 16:52; ☽⚼♂ 21:48

August 2016

LONGITUDE

Day	Sid.Time	☉	☽	☽ 12 hour	Mean☊	True☊	☿	♀	♂	⚳	♃	♄	⚷	♅	♆	♇
	h m s	° ' "	° ' "	° ' "	° '	° '	° '	° '	° '	° '	° '	° '	° '	° '	° '	° '
1 M	20 40 08	9♌10 39	15♋35 41	22♋29 02	14♍19.7	13♍05.6	1♍53.4	24♌17.6	29♏21.3	2♉49.5	22♍04.2	9♐54.2	24♓44.3	24♈30.4	11♓28.0	15♑38.0
2 Tu	20 44 04	10 08 05	29 18 42	6♌04 20	14 16.5	13R 00.6	3 23.2	25 31.3	29 43.3	2 59.0	22 15.3	9R 53.0	24R 42.6	24R 30.2	11R 26.6	15R 36.7
3 W	20 48 01	11 05 31	12♌45 38	19 22 26	14 13.3	12 56.6	4 51.1	26 45.0	0♐05.8	3 08.3	22 26.4	9 52.0	24 40.8	24 30.1	11 25.3	15 35.3
4 Th	20 51 58	12 02 59	25 54 36	2♍22 07	14 10.1	12 54.0	6 17.3	27 58.8	0 28.8	3 17.2	22 37.6	9 51.0	24 39.0	24 29.8	11 23.9	15 34.0
5 F	20 55 54	13 00 27	8♍45 01	15 03 29	14 07.0	12D 52.9	7 41.6	29 12.5	0 52.3	3 25.9	22 48.8	9 50.2	24 37.1	24 29.5	11 22.5	15 32.8
6 Sa	20 59 51	13 57 56	21 17 42	27 28 00	14 03.8	12 53.1	9 04.1	0♍26.2	1 16.2	3 34.3	23 00.1	9 49.4	24 35.2	24 29.2	11 21.1	15 31.5
7 Su	21 03 47	14 55 26	3♎34 44	9♎38 19	14 00.6	12 54.2	10 24.7	1 39.9	1 40.7	3 42.5	23 11.5	9 48.7	24 33.3	24 28.8	11 19.7	15 30.2
8 M	21 07 44	15 52 57	15 39 15	21 38 01	13 57.4	12 55.9	11 43.3	2 53.7	2 05.5	3 50.3	23 22.9	9 48.2	24 31.3	24 28.4	11 18.2	15 29.0
9 Tu	21 11 40	16 50 29	27 35 12	3♏31 21	13 54.2	12 57.5	13 00.0	4 07.4	2 30.8	3 57.9	23 34.4	9 47.7	24 29.3	24 28.0	11 16.8	15 27.8
10 W	21 15 37	17 48 02	9♏27 05	15 22 59	13 51.1	12R 58.6	14 14.6	5 21.1	2 56.6	4 05.1	23 45.9	9 47.3	24 27.3	24 27.4	11 15.3	15 26.6
11 Th	21 19 33	18 45 35	21 19 40	27 17 43	13 47.9	12 58.9	15 27.1	6 34.8	3 22.8	4 12.1	23 57.5	9 47.0	24 25.2	24 26.9	11 13.8	15 25.4
12 F	21 23 30	19 43 09	3♐17 45	9♐20 18	13 44.7	12 58.1	16 37.4	7 48.5	3 49.4	4 18.8	24 09.2	9 46.8	24 23.1	24 26.3	11 12.3	15 24.2
13 Sa	21 27 26	20 40 45	15 25 54	21 35 02	13 41.5	12 56.4	17 45.5	9 02.1	4 16.4	4 25.1	24 20.9	9D 46.8	24 20.9	24 25.6	11 10.8	15 23.1
14 Su	21 31 23	21 38 21	27 48 08	4♑05 35	13 38.4	12 53.9	18 51.3	10 15.8	4 43.8	4 31.2	24 32.7	9 46.8	24 18.7	24 24.9	11 09.3	15 21.9
15 M	21 35 20	22 35 58	10♑27 41	16 54 39	13 35.2	12 51.0	19 54.6	11 29.5	5 11.6	4 36.9	24 44.5	9 46.9	24 16.5	24 24.1	11 07.8	15 20.8
16 Tu	21 39 16	23 33 37	23 26 38	0♒03 40	13 32.0	12 48.1	20 55.3	12 43.1	5 39.7	4 42.4	24 56.4	9 47.1	24 14.3	24 23.3	11 06.2	15 19.7
17 W	21 43 13	24 31 16	6♒45 43	13 32 37	13 28.8	12 45.6	21 53.4	13 56.8	6 08.3	4 47.5	25 08.3	9 47.4	24 12.0	24 22.5	11 04.7	15 18.7
18 Th	21 47 09	25 28 57	20 24 09	27 19 59	13 25.6	12 43.8	22 48.6	15 10.4	6 37.2	4 52.3	25 20.3	9 47.8	24 09.7	24 21.6	11 03.1	15 17.6
19 F	21 51 06	26 26 39	4♓19 44	11♓22 55	13 22.5	12D 42.9	23 40.9	16 24.0	7 06.4	4 56.8	25 32.3	9 48.3	24 07.3	24 20.7	11 01.5	15 16.6
20 Sa	21 55 02	27 24 22	18 29 02	25 37 30	13 19.3	12 42.8	24 30.0	17 37.7	7 36.0	5 00.9	25 44.4	9 48.8	24 04.9	24 19.7	10 59.9	15 15.6
21 Su	21 58 59	28 22 07	2♈47 47	9♈59 18	13 16.1	12 43.4	25 15.8	18 51.3	8 06.0	5 04.7	25 56.5	9 49.5	24 02.5	24 18.7	10 58.4	15 14.6
22 M	22 02 55	29 19 53	17 11 29	24 23 48	13 12.9	12 44.3	25 58.2	20 04.9	8 36.2	5 08.2	26 08.7	9 50.3	24 00.1	24 17.6	10 56.8	15 13.6
23 Tu	22 06 52	0♍17 41	1♉35 45	8♉46 52	13 09.7	12 45.3	26 36.8	21 18.5	9 06.8	5 11.3	26 20.9	9 51.2	23 57.7	24 16.5	10 55.1	15 12.6
24 W	22 10 49	1 15 31	15 56 44	23 04 59	13 06.6	12 46.1	27 11.6	22 32.1	9 37.8	5 14.1	26 33.1	9 52.2	23 55.2	24 15.4	10 53.5	15 11.7
25 Th	22 14 45	2 13 22	0♊11 18	7♊15 24	13 03.4	12R 46.4	27 42.1	23 45.7	10 09.0	5 16.6	26 45.4	9 53.2	23 52.7	24 14.2	10 51.9	15 10.8
26 F	22 18 42	3 11 16	14 17 03	21 16 03	13 00.2	12 46.3	28 08.3	24 59.2	10 40.6	5 18.7	26 57.8	9 54.4	23 50.2	24 12.9	10 50.3	15 09.9
27 Sa	22 22 38	4 09 11	28 12 13	5♋05 24	12 57.0	12 45.7	28 29.8	26 12.8	11 12.5	5 20.4	27 10.1	9 55.7	23 47.6	24 11.6	10 48.6	15 09.1
28 Su	22 26 35	5 07 08	11♋55 29	18 42 20	12 53.9	12 44.9	28 46.4	27 26.4	11 44.6	5 21.8	27 22.5	9 57.0	23 45.1	24 10.3	10 47.0	15 08.2
29 M	22 30 31	6 05 07	25 25 53	2♌06 02	12 50.7	12 44.0	28 57.8	28 39.9	12 17.1	5 22.8	27 35.0	9 58.5	23 42.5	24 09.0	10 45.4	15 07.4
30 Tu	22 34 28	7 03 07	8♌42 43	15 15 54	12 47.5	12 43.3	29R 03.8	29 53.5	12 49.9	5 23.5	27 47.5	10 00.0	23 39.9	24 07.6	10 43.7	15 06.6
31 W	22 38 24	8♍01 10	21 45 33	28 11 40	12♍44.3	12♍42.8	29♍04.0	1♎07.0	13♐23.0	5♉23.8	28♍00.0	10♐01.7	23♓37.3	24♈06.1	10♓42.1	15♑05.9

1st of Month

Julian Day #
2457601.5
Obliquity
23°26'05"
SVP 5♓01'45"
GC 27♐04.3
Eris 23♈37.7[illegible]

Day	⚴
1	2♓40.6R
6	1 32.2R
11	0 19.4R
16	29♒03.7R
21	27 46.7R
26	26 30.1R
31	25 15.4R

Day	⚵
1	3♏00.7
6	3 54.7
11	4 53.4
16	5 56.4
21	7 03.5
26	8 14.3
31	9 28.7

Day	⚶
1	2♋29.5
6	4 30.5
11	6 29.9
16	8 27.8
21	10 23.9
26	12 18.2
31	14 10.4

DECLINATION and LATITUDE

Day	☉ Decl	☽ Decl	☽ Lat	☽12h Decl	☿ Decl	☿ Lat	♀ Decl	♀ Lat	♂ Decl	♂ Lat	⚳ Decl	⚳ Lat	♃ Decl	♃ Lat	♄ Decl	♄ Lat
1 M	17N57	18N10	4S23	17N36	11N22	0N37	14N49	1N29	22S48	2S52	2N09	10S57	4N11	1N08	20S18	1N39
2 Tu	17 42	16 46	3 36	15 43	10 42	0 29	14 24	1 29	22 53	2 52	2 10	10 59	4 07	1 08	20 18	1 39
3 W	17 26	14 28	2 37	13 02	10 03	0 20	13 59	1 29	22 58	2 52	2 10	11 02	4 02	1 08	20 18	1 39
4 Th	17 11	11 27	1 32	9 44	9 23	0 12	13 34	1 29	23 03	2 52	2 11	11 04	3 58	1 08	20 18	1 39
5 F	16 54	7 56	0 23	6 04	8 43	0 03	13 08	1 29	23 08	2 52	2 11	11 07	3 53	1 08	20 18	1 38
6 Sa	16 38	4 09	0N46	2 13	8 04	0S06	12 42	1 29	23 13	2 52	2 12	11 09	3 49	1 07	20 18	1 38
7 Su	16 21	0 17	1 51	1S39	7 25	0 16	12 16	1 29	23 18	2 52	2 12	11 12	3 44	1 07	20 18	1 38
8 M	16 04	3S32	2 50	5 23	6 47	0 25	11 49	1 29	23 23	2 52	2 12	11 14	3 39	1 07	20 18	1 38
9 Tu	15 47	7 10	3 41	8 52	6 08	0 35	11 22	1 28	23 28	2 51	2 12	11 17	3 35	1 07	20 19	1 37
10 W	15 30	10 29	4 23	11 59	5 31	0 45	10 55	1 28	23 33	2 51	2 12	11 19	3 30	1 07	20 19	1 37
11 Th	15 12	13 23	4 53	14 38	4 53	0 55	10 27	1 28	23 38	2 51	2 12	11 22	3 26	1 07	20 19	1 37
12 F	14 54	15 44	5 10	16 40	4 17	1 05	9 59	1 27	23 42	2 51	2 12	11 24	3 21	1 07	20 19	1 37
13 Sa	14 36	17 26	5 14	17 59	3 41	1 15	9 31	1 27	23 47	2 51	2 11	11 27	3 16	1 07	20 19	1 37
14 Su	14 17	18 21	5 04	18 29	3 06	1 26	9 03	1 26	23 52	2 50	2 11	11 30	3 11	1 07	20 19	1 36
15 M	13 59	18 23	4 39	18 03	2 31	1 36	8 34	1 25	23 57	2 50	2 10	11 32	3 07	1 07	20 20	1 36
16 Tu	13 40	17 28	3 59	16 39	1 58	1 47	8 05	1 24	24 02	2 50	2 10	11 35	3 02	1 07	20 20	1 36
17 W	13 21	15 35	3 06	14 17	1 25	1 57	7 36	1 24	24 07	2 50	2 09	11 37	2 57	1 07	20 20	1 36
18 Th	13 01	12 47	2 00	11 05	0 54	2 08	7 07	1 23	24 12	2 49	2 08	11 40	2 52	1 07	20 20	1 35
19 F	12 42	9 12	0 46	7 11	0 23	2 18	6 37	1 22	24 16	2 49	2 07	11 42	2 47	1 07	20 21	1 35
20 Sa	12 22	5 03	0S32	2 49	0S06	2 29	6 08	1 21	24 21	2 49	2 06	11 45	2 43	1 06	20 21	1 35
21 Su	12 02	0 33	1 49	1N44	0 33	2 39	5 38	1 20	24 26	2 48	2 05	11 48	2 38	1 06	20 21	1 35
22 M	11 42	3N59	2 59	6 11	0 59	2 49	5 08	1 18	24 30	2 48	2 03	11 50	2 33	1 06	20 22	1 35
23 Tu	11 22	8 17	3 59	10 16	1 24	2 59	4 38	1 17	24 34	2 48	2 02	11 53	2 28	1 06	20 22	1 34
24 W	11 02	12 05	4 43	13 43	1 47	3 09	4 07	1 16	24 39	2 47	2 00	11 55	2 23	1 06	20 22	1 34
25 Th	10 41	15 09	5 09	16 20	2 08	3 19	3 37	1 14	24 43	2 47	1 59	11 58	2 18	1 06	20 23	1 34
26 F	10 20	17 16	5 17	17 56	2 27	3 28	3 06	1 13	24 47	2 47	1 57	12 00	2 13	1 06	20 23	1 34
27 Sa	9 59	18 20	5 05	18 27	2 43	3 37	2 36	1 11	24 52	2 46	1 55	12 03	2 08	1 06	20 24	1 33
28 Su	9 38	18 18	4 37	17 53	2 57	3 45	2 05	1 10	24 56	2 46	1 53	12 05	2 03	1 06	20 24	1 33
29 M	9 17	17 14	3 53	16 20	3 09	3 53	1 34	1 08	24 60	2 45	1 51	12 08	1 58	1 06	20 24	1 33
30 Tu	8 55	15 13	2 58	13 55	3 18	4 00	1 04	1 07	25 03	2 45	1 49	12 10	1 53	1 06	20 25	1 33
31 W	8N34	12N27	1S54	10N51	3S24	4S06	0N33	1N05	25S07	2S44	1N47	12S13	1N48	1N06	20S25	1N33

Day	⚷ Decl	⚷ Lat	♅ Decl	♅ Lat	♆ Decl	♆ Lat	♇ Decl	♇ Lat
1	1N55	4N22	8N55	0S37	8S04	0S52	21S12	1N2[illegible]
6	1 52	4 22	8 55	0 37	8 07	0 52	21 13	1 1[illegible]
11	1 48	4 23	8 54	0 37	8 10	0 52	21 15	1 1[illegible]
16	1 44	4 23	8 52	0 38	8 12	0 52	21 16	1 1[illegible]
21	1 40	4 23	8 50	0 38	8 16	0 53	21 17	1 1[illegible]
26	1 35	4 24	8 48	0 38	8 19	0 53	21 18	1 1[illegible]
31	1N30	4N24	8N46	0S38	8S22	0S53	21S19	1N1[illegible]

Day	⚴ Decl	⚴ Lat	⚵ Decl	⚵ Lat	⚶ Decl	⚶ Lat	Eris Decl	Eris Lat
1	12N46	24N55	1S38	11N34	21N02	2S22	2S25	12S2[illegible]
6	12 11	24 41	2 05	11 24	21 04	2 18	2 25	12 2[illegible]
11	11 30	24 23	2 33	11 14	21 03	2 14	2 26	12 2[illegible]
16	10 44	23 59	3 01	11 05	21 01	2 09	2 27	12 2[illegible]
21	9 53	23 31	3 31	10 56	20 57	2 05	2 28	12 2[illegible]
26	8 58	22 58	4 00	10 48	20 53	1 60	2 29	12 2[illegible]
31	7N59	22N20	4S30	10N40	20N46	1S55	2S30	12S2[illegible]

Moon Phenomena

Max/0 Decl

dy	hr mn	
7	1:44	0 S
14	13:02	18S29
21	2:55	0 N
27	11:19	18N27

Perigee/Apogee

dy	hr m		kilometers
10	0:05	a	404262
22	1:15	p	367050

Max/0 Lat

dy	hr mn	
5	7:51	0 N
12	19:09	5N15
19	14:15	0 S
25	21:32	5S17

PH	dy	hr mn	
●	2	20:46	10♌58
☽	10	18:22	18♏32
○	18	9:28	25♒52
☾	25	3:42	2♊22

Void of Course Moon

Last Aspect				☽ Ingress		
2	0:45	♂	△	♌	2	1:13
4	4:14	♀	☌	♍	4	7:35
6	3:21	♃	☌	♎	6	16:58
8	17:42	♅	☍	♏	9	4:53
11	5:23	♃	⚹	♐	11	17:25
13	17:38	♃	□	♑	14	4:13
16	2:46	♃	△	♒	16	11:53
18	9:28	☉	☍	♓	18	16:35
20	12:22	♃	☍	♈	20	19:20
22	11:49	♅	☌	♉	22	21:20
24	19:39	☿	△	♊	24	23:41
27	0:31	☿	□	♋	27	3:07
29	6:24	☿	⚹	♌	29	8:13
31	4:21	♅	△	♍	31	15:23

DAILY ASPECTARIAN

1 M
☽☍♇ 0:04
☽∠☿ 2:32
♀△♅ 4:10
☉∥☽ 6:37
♀⚻⚷ 8:31
☽⚹♃ 11:26
☉⚼⚷ 13:40
☽□♅ 15:32
☽△⚷ 15:55
☽⚼♄ 16:13
☽⚺♀ 16:40
☿△⚳ 16:44
☉△♄ 17:50
☽⚼♆ 18:57

2 Tu
☽△♂ 0:45
☽□⚳ 6:35
☽⚺☿ 8:06
☽∠♃ 14:19
♂ ♐ 17:50
☽⚼⚷ 18:28
☽△♄ 18:48
☉☌☽ 20:46
☽⚻♆ 21:35

3 W
☽∥♀ 4:48
☽⚻♇ 5:06
☉⚻♆ 8:04
☽⚺♃ 17:52
☽△♅ 21:24
☽⚻⚷ 21:41

4 Th
☽☌♀ 4:14
♂∠♇ 5:07
☽⚼♇ 8:38
☽□♂ 8:44
☽△⚳ 13:53
☿∥♅ 17:07
☽∥♅ 17:34
☽∥☿ 17:41
☽☌☿ 21:46
☽#♆ 22:56

5 F
☽⚼♅ 1:24
☽□♄ 2:03
☽☍♆ 4:58
☉⚺☽ 8:45
☽△♇ 12:55
♀ ♍ 15:28
☽⚼⚳ 18:41
☿#♆ 22:30

6 Sa
♀⚼♇ 1:41
☽∥♃ 2:11
☽☌♃ 3:21
☽⚻♅ 6:11
☽☍⚷ 6:22
☿⚼♅ 7:23
☽∥⚳ 12:08
☿□♄ 13:19
☽∥⚷ 14:14
☉∠☽ 16:12
☽⚺♀ 19:49
☽⚹♂ 20:08

7 Su
☽⚻⚳ 0:15
♀□♂ 0:21
☽⚹♄ 12:20
☽#⚷ 13:16
☉⚻♇ 14:13
☽⚺☿ 15:12
☽⚻♆ 15:20
☽#⚳ 15:30
☿☍♆ 16:25
☽□♇ 23:40

8 M
☉⚹☽ 0:30
☽#♃ 0:45
☽∠♂ 2:59
☽∠♀ 5:00
☽⚺♃ 15:46
☽☍♅ 17:42
☽⚻⚷ 17:46
☽#☿ 18:04
☽∠♄ 18:22
♀△⚳ 20:34
☽⚼♆ 21:22

9 Tu
☽∠☿ 0:56
☽∥♆ 6:48
☽⚺♂ 10:20
☽#♅ 12:12
☽☍⚳ 13:02
☽⚹♀ 14:45
♅⚺⚷ 21:25
☽∠♃ 22:35

10 W
☽⚼⚷ 0:00
☽⚺♄ 0:41
☽#♀ 2:54
☽△♆ 3:39
☽⚹☿ 10:48
☽⚹♇ 12:06
☉□☽ 18:22
☿△♇ 23:26

11 Th
☽⚹♃ 5:23
☽△⚷ 6:12
☽⚻♅ 6:17
☉#☽ 15:52
☽∠♇ 18:14

12 F
☽☌♂ 1:05
☽⚻⚳ 2:03
⚴R♒ 7:04
☽□♀ 9:59
☽⚼♅ 12:11
☽☌♄ 12:52
☽□♆ 15:39
☽⚺♇ 23:54

13 Sa
♃☍⚷ 0:00
☽□☿ 5:00
♀⚼♅ 7:34
☽⚼⚳ 7:51
♃⚻♅ 9:03
♄D 9:51
♂⚻⚳ 9:58
☉△☽ 11:06
♀□♄ 14:32
☽□⚷ 17:18
☽△♅ 17:29
☽□♃ 17:38
☿∥♃ 19:24

14 Su
♀∥♅ 8:22
☽△⚳ 12:54
☽⚺♂ 13:42
☿⚼⚳ 16:33
♀☍♆ 17:04
☉⚼☽ 18:11
☽⚺♄ 22:43

15 M
☽⚹♆ 1:15
☽△♀ 2:08
☽☌♇ 9:05
☿∥⚳ 15:14
♀#♆ 18:00
☽∠♂ 18:43
☽△☿ 19:00

16 Tu
☉⚻☽ 0:14
☽⚹⚷ 1:27
☽□♅ 1:43
☽∠♄ 2:27
☽△♃ 2:46
☽∠♆ 4:50
☽⚼♀ 8:34
☿∥⚷ 10:00
☉⚻⚷ 16:16
☉△♅ 20:24
☽□⚳ 20:28
☽⚹♂ 22:51

17 W
☽⚼☿ 0:15
☽∠⚷ 4:19
☽⚹♄ 5:23
☽⚼♃ 6:05
☽⚺♆ 7:38
☽⚻♀ 13:58
☽⚺♇ 15:05
☉⚺♃ 19:27
☉#☽ 21:58

18 Th
♀△♇ 2:19
☽⚻☿ 4:28
☽⚺⚷ 6:30
☽⚹♅ 6:52
☽⚻♃ 8:41
☉☍☽ 9:28
☽∠♇ 17:04

19 F
☽⚹⚳ 1:04
☽#♅ 2:09
☽□♂ 4:54
☽∥♆ 5:48
☽∠♅ 8:32
☽□♄ 9:20
☽☌♆ 11:22
☿☍⚷ 12:08
☽#♀ 17:12
☽⚹♇ 18:34
☿⚻♅ 18:56
☽☍♀ 22:25

20 Sa
☽∠⚳ 2:35
☽☌⚷ 9:23
☽⚺♅ 9:49
☽☍☿ 10:42
☽☍♃ 12:22
☽#♃ 12:50
☽#⚳ 15:56
☉⚻☽ 16:04
☽#⚷ 18:07
☽∥☿ 24:00

21 Su
☽⚺⚳ 3:50
☽#☿ 6:27
☽△♂ 9:10
☽∥⚷ 11:38
☽△♄ 11:44
☽⚺♆ 13:37
☽∥⚳ 13:46
☽∥♃ 16:28
☉⚼☽ 18:54
☽□♇ 20:44

22 M
♀⚼⚳ 1:08
☽⚻♀ 5:16
☽∥♀ 5:33
☿☌♃ 9:06
☽⚼♂ 11:04
☽⚺⚷ 11:19
☽☌♅ 11:49
☽⚼♄ 12:45
☽∠♆ 14:33
☽⚻♃ 15:08
☽⚻☿ 15:19
☉ ♍ 16:40
☉△☽ 21:40
☉⚼♇ 21:56
☽#♆ 23:56

23 Tu
☽∥♅ 3:09
☽☌⚳ 6:01
♂⚼♅ 7:15
☽⚼♀ 8:36
☽∠⚷ 12:16
☽⚻♂ 13:01
☽⚻♄ 13:49
☿#⚷ 14:09
☽⚹♆ 15:33
☽⚼♃ 16:32
☉∥☽ 17:27
☽⚼☿ 17:27
☽△♇ 22:45

24 W
♂☌♄ 11:28
☽△♀ 12:07
☽⚹⚷ 13:22
☽⚺♅ 13:57
☿#⚳ 14:13
☽△♃ 18:07
☽△☿ 19:39
☽⚼♇ 23:59

25 Th
♀☍⚷ 2:13
☉□☽ 3:42
☽⚺⚳ 8:39
♀⚻♅ 9:09
☿#♃ 10:13
☽∠♅ 15:21
☽☍♄ 16:30
☽☍♂ 17:35
☽□♆ 18:07

26 F
☽⚻♇ 1:31
♂□♆ 6:57
☽∠⚳ 10:23
☽□⚷ 16:23
☽⚹♅ 17:04
☽□♀ 20:13
☿#♀ 20:14
☽□♃ 22:11

27 Sa
☽□☿ 0:31
☉⚹☽ 11:09
☽⚹⚳ 12:28
☽⚻♄ 20:31
☽△♆ 22:00
♀☌♃ 22:30
☽⚻♂ 23:40

28 Su
♀∥♃ 1:55
☽☍♇ 5:40
☉△⚳ 6:12
♀∥⚳ 10:01
☉∠☽ 15:38
☽△⚷ 20:56
☽□♅ 21:43
☽⚼♄ 23:11

29 M
☽⚼♆ 0:35
♀∥⚷ 1:45
☽⚼♂ 3:28
☽⚹♃ 3:55
☽⚹♀ 6:24
☽⚹☿ 6:24
☿☌♀ 6:33
☽□⚳ 17:57
☉⚺☽ 20:44
☽⚼⚷ 23:55

30 Tu
♀ ♎ 2:08
☽△♄ 2:21
☽⚻♆ 3:40
☽∠♃ 7:35
☽△♂ 7:52
☽∠☿ 9:49
☉∥♅ 10:26
☽⚻♇ 11:42
☽∠♀ 12:29
☿R 13:05

31 W
☽⚻⚷ 3:27
☽△♅ 4:21
⚳R 7:10
⚳∥♃ 11:01
☽⚺♃ 11:50
☉#♆ 12:39
☽⚺☿ 13:34
☽⚼♇ 15:33
☽⚺♀ 19:21

LONGITUDE

Day	Sid.Time	☉	☽	☽ 12 hour	Mean ☊	True ☊	☿	♀	♂	⚳	♃	♄	⚷	♅	♆	♇
	h m s	° ' "	° ' "	° ' "	° '	° '	° '	° '	° '	° '	° '	° '	° '	° '	° '	° '
Th	22 42 21	8♍59 14	4♍34 16	10♍53 25	12♍41.2	12♍42.6	28♍58.4	2♎20.6	13♐56.3	5♉23.7	28♍12.5	10♐03.4	23♓34.6	24♈04.6	10♓40.4	15♑05.1
F	22 46 18	9 57 19	17 09 11	23 21 42	12 38.0	12D 42.5	28R 46.6	3 34.1	14 30.0	5R 23.3	28 25.1	10 05.2	23R 32.0	24R 03.1	10R 38.8	15R 04.4
Sa	22 50 14	10 55 26	29 31 08	5♎37 40	12 34.8	12 42.6	28 28.6	4 47.6	15 03.9	5 22.5	28 37.7	10 07.2	23 29.3	24 01.5	10 37.1	15 03.7
Su	22 54 11	11 53 35	11♎41 33	17 43 05	12 31.6	12R 42.7	28 04.3	6 01.1	15 38.0	5 21.3	28 50.4	10 09.2	23 26.6	23 59.9	10 35.5	15 03.1
M	22 58 07	12 51 45	23 42 35	29 40 25	12 28.4	12 42.8	27 33.7	7 14.6	16 12.5	5 19.7	29 03.0	10 11.3	23 23.9	23 58.3	10 33.8	15 02.5
Tu	23 02 04	13 49 57	5♏36 58	11♏32 43	12 25.3	12 42.7	26 57.0	8 28.0	16 47.2	5 17.8	29 15.7	10 13.5	23 21.2	23 56.6	10 32.2	15 01.8
W	23 06 00	14 48 11	17 28 08	23 23 42	12 22.1	12 42.5	26 14.6	9 41.5	17 22.1	5 15.5	29 28.5	10 15.8	23 18.5	23 54.9	10 30.5	15 01.3
Th	23 09 57	15 46 26	29 19 57	5♐17 28	12 18.9	12 42.3	25 26.8	10 55.0	17 57.3	5 12.8	29 41.2	10 18.2	23 15.7	23 53.2	10 28.9	15 00.7
F	23 13 53	16 44 43	11♐16 47	17 18 29	12 15.7	12D 42.1	24 34.3	12 08.4	18 32.8	5 09.7	29 54.0	10 20.7	23 13.0	23 51.4	10 27.2	15 00.2
Sa	23 17 50	17 43 01	23 23 09	29 31 20	12 12.5	12 42.1	23 37.9	13 21.8	19 08.5	5 06.3	0♎06.8	10 23.3	23 10.3	23 49.6	10 25.6	14 59.7
Su	23 21 47	18 41 20	5♑43 34	12♑00 23	12 09.4	12 42.4	22 38.7	14 35.2	19 44.4	5 02.5	0 19.6	10 25.9	23 07.5	23 47.8	10 24.0	14 59.2
M	23 25 43	19 39 42	18 22 14	24 49 31	12 06.2	12 42.9	21 37.8	15 48.6	20 20.5	4 58.3	0 32.4	10 28.7	23 04.8	23 45.9	10 22.3	14 58.8
Tu	23 29 40	20 38 05	1♒22 35	8♒01 40	12 03.0	12 43.6	20 36.5	17 02.0	20 56.9	4 53.8	0 45.2	10 31.5	23 02.0	23 44.0	10 20.7	14 58.4
W	23 33 36	21 36 29	14 46 54	21 38 19	11 59.8	12 44.4	19 36.3	18 15.3	21 33.5	4 48.9	0 58.1	10 34.5	22 59.3	23 42.0	10 19.1	14 58.0
Th	23 37 33	22 34 55	28 35 47	5♓39 03	11 56.7	12R 45.0	18 38.5	19 28.6	22 10.2	4 43.6	1 11.0	10 37.5	22 56.5	23 40.1	10 17.5	14 57.6
F	23 41 29	23 33 23	12♓47 44	20 01 16	11 53.5	12 45.3	17 44.6	20 41.9	22 47.2	4 37.9	1 23.9	10 40.6	22 53.8	23 38.1	10 15.9	14 57.3
Sa	23 45 26	24 31 52	27 19 00	4♈40 08	11 50.3	12 45.0	16 56.0	21 55.2	23 24.4	4 31.9	1 36.8	10 43.8	22 51.0	23 36.1	10 14.3	14 57.0
Su	23 49 22	25 30 24	12♈03 47	19 29 00	11 47.1	12 44.0	16 14.0	23 08.5	24 01.8	4 25.6	1 49.7	10 47.0	22 48.2	23 34.0	10 12.7	14 56.7
M	23 53 19	26 28 57	26 54 49	4♉20 16	11 43.9	12 42.6	15 39.5	24 21.8	24 39.4	4 18.8	2 02.6	10 50.4	22 45.5	23 31.9	10 11.2	14 56.5
Tu	23 57 15	27 27 33	11♉44 24	19 06 22	11 40.8	12 40.8	15 13.6	25 35.0	25 17.2	4 11.7	2 15.5	10 53.8	22 42.7	23 29.8	10 09.6	14 56.3
W	0 01 12	28 26 11	26 25 25	3♊40 54	11 37.6	12 39.1	14 56.8	26 48.3	25 55.1	4 04.3	2 28.5	10 57.3	22 40.0	23 27.7	10 08.0	14 56.1
Th	0 05 09	29 24 51	10♊52 17	17 59 13	11 34.4	12 37.7	14D 49.6	28 01.5	26 33.3	3 56.5	2 41.4	11 01.0	22 37.3	23 25.5	10 06.5	14 55.9
F	0 09 05	0♎23 34	25 01 25	1♋58 45	11 31.2	12D 36.9	14 52.3	29 14.7	27 11.6	3 48.4	2 54.4	11 04.6	22 34.5	23 23.4	10 05.0	14 55.8
Sa	0 13 02	1 22 18	8♋51 11	15 38 46	11 28.1	12 37.0	15 04.9	0♏27.9	27 50.1	3 39.9	3 07.4	11 08.4	22 31.8	23 21.2	10 03.5	14 55.7
Su	0 16 58	2 21 05	22 21 37	28 59 56	11 24.9	12 37.8	15 27.2	1 41.0	28 28.8	3 31.2	3 20.3	11 12.3	22 29.1	23 19.0	10 02.0	14 55.7
M	0 20 55	3 19 54	5♌33 55	12♌03 48	11 21.7	12 39.2	15 59.0	2 54.2	29 07.7	3 22.0	3 33.3	11 16.2	22 26.4	23 16.7	10 00.5	14D 55.6
Tu	0 24 51	4 18 46	18 29 50	24 52 18	11 18.5	12 40.7	16 39.8	4 07.3	29 46.7	3 12.6	3 46.3	11 20.2	22 23.7	23 14.5	9 59.0	14 55.6
W	0 28 48	5 17 40	1♍11 25	7♍27 27	11 15.3	12R 41.9	17 29.2	5 20.5	0♑25.9	3 02.8	3 59.3	11 24.3	22 21.0	23 12.2	9 57.5	14 55.7
Th	0 32 44	6 16 35	13 40 37	19 51 07	11 12.2	12 42.3	18 26.4	6 33.6	1 05.3	2 52.8	4 12.2	11 28.4	22 18.4	23 09.9	9 56.1	14 55.7
F	0 36 41	7♎15 33	25 59 11	2♎05 00	11♍09.0	12♍41.6	19♍30.9	7♏46.7	1♑44.9	2♉42.4	4♎25.2	11♐32.7	22♓15.7	23♈07.6	9♓54.7	14♑55.8

1st of Month

Julian Day #
2457632.5
Obliquity
23°26'05"
SVP 5♓01'41"
GC 27♐04.3
Eris 23♈29.1R

Day	⚴
1	25♒00.9R
6	23 50.8R
11	22 46.2R
16	21 48.0R
21	20 57.4R
26	20 14.8R

	⚵
1	9♏43.9
6	11 02.1
11	12 23.3
16	13 47.1
21	15 13.3
26	16 41.9

	⚶
1	14♋32.6
6	16 21.9
11	18 08.7
16	19 52.7
21	21 33.5
26	23 11.0

DECLINATION and LATITUDE

Day	☉ Decl	☽ Decl	☽ Lat	☽ 12h Decl	☿ Decl	☿ Lat	♀ Decl	♀ Lat	♂ Decl	♂ Lat	⚳ Decl	⚳ Lat	♃ Decl	♃ Lat	♄ Decl	♄ Lat
Th	8N12	9N08	0S45	7N20	3S27	4S12	0N02	1N03	25S11	2S44	1N45	12S15	1N43	1N06	20S26	1N32
F	7 50	5 27	0N25	3 32	3 26	4 16	0S29	1 01	25 14	2 43	1 42	12 17	1 38	1 06	20 26	1 32
Sa	7 28	1 36	1 32	0S20	3 22	4 20	0 60	0 59	25 18	2 43	1 40	12 20	1 33	1 06	20 27	1 32
Su	7 06	2S16	2 34	4 09	3 14	4 22	1 31	0 57	25 21	2 42	1 37	12 22	1 28	1 06	20 27	1 32
M	6 44	5 58	3 28	7 44	3 03	4 22	2 02	0 55	25 24	2 42	1 34	12 24	1 23	1 06	20 28	1 32
Tu	6 21	9 24	4 13	10 59	2 47	4 21	2 33	0 53	25 27	2 41	1 32	12 27	1 18	1 06	20 28	1 31
W	5 59	12 27	4 47	13 47	2 28	4 19	3 03	0 51	25 30	2 41	1 29	12 29	1 13	1 06	20 29	1 31
Th	5 37	14 59	5 09	16 01	2 05	4 14	3 34	0 49	25 33	2 40	1 26	12 31	1 08	1 06	20 29	1 31
F	5 14	16 53	5 17	17 35	1 38	4 08	4 05	0 47	25 35	2 39	1 23	12 33	1 03	1 06	20 30	1 31
Sa	4 51	18 05	5 12	18 22	1 08	3 60	4 36	0 44	25 38	2 39	1 20	12 35	0 57	1 06	20 31	1 31
Su	4 28	18 27	4 52	18 18	0 36	3 49	5 06	0 42	25 40	2 38	1 17	12 37	0 52	1 06	20 31	1 30
M	4 06	17 55	4 18	17 18	0 01	3 37	5 37	0 39	25 42	2 38	1 14	12 39	0 47	1 06	20 32	1 30
Tu	3 43	16 26	3 30	15 21	0N36	3 23	6 07	0 37	25 44	2 37	1 10	12 41	0 42	1 06	20 32	1 30
W	3 20	14 01	2 29	12 29	1 14	3 08	6 37	0 35	25 46	2 36	1 07	12 43	0 37	1 06	20 33	1 30
Th	2 57	10 45	1 18	8 50	1 52	2 51	7 08	0 32	25 48	2 36	1 04	12 45	0 32	1 06	20 34	1 29
F	2 33	6 46	0S00	4 34	2 30	2 33	7 38	0 29	25 49	2 35	1 00	12 47	0 27	1 06	20 34	1 29
Sa	2 10	2 17	1 20	0N03	3 06	2 14	8 07	0 27	25 51	2 34	0 57	12 48	0 22	1 06	20 35	1 29
Su	1 47	2N23	2 35	4 42	3 41	1 54	8 37	0 24	25 52	2 34	0 53	12 50	0 16	1 06	20 35	1 29
M	1 24	6 56	3 41	9 04	4 12	1 34	9 07	0 21	25 53	2 33	0 49	12 52	0 11	1 06	20 36	1 29
Tu	1 01	11 03	4 31	12 51	4 41	1 14	9 36	0 19	25 53	2 32	0 46	12 53	0 06	1 06	20 37	1 28
W	0 37	14 26	5 03	15 46	5 05	0 55	10 05	0 16	25 54	2 32	0 42	12 55	0 01	1 06	20 38	1 28
Th	0 14	16 52	5 16	17 40	5 26	0 36	10 34	0 13	25 54	2 31	0 38	12 56	0S04	1 06	20 38	1 28
F	0S09	18 12	5 09	18 27	5 42	0 17	11 02	0 10	25 55	2 30	0 34	12 57	0 09	1 06	20 39	1 28
Sa	0 33	18 25	4 43	18 08	5 53	0N00	11 31	0 08	25 55	2 30	0 30	12 58	0 14	1 06	20 40	1 28
Su	0 56	17 35	4 03	16 48	5 59	0 17	11 59	0 05	25 54	2 29	0 27	12 60	0 19	1 06	20 40	1 28
M	1 19	15 47	3 11	14 36	6 01	0 32	12 27	0 02	25 54	2 28	0 23	13 01	0 25	1 06	20 41	1 27
Tu	1 43	13 14	2 10	11 43	5 58	0 46	12 55	0S01	25 53	2 27	0 19	13 01	0 30	1 06	20 42	1 27
W	2 06	10 04	1 03	8 19	5 51	0 59	13 22	0 04	25 53	2 27	0 15	13 02	0 35	1 06	20 43	1 27
Th	2 30	6 30	0N05	4 37	5 39	1 10	13 49	0 07	25 52	2 26	0 11	13 03	0 40	1 06	20 43	1 27
F	2S53	2N42	1N12	0N46	5N23	1N20	14S16	0S10	25S50	2S25	0N07	13S04	0S45	1N06	20S44	1N27

Day	⚷ Decl	⚷ Lat	♅ Decl	♅ Lat	♆ Decl	♆ Lat	♇ Decl	♇ Lat
1	1N29	4N24	8N45	0S38	8S23	0S53	21S20	1N16
6	1 24	4 24	8 42	0 38	8 26	0 53	21 21	1 15
11	1 18	4 23	8 39	0 38	8 29	0 53	21 21	1 15
16	1 13	4 23	8 35	0 38	8 32	0 53	21 22	1 14
21	1 07	4 23	8 31	0 38	8 35	0 53	21 23	1 13
26	1 01	4 22	8 27	0 38	8 38	0 53	21 24	1 13

Day	⚴ Decl	⚴ Lat	⚵ Decl	⚵ Lat	⚶ Decl	⚶ Lat	Eris Decl	Eris Lat
1	7N47	22N12	4S36	10N39	20N45	1S54	2S30	12S29
6	6 46	21 30	5 06	10 32	20 38	1 49	2 31	12 29
11	5 44	20 44	5 36	10 26	20 29	1 44	2 32	12 30
16	4 41	19 56	6 06	10 20	20 20	1 39	2 33	12 30
21	3 38	19 06	6 35	10 14	20 10	1 33	2 34	12 30
26	2 37	18 15	7 04	10 09	20 00	1 28	2 35	12 30

Moon Phenomena

Max/0 Decl

dy hr mn	
3 9:53	0 S
10 22:08	18S27
17 11:47	0 N
23 16:51	18N28
30 16:47	0 S

Max/0 Lat

dy hr mn	
1 15:29	0 N
9 2:49	5N17
15 23:56	0 S
22 2:51	5S16
28 22:07	0 N

Perigee/Apogee

dy hr m		kilometers
6 18:50	a	405054
18 17:08	p	361899

PH	dy hr mn	
●	1 9:04	9♍21
☉ (eclipse)	1 9:08	A 03'05"
☽	9 11:50	17♐13
○	16 19:06	24♓20
☽ (eclipse)	16 18:55	A 0.908
☾	23 9:57	0♋48

Void of Course Moon

Last Aspect			☽ Ingress		
2 22:14	♃	☌	♎	3	0:57
5 0:31	♅	☍	♏	5	12:40
8 0:44	♃	⚹	♐	8	1:21
10 0:52	♅	△	♑	10	12:56
12 10:01	♅	□	♒	12	21:30
14 15:32	♅	⚹	♓	15	2:24
16 19:06	☉	☍	♈	17	4:23
18 20:12	♂	△	♉	19	4:59
21 3:33	☉	△	♊	21	5:54
23 7:58	♀	△	♋	23	8:34
25 1:43	♅	□	♌	25	13:49
27 8:54	♅	△	♍	27	21:44
29 10:06	☿	☌	♎	30	7:53

DAILY ASPECTARIAN

☽△⚳ 1:34
☉⚼♅ 2:10
☽∥♅ 2:36
☽⋕♆ 5:05
☉∥☽ 6:58
☽⚼♅ 8:32
☉☌☽ 9:04
☽□♄ 10:26
☽☍♆ 11:34
☽□♂ 18:40
☽△♇ 20:01

☉□♄ 3:23
☽⚼⚳ 6:14
☽☍⚷ 12:17
☽⋕☿ 12:49
☽⚻♅ 13:19
☉☍♆ 16:39
☿☌♃ 17:19
☽☌☿ 22:01
☽☌♃ 22:14
☽∥⚳ 23:36
♂⚺♇ 23:55

☽∥♃ 0:18
☽∥⚷ 0:54
☽⋕♀ 3:17
♀⚻⚳ 11:13
☽⚻⚳ 11:29
☽☌♀ 11:31
☽∥♀ 18:35
☽⋕⚷ 18:51
☽⋕♃ 19:08
☽⋕⚳ 20:01
♀⋕⚷ 20:27
☽⚹♄ 20:56
☽⚻♆ 21:49
♀⋕♃ 22:09

4 Su
☉⚺☽ 0:26
♀⋕⚳ 4:33
☽∥☿ 5:55
☽□♇ 6:40
☽⚹♂ 8:14
♃∥⚷ 11:43
☽⚻⚷ 23:23

5 M
☽☍♅ 0:31
☽∠♄ 2:59
☽⚼♆ 3:43
☉⋕☽ 4:38
☽⚺☿ 7:23
☉∠☽ 9:05
☽⚺♃ 10:56
☽∠♂ 15:52
☽∥♆ 16:54
☽⋕♅ 18:53
☽☍⚳ 23:21

6 Tu
☽⚼⚷ 5:31
☽⚺♀ 6:26
☿∥♀ 7:08
☽⚺♄ 9:21
☽△♆ 9:56
☽∠☿ 12:07
☽∠♃ 17:49
☉⚹☽ 18:07
☽⚹♇ 19:03
☽⚺♂ 23:47

7 W
☉△♇ 5:21
♀⚹♄ 11:35
☽△⚷ 11:47
☽⚻♅ 13:01
♀⚻♆ 15:40
☽∠♀ 16:18
☽⚹☿ 16:40

8 Th
☽⚹♃ 0:44
☽∠♇ 1:22
☽⚻⚳ 11:48
☽⚼♅ 19:10
☽☌♄ 22:07
☽□♆ 22:21

9 F
☽⚹♀ 1:55
☽⚺♇ 7:25
♃ ♎ 11:19
☉□☽ 11:50
☿⋕⚳ 14:01
☿⋕⚷ 15:03
☽☌♂ 15:12
☽⚼⚳ 17:34
☿⚻♅ 18:59
☽□⚷ 23:35

10 Sa
☽□☿ 0:27
☽△♅ 0:52
⚳∥⚷ 5:11
☉⋕♀ 6:59
☿⋕♃ 9:46
☿☍⚷ 11:52
♄□♆ 13:05
☽□♃ 13:23
☽△⚳ 22:41

11 Su
♀□♇ 7:49
☽⚹♆ 8:55
☽⚺♄ 9:02
♂⚼⚳ 10:50
☽☌♇ 17:38
☽□♀ 18:41

12 M
☉△☽ 2:37
☽⚺♂ 3:52
☽△☿ 5:38
☉⚼⚳ 7:07
☽⚹⚷ 8:44
☽□♅ 10:01
☽∠♆ 12:59
☽∠♄ 13:15
☿□♂ 18:59
☽△♃ 22:51
☉☌☿ 23:41

13 Tu
☿∥♃ 3:22
☽□⚳ 6:20
☽⚼☿ 7:07
☉⚼☽ 8:19
☽∠♂ 8:40
☽∠⚷ 11:58
☽⚺♆ 16:06
☽⚹♄ 16:31
☿⚼⚳ 18:27
☿∥⚳ 19:53
☉□♂ 20:40

14 W
☽⚺♇ 0:20
☿∥⚷ 0:34
☽⚼♃ 2:07
☽△♀ 6:42
☽⚻☿ 7:54
☽⚹♂ 12:24
☉⚻☽ 12:51
☽⚺⚷ 14:18
☿⚺♀ 14:45
☽⚹♅ 15:32

15 Th
☽∠♇ 2:20
☽⚻♃ 4:29
☉☍⚷ 8:28
☽⚹⚳ 10:22
☽⚼♀ 10:57
☽⋕♅ 13:25
☽∥♆ 13:47
☽∠♅ 17:03
☽∥♀ 19:35
☽☌♆ 19:46
☽□♄ 20:27

16 F
☉∥☿ 1:27
☉⚻♅ 1:52
☽⚹♇ 3:36
♂□⚷ 3:56
☽☍☿ 7:47
☽∠⚳ 11:17
☽⚻♀ 14:19
☽☌⚷ 16:41
☽□♂ 17:18
☽⚺♅ 17:55
☉☍☽ 19:06
☽⋕☿ 20:14

17 Sa
☉⋕☽ 0:39
☽⋕⚷ 5:41
☽⋕⚳ 7:02
♂△♅ 7:06
☽☍♃ 7:08
☽⋕♃ 10:07
☽⚺⚳ 11:42
☽∥♃ 13:23
☽∥⚳ 16:23
♀⚻⚷ 17:36
☽∥⚷ 17:48
♀∥♆ 20:43
☽⚺♆ 21:00
☉∥☽ 21:09
♀⋕♅ 21:11
☽△♄ 21:55

18 Su
☽□♇ 4:40
☽⚻☿ 6:29
♅⋕♆ 7:04
☽∥☿ 7:34
♀☍♅ 8:07
☽⚺⚷ 17:19
☽☌♅ 18:33
☽☍♀ 19:31
☽△♂ 20:12
☽∠♆ 21:13
☽⚼♄ 22:16
☉⚻☽ 23:15

19 M
☽⚼☿ 5:52
☽⚻♃ 8:25
☽∥♅ 8:58
☽⋕♆ 9:07
☽☌⚳ 11:52
♀⚹♂ 11:54
☽⋕♀ 13:55
♀⚼♆ 15:51
☉∥⚷ 15:55
☽∠⚷ 17:29
☽⚹♆ 21:26
☽⚼♂ 21:32
☽⚻♄ 22:38

20 Tu
☉⚼☽ 1:15
☽△♇ 5:12
☽△☿ 5:33
♀∠♄ 6:28
☽⚼♃ 9:07
☽⚹⚷ 17:51
☉∥⚳ 18:25
☽⚺♅ 19:09
☽⚻♂ 23:08

21 W
☽⚻♀ 0:41
☿△♇ 1:27
☉△☽ 3:33
☽⚼♇ 5:48
☽△♃ 10:09
☽⚺⚳ 12:32
☽∠♅ 19:55
☽□♆ 22:43

22 Th
☽☍♄ 0:15
☽⚼♀ 3:57
☿ D 5:30
☽□☿ 6:39
☽⚻♇ 6:50
☉⋕♃ 8:21
☽∠⚳ 13:30
☉ ♎ 14:22
☽□⚷ 19:49
☽⚹♅ 21:13
☉∥♃ 23:47

23 F
☽☍♂ 3:55
☽△♀ 7:58
☿△♇ 8:52
☉□☽ 9:57
☽□♃ 13:50
☿∠♀ 14:26
♀ ♏ 14:52
☽⚹⚳ 15:01
☉⋕⚳ 21:59

24 Sa
☽△♆ 2:07
☽⚻♄ 4:03
☽☍♇ 10:44
☽⚹☿ 11:16

25 Su
☽△⚷ 0:13
☽□♅ 1:43
☽⚼♆ 4:48
☉⋕⚷ 6:01
☽⚼♄ 6:58
☽⚻♂ 11:38
⚳⚻♃ 11:47
☽∠☿ 15:14
☽□♀ 18:37
⚳⋕♃ 18:50
☉⚹☽ 19:34
☽□⚳ 20:01
☽⚹♃ 20:15

26 M
☉⚻⚳ 0:45
☽⚼⚷ 3:26
☉☌♃ 7:01
♀☍⚳ 8:06
☽⚻♆ 8:11
☽△♄ 10:35
♇ D 15:03
♀⚺♃ 15:36
☽⚼♂ 16:41
☽⚻♇ 17:20
☽⚺☿ 20:21

27 Tu
☽∠♃ 0:31
☉∠☽ 1:39
☽⋕♀ 2:15
☽⚻⚷ 7:18
♂ ♑ 8:08
☽△♅ 8:54
☉⚺♀ 19:15
☽⚼♇ 21:36
☽△♂ 22:29

28 W
☽△⚳ 3:30
☽⚺♃ 5:26
☉⚺☽ 8:31
☽⚹♀ 8:48
☽⋕♆ 9:47
☽∥♅ 11:22
☿⚼⚳ 12:21
☽⚼♅ 13:24
☽☍♆ 16:47
☽□♄ 19:43

29 Th
☽△♇ 2:26
☽∥☿ 5:53
☽⚼⚳ 8:03
☽☌☿ 10:06
♀⚼⚷ 14:12
☽☍⚷ 16:44
☽∠♀ 17:01
☽⚻♅ 18:25
☉⋕☽ 23:00

30 F
☽∥⚷ 11:00
☽⋕♃ 11:51
☽□♂ 11:59
☽⚻⚳ 13:03
☽∥⚳ 16:21
☽☌♃ 16:55
☽⋕⚳ 17:13
☽∥♃ 21:57
☽⋕⚷ 22:32

LONGITUDE

Day	Sid.Time	☉	☽	☽ 12 hour	Mean☊	True☊	☿	♀	♂	⚳	♃	♄	⚷	♅	♆	♇
	h m s	° ' "	° ' "	° ' "	° '	° '	° '	° '	° '	° '	° '	° '	° '	° '	° '	° '
1 Sa	0 40 38	8♎14 33	8♎08 45	14♎10 38	11♍05.8	12♍39.6	20♍42.0	8♏59.8	21♑24.6	2♉31.8	4♎38.2	11♐37.0	22♓13.1	23♈05.2	9♓53.3	14♑55.9
2 Su	0 44 34	9 13 35	20 10 51	26 09 35	11 02.6	12R 36.3	21 58.8	10 12.8	3 04.5	2R 20.9	4 51.1	11 41.4	22R 10.5	23R 02.9	9R 51.9	14 56.1
3 M	0 48 31	10 12 39	2♏07 04	8♏03 32	10 59.4	12 31.9	23 20.9	11 25.9	3 44.5	2 09.7	5 04.1	11 45.8	22 07.9	23 00.5	9 50.5	14 56.2
4 Tu	0 52 27	11 11 45	13 59 16	19 54 32	10 56.3	12 26.8	24 47.4	12 38.9	4 24.7	1 58.3	5 17.1	11 50.4	22 05.3	22 58.2	9 49.1	14 56.5
5 W	0 56 24	12 10 53	25 49 41	1♐45 04	10 53.1	12 21.5	26 17.8	13 51.9	5 05.0	1 46.6	5 30.0	11 55.0	22 02.8	22 55.8	9 47.8	14 56.7
6 Th	1 00 20	13 10 02	7♐41 06	13 38 11	10 49.9	12 16.7	27 51.3	15 04.9	5 45.5	1 34.7	5 42.9	11 59.7	22 00.2	22 53.4	9 46.5	14 57.0
7 F	1 04 17	14 09 14	19 36 49	25 37 28	10 46.7	12 12.9	29 27.6	16 17.8	6 26.1	1 22.5	5 55.8	12 04.4	21 57.7	22 51.0	9 45.2	14 57.3
8 Sa	1 08 13	15 08 27	1♑40 42	7♑47 01	10 43.6	12 10.5	1♎06.1	17 30.8	7 06.9	1 10.2	6 08.8	12 09.2	21 55.3	22 48.6	9 43.9	14 57.6
9 Su	1 12 10	16 07 42	13 57 02	20 11 16	10 40.4	12D 09.5	2 46.3	18 43.7	7 47.8	0 57.7	6 21.7	12 14.1	21 52.8	22 46.1	9 42.6	14 58.0
10 M	1 16 07	17 06 59	26 30 19	2♒54 42	10 37.2	12 09.9	4 27.9	19 56.6	8 28.8	0 45.0	6 34.5	12 19.1	21 50.4	22 43.7	9 41.4	14 58.4
11 Tu	1 20 03	18 06 18	9♒24 56	16 01 26	10 34.0	12 11.2	6 10.6	21 09.4	9 10.0	0 32.1	6 47.4	12 24.1	21 48.0	22 41.3	9 40.2	14 58.8
12 W	1 24 00	19 05 38	22 44 36	29 34 40	10 30.8	12 12.8	7 54.0	22 22.3	9 51.3	0 19.1	7 00.2	12 29.2	21 45.6	22 38.9	9 39.0	14 59.2
13 Th	1 27 56	20 05 01	6♓31 46	13♓35 52	10 27.7	12R 13.8	9 37.8	23 35.1	10 32.7	0 05.9	7 13.1	12 34.3	21 43.3	22 36.4	9 37.8	14 59.7
14 F	1 31 53	21 04 25	20 46 46	28 04 05	10 24.5	12 13.6	11 22.0	24 47.9	11 14.2	29♈52.6	7 25.9	12 39.5	21 40.9	22 34.0	9 36.7	15 00.2
15 Sa	1 35 49	22 03 50	5♈27 13	12♈55 21	10 21.3	12 11.7	13 06.3	26 00.6	11 55.9	29 39.2	7 38.6	12 44.8	21 38.7	22 31.5	9 35.6	15 00.8
16 Su	1 39 46	23 03 18	20 27 30	28 02 31	10 18.1	12 07.9	14 50.5	27 13.4	12 37.6	29 25.7	7 51.4	12 50.1	21 36.4	22 29.1	9 34.5	15 01.3
17 M	1 43 42	24 02 48	5♉39 08	13♉16 02	10 15.0	12 02.5	16 34.6	28 26.0	13 19.5	29 12.1	8 04.1	12 55.5	21 34.2	22 26.6	9 33.4	15 01.9
18 Tu	1 47 39	25 02 20	20 51 53	28 25 23	10 11.8	11 56.0	18 18.4	29 38.7	14 01.5	28 58.5	8 16.8	13 01.0	21 32.0	22 24.2	9 32.4	15 02.6
19 W	1 51 35	26 01 54	5♊55 21	13♊20 48	10 08.6	11 49.4	20 01.9	0♐51.4	14 43.5	28 44.8	8 29.5	13 06.5	21 29.9	22 21.8	9 31.4	15 03.2
20 Th	1 55 32	27 01 30	20 40 52	27 54 56	10 05.4	11 43.7	21 45.0	2 04.0	15 25.7	28 31.0	8 42.2	13 12.1	21 27.7	22 19.3	9 30.4	15 03.9
21 F	1 59 29	28 01 09	5♋02 34	12♋03 33	10 02.2	11 39.6	23 27.7	3 16.6	16 08.0	28 17.3	8 54.8	13 17.7	21 25.7	22 16.9	9 29.4	15 04.6
22 Sa	2 03 25	29 00 50	18 57 51	25 45 33	9 59.1	11D 37.3	25 09.9	4 29.1	16 50.4	28 03.5	9 07.4	13 23.4	21 23.6	22 14.5	9 28.5	15 05.4
23 Su	2 07 22	0♏00 33	2♌26 54	9♌02 15	9 55.9	11 36.8	26 51.6	5 41.7	17 32.9	27 49.7	9 20.0	13 29.1	21 21.6	22 12.1	9 27.5	15 06.2
24 M	2 11 18	1 00 19	15 32 01	21 56 38	9 52.7	11 37.6	28 32.8	6 54.2	18 15.5	27 36.0	9 32.5	13 34.9	21 19.7	22 09.6	9 26.7	15 07.0
25 Tu	2 15 15	2 00 06	28 16 37	4♍32 27	9 49.5	11 38.8	0♏13.4	8 06.7	18 58.2	27 22.2	9 45.0	13 40.8	21 17.7	22 07.2	9 25.8	15 07.8
26 W	2 19 11	2 59 56	10♍44 36	16 53 35	9 46.4	11R 39.5	1 53.6	9 19.1	19 41.0	27 08.6	9 57.4	13 46.7	21 15.8	22 04.9	9 25.0	15 08.7
27 Th	2 23 08	3 59 48	22 59 47	29 03 40	9 43.2	11 38.7	3 33.2	10 31.5	20 23.9	26 55.0	10 09.9	13 52.6	21 14.0	22 02.5	9 24.2	15 09.6
28 F	2 27 04	4 59 42	5♎05 34	11♎05 50	9 40.0	11 35.8	5 12.2	11 43.9	21 06.9	26 41.5	10 22.3	13 58.6	21 12.2	22 00.1	9 23.4	15 10.5
29 Sa	2 31 01	5 59 39	17 04 45	23 02 36	9 36.8	11 30.4	6 50.8	12 56.3	21 49.9	26 28.1	10 34.6	14 04.6	21 10.4	21 57.7	9 22.7	15 11.4
30 Su	2 34 58	6 59 37	28 59 36	4♏55 58	9 33.6	11 22.4	8 28.8	14 08.6	22 33.1	26 14.8	10 46.9	14 10.7	21 08.7	21 55.4	9 22.0	15 12.4
31 M	2 38 54	7♏59 37	10♏51 54	16 47 34	9♍30.5	11♍12.4	10♏06.3	15♐20.9	23♑16.4	26♈01.6	10♎59.2	14♐16.9	21♓07.0	21♈53.1	9♓21.3	15♑13.4

1st of Mon

Julian Day 2457662.5
Obliquity 23°26'05"
SVP 5♓01'3
GC 27♐04.
Eris 23♈13.

Day	⚴
1	19♒40.8
6	19 15.7
11	18 59.5
16	18 52.1
21	18 53.2
26	19 02.6
31	19 19.9

Day	⚵
1	18♏12.5
6	19 45.1
11	21 19.5
16	22 55.3
21	24 32.6
26	26 11.2
31	27 50.9

Day	⚶
1	24♋44.7
6	26 14.3
11	27 39.2
16	28 59.2
21	0♌13.8
26	1 22.3
31	2 24.3

DECLINATION and LATITUDE

Day	☉ Decl	☽ Decl	☽ Lat	☽12h Decl	☿ Decl	☿ Lat	♀ Decl	♀ Lat	♂ Decl	♂ Lat	⚳ Decl	⚳ Lat	♃ Decl	♃ Lat	♄ Decl	♄ Lat
1 Sa	3S16	1S10	2N15	3S04	5N03	1N29	14S42	0S13	25S49	2S24	0N03	13S04	0S50	1N06	20S45	1N26
2 Su	3 39	4 56	3 11	6 44	4 39	1 36	15 08	0 16	25 47	2 23	0S01	13 04	0 55	1 06	20 46	1 26
3 M	4 03	8 28	3 58	10 07	4 12	1 42	15 34	0 19	25 45	2 23	0 05	13 05	1 01	1 06	20 46	1 26
4 Tu	4 26	11 39	4 35	13 05	3 43	1 47	15 59	0 22	25 43	2 22	0 09	13 05	1 06	1 06	20 47	1 26
5 W	4 49	14 22	4 59	15 30	3 10	1 51	16 24	0 25	25 41	2 21	0 13	13 05	1 11	1 06	20 48	1 26
6 Th	5 12	16 28	5 11	17 16	2 36	1 54	16 48	0 28	25 39	2 20	0 17	13 05	1 16	1 06	20 49	1 25
7 F	5 35	17 53	5 10	18 18	1 59	1 56	17 13	0 31	25 36	2 19	0 20	13 05	1 21	1 06	20 49	1 25
8 Sa	5 58	18 31	4 54	18 31	1 21	1 56	17 36	0 34	25 33	2 18	0 24	13 04	1 26	1 06	20 50	1 25
9 Su	6 21	18 18	4 26	17 51	0 41	1 56	17 60	0 37	25 30	2 18	0 28	13 04	1 31	1 06	20 51	1 25
10 M	6 43	17 11	3 44	16 18	0S00	1 56	18 22	0 41	25 26	2 17	0 32	13 04	1 36	1 06	20 52	1 25
11 Tu	7 06	15 10	2 49	13 50	0 42	1 54	18 45	0 44	25 23	2 16	0 35	13 03	1 41	1 06	20 53	1 25
12 W	7 29	12 17	1 44	10 33	1 25	1 52	19 07	0 47	25 19	2 15	0 39	13 02	1 46	1 06	20 54	1 24
13 Th	7 51	8 38	0 31	6 34	2 08	1 49	19 28	0 50	25 15	2 14	0 43	13 01	1 51	1 06	20 54	1 24
14 F	8 13	4 22	0S46	2 04	2 52	1 46	19 49	0 53	25 10	2 13	0 46	13 00	1 56	1 06	20 55	1 24
15 Sa	8 36	0N17	2 03	2N40	3 36	1 43	20 09	0 56	25 06	2 12	0 49	12 59	2 01	1 06	20 56	1 24
16 Su	8 58	5 01	3 12	7 18	4 20	1 38	20 29	0 59	25 01	2 12	0 53	12 58	2 06	1 06	20 57	1 24
17 M	9 20	9 29	4 09	11 30	5 04	1 34	20 49	1 02	24 56	2 11	0 56	12 56	2 11	1 06	20 58	1 24
18 Tu	9 41	13 20	4 48	14 55	5 48	1 29	21 07	1 05	24 51	2 10	0 59	12 55	2 16	1 06	20 59	1 24
19 W	10 03	16 15	5 07	17 18	6 32	1 24	21 26	1 08	24 45	2 09	1 02	12 53	2 21	1 06	20 59	1 23
20 Th	10 25	18 02	5 05	18 29	7 16	1 18	21 43	1 11	24 40	2 08	1 05	12 51	2 26	1 06	21 00	1 23
21 F	10 46	18 37	4 44	18 28	7 59	1 13	22 01	1 14	24 34	2 07	1 08	12 49	2 31	1 07	21 01	1 23
22 Sa	11 07	18 02	4 06	17 21	8 42	1 07	22 17	1 16	24 27	2 06	1 11	12 47	2 36	1 07	21 02	1 23
23 Su	11 28	16 26	3 15	15 19	9 24	1 01	22 33	1 19	24 21	2 05	1 14	12 45	2 41	1 07	21 03	1 23
24 M	11 49	14 00	2 16	12 33	10 06	0 55	22 48	1 22	24 14	2 04	1 16	12 43	2 45	1 07	21 04	1 23
25 Tu	12 10	10 57	1 12	9 15	10 48	0 48	23 03	1 25	24 07	2 03	1 19	12 40	2 50	1 07	21 04	1 22
26 W	12 31	7 28	0 05	5 36	11 28	0 42	23 17	1 28	24 00	2 02	1 21	12 38	2 55	1 07	21 05	1 22
27 Th	12 51	3 42	1N01	1 47	12 09	0 35	23 31	1 30	23 53	2 01	1 23	12 35	2 60	1 07	21 06	1 22
28 F	13 11	0S09	2 02	2S04	12 48	0 29	23 43	1 33	23 45	2 00	1 25	12 32	3 05	1 07	21 07	1 22
29 Sa	13 31	3 58	2 58	5 49	13 27	0 22	23 56	1 36	23 38	1 59	1 27	12 29	3 09	1 07	21 08	1 22
30 Su	13 51	7 36	3 45	9 18	14 05	0 15	24 07	1 38	23 30	1 58	1 29	12 26	3 14	1 07	21 09	1 22
31 M	14S10	10S55	4N23	12S25	14S43	0N09	24S18	1S41	23S21	1S57	1S30	12S23	3S19	1N07	21S09	1N22

Day	⚷ Decl	⚷ Lat	♅ Decl	♅ Lat	♆ Decl	♆ Lat	♇ Decl	♇ Lat
1	0N55	4N22	8N23	0S38	8S40	0S53	21S25	1N
6	0 50	4 21	8 18	0 38	8 43	0 53	21 25	1
11	0 44	4 20	8 14	0 38	8 45	0 53	21 26	1
16	0 39	4 19	8 09	0 38	8 47	0 53	21 26	1
21	0 33	4 18	8 05	0 38	8 49	0 53	21 26	1
26	0 29	4 17	8 01	0 38	8 51	0 52	21 26	1
31	0N24	4N16	7N56	0S38	8S52	0S52	21S26	1N

Day	⚴ Decl	⚴ Lat	⚵ Decl	⚵ Lat	⚶ Decl	⚶ Lat	Eris Decl	Eris Lat
1	1N38	17N23	7S33	10N05	19N50	1S22	2S36	12S
6	0 41	16 31	8 01	10 01	19 40	1 15	2 37	12
11	0S13	15 39	8 28	9 58	19 30	1 09	2 38	12
16	1 03	14 49	8 54	9 55	19 21	1 02	2 39	12
21	1 50	13 59	9 19	9 52	19 13	0 54	2 40	12
26	2 33	13 11	9 43	9 50	19 06	0 46	2 41	12
31	3S13	12N24	10S06	9N49	19N00	0S38	2S42	12S

Moon Phenomena

Max/0 Decl
dy hr mn
8 6:02 18S33
14 22:33 0 N
20 23:49 18N37
27 23:04 0 S

Perigee/Apogee
dy hr m kilometers
4 11:04 a 406096
16 23:49 p 357861
31 19:27 a 406662

PH dy hr mn
● 1 0:13 8♎15
☽ 9 4:34 16♑19
○ 16 4:24 23♈14
☾ 22 19:15 29♋49
● 30 17:39 7♏44

Max/0 Lat
dy hr mn
6 9:12 5N12
13 9:42 0 S
19 9:25 5S09
26 1:47 0 N

Void of Course Moon

Last Aspect			☽ Ingres
2 5:44	♅	☍	♏ 2 19:
5 1:05	♅	⚻	♐ 5 8:
7 6:27	♅	△	♑ 7 20:
9 16:52	♅	□	♒ 10 6:
11 23:50	♅	⚹	♓ 12 12:
14 7:14	♀	△	♈ 14 15:
16 4:24	☉	☍	♉ 16 15:
17 14:48	♇	△	♊ 18 14:
20 11:18	☉	△	♋ 20 15:
22 19:15	☉	□	♌ 22 19:
24 12:22	♅	△	♍ 25 3:
26 18:34	♂	△	♎ 27 13:
29 10:10	♂	□	♏ 30 2:

DAILY ASPECTARIAN

1 Sa: ☉☌☽ 0:13; ☽⚺♀ 1:53; ♂△⚳ 3:24; ☽⚻♆ 3:27; ☽⚹♄ 6:56; ☽□♇ 13:30; ☉∥☽ 14:49; ♀△♆ 17:15; ♃⋕⚷ 19:10; ☽⋕☿ 22:22
2 Su: ☿☍⚷ 3:23; ☽⚻⚷ 3:59; ☽⚺☿ 4:04; ☽☍♅ 5:44; ☽⚼♆ 9:23; ☽∠♄ 13:09; ☉⚻♆ 15:12; ☿⚻♅ 18:20; ☽⋕♅ 23:08
3 M: ☽☍⚳ 0:05; ☽∥♆ 1:33; ☽⚹♂ 3:28; ☉⋕☿ 4:31; ☽⚺♃ 6:04; ♀⚺♄ 7:00; ☽⚼⚷ 10:05; ☽∠☿ 14:18; ☽△♆ 15:35; ☉⚺☽ 17:50; ☽⚺♄ 19:37; ☽☌♀ 20:59
4 Tu: ☽⚹♇ 1:56; ☽∠♂ 11:39; ☽∠♃ 13:00; ☽△⚷ 16:22; ☉⚹♄ 17:00; ☽⚻♅ 18:09
5 W: ☽⚹☿ 1:05; ☉∠☽ 3:00; ☽∠♇ 8:21; ☽⚻⚳ 11:51; ☽⚺♂ 19:52; ☽⚹♃ 19:57; ♀⚹♇ 21:23; ♂□♃ 21:46
6 Th: ☽⚼♅ 0:25; ☽□♆ 4:13; ☽∥♀ 6:21; ☽☌♄ 8:45; ☉⚹☽ 12:03; ☽⚺♇ 14:39; ☽⚺♀ 16:36; ☽⚼⚳ 17:37
7 F: ☽□⚷ 4:41; ☽△♅ 6:27; ☿ ♎ 7:57; ☉□♇ 19:34; ☿⋕♃ 21:04; ☽□☿ 22:41; ☽△⚳ 23:01
8 Sa: ☿⚻⚳ 0:53; ☽∠♀ 1:50; ☽□♃ 8:57; ☽☌♂ 11:19; ☽⚹♆ 15:47; ☽⚺♄ 20:39; ☿∥⚷ 20:41
9 Su: ☽☌♇ 1:58; ☉□☽ 4:34; ☽∥♀ 6:21; ☿⋕⚳ 6:55; ☽⚹♀ 10:12; ☽⚹⚷ 15:11; ☽□♅ 16:52; ☽∠♆ 20:34
10 M: ☽∠♄ 1:33; ☽□⚳ 7:50; ☽△☿ 17:08; ☽△♃ 19:06; ☽∠⚷ 19:13; ☿∥⚳ 19:47; ☿∠♀ 23:06; ☽⚺♂ 23:31
11 Tu: ☽⚺♆ 0:28; ☿⋕⚷ 1:00; ☽⚹♄ 5:29; ☿☌♃ 9:47; ☽⚺♇ 10:07; ♀△⚷ 12:18; ♀∠♃ 15:11; ☉△☽ 16:59; ♂⚹♆ 17:05; ☽⚺⚷ 22:16; ☽⚼♃ 22:40; ☽□♀ 23:17; ☽⚹♅ 23:50
12 W: ☽⚼☿ 0:19; ☽∠♂ 3:56; ♀⚻♅ 5:17; ☽∠♇ 12:43; ☽⚹⚳ 13:05; ☿∥♃ 13:21; ⚳⋕⚷ 20:02; ☉⚼☽ 21:20; ☽∥♆ 23:11; ☿⚻♆ 24:00
13 Th: ☽⚻♃ 1:12; ☽∠♅ 1:50; ☽⋕♅ 2:34; ☉∥☽ 4:15; ☽☌♆ 5:17; ☽⚻☿ 6:02; ☽⚹♂ 7:11; ☽□♄ 10:20; ⚳R♈ 10:42; ☽∠⚳ 14:18; ☽⚹♇ 14:21; ☿□♂ 21:01; ☉⋕♅ 21:53
14 F: ☉⚻☽ 0:31; ☽☌⚷ 1:29; ☽⚺♅ 2:57; ☽∥☿ 6:48; ☽△♀ 7:14; ☽∥♃ 12:27; ☉⚻⚷ 14:13; ☽⚺⚳ 14:44; ☽∥⚳ 18:25; ☿⚹♄ 18:48; ☽⋕⚷ 19:10
15 Sa: ☽∥⚷ 1:53; ☽⋕⚳ 2:45; ☽☍♃ 3:35; ☽⚺♆ 6:39; ☽⋕♃ 8:54; ☽⚼♀ 9:43; ☉☍♅ 10:44; ☽□♂ 10:55; ☽△♄ 11:47; ☉∥♆ 12:42; ☽☍☿ 13:54; ☽□♇ 15:21; ☽⋕☿ 19:49
16 Su: ☽⚺⚷ 1:49; ☿□♇ 2:30; ☽☌♅ 3:12; ☉☍☽ 4:24; ☽∠♆ 6:31; ♂⚺♄ 8:15; ☽⚻♀ 11:38; ☽⚼♄ 11:45; ☽☌⚳ 13:59; ☽∥♅ 16:33; ♀∠♂ 18:52; ☽⋕♆ 20:07; ☉⋕☽ 23:01
17 M: ☽∠⚷ 1:27; ☽⚻♃ 3:52; ☽⚹♆ 6:09; ☽⚻♄ 11:32; ♀∥♄ 11:56; ☉⚼♆ 12:08; ☽△♂ 12:40; ♀⚻⚳ 12:49; ☽△♇ 14:48; ☽⚻☿ 19:26; ⚴ D 19:32
18 Tu: ☽⚹⚷ 1:03; ☽⚺♅ 2:26; ☽⚼♃ 3:53; ♀ ♐ 7:02; ☉⚻☽ 7:05; ♀∠♇ 7:57; ☽⚺⚳ 12:41; ☽⚼♂ 13:36; ☽⚼♇ 14:36; ☽☍♀ 15:10; ☽⚼☿ 22:23
19 W: ♀∥♇ 0:25; ☽∠♅ 2:19; ☽△♃ 4:12; ☽□♆ 5:48; ☉⚼☽ 8:50; ♂☌♇ 11:24; ☽☍♄ 11:41; ☽∠⚳ 12:28; ☽⚻♇ 14:48; ☽⚻♂ 14:58; ☿⚻⚷ 20:03
20 Th: ⚶ ♌ 1:07; ☽□⚷ 1:17; ☽△☿ 2:00; ☽⚹♅ 2:42; ☿☍♅ 7:49; ☉△☽ 11:18; ☽⚹⚳ 12:48; ☽⚻♀ 20:44; ⚳⚼♄ 23:27
21 F: ☿⋕♅ 3:17; ☉☍⚳ 5:16; ☽□♃ 6:42; ☉∠♄ 7:21; ☽△♆ 7:35; ☽⚻♄ 14:14; ☿⚼♆ 14:21; ☽☍♇ 17:14; ☽☍♂ 20:05
22 Sa: ☽⚼♀ 1:00; ☽△⚷ 4:16; ☿∥♆ 4:25; ☽□♅ 5:45; ☽⚼♆ 9:42; ☽□☿ 12:31; ☽□⚳ 15:50; ☽⚼♄ 16:49; ☉□☽ 19:15; ☉ ♏ 23:47
23 Su: ☽△♀ 6:29; ☽⚼⚷ 7:05; ☿☍⚳ 12:07; ☽⚹♃ 12:45; ☽⚻♆ 12:46; ♃⚻♆ 13:34; ☽△♄ 20:21; ☽⚻♇ 23:13
24 M: ☿∠♄ 0:32; ♀⚼♅ 4:57; ☽⚻♂ 5:23; ☽⚻⚷ 10:49; ☽△♅ 12:22; ☉⋕☽ 15:50; ☽∠♃ 17:11; ☿ ♏ 20:47; ☽△⚳ 22:18
25 Tu: ☽⋕☿ 0:57; ☽⚼♇ 3:32; ☽⚹☿ 4:17; ☉⚹☽ 7:44; ☽⚼♂ 11:34; ☽⋕♆ 14:45; ☽⚼♅ 16:55; ☽∥♅ 20:22; ☽□♀ 20:56; ☽☍♆ 21:26; ☽⚺♃ 22:27
26 W: ♀□♆ 1:55; ☽⚼⚳ 2:40; ☽□♄ 5:57; ☽△♇ 8:35; ☽∠☿ 13:53; ♀⚹♃ 15:20; ☉∠☽ 15:26; ☽△♂ 18:34; ☽☍⚷ 20:32; ☽⚻♅ 22:07
27 Th: ☽⋕♃ 4:21; ☽⚻⚳ 7:36; ☽⋕⚳ 14:21; ☉☌☿ 16:18; ☽∥⚷ 20:18; ♀⚼⚳ 23:19; ☉⚺☽ 23:47
28 F: ☽⚺☿ 0:15; ☽⋕⚷ 1:50; ♀∥♂ 2:20; ♂⚹⚷ 2:51; ☽∥⚳ 7:59; ☽⚻♆ 8:34; ☽☌♃ 10:44; ☿⚼⚷ 14:20; ☽⚹♀ 14:45; ☽⚹♄ 17:55; ☽∥♃ 18:45; ☽□♇ 20:12
29 Sa: ♂□♅ 4:07; ☉⚼⚷ 4:12; ☉∥☿ 5:07; ☽⚻⚷ 8:13; ☽☍♅ 9:47; ☽□♂ 10:10; ☽⚼♆ 14:40; ☽☍⚳ 18:33
30 Su: ☽∠♀ 0:20; ☽∠♄ 0:23; ♀☌♄ 0:46; ☽⋕♅ 2:25; ☽∥♆ 8:52; ☿△♆ 12:58; ☽⚼⚷ 14:25; ☉☌☽ 17:39; ☽△♆ 20:57; ♀⚺♇ 21:28; ☽☌☿ 22:13
31 M: ☽⚺♃ 0:15; ☽⚺♄ 6:59; ☽⚹♇ 8:50; ☽⚺♀ 10:06; ☿⚺♃ 14:56; ☽△⚷ 20:43; ☽⚻♅ 22:14

LONGITUDE — November 2016

Day	Sid.Time	☉	☽	☽ 12 hour	Mean☊	True☊	☿	♀	♂	⚳	♃	♄	⚷	♅	♆	♇
	h m s	° ' "	° ' "	° ' "	° '	° '	° '	° '	° '	° '	° '	° '	° '	° '	° '	° '
1 Tu	2 42 51	8♏59 39	22♏43 09	28♏38 51	9♍27.3	11♍00.9	11♏43.4	16♐33.2	23♑59.7	25♈48.6	11♎11.4	14♐23.1	21♓05.4	21♈50.8	9♓20.6	15♑14.4
2 W	2 46 47	9 59 43	4♐34 51	10♐31 22	9 24.1	10R 49.0	13 20.0	17 45.4	24 43.1	25R 35.8	11 23.5	14 29.3	21R 03.8	21R 48.5	9R 20.0	15 15.5
3 Th	2 50 44	10 59 49	16 28 39	22 26 59	9 20.9	10 37.7	14 56.1	18 57.6	25 26.6	25 23.1	11 35.7	14 35.6	21 02.3	21 46.2	9 19.4	15 16.6
4 F	2 54 40	11 59 56	28 26 41	4♑28 05	9 17.8	10 28.1	16 31.8	20 09.8	26 10.2	25 10.7	11 47.7	14 41.9	21 00.8	21 43.9	9 18.9	15 17.7
5 Sa	2 58 37	13 00 05	10♑31 37	16 37 41	9 14.6	10 20.7	18 07.1	21 21.9	26 53.9	24 58.4	11 59.8	14 48.2	20 59.4	21 41.7	9 18.3	15 18.8
6 Su	3 02 33	14 00 16	22 46 47	28 59 26	9 11.4	10 15.9	19 41.9	22 33.9	27 37.6	24 46.3	12 11.7	14 54.6	20 58.0	21 39.5	9 17.9	15 20.0
7 M	3 06 30	15 00 28	5♒16 08	11♒37 27	9 08.2	10D 13.6	21 16.4	23 45.9	28 21.4	24 34.5	12 23.6	15 01.1	20 56.7	21 37.3	9 17.4	15 21.2
8 Tu	3 10 27	16 00 42	18 03 56	24 36 07	9 05.0	10 13.2	22 50.5	24 57.9	29 05.3	24 22.9	12 35.5	15 07.6	20 55.4	21 35.1	9 17.0	15 22.4
9 W	3 14 23	17 00 57	1♓14 28	7♓59 27	9 01.9	10R 13.6	24 24.2	26 09.8	29 49.2	24 11.6	12 47.3	15 14.1	20 54.1	21 33.0	9 16.6	15 23.7
10 Th	3 18 20	18 01 13	14 51 23	21 50 28	8 58.7	10 13.7	25 57.6	27 21.7	0♒33.2	24 00.6	12 59.0	15 20.6	20 52.9	21 30.9	9 16.2	15 24.9
11 F	3 22 16	19 01 31	28 56 48	6♈10 14	8 55.5	10 12.4	27 30.7	28 33.5	1 17.3	23 49.8	13 10.7	15 27.2	20 51.8	21 28.8	9 15.9	15 26.2
12 Sa	3 26 13	20 01 51	13♈30 26	20 56 50	8 52.3	10 08.7	29 03.4	29 45.3	2 01.4	23 39.3	13 22.3	15 33.8	20 50.7	21 26.7	9 15.6	15 27.5
13 Su	3 30 09	21 02 11	28 28 37	6♉04 45	8 49.2	10 02.2	0♐35.9	0♑57.0	2 45.6	23 29.1	13 33.9	15 40.4	20 49.7	21 24.7	9 15.3	15 28.9
14 M	3 34 06	22 02 34	13♉44 00	21 24 59	8 46.0	9 53.3	2 08.0	2 08.6	3 29.8	23 19.2	13 45.4	15 47.1	20 48.7	21 22.7	9 15.1	15 30.2
15 Tu	3 38 02	23 02 58	29 06 11	6♊46 06	8 42.8	9 42.8	3 39.8	3 20.2	4 14.1	23 09.6	13 56.8	15 53.8	20 47.7	21 20.7	9 14.9	15 31.6
16 W	3 41 59	24 03 24	14♊23 16	21 56 20	8 39.6	9 31.9	5 11.4	4 31.7	4 58.4	23 00.4	14 08.2	16 00.5	20 46.9	21 18.7	9 14.8	15 33.0
17 Th	3 45 56	25 03 51	29 24 08	6♋45 43	8 36.4	9 21.9	6 42.7	5 43.2	5 42.8	22 51.4	14 19.4	16 07.3	20 46.0	21 16.8	9 14.6	15 34.5
18 F	3 49 52	26 04 21	14♋00 23	21 07 40	8 33.3	9 13.9	8 13.7	6 54.6	6 27.3	22 42.8	14 30.7	16 14.1	20 45.3	21 14.9	9 14.5	15 35.9
19 Sa	3 53 49	27 04 52	28 07 20	4♌59 23	8 30.1	9 08.5	9 44.4	8 05.9	7 11.7	22 34.6	14 41.8	16 20.9	20 44.6	21 13.1	9 14.5	15 37.4
20 Su	3 57 45	28 05 24	11♌43 59	18 21 27	8 26.9	9 05.7	11 14.8	9 17.2	7 56.3	22 26.6	14 52.9	16 27.7	20 43.9	21 11.3	9D 14.5	15 38.9
21 M	4 01 42	29 05 59	24 52 15	1♍16 54	8 23.7	9D 04.8	12 44.9	10 28.4	8 40.8	22 19.1	15 03.9	16 34.6	20 43.3	21 09.5	9 14.5	15 40.5
22 Tu	4 05 38	0♐06 35	7♍36 00	13 50 09	8 20.6	9R 04.8	14 14.7	11 39.6	9 25.5	22 11.9	15 14.8	16 41.5	20 42.7	21 07.7	9 14.5	15 42.0
23 W	4 09 35	1 07 13	19 59 59	26 06 09	8 17.4	9 04.5	15 44.2	12 50.6	10 10.1	22 05.0	15 25.7	16 48.4	20 42.2	21 06.0	9 14.6	15 43.6
24 Th	4 13 31	2 07 53	2♎09 13	8♎09 48	8 14.2	9 02.6	17 13.3	14 01.6	10 54.8	21 58.6	15 36.4	16 55.3	20 41.8	21 04.3	9 14.7	15 45.1
25 F	4 17 28	3 08 34	14 08 25	20 05 34	8 11.0	8 58.3	18 42.0	15 12.6	11 39.6	21 52.5	15 47.1	17 02.3	20 41.4	21 02.7	9 14.9	15 46.7
26 Sa	4 21 25	4 09 17	26 01 41	1♏57 11	8 07.9	8 51.0	20 10.2	16 23.4	12 24.4	21 46.8	15 57.7	17 09.2	20 41.0	21 01.1	9 15.0	15 48.4
27 Su	4 25 21	5 10 01	7♏52 23	13 47 36	8 04.7	8 40.7	21 38.0	17 34.2	13 09.2	21 41.4	16 08.2	17 16.2	20 40.8	20 59.5	9 15.3	15 50.0
28 M	4 29 18	6 10 47	19 43 06	25 39 04	8 01.5	8 27.7	23 05.1	18 44.9	13 54.1	21 36.5	16 18.7	17 23.2	20 40.5	20 58.0	9 15.5	15 51.7
29 Tu	4 33 14	7 11 34	1♐35 42	7♐33 10	7 58.3	8 13.0	24 31.7	19 55.5	14 39.0	21 31.9	16 29.0	17 30.2	20 40.4	20 56.5	9 15.8	15 53.4
30 W	4 37 11	8♐12 23	13 31 35	19 31 07	7♍55.1	7♍57.7	25♐57.4	21♑06.0	15♒23.9	21♈27.8	16♎39.2	17♐37.3	20♓40.3	20♈55.1	9♓16.1	15♑55.1

1st of Month

Julian Day # 2457693.5
Obliquity 23°26'05"
SVP 5♓01'36"
GC 27♐04.5
Eris 22♈55.6R

Day	⚴
1	19♒24.3
6	19 50.5
11	20 23.8
16	21 03.6
21	21 49.4
26	22 40.9

Day	⚵
1	28♏10.9
6	29 51.8
11	1♐33.5
16	3 15.8
21	4 58.7
26	6 42.1

Day	⚶
1	2♌35.8
6	3 29.0
11	4 14.1
16	4 50.7
21	5 18.1
26	5 35.6

DECLINATION and LATITUDE

Day	☉ Decl	☽ Decl	☽ Lat	☽12h Decl	☿ Decl	☿ Lat	♀ Decl	♀ Lat	♂ Decl	♂ Lat	⚳ Decl	⚳ Lat	♃ Decl	♃ Lat	♄ Decl	♄ Lat
1 Tu	14S30	13S48	4N48	15S02	15S19	0N02	24S28	1S43	23S13	1S56	1S32	12S20	3S24	1N07	21S10	1N22
2 W	14 49	16 06	5 02	17 01	15 55	0S05	24 38	1 46	23 04	1 55	1 33	12 16	3 28	1 07	21 11	1 21
3 Th	15 07	17 44	5 02	18 17	16 30	0 12	24 46	1 48	22 55	1 54	1 34	12 13	3 33	1 08	21 12	1 21
4 F	15 26	18 37	4 49	18 44	17 04	0 18	24 54	1 50	22 46	1 53	1 36	12 09	3 38	1 08	21 13	1 21
5 Sa	15 44	18 39	4 23	18 21	17 37	0 25	25 02	1 53	22 37	1 52	1 36	12 06	3 42	1 08	21 14	1 21
6 Su	16 02	17 49	3 45	17 05	18 10	0 32	25 08	1 55	22 27	1 51	1 37	12 02	3 47	1 08	21 14	1 21
7 M	16 20	16 07	2 55	14 57	18 41	0 38	25 14	1 57	22 17	1 50	1 38	11 58	3 51	1 08	21 15	1 21
8 Tu	16 38	13 35	1 55	12 02	19 12	0 45	25 19	1 59	22 07	1 49	1 38	11 54	3 56	1 08	21 16	1 21
9 W	16 55	10 17	0 48	8 23	19 42	0 51	25 24	2 01	21 57	1 48	1 38	11 50	4 00	1 08	21 17	1 21
10 Th	17 12	6 20	0S25	4 10	20 10	0 57	25 28	2 03	21 46	1 47	1 38	11 46	4 05	1 08	21 18	1 20
11 F	17 28	1 55	1 38	0N25	20 38	1 03	25 31	2 05	21 36	1 46	1 38	11 42	4 09	1 08	21 19	1 20
12 Sa	17 45	2N46	2 47	5 07	21 04	1 09	25 33	2 07	21 25	1 45	1 38	11 37	4 14	1 08	21 19	1 20
13 Su	18 01	7 24	3 46	9 36	21 30	1 15	25 34	2 09	21 14	1 44	1 38	11 33	4 18	1 09	21 20	1 20
14 M	18 17	11 39	4 31	13 30	21 55	1 21	25 35	2 10	21 02	1 43	1 37	11 28	4 22	1 09	21 21	1 20
15 Tu	18 32	15 08	4 56	16 29	22 18	1 27	25 35	2 12	20 51	1 42	1 36	11 24	4 27	1 09	21 22	1 20
16 W	18 47	17 33	5 00	18 18	22 40	1 32	25 35	2 13	20 39	1 41	1 35	11 19	4 31	1 09	21 23	1 20
17 Th	19 02	18 43	4 43	18 48	23 02	1 37	25 33	2 15	20 27	1 40	1 34	11 15	4 35	1 09	21 23	1 20
18 F	19 16	18 35	4 08	18 04	23 22	1 43	25 32	2 16	20 15	1 39	1 33	11 10	4 39	1 09	21 24	1 20
19 Sa	19 30	17 17	3 19	16 16	23 41	1 47	25 28	2 17	20 03	1 38	1 32	11 05	4 44	1 09	21 25	1 19
20 Su	19 44	15 02	2 19	13 37	23 58	1 52	25 25	2 19	19 50	1 37	1 30	11 00	4 48	1 09	21 26	1 19
21 M	19 57	12 03	1 15	10 22	24 15	1 56	25 20	2 20	19 38	1 36	1 28	10 56	4 52	1 10	21 27	1 19
22 Tu	20 10	8 36	0 08	6 45	24 30	2 01	25 15	2 21	19 25	1 35	1 26	10 51	4 56	1 10	21 27	1 19
23 W	20 23	4 50	0N57	2 54	24 44	2 05	25 10	2 22	19 12	1 34	1 24	10 46	4 60	1 10	21 28	1 19
24 Th	20 35	0 58	1 59	0S59	24 57	2 08	25 03	2 22	18 59	1 33	1 22	10 41	5 04	1 10	21 29	1 19
25 F	20 47	2S54	2 54	4 47	25 08	2 11	24 56	2 23	18 45	1 32	1 19	10 36	5 08	1 10	21 30	1 19
26 Sa	20 58	6 37	3 41	8 23	25 18	2 14	24 48	2 24	18 32	1 31	1 17	10 31	5 12	1 10	21 30	1 19
27 Su	21 09	10 04	4 18	11 39	25 27	2 17	24 40	2 24	18 18	1 30	1 14	10 26	5 16	1 10	21 31	1 19
28 M	21 20	13 06	4 44	14 26	25 34	2 19	24 30	2 24	18 04	1 29	1 11	10 21	5 20	1 11	21 32	1 19
29 Tu	21 30	15 37	4 57	16 39	25 40	2 21	24 21	2 25	17 50	1 27	1 08	10 16	5 23	1 11	21 33	1 19
30 W	21S40	17S30	4N58	18S09	25S45	2S23	24S10	2S25	17S35	1S26	1S05	10S11	5S27	1N11	21S33	1N18

Day	⚷ Decl	⚷ Lat	♅ Decl	♅ Lat	♆ Decl	♆ Lat	♇ Decl	♇ Lat
1	0N23	4N16	7N55	0S38	8S52	0S52	21S26	1N08
6	0 19	4 14	7 51	0 38	8 53	0 52	21 26	1 07
11	0 15	4 13	7 47	0 38	8 54	0 52	21 26	1 07
16	0 12	4 12	7 44	0 38	8 54	0 52	21 26	1 06
21	0 10	4 10	7 40	0 38	8 54	0 52	21 26	1 05
26	0 07	4 09	7 37	0 37	8 54	0 52	21 26	1 05

Day	⚴ Decl	⚴ Lat	⚵ Decl	⚵ Lat	⚶ Decl	⚶ Lat	Eris Decl	Eris Lat
1	3S20	12N15	10S11	9N48	18N59	0S36	2S42	12S29
6	3 55	11 30	10 33	9 47	18 56	0 27	2 43	12 29
11	4 26	10 48	10 53	9 47	18 55	0 17	2 43	12 28
16	4 53	10 06	11 12	9 47	18 56	0 07	2 44	12 28
21	5 16	9 27	11 29	9 47	19 00	0N04	2 44	12 27
26	5 36	8 49	11 45	9 48	19 07	0 16	2 44	12 27

Moon Phenomena

Max/0 Decl
dy hr mn
4 13:07 18S44
11 9:53 0 N
17 9:26 18N48
24 5:55 0 S

Max/0 Lat
dy hr mn
2 12:24 5N04
9 15:56 0 S
15 16:33 5S01
22 2:50 0 N
29 13:04 4N59

Perigee/Apogee
dy hr m kilometers
14 11:21 p 356515
27 20:08 a 406554

PH dy hr mn
☽ 7 19:52 15♒50
○ 14 13:53 22♉38
☾ 21 8:34 29♌28
● 29 12:19 7♐43

Void of Course Moon

Last Aspect			☽ Ingress		
1	2:45	♂ ⚹	♐	1	14:44
3	10:36	♅ △	♑	4	3:06
6	9:58	♂ ☌	♒	6	13:56
8	13:56	♀ ⚹	♓	8	21:46
10	23:17	♀ □	♈	11	1:46
12	12:46	♅ ☌	♉	13	2:25
14	13:53	☉ ☍	♊	15	1:24
16	10:59	♅ ⚹	♋	17	0:58
18	22:04	☉ △	♌	19	3:16
21	8:34	☉ □	♍	21	9:35
22	17:43	♄ □	♎	23	19:43
25	13:53	♅ ☍	♏	26	8:03
27	21:49	♀ ⚹	♐	28	20:47

DAILY ASPECTARIAN

1 Tu: ☽⚹♂ 2:45; ☽⚻⚳ 6:09; ☽∠♃ 7:09; ☉∥☽ 7:37; ☉△♆ 8:18; ♂∠♆ 11:24; ☽∠♇ 15:15; ☽∥☿ 20:53

2 W: ☽⚼♅ 4:29; ☽□♆ 9:36; ☽∠♂ 11:03; ☽⚼⚳ 11:56; ☉⊻☽ 11:56; ☽⚹♃ 14:00; ☿⊻♄ 18:30; ☽☌♄ 20:10; ☽⊻☿ 20:25; ☽⊻♇ 21:35; ♂□⚳ 22:30

3 Th: ☿⚹♇ 5:11; ☽☌♀ 5:33; ☽□⚷ 9:09; ☽△♅ 10:36; ☽△⚳ 17:35; ☉⊻♃ 17:55; ☽⊻♂ 19:10; ☉∠☽ 20:51

4 F: ☽∠☿ 7:05; ♀□⚷ 16:40; ☽⚹♆ 21:35

5 Sa: ☽□♃ 2:57; ☉⚹☽ 5:19; ♀△♅ 6:25; ☽⊻♄ 8:30; ☽☌♇ 9:26; ☽⚹☿ 17:07; ☽∥☿ 19:09; ☽⚹⚷ 20:29; ☽□♅ 21:50; ☽⊻♀ 23:32

6 Su: ☽∠♆ 2:57; ☽□⚳ 3:48; ⚵ ♐ 9:41; ☽☌♂ 9:58; ☽∠♄ 13:53; ☿△⚷ 19:03; ☉∥☽ 21:50

7 M: ☉⊻♄ 0:16; ☽∠⚷ 1:17; ☿⚻♅ 5:12; ☽∠♀ 7:19; ☽⊻♆ 7:36; ☉⚹♇ 8:26; ☽△♃ 13:39; ♀△⚳ 13:57; ☽⚹♄ 18:30; ☽⊻♇ 19:00; ☉□☽ 19:52

8 Tu: ☽⊻⚷ 5:16; ☽⚹♅ 6:28; ☽□☿ 9:58; ☽⚹⚳ 11:26; ⚳∠♆ 13:02; ☽⚹♀ 13:56; ☽⚼♃ 17:41; ☿⚻⚳ 21:06; ☽⊻♂ 21:18; ☽∠♇ 22:29

9 W: ♂ ♒ 5:53; ☽∥♆ 8:52; ☽∠♅ 9:26; ☽∠⚳ 13:56; ☽☌♆ 14:15; ☽⋕♅ 15:29; ♂∠♄ 15:55; ☽⚻♃ 20:42

10 Th: ☽□♄ 0:51; ☽⚹♇ 0:58; ☽∠♂ 1:16; ☉△☽ 5:53; ☽☌⚷ 10:21; ☽⊻♅ 11:25; ☽∥♃ 12:18; ☽⊻⚳ 15:29; ♄⊻♇ 19:40; ☽△☿ 21:18; ☽□♀ 23:17

11 F: ☽∥⚳ 1:26; ☽⚹♂ 4:07; ☽⋕⚷ 8:35; ☉⚼☽ 9:05; ☽∥⚷ 11:10; ☿∠♃ 11:50; ☽⊻♆ 17:05; ☽⋕⚳ 18:14; ♂∥♇ 20:46; ☽☍♃ 23:47

12 Sa: ☽⚼☿ 1:00; ☽□♇ 3:10; ☽△♄ 3:21; ♀ ♑ 4:55; ☽⋕♃ 7:34; ♂∥♄ 11:00; ☉⚻☽ 11:17; ☽⊻⚷ 11:49; ☽☌♅ 12:46; ☿∥♂ 13:18; ☿∥♄ 14:25; ☿ ♐ 14:41; ☽☌⚳ 16:09; ☽∠♆ 17:17; ☉△⚷ 19:06; ☿∥♇ 20:28; ☿∠♇ 22:09

13 Su: ☽∥♅ 1:56; ☽⚼♄ 3:30; ☽⚻☿ 3:44; ☽△♀ 4:15; ☽□♂ 7:07; ☽⋕♆ 8:08; ☉⚻♅ 8:39; ☽∠⚷ 11:35; ☽⚹♆ 16:59

14 M: ☽⚻♃ 0:02; ☿⊻♀ 0:45; ☽△♇ 2:46; ☽⚻♄ 3:14; ☽⚼♀ 5:47; ☽⚹⚷ 11:03; ☽⊻♅ 11:55; ☉☍☽ 13:53; ☽⊻⚳ 14:49; ☽⚼♃ 23:45

15 Tu: ☽⚼♇ 2:14; ☉⚻⚳ 2:17; ☽⚻♀ 7:11; ☽☍☿ 7:55; ☽△♂ 8:26; ☽∠♅ 11:19; ☽∠⚳ 14:03; ☽□♆ 15:54; ☿⚹♂ 17:24; ☽△♃ 23:36

16 W: ☽⚻♇ 1:51; ☽☍♄ 2:35; ☽⚼♂ 9:19; ☽□⚷ 10:09; ☽⚹♅ 10:59; ☽⚹⚳ 13:34; ☉⚻☽ 16:30; ☿⚼♅ 17:20; ♀⊻♂ 23:39

17 Th: ♂∠⚷ 1:43; ☽⚻♂ 10:50; ☽☍♀ 11:12; ☽⚻☿ 13:18; ☽△♆ 16:05; ☿⚼⚳ 16:33; ☉⚼☽ 18:45

18 F: ☽□♃ 0:51; ☽☍♇ 2:40; ☽⚻♄ 3:46; ☽△⚷ 11:22; ☽□♅ 12:11; ☽□⚳ 14:34; ☿□♆ 16:05; ☽⚼♆ 17:19; ☽⚼☿ 17:28; ☉△☽ 22:04

19 Sa: ☽⚼♄ 5:39; ☽⚼⚷ 13:19; ☽☍♂ 16:50; ☽⚻♀ 19:12; ☽⚻♆ 19:32; ☽△☿ 23:01; ♀⚹♆ 23:04

20 Su: ♆ D 4:40; ♄∥♇ 5:06; ☽⚹♃ 5:45; ☉∥♂ 6:04; ☽⚻♇ 7:05; ☽△♄ 8:37; ☽⚻⚷ 16:20; ☽△♅ 17:09; ☽△⚳ 19:19

21 M: ☽⚼♀ 1:14; ☉□☽ 8:34; ☽∠♃ 9:51; ☽⚼♇ 10:53; ♂⊻♆ 18:07; ☽⚼♅ 21:12; ☉ ♐ 21:24; ☽⋕♆ 21:57; ☽⚼⚳ 23:14

22 Tu: ☽☍♆ 3:09; ☽⚻♂ 3:43; ☉∠♃ 3:58; ☽∥♅ 6:07; ☽△♀ 8:37; ☉∠♇ 14:23; ☽□☿ 14:33; ☽⊻♃ 14:57; ☽△♇ 15:39; ☽□♄ 17:43; ☿⚹♃ 18:20; ☽⋕♃ 23:02; ☿⊻♇ 23:50

23 W: ☽☍⚷ 1:23; ☽⚻♅ 2:09; ☽⚻⚳ 4:03; ☽⚼♂ 10:49; ☿☌♄ 18:45; ☽⋕⚳ 21:29; ☉⚹☽ 23:57

24 Th: ☽∥⚷ 5:05; ☽⋕⚷ 6:45; ☿∥♀ 8:19; ☽⚻♆ 14:10; ☽∥⚳ 14:14; ☽△♂ 18:41; ♃□♇ 23:02

25 F: ☽□♀ 2:23; ☽□♇ 3:18; ☽☌♃ 3:22; ☽⚹♄ 5:54; ☉∠☽ 8:49; ☽⚹☿ 10:29; ♀☌♇ 11:51; ☽⚻⚷ 13:12; ♀□♃ 13:46; ☽☍♅ 13:53; ☽∥♃ 14:29; ☽☍⚳ 15:28; ☽⚼♆ 20:24

26 Sa: ☽⋕♅ 6:44; ☿□⚷ 8:23; ☽∠♄ 12:32; ☿△♅ 13:39; ☽∥♆ 15:38; ♀⊻♄ 17:14; ☉⊻☽ 18:00; ☽⚼⚷ 19:33; ☽∠☿ 21:08

27 Su: ☿△⚳ 0:54; ☽△♆ 2:48; ☽□♂ 11:25; ☽⚹♇ 16:10; ☽⊻♃ 17:00; ☉⚼♅ 19:04; ☽⊻♄ 19:14; ☽⚹♀ 21:49

28 M: ☽△⚷ 1:56; ☽⚻♅ 2:31; ☽⚻⚳ 3:48; ☽⊻☿ 7:45; ☉⚼⚳ 9:26; ☉∥♇ 12:16; ☽∠♇ 22:34; ☽∠♃ 23:46

29 Tu: ☉∥♄ 5:47; ☽∠♀ 7:27; ☽⚼♅ 8:44; ☽⚼⚳ 9:53; ☉☌☽ 12:19; ♀⚹⚷ 15:15; ☽□♆ 15:27; ♀□♅ 20:21

30 W: ☽∥♂ 1:22; ☽⚹♂ 4:00; ☽⊻♇ 4:48; ☽⚹♃ 6:22; ♀□⚳ 7:02; ☽☌♄ 8:17; ☽□⚷ 14:18; ☽△♅ 14:46; ☽△⚳ 15:48; ☽⊻♀ 16:48; ♂⊻♇ 17:16

December 2016

LONGITUDE

Day	Sid.Time	☉	☽	☽ 12 hour	Mean☊	True☊	☿	♀	♂	⚳	♃	♄	⚷	♅	♆	♇
	h m s	° ' "	° ' "	° ' "	° '	° '	° '	° '	° '	° '	° '	° '	° '	° '	° '	° '
1 Th	4 41 07	9♐13 12	25♐31 52	1♑33 59	7♍52.0	7♍43.1	27♐22.4	22♑16.4	16♒08.9	21♈24.0	16♎49.4	17♐44.3	20♓40.2	20♈53.7	9♓16.5	15♑56.8
2 F	4 45 04	10 14 03	7♑37 39	13 43 03	7 48.8	7R 30.3	28 46.4	23 26.7	16 53.9	21R 20.7	16 59.5	17 51.3	20D 40.2	20R 52.3	9 16.9	15 58.5
3 Sa	4 49 00	11 14 55	19 50 24	25 59 58	7 45.6	7 20.2	0♑09.2	24 37.0	17 39.0	21 17.7	17 09.4	17 58.4	20 40.3	20 51.0	9 17.3	16 00.3
4 Su	4 52 57	12 15 48	2♒12 03	8♒27 00	7 42.4	7 13.2	1 30.7	25 47.1	18 24.0	21 15.1	17 19.3	18 05.5	20 40.4	20 49.7	9 17.8	16 02.1
5 M	4 56 54	13 16 42	14 45 11	21 07 03	7 39.3	7 09.3	2 50.8	26 57.1	19 09.1	21 12.9	17 29.1	18 12.6	20 40.6	20 48.5	9 18.3	16 03.8
6 Tu	5 00 50	14 17 36	27 33 00	4♓03 31	7 36.1	7D 07.7	4 09.1	28 07.0	19 54.3	21 11.1	17 38.7	18 19.6	20 40.8	20 47.3	9 18.8	16 05.6
7 W	5 04 47	15 18 31	10♓39 02	17 20 00	7 32.9	7R 07.5	5 25.3	29 16.8	20 39.4	21 09.8	17 48.3	18 26.7	20 41.1	20 46.2	9 19.3	16 07.5
8 Th	5 08 43	16 19 27	24 06 46	0♈59 39	7 29.7	7 07.4	6 39.2	0♒26.5	21 24.6	21 08.8	17 57.7	18 33.8	20 41.4	20 45.1	9 19.9	16 09.3
9 F	5 12 40	17 20 23	7♈58 52	15 04 29	7 26.6	7 06.1	7 50.4	1 36.0	22 09.8	21 08.2	18 07.1	18 40.9	20 41.8	20 44.1	9 20.6	16 11.1
10 Sa	5 16 36	18 21 21	22 16 23	29 34 19	7 23.4	7 02.5	8 58.4	2 45.4	22 55.0	21D 08.0	18 16.3	18 48.0	20 42.3	20 43.1	9 21.2	16 13.0
11 Su	5 20 33	19 22 18	6♉57 46	14♉26 02	7 20.2	6 56.2	10 02.8	3 54.7	23 40.2	21 08.2	18 25.4	18 55.1	20 42.8	20 42.1	9 21.9	16 14.9
12 M	5 24 29	20 23 17	21 58 11	29 33 06	7 17.0	6 47.3	11 03.0	5 03.8	24 25.4	21 08.7	18 34.5	19 02.2	20 43.4	20 41.2	9 22.7	16 16.8
13 Tu	5 28 26	21 24 16	7♊09 31	14♊46 04	7 13.8	6 36.6	11 58.4	6 12.8	25 10.6	21 09.7	18 43.4	19 09.3	20 44.0	20 40.4	9 23.4	16 18.7
14 W	5 32 23	22 25 16	22 21 20	29 53 57	7 10.7	6 25.3	12 48.2	7 21.7	25 55.9	21 11.0	18 52.2	19 16.4	20 44.7	20 39.5	9 24.2	16 20.6
15 Th	5 36 19	23 26 16	7♋22 39	14♋46 18	7 07.5	6 14.8	13 31.9	8 30.3	26 41.1	21 12.8	19 00.8	19 23.4	20 45.4	20 38.8	9 25.1	16 22.5
16 F	5 40 16	24 27 18	22 03 58	29 14 58	7 04.3	6 06.2	14 08.4	9 38.9	27 26.4	21 14.9	19 09.4	19 30.5	20 46.2	20 38.1	9 25.9	16 24.4
17 Sa	5 44 12	25 28 20	6♌18 47	13♌15 12	7 01.1	6 00.2	14 37.0	10 47.2	28 11.7	21 17.4	19 17.8	19 37.6	20 47.1	20 37.4	9 26.8	16 26.4
18 Su	5 48 09	26 29 23	20 04 08	26 45 44	6 58.0	5 56.9	14 56.7	11 55.4	28 57.0	21 20.2	19 26.2	19 44.7	20 48.0	20 36.8	9 27.8	16 28.3
19 M	5 52 05	27 30 27	3♍20 17	9♍48 13	6 54.8	5D 55.8	15R 06.7	13 03.4	29 42.3	21 23.4	19 34.4	19 51.7	20 48.9	20 36.3	9 28.7	16 30.3
20 Tu	5 56 02	28 31 32	16 10 02	22 26 20	6 51.6	5 56.1	15 06.2	14 11.3	0♓27.6	21 27.0	19 42.4	19 58.8	20 49.9	20 35.7	9 29.7	16 32.3
21 W	5 59 58	29 32 37	28 37 43	4♎44 52	6 48.4	5R 56.5	14 54.5	15 18.9	1 12.9	21 30.9	19 50.4	20 05.8	20 51.0	20 35.3	9 30.7	16 34.3
22 Th	6 03 55	0♑33 43	10♎48 25	16 49 04	6 45.3	5 55.9	14 31.2	16 26.4	1 58.2	21 35.2	19 58.2	20 12.8	20 52.1	20 34.9	9 31.8	16 36.3
23 F	6 07 52	1 34 50	22 47 25	28 44 07	6 42.1	5 53.4	13 56.1	17 33.7	2 43.5	21 39.9	20 05.8	20 19.8	20 53.3	20 34.5	9 32.9	16 38.3
24 Sa	6 11 48	2 35 58	4♏39 42	10♏34 43	6 38.9	5 48.4	13 09.6	18 40.8	3 28.8	21 44.9	20 13.4	20 26.8	20 54.5	20 34.2	9 34.0	16 40.3
25 Su	6 15 45	3 37 06	16 29 40	22 24 57	6 35.7	5 40.9	12 12.4	19 47.6	4 14.1	21 50.3	20 20.8	20 33.8	20 55.8	20 33.9	9 35.1	16 42.3
26 M	6 19 41	4 38 15	28 20 59	4♐18 06	6 32.6	5 31.0	11 05.8	20 54.3	4 59.5	21 56.0	20 28.1	20 40.8	20 57.1	20 33.7	9 36.3	16 44.3
27 Tu	6 23 38	5 39 25	10♐16 33	16 16 35	6 29.4	5 19.5	9 51.8	22 00.8	5 44.8	22 02.1	20 35.2	20 47.8	20 58.5	20 33.6	9 37.5	16 46.3
28 W	6 27 34	6 40 35	22 18 24	28 22 08	6 26.2	5 07.4	8 32.5	23 07.0	6 30.1	22 08.5	20 42.2	20 54.7	20 59.9	20 33.5	9 38.8	16 48.4
29 Th	6 31 31	7 41 45	4♑27 54	10♑35 48	6 23.0	4 55.7	7 10.7	24 13.0	7 15.4	22 15.2	20 49.1	21 01.6	21 01.4	20D 33.4	9 40.1	16 50.4
30 F	6 35 28	8 42 55	16 45 55	22 58 19	6 19.8	4 45.6	5 49.1	25 18.7	8 00.8	22 22.3	20 55.8	21 08.5	21 02.9	20 33.4	9 41.4	16 52.4
31 Sa	6 39 24	9♑44 06	29 13 04	5♒30 16	6♍16.7	4♍37.7	4♑30.3	26♒24.2	8♓46.1	22♈29.7	21♎02.3	21♐15.4	21♓04.5	20♈33.5	9♓42.7	16♑54.5

1st of Month

Julian Day # 2457723.5
Obliquity 23°26'04"
SVP 5♓01'32"
GC 27♐04.5
Eris 22♈40.5R

Day	⚴
1	23♒37.7
6	24 39.4
11	25 45.6
16	26 56.0
21	28 10.1
26	29 27.7
31	0♓48.6

Day	⚵
1	8♐25.7
6	10 09.5
11	11 53.2
16	13 36.8
21	15 20.2
26	17 03.2
31	18 45.6

Day	⚶
1	5♌42.4
6	5 38.3R
11	5 22.9R
16	4 56.2R
21	4 18.4R
26	3 29.8R
31	2 31.4R

DECLINATION and LATITUDE

Day	☉ Decl	☽ Decl	☽ Lat	☽12h Decl	☿ Decl	☿ Lat	♀ Decl	♀ Lat	♂ Decl	♂ Lat	⚳ Decl	⚳ Lat	♃ Decl	♃ Lat	♄ Decl	♄ Lat
1 Th	21S50	18S37	4N45	18S52	25S48	2S24	23S59	2S25	17S21	1S25	1S02	10S06	5S31	1N11	21S34	1N18
2 F	21 59	18 54	4 20	18 43	25 50	2 24	23 47	2 25	17 06	1 24	0 58	10 00	5 35	1 11	21 35	1 18
3 Sa	22 07	18 19	3 42	17 41	25 50	2 24	23 34	2 25	16 52	1 23	0 54	9 55	5 38	1 11	21 35	1 18
4 Su	22 16	16 51	2 53	15 49	25 49	2 24	23 21	2 25	16 37	1 22	0 51	9 50	5 42	1 12	21 36	1 18
5 M	22 23	14 34	1 55	13 08	25 47	2 22	23 07	2 24	16 22	1 21	0 47	9 45	5 46	1 12	21 37	1 18
6 Tu	22 31	11 32	0 50	9 46	25 43	2 21	22 53	2 24	16 06	1 20	0 43	9 40	5 49	1 12	21 38	1 18
7 W	22 38	7 52	0S19	5 50	25 37	2 18	22 38	2 23	15 51	1 19	0 38	9 35	5 53	1 12	21 38	1 18
8 Th	22 44	3 42	1 29	1 29	25 31	2 15	22 22	2 22	15 36	1 18	0 34	9 30	5 56	1 12	21 39	1 18
9 F	22 50	0N47	2 35	3N04	25 23	2 11	22 06	2 22	15 20	1 17	0 29	9 25	5 59	1 12	21 40	1 18
10 Sa	22 55	5 21	3 35	7 35	25 13	2 06	21 49	2 21	15 04	1 16	0 25	9 20	6 03	1 13	21 40	1 18
11 Su	23 01	9 43	4 21	11 44	25 03	1 60	21 32	2 20	14 48	1 15	0 20	9 14	6 06	1 13	21 41	1 18
12 M	23 05	13 34	4 51	15 11	24 51	1 53	21 14	2 18	14 32	1 14	0 15	9 09	6 09	1 13	21 41	1 18
13 Tu	23 09	16 33	5 01	17 38	24 39	1 45	20 56	2 17	14 16	1 13	0 10	9 04	6 12	1 13	21 42	1 18
14 W	23 13	18 24	4 50	18 50	24 25	1 36	20 37	2 16	13 60	1 12	0 05	8 59	6 16	1 13	21 43	1 18
15 Th	23 16	18 56	4 18	18 42	24 11	1 26	20 17	2 14	13 43	1 10	0N01	8 54	6 19	1 13	21 43	1 18
16 F	23 19	18 10	3 30	17 21	23 55	1 15	19 57	2 12	13 27	1 09	0 06	8 49	6 22	1 14	21 44	1 17
17 Sa	23 21	16 16	2 30	14 58	23 40	1 02	19 37	2 10	13 10	1 08	0 12	8 44	6 25	1 14	21 45	1 17
18 Su	23 23	13 28	1 23	11 50	23 24	0 48	19 16	2 09	12 53	1 07	0 17	8 39	6 28	1 14	21 45	1 17
19 M	23 25	10 04	0 14	8 13	23 08	0 33	18 55	2 06	12 36	1 06	0 23	8 34	6 31	1 14	21 46	1 17
20 Tu	23 26	6 17	0N54	4 20	22 51	0 17	18 33	2 04	12 19	1 05	0 29	8 29	6 34	1 14	21 46	1 17
21 W	23 26	2 21	1 58	0 22	22 35	0N01	18 11	2 02	12 02	1 04	0 35	8 24	6 36	1 15	21 47	1 17
22 Th	23 26	1S36	2 54	3S32	22 19	0 20	17 48	1 59	11 45	1 03	0 41	8 20	6 39	1 15	21 47	1 17
23 F	23 26	5 25	3 42	7 14	22 04	0 39	17 25	1 57	11 28	1 02	0 47	8 15	6 42	1 15	21 48	1 17
24 Sa	23 25	8 59	4 20	10 38	21 49	0 59	17 02	1 54	11 11	1 01	0 53	8 10	6 44	1 15	21 48	1 17
25 Su	23 23	12 11	4 47	13 36	21 34	1 18	16 38	1 51	10 53	0 60	0 60	8 05	6 47	1 15	21 49	1 17
26 M	23 21	14 54	5 01	16 02	21 21	1 38	16 14	1 48	10 36	0 59	1 06	8 00	6 50	1 16	21 50	1 17
27 Tu	23 19	16 60	5 02	17 47	21 08	1 56	15 49	1 45	10 18	0 58	1 13	7 56	6 52	1 16	21 50	1 17
28 W	23 16	18 23	4 50	18 46	20 56	2 14	15 24	1 41	10 00	0 57	1 20	7 51	6 54	1 16	21 51	1 17
29 Th	23 13	18 57	4 25	18 54	20 45	2 29	14 59	1 38	9 42	0 56	1 27	7 46	6 57	1 16	21 51	1 17
30 F	23 09	18 38	3 47	18 08	20 36	2 43	14 34	1 34	9 25	0 55	1 33	7 42	6 59	1 16	21 51	1 17
31 Sa	23S05	17S25	2N57	16S29	20S28	2N54	14S08	1S31	9S07	0S54	1N40	7S37	7S01	1N17	21S52	1N17

Day	⚷ Decl	⚷ Lat	♅ Decl	♅ Lat	♆ Decl	♆ Lat	♇ Decl	♇ Lat
1	0N06	4N07	7N35	0S37	8S53	0S52	21S25	1N04
6	0 05	4 06	7 32	0 37	8 52	0 52	21 25	1 04
11	0 04	4 05	7 31	0 37	8 51	0 52	21 24	1 03
16	0 04	4 03	7 29	0 37	8 50	0 52	21 24	1 03
21	0 05	4 02	7 28	0 37	8 48	0 51	21 23	1 02
26	0 06	4 00	7 28	0 36	8 46	0 51	21 22	1 02
31	0N07	3N59	7N28	0S36	8S43	0S51	21S21	1N01

Day	⚴ Decl	⚴ Lat	⚵ Decl	⚵ Lat	⚶ Decl	⚶ Lat	Eris Decl	Eris Lat
1	5S52	8N13	11S60	9N50	19N18	0N28	2S44	12S26
6	6 05	7 39	12 13	9 51	19 31	0 41	2 45	12 25
11	6 15	7 05	12 24	9 54	19 49	0 55	2 44	12 25
16	6 22	6 34	12 33	9 57	20 09	1 10	2 44	12 24
21	6 25	6 03	12 41	10 00	20 33	1 25	2 44	12 23
26	6 27	5 34	12 47	10 04	20 60	1 40	2 44	12 22
31	6S25	5N05	12S51	10N09	21N29	1N56	2S43	12S22

Moon Phenomena

Max/0 Decl

dy	hr mn	
1	20:03	18S54
8	19:52	0 N
14	21:53	18N56
21	14:13	0 S
29	3:28	18S58

Max/0 Lat

dy	hr mn	
6	17:36	0 S
12	23:22	5S01
19	4:48	0 N
26	14:14	5N03

Perigee/Apogee

dy	hr m		kilometers
12	23:43	p	358461
25	5:54	a	405870

PH	dy	hr mn	
☽	7	9:04	15♓42
○	14	0:07	22♊26
☾	21	1:57	29♍38
●	29	6:54	7♑59

Void of Course Moon

Last Aspect				☽ Ingress		
1	4:09	☿	☌	♑	1	8:53
3	10:17	♀	☌	♒	3	19:45
5	11:24	♅	⚹	♓	6	4:32
7	14:06	♄	□	♈	8	10:17
10	1:07	♂	⚹	♉	10	12:42
12	4:06	♂	□	♊	12	12:42
14	5:59	♂	△	♋	14	12:10
15	21:38	♅	□	♌	16	13:16
18	16:56	♂	☍	♍	18	17:53
21	1:57	☉	□	♎	21	2:41
22	19:33	♅	☍	♏	23	14:34
25	7:23	♀	□	♐	26	3:20
28	1:46	♀	⚹	♑	28	15:13
30	8:08	♃	□	♒	31	1:30

DAILY ASPECTARIAN

1 Th
☉□♆ 1:18
☽☌☿ 4:09
⚷ D 9:54
☽∠♂ 11:55
⚶ R 15:40

2 F
☽⚹♆ 3:16
♂△♃ 3:47
☉⚺☽ 5:37
☽☌♇ 16:28
♀∠♆ 17:14
☽□♃ 18:41
☽⚺♂ 19:26
☽⚺♄ 20:19
☿ ♑ 21:19

3 Sa
☽⚹⚷ 1:37
☽□♅ 1:58
☽□⚳ 2:50
☽∠♆ 8:41
☽☌♀ 10:17
♂⚹♄ 12:16
☉∠☽ 13:36
☽⚺☿ 22:31

4 Su
☽∠♄ 1:44
☽∥♂ 3:25
☽∠⚷ 6:41
☽⚺♆ 13:38
☉⚹☽ 20:57

5 M
☽⚺♇ 2:29
☽△♃ 5:14
☽∠☿ 6:31
☽⚹♄ 6:36
☽☌♂ 8:50
☽⚺⚷ 11:11
☽⚹♅ 11:24
☽⚹⚳ 12:09

6 Tu
☽⚺♀ 1:09
☽∠♇ 6:34
☽⚼♃ 9:31
☽⚹☿ 13:29
☽∠♅ 15:09
☽∠⚳ 15:52
☽∥♆ 17:44
☽☌♆ 21:36

7 W
☉∥♀ 0:22
♂⚺⚷ 0:54
☽⋕♅ 1:58
♂⚹♅ 3:31
☽∠♀ 7:10
☉□☽ 9:04
☽⚹♇ 9:52
☿∠♂ 11:31
☽∥♃ 11:34
☽⚻♃ 12:59
☽□♄ 14:06
♀ ♒ 14:52
♂⚹⚳ 15:46
☽☌⚷ 17:58
☽⚺♅ 18:05
☽⚺⚳ 18:47
☽⚺♂ 18:57
☉⚺♇ 19:53

8 Th
☽⚹♀ 12:03
☽∥⚳ 17:09
☽⋕⚷ 19:29
☽∥⚷ 20:14
☽⋕⚳ 22:28
☽∠♂ 22:31
☽□☿ 23:44

9 F
☽⚺♆ 2:19
☽□♇ 13:53
☉△☽ 17:00
☽☍♃ 17:17
☽△♄ 18:11
☽⚺⚷ 21:24
☽☌♅ 21:25
☉⚹♃ 21:40
☽☌⚳ 22:07

10 Sa
⚳ D 0:27
☽⚹♂ 1:07
☽∠♆ 3:26
☽⋕♃ 3:45
☿⚹♆ 8:27
☽∥♅ 11:39
☉☌♄ 11:52
♀∥♄ 12:12
♅⚺⚷ 12:37
☽□♀ 18:39
☽⚼♄ 19:02
☽⋕♆ 19:05
☉⚼☽ 19:30
☽∠⚷ 21:59

11 Su
♀∠♄ 0:09
☽⚹♆ 3:52
☽△☿ 5:20
♀∥♇ 10:38
☽△♇ 14:56
☽⚻♃ 18:33
☽⚻♄ 19:18
☉⚻☽ 21:18
☽⚺♅ 21:58
☽⚹⚷ 22:01
☽⚺⚳ 22:41

12 M
☽□♂ 4:06
☽⋕♂ 6:27
☽⚼☿ 6:54
☉△♅ 6:57
☉□⚷ 7:59
♀∠⚷ 13:52
☽⚼♇ 14:45
☉△⚳ 18:10
☽⚼♃ 18:32
☽∠♅ 21:40
☽△♀ 22:23
☽∠⚳ 22:26

13 Tu
☽□♆ 3:31
☽⚻☿ 8:03
☽⚻♇ 14:28
☽△♃ 18:26
☽☍♄ 19:05
☽⚹♅ 21:19
☽□⚷ 21:27
☽⚹⚳ 22:08

14 W
☽⚼♀ 0:01
☉☍☽ 0:07
⚳⋕⚷ 3:07
☽△♂ 5:59
☉∠♀ 11:14

15 Th
☽⚻♀ 1:58
☽△♆ 3:18
☽⚼♂ 7:21
☽☍☿ 10:26
☽☍♇ 14:39
⚳∥⚷ 15:37
☽□♃ 19:09
♀⚺♆ 19:25
☽⚻♄ 19:44
☽□♅ 21:38
☽△⚷ 21:51
☽□⚳ 22:39

16 F
☽⚼♆ 3:56
☉⚻☽ 4:16
☽⚻♂ 9:28
☽⚼♄ 21:06
☽⚼⚷ 23:06

17 Sa
☽⚻♆ 5:24
☉⚼☽ 7:44
☽☍♀ 8:24
☽⚻☿ 14:46
☽⚻♇ 17:38
☽⚹♃ 22:52
☽△♄ 23:25

18 Su
☉∥☿ 0:42
☽△♅ 0:58
☽⚻⚷ 1:18
☽△⚳ 2:16
☽⋕♂ 4:48
☉△☽ 12:28
☽☍♂ 16:56
☽⚼☿ 18:03
☽⚼♇ 20:38

19 M
☽∠♃ 2:18
☽⚼♅ 4:11
☽⚼⚳ 5:40
☽⋕♆ 8:12
♂ ♓ 9:24
☿ R 10:56
☽☍♆ 11:24
☿∠♂ 13:32
☽∥♅ 16:37
☽⚻♀ 19:53
☽△☿ 22:00
☽⋕♃ 22:21

20 Tu
☽△♇ 0:42
☽⚺♃ 6:50
☽□♄ 7:21
☽⚻♅ 8:27
☽☍⚷ 8:55
☽⚻⚳ 10:09
☿⚺♀ 16:59

21 W
☉□☽ 1:57
☽⚼♀ 3:38
☽⚻♂ 5:23
☽∥⚳ 10:25
☉ ♑ 10:45
♂∠♇ 11:52
☽∥⚷ 13:44
☽⋕⚷ 14:42
☽⋕⚳ 18:13
☽⚻♆ 21:27

22 Th
♀⚺♇ 3:37
☽□☿ 7:06
☽□♇ 11:36
☽△♀ 12:24
☽⚼♂ 13:08
☽☌♃ 18:31
☽⚹♄ 19:00
☽☍♅ 19:33
☽⚻⚷ 20:10
☽☍⚳ 21:43

23 F
☽⚼♆ 3:33
☽∥♃ 8:29
☽⋕♅ 13:33
☉⚹☽ 19:26
☽△♂ 21:27
☽∥♆ 22:32

24 Sa
☿∥♄ 0:26
☽∠♄ 1:37
☽⚼⚷ 2:32
☽△♆ 9:58
☽∥♂ 14:44
☽⚹☿ 15:59

25 Su
♄△♅ 0:22
☽⚹♇ 0:26
☉∠☽ 4:43
☽□♀ 7:23
☽⚺♃ 7:53
☽⚻♅ 8:15
☽⚺♄ 8:20
☽△⚷ 9:00
☽⚻⚳ 10:55
♀△♃ 13:24
♀⚹♅ 16:37
♀⚹♄ 18:34
☽∠☿ 19:51
☿∥♇ 21:27

26 M
♀⚺⚷ 1:02
☽∠♇ 6:51
☽∥♀ 11:58
☉⚺☽ 13:52
☽□♂ 14:17
☽∠♃ 14:29
☽⚼♅ 14:32
☽⚼⚳ 17:26
♂⚼♃ 18:00
♂∠♅ 18:05
♃☍♅ 18:36
☽□♆ 22:42
☽⚺☿ 23:15

27 Tu
♀⚹⚳ 0:32
☿⚹♆ 4:20
☉⚹♂ 8:08
☽⚺♇ 13:01
☽△♅ 20:32
☽⚹♃ 20:47
☽☌♄ 21:12
☽□⚷ 21:24
☽△⚳ 23:40

28 W
♀ ♓ 0:25
☽⚹♀ 1:46
☿∠♀ 4:10
☉☌☿ 18:48
♄□⚷ 23:06
☿⚹♂ 23:07
♂∠⚳ 23:52

29 Th
☽☌☿ 4:47
☽⚹♂ 5:50
☉☌☽ 6:54
♅ D 9:30
☽⚹♆ 10:12
☽∠♀ 10:13

30 F
☽☌♇ 0:13
☽□♅ 7:20
☽□♃ 8:08
☽⚹⚷ 8:18
☽⚺♄ 8:33
☽□⚳ 10:57
☽∠♂ 12:52
☽∠♆ 15:20
☽⚺♀ 18:05
☉⚹♆ 23:26

31 Sa
☽⚺☿ 9:11
♃⚻⚷ 10:59
☽∠⚷ 13:07
☽∠♄ 13:33
☽⚺♂ 19:21
☽⚺♆ 20:01
☉⚺☽ 21:47

LONGITUDE

Day	Sid.Time	☉	☽	☽ 12 hour	Mean ☊	True ☊	☿	♀	♂	⚳	♃	♄	⚷	♅	♆	♇
	h m s	° ' "	° ' "	° ' "	° '	° '	° '	° '	° '	° '	° '	° '	° '	° '	° '	° '
Su	6 43 21	10♑45 16	11♒50 00	18♒12 25	6♍13.5	4♍32.5	3♑16.6	27♒29.4	9♓31.4	22♈37.4	21♎08.7	21♐22.2	21♓06.2	20♈33.6	9♓44.0	16♑56.5
M	6 47 17	11 46 27	24 37 39	1♓05 53	6 10.3	4D 29.9	2R 10.1	28 34.4	10 16.7	22 45.5	21 15.0	21 29.0	21 07.9	20 33.8	9 45.4	16 58.6
Tu	6 51 14	12 47 37	7♓37 19	14 12 12	6 07.1	4 29.4	1 12.3	29 39.1	11 02.0	22 53.9	21 21.1	21 35.8	21 09.6	20 34.0	9 46.8	17 00.7
W	6 55 10	13 48 47	20 50 46	27 33 14	6 04.0	4 30.3	0 24.0	0♓43.4	11 47.3	23 02.5	21 27.1	21 42.6	21 11.4	20 34.3	9 48.3	17 02.7
Th	6 59 07	14 49 56	4♈19 51	11♈10 48	6 00.8	4R 31.4	29♐45.8	1 47.5	12 32.6	23 11.5	21 32.9	21 49.3	21 13.2	20 34.6	9 49.8	17 04.8
F	7 03 03	15 51 06	18 06 14	25 06 13	5 57.6	4 31.8	29 17.8	2 51.3	13 17.9	23 20.8	21 38.5	21 56.0	21 15.1	20 34.9	9 51.3	17 06.8
Sa	7 07 00	16 52 15	2♉10 43	9♉19 36	5 54.4	4 30.6	28 59.9	3 54.7	14 03.2	23 30.4	21 44.0	22 02.7	21 17.0	20 35.4	9 52.8	17 08.9
Su	7 10 56	17 53 23	16 32 35	23 49 15	5 51.3	4 27.5	28D 51.7	4 57.8	14 48.4	23 40.3	21 49.3	22 09.3	21 19.0	20 35.8	9 54.3	17 11.0
M	7 14 53	18 54 31	1♊09 02	8♊31 12	5 48.1	4 22.3	28 52.5	6 00.5	15 33.7	23 50.5	21 54.5	22 16.0	21 21.1	20 36.4	9 55.9	17 13.0
Tu	7 18 50	19 55 39	15 54 56	23 19 17	5 44.9	4 15.8	29 01.7	7 02.9	16 18.9	24 00.9	21 59.5	22 22.5	21 23.1	20 36.9	9 57.5	17 15.1
W	7 22 46	20 56 46	0♋43 14	8♋05 45	5 41.7	4 08.6	29 18.7	8 04.8	17 04.1	24 11.7	22 04.3	22 29.1	21 25.2	20 37.6	9 59.1	17 17.1
Th	7 26 43	21 57 53	15 25 47	22 42 24	5 38.6	4 01.9	29 42.8	9 06.4	17 49.3	24 22.7	22 09.0	22 35.6	21 27.4	20 38.3	10 00.8	17 19.2
F	7 30 39	22 58 59	29 54 44	7♌02 02	5 35.4	3 56.4	0♑13.4	10 07.6	18 34.4	24 34.0	22 13.5	22 42.0	21 29.6	20 39.0	10 02.4	17 21.3
Sa	7 34 36	24 00 05	14♌03 42	20 59 21	5 32.2	3 52.7	0 49.7	11 08.4	19 19.6	24 45.5	22 17.9	22 48.5	21 31.9	20 39.8	10 04.1	17 23.3
Su	7 38 32	25 01 11	27 48 41	4♍31 38	5 29.0	3D 51.0	1 31.3	12 08.7	20 04.7	24 57.3	22 22.1	22 54.9	21 34.2	20 40.6	10 05.9	17 25.4
M	7 42 29	26 02 16	11♍08 15	17 38 42	5 25.8	3 51.1	2 17.6	13 08.5	20 49.8	25 09.4	22 26.1	23 01.2	21 36.5	20 41.5	10 07.6	17 27.4
Tu	7 46 26	27 03 21	24 03 18	0♎22 26	5 22.7	3 52.4	3 08.1	14 08.0	21 34.9	25 21.7	22 29.9	23 07.5	21 38.9	20 42.4	10 09.4	17 29.4
W	7 50 22	28 04 26	6♎36 35	12 46 18	5 19.5	3 54.1	4 02.4	15 06.9	22 19.9	25 34.3	22 33.5	23 13.8	21 41.3	20 43.4	10 11.2	17 31.5
Th	7 54 19	29 05 31	18 52 09	24 54 44	5 16.3	3R 55.5	5 00.2	16 05.3	23 05.0	25 47.1	22 37.0	23 20.0	21 43.8	20 44.5	10 13.0	17 33.5
F	7 58 15	0♒06 35	0♏54 41	6♏52 37	5 13.1	3 56.1	6 01.0	17 03.2	23 50.0	26 00.2	22 40.3	23 26.2	21 46.3	20 45.5	10 14.8	17 35.5
Sa	8 02 12	1 07 39	12 49 11	18 44 58	5 10.0	3 55.3	7 04.6	18 00.6	24 35.0	26 13.5	22 43.5	23 32.3	21 48.8	20 46.7	10 16.6	17 37.6
Su	8 06 08	2 08 42	24 40 34	0♐36 31	5 06.8	3 52.9	8 10.7	18 57.5	25 20.0	26 27.1	22 46.4	23 38.4	21 51.4	20 47.9	10 18.5	17 39.6
M	8 10 05	3 09 46	6♐33 22	12 31 34	5 03.6	3 49.2	9 19.1	19 53.8	26 04.9	26 40.8	22 49.2	23 44.4	21 54.0	20 49.1	10 20.4	17 41.6
Tu	8 14 01	4 10 48	18 31 34	24 33 44	5 00.4	3 44.5	10 29.5	20 49.5	26 49.9	26 54.9	22 51.8	23 50.4	21 56.6	20 50.4	10 22.3	17 43.6
W	8 17 58	5 11 50	0♑38 25	6♑45 53	4 57.2	3 39.2	11 41.9	21 44.5	27 34.8	27 09.1	22 54.2	23 56.3	21 59.3	20 51.7	10 24.3	17 45.6
Th	8 21 55	6 12 52	12 56 21	19 09 59	4 54.1	3 34.2	12 56.0	22 39.0	28 19.7	27 23.6	22 56.4	24 02.2	22 02.1	20 53.1	10 26.2	17 47.5
F	8 25 51	7 13 52	25 26 55	1♒47 11	4 50.9	3 29.8	14 11.7	23 32.8	29 04.6	27 38.3	22 58.4	24 08.0	22 04.8	20 54.5	10 28.2	17 49.5
Sa	8 29 48	8 14 52	8♒10 50	14 37 51	4 47.7	3 26.5	15 28.9	24 25.9	29 49.4	27 53.2	23 00.3	24 13.8	22 07.6	20 56.0	10 30.2	17 51.5
Su	8 33 44	9 15 51	21 08 11	27 41 46	4 44.5	3D 24.6	16 47.4	25 18.3	0♈34.2	28 08.3	23 01.9	24 19.5	22 10.5	20 57.5	10 32.2	17 53.4
M	8 37 41	10 16 49	4♓18 31	10♓58 21	4 41.4	3 24.0	18 07.2	26 09.9	1 19.0	28 23.6	23 03.4	24 25.2	22 13.3	20 59.1	10 34.2	17 55.4
Tu	8 41 37	11♒17 46	17 41 09	24 26 50	4♍38.2	3♍24.6	19♑28.3	27♓00.8	2♈03.8	28♈39.2	23♎04.7	24♐30.8	22♓16.2	21♈00.7	10♓36.2	17♑57.3

1st of Month

Julian Day #
2457754.5
Obliquity
23°26'04"
SVP 5♓01'27"
GC 27♐04.6
Eris 22♈32.5R

Day	⚴
1	1♓05.2
6	2 29.6
11	3 56.7
16	5 26.2
21	6 57.8
26	8 31.5
31	10 07.0

Day	⚵
1	19♐06.0
6	20 47.5
11	22 28.1
16	24 07.7
21	25 46.0
26	27 23.0
31	28 58.4

Day	⚶
1	2♌18.7R
6	1 10.5R
11	29♋56.3R
16	28 38.2R
21	27 18.6R
26	26 00.1R
31	24 45.1R

DECLINATION and LATITUDE

Day	☉ Decl	☽ Decl	☽ Lat	☽ 12h Decl	☿ Decl	☿ Lat	♀ Decl	♀ Lat	♂ Decl	♂ Lat	⚳ Decl	⚳ Lat	♃ Decl	♃ Lat	♄ Decl	♄ Lat
Su	22S60	15S20	1N59	13S60	20S21	3N02	13S42	1S27	8S49	0S53	1N47	7S32	7S04	1N17	21S52	1N17
M	22 55	12 29	0 53	10 48	20 16	3 09	13 16	1 23	8 31	0 52	1 55	7 28	7 06	1 17	21 53	1 17
Tu	22 49	8 58	0S17	7 01	20 14	3 12	12 49	1 18	8 12	0 51	2 02	7 23	7 08	1 17	21 53	1 17
W	22 43	4 58	1 27	2 49	20 12	3 14	12 22	1 14	7 54	0 50	2 09	7 19	7 10	1 18	21 54	1 17
Th	22 37	0 38	2 34	1N36	20 13	3 13	11 55	1 10	7 36	0 49	2 16	7 15	7 12	1 18	21 54	1 17
F	22 30	3N49	3 33	6 01	20 15	3 11	11 28	1 05	7 18	0 48	2 24	7 10	7 14	1 18	21 55	1 17
Sa	22 22	8 09	4 21	10 11	20 19	3 07	11 01	1 00	6 59	0 47	2 31	7 06	7 15	1 18	21 55	1 17
Su	22 14	12 05	4 53	13 50	20 24	3 02	10 33	0 55	6 41	0 46	2 39	7 02	7 17	1 18	21 55	1 17
M	22 06	15 22	5 08	16 40	20 31	2 55	10 05	0 50	6 23	0 45	2 47	6 57	7 19	1 19	21 56	1 17
Tu	21 57	17 41	5 02	18 25	20 38	2 48	9 37	0 45	6 04	0 44	2 54	6 53	7 21	1 19	21 56	1 17
W	21 48	18 50	4 36	18 56	20 46	2 40	9 09	0 40	5 46	0 43	3 02	6 49	7 22	1 19	21 57	1 17
Th	21 39	18 42	3 52	18 10	20 54	2 32	8 41	0 34	5 27	0 42	3 10	6 45	7 24	1 19	21 57	1 17
F	21 29	17 20	2 53	16 15	21 03	2 23	8 13	0 29	5 08	0 41	3 18	6 40	7 25	1 20	21 57	1 17
Sa	21 18	14 55	1 45	13 24	21 12	2 14	7 44	0 23	4 50	0 40	3 26	6 36	7 27	1 20	21 58	1 17
Su	21 07	11 43	0 33	9 54	21 22	2 04	7 16	0 17	4 31	0 39	3 34	6 32	7 28	1 20	21 58	1 17
M	20 56	7 60	0N40	6 01	21 31	1 54	6 47	0 11	4 13	0 38	3 42	6 28	7 29	1 20	21 58	1 17
Tu	20 45	4 01	1 48	1 59	21 39	1 45	6 19	0 05	3 54	0 37	3 50	6 24	7 30	1 21	21 59	1 17
W	20 33	0S02	2 49	2S02	21 48	1 35	5 50	0N02	3 35	0 36	3 58	6 20	7 31	1 21	21 59	1 17
Th	20 20	3 59	3 41	5 52	21 55	1 25	5 22	0 08	3 17	0 35	4 07	6 16	7 33	1 21	21 59	1 17
F	20 07	7 41	4 22	9 25	22 03	1 15	4 53	0 15	2 58	0 34	4 15	6 13	7 34	1 21	21 60	1 17
Sa	19 54	11 03	4 51	12 34	22 09	1 06	4 24	0 22	2 39	0 33	4 23	6 09	7 34	1 22	21 60	1 17
Su	19 41	13 57	5 08	15 11	22 15	0 56	3 56	0 29	2 20	0 32	4 32	6 05	7 35	1 22	22 00	1 17
M	19 27	16 16	5 12	17 11	22 20	0 47	3 27	0 36	2 02	0 31	4 40	6 01	7 36	1 22	22 00	1 17
Tu	19 13	17 55	5 02	18 28	22 24	0 37	2 59	0 43	1 43	0 30	4 49	5 57	7 37	1 22	22 01	1 17
W	18 58	18 47	4 39	18 54	22 27	0 28	2 30	0 50	1 24	0 29	4 57	5 54	7 37	1 23	22 01	1 17
Th	18 43	18 47	4 02	18 27	22 29	0 19	2 02	0 58	1 06	0 28	5 06	5 50	7 38	1 23	22 01	1 17
F	18 28	17 53	3 13	17 05	22 30	0 11	1 34	1 06	0 47	0 27	5 14	5 46	7 39	1 23	22 01	1 17
Sa	18 12	16 03	2 14	14 49	22 30	0 02	1 05	1 13	0 28	0 26	5 23	5 43	7 39	1 23	22 02	1 17
Su	17 56	13 24	1 07	11 47	22 29	0S06	0 37	1 21	0 09	0 25	5 32	5 39	7 39	1 24	22 02	1 17
M	17 40	10 00	0S05	8 05	22 27	0 15	0 09	1 29	0N09	0 24	5 40	5 35	7 40	1 24	22 02	1 17
Tu	17S23	6S04	1S18	3S56	22S24	0S22	0N18	1N38	0N28	0S23	5N49	5S32	7S40	1N24	22S02	1N17

Day	⚷ Decl	⚷ Lat	♅ Decl	♅ Lat	♆ Decl	♆ Lat	♇ Decl	♇ Lat
1	0N08	3N59	7N28	0S36	8S43	0S51	21S21	1N01
6	0 10	3 57	7 29	0 36	8 40	0 51	21 20	1 00
11	0 13	3 56	7 30	0 36	8 37	0 51	21 20	0 60
16	0 16	3 55	7 32	0 36	8 33	0 51	21 19	0 60
21	0 20	3 54	7 34	0 35	8 30	0 51	21 18	0 59
26	0 24	3 53	7 36	0 35	8 26	0 51	21 17	0 59
31	0N29	3N52	7N39	0S35	8S23	0S51	21S16	0N58

Day	⚴ Decl	⚴ Lat	⚵ Decl	⚵ Lat	⚶ Decl	⚶ Lat	Eris Decl	Eris Lat
1	6S25	4N60	12S52	10N10	21N35	1N59	2S43	12S21
6	6 20	4 33	12 54	10 15	22 05	2 15	2 42	12 21
11	6 14	4 06	12 54	10 20	22 37	2 31	2 42	12 20
16	6 05	3 41	12 52	10 27	23 08	2 46	2 41	12 19
21	5 55	3 16	12 49	10 33	23 38	3 00	2 40	12 18
26	5 43	2 52	12 44	10 41	24 07	3 14	2 39	12 17
31	5S29	2N28	12S37	10N49	24N33	3N26	2S38	12S16

Moon Phenomena

Max/0 Decl
dy hr mn
5 3:24 0 N
11 9:28 18N56
17 23:47 0 S
25 12:03 18S54

Perigee/Apogee
dy hr m kilometers
10 5:54 p 363241
22 0:07 a 404914

Max/0 Lat
dy hr mn
2 18:15 0 S
9 5:05 5S08
15 10:47 0 N
22 18:33 5N12
29 22:22 0 S

PH dy hr mn
☽ 5 19:48 15♈40
○ 12 11:35 22♋27
☾ 19 22:15 0♏02
● 28 0:08 8♒15

Void of Course Moon

Last Aspect	☽ Ingress
2 8:00 ♀ ☌	♓ 2 9:58
4 16:15 ☿ □	♈ 4 16:21
6 18:43 ☿ △	♉ 6 20:19
8 2:24 ☉ △	♊ 8 22:07
10 21:40 ☿ ☍	♋ 10 22:50
12 11:35 ☉ ☍	♌ 13 0:09
14 15:18 ♄ △	♍ 15 3:53
17 6:11 ☉ △	♎ 17 11:17
19 8:56 ♄ ⚹	♏ 19 22:10
22 1:25 ♂ △	♐ 22 10:46
24 17:34 ♂ □	♑ 24 22:44
27 7:19 ♂ ⚹	♒ 27 8:38
29 5:53 ♄ ⚹	♓ 29 16:11
31 17:37 ♀ ☌	♈ 31 21:48

DAILY ASPECTARIAN

♂☌♆ 6:54
♂∥♆ 8:20
☽⚺♇ 9:39
☽∠☿ 11:08
☽⚹♅ 16:25
☽∥♀ 17:00
☽⚺⚷ 17:28
☽△♃ 17:39
☽⚹♄ 18:05
☽⚹⚳ 20:29

☉∠☽ 4:20
☽☌♀ 8:00
☽⚹☿ 12:59
☽∠♇ 13:40
☽∠♅ 20:14
☽⚼♃ 21:39

☽∠⚳ 0:31
☽∥♆ 1:46
☽☌♆ 3:57
☽∥♂ 5:10
☽☌♂ 6:37
♀ ♓ 7:48
☽⋕♅ 9:15
☉⚹☽ 10:14
☽∥♃ 11:13
☽⚹♇ 17:08
☿⚹♀ 19:42
☽⚺♅ 23:30

☽☌⚷ 0:37
☽⚻♃ 1:06
☽□♄ 1:34
☽⚺⚳ 3:59
☿R♐ 14:18
☽⋕⚳ 15:16
☽□☿ 16:15
☽⚺♀ 19:08

5 Th
☽⋕⚷ 2:32
☽∥⚷ 4:17
♀∠♇ 6:42
♂⋕♅ 9:31
☽⚺♆ 9:40
☽⚺♂ 15:12
☽∥⚳ 16:07
☉□☽ 19:48
☽□♇ 22:17
☽∠♀ 23:32

6 F
☽☌♅ 4:16
♂∥♃ 4:47
☽⚺⚷ 5:25
☽☍♃ 6:07
☽△♄ 6:38
☽☌⚳ 9:06
☽∠♆ 11:36
☽⋕♂ 17:53
☽∠♂ 18:25
☽△☿ 18:43
☽⋕♃ 18:56
☽∥♅ 20:14

7 Sa
☽⋕♆ 2:56
☽⚹♀ 3:09
☉☌♇ 6:46
☽∠⚷ 6:55
☽⚼♄ 8:15
☽⚹♆ 12:57
☽⋕♀ 15:16
☽⚼☿ 19:34
☽⚹♂ 20:58

8 Su
☽△♇ 1:04
☉△☽ 2:24
☽⚺♅ 6:42
☽⚹⚷ 7:54
☽⚻♃ 8:46
☽⚻♄ 9:20
☿ D 9:44
☽⚺⚳ 11:53
♀∠♅ 14:40
☽⚻☿ 20:16

9 M
☽⚼♇ 1:45
☉⚼☽ 4:50
☽∠♅ 7:16
☽□♀ 8:31
☽⚼♃ 9:26
☽∠⚳ 12:40
☽□♆ 14:19
♀⚼♃ 22:35

10 Tu
☽□♂ 0:41
☽⚻♇ 2:10
☉∥♄ 2:59
☉⚻☽ 6:59
☽⚹♅ 7:37
☽□⚷ 8:53
☽△♃ 9:54
☽☍♄ 10:33
☽⚹⚳ 13:17
☉□♅ 16:23
⚶R♋ 18:12
☽☍☿ 21:40

11 W
♂⚹♇ 7:16
☉⚹⚷ 11:36
☽△♀ 12:53
☽△♆ 15:07

12 Th
☽☍♇ 3:07
☽△♂ 4:09
♀∥♆ 4:21
☉□♃ 4:44
♀∠⚳ 7:47
☽□♅ 8:35
☽△⚷ 9:57
☽□♃ 11:08
☉☍☽ 11:35
☽⚻♄ 11:54
☿ ♑ 14:04
☽□⚳ 14:58
☽⚼♀ 15:25
☽⚼♆ 15:52
☉⚺♄ 16:34
♀☌♆ 21:55

13 F
☽⚻☿ 0:33
☽⚼♂ 6:30
☽⚼⚷ 11:07
☽⚼♄ 13:14
☽⚻♆ 17:09
☽⚻♀ 18:36
☉∥♇ 22:11

14 Sa
☽⚼☿ 3:12
☽⚻♇ 5:45
☉∥☿ 7:04
☽⚻♂ 9:38
♀⋕♅ 11:16
☽△♅ 11:27
☽⚻⚷ 12:59
☽⚹♃ 14:22
♀∥♃ 14:24
☽△♄ 15:18
☿∥♇ 17:05
☉⚻☽ 18:40
☽△⚳ 18:53
☉□⚳ 22:07

15 Su
☉∠♆ 1:54
☽△☿ 7:00
☽⚼♇ 8:14
☽⚼♅ 14:05
☽∠♃ 17:13
♂⚺♅ 19:30
⚳∠♆ 19:54
☽⋕♆ 20:31
☽☍♆ 22:09
☽⚼⚳ 22:11
☉⚼☽ 23:48

16 M
☽∥♅ 2:53
☽⋕♃ 3:08
☽☍♀ 3:59
☽⋕♀ 8:23
☽△♇ 11:41
☽⚻♅ 17:42
☽☍♂ 19:04
☽☍⚷ 19:28
☽⚺♃ 21:03
☽□♄ 22:14

17 Tu
☽⋕♂ 0:43
☽∥⚳ 1:00
♂☌⚷ 2:15
☽⚻⚳ 2:31
♂⋕⚳ 3:14
☉△☽ 6:11
☽□☿ 18:38
☽∥⚷ 22:01

18 W
☽⋕⚷ 1:33
☽⚻♆ 6:58
♂⚻♃ 7:52
☽⚻♀ 18:02
☽∥♂ 19:57
☽□♇ 21:24

19 Th
☽⋕⚳ 0:51
☽☍♅ 3:43
☽⚻⚷ 5:41
☽☌♃ 7:28
☽∥♀ 7:44
☽⚻♂ 8:55
☽⚹♄ 8:56
♂□♄ 9:17
☽⚼♆ 12:38
♃⋕♅ 13:09
☿∥♄ 13:14
☽☍⚳ 14:00
☉ ♒ 21:25
☉□☽ 22:15
☽⋕♅ 23:05
☽∥♃ 23:06

20 F
☽⚼♀ 2:30
☽∥♆ 5:36
☽⚹☿ 11:15
☽⚼⚷ 11:50
♀⚹♇ 13:58
☽∠♄ 15:17
☽⚼♂ 17:01
☽△♆ 18:51

21 Sa
♀⋕⚳ 0:41
☽⚹♇ 9:45
☽△♀ 11:25
☽⚻♅ 16:08
☽△⚷ 18:16
☽⚺♃ 20:08
☽∠☿ 20:39
☽⚺♄ 21:53

22 Su
☽△♂ 1:25
☽⚻⚳ 3:40
☽∠♇ 16:11
☉⚹☽ 16:31
☽⚼♅ 22:31

23 M
☽∠♃ 2:33
☽⚺☿ 6:09
☽□♆ 7:38
☽⚼⚳ 10:30
☿⚹♆ 21:30
☽⚺♇ 22:24

24 Tu
♀⚺♅ 0:25
☉∠☽ 1:25
♂⚺⚳ 3:53
☽△♅ 4:37
☽□♀ 4:57
☽□⚷ 6:50
☽⚹♃ 8:39
☽☌♄ 10:39
☽△⚳ 16:59
☽□♂ 17:34

25 W
♀☌⚷ 6:50
☉∥☽ 7:41
☉⚺☽ 9:45
☽⚹♆ 19:08
☽☌☿ 23:59

26 Th
☉∥☽ 5:40
♀⚻♃ 8:03
☽☌♇ 9:23
☽□♅ 15:19
☽⚹⚷ 17:33
☽□♃ 19:16
☽⚹♀ 20:06
☉∠⚷ 20:17
☽⚺♄ 21:29

27 F
☽∠♆ 0:02
☽□⚳ 4:14
☽⚹♂ 7:19
♀□♄ 17:51
☽∠⚷ 22:01

28 Sa
☉☌☽ 0:08
☽∠♄ 1:58
♂⋕⚷ 2:25
☽∠♀ 2:30
☽⚺♆ 4:21
♂ ♈ 5:40
☽∠♂ 13:07
☽⚺☿ 15:05
☽⚺♇ 18:01
☽⚹♅ 23:40

29 Su
☉∠♄ 1:36
☽⚺⚷ 1:55
☽△♃ 3:29
☽⚹♄ 5:53
☽⚺♀ 8:10
♀⋕⚷ 8:28
☽⚹⚳ 13:03
☽⚺♂ 18:16
☿☌♇ 20:22
☽∠♇ 21:29
☽∠☿ 21:37

30 M
♀⋕♂ 0:04
☽∠♅ 3:02
☽⚼♃ 6:46
☉⚺♆ 7:04
☽∥♆ 10:13
☽☌♆ 11:18
☉⚺☽ 11:39
☽∥♃ 14:34
☽⋕♅ 14:39
☽∠⚳ 16:40

31 Tu
☽⚹♇ 0:29
☽⋕⚳ 1:21
♂∥⚷ 1:32
☽⚹☿ 3:32
☽⚺♅ 5:56
☽☌⚷ 8:11
♀∥⚷ 9:30
☽⚻♃ 9:35
☽□♄ 12:12
☉∠☽ 16:30
☽☌♀ 17:37
☽⚺⚳ 19:48

February 2017

LONGITUDE

Day	Sid.Time	☉	☽	☽ 12 hour	Mean☊	True☊	☿	♀	♂	⚳	♃	♄	⚷	♅	♆	♇
	h m s	° ' "	° ' "	° ' "	° '	° '	° '	° '	° '	° '	° '	° '	° '	° '	° '	° '
1 W	8 45 34	12♒18 41	1♈15 19	8♈06 28	4♍35.0	3♍25.9	20♑50.4	27♓50.9	2♈48.5	28♈54.9	23♎05.8	24♐36.3	22♓19.2	21♈02.4	10♓38.3	17♑59.2
2 Th	8 49 30	13 19 35	15 00 14	21 56 30	4 31.8	3 27.4	22 13.6	28 40.1	3 33.2	29 10.8	23 06.7	24 41.8	22 22.1	21 04.1	10 40.3	18 01.1
3 F	8 53 27	14 20 28	28 55 09	5♉56 04	4 28.7	3 28.6	23 37.9	29 28.5	4 17.9	29 27.0	23 07.4	24 47.2	22 25.1	21 05.9	10 42.4	18 03.0
4 Sa	8 57 24	15 21 20	12♉59 04	20 04 00	4 25.5	3R 29.2	25 03.2	0♈16.0	5 02.5	29 43.3	23 07.9	24 52.6	22 28.2	21 07.7	10 44.5	18 04.9
5 Su	9 01 20	16 22 10	27 10 36	4♊18 35	4 22.3	3 28.9	26 29.4	1 02.5	5 47.2	29 59.8	23 08.3	24 57.9	22 31.2	21 09.5	10 46.6	18 06.8
6 M	9 05 17	17 22 59	11♊27 36	18 37 17	4 19.1	3 27.8	27 56.5	1 48.0	6 31.7	0♉16.5	23R 08.4	25 03.1	22 34.3	21 11.4	10 48.7	18 08.6
7 Tu	9 09 13	18 23 46	25 47 08	2♋56 41	4 15.9	3 26.2	29 24.5	2 32.6	7 16.3	0 33.4	23 08.4	25 08.3	22 37.4	21 13.3	10 50.9	18 10.5
8 W	9 13 10	19 24 32	10♋05 23	17 12 41	4 12.8	3 24.3	0♒53.4	3 16.0	8 00.8	0 50.4	23 08.1	25 13.4	22 40.6	21 15.3	10 53.0	18 12.3
9 Th	9 17 06	20 25 16	24 17 59	1♌20 45	4 09.6	3 22.5	2 23.2	3 58.3	8 45.3	1 07.6	23 07.7	25 18.4	22 43.7	21 17.3	10 55.2	18 14.1
10 F	9 21 03	21 25 59	8♌20 27	15 16 35	4 06.4	3 21.1	3 53.9	4 39.5	9 29.7	1 25.0	23 07.1	25 23.4	22 46.9	21 19.4	10 57.3	18 15.9
11 Sa	9 24 59	22 26 40	22 08 44	28 56 32	4 03.2	3D 20.3	5 25.4	5 19.5	10 14.1	1 42.6	23 06.3	25 28.3	22 50.1	21 21.5	10 59.5	18 17.7
12 Su	9 28 56	23 27 20	5♍39 43	12♍18 07	4 00.1	3 20.1	6 57.7	5 58.3	10 58.5	2 00.3	23 05.3	25 33.1	22 53.4	21 23.6	11 01.7	18 19.5
13 M	9 32 53	24 27 59	18 51 37	25 20 15	3 56.9	3 20.4	8 30.9	6 35.7	11 42.8	2 18.2	23 04.2	25 37.9	22 56.6	21 25.8	11 03.9	18 21.2
14 Tu	9 36 49	25 28 37	1♎44 06	8♎03 20	3 53.7	3 21.1	10 05.0	7 11.8	12 27.1	2 36.2	23 02.8	25 42.6	22 59.9	21 28.0	11 06.1	18 22.9
15 W	9 40 46	26 29 13	14 18 14	20 29 07	3 50.5	3 21.9	11 39.9	7 46.6	13 11.3	2 54.4	23 01.2	25 47.2	23 03.2	21 30.2	11 08.3	18 24.7
16 Th	9 44 42	27 29 48	26 36 23	2♏40 28	3 47.3	3 22.6	13 15.7	8 19.9	13 55.5	3 12.8	22 59.5	25 51.7	23 06.6	21 32.5	11 10.5	18 26.3
17 F	9 48 39	28 30 21	8♏41 53	14 41 09	3 44.2	3 23.1	14 52.4	8 51.6	14 39.7	3 31.3	22 57.6	25 56.2	23 09.9	21 34.9	11 12.8	18 28.0
18 Sa	9 52 35	29 30 54	20 38 49	26 35 29	3 41.0	3R 23.4	16 29.9	9 21.9	15 23.9	3 49.9	22 55.5	26 00.6	23 13.3	21 37.2	11 15.0	18 29.7
19 Su	9 56 32	0♓31 25	2♐31 43	8♐28 07	3 37.8	3 23.4	18 08.4	9 50.5	16 08.0	4 08.7	22 53.2	26 04.9	23 16.7	21 39.7	11 17.2	18 31.3
20 M	10 00 28	1 31 55	14 25 17	20 23 47	3 34.6	3 23.4	19 47.7	10 17.5	16 52.1	4 27.7	22 50.7	26 09.1	23 20.1	21 42.1	11 19.5	18 32.9
21 Tu	10 04 25	2 32 24	26 24 11	2♑27 01	3 31.5	3D 23.3	21 28.0	10 42.7	17 36.1	4 46.8	22 48.0	26 13.3	23 23.5	21 44.6	11 21.7	18 34.5
22 W	10 08 21	3 32 51	8♑32 46	14 41 54	3 28.3	3 23.2	23 09.2	11 06.2	18 20.1	5 06.0	22 45.2	26 17.4	23 26.9	21 47.1	11 24.0	18 36.1
23 Th	10 12 18	4 33 17	20 54 49	27 11 51	3 25.1	3 23.3	24 51.4	11 27.8	19 04.1	5 25.4	22 42.1	26 21.4	23 30.4	21 49.6	11 26.3	18 37.7
24 F	10 16 15	5 33 41	3♒33 17	9♒59 18	3 21.9	3 23.5	26 34.6	11 47.5	19 48.0	5 44.9	22 38.9	26 25.3	23 33.9	21 52.2	11 28.5	18 39.2
25 Sa	10 20 11	6 34 04	16 30 03	23 05 33	3 18.7	3 23.7	28 18.7	12 05.2	20 31.9	6 04.5	22 35.5	26 29.1	23 37.4	21 54.8	11 30.8	18 40.7
26 Su	10 24 08	7 34 25	29 45 44	6♓30 30	3 15.6	3R 23.9	0♓03.8	12 20.9	21 15.8	6 24.3	22 32.0	26 32.9	23 40.9	21 57.5	11 33.1	18 42.2
27 M	10 28 04	8 34 45	13♓19 36	20 12 45	3 12.4	3 23.8	1 49.9	12 34.5	21 59.6	6 44.2	22 28.2	26 36.5	23 44.4	22 00.2	11 35.4	18 43.7
28 Tu	10 32 01	9♓35 03	27 09 34	4♈09 38	3♍09.2	3♍23.4	3♓37.0	12♈45.9	22♈43.4	7♉04.2	22♎24.3	26♐40.1	23♓47.9	22♈02.9	11♓37.6	18♑45.2

1st of Mon
Julian Day 2457785.
Obliquity 23°26'05
SVP 5♓01'
GC 27♐04
Eris 22♈34

Day	⚴
1	10♓26.
6	12 03.
11	13 42.
16	15 22.
21	17 03.
26	18 46.

Day	⚵
1	29♐17.
6	0♑50.
11	2 21.
16	3 50.
21	5 16.
26	6 40.

Day	⚶
1	24♋30.
6	23 23.
11	22 24.
16	21 34.
21	20 55.
26	20 27.

DECLINATION and LATITUDE

Day	☉ Decl	☽ Decl	☽ Lat	☽ 12h Decl	☿ Decl	☿ Lat	♀ Decl	♀ Lat	♂ Decl	♂ Lat	⚳ Decl	⚳ Lat	♃ Decl	♃ Lat	♄ Decl	♄ Lat
1 W	17S06	1S45	2S28	0N28	22S19	0S30	0N46	1N46	0N46	0S22	5N58	5S28	7S40	1N24	22S02	1N17
2 Th	16 49	2N41	3 30	4 53	22 13	0 38	1 13	1 55	1 05	0 21	6 07	5 25	7 40	1 25	22 03	1 17
3 F	16 32	7 02	4 20	9 05	22 06	0 45	1 41	2 03	1 24	0 21	6 15	5 22	7 40	1 25	22 03	1 17
4 Sa	16 14	11 02	4 56	12 49	21 58	0 52	2 08	2 12	1 42	0 20	6 24	5 18	7 40	1 25	22 03	1 17
5 Su	15 56	14 26	5 14	15 50	21 49	0 59	2 34	2 21	2 01	0 19	6 33	5 15	7 40	1 25	22 03	1 17
6 M	15 37	16 59	5 13	17 53	21 38	1 05	3 01	2 30	2 19	0 18	6 42	5 12	7 40	1 26	22 03	1 17
7 Tu	15 19	18 30	4 52	18 49	21 26	1 11	3 27	2 39	2 38	0 17	6 51	5 08	7 40	1 26	22 03	1 17
8 W	14 60	18 50	4 14	18 33	21 13	1 17	3 53	2 49	2 56	0 16	6 60	5 05	7 39	1 26	22 04	1 17
9 Th	14 41	17 59	3 20	17 07	20 58	1 23	4 18	2 58	3 14	0 15	7 09	5 02	7 39	1 26	22 04	1 17
10 F	14 21	16 01	2 14	14 41	20 42	1 28	4 43	3 08	3 33	0 14	7 18	4 59	7 39	1 27	22 04	1 17
11 Sa	14 02	13 09	1 02	11 28	20 25	1 33	5 08	3 17	3 51	0 13	7 27	4 55	7 38	1 27	22 04	1 17
12 Su	13 42	9 38	0N13	7 42	20 06	1 38	5 32	3 27	4 09	0 13	7 36	4 52	7 37	1 27	22 04	1 17
13 M	13 22	5 43	1 25	3 40	19 46	1 42	5 56	3 37	4 27	0 12	7 45	4 49	7 37	1 27	22 04	1 18
14 Tu	13 02	1 37	2 31	0S26	19 25	1 46	6 20	3 47	4 45	0 11	7 54	4 46	7 36	1 28	22 04	1 18
15 W	12 41	2S26	3 28	4 24	19 03	1 50	6 43	3 57	5 03	0 10	8 03	4 43	7 35	1 28	22 04	1 18
16 Th	12 20	6 18	4 14	8 07	18 39	1 53	7 06	4 07	5 21	0 09	8 12	4 40	7 34	1 28	22 05	1 18
17 F	11 59	9 50	4 48	11 27	18 14	1 57	7 28	4 18	5 39	0 08	8 21	4 37	7 33	1 28	22 05	1 18
18 Sa	11 38	12 56	5 09	14 17	17 47	1 59	7 49	4 28	5 57	0 07	8 30	4 34	7 32	1 28	22 05	1 18
19 Su	11 17	15 29	5 17	16 31	17 19	2 02	8 10	4 39	6 15	0 07	8 39	4 31	7 31	1 29	22 05	1 18
20 M	10 56	17 22	5 11	18 03	16 50	2 04	8 30	4 49	6 32	0 06	8 48	4 28	7 30	1 29	22 05	1 18
21 Tu	10 34	18 31	4 52	18 47	16 19	2 05	8 50	4 60	6 50	0 05	8 57	4 25	7 29	1 29	22 05	1 18
22 W	10 12	18 50	4 20	18 40	15 47	2 06	9 09	5 10	7 07	0 04	9 06	4 22	7 28	1 29	22 05	1 18
23 Th	9 50	18 16	3 35	17 39	15 14	2 07	9 27	5 21	7 25	0 03	9 15	4 19	7 27	1 30	22 05	1 18
24 F	9 28	16 47	2 38	15 43	14 39	2 08	9 44	5 31	7 42	0 03	9 24	4 16	7 25	1 30	22 05	1 18
25 Sa	9 06	14 25	1 32	12 55	14 03	2 08	10 01	5 42	7 59	0 02	9 33	4 14	7 24	1 30	22 05	1 18
26 Su	8 44	11 14	0 20	9 23	13 26	2 07	10 17	5 52	8 17	0 01	9 42	4 11	7 22	1 30	22 05	1 18
27 M	8 21	7 24	0S55	5 17	12 47	2 06	10 32	6 03	8 34	0 00	9 51	4 08	7 21	1 30	22 05	1 18
28 Tu	7S58	3S05	2S08	0S50	12S07	2S05	10N46	6N13	8N51	0N01	10N00	4S05	7S19	1N31	22S05	1N18

Day	⚷ Decl	⚷ Lat	♅ Decl	♅ Lat	♆ Decl	♆ Lat	♇ Decl	♇ La
1	0N30	3N52	7N40	0S35	8S22	0S51	21S16	0N
6	0 35	3 51	7 44	0 35	8 18	0 51	21 15	0
11	0 41	3 50	7 47	0 35	8 14	0 51	21 14	0
16	0 46	3 49	7 52	0 35	8 09	0 51	21 13	0
21	0 52	3 48	7 56	0 34	8 05	0 51	21 13	0
26	0N59	3N48	8N01	0S34	8S01	0S51	21S12	0N

Day	⚴ Decl	⚴ Lat	⚵ Decl	⚵ Lat	⚶ Decl	⚶ Lat	Eris Decl	Eris La
1	5S26	2N24	12S35	10N51	24N38	3N28	2S38	12S
6	5 11	2 01	12 26	10 60	25 01	3 39	2 36	12
11	4 54	1 38	12 16	11 09	25 20	3 49	2 35	12
16	4 36	1 16	12 04	11 19	25 36	3 57	2 34	12
21	4 17	0 53	11 50	11 30	25 50	4 04	2 32	12
26	3S58	0N32	11S35	11N42	25N60	4N10	2S31	12S

Moon Phenomena

Max/0 Decl
dy hr mn
1 9:31 0 N
7 18:48 18N52
14 9:30 0 S
21 20:57 18S51
28 16:23 0 N

Max/0 Lat
dy hr mn
5 10:35 5S16
11 19:50 0 N
19 1:43 5N17
26 6:29 0 S

Perigee/Apogee
dy hr m kilometers
6 14:03 p 368816
18 21:23 a 404375

PH dy hr mn
☽ 4 4:20 15♉32
○ 11 0:34 22♌28
• 11 0:45 A 0.988
☾ 18 19:34 0♐20
● 26 14:59 8♓12
• 26 14:55 A 00'44"

Void of Course Moon

Last Aspect	☽ Ingress
2 16:51 ♄ △	♉ 3 1:
4 22:43 ♄ △	♊ 5 4:
6 22:55 ♄ ☍	♋ 7 7.
8 22:01 ♃ □	♌ 9 9:
11 5:53 ♄ △	♍ 11 13:
13 12:38 ♄ □	♎ 13 20:
16 1:55 ☉ △	♏ 16 6:
17 19:39 ♇ ⚹	♐ 18 18:
20 23:38 ♄ ☌	♑ 21 7
23 3:25 ♃ □	♒ 23 17:
25 18:12 ♄ ⚹	♓ 26 0:
27 23:09 ♄ □	♈ 28 4:

DAILY ASPECTARIAN

1 W
♀∥♂ 1:16
☽☌♂ 2:53
☿□♅ 3:33
☽#♀ 4:52
☽#♂ 4:59
☽#⚷ 6:47
♃#♅ 7:28
☽∥⚷ 12:15
☽∥♂ 14:43
☽∥♀ 15:12
☽⚺♆ 16:27
☉⚹☽ 20:51

2 Th
☿⚹⚷ 2:31
☽□♇ 5:14
☽☌♅ 10:31
☽⚺⚷ 12:47
☽□☿ 13:53
☽☍♃ 14:02
☿□♃ 15:17
☽△♄ 16:51
☽∠♆ 18:28
☽∥⚳ 19:28
♀⚺⚳ 22:50

3 F
☽☌⚳ 0:56
☽⚺♀ 1:01
☽#♃ 3:41
☽∥♅ 3:47
⚵ ♑ 6:48
☽#♆ 7:31
☽⚺♂ 9:43
☿∥♄ 10:18
☽∠⚷ 14:35
☉∠♀ 14:36
♀ ♈ 15:52
☽⚼♄ 18:41
☽⚹♆ 20:11
☿⚺♄ 20:51

4 Sa
☽∠♀ 4:06
☉□☽ 4:20
☽△♇ 8:40
☿∠♆ 11:50
☽∠♂ 12:37
☽⚺♅ 13:49
☽⚹⚷ 16:07
☽⚻♃ 17:11
☽⚻♄ 20:15
☽△☿ 22:43

5 Su
⚳ ♉ 0:18
☽⚺⚳ 4:51
☽⚹♀ 6:52
☽⚼♇ 10:01
☉#☽ 11:34
☽∠♅ 15:08
☽⚹♂ 15:16
☽⚼♃ 18:26
☽□♆ 22:55

6 M
☽⚼☿ 2:46
☽∠⚳ 6:31
♃ R 6:54
☉△☽ 10:41
☽⚻♇ 11:13
☽⚹♅ 16:20
☉⚺♇ 18:35
☽□⚷ 18:41
☽△♃ 19:34
☽☍♄ 22:55

7 Tu
☽⚻☿ 6:46
☽⚹⚳ 8:09
☿ ♒ 9:36
☽□♀ 11:56
☉⚼☽ 13:44
☿∥♇ 20:11
☽□♂ 20:19
☿□⚳ 23:00

8 W
☽△♆ 1:20
☽☍♇ 13:42
☉⚻☽ 16:55
☽□♅ 18:53
☽△⚷ 21:19
☽□♃ 22:01

9 Th
☽⚻♄ 1:43
☽⚼♆ 2:46
☽□⚳ 11:52
☽☍☿ 15:26
☽△♀ 17:21
☉⚹♅ 21:17
☽⚼⚷ 23:02

10 F
☽△♂ 2:06
☽⚼♄ 3:33
☽⚻♆ 4:31
☉#☽ 16:30
☽⚻♇ 17:15
☽⚼♀ 20:39
☿⚹♀ 21:20
☽△♅ 22:37

11 Sa
☉☍☽ 0:34
☽⚻⚷ 1:13
☽⚹♃ 1:41
☽⚼♂ 5:45
☽△♄ 5:53
☉⚺⚷ 9:48
☉△♃ 15:26
☽△⚳ 17:18
☽⚼♇ 19:48

12 Su
☽⚻♀ 0:35
☽⚼♅ 1:19
♂⚺♆ 1:50
☽⚻☿ 2:39
☽∠♃ 4:22
⚳#♃ 4:41
☽#♆ 8:56
☽☍♆ 9:43
☽⚻♂ 10:09
☽∥♅ 11:22
☽∥⚳ 12:14
☽#♃ 12:32
☿∠⚷ 14:53
☽⚼⚳ 21:04
☽∥♀ 22:45
☽△♇ 23:04

13 M
☽⚻♅ 4:45
☽∥♂ 6:55
☽☍⚷ 7:35
☽⚺♃ 7:46
☽⚼☿ 9:48
☉⚻☽ 11:16
☽□♄ 12:38
⚳∥♅ 13:17

14 Tu
☽⚻⚳ 1:41
☽∥⚷ 5:10
☉⚹♄ 5:59
☿∠♄ 10:01
☽☍♀ 10:52
☽#⚷ 13:53
♃⚻⚷ 14:17
☿⚺♆ 15:51
☽⚻♆ 17:53
☉⚼☽ 18:06
☽△☿ 18:11
☽☍♂ 21:43

15 W
☽□♇ 7:59
☽☍♅ 14:02
☽☌♃ 16:55
☽⚻⚷ 17:06
☽#♂ 17:24
⚳#♆ 18:43
☽⚹♄ 22:32
☽⚼♆ 23:09

16 Th
☉△☽ 1:55
☽#♀ 5:43
☽∥♃ 8:17
☽#♅ 10:18
☽∥♆ 12:12
☽#⚳ 13:03
☽☍⚳ 13:25
☿⚹♂ 18:16
☽⚼⚷ 22:56

17 F
☽⚻♀ 0:20
☽∠♄ 4:30
☽△♆ 5:03
♀#♃ 6:18
☽⚻♂ 12:44
☽□☿ 14:19
☉∥☽ 14:35
☽⚹♇ 19:39

18 Sa
☽⚻♅ 1:58
☽⚺♃ 4:35
☽△⚷ 5:13
♀∥♅ 5:22
☽⚼♀ 7:49
☽⚺♄ 10:53
☉ ♓ 11:32
☉□☽ 19:34
♀#♆ 20:41
☽⚼♂ 21:00

19 Su
☽∠♇ 2:01
☽⚻⚳ 3:21
☿⚺♇ 5:39
☽⚼♅ 8:23
☽∠♃ 10:47
☽△♀ 15:22
☽□♆ 17:45
☽∥☿ 17:55

20 M
☽△♂ 5:15
☽⚺♇ 8:19
☽⚼⚳ 10:24
☽⚹☿ 12:33
☽△♅ 14:40
☽⚹♃ 16:50
☽□⚷ 17:58
☽☌♄ 23:38

21 Tu
☿⚹♅ 4:03
☉∠♂ 5:25
☉⚹☽ 13:17
☽△⚳ 17:03
♀∥⚳ 17:05
☿△♃ 18:28
☽∠☿ 23:06

22 W
☉∠♇ 1:20
☿⚺⚷ 4:19
☽□♀ 5:09
☽⚹♆ 5:36
♂□♇ 9:04
☽☌♇ 19:36
☽□♂ 20:14
☉∠☽ 21:09
♀⚺♆ 22:00

23 Th
☽□♅ 1:46
♂#♃ 2:11
☽□♃ 3:25
☽⚹⚷ 4:59
☽⚺☿ 8:44
☽⚺♄ 10:27
☽∠♆ 10:35
☉#♀ 14:10
☿⚹♄ 21:46

24 F
☉#⚳ 3:13
☿∠♀ 3:39
☉⚺☽ 4:05
☽□⚳ 4:13
☉⚹⚳ 6:35
☽∠⚷ 9:24
☽∠♄ 14:44
☽⚺♆ 14:48
☽⚹♀ 15:42

25 Sa
♂∥♅ 1:11
♂#♆ 3:04
☽∥☿ 3:53
☽⚺♇ 3:59
☽⚹♂ 7:47
☉∠♅ 8:38
☽⚹♅ 9:54
☽△♃ 11:03
☽⚺⚷ 13:01
☽⚹♄ 18:12
♅#♆ 19:29
☽∠♀ 19:35
☉⚼♃ 23:05
☿ ♓ 23:08

26 Su
☽☌☿ 0:37
☽#♀ 5:56
☽∠♇ 7:02
☽#⚳ 9:39
☽⚹⚳ 12:07
☽∠♂ 12:13
☽∠♅ 12:50
☽⚼♃ 13:45
☉☌☽ 14:59
☉#♂ 16:20
☽#♂ 17:32
☉∥☽ 17:45
☽#♅ 20:14
☽∥♆ 20:25
☽☌♆ 20:57
☽⚺♀ 22:40

27 M
☽∥♃ 0:18
♂☌♅ 0:21
☽⚹♇ 9:26
♂☍♃ 14:26
☽∠⚳ 15:00
☽⚺♅ 15:09
☽⚻♃ 15:50
☽⚺♂ 15:55
☽☌⚷ 18:11
☉#♅ 19:06
☽□♄ 23:09
☉∥♆ 23:13

28 Tu
☿∠♇ 1:51
☽#⚷ 10:57
☽⚺☿ 12:42
☽⚺⚳ 17:23
☽∥⚷ 21:51
☉⚺☽ 22:52

LONGITUDE

Day	Sid.Time	☉	☽	☽ 12 hour	Mean ☊	True ☊	☿	♀	♂	⚳	♃	♄	⚷	♅	♆	♇
	h m s	° ' "	° ' "	° ' "	° '	° '	° '	° '	° '	° '	° '	° '	° '	° '	° '	° '
1 W	10 35 57	10♓35 19	11♈12 28	18♈17 34	3♍06.0	3♍22.7	5♓25.1	12♈55.1	23♈27.1	7♉24.3	22♎20.3	26♐43.6	23♓51.5	22♈05.6	11♓39.9	18♑46.6
2 Th	10 39 54	11 35 33	25 24 26	2♉32 31	3 02.9	3R 21.8	7 14.3	13 02.0	24 10.8	7 44.6	22R 16.0	26 47.0	23 55.0	22 08.4	11 42.2	18 48.0
3 F	10 43 50	12 35 45	9♉41 19	16 50 22	2 59.7	3 20.8	9 04.5	13 06.5	24 54.5	8 05.0	22 11.6	26 50.4	23 58.6	22 11.2	11 44.5	18 49.4
4 Sa	10 47 47	13 35 55	23 59 12	1♊07 26	2 56.5	3 19.9	10 55.6	13R 08.6	25 38.1	8 25.5	22 07.0	26 53.6	24 02.1	22 14.1	11 46.7	18 50.7
5 Su	10 51 44	14 36 03	8♊14 41	15 20 39	2 53.3	3D 19.3	12 47.8	13 08.4	26 21.7	8 46.1	22 02.3	26 56.7	24 05.7	22 16.9	11 49.0	18 52.1
6 M	10 55 40	15 36 09	22 25 02	29 27 37	2 50.1	3 19.4	14 41.0	13 05.6	27 05.2	9 06.8	21 57.4	26 59.8	24 09.3	22 19.8	11 51.3	18 53.4
7 Tu	10 59 37	16 36 12	6♋28 12	13♋26 35	2 47.0	3 20.0	16 35.1	13 00.3	27 48.7	9 27.6	21 52.4	27 02.8	24 12.9	22 22.7	11 53.6	18 54.7
8 W	11 03 33	17 36 14	20 22 37	27 16 09	2 43.8	3 21.0	18 30.1	12 52.5	28 32.2	9 48.6	21 47.2	27 05.6	24 16.5	22 25.7	11 55.9	18 55.9
9 Th	11 07 30	18 36 13	4♌07 03	10♌55 11	2 40.6	3 22.2	20 25.9	12 42.2	29 15.6	10 09.6	21 41.9	27 08.4	24 20.1	22 28.6	11 58.1	18 57.2
10 F	11 11 26	19 36 10	17 40 25	24 22 38	2 37.4	3 23.3	22 22.5	12 29.3	29 59.0	10 30.7	21 36.4	27 11.1	24 23.7	22 31.6	12 00.4	18 58.4
11 Sa	11 15 23	20 36 05	1♍01 43	7♍37 34	2 34.3	3R 23.8	24 19.7	12 14.0	0♉42.3	10 52.0	21 30.8	27 13.7	24 27.3	22 34.7	12 02.6	18 59.6
12 Su	11 19 19	21 35 59	14 10 04	20 39 10	2 31.1	3 23.5	26 17.5	11 56.2	1 25.5	11 13.3	21 25.1	27 16.2	24 30.9	22 37.7	12 04.9	19 00.7
13 M	11 23 16	22 35 50	27 04 48	3♎26 59	2 27.9	3 22.2	28 15.7	11 36.0	2 08.8	11 34.7	21 19.2	27 18.7	24 34.5	22 40.8	12 07.2	19 01.9
14 Tu	11 27 13	23 35 39	9♎45 43	16 01 05	2 24.7	3 19.9	0♈14.1	11 13.4	2 52.0	11 56.3	21 13.2	27 21.0	24 38.1	22 43.8	12 09.4	19 03.0
15 W	11 31 09	24 35 26	22 13 12	28 22 13	2 21.5	3 16.7	2 12.6	10 48.7	3 35.1	12 17.9	21 07.1	27 23.2	24 41.8	22 46.9	12 11.6	19 04.1
16 Th	11 35 06	25 35 11	4♏28 21	10♏31 53	2 18.4	3 13.0	4 10.8	10 21.8	4 18.2	12 39.6	21 00.9	27 25.4	24 45.4	22 50.1	12 13.9	19 05.1
17 F	11 39 02	26 34 55	16 33 08	22 32 27	2 15.2	3 09.3	6 08.5	9 53.0	5 01.3	13 01.4	20 54.5	27 27.4	24 49.0	22 53.2	12 16.1	19 06.1
18 Sa	11 42 59	27 34 37	28 30 17	4♐27 04	2 12.0	3 05.9	8 05.5	9 22.4	5 44.3	13 23.3	20 48.0	27 29.3	24 52.6	22 56.4	12 18.3	19 07.1
19 Su	11 46 55	28 34 17	10♐23 19	16 19 34	2 08.8	3 03.4	10 01.3	8 50.1	6 27.3	13 45.3	20 41.4	27 31.2	24 56.2	22 59.6	12 20.5	19 08.1
20 M	11 50 52	29 33 56	22 16 21	28 14 18	2 05.6	3D 02.0	11 55.6	8 16.3	7 10.2	14 07.3	20 34.8	27 33.0	24 59.8	23 02.8	12 22.7	19 09.1
21 Tu	11 54 48	0♈33 32	4♑13 58	10♑16 00	2 02.5	3 01.8	13 48.0	7 41.3	7 53.1	14 29.5	20 28.0	27 34.6	25 03.4	23 06.0	12 24.9	19 10.0
22 W	11 58 45	1 33 07	16 20 58	22 29 28	1 59.3	3 02.7	15 38.0	7 05.3	8 35.9	14 51.7	20 21.1	27 36.2	25 07.0	23 09.2	12 27.1	19 10.9
23 Th	12 02 42	2 32 40	28 42 05	4♒59 19	1 56.1	3 04.2	17 25.3	6 28.5	9 18.8	15 14.0	20 14.1	27 37.6	25 10.6	23 12.5	12 29.3	19 11.7
24 F	12 06 38	3 32 12	11♒21 39	17 49 29	1 52.9	3 05.9	19 09.3	5 51.1	10 01.5	15 36.4	20 07.1	27 39.0	25 14.2	23 15.8	12 31.4	19 12.6
25 Sa	12 10 35	4 31 41	24 23 09	1♓02 51	1 49.8	3R 07.2	20 49.8	5 13.4	10 44.3	15 58.9	19 59.9	27 40.3	25 17.8	23 19.1	12 33.6	19 13.4
26 Su	12 14 31	5 31 09	7♓48 41	14 40 37	1 46.6	3 07.4	22 26.1	4 35.7	11 27.0	16 21.4	19 52.7	27 41.4	25 21.4	23 22.4	12 35.7	19 14.2
27 M	12 18 28	6 30 35	21 38 28	28 41 55	1 43.4	3 06.1	23 57.9	3 58.2	12 09.6	16 44.1	19 45.4	27 42.5	25 24.9	23 25.7	12 37.9	19 14.9
28 Tu	12 22 24	7 29 59	5♈50 27	13♈03 29	1 40.2	3 03.1	25 24.8	3 21.1	12 52.2	17 06.8	19 38.1	27 43.5	25 28.5	23 29.0	12 40.0	19 15.6
29 W	12 26 21	8 29 21	20 20 13	27 39 49	1 37.0	2 58.6	26 46.4	2 44.7	13 34.8	17 29.5	19 30.7	27 44.3	25 32.0	23 32.3	12 42.1	19 16.3
30 Th	12 30 17	9 28 40	5♉01 20	12♉23 50	1 33.9	2 53.2	28 02.5	2 09.2	14 17.3	17 52.4	19 23.2	27 45.1	25 35.6	23 35.7	12 44.2	19 17.0
31 F	12 34 14	10♈27 58	19 46 19	27 07 52	1♍30.7	2♍47.5	29♈12.6	1♈34.8	14♉59.8	18♉15.3	19♎15.7	27♐45.8	25♓39.1	23♈39.1	12♓46.3	19♑17.6

1st of Month

Julian Day #
2457813.5
Obliquity
23°26'06"
SVP 5♓01'19"
GC 27♐04.7
Eris 22♈45.2

Day	⚴
1	19♓48.0
6	21 31.6
11	23 15.8
16	25 00.5
21	26 45.7
26	28 31.2
31	0♈16.9
	⚵
1	7♑29.0
6	8 47.6
11	10 02.7
16	11 14.1
21	12 21.3
26	13 24.1
31	14 22.0
	⚶
1	20♋16.6R
6	20 07.6R
11	20 10.0
16	20 23.5
21	20 47.5
26	21 21.5
31	22 04.8

DECLINATION and LATITUDE

Day	☉	☽		☽12h	☿		♀		♂		⚳		♃		♄	
	Decl	Decl	Lat	Decl	Decl	Lat	Decl	Lat	Decl	Lat	Decl	Lat	Decl	Lat	Decl	Lat
1 W	7S36	1N27	3S15	3N43	11S26	2S03	10N59	6N23	9N08	0N01	10N09	4S03	7S17	1N31	22S05	1N18
2 Th	7 13	5 57	4 10	8 05	10 43	2 01	11 11	6 34	9 25	0 02	10 18	3 60	7 15	1 31	22 05	1 18
3 F	6 50	10 07	4 50	12 00	9 59	1 58	11 22	6 44	9 41	0 03	10 27	3 57	7 14	1 31	22 05	1 18
4 Sa	6 27	13 43	5 12	15 13	9 13	1 55	11 32	6 53	9 58	0 04	10 36	3 54	7 12	1 31	22 05	1 19
5 Su	6 04	16 29	5 15	17 30	8 28	1 51	11 40	7 03	10 14	0 04	10 45	3 52	7 10	1 32	22 05	1 19
6 M	5 41	18 14	4 59	18 42	7 40	1 46	11 48	7 12	10 31	0 05	10 54	3 49	7 08	1 32	22 05	1 19
7 Tu	5 17	18 52	4 25	18 44	6 51	1 41	11 54	7 21	10 47	0 06	11 03	3 47	7 06	1 32	22 05	1 19
8 W	4 54	18 20	3 36	17 39	6 01	1 36	11 59	7 30	11 03	0 07	11 12	3 44	7 04	1 32	22 05	1 19
9 Th	4 30	16 43	2 35	15 33	5 10	1 30	12 02	7 38	11 20	0 07	11 21	3 41	7 02	1 32	22 05	1 19
10 F	4 07	14 10	1 26	12 37	4 18	1 23	12 05	7 46	11 35	0 08	11 30	3 39	6 59	1 33	22 05	1 19
11 Sa	3 43	10 54	0 13	9 04	3 25	1 16	12 05	7 53	11 51	0 09	11 39	3 36	6 57	1 33	22 05	1 19
12 Su	3 20	7 08	0N59	5 08	2 31	1 08	12 05	8 00	12 07	0 10	11 48	3 34	6 55	1 33	22 05	1 19
13 M	2 56	3 06	2 07	1 03	1 36	0 60	12 02	8 06	12 23	0 10	11 57	3 31	6 53	1 33	22 05	1 19
14 Tu	2 33	0S60	3 07	3S01	0 41	0 51	11 58	8 12	12 38	0 11	12 06	3 29	6 50	1 33	22 05	1 19
15 W	2 09	4 59	3 57	6 52	0N15	0 42	11 53	8 17	12 54	0 12	12 15	3 27	6 48	1 33	22 05	1 19
16 Th	1 45	8 41	4 36	10 23	1 11	0 32	11 46	8 21	13 09	0 13	12 23	3 24	6 45	1 33	22 05	1 19
17 F	1 22	11 58	5 01	13 26	2 07	0 21	11 38	8 24	13 24	0 13	12 32	3 22	6 43	1 34	22 05	1 19
18 Sa	0 58	14 44	5 13	15 53	3 03	0 10	11 28	8 27	13 39	0 14	12 41	3 19	6 40	1 34	22 05	1 19
19 Su	0 34	16 52	5 11	17 40	3 59	0N01	11 17	8 29	13 54	0 15	12 50	3 17	6 38	1 34	22 05	1 19
20 M	0 10	18 17	4 56	18 41	4 54	0 13	11 04	8 29	14 09	0 15	12 59	3 15	6 35	1 34	22 05	1 20
21 Tu	0N13	18 53	4 29	18 53	5 49	0 24	10 50	8 29	14 23	0 16	13 07	3 12	6 32	1 34	22 05	1 20
22 W	0 37	18 39	3 49	18 12	6 43	0 37	10 35	8 28	14 38	0 17	13 16	3 10	6 30	1 34	22 05	1 20
23 Th	1 01	17 31	2 57	16 37	7 36	0 49	10 19	8 26	14 52	0 17	13 25	3 08	6 27	1 34	22 05	1 20
24 F	1 24	15 30	1 56	14 10	8 27	1 01	10 01	8 23	15 06	0 18	13 33	3 05	6 24	1 34	22 05	1 20
25 Sa	1 48	12 38	0 48	10 55	9 16	1 14	9 43	8 20	15 20	0 19	13 42	3 03	6 22	1 34	22 05	1 20
26 Su	2 12	9 02	0S26	6 60	10 03	1 26	9 23	8 15	15 34	0 19	13 50	3 01	6 19	1 34	22 05	1 20
27 M	2 35	4 50	1 39	2 35	10 49	1 38	9 03	8 09	15 48	0 20	13 59	2 58	6 16	1 35	22 05	1 20
28 Tu	2 59	0 16	2 49	2N05	11 31	1 49	8 42	8 02	16 01	0 21	14 07	2 56	6 13	1 35	22 05	1 20
29 W	3 22	4N24	3 49	6 41	12 12	2 01	8 21	7 55	16 15	0 21	14 16	2 54	6 10	1 35	22 05	1 20
30 Th	3 45	8 53	4 35	10 56	12 49	2 11	7 59	7 47	16 28	0 22	14 24	2 52	6 07	1 35	22 05	1 20
31 F	4N09	12N49	5S02	14N30	13N24	2N22	7N38	7N38	16N41	0N22	14N33	2S50	6S05	1N35	22S05	1N20

Day	⚷		♅		♆		♇	
	Decl	Lat	Decl	Lat	Decl	Lat	Decl	Lat
1	1N02	3N47	8N04	0S34	7S58	0S51	21S12	0N56
6	1 09	3 47	8 10	0 34	7 54	0 51	21 11	0 56
11	1 16	3 46	8 15	0 34	7 50	0 51	21 11	0 55
16	1 23	3 46	8 21	0 34	7 46	0 51	21 10	0 55
21	1 30	3 46	8 27	0 34	7 41	0 51	21 10	0 55
26	1 37	3 46	8 33	0 34	7 37	0 51	21 10	0 54
31	1N43	3N46	8N39	0S34	7S33	0S51	21S09	0N54

Day	⚴		⚵		⚶		Eris	
	Decl	Lat	Decl	Lat	Decl	Lat	Decl	Lat
1	3S45	0N18	11S25	11N49	26N05	4N13	2S30	12S12
6	3 25	0S03	11 08	12 02	26 10	4 18	2 29	12 12
11	3 04	0 25	10 49	12 16	26 14	4 21	2 27	12 11
16	2 42	0 47	10 30	12 30	26 15	4 24	2 26	12 11
21	2 21	1 09	10 09	12 46	26 13	4 27	2 24	12 10
26	1 59	1 32	9 48	13 02	26 10	4 29	2 23	12 10
31	1S38	1S54	9S25	13N18	26N04	4N30	2S21	12S10

Moon Phenomena

Max/0 Decl		
dy	hr mn	
7	0:41	18N52
13	18:08	0 S
21	5:22	18S55
28	1:22	0 N

Perigee/Apogee			
dy	hr m		kilometers
3	7:35	p	369062
18	17:31	a	404648
30	12:34	p	363857

PH	dy	hr mn	
☽	5	11:34	15♊05
○	12	14:55	22♍13
☾	20	15:59	0♑14
●	28	2:58	7♈37

Max/0 Lat		
dy	hr mn	
4	15:46	5S17
11	4:18	0 N
18	9:14	5N14
25	15:42	0 S
31	21:18	5S10

Void of Course Moon

Last Aspect				☽ Ingress		
2	2:20	♄	△	♉	2	7:44
3	15:21	♇	△	♊	4	10:07
6	8:23	♂	✶	♋	6	12:55
8	15:00	♂	□	♌	8	16:47
10	17:07	♄	△	♍	10	22:08
13	2:37	☿	☍	♎	13	5:29
15	10:06	♄	✶	♏	15	15:12
17	21:58	☉	△	♐	18	3:01
20	10:39	♄	☌	♑	20	15:32
22	13:21	♅	□	♒	23	2:29
25	5:57	♄	✶	♓	25	10:08
27	10:20	♄	□	♈	27	14:12
29	12:08	♄	△	♉	29	15:49
30	23:13	♇	△	♊	31	16:41

DAILY ASPECTARIAN

1 W	☽⚺♆	0:47
	☽☌♀	2:56
	☿⋕♀	11:50
	☽□♇	12:50
	♂⚺⚷	14:32
	☽∠☿	17:52
	☽☌♅	18:29
	☽☍♃	18:44
	☉∥♃	21:03
	☽⚺⚷	21:29
	☽☌♂	21:49
	☿∠♅	22:41
2 Th	☿⚼♃	0:22
	☉∠☽	2:09
	☽∠♆	2:11
	☽△♄	2:20
	☉☌♆	2:45
	☉⋕☽	6:28
	☽⋕♃	7:14
	☿✶⚳	8:07
	☽⋕♆	11:13
	☿⋕⚳	11:19
	☽∥♅	12:04
	☽∥♂	21:11
	☽☌⚳	21:14
	☽∠⚷	22:48
	☽✶☿	22:49
	☽⋕☿	23:18
3 F	♃☍♅	1:17
	☽∥⚳	2:08
	☽✶♆	3:27
	☽⚼♄	3:37
	☉✶☽	5:15
	☽⚺♀	5:46
	☿⋕♂	7:00
	☽∥♀	8:10
	☉⚺♀	12:51
	☽△♇	15:21
	☿∠♂	17:48
	☽⚻♃	20:53
	☽⚺♅	21:03
4 Sa	☽✶⚷	0:05
	☽⚺♂	2:55
	☽⚻♄	4:54
	☽∠♀	7:00
	♀ R	9:10
	☿☌♆	11:11
	☽⚼♇	16:37
	☽⚼♃	21:59
	☽∠♅	22:22
5 Su	☽⚺⚳	0:54
	☿⚺♀	4:18
	☽∠♂	5:33
	☽□♆	6:03
	☽✶♀	8:15
	☽□☿	8:52
	☿⋕♅	9:22
	☉□☽	11:34
	♂∠♆	15:54
	☿∥♆	16:48
	☽⚻♇	18:00
	♂△♄	20:47
	☽△♃	23:13
	☽✶♅	23:51
6 M	☽∠⚳	2:57
	☽□⚷	2:58
	⚳∠⚷	3:30
	☽☍♄	7:49
	☽✶♂	8:23
	☿∥♃	16:28
7 Tu	☉☌☿	0:30
	☽✶⚳	5:16
	☽△♆	9:21
	⚶ D	9:33
	☽□♀	11:09
	☉△☽	18:49
	☽△☿	20:13
	☽☍♇	21:29
8 W	☽□♃	2:26
	☽□♅	3:35
	☿✶♇	5:26
	☽△⚷	6:48
	☽⚼♆	11:26
	☽⚻♄	11:44
	☽□♂	15:00
	☉⚼☽	23:02
9 Th	☽⚼☿	2:42
	♂∥⚳	6:03
	☉✶♇	8:34
	☽⚼⚷	9:14
	☽□⚳	10:56
	☽⚻♆	13:54
	☽⚼♄	14:13
	☽△♀	14:56
	☿⚻♃	14:58
10 F	♂ ♉	0:35
	☿⚺♅	1:56
	☽⚻♇	2:19
	☉⚻☽	3:43
	☽✶♃	6:59
	☽△♅	8:43
	☉∥☿	9:00
	☽⚻☿	9:50
	☽⚻⚷	12:05
	☽∥♀	15:48
	☽△♄	17:07
	☽⚼♀	17:17
	☽∥♂	17:54
	☽∥⚳	19:04
	☽△♂	23:23
11 Sa	☿☌⚷	1:36
	☽⚼♇	5:23
	☽∠♃	9:54
	☽⚼♅	11:57
	♀⚺♆	13:54
	☽∥♅	17:02
	☽△⚳	18:26
	☽⋕♆	19:50
	☽⚻♀	19:59
	☉⚻♃	20:02
	☽☍♆	20:09
	♀∥♂	20:21
	☿∠⚳	22:57
12 Su	☽⋕♃	1:22
	☽⚼♂	4:25
	☽△♇	8:58
	☿□♄	12:11
	☽⚺♃	13:19
	☉☍☽	14:55
	☽⚻♅	15:44
	☽☍⚷	19:17
	☽⚼⚳	23:02
13 M	☽□♄	0:26
	♀⚺⚳	0:41
	☉⋕☽	1:04
	☉⚺♅	2:05
	☽☍☿	2:37
	☿⋕⚷	7:36
	☽⚻♂	10:07
	☽∥⚷	10:25
	♀∥⚳	10:26
	☽⋕☿	11:15
	☿ ♈	21:08
	☽∥☿	22:30
14 Tu	☽⋕⚷	1:59
	☽☍♀	2:43
	☽⚻⚳	4:17
	☽⚻♆	4:36
	☉∥☽	8:22
	⚳✶♆	16:17
	☽□♇	17:53
	☽☌♃	21:53
15 W	☽☍♅	1:06
	☉☌⚷	2:42
	☽⚻⚷	4:51
	☉⚻☽	5:01
	⚳⚼♄	6:35
	☽⚼♆	9:44
	☽✶♄	10:06
	☽∥♃	11:23
	☽∥♆	17:50
	☽⋕♅	21:46
	☽⚻☿	23:19
	☽☍♂	23:39
16 Th	☿⚺♂	2:23
	☿∥⚷	5:17
	☉⋕☿	10:24
	☽⚼⚷	10:31
	☽⚻♀	11:14
	☉⚼☽	13:12
	☽△♆	15:26
	☽∠♄	15:48
	☽☍⚳	16:44
	☽⋕♀	21:30
	☉⋕⚷	21:35
17 F	☽⋕⚳	4:47
	☽✶♇	5:07
	☽⚺♃	8:39
	☽⚼☿	10:59
	☽⚻♅	12:45
	☽⋕♂	12:58
	☽⚼♀	16:02
	☽△⚷	16:39
	☉□♄	21:49
	☽⚺♄	21:57
	☉△☽	21:58
18 Sa	☽∠♇	11:21
	☿☌♀	12:28
	☽∠♃	14:36
	☽⚻♂	15:32
	☽⚼♅	19:08
	☽△♀	21:00
	☽△☿	23:07
19 Su	☽□♆	3:58
	☉∠⚳	7:00
	☽⚻⚳	7:01
	☽⚺♇	17:42
	☽✶♃	20:37
	☽⚼♂	23:47
20 M	☽△♅	1:34
	☽□⚷	5:31
	☿⚺♆	5:52
	☉ ♈	10:30
	☽☌♄	10:39
	☽⚼⚳	14:13
	☉□☽	15:59
	♀⚺♂	20:24
21 Tu	☽□♀	6:34
	☽△♂	7:44
	☿⚺⚳	11:15
	☽✶♆	16:18
	☿⋕♃	18:21
	☽△⚳	20:59
	☽□☿	22:21
22 W	☽☌♇	5:33
	☽□♃	7:46
	☽□♅	13:21
	☽✶⚷	17:10
	☽∠♆	21:40
	☽⚺♄	21:56
23 Th	☿⋕♆	1:56
	☉✶☽	7:59
	☽✶♀	14:07
	☽□♂	21:21
	☽∠⚷	21:53
24 F	☿□♇	0:46
	☿∥♅	2:03
	☽⚺♆	2:11
	☽∠♄	2:25
	☽⋕♂	3:29
	♂∠⚷	7:46
	☽□⚳	8:08
	☉∥⚷	10:10
	☿☍♃	12:46
	☉∠☽	14:24
	☽⚺♇	14:34
	☽△♃	16:04
	☽⋕⚳	16:16
	☽✶☿	16:35
	☽∠♀	16:45
	☽✶♅	22:03
25 Sa	☽⚺⚷	1:40
	☽✶♄	5:57
	☿∥♀	9:32
	☉☌♀	10:18
	☽∠♇	17:40
	☽⚺♀	18:34
	☽⋕☿	18:42
	☽⚼♃	18:52
	☉⚺☽	19:38
	☽⋕♀	21:37
	☽∠☿	23:15
26 Su	☽∠♅	1:00
	☽⋕♅	2:53
	☽✶♂	6:44
	☽☌♆	8:24
	☽∥♆	8:25
	☿☌♅	15:07
	☽✶⚳	15:20
	☽∥♃	16:02
	☽✶♇	19:53
	☽⚻♃	20:48
27 M	☽⚺♅	3:04
	☽⚺☿	4:26
	☽☌⚷	6:28
	☽∠♂	9:53
	☽□♄	10:20
	☉⋕☽	11:02
	♂✶♆	16:45
	☽⋕⚷	16:52
	☽∠⚳	17:35
	♂⚼♄	18:58
	☽☌♀	20:00
28 Tu	☿⚺⚷	1:06
	☉☌☽	2:58
	♀∥♅	7:08
	☽∥⚷	9:53
	☽⚺♆	11:23
	☽⚺♂	12:17
	☉∥☽	18:07
	☽⚺⚳	19:12
	☽□♇	22:15
	☽☍♃	22:39
29 W	☽☌♅	5:16
	♀∠⚳	6:12
	☽⚺⚷	8:33
	☽⋕♃	9:09
	☽☌☿	11:34
	☽∠♆	12:05
	☽△♄	12:08
	☽⋕♆	16:47
	☿∠♆	17:53
	☿△♄	18:18
	☽∥♀	19:27
	☽⚺♀	19:30
	☽∥♅	22:39
30 Th	♀ ♈	4:48
	☉⚺☽	7:46
	☽∠⚷	9:06
	☽✶♆	12:35
	☽⚼♄	12:35
	☽☌♂	15:50
	♃□♇	18:20
	☽∠♀	19:00
	☽☌⚳	21:28
	☽⚻♃	23:11
	☽△♇	23:13
31 F	☽∥☿	4:42
	♀⋕♆	4:43
	☽⚺♅	6:21
	☽✶⚷	9:37
	☉∠☽	9:57
	☽∥⚳	12:56
	☽⚻♄	13:02
	☽⚺☿	16:38
	☿ ♉	17:32
	☽✶♀	18:35
	☽⚼♃	23:28
	☽⚼♇	23:44

April 2017

LONGITUDE

Day	Sid.Time	☉	☽	☽ 12 hour	Mean☊	True☊	☿	♀	♂	⚳	♃	♄	⚷	♅	♆	♇
	h m s	° ' "	° ' "	° ' "	° '	° '	° '	° '	° '	° '	° '	° '	° '	° '	° '	° '
1 Sa	12 38 10	11♈27 13	4♊27 40	11♊44 56	1♍27.5	2♍42.5	0♉16.6	1♈01.8	15♉42.2	18♉38.3	19♎08.1	27♐46.3	25♓42.6	23♈42.4	12♓48.3	19♑18.2
2 Su	12 42 07	12 26 26	18 59 05	26 09 37	1 24.3	2R 38.7	1 14.3	0R 30.3	16 24.6	19 01.3	19R 00.5	27 46.8	25 46.1	23 45.8	12 50.4	19 18.8
3 M	12 46 04	13 25 37	3♋16 10	10♋18 32	1 21.2	2D 36.6	2 05.3	0 00.5	17 07.0	19 24.4	18 52.9	27 47.2	25 49.6	23 49.2	12 52.4	19 19.3
4 Tu	12 50 00	14 24 46	17 16 35	24 10 18	1 18.0	2 36.2	2 49.6	29♓32.6	17 49.3	19 47.6	18 45.2	27 47.4	25 53.1	23 52.6	12 54.4	19 19.8
5 W	12 53 57	15 23 52	0♌59 46	7♌45 06	1 14.8	2 37.0	3 27.1	29 06.7	18 31.5	20 10.8	18 37.6	27 47.6	25 56.5	23 56.0	12 56.4	19 20.3
6 Th	12 57 53	16 22 56	14 26 29	21 04 05	1 11.6	2 38.4	3 57.6	28 42.8	19 13.7	20 34.1	18 29.9	27R 47.7	26 00.0	23 59.4	12 58.4	19 20.8
7 F	13 01 50	17 21 57	27 38 08	4♍08 48	1 08.4	2R 39.4	4 21.2	28 21.2	19 55.9	20 57.5	18 22.2	27 47.7	26 03.4	24 02.8	13 00.4	19 21.2
8 Sa	13 05 46	18 20 56	10♍36 19	17 00 49	1 05.3	2 39.2	4 37.9	28 01.9	20 38.0	21 20.9	18 14.5	27 47.5	26 06.8	24 06.3	13 02.3	19 21.6
9 Su	13 09 43	19 19 53	23 22 29	29 41 27	1 02.1	2 37.1	4R 47.7	27 45.0	21 20.1	21 44.4	18 06.7	27 47.3	26 10.2	24 09.7	13 04.3	19 21.9
10 M	13 13 39	20 18 48	5♎57 48	12♎11 41	0 58.9	2 32.8	4 50.8	27 30.5	22 02.1	22 07.9	17 59.0	27 47.0	26 13.6	24 13.1	13 06.2	19 22.3
11 Tu	13 17 36	21 17 40	18 23 09	24 32 20	0 55.7	2 26.2	4 47.4	27 18.4	22 44.1	22 31.5	17 51.3	27 46.6	26 16.9	24 16.5	13 08.1	19 22.6
12 W	13 21 33	22 16 31	0♏39 17	6♏44 09	0 52.5	2 17.8	4 37.7	27 08.8	23 26.1	22 55.1	17 43.7	27 46.0	26 20.3	24 20.0	13 09.9	19 22.8
13 Th	13 25 29	23 15 20	12 47 04	18 48 09	0 49.4	2 08.2	4 22.1	27 01.7	24 08.0	23 18.8	17 36.0	27 45.4	26 23.6	24 23.4	13 11.8	19 23.1
14 F	13 29 26	24 14 07	24 47 39	0♐45 45	0 46.2	1 58.3	4 01.0	26 57.0	24 49.8	23 42.5	17 28.4	27 44.7	26 26.9	24 26.8	13 13.6	19 23.3
15 Sa	13 33 22	25 12 52	6♐42 45	12 38 59	0 43.0	1 49.0	3 34.8	26D 54.8	25 31.7	24 06.3	17 20.8	27 43.9	26 30.1	24 30.3	13 15.4	19 23.5
16 Su	13 37 19	26 11 35	18 34 48	24 30 38	0 39.8	1 41.2	3 04.2	26 55.0	26 13.4	24 30.1	17 13.2	27 43.0	26 33.4	24 33.7	13 17.2	19 23.6
17 M	13 41 15	27 10 16	0♑26 55	6♑24 12	0 36.7	1 35.3	2 29.8	26 57.5	26 55.2	24 54.0	17 05.7	27 42.0	26 36.6	24 37.1	13 19.0	19 23.7
18 Tu	13 45 12	28 08 56	12 22 59	18 23 52	0 33.5	1 31.7	1 52.3	27 02.3	27 36.9	25 17.9	16 58.2	27 40.9	26 39.8	24 40.6	13 20.8	19 23.8
19 W	13 49 08	29 07 34	24 27 28	0♒34 24	0 30.3	1D 30.2	1 12.5	27 09.5	28 18.5	25 41.9	16 50.8	27 39.7	26 43.0	24 44.0	13 22.5	19 23.9
20 Th	13 53 05	0♉06 11	6♒45 17	13 00 46	0 27.1	1 30.3	0 31.0	27 18.8	29 00.2	26 05.9	16 43.4	27 38.4	26 46.1	24 47.4	13 24.2	19R 23.9
21 F	13 57 02	1 04 46	19 21 25	25 47 50	0 23.9	1R 31.1	29♈48.8	27 30.3	29 41.7	26 30.0	16 36.1	27 37.0	26 49.3	24 50.9	13 25.9	19 23.9
22 Sa	14 00 58	2 03 19	2♓20 31	8♓59 51	0 20.8	1 31.5	29 06.5	27 43.9	0♊23.3	26 54.1	16 28.9	27 35.6	26 52.4	24 54.3	13 27.6	19 23.9
23 Su	14 04 55	3 01 50	15 46 10	22 39 37	0 17.6	1 30.6	28 25.1	27 59.5	1 04.8	27 18.2	16 21.7	27 34.0	26 55.4	24 57.7	13 29.2	19 23.8
24 M	14 08 51	4 00 20	29 40 12	6♈47 44	0 14.4	1 27.6	27 45.1	28 17.1	1 46.2	27 42.4	16 14.6	27 32.3	26 58.5	25 01.1	13 30.8	19 23.7
25 Tu	14 12 48	4 58 48	14♈01 49	21 21 51	0 11.2	1 22.1	27 07.2	28 36.5	2 27.6	28 06.7	16 07.6	27 30.6	27 01.5	25 04.5	13 32.4	19 23.6
26 W	14 16 44	5 57 14	28 47 01	6♉16 19	0 08.1	1 14.3	26 32.1	28 57.8	3 09.0	28 30.9	16 00.7	27 28.7	27 04.5	25 07.9	13 34.0	19 23.5
27 Th	14 20 41	6 55 39	13♉48 35	21 22 32	0 04.9	1 04.9	26 00.3	29 20.9	3 50.4	28 55.3	15 53.9	27 26.8	27 07.4	25 11.3	13 35.5	19 23.3
28 F	14 24 37	7 54 01	28 56 53	6♊30 17	0 01.7	0 55.0	25 32.1	29 45.6	4 31.7	29 19.6	15 47.2	27 24.8	27 10.4	25 14.7	13 37.1	19 23.1
29 Sa	14 28 34	8 52 22	14♊01 32	21 29 29	29♌58.5	0 45.8	25 08.1	0♈12.0	5 12.9	29 44.0	15 40.5	27 22.7	27 13.3	25 18.0	13 38.6	19 22.8
30 Su	14 32 30	9♉50 41	28 53 11	6♋11 54	29♌55.3	0♍38.4	24♈48.3	0♈40.0	5♊54.2	0♊08.4	15♎34.0	27♐20.5	27♓16.1	25♈21.4	13♓40.0	19♑22.6

1st of Month

Julian Day # 2457844.5
Obliquity 23°26'06"
SVP 5♓01'17"
GC 27♐04.8
Eris 23♈03.3

Day	⚴
1	0♈38.1
6	2 23.9
11	4 09.8
16	5 55.5
21	7 41.0
26	9 26.3

Day	⚵
1	14♑32.9
6	15 24.4
11	16 10.2
16	16 49.8
21	17 22.8
26	17 48.8

Day	⚶
1	22♋14.5
6	23 08.3
11	24 09.9
16	25 18.8
21	26 34.3
26	27 56.1

DECLINATION and LATITUDE

Day	☉ Decl	☽ Decl	☽ Lat	☽12h Decl	☿ Decl	☿ Lat	♀ Decl	♀ Lat	♂ Decl	♂ Lat	⚳ Decl	⚳ Lat	♃ Decl	♃ Lat	♄ Decl	♄ Lat
1 Sa	4N32	15N57	5S10	17N08	13N55	2N31	7N16	7N28	16N54	0N23	14N41	2S47	6S02	1N35	22S05	1N20
2 Su	4 55	18 02	4 58	18 38	14 24	2 40	6 54	7 18	17 07	0 24	14 49	2 45	5 59	1 35	22 05	1 20
3 M	5 18	18 57	4 27	18 57	14 49	2 47	6 32	7 07	17 20	0 24	14 58	2 43	5 56	1 35	22 05	1 20
4 Tu	5 41	18 40	3 41	18 06	15 10	2 54	6 10	6 55	17 32	0 25	15 06	2 41	5 53	1 35	22 04	1 21
5 W	6 04	17 17	2 43	16 13	15 29	2 60	5 49	6 44	17 45	0 26	15 14	2 39	5 50	1 35	22 04	1 21
6 Th	6 26	14 57	1 37	13 29	15 43	3 04	5 28	6 31	17 57	0 26	15 22	2 37	5 47	1 35	22 04	1 21
7 F	6 49	11 52	0 27	10 07	15 55	3 08	5 08	6 19	18 09	0 27	15 30	2 35	5 44	1 35	22 04	1 21
8 Sa	7 12	8 15	0N43	6 18	16 02	3 10	4 48	6 06	18 21	0 27	15 39	2 32	5 41	1 35	22 04	1 21
9 Su	7 34	4 18	1 49	2 16	16 06	3 10	4 30	5 52	18 32	0 28	15 47	2 30	5 38	1 35	22 04	1 21
10 M	7 56	0 14	2 50	1S48	16 06	3 09	4 12	5 39	18 44	0 28	15 55	2 28	5 35	1 35	22 04	1 21
11 Tu	8 18	3S48	3 41	5 45	16 03	3 07	3 54	5 26	18 55	0 29	16 03	2 26	5 33	1 35	22 04	1 21
12 W	8 40	7 37	4 21	9 24	15 56	3 04	3 38	5 12	19 06	0 30	16 10	2 24	5 30	1 35	22 04	1 21
13 Th	9 02	11 05	4 49	12 38	15 46	2 58	3 23	4 58	19 17	0 30	16 18	2 22	5 27	1 35	22 04	1 21
14 F	9 24	14 03	5 03	15 19	15 33	2 52	3 08	4 45	19 28	0 31	16 26	2 20	5 24	1 35	22 04	1 21
15 Sa	9 45	16 25	5 05	17 21	15 16	2 43	2 55	4 31	19 39	0 31	16 34	2 18	5 21	1 35	22 04	1 21
16 Su	10 07	18 05	4 53	18 38	14 56	2 34	2 43	4 18	19 49	0 32	16 42	2 16	5 18	1 35	22 04	1 21
17 M	10 28	18 58	4 28	19 06	14 34	2 23	2 31	4 04	19 59	0 32	16 49	2 14	5 15	1 35	22 04	1 21
18 Tu	10 49	19 01	3 52	18 43	14 10	2 10	2 21	3 51	20 09	0 33	16 57	2 12	5 13	1 34	22 04	1 21
19 W	11 10	18 11	3 05	17 27	13 43	1 57	2 12	3 38	20 19	0 33	17 05	2 10	5 10	1 34	22 03	1 21
20 Th	11 30	16 30	2 09	15 21	13 15	1 42	2 04	3 25	20 29	0 34	17 12	2 08	5 07	1 34	22 03	1 21
21 F	11 51	13 59	1 05	12 26	12 46	1 27	1 57	3 12	20 39	0 34	17 20	2 06	5 04	1 34	22 03	1 22
22 Sa	12 11	10 42	0S04	8 49	12 16	1 11	1 50	2 59	20 48	0 35	17 27	2 04	5 02	1 34	22 03	1 22
23 Su	12 31	6 46	1 15	4 36	11 45	0 54	1 45	2 47	20 57	0 36	17 34	2 02	4 59	1 34	22 03	1 22
24 M	12 51	2 20	2 24	0 00	11 15	0 38	1 41	2 35	21 06	0 36	17 42	2 00	4 57	1 34	22 03	1 22
25 Tu	13 11	2N22	3 26	4N44	10 46	0 20	1 38	2 23	21 15	0 37	17 49	1 58	4 54	1 34	22 03	1 22
26 W	13 30	7 03	4 16	9 17	10 17	0 03	1 36	2 11	21 23	0 37	17 56	1 56	4 51	1 34	22 03	1 22
27 Th	13 49	11 23	4 49	13 18	9 50	0S13	1 34	1 60	21 32	0 38	18 03	1 54	4 49	1 34	22 03	1 22
28 F	14 08	14 60	5 02	16 27	9 24	0 30	1 34	1 49	21 40	0 38	18 10	1 52	4 46	1 33	22 03	1 22
29 Sa	14 27	17 36	4 55	18 27	9 01	0 46	1 34	1 38	21 48	0 39	18 17	1 50	4 44	1 33	22 03	1 22
30 Su	14N46	18N59	4S27	19N11	8N39	1S02	1N36	1N27	21N56	0N39	18N24	1S49	4S42	1N33	22S03	1N22

Day	⚷ Decl	⚷ Lat	♅ Decl	♅ Lat	♆ Decl	♆ Lat	♇ Decl	♇ Lat
1	1N45	3N46	8N41	0S34	7S33	0S51	21S09	0N5
6	1 52	3 46	8 47	0 34	7 29	0 52	21 09	0 5
11	1 59	3 46	8 53	0 34	7 25	0 52	21 09	0 5
16	2 05	3 46	8 60	0 34	7 22	0 52	21 10	0 5
21	2 12	3 46	9 06	0 34	7 19	0 52	21 10	0 5
26	2 18	3 46	9 12	0 34	7 16	0 52	21 10	0 5

Day	⚴ Decl	⚴ Lat	⚵ Decl	⚵ Lat	⚶ Decl	⚶ Lat	Eris Decl	Eris Lat
1	1S34	1S59	9S21	13N22	26N03	4N30	2S21	12S0
6	1 13	2 22	8 58	13 40	25 55	4 32	2 20	12 0
11	0 52	2 45	8 35	13 58	25 45	4 32	2 18	12 0
16	0 32	3 09	8 12	14 17	25 35	4 33	2 17	12 0
21	0 13	3 33	7 48	14 37	25 19	4 34	2 16	12 0
26	0N05	3 58	7 25	14 57	25 03	4 34	2 14	12 0

Moon Phenomena

Max/0 Decl
dy hr mn
3 6:10 18N59
10 1:21 0 S
17 13:18 19S06
24 12:00 0 N
30 13:37 19N11

Max/0 Lat
dy hr mn
7 9:15 0 N
14 14:16 5N06
21 22:31 0 S
28 2:55 5S03

Perigee/Apogee
dy hr m kilometers
15 10:05 a 405474
27 16:22 p 359331

PH dy hr mn
☽ 3 18:41 14♋12
○ 11 6:09 21♎33
☾ 19 9:58 29♑32
● 26 12:17 6♉27

Void of Course Moon

Last Aspect	☽ Ingress
2 14:44 ♄ ☍	♋ 2 18:28
4 20:46 ♀ △	♌ 4 22:14
7 0:17 ♄ △	♍ 7 4:21
9 8:22 ♄ □	♎ 9 12:35
11 18:20 ♄ ✶	♏ 11 22:43
14 4:19 ♀ △	♐ 14 10:28
16 18:27 ♄ ☌	♑ 16 23:06
19 9:58 ☉ □	♒ 19 10:53
21 18:24 ♀ ✶	♓ 21 19:44
23 21:35 ♀ ☌	♈ 24 0:34
25 21:54 ♄ △	♉ 26 1:57
28 1:20 ♀ ✶	♊ 28 1:40
29 21:29 ♄ ☍	♋ 30 1:49

DAILY ASPECTARIAN

Day	Aspect	Time
1 Sa	♀ ∠ ♂	6:19
	☽ ∠ ♅	7:01
	☽ ∥ ♂	10:35
	☿ ⊻ ♀	11:54
	☉ ✶ ☽	12:21
	☽ □ ♆	13:47
	☽ ∠ ☿	19:07
	☽ ⊻ ♂	19:30
	⚳ ⊼ ♃	23:22
2 Su	☽ △ ♃	0:02
	☽ ⊻ ⚳	0:04
	☽ ⊼ ♇	0:33
	☽ ✶ ♅	8:01
	☉ ⊻ ♆	10:03
	☽ □ ⚷	11:23
	☽ ☍ ♄	14:44
	⚳ △ ♇	18:33
	☽ □ ♀	18:40
	☽ ✶ ☿	21:53
	☽ ∠ ♂	21:57
3 M	♀ R ♓	0:26
	☽ ∠ ⚳	1:59
	☿ ∥ ⚳	15:17
	☽ △ ♆	16:27
	☉ □ ☽	18:41
4 Tu	☽ ✶ ♂	1:00
	☽ □ ♃	2:32
	☽ ☍ ♇	3:34
	☽ ✶ ⚳	4:30
	☉ ⋕ ♃	11:16
	☽ □ ♅	11:32
	☽ △ ⚷	15:04
	☉ ∥ ♀	15:56
	☽ ∥ ♂	18:21
	☽ ⊼ ♄	18:21
	☽ ⚼ ♆	18:36
	☽ △ ♀	20:46
	♀ ⋕ ♃	22:34
5 W	♂ ⊼ ♃	2:54
	☽ □ ☿	4:32
	☽ ∥ ☿	17:29
	☽ ⚼ ⚷	17:47
	☽ ∥ ⚳	20:23
	☽ ⚼ ♄	21:02
	☽ ⊼ ♆	21:21
	☽ ⚼ ♀	22:44
6 Th	☉ △ ☽	3:47
	♂ △ ♇	4:02
	♄ R	5:07
	☽ ✶ ♃	7:16
	☽ ⊼ ♇	8:53
	☽ □ ♂	9:09
	☽ □ ⚳	11:26
	☽ △ ♅	17:24
	☽ ⊼ ⚷	21:06
7 F	☽ △ ♄	0:17
	☽ ⊼ ♀	1:17
	☉ ⚼ ☽	9:25
	☽ ∠ ♃	10:28
	☽ ⚼ ♇	12:23
	☽ △ ☿	12:41
	☽ ∥ ♅	20:22
	☽ ⚼ ♅	21:11
	☉ ☍ ♃	21:40
8 Sa	☽ ☍ ♆	4:33
	☽ ⋕ ♆	4:58
	☉ ∥ ☽	6:01
	☽ ⊻ ♃	14:10
	☉ ⊼ ☽	15:43
	☽ ⋕ ♃	15:56
	☽ △ ♇	16:25
	☉ ⋕ ♆	16:30
	☽ ⚼ ☿	17:10
	☽ △ ♂	19:55
	♀ □ ♄	20:29
	☽ △ ⚳	20:48
	☽ ∥ ♀	22:47
9 Su	☉ □ ♇	0:50
	☽ ⊼ ♅	1:30
	☽ ☍ ⚷	5:19
	☽ ☍ ♀	8:08
	☽ □ ♄	8:22
	☽ ∥ ⚷	13:56
	☽ ⊼ ☿	21:52
	☿ R	23:17
10 M	☽ ⚼ ♂	2:11
	☽ ⚼ ⚳	2:19
	♂ ☌ ⚳	7:28
	☽ ⋕ ⚷	12:58
	☽ ⊼ ♆	13:47
	☽ ☌ ♃	22:59
11 Tu	☽ ⋕ ♀	0:36
	☿ ∥ ⚳	1:18
	☽ □ ♇	1:56
	☉ ☍ ☽	6:09
	☽ ⊼ ⚳	8:20
	☽ ⊼ ♂	8:59
	☽ ∥ ♃	10:35
	☽ ☍ ♅	11:32
	☽ ⊼ ⚷	15:29
	☽ ⊼ ♀	17:11
	☽ ✶ ♄	18:20
	☽ ⚼ ♆	19:06
	☽ ∥ ♆	22:37
12 W	☽ ☍ ☿	7:41
	☉ ⋕ ☽	7:47
	☽ ⋕ ♅	8:39
	☉ ∥ ♅	16:47
	☽ ⚼ ⚷	21:13
	☽ ⚼ ♀	22:31
	☽ ∠ ♄	23:57
13 Th	☽ △ ♆	0:49
	☉ ⊻ ⚳	2:21
	☽ ⊻ ♃	9:30
	♂ ⊻ ♅	9:38
	☽ ✶ ♇	13:10
	☽ ☍ ⚳	21:45
	☉ ⊼ ☽	22:47
	☽ ⊼ ♅	23:18
14 F	☽ ☍ ♂	0:05
	☽ △ ⚷	3:20
	☽ △ ♀	4:19
	☉ ☌ ♅	5:31
	☽ ⊻ ♄	5:55
	☽ ⋕ ☿	12:50
	☽ ∠ ♃	15:17
	☽ ⊼ ☿	17:55
	☽ ∠ ♇	19:19
15 Sa	☽ ⋕ ⚳	1:50
	☽ ⚼ ♅	5:40
	☉ ⚼ ☽	7:43
	♀ D	10:19
	☽ □ ♆	13:16
	☽ ✶ ♃	21:17
	☽ ⚼ ☿	23:01
16 Su	☽ ⊻ ♇	1:39
	☉ ⊻ ♂	2:39
	⚳ ⊻ ♅	4:15
	☉ ⊻ ⚷	9:26
	☽ △ ♅	12:10
	☽ ⊼ ⚳	12:24
	♂ ✶ ⚷	12:25
	☽ □ ⚷	16:13
	☽ ⊼ ♂	16:26
	☉ △ ☽	16:47
	☽ □ ♀	16:55
	☉ ⊻ ♀	18:27
	☽ ☌ ♄	18:27
17 M	♀ ✶ ♂	1:27
	☽ △ ☿	3:56
	☉ △ ♄	12:45
	☽ ⚼ ⚳	19:41
18 Tu	☽ ⚼ ♂	0:30
	☽ ✶ ♆	1:56
	♂ ⊼ ♄	2:15
	☉ ∠ ♆	5:00
	☽ □ ♃	9:04
	☽ ☌ ♇	13:59
19 W	☽ □ ♅	0:33
	☽ △ ⚳	2:32
	☽ ✶ ⚷	4:28
	☽ ✶ ♀	5:22
	☽ ⊻ ♄	6:17
	♀ ∥ ⚷	6:48
	☽ ∠ ♆	7:43
	☽ △ ♂	8:02
	☉ □ ☽	9:58
	☽ □ ☿	12:32
	☽ ⋕ ⚳	16:02
	☉ ♉	21:28
20 Th	☉ ☌ ☿	5:55
	☽ ∠ ⚷	9:40
	☽ ∠ ♀	10:49
	☽ ∠ ♄	11:16
	☽ ⊻ ♆	12:46
	♇ R	12:50
	☿ R ♈	17:38
	☽ △ ♃	18:52
21 F	☽ ⊻ ♇	0:05
	☿ ⊻ ♂	2:01
	☽ ✶ ♅	10:17
	♂ ♊	10:33
	♀ □ ♄	11:10
	☽ ⋕ ☿	11:21
	☽ □ ⚳	13:43
	☽ ⊻ ⚷	13:57
	☉ ⋕ ☽	14:45
	☽ ✶ ♄	15:20
	☽ ⊻ ♀	15:25
	☽ ✶ ☿	18:24
	☽ □ ♂	20:14
	⚳ ✶ ⚷	22:03
	☽ ⚼ ♃	22:27
	☉ ✶ ☽	23:26
22 Sa	☉ ∥ ☿	2:11
	☽ ∠ ♇	3:44
	☽ ⋕ ♅	10:02
	☽ ∠ ♅	13:41
	☽ ☌ ♆	19:58
	☽ ∠ ☿	20:03
	☽ ∥ ♆	20:59
	☿ ∠ ♆	21:39
23 Su	☽ ⊼ ♃	1:02
	☉ ∠ ☽	4:16
	☽ ✶ ♇	6:20
	♂ ⚼ ♃	8:23
	☽ ∥ ♃	10:00
	☿ ⊻ ♀	10:40
	⚳ ⊼ ♄	14:39
	☽ ⊻ ♅	16:02
	☽ ☌ ⚷	19:24
	☽ □ ♄	20:23
	☽ ✶ ⚳	20:34
	☽ ⊻ ☿	20:53
	☽ ☌ ♀	21:35
24 M	☽ ⋕ ⚷	0:24
	☿ ⊻ ⚳	1:00
	☽ ⋕ ♀	3:25
	☽ ✶ ♂	3:44
	☉ ⊻ ☽	7:51
	☿ △ ♄	8:17
	♂ ⋕ ♇	11:27
	☽ ∥ ♀	20:19
	☽ ∠ ⚳	22:26
	☽ ⊻ ♆	23:11
	☽ ∥ ⚷	23:34
25 Tu	☽ ☍ ♃	3:25
	☿ ⊻ ⚷	3:29
	☽ ∠ ♂	5:55
	☽ □ ♇	8:47
	☽ ⋕ ♃	12:45
	☽ ☌ ♅	18:05
	☽ ☌ ☿	20:30
	☽ ⊻ ⚷	21:14
	☽ △ ♄	21:54
	☽ ⊻ ⚳	23:33
	☽ ∠ ♆	23:39
26 W	☽ ⊻ ♀	0:18
	☽ ⋕ ♆	1:08
	☽ ⊻ ♂	7:21
	☽ ∥ ♅	11:38
	☉ ☌ ☽	12:17
	☽ ∥ ☿	15:56
	☽ ∠ ⚷	21:19
	☽ ⚼ ♄	21:50
	☽ ✶ ♆	23:39
27 Th	☽ ∠ ♀	0:53
	☽ ⊼ ♃	3:17
	☽ △ ♇	8:51
	☉ ∥ ☽	17:07
	☽ ⊻ ♅	18:07
	☽ ⊻ ☿	18:45
	♂ ⚼ ♇	19:02
	☽ ✶ ⚷	21:11
	☽ ⊼ ♄	21:34
28 F	☽ ☌ ⚳	0:37
	☽ ✶ ♀	1:20
	☽ ⚼ ♃	2:54
	☽ ⚼ ♇	8:38
	☿ ∥ ♅	9:01
	☽ ☌ ♂	9:17
	♀ ♈	13:14
	☿ ☌ ♅	14:50
	☉ ⊻ ☽	15:12
	☽ ∠ ☿	17:56
	☽ ∠ ♅	18:02
	☽ □ ♆	23:23
29 Sa	☽ △ ♃	2:37
	☽ ⊼ ♇	8:36
	☽ ∥ ⚳	10:12
	⚳ ♊	15:43
	☉ ∠ ☽	16:58
	☽ ✶ ☿	17:30
	☽ ✶ ♅	18:14
	☽ □ ⚷	21:21
	☽ ☍ ♄	21:29
30 Su	☽ ⊻ ⚳	2:06
	☽ □ ♀	3:00
	☽ ⊻ ♂	12:05
	☉ ✶ ☽	19:21
	⚳ ⚼ ♃	19:52
	♄ □ ⚷	20:27
	♂ ⋕ ♄	21:45

LONGITUDE

Day	Sid.Time	☉	☽	☽ 12 hour	Mean ☊	True ☊	☿	♀	♂	⚳	♃	♄	⚷	♅	♆	♇
	h m s	° ' "	° ' "	° ' "	° '	° '	° '	° '	° '	° '	° '	° '	° '	° '	° '	° '
M	14 36 27	10♉48 58	13♋25 04	20♋32 18	29♌52.2	0♍33.3	24♈33.2	1♈09.5	6♊35.3	0♊32.9	15♎27.6	27♐18.2	27♓19.0	25♈24.8	13♓41.5	19♑22.3
Tu	14 40 24	11 47 13	27 33 27	4♌28 30	29 49.0	0R 30.7	24R 22.7	1 40.4	7 16.5	0 57.4	15R 21.3	27R 15.9	27 21.8	25 28.1	13 42.9	19R 22.0
W	14 44 20	12 45 26	11♌17 36	18 00 58	29 45.8	0D 30.0	24D 17.0	2 12.7	7 57.6	1 21.9	15 15.1	27 13.4	27 24.5	25 31.4	13 44.3	19 21.6
Th	14 48 17	13 43 36	24 38 56	1♍11 52	29 42.6	0R 30.2	24 16.0	2 46.4	8 38.6	1 46.5	15 09.0	27 10.9	27 27.3	25 34.7	13 45.7	19 21.2
F	14 52 13	14 41 45	7♍40 12	14 04 20	29 39.5	0 30.1	24 19.9	3 21.4	9 19.7	2 11.1	15 03.1	27 08.3	27 30.0	25 38.0	13 47.0	19 20.8
Sa	14 56 10	15 39 52	20 24 41	26 41 39	29 36.3	0 28.6	24 28.5	3 57.6	10 00.6	2 35.7	14 57.3	27 05.6	27 32.6	25 41.3	13 48.3	19 20.4
Su	15 00 06	16 37 56	2♎55 36	9♎06 53	29 33.1	0 24.8	24 41.8	4 35.0	10 41.6	3 00.3	14 51.6	27 02.8	27 35.3	25 44.6	13 49.6	19 19.9
M	15 04 03	17 35 59	15 15 49	21 22 38	29 29.9	0 18.2	24 59.6	5 13.6	11 22.5	3 25.0	14 46.1	27 00.0	27 37.8	25 47.8	13 50.8	19 19.4
Tu	15 07 59	18 34 00	27 27 35	3♏30 52	29 26.7	0 08.7	25 21.9	5 53.3	12 03.3	3 49.7	14 40.6	26 57.1	27 40.4	25 51.1	13 52.1	19 18.9
W	15 11 56	19 32 00	9♏32 40	15 33 09	29 23.6	29♌56.9	25 48.5	6 34.1	12 44.1	4 14.4	14 35.4	26 54.1	27 42.9	25 54.3	13 53.2	19 18.4
Th	15 15 53	20 29 57	21 32 26	27 30 42	29 20.4	29 43.6	26 19.3	7 15.9	13 24.9	4 39.2	14 30.2	26 51.0	27 45.4	25 57.5	13 54.4	19 17.8
F	15 19 49	21 27 54	3♐28 05	9♐24 46	29 17.2	29 29.7	26 54.1	7 58.7	14 05.6	5 04.0	14 25.3	26 47.9	27 47.8	26 00.7	13 55.6	19 17.2
Sa	15 23 46	22 25 49	15 20 55	21 16 47	29 14.0	29 16.6	27 32.8	8 42.5	14 46.3	5 28.8	14 20.4	26 44.7	27 50.2	26 03.9	13 56.7	19 16.6
Su	15 27 42	23 23 42	27 12 37	3♑08 42	29 10.9	29 05.1	28 15.3	9 27.2	15 27.0	5 53.6	14 15.8	26 41.5	27 52.6	26 07.0	13 57.7	19 15.9
M	15 31 39	24 21 34	9♑05 23	15 03 04	29 07.7	28 56.0	29 01.5	10 12.8	16 07.6	6 18.4	14 11.2	26 38.1	27 54.9	26 10.1	13 58.8	19 15.3
Tu	15 35 35	25 19 25	21 02 10	27 03 11	29 04.5	28 49.8	29 51.1	10 59.2	16 48.2	6 43.3	14 06.9	26 34.7	27 57.2	26 13.3	13 59.8	19 14.6
W	15 39 32	26 17 14	3♒06 38	9♒13 03	29 01.3	28 46.2	0♉44.1	11 46.4	17 28.8	7 08.2	14 02.6	26 31.3	27 59.5	26 16.3	14 00.8	19 13.8
Th	15 43 28	27 15 02	15 23 03	21 37 13	28 58.2	28 44.8	1 40.4	12 34.5	18 09.3	7 33.1	13 58.6	26 27.8	28 01.7	26 19.4	14 01.8	19 13.1
F	15 47 25	28 12 49	27 56 11	4♓20 33	28 55.0	28 44.6	2 39.9	13 23.2	18 49.8	7 58.1	13 54.7	26 24.2	28 03.8	26 22.5	14 02.7	19 12.3
Sa	15 51 22	29 10 35	10♓50 52	17 27 39	28 51.8	28 44.4	3 42.5	14 12.7	19 30.2	8 23.1	13 51.0	26 20.6	28 06.0	26 25.5	14 03.6	19 11.5
Su	15 55 18	0♊08 20	24 11 21	1♈02 17	28 48.6	28 43.1	4 48.0	15 02.9	20 10.6	8 48.0	13 47.4	26 16.9	28 08.0	26 28.5	14 04.5	19 10.7
M	15 59 15	1 06 04	8♈00 38	15 06 23	28 45.4	28 39.8	5 56.4	15 53.8	20 51.0	9 13.0	13 44.0	26 13.1	28 10.1	26 31.5	14 05.3	19 09.8
Tu	16 03 11	2 03 47	22 19 22	29 39 08	28 42.3	28 33.9	7 07.7	16 45.3	21 31.4	9 38.1	13 40.8	26 09.3	28 12.0	26 34.4	14 06.1	19 09.0
W	16 07 08	3 01 28	7♉05 03	14♉36 11	28 39.1	28 25.5	8 21.7	17 37.5	22 11.7	10 03.1	13 37.7	26 05.5	28 14.0	26 37.4	14 06.9	19 08.1
Th	16 11 04	3 59 09	22 11 26	29 49 32	28 35.9	28 15.3	9 38.5	18 30.2	22 52.0	10 28.2	13 34.8	26 01.6	28 15.9	26 40.3	14 07.6	19 07.2
F	16 15 01	4 56 48	7♊29 03	15♊08 33	28 32.7	28 04.5	10 57.8	19 23.5	23 32.2	10 53.3	13 32.1	25 57.6	28 17.8	26 43.1	14 08.4	19 06.2
Sa	16 18 57	5 54 27	22 46 32	0♋21 41	28 29.6	27 54.2	12 19.8	20 17.3	24 12.4	11 18.3	13 29.6	25 53.6	28 19.6	26 46.0	14 09.0	19 05.3
Su	16 22 54	6 52 04	7♋52 44	15 18 40	28 26.4	27 45.8	13 44.4	21 11.7	24 52.6	11 43.5	13 27.2	25 49.6	28 21.3	26 48.8	14 09.7	19 04.3
M	16 26 51	7 49 39	22 38 40	29 52 09	28 23.2	27 39.8	15 11.6	22 06.6	25 32.8	12 08.6	13 25.1	25 45.5	28 23.0	26 51.6	14 10.3	19 03.3
Tu	16 30 47	8 47 14	6♌58 46	13♌58 21	28 20.0	27 36.4	16 41.2	23 01.9	26 12.9	12 33.7	13 23.1	25 41.4	28 24.7	26 54.4	14 10.9	19 02.3
W	16 34 44	9♊44 47	20 50 58	27 36 46	28♌16.9	27♌35.2	18♉13.4	23♈57.8	26♊53.0	12♊58.9	13♎21.3	25♐37.3	28♓26.3	26♈57.1	14♓11.5	19♑01.2

1st of Month

Julian Day # 2457874.5
Obliquity 23°26'05"
SVP 5♓01'14"
GC 27♐04.9
Eris 23♈22.8

Day	⚴
1	11♈11.1
6	12 55.4
11	14 39.0
16	16 21.9
21	18 04.0
26	19 45.1
31	21 25.1

Day	⚵
1	18♑07.3
6	18 17.9
11	18 20.3R
16	18 14.3R
21	17 59.6R
26	17 36.2R
31	17 04.2R

Day	⚶
1	29♋23.5
6	0♌56.2
11	2 33.7
16	4 15.4
21	6 01.3
26	7 50.8
31	9 43.9

DECLINATION and LATITUDE

Day	☉ Decl	☽ Decl	☽ Lat	☽12h Decl	☿ Decl	☿ Lat	♀ Decl	♀ Lat	♂ Decl	♂ Lat	⚳ Decl	⚳ Lat	♃ Decl	♃ Lat	♄ Decl	♄ Lat
M	15N04	19N04	3S43	18N39	8N19	1S17	1N38	1N16	22N03	0N39	18N31	1S47	4S39	1N33	22S03	1N22
Tu	15 22	17 56	2 45	16 59	8 02	1 31	1 41	1 06	22 11	0 40	18 38	1 45	4 37	1 33	22 02	1 22
W	15 40	15 47	1 40	14 23	7 48	1 44	1 45	0 56	22 18	0 40	18 45	1 43	4 35	1 33	22 02	1 22
Th	15 57	12 49	0 31	11 06	7 36	1 57	1 49	0 47	22 25	0 41	18 52	1 41	4 33	1 32	22 02	1 22
F	16 15	9 17	0N38	7 22	7 26	2 09	1 54	0 37	22 32	0 41	18 59	1 39	4 31	1 32	22 02	1 22
Sa	16 32	5 23	1 43	3 22	7 19	2 19	2 00	0 28	22 38	0 42	19 05	1 37	4 28	1 32	22 02	1 22
Su	16 48	1 19	2 43	0S43	7 15	2 29	2 07	0 19	22 45	0 42	19 12	1 35	4 26	1 32	22 02	1 22
M	17 05	2S44	3 33	4 42	7 13	2 38	2 15	0 11	22 51	0 43	19 18	1 34	4 24	1 32	22 02	1 22
Tu	17 21	6 37	4 13	8 28	7 14	2 46	2 23	0 02	22 57	0 43	19 25	1 32	4 23	1 32	22 02	1 22
W	17 37	10 13	4 41	11 51	7 16	2 54	2 31	0S06	23 02	0 44	19 31	1 30	4 21	1 31	22 02	1 22
Th	17 52	13 22	4 57	14 44	7 22	3 00	2 41	0 14	23 08	0 44	19 37	1 28	4 19	1 31	22 02	1 22
F	18 08	15 57	4 59	16 59	7 29	3 05	2 50	0 21	23 13	0 44	19 44	1 26	4 17	1 31	22 02	1 22
Sa	18 22	17 51	4 48	18 31	7 38	3 10	3 01	0 29	23 19	0 45	19 50	1 24	4 15	1 31	22 01	1 22
Su	18 37	18 59	4 25	19 15	7 50	3 14	3 12	0 36	23 23	0 45	19 56	1 22	4 14	1 31	22 01	1 22
M	18 51	19 18	3 50	19 08	8 03	3 17	3 23	0 43	23 28	0 46	20 02	1 21	4 12	1 30	22 01	1 22
Tu	19 05	18 44	3 05	18 09	8 19	3 19	3 35	0 49	23 33	0 46	20 08	1 19	4 11	1 30	22 01	1 22
W	19 19	17 20	2 11	16 19	8 36	3 21	3 48	0 56	23 37	0 47	20 14	1 17	4 09	1 30	22 01	1 22
Th	19 32	15 06	1 10	13 42	8 54	3 21	4 01	1 02	23 41	0 47	20 20	1 15	4 08	1 30	22 01	1 22
F	19 46	12 07	0 04	10 23	9 15	3 21	4 14	1 08	23 45	0 47	20 26	1 13	4 07	1 29	22 01	1 22
Sa	19 58	8 29	1S04	6 27	9 36	3 20	4 28	1 14	23 49	0 48	20 31	1 12	4 06	1 29	22 01	1 22
Su	20 11	4 18	2 10	2 04	9 60	3 19	4 42	1 20	23 52	0 48	20 37	1 10	4 04	1 29	22 01	1 22
M	20 23	0N15	3 12	2N35	10 24	3 17	4 57	1 25	23 56	0 49	20 43	1 08	4 03	1 29	22 01	1 22
Tu	20 34	4 56	4 03	7 14	10 50	3 14	5 12	1 30	23 59	0 49	20 48	1 06	4 02	1 29	22 01	1 22
W	20 46	9 27	4 40	11 34	11 17	3 10	5 27	1 35	24 01	0 49	20 54	1 04	4 01	1 28	22 00	1 22
Th	20 56	13 30	4 59	15 13	11 45	3 06	5 43	1 40	24 04	0 50	20 59	1 02	4 00	1 28	22 00	1 22
F	21 07	16 41	4 57	17 51	12 14	3 02	5 58	1 45	24 07	0 50	21 04	1 01	3 60	1 28	22 00	1 22
Sa	21 17	18 42	4 33	19 12	12 44	2 56	6 15	1 49	24 09	0 50	21 09	0 59	3 59	1 28	22 00	1 22
Su	21 27	19 22	3 51	19 11	13 15	2 50	6 31	1 53	24 11	0 51	21 15	0 57	3 58	1 27	22 00	1 22
M	21 37	18 41	2 54	17 53	13 46	2 44	6 48	1 57	24 13	0 51	21 20	0 55	3 57	1 27	21 60	1 22
Tu	21 46	16 48	1 47	15 29	14 18	2 37	7 05	2 01	24 14	0 51	21 25	0 54	3 57	1 27	21 60	1 22
W	21N54	13N59	0S36	12N18	14N51	2S30	7N22	2S05	24N16	0N52	21N30	0S52	3S56	1N27	21S60	1N22

Day	⚷ Decl	⚷ Lat	♅ Decl	♅ Lat	♆ Decl	♆ Lat	♇ Decl	♇ Lat
1	2N24	3N47	9N18	0S34	7S13	0S52	21S11	0N52
6	2 30	3 47	9 24	0 34	7 11	0 52	21 11	0 51
11	2 35	3 48	9 30	0 34	7 08	0 53	21 12	0 51
16	2 41	3 48	9 36	0 34	7 06	0 53	21 13	0 51
21	2 45	3 49	9 41	0 34	7 05	0 53	21 14	0 50
26	2 50	3 49	9 47	0 34	7 04	0 53	21 15	0 50
31	2N54	3N50	9N52	0S34	7S02	0S53	21S16	0N50

Day	⚴ Decl	⚴ Lat	⚵ Decl	⚵ Lat	⚶ Decl	⚶ Lat	Eris Decl	Eris Lat
1	0N22	4S24	7S03	15N18	24N45	4N35	2S13	12S09
6	0 38	4 51	6 41	15 38	24 25	4 35	2 12	12 09
11	0 53	5 18	6 20	15 59	24 03	4 35	2 11	12 09
16	1 06	5 47	6 01	16 19	23 39	4 36	2 10	12 09
21	1 17	6 16	5 43	16 39	23 13	4 36	2 09	12 09
26	1 26	6 47	5 27	16 57	22 45	4 36	2 09	12 09
31	1N33	7S19	5S14	17N15	22N15	4N36	2S08	12S10

Moon Phenomena

Max/0 Decl
dy hr mn
7 7:47 0 S
14 20:41 19S18
21 22:45 0 N
27 23:54 19N22

Max/0 Lat
dy hr mn
4 10:44 0 N
11 16:11 5N00
19 1:31 0 S
25 9:22 5S00
31 11:58 0 N

Perigee/Apogee
dy hr m kilometers
12 19:51 a 406210
26 1:09 p 357208

PH dy hr mn
☽ 3 2:48 12♌52
○ 10 21:44 20♏24
☾ 19 0:34 28♒14
● 25 19:46 4♊47

Void of Course Moon

Last Aspect	☽ Ingress
1 20:24 ♅ □	♌ 2 4:13
4 4:36 ♄ △	♍ 4 9:48
6 12:43 ♄ □	♎ 6 18:21
8 23:00 ♄ ⚹	♏ 9 5:02
10 21:44 ☉ ☍	♐ 11 17:01
14 2:15 ♅ △	♑ 14 5:39
16 10:23 ♅ □	♒ 16 17:51
19 0:34 ☉ □	♓ 19 3:53
21 3:40 ♄ □	♈ 21 10:12
23 7:00 ♅ ☌	♉ 23 12:34
24 19:09 ♇ △	♊ 25 12:16
27 6:19 ♅ ⚹	♋ 27 11:26
29 7:00 ♅ □	♌ 29 12:13
31 11:15 ♂ ⚹	♍ 31 16:17

DAILY ASPECTARIAN

☽△♆ 0:28
☽□♃ 3:24
☽∠⚳ 3:41
☽☍♇ 10:01
☽∥⚳ 13:13
☽∠♂ 14:30
☽□☿ 18:36
☽□♅ 20:24
☽⚻♄ 23:30
☽△⚷ 23:40

☽⚼♆ 2:00
☽⚹⚳ 6:03
☽△♀ 7:24
☉⚼♄ 11:20
☉∠⚷ 14:58
☽⚹♂ 17:48
⚶ ♌ 23:58

☉∥☽ 0:58
☽⚼♄ 1:39
☽⚼⚷ 1:59
☉□☽ 2:48
☽⚻♆ 4:21
☽⚹♃ 7:00
☽⚼♀ 11:01
☽⚻♇ 14:25
☿ D 16:34
☽△☿ 23:18

☉⚹♆ 0:52
☽△♅ 1:42
☽△♄ 4:36
☽⚻⚷ 5:08
☽∠♃ 10:00
☽□⚳ 13:29
☽⚻♀ 15:36
☽⚼♇ 17:50
☽∥♅ 23:18

5 F
☿∠♂ 0:11
☽⚼☿ 3:08
☽□♂ 3:16
☽⚼♅ 5:34
☉⚻♃ 8:00
☽☍♆ 11:29
☽∥☿ 11:56
☽#♆ 13:08
☽⊻♃ 13:44
☉△☽ 14:16
☽△♇ 21:58

6 Sa
☽#♃ 5:28
☽⚻☿ 7:52
☽⚻♅ 10:07
☽□♄ 12:43
☽☍⚷ 13:41
☽∥⚷ 17:01
☽∥♀ 19:28
☉⚼☽ 21:17

7 Su
☽△⚳ 0:09
♂∠♅ 1:55
☽☍♀ 3:23
☽△♂ 15:57
☽#♀ 20:59
☽⚻♆ 21:13
☽#⚷ 22:50
☽☌♃ 23:02

8 M
☉⚻☽ 4:58
☽⚼⚳ 6:24
☽□♇ 7:57
☽∥♃ 10:05
☽☍☿ 19:43
☽☍♅ 20:48
☽⚹♄ 23:00
☽⚼♂ 23:09

9 Tu
☽⚻⚷ 0:25
☽⚼♆ 2:47
☽∥♆ 3:23
☽#☿ 3:53
☽⚻⚳ 13:04
☽⚻♀ 17:43
☊R♌ 18:08
☉△♇ 18:25
☽#♅ 18:52
⚵ R 23:07

10 W
⚳⚼♇ 3:45
☽∠♄ 4:41
☿☌♅ 5:21
☽⚼⚷ 6:21
☽⚻♂ 6:45
☽△♆ 8:41
♀∥⚷ 9:18
☽⊻♃ 10:00
☽⚹♇ 19:30
☉☍☽ 21:44

11 Th
☽⚼♀ 1:33
☽⚻♅ 8:55
☽⚻☿ 10:05
☽⊻♄ 10:37
☽△⚷ 12:32
☽∠♃ 15:54
♂□♆ 17:53
☿△♄ 20:15

12 F
☽∠♇ 1:39
☽☍⚳ 3:20
☽△♀ 9:42
♂△♃ 10:20
☽⚼♅ 15:18
☽⚼☿ 18:00
☽□♆ 21:09
☽⚹♃ 21:58
☽☍♂ 22:46

13 Sa
☽⊻♇ 7:56
☿⊻⚷ 10:41
☉#☽ 11:24
☉⚻☽ 15:36
☽△♅ 21:47
☽☌♄ 22:57

14 Su
☽□⚷ 1:21
☽△☿ 2:15
☽⚻⚳ 18:11
☿∠♆ 22:38

15 M
☉⚼☽ 0:35
☽□♀ 2:25
☽⚹♆ 9:52
☽□♃ 10:12
☽⚻♂ 15:01
☉#☽ 16:11
☽☌♇ 20:25

16 Tu
☽⚼⚳ 1:25
☿ ♉ 4:08
☉△☽ 9:18
☽□♅ 10:23
☽⊻♄ 11:00
☽⚹⚷ 13:50
☽∠♆ 15:53
☽□☿ 18:56
☽⚼♂ 22:41
☉⊻♅ 23:37

17 W
☉⚻♄ 5:30
☽△⚳ 8:12
♃⚻♆ 8:38
☽∠♄ 16:25
☽⚹♀ 18:10
☽∠⚷ 19:25
☽△♃ 21:17
☽⊻♆ 21:22

18 Th
☽△♂ 5:39
☽⊻♇ 7:23
♀#♃ 11:57
☉⚹⚷ 20:07
☽⚹♅ 21:02
☽⚹♄ 21:07

19 F
☽⊻⚷ 0:14
☉□☽ 0:34
☽∠♀ 0:55
☽⚼♃ 1:50
♄△♅ 6:16
☽⚹☿ 9:39
☽∠♇ 11:44
♂⚻♇ 13:07
♀☍♃ 14:13
☉⚼♃ 16:20
☽#♅ 16:35
☽#☿ 17:35
☽□⚳ 19:20
♀⊻♆ 19:31

20 Sa
☽∠♅ 1:04
☿∥♅ 4:13
☽⚻♃ 5:27
☽☌♆ 5:52
☽⊻♀ 6:32
☉∠♀ 6:38
☽∥♆ 8:18
☽⚹♇ 15:05
☽∠☿ 15:30
☽□♂ 16:30
☉ ♊ 20:32
☽#♀ 21:54

21 Su
☽∥♃ 1:14
☽□♄ 3:40
☽⊻♅ 4:03
☽☌⚷ 6:57
☽#⚷ 8:17
☉⚹☽ 11:13
☿∠♂ 19:33
☽⊻☿ 20:08

22 M
☽⚹⚳ 2:07
☽☍♃ 9:39
☽⊻♆ 10:18
☽∥⚷ 13:00
☽☌♀ 14:10
☉∠☽ 14:39
☽□♇ 18:45
☽#♃ 19:27
☽⚹♂ 22:37

23 Tu
☽∥♀ 1:28
☽∠⚳ 3:55
☽△♄ 6:16
☽☌♅ 7:00
☽⊻⚷ 9:39
☽∠♆ 11:07
☽#♆ 11:09
☉⊻☽ 17:01

24 W
☽∠♂ 0:11
☽∥♅ 1:35
☽☌☿ 2:14
☽⊻⚳ 4:53
☽⚼♄ 6:23
☽∠⚷ 9:51
☽⚻♃ 10:25
☽⚹♆ 11:14
☽∥☿ 11:42
☽⊻♀ 17:49
☽△♇ 19:09

25 Th
☽⊻♂ 1:07
☉⚼♇ 3:17
☽⚻♄ 6:01
☽⊻♅ 7:04
☽⚹⚷ 9:34
☽⚼♃ 10:01
☉∥⚳ 11:07
♀□♇ 16:23
☽⚼♇ 18:43
☽∠♀ 18:51
☉☌☽ 19:46
☿⊻⚳ 22:01
☿⚼♄ 23:56

26 F
☽☌⚳ 5:29
☽⊻☿ 5:59
☽∠♅ 6:39
☽△♃ 9:27
☽□♆ 10:26
☽⚻♇ 18:12
☉#♇ 18:56
☽⚹♀ 19:50

27 Sa
☽☌♂ 2:22
☽☍♄ 4:54
☽⚹♅ 6:19
☽∠☿ 7:56
☽□⚷ 8:47
☿∠⚷ 17:23
☿⚻♃ 19:18
☉⊻☽ 22:16

28 Su
⚳#♇ 3:35
⚳∠♅ 5:46
☽⊻⚳ 6:22
☿⚹♆ 7:05
☽□♃ 8:58
☽△♆ 10:09
☽⚹☿ 10:28
☽☍♇ 18:07
☽□♀ 23:04

29 M
☉∠☽ 0:19
☽⊻♂ 5:02
☽⚻♄ 5:08
♂☍♄ 6:56
☽□♅ 7:00
☽∠⚳ 7:40
☽△⚷ 9:32
☽⚼♆ 10:51
♀#♆ 21:09

30 Tu
☉⚹☽ 3:19
☽⚼♄ 6:19
☽∠♂ 7:37
☽⚹⚳ 9:52
☽⚹♃ 10:58
☽⚼⚷ 11:03
☽⚻♆ 12:22
☽∥☿ 18:17
☽□☿ 18:48
☽⚻♇ 20:48

31 W
♂⚹♅ 2:41
☽△♀ 5:55
☽△♄ 8:24
☽△♅ 10:51
☽⚹♂ 11:15
☿△♇ 12:04
☽∠♃ 13:18
☽⚻⚷ 13:30
☉#♄ 14:55
⚳△♃ 20:03
☽⚼♇ 23:31

June 2017

LONGITUDE

Day	Sid.Time	⊙	☽	☽ 12 hour	Mean☊	True☊	☿	♀	♂	⚳	♃	♄	⚷	♅	♆	♇
	h m s	° ' "	° ' "	° ' "	° '	° '	° '	° '	° '	° '	° '	° '	° '	° '	° '	° '
1 Th	16 38 40	10♊42 18	4♍16 05	10♍49 20	28♌13.7	27♌35.1	19♉48.1	24♈54.0	27♊33.0	13♊24.0	13♎19.6	25♐33.1	28♓27.9	26♈59.8	14♓12.0	19♑00.1
2 F	16 42 37	11 39 48	17 16 59	23 39 32	28 10.5	27R 35.1	21 25.2	25 50.8	28 13.0	13 49.2	13R 18.2	25R 28.9	28 29.5	27 02.5	14 12.5	18R 59.1
3 Sa	16 46 33	12 37 17	29 57 30	6♎11 27	28 07.3	27 33.9	23 04.9	26 47.9	28 53.0	14 14.4	13 16.9	25 24.7	28 30.9	27 05.2	14 12.9	18 58.0
4 Su	16 50 30	13 34 44	12♎21 51	18 29 14	28 04.1	27 30.7	24 47.0	27 45.5	29 32.9	14 39.5	13 15.8	25 20.4	28 32.4	27 07.8	14 13.3	18 56.8
5 M	16 54 26	14 32 11	24 34 01	0♏36 40	28 01.0	27 25.0	26 31.5	28 43.4	0♋12.8	15 04.7	13 14.9	25 16.1	28 33.7	27 10.4	14 13.7	18 55.7
6 Tu	16 58 23	15 29 36	6♏37 31	12 36 57	27 57.8	27 16.6	28 18.5	29 41.8	0 52.7	15 29.9	13 14.1	25 11.8	28 35.1	27 12.9	14 14.1	18 54.5
7 W	17 02 20	16 27 00	18 35 15	24 32 41	27 54.6	27 05.9	0♊08.0	0♉40.5	1 32.5	15 55.1	13 13.6	25 07.4	28 36.4	27 15.4	14 14.4	18 53.4
8 Th	17 06 16	17 24 23	0♐29 30	6♐25 55	27 51.4	26 53.8	1 59.8	1 39.6	2 12.3	16 20.3	13 13.2	25 03.1	28 37.6	27 17.9	14 14.7	18 52.2
9 F	17 10 13	18 21 45	12 22 06	18 18 16	27 48.3	26 41.3	3 54.0	2 39.0	2 52.1	16 45.6	13D 13.0	24 58.7	28 38.8	27 20.4	14 15.0	18 51.0
10 Sa	17 14 09	19 19 07	24 14 34	0♑11 13	27 45.1	26 29.3	5 50.4	3 38.8	3 31.9	17 10.8	13 13.0	24 54.3	28 39.9	27 22.8	14 15.2	18 49.7
11 Su	17 18 06	20 16 27	6♑08 23	12 06 19	27 41.9	26 18.8	7 49.1	4 39.0	4 11.6	17 36.0	13 13.2	24 49.9	28 41.0	27 25.2	14 15.4	18 48.5
12 M	17 22 02	21 13 47	18 05 14	24 05 25	27 38.7	26 10.6	9 49.9	5 39.4	4 51.3	18 01.3	13 13.5	24 45.5	28 42.1	27 27.5	14 15.5	18 47.2
13 Tu	17 25 59	22 11 07	0♒07 11	6♒10 52	27 35.6	26 05.1	11 52.8	6 40.2	5 30.9	18 26.5	13 14.0	24 41.1	28 43.0	27 29.8	14 15.7	18 46.0
14 W	17 29 56	23 08 26	12 16 52	18 25 37	27 32.4	26 02.0	13 57.4	7 41.2	6 10.5	18 51.8	13 14.7	24 36.7	28 44.0	27 32.1	14 15.8	18 44.7
15 Th	17 33 52	24 05 44	24 37 33	0♓53 09	27 29.2	26D 01.1	16 03.8	8 42.6	6 50.1	19 17.0	13 15.6	24 32.3	28 44.9	27 34.4	14 15.8	18 43.4
16 F	17 37 49	25 03 02	7♓12 56	13 37 25	27 26.0	26 01.4	18 11.7	9 44.2	7 29.7	19 42.3	13 16.6	24 27.8	28 45.7	27 36.6	14R 15.9	18 42.1
17 Sa	17 41 45	26 00 19	20 07 04	26 42 23	27 22.8	26R 02.1	20 20.9	10 46.2	8 09.3	20 07.5	13 17.9	24 23.4	28 46.5	27 38.7	14 15.9	18 40.7
18 Su	17 45 42	26 57 37	3♈23 47	10♈11 36	27 19.7	26 02.0	22 31.1	11 48.4	8 48.8	20 32.8	13 19.3	24 19.0	28 47.2	27 40.9	14 15.8	18 39.4
19 M	17 49 38	27 54 54	17 06 06	24 07 22	27 16.5	26 00.4	24 42.0	12 50.8	9 28.3	20 58.1	13 20.9	24 14.6	28 47.9	27 42.9	14 15.8	18 38.1
20 Tu	17 53 35	28 52 10	1♉15 23	8♉29 53	27 13.3	25 56.8	26 53.5	13 53.5	10 07.7	21 23.3	13 22.6	24 10.2	28 48.5	27 45.0	14 15.7	18 36.7
21 W	17 57 31	29 49 27	15 50 26	23 16 23	27 10.1	25 51.0	29 05.2	14 56.5	10 47.2	21 48.6	13 24.6	24 05.8	28 49.1	27 47.0	14 15.5	18 35.3
22 Th	18 01 28	0♋46 43	0♊46 53	8♊20 51	27 07.0	25 43.7	1♋16.9	15 59.6	11 26.6	22 13.9	13 26.7	24 01.4	28 49.6	27 49.0	14 15.4	18 33.9
23 F	18 05 25	1 44 00	15 57 07	23 34 19	27 03.8	25 35.7	3 28.2	17 03.1	12 06.0	22 39.1	13 28.9	23 57.0	28 50.1	27 50.9	14 15.2	18 32.6
24 Sa	18 09 21	2 41 16	1♋11 08	8♋46 11	27 00.6	25 28.1	5 39.0	18 06.7	12 45.3	23 04.4	13 31.4	23 52.6	28 50.5	27 52.8	14 15.0	18 31.2
25 Su	18 13 18	3 38 31	16 18 13	23 46 05	26 57.4	25 21.8	7 48.9	19 10.5	13 24.7	23 29.7	13 34.0	23 48.3	28 50.9	27 54.7	14 14.7	18 29.7
26 M	18 17 14	4 35 47	1♌08 48	8♌25 35	26 54.3	25 17.5	9 57.8	20 14.6	14 04.0	23 54.9	13 36.8	23 44.0	28 51.2	27 56.5	14 14.4	18 28.3
27 Tu	18 21 11	5 33 01	15 35 52	22 39 18	26 51.1	25D 15.4	12 05.5	21 18.8	14 43.3	24 20.2	13 39.8	23 39.7	28 51.4	27 58.2	14 14.1	18 26.9
28 W	18 25 07	6 30 15	29 35 43	6♍25 08	26 47.9	25 15.0	14 11.7	22 23.3	15 22.5	24 45.4	13 42.9	23 35.4	28 51.6	28 00.0	14 13.7	18 25.5
29 Th	18 29 04	7 27 29	13♍07 42	19 43 43	26 44.7	25 15.9	16 16.4	23 27.9	16 01.8	25 10.6	13 46.2	23 31.2	28 51.8	28 01.7	14 13.4	18 24.0
30 F	18 33 00	8♋24 42	26 13 34	2♎37 43	26♌41.6	25♌17.1	18♋19.4	24♉32.7	16♋41.0	25♊35.9	13♎49.7	23♐27.0	28♓51.9	28♈03.3	14♓12.9	18♑22.6

1st of Mont

Julian Day 2457905.5
Obliquity 23°26'05"
SVP 5♓01'0
GC 27♐05.
Eris 23♈40

Day	⚴
1	21♈44.9
6	23 23.2
11	25 00.1
16	26 35.3
21	28 08.7
26	29 40.1

Day	⚵
1	16♑56.8
6	16 14.9
11	15 25.5
16	14 29.4
21	13 27.5
26	12 21.3

Day	⚶
1	10♌06.9
6	12 03.7
11	14 03.3
16	16 05.6
21	18 10.4
26	20 17.6

DECLINATION and LATITUDE

Day	⊙ Decl	☽ Decl	☽ Lat	☽12h Decl	☿ Decl	☿ Lat	♀ Decl	♀ Lat	♂ Decl	♂ Lat	⚳ Decl	⚳ Lat	♃ Decl	♃ Lat	♄ Decl	♄ Lat
1 Th	22N03	10N29	0N35	8N35	15N24	2S22	7N39	2S08	24N17	0N52	21N35	0S50	3S56	1N26	21S60	1N22
2 F	22 11	6 36	1 42	4 34	15 58	2 14	7 57	2 11	24 18	0 53	21 39	0 48	3 56	1 26	21 60	1 22
3 Sa	22 18	2 30	2 43	0 26	16 32	2 05	8 14	2 14	24 19	0 53	21 44	0 46	3 55	1 26	21 59	1 22
4 Su	22 26	1S36	3 34	3S37	17 05	1 56	8 32	2 17	24 19	0 53	21 49	0 45	3 55	1 26	21 59	1 22
5 M	22 32	5 35	4 14	7 28	17 39	1 46	8 50	2 20	24 20	0 54	21 53	0 43	3 55	1 25	21 59	1 22
6 Tu	22 39	9 16	4 42	10 59	18 13	1 36	9 08	2 23	24 20	0 54	21 58	0 41	3 55	1 25	21 59	1 22
7 W	22 45	12 34	4 58	14 02	18 46	1 26	9 26	2 25	24 20	0 54	22 02	0 39	3 55	1 25	21 59	1 22
8 Th	22 50	15 21	5 01	16 30	19 19	1 16	9 45	2 27	24 19	0 55	22 07	0 37	3 55	1 24	21 59	1 22
9 F	22 56	17 28	4 50	18 16	19 52	1 05	10 03	2 29	24 19	0 55	22 11	0 36	3 55	1 24	21 59	1 22
10 Sa	23 00	18 51	4 27	19 15	20 23	0 54	10 21	2 31	24 18	0 55	22 15	0 34	3 56	1 24	21 59	1 22
11 Su	23 05	19 25	3 53	19 23	20 54	0 43	10 40	2 33	24 18	0 55	22 19	0 32	3 56	1 24	21 59	1 21
12 M	23 09	19 07	3 07	18 38	21 24	0 32	10 58	2 35	24 16	0 56	22 24	0 30	3 56	1 23	21 58	1 21
13 Tu	23 12	17 57	2 13	17 03	21 52	0 21	11 17	2 36	24 15	0 56	22 28	0 29	3 57	1 23	21 58	1 21
14 W	23 15	15 57	1 13	14 40	22 19	0 10	11 35	2 38	24 14	0 56	22 31	0 27	3 57	1 23	21 58	1 21
15 Th	23 18	13 12	0 07	11 34	22 44	0N01	11 54	2 39	24 12	0 57	22 35	0 25	3 58	1 23	21 58	1 21
16 F	23 21	9 47	0S60	7 52	23 07	0 12	12 12	2 40	24 10	0 57	22 39	0 23	3 59	1 22	21 58	1 21
17 Sa	23 22	5 50	2 05	3 42	23 27	0 22	12 30	2 41	24 08	0 57	22 43	0 21	3 59	1 22	21 58	1 21
18 Su	23 24	1 30	3 06	0N46	23 46	0 33	12 49	2 42	24 06	0 58	22 46	0 20	4 00	1 22	21 58	1 21
19 M	23 25	3N03	3 58	5 19	24 02	0 42	13 07	2 42	24 03	0 58	22 50	0 18	4 01	1 22	21 58	1 21
20 Tu	23 26	7 34	4 38	9 43	24 16	0 52	13 25	2 43	24 01	0 58	22 53	0 16	4 02	1 21	21 58	1 21
21 W	23 26	11 46	5 01	13 39	24 26	1 01	13 43	2 43	23 58	0 58	22 57	0 14	4 03	1 21	21 58	1 21
22 Th	23 26	15 21	5 04	16 47	24 34	1 09	14 01	2 43	23 55	0 59	23 00	0 12	4 04	1 21	21 57	1 21
23 F	23 25	17 56	4 47	18 47	24 40	1 16	14 19	2 44	23 52	0 59	23 03	0 11	4 05	1 20	21 57	1 21
24 Sa	23 24	19 17	4 09	19 26	24 42	1 23	14 36	2 43	23 48	0 59	23 06	0 09	4 06	1 20	21 57	1 20
25 Su	23 23	19 14	3 14	18 42	24 42	1 30	14 54	2 43	23 45	0 59	23 10	0 07	4 07	1 20	21 57	1 20
26 M	23 21	17 51	2 06	16 43	24 39	1 35	15 11	2 43	23 41	0 60	23 13	0 05	4 09	1 20	21 57	1 20
27 Tu	23 19	15 20	0 52	13 44	24 33	1 40	15 28	2 43	23 37	0 60	23 15	0 03	4 10	1 19	21 57	1 20
28 W	23 16	11 59	0N23	10 05	24 24	1 44	15 45	2 42	23 33	1 00	23 18	0 02	4 12	1 19	21 57	1 20
29 Th	23 13	8 05	1 35	6 02	24 13	1 47	16 01	2 42	23 28	1 00	23 21	0N00	4 13	1 19	21 57	1 20
30 F	23N10	3N56	2N39	1N50	23N60	1N50	16N18	2S41	23N24	1N01	23N24	0N02	4S15	1N19	21S57	1N20

Day	⚷ Decl	⚷ Lat	♅ Decl	♅ Lat	♆ Decl	♆ Lat	♇ Decl	♇ Lat
1	2N55	3N50	9N53	0S34	7S02	0S53	21S16	0N
6	2 58	3 51	9 57	0 34	7 02	0 54	21 17	0
11	3 01	3 52	10 01	0 34	7 01	0 54	21 19	0
16	3 04	3 52	10 05	0 34	7 01	0 54	21 20	0
21	3 06	3 53	10 09	0 34	7 02	0 54	21 21	0
26	3 07	3 54	10 12	0 34	7 02	0 54	21 23	0

Day	⚴ Decl	⚴ Lat	⚵ Decl	⚵ Lat	⚶ Decl	⚶ Lat	Eris Decl	Eris Lat
1	1N34	7S26	5S11	17N18	22N08	4N36	2S08	12S
6	1 39	7 60	5 01	17 33	21 36	4 37	2 07	12
11	1 41	8 35	4 54	17 45	21 01	4 37	2 07	12
16	1 40	9 12	4 50	17 55	20 25	4 37	2 07	12
21	1 36	9 51	4 49	18 01	19 47	4 38	2 07	12
26	1 29	10 31	4 52	18 04	19 07	4 38	2 06	12

Moon Phenomena

Max/0 Decl

dy hr mn	
3 14:34	0 S
11 3:37	19S26
18 7:58	0 N
24 11:09	19N26
30 22:27	0 S

Max/0 Lat

dy hr mn	
7 16:54	5N01
15 2:41	0 S
21 16:05	5S06
27 16:28	0 N

Perigee/Apogee

dy hr m		kilometers
8 22:19	a	406401
23 10:51	p	357942

PH	dy hr mn	
☽	1 12:43	11♍13
○	9 13:11	18♐53
☾	17 11:34	26♓28
●	24 2:32	2♋47

Void of Course Moon

Last Aspect			☽ Ingres	
2 21:50	♂	□	♎	3 0:
5 8:58	♀	☍	♏	5 10:
7 0:36	♇	✶	♐	7 23:
10 6:21	♅	△	♑	10 11:
12 18:46	♅	□	♒	12 23:
15 5:41	♅	✶	♓	15 10:
17 11:34	⊙	□	♈	17 17:
19 19:43	⊙	✶	♉	19 21:
21 4:27	♇	△	♊	21 22:
23 18:47	♅	✶	♋	23 22:
25 18:46	♅	□	♌	25 22:
27 21:13	♅	△	♍	28 0:
29 20:36	♀	△	♎	30 7:

DAILY ASPECTARIAN

1 Th	☽∥♅	3:55
	☽⚼♀	11:06
	⊙□☽	12:43
	☽⚼♅	14:13
	♀△♄	15:24
	☽∥♀	16:26
	☽⚺♃	16:36
	☽□⚳	17:20
	☽☍♆	18:16
	☽⋕♆	21:21
2 F	☽△♇	3:11
	☽△☿	8:56
	⊙∠♅	9:56
	♂□⚷	10:15
	☽□♄	15:22
	☽⋕♃	15:43
	☽⚻♀	17:28
	☽⚻♅	18:30
	☽☍⚷	21:14
	☽∥⚷	21:30
	☽□♂	21:50
	⚳□♆	22:36
3 Sa	♀☌♅	7:33
	⊙△♃	16:13
	☽⚼☿	18:09
4 Su	☽☌♃	1:45
	⊙△☽	2:34
	☽⚻♆	3:38
	☽△⚳	4:39
	☿⚻♄	7:26
	☽⋕⚷	8:00
	☽□♇	12:53
	☽∥♃	13:50
	⊙□♆	16:14
	♂ ♋	16:17
	♀⚺⚷	19:54
5 M	☽✶♄	1:23
	☽⚻☿	4:33
	☽☍♅	5:11
	☽⚻⚷	7:56
	☽☍♀	8:58
	☿⚺♅	8:59
	☽∥♆	9:11
	☽⚼♆	9:15
	⊙⚼☽	10:43
	☽⚼⚳	11:20
	☽△♂	11:52
	♀∠♆	12:33
	☽⋕♀	22:58
	☿⚼♃	23:02
6 Tu	⊙☌⚳	0:15
	☿✶⚷	3:42
	☽⋕♅	4:42
	⚳⋕♄	6:03
	☽∠♄	7:06
	♀ ♉	7:28
	☽⚺♃	13:14
	☽⚼⚷	13:58
	☽△♆	15:15
	☽⚻⚳	18:26
	⊙⚻☽	19:20
	☽⚼♂	19:39
	☿ ♊	22:16
7 W	☽✶♇	0:36
	♀∠⚳	10:23
	☽⚺♄	13:05
	☿⚺♀	14:55
	☽⚻♅	17:32
	☽∠♃	19:25
	☽△⚷	20:14
8 Th	☽⚻♀	2:34
	☽☍☿	3:37
	☽⚻♂	3:40
	☿⚺♂	4:06
	☽∠♇	6:49
	♀∥♅	19:43
	☿⚼♇	23:23
	☽⚼♅	23:56
9 F	☽✶♃	1:43
	☽□♆	3:48
	☽☍⚳	9:12
	☽⚼♀	11:39
	⊙⚻♇	11:58
	☽⚺♇	13:05
	⊙☍☽	13:11
	♃ D	14:04
	♀✶♂	15:42
10 Sa	☽☌♄	1:20
	☽△♅	6:21
	☽□⚷	8:57
	☽☍♂	19:51
	☽△♀	20:43
11 Su	☽⚻☿	4:04
	☽□♃	14:15
	☽✶♆	16:19
	☿⋕♇	20:05
	☽⚻⚳	23:52
12 M	☽☌♇	1:24
	⊙⚻☽	6:50
	☽⚺♄	13:15
	☽⚼☿	16:14
	☽□♅	18:46
	☽✶⚷	21:13
	☽∠♆	22:18
13 Tu	☿⋕♄	5:40
	☽⚼⚳	6:49
	☿∠♅	7:18
	☽⚻♂	11:18
	☽□♀	14:09
	⊙⚼☽	15:10
	☿△♃	15:46
	⚳⚻♇	17:36
	☽∠♄	18:47
14 W	☽△♃	1:53
	☽∠⚷	2:51
	☿□♆	3:30
	☽⚺♆	3:53
	☽△☿	3:57
	☽⚺♇	12:36
	☽△⚳	13:18
	☿∥⚳	14:22
	☽⚼♂	18:19
	⊙△☽	22:54
	☽✶♄	23:50
15 Th	☽✶♅	5:41
	☽⚼♃	6:59
	☽⚺⚷	7:55
	☽⋕♀	8:51
	⊙☍♄	10:19
	☽∠♇	17:22
	♀⚼♄	18:03
	☽⋕♅	21:59
16 F	☽△♂	0:33
	☽✶♀	5:09
	☿⚻♇	5:36
	☽∠♅	10:08
	♆ R	11:11
	☽⚻♃	11:22
	☽☌♆	13:12
	☽∥♆	17:02
	⊙∥☿	17:31
	☿☌⚳	20:56
	☽✶♇	21:22
17 Sa	☽□⚳	0:01
	☽□☿	0:30
	☽□♄	7:45
	☽∥♃	10:23
	☽∠♀	11:11
	⊙□☽	11:34
	☽⚺♅	13:44
	☽⋕⚷	15:27
	☽☌⚷	15:45
18 Su	☽□♂	10:04
	☽⚺♀	16:02
	☽☍♃	17:29
	⊙✶♅	18:48
	☽⚺♆	19:06
	☿☍♄	19:08
19 M	☽∥⚷	0:12
	☿∥♂	1:55
	☽□♇	2:38
	☽⋕♃	5:07
	☽✶⚳	6:50
	♀⚻♃	11:50
	☽△♄	12:08
	☽✶☿	15:21
	☽☌♅	18:07
	⊙∠♀	18:09
	⊙✶☽	19:43
	☽⚺⚷	19:54
	☽∠♆	20:40
	☽⋕♆	21:06
	♀∠⚷	22:04
	⊙□⚷	22:27
20 Tu	♀✶♆	8:27
	☽∠⚳	8:46
	☿✶♅	9:32
	☽⚼♄	13:02
	☽∥♅	14:25
	☽✶♂	15:22
	☽⚻♃	20:02
	☽∠☿	20:39
	☽∠⚷	20:42
	☿□⚷	21:03
	☽✶♆	21:26
	⊙∠☽	22:14
	☽☌♀	22:26
21 W	⊙ ♋	4:25
	☽△♇	4:27
	☽⚺⚳	9:56
	☿ ♋	9:59
	☽⚻♄	13:15
	☽∥♀	13:31
	⊙☌☿	14:15
	☽∠♂	16:46
	☿∠♀	17:56
	☽⚺♅	19:16
	☽⚼♃	20:16
	☽✶⚷	20:53
	⊙⚺☽	24:00
22 Th	☽⚺☿	0:56
	☽⚼♇	4:25
	☽⚺♂	17:39
	☽∠♅	19:06
	☽△♃	20:06
	☽□♆	21:19
23 F	☽⚺♀	1:52
	☽⚻♇	4:04
	☽☌⚳	10:51
	☽☍♄	12:32
	☽✶♅	18:47
	☽□⚷	20:18
24 Sa	⊙☌☽	2:32
	☽∠♀	3:16
	☽☌☿	8:14
	♀△♇	9:00
	☽☌♂	19:10
	☽□♃	19:37
	☽△♆	20:43
25 Su	☽☍♇	3:30
	☽✶♀	4:57
	♂□♃	6:08
	☽⚺⚳	11:54
	☽⚻♄	12:00
	⚳☍♄	15:08
	☽□♅	18:46
	☽△⚷	20:15
	☽⚼♆	20:53
26 M	⊙⚺☽	6:04
	♂△♆	6:19
	☽⚼♄	12:27
	☽∠⚳	13:12
	☽⚺☿	17:05
	☽✶♃	20:44
	☽⚼⚷	21:04
	☽⚻♆	21:42
	☽⚺♂	22:27
	☽∥♀	23:01
27 Tu	⚴ ♉	2:35
	☽⚻♇	4:49
	⊙∠☽	9:01
	☽□♀	10:31
	☽△♄	13:40
	☽✶⚳	15:21
	⊙∥⚳	16:03
	☿□♃	18:22
	☽△♅	21:13
	☽∠♃	22:28
	☽⚻⚷	22:43
	☽∠☿	23:11
28 W	☿△♆	0:23
	☽∠♂	1:26
	☽⚼♇	6:42
	☽∥♅	11:05
	⊙✶☽	13:05
	☿☌♂	19:52
	☽⚼♅	23:49
29 Th	♀⚻♄	1:08
	☽⚺♃	1:10
	☽☍♆	1:59
	☽✶♂	5:31
	☽⋕♆	6:07
	☽✶☿	6:45
	☽△♇	9:33
	☽□♄	18:53
	☽△♀	20:36
	☽⋕♃	22:15
	☽□⚳	22:48
30 F	♂∥⚳	0:02
	☿☍♇	0:37
	☽⚻♅	3:25
	☽∥⚷	4:34
	☽☍⚷	4:55

LONGITUDE

Day	Sid.Time	☉	☽	☽ 12 hour	Mean ☊	True ☊	☿	♀	♂	⚳	♃	♄	⚷	♅	♆	♇
	h m s	° ' "	° ' "	° ' "	° '	° '	° '	° '	° '	° '	° '	° '	° '	° '	° '	° '
1 Sa	18 36 57	9♋21 55	8♎56 41	15♎11 00	26♌38.4	25♌17.7	20♋20.7	25♉37.7	17♋20.1	26♊01.1	13♎53.3	23♐22.8	28♓51.9	28♈04.9	14♓12.5	18♑21.1
2 Su	18 40 54	10 19 08	21 21 15	27 27 58	26 35.2	25R 17.0	22 20.1	26 42.9	17 59.3	26 26.3	13 57.1	23R 18.6	28R 51.9	28 06.4	14R 12.0	18R 19.7
3 M	18 44 50	11 16 20	3♏31 42	9♏33 00	26 32.0	25 14.5	24 17.6	27 48.2	18 38.4	26 51.5	14 01.1	23 14.5	28 51.8	28 07.9	14 11.5	18 18.2
4 Tu	18 48 47	12 13 31	15 32 21	21 30 13	26 28.8	25 10.3	26 13.2	28 53.7	19 17.5	27 16.7	14 05.2	23 10.5	28 51.7	28 09.4	14 11.0	18 16.8
5 W	18 52 43	13 10 43	27 27 03	3♐23 15	26 25.7	25 04.4	28 06.8	29 59.4	19 56.6	27 41.9	14 09.5	23 06.4	28 51.6	28 10.8	14 10.4	18 15.3
6 Th	18 56 40	14 07 54	9♐19 10	15 15 08	26 22.5	24 57.5	29 58.4	1♊05.3	20 35.6	28 07.1	14 13.9	23 02.4	28 51.3	28 12.2	14 09.8	18 13.8
7 F	19 00 36	15 05 05	21 11 26	27 08 21	26 19.3	24 50.1	1♌48.0	2 11.3	21 14.7	28 32.2	14 18.5	22 58.5	28 51.1	28 13.5	14 09.2	18 12.3
8 Sa	19 04 33	16 02 17	3♑06 07	9♑04 58	26 16.1	24 43.1	3 35.6	3 17.5	21 53.7	28 57.4	14 23.3	22 54.6	28 50.7	28 14.8	14 08.5	18 10.9
9 Su	19 08 29	16 59 28	15 05 04	21 06 39	26 13.0	24 37.1	5 21.2	4 23.8	22 32.6	29 22.5	14 28.2	22 50.8	28 50.4	28 16.1	14 07.8	18 09.4
10 M	19 12 26	17 56 39	27 09 54	3♒15 00	26 09.8	24 32.6	7 04.8	5 30.3	23 11.6	29 47.7	14 33.2	22 47.0	28 49.9	28 17.2	14 07.1	18 07.9
11 Tu	19 16 23	18 53 51	9♒22 11	15 31 38	26 06.6	24 29.8	8 46.3	6 36.9	23 50.5	0♋12.8	14 38.4	22 43.2	28 49.5	28 18.4	14 06.4	18 06.4
12 W	19 20 19	19 51 03	21 43 36	27 58 21	26 03.4	24D 28.7	10 25.8	7 43.7	24 29.5	0 37.9	14 43.8	22 39.5	28 48.9	28 19.5	14 05.6	18 05.0
13 Th	19 24 16	20 48 15	4♓16 08	10♓37 16	26 00.3	24 29.0	12 03.4	8 50.6	25 08.3	1 03.0	14 49.3	22 35.9	28 48.3	28 20.6	14 04.8	18 03.5
14 F	19 28 12	21 45 28	17 02 01	23 30 44	25 57.1	24 30.3	13 38.9	9 57.7	25 47.2	1 28.0	14 54.9	22 32.3	28 47.7	28 21.6	14 04.0	18 02.0
15 Sa	19 32 09	22 42 41	0♈03 41	6♈41 12	25 53.9	24 31.8	15 12.3	11 04.9	26 26.1	1 53.1	15 00.7	22 28.8	28 47.0	28 22.5	14 03.1	18 00.6
16 Su	19 36 05	23 39 54	13 23 31	20 10 53	25 50.7	24R 33.1	16 43.8	12 12.2	27 04.9	2 18.1	15 06.6	22 25.3	28 46.3	28 23.4	14 02.2	17 59.1
17 M	19 40 02	24 37 09	27 03 27	4♉01 18	25 47.5	24 33.4	18 13.2	13 19.7	27 43.7	2 43.2	15 12.7	22 21.9	28 45.5	28 24.3	14 01.3	17 57.6
18 Tu	19 43 58	25 34 24	11♉04 23	18 12 35	25 44.4	24 32.6	19 40.5	14 27.3	28 22.5	3 08.2	15 18.9	22 18.6	28 44.7	28 25.1	14 00.4	17 56.2
19 W	19 47 55	26 31 39	25 25 35	2♊42 59	25 41.2	24 30.5	21 05.7	15 35.1	29 01.3	3 33.2	15 25.3	22 15.3	28 43.8	28 25.9	13 59.4	17 54.7
20 Th	19 51 52	27 28 56	10♊04 11	17 28 29	25 38.0	24 27.5	22 28.9	16 42.9	29 40.1	3 58.1	15 31.8	22 12.1	28 42.8	28 26.6	13 58.4	17 53.2
21 F	19 55 48	28 26 13	24 55 00	2♋22 47	25 34.8	24 24.0	23 49.8	17 50.9	0♌18.8	4 23.1	15 38.4	22 08.9	28 41.8	28 27.3	13 57.4	17 51.8
22 Sa	19 59 45	29 23 32	9♋50 49	17 18 01	25 31.7	24 20.7	25 08.6	18 59.1	0 57.5	4 48.0	15 45.1	22 05.9	28 40.8	28 27.9	13 56.4	17 50.4
23 Su	20 03 41	0♌20 50	24 43 22	2♌05 50	25 28.5	24 18.0	26 25.2	20 07.3	1 36.3	5 13.0	15 52.0	22 02.9	28 39.7	28 28.5	13 55.3	17 48.9
24 M	20 07 38	1 18 10	9♌24 30	16 38 36	25 25.3	24 16.3	27 39.5	21 15.6	2 15.0	5 37.8	15 59.1	21 59.9	28 38.6	28 29.0	13 54.2	17 47.5
25 Tu	20 11 34	2 15 29	23 47 26	0♍50 31	25 22.1	24D 15.7	28 51.4	22 24.1	2 53.6	6 02.7	16 06.2	21 57.1	28 37.4	28 29.5	13 53.1	17 46.1
26 W	20 15 31	3 12 50	7♍47 30	14 38 11	25 19.0	24 16.1	0♍00.8	23 32.6	3 32.3	6 27.5	16 13.5	21 54.3	28 36.2	28 29.9	13 52.0	17 44.7
27 Th	20 19 27	4 10 10	21 22 32	28 00 38	25 15.8	24 17.2	1 07.8	24 41.3	4 10.9	6 52.4	16 21.0	21 51.6	28 34.9	28 30.3	13 50.8	17 43.2
28 F	20 23 24	5 07 31	4♎32 41	10♎59 00	25 12.6	24 18.6	2 12.2	25 50.1	4 49.5	7 17.1	16 28.5	21 49.0	28 33.6	28 30.6	13 49.7	17 41.8
29 Sa	20 27 21	6 04 53	17 19 57	23 36 00	25 09.4	24 19.9	3 13.9	26 59.0	5 28.1	7 41.9	16 36.2	21 46.4	28 32.2	28 30.9	13 48.5	17 40.5
30 Su	20 31 17	7 02 15	29 47 38	5♏55 24	25 06.2	24R 20.7	4 12.8	28 07.9	6 06.7	8 06.6	16 44.0	21 44.0	28 30.8	28 31.1	13 47.2	17 39.1
31 M	20 35 14	7♌59 38	11♏59 50	18 01 30	25♌03.1	24♌20.8	5♍08.7	29♊17.0	6♌45.3	8♋31.3	16♎51.9	21♐41.6	28♓29.3	28♈31.3	13♓46.0	17♑37.7

1st of Month

Julian Day #
2457935.5
Obliquity
23°26'05"
SVP 5♓01'04"
GC 27♐05.0
Eris 23♈50.3

Day	⚴
1	1♉09.0
6	2 35.4
11	3 58.9
16	5 19.3
21	6 36.1
26	7 48.9
31	8 57.2

Day	⚵
1	11♑12.4R
6	10 02.3R
11	8 52.9R
16	7 45.8R
21	6 42.5R
26	5 44.7R
31	4 53.5R

Day	⚶
1	22♌27.0
6	24 38.3
11	26 51.5
16	29 06.4
21	1♍23.0
26	3 41.2
31	6 00.8

DECLINATION and LATITUDE

Day	☉ Decl	☽ Decl	☽ Lat	☽12h Decl	☿ Decl	☿ Lat	♀ Decl	♀ Lat	♂ Decl	♂ Lat	⚳ Decl	⚳ Lat	♃ Decl	♃ Lat	♄ Decl	♄ Lat
1 Sa	23N06	0S16	3N34	2S20	23N44	1N52	16N34	2S40	23N19	1N01	23N26	0N04	4S16	1N18	21S57	1N20
2 Su	23 02	4 21	4 17	6 19	23 27	1 53	16 50	2 39	23 14	1 01	23 29	0 06	4 18	1 18	21 56	1 20
3 M	22 57	8 11	4 47	9 58	23 07	1 53	17 06	2 38	23 09	1 01	23 31	0 08	4 20	1 18	21 56	1 19
4 Tu	22 52	11 38	5 05	13 10	22 45	1 53	17 21	2 37	23 04	1 02	23 34	0 09	4 22	1 18	21 56	1 19
5 W	22 47	14 34	5 09	15 49	22 22	1 52	17 36	2 36	22 58	1 02	23 36	0 11	4 24	1 17	21 56	1 19
6 Th	22 41	16 55	4 59	17 49	21 57	1 50	17 51	2 35	22 53	1 02	23 38	0 13	4 26	1 17	21 56	1 19
7 F	22 35	18 32	4 37	19 03	21 31	1 48	18 05	2 33	22 47	1 02	23 41	0 15	4 28	1 17	21 56	1 19
8 Sa	22 28	19 21	4 03	19 26	21 03	1 45	18 20	2 32	22 41	1 03	23 43	0 17	4 30	1 17	21 56	1 19
9 Su	22 21	19 18	3 18	18 57	20 34	1 42	18 33	2 30	22 35	1 03	23 45	0 19	4 32	1 16	21 56	1 19
10 M	22 14	18 23	2 23	17 35	20 05	1 38	18 47	2 29	22 29	1 03	23 47	0 21	4 34	1 16	21 56	1 19
11 Tu	22 06	16 36	1 21	15 24	19 34	1 33	18 60	2 27	22 22	1 03	23 49	0 22	4 36	1 16	21 56	1 18
12 W	21 58	14 01	0 15	12 28	19 02	1 28	19 13	2 25	22 15	1 03	23 50	0 24	4 38	1 16	21 56	1 18
13 Th	21 49	10 46	0S53	8 56	18 30	1 22	19 25	2 23	22 09	1 04	23 52	0 26	4 41	1 15	21 56	1 18
14 F	21 41	6 58	2 00	4 54	17 56	1 16	19 37	2 21	22 02	1 04	23 54	0 28	4 43	1 15	21 56	1 18
15 Sa	21 31	2 46	3 02	0 34	17 23	1 10	19 48	2 19	21 55	1 04	23 55	0 30	4 46	1 15	21 56	1 18
16 Su	21 22	1N39	3 56	3N53	16 49	1 02	19 59	2 17	21 47	1 04	23 57	0 32	4 48	1 15	21 55	1 18
17 M	21 12	6 06	4 38	8 15	16 14	0 55	20 10	2 15	21 40	1 04	23 58	0 34	4 51	1 14	21 55	1 18
18 Tu	21 01	10 19	5 05	12 15	15 39	0 47	20 20	2 12	21 32	1 05	23 60	0 36	4 53	1 14	21 55	1 17
19 W	20 51	14 02	5 13	15 38	15 04	0 39	20 30	2 10	21 24	1 05	24 01	0 38	4 56	1 14	21 55	1 17
20 Th	20 40	16 59	5 02	18 03	14 29	0 30	20 39	2 08	21 16	1 05	24 02	0 40	4 59	1 14	21 55	1 17
21 F	20 28	18 50	4 30	19 17	13 54	0 21	20 48	2 05	21 08	1 05	24 03	0 42	5 01	1 14	21 55	1 17
22 Sa	20 16	19 25	3 40	19 11	13 19	0 11	20 57	2 03	21 00	1 05	24 04	0 43	5 04	1 13	21 55	1 17
23 Su	20 04	18 38	2 35	17 45	12 44	0 02	21 04	1 60	20 52	1 05	24 05	0 45	5 07	1 13	21 55	1 17
24 M	19 52	16 36	1 21	15 11	12 09	0S08	21 12	1 57	20 43	1 06	24 06	0 47	5 10	1 13	21 55	1 16
25 Tu	19 39	13 33	0 03	11 44	11 35	0 19	21 19	1 55	20 34	1 06	24 07	0 49	5 13	1 13	21 55	1 16
26 W	19 26	9 47	1N14	7 44	11 00	0 29	21 25	1 52	20 26	1 06	24 08	0 51	5 16	1 12	21 55	1 16
27 Th	19 13	5 37	2 24	3 28	10 27	0 40	21 31	1 49	20 17	1 06	24 09	0 53	5 19	1 12	21 55	1 16
28 F	18 59	1 19	3 24	0S49	9 53	0 51	21 36	1 46	20 08	1 06	24 09	0 55	5 22	1 12	21 55	1 16
29 Sa	18 45	2S55	4 12	4 57	9 21	1 03	21 41	1 43	19 58	1 06	24 10	0 57	5 25	1 12	21 55	1 16
30 Su	18 31	6 55	4 47	8 47	8 49	1 14	21 45	1 40	19 49	1 07	24 10	0 59	5 28	1 12	21 55	1 15
31 M	18N16	10S32	5N09	12S10	8N18	1S26	21N48	1S37	19N39	1N07	24N11	1N01	5S32	1N11	21S55	1N15

Day	⚷ Decl	⚷ Lat	♅ Decl	♅ Lat	♆ Decl	♆ Lat	♇ Decl	♇ Lat
1	3N08	3N55	10N15	0S34	7S03	0S55	21S24	0N47
6	3 09	3 55	10 18	0 34	7 04	0 55	21 26	0 46
11	3 09	3 56	10 20	0 35	7 06	0 55	21 27	0 46
16	3 08	3 57	10 22	0 35	7 08	0 55	21 29	0 45
21	3 07	3 58	10 23	0 35	7 10	0 55	21 30	0 45
26	3 05	3 58	10 24	0 35	7 12	0 56	21 32	0 44
31	3N03	3N59	10N24	0S35	7S14	0S56	21S33	0N44

Day	⚴ Decl	⚴ Lat	⚵ Decl	⚵ Lat	⚶ Decl	⚶ Lat	Eris Decl	Eris Lat
1	1N19	11S14	4S58	18N03	18N25	4N39	2S06	12S12
6	1 05	11 60	5 08	17 59	17 41	4 39	2 07	12 12
11	0 47	12 47	5 21	17 50	16 56	4 40	2 07	12 13
16	0 25	13 37	5 37	17 37	16 09	4 40	2 07	12 13
21	0S01	14 30	5 56	17 21	15 21	4 41	2 08	12 14
26	0 32	15 26	6 18	17 02	14 32	4 42	2 08	12 14
31	1S07	16S25	6S42	16N40	13N41	4N42	2S09	12S15

Moon Phenomena

Max/0 Decl
dy hr mn
8 10:49 19S26
15 15:05 0 N
21 22:22 19N25
28 7:23 0 S

Max/0 Lat
dy hr mn
4 19:17 5N09
12 5:18 0 S
18 22:37 5S13
25 0:48 0 N

Perigee/Apogee
dy hr m kilometers
6 4:29 a 405934
21 17:19 p 361239

PH dy hr mn
☽ 1 0:52 9♎24
○ 9 4:08 17♑09
☾ 16 19:27 24♈26
● 23 9:47 0♌44
☽ 30 15:24 7♏39

Void of Course Moon

Last Aspect			☽ Ingress		
2 13:18	♅	☍	♏	2	17:00
5 1:35	☿	△	♐	5	5:09
7 14:13	♅	△	♑	7	17:46
10 2:13	♅	□	♒	10	5:36
12 12:42	♅	⚹	♓	12	15:53
14 17:02	♂	△	♈	14	23:53
17 2:20	♅	☌	♉	17	5:05
19 6:12	♂	⚹	♊	19	7:32
21 5:42	♅	⚹	♋	21	8:11
23 6:06	♅	□	♌	23	8:35
25 9:23	☿	☌	♍	25	10:33
27 6:32	♀	□	♎	27	15:38
29 21:31	♅	☍	♏	30	0:24

DAILY ASPECTARIAN

1 Sa
☉□☽ 0:52
☽⚼♀ 3:32
⚷ R 7:10
☽☌♃ 9:33
☽⚻♆ 10:07
♀⚺⚳ 14:04
☽#⚷ 16:43
☽□♂ 17:04
☽□♇ 18:07
☿∥⚳ 21:11
☽∥♃ 23:40

2 Su
☽□☿ 2:17
☽⚹♄ 3:48
☽△⚳ 10:20
☿⚻♄ 11:30
☽⚻♀ 11:33
♂☍♇ 12:03
☽☍♅ 13:18
☽⚻⚷ 14:46
☽⚼♆ 15:25
☽∥♆ 16:44
☿∥♂ 20:22

3 M
♀⚺♅ 7:24
☽∠♄ 9:20
☉∥☿ 13:52
☽#♅ 14:13
☉△☽ 16:47
☽⚼⚳ 17:13
☽⚼⚷ 20:38
☽⚺♃ 21:04
☽△♆ 21:17
♀⚹⚷ 23:16

4 Tu
♀⚼♃ 4:29
☽⚹♇ 5:30
☽△♂ 7:59
☽⚺♄ 15:17
☿⚺⚳ 17:11

5 W
♀ ♊ 0:13
☽⚻⚳ 0:31
☿□♅ 0:52
☽⚻♅ 1:29
☽△☿ 1:35
☉⚼☽ 1:36
☽△⚷ 2:51
☽∠♃ 3:28
♃⚻♆ 4:20
☽☍♀ 5:39
☿△⚷ 9:33
☽∠♇ 11:42
☿⚼♆ 13:33
☽⚼♂ 16:02

6 Th
☿ ♌ 0:21
☉△♆ 0:47
☿#♄ 0:54
☉□♃ 2:45
⚳⚹♅ 5:10
☽⚼♅ 7:52
☽□♆ 9:47
☽⚹♃ 10:00
☉⚻☽ 10:35
☽⚼☿ 13:32
☽#♀ 14:47
☽⚺♇ 17:59

7 F
☽⚻♂ 0:07
☽☌♄ 3:35
☿#♇ 4:12
☿⚹♀ 13:20
☽△♅ 14:13
☽☍⚳ 15:21
☽□⚷ 15:26
⚳□⚷ 17:45
♀⚼♇ 21:40

8 Sa
☽⚻♀ 0:25
☽⚻☿ 1:10
☽⚹♆ 22:06
☽□♃ 22:46

9 Su
☉☍☽ 4:08
☽☌♇ 6:07
☽⚼♀ 9:28
♂⚻♄ 10:10
☽⚺♄ 15:22
☽☍♂ 15:41
☽#♀ 17:26

10 M
☽□♅ 2:13
☽⚹⚷ 3:18
☽∠♆ 3:51
☉☍♇ 4:37
☽⚻⚳ 5:23
☿⚼♄ 9:34
⚳ ♋ 11:48
☽△♀ 18:04
☽∠♄ 20:47
☽☍☿ 22:39

11 Tu
☽∠⚷ 8:41
☽⚺♆ 9:14
☽△♃ 10:21
☽⚼⚳ 11:47
☽⚺♇ 16:58
☿∥♀ 18:16
☉⚻☽ 20:05

12 W
☽⚹♄ 1:47
☽⚻♂ 5:37
☉#♄ 6:39
☽⚹♅ 12:42
☽⚺⚷ 13:36
☽⚼♃ 15:28
☽△⚳ 17:40
☽∠♇ 21:42

13 Th
☽#♅ 2:50
☉⚼☽ 3:09
☽□♀ 9:29
☽⚼♂ 11:41
☽⚻☿ 16:47
☽∠♅ 17:08
☽☌♆ 18:28
☽⚻♃ 20:01
☽∥♆ 23:06

14 F
☽⚹♇ 1:51
☿⚼⚷ 2:14
☿⚻♆ 6:20
☉△☽ 9:27
☽□♄ 10:09
☽∥♃ 12:55
☽△♂ 17:02
☉⚻♄ 18:30
♂#♄ 20:33
☿⚹♃ 20:47
☽⚺♅ 20:55
☽☌⚷ 21:40
☽#⚷ 21:56

15 Sa
☽⚼☿ 0:18
☽□⚳ 3:25
☉#♇ 7:21
♀∠♂ 17:51
☽⚹♀ 21:41

16 Su
☽⚺♆ 1:09
☽☍♃ 3:04
☽△☿ 6:39
☽∥⚷ 7:56
☽□♇ 8:07
☿∠⚳ 12:43
☽△♄ 15:52
☽#♃ 17:06
☉□☽ 19:27
☿⚻♇ 19:51

17 M
☽□♂ 1:13
♀∠♅ 1:39
☽☌♅ 2:20
☽∠♀ 2:24
☽⚺⚷ 2:56
☽∠♆ 3:24
☽#♆ 5:45
☽⚹⚳ 10:04
♀□♆ 14:34
☽⚼♄ 17:38
⚶ ♍ 23:16

18 Tu
☽∥♅ 0:20
♂□♅ 1:38
☽∠⚷ 4:30
☽⚹♆ 4:57
☽⚺♀ 6:12
☽⚻♃ 7:12
♂#♇ 8:41
☽△♇ 11:31
☽∠⚳ 12:14
♂△⚷ 13:24
☽□☿ 16:02
☽⚻♄ 18:46
♀△♃ 20:10
♂⚼♆ 22:52

19 W
☉⚹☽ 1:57
☽⚺♅ 4:58
☽⚹⚷ 5:27
☽⚹♂ 6:12
☽∥☿ 6:26
☽⚼♃ 8:18
☽⚼♇ 12:18
☽⚺⚳ 13:46
☿△♄ 19:17

20 Th
☉∥♀ 0:17
☉∠☽ 4:11
☽∠♅ 5:29
☽□♆ 6:20
☽∠♂ 7:48
☽△♃ 8:55
☽☌♀ 11:40
♂ ♌ 12:21
☽⚻♇ 12:39
☽☍♄ 19:33
☽⚹☿ 22:05

21 F
♀⚻♇ 0:18
☉□♅ 0:27
☽⚹♅ 5:42
☉⚺☽ 6:03
☽□⚷ 6:04
☉△⚷ 6:26
☽⚺♂ 9:04
☉⚼♆ 12:50
☽☌⚳ 15:39

22 Sa
☽∠☿ 0:31
♀∥♂ 5:14
☽△♆ 6:35
☽□♃ 9:35
☽☍♇ 12:51
☉ ♌ 15:16
☽⚺♀ 15:56
☽⚻♄ 19:41

23 Su
☽⚺☿ 3:01
☽□♅ 6:06
☽△⚷ 6:23
☽⚼♆ 6:49
☉☌☽ 9:47
☽☌♂ 11:43
☽⚺⚳ 17:36
☽∠♀ 18:23
☽⚼♄ 20:03

24 M
☽⚼⚷ 7:00
☽⚻♆ 7:26
☽⚹♃ 11:00
☽⚻♇ 13:54
♀☍♄ 14:55
☿△♅ 16:34
☽∠⚳ 19:14
☿⚻⚷ 19:21
☽△♄ 20:54
☽⚹♀ 21:27

25 Tu
☽△♅ 7:59
☽⚻⚷ 8:12
☽☌☿ 9:23
☽∠♃ 12:34
☽⚼♇ 15:17
☽∥☿ 15:18
☉⚺☽ 15:30
☽⚺♂ 16:17
☽∥♅ 20:20
☽⚹⚳ 21:37
☿ ♍ 23:42

26 W
☽⚼♅ 10:00
☽☍♆ 10:38
☽⚺♃ 14:57
☽#♆ 15:04
☽△♇ 17:29
☉∠☽ 19:45
☽∠♂ 19:53

27 Th
☽□♄ 0:52
☉☌♂ 0:58
☽#♃ 1:42
☿∥♅ 2:01
♀#♇ 5:20
☿∠♃ 5:27
☽□♀ 6:32
☽⚻♅ 12:54
☽☍⚷ 13:01
☽∥⚷ 14:14
☽⚺☿ 19:18

28 F
☽⚹♂ 0:33
☉⚹☽ 1:10
☽□⚳ 5:15
☿⚼♇ 11:09
☽⚻♆ 17:20
☽☌♃ 22:36

29 Sa
☽□♇ 0:39
☽#⚷ 0:52
☽∠☿ 1:52
☽⚹♄ 8:28
☽∥♃ 15:02
☉⚼♄ 16:40
♅⚺⚷ 18:48
☽△♀ 20:26
☽⚻⚷ 21:31
☽☍♅ 21:31
☽⚼♆ 22:03

30 Su
☽∥♆ 2:02
♀□⚷ 7:46
♀⚹♅ 8:05
☽⚹☿ 9:22
☽#☿ 10:42
☽□♂ 13:04
☽∠♄ 13:33
☉□☽ 15:24
☽△⚳ 16:53
♂⚼♄ 21:50
☽#♅ 23:05

31 M
☽⚼⚷ 2:57
☽△♆ 3:30
☽⚼♀ 5:01
☽⚺♃ 9:48
☽⚹♇ 11:11
♀ ♋ 14:55
☽⚺♄ 19:17
☉⚺⚳ 23:15
☽⚼⚳ 23:50

August 2017

LONGITUDE

Day	Sid.Time	☉	☽	☽ 12 hour	Mean☊	True☊	☿	♀	♂	⚳	♃	♄	⚷	♅	♆	♇
	h m s	° ' "	° ' "	° ' "	° '	° '	° '	° '	° '	° '	° '	° '	° '	° '	° '	° '
1 Tu	20 39 10	8♌57 01	24♏00 59	29♏58 48	24♌59.9	24♌20.1	6♍01.6	0♋26.2	7♌23.8	8♋56.0	16♎59.9	21♐39.3	28♓27.8	28♈31.4	13♓44.7	17♑36.4
2 W	20 43 07	9 54 25	5♐55 31	11♐51 39	24 56.7	24R 18.9	6 51.4	1 35.5	8 02.4	9 20.6	17 08.1	21R 37.1	28R 26.2	28 31.5	13R 43.4	17R 35.0
3 Th	20 47 03	10 51 50	17 47 41	23 44 05	24 53.5	24 17.2	7 37.7	2 44.9	8 40.9	9 45.2	17 16.3	21 35.0	28 24.6	28R 31.6	13 42.1	17 33.7
4 F	20 51 00	11 49 15	29 41 16	5♑39 37	24 50.4	24 15.4	8 20.6	3 54.4	9 19.4	10 09.8	17 24.7	21 32.9	28 23.0	28 31.5	13 40.8	17 32.4
5 Sa	20 54 56	12 46 41	11♑39 32	17 41 18	24 47.2	24 13.7	8 59.9	5 03.9	9 57.9	10 34.4	17 33.2	21 31.0	28 21.3	28 31.5	13 39.5	17 31.1
6 Su	20 58 53	13 44 08	23 45 12	29 51 30	24 44.0	24 12.3	9 35.2	6 13.6	10 36.3	10 58.9	17 41.8	21 29.1	28 19.6	28 31.4	13 38.1	17 29.8
7 M	21 02 50	14 41 36	6♒00 25	12♒12 06	24 40.8	24 11.3	10 06.5	7 23.4	11 14.8	11 23.3	17 50.5	21 27.3	28 17.8	28 31.2	13 36.7	17 28.5
8 Tu	21 06 46	15 39 04	18 26 44	24 44 26	24 37.6	24D 10.9	10 33.6	8 33.3	11 53.2	11 47.8	17 59.3	21 25.6	28 16.0	28 31.0	13 35.3	17 27.2
9 W	21 10 43	16 36 34	1♓05 19	7♓29 27	24 34.5	24 10.9	10 56.3	9 43.2	12 31.6	12 12.2	18 08.3	21 24.0	28 14.2	28 30.7	13 33.9	17 26.0
10 Th	21 14 39	17 34 05	13 56 54	20 27 44	24 31.3	24 11.2	11 14.2	10 53.3	13 10.0	12 36.5	18 17.3	21 22.5	28 12.3	28 30.4	13 32.5	17 24.8
11 F	21 18 36	18 31 37	27 02 00	3♈39 43	24 28.1	24 11.7	11 27.4	12 03.5	13 48.4	13 00.9	18 26.4	21 21.1	28 10.4	28 30.1	13 31.0	17 23.5
12 Sa	21 22 32	19 29 10	10♈20 55	17 05 37	24 24.9	24 12.3	11 35.5	13 13.7	14 26.8	13 25.1	18 35.7	21 19.7	28 08.4	28 29.7	13 29.6	17 22.3
13 Su	21 26 29	20 26 45	23 53 47	0♉45 25	24 21.8	24 12.6	11R 38.4	14 24.1	15 05.2	13 49.4	18 45.0	21 18.5	28 06.4	28 29.2	13 28.1	17 21.2
14 M	21 30 25	21 24 21	7♉40 26	14 38 45	24 18.6	24 12.9	11 35.9	15 34.5	15 43.5	14 13.6	18 54.4	21 17.3	28 04.4	28 28.7	13 26.6	17 20.0
15 Tu	21 34 22	22 21 59	21 40 15	28 44 44	24 15.4	24R 12.9	11 27.9	16 45.0	16 21.9	14 37.8	19 04.0	21 16.3	28 02.3	28 28.2	13 25.1	17 18.8
16 W	21 38 19	23 19 39	5♊51 57	13♊01 37	24 12.2	24D 12.9	11 14.4	17 55.7	17 00.2	15 01.9	19 13.6	21 15.3	28 00.2	28 27.6	13 23.6	17 17.7
17 Th	21 42 15	24 17 20	20 13 22	27 26 45	24 09.0	24 12.9	10 55.3	19 06.4	17 38.6	15 26.0	19 23.4	21 14.4	27 58.1	28 27.0	13 22.1	17 16.6
18 F	21 46 12	25 15 02	4♋41 16	11♋56 22	24 05.9	24 13.0	10 30.6	20 17.2	18 16.9	15 50.0	19 33.2	21 13.7	27 55.9	28 26.3	13 20.5	17 15.5
19 Sa	21 50 08	26 12 47	19 11 26	26 25 50	24 02.7	24 13.1	10 00.6	21 28.1	18 55.2	16 14.0	19 43.1	21 13.0	27 53.7	28 25.5	13 19.0	17 14.4
20 Su	21 54 05	27 10 32	3♌38 53	10♌49 56	23 59.5	24 13.3	9 25.3	22 39.1	19 33.5	16 38.0	19 53.1	21 12.4	27 51.5	28 24.8	13 17.4	17 13.4
21 M	21 58 01	28 08 19	17 58 19	25 03 27	23 56.3	24R 13.5	8 45.3	23 50.1	20 11.8	17 01.9	20 03.2	21 11.9	27 49.2	28 23.9	13 15.9	17 12.3
22 Tu	22 01 58	29 06 08	2♍04 45	9♍01 46	23 53.2	24 13.5	8 01.0	25 01.2	20 50.0	17 25.7	20 13.4	21 11.5	27 46.9	28 23.1	13 14.3	17 11.3
23 W	22 05 54	0♍03 58	15 54 06	22 41 26	23 50.0	24 13.2	7 12.9	26 12.5	21 28.3	17 49.5	20 23.7	21 11.2	27 44.6	28 22.1	13 12.7	17 10.3
24 Th	22 09 51	1 01 49	29 23 36	6♎00 29	23 46.8	24 12.6	6 21.9	27 23.7	22 06.6	18 13.2	20 34.1	21 11.0	27 42.2	28 21.2	13 11.1	17 09.4
25 F	22 13 48	1 59 42	12♎32 06	18 58 35	23 43.6	24 11.6	5 28.8	28 35.0	22 44.8	18 36.9	20 44.5	21D 11.0	27 39.8	28 20.2	13 09.5	17 08.4
26 Sa	22 17 44	2 57 35	25 20 06	1♏36 56	23 40.4	24 10.6	4 34.5	29 46.6	23 23.0	19 00.5	20 55.1	21 10.9	27 37.4	28 19.1	13 07.8	17 07.5
27 Su	22 21 41	3 55 31	7♏49 27	13 58 04	23 37.3	24 09.5	3 40.2	0♌58.1	24 01.3	19 24.1	21 05.7	21 11.0	27 35.0	28 18.0	13 06.2	17 06.6
28 M	22 25 37	4 53 27	20 03 15	26 05 31	23 34.1	24 08.7	2 47.0	2 09.7	24 39.5	19 47.6	21 16.4	21 11.2	27 32.5	28 16.9	13 04.6	17 05.7
29 Tu	22 29 34	5 51 25	2♐05 24	8♐03 29	23 30.9	24D 08.3	1 56.0	3 21.3	25 17.7	20 11.0	21 27.1	21 11.5	27 30.0	28 15.7	13 03.0	17 04.8
30 W	22 33 30	6 49 24	14 00 19	19 56 31	23 27.7	24 08.3	1 08.3	4 33.1	25 55.8	20 34.4	21 38.0	21 11.9	27 27.5	28 14.4	13 01.3	17 04.0
31 Th	22 37 27	7♍47 24	25 52 39	1♑49 18	23♌24.6	24♌09.0	0♍25.1	5♌44.9	26♌34.0	20♋57.7	21♎48.9	21♐12.4	27♓25.0	28♈13.2	12♓59.7	17♑03.2

1st of Month

Julian Day #
2457966.5
Obliquity
23°26'05"
SVP 5♓01'00"
GC 27♐05.1
Eris 23♈51.5R

Day	⚴
1	9♉10.3
6	10 12.6
11	11 09.5
16	12 00.2
21	12 44.0
26	13 20.2
31	13 48.1

Day	⚵
1	4♑44.1R
6	4 02.3R
11	3 28.9R
16	3 04.4R
21	2 49.2R
26	2 43.2R
31	2 46.4

Day	⚶
1	6♍28.9
6	8 50.2
11	11 12.7
16	13 36.4
21	16 01.3
26	18 27.2
31	20 54.1

DECLINATION and LATITUDE

Day	☉ Decl	☽ Decl	☽ Lat	☽12h Decl	☿ Decl	☿ Lat	♀ Decl	♀ Lat	♂ Decl	♂ Lat	⚳ Decl	⚳ Lat	♃ Decl	♃ Lat	♄ Decl	♄ Lat
1 Tu	18N01	13S40	5N16	15S01	7N47	1S38	21N52	1S34	19N30	1N07	24N11	1N03	5S35	1N11	21S55	1N15
2 W	17 46	16 13	5 09	17 14	7 18	1 50	21 54	1 31	19 20	1 07	24 12	1 05	5 38	1 11	21 55	1 15
3 Th	17 30	18 04	4 50	18 42	6 50	2 02	21 56	1 28	19 10	1 07	24 12	1 07	5 41	1 11	21 55	1 15
4 F	17 14	19 08	4 18	19 22	6 22	2 14	21 57	1 25	18 60	1 07	24 12	1 09	5 45	1 11	21 55	1 15
5 Sa	16 58	19 22	3 34	19 09	5 57	2 26	21 58	1 22	18 50	1 07	24 12	1 12	5 48	1 10	21 56	1 14
6 Su	16 42	18 43	2 41	18 03	5 32	2 38	21 58	1 19	18 39	1 07	24 12	1 14	5 52	1 10	21 56	1 14
7 M	16 25	17 10	1 39	16 05	5 09	2 50	21 58	1 16	18 29	1 08	24 12	1 16	5 55	1 10	21 56	1 14
8 Tu	16 08	14 48	0 32	13 19	4 48	3 01	21 57	1 13	18 18	1 08	24 12	1 18	5 59	1 10	21 56	1 14
9 W	15 51	11 41	0S38	9 53	4 29	3 13	21 55	1 09	18 08	1 08	24 12	1 20	6 02	1 10	21 56	1 14
10 Th	15 34	7 58	1 47	5 56	4 12	3 24	21 53	1 06	17 57	1 08	24 12	1 22	6 06	1 09	21 56	1 14
11 F	15 16	3 49	2 52	1 38	3 57	3 35	21 51	1 03	17 46	1 08	24 12	1 24	6 10	1 09	21 56	1 13
12 Sa	14 58	0N35	3 49	2N49	3 44	3 46	21 47	0 60	17 35	1 08	24 11	1 26	6 13	1 09	21 56	1 13
13 Su	14 40	5 01	4 34	7 11	3 34	3 56	21 43	0 56	17 24	1 08	24 11	1 28	6 17	1 09	21 56	1 13
14 M	14 22	9 16	5 04	11 14	3 26	4 05	21 39	0 53	17 12	1 08	24 11	1 31	6 21	1 09	21 56	1 13
15 Tu	14 03	13 04	5 17	14 44	3 21	4 14	21 34	0 50	17 01	1 09	24 10	1 33	6 25	1 08	21 56	1 13
16 W	13 44	16 11	5 11	17 23	3 19	4 22	21 28	0 47	16 50	1 09	24 10	1 35	6 28	1 08	21 56	1 12
17 Th	13 25	18 20	4 45	18 59	3 20	4 28	21 22	0 43	16 38	1 09	24 09	1 37	6 32	1 08	21 57	1 12
18 F	13 06	19 20	4 02	19 21	3 24	4 34	21 15	0 40	16 26	1 09	24 08	1 39	6 36	1 08	21 57	1 12
19 Sa	12 47	19 03	3 02	18 26	3 31	4 38	21 07	0 37	16 14	1 09	24 08	1 42	6 40	1 08	21 57	1 12
20 Su	12 27	17 31	1 52	16 20	3 42	4 41	20 59	0 33	16 03	1 09	24 07	1 44	6 44	1 08	21 57	1 12
21 M	12 07	14 54	0 35	13 14	3 55	4 42	20 50	0 30	15 51	1 09	24 06	1 46	6 48	1 07	21 57	1 12
22 Tu	11 47	11 25	0N43	9 26	4 12	4 42	20 41	0 27	15 38	1 09	24 05	1 48	6 52	1 07	21 57	1 11
23 W	11 27	7 22	1 57	5 13	4 32	4 39	20 31	0 24	15 26	1 09	24 05	1 51	6 56	1 07	21 58	1 11
24 Th	11 06	3 02	3 03	0 51	4 54	4 35	20 21	0 20	15 14	1 09	24 04	1 53	6 60	1 07	21 58	1 11
25 F	10 46	1S19	3 57	3S26	5 19	4 29	20 10	0 17	15 01	1 09	24 03	1 55	7 04	1 07	21 58	1 11
26 Sa	10 25	5 29	4 37	7 27	5 46	4 21	19 58	0 14	14 49	1 09	24 02	1 58	7 08	1 07	21 58	1 11
27 Su	10 04	9 19	5 04	11 06	6 15	4 12	19 46	0 11	14 36	1 10	24 01	2 00	7 12	1 06	21 58	1 10
28 M	9 43	12 41	5 16	14 09	6 45	3 60	19 33	0 08	14 24	1 10	23 60	2 02	7 16	1 06	21 58	1 10
29 Tu	9 22	15 27	5 14	16 35	7 15	3 47	19 20	0 04	14 11	1 10	23 58	2 05	7 20	1 06	21 59	1 10
30 W	9 00	17 33	4 58	18 19	7 46	3 32	19 06	0 01	13 58	1 10	23 57	2 07	7 25	1 06	21 59	1 10
31 Th	8N39	18S53	4N29	19S15	8N16	3S16	18N52	0N02	13N45	1N10	23N56	2N10	7S29	1N06	21S59	1N10

Day	⚷ Decl	⚷ Lat	♅ Decl	♅ Lat	♆ Decl	♆ Lat	♇ Decl	♇ Lat
1	3N02	3N59	10N24	0S35	7S15	0S56	21S33	0N44
6	2 60	3 59	10 24	0 35	7 18	0 56	21 35	0 43
11	2 56	3 60	10 23	0 35	7 20	0 56	21 36	0 43
16	2 53	4 00	10 22	0 35	7 23	0 56	21 37	0 42
21	2 49	4 00	10 21	0 35	7 26	0 56	21 39	0 42
26	2 44	4 01	10 19	0 35	7 30	0 56	21 40	0 41
31	2N39	4N01	10N17	0S36	7S33	0S56	21S41	0N4

Day	⚴ Decl	⚴ Lat	⚵ Decl	⚵ Lat	⚶ Decl	⚶ Lat	Eris Decl	Eris Lat
1	1S15	16S38	6S47	16N35	13N30	4N43	2S09	12S15
6	1 57	17 41	7 12	16 10	12 38	4 43	2 09	12 1
11	2 44	18 47	7 40	15 44	11 44	4 44	2 10	12 16
16	3 36	19 57	8 08	15 16	10 50	4 45	2 11	12 16
21	4 34	21 10	8 36	14 48	9 54	4 46	2 12	12 17
26	5 38	22 27	9 05	14 19	8 58	4 47	2 13	12 17
31	6S47	23S47	9S34	13N50	8N01	4N48	2S14	12S17

Moon Phenomena

Max/0 Decl
dy hr mn
4 18:19 19S24
11 20:50 0 N
18 6:44 19N23
24 16:42 0 S

Max/0 Lat
dy hr mn
1 0:37 5N16
8 10:56 0 S
15 4:14 5S17
21 10:36 0 N
28 8:06 5N17

Perigee/Apogee
dy hr m kilometers
2 18:00 a 405024
18 13:21 p 366123
30 11:25 a 404306

PH dy hr mn
○ 7 18:12 15♒25
☍ 7 18:22 P 0.246
☾ 15 1:16 22♉25
● 21 18:31 28♌53
☌ 21 18:27 T 02'40"
☽ 29 8:14 6♐11

Void of Course Moon

Last Aspect	☽ Ingress
31 11:11 ♇ ⚹	♐ 1 12:02
3 21:40 ♅ △	♑ 4 0:38
6 9:23 ♅ □	♒ 6 12:17
8 19:09 ♅ ⚹	♓ 8 21:57
10 13:39 ♄ □	♈ 11 5:23
13 8:02 ♅ ☌	♉ 13 10:41
15 1:16 ☉ □	♊ 15 14:07
17 13:39 ♅ ⚹	♋ 17 16:14
19 15:18 ♅ □	♌ 19 17:56
21 18:31 ☉ ☌	♍ 21 20:26
23 20:03 ♀ ⚹	♎ 24 1:06
26 5:40 ♅ ☍	♏ 26 8:54
28 9:39 ♂ □	♐ 28 19:49
31 4:43 ♅ △	♑ 31 8:20

DAILY ASPECTARIAN

1 Tu ☽△⚷ 8:55; ☽⚻♅ 9:04; ☽⚻♀ 14:18; ☽∠♃ 16:15; ☽∠♇ 17:16

2 W ☿#♆ 1:58; ☽□☿ 2:01; ☽△♂ 4:31; ☽⚻⚳ 7:09; ☉△☽ 8:45; ☽⚼♅ 15:22; ♀#♄ 15:31; ☽□♆ 15:44; ☉#☽ 16:45; ☽⚹♃ 22:56; ☽⚺♇ 23:32

3 Th ♅R 5:32; ☽☌♄ 7:38; ☽⚼♂ 12:34; ☉⚼☽ 17:43; ☽#♂ 20:14; ☽□⚷ 21:23; ☽△♅ 21:40

4 F ☽☍♀ 9:23; ☽△☿ 18:23; ♃□♇ 18:49; ☽⚻♂ 20:25; ☽☍⚳ 21:45

5 Sa ☉⚻☽ 2:26; ☽⚹♆ 3:59; ☿#♃ 7:04; ☽☌♇ 11:38; ☽□♃ 11:52; ☉⚼⚷ 14:03; ☽⚺♄ 19:32; ☉⚻♆ 21:33

6 Su ☽#♂ 1:19; ☽⚼☿ 1:43; ☽⚹⚷ 8:59; ☽□♅ 9:23; ☽∠♆ 9:35

7 M ☽∠♄ 0:52; ☽⚻♀ 2:58; ☽⚻☿ 8:16; ☉#☽ 9:37; ☽☍♂ 10:42; ☽⚻⚳ 10:47; ☽∠⚷ 14:05; ♂⚺⚳ 14:41; ☽⚺♆ 14:41; ☉☍☽ 18:12; ☽⚺♇ 22:06; ☽△♃ 23:07

8 Tu ☽⚹♄ 5:41; ☽⚼♀ 10:44; ☽⚼⚳ 16:25; ☽⚺⚷ 18:38; ☽⚹♅ 19:09; ♀#♄ 20:07

9 W ☽∠♇ 2:31; ☽⚼♃ 3:54; ☽#♅ 8:42; ☽△♀ 17:46; ☽☍☿ 18:52; ☉⚻♇ 20:11; ☽△⚳ 21:26; ☽⚻♂ 22:29; ☽∠♅ 23:11; ☽☌♆ 23:15

10 Th ♂⚼⚷ 1:22; ☽∥♆ 3:48; ☽⚹♇ 6:23; ☉⚻☽ 7:13; ☽⚻♃ 8:06; ☿⚹♀ 9:04; ☽∥♃ 10:53; ♂⚻♆ 13:32; ☽□♄ 13:39; ☉⚹♃ 21:25; ☽#☿ 23:13

11 F ☽☌⚷ 2:04; ☽⚺♅ 2:40; ☽⚼♂ 3:23; ☽#⚷ 4:51; ☉⚼☽ 12:40; ♅∠♆ 21:50

12 Sa ☽⚻☿ 2:14; ⚳△♆ 4:08; ♀△♆ 5:18; ☽⚺♆ 5:36; ☽□♀ 5:37; ☽□⚳ 5:39; ♀☌⚳ 5:58; ☽△♂ 7:40; ☽□♇ 12:29; ☽∥⚷ 12:35; ☽☍♃ 14:50; ☽∥☿ 16:18; ☉△☽ 17:28; ☽△♄ 19:27

13 Su ☿R 1:01; ☽⚼☿ 4:49; ☽#♃ 7:03; ☽⚺⚷ 7:22; ☽∠♆ 8:00; ☽☌♅ 8:02; ☽#♆ 13:01; ☉△♄ 21:08; ☽⚼♄ 21:36

14 M ☽∥♅ 6:40; ☽△☿ 6:43; ♀⚺♂ 6:44; ♀#♇ 9:10; ☽∠⚷ 9:17; ☽⚹♆ 9:55; ☽⚹⚳ 11:37; ☽□♂ 14:31; ☽⚹♀ 14:50; ☽△♇ 16:35; ☽⚻♃ 19:31; ☽⚻♄ 23:19

15 Tu ☉□☽ 1:16; ☉∥☽ 6:20; ☽⚹⚷ 10:47; ♀☍♇ 11:18; ☽⚺♅ 11:32; ☽∠⚳ 13:53; ☽⚼♇ 18:00; ☽∠♀ 18:37; ☽⚼♃ 21:13

16 W ☽∥♂ 5:39; ☽□☿ 8:50; ♂⚻♇ 10:38; ☽□♆ 12:35; ☽∠♅ 12:43; ☽⚺⚳ 15:47; ☽⚻♇ 19:06; ☽⚹♂ 19:30; ☽⚺♀ 21:59; ☽△♃ 22:36

17 Th ☽☍♄ 1:42; ♀□♃ 6:41; ☉⚹☽ 7:14; ☽□⚷ 12:50; ☽⚹♅ 13:39; ☽∠♂ 21:34

18 F ☽⚹☿ 9:20; ☉∠☽ 9:52; ☽△♆ 14:18; ♀⚻♄ 18:56; ☽☌⚳ 18:58; ☽☍♇ 20:47; ☽⚺♂ 23:32

19 Sa ☽□♃ 0:53; ☽⚻♄ 3:21; ☽☌♀ 4:06; ☽∠☿ 9:17; ☉⚺☽ 12:28; ☽△⚷ 14:24; ☽⚼♆ 15:06; ☽□♅ 15:18

20 Su ☽⚼♄ 4:16; ☽⚺☿ 9:14; ☽⚼⚷ 15:21; ☽∥♂ 15:42; ☽⚻♆ 16:06; ☉⚻⚷ 16:22; ♂⚹♃ 16:43; ☽⚺⚳ 22:22; ☽⚻♇ 22:43; ☿∠♀ 22:59

21 M ☽⚹♃ 3:34; ☽☌♂ 3:56; ☽△♄ 5:27; ☉△♅ 6:23; ⚳☍♇ 10:06; ☽⚺♀ 10:50; ☽⚻⚷ 16:40; ☽△♅ 17:41; ☉☌☽ 18:31; ☉∥☽ 21:23

22 Tu ☽⚼♇ 0:11; ☽∠⚳ 0:37; ☽∠♃ 5:29; ☽∥♅ 6:34; ☽☌☿ 9:42; ♂△♄ 13:22; ☽∠♀ 15:01; ☽☍♆ 19:18; ☽⚼♅ 19:34; ☉ ♍ 22:21; ☽#♆ 23:26

23 W ☽△♇ 2:14; ☽#♃ 2:24; ☽⚹⚳ 3:29; ☽⚺♃ 8:02; ☽□♄ 9:20; ☽⚺♂ 10:19; ☽∥☿ 14:34; ☽⚹♀ 20:03; ☽☍⚷ 20:58; ☽⚻♅ 22:08

24 Th ☽∥⚷ 1:30; ☉⚺☽ 3:11; ♀△⚷ 6:01; ☽⚺☿ 11:52; ☽∠♂ 14:44; ♀⚼♆ 15:34; ☿∠♃ 18:06; ♀□♅ 19:03

25 F ☽⚻♆ 1:09; ☉⚼♇ 3:33; ☽#⚷ 8:04; ☽□♇ 8:33; ☉∠☽ 8:58; ☽□⚳ 11:41; ♄D 12:09; ☽∠☿ 13:51; ☽☌♃ 15:32; ☽⚹♄ 16:09; ☽⚹♂ 20:06

26 Sa ☽#☿ 1:55; ☽⚻⚷ 4:21; ♀ ♌ 4:31; ☽⚼♆ 5:19; ☽☍♅ 5:40; ☉∥♅ 6:45; ☽□♀ 9:22; ☽∥♃ 10:10; ☿∠⚳ 10:27; ☽∥♆ 12:16; ☉⚹☽ 15:49; ☽⚹☿ 16:30; ⚵D 17:15; ☉☌☿ 20:43; ☽∠♄ 20:49

27 Su ☉#☽ 4:35; ☽#♅ 6:43; ☽⚼⚷ 9:15; ☽△♆ 10:17; ♃⚹♄ 12:16; ☽⚹♇ 18:10; ☉∠⚳ 19:55; ☽△⚳ 23:28

28 M ☽⚺♄ 2:15; ☽⚺♃ 2:27; ☿⚺♀ 7:15; ☽□♂ 9:39; ☽#♂ 13:10; ☽△⚷ 14:51; ☽⚻♅ 16:21; ☿⚼♇ 19:39; ☽□☿ 23:42; ☽∠♇ 23:59

29 Tu ☽△♀ 2:49; ☿#♃ 4:44; ☽⚼⚳ 6:25; ☉□☽ 8:14; ☽∠♃ 8:54; ☿#♆ 13:02; ☉∠♃ 18:12; ☽□♆ 22:01; ☽⚼♅ 22:27

30 W ☽⚺♇ 6:11; ☽⚼♀ 12:28; ☽⚻⚳ 13:44; ☽☌♄ 14:33; ☽⚹♃ 15:40; ☽#♀ 23:31

31 Th ☽△♂ 1:28; ☽□⚷ 3:06; ☽△♅ 4:43; ☽△☿ 8:41; ♀⚼♄ 9:16; ☉∥☿ 10:42; ☿R♌ 15:29; ⚳⚻♄ 15:31; ☽⚻♀ 22:08

LONGITUDE

September 2017

Day	Sid.Time	☉	☽	☽ 12 hour	Mean☊	True☊	☿	♀	♂	⚳	♃	♄	⚷	♅	♆	♇
	h m s	° ' "	° ' "	° ' "	° '	° '	° '	° '	° '	° '	° '	° '	° '	° '	° '	° '
F	22 41 23	8♍45 26	7♑47 02	13♑46 22	23♌21.4	24♌10.1	29♌47.3	6♌56.8	27♌12.2	21♋21.0	21♎59.9	21♐13.0	27♓22.5	28♈11.9	12♓58.0	17♑02.4
Sa	22 45 20	9 43 30	19 47 49	25 51 51	23 18.2	24 11.4	29R 15.8	8 08.7	27 50.3	21 44.2	22 11.0	21 13.7	27R 19.9	28R 10.5	12R 56.4	17R 01.6
Su	22 49 16	10 41 34	1♒58 53	8♒09 18	23 15.0	24 12.7	28 51.5	9 20.8	28 28.5	22 07.3	22 22.1	21 14.5	27 17.3	28 09.1	12 54.8	17 00.9
M	22 53 13	11 39 40	14 23 25	20 41 29	23 11.8	24R 13.6	28 34.9	10 32.9	29 06.6	22 30.4	22 33.4	21 15.3	27 14.7	28 07.7	12 53.1	17 00.2
Tu	22 57 10	12 37 48	27 03 42	3♓30 11	23 08.7	24 13.9	28D 26.5	11 45.1	29 44.8	22 53.4	22 44.6	21 16.3	27 12.1	28 06.2	12 51.5	16 59.5
W	23 01 06	13 35 58	10♓00 58	16 36 03	23 05.5	24 13.2	28 26.7	12 57.3	0♍22.9	23 16.3	22 56.0	21 17.4	27 09.5	28 04.7	12 49.8	16 58.8
Th	23 05 03	14 34 09	23 15 19	29 58 37	23 02.3	24 11.5	28 35.6	14 09.6	1 01.0	23 39.1	23 07.4	21 18.6	27 06.8	28 03.1	12 48.2	16 58.2
F	23 08 59	15 32 21	6♈45 42	13♈36 19	22 59.1	24 09.0	28 53.4	15 22.0	1 39.1	24 01.9	23 18.9	21 19.8	27 04.1	28 01.6	12 46.5	16 57.6
Sa	23 12 56	16 30 36	20 30 08	27 26 46	22 55.9	24 05.9	29 20.0	16 34.5	2 17.2	24 24.6	23 30.4	21 21.2	27 01.5	27 59.9	12 44.9	16 57.0
Su	23 16 52	17 28 53	4♉25 53	11♉27 04	22 52.8	24 02.7	29 55.2	17 47.0	2 55.3	24 47.2	23 42.0	21 22.6	26 58.8	27 58.3	12 43.2	16 56.5
M	23 20 49	18 27 11	18 29 56	25 34 06	22 49.6	23 59.8	0♍38.8	18 59.6	3 33.4	25 09.8	23 53.7	21 24.2	26 56.1	27 56.6	12 41.6	16 55.9
Tu	23 24 45	19 25 32	2♊39 14	9♊44 59	22 46.4	23 57.8	1 30.4	20 12.3	4 11.5	25 32.2	24 05.4	21 25.8	26 53.4	27 54.8	12 39.9	16 55.4
W	23 28 42	20 23 55	16 51 03	23 57 08	22 43.2	23D 56.9	2 29.5	21 25.0	4 49.5	25 54.6	24 17.2	21 27.6	26 50.7	27 53.1	12 38.3	16 54.9
Th	23 32 39	21 22 20	1♋02 58	8♋08 19	22 40.1	23 57.2	3 35.8	22 37.9	5 27.6	26 16.9	24 29.0	21 29.4	26 48.0	27 51.3	12 36.7	16 54.5
F	23 36 35	22 20 48	15 12 56	22 16 36	22 36.9	23 58.3	4 48.7	23 50.7	6 05.7	26 39.1	24 40.9	21 31.3	26 45.2	27 49.4	12 35.0	16 54.1
Sa	23 40 32	23 19 17	29 19 02	6♌20 02	22 33.7	23 59.8	6 07.5	25 03.7	6 43.7	27 01.3	24 52.9	21 33.3	26 42.5	27 47.6	12 33.4	16 53.7
Su	23 44 28	24 17 49	13♌19 18	20 16 35	22 30.5	24R 01.0	7 31.8	26 16.7	7 21.8	27 23.3	25 04.9	21 35.5	26 39.8	27 45.7	12 31.8	16 53.3
M	23 48 25	25 16 22	27 11 35	4♍04 01	22 27.4	24 01.3	9 00.8	27 29.8	7 59.9	27 45.3	25 17.0	21 37.7	26 37.0	27 43.7	12 30.2	16 53.0
Tu	23 52 21	26 14 58	10♍53 36	17 40 01	22 24.2	24 00.2	10 34.1	28 42.9	8 37.9	28 07.1	25 29.1	21 40.0	26 34.3	27 41.8	12 28.6	16 52.7
W	23 56 18	27 13 36	24 23 01	1♎02 21	22 21.0	23 57.5	12 10.9	29 56.1	9 16.0	28 28.9	25 41.2	21 42.3	26 31.5	27 39.8	12 27.0	16 52.4
Th	0 00 14	28 12 15	7♎37 50	14 09 18	22 17.8	23 53.1	13 50.9	1♍09.4	9 54.0	28 50.5	25 53.4	21 44.8	26 28.8	27 37.8	12 25.4	16 52.2
F	0 04 11	29 10 57	20 36 40	26 59 53	22 14.6	23 47.5	15 33.4	2 22.7	10 32.0	29 12.1	26 05.7	21 47.4	26 26.1	27 35.7	12 23.9	16 51.9
Sa	0 08 08	0♎09 40	3♏19 01	9♏34 11	22 11.5	23 41.1	17 17.9	3 36.0	11 10.0	29 33.5	26 18.0	21 50.1	26 23.3	27 33.6	12 22.3	16 51.8
Su	0 12 04	1 08 25	15 45 34	21 53 25	22 08.3	23 34.8	19 04.1	4 49.5	11 48.1	29 54.9	26 30.4	21 52.8	26 20.6	27 31.5	12 20.8	16 51.6
M	0 16 01	2 07 12	27 58 05	3♐59 56	22 05.1	23 29.2	20 51.6	6 02.9	12 26.1	0♌16.1	26 42.7	21 55.7	26 17.9	27 29.4	12 19.2	16 51.5
Tu	0 19 57	3 06 01	9♐59 27	15 57 06	22 01.9	23 25.0	22 39.9	7 16.5	13 04.1	0 37.3	26 55.2	21 58.6	26 15.2	27 27.3	12 17.7	16 51.4
W	0 23 54	4 04 52	21 53 27	27 49 05	21 58.7	23 22.3	24 28.8	8 30.0	13 42.1	0 58.3	27 07.6	22 01.6	26 12.4	27 25.1	12 16.2	16 51.3
Th	0 27 50	5 03 44	3♑44 35	9♑40 35	21 55.6	23D 21.4	26 18.1	9 43.7	14 20.1	1 19.2	27 20.2	22 04.7	26 09.8	27 22.9	12 14.7	16D 51.3
F	0 31 47	6 02 38	15 37 45	21 36 41	21 52.4	23 21.9	28 07.4	10 57.3	14 58.1	1 40.0	27 32.7	22 07.9	26 07.1	27 20.7	12 13.2	16 51.2
Sa	0 35 43	7♎01 34	27 38 02	3♒42 25	21♌49.2	23♌23.2	29♍56.7	12♍11.1	15♍36.0	2♌00.7	27♎45.3	22♐11.2	26♓04.4	27♈18.4	12♓11.7	16♑51.3

1st of Month

Julian Day # 2457997.5
Obliquity 23°26'06"
SVP 5♓00'56"
GC 27♐05.2
Eris 23♈43.0R

Day	⚴
1	13♉52.6
6	14 09.5
11	14 16.4
16	14 12.4R
21	13 56.9R
26	13 29.3R

Day	⚵
1	2♏48.2
6	3 02.2
11	3 24.7
16	3 55.4
21	4 34.0
26	5 20.0

Day	⚶
1	21♍23.6
6	23 51.6
11	26 20.4
16	28 50.1
21	1♎20.5
26	3 51.6

DECLINATION and LATITUDE

Day	☉ Decl	☽ Decl	☽ Lat	☽ 12h Decl	☿ Decl	☿ Lat	♀ Decl	♀ Lat	♂ Decl	♂ Lat	⚳ Decl	⚳ Lat	♃ Decl	♃ Lat	♄ Decl	♄ Lat
F	8N17	19S23	3N49	19S19	8N45	2S59	18N37	0N05	13N32	1N10	23N55	2N12	7S33	1N06	21S59	1N09
Sa	7 55	19 01	2 59	18 30	9 13	2 41	18 21	0 08	13 19	1 10	23 54	2 14	7 37	1 06	21 60	1 09
Su	7 33	17 46	1 60	16 49	9 39	2 22	18 05	0 11	13 06	1 10	23 52	2 17	7 42	1 05	21 60	1 09
M	7 11	15 39	0 54	14 17	10 02	2 03	17 49	0 14	12 52	1 10	23 51	2 19	7 46	1 05	22 00	1 09
Tu	6 49	12 44	0S16	11 01	10 23	1 44	17 32	0 17	12 39	1 10	23 49	2 22	7 50	1 05	22 00	1 09
W	6 27	9 08	1 26	7 08	10 41	1 25	17 14	0 20	12 26	1 10	23 48	2 24	7 54	1 05	22 01	1 09
Th	6 04	5 01	2 33	2 50	10 55	1 06	16 56	0 23	12 12	1 10	23 47	2 27	7 59	1 05	22 01	1 08
F	5 42	0 35	3 33	1N42	11 06	0 48	16 38	0 25	11 59	1 10	23 45	2 30	8 03	1 05	22 01	1 08
Sa	5 19	3N58	4 22	6 11	11 14	0 31	16 19	0 28	11 45	1 10	23 44	2 32	8 08	1 05	22 01	1 08
Su	4 57	8 21	4 56	10 24	11 17	0 14	15 59	0 31	11 31	1 10	23 42	2 35	8 12	1 05	22 02	1 08
M	4 34	12 19	5 12	14 04	11 17	0N02	15 39	0 34	11 18	1 10	23 41	2 37	8 16	1 04	22 02	1 08
Tu	4 11	15 37	5 10	16 56	11 12	0 17	15 19	0 36	11 04	1 10	23 39	2 40	8 21	1 04	22 02	1 07
W	3 48	17 59	4 49	18 46	11 04	0 31	14 58	0 39	10 50	1 10	23 37	2 43	8 25	1 04	22 02	1 07
Th	3 25	19 15	4 11	19 26	10 52	0 44	14 37	0 41	10 36	1 10	23 36	2 45	8 30	1 04	22 03	1 07
F	3 02	19 18	3 17	18 53	10 37	0 56	14 16	0 44	10 22	1 10	23 34	2 48	8 34	1 04	22 03	1 07
Sa	2 39	18 09	2 11	17 09	10 17	1 06	13 54	0 46	10 08	1 10	23 32	2 51	8 39	1 04	22 03	1 07
Su	2 16	15 53	0 58	14 24	9 55	1 16	13 31	0 49	9 54	1 10	23 31	2 53	8 43	1 04	22 04	1 07
M	1 53	12 43	0N17	10 52	9 29	1 24	13 08	0 51	9 39	1 10	23 29	2 56	8 48	1 04	22 04	1 06
Tu	1 29	8 53	1 31	6 48	9 00	1 31	12 45	0 53	9 25	1 10	23 27	2 59	8 52	1 04	22 04	1 06
W	1 06	4 39	2 38	2 28	8 29	1 37	12 22	0 56	9 11	1 10	23 26	3 02	8 57	1 03	22 05	1 06
Th	0 43	0 16	3 35	1S54	7 55	1 42	11 58	0 58	8 57	1 10	23 24	3 05	9 01	1 03	22 05	1 06
F	0 20	4S02	4 20	6 05	7 19	1 46	11 33	0 60	8 42	1 10	23 22	3 08	9 06	1 03	22 05	1 06
Sa	0S04	8 03	4 51	9 55	6 41	1 48	11 09	1 02	8 28	1 10	23 20	3 10	9 10	1 03	22 06	1 05
Su	0 27	11 39	5 07	13 14	6 01	1 50	10 44	1 04	8 13	1 10	23 19	3 13	9 15	1 03	22 06	1 05
M	0 51	14 41	5 09	15 57	5 20	1 51	10 19	1 06	7 59	1 10	23 17	3 16	9 19	1 03	22 06	1 05
Tu	1 14	17 02	4 57	17 56	4 37	1 52	9 53	1 08	7 44	1 10	23 15	3 19	9 24	1 03	22 07	1 05
W	1 37	18 39	4 33	19 09	3 54	1 51	9 27	1 10	7 30	1 10	23 14	3 22	9 28	1 03	22 07	1 05
Th	2 01	19 26	3 57	19 31	3 09	1 50	9 01	1 11	7 15	1 10	23 12	3 25	9 33	1 03	22 07	1 05
F	2 24	19 22	3 10	19 00	2 24	1 48	8 35	1 13	7 00	1 10	23 10	3 28	9 37	1 03	22 08	1 04
Sa	2S47	18S25	2N15	17S37	1N39	1N46	8N08	1N15	6N45	1N10	23N08	3N31	9S42	1N02	22S08	1N04

Day	⚷ Decl	⚷ Lat	♅ Decl	♅ Lat	♆ Decl	♆ Lat	♇ Decl	♇ Lat
1	2N38	4N01	10N17	0S36	7S33	0S56	21S41	0N40
6	2 33	4 01	10 14	0 36	7 37	0 56	21 42	0 40
11	2 28	4 01	10 11	0 36	7 40	0 56	21 43	0 39
16	2 22	4 00	10 08	0 36	7 43	0 56	21 44	0 39
21	2 16	4 00	10 04	0 36	7 46	0 56	21 45	0 38
26	2 11	3 60	10 00	0 36	7 49	0 56	21 45	0 37

Day	⚴ Decl	⚴ Lat	⚵ Decl	⚵ Lat	⚶ Decl	⚶ Lat	Eris Decl	Eris Lat
1	7S02	24S04	9S40	13N45	7N49	4N48	2S14	12S17
6	8 17	25 27	10 08	13 16	6 51	4 49	2 15	12 18
11	9 38	26 53	10 36	12 48	5 53	4 50	2 16	12 18
16	11 03	28 22	11 02	12 20	4 55	4 51	2 17	12 18
21	12 33	29 51	11 28	11 54	3 56	4 52	2 18	12 18
26	14 05	31 20	11 52	11 28	2 57	4 53	2 19	12 18

Moon Phenomena

Max/0 Decl
dy hr mn
1 1:59 19S24
8 3:04 0 N
14 13:05 19N26
21 1:30 0 S
28 10:07 19S31

Max/0 Lat
dy hr mn
4 18:41 0 S
11 9:17 5S14
17 18:30 0 N
24 15:14 5N10

Perigee/Apogee
dy hr m kilometers
13 16:04 p 369859
27 6:46 a 404346

PH dy hr mn
○ 6 7:04 13♓53
☾ 13 6:26 20♊40
● 20 5:31 27♍27
☽ 28 2:55 5♑11

Void of Course Moon

Last Aspect	☽ Ingress
2 16:31 ♅ □	♒ 2 20:07
5 5:17 ♂ ☍	♓ 5 5:29
6 20:30 ♄ □	♈ 7 12:02
9 15:53 ☿ △	♉ 9 16:24
11 0:55 ♀ □	♊ 11 19:30
13 18:37 ♅ ✶	♋ 13 22:13
15 21:24 ♅ □	♌ 16 1:10
18 0:56 ♅ △	♍ 18 4:53
20 5:31 ☉ ☌	♎ 20 10:07
22 13:06 ♅ ☍	♏ 22 17:41
24 7:34 ☿ ✶	♐ 25 4:02
27 11:09 ♅ △	♑ 27 16:25
30 0:15 ♃ □	♒ 30 4:41

DAILY ASPECTARIAN

☉△☽ 2:08
♃∥♆ 2:28
♂⚻⚷ 6:03
☽⚼♂ 9:21
☽✶♆ 10:22
☽⚼☿ 13:25
☽☌♇ 18:30

☽⚺♄ 2:51
☽☍⚳ 3:58
☽□♃ 4:48
☉⚼☽ 10:36
♂△♅ 12:14
☽✶⚷ 14:50
☽∠♆ 16:03
☽□♅ 16:31
☉⋕♃ 16:31
☽⚻♂ 16:45
☽⚻☿ 18:04
☽⋕♀ 18:11
☉⋕♆ 22:36

☽∠♄ 8:18
☿☌♂ 9:39
☽☍♀ 15:50
☉⚻☽ 18:19
☽∠⚷ 19:54
☽⚺♆ 21:07

☽⚺♇ 4:59
⚳□♃ 6:06
☽✶♄ 13:05
☿∥♅ 13:55
☽△♃ 15:45
☽⚻⚳ 15:55

5 Tu
☽⚺⚷ 0:16
☽⋕♂ 0:38
☽✶♅ 1:57
☽☍☿ 2:34
☽☍♂ 5:17
☉☍♆ 5:29
♀⚼⚷ 8:40
☽∠♇ 9:11
♂ ♍ 9:36
☉⚼♅ 11:26
☿ D 11:30
☽⋕☿ 14:53
☽⋕♅ 17:05
☽⚼♃ 20:07
☽⚼⚳ 20:42
♀⚻♆ 21:34

6 W
☽☌♆ 5:08
☽∠♅ 5:35
☽⚻♀ 5:55
☉☍☽ 7:04
☽∥♃ 7:19
☽∥♆ 9:11
☽✶♇ 12:41
☉⋕☽ 17:30
☽□♄ 20:30
☽⚻♃ 23:46

7 Th
☽△⚳ 0:44
☽☌⚷ 6:53
☽⚺♅ 8:34
☽⚻☿ 9:43
☽⚼♀ 11:35
☽⋕⚷ 13:38
☽⚻♂ 14:32

8 F
☽⚺♆ 10:32
♂⚼♇ 11:29
☽⚼☿ 12:53
☽∥⚷ 16:17
☽△♀ 16:31
☉⚻☽ 16:32
☉⚺♀ 17:27
☽□♇ 17:50
☽⚼♂ 18:09

9 Sa
☽△♄ 1:29
☽☍♃ 5:17
☉∥☽ 6:44
☽□⚳ 6:57
♀⚻♇ 7:24
☉△♇ 10:46
☽⚺⚷ 11:14
☽∠♆ 12:30
☽☌♅ 12:56
☽△☿ 15:53
☽⋕♆ 20:04
☉⚼☽ 20:24
☽△♂ 21:17
☽⋕♃ 23:08

10 Su
☿ ♍ 2:53
☽⚼♄ 3:20
☽∥♅ 10:43
☽∠⚷ 12:52
☽✶♆ 14:08
☽∥☿ 17:25
☽∥♂ 17:50
☽△♇ 21:20
☉△☽ 23:55

11 M
☽□♀ 0:55
☿∥♂ 2:06
☽⚻♄ 4:57
☽⚻♃ 9:17
☽✶⚳ 11:37
☽✶⚷ 14:16
☽⚺♅ 15:59
⚴ R 17:47
☽∥♀ 21:51
☽□☿ 21:55
☽⚼♇ 22:46

12 Tu
☽□♂ 2:43
☿⚼♇ 10:27
☽⚼♃ 11:02
☽∠⚳ 13:41
☽□♆ 16:54
☽∠♅ 17:19

13 W
☽⚻♇ 0:07
♀△♄ 0:51
☉□☽ 6:26
☽☍♄ 7:48
☽✶♀ 8:26
☽△♃ 12:45
☽⚺⚳ 15:43
☽□⚷ 16:50
☽✶♅ 18:37

14 Th
☉□♄ 3:00
☽✶☿ 4:42
☽✶♂ 7:49
☽∠♀ 12:11
☽△♆ 19:33

15 F
☽☍♇ 2:52
⚳△⚷ 5:52
☽∠☿ 8:35
☽∠♂ 10:28
☽⚻♄ 10:44
☉✶☽ 13:01
☽⚺♀ 16:03
☽□♃ 16:20
☽△⚷ 19:34
♀✶♃ 19:45
☽☌⚳ 19:59
☽⚼♆ 21:00
☽□♅ 21:24

16 Sa
♂∥♅ 0:12
☿∥♅ 11:03
☽⚼♄ 12:25
☽⚺☿ 12:55
☽⚺♂ 13:17
☉∠☽ 16:34
☉∥⚷ 18:27
☿☌♂ 19:03
☽⚼⚷ 21:09
☽⚻♆ 22:38

17 Su
☿∥♂ 2:38
☽⚻♇ 6:09
♀⚻⚷ 7:18
⚳⚼♆ 8:39
☽△♄ 14:19
☉⚺☽ 20:24
☽✶♃ 20:38
☽∥♀ 20:44
⚳□♅ 22:28
☽⚻⚷ 23:00

18 M
☉⚺♃ 0:18
☽☌♀ 0:35
☽△♅ 0:56
☽⚺⚳ 1:00
♀△♅ 4:28
♀⚺⚳ 7:15
⚶ ♎ 7:51
☽⚼♇ 8:11
☽∥♅ 16:44
☽☌♂ 19:49
☽∥♂ 20:36
☿∠♃ 22:33
☽∥☿ 23:10
☽∠♃ 23:16
☽☌☿ 23:21

19 Tu
☽⋕♃ 0:05
☽☍♆ 2:47
☽⚼♅ 3:11
☽∠⚳ 4:02
☿⋕♃ 5:42
☽⋕♆ 6:35
☉☍⚷ 7:33
☽△♇ 10:36
☽□♄ 19:11

20 W
♀ ♍ 1:16
☽⚺♃ 2:23
☽☍⚷ 3:50
☿☍♆ 3:51
☉☌☽ 5:31
☽⚻♅ 5:53
☿⚼♅ 6:51
☽✶⚳ 7:35
☉⚻♅ 10:22
☽⚺♀ 11:01
☽∥⚷ 13:00
♂⋕♃ 18:19
☉∥☽ 21:21
☿∠⚳ 23:53

21 Th
☽⚺♂ 4:22
☉⋕☽ 4:59
☿⋕♆ 6:00
☽⚻♆ 8:47
☽⚺☿ 13:09
♀⚼♇ 13:58
☽⋕⚷ 14:02
☽□♇ 17:02
☽∠♀ 17:21

22 F
☉✶⚳ 0:44
☽✶♄ 2:13
☽∠♂ 9:43
☽☌♃ 10:28
☽⚻⚷ 10:54
☽⚼♆ 12:44
☽☍♅ 13:06
☽□⚳ 16:38
☽⋕☿ 16:45
☉⚺☽ 17:29
☿△♇ 18:02
☉ ♎ 20:03
☽∠☿ 21:45
☽∥♆ 22:21

23 Sa
☽✶♀ 0:36
☽⋕♂ 2:26
☽∠♄ 6:46
☽∥♃ 7:16
♂∠♃ 7:26
♃⚻⚷ 8:29
☽⋕♅ 12:51
☽⚼⚷ 15:28
☽✶♂ 15:54
☽△♆ 17:23
☽⋕♀ 18:16

24 Su
☉∠☽ 0:48
☽✶♇ 2:09
⚳ ♌ 5:46
☽✶☿ 7:34
☽⚺♄ 12:02
♂☍♆ 19:50
☽△⚷ 20:42
☽⚺♃ 21:28
☽⚻♅ 23:03

25 M
♂⚼♅ 2:00
☽△⚳ 4:42
☽∠♇ 7:44
☉✶☽ 8:59
☿□♄ 14:37
♂⋕♆ 16:21
♀∥♅ 17:07
☽□♀ 17:56

26 Tu
☽∠♃ 3:57
☽□♆ 4:37
☽⚼♅ 4:56
☽□♂ 6:32
☽⚼⚳ 11:41
☽⚺♇ 13:49
♀⋕♃ 23:15

27 W
☽☌♄ 0:17
☽□☿ 6:11
☽□⚷ 8:42
☽✶♃ 10:47
☽△♅ 11:09
♃⚼♆ 14:38
☽⚻⚳ 18:57
☿☍⚷ 22:13

28 Th
☉□☽ 2:55
♃☍♅ 4:26
☉⋕⚷ 7:30
☽△♀ 13:30
☿⚻♅ 13:57
☿⚺♃ 15:24
☽✶♆ 17:09
♇ D 19:37
☽△♂ 22:36

29 F
☉⋕☿ 0:04
☽☌♇ 2:28
☿∥⚷ 9:12
☽⚺♄ 13:06
☽✶⚷ 20:55
☽⚼♀ 23:00
☽∠♆ 23:08
☽□♅ 23:21

30 Sa
♀☍♆ 0:13
☽□♃ 0:15
☿ ♎ 0:43
♀⚼♅ 2:19
☽△☿ 5:23
☽⚼♂ 6:12
☽☍⚳ 8:55
♀∠♃ 13:25
♀⋕♆ 14:59
☽∠♄ 18:55
☉△☽ 20:07

October 2017

LONGITUDE

Day	Sid.Time	☉	☽	☽ 12 hour	Mean ☊	True ☊	☿	♀	♂	⚳	♃	♄	⚷	♅	♆	♇
	h m s	° ′ ″	° ′ ″	° ′ ″	° ′	° ′	° ′	° ′	° ′	° ′	° ′	° ′	° ′	° ′	° ′	° ′
1 Su	0 39 40	8♎00 32	9♒50 24	16♒02 33	21♌46.0	23♌24.7	1♎45.8	13♍24.9	16♍14.0	2♌21.2	27♎57.9	22♐14.6	26♓01.7	27♈16.2	12♓10.3	16♑51.3
2 M	0 43 36	8 59 31	22 19 20	28 41 11	21 42.9	23R 25.4	3 34.5	14 38.7	16 52.0	2 41.6	28 10.6	22 18.0	25R 59.1	27R 13.9	12R 08.9	16 51.4
3 Tu	0 47 33	9 58 32	5♓08 25	11♓41 15	21 39.7	23 24.7	5 22.7	15 52.6	17 30.0	3 01.9	28 23.2	22 21.6	25 56.4	27 11.6	12 07.4	16 51.5
4 W	0 51 30	10 57 35	18 19 49	25 04 07	21 36.5	23 22.0	7 10.4	17 06.5	18 07.9	3 22.1	28 36.0	22 25.2	25 53.8	27 09.3	12 06.0	16 51.6
5 Th	0 55 26	11 56 40	1♈53 59	8♈49 09	21 33.3	23 17.2	8 57.5	18 20.5	18 45.9	3 42.2	28 48.7	22 28.9	25 51.2	27 06.9	12 04.6	16 51.8
6 F	0 59 23	12 55 47	15 49 13	22 53 38	21 30.1	23 10.5	10 44.0	19 34.5	19 23.8	4 02.1	29 01.5	22 32.6	25 48.6	27 04.6	12 03.3	16 52.0
7 Sa	1 03 19	13 54 56	0♉01 46	7♉12 53	21 27.0	23 02.5	12 29.7	20 48.6	20 01.8	4 21.9	29 14.3	22 36.5	25 46.0	27 02.2	12 01.9	16 52.2
8 Su	1 07 16	14 54 07	14 26 11	21 40 53	21 23.8	22 54.1	14 14.8	22 02.7	20 39.7	4 41.5	29 27.1	22 40.4	25 43.5	26 59.9	12 00.6	16 52.5
9 M	1 11 12	15 53 20	28 56 10	6♊11 17	21 20.6	22 46.5	15 59.1	23 16.8	21 17.7	5 01.0	29 39.9	22 44.4	25 40.9	26 57.5	11 59.3	16 52.8
10 Tu	1 15 09	16 52 36	13♊25 33	20 38 20	21 17.4	22 40.4	17 42.7	24 31.0	21 55.6	5 20.4	29 52.8	22 48.5	25 38.4	26 55.1	11 58.0	16 53.1
11 W	1 19 05	17 51 53	27 49 10	4♋57 38	21 14.2	22 36.4	19 25.5	25 45.3	22 33.5	5 39.6	0♏05.7	22 52.7	25 36.0	26 52.7	11 56.7	16 53.5
12 Th	1 23 02	18 51 14	12♋03 28	19 06 27	21 11.1	22D 34.7	21 07.6	26 59.6	23 11.5	5 58.7	0 18.6	22 57.0	25 33.5	26 50.3	11 55.5	16 53.8
13 F	1 26 59	19 50 36	26 06 30	3♌03 33	21 07.9	22 34.6	22 49.0	28 14.0	23 49.4	6 17.6	0 31.6	23 01.3	25 31.1	26 47.9	11 54.3	16 54.3
14 Sa	1 30 55	20 50 01	9♌57 37	16 48 45	21 04.7	22R 35.4	24 29.6	29 28.4	24 27.4	6 36.4	0 44.6	23 05.7	25 28.6	26 45.4	11 53.1	16 54.7
15 Su	1 34 52	21 49 29	23 37 01	0♍22 28	21 01.5	22 35.8	26 09.5	0♎42.8	25 05.3	6 55.0	0 57.5	23 10.1	25 26.3	26 43.0	11 51.9	16 55.2
16 M	1 38 48	22 48 58	7♍05 09	13 45 06	20 58.4	22 34.8	27 48.8	1 57.3	25 43.2	7 13.4	1 10.5	23 14.7	25 23.9	26 40.5	11 50.7	16 55.7
17 Tu	1 42 45	23 48 30	20 22 20	26 56 49	20 55.2	22 31.5	29 27.3	3 11.8	26 21.2	7 31.7	1 23.6	23 19.3	25 21.6	26 38.1	11 49.6	16 56.2
18 W	1 46 41	24 48 04	3♎28 32	9♎57 25	20 52.0	22 25.5	1♏05.2	4 26.3	26 59.1	7 49.8	1 36.6	23 24.0	25 19.3	26 35.6	11 48.5	16 56.8
19 Th	1 50 38	25 47 40	16 23 24	22 46 25	20 48.8	22 16.8	2 42.4	5 40.9	27 37.0	8 07.8	1 49.6	23 28.7	25 17.0	26 33.2	11 47.4	16 57.3
20 F	1 54 34	26 47 18	29 06 25	5♏23 22	20 45.6	22 05.9	4 19.0	6 55.3	28 14.9	8 25.5	2 02.7	23 33.6	25 14.8	26 30.7	11 46.3	16 58.0
21 Sa	1 58 31	27 46 58	11♏37 15	17 48 06	20 42.5	21 53.7	5 55.0	8 10.2	28 52.9	8 43.1	2 15.7	23 38.5	25 12.6	26 28.3	11 45.3	16 58.6
22 Su	2 02 28	28 46 40	23 56 01	0♐01 06	20 39.3	21 41.3	7 30.4	9 24.9	29 30.8	9 00.5	2 28.8	23 43.4	25 10.4	26 25.8	11 44.3	16 59.3
23 M	2 06 24	29 46 24	6♐03 36	12 03 43	20 36.1	21 29.8	9 05.2	10 39.6	0♎08.7	9 17.7	2 41.9	23 48.5	25 08.2	26 23.4	11 43.3	17 00.0
24 Tu	2 10 21	0♏46 10	18 01 49	23 58 15	20 32.9	21 20.1	10 39.5	11 54.3	0 46.6	9 34.7	2 55.0	23 53.6	25 06.1	26 20.9	11 42.4	17 00.7
25 W	2 14 17	1 45 57	29 53 28	5♑47 57	20 29.8	21 12.9	12 13.1	13 09.1	1 24.5	9 51.5	3 08.1	23 58.7	25 04.1	26 18.5	11 41.4	17 01.5
26 Th	2 18 14	2 45 47	11♑42 16	17 36 59	20 26.6	21 08.4	13 46.3	14 23.9	2 02.4	10 08.2	3 21.2	24 04.0	25 02.1	26 16.1	11 40.6	17 02.3
27 F	2 22 10	3 45 38	23 32 45	29 30 12	20 23.4	21D 06.3	15 18.9	15 38.7	2 40.3	10 24.6	3 34.3	24 09.2	25 00.1	26 13.6	11 39.7	17 03.1
28 Sa	2 26 07	4 45 30	5♒30 00	11♒32 53	20 20.2	21 05.8	16 51.0	16 53.6	3 18.2	10 40.8	3 47.4	24 14.6	24 58.1	26 11.2	11 38.8	17 04.0
29 Su	2 30 03	5 45 25	17 39 30	23 50 32	20 17.1	21R 06.0	18 22.6	18 08.5	3 56.0	10 56.8	4 00.5	24 20.0	24 56.2	26 08.8	11 38.0	17 04.9
30 M	2 34 00	6 45 21	0♓06 36	6♓28 19	20 13.9	21 05.8	19 53.6	19 23.4	4 33.9	11 12.6	4 13.6	24 25.5	24 54.3	26 06.4	11 37.2	17 05.8
31 Tu	2 37 57	7♏45 18	12 56 11	19 30 37	20♌10.7	21♌04.0	21♏24.2	20♎38.3	5♎11.8	11♌28.2	4♏26.7	24♐31.0	24♓52.5	26♈04.0	11♓36.5	17♑06.7

1st of Mont[h]

Julian Day 2458027.5
Obliquity 23°26'06"
SVP 5♓00'5
GC 27♐05.
Eris 23♈27.

Day	⚴
1	12♉49.4
6	11 57.2
11	10 53.1
16	9 38.1
21	8 13.5
26	6 41.6
31	5 05.2

Day	⚵
1	6♑13.0
6	7 12.5
11	8 18.1
16	9 29.4
21	10 46.1
26	12 07.9
31	13 34.3

Day	⚶
1	6♎23.2
6	8 55.3
11	11 28.0
16	14 01.0
21	16 34.5
26	19 08.1
31	21 42.0

DECLINATION and LATITUDE

Day	☉ Decl	☽ Decl	☽ Lat	☽ 12h Decl	☿ Decl	☿ Lat	♀ Decl	♀ Lat	♂ Decl	♂ Lat	⚳ Decl	⚳ Lat	♃ Decl	♃ Lat	♄ Decl	♄ Lat
1 Su	3S11	16S37	1N13	15S23	0N52	1N43	7N41	1N16	6N31	1N10	23N07	3N34	9S47	1N02	22S08	1N04
2 M	3 34	13 58	0 06	12 22	0 06	1 40	7 14	1 18	6 16	1 10	23 05	3 38	9 51	1 02	22 09	1 04
3 Tu	3 57	10 36	1S03	8 40	0S40	1 36	6 47	1 19	6 01	1 10	23 03	3 41	9 56	1 02	22 09	1 04
4 W	4 20	6 37	2 10	4 26	1 27	1 32	6 20	1 20	5 46	1 10	23 02	3 44	10 00	1 02	22 10	1 04
5 Th	4 43	2 11	3 12	0N08	2 13	1 27	5 52	1 22	5 31	1 10	22 60	3 47	10 05	1 02	22 10	1 03
6 F	5 06	2N28	4 04	4 48	2 59	1 22	5 24	1 23	5 16	1 10	22 58	3 50	10 10	1 02	22 10	1 03
7 Sa	5 29	7 05	4 42	9 16	3 45	1 17	4 56	1 24	5 01	1 10	22 57	3 54	10 14	1 02	22 11	1 03
8 Su	5 52	11 21	5 03	13 15	4 31	1 11	4 28	1 25	4 46	1 10	22 55	3 57	10 19	1 02	22 11	1 03
9 M	6 15	14 58	5 04	16 27	5 17	1 06	3 59	1 26	4 31	1 10	22 53	4 00	10 23	1 02	22 11	1 03
10 Tu	6 38	17 40	4 46	18 36	6 02	0 60	3 31	1 27	4 16	1 10	22 52	4 04	10 28	1 02	22 12	1 03
11 W	7 00	19 15	4 11	19 34	6 46	0 54	3 02	1 28	4 01	1 10	22 50	4 07	10 32	1 02	22 12	1 02
12 Th	7 23	19 35	3 19	19 17	7 30	0 47	2 33	1 29	3 46	1 10	22 49	4 10	10 37	1 02	22 13	1 02
13 F	7 46	18 41	2 17	17 48	8 14	0 41	2 04	1 29	3 31	1 10	22 48	4 14	10 42	1 02	22 13	1 02
14 Sa	8 08	16 40	1 07	15 18	8 57	0 35	1 35	1 30	3 16	1 10	22 46	4 17	10 46	1 01	22 13	1 02
15 Su	8 30	13 44	0N05	11 59	9 40	0 28	1 06	1 31	3 01	1 10	22 45	4 21	10 51	1 01	22 14	1 02
16 M	8 52	10 06	1 17	8 05	10 22	0 21	0 37	1 31	2 46	1 10	22 43	4 25	10 55	1 01	22 14	1 02
17 Tu	9 14	5 60	2 23	3 51	11 03	0 15	0 08	1 31	2 31	1 10	22 42	4 28	10 60	1 01	22 15	1 02
18 W	9 36	1 40	3 20	0S30	11 44	0 08	0S22	1 32	2 16	1 10	22 41	4 32	11 04	1 01	22 15	1 01
19 Th	9 58	2S40	4 06	4 46	12 24	0 01	0 51	1 32	2 01	1 09	22 40	4 35	11 09	1 01	22 15	1 01
20 F	10 20	6 49	4 39	8 45	13 03	0S06	1 20	1 32	1 45	1 09	22 38	4 39	11 13	1 01	22 16	1 01
21 Sa	10 41	10 36	4 57	12 18	13 41	0 13	1 49	1 32	1 30	1 09	22 37	4 43	11 18	1 01	22 16	1 01
22 Su	11 02	13 52	5 02	15 17	14 19	0 19	2 19	1 33	1 15	1 09	22 36	4 47	11 23	1 01	22 16	1 01
23 M	11 23	16 31	4 53	17 33	14 56	0 26	2 48	1 33	0 60	1 09	22 35	4 50	11 27	1 01	22 17	1 01
24 Tu	11 44	18 24	4 30	19 03	15 32	0 33	3 17	1 32	0 45	1 09	22 34	4 54	11 32	1 01	22 17	1 01
25 W	12 05	19 29	3 57	19 43	16 08	0 40	3 46	1 32	0 30	1 09	22 34	4 58	11 36	1 01	22 18	1 00
26 Th	12 26	19 43	3 13	19 30	16 43	0 46	4 16	1 32	0 15	1 09	22 33	5 02	11 40	1 01	22 18	1 00
27 F	12 46	19 04	2 21	18 25	17 16	0 53	4 45	1 32	0S01	1 09	22 32	5 06	11 45	1 01	22 18	1 00
28 Sa	13 06	17 34	1 22	16 30	17 49	0 60	5 14	1 31	0 16	1 09	22 31	5 10	11 49	1 01	22 19	0 60
29 Su	13 26	15 15	0 18	13 48	18 21	1 06	5 43	1 31	0 31	1 09	22 31	5 14	11 54	1 01	22 19	0 60
30 M	13 46	12 10	0S48	10 23	18 52	1 12	6 11	1 30	0 46	1 08	22 30	5 18	11 58	1 01	22 19	0 60
31 Tu	14S06	8S26	1S53	6S22	19S22	1S19	6S40	1N30	1S01	1N08	22N30	5N22	12S03	1N01	22S20	0N60

Day	⚷ Decl	⚷ Lat	♅ Decl	♅ Lat	♆ Decl	♆ Lat	♇ Decl	♇ Lat
1	2N05	3N59	9N56	0S36	7S52	0S56	21S46	0N
6	1 59	3 59	9 52	0 36	7 54	0 56	21 46	0
11	1 53	3 58	9 48	0 36	7 57	0 56	21 47	0
16	1 48	3 57	9 44	0 36	7 59	0 56	21 47	0
21	1 43	3 56	9 39	0 36	8 01	0 56	21 47	0
26	1 38	3 55	9 35	0 36	8 03	0 56	21 47	0
31	1N33	3N54	9N30	0S36	8S04	0S56	21S47	0N

Day	⚴ Decl	⚴ Lat	⚵ Decl	⚵ Lat	⚶ Decl	⚶ Lat	Eris Decl	Eris Lat
1	15S39	32S48	12S15	11N03	1N58	4N54	2S20	12S
6	17 14	34 14	12 37	10 38	0 60	4 56	2 21	12
11	18 48	35 36	12 56	10 15	0 01	4 57	2 22	12
16	20 20	36 52	13 14	9 53	0S57	4 58	2 23	12
21	21 47	38 01	13 30	9 31	1 54	4 59	2 24	12
26	23 08	39 01	13 44	9 11	2 51	5 01	2 25	12
31	24S22	39S52	13S56	8N51	3S47	5N02	2S26	12S

Moon Phenomena

Max/0 Decl

dy	hr mn	
5	11:19	0 N
11	18:31	19N37
18	9:13	0 S
25	18:17	19S44

Perigee/Apogee

dy	hr m		kilometers
9	5:52	p	366856
25	2:20	a	405154

Max/0 Lat

dy	hr mn	
2	2:06	0 S
8	13:56	5S06
14	22:12	0 N
21	19:44	5N02
29	6:42	0 S

PH	dy	hr mn	
○	5	18:41	12♈43
☾	12	12:27	19♋22
●	19	19:13	26♎35
☽	27	22:23	4♒41

Void of Course Moon

Last Aspect			☽ Ingres[s]	
2 11:14	♃	△	♓	2 14:
4 7:20	♄	□	♈	4 20:
6 22:39	♃	☍	♉	6 23:
8 13:46	♀	△	♊	9 1:
10 22:26	♅	✱	♋	11 3:
13 4:01	♀	✱	♌	13 6:
15 5:29	♅	△	♍	15 11:
17 11:28	♂	☌	♎	17 17:
19 19:13	☉	☌	♏	20 1:
22 11:36	♂	✱	♐	22 11:
24 16:46	♅	△	♑	25 0:
27 5:24	♅	□	♒	27 13:
29 16:23	♅	✱	♓	29 23:

DAILY ASPECTARIAN

1 Su ☽∠⚷ 2:18 · ☽⚺♆ 4:31 · ☽⚻♀ 7:42 · ☿✱⚳ 9:37 · ☽⚻♂ 13:02 · ☽⚺♇ 13:34 · ☽⚼☿ 15:39 · ♂△♇ 23:38 · ☽✱♄ 23:57

2 M ☉⚼☽ 3:26 · ☽⚺⚷ 6:54 · ☽✱♅ 9:15 · ☽△♃ 11:14 · ☽∠♇ 17:55 · ♃⋕♅ 19:03 · ☽⚻⚳ 20:00

3 Tu ☽⚻☿ 0:31 · ☽∥♃ 4:11 · ☽⋕♅ 4:24 · ☉⚻☽ 9:36 · ☽☌♆ 12:46 · ☽∠♅ 12:53 · ☽⚼♃ 15:20 · ☽∥♆ 16:39 · ♀△♇ 19:10 · ☽✱♇ 21:22 · ☽☍♀ 21:35 · ☽☍♂ 23:38

4 W ☽⚼⚳ 0:04 · ☽⋕♀ 1:49 · ☽⋕♂ 5:00 · ☽□♄ 7:20 · ☉∥☽ 11:33 · ☽☌⚷ 13:25 · ☽⚺♅ 15:38 · ☿⋕⚷ 17:30 · ☽⚻♃ 18:31 · ♂∠⚳ 19:03 · ☽∥☿ 23:50

5 Th ☽⋕⚷ 0:56 · ☉⚻♆ 3:10 · ☽△⚳ 3:13 · ♀∠⚳ 9:38 · ☽☍☿ 14:02 · ♀☌♂ 16:54 · ☽⚺♆ 17:34 · ☉☍☽ 18:41 · ☽∥⚷ 21:31

6 F ☽□♇ 1:47 · ☽⋕☿ 3:12 · ☉⋕♂ 6:21 · ☽⚻♂ 6:22 · ☽⚻♀ 7:00 · ☉⋕♀ 8:15 · ☽△♄ 11:28 · ♀∥♂ 13:43 · ☽∥♀ 13:44 · ☽∥♂ 13:44 · ☉⋕☽ 14:51 · ☽⚺⚷ 16:52 · ☿⚻♆ 17:45 · ☽∠♆ 18:59 · ☽☌♅ 19:00 · ☽☍♃ 22:39

7 Sa ☽⋕♆ 4:32 · ♅∠♆ 7:15 · ☽□⚳ 7:25 · ☽⚼♂ 8:45 · ☽⚼♀ 10:34 · ☽⚼♄ 12:43 · ☽∥♅ 15:15 · ☽⋕♃ 17:49 · ☽∠⚷ 17:51 · ☽✱♆ 19:59 · ☿⋕♀ 22:49 · ☽⚻☿ 23:38

8 Su ☉⚻☽ 0:50 · ☽△♇ 4:03 · ☿⋕♂ 6:03 · ☽△♂ 10:47 · ♀□♄ 12:55 · ☽⚻♄ 13:42 · ☽△♀ 13:46 · ☽✱⚷ 18:38 · ☽⚺♅ 20:44 · ☉☌☿ 20:55

9 M ☽⚻♃ 1:13 · ☉⚼☽ 3:28 · ☽⚼☿ 3:51 · ☽⚼♇ 4:52 · ☽✱⚳ 10:17 · ☿□♇ 12:28 · ☽∠♅ 21:30 · ☽□♆ 21:35

10 Tu ☉□♇ 0:13 · ☽⚼♃ 2:27 · ☽⚻♇ 5:45 · ☉△☽ 6:09 · ☽△☿ 8:05 · ☽∠⚳ 11:46 · ♃ ♏ 13:21 · ☽□♂ 14:48 · ☽☍♄ 15:42 · ☽□♀ 20:13 · ☽□⚷ 20:18 · ♀☍⚷ 21:05 · ☽✱♅ 22:26

11 W ☽△♃ 3:53 · ☽⚺⚳ 13:29 · ♂□♄ 13:38 · ☉∥☿ 15:41 · ♀⚻♅ 21:05 · ☽△♆ 23:47

12 Th ☽☍♇ 8:14 · ☉□☽ 12:27 · ☿∥♆ 14:53 · ☽□☿ 17:34 · ☽⚻♄ 18:40 · ☽✱♂ 19:53 · ☽△⚷ 22:59

13 F ☽□♅ 1:11 · ☽⚼♆ 1:22 · ☿✱♄ 3:04 · ☽✱♀ 4:01 · ☽□♃ 7:44 · ♀∥⚷ 11:11 · ☉∥♆ 13:26 · ☽☌⚳ 18:01 · ☽⚼♄ 20:44 · ☽∠♂ 23:05 · ☿⚺♂ 23:08

14 Sa ☽⚼⚷ 0:54 · ☽⚻♆ 3:21 · ☽∠♀ 8:41 · ♀ ♎ 10:12 · ☽⚻♇ 12:11 · ☿⚻⚷ 13:50 · ☉✱☽ 20:35 · ☽△♄ 23:12

15 Su ☿⋕♅ 2:34 · ☽⚺♂ 2:44 · ☽⚻⚷ 3:13 · ☽✱☿ 5:08 · ☽△♅ 5:29 · ♀⚺♃ 5:46 · ☿☍♅ 7:53 · ☿⚼♆ 10:06 · ♂☍⚷ 12:29 · ☽✱♃ 13:15 · ☽⚺♀ 13:53 · ☽⚼♇ 14:46 · ☽⋕♃ 18:57 · ☽⋕☿ 22:36

16 M ☽⚺⚳ 0:15 · ☉∠☽ 1:25 · ☽∥♅ 2:16 · ☉⋕☽ 6:46 · ☽⚼♅ 8:14 · ☽☍♆ 8:33 · ☉✱♄ 11:14 · ☽∠☿ 11:46 · ☽⋕♆ 12:35 · ☽∠♃ 16:39 · ☽△♇ 17:45 · ☿∥♃ 21:54

17 Tu ☽∠⚳ 4:01 · ☽□♄ 5:24 · ☉⚺☽ 6:46 · ☿ ♏ 8:00 · ☽☍⚷ 9:04 · ♂⚻♅ 10:04 · ☽⚻♅ 11:24 · ☽☌♂ 11:28 · ☽⚺☿ 18:58 · ☽⚺♃ 20:30 · ☽∥♂ 20:34 · ☽∥⚷ 23:31

18 W ☽☌♀ 1:58 · ☉⋕♅ 5:54 · ☽⋕♀ 6:31 · ☽✱⚳ 8:15 · ☿☌♃ 8:55 · ☉⚻⚷ 12:06 · ☽∥♀ 12:37 · ☽⚻♆ 15:25 · ☽⋕⚷ 18:54 · ☽⋕♂ 20:34

19 Th ☽□♇ 1:04 · ☽✱♄ 13:25 · ☽⚻⚷ 16:42 · ☉☍♅ 17:36 · ☽☍♅ 19:05 · ☉☌☽ 19:13 · ☽⚼♆ 19:34 · ☽⚺♂ 22:17 · ☉⚼♆ 23:37

20 F ♂∥⚷ 3:07 · ☽☌♃ 5:42 · ☽∥♆ 7:21 · ☽☌☿ 11:24 · ♀⋕♂ 13:41 · ⚳⚼♄ 15:11 · ☽⚺♀ 16:36 · ☽⋕♅ 17:46 · ☽∠♄ 18:13 · ☽□⚳ 18:16 · ♀⋕⚷ 18:35 · ☽⚼⚷ 21:17

21 Sa ☽△♆ 0:16 · ☉∥☽ 0:39 · ☽∠♂ 4:37 · ☽∥♃ 4:56 · ☽✱♇ 10:24 · ♀✱⚳ 13:48 · ☽⚺♄ 23:35

22 Su ☽∠♀ 1:03 · ☽△⚷ 2:26 · ☽∥☿ 4:42 · ☽⚻♅ 4:54 · ☉⚺☽ 10:24 · ☽✱♂ 11:36 · ☽∠♇ 15:55 · ☽⚺♃ 17:11 · ♂ ♎ 18:30 · ☿∠♄ 19:30

23 M ☿□⚳ 3:52 · ☉∥♃ 5:16 · ☉ ♏ 5:28 · ☽△⚳ 6:37 · ☽⚺☿ 6:57 · ☽✱♀ 10:15 · ☽⚼♅ 10:37 · ☽□♆ 11:18 · ☿⚼⚷ 15:41 · ☉∠☽ 19:02 · ♀⚻♆ 20:13 · ☽⚺♇ 21:57 · ☽∠♃ 23:46

24 Tu ☉⚺♂ 0:28 · ☽☌♄ 11:56 · ☽⚼⚳ 13:33 · ☽□⚷ 14:15 · ☿△♆ 15:57 · ☽△♅ 16:46 · ☽∠☿ 17:46

25 W ☽□♂ 3:15 · ☉✱☽ 4:09 · ☽✱♃ 6:43 · ⚳⚼⚷ 16:07 · ☽⚻⚳ 20:44 · ☽✱♆ 23:57

26 Th ☽✱☿ 4:50 · ☽□♀ 6:07 · ☽☌♇ 10:50 · ☉☌♃ 18:11

27 F ☽⚺♄ 1:14 · ☽✱⚷ 2:56 · ☽□♅ 5:24 · ☽∠♆ 6:17 · ☽△♂ 19:22 · ☽□♃ 20:31 · ☽∥☿ 21:31 · ☉□☽ 22:23

28 Sa ♀□♇ 3:22 · ☿✱♇ 3:26 · ☿⚺♀ 3:43 · ☽∠♄ 7:30 · ☽∠⚷ 8:51 · ☽☍⚳ 10:31 · ☽⚺♆ 12:11 · ☽⚺♇ 22:52

29 Su ☽△♀ 1:03 · ☽□☿ 1:36 · ☽⚼♂ 2:37 · ♂⚺♃ 4:18 · ☽✱♄ 13:02 · ☉∥☽ 13:22 · ☽⚺⚷ 14:04 · ☿∠♂ 15:05 · ☽✱♅ 16:23

30 M ☽∥♃ 1:23 · ☽∠♇ 3:46 · ☽△♃ 7:55 · ☽⚻♂ 8:52 · ☽⚼♀ 8:58 · ☉△☽ 13:35 · ☽⋕♅ 17:29 · ☽∠♅ 20:34 · ☽⚻⚳ 21:14 · ☽☌♆ 21:33

31 Tu ☽∥♆ 2:11 · ☽✱♇ 7:39 · ☽∥♀ 9:14 · ☽⚼♃ 12:05 · ⚳⚻♆ 12:23 · ☽⚻♀ 15:29 · ☽△☿ 17:22 · ☉⚼☽ 19:17 · ☽□♄ 21:09 · ☽☌⚷ 21:36 · ☽⚺♅ 23:42

November 2017

LONGITUDE

Day	Sid.Time	☉	☽	☽ 12 hour	Mean☊	True☊	☿	♀	♂	⚳	♃	♄	⚷	♅	♆	♇
	h m s	° ' "	° ' "	° ' "	° '	° '	° '	° '	° '	° '	° '	° '	° '	° '	° '	° '
1 W	2 41 53	8♏45 18	26♓11 54	3♈00 13	20♌07.5	20♌59.8	22♏54.3	21♎53.3	5♎49.7	11♌43.5	4♏39.8	24♐36.6	24♓50.7	26♈01.6	11♓35.8	17♑07.7
2 Th	2 45 50	9 45 18	9♈55 32	16 57 39	20 04.3	20R 53.0	24 23.8	23 08.3	6 27.5	11 58.7	4 52.8	24 42.2	24R 49.0	25R 59.3	11R 35.1	17 08.7
3 F	2 49 46	10 45 21	24 06 10	1♉20 29	20 01.2	20 43.6	25 52.9	24 23.3	7 05.4	12 13.6	5 05.9	24 47.9	24 47.3	25 56.9	11 34.4	17 09.7
4 Sa	2 53 43	11 45 25	8♉39 49	16 03 14	19 58.0	20 32.4	27 21.5	25 38.3	7 43.2	12 28.2	5 19.0	24 53.7	24 45.6	25 54.6	11 33.8	17 10.7
5 Su	2 57 39	12 45 32	23 29 38	0♊57 51	19 54.8	20 20.6	28 49.5	26 53.3	8 21.1	12 42.7	5 32.0	24 59.5	24 44.0	25 52.3	11 33.2	17 11.8
6 M	3 01 36	13 45 40	8♊26 42	15 55 00	19 51.6	20 09.6	0♐17.0	28 08.4	8 58.9	12 56.9	5 45.1	25 05.3	24 42.5	25 50.0	11 32.6	17 12.9
7 Tu	3 05 32	14 45 50	23 21 41	0♋45 45	19 48.4	20 00.5	1 43.9	29 23.5	9 36.8	13 10.8	5 58.1	25 11.2	24 40.9	25 47.7	11 32.1	17 14.0
8 W	3 09 29	15 46 02	8♋06 23	15 22 58	19 45.3	19 54.1	3 10.2	0♏38.6	10 14.7	13 24.5	6 11.2	25 17.2	24 39.5	25 45.4	11 31.6	17 15.2
9 Th	3 13 26	16 46 16	22 34 59	29 42 10	19 42.1	19 50.4	4 36.0	1 53.8	10 52.5	13 38.0	6 24.2	25 23.2	24 38.0	25 43.2	11 31.1	17 16.3
10 F	3 17 22	17 46 32	6♌44 21	13♌41 32	19 38.9	19 49.1	6 01.0	3 08.9	11 30.4	13 51.2	6 37.2	25 29.3	24 36.7	25 41.0	11 30.7	17 17.6
11 Sa	3 21 19	18 46 51	20 33 48	27 21 21	19 35.7	19 48.9	7 25.3	4 24.1	12 08.2	14 04.1	6 50.1	25 35.4	24 35.3	25 38.8	11 30.2	17 18.8
12 Su	3 25 15	19 47 11	4♍04 25	10♍43 17	19 32.6	19 48.6	8 48.8	5 39.3	12 46.0	14 16.8	7 03.1	25 41.5	24 34.0	25 36.6	11 29.9	17 20.0
13 M	3 29 12	20 47 33	17 18 13	23 49 31	19 29.4	19 46.9	10 11.5	6 54.6	13 23.9	14 29.2	7 16.1	25 47.7	24 32.8	25 34.4	11 29.5	17 21.3
14 Tu	3 33 08	21 47 57	0♎17 27	6♎42 16	19 26.2	19 42.7	11 33.3	8 09.8	14 01.7	14 41.3	7 29.0	25 53.9	24 31.6	25 32.3	11 29.2	17 22.6
15 W	3 37 05	22 48 23	13 04 11	19 23 23	19 23.0	19 35.4	12 53.9	9 25.1	14 39.6	14 53.1	7 41.9	26 00.2	24 30.5	25 30.2	11 28.9	17 23.9
16 Th	3 41 01	23 48 50	25 39 59	1♏54 09	19 19.9	19 25.1	14 13.4	10 40.3	15 17.4	15 04.6	7 54.8	26 06.6	24 29.4	25 28.1	11 28.7	17 25.3
17 F	3 44 58	24 49 20	8♏05 56	14 15 26	19 16.7	19 12.3	15 31.7	11 55.6	15 55.2	15 15.8	8 07.6	26 12.9	24 28.4	25 26.0	11 28.5	17 26.7
18 Sa	3 48 54	25 49 51	20 22 44	26 27 52	19 13.5	18 58.0	16 48.4	13 11.0	16 33.0	15 26.8	8 20.4	26 19.3	24 27.4	25 24.0	11 28.3	17 28.1
19 Su	3 52 51	26 50 24	2♐30 58	8♐32 05	19 10.3	18 43.3	18 03.5	14 26.3	17 10.9	15 37.4	8 33.2	26 25.8	24 26.5	25 22.0	11 28.2	17 29.5
20 M	3 56 48	27 50 58	14 31 24	20 29 04	19 07.1	18 29.5	19 16.7	15 41.6	17 48.7	15 47.7	8 46.0	26 32.3	24 25.6	25 20.1	11 28.0	17 30.9
21 Tu	4 00 44	28 51 34	26 25 17	2♑20 20	19 04.0	18 17.7	20 27.7	16 57.0	18 26.5	15 57.7	8 58.7	26 38.8	24 24.8	25 18.1	11 28.0	17 32.4
22 W	4 04 41	29 52 11	8♑14 32	14 08 14	19 00.8	18 08.6	21 36.4	18 12.3	19 04.3	16 07.4	9 11.5	26 45.3	24 24.0	25 16.2	11D 27.9	17 33.9
23 Th	4 08 37	0♐52 49	20 01 52	25 55 54	18 57.6	18 02.5	22 42.3	19 27.7	19 42.1	16 16.7	9 24.1	26 51.9	24 23.3	25 14.4	11 27.9	17 35.4
24 F	4 12 34	1 53 29	1♒50 52	7♒47 20	18 54.4	17 59.3	23 45.0	20 43.1	20 19.9	16 25.8	9 36.8	26 58.5	24 22.6	25 12.5	11 28.0	17 36.9
25 Sa	4 16 30	2 54 09	13 45 54	19 47 14	18 51.3	17D 58.1	24 44.2	21 58.5	20 57.6	16 34.4	9 49.4	27 05.2	24 22.0	25 10.7	11 28.0	17 38.5
26 Su	4 20 27	3 54 51	25 52 00	2♓00 51	18 48.1	17R 58.2	25 39.4	23 13.9	21 35.4	16 42.8	10 01.9	27 11.9	24 21.5	25 09.0	11 28.1	17 40.0
27 M	4 24 24	4 55 34	8♓14 30	14 33 35	18 44.9	17 58.3	26 29.9	24 29.3	22 13.2	16 50.8	10 14.4	27 18.6	24 21.0	25 07.2	11 28.3	17 41.6
28 Tu	4 28 20	5 56 18	20 58 44	27 30 30	18 41.7	17 57.3	27 15.2	25 44.7	22 50.9	16 58.4	10 26.9	27 25.3	24 20.5	25 05.5	11 28.4	17 43.2
29 W	4 32 17	6 57 02	4♈09 23	10♈55 41	18 38.6	17 54.2	27 54.6	27 00.1	23 28.7	17 05.7	10 39.3	27 32.1	24 20.1	25 03.9	11 28.6	17 44.9
30 Th	4 36 13	7♐57 48	17 49 38	24 51 15	18♌35.4	17♌48.7	28♐27.3	28♏15.5	24♎06.4	17♌12.7	10♏51.7	27♐38.9	24♓19.8	25♈02.3	11♓28.9	17♑46.5

1st of Month

Julian Day # 2458058.5
Obliquity 23°26'06"
SVP 5♓00'51"
GC 27♐05.3
Eris 23♈09.5R

Day	⚴
1	4♉45.6R
6	3 07.8R
11	1 32.2R
16	0 02.1R
21	28♈40.5R
26	27 29.9R

Day	⚵
1	13♑52.2
6	15 23.8
11	16 59.4
16	18 38.8
21	20 21.7
26	22 07.9

Day	⚶
1	22♎12.7
6	24 46.7
11	27 20.6
16	29 54.5
21	2♏28.2
26	5 01.7

DECLINATION and LATITUDE

Day	☉ Decl	☽ Decl	☽ Lat	☽12h Decl	☿ Decl	☿ Lat	♀ Decl	♀ Lat	♂ Decl	♂ Lat	⚳ Decl	⚳ Lat	♃ Decl	♃ Lat	♄ Decl	♄ Lat
1 W	14S25	4S11	2S54	1S54	19S52	1S25	7S09	1N29	1S16	1N08	22N29	5N27	12S07	1N01	22S20	0N59
2 Th	14 44	0N26	3 48	2N48	20 20	1 31	7 37	1 29	1 31	1 08	22 29	5 31	12 12	1 01	22 21	0 59
3 F	15 03	5 10	4 29	7 30	20 47	1 36	8 05	1 28	1 46	1 08	22 29	5 35	12 16	1 01	22 21	0 59
4 Sa	15 22	9 44	4 54	11 51	21 18	1 42	8 33	1 27	2 01	1 08	22 29	5 39	12 20	1 01	22 21	0 59
5 Su	15 40	13 48	4 60	15 32	21 38	1 47	9 01	1 26	2 16	1 08	22 29	5 44	12 25	1 01	22 22	0 59
6 M	15 58	17 01	4 45	18 12	22 02	1 53	9 29	1 25	2 31	1 08	22 29	5 48	12 29	1 01	22 22	0 59
7 Tu	16 16	19 05	4 12	19 38	22 25	1 58	9 57	1 24	2 46	1 07	22 29	5 53	12 33	1 01	22 22	0 59
8 W	16 33	19 50	3 21	19 43	22 47	2 02	10 24	1 23	3 01	1 07	22 29	5 57	12 38	1 01	22 23	0 59
9 Th	16 51	19 16	2 19	18 31	23 08	2 07	10 51	1 22	3 16	1 07	22 30	6 02	12 42	1 01	22 23	0 58
10 F	17 08	17 29	1 09	16 12	23 28	2 11	11 18	1 21	3 31	1 07	22 30	6 06	12 46	1 01	22 23	0 58
11 Sa	17 24	14 42	0N04	13 01	23 46	2 15	11 44	1 20	3 46	1 07	22 31	6 11	12 50	1 01	22 24	0 58
12 Su	17 41	11 10	1 15	9 13	24 03	2 19	12 10	1 18	4 01	1 07	22 31	6 15	12 55	1 01	22 24	0 58
13 M	17 57	7 10	2 18	5 02	24 19	2 22	12 36	1 17	4 16	1 07	22 32	6 20	12 59	1 01	22 24	0 58
14 Tu	18 13	2 53	3 16	0 43	24 34	2 25	13 02	1 15	4 31	1 06	22 33	6 25	13 03	1 01	22 25	0 58
15 W	18 28	1S27	4 02	3S34	24 47	2 28	13 27	1 14	4 45	1 06	22 34	6 30	13 07	1 01	22 25	0 58
16 Th	18 43	5 39	4 35	7 39	24 59	2 30	13 52	1 12	5 00	1 06	22 35	6 35	13 11	1 01	22 25	0 58
17 F	18 58	9 34	4 54	11 21	25 10	2 32	14 17	1 11	5 15	1 06	22 36	6 39	13 15	1 01	22 25	0 57
18 Sa	19 13	13 01	4 60	14 32	25 19	2 33	14 42	1 09	5 30	1 06	22 38	6 44	13 20	1 01	22 26	0 57
19 Su	19 27	15 54	4 51	17 05	25 27	2 34	15 05	1 08	5 44	1 06	22 39	6 49	13 24	1 01	22 26	0 57
20 M	19 41	18 04	4 30	18 51	25 34	2 34	15 29	1 06	5 59	1 05	22 41	6 54	13 28	1 01	22 26	0 57
21 Tu	19 54	19 26	3 57	19 48	25 39	2 34	15 52	1 04	6 13	1 05	22 43	6 60	13 32	1 01	22 27	0 57
22 W	20 07	19 57	3 14	19 53	25 43	2 33	16 15	1 02	6 28	1 05	22 45	7 05	13 36	1 01	22 27	0 57
23 Th	20 20	19 36	2 22	19 05	25 45	2 31	16 37	1 00	6 42	1 05	22 47	7 10	13 40	1 01	22 27	0 57
24 F	20 32	18 22	1 24	17 27	25 46	2 29	16 59	0 59	6 57	1 05	22 49	7 15	13 44	1 01	22 27	0 57
25 Sa	20 44	16 20	0 22	15 02	25 45	2 25	17 21	0 57	7 11	1 04	22 51	7 20	13 48	1 01	22 28	0 57
26 Su	20 56	13 33	0S42	11 54	25 43	2 21	17 42	0 55	7 25	1 04	22 53	7 26	13 52	1 01	22 28	0 57
27 M	21 07	10 07	1 46	8 10	25 39	2 16	18 02	0 53	7 40	1 04	22 56	7 31	13 55	1 01	22 28	0 56
28 Tu	21 18	6 07	2 46	3 57	25 34	2 10	18 22	0 51	7 54	1 04	22 59	7 36	13 59	1 01	22 28	0 56
29 W	21 28	1 42	3 40	0N36	25 27	2 02	18 42	0 49	8 08	1 04	23 02	7 42	14 03	1 01	22 29	0 56
30 Th	21S38	2N57	4S23	5N17	25S19	1S54	19S01	0N46	8S22	1N03	23N05	7N47	14S07	1N01	22S29	0N56

Day	⚷ Decl	⚷ Lat	♅ Decl	♅ Lat	♆ Decl	♆ Lat	♇ Decl	♇ Lat
1	1N32	3N54	9N30	0S36	8S05	0S56	21S47	0N33
6	1 28	3 53	9 25	0 36	8 06	0 56	21 47	0 33
11	1 24	3 52	9 21	0 36	8 07	0 56	21 47	0 32
16	1 20	3 50	9 18	0 36	8 07	0 56	21 47	0 32
21	1 17	3 49	9 14	0 35	8 07	0 56	21 46	0 31
26	1 15	3 48	9 11	0 35	8 07	0 56	21 46	0 31

Day	⚴ Decl	⚴ Lat	⚵ Decl	⚵ Lat	⚶ Decl	⚶ Lat	Eris Decl	Eris Lat
1	24S36	40S00	13S58	8N47	3S58	5N03	2S26	12S17
6	25 38	40 39	14 08	8 28	4 53	5 04	2 27	12 17
11	26 31	41 06	14 15	8 10	5 46	5 06	2 27	12 16
16	27 13	41 23	14 20	7 53	6 38	5 07	2 28	12 16
21	27 43	41 31	14 22	7 36	7 29	5 09	2 28	12 15
26	28 03	41 29	14 23	7 20	8 19	5 10	2 28	12 15

Moon Phenomena

Max/0 Decl dy hr mn	
1 21:46	0 N
8 1:18	19N51
14 15:58	0 S
22 2:03	19S57
29 8:54	0 N

Perigee/Apogee dy hr m	kilometers
6 0:11 p	361438
21 18:55 a	406131

PH	dy hr mn	
○	4 5:24	11♉59
☾	10 20:38	18♌38
●	18 11:43	26♏19
☽	26 17:04	4♓38

Max/0 Lat dy hr mn	
4 19:08	5S00
10 22:42	0 N
17 21:22	5N00
25 8:23	0 S

Void of Course Moon

Last Aspect			☽ Ingress		
31 21:09	♄	□	♈	1	6:44
3 3:04	♅	☌	♉	3	9:47
5 9:30	☿	☍	♊	5	10:27
7 10:41	♀	△	♋	7	10:46
9 5:15	♅	□	♌	9	12:30
11 8:57	♅	△	♍	11	16:42
13 15:46	♄	□	♎	13	23:27
16 0:51	♄	⚹	♏	16	8:20
18 11:43	☉	☌	♐	18	19:00
21 0:28	♄	☌	♑	21	7:15
23 10:34	♅	□	♒	23	20:15
26 2:38	♄	⚹	♓	26	8:05
28 12:10	☿	□	♈	28	16:31
30 18:38	☿	△	♉	30	20:39

DAILY ASPECTARIAN

1 W
☽Q⚳ 0:57
☽#⚷ 13:57
☽‖♂ 14:28
☽⊼♃ 15:08
☽☍♂ 17:44
☉∠♄ 22:38
☽Q☿ 22:59
♂#⚷ 23:33
☉⊼☽ 23:41

2 Th
☉Q⚷ 1:26
☽⊻♆ 2:51
☽△⚳ 3:35
☿⊻♄ 5:17
☽‖⚷ 5:27
☽#♂ 5:48
☿△⚷ 6:38
☽□♇ 12:19
♄□⚷ 21:56
♀‖♆ 23:45

3 F
☽☍♀ 0:31
☿⊼♅ 1:04
☽⊻⚷ 1:08
☽△♄ 1:10
☽☌♅ 3:04
☽⊼☿ 3:18
☽∠♆ 4:07
♀⊼⚷ 7:31
♀⚹♄ 8:33
☽#♆ 15:06
☽#♀ 16:52
☽☍♃ 18:27
☉△♆ 19:24
☽⊼♂ 22:24
☽‖♅ 22:26

4 Sa
☽∠⚷ 1:47
☽Q♄ 2:01
☽⚹♆ 4:43
♀☍♅ 5:04
☉☍☽ 5:24
☽□⚳ 6:18
☽△♇ 13:50
☽#♃ 15:09
♀Q♆ 17:36
☉□⚳ 22:30
☽Q♂ 23:46

5 Su
☽⚹⚷ 1:59
☽⊼♄ 2:25
☽⊻♅ 3:49
☽⊼♀ 5:57
☿‖♇ 8:36
☽☍☿ 9:30
☽Q♇ 14:00
☉#☽ 14:25
☿ ♐ 19:20
☽⊼♃ 19:37
♀#♅ 20:56

6 M
☽△♂ 0:54
☽∠♅ 3:49
☽□♆ 4:58
☽⚹⚳ 7:21
☽Q♀ 8:14
☉⊼☽ 9:09
☽⊼♇ 14:06
☽Q♃ 20:05
☿‖♄ 20:34

7 Tu
☽□⚷ 2:08
☽☍♄ 2:58
☽⚹♅ 3:56
☿#⚳ 3:57
☽∠⚳ 7:56
☿∠♇ 8:28
☽△♀ 10:41
☉Q☽ 11:08
♀ ♏ 11:40
☽⊼☿ 15:03
☽△♃ 20:48

8 W
☽□♂ 3:40
☽△♆ 5:37
☽⊻⚳ 8:52
☉△☽ 13:35
☽☍♇ 15:08
☽Q☿ 18:28

9 Th
☽△⚷ 3:26
☽⊼♄ 4:45
☽□♅ 5:15
☽Q♆ 6:37
☉⚹♇ 12:13
☽□♀ 17:16
☽△☿ 22:37
☽□♃ 23:47

10 F
♂⊼♆ 0:11
☉#☽ 3:09
☽Q⚷ 4:56
☽Q♄ 6:30
☽⊼♆ 8:13
☽⚹♂ 8:36
☿⊻♃ 12:08
☽☌⚳ 12:29
☽⊼♇ 18:18
☉□☽ 20:38

11 Sa
☽⊼⚷ 7:05
☽△♄ 8:56
☽△♅ 8:57
♄△♅ 9:46
☽∠♂ 12:11
☽#♃ 12:54
☽#♀ 18:15
☽Q♇ 20:52

12 Su
☽⚹♀ 3:08
☽⚹♃ 5:27
☽□☿ 9:32
☽‖♅ 11:15
☽Q♅ 11:46
☽☍♆ 13:24
☽⊻♂ 16:30
☽#♆ 18:29
☽⊻⚳ 18:46

13 M
☽△♇ 0:06
☿Q♅ 6:31
☉⚹☽ 6:57
♀☌♃ 8:17
☽∠♃ 9:17
☽∠♀ 9:22
☽☍⚷ 13:19
☽⊼♅ 15:12
☽#♂ 15:27
☽□♄ 15:46
☿□♆ 22:49
☽∠⚳ 22:52

14 Tu
♀‖♃ 0:57
☽‖⚷ 8:28
☉∠☽ 13:13
☽⊻♃ 13:42
☽⊻♀ 16:21
☽⊼♆ 21:00
☽#⚷ 23:27
☽⚹☿ 23:38

15 W
♀Q⚷ 1:42
☽☌♂ 3:10
☽⚹⚳ 3:29
☽□♇ 8:14
♂⚹⚳ 12:22
☽‖♂ 19:59
☉⊻☽ 20:08
☽⊼⚷ 21:45
☽☍♅ 23:37

16 Th
☽⚹♄ 0:51
☽Q♆ 1:33
⚴R♈ 2:54
⚶ ♏ 4:17
☽∠☿ 7:38
♀∠♄ 9:07
☽‖♆ 14:53
♀△♆ 15:22
☉△⚷ 15:49
☿△⚳ 18:18
☽#♅ 22:13

17 F
☽☌♃ 0:03
☽Q⚷ 2:40
☽∠♄ 6:07
☽△♆ 6:34
☽☌♀ 8:18
☉⊼♅ 14:05
☽□⚳ 14:11
☿⚹♂ 14:25
☽⊻♂ 16:05
☽⊻☿ 16:11
☽⚹♇ 18:16

18 Sa
☽‖♃ 2:21
☽△⚷ 8:01
☽⊼♅ 9:52
☉☌☽ 11:43
☽⊻♄ 11:49
☿⊻♇ 12:51
☉⊻♄ 13:04
☽‖♀ 15:28
☽∠♂ 23:18
☽∠♇ 23:57

19 Su
☽⊻♃ 12:15
♂□♇ 12:17
☽Q♅ 15:37
☽□♆ 17:52

20 M
♀□⚳ 2:14
☽△⚳ 2:36
☽⊻♀ 2:38
☽⊻♇ 6:02
☽⚹♂ 6:59
☽☌☿ 10:38
☽∠♃ 18:58
☽□⚷ 19:56
☽△♅ 21:44

21 Tu
☽☌♄ 0:28
☉⊻☽ 5:24
☽Q⚳ 9:20
♀⚹♇ 11:30
☽∠♀ 12:33

22 W
☽⚹♃ 1:58
☉ ♐ 3:06
☽⚹♆ 6:34
♆ D 14:22
☉∠☽ 14:45
☽⊼⚳ 16:16
☽☌♇ 19:01
♃Q⚷ 22:30
☽⚹♀ 22:42
☽□♂ 23:17

23 Th
☽⊻☿ 5:59
☽⚹⚷ 8:51
♀⊻♂ 9:11
☽□♅ 10:34
☽∠♆ 13:05
☽⊻♄ 14:02

24 F
☉⚹☽ 0:06
☽‖♀ 14:47
☿□⚷ 14:55
☽∠⚷ 15:11
☽∠☿ 15:13
☽□♃ 15:57
☉∠♇ 17:38
☽⊻♆ 19:24
☽∠♄ 20:36

25 Sa
☿∠♃ 2:47
☽☍⚳ 5:41
☽⊻♇ 7:45
☿△♅ 10:57
☽△♂ 15:07
☽□♀ 18:13
☽⊻⚷ 21:02
☽‖♃ 21:40
☽⚹♅ 22:36
☽⚹☿ 23:33

26 Su
☽⚹♄ 2:38
☽∠♇ 13:18
☉□☽ 17:04
♀△⚷ 21:23
☽Q♂ 21:56

27 M
☽∠♅ 3:35
☽△♃ 3:53
☽#♅ 5:56
☽☌♆ 6:09
♀⊼♅ 11:49
☽‖♆ 12:21
☽‖♂ 14:14
☽⊼⚳ 16:28
☽⚹♇ 17:55

28 Tu
☽⊼♂ 3:38
☽☌⚷ 6:12
☿☌♄ 6:59
☽⊻♅ 7:34
☽Q♃ 8:22
☽△♀ 9:42
☽□♄ 11:57
☽□☿ 12:10
☽Q⚳ 20:16
♂‖♆ 22:13

29 W
☽#⚷ 2:32
☉△☽ 5:23
♀⊻♄ 11:12
☽⊼♃ 11:42
☽⊻♆ 12:58
☽‖⚷ 15:11
☽Q♀ 15:17
☽△⚳ 22:56
☽□♇ 23:55

30 Th
☿⊻♀ 6:01
♂⊼⚷ 8:27
☉Q☽ 9:28
☽⊻⚷ 11:06
☽☍♂ 11:14
☽☌♅ 12:17
☽∠♆ 14:45
☽△♄ 16:51
☉‖♇ 18:01
☽△☿ 18:38
☽⊼♀ 19:27

December 2017

LONGITUDE

Day	Sid.Time	☉	☽	☽ 12 hour	Mean☊	True☊	☿	♀	♂	⚳	♃	♄	⚷	♅	♆	♇
	h m s	° ' "	° ' "	° ' "	° '	° '	° '	° '	° '	° '	° '	° '	° '	° '	° '	° '
1 F	4 40 10	8♐58 35	2♉00 19	9♉16 27	18♌32.2	17♌40.7	28♐52.6	29♏30.9	24♎44.2	17♌19.3	11♏04.1	27♐45.7	24♓19.5	25♈00.7	11♓29.1	17♑48.2
2 Sa	4 44 06	9 59 23	16 39 00	24 07 05	18 29.0	17R 31.0	29 09.7	0♐46.3	25 21.9	17 25.5	11 16.4	27 52.5	24R 19.3	24R 59.2	11 29.4	17 49.9
3 Su	4 48 03	11 00 12	1♊39 38	9♊15 23	18 25.8	17 20.4	29R 17.7	2 01.8	25 59.6	17 31.3	11 28.6	27 59.4	24 19.2	24 57.7	11 29.8	17 51.6
4 M	4 51 59	12 01 02	16 53 00	24 31 04	18 22.7	17 10.4	29 15.8	3 17.2	26 37.3	17 36.8	11 40.8	28 06.3	24 19.1	24 56.2	11 30.2	17 53.3
5 Tu	4 55 56	13 01 53	2♋08 10	9♋43 01	18 19.5	17 02.1	29 03.3	4 32.7	27 15.0	17 41.9	11 53.0	28 13.2	24D 19.0	24 54.8	11 30.6	17 55.0
6 W	4 59 53	14 02 45	17 14 26	24 41 24	18 16.3	16 56.2	28 39.8	5 48.1	27 52.8	17 46.6	12 05.1	28 20.1	24 19.0	24 53.4	11 31.0	17 56.8
7 Th	5 03 49	15 03 39	2♌03 08	9♌19 02	18 13.1	16 53.1	28 05.0	7 03.6	28 30.5	17 51.0	12 17.1	28 27.1	24 19.1	24 52.1	11 31.5	17 58.6
8 F	5 07 46	16 04 34	16 28 44	23 32 02	18 10.0	16D 52.2	27 19.0	8 19.1	29 08.2	17 54.9	12 29.1	28 34.1	24 19.2	24 50.8	11 32.0	18 00.3
9 Sa	5 11 42	17 05 29	0♍28 56	7♍19 32	18 06.8	16 52.6	26 22.4	9 34.6	29 45.9	17 58.4	12 41.2	28 41.0	24 19.4	24 49.6	11 32.6	18 02.1
10 Su	5 15 39	18 06 27	14 04 06	20 42 56	18 03.6	16R 53.3	25 16.4	10 50.1	0♏23.5	18 01.5	12 52.9	28 48.0	24 19.6	24 48.4	11 33.1	18 04.0
11 M	5 19 35	19 07 25	27 16 24	3♎44 57	18 00.4	16 53.1	24 02.5	12 05.6	1 01.2	18 04.2	13 04.8	28 55.0	24 19.9	24 47.2	11 33.8	18 05.8
12 Tu	5 23 32	20 08 24	10♎08 59	16 28 57	17 57.3	16 50.9	22 43.0	13 21.1	1 38.9	18 06.5	13 16.5	29 02.1	24 20.2	24 46.1	11 34.4	18 07.6
13 W	5 27 28	21 09 25	22 45 14	28 58 15	17 54.1	16 46.4	21 20.4	14 36.6	2 16.6	18 08.4	13 28.2	29 09.1	24 20.6	24 45.1	11 35.1	18 09.5
14 Th	5 31 25	22 10 27	5♏08 22	11♏15 53	17 50.9	16 39.4	19 57.6	15 52.1	2 54.2	18 09.9	13 39.8	29 16.1	24 21.0	24 44.1	11 35.8	18 11.4
15 F	5 35 22	23 11 29	17 21 08	23 24 22	17 47.7	16 30.3	18 37.3	17 07.6	3 31.9	18 10.9	13 51.4	29 23.2	24 21.5	24 43.1	11 36.6	18 13.2
16 Sa	5 39 18	24 12 33	29 25 50	5♐25 43	17 44.5	16 20.0	17 22.1	18 23.1	4 09.5	18R 11.5	14 02.9	29 30.3	24 22.1	24 42.2	11 37.3	18 15.1
17 Su	5 43 15	25 13 37	11♐24 14	17 21 34	17 41.4	16 09.3	16 14.2	19 38.6	4 47.1	18 11.7	14 14.3	29 37.3	24 22.7	24 41.3	11 38.2	18 17.0
18 M	5 47 11	26 14 42	23 17 54	29 13 23	17 38.2	15 59.2	15 15.4	20 54.2	5 24.8	18 11.5	14 25.7	29 44.4	24 23.4	24 40.5	11 39.0	18 19.0
19 Tu	5 51 08	27 15 48	5♑08 14	11♑02 40	17 35.0	15 50.7	14 26.7	22 09.7	6 02.4	18 10.8	14 36.9	29 51.5	24 24.1	24 39.7	11 39.9	18 20.9
20 W	5 55 04	28 16 54	16 56 53	22 51 10	17 31.8	15 44.3	13 48.9	23 25.2	6 40.0	18 09.7	14 48.1	29 58.6	24 24.9	24 39.0	11 40.8	18 22.8
21 Th	5 59 01	29 18 01	28 45 49	4♒41 10	17 28.7	15 40.2	13 22.0	24 40.7	7 17.5	18 08.2	14 59.3	0♑05.7	24 25.7	24 38.3	11 41.8	18 24.8
22 F	6 02 57	0♑19 08	10♒37 35	16 35 30	17 25.5	15D 38.5	13 05.9	25 56.3	7 55.1	18 06.2	15 10.3	0 12.7	24 26.6	24 37.7	11 42.7	18 26.7
23 Sa	6 06 54	1 20 16	22 35 21	28 37 39	17 22.3	15 38.6	13D 00.2	27 11.8	8 32.7	18 03.8	15 21.3	0 19.8	24 27.6	24 37.1	11 43.8	18 28.7
24 Su	6 10 51	2 21 23	4♓42 56	10♓51 44	17 19.1	15 39.8	13 04.2	28 27.3	9 10.2	18 00.9	15 32.2	0 26.9	24 28.6	24 36.6	11 44.8	18 30.7
25 M	6 14 47	3 22 31	17 04 38	23 22 13	17 16.0	15 41.4	13 17.1	29 42.8	9 47.7	17 57.6	15 43.0	0 34.0	24 29.6	24 36.1	11 45.9	18 32.7
26 Tu	6 18 44	4 23 39	29 45 03	6♈13 41	17 12.8	15R 42.4	13 38.3	0♑58.4	10 25.2	17 53.9	15 53.7	0 41.1	24 30.8	24 35.7	11 47.0	18 34.7
27 W	6 22 40	5 24 47	12♈48 36	19 30 14	17 09.6	15 42.2	14 07.0	2 13.9	11 02.7	17 49.8	16 04.3	0 48.2	24 31.9	24 35.4	11 48.1	18 36.7
28 Th	6 26 37	6 25 55	26 18 55	3♉14 49	17 06.4	15 40.4	14 42.3	3 29.4	11 40.2	17 45.2	16 14.9	0 55.2	24 33.1	24 35.0	11 49.3	18 38.7
29 F	6 30 33	7 27 02	10♉17 59	17 28 18	17 03.3	15 36.9	15 23.6	4 44.9	12 17.7	17 40.2	16 25.3	1 02.3	24 34.4	24 34.8	11 50.5	18 40.7
30 Sa	6 34 30	8 28 10	24 45 23	2♊08 42	17 00.1	15 32.0	16 10.2	6 00.4	12 55.1	17 34.8	16 35.7	1 09.3	24 35.7	24 34.6	11 51.7	18 42.7
31 Su	6 38 26	9♑29 18	9♊37 28	17 10 42	16♌56.9	15♌26.4	17♐01.6	7♑15.9	13♏32.6	17♌29.0	16♏45.9	1♑16.4	24♓37.1	24♈34.4	11♓53.0	18♑44.7

1st of Month

Julian Day # 2458088.5
Obliquity 23°26'06"
SVP 5♓00'47"
GC 27♐05.4
Eris 22♈54.4R

Day	⚴	Day	⚵	Day	⚶
1	26♈32.3R	1	23♑57.1	1	7♏34.7
6	25 48.8R	6	25 49.1	6	10 07.2
11	25 20.2R	11	27 43.7	11	12 39.2
16	25 06.6R	16	29 40.9	16	15 10.4
21	25 08.1	21	1♒40.4	21	17 40.8
26	25 24.3	26	3 42.1	26	20 10.1
31	25 54.5	31	5 45.7	31	22 38.3

DECLINATION and LATITUDE

Day	☉ Decl	☽ Decl	☽ Lat	☽12h Decl	☿ Decl	☿ Lat	♀ Decl	♀ Lat	♂ Decl	♂ Lat	⚳ Decl	⚳ Lat	♃ Decl	♃ Lat	♄ Decl	♄ Lat
1 F	21S48	7N36	4S52	9N51	25S10	1S44	19S19	0N44	8S36	1N03	23N08	7N53	14S11	1N01	22S29	0N56
2 Sa	21 57	11 58	5 03	13 56	24 59	1 33	19 37	0 42	8 50	1 03	23 11	7 58	14 15	1 01	22 29	0 56
3 Su	22 05	15 42	4 54	17 12	24 46	1 20	19 55	0 40	9 04	1 03	23 15	8 04	14 18	1 01	22 29	0 56
4 M	22 14	18 25	4 24	19 18	24 32	1 06	20 12	0 38	9 18	1 03	23 18	8 09	14 22	1 01	22 30	0 56
5 Tu	22 21	19 50	3 35	20 01	24 16	0 51	20 28	0 35	9 31	1 02	23 22	8 15	14 26	1 01	22 30	0 56
6 W	22 29	19 49	2 31	19 17	23 59	0 34	20 43	0 33	9 45	1 02	23 26	8 21	14 29	1 01	22 30	0 56
7 Th	22 36	18 26	1 18	17 16	23 41	0 16	20 59	0 31	9 59	1 02	23 30	8 27	14 33	1 01	22 30	0 56
8 F	22 42	15 52	0 02	14 14	23 21	0N03	21 13	0 29	10 12	1 02	23 34	8 32	14 37	1 01	22 30	0 55
9 Sa	22 49	12 16	1N12	10 29	22 60	0 23	21 27	0 26	10 26	1 01	23 39	8 38	14 40	1 01	22 30	0 55
10 Su	22 54	8 25	2 20	6 18	22 38	0 44	21 40	0 24	10 39	1 01	23 43	8 44	14 44	1 01	22 31	0 55
11 M	22 59	4 07	3 19	1 56	22 14	1 04	21 53	0 22	10 53	1 01	23 48	8 50	14 47	1 01	22 31	0 55
12 Tu	23 04	0S15	4 06	2S25	21 51	1 23	22 05	0 19	11 06	1 00	23 53	8 56	14 51	1 01	22 31	0 55
13 W	23 08	4 31	4 39	6 34	21 27	1 42	22 16	0 17	11 19	1 00	23 58	9 02	14 54	1 02	22 31	0 55
14 Th	23 12	8 31	4 60	10 23	21 05	1 59	22 27	0 14	11 32	0 60	24 03	9 08	14 57	1 02	22 31	0 55
15 F	23 16	12 07	5 06	13 43	20 43	2 14	22 37	0 12	11 45	0 60	24 08	9 14	15 01	1 02	22 31	0 55
16 Sa	23 18	15 10	4 58	16 28	20 23	2 27	22 46	0 10	11 58	0 59	24 14	9 20	15 04	1 02	22 31	0 55
17 Su	23 21	17 34	4 37	18 29	20 06	2 38	22 55	0 07	12 11	0 59	24 19	9 26	15 07	1 02	22 31	0 55
18 M	23 23	19 12	4 04	19 42	19 52	2 47	23 03	0 05	12 24	0 59	24 25	9 32	15 11	1 02	22 31	0 55
19 Tu	23 24	19 60	3 21	20 03	19 40	2 53	23 10	0 02	12 37	0 58	24 31	9 38	15 14	1 02	22 31	0 55
20 W	23 25	19 54	2 29	19 32	19 32	2 56	23 16	0 00	12 49	0 58	24 37	9 44	15 17	1 02	22 32	0 55
21 Th	23 26	18 56	1 30	18 08	19 27	2 58	23 22	0S02	13 02	0 58	24 43	9 50	15 20	1 02	22 32	0 54
22 F	23 26	17 08	0 27	15 57	19 25	2 58	23 27	0 05	13 14	0 57	24 50	9 56	15 24	1 02	22 32	0 54
23 Sa	23 26	14 34	0S38	13 03	19 26	2 56	23 32	0 07	13 27	0 57	24 56	10 02	15 27	1 02	22 32	0 54
24 Su	23 25	11 21	1 42	9 32	19 30	2 53	23 35	0 10	13 39	0 57	25 03	10 08	15 30	1 02	22 32	0 54
25 M	23 24	7 36	2 42	5 33	19 35	2 49	23 38	0 12	13 51	0 56	25 10	10 14	15 33	1 02	22 32	0 54
26 Tu	23 22	3 25	3 37	1 13	19 43	2 44	23 40	0 14	14 03	0 56	25 17	10 21	15 36	1 02	22 32	0 54
27 W	23 19	1N02	4 22	3N19	19 52	2 38	23 42	0 17	14 15	0 56	25 24	10 27	15 39	1 03	22 32	0 54
28 Th	23 17	5 35	4 54	7 50	20 03	2 31	23 42	0 19	14 27	0 55	25 31	10 33	15 42	1 03	22 32	0 54
29 F	23 14	9 60	5 10	12 04	20 15	2 24	23 42	0 21	14 39	0 55	25 38	10 39	15 45	1 03	22 32	0 54
30 Sa	23 10	13 59	5 07	15 43	20 27	2 17	23 42	0 24	14 51	0 55	25 46	10 45	15 47	1 03	22 32	0 54
31 Su	23S06	17N12	4S44	18N25	20S40	2N09	23S40	0S26	15S02	0N54	25N53	10N51	15S50	1N03	22S32	0N54

Day	⚷ Decl	⚷ Lat	♅ Decl	♅ Lat	♆ Decl	♆ Lat	♇ Decl	♇ Lat
1	1N13	3N46	9N08	0S35	8S07	0S55	21S45	0N30
6	1 11	3 45	9 06	0 35	8 06	0 55	21 45	0 30
11	1 10	3 44	9 03	0 35	8 05	0 55	21 44	0 29
16	1 10	3 42	9 02	0 35	8 03	0 55	21 43	0 29
21	1 10	3 41	9 00	0 35	8 01	0 55	21 42	0 28
26	1 11	3 40	8 60	0 34	7 59	0 55	21 41	0 28
31	1N12	3N38	8N59	0S34	7S57	0S55	21S40	0N27

Day	⚴ Decl	⚴ Lat	⚵ Decl	⚵ Lat	⚶ Decl	⚶ Lat	Eris Decl	Eris Lat
1	28S11	41S19	14S20	7N05	9S07	5N12	2S29	12S14
6	28 10	41 03	14 16	6 50	9 53	5 14	2 29	12 14
11	27 59	40 41	14 09	6 35	10 37	5 16	2 29	12 13
16	27 39	40 15	13 60	6 21	11 19	5 18	2 28	12 12
21	27 11	39 46	13 48	6 08	11 59	5 19	2 28	12 12
26	26 37	39 14	13 34	5 54	12 37	5 21	2 28	12 11
31	25S57	38S40	13S18	5N42	13S13	5N23	2S27	12S10

Moon Phenomena

Max/0 Decl
dy hr mn
5 11:43 20N00
11 22:37 0 S
19 9:31 20S04
26 18:28 0 N

Perigee/Apogee
dy hr m kilometers
4 8:42 p 357497
19 1:31 a 406603

Max/0 Lat
dy hr mn
2 1:11 5S03
8 0:40 0 N
14 22:25 5N06
22 10:06 0 S
29 8:49 5S11

PH dy hr mn
○ 3 15:48 11♊40
☾ 10 7:53 18♍26
● 18 6:32 26♐31
☽ 26 9:21 4♈47

Void of Course Moon

Last Aspect			☽ Ingress	
2 1:55	♇	△	♊	2 21:22
4 19:14	♀	☍	♋	4 20:38
6 17:57	♂	□	♌	6 20:38
8 22:42	♂	⚹	♍	8 23:10
11 3:04	♄	□	♎	11 5:02
13 12:28	♄	⚹	♏	13 14:00
15 1:43	♇	⚹	♐	16 1:08
18 13:11	☉	☌	♑	18 13:35
20 15:38	♅	□	♒	21 2:30
23 10:14	♀	⚹	♓	23 14:43
25 2:49	♇	⚹	♈	26 0:28
27 20:58	♅	☌	♉	28 6:24
29 14:02	♇	△	♊	30 8:32

DAILY ASPECTARIAN

1 F
☽⋕♆ 2:41
☽⋕♂ 5:34
☽∥♅ 8:08
♀ ♐ 9:15
♂☍♅ 10:07
☽∠⚷ 12:05
☉⊼☽ 12:22
☽☍♃ 15:09
☽⚹♆ 15:37
☽⚼♄ 17:50
☽⚼☿ 19:54
☉⚼♅ 23:55

2 Sa
☽□⚳ 1:16
☽△♇ 1:55
☽⚹⚷ 12:19
☽⚺♅ 13:22
☽⋕♃ 14:14
☽⊼♂ 14:36
☽⊼♄ 18:08
☽⊼☿ 20:14
☉∠♂ 23:24

3 Su
☽☍♀ 0:38
☽⚼♇ 1:54
♃△♆ 2:21
♂⋕♅ 5:19
☿ R 7:35
☉□♆ 11:45
☽∠♅ 13:05
☉⚺♃ 14:02
☽⚼♂ 15:22
☽□♆ 15:32
☽⊼♃ 15:42
☉☍☽ 15:48
♀∠♇ 16:12
♂⚼♆ 19:24

4 M
☽⚹⚳ 1:09
☽⊼♇ 1:35
☽□⚷ 11:41
☽⚹♅ 12:38
☽⚼♃ 15:37
☽△♂ 15:58
☽☍♄ 17:47
☽☍☿ 19:14

5 Tu
☽∠⚳ 0:54
☽⊼♀ 4:09
⚷ D 9:48
☽△♆ 14:52
☽△♃ 15:39
☉⊼☽ 18:31

6 W
☽⚺⚳ 0:52
☽☍♇ 1:08
☉∥♄ 3:21
☽⚼♀ 6:15
☽△⚷ 11:24
☿☌♄ 12:06
☽□♅ 12:19
☽⚼♆ 14:58
☿⚹♂ 15:59
☽⊼☿ 17:47
☽□♂ 17:57
☽⊼♄ 18:04
☉⚼☽ 20:30
♂⚹♄ 21:22

7 Th
☽△♀ 9:02
☿⋕⚳ 11:08
☽⚼⚷ 12:00
☽⊼♆ 15:42
☽□♃ 17:12
☽⚼☿ 17:23
☽⚼♄ 19:04
☿∠♃ 20:06
☉△☽ 23:16

8 F
☽☌⚳ 2:26
☽⊼♇ 2:35
☽⋕♃ 9:12
☽⊼⚷ 13:21
☽△♅ 14:14
☽△☿ 17:22
☽△♄ 20:51
☽⚹♂ 22:42

9 Sa
☽⚼♇ 4:28
♀⚼♅ 4:42
♂ ♏ 9:00
☉∥☿ 9:47
☽⋕♂ 11:38
☽⚼♅ 16:24
☽□♀ 17:38
☽☍♆ 19:30
☽∥♅ 20:19
☽⚹♃ 21:51
☉△⚳ 21:58
☉⚺♇ 22:59

10 Su
☽⋕♆ 1:58
☽∠♂ 2:30
♀∥♇ 6:56
☽⚺⚳ 7:09
☽△♇ 7:13
☿∥♄ 7:19
☉□☽ 7:53
☿△♅ 9:30
♀□♆ 13:49
☿□⚷ 18:34
☽□☿ 18:36
☽☍⚷ 18:36
☽⊼♅ 19:26

11 M
☽∠♃ 1:30
☽□♄ 3:04
☽⚺♂ 7:17
☽∠⚳ 10:46
☿∥♀ 14:32
☽∥⚷ 16:10
♀⚺♃ 22:17

12 Tu
☽⊼♆ 2:41
☽⋕⚷ 5:05
☽⚺♃ 6:00
☽⚹♀ 6:43
☿∥♇ 7:20
☽⚹⚳ 15:08
☽□♇ 15:10
☉⚹☽ 20:40
☽⚹☿ 21:33

13 W
☉☌☿ 1:50
☽⊼⚷ 3:04
☽☍♅ 3:50
☽⚼♆ 7:23
☽⚹♄ 12:28
☽∠♀ 14:44
☽☌♂ 19:24
☽∥♆ 21:08
☽∠☿ 23:41

14 Th
☽⋕♅ 3:16
☉∠☽ 4:20
☽⚼⚷ 8:15
♀∥♄ 10:13
☽△♆ 12:40
☽☌♃ 16:59
☽∠♄ 18:05
☽∥♂ 21:15
☽⚺♀ 23:30

15 F
☿∠♂ 1:07
☽□⚳ 1:39
☽⚹♇ 1:43
☽⚺☿ 2:16
☿⚺♇ 7:17
☿△⚳ 8:07
☉⚺☽ 12:38
☽△⚷ 13:54
☿☌♀ 14:10
☽⊼♅ 14:35
♀△⚳ 20:18
♀⚺♇ 21:24
☽∥♃ 23:04

16 Sa
☽⚺♄ 0:09
☉□⚷ 3:48
☽∠♇ 7:40
☽⚺♂ 9:59
☉△♅ 11:29
⚵ ♒ 19:19
☽⚼♅ 20:33
⚳ R 22:30

17 Su
☽□♆ 0:28
♀∠♂ 5:23
☽⚺♃ 5:48
☽☌☿ 8:58
☽△⚳ 13:41
☽⚺♇ 13:54
☽∠♂ 17:50
☽☌♀ 18:35
⚴ D 23:37

18 M
☽□⚷ 2:13
☽△♅ 2:47
☉☌☽ 6:32
☽∠♃ 12:37
☽☌♄ 13:11
☽∥☿ 13:22
☿⚺♃ 19:35
☽⚼⚳ 20:02

19 Tu
☽⚹♂ 1:56
☽⚹♆ 13:17
☽⚺☿ 17:55
☽⚹♃ 19:34

20 W
☽⊼⚳ 2:28
☽☌♇ 2:55
♄ ♑ 4:50
☽∥☿ 12:59
☽⚺♀ 14:43
☽⚹⚷ 15:11
☽□♅ 15:38
♀□⚷ 19:11
☽∠♆ 19:48
☽∠☿ 23:13
♀△♅ 23:14

21 Th
☉⚺☽ 1:11
☽⚺♄ 2:44
☉ ♑ 16:29
☽□♂ 18:14
☉∥♀ 18:40
☉∠♃ 19:47
☉☌♄ 21:10
☽∠⚷ 21:37

22 F
☽∠♀ 0:42
☽⚺♆ 2:12
☽⚹☿ 4:55
☽□♃ 9:18
☽∠♄ 9:19
☉∠☽ 10:20
♃∠♄ 14:56
☽☍⚳ 14:59
☽⚺♇ 15:46
☽∥♃ 16:41

23 Sa
☿ D 1:51
☽⚺⚷ 3:44
☽⚹♅ 4:02
☽∥♂ 8:24
☽⚹♀ 10:14
☽⚹♄ 15:31
☉⚹☽ 18:56
☽∠♇ 21:38

24 Su
☽△♂ 9:10
☽∠♅ 9:34
♂⚼⚷ 12:06
☽☌♆ 13:44
☉⚼⚳ 14:45
☽⋕♅ 15:25
☽□☿ 16:32
☽△♃ 21:21
☽∥♆ 21:35

25 M
☽⊼⚳ 1:41
☽⚹♇ 2:49
♀ ♑ 5:27
☽☌⚷ 14:09
☽⚺♅ 14:19
☽⚼♂ 15:27
♀☌♄ 17:56
♀∠♃ 22:16

26 Tu
☽□♄ 1:45
☽⚼♃ 2:10
☽□♀ 2:31
☽⚼⚳ 5:50
☉□☽ 9:21
☽⋕⚷ 12:08
☽⊼♂ 20:39
☽⚺♆ 22:10

27 W
☽∥⚷ 0:47
☽△☿ 2:27
☽⊼♃ 5:57
☽△⚳ 8:58
☽□♇ 10:26
♀⚼⚳ 10:47
☽⚺⚷ 20:55
☽☌♅ 20:58

28 Th
☽∠♆ 0:53
♂△♆ 6:00
☽⚼☿ 6:11
☽△♄ 8:04
☽⋕♆ 12:46
☽△♀ 13:38
☽∥♅ 18:22
☉△☽ 18:48
☽∠⚷ 22:46

29 F
☽⚹♆ 2:36
☽☍♂ 3:31
♅⚺⚷ 5:48
☽⊼☿ 9:01
☽⚼♄ 9:42
☽☍♃ 10:23
☽□⚳ 12:15
☽△♇ 14:02
☽⚼♀ 17:16
☉⚼☽ 21:44
☽⚺♅ 23:42
☽⚹⚷ 23:44

30 Sa
☽⋕♂ 6:09
☽⊼♄ 10:29
☽⋕♃ 12:47
☽⚼♇ 14:33
☿⚺♃ 15:10
☽⊼♀ 19:53
☉⊼☽ 23:46
☽∠♅ 23:55

31 Su
☽□♆ 3:36
☽⊼♂ 6:30
☿△⚳ 10:51
☽⊼♃ 11:28
☽⚹⚳ 12:24
☽☍☿ 12:31
☽⊼♇ 14:31
☽⚹♅ 23:40
☽□⚷ 23:46

January 2018

LONGITUDE

Day	Sid.Time	☉	☽	☽ 12 hour	Mean☊	True☊	☿	♀	♂	⚳	♃	♄	⚷	♅	♆	♇
	h m s	° ' "	° ' "	° ' "	° '	° '	° '	° '	° '	° '	° '	° '	° '	° '	° '	° '
M	6 42 23	10♑30 26	24♊47 15	2♋25 50	16♌53.7	15♌21.0	17♐57.1	8♑31.4	14♏10.0	17♌22.7	16♏56.1	1♑23.4	24♓38.5	24♈34.3	11♓54.3	18♑46.7
Tu	6 46 20	11 31 34	10♋05 07	17 43 42	16 50.5	15R 16.5	18 56.4	9 46.9	14 47.4	17R 16.1	17 06.2	1 30.4	24 40.0	24D 34.2	11 55.6	18 48.8
W	6 50 16	12 32 41	25 20 16	2♌53 34	16 47.4	15 13.5	19 59.0	11 02.4	15 24.8	17 09.0	17 16.2	1 37.4	24 41.5	24 34.2	11 56.9	18 50.8
Th	6 54 13	13 33 49	10♌22 31	17 46 13	16 44.2	15D 12.2	21 04.6	12 17.9	16 02.2	17 01.5	17 26.0	1 44.4	24 43.1	24 34.3	11 58.3	18 52.9
F	6 58 09	14 34 57	25 03 55	2♍15 08	16 41.0	15 12.4	22 12.7	13 33.4	16 39.6	16 53.6	17 35.8	1 51.4	24 44.7	24 34.4	11 59.7	18 54.9
Sa	7 02 06	15 36 06	9♍19 32	16 16 59	16 37.8	15 13.6	23 23.2	14 48.9	17 17.0	16 45.4	17 45.5	1 58.4	24 46.4	24 34.5	12 01.1	18 56.9
Su	7 06 02	16 37 14	23 07 31	29 51 18	16 34.7	15 15.3	24 35.7	16 04.3	17 54.3	16 36.7	17 55.1	2 05.3	24 48.1	24 34.7	12 02.6	18 59.0
M	7 09 59	17 38 22	6♎28 37	12♎59 49	16 31.5	15R 16.6	25 50.2	17 19.8	18 31.6	16 27.7	18 04.5	2 12.3	24 49.9	24 35.0	12 04.1	19 01.0
Tu	7 13 55	18 39 31	19 25 21	25 45 42	16 28.3	15 17.1	27 06.3	18 35.3	19 08.9	16 18.3	18 13.9	2 19.2	24 51.7	24 35.3	12 05.6	19 03.1
W	7 17 52	19 40 39	2♏01 20	8♏12 49	16 25.1	15 16.4	28 23.9	19 50.8	19 46.2	16 08.5	18 23.1	2 26.0	24 53.6	24 35.6	12 07.1	19 05.1
Th	7 21 49	20 41 48	14 20 37	20 25 15	16 22.0	15 14.5	29 42.8	21 06.3	20 23.5	15 58.4	18 32.3	2 32.9	24 55.5	24 36.0	12 08.7	19 07.1
F	7 25 45	21 42 57	26 27 13	2♐26 57	16 18.8	15 11.5	1♑03.0	22 21.7	21 00.8	15 48.0	18 41.3	2 39.8	24 57.4	24 36.5	12 10.3	19 09.2
Sa	7 29 42	22 44 05	8♐24 54	14 21 27	16 15.6	15 07.8	2 24.4	23 37.2	21 38.0	15 37.2	18 50.2	2 46.6	24 59.4	24 37.0	12 11.9	19 11.2
Su	7 33 38	23 45 14	20 16 59	26 11 50	16 12.4	15 03.9	3 46.8	24 52.7	22 15.3	15 26.1	18 59.0	2 53.4	25 01.5	24 37.6	12 13.5	19 13.3
M	7 37 35	24 46 22	2♑06 19	8♑00 43	16 09.3	15 00.3	5 10.2	26 08.1	22 52.5	15 14.7	19 07.7	3 00.1	25 03.6	24 38.2	12 15.2	19 15.3
Tu	7 41 31	25 47 30	13 55 18	19 50 19	16 06.1	14 57.3	6 34.5	27 23.6	23 29.7	15 03.0	19 16.2	3 06.9	25 05.7	24 38.9	12 16.9	19 17.4
W	7 45 28	26 48 37	25 46 02	1♒42 39	16 02.9	14 55.2	7 59.6	28 39.1	24 06.8	14 51.0	19 24.7	3 13.6	25 07.9	24 39.6	12 18.6	19 19.4
Th	7 49 25	27 49 44	7♒40 25	13 39 34	15 59.7	14D 54.1	9 25.6	29 54.5	24 43.9	14 38.8	19 33.0	3 20.3	25 10.2	24 40.4	12 20.3	19 21.4
F	7 53 21	28 50 50	19 40 21	25 43 02	15 56.5	14 54.0	10 52.3	1♒10.0	25 21.1	14 26.3	19 41.1	3 26.9	25 12.4	24 41.2	12 22.1	19 23.5
Sa	7 57 18	29 51 56	1♓47 54	7♓55 14	15 53.4	14 54.7	12 19.7	2 25.4	25 58.1	14 13.5	19 49.2	3 33.5	25 14.8	24 42.1	12 23.8	19 25.5
Su	8 01 14	0♒53 01	14 05 21	20 18 36	15 50.2	14 55.8	13 47.9	3 40.8	26 35.2	14 00.6	19 57.1	3 40.1	25 17.1	24 43.0	12 25.6	19 27.5
M	8 05 11	1 54 05	26 35 19	2♈55 53	15 47.0	14 57.1	15 16.7	4 56.2	27 12.2	13 47.4	20 04.9	3 46.7	25 19.5	24 44.0	12 27.5	19 29.5
Tu	8 09 07	2 55 08	9♈20 40	15 50 00	15 43.8	14 58.3	16 46.2	6 11.6	27 49.2	13 34.1	20 12.5	3 53.2	25 21.9	24 45.0	12 29.3	19 31.5
W	8 13 04	3 56 10	22 24 16	29 03 45	15 40.7	14R 59.0	18 16.4	7 27.0	28 26.2	13 20.6	20 20.0	3 59.7	25 24.4	24 46.1	12 31.2	19 33.5
Th	8 17 00	4 57 11	5♉48 44	12♉39 24	15 37.5	14 59.2	19 47.2	8 42.4	29 03.2	13 07.0	20 27.4	4 06.1	25 26.9	24 47.2	12 33.0	19 35.5
F	8 20 57	5 58 11	19 35 53	26 38 10	15 34.3	14 59.0	21 18.6	9 57.8	29 40.1	12 53.2	20 34.6	4 12.5	25 29.5	24 48.4	12 35.0	19 37.5
Sa	8 24 53	6 59 10	3♊46 08	10♊59 32	15 31.1	14 58.3	22 50.8	11 13.1	0♐17.0	12 39.3	20 41.7	4 18.8	25 32.1	24 49.6	12 36.9	19 39.4
Su	8 28 50	8 00 07	18 17 56	25 40 47	15 27.9	14 57.5	24 23.5	12 28.5	0 53.8	12 25.3	20 48.7	4 25.2	25 34.7	24 50.9	12 38.8	19 41.4
M	8 32 47	9 01 04	3♋07 21	10♋36 46	15 24.8	14 56.8	25 56.9	13 43.8	1 30.7	12 11.3	20 55.5	4 31.4	25 37.4	24 52.2	12 40.8	19 43.4
Tu	8 36 43	10 02 00	18 08 03	25 40 08	15 21.6	14 56.2	27 31.0	14 59.1	2 07.5	11 57.2	21 02.2	4 37.7	25 40.1	24 53.6	12 42.8	19 45.3
W	8 40 40	11♒02 54	3♌11 55	10♌42 15	15♌18.4	14♌55.9	29♑05.7	16♒14.4	2♐44.3	11♌43.0	21♏08.7	4♑43.8	25♓42.8	24♈55.0	12♓44.8	19♑47.3

1st of Month

Julian Day #
2458119.5
Obliquity
23°26'06"
SVP 5♓00'42"
GC 27♐05.4
Eris 22♈46.2R

Day	⚴	Day	⚵	Day	⚶
1	26♈02.1	1	6♒10.7	1	23♏07.8
6	26 47.9	6	8 16.5	6	25 34.4
11	27 45.8	11	10 24.1	11	27 59.5
16	28 55.1	16	12 33.3	16	0♐22.9
21	0♉15.0	21	14 44.1	21	2 44.3
26	1 44.5	26	16 56.1	26	5 03.6
31	3 23.0	31	19 09.5	31	7 20.6

DECLINATION and LATITUDE

Day	☉ Decl	☽ Decl	☽ Lat	☽12h Decl	☿ Decl	☿ Lat	♀ Decl	♀ Lat	♂ Decl	♂ Lat	⚳ Decl	⚳ Lat	♃ Decl	♃ Lat	♄ Decl	♄ Lat
M	23S01	19N19	4S01	19N52	20S54	2N00	23S38	0S28	15S14	0N54	26N01	10N57	15S53	1N03	22S32	0N54
Tu	22 56	20 03	3 00	19 52	21 07	1 52	23 35	0 31	15 25	0 54	26 09	11 03	15 56	1 03	22 32	0 54
W	22 51	19 19	1 47	18 25	21 21	1 43	23 31	0 33	15 36	0 53	26 17	11 09	15 59	1 03	22 32	0 54
Th	22 45	17 13	0 26	15 44	21 34	1 34	23 27	0 35	15 48	0 53	26 24	11 14	16 01	1 03	22 32	0 54
F	22 38	14 01	0N54	12 06	21 47	1 26	23 22	0 37	15 59	0 52	26 32	11 20	16 04	1 03	22 32	0 54
Sa	22 31	10 03	2 09	7 54	21 59	1 17	23 16	0 39	16 10	0 52	26 40	11 26	16 06	1 03	22 32	0 54
Su	22 24	5 41	3 13	3 26	22 11	1 08	23 09	0 41	16 20	0 52	26 49	11 32	16 09	1 04	22 32	0 54
M	22 16	1 11	4 05	1S03	22 23	0 59	23 02	0 43	16 31	0 51	26 57	11 37	16 12	1 04	22 32	0 53
Tu	22 08	3S14	4 43	5 21	22 34	0 51	22 54	0 46	16 42	0 51	27 05	11 43	16 14	1 04	22 31	0 53
W	21 60	7 23	5 06	9 19	22 43	0 42	22 45	0 48	16 52	0 50	27 13	11 48	16 16	1 04	22 31	0 53
Th	21 50	11 08	5 14	12 49	22 52	0 34	22 36	0 50	17 03	0 50	27 22	11 54	16 19	1 04	22 31	0 53
F	21 41	14 23	5 08	15 44	23 01	0 25	22 26	0 51	17 13	0 49	27 30	11 59	16 21	1 04	22 31	0 53
Sa	21 31	16 57	4 49	17 58	23 08	0 17	22 15	0 53	17 23	0 49	27 38	12 04	16 24	1 04	22 31	0 53
Su	21 21	18 48	4 17	19 26	23 14	0 09	22 03	0 55	17 33	0 48	27 47	12 10	16 26	1 04	22 31	0 53
M	21 10	19 50	3 35	20 02	23 19	0 01	21 51	0 57	17 43	0 48	27 55	12 15	16 28	1 04	22 31	0 53
Tu	20 59	20 00	2 43	19 45	23 23	0S07	21 38	0 59	17 53	0 47	28 04	12 20	16 30	1 05	22 31	0 53
W	20 47	19 17	1 44	18 36	23 26	0 15	21 25	1 01	18 02	0 47	28 12	12 25	16 32	1 05	22 31	0 53
Th	20 36	17 42	0 40	16 37	23 28	0 23	21 11	1 02	18 12	0 46	28 20	12 29	16 35	1 05	22 31	0 53
F	20 23	15 20	0S26	13 53	23 29	0 29	20 56	1 04	18 21	0 46	28 29	12 34	16 37	1 05	22 30	0 53
Sa	20 11	12 16	1 32	10 31	23 28	0 36	20 41	1 06	18 30	0 45	28 37	12 38	16 39	1 05	22 30	0 53
Su	19 57	8 38	2 35	6 39	23 26	0 43	20 25	1 07	18 40	0 45	28 45	12 43	16 41	1 05	22 30	0 53
M	19 44	4 35	3 31	2 27	23 23	0 50	20 08	1 09	18 49	0 44	28 53	12 47	16 43	1 05	22 30	0 53
Tu	19 30	0 15	4 18	1N58	23 19	0 56	19 51	1 10	18 57	0 44	29 01	12 51	16 45	1 05	22 30	0 53
W	19 16	4N11	4 53	6 22	23 13	1 02	19 33	1 11	19 06	0 43	29 09	12 55	16 46	1 06	22 30	0 53
Th	19 01	8 31	5 13	10 35	23 06	1 08	19 15	1 13	19 15	0 43	29 17	12 59	16 48	1 06	22 29	0 53
F	18 47	12 33	5 16	14 21	22 58	1 14	18 56	1 14	19 23	0 42	29 25	13 03	16 50	1 06	22 29	0 53
Sa	18 31	15 59	5 01	17 22	22 48	1 19	18 37	1 15	19 32	0 42	29 32	13 07	16 52	1 06	22 29	0 53
Su	18 16	18 31	4 26	19 21	22 38	1 25	18 17	1 17	19 40	0 41	29 40	13 10	16 53	1 06	22 29	0 53
M	17 60	19 52	3 32	20 02	22 25	1 30	17 57	1 18	19 48	0 40	29 47	13 13	16 55	1 06	22 29	0 53
Tu	17 44	19 50	2 24	19 17	22 12	1 34	17 36	1 19	19 56	0 40	29 54	13 17	16 57	1 06	22 29	0 53
W	17S27	18N23	1S05	17N10	21S57	1S39	17S14	1S20	20S04	0N39	30N01	13N20	16S58	1N07	22S28	0N53

Day	⚷ Decl	⚷ Lat	♅ Decl	♅ Lat	♆ Decl	♆ Lat	♇ Decl	♇ Lat
1	1N13	3N38	8N59	0S34	7S56	0S55	21S40	0N27
6	1 15	3 37	8 60	0 34	7 54	0 55	21 39	0 27
11	1 17	3 36	9 00	0 34	7 51	0 55	21 38	0 26
16	1 20	3 35	9 02	0 34	7 48	0 55	21 37	0 26
21	1 24	3 34	9 03	0 33	7 44	0 54	21 36	0 25
26	1 28	3 32	9 05	0 33	7 40	0 54	21 35	0 25
31	1N32	3N31	9N08	0S33	7S37	0S54	21S34	0N24

Day	⚴ Decl	⚴ Lat	⚵ Decl	⚵ Lat	⚶ Decl	⚶ Lat	Eris Decl	Eris Lat
1	25S48	38S33	13S15	5N39	13S20	5N24	2S27	12S10
6	25 02	37 58	12 56	5 27	13 52	5 26	2 27	12 09
11	24 12	37 23	12 35	5 14	14 23	5 28	2 26	12 08
16	23 18	36 48	12 12	5 02	14 51	5 30	2 25	12 07
21	22 21	36 12	11 46	4 51	15 17	5 32	2 24	12 06
26	21 22	35 37	11 19	4 39	15 40	5 34	2 23	12 06
31	20S21	35S03	10S50	4N28	16S00	5N36	2S22	12S05

Moon Phenomena

Max/0 Decl

dy	hr mn	
1	23:59	20N03
8	6:21	0 S
15	16:34	20S03
23	1:24	0 N
29	11:33	20N01

Max/0 Lat

dy	hr mn	
4	7:50	0 N
11	1:44	5N14
18	14:29	0 S
25	16:05	5S18
31	18:48	0 N

Perigee/Apogee

dy	hr m		kilometers
1	22:03	p	356566
15	2:13	a	406464
30	9:56	p	358998

PH	dy	hr mn	
○	2	2:25	11♋38
☾	8	22:26	18♎36
●	17	2:18	26♑54
☽	24	22:22	4♉53
○	31	13:28	11♌37
•	31	13:31	T 1.316

Void of Course Moon

Last Aspect			☽ Ingress		
31 23:40	♅	⚹	♋	1	8:11
2 22:47	♅	□	♌	3	7:24
4 23:11	♅	△	♍	5	8:13
7 2:52	☿	□	♎	7	12:16
9 16:14	☿	⚹	♏	9	20:07
11 14:54	♀	⚹	♐	12	7:05
14 8:49	♅	△	♑	14	19:43
17 6:31	♀	☌	♒	17	8:33
19 11:53	♂	□	♓	19	20:28
22 1:14	♂	△	♈	22	6:28
24 4:17	♅	☌	♉	24	13:41
26 3:18	☿	△	♊	26	17:41
28 10:40	♅	⚹	♋	28	18:59
30 16:41	☿	☍	♌	30	18:54

DAILY ASPECTARIAN

☽⚼♂ 7:10
☽☍♄ 10:27
☽⚼♃ 11:21
☽∠⚳ 11:50
☿⚺♇ 20:52
☽☍♀ 23:29

☉☍☽ 2:25
☽△♆ 2:54
☽△♂ 7:42
☉⚹♆ 9:38
☽△♃ 11:08
☽⚺⚳ 11:11
☽☍♇ 13:44
⚳□♃ 13:57
♅D 14:12
☽⚻☿ 14:55
☽□♅ 22:47
☽△⚷ 22:59

☽⚼♆ 2:33
☽⚻♄ 10:03
☽⚼☿ 16:32
♀⚹♆ 17:39
☽⚼⚷ 22:56

☽⚻♆ 2:35
☽⚻♀ 3:24
☉⚻☽ 5:32
☽□♂ 9:35
☽#♃ 9:39
☽⚼♄ 10:24
☿∥♇ 10:38
☽☌⚳ 10:42
☽#♂ 10:53
☽□♃ 11:35
☽⚻♇ 13:51
☽△☿ 18:53
☽△♅ 23:11
☽⚻⚷ 23:28

5 F
⚳⚼♄ 3:33
☽⚼♀ 6:22
♂□⚳ 7:25
☉⚼☽ 8:06
♂∠♄ 9:20
☽△♄ 11:26
☽⚼♇ 14:50
♂∥♃ 15:08
☉∥♄ 22:59

6 Sa
☽⚼♅ 0:26
☽☍♆ 4:38
☽∥♅ 5:59
☽△♀ 10:24
☉△☽ 11:41
☽#♆ 12:05
☽⚺⚳ 12:42
☽⚹♂ 14:24
☽⚹♃ 14:45
☽△♇ 16:42
☿△♅ 23:40
☉⚻⚳ 23:50

7 Su
♂☌♃ 0:40
☽⚻♅ 2:35
☽□☿ 2:52
☽☍⚷ 2:59
☿□⚷ 4:08
♀⚻⚳ 9:13
☽∠⚳ 15:00
☉∥☿ 15:50
☽□♄ 16:10
☽∠♃ 17:44
☽∠♂ 18:22
☽∥⚷ 23:36

8 M
☽⚻♆ 10:18
☉⚹♃ 12:08
☽#⚷ 13:12
♀⚹♃ 16:14
☽⚹⚳ 18:14
☿∥♄ 19:19
♂⚹♇ 20:00
☽⚺♃ 21:44
☽□♀ 22:16
☉□☽ 22:26
☽□♇ 23:18
☽⚺♂ 23:28

9 Tu
☉☌♀ 7:03
♀☌♇ 9:04
☉☌♇ 9:34
☽☍♅ 9:46
☽⚻⚷ 10:19
☽⚼♆ 14:34
☽⚹☿ 16:14
♀⚹♂ 21:09

10 W
☽⚹♄ 0:48
☿∥♀ 2:10
☽∥♆ 2:53
☉⚹♂ 5:38
☽#♅ 10:02
☽⚼⚷ 15:19
☽△♆ 19:40

11 Th
☽∠☿ 0:49
☽□⚳ 3:10
☿ ♑ 5:10
☽∠♄ 6:23
☽☌♃ 8:23
☽⚹♇ 9:27
♀∥♄ 10:41
☽☌♂ 12:35
☉⚹☽ 13:42
☽⚹♀ 14:54
☿⚼⚳ 20:02
☽⚻♅ 20:19
☽△⚷ 21:00

12 F
☉∥♇ 7:09
☽⚺☿ 10:22
☽⚺♄ 12:33
☽∠♇ 15:28
☽∥♃ 18:12
☉∠☽ 22:30

13 Sa
☽∠♀ 0:28
☽⚼♅ 2:26
☽∥♂ 5:17
☿☌♄ 7:04
☽□♆ 7:39
☽△⚳ 14:20
♀□♅ 19:10
☽⚺♃ 21:20
☽⚺♇ 21:51

14 Su
♀⚹⚷ 2:53
☿∠♃ 3:56
☽⚺♂ 4:13
☉⚺☽ 7:42
☽△♅ 8:49
☽□⚷ 9:39
☽⚺♀ 10:26
☽⚼⚳ 20:17
☉□♅ 20:46

15 M
☽☌♄ 1:50
☽∠♃ 4:10
⚶ ♐ 4:46
☉⚹⚷ 7:01
☽☌☿ 7:04
☽∠♂ 12:22
☽⚹♆ 20:40
♀∠♆ 21:48

16 Tu
♀∥♇ 1:51
☽⚻⚳ 2:15
♃⚹♇ 4:15
☽☌♇ 10:55
☽⚹♃ 10:59
☽⚹♂ 20:28
☽□♅ 21:46
☽⚹⚷ 22:43

17 W
☉☌☽ 2:18
☽∠♆ 3:07
☽☌♀ 6:31
☉∠♆ 12:06
☽⚺♄ 15:12
☽∥♂ 18:15
♂⚻♅ 21:38

18 Th
♀ ♒ 1:45
☽⚺☿ 4:00
☽∠⚷ 5:02
☿∠♂ 8:56
☽⚺♆ 9:23
☽∥♃ 12:11
☽☍⚳ 13:44
♂△⚷ 18:03
☽∠♄ 21:32
☽⚺♇ 23:26

19 F
☽□♃ 0:02
☽⚹♅ 9:58
☽⚺⚷ 11:02
☽□♂ 11:53
☽∠☿ 13:59
☉⚺☽ 19:51

20 Sa
☿⚹♆ 1:09
☽⚺♀ 1:22
⚴ ♉ 2:36
☉ ♒ 3:10
☽⚹♄ 3:30
☽∠♇ 5:10
☽∠♅ 15:30
☽☌♆ 20:46
☽#♅ 21:26
☽⚹☿ 23:22
♀⚺♄ 23:46
☽⚻⚳ 23:51

21 Su
☿⚻⚳ 3:00
☉∠☽ 3:47
☽∥♆ 5:34
☽∠♀ 9:52
☽⚹♇ 10:23
☽△♃ 11:26
☽⚺♅ 20:28
☽☌⚷ 21:35

22 M
☽△♂ 1:14
☽⚼⚳ 4:06
☉⚹☽ 10:56
☽□♄ 13:42
☽⚼♃ 16:12
☽⚹♀ 17:29
☽#⚷ 17:40

23 Tu
☽⚺♆ 5:51
☽⚼♂ 6:46
☽△⚳ 7:42
☽∥⚷ 9:06
☽□☿ 15:30
☽□♇ 18:48
☽⚻♃ 20:12

24 W
☉⚺♄ 1:32
☽☌♅ 4:17
☽⚺⚷ 5:27
☽∠♆ 9:15
☉∥♂ 10:10
☽⚻♂ 11:24
☽#♆ 19:18
☿☌♇ 20:51
☽△♄ 20:57
☉□☽ 22:22

25 Th
♀∥♂ 0:15
☽∥♅ 3:11
☽□♀ 5:37
☽∠⚷ 8:10
☿⚹♃ 11:29
☽⚹♆ 11:50
☽□⚳ 12:35
☽⚼♄ 23:20

26 F
☽△♇ 0:03
☽☍♃ 1:42
☽△☿ 3:18
☽⚺♅ 8:54
☽⚹⚷ 10:05
♀∠⚷ 10:28
♂ ♐ 12:57
☽☍♂ 17:53

27 Sa
☽⚻♄ 0:55
☽⚼♇ 1:29
⚳⚻♆ 3:40
☉△☽ 5:46
☽#♃ 7:27
☽⚼☿ 7:36
☽∠♅ 10:05
☽△♀ 13:32
☽⚹⚳ 14:31
☽□♆ 14:42
☉#☽ 21:26
☽#♀ 21:42
♀☍⚳ 23:09

28 Su
☽⚻♇ 2:17
♀⚺♆ 3:23
☽⚻♃ 4:08
☉∥♀ 6:04
☿□♅ 7:09
☉⚼☽ 8:13
☽⚹♅ 10:40
☽⚻☿ 11:04
☽□⚷ 11:52
☽∠⚳ 14:35
☽⚼♀ 16:17
☿∥♄ 17:25
☿⚹⚷ 18:51
☽⚻♂ 21:18
☽#♂ 21:34

29 M
☽☍♄ 2:16
☽⚼♃ 4:32
☉⚻☽ 10:08
☽⚺⚳ 14:18
☽△♆ 15:20
☽⚻♀ 18:31
☽#♂ 21:01
☽⚼♂ 22:19

30 Tu
☽☍♇ 2:35
☿∠♆ 3:03
☽△♃ 4:39
☽□♅ 10:47
☽△⚷ 12:02
☽⚼♆ 15:17
☉∠⚷ 15:43
☽☍☿ 16:41
☽△♂ 23:14

31 W
☽⚻♄ 2:28
☉#☽ 10:33
☽⚼⚷ 12:03
☉☍⚳ 12:50
☽#♀ 13:09
☽☌⚳ 13:25
☉☍☽ 13:28
☽#♃ 13:35
☿ ♒ 13:40
☽⚻♆ 15:19
♀∥♃ 16:14
☽☍♀ 22:49

February 2018

LONGITUDE

Day	Sid.Time	☉	☽	☽ 12 hour	Mean ☊	True ☊	☿	♀	♂	⚳	♃	♄	⚷	♅	♆	♇
	h m s	° ' "	° ' "	° ' "	° '	° '	° '	° '	° '	° '	° '	° '	° '	° '	° '	° '
1 Th	8 44 36	12♒03 47	18♌10 03	25♌34 18	15♌15.2	14♌55.9	0♒41.2	17♒29.7	3♐21.0	11♌28.9	21♏15.1	4♑50.0	25♓45.6	24♈56.5	12♓46.8	19♑49.2
2 F	8 48 33	13 04 40	2♍54 05	10♍08 38	15 12.1	14 56.0	2 17.3	18 45.0	3 57.8	11R 14.7	21 21.3	4 56.1	25 48.4	24 58.0	12 48.8	19 51.1
3 Sa	8 52 29	14 05 31	17 17 21	24 19 46	15 08.9	14R 56.1	3 54.1	20 00.3	4 34.5	11 00.5	21 27.4	5 02.1	25 51.3	24 59.6	12 50.8	19 53.0
4 Su	8 56 26	15 06 21	1♎15 36	8♎04 44	15 05.7	14 56.1	5 31.6	21 15.5	5 11.2	10 46.4	21 33.3	5 08.1	25 54.1	25 01.2	12 52.9	19 54.9
5 M	9 00 22	16 07 11	14 47 11	21 23 06	15 02.5	14 56.0	7 09.8	22 30.8	5 47.8	10 32.4	21 39.1	5 14.1	25 57.0	25 02.8	12 55.0	19 56.8
6 Tu	9 04 19	17 07 59	27 52 45	4♏16 31	14 59.4	14 55.9	8 48.3	23 46.0	6 24.4	10 18.4	21 44.7	5 19.9	26 00.0	25 04.5	12 57.0	19 58.7
7 W	9 08 16	18 08 47	10♏34 50	16 48 11	14 56.2	14D 55.7	10 28.6	25 01.3	7 01.0	10 04.5	21 50.1	5 25.8	26 02.9	25 06.3	12 59.1	20 00.5
8 Th	9 12 12	19 09 33	22 57 07	29 02 12	14 53.0	14 55.7	12 09.1	26 16.5	7 37.5	9 50.6	21 55.4	5 31.6	26 05.9	25 08.1	13 01.3	20 02.4
9 F	9 16 09	20 10 19	5♐04 01	11♐03 08	14 49.8	14 55.9	13 50.5	27 31.7	8 14.1	9 37.0	22 00.5	5 37.3	26 08.9	25 09.9	13 03.4	20 04.2
10 Sa	9 20 05	21 11 04	17 00 10	22 55 38	14 46.6	14 56.4	15 32.6	28 46.9	8 50.5	9 23.4	22 05.5	5 43.0	26 12.0	25 11.8	13 05.5	20 06.0
11 Su	9 24 02	22 11 48	28 50 06	4♑44 06	14 43.5	14 57.1	17 15.5	0♓02.1	9 27.0	9 10.1	22 10.3	5 48.6	26 15.1	25 13.7	13 07.7	20 07.8
12 M	9 27 58	23 12 30	10♑38 05	16 32 31	14 40.3	14 58.0	18 59.3	1 17.2	10 03.4	8 56.9	22 14.9	5 54.2	26 18.2	25 15.7	13 09.8	20 09.6
13 Tu	9 31 55	24 13 12	22 27 49	28 24 23	14 37.1	14 58.9	20 43.9	2 32.4	10 39.7	8 43.9	22 19.4	5 59.7	26 21.3	25 17.7	13 12.0	20 11.4
14 W	9 35 51	25 13 52	4♒22 32	10♒22 35	14 33.9	14R 59.6	22 29.4	3 47.5	11 16.1	8 31.1	22 23.7	6 05.1	26 24.5	25 19.7	13 14.2	20 13.1
15 Th	9 39 48	26 14 31	16 24 48	22 29 25	14 30.8	14 59.8	24 15.7	5 02.6	11 52.3	8 18.6	22 27.8	6 10.5	26 27.7	25 21.8	13 16.4	20 14.8
16 F	9 43 45	27 15 08	28 36 38	4♓46 38	14 27.6	14 59.4	26 02.8	6 17.7	12 28.6	8 06.2	22 31.8	6 15.8	26 30.9	25 23.9	13 18.6	20 16.6
17 Sa	9 47 41	28 15 44	10♓59 33	17 15 30	14 24.4	14 58.3	27 50.8	7 32.8	13 04.7	7 54.2	22 35.6	6 21.1	26 34.1	25 26.1	13 20.8	20 18.3
18 Su	9 51 38	29 16 18	23 34 36	29 56 57	14 21.2	14 56.5	29 39.6	8 47.9	13 40.9	7 42.4	22 39.2	6 26.3	26 37.4	25 28.3	13 23.0	20 19.9
19 M	9 55 34	0♓16 51	6♈22 36	12♈51 39	14 18.0	14 54.3	1♓29.2	10 03.0	14 17.0	7 31.0	22 42.6	6 31.4	26 40.6	25 30.6	13 25.2	20 21.6
20 Tu	9 59 31	1 17 22	19 24 10	26 00 12	14 14.9	14 51.9	3 19.5	11 18.0	14 53.0	7 19.8	22 45.9	6 36.5	26 43.9	25 32.9	13 27.5	20 23.3
21 W	10 03 27	2 17 51	2♉39 50	9♉23 05	14 11.7	14 49.7	5 10.6	12 33.0	15 29.0	7 08.9	22 49.0	6 41.5	26 47.3	25 35.2	13 29.7	20 24.9
22 Th	10 07 24	3 18 19	16 10 02	23 00 41	14 08.5	14 48.1	7 02.4	13 48.0	16 04.9	6 58.4	22 51.8	6 46.4	26 50.6	25 37.6	13 32.0	20 26.5
23 F	10 11 20	4 18 44	29 55 02	6♊53 03	14 05.3	14D 47.3	8 54.8	15 03.0	16 40.8	6 48.2	22 54.6	6 51.2	26 54.0	25 40.0	13 34.2	20 28.1
24 Sa	10 15 17	5 19 08	13♊54 41	20 59 47	14 02.2	14 47.5	10 47.7	16 17.9	17 16.7	6 38.4	22 57.1	6 56.0	26 57.3	25 42.4	13 36.5	20 29.7
25 Su	10 19 14	6 19 29	28 08 09	5♋19 31	13 59.0	14 48.4	12 41.0	17 32.8	17 52.5	6 28.9	22 59.5	7 00.8	27 00.7	25 44.9	13 38.7	20 31.2
26 M	10 23 10	7 19 49	12♋33 32	19 49 46	13 55.8	14 49.9	14 34.6	18 47.7	18 28.2	6 19.8	23 01.6	7 05.4	27 04.1	25 47.4	13 41.0	20 32.7
27 Tu	10 27 07	8 20 07	27 07 40	4♌26 37	13 52.6	14 51.2	16 28.3	20 02.6	19 03.9	6 11.1	23 03.6	7 10.0	27 07.6	25 49.9	13 43.3	20 34.2
28 W	10 31 03	9♓20 22	11♌45 57	19 04 54	13♌49.4	14♌51.9	18♓21.9	21♓17.4	19♐39.5	6♌02.8	23♏05.4	7♑14.5	27♓11.0	25♈52.5	13♓45.5	20♑35.7

1st of Mon

Julian Day
2458150.
Obliquity
23°26'06
SVP 5♓00'
GC 27♐05
Eris 22♈48

Day	⚴
1	3♉43.
6	5 31.
11	7 27.
16	9 29.
21	11 38.
26	13 52.

Day	⚵
1	19♒36.
6	21 51.
11	24 06.
16	26 23.
21	28 41.
26	0♓59.

Day	⚶
1	7♐47.
6	10 01.
11	12 12.
16	14 20.
21	16 24.
26	18 24.

DECLINATION and LATITUDE

Day	☉ Decl	☽ Decl	☽ Lat	☽12h Decl	☿ Decl	☿ Lat	♀ Decl	♀ Lat	♂ Decl	♂ Lat	⚳ Decl	⚳ Lat	♃ Decl	♃ Lat	♄ Decl	♄ Lat
1 Th	17S10	15N40	0N18	13N55	21S40	1S43	16S52	1S21	20S11	0N39	30N08	13N22	16S60	1N07	22S28	0N53
2 F	16 53	11 58	1 38	9 51	21 23	1 47	16 30	1 22	20 19	0 38	30 15	13 25	17 01	1 07	22 28	0 53
3 Sa	16 36	7 38	2 50	5 21	21 03	1 50	16 07	1 23	20 26	0 37	30 22	13 28	17 03	1 07	22 28	0 53
4 Su	16 18	3 01	3 50	0 42	20 43	1 53	15 44	1 23	20 33	0 37	30 28	13 30	17 04	1 07	22 27	0 53
5 M	16 00	1S36	4 35	3S50	20 21	1 56	15 20	1 24	20 41	0 36	30 34	13 32	17 05	1 07	22 27	0 53
6 Tu	15 42	5 59	5 04	8 02	19 57	1 58	14 56	1 25	20 48	0 35	30 41	13 35	17 07	1 07	22 27	0 53
7 W	15 23	9 58	5 17	11 46	19 33	2 01	14 31	1 25	20 54	0 35	30 46	13 36	17 08	1 08	22 27	0 53
8 Th	15 04	13 26	5 15	14 55	19 06	2 02	14 06	1 26	21 01	0 34	30 52	13 38	17 09	1 08	22 27	0 53
9 F	14 45	16 15	4 59	17 23	18 39	2 04	13 41	1 26	21 08	0 33	30 58	13 40	17 10	1 08	22 26	0 53
10 Sa	14 26	18 20	4 30	19 04	18 10	2 05	13 15	1 27	21 14	0 33	31 03	13 41	17 12	1 08	22 26	0 53
11 Su	14 07	19 36	3 49	19 56	17 39	2 05	12 49	1 27	21 20	0 32	31 08	13 43	17 13	1 08	22 26	0 53
12 M	13 47	20 02	2 60	19 54	17 07	2 06	12 23	1 27	21 26	0 31	31 13	13 44	17 14	1 08	22 26	0 53
13 Tu	13 27	19 33	2 02	18 60	16 34	2 05	11 56	1 28	21 32	0 30	31 17	13 45	17 15	1 08	22 25	0 53
14 W	13 07	18 13	0 59	17 14	15 59	2 05	11 29	1 28	21 38	0 30	31 22	13 45	17 16	1 09	22 25	0 53
15 Th	12 46	16 02	0S08	14 40	15 22	2 04	11 01	1 28	21 44	0 29	31 26	13 46	17 17	1 09	22 25	0 53
16 F	12 25	13 07	1 15	11 26	14 45	2 02	10 34	1 28	21 49	0 28	31 30	13 47	17 17	1 09	22 25	0 53
17 Sa	12 05	9 35	2 19	7 38	14 06	1 60	10 06	1 28	21 55	0 27	31 34	13 47	17 18	1 09	22 24	0 53
18 Su	11 44	5 35	3 18	3 27	13 25	1 57	9 37	1 28	21 60	0 27	31 37	13 47	17 19	1 09	22 24	0 53
19 M	11 22	1 15	4 08	0N58	12 43	1 54	9 09	1 27	22 05	0 26	31 40	13 47	17 20	1 09	22 24	0 53
20 Tu	11 01	3N11	4 45	5 24	12 00	1 50	8 40	1 27	22 10	0 25	31 43	13 47	17 20	1 10	22 23	0 53
21 W	10 39	7 33	5 09	9 39	11 16	1 46	8 11	1 27	22 15	0 24	31 46	13 47	17 21	1 10	22 23	0 53
22 Th	10 18	11 38	5 16	13 29	10 30	1 42	7 42	1 27	22 19	0 23	31 49	13 47	17 22	1 10	22 23	0 53
23 F	9 56	15 10	5 05	16 39	9 43	1 36	7 13	1 26	22 24	0 22	31 51	13 47	17 22	1 10	22 23	0 53
24 Sa	9 34	17 54	4 36	18 53	8 55	1 30	6 43	1 26	22 28	0 22	31 53	13 46	17 23	1 10	22 23	0 53
25 Su	9 11	19 35	3 50	19 59	8 05	1 24	6 14	1 25	22 32	0 21	31 55	13 45	17 23	1 10	22 22	0 53
26 M	8 49	20 02	2 49	19 46	7 15	1 17	5 44	1 24	22 36	0 20	31 57	13 44	17 24	1 10	22 22	0 53
27 Tu	8 27	19 09	1 36	18 13	6 24	1 09	5 14	1 24	22 40	0 19	31 58	13 43	17 24	1 11	22 22	0 53
28 W	8S04	16N59	0S17	15N28	5S32	1S00	4S43	1S23	22S44	0N18	31N59	13N42	17S24	1N11	22S22	0N53

Day	⚷ Decl	⚷ Lat	♅ Decl	♅ Lat	♆ Decl	♆ Lat	♇ Decl	♇ La
1	1N33	3N31	9N08	0S33	7S36	0S54	21S34	0N
6	1 38	3 30	9 12	0 33	7 32	0 54	21 33	0
11	1 43	3 30	9 15	0 33	7 28	0 54	21 32	0
16	1 48	3 29	9 19	0 33	7 24	0 54	21 32	0
21	1 54	3 28	9 23	0 33	7 19	0 54	21 31	0
26	2N00	3N27	9N28	0S32	7S15	0S54	21S30	0N

Day	⚴ Decl	⚴ Lat	⚵ Decl	⚵ Lat	⚶ Decl	⚶ Lat	Eris Decl	Eris La
1	20S09	34S56	10S44	4N25	16S04	5N36	2S22	12S
6	19 06	34 23	10 13	4 14	16 22	5 39	2 21	12
11	18 03	33 49	9 40	4 03	16 37	5 41	2 19	12
16	16 59	33 17	9 05	3 52	16 50	5 43	2 18	12
21	15 55	32 45	8 29	3 40	17 01	5 45	2 17	12
26	14S50	32S14	7S51	3N29	17S10	5N47	2S15	12S

Moon Phenomena

Max/0 Decl

dy	hr mn	
4	15:38	0 S
11	23:28	20S02
19	6:49	0 N
25	20:22	20N03

Max/0 Lat

dy	hr mn	
7	8:22	5N18
14	21:12	0 S
21	21:41	5S16
28	5:05	0 N

Perigee/Apogee

dy	hr m		kilometers
11	14:18	a	405699
27	14:43	p	363935

PH	dy	hr mn	
☾	7	15:55	18♏49
●	15	21:06	27♒08
●	15	20:53	P 0.599
☽	23	8:10	4♊39

Void of Course Moon

Last Aspect			☽ Ingre
1 11:00	♅	△	♍ 1 19:
3 7:08	♃	✶	♎ 3 21:
5 18:47	♅	☍	♏ 6 3:
8 7:17	♀	□	♐ 8 13
10 16:39	♅	△	♑ 11 2
13 5:44	♅	□	♒ 13 15.
15 21:06	☉	☌	♓ 16 2:
17 22:15	♃	△	♈ 18 12:
20 11:12	♅	☌	♉ 20 19:
22 11:47	♃	☍	♊ 23 0
24 19:59	♅	✶	♋ 25 3
26 21:52	♅	□	♌ 27 4:

DAILY ASPECTARIAN

1 Th
☽⚻♇ 2:41
☽⚼♄ 2:43
☽□♃ 5:01
☿∥♇ 8:29
☽△♅ 11:00
☽⚻⚷ 12:21
☉∥♃ 13:41
☉⚺♆ 17:32
☽⚻☿ 22:52

2 F
☽□♂ 1:50
☽⚼♇ 3:13
☽△♄ 3:23
☽⚼♅ 11:44
☽⚺⚳ 13:37
☽∥♅ 15:50
☽☍♆ 16:30
☉⚻☽ 18:12
♀⚺♇ 21:37

3 Sa
☽⋕♆ 0:20
♀∠♄ 0:38
☽⚼☿ 3:05
☽△♇ 4:25
☽⚻♀ 5:03
☽✶♃ 7:08
♂∠♇ 12:47
⚳⚼⚷ 13:08
☽⚻♅ 13:10
☽∠⚳ 14:39
☽☍⚷ 14:41
☿✶♂ 15:58
☿⚺♄ 17:52
♂⚺♄ 21:37
☉⚼☽ 21:50

4 Su
♀□♃ 6:08
☽□♄ 6:51
☽✶♂ 7:13
☽∥⚷ 7:20
☿∥♂ 7:48
☽△☿ 8:31
☽∠♃ 9:22
☽⚼♀ 9:40
☽✶⚳ 16:31
☽⚻♆ 20:38

5 M
☽⋕⚷ 0:05
☉△☽ 2:37
☽□♇ 9:23
☽∠♂ 11:27
☽⚺♃ 12:35
☽△♀ 15:34
☽☍♅ 18:47
☽⚻⚷ 20:30

6 Tu
☽⚼♆ 0:08
☽∥♆ 8:59
☽✶♄ 14:07
☽⚺♂ 16:51
☿☍⚳ 18:55
☽⋕♅ 19:08
☽□⚳ 23:03
☽□☿ 23:46

7 W
☽⚼⚷ 0:54
♀✶♅ 1:38
☽△♆ 4:38
☿∠⚷ 8:28
☉□☽ 15:55
☽✶♇ 18:17
☽∠♄ 19:13
♀⚺⚷ 20:29
☽☌♃ 21:58

8 Th
☽⚻♅ 4:18
☽∥♀ 4:37
☽△⚷ 6:13
☽□♀ 7:17
☉∥☽ 11:59
☿⚺♆ 12:38
☉⚺♇ 21:30

9 F
☽∠♇ 0:00
☽⚺♄ 1:07
☽☌♂ 6:41
☽△⚳ 8:57
☽∥♃ 9:45
☽⚼♅ 10:15
☉∠♄ 11:46
☽□♆ 16:05
☽✶☿ 20:33
☽∥☿ 22:11

10 Sa
☽⚺♇ 6:17
☉✶☽ 9:15
☽⚺♃ 10:23
☽⚼⚳ 14:42
♂△⚳ 15:51
☽△♅ 16:39
☽□⚷ 18:44
♀ ♓ 23:21
☉□♃ 23:22

11 Su
☽✶♀ 2:44
☽∠☿ 8:09
☽☌♄ 14:18
☽∠♃ 17:04
☉∠☽ 18:36
☿∥♃ 19:13
☽⚻⚳ 20:38
☽⚺♂ 22:46

12 M
☽✶♆ 5:09
♂⚼♅ 8:35
☽∠♀ 12:51
☿⚺♇ 16:25
☽☌♇ 19:23
☽⚺☿ 19:53
♂∥♇ 22:58
☽✶♃ 23:43

13 Tu
☿∠♄ 3:48
☉⚺☽ 3:53
☽□♅ 5:44
☽∠♂ 6:49
☽✶⚷ 7:54
☽∠♆ 11:37
☿□♃ 22:40
☽⚺♀ 22:42

14 W
☉✶♅ 2:24
☽⚺♄ 3:27
☽☍⚳ 8:09
☽∥♃ 11:31
☽∠⚷ 14:07
☽✶♂ 14:30
☽⚺♆ 17:45

15 Th
♀∠♇ 4:00
☉⚺⚷ 5:30
☽⚺♇ 7:36
☽∥☿ 7:45
☽∠♄ 9:29
☽□♃ 12:01
☿✶♅ 15:08
☽✶♅ 17:42
☽☌☿ 18:07
☽⚺⚷ 19:53
☉☌☽ 21:06
♀✶♄ 23:21

16 F
☉∥☽ 5:39
☿⚺⚷ 6:27
☽∠♇ 13:00
☽✶♄ 14:59
☽☌♀ 16:37
☽⚻⚳ 18:08
☽∥♀ 20:19
☽∠♅ 22:56

17 Sa
☽⋕♅ 1:37
☽□♂ 4:13
☽☌♆ 4:32
♀⚻⚳ 5:54
♂□♆ 11:21
☉☌☿ 12:28
☽∥♆ 13:33
☽✶♇ 17:50
☽△♃ 22:15
☽⚼⚳ 22:23

18 Su
☽⚺♅ 3:35
☿ ♓ 4:29
☽☌⚷ 5:46
☉⚺☽ 11:39
☽⚺☿ 13:22
♀⋕♅ 13:50
☉ ♓ 17:19
☽⋕⚷ 20:42

19 M
☽□♄ 0:16
☽△⚳ 2:05
☽⚼♃ 2:29
☽⚺♀ 7:32
♀∠♅ 9:07
☽⚺♆ 13:04
☽△♂ 15:19
☽∥⚷ 16:57
☉∠☽ 17:50
☽∠☿ 21:43

20 Tu
☽□♇ 1:48
☽⚻♃ 6:09
☽☌♅ 11:12
☽⚺⚷ 13:22
☽∠♀ 13:50
☽∠♆ 16:29
☽⚼♂ 19:54
☽⋕♆ 22:42
☉✶☽ 23:17

21 W
☿∠♇ 3:07
☽⋕♀ 3:13
☽✶☿ 5:13
☽△♄ 7:15
☽□⚳ 7:55
☽∥♅ 10:32
☽∠⚷ 16:20
☉⋕☽ 16:32
☽⋕☿ 18:12
♀☌♆ 18:43
☽✶♆ 19:20
☽✶♀ 19:24
☿✶♄ 20:24
☿⚻⚳ 23:13
☽⚻♂ 23:51

22 Th
☽△♇ 7:31
☽⚼♄ 9:54
☽☍♃ 11:47
☉∥☿ 11:47
☽⚺♅ 16:36
☽✶⚷ 18:45
⚳⚻♄ 19:07
♂∥♄ 19:48
♀∥♆ 19:53

23 F
☉□☽ 8:10
☿⋕♅ 8:46
☽⚼♇ 9:35
☽✶⚳ 11:43
☽⚻♄ 12:01
☽□☿ 17:52
☽∠♅ 18:31
☽⋕♃ 18:43
⚵ ♓ 20:12
☿∠♅ 22:51
☽□♆ 23:29

24 Sa
☉∠♇ 4:18
☽□♀ 4:27
☽☍♂ 5:58
☉⋕♅ 8:03
☽⚻♇ 11:10
☽∠⚳ 12:56
☽⚻♃ 15:20
☽✶♅ 19:59
☽□⚷ 22:07

25 Su
☉⚻⚳ 3:15
♀□♂ 12:03
☿☌♆ 12:27
☽⚺⚳ 13:47
☉△☽ 14:41
☽☍♄ 14:53
☽⚼♃ 16:28
☉✶♄ 17:47
☿∥♆ 23:54

26 M
☽△♆ 1:52
☽△☿ 3:50
☽⚻♂ 10:11
☽△♀ 11:16
☽☍♇ 13:12
☽△♃ 17:18
☉⚼☽ 17:18
☽□♅ 21:52
☽△⚷ 24:00

27 Tu
☽⚼♆ 2:37
☽⚼☿ 8:11
♀✶♇ 10:21
☽⚼♂ 11:52
☽⚼♀ 14:11
☽☌⚳ 14:43
☽⚻♄ 16:33
☉⚻☽ 19:44
♀⚼⚳ 19:45
☽⋕♃ 20:15

28 W
☽⚼⚷ 0:41
☽⚻♆ 3:17
☽⚻☿ 12:26
☽△♂ 13:30
☽⚻♇ 14:31
☽⚻♀ 17:05
☽⚼♄ 17:17
☽□♃ 18:37
☽△♅ 23:14
☿□♂ 23:57

LONGITUDE

Day	Sid.Time	☉	☽	☽ 12 hour	Mean☊	True☊	☿	♀	♂	⚳	♃	♄	⚷	♅	♆	♇
	h m s	° ' "	° ' "	° ' "	° '	° '	° '	° '	° '	° '	° '	° '	° '	° '	° '	° '
1 Th	10 35 00	10♓20 36	26♌22 41	3♍38 30	13♌46.3	14♌51.6	20♓15.3	22♓32.3	20♐15.1	5♌54.8	23♏07.1	7♑18.9	27♓14.4	25♈55.1	13♓47.8	20♑37.2
2 F	10 38 56	11 20 48	10♍51 33	18 01 07	13 43.1	14R 49.8	22 08.0	23 47.1	20 50.6	5R 47.2	23 08.5	7 23.2	27 17.9	25 57.8	13 50.1	20 38.6
3 Sa	10 42 53	12 20 58	25 06 29	2♎07 05	13 39.9	14 46.7	23 59.9	25 01.8	21 26.1	5 40.1	23 09.8	7 27.5	27 21.4	26 00.5	13 52.4	20 40.1
4 Su	10 46 49	13 21 07	9♎02 25	15 52 08	13 36.7	14 42.5	25 50.5	26 16.6	22 01.5	5 33.3	23 10.8	7 31.7	27 24.9	26 03.2	13 54.7	20 41.5
5 M	10 50 46	14 21 13	22 36 00	29 13 56	13 33.6	14 37.8	27 39.6	27 31.3	22 36.9	5 27.0	23 11.7	7 35.8	27 28.4	26 05.9	13 56.9	20 42.8
6 Tu	10 54 43	15 21 18	5♏45 57	12♏12 12	13 30.4	14 33.1	29 26.6	28 46.0	23 12.2	5 21.1	23 12.4	7 39.8	27 31.9	26 08.7	13 59.2	20 44.2
7 W	10 58 39	16 21 22	18 32 57	24 48 34	13 27.2	14 29.1	1♈11.2	0♈00.7	23 47.4	5 15.6	23 12.9	7 43.8	27 35.4	26 11.5	14 01.5	20 45.5
8 Th	11 02 36	17 21 24	0♐59 28	7♐06 10	13 24.0	14 26.3	2 52.8	1 15.4	24 22.6	5 10.5	23 13.2	7 47.7	27 38.9	26 14.3	14 03.8	20 46.8
9 F	11 06 32	18 21 24	13 09 13	19 09 14	13 20.8	14D 24.9	4 30.9	2 30.0	24 57.7	5 05.9	23R 13.4	7 51.5	27 42.5	26 17.2	14 06.0	20 48.1
10 Sa	11 10 29	19 21 23	25 06 48	1♑02 35	13 17.7	14 24.9	6 05.0	3 44.6	25 32.8	5 01.7	23 13.3	7 55.2	27 46.0	26 20.0	14 08.3	20 49.4
11 Su	11 14 25	20 21 20	6♑57 14	12 51 22	13 14.5	14 26.0	7 34.6	4 59.2	26 07.8	4 57.9	23 13.1	7 58.8	27 49.6	26 23.0	14 10.6	20 50.6
12 M	11 18 22	21 21 15	18 45 38	24 40 37	13 11.3	14 27.8	8 59.1	6 13.7	26 42.7	4 54.5	23 12.6	8 02.4	27 53.1	26 25.9	14 12.8	20 51.8
13 Tu	11 22 18	22 21 09	0♒36 54	6♒35 02	13 08.1	14 29.4	10 18.0	7 28.3	27 17.5	4 51.6	23 12.0	8 05.8	27 56.7	26 28.9	14 15.1	20 53.0
14 W	11 26 15	23 21 01	12 35 31	18 38 46	13 05.0	14R 30.3	11 30.8	8 42.8	27 52.3	4 49.1	23 11.2	8 09.2	28 00.3	26 31.9	14 17.4	20 54.1
15 Th	11 30 12	24 20 51	24 45 13	0♓55 10	13 01.8	14 29.7	12 37.1	9 57.3	28 26.9	4 47.1	23 10.2	8 12.5	28 03.8	26 34.9	14 19.6	20 55.3
16 F	11 34 08	25 20 39	7♓08 52	13 26 32	12 58.6	14 27.3	13 36.5	11 11.7	29 01.5	4 45.5	23 09.0	8 15.7	28 07.4	26 37.9	14 21.9	20 56.4
17 Sa	11 38 05	26 20 26	19 48 17	26 14 07	12 55.4	14 22.9	14 28.5	12 26.2	29 36.0	4 44.3	23 07.6	8 18.8	28 11.0	26 41.0	14 24.1	20 57.4
18 Su	11 42 01	27 20 10	2♈44 03	9♈17 58	12 52.2	14 16.6	15 12.9	13 40.6	0♑10.5	4 43.6	23 06.0	8 21.8	28 14.6	26 44.1	14 26.4	20 58.5
19 M	11 45 58	28 19 53	15 55 41	22 37 02	12 49.1	14 09.2	15 49.4	14 54.9	0 44.8	4D 43.3	23 04.3	8 24.8	28 18.2	26 47.2	14 28.6	20 59.5
20 Tu	11 49 54	29 19 33	29 21 44	6♉09 32	12 45.9	14 01.3	16 17.9	16 09.3	1 19.1	4 43.4	23 02.3	8 27.6	28 21.7	26 50.3	14 30.8	21 00.5
21 W	11 53 51	0♈19 11	13♉00 06	19 53 10	12 42.7	13 53.9	16 38.2	17 23.6	1 53.2	4 44.0	23 00.2	8 30.4	28 25.3	26 53.4	14 33.0	21 01.5
22 Th	11 57 47	1 18 47	26 48 27	3♊45 40	12 39.5	13 47.8	16 50.4	18 37.9	2 27.3	4 45.0	22 57.9	8 33.0	28 28.9	26 56.6	14 35.2	21 02.4
23 F	12 01 44	2 18 21	10♊44 34	17 44 56	12 36.3	13 43.6	16R 54.5	19 52.1	3 01.3	4 46.5	22 55.4	8 35.6	28 32.5	26 59.8	14 37.4	21 03.3
24 Sa	12 05 40	3 17 53	24 46 35	1♋49 21	12 33.2	13D 41.6	16 50.7	21 06.4	3 35.2	4 48.3	22 52.8	8 38.1	28 36.0	27 03.0	14 39.6	21 04.2
25 Su	12 09 37	4 17 22	8♋53 04	15 57 35	12 30.0	13 41.3	16 39.3	22 20.5	4 09.0	4 50.6	22 49.9	8 40.5	28 39.6	27 06.2	14 41.8	21 05.1
26 M	12 13 34	5 16 49	23 02 45	0♌08 23	12 26.8	13 42.2	16 20.6	23 34.7	4 42.6	4 53.3	22 46.9	8 42.8	28 43.2	27 09.5	14 44.0	21 05.9
27 Tu	12 17 30	6 16 14	7♌14 17	14 20 11	12 23.6	13R 43.1	15 55.3	24 48.8	5 16.2	4 56.4	22 43.7	8 45.0	28 46.7	27 12.7	14 46.1	21 06.7
28 W	12 21 27	7 15 36	21 25 49	28 30 49	12 20.5	13 43.0	15 23.8	26 02.9	5 49.7	4 59.9	22 40.3	8 47.1	28 50.3	27 16.0	14 48.3	21 07.5
29 Th	12 25 23	8 14 56	5♍34 47	12♍37 18	12 17.3	13 41.0	14 47.1	27 16.9	6 23.1	5 03.8	22 36.8	8 49.1	28 53.8	27 19.3	14 50.4	21 08.2
30 F	12 29 20	9 14 13	19 37 52	26 36 01	12 14.1	13 36.5	14 05.8	28 30.9	6 56.4	5 08.2	22 33.1	8 51.0	28 57.4	27 22.6	14 52.5	21 08.9
31 Sa	12 33 16	10♈13 29	3♎31 13	10♎23 02	12♌10.9	13♌29.6	13♈20.9	29♈44.9	7♑29.6	5♌12.9	22♏29.2	8♑52.8	29♓00.9	27♈25.9	14♓54.6	21♑09.6

1st of Month

Julian Day # 2458178.5
Obliquity 23°26'07"
SVP 5♓00'33"
GC 27♐05.6
Eris 22♈58.7

Day	⚴
1	15♉16.0
6	17 38.4
11	20 05.2
16	22 36.3
21	25 11.0
26	27 49.2
31	0♊30.3

Day	⚵
1	2♓23.4
6	4 43.1
11	7 03.4
16	9 24.4
21	11 45.8
26	14 07.7
31	16 29.9

Day	⚶
1	19♐34.3
6	21 27.3
11	23 15.5
16	24 58.2
21	26 34.8
26	28 04.8
31	29 27.7

DECLINATION and LATITUDE

Day	☉ Decl	☽ Decl	☽ Lat	☽12h Decl	☿ Decl	☿ Lat	♀ Decl	♀ Lat	♂ Decl	♂ Lat	⚳ Decl	⚳ Lat	♃ Decl	♃ Lat	♄ Decl	♄ Lat
1 Th	7S41	13N43	1N03	11N45	4S39	0S51	4S13	1S22	22S48	0N17	32N00	13N41	17S24	1N11	22S22	0N53
2 F	7 18	9 37	2 18	7 23	3 46	0 42	3 43	1 21	22 51	0 16	32 01	13 40	17 24	1 11	22 21	0 53
3 Sa	6 56	5 03	3 23	2 41	2 52	0 32	3 12	1 20	22 54	0 15	32 02	13 38	17 25	1 11	22 21	0 53
4 Su	6 33	0 19	4 15	2S01	1 58	0 21	2 42	1 19	22 58	0 14	32 02	13 37	17 25	1 11	22 21	0 53
5 M	6 09	4S18	4 50	6 29	1 04	0 09	2 11	1 18	23 01	0 13	32 02	13 36	17 25	1 12	22 21	0 53
6 Tu	5 46	8 34	5 09	10 32	0 11	0N02	1 40	1 17	23 04	0 12	32 02	13 34	17 25	1 12	22 20	0 53
7 W	5 23	12 20	5 12	13 59	0N42	0 15	1 09	1 16	23 06	0 11	32 02	13 32	17 25	1 12	22 20	0 53
8 Th	4 60	15 27	5 00	16 44	1 34	0 27	0 39	1 15	23 09	0 10	32 02	13 30	17 25	1 12	22 20	0 53
9 F	4 36	17 50	4 35	18 43	2 25	0 40	0 08	1 13	23 11	0 09	32 01	13 28	17 25	1 12	22 20	0 53
10 Sa	4 13	19 23	3 58	19 51	3 14	0 54	0N23	1 12	23 14	0 08	32 00	13 26	17 24	1 12	22 19	0 53
11 Su	3 49	20 05	3 11	20 05	4 02	1 07	0 54	1 10	23 16	0 07	31 59	13 24	17 24	1 12	22 19	0 53
12 M	3 26	19 53	2 16	19 27	4 48	1 20	1 25	1 09	23 18	0 06	31 58	13 22	17 24	1 13	22 19	0 53
13 Tu	3 02	18 48	1 15	17 56	5 31	1 34	1 56	1 07	23 20	0 04	31 57	13 20	17 24	1 13	22 19	0 53
14 W	2 38	16 51	0 10	15 36	6 12	1 47	2 27	1 06	23 22	0 03	31 55	13 18	17 23	1 13	22 18	0 53
15 Th	2 15	14 08	0S56	12 31	6 49	1 60	2 57	1 04	23 23	0 02	31 53	13 15	17 23	1 13	22 18	0 53
16 F	1 51	10 44	1 60	8 50	7 24	2 12	3 28	1 02	23 25	0 01	31 52	13 13	17 22	1 13	22 18	0 53
17 Sa	1 27	6 47	2 60	4 40	7 55	2 24	3 59	1 01	23 26	0S00	31 50	13 10	17 22	1 13	22 18	0 53
18 Su	1 04	2 27	3 52	0 12	8 23	2 36	4 29	0 59	23 28	0 01	31 47	13 08	17 22	1 13	22 18	0 53
19 M	0 40	2N05	4 32	4N21	8 47	2 46	4 60	0 57	23 29	0 03	31 45	13 05	17 21	1 14	22 17	0 53
20 Tu	0 16	6 35	4 58	8 46	9 07	2 56	5 30	0 55	23 30	0 04	31 42	13 03	17 20	1 14	22 17	0 53
21 W	0N08	10 50	5 08	12 47	9 22	3 04	6 01	0 53	23 31	0 05	31 40	13 00	17 20	1 14	22 17	0 53
22 Th	0 31	14 34	5 00	16 09	9 34	3 11	6 31	0 51	23 31	0 07	31 37	12 58	17 19	1 14	22 17	0 53
23 F	0 55	17 31	4 35	18 38	9 41	3 17	7 01	0 49	23 32	0 08	31 34	12 55	17 18	1 14	22 17	0 53
24 Sa	1 19	19 27	3 53	19 59	9 43	3 22	7 30	0 47	23 32	0 09	31 31	12 52	17 17	1 14	22 17	0 53
25 Su	1 42	20 12	2 56	20 06	9 42	3 25	8 00	0 45	23 33	0 11	31 28	12 49	17 17	1 14	22 16	0 53
26 M	2 06	19 41	1 49	18 56	9 36	3 26	8 30	0 43	23 33	0 12	31 24	12 47	17 16	1 15	22 16	0 53
27 Tu	2 29	17 54	0 35	16 35	9 26	3 26	8 59	0 40	23 33	0 13	31 21	12 44	17 15	1 15	22 16	0 53
28 W	2 53	15 01	0N41	13 13	9 12	3 24	9 28	0 38	23 33	0 15	31 17	12 41	17 14	1 15	22 16	0 53
29 Th	3 16	11 14	1 55	9 07	8 54	3 20	9 57	0 36	23 33	0 16	31 13	12 38	17 13	1 15	22 16	0 53
30 F	3 40	6 52	3 00	4 33	8 33	3 14	10 25	0 34	23 33	0 18	31 10	12 35	17 12	1 15	22 16	0 53
31 Sa	4N03	2N11	3N54	0S11	8N08	3N07	10N54	0S31	23S33	0S19	31N06	12N33	17S11	1N15	22S15	0N53

Day	⚷ Decl	⚷ Lat	♅ Decl	♅ Lat	♆ Decl	♆ Lat	♇ Decl	♇ Lat
1	2N04	3N27	9N31	0S32	7S12	0S54	21S30	0N22
6	2 11	3 27	9 36	0 32	7 08	0 54	21 29	0 22
11	2 17	3 26	9 41	0 32	7 04	0 54	21 28	0 21
16	2 24	3 26	9 46	0 32	6 59	0 55	21 28	0 21
21	2 31	3 25	9 52	0 32	6 55	0 55	21 28	0 20
26	2 38	3 25	9 58	0 32	6 51	0 55	21 27	0 20
31	2N45	3N25	10N04	0S32	6S47	0S55	21S27	0N19

Day	⚴ Decl	⚴ Lat	⚵ Decl	⚵ Lat	⚶ Decl	⚶ Lat	Eris Decl	Eris Lat
1	14S12	31S55	7S28	3N22	17S15	5N48	2S14	12S01
6	13 09	31 25	6 49	3 11	17 21	5 50	2 13	12 00
11	12 06	30 55	6 08	2 60	17 25	5 51	2 12	11 60
16	11 04	30 25	5 26	2 48	17 28	5 53	2 10	11 59
21	10 04	29 56	4 44	2 37	17 29	5 54	2 09	11 59
26	9 05	29 27	4 01	2 25	17 30	5 55	2 07	11 58
31	8S08	28S58	3S17	2N13	17S30	5N56	2S06	11S58

Moon Phenomena

Max/0 Decl
dy hr mn
4 1:39 0 S
11 6:36 20S07
18 13:03 0 N
25 1:59 20N13
31 11:04 0 S

Max/0 Lat
dy hr mn
6 16:22 5N13
14 3:48 0 S
21 1:26 5S08
27 10:58 0 N

Perigee/Apogee
dy hr m kilometers
11 9:12 a 404676
26 17:18 p 369106

PH dy hr mn
○ 2 0:52 11♍23
☾ 9 11:21 18♐50
● 17 13:13 26♓53
☽ 24 15:36 3♋57
○ 31 12:38 10♎45

Void of Course Moon

Last Aspect	☽ Ingress
28 23:14 ♅ △	♍ 1 5:59
2 23:51 ♀ ☍	♎ 3 8:22
5 6:20 ♅ ☍	♏ 5 13:24
7 8:56 ♃ ☌	♐ 7 22:04
10 2:29 ♅ △	♑ 10 9:53
12 15:37 ♅ □	♒ 12 22:46
15 7:34 ♂ ⚹	♓ 15 10:13
17 13:13 ☉ ☌	♈ 17 18:58
19 19:30 ♂ △	♉ 20 1:08
21 17:22 ♃ ☍	♊ 22 5:31
24 3:53 ♅ ⚹	♋ 24 8:54
26 6:59 ♅ □	♌ 26 11:46
28 9:55 ♅ △	♍ 28 14:31
30 5:00 ♃ ⚹	♎ 30 17:53

DAILY ASPECTARIAN

1 Th: ☽⊼⚷ 1:26; ☿⚹♇ 4:43; ☿⚼⚳ 7:52; ♀△♃ 11:23; ☉∠♅ 14:24; ☽⚼♇ 15:18; ♂⊻♇ 15:33; ☽⊻⚳ 15:38; ☽△♄ 18:11; ♂⚼⚳ 22:06

2 F: ☽⚼♅ 0:10; ☽∥♅ 0:32; ☉☍☽ 0:52; ☿∥♀ 2:59; ☽☍♆ 4:59; ☉∥♆ 7:30; ☽#♆ 13:01; ☿△♃ 13:06; ☉#☽ 13:29; ☽△♇ 16:27; ☽∠⚳ 16:32; ☽□♂ 17:30; ☽⚹♃ 20:41; ☽☍☿ 21:50; ☽☍♀ 23:51

3 Sa: ☽⊼♅ 1:32; ☽☍⚷ 3:51; ☽#♀ 10:33; ☽#☿ 13:42; ☽∥⚷ 14:52; ☽⚹⚳ 17:59; ♀⊻♅ 19:32; ☿#⚷ 19:42; ☽□♄ 21:21; ☽∠♃ 22:30

4 Su: ☿⊻♅ 2:50; ☉⊼☽ 8:10; ☽⊼♆ 8:34; ☽∥☿ 9:52; ☽#⚷ 12:41; ☉☌♆ 13:55; ☽∥♀ 13:59; ☿☌♀ 18:06; ☽□♇ 20:37; ☿☌⚷ 21:26; ♀☌⚷ 23:01

5 M: ☽⚹♂ 0:02; ☽⊻♃ 1:04; ♀#⚷ 1:11; ☽☍♅ 6:20; ☽⊼⚷ 8:50; ☉∥☽ 9:20; ☽⊼♀ 9:49; ☽⊼☿ 10:35; ☽⚼♆ 11:31; ☉⚼☽ 13:14; ☽∥♆ 15:41; ☽□⚳ 23:14

6 Tu: ♂⊻♃ 0:09; ☽⚹♄ 3:32; ☽∠♂ 4:44; ☽#♅ 6:11; ☿ ♈ 7:35; ☽⚼⚷ 12:41; ☽△♆ 15:24; ☽⚼♀ 16:34; ☽⚼☿ 18:48; ☉△☽ 19:29; ♀ ♈ 23:47

7 W: ☽⚹♇ 4:13; ☿#♀ 7:56; ☽∠♄ 8:02; ☽☌♃ 8:56; ☽⊻♂ 10:32; ☽⊼♅ 14:44; ☽△⚷ 17:28

8 Th: ☽△♀ 0:35; ☽△☿ 4:16; ☽△⚳ 8:09; ☽∠♇ 9:25; ☽⊻♄ 13:26; ☿∥⚷ 19:01; ☽∥♃ 19:07; ☽⚼♅ 20:16

9 F: ☽□♆ 1:54; ♃ R 4:47; ☿△⚳ 8:24; ☉□☽ 11:21; ☽⚼⚳ 13:49; ☽⊻♇ 15:20; ☽⊻♃ 20:11

10 Sa: ☽☌♂ 0:55; ☽△♅ 2:29; ☽□⚷ 5:23; ☉⚼⚳ 15:09; ☽□♀ 19:32; ☉#☿ 19:41; ☽⊼⚳ 19:59; ♀△⚳ 23:36

11 Su: ☽□☿ 1:27; ☽☌♄ 2:06; ☽∠♃ 2:34; ☿□♄ 7:01; ☿⚼♃ 10:41; ♂△♅ 11:24; ☉⚹♇ 11:57; ☽⚹♆ 14:44

12 M: ☽☌♇ 4:17; ☉⚹☽ 5:45; ☽⚹♃ 9:01; ☽□♅ 15:37; ☽⊻♂ 16:57; ☽⚹⚷ 18:35; ☽∠♆ 21:14

13 Tu: ☽☍⚳ 8:31; ♀□♄ 12:40; ♀⚼♃ 13:56; ☉∠☽ 14:46; ☽⊻♄ 15:06; ☽⚹♀ 15:22; ☽∥♃ 18:18; ♀∥⚷ 19:34; ☉△♃ 20:07; ☽⚹☿ 21:37

14 W: ☽∠♂ 0:35; ☽∠⚷ 0:50; ☽⊻♆ 3:23; ☉#♀ 5:09; ♂□⚷ 6:11; ♃∠♄ 11:04; ☉#⚷ 16:25; ☽⊻♇ 16:28; ☽□♃ 20:54; ☽∠♄ 20:58; ☉⊻☽ 23:08

15 Th: ☽∠♀ 0:26; ☽⚹♅ 3:35; ☽∠☿ 6:06; ☽⊻⚷ 6:29; ☿#♆ 7:07; ☽⚹♂ 7:34; ☽⊼⚳ 19:25; ☽∠♇ 21:41

16 F: ☽⚹♄ 2:08; ☽#♅ 6:08; ☽⊻♀ 8:34; ☽∠♅ 8:36; ☽⊻☿ 13:15; ☽☌♆ 13:47; ☽#☿ 18:07; ☿⊻♆ 21:45; ☽∥♆ 22:55; ☽⚼⚳ 23:53

17 Sa: ☽⚹♇ 2:10; ☽△♃ 6:12; ☉⊻♅ 8:42; ☽⊻♅ 12:53; ☉☌☽ 13:13; ☽#♀ 14:05; ☽☌⚷ 15:41; ♂ ♑ 16:41; ☽□♂ 19:04

18 Su: ☽#⚷ 0:03; ☽△⚳ 3:39; ☉∥☽ 8:09; ☽⚼♃ 9:48; ☽□♄ 10:20; ♀⊻♆ 15:14; ☉#☽ 17:08; ☽⊻♆ 21:22; ☽☌♀ 21:59; ☉☌⚷ 23:16; ☽☌☿ 23:48

19 M: ☽∥⚷ 2:03; ⚳ D 4:13; ☽□♇ 9:06; ☽⊼♃ 12:47; ☽∥♀ 17:24; ☽☌♅ 19:30; ☽⊻⚷ 22:13; ☉⊻☽ 23:56

20 Tu: ☽∠♆ 0:16; ☽#♆ 1:52; ☽△♂ 3:37; ☿☌♀ 4:04; ☽□⚳ 9:29; ☽∥☿ 14:56; ☽△♄ 16:06; ☉ ♈ 16:17; ☽∥♅ 18:17

21 W: ☽∠⚷ 0:44; ☽⚹♆ 2:43; ☉∠☽ 4:22; ☽⊻☿ 6:28; ☽⚼♂ 7:04; ☽⊻♀ 8:25; ☽△♇ 14:00; ☽☍♃ 17:22; ☽⚼♄ 18:21

22 Th: ☽⊻♅ 0:14; ☽⚹⚷ 2:54; ☉⚹☽ 8:23; ☽∠☿ 8:46; ☽⊼♂ 10:10; ☽∠♀ 12:55; ☽⚹⚳ 13:44; ☽⚼♇ 15:56; ♀#♆ 18:31; ☽⊼♄ 20:18; ☽#♃ 21:59

23 F: ☿ R 0:18; ☽∠♅ 2:10; ☽□♆ 6:40; ☽⚹☿ 10:32; ☽∠⚳ 15:30; ☽⚹♀ 17:08; ☽⊼♇ 17:40; ☽⊼♃ 20:46; ♀□♇ 23:18

24 Sa: ☽⚹♅ 3:53; ☽□⚷ 6:33; ☉□☽ 15:36; ☽☍♂ 15:37; ☉□♂ 16:09; ☽⊻⚳ 17:07; ☽⚼♃ 22:13; ☽☍♄ 23:39

25 Su: ♀⊼♃ 9:09; ☽△♆ 9:53; ☽□☿ 12:55; ☉△⚳ 14:02; ☽☍♇ 20:42; ☽△♃ 23:33

26 M: ☽□♀ 0:59; ☽□♅ 6:59; ♂⊼⚳ 8:21; ☽△⚷ 9:38; ☽⚼♆ 11:20; ☽☌⚳ 20:06; ☽⊼♂ 20:32; ☉△☽ 22:15

27 Tu: ☽⊼♄ 2:34; ☽#♃ 6:15; ☉∥⚷ 10:30; ☽⚼⚷ 11:06; ☽⊼♆ 12:46; ☽△☿ 14:11; ☿∥♀ 15:12; ☽⚼♂ 22:56; ☽⊼♇ 23:29

28 W: ☉⚼☽ 1:31; ☽□♃ 2:06; ☽⚼♄ 4:00; ☽△♀ 8:34; ☉⚼♃ 9:27; ☽△♅ 9:55; ☽⊼⚷ 12:36; ☽⚼☿ 14:35; ☿⊻♆ 22:03; ☽⊻⚳ 23:07

29 Th: ♀☌♅ 0:48; ☽⚼♇ 0:57; ☽△♂ 1:26; ♀∥♅ 4:07; ☉⊼☽ 4:53; ☽△♄ 5:31; ☽∥♀ 6:38; ☽∥♅ 6:55; ☽⚼♅ 11:32; ☽⚼♀ 12:31; ☽∥☿ 14:17; ☉□♄ 14:17; ☽⊼☿ 14:58; ☽☍♆ 15:50

30 F: ☽#♆ 0:22; ☽∠⚳ 0:52; ⚴ ♊ 1:36; ☽△♇ 2:37; ☽⚹♃ 5:00; ♀⊻⚷ 9:01; ☽⊼♅ 13:24; ☉∥☽ 15:16; ☽☍⚷ 16:09; ☽⊼♀ 16:48; ☽∥⚷ 21:11; ♂∠♃ 23:46

31 Sa: ☽⚹⚳ 2:58; ♀∠♆ 3:16; ♀ ♉ 4:55; ☽∠♃ 6:53; ☽□♂ 7:13; ☽□♄ 9:23; ☉☍☽ 12:38; ☽☍☿ 16:17; ☽⊼♆ 20:02

April 2018

LONGITUDE

Day	Sid.Time	☉	☽	☽ 12 hour	Mean☊	True☊	☿	♀	♂	⚳	♃	♄	⚷	♅	♆	♇
	h m s	° ' "	° ' "	° ' "	° '	° '	° '	° '	° '	° '	° '	° '	° '	° '	° '	° '
1 Su	12 37 13	11♈12 42	17♎10 59	23♎54 44	12♌07.7	13♌20.6	12♈33.4	0♉58.8	8♑02.6	5♌18.0	22♏25.2	8♑54.5	29♓04.4	27♈29.2	14♓56.7	21♑10.3
2 M	12 41 09	12 11 54	0♏33 56	7♏08 24	12 04.6	13R 10.4	11R 44.3	2 12.7	8 35.6	5 23.5	22R 21.0	8 56.2	29 07.9	27 32.6	14 58.8	21 10.9
3 Tu	12 45 06	13 11 03	13 37 59	20 02 41	12 01.4	13 00.1	10 54.6	3 26.5	9 08.5	5 29.3	22 16.6	8 57.7	29 11.4	27 35.9	15 00.9	21 11.5
4 W	12 49 03	14 10 11	26 22 35	2♐37 51	11 58.2	12 50.6	10 05.2	4 40.4	9 41.2	5 35.6	22 12.1	8 59.1	29 14.9	27 39.3	15 02.9	21 12.1
5 Th	12 52 59	15 09 17	8♐48 47	14 55 45	11 55.0	12 42.8	9 17.2	5 54.2	10 13.8	5 42.2	22 07.4	9 00.5	29 18.4	27 42.6	15 05.0	21 12.6
6 F	12 56 56	16 08 21	20 59 10	26 59 34	11 51.9	12 37.3	8 31.4	7 07.9	10 46.3	5 49.2	22 02.6	9 01.7	29 21.8	27 46.0	15 07.0	21 13.1
7 Sa	13 00 52	17 07 23	2♑57 30	8♑53 35	11 48.7	12 34.1	7 48.5	8 21.6	11 18.6	5 56.5	21 57.6	9 02.9	29 25.3	27 49.4	15 09.0	21 13.6
8 Su	13 04 49	18 06 23	14 48 27	20 42 47	11 45.5	12D 33.0	7 09.2	9 35.3	11 50.9	6 04.2	21 52.5	9 03.9	29 28.7	27 52.8	15 11.0	21 14.1
9 M	13 08 45	19 05 22	26 37 14	2♒32 30	11 42.3	12 33.1	6 34.0	10 49.0	12 23.0	6 12.3	21 47.2	9 04.9	29 32.1	27 56.2	15 13.0	21 14.5
10 Tu	13 12 42	20 04 19	8♒29 17	14 28 12	11 39.1	12R 33.6	6 03.4	12 02.6	12 54.9	6 20.7	21 41.8	9 05.7	29 35.5	27 59.6	15 14.9	21 14.9
11 W	13 16 38	21 03 14	20 29 55	26 35 01	11 36.0	12 33.4	5 37.7	13 16.2	13 26.7	6 29.5	21 36.2	9 06.5	29 38.9	28 03.0	15 16.9	21 15.2
12 Th	13 20 35	22 02 08	2♓44 01	8♓57 26	11 32.8	12 31.5	5 17.1	14 29.7	13 58.4	6 38.6	21 30.5	9 07.1	29 42.3	28 06.5	15 18.8	21 15.6
13 F	13 24 32	23 00 59	15 15 37	21 38 54	11 29.6	12 27.2	5 01.7	15 43.2	14 29.9	6 48.0	21 24.7	9 07.7	29 45.7	28 09.9	15 20.7	21 15.9
14 Sa	13 28 28	23 59 49	28 07 28	4♈41 25	11 26.4	12 20.4	4 51.7	16 56.7	15 01.2	6 57.8	21 18.8	9 08.1	29 49.0	28 13.3	15 22.6	21 16.1
15 Su	13 32 25	24 58 37	11♈20 42	18 05 09	11 23.2	12 11.0	4D 47.0	18 10.1	15 32.4	7 07.9	21 12.7	9 08.5	29 52.3	28 16.8	15 24.5	21 16.4
16 M	13 36 21	25 57 23	24 54 31	1♉48 23	11 20.1	12 00.0	4 47.6	19 23.5	16 03.4	7 18.3	21 06.5	9 08.7	29 55.6	28 20.2	15 26.3	21 16.6
17 Tu	13 40 18	26 56 07	8♉46 16	15 47 45	11 16.9	11 48.2	4 53.3	20 36.9	16 34.3	7 29.0	21 00.2	9 08.9	29 58.9	28 23.6	15 28.1	21 16.8
18 W	13 44 14	27 54 49	22 51 43	29 58 01	11 13.7	11 36.9	5 04.1	21 50.2	17 05.0	7 40.1	20 53.7	9R 08.9	0♈02.1	28 27.1	15 29.9	21 16.9
19 Th	13 48 11	28 53 29	7♊05 49	14♊14 29	11 10.5	11 27.4	5 19.7	23 03.5	17 35.5	7 51.5	20 47.2	9 08.9	0 05.4	28 30.5	15 31.7	21 17.0
20 F	13 52 07	29 52 07	21 23 27	28 32 13	11 07.4	11 20.3	5 40.1	24 16.7	18 05.8	8 03.1	20 40.6	9 08.8	0 08.6	28 34.0	15 33.5	21 17.1
21 Sa	13 56 04	0♉50 43	5♋40 19	12♋47 26	11 04.2	11 16.1	6 04.9	25 29.9	18 35.9	8 15.1	20 33.9	9 08.5	0 11.8	28 37.4	15 35.2	21 17.2
22 Su	14 00 01	1 49 16	19 53 18	26 57 42	11 01.0	11D 14.3	6 34.1	26 43.1	19 05.9	8 27.4	20 27.0	9 08.2	0 14.9	28 40.9	15 37.0	21R 17.2
23 M	14 03 57	2 47 48	4♌00 31	11♌01 40	10 57.8	11R 13.9	7 07.5	27 56.2	19 35.6	8 39.9	20 20.1	9 07.7	0 18.1	28 44.3	15 38.7	21 17.2
24 Tu	14 07 54	3 46 17	18 01 06	24 58 45	10 54.7	11 13.9	7 44.9	29 09.2	20 05.2	8 52.7	20 13.1	9 07.2	0 21.2	28 47.7	15 40.3	21 17.2
25 W	14 11 50	4 44 44	1♍54 36	8♍48 35	10 51.5	11 12.8	8 26.0	0♊22.3	20 34.5	9 05.9	20 06.1	9 06.6	0 24.3	28 51.2	15 42.0	21 17.2
26 Th	14 15 47	5 43 09	15 40 37	22 30 34	10 48.3	11 09.6	9 10.8	1 35.2	21 03.7	9 19.2	19 58.9	9 05.9	0 27.4	28 54.6	15 43.6	21 17.1
27 F	14 19 43	6 41 31	29 18 19	6♎03 40	10 45.1	11 03.6	9 59.1	2 48.1	21 32.7	9 32.9	19 51.7	9 05.0	0 30.4	28 58.0	15 45.2	21 17.0
28 Sa	14 23 40	7 39 52	12♎46 24	19 26 19	10 41.9	10 54.7	10 50.7	4 01.0	22 01.4	9 46.8	19 44.4	9 04.1	0 33.4	29 01.4	15 46.8	21 16.8
29 Su	14 27 36	8 38 11	26 03 10	2♏36 45	10 38.8	10 43.5	11 45.5	5 13.8	22 29.9	10 01.0	19 37.1	9 03.1	0 36.4	29 04.8	15 48.4	21 16.6
30 M	14 31 33	9♉36 27	9♏06 52	15 33 21	10♌35.6	10♌30.7	12♈43.3	6♊26.6	22♑58.2	10♌15.4	19♏29.7	9♑02.0	0♈39.3	29♈08.2	15♓49.9	21♑16.4

1st of Month

Julian Day # 2458209.5
Obliquity 23°26'07"
SVP 5♓00'31"
GC 27♐05.6
Eris 23♈16.7

Day	⚴
1	1♊02.8
6	3 47.1
11	6 33.8
16	9 22.5
21	12 13.1
26	15 05.2

Day	⚵
1	16♓58.4
6	19 21.0
11	21 43.9
16	24 07.0
21	26 30.3
26	28 53.5

Day	⚶
1	29♐43.4
6	0♑57.0
11	2 02.0
16	2 57.6
21	3 43.2
26	4 18.0

DECLINATION and LATITUDE

Day	☉ Decl	☽ Decl	☽ Lat	☽12h Decl	☿ Decl	☿ Lat	♀ Decl	♀ Lat	♂ Decl	♂ Lat	⚳ Decl	⚳ Lat	♃ Decl	♃ Lat	♄ Decl	♄ Lat
1 Su	4N26	2S32	4N34	4S49	7N42	2N58	11N22	0S29	23S32	0S21	31N02	12N30	17S10	1N15	22S15	0N53
2 M	4 49	7 01	4 57	9 07	7 13	2 48	11 50	0 26	23 32	0 22	30 57	12 27	17 08	1 15	22 15	0 53
3 Tu	5 12	11 05	5 04	12 54	6 42	2 36	12 17	0 24	23 31	0 24	30 53	12 24	17 07	1 15	22 15	0 53
4 W	5 35	14 32	4 56	15 60	6 11	2 23	12 45	0 21	23 30	0 25	30 49	12 21	17 06	1 16	22 15	0 53
5 Th	5 58	17 15	4 34	18 19	5 39	2 09	13 12	0 19	23 29	0 27	30 44	12 18	17 05	1 16	22 15	0 53
6 F	6 21	19 09	3 59	19 46	5 07	1 54	13 38	0 16	23 28	0 29	30 39	12 15	17 03	1 16	22 15	0 53
7 Sa	6 43	20 09	3 15	20 19	4 36	1 38	14 04	0 14	23 27	0 30	30 35	12 12	17 02	1 16	22 15	0 53
8 Su	7 06	20 15	2 23	19 58	4 06	1 22	14 30	0 11	23 26	0 32	30 30	12 09	17 01	1 16	22 15	0 53
9 M	7 28	19 27	1 24	18 43	3 37	1 06	14 56	0 08	23 25	0 34	30 25	12 06	16 59	1 16	22 15	0 53
10 Tu	7 51	17 47	0 22	16 39	3 10	0 49	15 21	0 06	23 24	0 35	30 20	12 04	16 58	1 16	22 14	0 53
11 W	8 13	15 19	0S42	13 49	2 44	0 33	15 46	0 03	23 22	0 37	30 15	12 01	16 56	1 16	22 14	0 53
12 Th	8 35	12 08	1 45	10 18	2 22	0 17	16 11	0 00	23 21	0 39	30 09	11 58	16 55	1 16	22 14	0 53
13 F	8 57	8 20	2 45	6 15	2 01	0 01	16 35	0N02	23 19	0 41	30 04	11 55	16 53	1 16	22 14	0 53
14 Sa	9 18	4 04	3 37	1 48	1 43	0S14	16 58	0 05	23 18	0 43	29 59	11 52	16 52	1 16	22 14	0 53
15 Su	9 40	0N30	4 19	2N50	1 27	0 29	17 22	0 08	23 16	0 44	29 53	11 49	16 50	1 16	22 14	0 53
16 M	10 01	5 10	4 48	7 27	1 15	0 43	17 44	0 10	23 14	0 46	29 47	11 46	16 48	1 16	22 14	0 53
17 Tu	10 23	9 40	5 01	11 46	1 04	0 57	18 07	0 13	23 12	0 48	29 42	11 43	16 47	1 16	22 14	0 53
18 W	10 44	13 43	4 56	15 29	0 57	1 10	18 29	0 16	23 10	0 50	29 36	11 40	16 45	1 16	22 14	0 53
19 Th	11 05	17 01	4 32	18 35	0 52	1 22	18 50	0 19	23 08	0 52	29 30	11 37	16 43	1 16	22 14	0 53
20 F	11 25	19 18	3 52	20 00	0 49	1 34	19 11	0 21	23 06	0 54	29 24	11 35	16 41	1 17	22 14	0 53
21 Sa	11 46	20 23	2 56	20 25	0 49	1 44	19 31	0 24	23 04	0 56	29 18	11 32	16 40	1 17	22 14	0 53
22 Su	12 06	20 08	1 51	19 32	0 51	1 54	19 51	0 27	23 02	0 58	29 12	11 29	16 38	1 17	22 14	0 53
23 M	12 26	18 38	0 38	17 27	0 56	2 04	20 11	0 30	23 00	1 00	29 06	11 26	16 36	1 17	22 14	0 53
24 Tu	12 46	15 60	0N36	14 20	1 03	2 12	20 30	0 32	22 58	1 03	28 59	11 23	16 34	1 17	22 14	0 53
25 W	13 06	12 28	1 47	10 26	1 12	2 20	20 48	0 35	22 56	1 05	28 53	11 20	16 32	1 17	22 14	0 53
26 Th	13 26	8 17	2 51	6 02	1 23	2 27	21 06	0 38	22 53	1 07	28 47	11 18	16 30	1 17	22 14	0 53
27 F	13 45	3 43	3 45	1 22	1 36	2 34	21 23	0 41	22 51	1 09	28 40	11 15	16 28	1 17	22 14	0 53
28 Sa	14 04	0S58	4 25	3S17	1 51	2 39	21 39	0 43	22 49	1 12	28 34	11 12	16 26	1 17	22 14	0 53
29 Su	14 23	5 33	4 51	7 43	2 08	2 44	21 55	0 46	22 46	1 14	28 27	11 09	16 24	1 17	22 14	0 53
30 M	14N41	9S47	5N00	11S43	2N26	2S49	22N11	0N49	22S44	1S16	28N20	11N07	16S22	1N17	22S15	0N53

Day	⚷ Decl	⚷ Lat	♅ Decl	♅ Lat	♆ Decl	♆ Lat	♇ Decl	♇ Lat
1	2N46	3N25	10N05	0S32	6S46	0S55	21S27	0N19
6	2 53	3 25	10 11	0 32	6 42	0 55	21 27	0 19
11	2 60	3 25	10 17	0 32	6 39	0 55	21 27	0 18
16	3 06	3 25	10 23	0 32	6 35	0 55	21 27	0 18
21	3 13	3 25	10 30	0 31	6 32	0 55	21 28	0 18
26	3 19	3 25	10 36	0 31	6 29	0 55	21 28	0 17

Day	⚴ Decl	⚴ Lat	⚵ Decl	⚵ Lat	⚶ Decl	⚶ Lat	Eris Decl	Eris Lat
1	7S56	28S52	3S08	2N10	17S30	5N56	2S05	11S58
6	7 01	28 23	2 24	1 58	17 30	5 56	2 04	11 58
11	6 08	27 54	1 40	1 45	17 29	5 56	2 03	11 57
16	5 17	27 25	0 55	1 32	17 29	5 55	2 01	11 57
21	4 29	26 57	0 11	1 19	17 30	5 53	1 60	11 57
26	3 43	26 28	0N33	1 05	17 31	5 51	1 59	11 57

Moon Phenomena

Max/0 Decl
dy hr mn
7 14:37 20S19
14 21:23 0 N
21 7:35 20N26
27 19:02 0 S

Max/0 Lat
dy hr mn
2 22:57 5N04
10 8:11 0 S
17 5:01 5S01
23 12:22 0 N
30 2:28 5N00

Perigee/Apogee
dy hr m kilometers
8 5:26 a 404142
20 14:43 p 368714

PH dy hr mn
☾ 8 7:19 18♑24
● 16 1:58 26♈02
☽ 22 21:47 2♌42
○ 30 0:59 9♏39

Void of Course Moon

Last Aspect	☽ Ingress
1 18:30 ♅ ☍	♏ 1 22:58
3 16:07 ♃ ☌	♐ 4 6:56
6 13:37 ♅ △	♑ 6 18:02
9 2:41 ♅ □	♒ 9 6:51
11 14:57 ♅ ⚹	♓ 11 18:41
13 11:28 ♃ △	♈ 14 3:27
16 6:00 ♅ ☌	♉ 16 8:52
17 22:06 ♀ ☌	♊ 18 12:03
20 12:06 ♅ ⚹	♋ 20 14:28
22 14:59 ♅ □	♌ 22 17:10
24 18:41 ♅ △	♍ 24 20:41
26 9:51 ♇ △	♎ 27 1:14
29 5:33 ♅ ☍	♏ 29 7:13

DAILY ASPECTARIAN

1 Su
☽ # ⚷ 1:14
☽ □ ♇ 7:06
☽ ⚺ ♃ 9:17
☉ # ☽ 10:54
☉ ☌ ☿ 17:54
☽ ☍ ♅ 18:30
☽ ⚻ ⚷ 21:23
☽ ∥ ♆ 22:32
☽ ⚼ ♆ 22:56

2 M
☽ # ☿ 0:57
⚶ ♑ 1:55
☽ ☍ ♀ 3:18
☽ □ ⚳ 8:52
☽ ⚹ ♂ 15:19
☽ ⚹ ♄ 15:20
♂ ☌ ♄ 15:45
☽ # ♅ 18:01
☽ ⚻ ☿ 19:15
☿ # ♆ 22:02
☉ ⚻ ☽ 23:06

3 Tu
☽ ⚼ ⚷ 1:02
☽ △ ♆ 2:35
☽ # ♀ 9:02
☽ ⚹ ♇ 14:10
☽ ☌ ♃ 16:07
☽ ∠ ♄ 19:27
☽ ∠ ♂ 20:38
☽ ⚼ ☿ 21:42

4 W
☽ ⚻ ♅ 2:27
☽ △ ⚷ 5:31
☉ ⚼ ☽ 5:48
☿ □ ♂ 7:06
☉ ∥ ☿ 15:38
☽ ⚻ ♀ 17:43
☽ △ ⚳ 17:54
☽ ∠ ♇ 18:56
♀ □ ⚳ 19:43
☉ ⚺ ♆ 22:11
☽ ∥ ♃ 22:12

5 Th
☽ ⚺ ♄ 0:23
☽ △ ☿ 0:52
☽ ⚺ ♂ 2:54
☽ ⚼ ♅ 7:40
☿ □ ♄ 8:23
☽ □ ♆ 12:20
☉ △ ☽ 13:33
☽ ⚼ ⚳ 23:40

6 F
☽ ⚺ ♇ 0:28
☽ ⚺ ♃ 2:05
☽ ⚼ ♀ 2:32
☽ △ ♅ 13:37
☽ □ ⚷ 16:51
☿ ⚺ ♀ 17:07
☉ # ♆ 22:09

7 Sa
☽ ⚻ ⚳ 6:06
☽ ∠ ♃ 8:02
☽ □ ☿ 9:16
☽ △ ♀ 12:11
☽ ☌ ♄ 12:20
♀ △ ♄ 13:38
☽ ☌ ♂ 17:42

8 Su
☽ ⚹ ♆ 0:46
☉ □ ☽ 7:19
☿ ⚼ ♃ 12:57
☽ ☌ ♇ 13:04
☽ ⚹ ♃ 14:15

9 M
☽ □ ♅ 2:41
☽ ⚹ ⚷ 5:56
☽ ∠ ♆ 7:19
☿ △ ⚳ 13:00
☽ ⚹ ☿ 19:17
☽ ☍ ⚳ 19:38

10 Tu
☽ ⚺ ♄ 1:13
☽ □ ♀ 7:57
☽ ∥ ♃ 9:00
☽ ⚺ ♂ 9:18
☿ ∥ ⚷ 10:06
☽ ∠ ⚷ 12:18
☽ ⚺ ♆ 13:36
☽ # ♀ 20:38

11 W
☽ ∠ ☿ 0:15
☉ ⚹ ☽ 1:12
☽ ⚺ ♇ 1:30
☽ □ ♃ 2:10
☉ □ ♇ 4:55
♀ △ ♂ 6:04
☽ ∠ ♄ 7:08
☉ ⚻ ♃ 12:16
☽ ⚹ ♅ 14:57
☽ ∠ ♂ 16:21
☽ ⚺ ⚷ 18:05

12 Th
♀ ∠ ⚷ 4:19
☽ ⚺ ☿ 4:49
☽ ∠ ♇ 6:49
☽ ⚻ ⚳ 7:39
☉ ∠ ☽ 9:01
☽ # ♅ 11:54
☽ ⚹ ♄ 12:19
♀ ⚹ ♆ 16:27
☽ ∠ ♅ 20:01
☉ # ☽ 20:40
☽ ⚹ ♂ 22:30

13 F
☽ ☌ ♆ 0:10
☽ ⚹ ♀ 0:58
☽ ∥ ♆ 9:56
☽ ⚹ ♇ 11:17
☽ △ ♃ 11:28
☽ ⚼ ⚳ 12:26
☉ ⚺ ☽ 15:45
♀ # ♃ 17:23

14 Sa
☽ ⚺ ♅ 0:11
☽ ☌ ⚷ 3:07
☽ # ⚷ 5:21
☽ ∠ ♀ 7:43
♃ ⚹ ♇ 9:59
☽ ☌ ☿ 12:13
☽ # ☿ 13:14
☽ ⚼ ♃ 14:50
☽ △ ⚳ 16:19
♂ ⚹ ♆ 17:28
☽ □ ♄ 20:02

15 Su
☽ ∥ ☿ 4:40
☽ ⚺ ♆ 7:16
☽ □ ♂ 7:47
☿ D 9:22
☽ ∥ ⚷ 13:18
☽ ⚺ ♀ 13:21
☽ ⚻ ♃ 17:23
☽ □ ♇ 17:38

16 M
☉ ☌ ☽ 1:58
☽ ☌ ♅ 6:00
☽ # ♆ 7:24
☿ ∠ ♀ 8:21
☽ ⚺ ⚷ 8:47
☽ ∠ ♆ 9:39
☽ ⚺ ☿ 17:16
☽ □ ⚳ 21:46

17 Tu
☽ △ ♄ 0:39
☉ ∥ ♅ 2:20
☽ ∥ ♅ 4:12
☉ ∥ ☽ 4:22
♀ ☍ ♃ 7:01
⚷ ♈ 8:13
☽ ∠ ⚷ 10:39
☽ ⚹ ♆ 11:28
♀ △ ♇ 13:05
☽ △ ♂ 13:50
☽ ∠ ☿ 19:12
☽ ☍ ♃ 20:42
☽ △ ♇ 21:19
☽ ☌ ♀ 22:06

18 W
♄ R 1:48
☽ ⚼ ♄ 2:11
☉ ⚺ ☽ 9:10
☽ ⚺ ♅ 9:29
☽ ⚹ ⚷ 12:10
☉ ☌ ♅ 14:01
☽ ⚼ ♂ 16:08
☽ ⚹ ☿ 20:58
☽ # ♃ 21:33
☽ ⚼ ♇ 22:38

19 Th
☽ ⚹ ⚳ 1:18
☽ ⚻ ♄ 3:27
☽ ∠ ♅ 10:49
☉ ∠ ☽ 12:15
☽ □ ♆ 14:11
☽ ⚻ ♂ 18:16
♀ ⚼ ♄ 21:24
☽ ∥ ♀ 21:57
☽ ⚻ ♃ 22:49
☽ ⚻ ♇ 23:49

20 F
☿ ⚼ ♃ 0:25
☽ ∠ ⚳ 2:50
☉ ♉ 3:14
☽ ⚺ ♀ 5:18
☉ ⚺ ⚷ 7:08
☽ ⚹ ♅ 12:06
☽ □ ⚷ 14:45
☉ ⚹ ☽ 15:17
☉ ∠ ♆ 17:28
☽ ⚼ ♃ 23:49

21 Sa
☽ □ ☿ 0:43
☽ ⚺ ⚳ 4:24
☽ ☍ ♄ 5:51
☽ ∠ ♀ 8:54
☽ △ ♆ 16:46
☽ ☍ ♂ 22:37

22 Su
☽ △ ♃ 0:57
☽ ☍ ♇ 2:22
☽ ∥ ♀ 5:02
☽ ⚹ ♀ 12:41
☽ □ ♅ 14:59
♇ R 15:27
☽ △ ⚷ 17:40
☽ ⚼ ♆ 18:15
☉ □ ☽ 21:47

23 M
☽ △ ☿ 5:34
☽ ☌ ⚳ 8:05
☽ ⚻ ♄ 8:45
♀ ⚺ ♅ 16:35
☽ ⚼ ⚷ 19:24
☽ # ♃ 19:27
☽ ⚻ ♆ 19:58

24 Tu
☽ ⚻ ♂ 3:41
☽ □ ♃ 3:45
♂ ⚹ ♃ 5:14
☽ ⚻ ♇ 5:38
☽ ⚼ ☿ 8:33
☽ ⚼ ♄ 10:31
♀ ♊ 16:41
☽ △ ♅ 18:41
☉ ∥ ☽ 20:19
☽ □ ♀ 21:04
☽ ⚻ ⚷ 21:23

25 W
♀ ⚹ ⚷ 0:42
⚳ ⚻ ♄ 1:16
☉ △ ☽ 5:18
☽ ⚼ ♂ 6:36
☽ ⚼ ♇ 7:36
☽ ∥ ♅ 11:08
☽ ⚻ ☿ 11:59
☽ △ ♄ 12:31
☽ ⚺ ⚳ 12:42
☽ ⚼ ♅ 20:54
☿ □ ♄ 21:29

26 Th
☽ ☍ ♆ 0:05
☿ △ ⚳ 6:03
☽ ⚹ ♃ 7:29
☉ ⚼ ☽ 9:32
☽ # ♆ 9:39
☽ △ ♂ 9:48
☽ △ ♇ 9:51
♂ ☌ ♇ 11:01
☽ ∠ ⚳ 15:27
☽ ⚻ ♅ 23:24

27 F
☽ ∥ ⚷ 1:56
☽ ☍ ⚷ 2:08
☽ △ ♀ 6:49
♀ # ♇ 7:51
☽ ∠ ♃ 9:47
☽ ∥ ☿ 10:20
☉ ⚻ ☽ 14:09
☽ □ ♄ 17:22
☽ ⚹ ⚳ 18:33
☽ ☍ ☿ 20:18

28 Sa
☽ # ☿ 4:48
☽ ⚻ ♆ 5:25
⚵ ♈ 7:45
☽ ⚼ ♀ 12:22
☽ ⚺ ♃ 12:26
☽ # ⚷ 12:28
☽ □ ♇ 15:20
☽ □ ♂ 17:18

29 Su
☽ ∥ ♆ 4:56
☽ ☍ ♅ 5:33
☽ ⚻ ⚷ 8:21
☽ ⚼ ♆ 8:42
☉ △ ♄ 10:05
☽ ⚻ ♀ 18:33
♀ ⚼ ♇ 20:39
☽ ⚹ ♄ 23:51

30 M
☉ ☍ ☽ 0:59
☽ □ ⚳ 2:10
☽ # ♅ 5:26
♀ # ♄ 6:06
☽ ⚻ ☿ 7:16
☽ ⚼ ⚷ 12:14
☽ △ ♆ 12:33
☽ ☌ ♃ 19:13
☉ □ ⚳ 21:26
☽ ⚹ ♇ 22:45

LONGITUDE

Day	Sid.Time	☉	☽	☽ 12 hour	Mean ☊	True ☊	☿	♀	♂	⚳	♃	♄	⚷	♅	♆	♇
	h m s	° ' "	° ' "	° ' "	° '	° '	° '	° '	° '	° '	° '	° '	° '	° '	° '	° '
Tu	14 35 29	10♉34 42	21♏56 06	28♏15 04	10♌32.4	10♌17.6	13♈44.2	7♊39.4	23♑26.3	10♌30.1	19♏22.3	9♑00.8	0♈42.3	29♈11.6	15♓51.4	21♑16.2
W	14 39 26	11 32 56	4♐30 16	10♐41 48	10 29.2	10R 05.3	14 47.8	8 52.0	23 54.1	10 45.0	19R 14.8	8R 59.5	0 45.1	29 15.0	15 52.9	21R 15.9
Th	14 43 23	12 31 08	16 49 49	22 54 34	10 26.1	9 55.0	15 54.2	10 04.7	24 21.7	11 00.1	19 07.3	8 58.1	0 48.0	29 18.4	15 54.4	21 15.7
F	14 47 19	13 29 18	28 56 21	4♑55 35	10 22.9	9 47.1	17 03.2	11 17.3	24 49.1	11 15.5	18 59.7	8 56.7	0 50.8	29 21.7	15 55.8	21 15.3
Sa	14 51 16	14 27 27	10♑52 42	16 48 12	10 19.7	9 42.0	18 14.7	12 29.8	25 16.2	11 31.2	18 52.1	8 55.1	0 53.6	29 25.1	15 57.2	21 15.0
Su	14 55 12	15 25 34	22 42 39	28 36 39	10 16.5	9 39.3	19 28.7	13 42.3	25 43.0	11 47.0	18 44.5	8 53.4	0 56.4	29 28.4	15 58.6	21 14.6
M	14 59 09	16 23 40	4♒30 50	10♒25 53	10 13.3	9D 38.5	20 45.2	14 54.8	26 09.6	12 03.1	18 36.9	8 51.7	0 59.2	29 31.8	15 59.9	21 14.2
Tu	15 03 05	17 21 44	16 22 29	22 21 18	10 10.2	9R 38.5	22 04.0	16 07.2	26 35.9	12 19.4	18 29.3	8 49.9	1 01.9	29 35.1	16 01.2	21 13.8
W	15 07 02	18 19 47	28 23 03	4♓28 23	10 07.0	9 38.2	23 25.0	17 19.6	27 01.9	12 35.9	18 21.6	8 47.9	1 04.5	29 38.4	16 02.5	21 13.3
Th	15 10 58	19 17 49	10♓37 58	16 52 21	10 03.8	9 36.6	24 48.4	18 31.9	27 27.6	12 52.7	18 14.0	8 45.9	1 07.2	29 41.7	16 03.8	21 12.9
F	15 14 55	20 15 49	23 12 06	29 37 39	10 00.6	9 32.9	26 13.9	19 44.1	27 53.0	13 09.6	18 06.3	8 43.8	1 09.8	29 45.0	16 05.1	21 12.4
Sa	15 18 52	21 13 48	6♈09 20	12♈47 24	9 57.5	9 26.7	27 41.7	20 56.4	28 18.1	13 26.8	17 58.7	8 41.6	1 12.3	29 48.3	16 06.3	21 11.8
Su	15 22 48	22 11 45	19 31 54	26 22 46	9 54.3	9 18.1	29 11.6	22 08.5	28 42.9	13 44.1	17 51.0	8 39.4	1 14.8	29 51.5	16 07.4	21 11.3
M	15 26 45	23 09 41	3♉19 46	10♉22 31	9 51.1	9 07.6	0♉43.7	23 20.7	29 07.3	14 01.7	17 43.4	8 37.0	1 17.3	29 54.7	16 08.6	21 10.7
Tu	15 30 41	24 07 36	17 30 25	24 42 47	9 47.9	8 56.4	2 17.8	24 32.7	29 31.4	14 19.5	17 35.8	8 34.6	1 19.8	29 58.0	16 09.7	21 10.0
W	15 34 38	25 05 30	1♊58 47	9♊17 32	9 44.7	8 45.6	3 54.1	25 44.8	29 55.2	14 37.4	17 28.3	8 32.0	1 22.2	0♉01.2	16 10.8	21 09.4
Th	15 38 34	26 03 22	16 38 02	23 59 21	9 41.6	8 36.4	5 32.6	26 56.7	0♒18.6	14 55.6	17 20.8	8 29.4	1 24.6	0 04.3	16 11.9	21 08.7
F	15 42 31	27 01 12	1♋20 35	8♋40 50	9 38.4	8 29.6	7 13.1	28 08.7	0 41.6	15 13.9	17 13.3	8 26.8	1 26.9	0 07.5	16 12.9	21 08.0
Sa	15 46 27	27 59 01	15 59 24	23 15 37	9 35.2	8 25.5	8 55.7	29 20.5	1 04.3	15 32.5	17 05.9	8 24.0	1 29.2	0 10.7	16 13.9	21 07.3
Su	15 50 24	28 56 48	0♌28 59	7♌39 08	9 32.0	8D 23.8	10 40.4	0♋32.3	1 26.6	15 51.2	16 58.5	8 21.2	1 31.5	0 13.8	16 14.9	21 06.6
M	15 54 21	29 54 33	14 45 48	21 48 50	9 28.9	8 23.7	12 27.3	1 44.1	1 48.5	16 10.0	16 51.2	8 18.3	1 33.7	0 16.9	16 15.9	21 05.8
Tu	15 58 17	0♊52 17	28 48 10	5♍43 48	9 25.7	8R 24.0	14 16.2	2 55.8	2 10.0	16 29.1	16 43.9	8 15.3	1 35.9	0 20.0	16 16.8	21 05.0
W	16 02 14	1 49 59	12♍35 48	19 24 16	9 22.5	8 23.6	16 07.3	4 07.4	2 31.1	16 48.3	16 36.7	8 12.2	1 38.0	0 23.0	16 17.7	21 04.2
Th	16 06 10	2 47 40	26 09 16	2♎50 56	9 19.3	8 21.3	18 00.4	5 18.9	2 51.8	17 07.7	16 29.6	8 09.1	1 40.1	0 26.1	16 18.5	21 03.4
F	16 10 07	3 45 19	9♎29 21	16 04 36	9 16.2	8 16.7	19 55.6	6 30.4	3 12.1	17 27.3	16 22.6	8 05.9	1 42.1	0 29.1	16 19.4	21 02.5
Sa	16 14 03	4 42 56	22 36 46	29 05 53	9 13.0	8 09.7	21 52.8	7 41.9	3 32.0	17 47.0	16 15.6	8 02.7	1 44.1	0 32.1	16 20.1	21 01.6
Su	16 18 00	5 40 32	5♏31 58	11♏55 04	9 09.8	8 00.5	23 52.0	8 53.2	3 51.4	18 06.8	16 08.7	7 59.3	1 46.1	0 35.0	16 20.9	21 00.7
M	16 21 56	6 38 07	18 15 11	24 32 19	9 06.6	7 50.0	25 53.1	10 04.5	4 10.4	18 26.9	16 01.9	7 56.0	1 48.0	0 38.0	16 21.6	20 59.8
Tu	16 25 53	7 35 40	0♐46 31	6♐57 50	9 03.4	7 39.2	27 56.1	11 15.8	4 28.9	18 47.0	15 55.2	7 52.5	1 49.9	0 40.9	16 22.3	20 58.8
W	16 29 50	8 33 13	13 06 19	19 12 06	9 00.3	7 29.0	0♊00.9	12 26.9	4 46.9	19 07.3	15 48.6	7 49.0	1 51.7	0 43.8	16 23.0	20 57.9
Th	16 33 46	9♊30 44	25 15 20	1♑16 11	8♌57.1	7♌20.5	2♊07.2	13♋38.0	5♒04.5	19♌27.8	15♏42.1	7♑45.4	1♈53.5	0♉46.7	16♓23.6	20♑56.9

1st of Month

Julian Day # 2458239.5
Obliquity 23°26'07"
SVP 5♓00'28"
GC 27♐05.7
Eris 23♈36.2

Day	⚴	Day	⚵	Day	⚶
1	17♊58.5	1	1♈16.7	1	4♑41.6
6	20 52.9	6	3 39.8	6	4 53.5
11	23 48.2	11	6 02.8	11	4 53.0R
16	26 44.2	16	8 25.6	16	4 40.1R
21	29 40.6	21	10 48.1	21	4 14.9R
26	2♋37.3	26	13 10.1	26	3 38.0R
31	5 34.0	31	15 31.6	31	2 50.4R

DECLINATION and LATITUDE

Day	☉ Decl	☽ Decl	☽ Lat	☽12h Decl	☿ Decl	☿ Lat	♀ Decl	♀ Lat	♂ Decl	♂ Lat	⚳ Decl	⚳ Lat	♃ Decl	♃ Lat	♄ Decl	♄ Lat
Tu	14N60	13S30	4N54	15S07	2N46	2S52	22N26	0N51	22S41	1S19	28N13	11N04	16S20	1N16	22S15	0N53
W	15 18	16 33	4 34	17 46	3 08	2 55	22 40	0 54	22 39	1 21	28 07	11 01	16 18	1 16	22 15	0 53
Th	15 36	18 47	4 01	19 34	3 32	2 57	22 53	0 56	22 37	1 23	27 60	10 59	16 16	1 16	22 15	0 53
F	15 53	20 08	3 18	20 28	3 56	2 59	23 06	0 59	22 34	1 26	27 53	10 56	16 14	1 16	22 15	0 53
Sa	16 10	20 34	2 26	20 26	4 23	2 60	23 18	1 02	22 32	1 28	27 46	10 53	16 12	1 16	22 15	0 53
Su	16 27	20 04	1 29	19 29	4 50	3 00	23 30	1 04	22 29	1 31	27 38	10 51	16 10	1 16	22 15	0 53
M	16 44	18 41	0 27	17 41	5 19	3 00	23 41	1 07	22 27	1 34	27 31	10 48	16 08	1 16	22 15	0 53
Tu	17 01	16 30	0S36	15 07	5 49	2 59	23 51	1 09	22 24	1 36	27 24	10 46	16 06	1 16	22 15	0 53
W	17 17	13 34	1 38	11 51	6 21	2 58	24 01	1 11	22 22	1 39	27 17	10 43	16 04	1 16	22 16	0 53
Th	17 33	9 60	2 37	8 00	6 53	2 56	24 10	1 14	22 20	1 42	27 09	10 41	16 02	1 16	22 16	0 53
F	17 49	5 54	3 29	3 42	7 26	2 53	24 18	1 16	22 17	1 44	27 02	10 38	16 00	1 16	22 16	0 53
Sa	18 04	1 26	4 13	0N54	8 01	2 50	24 26	1 19	22 15	1 47	26 54	10 35	15 58	1 16	22 16	0 53
Su	18 19	3N15	4 44	5 36	8 36	2 46	24 33	1 21	22 13	1 50	26 47	10 33	15 56	1 16	22 16	0 53
M	18 34	7 55	5 00	10 09	9 12	2 41	24 39	1 23	22 10	1 53	26 39	10 31	15 54	1 16	22 16	0 53
Tu	18 48	12 17	4 58	14 15	9 49	2 36	24 45	1 25	22 08	1 56	26 31	10 28	15 52	1 16	22 16	0 53
W	19 02	16 01	4 38	17 33	10 27	2 31	24 49	1 27	22 06	1 59	26 23	10 26	15 50	1 15	22 17	0 53
Th	19 16	18 49	3 58	19 45	11 05	2 25	24 53	1 29	22 04	2 02	26 15	10 23	15 48	1 15	22 17	0 53
F	19 29	20 22	3 03	20 38	11 44	2 19	24 57	1 31	22 02	2 05	26 07	10 21	15 46	1 15	22 17	0 53
Sa	19 42	20 33	1 56	20 07	12 23	2 12	24 59	1 33	22 00	2 08	25 59	10 18	15 44	1 15	22 17	0 53
Su	19 55	19 22	0 42	18 17	13 03	2 04	25 01	1 35	21 58	2 11	25 51	10 16	15 42	1 15	22 17	0 53
M	20 08	16 57	0N34	15 17	13 43	1 56	25 03	1 37	21 56	2 15	25 43	10 14	15 40	1 15	22 18	0 53
Tu	20 20	13 33	1 46	11 35	14 24	1 48	25 03	1 39	21 55	2 18	25 35	10 11	15 38	1 15	22 18	0 53
W	20 31	9 28	2 52	7 16	15 04	1 39	25 03	1 41	21 53	2 21	25 27	10 09	15 37	1 15	22 18	0 53
Th	20 43	4 59	3 46	2 40	15 45	1 30	25 02	1 43	21 51	2 24	25 19	10 07	15 35	1 14	22 18	0 53
F	20 54	0 20	4 27	1S59	16 25	1 21	25 01	1 44	21 50	2 28	25 10	10 05	15 33	1 14	22 18	0 53
Sa	21 05	4S16	4 53	6 28	17 05	1 11	24 58	1 46	21 49	2 31	25 02	10 02	15 31	1 14	22 19	0 53
Su	21 15	8 35	5 03	10 36	17 45	1 01	24 55	1 47	21 47	2 35	24 53	10 00	15 29	1 14	22 19	0 53
M	21 25	12 28	4 59	14 12	18 24	0 51	24 52	1 49	21 46	2 38	24 45	9 58	15 27	1 14	22 19	0 53
Tu	21 34	15 45	4 40	17 06	19 03	0 40	24 47	1 50	21 45	2 42	24 36	9 56	15 26	1 14	22 19	0 53
W	21 44	18 16	4 08	19 13	19 40	0 30	24 42	1 51	21 44	2 45	24 28	9 54	15 24	1 13	22 20	0 53
Th	21N52	19S56	3N25	20S26	20N16	0S19	24N36	1N53	21S44	2S49	24N19	9N51	15S22	1N13	22S20	0N53

Day	⚷ Decl	⚷ Lat	♅ Decl	♅ Lat	♆ Decl	♆ Lat	♇ Decl	♇ Lat
1	3N25	3N25	10N42	0S31	6S26	0S56	21S29	0N17
6	3 31	3 26	10 48	0 31	6 23	0 56	21 29	0 16
11	3 37	3 26	10 53	0 31	6 21	0 56	21 30	0 16
16	3 42	3 27	10 59	0 31	6 19	0 56	21 31	0 15
21	3 47	3 27	11 05	0 32	6 17	0 56	21 32	0 15
26	3 52	3 27	11 10	0 32	6 16	0 57	21 33	0 15
31	3N56	3N28	11N15	0S32	6S14	0S57	21S34	0N14

Day	⚴ Decl	⚴ Lat	⚵ Decl	⚵ Lat	⚶ Decl	⚶ Lat	Eris Decl	Eris Lat
1	2S59	25S59	1N17	0N51	17S34	5N47	1S58	11S57
6	2 19	25 29	2 01	0 36	17 39	5 42	1 56	11 57
11	1 41	25 00	2 44	0 21	17 45	5 36	1 55	11 57
16	1 06	24 31	3 26	0 05	17 54	5 28	1 55	11 57
21	0 35	24 01	4 06	0S11	18 04	5 18	1 54	11 57
26	0 06	23 31	4 46	0 28	18 17	5 06	1 53	11 58
31	0N19	23S01	5N24	0S46	18S32	4N52	1S52	11S58

Moon Phenomena

Max/0 Decl dy hr mn	Perigee/Apogee dy hr m kilometers
4 23:06 20S34	6 0:28 a 404457
12 7:22 0 N	17 21:17 p 363778
18 15:10 20N39	
25 1:42 0 S	

Max/0 Lat dy hr mn	PH dy hr mn
7 10:24 0 S	☾ 8 2:10 17♒27
14 9:43 5S02	● 15 11:49 24♉36
20 13:15 0 N	☽ 22 3:50 1♍02
27 4:31 5N04	○ 29 14:21 8♐10

Void of Course Moon

Last Aspect	☽ Ingress
1 2:57 ♂ ✶	♐ 1 15:21
4 0:51 ☿ △	♑ 4 2:07
6 13:49 ♅ △	♒ 6 14:50
9 2:30 ♅ ✶	♓ 9 3:12
11 9:03 ♂ ✶	♈ 11 12:41
13 18:06 ♅ ☌	♉ 13 18:16
15 20:31 ♂ △	♊ 15 20:44
17 18:19 ♀ ☌	♋ 17 21:48
19 21:15 ☉ ✶	♌ 19 23:12
21 3:31 ♃ □	♍ 22 2:04
23 14:56 ♇ △	♎ 24 6:53
25 21:05 ♇ □	♏ 26 13:41
28 17:26 ☿ ☍	♐ 28 22:30
30 6:27 ♆ □	♑ 31 9:28

DAILY ASPECTARIAN

☽✶♂ 2:57
☽∠♄ 3:56
☉⋕☽ 12:13
☽⚻♅ 13:52
☽⚼☿ 14:06
☽△⚷ 16:46
☽∥♃ 21:53
♀⋕♂ 22:59

♀⚼♂ 1:07
♀⚻♄ 2:25
☽∠♇ 3:24
☽⚺♄ 8:40
☽∠♂ 8:50
☽☍♀ 9:22
☽△⚳ 12:21
☉⚻☽ 14:50
☽⚼♅ 19:02
☿∥⚷ 19:57
☽△☿ 22:00
☽□♆ 22:11

☿⚺♆ 0:04
☽⚺♃ 4:28
☽⚺♇ 8:44
☽⚺♂ 15:28
☽⚼⚳ 18:32
☉⚼☽ 23:01
♀✶⚳ 23:16

☽△♅ 0:51
☽□⚷ 3:50
☽∠♃ 10:01
☽☌♄ 20:03

☽⚻⚳ 1:20
Sa ☉⋕♃ 2:33
☽⚻♀ 3:39
☉△☽ 7:53
☽✶♆ 10:18
☿⚻♃ 11:06
☽✶♃ 16:01
☽□☿ 16:39
☽☌♇ 21:01

6 Su ☽☌♂ 6:21
☉∠⚷ 13:23
☽⚼♀ 13:35
☽□♅ 13:49
☉✶♆ 13:58
♀∠♅ 16:00
☽✶⚷ 16:48
☽∠♆ 16:51

7 M ☽⚺♄ 8:48
☿□♇ 8:53
☽☍⚳ 15:38
☉⋕☽ 19:31
♀□♆ 21:59
☽⚺♆ 23:17
☽∠⚷ 23:18
☽△♀ 23:26

8 Tu ☉□☽ 2:10
☽∥♃ 3:34
☽□♃ 4:12
⚶ R 7:50
☽⚺♇ 9:45
☽✶☿ 12:52
☽∠♄ 14:54
☽⚺♂ 21:13

9 W ☉☍♃ 0:40
☿⋕♆ 0:58
☽✶♅ 2:30
☽⚺⚷ 5:20
☽∠♇ 15:25
☽⋕♅ 18:27
♀⚻♃ 18:37
☽✶♄ 20:23
☽∠☿ 22:12

10 Th ☽∠♂ 3:39
☽⚻⚳ 4:26
☽∠♅ 7:52
☽☌♆ 10:28
☽△♃ 14:27
☽⋕☿ 16:19
☽□♀ 16:46
☉✶☽ 18:00
☽✶♇ 20:14
☽∥♆ 21:29

11 F ☽⚺☿ 6:24
☽✶♂ 9:03
☽⚼⚳ 9:29
☽⚺♅ 12:17
☽⋕⚷ 12:25
♂∥♄ 14:18
☽☌⚷ 14:53
☽⚼♃ 18:14
☉△♇ 23:11

12 Sa ☉∠☽ 0:09
☽□♄ 4:36
♀⚻♇ 5:06
☽△⚳ 13:28
☿□♂ 13:31
☽⚺♆ 17:57
☽⚻♃ 21:03

13 Su ☽∥⚷ 2:02
☽□♇ 2:55
☽✶♀ 5:02
☉⚺☽ 5:03
☉⚺♀ 5:26
☿☌♅ 10:51
☿ ♉ 12:41
☽⋕♆ 15:45
☽□♂ 16:32
☽☌♅ 18:06
☽☌☿ 18:58
☽∠♆ 20:14
☽⚺⚷ 20:29

14 M ☿∠♆ 6:29
☽∥☿ 7:56
☿⚺⚷ 8:53
☽△♄ 9:00
☽∠♀ 9:21
☉⚼♄ 10:52
☽∥♅ 16:29
☽□⚳ 18:33
☽✶♆ 21:45
☽∠⚷ 22:01

15 Tu ☽☍♃ 0:09
☽△♇ 6:06
☽⚼♄ 10:05
☉☌☽ 11:49
☽⚺♀ 12:47
♅ ♉ 15:18
☽△♂ 20:31
☽⚺♅ 20:46
☽⋕♃ 22:43
☽✶⚷ 23:00

16 W ☽⚺☿ 3:33
♂ ♒ 4:56
☽⚼♇ 6:51
♂□♅ 7:05
☽⚻♄ 10:44
☿∥♅ 20:52
☽✶⚳ 21:09
☽∠♅ 21:26
☽⚼♂ 21:47
☽□♆ 23:17

17 Th ☽⚻♃ 1:09
☉∥☽ 6:00
☽∠☿ 7:11
☽⚻♇ 7:21
☉⚺☽ 16:27
☽☌♀ 18:19
☽✶♅ 22:00
☽∠⚳ 22:09
☽⚻♂ 22:55

18 F ☽□⚷ 0:10
☽⚼♃ 1:25
☽✶☿ 10:52
☽☍♄ 11:35
☿△♄ 16:50
☉∠☽ 18:43
☽⚺⚳ 23:15

19 Sa ☽△♆ 0:24
☽△♃ 1:49
☽☍♇ 8:27
♂∠♆ 10:51
♀ ♋ 13:12
☉∥☽ 16:45
♀✶♅ 17:31
☉✶☽ 21:15
☽□♅ 23:35

20 Su ☽⚺♀ 0:06
☽⚼♆ 1:17
☽☍♂ 1:39
☽△⚷ 1:45
♂✶⚷ 5:57
♀∠⚳ 8:33
☽⚻♄ 13:08
☽□☿ 19:32
♀□⚷ 20:25

21 M ♀⚻♂ 2:07
♀⚼♃ 2:10
☉ ♊ 2:16
☽☌⚳ 2:26
☽⚻♆ 2:33
☽⚼⚷ 3:04
☽□♃ 3:31
☽∠♀ 3:39
⚳⚻♆ 7:45
☽⋕♃ 9:48
☉⚺♅ 9:49
☽⚻♇ 10:46
⚴ ♋ 13:10
☽⚼♄ 14:30
☽∥☿ 19:22

22 Tu ☽△♅ 2:39
☉□☽ 3:50
☽⚻⚷ 4:51
☽⚻♂ 5:58
☽✶♀ 7:49
⚳⚼⚷ 9:32
☽⚼♇ 12:36
⚳□♃ 13:29
☽∥♅ 14:46
☽△♄ 16:20
☉✶⚷ 18:49
♃⚼⚷ 20:43

23 W ☿✶♆ 2:15
☽⚼♅ 4:55
☿☍♃ 5:55
☽☍♆ 6:31
☿∠⚷ 6:41
☽✶♃ 7:00
☽△☿ 7:11
☽⚺⚳ 7:35
☽⚼♂ 8:54
☿□⚳ 10:34
☽△♇ 14:56
☽⋕♆ 17:15
☿⋕♃ 18:14

24 Th ☉△♂ 2:40
☽∥⚷ 5:56
☽⚻♅ 7:41
☽∠♃ 9:29
☽☍⚷ 9:54
☽∠⚳ 10:58
☽△♂ 12:20
☉△☽ 12:50
☽⚼☿ 14:21
☽□♀ 18:04
☽□♄ 21:29

25 F ♃△♆ 9:53
☽⚺♃ 12:26
☽⚻♆ 12:28
☿△♇ 13:39
☽✶⚳ 14:54
☉⚼☽ 18:15
☽□♇ 21:05
☽⋕⚷ 21:52
☽⚻☿ 22:25

26 Sa ♀☍♄ 6:41
☽∥♆ 10:50
☿⚼♄ 13:44
☽☍♅ 14:44
♀∥⚳ 15:09
☽⚼♆ 16:11
☽⚻⚷ 16:57
☽□♂ 20:47

27 Su ☉⚻☽ 0:17
☿∠♀ 0:36
☽✶♄ 4:35
☽△♀ 6:56
☉⚼♇ 8:17
☽⋕♅ 15:43
☽☌♃ 19:49
☽△♆ 20:24
☽⚼⚷ 21:14

28 M ☽□⚳ 0:23
☽✶♇ 5:13
☽∠♄ 8:53
☽⚼♀ 14:24
☽☍☿ 17:26
☽∥♃ 21:27
☉⋕♇ 22:30
☽⚻♅ 23:49

29 Tu ☽△⚷ 2:03
☉⚻♄ 6:38
☽✶♂ 7:21
☽∠♇ 10:04
☽⚺♄ 13:43
☉☍☽ 14:21
☽⚻♀ 22:35
☿ ♊ 23:50

30 W ☉⋕♂ 1:51
☽⚼♅ 5:11
☽⚺♃ 5:16
☽□♆ 6:27
☿⚺♅ 8:23
☽△⚳ 12:11
☽∠♂ 13:29
☽⚺♇ 15:28
☿✶⚷ 21:23

31 Th ☽∠♃ 10:46
☽△♅ 11:04
☽□⚷ 13:17
☽⚻☿ 16:40
☽⚼⚳ 18:57
☽⚺♂ 20:07

June 2018

LONGITUDE

Day	Sid.Time	☉	☽	☽ 12 hour	Mean☊	True☊	☿	♀	♂	⚳	♃	♄	⚷	♅	♆	♇
	h m s	° ' "	° ' "	° ' "	° '	° '	° '	° '	° '	° '	° '	° '	° '	° '	° '	° '
1 F	16 37 43	10♊28 14	7♑14 55	13♑11 50	8♌53.9	7♌14.1	4♊15.0	14♋49.1	5♒21.6	19♌48.4	15♏35.7	7♑41.8	1♈55.3	0♉49.5	16♓24.2	20♑55.9
2 Sa	16 41 39	11 25 44	19 07 15	25 01 36	8 50.7	7R 10.0	6 24.2	16 00.0	5 38.2	20 09.2	15R 29.5	7R 38.1	1 57.0	0 52.3	16 24.8	20R 54.8
3 Su	16 45 36	12 23 12	0♒55 17	6♒48 50	8 47.6	7D 08.2	8 34.4	17 10.9	5 54.2	20 30.1	15 23.3	7 34.4	1 58.6	0 55.1	16 25.4	20 53.8
4 M	16 49 32	13 20 40	12 42 45	18 37 38	8 44.4	7 08.2	10 45.4	18 21.8	6 09.8	20 51.1	15 17.2	7 30.6	2 00.2	0 57.9	16 25.9	20 52.7
5 Tu	16 53 29	14 18 06	24 34 04	0♓32 42	8 41.2	7 09.1	12 57.1	19 32.5	6 24.8	21 12.2	15 11.3	7 26.8	2 01.8	1 00.6	16 26.3	20 51.6
6 W	16 57 25	15 15 33	6♓34 10	12 39 06	8 38.0	7R 10.1	15 09.2	20 43.2	6 39.2	21 33.5	15 05.5	7 22.9	2 03.3	1 03.3	16 26.8	20 50.5
7 Th	17 01 22	16 12 58	18 48 10	25 02 00	8 34.9	7 10.4	17 21.3	21 53.8	6 53.0	21 54.9	14 59.8	7 19.0	2 04.7	1 05.9	16 27.2	20 49.4
8 F	17 05 19	17 10 23	1♈21 10	7♈46 13	8 31.7	7 09.3	19 33.2	23 04.4	7 06.3	22 16.5	14 54.3	7 15.0	2 06.2	1 08.6	16 27.6	20 48.2
9 Sa	17 09 15	18 07 47	14 17 36	20 55 40	8 28.5	7 06.4	21 44.7	24 14.8	7 19.0	22 38.1	14 48.9	7 11.0	2 07.5	1 11.2	16 27.9	20 47.1
10 Su	17 13 12	19 05 11	27 40 40	4♉32 40	8 25.3	7 01.6	23 55.5	25 25.2	7 31.1	22 59.9	14 43.6	7 06.9	2 08.8	1 13.7	16 28.2	20 45.9
11 M	17 17 08	20 02 34	11♉31 37	18 37 15	8 22.1	6 55.4	26 05.3	26 35.6	7 42.5	23 21.9	14 38.4	7 02.8	2 10.1	1 16.3	16 28.5	20 44.7
12 Tu	17 21 05	20 59 57	25 49 08	3♊06 37	8 19.0	6 48.3	28 13.8	27 45.8	7 53.3	23 43.9	14 33.5	6 58.7	2 11.3	1 18.8	16 28.7	20 43.5
13 W	17 25 01	21 57 19	10♊28 56	17 55 08	8 15.8	6 41.5	0♋21.0	28 56.0	8 03.5	24 06.1	14 28.6	6 54.5	2 12.5	1 21.3	16 29.0	20 42.2
14 Th	17 28 58	22 54 40	25 24 09	2♋54 51	8 12.6	6 35.7	2 26.6	0♌06.1	8 13.0	24 28.3	14 23.9	6 50.3	2 13.6	1 23.7	16 29.1	20 41.0
15 F	17 32 55	23 52 01	10♋26 06	17 56 45	8 09.4	6 31.5	4 30.5	1 16.1	8 21.8	24 50.7	14 19.4	6 46.1	2 14.7	1 26.1	16 29.3	20 39.7
16 Sa	17 36 51	24 49 21	25 25 46	2♌52 12	8 06.3	6D 29.3	6 32.5	2 26.0	8 29.9	25 13.2	14 15.0	6 41.8	2 15.7	1 28.5	16 29.4	20 38.4
17 Su	17 40 48	25 46 40	10♌15 12	17 34 08	8 03.1	6 28.9	8 32.4	3 35.9	8 37.4	25 35.8	14 10.8	6 37.6	2 16.7	1 30.8	16 29.5	20 37.2
18 M	17 44 44	26 43 59	24 48 27	1♍57 48	7 59.9	6 29.8	10 30.4	4 45.6	8 44.2	25 58.5	14 06.7	6 33.2	2 17.6	1 33.1	16R 29.5	20 35.9
19 Tu	17 48 41	27 41 16	9♍01 58	16 00 50	7 56.7	6 31.1	12 26.2	5 55.3	8 50.3	26 21.3	14 02.8	6 28.9	2 18.5	1 35.4	16 29.6	20 34.5
20 W	17 52 37	28 38 33	22 54 26	29 42 49	7 53.6	6R 32.1	14 19.8	7 04.8	8 55.7	26 44.3	13 59.1	6 24.6	2 19.3	1 37.6	16 29.5	20 33.2
21 Th	17 56 34	29 35 49	6♎26 11	13♎04 43	7 50.4	6 32.0	16 11.2	8 14.3	9 00.3	27 07.3	13 55.5	6 20.2	2 20.1	1 39.8	16 29.5	20 31.9
22 F	18 00 30	0♋33 04	19 38 41	26 08 20	7 47.2	6 30.4	18 00.3	9 23.6	9 04.3	27 30.4	13 52.1	6 15.8	2 20.8	1 41.9	16 29.4	20 30.5
23 Sa	18 04 27	1 30 18	2♏33 55	8♏55 44	7 44.0	6 27.3	19 47.1	10 32.9	9 07.5	27 53.6	13 48.9	6 11.4	2 21.4	1 44.0	16 29.3	20 29.2
24 Su	18 08 24	2 27 32	15 14 02	21 29 05	7 40.8	6 22.9	21 31.7	11 42.1	9 10.0	28 16.9	13 45.8	6 07.0	2 22.0	1 46.1	16 29.1	20 27.8
25 M	18 12 20	3 24 45	27 41 05	3♐50 19	7 37.7	6 17.6	23 14.0	12 51.1	9 11.8	28 40.3	13 42.9	6 02.6	2 22.6	1 48.1	16 29.0	20 26.4
26 Tu	18 16 17	4 21 58	9♐56 58	16 01 15	7 34.5	6 12.1	24 53.9	14 00.1	9R 12.8	29 03.8	13 40.2	5 58.2	2 23.1	1 50.1	16 28.8	20 25.0
27 W	18 20 13	5 19 10	22 03 23	28 03 35	7 31.3	6 07.0	26 31.5	15 08.9	9 13.1	29 27.4	13 37.6	5 53.8	2 23.6	1 52.1	16 28.5	20 23.6
28 Th	18 24 10	6 16 22	4♑02 04	9♑59 02	7 28.1	6 02.7	28 06.9	16 17.6	9 12.6	29 51.0	13 35.3	5 49.4	2 24.0	1 54.0	16 28.2	20 22.2
29 F	18 28 06	7 13 34	15 54 46	21 49 30	7 25.0	5 59.8	29 39.8	17 26.2	9 11.4	0♍14.8	13 33.1	5 45.0	2 24.3	1 55.9	16 27.9	20 20.8
30 Sa	18 32 03	8♋10 46	27 43 33	3♒37 12	7♌21.8	5♌58.2	1♌10.4	18♌34.7	9♒09.4	0♍38.6	13♏31.1	5♑40.5	2♈24.6	1♉57.7	16♓27.6	20♑19.4

1st of Mon
Julian Day 2458270.
Obliquity 23°26'07
SVP 5♓00'
GC 27♐05
Eris 23♈53

Day	⚴
1	6♋09.
6	9 06.
11	12 02.
16	14 58.
21	17 54.
26	20 48.

Day	⚵
1	15♈59.
6	18 20.
11	20 40.
16	22 59.
21	25 17.
26	27 34.

Day	⚶
1	2♑39.
6	1 41.
11	0 35.
16	29♐25.
21	28 12.
26	27 01.

DECLINATION and LATITUDE

Day	☉ Decl	☽ Decl	☽ Lat	☽12h Decl	☿ Decl	☿ Lat	♀ Decl	♀ Lat	♂ Decl	♂ Lat	⚳ Decl	⚳ Lat	♃ Decl	♃ Lat	♄ Decl	♄ Lat
1 F	22N01	20S41	2N33	20S43	20N51	0S08	24N30	1N54	21S43	2S53	24N10	9N49	15S21	1N13	22S20	0N53
2 Sa	22 09	20 30	1 35	20 04	21 25	0N02	24 23	1 55	21 42	2 56	24 01	9 47	15 19	1 13	22 20	0 53
3 Su	22 17	19 24	0 33	18 32	21 57	0 13	24 15	1 56	21 42	3 00	23 52	9 45	15 17	1 13	22 21	0 53
4 M	22 24	17 28	0S30	16 13	22 26	0 23	24 06	1 57	21 42	3 04	23 43	9 43	15 16	1 12	22 21	0 53
5 Tu	22 31	14 47	1 33	13 12	22 54	0 34	23 57	1 57	21 42	3 08	23 34	9 41	15 14	1 12	22 21	0 53
6 W	22 37	11 27	2 32	9 34	23 20	0 43	23 47	1 58	21 42	3 12	23 25	9 39	15 13	1 12	22 21	0 53
7 Th	22 43	7 35	3 25	5 29	23 43	0 53	23 37	1 59	21 42	3 16	23 16	9 37	15 11	1 12	22 22	0 52
8 F	22 49	3 18	4 11	1 02	24 03	1 02	23 26	1 60	21 43	3 20	23 07	9 35	15 10	1 12	22 22	0 52
9 Sa	22 54	1N16	4 45	3N35	24 21	1 10	23 14	2 00	21 43	3 24	22 58	9 33	15 08	1 11	22 22	0 52
10 Su	22 59	5 54	5 04	8 11	24 36	1 18	23 01	2 00	21 44	3 28	22 49	9 31	15 07	1 11	22 22	0 52
11 M	23 04	10 24	5 08	12 31	24 48	1 25	22 48	2 01	21 45	3 32	22 39	9 29	15 06	1 11	22 23	0 52
12 Tu	23 08	14 29	4 52	16 15	24 57	1 32	22 35	2 01	21 47	3 36	22 30	9 27	15 05	1 11	22 23	0 52
13 W	23 11	17 47	4 17	19 01	25 04	1 38	22 21	2 01	21 48	3 41	22 21	9 25	15 03	1 11	22 23	0 52
14 Th	23 15	19 57	3 24	20 32	25 08	1 43	22 06	2 01	21 49	3 45	22 11	9 23	15 02	1 10	22 23	0 52
15 F	23 18	20 45	2 17	20 36	25 09	1 48	21 51	2 01	21 51	3 49	22 02	9 21	15 01	1 10	22 24	0 52
16 Sa	23 20	20 04	0 60	19 12	25 08	1 51	21 35	2 01	21 53	3 53	21 52	9 19	14 60	1 10	22 24	0 52
17 Su	23 22	17 60	0N20	16 31	25 04	1 54	21 18	2 01	21 55	3 58	21 42	9 17	14 59	1 10	22 24	0 52
18 M	23 24	14 47	1 38	12 52	24 57	1 57	21 01	2 00	21 58	4 02	21 33	9 15	14 58	1 09	22 25	0 52
19 Tu	23 25	10 46	2 48	8 34	24 49	1 58	20 44	2 00	22 00	4 07	21 23	9 14	14 57	1 09	22 25	0 52
20 W	23 26	6 16	3 46	3 56	24 38	1 59	20 26	1 60	22 03	4 11	21 13	9 12	14 56	1 09	22 25	0 52
21 Th	23 26	1 35	4 30	0S46	24 25	1 59	20 07	1 59	22 06	4 15	21 03	9 10	14 55	1 09	22 25	0 52
22 F	23 26	3S05	4 58	5 19	24 10	1 58	19 48	1 58	22 10	4 20	20 54	9 08	14 55	1 08	22 26	0 52
23 Sa	23 26	7 29	5 11	9 33	23 54	1 57	19 28	1 57	22 13	4 24	20 44	9 06	14 54	1 08	22 26	0 52
24 Su	23 25	11 29	5 08	13 17	23 36	1 55	19 08	1 57	22 17	4 29	20 34	9 05	14 53	1 08	22 26	0 51
25 M	23 23	14 55	4 51	16 23	23 16	1 52	18 48	1 56	22 20	4 33	20 24	9 03	14 53	1 08	22 27	0 51
26 Tu	23 22	17 39	4 20	18 43	22 55	1 48	18 27	1 54	22 24	4 38	20 14	9 01	14 52	1 07	22 27	0 51
27 W	23 20	19 35	3 38	20 12	22 33	1 44	18 06	1 53	22 29	4 42	20 04	8 59	14 51	1 07	22 27	0 51
28 Th	23 17	20 36	2 46	20 46	22 10	1 40	17 44	1 52	22 33	4 47	19 54	8 58	14 51	1 07	22 27	0 51
29 F	23 14	20 42	1 48	20 24	21 45	1 34	17 21	1 50	22 38	4 51	19 43	8 56	14 51	1 07	22 28	0 51
30 Sa	23N11	19S52	0N45	19S08	21N20	1N28	16N59	1N49	22S43	4S56	19N33	8N54	14S50	1N06	22S28	0N51

Day	⚷ Decl	⚷ Lat	♅ Decl	♅ Lat	♆ Decl	♆ Lat	♇ Decl	♇ Lat
1	3N57	3N28	11N16	0S32	6S14	0S57	21S35	0N
6	4 00	3 29	11 21	0 32	6 13	0 57	21 36	0
11	4 04	3 29	11 25	0 32	6 13	0 57	21 37	0
16	4 07	3 30	11 29	0 32	6 13	0 57	21 39	0
21	4 09	3 31	11 33	0 32	6 13	0 58	21 40	0
26	4 11	3 31	11 37	0 32	6 13	0 58	21 42	0

Day	⚴ Decl	⚴ Lat	⚵ Decl	⚵ Lat	⚶ Decl	⚶ Lat	Eris Decl	Eris Lat
1	0N24	22S55	5N32	0S49	18S35	4N49	1S52	11S
6	0 46	22 24	6 08	1 08	18 52	4 33	1 52	11
11	1 04	21 54	6 43	1 28	19 11	4 15	1 51	11
16	1 20	21 23	7 16	1 48	19 31	3 55	1 51	11
21	1 32	20 52	7 46	2 10	19 52	3 33	1 51	11
26	1 41	20 21	8 15	2 32	20 14	3 10	1 51	11

Moon Phenomena

Max/0 Decl

dy	hr mn	
1	7:07	20S44
8	17:27	0 N
15	0:41	20N45
21	8:04	0 S
28	14:29	20S46

Max/0 Lat

dy	hr mn	
3	12:40	0 S
10	16:13	5S08
16	17:52	0 N
23	7:16	5N12
30	16:47	0 S

Perigee/Apogee

dy	hr m		kilometers
2	16:38	a	405316
14	23:53	p	359503
30	2:45	a	406061

PH	dy	hr mn	
☾	6	18:33	16♓00
●	13	19:44	22♊44
☽	20	10:52	29♍04
○	28	4:54	6♑28

Void of Course Moon

Last Aspect				☽ Ingre		
2	3:38	♇	☌	♒	2	22:
4	5:11	♃	□	♓	5	10:
7	6:36	♀	△	♈	7	21:
9	19:38	♀	□	♉	10	4
12	3:30	♀	⚹	♊	12	6
13	19:44	☉	☌	♋	14	7
15	16:20	♇	☍	♌	16	7:
18	3:27	☉	⚹	♍	18	8:
20	10:52	☉	□	♎	20	12:
22	1:35	♇	□	♏	22	19:
24	14:01	☿	△	♐	25	4:
26	12:54	♆	□	♑	27	15:
29	8:59	♇	☌	♒	30	4

DAILY ASPECTARIAN

1 F: ☽☌♄ 0:54; ☉⚻☽ 7:04; ☿△♂ 14:14; ♀△♃ 14:30; ☽⚹♃ 16:42; ☽☍♀ 16:58; ☽⚹♆ 18:30; ☿⚼♇ 18:37

2 Sa: ☽⚻⚳ 2:09; ☽☌♇ 3:38; ☽⚼☿ 5:40; ☿⋕♇ 7:24; ♀△♆ 8:27; ☿⋕♂ 12:58; ☿⚻♄ 13:17; ☉⚼☽ 16:10; ☽□♅ 24:00

3 Su: ☽∠♆ 1:01; ☽⚹⚷ 2:09; ☽☌♂ 10:23; ☽⚺♄ 13:29; ☉⋕♄ 13:31; ☽△☿ 19:07; ☿⋕♄ 19:15; ☉∥☿ 21:04

4 M: ☉△☽ 1:24; ⚳⚻♇ 1:46; ☽□♃ 5:11; ☽⚺♆ 7:33; ☽∠⚷ 8:44; ☽⚻♀ 12:44; ☽⚺♇ 16:32; ☽☍⚳ 17:00; ☽∠♄ 19:45; ☽∥♃ 20:20

5 Tu: ☽⚹♅ 12:59; ☽⚺⚷ 15:00; ☉⚻♃ 20:11; ☽⚼♀ 22:08; ☽∠♇ 22:34; ☿⚻♃ 23:22

6 W: ☽⚺♂ 0:10; ☽⋕♅ 0:42; ☽⚹♄ 1:36; ☉☌☿ 2:03; ♀☍♇ 2:26; ☿∥⚳ 4:08; ☿∠♅ 10:02; ☿□♆ 14:08; ☽△♃ 16:39; ☉□☽ 18:33; ☽∠♅ 18:43; ☽☌♆ 19:26; ☿∥♀ 19:36; ☽□☿ 20:35; ☉∠♅ 20:55

7 Th: ♀⚺⚳ 0:32; ☽⚹♇ 3:54; ☉□♆ 5:59; ☽∠♂ 6:04; ☽⚻⚳ 6:12; ☽△♀ 6:36; ☽∥♆ 7:49; ☽⋕⚷ 20:01; ☽⚼♃ 21:17; ⚳⚼♄ 22:37; ☽⚺♅ 23:36

8 F: ☽☌⚷ 1:25; ☽⚹♂ 10:57; ☽□♄ 10:59; ☽⚼⚳ 11:24; ♂⚺♄ 12:23; ☿⚻♇ 13:33

9 Sa: ☽⚻♃ 0:57; ☽⚺♆ 3:57; ☉∥⚳ 6:06; ☿⚼♂ 6:56; ☉⚹☽ 7:30; ☽□♇ 11:43; ☿⚹⚳ 11:44; ☽∥⚷ 14:23; ☽△⚳ 15:28; ☽⚹☿ 16:04; ☽□♀ 19:38

10 Su: ☽⋕♆ 1:38; ☉∥♀ 3:06; ☽☌♅ 6:15; ☽∠♆ 6:39; ☽⚺⚷ 7:51; ☉∠☽ 12:02; ☽△♄ 16:22; ☽□♂ 17:22; ☽∠☿ 23:07

11 M: ☽☍♃ 5:15; ☽∥♅ 5:41; ☽⚹♆ 8:23; ☽∠⚷ 9:34; ☿⚺♀ 12:24; ☉⚺☽ 15:25; ☽△♇ 15:32; ☉⚻♇ 17:15; ☽⚼♄ 17:39; ☽□⚳ 20:27

12 Tu: ☽⚹♀ 3:30; ☽⋕♃ 3:53; ☽⚺☿ 4:40; ☽⚺♅ 9:05; ☽⚹⚷ 10:30; ☿⚼♃ 14:26; ☽⚼♇ 16:15; ⚳⋕♄ 17:31; ☽⚻♄ 18:13; ♀⋕♄ 19:52; ☿ ♋ 20:01; ☽△♂ 20:01

13 W: ♀∥⚳ 0:27; ☽∠♀ 6:03; ☽⚻♃ 6:25; ☽∠♅ 9:30; ☽□♆ 9:41; ☿⚹♅ 11:42; ⚶R♐ 13:16; ☽⚻♇ 16:27; ☉☌☽ 19:44; ☽⚼♂ 20:28; ☿□⚷ 21:29; ♀ ♌ 21:55; ☽⚹⚳ 22:28

14 Th: ☽⚼♃ 6:21; ☽⚺♀ 8:09; ☉⚼♂ 9:05; ☽⚹♅ 9:36; ☽□⚷ 10:55; ☽☌☿ 13:03; ☽☍♄ 18:11; ☽⚻♂ 20:40; ♀⋕♂ 23:00; ☽∠⚳ 23:02

15 F: ♀□♅ 3:34; ♀⚼♆ 4:32; ☽△♃ 6:11; ☽△♆ 9:40; ☽☍♇ 16:20; ♀⋕♇ 18:16; ♀△⚷ 20:25; ♂⋕⚳ 21:27; ☉⚺☽ 22:57; ☽⚺⚳ 23:39

16 Sa: ☿☍♄ 1:48; ♅∠♆ 9:42; ☽⚼♆ 9:46; ☽□♅ 9:46; ☽△⚷ 11:02; ☽☌♀ 12:15; ☉⚹⚳ 16:29; ☽⚻♄ 18:07; ☽⚺☿ 20:46; ☽☍♂ 21:19

17 Su: ☉∠☽ 0:55; ☿⚻♂ 1:04; ☽□♃ 6:24; ⚳⋕♇ 8:37; ☽⚻♆ 10:14; ☽⚼⚷ 11:32; ☽⚻♇ 17:01; ☽⚼♄ 18:37; ☽⋕♃ 22:50

18 M: ☽∠☿ 1:21; ☽☌⚳ 2:00; ☉⚹☽ 3:27; ☿∠⚳ 7:12; ☽△♅ 11:20; ☽⚻⚷ 12:34; ☽⚼♇ 18:07; ☽⚺♀ 18:14; ☽△♄ 19:41; ☽∥♅ 19:47; ♆R 23:28; ☽⚻♂ 23:40

19 Tu: ☽⚹☿ 6:45; ☽⚹♃ 8:34; ♀⚻♄ 10:56; ☽☍♆ 12:50; ☽⚼♅ 13:02; ☿△♃ 19:44; ☽△♇ 19:54; ☽∠♀ 22:25

20 W: ☽⋕♆ 0:18; ☽⚼♂ 1:48; ☽⚺⚳ 6:56; ☉⚼♃ 8:05; ☽∠♃ 10:40; ☉□☽ 10:52; ☽∥⚷ 10:56; ☽⚻♅ 15:27; ☽☍⚷ 16:39; ☽□♄ 23:49

21 Th: ☽⚹♀ 3:33; ☿△♆ 4:00; ☽△♂ 4:39; ☉ ♋ 10:08; ☽∠⚳ 10:34; ☽⚺♃ 13:29; ♀☍♂ 16:55; ☽⚻♆ 18:13; ☽□☿ 20:31

22 F: ☽□♇ 1:35; ☽⋕⚷ 5:43; ☽⚹⚳ 15:00; ☽∥♆ 16:54; ☉△☽ 21:51; ☽⚼♆ 21:59; ☽☍♅ 22:26; ☽⚻⚷ 23:37

23 Sa: ☉⚹♅ 5:59; ☽⚹♄ 6:47; ☿☍♇ 9:28; ☽□♂ 12:25; ☽□♀ 16:35; ☽☌♃ 21:12; ☉□⚷ 21:40

24 Su: ☽⋕♅ 0:39; ☽△♆ 2:24; ☽⚼⚷ 4:05; ☉⚼☽ 4:37; ☽⚹♇ 10:01; ☽∠♄ 11:14; ☽△☿ 14:01; ☉∥☿ 14:46; ☽∥♃ 23:40

25 M: ☽□⚳ 1:59; ☽⚻♅ 8:03; ☽△⚷ 9:09; ☉⚻☽ 12:06; ☽∠♇ 15:07; ☽⚺♄ 16:13; ♀□♃ 17:20; ☽⚹♂ 22:33; ☽⚼☿ 23:53

26 Tu: ☽⚺♃ 7:19; ☽⋕♀ 7:25; ☽△♀ 8:50; ☽□♆ 12:54; ☽⚼♅ 13:39; ♂∥♄ 14:10; ☽⚺♇ 20:42; ♂R 21:06

27 W: ☿⋕♂ 3:46; ☽∠♂ 4:19; ☿⋕♄ 6:08; ☽⋕⚳ 7:45; ☽⚻☿ 10:18; ☽∠♃ 13:06; ☉☍♄ 13:29; ☽△⚳ 15:18; ☽⚼♀ 17:54; ☽△♅ 19:42; ☽□⚷ 20:43

28 Th: ☽☌♄ 3:35; ♀⚻♆ 3:42; ☉☍☽ 4:54; ⚳ ♍ 9:05; ☽⚺♂ 10:25; ☽⚹♃ 19:14; ☽⚼⚳ 22:36; ♀⚼⚷ 23:20

29 F: ☽⚹♆ 1:07; ☿⋕♇ 2:36; ☽⚻♀ 3:25; ☿ ♌ 5:17; ☽☌♇ 8:59; ☿⚺⚳ 12:27

30 Sa: ☿⚼♆ 4:36; ☽⚻⚳ 6:09; ☽⋕⚳ 6:20; ☽∠♆ 7:36; ☽☍☿ 8:02; ☽□♅ 8:39; ☽⚹⚷ 9:32; ☿□♅ 13:03; ☽⚺♄ 16:05; ☿△⚷ 20:11; ☉⚻☽ 23:09; ☽☌♂ 23:11; ☉⚻♂ 23:30

LONGITUDE

Day	Sid.Time	☉	☽	☽ 12 hour	Mean☊	True☊	☿	♀	♂	⚳	♃	♄	⚷	♅	♆	♇
	h m s	° ' "	° ' "	° ' "	° '	° '	° '	° '	° '	° '	° '	° '	° '	° '	° '	° '
1 Su	18 35 59	9♋07 57	9♒30 48	15♒24 45	7♌18.6	5♌57.9	2♌38.7	19♌43.1	9♒06.7	1♍02.5	13♏29.2	5♑36.1	2♈24.9	1♉59.5	16♓27.2	20♑18.0
2 M	18 39 56	10 05 09	21 19 26	27 15 18	7 15.4	5 58.7	4 04.5	20 51.3	9R 03.2	1 26.5	13R 27.6	5R 31.7	2 25.1	2 01.2	16R 26.8	20R 16.5
3 Tu	18 43 53	11 02 21	3♓12 49	9♓12 29	7 12.3	6 00.2	5 28.0	21 59.5	8 59.0	1 50.6	13 26.1	5 27.3	2 25.2	2 03.0	16 26.4	20 15.1
4 W	18 47 49	11 59 32	15 14 49	21 20 22	7 09.1	6 01.9	6 48.9	23 07.5	8 54.0	2 14.7	13 24.8	5 23.0	2 25.3	2 04.6	16 26.0	20 13.6
5 Th	18 51 46	12 56 44	27 29 41	3♈43 18	7 05.9	6 03.2	8 07.4	24 15.4	8 48.3	2 39.0	13 23.6	5 18.6	2R 25.3	2 06.2	16 25.5	20 12.2
6 F	18 55 42	13 53 56	10♈01 46	16 25 36	7 02.7	6R 04.0	9 23.4	25 23.1	8 41.8	3 03.3	13 22.7	5 14.2	2 25.3	2 07.8	16 24.9	20 10.7
7 Sa	18 59 39	14 51 08	22 55 16	29 31 11	6 59.5	6 03.8	10 36.7	26 30.8	8 34.6	3 27.6	13 21.9	5 09.9	2 25.2	2 09.3	16 24.4	20 09.3
8 Su	19 03 35	15 48 21	6♉13 39	13♉02 56	6 56.4	6 02.7	11 47.4	27 38.3	8 26.7	3 52.1	13 21.3	5 05.6	2 25.1	2 10.8	16 23.8	20 07.8
9 M	19 07 32	16 45 34	19 59 05	27 02 05	6 53.2	6 00.9	12 55.4	28 45.6	8 18.0	4 16.6	13 20.9	5 01.3	2 25.0	2 12.3	16 23.2	20 06.3
10 Tu	19 11 28	17 42 48	4♊11 42	11♊27 33	6 50.0	5 58.7	14 00.5	29 52.9	8 08.7	4 41.2	13D 20.7	4 57.0	2 24.7	2 13.7	16 22.6	20 04.9
11 W	19 15 25	18 40 02	18 49 02	26 15 26	6 46.8	5 56.5	15 02.8	1♍00.0	7 58.7	5 05.9	13 20.7	4 52.8	2 24.5	2 15.0	16 21.9	20 03.4
12 Th	19 19 22	19 37 16	3♋45 49	11♋19 08	6 43.7	5 54.6	16 02.1	2 06.9	7 48.1	5 30.7	13 20.8	4 48.6	2 24.1	2 16.3	16 21.2	20 01.9
13 F	19 23 18	20 34 31	18 54 16	26 29 59	6 40.5	5 53.4	16 58.4	3 13.7	7 36.8	5 55.5	13 21.1	4 44.4	2 23.8	2 17.6	16 20.5	20 00.5
14 Sa	19 27 15	21 31 46	4♌05 07	11♌38 29	6 37.3	5D 52.9	17 51.4	4 20.4	7 24.9	6 20.4	13 21.6	4 40.3	2 23.3	2 18.8	16 19.7	19 59.0
15 Su	19 31 11	22 29 01	19 08 59	26 35 40	6 34.1	5 53.2	18 41.1	5 26.9	7 12.5	6 45.3	13 22.3	4 36.2	2 22.8	2 20.0	16 18.9	19 57.6
16 M	19 35 08	23 26 16	3♍57 42	11♍14 25	6 31.0	5 53.9	19 27.3	6 33.2	6 59.5	7 10.3	13 23.2	4 32.1	2 22.3	2 21.1	16 18.1	19 56.1
17 Tu	19 39 04	24 23 31	18 25 18	25 30 03	6 27.8	5 54.8	20 10.0	7 39.4	6 46.1	7 35.4	13 24.3	4 28.1	2 21.7	2 22.2	16 17.3	19 54.6
18 W	19 43 01	25 20 47	2♎28 28	9♎20 30	6 24.6	5 55.7	20 48.9	8 45.4	6 32.1	8 00.5	13 25.5	4 24.1	2 21.1	2 23.2	16 16.4	19 53.2
19 Th	19 46 57	26 18 02	16 06 15	22 45 55	6 21.4	5R 56.2	21 23.9	9 51.2	6 17.8	8 25.7	13 26.9	4 20.1	2 20.4	2 24.2	16 15.5	19 51.7
20 F	19 50 54	27 15 18	29 19 45	5♏48 06	6 18.3	5 56.3	21 54.9	10 56.9	6 03.0	8 51.0	13 28.5	4 16.2	2 19.6	2 25.1	16 14.6	19 50.2
21 Sa	19 54 51	28 12 34	12♏11 21	18 29 54	6 15.1	5 56.1	22 21.7	12 02.3	5 48.0	9 16.3	13 30.2	4 12.4	2 18.8	2 26.0	16 13.6	19 48.8
22 Su	19 58 47	29 09 50	24 44 11	0♐54 40	6 11.9	5 55.5	22 44.1	13 07.6	5 32.6	9 41.6	13 32.2	4 08.6	2 18.0	2 26.8	16 12.7	19 47.3
23 M	20 02 44	0♌07 06	7♐01 45	13 05 54	6 08.7	5 54.8	23 02.0	14 12.7	5 16.9	10 07.1	13 34.3	4 04.8	2 17.1	2 27.6	16 11.7	19 45.9
24 Tu	20 06 40	1 04 23	19 07 29	25 06 56	6 05.5	5 54.2	23 15.3	15 17.5	5 01.0	10 32.5	13 36.6	4 01.1	2 16.2	2 28.4	16 10.6	19 44.5
25 W	20 10 37	2 01 40	1♑04 37	7♑00 52	6 02.4	5 53.6	23 23.7	16 22.2	4 44.9	10 58.0	13 39.1	3 57.5	2 15.2	2 29.1	16 09.6	19 43.0
26 Th	20 14 33	2 58 58	12 56 04	18 50 30	5 59.2	5 53.3	23R 27.3	17 26.6	4 28.7	11 23.6	13 41.7	3 53.9	2 14.1	2 29.7	16 08.5	19 41.6
27 F	20 18 30	3 56 16	24 44 30	0♒38 21	5 56.0	5D 53.1	23 25.8	18 30.9	4 12.4	11 49.2	13 44.5	3 50.4	2 13.1	2 30.3	16 07.4	19 40.2
28 Sa	20 22 26	4 53 35	6♒32 20	12 26 46	5 52.8	5 53.1	23 19.3	19 34.9	3 56.0	12 14.9	13 47.5	3 46.9	2 11.9	2 30.9	16 06.3	19 38.8
29 Su	20 26 23	5 50 55	18 21 53	24 18 01	5 49.7	5R 53.1	23 07.7	20 38.6	3 39.6	12 40.6	13 50.6	3 43.5	2 10.7	2 31.4	16 05.2	19 37.4
30 M	20 30 20	6 48 15	0♓15 27	6♓14 28	5 46.5	5 53.0	22 51.1	21 42.2	3 23.2	13 06.4	13 54.0	3 40.2	2 09.5	2 31.8	16 04.0	19 36.0
31 Tu	20 34 16	7♌45 36	12 15 25	18 18 37	5♌43.3	5♌52.9	22♌29.6	22♍45.5	3♒06.9	13♍32.2	13♏57.4	3♑36.9	2♈08.2	2♉32.2	16♓02.8	19♑34.6

1st of Month

Julian Day #
2458300.5
Obliquity
23°26'07"
SVP 5♓00'18"
GC 27♐05.9
Eris 24♈03.9

Day	⚴
1	23♋43.0
6	26 36.3
11	29 28.8
16	2♌20.2
21	5 10.6
26	7 59.8
31	10 47.7

Day	⚵
1	29♈50.1
6	2♉04.1
11	4 16.2
16	6 26.3
21	8 33.9
26	10 38.9
31	12 40.9

Day	⚶
1	25♐53.3R
6	24 51.3R
11	23 57.2R
16	23 12.9R
21	22 39.7R
26	22 18.2R
31	22 08.7R

DECLINATION and LATITUDE

Day	☉ Decl	☽ Decl	☽ Lat	☽12h Decl	☿ Decl	☿ Lat	♀ Decl	♀ Lat	♂ Decl	♂ Lat	⚳ Decl	⚳ Lat	♃ Decl	♃ Lat	♄ Decl	♄ Lat
1 Su	23N07	18S11	0S20	17S02	20N54	1N22	16N36	1N47	22S48	5S00	19N23	8N53	14S50	1N06	22S28	0N51
2 M	23 03	15 43	1 24	14 13	20 27	1 15	16 12	1 46	22 53	5 05	19 13	8 51	14 50	1 06	22 28	0 51
3 Tu	22 59	12 34	2 25	10 47	19 59	1 07	15 49	1 44	22 58	5 09	19 02	8 49	14 50	1 06	22 29	0 51
4 W	22 54	8 53	3 20	6 52	19 31	0 59	15 24	1 42	23 04	5 13	18 52	8 48	14 49	1 05	22 29	0 51
5 Th	22 48	4 47	4 07	2 36	19 03	0 51	15 00	1 40	23 10	5 18	18 42	8 46	14 49	1 05	22 29	0 50
6 F	22 43	0 23	4 44	1N52	18 34	0 41	14 35	1 37	23 15	5 22	18 31	8 45	14 49	1 05	22 30	0 50
7 Sa	22 36	4N09	5 08	6 24	18 05	0 32	14 10	1 35	23 21	5 26	18 21	8 43	14 49	1 05	22 30	0 50
8 Su	22 30	8 37	5 16	10 46	17 36	0 22	13 45	1 33	23 27	5 30	18 10	8 42	14 49	1 04	22 30	0 50
9 M	22 23	12 48	5 07	14 42	17 07	0 11	13 19	1 30	23 34	5 34	17 60	8 40	14 49	1 04	22 30	0 50
10 Tu	22 16	16 25	4 39	17 54	16 38	0 01	12 53	1 28	23 40	5 38	17 49	8 38	14 50	1 04	22 31	0 50
11 W	22 08	19 07	3 52	20 01	16 09	0S11	12 27	1 25	23 46	5 42	17 38	8 37	14 50	1 04	22 31	0 50
12 Th	22 00	20 34	2 49	20 46	15 40	0 22	11 60	1 22	23 53	5 46	17 28	8 35	14 50	1 03	22 31	0 50
13 F	21 52	20 34	1 33	20 00	15 12	0 34	11 33	1 19	23 60	5 50	17 17	8 34	14 51	1 03	22 31	0 50
14 Sa	21 43	19 04	0 10	17 48	14 44	0 47	11 06	1 16	24 06	5 53	17 06	8 32	14 51	1 03	22 32	0 50
15 Su	21 34	16 14	1N13	14 25	14 17	0 59	10 39	1 13	24 13	5 57	16 55	8 31	14 51	1 03	22 32	0 49
16 M	21 24	12 23	2 30	10 11	13 50	1 12	10 11	1 10	24 19	6 00	16 45	8 29	14 52	1 02	22 32	0 49
17 Tu	21 14	7 52	3 35	5 29	13 25	1 25	9 44	1 07	24 26	6 04	16 34	8 28	14 52	1 02	22 32	0 49
18 W	21 04	3 04	4 25	0 39	12 60	1 39	9 16	1 03	24 33	6 07	16 23	8 27	14 53	1 02	22 33	0 49
19 Th	20 53	1S44	4 59	4S04	12 36	1 52	8 47	0 59	24 39	6 10	16 12	8 25	14 54	1 01	22 33	0 49
20 F	20 42	6 19	5 15	8 27	12 13	2 06	8 19	0 56	24 46	6 13	16 01	8 24	14 54	1 01	22 33	0 49
21 Sa	20 31	10 29	5 16	12 22	11 51	2 20	7 51	0 52	24 52	6 15	15 50	8 22	14 55	1 01	22 33	0 49
22 Su	20 19	14 05	5 01	15 38	11 31	2 33	7 22	0 48	24 59	6 18	15 39	8 21	14 56	1 01	22 34	0 49
23 M	20 07	17 00	4 32	18 11	11 12	2 47	6 53	0 44	25 05	6 20	15 28	8 20	14 57	1 00	22 34	0 49
24 Tu	19 55	19 08	3 52	19 53	10 55	3 01	6 25	0 40	25 11	6 22	15 17	8 18	14 58	1 00	22 34	0 48
25 W	19 42	20 24	3 02	20 41	10 40	3 14	5 56	0 36	25 17	6 24	15 06	8 17	14 59	0 60	22 34	0 48
26 Th	19 29	20 45	2 04	20 34	10 26	3 27	5 27	0 32	25 23	6 26	14 55	8 15	14 60	0 60	22 35	0 48
27 F	19 16	20 10	1 02	19 32	10 15	3 39	4 57	0 27	25 29	6 28	14 44	8 14	15 01	0 59	22 35	0 48
28 Sa	19 02	18 42	0S04	17 39	10 06	3 52	4 28	0 23	25 34	6 30	14 33	8 13	15 02	0 59	22 35	0 48
29 Su	18 48	16 25	1 09	15 00	9 59	4 03	3 59	0 18	25 39	6 31	14 21	8 12	15 03	0 59	22 35	0 48
30 M	18 34	13 26	2 11	11 43	9 54	4 14	3 30	0 13	25 45	6 32	14 10	8 10	15 04	0 59	22 35	0 48
31 Tu	18N20	9S52	3S09	7S55	9N52	4S23	3N00	0N08	25S49	6S33	13N59	8N09	15S06	0N58	22S36	0N48

Day	⚷ Decl	⚷ Lat	♅ Decl	♅ Lat	♆ Decl	♆ Lat	♇ Decl	♇ Lat
1	4N12	3N32	11N40	0S32	6S14	0S58	21S43	0N11
6	4 13	3 32	11 43	0 32	6 15	0 58	21 45	0 11
11	4 13	3 33	11 45	0 32	6 17	0 58	21 46	0 10
16	4 13	3 34	11 47	0 32	6 18	0 59	21 48	0 10
21	4 12	3 34	11 48	0 32	6 20	0 59	21 49	0 09
26	4 10	3 35	11 50	0 33	6 22	0 59	21 51	0 09
31	4N09	3N35	11N50	0S33	6S25	0S59	21S52	0N08

Day	⚴ Decl	⚴ Lat	⚵ Decl	⚵ Lat	⚶ Decl	⚶ Lat	Eris Decl	Eris Lat
1	1N47	19S50	8N40	2S56	20S36	2N47	1S51	12S00
6	1 50	19 19	9 03	3 21	20 58	2 22	1 51	12 01
11	1 51	18 47	9 23	3 47	21 19	1 58	1 51	12 01
16	1 48	18 16	9 40	4 14	21 41	1 35	1 51	12 02
21	1 43	17 44	9 53	4 43	22 02	1 12	1 52	12 02
26	1 36	17 13	10 02	5 14	22 23	0 50	1 52	12 03
31	1N26	16S41	10N08	5S46	22S43	0N29	1S53	12S03

Moon Phenomena

Max/0 Decl

dy	hr mn	
6	2:03	0 N
12	12:02	20N45
18	15:16	0 S
25	20:56	20S45

Perigee/Apogee

dy	hr m		kilometers
13	8:21	p	357436
27	5:48	a	406223

Max/0 Lat

dy	hr mn	
7	23:45	5S16
14	2:51	0 N
20	12:16	5N17
27	22:41	0 S

PH	dy	hr mn	
☾	6	7:52	14♈13
●	13	2:49	20♋41
☊	13	3:02	P 0.337
☽	19	19:53	27♎05
○	27	20:22	4♒45
☋	27	20:23	T 1.609

Void of Course Moon

Last Aspect			☽ Ingress	
1 22:57	♀	☍	♓	2 17:32
4 9:48	♇	⚹	♈	5 4:51
7 7:10	♀	△	♉	7 12:52
9 16:11	♀	□	♊	9 16:59
10 20:01	♆	□	♋	11 18:00
13 2:49	☉	☌	♌	13 17:32
14 23:13	☿	☌	♍	15 17:32
17 10:51	☉	⚹	♎	17 19:43
19 19:53	☉	□	♏	20 1:14
22 9:19	☉	△	♐	22 10:13
24 8:23	☿	△	♑	24 21:50
26 13:42	♇	☌	♒	27 10:42
29 9:26	☿	☍	♓	29 23:29

DAILY ASPECTARIAN

1 Su ☽□♃ 8:04; ⚵ ♉ 8:47; ♀⚻♇ 12:00; ☽⚺♆ 14:07; ☽∠⚷ 16:04; ♀⚼♄ 17:31; ☽⋕♀ 18:57; ☽⚺♇ 21:53; ☽∠♄ 22:24; ☽☍♀ 22:57

2 M ☽∥♃ 7:15; ☉⚼☽ 8:17; ☽☍⚳ 21:09; ☽⚹♅ 21:39; ☽⚺⚷ 22:24; ☿⚻♄ 23:50

3 Tu ☉⋕♂ 0:45; ☽∠♇ 4:05; ☽⚹♄ 4:28; ☽⚻☿ 5:06; ☽⋕♅ 6:05; ☽⚺♂ 11:28; ⚳△♅ 13:14; ☉△☽ 16:59; ☽△♃ 20:22

4 W ☽☌♆ 2:21; ☽∠♅ 3:37; ☽⚹♇ 9:48; ⚳⚻⚷ 10:30; ☽⚼☿ 14:29; ☽∥♆ 15:37; ☽∠♂ 16:53; ☽⚻♀ 17:04

5 Th ☽⚼♃ 1:44; ☽⋕⚷ 3:10; ⚷ R 4:47; ☽⚺♅ 8:55; ☽☌⚷ 9:30; ☽⚻⚳ 10:17; ♀⋕♃ 10:27; ☉△♃ 11:06; ☿☍♂ 11:50; ☽□♄ 14:57; ☽⚹♂ 21:30; ☽△☿ 22:39

6 F ☽⚼♀ 0:44; ☿∥⚳ 3:46; ☽⚻♃ 6:18; ☉□☽ 7:52; ☽⚺♆ 11:58; ☽⚼⚳ 15:31; ☽□♇ 18:55

7 Sa ☽∥⚷ 0:22; ☽△♀ 7:10; ☽⋕♆ 11:14; ☽∠♆ 15:23; ☽☌♅ 16:46; ☽⚺⚷ 17:13; ☽△⚳ 19:40; ☽△♄ 22:00; ☉⋕♄ 23:35

8 Su ☽□♂ 3:53; ☽□☿ 10:42; ☽☍♃ 12:32; ☉△♆ 14:43; ☽∥♅ 17:35; ☽⚹♆ 17:48; ☉⚹☽ 18:02; ☽∠⚷ 19:35

9 M ☽⚼♄ 0:04; ☽△♇ 0:12; ☽∥♀ 2:48; ☿□♃ 9:15; ☽⋕♃ 12:49; ☽□♀ 16:11; ☽⚺♅ 20:43; ☽⚹⚷ 21:02; ☉∠☽ 21:21

10 Tu ☽□⚳ 0:51; ☽⚻♄ 1:15; ☽∥☿ 1:24; ☽⚼♇ 1:28; ♀ ♍ 2:33; ☽△♂ 6:28; ☽∥⚳ 10:36; ⚳△♄ 13:07; ☽⚻♃ 15:05; ♃ D 17:04; ☽⚹☿ 17:25; ☽□♆ 20:01; ☽∠♅ 21:27; ⚳⚼♇ 21:43; ☉⚺☽ 23:44

11 W ☽⚻♇ 2:00; ☽⚼♂ 6:39; ☽⚼♃ 15:21; ☽∠☿ 19:21; ☽⚹♀ 21:10; ☽⚹♅ 21:37; ⚴ ♌ 21:48; ☽□⚷ 21:50

12 Th ☽☍♄ 1:39; ☽⚹⚳ 2:52; ♀△♅ 3:27; ♀⚻⚷ 6:09; ☽⚻♂ 6:21; ☿⚻♆ 7:53; ☉☍♇ 10:05; ♀∥♅ 12:53; ☽△♃ 15:13; ☽△♆ 19:57; ☽⚺☿ 20:45; ☽∠♀ 22:51

13 F ☽☍♇ 1:44; ☉☌☽ 2:49; ☽∠⚳ 3:17; ☿⚼⚷ 11:13; ☉⋕♇ 12:52; ☉∠⚳ 15:32; ☿⋕♃ 18:14; ☽⚼♆ 19:38; ☽□♅ 21:11; ☽△⚷ 21:19

14 Sa ☽⚺♀ 0:26; ☽⚻♄ 0:55; ☽⚺⚳ 3:40; ☽☍♂ 5:13; ♀△♄ 6:45; ♀⚼♇ 13:38; ☽□♃ 14:45; ☽∥⚳ 18:40; ☽⚻♆ 19:28; ☽⚼⚷ 21:10; ☽☌☿ 23:13

15 Su ☽⚼♄ 0:43; ☽⚻♇ 1:18; ☉⚺☽ 5:44; ☽⋕♃ 9:10; ☽∥☿ 14:25; ♂⚻⚳ 17:13; ☽△♅ 21:22; ☽⚻⚷ 21:24

16 M ☽△♄ 0:56; ☽⚼♇ 1:36; ☿⚼♄ 2:22; ☽∥♅ 3:19; ☽☌♀ 4:36; ☽⚻♂ 4:54; ☽☌⚳ 5:26; ☉∠☽ 7:53; ♀⚻♂ 7:57; ☽∥♀ 13:20; ☿⚻♇ 15:25; ☽⚹♃ 15:35; ♅⚺⚷ 17:11; ☽☍♆ 20:25; ♀☌⚳ 21:40; ☽⚼♅ 22:14

17 Tu ☽△♇ 2:30; ☽⚺☿ 3:05; ☽⚼♂ 5:34; ☽⋕♆ 7:53; ☉⚹☽ 10:51; ☽∠♃ 17:00; ☽∥⚷ 18:22; ☽☍⚷ 23:47; ☽⚻♅ 23:51

18 W ☽□♄ 3:20; ☽∠☿ 6:05; ☽△♂ 6:57; ☽⚺⚳ 9:58; ☽⚺♀ 11:56; ☽⚺♃ 19:15

19 Th ☽⚻♆ 0:17; ☽□♇ 6:44; ☽⚹☿ 9:56; ☽⋕⚷ 12:44; ☽∠⚳ 13:38; ☽∠♀ 17:14; ☉□☽ 19:53

20 F ☽∥♆ 0:06; ☽⚼♆ 3:32; ☽⚻⚷ 5:32; ☽☍♅ 5:43; ☽⚹♄ 9:06; ☽⋕♀ 10:05; ☽□♂ 12:14; ☽⚹⚳ 18:19; ☽⚹♀ 23:41

21 Sa ☽☌♃ 2:30; ☿∥♅ 3:09; ☽△♆ 7:39; ☽⋕☿ 7:57; ☽⋕♅ 8:24; ☽⚼⚷ 9:44; ☽∠♄ 13:17; ☽⚹♇ 14:29; ☽□☿ 20:02

22 Su ☽∥♃ 6:25; ☉△☽ 9:19; ♀⚹♃ 9:22; ☽⋕⚳ 11:24; ☽△⚷ 14:42; ☽⚻♅ 15:01; ☽⚺♄ 18:14; ☽∠♇ 19:33; ☽⚹♂ 20:38; ☉ ♌ 21:01

23 M ☽□⚳ 6:19; ☽⚺♃ 12:59; ☽□♀ 15:36; ☉⚼☽ 17:23; ☽□♆ 18:08; ☽⚼♅ 20:42

24 Tu ☽⚺♇ 1:14; ☽∠♂ 1:45; ☉⚼♆ 2:34; ♀⋕♆ 2:36; ☽△☿ 8:23; ☉⋕☽ 10:51; ☽∠♃ 19:06; ♀☍♆ 19:24

25 W ☉⚻☽ 2:05; ☽□⚷ 2:22; ☽△♅ 2:51; ☉△⚷ 5:34; ☽☌♄ 5:47; ☽⚺♂ 7:15; ☉□♅ 11:37; ⚳⋕♃ 14:03; ☽⚼☿ 14:53; ☽△⚳ 20:45

26 Th ♀⚼♅ 1:10; ☽⚹♃ 1:33; ☿ R 5:03; ☽⚹♆ 6:30; ☽△♀ 10:04; ☽☌♇ 13:42; ☽⚻☿ 21:21; ☉⚻♄ 21:41

27 F ☽⚼⚳ 4:23; ☉☍♂ 5:14; ♀⚼♂ 12:23; ☽∠♆ 12:58; ☽⚹⚷ 15:11; ☽□♅ 15:49; ☽⚺♄ 18:25; ☉⋕☽ 18:43; ☽☌♂ 18:49; ☽⚼♀ 19:37; ☉☍☽ 20:22

28 Sa ♀△♇ 1:27; ☽⚻⚳ 12:02; ☽□♃ 14:48; ♀∥⚷ 15:20; ♂⚺♄ 16:41; ☽⚺♆ 19:23; ☽∠⚷ 21:36

29 Su ☽∠♄ 0:44; ☽⚺♇ 2:33; ☽⚻♀ 5:04; ☽☍☿ 9:26; ☽∥♃ 11:29; ☽⋕⚳ 18:08

30 M ☽⚺⚷ 3:49; ☽⚹♅ 4:34; ☽⚺♂ 6:09; ☽⚹♄ 6:49; ☽∠♇ 8:42; ☽⋕♅ 11:08; ☉⚻☽ 14:16; ☿⚺♀ 19:36

31 Tu ☽⋕☿ 0:04; ☉∠♀ 0:30; ☽☍⚳ 2:38; ☽△♃ 3:24; ☽☌♆ 7:31; ☽∠♅ 10:29; ☽∠♂ 11:22; ☽⚹♇ 14:28; ☽⚻☿ 19:33; ☽∥♆ 20:49; ☉⚼☽ 22:32; ☽☍♀ 22:43

August 2018

LONGITUDE

Day	Sid.Time	☉	☽	☽ 12 hour	Mean☊	True☊	☿	♀	♂	⚳	♃	♄	⚷	♅	♆	♇
	h m s	° ' "	° ' "	° ' "	° '	° '	° '	° '	° '	° '	° '	° '	° '	° '	° '	° '
1 W	20 38 13	8♌42 58	24♓24 24	0♈33 09	5♌40.1	5♌52.6	22♌03.3	23♍48.5	2♒50.7	13♍58.1	14♏01.1	3♑33.7	2♈06.9	2♉32.6	16♓01.6	19♑33.3
2 Th	20 42 09	9 40 21	6♈45 15	13 01 03	5 36.9	5R 52.2	21R 32.5	24 51.3	2R 34.7	14 24.0	14 04.9	3R 30.6	2R 05.6	2 32.9	16R 00.3	19R 31.9
3 F	20 46 06	10 37 46	19 20 58	25 45 22	5 33.8	5 51.8	20 57.6	25 53.9	2 18.8	14 49.9	14 08.9	3 27.5	2 04.1	2 33.1	15 59.1	19 30.6
4 Sa	20 50 02	11 35 11	2♉14 38	8♉49 06	5 30.6	5D 51.5	20 19.0	26 56.2	2 03.3	15 15.9	14 13.0	3 24.5	2 02.7	2 33.3	15 57.8	19 29.2
5 Su	20 53 59	12 32 38	15 29 05	22 14 50	5 27.4	5 51.4	19 37.1	27 58.2	1 48.0	15 41.9	14 17.3	3 21.6	2 01.2	2 33.5	15 56.5	19 27.9
6 M	20 57 55	13 30 06	29 06 31	6♊04 13	5 24.2	5 51.7	18 52.8	28 59.1	1 33.0	16 08.0	14 21.8	3 18.7	1 59.6	2 33.6	15 55.2	19 26.6
7 Tu	21 01 52	14 27 35	13♊07 55	20 17 29	5 21.1	5 52.2	18 06.6	0♎01.3	1 18.4	16 34.2	14 26.4	3 15.9	1 58.0	2R 33.6	15 53.9	19 25.3
8 W	21 05 49	15 25 06	27 32 35	4♋52 48	5 17.9	5 53.0	17 19.3	1 02.5	1 04.3	17 00.3	14 31.2	3 13.2	1 56.4	2 33.7	15 52.5	19 24.0
9 Th	21 09 45	16 22 37	12♋17 31	19 45 59	5 14.7	5 53.7	16 31.9	2 03.3	0 50.5	17 26.5	14 36.2	3 10.6	1 54.7	2 33.6	15 51.2	19 22.7
10 F	21 13 42	17 20 11	27 17 18	4♌50 28	5 11.5	5R 54.3	15 45.1	3 03.9	0 37.3	17 52.8	14 41.3	3 08.0	1 53.0	2 33.5	15 49.8	19 21.5
11 Sa	21 17 38	18 17 45	12♌24 23	19 57 54	5 08.4	5 54.3	14 59.9	4 04.1	0 24.6	18 19.1	14 46.5	3 05.6	1 51.3	2 33.4	15 48.4	19 20.2
12 Su	21 21 35	19 15 20	27 29 52	4♍59 10	5 05.2	5 53.7	14 17.2	5 04.0	0 12.5	18 45.4	14 51.9	3 03.2	1 49.5	2 33.2	15 46.9	19 19.0
13 M	21 25 31	20 12 57	12♍24 46	19 45 45	5 02.0	5 52.4	13 37.8	6 03.5	0 01.0	19 11.7	14 57.5	3 00.9	1 47.6	2 33.0	15 45.5	19 17.8
14 Tu	21 29 28	21 10 34	27 01 20	4♎10 53	4 58.8	5 50.6	13 02.6	7 02.7	29♑50.2	19 38.1	15 03.2	2 58.7	1 45.7	2 32.7	15 44.1	19 16.6
15 W	21 33 24	22 08 13	11♎14 00	18 10 23	4 55.6	5 48.6	12 32.3	8 01.5	29 40.0	20 04.6	15 09.1	2 56.5	1 43.8	2 32.3	15 42.6	19 15.4
16 Th	21 37 21	23 05 52	24 59 55	1♏42 41	4 52.5	5 46.7	12 07.5	9 00.0	29 30.5	20 31.0	15 15.1	2 54.5	1 41.9	2 31.9	15 41.1	19 14.2
17 F	21 41 18	24 03 33	8♏18 51	14 48 41	4 49.3	5 45.3	11 48.9	9 58.0	29 21.7	20 57.5	15 21.2	2 52.5	1 39.9	2 31.5	15 39.6	19 13.1
18 Sa	21 45 14	25 01 14	21 12 36	27 31 03	4 46.1	5D 44.6	11 36.9	10 55.6	29 13.7	21 24.0	15 27.5	2 50.6	1 37.9	2 31.0	15 38.1	19 11.9
19 Su	21 49 11	25 58 57	3♐44 32	9♐53 35	4 42.9	5 44.8	11D 31.9	11 52.8	29 06.4	21 50.6	15 34.0	2 48.9	1 35.8	2 30.5	15 36.6	19 10.8
20 M	21 53 07	26 56 41	15 58 48	22 00 44	4 39.8	5 45.7	11 34.3	12 49.6	28 59.9	22 17.1	15 40.5	2 47.2	1 33.7	2 29.9	15 35.0	19 09.7
21 Tu	21 57 04	27 54 25	27 59 58	3♑57 03	4 36.6	5 47.2	11 44.1	13 45.9	28 54.2	22 43.8	15 47.3	2 45.6	1 31.6	2 29.3	15 33.5	19 08.7
22 W	22 01 00	28 52 11	9♑52 31	15 46 53	4 33.4	5 48.8	12 01.6	14 41.7	28 49.3	23 10.4	15 54.1	2 44.0	1 29.4	2 28.6	15 31.9	19 07.6
23 Th	22 04 57	29 49 59	21 40 39	27 34 15	4 30.2	5 50.2	12 26.8	15 37.0	28 45.2	23 37.1	16 01.1	2 42.6	1 27.2	2 27.9	15 30.4	19 06.6
24 F	22 08 53	0♍47 47	3♒28 07	9♒22 37	4 27.0	5R 50.9	12 59.6	16 31.8	28 41.8	24 03.7	16 08.3	2 41.3	1 25.0	2 27.1	15 28.8	19 05.6
25 Sa	22 12 50	1 45 37	15 18 08	21 14 57	4 23.9	5 50.6	13 40.0	17 26.1	28 39.3	24 30.4	16 15.5	2 40.0	1 22.7	2 26.3	15 27.2	19 04.6
26 Su	22 16 47	2 43 28	27 13 22	3♓13 38	4 20.7	5 48.9	14 27.8	18 19.9	28 37.6	24 57.2	16 22.9	2 38.9	1 20.4	2 25.5	15 25.6	19 03.6
27 M	22 20 43	3 41 21	9♓15 58	15 20 36	4 17.5	5 46.0	15 22.7	19 13.1	28D 36.7	25 23.9	16 30.4	2 37.8	1 18.1	2 24.6	15 24.0	19 02.7
28 Tu	22 24 40	4 39 15	21 27 40	27 37 23	4 14.3	5 41.9	16 24.6	20 05.7	28 36.7	25 50.7	16 38.1	2 36.9	1 15.8	2 23.6	15 22.4	19 01.7
29 W	22 28 36	5 37 10	3♈49 53	10♈05 19	4 11.2	5 37.0	17 33.1	20 57.7	28 37.4	26 17.5	16 45.9	2 36.0	1 13.4	2 22.6	15 20.8	19 00.8
30 Th	22 32 33	6 35 08	16 23 52	22 45 40	4 08.0	5 31.9	18 47.8	21 49.0	28 39.0	26 44.4	16 53.8	2 35.2	1 11.0	2 21.6	15 19.1	18 59.9
31 F	22 36 29	7♍33 07	29 10 52	5♉39 39	4♌04.8	5♌27.2	20♌08.4	22♎39.8	28♑41.3	27♍11.2	17♏01.8	2♑34.6	1♈08.6	2♉20.5	15♓17.5	18♑59.1

1st of Month

Julian Day # 2458331.5
Obliquity 23°26'07"
SVP 5♓00'14"
GC 27♐05.9
Eris 24♈05.2R

Day	⚴	Day	⚵	Day	⚶
1	11♌21.2	1	13♉04.9	1	22♐08.3R
6	14 07.6	6	15 02.8	6	22 13.2
11	16 52.8	11	16 56.7	11	22 29.7
16	19 36.6	16	18 46.2	16	22 57.6
21	22 19.0	21	20 30.6	21	23 36.2
26	24 59.9	26	22 09.4	26	24 24.8
31	27 39.3	31	23 42.0	31	25 22.5

DECLINATION and LATITUDE

Day	☉ Decl	☽ Decl	☽ Lat	☽12h Decl	☿ Decl	☿ Lat	♀ Decl	♀ Lat	♂ Decl	♂ Lat	⚳ Decl	⚳ Lat	♃ Decl	♃ Lat	♄ Decl	♄ Lat
1 W	18N05	5S52	3S58	3S45	9N52	4S32	2N31	0N03	25S54	6S34	13N48	8N08	15S07	0N58	22S36	0N47
2 Th	17 50	1 34	4 38	0N38	9 54	4 40	2 01	0S02	25 58	6 34	13 36	8 06	15 08	0 58	22 36	0 47
3 F	17 34	2N52	5 05	5 06	9 59	4 46	1 32	0 07	26 03	6 35	13 25	8 05	15 10	0 58	22 36	0 47
4 Sa	17 18	7 17	5 17	9 25	10 07	4 51	1 02	0 12	26 06	6 35	13 14	8 04	15 11	0 57	22 37	0 47
5 Su	17 02	11 29	5 13	13 25	10 17	4 54	0 33	0 17	26 10	6 35	13 03	8 03	15 13	0 57	22 37	0 47
6 M	16 46	15 12	4 52	16 48	10 29	4 55	0 03	0 23	26 13	6 35	12 51	8 01	15 14	0 57	22 37	0 47
7 Tu	16 29	18 11	4 13	19 18	10 43	4 55	0S26	0 28	26 16	6 34	12 40	8 00	15 16	0 57	22 37	0 47
8 W	16 13	20 07	3 17	20 37	10 59	4 53	0 56	0 34	26 19	6 34	12 28	7 59	15 18	0 56	22 37	0 46
9 Th	15 56	20 45	2 07	20 31	11 17	4 49	1 25	0 39	26 21	6 33	12 17	7 58	15 19	0 56	22 38	0 46
10 F	15 38	19 55	0 48	18 57	11 36	4 43	1 55	0 45	26 24	6 32	12 06	7 57	15 21	0 56	22 38	0 46
11 Sa	15 21	17 39	0N36	16 03	11 57	4 35	2 24	0 51	26 25	6 31	11 54	7 55	15 23	0 56	22 38	0 46
12 Su	15 03	14 10	1 57	12 04	12 18	4 26	2 53	0 57	26 27	6 30	11 43	7 54	15 25	0 55	22 38	0 46
13 M	14 45	9 49	3 09	7 25	12 39	4 15	3 22	1 03	26 28	6 29	11 31	7 53	15 26	0 55	22 38	0 46
14 Tu	14 26	4 57	4 07	2 28	13 01	4 02	3 51	1 09	26 29	6 27	11 20	7 52	15 28	0 55	22 39	0 46
15 W	14 08	0S02	4 48	2S29	13 23	3 49	4 20	1 15	26 30	6 25	11 08	7 51	15 30	0 55	22 39	0 46
16 Th	13 49	4 51	5 11	7 08	13 44	3 34	4 49	1 22	26 30	6 24	10 57	7 50	15 32	0 55	22 39	0 45
17 F	13 30	9 17	5 16	11 18	14 04	3 18	5 18	1 28	26 30	6 22	10 45	7 49	15 34	0 54	22 39	0 45
18 Sa	13 11	13 09	5 05	14 50	14 23	3 02	5 46	1 35	26 30	6 20	10 34	7 47	15 36	0 54	22 39	0 45
19 Su	12 51	16 19	4 39	17 37	14 41	2 44	6 15	1 41	26 29	6 17	10 22	7 46	15 38	0 54	22 39	0 45
20 M	12 32	18 41	4 02	19 33	14 57	2 27	6 43	1 48	26 28	6 15	10 11	7 45	15 40	0 54	22 40	0 45
21 Tu	12 12	20 11	3 14	20 36	15 12	2 09	7 11	1 55	26 27	6 13	9 59	7 44	15 43	0 53	22 40	0 45
22 W	11 52	20 46	2 18	20 42	15 24	1 51	7 39	2 01	26 25	6 10	9 47	7 43	15 45	0 53	22 40	0 44
23 Th	11 32	20 25	1 17	19 54	15 34	1 33	8 07	2 08	26 24	6 07	9 36	7 42	15 47	0 53	22 40	0 44
24 F	11 11	19 10	0 13	18 13	15 42	1 16	8 35	2 15	26 22	6 05	9 24	7 41	15 49	0 53	22 40	0 44
25 Sa	10 51	17 04	0S52	15 44	15 47	0 59	9 02	2 22	26 20	6 02	9 13	7 40	15 52	0 53	22 40	0 44
26 Su	10 30	14 14	1 55	12 34	15 49	0 42	9 29	2 29	26 17	5 59	9 01	7 39	15 54	0 52	22 41	0 44
27 M	10 09	10 46	2 53	8 51	15 48	0 26	9 56	2 36	26 14	5 56	8 50	7 38	15 56	0 52	22 41	0 44
28 Tu	9 48	6 49	3 45	4 43	15 45	0 11	10 22	2 43	26 11	5 53	8 38	7 37	15 59	0 52	22 41	0 44
29 W	9 27	2 33	4 26	0 20	15 38	0N04	10 49	2 51	26 08	5 50	8 26	7 36	16 01	0 52	22 41	0 43
30 Th	9 06	1N54	4 55	4N08	15 28	0 18	11 15	2 58	26 05	5 47	8 15	7 35	16 03	0 51	22 41	0 43
31 F	8N44	6N20	5S10	8N29	15N15	0N30	11S41	3S05	26S01	5S43	8N03	7N34	16S06	0N51	22S41	0N43

Day	⚷ Decl	⚷ Lat	♅ Decl	♅ Lat	♆ Decl	♆ Lat	♇ Decl	♇ Lat
1	4N08	3N35	11N51	0S33	6S25	0S59	21S53	0N0
6	4 06	3 36	11 51	0 33	6 28	0 59	21 54	0 0
11	4 03	3 36	11 51	0 33	6 31	0 59	21 55	0 0
16	3 59	3 37	11 50	0 33	6 34	0 60	21 57	0 0
21	3 55	3 37	11 49	0 33	6 37	0 60	21 58	0 0
26	3 51	3 37	11 48	0 33	6 40	0 60	21 59	0 0
31	3N47	3N37	11N46	0S33	6S43	0S60	22S00	0N0

Day	⚴ Decl	⚴ Lat	⚵ Decl	⚵ Lat	⚶ Decl	⚶ Lat	Eris Decl	Eris Lat
1	1N24	16S35	10N09	5S53	22S47	0N25	1S53	12S0
6	1 11	16 03	10 10	6 27	23 07	0 06	1 54	12 0
11	0 56	15 31	10 07	7 04	23 26	0S13	1 54	12 0
16	0 40	14 59	9 59	7 42	23 44	0 29	1 55	12 0
21	0 22	14 27	9 47	8 23	24 02	0 45	1 56	12 0
26	0 02	13 56	9 30	9 06	24 19	0 60	1 57	12 0
31	0S19	13S23	9N08	9S51	24S34	1S13	1S58	12S0

Moon Phenomena

Max/0 Decl

dy	hr mn	
2	8:32	0 N
8	22:44	20N45
14	23:52	0 S
22	2:51	20S46
29	13:48	0 N

Max/0 Lat

dy	hr mn	
4	6:35	5S18
10	13:42	0 N
16	19:24	5N16
24	4:51	0 S
31	11:34	5S12

Perigee/Apogee

dy	hr m		kilometers
10	18:16	p	358082
23	11:24	a	405745

PH	dy	hr mn	
☾	4	18:19	12♉19
●	11	9:59	18♌42
●	11	9:47	P 0.737
☽	18	7:50	25♏20
○	26	11:57	3♓12

Void of Course Moon

Last Aspect				☽ Ingress		
31	22:43	♀ ☍		♈	1	10:56
3	2:53	☿ △		♉	3	19:52
5	23:48	♀ △		♊	6	1:33
7	7:56	☿ ⚹		♋	8	4:02
9	11:22	♇ ☍		♌	10	4:19
11	9:59	☉ ☌		♍	12	4:00
14	4:38	♂ △		♎	14	4:58
16	7:57	♂ □		♏	16	8:55
18	15:08	♂ ⚹		♐	18	16:46
20	23:48	☉ △		♑	21	4:02
23	14:20	♂ ☌		♒	23	16:57
25	4:40	♀ △		♓	26	5:34
28	13:56	♂ ⚹		♈	28	16:36
30	23:05	♂ □		♉	31	1:31

DAILY ASPECTARIAN

1 W
⚳⚹♃ 3:17
☽⚼♃ 9:04
☽⋕⚷ 9:51
⚶ D 10:40
☽☌⚷ 15:00
☽⚺♅ 15:52
☽⚹♂ 16:06
☽□♄ 17:46
☽⋕♀ 21:14
☽⚼☿ 23:37

2 Th
♂□♅ 2:40
☉△☽ 6:04
☽⚻♃ 14:06
☽⚻⚳ 15:09
☽∥♀ 17:30
☽⚺♆ 17:39

3 F
☽□♇ 0:18
☽△☿ 2:53
☽∥⚷ 6:44
☽⚻♀ 13:20
☽⋕♆ 19:22
☽⚼⚳ 20:14
☽∠♆ 21:39
☽⚺⚷ 23:38
☽□♂ 23:39

4 Sa
☽☌♅ 0:34
♂⚹⚷ 0:59
☽△♄ 2:08
☽∥☿ 16:37
☉□☽ 18:19
☽⚼♀ 19:07
☽☍♃ 21:51

5 Su
☽△⚳ 0:24
☽⚹♆ 0:49
☽∥♅ 2:14
☽∠⚷ 2:44
☽⚼♄ 5:06
☿⚻♇ 5:16
☽□☿ 6:59
☽△♇ 7:04
☽∥⚳ 9:10
⚳☍♆ 12:47
☽△♀ 23:48

6 M
☽⋕♃ 0:16
☽△♂ 4:09
☽⚹⚷ 4:59
☽⚺♅ 5:58
☽⚻♄ 7:14
☽⚼♇ 9:12
♀∠♃ 9:14
☉∥☽ 10:43
♂⚼⚳ 14:42
☿⚼♄ 18:54
☉□♃ 23:29
♀ ♎ 23:29

7 Tu
☽⚻♃ 2:13
☉⚹☽ 2:24
☽□♆ 4:39
☽⚼♂ 5:15
☽□⚳ 5:58
☽∠♅ 7:26
☽⚹☿ 7:56
☽⚻♇ 10:32
♅ R 16:50

8 W
♀△♂ 0:34
☽⚼♃ 3:16
☉∠☽ 5:03
☽⚻♂ 5:42
☽□♀ 6:10
☿⚺⚳ 6:11
☽□⚷ 7:12
☽∠☿ 7:26
☽⚹♅ 8:13
☽☍♄ 9:16
☉⚻♆ 11:11
☿⚼⚷ 12:00
☿∠♀ 17:01
♀☍⚷ 20:41
♂∠♆ 22:46

9 Th
☉☌☿ 2:07
☽△♃ 3:44
☽△♆ 5:43
⚳⚼♅ 6:28
☽⚺☿ 6:29
☉⚺☽ 7:01
☽⚹⚳ 8:32
☽☍♇ 11:22
♀⚻♅ 11:58
☉⚼⚷ 13:00
☿⚻♆ 21:30

10 F
♀□♄ 1:35
☽☍♂ 5:14
☽⚼♆ 5:37
☽△⚷ 7:17
☽□♅ 8:23
☽∠⚳ 9:09
☽⚻♄ 9:16
☽⚹♀ 9:50
☿∥♅ 16:57
☉⚼♄ 19:08
☉⋕♃ 21:16
☿∥⚳ 22:05

11 Sa
☉⚺⚳ 1:00
☽□♃ 3:47
☽☌☿ 3:55
☽⚻♆ 5:23
☿□♃ 6:33
☽⚼⚷ 7:03
⚳∥♅ 7:26
☽⚼♄ 9:00
☽⚺⚳ 9:40
☉☌☽ 9:59
☽⚻♇ 10:59
☽∠♀ 11:19
☽⋕♃ 16:17
☉∥☽ 18:06

12 Su
☉⚻♇ 1:29
☽⚻♂ 4:17
☽⚻⚷ 6:55
☽△♅ 8:05
☽△♄ 8:52
☽∥☿ 9:57
☽⚼♇ 10:55
☽⚺♀ 13:00
☽∥♅ 13:16
☽∥⚳ 14:36

13 M
☽⚺☿ 1:54
♂R♑ 2:15
☽⚹♃ 4:10
☽⚼♂ 4:11
⚳△♇ 5:15
☽☍♆ 5:26
☽⚼♅ 8:22
☽△♇ 11:13
☽☌⚳ 11:25
☉⚺☽ 13:39
☽⋕♆ 16:21

14 Tu
☽∠☿ 1:38
☽∥⚷ 4:34
☽△♂ 4:38
☽⋕♀ 4:50
☽∠♃ 5:06
♀⋕⚷ 7:33
☽☍⚷ 7:55
☽⚻♅ 9:14
☽□♄ 9:57
☉∠☽ 16:30
☽☌♀ 18:07

15 W
☽⚹☿ 2:10
☽⚺♃ 6:48
☽⚻♆ 7:42
☽□♇ 13:52
☽⚺⚳ 15:50
☽⋕⚷ 19:36
☉⚹☽ 20:23
☽∥♀ 23:49

16 Th
☉∥☿ 3:08
☽□♂ 7:57
☽∥♆ 8:58
☽⚼♆ 10:08
☽⚻⚷ 11:57
☽☍♅ 13:29
☽⚹♄ 14:08
☽∠⚳ 19:33

17 F
☽⚺♀ 3:17
☽□☿ 6:19
☽⋕⚳ 8:16
☽☌♃ 13:07
☽△♆ 13:33
☽⋕♅ 15:20
☽⚼⚷ 15:25
☽∠♄ 17:41
☽⚹♇ 20:13

18 Sa
☉⋕☽ 0:11
☽⚹⚳ 0:22
☉□☽ 7:50
☽⋕☿ 9:37
☽∠♀ 9:42
☽⚹♂ 15:08
☿⚹♀ 15:36
☽∥♃ 18:16
☽△⚷ 19:52
☽⚻♅ 21:37
☽⚺♄ 22:12

19 Su
☽∠♇ 0:51
☿ D 4:25
♃△♆ 7:45
☽△☿ 15:14
☽⚹♀ 17:15
♀∥♆ 17:42
☽∠♂ 20:07
☽□♆ 23:13
☽⚺♃ 23:24

20 M
☽⚼♅ 3:01
☽⚺♇ 6:19
☽□⚳ 13:02
☽⚼☿ 21:25
☉△☽ 23:48

21 Tu
☽⚺♂ 1:48
☽∠♃ 5:40
☽□⚷ 7:05
☽△♅ 9:02
☽☌♄ 9:34
☉⚻♂ 22:53

22 W
☉∥♅ 3:48
☽⚻☿ 4:31
☉⚼☽ 8:50
☽□♀ 10:37
☽⚹♆ 11:28
☽⚹♃ 12:22
☽☌♇ 18:47
♀⚻♆ 21:11

23 Th
☽△⚳ 4:06
☉ ♍ 4:10
♀⚺♃ 12:05
☽☌♂ 14:20
☽∠♆ 17:56
☉⚻☽ 18:05
☽⚹⚷ 19:50
☽□♅ 21:56
☽⚺♄ 22:25

24 F
☽⚼⚳ 11:48
☉⚻⚷ 14:52
☽☍☿ 20:29

25 Sa
☽⚺♆ 0:18
☽□♃ 1:57
☽∠⚷ 2:10
☽△♀ 4:40
☽∠♄ 4:46
♀⋕⚳ 6:44
☽⚺♇ 7:37
☽∥♃ 10:48
☽⋕☿ 11:27
☉△♅ 16:39
♃⚼⚷ 17:54
☽⚻⚳ 19:16
☉△♄ 22:08

26 Su
☽⚺♂ 2:48
☽⚺⚷ 8:13
☽⚹♅ 10:23
☽⚹♄ 10:50
☉☍☽ 11:57
☽⚼♀ 13:11
☽∠♇ 13:38
☽⋕♅ 17:18
♀□♇ 19:22

27 M
☿⚻♆ 0:30
☉⋕☽ 4:19
☽∥♀ 4:46
☉⋕♀ 6:43
☽∠♂ 8:35
☉⚼♇ 8:42
☽☌♆ 12:05
☽⋕⚳ 12:45
☽⚻☿ 13:09
♂ D 14:06
☽△♃ 14:26
☽∠♅ 16:02
☽⚹♇ 19:15
☿⚼⚷ 20:51
☽⚻♀ 21:07

28 Tu
☽∥♆ 0:49
☿□♃ 5:33
☽☍⚳ 8:52
☽⚹♂ 13:56
☽⋕⚷ 17:02
☽☌⚷ 18:59
☽⚼♃ 19:58
☽⚺♅ 21:12
☽⚼☿ 21:16
☽□♄ 21:38

29 W
☿⚼♄ 0:58
☉⚻☽ 3:44
☽⚺♆ 21:58

30 Th
☽⚻♃ 0:57
☿⚻♇ 3:41
☽□♇ 4:55
☽△☿ 5:03
☽∥⚷ 10:08
☉⚼☽ 10:36
☽☍♀ 10:57
☽⚻⚳ 20:09
☽□♂ 23:05

31 F
☽∠♆ 2:04
☽⋕♆ 2:05
☽⚺⚷ 3:38
♀⋕♅ 4:39
☽☌♅ 5:52
☽△♄ 6:18
☽∥⚳ 9:07
☉∥☽ 12:20
☉△☽ 16:43
☉∠♀ 20:10

LONGITUDE

September 2018

Day	Sid.Time	☉	☽	☽ 12 hour	Mean ☊	True ☊	☿	♀	♂	⚳	♃	♄	⚷	♅	♆	♇
	h m s	° ' "	° ' "	° ' "	° '	° '	° '	° '	° '	° '	° '	° '	° '	° '	° '	° '
Sa	22 40 26	8♍31 08	12♉12 10	18♉48 36	4♌01.6	5♌23.5	21♌34.4	23♎29.8	28♑44.5	27♍38.1	17♏09.9	2♑34.0	1♈06.1	2♉19.4	15♓15.9	18♑58.3
Su	22 44 22	9 29 11	25 29 07	2♊13 51	3 58.4	5R 21.1	23 05.3	24 19.2	28 48.5	28 05.0	17 18.2	2R 33.5	1R 03.7	2R 18.2	15R 14.2	18R 57.4
M	22 48 19	10 27 16	9♊02 58	15 56 33	3 55.3	5D 20.2	24 40.6	25 07.8	28 53.2	28 31.9	17 26.6	2 33.1	1 01.2	2 17.0	15 12.6	18 56.6
Tu	22 52 15	11 25 23	22 54 39	29 57 15	3 52.1	5 20.7	26 19.8	25 55.7	28 58.8	28 58.8	17 35.1	2 32.8	0 58.7	2 15.7	15 11.0	18 55.9
W	22 56 12	12 23 32	7♋04 17	14♋15 33	3 48.9	5 21.9	28 02.5	26 42.8	29 05.2	29 25.8	17 43.8	2 32.6	0 56.1	2 14.4	15 09.3	18 55.1
Th	23 00 09	13 21 43	21 30 45	28 49 29	3 45.7	5R 23.2	29 48.1	27 29.2	29 12.3	29 52.7	17 52.5	2D 32.5	0 53.6	2 13.1	15 07.7	18 54.4
F	23 04 05	14 19 56	6♌11 11	13♌35 12	3 42.6	5 23.8	1♍36.2	28 14.7	29 20.2	0♎19.7	18 01.4	2 32.5	0 51.0	2 11.7	15 06.0	18 53.7
Sa	23 08 02	15 18 10	21 00 44	28 26 55	3 39.4	5 22.9	3 26.2	28 59.3	29 28.9	0 46.8	18 10.4	2 32.6	0 48.4	2 10.3	15 04.4	18 53.1
Su	23 11 58	16 16 27	5♍52 45	13♍17 15	3 36.2	5 20.1	5 17.8	29 43.1	29 38.4	1 13.8	18 19.4	2 32.8	0 45.8	2 08.8	15 02.7	18 52.4
M	23 15 55	17 14 45	20 39 24	27 58 14	3 33.0	5 15.4	7 10.6	0♏25.9	29 48.6	1 40.8	18 28.6	2 33.1	0 43.2	2 07.3	15 01.0	18 51.8
Tu	23 19 51	18 13 06	5♎12 51	12♎22 28	3 29.8	5 09.1	9 04.2	1 07.7	29 59.6	2 07.9	18 37.9	2 33.5	0 40.5	2 05.8	14 59.4	18 51.2
W	23 23 48	19 11 28	19 26 26	26 24 15	3 26.7	5 02.1	10 58.3	1 48.5	0♒11.3	2 34.9	18 47.4	2 34.0	0 37.9	2 04.2	14 57.7	18 50.7
Th	23 27 44	20 09 51	3♏15 36	10♏00 20	3 23.5	4 55.2	12 52.7	2 28.2	0 23.7	3 02.0	18 56.9	2 34.6	0 35.2	2 02.6	14 56.1	18 50.1
F	23 31 41	21 08 16	16 38 27	23 10 04	3 20.3	4 49.3	14 47.0	3 06.9	0 36.8	3 29.1	19 06.5	2 35.3	0 32.6	2 00.9	14 54.4	18 49.6
Sa	23 35 38	22 06 43	29 35 30	5♐55 06	3 17.1	4 44.9	16 41.1	3 44.4	0 50.7	3 56.2	19 16.2	2 36.1	0 29.9	1 59.3	14 52.8	18 49.2
Su	23 39 34	23 05 12	12♐09 21	18 18 49	3 13.9	4D 42.4	18 34.9	4 20.7	1 05.2	4 23.3	19 26.1	2 37.0	0 27.2	1 57.5	14 51.2	18 48.7
M	23 43 31	24 03 42	24 24 04	0♑25 45	3 10.8	4 41.7	20 28.1	4 55.7	1 20.5	4 50.4	19 36.0	2 38.0	0 24.5	1 55.8	14 49.5	18 48.3
Tu	23 47 27	25 02 14	6♑24 32	12 21 03	3 07.6	4 42.3	22 20.7	5 29.5	1 36.4	5 17.6	19 46.0	2 39.1	0 21.8	1 54.0	14 47.9	18 47.9
W	23 51 24	26 00 47	18 15 58	24 09 56	3 04.4	4 43.5	24 12.6	6 01.9	1 52.9	5 44.7	19 56.1	2 40.2	0 19.1	1 52.1	14 46.3	18 47.5
Th	23 55 20	26 59 23	0♒03 34	5♒57 27	3 01.2	4R 44.5	26 03.7	6 32.9	2 10.1	6 11.9	20 06.3	2 41.5	0 16.4	1 50.3	14 44.7	18 47.2
F	23 59 17	27 57 59	11 52 09	17 48 10	2 58.1	4 44.3	27 54.0	7 02.4	2 27.9	6 39.0	20 16.6	2 42.9	0 13.6	1 48.4	14 43.1	18 46.9
Sa	0 03 13	28 56 38	23 45 57	29 45 57	2 54.9	4 42.3	29 43.3	7 30.4	2 46.2	7 06.2	20 27.0	2 44.4	0 10.9	1 46.5	14 41.5	18 46.6
Su	0 07 10	29 55 18	5♓48 28	11♓53 50	2 51.7	4 38.0	1♎31.8	7 56.9	3 05.2	7 33.3	20 37.5	2 45.9	0 08.2	1 44.5	14 39.9	18 46.4
M	0 11 07	0♎54 00	18 02 15	24 13 55	2 48.5	4 31.3	3 19.3	8 21.7	3 24.8	8 00.5	20 48.1	2 47.6	0 05.5	1 42.5	14 38.4	18 46.1
Tu	0 15 03	1 52 44	0♈28 55	6♈47 19	2 45.3	4 22.5	5 05.9	8 44.8	3 44.9	8 27.6	20 58.8	2 49.3	0 02.7	1 40.5	14 36.8	18 45.9
W	0 19 00	2 51 30	13 09 08	19 34 19	2 42.2	4 12.3	6 51.5	9 06.1	4 05.6	8 54.8	21 09.5	2 51.2	0 00.0	1 38.5	14 35.2	18 45.8
Th	0 22 56	3 50 18	26 02 48	2♉34 30	2 39.0	4 01.7	8 36.2	9 25.6	4 26.8	9 22.0	21 20.3	2 53.1	29♓57.3	1 36.4	14 33.7	18 45.6
F	0 26 53	4 49 09	9♉09 16	15 47 02	2 35.8	3 51.6	10 19.9	9 43.3	4 48.5	9 49.1	21 31.2	2 55.2	29 54.6	1 34.3	14 32.2	18 45.5
Sa	0 30 49	5 48 01	22 27 39	29 11 04	2 32.6	3 43.1	12 02.8	9 59.0	5 10.8	10 16.3	21 42.2	2 57.3	29 51.9	1 32.2	14 30.6	18 45.4
Su	0 34 46	6♎46 56	5♊57 09	12♊45 54	2♌29.5	3♌36.9	13♎44.7	10♏12.7	5♒33.5	10♎43.5	21♏53.3	2♑59.5	29♓49.2	1♉30.0	14♓29.1	18♑45.4

1st of Month

Julian Day #
2458362.5
Obliquity
23°26'08"
SVP 5♓00'10"
GC 27♐06.0
Eris 23♈56.9R

Day	⚴
1	28♌11.0
6	0♍48.6
11	3 24.6
16	5 58.9
21	8 31.6
26	11 02.4

	⚵
1	23♉59.7
6	25 23.8
11	26 39.8
16	27 46.8
21	28 44.2
26	29 30.9

	⚶
1	25♐35.1
6	26 43.1
11	27 58.9
16	29 21.9
21	0♑51.5
26	2 27.0

DECLINATION and LATITUDE

Day	☉ Decl	☽ Decl	☽ Lat	☽ 12h Decl	☿ Decl	☿ Lat	♀ Decl	♀ Lat	♂ Decl	♂ Lat	⚳ Decl	⚳ Lat	♃ Decl	♃ Lat	♄ Decl	♄ Lat
Sa	8N22	10N34	5S10	12N32	14N59	0N42	12S06	3S13	25S57	5S40	7N52	7N33	16S08	0N51	22S42	0N43
Su	8 01	14 23	4 53	16 03	14 40	0 53	12 32	3 20	25 53	5 37	7 40	7 32	16 11	0 51	22 42	0 43
M	7 39	17 31	4 20	18 45	14 17	1 03	12 56	3 28	25 49	5 33	7 28	7 31	16 14	0 51	22 42	0 43
Tu	7 17	19 44	3 31	20 25	13 52	1 12	13 21	3 35	25 44	5 30	7 17	7 30	16 16	0 50	22 42	0 43
W	6 55	20 47	2 28	20 48	13 24	1 20	13 45	3 43	25 39	5 26	7 05	7 29	16 19	0 50	22 42	0 42
Th	6 32	20 29	1 15	19 48	12 54	1 27	14 09	3 50	25 34	5 23	6 54	7 28	16 21	0 50	22 42	0 42
F	6 10	18 48	0N04	17 27	12 21	1 33	14 33	3 58	25 29	5 19	6 42	7 27	16 24	0 50	22 43	0 42
Sa	5 47	15 49	1 24	13 55	11 46	1 38	14 56	4 05	25 24	5 16	6 31	7 26	16 27	0 50	22 43	0 42
Su	5 25	11 48	2 38	9 30	11 08	1 42	15 19	4 13	25 18	5 12	6 19	7 25	16 29	0 49	22 43	0 42
M	5 02	7 05	3 41	4 35	10 29	1 45	15 41	4 21	25 13	5 08	6 07	7 24	16 32	0 49	22 43	0 42
Tu	4 39	2 02	4 28	0S31	9 49	1 47	16 03	4 28	25 07	5 05	5 56	7 23	16 35	0 49	22 43	0 42
W	4 17	3S01	4 58	5 26	9 07	1 48	16 25	4 36	25 01	5 01	5 44	7 22	16 38	0 49	22 43	0 41
Th	3 54	7 45	5 09	9 56	8 24	1 48	16 46	4 44	24 54	4 58	5 33	7 22	16 40	0 49	22 43	0 41
F	3 31	11 58	5 03	13 50	7 39	1 48	17 06	4 51	24 48	4 54	5 21	7 21	16 43	0 49	22 44	0 41
Sa	3 08	15 29	4 41	16 57	6 54	1 47	17 26	4 59	24 41	4 50	5 10	7 20	16 46	0 48	22 44	0 41
Su	2 45	18 11	4 06	19 12	6 08	1 46	17 46	5 06	24 34	4 47	4 58	7 19	16 49	0 48	22 44	0 41
M	2 21	19 59	3 20	20 32	5 22	1 44	18 05	5 14	24 27	4 43	4 47	7 18	16 52	0 48	22 44	0 41
Tu	1 58	20 50	2 27	20 54	4 35	1 41	18 24	5 21	24 20	4 39	4 35	7 17	16 54	0 48	22 44	0 41
W	1 35	20 44	1 28	20 21	3 48	1 38	18 42	5 29	24 13	4 36	4 24	7 16	16 57	0 48	22 44	0 40
Th	1 12	19 43	0 25	18 53	3 00	1 34	18 59	5 36	24 05	4 32	4 12	7 15	17 00	0 48	22 44	0 40
F	0 49	17 50	0S38	16 36	2 13	1 30	19 16	5 44	23 58	4 29	4 01	7 15	17 03	0 47	22 44	0 40
Sa	0 25	15 11	1 41	13 35	1 25	1 26	19 32	5 51	23 50	4 25	3 49	7 14	17 06	0 47	22 44	0 40
Su	0 02	11 50	2 39	9 58	0 38	1 21	19 48	5 58	23 42	4 21	3 38	7 13	17 09	0 47	22 45	0 40
M	0S21	7 58	3 31	5 52	0S09	1 16	20 02	6 05	23 34	4 18	3 27	7 12	17 12	0 47	22 45	0 40
Tu	0 45	3 41	4 13	1 27	0 57	1 11	20 16	6 12	23 26	4 14	3 15	7 11	17 15	0 47	22 45	0 40
W	1 08	0N50	4 44	3N07	1 43	1 05	20 30	6 19	23 17	4 11	3 04	7 11	17 18	0 46	22 45	0 39
Th	1 32	5 23	5 01	7 36	2 30	0 59	20 42	6 25	23 09	4 07	2 53	7 10	17 21	0 46	22 45	0 39
F	1 55	9 45	5 03	11 49	3 16	0 53	20 54	6 32	22 60	4 04	2 41	7 09	17 24	0 46	22 45	0 39
Sa	2 18	13 44	4 48	15 30	4 02	0 47	21 05	6 38	22 51	4 00	2 30	7 08	17 27	0 46	22 45	0 39
Su	2S42	17N04	4S18	18N25	4S48	0N41	21S15	6S44	22S42	3S57	2N19	7N07	17S30	0N46	22S45	0N39

Day	⚷ Decl	⚷ Lat	♅ Decl	♅ Lat	♆ Decl	♆ Lat	♇ Decl	♇ Lat
1	3N46	3N37	11N45	0S33	6S44	0S60	22S01	0N05
6	3 41	3 37	11 43	0 33	6 47	0 60	22 02	0 05
11	3 35	3 37	11 41	0 33	6 50	0 60	22 02	0 04
16	3 30	3 37	11 38	0 33	6 53	1 00	22 03	0 04
21	3 24	3 37	11 35	0 34	6 56	1 00	22 04	0 03
26	3 19	3 36	11 31	0 34	6 59	1 00	22 05	0 03

Day	⚴ Decl	⚴ Lat	⚵ Decl	⚵ Lat	⚶ Decl	⚶ Lat	Eris Decl	Eris Lat
1	0S23	13S17	9N03	10S00	24S37	1S16	1S58	12S05
6	0 46	12 45	8 36	10 48	24 52	1 28	1 59	12 06
11	1 09	12 13	8 04	11 39	25 05	1 39	2 00	12 06
16	1 33	11 40	7 26	12 32	25 16	1 50	2 01	12 06
21	1 58	11 08	6 44	13 26	25 26	1 60	2 02	12 06
26	2 22	10 35	5 58	14 23	25 33	2 09	2 03	12 06

Moon Phenomena

Max/0 Decl

dy	hr mn	
5	6:49	20N50
11	9:36	0 S
18	9:33	20S55
25	19:39	0 N

Max/0 Lat

dy	hr mn	
6	22:43	0 N
13	2:51	5N09
20	9:32	0 S
27	14:30	5S04

Perigee/Apogee

dy	hr m		kilometers
8	1:08	p	361351
20	0:49	a	404876

PH	dy	hr mn	
☾	3	2:39	10♊34
●	9	18:03	17♍00
☽	16	23:16	24♐02
○	25	2:54	2♈00

Void of Course Moon

Last Aspect				☽ Ingress		
2	5:58	♂	△	♊	2	8:03
4	6:38	☿	⚹	♋	4	12:05
6	12:44	♂	☍	♌	6	13:55
8	13:32	♀	⚹	♍	8	14:30
10	15:14	♂	△	♎	10	15:21
11	22:59	♇	□	♏	12	18:16
14	8:55	☉	⚹	♐	15	0:46
16	23:16	☉	□	♑	17	11:09
19	17:11	☉	△	♒	19	23:53
21	17:14	♃	□	♓	22	12:28
24	5:27	♃	△	♈	24	23:05
26	10:29	♇	□	♉	27	7:17
28	22:37	♃	☍	♊	29	13:27

DAILY ASPECTARIAN

☽⚼⚳ 0:49
☽⚹♆ 5:34
☽∠⚷ 7:04
☽∥♅ 7:08
☽☍♃ 9:07
☽⚼♄ 9:45
☽#♀ 10:25
☽△♇ 12:17
☽□☿ 19:09
☽⊼♀ 21:47

☽∥☿ 1:46
☽△⚳ 4:48
☽△♂ 5:58
☽⚹⚷ 9:54
☽⊻♅ 12:07
☽⊼♄ 12:34
☽#♃ 13:13
☽⚼♇ 15:02

☽⚼♀ 2:00
☉□☽ 2:39
☽⚼♂ 8:29
☽□♆ 10:43
☿⚹♀ 12:59
☽∠♅ 14:18
☽⊼♃ 14:45
☽⊼♇ 17:10
♃∠♄ 17:43
☉∥⚳ 23:43
♂△⚳ 23:59

☽△♀ 5:28
☽⚹☿ 6:38
☽⊼♂ 10:25
☽□⚳ 10:41
♀ ♍ 10:53
☽□⚷ 13:42
☿#♀ 14:27
☽⚹♅ 15:53
☽☍♄ 16:23
☽⚼♃ 16:37

5 W
☉#♆ 8:50
☉⚹☽ 9:32
☽∠☿ 11:21
☽△♆ 13:28
☿⊼♂ 15:19
☽△♃ 17:56
☽☍♇ 19:42

6 Th
☿⊻⚳ 1:23
☿ ♍ 2:40
⚳ ♎ 6:27
☽□♀ 10:21
♄ D 11:10
☉∠☽ 12:02
☽☍♂ 12:44
⚳#♆ 13:28
☽⚼♆ 14:06
☽⚹⚳ 14:09
☿⊼⚷ 14:16
☽△⚷ 15:20
☽⊻☿ 15:29
☽□♅ 17:31
☽⊼♄ 18:04

7 F
☉⚼♂ 0:09
☿△♅ 7:42
☿△♄ 12:21
☉⊻☽ 14:08
☽⊼♆ 14:25
☽∠⚳ 15:17
☽⚼⚷ 15:37
☽⚼♄ 18:24
☉☍♆ 18:28
☽□♃ 19:22
☽#♃ 19:41
☽⊼♇ 20:34

8 Sa
⚳☍⚷ 1:21
☿∥♅ 2:19
☽#♀ 5:15
☿⚼♇ 5:46
☽⚹♀ 13:32
☽⊼♂ 13:49
☽⊼⚷ 15:46
☽⊻⚳ 16:15
☽△♅ 17:59
☽△♄ 18:37
♀□♂ 20:39
☽⚼♇ 20:46
☽☌☿ 22:55

9 Su
☽∥♅ 0:35
☽∥☿ 4:07
♀ ♏ 9:26
♀⚼♆ 10:33
☽⚼♂ 14:22
☽☍♆ 14:50
☽∠♀ 15:03
☉☌☽ 18:03
☽⚼♅ 18:15
☽⚹♃ 20:24
☉⚼♅ 21:02
☽△♇ 21:05

10 M
☽#♆ 1:16
☽∥⚳ 4:50
♀⊼⚷ 9:18
☉∥☽ 10:37
☽△♂ 15:14
☽☍⚷ 16:29
☽∥⚷ 16:39
☽⊻♀ 16:53
☽☌⚳ 18:43
☽⊼♅ 18:50
☽□♄ 19:35
☽∠♃ 21:20
⚳⊼♅ 22:16
♂∠♆ 23:42

11 Tu
♂ ♒ 0:57
☽⊻☿ 7:26
☉⚹♃ 12:11
☉△♇ 15:32
☽⊼♆ 16:24
☽⊻♃ 22:52
☽□♇ 22:59
⚳□♄ 23:10
☉⊻☽ 23:33

12 W
☽#⚷ 2:44
☉#☽ 5:46
♃⚹♇ 7:56
♀☍♅ 9:03
☽#⚳ 13:01
☽∠☿ 13:03
♀∥♃ 16:53
☽⚼♆ 18:10
☽□♂ 18:53
☽∥♆ 19:16
☽⊼⚷ 19:19
☽☍♅ 21:52
☽☌♀ 22:32
☽⚹♄ 22:48
☽⊻⚳ 23:35

13 Th
☽#☿ 2:57
☉∠☽ 3:38
♀⚹♄ 3:59
♂⚹⚷ 17:36
☽⚹☿ 20:03
☽△♆ 20:51
☽⚼⚷ 22:00
☽#♅ 22:02
☉∥⚷ 22:29

14 F
☿☍♆ 1:33
☽∠♄ 1:44
☽∠⚳ 3:30
☽⚹♇ 4:00
☽☌♃ 4:34
☉⚹☽ 8:55
☿⚼♂ 11:54

15 Sa
☿#♆ 0:48
☽△⚷ 1:42
☽⚹♂ 2:25
☿⚼♅ 3:46
☽⊼♅ 4:31
☽⊻♄ 5:42
☽∠♇ 8:00
☽⊻♀ 8:15
☽⚹⚳ 8:32
☽∥♃ 10:37
☽∥♀ 19:04

16 Su
☿△♇ 2:55
⚳∠♃ 3:48
☽□♆ 5:14
♀⊻⚳ 7:33
☽∠♂ 7:48
☽⚼♅ 9:20
☿⚹♃ 11:52
☽⊻♇ 12:58
☿∠♀ 14:05
☽⊻♃ 14:24
☽∠♀ 14:44
☽□☿ 14:49
☉□☽ 23:16

17 M
☽□⚷ 11:55
☽⊻♂ 14:08
☽△♅ 14:58
☽☌♄ 16:26
☽∠♃ 20:39
☽□⚳ 21:40
☽⚹♀ 22:04
☿∥⚳ 23:52

18 Tu
⚶ ♑ 4:04
☽⚹♆ 16:55
♂□♅ 23:02

19 W
☽☌♇ 1:04
☽⚹♃ 3:27
☿∥⚷ 11:02
☽△☿ 14:21
☉△☽ 17:11
☽∠♆ 23:22

20 Th
☽⚹⚷ 0:26
☽□♅ 3:37
☽☌♂ 4:24
☽⊻♄ 5:22
☽∥♀ 9:16
☽△⚳ 12:59
☽□♀ 13:47

21 F
☉☌☿ 1:53
☉⚼☽ 2:25
☽⚼☿ 2:28
☽⊻♆ 5:45
☽∠⚷ 6:46
☽∥♃ 7:41
☽∠♄ 11:51
☽⊻♇ 13:58
☽□♃ 17:14
☽⚼⚳ 20:32
♂⊻♄ 21:21

22 Sa
☿ ♎ 3:41
☿☍⚷ 5:56
☉⊼☽ 11:17
☽⊻⚷ 12:47
☽⊼☿ 14:01
☽⚹♅ 15:57
☽⚹♄ 17:57
☽⊻♂ 18:28
☽∠♇ 19:58

23 Su
☽#♅ 1:54
☉ ♎ 1:55
☿⊼♅ 2:47
☽⊼⚳ 3:35
☽△♀ 4:23
☉☍⚷ 5:02
☉#☿ 13:31
☿□♄ 16:47
☽☌♆ 17:23
☽∠♅ 21:25

24 M
☽∠♂ 0:45
☽⚹♇ 1:25
☿△♂ 1:31
☽△♃ 5:27
☽∥♆ 5:42
☽⚼♀ 10:39
☉∥☿ 12:11
⚳∥⚷ 13:28
☉⊼♅ 19:10
☽☌⚷ 23:10

25 Tu
☽#⚷ 1:55
☽⊻♅ 2:16
☽#⚳ 2:24
☉☍☽ 2:54
☽□♄ 4:29
☽⚹♂ 6:24
☽☍☿ 10:13
☽⚼♃ 10:37
☽∥☿ 12:30
☿∠♃ 13:21
☉∥☽ 14:27
☽☍⚳ 15:43
☽⊼♀ 16:10
☉□♄ 23:52

26 W
⚷R♓ 0:10
☉#☽ 1:47
☽⊻♆ 2:41
☽#☿ 5:41
☽□♇ 10:29
☽∥⚳ 11:18
☽∥⚷ 13:00
☽⊼♃ 15:10

27 Th
☽∠♆ 6:28
☽⊻⚷ 7:10
☽#♆ 8:45
☿#⚳ 9:22
♀⊻⚳ 9:48
☽☌♅ 10:12
☽△♄ 12:36
☿⊻♀ 13:49
☿☌⚳ 14:19
☉⊼☽ 15:28
☽□♂ 15:51
☉△♂ 23:36
☿#⚷ 23:58

28 F
☽☍♀ 1:03
☽⊼⚳ 1:15
☽⊼☿ 2:27
☽⚹♆ 9:44
☽∥♅ 10:05
☽∠⚷ 10:23
☽⚼♄ 15:53
☽△♇ 17:21
☉⚼☽ 20:47
☽☍♃ 22:37

29 Sa
☽⚼⚳ 5:12
☉#⚳ 8:11
☽⚼☿ 9:23
☽⚹⚷ 13:10
♂∥♄ 15:13
☽⊻♅ 16:08
☽⊼♄ 18:45
☽⚼♇ 20:07
☽△♂ 23:17
⚵ ♊ 23:40

30 Su
☉△☽ 1:35
☉∠♃ 3:12
☽#♃ 3:40
☽⊼♀ 7:38
☽△⚳ 8:42
☿⊼♆ 10:23
☽□♆ 15:00
☽△☿ 15:39
☽∠♅ 18:30
☽⊼♇ 22:29

October 2018

LONGITUDE

Day	Sid.Time	☉	☽	☽ 12 hour	Mean☊	True☊	☿	♀	♂	⚳	♃	♄	⚷	♅	♆	♇
	h m s	° ' "	° ' "	° ' "	° '	° '	° '	° '	° '	° '	° '	° '	° '	° '	° '	° '
1 M	0 38 42	7♎45 53	19♊37 14	26♊31 10	2♌26.3	3♌33.2	15♎25.7	10♏24.4	5♒56.8	11♎10.7	22♏04.4	3♑01.8	29♓46.5	1♉27.9	14♓27.6	18♑45.4
2 Tu	0 42 39	8 44 52	3♋27 41	10♋26 46	2 23.1	3D 31.8	17 05.8	10 34.0	6 20.5	11 37.9	22 15.7	3 04.2	29R 43.8	1R 25.7	14R 26.2	18D 45.4
3 W	0 46 36	9 43 54	17 28 23	24 32 29	2 19.9	3 31.8	18 45.1	10 41.4	6 44.7	12 05.0	22 27.0	3 06.7	29 41.1	1 23.4	14 24.7	18 45.4
4 Th	0 50 32	10 42 58	1♌38 57	8♌47 38	2 16.7	3R 32.2	20 23.5	10 46.7	7 09.3	12 32.2	22 38.4	3 09.3	29 38.5	1 21.2	14 23.3	18 45.5
5 F	0 54 29	11 42 04	15 58 16	23 10 31	2 13.6	3 31.7	22 01.2	10R 49.6	7 34.4	12 59.4	22 49.8	3 12.0	29 35.8	1 19.0	14 21.8	18 45.6
6 Sa	0 58 25	12 41 12	0♍23 56	7♍38 00	2 10.4	3 29.2	23 37.9	10 50.3	8 00.0	13 26.6	23 01.4	3 14.8	29 33.2	1 16.7	14 20.4	18 45.7
7 Su	1 02 22	13 40 23	14 52 04	22 05 27	2 07.2	3 24.0	25 13.9	10 48.7	8 26.0	13 53.8	23 12.9	3 17.6	29 30.6	1 14.4	14 19.0	18 45.9
8 M	1 06 18	14 39 36	29 17 23	6♎27 07	2 04.0	3 16.0	26 49.2	10 44.7	8 52.4	14 20.9	23 24.6	3 20.6	29 27.9	1 12.1	14 17.7	18 46.1
9 Tu	1 10 15	15 38 51	13♎33 51	20 36 52	2 00.9	3 05.6	28 23.6	10 38.3	9 19.2	14 48.1	23 36.4	3 23.6	29 25.3	1 09.7	14 16.3	18 46.3
10 W	1 14 11	16 38 08	27 35 31	4♏29 13	1 57.7	2 54.0	29 57.3	10 29.5	9 46.5	15 15.2	23 48.2	3 26.8	29 22.8	1 07.4	14 14.9	18 46.5
11 Th	1 18 08	17 37 27	11♏17 34	18 00 13	1 54.5	2 42.2	1♏30.3	10 18.3	10 14.1	15 42.4	24 00.0	3 30.0	29 20.2	1 05.0	14 13.6	18 46.8
12 F	1 22 04	18 36 48	24 37 02	1♐07 59	1 51.3	2 31.5	3 02.5	10 04.7	10 42.1	16 09.5	24 12.0	3 33.3	29 17.7	1 02.6	14 12.3	18 47.1
13 Sa	1 26 01	19 36 11	7♐33 11	13 52 52	1 48.1	2 22.9	4 34.0	9 48.8	11 10.5	16 36.7	24 23.9	3 36.7	29 15.2	1 00.2	14 11.0	18 47.5
14 Su	1 29 58	20 35 36	20 07 22	26 17 09	1 45.0	2 16.8	6 04.8	9 30.5	11 39.3	17 03.8	24 36.0	3 40.1	29 12.7	0 57.8	14 09.8	18 47.9
15 M	1 33 54	21 35 03	2♑22 42	8♑24 39	1 41.8	2 13.3	7 34.9	9 09.9	12 08.5	17 30.9	24 48.1	3 43.7	29 10.2	0 55.4	14 08.6	18 48.3
16 Tu	1 37 51	22 34 31	14 23 36	20 20 13	1 38.6	2D 11.9	9 04.3	8 47.2	12 38.0	17 58.0	25 00.3	3 47.3	29 07.7	0 53.0	14 07.3	18 48.7
17 W	1 41 47	23 34 02	26 15 13	2♒09 16	1 35.4	2R 11.8	10 32.9	8 22.3	13 07.8	18 25.1	25 12.5	3 51.1	29 05.3	0 50.6	14 06.2	18 49.2
18 Th	1 45 44	24 33 34	8♒03 06	13 57 22	1 32.3	2 11.7	12 00.8	7 55.4	13 38.0	18 52.2	25 24.8	3 54.9	29 02.9	0 48.2	14 05.0	18 49.6
19 F	1 49 40	25 33 07	19 52 45	25 49 54	1 29.1	2 10.7	13 28.0	7 26.7	14 08.4	19 19.2	25 37.1	3 58.8	29 00.6	0 45.7	14 03.8	18 50.2
20 Sa	1 53 37	26 32 43	1♓49 22	7♓51 43	1 25.9	2 07.7	14 54.4	6 56.2	14 39.2	19 46.3	25 49.5	4 02.7	28 58.2	0 43.3	14 02.7	18 50.7
21 Su	1 57 33	27 32 20	13 57 25	20 06 53	1 22.7	2 02.2	16 20.1	6 24.2	15 10.3	20 13.3	26 02.0	4 06.8	28 55.9	0 40.8	14 01.6	18 51.3
22 M	2 01 30	28 31 59	26 20 26	2♈38 19	1 19.5	1 53.8	17 45.0	5 50.9	15 41.7	20 40.3	26 14.4	4 10.9	28 53.6	0 38.4	14 00.6	18 51.9
23 Tu	2 05 27	29 31 40	9♈00 40	15 27 32	1 16.4	1 43.0	19 09.0	5 16.4	16 13.4	21 07.3	26 27.0	4 15.1	28 51.4	0 35.9	13 59.5	18 52.5
24 W	2 09 23	0♏31 22	21 58 54	28 34 36	1 13.2	1 30.3	20 32.2	4 41.0	16 45.3	21 34.3	26 39.6	4 19.4	28 49.1	0 33.4	13 58.5	18 53.2
25 Th	2 13 20	1 31 07	5♉14 25	11♉58 04	1 10.0	1 17.1	21 54.5	4 04.9	17 17.5	22 01.2	26 52.2	4 23.7	28 47.0	0 31.0	13 57.5	18 53.9
26 F	2 17 16	2 30 54	18 45 12	25 35 24	1 06.8	1 04.5	23 15.8	3 28.4	17 50.0	22 28.2	27 04.8	4 28.1	28 44.8	0 28.5	13 56.5	18 54.6
27 Sa	2 21 13	3 30 42	2♊28 17	9♊23 25	1 03.6	0 53.7	24 36.1	2 51.6	18 22.7	22 55.1	27 17.6	4 32.6	28 42.7	0 26.1	13 55.6	18 55.4
28 Su	2 25 09	4 30 33	16 20 24	23 18 54	1 00.5	0 45.5	25 55.3	2 15.0	18 55.7	23 22.0	27 30.3	4 37.2	28 40.6	0 23.6	13 54.7	18 56.2
29 M	2 29 06	5 30 27	0♋18 33	7♋19 07	0 57.3	0 40.4	27 13.4	1 38.6	19 28.9	23 48.9	27 43.1	4 41.8	28 38.6	0 21.2	13 53.8	18 57.0
30 Tu	2 33 02	6 30 22	14 20 23	21 22 10	0 54.1	0 38.0	28 30.2	1 02.9	20 02.4	24 15.7	27 56.0	4 46.6	28 36.5	0 18.7	13 52.9	18 57.8
31 W	2 36 59	7♏30 19	28 24 21	5♌26 49	0♌50.9	0♌37.4	29♏45.5	0♏27.9	20♒36.1	24♎42.6	28♏08.8	4♑51.4	28♓34.6	0♉16.3	13♓52.1	18♑58.7

1st of Mon

Julian Day 2458392.
Obliquity 23°26'08
SVP 5♓00'
GC 27♐06
Eris 23♈41.

Day	⚴
1	13♍31.
6	15 58.
11	18 24.
16	20 47.
21	23 08.
26	25 27.
31	27 44.
	⚵
1	0♊06.
6	0 29.
11	0 38.
16	0 35.
21	0 18.
26	29♉48.
31	29 06.
	⚶
1	4♑08.
6	5 53.
11	7 44.
16	9 39.
21	11 37.
26	13 39.
31	15 45.

DECLINATION and LATITUDE

Day	☉ Decl	☽ Decl	☽ Lat	☽ 12h Decl	☿ Decl	☿ Lat	♀ Decl	♀ Lat	♂ Decl	♂ Lat	⚳ Decl	⚳ Lat	♃ Decl	♃ Lat	♄ Decl	♄ Lat
1 M	3S05	19N31	3S32	20N20	5S33	0N34	21S24	6S49	22S33	3S53	2N08	7N07	17S33	0N46	22S45	0N39
2 Tu	3 28	20 50	2 33	21 02	6 17	0 28	21 32	6 55	22 23	3 50	1 56	7 06	17 36	0 46	22 45	0 39
3 W	3 51	20 54	1 25	20 26	7 01	0 21	21 40	6 60	22 14	3 46	1 45	7 05	17 39	0 45	22 46	0 38
4 Th	4 14	19 38	0 10	18 30	7 45	0 14	21 46	7 04	22 04	3 43	1 34	7 04	17 42	0 45	22 46	0 38
5 F	4 38	17 06	1N06	15 24	8 28	0 07	21 51	7 09	21 55	3 40	1 23	7 04	17 45	0 45	22 46	0 38
6 Sa	5 01	13 29	2 18	11 21	9 10	0 00	21 55	7 13	21 45	3 36	1 12	7 03	17 48	0 45	22 46	0 38
7 Su	5 24	9 03	3 21	6 37	9 52	0S07	21 58	7 16	21 35	3 33	1 01	7 02	17 51	0 45	22 46	0 38
8 M	5 47	4 07	4 11	1 34	10 33	0 14	21 59	7 20	21 24	3 30	0 50	7 02	17 54	0 45	22 46	0 38
9 Tu	6 09	0S59	4 45	3S30	11 14	0 21	21 60	7 22	21 14	3 26	0 38	7 01	17 57	0 45	22 46	0 38
10 W	6 32	5 56	5 00	8 17	11 53	0 28	21 59	7 24	21 03	3 23	0 27	7 00	18 00	0 44	22 46	0 37
11 Th	6 55	10 29	4 58	12 32	12 33	0 35	21 57	7 26	20 53	3 20	0 17	6 59	18 03	0 44	22 46	0 37
12 F	7 18	14 24	4 40	16 03	13 11	0 42	21 53	7 27	20 42	3 17	0 06	6 59	18 06	0 44	22 46	0 37
13 Sa	7 40	17 30	4 07	18 43	13 49	0 49	21 48	7 27	20 31	3 13	0S05	6 58	18 09	0 44	22 46	0 37
14 Su	8 02	19 41	3 24	20 25	14 25	0 56	21 42	7 27	20 20	3 10	0 16	6 57	18 12	0 44	22 46	0 37
15 M	8 25	20 54	2 31	21 08	15 02	1 03	21 34	7 26	20 09	3 07	0 27	6 57	18 16	0 44	22 46	0 37
16 Tu	8 47	21 07	1 33	20 52	15 37	1 10	21 25	7 24	19 57	3 04	0 38	6 56	18 19	0 44	22 46	0 37
17 W	9 09	20 23	0 32	19 40	16 11	1 16	21 14	7 21	19 46	3 01	0 49	6 55	18 22	0 43	22 46	0 37
18 Th	9 31	18 45	0S31	17 38	16 45	1 23	21 02	7 18	19 34	2 58	0 59	6 55	18 25	0 43	22 46	0 36
19 F	9 53	16 19	1 32	14 49	17 18	1 29	20 49	7 14	19 22	2 55	1 10	6 54	18 28	0 43	22 46	0 36
20 Sa	10 14	13 10	2 30	11 21	17 50	1 36	20 34	7 09	19 10	2 52	1 21	6 54	18 31	0 43	22 46	0 36
21 Su	10 36	9 25	3 22	7 21	18 21	1 42	20 18	7 03	18 58	2 49	1 31	6 53	18 34	0 43	22 46	0 36
22 M	10 57	5 12	4 05	2 58	18 51	1 48	20 00	6 56	18 46	2 46	1 42	6 52	18 37	0 43	22 46	0 36
23 Tu	11 18	0 41	4 37	1N39	19 20	1 54	19 41	6 49	18 34	2 43	1 52	6 52	18 40	0 43	22 46	0 36
24 W	11 39	3N59	4 56	6 18	19 48	1 60	19 21	6 41	18 21	2 40	2 03	6 51	18 43	0 43	22 46	0 36
25 Th	12 00	8 33	4 59	10 44	20 15	2 05	19 00	6 31	18 09	2 37	2 13	6 50	18 46	0 42	22 46	0 36
26 F	12 21	12 48	4 46	14 44	20 41	2 10	18 38	6 22	17 56	2 35	2 24	6 50	18 49	0 42	22 46	0 35
27 Sa	12 41	16 28	4 16	17 58	21 06	2 15	18 16	6 11	17 43	2 32	2 34	6 49	18 52	0 42	22 46	0 35
28 Su	13 01	19 14	3 31	20 13	21 30	2 20	17 52	5 60	17 30	2 29	2 44	6 49	18 55	0 42	22 46	0 35
29 M	13 21	20 53	2 33	21 14	21 53	2 25	17 28	5 48	17 17	2 26	2 55	6 48	18 58	0 42	22 46	0 35
30 Tu	13 41	21 15	1 25	20 56	22 15	2 29	17 04	5 35	17 04	2 23	3 05	6 48	19 01	0 42	22 46	0 35
31 W	14S01	20N17	0S12	19N19	22S35	2S33	16S39	5S22	16S51	2S21	3S15	6N47	19S04	0N42	22S46	0N35

Day	⚷ Decl	⚷ Lat	♅ Decl	♅ Lat	♆ Decl	♆ Lat	♇ Decl	♇ Lat
1	3N13	3N36	11N27	0S34	7S02	1S00	22S05	0N
6	3 07	3 36	11 23	0 34	7 05	0 60	22 06	0
11	3 01	3 35	11 19	0 34	7 08	0 60	22 06	0
16	2 56	3 34	11 15	0 34	7 10	0 60	22 06	0
21	2 50	3 33	11 11	0 34	7 12	0 60	22 06	0
26	2 45	3 33	11 07	0 34	7 14	0 60	22 06	0S
31	2N40	3N32	11N03	0S34	7S16	0S60	22S06	0S

Day	⚴ Decl	⚴ Lat	⚵ Decl	⚵ Lat	⚶ Decl	⚶ Lat	Eris Decl	Eris Lat
1	2S48	10S02	5N08	15S22	25S39	2S17	2S04	12S
6	3 12	9 28	4 14	16 21	25 43	2 25	2 05	12
11	3 37	8 55	3 17	17 21	25 44	2 32	2 06	12
16	4 01	8 21	2 18	18 20	25 43	2 39	2 07	12
21	4 25	7 46	1 19	19 18	25 40	2 45	2 08	12
26	4 47	7 11	0 19	20 13	25 34	2 51	2 09	12
31	5S08	6S35	0S38	21S03	25S26	2S56	2S10	12S

Moon Phenomena

Max/0 Decl
dy hr mn
2 13:06 21N02
8 19:23 0 S
15 17:28 21S09
23 3:31 0 N
29 18:44 21N17

Max/0 Lat
dy hr mn
4 3:11 0 N
10 9:04 5N02
17 12:06 0 S
24 17:04 5S00
31 3:47 0 N

Perigee/Apogee
dy hr m kilometers
5 22:34 p 366393
17 19:24 a 404226
31 20:16 p 370204

PH dy hr mn
☾ 2 9:47 9♋09
● 9 3:48 15♎48
☽ 16 18:03 23♑19
○ 24 16:46 1♉13
☾ 31 16:41 8♌12

Void of Course Moon

Last Aspect			☽ Ingress		
30 15:39	☿	△	♋	1	18:
3 8:34	♃	△	♌	3	21:
5 11:35	♃	□	♍	5	23:
7 14:04	♃	⚹	♎	8	1:
9 8:51	♇	□	♏	10	4:
11 23:13	♃	☌	♐	12	9:
14 0:59	☉	⚹	♑	14	19:
16 21:50	♃	⚹	♒	17	7:
19 12:28	☉	△	♓	19	20:
21 23:48	♃	△	♈	22	6:
23 18:19	♇	□	♉	24	14:
26 14:50	♃	☍	♊	26	19:
28 4:39	♂	△	♋	28	23:
31 2:32	☿	△	♌	31	2:

DAILY ASPECTARIAN

1 M
♇ D 2:04
☽ ⚼ ♂ 2:23
☽ ⚻ ♃ 4:20
☉ ⋕ ⚷ 7:53
☽ ⚼ ♀ 10:12
☽ □ ⚷ 17:35
☽ ⚹ ♅ 20:30
☽ ☍ ♄ 23:19

2 Tu
☽ ⚻ ♂ 5:06
☽ ⚼ ♃ 6:38
☉ □ ☽ 9:47
☽ △ ♀ 12:19
☽ □ ⚳ 14:30
☽ △ ♆ 18:47

3 W
☿ □ ♇ 0:05
☿ ∥ ♆ 1:07
☽ ☍ ♇ 2:11
☽ □ ☿ 2:28
☽ △ ♃ 8:34
☽ ⚼ ♆ 20:12
☽ △ ⚷ 20:38
♂ ∥ ♇ 21:08
☽ □ ♅ 23:30

4 Th
☉ ⚺ ♀ 1:37
☽ ⚻ ♄ 2:33
☽ ☍ ♂ 9:32
☽ □ ♀ 15:23
☉ ⚹ ☽ 16:20
☽ ⋕ ♃ 18:48
☽ ⚹ ⚳ 18:52
☽ ⚻ ♆ 21:19
☽ ⚼ ⚷ 21:43

5 F
☽ ⚼ ♄ 3:44
☽ ⚻ ♇ 4:39
♀ ∥ ♂ 5:59
☽ ⚹ ☿ 11:21
☽ □ ♃ 11:35
☿ ⚺ ♃ 13:40
♀ R 19:06
☉ ∠ ☽ 19:10
☽ ∠ ⚳ 20:39
☽ ⚻ ⚷ 22:36

6 Sa
☽ △ ♅ 1:27
☽ △ ♄ 4:44
☽ ⚼ ♇ 5:35
☽ ∥ ♅ 11:47
☽ ⚻ ♂ 13:00
☽ ∠ ☿ 15:21
☽ ⚹ ♀ 17:17
☽ ⋕ ☿ 20:20
☉ ⚺ ☽ 21:52
☽ ⚺ ⚳ 22:20
☽ ☍ ♆ 23:05

7 Su
☽ ⚼ ♅ 2:16
☽ △ ♇ 6:28
☽ ⋕ ♆ 9:42
☉ ☌ ⚳ 10:01
☽ ⚹ ♃ 14:04
☽ ⚼ ♂ 14:41
☉ ⚻ ♆ 15:18
☉ ⋕ ☽ 16:39
☽ ∠ ♀ 18:07
☽ ⚺ ☿ 19:22
⚳ ⚻ ♆ 21:15

8 M
☽ ☍ ⚷ 0:18
☽ ⚻ ♅ 3:11
☽ ∥ ⚷ 4:56
☽ □ ♄ 6:48
☽ ∠ ♃ 15:30
☽ ∥ ⚳ 16:05
☽ △ ♂ 16:36
☽ ⚺ ♀ 19:06
☽ ⋕ ⚳ 22:28

9 Tu
☽ ⚻ ♆ 1:12
☽ ☌ ⚳ 2:10
☉ ☌ ☽ 3:48
☿ ⋕ ♅ 4:21
☽ □ ♇ 8:51
☽ ⋕ ⚷ 9:53
☿ ⚼ ♆ 13:17
☿ ⚻ ⚷ 15:22
☽ ⚺ ♃ 17:22

10 W
☿ ♏ 0:41
☽ ⚼ ♆ 2:52
☽ ⚻ ⚷ 3:05
☉ ∥ ☽ 3:17
☽ ☌ ☿ 4:37
☽ ∥ ♆ 6:00
☽ ☍ ♅ 6:07
☽ ⚹ ♄ 10:13
☿ ☍ ♅ 17:37
☽ □ ♂ 22:03
☽ ☌ ♀ 22:16

11 Th
♀ □ ♂ 2:30
☽ ⋕ ♅ 4:48
☽ △ ♆ 5:13
☽ ⚼ ⚷ 5:24
☽ ⚺ ⚳ 8:09
☉ ⚺ ☽ 12:14
☽ ∠ ♄ 12:57
☽ ⚹ ♇ 13:24
☉ ∥ ♆ 13:48
☽ ∥ ☿ 14:29
☽ ☌ ♃ 23:13

12 F
⚵ R 4:06
☉ □ ♇ 4:12
☿ ⚹ ♄ 8:21
☽ △ ⚷ 8:34
☽ ⚻ ♅ 11:48
☽ ∠ ⚳ 12:29
☽ ⚺ ♄ 16:35
☽ ∠ ♇ 16:57
☽ ⚺ ☿ 17:39
☉ ∠ ☽ 18:00

13 Sa
☽ ⚺ ♀ 4:10
☽ ∥ ♃ 6:22
☽ ⚹ ♂ 7:07
☽ □ ♆ 12:34
☽ ⚼ ♅ 16:01
☽ ⚹ ⚳ 17:53
☽ ⚺ ♇ 21:26

14 Su
☉ ⚹ ☽ 0:59
☽ ∠ ☿ 2:07
☽ ∠ ♀ 8:18
☽ ⚺ ♃ 8:51
☽ ∥ ♂ 9:08
☽ ∠ ♂ 13:15
☽ □ ⚷ 17:41
☽ △ ♅ 21:08

15 M
☽ ☌ ♄ 2:41
☽ ⚹ ☿ 11:49
☽ ⚹ ♀ 13:06
☽ ∠ ♃ 15:02
☽ ⚺ ♂ 20:18
☿ ☌ ♀ 20:22
☽ ⚹ ♆ 23:27

16 Tu
☽ □ ⚳ 7:29
☽ ☌ ♇ 8:55
☉ □ ☽ 18:03
☽ ⚹ ♃ 21:50

17 W
☽ ⚹ ⚷ 5:45
☽ ∠ ♆ 5:47
☽ □ ♅ 9:18
☽ ∥ ♂ 12:06
☽ ⚺ ♄ 15:32
⚳ □ ♇ 21:44
☽ □ ♀ 23:45

18 Th
☽ ∥ ♃ 3:46
☽ □ ☿ 9:11
☽ ☌ ♂ 11:51
☽ ∠ ⚷ 12:09
☽ ⚺ ♆ 12:14
☽ ∥ ☿ 16:41
♂ ∠ ⚷ 18:16
♂ ⚺ ♆ 20:31
☽ ⚺ ♇ 21:53
☽ ∠ ♄ 22:10
☽ △ ⚳ 22:50

19 F
☉ ⚺ ♃ 2:02
☿ ⚼ ⚷ 8:47
☿ △ ♆ 9:48
☽ □ ♃ 11:47
☉ △ ☽ 12:28
☿ □ ♂ 17:24
☽ ⚺ ⚷ 18:19
☽ ⚹ ♅ 21:48

20 Sa
☽ ∠ ♇ 4:02
☽ ⚹ ♄ 4:27
☽ ⚼ ⚳ 6:06
☽ △ ♀ 9:45
☽ ⋕ ♅ 13:02
☉ ∥ ☽ 17:23
☉ ⚼ ☽ 20:58

21 Su
☽ ☌ ♆ 0:08
☽ ⚺ ♂ 2:29
☽ ∠ ♅ 3:22
☽ △ ☿ 5:15
☽ ⚹ ♇ 9:34
☿ ∥ ♃ 11:26
☽ ⚻ ⚳ 12:40
☽ ∥ ♆ 12:51
☽ ⚼ ♀ 13:53
☿ ∥ ♂ 21:18
☽ △ ♃ 23:48

22 M
☉ ⚻ ☽ 4:33
☽ ☌ ⚷ 4:52
☽ ⚺ ♅ 8:11
☉ ⚻ ⚷ 8:23
☽ ∠ ♂ 8:40
☉ ⚼ ♆ 11:18
☽ ⋕ ⚷ 12:50
☽ ⚼ ☿ 13:44
☉ ⋕ ♅ 14:15
♂ ∥ ♃ 14:37
☽ □ ♄ 15:00
☽ ⚻ ♀ 17:17
☽ ∥ ⚳ 18:00
☿ ⚹ ♇ 19:15

23 Tu
☿ ∠ ♄ 1:50
☽ ⚼ ♃ 4:38
☽ ⚺ ♆ 9:16
☿ ∥ ♀ 10:40
☉ ♏ 11:24
☽ ⋕ ⚳ 13:41
☽ ⚹ ♂ 13:59
☽ ∥ ⚷ 17:53
☽ □ ♇ 18:19
☽ ⚻ ☿ 21:02
☽ ☍ ⚳ 23:13

24 W
☉ ☍ ♅ 0:48
⚵ R♉ 7:57
☽ ⚻ ♃ 8:40
☽ ⚺ ⚷ 12:24
☽ ∠ ♆ 12:42
♀ ⚹ ♄ 12:53
☽ ☌ ♅ 15:32
☉ ☍ ☽ 16:46
☽ ⋕ ♆ 16:55
☽ ☍ ♀ 22:01
☽ △ ♄ 22:29

25 Th
☿ ⚺ ⚳ 2:57
♀ ∥ ♃ 14:03
☽ ∥ ♅ 14:08
☽ ∠ ⚷ 15:11
☽ ⚹ ♆ 15:31
☉ ⋕ ☽ 20:59
☽ □ ♂ 22:19

26 F
☽ △ ♇ 0:17
☽ ⚼ ♄ 1:16
☽ ⚻ ⚳ 6:45
☽ ☍ ☿ 8:47
☉ ☌ ♀ 14:17
☽ ☍ ♃ 14:50
☽ ⚹ ⚷ 17:28
☽ ⚺ ♅ 20:28

27 Sa
☽ ⚻ ♀ 0:39
☉ ⚻ ☽ 1:57
☽ ⚼ ♇ 2:32
☽ ⚻ ♄ 3:37
☽ ⋕ ♂ 9:12
☽ ⚼ ⚳ 9:46
☽ ⋕ ♀ 12:45
☽ □ ♆ 19:49
☽ ⋕ ♃ 20:40
⚳ ⋕ ⚷ 21:13
☽ ∠ ♅ 22:22

28 Su
♂ ⚺ ♇ 0:20
☽ ⚼ ♀ 1:30
☉ ⚹ ♄ 2:53
☽ ⚻ ♇ 4:29
☽ △ ♂ 4:39
☉ ⚼ ☽ 5:53
☽ △ ⚳ 12:29
☽ ⚻ ☿ 18:10
☽ ⚻ ♃ 19:29
☽ □ ⚷ 21:09

29 M
☽ ⚹ ♅ 0:04
☽ △ ♀ 2:12
☽ ⚼ ♂ 7:27
☽ ☍ ♄ 7:33
☉ △ ☽ 9:35
♂ ∠ ♄ 10:48
☿ ☌ ♃ 11:06
☿ ∥ ♇ 14:35
☽ ⚼ ♃ 21:34
☽ ⚼ ☿ 22:26
☽ △ ♆ 23:13
♀ ∥ ♂ 23:42

30 Tu
☿ △ ⚷ 1:58
☽ ☍ ♇ 7:54
☽ ⚻ ♂ 10:08
☽ □ ⚳ 17:29
☽ △ ♃ 23:33

31 W
☽ △ ⚷ 0:17
☽ ⚼ ♆ 0:47
☽ △ ☿ 2:32
☽ □ ♅ 3:10
☽ □ ♀ 3:22
☿ ♐ 4:39
♀ ☍ ♅ 8:46
☿ ⚺ ♀ 9:22
☿ ⚻ ♅ 9:37
☽ ⚻ ♄ 11:03
☿ ∥ ♄ 13:42
☽ ⋕ ♃ 14:19
☉ □ ☽ 16:41
♀ R♎ 19:43

LONGITUDE

Day	Sid.Time	☉	☽	☽ 12 hour	Mean ☊	True ☊	☿	♀	♂	⚳	♃	♄	⚷	♅	♆	♇
	h m s	° ' "	° ' "	° ' "	° '	° '	° '	° '	° '	° '	° '	° '	° '	° '	° '	° '
1 Th	2 40 56	8♏30 19	12♌29 31	19♌32 21	0♌47.8	0♌37.4	0♐59.4	29♎54.0	21♒10.0	25♎09.4	28♏21.7	4♑56.2	28♓32.6	0♉13.9	13♓51.3	18♑59.6
2 F	2 44 52	9 30 21	26 35 13	3♍37 58	0 44.6	0R 36.6	2 11.6	29R 21.4	21 44.1	25 36.2	28 34.7	5 01.1	28R 30.7	0R 11.5	13R 50.6	19 00.5
3 Sa	2 48 49	10 30 25	10♍40 28	17 42 27	0 41.4	0 33.8	3 21.9	28 50.2	22 18.4	26 03.0	28 47.7	5 06.1	28 28.9	0 09.0	13 49.8	19 01.5
4 Su	2 52 45	11 30 31	24 43 38	1♎43 40	0 38.2	0 28.3	4 30.2	28 20.6	22 53.0	26 29.7	29 00.7	5 11.2	28 27.1	0 06.6	13 49.1	19 02.4
5 M	2 56 42	12 30 39	8♎42 10	15 38 41	0 35.1	0 19.9	5 36.2	27 52.9	23 27.8	26 56.4	29 13.7	5 16.3	28 25.3	0 04.3	13 48.4	19 03.4
6 Tu	3 00 38	13 30 49	22 32 46	29 23 55	0 31.9	0 09.0	6 39.7	27 27.1	24 02.7	27 23.1	29 26.8	5 21.5	28 23.6	0 01.9	13 47.8	19 04.5
7 W	3 04 35	14 31 01	6♏11 44	12♏55 45	0 28.7	29♋56.6	7 40.3	27 03.3	24 37.9	27 49.8	29 39.9	5 26.7	28 21.9	29♈59.5	13 47.2	19 05.5
8 Th	3 08 31	15 31 15	19 35 39	26 11 08	0 25.5	29 44.0	8 37.7	26 41.8	25 13.3	28 16.4	29 53.1	5 32.1	28 20.2	29 57.2	13 46.6	19 06.6
9 F	3 12 28	16 31 31	2♐42 01	9♐08 11	0 22.3	29 32.4	9 31.5	26 22.5	25 48.8	28 43.0	0♐06.2	5 37.4	28 18.6	29 54.8	13 46.0	19 07.7
10 Sa	3 16 25	17 31 48	15 29 39	21 46 31	0 19.2	29 22.9	10 21.3	26 05.5	26 24.5	29 09.6	0 19.4	5 42.9	28 17.1	29 52.5	13 45.5	19 08.9
11 Su	3 20 21	18 32 08	27 58 59	4♑07 21	0 16.0	29 15.9	11 06.5	25 50.9	27 00.5	29 36.1	0 32.6	5 48.4	28 15.6	29 50.2	13 45.0	19 10.0
12 M	3 24 18	19 32 28	10♑11 58	16 13 19	0 12.8	29 11.8	11 46.8	25 38.8	27 36.5	0♏02.6	0 45.9	5 54.0	28 14.1	29 47.9	13 44.5	19 11.2
13 Tu	3 28 14	20 32 50	22 11 54	28 08 18	0 09.6	29D 10.0	12 21.3	25 29.1	28 12.8	0 29.1	0 59.1	5 59.6	28 12.7	29 45.7	13 44.1	19 12.4
14 W	3 32 11	21 33 14	4♒03 08	9♒57 03	0 06.5	29 09.8	12 49.6	25 21.9	28 49.2	0 55.5	1 12.4	6 05.2	28 11.3	29 43.4	13 43.7	19 13.7
15 Th	3 36 07	22 33 39	15 50 43	21 44 50	0 03.3	29R 10.3	13 10.9	25 17.1	29 25.8	1 21.9	1 25.7	6 11.0	28 10.0	29 41.2	13 43.4	19 14.9
16 F	3 40 04	23 34 05	27 40 07	3♓37 13	0 00.1	29 10.4	13 24.4	25D 14.8	0♓02.5	1 48.2	1 39.0	6 16.8	28 08.7	29 39.0	13 43.0	19 16.2
17 Sa	3 44 00	24 34 33	9♓36 50	15 39 36	29♋56.9	29 09.1	13R 29.5	25 14.9	0 39.4	2 14.6	1 52.3	6 22.6	28 07.5	29 36.9	13 42.8	19 17.5
18 Su	3 47 57	25 35 01	21 46 07	27 56 57	29 53.8	29 05.6	13 25.4	25 17.4	1 16.4	2 40.8	2 05.6	6 28.5	28 06.3	29 34.7	13 42.5	19 18.9
19 M	3 51 54	26 35 32	4♈12 33	10♈33 18	29 50.6	28 59.8	13 11.5	25 22.3	1 53.5	3 07.1	2 19.0	6 34.4	28 05.2	29 32.6	13 42.3	19 20.2
20 Tu	3 55 50	27 36 03	16 59 32	23 31 23	29 47.4	28 51.7	12 47.3	25 29.5	2 30.8	3 33.2	2 32.3	6 40.4	28 04.1	29 30.5	13 42.1	19 21.6
21 W	3 59 47	28 36 36	0♉08 57	6♉52 09	29 44.2	28 41.9	12 12.6	25 39.0	3 08.2	3 59.4	2 45.7	6 46.4	28 03.1	29 28.4	13 41.9	19 23.0
22 Th	4 03 43	29 37 10	13 40 46	20 34 29	29 41.0	28 31.4	11 27.4	25 50.7	3 45.7	4 25.5	2 59.1	6 52.5	28 02.1	29 26.4	13 41.8	19 24.5
23 F	4 07 40	0♐37 46	27 32 51	4♊35 20	29 37.9	28 21.4	10 32.0	26 04.5	4 23.4	4 51.5	3 12.5	6 58.7	28 01.2	29 24.4	13 41.7	19 25.9
24 Sa	4 11 36	1 38 23	11♊41 16	18 49 58	29 34.7	28 12.8	9 27.5	26 20.5	5 01.1	5 17.5	3 25.8	7 04.8	28 00.4	29 22.4	13 41.7	19 27.4
25 Su	4 15 33	2 39 02	26 00 44	3♋12 51	29 31.5	28 06.4	8 15.2	26 38.6	5 39.0	5 43.5	3 39.2	7 11.1	27 59.6	29 20.5	13D 41.6	19 28.9
26 M	4 19 29	3 39 42	10♋25 37	17 38 26	29 28.3	28 02.7	6 57.2	26 58.6	6 17.0	6 09.4	3 52.6	7 17.3	27 58.8	29 18.6	13 41.6	19 30.4
27 Tu	4 23 26	4 40 23	24 50 42	2♌01 58	29 25.2	28D 01.3	5 35.7	27 20.6	6 55.1	6 35.3	4 06.0	7 23.6	27 58.1	29 16.7	13 41.7	19 31.9
28 W	4 27 23	5 41 07	9♌11 49	16 19 55	29 22.0	28 01.7	4 13.4	27 44.5	7 33.3	7 01.1	4 19.4	7 30.0	27 57.4	29 14.9	13 41.8	19 33.5
29 Th	4 31 19	6 41 51	23 26 04	0♍30 04	29 18.8	28 02.7	2 53.1	28 10.1	8 11.5	7 26.9	4 32.9	7 36.4	27 56.9	29 13.0	13 41.9	19 35.1
30 F	4 35 16	7♐42 38	7♍31 48	14 31 11	29♋15.6	28♋03.3	1♐37.6	28♎37.5	8♓49.9	7♏52.6	4♐46.3	7♑42.8	27♓56.3	29♈11.3	13♓42.1	19♑36.7

1st of Month
Julian Day # 2458423.5
Obliquity 23°26'08"
SVP 5♓00'04"
GC 27♐06.1
Eris 23♈23.5R

Day	⚴
1	28♍11.2
6	0♎24.9
11	2 35.9
16	4 44.2
21	6 49.4
26	8 51.4

Day	⚵
1	28♉57.3R
6	28 03.2R
11	27 01.4R
16	25 55.0R
21	24 47.3R
26	23 41.7R

Day	⚶
1	16♑10.3
6	18 18.9
11	20 30.0
16	22 43.6
21	24 59.1
26	27 16.6

DECLINATION and LATITUDE

Day	☉ Decl	☽ Decl	☽ Lat	☽ 12h Decl	☿ Decl	☿ Lat	♀ Decl	♀ Lat	♂ Decl	♂ Lat	⚳ Decl	⚳ Lat	♃ Decl	♃ Lat	♄ Decl	♄ Lat
1 Th	14S20	18N03	1N02	16N31	22S54	2S36	16S14	5S08	16S37	2S18	3S25	6N46	19S07	0N42	22S46	0N35
2 F	14 39	14 44	2 13	12 44	23 12	2 39	15 50	4 54	16 24	2 15	3 35	6 46	19 10	0 42	22 46	0 35
3 Sa	14 58	10 34	3 15	8 16	23 28	2 42	15 25	4 40	16 10	2 13	3 45	6 45	19 13	0 42	22 46	0 34
4 Su	15 17	5 51	4 05	3 22	23 44	2 44	15 01	4 25	15 56	2 10	3 55	6 45	19 16	0 41	22 46	0 34
5 M	15 35	0 51	4 40	1S40	23 57	2 46	14 37	4 10	15 42	2 08	4 05	6 44	19 19	0 41	22 46	0 34
6 Tu	15 54	4S09	4 59	6 34	24 10	2 47	14 13	3 55	15 28	2 05	4 15	6 44	19 22	0 41	22 46	0 34
7 W	16 11	8 52	4 59	11 03	24 20	2 47	13 50	3 40	15 14	2 03	4 25	6 43	19 24	0 41	22 45	0 34
8 Th	16 29	13 04	4 44	14 55	24 29	2 47	13 28	3 25	14 60	2 00	4 35	6 43	19 27	0 41	22 45	0 34
9 F	16 46	16 34	4 13	17 59	24 37	2 46	13 07	3 10	14 45	1 58	4 45	6 42	19 30	0 41	22 45	0 34
10 Sa	17 04	19 10	3 30	20 06	24 43	2 45	12 47	2 54	14 31	1 55	4 54	6 42	19 33	0 41	22 45	0 34
11 Su	17 20	20 47	2 38	21 13	24 47	2 42	12 28	2 39	14 16	1 53	5 04	6 41	19 36	0 41	22 45	0 34
12 M	17 37	21 24	1 39	21 19	24 49	2 39	12 09	2 24	14 02	1 50	5 14	6 41	19 39	0 41	22 45	0 33
13 Tu	17 53	20 60	0 37	20 26	24 49	2 34	11 52	2 10	13 47	1 48	5 23	6 40	19 41	0 41	22 45	0 33
14 W	18 09	19 40	0S26	18 40	24 47	2 28	11 36	1 55	13 32	1 46	5 33	6 40	19 44	0 40	22 45	0 33
15 Th	18 24	17 29	1 28	16 07	24 43	2 21	11 21	1 41	13 17	1 43	5 42	6 39	19 47	0 40	22 44	0 33
16 F	18 40	14 34	2 26	12 52	24 36	2 13	11 07	1 27	13 02	1 41	5 51	6 39	19 50	0 40	22 44	0 33
17 Sa	18 55	11 02	3 18	9 04	24 27	2 03	10 54	1 13	12 47	1 39	6 01	6 38	19 53	0 40	22 44	0 33
18 Su	19 09	6 59	4 03	4 49	24 16	1 52	10 43	0 60	12 31	1 36	6 10	6 38	19 55	0 40	22 44	0 33
19 M	19 23	2 34	4 37	0 16	24 01	1 40	10 32	0 47	12 16	1 34	6 19	6 37	19 58	0 40	22 44	0 33
20 Tu	19 37	2N05	4 58	4N26	23 44	1 25	10 23	0 34	12 00	1 32	6 28	6 37	20 01	0 40	22 43	0 33
21 W	19 51	6 46	5 04	9 03	23 24	1 10	10 15	0 22	11 45	1 30	6 37	6 36	20 03	0 40	22 43	0 33
22 Th	20 04	11 16	4 54	13 21	23 01	0 52	10 08	0 10	11 29	1 28	6 46	6 36	20 06	0 40	22 43	0 32
23 F	20 17	15 17	4 26	17 01	22 35	0 34	10 02	0N02	11 13	1 25	6 55	6 36	20 09	0 40	22 43	0 32
24 Sa	20 29	18 31	3 42	19 44	22 06	0 14	9 58	0 13	10 58	1 23	7 04	6 35	20 11	0 40	22 43	0 32
25 Su	20 41	20 40	2 43	21 15	21 35	0N06	9 54	0 24	10 42	1 21	7 13	6 35	20 14	0 40	22 42	0 32
26 M	20 53	21 29	1 33	21 21	21 02	0 27	9 51	0 35	10 26	1 19	7 22	6 34	20 16	0 40	22 42	0 32
27 Tu	21 04	20 53	0 17	20 03	20 28	0 47	9 50	0 45	10 10	1 17	7 30	6 34	20 19	0 39	22 42	0 32
28 W	21 15	18 55	0N60	17 29	19 54	1 07	9 49	0 54	9 54	1 15	7 39	6 34	20 22	0 39	22 42	0 32
29 Th	21 25	15 47	2 13	13 53	19 20	1 25	9 50	1 04	9 38	1 13	7 47	6 33	20 24	0 39	22 41	0 32
30 F	21S36	11N47	3N16	9N32	18S49	1N42	9S51	1N13	9S21	1S11	7S56	6N33	20S27	0N39	22S41	0N32

Day	⚷ Decl	⚷ Lat	♅ Decl	♅ Lat	♆ Decl	♆ Lat	♇ Decl	♇ Lat
1	2N39	3N31	11N02	0S34	7S16	0S60	22S06	0S01
6	2 35	3 30	10 58	0 33	7 17	0 60	22 06	0 01
11	2 31	3 29	10 54	0 33	7 18	0 59	22 06	0 02
16	2 27	3 28	10 50	0 33	7 19	0 59	22 05	0 02
21	2 24	3 27	10 46	0 33	7 19	0 59	22 05	0 03
26	2 21	3 26	10 43	0 33	7 19	0 59	22 04	0 03

Day	⚴ Decl	⚴ Lat	⚵ Decl	⚵ Lat	⚶ Decl	⚶ Lat	Eris Decl	Eris Lat
1	5S13	6S28	0S49	21S12	25S24	2S57	2S10	12S05
6	5 32	5 51	1 42	21 56	25 12	3 03	2 11	12 05
11	5 50	5 14	2 29	22 32	24 58	3 08	2 11	12 05
16	6 06	4 35	3 10	22 60	24 41	3 12	2 12	12 04
21	6 19	3 56	3 42	23 18	24 21	3 17	2 12	12 04
26	6 30	3 15	4 05	23 28	23 59	3 21	2 12	12 03

Moon Phenomena

Max/0 Decl

dy	hr mn	
5	4:01	0 S
12	2:14	21S24
19	13:20	0 N
26	1:39	21N29

Max/0 Lat

dy	hr mn	
6	13:09	5N01
13	14:05	0 S
20	21:30	5S05
27	5:19	0 N

Perigee/Apogee

dy	hr m		kilometers
14	16:01	a	404337
26	12:14	p	366622

PH	dy	hr mn	
●	7	16:03	15♏11
☽	15	14:55	23♒11
○	23	5:40	0♊52
☾	30	0:20	7♍43

Void of Course Moon

Last Aspect				☽ Ingress		
2	4:33	♀	✶	♍	2	5:49
4	7:27	♃	✶	♎	4	9:02
6	8:20	♀	☌	♏	6	13:03
8	10:43	♂	□	♐	8	19:01
11	3:36	♅	△	♑	11	3:56
13	15:14	♅	□	♒	13	15:46
16	4:00	♅	✶	♓	16	4:43
18	8:05	☉	△	♈	18	15:57
20	22:47	♅	☌	♉	20	23:44
22	10:00	♇	△	♊	23	4:12
25	5:32	♅	✶	♋	25	6:39
27	7:23	♅	□	♌	27	8:36
29	9:48	♅	△	♍	29	11:09

DAILY ASPECTARIAN

1 Th: ☽⚼⚷ 1:47; ☽⚻♆ 2:19; ☽⚻♇ 11:05; ☽#♂ 12:02; ☽⚼♄ 12:45; ☽☍♂ 15:23; ☽#♀ 15:50; ♃△⚷ 17:36; ☽✶⚳ 22:16

2 F: ☉#☽ 0:26; ☽⚻⚷ 3:16; ☽□♃ 3:27; ☽✶♀ 4:33; ☽△♅ 6:07; ☽□☿ 10:25; ☽⚼♇ 12:39; ☽△♄ 14:27; ☽∥♅ 21:40; ☉✶☽ 23:42

3 Sa: ♀⚼♆ 0:18; ☽∠⚳ 0:40; ♀⚺♃ 1:23; ☽∠♀ 5:12; ☽☍♆ 5:23; ☽⚼♅ 7:37; ☿∠♇ 14:00; ☽△♇ 14:16; ☉∥♀ 14:50; ☽#♆ 16:56; ♀⚻⚷ 18:18; ☽⚻♂ 20:43

4 Su: ☽⚺⚳ 3:08; ☉∠☽ 3:17; ☽⚺♀ 5:59; ☽☍⚷ 6:22; ☽✶♃ 7:27; ☽#⚳ 9:00; ☽⚻♅ 9:12; ☽∥⚷ 15:39; ☿⚺♄ 16:03; ☽□♄ 18:03; ☽✶☿ 18:13; ☽⚼♂ 23:34

5 M: ♀ ♎ 1:31; ☉∥♂ 5:05; ☉⚺☽ 7:05; ☽⚻♆ 8:49; ☽∠♃ 9:42; ☽#⚷ 16:24; ☽□♇ 17:57; ☉⚼⚷ 21:11; ☽∠☿ 22:20

6 Tu: ☽∥⚳ 0:32; ♀☌⚳ 1:51; ☽△♂ 2:44; ☉△♆ 6:41; ☽☌♀ 8:20; ☽☌⚳ 8:45; ☽⚻⚷ 10:13; ☽⚼♆ 10:56; ☽⚺♃ 12:17; ☽☍♅ 13:04; ☽∥♆ 15:44; ☊R ♋ 17:38; ♅R ♈ 19:01; ☽✶♄ 22:40

7 W: ☽⚺☿ 2:49; ☽#♅ 11:22; ☽⚼⚷ 12:45; ☽△♆ 13:32; ☉☌☽ 16:03; ☽✶♇ 23:07

8 Th: ☽∠♄ 1:43; ☽∥♀ 2:17; ⚳⚻⚷ 3:14; ♃⚻♅ 6:21; ☽□♂ 10:43; ☽∥♂ 11:44; ☽⚺♀ 12:37; ♃ ♐ 12:40; ☽△⚷ 15:55; ☽⚺⚳ 16:23; ☽⚻♅ 18:52; ☽☌♃ 19:07

9 F: ☉∥☽ 1:53; ☽∠♇ 2:39; ⚳⚼♆ 2:39; ☽⚺♄ 5:28; ☽☌☿ 13:38; ♀△♂ 15:13; ☽∠♀ 15:51; ☽□♆ 20:43; ☽∠⚳ 21:23; ☽⚼♅ 22:50

10 Sa: ☉⚺☽ 4:13; ☽∥♃ 4:40; ☽⚺♇ 6:58; ☿∠♀ 17:27; ☽✶♀ 19:56; ☽✶♂ 22:01

11 Su: ☽□⚷ 0:32; ☽✶⚳ 3:16; ☽△♅ 3:36; ☽⚺♃ 5:05; ⚳☍♅ 11:45; ☉∠☽ 11:49; ☉✶♇ 15:23; ☽☌♄ 15:26; ⚳ ♏ 21:38

12 M: ☽⚺☿ 3:19; ☽∠♂ 5:02; ☽✶♆ 7:03; ☽∠♃ 11:18; ☽☌♇ 17:58; ☉✶☽ 20:22; ♂⚺⚷ 23:56

13 Tu: ☽□♀ 6:33; ☽∠☿ 10:53; ☉∠♄ 11:43; ☽✶⚷ 12:07; ☽⚺♂ 12:48; ☽∠♆ 13:12; ☽□♅ 15:14; ☽□⚳ 17:24; ☽✶♃ 18:07; ☽∥♃ 22:59

14 W: ☽⚺♄ 4:10; ☉∥☽ 15:45; ☽✶☿ 18:26; ☽∠⚷ 18:33; ☽⚺♆ 19:41

15 Th: ⚳⚺♃ 6:56; ☽⚺♇ 6:56; ♂✶♅ 9:32; ☽∠♄ 10:57; ☉□☽ 14:55; ☽△♀ 19:06; ♂ ♓ 22:22

16 F: ☽⚺⚷ 0:58; ☽✶♅ 4:00; ☽☌♂ 5:03; ☽□♃ 8:11; ☽△⚳ 8:40; ♀ D 10:52; ☽∥♂ 11:44; ☽∠♇ 13:20; ☽✶♄ 17:29

17 Sa: ☽∥♀ 0:49; ☽⚼♀ 1:16; ☽#♅ 1:20; ☿ R 1:33; ☽□☿ 7:42; ☽☌♆ 8:09; ☽∠♅ 9:54; ♀#♅ 11:27; ☽⚼⚳ 15:41; ☉⚺♀ 16:36; ☽✶♇ 19:11; ☽∥♆ 22:06

18 Su: ☽∥⚳ 4:25; ☽⚻♀ 6:54; ☉△☽ 8:05; ☽☌⚷ 12:17; ☽⚺♅ 15:06; ☽⚺♂ 19:21; ☽△♃ 20:19; ☽⚻⚳ 21:51

19 M: ☽#⚷ 0:47; ☽□♄ 4:32; ☉⚼☽ 15:08; ☽△☿ 16:27; ☽⚺♆ 17:53

20 Tu: ☽∠♂ 1:01; ☽⚼♃ 1:02; ♂□♃ 1:32; ☽∥⚷ 1:38; ☽□♇ 4:23; ☉△⚷ 10:57; ☽☍♀ 15:46; ☽⚼☿ 18:57; ☽⚺⚷ 20:13; ☉⚻☽ 21:00; ☽∠♆ 21:23; ☽☌♅ 22:47; ☽#⚳ 23:13

21 W: ☽#♆ 2:52; ☽⚻♃ 4:46; ☽✶♂ 5:37; ☽☍⚳ 7:06; ☽△♄ 11:55; ☽#♀ 17:58; ☉⚻♅ 19:53; ☽⚻☿ 20:19; ☽∥♅ 21:13; ☽∠⚷ 22:52

22 Th: ☽✶♆ 0:02; ☽#♂ 1:12; ☉∥♃ 4:51; ☉ ♐ 9:03; ☽△♇ 10:00; ☿∠♀ 13:13; ☽⚼♄ 14:21; ☿∥♄ 16:48; ☽⚻♀ 21:26

23 F: ☽✶⚷ 0:49; ♂∠♇ 1:40; ☽⚺♅ 3:10; ☉☍☽ 5:40; ☽☍♃ 9:49; ☽⚼♇ 11:45; ☽□♂ 12:12; ☽⚻⚳ 12:51; ☽⚻♄ 16:10; ☽☍☿ 20:31; ☽⚼♀ 23:24

24 Sa: ☿∥♇ 1:21; ☽□♆ 3:23; ☽∠♅ 4:31; ☽⚻♇ 13:04; ☽⚼⚳ 14:54; ☽#♃ 17:46; ♂#♅ 21:35

25 Su: ☉#☽ 0:31; ☽△♀ 1:05; ♆ D 1:09; ☽□⚷ 3:18; ☽✶♅ 5:32; ♂△⚳ 8:58; ☉⚻☽ 11:54; ☽⚻♃ 12:56; ☽#☿ 13:13; ☽△⚳ 16:41; ☽△♂ 16:47; ⚳∥♆ 17:33; ☿⚺♄ 18:23; ☽⚻☿ 18:43; ☽☍♄ 18:45

26 M: ☉∥☿ 4:45; ☽△♆ 5:26; ☉☌♃ 6:34; ☿□♂ 8:07; ☿⚺⚳ 10:44; ☽⚼♃ 14:17; ☉⚼☽ 14:44; ☽☍♇ 15:08; ☽⚼☿ 17:32; ☽⚼♂ 18:54; ☉∠♇ 20:34; ☉#☽ 20:38

27 Tu: ☽□♀ 4:17; ☽△⚷ 5:12; ☿∥♃ 5:43; ☽⚼♆ 6:25; ☽□♅ 7:23; ☽#♃ 8:25; ☉☌☿ 9:16; ☽#☿ 9:44; ☽△♃ 15:42; ☽△☿ 16:23; ☉△☽ 17:40; ☿∠♇ 18:14; ☽□⚳ 20:14; ☽⚻♂ 21:07; ☽⚻♄ 21:08; ♂✶♄ 21:32; ☿☌♃ 22:28

28 W: ☽⚼⚷ 6:19; ♀∥♂ 6:37; ☽⚻♆ 7:34; ♀⚻⚷ 12:04; ☽⚻♇ 17:29; ☽⚼♄ 22:35

29 Th: ♃∠♇ 4:29; ☽⚻⚷ 7:39; ☽✶♀ 8:18; ☽△♅ 9:48; ⚳✶♄ 11:48; ☽□☿ 14:44; ☽⚼♇ 19:00; ☽□♃ 19:12

30 F: ☉⚺♄ 0:05; ☽△♄ 0:19; ☉□☽ 0:20; ☽✶⚳ 0:37; ☽☍♂ 2:20; ♀⚼♆ 3:52; ☽∥♅ 6:02; ☉⚺⚳ 6:49; ☽#♀ 10:18; ☽☍♆ 10:36; ☽∠♀ 10:50; ☽⚼♅ 11:24; ☽#♂ 13:45; ☽#⚳ 19:38; ☽△♇ 20:50; ☽#♆ 23:19

December 2018

LONGITUDE

Day	Sid.Time	☉	☽	☽ 12 hour	Mean☊	True☊	☿	♀	♂	⚳	♃	♄	⚷	♅	♆	♇
	h m s	° ' "	° ' "	° ' "	° '	° '	° '	° '	° '	° '	° '	° '	° '	° '	° '	° '
1 Sa	4 39 12	8♐43 25	21♍28 08	28♍22 37	29♋12.5	28♋02.5	0♐29.1	29♎06.6	9♓28.4	8♏18.3	4♐59.7	7♑49.3	27♓55.8	29♈09.5	13♓42.2	19♑38.3
2 Su	4 43 09	9 44 15	5♎14 34	12♎03 56	29 09.3	27R 59.7	29♏29.5	29 37.3	10 07.0	8 43.9	5 13.1	7 55.8	27R 55.4	29R 07.8	13 42.5	19 39.9
3 M	4 47 05	10 45 06	18 50 38	25 34 34	29 06.1	27 54.6	28R 40.3	0♏09.5	10 45.6	9 09.4	5 26.4	8 02.3	27 55.0	29 06.2	13 42.7	19 41.5
4 Tu	4 51 02	11 45 58	2♏15 39	8♏53 43	29 02.9	27 47.8	28 02.2	0 43.2	11 24.4	9 34.9	5 39.8	8 08.9	27 54.7	29 04.5	13 43.0	19 43.2
5 W	4 54 58	12 46 51	15 28 42	22 00 25	28 59.7	27 39.7	27 35.6	1 18.4	12 03.2	10 00.4	5 53.2	8 15.5	27 54.4	29 02.9	13 43.3	19 44.9
6 Th	4 58 55	13 47 46	28 28 48	4♐53 45	28 56.6	27 31.4	27D 20.5	1 54.9	12 42.2	10 25.7	6 06.6	8 22.1	27 54.2	29 01.4	13 43.7	19 46.6
7 F	5 02 52	14 48 42	11♐15 13	17 33 09	28 53.4	27 23.7	27 16.3	2 32.8	13 21.2	10 51.1	6 19.9	8 28.8	27 54.0	28 59.9	13 44.1	19 48.3
8 Sa	5 06 48	15 49 39	23 47 37	29 58 40	28 50.2	27 17.5	27 22.5	3 11.9	14 00.3	11 16.3	6 33.3	8 35.5	27 53.9	28 58.4	13 44.5	19 50.1
9 Su	5 10 45	16 50 37	6♑06 27	12♑11 09	28 47.0	27 13.1	27 38.3	3 52.3	14 39.5	11 41.5	6 46.6	8 42.3	27D 53.9	28 57.0	13 45.0	19 51.8
10 M	5 14 41	17 51 36	18 13 01	24 12 23	28 43.9	27D 10.8	28 02.8	4 33.8	15 18.7	12 06.6	6 59.9	8 49.0	27 53.9	28 55.6	13 45.5	19 53.6
11 Tu	5 18 38	18 52 35	0♒09 37	6♒05 06	28 40.7	27 10.4	28 35.3	5 16.5	15 58.1	12 31.7	7 13.2	8 55.8	27 53.9	28 54.3	13 46.0	19 55.4
12 W	5 22 34	19 53 35	11 59 21	17 52 52	28 37.5	27 11.4	29 14.8	6 00.2	16 37.5	12 56.7	7 26.5	9 02.6	27 54.1	28 53.0	13 46.6	19 57.2
13 Th	5 26 31	20 54 36	23 46 32	29 39 57	28 34.3	27 13.1	0♐00.5	6 45.0	17 16.9	13 21.6	7 39.8	9 09.5	27 54.2	28 51.7	13 47.2	19 59.0
14 F	5 30 27	21 55 38	5♓34 43	11♓31 09	28 31.2	27 14.9	0 51.9	7 30.8	17 56.5	13 46.4	7 53.0	9 16.4	27 54.5	28 50.5	13 47.8	20 00.8
15 Sa	5 34 24	22 56 40	17 29 54	23 31 37	28 28.0	27R 16.0	1 48.0	8 17.5	18 36.0	14 11.2	8 06.2	9 23.2	27 54.8	28 49.3	13 48.5	20 02.7
16 Su	5 38 21	23 57 42	29 36 56	5♈46 28	28 24.8	27 16.0	2 48.5	9 05.2	19 15.7	14 35.9	8 19.4	9 30.1	27 55.1	28 48.2	13 49.2	20 04.5
17 M	5 42 17	24 58 45	12♈00 48	18 20 28	28 21.6	27 14.5	3 52.7	9 53.7	19 55.4	15 00.5	8 32.6	9 37.1	27 55.5	28 47.1	13 49.9	20 06.4
18 Tu	5 46 14	25 59 48	24 45 55	1♉17 32	28 18.4	27 11.7	5 00.1	10 43.1	20 35.2	15 25.1	8 45.7	9 44.0	27 56.0	28 46.1	13 50.7	20 08.3
19 W	5 50 10	27 00 51	7♉55 34	14 40 11	28 15.3	27 07.6	6 10.4	11 33.4	21 15.0	15 49.5	8 58.8	9 51.0	27 56.5	28 45.1	13 51.5	20 10.2
20 Th	5 54 07	28 01 55	21 31 22	28 28 58	28 12.1	27 03.0	7 23.2	12 24.4	21 54.8	16 13.9	9 11.9	9 58.0	27 57.0	28 44.2	13 52.3	20 12.1
21 F	5 58 03	29 03 00	5♊32 41	12♊42 02	28 08.9	26 58.5	8 38.2	13 16.2	22 34.7	16 38.2	9 25.0	10 05.0	27 57.7	28 43.3	13 53.2	20 14.0
22 Sa	6 02 00	0♑04 05	19 56 26	27 15 05	28 05.7	26 54.6	9 55.1	14 08.8	23 14.6	17 02.4	9 38.0	10 12.0	27 58.3	28 42.5	13 54.1	20 15.9
23 Su	6 05 56	1 05 10	4♋37 10	12♋01 43	28 02.6	26 51.9	11 13.7	15 02.0	23 54.6	17 26.6	9 51.0	10 19.0	27 59.1	28 41.7	13 55.0	20 17.8
24 M	6 09 53	2 06 16	19 27 45	26 54 16	27 59.4	26D 50.6	12 33.8	15 56.0	24 34.7	17 50.6	10 03.9	10 26.0	27 59.8	28 41.0	13 56.0	20 19.8
25 Tu	6 13 50	3 07 22	4♌20 19	11♌44 59	27 56.2	26 50.6	13 55.1	16 50.6	25 14.7	18 14.6	10 16.9	10 33.1	28 00.7	28 40.3	13 57.0	20 21.7
26 W	6 17 46	4 08 29	19 07 27	26 27 02	27 53.0	26 51.5	15 17.7	17 45.9	25 54.8	18 38.5	10 29.7	10 40.1	28 01.6	28 39.7	13 58.0	20 23.7
27 Th	6 21 43	5 09 36	3♍43 07	10♍55 15	27 49.9	26 53.0	16 41.2	18 41.8	26 34.9	19 02.3	10 42.6	10 47.2	28 02.5	28 39.1	13 59.1	20 25.7
28 F	6 25 39	6 10 44	18 03 05	25 06 24	27 46.7	26 54.3	18 05.7	19 38.2	27 15.1	19 26.0	10 55.4	10 54.3	28 03.5	28 38.5	14 00.2	20 27.6
29 Sa	6 29 36	7 11 53	2♎05 04	8♎59 03	27 43.5	26R 55.1	19 31.0	20 35.3	27 55.3	19 49.6	11 08.1	11 01.3	28 04.6	28 38.1	14 01.3	20 29.6
30 Su	6 33 32	8 13 01	15 48 22	22 33 08	27 40.3	26 55.0	20 57.1	21 32.9	28 35.5	20 13.1	11 20.9	11 08.4	28 05.7	28 37.6	14 02.5	20 31.6
31 M	6 37 29	9♑14 11	29 13 29	5♏49 34	27♋37.2	26♋54.0	22♐23.8	22♏31.0	29♓15.8	20♏36.5	11♐33.5	11♑15.5	28♓06.8	28♈37.2	14♓03.6	20♑33.6

1st of Month

Julian Day # 2458453.5
Obliquity 23°26'08"
SVP 5♓00'00"
GC 27♐06.2
Eris 23♈08.3R

Day	⚴
1	10♎50.1
6	12 45.2
11	14 36.2
16	16 23.0
21	18 05.1
26	19 42.3
31	21 14.0

Day	⚵
1	22♉41.2R
6	21 48.9R
11	21 07.1R
16	20 37.9R
21	20 22.2R
26	20 20.4
31	20 32.6

Day	⚶
1	29♑35.8
6	1♒56.6
11	4 18.8
16	6 42.2
21	9 06.6
26	11 32.0
31	13 58.3

DECLINATION and LATITUDE

Day	☉ Decl	☽ Decl	☽ Lat	☽12h Decl	☿ Decl	☿ Lat	♀ Decl	♀ Lat	♂ Decl	♂ Lat	⚳ Decl	⚳ Lat	♃ Decl	♃ Lat	♄ Decl	♄ Lat
1 Sa	21S45	7N11	4N08	4N45	18S20	1N57	9S53	1N22	9S05	1S09	8S04	6N32	20S29	0N39	22S41	0N32
2 Su	21 54	2 16	4 44	0S13	17 55	2 10	9 56	1 30	8 49	1 07	8 13	6 32	20 32	0 39	22 41	0 31
3 M	22 03	2S41	5 04	5 06	17 34	2 21	9 60	1 38	8 32	1 05	8 21	6 32	20 34	0 39	22 40	0 31
4 Tu	22 12	7 27	5 07	9 41	17 18	2 29	10 04	1 46	8 16	1 03	8 29	6 31	20 36	0 39	22 40	0 31
5 W	22 20	11 47	4 54	13 44	17 06	2 35	10 10	1 53	7 59	1 01	8 37	6 31	20 39	0 39	22 40	0 31
6 Th	22 27	15 31	4 25	17 05	16 58	2 40	10 16	1 60	7 42	0 60	8 45	6 31	20 41	0 39	22 39	0 31
7 F	22 34	18 26	3 43	19 34	16 55	2 42	10 22	2 07	7 26	0 58	8 53	6 30	20 44	0 39	22 39	0 31
8 Sa	22 41	20 26	2 51	21 04	16 55	2 43	10 30	2 13	7 09	0 56	9 01	6 30	20 46	0 39	22 39	0 31
9 Su	22 47	21 26	1 52	21 32	16 59	2 42	10 38	2 19	6 52	0 54	9 09	6 29	20 48	0 39	22 38	0 31
10 M	22 53	21 24	0 49	21 00	17 07	2 41	10 46	2 25	6 36	0 52	9 17	6 29	20 50	0 39	22 38	0 31
11 Tu	22 58	20 23	0S16	19 32	17 17	2 38	10 55	2 30	6 19	0 51	9 25	6 29	20 53	0 39	22 38	0 31
12 W	23 03	18 28	1 20	17 14	17 29	2 34	11 05	2 35	6 02	0 49	9 33	6 28	20 55	0 39	22 37	0 31
13 Th	23 07	15 48	2 20	14 13	17 43	2 29	11 15	2 40	5 45	0 47	9 40	6 28	20 57	0 38	22 37	0 30
14 F	23 11	12 29	3 15	10 37	17 59	2 24	11 25	2 45	5 28	0 45	9 48	6 28	20 59	0 38	22 36	0 30
15 Sa	23 15	8 38	4 01	6 34	18 16	2 18	11 36	2 49	5 11	0 44	9 55	6 28	21 01	0 38	22 36	0 30
16 Su	23 18	4 24	4 38	2 10	18 34	2 11	11 47	2 53	4 54	0 42	10 02	6 27	21 04	0 38	22 36	0 30
17 M	23 20	0N06	5 02	2N25	18 53	2 04	11 59	2 57	4 37	0 40	10 10	6 27	21 06	0 38	22 35	0 30
18 Tu	23 22	4 44	5 13	7 02	19 12	1 57	12 11	3 00	4 19	0 39	10 17	6 27	21 08	0 38	22 35	0 30
19 W	23 24	9 17	5 08	11 28	19 32	1 50	12 23	3 04	4 02	0 37	10 24	6 26	21 10	0 38	22 34	0 30
20 Th	23 25	13 33	4 45	15 28	19 52	1 42	12 35	3 07	3 45	0 36	10 31	6 26	21 12	0 38	22 34	0 30
21 F	23 26	17 12	4 06	18 41	20 11	1 34	12 48	3 10	3 28	0 34	10 38	6 26	21 14	0 38	22 33	0 30
22 Sa	23 26	19 55	3 09	20 49	20 31	1 26	13 01	3 12	3 11	0 32	10 45	6 25	21 16	0 38	22 33	0 30
23 Su	23 26	21 22	1 59	21 33	20 50	1 18	13 14	3 15	2 53	0 31	10 52	6 25	21 18	0 38	22 33	0 30
24 M	23 25	21 21	0 41	20 47	21 08	1 10	13 28	3 17	2 36	0 29	10 59	6 25	21 20	0 38	22 32	0 30
25 Tu	23 24	19 50	0N41	18 34	21 26	1 02	13 41	3 19	2 19	0 28	11 05	6 25	21 22	0 38	22 32	0 29
26 W	23 22	16 59	1 60	15 09	21 43	0 54	13 55	3 20	2 02	0 26	11 12	6 24	21 24	0 38	22 31	0 29
27 Th	23 20	13 05	3 10	10 52	22 00	0 46	14 09	3 22	1 44	0 25	11 19	6 24	21 25	0 38	22 31	0 29
28 F	23 17	8 30	4 06	6 03	22 16	0 38	14 23	3 23	1 27	0 24	11 25	6 24	21 27	0 38	22 30	0 29
29 Sa	23 14	3 34	4 47	1 03	22 31	0 31	14 37	3 24	1 10	0 22	11 32	6 24	21 29	0 38	22 30	0 29
30 Su	23 11	1S27	5 10	3S54	22 45	0 23	14 51	3 25	0 53	0 21	11 38	6 23	21 31	0 38	22 29	0 29
31 M	23S07	6S16	5N16	8S33	22S58	0N15	15S05	3N26	0S35	0S19	11S44	6N23	21S33	0N38	22S29	0N29

Day	⚷ Decl	⚷ Lat	♅ Decl	♅ Lat	♆ Decl	♆ Lat	♇ Decl	♇ Lat
1	2N18	3N25	10N40	0S33	7S19	0S59	22S03	0S03
6	2 17	3 23	10 37	0 33	7 18	0 59	22 03	0 04
11	2 15	3 22	10 34	0 33	7 17	0 59	22 02	0 04
16	2 15	3 21	10 32	0 33	7 16	0 59	22 01	0 05
21	2 15	3 20	10 31	0 32	7 14	0 58	21 60	0 05
26	2 15	3 19	10 30	0 32	7 12	0 58	21 59	0 06
31	2N16	3N17	10N29	0S32	7S10	0S58	21S58	0S06

Day	⚴ Decl	⚴ Lat	⚵ Decl	⚵ Lat	⚶ Decl	⚶ Lat	Eris Decl	Eris Lat
1	6S38	2S33	4S19	23S28	23S34	3S25	2S13	12S02
6	6 43	1 49	4 23	23 20	23 07	3 29	2 13	12 02
11	6 44	1 04	4 17	23 04	22 37	3 32	2 13	12 01
16	6 42	0 17	4 02	22 42	22 05	3 36	2 13	12 00
21	6 36	0N32	3 39	22 15	21 30	3 40	2 12	11 60
26	6 25	1 24	3 09	21 43	20 53	3 43	2 12	11 59
31	6S09	2N17	2S33	21S08	20S14	3S46	2S11	11S58

Moon Phenomena

Max/0 Decl

dy	hr mn	
2	10:57	0 S
9	11:07	21S32
16	23:27	0 N
23	11:49	21N33
29	17:02	0 S

Max/0 Lat

dy	hr mn	
3	16:06	5N08
10	17:59	0 S
18	4:25	5S13
24	11:54	0 N
30	19:53	5N16

Perigee/Apogee

dy	hr m		kilometers
12	12:26	a	405175
24	9:47	p	361065

PH	dy	hr mn	
●	7	7:22	15♐07
☽	15	11:50	23♓27
○	22	17:50	0♋49
☾	29	9:35	7♎36

Void of Course Moon

Last Aspect			☽ Ingress		
1	14:35 ☿	⚹	♎	1	14:50
3	18:17 ♅	☍	♏	3	19:56
5	21:54 ☿	☌	♐	6	2:50
8	10:01 ♅	△	♑	8	12:03
10	21:28 ♅	□	♒	10	23:41
13	10:21 ♅	⚹	♓	13	12:41
15	11:50 ☉	□	♈	16	0:45
18	7:22 ♅	☌	♉	18	9:38
20	0:43 ♂	⚹	♊	20	14:36
22	14:22 ♅	⚹	♋	22	16:29
24	14:51 ♅	□	♌	24	17:00
26	15:38 ♅	△	♍	26	17:51
28	16:28 ♂	☍	♎	28	20:24
30	22:55 ♅	☍	♏	31	1:24

DAILY ASPECTARIAN

1 Sa: ♀☍♅ 2:14; ☽∠⚳ 3:17; ☽☍⚷ 11:13; ☿R♏ 11:13; ☽⚻♅ 13:20; ☽⚺♀ 13:47; ☽⚹☿ 14:35; ⚶ ♒ 20:44; ☿⚺♀ 21:51; ☽∥⚷ 23:51; ☽⚹♃ 23:57

2 Su: ☽□♄ 4:45; ☽⚺⚳ 6:19; ☉⚹☽ 8:32; ☽⚻♂ 8:59; ☿⚻♅ 10:17; ☽⚻♆ 14:54; ☽∠☿ 15:19; ♀ ♏ 17:03; ☽#⚷ 22:06; ☉∥♇ 23:26

3 M: ☉□♂ 0:35; ☽□♇ 1:31; ☽∠♃ 2:53; ♂∥⚳ 10:51; ☽⚼♂ 12:57; ☉∠☽ 13:19; ☽⚻⚷ 16:11; ☽⚺☿ 16:43; ☽⚼♆ 17:37; ☽☍♅ 18:17; ☽☌♀ 21:06; ☽∥♆ 23:17

4 Tu: ☽∥♂ 4:04; ☽∥⚳ 5:41; ☿△⚷ 5:55; ☽⚺♃ 6:15; ☽⚹♄ 10:44; ☽☌⚳ 13:41; ☽∥♀ 14:28; ☽#♅ 17:17; ☽△♂ 17:25; ☉⚺☽ 18:40; ☽⚼⚷ 19:18; ☽△♆ 20:47

5 W: ☽⚹♇ 7:51; ☽∠♄ 14:26; ☽☌☿ 21:54; ☉□♆ 22:23; ☽△⚷ 22:56

6 Th: ☽⚻♅ 1:01; ☉⚼♅ 5:14; ☽⚺♀ 6:44; ☽∥☿ 10:48; ☽∠♇ 11:48; ☽☌♃ 14:32; ☽⚺♄ 18:42; ☿D 21:25; ☽⚺⚳ 23:13

7 F: ☽□♂ 4:12; ☽□♆ 4:43; ☽⚼♅ 5:12; ☉☌☽ 7:22; ♂∥♆ 11:20; ☽∠♀ 12:39; ♂☌♆ 14:12; ☉∥♄ 15:59; ☽⚺♇ 16:21; ♂∠♅ 22:53

8 Sa: ☽∠⚳ 4:58; ☽∥♃ 5:52; ☽⚺☿ 7:03; ☽□⚷ 7:57; ☽△♅ 10:01; ♀#♅ 17:52; ☽⚹♀ 19:21

9 Su: ☽⚺♃ 1:20; ☽☌♄ 5:10; ⚷D 7:53; ☽⚹⚳ 11:25; ☽∠☿ 13:19; ☽⚹♆ 15:07; ☿△⚷ 16:08; ☽⚹♂ 17:53; ☉⚺☽ 23:13

10 M: ☽☌♇ 3:22; ☽∠♃ 7:43; ☽∥♃ 15:05; ☽⚹⚷ 19:26; ☽⚹☿ 20:39; ☽∠♆ 21:11; ☽□♅ 21:28

11 Tu: ☽∠♂ 1:44; ☉∠☽ 8:14; ☽□♀ 11:02; ☿⚻♅ 11:39; ☽⚹♃ 14:35; ☽⚺♄ 17:57; ⚳⚼⚷ 21:29

12 W: ☉⚺♇ 1:28; ☽∠⚷ 1:51; ☽□⚳ 2:01; ☽⚺♆ 3:38; ☽∥☿ 8:53; ☽⚺♂ 10:00; ☽⚺♇ 16:16; ☉⚹☽ 17:37; ☿ ♐ 23:44

13 Th: ☽∠♄ 0:48; ☽⚺⚷ 8:25; ☽⚹♅ 10:21; ☽□☿ 13:40; ☽∠♇ 22:51

14 F: ⚳△♆ 1:22; ☽△♀ 4:11; ☽□♃ 4:45; ☽∥♀ 6:37; ☽⚹♄ 7:33; ☽#♅ 12:25; ♀⚺♃ 16:00; ☽∥⚳ 16:33; ☽☌♆ 16:36; ☽∠♅ 16:39; ☽△⚳ 17:08

15 Sa: ☽☌♂ 2:20; ☽⚹♇ 5:06; ☽∥♆ 7:58; ♅∠♆ 11:13; ☉□☽ 11:50; ☽⚼♀ 12:20; ☽☌⚷ 20:40; ☽∥♂ 21:06; ☽⚺♅ 22:25; ☽⚼⚳ 23:58

16 Su: ☽△☿ 6:49; ☽#⚷ 11:36; ☉∠♀ 14:09; ♀⚹♄ 14:28; ☽△♃ 17:14; ☽□♄ 19:22; ☽⚻♀ 19:40

17 M: ☽⚺♆ 3:28; ☽⚻⚳ 5:54; ♂⚹♇ 6:58; ☽∥⚷ 11:07; ☽⚼☿ 14:15; ☽□♇ 15:21; ☽⚺♂ 15:47; ☽#♂ 22:01; ☽⚼♃ 22:06

18 Tu: ☉△☽ 2:28; ☿∠♇ 2:55; ☽⚺⚷ 5:51; ☽☌♅ 7:22; ☽∠♆ 7:32; ☽#♆ 13:09; ☽⚻☿ 20:32; ☽∠♂ 20:50

19 W: ☽⚻♃ 1:55; ☽△♄ 3:28; ☽#⚳ 6:13; ☽∥♅ 6:43; ☽☍♀ 6:55; ☉⚼☽ 7:53; ☽∠⚷ 8:57; ☽⚹♆ 10:35; ☽☍⚳ 14:28; ☽#♀ 18:05; ☽△♇ 21:42; ☉□⚷ 22:03; ⚳#♅ 23:48

20 Th: ☽⚹♂ 0:43; ☽⚼♄ 6:01; ☽⚹⚷ 11:06; ☉⚻☽ 12:06; ☽⚺♅ 12:25; ♀⚼⚷ 15:20; ☉△♅ 16:23; ☽⚼♇ 23:28

21 F: ☽☍☿ 5:43; ☽☍♃ 6:37; ☽⚻♄ 7:41; ☽∠♅ 13:41; ☽⚻♀ 13:47; ☽□♆ 13:59; ♀△♆ 17:13; ☿☌♃ 17:38; ☽⚻⚳ 19:04; ☉ ♑ 22:24

22 Sa: ☽⚻♇ 0:32; ☽□♂ 5:42; ☿⚺♄ 5:42; ☽#☿ 9:16; ☽□⚷ 13:11; ☽⚹♅ 14:22; ☽⚼♀ 16:04; ☉☍☽ 17:50; ☽⚼⚳ 20:22; ☽#♃ 21:54

23 Su: ☽⚻♃ 8:36; ☽☍♄ 9:18; ☽⚻☿ 11:45; ☽△♆ 15:04; ☽△♀ 17:56; ☽△⚳ 21:19

24 M: ☽#♃ 0:42; ☽☍♇ 1:24; ⚵D 2:57; ☽#☿ 4:17; ☽△♂ 8:38; ☽⚼♃ 9:10; ☽△⚷ 13:47; ☽⚼☿ 14:22; ☽□♅ 14:51; ☽⚼♆ 15:17; ☿∥♃ 17:22; ☿⚼♅ 19:41; ☉⚻☽ 21:53

25 Tu: ☿□♆ 0:33; ☉∠⚳ 4:40; ♂#⚷ 5:33; ☽△♃ 9:46; ☽⚼♂ 10:01; ☽⚻♄ 10:08; ☽⚼⚷ 14:04; ☽⚻♆ 15:36; ☽△☿ 17:07; ☽□♀ 21:38; ☽□⚳ 23:11

26 W: ☉⚼☽ 0:02; ☽⚻♇ 2:05; ☽⚼♄ 10:48; ☽⚻♂ 11:39; ☽⚻⚷ 14:37; ☽△♅ 15:38; ☽#♀ 18:17; ☿∥♇ 22:03

27 Th: ☉△☽ 2:34; ☽⚼♇ 2:51; ☽#⚳ 9:25; ☽□♃ 11:49; ☽△♄ 11:52; ☽∥♅ 13:55; ♀☌⚳ 15:05; ☽⚼♅ 16:34; ☽☍♆ 17:10; ♃⚺♄ 19:19

28 F: ☽□☿ 0:05; ☽⚹⚳ 2:24; ☽⚹♀ 2:53; ☽△♇ 4:06; ☽#♆ 6:30; ☽☍♂ 16:28; ☽☍⚷ 17:05; ☽⚻♅ 18:03; ♀⚹♇ 21:32; ☿∥♄ 22:01

29 Sa: ☽∠⚳ 4:54; ♂☌⚷ 5:42; ☽∥⚷ 6:13; ☽∠♀ 6:32; ☿⚺⚳ 7:10; ☉□☽ 9:35; ☽#♂ 12:09; ☽□♄ 15:42; ☽⚹♃ 16:01; ☿⚺♇ 16:45; ☽⚻♆ 20:53; ☽∥♂ 21:24

30 Su: ♂⚺♅ 1:15; ☽#⚷ 4:00; ☽⚺⚳ 8:04; ☽□♇ 8:24; ☽⚹☿ 10:14; ☽⚺♀ 11:00; ☽∠♃ 19:07; ⚳⚹♇ 20:43; ☽⚻⚷ 21:59; ☽☍♅ 22:55; ☽⚼♆ 23:42

31 M: ☽⚻♂ 0:04; ☽∥♆ 4:40; ☿⚺♀ 6:01; ☉∥☿ 12:37; ☽∠☿ 16:44; ☉⚹☽ 19:48; ☽⚹♄ 22:10; ☽#♅ 22:45; ☽⚺♃ 22:54

LONGITUDE

y	Sid.Time	☉	☽	☽ 12 hour	Mean☊	True☊	☿	♀	♂	⚳	♃	♄	⚷	♅	♆	♇
	h m s	° ' "	° ' "	° ' "	° '	° '	° '	° '	° '	° '	° '	° '	° '	° '	° '	° '
u	6 41 26	10♑15 21	12♏21 35	18♏49 44	27♋34.0	26♋52.2	23♐51.2	23♏29.6	29♓56.1	20♏59.9	11♐46.2	11♑22.6	28♓08.0	28♈36.9	14♓04.8	20♑35.6
V	6 45 22	11 16 31	25 14 11	1♐35 10	27 30.8	26R 50.0	25 19.2	24 28.7	0♈36.4	21 23.1	11 58.7	11 29.7	28 09.3	28R 36.6	14 06.1	20 37.6
h	6 49 19	12 17 42	7♐52 52	14 07 28	27 27.6	26 47.6	26 47.7	25 28.3	1 16.7	21 46.2	12 11.3	11 36.8	28 10.6	28 36.4	14 07.4	20 39.6
	6 53 15	13 18 52	20 19 08	26 28 04	27 24.4	26 45.5	28 16.7	26 28.4	1 57.1	22 09.2	12 23.7	11 43.9	28 12.0	28 36.2	14 08.7	20 41.6
Sa	6 57 12	14 20 03	2♑34 27	8♑38 27	27 21.3	26 43.9	29 46.2	27 28.8	2 37.5	22 32.1	12 36.2	11 51.0	28 13.4	28 36.1	14 10.0	20 43.7
Su	7 01 08	15 21 14	14 40 17	20 40 08	27 18.1	26 42.9	1♑16.2	28 29.7	3 18.0	22 54.9	12 48.5	11 58.1	28 14.9	28D 36.0	14 11.4	20 45.7
M	7 05 05	16 22 25	26 38 13	2♒34 48	27 14.9	26D 42.6	2 46.7	29 31.0	3 58.4	23 17.6	13 00.9	12 05.1	28 16.4	28 36.0	14 12.8	20 47.7
u	7 09 01	17 23 36	8♒30 08	14 24 32	27 11.7	26 42.9	4 17.6	0♐32.6	4 38.9	23 40.2	13 13.1	12 12.2	28 18.0	28 36.0	14 14.2	20 49.7
V	7 12 58	18 24 46	20 18 17	26 11 47	27 08.6	26 43.5	5 48.9	1 34.7	5 19.4	24 02.6	13 25.3	12 19.3	28 19.6	28 36.1	14 15.6	20 51.8
h	7 16 55	19 25 56	2♓05 23	7♓59 33	27 05.4	26 44.3	7 20.7	2 37.0	6 00.0	24 25.0	13 37.5	12 26.4	28 21.2	28 36.3	14 17.1	20 53.8
	7 20 51	20 27 06	13 54 43	19 51 21	27 02.2	26 45.1	8 52.9	3 39.8	6 40.5	24 47.2	13 49.5	12 33.4	28 23.0	28 36.5	14 18.6	20 55.8
Sa	7 24 48	21 28 15	25 50 00	1♈51 11	26 59.0	26 45.8	10 25.6	4 42.8	7 21.1	25 09.3	14 01.6	12 40.5	28 24.7	28 36.7	14 20.1	20 57.8
Su	7 28 44	22 29 23	7♈55 28	14 03 23	26 55.9	26 46.2	11 58.7	5 46.2	8 01.6	25 31.3	14 13.5	12 47.5	28 26.5	28 37.0	14 21.7	20 59.9
M	7 32 41	23 30 31	20 15 31	26 32 25	26 52.7	26R 46.3	13 32.3	6 49.9	8 42.2	25 53.1	14 25.4	12 54.5	28 28.4	28 37.3	14 23.2	21 01.9
u	7 36 37	24 31 39	2♉54 37	9♉22 34	26 49.5	26 46.3	15 06.3	7 53.9	9 22.8	26 14.9	14 37.2	13 01.5	28 30.3	28 37.7	14 24.8	21 03.9
V	7 40 34	25 32 45	15 56 44	22 37 25	26 46.3	26 46.2	16 40.9	8 58.1	10 03.4	26 36.5	14 48.9	13 08.5	28 32.3	28 38.2	14 26.5	21 06.0
h	7 44 30	26 33 51	29 24 55	6♊19 19	26 43.1	26D 46.2	18 15.9	10 02.7	10 44.1	26 57.9	15 00.6	13 15.5	28 34.3	28 38.7	14 28.1	21 08.0
	7 48 27	27 34 56	13♊20 37	20 28 38	26 40.0	26 46.2	19 51.4	11 07.5	11 24.7	27 19.3	15 12.3	13 22.4	28 36.3	28 39.3	14 29.8	21 10.0
Sa	7 52 24	28 36 01	27 43 02	5♋03 17	26 36.8	26 46.3	21 27.4	12 12.6	12 05.3	27 40.5	15 23.7	13 29.4	28 38.4	28 39.9	14 31.5	21 12.0
Su	7 56 20	29 37 05	12♋28 41	19 58 21	26 33.6	26R 46.5	23 04.0	13 18.0	12 45.9	28 01.5	15 35.2	13 36.3	28 40.5	28 40.5	14 33.2	21 14.0
	8 00 17	0♒38 08	27 31 16	5♌06 20	26 30.4	26 46.6	24 41.1	14 23.6	13 26.6	28 22.4	15 46.6	13 43.2	28 42.7	28 41.2	14 35.0	21 16.0
u	8 04 13	1 39 10	12♌42 19	20 18 02	26 27.3	26 46.5	26 18.8	15 29.4	14 07.2	28 43.2	15 57.9	13 50.1	28 44.9	28 42.0	14 36.7	21 18.1
V	8 08 10	2 40 12	27 52 14	5♍23 48	26 24.1	26 46.0	27 57.0	16 35.5	14 47.9	29 03.9	16 09.1	13 56.9	28 47.2	28 42.8	14 38.5	21 20.1
h	8 12 06	3 41 13	12♍51 42	20 15 03	26 20.9	26 45.3	29 35.9	17 41.8	15 28.5	29 24.4	16 20.2	14 03.8	28 49.5	28 43.7	14 40.4	21 22.0
	8 16 03	4 42 13	27 33 07	4♎45 21	26 17.7	26 44.4	1♒15.3	18 48.4	16 09.1	29 44.7	16 31.3	14 10.6	28 51.8	28 44.6	14 42.2	21 24.0
Sa	8 19 59	5 43 13	11♎51 22	18 50 57	26 14.6	26 43.6	2 55.4	19 55.1	16 49.8	0♐04.9	16 42.2	14 17.4	28 54.2	28 45.6	14 44.0	21 26.0
Su	8 23 56	6 44 12	25 44 03	2♏30 45	26 11.4	26D 42.9	4 36.1	21 02.1	17 30.4	0 24.9	16 53.1	14 24.1	28 56.6	28 46.6	14 45.9	21 28.0
M	8 27 53	7 45 11	9♏11 14	15 45 48	26 08.2	26 42.7	6 17.4	22 09.2	18 11.1	0 44.8	17 03.9	14 30.8	28 59.1	28 47.7	14 47.8	21 30.0
u	8 31 49	8 46 10	22 14 47	28 38 36	26 05.0	26 43.1	7 59.4	23 16.6	18 51.7	1 04.6	17 14.6	14 37.5	29 01.6	28 48.8	14 49.7	21 31.9
V	8 35 46	9 47 07	4♐57 41	11♐12 28	26 01.8	26 43.9	9 42.1	24 24.1	19 32.3	1 24.1	17 25.2	14 44.2	29 04.1	28 49.9	14 51.6	21 33.9
h	8 39 42	10♒48 04	17 23 26	23 31 01	25♋58.7	26♋45.2	11♒25.4	25♐31.8	20♈13.0	1♐43.5	17♐35.7	14♑50.8	29♓06.7	28♈51.2	14♓53.6	21♑35.8

1st of Month

Julian Day # 2458484.5
Obliquity 23°26'08"
SVP 4♓59'55"
GC 27♐06.3
Eris 23♈00.0R

Day	⚴
1	21♎31.7
6	22 56.3
11	24 14.4
16	25 25.3
21	26 28.6
26	27 23.6
31	28 09.5

Day	⚵
1	20♉36.6
6	21 05.1
11	21 46.5
16	22 40.0
21	23 44.7
26	24 59.4
31	26 23.3

Day	⚶
1	14♒27.6
6	16 54.7
11	19 22.4
16	21 50.5
21	24 18.9
26	26 47.6
31	29 16.5

DECLINATION and LATITUDE

y	☉ Decl	☽ Decl	☽ Lat	☽12h Decl	☿ Decl	☿ Lat	♀ Decl	♀ Lat	♂ Decl	♂ Lat	⚳ Decl	⚳ Lat	♃ Decl	♃ Lat	♄ Decl	♄ Lat
u	23S02	10S42	5N05	12S43	23S10	0N07	15S19	3N26	0S18	0S18	11S50	6N23	21S34	0N38	22S28	0N29
V	22 57	14 34	4 38	16 14	23 21	0S00	15 33	3 27	0 01	0 17	11 56	6 23	21 36	0 38	22 27	0 29
h	22 52	17 41	3 59	18 56	23 31	0 07	15 47	3 27	0N17	0 15	12 02	6 22	21 38	0 38	22 27	0 29
	22 46	19 57	3 08	20 43	23 40	0 15	16 00	3 27	0 34	0 14	12 08	6 22	21 39	0 38	22 26	0 29
Sa	22 40	21 15	2 10	21 31	23 48	0 22	16 14	3 27	0 51	0 13	12 14	6 22	21 41	0 38	22 26	0 29
Su	22 33	21 32	1 06	21 18	23 54	0 29	16 28	3 27	1 08	0 11	12 20	6 22	21 43	0 38	22 25	0 29
M	22 26	20 49	0 00	20 07	23 60	0 35	16 41	3 26	1 26	0 10	12 26	6 22	21 44	0 38	22 25	0 29
u	22 18	19 11	1S05	18 03	24 04	0 42	16 55	3 25	1 43	0 09	12 31	6 21	21 46	0 38	22 24	0 29
V	22 10	16 44	2 07	15 14	24 07	0 48	17 08	3 25	2 00	0 07	12 37	6 21	21 47	0 37	22 24	0 28
h	22 02	13 36	3 04	11 49	24 08	0 55	17 21	3 24	2 17	0 06	12 43	6 21	21 49	0 37	22 23	0 28
	21 53	9 55	3 54	7 55	24 09	1 01	17 34	3 23	2 34	0 05	12 48	6 21	21 50	0 37	22 22	0 28
Sa	21 43	5 50	4 33	3 41	24 08	1 06	17 46	3 22	2 52	0 04	12 53	6 21	21 52	0 37	22 22	0 28
Su	21 34	1 28	5 01	0N46	24 06	1 12	17 59	3 20	3 09	0 03	12 59	6 20	21 53	0 37	22 21	0 28
M	21 23	3N02	5 16	5 17	24 02	1 17	18 11	3 19	3 26	0 01	13 04	6 20	21 54	0 37	22 21	0 28
u	21 13	7 31	5 16	9 42	23 57	1 23	18 23	3 17	3 43	0 00	13 09	6 20	21 56	0 37	22 20	0 28
V	21 02	11 48	5 01	13 48	23 50	1 27	18 34	3 16	3 60	0N01	13 14	6 20	21 57	0 37	22 19	0 28
h	20 50	15 39	4 28	17 20	23 43	1 32	18 45	3 14	4 17	0 02	13 19	6 20	21 58	0 37	22 19	0 28
	20 38	18 46	3 39	19 57	23 33	1 36	18 56	3 12	4 34	0 03	13 24	6 19	21 60	0 37	22 18	0 28
Sa	20 26	20 50	2 35	21 22	23 23	1 41	19 07	3 10	4 51	0 04	13 28	6 19	22 01	0 37	22 17	0 28
Su	20 14	21 33	1 19	21 20	23 11	1 44	19 17	3 08	5 07	0 05	13 33	6 19	22 02	0 37	22 17	0 28
M	20 01	20 43	0N04	19 44	22 57	1 48	19 27	3 05	5 24	0 06	13 38	6 19	22 03	0 37	22 16	0 28
u	19 47	18 24	1 27	16 44	22 42	1 51	19 37	3 03	5 41	0 08	13 42	6 19	22 05	0 37	22 16	0 28
V	19 34	14 47	2 45	12 37	22 26	1 54	19 46	3 01	5 58	0 09	13 47	6 19	22 06	0 37	22 15	0 28
h	19 20	10 15	3 49	7 47	22 08	1 57	19 55	2 58	6 14	0 10	13 51	6 18	22 07	0 37	22 14	0 28
	19 05	5 13	4 38	2 37	21 49	1 59	20 03	2 55	6 31	0 11	13 56	6 18	22 08	0 37	22 14	0 27
Sa	18 50	0 02	5 07	2S32	21 28	2 01	20 11	2 53	6 48	0 12	13 60	6 18	22 09	0 37	22 13	0 27
Su	18 35	5S01	5 18	7 23	21 06	2 03	20 18	2 50	7 04	0 13	14 04	6 18	22 10	0 37	22 12	0 27
M	18 20	9 39	5 10	11 46	20 42	2 04	20 25	2 47	7 20	0 14	14 08	6 18	22 11	0 37	22 12	0 27
u	18 04	13 42	4 47	15 28	20 16	2 05	20 32	2 44	7 37	0 15	14 12	6 18	22 12	0 37	22 11	0 27
V	17 48	17 02	4 10	18 22	19 49	2 05	20 38	2 41	7 53	0 16	14 16	6 17	22 13	0 37	22 10	0 27
h	17S31	19S29	3N22	20S22	19S21	2S05	20S44	2N38	8N09	0N17	14S20	6N17	22S14	0N37	22S10	0N27

Day	⚷ Decl	⚷ Lat	♅ Decl	♅ Lat	♆ Decl	♆ Lat	♇ Decl	♇ Lat
1	2N16	3N17	10N29	0S32	7S09	0S58	21S58	0S06
6	2 18	3 16	10 29	0 32	7 07	0 58	21 57	0 07
11	2 20	3 15	10 29	0 32	7 04	0 58	21 55	0 07
16	2 23	3 14	10 30	0 31	7 01	0 58	21 54	0 08
21	2 26	3 13	10 31	0 31	6 58	0 58	21 53	0 08
26	2 30	3 12	10 33	0 31	6 54	0 58	21 52	0 09
31	2N34	3N11	10N35	0S31	6S50	0S58	21S51	0S09

Day	⚴ Decl	⚴ Lat	⚵ Decl	⚵ Lat	⚶ Decl	⚶ Lat	Eris Decl	Eris Lat
1	6S06	2N29	2S25	21S01	20S06	3S47	2S11	11S58
6	5 44	3 26	1 42	20 14	19 25	3 50	2 11	11 57
11	5 17	4 26	0 55	19 45	18 42	3 53	2 10	11 56
16	4 43	5 29	0 05	19 06	17 57	3 57	2 09	11 56
21	4 04	6 35	0N47	18 27	17 11	3 60	2 08	11 55
26	3 18	7 45	1 41	17 49	16 23	4 03	2 07	11 54
31	2S25	8N58	2N36	17S11	15S34	4S06	2S06	11S53

Moon Phenomena

Max/0 Decl
dy hr mn
5 18:48 21S33
13 7:53 0 N
19 23:33 21N33
26 0:07 0 S

Perigee/Apogee
dy hr m kilometers
9 4:28 a 406117
21 20:12 p 357345

PH dy hr mn
● 6 1:29 15♑25
● 6 1:43 P 0.715
☽ 14 6:47 23♈48
○ 21 5:17 0♌52
● 21 5:13 T 1.195
☾ 27 21:12 7♏38

Max/0 Lat
dy hr mn
7 0:09 0 S
14 12:27 5S18
20 22:49 0 N
27 1:40 5N18

Void of Course Moon

Last Aspect	☽ Ingress
1 22:27 ♀ ☌	♐ 2 9:00
4 17:43 ☿ ☌	♑ 4 18:56
7 6:21 ☿ ⚹	♒ 7 6:47
9 16:54 ♅ ⚹	♓ 9 19:45
11 14:26 ☉ ⚹	♈ 12 8:19
14 15:57 ♅ ☌	♉ 14 18:32
16 18:35 ☉ △	♊ 17 1:01
19 1:34 ♅ ⚹	♋ 19 3:45
21 1:51 ♅ □	♌ 21 3:56
23 1:21 ♅ △	♍ 23 3:23
24 13:52 ♇ △	♎ 25 4:04
27 5:22 ♅ ☍	♏ 27 7:32
28 22:40 ♇ ⚹	♐ 29 14:34

DAILY ASPECTARIAN

☽⚼⚷ 1:26
♂ ♈ 2:21
☽△♆ 3:11
☽⚼♂ 5:01
☽∥⚳ 6:51
☽⚹♇ 15:20
☽☌⚳ 16:33
☽☌♀ 22:27

☽⊻☿ 0:11
☉∠☽ 2:08
☽∠♄ 2:24
☽△⚷ 5:31
☉☌♄ 5:51
☽⊼♅ 6:22
☽∥♀ 7:25
☽△♂ 10:43
☽∠♇ 19:45
☉⊻♃ 20:50

☽⊻♄ 7:14
☽☌♃ 8:24
☉⊻☽ 9:14
☽⚼♅ 11:00
☽□♆ 12:01
☿□⚷ 22:43

☽⊻♇ 0:44
☽⊻⚳ 3:41
☿△♅ 5:14
♀∠♄ 7:00
☽⊻♀ 13:05
☽□⚷ 15:25
☽△♅ 16:11
☽☌☿ 17:43
☉⚹♆ 19:58

5 Sa ☽□♂ 0:06
☿ ♑ 3:41
☽∠⚳ 10:08
♀△⚷ 18:01
☽☌♄ 18:33
☽⊻♃ 20:13
☽∠♀ 21:26
☽⚹♆ 23:02

6 Su ☉☌☽ 1:29
♀⊼♅ 2:29
☽☌♇ 12:13
☽⚹⚳ 17:03
♅ D 20:28

7 M ☽∠♃ 2:50
☽⚹⚷ 3:18
☽□♅ 3:58
☉∥♄ 4:11
☽∠♆ 5:12
☽⚹♀ 6:21
♀ ♐ 11:19
☽⊻☿ 14:13
☽⚹♂ 15:43

8 Tu ☽⊻♄ 7:36
☽⚹♃ 9:45
☽∠⚷ 9:46
☿□♂ 10:06
☽⊻♆ 11:40
☉⊻☽ 19:47
☽∥♀ 20:46

9 W ☽∠♂ 0:02
☽⊻♇ 1:08
☽∠☿ 1:12
☽□⚳ 7:52
☽∠♄ 14:26
☽⊻⚷ 16:23
☽⚹♅ 16:54
♃⚼♅ 21:34

10 Th ☽□♀ 1:11
♂∥⚷ 3:28
☉∠☽ 5:13
☽∥⚳ 5:56
☽∠♇ 7:46
☽⊻♂ 8:26
☽⚹☿ 12:17
☉∥♇ 16:40
☽#♅ 20:29
☽⚹♄ 21:14
☽∠♅ 23:23
☽□♃ 23:49

11 F ☽☌♆ 0:48
☉∥♃ 5:45
☉☌♇ 11:39
☽⚹♇ 14:12
☉⚹☽ 14:26
☽∥♆ 16:59
☿∠⚳ 18:29
☽△⚳ 22:36

12 Sa ☽☌⚷ 5:10
☽⊻♅ 5:33
☽#♂ 15:28
☽#⚷ 19:14
☽△♀ 19:21

13 Su ☽☌♂ 0:13
☽⚼⚳ 5:15
♀∠♇ 5:20
☽□☿ 9:06
☽□♄ 9:38
☽△♃ 12:32
☽⊻♆ 12:37
☿☌♄ 13:32
♃□♆ 18:59
☽∥⚷ 20:26

14 M ☽□♇ 1:29
☽∥♂ 2:15
☽⚼♀ 3:18
♃∥♇ 5:07
☉□☽ 6:47
☽⊼⚳ 11:04
☿⚹♆ 13:14
☿⊻♃ 15:31
☽⊻⚷ 15:42
☽☌♅ 15:57
☽∠♆ 17:25
☽⚼♃ 17:44
☽#♆ 21:20

15 Tu ☽⊼♀ 10:06
☽⊻♂ 12:40
☽∥♅ 16:28
☽△♄ 18:51
☽∠⚷ 19:37
☽⚹♆ 21:16
☽⊼♃ 21:55

16 W ☽△☿ 1:31
☽#⚳ 8:39
☽△♇ 9:18
☽∠♂ 17:11
☉△☽ 18:35
☽☍⚳ 19:35
☽⚼♄ 21:57
☽⚹⚷ 22:31
☽⊻♅ 22:39

17 Th ☽⚼☿ 7:35
☽⚼♇ 11:42
☉⚹⚳ 14:32
☽☍♀ 19:55
☽⚹♂ 20:33
☉⚼☽ 22:36

18 F ☽⊼♄ 0:03
☽∠♅ 0:32
☽#♀ 1:38
☽□♆ 1:57
☽☍♃ 3:11
☽⊼☿ 12:20
☽⊼♇ 13:11
♀△♂ 16:51
☉#☽ 18:40
☿☌♇ 20:05
☽⊼⚳ 23:56

19 Sa ☉⚹⚷ 0:58
☽□⚷ 1:31
☉□♅ 1:32
☽⚹♅ 1:34
☉⊼☽ 1:34
☉∠♆ 22:27

20 Su ♅⊻⚷ 0:04
☽□♂ 0:29
☽⚼⚳ 0:54
☽⊼♀ 1:26
☽☍♄ 1:50
☽△♆ 3:20
☽⊼♃ 5:03
♀⊻♄ 7:30
♀⚼♅ 8:21
☉ ♒ 9:01
☽☍♇ 14:02
☽☍☿ 18:57
♂⚼⚳ 18:58

21 M ☽△⚳ 1:23
☽□♅ 1:51
☽△⚷ 1:53
☽⚼♀ 3:12
☽⚼♆ 3:16
☉∠♃ 4:05
♀□♆ 4:16
☽⚼♃ 5:13
☉☍☽ 5:17
☉#☽ 10:01
♂□♄ 11:49
☽#♀ 13:51
⚳⊼♅ 22:32

22 Tu ☽⚼⚷ 1:39
☽⊼♄ 1:48
⚳△⚷ 2:12
☽△♂ 2:20
☽⊼♆ 3:01
☽△♀ 4:45
☽△♃ 5:13
☉∥♀ 11:06
⚳∠♄ 11:55
♀☌♃ 12:27
☽⊼♇ 13:37
♂⊻♆ 18:14

23 W ☽⊼☿ 0:09
☽△♅ 1:21
☽⊼⚷ 1:28
☽⚼♄ 1:44
☽□⚳ 1:57
☽⚼♂ 3:13
☽#⚳ 5:35
☉⊼☽ 8:12
☿□♅ 11:14
☿⚹⚷ 12:29
☽⚼♇ 13:32
☿∥♄ 15:41
☿⚹⚳ 20:30
☽∥♅ 22:38

24 Th ☿∠♆ 1:07
☿∥♃ 1:19
☽⚼♅ 1:24
☽△♄ 1:57
☽☍♆ 2:56
☽⚼☿ 3:10
☽⊼♂ 4:26
☽□♃ 5:42
☿ ♒ 5:50
☽□♀ 8:29
☉⚼☽ 10:09
☽△♇ 13:52
☽#♆ 16:05
☽∥♂ 18:15
☿∥♇ 19:36

25 F ☽⊼♅ 1:59
☽☍⚷ 2:11
☽⚹⚳ 3:43
☿∠♃ 4:19
☽△☿ 6:57
☽∥⚷ 12:37
☉△☽ 12:50
♂△♃ 17:54
⚳ ♐ 18:09

26 Sa ☽□♄ 4:11
☽⊼♆ 4:56
☽∠⚳ 5:39
☽⚹♃ 8:25
☽☍♂ 8:57
♂#♆ 9:00
☽#⚷ 11:53
☽⚹♀ 15:04
☽□♇ 16:31

27 Su ☽☍♅ 5:22
☽⊼⚷ 5:41
☽⚼♆ 7:08
☽⊻⚳ 8:29
☽∥♆ 9:24
♀⊻♇ 9:33
☽#♂ 10:59
☽∠♃ 11:02
☽□☿ 18:01
☽∠♀ 19:59
☉□☽ 21:12

28 M ♃∥♄ 3:08
☽#♅ 5:05
☽⚼⚷ 8:46
☽⚹♄ 9:47
☽△♆ 10:15
☿∥♀ 12:18
☽⊻♃ 14:36
☽⊼♂ 17:22
☽⚹♇ 22:40

29 Tu ☽⊻♀ 2:06
☽∥⚳ 3:22
☿∠♀ 11:45
☽⊼♅ 12:20
☽△⚷ 12:46
☽∠♄ 13:59
☽☌⚳ 17:03
☽⚼♂ 23:09

30 W ☉☌☿ 2:53
☽∠♇ 3:05
☉∥☽ 6:01
☉⚹☽ 10:05
☽⚹☿ 10:33
☽⚼♅ 17:06
☽⊻♄ 19:00
☽□♆ 19:08
☽∥☿ 22:41

31 Th ☽☌♃ 0:24
☽△♂ 5:51
☽⊻♇ 8:15
♄⚹♆ 14:16
☽☌♀ 17:36
☉∠☽ 18:00
☽∥♀ 19:27
☽∠☿ 20:41
☽△♅ 22:34
☽□⚷ 23:08

February 2019

LONGITUDE

Day	Sid.Time	☉	☽	☽ 12 hour	Mean ☊	True ☊	☿	♀	♂	⚳	♃	♄	⚷	♅	♆	♇
	h m s	° ' "	° ' "	° ' "	° '	° '	° '	° '	° '	° '	° '	° '	° '	° '	° '	° '
1 F	8 43 39	11♒49 01	29♐35 40	5♑37 46	25♋55.5	26♋46.6	13♒09.4	26♐39.7	20♈53.6	2♐02.8	17♐46.2	14♑57.4	29♓09.3	28♈52.4	14♓55.6	21♑37.8
2 Sa	8 47 35	12 49 56	11♑37 44	17 35 55	25 52.3	26 47.8	14 54.0	27 47.7	21 34.3	2 21.8	17 56.5	15 04.0	29 12.0	28 53.7	14 57.6	21 39.7
3 Su	8 51 32	13 50 51	23 32 41	29 28 19	25 49.1	26R 48.4	16 39.3	28 55.9	22 14.9	2 40.7	18 06.7	15 10.5	29 14.7	28 55.1	14 59.6	21 41.6
4 M	8 55 28	14 51 44	5♒23 07	11♒17 23	25 46.0	26 48.2	18 25.1	0♑04.3	22 55.6	2 59.4	18 16.8	15 17.0	29 17.4	28 56.5	15 01.6	21 43.5
5 Tu	8 59 25	15 52 37	17 11 21	23 05 17	25 42.8	26 46.9	20 11.6	1 12.8	23 36.2	3 18.0	18 26.9	15 23.5	29 20.1	28 58.0	15 03.6	21 45.4
6 W	9 03 22	16 53 28	28 59 26	4♓54 03	25 39.6	26 44.6	21 58.6	2 21.4	24 16.8	3 36.3	18 36.8	15 29.9	29 22.9	28 59.5	15 05.7	21 47.3
7 Th	9 07 18	17 54 18	10♓49 22	16 45 40	25 36.4	26 41.4	23 46.1	3 30.2	24 57.4	3 54.5	18 46.6	15 36.3	29 25.8	29 01.0	15 07.7	21 49.1
8 F	9 11 15	18 55 06	22 43 13	28 42 20	25 33.3	26 37.6	25 34.1	4 39.1	25 38.1	4 12.5	18 56.3	15 42.6	29 28.6	29 02.6	15 09.8	21 51.0
9 Sa	9 15 11	19 55 54	4♈43 20	10♈46 33	25 30.1	26 33.6	27 22.3	5 48.1	26 18.7	4 30.2	19 05.9	15 48.9	29 31.5	29 04.3	15 11.9	21 52.8
10 Su	9 19 08	20 56 39	16 52 23	23 01 13	25 26.9	26 29.8	29 10.8	6 57.2	26 59.3	4 47.8	19 15.4	15 55.2	29 34.4	29 06.0	15 14.0	21 54.7
11 M	9 23 04	21 57 24	29 13 28	5♉29 33	25 23.7	26 26.9	0♓59.5	8 06.5	27 39.9	5 05.2	19 24.7	16 01.4	29 37.4	29 07.7	15 16.1	21 56.5
12 Tu	9 27 01	22 58 06	11♉49 57	18 15 05	25 20.5	26D 25.1	2 48.0	9 15.9	28 20.5	5 22.4	19 34.0	16 07.6	29 40.3	29 09.5	15 18.3	21 58.3
13 W	9 30 57	23 58 47	24 45 24	1♊21 17	25 17.4	26 24.5	4 36.4	10 25.4	29 01.1	5 39.4	19 43.1	16 13.7	29 43.3	29 11.3	15 20.4	22 00.1
14 Th	9 34 54	24 59 27	8♊03 08	14 51 13	25 14.2	26 25.2	6 24.3	11 35.0	29 41.6	5 56.2	19 52.2	16 19.7	29 46.4	29 13.2	15 22.6	22 01.8
15 F	9 38 51	26 00 04	21 45 47	28 46 54	25 11.0	26 26.6	8 11.5	12 44.7	0♉22.2	6 12.7	20 01.1	16 25.8	29 49.4	29 15.1	15 24.7	22 03.6
16 Sa	9 42 47	27 00 41	5♋54 34	13♋08 35	25 07.8	26 28.1	9 57.7	13 54.5	1 02.7	6 29.1	20 09.8	16 31.7	29 52.5	29 17.1	15 26.9	22 05.3
17 Su	9 46 44	28 01 15	20 28 36	27 54 04	25 04.7	26R 29.2	11 42.6	15 04.4	1 43.3	6 45.2	20 18.5	16 37.7	29 55.7	29 19.1	15 29.1	22 07.1
18 M	9 50 40	29 01 48	5♌24 14	12♌58 12	25 01.5	26 29.0	13 25.7	16 14.4	2 23.8	7 01.2	20 27.0	16 43.5	29 58.8	29 21.1	15 31.3	22 08.8
19 Tu	9 54 37	0♓02 18	20 34 51	28 12 58	24 58.3	26 27.2	15 06.7	17 24.5	3 04.3	7 16.9	20 35.5	16 49.4	0♈02.0	29 23.2	15 33.5	22 10.5
20 W	9 58 33	1 02 48	5♍51 15	13♍28 21	24 55.1	26 23.8	16 45.0	18 34.7	3 44.7	7 32.3	20 43.7	16 55.1	0 05.1	29 25.3	15 35.7	22 12.1
21 Th	10 02 30	2 03 15	21 02 58	28 33 52	24 51.9	26 18.9	18 20.1	19 45.0	4 25.2	7 47.6	20 51.9	17 00.8	0 08.3	29 27.5	15 38.0	22 13.8
22 F	10 06 26	3 03 42	5♎59 57	13♎20 16	24 48.8	26 13.3	19 51.5	20 55.4	5 05.6	8 02.6	20 59.9	17 06.5	0 11.6	29 29.7	15 40.2	22 15.4
23 Sa	10 10 23	4 04 06	20 34 06	27 40 57	24 45.6	26 07.7	21 18.5	22 05.8	5 46.1	8 17.4	21 07.8	17 12.1	0 14.8	29 31.9	15 42.4	22 17.0
24 Su	10 14 20	5 04 30	4♏40 29	11♏32 37	24 42.4	26 02.9	22 40.5	23 16.4	6 26.5	8 31.9	21 15.6	17 17.6	0 18.1	29 34.2	15 44.7	22 18.6
25 M	10 18 16	6 04 52	18 17 24	24 55 04	24 39.2	25 59.6	23 56.9	24 27.0	7 06.9	8 46.2	21 23.2	17 23.1	0 21.4	29 36.5	15 46.9	22 20.2
26 Tu	10 22 13	7 05 12	1♐25 58	7♐50 34	24 36.1	25D 58.0	25 07.0	25 37.8	7 47.2	9 00.3	21 30.7	17 28.5	0 24.7	29 38.9	15 49.2	22 21.8
27 W	10 26 09	8 05 32	14 09 24	20 23 01	24 32.9	25 58.0	26 10.2	26 48.6	8 27.6	9 14.1	21 38.0	17 33.9	0 28.0	29 41.3	15 51.4	22 23.3
28 Th	10 30 06	9♓05 50	26 32 03	2♑37 07	24♋29.7	25♋59.2	27♓06.0	27♑59.4	9♉08.0	9♐27.6	21♐45.3	17♑39.2	0♈31.4	29♈43.7	15♓53.7	22♑24.8

1st of Mon

Julian Day
2458515.
Obliquity
23°26'08"
SVP 4♓59'5
GC 27♐06
Eris 23♈02

Day	⚴
1	28♎17.
6	28 51.
11	29 15.
16	29 27.
21	29 28.0
26	29 16.

Day	⚵
1	26♉41.
6	28 15.0
11	29 56.
16	1♊43.
21	3 37.
26	5 35.

Day	⚶
1	29♒46.
6	2♓15.
11	4 44.
16	7 12.
21	9 41.
26	12 09.

DECLINATION and LATITUDE

Day	☉ Decl	☽ Decl	☽ Lat	☽ 12h Decl	☿ Decl	☿ Lat	♀ Decl	♀ Lat	♂ Decl	♂ Lat	⚳ Decl	⚳ Lat	♃ Decl	♃ Lat	♄ Decl	♄ Lat
1 F	17S15	21S01	2N25	21S24	18S51	2S05	20S49	2N35	8N25	0N17	14S24	6N17	22S15	0N37	22S09	0N27
2 Sa	16 57	21 33	1 23	21 26	18 20	2 04	20 54	2 31	8 42	0 18	14 28	6 17	22 16	0 37	22 08	0 27
3 Su	16 40	21 05	0 18	20 30	17 47	2 02	20 58	2 28	8 58	0 19	14 32	6 17	22 17	0 37	22 08	0 27
4 M	16 22	19 41	0S47	18 39	17 13	2 00	21 01	2 25	9 14	0 20	14 35	6 17	22 18	0 37	22 07	0 27
5 Tu	16 04	17 26	1 50	16 02	16 37	1 58	21 04	2 21	9 29	0 21	14 39	6 17	22 19	0 37	22 06	0 27
6 W	15 46	14 27	2 49	12 44	15 60	1 55	21 07	2 18	9 45	0 22	14 42	6 16	22 20	0 37	22 05	0 27
7 Th	15 28	10 54	3 40	8 56	15 21	1 52	21 09	2 14	10 01	0 23	14 46	6 16	22 21	0 37	22 05	0 27
8 F	15 09	6 53	4 21	4 46	14 41	1 47	21 10	2 11	10 17	0 24	14 49	6 16	22 21	0 37	22 04	0 27
9 Sa	14 50	2 36	4 52	0 23	13 60	1 43	21 11	2 07	10 32	0 25	14 53	6 16	22 22	0 37	22 03	0 27
10 Su	14 31	1N51	5 10	4N05	13 17	1 38	21 12	2 04	10 48	0 25	14 56	6 16	22 23	0 37	22 03	0 27
11 M	14 11	6 18	5 14	8 28	12 33	1 32	21 12	1 60	11 03	0 26	14 59	6 16	22 24	0 37	22 02	0 27
12 Tu	13 52	10 34	5 03	12 35	11 48	1 25	21 11	1 56	11 18	0 27	15 02	6 15	22 24	0 37	22 01	0 27
13 W	13 32	14 28	4 37	16 13	11 02	1 18	21 10	1 52	11 33	0 28	15 05	6 15	22 25	0 37	22 01	0 27
14 Th	13 11	17 47	3 55	19 07	10 15	1 10	21 08	1 49	11 49	0 29	15 08	6 15	22 26	0 37	21 60	0 26
15 F	12 51	20 12	2 59	20 60	9 27	1 02	21 05	1 45	12 04	0 29	15 11	6 15	22 26	0 37	21 59	0 26
16 Sa	12 30	21 28	1 51	21 35	8 38	0 52	21 02	1 41	12 18	0 30	15 14	6 15	22 27	0 37	21 59	0 26
17 Su	12 10	21 20	0 33	20 42	7 49	0 42	20 59	1 37	12 33	0 31	15 17	6 15	22 28	0 37	21 58	0 26
18 M	11 49	19 42	0N49	18 20	7 00	0 32	20 54	1 33	12 48	0 32	15 19	6 14	22 28	0 37	21 57	0 26
19 Tu	11 27	16 39	2 08	14 40	6 11	0 20	20 50	1 29	13 03	0 32	15 22	6 14	22 29	0 37	21 57	0 26
20 W	11 06	12 26	3 19	10 01	5 22	0 08	20 44	1 25	13 17	0 33	15 25	6 14	22 29	0 37	21 56	0 26
21 Th	10 45	7 27	4 15	4 47	4 33	0N04	20 38	1 22	13 31	0 34	15 27	6 14	22 30	0 37	21 55	0 26
22 F	10 23	2 05	4 52	0S36	3 45	0 17	20 32	1 18	13 46	0 35	15 30	6 14	22 31	0 37	21 55	0 26
23 Sa	10 01	3S15	5 10	5 48	2 58	0 31	20 25	1 14	13 60	0 35	15 32	6 13	22 31	0 37	21 54	0 26
24 Su	9 39	8 14	5 08	10 32	2 13	0 45	20 17	1 10	14 14	0 36	15 35	6 13	22 32	0 37	21 53	0 26
25 M	9 17	12 39	4 48	14 35	1 30	0 59	20 09	1 06	14 28	0 37	15 37	6 13	22 32	0 37	21 53	0 26
26 Tu	8 54	16 18	4 14	17 48	0 49	1 14	19 60	1 02	14 42	0 37	15 39	6 13	22 33	0 37	21 52	0 26
27 W	8 32	19 03	3 28	20 04	0 10	1 29	19 51	0 58	14 55	0 38	15 42	6 12	22 33	0 37	21 51	0 26
28 Th	8S09	20S50	2N33	21S21	0N26	1N43	19S41	0N54	15N09	0N39	15S44	6N12	22S33	0N37	21S51	0N26

Day	⚷ Decl	⚷ Lat	♅ Decl	♅ Lat	♆ Decl	♆ Lat	♇ Decl	♇ La
1	2N35	3N10	10N35	0S31	6S49	0S58	21S51	0S
6	2 39	3 10	10 38	0 31	6 46	0 58	21 50	0
11	2 44	3 09	10 41	0 31	6 41	0 58	21 49	0
16	2 49	3 08	10 45	0 30	6 37	0 58	21 48	0
21	2 55	3 07	10 48	0 30	6 33	0 58	21 47	0
26	3N01	3N07	10N53	0S30	6S29	0S58	21S46	0S

Day	⚴ Decl	⚴ Lat	⚵ Decl	⚵ Lat	⚶ Decl	⚶ Lat	Eris Decl	Eris La
1	2S14	9N14	2N47	17S03	15S24	4S07	2S06	11S
6	1 13	10 31	3 43	16 26	14 33	4 10	2 05	11
11	0 05	11 53	4 38	15 50	13 42	4 13	2 04	11
16	1N10	13 17	5 32	15 15	12 49	4 16	2 02	11
21	2 32	14 45	6 26	14 42	11 56	4 19	2 01	11
26	4N00	16N14	7N17	14S09	11S02	4S22	1S60	11S

Moon Phenomena

Max/0 Decl
dy hr mn
2 0:41 21S33
9 14:02 0 N
16 9:54 21N35
22 9:19 0 S

Max/0 Lat
dy hr mn
3 6:37 0 S
10 18:42 5S14
17 9:44 0 N
23 9:17 5N11

Perigee/Apogee
dy hr m kilometers
5 9:31 a 406556
19 9:00 p 356766

PH dy hr mn
● 4 21:05 15♒45
☽ 12 22:27 23♉55
○ 19 15:55 0♍42
☾ 26 11:29 7♐34

Void of Course Moon

Last Aspect	☽ Ingres
31 22:34 ♅ △	♑ 1 0:
3 10:54 ♅ □	♒ 3 13:
6 0:00 ♅ ⚹	♓ 6 2:
7 22:15 ♇ ⚹	♈ 8 14:
10 23:49 ♅ ☌	♉ 11 1:
12 22:27 ☉ □	♊ 13 9:
15 12:50 ♅ ⚹	♋ 15 14:
17 14:18 ♅ □	♌ 17 15:
19 13:52 ♅ △	♍ 19 14:
21 1:53 ♇ △	♎ 21 14:
23 15:12 ♅ ☍	♏ 23 15:
25 12:15 ♀ ⚹	♐ 25 21:
28 6:18 ♅ △	♑ 28 6:

DAILY ASPECTARIAN

1 F	☽ ⊻ ⚳	5:00
	⚶ ♓	11:05
	☿ ∠ ⚷	14:08
2 Sa	☿ ⊻ ♆	0:50
	☿ ⊻ ♄	2:26
	☉ ⊻ ☽	2:38
	♂ □ ♇	3:21
	☽ ⚹ ♆	6:42
	☽ ☌ ♄	6:58
	☉ ∠ ♀	7:23
	☽ ⊻ ☿	7:42
	☽ ∠ ⚳	11:50
	☽ ⊻ ♃	12:52
	☽ ☌ ♇	20:15
	☽ □ ♂	21:13
	♀ △ ♅	23:43
3 Su	☽ ∥ ♀	2:48
	♀ □ ⚷	6:52
	☉ ∠ ⚷	9:50
	☽ □ ♅	10:54
	☽ ⚹ ⚷	11:35
	☽ ⊻ ♀	12:04
	☽ ∠ ♆	13:06
	☽ ⚹ ⚳	19:00
	☽ ∠ ♃	19:40
	☿ ⚹ ♃	21:56
	♀ ♑	22:30
4 M	☉ ⊻ ♆	4:01
	☉ ⊻ ♄	11:10
	☽ ∠ ⚷	18:10
	☽ ⊻ ♆	19:39
	☽ ⊻ ♄	20:19
	☉ ☌ ☽	21:05
	☽ ∠ ♀	21:48
5 Tu	☽ ⚹ ♃	2:36
	☽ ☌ ☿	7:12
	☽ ∥ ☿	9:06
	☽ ⊻ ♇	9:19
	☉ ∥ ☽	12:55
	☽ ⚹ ♂	13:51
	☿ ⊻ ♇	21:25
	☽ ∥ ⚳	22:11
6 W	☽ ⚹ ♅	0:00
	☽ ⊻ ⚷	0:48
	☽ ∠ ♄	3:06
	☽ ⚹ ♀	7:34
	☽ □ ⚳	9:37
	☽ ∠ ♇	15:52
	☉ ∥ ☿	16:03
	☽ ∠ ♂	22:09
7 Th	☽ ∦ ♅	1:33
	☽ ∦ ♂	5:07
	☽ ∠ ♅	6:28
	☽ ☌ ♆	8:44
	☽ ⚹ ♄	9:45
	♀ ⊻ ⚳	11:29
	☉ ⊻ ☽	15:38
	☽ □ ♃	16:17
	☿ ∥ ⚳	19:28
	☽ ⚹ ♇	22:15
8 F	☉ ⚹ ♃	0:33
	☽ ∥ ♆	0:54
	☿ ⚹ ♂	1:26
	☽ ⊻ ♂	6:12
	☽ ⊻ ☿	6:44
	☽ ⊻ ♅	12:42
	☽ ☌ ⚷	13:36
	☉ ∥ ⚳	21:18
	☽ ∦ ⚷	23:24
	☽ △ ⚳	23:33
9 Sa	☉ ∠ ☽	0:27
	☽ □ ♀	2:22
	♂ ∥ ♅	12:29
	☽ ∠ ☿	17:47
	☽ ⊻ ♆	20:46
	☽ □ ♄	22:07
	☿ ⚹ ♅	22:54
10 Su	☽ ∥ ⚷	4:40
	☽ △ ♃	4:43
	☿ ⊻ ⚷	5:21
	☽ ⚼ ⚳	5:52
	☉ ⚹ ☽	8:40
	☽ □ ♇	9:52
	☿ ♓	10:52
	☽ ☌ ♂	20:49
	☉ ⊻ ♇	23:38
	☽ ☌ ♅	23:49
11 M	☿ ∠ ♄	0:27
	☽ ⊻ ⚷	0:46
	☽ ∠ ♆	2:01
	☽ ∦ ♆	2:09
	☽ ⚹ ☿	3:58
	⚵ ♊	4:22
	☽ ⚼ ♃	10:04
	☽ ⚻ ⚳	11:29
	☽ △ ♀	18:40
12 Tu	☽ ∥ ♅	0:44
	☽ ∥ ♂	4:36
	☽ ∠ ⚷	5:21
	☽ ∦ ☿	6:05
	☽ ⚹ ♆	6:32
	☽ △ ♄	8:06
	☿ ∦ ♂	11:39
	☽ ⚻ ♃	14:37
	☉ ∦ ☽	18:22
	☽ △ ♇	18:56
	☉ □ ☽	22:27
13 W	☽ ⚼ ♀	1:20
	☽ ∦ ⚳	4:08
	♂ ☌ ♅	6:22
	☽ ⊻ ♅	8:06
	☽ ⊻ ♂	8:11
	☽ ⚹ ⚷	9:05
	☿ ∦ ♅	9:46
	☽ ⚼ ♄	11:52
	☿ □ ⚳	16:35
	☽ ☍ ⚳	20:09
	☽ □ ☿	20:37
	☽ ⚼ ♇	22:11
14 Th	♂ ⊻ ⚷	3:03
	☽ ⚻ ♀	6:50
	☿ ∠ ♇	8:31
	♂ ♉	10:52
	☽ ∠ ♅	10:55
	☽ ∠ ♂	12:20
	☽ □ ♆	12:57
	☽ ⚻ ♄	14:41
	☽ ☍ ♃	20:57
15 F	☽ ⚻ ♇	0:31
	♂ ∠ ♆	1:36
	☉ △ ☽	7:50
	☽ ⚹ ♅	12:50
	☽ ∦ ♀	13:20
	☽ □ ⚷	13:49
	☽ ⚹ ♂	15:25
16 Sa	☽ ⚻ ⚳	0:59
	☽ △ ☿	7:40
	☉ ∦ ♂	8:03
	☉ ⚼ ☽	10:53
	☽ ☍ ♀	14:24
	☽ △ ♆	15:50
	☽ ☍ ♄	17:41
	☽ ⚻ ♃	23:43
17 Su	☽ ⚼ ⚳	2:07
	☽ ☍ ♇	2:40
	☽ ∦ ♀	7:59
	♀ ⚹ ♆	8:45
	☽ ⚼ ☿	11:24
	☉ ⚻ ☽	13:04
	☽ □ ♅	14:18
	☽ △ ⚷	15:18
	☽ ⚼ ♆	16:11
	☽ □ ♂	18:59
18 M	☽ ⚼ ♃	0:05
	☽ △ ⚳	2:37
	☉ ⚹ ♅	7:56
	⚷ ♈	9:11
	♀ ☌ ♄	10:53
	☿ ∥ ♆	12:07
	⚳ ∠ ♇	12:59
	☿ ∠ ♅	13:22
	☽ ⚻ ☿	14:19
	☽ ⚼ ⚷	15:14
	☽ ⚻ ♆	16:04
	⚴ R	16:41
	☽ ⚻ ♄	18:03
	☽ ⚻ ♀	18:35
	☉ ♓	23:05
	☉ ⊻ ⚷	23:51
19 Tu	☽ △ ♃	0:01
	☽ ⚻ ♇	2:31
	☿ ☌ ♆	6:38
	☽ ∦ ⚳	7:51
	☽ △ ♅	13:52
	☽ ⚻ ⚷	14:54
	☉ ☍ ☽	15:55
	☽ ⚼ ♄	17:47
	☽ ∥ ♂	19:48
	☽ ⚼ ♀	20:08
	☽ △ ♂	20:32
20 W	☽ ⚼ ♇	2:07
	☿ ⚹ ♄	2:40
	☽ □ ⚳	2:42
	☉ ∦ ☽	7:15
	☽ ∥ ♅	8:13
	☽ ⚼ ♅	13:32
	☽ ☍ ♆	15:24
	☽ △ ♄	17:33
	☽ ☍ ☿	19:12
	☉ ∦ ♅	19:51
	☽ ⚼ ♂	21:17
	☽ △ ♀	21:46
	☉ ∠ ♄	22:56
	☽ □ ♃	23:42
21 Th	☽ △ ♇	1:53
	☽ ∦ ♆	4:06
	☽ ⚻ ♅	13:28
	☽ ☍ ⚷	14:35
	☽ ∦ ☿	15:22
	☉ ⚻ ☽	18:54
	☽ ∥ ⚷	20:15
	☽ ⚻ ♂	22:28
22 F	♀ ⊻ ♃	1:45
	☽ ⚹ ⚳	3:23
	☿ ∠ ♂	7:03
	☽ ⚻ ♆	15:54
	☽ □ ♄	18:21
	☿ □ ♃	20:41
	☉ ⚼ ☽	21:18
	☽ ∦ ⚷	22:40
	☽ ∥ ☿	22:55
23 Sa	☿ ∦ ⚷	0:28
	☽ ⚹ ♃	0:57
	☽ ⚻ ☿	1:22
	☽ □ ♀	2:48
	☽ □ ♇	2:53
	♀ ☌ ♇	3:54
	☽ ∠ ⚳	4:39
	☽ ☍ ♅	15:12
	☽ ∥ ♆	15:26
	♂ ⚼ ♃	16:00
	☽ ⚻ ⚷	16:27
	☽ ⚼ ♆	17:13
	☿ ⚹ ♇	17:19
24 Su	☉ △ ☽	0:45
	☽ ∠ ♃	2:47
	☽ ☍ ♂	3:13
	☽ ⚼ ☿	5:46
	♀ ∠ ⚳	6:38
	☉ ∥ ☽	6:44
	☽ ⊻ ⚳	6:50
	☽ ∦ ♅	13:46
	☽ ⚼ ⚷	18:44
	☽ △ ♆	19:30
	☽ ⚹ ♄	22:22
25 M	☽ ⊻ ♃	5:38
	☽ ⚹ ♇	7:19
	☽ △ ☿	11:15
	☽ ∦ ♂	11:59
	☽ ⚹ ♀	12:15
	☽ ∥ ⚳	19:17
	☽ ⚻ ♅	20:41
	☽ △ ⚷	22:06
26 Tu	☽ ∠ ♄	1:57
	☉ ∠ ♇	6:46
	☽ ∠ ♇	11:07
	☉ □ ☽	11:29
	☽ ⚻ ♂	12:34
	☽ ☌ ⚳	14:28
	☽ ∠ ♀	19:03
27 W	☽ ⚼ ♅	1:01
	☽ □ ♆	3:16
	☽ ⊻ ♄	6:36
	☽ ∥ ♀	8:21
	☽ ☌ ♃	14:34
	☽ ⊻ ♇	15:56
	☽ ⚼ ♂	19:02
28 Th	☽ □ ☿	1:12
	☉ ⚹ ♂	2:34
	☽ ⊻ ♀	3:10
	☽ △ ♅	6:18
	☽ □ ⚷	7:53
	☉ □ ⚳	11:10
	♂ ⚻ ⚳	17:30

LONGITUDE

Day	Sid.Time	☉	☽	☽ 12 hour	Mean ☊	True ☊	☿	♀	♂	⚳	♃	♄	⚷	♅	♆	♇
	h m s	° ' "	° ' "	° ' "	° '	° '	° '	° '	° '	° '	° '	° '	° '	° '	° '	° '
1 F	10 34 02	10♓06 06	8♑38 49	14♑37 47	24♋26.5	26♋00.7	27♓53.7	29♑10.4	9♉48.3	9♐40.9	21♐52.3	17♑44.4	0♈34.8	29♈46.2	15♓56.0	22♑26.3
2 Sa	10 37 59	11 06 21	20 34 34	26 29 45	24 23.3	26R 01.9	28 32.9	0♒21.4	10 28.6	9 54.0	21 59.2	17 49.6	0 38.1	29 48.7	15 58.2	22 27.8
3 Su	10 41 55	12 06 34	2♒23 48	8♒17 14	24 20.2	26 01.8	29 03.3	1 32.5	11 08.9	10 06.7	22 06.0	17 54.7	0 41.5	29 51.2	16 00.5	22 29.3
4 M	10 45 52	13 06 46	14 10 27	20 03 51	24 17.0	25 59.8	29 24.4	2 43.6	11 49.2	10 19.2	22 12.7	17 59.7	0 45.0	29 53.8	16 02.8	22 30.7
5 Tu	10 49 49	14 06 56	25 57 46	1♓52 30	24 13.8	25 55.6	29R 36.2	3 54.8	12 29.5	10 31.4	22 19.1	18 04.7	0 48.4	29 56.4	16 05.1	22 32.1
6 W	10 53 45	15 07 04	7♓48 18	13 45 26	24 10.6	25 49.0	29 38.7	5 06.1	13 09.8	10 43.4	22 25.5	18 09.6	0 51.8	29 59.1	16 07.3	22 33.5
7 Th	10 57 42	16 07 10	19 44 04	25 44 23	24 07.5	25 40.5	29 31.9	6 17.4	13 50.0	10 55.0	22 31.6	18 14.4	0 55.3	0♉01.7	16 09.6	22 34.9
8 F	11 01 38	17 07 14	1♈46 33	7♈50 42	24 04.3	25 30.6	29 16.2	7 28.7	14 30.2	11 06.4	22 37.6	18 19.2	0 58.7	0 04.4	16 11.9	22 36.2
9 Sa	11 05 35	18 07 17	13 57 00	20 05 36	24 01.1	25 20.2	28 52.0	8 40.1	15 10.4	11 17.4	22 43.5	18 23.9	1 02.2	0 07.2	16 14.2	22 37.5
10 Su	11 09 31	19 07 17	26 16 39	2♉30 22	23 57.9	25 10.3	28 20.0	9 51.6	15 50.6	11 28.2	22 49.2	18 28.5	1 05.7	0 09.9	16 16.4	22 38.8
11 M	11 13 28	20 07 16	8♉46 55	15 06 34	23 54.7	25 01.9	27 40.9	11 03.1	16 30.8	11 38.7	22 54.7	18 33.0	1 09.2	0 12.7	16 18.7	22 40.1
12 Tu	11 17 24	21 07 12	21 29 33	27 56 09	23 51.6	24 55.5	26 55.8	12 14.7	17 11.0	11 48.8	23 00.1	18 37.5	1 12.7	0 15.6	16 21.0	22 41.3
13 W	11 21 21	22 07 06	4♊26 40	11♊01 26	23 48.4	24 51.7	26 05.7	13 26.3	17 51.1	11 58.7	23 05.3	18 41.9	1 16.2	0 18.4	16 23.3	22 42.6
14 Th	11 25 17	23 06 58	17 40 43	24 24 52	23 45.2	24D 50.1	25 11.9	14 37.9	18 31.2	12 08.2	23 10.4	18 46.2	1 19.7	0 21.3	16 25.5	22 43.8
15 F	11 29 14	24 06 48	1♋14 06	8♋08 40	23 42.0	24 50.1	24 15.6	15 49.6	19 11.3	12 17.5	23 15.3	18 50.5	1 23.3	0 24.2	16 27.8	22 44.9
16 Sa	11 33 11	25 06 35	15 08 42	22 14 14	23 38.9	24R 50.8	23 18.2	17 01.3	19 51.4	12 26.4	23 20.0	18 54.6	1 26.8	0 27.2	16 30.1	22 46.1
17 Su	11 37 07	26 06 21	29 25 11	6♌41 19	23 35.7	24 51.0	22 20.9	18 13.1	20 31.4	12 35.0	23 24.6	18 58.7	1 30.3	0 30.1	16 32.3	22 47.2
18 M	11 41 04	27 06 04	14♌02 14	21 27 22	23 32.5	24 49.6	21 24.9	19 24.9	21 11.4	12 43.3	23 29.0	19 02.7	1 33.9	0 33.1	16 34.6	22 48.3
19 Tu	11 45 00	28 05 44	28 55 56	6♍27 02	23 29.3	24 45.7	20 31.3	20 36.7	21 51.4	12 51.3	23 33.2	19 06.7	1 37.4	0 36.1	16 36.8	22 49.4
20 W	11 48 57	29 05 23	13♍59 35	21 32 22	23 26.1	24 39.3	19 41.1	21 48.6	22 31.4	12 58.9	23 37.3	19 10.5	1 41.0	0 39.1	16 39.1	22 50.4
21 Th	11 52 53	0♈04 59	29 04 11	6♎33 44	23 23.0	24 30.5	18 55.1	23 00.5	23 11.4	13 06.2	23 41.1	19 14.3	1 44.5	0 42.2	16 41.3	22 51.4
22 F	11 56 50	1 04 33	13♎59 51	21 21 24	23 19.8	24 20.3	18 13.9	24 12.5	23 51.3	13 13.1	23 44.8	19 18.0	1 48.1	0 45.3	16 43.5	22 52.4
23 Sa	12 00 46	2 04 06	28 37 28	5♏47 15	23 16.6	24 09.9	17 38.0	25 24.5	24 31.2	13 19.7	23 48.4	19 21.6	1 51.6	0 48.4	16 45.7	22 53.4
24 Su	12 04 43	3 03 36	12♏50 14	19 46 01	23 13.4	24 00.6	17 07.8	26 36.5	25 11.1	13 26.0	23 51.7	19 25.1	1 55.2	0 51.5	16 47.9	22 54.3
25 M	12 08 40	4 03 05	26 34 28	3♐15 39	23 10.2	23 53.1	16 43.5	27 48.6	25 51.0	13 31.9	23 54.9	19 28.5	1 58.7	0 54.7	16 50.1	22 55.2
26 Tu	12 12 36	5 02 32	9♐49 44	16 17 05	23 07.1	23 48.1	16 25.3	29 00.7	26 30.8	13 37.5	23 57.9	19 31.9	2 02.3	0 57.8	16 52.3	22 56.1
27 W	12 16 33	6 01 57	22 38 10	28 53 31	23 03.9	23 45.4	16 13.0	0♓12.8	27 10.6	13 42.7	24 00.8	19 35.2	2 05.8	1 01.0	16 54.5	22 57.0
28 Th	12 20 29	7 01 21	5♑03 46	11♑09 35	23 00.7	23D 44.6	16D 06.7	1 25.0	27 50.4	13 47.5	24 03.4	19 38.3	2 09.4	1 04.2	16 56.7	22 57.8
29 F	12 24 26	8 00 42	17 11 38	23 10 37	22 57.5	23R 44.8	16 06.2	2 37.2	28 30.2	13 52.0	24 05.9	19 41.4	2 12.9	1 07.4	16 58.9	22 58.6
30 Sa	12 28 22	9 00 02	29 07 12	5♒02 05	22 54.4	23 44.8	16 11.4	3 49.4	29 10.0	13 56.1	24 08.2	19 44.4	2 16.4	1 10.7	17 01.0	22 59.4
31 Su	12 32 19	9♈59 21	10♒55 53	16 49 12	22♋51.2	23♋43.5	16♓22.0	5♓01.7	29♉49.7	13♐59.9	24♐10.3	19♑47.4	2♈20.0	1♉13.9	17♓03.2	23♑00.1

1st of Month

Julian Day # 2458543.5
Obliquity 23°26'09"
SVP 4♓59'46"
GC 27♐06.4
Eris 23♈12.2

Day	⚴
1	29♎02.9R
6	28 30.7R
11	27 45.8R
16	26 48.9R
21	25 41.0R
26	24 23.6R
31	22 58.4R

Day	⚵
1	6♊49.1
6	8 54.5
11	11 03.6
16	13 15.9
21	15 30.9
26	17 48.2
31	20 07.6

Day	⚶
1	13♓38.4
6	16 06.0
11	18 33.1
16	20 59.7
21	23 25.6
26	25 50.8
31	28 15.2

DECLINATION and LATITUDE

Day	☉ Decl	☽ Decl	☽ Lat	☽ 12h Decl	☿ Decl	☿ Lat	♀ Decl	♀ Lat	♂ Decl	♂ Lat	⚳ Decl	⚳ Lat	♃ Decl	♃ Lat	♄ Decl	♄ Lat
1 F	7S47	21S36	1N33	21S37	0N58	1N58	19S30	0N50	15N22	0N39	15S46	6N12	22S34	0N37	21S50	0N26
2 Sa	7 24	21 22	0 30	20 54	1 27	2 12	19 19	0 46	15 36	0 40	15 48	6 12	22 34	0 37	21 49	0 26
3 Su	7 01	20 11	0S34	19 15	1 51	2 26	19 07	0 42	15 49	0 41	15 50	6 11	22 35	0 37	21 49	0 26
4 M	6 38	18 07	1 37	16 47	2 12	2 39	18 55	0 39	16 02	0 41	15 52	6 11	22 35	0 37	21 48	0 26
5 Tu	6 15	15 17	2 34	13 37	2 28	2 51	18 43	0 35	16 15	0 42	15 54	6 11	22 35	0 38	21 48	0 26
6 W	5 52	11 49	3 26	9 54	2 39	3 02	18 29	0 31	16 28	0 42	15 56	6 11	22 36	0 38	21 47	0 26
7 Th	5 29	7 52	4 08	5 45	2 45	3 12	18 16	0 27	16 40	0 43	15 58	6 10	22 36	0 38	21 46	0 26
8 F	5 05	3 35	4 40	1 21	2 47	3 21	18 01	0 23	16 53	0 44	15 60	6 10	22 36	0 38	21 46	0 26
9 Sa	4 42	0N54	4 60	3N09	2 44	3 28	17 47	0 20	17 05	0 44	16 01	6 10	22 37	0 38	21 45	0 25
10 Su	4 18	5 23	5 06	7 35	2 36	3 33	17 31	0 16	17 17	0 45	16 03	6 09	22 37	0 38	21 45	0 25
11 M	3 55	9 44	4 57	11 47	2 23	3 37	17 15	0 12	17 30	0 45	16 05	6 09	22 37	0 38	21 44	0 25
12 Tu	3 31	13 43	4 34	15 31	2 07	3 38	16 59	0 09	17 42	0 46	16 07	6 09	22 37	0 38	21 43	0 25
13 W	3 08	17 09	3 56	18 35	1 46	3 37	16 42	0 05	17 53	0 46	16 08	6 08	22 38	0 38	21 43	0 25
14 Th	2 44	19 47	3 05	20 44	1 23	3 35	16 25	0 01	18 05	0 47	16 10	6 08	22 38	0 38	21 42	0 25
15 F	2 20	21 23	2 03	21 43	0 56	3 30	16 07	0S02	18 17	0 47	16 11	6 07	22 38	0 38	21 42	0 25
16 Sa	1 57	21 43	0 52	21 22	0 28	3 24	15 49	0 06	18 28	0 48	16 13	6 07	22 38	0 38	21 41	0 25
17 Su	1 33	20 40	0N24	19 37	0S03	3 15	15 31	0 09	18 39	0 48	16 14	6 07	22 39	0 38	21 41	0 25
18 M	1 09	18 13	1 41	16 31	0 34	3 05	15 12	0 12	18 50	0 49	16 16	6 06	22 39	0 38	21 40	0 25
19 Tu	0 45	14 31	2 51	12 17	1 05	2 54	14 52	0 16	19 01	0 49	16 17	6 06	22 39	0 38	21 40	0 25
20 W	0 22	9 51	3 51	7 15	1 36	2 42	14 32	0 19	19 12	0 50	16 19	6 05	22 39	0 38	21 39	0 25
21 Th	0N02	4 34	4 34	1 49	2 07	2 28	14 12	0 22	19 23	0 50	16 20	6 05	22 39	0 38	21 39	0 25
22 F	0 26	0S56	4 58	3S39	2 36	2 14	13 51	0 26	19 33	0 51	16 22	6 04	22 40	0 38	21 38	0 25
23 Sa	0 49	6 16	5 02	8 47	3 03	1 59	13 30	0 29	19 44	0 51	16 23	6 04	22 40	0 38	21 38	0 25
24 Su	1 13	11 08	4 47	13 17	3 29	1 44	13 09	0 32	19 54	0 52	16 24	6 03	22 40	0 38	21 37	0 25
25 M	1 37	15 14	4 16	16 58	3 53	1 29	12 47	0 35	20 04	0 52	16 26	6 02	22 40	0 38	21 37	0 25
26 Tu	2 00	18 26	3 31	19 39	4 14	1 13	12 24	0 38	20 14	0 53	16 27	6 02	22 40	0 38	21 36	0 25
27 W	2 24	20 37	2 37	21 18	4 33	0 58	12 02	0 41	20 23	0 53	16 28	6 01	22 40	0 38	21 36	0 25
28 Th	2 47	21 43	1 38	21 52	4 49	0 43	11 39	0 44	20 33	0 53	16 29	6 00	22 40	0 38	21 35	0 25
29 F	3 11	21 45	0 35	21 24	5 03	0 28	11 16	0 46	20 42	0 54	16 31	5 60	22 40	0 38	21 35	0 25
30 Sa	3 34	20 48	0S29	19 58	5 15	0 13	10 52	0 49	20 51	0 54	16 32	5 59	22 40	0 38	21 35	0 25
31 Su	3N57	18S56	1S30	17S41	5S23	0S01	10S28	0S52	21N00	0N55	16S33	5N58	22S41	0N38	21S34	0N25

Day	⚷ Decl	⚷ Lat	♅ Decl	♅ Lat	♆ Decl	♆ Lat	♇ Decl	♇ Lat
1	3N05	3N06	10N55	0S30	6S26	0S58	21S46	0S12
6	3 11	3 06	10 60	0 30	6 22	0 58	21 45	0 12
11	3 17	3 05	11 05	0 30	6 17	0 58	21 44	0 13
16	3 24	3 05	11 10	0 30	6 13	0 58	21 44	0 13
21	3 31	3 04	11 15	0 30	6 09	0 58	21 43	0 14
26	3 38	3 04	11 21	0 30	6 04	0 58	21 43	0 14
31	3N44	3N04	11N26	0S30	6S00	0S58	21S43	0S15

Day	⚴ Decl	⚴ Lat	⚵ Decl	⚵ Lat	⚶ Decl	⚶ Lat	Eris Decl	Eris Lat
1	4N56	17N09	7N48	13S50	10S30	4S24	1S59	11S49
6	6 33	18 41	8 36	13 19	9 35	4 28	1 57	11 49
11	8 13	20 12	9 23	12 50	8 41	4 31	1 56	11 48
16	9 56	21 42	10 07	12 21	7 46	4 34	1 54	11 48
21	11 40	23 09	10 49	11 54	6 51	4 38	1 53	11 47
26	13 22	24 31	11 28	11 28	5 57	4 41	1 51	11 47
31	15N02	25N47	12N04	11S02	5S03	4S45	1S50	11S46

Moon Phenomena

Max/0 Decl

dy hr mn	
1 6:16	21S38
8 19:14	0 N
15 18:09	21N46
21 19:54	0 S
28 12:57	21S52

Max/0 Lat

dy hr mn	
2 11:04	0 S
9 21:57	5S06
16 16:23	0 N
22 16:48	5N03
29 13:10	0 S

Perigee/Apogee

dy hr m		kilometers
4 11:28	a	406391
19 19:59	p	359379

PH	dy hr mn	
●	6 16:05	15♓47
☽	14 10:28	23♊33
○	21 1:44	0♎09
☾	28 4:11	7♑12

Void of Course Moon

Last Aspect			☽ Ingress	
2 18:48	♅	□	♒	2 19:07
5 8:06	♅	⚹	♓	5 8:12
7 19:09	☿	☌	♈	7 20:29
9 17:15	♃	△	♉	10 7:11
12 9:32	☿	⚹	♊	12 15:49
14 12:32	☿	□	♋	14 21:50
16 18:04	☉	△	♌	17 0:58
18 15:20	♃	△	♍	19 1:42
20 15:23	♃	□	♎	21 1:29
22 18:11	♀	△	♏	23 2:17
25 2:25	♀	□	♐	25 6:07
27 2:38	♃	☌	♑	27 14:09
30 0:06	♂	△	♒	30 1:47

DAILY ASPECTARIAN

1 F	☽ ⊻ ⚳	2:07
	☽ △ ♂	2:27
	☉ ⚹ ☽	3:11
	♀ □ ♅	12:33
	☽ ⚹ ♆	14:40
	♀ ♒	16:46
	☽ ☌ ♄	18:24
2 Sa	☽ ⊻ ♃	2:53
	☽ ☌ ♇	3:50
	♀ ⚹ ⚷	5:57
	☽ ∠ ⚳	8:55
	☉ ∠ ☽	12:15
	♀ ∠ ♆	12:51
	☽ ⚹ ☿	16:56
	☽ □ ♅	18:48
	☽ ⚹ ⚷	20:31
	☽ ∠ ♆	21:10
	☽ ☌ ♀	22:04
3 Su	♂ # ⚳	2:49
	☽ ∠ ♃	9:40
	☽ ∥ ♀	14:50
	☽ ⚹ ⚳	16:00
	☽ □ ♂	18:55
	☉ ⊻ ☽	21:38
4 M	☽ ∠ ☿	0:29
	☽ ∠ ⚷	3:14
	☽ ⊻ ♆	3:50
	☽ ⊻ ♄	7:50
	☉ ∥ ♆	15:53
	☽ ⚹ ♃	16:31
	☽ # ♂	16:59
	☽ ⊻ ♇	17:01
	☽ ∥ ⚳	19:17
5 Tu	☽ ⊻ ☿	7:27
	☽ ⚹ ♅	8:06
	☽ ⊻ ⚷	9:53
	☽ ∠ ♄	14:32
	☽ ⊻ ♀	17:55
	☿ R	18:21
	☉ ∠ ♅	20:40
	☽ ∠ ♇	23:30
6 W	☽ # ♅	5:13
	☽ □ ⚳	5:59
	♅ ♉	8:28
	☽ ⚹ ♂	11:27
	☽ ∠ ♅	14:31
	☉ ☌ ☽	16:05
	☽ ☌ ♆	16:48
	☽ ⚹ ♄	20:59
7 Th	☉ ☌ ♆	1:01
	☽ ∠ ♀	3:27
	☽ □ ♃	5:38
	☽ ⚹ ♇	5:42
	☽ ∥ ♆	8:44
	☉ ∥ ☽	14:55
	♃ ⊻ ♇	16:34
	☿ ∠ ♂	18:19
	☽ ☌ ☿	19:09
	☽ ∠ ♂	19:14
	☽ ⊻ ♅	20:37
	☽ ☌ ⚷	22:25
8 F	☽ # ⚷	1:55
	♀ ∠ ♃	3:16
	☽ # ☿	4:20
	☽ ⚹ ♀	12:30
	☽ △ ⚳	18:42
9 Sa	☽ ⊻ ♂	2:32
	☽ ⊻ ♆	4:29
	☉ ⚹ ♄	7:11
	☽ □ ♄	8:45
	☉ ⊻ ☽	8:53
	☽ ∥ ☿	9:32
	☽ ∥ ⚷	12:34
	☽ □ ♇	16:57
	☽ △ ♃	17:15
	☉ # ☽	18:38
10 Su	☽ ⚼ ⚳	0:23
	♄ ∥ ♇	3:00
	☽ ⊻ ☿	3:47
	☽ # ♆	4:56
	☽ ☌ ♅	7:32
	☽ ⊻ ⚷	9:20
	☽ ∠ ♆	9:40
	♂ ∠ ⚷	9:52
	♀ # ♂	11:51
	♂ ⚹ ♆	16:21
	☉ ∠ ☽	16:24
	☽ ⚼ ♃	22:20
11 M	☽ □ ♀	4:46
	☽ ⊼ ⚳	5:31
	☽ ∠ ☿	7:01
	☽ ∥ ♅	7:51
	♀ ⚹ ⚳	13:55
	☽ ∠ ⚷	14:02
	☽ ⚹ ♆	14:19
	☽ ☌ ♂	15:28
	☽ △ ♄	18:35
	☿ ∠ ♀	20:11
	☉ ⚹ ☽	23:15
12 Tu	☽ △ ♇	2:14
	☽ ⊼ ♃	2:51
	☽ ⚹ ☿	9:32
	☉ # ⚷	12:02
	☽ # ⚳	16:18
	☽ ⊻ ♅	16:21
	☽ ⚹ ⚷	18:08
	☽ # ♀	20:50
	☽ ⚼ ♄	22:37
13 W	☽ ⚼ ♇	5:59
	☽ ∥ ♂	6:23
	☽ ☍ ⚳	13:54
	☉ ⚹ ♇	14:30
	☽ △ ♀	17:59
	☽ ∠ ♅	19:49
	☽ □ ♆	21:45
14 Th	☉ □ ♃	1:30
	☽ ⊻ ♂	1:35
	☽ ⊼ ♄	1:58
	☽ ⊼ ♇	9:01
	☽ ☍ ♃	9:52
	♂ △ ♄	10:03
	☉ □ ☽	10:28
	☽ □ ☿	12:32
	♀ ∥ ⚳	19:01
	☽ ⚹ ♅	22:32
	☽ ⚼ ♀	23:13
15 F	☽ □ ⚷	0:16
	☉ ☌ ☿	1:49
	☽ ∠ ♂	5:25
	♀ ∠ ⚷	11:51
	♀ ⊻ ♆	13:12
	☽ ⊼ ⚳	19:20
	☽ # ♇	23:08
	☽ # ♇	23:08
	☿ □ ♃	23:18
16 Sa	☽ # ♄	1:59
	☽ # ♄	2:05
	☽ △ ♆	2:19
	☽ ⊼ ♀	3:29
	☽ ☍ ♄	6:25
	☽ ⚹ ♂	8:23
	☽ ☍ ♇	12:54
	☽ △ ☿	12:55
	☿ ⚹ ♇	13:09
	☽ ⊼ ♃	13:55
	☉ △ ☽	18:04
	☽ ⚼ ⚳	20:55
17 Su	☽ □ ♅	1:48
	☽ △ ⚷	3:28
	☽ ⚼ ♆	3:31
	☽ ⚼ ☿	12:17
	☽ ⚼ ♃	14:54
	♀ ⊻ ♄	16:10
	☽ ∥ ♂	19:16
	☉ ⚼ ☽	20:37
	☽ △ ⚳	21:50
18 M	☿ ⚹ ♂	3:24
	☽ ⚼ ⚷	4:07
	☽ ⊼ ♆	4:08
	☽ ⊼ ♄	8:09
	☽ ☍ ♀	9:28
	☽ ⊼ ☿	11:15
	☽ □ ♂	12:07
	☽ # ⚳	13:28
	☽ ⊼ ♇	14:11
	☽ △ ♃	15:20
	☉ ∥ ☿	15:25
	☽ # ♀	21:49
	☉ ⊼ ☽	22:34
	☿ ⊻ ♀	22:57
19 Tu	☽ △ ♅	2:41
	☽ ⊼ ⚷	4:19
	☽ ⚼ ♄	8:18
	☽ ⚼ ♇	14:12
	☽ ∥ ♅	17:16
	☽ □ ⚳	22:23
20 W	☽ ⚼ ♅	2:39
	☽ ☍ ♆	4:14
	☽ △ ♄	8:16
	☽ ☍ ☿	8:36
	♂ △ ♇	11:42
	☽ ⊼ ♀	13:30
	☽ △ ♇	14:05
	☽ △ ♂	14:12
	☿ ⚹ ♄	14:28
	☽ □ ♃	15:23
	☽ # ♆	16:58
	♀ ⊻ ♇	20:55
	☉ ♈	22:00
21 Th	☉ ☍ ☽	1:44
	☽ ⊼ ♅	2:37
	☽ ☍ ⚷	4:17
	☽ ∥ ⚷	4:35
	♀ □ ♂	8:08
	☽ # ☿	9:49
	♀ ⚹ ♃	14:18
	☽ ⚼ ♂	15:18
	☽ ⚼ ♀	15:35
	☉ ⊻ ♅	15:49
	☉ ∥ ☽	18:26
	♂ ⊼ ♃	19:44
	☉ # ☽	21:36
	☽ ⚹ ⚳	22:44
22 F	☽ ⊼ ♆	4:27
	☽ ⊼ ☿	6:36
	☽ ∥ ☿	8:01
	☽ □ ♄	8:40
	☽ # ⚷	11:33
	☽ □ ♇	14:31
	☽ ⚹ ♃	16:00
	☽ ⊼ ♂	16:53
	☽ △ ♀	18:11
	☉ ☌ ⚷	18:39
	☽ ∥ ♆	23:16
	☽ ∠ ⚳	23:30
23 Sa	☽ ☍ ♅	3:39
	☽ ⚼ ♆	5:15
	☽ ⊼ ⚷	5:25
	☉ ⊼ ☽	6:11
	☽ ⚼ ☿	6:27
	☽ ∠ ♃	17:11
24 Su	☽ # ♅	0:59
	☽ ⊻ ⚳	1:02
	☿ # ⚷	5:48
	☽ △ ♆	6:51
	☽ ⚼ ⚷	7:05
	☽ △ ☿	7:11
	☉ ⚼ ☽	9:44
	☽ ∥ ♀	10:16
	☽ ⚹ ♄	11:26
	☿ ☌ ♆	17:29
	☽ ⚹ ♇	17:32
	☽ ⊻ ♃	19:16
	☽ ☍ ♂	22:39
25 M	☽ □ ♀	2:25
	☽ ⊼ ♅	7:47
	☽ ∥ ⚳	8:08
	☽ △ ⚷	9:44
	☽ ∠ ♄	14:16
	☉ △ ☽	14:31
	☽ ∠ ♇	20:31
26 Tu	☽ ☌ ⚳	7:05
	☽ ⚼ ♅	11:27
	☽ □ ☿	12:03
	☽ □ ♆	13:08
	☽ ⊻ ♄	18:11
	♀ ♓	19:44
	☽ # ♂	20:33
27 W	☽ ⊻ ♇	0:36
	☽ ☌ ♃	2:38
	☽ ⊼ ♂	9:11
	☽ ⚹ ♀	16:07
	☽ △ ♅	16:11
	♀ ⚹ ♅	16:46
	☽ □ ⚷	18:18
	☽ ∥ ♄	19:39
28 Th	☽ ∥ ♇	0:14
	☉ □ ☽	4:11
	☿ ∠ ♅	11:40
	☿ D	14:00
	♀ ⊻ ⚷	15:31
	♀ # ♅	15:44
	☽ ⚼ ♂	16:13
	☽ ⊻ ⚳	17:20
	☽ ⚹ ☿	21:49
	☽ ⚹ ♆	23:34
29 F	☽ ∠ ♀	0:57
	☽ ∥ ♇	1:48
	☽ ☌ ♄	5:01
	☽ ∥ ♄	6:47
	☽ ☌ ♇	11:37
	☽ ⊻ ♃	13:54
	☿ ∠ ♅	19:51
	☽ # ♂	23:08
	☽ ∠ ⚳	23:37
30 Sa	☽ △ ♂	0:06
	☽ □ ♅	4:11
	☽ ∠ ☿	4:15
	☽ ∠ ♆	5:53
	☽ ⚹ ⚷	6:25
	☉ ∥ ⚷	9:44
	☽ ⊻ ♀	10:37
	♀ ∠ ♄	19:03
	☽ ∠ ♃	20:24
	☉ ⚹ ☽	21:54
31 Su	♂ ♊	6:13
	☽ ⚹ ⚳	6:17
	☽ ⊻ ☿	11:18
	☽ ⊻ ♆	12:31
	☽ ∠ ⚷	13:07
	☽ ⊻ ♄	18:07
	☽ ∥ ⚳	21:33

April 2019

LONGITUDE

Day	Sid.Time	☉	☽	☽ 12 hour	Mean ☊	True ☊	☿	♀	♂	⚳	♃	♄	⚷	♅	♆	♇
	h m s	° ' "	° ' "	° ' "	° '	° '	° '	° '	° '	° '	° '	° '	° '	° '	° '	° '
1 M	12 36 15	10♈58 37	22♒42 37	28♒36 39	22♋48.0	23♋40.1	16♓37.8	6♓14.0	0♊29.4	14♐03.2	24♐12.2	19♑50.2	2♈23.5	1♉17.2	17♓05.3	23♑00.8
2 Tu	12 40 12	11 57 51	4♓31 45	10♓28 19	22 44.8	23R 34.0	16 58.6	7 26.3	1 09.1	14 06.2	24 13.9	19 52.9	2 27.0	1 20.5	17 07.4	23 01.5
3 W	12 44 09	12 57 04	16 26 44	22 27 15	22 41.7	23 25.0	17 24.1	8 38.6	1 48.8	14 08.8	24 15.4	19 55.6	2 30.5	1 23.8	17 09.5	23 02.1
4 Th	12 48 05	13 56 14	28 30 08	4♈35 34	22 38.5	23 13.5	17 54.1	9 51.0	2 28.5	14 11.0	24 16.8	19 58.1	2 34.0	1 27.1	17 11.6	23 02.8
5 F	12 52 02	14 55 23	10♈43 39	16 54 30	22 35.3	23 00.3	18 28.3	11 03.3	3 08.1	14 12.8	24 18.0	20 00.6	2 37.5	1 30.4	17 13.7	23 03.4
6 Sa	12 55 58	15 54 29	23 08 08	29 24 36	22 32.1	22 46.4	19 06.6	12 15.7	3 47.7	14 14.3	24 18.9	20 02.9	2 41.0	1 33.8	17 15.7	23 03.9
7 Su	12 59 55	16 53 34	5♉43 53	12♉05 58	22 28.9	22 33.0	19 48.8	13 28.2	4 27.3	14 15.3	24 19.7	20 05.2	2 44.4	1 37.1	17 17.8	23 04.5
8 M	13 03 51	17 52 36	18 30 52	24 58 33	22 25.8	22 21.4	20 34.5	14 40.6	5 06.9	14 16.0	24 20.3	20 07.4	2 47.9	1 40.5	17 19.8	23 05.0
9 Tu	13 07 48	18 51 36	1♊29 04	8♊02 27	22 22.6	22 12.3	21 23.7	15 53.0	5 46.5	14R 16.3	24 20.7	20 09.5	2 51.3	1 43.9	17 21.8	23 05.5
10 W	13 11 44	19 50 34	14 38 46	21 18 07	22 19.4	22 06.3	22 16.1	17 05.5	6 26.0	14 16.1	24R 21.0	20 11.5	2 54.8	1 47.3	17 23.8	23 05.9
11 Th	13 15 41	20 49 30	28 00 39	4♋46 29	22 16.2	22 03.0	23 11.6	18 18.0	7 05.5	14 15.6	24 21.0	20 13.4	2 58.2	1 50.7	17 25.8	23 06.3
12 F	13 19 37	21 48 24	11♋35 46	18 28 39	22 13.0	22 01.9	24 10.0	19 30.5	7 45.0	14 14.7	24 20.9	20 15.2	3 01.6	1 54.1	17 27.8	23 06.7
13 Sa	13 23 34	22 47 15	25 25 15	2♌25 37	22 09.9	22 01.8	25 11.2	20 43.0	8 24.5	14 13.4	24 20.5	20 16.9	3 05.0	1 57.5	17 29.7	23 07.1
14 Su	13 27 31	23 46 04	9♌29 47	16 37 39	22 06.7	22 01.4	26 15.1	21 55.5	9 03.9	14 11.7	24 20.0	20 18.5	3 08.4	2 00.9	17 31.7	23 07.4
15 M	13 31 27	24 44 51	23 49 00	1♍03 34	22 03.5	21 59.4	27 21.6	23 08.1	9 43.3	14 09.7	24 19.3	20 20.0	3 11.7	2 04.3	17 33.6	23 07.7
16 Tu	13 35 24	25 43 35	8♍20 51	15 40 16	22 00.3	21 55.0	28 30.5	24 20.6	10 22.7	14 07.2	24 18.4	20 21.5	3 15.1	2 07.7	17 35.5	23 08.0
17 W	13 39 20	26 42 17	23 01 07	0♎22 33	21 57.2	21 47.8	29 41.7	25 33.2	11 02.1	14 04.3	24 17.3	20 22.8	3 18.4	2 11.2	17 37.4	23 08.2
18 Th	13 43 17	27 40 57	7♎43 38	15 03 23	21 54.0	21 38.2	0♈55.3	26 45.8	11 41.5	14 01.0	24 16.0	20 24.0	3 21.7	2 14.6	17 39.2	23 08.4
19 F	13 47 13	28 39 35	22 20 50	29 35 01	21 50.8	21 26.9	2 11.0	27 58.4	12 20.8	13 57.4	24 14.6	20 25.1	3 25.0	2 18.0	17 41.0	23 08.6
20 Sa	13 51 10	29 38 11	6♏45 03	13♏50 11	21 47.6	21 15.3	3 28.9	29 11.0	13 00.1	13 53.4	24 12.9	20 26.2	3 28.3	2 21.5	17 42.9	23 08.8
21 Su	13 55 06	0♉36 45	20 49 46	27 43 20	21 44.4	21 04.6	4 48.8	0♈23.6	13 39.3	13 49.0	24 11.1	20 27.1	3 31.5	2 24.9	17 44.7	23 08.9
22 M	13 59 03	1 35 17	4♐30 36	11♐11 26	21 41.3	20 55.7	6 10.8	1 36.3	14 18.6	13 44.2	24 09.1	20 27.9	3 34.7	2 28.4	17 46.4	23 09.0
23 Tu	14 03 00	2 33 48	17 45 51	24 14 01	21 38.1	20 49.5	7 34.7	2 48.9	14 57.8	13 39.0	24 06.9	20 28.7	3 37.9	2 31.8	17 48.2	23 09.1
24 W	14 06 56	3 32 17	0♑36 16	6♑52 59	21 34.9	20 45.8	9 00.6	4 01.6	15 37.1	13 33.4	24 04.5	20 29.3	3 41.1	2 35.2	17 49.9	23R 09.1
25 Th	14 10 53	4 30 44	13 04 40	19 11 55	21 31.7	20D 44.3	10 28.4	5 14.3	16 16.2	13 27.5	24 02.0	20 29.9	3 44.3	2 38.7	17 51.6	23 09.1
26 F	14 14 49	5 29 09	25 15 20	1♒15 34	21 28.6	20R 44.1	11 58.1	6 27.0	16 55.4	13 21.2	23 59.3	20 30.3	3 47.4	2 42.1	17 53.3	23 09.1
27 Sa	14 18 46	6 27 33	7♒13 19	13 09 15	21 25.4	20 44.3	13 29.6	7 39.7	17 34.6	13 14.5	23 56.4	20 30.7	3 50.5	2 45.6	17 55.0	23 09.0
28 Su	14 22 42	7 25 56	19 04 24	24 58 25	21 22.2	20 43.7	15 03.0	8 52.5	18 13.7	13 07.5	23 53.3	20 30.9	3 53.6	2 49.0	17 56.6	23 09.0
29 M	14 26 39	8 24 17	0♓52 57	6♓48 17	21 19.0	20 41.4	16 38.2	10 05.2	18 52.8	13 00.1	23 50.0	20 31.1	3 56.7	2 52.5	17 58.3	23 08.8
30 Tu	14 30 35	9♉22 36	12 44 59	18 43 33	21♋15.9	20♋36.7	18♈15.3	11♈18.0	19♊31.9	12♐52.3	23♐46.6	20♑31.1	3♈59.7	2♉55.9	17♓59.9	23♑08.7

1st of Month

Julian Day # 2458574.5
Obliquity 23°26'09"
SVP 4♓59'43"
GC 27♐06.5
Eris 23♈30.1

Day	⚴
1	22♎40.7R
6	21 09.4R
11	19 36.0R
16	18 03.5R
21	16 34.6R
26	15 11.7R

Day	⚵
1	20♊35.7
6	22 57.1
11	25 20.0
16	27 44.0
21	0♋08.9
26	2 34.5

Day	⚶
1	28♓44.0
6	1♈07.4
11	3 29.9
16	5 51.3
21	8 11.6
26	10 30.7

DECLINATION and LATITUDE

Day	☉ Decl	☽ Decl	☽ Lat	☽ 12h Decl	☿ Decl	☿ Lat	♀ Decl	♀ Lat	♂ Decl	♂ Lat	⚳ Decl	⚳ Lat	♃ Decl	♃ Lat	♄ Decl	♄ Lat
1 M	4N21	16S16	2S27	14S40	5S30	0S14	10S04	0S54	21N09	0N55	16S34	5N57	22S41	0N38	21S34	0N25
2 Tu	4 44	12 55	3 18	11 02	5 34	0 27	9 40	0 57	21 18	0 56	16 35	5 57	22 41	0 38	21 33	0 25
3 W	5 07	9 03	4 01	6 57	5 35	0 40	9 15	0 59	21 26	0 56	16 36	5 56	22 41	0 38	21 33	0 25
4 Th	5 30	4 46	4 33	2 32	5 34	0 51	8 50	1 02	21 34	0 56	16 38	5 55	22 41	0 38	21 33	0 25
5 F	5 53	0 15	4 53	2N03	5 31	1 03	8 25	1 04	21 42	0 57	16 39	5 54	22 41	0 38	21 32	0 24
6 Sa	6 16	4N20	5 00	6 37	5 26	1 13	7 59	1 07	21 50	0 57	16 40	5 53	22 41	0 38	21 32	0 24
7 Su	6 38	8 50	4 52	10 58	5 19	1 24	7 33	1 09	21 58	0 57	16 41	5 52	22 41	0 38	21 32	0 24
8 M	7 01	13 00	4 30	14 55	5 10	1 33	7 07	1 11	22 06	0 58	16 42	5 51	22 41	0 38	21 32	0 24
9 Tu	7 23	16 39	3 53	18 11	4 58	1 42	6 41	1 13	22 13	0 58	16 43	5 50	22 41	0 38	21 31	0 24
10 W	7 46	19 31	3 04	20 35	4 45	1 50	6 15	1 15	22 20	0 58	16 44	5 49	22 41	0 38	21 31	0 24
11 Th	8 08	21 22	2 03	21 51	4 30	1 58	5 48	1 17	22 27	0 59	16 45	5 48	22 41	0 38	21 31	0 24
12 F	8 30	22 01	0 55	21 51	4 14	2 05	5 22	1 19	22 34	0 59	16 46	5 46	22 41	0 38	21 31	0 24
13 Sa	8 52	21 21	0N18	20 30	3 55	2 11	4 55	1 20	22 41	0 59	16 47	5 45	22 41	0 38	21 30	0 24
14 Su	9 13	19 20	1 31	17 51	3 35	2 17	4 28	1 22	22 47	0 60	16 48	5 44	22 41	0 38	21 30	0 24
15 M	9 35	16 05	2 39	14 04	3 14	2 22	4 00	1 24	22 54	1 00	16 49	5 43	22 41	0 38	21 30	0 24
16 Tu	9 56	11 49	3 39	9 23	2 50	2 27	3 33	1 25	22 60	1 00	16 51	5 41	22 41	0 38	21 30	0 24
17 W	10 18	6 49	4 24	4 08	2 26	2 31	3 06	1 27	23 06	1 01	16 52	5 40	22 41	0 38	21 30	0 24
18 Th	10 39	1 24	4 52	1S20	1 60	2 35	2 38	1 28	23 12	1 01	16 53	5 38	22 41	0 38	21 29	0 24
19 F	10 60	4S03	5 00	6 41	1 32	2 38	2 10	1 29	23 17	1 01	16 54	5 37	22 41	0 38	21 29	0 24
20 Sa	11 21	9 12	4 50	11 34	1 04	2 40	1 43	1 31	23 22	1 02	16 55	5 35	22 41	0 38	21 29	0 24
21 Su	11 41	13 45	4 22	15 43	0 34	2 42	1 15	1 32	23 28	1 02	16 56	5 34	22 40	0 38	21 29	0 24
22 M	12 01	17 27	3 39	18 56	0 02	2 43	0 47	1 33	23 33	1 02	16 57	5 32	22 40	0 38	21 29	0 24
23 Tu	12 22	20 08	2 45	21 03	0N30	2 44	0 19	1 34	23 37	1 02	16 58	5 30	22 40	0 38	21 29	0 24
24 W	12 42	21 41	1 45	22 03	1 04	2 44	0N09	1 35	23 42	1 03	16 59	5 29	22 40	0 38	21 29	0 24
25 Th	13 01	22 07	0 41	21 56	1 38	2 43	0 37	1 36	23 46	1 03	17 00	5 27	22 40	0 38	21 29	0 24
26 F	13 21	21 29	0S24	20 47	2 14	2 42	1 05	1 36	23 51	1 03	17 01	5 25	22 40	0 38	21 29	0 24
27 Sa	13 40	19 51	1 26	18 43	2 51	2 41	1 33	1 37	23 55	1 03	17 02	5 23	22 40	0 38	21 29	0 24
28 Su	13 59	17 23	2 24	15 53	3 29	2 39	2 01	1 38	23 58	1 04	17 04	5 21	22 40	0 38	21 29	0 24
29 M	14 18	14 13	3 16	12 24	4 08	2 36	2 29	1 38	24 02	1 04	17 05	5 19	22 40	0 38	21 29	0 24
30 Tu	14N37	10S28	3S59	8S24	4N48	2S33	2N57	1S39	24N05	1N04	17S06	5N17	22S39	0N38	21S29	0N24

Day	⚷ Decl	⚷ Lat	♅ Decl	♅ Lat	♆ Decl	♆ Lat	♇ Decl	♇ Lat
1	3N46	3N04	11N28	0S29	5S59	0S58	21S43	0S15
6	3 53	3 04	11 33	0 29	5 55	0 58	21 43	0 16
11	3 59	3 04	11 39	0 29	5 52	0 58	21 43	0 16
16	4 06	3 04	11 45	0 29	5 48	0 58	21 43	0 16
21	4 13	3 04	11 51	0 29	5 45	0 59	21 44	0 17
26	4 19	3 04	11 57	0 29	5 41	0 59	21 44	0 17

Day	⚴ Decl	⚴ Lat	⚵ Decl	⚵ Lat	⚶ Decl	⚶ Lat	Eris Decl	Eris Lat
1	15N21	26N01	12N10	10S57	4S52	4S46	1S50	11S46
6	16 54	27 08	12 43	10 33	3 59	4 49	1 48	11 46
11	18 20	28 07	13 12	10 10	3 06	4 53	1 47	11 46
16	19 38	28 56	13 38	9 47	2 13	4 57	1 46	11 46
21	20 46	29 36	14 01	9 25	1 22	5 01	1 44	11 45
26	21 44	30 07	14 20	9 04	0 31	5 05	1 43	11 45

Moon Phenomena

Max/0 Decl
dy hr mn
5 1:20 0 N
12 0:02 22N01
18 6:09 0 S
24 21:24 22S08

Perigee/Apogee
dy hr m kilometers
1 0:11 a 405577
16 22:14 p 364205
28 18:27 a 404581

Max/0 Lat
dy hr mn
5 23:24 5S00
12 18:09 0 N
18 22:44 5N01
25 15:03 0 S

PH dy hr mn
● 5 8:52 15♈17
☽ 12 19:07 22♋35
○ 19 11:13 29♎07
☾ 26 22:19 6♒23

Void of Course Moon

Last Aspect		☽ Ingress
1 3:03	♃ ✱	♓ 1 14:49
3 15:37	♃ □	♈ 4 2:58
6 2:16	♃ △	♉ 6 13:07
8 8:30	♇ △	♊ 8 21:16
10 17:28	♃ ☍	♋ 11 3:32
12 23:34	♀ △	♌ 13 7:51
15 1:40	☉ △	♍ 15 10:15
17 4:30	♀ ☍	♎ 17 11:23
19 11:13	☉ ☍	♏ 19 12:42
21 4:01	♇ ✱	♐ 21 16:00
23 11:45	♃ ☌	♑ 23 22:51
25 19:49	♇ ☌	♒ 26 9:28
28 9:45	♃ ✱	♓ 28 22:13

DAILY ASPECTARIAN

1 M ☽⊻♇ 0:37 · ☽✱♃ 3:03 · ☉∠☽ 7:15 · ☽□♂ 16:45 · ☽✱♅ 17:31 · ☽⊻⚷ 19:46

2 Tu ☽∠♄ 0:43 · ☽☌♀ 6:33 · ☽∠♇ 7:04 · ♂⊻♅ 7:30 · ☽#♅ 9:14 · ☿☌♆ 9:37 · ♀∠♇ 11:48 · ☉⊻☽ 16:21 · ☽□⚳ 19:22 · ☽∥♀ 22:41 · ☽∠♅ 23:54

3 W ☽☌♆ 1:26 · ☽☌☿ 1:59 · ☽✱♄ 6:59 · ☽✱♇ 13:10 · ⚶ ♈ 15:29 · ☽□♃ 15:37 · ☽∥♆ 17:32 · ☽∥☿ 19:36 · ♂#♄ 19:38 · ☉#☽ 20:22

4 Th ♂✱⚷ 3:41 · ☉#☿ 4:16 · ☽#⚷ 5:03 · ☽⊻♅ 5:51 · ☉△⚳ 6:12 · ☽☌⚷ 8:03 · ☽✱♂ 8:17

5 F ☽⊻♀ 0:43 · ♂#♇ 1:15 · ☉#♆ 3:35 · ☽△⚳ 6:48 · ☉☌☽ 8:52 · ☽⊻♆ 12:39 · ☽∠♂ 15:11 · ☽⊻☿ 15:49 · ☽□♄ 18:03 · ☽∥⚷ 21:33 · ☽□♇ 23:52

6 Sa ☽△♃ 2:16 · ☽#☿ 5:37 · ☽#♆ 8:19 · ☽∠♀ 8:45 · ☉∥☽ 11:03 · ☽⚼⚳ 11:41 · ☽☌♅ 16:10 · ☽∠♆ 17:28 · ☽#♀ 17:40 · ☽⊻⚷ 18:18 · ☽⊻♂ 21:27 · ☽∠☿ 22:09

7 Su ☽⚼♃ 6:48 · ☿✱♄ 9:19 · ☉⊻♆ 10:12 · ☽∥♅ 15:34 · ♀□⚳ 15:48 · ☽⊼⚳ 16:04 · ☽✱♀ 16:05 · ☽✱♆ 21:47 · ☽∠⚷ 22:40 · ☉⊻☽ 22:43

8 M ♂⚼♄ 0:19 · ☽△♄ 3:00 · ☉#♀ 3:15 · ☽✱☿ 4:05 · ☽△♇ 8:30 · ☽⊼♃ 10:50

9 Tu ☽⊻♅ 0:27 · ☽#⚳ 0:31 · ☽✱⚷ 2:32 · ⚳ R 4:36 · ☉∠☽ 4:43 · ☽⚼♄ 6:45 · ☽☌♂ 8:17 · ☽⚼♇ 12:06 · ♀∠♅ 17:39 · ☽☍⚳ 23:19

10 W ☽∠♅ 3:53 · ☽□♀ 4:52 · ☽□♆ 4:59 · ♀☌♆ 6:14 · ☉□♄ 8:48 · ☽⊼♄ 10:02 · ☉✱☽ 10:07 · ☽□☿ 14:44 · ☽⊼♇ 15:14 · ♃ R 17:02 · ☽☍♃ 17:28 · ♀∥♆ 20:52 · ☿✱♇ 21:47

11 Th ☽#♄ 2:57 · ☽✱♅ 6:51 · ☽#♇ 7:50 · ☽□⚷ 8:51 · ☽⊻♂ 16:54

12 F ☿□♃ 4:19 · ☽⊼⚳ 4:38 · ☽△♆ 10:16 · ♂⚼♇ 13:20 · ☽△♀ 15:06 · ☽☍♄ 15:07 · ♀✱♄ 15:09 · ☿#⚷ 15:59 · ☽#♇ 16:00 · ☉□☽ 19:07 · ☽☍♇ 20:02 · ☽∠♂ 20:22 · ☽#♄ 20:55 · ☽⊼♃ 22:09 · ☽△☿ 23:34 · ♂#♃ 23:39

13 Sa ☽⚼⚳ 6:31 · ☉□♇ 8:08 · ☽□♅ 11:15 · ☽⚼♆ 12:09 · ☽△⚷ 13:10 · ☽⚼♀ 19:15 · ☽✱♂ 23:14 · ☽⚼♃ 23:43

14 Su ☽⚼☿ 3:13 · ☽△⚳ 7:54 · ☽⊼♆ 13:32 · ☉△♃ 13:42 · ☽⚼⚷ 14:35 · ☽⊼♄ 18:11 · ☽#⚳ 19:14 · ♀#⚷ 20:27 · ☉∠♂ 22:08 · ☽⊼♀ 22:46 · ☽⊼♇ 22:51 · ♀✱♇ 23:53

15 M ☽△♃ 0:50 · ☉△☽ 1:40 · ☽⊼☿ 6:23 · ☽△♅ 13:43 · ☽⊼⚷ 15:35 · ☽⚼♄ 19:05 · ♀□♃ 23:16 · ☽⚼♇ 23:39

16 Tu ☽∥♅ 0:19 · ☽□♂ 3:29 · ☉⚼☽ 4:11 · ☉∥☽ 8:41 · ☽□⚳ 9:26 · ☽⚼♅ 14:26 · ☽☍♆ 15:10 · ☽△♄ 19:41

17 W ☽△♇ 0:12 · ☽□♃ 2:04 · ☽☍♀ 4:30 · ☽#♆ 4:38 · ☿ ♈ 6:02 · ☉⊼☽ 6:26 · ☽☍☿ 11:52 · ☽∥⚷ 12:01 · ☽⊼♅ 15:01 · ☽☍⚷ 16:51 · ☽#♀ 18:07 · ☽#☿ 21:11

18 Th ☽△♂ 6:47 · ☽✱⚳ 10:15 · ☽∥☿ 13:46 · ☽⊼♆ 16:18 · ☽∥♀ 16:20 · ☽□♄ 20:49

19 F ☽#⚷ 0:32 · ☽□♇ 1:19 · ☿⊻♅ 2:18 · ☽✱♃ 3:08 · ☉⚼⚳ 6:51 · ☽∥♆ 7:46 · ☽⚼♂ 8:40 · ☽⊼♀ 10:10 · ☽∠⚳ 10:54 · ☉☍☽ 11:13 · ☽☍♅ 16:36 · ☽⚼♆ 17:13 · ☽⊼☿ 17:57 · ☽⊼⚷ 18:28 · ☿☌⚷ 23:48

20 Sa ☽∠♃ 4:09 · ☉ ♉ 8:56 · ☽⊼♂ 11:06 · ☉#☽ 11:42 · ☽⊻⚳ 12:02 · ☽#♅ 13:28 · ☽⚼♀ 13:47 · ♀ ♈ 16:12 · ⚵ ♋ 16:39 · ☽△♆ 18:41 · ☽⚼⚷ 20:01 · ☽⚼☿ 22:04 · ☽✱♄ 23:21

21 Su ☽✱♇ 4:01 · ♂☍⚳ 5:15 · ☽⊻♃ 5:48 · ☉∥♅ 12:29 · ☽△♀ 18:20 · ☉⊼☽ 18:25 · ☽∥⚳ 20:19 · ☽⊼♅ 20:22 · ☉⊻♀ 22:20 · ☽△⚷ 22:20

22 M ☽∠♄ 1:42 · ☽△☿ 3:20 · ☽∠♇ 6:31 · ☽☌⚳ 16:31 · ♀⊻♅ 18:04 · ☽☍♂ 18:36 · ☿#♀ 19:41 · ☉☌♅ 23:08 · ☽⚼♅ 23:34 · ☉⚼☽ 23:36

23 Tu ☽□♆ 0:04 · ☽⊻♄ 5:01 · ☉∠♆ 6:05 · ☽⊻♇ 9:59 · ☽☌♃ 11:45 · ♀☌⚷ 16:56 · ☽∥♄ 19:29

24 W ☽∥♇ 1:00 · ☽△♅ 3:47 · ☉⊻⚷ 3:51 · ☽□⚷ 5:54 · ☉△☽ 6:03 · ☽□♀ 7:13 · ☽□☿ 18:15 · ♇ R 18:49

25 Th ☽⊻⚳ 0:44 · ☽⊼♂ 6:36 · ☽✱♆ 9:23 · ☽☌♄ 14:34 · ☽∥♇ 17:57 · ☽☌♇ 19:49 · ☽⊻♃ 21:29 · ☽∥♄ 23:52

26 F ☽∠⚳ 6:07 · ☽⚼♂ 14:06 · ☽□♅ 14:58 · ☽∠♆ 15:18 · ☽✱⚷ 17:10 · ☿△⚳ 20:20 · ☉□☽ 22:19

27 Sa ☽✱♀ 0:59 · ☽∠♃ 3:27 · ♂∠♅ 7:24 · ☽✱⚳ 12:04 · ♂□♆ 13:05 · ☽✱☿ 14:36 · ☽⊻♆ 21:43 · ☽△♂ 22:12 · ☽∠⚷ 23:39

28 Su ☽∥⚳ 2:44 · ☽⊻♄ 2:56 · ☽⊻♇ 8:17 · ☽✱♃ 9:45 · ☽∠♀ 10:53 · ☉#☽ 23:26

29 M ☽∠☿ 1:46 · ☽✱♅ 4:04 · ☽⊻⚷ 6:14 · ☿∥⚷ 9:16 · ☽∠♄ 9:24 · ☉⚼♃ 10:00 · ☽#♅ 14:24 · ☽∠♇ 14:43 · ☉✱☽ 16:36 · ☿⊻♆ 20:10 · ☽⊻♀ 20:45

30 Tu ☽□⚳ 0:15 · ♄ R 0:55 · ☽∠♅ 10:28 · ☽☌♆ 10:34 · ☽⊻☿ 12:48 · ☽□♂ 14:24 · ☽✱♄ 15:35 · ☽✱♇ 20:49 · ☽□♃ 21:58

LONGITUDE

y	Sid.Time	☉	☽	☽ 12 hour	Mean☊	True☊	☿	♀	♂	⚳	♃	♄	⚷	♅	♆	♇
	h m s	° ' "	° ' "	° ' "	° '	° '	° '	° '	° '	° '	° '	° '	° '	° '	° '	° '
V	14 34 32	10♉20 54	24♓44 29	0♈48 10	21♋12.7	20♋29.6	19♈54.1	12♈30.7	20♊11.0	12♐44.2	23♐43.0	20♑31.1	4♈02.8	2♉59.3	18♓01.4	23♑08.5
h	14 38 29	11 19 10	6♈54 57	13 05 06	21 09.5	20R 20.1	21 34.8	13 43.5	20 50.0	12R 35.8	23R 39.2	20R 30.9	4 05.7	3 02.7	18 03.0	23R 08.3
	14 42 25	12 17 24	19 18 47	25 36 10	21 06.3	20 08.9	23 17.3	14 56.3	21 29.1	12 27.0	23 35.2	20 30.7	4 08.7	3 06.2	18 04.5	23 08.1
a	14 46 22	13 15 37	1♉57 17	8♉22 06	21 03.1	19 57.1	25 01.6	16 09.1	22 08.1	12 17.9	23 31.1	20 30.4	4 11.6	3 09.6	18 06.0	23 07.9
u	14 50 18	14 13 48	14 50 34	21 22 34	21 00.0	19 45.6	26 47.8	17 21.9	22 47.1	12 08.5	23 26.9	20 29.9	4 14.5	3 13.0	18 07.5	23 07.6
1	14 54 15	15 11 57	27 57 55	4♊36 26	20 56.8	19 35.7	28 35.8	18 34.7	23 26.1	11 58.8	23 22.4	20 29.4	4 17.4	3 16.4	18 08.9	23 07.3
u	14 58 11	16 10 05	11♊17 55	18 02 10	20 53.6	19 28.0	0♉25.6	19 47.5	24 05.1	11 48.8	23 17.8	20 28.8	4 20.2	3 19.8	18 10.3	23 06.9
V	15 02 08	17 08 11	24 48 59	1♋38 12	20 50.4	19 23.0	2 17.3	21 00.4	24 44.0	11 38.5	23 13.1	20 28.0	4 23.0	3 23.1	18 11.7	23 06.6
h	15 06 04	18 06 16	8♋29 40	15 23 15	20 47.3	19D 20.6	4 10.8	22 13.2	25 22.9	11 27.9	23 08.2	20 27.2	4 25.8	3 26.5	18 13.1	23 06.2
	15 10 01	19 04 18	22 18 52	29 16 26	20 44.1	19 20.1	6 06.1	23 26.0	26 01.9	11 17.1	23 03.1	20 26.3	4 28.6	3 29.9	18 14.4	23 05.7
a	15 13 58	20 02 18	6♌15 51	13♌17 05	20 40.9	19 20.7	8 03.3	24 38.9	26 40.7	11 06.0	22 57.9	20 25.3	4 31.3	3 33.2	18 15.7	23 05.3
u	15 17 54	21 00 17	20 20 02	27 24 35	20 37.7	19R 21.2	10 02.2	25 51.7	27 19.6	10 54.7	22 52.6	20 24.2	4 33.9	3 36.5	18 17.0	23 04.8
1	15 21 51	21 58 13	4♍30 34	11♍37 46	20 34.5	19 20.5	12 02.9	27 04.6	27 58.5	10 43.1	22 47.1	20 23.0	4 36.6	3 39.9	18 18.3	23 04.3
u	15 25 47	22 56 08	18 45 55	25 54 39	20 31.4	19 17.9	14 05.3	28 17.4	28 37.3	10 31.3	22 41.5	20 21.7	4 39.2	3 43.2	18 19.5	23 03.8
V	15 29 44	23 54 01	3♎03 33	10♎12 06	20 28.2	19 13.1	16 09.3	29 30.3	29 16.1	10 19.3	22 35.8	20 20.3	4 41.8	3 46.5	18 20.7	23 03.2
h	15 33 40	24 51 52	17 19 45	24 25 56	20 25.0	19 06.3	18 14.8	0♉43.2	29 54.9	10 07.2	22 29.9	20 18.8	4 44.3	3 49.7	18 21.9	23 02.6
	15 37 37	25 49 42	1♏30 00	8♏31 20	20 21.8	18 58.1	20 21.7	1 56.0	0♋33.6	9 54.8	22 23.9	20 17.2	4 46.8	3 53.0	18 23.0	23 02.0
a	15 41 33	26 47 30	15 29 23	22 23 36	20 18.7	18 49.6	22 29.9	3 08.9	1 12.4	9 42.3	22 17.8	20 15.6	4 49.3	3 56.2	18 24.1	23 01.4
u	15 45 30	27 45 16	29 13 30	5♐58 44	20 15.5	18 41.7	24 39.3	4 21.8	1 51.1	9 29.7	22 11.5	20 13.8	4 51.7	3 59.5	18 25.2	23 00.7
1	15 49 27	28 43 01	12♐39 02	19 14 13	20 12.3	18 35.2	26 49.5	5 34.7	2 29.8	9 16.9	22 05.2	20 12.0	4 54.1	4 02.7	18 26.3	23 00.0
u	15 53 23	29 40 45	25 44 15	2♑09 11	20 09.1	18 30.8	29 00.5	6 47.6	3 08.5	9 03.9	21 58.7	20 10.1	4 56.4	4 05.9	18 27.3	22 59.3
V	15 57 20	0♊38 28	8♑29 12	14 44 32	20 06.0	18D 28.4	1♊11.9	8 00.6	3 47.2	8 50.9	21 52.2	20 08.1	4 58.7	4 09.1	18 28.3	22 58.6
h	16 01 16	1 36 09	20 55 32	27 02 38	20 02.8	18 27.9	3 23.5	9 13.5	4 25.8	8 37.8	21 45.5	20 06.0	5 01.0	4 12.2	18 29.2	22 57.8
	16 05 13	2 33 50	3♒06 19	9♒07 07	19 59.6	18 28.8	5 35.1	10 26.5	5 04.5	8 24.6	21 38.8	20 03.8	5 03.3	4 15.4	18 30.2	22 57.1
a	16 09 09	3 31 29	15 05 36	21 02 23	19 56.4	18 30.2	7 46.3	11 39.4	5 43.1	8 11.3	21 31.9	20 01.5	5 05.5	4 18.5	18 31.1	22 56.3
u	16 13 06	4 29 07	26 58 05	2♓53 21	19 53.2	18R 31.3	9 56.9	12 52.4	6 21.7	7 57.9	21 25.0	19 59.2	5 07.6	4 21.6	18 32.0	22 55.4
1	16 17 02	5 26 44	8♓48 48	14 45 06	19 50.1	18 31.6	12 06.6	14 05.4	7 00.3	7 44.6	21 18.0	19 56.8	5 09.7	4 24.6	18 32.8	22 54.6
u	16 20 59	6 24 20	20 42 51	26 42 39	19 46.9	18 30.3	14 15.2	15 18.4	7 38.9	7 31.2	21 10.9	19 54.3	5 11.8	4 27.7	18 33.6	22 53.7
V	16 24 56	7 21 56	2♈45 02	8♈50 31	19 43.7	18 27.4	16 22.4	16 31.4	8 17.4	7 17.8	21 03.7	19 51.7	5 13.8	4 30.7	18 34.4	22 52.8
h	16 28 52	8 19 30	14 59 35	21 12 36	19 40.5	18 22.9	18 28.0	17 44.4	8 56.0	7 04.4	20 56.4	19 49.0	5 15.8	4 33.7	18 35.1	22 51.9
	16 32 49	9♊17 04	27 29 54	3♉51 43	19♋37.4	18♋17.2	20♊31.7	18♉57.4	9♋34.5	6♐51.0	20♐49.1	19♑46.2	5♈17.8	4♉36.7	18♓35.9	22♑50.9

1st of Month

Julian Day # 2458604.5
Obliquity 23°26'09"
SVP 4♓59'40"
GC 27♐06.6
Eris 23♈49.6

Day	⚴
1	13♎56.9R
6	12 51.9R
11	11 58.1R
16	11 16.2R
21	10 46.4R
26	10 28.6R
31	10 22.5R

Day	⚵
1	5♋00.8
6	7 27.5
11	9 54.5
16	12 21.6
21	14 48.8
26	17 15.8
31	19 42.8

Day	⚶
1	12♈48.6
6	15 05.1
11	17 20.2
16	19 33.7
21	21 45.6
26	23 55.7
31	26 04.0

DECLINATION and LATITUDE

y	☉ Decl	☽ Decl	☽ Lat	☽12h Decl	☿ Decl	☿ Lat	♀ Decl	♀ Lat	♂ Decl	♂ Lat	⚳ Decl	⚳ Lat	♃ Decl	♃ Lat	♄ Decl	♄ Lat
V	14N55	6S16	4S33	4S02	5N28	2S30	3N25	1S39	24N09	1N04	17S07	5N15	22S39	0N38	21S29	0N23
h	15 13	1 46	4 54	0N33	6 10	2 25	3 53	1 40	24 12	1 05	17 08	5 13	22 39	0 38	21 29	0 23
	15 31	2N54	5 02	5 13	6 52	2 21	4 21	1 40	24 14	1 05	17 09	5 10	22 39	0 38	21 29	0 23
a	15 49	7 31	4 56	9 46	7 35	2 16	4 49	1 40	24 17	1 05	17 10	5 08	22 39	0 38	21 29	0 23
u	16 06	11 55	4 34	13 57	8 19	2 10	5 17	1 40	24 20	1 05	17 12	5 06	22 39	0 38	21 29	0 23
1	16 24	15 50	3 58	17 32	9 03	2 04	5 44	1 40	24 22	1 06	17 13	5 03	22 38	0 38	21 29	0 23
u	16 40	19 01	3 08	20 16	9 48	1 57	6 12	1 40	24 24	1 06	17 14	5 01	22 38	0 38	21 30	0 23
V	16 57	21 13	2 07	21 52	10 33	1 50	6 39	1 40	24 26	1 06	17 15	4 58	22 38	0 38	21 30	0 23
h	17 13	22 12	0 58	22 12	11 18	1 42	7 07	1 40	24 27	1 06	17 16	4 56	22 38	0 38	21 30	0 23
	17 29	21 51	0N16	21 10	12 04	1 34	7 34	1 39	24 29	1 06	17 17	4 53	22 38	0 38	21 30	0 23
a	17 45	20 09	1 29	18 49	12 50	1 26	8 01	1 39	24 30	1 06	17 19	4 50	22 37	0 38	21 30	0 23
u	18 00	17 12	2 38	15 20	13 37	1 17	8 28	1 39	24 31	1 07	17 20	4 48	22 37	0 38	21 30	0 23
1	18 15	13 14	3 37	10 56	14 23	1 08	8 54	1 38	24 32	1 07	17 21	4 45	22 37	0 37	21 31	0 23
u	18 30	8 29	4 24	5 55	15 08	0 58	9 21	1 37	24 33	1 07	17 22	4 42	22 37	0 37	21 31	0 23
V	18 45	3 17	4 54	0 36	15 54	0 48	9 47	1 37	24 33	1 07	17 24	4 39	22 36	0 37	21 31	0 23
h	18 59	2S06	5 06	4S45	16 39	0 38	10 13	1 36	24 33	1 07	17 25	4 36	22 36	0 37	21 31	0 23
	19 13	7 19	4 59	9 47	17 23	0 28	10 39	1 35	24 34	1 08	17 26	4 33	22 36	0 37	21 32	0 23
a	19 26	12 07	4 34	14 15	18 07	0 17	11 05	1 35	24 33	1 08	17 27	4 30	22 36	0 37	21 32	0 23
u	19 39	16 11	3 53	17 53	18 49	0 07	11 30	1 34	24 33	1 08	17 29	4 27	22 35	0 37	21 32	0 23
1	19 52	19 19	3 01	20 30	19 30	0N04	11 55	1 33	24 33	1 08	17 30	4 23	22 35	0 37	21 33	0 23
u	20 05	21 23	1 59	21 58	20 10	0 14	12 20	1 32	24 32	1 08	17 31	4 20	22 35	0 37	21 33	0 23
V	20 17	22 16	0 54	22 17	20 48	0 25	12 45	1 31	24 31	1 08	17 33	4 17	22 34	0 37	21 33	0 22
h	20 29	22 02	0S13	21 21	21 24	0 35	13 09	1 29	24 30	1 08	17 34	4 13	22 34	0 37	21 34	0 22
	20 40	20 44	1 18	19 44	21 58	0 45	13 33	1 28	24 29	1 08	17 35	4 10	22 34	0 37	21 34	0 22
a	20 51	18 31	2 19	17 07	22 30	0 55	13 57	1 27	24 27	1 09	17 37	4 07	22 33	0 37	21 34	0 22
u	21 02	15 33	3 13	13 49	22 59	1 04	14 20	1 26	24 26	1 09	17 38	4 03	22 33	0 37	21 35	0 22
1	21 12	11 57	3 59	9 58	23 26	1 13	14 43	1 24	24 24	1 09	17 39	3 59	22 33	0 37	21 35	0 22
u	21 22	7 53	4 35	5 43	23 51	1 21	15 06	1 23	24 22	1 09	17 41	3 56	22 32	0 36	21 36	0 22
V	21 32	3 28	4 59	1 11	24 12	1 28	15 28	1 21	24 20	1 09	17 42	3 52	22 32	0 36	21 36	0 22
h	21 41	1N09	5 09	3N29	24 31	1 35	15 50	1 20	24 17	1 09	17 44	3 49	22 31	0 36	21 37	0 22
	21N50	5N49	5S06	8N07	24N47	1N42	16N12	1S18	24N15	1N09	17S45	3N45	22S31	0N36	21S37	0N22

Day	⚷ Decl	⚷ Lat	♅ Decl	♅ Lat	♆ Decl	♆ Lat	♇ Decl	♇ Lat
1	4N25	3N04	12N03	0S29	5S38	0S59	21S45	0S18
6	4 31	3 04	12 09	0 29	5 36	0 59	21 45	0 18
11	4 37	3 04	12 14	0 29	5 33	0 59	21 46	0 19
16	4 42	3 04	12 20	0 29	5 31	0 59	21 47	0 19
21	4 47	3 05	12 26	0 29	5 29	0 60	21 48	0 20
26	4 52	3 05	12 31	0 29	5 27	0 60	21 49	0 20
31	4N57	3N06	12N36	0S29	5S26	1S00	21S51	0S21

Day	⚴ Decl	⚴ Lat	⚵ Decl	⚵ Lat	⚶ Decl	⚶ Lat	Eris Decl	Eris Lat
1	22N31	30N30	14N37	8S44	0N18	5S09	1S42	11S45
6	23 08	30 44	14 50	8 25	1 07	5 14	1 41	11 45
11	23 35	30 52	14 59	8 06	1 54	5 18	1 40	11 45
16	23 52	30 55	15 06	7 48	2 40	5 23	1 39	11 46
21	24 01	30 52	15 09	7 30	3 24	5 28	1 38	11 46
26	24 02	30 46	15 09	7 13	4 07	5 33	1 37	11 46
31	23N55	30N36	15N07	6S57	4N48	5S39	1S37	11S46

Moon Phenomena

Max/0 Decl
dy hr mn
2 9:07 0 N
9 5:40 22N15
15 14:38 0 S
22 6:36 22S19
29 18:06 0 N

Max/0 Lat
dy hr mn
3 1:30 5S02
9 18:51 0 N
16 2:51 5N06
22 19:13 0 S
30 6:29 5S10

Perigee/Apogee
dy hr m kilometers
13 21:52 p 369009
26 13:30 a 404135

PH dy hr mn
● 4 22:47 14♉11
☽ 12 1:13 21♌03
○ 18 21:13 27♏39
☾ 26 16:35 5♓09

Void of Course Moon

Last Aspect	☽ Ingress
30 21:58 ♃ □	♈ 1 10:25
3 8:48 ♀ ☌	♉ 3 20:19
5 15:11 ♇ △	♊ 6 3:41
7 23:51 ♂ ☌	♋ 8 9:08
10 2:07 ♀ □	♌ 10 13:15
12 12:26 ♂ ✱	♍ 12 16:23
14 17:20 ♂ □	♎ 14 18:52
16 9:39 ♇ □	♏ 16 21:27
18 21:13 ☉ ☍	♐ 19 1:22
20 17:06 ♃ ☌	♑ 21 7:57
23 3:59 ♇ ☌	♒ 23 17:50
25 12:52 ♃ ✱	♓ 26 6:09
28 4:22 ♇ ✱	♈ 28 18:33
30 15:09 ♇ □	♉ 31 4:44

DAILY ASPECTARIAN

☉∠☽ 1:19
☽∥♆ 3:24
☽#☿ 3:43
♀△⚳ 4:00
☿#♆ 5:44
☿✱♂ 6:39
☿□♄ 8:51
☽#⚷ 9:56
♂⚻♄ 12:19
☽#♀ 13:51
☽⚺♅ 16:23
☽☌⚷ 18:27

♅∠♆ 2:51
☉⚺☽ 9:18
☽△⚳ 10:56
☽☌♀ 14:40
☽⚺♆ 21:37
☿□♇ 21:52

☽□♄ 2:18
☉⚻⚳ 3:26
☿△♃ 4:00
☽✱♂ 4:23
♀∥⚷ 5:52
☽□♇ 7:18
☽∥⚷ 8:05
☽△♃ 8:07
☽∥♀ 8:20
☽☌☿ 8:48
☽#♆ 14:02
☽⚼⚳ 15:19

☽∥☿ 0:24
☽∠♆ 2:09
☽☌♅ 2:16
☽⚺⚷ 4:13
☽∠♂ 10:13
☽⚼♃ 12:13
☽⚻⚳ 19:04
☉☌☽ 22:47

5 Su ☽∥♅ 1:14
☿⚼⚳ 4:15
☽⚺♀ 5:07
☽✱♆ 6:03
☽∠⚷ 8:07
☽△♄ 10:23
♂⚻♇ 12:30
☽△♇ 15:11
♀⚺♆ 15:19
☽⚺♂ 15:20
☽⚻♃ 15:42
♀#♆ 16:34
♂☍♃ 21:58

6 M ☽⚺☿ 1:20
☉∥☽ 4:06
☽#⚳ 9:38
☽⚺♅ 9:38
☽∠♀ 11:10
☽✱⚷ 11:28
☽⚼♄ 13:35
☽⚼♇ 18:18
☿ ♉ 18:26

7 Tu ☽☍⚳ 0:54
☽∠☿ 8:32
☉⚺☽ 9:21
☽□♆ 12:16
☽∠♅ 12:34
♀□♄ 13:27
☽⚻♄ 16:19
☽✱♀ 16:36
☽⚻♇ 20:59
☽☍♃ 21:12
☽☌♂ 23:51

8 W ☽#♄ 4:25
☽#♇ 9:30
☿∠♆ 11:42
☉∠☽ 13:51
☿☌♅ 14:24
☽✱♅ 15:08
☽✱☿ 15:15
☽□⚷ 16:52

9 Th ☉✱♆ 2:53
☿⚺⚷ 3:13
☉#⚳ 4:47
☽⚻⚳ 5:07
♃⚺♇ 10:31
☽△♆ 16:56
♀△♃ 16:57
♀□♇ 17:21
☉✱☽ 17:58
☽☍♄ 20:46

10 F ☽⚻♃ 1:16
☽☍♇ 1:21
☽#♇ 1:49
☽□♀ 2:07
☿∥♅ 4:49
☽⚺♂ 6:44
☽#♄ 6:45
☽⚼⚳ 6:46
☉∠⚷ 10:32
☽⚼♆ 18:51
☽□♅ 19:20
☽△⚷ 21:00
☿⚼♃ 22:57

11 Sa ☽⚼♃ 2:54
☽□☿ 3:34
☽△⚳ 8:10
☉△♄ 9:20
☽∠♂ 9:42
☉∥☽ 18:41
☽⚻♆ 20:31
☽⚼⚷ 22:41
☽#⚳ 23:07

12 Su ☽⚻♄ 0:07
♀⚼⚳ 0:50
☉□☽ 1:13
☽△♃ 4:17
☽⚻♇ 4:40
☿⚻⚳ 9:33
☽△♀ 10:15
☽✱♂ 12:26
☽∥☿ 18:34
☽△♅ 22:34

13 M ☽⚻⚷ 0:10
☽⚼♄ 1:28
☽∥♅ 5:03
☽⚼♇ 6:00
☽□⚳ 10:19
☽⚼♀ 13:56
☽△☿ 14:49
☿∠♂ 16:01
☉⚻♃ 18:29
☽∥♀ 20:12
☽☍♆ 23:16
☽⚼♅ 23:55

14 Tu ☽△♄ 2:41
☉△♇ 3:08
☽□♃ 6:33
☽△♇ 7:13
☉△☽ 7:31
☽#♆ 13:49
♀✱♂ 13:59
☽□♂ 17:20
☽⚻♀ 17:29
☽∥⚷ 17:39
☽⚼☿ 20:15

15 W ☽⚻♅ 1:12
☽☍⚷ 2:45
♀ ♉ 9:47
☉⚼☽ 10:31
☽✱⚳ 12:02

16 Th ☿✱♆ 1:21
☽⚻♆ 1:45
☽⚻☿ 1:49
♂ ♋ 3:10
☽□♄ 5:02
☽✱♃ 8:40
☽□♇ 9:39
☽#⚷ 11:51
☽∠⚳ 12:59
☉⚻☽ 13:40
☽∥♆ 15:31
☿∠⚷ 17:17
☽△♂ 22:19
☿△♄ 23:10

17 F ☽☍♀ 0:49
☿#⚳ 1:32
☽⚼♆ 3:13
☽☍♅ 4:05
☽⚻⚷ 5:37
☽∠♃ 10:00
☽⚺⚳ 14:11
☽#♀ 18:02
☿⚻♃ 21:50

18 Sa ☽⚼♂ 1:18
☽#♅ 1:25
☽△♆ 5:03
♀∠♆ 5:05
☿△♇ 5:49
☽⚼⚷ 7:32
☽✱♄ 8:16
☽⚺♃ 11:45
☽✱♇ 13:05
☽☍☿ 14:27
♀☌♅ 16:18
☉☍☽ 21:13

19 Su ☽⚻♂ 4:53
☽⚻♅ 8:29
☽∥⚳ 9:03
☽⚻♀ 10:01
☽△⚷ 10:02
♀⚺⚷ 10:10
☽∠♄ 10:38
☽∠♇ 15:38
☽☌⚳ 18:01

20 M ☽#☿ 2:18
☉#☽ 5:47
☽□♆ 10:33
☽⚼♅ 11:42
☽⚺♄ 13:44
☽⚼♀ 15:57
☽☌♃ 17:06
☽⚺♇ 18:55
☉∥☿ 19:16

21 Tu ☽∥♄ 2:59
♀⚼♃ 3:21
♀∥♅ 5:22
☽⚻☿ 7:21
☉⚻☽ 7:57
☉ ♊ 8:00
☽∥♇ 8:02
☿ ♊ 10:53
☉☌☿ 13:08
☽☍♂ 14:36
☽△♅ 15:44
☽□⚷ 17:19
☽△♀ 23:00

22 W ☽⚺⚳ 0:41
♀⚻⚳ 14:02
♂✱♅ 14:47
☉⚼☽ 14:53
☽⚼☿ 18:00
☽✱♆ 19:15
☽☌♄ 22:24

23 Th ☽⚺♃ 1:37
☽☌♇ 3:59
☽∠⚳ 5:12
☽∥♇ 5:38
☿#♄ 6:42
☿⚺♅ 9:06
☽#☿ 9:31
☽∥♄ 10:49
☿⚺♂ 16:06
☿#♇ 17:16
☿✱⚷ 18:06
☿⚼♄ 18:23
☉△☽ 22:50
♂□⚷ 23:12

24 F ☉#☽ 0:45
☽∠♆ 0:48
☽□♅ 2:18
☽✱⚷ 3:54
☽⚻♂ 4:09
☽△☿ 6:02
☽∠♃ 6:59
☽✱⚳ 10:23
☽□♀ 16:18

25 Sa ☿⚼♇ 1:49
☿#♃ 2:37
☿☍⚳ 4:09
☽⚺♆ 6:55
☽∥⚳ 7:54
☽⚺♄ 9:55
☽∠⚷ 10:07
☽⚼♂ 12:00
☽✱♃ 12:52
☽⚺♇ 15:49
☉⚺♅ 20:41

26 Su ⚳∠♇ 4:50
☽#♀ 7:38
☉⚼♄ 12:02
☽✱♅ 15:03
☽∠♄ 16:12
☉□☽ 16:35
☽⚺⚷ 16:35
☉✱⚷ 16:39
☽△♂ 20:08
☽#♅ 20:23
☽□⚳ 21:52
☽∠♇ 22:10

27 M ☽□☿ 8:08
☽✱♀ 11:53
☽☌♆ 19:40
♂⚻⚳ 20:27
☽∠♅ 21:28
☽✱♄ 22:23

28 Tu ☽□♃ 0:56
☽✱♇ 4:22
☽∥♆ 13:28
☽#⚷ 16:20
☽∠♀ 21:18
☉☍⚳ 22:36

29 W ☽⚺♅ 3:30
☿⚺♀ 4:02
☽☌⚷ 4:55
☿∥♂ 7:50
☽△⚳ 8:48
☉✱☽ 9:53
☉#♄ 10:41
☽□♂ 11:31
☉⚼♇ 12:40

30 Th ☿□♆ 1:23
☽⚺♀ 5:54
☽⚺♆ 6:57
☽✱☿ 8:04
☽□♄ 9:17
☽△♃ 11:22
☿∠♅ 13:01
☽⚼⚳ 13:25
☽□♇ 15:09
☿⚻♄ 15:20
♀✱♆ 16:51
☉∠☽ 17:23
☽∥⚷ 19:29
☽#♆ 22:01

31 F ☉#♇ 0:42
⚴ D 2:53
☿☍♃ 3:13
☽∠♆ 11:31
☽☌♅ 13:27
☽⚺⚷ 14:43
♀△♄ 15:27
☽⚼♃ 15:31
☽⚻⚳ 17:17
☽∠☿ 17:57
☉⚺♂ 22:03
☽✱♂ 23:50
☉⚺☽ 23:53

June 2019

LONGITUDE

Day	Sid.Time	☉	☽	☽ 12 hour	Mean☊	True☊	☿	♀	♂	⚳	♃	♄	⚷	♅	♆	♇
	h m s	° ' "	° ' "	° ' "	° '	° '	° '	° '	° '	° '	° '	° '	° '	° '	° '	° '
1 Sa	16 36 45	10♊14 36	10♉18 14	16♉49 31	19♋34.2	18♋10.8	22♊33.5	20♉10.4	10♋13.1	6♐37.7	20♐41.8	19♑43.4	5♈19.7	4♉39.7	18♓36.5	22♑50.0
2 Su	16 40 42	11 12 08	23 25 31	0♊06 10	19 31.0	18R 04.6	24 33.1	21 23.5	10 51.6	6R 24.4	20R 34.3	19R 40.5	5 21.5	4 42.6	18 37.2	22R 49.0
3 M	16 44 38	12 09 39	6♊51 13	13 40 27	19 27.8	17 59.2	26 30.5	22 36.5	11 30.1	6 11.2	20 26.9	19 37.5	5 23.3	4 45.5	18 37.8	22 48.0
4 Tu	16 48 35	13 07 09	20 33 29	27 29 56	19 24.6	17 55.3	28 25.6	23 49.6	12 08.6	5 58.1	20 19.4	19 34.5	5 25.1	4 48.4	18 38.4	22 47.0
5 W	16 52 31	14 04 38	4♋29 23	11♋31 22	19 21.5	17D 53.0	0♋18.2	25 02.7	12 47.0	5 45.1	20 11.8	19 31.4	5 26.8	4 51.3	18 39.0	22 45.9
6 Th	16 56 28	15 02 06	18 35 26	25 41 07	19 18.3	17 52.3	2 08.2	26 15.7	13 25.5	5 32.2	20 04.2	19 28.2	5 28.5	4 54.1	18 39.5	22 44.9
7 F	17 00 25	15 59 32	2♌47 59	9♌55 37	19 15.1	17 52.9	3 55.8	27 28.8	14 03.9	5 19.5	19 56.6	19 24.9	5 30.1	4 56.9	18 40.0	22 43.8
8 Sa	17 04 21	16 56 58	17 03 38	24 11 42	19 11.9	17 54.3	5 40.7	28 41.9	14 42.4	5 06.8	19 49.0	19 21.6	5 31.7	4 59.7	18 40.4	22 42.7
9 Su	17 08 18	17 54 22	1♍19 29	8♍26 42	19 08.8	17 55.6	7 23.0	29 55.0	15 20.8	4 54.4	19 41.4	19 18.2	5 33.3	5 02.4	18 40.9	22 41.5
10 M	17 12 14	18 51 46	15 33 04	22 38 20	19 05.6	17R 56.4	9 02.6	1♊08.1	15 59.2	4 42.1	19 33.7	19 14.8	5 34.7	5 05.1	18 41.3	22 40.4
11 Tu	17 16 11	19 49 08	29 42 16	6♎44 37	19 02.4	17 56.1	10 39.6	2 21.2	16 37.6	4 30.0	19 26.0	19 11.3	5 36.2	5 07.8	18 41.6	22 39.2
12 W	17 20 07	20 46 28	13♎45 08	20 43 36	18 59.2	17 54.6	12 13.8	3 34.4	17 15.9	4 18.1	19 18.4	19 07.7	5 37.6	5 10.5	18 41.9	22 38.1
13 Th	17 24 04	21 43 48	27 39 46	4♏33 22	18 56.1	17 51.9	13 45.4	4 47.5	17 54.3	4 06.4	19 10.7	19 04.1	5 38.9	5 13.1	18 42.2	22 36.9
14 F	17 28 00	22 41 07	11♏24 11	18 11 58	18 52.9	17 48.6	15 14.1	6 00.6	18 32.6	3 55.0	19 03.1	19 00.4	5 40.2	5 15.7	18 42.5	22 35.7
15 Sa	17 31 57	23 38 26	24 56 30	1♐37 35	18 49.7	17 45.0	16 40.2	7 13.8	19 11.0	3 43.8	18 55.5	18 56.7	5 41.5	5 18.2	18 42.7	22 34.5
16 Su	17 35 54	24 35 43	8♐15 03	14 48 45	18 46.5	17 41.7	18 03.4	8 27.0	19 49.3	3 32.8	18 47.9	18 52.9	5 42.7	5 20.8	18 42.9	22 33.2
17 M	17 39 50	25 33 00	21 18 36	27 44 33	18 43.4	17 39.1	19 23.7	9 40.1	20 27.6	3 22.1	18 40.3	18 49.1	5 43.8	5 23.3	18 43.1	22 32.0
18 Tu	17 43 47	26 30 16	4♑06 37	10♑24 51	18 40.2	17 37.5	20 41.2	10 53.3	21 05.9	3 11.6	18 32.8	18 45.2	5 44.9	5 25.7	18 43.2	22 30.7
19 W	17 47 43	27 27 31	16 39 24	22 50 25	18 37.0	17D 36.9	21 55.8	12 06.5	21 44.2	3 01.4	18 25.3	18 41.3	5 46.0	5 28.1	18 43.3	22 29.4
20 Th	17 51 40	28 24 47	28 58 09	5♒02 53	18 33.8	17 37.3	23 07.4	13 19.8	22 22.5	2 51.5	18 17.8	18 37.3	5 47.0	5 30.5	18 43.4	22 28.1
21 F	17 55 36	29 22 01	11♒04 59	17 04 48	18 30.7	17 38.3	24 16.0	14 33.0	23 00.7	2 41.8	18 10.4	18 33.3	5 48.0	5 32.9	18R 43.4	22 26.8
22 Sa	17 59 33	0♋19 16	23 02 47	28 59 25	18 27.5	17 39.7	25 21.4	15 46.3	23 39.0	2 32.5	18 03.1	18 29.3	5 48.9	5 35.2	18 43.4	22 25.5
23 Su	18 03 30	1 16 30	4♓55 12	10♓50 39	18 24.3	17 41.1	26 23.7	16 59.5	24 17.2	2 23.5	17 55.8	18 25.2	5 49.7	5 37.5	18 43.4	22 24.2
24 M	18 07 26	2 13 44	16 46 21	22 42 52	18 21.1	17 42.2	27 22.7	18 12.8	24 55.4	2 14.8	17 48.5	18 21.0	5 50.5	5 39.7	18 43.4	22 22.9
25 Tu	18 11 23	3 10 58	28 40 48	4♈40 42	18 17.9	17R 42.8	28 18.4	19 26.1	25 33.7	2 06.4	17 41.4	18 16.9	5 51.3	5 41.9	18 43.3	22 21.5
26 W	18 15 19	4 08 11	10♈43 10	16 48 46	18 14.8	17 42.8	29 10.6	20 39.4	26 11.9	1 58.3	17 34.3	18 12.7	5 52.0	5 44.1	18 43.1	22 20.1
27 Th	18 19 16	5 05 25	22 58 02	29 11 29	18 11.6	17 42.1	29 59.3	21 52.8	26 50.1	1 50.5	17 27.2	18 08.4	5 52.6	5 46.2	18 43.0	22 18.8
28 F	18 23 12	6 02 39	5♉29 33	11♉52 39	18 08.4	17 41.0	0♌44.4	23 06.1	27 28.3	1 43.1	17 20.3	18 04.2	5 53.2	5 48.3	18 42.8	22 17.4
29 Sa	18 27 09	6 59 53	18 21 06	24 55 08	18 05.2	17 39.7	1 25.6	24 19.5	28 06.5	1 36.0	17 13.4	17 59.9	5 53.8	5 50.4	18 42.6	22 16.0
30 Su	18 31 05	7♋57 06	1♊34 54	8♊20 24	18♋02.1	17♋38.4	2♌03.0	25♊32.9	28♋44.7	1♐29.3	17♐06.7	17♑55.6	5♈54.3	5♉52.4	18♓42.3	22♑14.6

1st of Mo
Julian Da
2458635.
Obliquit
23°26'09
SVP 4♓59'
GC 27♐0
Eris 24♈0

Day	⚴
1	10♎22
6	10 30
11	10 48
16	11 16
21	11 54.
26	12 40.

Day	⚵
1	20♋12
6	22 38.
11	25 05.
16	27 31.
21	29 56
26	2♌21

Day	⚶
1	26♈29.
6	28 35.
11	0♉39.
16	2 40
21	4 39.
26	6 35.

DECLINATION and LATITUDE

Day	☉ Decl	☽ Decl	☽ Lat	☽12h Decl	☿ Decl	☿ Lat	♀ Decl	♀ Lat	♂ Decl	♂ Lat	⚳ Decl	⚳ Lat	♃ Decl	♃ Lat	♄ Decl	♄ Lat
1 Sa	21N59	10N21	4S47	12N30	25N01	1N48	16N33	1S17	24N12	1N09	17S47	3N41	22S31	0N36	21S38	0N22
2 Su	22 07	14 32	4 14	16 24	25 12	1 52	16 54	1 15	24 09	1 09	17 48	3 37	22 30	0 36	21 38	0 22
3 M	22 15	18 05	3 25	19 32	25 20	1 57	17 15	1 13	24 06	1 10	17 50	3 34	22 30	0 36	21 38	0 22
4 Tu	22 22	20 43	2 23	21 36	25 26	2 00	17 34	1 11	24 02	1 10	17 51	3 30	22 29	0 36	21 39	0 22
5 W	22 29	22 09	1 12	22 22	25 29	2 03	17 54	1 09	23 59	1 10	17 53	3 26	22 29	0 36	21 39	0 22
6 Th	22 36	22 13	0N04	21 42	25 30	2 05	18 13	1 08	23 55	1 10	17 54	3 22	22 28	0 36	21 40	0 22
7 F	22 42	20 50	1 21	19 39	25 28	2 06	18 32	1 06	23 51	1 10	17 56	3 18	22 28	0 35	21 41	0 22
8 Sa	22 48	18 09	2 33	16 22	25 25	2 06	18 50	1 04	23 47	1 10	17 58	3 14	22 28	0 35	21 41	0 21
9 Su	22 53	14 22	3 36	12 09	25 19	2 06	19 07	1 02	23 43	1 10	17 59	3 10	22 27	0 35	21 42	0 21
10 M	22 58	9 46	4 25	7 16	25 12	2 05	19 25	0 60	23 38	1 10	18 01	3 06	22 27	0 35	21 42	0 21
11 Tu	23 03	4 40	4 58	2 02	25 03	2 03	19 41	0 58	23 34	1 10	18 03	3 02	22 26	0 35	21 43	0 21
12 W	23 07	0S37	5 13	3S15	24 52	2 00	19 57	0 56	23 29	1 10	18 05	2 58	22 26	0 35	21 43	0 21
13 Th	23 11	5 50	5 09	8 19	24 40	1 57	20 13	0 53	23 24	1 10	18 06	2 55	22 25	0 35	21 44	0 21
14 F	23 14	10 41	4 48	12 55	24 26	1 53	20 28	0 51	23 19	1 10	18 08	2 51	22 25	0 35	21 44	0 21
15 Sa	23 17	14 57	4 10	16 47	24 11	1 48	20 42	0 49	23 14	1 10	18 10	2 47	22 24	0 34	21 45	0 21
16 Su	23 20	18 23	3 20	19 44	23 54	1 42	20 56	0 47	23 08	1 10	18 12	2 43	22 24	0 34	21 46	0 21
17 M	23 22	20 49	2 20	21 38	23 37	1 36	21 10	0 45	23 02	1 11	18 14	2 39	22 23	0 34	21 46	0 21
18 Tu	23 23	22 09	1 14	22 22	23 19	1 29	21 23	0 42	22 57	1 11	18 16	2 35	22 23	0 34	21 47	0 21
19 W	23 25	22 19	0 05	21 59	22 59	1 22	21 35	0 40	22 51	1 11	18 18	2 31	22 22	0 34	21 47	0 21
20 Th	23 26	21 23	1S02	20 32	22 40	1 13	21 46	0 38	22 44	1 11	18 20	2 27	22 22	0 34	21 48	0 21
21 F	23 26	19 28	2 06	18 11	22 19	1 04	21 57	0 35	22 38	1 11	18 22	2 23	22 21	0 34	21 49	0 21
22 Sa	23 26	16 43	3 03	15 05	21 58	0 55	22 08	0 33	22 32	1 11	18 24	2 19	22 21	0 33	21 49	0 21
23 Su	23 26	13 19	3 52	11 24	21 36	0 45	22 18	0 31	22 25	1 11	18 26	2 15	22 20	0 33	21 50	0 20
24 M	23 25	9 23	4 32	7 17	21 15	0 34	22 27	0 28	22 18	1 11	18 28	2 11	22 20	0 33	21 51	0 20
25 Tu	23 24	5 06	4 59	2 51	20 52	0 23	22 35	0 26	22 11	1 11	18 30	2 07	22 19	0 33	21 51	0 20
26 W	23 22	0 35	5 14	1N44	20 30	0 11	22 43	0 23	22 04	1 11	18 33	2 03	22 19	0 33	21 52	0 20
27 Th	23 20	4N03	5 15	6 21	20 08	0S01	22 50	0 21	21 57	1 11	18 35	1 59	22 18	0 33	21 52	0 20
28 F	23 18	8 37	5 01	10 49	19 46	0 14	22 57	0 18	21 49	1 11	18 37	1 55	22 18	0 32	21 53	0 20
29 Sa	23 15	12 55	4 32	14 55	19 24	0 27	23 03	0 16	21 42	1 11	18 40	1 51	22 17	0 32	21 54	0 20
30 Su	23N12	16N45	3S48	18N23	19N02	0S41	23N08	0S14	21N34	1N11	18S42	1N47	22S17	0N32	21S54	0N20

Day	⚷ Decl	⚷ Lat	♅ Decl	♅ Lat	♆ Decl	♆ Lat	♇ Decl	♇ La
1	4N57	3N06	12N37	0S29	5S26	1S00	21S51	0
6	5 01	3 06	12 42	0 29	5 25	1 00	21 52	0
11	5 05	3 07	12 46	0 29	5 24	1 01	21 54	0
16	5 08	3 07	12 50	0 29	5 24	1 01	21 55	0
21	5 10	3 08	12 54	0 29	5 24	1 01	21 57	0
26	5 12	3 08	12 58	0 30	5 24	1 01	21 58	0

Day	⚴ Decl	⚴ Lat	⚵ Decl	⚵ Lat	⚶ Decl	⚶ Lat	Eris Decl	Eris La
1	23N53	30N34	15N06	6S53	4N56	5S40	1S36	11
6	23 39	30 22	14 60	6 38	5 35	5 45	1 36	11
11	23 20	30 08	14 51	6 22	6 13	5 51	1 36	11
16	22 56	29 53	14 39	6 07	6 48	5 57	1 35	11
21	22 28	29 37	14 24	5 53	7 22	6 03	1 35	11
26	21 57	29 22	14 08	5 39	7 53	6 10	1 35	11

Moon Phenomena

Max/0 Decl

dy	hr mn	
5	13:02	22N21
11	21:11	0 S
18	15:32	22S23
26	3:00	0 N

Max/0 Lat

dy	hr mn	
5	22:47	0 N
12	7:04	5N13
19	1:52	0 S
26	13:46	5S16

Perigee/Apogee

dy	hr m		kilometers
7	23:21	p	368504
23	7:47	a	404546

PH	dy	hr mn	
●	3	10:03	12♊34
☽	10	6:00	19♍06
○	17	8:32	25♐53
☾	25	9:48	3♈34

Void of Course Moo

Last Aspect				☽ Ingre		
1	22:54	♇	△	♊	2	11
4	15:43	☿	☌	♋	4	16
6	14:11	♀	⚹	♌	6	19
8	21:24	♀	□	♍	8	21
10	12:03	♇	△	♎	11	0
12	15:16	♇	□	♏	13	4
14	19:47	♇	⚹	♐	15	9
17	8:32	☉	☍	♑	17	16
19	11:20	☿	☍	♒	20	2
21	14:03	♃	⚹	♓	22	14
24	23:11	☿	△	♈	25	2
27	7:52	♂	□	♉	27	13
29	18:39	♂	⚹	♊	29	21

DAILY ASPECTARIAN

1 Sa
♀∠⚷ 3:07
☿⊼♇ 3:15
♀⊼♃ 9:21
☽∥♅ 12:40
☽⚹♆ 15:16
☽△♄ 17:13
☽∠⚷ 18:26
☽⊼♃ 18:53
☽☌♀ 19:57
☽△♇ 22:54

2 Su
☽⊻☿ 2:23
☽∠♂ 4:37
☽∥♀ 17:06
☽⚼♄ 20:04
☽⊻♅ 20:17
☽⚹⚷ 21:24
☽#⚳ 22:04
☽☍⚳ 22:50

3 M
☽⚼♇ 1:40
♀△♇ 3:43
☽⊻♂ 8:36
☉☌☽ 10:03
☽□♆ 20:40
☽⊼♄ 22:18
☽∠♅ 22:41
☽☍♃ 23:36

4 Tu
☽⊼♇ 3:51
☽⊻♀ 6:12
☽#♄ 13:01
☽☌☿ 15:43
☽#♇ 16:57
☿ ♋ 20:06
♀#⚳ 22:29
☉#♃ 23:03

5 W
☽⚹♅ 0:38
☽□⚷ 1:38
☽⊼⚳ 2:08
☽∠♀ 10:23
☽☌♂ 14:49
☉⊻☽ 17:32

6 Th
☽△♆ 0:07
☽☍♄ 1:29
☽⊼♃ 2:29
☽⚼⚳ 3:15
⚳△⚷ 6:10
☽☍♇ 7:02
☽#♇ 8:44
☽#♄ 12:27
☽⚹♀ 14:11
☉∠☽ 20:44
♃⚼♅ 23:20

7 F
☽⚼♆ 1:28
☽⊻☿ 2:10
☽⚼♃ 3:35
☽□♅ 3:38
☽△⚳ 4:11
☽△⚷ 4:34
☿⚹♅ 14:18
☿⊼⚳ 17:02
☽∥♀ 19:17
☽⊻♂ 19:51
☿□⚷ 21:54
☉⚹☽ 23:48

8 Sa
☽#⚳ 1:20
☽⊼♆ 2:43
☽⊼♄ 3:51
☽△♃ 4:36
☽⚼⚷ 5:51
☽∠☿ 6:55
☽⊼♇ 9:29
⚳⊼♅ 11:16
☽□♀ 21:24
☽∠♂ 22:17

9 Su
♀ ♊ 1:38
☽⚼♄ 5:00
☽□⚳ 5:57
☽△♅ 6:17
☽⊼⚷ 7:08
☽∥♅ 8:50
⚶ ♉ 9:56
☽⚼♇ 10:43
☽⚹☿ 11:34
♀∠♂ 17:49
☉□♆ 19:35

10 M
☽⚹♂ 0:46
☽☍♆ 5:19
☉□☽ 6:00
☽△♄ 6:14
☽□♃ 6:44
☽⚼♅ 7:42
☉⊼♄ 9:05
☽△♇ 12:03
☉☍♃ 15:29
☽#♆ 20:39
☽∥⚷ 22:08

11 Tu
☽△♀ 4:56
☽⚹⚳ 8:03
☉∠♅ 8:12
☽⊼♅ 9:16
☽☍⚷ 10:04
☽□☿ 21:04

12 W
☽□♂ 6:20
☽⊼♆ 8:30
☽⚼♀ 9:05
☽□♄ 9:12
☽∠⚳ 9:25
☽⚹♃ 9:28
♀⚼♄ 10:26
♀☍⚳ 12:23
☉△☽ 12:58
☽□♇ 15:16
☽#⚷ 20:34
☽∥♆ 21:58

13 Th
⚳∠♄ 7:08
♀⊻♅ 8:42
☽⚼♆ 10:31
☽⊻⚳ 11:04
☽∠♃ 11:14
☽☍♅ 13:12
☽⊼♀ 13:37
☽⊼⚷ 13:56
☉⚼☽ 16:59
♀⚹⚷ 17:11
☉⊼♇ 21:46

14 F
♂△♆ 6:12
☽△☿ 7:34
♂⚼⚳ 10:48
☽#♅ 11:30
☽△♆ 12:54
☽△♂ 13:14
☽⚹♄ 13:22
☽⊻♃ 13:23
☉∥♂ 13:52
♂☍♄ 15:51
♂⊼♃ 15:54
☽⚼⚷ 16:25
♃⊻♄ 16:29
☽⚹♇ 19:47
☉⊼☽ 21:30

15 Sa
♀⚼♇ 6:40
☽⚼☿ 13:30
☽☌⚳ 15:35
☽∠♄ 16:07
☽⚼♂ 17:28
☽⊼♅ 18:42
☽△⚷ 19:23
☽∥⚳ 22:28
☽∠♇ 22:44

16 Su
☽☍♀ 0:24
☿⚼⚳ 7:40
☿△♆ 11:44
☿⊼♃ 12:03
☿☍♄ 14:02
♃□♆ 15:23
☽☌♃ 19:10
☽□♆ 19:12
☽⊻♄ 19:24
☽⊼☿ 20:03
☽⚼♅ 22:17
☽⊼♂ 22:21

17 M
☽⊻♇ 2:16
☽#♀ 5:16
☉☍☽ 8:32
☽∥♄ 14:54
☽∥♇ 18:11
☉∥☿ 18:24
☽⊻⚳ 22:17

18 Tu
☽△♅ 2:30
☽□⚷ 3:07
♄⚹♆ 11:48
☽⊼♀ 14:18
☿☌♂ 16:06
☽∥♃ 18:21
☽∥♃ 18:21

19 W
☽∠⚳ 2:36
☽⊻♃ 3:23
☽☌♄ 3:55
☽⚹♆ 4:00
☽☍♂ 10:23
☿☍♇ 10:57
☽☌♇ 11:18
☽☍☿ 11:20
☽∥♇ 12:55
☿∥♂ 15:40
☽∥♄ 16:08
☽#♀ 17:41
☽⚼♀ 22:36
☉⊼☽ 22:49

20 Th
♂☍♇ 3:27
♀#♄ 3:42
☽⚹⚳ 7:34
☽∠♃ 8:27
☽∠♆ 9:23
☽□♅ 12:57
☽⚹⚷ 13:29
☿#♃ 21:26
♀#♇ 22:19

21 F
⚵ ♌ 2:38
☉⚼☽ 7:08
☽△♀ 7:43
☽∥⚳ 10:17
☽⚹♃ 14:03
♆ R 14:37
☽⊻♄ 14:53
☽⊻♆ 15:18
☉ ♋ 15:55
☿∥♀ 16:26
☽∠⚷ 19:30
☽⊻♇ 22:45

22 Sa
☿#♇ 0:59
☽⊼♂ 1:17
☽⊼☿ 5:07
☿#♄ 9:22
☉△☽ 15:59
☽□⚳ 18:57
☽∠♄ 20:59

23 Su
☽⚹♅ 1:26
☽⊻⚷ 1:51
☽#♅ 2:26
☽∠♇ 5:01
♀#♃ 6:15
☽⚼♂ 9:21
♀∥♂ 10:54
☽⚼☿ 14:19
♀☍♃ 16:46
♂#♃ 18:02

24 M
☉⊼⚳ 0:23
☽□♃ 2:04
♀⊼♄ 2:33
☽⚹♄ 3:10
☽□♀ 3:15
☽☌♆ 3:56
☽∠♅ 7:53
♀□♆ 10:00
☽⚹♇ 11:18
☽△♂ 17:23
☽∥♆ 22:22
☽△☿ 23:11
☽#⚷ 23:27

25 Tu
☽△⚳ 6:47
☉□☽ 9:48
☽⊻♅ 14:05
☽☌⚷ 14:22

26 W
♀∠♅ 1:35
☽⚼⚳ 12:11
☽△♃ 13:21
☽□♄ 14:39
☽⊻♆ 15:44
♂#♇ 17:52
☽⚹♀ 21:39
☽□♇ 22:44

27 Th
☿ ♌ 0:21
☽∥⚷ 6:05
☽#♆ 7:04
☽□♂ 7:52
♀⊼♇ 8:21
♂#♄ 12:22
☽□☿ 14:24
☽⊼⚳ 16:54
☉⚹♅ 17:46
☽⚼♃ 18:04
☉□⚷ 20:01
☽∠♆ 20:38

28 F
☽☌♅ 0:36
☽⊻⚷ 0:45
☉⚹☽ 1:08
☽∠♀ 5:27
☽⊼♃ 21:56
☽△♄ 23:21

29 Sa
☽∥♅ 0:27
☽⚹♆ 0:39
☽∠⚷ 4:40
☿△⚳ 5:29
☽△♇ 7:10
☉∠☽ 7:12
☽⊻♀ 12:02
☽⚹♂ 18:39
☽☍⚳ 23:50

30 Su
☽⚹☿ 0:52
☿⚼♃ 2:08
☽⚼♄ 2:23
☽⊻♅ 7:39
☽⚹⚷ 7:42
☽⚼♇ 10:03
☉∥♀ 10:52
☉⊻☽ 12:10
☽#⚳ 14:43
☽∥☿ 15:25
☿#⚳ 20:34
☽∠♂ 22:31

LONGITUDE

July 2019

Day	Sid.Time	☉	☽	☽ 12 hour	Mean ☊	True ☊	☿	♀	♂	⚳	♃	♄	⚷	♅	♆	♇
	h m s	° ' "	° ' "	° ' "	° '	° '	° '	° '	° '	° '	° '	° '	° '	° '	° '	° '
1 M	18 35 02	8♋54 20	15♊11 35	22♊08 13	17♋58.9	17♋37.4	2♌36.3	26♊46.3	29♋22.9	1♐23.0	17♐00.0	17♑51.3	5♈54.7	5♉54.4	18♓42.0	22♑13.2
2 Tu	18 38 59	9 51 34	29 09 59	6♋16 27	17 55.7	17R 36.7	3 05.5	27 59.7	0♌01.0	1R 16.9	16R 53.5	17R 46.9	5 55.1	5 56.3	18R 41.7	22R 11.8
3 W	18 42 55	10 48 48	13♋27 03	20 41 08	17 52.5	17D 36.4	3 30.5	29 13.1	0 39.2	1 11.3	16 47.0	17 42.6	5 55.5	5 58.2	18 41.4	22 10.4
4 Th	18 46 52	11 46 01	27 58 00	5♌16 51	17 49.4	17 36.5	3 51.1	0♋26.6	1 17.4	1 06.0	16 40.6	17 38.2	5 55.8	6 00.1	18 41.0	22 09.0
5 F	18 50 48	12 43 15	12♌36 55	19 57 22	17 46.2	17 36.7	4 07.2	1 40.0	1 55.6	1 01.1	16 34.4	17 33.8	5 56.0	6 01.9	18 40.6	22 07.5
6 Sa	18 54 45	13 40 28	27 17 27	4♍36 26	17 43.0	17 37.1	4 18.8	2 53.5	2 33.7	0 56.5	16 28.3	17 29.4	5 56.2	6 03.7	18 40.1	22 06.1
7 Su	18 58 41	14 37 41	11♍53 38	19 08 28	17 39.8	17 37.4	4R 25.7	4 07.0	3 11.9	0 52.3	16 22.3	17 25.0	5 56.3	6 05.4	18 39.6	22 04.6
8 M	19 02 38	15 34 54	26 20 26	3♎29 07	17 36.6	17 37.6	4 27.9	5 20.5	3 50.0	0 48.5	16 16.4	17 20.5	5R 56.4	6 07.1	18 39.1	22 03.2
9 Tu	19 06 34	16 32 06	10♎34 12	17 35 27	17 33.5	17R 37.7	4 25.4	6 34.0	4 28.1	0 45.1	16 10.7	17 16.1	5 56.4	6 08.7	18 38.6	22 01.7
10 W	19 10 31	17 29 19	24 32 42	1♏25 53	17 30.3	17D 37.7	4 18.2	7 47.6	5 06.2	0 42.0	16 05.1	17 11.7	5 56.4	6 10.3	18 38.0	22 00.3
11 Th	19 14 28	18 26 31	8♏14 58	14 59 57	17 27.1	17 37.7	4 06.4	9 01.1	5 44.4	0 39.3	15 59.6	17 07.3	5 56.3	6 11.9	18 37.4	21 58.8
12 F	19 18 24	19 23 43	21 40 56	28 17 58	17 23.9	17 37.9	3 50.0	10 14.7	6 22.5	0 37.0	15 54.3	17 02.8	5 56.2	6 13.4	18 36.8	21 57.4
13 Sa	19 22 21	20 20 55	4♐51 11	11♐20 42	17 20.8	17 38.1	3 29.3	11 28.2	7 00.6	0 35.1	15 49.1	16 58.4	5 56.0	6 14.8	18 36.2	21 55.9
14 Su	19 26 17	21 18 07	17 46 38	24 09 10	17 17.6	17 38.4	3 04.5	12 41.8	7 38.7	0 33.5	15 44.0	16 54.0	5 55.8	6 16.3	18 35.5	21 54.5
15 M	19 30 14	22 15 19	0♑28 25	6♑44 32	17 14.4	17 38.8	2 35.9	13 55.4	8 16.8	0 32.3	15 39.1	16 49.6	5 55.5	6 17.6	18 34.8	21 53.0
16 Tu	19 34 10	23 12 32	12 57 41	19 08 03	17 11.2	17R 39.0	2 03.8	15 09.1	8 54.9	0 31.4	15 34.4	16 45.3	5 55.2	6 19.0	18 34.0	21 51.6
17 W	19 38 07	24 09 44	25 15 47	1♒21 05	17 08.1	17 38.9	1 28.8	16 22.7	9 32.9	0D 31.0	15 29.8	16 40.9	5 54.8	6 20.3	18 33.3	21 50.1
18 Th	19 42 03	25 06 58	7♒24 09	13 25 14	17 04.9	17 38.5	0 51.3	17 36.4	10 11.0	0 30.9	15 25.4	16 36.5	5 54.3	6 21.5	18 32.5	21 48.6
19 F	19 46 00	26 04 11	19 24 33	25 22 25	17 01.7	17 37.7	0 11.9	18 50.1	10 49.1	0 31.1	15 21.1	16 32.2	5 53.8	6 22.7	18 31.6	21 47.2
20 Sa	19 49 57	27 01 25	1♓19 06	7♓14 58	16 58.5	17 36.6	29♋31.4	20 03.8	11 27.2	0 31.7	15 16.9	16 27.9	5 53.3	6 23.8	18 30.8	21 45.7
21 Su	19 53 53	27 58 40	13 10 21	19 05 40	16 55.3	17 35.2	28 50.2	21 17.5	12 05.2	0 32.7	15 13.0	16 23.6	5 52.7	6 24.9	18 29.9	21 44.3
22 M	19 57 50	28 55 55	25 01 21	0♈57 50	16 52.2	17 33.7	28 09.3	22 31.2	12 43.3	0 34.0	15 09.2	16 19.3	5 52.1	6 26.0	18 29.0	21 42.8
23 Tu	20 01 46	29 53 11	6♈55 38	12 55 14	16 49.0	17 32.4	27 29.2	23 45.0	13 21.4	0 35.7	15 05.6	16 15.1	5 51.4	6 27.0	18 28.1	21 41.4
24 W	20 05 43	0♌50 27	18 57 09	25 01 57	16 45.8	17 31.5	26 50.7	24 58.8	13 59.4	0 37.7	15 02.1	16 10.9	5 50.6	6 27.9	18 27.1	21 40.0
25 Th	20 09 39	1 47 45	1♉10 11	7♉22 21	16 42.6	17D 31.1	26 14.6	26 12.6	14 37.5	0 40.1	14 58.8	16 06.7	5 49.8	6 28.9	18 26.1	21 38.5
26 F	20 13 36	2 45 04	13 39 02	20 00 42	16 39.5	17 31.4	25 41.5	27 26.4	15 15.6	0 42.9	14 55.7	16 02.5	5 49.0	6 29.7	18 25.1	21 37.1
27 Sa	20 17 32	3 42 23	26 27 49	3♊00 48	16 36.3	17 32.3	25 12.0	28 40.2	15 53.7	0 46.0	14 52.7	15 58.4	5 48.1	6 30.5	18 24.1	21 35.7
28 Su	20 21 29	4 39 43	9♊39 59	16 25 35	16 33.1	17 33.5	24 46.8	29 54.1	16 31.7	0 49.4	14 50.0	15 54.3	5 47.2	6 31.3	18 23.0	21 34.3
29 M	20 25 26	5 37 05	23 17 45	0♋16 27	16 29.9	17 34.7	24 26.2	1♌08.0	17 09.8	0 53.1	14 47.4	15 50.3	5 46.2	6 32.0	18 21.9	21 32.8
30 Tu	20 29 22	6 34 27	7♋21 32	14 32 41	16 26.8	17R 35.7	24 10.8	2 21.9	17 47.9	0 57.3	14 45.0	15 46.3	5 45.1	6 32.7	18 20.8	21 31.5
31 W	20 33 19	7♌31 51	21 49 25	29 11 04	16♋23.6	17♋35.8	24♋01.0	3♌35.8	18♌26.0	1♐01.7	14♐42.7	15♑42.3	5♈44.0	6♉33.3	18♓19.7	21♑30.1

1st of Month

Julian Day # 2458665.5
Obliquity 23°26'09"
SVP 4♓59'31"
GC 27♐06.7
Eris 24♈17.6

Day	⚴
1	13♎33.8
6	14 34.9
11	15 42.6
16	16 56.3
21	18 15.6
26	19 39.9
31	21 08.8

Day	⚵
1	4♌46.3
6	7 10.3
11	9 33.6
16	11 56.2
21	14 18.0
26	16 39.0
31	18 59.3

Day	⚶
1	8♉28.5
6	10 18.6
11	12 05.2
16	13 48.3
21	15 27.4
26	17 02.3
31	18 32.5

DECLINATION and LATITUDE

Day	☉ Decl	☽ Decl	☽ Lat	☽ 12h Decl	☿ Decl	☿ Lat	♀ Decl	♀ Lat	♂ Decl	♂ Lat	⚳ Decl	⚳ Lat	♃ Decl	♃ Lat	♄ Decl	♄ Lat
1 M	23N08	19N48	2S50	20N56	18N41	0S55	23N13	0S11	21N26	1N11	18S45	1N44	22S16	0N32	21S55	0N20
2 Tu	23 04	21 45	1 41	22 15	18 20	1 09	23 17	0 09	21 18	1 11	18 47	1 40	22 16	0 32	21 56	0 20
3 W	22 60	22 22	0 23	22 07	18 00	1 24	23 20	0 06	21 10	1 11	18 50	1 36	22 15	0 32	21 56	0 20
4 Th	22 55	21 30	0N57	20 30	17 41	1 39	23 22	0 04	21 01	1 11	18 52	1 32	22 15	0 31	21 57	0 20
5 F	22 50	19 10	2 14	17 31	17 23	1 54	23 24	0 01	20 53	1 11	18 55	1 29	22 14	0 31	21 58	0 19
6 Sa	22 44	15 35	3 23	13 25	17 05	2 09	23 25	0N01	20 44	1 11	18 58	1 25	22 14	0 31	21 58	0 19
7 Su	22 38	11 04	4 18	8 34	16 49	2 25	23 26	0 04	20 35	1 11	19 00	1 21	22 14	0 31	21 59	0 19
8 M	22 32	5 59	4 56	3 19	16 33	2 40	23 26	0 06	20 26	1 11	19 03	1 18	22 13	0 31	21 60	0 19
9 Tu	22 25	0 39	5 15	2S01	16 19	2 55	23 25	0 08	20 17	1 11	19 06	1 14	22 13	0 31	22 00	0 19
10 W	22 18	4S37	5 15	7 09	16 06	3 10	23 23	0 11	20 08	1 11	19 09	1 10	22 12	0 30	22 01	0 19
11 Th	22 10	9 34	4 57	11 50	15 55	3 24	23 21	0 13	19 58	1 11	19 12	1 07	22 12	0 30	22 02	0 19
12 F	22 02	13 57	4 23	15 52	15 45	3 38	23 18	0 16	19 49	1 11	19 15	1 03	22 12	0 30	22 02	0 19
13 Sa	21 54	17 34	3 36	19 02	15 37	3 51	23 14	0 18	19 39	1 11	19 18	0 60	22 11	0 30	22 03	0 19
14 Su	21 45	20 15	2 38	21 12	15 31	4 04	23 10	0 20	19 29	1 10	19 21	0 56	22 11	0 30	22 03	0 19
15 M	21 36	21 52	1 34	22 16	15 26	4 15	23 05	0 23	19 20	1 10	19 24	0 53	22 10	0 29	22 04	0 19
16 Tu	21 26	22 22	0 26	22 12	15 23	4 26	22 59	0 25	19 10	1 10	19 27	0 50	22 10	0 29	22 05	0 19
17 W	21 17	21 46	0S42	21 05	15 21	4 35	22 53	0 27	18 59	1 10	19 30	0 46	22 10	0 29	22 05	0 18
18 Th	21 06	20 09	1 47	18 60	15 22	4 43	22 46	0 29	18 49	1 10	19 33	0 43	22 10	0 29	22 06	0 18
19 F	20 56	17 38	2 47	16 06	15 24	4 49	22 38	0 32	18 39	1 10	19 37	0 40	22 09	0 29	22 07	0 18
20 Sa	20 45	14 25	3 39	12 35	15 28	4 54	22 30	0 34	18 28	1 10	19 40	0 36	22 09	0 29	22 07	0 18
21 Su	20 34	10 38	4 21	8 35	15 33	4 57	22 21	0 36	18 17	1 10	19 43	0 33	22 09	0 28	22 08	0 18
22 M	20 22	6 27	4 52	4 15	15 40	4 58	22 11	0 38	18 07	1 10	19 47	0 30	22 09	0 28	22 08	0 18
23 Tu	20 10	2 01	5 11	0N16	15 48	4 58	22 01	0 40	17 56	1 10	19 50	0 27	22 08	0 28	22 09	0 18
24 W	19 58	2N33	5 16	4 49	15 57	4 56	21 50	0 42	17 45	1 10	19 54	0 24	22 08	0 28	22 10	0 18
25 Th	19 45	7 04	5 07	9 17	16 07	4 52	21 38	0 44	17 33	1 10	19 57	0 21	22 08	0 28	22 10	0 18
26 F	19 33	11 25	4 44	13 27	16 19	4 46	21 26	0 46	17 22	1 10	20 01	0 18	22 08	0 27	22 11	0 18
27 Sa	19 19	15 22	4 06	17 08	16 31	4 39	21 13	0 48	17 11	1 10	20 04	0 15	22 08	0 27	22 11	0 17
28 Su	19 06	18 41	3 14	20 02	16 44	4 31	20 59	0 50	16 59	1 10	20 08	0 12	22 08	0 27	22 12	0 17
29 M	18 52	21 06	2 10	21 52	16 57	4 21	20 45	0 52	16 48	1 10	20 11	0 09	22 07	0 27	22 13	0 17
30 Tu	18 38	22 18	0 56	22 22	17 10	4 10	20 30	0 54	16 36	1 09	20 15	0 06	22 07	0 27	22 13	0 17
31 W	18N23	22N03	0N23	21N21	17N24	3S58	20N15	0N56	16N24	1N09	20S19	0N03	22S07	0N26	22S14	0N17

Day	⚷ Decl	⚷ Lat	♅ Decl	♅ Lat	♆ Decl	♆ Lat	♇ Decl	♇ Lat
1	5N14	3N09	13N01	0S30	5S25	1S01	21S60	0S24
6	5 15	3 09	13 04	0 30	5 26	1 02	22 02	0 24
11	5 16	3 10	13 07	0 30	5 27	1 02	22 03	0 25
16	5 16	3 10	13 09	0 30	5 28	1 02	22 05	0 25
21	5 15	3 11	13 11	0 30	5 30	1 02	22 06	0 26
26	5 14	3 11	13 13	0 30	5 32	1 02	22 08	0 26
31	5N13	3N12	13N14	0S30	5S35	1S03	22S10	0S27

Day	⚴ Decl	⚴ Lat	⚵ Decl	⚵ Lat	⚶ Decl	⚶ Lat	Eris Decl	Eris Lat
1	21N23	29N05	13N48	5S25	8N23	6S16	1S35	11S48
6	20 46	28 49	13 27	5 12	8 50	6 24	1 35	11 49
11	20 08	28 34	13 03	4 59	9 15	6 31	1 35	11 49
16	19 27	28 19	12 38	4 46	9 38	6 39	1 35	11 50
21	18 46	28 04	12 10	4 34	9 58	6 47	1 36	11 50
26	18 03	27 50	11 41	4 22	10 17	6 55	1 36	11 51
31	17N20	27N36	11N10	4S10	10N32	7S04	1S37	11S51

Moon Phenomena

Max/0 Decl

dy	hr mn	
2	22:18	22N23
9	2:54	0 S
15	22:52	22S22
23	10:38	0 N
30	8:05	22N23

Max/0 Lat

dy	hr mn	
3	6:54	0 N
9	12:05	5N17
16	9:07	0 S
23	21:12	5S16
30	17:03	0 N

Perigee/Apogee

dy	hr m		kilometers
5	4:54	p	363728
20	23:59	a	405481

PH	dy	hr mn	
●	2	19:17	10♋38
(eclipse)	2	19:24	T 04'33"
☽	9	10:56	16♎58
○	16	21:39	24♑04
(eclipse)	16	21:32	P 0.653
☾	25	1:19	1♉51

Void of Course Moon

Last Aspect			☽ Ingress		
1 21:49	♀	☌	♋	2	1:25
3 14:26	♇	☍	♌	4	3:20
5 6:26	♃	△	♍	6	4:26
7 16:51	♇	△	♎	8	6:08
9 19:37	♇	□	♏	10	9:30
12 0:30	♇	⚹	♐	12	15:06
14 1:31	♆	□	♑	14	23:06
16 21:39	☉	☍	♒	17	9:20
18 15:55	♃	⚹	♓	19	21:20
22 8:35	☉	△	♈	22	10:03
24 14:49	☿	□	♉	24	21:43
27 4:29	♀	⚹	♊	27	6:30
28 15:25	♆	□	♋	29	11:32
31 3:34	☿	☌	♌	31	13:19

DAILY ASPECTARIAN

1 M: ☽☍♃ 3:07, ☽∠☿ 4:21, ☽⚻♄ 4:36, ♅⚺⚷ 5:26, ☽□♆ 6:05, ☽∠♅ 9:54, ☽⚻♇ 12:07, ☽∥♂ 17:18, ☽☌♀ 21:49, ♂ ♌ 23:20

2 Tu: ☽⚺♂ 1:31, ☽⋕♄ 3:24, ☽⚻⚳ 3:34, ☽⋕♇ 5:04, ☽⚺☿ 6:51, ☽□⚷ 11:24, ☽⚹♅ 11:28, ☽⋕♃ 12:36, ☉☌☽ 19:17

3 W: ☽⚼⚳ 4:31, ☽⚻♃ 5:30, ☽☍♄ 7:02, ☽⋕♃ 7:45, ☽△♆ 8:42, ☿⚼♆ 11:47, ☽☍♇ 14:26, ☽⋕♇ 14:42, ♀ ♋ 15:19, ☽⋕♄ 16:09, ♂△⚳ 17:41

4 Th: ☽⚺♀ 4:26, ☽△⚳ 5:07, ☽☌♂ 5:42, ☽⚼♃ 6:03, ☽∥♂ 6:46, ☽⚼♆ 9:23, ☽☌☿ 9:51, ♀⚻⚳ 12:04, ♂⚼♃ 12:34, ☽△⚷ 13:04, ☽□♅ 13:12

5 F: ☉⚺☽ 0:11, ☽⋕⚳ 1:57, ☽△♃ 6:26, ☽∠♀ 7:14, ☽⚻♄ 8:03, ☽⚻♆ 9:54, ♀⚺♂ 10:33, ☽⚼⚷ 13:36, ☽∥☿ 14:02, ☽⚻♇ 15:31

6 Sa: ☉∠☽ 2:25, ☽□⚳ 5:57, ☽⚼♄ 8:29, ☽⚺♂ 9:02, ☽⚹♀ 10:01, ☽⚺☿ 11:38, ☽∥♅ 13:48, ☽⚻⚷ 14:11, ☽△♅ 14:25, ☽⚼♇ 16:05

7 Su: ☉⚹☽ 4:50, ☿⚺♀ 6:27, ☽□♃ 7:21, ☽△♄ 9:05, ☽∠♂ 10:55, ☽☍♆ 11:12, ☽∠☿ 12:32, ☽⚼♅ 15:16, ☽△♇ 16:51, ♂⚼♆ 17:16, ☿ R 23:16

8 M: ☽⋕♆ 2:28, ☽∥⚷ 3:16, ☉⚼⚳ 5:23, ☽⚹⚳ 7:28, ♀□⚷ 11:43, ☽⚹♂ 13:11, ☽⚹☿ 13:38, ♀⚹♅ 15:33, ☉⚻♃ 15:49, ☽☍⚷ 16:09, ☽⚻♅ 16:29, ☽□♀ 16:34, ☿☌♂ 22:28, ⚷ R 23:41

9 Tu: ☽∠⚳ 8:49, ☽⚹♃ 9:31, ☉□☽ 10:56, ☽□♄ 11:23, ☽⚻♆ 13:48, ☉☍♄ 17:08, ☽□♇ 19:37

10 W: ☽⋕⚷ 2:59, ☽∥♆ 3:51, ☽⚺⚳ 10:41, ☽∠♃ 11:19, ☽⚼♆ 15:51, ☽□☿ 16:49, ☉⋕♃ 17:42, ☽□♂ 19:21, ☽⚻⚷ 19:55, ☽☍♅ 20:22

11 Th: ☽△♀ 1:30, ☉△♆ 4:32, ♂△⚷ 7:30, ☽⚺♃ 13:41, ☽⚹♄ 15:43, ♂□♅ 18:02, ☽△♆ 18:29, ☽⋕♅ 19:12, ☉△☽ 19:34, ☉⋕♇ 19:49, ☽⚼⚷ 22:39, ☉⋕♄ 23:29

12 F: ☽⚹♇ 0:30, ☽⚼♀ 7:06, ☽⋕☿ 10:53, ☽☌⚳ 16:11, ☿⚼♆ 16:20, ☽∠♄ 18:45, ☽△☿ 21:34

13 Sa: ☉⚼☽ 0:59, ☽△⚷ 1:59, ☽⚻♅ 2:34, ☽∠♇ 3:49, ☽△♂ 4:11, ☽⚻♀ 13:31, ☽∥⚳ 14:41, ☽⋕♂ 16:44, ☽☌♃ 20:12, ☽⚺♄ 22:22

14 Su: ☽⚼☿ 0:32, ☽□♆ 1:31, ☽⚼♅ 6:34, ☉⚻☽ 7:09, ☽⚺♇ 7:45, ☽⚼♂ 9:38, ☉☍♇ 14:52, ♂⋕⚳ 16:18, ☉⋕☽ 19:08

15 M: ☽⚺⚳ 0:07, ☽⚻☿ 3:54, ☽∥♄ 5:07, ☽∥♇ 5:16, ☽∥♃ 8:24, ☽□⚷ 10:26, ☽△♅ 11:10, ☽⚻♂ 15:46

16 Tu: ♄∥♇ 3:30, ☽☍♀ 4:43, ☽∠⚳ 4:58, ☽⚺♃ 5:02, ♀⚼⚳ 7:14, ☽☌♄ 7:19, ♀⚻♃ 7:45, ☽⚹♆ 10:53, ☽∥♃ 13:26, ☽∥♄ 16:05, ☽∥♇ 16:09, ☽☌♇ 17:17, ☉☍☽ 21:39

17 W: ♀☍♄ 5:35, ☉⋕☽ 10:03, ☽∠♃ 10:15, ☽⚹⚳ 10:21, ☽☍☿ 11:40, ☽∠♆ 16:21, ⚳ D 19:07, ☽⚹⚷ 21:02, ☽□♅ 21:55

18 Th: ☽☍♂ 5:51, ☽∥⚳ 6:17, ☿△⚳ 12:32, ☽⋕♂ 14:39, ☽⚹♃ 15:55, ☿⚼♃ 17:52, ♀△♆ 18:04, ☽⚺♄ 18:16, ☽⚺♆ 22:14, ☽⚻♀ 22:43

19 F: ☽∠⚷ 2:59, ☽⚺♇ 4:46, ☿R♋ 7:07, ☉⚻☽ 14:34, ☽⋕☿ 16:51, ☽⚻☿ 20:34, ☽□⚳ 22:24

20 Sa: ☽∠♄ 0:18, ☽⋕♅ 8:09, ☽⚼♀ 8:27, ☽⚺⚷ 9:14, ☽⚹♅ 10:17, ☽∠♇ 11:00, ☽⚻♂ 21:41, ☉⚼☽ 23:34

21 Su: ☽⚼☿ 1:16, ☽□♃ 4:07, ☽⚹♄ 6:29, ♀☍♇ 8:33, ☽☌♆ 10:47, ☉☌☿ 12:35, ☽∠♅ 16:44, ☽⚹♇ 17:19, ☽△♀ 18:21

22 M: ♃∥♄ 2:10, ☽∥♆ 5:09, ♀⋕♄ 5:28, ♀⋕♃ 5:45, ☽⚼♂ 5:46, ☽△☿ 5:59, ☽⋕⚷ 6:35, ☉△☽ 8:35, ♀⋕♇ 9:33, ☽△⚳ 11:13, ☽☌⚷ 21:51, ☽⚺♅ 23:02

23 Tu: ☉ ♌ 2:52, ☉⚼♃ 4:53, ☽△♂ 13:35, ☽△♃ 16:15, ☽⚼⚳ 17:23, ☉△⚳ 18:28, ☽□♄ 18:32, ☽⚺♆ 23:01

24 W: ☽□♇ 5:21, ☉⋕⚳ 6:44, ☽□♀ 13:14, ☽∥⚷ 14:14, ☽□☿ 14:49, ☽⋕♆ 15:45, ☽⚼♃ 21:42, ☽⚻⚳ 23:01

25 Th: ☿☌♀ 0:27, ☉□☽ 1:19, ☽∠♆ 4:24, ☽⚺⚷ 9:01, ☽☌♅ 10:18, ♂△♃ 12:24, ♃∥♇ 12:55

26 F: ☽⚻♃ 2:25, ☽□♂ 3:13, ☽△♄ 4:30, ☽⚹♆ 9:00, ☽∥♅ 10:33, ☽∠⚷ 13:29, ☽△♇ 14:59, ☉⚼♆ 16:28, ☽⚹☿ 21:45

27 Sa: ♂⚻♄ 2:42, ☽⚹♀ 4:29, ☽☍⚳ 7:56, ☽∥☿ 8:10, ☽⚼♄ 8:14, ☽∥♂ 11:43, ☉⚹☽ 14:17, ☽⚹⚷ 17:02, ☽⚺♅ 18:21, ☽⚼♇ 18:27, ♀⚼♃ 22:42

28 Su: ☽∠☿ 0:12, ♀ ♌ 1:55, ☉∥☽ 3:09, ☽☍♃ 9:09, ☽∠♀ 10:14, ☽⚻♄ 11:02, ☽⚹♂ 12:46, ☽⋕⚳ 13:22, ☿∥♂ 15:09, ⚳∠♄ 15:18, ☽□♆ 15:25, ♀△⚳ 18:55, ☉∠☽ 19:00, ☽∥♀ 20:11, ☽∠♅ 20:56, ☽⚻♇ 20:58

29 M: ☽⚺☿ 1:56, ☉△⚷ 3:44, ☽⚻⚳ 13:06, ☽⚺♀ 14:45, ☽∠♂ 15:56, ☽⋕♃ 18:02, ☽⋕♇ 18:54, ☽⋕♄ 20:50, ☽⋕♄ 20:57, ☽□⚷ 21:18, ☉⚺☽ 22:35, ☽⚹♅ 22:38, ☉□♅ 23:15

30 Tu: ☽⚻♃ 12:18, ☽☍♄ 13:58, ☽⚼⚳ 14:24, ☽⚺♂ 18:10, ☽△♆ 18:16, ♀⚼♆ 18:51, ♀⋕⚳ 19:13, ♂⚻♆ 20:10, ☽⋕♇ 21:06, ☽⋕♃ 22:10, ☽☍♇ 23:28

31 W: ☽☌☿ 3:34, ☽⚼♃ 12:49, ☽△⚳ 15:04, ☽⚼♆ 18:41, ☽☌♀ 20:52, ☽△⚷ 22:33, ☽⋕⚳ 23:03, ☽□♅ 23:55

August 2019

LONGITUDE

Day	Sid.Time	☉	☽	☽ 12 hour	Mean☊	True☊	☿	♀	♂	⚳	♃	♄	⚷	♅	♆	♇
	h m s	° ' "	° ' "	° ' "	° '	° '	° '	° '	° '	° '	° '	° '	° '	° '	° '	° '
1 Th	20 37 15	8♌29 15	6♌36 50	14♌05 46	16♋20.4	17♋35.0	23♋56.9	4♌49.8	19♌04.0	1♐06.5	14♐40.7	15♑38.4	5♈42.9	6♉33.9	18♓18.5	21♑28.7
2 F	20 41 12	9 26 40	21 36 48	29 08 48	16 17.2	17R 33.2	23D 59.0	6 03.7	19 42.1	1 11.6	14R 38.8	15R 34.6	5R 41.7	6 34.4	18R 17.4	21R 27.3
3 Sa	20 45 08	10 24 06	6♍40 39	14♍11 11	16 14.0	17 30.6	24 07.3	7 17.7	20 20.2	1 17.0	14 37.1	15 30.7	5 40.5	6 34.9	18 16.2	21 25.9
4 Su	20 49 05	11 21 32	21 39 20	29 04 09	16 10.9	17 27.5	24 22.1	8 31.7	20 58.3	1 22.7	14 35.6	15 27.0	5 39.2	6 35.3	18 14.9	21 24.6
5 M	20 53 01	12 18 59	6♎24 48	13♎40 35	16 07.7	17 24.5	24 43.3	9 45.7	21 36.4	1 28.8	14 34.3	15 23.3	5 37.9	6 35.7	18 13.7	21 23.2
6 Tu	20 56 58	13 16 27	20 51 01	27 55 44	16 04.5	17 22.1	25 11.0	10 59.7	22 14.4	1 35.2	14 33.2	15 19.6	5 36.5	6 36.0	18 12.4	21 21.9
7 W	21 00 55	14 13 55	4♏54 34	11♏47 27	16 01.3	17D 20.7	25 45.3	12 13.7	22 52.5	1 41.9	14 32.2	15 16.0	5 35.1	6 36.3	18 11.1	21 20.6
8 Th	21 04 51	15 11 25	18 34 29	25 15 50	15 58.2	17 20.4	26 26.0	13 27.8	23 30.6	1 48.9	14 31.5	15 12.5	5 33.6	6 36.5	18 09.8	21 19.3
9 F	21 08 48	16 08 55	1♐51 46	8♐22 36	15 55.0	17 21.2	27 13.1	14 41.9	24 08.7	1 56.2	14 30.9	15 09.0	5 32.1	6 36.7	18 08.5	21 18.0
10 Sa	21 12 44	17 06 26	14 48 42	21 10 27	15 51.8	17 22.7	28 06.6	15 55.9	24 46.8	2 03.8	14 30.5	15 05.6	5 30.6	6 36.8	18 07.2	21 16.7
11 Su	21 16 41	18 03 57	27 28 15	3♑42 28	15 48.6	17 24.3	29 06.3	17 10.0	25 24.9	2 11.7	14D 30.3	15 02.3	5 29.0	6 36.9	18 05.8	21 15.4
12 M	21 20 37	19 01 30	9♑53 30	16 01 43	15 45.5	17R 25.4	0♌12.0	18 24.1	26 03.0	2 19.8	14 30.3	14 59.0	5 27.4	6R 36.9	18 04.4	21 14.2
13 Tu	21 24 34	19 59 03	22 07 27	28 11 00	15 42.3	17 25.6	1 23.5	19 38.3	26 41.0	2 28.3	14 30.5	14 55.8	5 25.7	6 36.9	18 03.0	21 12.9
14 W	21 28 30	20 56 38	4♒12 42	10♒12 47	15 39.1	17 24.3	2 40.7	20 52.4	27 19.1	2 37.1	14 30.8	14 52.6	5 24.0	6 36.8	18 01.6	21 11.7
15 Th	21 32 27	21 54 14	16 11 32	22 09 10	15 35.9	17 21.3	4 03.2	22 06.5	27 57.2	2 46.1	14 31.4	14 49.5	5 22.2	6 36.7	18 00.2	21 10.5
16 F	21 36 24	22 51 50	28 05 55	4♓02 01	15 32.7	17 16.7	5 30.9	23 20.7	28 35.3	2 55.4	14 32.1	14 46.5	5 20.4	6 36.5	17 58.8	21 09.3
17 Sa	21 40 20	23 49 28	9♓57 42	15 53 10	15 29.6	17 10.7	7 03.3	24 34.9	29 13.4	3 04.9	14 33.0	14 43.6	5 18.6	6 36.3	17 57.3	21 08.1
18 Su	21 44 17	24 47 08	21 48 42	27 44 32	15 26.4	17 04.0	8 40.1	25 49.1	29 51.5	3 14.8	14 34.1	14 40.7	5 16.7	6 36.1	17 55.8	21 07.0
19 M	21 48 13	25 44 49	3♈40 58	9♈38 18	15 23.2	16 57.0	10 20.9	27 03.3	0♍29.7	3 24.9	14 35.4	14 38.0	5 14.8	6 35.7	17 54.3	21 05.8
20 Tu	21 52 10	26 42 31	15 36 54	21 37 08	15 20.0	16 50.6	12 05.4	28 17.5	1 07.8	3 35.2	14 36.8	14 35.2	5 12.9	6 35.4	17 52.8	21 04.7
21 W	21 56 06	27 40 15	27 39 25	3♉44 10	15 16.8	16 45.4	13 53.1	29 31.8	1 45.9	3 45.8	14 38.5	14 32.6	5 10.9	6 35.0	17 51.3	21 03.6
22 Th	22 00 03	28 38 00	9♉51 52	16 03 00	15 13.7	16 41.8	15 43.6	0♍46.0	2 24.0	3 56.7	14 40.3	14 30.1	5 08.9	6 34.5	17 49.8	21 02.5
23 F	22 03 59	29 35 47	22 18 05	28 37 38	15 10.5	16D 39.9	17 36.4	2 00.3	3 02.2	4 07.8	14 42.3	14 27.6	5 06.8	6 34.0	17 48.2	21 01.4
24 Sa	22 07 56	0♍33 36	5♊02 09	11♊32 09	15 07.3	16 39.7	19 31.2	3 14.6	3 40.3	4 19.1	14 44.5	14 25.2	5 04.7	6 33.4	17 46.7	21 00.4
25 Su	22 11 53	1 31 27	18 08 04	24 50 19	15 04.1	16 40.7	21 27.6	4 28.9	4 18.5	4 30.7	14 46.9	14 22.9	5 02.6	6 32.8	17 45.1	20 59.3
26 M	22 15 49	2 29 19	1♋39 13	8♋34 58	15 01.0	16 41.9	23 25.1	5 43.2	4 56.7	4 42.5	14 49.4	14 20.7	5 00.4	6 32.2	17 43.5	20 58.3
27 Tu	22 19 46	3 27 14	15 37 39	22 47 12	14 57.8	16R 42.6	25 23.4	6 57.6	5 34.9	4 54.6	14 52.1	14 18.5	4 58.2	6 31.5	17 42.0	20 57.3
28 W	22 23 42	4 25 10	0♌03 19	7♌25 32	14 54.6	16 41.9	27 22.2	8 11.9	6 13.0	5 06.9	14 55.0	14 16.5	4 56.0	6 30.7	17 40.4	20 56.4
29 Th	22 27 39	5 23 07	14 53 11	22 25 22	14 51.4	16 39.2	29 21.2	9 26.3	6 51.2	5 19.4	14 58.1	14 14.5	4 53.8	6 29.9	17 38.8	20 55.4
30 F	22 31 35	6 21 07	0♍01 00	7♍38 51	14 48.3	16 34.3	1♍20.2	10 40.7	7 29.4	5 32.2	15 01.4	14 12.6	4 51.5	6 29.1	17 37.2	20 54.5
31 Sa	22 35 32	7♍19 07	15 17 34	22 55 46	14♋45.1	16♋27.7	3♍18.9	11♍55.1	8♍07.7	5♐45.2	15♐04.8	14♑10.8	4♈49.2	6♉28.2	17♓35.6	20♑53.6

1st of Month

Julian Day # 2458696.5
Obliquity 23°26'10"
SVP 4♓59'26"
GC 27♐06.8
Eris 24♈19.1R

Day	⚴	⚵	⚶
1	21♎27.1	19♌27.3	18♉49.9
6	23 01.2	21 46.6	20 14.0
11	24 39.0	24 04.9	21 32.4
16	26 20.2	26 22.3	22 44.9
21	28 04.6	28 38.6	23 50.7
26	29 51.9	0♍54.0	24 49.5
31	1♏41.9	3 08.3	25 40.6

DECLINATION and LATITUDE

Day	☉ Decl	☽ Decl	☽ Lat	☽12h Decl	☿ Decl	☿ Lat	♀ Decl	♀ Lat	♂ Decl	♂ Lat	⚳ Decl	⚳ Lat	♃ Decl	♃ Lat	♄ Decl	♄ Lat
1 Th	18N08	20N17	1N43	18N51	17N38	3S44	19N59	0N58	16N12	1N09	20S23	0N00	22S07	0N26	22S14	0N17
2 F	17 53	17 05	2 57	15 02	17 51	3 30	19 43	0 59	16 00	1 09	20 26	0S03	22 07	0 26	22 15	0 17
3 Sa	17 38	12 45	3 58	10 16	18 04	3 16	19 26	1 01	15 48	1 09	20 30	0 06	22 07	0 26	22 15	0 17
4 Su	17 22	7 38	4 43	4 56	18 17	3 00	19 08	1 03	15 36	1 09	20 34	0 08	22 07	0 26	22 16	0 17
5 M	17 06	2 10	5 08	0S35	18 29	2 45	18 50	1 04	15 23	1 09	20 38	0 11	22 07	0 25	22 16	0 17
6 Tu	16 50	3S18	5 13	5 56	18 39	2 29	18 31	1 06	15 11	1 09	20 42	0 14	22 07	0 25	22 17	0 17
7 W	16 33	8 27	4 59	10 50	18 49	2 13	18 12	1 07	14 58	1 09	20 46	0 16	22 07	0 25	22 17	0 16
8 Th	16 17	13 02	4 29	15 04	18 58	1 56	17 52	1 09	14 46	1 09	20 50	0 19	22 08	0 25	22 18	0 16
9 F	15 60	16 52	3 44	18 27	19 05	1 40	17 32	1 10	14 33	1 08	20 54	0 22	22 08	0 25	22 18	0 16
10 Sa	15 42	19 46	2 49	20 50	19 10	1 24	17 12	1 11	14 20	1 08	20 58	0 24	22 08	0 25	22 19	0 16
11 Su	15 25	21 38	1 47	22 09	19 14	1 08	16 50	1 12	14 07	1 08	21 02	0 27	22 08	0 24	22 19	0 16
12 M	15 07	22 23	0 41	22 21	19 15	0 52	16 29	1 14	13 54	1 08	21 06	0 29	22 08	0 24	22 20	0 16
13 Tu	14 49	22 02	0S26	21 29	19 15	0 37	16 07	1 15	13 41	1 08	21 10	0 32	22 08	0 24	22 20	0 16
14 W	14 31	20 40	1 30	19 38	19 12	0 22	15 44	1 16	13 28	1 08	21 14	0 34	22 09	0 24	22 21	0 16
15 Th	14 12	18 22	2 30	16 56	19 06	0 08	15 21	1 17	13 15	1 08	21 18	0 37	22 09	0 24	22 21	0 16
16 F	13 54	15 19	3 23	13 33	18 58	0N05	14 58	1 18	13 01	1 08	21 23	0 39	22 09	0 23	22 22	0 15
17 Sa	13 35	11 39	4 07	9 38	18 48	0 18	14 34	1 19	12 48	1 07	21 27	0 41	22 09	0 23	22 22	0 15
18 Su	13 15	7 32	4 40	5 22	18 34	0 30	14 10	1 20	12 34	1 07	21 31	0 44	22 10	0 23	22 23	0 15
19 M	12 56	3 09	5 01	0 53	18 18	0 41	13 45	1 20	12 21	1 07	21 35	0 46	22 10	0 23	22 23	0 15
20 Tu	12 37	1N23	5 09	3N39	17 60	0 52	13 20	1 21	12 07	1 07	21 39	0 48	22 10	0 23	22 23	0 15
21 W	12 17	5 54	5 04	8 07	17 38	1 01	12 55	1 22	11 53	1 07	21 44	0 51	22 11	0 22	22 24	0 15
22 Th	11 57	10 10	4 45	12 19	17 14	1 10	12 29	1 22	11 39	1 07	21 48	0 53	22 11	0 22	22 24	0 15
23 F	11 37	14 17	4 12	16 06	16 47	1 17	12 03	1 23	11 26	1 07	21 52	0 55	22 12	0 22	22 24	0 15
24 Sa	11 16	17 45	3 26	19 13	16 18	1 24	11 37	1 24	11 12	1 06	21 56	0 57	22 12	0 22	22 25	0 15
25 Su	10 56	20 27	2 28	21 25	15 46	1 30	11 10	1 24	10 58	1 06	22 01	0 59	22 12	0 22	22 25	0 15
26 M	10 35	22 05	1 21	22 26	15 12	1 35	10 43	1 24	10 43	1 06	22 05	1 01	22 13	0 22	22 25	0 14
27 Tu	10 14	22 25	0 06	22 08	14 36	1 39	10 16	1 25	10 29	1 06	22 09	1 03	22 13	0 21	22 26	0 14
28 W	9 53	21 18	1N11	20 10	13 59	1 42	9 48	1 25	10 15	1 06	22 13	1 06	22 14	0 21	22 26	0 14
29 Th	9 32	18 41	2 26	16 52	13 19	1 44	9 21	1 25	10 01	1 06	22 18	1 08	22 14	0 21	22 26	0 14
30 F	9 11	14 46	3 31	12 24	12 39	1 46	8 52	1 25	9 46	1 06	22 22	1 10	22 15	0 21	22 27	0 14
31 Sa	8N49	9N50	4N23	7N07	11N56	1N46	8N24	1N25	9N32	1N05	22S26	1S12	22S16	0N21	22S27	0N14

Day	⚷ Decl	⚷ Lat	♅ Decl	♅ Lat	♆ Decl	♆ Lat	♇ Decl	♇ Lat
1	5N12	3N12	13N14	0S30	5S35	1S03	22S10	0S27
6	5 10	3 12	13 14	0 30	5 38	1 03	22 11	0 27
11	5 07	3 12	13 15	0 30	5 40	1 03	22 13	0 28
16	5 04	3 13	13 14	0 30	5 43	1 03	22 14	0 28
21	5 01	3 13	13 14	0 31	5 46	1 03	22 16	0 29
26	4 57	3 13	13 13	0 31	5 49	1 03	22 17	0 29
31	4N52	3N13	13N12	0S31	5S52	1S03	22S18	0S30

Day	⚴ Decl	⚴ Lat	⚵ Decl	⚵ Lat	⚶ Decl	⚶ Lat	Eris Decl	Eris Lat
1	17N11	27N33	11N04	4S07	10N35	7S06	1S37	11S51
6	16 28	27 21	10 31	3 56	10 48	7 15	1 38	11 52
11	15 44	27 09	9 58	3 45	10 59	7 25	1 38	11 52
16	14 60	26 58	9 23	3 33	11 07	7 34	1 39	11 52
21	14 16	26 47	8 47	3 22	11 13	7 45	1 40	11 53
26	13 32	26 37	8 10	3 12	11 17	7 55	1 41	11 53
31	12N49	26N28	7N32	3S01	11N18	8S06	1S42	11S54

Moon Phenomena

Max/0 Decl
dy hr mn
5 9:28 0 S
12 4:19 22S24
19 16:42 0 N
26 17:56 22N28

Max/0 Lat
dy hr mn
5 18:16 5N14
12 14:45 0 S
20 2:24 5S10
27 1:50 0 N

Perigee/Apogee
dy hr m kilometers
2 7:06 p 359402
17 10:50 a 406245
30 16:00 p 357181

PH dy hr mn
● 1 3:13 8♌37
☽ 7 17:32 14♏56
○ 15 12:30 22♒24
☾ 23 14:57 0♊12
● 30 10:38 6♍47

Void of Course Moon

Last Aspect		☽ Ingress
1 20:49	♂ ☌	♍ 2 13:22
4 4:28	☿ ⚹	♎ 4 13:31
6 7:37	☿ □	♏ 6 15:33
8 14:59	☿ △	♐ 8 20:36
10 19:52	☉ △	♑ 11 4:51
12 22:13	♇ ☌	♒ 13 15:37
16 1:03	☉ ☍	♓ 16 3:51
17 22:36	♇ ⚹	♈ 18 16:34
21 4:08	☉ △	♉ 21 4:38
22 21:34	♇ △	♊ 23 14:35
25 7:00	☿ ⚹	♋ 25 21:06
27 8:56	♇ ☍	♌ 27 23:55
29 0:08	♃ △	♍ 29 23:58
31 8:47	♇ △	♎ 31 23:09

DAILY ASPECTARIAN

1 Th	☽∥♀ 2:59, ☉☌☽ 3:13, ☿ D 3:58, ☽△♃ 12:54, ☽⚻♄ 14:24, ♀△⚷ 16:59, ☉∥☽ 18:21, ☽⚻♆ 18:42, ☽∥☿ 19:17, ☽☌♂ 20:49, ☽⚼⚷ 22:32, ☽⚻♇ 23:45
2 F	☉∥☿ 1:41, ☽⚺☿ 3:48, ☽∥♂ 6:51, ♀□♅ 10:02, ☽⚼♄ 14:13, ☽□⚳ 15:21, ☽∥♅ 21:30, ☽⚻⚷ 22:24, ☽⚼♇ 23:37, ☽△♅ 23:51
3 Sa	☽⚺♀ 1:04, ☽∠☿ 3:57, ☉⚺☽ 6:21, ♂⚼⚷ 12:23, ☽□♃ 12:40, ☽△♄ 14:04, ☽☍♆ 18:32, ☽⚺♂ 22:51, ☽△♇ 23:36, ☽⚼♅ 23:54
4 Su	☽∠♀ 3:18, ☽⚹☿ 4:28, ☉∠☽ 8:08, ☽#♆ 9:01, ☽∥⚷ 10:54, ☽⚹⚳ 15:52, ♂⚻♇ 16:00, ☽☍⚷ 22:43
5 M	☽⚻♅ 0:18, ☽∠♂ 0:20, ☽⚹♀ 6:02, ☉⚹☽ 10:26, ☽⚹♃ 13:28, ☽□♄ 14:47, ☽∠⚳ 16:48, ☿∥♀ 17:21, ☽⚻♆ 19:34
6 Tu	☽□♇ 0:52, ☽⚹♂ 2:27, ☽□☿ 7:37, ☽#⚷ 8:29, ☽∥♆ 10:38, ☽∠♃ 14:46, ☽⚺⚳ 18:25, ☽⚼♆ 21:02
7 W	☽⚻⚷ 1:10, ☽☍♅ 2:56, ☉△♃ 7:32, ☽□♀ 14:02, ☽⚺♃ 16:49, ☉□☽ 17:32, ☽⚹♄ 18:03, ☽△♆ 23:16
8 Th	☉⚻♄ 0:26, ☽#♅ 1:09, ☽⚼⚷ 3:32, ☽⚹♇ 4:54, ☽□♂ 9:17, ☽#♂ 9:37, ☽△☿ 14:59, ☉#☽ 18:27, ♀△♃ 20:29, ☽∠♄ 20:53
9 F	☽☌⚳ 0:08, ☽#♀ 4:25, ☽△⚷ 6:44, ☽∠♇ 8:09, ♀⚻♄ 8:25, ☽⚻♅ 8:44, ☽#☿ 18:06, ☽⚼☿ 20:34, ☽☌♃ 23:26
10 Sa	☽⚺♄ 0:32, ☽△♀ 2:20, ☉△☽ 4:40, ☽□♆ 6:13, ☽⚺♇ 12:11, ☽⚼♅ 12:50, ☽∥⚳ 14:20, ☽△♂ 19:52
11 Su	☉⚻♆ 0:45, ☽⚻☿ 3:25, ☿⚼♃ 9:02, ☽⚺⚳ 9:11, ☽⚼♀ 10:01, ☉⚼☽ 11:40, ☽∥♃ 11:46, ♃ D 13:38, ☽∥♇ 14:36, ☽□⚷ 15:24, ☽△♅ 17:38, ♀⚻♆ 17:44, ☽∥♄ 19:40, ☿ ♌ 19:47, ☽∥♄ 19:47
12 M	☽⚼♂ 2:23, ♅ R 2:28, ☽⚺♃ 9:01, ☽☌♄ 9:54, ☽∠⚳ 14:44, ☽⚹♆ 15:59, ☽∥♇ 18:08, ☽⚻♀ 18:33, ☉⚻☽ 19:25, ☽∥♃ 21:05, ☽☌♇ 22:13
13 Tu	☽⚻♂ 9:31, ☉⚼⚷ 10:47, ☽∠♃ 14:38, ♀⚼⚷ 15:01, ☽∥⚳ 16:14, ☽☍☿ 20:34, ☽⚹⚳ 20:47, ☽∠♆ 21:39, ☿△⚳ 22:46
14 W	☽⚹⚷ 2:22, ☽□♅ 4:48, ☿⚼♆ 6:07, ☉☌♀ 6:09, ♀⚻♇ 6:09, ☉⚻♇ 6:09, ☽#☿ 16:56, ☽⚹♃ 20:39, ☽⚺♄ 21:16, ♂∥♅ 23:59
15 Th	☽⚺♆ 3:38, ☽∠⚷ 8:23, ☽⚺♇ 10:01, ☉☍☽ 12:30, ☽☍♀ 13:18, ☿△⚷ 21:16
16 F	☽☍♂ 1:03, ☽#♀ 2:46, ☽∠♄ 3:22, ☽□⚳ 9:53, ☉#☽ 10:38, ☽#♅ 13:58, ☽⚺⚷ 14:36, ☽∠♇ 16:16, ☽#♂ 16:22, ☿□♅ 17:09, ☽⚹♅ 17:12, ☽⚻☿ 17:13
17 Sa	☽□♃ 9:18, ☽⚹♄ 9:37, ☽☌♆ 16:09, ♂⚼♄ 17:40, ☽⚹♇ 22:36, ☽∠♅ 23:34
18 Su	☉∥♅ 1:31, ☽⚼☿ 4:22, ♂ ♍ 5:19, ☉⚻☽ 6:33, ☽⚻♀ 9:03, ☽∥♆ 9:57, ☽#⚷ 13:47, ☽⚻♂ 17:12, ☽△⚳ 23:27
19 M	☽☌⚷ 3:09, ☽⚺♅ 5:52, ♃⚺♄ 14:48, ☉⚼☽ 15:29, ☽△☿ 15:42, ☽⚼♀ 18:48, ☽□♄ 21:57, ☽△♃ 21:59
20 Tu	☽⚼♂ 1:05, ☽⚺♆ 4:32, ♀∥♅ 5:52, ☽⚼⚳ 6:02, ☽□♇ 10:54, ☽∥⚷ 19:14, ☽#♆ 23:16
21 W	☉△☽ 0:02, ♀⚼♄ 0:16, ☽⚼♃ 3:56, ☽△♀ 4:08, ☿⚻♄ 8:27, ☽△♂ 8:34, ♀ ♍ 9:08, ☿△♃ 10:06, ☽∠♆ 10:15, ☽⚻⚳ 12:14, ☽⚺⚷ 14:48, ☽☌♅ 17:35
22 Th	☽∥♂ 7:37, ☽△♄ 8:59, ☉∥☽ 9:01, ☽⚻♃ 9:22, ☽∥♀ 11:42, ☽□☿ 13:23, ☽⚹♆ 15:24, ☽∥♅ 17:26, ☽∠⚷ 19:50, ☉⚼♄ 20:44, ☽△♇ 21:34
23 F	☿⚻♆ 2:27, ☉ ♍ 10:03, ☽⚼♄ 13:32, ☽∥☿ 14:42, ☉□☽ 14:57, ☽□♀ 20:18, ☽□♂ 21:20, ☽☍⚳ 22:39
24 Sa	⚵ ♍ 0:02, ☽⚹⚷ 0:05, ☽⚼♇ 1:48, ☽⚺♅ 2:49, ☿⚼⚷ 6:49, ♀☌♂ 17:06, ☽⚻♄ 17:13, ☽☍♃ 17:54, ☉∥♂ 17:58, ☿⚻♇ 18:15, ☽□♆ 23:19
25 Su	♀□⚳ 0:42, ☽⚻♇ 5:08, ☽∠♅ 6:08, ☽⚹☿ 7:00, ♀⚻⚷ 10:34, ♂□⚳ 11:06, ♀∥♂ 23:29, ☽#⚳ 23:57
26 M	☉⚹☽ 1:34, ♂⚻⚷ 2:14, ☽#♃ 3:27, ♀⚼♇ 4:49, ☽⚻⚳ 5:24, ☽#♇ 5:27, ☽□⚷ 5:49, ☽⚹♂ 6:00, ☽⚹♀ 7:45, ☽⚹♅ 8:28, ⚴ ♏ 8:57, ☽∠☿ 13:38, ♀△♅ 15:40, ☽☍♄ 21:46, ☽⚻♃ 22:43, ☽#♄ 23:36, ☽#♄ 23:36
27 Tu	☽△♆ 3:29, ☉∠☽ 5:06, ☉∥♀ 5:41, ☽#♇ 5:51, ⚳△⚷ 6:02, ☽⚼⚳ 7:18, ☽#♃ 7:38, ☽∠♂ 8:42, ☽#⚳ 8:52, ☽☍♇ 8:56, ☽∠♀ 11:37, ♂⚼♇ 13:47, ☽⚺☿ 18:53, ☽⚼♃ 23:46
28 W	⚳∥♃ 2:48, ☽⚼♆ 4:16, ☉⚺☽ 7:37, ☽△⚷ 7:56, ☽△⚳ 8:22, ☽⚺♂ 10:30, ☽□♅ 10:31, ♂△♅ 10:54, ☉⚻⚷ 12:18, ☽⚺♀ 14:27, ☉□⚳ 22:03, ⚳∥♇ 22:38, ☿⚼♄ 22:40, ☽⚻♄ 22:58
29 Th	☽△♃ 0:08, ☿∥♅ 4:20, ☽⚻♆ 4:24, ☿ ♍ 7:49, ☽⚼⚷ 7:58, ☽⚻♇ 9:37, ☉⚼♇ 13:10, ☽⚼♄ 22:44
30 F	☽☌☿ 2:23, ☉△♅ 3:16, ☽⚻⚷ 7:36, ☽∥♅ 8:04, ☽□⚳ 8:48, ☽⚼♇ 9:16, ☽△♅ 10:10, ☉☌☽ 10:38, ☽☌♂ 12:16, ☽∥☿ 12:34, ☽☌♀ 18:14, ☽△♄ 22:15, ☽□♃ 23:40
31 Sa	☽∥♂ 1:24, ☽☍♆ 3:36, ⚳∥♄ 4:16, ☉∥☽ 4:50, ☽∥♀ 6:58, ☽△♇ 8:47, ☽⚼♅ 9:42, ⚳∠♇ 14:24, ☽#♆ 17:16, ☿⚻⚷ 17:58, ☽∥⚷ 21:37

LONGITUDE

Day	Sid.Time	☉	☽	☽ 12 hour	Mean☊	True☊	☿	♀	♂	⚳	♃	♄	⚷	♅	♆	♇
	h m s	° ' "	° ' "	° ' "	° '	° '	° '	° '	° '	° '	° '	° '	° '	° '	° '	° '
Su	22 39 28	8♍17 10	0♎32 05	8♎05 10	14♋41.9	16♋20.0	5♍17.1	13♍09.5	8♍45.9	5♐58.4	15♐08.4	14♑09.1	4♈46.8	6♉27.3	17♓33.9	20♑52.7
M	22 43 25	9 15 14	15 33 54	22 57 15	14 38.7	16R 12.2	7 14.6	14 23.9	9 24.1	6 11.8	15 12.2	14R 07.5	4R 44.4	6R 26.3	17R 32.3	20R 51.8
Tu	22 47 22	10 13 19	0♏14 27	7♏24 57	14 35.5	16 05.5	9 11.4	15 38.3	10 02.3	6 25.4	15 16.2	14 06.0	4 42.1	6 25.3	17 30.7	20 51.0
W	22 51 18	11 11 26	14 28 22	21 24 36	14 32.4	16 00.5	11 07.4	16 52.7	10 40.6	6 39.2	15 20.3	14 04.6	4 39.6	6 24.2	17 29.0	20 50.2
Th	22 55 15	12 09 34	28 13 40	4♐55 47	14 29.2	15 57.6	13 02.4	18 07.2	11 18.8	6 53.3	15 24.6	14 03.2	4 37.2	6 23.1	17 27.4	20 49.4
F	22 59 11	13 07 44	11♐31 18	18 00 36	14 26.0	15D 56.7	14 56.4	19 21.6	11 57.1	7 07.5	15 29.0	14 02.0	4 34.7	6 21.9	17 25.7	20 48.6
Sa	23 03 08	14 05 55	24 24 14	0♑42 42	14 22.8	15 57.1	16 49.3	20 36.0	12 35.3	7 22.0	15 33.7	14 00.8	4 32.2	6 20.7	17 24.1	20 47.9
Su	23 07 04	15 04 07	6♑56 36	13 06 30	14 19.7	15R 57.9	18 41.2	21 50.5	13 13.6	7 36.6	15 38.5	13 59.8	4 29.7	6 19.5	17 22.4	20 47.2
M	23 11 01	16 02 22	19 12 56	25 16 29	14 16.5	15 58.1	20 31.9	23 05.0	13 51.9	7 51.4	15 43.4	13 58.8	4 27.2	6 18.2	17 20.8	20 46.5
Tu	23 14 57	17 00 37	1♒17 38	7♒16 52	14 13.3	15 56.8	22 21.5	24 19.4	14 30.2	8 06.4	15 48.5	13 58.0	4 24.7	6 16.9	17 19.1	20 45.8
W	23 18 54	17 58 54	13 14 38	19 11 19	14 10.1	15 53.3	24 09.9	25 33.9	15 08.5	8 21.6	15 53.8	13 57.2	4 22.1	6 15.5	17 17.5	20 45.2
Th	23 22 51	18 57 13	25 07 17	1♓02 49	14 06.9	15 47.2	25 57.2	26 48.4	15 46.8	8 37.0	15 59.3	13 56.6	4 19.5	6 14.1	17 15.8	20 44.6
F	23 26 47	19 55 34	6♓58 13	12 53 44	14 03.8	15 38.5	27 43.4	28 02.9	16 25.1	8 52.6	16 04.9	13 56.0	4 16.9	6 12.7	17 14.2	20 44.0
Sa	23 30 44	20 53 56	18 49 33	24 45 53	14 00.6	15 27.7	29 28.4	29 17.4	17 03.5	9 08.3	16 10.6	13 55.5	4 14.3	6 11.2	17 12.5	20 43.4
Su	23 34 40	21 52 20	0♈42 53	6♈40 46	13 57.4	15 15.4	1♎12.4	0♎31.9	17 41.8	9 24.2	16 16.5	13 55.1	4 11.7	6 09.6	17 10.9	20 42.9
M	23 38 37	22 50 46	12 39 40	18 39 47	13 54.2	15 02.8	2 55.2	1 46.4	18 20.2	9 40.3	16 22.6	13 54.9	4 09.0	6 08.1	17 09.2	20 42.4
Tu	23 42 33	23 49 14	24 41 19	0♉44 29	13 51.0	14 50.9	4 37.0	3 00.9	18 58.5	9 56.5	16 28.8	13 54.7	4 06.4	6 06.5	17 07.6	20 41.9
W	23 46 30	24 47 44	6♉49 32	12 56 46	13 47.9	14 40.7	6 17.7	4 15.4	19 36.9	10 12.9	16 35.1	13D 54.6	4 03.7	6 04.8	17 06.0	20 41.4
Th	23 50 26	25 46 16	19 06 30	25 19 05	13 44.7	14 32.9	7 57.4	5 29.9	20 15.3	10 29.5	16 41.6	13 54.6	4 01.0	6 03.1	17 04.3	20 41.0
F	23 54 23	26 44 51	1♊34 54	7♊54 25	13 41.5	14 27.8	9 36.0	6 44.4	20 53.7	10 46.2	16 48.3	13 54.7	3 58.4	6 01.4	17 02.7	20 40.6
Sa	23 58 19	27 43 27	14 18 02	20 46 14	13 38.3	14 25.2	11 13.7	7 59.0	21 32.1	11 03.1	16 55.1	13 54.9	3 55.7	5 59.7	17 01.1	20 40.2
Su	0 02 16	28 42 06	27 19 27	3♋58 09	13 35.2	14D 24.5	12 50.3	9 13.5	22 10.6	11 20.1	17 02.1	13 55.2	3 53.0	5 57.9	16 59.5	20 39.9
M	0 06 13	29 40 47	10♋42 43	17 33 29	13 32.0	14R 24.6	14 26.0	10 28.1	22 49.0	11 37.3	17 09.2	13 55.6	3 50.3	5 56.1	16 57.9	20 39.6
Tu	0 10 09	0♎39 30	24 30 41	1♌34 26	13 28.8	14 24.4	16 00.7	11 42.6	23 27.5	11 54.7	17 16.4	13 56.2	3 47.6	5 54.2	16 56.3	20 39.3
W	0 14 06	1 38 16	8♌44 42	16 01 14	13 25.6	14 22.6	17 34.4	12 57.2	24 06.0	12 12.2	17 23.8	13 56.8	3 44.9	5 52.3	16 54.7	20 39.1
Th	0 18 02	2 37 04	23 23 38	0♍51 15	13 22.4	14 18.3	19 07.2	14 11.8	24 44.5	12 29.8	17 31.3	13 57.5	3 42.1	5 50.4	16 53.1	20 38.8
F	0 21 59	3 35 54	8♍23 14	15 58 29	13 19.3	14 11.4	20 39.1	15 26.3	25 23.0	12 47.6	17 38.9	13 58.3	3 39.4	5 48.5	16 51.5	20 38.6
Sa	0 25 55	4 34 46	23 35 47	1♎13 47	13 16.1	14 01.9	22 10.0	16 40.9	26 01.5	13 05.5	17 46.7	13 59.2	3 36.7	5 46.5	16 50.0	20 38.4
Su	0 29 52	5 33 40	8♎51 02	16 26 09	13 12.9	13 51.0	23 40.0	17 55.5	26 40.0	13 23.6	17 54.7	14 00.2	3 34.0	5 44.5	16 48.4	20 38.3
M	0 33 48	6♎32 36	23 57 46	1♏24 42	13♋09.7	13♋39.8	25♎09.0	19♎10.1	27♍18.6	13♐41.8	18♐02.7	14♑01.3	3♈31.3	5♉42.4	16♓46.9	20♑38.2

1st of Month

Julian Day # 2458727.5
Obliquity 23°26'10"
SVP 4♓59'22"
GC 27♐06.8
Eris 24♈10.9R

Day	⚴
1	2♏04.2
6	3 57.0
11	5 52.0
16	7 49.0
21	9 47.7
26	11 48.1

Day	⚵
1	3♍35.0
6	5 47.8
11	7 59.4
16	10 09.7
21	12 18.5
26	14 26.0

Day	⚶
1	25♉49.8
6	26 30.7
11	27 02.6
16	27 24.9
21	27 37.0
26	27 38.5R

DECLINATION and LATITUDE

Day	☉ Decl	☽ Decl	☽ Lat	☽12h Decl	☿ Decl	☿ Lat	♀ Decl	♀ Lat	♂ Decl	♂ Lat	⚳ Decl	⚳ Lat	♃ Decl	♃ Lat	♄ Decl	♄ Lat
Su	8N28	4N18	4N55	1N26	11N13	1N46	7N56	1N25	9N17	1N05	22S31	1S14	22S16	0N21	22S27	0N14
M	8 06	1S25	5 06	4S13	10 29	1 46	7 27	1 25	9 03	1 05	22 35	1 16	22 17	0 20	22 28	0 14
Tu	7 44	6 55	4 57	9 29	9 44	1 44	6 58	1 25	8 48	1 05	22 39	1 18	22 17	0 20	22 28	0 14
W	7 22	11 53	4 30	14 05	8 58	1 43	6 29	1 25	8 34	1 05	22 43	1 20	22 18	0 20	22 28	0 14
Th	6 60	16 04	3 47	17 49	8 12	1 40	5 59	1 24	8 19	1 04	22 48	1 21	22 19	0 20	22 28	0 13
F	6 38	19 18	2 54	20 30	7 26	1 37	5 30	1 24	8 04	1 04	22 52	1 23	22 19	0 20	22 29	0 13
Sa	6 15	21 26	1 53	22 05	6 39	1 34	5 00	1 23	7 49	1 04	22 56	1 25	22 20	0 19	22 29	0 13
Su	5 53	22 27	0 48	22 32	5 51	1 30	4 30	1 23	7 34	1 04	23 00	1 27	22 21	0 19	22 29	0 13
M	5 30	22 21	0S17	21 53	5 04	1 26	4 00	1 22	7 20	1 04	23 05	1 29	22 21	0 19	22 29	0 13
Tu	5 08	21 11	1 21	20 15	4 16	1 21	3 30	1 22	7 05	1 04	23 09	1 31	22 22	0 19	22 29	0 13
W	4 45	19 05	2 20	17 43	3 29	1 16	3 00	1 21	6 50	1 03	23 13	1 32	22 23	0 19	22 30	0 13
Th	4 22	16 10	3 13	14 28	2 42	1 11	2 30	1 20	6 35	1 03	23 17	1 34	22 23	0 19	22 30	0 13
F	3 59	12 37	3 57	10 38	1 54	1 05	1 60	1 20	6 20	1 03	23 21	1 36	22 24	0 18	22 30	0 13
Sa	3 36	8 34	4 30	6 24	1 07	0 60	1 29	1 19	6 04	1 03	23 26	1 38	22 25	0 18	22 30	0 13
Su	3 13	4 11	4 52	1 55	0 20	0 54	0 59	1 18	5 49	1 03	23 30	1 39	22 26	0 18	22 30	0 12
M	2 50	0N22	5 01	2N40	0S26	0 47	0 28	1 17	5 34	1 02	23 34	1 41	22 26	0 18	22 30	0 12
Tu	2 27	4 57	4 57	7 12	1 13	0 41	0S02	1 16	5 19	1 02	23 38	1 43	22 27	0 18	22 30	0 12
W	2 04	9 23	4 40	11 29	1 59	0 34	0 33	1 15	5 04	1 02	23 42	1 44	22 28	0 18	22 31	0 12
Th	1 41	13 30	4 09	15 23	2 44	0 27	1 04	1 13	4 48	1 02	23 46	1 46	22 29	0 18	22 31	0 12
F	1 18	17 06	3 26	18 39	3 29	0 21	1 34	1 12	4 33	1 01	23 50	1 48	22 30	0 17	22 31	0 12
Sa	0 54	19 59	2 32	21 05	4 14	0 14	2 05	1 11	4 18	1 01	23 54	1 49	22 30	0 17	22 31	0 12
Su	0 31	21 55	1 29	22 28	4 58	0 06	2 35	1 10	4 02	1 01	23 58	1 51	22 31	0 17	22 31	0 12
M	0 08	22 41	0 20	22 34	5 42	0S01	3 06	1 08	3 47	1 01	24 02	1 53	22 32	0 17	22 31	0 12
Tu	0S16	22 05	0N53	21 16	6 25	0 08	3 36	1 07	3 31	1 01	24 06	1 54	22 33	0 17	22 31	0 12
W	0 39	20 05	2 05	18 34	7 08	0 15	4 07	1 05	3 16	1 00	24 10	1 56	22 34	0 17	22 31	0 11
Th	1 02	16 43	3 11	14 35	7 50	0 23	4 37	1 04	3 01	1 00	24 14	1 57	22 35	0 16	22 31	0 11
F	1 26	12 12	4 04	9 36	8 32	0 30	5 07	1 02	2 45	0 60	24 18	1 59	22 36	0 16	22 31	0 11
Sa	1 49	6 51	4 42	3 60	9 13	0 37	5 38	1 00	2 30	0 60	24 21	2 00	22 36	0 16	22 31	0 11
Su	2 13	1 05	4 59	1S50	9 53	0 45	6 08	0 59	2 14	0 59	24 25	2 02	22 37	0 16	22 31	0 11
M	2S36	4S43	4N56	7S29	10S33	0S52	6S38	0N57	1N58	0N59	24S29	2S03	22S38	0N16	22S31	0N11

Day	⚷ Decl	⚷ Lat	♅ Decl	♅ Lat	♆ Decl	♆ Lat	♇ Decl	♇ Lat
1	4N51	3N13	13N11	0S31	5S53	1S03	22S18	0S30
6	4 47	3 13	13 09	0 31	5 56	1 03	22 19	0 30
11	4 42	3 13	13 07	0 31	5 60	1 03	22 20	0 30
16	4 36	3 13	13 05	0 31	6 03	1 04	22 21	0 31
21	4 31	3 13	13 02	0 31	6 06	1 04	22 22	0 31
26	4 25	3 13	12 59	0 31	6 09	1 04	22 22	0 32

Day	⚴ Decl	⚴ Lat	⚵ Decl	⚵ Lat	⚶ Decl	⚶ Lat	Eris Decl	Eris Lat
1	12N41	26N27	7N25	2S59	11N18	8S08	1S42	11S54
6	11 59	26 19	6 46	2 48	11 16	8 20	1 43	11 54
11	11 18	26 11	6 08	2 38	11 12	8 31	1 44	11 54
16	10 37	26 05	5 29	2 28	11 06	8 42	1 45	11 54
21	9 58	25 59	4 49	2 17	10 58	8 53	1 46	11 54
26	9 20	25 54	4 10	2 07	10 48	9 03	1 47	11 55

Moon Phenomena

Max/0 Decl		
dy	hr mn	
1	18:02	0 S
8	9:36	22S32
15	22:03	0 N
23	1:43	22N41
29	4:26	0 S

Max/0 Lat		
dy	hr mn	
2	0:53	5N06
8	17:37	0 S
16	4:39	5S02
23	6:31	0 N
29	7:43	5N00

Perigee/Apogee			
dy	hr m		kilometers
13	13:33	a	406378
28	2:12	p	357804

PH	dy	hr mn	
☽	6	3:12	13♐15
○	14	4:34	21♓05
☾	22	2:42	28♊49
●	28	18:28	5♎20

Void of Course Moon

Last Aspect				☽ Ingress		
2	8:35	♇	□	♏	2	23:36
4	10:59	♇	⚹	♐	5	3:09
6	16:04	♀	□	♑	7	10:38
9	8:31	♀	△	♒	9	21:25
11	5:24	♃	⚹	♓	12	9:53
14	4:34	☉	☍	♈	14	22:34
16	16:04	♇	□	♉	17	10:32
19	13:58	☉	△	♊	19	20:59
22	2:42	☉	□	♋	22	4:51
23	22:06	♂	⚹	♌	24	9:21
25	16:15	☿	⚹	♍	26	10:38
28	3:59	♂	☌	♎	28	10:04
30	2:07	☿	☌	♏	30	9:43

DAILY ASPECTARIAN

☽☍⚷ 6:43
☿⚼♇ 7:12
☽⚺☿ 8:40
☽⚹⚳ 8:46
☽⚻♅ 9:23
☿□⚳ 9:30
☉⚺☽ 13:10
☽⚺♂ 13:40
☿△♅ 14:12
♀△♄ 18:50
☽□♄ 21:41
☽⚺♀ 21:57
☽⚹♃ 23:25

☽⚻♆ 3:11
☽□♇ 8:35
☽∠⚳ 9:17
☉☌♂ 10:44
☽∠☿ 12:30
☽⋕⚷ 14:43
☽∠♂ 15:02
☉∠☽ 15:08
♀□♃ 16:27
☽∥♆ 19:28
⚳⚻♅ 23:48

☽∠♃ 0:03
☽⋕♀ 0:13
☽∠♀ 0:43
☉⋕☽ 3:31
☽⚼♆ 3:46
☽⚻⚷ 7:25
☽⋕♂ 8:22
☽☍♅ 10:19
☽⚺⚳ 10:30
☽⋕☿ 11:29
☿☌♂ 15:41
☽⚹♂ 17:13
☽⚹☿ 17:23
☉⚹☽ 17:59
☽⚹♄ 23:19

4 W
☽⚺♃ 1:30
☉☌☿ 1:41
☽⚹♀ 4:33
☽△♆ 5:10
☽⋕♅ 6:52
☽⚼⚷ 8:56
☽⚹♇ 10:59
♀☍♆ 11:27
☿∥♂ 18:57

5 Th
☽∠♄ 1:28
♀⋕♆ 2:55
☽△⚷ 11:24
☿△♄ 12:38
☽∠♇ 13:36
☽⚻♅ 14:37
☽☌⚳ 15:50

6 F
☽□♂ 0:50
♃∥♇ 0:56
☉□☽ 3:12
☽⚺♄ 4:37
☿□♃ 7:12
☽☌♃ 7:21
☽□☿ 7:22
☽□♆ 10:54
☽□♀ 16:04
☽⚺♇ 17:13
☽⚼♅ 18:15
☉△♄ 21:57

7 Sa
♀△♇ 3:47
☿☍♆ 7:20
♀∥⚷ 12:08
♀⚼♅ 14:10
☽∥♇ 18:44
☉⋕♆ 19:03
☽∥♃ 19:14
☽□⚷ 19:17
☿⋕♆ 20:49
☉∥☿ 22:28
☽△♅ 22:48

8 Su
☽⚺⚳ 1:19
☽∥♄ 1:53
☽∥♄ 1:53
☽△♂ 12:54
☽☌♄ 13:43
☉□♃ 15:28
☽⚺♃ 17:05
☉△☽ 17:12
☽⚹♆ 20:19
☽∥♃ 23:42

9 M
☽∥♇ 0:35
☽△☿ 3:04
☽☌♇ 3:05
☿△♇ 3:10
♂△♄ 4:15
☽∠⚳ 7:21
☽△♀ 8:31
☿⚼♅ 10:00
☿∥⚷ 10:30
☽⚼♂ 20:13
☽∠♃ 23:01

10 Tu
☉⚼☽ 1:34
☽∠♆ 2:03
☽⚹⚷ 6:13
☉☍♆ 7:25
☽□♅ 9:58
☽⚹⚳ 13:57
☽⚼☿ 14:20
☽⚼♀ 17:59

11 W
☽⚺♄ 1:26
☉∥⚷ 3:47
☽⚻♂ 4:03
☽⚹♃ 5:24
☽⚺♆ 8:09
☉⚻☽ 10:25
☽∠⚷ 12:19
☽⚺♇ 15:09

12 Th
☽⚻☿ 1:59
☽⚻♀ 3:49
☽∠♄ 7:44
♂□♃ 9:07
☿∥♀ 16:29
☽⚺⚷ 18:34
☽⋕♅ 20:53
☽∠♇ 21:30
☽⚹♅ 22:28

13 F
☽□⚳ 3:57
☽⚹♄ 14:05
☿☌♀ 15:12
☽□♃ 18:36
☉△♇ 19:43
☽☍♂ 20:13
☽☌♆ 20:44

14 Sa
☽⚹♇ 3:50
♂⋕♆ 4:18
☉☍☽ 4:34
☽∠♅ 4:46
♂☍♆ 5:27
☉⚼♅ 6:54
☿ ♎ 7:16
♀ ♎ 13:44
☽∥♆ 14:02
☽⋕♂ 14:39
☽⋕⚷ 21:39
☽☍♀ 23:35

15 Su
☽☍☿ 1:09
☉⋕☽ 5:35
☽☌⚷ 6:59
☽⚺♅ 10:56
☽△⚳ 17:52
☽⋕♀ 19:03
☽∥☿ 20:23

16 M
☽⋕☿ 0:25
☽∥♀ 0:28
☿⋕♀ 0:36
☽□♄ 2:31
☽△♃ 7:30
☽⚺♆ 8:58
☉∥☽ 11:54
☽⚻♂ 11:59
☽□♇ 16:04
☿☍⚷ 16:56
☽∥⚷ 22:06
☉⚻☽ 22:07

17 Tu
☽⚼⚳ 0:31
☽∥♂ 1:51
☽⋕♆ 5:55
☽⚼♃ 13:35
☽∠♆ 14:42
☽⚻♀ 18:22
☽⚺⚷ 18:35
☽⚼♂ 19:24
♀☍⚷ 20:22
☿⚻♅ 20:58
☽☌♅ 22:32
☽⚻☿ 22:47

18 W
☉⋕☿ 1:55
☉⚼☽ 6:20
☽⚻⚳ 6:49
♄ D 8:48
☽△♄ 13:53
☽⚻♃ 19:16
☽⚹♆ 20:03
☽∥♅ 21:16
☽∠⚷ 23:49

19 Th
☽△♂ 2:21
☽⚼♀ 3:00
☽△♇ 3:03
☽⚼☿ 8:35
♀⚻♅ 10:28
☉△☽ 13:58
♂△♇ 15:55
☉⋕♀ 16:36
☽⚼♄ 18:54

20 F
♂∥⚷ 1:53
☽⚹⚷ 4:32
♂⚼♅ 4:37
☽⚼♇ 7:47
☽⚺♅ 8:25
☽△♀ 10:52
☽△☿ 17:25
☽☍⚳ 17:47
☿⚹⚳ 20:50
☽⚻♄ 23:17

21 Sa
☿⋕♂ 1:28
☽☍♃ 4:55
☽□♆ 5:03
☿⋕⚷ 8:51
♃∥♄ 11:33
☽⚻♇ 11:49
☽∠♅ 12:23
☽□♂ 14:06
♃□♆ 16:45

22 Su
☉□☽ 2:42
☽⋕♇ 9:20
☽□⚷ 11:48
☽⋕♄ 13:58
☽⋕♃ 14:30
☽⚹♅ 15:32
☿□♄ 16:20
☽□♀ 23:32

23 M
☽⚻⚳ 1:38
☽☍♄ 5:40
☽□☿ 7:24
☉ ♎ 7:51
☽△♆ 10:57
☽⚻♃ 11:24
☽⋕♃ 12:33
☽⋕♄ 13:32
☿∥♆ 14:13
☽☍♇ 17:22
☽⋕♇ 17:59
♀⋕♂ 21:26
☽⚹♂ 22:06

24 Tu
⚶ R 3:44
☽⚼⚳ 4:11
♀⚹⚳ 5:04
☉⚹☽ 11:14
☽⚼♆ 12:35
☽⚼♃ 13:17
☿⚻♆ 13:58
☽△⚷ 15:41
☽□♅ 19:13
☿⚹♃ 21:02

25 W
☽∠♂ 0:37
☽△⚳ 5:50
☽⚹♀ 7:36
☽⚻♄ 8:36
☽⚻♆ 13:26
☉∠☽ 13:56
☽△♃ 14:22
♀⋕⚷ 14:51
☽⚹☿ 16:15
☽⚼⚷ 16:24
♀□♄ 19:21
☽⚻♇ 19:33

26 Th
☽⚺♂ 2:16
☽⚼♄ 8:58
☽∠♀ 10:11
☉⚺☽ 15:51
☽⚻⚷ 16:30
☽∠☿ 19:10
☽⚼♇ 19:38
☽△♅ 19:55
☽∥♅ 20:14
☿□♇ 23:53

27 F
☉☍⚷ 1:23
☽□⚳ 7:07
☽△♄ 8:51
☽⚺♀ 12:09
☽☍♆ 13:22
☽□♃ 14:46
☽⋕☿ 14:54
☽△♇ 19:21
☽⚼♅ 19:34
☽⚺☿ 21:30

28 Sa
♀⚻♆ 2:51
☽⋕♆ 2:53
☽☌♂ 3:59
☽⋕♀ 4:47
☽∥⚷ 10:26
☽☍⚷ 15:42
☉☌☽ 18:28
☽∥♂ 19:03
☽⚻♅ 19:07
☉⋕☽ 19:39
♀⚹♃ 23:42

29 Su
☉⋕♂ 0:54
♀∥♆ 2:46
☉⚻♅ 4:15
☽⚹⚳ 7:20
☽□♄ 8:09
☽⚻♆ 12:34
☽⋕♂ 13:03
☽⚹♃ 14:28
☉∥☽ 14:30
☽☌♀ 15:39
☽□♇ 18:41
☽⋕⚷ 22:27

30 M
☽☌☿ 2:07
☽⚺♂ 5:37
☽∥♆ 6:22
☽∠⚳ 7:46
☽∥♀ 9:03
☽⚼♆ 12:35
☽∠♃ 14:47
☽⚻⚷ 15:23
☽☍♅ 18:57
☉⚺☽ 21:49

October 2019

LONGITUDE

Day	Sid.Time	☉	☽	☽ 12 hour	Mean☊	True☊	☿	♀	♂	⚳	♃	♄	⚷	♅	♆	♇
	h m s	° ' "	° ' "	° ' "	° '	° '	° '	° '	° '	° '	° '	° '	° '	° '	° '	° '
1 Tu	0 37 45	7♎31 34	8♏45 55	16♏00 37	13♋06.6	13♋29.7	26♎37.2	20♎24.7	27♍57.2	14♐00.2	18♐10.9	14♑02.5	3♈28.6	5♉40.4	16♓45.3	20♑38.1
2 W	0 41 42	8 30 34	23 08 13	0♐08 24	13 03.4	13R 21.7	28 04.3	21 39.3	28 35.7	14 18.6	18 19.2	14 03.8	3R 25.9	5R 38.3	16R 43.8	20R 38.0
3 Th	0 45 38	9 29 36	7♐01 02	13 46 11	13 00.2	13 16.3	29 30.6	22 53.9	29 14.3	14 37.3	18 27.7	14 05.1	3 23.2	5 36.1	16 42.3	20D 38.0
4 F	0 49 35	10 28 39	20 24 07	26 55 13	12 57.0	13 13.4	0♏55.8	24 08.5	29 52.9	14 56.0	18 36.3	14 06.6	3 20.5	5 34.0	16 40.8	20 38.0
5 Sa	0 53 31	11 27 45	3♑19 57	9♑38 54	12 53.8	13 12.5	2 20.1	25 23.0	0♎31.6	15 14.9	18 45.0	14 08.2	3 17.8	5 31.8	16 39.4	20 38.1
6 Su	0 57 28	12 26 52	15 52 41	22 01 58	12 50.7	13 12.4	3 43.3	26 37.6	1 10.2	15 33.8	18 53.8	14 09.9	3 15.1	5 29.6	16 37.9	20 38.1
7 M	1 01 24	13 26 01	28 07 22	4♒09 34	12 47.5	13 12.0	5 05.4	27 52.2	1 48.9	15 53.0	19 02.7	14 11.7	3 12.5	5 27.4	16 36.5	20 38.2
8 Tu	1 05 21	14 25 11	10♒09 12	16 06 52	12 44.3	13 10.1	6 26.5	29 06.8	2 27.5	16 12.2	19 11.8	14 13.6	3 09.8	5 25.2	16 35.1	20 38.4
9 W	1 09 17	15 24 24	22 03 08	27 58 31	12 41.1	13 06.0	7 46.4	0♏21.4	3 06.2	16 31.5	19 21.0	14 15.6	3 07.2	5 22.9	16 33.7	20 38.5
10 Th	1 13 14	16 23 38	3♓53 31	9♓48 33	12 38.0	12 59.0	9 05.2	1 36.0	3 44.9	16 51.0	19 30.3	14 17.6	3 04.5	5 20.7	16 32.3	20 38.7
11 F	1 17 11	17 22 54	15 44 00	21 40 10	12 34.8	12 49.1	10 22.6	2 50.5	4 23.6	17 10.5	19 39.7	14 19.8	3 01.9	5 18.4	16 30.9	20 38.9
12 Sa	1 21 07	18 22 12	27 37 21	3♈35 47	12 31.6	12 36.9	11 38.8	4 05.1	5 02.3	17 30.2	19 49.2	14 22.0	2 59.3	5 16.0	16 29.6	20 39.1
13 Su	1 25 04	19 21 32	9♈35 39	15 37 05	12 28.4	12 23.1	12 53.5	5 19.7	5 41.0	17 50.0	19 58.8	14 24.4	2 56.8	5 13.7	16 28.2	20 39.4
14 M	1 29 00	20 20 54	21 40 15	27 45 13	12 25.2	12 08.9	14 06.6	6 34.3	6 19.8	18 09.9	20 08.6	14 26.8	2 54.2	5 11.4	16 26.9	20 39.7
15 Tu	1 32 57	21 20 18	3♉52 06	10♉00 59	12 22.1	11 55.3	15 18.2	7 48.8	6 58.6	18 29.9	20 18.4	14 29.3	2 51.6	5 09.0	16 25.6	20 40.1
16 W	1 36 53	22 19 44	16 11 59	22 25 13	12 18.9	11 43.6	16 28.0	9 03.4	7 37.4	18 50.0	20 28.4	14 32.0	2 49.1	5 06.6	16 24.4	20 40.4
17 Th	1 40 50	23 19 12	28 40 49	4♊58 58	12 15.7	11 34.6	17 35.8	10 18.0	8 16.2	19 10.2	20 38.5	14 34.7	2 46.6	5 04.2	16 23.1	20 40.8
18 F	1 44 46	24 18 43	11♊19 51	17 43 42	12 12.5	11 28.5	18 41.6	11 32.5	8 55.0	19 30.4	20 48.6	14 37.5	2 44.1	5 01.8	16 21.9	20 41.2
19 Sa	1 48 43	25 18 15	24 10 49	0♋41 29	12 09.4	11 25.2	19 45.2	12 47.1	9 33.8	19 50.8	20 58.9	14 40.4	2 41.7	4 59.4	16 20.7	20 41.7
20 Su	1 52 39	26 17 50	7♋16 00	13 54 42	12 06.2	11D 24.1	20 46.2	14 01.7	10 12.7	20 11.3	21 09.3	14 43.4	2 39.2	4 57.0	16 19.5	20 42.2
21 M	1 56 36	27 17 28	20 37 55	27 25 54	12 03.0	11R 24.2	21 44.5	15 16.2	10 51.6	20 31.9	21 19.8	14 46.4	2 36.8	4 54.6	16 18.3	20 42.7
22 Tu	2 00 33	28 17 08	4♌18 54	11♌17 06	11 59.8	11 24.2	22 39.8	16 30.8	11 30.5	20 52.6	21 30.3	14 49.6	2 34.5	4 52.1	16 17.2	20 43.2
23 W	2 04 29	29 16 49	18 20 32	25 29 09	11 56.6	11 22.8	23 31.7	17 45.4	12 09.4	21 13.4	21 41.0	14 52.9	2 32.1	4 49.7	16 16.1	20 43.8
24 Th	2 08 26	0♏16 34	2♍42 44	10♍00 55	11 53.5	11 19.3	24 20.0	19 00.0	12 48.4	21 34.3	21 51.8	14 56.2	2 29.8	4 47.2	16 15.0	20 44.4
25 F	2 12 22	1 16 20	17 23 07	24 48 35	11 50.3	11 13.1	25 04.2	20 14.5	13 27.3	21 55.2	22 02.6	14 59.6	2 27.5	4 44.8	16 14.0	20 45.0
26 Sa	2 16 19	2 16 09	2♎16 27	9♎45 39	11 47.1	11 04.5	25 43.9	21 29.1	14 06.3	22 16.3	22 13.6	15 03.1	2 25.2	4 42.3	16 12.9	20 45.7
27 Su	2 20 15	3 15 59	17 15 01	24 43 23	11 43.9	10 54.4	26 18.6	22 43.7	14 45.3	22 37.4	22 24.6	15 06.7	2 22.9	4 39.8	16 11.9	20 46.4
28 M	2 24 12	4 15 52	2♏09 32	9♏32 20	11 40.8	10 43.9	26 47.8	23 58.3	15 24.3	22 58.6	22 35.8	15 10.4	2 20.7	4 37.4	16 10.9	20 47.1
29 Tu	2 28 08	5 15 47	16 50 44	24 03 52	11 37.6	10 34.2	27 10.9	25 12.8	16 03.4	23 19.9	22 47.0	15 14.2	2 18.6	4 34.9	16 10.0	20 47.8
30 W	2 32 05	6 15 44	1♐11 01	8♐11 40	11 34.4	10 26.5	27 27.4	26 27.4	16 42.4	23 41.3	22 58.3	15 18.0	2 16.4	4 32.4	16 09.0	20 48.6
31 Th	2 36 02	7♏15 42	15 05 30	21 52 23	11♋31.2	10♋21.2	27♏36.5	27♏42.0	17♎21.5	24♐02.7	23♐09.7	15♑21.9	2♈14.3	4♉30.0	16♓08.2	20♑49.4

1st of Mo

Julian Da 2458757
Obliquit 23°26'11
SVP 4♓59'
GC 27♐0
Eris 23♈55

Day	⚴
1	13♏49
6	15 53
11	17 57
16	20 02
21	22 09
26	24 16.
31	26 23.

Day	⚵
1	16♍31
6	18 36
11	20 38.
16	22 39.
21	24 37.
26	26 34.
31	28 28

Day	⚶
1	27♉28.
6	27 07.
11	26 35.
16	25 53
21	25 00.
26	23 58
31	22 49.

DECLINATION and LATITUDE

Day	☉ Decl	☽ Decl	☽ Lat	☽12h Decl	☿ Decl	☿ Lat	♀ Decl	♀ Lat	♂ Decl	♂ Lat	⚳ Decl	⚳ Lat	♃ Decl	♃ Lat	♄ Decl	♄ Lat
1 Tu	2S59	10S07	4N32	12S34	11S12	0S60	7S07	0N55	1N43	0N59	24S33	2S05	22S39	0N16	22S31	0N11
2 W	3 22	14 49	3 52	16 49	11 50	1 07	7 37	0 53	1 27	0 59	24 36	2 06	22 40	0 16	22 31	0 11
3 Th	3 46	18 32	2 59	19 59	12 27	1 14	8 07	0 51	1 12	0 58	24 40	2 08	22 41	0 15	22 31	0 11
4 F	4 09	21 08	1 57	21 59	13 04	1 21	8 36	0 49	0 56	0 58	24 44	2 09	22 42	0 15	22 31	0 11
5 Sa	4 32	22 32	0 52	22 46	13 40	1 29	9 05	0 47	0 41	0 58	24 47	2 11	22 43	0 15	22 31	0 10
6 Su	4 55	22 44	0S14	22 24	14 15	1 36	9 34	0 45	0 25	0 58	24 51	2 12	22 43	0 15	22 31	0 10
7 M	5 18	21 48	1 18	20 58	14 50	1 42	10 03	0 43	0 09	0 57	24 54	2 14	22 44	0 15	22 31	0 10
8 Tu	5 41	19 54	2 17	18 37	15 23	1 49	10 31	0 41	0S06	0 57	24 58	2 15	22 45	0 15	22 31	0 10
9 W	6 04	17 09	3 10	15 30	15 56	1 56	10 59	0 39	0 22	0 57	25 01	2 16	22 46	0 15	22 30	0 10
10 Th	6 27	13 42	3 54	11 47	16 27	2 02	11 27	0 37	0 38	0 57	25 04	2 18	22 47	0 14	22 30	0 10
11 F	6 49	9 44	4 27	7 35	16 58	2 09	11 55	0 34	0 53	0 56	25 08	2 19	22 48	0 14	22 30	0 10
12 Sa	7 12	5 22	4 50	3 06	17 28	2 15	12 22	0 32	1 09	0 56	25 11	2 21	22 49	0 14	22 30	0 10
13 Su	7 35	0 47	4 59	1N33	17 56	2 21	12 50	0 30	1 24	0 56	25 14	2 22	22 49	0 14	22 30	0 10
14 M	7 57	3N52	4 56	6 11	18 24	2 26	13 16	0 28	1 40	0 55	25 17	2 23	22 50	0 14	22 30	0 10
15 Tu	8 19	8 26	4 38	10 38	18 50	2 32	13 43	0 25	1 56	0 55	25 21	2 25	22 51	0 14	22 30	0 09
16 W	8 41	12 43	4 08	14 42	19 16	2 37	14 09	0 23	2 11	0 55	25 24	2 26	22 52	0 14	22 29	0 09
17 Th	9 04	16 31	3 25	18 11	19 40	2 42	14 35	0 20	2 27	0 54	25 27	2 27	22 53	0 14	22 29	0 09
18 F	9 25	19 38	2 32	20 51	20 03	2 46	15 01	0 18	2 42	0 54	25 30	2 29	22 54	0 13	22 29	0 09
19 Sa	9 47	21 49	1 30	22 30	20 24	2 50	15 26	0 15	2 58	0 54	25 33	2 30	22 55	0 13	22 29	0 09
20 Su	10 09	22 52	0 22	22 56	20 44	2 54	15 50	0 13	3 13	0 54	25 35	2 31	22 55	0 13	22 28	0 09
21 M	10 30	22 39	0N49	22 03	21 03	2 57	16 15	0 10	3 29	0 53	25 38	2 33	22 56	0 13	22 28	0 09
22 Tu	10 52	21 06	1 58	19 49	21 20	2 60	16 39	0 08	3 44	0 53	25 41	2 34	22 57	0 13	22 28	0 09
23 W	11 13	18 13	3 03	16 20	21 35	3 02	17 02	0 05	3 60	0 53	25 44	2 35	22 58	0 13	22 28	0 09
24 Th	11 34	14 11	3 57	11 48	21 48	3 03	17 25	0 03	4 15	0 52	25 46	2 37	22 59	0 13	22 27	0 09
25 F	11 55	9 14	4 37	6 30	22 00	3 04	17 48	0 00	4 31	0 52	25 49	2 38	22 59	0 13	22 27	0 09
26 Sa	12 16	3 40	4 59	0 46	22 10	3 04	18 10	0S02	4 46	0 52	25 52	2 39	23 00	0 13	22 27	0 08
27 Su	12 36	2S09	5 00	5S01	22 17	3 03	18 32	0 05	5 01	0 51	25 54	2 40	23 01	0 12	22 26	0 08
28 M	12 56	7 49	4 42	10 28	22 22	3 01	18 53	0 08	5 17	0 51	25 56	2 42	23 02	0 12	22 26	0 08
29 Tu	13 16	12 57	4 04	15 14	22 25	2 58	19 14	0 10	5 32	0 51	25 59	2 43	23 02	0 12	22 26	0 08
30 W	13 36	17 15	3 12	18 60	22 25	2 54	19 34	0 13	5 47	0 50	26 01	2 44	23 03	0 12	22 25	0 08
31 Th	13S56	20S27	2N10	21S35	22S22	2S49	19S54	0S15	6S03	0N50	26S03	2S45	23S04	0N12	22S25	0N08

Day	⚷ Decl	⚷ Lat	♅ Decl	♅ Lat	♆ Decl	♆ Lat	♇ Decl	♇ La
1	4N19	3N12	12N55	0S31	6S12	1S04	22S23	0
6	4 14	3 12	12 52	0 31	6 15	1 03	22 23	0
11	4 08	3 11	12 48	0 31	6 18	1 03	22 23	0
16	4 02	3 11	12 44	0 31	6 20	1 03	22 24	0
21	3 57	3 10	12 40	0 31	6 23	1 03	22 24	0
26	3 51	3 09	12 36	0 31	6 25	1 03	22 23	0
31	3N46	3N09	12N32	0S31	6S26	1S03	22S23	0

Day	⚴ Decl	⚴ Lat	⚵ Decl	⚵ Lat	⚶ Decl	⚶ Lat	Eris Decl	Eris La
1	8N44	25N50	3N31	1S57	10N36	9S13	1S48	11
6	8 09	25 46	2 52	1 47	10 23	9 23	1 49	11
11	7 36	25 44	2 14	1 37	10 08	9 30	1 50	11
16	7 04	25 42	1 36	1 26	9 52	9 37	1 51	11
21	6 34	25 40	0 58	1 16	9 36	9 41	1 52	11
26	6 07	25 40	0 22	1 06	9 20	9 43	1 53	11
31	5N41	25N40	0S14	0S55	9N04	9S43	1S54	11

Moon Phenomena

Max/0 Decl
dy hr mn
5 16:04 22S47
13 4:03 0 N
20 8:05 22N57
26 15:09 0 S

Perigee/Apogee
dy hr m kilometers
10 18:32 a 405899
26 10:38 p 361315

Max/0 Lat
dy hr mn
5 18:51 0 S
13 5:25 5S00
20 7:29 0 N
26 14:00 5N02

PH dy hr mn
☽ 5 16:48 12♑09
○ 13 21:09 20♈14
☾ 21 12:40 27♋49
● 28 3:40 4♏25

Void of Course Moo

Last Aspect	☽ Ingre
2 9:47 ♂ ⚹	♐ 2 11
4 7:35 ♀ ⚹	♑ 4 17
6 23:27 ☉ ⚹	♒ 7 3
8 18:28 ♃ ⚹	♓ 9 16
11 9:56 ♇ ⚹	♈ 12 4
13 22:00 ♇ □	♉ 14 16
16 8:39 ♇ △	♊ 17 2
19 2:15 ☉ □	♋ 19 10
21 12:40 ☉ □	♌ 21 16
23 9:15 ☿ □	♍ 23 19
25 13:01 ☿ ⚹	♎ 25 20
27 8:23 ♃ ⚹	♏ 27 20
29 17:36 ☿ ☌	♐ 29 22

DAILY ASPECTARIAN

1 Tu
⚳⊻♄ 3:12
♀□♇ 4:19
☽∥☿ 5:54
☽∠♂ 7:14
☽⚹♄ 8:44
☽⊻⚳ 8:51
☽△♆ 13:13
☽#♅ 13:46
☽⊻♃ 15:47
☽⚼⚷ 16:05
☽⚹♇ 19:46
☽⊻♀ 21:15

2 W
☉∠☽ 0:41
☽⊻☿ 9:25
☽⚹♂ 9:47
☽∠♄ 10:10
☿⊻♂ 15:46
☽△⚷ 17:40
☽⊼♅ 21:31
☽∠♇ 21:34

3 Th
☽∠♀ 1:43
☿∠⚳ 2:24
☉⚹☽ 4:43
♇ D 6:40
☿ ♏ 8:15
☽⊻♄ 12:35
☽☌⚳ 13:51
☽∠☿ 14:55
☿#♅ 17:02
☽□♆ 17:15
☽☌♃ 20:41

4 F
☽⚼♅ 0:18
☽⊻♇ 0:25
♂ ♎ 4:23
☉#⚷ 7:01
☽⚹♀ 7:35
☿⚼♆ 12:34
☽□♂ 18:27
☽∥♇ 20:09
☽⚹☿ 21:53
☽∥♄ 23:35
☽□⚷ 23:56

5 Sa
☽△♅ 4:09
☿⊼⚷ 16:06
☉□☽ 16:48
☽☌♄ 20:41
☽⊻⚳ 23:23

6 Su
☽∥♃ 0:09
☽∥♃ 0:09
☽⚹♆ 1:28
☿∠♃ 3:25
☽⊻♃ 5:56
☽∥♄ 8:49
☽☌♇ 9:16
☽∥♇ 12:19
☽□♀ 23:27

7 M
☽∠⚳ 5:37
☿☍♅ 6:18
☽∠♆ 6:54
☽△♂ 7:44
☽⚹⚷ 10:04
☽∠♃ 11:55
☽□♅ 14:33
☽□☿ 15:37
☉□♄ 19:08

8 Tu
☽⊻♄ 8:13
☉△☽ 9:21
☽⚹⚳ 12:31
☽⊻♆ 12:55
☽⚼♂ 15:33
☽∠⚷ 16:05
♀ ♏ 17:07
☽⚹♃ 18:28
☽⊻♇ 21:09

9 W
♂☍⚷ 0:34
⚳□♆ 2:29
☽∥☿ 7:46
☉∥♆ 13:45
☽∠♄ 14:39
☉⚼☽ 18:28
☽△♀ 18:48
☽⊻⚷ 22:21
♀⚼♆ 22:50
☽⊼♂ 23:41

10 Th
☽⚹♅ 2:56
☉⊼♆ 3:25
☽∠♇ 3:33
☽#♅ 5:40
♀∠⚳ 6:32
☽△☿ 11:50
☽∥♀ 12:29
☉⚹⚳ 16:31
☽⚹♄ 21:09

11 F
☽☌♆ 1:35
☽□⚳ 3:00
♀⊼⚷ 3:33
☉⊼☽ 3:38
☽⚼♀ 4:46
☽□♃ 8:03
☽∠♅ 9:13
☽⚹♇ 9:56
☉∥☽ 14:55
☽∥♆ 19:01
☽⚼☿ 21:48

12 Sa
☽#⚷ 6:42
♂⊼♅ 8:02
☽☌⚷ 10:45
☽⊼♀ 14:29
☽⊻♅ 15:18
☽☍♂ 15:44
♀∠♃ 16:18
☽∥♂ 20:58
♀#♅ 21:18
♀☍♅ 22:08

13 Su
☽⊼☿ 7:19
☽□♄ 9:37
☽#♂ 11:57
☽⊻♆ 13:40
♀⊻♂ 14:18
☽△⚳ 16:52
☉⚹♃ 18:03
☽△♃ 20:56
☉☍☽ 21:09
☽□♇ 22:00

14 M
☽∥⚷ 1:03
♃⚼♅ 5:27
☿⚹♄ 6:57
☉□♇ 7:39
☽#♆ 12:47
☽∠♆ 19:14
☽⊻⚷ 22:02
☽⚼⚳ 23:15
☉#☽ 23:20

15 Tu
☽☌♅ 2:30
☽⚼♃ 2:51
☽⊼♂ 6:25
☽☍♀ 8:34
☽△♄ 20:46
☿△♆ 22:46

16 W
☽∥♅ 0:05
☽⚹♆ 0:24
☽☍☿ 0:34
☽∠⚷ 3:07
☽⊼⚳ 5:14
☽⊼♃ 8:22
☽△♇ 8:39
☽#♀ 9:42
☉⊼☽ 12:51
☽⚼♂ 13:04

17 Th
☽⚼♄ 1:43
☿⚼⚷ 3:44
♃⊻♇ 5:46
☽⚹⚷ 7:47
☽⊻♅ 12:08
☽⚼♇ 13:20
☽△♂ 19:12
☉⚼☽ 19:52

18 F
☽⊼♀ 0:26
☽#☿ 4:30
☽⊼♄ 6:13
☽□♆ 9:26
☽⊼☿ 15:03
☽☍⚳ 15:44
☽∠♅ 16:15
☽⊼♇ 17:32
☽☍♃ 17:59

19 Sa
☉△☽ 2:15
☿⊻⚳ 3:16
☽⚼♀ 7:22
⚳⚼♅ 8:59
☽#♇ 9:53
☽#♄ 11:39
☽□⚷ 15:37
☽⚹♅ 19:48
☽⚼☿ 21:03
☿⚹♇ 22:22

20 Su
☽#♃ 3:53
☽□♂ 5:36
☿⊻♃ 11:24
☽#♃ 11:45
☽△♀ 13:28
☽☍♄ 13:30
♀⚹♄ 14:00
☽△♆ 16:18
☽⊼⚳ 23:49

21 M
☽☍♇ 0:08
☽⊼♃ 1:15
☽△☿ 2:07
☽#♄ 4:23
☽#♇ 5:56
☉□☽ 12:40
⚳⊻♇ 12:49
☽⚼♆ 18:45
♀△♆ 19:41
☽△⚷ 20:59
☽#☿ 21:42

22 Tu
☽□♅ 0:57
☽⚼⚳ 2:46
☽⚼♃ 3:50
☽⚹♂ 12:59
♂#⚷ 16:31
☽⊼♄ 18:07
♀⚼⚷ 19:51
☽⊼♆ 20:30
☽⚼⚷ 22:38
☽□♀ 22:55

23 W
☽⊼♇ 4:02
☽△⚳ 4:59
☽△♃ 5:42
☽#♀ 7:01
☽□☿ 9:15
☽∠♂ 15:29
☉ ♏ 17:21
☽⚼♄ 19:23
☉⚹☽ 19:40
☽⊼⚷ 23:39

24 Th
☽△♅ 3:25
☽⚼♇ 4:59
☽∥♅ 7:59
☉#☽ 12:17
☽⊻♂ 17:19
☽△♄ 20:06
☉∠☽ 22:04
☽☍♆ 22:08
☉⚼♆ 23:04

25 F
☽⚼♅ 3:49
☽⚹♀ 5:03
☽△♇ 5:27
☽□⚳ 7:31
☽□♃ 7:38
♀⚹♇ 9:54
☽#♆ 12:24
☽⚹☿ 13:01
⚳☌♃ 17:39
☽#♂ 19:34
☽∥⚷ 23:11
☉⊻☽ 23:59

26 Sa
☽☍⚷ 0:14
☉⊼⚷ 3:30
☽⊼♅ 3:53
☽∠♀ 7:22
☽∠☿ 14:07
♀⊻♃ 16:48
☽☌♂ 19:49
☽□♄ 20:33
♀⊻⚳ 21:10
☽⊼♆ 22:19
☉#♅ 23:02

27 Su
☽□♇ 5:39
☽#⚷ 7:02
☽⚹♃ 8:23
☽⚹⚳ 8:50
☽⊻♀ 9:35
☽∥♂ 12:35
♂□♄ 14:32
☽⊻☿ 15:04
☽∥♆ 17:58
☽⚼♆ 22:25

28 M
☽⊼⚷ 0:18
☉☌☽ 3:40
☽☍♅ 3:59
☉☍♅ 8:16
☿∥♇ 8:30
☽∠♃ 8:57
☽∠⚳ 9:41
☽⚹♄ 21:20
☽#♅ 22:01
☽⊻♂ 22:38
☽△♆ 22:53

29 Tu
☽⚼⚷ 0:46
☉∥☽ 1:44
♂⊼♆ 3:58
☽⚹♇ 6:33
☽⊻♃ 9:59
☽⊻⚳ 11:03
☽☌♀ 15:15
☽☌☿ 17:36
☽∠♄ 22:30

30 W
☽∠♂ 0:56
☽△⚷ 1:51
☽⊼♅ 5:42
☽∠♇ 7:54
☉⊻☽ 9:21
☿∥♇ 14:01
☽∥♀ 18:30
☿☌♀ 22:06

31 Th
☽⊻♄ 0:29
☽□♆ 1:50
☽⚹♂ 4:11
☽⚼♅ 7:45
☽⊻♇ 10:08
☉∠☽ 13:43
☽☌♃ 14:31
☿ R 15:43
☽☌⚳ 16:20
☽∥☿ 21:55
☽⊻☿ 22:21
☽∥♇ 23:59

LONGITUDE — November 2019

Day	Sid.Time	☉	☽	☽ 12 hour	Mean☊	True☊	☿	♀	♂	⚳	♃	♄	⚷	♅	♆	♇
	h m s	° ' "	° ' "	° ' "	° '	° '	° '	° '	° '	° '	° '	° '	° '	° '	° '	° '
1 F	2 39 58	8♏15 43	28♐32 23	5♑05 41	11♋28.0	10♋18.5	27♏37.8	28♏56.5	18♎00.6	24♐24.3	23♐21.2	15♑25.9	2♈12.2	4♉27.5	16♓07.3	20♑50.2
2 Sa	2 43 55	9 15 45	11♑32 38	17 53 41	11 24.9	10D 17.9	27R 30.5	0♐11.1	18 39.7	24 45.9	23 32.7	15 30.0	2R 10.2	4R 25.1	16R 06.4	20 51.1
3 Su	2 47 51	10 15 48	24 09 20	0♒20 12	11 21.7	10 18.4	27 14.3	1 25.6	19 18.8	25 07.6	23 44.3	15 34.2	2 08.2	4 22.6	16 05.6	20 52.0
4 M	2 51 48	11 15 53	6♒26 54	12 30 05	11 18.5	10R 19.2	26 48.6	2 40.2	19 58.0	25 29.4	23 56.1	15 38.4	2 06.2	4 20.2	16 04.9	20 52.9
5 Tu	2 55 44	12 16 00	18 30 24	24 28 32	11 15.3	10 19.0	26 13.2	3 54.7	20 37.1	25 51.2	24 07.8	15 42.8	2 04.3	4 17.7	16 04.1	20 53.8
6 W	2 59 41	13 16 08	0♓25 07	6♓20 46	11 12.2	10 17.2	25 28.3	5 09.3	21 16.3	26 13.1	24 19.7	15 47.1	2 02.4	4 15.3	16 03.4	20 54.8
7 Th	3 03 37	14 16 18	12 16 04	18 11 33	11 09.0	10 13.2	24 34.1	6 23.8	21 55.5	26 35.1	24 31.6	15 51.6	2 00.6	4 12.9	16 02.7	20 55.8
8 F	3 07 34	15 16 30	24 07 44	0♈05 05	11 05.8	10 06.8	23 31.4	7 38.3	22 34.7	26 57.1	24 43.7	15 56.2	1 58.8	4 10.5	16 02.0	20 56.8
9 Sa	3 11 31	16 16 42	6♈03 58	12 04 44	11 02.6	9 58.5	22 21.5	8 52.8	23 13.9	27 19.2	24 55.7	16 00.8	1 57.0	4 08.1	16 01.4	20 57.8
0 Su	3 15 27	17 16 57	18 07 42	24 13 04	10 59.4	9 48.7	21 06.0	10 07.3	23 53.2	27 41.4	25 07.9	16 05.5	1 55.3	4 05.7	16 00.8	20 58.9
1 M	3 19 24	18 17 13	0♉21 01	6♉31 42	10 56.3	9 38.5	19 47.1	11 21.8	24 32.4	28 03.6	25 20.1	16 10.2	1 53.6	4 03.3	16 00.2	21 00.0
2 Tu	3 23 20	19 17 31	12 45 11	19 01 31	10 53.1	9 28.8	18 27.2	12 36.3	25 11.7	28 25.9	25 32.4	16 15.1	1 52.0	4 01.0	15 59.7	21 01.1
3 W	3 27 17	20 17 50	25 20 43	1♊42 47	10 49.9	9 20.5	17 08.8	13 50.8	25 51.0	28 48.2	25 44.7	16 20.0	1 50.4	3 58.6	15 59.2	21 02.3
4 Th	3 31 13	21 18 12	8♊07 42	14 35 26	10 46.7	9 14.2	15 54.5	15 05.2	26 30.4	29 10.7	25 57.1	16 24.9	1 48.9	3 56.3	15 58.7	21 03.5
5 F	3 35 10	22 18 35	21 05 59	27 39 20	10 43.6	9 10.3	14 46.7	16 19.7	27 09.7	29 33.1	26 09.6	16 30.0	1 47.4	3 54.0	15 58.3	21 04.7
6 Sa	3 39 06	23 18 59	4♋15 31	10♋54 32	10 40.4	9D 08.7	13 47.5	17 34.2	27 49.1	29 55.7	26 22.1	16 35.1	1 45.9	3 51.7	15 57.9	21 05.9
7 Su	3 43 03	24 19 26	17 36 27	24 21 19	10 37.2	9 08.8	12 58.2	18 48.6	28 28.5	0♑18.2	26 34.7	16 40.2	1 44.5	3 49.4	15 57.5	21 07.1
8 M	3 47 00	25 19 55	1♌09 13	8♌00 14	10 34.0	9 10.0	12 20.1	20 03.1	29 07.9	0 40.9	26 47.4	16 45.5	1 43.2	3 47.2	15 57.1	21 08.4
9 Tu	3 50 56	26 20 25	14 54 23	21 51 44	10 30.9	9R 11.3	11 53.6	21 17.5	29 47.4	1 03.6	27 00.1	16 50.8	1 41.9	3 45.0	15 56.8	21 09.7
0 W	3 54 53	27 20 57	28 52 14	5♍55 50	10 27.7	9 11.8	11D 38.8	22 32.0	0♏26.8	1 26.3	27 12.8	16 56.1	1 40.6	3 42.7	15 56.6	21 11.0
1 Th	3 58 49	28 21 31	13♍02 23	20 11 37	10 24.5	9 10.8	11 35.4	23 46.4	1 06.3	1 49.1	27 25.6	17 01.6	1 39.4	3 40.6	15 56.3	21 12.4
2 F	4 02 46	29 22 07	27 23 13	4♎36 43	10 21.3	9 08.0	11 42.9	25 00.8	1 45.8	2 12.0	27 38.5	17 07.0	1 38.2	3 38.4	15 56.1	21 13.8
3 Sa	4 06 42	0♐22 44	11♎51 35	19 07 11	10 18.1	9 03.6	12 00.6	26 15.2	2 25.3	2 34.9	27 51.4	17 12.6	1 37.1	3 36.3	15 55.9	21 15.1
4 Su	4 10 39	1 23 23	26 22 48	3♏37 39	10 15.0	8 57.9	12 27.6	27 29.7	3 04.9	2 57.8	28 04.4	17 18.2	1 36.1	3 34.2	15 55.8	21 16.6
5 M	4 14 35	2 24 04	10♏50 57	18 01 54	10 11.8	8 51.9	13 03.1	28 44.1	3 44.5	3 20.8	28 17.4	17 23.8	1 35.1	3 32.1	15 55.7	21 18.0
6 Tu	4 18 32	3 24 46	25 09 43	2♐13 44	10 08.6	8 46.3	13 46.0	29 58.5	4 24.1	3 43.8	28 30.5	17 29.6	1 34.1	3 30.0	15 55.6	21 19.5
7 W	4 22 29	4 25 30	9♐13 20	16 08 01	10 05.4	8 41.9	14 35.7	1♑12.9	5 03.7	4 06.9	28 43.6	17 35.3	1 33.2	3 28.0	15D 55.6	21 20.9
8 Th	4 26 25	5 26 15	22 57 24	29 41 14	10 02.3	8 39.2	15 31.2	2 27.3	5 43.3	4 30.1	28 56.8	17 41.2	1 32.3	3 26.0	15 55.6	21 22.4
9 F	4 30 22	6 27 02	6♑19 25	12♑51 58	9 59.1	8D 38.1	16 31.9	3 41.6	6 23.0	4 53.2	29 10.0	17 47.0	1 31.5	3 24.1	15 55.6	21 24.0
0 Sa	4 34 18	7♐27 49	19 18 59	25 40 44	9♋55.9	8♋38.5	17♏37.0	4♑56.0	7♏02.6	5♑16.5	29♐23.2	17♑53.0	1♈30.8	3♉22.1	15♓55.7	21♑25.5

1st of Month

Julian Day #
2458788.5
Obliquity
23°26'10"
SVP 4♓59'16"
GC 27♐07.0
Eris 23♈37.6R

Day	⚴
1	26♏49.3
6	28 57.5
11	1♐06.1
16	3 15.0
21	5 24.0
26	7 33.1

Day	⚵
1	28♍50.7
6	0♎41.8
11	2 30.1
16	4 15.6
21	5 57.9
26	7 36.9

Day	⚶
1	22♉34.9R
6	21 19.5R
11	20 01.5R
16	18 43.2R
21	17 27.0R
26	16 15.2R

DECLINATION and LATITUDE

Day	☉ Decl	☽ Decl	☽ Lat	☽12h Decl	☿ Decl	☿ Lat	♀ Decl	♀ Lat	♂ Decl	♂ Lat	⚳ Decl	⚳ Lat	♃ Decl	♃ Lat	♄ Decl	♄ Lat
1 F	14S16	22S23	1N02	22S53	22S16	2S42	20S13	0S18	6S18	0N50	26S06	2S47	23S05	0N12	22S25	0N08
2 Sa	14 35	23 03	0S07	22 55	22 06	2 34	20 31	0 21	6 33	0 49	26 08	2 48	23 05	0 12	22 24	0 08
3 Su	14 54	22 29	1 13	21 47	21 53	2 24	20 49	0 23	6 48	0 49	26 10	2 49	23 06	0 11	22 24	0 08
4 M	15 12	20 50	2 15	19 40	21 36	2 13	21 07	0 26	7 03	0 49	26 12	2 50	23 07	0 11	22 24	0 08
5 Tu	15 31	18 17	3 10	16 43	21 15	2 00	21 24	0 28	7 18	0 48	26 14	2 52	23 07	0 11	22 23	0 08
6 W	15 49	14 59	3 55	13 07	20 50	1 46	21 40	0 31	7 33	0 48	26 16	2 53	23 08	0 11	22 23	0 07
7 Th	16 07	11 07	4 30	9 01	20 21	1 29	21 56	0 34	7 48	0 48	26 18	2 54	23 08	0 11	22 22	0 07
8 F	16 25	6 50	4 54	4 34	19 48	1 12	22 11	0 36	8 03	0 47	26 19	2 55	23 09	0 11	22 22	0 07
9 Sa	16 42	2 15	5 05	0N05	19 12	0 53	22 25	0 39	8 18	0 47	26 21	2 57	23 10	0 11	22 21	0 07
0 Su	16 59	2N27	5 02	4 48	18 33	0 33	22 39	0 41	8 33	0 46	26 23	2 58	23 10	0 11	22 21	0 07
1 M	17 16	7 07	4 46	9 24	17 52	0 12	22 52	0 44	8 48	0 46	26 24	2 59	23 11	0 10	22 20	0 07
2 Tu	17 33	11 36	4 16	13 41	17 11	0N09	23 04	0 46	9 02	0 46	26 26	3 00	23 11	0 10	22 20	0 07
3 W	17 49	15 39	3 33	17 26	16 29	0 29	23 16	0 49	9 17	0 45	26 27	3 01	23 12	0 10	22 19	0 07
4 Th	18 05	19 02	2 39	20 25	15 49	0 49	23 27	0 51	9 32	0 45	26 29	3 03	23 12	0 10	22 19	0 07
5 F	18 21	21 33	1 36	22 23	15 12	1 07	23 37	0 54	9 46	0 45	26 30	3 04	23 13	0 10	22 18	0 07
6 Sa	18 36	22 56	0 26	23 09	14 39	1 24	23 47	0 56	10 01	0 44	26 31	3 05	23 13	0 10	22 18	0 07
7 Su	18 51	23 02	0N46	22 35	14 10	1 38	23 56	0 58	10 15	0 44	26 32	3 06	23 14	0 10	22 17	0 07
8 M	19 06	21 47	1 56	20 40	13 46	1 51	24 04	1 01	10 29	0 43	26 33	3 07	23 14	0 10	22 17	0 06
9 Tu	19 20	19 15	3 01	17 32	13 28	2 02	24 12	1 03	10 44	0 43	26 34	3 09	23 15	0 10	22 16	0 06
0 W	19 34	15 34	3 57	13 21	13 15	2 11	24 19	1 05	10 58	0 43	26 35	3 10	23 15	0 09	22 16	0 06
1 Th	19 48	10 57	4 39	8 23	13 07	2 18	24 25	1 08	11 12	0 42	26 36	3 11	23 15	0 09	22 15	0 06
2 F	20 01	5 41	5 04	2 54	13 04	2 23	24 30	1 10	11 26	0 42	26 37	3 12	23 16	0 09	22 14	0 06
3 Sa	20 14	0 04	5 10	2S46	13 07	2 27	24 35	1 12	11 40	0 41	26 38	3 13	23 16	0 09	22 14	0 06
4 Su	20 26	5S35	4 56	8 18	13 13	2 29	24 39	1 14	11 54	0 41	26 39	3 15	23 16	0 09	22 13	0 06
5 M	20 38	10 54	4 23	13 20	13 23	2 29	24 42	1 16	12 08	0 40	26 39	3 16	23 17	0 09	22 12	0 06
6 Tu	20 50	15 35	3 35	17 34	13 36	2 29	24 44	1 18	12 21	0 40	26 40	3 17	23 17	0 09	22 12	0 06
7 W	21 01	19 18	2 34	20 44	13 53	2 27	24 46	1 20	12 35	0 40	26 40	3 18	23 17	0 09	22 11	0 06
8 Th	21 12	21 50	1 25	22 37	14 11	2 24	24 47	1 22	12 49	0 39	26 41	3 19	23 17	0 09	22 10	0 06
9 F	21 23	23 04	0 13	23 12	14 32	2 21	24 47	1 24	13 02	0 39	26 41	3 20	23 17	0 09	22 10	0 06
0 Sa	21S33	23S00	0S58	22S31	14S54	2N16	24S47	1S26	13S16	0N38	26S41	3S22	23S18	0N08	22S09	0N06

Day	⚷ Decl	⚷ Lat	♅ Decl	♅ Lat	♆ Decl	♆ Lat	♇ Decl	♇ Lat
1	3N45	3N08	12N31	0S31	6S27	1S03	22S23	0S34
6	3 41	3 07	12 27	0 31	6 28	1 03	22 23	0 35
11	3 36	3 07	12 23	0 31	6 29	1 03	22 22	0 35
16	3 32	3 06	12 19	0 31	6 30	1 03	22 22	0 36
21	3 29	3 04	12 16	0 31	6 30	1 03	22 21	0 36
26	3 26	3 03	12 12	0 31	6 31	1 03	22 21	0 36

Day	⚴ Decl	⚴ Lat	⚵ Decl	⚵ Lat	⚶ Decl	⚶ Lat	Eris Decl	Eris Lat
1	5N36	25N41	0S21	0S53	9N01	9S42	1S54	11S54
6	5 13	25 42	0 55	0 42	8 46	9 38	1 55	11 53
11	4 52	25 44	1 28	0 31	8 33	9 32	1 55	11 53
16	4 33	25 47	1 60	0 20	8 22	9 22	1 56	11 52
21	4 17	25 51	2 30	0 08	8 14	9 10	1 56	11 52
26	4 03	25 56	2 58	0N04	8 08	8 55	1 56	11 51

Moon Phenomena

Max/0 Decl
dy hr mn
2 0:29 23S03
9 11:33 0 N
16 13:57 23N09
23 0:16 0 S
29 10:34 23S12

Perigee/Apogee
dy hr m kilometers
7 8:35 a 405057
23 7:38 p 366718

Max/0 Lat
dy hr mn
1 21:41 0 S
9 7:41 5S05
16 8:50 0 N
22 19:31 5N10
29 4:14 0 S

PH dy hr mn
☽ 4 10:24 11♒42
○ 12 13:36 19♉52
☾ 19 21:12 27♌14
● 26 15:07 4♐03

Void of Course Moon

Last Aspect		☽ Ingress
31 14:31	♃ ☌	♑ 1 2:39
3 5:48	♅ ✶	♒ 3 11:21
5 14:38	♀ □	♓ 5 23:09
8 1:14	♃ □	♈ 8 11:50
10 14:02	♃ △	♉ 10 23:19
12 15:49	♇ △	♊ 13 8:47
15 11:41	♂ △	♋ 15 16:16
17 20:16	♂ □	♌ 17 21:58
19 21:12	☉ □	♍ 20 1:56
22 3:33	☉ ✶	♎ 22 4:21
24 2:51	♃ ✶	♏ 24 5:59
25 17:31	♇ ✶	♐ 26 8:12
28 10:51	♃ ☌	♑ 28 12:34
30 3:58	♇ ☌	♒ 30 20:14

DAILY ASPECTARIAN

1 F: ☽∥♄ 0:27; ☽⚺♀ 0:48; ☉∠♃ 2:41; ☽□⚷ 6:40; ☽△♅ 10:48; ♂∥♆ 14:11; ☉✶☽ 19:22; ♀ ♐ 20:26

2 Sa: ☽∠☿ 1:47; ♀∠♄ 6:27; ☽☌♄ 7:30; ☽∠♀ 7:36; ☽✶♆ 8:36; ☽□♂ 14:12; ☽☌♇ 17:40; ☉∠⚳ 18:52; ☽⚺♃ 23:11

3 Su: ☽∥♄ 1:43; ☽⚺⚳ 1:56; ☽∥♇ 1:59; ☽✶☿ 5:48; ☽∥☿ 12:39; ♀△⚷ 13:21; ☽∠♆ 13:28; ☽✶⚷ 15:29; ☽✶♀ 15:44; ☽□♅ 19:51; ☽∥♀ 21:13

4 M: ⚵ ♎ 2:29; ☽∠♃ 5:00; ☽∠⚳ 8:15; ☉□☽ 10:24; ☽⚺♄ 18:22; ☿∥♀ 18:43; ☽⚺♆ 19:07; ☽∠⚷ 21:08

5 Tu: ☽△♂ 4:29; ☽⚺♇ 4:48; ♀⚻♅ 7:10; ☿⚺⚳ 8:17; ♄∥♇ 10:11; ♂□♇ 10:29; ☽✶♃ 11:30; ☽□☿ 14:38; ☽✶⚳ 15:15; ☉∥☽ 18:48

6 W: ☽∠♄ 0:45; ☽⚺⚷ 3:16; ☽✶♅ 7:44; ☽□♀ 10:42; ☽∠♇ 11:08; ☽⚼♂ 12:32; ♀∠♇ 14:51; ☽⋕♅ 16:07

7 Th: ☿⚺♃ 0:49; ☉△☽ 4:26; ☽✶♄ 7:19; ☽☌♆ 7:39; ☽∠♅ 14:01; ☽✶♇ 17:34; ☽∥♂ 17:41; ☽⚻♂ 20:41; ♀∠♂ 21:33; ☽△☿ 22:53

8 F: ☽□♃ 1:14; ☽∥♆ 1:53; ☽□⚳ 5:52; ♀ ♐ 10:19; ☿⚺♂ 12:39; ☉⚼☽ 13:31; ☽☌⚷ 15:46; ☽⋕⚷ 16:51; ☉✶♄ 17:07; ☉△♆ 17:57; ♀∥♄ 18:10; ☽⚺♅ 20:09; ♀∥♇ 20:12

9 Sa: ☽⚼☿ 2:21; ♄✶♆ 2:47; ☽△♀ 6:16; ☉⚼⚷ 15:37; ☽⚺♆ 19:49; ☽□♄ 19:56; ☉⚻☽ 22:11

10 Su: ☿✶♇ 2:10; ☽⚻☿ 5:18; ☽□♇ 5:38; ☽∥⚷ 5:57; ☽☍♂ 11:59; ☽△♃ 14:02; ☽⚼♀ 15:20; ☽△⚳ 19:23; ☽⋕♆ 20:41

11 M: ☽∠♆ 1:16; ☽⚺⚷ 3:00; ☽☌♅ 7:11; ☽⋕♂ 9:17; ☉∥☿ 14:52; ☉☌☿ 15:23; ☽⚼♃ 19:40; ☽⚻♀ 23:41

12 Tu: ☽⚼⚳ 1:21; ☽∥♅ 4:23; ☽✶♆ 6:13; ☽△♄ 6:45; ☽∠⚷ 7:52; ☽☍☿ 9:52; ☉☍☽ 13:36; ♀∥♃ 15:01; ☽△♇ 15:49; ♂✶♃ 18:22

13 W: ☽⚻♃ 0:46; ☽⚻♂ 1:00; ☽⋕☿ 4:38; ☿⚼⚷ 5:54; ☽⚻⚳ 6:44; ☽⚼♄ 11:22; ☽✶⚷ 12:13; ☿✶♄ 14:36; ☉⋕☽ 16:01; ☽⚺♅ 16:12; ☉✶♇ 18:02; ☽⚼♇ 20:08; ☿△♆ 22:35

14 Th: ☽⚼♂ 6:37; ☿⚺♀ 8:10; ☽⚻☿ 13:15; ☽☍♀ 14:17; ☽□♆ 14:33; ☽⚻♄ 15:28; ♀□♆ 17:08; ☽∠♅ 19:58; ☽⚻♇ 23:58

15 F: ☉⚻☽ 2:24; ♀⚺♄ 3:33; ☿∠⚳ 3:49; ☽☍♃ 9:25; ☽⋕♄ 10:36; ☽△♂ 11:41; ☽⋕♇ 11:41; ☽⚼☿ 14:44; ☽☍⚳ 15:55; ☽□⚷ 19:29; ☽✶♅ 23:17

16 Sa: ⚳ ♑ 4:37; ☉⚼☽ 7:56; ☽△☿ 16:09; ☽△♆ 21:03; ☽☍♄ 22:19

17 Su: ♀⚼♅ 0:15; ☽⚻♀ 2:22; ☽☍♇ 6:16; ☉△☽ 12:54; ☽⋕♇ 15:48; ☽⚻♃ 16:11; ☽⋕♄ 17:07; ☽□♂ 20:16; ☽⚻⚳ 23:09; ☽⚼♆ 23:39

18 M: ☽△⚷ 1:00; ☽□♅ 4:37; ☽⚼♀ 7:31; ☽⚼♃ 18:53; ☽□☿ 18:54; ☿∠♃ 19:29; ♀⚺♇ 21:26; ☉⋕☽ 23:25

19 Tu: ☽⚻♆ 1:48; ☽⚼⚳ 2:03; ☽⚼⚷ 3:06; ☽⚻♄ 3:23; ♂ ♏ 7:41; ☽⚻♇ 10:49; ☽△♀ 12:06; ☉⚺♃ 19:55; ☽△♃ 21:08; ☉□☽ 21:12

20 W: ☽✶♂ 2:49; ☽△⚳ 4:30; ☽⚻⚷ 4:46; ☽⚼♄ 5:15; ☽△♅ 8:13; ☽⚼♇ 12:27; ☽⋕☿ 12:58; ⚳□⚷ 14:18; ☽∥♅ 17:33; ♂⚼♆ 17:58; ☿ D 19:15; ☽✶☿ 21:33; ☽⋕♂ 22:51

21 Th: ☽☍♆ 4:52; ☽∠♂ 5:24; ☽△♄ 6:44; ☽⚼♅ 9:26; ☽△♇ 13:43; ♂⚻⚷ 19:32; ☽□♀ 19:40; ☽⋕♆ 20:22; ☽∠☿ 22:52

22 F: ☽□♃ 0:26; ☉✶☽ 3:33; ☽☍⚷ 7:03; ☽⚺♂ 7:37; ☽□⚳ 8:13; ☽∥⚷ 9:34; ☽⚻♅ 10:22; ☉ ♐ 15:00

23 Sa: ☽⚺☿ 0:15; ☉∠☽ 6:15; ☽⚻♆ 6:44; ☽□♄ 8:54; ♂✶⚳ 13:45; ☽⋕⚷ 14:53; ☽□♇ 15:33; ☿∠♀ 22:52

24 Su: ☽✶♀ 2:01; ☽✶♃ 2:51; ☽∥♆ 4:04; ☉△⚷ 4:56; ☽⚼♆ 7:32; ☽⚻⚷ 8:38; ☉⚺☽ 8:55; ☽✶⚳ 11:12; ☽☌♂ 11:37; ☽☍♅ 11:52; ♀☌♃ 13:35; ♂☍♅ 16:52; ☉∠♄ 23:54

25 M: ☽☌☿ 3:51; ☽∠♃ 4:08; ☽∠♀ 5:16; ☽∥♂ 6:13; ☽⋕♅ 6:19; ♂⋕♅ 8:26; ☽△♆ 8:29; ☽⚼⚷ 9:34; ⚳△♅ 10:47; ☽✶♄ 11:01; ☿∠♃ 12:13; ☽∥☿ 12:48; ☽∠⚳ 12:52; ☽✶♇ 17:31

26 Tu: ♀ ♑ 0:30; ☉⚻♅ 2:01; ☽⚺♃ 5:45; ☽⚺♀ 8:57; ☽△⚷ 10:52; ☉⚺⚳ 12:10; ☽∠♄ 12:32; ☽⚻♅ 14:08; ☽⚺⚳ 14:59; ☉☌☽ 15:07; ☽⚺♂ 16:29; ☽∠♇ 19:03

27 W: ♀□⚷ 6:29; ☽⚺☿ 9:58; ☽□♆ 11:38; ♆ D 12:33; ☽⚺♄ 14:39; ☽⚼♅ 16:03; ☉∥☽ 16:09; ☽∠♂ 19:51; ☽⚺♇ 21:12

28 Th: ☽∥♄ 4:30; ☽∥♇ 7:02; ☿△♆ 9:52; ☽☌♃ 10:51; ☽∠☿ 14:35; ☽□⚷ 15:19; ♀△♅ 18:29; ☽△♅ 18:42; ☽☌♀ 18:44; ☉⚺♂ 19:22; ☽☌⚳ 21:19; ☉∠♇ 22:45; ☿⚼⚷ 23:53

29 F: ☽✶♂ 0:07; ☉⚺☽ 0:15; ☽✶♆ 17:41; ☽✶☿ 20:31; ☽☌♄ 21:18

30 Sa: ☽☌♇ 3:58; ☿✶♄ 6:14; ☉∠☽ 6:26; ♀☌⚳ 9:37; ☽∥♇ 15:11; ☽∥♄ 18:15; ☽⚺♃ 19:25; ☽∠♆ 22:01; ☽✶⚷ 23:07

December 2019

LONGITUDE

Day	Sid.Time	☉	☽	☽ 12 hour	Mean☊	True ☊	☿	♀	♂	⚳	♃	♄	⚷	♅	♆	♇
	h m s	° ' "	° ' "	° ' "	° '	° '	° '	° '	° '	° '	° '	° '	° '	° '	° '	° '
1 Su	4 38 15	8♐28 38	1♒57 32	8♒09 47	9♋52.7	8♋39.9	18♏45.9	6♑10.3	7♏42.3	5♑39.7	29♐36.5	17♑59.0	1♈30.1	3♉20.2	15♓55.8	21♑27.1
2 M	4 42 11	9 29 27	14 17 59	20 22 38	9 49.6	8 41.8	19 58.2	7 24.7	8 22.0	6 03.0	29 49.8	18 05.0	1R 29.5	3R 18.4	15 55.9	21 28.6
3 Tu	4 46 08	10 30 18	26 24 19	2♓23 38	9 46.4	8 43.4	21 13.4	8 39.0	9 01.6	6 26.3	0♑03.1	18 11.1	1 28.9	3 16.6	15 56.1	21 30.2
4 W	4 50 05	11 31 09	8♓21 11	14 17 35	9 43.2	8R 44.2	22 31.0	9 53.3	9 41.5	6 49.7	0 16.5	18 17.2	1 28.3	3 14.8	15 56.3	21 31.9
5 Th	4 54 01	12 32 01	20 13 29	26 09 28	9 40.0	8 43.9	23 50.7	11 07.6	10 21.3	7 13.1	0 30.0	18 23.4	1 27.9	3 13.0	15 56.5	21 33.5
6 F	4 57 58	13 32 54	2♈06 08	8♈04 03	9 36.9	8 42.5	25 12.2	12 21.8	11 01.0	7 36.5	0 43.4	18 29.6	1 27.4	3 11.3	15 56.8	21 35.2
7 Sa	5 01 54	14 33 48	14 03 43	20 05 40	9 33.7	8 39.9	26 35.2	13 36.1	11 40.9	8 00.0	0 56.9	18 35.9	1 27.1	3 09.6	15 57.1	21 36.8
8 Su	5 05 51	15 34 42	26 10 19	2♉18 04	9 30.5	8 36.5	27 59.6	14 50.3	12 20.7	8 23.5	1 10.4	18 42.2	1 26.8	3 08.0	15 57.5	21 38.5
9 M	5 09 47	16 35 37	8♉29 15	14 44 08	9 27.3	8 32.8	29 25.1	16 04.5	13 00.5	8 47.0	1 23.9	18 48.5	1 26.5	3 06.4	15 57.8	21 40.2
10 Tu	5 13 44	17 36 34	21 02 54	27 25 42	9 24.1	8 29.2	0♐51.6	17 18.7	13 40.4	9 10.6	1 37.5	18 54.9	1 26.3	3 04.8	15 58.3	21 41.9
11 W	5 17 40	18 37 31	3♊52 36	10♊23 34	9 21.0	8 26.2	2 18.9	18 32.9	14 20.3	9 34.1	1 51.1	19 01.4	1 26.2	3 03.3	15 58.7	21 43.7
12 Th	5 21 37	19 38 29	16 58 34	23 37 28	9 17.8	8 24.1	3 46.9	19 47.0	15 00.2	9 57.7	2 04.7	19 07.8	1 26.1	3 01.8	15 59.2	21 45.4
13 F	5 25 34	20 39 27	0♋20 05	7♋06 11	9 14.6	8D 23.0	5 15.5	21 01.1	15 40.1	10 21.4	2 18.4	19 14.3	1D 26.0	3 00.4	15 59.7	21 47.2
14 Sa	5 29 30	21 40 27	13 55 31	20 47 48	9 11.4	8 22.9	6 44.7	22 15.2	16 20.1	10 45.0	2 32.0	19 20.9	1 26.0	2 59.0	16 00.3	21 49.0
15 Su	5 33 27	22 41 27	27 42 44	4♌40 01	9 08.3	8 23.6	8 14.3	23 29.3	17 00.0	11 08.7	2 45.7	19 27.5	1 26.1	2 57.6	16 00.8	21 50.8
16 M	5 37 23	23 42 29	11♌39 21	18 40 25	9 05.1	8 24.7	9 44.4	24 43.4	17 40.1	11 32.4	2 59.4	19 34.1	1 26.2	2 56.3	16 01.5	21 52.6
17 Tu	5 41 20	24 43 31	25 42 57	2♍46 38	9 01.9	8 25.9	11 14.8	25 57.4	18 20.1	11 56.2	3 13.1	19 40.7	1 26.4	2 55.0	16 02.1	21 54.4
18 W	5 45 16	25 44 34	9♍51 12	16 56 24	8 58.7	8 26.8	12 45.5	27 11.9	19 00.1	12 19.9	3 26.9	19 47.4	1 26.7	2 53.8	16 02.8	21 56.3
19 Th	5 49 13	26 45 39	24 01 58	1♎07 38	8 55.6	8R 27.2	14 16.6	28 25.4	19 40.2	12 43.7	3 40.6	19 54.1	1 27.0	2 52.6	16 03.5	21 58.1
20 F	5 53 09	27 46 44	8♎13 08	15 18 10	8 52.4	8 27.1	15 47.9	29 39.3	20 20.3	13 07.5	3 54.4	20 00.9	1 27.3	2 51.5	16 04.3	22 00.0
21 Sa	5 57 06	28 47 50	22 22 28	29 25 43	8 49.2	8 26.4	17 19.4	0♒53.3	21 00.4	13 31.3	4 08.2	20 07.6	1 27.7	2 50.4	16 05.1	22 01.9
22 Su	6 01 03	29 48 56	6♏27 36	13♏27 47	8 46.0	8 25.5	18 51.3	2 07.2	21 40.5	13 55.1	4 22.0	20 14.4	1 28.2	2 49.4	16 05.9	22 03.7
23 M	6 04 59	0♑50 04	20 25 56	27 21 42	8 42.8	8 24.4	20 23.3	3 21.0	22 20.7	14 19.0	4 35.8	20 21.2	1 28.7	2 48.4	16 06.7	22 05.6
24 Tu	6 08 56	1 51 12	4♐14 45	11♐04 46	8 39.7	8 23.6	21 55.6	4 34.9	23 00.9	14 42.9	4 49.6	20 28.1	1 29.2	2 47.4	16 07.6	22 07.6
25 W	6 12 52	2 52 21	17 51 27	24 34 33	8 36.5	8 23.0	23 28.2	5 48.7	23 41.1	15 06.8	5 03.4	20 35.0	1 29.9	2 46.5	16 08.5	22 09.5
26 Th	6 16 49	3 53 31	1♑13 49	7♑49 06	8 33.3	8D 22.7	25 01.0	7 02.5	24 21.3	15 30.7	5 17.2	20 41.9	1 30.6	2 45.7	16 09.5	22 11.4
27 F	6 20 45	4 54 41	14 20 18	20 47 20	8 30.1	8 22.7	26 34.0	8 16.3	25 01.5	15 54.6	5 31.1	20 48.8	1 31.3	2 44.9	16 10.5	22 13.3
28 Sa	6 24 42	5 55 51	27 10 14	3♒29 04	8 27.0	8 22.8	28 07.2	9 30.2	25 41.8	16 18.5	5 44.9	20 55.7	1 32.1	2 44.1	16 11.5	22 15.3
29 Su	6 28 38	6 57 01	9♒44 01	15 55 15	8 23.8	8 23.0	29 40.7	10 43.7	26 22.1	16 42.5	5 58.7	21 02.7	1 32.9	2 43.4	16 12.5	22 17.2
30 M	6 32 35	7 58 11	22 03 05	28 07 50	8 20.6	8R 23.1	1♑14.5	11 57.3	27 02.4	17 06.4	6 12.6	21 09.7	1 33.8	2 42.8	16 13.6	22 19.2
31 Tu	6 36 32	8♑59 21	4♓09 53	10♓09 42	8♋17.4	8♋23.1	2♑48.6	13♒10.9	27♏42.7	17♑30.4	6♑26.4	21♑16.7	1♈34.8	2♉42.2	16♓14.7	22♑21.2

1st of Month

Julian Day # 2458818.5
Obliquity 23°26'10"
SVP 4♓59'12"
GC 27♐07.0
Eris 23♈22.3R

Day	⚴	Day	⚵	Day	⚶
1	9♐42.1	1	9♎12.2	1	15♉09.9R
6	11 50.8	6	10 43.5	6	14 13.1R
11	13 59.1	11	12 10.5	11	13 25.8R
16	16 07.0	16	13 33.0	16	12 49.1R
21	18 14.3	21	14 50.6	21	12 23.4R
26	20 20.8	26	16 02.8	26	12 09.0R
31	22 26.5	31	17 09.2	31	12 05.7

DECLINATION and LATITUDE

Day	☉ Decl	☽ Decl	☽ Lat	☽ 12h Decl	☿ Decl	☿ Lat	♀ Decl	♀ Lat	♂ Decl	♂ Lat	⚳ Decl	⚳ Lat	♃ Decl	♃ Lat	♄ Decl	♄ Lat
1 Su	21S43	21S44	2S04	20S43	15S18	2N12	24S45	1S28	13S29	0N38	26S42	3S23	23S18	0N08	22S08	0N05
2 M	21 52	19 27	3 03	17 60	15 42	2 06	24 43	1 30	13 42	0 37	26 42	3 24	23 18	0 08	22 08	0 05
3 Tu	22 01	16 21	3 52	14 33	16 07	2 01	24 40	1 31	13 55	0 37	26 42	3 25	23 18	0 08	22 07	0 05
4 W	22 10	12 37	4 31	10 35	16 33	1 54	24 37	1 33	14 08	0 36	26 42	3 26	23 18	0 08	22 06	0 05
5 Th	22 18	8 26	4 58	6 13	16 59	1 48	24 32	1 34	14 21	0 36	26 42	3 28	23 18	0 08	22 05	0 05
6 F	22 25	3 56	5 12	1 37	17 25	1 41	24 27	1 36	14 34	0 36	26 42	3 29	23 18	0 08	22 05	0 05
7 Sa	22 33	0N44	5 13	3N06	17 52	1 34	24 21	1 37	14 47	0 35	26 41	3 30	23 18	0 08	22 04	0 05
8 Su	22 39	5 27	4 59	7 46	18 17	1 27	24 15	1 39	14 59	0 35	26 41	3 31	23 18	0 08	22 03	0 05
9 M	22 46	10 02	4 32	12 13	18 43	1 20	24 08	1 40	15 12	0 34	26 41	3 32	23 18	0 08	22 02	0 05
10 Tu	22 52	14 17	3 52	16 12	19 08	1 13	23 60	1 41	15 24	0 34	26 40	3 34	23 18	0 07	22 01	0 05
11 W	22 57	17 60	2 59	19 33	19 33	1 05	23 51	1 43	15 37	0 33	26 40	3 35	23 18	0 07	22 01	0 05
12 Th	23 02	20 53	1 55	21 56	19 57	0 58	23 41	1 44	15 49	0 33	26 39	3 36	23 18	0 07	21 60	0 05
13 F	23 06	22 42	0 44	23 08	20 21	0 50	23 31	1 45	16 01	0 32	26 38	3 37	23 18	0 07	21 59	0 05
14 Sa	23 10	23 13	0N31	22 57	20 44	0 43	23 20	1 46	16 13	0 32	26 38	3 38	23 18	0 07	21 58	0 04
15 Su	23 14	22 20	1 45	21 22	21 06	0 36	23 09	1 47	16 25	0 31	26 37	3 40	23 18	0 07	21 57	0 04
16 M	23 17	20 04	2 54	18 28	21 27	0 28	22 57	1 48	16 37	0 31	26 36	3 41	23 17	0 07	21 56	0 04
17 Tu	23 20	16 36	3 53	14 29	21 47	0 21	22 44	1 48	16 48	0 30	26 35	3 42	23 17	0 07	21 55	0 04
18 W	23 22	12 10	4 38	9 41	22 06	0 13	22 30	1 49	16 60	0 30	26 34	3 43	23 17	0 07	21 55	0 04
19 Th	23 24	7 04	5 07	4 21	22 24	0 06	22 16	1 50	17 11	0 29	26 33	3 44	23 17	0 07	21 54	0 04
20 F	23 25	1 35	5 17	1S11	22 42	0S01	22 01	1 50	17 22	0 28	26 32	3 46	23 16	0 06	21 53	0 04
21 Sa	23 26	3S57	5 07	6 39	22 58	0 08	21 45	1 51	17 33	0 28	26 31	3 47	23 16	0 06	21 52	0 04
22 Su	23 26	9 16	4 40	11 45	23 13	0 15	21 29	1 51	17 44	0 27	26 29	3 48	23 16	0 06	21 51	0 04
23 M	23 26	14 04	3 56	16 11	23 27	0 22	21 13	1 51	17 55	0 27	26 28	3 49	23 15	0 06	21 50	0 04
24 Tu	23 25	18 04	2 58	19 42	23 40	0 28	20 55	1 52	18 06	0 26	26 27	3 51	23 15	0 06	21 49	0 04
25 W	23 24	21 02	1 51	22 04	23 52	0 35	20 37	1 52	18 17	0 26	26 25	3 52	23 14	0 06	21 48	0 04
26 Th	23 22	22 46	0 40	23 09	24 02	0 41	20 19	1 52	18 27	0 25	26 24	3 53	23 14	0 06	21 47	0 04
27 F	23 21	23 13	0S33	22 57	24 11	0 48	19 60	1 52	18 37	0 25	26 22	3 54	23 13	0 06	21 46	0 03
28 Sa	23 18	22 24	1 42	21 33	24 19	0 54	19 40	1 52	18 47	0 24	26 20	3 56	23 13	0 06	21 45	0 03
29 Su	23 15	20 28	2 45	19 08	24 26	0 60	19 20	1 51	18 58	0 23	26 18	3 57	23 12	0 06	21 44	0 03
30 M	23 12	17 37	3 39	15 54	24 31	1 05	18 59	1 51	19 07	0 23	26 17	3 58	23 12	0 06	21 43	0 03
31 Tu	23S08	14S03	4S22	12S04	24S35	1S11	18S38	1S51	19S17	0N22	26S15	3S59	23S11	0N05	21S42	0N03

Day	⚷ Decl	⚷ Lat	♅ Decl	♅ Lat	♆ Decl	♆ Lat	♇ Decl	♇ Lat
1	3N23	3N02	12N09	0S30	6S30	1S02	22S20	0S37
6	3 21	3 01	12 06	0 30	6 30	1 02	22 19	0 37
11	3 19	3 00	12 03	0 30	6 29	1 02	22 18	0 37
16	3 18	2 59	12 01	0 30	6 28	1 02	22 17	0 38
21	3 18	2 58	11 59	0 30	6 26	1 02	22 16	0 38
26	3 18	2 57	11 58	0 30	6 25	1 02	22 15	0 39
31	3N19	2N56	11N57	0S30	6S22	1S02	22S14	0S39

Day	⚴ Decl	⚴ Lat	⚵ Decl	⚵ Lat	⚶ Decl	⚶ Lat	Eris Decl	Eris Lat
1	3N52	26N01	3S24	0N16	8N06	8S39	1S57	11S51
6	3 43	26 08	3 49	0 28	8 08	8 20	1 57	11 50
11	3 37	26 15	4 11	0 41	8 13	8 01	1 57	11 49
16	3 33	26 24	4 30	0 55	8 22	7 40	1 57	11 49
21	3 32	26 33	4 48	1 09	8 34	7 20	1 56	11 48
26	3 34	26 43	5 02	1 23	8 49	6 59	1 56	11 47
31	3N39	26N54	5S13	1N38	9N08	6S38	1S56	11S46

Moon Phenomena

Max/0 Decl
dy hr mn
6 20:14 0 N
13 21:09 23N13
20 6:52 0 S
26 20:18 23S14

Max/0 Lat
dy hr mn
6 13:15 5S14
13 14:16 0 N
20 0:16 5N17
26 13:02 0 S

Perigee/Apogee
dy hr m kilometers
5 4:03 a 404445
18 20:18 p 370264

PH	dy	hr mn	
☽	4	6:59	11♓49
○	12	5:13	19♊52
☾	19	4:58	26♍58
●	26	5:14	4♑07
●	26	5:19	A 03'39"

Void of Course Moon

Last Aspect			☽ Ingress		
2 12:28	☿	□	♓	3	7:12
5 8:16	☿	△	♈	5	19:46
7 15:03	♇	□	♉	8	7:30
10 1:14	♇	△	♊	10	16:48
12 5:13	☉	☍	♋	12	23:24
14 15:58	♀	☍	♌	15	3:57
16 22:11	☉	△	♍	17	7:17
19 8:08	♀	△	♎	19	10:06
21 11:47	☉	⚹	♏	21	12:58
23 3:28	♂	☌	♐	23	16:35
25 11:19	☿	☌	♑	25	21:46
27 21:04	♂	⚹	♒	28	5:22
30 10:25	♂	□	♓	30	15:43

DAILY ASPECTARIAN

1 Su
☉∥☽ 0:17
☽□♅ 2:39
☽⚺⚳ 7:23
☽⚺♀ 9:02
☽□♂ 11:44
☉⚹☽ 13:45

2 M
☽∠♃ 1:04
☽⚺♆ 3:13
☽∠⚷ 4:19
☽⚺♄ 7:31
☽□☿ 12:28
☽∠⚳ 13:47
☽⚺♇ 14:13
☽∠♀ 17:52
♃ ♑ 18:21

3 Tu
☽∥☿ 1:25
☿⚹♇ 5:24
☿∠⚳ 5:50
☽⚹♃ 7:26
☽⚺⚷ 10:10
☽∠♄ 13:42
☽⚹♅ 13:44
☉∥♄ 14:33
☽∥♂ 15:10
♀⚹♂ 15:48
☽∠♇ 20:19
☽⚹⚳ 20:49

4 W
☽△♂ 2:52
☽#♅ 3:02
☽⚹♀ 3:28
☉□☽ 6:59
☽☌♆ 15:20
☽∠♅ 19:57
☽⚹♄ 20:15

5 Th
☽⚹♇ 2:42
☉∥♇ 3:58
☽△☿ 8:16
☽∥♆ 10:28
☽⚼♂ 10:59
☽□♃ 21:10
☽☌⚷ 22:42

6 F
☽⚺♅ 2:11
☽#⚷ 3:02
☽□⚳ 11:27
☽⚼☿ 18:24
☽⚻♂ 18:58
☽□♀ 22:58

7 Sa
☉△☽ 1:06
☽⚺♆ 3:46
☽□♄ 9:07
☽∥⚷ 13:14
☽□♇ 15:03

8 Su
☽⚻☿ 4:03
☽#♆ 5:23
☉□♆ 9:01
☽∠♆ 9:23
☉⚼☽ 9:25
☽△♃ 9:59
☽⚺⚷ 10:20
☽☌♅ 13:35
♀⚹♆ 21:50

9 M
☽△⚳ 0:35
♃□⚷ 4:28
☽☍♂ 9:11
☿ ♐ 9:43
☽∥♅ 11:12
☽⚹♆ 14:21
☽∠⚷ 15:15
☽⚼♃ 15:27
☽△♀ 16:08
☉⚻☽ 16:54
☽△♄ 19:55

10 Tu
☽△♇ 1:14
☽⚼⚳ 6:05
☽#♂ 7:12
☿△⚷ 9:33
☉⚼♅ 10:51
☿⚺♃ 14:59
☽⚹⚷ 19:28
☽⚻♃ 20:11
☽☍☿ 20:44
☽⚺♅ 22:29
☽⚼♀ 23:20

11 W
☽⚼♄ 0:16
☽⚼♇ 5:17
☉⚺♀ 8:27
♀☌♄ 10:06
☉⚺♄ 10:30
☽⚻⚳ 10:49
☿⚻♅ 11:56
☽#☿ 13:56
☽⚻♂ 20:14
☽□♆ 22:12

12 Th
☽∠♅ 1:54
☽⚻♄ 3:56
☉☍☽ 5:13
☽⚻♀ 5:36
☿∠♄ 6:08
☽⚻♇ 8:40
☽#♄ 12:39
☽#♇ 17:01

13 F
☽⚼♂ 0:38
☽□⚷ 1:57
☽☍♃ 3:34
⚷ D 3:49
☽⚹♅ 4:44
☽⚻☿ 9:49
♂△♆ 11:56
♀☌♇ 15:17
☽☍⚳ 18:16

14 Sa
☿∠♇ 1:11
☉#☽ 2:52
☉#☽ 3:02
☉⚺♇ 3:28
♂⚼⚷ 3:35
☽△♆ 3:39
☽△♂ 4:26
♀∥♃ 5:42
☽☍♄ 9:33
☽☍♇ 13:48
☉⚻☽ 14:36
☽⚼☿ 15:18
☉∥♀ 15:39
☽☍♀ 15:58

15 Su
☽#♇ 0:38
☽#♄ 5:12
☽⚼♆ 5:43
☽△⚷ 6:26
☽⚻♃ 8:52
☽□♅ 9:03
☽#☿ 12:49
☉⚼☽ 18:33
♃△♅ 19:02
☽△☿ 20:19
☿∠♀ 22:30
☽⚻⚳ 23:48

16 M
☉∥♃ 0:54
☽⚻♆ 7:29
☽⚼⚷ 8:11
☽□♂ 10:48
☽⚼♃ 11:01
☽⚻♄ 13:38
☽⚻♇ 17:30
♂∠♃ 17:40
☉△☽ 22:11
☽#♂ 22:48

17 Tu
☽⚻♀ 0:27
☽⚼⚳ 2:08
☽⚻⚷ 9:44
☿∥♄ 10:03
☽△♅ 12:13
☽△♃ 12:58
☿⚺⚳ 14:50
☽⚼♄ 15:21
☽⚼♇ 19:03

18 W
☽∥♅ 0:47
☽△⚳ 4:19
☽⚼♀ 4:20
☽□☿ 5:31
☽☍♆ 10:30
☿∥♇ 13:15
☽⚼♅ 13:36
☽⚹♂ 16:15
☽△♄ 16:57
☿∥♀ 17:37
☽△♇ 20:30
♀∥♇ 23:16

19 Th
☽#♆ 2:44
☉□☽ 4:58
☽△♀ 8:08
♂⚹♄ 10:01
☽☍⚷ 12:33
☽⚻♅ 14:56
☽□♃ 16:35
☽∥⚷ 16:35
☽∠♂ 18:53

20 F
☿□♆ 4:20
♀ ♒ 6:43
☽□⚳ 8:33
☽⚻♆ 13:19
♀∥♄ 13:39
☽⚹☿ 14:23
☽□♄ 20:09
☽#⚷ 21:09
☽⚺♂ 21:34
☽□♇ 23:25

21 Sa
♀∠♆ 3:52
☿⚼♅ 8:00
☽∥♆ 11:01
♀⚹⚷ 11:15
☉⚹☽ 11:47
☽⚼♆ 14:50
☽⚻⚷ 15:28
☽□♀ 15:53
☽☍♅ 17:48
☽∠☿ 19:00
☽⚹♃ 20:22

22 Su
☿∥♃ 4:10
☉ ♑ 4:21
☽#♅ 13:09
☽⚹⚳ 13:09
♀□♅ 13:32
♂⚹♇ 14:34
☉∠☽ 15:27
☽△♆ 16:33
☽⚼⚷ 17:11
☉∥☿ 22:15
☽∠♃ 22:32
☿⚺♄ 23:25
☽⚹♄ 23:52
☽⚺☿ 23:55

23 M
☽⚹♇ 2:53
☽☌♂ 3:28
☉□⚷ 15:18
☽∠⚳ 15:51
☽△⚷ 19:11
☉⚺☽ 19:29
☽⚻♅ 21:28

24 Tu
☽∥♂ 0:12
☽⚹♀ 0:39
☽⚺♃ 1:02
☽∠♄ 2:09
☿⚺♇ 3:09
☽∠♇ 5:03
♀⚺♃ 5:52
☽⚺⚳ 18:59
☽∥♀ 20:26
☽□♆ 20:57
☉△♅ 21:45
☽⚼♅ 23:51

25 W
☽⚺♄ 4:54
☽∠♀ 5:48
☿⚺♂ 5:54
☽⚺♇ 7:41
☽∥♄ 8:32
☽⚺♂ 10:57
☽☌☿ 11:19
☽∥♇ 14:41

26 Th
☽□⚷ 0:30
☽△♅ 2:47
☉☌☽ 5:14
☽☌♃ 7:30
☽⚺♀ 11:40
☽∠♂ 15:37
☽∥♃ 21:04
☽∥♃ 21:04

27 F
☽☌⚳ 3:00
☽⚹♆ 3:24
☽☌♄ 12:09
☽☌♇ 14:43
⚳⚹♆ 16:39
☉☌♃ 18:26
☽⚹♂ 21:04

28 Sa
☽⚺☿ 2:03
☽∥♇ 2:36
☽∠♆ 7:38
☽⚹⚷ 8:17
☽∥♄ 9:37
☽□♅ 10:34
☽⚺♃ 16:38
☉⚺☽ 18:10

29 Su
☽☌♀ 2:08
☿ ♑ 4:56
☽∠☿ 10:58
☽∥♀ 11:50
☽⚺♆ 12:35
☽∥♂ 12:47
☽∠⚷ 13:14
☽⚺⚳ 13:59
♀∥♂ 17:25
☽⚺♄ 22:14
☽∠♃ 22:19
⚶ D 22:41
☉∥♃ 22:54

30 M
☽⚺♇ 0:32
☉∠☽ 1:58
☿□⚷ 4:59
☽□♂ 10:25
☽⚺⚷ 18:51
☽∠⚳ 20:35
☽⚹☿ 20:54
☽⚹♅ 21:05
☿△♅ 22:23

31 Tu
☽∠♄ 4:16
☽⚹♃ 4:38
☽∠♇ 6:23
☉⚹☽ 10:33
☽#♅ 12:44
☽⚺♀ 20:08

LONGITUDE

January 2020

Day	Sid.Time	☉	☽	☽ 12 hour	Mean ☊	True ☊	☿	♀	♂	⚳	♃	♄	⚷	♅	♆	♇
	h m s	° ' "	° ' "	° ' "	° '	° '	° '	° '	° '	° '	° '	° '	° '	° '	° '	° '
W	6 40 28	10♑00 31	16♓07 44	22♓04 31	8♋14.3	8♋23.0	4♑22.9	14♒24.5	28♏23.0	17♑54.3	6♑40.2	21♑23.7	1♈35.8	2♉41.6	16♓15.9	22♑23.1
Th	6 44 25	11 01 41	28 00 35	3♈56 32	8 11.1	8R 22.8	5 57.6	15 38.0	29 03.4	18 18.3	6 54.0	21 30.7	1 36.8	2R 41.1	16 17.0	22 25.1
F	6 48 21	12 02 51	9♈52 55	15 50 21	8 07.9	8D 22.7	7 32.5	16 51.5	29 43.8	18 42.3	7 07.9	21 37.8	1 37.9	2 40.7	16 18.2	22 27.1
Sa	6 52 18	13 04 01	21 49 26	27 50 45	8 04.7	8 22.8	9 07.8	18 04.9	0♐24.2	19 06.2	7 21.7	21 44.8	1 39.1	2 40.3	16 19.5	22 29.1
Su	6 56 14	14 05 10	3♉54 51	10♉02 19	8 01.6	8 23.1	10 43.5	19 18.3	1 04.6	19 30.2	7 35.5	21 51.9	1 40.3	2 40.0	16 20.7	22 31.1
M	7 00 11	15 06 19	16 13 39	22 29 18	7 58.4	8 23.7	12 19.4	20 31.6	1 45.0	19 54.2	7 49.3	21 58.9	1 41.6	2 39.7	16 22.0	22 33.1
Tu	7 04 07	16 07 28	28 49 41	5♊15 08	7 55.2	8 24.5	13 55.8	21 44.9	2 25.5	20 18.2	8 03.0	22 06.0	1 42.9	2 39.4	16 23.3	22 35.1
W	7 08 04	17 08 36	11♊45 54	18 22 09	7 52.0	8 25.3	15 32.6	22 58.1	3 05.9	20 42.2	8 16.8	22 13.1	1 44.3	2 39.2	16 24.7	22 37.1
Th	7 12 01	18 09 45	25 03 56	1♋51 11	7 48.8	8R 26.0	17 09.8	24 11.3	3 46.4	21 06.1	8 30.6	22 20.2	1 45.7	2 39.1	16 26.1	22 39.1
F	7 15 57	19 10 53	8♋43 44	15 41 18	7 45.7	8 26.2	18 47.3	25 24.4	4 26.9	21 30.1	8 44.3	22 27.3	1 47.2	2 39.0	16 27.5	22 41.1
Sa	7 19 54	20 12 00	22 43 29	29 49 45	7 42.5	8 25.9	20 25.4	26 37.4	5 07.5	21 54.1	8 58.0	22 34.4	1 48.7	2D 39.0	16 28.9	22 43.1
Su	7 23 50	21 13 08	6♌59 30	14♌12 04	7 39.3	8 24.9	22 03.8	27 50.4	5 48.0	22 18.1	9 11.7	22 41.5	1 50.3	2 39.0	16 30.4	22 45.1
M	7 27 47	22 14 15	21 26 44	28 42 42	7 36.1	8 23.4	23 42.7	29 03.3	6 28.6	22 42.1	9 25.4	22 48.6	1 51.9	2 39.1	16 31.9	22 47.2
Tu	7 31 43	23 15 22	5♍59 14	13♍15 36	7 33.0	8 21.4	25 22.1	0♓16.2	7 09.2	23 06.0	9 39.1	22 55.7	1 53.6	2 39.2	16 33.4	22 49.2
W	7 35 40	24 16 28	20 31 06	27 45 07	7 29.8	8 19.5	27 01.9	1 29.0	7 49.9	23 30.0	9 52.7	23 02.8	1 55.3	2 39.4	16 34.9	22 51.2
Th	7 39 36	25 17 35	4♎57 06	12♎06 37	7 26.6	8 17.9	28 42.2	2 41.7	8 30.5	23 53.9	10 06.4	23 10.0	1 57.0	2 39.6	16 36.5	22 53.2
F	7 43 33	26 18 41	19 13 18	26 16 52	7 23.4	8D 17.0	0♒23.0	3 54.3	9 11.2	24 17.9	10 20.0	23 17.1	1 58.8	2 39.9	16 38.1	22 55.2
Sa	7 47 30	27 19 48	3♏17 09	10♏14 01	7 20.3	8 16.9	2 04.2	5 06.9	9 51.9	24 41.8	10 33.5	23 24.2	2 00.7	2 40.2	16 39.7	22 57.2
Su	7 51 26	28 20 54	17 07 25	23 57 20	7 17.1	8 17.7	3 45.8	6 19.5	10 32.6	25 05.8	10 47.1	23 31.3	2 02.6	2 40.6	16 41.3	22 59.2
M	7 55 23	29 22 00	0♐43 49	7♐26 54	7 13.9	8 19.1	5 27.9	7 31.9	11 13.3	25 29.7	11 00.6	23 38.4	2 04.5	2 41.1	16 43.0	23 01.2
Tu	7 59 19	0♒23 05	14 06 39	20 43 09	7 10.7	8 20.7	7 10.3	8 44.3	11 54.1	25 53.6	11 14.1	23 45.5	2 06.5	2 41.5	16 44.7	23 03.2
W	8 03 16	1 24 10	27 16 28	3♑46 39	7 07.6	8R 21.9	8 53.1	9 56.6	12 34.9	26 17.6	11 27.6	23 52.5	2 08.6	2 42.1	16 46.4	23 05.2
Th	8 07 12	2 25 15	10♑13 46	16 37 53	7 04.4	8 22.3	10 36.2	11 08.8	13 15.7	26 41.5	11 41.0	23 59.6	2 10.7	2 42.7	16 48.1	23 07.2
F	8 11 09	3 26 19	22 59 03	29 17 18	7 01.2	8 21.5	12 19.5	12 21.0	13 56.5	27 05.3	11 54.4	24 06.7	2 12.8	2 43.3	16 49.9	23 09.2
Sa	8 15 06	4 27 23	5♒32 43	11♒45 21	6 58.0	8 19.2	14 02.9	13 33.0	14 37.3	27 29.2	12 07.8	24 13.7	2 15.0	2 44.0	16 51.7	23 11.2
Su	8 19 02	5 28 25	17 55 19	24 02 42	6 54.9	8 15.6	15 46.4	14 45.0	15 18.2	27 53.1	12 21.1	24 20.8	2 17.2	2 44.8	16 53.5	23 13.2
M	8 22 59	6 29 27	0♓07 41	6♓10 25	6 51.7	8 10.8	17 29.8	15 56.9	15 59.0	28 16.9	12 34.4	24 27.8	2 19.5	2 45.6	16 55.3	23 15.2
Tu	8 26 55	7 30 27	12 11 08	18 10 07	6 48.5	8 05.4	19 12.9	17 08.7	16 39.9	28 40.7	12 47.6	24 34.8	2 21.7	2 46.5	16 57.1	23 17.1
W	8 30 52	8 31 27	24 07 39	0♈04 06	6 45.3	7 59.9	20 55.6	18 20.4	17 20.8	29 04.5	13 00.8	24 41.8	2 24.1	2 47.4	16 59.0	23 19.1
Th	8 34 48	9 32 25	5♈59 52	11 55 24	6 42.1	7 54.9	22 37.7	19 32.0	18 01.7	29 28.3	13 14.0	24 48.7	2 26.5	2 48.3	17 00.9	23 21.0
F	8 38 45	10♒33 23	17 51 10	23 47 42	6♋39.0	7♋51.1	24♒18.9	20♓43.5	18♐42.7	29♑52.1	13♑27.1	24♑55.7	2♈28.9	2♉49.3	17♓02.8	23♑23.0

1st of Month

Julian Day # 2458849.5
Obliquity 23°26'10"
SVP 4♓59'06"
GC 27♐07.1
Eris 23♈13.9R

Day	⚴
1	22♐51.6
6	24 56.0
11	26 59.2
16	29 01.0
21	1♑01.5
26	3 00.2
31	4 57.1

Day	⚵
1	17♎21.8
6	18 20.7
11	19 12.9
16	19 57.9
21	20 35.3
26	21 04.5
31	21 25.1

Day	⚶
1	12♉06.4
6	12 16.3
11	12 36.5
16	13 06.4
21	13 45.5
26	14 33.1
31	15 28.6

DECLINATION and LATITUDE

Day	☉ Decl	☽ Decl	☽ Lat	☽12h Decl	☿ Decl	☿ Lat	♀ Decl	♀ Lat	♂ Decl	♂ Lat	⚳ Decl	⚳ Lat	♃ Decl	♃ Lat	♄ Decl	♄ Lat
W	23S04	9S59	4S54	7S48	24S38	1S16	18S16	1S50	19S27	0N22	26S13	4S01	23S11	0N05	21S41	0N03
Th	22 59	5 34	5 12	3 16	24 40	1 21	17 54	1 50	19 36	0 21	26 11	4 02	23 10	0 05	21 40	0 03
F	22 53	0 57	5 17	1N24	24 40	1 26	17 31	1 49	19 45	0 20	26 09	4 03	23 10	0 05	21 39	0 03
Sa	22 48	3N44	5 08	6 03	24 38	1 31	17 08	1 48	19 55	0 20	26 06	4 04	23 09	0 05	21 38	0 03
Su	22 41	8 20	4 46	10 33	24 35	1 36	16 44	1 48	20 03	0 19	26 04	4 06	23 08	0 05	21 37	0 03
M	22 35	12 41	4 11	14 43	24 31	1 40	16 20	1 47	20 12	0 19	26 02	4 07	23 07	0 05	21 36	0 03
Tu	22 28	16 36	3 22	18 19	24 26	1 44	15 55	1 46	20 21	0 18	25 60	4 08	23 07	0 05	21 35	0 03
W	22 20	19 50	2 23	21 07	24 18	1 47	15 30	1 45	20 29	0 17	25 57	4 10	23 06	0 05	21 34	0 03
Th	22 12	22 07	1 13	22 49	24 10	1 51	15 05	1 44	20 38	0 17	25 55	4 11	23 05	0 05	21 33	0 03
F	22 04	23 11	0N02	23 11	23 60	1 54	14 39	1 42	20 46	0 16	25 52	4 12	23 04	0 04	21 32	0 02
Sa	21 55	22 48	1 18	22 04	23 48	1 57	14 13	1 41	20 54	0 15	25 50	4 14	23 04	0 04	21 30	0 02
Su	21 46	20 58	2 31	19 31	23 35	1 59	13 47	1 40	21 02	0 15	25 47	4 15	23 03	0 04	21 29	0 02
M	21 36	17 45	3 36	15 43	23 21	2 01	13 20	1 38	21 09	0 14	25 44	4 16	23 02	0 04	21 28	0 02
Tu	21 26	13 27	4 27	10 59	23 04	2 03	12 53	1 36	21 17	0 14	25 41	4 18	23 01	0 04	21 27	0 02
W	21 15	8 22	5 01	5 38	22 47	2 04	12 25	1 35	21 24	0 13	25 38	4 19	23 00	0 04	21 26	0 02
Th	21 05	2 51	5 15	0 03	22 28	2 05	11 57	1 33	21 31	0 12	25 36	4 20	22 59	0 04	21 25	0 02
F	20 53	2S44	5 10	5S28	22 07	2 06	11 29	1 31	21 38	0 12	25 33	4 22	22 58	0 04	21 24	0 02
Sa	20 41	8 07	4 46	10 38	21 45	2 06	11 01	1 29	21 45	0 11	25 30	4 23	22 57	0 04	21 23	0 02
Su	20 29	13 00	4 06	15 11	21 21	2 06	10 32	1 27	21 51	0 10	25 27	4 24	22 56	0 04	21 21	0 02
M	20 17	17 09	3 13	18 53	20 55	2 05	10 03	1 25	21 58	0 09	25 23	4 26	22 55	0 04	21 20	0 02
Tu	20 04	20 21	2 10	21 31	20 28	2 04	9 34	1 23	22 04	0 09	25 20	4 27	22 54	0 03	21 19	0 02
W	19 51	22 24	1 01	22 58	19 60	2 02	9 05	1 20	22 10	0 08	25 17	4 29	22 53	0 03	21 18	0 02
Th	19 37	23 13	0S10	23 09	19 30	1 60	8 35	1 18	22 16	0 07	25 14	4 30	22 52	0 03	21 17	0 02
F	19 23	22 47	1 19	22 08	18 59	1 57	8 05	1 15	22 22	0 07	25 10	4 31	22 51	0 03	21 16	0 01
Sa	19 09	21 12	2 24	20 02	18 26	1 54	7 35	1 13	22 27	0 06	25 07	4 33	22 50	0 03	21 15	0 01
Su	18 54	18 38	3 20	17 02	17 51	1 50	7 05	1 10	22 32	0 05	25 03	4 34	22 49	0 03	21 13	0 01
M	18 39	15 16	4 06	13 21	17 16	1 45	6 35	1 08	22 38	0 04	24 60	4 36	22 48	0 03	21 12	0 01
Tu	18 23	11 19	4 41	9 11	16 39	1 40	6 04	1 05	22 42	0 04	24 56	4 37	22 46	0 03	21 11	0 01
W	18 08	6 58	5 03	4 42	16 00	1 34	5 33	1 02	22 47	0 03	24 53	4 39	22 45	0 03	21 10	0 01
Th	17 52	2 23	5 12	0 04	15 21	1 28	5 03	0 59	22 52	0 02	24 49	4 40	22 44	0 03	21 09	0 01
F	17S35	2N16	5S07	4N35	14S41	1S20	4S32	0S56	22S56	0N01	24S45	4S41	22S43	0N03	21S08	0N01

Day	⚷ Decl	⚷ Lat	♅ Decl	♅ Lat	♆ Decl	♆ Lat	♇ Decl	♇ Lat
1	3N19	2N55	11N57	0S30	6S22	1S02	22S13	0S39
6	3 20	2 54	11 56	0 29	6 19	1 01	22 12	0 40
11	3 22	2 53	11 56	0 29	6 17	1 01	22 11	0 40
16	3 24	2 52	11 56	0 29	6 14	1 01	22 10	0 40
21	3 27	2 51	11 57	0 29	6 10	1 01	22 08	0 41
26	3 31	2 50	11 58	0 29	6 07	1 01	22 07	0 41
31	3N34	2N49	12N00	0S29	6S03	1S01	22S06	0S42

Day	⚴ Decl	⚴ Lat	⚵ Decl	⚵ Lat	⚶ Decl	⚶ Lat	Eris Decl	Eris Lat
1	3N40	26N57	5S15	1N41	9N12	6S34	1S55	11S46
6	3 48	27 09	5 23	1 57	9 34	6 14	1 55	11 45
11	3 58	27 23	5 27	2 14	9 59	5 55	1 54	11 45
16	4 11	27 37	5 28	2 31	10 26	5 36	1 53	11 44
21	4 27	27 53	5 25	2 49	10 54	5 18	1 53	11 43
26	4 46	28 10	5 19	3 08	11 25	5 01	1 52	11 42
31	5N07	28N28	5S08	3N28	11N56	4S44	1S51	11S42

Moon Phenomena

Max/0 Decl

dy	hr mn	
3	4:52	0 N
10	5:56	23N13
16	12:13	0 S
23	3:29	23S13
30	12:19	0 N

Max/0 Lat

dy	hr mn	
2	21:00	5S17
9	23:30	0 N
16	5:31	5N16
22	20:33	0 S
30	3:50	5S12

Perigee/Apogee

dy	hr m		kilometers
2	1:23	a	404580
13	20:31	p	365960
29	21:33	a	405392

PH	dy	hr mn	
☽	3	4:47	12♈15
○	10	19:22	20♋00
◐	10	19:11	A 0.895
☾	17	13:00	26♎52
●	24	21:43	4♒22

Void of Course Moon

Last Aspect				☽ Ingress		
2	2:15	♂	△	♈	2	4:02
4	1:19	♇	□	♉	4	16:16
6	12:09	♇	△	♊	7	2:12
8	22:17	♀	△	♋	9	8:44
10	23:59	♇	☍	♌	11	12:17
13	13:43	♀	☍	♍	13	14:08
15	12:13	☿	△	♎	15	15:44
17	13:00	☉	□	♏	17	18:22
19	21:23	☉	⚹	♐	19	22:42
21	4:47	♆	□	♑	22	5:01
24	2:10	♄	☌	♒	24	13:22
25	19:08	☿	☌	♓	26	23:45
29	1:10	♄	⚹	♈	29	11:52

DAILY ASPECTARIAN

☽☌♆ 0:16
☽∠♅ 3:09
☽⚹⚳ 3:42
☽⚹♄ 10:44
☽⚹♇ 12:40
☽∥♆ 19:46

☽△♂ 2:15
☽∠♀ 5:55
☽☌⚷ 7:18
☽⚺♅ 9:27
☽⋕⚷ 11:44
♀⚺♆ 12:57
☿☌♃ 16:43
☽□♃ 18:20
☽□☿ 18:33
♀∠⚷ 19:30

☉□☽ 4:47
♂ ♐ 9:39
☽⚼♂ 10:21
☽⚺♆ 12:57
☽⚹♀ 15:39
☽□⚳ 18:22
☽∥⚷ 21:56
☽□♄ 23:51

☽□♇ 1:19
☽⋕♆ 13:30
☽⚻♂ 18:04
☽∠♆ 18:55
☽⚺⚷ 19:34
☽☌♅ 21:32

♀⚺⚳ 5:47
☽△♃ 7:21
☽△☿ 15:19
☽∥♅ 19:43
☉△☽ 21:38
♂△⚷ 21:54

6 M
☽⚹♆ 0:16
☽∠⚷ 0:54
☽△⚳ 7:18
☽□♀ 9:09
☽△♄ 11:08
☽△♇ 12:09
☽⚼♃ 12:52
☽⋕♀ 20:00

7 Tu
☽⚼☿ 0:13
☉⚼☽ 4:41
☽⚹⚷ 5:25
☉⚹♆ 6:22
☽☍♂ 7:07
☽⚺♅ 7:10
♀⚺♄ 7:40
♂⚻♅ 8:15
☽⚼⚳ 12:29
☽⚼♄ 15:34
☽⚼♇ 16:21
♀⚺♇ 16:55
☽⚻♃ 17:29

8 W
☽⋕♂ 6:08
♀∠♃ 7:33
☽⚻☿ 7:51
☽□♆ 8:28
☉⚻☽ 10:36
☽∠♅ 10:42
☿⚹♆ 13:04
☽⚻⚳ 16:42
☽⋕♄ 16:45
☽⚻♄ 19:05
☽⚻♇ 19:41
☽△♀ 22:17

9 Th
☽⋕♇ 0:58
☉⋕☽ 1:06
☉∥♇ 2:47
☽□⚷ 11:52
☽⚹♅ 13:24
☽⚻♂ 16:10
☽⋕♃ 19:22

10 F
☽☍♃ 0:01
☽⚼♀ 3:11
☽△♆ 13:20
☉☌☿ 15:21
☿∠♂ 16:33
☽⋕♃ 17:03
☉∠♂ 18:44
☽⚼♂ 19:21
☉☍☽ 19:22
☽☍☿ 19:34
☽☍⚳ 22:34
☽☍♄ 23:44
☽☍♇ 23:59

11 Sa
♅ D 1:50
☽⚻♀ 7:13
☽⋕♇ 10:28
☽⚼♆ 14:48
☉⋕☽ 15:00
☽△⚷ 15:21
☽□♅ 16:44
☽⋕♄ 18:42
☽△♂ 21:55
☽⋕♂ 23:26

12 Su
☽⚻♃ 3:44
☿☌⚳ 4:35
☿☌♄ 9:52
☿☌♇ 10:15
☽⚻♆ 15:51
☽⚼⚷ 16:24
♄☌♇ 17:00

13 M
☉⚻☽ 1:24
☽⚻⚳ 2:08
☽⚻♇ 2:13
☽⚻♄ 2:17
☽⚻☿ 4:14
☽⚼♃ 5:00
⚳☌♇ 5:34
⚳☌♄ 9:22
☉☌♇ 13:22
☽☍♀ 13:43
☉☌♄ 15:17
☽⚻⚷ 17:14
☉☌⚳ 17:58
☽△♅ 18:30
♀ ♓ 18:40
☉∥♄ 20:58

14 Tu
☽□♂ 2:01
☽⚼♇ 3:02
☽⋕♀ 3:08
☽⚼♄ 3:14
☽⚼⚳ 3:35
☉⚼☽ 4:01
☿∥♃ 5:09
☽△♃ 6:08
☽∥♅ 7:26
☽⚼☿ 8:10
☉∥♂ 12:27
☽☍♆ 17:29
☽⚼♅ 19:16

15 W
♂∠♇ 0:49
☽△♇ 3:53
☽△♄ 4:14
☽△⚳ 5:05
♂∥♄ 5:39
☉△☽ 6:42
♀⚺⚷ 8:53
♂∠♄ 9:18
☽⋕♆ 9:25
☽△☿ 12:13
☽☍⚷ 18:59
☽⚻♀ 19:53
☽⚻♅ 20:10
☽∥⚷ 21:38
♀⚹♅ 23:19

16 Th
♀⋕♅ 0:58
☽⚹♂ 6:15
☽□♃ 8:46
☿ ♒ 18:32
☽⚻♆ 19:37
☿∥♇ 21:11
☽⚼♀ 23:25

17 F
☽⋕⚷ 2:57
☽□♇ 6:17
☽□♄ 6:57
☽∠♂ 8:51
☽□⚳ 8:52
♂∠⚳ 9:39
☉□☽ 13:00
☽∥♆ 15:17
☿∠♆ 18:06
☽⚼♆ 21:12
☽□☿ 21:37
☽⚻⚷ 21:48
☽☍♅ 22:56
☿⚹⚷ 23:09
☿∥♂ 23:45

18 Sa
☽△♀ 3:27
☿□♅ 8:33
⚴ ♑ 10:34
☽⚺♂ 11:57
☽∥♀ 12:37
☽⚹♃ 12:46
☽⋕♅ 18:30
☿∥♄ 23:13
☽△♆ 23:14
☽⚼⚷ 23:52

19 Su
☽⚹♇ 10:19
☽⚹♄ 11:20
♂⚺♃ 12:47
☽⚹⚳ 14:26
☽∠♃ 15:29
☉⚹☽ 21:23

20 M
☽△⚷ 2:24
☽⚻♅ 3:29
☽⚹☿ 9:41
♀∠♇ 10:00
☽∠♇ 13:04
☽□♀ 13:21
☽∠♄ 14:16
☉ ♒ 14:56
☽∠⚳ 18:01
☽⚺♃ 18:43
☽☌♂ 19:48
☉∥☽ 21:43

21 Tu
♀∠♄ 0:26
☽∥☿ 1:01
☉∠☽ 2:30
☽□♆ 4:47
☽⚼♅ 6:30
☽∥♄ 9:40
♂∥♇ 16:09
☽⚺♇ 16:18
☽∠☿ 16:51
☽⚺♄ 17:43
☽∥♇ 19:59
☽∥♂ 20:15
☽⚺⚳ 22:08

22 W
☉⚺☽ 8:15
☉∠♆ 8:59
☽□⚷ 9:00
☽∥♃ 9:48
☽△♅ 10:01
☉∥☿ 13:51
☉⚹⚷ 18:04

23 Th
☽⚺☿ 0:48
☽⚹♀ 1:53
☽☌♃ 2:46
☽⚺♂ 5:59
☉□♅ 6:56
☽⚹♆ 12:21
♀⚹♃ 13:08
♀∠⚳ 16:13
☿⚺♃ 17:18
☽∥♃ 22:21

24 F
☽☌♇ 0:19
☿⚺♀ 1:08
☽☌♄ 2:10
☽∥♂ 7:45
☽☌⚳ 8:03
☽∠♀ 9:11
☽∠♂ 11:59
☽∥♇ 12:02
☽∠♆ 16:54
☽⚹⚷ 17:39
☽□♅ 18:36
☉☌☽ 21:43
☽∥♄ 23:31

25 Sa
☽⚺♃ 12:57
☿⚹♂ 13:11
☽⚺♀ 17:09
☽⚹♂ 18:36
☽☌☿ 19:08
☉∥☽ 21:36
☽⚺♆ 21:59
☽∠⚷ 22:45

26 Su
☽∥☿ 7:19
☽⚺♇ 10:24
☽⚺♄ 12:43
☿⚺♆ 15:51
☽∠♃ 18:51
☽⚺⚳ 20:14
☿∠⚷ 21:33

27 M
♀□♂ 1:38
☽⚺⚷ 4:22
☽⚹♅ 5:13
☉⚺☽ 13:48
☽∠♇ 16:11
☽∠♄ 18:44
♀☌♆ 20:01
☽⋕♅ 20:07
♀∥♆ 23:02

28 Tu
☽⚹♃ 1:14
☽∠⚳ 3:06
☽□♂ 9:31
☽☌♆ 9:35
♂□♆ 10:35
☽☌♀ 11:03
☽∠♅ 11:13
♀∠♅ 12:47
♂∥♃ 16:10
☽⚺☿ 16:28
☽⚹♇ 22:22
☉∠☽ 22:40

29 W
☽⚹♄ 1:10
☽∥♆ 4:44
☽∥♀ 8:25
☽⚹⚳ 10:20
♂⚼♅ 15:56
☽☌⚷ 16:47
☽⚺♅ 17:32
☽⋕⚷ 17:56

30 Th
☽∠☿ 3:51
☉⚹☽ 7:51
☿⚺♇ 10:27
☽□♃ 14:56
☽⚺♆ 22:22

31 F
☽△♂ 1:50
☽⚺♀ 6:27
☽∥⚷ 6:47
⚳ ♒ 8:02
☿⚺♄ 9:27
☽⋕♀ 10:32
☽□♇ 11:12
☽□♄ 14:25
☽⚹☿ 15:11
☽⋕♆ 19:38

February 2020

LONGITUDE

Day	Sid.Time	☉	☽	☽ 12 hour	Mean☊	True☊	☿	♀	♂	⚳	♃	♄	⚷	♅	♆	♇
	h m s	° ' "	° ' "	° ' "	° '	° '	° '	° '	° '	° '	° '	° '	° '	° '	° '	° '
1 Sa	8 42 41	11♒34 19	29♈45 34	5♉45 20	6♋35.8	7♋48.7	25♒58.9	21♓54.9	19♐23.6	0♒15.8	13♑40.1	25♑02.6	2♈31.3	2♉50.4	17♓04.7	23♑24.9
2 Su	8 46 38	12 35 14	11♉47 36	17 52 59	6 32.6	7D 47.8	27 37.4	23 06.2	20 04.6	0 39.5	13 53.2	25 09.5	2 33.8	2 51.5	17 06.7	23 26.9
3 M	8 50 34	13 36 07	24 02 07	0♊15 34	6 29.4	7 48.4	29 14.0	24 17.4	20 45.6	1 03.2	14 06.1	25 16.4	2 36.4	2 52.6	17 08.6	23 28.8
4 Tu	8 54 31	14 36 59	6♊33 57	12 57 46	6 26.2	7 49.8	0♓48.2	25 28.5	21 26.6	1 26.8	14 19.0	25 23.3	2 39.0	2 53.9	17 10.6	23 30.7
5 W	8 58 28	15 37 50	19 27 31	26 03 36	6 23.1	7 51.5	2 19.5	26 39.5	22 07.6	1 50.5	14 31.9	25 30.1	2 41.6	2 55.1	17 12.6	23 32.6
6 Th	9 02 24	16 38 40	2♋46 19	9♋35 48	6 19.9	7R 52.6	3 47.4	27 50.3	22 48.6	2 14.1	14 44.7	25 36.9	2 44.2	2 56.4	17 14.6	23 34.5
7 F	9 06 21	17 39 28	16 32 07	23 35 07	6 16.7	7 52.3	5 11.3	29 01.0	23 29.7	2 37.7	14 57.5	25 43.7	2 46.9	2 57.8	17 16.6	23 36.3
8 Sa	9 10 17	18 40 15	0♌44 27	7♌59 39	6 13.5	7 50.3	6 30.5	0♈11.6	24 10.8	3 01.2	15 10.2	25 50.5	2 49.6	2 59.2	17 18.7	23 38.2
9 Su	9 14 14	19 41 00	15 19 59	22 44 36	6 10.4	7 46.3	7 44.2	1 22.0	24 51.9	3 24.7	15 22.9	25 57.2	2 52.4	3 00.6	17 20.7	23 40.1
10 M	9 18 10	20 41 44	0♍12 29	7♍42 30	6 07.2	7 40.5	8 51.8	2 32.3	25 33.0	3 48.2	15 35.4	26 03.9	2 55.1	3 02.1	17 22.8	23 41.9
11 Tu	9 22 07	21 42 27	15 13 28	22 44 11	6 04.0	7 33.6	9 52.5	3 42.5	26 14.1	4 11.7	15 48.0	26 10.6	2 57.9	3 03.7	17 24.9	23 43.7
12 W	9 26 04	22 43 09	0♎13 28	7♎40 14	6 00.8	7 26.6	10 45.5	4 52.6	26 55.3	4 35.1	16 00.4	26 17.2	3 00.8	3 05.3	17 27.0	23 45.6
13 Th	9 30 00	23 43 49	15 03 34	22 22 40	5 57.7	7 20.3	11 30.2	6 02.5	27 36.5	4 58.5	16 12.8	26 23.8	3 03.7	3 06.9	17 29.1	23 47.4
14 F	9 33 57	24 44 28	29 36 55	6♏45 53	5 54.5	7 15.7	12 05.8	7 12.2	28 17.7	5 21.9	16 25.2	26 30.4	3 06.6	3 08.6	17 31.2	23 49.1
15 Sa	9 37 53	25 45 06	13♏49 19	20 47 07	5 51.3	7D 13.1	12 31.8	8 21.8	28 58.9	5 45.2	16 37.5	26 36.9	3 09.5	3 10.3	17 33.4	23 50.9
16 Su	9 41 50	26 45 43	27 39 18	4♐26 02	5 48.1	7 12.4	12 47.8	9 31.3	29 40.1	6 08.5	16 49.7	26 43.4	3 12.5	3 12.1	17 35.5	23 52.7
17 M	9 45 46	27 46 19	11♐07 34	17 44 11	5 44.9	7 13.0	12R 53.4	10 40.6	0♑21.4	6 31.7	17 01.8	26 49.9	3 15.5	3 13.9	17 37.7	23 54.4
18 Tu	9 49 43	28 46 54	24 16 14	0♑44 05	5 41.8	7 14.2	12 48.6	11 49.8	1 02.6	6 55.0	17 13.9	26 56.3	3 18.5	3 15.8	17 39.9	23 56.1
19 W	9 53 39	29 47 28	7♑08 05	13 28 37	5 38.6	7R 14.8	12 33.4	12 58.8	1 43.9	7 18.1	17 25.9	27 02.7	3 21.5	3 17.7	17 42.1	23 57.9
20 Th	9 57 36	0♓48 00	19 46 00	26 00 32	5 35.4	7 13.9	12 08.3	14 07.6	2 25.2	7 41.3	17 37.8	27 09.0	3 24.6	3 19.6	17 44.3	23 59.6
21 F	10 01 33	1 48 31	2♒12 31	8♒22 12	5 32.2	7 10.8	11 33.8	15 16.3	3 06.6	8 04.4	17 49.7	27 15.3	3 27.7	3 21.6	17 46.5	24 01.2
22 Sa	10 05 29	2 49 00	14 29 46	20 35 26	5 29.1	7 05.1	10 50.9	16 24.8	3 47.9	8 27.4	18 01.5	27 21.6	3 30.8	3 23.6	17 48.7	24 02.9
23 Su	10 09 26	3 49 28	26 39 21	2♓41 39	5 25.9	6 56.7	10 00.6	17 33.1	4 29.3	8 50.5	18 13.2	27 27.8	3 34.0	3 25.7	17 50.9	24 04.5
24 M	10 13 22	4 49 54	8♓42 30	14 42 02	5 22.7	6 46.2	9 04.3	18 41.2	5 10.6	9 13.4	18 24.8	27 33.9	3 37.2	3 27.8	17 53.1	24 06.2
25 Tu	10 17 19	5 50 19	20 40 23	26 37 43	5 19.5	6 34.4	8 03.6	19 49.2	5 52.0	9 36.3	18 36.3	27 40.0	3 40.4	3 30.0	17 55.4	24 07.8
26 W	10 21 15	6 50 42	2♈34 14	8♈30 08	5 16.3	6 22.3	6 59.9	20 57.0	6 33.4	9 59.2	18 47.8	27 46.1	3 43.6	3 32.2	17 57.6	24 09.4
27 Th	10 25 12	7 51 02	14 25 41	20 21 10	5 13.2	6 10.9	5 54.9	22 04.5	7 14.8	10 22.0	18 59.1	27 52.1	3 46.8	3 34.4	17 59.8	24 10.9
28 F	10 29 08	8 51 21	26 16 56	2♉13 21	5 10.0	6 01.2	4 50.3	23 11.9	7 56.2	10 44.8	19 10.4	27 58.1	3 50.1	3 36.7	18 02.1	24 12.5
29 Sa	10 33 05	9♓51 39	8♉10 53	14 10 00	5♋06.8	5♋53.9	3♓47.6	24♈19.0	8♑37.6	11♒07.5	19♑21.6	28♑04.0	3♈53.4	3♉39.0	18♓04.3	24♑14.0

1st of Mo
Julian Da
2458880
Obliquit
23°26'11
SVP 4♓59
GC 27♐0
Eris 23♈1

Day	⚴
1	5♑20
6	7 14
11	9 06
16	10 56
21	12 43.
26	14 27.

Day	⚵
1	21♎28
6	21 37
11	21 38.
16	21 29.
21	21 10.
26	20 42.

Day	⚶
1	15♉40.
6	16 44.
11	17 55.
16	19 12.
21	20 34.
26	22 01.

DECLINATION and LATITUDE

Day	☉ Decl	☽ Decl	☽ Lat	☽ 12h Decl	☿ Decl	☿ Lat	♀ Decl	♀ Lat	♂ Decl	♂ Lat	⚳ Decl	⚳ Lat	♃ Decl	♃ Lat	♄ Decl	♄ Lat
1 Sa	17S19	6N52	4S49	9N06	13S59	1S12	4S01	0S53	23S00	0N01	24S42	4S43	22S42	0N02	21S06	0N01
2 Su	17 02	11 16	4 19	13 20	13 17	1 03	3 30	0 49	23 04	0S00	24 38	4 44	22 40	0 02	21 05	0 01
3 M	16 44	15 17	3 36	17 06	12 35	0 54	2 58	0 46	23 08	0 01	24 34	4 46	22 39	0 02	21 04	0 01
4 Tu	16 27	18 44	2 42	20 11	11 52	0 43	2 27	0 43	23 11	0 02	24 30	4 47	22 38	0 02	21 03	0 01
5 W	16 09	21 23	1 39	22 19	11 09	0 32	1 56	0 39	23 15	0 03	24 26	4 49	22 37	0 02	21 02	0 01
6 Th	15 51	22 57	0 28	23 15	10 26	0 20	1 24	0 36	23 18	0 03	24 22	4 50	22 35	0 02	21 00	0 01
7 F	15 32	23 11	0N47	22 46	9 43	0 07	0 53	0 32	23 21	0 04	24 18	4 52	22 34	0 02	20 59	0 00
8 Sa	15 14	21 57	2 01	20 47	9 02	0N06	0 22	0 28	23 23	0 05	24 14	4 54	22 33	0 02	20 58	0 00
9 Su	14 55	19 14	3 09	17 23	8 21	0 20	0N10	0 25	23 26	0 06	24 10	4 55	22 31	0 02	20 57	0 00
10 M	14 36	15 13	4 05	12 49	7 42	0 35	0 41	0 21	23 28	0 07	24 06	4 57	22 30	0 02	20 56	0 00
11 Tu	14 16	10 12	4 45	7 27	7 05	0 50	1 13	0 17	23 30	0 07	24 02	4 58	22 29	0 01	20 55	0 00
12 W	13 56	4 35	5 06	1 40	6 31	1 06	1 44	0 13	23 32	0 08	23 58	4 60	22 27	0 01	20 53	0 00
13 Th	13 37	1S14	5 05	4S06	5 59	1 22	2 16	0 09	23 34	0 09	23 53	5 01	22 26	0 01	20 52	0 00
14 F	13 16	6 53	4 45	9 33	5 30	1 38	2 47	0 05	23 36	0 10	23 49	5 03	22 24	0 01	20 51	0S00
15 Sa	12 56	12 02	4 08	14 21	5 06	1 54	3 18	0 01	23 37	0 11	23 45	5 05	22 23	0 01	20 50	0 00
16 Su	12 35	16 26	3 17	18 17	4 45	2 10	3 49	0N03	23 38	0 12	23 41	5 06	22 22	0 01	20 49	0 00
17 M	12 15	19 52	2 16	21 10	4 29	2 26	4 20	0 07	23 39	0 13	23 36	5 08	22 20	0 01	20 48	0 00
18 Tu	11 54	22 10	1 09	22 51	4 17	2 40	4 51	0 12	23 39	0 13	23 32	5 10	22 19	0 01	20 46	0 00
19 W	11 33	23 14	0 01	23 18	4 10	2 54	5 22	0 16	23 40	0 14	23 27	5 11	22 17	0 01	20 45	0 00
20 Th	11 11	23 05	1S07	22 07	4 08	3 07	5 53	0 20	23 40	0 15	23 23	5 13	22 16	0 01	20 44	0 00
21 F	10 50	21 46	2 10	20 43	4 11	3 18	6 24	0 25	23 40	0 16	23 18	5 15	22 14	0 01	20 43	0 01
22 Sa	10 28	19 26	3 06	17 57	4 18	3 27	6 54	0 29	23 40	0 17	23 14	5 16	22 13	0 00	20 42	0 01
23 Su	10 06	16 16	3 52	14 25	4 30	3 34	7 25	0 34	23 40	0 18	23 09	5 18	22 12	0 00	20 41	0 01
24 M	9 44	12 27	4 28	10 21	4 47	3 39	7 55	0 38	23 39	0 19	23 05	5 20	22 10	0 00	20 40	0 01
25 Tu	9 22	8 10	4 52	5 54	5 06	3 42	8 25	0 43	23 38	0 20	23 00	5 22	22 09	0 00	20 38	0 01
26 W	8 60	3 36	5 02	1 16	5 29	3 43	8 55	0 48	23 37	0 21	22 56	5 23	22 07	0 00	20 37	0 01
27 Th	8 37	1N04	5 00	3N25	5 54	3 42	9 24	0 52	23 36	0 22	22 51	5 25	22 06	0S00	20 36	0 01
28 F	8 15	5 43	4 45	7 59	6 21	3 38	9 54	0 57	23 35	0 23	22 46	5 27	22 04	0 00	20 35	0 01
29 Sa	7S52	10N11	4S17	12N17	6S49	3N33	10N23	1N02	23S33	0S24	22S42	5S29	22S03	0S00	20S34	0S01

Day	⚷ Decl	⚷ Lat	♅ Decl	♅ Lat	♆ Decl	♆ Lat	♇ Decl	♇ La
1	3N35	2N49	12N00	0S29	6S02	1S01	22S06	0
6	3 40	2 48	12 03	0 28	5 58	1 01	22 05	0
11	3 44	2 47	12 05	0 28	5 54	1 01	22 03	0
16	3 49	2 47	12 08	0 28	5 50	1 01	22 02	0
21	3 55	2 46	12 12	0 28	5 46	1 01	22 01	0
26	4N00	2N45	12N15	0S28	5S42	1S01	22S01	0

Day	⚴ Decl	⚴ Lat	⚵ Decl	⚵ Lat	⚶ Decl	⚶ Lat	Eris Decl	Eris La
1	5N11	28N32	5S06	3N32	12N03	4S41	1S50	11
6	5 35	28 52	4 50	3 52	12 36	4 25	1 49	11
11	6 02	29 13	4 31	4 14	13 09	4 11	1 48	11
16	6 31	29 35	4 07	4 35	13 44	3 56	1 47	11
21	7 02	29 59	3 40	4 57	14 18	3 43	1 45	11
26	7N35	30N23	3S09	5N20	14N53	3S30	1S44	11

Moon Phenomena

Max/0 Decl
dy hr mn
6 16:15 23N16
12 18:54 0 S
19 8:53 23S19
26 18:30 0 N

Max/0 Lat
dy hr mn
6 9:00 0 N
12 11:33 5N08
19 0:13 0 S
26 7:33 5S03

Perigee/Apogee
dy hr m kilometers
10 20:40 p 360463
26 11:35 a 406278

PH dy hr mn
☽ 2 1:43 12♉40
○ 9 7:34 20♌00
☾ 15 22:18 26♏41
● 23 15:33 4♓29

Void of Course Moo

Last Aspect	☽ Ingre
31 15:11 ☿ ✶	♉ 1 0
3 11:29 ☿ □	♊ 3 11
5 14:21 ♀ □	♋ 5 19
7 15:44 ♄ ☍	♌ 7 22
9 16:10 ♂ △	♍ 9 23
11 18:27 ♂ □	♎ 11 23
13 21:41 ♂ ✶	♏ 14 0
15 22:21 ♄ ✶	♐ 16 4
18 9:04 ☉ ✶	♑ 18 10
20 14:19 ♄ ☌	♒ 20 19
22 4:09 ♀ ✶	♓ 23 6
25 14:13 ♄ ✶	♈ 25 18
28 3:26 ♄ □	♉ 28 7

DAILY ASPECTARIAN

1 Sa
☽□⚳ 1:03
☽∠♆ 4:40
☽⚺⚷ 5:33
☽☌♅ 6:11
☽⚼♂ 9:50
☽∠♀ 15:53
♀⋕⚷ 19:06

2 Su
☉□☽ 1:43
☽△♃ 4:13
☽∥♅ 4:18
♀✶♇ 7:08
☽⋕☿ 10:00
☽✶♆ 10:31
☽∠⚷ 11:25
☽⚻♂ 17:15
☿∠♃ 21:43
☽△♇ 22:55

3 M
☽✶♀ 0:33
☽△♄ 2:25
☉⋕☽ 8:48
☽⚼♃ 9:57
☽□☿ 11:29
☿ ♓ 11:39
☽△⚳ 13:57
☉⚺♃ 15:01
☽✶⚷ 16:32
☽⚺♅ 17:02
☿⋕♅ 18:29
♀✶♄ 22:03

4 Tu
☽⚼♇ 3:41
☽⚼♄ 7:15
☿⚺⚳ 13:34
☽⚻♃ 14:46
☉△☽ 16:21
☽⚼⚳ 19:02
☽□♆ 19:51
☽⋕♄ 20:14
☽∠♅ 21:10

5 W
☽☍♂ 5:08
☿⚺⚷ 6:06
☽⚻♇ 7:28
☽⋕♇ 8:37
☿✶♅ 9:44
☽⚻♄ 11:05
☽□♀ 14:21
☽⋕♃ 16:39
☉⚼☽ 21:50
☽⚻⚳ 23:01
☽□⚷ 23:56

6 Th
☽✶♅ 0:18
⚳∠♆ 0:36
☽△☿ 2:01
☉⚺♆ 14:41
☽☍♃ 21:15

7 F
☽△♆ 1:16
☉⚻☽ 2:04
☉∠⚷ 3:04
♂⚺♇ 4:04
☽⚼☿ 6:54
⚳✶⚷ 10:37
☽☍♇ 12:04
☽⚻♂ 12:27
☽⋕♃ 15:38
☽☍♄ 15:44
♀ ♈ 20:04
⚳□♅ 21:48
☽⋕♇ 22:34
☽△♀ 23:00

8 Sa
☽⚼♆ 2:37
☽△⚷ 3:29
☽□♅ 3:44
☽☍⚳ 3:54
☽⋕♄ 10:18
☽⚻☿ 10:27
☽⚼♂ 14:38
⚵ R 18:00

9 Su
☽⚻♃ 0:05
☽⚼♀ 1:50
☽⚻♆ 3:17
☽⚼⚷ 4:08
☉☍☽ 7:34
☽⚻♇ 13:31
☽△♂ 16:10
☽⚻♄ 17:18
☿∠♇ 20:13

10 M
☽⚼♃ 0:37
☉⋕☽ 3:28
☽⚻♀ 4:03
☽⚻⚷ 4:21
☽△♅ 4:32
☽⚻⚳ 5:55
♀☌⚷ 8:07
♀⚺♅ 10:25
☽⚼♇ 13:37
☽☍☿ 14:52
☽∥♅ 15:25
☽⚼♄ 17:29
♂⚺♄ 21:31

11 Tu
☽△♃ 0:56
☽☍♆ 3:30
☽⚼♅ 4:32
☽⚼⚳ 6:31
☉⚻☽ 11:06
☽△♇ 13:37
♀✶⚳ 15:00
☽⋕☿ 15:04
☽△♄ 17:38
☽□♂ 18:27
☽⋕♆ 18:32

12 W
☽∥⚷ 3:25
☽☍⚷ 4:30
☽⚻♅ 4:37
☽△⚳ 7:12
☽☍♀ 8:07
☽∥♀ 10:47
☉⚼☽ 12:58
☽⚻☿ 17:56
☿∠♄ 19:34

13 Th
☉⚺♇ 1:27
☽□♃ 1:55
☽⚻♆ 3:58
☽⋕♀ 4:41
☿∥♆ 5:06
☽⋕⚷ 10:38
☽□♇ 14:22
☉△☽ 15:18
☽∥☿ 18:27
☽□♄ 18:47
☽∥♆ 19:34
☽⚼☿ 19:39
☽✶♂ 21:41

14 F
☽⚼♆ 4:52
☽⚻⚷ 5:52
☽☍♅ 5:55
☽□⚳ 9:55
☽⚻♀ 13:53
☽△☿ 21:44

15 Sa
☽∠♂ 0:17
☽⋕♅ 0:26
☉∥☽ 4:13
☽✶♃ 4:53
☽△♆ 6:26
☽⚼⚷ 7:29
♅⚺⚷ 16:11
☽✶♇ 17:22
☽⚼♀ 18:00
☉□☽ 22:18
☽✶♄ 22:21
☉⚺♄ 22:58

16 Su
♀∥⚷ 0:05
☽⚺♂ 3:44
☽∠♃ 7:29
☽⚻♅ 9:50
☽△⚷ 9:51
♂ ♑ 11:34
♂∥⚳ 12:13
☽✶⚳ 15:30
☽∠♇ 20:00
☽△♀ 23:07

17 M
☿ R 0:53
☽∠♄ 1:17
☽□☿ 3:11
☿⋕♀ 4:22
☉⋕♅ 6:29
☽∥♄ 8:16
☽⚺♃ 10:53
☽□♆ 11:50
☽⚼♅ 12:56
☽∠⚳ 19:32
☽∥♇ 22:17
☽⚺♇ 23:23

18 Tu
☽∥♃ 2:14
☽⚺♄ 4:59
☉✶☽ 9:04
☽☌♂ 13:17
☽△♅ 16:46
☽□⚷ 16:53
☿⚺♀ 17:04

19 W
☽⚺⚳ 0:20
☉ ♓ 4:58
☽✶☿ 9:58
☽□♀ 12:10
☉∠☽ 15:46
♀⋕♆ 19:15
☽☌♃ 19:51
☽✶♆ 20:06
☿∠♄ 23:32

20 Th
☽☌♇ 8:08
☽∠☿ 13:35
☽☌♄ 14:19
♃✶♆ 15:57
☽∥♃ 17:16
☽∥♇ 20:34
☉⚺☽ 23:09

21 F
☽∠♆ 1:06
☽⚺♂ 1:51
☽□♅ 2:15
☽✶⚷ 2:27
♂△♅ 9:11
☽☌⚳ 11:47
☽∥♄ 12:10
♂□⚷ 13:17
☽⚺☿ 17:16

22 Sa
☽✶♀ 4:09
☉∠♃ 6:08
☽⚺♆ 6:32
☽⚺♃ 7:03
☽∠⚷ 7:56
☽∠♂ 8:58
☉✶♅ 14:14
☉⚺⚷ 17:31
☽⚺♇ 18:53

23 Su
☽⚺♄ 1:37
♀⚺♆ 6:28
☽∠♀ 12:56
☽∠♃ 13:16
☽✶♅ 13:30
☽⚺⚷ 13:48
☉☌☽ 15:33
☽✶♂ 16:31
♀□♃ 17:00
☿⚺⚳ 21:20
☿∠♇ 23:17

24 M
☽☌☿ 0:40
☽∠♇ 0:47
☽⚺⚳ 1:04
☽⋕♅ 1:15
☽∠♄ 7:47
☉∥☽ 16:50
☽☌♆ 18:27
☽∠♅ 19:37
☽✶♃ 19:46
☽⚺♀ 22:06
☽⋕♀ 22:47

25 Tu
☉✶♂ 2:07
☽✶♇ 6:59
☽∠⚳ 8:11
☽∥♆ 13:06
☽✶♄ 14:13
☽∥☿ 15:00
☽⋕⚷ 21:55

26 W
☉☌☿ 1:46
☽⚺♅ 1:58
☽☌⚷ 2:21
☉⋕♀ 2:21
☿✶♂ 6:00
☽⚺☿ 8:13
☽□♂ 8:34
☉⚺☽ 9:27
☿∠♀ 11:24
☿∥♆ 11:54
☽✶⚳ 15:30

27 Th
☽⚺♆ 7:15
☽□♃ 9:23
☽∠☿ 12:03
☽∥⚷ 15:16
☽☌♀ 17:07
☉∠☽ 18:38
☽□♇ 19:48
☽⋕♆ 23:43

28 F
☽□♄ 3:26
☽⋕☿ 3:42
☉∠♇ 8:37
☉⋕☽ 12:24
☿∠♃ 12:51
☽∠♆ 13:41
☽☌♅ 14:51
☽⚺⚷ 15:19
☽✶☿ 15:52
☿⚺⚷ 21:51
♀□♇ 22:09

29 Sa
☽△♂ 0:57
☽∥♀ 1:19
☿✶♅ 3:14
☉✶☽ 3:41
☽□⚳ 6:06
☽∥♅ 12:05
☽✶♆ 19:51
☽∠⚷ 21:31
☽△♃ 22:42

LONGITUDE

Day	Sid.Time	☉	☽	☽ 12 hour	Mean ☊	True ☊	☿	♀	♂	⚳	♃	♄	⚷	♅	♆	♇
	h m s	° ' "	° ' "	° ' "	° '	° '	° '	° '	° '	° '	° '	° '	° '	° '	° '	° '
1 Su	10 37 01	10♓51 54	20♉11 12	26♉15 05	5♋03.6	5♋49.2	2♓48.0	25♈26.0	9♑19.0	11♒30.2	19♑32.7	28♑09.9	3♈56.7	3♉41.4	18♓06.6	24♑15.5
2 M	10 40 58	11 52 07	2♊22 12	8♊33 12	5 00.5	5D 47.0	1R 52.7	26 32.7	10 00.5	11 52.8	19 43.7	28 15.7	4 00.0	3 43.8	18 08.9	24 17.0
3 Tu	10 44 55	12 52 18	14 48 40	21 09 16	4 57.3	5 46.5	1 02.6	27 39.1	10 42.0	12 15.4	19 54.6	28 21.4	4 03.3	3 46.2	18 11.1	24 18.5
4 W	10 48 51	13 52 27	27 35 34	4♋08 07	4 54.1	5R 46.9	0 18.4	28 45.4	11 23.4	12 37.9	20 05.4	28 27.1	4 06.7	3 48.7	18 13.4	24 19.9
5 Th	10 52 48	14 52 34	10♋47 26	17 33 53	4 50.9	5 47.0	29♒40.6	29 51.4	12 04.9	13 00.3	20 16.2	28 32.8	4 10.0	3 51.2	18 15.7	24 21.3
6 F	10 56 44	15 52 39	24 27 45	1♌29 08	4 47.7	5 45.6	29 09.5	0♉57.1	12 46.4	13 22.7	20 26.8	28 38.4	4 13.4	3 53.7	18 18.0	24 22.7
7 Sa	11 00 41	16 52 42	8♌37 56	15 53 52	4 44.6	5 42.0	28 45.2	2 02.6	13 27.9	13 45.1	20 37.3	28 43.9	4 16.8	3 56.3	18 20.3	24 24.1
8 Su	11 04 37	17 52 42	23 16 25	0♍44 48	4 41.4	5 35.6	28 27.7	3 07.8	14 09.4	14 07.3	20 47.8	28 49.4	4 20.2	3 58.9	18 22.5	24 25.5
9 M	11 08 34	18 52 41	8♍18 01	15 54 53	4 38.2	5 26.8	28 17.0	4 12.8	14 51.0	14 29.6	20 58.1	28 54.8	4 23.7	4 01.5	18 24.8	24 26.8
10 Tu	11 12 30	19 52 38	23 34 02	1♎14 00	4 35.0	5 16.3	28D 12.8	5 17.4	15 32.5	14 51.7	21 08.3	29 00.1	4 27.1	4 04.2	18 27.1	24 28.1
11 W	11 16 27	20 52 32	8♎53 19	16 30 33	4 31.9	5 05.4	28 14.9	6 21.8	16 14.1	15 13.8	21 18.4	29 05.4	4 30.5	4 06.9	18 29.4	24 29.4
12 Th	11 20 24	21 52 25	24 04 21	1♏33 33	4 28.7	4 55.4	28 23.0	7 25.9	16 55.7	15 35.8	21 28.4	29 10.7	4 34.0	4 09.6	18 31.6	24 30.7
13 F	11 24 20	22 52 16	8♏57 14	16 14 38	4 25.5	4 47.3	28 36.9	8 29.6	17 37.3	15 57.8	21 38.4	29 15.8	4 37.5	4 12.4	18 33.9	24 31.9
14 Sa	11 28 17	23 52 05	23 25 18	0♐28 57	4 22.3	4 41.9	28 56.1	9 33.1	18 18.9	16 19.7	21 48.2	29 20.9	4 40.9	4 15.1	18 36.2	24 33.1
15 Su	11 32 13	24 51 53	7♐25 32	14 15 09	4 19.1	4 39.0	29 20.5	10 36.2	19 00.5	16 41.5	21 57.8	29 25.9	4 44.4	4 18.0	18 38.4	24 34.3
16 M	11 36 10	25 51 39	20 58 06	27 34 44	4 16.0	4D 38.1	29 49.6	11 39.1	19 42.1	17 03.3	22 07.4	29 30.9	4 47.9	4 20.8	18 40.7	24 35.5
17 Tu	11 40 06	26 51 24	4♑05 29	10♑30 53	4 12.8	4R 38.1	0♓23.3	12 41.5	20 23.8	17 25.0	22 16.9	29 35.8	4 51.4	4 23.7	18 43.0	24 36.6
18 W	11 44 03	27 51 06	16 51 28	23 07 44	4 09.6	4 37.7	1 01.2	13 43.7	21 05.4	17 46.6	22 26.2	29 40.6	4 54.9	4 26.6	18 45.2	24 37.7
19 Th	11 47 59	28 50 47	29 20 15	5♒29 30	4 06.4	4 35.8	1 43.0	14 45.5	21 47.1	18 08.2	22 35.5	29 45.4	4 58.5	4 29.5	18 47.5	24 38.8
20 F	11 51 56	29 50 27	11♒35 58	17 40 05	4 03.3	4 31.4	2 28.5	15 46.9	22 28.8	18 29.6	22 44.6	29 50.1	5 02.0	4 32.5	18 49.7	24 39.9
21 Sa	11 55 53	0♈50 04	23 42 14	29 42 47	4 00.1	4 24.0	3 17.5	16 47.9	23 10.5	18 51.0	22 53.5	29 54.7	5 05.5	4 35.5	18 52.0	24 40.9
22 Su	11 59 49	1 49 39	5♓42 01	11♓40 12	3 56.9	4 13.7	4 09.8	17 48.6	23 52.1	19 12.4	23 02.4	29 59.3	5 09.0	4 38.5	18 54.2	24 41.9
23 M	12 03 46	2 49 13	17 37 35	23 34 21	3 53.7	4 00.9	5 05.1	18 48.9	24 33.8	19 33.6	23 11.1	0♒03.7	5 12.6	4 41.5	18 56.5	24 42.9
24 Tu	12 07 42	3 48 44	29 30 41	5♈26 45	3 50.5	3 46.4	6 03.4	19 48.7	25 15.5	19 54.8	23 19.7	0 08.1	5 16.1	4 44.6	18 58.7	24 43.9
25 W	12 11 39	4 48 14	11♈22 41	17 18 41	3 47.4	3 31.5	7 04.3	20 48.1	25 57.2	20 15.8	23 28.2	0 12.4	5 19.6	4 47.7	19 00.9	24 44.8
26 Th	12 15 35	5 47 41	23 14 54	29 11 31	3 44.2	3 17.4	8 07.9	21 47.1	26 38.9	20 36.8	23 36.6	0 16.7	5 23.2	4 50.8	19 03.1	24 45.7
27 F	12 19 32	6 47 07	5♉08 46	11♉06 55	3 41.0	3 05.2	9 13.9	22 45.6	27 20.6	20 57.8	23 44.8	0 20.8	5 26.7	4 53.9	19 05.3	24 46.6
28 Sa	12 23 28	7 46 30	17 06 14	23 07 05	3 37.8	2 55.6	10 22.2	23 43.7	28 02.3	21 18.6	23 52.9	0 24.9	5 30.2	4 57.0	19 07.5	24 47.4
29 Su	12 27 25	8 45 51	29 09 49	5♊14 53	3 34.6	2 49.0	11 32.8	24 41.2	28 44.0	21 39.3	24 00.8	0 28.9	5 33.7	5 00.2	19 09.7	24 48.2
30 M	12 31 21	9 45 10	11♊22 44	17 33 54	3 31.5	2 45.2	12 45.5	25 38.3	29 25.7	22 00.0	24 08.6	0 32.9	5 37.3	5 03.4	19 11.8	24 49.0
31 Tu	12 35 18	10♈44 26	23 48 53	0♋08 16	3♋28.3	2♋43.8	14♓00.3	26♉34.8	0♒07.4	22♒20.5	24♑16.3	0♒36.7	5♈40.8	5♉06.6	19♓14.0	24♑49.8

1st of Month

Julian Day # 2458909.5
Obliquity 23°26'12"
SVP 4♓58'58"
GC 27♐07.3
Eris 23♈26.3

Day	⚴
1	15♑48.1
6	17 26.1
11	19 00.4
16	20 30.8
21	21 56.8
26	23 18.1
31	24 34.2

Day	⚵
1	20♎13.0R
6	19 28.7R
11	18 36.4R
16	17 37.3R
21	16 32.7R
26	15 23.9R
31	14 12.8R

Day	⚶
1	23♉14.2
6	24 49.2
11	26 27.9
16	28 10.1
21	29 55.4
26	1♊43.6
31	3 34.4

DECLINATION and LATITUDE

Day	☉ Decl	☽ Decl	☽ Lat	☽ 12h Decl	☿ Decl	☿ Lat	♀ Decl	♀ Lat	♂ Decl	♂ Lat	⚳ Decl	⚳ Lat	♃ Decl	♃ Lat	♄ Decl	♄ Lat
1 Su	7S29	14N18	3S38	16N10	7S17	3N25	10N52	1N07	23S31	0S25	22S37	5S31	22S01	0S00	20S33	0S01
2 M	7 07	17 53	2 48	19 26	7 45	3 16	11 21	1 12	23 29	0 26	22 32	5 32	21 60	0 00	20 32	0 01
3 Tu	6 44	20 46	1 49	21 52	8 13	3 05	11 50	1 16	23 27	0 27	22 28	5 34	21 58	0 01	20 31	0 01
4 W	6 21	22 41	0 43	23 14	8 39	2 54	12 18	1 21	23 24	0 28	22 23	5 36	21 57	0 01	20 30	0 01
5 Th	5 57	23 26	0N27	23 19	9 04	2 41	12 46	1 26	23 22	0 29	22 18	5 38	21 55	0 01	20 28	0 02
6 F	5 34	22 49	1 37	21 58	9 27	2 28	13 14	1 31	23 19	0 30	22 13	5 40	21 54	0 01	20 27	0 02
7 Sa	5 11	20 45	2 45	19 11	9 49	2 14	13 41	1 36	23 16	0 31	22 09	5 42	21 52	0 01	20 26	0 02
8 Su	4 47	17 16	3 43	15 04	10 08	2 00	14 08	1 41	23 12	0 32	22 04	5 44	21 51	0 01	20 25	0 02
9 M	4 24	12 36	4 28	9 55	10 25	1 46	14 35	1 46	23 09	0 33	21 59	5 46	21 49	0 01	20 24	0 02
10 Tu	4 01	7 04	4 55	4 06	10 40	1 32	15 01	1 51	23 05	0 34	21 54	5 47	21 48	0 01	20 23	0 02
11 W	3 37	1 05	5 00	1S57	10 52	1 17	15 28	1 56	23 01	0 35	21 49	5 49	21 46	0 01	20 22	0 02
12 Th	3 13	4S55	4 45	7 48	11 03	1 03	15 53	2 01	22 57	0 36	21 45	5 51	21 45	0 02	20 21	0 02
13 F	2 50	10 32	4 10	13 05	11 11	0 50	16 19	2 06	22 53	0 37	21 40	5 53	21 43	0 02	20 20	0 02
14 Sa	2 26	15 24	3 19	17 29	11 17	0 36	16 44	2 11	22 49	0 38	21 35	5 55	21 42	0 02	20 19	0 02
15 Su	2 02	19 16	2 19	20 46	11 21	0 23	17 09	2 16	22 44	0 39	21 30	5 57	21 41	0 02	20 18	0 02
16 M	1 39	21 56	1 12	22 48	11 22	0 10	17 33	2 20	22 39	0 40	21 25	5 59	21 39	0 02	20 17	0 02
17 Tu	1 15	23 20	0 03	23 32	11 22	0S02	17 57	2 25	22 34	0 41	21 21	6 02	21 38	0 02	20 16	0 02
18 W	0 51	23 26	1S04	23 02	11 20	0 14	18 21	2 30	22 29	0 42	21 16	6 04	21 36	0 02	20 15	0 03
19 Th	0 28	22 21	2 07	21 24	11 15	0 25	18 44	2 35	22 23	0 43	21 11	6 06	21 35	0 02	20 15	0 03
20 F	0 04	20 13	3 02	18 48	11 09	0 36	19 07	2 40	22 18	0 44	21 06	6 08	21 34	0 02	20 14	0 03
21 Sa	0N20	17 12	3 48	15 26	11 01	0 47	19 29	2 45	22 12	0 46	21 01	6 10	21 32	0 03	20 13	0 03
22 Su	0 44	13 30	4 24	11 27	10 52	0 57	19 51	2 50	22 06	0 47	20 57	6 12	21 31	0 03	20 12	0 03
23 M	1 07	9 18	4 47	7 03	10 40	1 06	20 13	2 54	21 59	0 48	20 52	6 14	21 29	0 03	20 11	0 03
24 Tu	1 31	4 45	4 58	2 25	10 27	1 15	20 34	2 59	21 53	0 49	20 47	6 16	21 28	0 03	20 10	0 03
25 W	1 55	0 03	4 56	2N19	10 12	1 23	20 54	3 04	21 46	0 50	20 42	6 19	21 27	0 03	20 09	0 03
26 Th	2 18	4N40	4 42	6 59	9 56	1 31	21 15	3 09	21 40	0 51	20 38	6 21	21 25	0 03	20 08	0 03
27 F	2 42	9 14	4 14	11 25	9 38	1 39	21 34	3 13	21 33	0 52	20 33	6 23	21 24	0 03	20 08	0 03
28 Sa	3 05	13 29	3 36	15 26	9 19	1 46	21 54	3 18	21 26	0 54	20 28	6 25	21 23	0 03	20 07	0 03
29 Su	3 28	17 15	2 47	18 53	8 58	1 52	22 12	3 22	21 18	0 55	20 23	6 28	21 22	0 03	20 06	0 03
30 M	3 52	20 19	1 50	21 32	8 36	1 58	22 31	3 27	21 11	0 56	20 19	6 30	21 20	0 04	20 05	0 04
31 Tu	4N15	22N31	0S47	23N12	8S12	2S04	22N48	3N31	21S03	0S57	20S14	6S32	21S19	0S04	20S05	0S04

Day	⚷ Decl	⚷ Lat	♅ Decl	♅ Lat	♆ Decl	♆ Lat	♇ Decl	♇ Lat
1	4N05	2N45	12N19	0S28	5S38	1S01	21S60	0S45
6	4 11	2 44	12 23	0 28	5 34	1 01	21 59	0 45
11	4 18	2 44	12 27	0 28	5 29	1 01	21 58	0 46
16	4 24	2 43	12 32	0 27	5 25	1 01	21 58	0 47
21	4 31	2 43	12 37	0 27	5 21	1 01	21 57	0 47
26	4 38	2 42	12 42	0 27	5 16	1 01	21 57	0 48
31	4N44	2N42	12N48	0S27	5S12	1S01	21S57	0S48

Day	⚴ Decl	⚴ Lat	⚵ Decl	⚵ Lat	⚶ Decl	⚶ Lat	Eris Decl	Eris Lat
1	8N03	30N44	2S41	5N38	15N20	3S21	1S43	11S37
6	8 40	31 12	2 04	5 60	15 55	3 09	1 41	11 37
11	9 19	31 41	1 24	6 21	16 28	2 58	1 40	11 36
16	9 59	32 11	0 43	6 42	17 02	2 48	1 38	11 36
21	10 41	32 43	0 00	7 02	17 34	2 37	1 37	11 35
26	11 24	33 16	0N43	7 21	18 06	2 28	1 35	11 35
31	12N09	33N50	1N26	7N38	18N36	2S18	1S34	11S35

Moon Phenomena

Max/0 Decl

dy	hr mn	
5	1:26	23N27
11	4:16	0 S
17	14:03	23S32
25	0:14	0 N

Max/0 Lat

dy	hr mn	
4	15:00	0 N
10	18:16	5N01
17	1:01	0 S
24	8:26	4S59
31	16:52	0 N

Perigee/Apogee

dy	hr m		kilometers
10	6:23	p	357126
24	15:22	a	406692

PH	dy	hr mn	
☽	2	19:59	12♊42
○	9	17:49	19♍37
☾	16	9:35	26♐16
●	24	9:29	4♈12

Void of Course Moon

Last Aspect				☽ Ingress		
1	15:53	♄	△	♊	1	19:22
4	2:21	♀	✶	♋	4	4:26
6	7:13	♄	☍	♌	6	9:29
8	8:14	☿	☍	♍	8	10:48
10	8:33	♄	△	♎	10	10:04
12	8:13	♄	□	♏	12	9:29
14	10:07	♄	✶	♐	14	11:10
16	9:35	☉	□	♑	16	16:26
19	0:49	♄	☌	♒	19	1:17
20	9:01	♀	□	♓	21	12:34
23	14:52	♂	✶	♈	24	0:59
26	7:18	♂	□	♉	26	13:38
28	23:06	♂	△	♊	29	1:39
30	15:11	♆	□	♋	31	11:44

DAILY ASPECTARIAN

1 Su	☉∥☿	5:49
	☽△♇	8:05
	☽⚼♂	8:41
	☽⚺♀	11:26
	☽△♄	15:53
	☽□☿	23:06
	♃∥♇	23:45
2 M	☉⚺⚳	0:27
	☽⚺♅	2:40
	☽✶⚷	3:11
	☽⚼♃	4:40
	☽⚼♇	13:26
	☽⚻♂	15:40
	☽△⚳	18:58
	☽∠♀	19:29
	☉□☽	19:59
	☽⚼♄	21:12
	☽#♄	21:34
3 Tu	☽□♆	6:25
	☽∠♅	7:32
	☽⚻♃	9:48
	☉∠♄	12:51
	☽#♃	13:13
	☽#♇	13:39
	♀□♄	16:46
	☽⚻♇	17:56
	☽#⚳	19:16
4 W	☽⚼⚳	0:04
	☽⚻♄	1:36
	☽✶♀	2:21
	♀∥♅	2:56
	☽△☿	4:45
	☿R♒	11:09
	☽✶♅	11:27
	☽□⚷	12:00
	☽#♂	18:02
	☿✶♀	21:25
5 Th	☽☍♂	2:26
	♀ ♉	3:08
	☽⚻⚳	4:04
	☉∠♀	4:56
	☽⚼☿	6:38
	☉△☽	7:50
	☽#♂	10:34
	☽△♆	13:15
	☽☍♃	16:57
	☽☍♇	23:51
6 F	☉∥♆	0:30
	☽☍♄	7:13
	☽⚻☿	7:48
	☽#⚳	9:16
	☽#♇	11:47
	☉⚼☽	11:48
	☽□♀	12:01
	☽#♃	12:57
	☽⚼♆	15:06
	☽□♅	16:07
	☽△⚷	16:41
7 Sa	☿⚺♄	1:09
	☽#♄	2:36
	☿∠♂	6:44
	☽⚻♂	8:24
	☽☍⚳	8:42
	☉⚻☽	14:36
	☽⚻♆	16:02
	☽⚼⚷	17:35
	☽⚻♃	19:56
	♂⚺⚳	21:23
8 Su	☽⚻♇	1:52
	♀∠♆	5:37
	☽☍☿	8:14
	☽⚻♄	8:59
	☽⚼♂	9:55
	☉☌♆	12:24
	☽∥♀	15:16
	☽△♀	17:01
	☽△♅	17:12
	☽⚻⚷	17:47
	♀☌♅	19:39
	☽⚼♃	20:16
9 M	☽∥♅	0:48
	⚳∥♇	1:46
	☽⚼♇	1:49
	☉∠♅	3:42
	♀⚺⚷	4:16
	☉#⚷	8:34
	☽⚼♄	8:54
	☽#☿	9:23
	☽⚻⚳	10:00
	☽△♂	10:49
	☽☍♆	15:58
	☽⚼♅	16:56
	☉☍☽	17:49
	☽⚼♀	18:29
	☽△♃	20:09
10 Tu	☽△♇	1:25
	☿D	3:49
	☽#♆	6:23
	☽⚻☿	7:16
	☽△♄	8:33
	☽⚼⚳	10:06
	☽∥⚷	11:16
	☉#☽	13:14
	☽⚻♅	16:29
	☽☍⚷	17:06
	☽⚻♀	19:44
11 W	☽⚼☿	6:54
	☽△⚳	10:14
	☽□♂	12:07
	☉✶♃	12:28
	☽⚻♆	15:10
	☉∥☽	17:32
	☽□♃	19:49
	☉⚻☽	20:15
	☽#⚷	21:31
	⚳∥♃	22:00
12 Th	☽□♇	0:42
	☽∥♆	2:15
	☽△☿	6:59
	☽□♄	8:13
	☽⚼♆	15:13
	☽☍♅	16:15
	☽⚻⚷	16:56
	☉⚼☽	22:06
	☽☍♀	23:11
13 F	☽∥☿	3:01
	☽#♅	9:09
	☽□⚳	11:50
	☽✶♂	15:01
	☽△♆	15:54
	☽⚼⚷	17:42
	☽✶♃	21:15
14 Sa	☉△☽	0:49
	☽✶♇	1:55
	☽#♀	8:23
	☽□☿	9:37
	☽✶♄	10:07
	♂✶♆	10:33
	☉✶♇	16:48
	☽∠♂	17:46
	☽⚻♅	18:33
	☽△⚷	19:19
	☽∠♃	23:11
15 Su	☽∠♇	3:45
	☿⚺♄	5:51
	☽⚻♀	6:02
	☽∥♄	8:02
	☽∠♄	12:24
	☽✶⚳	16:47
	☽∥⚳	18:34
	☽□♆	19:53
	☽∥♃	20:50
	☽⚼♅	21:05
	☽⚺♂	21:36
16 M	☽∥♇	0:20
	☽⚺♃	2:07
	☽⚺♇	6:34
	☿ ♓	7:44
	☽∥♂	9:10
	☉□☽	9:35
	☽⚼♀	11:12
	☽⚺♄	15:39
	☽✶☿	16:50
	☽∠⚳	20:49
17 Tu	☽△♅	0:34
	☽□⚷	1:26
	☽△♀	17:32
	☽∠☿	22:19
18 W	☽⚺⚳	1:48
	☽✶♆	3:38
	☽☌♂	8:34
	☽☌♃	10:48
	☽☌♇	14:55
	☉✶☽	22:58
	☽∥♂	23:24
19 Th	☽☌♄	0:49
	☽⚺☿	4:55
	☽∥♇	5:19
	☽∠♆	8:42
	☽∥♃	10:03
	☽□♅	10:05
	☽✶⚷	11:02
	☽∥⚳	14:55
	☉✶♄	23:51
	☽∥♄	23:52
20 F	☉ ♈	3:51
	☉∠☽	6:58
	☽#♀	8:26
	☽□♀	9:01
	♂☌♃	11:36
	☽☌⚳	14:03
	☽⚺♆	14:21
	☽∠⚷	16:47
	☽⚺♃	22:22
	☽⚺♂	22:53
21 Sa	⚳⚺♆	1:12
	☽⚺♇	1:57
	⚶ ♊	5:11
	☽⚺♄	12:29
	☉⚺☽	15:32
	☽☌☿	20:40
	☽✶♅	21:52
	☽⚺⚷	22:53
22 Su	♄ ♒	3:59
	☽∠♃	4:45
	☽#♅	5:06
	☽∠♂	6:46
	☽∠♇	8:03
	☿✶♅	13:20
	☽∥☿	16:02
	☽∠♄	18:48
	♀#♄	22:11
23 M	☽✶♀	2:37
	☽☌♆	2:40
	♀✶♆	3:09
	☿⚺⚷	3:20
	☽⚺⚳	4:01
	☽∠♅	4:11
	♂☌♇	5:22
	♂∥♇	7:59
	☽✶♃	11:21
	☽✶♇	14:20
	☽✶♂	14:52
	☽∥♆	21:10
24 Tu	☽#⚷	0:53
	☽✶♄	1:16
	♀□⚳	3:47
	☉☌☽	9:29
	☽⚺♅	10:37
	☽∠⚳	11:15
	☽∠♀	11:42
	☽☌⚷	11:42
	♀∠⚷	11:44
	♀#⚳	12:33
	☽⚺☿	14:28
	☉#☽	15:17
	☉⚺♅	23:45
25 W	⚳∠⚷	5:11
	☉∥☽	10:48
	☉☌⚷	13:28
	☽⚺♆	15:30
	☉∠⚳	17:14
	☽✶⚳	18:31
	☽⚺♀	20:47
	☽∠☿	23:44
	☽∥⚷	23:46
26 Th	☽□♃	0:44
	☽□♇	3:04
	☽#♆	3:05
	☽□♂	7:18
	☿∠♃	12:02
	♀#♃	12:24
	☽□♄	14:16
	☽∠♆	21:52
	♀#♂	22:34
	☽☌♅	23:30
27 F	☽⚺⚷	0:36
	☽#☿	2:01
	☉⚺☽	3:36
	☽✶☿	9:04
	☿∠♇	11:43
	☽∥♅	19:36
28 Sa	☽✶♆	4:03
	♀△♃	4:25
	♀#♇	4:28
	☽∠⚷	6:49
	☽□⚳	8:39
	♂∥♃	10:33
	☉∠☽	12:20
	☽△♃	13:40
	☽☌♀	14:21
	☽△♇	15:21
	☽△♂	23:06
29 Su	☽△♄	2:37
	♀△♇	2:58
	☽⚺♅	11:34
	☽✶⚷	12:41
	☽⚼♃	19:35
	☉✶☽	20:33
	☽⚼♇	20:57
	☽#♄	21:56
	☽#⚳	23:55
30 M	☽□☿	2:59
	☽⚼♂	6:17
	☽#♂	7:47
	☽⚼♄	8:09
	☽#♃	9:47
	☽□♆	15:11
	☽#♇	16:42
	☽∠♅	16:52
	♂ ♒	19:44
	☽△⚳	21:06
31 Tu	☽⚻♃	0:53
	☽⚻♇	1:56
	☽⚺♀	5:41
	☽∥♀	5:44
	☽⚻♂	12:40
	☽⚻♄	12:57
	♂☌♄	18:32
	☽✶♅	21:25
	☽□⚷	22:30

April 2020

LONGITUDE

Day	Sid.Time	☉	☽	☽ 12 hour	Mean ☊	True ☊	☿	♀	♂	⚳	♃	♄	⚷	♅	♆	♇
	h m s	° ' "	° ' "	° ' "	° '	° '	° '	° '	° '	° '	° '	° '	° '	° '	° '	° '
1 W	12 39 15	11♈43 40	6♋32 36	13♋02 27	3♋25.1	2♋43.6	15♓17.0	27♉30.8	0♒49.1	22♒41.0	24♑23.8	0♒40.5	5♈44.3	5♉09.8	19♓16.1	24♑50.5
2 Th	12 43 11	12 42 52	19 38 19	26 20 40	3 21.9	2R 43.5	16 35.6	28 26.2	1 30.8	23 01.4	24 31.2	0 44.2	5 47.8	5 13.1	19 18.3	24 51.2
3 F	12 47 08	13 42 02	3♌09 53	10♌06 13	3 18.8	2 42.3	17 56.0	29 21.1	2 12.5	23 21.6	24 38.4	0 47.8	5 51.3	5 16.3	19 20.4	24 51.9
4 Sa	12 51 04	14 41 09	17 09 47	24 20 31	3 15.6	2 39.1	19 18.2	0♊15.3	2 54.2	23 41.8	24 45.5	0 51.3	5 54.8	5 19.6	19 22.5	24 52.6
5 Su	12 55 01	15 40 14	1♍38 07	9♍02 05	3 12.4	2 33.2	20 42.2	1 08.9	3 35.9	24 01.9	24 52.5	0 54.7	5 58.3	5 22.9	19 24.6	24 53.2
6 M	12 58 57	16 39 16	16 31 40	24 05 54	3 09.2	2 25.0	22 07.9	2 01.9	4 17.6	24 21.9	24 59.3	0 58.1	6 01.8	5 26.2	19 26.7	24 53.8
7 Tu	13 02 54	17 38 17	1♎43 35	9♎23 21	3 06.1	2 14.9	23 35.3	2 54.1	4 59.3	24 41.8	25 05.9	1 01.3	6 05.3	5 29.5	19 28.8	24 54.4
8 W	13 06 50	18 37 15	17 03 47	24 43 23	3 02.9	2 04.3	25 04.3	3 45.7	5 41.0	25 01.5	25 12.4	1 04.5	6 08.8	5 32.8	19 30.8	24 54.9
9 Th	13 10 47	19 36 11	2♏20 41	9♏54 21	2 59.7	1 54.4	26 34.9	4 36.5	6 22.7	25 21.2	25 18.8	1 07.6	6 12.2	5 36.1	19 32.8	24 55.4
10 F	13 14 44	20 35 05	17 23 12	24 46 15	2 56.5	1 46.4	28 07.1	5 26.6	7 04.4	25 40.8	25 25.0	1 10.6	6 15.7	5 39.5	19 34.9	24 55.9
11 Sa	13 18 40	21 33 58	2♐02 46	9♐12 12	2 53.3	1 40.8	29 41.0	6 15.9	7 46.1	26 00.3	25 31.0	1 13.5	6 19.1	5 42.9	19 36.9	24 56.3
12 Su	13 22 37	22 32 48	16 14 18	23 08 59	2 50.2	1 37.8	1♈16.4	7 04.5	8 27.8	26 19.6	25 36.9	1 16.3	6 22.5	5 46.2	19 38.9	24 56.7
13 M	13 26 33	23 31 37	29 56 22	6♑36 41	2 47.0	1D 36.9	2 53.4	7 52.2	9 09.6	26 38.9	25 42.7	1 19.1	6 26.0	5 49.6	19 40.8	24 57.1
14 Tu	13 30 30	24 30 24	13♑10 21	19 37 50	2 43.8	1R 37.2	4 32.0	8 39.0	9 51.2	26 58.0	25 48.2	1 21.7	6 29.4	5 53.0	19 42.8	24 57.5
15 W	13 34 26	25 29 10	25 59 39	2♒16 24	2 40.6	1 37.5	6 12.2	9 24.9	10 32.9	27 17.0	25 53.7	1 24.3	6 32.8	5 56.4	19 44.8	24 57.8
16 Th	13 38 23	26 27 54	8♒28 39	14 37 01	2 37.5	1 36.8	7 53.9	10 10.0	11 14.6	27 35.9	25 58.9	1 26.7	6 36.1	5 59.8	19 46.7	24 58.1
17 F	13 42 19	27 26 36	20 42 05	26 44 24	2 34.3	1 34.1	9 37.3	10 54.0	11 56.3	27 54.7	26 04.0	1 29.1	6 39.5	6 03.3	19 48.6	24 58.4
18 Sa	13 46 16	28 25 16	2♓44 30	8♓42 52	2 31.1	1 29.0	11 22.2	11 37.1	12 38.0	28 13.4	26 08.9	1 31.4	6 42.8	6 06.7	19 50.5	24 58.7
19 Su	13 50 13	29 23 55	14 39 58	20 36 11	2 27.9	1 21.4	13 08.8	12 19.2	13 19.6	28 31.9	26 13.6	1 33.6	6 46.1	6 10.1	19 52.3	24 58.9
20 M	13 54 09	0♉22 31	26 31 53	2♈27 24	2 24.7	1 11.7	14 57.0	13 00.1	14 01.3	28 50.3	26 18.2	1 35.7	6 49.5	6 13.6	19 54.2	24 59.1
21 Tu	13 58 06	1 21 06	8♈23 00	14 18 57	2 21.6	1 00.6	16 46.8	13 40.0	14 42.9	29 08.6	26 22.6	1 37.7	6 52.7	6 17.0	19 56.0	24 59.2
22 W	14 02 02	2 19 39	20 15 27	26 12 42	2 18.4	0 49.1	18 38.2	14 18.7	15 24.5	29 26.8	26 26.9	1 39.6	6 56.0	6 20.4	19 57.8	24 59.3
23 Th	14 05 59	3 18 11	2♉10 53	8♉10 10	2 15.2	0 38.1	20 31.3	14 56.2	16 06.1	29 44.8	26 30.9	1 41.4	6 59.3	6 23.9	19 59.6	24 59.4
24 F	14 09 55	4 16 40	14 10 43	20 12 42	2 12.0	0 28.6	22 26.0	15 32.5	16 47.6	0♓02.7	26 34.8	1 43.1	7 02.5	6 27.3	20 01.4	24 59.5
25 Sa	14 13 52	5 15 08	26 16 20	2♊21 48	2 08.8	0 21.3	24 22.3	16 07.5	17 29.2	0 20.5	26 38.5	1 44.7	7 05.7	6 30.8	20 03.1	24R 59.5
26 Su	14 17 48	6 13 33	8♊29 21	14 39 15	2 05.7	0 16.5	26 20.2	16 41.1	18 10.7	0 38.1	26 42.0	1 46.2	7 08.9	6 34.3	20 04.8	24 59.5
27 M	14 21 45	7 11 57	20 51 48	27 07 20	2 02.5	0D 14.1	28 19.7	17 13.3	18 52.2	0 55.6	26 45.4	1 47.7	7 12.1	6 37.7	20 06.5	24 59.5
28 Tu	14 25 42	8 10 19	3♋26 11	9♋48 45	1 59.3	0 13.6	0♉20.8	17 44.1	19 33.7	1 12.9	26 48.6	1 49.0	7 15.2	6 41.2	20 08.2	24 59.5
29 W	14 29 38	9 08 39	16 15 26	22 46 37	1 56.1	0 14.4	2 23.3	18 13.4	20 15.1	1 30.1	26 51.6	1 50.2	7 18.3	6 44.6	20 09.9	24 59.4
30 Th	14 33 35	10♉06 56	29 22 43	6♌04 03	1♋53.0	0♋15.5	4♉27.3	18♊41.1	20♒56.6	1♓47.2	26♑54.4	1♒51.4	7♈21.4	6♉48.1	20♓11.5	24♑59.3

1st of Month

Julian Day #
2458940.5
Obliquity
23°26'12"
SVP 4♓58'55
GC 27♐07.3
Eris 23♈44.3

Day	⚴
1	24♑48.8
6	25 58.3
11	27 01.8
16	27 58.9
21	28 49.0
26	29 31.6

Day	⚵
1	13♎58.5R
6	12 47.2R
11	11 37.5R
16	10 31.0R
21	9 29.4R
26	8 33.8R

Day	⚶
1	3♊56.9
6	5 50.5
11	7 46.1
16	9 43.7
21	11 42.9
26	13 43.8

DECLINATION and LATITUDE

Day	☉ Decl	☽ Decl	☽ Lat	☽ 12h Decl	☿ Decl	☿ Lat	♀ Decl	♀ Lat	♂ Decl	♂ Lat	⚳ Decl	⚳ Lat	♃ Decl	♃ Lat	♄ Decl	♄ Lat
1 W	4N38	23N37	0N20	23N42	7S47	2S09	23N06	3N35	20S55	0S58	20S09	6S35	21S18	0S04	20S04	0S04
2 Th	5 01	23 27	1 28	22 52	7 20	2 13	23 23	3 40	20 47	0 59	20 05	6 37	21 17	0 04	20 03	0 04
3 F	5 24	21 56	2 34	20 40	6 52	2 17	23 39	3 44	20 39	1 01	20 00	6 39	21 16	0 04	20 02	0 04
4 Sa	5 47	19 03	3 32	17 08	6 23	2 21	23 55	3 48	20 31	1 02	19 56	6 42	21 14	0 04	20 02	0 04
5 Su	6 10	14 55	4 19	12 27	5 53	2 24	24 10	3 52	20 22	1 03	19 51	6 44	21 13	0 04	20 01	0 04
6 M	6 33	9 46	4 50	6 54	5 22	2 26	24 25	3 56	20 13	1 04	19 47	6 47	21 12	0 04	20 00	0 04
7 Tu	6 55	3 55	5 01	0 52	4 49	2 28	24 39	3 60	20 05	1 06	19 42	6 49	21 11	0 05	20 00	0 04
8 W	7 18	2S13	4 51	5S16	4 15	2 30	24 53	4 04	19 56	1 07	19 38	6 52	21 10	0 05	19 59	0 04
9 Th	7 40	8 13	4 20	11 01	3 40	2 31	25 06	4 07	19 46	1 08	19 33	6 54	21 09	0 05	19 59	0 04
10 F	8 02	13 38	3 32	16 01	3 04	2 31	25 19	4 11	19 37	1 09	19 29	6 57	21 08	0 05	19 58	0 04
11 Sa	8 24	18 07	2 30	19 55	2 26	2 31	25 31	4 14	19 28	1 11	19 25	6 59	21 07	0 05	19 57	0 05
12 Su	8 46	21 23	1 21	22 31	1 48	2 31	25 43	4 17	19 18	1 12	19 20	7 02	21 06	0 05	19 57	0 05
13 M	9 08	23 17	0 09	23 43	1 08	2 30	25 54	4 21	19 08	1 13	19 16	7 04	21 05	0 05	19 56	0 05
14 Tu	9 30	23 48	1S01	23 33	0 28	2 28	26 05	4 24	18 58	1 14	19 12	7 07	21 04	0 06	19 56	0 05
15 W	9 51	23 00	2 06	22 10	0N14	2 26	26 15	4 27	18 48	1 16	19 08	7 10	21 03	0 06	19 55	0 05
16 Th	10 13	21 05	3 03	19 45	0 56	2 23	26 25	4 29	18 38	1 17	19 03	7 12	21 03	0 06	19 55	0 05
17 F	10 34	18 13	3 50	16 30	1 40	2 20	26 34	4 32	18 28	1 18	18 59	7 15	21 02	0 06	19 55	0 05
18 Sa	10 55	14 38	4 26	12 38	2 24	2 17	26 42	4 34	18 17	1 20	18 55	7 18	21 01	0 06	19 54	0 05
19 Su	11 16	10 30	4 51	8 17	3 09	2 13	26 50	4 37	18 07	1 21	18 51	7 20	21 00	0 06	19 54	0 05
20 M	11 36	6 00	5 02	3 40	3 55	2 08	26 58	4 39	17 56	1 22	18 47	7 23	20 60	0 06	19 53	0 05
21 Tu	11 57	1 17	5 01	1N06	4 42	2 03	27 05	4 41	17 45	1 24	18 43	7 26	20 59	0 06	19 53	0 05
22 W	12 17	3N30	4 46	5 51	5 30	1 57	27 11	4 43	17 34	1 25	18 39	7 29	20 58	0 07	19 53	0 05
23 Th	12 37	8 10	4 19	10 25	6 18	1 51	27 17	4 44	17 23	1 26	18 36	7 32	20 58	0 07	19 52	0 06
24 F	12 57	12 35	3 41	14 38	7 07	1 45	27 23	4 45	17 12	1 28	18 32	7 35	20 57	0 07	19 52	0 06
25 Sa	13 16	16 32	2 51	18 17	7 56	1 38	27 28	4 47	17 00	1 29	18 28	7 37	20 56	0 07	19 52	0 06
26 Su	13 36	19 51	1 54	21 11	8 46	1 30	27 32	4 47	16 49	1 30	18 24	7 40	20 56	0 07	19 51	0 06
27 M	13 55	22 17	0 50	23 08	9 36	1 22	27 36	4 48	16 37	1 32	18 21	7 43	20 55	0 07	19 51	0 06
28 Tu	14 14	23 41	0N17	23 56	10 26	1 14	27 40	4 49	16 25	1 33	18 17	7 46	20 55	0 07	19 51	0 06
29 W	14 32	23 51	1 25	23 27	11 17	1 05	27 42	4 49	16 14	1 34	18 14	7 49	20 54	0 08	19 51	0 06
30 Th	14N51	22N44	2N30	21N40	12N08	0S56	27N45	4N49	16S02	1S36	18S10	7S52	20S54	0S08	19S51	0S06

Day	⚷ Decl	⚷ Lat	♅ Decl	♅ Lat	♆ Decl	♆ Lat	♇ Decl	♇ Lat
1	4N46	2N42	12N49	0S27	5S11	1S01	21S57	0S4
6	4 52	2 42	12 54	0 27	5 07	1 01	21 57	0 4
11	4 59	2 42	13 00	0 27	5 03	1 02	21 57	0 4
16	5 06	2 42	13 06	0 27	4 60	1 02	21 57	0 5
21	5 12	2 42	13 11	0 27	4 56	1 02	21 58	0 5
26	5 19	2 42	13 17	0 27	4 53	1 02	21 58	0 5

Day	⚴ Decl	⚴ Lat	⚵ Decl	⚵ Lat	⚶ Decl	⚶ Lat	Eris Decl	Eris Lat
1	12N18	33N57	1N34	7N41	18N42	2S17	1S34	11S3
6	13 03	34 33	2 15	7 55	19 11	2 08	1 32	11 3
11	13 50	35 11	2 53	8 08	19 38	1 59	1 31	11 3
16	14 36	35 49	3 29	8 18	20 05	1 51	1 30	11 3
21	15 23	36 29	4 01	8 27	20 29	1 43	1 28	11 3
26	16 09	37 09	4 28	8 34	20 52	1 35	1 27	11 3

Moon Phenomena

Max/0 Decl dy hr mn		
1	9:12	23N42
7	15:21	0 S
13	21:08	23S48
21	6:27	0 N
28	15:26	23N56

Max/0 Lat dy hr mn		
7	0:35	5N01
13	3:00	0 S
20	9:18	5S03
27	17:55	0 N

Perigee/Apogee dy hr m		kilometers
7 18:18	p	356910
20 19:02	a	406462

PH	dy hr mn	
☽	1 10:22	12♋09
○	8 2:36	18♎44
☾	14 22:57	25♑27
●	23 2:27	3♉24
☽	30 20:39	10♌57

Void of Course Moon

Last Aspect			☽ Ingress	
2 16:50	♀	✱	♌	2 18:2
3 19:30	☉	△	♍	4 21:2
6 13:30	♃	△	♎	6 21:1
8 12:51	♃	□	♏	8 20:1
10 19:36	☿	△	♐	10 20:3
12 11:47	☉	△	♑	13 0:0
14 23:49	♃	☌	♒	15 7:3
17 14:35	☉	✱	♓	17 18:3
19 23:32	♃	✱	♈	20 7:0
22 12:33	♃	□	♉	22 19:3
25 0:44	♃	△	♊	25 7:2
27 17:01	☿	✱	♋	27 17:2
29 19:31	♃	☍	♌	30 1:0

DAILY ASPECTARIAN

1 W
☽⚼⚳ 2:11
☿∠♄ 7:36
☉∥⚷ 8:09
☉□☽ 10:22
☽∠♀ 11:52
☽△☿ 17:52
☿∠♂ 20:58
☽△♆ 23:24

2 Th
☽∥♀ 1:34
☽⚻⚳ 6:14
☽☍♃ 8:50
☉#♆ 9:08
☽☍♇ 9:21
⚳∥♄ 10:54
☽✱♀ 16:50
☽☍♄ 19:50
☽☍♂ 22:14
☽⚼☿ 23:33
☽#♇ 23:51

3 F
☽⚼♆ 2:03
☽□♅ 3:41
☽△⚷ 4:42
☽#♃ 6:47
☽#♂ 12:40
☽#♄ 16:58
♀ ♊ 17:12
☽#⚳ 17:36
☉△☽ 19:30

4 Sa
☿☌♆ 1:16
☽⚻♆ 3:44
☽⚻☿ 3:59
☽⚼⚷ 6:19
☽☍⚳ 11:11
☽⚻♃ 12:47
☽⚻♇ 12:54
☉#☿ 16:24
♀△♄ 17:11
☿∠♅ 18:17
☉⚼☽ 22:19
☽⚻♄ 22:49
☽□♀ 23:09

5 Su
♃☌♇ 2:46
☽⚻♂ 3:21
☽△♅ 6:07
☽⚻⚷ 7:05
☽∥♅ 9:54
☽⚼♇ 13:23
☽⚼♃ 13:27
☽⚼♄ 23:06

6 M
☉⚻☽ 0:13
☽⚼♂ 4:36
☽☍♆ 4:39
♂∠♆ 5:29
☽⚼♅ 6:14
☽☍☿ 9:50
☿∥♆ 10:55
☉∥☽ 12:39
☽⚻⚳ 12:42
☽△♇ 13:16
☽△♃ 13:30
☽#♆ 19:15
☽#☿ 20:05
☽∥⚷ 20:08
☿#⚷ 20:36
☽△♄ 22:53

7 Tu
☽△♀ 1:57
☽△♂ 5:21
☽⚻♅ 5:55
☽☍⚷ 6:52
☽⚼⚳ 12:45
♂∥♄ 14:02
⚳⚺♇ 15:42
♂□♅ 18:52
☿✱♇ 21:29
☿⚺⚳ 23:04

8 W
☿✱♃ 2:21
☉☍☽ 2:36
☽⚼♀ 2:49
☽⚻♆ 3:51
☽∥☿ 7:17
☽#⚷ 10:41
☽∥♆ 11:19
☽□♇ 12:19
☽△⚳ 12:45
☽□♃ 12:51
☽⚻☿ 13:55
♂✱⚷ 17:25
⚳⚺♃ 19:38
☉#☽ 21:37
☽□♄ 22:04
☉⚺♆ 22:35

9 Th
☉∠♀ 0:59
☽⚼♆ 3:30
☽⚻♀ 3:48
☽☍♅ 5:11
☽⚻⚷ 6:08
☽□♂ 6:42
☽⚼☿ 16:21
☽#♅ 20:55

10 F
☽△♆ 3:33
☉⚻☽ 5:33
☽⚼⚷ 6:18
♀⚺♅ 6:41
☽✱♇ 12:16
☽✱♃ 13:09
☽□⚳ 13:48
☽△☿ 19:36
☽✱♄ 22:38

11 Sa
♀✱⚷ 1:40
☿ ♈ 4:49
☽⚻♅ 6:09
☽△⚷ 7:10
☽☍♀ 7:29
☉⚼☽ 8:07
☽∥⚳ 8:15
☽∥♂ 8:23
☽✱♂ 10:04
☽∥♄ 12:17
☽∠♇ 13:15
♂∥⚳ 14:14
☽∠♃ 14:20
☽∥♃ 21:29
☿✱♄ 23:59

12 Su
☽∠♄ 0:03
☽∥♇ 5:35
☽□♆ 5:54
☽⚼♅ 7:53
☉△☽ 11:47
☽∠♂ 13:13
☽⚺♇ 15:10
☽⚺♃ 16:27
☽✱⚳ 18:01

13 M
♆#⚷ 0:25
☽⚺♄ 2:28
☽□☿ 6:01
☽△♅ 10:38
☽□⚷ 11:44
☽⚻♀ 15:11
☽⚺♂ 17:34
☽∠⚳ 21:43

14 Tu
☉□♇ 11:08
☽✱♆ 12:11
☿⚺♅ 20:07
☽⚼♀ 20:49
☽☌♇ 22:03
☉□☽ 22:57
☽☌♃ 23:49

15 W
☽⚺⚳ 2:31
☿☌⚷ 5:03
☽☌♄ 10:22
☉□♃ 11:00
☽∥♇ 14:38
☽∠♆ 16:49
♀⚼♇ 17:36
☽□♅ 19:10
☽✱⚷ 20:21
☽✱☿ 22:42

16 Th
☽∥♃ 0:23
☽△♀ 3:30
☽☌♂ 5:43
☽∥♄ 10:41
☽∥⚳ 18:04
☽∥♂ 22:07
☽⚺♆ 22:14

17 F
☽∠⚷ 1:54
♀⚼♃ 6:12
☽⚺♇ 8:29
☽∠☿ 9:06
☽⚺♃ 10:44
☉✱☽ 14:35
☽☌⚳ 14:43
☉✱⚳ 16:52
☽⚺♄ 21:33

18 Sa
☿✱♀ 5:37
☽✱♅ 6:48
☽⚺⚷ 8:01
☽#♅ 9:00
☽∠♇ 14:33
☽∠♃ 17:01
☽□♀ 18:58
☉#☽ 20:07
☽⚺☿ 20:23
☽⚺♂ 21:08
☉∠☽ 23:25

19 Su
☽∠♄ 3:50
☿✱♂ 3:56
☿∠⚳ 6:14
☽☌♆ 10:33
☽∠♅ 13:12
☉ ♉ 14:47
☽✱♇ 20:52
☽✱♃ 23:32

20 M
☽#⚷ 4:12
☽⚺⚳ 4:48
☽∠♂ 5:21
☽∥♆ 5:27
☉⚺☽ 8:29
☽#☿ 9:10
☽✱♄ 10:17
☽⚺♅ 19:44
☽☌⚷ 20:56

21 Tu
☉□♄ 7:01
☿#♆ 7:02
☽✱♀ 11:18
☽∠⚳ 11:57
☽✱♂ 13:36
☿∥⚷ 15:45
☽☌☿ 20:07
☽⚺♆ 23:24

22 W
☽#♆ 7:14
☽∥⚷ 8:50
☽□♇ 9:32
☽∥☿ 12:14
☽□♃ 12:33
☿⚺♆ 17:12
☽✱⚳ 18:59
☽∠♀ 19:15
☽□♄ 23:01

23 Th
☉☌☽ 2:27
☽∠♆ 5:39
☽☌♅ 8:30
☽⚺⚷ 9:41
⚳ ♓ 20:21

24 F
☉∥☽ 2:16
☽⚺♀ 2:51
☽∥♅ 3:51
☽□♂ 5:32
☽✱♆ 11:39
☽∠⚷ 15:42
☉∠♆ 18:55
☽⚺☿ 19:31
☽△♇ 21:28
☉∥♅ 23:37

25 Sa
☽△♃ 0:44
☽#♂ 2:56
☿□♇ 7:37
☽□⚳ 8:13
☽△♄ 10:48
☽#⚳ 13:06
♇ R 18:55
☉⚺☽ 19:12
☽⚺♅ 20:14
☽✱⚷ 21:22

26 Su
☽#♄ 0:08
☽⚼♇ 2:56
♀⚼♄ 3:55
☿□♃ 4:32
☽⚼♃ 6:17
☽∠☿ 6:37
☉☌♅ 9:02
☽#♃ 9:32
☽⚼♄ 16:08
☽☌♀ 16:40
☽△♂ 19:56
☽#♇ 20:16
☽□♆ 22:33

27 M
☉⚺⚷ 0:03
☽∠♅ 1:29
☉∠☽ 2:47
☽⚻♇ 7:56
☽⚻♃ 11:21
☽✱☿ 17:01
☽△⚳ 19:42
☿ ♉ 19:54
☽⚻♄ 20:56

28 Tu
☽⚼♂ 2:15
☽✱♅ 6:10
☽□⚷ 7:14
☉✱☽ 9:40
☿✱⚳ 11:55
☿□♄ 17:29
♂⚺♆ 20:49

29 W
☽⚼⚳ 0:28
☽⚺♀ 3:46
☽△♆ 7:13
☽⚻♂ 7:47
☿∠♀ 12:34
☽☍♇ 16:02
☽☍♃ 19:31

30 Th
♀ ♒ 0:31
☽⚻⚳ 4:26
☽☍♄ 4:28
⚳⚺♄ 6:21
☽∠♀ 8:00
☿∠♆ 8:36
☽#♇ 8:49
☽⚼♆ 10:28
☽□☿ 10:48
☽□♅ 13:22
☽△⚷ 14:21
☽#♃ 19:03
☉□☽ 20:39

LONGITUDE

Day	Sid.Time	☉	☽	☽ 12 hour	Mean☊	True☊	☿	♀	♂	⚳	♃	♄	⚷	♅	♆	♇
	h m s	° ' "	° ' "	° ' "	° '	° '	° '	° '	° '	° '	° '	° '	° '	° '	° '	° '
	14 37 31	11♉05 12	12♌50 58	19♌43 41	1♋49.8	0♋15.9	6♉32.6	19♊07.1	21♒38.0	2♓04.1	26♑57.0	1♒52.4	7♈24.5	6♉51.5	20♓13.1	24♑59.1
a	14 41 28	12 03 25	26 42 20	3♍46 56	1 46.6	0R 14.9	8 39.2	19 31.5	22 19.4	2 20.8	26 59.5	1 53.3	7 27.5	6 55.0	20 14.7	24R 59.0
u	14 45 24	13 01 36	10♍57 21	18 13 16	1 43.4	0 12.0	10 46.8	19 54.1	23 00.7	2 37.4	27 01.7	1 54.2	7 30.5	6 58.4	20 16.3	24 58.8
	14 49 21	13 59 46	25 34 12	2♎59 29	1 40.3	0 07.3	12 55.4	20 14.8	23 42.0	2 53.8	27 03.8	1 54.9	7 33.5	7 01.8	20 17.8	24 58.6
u	14 53 17	14 57 53	10♎28 15	17 59 31	1 37.1	0 01.3	15 04.7	20 33.7	24 23.3	3 10.1	27 05.7	1 55.6	7 36.5	7 05.3	20 19.3	24 58.3
/	14 57 14	15 55 58	25 32 07	3♏04 52	1 33.9	29♊54.7	17 14.6	20 50.7	25 04.6	3 26.2	27 07.4	1 56.1	7 39.4	7 08.7	20 20.8	24 58.0
h	15 01 11	16 54 02	10♏36 32	18 05 54	1 30.7	29 48.4	19 24.7	21 05.7	25 45.8	3 42.2	27 08.9	1 56.6	7 42.3	7 12.1	20 22.2	24 57.7
	15 05 07	17 52 04	25 31 50	2♐53 20	1 27.5	29 43.3	21 34.9	21 18.6	26 27.1	3 58.0	27 10.3	1 56.9	7 45.2	7 15.5	20 23.7	24 57.4
a	15 09 04	18 50 04	10♐09 33	17 19 49	1 24.4	29 40.0	23 44.9	21 29.3	27 08.2	4 13.6	27 11.4	1 57.2	7 48.1	7 18.9	20 25.1	24 57.0
u	15 13 00	19 48 03	24 23 39	1♑20 45	1 21.2	29D 38.6	25 54.4	21 38.0	27 49.4	4 29.1	27 12.4	1 57.3	7 50.9	7 22.3	20 26.5	24 56.6
	15 16 57	20 46 01	8♑11 02	14 54 31	1 18.0	29 38.7	28 03.1	21 44.4	28 30.5	4 44.4	27 13.2	1R 57.4	7 53.7	7 25.7	20 27.8	24 56.2
u	15 20 53	21 43 57	21 31 24	28 02 00	1 14.8	29 39.9	0♊10.7	21 48.5	29 11.6	4 59.5	27 13.8	1 57.4	7 56.4	7 29.1	20 29.2	24 55.8
/	15 24 50	22 41 52	4♒26 42	10♒45 59	1 11.7	29 41.4	2 16.9	21R 50.3	29 52.6	5 14.4	27 14.2	1 57.3	7 59.2	7 32.4	20 30.5	24 55.3
h	15 28 46	23 39 46	17 00 22	23 10 25	1 08.5	29R 42.6	4 21.5	21 49.8	0♓33.6	5 29.2	27R 14.4	1 57.0	8 01.8	7 35.8	20 31.7	24 54.8
	15 32 43	24 37 38	29 16 43	5♓19 51	1 05.3	29 42.7	6 24.2	21 46.9	1 14.6	5 43.8	27 14.4	1 56.7	8 04.5	7 39.1	20 33.0	24 54.3
a	15 36 40	25 35 29	11♓20 25	17 18 57	1 02.1	29 41.4	8 24.7	21 41.6	1 55.5	5 58.1	27 14.2	1 56.3	8 07.1	7 42.5	20 34.2	24 53.7
u	15 40 36	26 33 19	23 16 02	29 12 10	0 59.0	29 38.6	10 23.0	21 33.9	2 36.4	6 12.3	27 13.9	1 55.8	8 09.7	7 45.8	20 35.4	24 53.2
	15 44 33	27 31 08	5♈07 50	11♈03 30	0 55.8	29 34.5	12 18.8	21 23.8	3 17.2	6 26.3	27 13.3	1 55.1	8 12.3	7 49.1	20 36.5	24 52.6
u	15 48 29	28 28 55	16 59 35	22 56 26	0 52.6	29 29.6	14 12.0	21 11.3	3 57.9	6 40.2	27 12.6	1 54.4	8 14.8	7 52.4	20 37.7	24 51.9
/	15 52 26	29 26 42	28 54 25	4♉53 48	0 49.4	29 24.3	16 02.4	20 56.4	4 38.7	6 53.8	27 11.6	1 53.6	8 17.3	7 55.7	20 38.8	24 51.3
h	15 56 22	0♊24 27	10♉54 53	16 57 52	0 46.2	29 19.2	17 50.0	20 39.1	5 19.3	7 07.2	27 10.5	1 52.7	8 19.7	7 58.9	20 39.8	24 50.6
	16 00 19	1 22 11	23 02 57	29 10 20	0 43.1	29 14.8	19 34.6	20 19.5	5 59.9	7 20.4	27 09.2	1 51.7	8 22.1	8 02.2	20 40.9	24 49.9
a	16 04 15	2 19 53	5♊20 09	11♊32 33	0 39.9	29 11.7	21 16.2	19 57.6	6 40.4	7 33.4	27 07.7	1 50.6	8 24.5	8 05.4	20 41.9	24 49.2
u	16 08 12	3 17 34	17 47 40	24 05 37	0 36.7	29D 09.9	22 54.7	19 33.6	7 20.9	7 46.2	27 06.0	1 49.4	8 26.9	8 08.6	20 42.9	24 48.4
	16 12 09	4 15 15	0♋26 32	6♋50 34	0 33.5	29 09.4	24 30.1	19 07.5	8 01.2	7 58.7	27 04.2	1 48.1	8 29.2	8 11.8	20 43.8	24 47.6
u	16 16 05	5 12 53	13 17 50	19 48 28	0 30.4	29 10.0	26 02.4	18 39.4	8 41.6	8 11.1	27 02.1	1 46.8	8 31.4	8 15.0	20 44.7	24 46.8
/	16 20 02	6 10 31	26 22 38	3♌00 27	0 27.2	29 11.3	27 31.4	18 09.5	9 21.8	8 23.2	26 59.8	1 45.3	8 33.6	8 18.1	20 45.6	24 46.0
h	16 23 58	7 08 06	9♌42 04	16 27 37	0 24.0	29 12.8	28 57.2	17 37.9	10 02.0	8 35.1	26 57.4	1 43.7	8 35.8	8 21.3	20 46.5	24 45.2
	16 27 55	8 05 41	23 17 10	0♍10 47	0 20.8	29 13.9	0♋19.7	17 04.8	10 42.1	8 46.8	26 54.8	1 42.1	8 38.0	8 24.4	20 47.3	24 44.3
a	16 31 51	9 03 14	7♍08 28	14 10 08	0 17.7	29R 14.5	1 38.9	16 30.3	11 22.1	8 58.2	26 52.0	1 40.3	8 40.0	8 27.5	20 48.1	24 43.4
u	16 35 48	10♊00 45	21 15 40	28 24 49	0♋14.5	29♊14.2	2♋54.7	15♊54.8	12♓02.0	9♓09.4	26♑49.0	1♒38.5	8♈42.1	8♉30.5	20♓48.9	24♑42.5

1st of Month

Julian Day #
2458970.5
Obliquity
23°26'12"
SVP 4♓58'51"
GC 27♐07.4
Eris 24♈03.8

Day	⚴
1	0♒06.1
6	0 32.1
11	0 49.2
16	0 56.8
21	0 54.5R
26	0 41.9R
31	0 19.0R
	⚵
1	7♎45.5R
6	7 05.1R
11	6 33.0R
16	6 09.5R
21	5 54.7R
26	5 48.6R
31	5 50.9
	⚶
1	15♊46.1
6	17 49.6
11	19 54.3
16	22 00.0
21	24 06.6
26	26 14.2
31	28 22.4

DECLINATION and LATITUDE

y	☉ Decl	☽ Decl	☽ Lat	☽12h Decl	☿ Decl	☿ Lat	♀ Decl	♀ Lat	♂ Decl	♂ Lat	⚳ Decl	⚳ Lat	♃ Decl	♃ Lat	♄ Decl	♄ Lat
	15N09	20N17	3N29	18N36	12N58	0S46	27N47	4N48	15S50	1S37	18S07	7S55	20S54	0S08	19S51	0S06
a	15 27	16 38	4 17	14 24	13 49	0 36	27 48	4 47	15 37	1 39	18 04	7 58	20 53	0 08	19 50	0 06
u	15 45	11 56	4 51	9 17	14 38	0 26	27 49	4 46	15 25	1 40	18 01	8 02	20 53	0 08	19 50	0 06
	16 02	6 27	5 07	3 31	15 28	0 16	27 49	4 45	15 13	1 41	17 58	8 05	20 53	0 08	19 50	0 07
u	16 19	0 30	5 03	2S32	16 16	0 05	27 49	4 43	15 00	1 43	17 54	8 08	20 53	0 08	19 50	0 07
/	16 36	5S33	4 38	8 29	17 04	0N05	27 48	4 41	14 48	1 44	17 51	8 11	20 52	0 09	19 50	0 07
h	16 53	11 18	3 54	13 55	17 50	0 16	27 47	4 39	14 35	1 46	17 49	8 14	20 52	0 09	19 50	0 07
	17 09	16 19	2 54	18 27	18 35	0 26	27 45	4 36	14 23	1 47	17 46	8 18	20 52	0 09	19 50	0 07
a	17 25	20 16	1 44	21 44	19 18	0 37	27 42	4 33	14 10	1 49	17 43	8 21	20 52	0 09	19 50	0 07
u	17 41	22 51	0 28	23 35	19 59	0 47	27 39	4 29	13 57	1 50	17 40	8 24	20 52	0 09	19 50	0 07
	17 57	23 57	0S46	23 58	20 39	0 57	27 36	4 25	13 44	1 51	17 38	8 27	20 52	0 09	19 50	0 07
u	18 12	23 38	1 56	22 58	21 16	1 06	27 31	4 21	13 31	1 53	17 35	8 31	20 52	0 10	19 50	0 07
/	18 27	22 01	2 58	20 49	21 51	1 16	27 26	4 16	13 18	1 54	17 33	8 34	20 52	0 10	19 51	0 07
h	18 41	19 23	3 49	17 44	22 24	1 24	27 21	4 10	13 05	1 56	17 30	8 38	20 52	0 10	19 51	0 07
	18 55	15 55	4 29	13 57	22 54	1 33	27 15	4 04	12 51	1 57	17 28	8 41	20 52	0 10	19 51	0 08
a	19 09	11 52	4 56	9 41	23 21	1 40	27 08	3 58	12 38	1 59	17 26	8 45	20 53	0 10	19 51	0 08
u	19 23	7 25	5 10	5 05	23 46	1 47	27 01	3 51	12 25	2 00	17 24	8 48	20 53	0 10	19 51	0 08
	19 36	2 42	5 10	0 19	24 08	1 53	26 53	3 44	12 11	2 02	17 22	8 52	20 53	0 10	19 51	0 08
u	19 49	2N06	4 57	4N29	24 28	1 59	26 44	3 36	11 58	2 03	17 20	8 55	20 53	0 11	19 52	0 08
/	20 02	6 51	4 32	9 09	24 45	2 04	26 34	3 27	11 44	2 05	17 18	8 59	20 54	0 11	19 52	0 08
h	20 14	11 24	3 54	13 32	24 60	2 08	26 24	3 18	11 31	2 06	17 16	9 03	20 54	0 11	19 52	0 08
	20 26	15 33	3 05	17 25	25 12	2 11	26 13	3 09	11 17	2 08	17 15	9 06	20 54	0 11	19 53	0 08
a	20 38	19 06	2 07	20 36	25 22	2 13	26 01	2 59	11 04	2 09	17 13	9 10	20 55	0 11	19 53	0 08
u	20 49	21 51	1 02	22 51	25 30	2 15	25 49	2 48	10 50	2 11	17 12	9 14	20 55	0 11	19 53	0 08
	20 60	23 33	0N07	23 58	25 35	2 16	25 36	2 37	10 36	2 12	17 11	9 18	20 56	0 12	19 54	0 09
u	21 10	24 03	1 17	23 48	25 38	2 16	25 22	2 25	10 22	2 14	17 09	9 21	20 56	0 12	19 54	0 09
/	21 20	23 14	2 24	22 20	25 40	2 15	25 07	2 13	10 09	2 15	17 08	9 25	20 57	0 12	19 55	0 09
h	21 30	21 06	3 25	19 35	25 39	2 13	24 52	2 01	9 55	2 17	17 07	9 29	20 58	0 12	19 55	0 09
	21 39	17 46	4 15	15 42	25 37	2 11	24 36	1 48	9 41	2 18	17 07	9 33	20 58	0 12	19 55	0 09
a	21 48	13 24	4 52	10 54	25 33	2 07	24 20	1 35	9 27	2 20	17 06	9 37	20 59	0 12	19 56	0 09
u	21N57	8N15	5N12	5N27	25N27	2N03	24N02	1N21	9S13	2S21	17S05	9S41	20S60	0S13	19S56	0S09

Day	⚷ Decl	⚷ Lat	♅ Decl	♅ Lat	♆ Decl	♆ Lat	♇ Decl	♇ Lat
1	5N25	2N42	13N23	0S27	4S50	1S02	21S59	0S52
6	5 31	2 42	13 28	0 27	4 47	1 02	21 60	0 52
11	5 37	2 42	13 34	0 27	4 44	1 03	22 01	0 53
16	5 42	2 42	13 39	0 27	4 42	1 03	22 02	0 54
21	5 47	2 42	13 45	0 27	4 40	1 03	22 03	0 54
26	5 52	2 43	13 50	0 27	4 38	1 03	22 04	0 55
31	5N57	2N43	13N55	0S27	4S37	1S03	22S05	0S55

Day	⚴ Decl	⚴ Lat	⚵ Decl	⚵ Lat	⚶ Decl	⚶ Lat	Eris Decl	Eris Lat
1	16N55	37N50	4N52	8N38	21N13	1S28	1S26	11S34
6	17 39	38 31	5 10	8 42	21 32	1 21	1 25	11 34
11	18 22	39 12	5 25	8 43	21 50	1 14	1 24	11 34
16	19 03	39 52	5 34	8 44	22 05	1 07	1 23	11 34
21	19 41	40 32	5 40	8 43	22 19	0 60	1 22	11 34
26	20 16	41 10	5 41	8 42	22 30	0 53	1 21	11 34
31	20N47	41N46	5N38	8N40	22N39	0S47	1S21	11S34

Moon Phenomena

Max/0 Decl
dy hr mn
5 1:59 0 S
11 6:11 24S00
18 13:32 0 N
25 21:22 24N03

Perigee/Apogee
dy hr m kilometers
6 2:52 p 359656
18 7:44 a 405582

Max/0 Lat
dy hr mn
4 7:14 5N08
10 9:03 0 S
17 12:50 5S11
24 21:35 0 N
31 13:23 5N15

PH dy hr mn
○ 7 10:46 17♏20
☾ 14 14:04 24♒14
● 22 17:40 2♊05
☽ 30 3:31 9♍12

Void of Course Moon

Last Aspect			☽ Ingress		
1 16:05	♂	☍	♍	2	5:36
4 2:26	♃	△	♎	4	7:11
6 2:32	♃	□	♏	6	7:06
8 2:40	♃	⚹	♐	8	7:16
10 6:12	♂	⚹	♑	10	9:40
12 10:31	♃	☌	♒	12	15:40
14 14:04	☉	□	♓	15	1:26
17 8:00	♃	⚹	♈	17	13:37
19 20:34	♃	□	♉	20	2:12
22 8:02	♃	△	♊	22	13:37
24 11:11	☿	☌	♋	24	23:10
27 1:07	♃	☍	♌	27	6:34
28 13:31	♀	⚹	♍	29	11:41
31 9:18	♃	△	♎	31	14:39

DAILY ASPECTARIAN

☽⋕♄ 3:24
☿☌♅ 3:42
☿⚺⚷ 10:06
☽⚹♀ 11:17
☿∥♅ 11:56
☽⚻♆ 12:52
☽⋕⚳ 15:20
☽☍♂ 16:05
☽⚼⚷ 16:41
☽⚻♇ 21:03

☽⚻♃ 0:29
♂∠⚷ 5:07
☽⋕♂ 5:52
☉∥☽ 6:07
☉⋕♂ 8:15
☽⚻♄ 8:49
☽☍⚳ 9:46
☽∥☿ 12:45
☽∥♅ 16:57
☽△♅ 17:20
☽⚻⚷ 18:14
☽⚼♇ 22:23
☽△☿ 23:39

☽⚼♃ 1:47
☉△☽ 3:41
☽⚼♄ 9:50
☽□♀ 15:07
☽☍♆ 15:23
☿⋕♂ 18:11
☽⚼♅ 18:13
☽⚻♂ 20:49
☽△♇ 23:02

4 M ☽△♃ 2:26
♀□♆ 3:54
☽∥⚷ 4:02
☽⚼☿ 4:28
☉⚼☽ 5:56
☽⋕♆ 6:49
☽△♄ 10:16
☽⚻⚳ 12:04
☽⚻♅ 18:34
☽☍⚷ 19:24
☉☌☿ 21:42
☽⚼♂ 22:11

5 Tu ☉∥☿ 2:32
☊R♊ 4:41
☉⚻☽ 7:40
☽⚻☿ 8:35
☽⚼⚳ 12:30
☽⚻♆ 15:44
☽△♀ 16:24
♂⚺♇ 20:12
☽∥♆ 20:54
☽□♇ 23:06
☽△♂ 23:14
☽⋕⚷ 23:51

6 W ☽□♃ 2:32
☽□♄ 10:11
☽△⚳ 12:48
☽⚼♆ 15:38
☽⚼♀ 16:41
☽☍♅ 18:33
☽⚻⚷ 19:21
☿⋕⚳ 23:21

7 Th ☽⋕♅ 10:00
☿⚹♆ 10:43
☉☍☽ 10:46
☽∥♂ 14:35
☽△♆ 15:41
☽☍☿ 16:31
☽⚻♀ 17:05
☽⚼⚷ 19:29
☿⚺♀ 20:40
☽⚹♇ 23:04

8 F ☽□♂ 1:34
☽⚹♃ 2:40
☉⋕☽ 4:49
☽∥⚳ 7:52
☽⚹♄ 10:28
☿∠⚷ 13:15
☽□⚳ 14:01
☽⋕☿ 15:49
☽⚻♅ 19:16
☽△⚷ 20:05
☽∥♄ 21:00
☽∠♇ 23:39

9 Sa ♂⚺♃ 1:55
☽∠♃ 3:23
☽∥♃ 4:37
☽∠♄ 11:22
☿△♇ 13:18
☽∥♇ 14:39
☉⚻☽ 15:36
☽□♆ 17:15
☿⋕♄ 18:36
☽☍♀ 19:15
☽⚼♅ 20:32
☉⋕⚳ 22:53

10 Su ☽⚺♇ 0:57
☽⚻☿ 3:04
☽⚺♃ 4:50
☽⚹♂ 6:12
☽⚺♄ 13:04
☿△♃ 14:37
☉⚹♆ 16:17
☽⚹⚳ 17:49
☉⚼☽ 19:25
☽△♅ 22:40
☽□⚷ 23:29

11 M ♄R 4:10
☿□♂ 7:34
☿⋕♃ 8:20
☽∠♂ 10:00
☽⚼☿ 10:19
♂⋕♅ 16:57
☽∠⚳ 21:09
☿ ♊ 21:59
☽⚹♆ 22:06

12 Tu ☉△☽ 0:25
☽⚻♀ 0:31
☉⚺♀ 1:59
☽☌♇ 6:15
☽☌♃ 10:31
☽⚺♂ 14:57
☽△☿ 19:08
☽☌♄ 19:19
☿△♄ 20:15

13 W ☽∥♇ 0:06
☽⋕☿ 1:31
☽⚺⚳ 1:32
☽∠♆ 2:01
♂ ♓ 4:18
☽⚼♀ 4:32
☽□♅ 5:53
☽⚹⚷ 6:44
♀R 6:46
☿⋕♇ 7:09
☉∠⚷ 7:31
☽∥♃ 11:31
☽∥♄ 20:17

14 Th ☉⋕☽ 4:51
☽⚺♆ 6:51
☽△♀ 9:21
☽∠⚷ 11:46
☽∥⚳ 13:43
☉□☽ 14:04
♃R 14:33
☿□⚳ 14:59
☽⚺♇ 15:24
☽⚺♃ 19:59

15 F ☽☌♂ 4:07
☽⚺♄ 5:16
☉△♇ 6:51
☽☌⚳ 13:03
☽⋕♅ 13:48
☿⚺♅ 15:18
☽⚹♅ 16:42
☽□☿ 16:59
☽⚺⚷ 17:32
☽∥♂ 19:25
☿⚹⚷ 20:23
☽∠♇ 21:07

16 Sa ♂⚺♄ 0:26
☽∠♃ 1:48
☽∠♄ 11:14
☿⚼♇ 17:55
☽☌♆ 18:35
☽□♀ 20:36
☽∠♅ 22:59

17 Su ☽⚹♇ 3:16
☉⚹☽ 7:14
☽⚹♃ 8:00
⚴R 8:30
☽⋕⚷ 8:42
☽∥♆ 14:00
☉△♃ 16:41
☽⚹♄ 17:30
☽⚺♂ 20:02
☿⚼♃ 22:51

18 M ☽⚺⚳ 2:42
☽⚺♅ 5:28
☽☌⚷ 6:15
☉∠☽ 16:17
☽⚹☿ 17:18

19 Tu ☽∠♂ 4:13
☉⋕♄ 4:56
☽⚺♆ 7:21
☽⚹♀ 8:18
☽∠⚳ 9:37
☽⋕♆ 12:56
☽□♇ 15:52
☽∥⚷ 18:29
☽□♃ 20:34

20 W ☉⚺☽ 1:10
☽∠☿ 5:03
☽□♄ 5:59
☿⚼♄ 11:15
☽⚹♂ 12:11
☽∠♆ 13:31
☽∠♀ 13:46
☉ ♊ 13:50
☽⚹⚳ 16:18
☽☌♅ 18:08
☽⚺⚷ 18:50
♀□♆ 23:04

21 Th ☽⋕♂ 0:37
☽∥♅ 13:17
☽⚺☿ 16:02
☽⚺♀ 18:47
☽⚹♆ 19:20

22 F ☽∠⚷ 0:38
☽△♇ 3:30
☽△♃ 8:02
☿☌♀ 8:42
☽⋕⚳ 10:48
☉△♄ 12:03
☿□♆ 15:44
☽△♄ 17:13
☉☌☽ 17:40

23 Sa ☽□♂ 2:45
☽□⚳ 4:23
☽⚺♅ 5:22
☽⚹⚷ 5:58
☽⋕♄ 6:03
☽⚼♇ 8:40
☽⚼♃ 13:06
☉∥☽ 13:12
☽⋕♃ 14:55
☽⚼♄ 22:09

24 Su ☽⋕♇ 2:18
☽☌♀ 3:16
☿∠♅ 3:34
☽□♆ 5:35
☽∠♅ 10:14
☽☌☿ 11:11
☽⚻♇ 13:20
☉⋕♃ 15:24
☽⚻♃ 17:39
♂☌⚳ 21:50

25 M ☿∥♀ 1:07
☽⚻♄ 2:33
☿⚻♇ 4:27
♂⚹♅ 6:49
☉⚺☽ 7:44
☽△⚳ 14:21
☽⚹♅ 14:35
☽△♂ 14:59
☽□⚷ 15:07
♂⚺⚷ 17:36

26 Tu ☽⚺♀ 9:32
⚳⚹♅ 10:23
☽△♆ 13:44
☉∠☽ 13:45
☿⚻♃ 15:36
☽⚼⚳ 18:28
☽⚼♂ 20:08
☽☍♇ 21:04

27 W ☽☍♃ 1:07
☽⚺☿ 2:20
⚵D 2:52
☽☍♄ 9:43
☽∠♀ 11:49
♂∠♇ 14:10
☽⋕♇ 14:46
☽⚼♆ 16:58
☉⚹☽ 19:04
☉∥☽ 20:40
☽□♅ 21:35
☽⚻⚳ 21:59
☽△⚷ 22:01

28 Th ☽⚻♂ 0:37
☽⋕♃ 1:14
⚳⚺⚷ 1:47
☽∠☿ 8:26
☽⋕♄ 9:31
☽⚹♀ 13:31
☿ ♋ 18:10
☽⚻♆ 19:37

29 F ☽⚼⚷ 0:36
☽⚻♇ 2:32
☽⋕⚳ 4:00
☽⚻♃ 6:18
☉⚺♅ 8:14
☽⚹☿ 13:34
☉⚹⚷ 13:58
☽⚻♄ 14:36
♀⚼♄ 16:44
☉□⚳ 21:24
☽∥♅ 21:31

30 Sa ☿⚻♄ 0:26
☽△♅ 2:16
☽⚻⚷ 2:37
☽☍⚳ 3:11
☉□☽ 3:31
☽⚼♇ 4:25
☽☍♂ 7:35
☽⚼♃ 8:03
☽□♀ 15:20
☽⚼♄ 16:13
☉⚼♇ 16:30
♂∠♃ 16:45
☽⋕♂ 19:29
☽☍♆ 23:15

31 Su ☽⚼♅ 3:48
☽△♇ 5:47
☽△♃ 9:18
☽∥⚷ 9:52
☽⋕♆ 15:31
☽△♄ 17:21
☽□☿ 21:17

June 2020

LONGITUDE

Day	Sid.Time	☉	☽	☽ 12 hour	Mean☊	True☊	☿	♀	♂	⚳	♃	♄	⚷	♅	♆	♇
	h m s	° ' "	° ' "	° ' "	° '	° '	° '	° '	° '	° '	° '	° '	° '	° '	° '	° '
1 M	16 39 44	10♊58 15	5♎37 14	12♎52 30	0♋11.3	29♊13.0	4♋07.1	15♊18.3	12♓41.9	9♓20.4	26♑45.9	1♒36.6	8♈44.1	8♉33.6	20♓49.6	24♑41.6
2 Tu	16 43 41	11 55 44	20 10 03	27 29 14	0 08.1	29R 11.3	5 16.0	14R 41.2	13 21.6	9 31.1	26R 42.6	1R 34.6	8 46.1	8 36.6	20 50.3	24R 40.6
3 W	16 47 38	12 53 12	4♏49 22	12♏09 37	0 04.9	29 09.2	6 21.4	14 03.6	14 01.3	9 41.6	26 39.1	1 32.5	8 48.0	8 39.6	20 51.0	24 39.6
4 Th	16 51 34	13 50 38	19 29 10	26 47 12	0 01.8	29 07.3	7 23.2	13 25.8	14 40.9	9 51.9	26 35.4	1 30.3	8 49.9	8 42.6	20 51.6	24 38.6
5 F	16 55 31	14 48 03	4♐02 52	11♐15 24	29♊58.6	29 05.8	8 21.3	12 48.1	15 20.5	10 01.9	26 31.6	1 28.1	8 51.7	8 45.5	20 52.2	24 37.6
6 Sa	16 59 27	15 45 28	18 24 06	25 28 22	29 55.4	29D 05.0	9 15.7	12 10.7	15 59.9	10 11.6	26 27.6	1 25.7	8 53.5	8 48.5	20 52.8	24 36.6
7 Su	17 03 24	16 42 51	2♑27 41	9♑21 41	29 52.2	29 04.8	10 06.2	11 33.9	16 39.2	10 21.1	26 23.4	1 23.3	8 55.3	8 51.4	20 53.3	24 35.5
8 M	17 07 20	17 40 14	16 10 06	22 52 48	29 49.1	29 05.2	10 52.8	10 57.9	17 18.5	10 30.4	26 19.1	1 20.8	8 57.0	8 54.2	20 53.8	24 34.5
9 Tu	17 11 17	18 37 36	29 29 47	6♒01 10	29 45.9	29 06.0	11 35.5	10 22.8	17 57.6	10 39.3	26 14.6	1 18.2	8 58.7	8 57.1	20 54.3	24 33.4
10 W	17 15 13	19 34 58	12♒27 07	18 47 56	29 42.7	29 06.9	12 14.0	9 49.0	18 36.7	10 48.0	26 09.9	1 15.6	9 00.3	8 59.9	20 54.8	24 32.3
11 Th	17 19 10	20 32 18	25 04 00	1♓15 44	29 39.5	29 07.8	12 48.4	9 16.7	19 15.6	10 56.5	26 05.1	1 12.8	9 01.9	9 02.7	20 55.2	24 31.1
12 F	17 23 07	21 29 39	7♓23 36	13 28 08	29 36.4	29 08.3	13 18.5	8 45.9	19 54.5	11 04.6	26 00.1	1 10.0	9 03.4	9 05.5	20 55.6	24 30.0
13 Sa	17 27 03	22 26 58	19 29 53	25 29 25	29 33.2	29R 08.6	13 44.2	8 16.9	20 33.2	11 12.5	25 55.0	1 07.1	9 04.9	9 08.2	20 55.9	24 28.8
14 Su	17 31 00	23 24 18	1♈27 16	7♈24 03	29 30.0	29 08.5	14 05.6	7 49.8	21 11.8	11 20.1	25 49.7	1 04.2	9 06.3	9 10.9	20 56.2	24 27.6
15 M	17 34 56	24 21 37	13 20 19	19 16 36	29 26.8	29 08.2	14 22.4	7 24.8	21 50.3	11 27.4	25 44.3	1 01.1	9 07.7	9 13.6	20 56.5	24 26.4
16 Tu	17 38 53	25 18 55	25 13 27	1♉11 21	29 23.7	29 07.8	14 34.8	7 01.9	22 28.6	11 34.5	25 38.8	0 58.0	9 09.0	9 16.2	20 56.8	24 25.2
17 W	17 42 49	26 16 13	7♉10 48	13 12 14	29 20.5	29 07.4	14 42.5	6 41.2	23 06.8	11 41.2	25 33.1	0 54.8	9 10.3	9 18.8	20 57.0	24 24.0
18 Th	17 46 46	27 13 31	19 16 02	25 22 34	29 17.3	29 07.1	14R 45.7	6 22.8	23 44.9	11 47.6	25 27.3	0 51.6	9 11.5	9 21.4	20 57.2	24 22.8
19 F	17 50 42	28 10 49	1♊32 07	7♊44 59	29 14.1	29D 07.0	14 44.4	6 06.7	24 22.9	11 53.8	25 21.3	0 48.3	9 12.7	9 24.0	20 57.3	24 21.5
20 Sa	17 54 39	29 08 06	14 01 20	20 21 21	29 10.9	29 07.0	14 38.7	5 53.0	25 00.7	11 59.6	25 15.2	0 44.9	9 13.9	9 26.5	20 57.4	24 20.2
21 Su	17 58 36	0♋05 23	26 45 08	3♋12 43	29 07.8	29R 07.0	14 28.5	5 41.7	25 38.3	12 05.1	25 09.0	0 41.5	9 15.0	9 29.0	20 57.5	24 18.9
22 M	18 02 32	1 02 39	9♋44 07	16 19 19	29 04.6	29 06.9	14 14.2	5 32.8	26 15.8	12 10.4	25 02.7	0 38.0	9 16.0	9 31.4	20 57.6	24 17.7
23 Tu	18 06 29	1 59 55	22 58 11	29 40 39	29 01.4	29 06.8	13 55.9	5 26.3	26 53.2	12 15.3	24 56.2	0 34.4	9 17.0	9 33.8	20R 57.6	24 16.3
24 W	18 10 25	2 57 10	6♌26 32	13♌15 39	28 58.2	29 06.5	13 33.9	5 22.1	27 30.3	12 19.8	24 49.7	0 30.8	9 18.0	9 36.2	20 57.6	24 15.0
25 Th	18 14 22	3 54 25	20 07 50	27 02 49	28 55.1	29 06.0	13 08.4	5D 20.3	28 07.3	12 24.1	24 43.0	0 27.1	9 18.9	9 38.5	20 57.6	24 13.7
26 F	18 18 18	4 51 40	4♍00 25	11♍00 21	28 51.9	29 05.4	12 39.9	5 20.8	28 44.2	12 28.0	24 36.3	0 23.4	9 19.7	9 40.8	20 57.5	24 12.4
27 Sa	18 22 15	5 48 53	18 02 22	25 06 12	28 48.7	29 04.9	12 08.8	5 23.6	29 20.8	12 31.6	24 29.4	0 19.6	9 20.5	9 43.1	20 57.4	24 11.0
28 Su	18 26 12	6 46 07	2♎11 34	9♎18 12	28 45.5	29D 04.6	11 35.7	5 28.6	29 57.3	12 34.9	24 22.4	0 15.7	9 21.2	9 45.3	20 57.2	24 09.6
29 M	18 30 08	7 43 19	16 25 45	23 33 56	28 42.4	29 04.7	11 00.9	5 35.7	0♈33.6	12 37.9	24 15.4	0 11.9	9 21.9	9 47.5	20 57.0	24 08.3
30 Tu	18 34 05	8♋40 31	0♏42 24	7♏50 46	28♊39.2	29♊05.2	10♋25.1	5♊45.1	1♈09.7	12♓40.5	24♑08.3	0♒07.9	9♈22.6	9♉49.7	20♓56.8	24♑06.9

1st of Mo

Julian Da
2459001
Obliquit
23°26'12
SVP 4♓58'
GC 27♐0
Eris 24♈2

Day	⚴
1	0♒13
6	29♑37
11	28 52
16	27 58
21	26 54
26	25 43.

	⚵
1	5♎52
6	6 04
11	6 23.
16	6 50.
21	7 23.
26	8 03

	⚶
1	28♊48.
6	0♋57.
11	3 06.
16	5 16.
21	7 27
26	9 38

DECLINATION and LATITUDE

Day	☉ Decl	☽ Decl	☽ Lat	☽12h Decl	☿ Decl	☿ Lat	♀ Decl	♀ Lat	♂ Decl	♂ Lat	⚳ Decl	⚳ Lat	♃ Decl	♃ Lat	♄ Decl	♄ Lat
1 M	22N05	2N34	5N13	0S23	25N20	1N58	23N45	1N08	8S59	2S23	17S05	9S45	21S01	0S13	19S57	0S09
2 Tu	22 13	3S20	4 54	6 15	25 12	1 52	23 27	0 54	8 45	2 24	17 04	9 49	21 01	0 13	19 57	0 09
3 W	22 20	9 06	4 16	11 49	25 02	1 46	23 08	0 40	8 31	2 26	17 04	9 53	21 02	0 13	19 58	0 09
4 Th	22 28	14 22	3 22	16 42	24 52	1 38	22 50	0 25	8 18	2 27	17 04	9 57	21 03	0 13	19 59	0 09
5 F	22 34	18 46	2 14	20 31	24 40	1 30	22 31	0 11	8 04	2 29	17 04	10 01	21 04	0 13	19 59	0 10
6 Sa	22 41	21 57	0 59	23 02	24 27	1 21	22 12	0S03	7 50	2 30	17 04	10 05	21 05	0 14	19 60	0 10
7 Su	22 46	23 43	0S19	24 03	24 14	1 11	21 53	0 17	7 36	2 32	17 04	10 09	21 06	0 14	20 00	0 10
8 M	22 52	23 60	1 33	23 36	23 60	1 00	21 34	0 31	7 22	2 33	17 04	10 14	21 07	0 14	20 01	0 10
9 Tu	22 57	22 52	2 40	21 50	23 45	0 49	21 16	0 45	7 08	2 35	17 05	10 18	21 08	0 14	20 02	0 10
10 W	23 02	20 33	3 38	19 01	23 29	0 37	20 57	0 58	6 54	2 36	17 05	10 22	21 09	0 14	20 02	0 10
11 Th	23 06	17 17	4 23	15 23	23 14	0 24	20 39	1 12	6 40	2 38	17 06	10 27	21 10	0 14	20 03	0 10
12 F	23 10	13 21	4 54	11 11	22 57	0 11	20 22	1 25	6 26	2 39	17 07	10 31	21 11	0 15	20 04	0 10
13 Sa	23 13	8 56	5 12	6 38	22 41	0S03	20 05	1 37	6 12	2 41	17 08	10 35	21 12	0 15	20 05	0 10
14 Su	23 16	4 16	5 16	1 52	22 24	0 17	19 49	1 50	5 59	2 42	17 09	10 40	21 13	0 15	20 05	0 10
15 M	23 19	0N33	5 07	2N57	22 07	0 32	19 33	2 01	5 45	2 44	17 10	10 44	21 14	0 15	20 06	0 11
16 Tu	23 21	5 20	4 45	7 41	21 51	0 48	19 18	2 13	5 31	2 45	17 11	10 48	21 16	0 15	20 07	0 11
17 W	23 23	9 58	4 10	12 11	21 34	1 04	19 04	2 24	5 17	2 47	17 13	10 53	21 17	0 15	20 08	0 11
18 Th	23 24	14 17	3 23	16 15	21 17	1 20	18 50	2 34	5 04	2 48	17 14	10 57	21 18	0 16	20 08	0 11
19 F	23 25	18 04	2 27	19 42	21 01	1 37	18 38	2 44	4 50	2 50	17 16	11 02	21 19	0 16	20 09	0 11
20 Sa	23 26	21 07	1 23	22 17	20 45	1 53	18 26	2 53	4 36	2 51	17 18	11 06	21 21	0 16	20 10	0 11
21 Su	23 26	23 11	0 13	23 47	20 30	2 10	18 16	3 02	4 23	2 53	17 20	11 11	21 22	0 16	20 11	0 11
22 M	23 26	24 03	0N59	23 60	20 15	2 26	18 06	3 11	4 09	2 54	17 22	11 16	21 23	0 16	20 12	0 11
23 Tu	23 25	23 35	2 08	22 51	20 01	2 42	17 57	3 19	3 56	2 56	17 25	11 20	21 25	0 16	20 13	0 11
24 W	23 24	21 46	3 12	20 22	19 47	2 58	17 49	3 26	3 42	2 57	17 27	11 25	21 26	0 17	20 13	0 11
25 Th	23 23	18 40	4 06	16 42	19 35	3 14	17 41	3 33	3 29	2 59	17 30	11 29	21 27	0 17	20 14	0 12
26 F	23 21	14 29	4 47	12 04	19 23	3 28	17 35	3 40	3 16	3 00	17 32	11 34	21 29	0 17	20 15	0 12
27 Sa	23 19	9 30	5 11	6 47	19 12	3 42	17 30	3 46	3 03	3 02	17 35	11 39	21 30	0 17	20 16	0 12
28 Su	23 16	3 58	5 16	1 05	19 02	3 55	17 25	3 52	2 49	3 03	17 38	11 43	21 31	0 17	20 17	0 12
29 M	23 13	1S48	5 02	4S41	18 53	4 06	17 21	3 57	2 36	3 05	17 41	11 48	21 33	0 17	20 18	0 12
30 Tu	23N09	7S30	4N30	10S13	18N46	4S17	17N18	4S02	2S23	3S06	17S45	11S53	21S34	0S18	20S19	0S12

Day	⚷ Decl	⚷ Lat	♅ Decl	♅ Lat	♆ Decl	♆ Lat	♇ Decl	♇ La
1	5N58	2N43	13N56	0S27	4S36	1S03	22S06	0
6	6 02	2 43	14 01	0 27	4 35	1 04	22 07	0
11	6 05	2 44	14 05	0 27	4 35	1 04	22 09	0
16	6 08	2 44	14 09	0 27	4 34	1 04	22 10	0
21	6 11	2 44	14 13	0 27	4 34	1 04	22 12	0
26	6 13	2 45	14 17	0 27	4 34	1 05	22 13	0

Day	⚴ Decl	⚴ Lat	⚵ Decl	⚵ Lat	⚶ Decl	⚶ Lat	Eris Decl	Eris La
1	20N53	41N52	5N37	8N40	22N41	0S45	1S21	11
6	21 19	42 25	5 30	8 37	22 47	0 39	1 20	11
11	21 40	42 53	5 20	8 35	22 52	0 32	1 20	11
16	21 55	43 17	5 07	8 31	22 54	0 26	1 19	11
21	22 04	43 35	4 51	8 28	22 54	0 20	1 19	11
26	22 06	43 47	4 33	8 25	22 52	0 14	1 19	11

Moon Phenomena

Max/0 Decl

dy	hr mn	
1	10:27	0 S
7	16:30	24S04
14	21:17	0 N
22	3:47	24N04
28	16:31	0 S

Max/0 Lat

dy	hr mn	
6	18:11	0 S
13	19:23	5S17
21	4:25	0 N
27	18:50	5N17

Perigee/Apogee

dy	hr m		kilometers
3	3:30	p	364367
15	0:50	a	404595
30	2:13	p	368958

PH	dy	hr mn	
○	5	19:14	15♐34
(lunar eclipse)	5	19:26	A 0.568
☾	13	6:25	22♓42
●	21	6:43	0♋21
(solar eclipse)	21	6:41	A 00'38"
☽	28	8:17	7♎06

Void of Course Moo

Last Aspect	☽ Ingre
2 10:41 ♃ □	♏ 2 16
4 11:38 ♃ ⚹	♐ 4 17
6 4:12 ♆ □	♑ 6 19
8 18:07 ♃ ☌	♒ 9 0
10 14:36 ☉ △	♓ 11 9
13 12:46 ♃ ⚹	♈ 13 21
16 0:51 ♃ □	♉ 16 9
18 12:03 ♃ △	♊ 18 21
20 21:49 ♂ □	♋ 21 6
23 7:21 ♂ △	♌ 23 12
24 5:35 ♅ □	♍ 25 17
27 20:03 ♂ ☍	♎ 27 20
29 13:03 ♃ □	♏ 29 22

DAILY ASPECTARIAN

1 M ☉⋕♇ 1:16; ☽⚻♅ 4:53; ☽☍⚷ 5:10; ☽⚻⚳ 6:14; ☉△☽ 9:29; ☽⚻♂ 12:16; ☽△♀ 15:21; ☉⚼♃ 18:48

2 Tu ☽⚻♆ 1:06; ☽∥♆ 5:11; ☽⚼⚳ 7:13; ☽□♇ 7:23; ☽□♃ 10:41; ☽⋕⚷ 10:51; ☉⚼☽ 11:52; ☽⚼♂ 14:04; ☽⚼♀ 14:58; ☽□♄ 18:39; ⚳∠♇ 19:47; ☽∥♂ 21:38

3 W ♀□♂ 0:42; ⚴R♑ 0:56; ☽⚼♆ 1:41; ☽△☿ 2:42; ☽☍♅ 6:18; ☽⚻⚷ 6:31; ☽△⚳ 8:04; ☉⚻☽ 14:07; ☽⚻♀ 14:29; ☽△♂ 15:45; ☉☌♀ 17:45; ⚶ ♋ 18:56; ☽⋕♅ 22:07

4 Th ☽△♆ 2:15; ☽⚼☿ 5:06; ☽⚼⚷ 7:09; ☽⚹♇ 8:28; ☽⚹♃ 11:38; ☽∥⚳ 14:02; ☽⚹♄ 19:44; ☉∥♀ 20:57

5 F ☽⚻☿ 7:39; ☽⚻♅ 7:52; ☽△⚷ 8:01; ☽∥♄ 8:09; ☽∠♇ 9:16; ☽□⚳ 10:04; ☿⚹♅ 11:06; ☽∠♃ 12:24; ☿□⚷ 13:42; ☽☍♀ 13:59; ☽∥♃ 16:19; ☉☍☽ 19:14; ☽□♂ 19:45; ☽∠♄ 20:41

6 Sa ☽∥♇ 1:36; ☽⋕♀ 2:09; ☽□♆ 4:12; ♀⋕♇ 6:20; ☉⋕☽ 8:01; ☽⚼♅ 9:12; ☽⚺♇ 10:31; ☽⚺♃ 13:37; ♂∠♄ 14:51; ☉⚼♄ 16:10; ☉□♂ 19:12; ☽⚺♄ 22:09

7 Su ♀⚼♃ 7:52; ☿△⚳ 9:18; ☽△♅ 11:09; ☽□⚷ 11:15; ☽⚹⚳ 13:54; ☽☍☿ 14:07; ☽⚻♀ 15:12

8 M ☽⋕☿ 0:22; ☽⋕☿ 0:24; ☿⚺♀ 1:30; ☽⚹♂ 2:08; ☉⚻☽ 2:53; ☽⚹♆ 8:27; ♀□⚳ 14:54; ☽☌♇ 15:02; ☽⚼♀ 16:50; ☽∠⚳ 16:56; ☽☌♃ 18:07; ☉⋕☽ 22:55

9 Tu ☽☌♄ 3:18; ☽∠♂ 6:41; ☉⚼☽ 8:11; ☽∥♇ 8:52; ♀⋕♃ 9:45; ☽∠♆ 11:48; ☽□♅ 17:31; ☽⚹⚷ 17:32; ☽∥♃ 18:43; ☽△♀ 19:16; ☽⋕♀ 19:57; ☽⚺⚳ 20:52; ☽⚻☿ 23:34

10 W ☽∥♄ 4:07; ♅⚺⚷ 7:22; ☽⚺♂ 12:17; ♀⚼♇ 12:45; ☉△☽ 14:36; ☽⚺♆ 16:02; ☽∠⚷ 22:00; ☽⚺♇ 22:57

11 Th ☽∥⚳ 1:13; ☽⚺♃ 1:57; ☽⚼☿ 5:32; ☉∥☿ 9:05; ☉□♆ 9:39; ♀⚺♅ 9:51; ♀⚹⚷ 10:51; ☽⚺♄ 11:52; ⚳∠♃ 15:44; ☽⋕♅ 19:39

12 F ☽□♀ 2:36; ☽⚺⚷ 3:17; ☽⚹♅ 3:21; ☽∠♇ 4:09; ☽∠♃ 7:04; ☽☌⚳ 7:21; ☽△☿ 12:08; ☽∠♄ 17:17

13 Sa ♀⋕♄ 0:35; ☽☌♂ 2:14; ☽☌♆ 2:52; ☉□☽ 6:25; ☽∠♅ 9:19; ♂⋕⚷ 9:48; ☽⚹♇ 9:57; ☽⚹♃ 12:46; ♂☌♆ 14:14; ☽⋕⚷ 14:37; ☽∥♂ 14:52; ☽∥♆ 22:26; ☽⚹♄ 23:14

14 Su ☽⚹♀ 12:25; ☽☌⚷ 15:28; ☽⚺♅ 15:39; ☽⚺⚳ 20:10; ☉∠♅ 20:28; ☿⋕♇ 20:36

15 M ☉⚻♇ 1:59; ☽□☿ 2:08; ☽⚺♆ 15:22; ☽∠♀ 17:45; ☽⚺♂ 18:09; ☽⋕♆ 20:07; ☽□♇ 22:23

16 Tu ☉⚹☽ 0:12; ☽□♃ 0:51; ☽⋕♂ 0:51; ☽∠⚳ 2:45; ☽∥⚷ 4:04; ☉⚻♃ 7:34; ☽□♄ 11:30; ☽∠♆ 21:32; ☽⚺♀ 23:02

17 W ☽∠♂ 1:58; ☽⚺⚷ 3:59; ☽☌♅ 4:16; ☉∠☽ 8:51; ☽⚹⚳ 9:04; ☽⚹☿ 15:04; ☿⋕♃ 23:09; ☽∥♅ 23:27

18 Th ☽⚹♆ 3:19; ☿ R 4:59; ☽⚹♂ 9:18; ☽∠⚷ 9:42; ☽△♇ 10:02; ☽△♃ 12:03; ☉⚺☽ 16:56; ☽⋕⚳ 18:33; ☽∠☿ 20:32; ☽△♄ 22:35; ♂⚹♇ 23:10

19 F ♂∠♅ 0:44; ☽∥♀ 3:47; ☽☌♀ 8:41; ☽⚹⚷ 14:50; ☽⚼♇ 15:04; ☽⚺♅ 15:13; ☽⋕♄ 15:45; ☽⚼♃ 16:52; ☽□⚳ 20:06; ☽∥☿ 21:05

20 Sa ☽⚺☿ 1:10; ☽⋕♃ 2:13; ☽⚼♄ 3:16; ♂∥♆ 3:50; ♂⚹♃ 7:57; ☽⋕♇ 11:00; ☽□♆ 13:08; ☽⚻♇ 19:27; ☽∠♅ 19:45; ☽⚻♃ 21:02; ☉ ♋ 21:45; ☽□♂ 21:49

21 Su ☉∥☽ 4:29; ☉☌☽ 6:43; ☽⚻♄ 7:18; ☉⚻♄ 14:15; ☽⚺♀ 16:23; ☽□⚷ 23:08; ☽⚹♅ 23:37

22 M ☽△⚳ 4:29; ☿⋕♄ 5:18; ☽☌☿ 8:02; ☽∠♀ 19:28; ☽△♆ 20:23

23 Tu ☽☍♇ 2:20; ☉∥☽ 3:16; ☽☍♃ 3:30; ♆ R 4:32; ☽△♂ 7:21; ☽⚼⚳ 7:43; ☽☍♄ 13:32; ☉⚺☽ 17:21; ☽⋕♇ 19:26; ☽⚹♀ 22:07; ☽⚼♆ 23:09

24 W ☽⋕♃ 3:04; ☽△⚷ 5:03; ☽□♅ 5:35; ☽⚻⚳ 10:25; ☽⚼♂ 11:11; ☽⚺☿ 12:10; ☽⋕♄ 12:59; ☽∥☿ 17:23; ☉∠☽ 21:43

25 Th ☽⚻♆ 1:27; ☽∥♀ 6:18; ♀ D 6:49; ☽⚻♇ 7:06; ☽⋕⚳ 7:14; ☽⚼⚷ 7:17; ☽⚻♃ 7:54; ☽∠☿ 13:26; ☽⚻♂ 14:30; ☽⚻♄ 17:48

26 F ☽∥♅ 1:03; ☉⚹☽ 1:35; ☽□♀ 2:18; ♀⋕⚳ 7:27; ☿△⚳ 8:23; ☽⚼♇ 8:54; ☽⚻⚷ 9:08; ☽⚼♃ 9:31; ☽△♅ 9:46; ☉⚺♀ 12:43; ☽⚹☿ 14:19; ☽☍⚳ 14:34; ☽⚼♄ 19:24

27 Sa ☽☍♆ 4:58; ☽△♇ 10:25; ☽△♃ 10:52; ☽⚼♅ 11:23; ☽∥⚷ 14:21; ☽☍♂ 20:03; ☽△♄ 20:45; ☽⋕♆ 21:25

28 Su ♂ ♈ 1:46; ☽⋕♂ 4:58; ☽△♀ 5:35; ☉□☽ 8:17; ♂⚹♄ 11:00; ☽☍⚷ 12:06; ☽⚻♅ 12:48; ☽□☿ 15:15; ☽⚻⚳ 17:35

29 M ☽∥♂ 3:12; ☽⚼♀ 7:05; ☽⚻♆ 7:36; ☽∥♆ 11:34; ☽□♇ 12:56; ☽□♃ 13:03; ☽⋕⚷ 18:36; ☽⚼⚳ 18:53; ☽□♄ 23:02

30 Tu ☽⚻♂ 0:48; ♃☌♇ 5:48; ☽⚻♀ 8:35; ☽⚼♆ 8:48; ☉△☽ 14:21; ☽⚻⚷ 14:35; ☽☍♅ 15:22; ☽△☿ 15:40; ☉□⚷ 17:50; ☽△⚳ 20:11; ☿⚹♅ 22:14

LONGITUDE

Day	Sid.Time	☉	☽	☽ 12 hour	Mean☊	True☊	☿	♀	♂	⚳	♃	♄	⚷	♅	♆	♇
	h m s	° ' "	° ' "	° ' "	° '	° '	° '	° '	° '	° '	° '	° '	° '	° '	° '	° '
W	18 38 01	9♋37 43	14♏58 41	22♏05 45	28♊36.0	29♊05.9	9♋49.0	5♊56.5	1♈45.7	12♓42.8	24♑01.1	0♒04.0	9♈23.2	9♉51.8	20♓56.6	24♑05.5
Th	18 41 58	10 34 55	29 11 32	6♐15 38	28 32.8	29 06.8	9R 13.0	6 09.9	2 21.4	12 44.7	23R 53.8	29♑59.9	9 23.7	9 53.9	20R 56.3	24R 04.1
F	18 45 54	11 32 06	13♐17 38	20 17 05	28 29.7	29 07.6	8 38.0	6 25.3	2 57.0	12 46.4	23 46.5	29R 55.9	9 24.2	9 55.9	20 56.0	24 02.7
Sa	18 49 51	12 29 17	27 13 37	4♑06 51	28 26.5	29R 08.0	8 04.3	6 42.7	3 32.3	12 47.6	23 39.1	29 51.8	9 24.6	9 57.9	20 55.7	24 01.3
Su	18 53 47	13 26 28	10♑56 26	17 42 04	28 23.3	29 07.7	7 32.7	7 01.9	4 07.5	12 48.6	23 31.7	29 47.7	9 25.0	9 59.9	20 55.3	23 59.9
M	18 57 44	14 23 39	24 33 33	1♒00 40	28 20.1	29 06.7	7 03.8	7 22.9	4 42.4	12 49.1	23 24.2	29 43.5	9 25.3	10 01.8	20 54.9	23 58.5
Tu	19 01 41	15 20 49	7♒33 21	14 01 32	28 17.0	29 05.0	6 37.9	7 45.6	5 17.1	12R 49.4	23 16.6	29 39.3	9 25.6	10 03.7	20 54.5	23 57.0
W	19 05 37	16 18 01	20 25 18	26 44 44	28 13.8	29 02.7	6 15.6	8 10.0	5 51.6	12 49.3	23 09.0	29 35.1	9 25.8	10 05.5	20 54.1	23 55.6
Th	19 09 34	17 15 12	3♓00 03	9♓11 31	28 10.6	29 00.1	5 57.4	8 36.1	6 25.9	12 48.8	23 01.4	29 30.8	9 26.0	10 07.3	20 53.6	23 54.2
F	19 13 30	18 12 23	15 19 26	21 24 13	28 07.4	28 57.6	5 43.5	9 03.7	7 00.0	12 48.0	22 53.7	29 26.5	9 26.1	10 09.1	20 53.1	23 52.7
Sa	19 17 27	19 09 35	27 26 17	3♈26 07	28 04.2	28 55.5	5 34.2	9 32.9	7 33.7	12 46.8	22 46.0	29 22.2	9R 26.2	10 10.8	20 52.5	23 51.3
Su	19 21 23	20 06 48	9♈24 15	15 21 13	28 01.1	28D 54.1	5D 29.9	10 03.5	8 07.3	12 45.2	22 38.3	29 17.9	9 26.2	10 12.4	20 51.9	23 49.8
M	19 25 20	21 04 01	21 17 36	27 13 59	27 57.9	28 53.6	5 30.7	10 35.4	8 40.6	12 43.3	22 30.6	29 13.5	9 26.2	10 14.1	20 51.3	23 48.4
Tu	19 29 16	22 01 14	3♉10 57	9♉09 07	27 54.7	28 54.1	5 36.7	11 08.8	9 13.6	12 41.1	22 22.9	29 09.1	9 26.1	10 15.6	20 50.7	23 46.9
W	19 33 13	22 58 28	15 09 03	21 11 20	27 51.5	28 55.3	5 48.1	11 43.4	9 46.3	12 38.5	22 15.1	29 04.7	9 26.0	10 17.2	20 50.0	23 45.5
Th	19 37 10	23 55 43	27 16 30	3♊25 03	27 48.4	28 56.9	6 04.9	12 19.3	10 18.8	12 35.5	22 07.4	29 00.3	9 25.8	10 18.7	20 49.3	23 44.0
F	19 41 06	24 52 58	9♊37 28	15 54 07	27 45.2	28 58.5	6 27.3	12 56.4	10 50.9	12 32.2	21 59.7	28 55.9	9 25.6	10 20.1	20 48.6	23 42.6
Sa	19 45 03	25 50 14	22 15 23	28 41 29	27 42.0	28R 59.5	6 55.1	13 34.7	11 22.8	12 28.5	21 52.0	28 51.5	9 25.3	10 21.5	20 47.8	23 41.1
Su	19 48 59	26 47 30	5♋12 38	11♋48 53	27 38.8	28 59.5	7 28.5	14 14.0	11 54.4	12 24.4	21 44.3	28 47.1	9 24.9	10 22.9	20 47.1	23 39.7
M	19 52 56	27 44 48	18 30 14	25 16 33	27 35.6	28 58.2	8 07.3	14 54.4	12 25.6	12 20.0	21 36.6	28 42.6	9 24.5	10 24.2	20 46.3	23 38.2
Tu	19 56 52	28 42 05	2♌07 37	9♌03 04	27 32.5	28 55.6	8 51.5	15 35.9	12 56.5	12 15.3	21 29.0	28 38.2	9 24.1	10 25.5	20 45.4	23 36.8
W	20 00 49	29 39 23	16 02 31	23 05 26	27 29.3	28 51.8	9 41.2	16 18.3	13 27.1	12 10.1	21 21.3	28 33.7	9 23.6	10 26.7	20 44.6	23 35.4
Th	20 04 45	0♌36 42	0♍11 15	7♍19 23	27 26.1	28 47.2	10 36.2	17 01.6	13 57.3	12 04.7	21 13.8	28 29.3	9 23.1	10 27.9	20 43.7	23 33.9
F	20 08 42	1 34 00	14 29 10	21 40 00	27 22.9	28 42.5	11 36.4	17 45.9	14 27.2	11 58.8	21 06.3	28 24.9	9 22.5	10 29.0	20 42.7	23 32.5
Sa	20 12 39	2 31 20	28 51 15	6♎02 21	27 19.8	28 38.4	12 41.8	18 31.1	14 56.7	11 52.7	20 58.8	28 20.4	9 21.8	10 30.1	20 41.8	23 31.1
Su	20 16 35	3 28 39	13♎12 48	20 22 09	27 16.6	28 35.5	13 52.3	19 17.0	15 25.9	11 46.2	20 51.4	28 16.0	9 21.1	10 31.1	20 40.8	23 29.6
M	20 20 32	4 25 59	27 30 01	4♏36 06	27 13.4	28D 34.0	15 07.8	20 03.8	15 54.7	11 39.3	20 44.0	28 11.6	9 20.3	10 32.1	20 39.8	23 28.2
Tu	20 24 28	5 23 20	11♏40 08	18 41 58	27 10.2	28 34.0	16 28.1	20 51.4	16 23.1	11 32.2	20 36.8	28 07.2	9 19.5	10 33.0	20 38.8	23 26.8
W	20 28 25	6 20 40	25 41 26	2♐38 26	27 07.1	28 35.0	17 53.2	21 39.7	16 51.2	11 24.7	20 29.6	28 02.8	9 18.7	10 33.9	20 37.8	23 25.4
Th	20 32 21	7 18 02	9♐32 53	16 24 45	27 03.9	28 36.4	19 22.8	22 28.8	17 18.8	11 16.8	20 22.4	27 58.5	9 17.8	10 34.7	20 36.7	23 24.0
F	20 36 18	8♌15 24	23 13 55	0♑00 22	27♊00.7	28♊37.4	20♋56.7	23♊18.6	17♈46.1	11♓08.7	20♑15.4	27♑54.2	9♈16.8	10♉35.5	20♓35.6	23♑22.6

1st of Month

Julian Day #
2459031.5
Obliquity
23°26'12"
SVP 4♓58'41"
GC 27♐07.5
Eris 24♈31.5

Day	⚴	⚵	⚶
1	24♑27.3R	8♎48.9	11♋49.3
6	23 06.8R	9 39.9	14 00.6
11	21 44.1R	10 35.9	16 12.1
16	20 21.3R	11 36.4	18 23.8
21	19 00.4R	12 41.3	20 35.5
26	17 43.5R	13 50.2	22 47.2
31	16 32.2R	15 02.7	24 58.8

DECLINATION and LATITUDE

Day	☉ Decl	☽ Decl	☽ Lat	☽12h Decl	☿ Decl	☿ Lat	♀ Decl	♀ Lat	♂ Decl	♂ Lat	⚳ Decl	⚳ Lat	♃ Decl	♃ Lat	♄ Decl	♄ Lat
W	23N05	12S49	3N41	15S13	18N39	4S26	17N15	4S06	2S10	3S08	17S48	11S57	21S36	0S18	20S20	0S12
Th	23 01	17 24	2 38	19 20	18 34	4 34	17 14	4 10	1 58	3 09	17 52	12 02	21 37	0 18	20 21	0 12
F	22 56	20 58	1 27	22 16	18 30	4 40	17 13	4 13	1 45	3 11	17 55	12 07	21 38	0 18	20 22	0 12
Sa	22 51	23 14	0 11	23 50	18 28	4 44	17 13	4 17	1 32	3 12	17 59	12 12	21 40	0 18	20 23	0 12
Su	22 45	24 04	1S05	23 56	18 26	4 47	17 13	4 20	1 20	3 14	18 03	12 16	21 41	0 18	20 24	0 12
M	22 40	23 27	2 15	22 39	18 27	4 49	17 14	4 22	1 07	3 15	18 07	12 21	21 43	0 18	20 25	0 13
Tu	22 33	21 33	3 16	20 10	18 28	4 49	17 15	4 24	0 55	3 17	18 12	12 26	21 44	0 19	20 26	0 13
W	22 27	18 34	4 06	16 46	18 31	4 47	17 17	4 26	0 42	3 18	18 16	12 31	21 46	0 19	20 27	0 13
Th	22 19	14 48	4 43	12 42	18 35	4 44	17 20	4 28	0 30	3 20	18 21	12 35	21 47	0 19	20 28	0 13
F	22 12	10 29	5 06	8 11	18 40	4 39	17 23	4 29	0 18	3 21	18 25	12 40	21 48	0 19	20 29	0 13
Sa	22 04	5 50	5 15	3 26	18 46	4 33	17 26	4 30	0 06	3 23	18 30	12 45	21 50	0 19	20 30	0 13
Su	21 56	1 01	5 09	1N24	18 53	4 26	17 30	4 31	0N06	3 24	18 35	12 50	21 51	0 19	20 31	0 13
M	21 47	3N48	4 51	6 10	19 01	4 18	17 34	4 31	0 18	3 25	18 40	12 54	21 53	0 19	20 32	0 13
Tu	21 38	8 29	4 20	10 44	19 11	4 09	17 38	4 31	0 29	3 27	18 45	12 59	21 54	0 20	20 33	0 13
W	21 29	12 54	3 38	14 57	19 20	3 59	17 43	4 31	0 41	3 28	18 50	13 04	21 55	0 20	20 34	0 13
Th	21 19	16 52	2 45	18 37	19 31	3 47	17 48	4 31	0 52	3 30	18 56	13 08	21 57	0 20	20 35	0 13
F	21 09	20 10	1 44	21 31	19 41	3 36	17 53	4 30	1 03	3 31	19 01	13 13	21 58	0 20	20 36	0 14
Sa	20 59	22 36	0 37	23 24	19 52	3 23	17 58	4 30	1 15	3 32	19 07	13 17	21 60	0 20	20 37	0 14
Su	20 48	23 54	0N34	24 04	20 04	3 10	18 03	4 29	1 26	3 34	19 13	13 22	22 01	0 20	20 38	0 14
M	20 37	23 53	1 45	23 21	20 15	2 57	18 09	4 28	1 36	3 35	19 19	13 27	22 02	0 20	20 39	0 14
Tu	20 25	22 28	2 51	21 14	20 26	2 43	18 15	4 26	1 47	3 36	19 25	13 31	22 04	0 21	20 40	0 14
W	20 13	19 40	3 49	17 48	20 37	2 28	18 20	4 25	1 58	3 38	19 31	13 36	22 05	0 21	20 41	0 14
Th	20 01	15 40	4 34	13 18	20 47	2 14	18 26	4 23	2 08	3 39	19 37	13 40	22 06	0 21	20 41	0 14
F	19 49	10 45	5 02	8 02	20 57	1 59	18 32	4 21	2 18	3 40	19 43	13 44	22 08	0 21	20 42	0 14
Sa	19 36	5 13	5 11	2 20	21 06	1 45	18 38	4 19	2 29	3 42	19 50	13 49	22 09	0 21	20 43	0 14
Su	19 23	0S35	5 01	3S29	21 13	1 30	18 44	4 17	2 39	3 43	19 56	13 53	22 10	0 21	20 44	0 14
M	19 09	6 20	4 33	9 06	21 20	1 15	18 50	4 15	2 48	3 45	20 03	13 57	22 11	0 21	20 45	0 14
Tu	18 55	11 43	3 48	14 11	21 25	1 01	18 55	4 13	2 58	3 46	20 09	14 01	22 13	0 21	20 46	0 15
W	18 41	16 26	2 49	18 27	21 28	0 47	19 01	4 10	3 08	3 47	20 16	14 05	22 14	0 22	20 47	0 15
Th	18 27	20 12	1 42	21 39	21 30	0 33	19 06	4 07	3 17	3 48	20 23	14 09	22 15	0 22	20 48	0 15
F	18N12	22S47	0N29	23S34	21N29	0S19	19N12	4S05	3N26	3S49	20S29	14S13	22S16	0S22	20S49	0S15

Day	⚷ Decl	⚷ Lat	♅ Decl	♅ Lat	♆ Decl	♆ Lat	♇ Decl	♇ Lat
1	6N15	2N45	14N20	0S27	4S35	1S05	22S15	0S59
6	6 16	2 46	14 24	0 27	4 36	1 05	22 17	0 59
11	6 17	2 46	14 26	0 27	4 37	1 05	22 19	0 60
16	6 17	2 46	14 29	0 27	4 38	1 05	22 20	1 00
21	6 17	2 47	14 31	0 27	4 40	1 06	22 22	1 01
26	6 16	2 47	14 32	0 27	4 42	1 06	22 24	1 01
31	6N15	2N48	14N34	0S28	4S44	1S06	22S25	1S01

Day	⚴ Decl	⚴ Lat	⚵ Decl	⚵ Lat	⚶ Decl	⚶ Lat	Eris Decl	Eris Lat
1	22N02	43N53	4N12	8N22	22N47	0S07	1S19	11S37
6	21 50	43 52	3 49	8 19	22 41	0 01	1 19	11 37
11	21 32	43 43	3 25	8 16	22 32	0N05	1 19	11 38
16	21 07	43 27	2 59	8 13	22 22	0 11	1 19	11 38
21	20 35	43 03	2 31	8 10	22 09	0 18	1 20	11 38
26	19 57	42 32	2 02	8 08	21 54	0 24	1 20	11 39
31	19N14	41N55	1N33	8N06	21N38	0N30	1S21	11S39

Moon Phenomena

Max/0 Decl
dy hr mn
5 1:27 24S04
12 5:03 0 N
19 11:52 24N04
25 21:35 0 S

Perigee/Apogee
dy hr m kilometers
12 19:34 a 404198
25 5:02 p 368361

Max/0 Lat
dy hr mn
4 3:19 0 S
11 2:57 5S15
18 12:34 0 N
24 23:49 5N11
31 9:33 0 S

PH dy hr mn
○ 5 4:46 13♑38
● 5 4:31 A 0.354
☾ 12 23:30 21♈03
● 20 17:34 28♋27
☽ 27 12:34 4♏56

Void of Course Moon

Last Aspect		☽ Ingress
2 1:22	♄ ⚹	♐ 2 1:22
3 13:07	♆ □	♑ 4 4:49
6 9:36	♄ ☌	♒ 6 10:09
7 4:39	♅ □	♓ 8 18:14
11 3:50	♄ ⚹	♈ 11 5:07
13 15:55	♄ □	♉ 13 17:35
16 3:22	♄ △	♊ 16 5:20
17 21:16	♆ □	♋ 18 14:25
20 17:56	♄ ☍	♌ 20 20:17
22 0:28	♀ ⚹	♍ 22 23:41
24 23:09	♀ △	♎ 25 1:55
27 1:10	♄ □	♏ 27 4:13
29 4:02	♄ ⚹	♐ 29 7:26
31 0:09	♀ ☍	♑ 31 11:59

DAILY ASPECTARIAN

1 W: ☉☌☿ 2:54; ☽⚼♂ 3:08; ☉⚹♅ 6:08; ☽#♅ 7:33; ☽△♆ 10:03; ☽⚹♃ 15:07; ☽⚹♇ 15:21; ☽⚼⚷ 15:53; ☽⚼☿ 15:55; ☿□⚷ 16:57; ☉⚼☽ 17:27; ☽#♀ 23:01; ♄R♑ 23:39

2 Th: ☽⚹♄ 1:22; ☽∥⚳ 2:46; ☽△♂ 5:36; ☽#☿ 6:56; ☽☍♀ 12:03; ☽∠♃ 16:21; ☽⚻☿ 16:21; ☽∠♇ 16:45; ☽△⚷ 17:21; ☽⚻♅ 18:15; ☽∥♄ 19:19; ☉⚻☽ 20:46; ☽□⚳ 23:06

3 F: ☽∠♄ 2:47; ☽∥♃ 5:55; ☽∥♇ 12:00; ☽□♆ 13:07; ☽⚺♃ 17:52; ☽⚺♇ 18:27; ☉#☽ 18:57; ☽⚼♅ 20:04

4 Sa: ☽⚺♄ 4:34; ☉△⚳ 7:51; ☽□♂ 11:29; ☽⚻♀ 16:57; ☽☍☿ 18:14; ☽□⚷ 21:19; ☽△♅ 22:20

5 Su: ☽⚹⚳ 3:18; ☉☍☽ 4:46; ☿⚺♀ 14:46; ☽⚹♆ 17:45; ☽⚼♀ 20:17; ☽☌♃ 22:14; ☽☌♇ 23:15

6 M: ☽∠⚳ 6:12; ☽☌♄ 9:36; ☉#☽ 12:29; ☽∥♇ 16:16; ☽⚹♂ 19:38; ☽∠♆ 20:58; ☽∥♃ 22:07; ☽⚻☿ 22:21

7 Tu: ☽△♀ 0:23; ☽⚹⚷ 3:27; ⚳ R 4:02; ☽□♅ 4:39; ☽⚺⚳ 9:46; ☽∥♄ 9:52; ☉⚻☽ 15:38; ♀⚼♃ 23:15

8 W: ☽#☿ 0:24; ☽∠♂ 0:52; ☽⚺♆ 0:54; ☽⚼☿ 1:33; ☽∥⚳ 2:04; ☽⚺♃ 5:07; ☽⚺♇ 6:37; ☽∠⚷ 7:36; ☽#♀ 8:35; ☿□♂ 10:43; ☽⚺♄ 17:20; ☉⚼☽ 22:26

9 Th: ☽#♅ 2:12; ☉#♇ 4:37; ☽△☿ 5:36; ☽⚺♂ 6:57; ☽∠♃ 9:38; ☽□♀ 11:16; ☽∠♇ 11:25; ☽⚺⚷ 12:28; ☽⚹♅ 13:51; ♀⚼♇ 15:05; ☽☌⚳ 19:03; ☽∠♄ 22:17

10 F: ☉△☽ 6:10; ☽☌♆ 10:58; ☽⚹♃ 14:48; ☽⚹♇ 16:53; ♀⚹⚷ 18:38; ☽∠♅ 19:29; ☽#⚷ 21:42

11 Sa: ☽⚹♄ 3:50; ☽∥♆ 6:06; ☽□☿ 16:10; ⚷ R 21:10; ☽☌♂ 21:17

12 Su: ☽☌⚷ 0:04; ☽⚹♀ 1:23; ☽⚺♅ 1:37; ☽#♂ 4:24; ☽∥♂ 5:46; ☽⚺⚳ 6:44; ♀⚺♅ 7:13; ☿ D 8:27; ☉#♃ 11:02; ☉△♆ 18:44; ☽⚺♆ 23:07; ☉□☽ 23:30

13 M: ☽□♃ 2:26; ☽#♆ 4:08; ☽□♇ 5:04; ☽∠♀ 9:06; ☽∥⚷ 12:35; ☽∠⚳ 12:57; ☽□♄ 15:55

14 Tu: ☽⚹☿ 4:57; ☽∠♆ 5:21; ☉☍♃ 8:00; ♂☌⚷ 9:09; ☽⚺⚷ 12:34; ☽⚺♂ 12:44; ☽☌♅ 14:15; ☽⚺♀ 16:48; ☽⚹⚳ 19:00

15 W: ☽∥♅ 9:09; ☽⚹♆ 11:17; ☽∠☿ 11:29; ☽△♃ 13:57; ☉⚹☽ 16:51; ☽△♇ 17:03; ☽∠⚷ 18:24; ☉☍♇ 19:14; ☽∠♂ 19:58; ♂⚺♅ 23:56

16 Th: ☽△♄ 3:22; ☽∥♀ 6:22; ♀□⚳ 9:43; ☽#⚳ 14:45; ☽⚺☿ 17:41; ☽⚼♃ 18:59; ☽∥☿ 19:52; ☽⚼♇ 22:15; ☽⚹⚷ 23:37

17 F: ☉∠☽ 0:32; ☽⚺♅ 1:22; ☽⚹♂ 2:27; ☽#♄ 3:35; ☽□⚳ 5:33; ☽☌♀ 6:41; ☉∥☽ 8:02; ☽⚼♄ 8:12; ☽#♃ 16:55; ☽#♇ 21:00; ☽□♆ 21:16; ☽⚻♃ 23:16

18 Sa: ☽⚻♇ 2:40; ☽∠♅ 5:49; ☉⚺☽ 7:14; ♀⚼♄ 9:17; ☽⚻♄ 12:14

19 Su: ☽☌☿ 4:20; ☽□⚷ 7:39; ☽⚹♅ 9:25; ☽□♂ 12:40; ☽△⚳ 13:00; ☉⚼⚳ 14:23; ☽⚺♀ 17:13; ☉#♄ 20:13; ♂⚺⚳ 20:15

20 M: ☽△♆ 4:02; ☽☍♃ 5:28; ☽☍♇ 9:06; ☽⚼⚳ 15:32; ☉☌☽ 17:34; ☽☍♄ 17:56; ☽∠♀ 21:11; ☉☍♄ 22:29; ☉∥☿ 22:54

21 Tu: ☽#♇ 1:04; ☽#♃ 4:15; ☽⚼♆ 6:18; ☽⚺☿ 12:23; ☽△⚷ 12:36; ☽□♅ 14:23; ☿□⚷ 15:52; ☽#♄ 16:34; ☽∥☿ 17:22; ☽⚻⚳ 17:24; ☽△♂ 19:24; ☉∥☽ 19:44

22 W: ☽⚹♀ 0:28; ☽#⚳ 1:02; ☽⚻♆ 8:00; ☽∥♀ 8:30; ☉ ♌ 8:38; ☽⚻♃ 8:58; ☿#♄ 9:04; ☽⚻♇ 12:49; ☽⚼⚷ 14:12; ☽∠☿ 15:42; ☿⚹♅ 20:26; ☽⚻♄ 21:09; ☽⚼♂ 21:51

23 Th: ☉⚺☽ 0:46; ☽∥♅ 5:56; ☽⚼♃ 10:05; ☽⚼♇ 14:04; ☽⚻⚷ 15:27; ☽△♅ 17:17; ☽⚹☿ 18:48; ☽☍⚳ 19:50; ☽⚼♄ 22:13; ☽⚻♂ 23:57

24 F: ☉∠☽ 3:44; ☽□♀ 5:47; ☉#⚳ 6:44; ☿△⚳ 7:43; ☽☍♆ 10:24; ☽△♃ 10:58; ☽△♇ 15:06; ☽⚼♅ 18:24; ☽∥⚷ 19:33; ☽△♄ 23:09

25 Sa: ☽#♆ 2:11; ☉⚹☽ 6:34; ☽∥♂ 11:04; ☽☍⚷ 17:33; ☽⚻♅ 19:29; ☽⚻⚳ 21:36

26 Su: ☽□☿ 1:12; ☽☍♂ 3:51; ☽#♂ 8:44; ☽△♀ 10:46; ☽⚻♆ 12:31; ☽□♃ 12:43; ☽∥♆ 17:06; ☽□♇ 17:13; ☽⚼⚳ 22:35; ☽#⚷ 23:42

27 M: ☽□♄ 1:10; ☉□☽ 12:34; ☽⚼♀ 13:32; ☽⚼♆ 13:47; ♃⚹♆ 16:08; ♀⚻♃ 17:37; ♀□♆ 17:49; ☽⚻⚷ 20:01; ☿□♂ 21:47; ☽☍♅ 22:06; ☽△⚳ 23:47; ☉∥♀ 23:52

28 Tu: ☉⚼♆ 6:22; ☽⚻♂ 8:19; ☽△☿ 9:05; ☽#♅ 13:55; ☽⚹♃ 15:09; ☽△♆ 15:19; ☽⚻♀ 16:39; ☽⚹♇ 20:06; ☽⚼⚷ 21:38

29 W: ☽⚹♄ 4:02; ☽⚼♂ 11:00; ☉#☽ 12:41; ☽⚼☿ 13:55; ☽#♀ 16:04; ☽∠♃ 16:48; ☉△☽ 19:48; ☽∠♇ 22:00; ☽△⚷ 23:34

30 Th: ☽∥⚳ 1:22; ☽⚻♅ 1:48; ☽□⚳ 3:00; ☽∥♄ 4:43; ☽∠♄ 5:57; ☽#☿ 10:36; ☽△♂ 14:03; ☿☍♃ 14:18; ☽∥♃ 18:07; ☿△♆ 18:46; ☽⚺♃ 18:48; ☽□♆ 19:21; ☽⚻☿ 19:26; ☽∥♇ 19:50

31 F: ☉⚼☽ 0:03; ☽☍♀ 0:09; ☽⚺♇ 0:15; ♀⚻♇ 1:52; ☽⚼♅ 4:11; ☽⚺♄ 8:13; ☉∠♀ 10:49

August 2020

LONGITUDE

Day	Sid.Time	☉	☽	☽ 12 hour	Mean☊	True☊	☿	♀	♂	⚳	♃	♄	⚷	♅	♆	♇
	h m s	° ' "	° ' "	° ' "	° '	° '	° '	° '	° '	° '	° '	° '	° '	° '	° '	° '
1 Sa	20 40 14	9♌12 46	6♑44 01	13♑24 46	26♊57.5	28♊37.2	22♋34.8	24♊09.1	18♈12.9	11♓00.3	20♑08.5	27♑49.8	9♈15.9	10♉36.3	20♓34.5	23♑21.2
2 Su	20 44 11	10 10 10	20 02 33	26 37 16	26 54.4	28R 35.3	24 16.8	25 00.2	18 39.3	10R 51.5	20R 01.6	27R 45.6	9R 14.8	10 37.0	20R 33.3	23R 19.8
3 M	20 48 08	11 07 34	3♒08 50	9♒37 10	26 51.2	28 31.4	26 02.4	25 52.0	19 05.3	10 42.5	19 54.9	27 41.3	9 13.7	10 37.6	20 32.2	23 18.5
4 Tu	20 52 04	12 04 58	16 02 12	22 23 54	26 48.0	28 25.6	27 51.3	26 44.3	19 30.8	10 33.1	19 48.2	27 37.1	9 12.6	10 38.2	20 31.0	23 17.1
5 W	20 56 01	13 02 24	28 42 15	4♓57 18	26 44.8	28 18.4	29 43.2	27 37.3	19 55.9	10 23.5	19 41.6	27 32.9	9 11.4	10 38.7	20 29.8	23 15.8
6 Th	20 59 57	13 59 51	11♓09 09	17 17 53	26 41.6	28 10.2	1♌37.8	28 30.9	20 20.5	10 13.6	19 35.2	27 28.7	9 10.2	10 39.2	20 28.5	23 14.4
7 F	21 03 54	14 57 19	23 23 45	29 26 58	26 38.5	28 02.1	3 34.6	29 25.0	20 44.7	10 03.4	19 28.9	27 24.6	9 08.9	10 39.7	20 27.3	23 13.1
8 Sa	21 07 50	15 54 48	5♈27 50	11♈26 44	26 35.3	27 54.8	5 33.4	0♋19.7	21 08.3	9 53.0	19 22.7	27 20.5	9 07.5	10 40.1	20 26.0	23 11.8
9 Su	21 11 47	16 52 18	17 24 04	23 20 19	26 32.1	27 49.0	7 33.8	1 14.9	21 31.5	9 42.3	19 16.6	27 16.4	9 06.2	10 40.4	20 24.7	23 10.5
10 M	21 15 43	17 49 50	29 15 59	5♉11 38	26 28.9	27 45.0	9 35.3	2 10.6	21 54.1	9 31.3	19 10.6	27 12.4	9 04.8	10 40.7	20 23.4	23 09.2
11 Tu	21 19 40	18 47 23	11♉07 50	17 05 12	26 25.7	27D 43.0	11 37.7	3 06.9	22 16.2	9 20.2	19 04.8	27 08.4	9 03.3	10 41.0	20 22.1	23 07.9
12 W	21 23 37	19 44 57	23 04 23	29 06 00	26 22.6	27 42.7	13 40.6	4 03.5	22 37.8	9 08.8	18 59.1	27 04.5	9 01.8	10 41.2	20 20.7	23 06.6
13 Th	21 27 33	20 42 33	5♊10 43	11♊19 09	26 19.4	27 43.5	15 43.7	5 00.7	22 58.8	8 57.1	18 53.5	27 00.6	9 00.2	10 41.3	20 19.4	23 05.4
14 F	21 31 30	21 40 10	17 31 54	23 49 31	26 16.2	27R 44.5	17 46.7	5 58.3	23 19.2	8 45.3	18 48.1	26 56.8	8 58.7	10 41.5	20 18.0	23 04.1
15 Sa	21 35 26	22 37 49	0♋12 33	6♋41 23	26 13.0	27 44.9	19 49.5	6 56.3	23 39.0	8 33.3	18 42.8	26 53.0	8 57.0	10R 41.5	20 16.6	23 02.9
16 Su	21 39 23	23 35 30	13 16 21	19 57 42	26 09.9	27 43.7	21 51.8	7 54.8	23 58.3	8 21.1	18 37.7	26 49.3	8 55.3	10 41.5	20 15.1	23 01.7
17 M	21 43 19	24 33 11	26 45 29	3♌39 37	26 06.7	27 40.4	23 53.3	8 53.6	24 16.9	8 08.7	18 32.7	26 45.6	8 53.6	10 41.5	20 13.7	23 00.5
18 Tu	21 47 16	25 30 55	10♌39 54	17 45 54	26 03.5	27 34.8	25 54.1	9 52.9	24 34.9	7 56.2	18 27.9	26 42.0	8 51.9	10 41.4	20 12.3	22 59.4
19 W	21 51 12	26 28 39	24 57 03	2♍12 37	26 00.3	27 27.2	27 53.8	10 52.5	24 52.3	7 43.5	18 23.3	26 38.4	8 50.1	10 41.2	20 10.8	22 58.2
20 Th	21 55 09	27 26 25	9♍31 44	16 53 27	25 57.2	27 18.2	29 52.5	11 52.5	25 09.0	7 30.7	18 18.8	26 34.9	8 48.2	10 41.0	20 09.3	22 57.1
21 F	21 59 06	28 24 12	24 16 44	1♎40 33	25 54.0	27 08.9	1♍50.1	12 52.8	25 25.0	7 17.8	18 14.4	26 31.5	8 46.3	10 40.8	20 07.8	22 55.9
22 Sa	22 03 02	29 22 01	9♎03 53	16 25 49	25 50.8	27 00.5	3 46.5	13 53.5	25 40.3	7 04.8	18 10.3	26 28.1	8 44.4	10 40.5	20 06.3	22 54.8
23 Su	22 06 59	0♍19 50	23 45 31	1♏02 16	25 47.6	26 53.9	5 41.6	14 54.5	25 55.0	6 51.7	18 06.3	26 24.8	8 42.5	10 40.1	20 04.8	22 53.7
24 M	22 10 55	1 17 41	8♏15 31	15 24 51	25 44.4	26 49.6	7 35.4	15 55.9	26 09.0	6 38.5	18 02.4	26 21.6	8 40.5	10 39.7	20 03.2	22 52.7
25 Tu	22 14 52	2 15 33	22 30 00	29 30 50	25 41.3	26D 47.5	9 27.9	16 57.6	26 22.2	6 25.2	17 58.8	26 18.4	8 38.5	10 39.3	20 01.7	22 51.6
26 W	22 18 48	3 13 26	6♐27 19	13♐19 32	25 38.1	26 47.2	11 19.1	17 59.5	26 34.7	6 11.9	17 55.3	26 15.3	8 36.4	10 38.8	20 00.1	22 50.6
27 Th	22 22 45	4 11 21	20 07 35	26 51 40	25 34.9	26R 47.6	13 08.9	19 01.8	26 46.5	5 58.6	17 52.0	26 12.3	8 34.3	10 38.3	19 58.6	22 49.6
28 F	22 26 41	5 09 17	3♑31 58	10♑08 42	25 31.7	26 47.6	14 57.5	20 04.4	26 57.6	5 45.3	17 48.9	26 09.3	8 32.2	10 37.7	19 57.0	22 48.6
29 Sa	22 30 38	6 07 14	16 42 05	23 12 19	25 28.6	26 46.0	16 44.7	21 07.3	27 07.9	5 31.9	17 46.0	26 06.5	8 30.0	10 37.1	19 55.4	22 47.6
30 Su	22 34 35	7 05 12	29 39 32	6♒03 55	25 25.4	26 42.0	18 30.7	22 10.4	27 17.4	5 18.6	17 43.2	26 03.7	8 27.8	10 36.4	19 53.8	22 46.7
31 M	22 38 31	8♍03 12	12♒25 33	18 44 33	25♊22.2	26♊35.2	20♍15.3	23♋13.9	27♈26.2	5♓05.3	17♑40.7	26♑00.9	8♈25.6	10♉35.7	19♓52.2	22♑45.8

1st of Month

Julian Day # 2459062.5
Obliquity 23°26'12"
SVP 4♓58'36"
GC 27♐07.6
Eris 24♈32.9

Day	⚴
1	16♑18.8R
6	15 16.2R
11	14 21.9R
16	13 36.7R
21	13 01.0R
26	12 35.2R
31	12 19.2R

Day	⚵
1	15♎17.6
6	16 34.0
11	17 53.4
16	19 15.6
21	20 40.4
26	22 07.5
31	23 36.6

Day	⚶
1	25♋25.1
6	27 36.5
11	29 47.7
16	1♌58.6
21	4 09.1
26	6 19.1
31	8 28.6

DECLINATION and LATITUDE

Day	☉ Decl	☽ Decl	☽ Lat	☽12h Decl	☿ Decl	☿ Lat	♀ Decl	♀ Lat	♂ Decl	♂ Lat	⚳ Decl	⚳ Lat	♃ Decl	♃ Lat	♄ Decl	♄ Lat
1 Sa	17N57	23S60	0S44	24S05	21N27	0S06	19N17	4S02	3N35	3S51	20S36	14S17	22S17	0S22	20S50	0S15
2 Su	17 42	23 49	1 53	23 13	21 22	0N06	19 22	3 59	3 44	3 52	20 43	14 21	22 18	0 22	20 51	0 15
3 M	17 26	22 18	2 56	21 06	21 14	0 18	19 27	3 55	3 53	3 53	20 50	14 25	22 19	0 22	20 52	0 15
4 Tu	17 10	19 39	3 48	17 58	21 04	0 30	19 32	3 52	4 01	3 54	20 57	14 29	22 21	0 22	20 53	0 15
5 W	16 54	16 06	4 28	14 04	20 52	0 40	19 36	3 49	4 10	3 55	21 04	14 32	22 22	0 22	20 54	0 15
6 Th	16 38	11 55	4 54	9 39	20 37	0 50	19 40	3 45	4 18	3 56	21 11	14 36	22 23	0 22	20 55	0 15
7 F	16 21	7 18	5 06	4 55	20 19	0 60	19 44	3 42	4 26	3 58	21 18	14 39	22 24	0 23	20 56	0 15
8 Sa	16 04	2 30	5 05	0 03	19 59	1 08	19 48	3 38	4 33	3 59	21 25	14 42	22 25	0 23	20 57	0 15
9 Su	15 47	2N22	4 50	4N46	19 36	1 15	19 51	3 34	4 41	3 60	21 32	14 45	22 26	0 23	20 57	0 16
10 M	15 29	7 07	4 22	9 24	19 10	1 22	19 54	3 31	4 48	4 01	21 39	14 49	22 27	0 23	20 58	0 16
11 Tu	15 11	11 37	3 44	13 44	18 42	1 28	19 57	3 27	4 56	4 02	21 46	14 52	22 27	0 23	20 59	0 16
12 W	14 53	15 43	2 55	17 33	18 12	1 33	19 60	3 23	5 03	4 03	21 54	14 54	22 28	0 23	20 60	0 16
13 Th	14 35	19 13	1 58	20 42	17 40	1 37	20 02	3 19	5 10	4 04	22 01	14 57	22 29	0 23	21 01	0 16
14 F	14 17	21 57	0 55	22 57	17 06	1 40	20 04	3 15	5 16	4 05	22 08	14 60	22 30	0 23	21 02	0 16
15 Sa	13 58	23 39	0N13	24 04	16 30	1 43	20 05	3 11	5 23	4 05	22 15	15 02	22 31	0 23	21 02	0 16
16 Su	13 39	24 08	1 22	23 52	15 52	1 44	20 06	3 06	5 29	4 06	22 21	15 05	22 32	0 23	21 03	0 16
17 M	13 20	23 14	2 29	22 15	15 13	1 45	20 06	3 02	5 35	4 07	22 28	15 07	22 32	0 23	21 04	0 16
18 Tu	13 01	20 54	3 28	19 13	14 33	1 46	20 07	2 58	5 40	4 08	22 35	15 09	22 33	0 24	21 05	0 16
19 W	12 41	17 14	4 17	14 58	13 51	1 45	20 06	2 54	5 46	4 09	22 42	15 11	22 34	0 24	21 05	0 16
20 Th	12 22	12 28	4 49	9 46	13 08	1 44	20 06	2 49	5 51	4 10	22 49	15 13	22 35	0 24	21 06	0 16
21 F	12 02	6 55	5 03	3 58	12 25	1 43	20 05	2 45	5 56	4 10	22 55	15 15	22 35	0 24	21 07	0 16
22 Sa	11 42	0 58	4 57	2S03	11 41	1 40	20 03	2 40	6 01	4 11	23 02	15 17	22 36	0 24	21 08	0 16
23 Su	11 21	5S01	4 31	7 54	10 56	1 38	20 01	2 36	6 06	4 12	23 08	15 18	22 37	0 24	21 08	0 17
24 M	11 01	10 39	3 48	13 14	10 11	1 34	19 59	2 31	6 10	4 12	23 14	15 20	22 37	0 24	21 09	0 17
25 Tu	10 40	15 37	2 52	17 46	9 25	1 31	19 56	2 27	6 15	4 13	23 21	15 21	22 38	0 24	21 10	0 17
26 W	10 19	19 39	1 46	21 13	8 39	1 27	19 52	2 22	6 19	4 13	23 27	15 22	22 38	0 24	21 10	0 17
27 Th	9 58	22 29	0 35	23 24	7 53	1 22	19 49	2 18	6 22	4 14	23 33	15 23	22 39	0 24	21 11	0 17
28 F	9 37	23 59	0S36	24 13	7 07	1 17	19 44	2 13	6 26	4 14	23 39	15 24	22 39	0 24	21 12	0 17
29 Sa	9 16	24 06	1 44	23 40	6 20	1 12	19 40	2 09	6 29	4 15	23 44	15 24	22 40	0 24	21 12	0 17
30 Su	8 54	22 54	2 45	21 51	5 34	1 06	19 34	2 04	6 32	4 15	23 50	15 25	22 40	0 24	21 13	0 17
31 M	8N33	20S32	3S37	18S59	4N47	1N01	19N29	1S59	6N35	4S15	23S55	15S25	22S40	0S25	21S13	0S17

Day	⚷ Decl	⚷ Lat	♅ Decl	♅ Lat	♆ Decl	♆ Lat	♇ Decl	♇ Lat
1	6N14	2N48	14N34	0S28	4S45	1S06	22S26	1S0
6	6 12	2 48	14 35	0 28	4 47	1 06	22 27	1 0
11	6 10	2 48	14 35	0 28	4 50	1 06	22 29	1 0
16	6 07	2 49	14 35	0 28	4 53	1 06	22 30	1 0
21	6 04	2 49	14 35	0 28	4 56	1 07	22 32	1 0
26	5 60	2 49	14 34	0 28	4 59	1 07	22 33	1 0
31	5N56	2N49	14N33	0S28	5S02	1S07	22S34	1S0

Day	⚴ Decl	⚴ Lat	⚵ Decl	⚵ Lat	⚶ Decl	⚶ Lat	Eris Decl	Eris Lat
1	19N04	41N47	1N27	8N05	21N34	0N32	1S21	11S3
6	18 15	41 03	0 56	8 03	21 16	0 38	1 22	11 4
11	17 23	40 15	0 25	8 02	20 55	0 45	1 22	11 4
16	16 27	39 22	0S07	8 00	20 33	0 52	1 23	11 4
21	15 29	38 26	0 40	7 59	20 10	0 58	1 24	11 4
26	14 29	37 28	1 13	7 58	19 45	1 05	1 25	11 4
31	13N29	36N29	1S45	7N58	19N19	1N13	1S26	11S4

Moon Phenomena

Max/0 Decl
dy hr mn
1 8:42 24S05
8 12:17 0 N
15 20:47 24N09
22 3:50 0 S
28 14:07 24S13

Max/0 Lat
dy hr mn
7 9:05 5S07
14 19:24 0 N
21 4:29 5N04
27 11:54 0 S

Perigee/Apogee
dy hr m kilometers
9 13:53 a 404657
21 10:57 p 363516

PH dy hr mn
○ 3 16:00 11♒46
☾ 11 16:46 19♉28
● 19 2:43 26♌35
☽ 25 17:59 2♐59

Void of Course Moon

Last Aspect			☽ Ingress		
2 14:01	♄	☌	♒	2	18:1
4 21:47	♀	△	♓	5	2:2
7 12:55	♀	□	♈	7	13:0
9 19:51	♄	□	♉	10	1:2
12 7:56	♄	△	♊	12	13:4
14 11:20	♂	⚹	♋	14	23:3
17 0:00	♄	☍	♌	17	5:4
19 5:39	☿	☌	♍	19	8:2
21 3:38	♄	△	♎	21	9:1
23 4:21	♄	□	♏	23	10:1
25 6:28	♄	⚹	♐	25	12:5
27 12:01	♂	△	♑	27	17:3
29 19:32	♂	□	♒	30	0:3

DAILY ASPECTARIAN

1 Sa ☉△⚷ 1:16; ☽□⚷ 4:32; ☉⚻☽ 4:47; ☽△♅ 6:57; ☽⚹⚳ 7:35; ☿☍♇ 10:53; ☽□♂ 21:24; ☽☌♃ 23:58
2 Su ☽⚹♆ 0:56; ☽☌♇ 5:59; ☽☍☿ 8:54; ☽⚻♀ 9:40; ☽∠⚳ 10:29; ☉□♅ 11:20; ☽☌♄ 14:01; ☉⚻⚳ 14:57; ♀∠♅ 17:18; ☿⚺♀ 19:28; ☿⚼⚳ 19:54; ☽∥♇ 22:24; ☽∥♃ 23:44
3 M ☽∠♆ 4:25; ⚳∥♄ 7:47; ☽⚹⚷ 11:15; ☽⫲☿ 11:25; ⚳⚹♅ 11:50; ☽∥⚳ 13:48; ☽⚺⚳ 13:52; ☽□♅ 13:53; ☽∥♄ 14:01; ☽⚼♀ 15:22; ☉☍☽ 16:00; ☿☍♄ 21:01
4 Tu ☽⫲♀ 0:54; ☽⚹♂ 6:46; ☽⚺♃ 7:02; ☽⚺♆ 8:26; ☿⫲⚳ 9:34; ♂□♃ 13:08; ☽⚺♇ 13:39; ☽∠⚷ 15:25; ☉⫲☽ 18:38; ☿⫲♄ 20:58; ☽△♀ 21:47; ☽⚺♄ 21:48; ♀⚻♄ 22:08
5 W ☽⚻☿ 2:17; ☿ ♌ 3:33; ☽⫲♅ 9:05; ☽∠♃ 11:24; ☽∠♂ 12:22; ☽∠♇ 18:22; ☽⚺⚷ 20:09; ☽☌⚳ 22:14; ☽⚹♅ 23:02
6 Th ☽∠♄ 2:34; ☉⚻☽ 6:01; ♂⚺♆ 7:32; ☽⚼☿ 12:42; ☽⚹♃ 16:21; ☽☌♆ 18:13; ☽⚺♂ 18:36; ☽⚹♇ 23:39
7 F ☽∠♅ 4:29; ☽⫲⚷ 5:36; ☽⚹♄ 7:54; ☽∥♆ 12:34; ☽□♀ 12:55; ☽⫲♂ 14:03; ☉⚼☽ 14:08; ♀ ♋ 15:22; ☿⚼♆ 22:32
8 Sa ☽△☿ 0:13; ☽☌⚷ 7:20; ☽⚺⚳ 8:44; ☿∥♀ 9:54; ☽⚺♅ 10:27; ☉△☽ 22:50
9 Su ☽□♃ 3:45; ☽⚺♆ 6:04; ☽☌♂ 8:36; ☽□♇ 11:39; ☽∥♂ 11:54; ☽⫲♆ 12:16; ☽∠⚳ 14:33; ☿△⚷ 18:04; ☽∥⚷ 19:10; ☽□♄ 19:51; ☿⚻⚳ 23:17
10 M ♂⫲♆ 3:07; ☽⚹♀ 6:24; ☽∠♆ 12:22; ☿□♅ 12:53; ☽⚺⚷ 19:49; ☽⚹⚳ 20:26; ☽☌♅ 23:06
11 Tu ☽□☿ 1:13; ☉⚻♃ 6:36; ⚶ ♌ 11:18; ☽∠♀ 15:16; ☽△♃ 15:53; ☉□☽ 16:46; ☽∥♅ 17:07; ☽⚹♆ 18:33; ☉∥☽ 19:18; ☽⚺♂ 23:05
12 W ☽△♇ 0:04; ☽∠⚷ 1:54; ☽△♄ 7:56; ☽∥☿ 14:17; ☉⚻♆ 14:34; ⚳⚺⚷ 16:39; ☽⚼♃ 21:29; ☽⚺♀ 23:39; ☉∥♅ 23:51
13 Th ♃∥♇ 5:22; ☽∠♂ 5:39; ☽⚼♇ 5:42; ☽∥♀ 6:26; ♂□♇ 7:15; ☽□⚳ 7:16; ☽⚹⚷ 7:28; ☽⚺♅ 10:47; ☽⚼♄ 13:16; ☽⫲♄ 14:55
14 F ☽⚹☿ 0:34; ☽⫲⚳ 2:04; ☽⚻♃ 2:25; ☽□♆ 5:17; ☽⫲♇ 6:13; ☽⫲♃ 6:20; ☉⚹☽ 8:34; ☽⚻♇ 10:33; ☽⚹♂ 11:20; ☿⚻♃ 11:30; ☽∠♅ 15:32; ☽⚻♄ 17:48; ♂∠⚳ 19:39
15 Sa ☿⚻♆ 5:15; ☽∠☿ 10:09; ☉⚻♇ 10:14; ☽☌♀ 13:27; ♅ R 14:28; ☉∠☽ 14:49; ☽△⚳ 15:11; ☽□⚷ 16:06; ☽⚹♅ 19:19
16 Su ☉⚼⚷ 8:01; ♀△⚳ 8:53; ☽☍♃ 9:34; ☽△♆ 12:30; ☿⚻♇ 13:40; ☉△♂ 14:03; ☽☍♇ 17:25; ☽⚼⚳ 17:44; ☽⚺☿ 18:05; ☽□♂ 19:33; ☉⚺☽ 19:50; ♀□⚷ 24:00
17 M ☽☍♄ 0:00; ☿⚼⚷ 0:04; ☿∠♀ 0:07; ☿△♂ 5:30; ⚳∥♇ 7:56; ☽⫲♃ 8:44; ☽⫲⚳ 9:05; ☽⫲♇ 9:08; ☽⚼♆ 14:40; ☉☌☿ 15:08; ⚳∥♃ 16:19; ⚳∠♇ 17:22; ☽⚻⚳ 19:25; ☽△⚷ 20:56; ☿∥♅ 22:20; ☽⚺♀ 22:34; ☽⫲♄ 22:34
18 Tu ☽□♅ 0:03; ☽∥♀ 5:55; ☿⚻♄ 9:18; ☽⚻♃ 13:06; ☽⚻♆ 16:04; ♀⚹♅ 19:29; ☽⚻♇ 20:43; ☽⚼⚷ 22:09; ☽△♂ 23:52
19 W ☽∠♀ 1:39; ☉☌☽ 2:43; ☽⚻♄ 2:47; ☉⚻♄ 3:50; ☽☌☿ 5:39; ☽⚼♃ 13:52; ☽∥♅ 13:52; ☽∥☿ 20:19; ☽☍⚳ 20:45; ☽⚼♇ 21:25; ☽⚻⚷ 22:49
20 Th ☉∥☽ 0:29; ☽⚼♂ 1:02; ☿ ♍ 1:31; ☽△♅ 1:53; ☽⚼♄ 3:20; ☽⚹♀ 4:07; ☽△♃ 14:15; ☽☍♆ 17:17; ☽△♇ 21:49
21 F ☽⚻♂ 1:53; ☽⚼♅ 2:16; ☽∥⚷ 3:30; ☽△♄ 3:38; ☽∥♂ 3:56; ☉⚺☽ 7:09; ☽⫲♆ 8:05; ☽⚺☿ 14:07; ☿⚼♃ 16:46; ☽⚻⚳ 20:49; ☉∥☿ 23:22; ☽☍⚷ 23:28
22 Sa ☽⚻♅ 2:37; ♂∥⚷ 7:02; ☽□♀ 8:27; ☉∠☽ 9:14; ☽□♃ 14:47; ☉ ♍ 15:46; ☽⚻♆ 17:59; ☽∠☿ 18:13; ☽⚼⚳ 20:56; ☽□♇ 22:35; ☽∥♆ 23:44
23 Su ☽☍♂ 3:36; ☽⫲⚷ 4:12; ☽□♄ 4:21; ☽⫲♂ 4:32; ☉⚹☽ 11:36; ☿☍⚳ 13:13; ☽⚼♆ 18:40; ☽△⚳ 21:21; ☽⫲☿ 22:10; ☽⚹☿ 22:43
24 M ☽⚻⚷ 0:42; ☉⫲☽ 1:32; ☿⚼♇ 3:38; ☽☍♅ 4:01; ☿⚻⚷ 13:37; ☽△♀ 13:53; ☽⚹♃ 16:22; ♂□♄ 18:21; ☽⫲♅ 18:36; ☽△♆ 19:49
25 Tu ☽⚹♇ 0:37; ☽⚼⚷ 1:56; ☽⚹♄ 6:28; ☽⚻♂ 6:43; ☿△♅ 15:19; ☉⚼♃ 16:54; ☽⚼♀ 17:31; ☽∠♃ 17:54; ☉□☽ 17:59; ♀☍♃ 22:27; ☿⚼♄ 23:12; ☽□⚳ 23:34
26 W ☽⫲♀ 1:36; ☽∠♇ 2:25; ☽△⚷ 3:44; ☿⚼♂ 3:49; ☽⚻♅ 7:18; ☽∠♄ 8:20; ☽⚼♂ 9:04; ☽□☿ 9:48; ☽∥♄ 11:39; ☽⚺♃ 20:01; ☽⚻♀ 21:54; ☽□♆ 23:44
27 Th ☽∥♇ 0:47; ☽∥♃ 1:52; ☽⚺♇ 4:47; ☽⚼♅ 9:48; ☽⚺♄ 10:47; ☽△♂ 12:01; ☽∥⚳ 15:30; ♀△♆ 21:14
28 F ☉△☽ 3:10; ☽⚹⚳ 3:57; ☽□⚷ 9:03; ☉☍⚳ 12:07; ☽△♅ 12:52; ♀⚼⚳ 12:53; ☿∥♂ 19:35; ☉∠♀ 23:47
29 Sa ☽△☿ 0:06; ☽☌♃ 1:57; ☽⚹♆ 5:55; ☽∠⚳ 6:56; ☉⚼☽ 8:48; ☽☍♀ 8:52; ☽∥⚳ 9:39; ☽☌♇ 11:13; ☿∥⚷ 11:58; ☿△♃ 13:29; ☽☌♄ 17:19; ☽□♂ 19:32
30 Su ☽∥♃ 3:01; ☽∥♇ 4:17; ☽⚼☿ 8:21; ☽∠♆ 9:47; ☽⚺⚳ 10:24; ♀☍♇ 13:32; ☉⚻☽ 15:04; ☿⫲♆ 16:27; ☽⚹⚷ 16:28; ☉⚼♇ 16:54; ☽∥♄ 18:04; ☿☍♆ 18:45; ☽□♅ 20:32
31 M ☽⫲♀ 8:39; ☉⚻⚷ 8:56; ☽⚺♃ 9:56; ☽⚺♆ 14:07; ☽⚻☿ 17:15; ☽⚺♇ 19:39; ☽∠⚷ 20:53; ☽⚻♀ 22:29

LONGITUDE

September 2020

Day	Sid.Time	☉	☽	☽ 12 hour	Mean ☊	True ☊	☿	♀	♂	⚳	♃	♄	⚷	♅	♆	♇
	h m s	° ′ ″	° ′ ″	° ′ ″	° ′	° ′	° ′	° ′	° ′	° ′	° ′	° ′	° ′	° ′	° ′	° ′
u	22 42 28	9♍01 13	25♒00 58	1♓14 52	25♊19.0	26♊25.7	21♍58.7	24♋17.6	27♈34.1	4♓52.0	17♑38.3	25♑58.3	8♈23.4	10♉34.9	19♓50.6	22♑44.9
/	22 46 24	9 59 16	7♓26 20	13 35 23	25 15.8	26R 14.1	23 40.8	25 21.5	27 41.3	4R 38.8	17R 36.1	25R 55.7	8R 21.1	10R 34.1	19R 49.0	22R 44.0
h	22 50 21	10 57 20	19 42 06	25 46 35	25 12.7	26 01.1	25 21.7	26 25.8	27 47.7	4 25.7	17 34.1	25 53.3	8 18.8	10 33.2	19 47.3	22 43.1
	22 54 17	11 55 26	1♈48 58	7♈49 23	25 09.5	25 48.0	27 01.3	27 30.3	27 53.2	4 12.6	17 32.2	25 50.9	8 16.4	10 32.3	19 45.7	22 42.3
a	22 58 14	12 53 34	13 48 03	19 45 13	25 06.3	25 35.9	28 39.7	28 35.0	27 57.9	3 59.6	17 30.6	25 48.5	8 14.1	10 31.3	19 44.1	22 41.5
u	23 02 10	13 51 44	25 41 12	1♉36 19	25 03.1	25 25.7	0♎17.0	29 40.0	28 01.7	3 46.8	17 29.2	25 46.3	8 11.7	10 30.3	19 42.4	22 40.7
I	23 06 07	14 49 56	7♉31 01	13 25 45	25 00.0	25 17.9	1 53.0	0♌45.2	28 04.7	3 34.0	17 27.9	25 44.1	8 09.2	10 29.3	19 40.8	22 39.9
u	23 10 04	15 48 09	19 21 01	25 17 22	24 56.8	25 12.9	3 27.9	1 50.7	28 06.9	3 21.4	17 26.8	25 42.1	8 06.8	10 28.2	19 39.1	22 39.2
/	23 14 00	16 46 25	1♊15 25	7♊15 46	24 53.6	25 10.3	5 01.6	2 56.3	28R 08.1	3 08.9	17 26.0	25 40.1	8 04.3	10 27.0	19 37.5	22 38.4
h	23 17 57	17 44 43	13 19 05	19 26 03	24 50.4	25 09.5	6 34.1	4 02.3	28 08.5	2 56.6	17 25.3	25 38.2	8 01.9	10 25.8	19 35.8	22 37.8
	23 21 53	18 43 03	25 37 18	1♋53 31	24 47.2	25 09.5	8 05.5	5 08.4	28 08.0	2 44.4	17 24.8	25 36.4	7 59.4	10 24.6	19 34.2	22 37.1
a	23 25 50	19 41 25	8♋15 19	14 43 17	24 44.1	25 09.1	9 35.8	6 14.7	28 06.6	2 32.5	17 24.5	25 34.7	7 56.8	10 23.3	19 32.5	22 36.4
u	23 29 46	20 39 49	21 17 52	27 59 30	24 40.9	25 07.3	11 04.8	7 21.3	28 04.3	2 20.7	17D 24.4	25 33.1	7 54.3	10 22.0	19 30.9	22 35.8
I	23 33 43	21 38 15	4♌48 25	11♌44 43	24 37.7	25 03.1	12 32.8	8 28.0	28 01.2	2 09.1	17 24.5	25 31.6	7 51.7	10 20.7	19 29.2	22 35.2
u	23 37 39	22 36 43	18 48 19	25 58 53	24 34.5	24 56.3	13 59.5	9 35.0	27 57.1	1 57.8	17 24.8	25 30.1	7 49.1	10 19.3	19 27.6	22 34.7
/	23 41 36	23 35 13	3♍15 56	10♍38 43	24 31.4	24 47.0	15 25.1	10 42.1	27 52.2	1 46.6	17 25.2	25 28.8	7 46.5	10 17.8	19 25.9	22 34.1
h	23 45 33	24 33 45	18 06 17	25 37 30	24 28.2	24 36.1	16 49.4	11 49.5	27 46.3	1 35.8	17 25.9	25 27.6	7 43.9	10 16.4	19 24.3	22 33.6
	23 49 29	25 32 20	3♎11 08	10♎45 51	24 25.0	24 24.7	18 12.6	12 57.0	27 39.7	1 25.1	17 26.8	25 26.4	7 41.3	10 14.8	19 22.6	22 33.1
a	23 53 26	26 30 55	18 20 19	25 53 14	24 21.8	24 14.1	19 34.4	14 04.7	27 32.1	1 14.8	17 27.8	25 25.4	7 38.7	10 13.3	19 21.0	22 32.7
u	23 57 22	27 29 33	3♏23 25	10♏49 51	24 18.6	24 05.6	20 55.0	15 12.5	27 23.7	1 04.7	17 29.1	25 24.4	7 36.0	10 11.7	19 19.3	22 32.3
I	0 01 19	28 28 13	18 11 42	25 28 19	24 15.5	23 59.8	22 14.2	16 20.6	27 14.5	0 54.8	17 30.5	25 23.5	7 33.3	10 10.1	19 17.7	22 31.9
u	0 05 15	29 26 54	2♐39 17	9♐44 19	24 12.3	23 56.6	23 32.1	17 28.8	27 04.6	0 45.3	17 32.2	25 22.8	7 30.7	10 08.4	19 16.1	22 31.5
/	0 09 12	0♎25 37	16 43 23	23 36 32	24 09.1	23D 55.5	24 48.4	18 37.1	26 53.8	0 36.1	17 34.0	25 22.1	7 28.0	10 06.7	19 14.5	22 31.1
h	0 13 08	1 24 22	0♑23 58	7♑05 57	24 05.9	23R 55.5	26 03.3	19 45.7	26 42.3	0 27.2	17 36.0	25 21.6	7 25.3	10 04.9	19 12.9	22 30.8
	0 17 05	2 23 08	13 42 49	20 14 57	24 02.8	23 55.1	27 16.6	20 54.4	26 30.0	0 18.6	17 38.2	25 21.1	7 22.6	10 03.2	19 11.2	22 30.5
a	0 21 01	3 21 56	26 42 45	3♒06 35	23 59.6	23 53.4	28 28.2	22 03.2	26 17.1	0 10.3	17 40.6	25 20.7	7 19.9	10 01.3	19 09.7	22 30.3
u	0 24 58	4 20 46	9♒26 51	15 43 54	23 56.4	23 49.2	29 38.0	23 12.2	26 03.4	0 02.3	17 43.2	25 20.5	7 17.2	9 59.5	19 08.1	22 30.0
I	0 28 55	5 19 38	21 58 02	28 09 33	23 53.2	23 42.2	0♏45.9	24 21.3	25 49.2	29♒54.7	17 46.0	25 20.3	7 14.5	9 57.6	19 06.5	22 29.8
u	0 32 51	6 18 31	4♓18 43	10♓25 44	23 50.0	23 32.4	1 51.8	25 30.6	25 34.3	29 47.4	17 49.0	25D 20.2	7 11.8	9 55.7	19 04.9	22 29.7
/	0 36 48	7♎17 26	16 30 47	22 34 04	23♊46.9	23♊20.4	2♏55.5	26♌40.1	25♈18.8	29♒40.4	17♑52.1	25♑20.3	7♈09.1	9♉53.8	19♓03.4	22♑29.5

1st of Month

Julian Day #
2459093.5
Obliquity
23°26'13"
SVP 4♓58'32"
GC 27♐07.7
Eris 24♈24.5R

Day	⚴
1	12♑17.1R
6	12 12.4R
11	12 16.8
16	12 29.9
21	12 51.2
26	13 20.3

Day	⚵
1	23♎54.7
6	25 26.1
11	26 59.3
16	28 34.1
21	0♏10.2
26	1 47.6

Day	⚶
1	8♌54.4
6	11 03.0
11	13 10.9
16	15 17.9
21	17 23.9
26	19 28.7

DECLINATION and LATITUDE

Day	☉ Decl	☽ Decl	☽ Lat	☽ 12h Decl	☿ Decl	☿ Lat	♀ Decl	♀ Lat	♂ Decl	♂ Lat	⚳ Decl	⚳ Lat	♃ Decl	♃ Lat	♄ Decl	♄ Lat
u	8N11	17S13	4S17	15S16	4N01	0N54	19N22	1S55	6N38	4S15	24S00	15S25	22S41	0S25	21S14	0S17
/	7 49	13 11	4 45	10 58	3 15	0 48	19 16	1 50	6 40	4 15	24 06	15 26	22 41	0 25	21 14	0 17
h	7 27	8 39	4 59	6 16	2 29	0 41	19 08	1 45	6 43	4 16	24 11	15 26	22 41	0 25	21 15	0 17
	7 05	3 51	4 59	1 24	1 43	0 35	19 01	1 41	6 44	4 16	24 15	15 25	22 42	0 25	21 15	0 17
a	6 43	1N03	4 46	3N29	0 57	0 28	18 52	1 36	6 46	4 15	24 20	15 25	22 42	0 25	21 16	0 17
u	6 21	5 53	4 20	8 13	0 12	0 21	18 44	1 32	6 48	4 15	24 24	15 25	22 42	0 25	21 16	0 17
I	5 58	10 29	3 44	12 40	0S33	0 13	18 34	1 27	6 49	4 15	24 29	15 24	22 43	0 25	21 17	0 18
u	5 36	14 43	2 57	16 38	1 17	0 06	18 25	1 22	6 50	4 15	24 33	15 23	22 43	0 25	21 17	0 18
/	5 13	18 24	2 03	19 59	2 01	0S02	18 14	1 18	6 51	4 15	24 37	15 22	22 43	0 25	21 18	0 18
h	4 51	21 22	1 02	22 31	2 45	0 09	18 04	1 13	6 51	4 14	24 41	15 22	22 43	0 25	21 18	0 18
	4 28	23 24	0N02	24 01	3 28	0 17	17 52	1 09	6 51	4 14	24 44	15 20	22 43	0 25	21 19	0 18
a	4 05	24 19	1 09	24 18	4 11	0 25	17 41	1 04	6 52	4 13	24 47	15 19	22 43	0 25	21 19	0 18
u	3 42	23 57	2 13	23 14	4 53	0 33	17 28	0 59	6 51	4 12	24 51	15 18	22 43	0 25	21 19	0 18
I	3 19	22 11	3 13	20 47	5 35	0 41	17 16	0 55	6 51	4 12	24 54	15 16	22 43	0 25	21 20	0 18
u	2 56	19 02	4 03	16 59	6 16	0 49	17 02	0 51	6 50	4 11	24 56	15 15	22 43	0 25	21 20	0 18
/	2 33	14 39	4 40	12 04	6 56	0 57	16 49	0 46	6 49	4 10	24 59	15 13	22 43	0 25	21 20	0 18
h	2 10	9 17	4 58	6 20	7 36	1 04	16 34	0 42	6 48	4 09	25 01	15 11	22 43	0 25	21 21	0 18
	1 46	3 16	4 57	0 10	8 15	1 12	16 20	0 37	6 47	4 08	25 03	15 09	22 43	0 25	21 21	0 18
a	1 23	2S57	4 34	6S01	8 54	1 20	16 05	0 33	6 46	4 06	25 05	15 07	22 43	0 25	21 21	0 18
u	0 60	8 59	3 53	11 48	9 32	1 28	15 49	0 29	6 44	4 05	25 07	15 05	22 43	0 26	21 21	0 18
I	0 37	14 25	2 57	16 48	10 08	1 36	15 33	0 24	6 42	4 03	25 09	15 03	22 43	0 26	21 21	0 18
u	0 13	18 54	1 50	20 41	10 45	1 44	15 16	0 20	6 40	4 02	25 10	15 00	22 43	0 26	21 22	0 18
V	0S10	22 09	0 38	23 15	11 20	1 51	14 59	0 16	6 38	4 00	25 11	14 58	22 42	0 26	21 22	0 18
h	0 34	24 00	0S34	24 24	11 54	1 59	14 42	0 12	6 35	3 58	25 12	14 55	22 42	0 26	21 22	0 18
	0 57	24 26	1 43	24 07	12 28	2 06	14 24	0 08	6 33	3 57	25 13	14 53	22 42	0 26	21 22	0 19
a	1 20	23 30	2 44	22 34	13 00	2 13	14 06	0 04	6 30	3 54	25 13	14 50	22 42	0 26	21 22	0 19
u	1 44	21 21	3 36	19 54	13 32	2 21	13 47	0N00	6 27	3 52	25 14	14 47	22 41	0 26	21 22	0 19
I	2 07	18 13	4 16	16 21	14 02	2 27	13 28	0 04	6 24	3 50	25 14	14 44	22 41	0 26	21 22	0 19
u	2 30	14 20	4 44	12 10	14 32	2 34	13 09	0 08	6 21	3 48	25 14	14 41	22 41	0 26	21 23	0 19
V	2S54	9S54	4S58	7S33	14S60	2S41	12N49	0N12	6N18	3S45	25S13	14S38	22S40	0S26	21S23	0S19

Day	⚷ Decl	⚷ Lat	♅ Decl	♅ Lat	♆ Decl	♆ Lat	♇ Decl	♇ Lat
1	5N55	2N49	14N33	0S28	5S03	1S07	22S34	1S04
6	5 50	2 49	14 32	0 28	5 06	1 07	22 35	1 04
11	5 45	2 49	14 30	0 28	5 09	1 07	22 36	1 05
16	5 40	2 49	14 28	0 28	5 13	1 07	22 37	1 05
21	5 35	2 49	14 25	0 28	5 16	1 07	22 38	1 05
26	5 29	2 48	14 22	0 28	5 19	1 07	22 38	1 06

Day	⚴ Decl	⚴ Lat	⚵ Decl	⚵ Lat	⚶ Decl	⚶ Lat	Eris Decl	Eris Lat
1	13N16	36N17	1S52	7N58	19N13	1N14	1S26	11S42
6	12 16	35 16	2 25	7 57	18 45	1 21	1 27	11 42
11	11 16	34 16	2 58	7 58	18 17	1 29	1 28	11 42
16	10 17	33 15	3 31	7 58	17 47	1 37	1 29	11 42
21	9 19	32 16	4 03	7 59	17 17	1 45	1 30	11 43
26	8 23	31 18	4 35	7 60	16 46	1 53	1 31	11 43

Moon Phenomena

Max/0 Decl
dy hr mn
4 18:51 0 N
12 5:18 24N21
18 12:37 0 S
24 19:18 24S27

Max/0 Lat
dy hr mn
3 12:16 5S00
10 23:07 0 N
17 10:12 5N00
23 12:34 0 S
30 13:19 5S00

Perigee/Apogee
dy hr m kilometers
6 6:27 a 405606
18 13:52 p 359087

PH dy hr mn
○ 2 5:23 10♓12
☾ 10 9:27 18♊08
● 17 11:01 25♍01
☽ 24 1:56 1♑29

Void of Course Moon

Last Aspect				☽ Ingress		
1	4:57	♂	✶	♓	1	9:35
3	14:35	♀	△	♈	3	20:23
6	4:46	♂	☌	♉	6	8:45
8	12:48	♄	△	♊	8	21:29
11	4:49	♂	✶	♋	11	8:24
13	12:06	♂	□	♌	13	15:34
15	15:11	♂	△	♍	15	18:38
17	11:43	♄	△	♎	17	18:57
19	14:30	♂	☍	♏	19	18:34
21	18:14	☉	✶	♐	21	19:33
23	17:33	♂	△	♑	23	23:17
26	3:37	☿	□	♒	26	6:09
28	7:19	♂	✶	♓	28	15:35

DAILY ASPECTARIAN

☽⊻♄ 1:50
☽✶♂ 4:57
☿△♇ 10:43
☽∠♃ 14:39
☽⫲♅ 16:15
☽☌⚳ 18:40

☽∠♇ 0:34
☽⊻⚷ 1:46
☉☍☽ 5:23
☽✶♅ 6:05
☽⚼♀ 6:14
☽∠♄ 6:47
☽∠♂ 10:20
♀☍♄ 12:19
☉△♅ 14:10
☽✶♃ 19:49
☉⚼♄ 22:23

☽☌♆ 0:10
☿⚼♅ 2:44
☽✶♇ 5:57
☉⫲☽ 6:35
☿△♄ 7:24
☽⫲♂ 9:46
☽∠♅ 11:33
☽✶♄ 12:11
☽☍☿ 12:58
☽⫲⚷ 13:59
☽△♀ 14:35
☽⊻♂ 16:08
☽∥♆ 17:57

☽⊻⚳ 4:41
♀□♂ 9:13
☽⫲☿ 12:23
☽☌⚷ 12:52
☿⊼♂ 13:16
☽⊻♅ 17:25
☿✶♀ 20:33
☉∥♂ 20:57
☉⊼☽ 22:01
☽∥☿ 23:35

5 Sa
☉⚼♂ 1:55
☽□♃ 7:27
☽∠⚳ 10:17
☽⊻♆ 11:56
☽□♇ 17:55
☿ ♎ 19:47
☽⫲♆ 20:03
☽∥⚷ 23:46

6 Su
☽□♄ 0:10
⚴ D 1:07
☉∥☽ 2:11
☽∥♂ 4:39
☽☌♂ 4:46
☉⚼☽ 7:01
♀ ♌ 7:23
☽□♀ 8:53
☽⊼☿ 10:47
☽✶⚳ 16:07
☽∠♆ 18:15

7 M
☽⊻⚷ 1:17
☽☌♅ 6:01
☉∥⚷ 10:10
☉△☽ 16:10
☽△♃ 20:09
☽⚼☿ 21:56
☿⊼⚳ 22:32
☽∥♅ 22:47

8 Tu
☽✶♆ 0:37
☽△♇ 6:40
☽∠⚷ 7:35
☽△♄ 12:48
☽⊻♂ 17:43
☽∥♀ 22:53

9 W
☽⚼♃ 2:21
☽✶♀ 3:43
☽□⚳ 3:43
♀⊼⚳ 3:51
☉⫲♆ 5:27
☽△☿ 8:39
☽⚼♇ 12:44
☽✶⚷ 13:34
☉△♃ 16:05
☽⊻♅ 18:18
☽⚼♄ 18:43
♂ R 22:24
☽⫲♄ 23:25
☽∠♂ 23:39

10 Th
☽⊼♃ 8:04
☉□☽ 9:27
♀⚼♆ 11:54
☽□♆ 12:17
☽∠♀ 12:20
☽⫲♇ 13:03
☽⫲♃ 14:28
☽⊼♇ 18:12
☿☍⚷ 22:25
☽∠♅ 23:36
☽⊼♄ 23:58

11 F
☽✶♂ 4:49
☽△⚳ 13:24
☽⊻♀ 19:52
☉☍♆ 20:27
☉⫲☿ 21:46
☽□⚷ 23:25

12 Sa
☽□☿ 2:50
☽✶♅ 3:58
☿⊼♅ 12:36
⚳∠♃ 16:23
☽⚼⚳ 16:55
☽☍♃ 16:55
☽△♆ 20:46
☉✶☽ 22:46

13 Su
♃ D 0:42
☽☍♇ 2:21
☽☍♄ 7:38
☿∥♆ 10:09
♀△⚷ 11:26
☽□♂ 12:06
☽⫲♃ 18:22
☽⊼⚳ 19:25
☽⫲♇ 19:36
☽⚼♆ 23:27

14 M
☉∠☽ 3:26
☿⫲⚷ 4:12
☽△⚷ 5:18
☽☌♀ 6:55
☽⫲♄ 7:36
☽□♅ 9:35
☽✶☿ 14:55
☽⊼♃ 21:39
☉△♇ 23:10

15 Tu
☽⊼♆ 1:06
☽⊼♇ 6:20
☽⚼⚷ 6:43
☉⊻☽ 6:51
☽⊼♄ 11:11
☽∥♀ 12:19
☽△♂ 15:11
♀□♅ 15:31
☽∠☿ 18:49
☿⫲♂ 20:00
☽☍⚳ 21:35
☽⚼♃ 22:37

16 W
☽∥♅ 0:54
☽⚼♇ 7:01
☽⊼⚷ 7:20
☽△♅ 11:25
☽⚼♄ 11:43
☽⊻♀ 13:05
☽⚼♂ 15:29
☿⚼⚳ 20:32
☽⊻☿ 21:44
☽△♃ 22:55

17 Th
☽☍♆ 2:05
☽⫲☿ 6:11
☽△♇ 7:07
☽∥♂ 10:07
☿□♃ 10:36
☉☌☽ 11:01
☽⚼♅ 11:25
☽△♄ 11:43
☽∥⚷ 14:44
☽∠♀ 15:02
☽⊼♂ 15:18
☽⫲♆ 16:21
☉⚼♅ 17:01
☽⊼⚳ 21:14
☉△♄ 21:37

18 F
☉∥☽ 6:11
☽☍⚷ 7:07
☽⊼♅ 11:10
☽✶♀ 16:42
☉⫲☽ 18:18
☿⊼♆ 20:07
☽⚼⚳ 20:43
☽□♃ 22:37

19 Sa
☽⊼♆ 1:36
☽☌☿ 2:09
☽□♇ 6:41
☽∥♆ 8:56
☽⫲⚷ 10:22
☽□♄ 11:15
☉⊻☽ 13:54
☽☍♂ 14:30
☽⫲♂ 14:53
☽△⚳ 20:20
☉⊼♂ 21:56

20 Su
☽⚼♆ 1:30
☽∥☿ 2:31
☽⊼⚷ 6:45
☽☍♅ 10:57
⚵ ♏ 11:20
☉∠☽ 15:44
☽□♀ 20:43
☽✶♃ 22:52

21 M
☽⫲♅ 0:01
☽△♆ 1:48
☽⫲♀ 5:16
☿□♇ 5:22
☽✶♇ 7:08
☽⚼⚷ 7:09
☽⊻☿ 7:18
☽✶♄ 11:52
☽⊼♂ 14:47
☉✶☽ 18:14
☽□⚳ 20:51
☽∠♃ 23:48

22 Tu
♀⊼♃ 1:14
☽△⚷ 8:11
☽∠♇ 8:14
☽∠☿ 10:57
☽⊼♅ 12:40
☽∠♄ 13:05
☉ ♎ 13:32
☽⚼♂ 15:48
☽∥♄ 17:15

23 W
☽⊻♃ 1:28
☽△♀ 3:35
☉⊼⚳ 3:43
☽□♆ 4:22
☽∥♇ 4:50
☽∥♃ 5:37
☽⊻♇ 10:05
☿□♄ 10:39
♀⊼♆ 12:47
☽⚼♅ 14:37
☽⊻♄ 15:05
☽✶☿ 15:32
☽△♂ 17:33

24 Th
☽✶⚳ 0:06
☉□☽ 1:56
☽⚼♀ 8:31
☿☍♂ 10:54
☽□⚷ 12:32
☽△♅ 17:21

25 F
♀∥♅ 1:41
☽∠⚳ 2:53
☽☌♃ 7:13
☽✶♆ 10:01
☽⊼♀ 14:30
☽☌♇ 16:11
☽☌♄ 21:27
☽□♂ 23:13

26 Sa
☽□☿ 3:37
♀⚼⚷ 5:36
☽⊻⚳ 6:24
♀⊼♇ 9:23
☽∥♃ 10:30
☽∥♇ 11:08
☉△☽ 13:31
☽∠♆ 13:57
☽✶⚷ 19:55
☽∥♄ 23:49

27 Su
☽□♅ 1:02
⚳ R♒ 7:09
☿⫲♀ 7:19
☿△⚳ 7:38
☿ ♏ 7:42
☽⊻♃ 15:53
☽⊻♆ 18:30
☉⚼☽ 20:34

28 M
☽∠⚷ 0:32
☽⊻♇ 1:01
☽☍♀ 5:06
☽⊻♄ 6:31
☽✶♂ 7:19
☿⫲♅ 14:55
☽☌⚳ 15:15
☽△☿ 18:45
♀⊼♄ 20:24
☽∠♃ 21:04
☽∥☿ 22:59
☽⫲♅ 23:56

29 Tu
♀△♂ 1:02
☉⊼☽ 4:15
♄ D 5:13
☽⊻⚷ 5:38
☽∠♇ 6:14
☽⫲♀ 7:15
☽✶♅ 10:59
☽∠♄ 11:49
☽∠♂ 12:02
☉☍⚷ 20:45
♂□♄ 21:51

30 W
☽✶♃ 2:42
☽⚼☿ 3:03
☽☌♆ 5:01
☽✶♇ 11:51
☽∠♅ 16:35
☽⊻♂ 17:05
☽✶♄ 17:31
☽⫲♂ 18:28
☽⊼♀ 22:18
☽⫲⚷ 22:43
☽∥♆ 22:51

October 2020

LONGITUDE

Day	Sid.Time	☉	☽	☽ 12 hour	Mean ☊	True ☊	☿	♀	♂	⚳	♃	♄	⚷	♅	♆	♇
	h m s	° ' "	° ' "	° ' "	° '	° '	° '	° '	° '	° '	° '	° '	° '	° '	° '	° '
1 Th	0 40 44	8♎16 23	28♓35 42	4♈35 51	23♊43.7	23♊07.0	3♏56.9	27♌49.7	25♈02.8	29♒33.8	17♑55.4	25♑20.4	7♈06.4	9♉51.8	19♓01.8	22♑29.4
2 F	0 44 41	9 15 22	10♈34 38	16 32 14	23 40.5	22R 53.5	4 55.7	28 59.4	24R 46.3	29R 27.5	17 58.9	25 20.6	7R 03.7	9R 49.8	19R 00.3	22R 29.3
3 Sa	0 48 37	10 14 23	22 28 47	28 24 29	23 37.3	22 40.8	5 51.8	0♍09.3	24 29.4	29 21.6	18 02.6	25 20.9	7 01.0	9 47.8	18 58.8	22 29.2
4 Su	0 52 34	11 13 26	4♉19 34	10♉14 16	23 34.1	22 30.1	6 44.9	1 19.3	24 11.9	29 16.0	18 06.5	25 21.4	6 58.3	9 45.7	18 57.3	22D 29.2
5 M	0 56 30	12 12 32	16 08 54	22 03 49	23 31.0	22 21.9	7 34.8	2 29.4	23 54.2	29 10.8	18 10.5	25 21.9	6 55.6	9 43.6	18 55.8	22 29.2
6 Tu	1 00 27	13 11 39	27 59 23	3♊56 03	23 27.8	22 16.5	8 21.2	3 39.7	23 36.0	29 05.9	18 14.8	25 22.5	6 52.9	9 41.5	18 54.3	22 29.2
7 W	1 04 24	14 10 49	9♊54 17	15 54 38	23 24.6	22 13.7	9 03.8	4 50.2	23 17.6	29 01.4	18 19.2	25 23.2	6 50.2	9 39.3	18 52.8	22 29.3
8 Th	1 08 20	15 10 01	21 57 39	28 03 56	23 21.4	22D 13.0	9 42.1	6 00.7	22 58.9	28 57.3	18 23.7	25 24.1	6 47.5	9 37.2	18 51.4	22 29.4
9 F	1 12 17	16 09 16	4♋14 06	10♋28 47	23 18.3	22 13.4	10 15.9	7 11.4	22 40.0	28 53.5	18 28.5	25 25.0	6 44.8	9 35.0	18 50.0	22 29.5
10 Sa	1 16 13	17 08 32	16 48 35	23 14 08	23 15.1	22R 13.7	10 44.6	8 22.2	22 21.0	28 50.1	18 33.4	25 26.0	6 42.2	9 32.8	18 48.5	22 29.6
11 Su	1 20 10	18 07 51	29 45 58	6♌24 35	23 11.9	22 13.1	11 07.9	9 33.1	22 01.8	28 47.1	18 38.5	25 27.1	6 39.5	9 30.5	18 47.1	22 29.8
12 M	1 24 06	19 07 13	13♌10 22	20 03 34	23 08.7	22 10.6	11 25.3	10 44.2	21 42.6	28 44.4	18 43.8	25 28.4	6 36.9	9 28.3	18 45.8	22 30.0
13 Tu	1 28 03	20 06 36	27 04 19	4♍12 29	23 05.6	22 05.8	11 36.2	11 55.3	21 23.4	28 42.1	18 49.2	25 29.7	6 34.3	9 26.0	18 44.4	22 30.3
14 W	1 31 59	21 06 02	11♍27 47	18 49 42	23 02.4	21 58.7	11R 40.2	13 06.6	21 04.2	28 40.2	18 54.8	25 31.1	6 31.7	9 23.7	18 43.1	22 30.5
15 Th	1 35 56	22 05 30	26 17 26	3♎50 02	22 59.2	21 50.1	11 36.7	14 18.0	20 45.2	28 38.6	19 00.6	25 32.6	6 29.1	9 21.4	18 41.7	22 30.8
16 F	1 39 53	23 05 01	11♎26 17	19 04 53	22 56.0	21 40.8	11 25.4	15 29.5	20 26.3	28 37.4	19 06.5	25 34.2	6 26.5	9 19.1	18 40.4	22 31.1
17 Sa	1 43 49	24 04 33	26 44 24	4♏23 25	22 52.8	21 32.2	11 05.7	16 41.1	20 07.6	28 36.6	19 12.6	25 35.9	6 24.0	9 16.7	18 39.2	22 31.5
18 Su	1 47 46	25 04 07	12♏00 32	19 34 28	22 49.7	21 25.2	10 37.6	17 52.8	19 49.1	28D 36.1	19 18.9	25 37.7	6 21.4	9 14.3	18 37.9	22 31.9
19 M	1 51 42	26 03 44	27 04 05	4♐28 27	22 46.5	21 20.5	10 00.7	19 04.6	19 31.0	28 36.1	19 25.3	25 39.6	6 18.9	9 12.0	18 36.7	22 32.3
20 Tu	1 55 39	27 03 22	11♐46 51	18 58 48	22 43.3	21D 18.2	9 15.4	20 16.5	19 13.3	28 36.4	19 31.9	25 41.7	6 16.4	9 09.6	18 35.4	22 32.7
21 W	1 59 35	28 03 02	26 03 59	3♑02 20	22 40.1	21 17.9	8 21.8	21 28.4	18 55.9	28 37.0	19 38.6	25 43.8	6 13.9	9 07.2	18 34.3	22 33.2
22 Th	2 03 32	29 02 44	9♑53 53	16 38 50	22 37.0	21 18.8	7 20.9	22 40.5	18 39.0	28 38.0	19 45.5	25 46.0	6 11.5	9 04.8	18 33.1	22 33.7
23 F	2 07 28	0♏02 28	23 17 31	29 50 19	22 33.8	21R 19.7	6 13.6	23 52.7	18 22.6	28 39.4	19 52.5	25 48.3	6 09.1	9 02.3	18 31.9	22 34.3
24 Sa	2 11 25	1 02 13	6♒17 40	12♒40 03	22 30.6	21 19.8	5 01.4	25 05.0	18 06.7	28 41.2	19 59.7	25 50.6	6 06.7	8 59.9	18 30.8	22 34.8
25 Su	2 15 22	2 02 00	18 57 57	25 11 53	22 27.4	21 18.1	3 46.2	26 17.3	17 51.3	28 43.3	20 07.1	25 53.1	6 04.3	8 57.4	18 29.7	22 35.4
26 M	2 19 18	3 01 48	1♓22 18	7♓29 40	22 24.2	21 14.4	2 30.2	27 29.7	17 36.6	28 45.7	20 14.6	25 55.7	6 01.9	8 55.0	18 28.7	22 36.0
27 Tu	2 23 15	4 01 38	13 34 25	19 36 56	22 21.1	21 08.6	1 15.5	28 42.2	17 22.5	28 48.5	20 22.2	25 58.4	5 59.6	8 52.5	18 27.6	22 36.7
28 W	2 27 11	5 01 30	25 37 36	1♈36 44	22 17.9	21 01.0	0 04.5	29 54.8	17 09.0	28 51.7	20 30.0	26 01.1	5 57.3	8 50.1	18 26.6	22 37.3
29 Th	2 31 08	6 01 24	7♈34 38	13 31 34	22 14.7	20 52.4	28♎59.4	1♎07.5	16 56.2	28 55.2	20 37.9	26 04.0	5 55.1	8 47.6	18 25.6	22 38.1
30 F	2 35 04	7 01 19	19 27 47	25 23 30	22 11.5	20 43.6	28 02.2	2 20.3	16 44.1	28 59.0	20 46.0	26 06.9	5 52.8	8 45.1	18 24.6	22 38.8
31 Sa	2 39 01	8♏01 17	1♉18 56	7♉14 18	22♊08.4	20♊35.4	27♎14.4	3♎33.1	16♈32.6	29♒03.2	20♑54.2	26♑09.9	5♈50.6	8♉42.7	18♓23.7	22♑39.5

1st of Mo[nth]

Julian Da[y]
2459123
Obliquit[y]
23°26'13
SVP 4♓58'
GC 27♐0
Eris 24♈09

Day	⚴
1	13♑56
6	14 39
11	15 28
16	16 23
21	17 22
26	18 27
31	19 36

Day	⚵
1	3♏26
6	5 05
11	6 45
16	8 26
21	10 08
26	11 50
31	13 32

Day	⚶
1	21♌32
6	23 34
11	25 34
16	27 33
21	29 29
26	1♍23
31	3 15

DECLINATION and LATITUDE

Day	☉ Decl	☽ Decl	☽ Lat	☽12h Decl	☿ Decl	☿ Lat	♀ Decl	♀ Lat	♂ Decl	♂ Lat	⚳ Decl	⚳ Lat	♃ Decl	♃ Lat	♄ Decl	♄ Lat
1 Th	3S17	5S08	4S59	2S41	15S27	2S47	12N28	0N16	6N14	3S43	25S13	14S35	22S40	0S26	21S23	0S19
2 F	3 40	0 13	4 47	2N15	15 52	2 53	12 08	0 19	6 11	3 40	25 12	14 32	22 39	0 26	21 23	0 19
3 Sa	4 03	4N42	4 22	7 06	16 16	2 58	11 46	0 23	6 07	3 37	25 11	14 29	22 39	0 26	21 23	0 19
4 Su	4 26	9 25	3 45	11 40	16 39	3 03	11 25	0 26	6 04	3 34	25 10	14 25	22 39	0 26	21 23	0 19
5 M	4 50	13 48	2 59	15 49	16 60	3 08	11 03	0 30	5 60	3 31	25 09	14 22	22 38	0 26	21 23	0 19
6 Tu	5 13	17 41	2 05	19 22	17 19	3 12	10 41	0 33	5 56	3 28	25 08	14 18	22 37	0 26	21 22	0 19
7 W	5 35	20 52	1 05	22 08	17 36	3 16	10 18	0 37	5 53	3 25	25 06	14 15	22 37	0 26	21 22	0 19
8 Th	5 58	23 10	0 01	23 56	17 51	3 19	9 56	0 40	5 49	3 21	25 04	14 11	22 36	0 26	21 22	0 19
9 F	6 21	24 26	1N04	24 37	18 04	3 21	9 32	0 43	5 45	3 18	25 03	14 08	22 36	0 26	21 22	0 19
10 Sa	6 44	24 29	2 07	24 01	18 15	3 23	9 09	0 47	5 41	3 15	25 00	14 04	22 35	0 26	21 22	0 19
11 Su	7 07	23 14	3 06	22 06	18 23	3 23	8 45	0 50	5 38	3 11	24 58	14 01	22 34	0 26	21 22	0 19
12 M	7 29	20 39	3 57	18 53	18 28	3 23	8 21	0 53	5 34	3 07	24 56	13 57	22 34	0 26	21 22	0 19
13 Tu	7 52	16 48	4 36	14 28	18 31	3 22	7 57	0 56	5 30	3 03	24 53	13 53	22 33	0 26	21 21	0 19
14 W	8 14	11 52	4 59	9 05	18 30	3 20	7 32	0 58	5 27	2 60	24 50	13 50	22 32	0 26	21 21	0 19
15 Th	8 36	6 07	5 04	3 02	18 25	3 16	7 07	1 01	5 23	2 56	24 47	13 46	22 31	0 26	21 21	0 20
16 F	8 58	0S07	4 47	3S18	18 17	3 11	6 42	1 04	5 20	2 52	24 44	13 42	22 31	0 26	21 21	0 20
17 Sa	9 20	6 26	4 09	9 28	18 04	3 04	6 17	1 07	5 16	2 48	24 41	13 38	22 30	0 26	21 20	0 20
18 Su	9 42	12 21	3 14	15 02	17 48	2 56	5 51	1 09	5 13	2 44	24 38	13 34	22 29	0 26	21 20	0 20
19 M	10 04	17 27	2 06	19 34	17 27	2 46	5 25	1 12	5 10	2 40	24 34	13 30	22 28	0 26	21 20	0 20
20 Tu	10 25	21 21	0 51	22 46	17 01	2 34	4 59	1 14	5 07	2 35	24 30	13 27	22 27	0 27	21 20	0 20
21 W	10 47	23 48	0S26	24 27	16 31	2 21	4 33	1 16	5 05	2 31	24 27	13 23	22 26	0 27	21 19	0 20
22 Th	11 08	24 42	1 38	24 35	15 56	2 06	4 07	1 19	5 02	2 27	24 23	13 19	22 25	0 27	21 19	0 20
23 F	11 29	24 07	2 43	23 19	15 18	1 49	3 40	1 21	5 00	2 23	24 18	13 15	22 24	0 27	21 18	0 20
24 Sa	11 50	22 13	3 38	20 51	14 37	1 30	3 13	1 23	4 58	2 19	24 14	13 11	22 23	0 27	21 18	0 20
25 Su	12 11	19 15	4 20	17 28	13 53	1 11	2 46	1 25	4 56	2 14	24 10	13 07	22 22	0 27	21 18	0 20
26 M	12 31	15 29	4 50	13 23	13 08	0 51	2 19	1 27	4 54	2 10	24 05	13 03	22 21	0 27	21 17	0 20
27 Tu	12 52	11 09	5 05	8 49	12 23	0 30	1 52	1 29	4 53	2 06	24 01	12 59	22 20	0 27	21 17	0 20
28 W	13 12	6 26	5 07	3 59	11 39	0 09	1 25	1 30	4 52	2 02	23 56	12 55	22 19	0 27	21 16	0 20
29 Th	13 32	1 31	4 55	0N58	10 57	0N11	0 57	1 32	4 51	1 57	23 51	12 51	22 18	0 27	21 16	0 20
30 F	13 51	3N27	4 30	5 53	10 18	0 30	0 30	1 33	4 50	1 53	23 46	12 47	22 16	0 27	21 15	0 20
31 Sa	14S11	8N16	3S54	10N35	9S44	0N48	0N02	1N35	4N50	1S49	23S41	12S43	22S15	0S27	21S15	0S20

Day	⚷ Decl	⚷ Lat	♅ Decl	♅ Lat	♆ Decl	♆ Lat	♇ Decl
1	5N24	2N48	14N19	0S28	5S22	1S07	22S39
6	5 18	2 48	14 16	0 28	5 25	1 07	22 39
11	5 12	2 47	14 13	0 28	5 28	1 07	22 39
16	5 06	2 47	14 09	0 28	5 30	1 07	22 39
21	5 01	2 46	14 05	0 28	5 33	1 07	22 39
26	4 56	2 45	14 01	0 28	5 35	1 07	22 39
31	4N50	2N45	13N57	0S28	5S37	1S07	22S39

Day	⚴ Decl	⚴ Lat	⚵ Decl	⚵ Lat	⚶ Decl	⚶ Lat	Eris Decl
1	7N30	30N21	5S07	8N01	16N15	2N02	1S32
6	6 38	29 26	5 38	8 03	15 43	2 11	1 33
11	5 50	28 32	6 08	8 05	15 11	2 20	1 34
16	5 04	27 41	6 37	8 07	14 40	2 30	1 35
21	4 21	26 51	7 06	8 10	14 09	2 40	1 36
26	3 41	26 04	7 34	8 13	13 38	2 51	1 37
31	3N04	25N18	8S00	8N16	13N08	3N02	1S38

Moon Phenomena

Max/0 Decl

dy hr mn	
2 1:01	0 N
9 13:07	24N37
15 23:32	0 S
22 1:59	24S42
29 7:18	0 N

Max/0 Lat

dy hr mn	
8 0:31	0 N
14 17:01	5N04
20 15:55	0 S
27 14:55	5S08

Perigee/Apogee

dy hr m		kilometers
3 17:22	a	406322
16 23:47	p	356912
30 18:44	a	406395

PH	dy hr mn	
○	1 21:06	9♈08
☾	10 0:41	17♋10
●	16 19:32	23♎53
☽	23 13:24	0♒36
○	31 14:50	8♉38

Void of Course Moon

Last Aspect			☽ Ingre[ss]
30 17:31	♄	⚹	♈ 1 2
3 5:48	♄	□	♉ 3 15
5 18:42	♄	△	♊ 6 4
8 1:58	♂	⚹	♋ 8 15
10 16:05	♄	☍	♌ 11 0
12 14:31	♂	△	♍ 13 4
14 22:48	♄	△	♎ 15 5
16 22:13	♄	□	♏ 17 5
18 21:44	♄	⚹	♐ 19 4
21 3:39	☉	⚹	♑ 21 6
23 4:36	♄	☌	♒ 23 12
24 21:55	♂	⚹	♓ 25 21
28 0:47	♄	⚹	♈ 28 8
30 16:14	☿	☍	♉ 30 21

DAILY ASPECTARIAN

1 Th ☽⚺⚳ 1:55 · ☿⚼♆ 1:56 · ☉∥☽ 8:24 · ☽⚻☿ 11:40 · ☽☌⚷ 16:58 · ♆⋕⚷ 21:04 · ☉☍☽ 21:06 · ☽⚺♅ 22:30

2 F ☽⚼♀ 7:37 · ☽∠⚳ 7:45 · ♀☍⚳ 8:53 · ☉⚻♅ 13:32 · ☽□♃ 15:00 · ☽⚺♆ 16:57 · ☉⋕☽ 20:33 · ♀ ♍ 20:49

3 Sa ☽□♇ 0:01 · ☽∥⚷ 3:15 · ☽⋕♆ 3:26 · ☽☌♂ 3:58 · ☽□♄ 5:48 · ☽∥♂ 7:00 · ♃∥♇ 11:04 · ☽⚹⚳ 13:49 · ☽△♀ 17:14 · ☽∠♆ 23:15

4 Su ☽☍☿ 5:18 · ☽⚺⚷ 5:21 · ☿⚻⚷ 5:56 · ☽∥♀ 9:49 · ☽☌♅ 11:00 · ♇ D 13:34 · ☉⚻☽ 15:17

5 M ☽∥♅ 2:44 · ☽△♃ 4:08 · ☽⚹♆ 5:38 · ☽∠⚷ 11:41 · ☽△♇ 12:52 · ♀⚼♃ 14:56 · ☽⚺♂ 15:20 · ☽△♄ 18:42 · ☽⋕☿ 21:21

6 Tu ☉⚼☽ 0:27 · ☽□⚳ 2:14 · ☉⋕⚷ 5:16 · ☽⚼♃ 10:41 · ☽□♀ 12:42 · ☉∥♆ 13:18 · ☽⚹⚷ 17:52 · ☽⚼♇ 19:09 · ☉⚼⚳ 20:27 · ☽∠♂ 20:51 · ☽⚻☿ 22:13 · ☽⚺♅ 23:30

7 W ☽⚼♄ 0:58 · ☽⋕♄ 4:34 · ☉△☽ 9:19 · ☉⋕♂ 15:20 · ☽⚻♃ 16:54 · ☽⋕♃ 17:08 · ☽⋕♇ 17:37 · ☽□♆ 17:52 · ☿☍♅ 20:57

8 Th ☽⚻♇ 1:03 · ☽⚹♂ 1:58 · ☽∠♅ 5:14 · ☽⚼☿ 5:41 · ☽⚻♄ 6:47 · ☽△⚳ 13:40 · ♀⚻⚷ 15:19

9 F ☽□⚷ 4:50 · ♀⚼♇ 6:09 · ☽⚹♀ 6:17 · ♀⚼♂ 7:39 · ☽⚹♅ 10:15 · ☽△☿ 12:04 · ♂□♇ 13:10 · ☽⚼⚳ 18:24

10 Sa ☉□☽ 0:41 · ☽☍♃ 3:18 · ☽△♆ 3:45 · ☽□♂ 10:06 · ☽☍♇ 10:38 · ☽∠♀ 13:29 · ☽☍♄ 16:05 · ☽⚻⚳ 22:13 · ♀△♅ 23:10

11 Su ☽⋕♇ 6:35 · ☽⚼♆ 7:16 · ☽⋕♃ 7:26 · ☽△⚷ 12:24 · ☉□♃ 13:36 · ☉⚻♆ 15:32 · ☽□♅ 17:29 · ☽⋕♄ 18:26 · ♀⚼♄ 18:34 · ☽⚺♀ 19:17 · ☽□☿ 20:51

12 M ♃⚹♆ 7:07 · ☽⚻♆ 9:44 · ☽⚻♃ 9:46 · ☉⚹☽ 11:10 · ☽⋕☿ 14:17 · ☽△♂ 14:31 · ☽⚼⚷ 14:38 · ☽⚻♇ 16:12 · ☿⚹♀ 16:40 · ☽⚻♄ 21:19

13 Tu ☉⋕♀ 2:39 · ☽☍⚳ 2:45 · ♂⋕♆ 8:26 · ☽⚼♃ 11:25 · ☽∥♅ 13:22 · ☉∠☽ 14:30 · ☽⚼♂ 15:17 · ☽⚻⚷ 15:53 · ☽⚼♇ 17:29 · ☽△♅ 20:36 · ☽⚼♄ 22:27 · ☉☍♂ 23:27

14 W ☽⚹☿ 0:20 · ☿ R 1:05 · ☽☌♀ 2:56 · ☽☍♆ 11:48 · ☽△♃ 12:13 · ☉⋕☽ 14:34 · ☽⚻♂ 15:18 · ☉⚺☽ 16:47 · ☽△♇ 17:56 · ☽∥♀ 19:41 · ☽⚼♅ 20:55 · ☽△♄ 22:48

15 Th ☽∠☿ 0:31 · ☽⋕♆ 2:26 · ☽∥♂ 2:54 · ☽⚻⚳ 3:45 · ☽∥⚷ 3:54 · ☉□♇ 10:16 · ☽☍⚷ 16:09 · ☽⚻♅ 20:40 · ☽⚺☿ 23:59

16 F ☽⚼⚳ 3:26 · ☽⚺♀ 6:54 · ☽⚻♆ 11:21 · ☽□♃ 12:07 · ☽☍♂ 13:51 · ☽□♇ 17:24 · ☽⋕⚷ 18:51 · ☉☌☽ 19:32 · ☽⋕♂ 19:35 · ☽∥♆ 20:27 · ☽□♄ 22:13 · ☽⋕♀ 23:27

17 Sa ☽△⚳ 2:56 · ☽∠♀ 8:25 · ☽⚼♆ 10:50 · ☉∥☽ 12:14 · ☽⚻⚷ 15:07 · ☽☍♅ 19:38 · ☽☌☿ 21:53

18 Su ☽⋕♅ 7:48 · ☽⚹♀ 10:06 · ☽△♆ 10:29 · ☽⚹♃ 11:40 · ☽⚻♂ 12:09 · ☉□♄ 13:59 · ☽⚼⚷ 14:48 · ♀☍♆ 14:50 · ☽⚹♇ 16:44 · ⚳ D 17:01 · ♀⋕♆ 18:09 · ☽⚹♄ 21:44 · ☉⚺☽ 22:16 · ☽∥☿ 23:57

19 M ☽□⚳ 2:28 · ♂□♃ 5:39 · ♀⚻♂ 7:04 · ♀△♃ 7:36 · ☽⚼♂ 11:50 · ☽∠♃ 12:00 · ☽△⚷ 14:58 · ♀∥♂ 15:32 · ☽∠♇ 17:01 · ☽⚻♅ 19:41 · ☽⚺☿ 20:03 · ♀∥⚷ 21:21 · ☽∠♄ 22:12 · ☽∥♄ 23:47

20 Tu ☉∠☽ 0:29 · ☿☍♅ 2:55 · ☽∥♃ 8:58 · ☽∥♇ 10:53 · ☽□♆ 11:20 · ☽△♂ 12:10 · ☽⚺♃ 13:02 · ☽□♀ 15:29 · ☽⚺♇ 18:02 · ☽∠☿ 19:41 · ☽⚼♅ 20:42 · ☽⚺♄ 23:25

21 W ☉⚹☽ 3:39 · ☽⚹⚳ 4:22 · ☽∥⚳ 11:11 · ☉△⚳ 13:53 · ☽□⚷ 17:31 · ☽⚹☿ 19:50 · ☿∠♀ 20:32 · ♀△♇ 21:43 · ☽△♅ 22:34

22 Th ☽∠⚳ 6:38 · ⚶ ♍ 7:39 · ♂⚺♆ 9:11 · ☽□♂ 15:17 · ☽⚹♆ 15:24 · ☽☌♃ 17:45 · ☽∥⚳ 19:39 · ☽☌♇ 22:41 · ☉ ♏ 23:01

23 F ☽△♀ 1:11 · ☿⚻⚷ 1:36 · ♀⚼♅ 3:06 · ☽☌♄ 4:36 · ☽⚺⚳ 9:51 · ☉□☽ 13:24 · ☽∠♆ 18:49 · ☽∥♇ 19:34 · ☽□☿ 21:50 · ☽∥♃ 22:16 · ☽⚹⚷ 23:39

24 Sa ☽□♅ 5:03 · ♂∥⚷ 6:20 · ☽⚼♀ 7:52 · ☽∥♄ 8:17 · ♀△♄ 15:42 · ☿⋕♅ 19:04 · ☽⚹♂ 21:55 · ☽⚺♆ 23:06

25 Su ☽⚺♃ 2:14 · ☽∠⚷ 4:02 · ☿⚼♆ 5:17 · ☽⚺♇ 6:58 · ☽⚺♄ 13:23 · ☽⚻♀ 15:38 · ☉☌☿ 18:24 · ☽☌⚳ 18:54

26 M ☽△☿ 2:00 · ☽∠♂ 2:22 · ☉△☽ 3:32 · ☽∠♃ 7:39 · ☽⋕♅ 8:27 · ☽⚺⚷ 9:06 · ☉⚼♆ 10:35 · ☽∠♇ 12:13 · ☉∥☿ 13:23 · ☽⚹♅ 14:45 · ☉∥☽ 15:29 · ☽∥☿ 16:07 · ☽∠♄ 18:50

27 Tu ♀⚻⚳ 2:10 · ☽⚼☿ 4:50 · ☽⚺♂ 7:24 · ☽☌♆ 9:41 · ☉⚼☽ 11:48 · ☽⚹♃ 13:39 · ☽⚹♇ 17:59 · ☽∠♅ 20:26

28 W ☽⚹♄ 0:47 · ☿R♎ 1:35 · ☿⚺♀ 1:39 · ♀ ♎ 1:42 · ☽∥♆ 4:07 · ☽⚺⚳ 6:31 · ☽⋕⚷ 7:35 · ☽⋕♂ 7:44 · ☽⚻☿ 8:09 · ☽☍♀ 9:33 · ☉⚻☽ 20:35 · ☽☌⚷ 20:40 · ☉⚻⚷ 21:33

29 Th ☿△⚳ 1:34 · ☽⚺♅ 2:27 · ☽⋕♀ 2:56 · ☽∥♀ 10:55 · ☽∠⚳ 12:52 · ☽☌♂ 18:34 · ☽⚺♆ 21:52

30 F ☽□♃ 2:40 · ☽□♇ 6:27 · ☽∥♂ 6:48 · ☽∥⚷ 6:55 · ☉⋕♅ 8:00 · ☽⋕♆ 10:38 · ☽□♄ 13:31 · ☽☍☿ 16:14 · ☽⚹⚳ 19:23

31 Sa ☽∠♆ 4:12 · ☽⚻♀ 5:03 · ☽⋕☿ 6:49 · ☽⚺⚷ 9:09 · ☉☍☽ 14:50 · ☽☌♅ 14:56 · ☉☍♅ 15:54

LONGITUDE

Day	Sid.Time	☉	☽	☽ 12 hour	Mean ☊	True ☊	☿	♀	♂	⚳	♃	♄	⚷	♅	♆	♇
	h m s	° ' "	° ' "	° ' "	° '	° '	° '	° '	° '	° '	° '	° '	° '	° '	° '	° '
1 Su	2 42 57	9♏01 16	13♉09 47	19♉05 37	22♊05.2	20♊28.5	26♎37.2	4♎46.0	16♈22.0	29♒07.7	21♑02.5	26♑13.1	5♈48.5	8♉40.2	18♓22.8	22♑40.3
2 M	2 46 54	10 01 17	25 02 00	0♊59 13	22 02.0	20R 23.5	26R 11.3	5 59.1	16R 12.0	29 12.6	21 11.0	26 16.3	5R 46.3	8R 37.7	18R 21.9	22 41.2
3 Tu	2 50 50	11 01 20	6♊57 31	12 57 12	21 58.8	20 20.5	25D 57.0	7 12.1	16 02.9	29 17.7	21 19.6	26 19.6	5 44.2	8 35.3	18 21.0	22 42.0
4 W	2 54 47	12 01 25	18 58 36	25 02 05	21 55.6	20D 19.5	25 54.2	8 25.3	15 54.4	29 23.2	21 28.4	26 22.9	5 42.2	8 32.8	18 20.2	22 42.9
5 Th	2 58 44	13 01 32	1♋08 02	7♋16 54	21 52.5	20 20.0	26 02.6	9 38.5	15 46.8	29 29.0	21 37.2	26 26.4	5 40.2	8 30.3	18 19.4	22 43.8
6 F	3 02 40	14 01 42	13 29 07	19 45 10	21 49.3	20 21.5	26 21.5	10 51.8	15 40.0	29 35.2	21 46.3	26 30.0	5 38.2	8 27.9	18 18.6	22 44.7
7 Sa	3 06 37	15 01 53	26 05 31	2♌30 40	21 46.1	20 23.1	26 50.1	12 05.2	15 33.9	29 41.6	21 55.4	26 33.6	5 36.2	8 25.4	18 17.9	22 45.7
8 Su	3 10 33	16 02 06	9♌01 05	15 37 12	21 42.9	20R 24.3	27 27.7	13 18.6	15 28.7	29 48.4	22 04.7	26 37.3	5 34.3	8 23.0	18 17.2	22 46.6
9 M	3 14 30	17 02 21	22 19 22	29 07 54	21 39.8	20 24.4	28 13.4	14 32.1	15 24.2	29 55.5	22 14.0	26 41.1	5 32.4	8 20.5	18 16.5	22 47.7
10 Tu	3 18 26	18 02 38	6♍03 00	13♍04 42	21 36.6	20 23.1	29 06.2	15 45.7	15 20.5	0♓02.9	22 23.6	26 45.0	5 30.6	8 18.1	18 15.9	22 48.7
11 W	3 22 23	19 02 58	20 12 56	27 27 26	21 33.4	20 20.4	0♏05.3	16 59.3	15 17.7	0 10.5	22 33.2	26 49.0	5 28.8	8 15.7	18 15.3	22 49.7
12 Th	3 26 20	20 03 19	4♎47 43	12♎13 08	21 30.2	20 16.5	1 09.9	18 13.0	15 15.7	0 18.5	22 42.9	26 53.1	5 27.0	8 13.3	18 14.7	22 50.8
13 F	3 30 16	21 03 42	19 42 52	27 15 53	21 27.1	20 12.2	2 19.3	19 26.8	15 14.4	0 26.8	22 52.8	26 57.2	5 25.3	8 10.9	18 14.1	22 51.9
14 Sa	3 34 13	22 04 07	4♏51 02	12♏27 06	21 23.9	20 08.1	3 32.8	20 40.6	15D 14.0	0 35.4	23 02.8	27 01.4	5 23.7	8 08.5	18 13.6	22 53.1
15 Su	3 38 09	23 04 34	20 02 48	27 36 50	21 20.7	20 04.8	4 49.7	21 54.4	15 14.4	0 44.2	23 12.9	27 05.7	5 22.1	8 06.1	18 13.1	22 54.3
16 M	3 42 06	24 05 02	5♐08 02	12♐35 17	21 17.5	20 02.7	6 09.7	23 08.4	15 15.6	0 53.4	23 23.1	27 10.1	5 20.5	8 03.8	18 12.6	22 55.4
17 Tu	3 46 02	25 05 32	19 57 39	27 14 21	21 14.3	20D 02.1	7 32.2	24 22.3	15 17.6	1 02.8	23 33.4	27 14.5	5 18.9	8 01.4	18 12.2	22 56.7
18 W	3 49 59	26 06 04	4♑24 50	11♑28 41	21 11.2	20 02.6	8 56.7	25 36.3	15 20.3	1 12.5	23 43.9	27 19.0	5 17.5	7 59.1	18 11.8	22 57.9
19 Th	3 53 55	27 06 37	18 25 42	25 15 50	21 08.0	20 03.9	10 23.1	26 50.4	15 23.9	1 22.5	23 54.4	27 23.7	5 16.0	7 56.8	18 11.5	22 59.2
20 F	3 57 52	28 07 11	1♒59 12	8♒36 01	21 04.8	20 05.5	11 50.9	28 04.5	15 28.2	1 32.7	24 05.1	27 28.3	5 14.6	7 54.5	18 11.2	23 00.5
21 Sa	4 01 49	29 07 46	15 06 38	21 31 27	21 01.6	20 06.8	13 19.9	29 18.6	15 33.3	1 43.3	24 15.9	27 33.1	5 13.3	7 52.3	18 10.9	23 01.8
22 Su	4 05 45	0♐08 23	27 50 57	4♓05 39	20 58.5	20R 07.4	14 49.9	0♏32.8	15 39.1	1 54.0	24 26.7	27 37.9	5 12.0	7 50.0	18 10.6	23 03.1
23 M	4 09 42	1 09 00	10♓16 05	16 22 47	20 55.3	20 07.1	16 20.8	1 47.1	15 45.7	2 05.1	24 37.7	27 42.8	5 10.8	7 47.8	18 10.4	23 04.5
24 Tu	4 13 38	2 09 39	22 26 19	28 27 13	20 52.1	20 05.9	17 52.3	3 01.3	15 53.0	2 16.4	24 48.7	27 47.7	5 09.6	7 45.6	18 10.2	23 05.8
25 W	4 17 35	3 10 19	4♈26 00	10♈23 09	20 48.9	20 03.9	19 24.3	4 15.6	16 01.0	2 27.9	24 59.9	27 52.8	5 08.4	7 43.4	18 10.0	23 07.2
26 Th	4 21 31	4 11 00	16 19 10	22 14 27	20 45.8	20 01.6	20 56.7	5 30.0	16 09.7	2 39.7	25 11.2	27 57.9	5 07.3	7 41.3	18 09.9	23 08.7
27 F	4 25 28	5 11 42	28 09 26	4♉04 29	20 42.6	19 59.0	22 29.5	6 44.3	16 19.1	2 51.7	25 22.5	28 03.0	5 06.3	7 39.2	18 09.8	23 10.1
28 Sa	4 29 24	6 12 26	9♉59 55	15 56 04	20 39.4	19 56.7	24 02.5	7 58.8	16 29.2	3 04.0	25 33.9	28 08.2	5 05.3	7 37.1	18 09.8	23 11.6
29 Su	4 33 21	7 13 10	21 53 13	27 51 37	20 36.2	19 54.9	25 35.7	9 13.2	16 39.9	3 16.5	25 45.5	28 13.5	5 04.3	7 35.0	18D 09.8	23 13.0
30 M	4 37 18	8♐13 56	3♊51 30	9♊53 05	20♊33.0	19♊53.8	27♏09.1	10♏27.7	16♈51.2	3♓29.2	25♑57.1	28♑18.9	5♈03.4	7♉33.0	18♓09.8	23♑14.6

1st of Month

Julian Day # 2459154.5
Obliquity 23°26'13"
SVP 4♓58'26"
GC 27♐07.8
Eris 23♈51.2R

Day	⚴	⚵	⚶
1	19♑50.9	13♏53.3	3♍37.3
6	21 04.7	15 35.8	5 25.3
11	22 22.1	17 18.4	7 10.2
16	23 42.7	19 01.0	8 51.4
21	25 06.4	20 43.3	10 28.6
26	26 32.7	22 25.2	12 01.3

DECLINATION and LATITUDE

Day	☉ Decl	☽ Decl	☽ Lat	☽ 12h Decl	☿ Decl	☿ Lat	♀ Decl	♀ Lat	♂ Decl	♂ Lat	⚳ Decl	⚳ Lat	♃ Decl	♃ Lat	♄ Decl	♄ Lat
1 Su	14S30	12N48	3S08	14N54	9S15	1N05	0S25	1N36	4N49	1S45	23S35	12S40	22S14	0S27	21S14	0S20
2 M	14 49	16 52	2 13	18 40	8 52	1 20	0 53	1 38	4 49	1 41	23 30	12 36	22 13	0 27	21 14	0 20
3 Tu	15 08	20 17	1 12	21 41	8 35	1 33	1 21	1 39	4 50	1 37	23 25	12 32	22 11	0 27	21 13	0 20
4 W	15 27	22 51	0 07	23 46	8 23	1 44	1 49	1 40	4 50	1 32	23 19	12 28	22 10	0 27	21 12	0 20
5 Th	15 45	24 25	0N59	24 45	8 17	1 54	2 16	1 41	4 51	1 28	23 13	12 24	22 09	0 27	21 12	0 20
6 F	16 03	24 48	2 03	24 31	8 17	2 01	2 44	1 42	4 52	1 24	23 08	12 20	22 07	0 27	21 11	0 21
7 Sa	16 21	23 55	3 03	23 00	8 22	2 07	3 12	1 43	4 53	1 20	23 02	12 16	22 06	0 27	21 11	0 21
8 Su	16 38	21 47	3 55	20 15	8 31	2 12	3 40	1 44	4 55	1 17	22 56	12 13	22 04	0 27	21 10	0 21
9 M	16 55	18 25	4 36	16 19	8 44	2 15	4 08	1 44	4 57	1 13	22 49	12 09	22 03	0 27	21 09	0 21
10 Tu	17 12	13 59	5 03	11 25	9 01	2 17	4 35	1 45	4 59	1 09	22 43	12 05	22 01	0 27	21 09	0 21
11 W	17 29	8 40	5 13	5 45	9 21	2 17	5 03	1 45	5 01	1 05	22 37	12 01	21 60	0 27	21 08	0 21
12 Th	17 45	2 44	5 03	0S22	9 44	2 17	5 31	1 46	5 04	1 02	22 31	11 58	21 58	0 27	21 07	0 21
13 F	18 01	3S30	4 33	6 36	10 09	2 15	5 58	1 46	5 07	0 58	22 24	11 54	21 57	0 27	21 06	0 21
14 Sa	18 17	9 38	3 43	12 31	10 37	2 13	6 26	1 46	5 10	0 54	22 18	11 50	21 55	0 27	21 06	0 21
15 Su	18 32	15 13	2 37	17 40	11 05	2 10	6 53	1 47	5 13	0 51	22 11	11 46	21 53	0 27	21 05	0 21
16 M	18 47	19 49	1 21	21 38	11 35	2 06	7 20	1 47	5 17	0 47	22 04	11 43	21 52	0 27	21 04	0 21
17 Tu	19 02	23 03	0 00	24 04	12 06	2 02	7 47	1 47	5 21	0 44	21 57	11 39	21 50	0 27	21 03	0 21
18 W	19 17	24 40	1S18	24 51	12 37	1 58	8 14	1 47	5 25	0 41	21 50	11 36	21 48	0 27	21 02	0 21
19 Th	19 31	24 39	2 30	24 04	13 09	1 52	8 41	1 47	5 29	0 37	21 43	11 32	21 46	0 27	21 01	0 21
20 F	19 44	23 08	3 31	21 55	13 42	1 47	9 08	1 46	5 34	0 34	21 36	11 28	21 45	0 27	21 01	0 21
21 Sa	19 58	20 25	4 19	18 42	14 14	1 41	9 34	1 46	5 39	0 31	21 29	11 25	21 43	0 27	20 60	0 21
22 Su	20 11	16 47	4 52	14 43	14 46	1 35	10 01	1 46	5 44	0 28	21 22	11 21	21 41	0 28	20 59	0 21
23 M	20 23	12 31	5 11	10 12	15 19	1 28	10 27	1 45	5 49	0 25	21 15	11 18	21 39	0 28	20 58	0 21
24 Tu	20 36	7 50	5 15	5 23	15 51	1 22	10 53	1 45	5 55	0 22	21 07	11 14	21 37	0 28	20 57	0 21
25 W	20 47	2 55	5 06	0 26	16 22	1 15	11 18	1 44	6 00	0 19	20 60	11 11	21 35	0 28	20 56	0 21
26 Th	20 59	2N03	4 43	4N31	16 53	1 08	11 44	1 43	6 06	0 16	20 52	11 08	21 33	0 28	20 55	0 21
27 F	21 10	6 57	4 09	9 19	17 24	1 02	12 09	1 43	6 13	0 13	20 45	11 04	21 31	0 28	20 54	0 21
28 Sa	21 21	11 36	3 23	13 47	17 54	0 55	12 34	1 42	6 19	0 11	20 37	11 01	21 29	0 28	20 53	0 22
29 Su	21 31	15 50	2 29	17 45	18 23	0 47	12 58	1 41	6 26	0 08	20 29	10 57	21 27	0 28	20 52	0 22
30 M	21S41	19N29	1S28	21N01	18S52	0N40	13S23	1N40	6N32	0S05	20S21	10S54	21S25	0S28	20S51	0S22

Day	⚷ Decl	⚷ Lat	♅ Decl	♅ Lat	♆ Decl	♆ Lat	♇ Decl	♇ Lat
1	4N49	2N44	13N57	0S28	5S37	1S07	22S39	1S08
6	4 45	2 44	13 53	0 28	5 38	1 06	22 38	1 08
11	4 40	2 43	13 49	0 28	5 40	1 06	22 38	1 08
16	4 36	2 42	13 45	0 28	5 41	1 06	22 37	1 09
21	4 32	2 41	13 41	0 28	5 41	1 06	22 36	1 09
26	4 29	2 40	13 38	0 28	5 41	1 06	22 35	1 09

Day	⚴ Decl	⚴ Lat	⚵ Decl	⚵ Lat	⚶ Decl	⚶ Lat	Eris Decl	Eris Lat
1	2N56	25N09	8S05	8N17	13N02	3N04	1S38	11S42
6	2 23	24 26	8 31	8 21	12 33	3 16	1 39	11 41
11	1 53	23 45	8 55	8 25	12 06	3 28	1 39	11 41
16	1 25	23 05	9 17	8 30	11 40	3 41	1 40	11 40
21	1 01	22 28	9 39	8 35	11 15	3 55	1 40	11 40
26	0 40	21 52	9 59	8 40	10 53	4 09	1 40	11 39

Moon Phenomena

Max/0 Decl
dy hr mn
5 19:36 24N49
12 10:34 0 S
18 11:34 24S51
25 14:04 0 N

Max/0 Lat
dy hr mn
4 2:41 0 N
11 0:03 5N13
17 0:08 0 S
23 19:24 5S16

Perigee/Apogee
dy hr m kilometers
14 11:44 p 357842
27 0:29 a 405894

PH dy hr mn
☾ 8 13:47 16♌37
● 15 5:08 23♏18
☽ 22 4:46 0♓20
○ 30 9:31 8♊38
☍ 30 9:44 A 0.828

Void of Course Moon

Last Aspect				☽ Ingress		
2	2:31	♄	△	♊	2	10:01
4	13:50	☿	△	♋	4	21:47
7	1:28	☿	□	♌	7	7:19
9	11:06	☿	⚹	♍	9	13:31
11	11:00	♄	△	♎	11	16:11
13	11:34	♄	□	♏	13	16:20
15	11:14	♄	⚹	♐	15	15:48
17	7:56	♀	⚹	♑	17	16:36
19	16:31	☉	⚹	♒	19	20:26
21	0:50	♂	⚹	♓	22	4:07
24	10:46	♄	⚹	♈	24	15:06
26	23:47	♄	□	♉	27	3:44
29	12:50	♄	△	♊	29	16:17

DAILY ASPECTARIAN

1 Su
♂ ∥ ⚷ 2:38
☽ ⚺ ♂ 6:24
☽ ∥ ♅ 6:24
☉ # ☽ 10:27
☽ ⚹ ♆ 10:33
☽ ⚼ ♀ 14:53
☽ ∠ ⚷ 15:25
☽ △ ♃ 16:08
☿ □ ♄ 19:07
☽ △ ♇ 19:15
♀ ☍ ⚷ 19:56

2 M
☽ ⚻ ☿ 2:16
☽ △ ♄ 2:31
☽ □ ⚳ 8:29
☽ ∠ ♂ 12:16
☽ ⚹ ⚷ 21:33
☽ ⚼ ♃ 22:43

3 Tu
☽ △ ♀ 0:33
☽ ⚼ ♇ 1:29
☽ ⚺ ♅ 3:15
☽ # ♄ 7:45
☽ ⚼ ☿ 7:55
☽ ⚼ ♄ 8:47
☉ ⚻ ☽ 8:53
☽ # ♃ 16:42
☿ D 17:53
☽ ⚹ ♂ 17:58
☽ # ♇ 21:34
☽ □ ♆ 22:44

4 W
♀ ⚻ ♅ 2:23
☽ ⚻ ♃ 5:01
☽ # ⚳ 5:21
☽ ⚻ ♇ 7:25
☽ ∠ ♅ 9:02
☽ △ ☿ 13:50
☽ ⚻ ♄ 14:44
☉ ⚼ ☽ 17:21
☽ △ ⚳ 20:44

5 Th
☽ □ ⚷ 8:50
☽ ⚹ ♅ 14:20
☽ □ ♀ 18:23

6 F
☉ △ ☽ 1:08
☽ ⚼ ⚳ 2:08
☽ □ ♂ 4:09
☿ □ ♄ 9:13
☽ △ ♆ 9:14
☽ ☍ ♃ 16:02
☽ ☍ ♇ 17:42

7 Sa
☽ ☍ ♄ 0:53
☽ □ ☿ 1:28
☽ ⚻ ⚳ 6:49
☉ ⚻ ♂ 11:42
☽ # ⚳ 12:19
☽ ⚼ ♆ 13:27
☽ # ♇ 15:57
☽ △ ⚷ 17:41
☽ # ♃ 21:20
☽ □ ♅ 22:50

8 Su
☽ # ♄ 5:04
☽ ⚹ ♀ 8:37
☽ △ ♂ 11:40
☉ □ ☽ 13:47
☽ ⚻ ♆ 16:47
☽ ⚼ ⚷ 20:50
☽ ⚻ ♃ 23:50

9 M
☽ ⚻ ♇ 0:50
☽ ⚻ ♄ 7:45
☉ # ☽ 8:11
♀ ⚼ ⚳ 8:28
☽ ⚹ ☿ 11:06
☽ ☍ ⚳ 13:30
☽ ∠ ♀ 13:57
☽ ⚼ ♂ 14:09
⚳ ♓ 14:49
♀ ☍ ♂ 16:10
☽ ⚻ ⚷ 23:04

10 Tu
☽ ∥ ♅ 0:46
☽ ⚼ ♃ 2:20
☽ ⚼ ♇ 3:02
☽ △ ♅ 3:51
♀ # ⚷ 4:43
☉ △ ♆ 5:13
☽ ⚼ ♄ 9:47
☽ ∠ ☿ 14:44
☽ ⚻ ♂ 15:46
☽ ⚺ ♀ 18:05
☽ ☍ ♆ 20:43
☽ # ☿ 21:14
⚳ ∥ ♇ 21:42
☉ ⚹ ☽ 21:54
☿ ♏ 21:57
♀ # ♂ 22:15

11 W
☿ △ ⚳ 2:19
☽ △ ♃ 3:56
☽ △ ♇ 4:21
☽ ⚼ ♅ 5:03
☽ △ ♄ 11:00
☽ # ♆ 12:22
☽ # ♀ 13:46
☽ ∥ ♂ 14:51
☽ ∥ ⚷ 16:24
☽ ⚻ ⚳ 16:37
♂ ∠ ⚳ 17:02
☽ ⚺ ☿ 17:36

12 Th
☉ ∠ ☽ 0:27
♀ ⚻ ♆ 0:32
☽ ☍ ⚷ 1:04
☽ ⚻ ♅ 5:32
♀ ∥ ♆ 8:03
☉ ⚼ ⚷ 9:10
☽ ☍ ♂ 16:51
☽ ⚼ ⚳ 17:07
☽ ⚻ ♆ 21:38
♃ ☌ ♇ 21:40
☽ ☌ ♀ 23:32

13 F
☉ ⚺ ☽ 2:18
☽ # ⚷ 4:22
☽ □ ♇ 5:01
☽ □ ♃ 5:06
☽ # ♂ 6:15
☽ ∥ ♆ 8:21
☽ ∥ ♀ 10:17
☽ □ ♄ 11:34
☽ △ ⚳ 17:12
☿ ⚼ ♆ 17:54
☽ ⚼ ♆ 21:26
☽ ☌ ☿ 21:45

14 Sa
♂ D 0:37
☽ ⚻ ⚷ 0:51
☽ ∥ ☿ 4:19
☽ ☍ ♅ 5:11
☽ ⚻ ♂ 16:24
☽ # ♅ 17:24
☉ ⚹ ♇ 19:49
☽ △ ♆ 21:07

15 Su
☽ ⚼ ⚷ 0:30
☽ ⚺ ♀ 3:12
☉ ⚹ ♃ 3:59
☽ ⚹ ♇ 4:32
☽ ⚹ ♃ 5:04
☉ ☌ ☽ 5:08
☿ ⚻ ⚷ 9:37
☽ ⚹ ♄ 11:14
☽ ⚼ ♂ 16:12
☽ □ ⚳ 17:09
☉ ∥ ☽ 17:39
♀ □ ♇ 19:44

16 M
☽ △ ⚷ 0:20
☽ ⚺ ☿ 1:49
☽ ∠ ♇ 4:29
☽ ⚻ ♅ 4:41
☽ ∠ ♀ 5:16
☽ ∠ ♃ 5:17
♀ □ ♃ 5:34
☽ ∥ ♄ 7:59
☽ ∠ ♄ 11:23
☽ ∥ ♃ 13:40
☽ ∥ ⚳ 14:52
☽ △ ♂ 16:22
☽ ∥ ♇ 19:58
☽ □ ♆ 21:08

17 Tu
☽ ∠ ☿ 4:41
☽ ⚺ ♇ 4:54
☽ ⚼ ♅ 5:01
☽ ⚺ ♃ 5:59
☽ ⚹ ♀ 7:56
☿ ☍ ♅ 8:09
☉ ⚺ ☽ 9:05
☽ ⚺ ♄ 12:04
☽ ⚹ ⚳ 18:33

18 W
☽ □ ⚷ 1:29
☽ △ ♅ 6:02
☽ ⚹ ☿ 8:33
⚳ ∥ ♃ 10:24
☉ ∠ ☽ 12:14
☽ □ ♂ 18:43
☽ ∠ ⚳ 20:23
☽ ⚹ ♆ 23:35

19 Th
☉ ⚹ ♄ 7:19
☽ ☌ ♇ 8:00
☽ ☌ ♃ 9:44
♀ □ ♄ 11:30
☽ ☌ ♄ 15:52
☽ □ ♀ 16:17
☉ ⚹ ☽ 16:31
☽ ⚺ ⚳ 23:12

20 F
☿ # ♅ 0:24
☽ ∠ ♆ 2:10
☉ ⚺ ♀ 4:46
☽ ∥ ♇ 5:35
☽ ⚹ ⚷ 5:53
☽ □ ♅ 10:42
☽ ∥ ♃ 13:38
☽ ∥ ⚳ 15:17
☽ ∥ ♄ 19:35
☽ □ ☿ 20:17

21 Sa
☽ ⚹ ♂ 0:50
☉ ∥ ☽ 3:08
☽ ⚺ ♆ 5:43
☽ ∠ ⚷ 9:32
♂ # ♆ 11:33
♀ ♏ 13:23
☽ ⚺ ♇ 14:52
☽ ⚺ ♃ 17:26
☉ ♐ 20:41
☽ ⚺ ♄ 23:35

22 Su
☉ □ ☽ 4:46
☽ ∠ ♂ 5:25
☽ △ ♀ 5:44
☽ ☌ ⚳ 7:53
☽ ∥ ☿ 10:21
☉ ⚼ ♂ 13:37
☿ ⚻ ♂ 14:01
☽ ⚺ ⚷ 14:07
☽ # ♅ 17:46
☽ ⚹ ♅ 19:12
☽ ∠ ♇ 19:43
☽ ∠ ♃ 22:44

23 M
☽ ∠ ♄ 4:49
♀ △ ⚳ 6:52
☽ ∥ ♀ 9:52
☽ ⚺ ♂ 10:53
☽ △ ☿ 13:39
☽ ⚼ ♀ 14:15
☽ ☌ ♆ 15:32

24 Tu
☽ ∠ ♅ 0:38
☽ ⚹ ♇ 1:19
♀ ⚼ ♆ 2:52
☉ □ ⚳ 3:16
☿ △ ♆ 4:41
☽ ⚹ ♃ 4:48
☽ # ♂ 9:16
☽ ∥ ♆ 10:32
☽ ⚹ ♄ 10:46
☽ # ⚷ 16:21
☽ ⚺ ⚳ 19:59
☉ △ ☽ 21:14
☽ ⚻ ♀ 23:37
☽ ⚼ ☿ 23:56

25 W
☽ ☌ ⚷ 1:25
☽ ⚺ ♅ 6:36
☿ ⚼ ⚷ 11:20
⚳ ∥ ♄ 13:58
☉ ∥ ⚳ 15:39
☉ ∥ ♄ 16:33
♀ ⚻ ⚷ 16:48
☽ ☌ ♂ 23:41

26 Th
☽ ∠ ⚳ 2:46
☽ ⚺ ♆ 3:44
☉ ⚼ ☽ 6:21
☽ ⚻ ☿ 10:47
☽ ∥ ⚷ 11:48
☽ □ ♇ 13:52
☽ # ♆ 17:46
☽ □ ♃ 18:16
☽ ∥ ♂ 20:16
☉ △ ⚷ 21:53
☽ □ ♄ 23:47

27 F
☽ ⚹ ⚳ 9:42
☽ ∠ ♆ 10:09
☿ ⚹ ♇ 10:40
☽ ⚺ ⚷ 14:04
☉ ⚻ ☽ 15:36
♀ ☍ ♅ 17:12
☽ ☌ ♅ 19:12
☽ ☍ ♀ 19:26

28 Sa
☽ # ♀ 5:48
☽ ∥ ♅ 11:02
☽ ⚺ ♂ 13:19
☉ ∥ ♃ 16:05
☽ ⚹ ♆ 16:30
☽ ∠ ⚷ 20:21

29 Su
♆ D 0:37
☽ △ ♇ 2:41
☿ ⚹ ♃ 2:52
☽ △ ♃ 7:55
☉ ⚻ ♅ 8:21
☽ ☍ ☿ 8:34
☽ △ ♄ 12:50
☽ # ☿ 18:52
☽ ∠ ♂ 19:56
☽ □ ⚳ 23:15

30 M
☉ ∠ ♇ 0:15
☽ ⚹ ⚷ 2:23
☽ # ⚳ 6:21
☽ ⚺ ♅ 7:20
☽ ⚼ ♇ 8:45
☉ ☍ ☽ 9:31
☽ # ♄ 10:31
♀ # ♅ 12:21
☽ ⚼ ♃ 14:21
☽ ⚻ ♀ 14:39
☽ # ♃ 15:09
☉ # ☽ 18:53
☽ ⚼ ♄ 18:57
☿ ⚹ ♄ 19:02

December 2020

LONGITUDE

Day	Sid.Time	☉	☽	☽ 12 hour	Mean☊	True☊	☿	♀	♂	⚳	♃	♄	⚷	♅	♆	♇
	h m s	° ' "	° ' "	° ' "	° '	° '	° '	° '	° '	° '	° '	° '	° '	° '	° '	° '
1 Tu	4 41 14	9♐14 43	15♊56 35	22♊02 11	20♊29.9	19♊53.3	28♏42.5	11♏42.2	17♈03.2	3♓42.2	26♑08.8	28♑24.3	5♈02.6	7♉31.0	18♓09.8	23♑16.1
2 W	4 45 11	10 15 31	28 10 06	4♋20 30	20 26.7	19D 53.3	0♐16.1	12 56.8	17 15.8	3 55.3	26 20.6	28 29.8	5R 01.8	7R 29.0	18 09.9	23 17.6
3 Th	4 49 07	11 16 21	10♋33 37	16 49 38	20 23.5	19 53.9	1 49.7	14 11.4	17 29.0	4 08.7	26 32.5	28 35.3	5 01.1	7 27.1	18 10.0	23 19.2
4 F	4 53 04	12 17 11	23 08 47	29 31 16	20 20.3	19 54.6	3 23.4	15 26.0	17 42.7	4 22.4	26 44.4	28 40.9	5 00.4	7 25.2	18 10.2	23 20.8
5 Sa	4 57 00	13 18 03	5♌57 19	12♌27 10	20 17.2	19 55.4	4 57.1	16 40.7	17 57.1	4 36.2	26 56.5	28 46.6	4 59.8	7 23.3	18 10.4	23 22.4
6 Su	5 00 57	14 18 57	19 01 02	25 39 09	20 14.0	19 56.0	6 30.8	17 55.4	18 12.0	4 50.2	27 08.6	28 52.3	4 59.2	7 21.5	18 10.6	23 24.0
7 M	5 04 53	15 19 51	2♍21 41	9♍08 49	20 10.8	19 56.4	8 04.5	19 10.1	18 27.5	5 04.5	27 20.8	28 58.1	4 58.7	7 19.7	18 10.9	23 25.7
8 Tu	5 08 50	16 20 47	16 00 39	22 57 14	20 07.6	19R 56.5	9 38.3	20 24.9	18 43.4	5 18.9	27 33.1	29 03.9	4 58.2	7 17.9	18 11.2	23 27.3
9 W	5 12 47	17 21 44	29 58 32	7♎04 26	20 04.5	19 56.4	11 12.1	21 39.7	19 00.0	5 33.6	27 45.4	29 09.8	4 57.8	7 16.1	18 11.5	23 29.0
10 Th	5 16 43	18 22 42	14♎14 43	21 29 01	20 01.3	19 56.3	12 45.9	22 54.5	19 17.0	5 48.4	27 57.9	29 15.7	4 57.4	7 14.4	18 11.8	23 30.7
11 F	5 20 40	19 23 42	28 46 54	6♏07 46	19 58.1	19D 56.2	14 19.8	24 09.3	19 34.5	6 03.5	28 10.4	29 21.7	4 57.1	7 12.8	18 12.2	23 32.4
12 Sa	5 24 36	20 24 43	13♏30 55	20 55 34	19 54.9	19 56.2	15 53.7	25 24.2	19 52.6	6 18.7	28 22.9	29 27.7	4 56.9	7 11.2	18 12.7	23 34.1
13 Su	5 28 33	21 25 44	28 20 50	5♐45 47	19 51.8	19 56.3	17 27.7	26 39.0	20 11.1	6 34.2	28 35.6	29 33.8	4 56.7	7 09.6	18 13.1	23 35.8
14 M	5 32 29	22 26 47	13♐09 28	20 30 56	19 48.6	19R 56.4	19 01.7	27 53.9	20 30.1	6 49.8	28 48.3	29 40.0	4 56.6	7 08.1	18 13.6	23 37.6
15 Tu	5 36 26	23 27 51	27 49 17	5♑03 42	19 45.4	19 56.4	20 35.9	29 08.9	20 49.6	7 05.6	29 01.1	29 46.1	4D 56.5	7 06.6	18 14.2	23 39.4
16 W	5 40 22	24 28 55	12♑13 27	19 17 58	19 42.2	19 56.1	22 10.1	0♐23.8	21 09.5	7 21.6	29 13.9	29 52.4	4 56.5	7 05.1	18 14.7	23 41.2
17 Th	5 44 19	25 30 00	26 16 45	3♒09 30	19 39.1	19 55.6	23 44.5	1 38.8	21 29.9	7 37.8	29 26.8	29 58.7	4 56.5	7 03.7	18 15.4	23 43.0
18 F	5 48 16	26 31 06	9♒56 01	16 36 18	19 35.9	19 54.9	25 19.0	2 53.7	21 50.7	7 54.1	29 39.8	0♒05.0	4 56.6	7 02.3	18 16.0	23 44.8
19 Sa	5 52 12	27 32 11	23 10 26	29 38 36	19 32.7	19 53.9	26 53.6	4 08.7	22 11.9	8 10.6	29 52.8	0 11.4	4 56.7	7 01.0	18 16.7	23 46.6
20 Su	5 56 09	28 33 17	6♓01 07	12♓18 24	19 29.5	19 53.0	28 28.4	5 23.7	22 33.6	8 27.3	0♒05.9	0 17.8	4 56.9	6 59.7	18 17.4	23 48.4
21 M	6 00 05	29 34 23	18 30 54	24 39 07	19 26.3	19D 52.4	0♑03.4	6 38.7	22 55.6	8 44.2	0 19.1	0 24.2	4 57.2	6 58.5	18 18.1	23 50.3
22 Tu	6 04 02	0♑35 30	0♈43 38	6♈45 01	19 23.2	19 52.1	1 38.6	7 53.8	23 18.0	9 01.2	0 32.3	0 30.7	4 57.5	6 57.3	18 18.9	23 52.1
23 W	6 07 58	1 36 37	12 43 52	18 40 48	19 20.0	19 52.4	3 13.9	9 08.8	23 40.8	9 18.3	0 45.5	0 37.2	4 57.8	6 56.1	18 19.7	23 54.0
24 Th	6 11 55	2 37 43	24 36 23	0♉31 14	19 16.8	19 53.2	4 49.5	10 23.8	24 04.0	9 35.7	0 58.8	0 43.8	4 58.2	6 55.0	18 20.5	23 55.9
25 F	6 15 51	3 38 50	6♉25 54	12 20 56	19 13.6	19 54.5	6 25.3	11 38.9	24 27.5	9 53.1	1 12.2	0 50.4	4 58.7	6 54.0	18 21.4	23 57.8
26 Sa	6 19 48	4 39 58	18 16 50	24 14 05	19 10.5	19 55.9	8 01.3	12 54.0	24 51.4	10 10.8	1 25.6	0 57.0	4 59.2	6 53.0	18 22.3	23 59.7
27 Su	6 23 45	5 41 05	0♊13 07	6♊14 20	19 07.3	19 57.2	9 37.6	14 09.1	25 15.6	10 28.5	1 39.0	1 03.7	4 59.8	6 52.0	18 23.2	24 01.6
28 M	6 27 41	6 42 13	12 18 04	18 24 36	19 04.1	19R 58.1	11 14.1	15 24.1	25 40.2	10 46.5	1 52.5	1 10.4	5 00.5	6 51.1	18 24.2	24 03.5
29 Tu	6 31 38	7 43 20	24 34 12	0♋47 03	19 00.9	19 58.2	12 50.9	16 39.2	26 05.0	11 04.5	2 06.1	1 17.1	5 01.2	6 50.2	18 25.2	24 05.5
30 W	6 35 34	8 44 28	7♋03 18	13 23 02	18 57.8	19 57.3	14 28.0	17 54.4	26 30.2	11 22.7	2 19.7	1 23.9	5 01.9	6 49.4	18 26.2	24 07.4
31 Th	6 39 31	9♑45 36	19 46 19	26 13 08	18♊54.6	19♊55.5	16♑05.3	19♐09.5	26♈55.7	11♓41.1	2♒33.3	1♒30.7	5♈02.7	6♉48.7	18♓27.3	24♑09.3

1st of Month

Julian Day #
2459184.5
Obliquity
23°26'13"
SVP 4♓58'21
GC 27♐07.9
Eris 23♈35.9

Day	⚴
1	28♑01.3
6	29 32.2
11	1♒04.9
16	2 39.5
21	4 15.5
26	5 52.9
31	7 31.3

Day	⚵
1	24♏06.6
6	25 47.4
11	27 27.4
16	29 06.4
21	0♐44.4
26	2 21.0
31	3 56.1

Day	⚶
1	13♍29.1
6	14 51.4
11	16 07.8
16	17 17.6
21	18 20.0
26	19 14.5
31	20 00.4

DECLINATION and LATITUDE

Day	☉ Decl	☽ Decl	☽ Lat	☽ 12h Decl	☿ Decl	☿ Lat	♀ Decl	♀ Lat	♂ Decl	♂ Lat	⚳ Decl	⚳ Lat	♃ Decl	♃ Lat	♄ Decl	♄ Lat
1 Tu	21S50	22N20	0S22	23N24	19S20	0N33	13S47	1N39	6N39	0S03	20S14	10S51	21S22	0S28	20S50	0S22
2 W	21 59	24 11	0N46	24 41	19 47	0 26	14 10	1 38	6 46	0 00	20 06	10 48	21 20	0 28	20 49	0 22
3 Th	22 08	24 53	1 52	24 46	20 13	0 19	14 34	1 36	6 54	0N02	19 58	10 44	21 18	0 28	20 48	0 22
4 F	22 16	24 19	2 54	23 33	20 38	0 12	14 57	1 35	7 01	0 04	19 50	10 41	21 16	0 28	20 47	0 22
5 Sa	22 24	22 28	3 49	21 06	21 02	0 05	15 19	1 34	7 09	0 07	19 42	10 38	21 14	0 28	20 46	0 22
6 Su	22 31	19 26	4 33	17 30	21 25	0S02	15 41	1 33	7 17	0 09	19 33	10 35	21 11	0 28	20 44	0 22
7 M	22 38	15 20	5 03	12 57	21 48	0 09	16 03	1 31	7 24	0 11	19 25	10 32	21 09	0 28	20 43	0 22
8 Tu	22 44	10 23	5 17	7 39	22 09	0 15	16 25	1 30	7 33	0 13	19 17	10 29	21 07	0 28	20 42	0 22
9 W	22 50	4 47	5 13	1 50	22 29	0 22	16 46	1 28	7 41	0 16	19 09	10 26	21 04	0 28	20 41	0 22
10 Th	22 56	1S10	4 50	4S11	22 48	0 29	17 06	1 26	7 49	0 18	19 00	10 23	21 02	0 28	20 40	0 22
11 F	23 01	7 11	4 08	10 06	23 06	0 35	17 26	1 25	7 58	0 20	18 52	10 20	20 59	0 28	20 39	0 22
12 Sa	23 05	12 53	3 09	15 30	23 23	0 41	17 46	1 23	8 06	0 22	18 43	10 17	20 57	0 28	20 37	0 22
13 Su	23 10	17 53	1 57	19 59	23 38	0 48	18 05	1 21	8 15	0 24	18 35	10 14	20 54	0 28	20 36	0 22
14 M	23 13	21 45	0 38	23 09	23 53	0 54	18 24	1 19	8 24	0 25	18 26	10 11	20 52	0 28	20 35	0 22
15 Tu	23 17	24 09	0S44	24 43	24 06	0 60	18 42	1 17	8 33	0 27	18 17	10 08	20 49	0 28	20 34	0 22
16 W	23 19	24 53	2 01	24 37	24 18	1 05	19 00	1 16	8 42	0 29	18 09	10 05	20 46	0 29	20 32	0 22
17 Th	23 22	23 59	3 08	22 59	24 28	1 11	19 17	1 14	8 51	0 31	17 60	10 02	20 44	0 29	20 31	0 22
18 F	23 23	21 40	4 03	20 04	24 37	1 16	19 34	1 12	9 01	0 32	17 51	9 60	20 41	0 29	20 30	0 23
19 Sa	23 25	18 15	4 43	16 14	24 45	1 21	19 50	1 09	9 10	0 34	17 42	9 57	20 38	0 29	20 29	0 23
20 Su	23 26	14 04	5 08	11 47	24 52	1 26	20 06	1 07	9 20	0 36	17 33	9 54	20 36	0 29	20 27	0 23
21 M	23 26	9 24	5 17	6 57	24 57	1 31	20 21	1 05	9 29	0 37	17 24	9 51	20 33	0 29	20 26	0 23
22 Tu	23 26	4 28	5 11	1 58	25 01	1 36	20 35	1 03	9 39	0 39	17 15	9 49	20 30	0 29	20 25	0 23
23 W	23 26	0N32	4 52	3N02	25 04	1 40	20 49	1 01	9 49	0 40	17 06	9 46	20 27	0 29	20 23	0 23
24 Th	23 25	5 29	4 21	7 53	25 05	1 44	21 02	0 59	9 59	0 42	16 57	9 43	20 25	0 29	20 22	0 23
25 F	23 23	10 13	3 38	12 28	25 05	1 48	21 15	0 56	10 09	0 43	16 48	9 41	20 22	0 29	20 20	0 23
26 Sa	23 21	14 36	2 47	16 36	25 03	1 51	21 27	0 54	10 19	0 45	16 39	9 38	20 19	0 29	20 19	0 23
27 Su	23 19	18 27	1 47	20 07	24 60	1 55	21 38	0 52	10 29	0 46	16 30	9 36	20 16	0 29	20 18	0 23
28 M	23 16	21 34	0 42	22 47	24 55	1 58	21 49	0 49	10 39	0 47	16 21	9 33	20 13	0 29	20 16	0 23
29 Tu	23 13	23 45	0N25	24 25	24 49	2 00	21 59	0 47	10 50	0 49	16 11	9 31	20 10	0 29	20 15	0 23
30 W	23 09	24 48	1 33	24 51	24 41	2 03	22 09	0 44	10 60	0 50	16 02	9 28	20 07	0 29	20 13	0 23
31 Th	23S05	24N34	2N37	23N58	24S32	2S05	22S18	0N42	11N10	0N51	15S53	9S26	20S04	0S29	20S12	0S23

Day	⚷ Decl	⚷ Lat	♅ Decl	♅ Lat	♆ Decl	♆ Lat	♇ Decl	♇ Lat
1	4N26	2N39	13N35	0S28	5S41	1S06	22S34	1S0
6	4 24	2 38	13 32	0 28	5 41	1 06	22 33	1 1
11	4 22	2 37	13 29	0 28	5 40	1 05	22 32	1 1
16	4 21	2 36	13 27	0 27	5 39	1 05	22 31	1 1
21	4 20	2 35	13 25	0 27	5 38	1 05	22 30	1 1
26	4 20	2 34	13 23	0 27	5 36	1 05	22 29	1 1
31	4N21	2N33	13N22	0S27	5S34	1S05	22S27	1S1

Day	⚴ Decl	⚴ Lat	⚵ Decl	⚵ Lat	⚶ Decl	⚶ Lat	Eris Decl	Eris Lat
1	0N21	21N18	10S17	8N46	10N34	4N24	1S41	11S3
6	0 06	20 46	10 34	8 53	10 16	4 41	1 41	11 3
11	0S07	20 15	10 49	9 00	10 02	4 57	1 41	11 3
16	0 17	19 46	11 02	9 08	9 51	5 15	1 41	11 3
21	0 24	19 18	11 14	9 16	9 44	5 34	1 40	11 3
26	0 29	18 51	11 24	9 24	9 41	5 54	1 40	11 3
31	0S31	18N26	11S32	9N34	9N42	6N15	1S40	11S3

Moon Phenomena

Max/0 Decl
dy hr mn
3 1:16 24N53
9 19:22 0 S
15 22:41 24S53
22 21:25 0 N
30 7:51 24N52

Max/0 Lat
dy hr mn
1 7:47 0 N
8 6:45 5N18
14 11:04 0 S
21 2:37 5S17
28 15:03 0 N

Perigee/Apogee
dy hr m kilometers
12 20:53 p 361774
24 16:36 a 405010

PH dy hr mn
☾ 8 0:38 16♍22
● 14 16:18 23♐08
● 14 16:15 T 02'10"
☽ 21 23:42 0♈35
○ 30 3:29 8♋53

Void of Course Moon

Last Aspect				☽ Ingress		
1	4:23	♆	□	♋	2	3:3
4	10:30	♄	☍	♌	4	12:5
5	22:29	♂	△	♍	6	19:4
8	22:36	♄	△	♎	9	0:0
11	0:57	♄	□	♏	11	2:0
13	1:59	♄	✱	♐	13	2:4
14	16:18	☉	☌	♑	15	3:3
17	5:36	♃	☌	♒	17	6:2
19	8:46	☉	✱	♓	19	12:4
21	10:26	♇	✱	♈	21	22:3
23	22:52	♂	☌	♉	24	10:5
26	11:33	♇	△	♊	26	23:3
29	3:02	♂	✱	♋	29	10:2
31	13:46	♂	□	♌	31	18:5

DAILY ASPECTARIAN

1 Tu
☽✱♂ 2:14
☽#♇ 2:29
☽□♆ 4:23
☽∠♅ 12:54
☽⚻♇ 14:27
☿ ♐ 19:52
☽⚻♃ 20:23
☽⚼♀ 23:31

2 W
☽⚻♄ 0:39
☽⚻☿ 4:41
☽△⚳ 11:24
☽□⚷ 13:19
☿∥⚳ 13:20
☽✱♅ 18:02

3 Th
☉⚻☽ 1:29
☽△♀ 7:44
☉∠♃ 7:55
☿⚼♂ 11:46
☽□♂ 13:30
☽⚼☿ 13:42
☽△♆ 14:33
☽⚼⚳ 16:43

4 F
☽☍♇ 0:23
☽☍♃ 6:53
☿∥♄ 8:10
☉⚼☽ 8:29
☽☍♄ 10:30
☿□⚳ 17:43
☽⚼♆ 18:49
☽⚻⚳ 21:27
☽△☿ 21:53
☽△⚷ 22:13
☽#♇ 23:10

5 Sa
☿△⚷ 0:41
☉#☽ 0:45
☽□♅ 2:39
☿∥♃ 10:34
☽#☿ 11:02
☽#♃ 11:06
☉∠♄ 12:24
☽#♄ 14:41
☉△☽ 14:42
♂⚺♆ 21:45
☽□♀ 21:48
☽⚻♆ 22:28
☽△♂ 22:29
☽#⚳ 23:09

6 Su
☽⚼⚷ 1:46
♀△♆ 4:54
♀⚻♂ 6:42
☽⚻♇ 7:57
☉∥♇ 8:05
☿⚻♅ 12:44
⚳⚺⚷ 14:37
☽⚻♃ 14:54
☽⚻♄ 17:54
☽#♀ 20:28

7 M
☽⚼♂ 1:59
☽⚻⚷ 4:38
☽☍⚳ 4:54
☿∠♇ 5:30
☽△♅ 8:47
☽∥♅ 9:15
☽⚼♇ 10:45
☽□☿ 11:25
⚴ ♒ 12:15
♀⚼⚷ 15:30
☽⚼♃ 17:53
☽⚼♄ 20:35

8 Tu
☉□☽ 0:38
☽☍♆ 3:46
☽⚻♂ 4:48
☽✱♀ 8:23
☽⚼♅ 10:51
☽∥♂ 12:09
☽△♇ 12:53
☽△♃ 20:10
☽#♆ 20:20
☽△♄ 22:36

9 W
☽∥⚷ 1:41
☿∥♇ 4:33
☽☍⚷ 8:26
☽⚻⚳ 9:37
☽⚻♅ 12:18
☽∠♀ 12:23
☉□♆ 19:42
☽✱☿ 21:14

10 Th
☿∠♃ 3:32
☽⚻♆ 6:34
☉✱☽ 7:23
☽☍♂ 8:32
☽⚼⚳ 11:04
♀✱♇ 11:53
☽#⚷ 12:44
☉∥☿ 14:20
☽□♇ 15:22
☽⚺♀ 15:41
☽∥♆ 17:55
☽□♃ 22:59

11 F
☿∠♄ 0:31
☽□♄ 0:57
☽∠☿ 1:00
☽#♂ 3:15
☉△♂ 6:02
☽⚼♆ 7:14
☉∠☽ 9:51
☽⚻⚷ 10:05
☽△⚳ 12:05
☽☍♅ 13:44

12 Sa
☽#♅ 2:37
☽⚺☿ 4:19
☽△♆ 7:37
☽⚼⚷ 10:25
☽⚻♂ 10:31
☉⚺☽ 11:59
☽✱♇ 16:18
☽☌♀ 21:00

13 Su
☽✱♃ 0:24
☽∥♀ 1:11
☽✱♄ 1:59
☽∥⚳ 3:39
☽△⚷ 10:40
☽⚼♂ 11:18
☿□♆ 11:40
☽□⚳ 13:33
☽⚻♅ 14:14
☽∥♄ 15:51
☽∠♇ 16:38
☉⚼♅ 16:49
☽∥♃ 17:44

14 M
☽∠♃ 1:04
♀∥⚳ 1:47
☽∠♄ 2:28
☽∥♇ 6:14
☽□♆ 8:16
☽☌☿ 10:43
☽△♂ 12:15
☉∥☽ 13:05
☽⚼♅ 14:38
☉☌☽ 16:18
☽⚺♇ 17:08
♀✱♃ 20:59
☽∥☿ 23:07

15 Tu
⚳✱♅ 1:19
☽⚺♃ 2:00
☽⚺♀ 2:24
☽⚺♄ 3:14
☿△♂ 4:25
☉⚺♇ 4:40
☽□⚷ 11:48
♀✱♄ 13:01
☽△♅ 15:23
☽✱⚳ 15:41
♀ ♐ 16:22
⚷ D 22:18
☿⚼♅ 22:44

16 W
☽∠♀ 5:53
☽✱♆ 10:13
☽□♂ 15:33
☽∥☿ 16:34
☽∠⚳ 17:35
☽⚺☿ 19:04
☽☌♇ 19:34
☉⚺☽ 22:33
☿⚺♇ 23:36

17 Th
♄ ♒ 5:05
☽☌♃ 5:36
☽☌♄ 6:29
☉∥☽ 7:43
☽✱♀ 10:17
☽∠♆ 12:11
☽✱⚷ 15:09
☽∥♇ 16:33
☽□♅ 18:52
☽⚺⚳ 20:18

18 F
☽∠☿ 0:46
☉∠☽ 3:04
☽∥♃ 7:41
☽∥♄ 9:01
☽∥♀ 14:23
☽⚺♆ 15:02
⚵ ♐ 17:26
☽∠⚷ 18:05
☽✱♂ 22:09

19 Sa
☽⚺♇ 1:07
☽∥⚳ 3:29
☽✱☿ 7:50
☉✱☽ 8:46
☽⚺♃ 12:40
☽⚺♄ 13:08
♃ ♒ 13:08
♀△⚷ 15:24
☽⚺⚷ 21:58
☽□♀ 22:41

20 Su
☽✱♅ 1:51
☽∠♂ 3:01
☉☌☿ 3:27
☽#♅ 3:29
☽☌⚳ 4:44
☽∠♇ 5:19
☽∠♃ 17:41
☽∠♄ 17:55
☿ ♑ 23:08
☽#♂ 23:34
☽☌♆ 23:35

21 M
☿⚺♃ 4:36
☿⚺♄ 5:38
♀⚻♅ 6:13
☽∠♅ 6:44
♀∥♄ 7:45
☽⚺♂ 8:53
⚳∠♇ 9:45
☉ ♑ 10:03
☽✱♇ 10:26
♀∥♃ 16:56
♃☌♄ 18:22
☽∥♆ 18:29
☉⚺♄ 21:53
☉⚺♃ 22:23
☽✱♄ 23:34
☽✱♃ 23:37
☉□☽ 23:42

22 Tu
☽#⚷ 0:39
☽□☿ 2:06
☽☌⚷ 8:25
♀⚼♂ 11:08
☽⚺♅ 12:23
☽△♀ 15:58
☽⚺⚳ 16:57
♀∠♇ 19:09

23 W
♀□⚳ 3:57
☽⚺♆ 11:18
♂□♇ 14:54
☽∥⚷ 18:22
☽□♇ 22:38
☽☌♂ 22:52
☽∠⚳ 23:58

24 Th
☽#♆ 0:37
☽⚼♀ 1:48
☿□⚷ 2:12
☽□♄ 12:32
☽□♃ 13:11
☽∠♆ 17:45
☉△☽ 17:49
☽⚺⚷ 21:03
☽∥♂ 23:36
☽△☿ 23:59

25 F
☽☌♅ 0:57
☿△♅ 7:06
☽✱⚳ 7:11
☽⚻♀ 11:50
☽∥♅ 17:04
♃∥♄ 18:52

26 Sa
☽✱♆ 0:11
☉⚼☽ 3:04
☽∠⚷ 3:27
☉□⚷ 7:38
☽⚼☿ 11:03
☽△♇ 11:33
☽#⚳ 11:50
☽⚺♂ 13:43

27 Su
☽△♄ 1:42
☽△♃ 2:55
☽✱⚷ 9:32
☉⚻☽ 11:54
☽#♃ 12:58
☽⚺♅ 13:14
☽#♄ 13:19
☿✱⚳ 15:33
☽⚼♇ 17:35
☽∠♂ 20:40
☽□⚳ 20:55
☽⚻☿ 21:35

28 M
☽#♀ 2:29
☉△♅ 3:27
☽☍♀ 6:48
☽⚼♄ 7:41
☽#♇ 8:36
☽⚼♃ 9:10
☽□♆ 12:00
♀∠♄ 16:14
☉#☽ 17:06
☽∠♅ 18:42
♂∠⚳ 22:13
☽⚻♇ 23:04

29 Tu
☽✱♂ 3:02
♀∠♃ 10:28
☽⚻♄ 13:05
☽⚻♃ 14:48
☽#☿ 20:01
☽□⚷ 20:08
☽✱♅ 23:34

30 W
☉☍☽ 3:29
☽△⚳ 8:25
♀□♆ 10:20
☽☍☿ 16:05
☽△♆ 21:32
☽⚻♀ 22:44

31 Th
☽#☿ 1:18
☽☍♇ 8:11
☽⚼⚳ 13:10
☽□♂ 13:46
☽☍♄ 21:58

Books by Neil F. Michelsen

The American Ephemeris 1931-1980 & Book of Tables
The American Ephemeris 1901-1930
The American Ephemeris 1941-1950
The American Ephemeris 1951-1960
The American Ephemeris 1961-1970
The American Ephemeris 1971-1980
The American Ephemeris 1981-1990
The American Ephemeris 1991-2000
The American Ephemeris for the 20th Century, 1900 to 2000 at Noon
The American Ephemeris for the 20th Century, 1900 to 2000 at Midnight
The American Ephemeris for the 21st Century, 2000 to 2050 at Noon
The American Ephemeris for the 21st Century, 2000 to 2050 at Midnight
The American Sidereal Ephemeris 1976-2000
*The American Sidereal Ephemeris 2001-2025**
The American Heliocentric Ephemeris 1901-2000
*The American Heliocentric Ephemeris 2001-2050**
The American Midpoint Ephemeris 1986-1990
The American Midpoint Ephemeris 1990-1995
*The American Midpoint Ephemeris 1996-2000**
*The American Midpoint Ephemeris 2001-2005**
The American Book of Tables
The Koch Book of Tables
The Michelsen Book of Tables
The Uranian Transneptune Ephemeris 1850-2050
Comet Halley Ephemeris 1901-1996
Search for the Christmas Star (with Maria Kay Simms)
The Asteroid Ephemeris (with Zipporah Dobyns and Rique Pottenger)
Tables of Planetary Phenomena

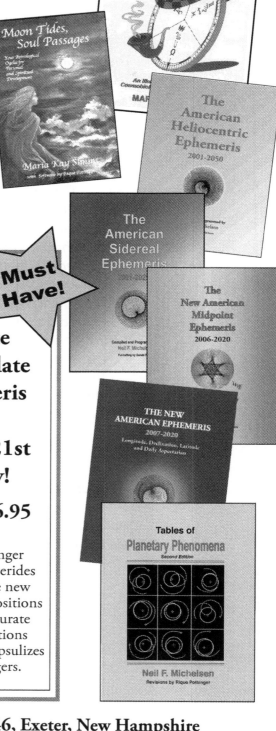